Rugged Hills, Gentle Folk

My Friends & Neighbors in the Big Pine Valley

Stories and Photos by
William J. Weber

In tender, warmhearted pictures and prose, retired veterinarian William J. Weber shows what rural life is like in the Big Pine Valley of North Carolina. Meet Uncle Bass, Clyde, Ruby-Noah, Eulala and many others. Find out how they "head up" a spring, make molasses and bring in hay the old-fashioned way. Also meet "Mike" the old red mule, "Drumstix" the 14-year-old rooster and "Bitsy" the determined little lamb.

Published by Country Books/Reiman Publications

RUGGED HILLS, GENTLE FOLK
My Friends & Neighbors in the Big Pine Valley

Publisher: Roy J. Reiman
Editor: Nick Pabst
Associate Editors: Rick Van Etten,
Kristine Krueger, Henry de Fiebre
Art Director: Gail Engeldahl
Design Director: Jim Sibilski
Production Assistants: Ellen Lloyd, Judy Pope, Julie Wagner
Photo Coordinator: Trudi Bellin

5400 S. 60th St., Greendale WI 53129

Country Books
International Standard Book Number: 0-89821-134-4
Library of Congress Catalog Card Number: 94-69754

For additional copies of this book or information on other Reiman Publications books or magazines, write:
Country Books, P.O. Box 990, Greendale WI 53129.

Credit card orders call toll-free 1-800/558-1013

On the cover: Fall in the Big Pine Valley. Inset photos (clockwise from top right), Clara showing Barbara how to churn butter; danaus plexippus; Clem resting after working at the boiler box; Jerry; "Drumstix" the rooster; Alastair pitching hay. **Above**: Ronnie and "Gyp" in the tobacco patch. **At right**: Mary walking by the old Davis place. **On table of contents pages:** Clyde and corn shocks.

*I especially
want to thank
Leonard Buckner
and his family,
Wade and Clara Massey,
Don and Geraldine Wild,
Dayton and Almarie Wild,
and all my friends and neighbors
in the Big Pine Valley
of North Carolina
for their help.
This is their book.*

WJW

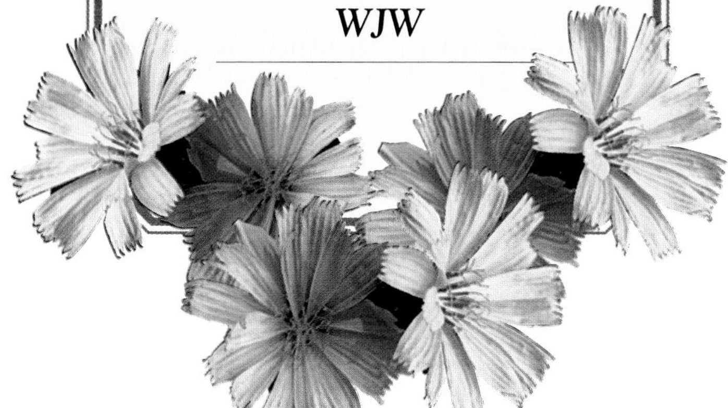

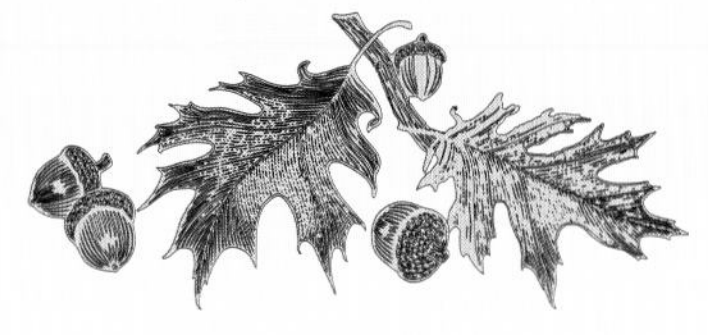

CONTENTS

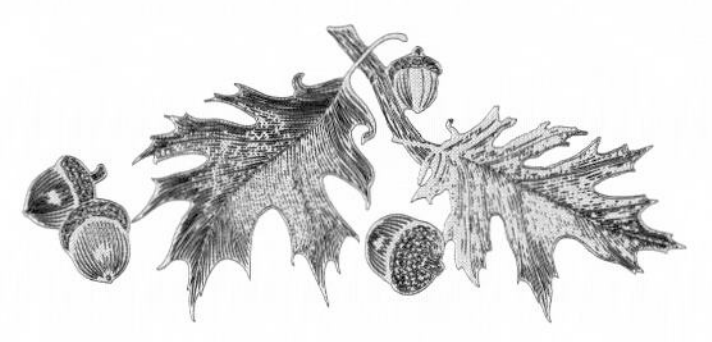

CONTENTS

Chapter 1

This Is Where Our Hearts Are

Big Pine Valley

Big Pine Creek, which gives its name to this secluded valley in western North Carolina where I live, meanders for nearly 10 miles between tall forested hills and a passel of small farms. The farms are mostly under 60 acres and many are still tilled with a horse or mule. They are owned by folks whose families have wrested a living from these steep hillsides for generations.

At its start, Big Pine Creek has two forks, the north and the south. They twist and tumble about a mile to where they meet and become one at the North Fork Baptist Church. From there to French Broad River at the valley's mouth is 8 miles. In that distance, the road crosses the creek nine times—not that many if you consider that in the old days, you had to ford the winding creek 23 times to get back home from town.

The Big Pine Valley itself is hewed from the Walnut Mountains, which are part of the picturesque Blue Ridge Mountains. Despite years of tobacco growing, the heavy brown soil in the valley is still rich and fertile. It's said that tobacco leeches nutrients from the soil, but in this valley you can plant a whittled stick in the ground and before you know it, it'll be growing leaves and branches.

That's partly because of the soil itself, which clings to the hillsides as stubbornly as the people who live here. It's also because of what these people put back into the soil, not just in fertilizer but in love. These folks—my friends and neighbors—have made caring for the land and each other their way of life.

They work hard, putting in 6 long days a week to grow most of the food they will need in a year for themselves and their livestock. In a way, Big Pine Creek is a fitting symbol for the valley. Though it constantly struggles against the rugged hills to maintain its course, the creek is never drained of its beauty.

The progression of seasons in the valley is vivid. Spring bursts forth with bright blossoms and bird songs. Summer is rich with lush greens, hot sunny days, katydid songs and evenings full of flickering lightning bugs. Fall lights up the valley with rich reds, yellows and oranges. And winter sometimes cloaks the hills with soft white snow, though it soon melts away.

My wife, Barbara, and I found this valley almost 20 years ago. Our two sons were grown, and I would soon retire from my veterinary practice in Florida, so we looked for a scenic area to live where I could grow fruit trees, have a garden and raise a few sheep.

We have all that now, but we also have much more. Besides scenic beauty, our livestock and bountiful good-tasting fruit and vegetables, we have our unique friends and neighbors, the farmers

Earl Roberts prepares his ground in the spring for tobacco (above left) while the North Fork Baptist Church welcomes folks to the Big Pine Valley (right). Inset: a Carolina chickadee takes a break while looking for a nest site.

who make up the majority of folks in the valley.

There are actually fewer people living here now than 100 years ago. In fact, old-timers say that forests are slowly reclaiming farmland that's being left untilled because there aren't enough folks to work it. That's because subsistence farming is about all there is to do, so young folks tend to go elsewhere if they're interested in money.

Those of our friends and neighbors who are getting on in years headed to Detroit and jobs in the auto plants when they themselves were young. The ones who couldn't get the valley out of their systems eventually came back to toil on the hillsides.

Their primary cash crops are tobacco, cattle and sawmill logs. Despite the urgent need to plow and plant, hoe and harvest, they always have time to visit. Everyone waves as they pass in cars or see a friend working in the field. When someone is injured or sick, neighbors have "a workin' " and put up his hay or cut his tobacco or put a new roof on a widow's house as they recently did for Ruby-Noah. These things are important here.

Sunday morning is the time for meeting at our small North Fork Baptist Church. It has always been an important influence on the people of the community. Activities such as

In the old days, folks had to ford Big Pine Creek 23 times to get up or down the valley. Today in less than 9 miles, nine bridges cross the creek. At left is one of the homes in Big Pine Valley that still has no electricity or plumbing.

Paul and Grace's home is well up the cove (above). That's Paul, his neighbor Jim and dog "Sunny" on the porch at right. Cherries and an indigo bunting provide dollop of bright color (top right).

Homecoming, workin's for someone in need, Christmas plays and Bible school all help bind the folks in the valley together.

Traveling up the road after crossing the French Broad River is almost like going back in time. Some families farm with teams, keep a cow for butter and milk and raise a hog to butcher in the fall. Women fill the cellar with canned green beans, pickles, applesauce, cherries, peaches, jams, jellies and tomatoes.

All the families put boxes of potatoes in a cool cellar and store squashes, apples and cabbages for use in the winter. Hardy and independent, they believe in providing for themselves. In addition, in the Big Pine Valley, a man's word is still worth more than a written contract.

This is a place where you can leave your doors unlocked when you go to town. You can also leave the windows down in your car and the keys in the ignition while you're in church or visiting. This is a community where the hammer you laid down when you were fixing the mailbox on the road will still be there next week when you finally remember where you had it last.

I've read about how newcomers to a rural area are not accepted by the old-time residents. Here it is a little different. Generally, old-timers will adopt the folks who move in near them. Don and Geraldine adopted us. Leonard and Alma adopted Frank and Barbara. Clem and Ruby adopted Neil and Pat, and Wade and Clara were there to help Jim and Mary.

I guess you can tell we like this secluded valley and its people. They have accepted us and made us feel at home. You'll have to go a long way to find a prettier place to live or better folks for neighbors.

I hope you will become better acquainted with our friends and neighbors—and the valley in general—as you go through this book. Maybe you'll see why this is now the place where our hearts are.

Leonard bales hay in steep hillside field typical of Big Pine Valley (left). Above, "Felix", the Weber cat, takes it easy, storing up energy in case he has to do something. Rambling rose and old chimney are about all that's left of early home (below).

On sunny hillside at left, farmers once grew rows of corn along each of the little terraces. Colorful blossom above is a rhododendron. Below: Barbara visits Wade and "Roscoe". When Wade was married, he and his brother Clyde built this house, then built one for Clyde.

Wade stands with hoe in tobacco patch (above) while Chad and Allan "plow". Folks in the Big Pine Valley refer to weeding or cultivating as plowing. At left, a goldfinch sits among wild azalea buds. Right: The Evan Roberts cabin, built in the 1830's, is the oldest in the valley.

In his 90's, "Mr. Mac" poses in front of his old store with Dayton, the valley's mailman (right). Below, bee pollinates apple blossoms. Bottom: Barbara Weber's summer harvest lines cellar shelves ready for winter; Spitzberg apples are one variety grown in the valley.

"Snowflake" (with her calf at left) got her name because she was born during a snowstorm. Thad gets a free ride on Dad's workhorse (right) while Levi heads home for dinner (below).

Peaches from a Weber tree (above) will taste good on breakfast cereal. Below, black-eyed Susans are among many valley wildflowers. One of Wade's haystacks (right) has a locust pole in the center to keep it on the hillside. When Gerald took sick, he and Betty Lou (bottom) couldn't "hand" their tobacco, so neighbors held "a workin'" and did it for them.

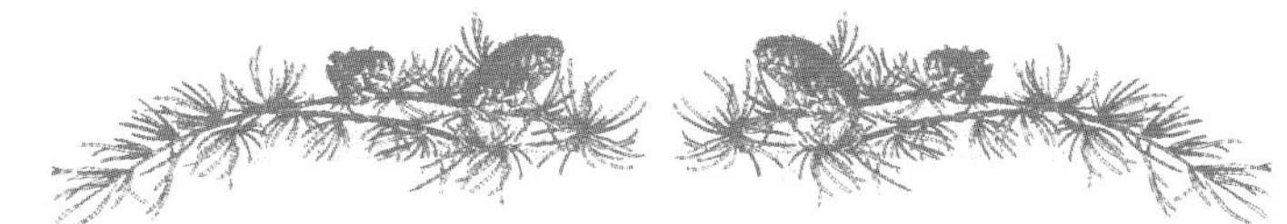

Friends & Neighbors

Once old-timers in the valley adopt you, there's nothing they won't do for you. They'll bring you tomatoes, cabbages, flowers and other plants for your garden. When you're haying, they'll come over and help out.

If you try to do something nice to repay them, the effort is always returned twofold. You can never catch up in favors returned, let alone get ahead. Don and Geraldine Wild are typical of the best of friends and neighbors.

We bought our farm from Don and Geraldine. It had been the upper part of their farm, so they became our closest neighbors and among our best friends. At the time of the purchase, Don was in his late 60's and wanted to sell some land and slow down a little. He estimated the land we wanted to buy at 50 acres, more or less.

Later we had the land surveyed and discovered we'd gotten 64 acres. Instead of feeling they'd been paid too little money, Geraldine said, "I'm so glad! I'd have felt terrible if you'd ended up with only 50 acres." That's the kind of folks they are—always giving more than they receive.

Don is one of the few people I know who has actually lived according to the Golden Rule. Before he retired and moved down off the hill into town, he was the one the widows called for help. Ruby-Noah called him when her spring stopped up. Eulala would hint about her garden needing to be tilled. Don always took them to the doctor or the store. No matter how busy he was, he'd pick up groceries for a family that didn't have a car. Beside him and always doing more than her part was his gentle wife, Geraldine.

Don Wild, born and raised in the Big Pine Valley, sold part of his farm to Bill and Barbara, then helped them build their house.

As a fourth-generation farmer in the Big Pine Valley, Don worked hard all his life scratching a living from the soil. Rising before dawn, he milked his cows for the cheese plant, raised a few beef cattle, fattened a couple of hogs, kept a flock of chickens, grew corn and tobacco and put up hay. His work was important to him, but so are his children and grandchildren, his friends and his church.

He taught me a lot about valley traditions. He also taught me practical things about gardening, fencing, cutting firewood and heading up a spring. He showed me how to "burst a tree for stakes" and where to plant my potatoes. When I had potato bugs or bean beetles, he showed me how to get rid of them.

Our younger son, John, came in the summer when he was out of college to help build our house. He especially enjoyed Geraldine's cooking and one Sunday he counted the various dishes on her table. "Sixteen, and two desserts, not including the biscuits and corn bread!" he exclaimed, while Geraldine blushed with pride.

"Let's see," continued John, "there are three salads, potatoes fixed two ways, green beans, peas, turnips, sweet corn, applesauce, pickled beets, cabbage, little sweet pickles, cucumbers, pork chops and baked steak. And everything is so good." He then made himself one of Geraldine's favorites when he told her, "I can't eat any more, but those biscuits are so good, I'd sure like to put a couple in my shirt pocket for later if that's all right."

While we helped Don a little, he helped us a lot over the years. Anytime we had a big job on the house, Don would show up to lend a hand. I would point out that he had his own work to do but that never stopped him. He helped mix cement, frame up walls, nail on siding and roof panels, and put oak boards on the porch frame. He was a pleasant companion and a good worker.

But he refused any payment, saying, "This is what neighbors are for." We ran our cows together and helped each other put up hay. I helped him "pull" corn in the fall. Since I was a veterinarian, I could vaccinate his cows and calves, dog and cat, and offer free veterinary help when needed. It was the one place where I could really help him.

When Don told us a couple of years ago that he was moving in to town to be near his daughters, we felt a great loss. He was sneaking up on 80 and had some health problems, so we understood. We still visit him and Geraldine, and they visit us, but we sure do miss them as neighbors.

Also among our good friends and neighbors are Wade and Clara Massey. Wade and his brother Clyde always helped when either Don or I was putting up hay. Of course, they refused any payment, too. Since both farmed with teams, they didn't have any way to bale their hay. Instead, they usually put it in stacks, especially in steep fields.

When Bill and Barbara found the little hillside farm of their dreams, it took five summers for them to build a house by hand (above and left). Now they have friends like Grace, who keeps wood for her cookstove in one of the neatest piles Bill has seen anywhere (above left). Coneflowers (far left) add color to the Webers' yard.

Wade mows hay (inset) and does his other farming with horses. His farm is over on Sugar Camp (above), one of the coves in the Big Pine Valley.

In an effort to be as good a neighbor as they were, I would take my tractor into their field after they'd mowed and "kick" the hay, fluffing it up so it would dry faster. Then Don would come in and bale for them, and we would both help them get the bales in the barn. We became a good haying crew, working together and getting a lot more done.

Barbara and I enjoy hearing Wade and Clara talk about the early days in the valley. They were both born and raised here. Shortly after they were married, Wade used his savings of $701 to buy 28 acres where they now live alongside the creek.

"It was all I had, but there was an old house on the place," Wade says. "Clara and I lived in that house and made out all right for about 3 years till I'd saved up enough to build a new house.

"I couldn't find a contractor, so my brother Clyde and I just started building it ourselves. When we didn't know how to do something, we'd go find someone to ask. I guess we just didn't know any better, but we built the house. It cost me $2,000—all I had—so we were broke again."

That was about 50 years ago. Wade and Clara still live in the house he and Clyde built. Wade grows a large tobacco crop and also has corn and hay. He raises cattle and has a big garden near the house.

Every year he harvests about 75 bushels of potatoes for winter storage. With just himself and Clara to feed, there's no way all those potatoes will be eaten by spring. When I once teased Wade about growing so many, he answered, "Better to have some extra because you never know when that might be all you have to eat."

Even though Barbara and I grow potatoes, too, Wade always offers us some for eating and for seed in the spring. He also shares his potatoes with other families he knows can use them.

Wade didn't just help us…he helped Jim and Mary, too. He taught them about growing their tobacco and helped them put up their hay. He is a good neighbor and enjoys helping folks.

Clyde was in his late 70's when we first met him, but he still worked hard. He had no car, so he walked everywhere, whether it was to help us farm or work his own fields or visit with neighbors. One morning he came walking up to our house with a young rooster under his arm.

"Knew you had some hens and thought you could probably use a rooster," he explained as he sat down to visit a few minutes. We wouldn't have been able to refuse that rooster even if we'd wanted to. We named the rooster "Drumstix" and he became one of our favorite pets.

Clyde also helped Kella and Novena when Kella got sick and went into the hospital for surgery. Every morning early, Clyde walked up to Kella's place to split wood for Novena's stove and to feed and care for the stock. That's just the way Clyde was.

As a young man, he was one of those who left the valley to seek his fortune. He went over to Tennessee and worked as a logger when they were clearing land for Fontana Dam. He came back for a while and then went to the auto plants in Detroit. When he finally returned to the valley for good, he got married and bought land next to Wade. The two of them built Clyde's house.

It was funny to see them work their farms together. As brothers, they were linked by both blood and spirit. But each had his own way of doing things, which made for more than a few warm discussions. Clyde liked mules and Wade liked horses, so they'd argue the merits of both regularly.

Once I was helping them get in some thick, heavy hay. Wade was riding the mower and Clyde was following behind with a pitchfork. Clyde's job was to move some of the hay over so it wouldn't clog the mower the next time around. Wade stopped to let the horses rest for a few minutes and we three sat down in the grass.

Wade said, " 'Mike' and 'Trigger' are 20 years old now. Like me, they need to rest a little more often." He'd had them since they were colts and it was obvious they meant a great deal to him.

"A good pair of mules and you wouldn't have to sit and rest like this," agitated Clyde.

"Now, Clyde," Wade retorted, "you know that when they were young, Mike and Trigger were as good a team as there was, horse or mule. They could work all day without slowing a bit."

Clyde was quiet a minute. Then he conceded, "Yes, they *could*

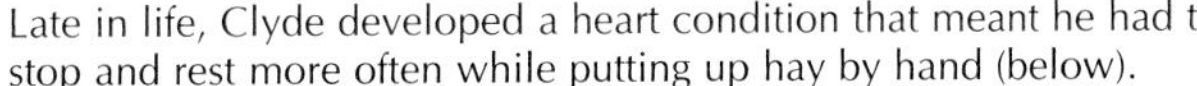

Late in life, Clyde developed a heart condition that meant he had to stop and rest more often while putting up hay by hand (below).

work when they were young. I guess that when measured in their years, they are a lot older than we are."

Wade climbed back on the mower and clucked to the horses. I watched him and Clyde take off across the slope and had to laugh to myself. I'd worked with both and knew they could still work most of us younger guys into the ground.

When Clyde was in his 80's, he developed a heart condition. Some nights it got so bad he had to sleep sitting up. Nonetheless, he still showed up to hay with us. He'd work so hard it would scare me. When I couldn't stand it any longer, I'd say, "Clyde, slow down and rest for a bit...we don't want you falling over dead here in the hay field."

His reply was always the same: "Can't think of a place I'd rather die." He accepted no sympathy or favors and insisted on doing his share.

Toward the end of his life, Clyde had only one mule left to plow his little patches of corn and tobacco. The mule got to eat most of the corn, but the chickens got some, too.

Clyde loved the early mornings. He'd get up in the dark and walk up the little hill from his house to the barn to feed his mule a couple ears of corn. He talked to the mule and patted him as he ate. They were quite a pair, Clyde and that mule!

One morning in November several years back, a friend found Clyde lying on the frozen ground. He'd walked up the hill to feed the mule just like always, but his old heart had given out as he was lifting the rails off the gate. He still had two ears of corn in his hand.

I guess Clyde died exactly the way he wanted to. I still have a few things around our place that remind me of him. There's those fence stakes he split out of hard yellow locust, then sharpened with his ax. And there's the wood handle he carved for my cant hook.

Clyde also gave me a little hemlock seedling that's now a tall healthy tree. A lot of us in the Big Pine Valley think Clyde was the very best kind of friend and neighbor.

Earl Roberts, in his 60's, is another good friend and neighbor. He lives about halfway down the creek with his wife, Viola. Earl still farms with horses. He is the first man in the valley to put out his tobacco, and it always looks good. Part of traveling down the valley road is checking everyone's garden and tobacco. This is not a malicious evaluation, but rather to see how your crops are doing compared to others in the valley.

Earl's tobacco is always greener and growing better than most along the road. I've watched Earl work his horse cultivating tobacco. He is a lot like Wade in that he talks to his horse all the time they are working. And the horse seems to acknowledge and respond to the suggestions Earl makes.

It is a pleasure to see them do a great deal of work in a short time. Earl's plots are small and, as he says, "With a horse I can plant right out to the edge. A tractor needs room to turn around, but 'Tony' can go out to the end, turn and never step on a plant."

Tobacco is the primary—if not only—source of cash in the valley. Farmers use the cash to buy what they can't produce themselves. In the fall, they hang tobacco in the barn to cure (above).

Both Earl and Viola are strong supporters of the volunteer fire department. Last year, as a fund-raiser, the fire department decided to grow some tobacco.

One patch was down near Earl's house. The plan was that folks would donate a little time and effort and, with all their help, the job would be done. The fire department would earn several thousand dollars to pay some of its insurance and other costs.

Earl knew when the tobacco should be worked, and instead of calling the volunteers, he and Viola just took care of it themselves. They raised the tobacco for the department.

When the department has a yard sale, a supper or a workin', you

"Our place is all hills," says Bill. "There's nowhere flat enough to set a glass of water without spilling it." The field at right, where Bill is raking hay, is an example. Earl, sporting a volunteer fire department cap above, is one of many valley folks who give freely of their time to help neighbors and the community. Below: fall asters.

can count on Earl and Viola being there to help. During the big snowstorm some years back, when for days no traffic could move up Big Pine Road, Earl went out with his horses and opened driveways for all his neighbors. He made certain they had food and firewood before he left.

One of his neighbors, Elizabeth, lives alone. Earl checked on her regularly to be sure she was all right. When he found she had not gotten in her wood that fall, he and Viola went up and cut enough to get her through the winter.

Earl and Viola grow Christmas trees as well as tobacco. Every year in November when it's time to buy Christmas trees, folks start coming out from Asheville to see Earl and pick out their trees.

It's enjoyable for them to come out to the country, and enjoyable for Earl, too—he likes visiting with his customers. He can count on the same folks coming every year. It has become part of the ritual of the season.

Since Don moved to town, I have become part of Leonard Buckner's haying crew. His crew consists of his son Ronnie; Ronnie's boys, Brandon and Bryan, when they are home; Jim, one of our neighbors; Wade; and me. We help Leonard put up his hay and he helps Wade and me put up ours.

It is a pretty congenial group that works together well. There is a lot of kidding and storytelling as the hay is baled, piled on trailers and stored in the barns. The fields are pretty small—in an afternoon, we will put up 500 bales. For the season, Leonard puts up about 5,000 bales as winter feed.

Ronnie and I run cows together. So part of the hay is winter feed for *our* cows. Ronnie, with three young'uns—two of them in college—has to work hard just to keep up. He works full-time at the supermarket in town and farms full-time growing tobacco, hemlock trees and hay, as well as keeping cows.

All of Leonard's family works right along with him. His grown daughters make time in their lives to come home to help plant and cut the tobacco, and to hang it in the barn. It is not unusual to see three generations of the family out hoeing in the field. Ronnie cultivates with "Gyp", Leonard's horse, while the rest clean all the weeds from the field with hoes.

Leonard works almost as hard for the North Fork Church as he does on the farm. He's been a deacon as long as we have been here. You can count on it: If the church needs painting or other work, Leonard will be there. He will also be in the choir every Sunday, singing with his friends and neighbors.

We enjoy going by his home and visiting on Sunday afternoons.

Horse-pulled rake, abandoned for a tractor, rusts amid dogwood (below left). Below: a great-tasting mountain-grown tomato and some daisies.

He remembers well what it was like growing up here in the valley. His stories of working, hunting, logging and "courting" Bass' daughter, Alma, who became his wife, make life in the valley as it was back then come alive.

There are many more friends and neighbors to tell about. Last August our mailman, Dayton, began leaving big ripe tomatoes from his garden in our mailbox. He'd heard that my crop of tomatoes had been ruined by "blight", so from then till the first hard frost killed all his healthy green vines, Dayton left tomatoes amongst our letters and packages.

Bruce and Brenda, Dean and Mary Ann, Gerald and Betty Lou, Ray and Margaret, Leonard and Faye, Roy and Janice—they're all the kind of friends and neighbors that make living in the Big Pine Valley so wonderful!

Bill hoes between rows of sweet corn, beans, cukes and tomatoes (below) while a swallowtail lights on a zinnia (right).

Bright fall colors light up Bill and Barbara's farm in the Big Pine Valley (left). Uncle Bass, who taught Bill so much about the history and customs of the valley, inspects his crop of broomcorn (above).

Viola exhibits one of her quilts (above). The pattern—a favorite of hers—is Double Wedding Ring. The many quilters in the valley not only carry on an old tradition but see quilting as a chance to have a friendly get-together. Meanwhile, bees like the one on a cosmos (upper right) and tobacco farmers (right) go about their busy days. In August, tobacco stalks are speared on sticks and left hanging in the field to begin to cure.

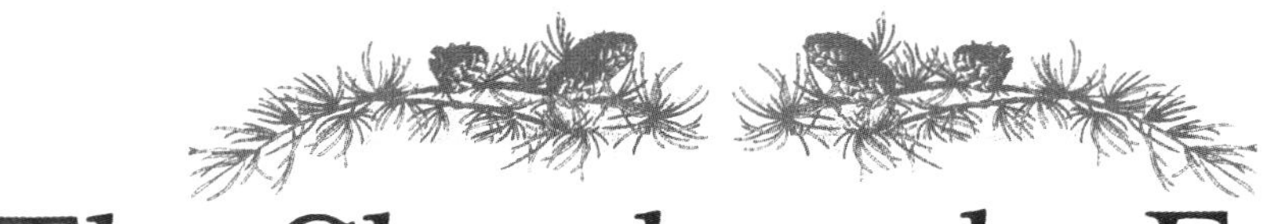

The Church at the Forks

The first Church at the Forks was built of logs...the second of pine planks painted white (above). Today the walls are brick, but the little church remains the center of valley life.

Way back in 1867, a small group of Big Pine Valley families started meeting for church in Absolom Buckner's house. Absolom was Leonard's great-great-granddad. Soon, this group decided to build a log church on 2 acres of donated land at the confluence of the north and south forks of Big Pine Creek.

Ever since, folks have called it the "Church at the Forks", even though its formal name is North Fork Baptist Church. Later when the road was built up the valley, it split at the church and skirted around Fork Mountain, with the north fork ending up at Ducket's Top and the south fork below Dick's Knob.

Thus did the little Church at the Forks become both a geographic and spiritual center in the valley. The upstairs was used as the valley's first school, and when there was a reason for folks to gather, they did so in the church.

Most important, the Church at the Forks was a source of courage for the families who clung to the valley even in the hardest of times. There were church meetings twice on Sundays, once in the morning and once in the evening. There were also meetings on Wednesday and Saturday evenings.

When someone died, all the men would come to the church cemetery and together dig the grave. No fee has ever been charged for members of the congregation to be buried in the church's pretty little cemetery. That even applies to folks who once lived in Big Pine Valley but moved away.

In 1903, the little log church burned to the ground. That's when the present church was built. This time it was made of heart-pine siding and painted white. Another building was erected nearby as a school. Years later, when yellow buses began hauling valley kids to classes elsewhere, the old school building was sold for $400.

When Barbara and I first came to the valley, the little Church at the Forks was still white, but the wood siding had become hard and brittle and very difficult to paint. A few years later, the congregation decided to hire a contractor to cover the wood with brick.

I've always missed the white wood, even if it didn't hold paint too well anymore. Once when I mentioned this to Leonard, he said, "I guess we all miss the little white church. But you know that painting the outside every couple years was getting harder and harder.

"We old guys don't like getting up on top of those ladders any longer, and we don't have too many younger men in church to take over the job."

On our first visit to the little Church at the Forks, we were the guests of Don Wild, one of the deacons. His great-grandfather, Jacob, was a preacher and the first of the Wilds to come to the Big Pine Valley. Jacob helped cut and mill the logs for the first church and also preached there.

After the fire in 1903, Don's grandfather, George, helped build the present church and paint it white. A few years later, he decided to supply both the church and his house just across the creek with electricity. He dammed up the creek and installed an "overshot" waterwheel—one where the water comes down a long race or flume from higher up the creek, then pours over the wheel from the top.

The waterwheel supplied the power for a generator, which lit the church for evening meetings and also replaced the oil lamps in George's own house. Once George had power, he bought his wife an electric churn and washing machine.

A few years later, George replaced the waterwheel with a newfan-

Uncle Bass' headstone (left) marks where he was put to rest at 94. Even today, the men of the valley come to the cemetery when a new grave needs digging (top left). Above: Leonard Buckner and his wife, Alma, enjoy Homecoming, as important an event at the Church at the Forks as Sunday meeting and "workin's".

gled turbine and supplied electricity to some of his neighbors' houses. Still not satisfied, he then installed crank phones in his and his neighbors' houses, stringing phone wires between fence posts and trees.

One of the most important events at the Church at the Forks has always been what folks call Homecoming. Held in early summer after all the planting is done, it is more important than most other holidays, including the Fourth of July. Homecoming is a time when families with relatives in the church cemetery come to honor them and to decorate their graves. It's a family time, a time for remembering, when even folks who have moved away come back to visit.

Over the years, the flowers on the graves have changed from wild purple rhododendrons, orange daylilies, white daisies and other native flowers to longer-lasting silk and plastic arrangements. In our first summer here, we visited the cemetery on the evening before Homecoming with Jerry, one of our neighbors.

Crippled since birth, Jerry uses two canes to walk. He is still very active and farms with his dad. As we passed his mother's grave, we saw a quart jar with a beautiful white cloud of wild daisies pressed against the gray headstone.

Before we could say a word, Jerry reached for the jar and pitched the flowers into the nearby ravine. "They just don't look good enough," was his choked explanation.

He had picked the flowers in the dim light of dawn and carried them up the hill to the grave. But now he felt they couldn't compete with the brighter artificial flowers on nearby graves. To Barbara and

There's more than enough food for even the heartiest appetites at Homecoming (right). After decorating the graves of their relatives (below), Big Pine Valley folks attend church services, then visit with friends, some of whom they see only at this annual get-together.

me, they were more beautiful, but our words would not console him.

On Homecoming Sunday, families go to the cemetery to talk and visit. They wander among the stones, exchanging remembrances. Then they go inside to worship together in the little Church at the Forks. They can count on an uplifting message from the preacher and some enjoyable music from the choir.

After the service, they eat at food-laden tables placed in the shade of the big maple trees just behind the church. There is more great home-cooked food than three times as many people could possibly eat. Chicken, hams, meat loaf, all sorts of casseroles, more varieties of vegetables fixed in tasty ways than can be described—these women are great cooks!

Salads, breads, puddings, cakes, and pies compete for space both on the tables and on the crowded dinner plates. Going back for seconds is mandatory, and thirds, if you are able, are appreciated by the cooks.

Then, while volunteers clean up the tables, most folks go back into the church for an hour or so of singing. The congregation, choir, quartets and soloists contribute in turn. Afterward, families return to their home place for more visiting.

Every year Alma's brother Rex and his wife, Shirley, like members of many other families, come all the way from Michigan for Homecoming. "It's the only time we can get together and enjoy each other's company," Rex says.

Homecoming, Bible school in summer, the Christmas play, an Easter sunrise service on the hill and "workin's"—they're all an important part of the little Church at the Forks.

Some things you're likely to see at Homecoming: Folks like Rex and Shirley (above), who return every year to the Big Pine Valley from out of state just for this occasion...Connie and Kay decorating the altar with wildflowers...a luna moth spreading its delicate wings.

Mail carrier Dayton Wild took the photo above of Fork Mountain with Don's corn shocks lining the road. It's here near the church that Big Pine Road splits to go around Fork Mountain. Below, the Church at the Forks decked out in the bricks that replaced the old pine siding. Weather vane atop the church (right) features Gabriel blowing a horn.

Wisdom & Folklore

One way to get to know a people is to listen to their sayings and learn their folklore. Most of the sayings I've heard here in the Big Pine Valley contain a kind of wisdom that is as much a part of the valley as the crops that grow on the hillsides.

I've been told, for example, that "the best time to build a rail fence is during a new moon. If you put the bottom rail down then, it won't rot into the ground."

In the early days, fences were made with rails split from chestnut trunks. Chestnut was considered the most durable wood and you could count on it to split into nice straight rails. Typically, these fences were eight to 10 rails high and were used to pen horses, cattle and hogs.

Potatoes, too, were planted according to phases of the moon and signs of the zodiac. "Planting when the moon is full is best," the saying goes. "Don't plant when the signs are in the feet or the potatoes will grow lots of little toes. If you plant on a new moon, you'll get all vines and no potatoes."

Before Barbara and I moved into the valley, Geraldine used to write us nice folksy letters. The way she described the valley made us long even more for it. In one letter, she was talking about what folks here call "the grassland"—a 40- or 50-acre patch of treeless meadow on top of one of the mountains that's good for grazing cattle.

"The grassland with its white snowy face has really glistened in the sunlight all during February," she wrote. "One night last week we had a thunderstorm and all the old-timers say that means we'll have a frost on that same date in May."

Old-timers believe they can predict fall's first frost by when katydids start singing in summer.

In another letter, Geraldine wrote, "The two guinea hens that Smithy gave us hollered all day yesterday. Mama always told us that the weather was going to change when the guineas began to chant 'pat-e-rack, pat-e-rack'."

I've also heard from others in the valley—Wade, Ruby-Ray, Clyde Davis, Kella—many more tidbits of folklore and local wisdom:

"When the trees turn their leaves up so you can see the undersides, it's about to rain. The number of fogs in August indicate the number of snows in winter; not much fog, light snow. The first frost of fall comes 9 weeks after you hear the first katydid sing.

"If the ice in November will bear a duck, there will be nothing after but slush and mud. Fair on September 1, fair for the month. September dries up wells or washes out bridges. Listen, the creek is making more noise, so it's going to rain!"

Of course, some sayings have more to do with the behavior of humans than the behavior of nature. Here are some of Don's favorites:

"Beware the man whose overalls show more wear on the seat than the front. Two inches can make a great deal of difference, especially if it's on the end of your nose. A man's never so tired he can't lift a hand to wave 'hello'."

A custom that I really appreciate has to do with how folks sometimes refer to each other. As you might imagine, in a close-knit community made up of people whose families go back generations, there are lots of folks with the same first name.

Because everyone around here is on a first-name basis, it can be hard to keep track of who's being referred to in a conversation. For example, I know a number of women named Ruby. Each attaches her husband's name to her own to help keep track of who's who.

Ruby-Noah is Noah's wife, Ruby-Clem, Clem's wife and Ruby-Ray, Ray's wife.

When we first moved here, Ruby-Noah introduced us to an expression that took us a while to figure out. Eventually, however, I realized that when she said "blinked milk" she meant milk that had gone a little sour. "My father truly enjoyed blinked milk," Ruby-Noah told me. "He'd put it on a big piece of corn bread for supper."

Another expression that really had me perplexed when I heard it was "ball-hootin' ". It turned out to mean a tractor—or some other object—sliding off one of our many steep hillsides. Because the fields are so steep, a tractor will sometimes get to sliding even though the brakes work fine. On ground that's wet or soft, the wheels might not get enough traction and the tractor will go ball-hootin' downhill. At such a time, there's nothing you can do but hang on and pray.

It wasn't as hard to figure out what Dayton meant when he said that whenever his dad saw him "loafering" near the house, he'd whistle from the field. Then Dayton would have to grab a hoe and start chopping weeds out of the tobacco or corn.

One thing I still can't get used to, however, is how folks in the valley use the word "evening". If Ruby-Clem says, "I'm going to town this evening," she means she could be leaving anytime after noon. Evening starts a lot earlier here and includes the whole afternoon.

There are many more interesting sayings and expressions in the Big Pine Valley. Most have at least a nugget of truth or practicality, but I enjoy them as much for their colorful expression as for their wisdom.

Maybe the one I like best, though, is the one I hear most: "Come with us and we'll go on home and get a bite to eat."

Geraldine (at left with husband Don) taught Bill valley wisdom and folklore. Among her sayings: "Thunder in February means frost on the same date in May." Other old-timers like Kella (above) and Uncle Bass, crossing the creek on his "foot log" (right), helped Bill learn the ways of nature and people in the valley.

Chapter 2

The Changing Seasons

Firewood

Getting in firewood is as much a part of the fall ritual in the Big Pine Valley as pulling corn or making molasses. On the first cold crisp day in late September, you suddenly hear the high-pitched whine of chain saws coming from all over the valley.

Most families still heat with wood, and many use wood stoves for cooking. On chilly mornings, the women look forward to working in the warm kitchen.

Hardwood forests line the steep slopes of the valley, so there are always plenty of dead trees for firewood. Nature helps out when, during summer storms, lightning strikes kill a number of trees. The following spring, with the ground wet and spongy, frisky winds can shake a big hickory or oak loose, causing it to tumble and become that fall's firewood.

Today, most of us use tractors to reach our selected firewood trees. The small branches are immediately trimmed off. We leave the large limbs on to "grab" the hillside, keeping the tree from rolling as we work it down the slope. On the steepest ground, horses bring out the trees. If you don't have a horse, your neighbor does and will be glad to help.

When we get our felled trees home, we first cut the trunks into chunks about 18 inches long and 12 to 16 inches in diameter. These make good "night sticks"—logs that are put in the fire last to give heat all night long. In olden times, these large logs were placed way in the back of the fireplace at night and were called "back sticks".

The rest of the trunk is split into manageable pieces using wedges and a sledge. The sound of wood cracking accompanies the ringing of the metal sledge. Each chunk of wood may be split and split again, depending on whether it is to be used for starting the fire or to provide longer-lasting heat.

For the kitchen stove, wood is cut into pieces about 12 inches long and only about an inch or 2 in diameter. The stove wood is stacked on the back porch or placed in a shed where it dries thoroughly. That way it burns readily and gives off its heat quickly. Locust, hickory and oak are the choices for good stove wood. Hard dense woods, they provide a lot of heat without making a great pile of ashes.

Generally, several live trees are included in the winter wood supply. That's because a green log, once you get it started, will burn longer. In the Big Pine Valley, having a generous supply of firewood stacked near the house for winter is as important as stocking the cellar with canned fruits and vegetables, or filling the barn with hay.

Getting in firewood means getting out not just the chain saw (right) but tools like those in inset photo at top right: a log lifter, cant hook, splitting maul, steel wedges and big wedges called "gluts". Above left: Splitting maul finishes job started with a wedge.

Most firewood is cut from dead trees, many killed by lightning. Wade snags just such a tree out of a hollow with the help of "Jeffrey" (below). Large branches are left on trees to keep them from rolling down steep hillsides (left). Once trunks are sawed into blocks, wedges are set to split the blocks (right) while a tire holds the blocks in place.

Some folks still dry their firewood the old-fashioned way—in a covered stack called a "pigpen" (above). Nowadays, most folks in the Big Pine Valley use horses when the trees are on terrain too steep or boggy for tractors. But the journey from hillside to home usually is made by modern convenience (top). In the end, the true test of good firewood is how well it burns, and Bill and Barbara have a good blaze going in the living room stove they use for heat (right).

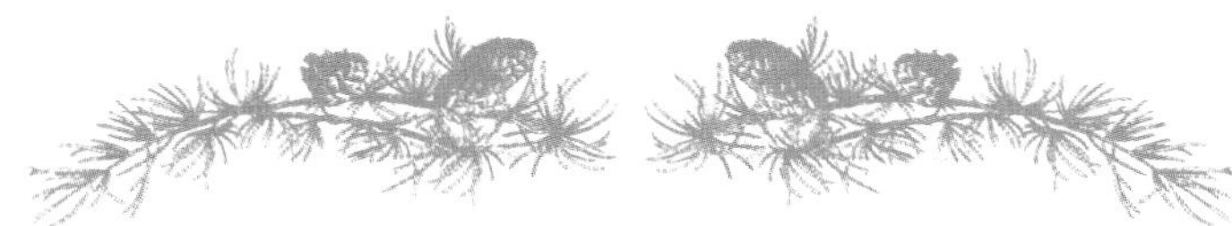

Fall Is Here Again

Tobacco is in the barns, the cover crop of rye has been disked into the ground and the cornstalks are turning yellow. Here and there, fall colors are beginning to appear on the hills. Buckeye trees are the first to show gold in their leaves, followed by walnuts and hickories.

It is amazing how we look forward to this change of seasons each year. You'd think it would be old stuff after so many times around. Brisk mornings, cool days, rich blue skies—fall is here again!

In the Big Pine Valley, the colors are spectacular. With the first frost of September, the changing leaves become one of the regular topics of conversation...along with the price of corn and cattle.

"You know, I think it's been too dry this summer to get the best color," you'll hear someone say. Or: "We've had so much rain the leaves will drop early this year."

Someone else may counter: "No, it should be a good color year...just not as good as 2 years ago." Opinions about how the leaves will turn—and when they'll reach their peak—are as varied as the path of milkweed seeds on September's blustery breezes.

As I drive the road that follows Big Pine Creek, I am an avid leaf watcher. I look for the smallest hint of change, trying to rush the season. Blue asters, called "frost weed" by folks here, and yellow goldenrod add their color to the hills. Less noticeably, the witch hazel trees bloom with yellow string-like flowers. That's the only tree I know that *blooms* in fall.

In a good year, the red dogwood berries, wild rose hips, spicebush berries, wild grapes, greenbrier berries, hickory nuts, walnuts and plentiful fat acorns assure the wildlife a bountiful supply of food. It's fun to watch the squirrels work in the big white oak below the house. They ignore the acorns on the ground and others that are easy to get, and go instead out on the very tips of branches for just the right one. When winter draws closer, they won't be as particular and will start burying all they can find.

The blue jays enjoy the acorns, too, but they don't bother storing any. They grab an acorn with their strong beaks and tear it loose from the tree. Moving to a sturdy branch, they clasp the acorn tightly against the limb with their toes and hammer it with that sharp beak. Three or four strokes and the nut is out of the shell and quickly swallowed.

The days are noticeably shorter as September moves to October. These shorter days send a signal to the tree that its year is over. The green chlorophyll fades from the leaves, allowing the underlying colors to show through. Yellows, oranges, reds, purples, tans and browns appear, making fall vivid.

Beech, birch, black cherry, locust, sycamore and poplar take on shades of yellow. Ash, sourwood and black gums turn reddish-purple. But the maples are the "stars". Some are bright yellow and orange while others are cloaked with shimmering red leaves. As Garrison

Fall brings vivid colors to a hillside seen from Troublesome Gap Road (above). Inset: Old-timers cut the tops off cornstalks so ears dry sooner. The tops of stalks are used as fodder to feed livestock.

Keillor puts it, it's "a red so brilliant that Crayola never put it in crayons for fear the children would color outside the lines".

Most of the oaks are russet or brown, but they add interesting contrast to the hillsides with their own hues and shades. The large vistas of changing colors challenge you to notice what's happening with individual trees. This is the time to wander the hills collecting walnuts, ginseng and hickory nuts. Folks hereabouts refer to ginseng as "sang". In fall, sang decorates itself with bright red berries.

The wonderful musky aroma of woods and fallen leaves fills the valley. It is more noticeable after a light rain or as you scuffle through the woods stirring up leafy windrows. Occasionally, the wispy smell of wood smoke drifts up the hill.

Henry David Thoreau put it better than I can: "It is pleasant to walk over the beds of these fresh, crisp and rustling leaves of a thousand hues. How beautifully they go to their graves."

In November, the cold winds tear the last of the leaves loose and the trees are left standing as stark black silhouettes waiting patiently for another spring.

By now, the tobacco has been compressed into bales and carried to the sale barns. All the corn is in the cribs to dry, and the people and the land seem to rest. There will still be chores to do, but the hectic season of work is over till next spring.

When Tessie Wild attended the Presbyterian school here in the valley back in the early 1900's, she learned a little poem about fall being over. Tessie passed the poem on to her children, and her son, Dayton, passed it on to me:

Come little leaves, said the wind one day,
Come over the meadows with me and play.
Put on your dresses of red and gold;
Summer is gone and the day's growing cold.
Come little leaves! said the wind's loud call,
Down they came, fluttering one and all.
Over the fields they danced and flew,
Singing the songs that only they knew.
Dancing and flying, the little leaves went.
For winter was calling and they were content.

Ginseng—called "sang" in the Big Pine Valley—develops red berries in the fall. You can see them in photo snapped by Dayton Wild (above). Perhaps most colorful of all, however, are maples like one at right. Troublesome Gap Road (opposite page) runs through a tunnel of color. Small photos: a common but seldom seen flying squirrel gets its nest ready for winter...tufted titmouse peers out at the world...fall asters display their feathery finery.

Fall finds Bill picking liberty apples in his orchard (top) while scarecrow (top left) does *his* job. Sugar Camp Creek (left) is one of the tributaries to Big Pine Creek.

Old Davis cabin—abandoned by a family that moved elsewhere in search of its dream—nonetheless adds to scenic beauty of the valley (top). Hillside pasture (right) and grazing sheep (above) are both on Bill and Barbara's farm. Those are black-eyed Susans at top right.

Gathering potatoes to store in the cellar for winter is a major autumn activity (right). At far right, Don's pig checks out the gate to see whether it can be opened. The colorful trees above are on the Weber farm.

A browsing buck works its way warily through the woods looking for morsels (above). Fall weeds glisten in light of early morning mist (left). Right: A view of Big Pine Valley from Sugar Camp Road.

Fall is apple cider and walnut time. Above, hulled walnuts are gathered for cracking, then stored in jars in the freezer to await use in cakes and cookies. Meanwhile, apples are hauled in from the orchard (right), washed, quartered and run through a cider press like the one Mary's turning below, with help from Joan and Milton. The press once belonged to Bill's dad.

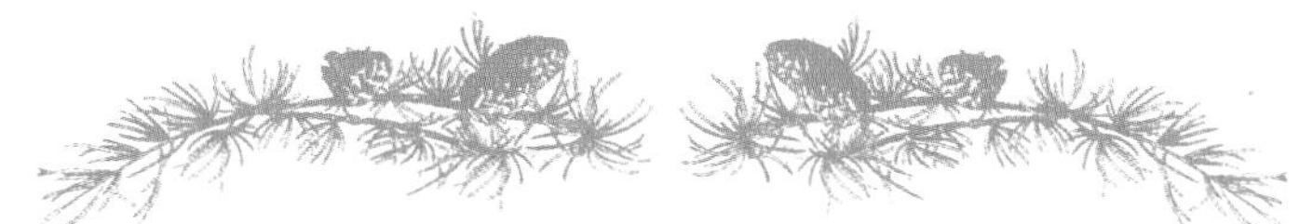

Winter's for Resting

During winter, the soil and people of Big Pine Valley get to rest. There are still chores to do—bales of hay must be carried from the barn to feed the always-hungry cows. Horses must be fed, eggs gathered and firewood carried in. Those who still have a cow must milk twice daily.

On warm days, equipment is pulled out of the shed and repaired or painted. A load of corn can be taken to the mill and "scrushed"—our word for running the ears with the kernels still on them through a hammer mill to get cobmeal for the cattle.

Many winter days are nice enough to do repair work on the barn, nailing up loose boards or replacing the ones that no longer hold the weather out. Around here, though, no one paints their barns; they are allowed to just weather to a steel gray.

The young people in the church put on a Christmas play. Rehearsals are an excuse for getting together and enjoying each other's company. After the play is over, the youngsters tour the valley singing Christmas carols and delivering baskets of fruit to the elderly.

When Barbara and I aren't here, we look forward to Geraldine's letters describing winter in the valley. "The holidays are over, the snow is gone and everything is so quiet and still," she wrote in one. "I don't think I've ever seen such a beautiful snow as the one we had on Christmas Day.

"The tree branches were bent down and it was a winter wonderland! If it hadn't been for having to cook dinner, I would have loved to walk and walk in it."

Snowy roads and hills *can* make valley life harder. Mostly, however, winter gets folks to snuggle up to a warm fire.

By the first of the year, even the most determined oak trees have given up the last of their leaves. In another of her letters, Geraldine wrote, "The wind is really howling around the house corners this morning. It may be warning us that cold weather is on the way."

When it does get cold—most often in January—temperatures can fall below zero. One winter, radio and television stations began issuing storm warnings on a Friday. By 10 a.m. Saturday, everyone knew the valley was going to have a huge snowfall.

Ronnie and Greg both worked in town at the supermarket at the time. When they were told by the manager to head for home, they set out in Ronnie's pickup. The farther up the valley they came, the deeper and heavier the snow got. About halfway home, some fallen trees blocked the road. Both men—young and strong—left the truck and started walking.

A mile up the road, a neighbor saw them passing and invited them in to warm up. While they were drinking hot coffee, the neighbor offered them some warm dry clothes for the rest of their walk.

Re-outfitted in heavy socks, boots, insulated coveralls, gloves and hats, Ronnie and Greg struck out again in snow up to their thighs. They stopped and rested at several homes as they struggled up the road.

When they finally got to Greg's folks' house at dark, both were exhausted. Ronnie still had another mile and a half to go to get home. He knew there was no way he could do it in the snow that was by then almost waist deep.

Telephones were out and he couldn't let his wife, Deborah, know he was safe. He'd called her before leaving the store, so she knew he was somewhere en route. She worried all night while he was sleeping safely. In the morning, he pushed out into the snow and covered the mile and a half home—in 3 hours.

Everyone did what they could to help neighbors. Dean fed Ronnie's cows because they were close to his house. Jimmy fed Wade's for the same reason. Volunteers from the fire department made their way on horseback to see that older folks living alone were warm and had food. Eventually every cove and hollow was checked.

For 3 days, even the snowplows couldn't get up Big Pine Road. Volunteers cleared away downed trees, but deep snow—and other priorities—kept the plows from clearing the road in this remote valley.

Slowly things returned to normal. The road was cleared, power restored and phones turned on again. The valley had survived the big 36-inch snow, giving everyone a topic of conversation for many months afterward.

Wintertime can be beautiful with new snow and a warm snug home. It can also be a time when even the smallest chores become difficult. Mostly, however, it is when all of us rest and build up energy for the spring farming that's just around the corner.

Bright winter scene was captured on film by Dayton as he delivered the mail one morning.

Wild turkeys like the one below have recently wintered in Eugene's field. Both Troublesome Gap Road (above) and Troublesome Gap Mountain (right) provide pretty winter scenery.

Kella's farm gets its first snow of the year (above). At right, it's a snowy Sunday morning at the Church at the Forks. Left: dogwood berries and titmouse out on a limb.

The view of the south fork of Big Pine Valley under a thin mantle of snow (above) is from Bill and Barbara's upper pasture. Fraser firs at left are on Smithy's Christmas tree farm. Dayton snapped photo of the old Baker place at right. It was built back in the days when winter cold easily found its way inside.

Above and right: Two more of Dayton's photos, taken along his 120-mile route with its 500 mailboxes. That's Almarie's dad, Curtis, and his horse hauling hay out to his cattle. Bill shot wintry scene at left.

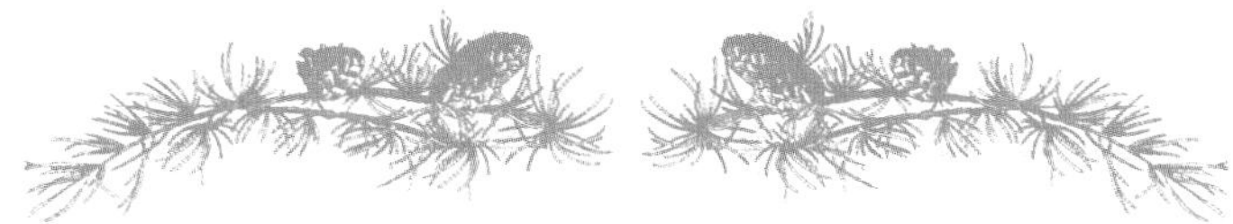

Spring Comes in Little Spurts

Grass starts growing while the trees are still stark and gray. Then, before there's much green anywhere, white bloodroot flowers appear. They are followed closely by yellow daffodils popping out of the ground.

Near our house and along the road, dogwoods deck themselves in white blossoms. Year after year, spring seems to come to the Big Pine Valley in little spurts.

From our porch, we make a point of counting the dogwoods in bloom. The fewest we can remember counting at one time is 23. Right along with the dogwoods come the redbuds...then the poplars and locusts. Locusts, too, sport white flowers, though they hang in grape-like clusters.

Day by day, as the rest of the trees leaf out, we watch a wave of green move slowly up the valley. It takes several weeks for the wave to reach the ridge tops.

The cows are moved into summer pasture from the barn lots where they have been fed all winter. They wander over the whole pasture checking to see if any hidden treasures of tasty vegetation have appeared since they left last fall. You can see how much they enjoy the tender new grasses after their winter diet of hay.

Warm spring weather moves the farmers in the valley into action, too. Tractors are serviced and horses groomed while the fields dry out enough to plow. During this time, fields are mentally planted in corn, tomatoes and tobacco.

Soon you can smell newly turned earth as you drive down Big Pine Road. Horses seem as eager as men to get into the fields after the inactivity of winter.

The wild azaleas that we planted next to the house suddenly burst into orange blooms. Along the roadside, azaleas that are still wild add to the season's first bright spots of color.

Early spring is when we expect our sheep to have their lambs. We watch them closely, ready to help if there is a problem in birth. We enjoy seeing these fluffy babies following their mothers in the pasture near the house. Soon they are playing together like small children—running, jumping and hollering to their mothers.

Wrens, filling the air with song, inspect nest sites near the porch. Every morning we awaken to a variety of bird songs, each signaling a claim to territory or a search for a mate. The phoebes start their nests on the shelf under the eaves...barn swallows dart in and out of the barn, building nests. Bluebirds sing near the nest boxes we have put up in the pasture.

Yes, it really is spring!

Apple, plum and cherry trees, all in full bloom, look like white clouds in the yard. They stand out even more against the pink blossoms of the peach tree. When the petals begin to drop, it's time to spray this year's fruit crop.

I wanted to be a purist when we moved here—no spray on any of my 100-plus fruit trees. Reality soon set in, however: Our two apricot trees weren't producing any fruit. As an experiment, we decided to spray one of the two trees with a mild insecticide and fungicide.

That year the tree that was sprayed every 2 weeks till early summer produced 3 bushels of apricots to can, eat and give to friends. The unsprayed tree yielded only three apricots. And as those ripened and changed color, brown spots appeared on the surface. Before they ever matured, the whole fruit was rotten.

When Barbara noticed that a third of the cherries she was pitting had worms, these trees were also added to the spray schedule. The six plum trees were soon sprayed as well.

As we saw the good results of our spraying, the peach and apple trees were added to the list. Now we had an abundance of fruit of all kinds, including grapes. It required a little more effort on my part, but the harvest of cherries in late spring, peaches in summer and apples

The smell of fresh earth being prepared for planting (right) is one of the sure signs that spring has arrived in the Big Pine Valley. Another is new lambs like the twins above born on Smithy's farm.

in fall made it all worthwhile...and I'm no longer a purist.

With the garden started, the fruit trees taken care of, and the cows "shedding off" and growing sleek, it is time to think "hay". There's usually plenty of moisture in the ground during winter and spring, so hay grows rapidly. The first cutting is after the middle of May. Frequent spring showers make it a challenge to guess the best time to mow.

Everyone wants to put the best possible hay in the barn. We listen to the weather reports, compare notes and then, when the forecast looks fair for a few days, mow. If we are lucky, the hay cures without being rained on. If it *is* rained on, it is fluffed up with the "kicker" to speed drying and we try again the next day.

When folks in the valley aren't putting up hay, they are planting corn and tobacco. Corn is for feeding stock, tobacco is for cash. Planting tobacco usually involves the whole family.

Plants from the bed started in early spring are pulled and placed in containers. It requires a lot of plants since about 5,000 per acre are put in. Actual planting takes four people.

One drives the tractor and two sit on the "baccer setter", feeding plants into the machine that waters the plants and puts them in the ground. The fourth person follows down each row to set out plants where the setter missed and straighten any that were planted poorly.

By the time we are cutting hay and the tobacco is planted, the wildflowers are blooming everywhere. Violets, wild geraniums, trilliums, wild iris—all add color to the creek banks and grassy slopes.

The whole valley is lush and green...the promise of spring has been kept again!

Black bear cub finds a comfortable perch in a tree (left). Above: A misty spring morning begins with sheep grazing between walnut and sycamore trees.

Other signs of spring (clockwise from bottom left): wild geraniums, buttercups, apple blossoms, mountain laurel, morning glories, violets and wild strawberries. In the center of this wreath of flower photos is a delicate whitetail fawn.

To plant tobacco (above), Connie and Kay ride the "baccer setter" while Leonard drives the tractor. The baccer setter places the plants—started earlier in a separate bed—in the ground. Putting up and painting bluebird houses (top right) is a springtime chore. Right: A robin feeds its young.

A sparrow chirps its welcome to spring (above) while cherries grow practically before your eyes (above right). At far right, Maggie, Judy and Smithy's daughter, feeds her two orphan lambs. Flame azaleas (below) contribute color to a Big Pine Valley spring. Right: A wren sits on the front porch of a house that's strictly for the birds.

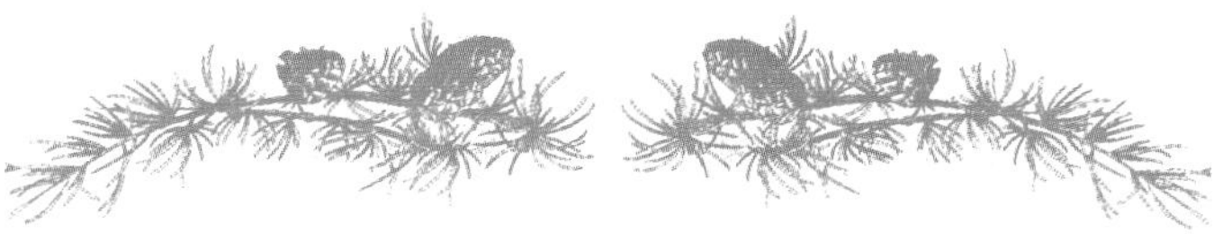

Summertime

Although the days are hot and humid during summer in the Big Pine Valley, a blanket always feels good at bedtime. In the evening when the sun disappears behind the west wall of the valley, things cool down quickly. But in the heat of the long days, you can see corn and tobacco grow taller by the hour.

There is much work to do as summer gets under way, and farmers stretch their days to 12 hours or more. Corn and tobacco must be hoed; the second crop of hay is about ready to bring in. Hay can usually be baled 2 days after it's mowed...unless, of course, it gets rained on.

Rain comes mostly in brief scattered thundershowers. From our place on the east side of the valley, we can see the Duckett fire tower high on a ridge to the southwest. Built many years ago of stone, it is still used in dry months.

When dark clouds roll around the Duckett tower, you can bet that it will be raining at our place soon. If you don't have hay down, it's nice to sit in a rocker on the porch and watch the rain march across the valley toward us. You can hear it coming as the big drops beat on the tree leaves.

The rain takes some of the moist haze of transpiration out of the air, making the valley smell clean and sweet. Besides cooling everything off, a shower helps the vegetables in the garden.

Summertime is garden time. Fresh sweet corn picked just before dinner...vine-ripe mountain-grown tomatoes warmed by the sun...cabbages getting ready for their conversion to sauerkraut... cucumbers just begging to be made into pickles—our garden is a joy from the moment we turn the soil and poke seeds into the ground till we finish harvesting it row by row.

When I first started gardening here, I never put any flowers in. If I couldn't eat it, I wasn't going to plant it. As time went on, I began to put a few flowers in where early crops were harvested. Barbara and I both enjoyed them so much that they are now a part of our regular garden, adding bits of bright color here and there among the vegetables.

Summertime is also the time for fruit. We grow both red and black raspberries, blueberries, cherries,

plums, apricots and peaches. Fresh fruit on cereal is part of every summertime breakfast. Even after we share our fruit with friends and neighbors, there is plenty for freezing, canning or making jams, jellies and pies.

I enjoy going to the basement to look at the results of Barbara's summer canning. Neat rows of jars line the shelves. There are jams ranging in color from the bright orange of peaches to the dark purple of blackberries. There are also quarts of green beans, pickles and white sauerkraut.

Summer is the time of wildflowers, too. Clematis, commonly called virgin's bower, drapes the fences with white blooms that the bees from our hives really love. Daisies spring up all over the pasture above the house. They must not taste good to the cows because the cows never bother them.

When the daisies are in full bloom, one of our neighbors across the valley likes to say that it looks like snow has just fallen in that one pasture.

Orange daylilies and white flags of elderberry line the creek banks. Red fire-pink and bee balm lay claim to the sunny roadside spots. Everywhere you look, you see blossoms.

When the sourwood trees bloom, it is almost time to "take off" honey from our hives. We never take honey after the 10th of August because the bees need time to put away their winter food supply.

As summer passes the halfway point, a new phrase creeps into conversations folks have about their corn, tobacco or garden. "Well," someone will say, "the corn is 'laid-by' for this year."

What they mean is that there will be no more hoeing or cultivating. Crops are now tall enough so that they won't be crowded out by weeds. Any weeds growing in the rows will be left where they are.

That certainly doesn't mean work is finished ...late summer is when tobacco is cut. The heavy butts of the plants are speared on sticks, five plants to a stick. Then the sticks are hauled to the barn and hung from tier poles. In late August, handing the heavy sticks up to the top of the barn is hot, heavy work.

By this time, we are all looking forward to the brisk days of fall. When we see the joe-pye weed starting to bloom, we know crisp mornings and deep blue skies are just around the corner!

During August, neighbors help Don rake and bale hay on a piece of his bottomland (left). Inset: Rufous-sided towhee makes its nest near Bill and Barbara's house.

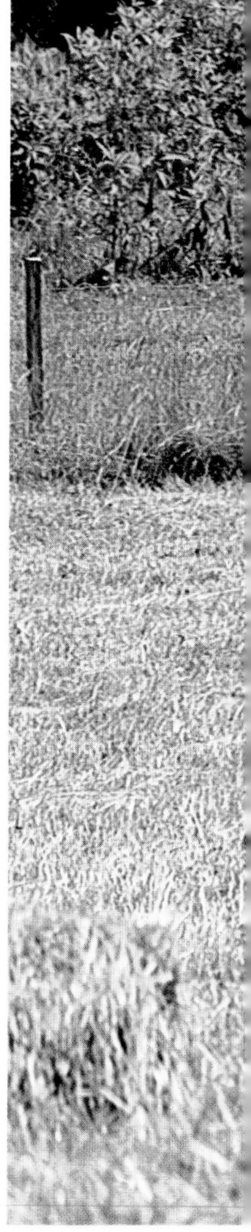

One of Gerald's big jobs in summer is picking his tomatoes (left). Few things are as tasty as a sun-ripened tomato fresh from the garden like the one at bottom left. The feathered friend at bottom middle is a catbird. Below: bee balm.

Neighbors often form crews among themselves when it comes time to hay in the Big Pine Valley. The same crew gathers hay on Bill's place (left) and in Leonard and Ronnie's field (below). At this time of year, fluffy milkweed is delicate and fine (right).

"Mr. Mac", still chopping wood at 92 (left), grew up in the valley and used to run one of the little country stores along the creek. Those are Ronnie's hemlock trees in photo at top. Sunflowers (above) grow big in mountain air.

On a warm summer day, a groundhog enjoys the scenery between munches (right). Below, healthy peppers, onions and cabbages—each destined for a Big Pine Valley table—fill a summer garden. At left, a bee seems to have decided that the cosmos makes a fine picnic table. Far left: dwarf wild iris.

Chapter 3

How It Was Way Back When

Simple Pleasures

One of my favorite Big Pine Valley pastimes is sitting and listening to Clem, Ruby-Noah, Wade, Kella, Don, Leonard, Nina and the others talking about the past. Their stories, like the deep roots of a tall tree, help bind Barbara and me to this valley.

It's not an easy matter to say just when and how the history of a place begins. Certainly, you *could* go back well beyond human memory and talk about how these mountains were formed and the Big Pine Valley was carved from them. You could also talk about how the trees, flowers, birds and animals got here.

For me, an important part of the history of the Big Pine Valley starts a few centuries back when the Cherokee Indians developed a trading path along the banks of what would later become known as the French Broad River.

The French Broad runs northwest to Tennessee right past the mouth of this valley. There it gathers up the swirling waters of Big Pine Creek, carrying them on a journey that eventually ends in the Gulf of Mexico.

When settlers arrived here in the 1700's, they began using the Cherokee's trail along the French Broad for commerce. Soon they were herding thousands of turkeys, ducks, hogs and cattle upstream along the trail from farms in Kentucky and Tennessee to markets in South Carolina and Georgia.

The biggest flocks of turkeys usually appeared on the trail in the fall. Each was led by an old "master gobbler" strutting along out front. The flock was herded by several drovers on the sides and in the rear.

Livestock on the trail—soon known as the Buncombe Turnpike—increased so much that one year, 110,000 hogs headed south passed the mouth of Big Pine Creek in a *single month*!

All this traffic led to the development of "stock stands"—small inns where livestock was fed and travelers could spend the night. The stock stands were about 10 miles apart—the distance hogs could be herded in a day.

One of the most legendary of the stock stands was at Barnard, a little community just across the French Broad from the mouth of Big Pine Creek. In those days, you had to cross from Big Pine Creek to Barnard on a small ferry.

Tales are told of robberies and murders occurring at that stock stand. More than a few bodies were supposedly dumped into the river as a way of getting rid of the evidence.

Because the livestock on the Buncombe required huge

Life could be hard for Big Pine Valley kids, who often worked in the fields by age 5. But, like Shannon and Stacy (above left), they also *played* in the fields. Right: On a Sunday afternoon, Kay, Barbara, Alma, Leonard and Jim discuss the past.

None of the old mills that once ground corn for valley farmers still operate...but a few retain a ghostly presence.

amounts of corn and grain for feed, folks began farming the steep hillsides of places like Big Pine Valley. Unfortunately, when the railroad came through in the late 1800's, it eliminated the need for all that farm produce...and the hard life in the Big Pine Valley got a little harder.

Many of our older friends and neighbors who grew up here remember just how hard life could be. Leonard says that when he was about 5 and old enough to handle a hoe, he went to work in the fields with his dad and brothers. Each morning, his dad would wake up him and his brothers at 4 a.m. They ate breakfast and fed the stock in the dark. Only when they'd walked most of the way up the hillside to "tend crops" did gray light begin to fill the sky and valley.

They spent all day in the fields, working their steep acres by hand and mule. About the only break they took was to eat the lunch of sweet milk, biscuits, meat and beans they'd brought with them.

Kids back then pretty much grew up in those hillside fields. When they were too young to work, their parents took them along to keep an eye on them. Later, both the boys and girls joined their parents tilling, hoeing, cutting and picking.

Children were valued in those days not just because they were part of the family, but because they could help get all the hard work done. Boys worked on the harvest, got in the firewood and learned to handle a team at an early age. They fed stock, hauled logs and did most of the heavier chores.

Girls helped cook, make soap, wash clothes and milk. They also learned to knit, sew and quilt. Once a week, the women left the fields for the day to wash clothes and bedding. They built fires under big cast-iron pots in their yards, then went to work with "rub boards" and lye soap.

Corn was the most important crop—it fed both humans and livestock. There were usually cornfield beans growing up the cornstalks as if the stalks were trellises. When the bean vines hung heavy with full green pods, the older children picked them.

The beans could be eaten fresh, canned or dried. When they were dried, everyone had to help out. They sat in a circle around a big pile of beans and used needles and heavy thread to string the beans up in chains that they called "leather britches".

The leather britches were then hung from the kitchen ceiling to dry. During the winter, the beans were shelled out and cooked with pieces of fat meat.

A child's life was not *all* work and no play, of course. When the corn and tobacco plants were big enough to hide behind, kids found time to chase each other up and down the rows.

Sundays, they played follow-the-leader by climbing up the high tier-poles in the barn where the tobacco was hung. Or they went swimming in the creek or climbed through the hills looking for plum, peach and chestnut trees.

Ruby-Noah recalls that chestnuts were good to eat raw and could often be traded at school for candy. "We had this one chestnut grove with about 30 trees in it," she remembers. "Daddy kept the grass mowed under those trees so it would be easy for us kids to pick up the nuts when they fell to the ground.

"It was up to us young'uns to gather the nuts and put them in burlap bags. Then Daddy took the bags to town in the wagon and sold them. He'd give us the money, which was the only time we ever had a few extra cents.

"There was a big difference in how the nuts from various trees tasted. We'd put the sweetest nuts from our favorite tree in a poke and save them for our own use. In the evening, we'd sit by the fire and roast some. First, though, Daddy cut an X in the shell of each one so it wouldn't explode when it got hot.

"After we were finished picking chestnuts in the grove, Daddy let the hogs in there. Those hogs sure did like chestnuts! I guess we all did. It was a big loss when the blight came through here in the '40's and killed off all our chestnut trees."

In the fall when school started, kids were sent off down the mountain with a lunch that included a jar of sweet milk that was kept in a spring to cool, a biscuit with a piece of meat, or some corn bread with jelly. Later in the fall, school let out for a few weeks so the kids could pick corn and harvest fodder.

One diversion for the boys was making and shooting "bean flips" or slingshots. They cut them from a choice crotch of a rhododendron shrub. According to Paul, a boy who had a steady hand and a good eye could use his bean flip to add a little extra meat to the family dinner pot.

Uncle Bass said that when he was a boy, all able-bodied males, regardless of age, had to spend 8 days a year working on the valley's roads. "That was how we paid our road tax," explained Uncle Bass. "I helped build the road up Big Pine...we all did.

"That way we got the roads we needed. Not good roads, mind you, but good enough to get a horse and wagon to town and back."

Actually, folks seldom had to go *all* the way to town for what they needed. Located here and there along Big Pine Creek were a handful of little stores like Jake Worley's and the one owned by Don Wild's folks at the forks of Big Pine Creek.

Jake's granddaughter Nina remembers regularly stopping at his store after school. "Grandpa would be weighing coffee, sugar and pinto beans," she says.

"I can still see the bolts of cloth, Star Brand shoes, bags of hog

Wild daisies still cover the hillsides in summer (above). What's changed is that this old hay rake has gone out of style.

Just as in the old days, a fodder shock (above) is made up of the tops of cornstalks that are stacked in the field to dry.

bran, plain flour, stovepipes, chewing tobacco, nail kegs, horseshoes, buckets of Royal Aster lard and all the patent medicines lined up neatly. I especially remember the candy in the display case and the warm bottles of soda pop."

The stores along the creek were all essentially the same—they each took care of the same needs. Yet each was also unique and had its own character.

Don's folks didn't spend much time in their store. When someone needed something, they pulled a rope that rang a big bell on top of a pole near the store.

A family member, hearing the bell, would come in from the field to take care of the customer. Don's folks also ran a corn mill and ground corn for local families every Saturday morning.

Don remembers that at first the mill was powered by a steam engine with a large boiler right in the building. The same steam engine was used by his grandfather to power the sawmill just behind the corn mill.

Later, when Don was older, his dad bought a new steel-wheeled tractor and the mill was run off the big flywheel. The tractor was hooked to the mill with a 6-inch-wide, four-ply belt that was 54 feet long.

"Dad sure did think a lot of that belt," Don recalls. "He made sure we always took really good care of it. When we were done grinding corn, we had to roll it up and put it away in a dry place. You know, that tractor was the first one in the Big Pine Valley."

Every Saturday, a member of each family in the valley came to one of the several mills along the creek. Everyone had a favorite mill and always took their corn there. Even though Uncle Bass lived closer to the Wilds' mill, he went farther down the creek for what he thought was more finely ground meal.

Folks rode to the mills in wagons, on mules or horseback and carried shelled corn in a sack. This was called a "turn of corn". After each turn of corn was ground, the miller would take a small amount as payment. That amount was

Timeless scenes: John and James enjoy playing in the creek (below) while Brook and Beth sit with "Trouble", a Border collie (left). Inset: "Bean flips", or slingshots, were made by Big Pine Valley boys from a rhododendron crotch.

specified by law, and an accurate scoop was supplied by the state. The payment was known as the "miller's toll". No toll was ever taken from families who didn't have much corn.

One regular source of supplies for folks in the Big Pine Valley was the peddlers who arrived in wagons or trucks once a week. They carried salt, pepper, other seasonings, coffee, flour, thread, needles, snuff, sacks of dried beans, pocketknives, bullets, bags of feed for dairy cows and hogs, chewing gum and a whole host of other treasures. Folks traded chickens, eggs, butter, chestnuts, molasses and walnuts for what they needed.

The 25-pound flour sacks were made of cotton and all came with different flower patterns printed on them. The women purchased sacks with the same patterns on them till they had enough material to make a dress, shirts for the children or an apron. Any little pieces left over were saved for making quilts in the winter.

Most of the early houses in the Big Pine Valley were hard to heat and, like the one above, have been abandoned. At left, Brook concentrates on hanging a hummingbird feeder from a porch nail.

White flour sacks were used for making pillowcases, diapers and backing for quilts. The peddler also carried kerosene to light lamps in the house. The kerosene was in a little tank under the back of the peddler's wagon or truck. Every home had a gallon container for lamp oil that was filled out of a spout in the peddler's tank.

Once I asked Leonard what both his best and worst memories of growing up in the Big Pine Valley were. He thought a few minutes, then said, "I remember one time when something good and something bad happened on the same day.

"I was only about 5 years old. For the first time my dad let me go with him on the wagon when he went down to the train station by the river to sell a load of acid wood. I was thrilled!

"About halfway down, when we went by Jake Worley's store, a feller Dad knew was 'loafering' outside. He spoke to Dad and said, 'That's a good-lookin' boy ridin' with you. What will you take for him?'

"My dad said, 'Why, I'll just give him to you on my way back up.' As soon as we were out of sight, I burst into tears. I cried that I didn't want to go with that man.

"Daddy put his arm around me and said that I should have known he was just teasing. I guess that was the worst part of the day.

"Then later, just when we crossed the bridge over the river to the train tracks, the train came in. It was the first one I had ever seen and it scared me to death. It puffed and made lots of noise. When the train left and Daddy told me I could drive the team of mules all the way home, I guess that was the best part of the day."

Whenever I listen to my Big Pine Valley friends and neighbors swap tales about the old days, I realize just how difficult those days were. Houses were cold, diets marginal, medical care almost non-existent. Work was hard and constant—long 12-hours days all summer and fall were the norm.

In late autumn, shelling corn, getting in firewood and "handing" tobacco could leave fingers and toes more than a little cold. (Years ago, farmers bunched their tobacco into "hands" of seven or so leaves, then bound them with a leaf on a flat oak basket for market—a job that took many hours in a cold dimly lit barn.)

Yet many of the stories I've heard about those days are told with warmth and have happy endings. True, children back then didn't have much…but they enjoyed the simplest of pleasures.

Dayton, Wade and Leonard all remember Christmas Eve the same way. "Each youngster hung a little quart-sized syrup pail on a hook at the fireplace," recalls Dayton.

"On Christmas morning, all us kids rushed to see what was in our pail. There would usually be an orange and a few pieces of hard candy. We were so happy, you'd have thought we'd each gotten a $100 bill!"

I feel lucky that we no longer face the hardships many of my friends and neighbors did. But I am reminded by their stories that love and tenderness can help almost anyone through even the toughest of times.

Ray and Margaret (top left), who just celebrated their 50th wedding anniversary, both grew up in the valley. By talking to folks like them, Bill and Barbara have learned many of the stories that lurk in the shadows of old buildings like the barn above.

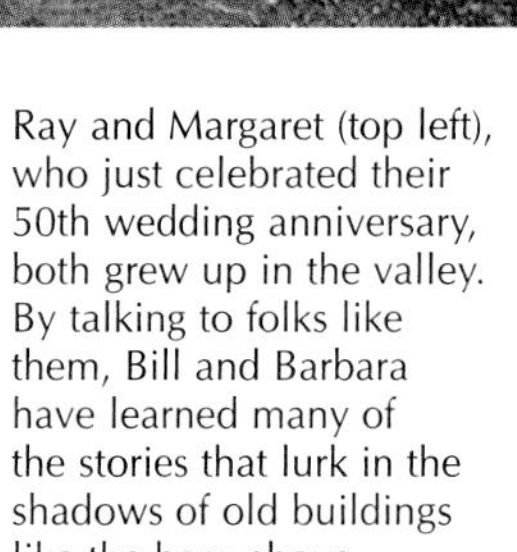

Simple pleasures like using a carrot on a stick to get a burro moving (left) and cuddling a lamb (right) can be appreciated by kids no matter what era they live in.

Folks in the Big Pine Valley seldom paint their barns, preferring to let them turn steel gray in the weather. Perhaps because of that, an antique latch has been left on the barn door above. All that's left of the old mill at right is the concrete base the waterwheel turned on. Building on the left was Jake Worley's store. Top right: Shannon takes time to smell some Big Pine Valley flowers.

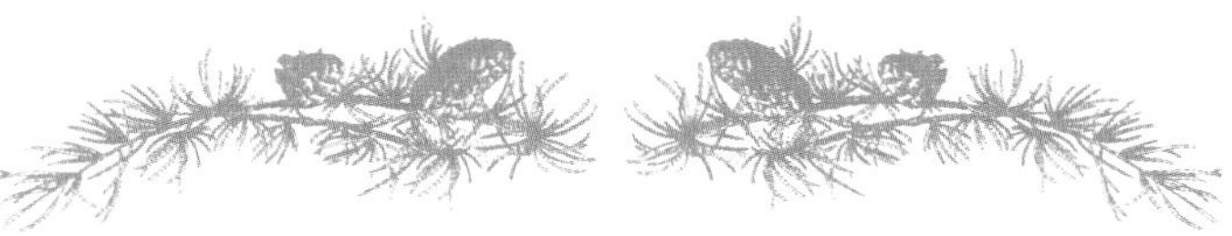

Geraldine

One day when I stopped by Geraldine's house, I found her working on a quilt for a great-granddaughter. Besides being a wonderful cook, Geraldine is a fine seamstress and quilter. She is always making things for her family.

When I asked her to repeat a story about her father that she'd first told me at least 10 years earlier, she looked up from her quilting in surprise. "That's very strange," she said. "Last week out of the blue I got to thinking about that story. I decided I really ought to write it down…and now here you are, asking for it!"

The story is about Geraldine's father and a little white dog. I liked it so much the first time I heard it that I thought it should be included in this book. I wanted Geraldine to tell it to me again so that I would get it right.

She put down her quilting and brought me a few pieces of paper with her clear, meticulous handwriting on them. Here's what she had written:

Don and Geraldine stand with their daughter, Donna Jean, before taking the short walk to church on Sunday.

I grew up in a small farming community. We six children were very lucky—we had good parents who taught us to work hard and put Christ first in our lives. We ate simple food from the garden and big juicy apples from the orchard. We also drank plenty of cold spring water.

We were happy and healthy and seldom went to a doctor. My mother was a firm believer in old-time home remedies. We drank gallons of catnip and pennyroyal tea, which tasted good. But I didn't much like the sulfur and molasses Mama fed us in early spring as a blood tonic.

Once my brother had an earache and a hacking cough that kept lingering. For once, Mama's home remedies had failed and she and Daddy decided it was time to get some medicine from a doctor. The nearest one lived on the other side of the mountain. Daddy saddled up ol' "Frank" and left early so he could get back before dark.

The "road" across the mountain was really just a narrow winding trail. The horse plodded slowly up it with the bushes slapping him in the face. All along the way, the horse's feet sent loose rocks tumbling down the mountain into a deep hollow.

Daddy had to travel very slowly and carefully. Finally, he reached the other side of the mountain. But then he couldn't see the doctor right away because a man had been shot and needed immediate attention.

After a long wait, Daddy finally saw the doctor and got some medicine. It was about dark when he and ol' Frank started home. Daddy tucked the medicine safely in his overall pocket.

When he got to the start of the mountain trail, Daddy had a sinking feeling in his stomach. The mountain loomed up before him, steep, high and dark. How could he ever find his way through the bushes? Daddy wondered. But he did what he always

Mist curls around the kind of steep rugged hill (left) that Geraldine's dad once crossed in the dark—with help from a surprising source—to get medicine from the doctor. Above: Geraldine's roses started as a cutting from her grandmother's favorite rosebush.

did—bowed his head and asked the Lord to show him the way. Feeling better and with a surge of faith, he told ol' Frank to "giddyap" and bravely started up that mountain again.

He hadn't gone but a few feet when suddenly, without any warning, a little white dog came running out of the bushes. The dog started right up that mountain ahead of Daddy and ol' Frank. It was as if the dog knew the way.

Daddy could just dimly see the little fellow, but he followed him on and on, up and up! And, do you know?—that dog led them safely home without a light!

The next morning, we hunted the place over for the little white dog...but he was nowhere to be found. He had disappeared in the same way he had appeared.

Daddy always said, "The Lord answered my prayer and sent me the little white dog." I believe He did, too! As we travel along the road of life—with all our troubles, disappointments and worries—He will lead us safely home. All we have to do is ask.

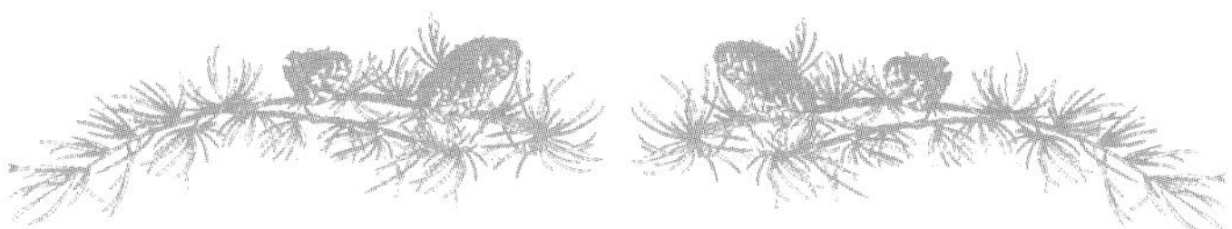

Logging

Farmers in the Big Pine Valley have long counted on logging for a little extra cash. In the early days, they themselves did the logging. Today, it's mostly done by contract loggers.

When the farmers first started logging, they had large stands of virgin oak, poplar and chestnuts to cut into. Heavy steam engines were dragged up the mountainsides to power the sawmills that were set up in the coves where the timber was being cut.

Teams of horses or mules dragged the logs to the edge of the steep hills. Then the logs were sent sliding on their own momentum down the hills to the valley floor.

Both Dayton's grandfather and father did a lot of logging. They told him about using six yoke of steers and a block and tackle to drag a steam engine and boiler up a mountain. The trail was so steep that the chain holding the engine broke.

There were several minor injuries when the engine slid back down the mountain. But the men persisted and eventually got the mill set up near the top of Fork Mountain. (Dayton's father liked using steers because he said they could work on steeper, softer ground than horses or mules.)

Clyde was a logger back in 1922 when land was being cleared for Fontana Dam in Tennessee. "I was just 17, and I guess I thought it would be an adventure," Clyde explained. "After we hired on, we walked 17 miles into camp where old railroad freight cars had been made into bunkhouses.

"We worked 10-hour days, 6 days a week, and earned $2.90 a day. That's less than $18 a week...*and* we were supposed to get out 40 logs a day. I lasted 2 years."

Here in the valley, logging occurred from February to October. Farmers went up into the woods whenever they could get time away from their crops and chores. When there wasn't a market for the logs here, they were hauled down twisting, winding Big Pine Road to the train. The train would take them to a mill in Asheville or over to Tennessee.

Wrestling logs off the steep hillsides required skill and hard work, and was more than a little dangerous. As many as 20 logs were hooked together with chains called "trailer grabs". These grabs swiveled, allowing the logs to turn and twist as they came sliding downhill.

Leonard once explained the details for me. "Uncle Al really liked to log," he said. "I'd drive the mules and he'd 'nose' the logs with an ax so they'd slide good. Then he'd set the grabs with a hammer or 'skip'.

"A skip had a steel mallet-like head on one end and a sharp point on the other. You used the hammer to set the grabs and the pointed end to pry them loose. The handle had a hole with a loop of rope threaded through it. That way you could just hang the skip from the hames on the horses' harness when you weren't using it.

"When the trailer was ready, you hooked your team to the first log with a 'J-grab'. It was called a J-grab because it kinda looked like the letter 'J'. It was made so that when the team pulled straight, the J-hook held.

"But as soon as the string of logs started to slide downhill on its own, you'd turn the team to either the right or left and the hook would automatically come loose.

"We always cut a trail where the team could turn out of the way. As the logs started to run, you hollered to your team, 'Jay...jay...jay!'

Logging today is done with machines. Years ago, "grabs" and "J-hooks" were used. At top, Don holds the grabs his father and grandfather used. Top left: Blocks of firewood illustrate how strings of logs, connected with grabs, were hitched to a team.

They knew the routine and scrambled up out of the way. We had one little mare that was kinda slow. She didn't 'jay' fast enough and the bunch of logs caught up to her. They hit her in her back legs and pulled both her shoes off. It sprained her legs and she could hardly walk for about 2 weeks.

"When we finally got her back in the woods, you couldn't believe how fast she got out of the way when you hollered 'jay'!"

Leonard chuckled at the memory, then continued: "When the ground was flat, it was hard for the team to pull the logs. So we made what we called a 'corduroy road'. We cut a bunch of short, small logs about 6 or 8 inches in diameter and laid them on the ground about 2 foot apart. They acted like rollers. Boy, those logs would really move when they hit the corduroy road!

"We always cut a path down the hill for the string of logs to slide down. We'd put in some stakes to turn the string wherever it might try to leave the path. Once the logs started sliding, the clanking of the grabs between the logs sounded like a little freight train coming down the mountain.

"The logs got going faster and faster the farther they slid down the hill. I never got tired of seeing a string of logs go ball-hootin' all the way to the road. But the logs sure did make a mess when they hit the road. They'd end up in a big pile.

"We'd go down to the pile and knock the grabs loose with the skip. Then with 'peaveys' and 'cant hooks', we'd make a neat new pile. Later the logs were loaded and hauled to the railroad. Dad and I sold ours to a man who made boxes and caskets over in Asheville. He knew we had good logs and gave us a good price. It was an all-day job just to take a load down to the train.

"Back then, we had some nice big trees. Poplars, oaks and chestnuts sometimes got better than 6 feet at the butt. You don't see trees like that here anymore. When the chestnuts all died from that blight in the '40's, we kept on cutting them for saw logs. Later they started falling down and we still cut them up and hauled them out. Trees like that made what we called 'acid wood'.

"We cut them into 5-foot lengths and put a cord of wood on a wagon and hauled it down to the railroad. I remember Dad said they got $15 a load. I never was sure what they used acid wood for."

For a long moment, Leonard was silent. He rocked his chair back on its two rear legs and stared out across the steep hills of Big Pine Valley. A look spread over his face like he had just taken a bite of something good and was savoring it.

Then he suddenly turned back to me and said, "It was sure something to watch a good team of horses or mules work a string of logs down off the mountain. Wish you could have been here to see it!"

As we sat there, a little breeze fluttered along the porch carrying the smell of thick woods warmed by the sun. I always like listening to Leonard, Dayton, Clyde and the others talk about the past. But it really made me feel good when Leonard said he wished I could have been around to share something special.

"I wish I could have been here, too," I said. "I truly wish I could have."

Using firewood, Clyde (far left) demonstrates how "trailer grabs" were hammered into logs with a "skip". A "J-hook", like the one at left, was used to hitch a team to the string of logs. It automatically pulled loose when the logs began to slide downhill and the team turned off to one side to get out of the way.

Carrying the Mail

Ruby-Noah told me about how her father, Zeb Davis, carried the mail on horseback 70 years ago. It took half a day to ride 9 miles down the rutted dirt road to the railroad track at Barnard.

There Zeb would meet train No. 12 at 12:30 p.m. and exchange the outgoing mail sack for the incoming one. Ruby chuckled and said, "You know, things may have been slower back then, but Daddy could take an order for Sears down with him one morning and bring back a package the next evening. All the way from Atlanta! Can you imagine that?"

One of her most vivid memories is of her father getting home during a sleet storm: "Mama used a piece of stove wood to beat on his stirrups and break the ice loose so he could get his feet out."

Mailmen back then left the mail at the three or four stores along Big Pine Creek that also served as post offices. It was still this way when Kella started delivering the mail in July of 1940. He used a horse several times a year in snowy weather when his pickup truck couldn't make it, but on most days the pickup made the trip down and back.

The road was not paved and Kella had to ford the creek more than 20 times going just one way. His route included both North and South Forks, Doe Branch and Anderson Branch. Kella's contract said he had to make six round-trips a week. In all those years, he remembers missing only one day, and that was because of heavy snow.

Delivering the mail in the Big Pine Valley has always involved getting to know the folks along the route. Here Dayton chats with Jim and Mary.

In the old days, the mailmen bid to deliver the mail for a 4-year period. When Kella got his first 4 years, he bid 99 cents a day. Gasoline cost him 20 cents a gallon, and after expenses, he didn't clear much.

Kella carried the mail for 25 years, 6 months and 15 days. As an independent contractor, he had no health insurance or retirement plan, and still receives just his Social Security.

Our mailman today is Dayton. He lives at the end of our road. Everyone along his route considers him a friend. We know we will get our mail whether it is properly addressed or not.

Dayton knows all the dogs along the route by name and they never bark at him. He also gets out of his car to check on older folks if he hasn't seen them for a day or so. In some of the remote parts of his route, he's often the only person they see for a week or more at a time.

Dayton's route covers 120 miles and has 500 mailboxes. He still travels a lot of unpaved roads and wears out a car about every 2 years. Little children he knew when he started his route are now grown and married and have children of their own.

"Sure I get tired sometimes and want to quit," Dayton says. "Then I'll find some homemade cookies in a mailbox with the flag up. Or I'll get a card of appreciation. That makes me want to keep on.

"Sometimes when the leaves are pretty or a doe and fawn cross the road ahead of me, I can't think of any other place I'd rather be."

Much of Dayton's mail route is unpaved, as the sign above between Beth and Brook demonstrates. At right, Dayton stops at a box in front of the Henderson place. He has to know exactly where a mailbox is, or he might miss it in the snow, as his photo at top shows.

Kella (top) occasionally delivered mail by horse. When he used his pickup, he had to ford the creek 40 times a day. Today, Dayton knows all the kids and dogs on his route by name. He snapped the photo above of Timmy and "Peggy" in 1980. Timmy is now married.

Quilting

Quilting is an important part of our heritage in the Big Pine Valley. Back in the early days, every house had a quilting frame hanging from the ceiling in the main room.

Whenever the quilt wasn't being worked on, it was rolled up on poles that were part of the frame, then hoisted to the ceiling where it would be out of the way. Most quilting was done in winter when there were fewer chores.

Not only was quilting an opportunity to make something that was both useful and beautiful...it also provided a chance for women to get together and swap information. While they quilted, mothers and daughters shared confidences and talked about their lives; neighbors exchanged news about their children, households and valley events.

Today, Margaret and Viola are known as two of the best quilters in the valley. They use traditional patterns in their quilts, such as Log Cabin, Double Wedding Ring and Ohio Star. Margaret especially favors variations of Carolina Lily and Field of Diamonds. Viola likes Log Cabin, but is making a Double Wedding Ring that will be raffled off to raise money for the volunteer fire department.

Margaret displays the Carolina Lily quilt she made to be raffled off as a fund-raiser for the volunteer fire department.

She is getting help from a neighbor, Judy, who has pieced the top as her contribution to the project. The person who ends up winning the quilt will become the owner of some very fine handwork.

The first quilts made in the valley were strictly functional, intended to cover you up and keep you warm. There wasn't much concern for how they looked when winter winds were howling down chimneys and slicing through chinks in the rough log walls.

Soon, however, women realized that quilting was a chance to express themselves, and they began to be more creative. Those early quilts were often pieced together from whatever was available—small scraps left over from making clothes or curtains...maybe even the clothes themselves once they were worn out.

A quilt can follow a set design or pattern and still reflect the personality and taste of the quilter. The colors and fabrics that are chosen for the top are like an artist's palette. And the thousands of stitches a quilter must make are judged for their size, delicacy and neatness.

Quilts have three basic elements: the "batting" or middle layer that provides warmth; the "top", which is decorative and made of colorful materials and designs; and the "backing" or bottom layer that helps hold it all together.

Margaret remembers when she was a girl, some folks were lucky enough to have the money to buy heavy cotton pads for batting. Those who didn't often used old blankets or tow sacks. Tow sacks were burlap bags that quilters boiled to make them soft and get the odor out.

"Backing was made from old sheets, white flour sacks or unbleached muslin," recalls Margaret. "We still use a cotton sheet or unbleached muslin today...though usually the sheet is new. And few people have to use flour sacks anymore. Today's batting is usually a thick sheet of polyester that's easy to work with and can be washed."

In the old days, women lowered the frames from the ceiling to a height that allowed them to sit around the quilt in chairs with their knees underneath it. Now many valley quilters buy hardwood quilting frames with adjustable legs and all sorts of other options.

Early-day frames consisted of two poles or boards called "rails". They were a little longer than the quilt that was to be worked, and the three layers of the quilt were basted to them. When the quilt was raised to the ceiling for storage, it was often at least partially rolled up on the rails to save space.

When the quilt was lowered again, "spreaders" were attached to

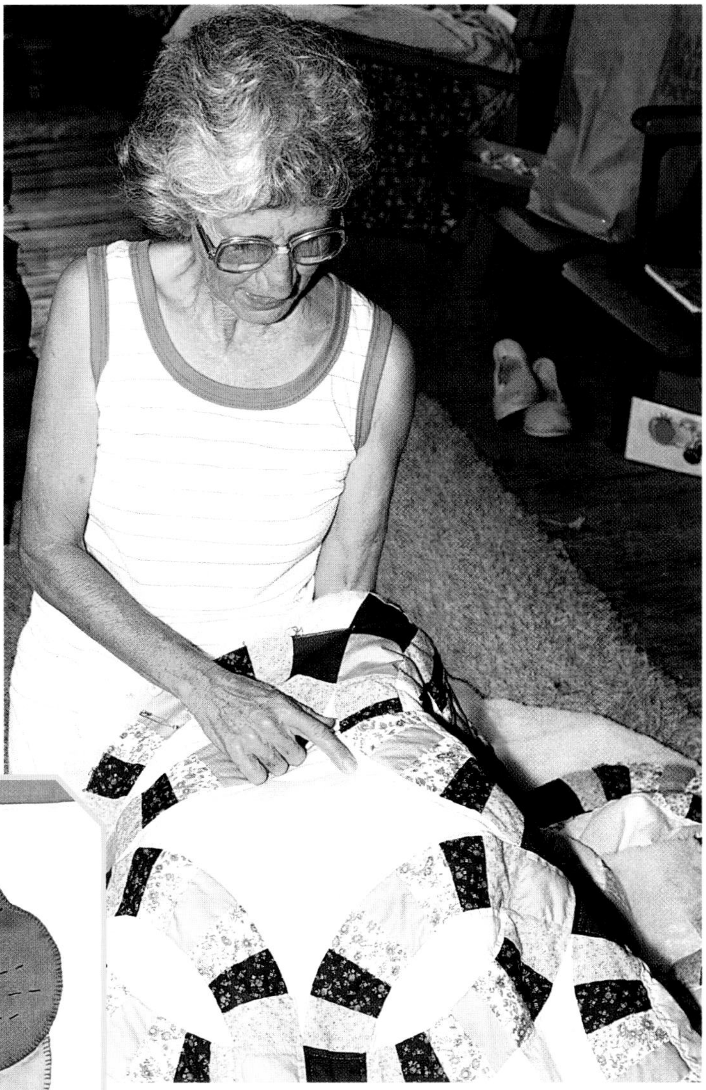

Viola works on one of her Double Wedding Ring quilts (far right), while a quilt made by Elizabeth (bottom right) depicts a Big Pine Valley scene. At right are Margaret's Field of Diamonds pattern and her pansy quilt. Above: Ohio star quilt made during a long winter years ago.

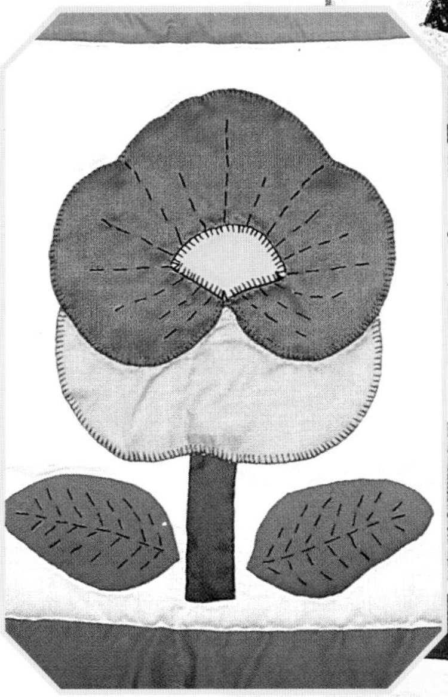

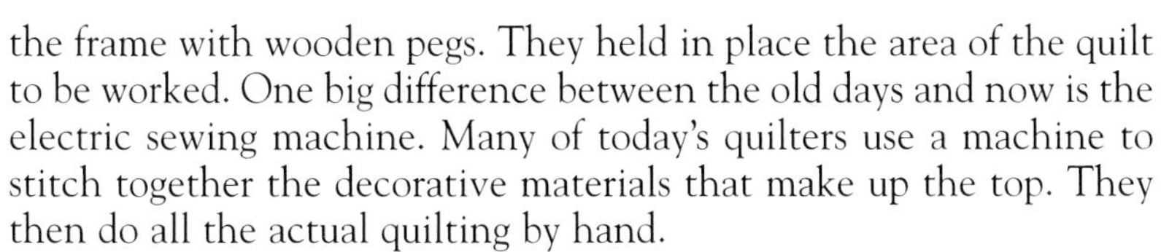

the frame with wooden pegs. They held in place the area of the quilt to be worked. One big difference between the old days and now is the electric sewing machine. Many of today's quilters use a machine to stitch together the decorative materials that make up the top. They then do all the actual quilting by hand.

"Quilting" is the process of stitching the top, batting and backing together. It can be tedious, difficult work, especially when the materials are hard to push a needle through. Yet, to complete a quilt, a quilter must do just that thousands of times over.

It kind of makes you appreciate even more the comfort of sleeping under a Big Pine Valley quilt!

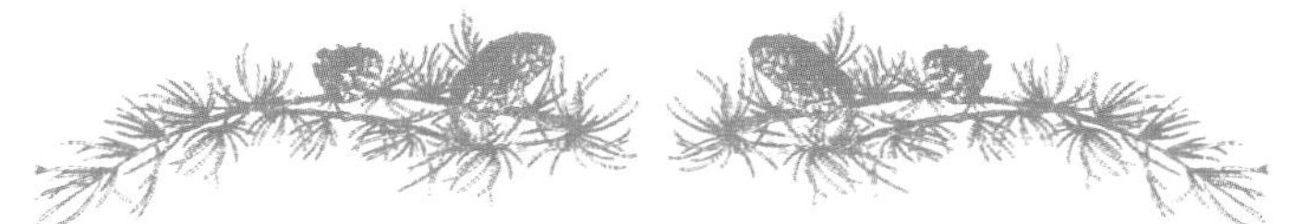

Radios & Talkin' Machines

Folks in the Big Pine Valley have always loved music, whether they were making it or listening to it. When the first record players arrived here better than three-quarters of a century ago, they were an immediate hit. Called "talkin' machines", they were hand-cranked and played 78-rpm records.

One of the most popular tunes performed today by the valley's many musicians, *Wildwood Flower*, was introduced way back then by a record. The talkin' machines, and the few battery-powered radios that arrived later, changed valley life in little ways, making it more pleasant and leading to new habits. Folks traded their small record collections back and forth till eventually everyone in the valley had heard every record.

When they arrived, the radios were run on wet cell batteries. Whenever the batteries got weak, they were put in a burlap bag and, with rocks for ballast, slung over the back of a mule or horse. Kids would then take the batteries down to Wilds' store along Big Pine Creek to be recharged.

"After my dad slung the sack over the saddle on our mule, he'd sit me up there, too," remembers Leonard. "Then I'd ride the mule down to Wilds'. They had that direct-current generator that was turned by the turbines in the creek.

"They used the generator to charge lights in their house and in the little Church at the Forks. Don's older brother, Roy, would hook up our radio battery to the generator and I'd leave it there for about 2 days. Then I'd ride the mule back again to pick up the battery. I was about 5 years old when I started doing this. I really thought I was something going down to the forks alone like that."

On Saturday nights, folks who couldn't afford a radio would gather at a house that had one and everyone listened to the Grand Ole Opry on Nashville's WSM radio station. There were other favorite programs, too—*First Nighter*, *One Man's Family* and *Mr. Keene, Tracer of Lost Persons* among them. Listening to records or the radio became a cherished family activity.

Folks who had radios carefully selected programs so as not to run down the battery too soon. Even so, Leonard remembers that he had to take their battery down to George Wild's about once a week.

Dayton adds, "You could always tell who owned a radio because they had two tall poles about 50 feet apart outside their house. There was a copper wire stretched between the poles as an antenna. Each end of the antenna was fastened to a glass insulator. Another wire ran from the antenna into the radio. You also had to run a ground wire to a metal stake.

"It was a lot of bother charging batteries and putting up antennas, but we sure felt it was worth it. Later on, you could buy dry cell batteries from the store in town, but you couldn't recharge them. When power finally came to the valley in 1948, we used the same radios with a little converter that changed the alternating current to the direct current the radio used.

"The first two radios in the valley were old Atwater Kents. Don's grandfather had one and my Uncle Kella over on Sugar Camp Creek had the other. To tune in a particular station, you had to turn three dials to the same number. They had that great big horn on top that the sound came out of. I've still got Uncle Kella's Atwater Kent and I guess Roy Wild still has Uncle George's."

Folks in the Big Pine Valley may not have had much by way of worldly possessions, but they enjoyed what they had, especially when it came to radios and talkin' machines.

Dayton (above) holds the tube and wire once used to hook up this old Atwater Kent—one of the first two radios in the valley—to a battery that had to be carried by mule down to the store for recharging.

Old-time radios are the topic of discussion between Jim (back to camera), Paul, Dayton and Grace (partially visible on Jim's left). During the conversation, Paul suddenly decided to give Dayton the two old battery-operated models shown above and at far left.

Chapter 4

Some Other Good Friends

Drumstix

As you probably realize by now, not all of our friends and neighbors in the Big Pine Valley are two-legged. Among those that *are* is a short little guy that wears feathers and a red crown and who goes by the name "Drumstix".

I'd like you to meet him as well as some of our other non-human friends. Drumstix is a rooster who has been a member of our family for more than 14 years. He was a present from Clyde. When Clyde walked up the lane carrying Drumstix under his arm, I immediately thought of all the ornery roosters we'd had in the past.

We've raised chickens for 30 years. They've been allowed to roam free around our home, but we've kept them fenced out of the garden. Our sons remember that as boys they were sometimes chased across the yard by roosters.

When I mentioned this to Clyde, he said, "Well, if this one doesn't work out, you can always eat him." Figuring that would be this rooster's ultimate fate, we named him Drumstix.

But Drumstix turned out to be the best rooster we ever had. He's never tried to intimidate a child or be aggressive toward anyone. Whenever I am working outside, he comes over and sits near me till I finish whatever I'm doing.

The mountains of North Carolina are a good place for a chicken to grow up. There are lots of green plants, grasshoppers, crickets and other bugs to eat. Unfortunately, there are also lots of predators here, too. Raccoons, opossums, skunks and foxes think chickens make about the best midnight snack there is.

Each evening when the chickens go in to roost, we close up the coop to keep predators out. One night, however, I forgot. A few hours later, I was awakened when I heard a chicken really "cutting a shine". (That's Big Pine Valley-ese for screaming and hollering.)

I jumped out of bed, pulled on my slippers, grabbed a flashlight and ran out into the night. What I found was a fox dragging Drumstix down the hill. When Drumstix saw me, he struggled even harder and hollered even louder. I shined the flashlight on the fox and shouted, "Turn loose that chicken, you varmint!"

And the fox did. Drumstix came streaking back up the hill, leaving a trail of white feathers. When he reached me, he huddled up against my feet. I picked him up and checked him over. He didn't seem to be hurt badly, so I put him back in the coop. This time—and always thereafter—I made good and sure the door was latched securely.

Each winter for many years, we've taken Drumstix and the other chickens with us to Florida for a few months. Before I had completely retired, my veterinary practice was down there. We always load up a little trailer behind the car with cats, dogs and

chickens and head south during the winter months.

Drumstix has gone back and forth so many times, I think he knows the way. When we reach Florida, he climbs nonchalantly out of the trailer, goes to get a drink of water and heads for the chicken coop. He jumps up on the same perch he's used year after year and goes to sleep.

I figure a rooster that's 14 in people years is really about 100 in chicken years. No wonder Drumstix needs a good snooze after that long ride—he's getting to be a real old-timer.

He always seems eager to get back to the Big Pine Valley each spring. Even at his age and with a touch of arthritis, he still gets up at the crack of dawn and crows loudly. I think he's letting all the young roosters in the valley know he's senior chicken around here.

I guess Drumstix is the only rooster from these parts who winters in Florida. Maybe that's why he's lived so long.

At 14, "Drumstix" is senior chicken in the Big Pine Valley. He still takes his responsibilities seriously and crows every morning at dawn. That's him at far left and above with a hen and some chicks on the Weber porch. Above right, a chick peeks out from under mother's protective wings. At right is a chicken coop, Big Pine Valley style. This one belongs to Paul and is made of logs chinked with mud.

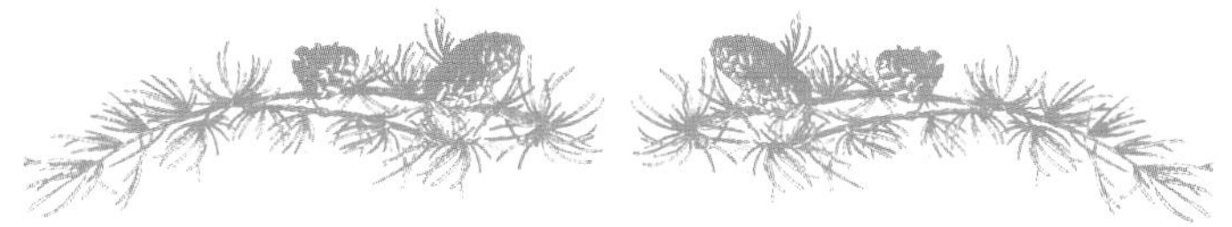

Bitsy

Small drops of chilly rain were falling from the gray April sky the day "Goldie" decided to give birth to a vigorous male lamb. After a few seconds of coughing and sneezing, the lamb struggled to his feet and started looking for his first warm breakfast.

Goldie stood patiently as the inept little lamb nuzzled along her underside looking for the nourishment that instinct told him was there. You could see his satisfaction when at last he found what he was looking for.

Goldie continued to clean him up even after he'd finished nursing and settled down into the hay for his very first nap. Then Goldie left her new lamb and made a nest for herself in the hay. Several big contractions later, another little lamb popped out.

Smaller and not nearly as active, this one seemed content to just lie patiently as its mother washed it. "What a little bit of a thing she is," Barbara exclaimed. And suddenly this second lamb had its name: "Little Bit", soon shortened to "Bitsy".

When Bitsy didn't show much interest in nursing, we lifted her up and showed her where breakfast could be found. After nursing, she seemed much more lively and followed Goldie and her brother out into the chilly drizzle.

In a few days, Bitsy was as frisky as any lamb in the pasture. She was even quicker and more agile than her larger brother. For a week, both lambs did fine. Then one morning I noticed Bitsy limping a little.

"I guess Goldie must have stepped on her," I said to Barbara. "She'll be better in a couple of days."

But she wasn't. The next day, Bitsy was practically dragging her left rear leg. The day after that, she could barely walk…and the day after *that*, she couldn't even get up at all.

"Bitsy" grew up inside the Weber yard, not the sheep pasture. Even now as a mature ewe, she's spoiled, admits Bill.

As I held her up to nurse, I examined her with my fingers. The back legs felt just fine, but she was sensitive at a spot on her back just in front of her tail. Still convinced that it was an injury, I didn't get a thermometer to check her temperature. Nor did I do a more thorough examination.

The next day, I again felt her legs and back while I was helping her nurse. This time I found some swelling. Not sure why it was there, I watched her another day.

Finally I understood the problem: There was an abscess under her skin. The infection had put pressure on the nerves controlling her legs and that had caused the increasing paralysis.

I cleaned the skin with an iodine disinfectant and used a sterile scalpel to cut through the skin over the swelling. Thick creamy "yuck" oozed out of the wound. I gently massaged the area to make sure all the yuck was gone, then flushed the wound with disinfectant. Lastly, I gave Bitsy an injection of two antibiotics.

All during this work, I talked to the patient little lamb. "Bitsy, this is my fault," I said. "I should have considered that there might be an infection, but I didn't. I hope we can get you well. You know we'll try our level best."

With the abscess opened, Bitsy seemed to feel better. She was more alert…but she was still paralyzed. "I guess we'll just have to put her into rehabilitation therapy to try and get her walking again," I told Barbara.

Since Bitsy could no longer keep up, Goldie disowned her. That's the way it is with nature—once a critter is weakened, it becomes a burden for the other animals and is often abandoned. Goldie wouldn't even let Bitsy nurse.

So Bitsy became a bottle baby. Because she couldn't walk, we helped her choose a spot in the grass near the house to spend her daytime hours. Three times a day I would go out and give her a bottle.

Then, with some soft straps under her pelvis and between her legs, I'd lift her up and try to make her stand. Sometimes the straps slipped and Bitsy would fall to the ground.

"This isn't going to do," I told Barbara. "Can you maybe take an old towel and sew Bitsy a little sling? You know—four holes for her legs and a place on the top of each side where I can fasten something to hold her up?"

Barbara had me take Bitsy's measurements—the distance from front to rear legs and between left and right legs. With that, Barbara made Bitsy the best sling you ever saw.

Bitsy seemed to enjoy the sling…she picked at tender grass sprouts while I supported her. But after 20 minutes of bending over, *my* back was killing me.

As an alternative, I started using an old pair of my suspenders to hang the sling from a low limb of an apple tree. That way, Bitsy could "stand" by herself as long as she wanted. In the beginning, that was for about half an hour at a time. When she would tire and begin to struggle, we'd let her lie back on the ground.

Soon she was pushing herself about while in the sling, reaching for the grain in her bowl and the grasses that were just beyond reach. This was enough encouragement to make us want to continue. Besides, we had come to really like and appreciate this woolly little fighter that wouldn't give up.

Three weeks later, she had outgrown her first sling. Barbara made her a new one of heavy duck material and added a better pair of my suspenders. Barbara also rigged the new suspenders to a handle so we could walk Bitsy about without having to bend over.

While in the sling, Bitsy would make walking movements with both back legs. She couldn't support her weight on her own, however. When she wasn't in the sling, she pulled herself around on the grass with her front legs, pushing with her hind legs.

Finally the day came when we saw her standing without help. She was wobbly and kept falling down. But then she'd get right back up and graze. Whenever she got tired, she would lie in the shade and chew her cud. Each day she got a little better and a little stronger.

Of course, she was spoiled and expected us to bring her little treats each time we came out of the house. But she still knew she was a sheep. One evening as the sun was going down, Bitsy wobbled over to the fence near the other sheep.

She found a spot where the fence didn't quite touch the ground and slithered under it. From then on, Bitsy would slip under the fence and spend the night in the pasture with the other sheep.

In the mornings, she'd be waiting at the pasture gate for me to let her out and back into the yard. She always slipped under the fence to let herself *into* the pasture, never out.

That all happened several years ago. Bitsy is still with us. She's smaller than she should be and wobbles some when she tries to walk fast.

But when it comes time for feeding, Bitsy holds her own against the other sheep. She is still just as spoiled…and she's still our favorite. That's because she never gave up and always seemed to appreciate our efforts.

After her surgery, Bitsy had to learn to walk all over again. To teach her, Barbara made a sling from an old towel and a pair of suspenders. Then Bill hung the sling from the low branch of an apple tree (left). Right: Before getting her infection, Bitsy and Goldie enjoyed some quality pasture time together.

Ol' Mike

Lately I've been stopping by fairly often to see Kella and his big red mule, "Mike". Kella just turned 80, but he still works his farm every day. Mike is about 30 and getting up there in years, too.

"Mike and I are both getting pretty wore out," Kella admitted on my most recent visit. We were walking down to the barn to hitch up Mike so Kella could cultivate the garden just above his house. I could tell from the way he talked that something was weighing heavily on his mind, and it probably had to do with Mike.

The reason I've been stopping by so often is to check on Mike—he's had some swellings on his belly and lower neck. I think the swellings are allergies; that's what I've treated him for and they've gone away.

But the swellings worry Kella. He thinks they are a sign that Mike is reaching the end of his working days. Also, like most old-timers in the Big Pine Valley, Kella is fiercely independent; he's convinced that asking me to check on Mike is an imposition, even though I keep assuring him it's not.

At the door of the barn, Kella said quietly, "Come on now, Mike. It's time to get some work done." There was a rustling back in the barn where Mike had been resting in the shade. He came to the door and voluntarily tucked his head and long ears into the bridle Kella held up.

You could tell these two had worked together for a long time—each seemed to know what to expect of the other. I patted Mike on his big shoulder and said to Kella, "You know, this is the best-behaved and most even-tempered mule I have ever seen."

"He *has* been a good one, that's for sure," Kella replied as he harnessed Mike. Then we headed up the hill to where the cultivator was lying. Mike followed along without being led.

When we reached the cultivator, Kella hooked Mike's trace chains to the singletree. Then he laid the cultivator on its side...no sense tearing up any ground on the way to the garden, he explained.

At the garden, Kella lifted the cultivator and moved it over to the edge of a row of potatoes. When he clucked once, Mike leaned into the harness and the two partners headed off down the row.

Kella always has a good big garden. Along with the potatoes, there are lots of tomatoes on dark green vines, as well as corn and beans. He plants more than enough to get him and his wife, Novena, through even the toughest winter.

When Kella and Mike returned to the end of the garden where I was standing, Kella said, "Watch ol' Mike now. When he turns, he won't step on a single tater."

He was right—Mike made the turn without any guidance, carefully avoiding the plants. As the two of them worked their way up and down the rows, I stood there thinking about why Kella had been so quiet and serious when he talked about Mike. Suddenly I understood. Here in the Big Pine Valley, farmers have traditionally kept animals only as long as they provide a decent return. That's understandable—when you have to scratch out a living, you can't afford much sentiment.

If an old mule can't pull his weight anymore, it's hard to justify keeping him around and giving him a share of the precious hay or corn crop. It's even worse if you have to have a vet stop by occasionally and tend to swellings on the mule's belly. So that's what Kella must have been worrying about—whether to keep ol' Mike or not.

It was obvious how Kella felt about ol' Mike...the two of them had been companions for 3 decades. Maybe Kella would decide to break with tradition; maybe he'd keep ol' Mike and the two of them would retire together. With a little practice, they might get as good at taking it easy as they have been at working!

That way, I'd be back for lots more visits with Mike and Kella—something I'd like a lot.

While Kella is gearing up "Mike", he worries about whether the old red mule has very many days of work left in him.

Bill likes making house calls on ol' Mike. Kella and Mike have been working together for 30 years and each knows what to expect of the other. But life can be hard in the Big Pine Valley, with little room for sentimentality.

Woolly Mowers

Even before we moved to the Big Pine Valley, I dreamed of having sheep. In my dream, the sheep would mow the couple of acres of grass around the house and under my 104 fruit trees. I dreamed that they would be small sheep, built close to the ground so they couldn't reach up and eat the fruit off my trees. Because they were going to be small, they would be a lot easier to handle.

I also dreamed they would have soft fine wool and I convinced Barbara that I could shear them. Of course, in the dream she would then spin the wool and knit us lots of beautiful sweaters.

Well, we've had sheep for more than a decade now—plenty of time for me to realize that my sheep-dream was not very realistic. But as so often happens in this valley, the reality turned out to be better than the dream.

During the first few years we were here, we concentrated on getting our house built. Once that task was pretty much finished, I figured it was time to pursue my sheep-dream. After some study, we chose Corriedale sheep because they are relatively small and noted for having fine wool.

I found a Corriedale breeder in the state, and one June day he delivered our four new woolly mowers to the farm. Before the little truck arrived, our son, John, and I checked the fence again to be sure it was tight and true.

We'd fenced an acre or so around the south side of the house and included about 12 of the fruit trees. We wanted the sheep close by so they could get used to us and so I could see how they did as mowing machines.

When the truck pulled up to our gate, I eagerly climbed up on the side to see our new babies. They had been born early in the year and weighed about 60 pounds each. They were even more excited than we were…or rather, I should say they were pretty scared.

Separated from their mothers, loaded in this strange vehicle, carried down a noisy highway for a hundred miles, and now facing these strange people who stared at them and made funny noises—no wonder they were uneasy.

Naturally, I wanted to help unload them—I could hardly wait to get my hands on these soft, woolly, lovable, little critters. As the first one bolted for the truck's sliding gate, I grabbed it by the wool with both hands to slow it down. The former owner took the lamb from me and lowered it to the ground.

Then he looked at me and in a gentle voice said, "You wouldn't like someone to grab you by the hair on your head, would you? It hurts them, just as it hurts you."

Then he showed me that if you are gentle and don't make sudden moves, you can restrain a lamb without creating much fuss or fear. Properly chastened, I had just had my first lesson in handling sheep.

After the truck left, John, Barbara and I went into the small pasture to try to make friends with our new sheep. They wouldn't have anything to do with us. They moved to the farthest point in the pen. They explored the fence all around and sampled some grass. But they were obviously still frightened.

We left them to quiet down and rest after their big trip. Later in the day, I took a little ground feed into the pen and placed it in their trough. Hesitantly, they came up to the trough and daintily nibbled a little bit. They still didn't want us too close.

The next few days, we became better acquainted. We still couldn't tell them apart, except for the wether, which was obvious. We started calling him "Bert" and explained to him he was supposed to be a woolly mowing machine, not lamb chops.

Even though they were on good pasture, I nonetheless fed them a little grain each day. It was a good way to get them to come to me and

When they got to know their "woolly mowers" better, the Webers realized "Emily" (below with her lamb) was a born tattletale.

Among Bill and Barbara's friends and neighbors are some of the non-human variety. At left are a tiger swallowtail on some butterfly weed, a cottontail rabbit, a southern toad and a red squirrel. Above, a raccoon licks its paw, while a bobwhite quail stays put in some grassy cover (top right) and a wild turkey (below) makes its presence known. Right: Whitetail doe and her fawn peer warily out of the woods.

CHAPTER 5

A KNACK FOR MAKING THINGS

Uncle Bass' Cornmeal

A century ago when folks in the Big Pine Valley said "bread", they usually meant *corn* bread. Back then, they always made cornmeal from white corn; yellow corn was for feeding chickens and livestock.

Today, we make cornmeal from both white and yellow corn. Either way, it's best ground fresh because old cornmeal smells musty and its oils turn rancid...unless, of course, you can freeze it.

In the old days, many farmers also grew wheat. They had that ground into flour to make breakfast biscuits. When loaves of bread made from wheat flour first appeared in the valley, they were called "light bread". If folks wanted light bread but didn't grow their own wheat, they had to buy flour from a peddler or at the little community stores along Big Pine Creek.

I got my first white corn seeds from Uncle Bass, who was in his 80's by then. He was still slender as a stick and tough as barbed wire. His family had been growing this same variety of white corn for at least 100 years. Each year, they kept the best ears back for the next year's seeds.

After all those years of selection, Uncle Bass' corn loved the soil of the Big Pine Valley. His corn grew 8 feet tall and generally set two large ears on each stalk. It learned to tolerate the heavy rains of spring and the hot dry spells of late summer. At harvest, there were seldom any signs of corn earworms or other insect damage. Uncle Bass' white corn had adapted well.

While he was still alive, Bass gave Barbara and me about a bushel of his best ears each year. He also taught me most of what I know about cornmeal and its history in the valley. Between the bushel he gave me and the corn I was already growing, I always had plenty to grind. Unfortunately, there weren't any mills left in the valley, so I set up a tiny one of my own.

My small mill only grinds about a quart of cornmeal at a time. It works on the same principle as the larger mills, but is powered by an electric motor instead of a waterwheel. In a couple of hours, I can grind all the cornmeal we need in a year. Naturally I think our meal is healthier and better tasting than store-bought.

In the old days, corn was dried in a slatted crib before it could be shelled and ground. The crib allowed air to circulate between the ears. Today I dry my corn in a homemade dehydrator, then shell it. It's usually ready for grinding a week or so after picking.

The sheller I use was a gift from Ruby-Noah. It's old-fashioned and has a hand crank. For me, shelling and grinding corn into

Uncle Bass' family has been raising white corn in the Big Pine Valley for more than 100 years—that's some of it drying in a crib (inset). At right, Bass strips seed from broomcorn to use as chicken feed. Above left: Brook takes shelled corn out of Bill's homemade dehydrator for milling.

meal is part of getting ready for winter...like drying apples or going up in the woods to cut firewood.

In the old days, corn was ground 1 day a week all year long. Everyone wanted fresh ground meal for their corn bread, so on Saturdays, someone in the family put shelled corn in a cotton sack and took it to the mill.

At one time, there were seven corn mills along the 8 miles of Big Pine Creek. All were powered by waterwheels, except for Don's folks' mill; it used a steam engine and, later, a tractor with a flywheel and belt. Only one mill about halfway down the creek had the type of millstones needed to grind wheat.

"Stone-ground" cornmeal is called that because it is ground between two millstones. One stone is fixed solidly in place and the other turns. Corn is usually fed through a hole in the center of the upper stone. Grooves chipped into the mill wheel's surface radiate out from the center like spokes.

The corn falls into these grooves and centrifugal force carries it toward the edge of the stones. The grooves become shallow and disappear the closer they get to the edge. Thus the meal is ground finer and finer as it is pushed outward. The fineness of the finished product depends on how far the stones are set apart.

Old-time millers would pick up a pinch of meal between thumb and forefinger and roll it around to test for proper fineness. Housewives of that day wanted their cornmeal finely ground. I, too, use the finger test to check my meal for fineness.

The stones on my little mill are only about 6 inches in diameter. That compares to the 12- to 36-inch stones of the old mills. One reason I prefer my home-ground cornmeal over store-bought is that commercial meal has had the fibrous hulls removed. The hull contains the bran, or fiber, and the "germ". The germ is the embryo of the new corn plant and is rich in protein and vitamins. I think the germ adds flavor to the cornmeal. Since we package all our meal in plastic bags to be stored in the freezer, the corn oils stay fresh-tasting, too.

In the old days, the miller used a large sieve with wooden sides and a fine-mesh flat bottom to sift his meal. All the coarse bits and the bran from the hull were sifted out and used for hog and horse feed.

We sift our meal, too, using a regular kitchen flour sifter. But all the bran and coarse grinds we collect are put through again with the next batch of corn. Uncle Bass was never convinced that it was a good idea to save the bran. Even he had to admit, however, that the meal tasted good with the bran. Because I ground more meal than we could use, I always took a good bit up to him to repay him for his corn.

After one of our visits, Bass took time to ride down the road along the creek and show me where all the old mills used to be. Several have burned down, but most are still there weathering away.

At each mill site, Bass brought the past alive by pointing out where the millraces came down the hill carrying water to the wheels and telling me about the families who ran the mills. He also told me technical facts like what kind of wheel each mill had.

Bass is gone now...he died at 93. But I can't help thinking about Bass whenever I grind corn. For as long as I knew him, he never hesitated to speak his mind. Bass was one of those few folks who say what

Three kinds of cornmeal are in the jars next to Bill below (from left)—yellow corn, white corn and sweet corn. At right is shelled corn ready to go through Bill's electric mill. Far right: stone mill wheel once used for grinding corn.

There's no longer any smoke coming from the house where Uncle Bass lived all his life. Bill took this photo so Bass could have it in the hospital.

they mean and mean what they say. Sometimes he sprinkled in a cuss word or two for emphasis or conviction. That always embarrassed his daughter, Alma, who would chide him gently.

Bass—like most all the old-timers in the Big Pine Valley—believed first and foremost that a person should be independent and self-reliant. Coming in a close second was his belief that neighbors should help neighbors. Bass really wasn't my uncle, but it always felt like he was. Thirty years older than me, he reminded me of my dad, which might be part of the reason we got along so well.

To Bass, dying was part of living and he had no fear of it. While he was still able to, he helped others deal with death. When someone in the valley died, the family called on Bass. "Some of us men would make the coffin out of whatever kind of wood there was," he said. "If it was a man who'd died, we'd help clean him up, shave him and put him in his best clothes.

"Then we'd put him in the new coffin and sit with the family all night. Neighbors came to visit, and even though it was a time of sadness, it was also a time of remembering. We'd all sit around and talk about the things we'd done together.

"In the morning, we carried the coffin to the Church at the Forks, where the preacher said some words. Then we went to the cemetery, where the men had dug the grave. After the preacher said a few more words, we'd lower the coffin and cover it with some good rich dirt."

When he went in the hospital the last time, Uncle Bass knew he wouldn't be coming back. He asked me to take a picture of his house so he could have it with him. It was the house where he'd lived all his life, but now there wasn't any smoke coming from the chimney.

The other request Bass made was of Leonard, Alma's husband. "You know, Leonard, I can't eat this hospital food," Bass said. "I could sure use some squirrel gravy on a nice fat biscuit. Now that would be a mighty fine meal!"

Leonard went home, got his gun and went out to the woods. He shot a squirrel and Alma made the gravy and biscuits. They took the food to the hospital and fed Uncle Bass, one spoonful at a time.

Bass couldn't eat much anymore, but he sure enjoyed what he did eat that day. When he died, it wasn't quite like the old days in one of the hillside cabins. We *did* sit around and talk about the past, but there was a funeral home to take care of the details.

As always, however, the men dug the grave at the Church at the Forks. Then they lowered Bass into the ground next to his wife, Kitty. Now each time I drive down the creek, I remember Bass telling me how they used to grind corn and make meal in the old days. And each spring, I put in some of that white corn that's descended from when Uncle Bass' family first started planting it here in the Big Pine Valley.

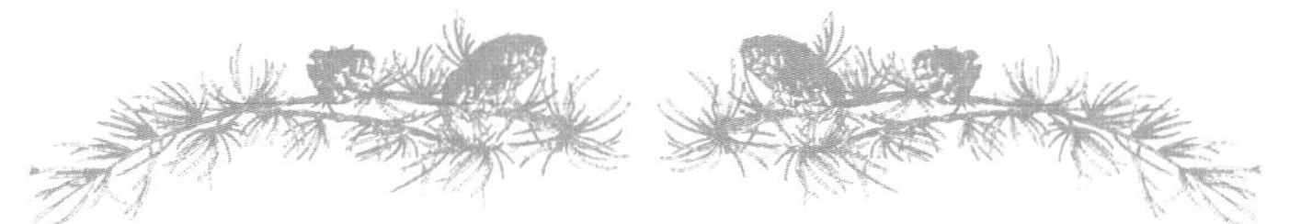

Stakes & Tortoises

Here in the valley, fence posts are called "stakes". The best stakes are split from the yellow heart of black locust trees. With wood from a good sound locust, stakes can last 30 years. As Clyde once put it, "Locust stakes will last you longer than one of them steel posts you can buy."

While we were building our house, a large locust blew down in a hollow just north of the house site. We were too busy to do anything, so the tree just lay there for over a year. Finally one cool fall day when we had a break, we decided it was time to cut up the locust.

Don came up to help. We cut up the limbs for the cookstove and for heating. Then we went to work on the trunk, measuring off 60-inch lengths to be split into stakes. Some farmers make their stakes 72 inches long.

I'm kinda short, and the longer stakes are too tall for me to drive into the ground with my sledge. We used Don's ax as the measuring stick—its handle and bit are exactly 36 inches long. A little less than two ax lengths turned out to be just right for my stakes.

A quick chop with Don's ax marked where the trunk would be cut with the chain saw. Then the "wedge and sledge" work began. Wedges were driven into the log, forcing it to crack along its length. Finally, with a rending groan, the log split in half.

Our fallen locust tree yielded 126 stakes and two cords of firewood. That old tree had plenty to be proud of!

One of the characteristics of locust logs is that they split nice and clean and straight. After a log has been split enough times so each piece is down to stake thickness, the pieces are sharpened on one end. Old-timers like Clyde use an ax to sharpen their stakes, but I find a chain saw is quicker and easier.

Stakes are sharpened so they can be pounded into the ground rather than set in postholes. All the rocks in our soil make it about impossible to dig a posthole.

Instead, we use a big steel crowbar to poke and gouge a little "pilot hole" into the ground. Then we stick in the sharp end of the stake and begin pounding it down with a sledge. On the way into the earth, the stake actually forces the smaller rocks out of its way. Don uses a 12-pound sledge, Ronnie a 16-pounder. They're out of my league; I work with an 8-pounder.

A North Carolina box turtle surprised Bill by tumbling down the hill while he was pounding in stakes, or fence posts.

I used the stakes we made from the fallen locust to strengthen the fence around the pasture and to close off a steep hillside where the cows' hooves were causing bad erosion. Don lent me "Pearl", his horse, and a sled to carry the stakes up the hill.

While I was pounding stakes into the steep eroded area, I suddenly heard a thumping sound like a rock rolling down the hill. I turned to see if I would have to jump out of the way. To my amazement, there was a large tortoise tumbling end over end right toward me. It stopped upside down near my feet.

I set the sledge to one side and reached down to turn the crusted varmint right side up. Before I could help, he extended his neck and, with a big heave, turned himself over. Then he swung his head around and calmly looked me over. He seemed quite composed for having just tumbled down a long steep hillside. The red irises of his eyes added bright spots of color to his dark head, indicating he was a male.

After a moment, he turned and slowly started across another steep slope. Before he got two steps, I picked him up. "Dummy, you'll fall again if you go across there," I scolded. "Let me give you a hand."

A tortoise usually pulls in his legs and head and closes up his shell tightly when you pick him up. Not this gentleman. He just sat placidly in my gloved hands and didn't seem a bit worried. His legs dangled over my hand and he extended his neck and lifted his head to better look me over.

I carried him to a flatter grassy part of the hill and placed him in the shade of a weedy bush. The last I saw of him, he seemed happy and content.

Now, this incident with the tortoise has nothing to do with making stakes and putting in fence. It *does* provide an example of the enjoyable breaks that come mixed in with work when you live here in the Big Pine Valley.

The day I helped that tortoise was many years ago. Since then, the eroded part of the hill that I fenced off has healed and I've pulled the stakes out. Today when I walk across there, I say a silent thanks to my neighbors for helping me cut up that big locust and to Pearl for hauling the stakes up here.

I also chuckle about a tortoise that could tumble clear down the hill and not be the least upset about it.

Don, Bill and Bill's son, John, "burst a tree" to make stakes for building fence. John "wedges" a portion of the trunk to split it while Don trims and sharpens the stakes (bottom). At left, Bill drives a new stake into the rocky ground with a sledge. Clyde always claimed that a good stake like the one at right would outlast a modern steel post.

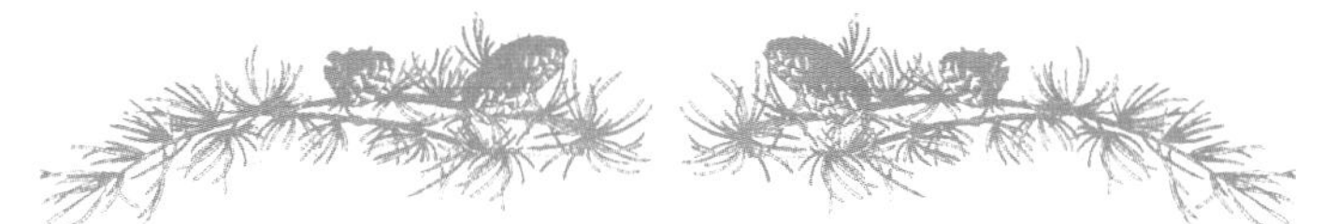

Old-Fashioned Haystacks

Dogwoods, decked out in pretty fall berries, frame four of the stacks Wade made on Clyde's farm. Locust poles in the center help hold stacks in place on steep slopes.

There are two main reasons why my friend Wade Massey has never owned a tractor. First, his hillside land is too steep to operate a tractor on safely. Second, he prefers working his farm with horses and by hand.

His two horses are named "Jeffrey" and "Dixie". Jeffrey is the older of the two and Wade expects him to be the leader. "Come on, Jeffrey, get in there and show Dixie how a real horse pulls," Wade will say. "You're not tired yet. Let's get this done so we can quit for lunch."

One of the best times to visit Wade is during haying season. That's when you can watch a good team in action and also see the art that goes into building a haystack, which looks simple, but isn't. Wade generally cuts hay twice a year, once in June and again in early August.

He mows in the morning just as soon as the dew is dry. "It's cooler then and the horses don't get so hot," he explains. Even so, both Wade and the horses work up a good sweat operating the chattering mower on the steep hills.

Wade doesn't like to get too much hay down at one time because it might rain. He *claims* that at 77 he's slowing down and can't put up as much hay in a day as he used to. I'm not sure I believe that because I've seen Wade outwork much younger men.

After mowing, Wade and his team rake the hay into heavy windrows. Jeffrey and Dixie seem to know just what is expected of them. Windrows close to the stack site are pulled into the site by the horses. Hay farther away is forked onto a sled and dragged over to the stack.

Wade starts each stack by digging a hole about 2 feet deep and planting a heavy locust pole that stands up about 10 to 12 feet. The pole will be in the center of the stack to help keep it from tipping over on the hillside as it dries and settles. The pole also helps make a well-rounded stack that will shed water.

Wade is regarded as a master stack-builder. As neighbors who are helping bring the hay in, Wade establishes the size of the stack by scattering forkfuls of hay in a circle around the pole. Adding more hay, he walks on it, packing it down and keeping the stack smooth and level as it goes up.

"I can tell by how the stack feels under my feet where I need to put more hay," he says, talking as he works. "Dad always said

Wade mows hay the old way (right) while Clyde follows along behind, moving thick hay so it won't jam mower on the next round. Below: Wade raking hay.

Getting in hay on the steep slopes of Wade's farm entails lots of hand labor. First, Wade starts a stack—in this case with help from older brother Clyde (right). Next, neighbors help Wade haul hay pitched by hand onto a sled into the stack (above). Then Clyde and Levi pitch hay from sled to stack (far right). As stack grows, Jim tosses hay up to Wade (inset).

if you can't talk and work, quit talking."

As the stack grows, someone forks the hay up to Wade and he places it where he feels it should go. When the stack gets up about 8 feet tall, he begins topping it off. He places the final forks of hay so they overlap like shingles. When the top is finished, Wade sits down and slides off the stack to the ground.

He stands back to admire his handiwork and says, "We used to make the stacks a lot taller. But that was when we were all younger. I guess when Levi, Ray, Kella and I are gone, they won't put up hay this way anymore."

At first, I thought Wade might be right. His older brother, Clyde, is already gone. And while some folks still use horses, they also use tractors and balers to make hay. I'll hate to see the day when there are no haystacks in the Big Pine Valley like the ones Wade makes.

There is still some hope, however. Allan Payne, in his early 40's, does a lot of farm work with two teams. He has three boys and they all like horses. The two older boys—both in their teens—drive a team as well as any man.

One day I stopped to watch Allan and his 16-year-old, Chad. They each had a horse and cultivator and were "plowing" tobacco. When they stopped for a breather at the end of the row, I asked Allan, owner of two John Deere tractors, how much he used the horses.

"We do fieldwork on steep ground with horses," he replied. "We use horses for mowing and raking hay and getting hay into the baler. Horses are better than a tractor for cultivating tobacco and corn. I also use horses to haul rocks out of a field on a sled.

"When the ground is soft in the early spring, horses are the best way to get manure into the fields. I wouldn't use anything but a horse to dig my potatoes in the fall. Now that I think about it, I guess I'd give up my tractors before I'd give up my horses."

Well, maybe with Allan, Chad and his brother Brad farming here, horses won't disappear from the Big Pine Valley for a while yet...and there still might be a few little handmade stacks with poles sticking out of the center.

Wade and Don (left) finish off a stack. Before sliding down to the ground, Wade places forkfuls of hay on top of one another like shingles so that the stack is smooth, rounded and rain-resistant.

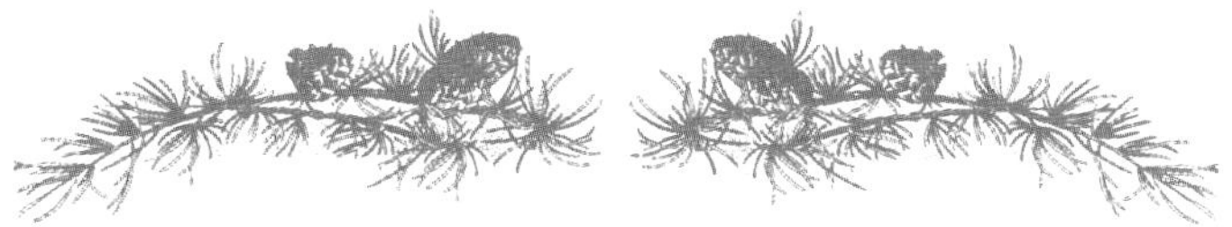

Sauerkraut

Part of summertime is the making of sauerkraut. Barbara cans tomatoes and makes relish and pickles, but I make the "kraut". Of course, it starts with planting cabbage in the early spring.

We choose almost any hybrid cabbage. I usually plant seeds and then transplant the young plants. But sometimes, neighbors will want to share their extra plants. I usually get a late start on mine, so I welcome the donation. My only consideration is that I like using cabbage that's nice and white inside. It just doesn't look right to have green kraut.

This spring we planted a generic hybrid cabbage. We had lots of rain, so the cabbages grew fast and got very large. We made our kraut the latter part of July, when the cabbages got so large that some started splitting.

I cut about a dozen heads, stripped their outer leaves and cleaned them in the garden. That way I could just leave the extra parts out there to compost. Then I washed the heads well and quartered them.

Most folks here in the valley make their kraut in earthen crocks. I make mine in a plastic, food-quality honey container. I keep bees, but usually have extra 5-gallon honey pails left to use for kraut and garlic dill pickles.

The cabbage must be shredded or chopped before it is placed in the container to ferment. Most folks use homemade chopping tools, and I did, too, until Jim found me a regular kraut shredder at an antique shop. It works very well and makes a finer kraut with long strands. When the cabbage is chopped, it makes smaller chunks. Either way, it still tastes good.

I shred 5 pounds of cabbage at a time—usually about two heads. I can pretty well judge the amount, but I always weigh it to be sure. I then mix in 3 tablespoons of plain —not iodized—salt.

The cabbage is placed in the 5-gallon pail, where it will stay for the next 2 to 3 weeks. The pail can hold 35 pounds of cabbage. As each 5 pounds is added to the pail, I tamp it down to eliminate the air pockets. To make good kraut, you must eliminate all air and seal the surface. I use a homemade wooden tamper cut from a dogwood log.

Tamping the cabbage also crushes it slightly, releasing the juices and forming brine, which is necessary for fermentation. I cap the pail with a flat pine board cut to fit snugly. I then place a rock on the cap to hold the wood down and cover the whole arrangement with a towel. Before I start shredding cabbage, I sterilize the rock and all the utensils in a weak bleach solution.

The longer the kraut stays in the pail or crock, the more sour it becomes. Don just lets his stay for 4 or 5 days; mine stays 2 to 3 weeks. The only way to know for sure when to take the kraut out is to taste it. If it's sour enough, can it. If not, seal it back up.

To can, I bring my pail up from the basement and pour the contents into Barbara's big kettle. She brings the whole mass to a boil and then ladles it into clean quart jars. The lids are placed on the jars and hand-tightened. Then the sealed jars are placed in boiling water for 20 minutes. Now it will keep all winter and you can have kraut anytime.

To make kraut, Bill shreds cabbage into one of the pails he would otherwise use for honey from his bees.

While kraut makes a good dish with almost any meal, Don is the only one I know who likes it for breakfast. "Nothing beats some of Geraldine's hot biscuits with good chicken gravy and a little sauerkraut on the side," he says.

I may not agree with him about kraut for breakfast, but he's sure right about Geraldine's scrumptious biscuits and gravy. When she makes chicken gravy, there is almost a whole chicken in it. One thing about Don's kraut: it isn't that sour and offers a little change of pace.

Barbara doesn't like kraut as much as I do, but she *does* go for sauerkraut salad. Here's her recipe:

- 1 *cup sugar*
- 1/2 *cup vinegar*
- 1 *quart sauerkraut*
- 1 *cup diced celery*
- 1 *cup diced onion*
- 1 *green pepper, diced*
- 1 *or 2 pimientos, diced*

Dissolve sugar in heated vinegar. In a large bowl, mix everything and let stand overnight to blend. It can then be transferred into smaller containers.

Kept refrigerated, it lasts a long time... except at our house! We all like Barbara's kraut salad, so it doesn't last long at all.

Cabbage (above) is from the Weber garden and will make about 10 pounds of kraut. After cleaning and cutting the cabbage, Bill mixes it with salt (left). He then packs the cabbage down with his homemade dogwood tamper (top right) and places a rock on the lid to keep cabbage airtight (bottom right). Valley tradition holds that the rock should be flint or quartz. That's his shredder and tamper at far right.

HONEY

HONEY

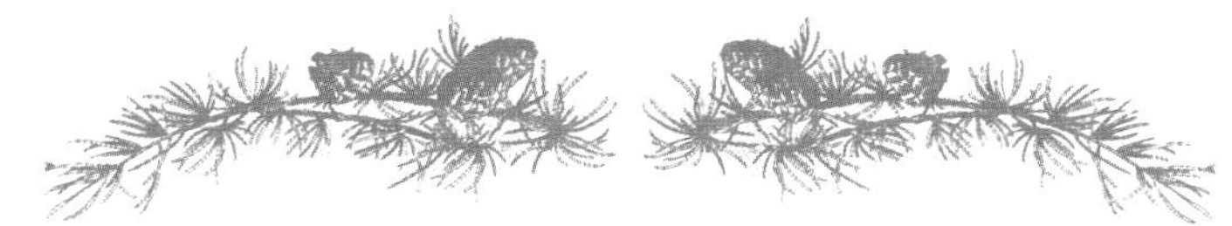

Heading Up a Spring

Most folks in the Big Pine Valley use a spring for their household water…and it's the best-tasting water in the world! If the spring is above the house, you get good water pressure from gravity alone.

When a spring is particularly good, it's called a "bold spring". Our place had a bold spring bubbling up under the roots of a sycamore tree …but it was downhill from where we wanted to build our house.

To avoid carrying or pumping water, we decided to look for another spring above the house. The first one we chose caused Don to ride to our rescue again. "You know," he admonished gently. "That spring you've picked looks good now, but it might go dry in the middle of the summer. Why don't you look at the spring up by the grove of walnut trees? It's always been a dependable spring."

So son John and I hiked up there and found water coming out of a clay bank. We followed the trickle down through the trees to where it drained into a little brook or "branch".

"Well, John, it looks like a nice spring all right," I said. "But I don't really know what do with it." When I asked Don, he said, "There's not much to capturing a spring. I'll just come up there in the morning and show you how. You get your tools ready—a couple of shovels and a pick—and we'll make us up some cement."

Once you've found what Big Pine Valley folks call a "bold spring", you "capture" it by doing such things as cementing up the floor of the spring.

We had scarcely finished breakfast the next morning when Don drove up in his truck. He had a hoe, a bag of coarse river sand for making cement and a few hand tools. We gathered our tools and bag of cement and, like loaded pack mules, trudged up the hill to the spring.

"First thing we got to do is find where the water gathers," Don explained. "You don't want just the trickle…you want the *source*. So let's dig back into the bank."

John and I were willing workers. With pick and shovel, we followed the water about 4 feet into the hillside. There we found it coming from under a big rock in a single stream about an inch in diameter.

"That looks good," Don said. "We can head 'er up right here." I didn't have the foggiest idea what he was talking about, but it soon became clear. "What we need to do is kinda 'pond' up that water. You know—dam it up and lead it into the hose that will take it to your reservoir.

"You always want to use a little reservoir so you can build up some surplus water. That way when you use a lot of water like in washing clothes, you won't run out. Looks like you got a bold spring here and you'll have plenty of water. Let's head it up before we worry about the reservoir.

"That big rock will make a good bottom. We'll mix up some cement to smooth it over. Then we'll lay this plastic pipe on the rock and make a dam to hold the water back. We call the dam a 'leaf', but I'm not sure why.

"Way back when, we used clay mud to make the bottom and sides and a good chestnut plank for the leaf. But sooner or later even chestnut rotted out. The cement lasts a whole lot longer."

We temporarily diverted the water so it didn't wash out the cement in our dam. Then we quickly formed the basin and leaf. They were about 6 inches high and 4 inches thick. Because our spring came out of rock and was down in the ground at least 4 or 5 feet, Don said we wouldn't get any seepage from surface water in a rain.

The next day, Don came up with a piece of metal roofing and a couple of chestnut boards. We used these and a small door I had made to close the spring in. With a door, we could open the little "springhouse" and check on things. When we were finished, I felt proud watching the water come out of the pipe.

Then we went to work on our reservoir. We created it by building a dam several feet high in the cleft of some boulders. The dam consisted of flat rocks laid on top of one another and some cement. The plastic water pipe came out the bottom.

"You'll need a strainer on that pipe in the spring so you won't get craw dads or salamanders in your coffee water," Don laughed. The third day, Don brought his workhorse, "Pearl", and a couple of plows to dig a trench for the pipe between the reservoir and the house. He used a turning plow to loosen the sod and a bull-tongue plow to deepen the ditch.

A bull-tongue plow looks like a spade turned backward. One pass with the turning plow and two with the bull-tongue and we had a pretty good ditch to lay pipe in.

Don and his two plows certainly saved John and me a lot of time and work! In just a few hours, we had our pipe laid and Don was driving Pearl toward home with our shouted thanks following him down the side of the valley.

Just for fun that evening, John did some calculations. He measured the angle from house to reservoir and, knowing the distance to the reservoir, figured that it was 130 feet higher than the house. Each foot of elevation provides about a half pound of water pressure...so we had about 60 pounds of pressure at the house.

Then, using the formula in one of his math books, he figured out the volume of water in 440 feet of 2-inch pipe. We had a little over 60 gallons stored in the pipe alone!

That convinced us we had indeed captured the right spring!

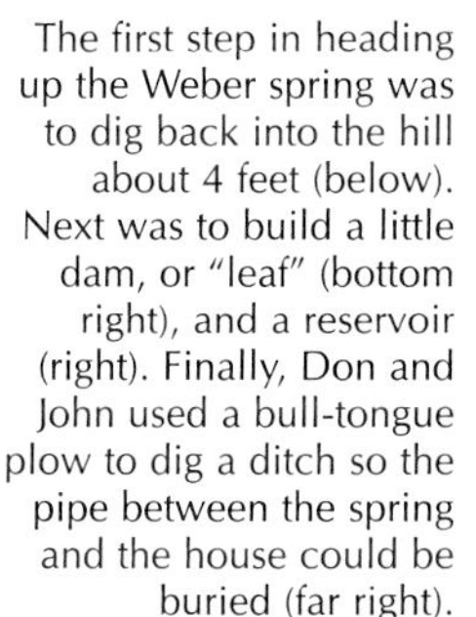

The first step in heading up the Weber spring was to dig back into the hill about 4 feet (below). Next was to build a little dam, or "leaf" (bottom right), and a reservoir (right). Finally, Don and John used a bull-tongue plow to dig a ditch so the pipe between the spring and the house could be buried (far right).

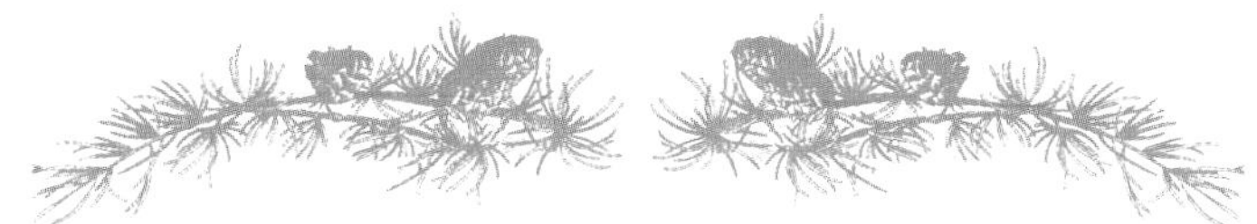

Molasses

In early fall when the leaves begin to show their first hint of yellow, my friends and neighbors start talking about "makin' molasses". Some things here are done just as they were more than 100 years ago.

The process of makin' molasses really begins when the tiny sorghum seed, saved from last year's crop, is planted in the spring. Sorghum is "tended" much the same as corn, with lots of cultivating and hoeing between the rows. Folks say that sorghum planted in heavy red clay makes the sweetest cane and the lightest color molasses.

Not every family makes molasses, and even those that do sometimes can't. Last year the ground was so cold and wet the seed never did come up.

I first watched Leonard and Alma's family makin' molasses shortly after we arrived in the valley. Theirs is a family operation and makin' molasses always turns into a big reunion. Everyone, however young or old, gets into the act. They try to schedule the molasses makin' before the first frost...cold weather makes the cane tough and the long flat leaves harder to strip from the stalks.

The cane is cut in the field, piled on a wagon and hauled to the barn. There the stalks are stripped and crushed in a mill. The mill has two heavy steel rollers that squeeze out the sweet juice. The rollers are turned by a horse that circles monotonously round and round, pulling a long pole called a "sweep".

As the horse's human helper feeds the cane into the mill, the green juice spurts from the cane and drains out a spout. The juice passes through a cloth that filters out the grassy fibers. Then the juice is collected in a bucket.

Kay feeds sorghum cane into the mill, which crushes the cane between two heavy steel rollers, producing sweet juice.

"Gyp", Leonard's gray horse, and "Nell", Clem's buckskin, take turns trudging around the circle. They get constant encouragement from whoever is feeding the mill.

At that first molasses makin', Alma's father, Bass, told me, "One time when we were makin' 'lasses at home, we decided the mule needed a rest from pulling the sweep. We hitched up an old ox that we used for dragging logs out of the woods. "That rascal made about six turns around the mill and got dizzy. He staggered so much we had to quick cut him loose before he tore the whole rig up."

Later, as Kay was feeding the mill, Leonard came over and said, "You may think this is easy work, but it definitely is not. One time Grandpa lost a finger that he got caught in this very same mill." In a louder voice, Leonard added, "Watch what you're doing there, Kay. Remember Grandpa's finger!"

Then I watched Ronnie carry the full bucket of juice over to the boiler-pan, where the juice is concentrated and made into molasses. It is a large flat pan about 6 inches deep, 30 inches wide and 6 feet long.

It rests on two long rock walls that make up the "furnace". Long and narrow like the pan, the furnace is designed so the fire heats everything evenly. Dead locust wood, poplar or oak is used for fuel to boil the juice.

As Ronnie poured the juice in the pan, which was almost full already, Leonard checked the fire, then came back to where we were standing. "In the old days, Dad used chestnut wood," he explained. "It burned at just the right temperature.

"Now the chestnut trees are gone—either killed by blight or logged out—and we use a lot of locust wood. It burns too hot, so we cool the fire down every so often with a spray of water from that garden hose. You can see from how the juice is boiling whether it is getting too hot."

Then he added, "That pan holds about 60 gallons of juice. When it cooks down in 6 or 8 hours, the molasses will be taken off and we'll have about 10 gallons of sweetnin'. If we let the fire get too hot, the molasses will be dark and the juice is apt to boil over. When that happens, the molasses will be too dark.

"On the other hand, if the fire isn't hot enough, you got to boil it forever to get the water off. I guess this is a lot of work to get a little sweet syrup."

As we watched Connie Sue skimming the boiling juice, Bass told me, “When I was young, ’lasses and honey were the only sweeteners any of us had. Sugar could be bought, but in those days money was scarce. We had a couple of stands of bees, but what honey we got we saved for when the preacher came for dinner.”

In the pan, a green scum formed on the surface as the juice boiled. Alma used a flat-bottomed scoop on a long stick to collect and remove the “skimmings”. Skimmings have to be removed all during the 6 to 8 hours of boiling. Alma told me, “If you don’t get this green scum off, the finished syrup will taste grassy.”

I later found out that this scum is a combination of chlorophyll, starch, dextrin, vegetable tissue, pectin and gluten. I also learned that the juice, which starts out with about 15 percent sugar, ends up after the boiling with about 70 percent. The tangy bite of molasses is due mainly to its high iron content, but also to some organic acids formed during the boiling.

There are many ways of determining when the molasses is finished cooking, none of them all that scientific. Clem went over and consulted with Alma on that subject. Their “test” was to watch how the hot molasses came off the scoop. If it flowed into a wide sheet, it was about ready. They also looked to see if there was a long thin string of it stretching from the scoop back to the pan.

“She looks ready,” Clem finally said, nodding.

Connie Sue applied a test of her own. She placed a cool bit of syrup between her thumb and second finger, then watched to see how far the string stretched when she spread thumb and finger apart. The string finally broke and formed a little corkscrew on her thumb, another important indicator.

“She’s ready,” Connie Sue said, smiling.

Leonard noted how the syrup boiled. “See there,” he said. “The bubbles of steam break through the thick syrup on the surface and leave little holes that last just an instant. Then the syrup forms what looks like the brims of hats or caps around the holes. That’s why we say the molasses is ‘bustin’ caps’. Yep, she’s ready, all right.”

Six-year-old Brandon had his own test. He dipped a short piece of cane stalk into the pan and tasted the warm syrup. “Sure ’nough,” he agreed. “She’s ready.” With this final confirmation, four of the men moved to the wooden handles on each end of the pan and lifted it off the fire.

They set it on two logs that tilted the pan slightly so the syrup ran into one end. Alma and Ronnie’s wife, Deborah, scooped the molasses out with saucepans. They poured it through a clean cheesecloth filter in a large funnel and golden syrup flowed out into clean jugs.

Alma’s brother Diedrick cuts cane (left). The harvested cane is loaded on a wagon (below) and hauled to the barn, where the stalks are stripped and crushed.

The youngsters used sharpened paddle-sticks cut from short pieces of cane to scrape sticky syrup from the bottom of the pan. I followed suit and got my first taste of Big Pine Valley sorghum molasses.

Ever since, Barbara and I have always looked forward to fall and talk of makin' molasses. It's partly the sights, sounds and wonderful aromas of producing something good for the table. It's also partly the chance to get together with friends and neighbors and share some of the valley's heritage.

Maybe what I like most, though, is watching the children. All during the process of making molasses, they are encouraged to help, even when the job might get done quicker and easier without them.

The kids strip cane and carry stalks to the mill. They bring wood and, under watchful eyes, feed the fire. They try their hand at skimming with the wide flat scoop. And they get to taste the syrup as it boils.

They have fun and enjoy themselves, but you can also see by the look on their faces that they are serious about learning. This is how one generation passes what it knows on to the next.

The kids may not know it yet, but by sampling the sweet syrup and stoking the fire under the pan, they are taking their first steps toward becoming teachers themselves.

Alma and Connie Sue (left) pour molasses from the pan into jars after the juice has boiled 6 to 8 hours. When boiling is completed, Clem scrapes a sample from the pan to taste (top). Above: With Leonard watching, Alma makes a finger test to see if syrup is ready.

Makin' molasses can be hot work, as Clem and Leonard, skimming in the photo below, can attest. At left, Clem strips leaves from cane stalks.

While "Nell" plods round and round turning the sweep, Leonard feeds cane stalks into the mill. Inset: Stalks enter the steel rollers in the mill, well on their way toward producing some fine Big Pine Valley sweets.

2853 DP
2854 DP
2853 DP
2854 DP
9688 AB

Newcomers

Even though Barbara and I have lived in the Big Pine Valley for 20 years, we still consider ourselves newcomers. There are other newcomers here, too. Like us, they "discovered" the valley while in pursuit of a special dream.

We arrived from Florida looking for a little parcel of fertile hillside land where we could grow vegetables and fruit that tasted just like what I remember as a boy growing up in Ohio. We were also looking for a place with old-fashioned values.

We were lucky. We found our dream—and more—here in the Big Pine Valley. But that's not always how it works out for newcomers who sometimes expect farming to be a whole lot easier than it is.

In reality, subsistence farming demands a lot of a person. Having to produce most of what you need can break, as well as mend, your spirit. Getting in hay for your stock, cutting winter firewood, constantly maintaining your spring and your buildings—these things are often more than a newcomer bargained for.

One day you hear that a place is up for sale again. The newcomers who lived there for such a short time have left to pursue their dream elsewhere.

Still, there are those who stay and ultimately thrive. At first, the valley may seem to defeat them, but then they change and grow. Across the valley from our place, perched on a steep hillside where we can see their lights at night and they can see ours, are Frank and Barbara.

Frank was a tool and die maker for a company that built airplanes in Florida. Barbara sold real estate. With their children grown and gone, Frank took early retirement. The two of them set off in pursuit of their dream and eventually found their way here.

Frank remodeled the old house on the place they bought and converted the barn into a workshop for his tools and machines. In the beginning, Frank and Barbara floundered a little. They bought cows, a bull and a tractor. They put up hay and spent a great deal of time building and repairing fences around their 50 acres.

But Frank, wanting to spend more time in his shop, began to resent the fencing and haying. After 6 or 7 years, they sold the tractor, the cows and the bull. They quit worrying about hay and fences and gradually switched over to the work they enjoyed.

Now Frank spends 10 hours a day in his barn shop, carefully turning pieces of wood into carousel horses or wonderful likenesses of wild birds. As he once carved steel, he now fashions wood. Barbara, the extrovert of the two, needed more people contact; today she works as a business agent for a local whitewater rafting company.

Smithy and Judy came from Texas. For generations, Smithy's family had been ranchers, farmers and bankers. They measured their ranches Texas style—in square miles, not acres. But Smithy

Elizabeth is one of those folks who've found their dream in the Big Pine Valley—though it's taken considerable perseverance. She relies on her large garden for much of her food. At far left, she gets "help" from her dog as she picks strawberries.

had an itch to try something different, to live in a space that wasn't as vast and hard to fill.

Judy grew up in North Carolina, so they gravitated to the Big Pine Valley. They found and fixed up an old log cabin beside the creek. They also bought 100 acres so they could raise horses and children.

It took several years and a son and a daughter before their dream began to jell. They quit putting up hay and tobacco and started raising Christmas trees. Now Smithy spends his days trimming, fertilizing and mowing around his trees.

Then there's Elizabeth, who's in her 60's. She grew up in Germany during the hard times of World War II. Now she lives alone on her little farm with her chickens, dairy goats and sheep.

Neighbors help her get in hay and firewood, and in exchange she gives them some of her goat cheese. She lives partly on determination and partly on the food she cans from her big garden. Elizabeth is one of those who refuses to let go of her dream, which is to survive alone on her land.

Also among the newcomers are Alastair and Allegra. He's from Scotland and she's a North Carolina native. They met in New York City, where she was a teacher and he was a carpenter. On a visit to the Big Pine Valley, they found there was considerable demand for good carpentry.

So when they moved here, Alastair immediately had a way to make a living. Allegra got a job teaching and they rented a house from Ray and Margaret. Eventually, they bought a parcel of beautiful land where they hoped to someday build a home.

When the volunteer fire department was organized, both Alastair and Allegra became fire fighters. They took special courses and learned to be "first responders" for medical emergencies in the valley. Folks usually call them instead of 911.

Last year on Thanksgiving night, Alastair and Allegra woke up to the smell of smoke. They tumbled out of bed and found flames consuming the upper part of the house. The fire truck arrived quickly, but the strong dry wind and lack of water made it impossible to get the fire out.

They lost everything—Alastair's carpentry tools as well as their clothes, cooking utensils, books and cash. Before the ashes cooled, offers of help started coming in. They were given a house to live in temporarily...and clothes, food, tools, pots and pans, furniture, bedding.

One of the volunteer firemen handed fire chief Dan five new $100 bills and asked that they be passed on anonymously to Alastair. Others helped the couple build a new house on the land they had bought earlier. Out of disaster emerged the home they had long hoped to build.

Alastair and Allegra had given to the valley and now the valley was giving back to them. That's the way the valley is—it can fight you or nurture you. You just have to be determined enough to stay with it.

Others have found their dream in this valley, too. Mary and Jim work with their horses and their garden...Steve and Diane grow herbs commercially...Dan and Shirley work with the volunteer fire department...John makes guitars that are works of art with silver and mother-of-pearl inlays...David and Jane are successful sculptors.

Newcomers are part of the story of the Big Pine Valley. They are enriching life in the valley even as the valley enriches their lives.

Alastair and Allegra (below) stand near the house they're building after fire destroyed the one they were renting. At right: Alastair and "Smokey" put up some hay, then he mulches zinnias in the garden.

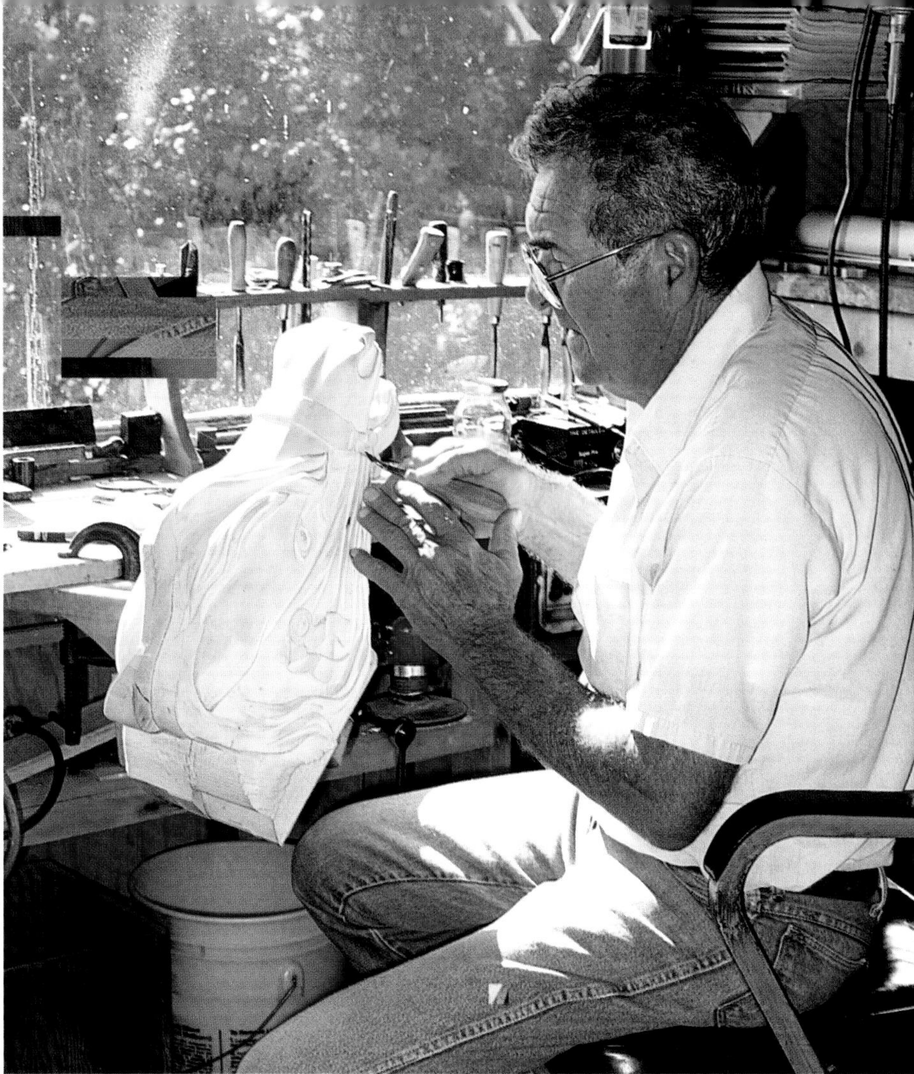

After farming for a few years, Frank decided to devote all his time to carving carousel horses and wild birds. In his barn, he works on a horse's head (top right) and examines finished horses (right). Originally, he painted the completed horses (above).

When they first moved to the Big Pine Valley, Smithy and Judy (left) grew traditional crops of hay and tobacco. Eventually, however, they discovered they'd rather be Christmas tree farmers. That's Smithy planting Fraser firs (below) and using boughs from culled trees to make wreaths (far left).

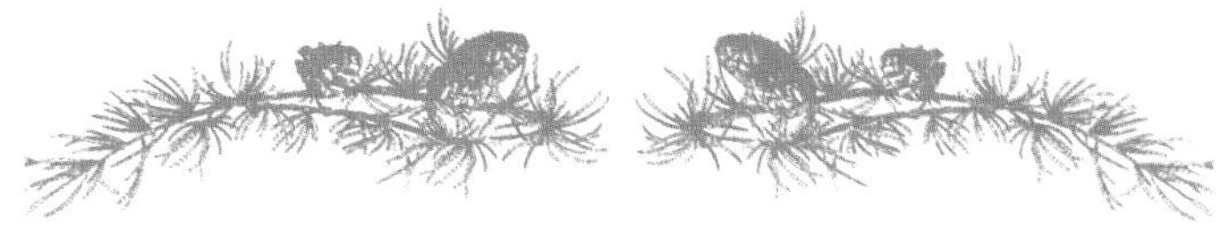

Pickin' & Fiddlin'

Stay in the Big Pine Valley very long and you'll hear the music of banjos, fiddles, dulcimers and guitars coming from someone's porch or backyard. Music and musicians are part of the life and heritage of the valley.

When you first encounter a Big Pine Valley musician, it'll likely be in his or her workaday role as a farmer, mechanic, mail carrier or store clerk. It isn't till Sunday afternoons that these musicians have the time to get together for a cookout and a few hours of serious pickin' and fiddlin'.

Ronnie enjoys getting together with friends and neighbors for a Sunday afternoon barbecue and some serious banjo pickin'.

The first time I met Dayton was over at his place shortly after we moved to the valley. He had an auto repair shop in his garage and the gearshift in my car had gotten loose. As often happens in this valley, it took a while for us to get around to discussing the business at hand.

First we had to sit by Dayton's homemade stove and talk about the weather and growing potatoes. Then he showed me a fiddle he'd just bought at a bargain price. The previous owner had stuck a couple of wood screws into the fiddle's neck, wrecking the fingerboard.

Dayton had fixed the fingerboard with some pieces of ebony and also replaced the tuning pegs. Naturally, pointing all this out led Dayton to pick up his bow and play a few tunes for me. His music was wonderful, something I hadn't exactly expected to encounter as part of getting the gearshift on my car fixed.

Then he put the fiddle down and picked up an old guitar he'd purchased at a gas station for $35. "This is my pride and joy," he said. "It's a D-18 Martin. I'd like to refinish it, but I'm afraid that might ruin its tone."

With that, he propped his foot up on a toolbox, placed the guitar on his knee and began to pick. The notes flowed out of that old guitar and filled the shop with sweet toe-tappin' music. It was grand.

When we finally did get around to the gearshift, Dayton grabbed a wrench and crawled under the car. He wiggled a few things, but couldn't find what was wrong. Then he got up and opened the hood. That's when he nodded to himself and tightened a nut with his wrench.

"Okay, now try 'er," he said. I did and the gearshift worked great. When I offered to pay him, Dayton not only refused, he "countered" with an invitation to a cookout the following Sunday. That's where Barbara and I were introduced to homemade mountain music.

Since then, we have visited back and forth many times and always look forward to hearing the boys make their music. Now Dayton's son, Timmy, is grown and has discovered he's got the same way with the strings of a guitar as his dad. There's nothing quite like listening to Dayton, Bruce, Timmy, Carmen, Ronnie, Warren, Jim and Steve carrying on the Big Pine Valley tradition of making fine music in the backyard.

Like Dayton, these folks all have other jobs, but they live for their music. Besides repairing cars and farming, Dayton also turned out to be our mailman.

Many valley musicians learn to play their stringed instruments without ever taking a lesson. Some also make their instruments. John lives just up the mountain from our house and not only plays a mean guitar, but makes one, too. Each of his guitars is a work of art—rich and mellow to listen to and, with inlaid silver and mother-of-pearl, beautiful to behold.

Of course, not all the talented musicians around here are men. Bruce's daughters flood the valley with music from their keyboard. And in church on Sunday mornings, two other women, Brenda and Deborah, play music for hymns on the organ and piano.

Sometimes, too, Brenda and her daughter, Beth Ann, will sing a duet with voices that are pure and true. At such times, the music spills out of the little Church at the Forks and runs right up the hill to the sky.

Dayton's porch becomes a music stage as (from left to right above) Tim, Ronnie, Dayton, Carmen and Warren pick and strum an afternoon away. Tim has both a friend and his guitar on his lap at left. Right: Beth Ann on the keyboard.

That's Jim stringin' along on his mandolin at top left. Above, John shows one of the beautiful guitars he makes. They are often decorated with inlaid silver and mother-of-pearl. Left: Dayton gets all he can out of his guitar while Bruce plays alongside him.

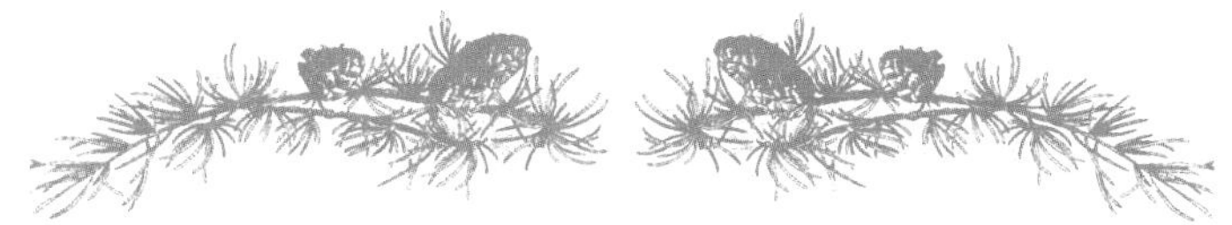

Sugar & Shoes

Tobacco—today a controversial crop—is not only the economic mainstay of the Big Pine Valley, but an important part of its culture and spirit. When Barbara and I first moved here 2 decades ago, I had already quit smoking and become anti-tobacco.

I haven't changed my mind about smoking, but I have learned to respect and appreciate what goes into growing tobacco. For most farmers in the Big Pine Valley, tobacco is the primary—if not *only*—source of cash. Raising burley is backbreaking work, but it returns good money for the effort.

With the cash they earn, farmers buy the things they need but can't produce themselves—sugar, shoes, a washing machine, a car. So without tobacco, folks here would face real hardship.

Like any effort that demands a lot of you, growing tobacco teaches you something about yourself. Much of the work involves doing things by hand, from getting the plants in the ground each spring to hanging the leaves in the barn in tiers to dry each fall.

In between, entire families may spend weeks in the tobacco patch hoeing out the weeds, snipping off the pretty pink and white tops of the tobacco plants, hanging the leaves on "baccer sticks" to cure and loading the tobacco on wagons.

In the fall when barns are cold and dank, you can find the same families "handing" their tobacco—sorting it and getting it ready to bale. Then the bales are lugged off to market and sold. That's when the family says its thanks for the annual miracle that converts earth, water and air first into plants, then into a new pair of work gloves or a small toy for a child at Christmas.

Growing tobacco not only makes a person appreciative; it instills a strong work ethic. And a strong work ethic is a good foundation for a lot of the other admirable values that bind families and community together.

There are few things prettier in summer than a tobacco patch with its big green leaves ruffled by a breeze. The movement of sunlight and shade through the patch makes a hillside look as if it's awash with waves of green.

What will happen if tobacco can no longer be grown in the Big Pine Valley? It's hard to say, of course. There would be adversity, that's for sure. But then folks here are used to that. Fiercely independent, they might just come up with some other way to earn the cash they need.

They have already experimented with growing tomatoes, broccoli, green beans, alfalfa and other commercial crops. But those have all fallen short when it comes to producing dependable income. Valley farmers don't have any trouble growing the crops, but then they can't sell them at a profit.

Ironically, the very strength and determination they have learned from growing tobacco may be what gets my friends and neighbors through an uncertain future.

Tobacco takes backbreaking work to produce, but in the Big Pine Valley, it pays for some of the necessities of life. It also adds to the beauty of the valley—thickening the hillside foliage, as Chad's "baccer" patch is doing at top left, growing in the field and drying in the barn (left) and, after it's cut, catching the sun while hanging on sticks in Alan's field (inset). Above: Don, carrying "baccer sticks", gets ready to spear some more leaves.

From setting the plants in the ground each spring to stripping leaves from the stalks in the fall (below), growing tobacco is a family affair on the Buckner place. The Buckner gals are Deborah, Kaye and Amy. Above, Noah checks plants on his place to see if they're ready to be topped. At left, tobacco being hung on tier poles in the barn to cure.

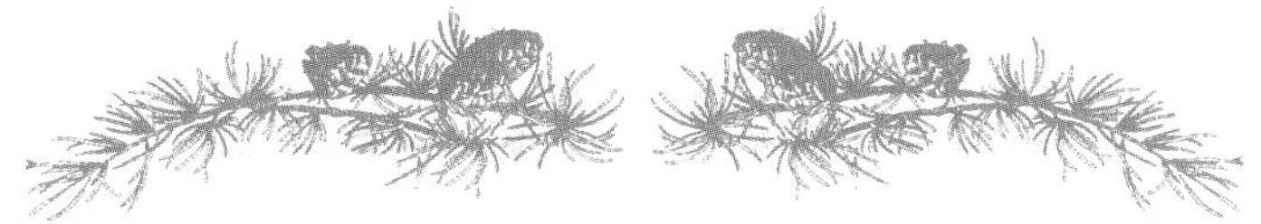

Saltin' Cows

There are so many more things to tell you about the Big Pine Valley. The longer we live here, the more we find to learn about, enjoy and appreciate.

Obviously, the valley is first and foremost a physical place. You can walk over its steep hills, through its woods and alongside the clear rushing waters of its creeks. You can inhale the sweetness of its spring flowers and the pungency of its rain-soaked leaves in the fall. With your hands, you can touch the bark of its trees, the rocks of its mountains and the rich heavy soil of its tilled fields.

You can hear its sounds, too. There are the soft breezes that rustle the cornstalks and tobacco leaves, and the cold winter winds that howl over "the bald" and down through the coves. There are birds that sing, frogs that croak and foxes that bark.

But the valley is more than a physical place, more than something that affects your senses. Live here very long and you will realize that it is a place of the spirit, too. You can see that not only in its many profound mysteries, but in its people. After all, much of who and what the people are comes from having been born and raised here.

In its way, the valley helped teach them many of the important things they know about life. Like a parent, the valley can be tender as well as hard, giving as well as taking. Its children have had to learn to be strong, to endure, to work hard and never give up. But they have also learned to drop whatever they are doing to lend a hand to those in need.

When Barbara and I moved here 20 years ago, we knew there were a lot of things we would have to learn. We didn't know the physical valley very well yet and we certainly didn't know much about its traditions and ways. As a retired veterinarian, I *did* know a bit about livestock. But there is always more to learn about that, too.

Since moving to the Big Pine Valley, Bill has learned many lessons, including the benefits of *not* giving his cows a block of salt.

Fortunately, I had a good person to teach me—a man who could show me both the valley's physical and spiritual dimensions. He was my friend and neighbor, Don Wild. Don didn't just teach me facts...he opened my eyes to a whole new way of thinking and doing.

He seemed to always work in harmony with people, with animals, with the land. He didn't so much offer advice—or even suggestions—as alternatives to choose between. He always started out by saying, "Maybe if you tried..." or by asking, "Have you thought of...?"

It took 5 years of work during the summers to finish and move into our house. During that time, Don was always there to help if we needed him. Even though he was still farming back then, he came up most days to see how we were doing. Without being asked, he helped mix cement and raise our walls.

He wouldn't let us pay him, but in return I could do the veterinary work on his cows, cats and dog. Our son, John, and I helped him put up his hay and get in firewood. We three worked as a team on any of the farm jobs Don needed extra hands for.

The first year after we started helping him, he insisted on giving John a cow. John and I objected, but Don wouldn't listen. The next year he gave *me* a cow. These two animals were the start of our small herd. We often ran our cows with Don's and when either his or ours needed to be worked, we did it together.

Even though I had worked with cows, Don was soon teaching me things there, too. One example was when Don salted his cows. Once a week during summer, I would hear him coming up through his fields toward our pasture hollering, "Hooooooooo, cows; fooooooooo, cows".

His voice echoed off the hillsides, and before long the cows and calves—and even the big bull—would come galloping out of the woods and down the hills toward him. He would stop by a big flat rock and, as the cattle gathered 'round, toss handfuls of coarse salt on the rock. While they ravenously licked up the salt, he moved among them, talking to them, calling some by name and petting the more gentle ones.

Then he would continue up the hill, cross through the fence and come to our pasture near the house. He'd call several times and our cows would run down the steep hillsides to where he was waiting. They, too, wanted their salt.

One day I couldn't stand it any longer. "Don," I said. "You know it would save you a lot of time and work if you just put a couple of salt blocks out in each pasture. We could fix up some sheltered feeders, then you wouldn't have to walk clear up here every week."

At first he didn't answer. He just moved among my cows, patting one here and talking to another there. Finally he looked at me over the backs of the cows and said in his quiet way, "You know, Bill, maybe you're right. But I like to see and touch all my cows on a regular basis.

"That way I can be sure they aren't coming down with pinkeye or something else. I can also make sure one of 'em hasn't fallen through a fence somewhere and injured herself or gotten lost.

"Now, if I was to walk through these hills and woods lookin' for all my cows, that *would* take me a lot of time and work. Even if I found them all, some would be a little skittish for lack of being worked and talked to and petted.

"So the best thing is to use the salt to train 'em so they come when

I holler. Not only do I get to see each cow up close every week; if I ever want to work 'em, I just holler and they come a runnin'."

The next week when he came up through his pasture saltin' cows, I met him at my fence. As we walked toward my saltin' rock, I said, "Don, let me holler this time. I think my cows need to learn my voice if I'm going to get them to come when I call."

Don just smiled. "Good idea," he said.

That was over 15 years ago. Since then, Don has seen his 80th birthday come and go. He doesn't hike these hills like he used to, but every week you can still hear, "Hooooooooooo, cows; fooooooooo, cows" echoing off the sides of the valley.

Maybe it doesn't sound as good as when Don did it. But after only 20 years in the Big Pine Valley, I'm still learning.

There's a nice flat saltin' rock in the pasture just above Bill and Barbara's house (left). Once Don taught him the wisdom of using that rock, Bill discovered he liked to stand there each week and holler (below). Opposite: "Snowflake" as a young heifer (inset) and cows grazing in Webers' steep pasture.

Dedication

To my wife Jacki for her extraordinary support, including making numerous suggestions and putting up with the evenings and weekends I was working on this book.

ALAN AGRESTI

To Corey and Cody, who have shown me the joys of motherhood, and to my husband, Dale, for being a dear friend and a dedicated father to our boys. You have always been my biggest supporters.

CHRIS FRANKLIN

To my wife Sophia and our children Franziska, Florentina, Maximilian, and Mattheus, who are a bunch of fun to be with, and to Jean-Luc Picard for inspiring me.

BERNHARD KLINGENBERG

Contents

An Introduction to the Web Apps

The book's website, www.pearsonhighered.com/AFK, links to several new and interactive web-based applets (or web apps) that run in a browser. These apps are designed to help students understand a wide range of statistical concepts and carry out statistical inference. Many of these apps are featured (often including screenshots) in Activities throughout the book. The apps allow saving output (such as graphs or tables) for potential inclusion in homework or projects.

- The **Random Numbers** app generates uniform random numbers (with or without replacement) from a user-defined range of integer values and simulates flipping a (potentially biased) coin.

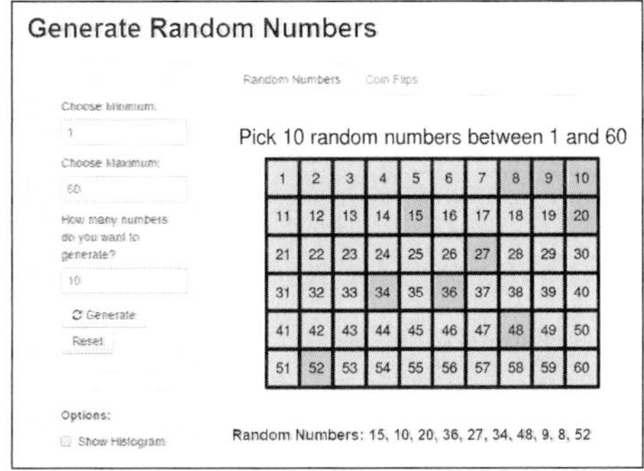

- The **Mean vs. Median** app allows users to add or delete points from a dot plot as the users explore the effect of outliers or skew on these two statistics.
- The **Explore Categorical Data** and **Explore Quantitative Data** apps provide basic statistics and plots for user-supplied data.
- The **Explore Linear Regression** app allows users to add or delete points from a scatterplot and observe how the regression line changes for different patterns or is affected by outliers. The **Fit Linear Regression** app allows users to supply their own data, fit a linear regression model and explore residuals.
- The **Guess the Correlation** app lets users guess the correlation for a given scatterplot (and find the correlation between guesses and the true values).
- The **Binomial, Normal, *t*-, Chi-square, and F Distribution** apps visually explore the meaning of parameters for these distributions. Users can also find probabilities and percentiles and check them visually on the graph.

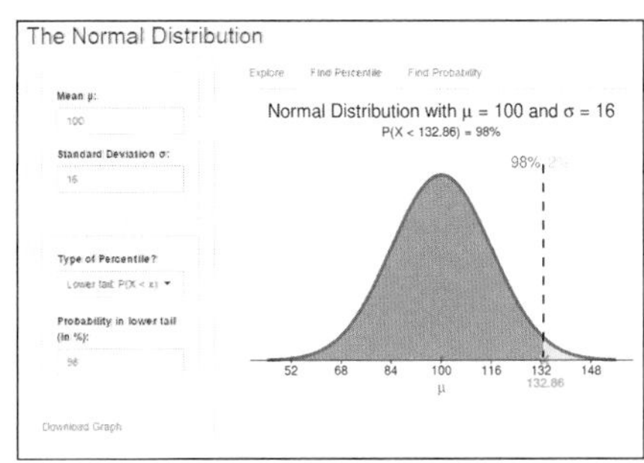

- The various **Sampling Distribution** apps generate sampling distributions of the sample proportion or the sample mean. These apps let users generate samples of various sizes from a wide range of distributions such as skewed, uniform, bell-shaped, bimodal, or custom-built. The apps display the population distribution, the data distribution of a randomly generated sample, and the sampling distribution of the sample mean or proportion. With the (repeated) click on a button, one can see how the sampling distribution builds up one simulated random sample at a time and, for large sample sizes, assumes a bell shape. Users can move sliders for sample size and various population parameters to see the effect on the sampling distribution. Chapter 7 shows many screenshots of these apps.
- The **Inference for a Proportion** and the **Inference for a Mean** app carry out statistical inference. They provide graphs, confidence intervals and results from z- or t-tests for data supplied in summary or original form.
- The **Explore Coverage** app uses simulation to demonstrate the concept of the confidence coefficient, both

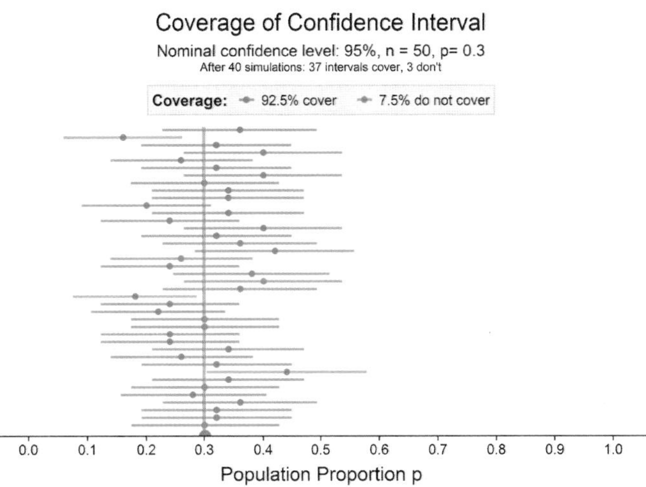

for confidence intervals for the proportion and for the mean. Different sliders for true population parameter, sample size or confidence coefficient show their effect on coverage and width of confidence intervals.

- The **Errors and Power** app explores Type I and Type II errors and the concept of power visually and interactively. Users can move sliders to connect these concepts to sample size, significance level, and true parameter value for one-sample tests about proportions or means.
- The **Inference Comparing Proportions** and the **Inference Comparing Means** apps construct appropriate graphs for a visual comparison and carry out two-sample inference. Confidence intervals and results of hypotheses tests for two independent (or two dependent) samples are displayed. Data can be supplied in summary or original form.
- The **Bootstrap** app finds a bootstrap confidence interval for a mean, median, or standard deviation.
- The **Permutation Test** (cont. data) app compares quantitative responses between two groups using a permutation approach. By repeatedly clicking a button, the sampling distribution using permutations is generated step-by-step, which is useful when first introducing the topic. Both the original and the (randomly) permuted datasets are shown.
- The **Permutation Test for Independence** app tests for independence in contingency tables using the permutation sampling distribution of the Chi-squared statistic X^2. It displays the original contingency table and bar chart along with the table and chart for the permuted dataset, as well as the sampling distribution of X^2.
- The **Fisher Exact Test** app can be used for exact inference in 2×2 contingency tables.
- The **ANOVA (One-Way)** app allows comparison of several means, including post-hoc pairwise multiple comparisons.

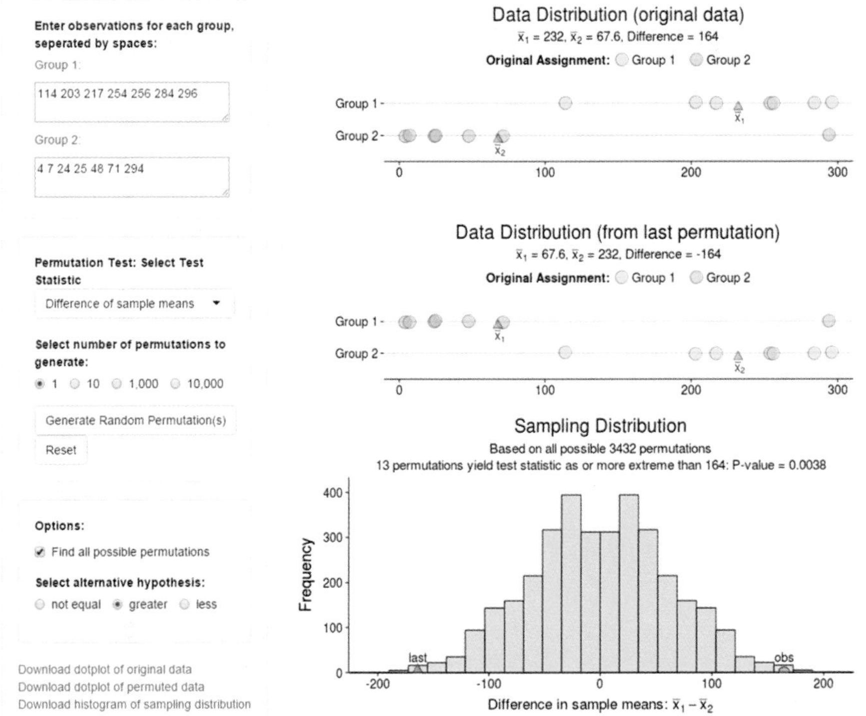

Preface

We have each taught introductory statistics for many years, and we have witnessed the welcome evolution from the traditional formula-driven mathematical statistics course to a concept-driven approach. This concept-driven approach places more emphasis on why statistics is important in the real world and places less emphasis on mathematical probability. One of our goals in writing this book was to help make the conceptual approach more interesting and more readily accessible to students. At the end of the course, we want students to look back at their statistics course and realize that they learned practical concepts that will serve them well for the rest of their lives.

We also want students to come to appreciate that in practice, assumptions are not perfectly satisfied, models are not exactly correct, distributions are not exactly normally distributed, and different factors should be considered in conducting a statistical analysis. The title of our book reflects the experience of data analysts, who soon realize that statistics is an art as well as a science.

What's New in This Edition

Our goal in writing the fourth edition of our textbook was to improve the student and instructor user experience. We have:

- Clarified terminology and streamlined writing throughout the text to improve ease of reading and facilitate comprehension.
- Used real data and real examples to illustrate almost all concepts discussed. Throughout the book, within three to five consecutive pages, an example is presented that depicts a real-world scenario to illustrate the statistical concept discussed.
- Introduced new web-based applets (referred to as *web apps* or *apps*) illustrating and helping students interact with key statistical concepts and techniques. These apps invite students to explore consequences of changing parameters and to carry out statistical inference. Among other relevant concepts and techniques, students are introduced to:
  - Sampling distributions
  - Central limit theorem
  - Bootstrapping for interval estimation (Chapter 8)
  - Randomization or permutation tests for significance testing (Chapter 10 for difference in two means and Chapter 11 for two categorical variables).
- Inserted brief overviews to set the stage for each chapter, introducing students to chapter concepts and helping them see how previous chapters' concepts, tools, and techniques are related.
- Included computer output from the most recent versions of MINITAB and the TI calculator.
- Expanded Chapter 1, providing key terminology to establish a foundation to understand the big picture of the statistical investigative process—the importance of asking good statistical questions, designing an appropriate study, performing descriptive and inferential analysis, and making a conclusion.

- Reflected the latest trends in statistical education, including:
  - Measures of association for categorical variables in Chapter 3
  - Permutation testing in Chapters 10 and 11
  - Updated coverage of McNemar's test in Chapter 10 (previously Chapter 11)
- Moved important coverage of risk difference and relative risk to Chapter 3 (instead of first introducing these measures in Chapter 11). We believe that understanding these two statistics is a necessary part of statistical literacy for the everyday citizen as they are pervasive in mass media and the medical literature.
- Updated or replaced over 25 percent of the exercises and examples. In addition, we have updated all General Social Services (GSS) data with the most current data available.

Our Approach

In 2005, the American Statistical Association (ASA) endorsed guidelines and recommendations for the introductory statistics course as described in the report, "Guidelines for Assessment and Instruction in Statistics Education (GAISE) for the College Introductory Course" (www.amstat.org/education/gaise). The report states that the overreaching goal of all introductory statistics courses is to produce statistically educated students, which means that students should develop statistical literacy and the ability to think statistically. The report gives six key recommendations for the college introductory course:

- Emphasize statistical literacy and develop statistical thinking.
- Use real data.
- Stress conceptual understanding rather than mere knowledge of procedures.
- Foster active learning in the classroom.
- Use technology for developing concepts and analyzing data.
- Use assessment to evaluate and improve student learning.

We wholeheartedly endorse these recommendations, and our textbook takes every opportunity to support these guidelines.

Ask and Answer Interesting Questions

In presenting concepts and methods, we encourage students to think about the data and the appropriate analyses by posing questions. Our approach, learning by framing questions, is carried out in various ways, including (1) presenting a structured approach to examples that separates the question and the analysis from the scenario presented, (2) providing homework problems that encourage students to think and write, and (3) asking questions in the figure captions that are answered in the Chapter Review.

Present Concepts Clearly

Students have told us that this book is more "readable" and interesting than other introductory statistics texts because of the wide variety of intriguing real data examples and exercises. We have simplified our prose wherever possible, without sacrificing any of the accuracy that instructors expect in a textbook.

A serious source of confusion for students is the multitude of inference methods that derive from the many combinations of confidence intervals and tests, means and proportions, large sample and small sample, variance known and unknown, two-sided and one-sided inference, independent and dependent samples, and so on. We emphasize the most important cases for practical application of inference: large sample, variance unknown, two-sided inference, and independent samples. The many other cases are also covered (except for known variances), but more briefly, with the exercises focusing mainly on the way inference is commonly conducted in practice. We present the traditional probability distribution–based inference but now also include inference using simulation through bootstrapping and permutation tests.

Connect Statistics to the Real World

We believe it's important for students to be comfortable with analyzing a balance of both quantitative and categorical data so students can work with the data they most often see in the world around them. Every day in the media, we see and hear percentages and rates used to summarize results of opinion polls, outcomes of medical studies, and economic reports. As a result, we have increased the attention paid to the analysis of proportions. For example, we use contingency tables early in the text to illustrate the concept of association between two categorical variables and to show the potential influence of a lurking variable.

Organization of the Book

The statistical investigative process has the following components: (1) asking a statistical question; (2) designing an appropriate study to collect data; (3) analyzing the data; and (4) interpreting the data and making conclusions to answer the statistical questions. With this in mind, the book is organized into four parts.

Part 1 focuses on gathering and exploring data. This equates to components 1, 2, and 3, when the data is analyzed descriptively (both for one variable and the association between two variables).

Part 2 covers probability, probability distributions, and the sampling distribution. This equates to component 3, when the student learns the underlying probability necessary to make the step from analyzing the data descriptively to analyzing the data inferentially (for example, understanding sampling distributions to develop the concept of a margin of error and a P-value).

Part 3 covers inferential statistics. This equates to components 3 and 4 of the statistical investigative process. The students learn how to form confidence intervals and conduct significance tests and then make appropriate conclusions answering the statistical question of interest.

Part 4 covers analyzing associations (inferentially) and looks at extended statistical methods.

The chapters are written in such a way that instructors can teach out of order. For example, after Chapter 1, an instructor could easily teach Chapter 4, Chapter 2, and Chapter 3. Alternatively, an instructor may teach Chapters 5, 6, and 7 after Chapters 1 and 4. Sample syllabi are available from the book's website.

Features of the Fourth Edition

Promoting Student Learning

To motivate students to think about the material, ask appropriate questions, and develop good problem-solving skills, we have created special features that distinguish this text.

Student Support

To draw students to important material we highlight key definitions, guidelines, procedures, "In Practice" remarks, and other summaries in boxes throughout the text. In addition, we have four types of margin notes:

- **In Words:** This feature explains, in plain language, the definitions and symbolic notation found in the body of the text (which, for technical accuracy, must be more formal).
- **Caution:** These margin boxes alert students to areas to which they need to pay special attention, particularly where they are prone to make mistakes or incorrect assumptions.
- **Recall:** As the student progresses through the book, concepts are presented that depend on information learned in previous chapters. The Recall margin boxes direct the reader back to a previous presentation in the text to review and reinforce concepts and methods already covered.
- **Did You Know:** These margin boxes provide information that helps with the contextual understanding of the statistical question under consideration.

Graphical Approach

Because many students are visual learners, we have taken extra care to make the **text figures** informative. We've annotated many of the figures with labels that clearly identify the noteworthy aspects of the illustration. Further, most figure captions include a question (answered in the Chapter Review) designed to challenge the student to interpret and think about the information being communicated by the graphic. The graphics also feature a pedagogical use of color to help students recognize patterns and distinguish between statistics and parameters. The use of color is explained in the very front of the book for easy reference.

Hands-On Activities and Simulations

Each chapter contains diverse and dynamic activities that allow students to become familiar with a number of statistical methodologies and tools. The instructor can elect to carry out the activities in class, outside of class, or a combination of both. The activity often involves simulation, commonly using a web app available through the book's website or MyStatLab. Similar activities can also be found within MyStatLab™. These hands-on activities and simulations encourage students to learn by doing.

Connection to History: On the Shoulders of . . .

We believe that knowledge pertaining to the evolution and history of the statistics discipline is relevant to understanding the methods we use for designing studies and analyzing data. Throughout the text, several chapters feature a spotlight on people who have made major contributions to the statistics discipline. These spotlights are titled **On the Shoulders of . . .**

Real-World Connections

Chapter-Opening Example

Each chapter begins with a **high-interest example** that raises key questions and establishes themes that are woven throughout the chapter. Illustrated with engaging photographs, this example is designed to grab students' attention and draw them into the chapter. The issues discussed in the chapter's opening example are referred to and revisited in examples within the chapter. All chapter-opening examples use real data from a variety of applications.

Statistics: In Practice

We realize that there is a difference between proper academic statistics and what is actually done in practice. Data analysis in practice is an art as well as a science. Although statistical theory has foundations based on precise assumptions and conditions, in practice the real world is not so simple. **In Practice** boxes and text references alert students to the way statisticians actually analyze data in practice. These comments are based on our extensive consulting experience and research and by observing what well-trained statisticians do in practice.

Exercises and Examples

Innovative Example Format

Recognizing that the worked examples are the major vehicle for engaging and teaching students, we have developed a unique structure to help students learn to model the question-posing and investigative thought process required to examine issues intelligently using statistics. The five components are as follows:

- **Picture the Scenario** presents background information so students can visualize the situation. This step places the data to be investigated in context and often provides a link to previous examples.
- **Questions to Explore** reference the information from the scenario and pose questions to help students focus on what is to be learned from the example and what types of questions are useful to ask about the data.
- **Think It Through** is the heart of each example. Here, the questions posed are investigated and answered using appropriate statistical methods. Each solution is clearly matched to the question so students can easily find the response to each Question to Explore.
- **Insight** clarifies the central ideas investigated in the example and places them in a broader context that often states the conclusions in less technical terms. Many of the Insights also provide connections between seemingly disparate topics in the text by referring to concepts learned previously and/or foreshadowing techniques and ideas to come.

- **Try Exercise:** Each example concludes by directing students to an end-of-section exercise that allows immediate practice of the concept or technique within the example.

Concept tags are included with each example so that students can easily identify the concept demonstrated in the example.

Relevant and Engaging Exercises

The text contains a strong emphasis on real data in both the examples and exercises. We have updated the exercise sets in the fourth edition to ensure that students have ample opportunity to practice techniques and apply the concepts. Nearly all of the chapters contain more than 100 exercises, and more than 25 percent of the exercises are new to this edition or have been updated with current data. These exercises are realistic and ask students to provide interpretations of the data or scenario rather than merely to find a numerical solution. We show how statistics addresses a wide array of applications, including opinion polls, market research, the environment, and health and human behavior. Because we believe that most students benefit more from focusing on the underlying concepts and interpretations of data analyses than from the actual calculations, the exercises often show summary statistics and printouts and ask what can be learned from them.

We have exercises in three places:

- **At the end of each section.** These exercises provide immediate reinforcement and are drawn from concepts within the section.

- **At the end of each chapter.** This more comprehensive set of exercises draws from all concepts across all sections within the chapter.
- **Part Reviews.** These exercises draw connections among a part's chapters and summarize the overarching themes and concepts. Part exercises reinforce primary learning objectives. These are all available at the book's website and in MyStatLab.

Each exercise has a descriptive label. Exercises for which technology is recommended (such as using software or an app to carry out the analysis) are indicated with the TECH icon. Larger data sets used in examples and exercises are referenced in the text, listed in the back endpapers, and made available on the book's website. The exercises are divided into the following three categories:

- **Practicing the Basics** are the section exercises and the first group of end-of-chapter exercises; they reinforce basic application of the methods.
- **Concepts and Investigations** exercises require the student to explore real data sets and carry out investigations for mini-projects. They may ask students to explore concepts and related theory or be extensions of the chapter's methods. This section contains some multiple-choice and true-false exercises to help students check their understanding of the basic concepts and prepare for tests. A few more difficult, optional exercises (highlighted with the ◆◆ icon) are included to present some additional concepts and methods. Concepts and Investigations exercises are found in the end-of-chapter exercises.
- **Student Activities** are designed for group work based on investigations each of the students performs on a team. Student Activities are found in the end-of-chapter exercises, and additional activities may be found within chapters as well.

Technology Integration

Up-to-Date Use of Technology

The availability of technology enables instruction that is less calculation-based and more concept-oriented. Output from software applications and calculators is displayed throughout the textbook, and discussion focuses on interpretation of the output rather than on the keystrokes needed to create the output. Although most of our output is from MINITAB® and the TI calculators, we also show screen captures from IBM® SPSS® and Microsoft Excel® as appropriate. Technology-specific resources containing keystroke information are available with this text. See the supplements listing for more information.

Web Apps

Web apps referred to in the text are found on the book's website (www.pearsonhighered.com/AFK) and in MyStatLab. These apps have great value because they demonstrate concepts to students visually. For example, creating a sampling distribution is accomplished more readily with a dynamic and interactive web app than with a static text figure. (Description and list of the apps may be found on page vii.)

Data Sets

We use a wealth of real data sets throughout the textbook. These data sets are available on the www.pearsonhighered.com/AFK website. The same data set is often used in several chapters, helping reinforce the four components of the statistical investigative process and allowing the students to see the big picture of statistical reasoning. Exercises requiring students to download the data set from the book's website are noted with this icon: TECH

Statistical Software

To help students learn the statistical process, a variety of software options are available to be bundled with this text. For a complete list of the software options, please contact your Pearson Education sales representative.

Learning Catalytics

Learning Catalytics is a web-based engagement and assessment tool. As a "bring-your-own-device" direct response system, Learning Catalytics offers a diverse library of dynamic question types that allow students to interact with and think critically about statistical concepts. As a real-time resource, instructors can take advantage of critical teaching moments both in the classroom or through assignable and gradeable homework.

UPDATED! Example-Level Videos

Select examples from the text have guided videos. These updated videos provide excellent support for students who require additional assistance or want reinforcement on topics and concepts learned in class.

MyStatLab™ Online Course (access code required)

MyStatLab is a course management system that delivers **proven results** in helping individual students succeed.

- MyStatLab can be successfully implemented in any environment—lab-based, hybrid, fully online, traditional—and demonstrates the quantifiable difference that integrated usage has on student retention, subsequent success, and overall achievement.
- MyStatLab's comprehensive online gradebook automatically tracks students' results on tests, quizzes, homework, and in the study plan. Instructors can use the gradebook to intervene if students have trouble or to provide positive feedback. Data can be easily exported to a variety of spreadsheet programs, such as Microsoft Excel.

MyStatLab provides **engaging experiences** that personalize, stimulate, and measure learning for each student.

- **Tutorial Exercises with Multimedia Learning Aids:** The homework and practice exercises in MyStatLab align with the exercises in the textbook, and they regenerate algorithmically to give students unlimited opportunity for practice and mastery. Exercises offer immediate helpful feedback, guided solutions, sample problems, animations, videos, and eText clips for extra help at point-of-use.
- **Getting Ready for Statistics:** A library of questions now appears within each MyStatLab course to offer the developmental math topics students need for the course. These can be assigned as a prerequisite to other assignments if desired.
- **Conceptual Question Library:** In addition to algorithmically regenerated questions that are aligned with your textbook, a library of 1,000 Conceptual Questions is available in the assessment managers that require students to apply their statistical understanding.
- **StatCrunch:** MyStatLab includes a web-based statistical software, StatCrunch, within the online assessment platform so that students can easily analyze data sets from exercises and the text. In addition, MyStatLab includes access to **www.StatCrunch.com**, a website where users can access more than 20,000 shared data sets, conduct online surveys, perform complex analyses using the powerful statistical software, and generate compelling reports.
- **Integration of Statistical Software:** Knowing that students often use external statistical software, we make it easy to copy our data sets, both from the

ebook and MyStatLab questions, into software like StatCrunch, MINITAB, Excel, and more. Students have access to a variety of support—Technology Instruction Videos and Technology Study Cards—to learn how to use statistical software effectively.

- **Expert Tutoring:** Although many students describe the whole of MyStatLab as "like having your own personal tutor," students also have access to live tutoring from Pearson. Qualified statistics instructors provide tutoring sessions for students via MyStatLab.

And, MyStatLab comes from a **trusted partner** with educational expertise and an eye on the future.

Knowing that you are using a Pearson product means knowing that you are using quality content. That means that our eTexts are accurate, that our assessment tools work, and that our questions are error-free. And whether you are just getting started with MyStatLab, or have a question along the way, we're here to help you learn about our technologies and how to incorporate them into your course.

To learn more about how MyStatLab combines proven learning applications with powerful assessment, visit **www.mystatlab.com** or contact your Pearson representative.

MathXL® for Statistics Online Course (access code required)

MathXL® is the homework and assessment engine that runs MyStatLab. (MyStatLab is MathXL plus a learning management system.) For this edition, the authors analyzed aggregated student usage and performance data from MyStatLab for the previous edition of this text. This analysis helped improve the quality and quantity of exercises that matter the most to instructors and students. With MathXL for Statistics, instructors can:

- Create, edit, and assign online homework and tests using algorithmically generated exercises correlated at the objective level to the textbook.
- Create and assign their own online exercises and import TestGen tests for added flexibility.
- Maintain records of all student work, tracked in MathXL's online gradebook.

With MathXL for Statistics, students can:

- Take chapter tests in MathXL and receive personalized study plans and/or personalized homework assignments based on their test results.
- Use the study plan and/or the homework to link directly to tutorial exercises for the objectives they need to study.
- Access supplemental animations and video clips directly from selected exercises.
- Easily copy our data sets, both from the eText and the MyStatLab questions, into software like StatCrunch, MINITAB, Excel, and more because we know that students often use external statistical software.

MathXL for Statistics is available to qualified adopters. For more information, visit our website at www.mathxl.com or contact your Pearson representative.

StatCrunch®

StatCrunch® is powerful web-based statistical software that allows users to perform complex analyses, share data sets, and generate compelling reports of their data. The vibrant online community offers more than 20,000 data sets for instructors to use and students to analyze.

- **Collect.** Users can upload their own data to StatCrunch or search a large library of publicly shared data sets, spanning almost any topic of interest. Also, an online survey tool allows users to collect data quickly through web-based surveys.

- **Crunch.** A full range of numerical and graphical methods allows users to analyze and gain insights from any data set. Interactive graphics help users understand statistical concepts and are available for export to enrich reports with visual representations of data.
- **Communicate.** Reporting options help users create a wide variety of visually appealing representations of their data.

Full access to StatCrunch is available with a MyStatLab kit, and StatCrunch is available by itself to qualified adopters. For more information, visit our website at www.statcrunch.com or contact your Pearson representative.

XLSTAT for Pearson

Used by leading businesses and universities, XLSTAT is a Microsoft Excel® add-in that offers a wide variety of functions to enhance the analytical capabilities of Excel, making it the ideal tool for your everyday data analysis and statistics requirements. XLSTAT is compatible with all Excel versions (except Mac 2008). Available for bundling with the text (ISBN-10: 0-321-75932-X; ISBN-13: 978-0-321-75932-0).

For more information, please contact your local Pearson Education Sales Representative.

An Invitation Rather Than a Conclusion

We hope that students using this textbook will gain a lasting appreciation for the vital role the art and science of statistics plays in analyzing data and helping us make decisions in our lives. Our major goals for this textbook are that students learn how to:

- Recognize that we are surrounded by data and the importance of becoming statistically literate to interpret these data and make informed decisions based on data.
- Become critical readers of studies summarized in mass media and of research papers that quote statistical results.
- Produce data that can provide answers to properly posed questions.
- Appreciate how probability helps us understand randomness in our lives and grasp the crucial concept of a sampling distribution and how it relates to inference methods.
- Choose appropriate descriptive and inferential methods for examining and analyzing data and drawing conclusions.
- Communicate the conclusions of statistical analyses clearly and effectively.
- Understand the limitations of most research, either because it was based on an observational study rather than a randomized experiment or survey or because a certain lurking variable was not measured that could have explained the observed associations.

We are excited about sharing the insights that we have learned from our experience as teachers and from our students through this text. Many students still enter statistics classes on the first day with dread because of its reputation as a dry, sometimes difficult, course. It is our goal to inspire a classroom environment that is filled with creativity, openness, realistic applications, and learning that students find inviting and rewarding. We hope that this textbook will help the instructor and the students experience a rewarding introductory course in statistics.

BREAKTHROUGH
To improving results

Resources for Success

MyStatLab™ Online Course for *Statistics: The Art and Science of Learning from Data* by Agresti, Franklin, and Klingenberg

(access code required)

MyStatLab is available to accompany Pearson's market leading text offerings. To give students a consistent tone, voice, and teaching method, each text's flavor and approach is tightly integrated throughout the accompanying MyStatLab course, making learning the material as seamless as possible.

Technology Tutorials and Study Cards

Technology tutorials provide brief video walkthroughs and step-by-step instructional study cards on common statistical procedures for MINITAB®, Excel®, and the TI family of graphing calculators.

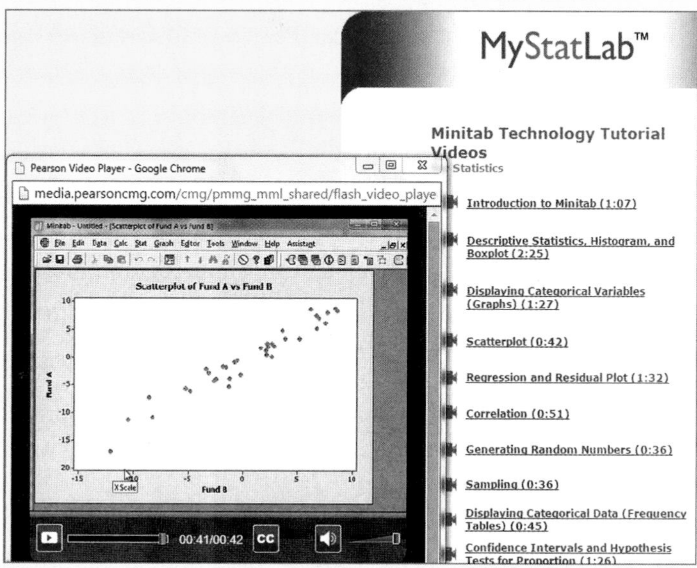

Example-Level Resources

Students looking for additional support can use the example-based videos to help solve problems, provide reinforcement on topics and concepts learned in class, and support their learning.

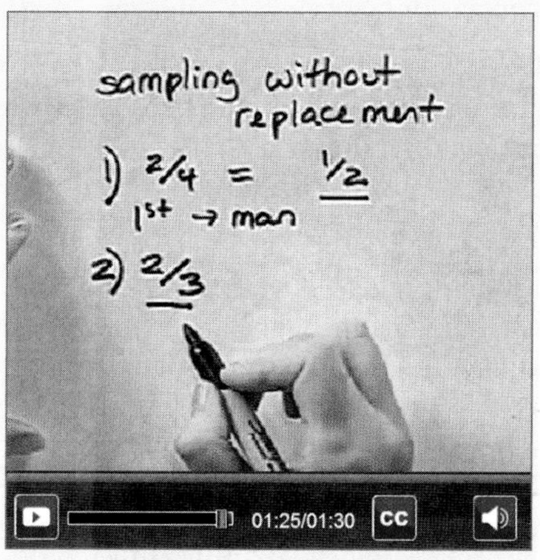

New! Apps: Examples, Exercises, and Simulations

Author-created web apps allow students to interact with key statistical concepts and techniques, including statistical distributions, inference for one and two samples, permutation tests, bootstrapping, and sampling distributions. Students can explore consequences of changing parameters and carry out simulations to explore coverage, or simply obtain descriptive statistics or a proper statistical graph. All these in a highly user-friendly and well designed app, where results can be downloaded for inclusion in homework or projects.

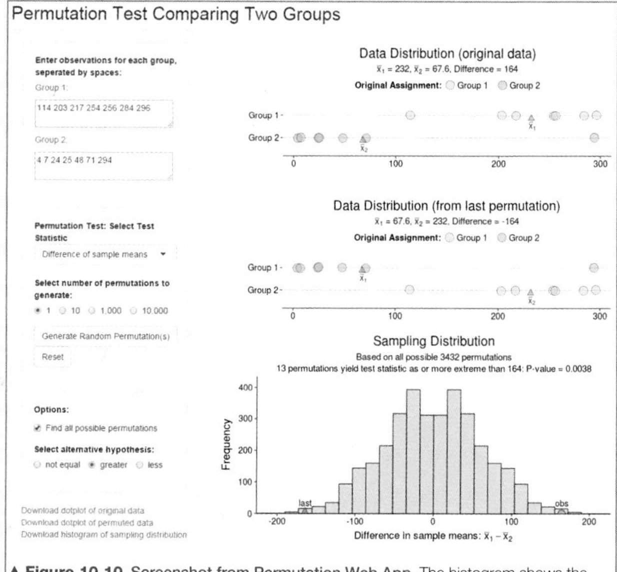

▲ **Figure 10.10** Screenshot from Permutation Web App. The histogram shows the permutation sampling distribution of the difference between sample means. This sampling distribution is obtained by considering all possible ways of dividing the responses of the 14 dogs into two groups of size 7 and computing the difference in sample means for each. The semi-circle in the right tail indicates the actually observed difference. (The dot plots above the histogram show the original data and the data after a random permutation, in this case, the permutation when all dogs in Group 1 are switched with all dogs from Group 2) **Question** Is the observed difference extreme?

www.mystatlab.com

Resources for Success

Instructor Resources

Additional resources can be downloaded from **www.pearsonhighered.com**, or hardcopy resources can be ordered from your sales representative.

Text-specific website, www.pearsonhighered.com/AFK
New to this edition, students and instructors will have a full library of resources, including apps developed for in-text activities, data sets (.csv, TI-83/84 Plus C, and .txt), and instructor-to-instructor videos.

Instructor's Edition (IE) contains comprehensive Instructor's Notes for each chapter. Broken down by section, they offer a valuable introduction to each chapter by presenting learning objectives (which could be shared with students), the author's rationale for content and presentation decisions made in the chapter, tips for introducing complex material, common pitfalls students encounter, additional examples and activities to use in class, and suggestions for how to integrate web apps and activities effectively. Short answers to all of the exercises are given in the Answer Appendix. Full solutions to all of the exercises are in the Instructor's Solutions Manual.

Updated! Instructor to Instructor Videos provide an opportunity for adjuncts, part-timers, TAs, or other instructors who are new to teaching from this text or have limited class prep time to learn about the book's approach and coverage from the authors. The videos focus on those topics that have proven to be most challenging to students. The authors offer suggestions, pointers, and ideas about how to present these topics and concepts effectively based on their many years of teaching introductory statistics. They also share insights on how to help students use the textbook in the most effective way to realize success in the course. The videos are available for download from Pearson's online catalog at www.pearsonhighered.com/irc and through MyStatLab.

Instructor's Solutions Manual, by James Lapp, contains fully worked solutions to every textbook exercise. Available for download from Pearson's online catalog at www.pearsonhighered.com/irc and through MyStatLab.

Answers to the Student Laboratory Manual are available for download from Pearson's online catalog at www.pearsonhighered.com/irc and through MyStatLab.

PowerPoint Lecture Slides are fully editable and printable slides that follow the textbook. These slides can be used during lectures or posted to a website in an online course. The PowerPoint Lecture Slides are available from Pearson's online catalog at www.pearsonhighered.com/irc and through MyStatLab.

TestGen® (www.pearsoned.com/testgen) enables instructors to build, edit, print, and administer tests using a computerized bank of questions developed to cover all the objectives of the text. TestGen is algorithmically based, allowing instructors to create multiple but equivalent versions of the same question or test with the click of a button. Instructors can also modify test bank questions or add new questions. The software and test bank are available for download from Pearson's online catalog at www.pearsonhighered.com/irc and through MyStatLab.

The Online Test Bank is a test bank derived from TestGen®. It includes multiple choice and short answer questions for each section of the text, along with the answer keys. Available for download from Pearson's online catalog at www.pearsonhighered.com/irc and through MyStatLab.

Student Resources

Additional resources to help student success.

Text-specific website, www.pearsonhighered.com/AFK
New to this edition, students and instructors will have a full library of resources, including apps developed for in-text activities and data sets (.csv, TI-83/84 Plus C, and .txt).

Student's Solutions Manual, by James Lapp, contains fully worked solutions to odd-numbered exercises. (ISBN-10: 0-13-386084-1; ISBN-13: 978-0-13-386084-9)

Updated! Example-level videos explain how to work examples from the text. The videos provide excellent support for students who require additional assistance or want reinforcement on topics and concepts learned in class (available in MyStatLab).

Student Laboratory Workbook, by Megan Mocko (University of Florida) and Maria Ripol (University of Florida), is a study tool for the first ten chapters of the text. This workbook provides section-by-section review and practice and additional activities that cover fundamental statistical topics (ISBN-10: 0-13-386089-2; ISBN-13: 978-0-13-386089-4).

Study Cards for Statistics Software This series of study cards, available for Excel®, MINITAB®, JMP®, SPSS®, R®, StatCrunch®, and the TI family of graphing calculators provides students with easy, step-by-step guides to the most common statistics software. Visit www.myPearsonStore.com for more information.

Acknowledgments

We are indebted to the following individuals, who provided valuable feedback for the fourth edition:

Evelyn Bailey, *Oxford College of Emory University*
Erica Bernstein, *University of Hawaii at Hilo*
Phyllis Curtiss, *Grand Valley State*
Katherine C. Earles, *Wichita State University*
Rob Eby, *Blinn College—Bryan Campus*
Matthew Jones, *Austin Perry Statue University*
Ann Kalinoskii, *San Jose University*
Michael Roty, *Mercer University*
Ping-Shou Zhong, *Michigan State University*

We are also indebted to the many reviewers, class testers, and students who gave us invaluable feedback and advice on how to improve the quality of the book.

ARIZONA Russel Carlson, University of Arizona; Peter Flanagan-Hyde, Phoenix Country Day School ■ **CALIFORINIA** James Curl, Modesto Junior College; Christine Drake, University of California at Davis; Mahtash Esfandiari, UCLA; Brian Karl Finch, San Diego State University; Dawn Holmes, University of California Santa Barbara; Rob Gould, UCLA; Rebecca Head, Bakersfield College; Susan Herring, Sonoma State University; Colleen Kelly, San Diego State University; Marke Mavis, Butte Community College; Elaine McDonald, Sonoma State University; Corey Manchester, San Diego State University; Amy McElroy, San Diego State University; Helen Noble, San Diego State University; Calvin Schmall, Solano Community College ■ **COLORADO** David Most, Colorado State University ■ **CONNECTICUT** Paul Bugl, University of Hartford; Anne Doyle, University of Connecticut; Pete Johnson, Eastern Connecticut State University; Dan Miller, Central Connecticut State University; Kathleen McLaughlin, University of Connecticut; Nalini Ravishanker, University of Connecticut; John Vangar, Fairfield University; Stephen Sawin, Fairfield University ■ **DISTRICT OF COLUMBIA** Hans Engler, Georgetown University; Mary W. Gray, American University; Monica Jackson, American University ■ **FLORIDA** Nazanin Azarnia, Santa Fe Community College; Brett Holbrook; James Lang, Valencia Community College; Karen Kinard, Tallahassee Community College; Megan Mocko, University of Florida; Maria Ripol, University of Florida; James Smart, Tallahassee Community College; Latricia Williams, St. Petersburg Junior College, Clearwater; Doug Zahn, Florida State University ■ **GEORGIA** Carrie Chmielarski, University of Georgia; Ouida Dillon, Oconee County High School; Kim Gilbert, University of Georgia; Katherine Hawks, Meadowcreek High School; Todd Hendricks, Georgia Perimeter College; Charles LeMarsh, Lakeside High School; Steve Messig, Oconee County High School; Broderick Oluyede, Georgia Southern University; Chandler Pike, University of Georgia; Kim Robinson, Clayton State University; Jill Smith, University of Georgia; John Seppala, Valdosta State University; Joseph Walker, Georgia State University ■ **IOWA** John Cryer, University of Iowa; Kathy Rogotzke, North Iowa Community College; R. P. Russo, University of Iowa; William Duckworth, Iowa State University ■ **ILLINOIS** Linda Brant Collins, University of Chicago; Dagmar Budikova, Illinois State University; Ellen Fireman, University of Illinois; Jinadasa Gamage, Illinois State; University; Richard Maher, Loyola University Chicago; Cathy Poliak, Northern Illinois University; Daniel Rowe, Heartland Community College ■ **KANSAS** James Higgins, Kansas State University; Michael Mosier, Washburn University ■ **KENTUCKY** Lisa Kay, Eastern Kentucky University

■ **MASSACHUSETTS** Richard Cleary, Bentley University; Katherine Halvorsen, Smith College; Xiaoli Meng, Harvard University; Daniel Weiner, Boston University ■ **MICHIGAN** Kirk Anderson, Grand Valley State University; Phyllis Curtiss, Grand Valley State University; Roy Erickson, Michigan State University; Jann-Huei Jinn, Grand Valley State University; Sango Otieno, Grand Valley State University; Alla Sikorskii, Michigan State University; Mark Stevenson, Oakland Community College; Todd Swanson, Hope College; Nathan Tintle, Hope College ■ **MINNESOTA** Bob Dobrow, Carleton College; German J. Pliego, University of St.Thomas; Peihua Qui, University of Minnesota; Engin A. Sungur, University of Minnesota–Morris ■ **MISSOURI** Lynda Hollingsworth, Northwest Missouri State University; Robert Paige, Missouri University of Science and Technology; Larry Ries, University of Missouri–Columbia; Suzanne Tourville, Columbia College ■ **MONTANA** Jeff Banfield, Montana State University ■ **NEW JERSEY** Harold Sackrowitz, Rutgers, The State University of New Jersey; Linda Tappan, Montclair State University ■ **NEW MEXICO** David Daniel, New Mexico State University ■ **NEW YORK** Brooke Fridley, Mohawk Valley Community College; Martin Lindquist, Columbia University; Debby Lurie, St. John's University; David Mathiason, Rochester Institute of Technology; Steve Stehman, SUNY ESF; Tian Zheng, Columbia University ■ **NEVADA**: Alison Davis, University of Nevada–Reno ■ **NORTH CAROLINA** Pamela Arroway, North Carolina State University; E. Jacquelin Dietz, North Carolina State University; Alan Gelfand, Duke University; Gary Kader, Appalachian State University; Scott Richter, UNC Greensboro; Roger Woodard, North Carolina State University ■ **NEBRASKA** Linda Young, University of Nebraska ■ **OHIO** Jim Albert, Bowling Green State University; John Holcomb, Cleveland State University; Jackie Miller, The Ohio State University; Stephan Pelikan, University of Cincinnati; Teri Rysz, University of Cincinnati; Deborah Rumsey, The Ohio State University; Kevin Robinson, University of Akron; Dottie Walton, Cuyahoga Community College - Eastern Campus ■ **OREGON** Michael Marciniak, Portland Community College; Henry Mesa, Portland Community College, Rock Creek; Qi-Man Shao, University of Oregon; Daming Xu, University of Oregon ■ **PENNSYLVANIA** Winston Crawley, Shippensburg University; Douglas Frank, Indiana University of Pennsylvania; Steven Gendler, Clarion University; Bonnie A. Green, East Stroudsburg University; Paul Lupinacci, Villanova University; Deborah Lurie, Saint Joseph's University; Linda Myers, Harrisburg Area Community College; Tom Short, Villanova University; Kay Somers, Moravian College; Sister Marcella Louise Wallowicz, Holy Family University ■ **SOUTH CAROLINA** Beverly Diamond, College of Charleston; Martin Jones, College of Charleston; Murray Siegel, The South Carolina Governor's School for Science and Mathematics; ■ **SOUTH DAKOTA** Richard Gayle, Black Hills State University; Daluss Siewert, Black Hills State University; Stanley Smith, Black Hills State University ■ **TENNESSEE** Bonnie Daves, Christian Academy of Knoxville; T. Henry Jablonski, Jr., East Tennessee State University; Robert Price, East Tennessee State University; Ginger Rowell, Middle Tennessee State University; Edith Seier, East Tennessee State University ■ **TEXAS** Larry Ammann, University of Texas, Dallas; Tom Bratcher, Baylor University; Jianguo Liu, University of North Texas; Mary Parker, Austin Community College; Robert Paige, Texas Tech University; Walter M. Potter, Southwestern University; Therese Shelton, Southwestern University; James Surles, Texas Tech University; Diane Resnick, University of Houston-Downtown ■ **UTAH** Patti Collings, Brigham Young University; Carolyn Cuff, Westminster College; Lajos Horvath, University of Utah; P. Lynne Nielsen, Brigham Young University ■ **VIRGINIA** David Bauer, Virginia Commonwealth University; Ching-Yuan Chiang, James Madison University; Jonathan Duggins, Virginia Tech; Steven Garren, James Madison University; Hasan Hamdan, James Madison University; Debra Hydorn, Mary Washington College; Nusrat Jahan, James Madison University; D'Arcy Mays, Virginia Commonwealth University; Stephanie Pickle, Virginia Polytechnic Institute and State University

■ **WASHINGTON** Rich Alldredge, Washington State University; Brian T. Gill, Seattle Pacific University; June Morita, University of Washington ■ WISCONSIN Brooke Fridley, University of Wisconsin–LaCrosse; Loretta Robb Thielman, University of Wisconsin–Stoutt. ■ **WYOMING** Burke Grandjean, University of Wyoming ■ **CANADA** Mike Kowalski, University of Alberta; David Loewen, University of Manitoba

We appreciate all of the thoughtful contributions to the fourth edition by Michael Posner. We also thank the following individuals, who made invaluable contributions to the third edition:

Ellen Breazel, *Clemson University*

Linda Dawson, *Washington State University, Tacoma*

Bernadette Lanciaux, *Rochester Institute of Technology*

Scott Nickleach, *Sonoma State University*

The detailed assessment of the text fell to our accuracy checkers, Ann Cannon and Joan Sanuik.

Thank you to James Lapp, who took on the task of revising the solutions manuals to reflect the many changes to the fourth edition. We also want to thank Jackie Miller (Ohio State University) for her contributions to the Instructor's Notes, and our student technology manual and workbook authors, Megan Mocko (University of Florida) and Maria Ripol (University of Florida).

We would like to thank the Pearson team who has given countless hours in developing this text; without their guidance and assistance, the text would not have come to completion. We thank Suzanna Bainbridge, Rachel Reeve, Danielle Simbajon, Justin Billing, Jean Choe, Tiffany Bitzel, Andrew Noble, Jennifer Myers, and especially Joe Vetere. We also thank Kristin Jobe, Senior Project Manager at Integra-Chicago, for keeping this book on track throughout production.

Alan Agresti would like to thank those who have helped us in some way, often by suggesting data sets or examples. These include Anna Gottard, Wolfgang Jank, Bernhard Klingenberg, René Lee-Pack, Jacalyn Levine, Megan Lewis, Megan Meece, Dan Nettleton, Yongyi Min, and Euijung Ryu. Many thanks also to Tom Piazza for his help with the General Social Survey. Finally, Alan Agresti would like to thank his wife Jacki Levine for her extraordinary support throughout the writing of this book. Besides putting up with the evenings and weekends he was working on this book, she offered numerous helpful suggestions for examples and for improving the writing.

Chris Franklin gives a special thank you to her husband and sons, Dale, Corey, and Cody Green. They have patiently sacrificed spending many hours with their spouse and mom as she has worked on this book through four editions. A special thank you also to her parents Grady and Helen Franklin and her two brothers, Grady and Mark, who have always been there for their daughter and sister. Chris also appreciates the encouragement and support of her colleagues and her many students who used the book, offering practical suggestions for improvement. Finally, Chris thanks her coauthors Alan and Bernhard for the amazing journey of writing a textbook together.

Bernhard Klingenberg wants to thank his statistics teachers in Graz, Austria; Sheffield, UK; and Gainesville, Florida, who showed him all the fascinating facets of statistics throughout his education. Thanks also to the Department of Mathematics & Statistics at Williams College for being such a wonderful place to work. Finally, thanks to Chris Franklin and Alan Agresti for a wonderful and inspiring collaboration.

ALAN AGRESTI, *Gainesville, Florida*

CHRISTINE FRANKLIN, *Athens, Georgia*

BERNHARD KLINGENBERG, *Williamstown, Massachusetts*

About the Authors

Alan Agresti is Distinguished Professor Emeritus in the Department of Statistics at the University of Florida. He taught statistics there for 38 years, including the development of three courses in statistical methods for social science students and three courses in categorical data analysis. He is author of more than 100 refereed articles and six texts, including *Statistical Methods for the Social Sciences* (with Barbara Finlay, Prentice Hall, 4th edition, 2009) and *Categorical Data Analysis* (Wiley, 3rd edition, 2013). He is a Fellow of the American Statistical Association and recipient of an Honorary Doctor of Science from De Montfort University in the UK. He has held visiting positions at Harvard University, Boston University, the London School of Economics, and Imperial College and has taught courses or short courses for universities and companies in about 30 countries worldwide. He has also received teaching awards from the University of Florida and an excellence in writing award from John Wiley & Sons.

Christine Franklin is a Senior Lecturer and Lothar Tresp Honoratus Honors Professor in the Department of Statistics at the University of Georgia. She has been teaching statistics for more than 35 years at the college level. Chris has been actively involved at the national and state level with promoting statistical education at Pre-K–16 since the 1980s. She is a past Chief Reader for AP Statistic. Chris served as the lead writer for the ASA-endorsed Guidelines for Assessment and Instruction in Statistics Education (GAISE) Report: A Pre- K–12 Curriculum Framework and chaired the ASA Statistical Education of Teachers (SET) Report. Chris has been honored by her selection as a Fellow of the American Statistical Association, recipient of the 2006 Mu Sigma Rho National Statistical Education Award, the 2013 USCOTS Lifetime Achievement Award, the 2014 ASA Founders Award, a 2014–2015 U.S. Fulbright Scholar, and numerous teaching and advising awards at the University of Georgia. Most important for Chris is her family, who love to hike and attend baseball games together.

Bernhard Klingenberg is Associate Professor of Statistics in the Department of Mathematics & Statistics at Williams College, where he has been teaching introductory and advanced statistics classes for the past 11 years. In 2013, Bernhard was instrumental in creating an undergraduate major in statistics at Williams, one of the first for a liberal arts college. A native of Austria, Bernhard frequently returns there to hold visiting positions at universities and gives short courses on categorical data analysis in Europe and the United States. He has published several peer-reviewed articles in statistical journals and consults regularly with academia and industry. Bernhard enjoys photography (some of his pictures appear in this book), scuba diving, and time with his wife and four children.

Gathering and Exploring Data

PART

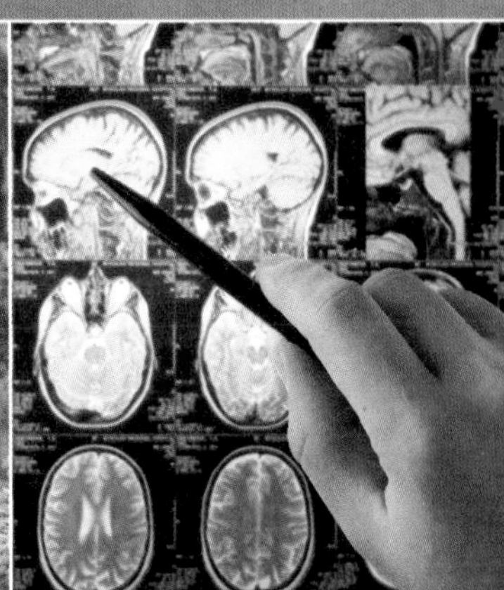

CHAPTER

1

Statistics: The Art and Science of Learning from Data

Example 1

How Statistics Helps Us Learn About the World

Picture the Scenario

In this book, you will explore a wide variety of everyday scenarios. For example, you will evaluate media reports about opinion surveys, medical research studies, the state of the economy, and environmental issues. You'll face financial decisions such as choosing between an investment with a sure return and one that could make you more money but could possibly cost you your entire investment. You'll learn how to analyze the available information to answer necessary questions in such scenarios. One purpose of this book is to show you why an understanding of statistics is essential for making good decisions in an uncertain world.

Questions to Explore

This book will show you how to collect appropriate information and how to apply statistical methods so you can better evaluate that information and answer the questions posed. Here are some examples of questions we'll investigate in coming chapters:

- How can you evaluate evidence about global warming?
- Are cell phones dangerous to your health?
- What's the chance your tax return will be audited?
- How likely are you to win the lottery?
- Is there bias against women in appointing managers?
- What 'hot streaks' should you expect in basketball?
- How can you analyze whether a diet really works?
- How can you predict the selling price of a house?

Thinking Ahead

Each chapter uses questions like these to introduce a topic and then introduces tools for making sense of the available information. We'll see that **statistics** is the art and science of designing studies and analyzing the information that those studies produce.

In the business world, managers use statistics to analyze results of marketing studies about new products, to help predict sales, and to measure employee performance. In finance, statistics is used to study stock returns and investment opportunities. Medical studies use statistics to evaluate whether new ways to treat disease are better than existing ways. In fact, most professional occupations today rely heavily on statistical methods. In a competitive job market, understanding statistics provides an important advantage.

But it's important to understand statistics even if you will never use it in your job. Understanding statistics can help you make better choices. Why? Because every day you are bombarded with statistical information from news reports, advertisements, political campaigns, and surveys. How do you know what to heed and what to ignore? An understanding of the statistical reasoning—and in some cases statistical misconceptions—underlying these pronouncements will help. For instance, this book will enable you to evaluate claims about medical research studies more effectively so that you know when you should be skeptical. For example, does taking an aspirin daily truly lessen the chance of having a heart attack?

We realize that you are probably not reading this book in the hope of becoming a statistician. (That's too bad, because there's a severe shortage of statisticians—more jobs than trained people. And with the ever-increasing ways in which statistics is being applied, it's an exciting time to be a statistician.) You may even suffer from math phobia. Please be assured that to learn the main concepts of statistics, logical thinking and perseverance are more important than high-powered math skills. Don't be frustrated if learning comes slowly and you need to read about a topic a few times before it starts to make sense. Just as you would not expect to sit through a single foreign language class session and be able to speak that language fluently, the same is true with the language of statistics. It takes time and practice. But we promise that your hard work will be rewarded. Once you have completed even part of this text, you will understand much better how to make sense of statistical information and, hence, the world around you.

1.1 Using Data to Answer Statistical Questions

Does a low-carbohydrate diet result in significant weight loss? Are people more likely to stop at a Starbucks if they've seen a recent Starbucks TV commercial? Information gathering is at the heart of investigating answers to such questions. The information we gather with experiments and surveys is collectively called **data**.

For instance, consider an experiment designed to evaluate the effectiveness of a low-carbohydrate diet. The data might consist of the following measurements for the people participating in the study: weight at the beginning of the study, weight at the end of the study, number of calories of food eaten per day, carbohydrate intake per day, body-mass index (BMI) at the start of the study, and gender. A marketing survey about the effectiveness of a TV ad for Starbucks could collect data on the percentage of people who went to a Starbucks since the ad aired and analyze how it compares for those who saw the ad and those who did not see it.

Defining Statistics

You already have a sense of what the word *statistics* means. You hear statistics quoted about sports events (number of points scored by each player on a basketball team), statistics about the economy (median income, unemployment rate), and statistics about opinions, beliefs, and behaviors (percentage of students who indulge in binge drinking). In this sense, a statistic is merely a number calculated from data. But statistics as a field is a way of thinking about data and quantifying uncertainty, not a maze of numbers and messy formulas.

Statistics

Statistics is the art and science of designing studies and analyzing the data that those studies produce. Its ultimate goal is translating data into knowledge and understanding of the world around us. In short, *statistics is the art and science of learning from data.*

Statistical methods help us investigate questions in an objective manner. Statistical problem solving is an investigative process that involves four components: (1) formulate a statistical question, (2) collect data, (3) analyze data, and (4) interpret results. The following examples ask questions that we'll learn how to answer using statistical investigations.

Scenario 1: Predicting an Election Using an Exit Poll In elections, television networks often declare the winner well before all the votes have been counted. They do this using exit polling, interviewing voters after they leave the voting booth. Using an exit poll, a network can often predict the winner after learning how several thousand people voted, out of possibly millions of voters.

The 2010 California gubernatorial race pitted Democratic candidate Jerry Brown against Republican candidate Meg Whitman. A TV exit poll used to project the outcome reported that 53.1% of a sample of 3889 voters said they had voted for Jerry Brown.[1] Was this sufficient evidence to project Brown as the winner, even though information was available from such a small portion of the more than 9.5 million voters in California? We'll learn how to answer that question in this book.

Scenario 2: Making Conclusions in Medical Research Studies Statistical reasoning is at the foundation of the analyses conducted in most medical research studies. Let's consider three examples of how statistics can be relevant.

Heart disease is the most common cause of death in industrialized nations. In the United States and Canada, nearly 30% of deaths yearly are due to heart disease, mainly heart attacks. Does regular aspirin intake reduce deaths from heart attacks? Harvard Medical School conducted a landmark study to investigate. The people participating in the study regularly took either an aspirin or a placebo (a pill with no active ingredient). Of those who took aspirin, 0.9% had heart attacks during the study. Of those who took the placebo, 1.7% had heart attacks, nearly twice as many.

Can you conclude that it's beneficial for people to take aspirin regularly? Or, could the observed difference be explained by how it was decided which people would receive aspirin and which would receive the placebo? For instance, might those who took aspirin have had better results merely because they were healthier, on average, than those who took the placebo? Or, did those taking aspirin have a better diet or exercise more regularly, on average?

For years there has been controversy about whether regular intake of large doses of vitamin C is beneficial. Some studies have suggested that it is. But some scientists have criticized those studies' designs, claiming that the subsequent statistical analysis was meaningless. How do we know when we can trust the statistical results in a medical study that is reported in the media?

---

[1]*Source:* Data from www.cnn.com/ELECTION/2010/results/polls/.

Suppose you wanted to investigate whether, as some have suggested, heavy use of cell phones makes you more likely to get brain cancer. You could pick half the students from your school and tell them to use a cell phone each day for the next 50 years, and tell the other half never to use a cell phone. Fifty years from now you could see whether more users than nonusers of cell phones got brain cancer. Obviously it would be impractical to carry out such a study. And who wants to wait 50 years to get the answer? Years ago, a British statistician figured out how to study whether a particular type of behavior has an effect on cancer, using already available data. He did this to answer a then controversial question: Does smoking cause lung cancer? How did he do this?

This book will show you how to answer questions like these. You'll learn when you can trust the results from studies reported in the media and when you should be skeptical.

Scenario 3: Using a Survey to Investigate People's Beliefs How similar are your opinions and lifestyle to those of others? It's easy to find out. Every other year, the National Opinion Research Center at the University of Chicago conducts the General Social Survey (GSS). This survey of a few thousand adult Americans provides data about the opinions and behaviors of the American public. You can use it to investigate how adult Americans answer a wide diversity of questions, such as, "Do you believe in life after death?" "Would you be willing to pay higher prices in order to protect the environment?" "How much TV do you watch per day?" and "How many sexual partners have you had in the past year?" Similar surveys occur in other countries, such as the Eurobarometer survey within the European Union. We'll use data from such surveys to illustrate the proper application of statistical methods.

Reasons for Using Statistical Methods

The scenarios just presented illustrate the three main components of statistics for answering a statistical question:

- **Design:** Stating the goal and/or statistical question of interest and planning how to obtain data that will address them
- **Description:** Summarizing and analyzing the data that are obtained
- **Inference:** Making decisions and predictions based on the data for answering the statistical question

Design refers to planning how to obtain data that will efficiently shed light on the statistical question of interest. How could you conduct an experiment to determine reliably whether regular large doses of vitamin C are beneficial? In marketing, how do you select the people to survey so you'll get data that provide good predictions about future sales?

Description means exploring and summarizing patterns in the data. Files of raw data are often huge. For example, over time the General Social Survey has collected data about hundreds of characteristics on many thousands of people. Such raw data are not easy to assess—we simply get bogged down in numbers. It is more informative to use a few numbers or a graph to summarize the data, such as an average amount of TV watched or a graph displaying how number of hours of TV watched per day relates to number of hours per week exercising.

In Words

The verb **infer** means to arrive at a decision or prediction by reasoning from known evidence. **Statistical inference** does this using data as evidence.

Inference means making decisions or predictions based on the data. Usually the decision or prediction refers to a larger group of people, not merely those in the study. For instance, in the exit poll described in Scenario 1, of 3889 voters sampled, 53.1% said they voted for Jerry Brown. Using these data, we can predict (infer) that a majority of the 9.5 million voters voted for him. Stating the percentages for the sample of 3889 voters is *description*, whereas predicting the outcome for all 9.5 million voters is *inference*.

Statistical description and inference are complementary ways of analyzing data. Statistical description provides useful summaries and helps you find patterns in the data; inference helps you make predictions and decide whether observed patterns are meaningful. You can use both to investigate questions that are important to society. For instance, "Has there been global warming over the past decade?" "Is having the death penalty available for punishment associated with a reduction in violent crime?" "Does student performance in school depend on the amount of money spent per student, the size of the classes, or the teachers' salaries?"

Long before we analyze data, we need to give careful thought to posing the questions to be answered by that analysis. The nature of these questions has an impact on all stages—design, description, and inference. For example, in an exit poll, do we just want to predict which candidate won, or do we want to investigate *why* by analyzing how voters' opinions about certain issues related to how they voted? We'll learn how questions such as these and the ones posed in the previous paragraph can be phrased in terms of statistical summaries (such as percentages and means) so that we can use data to investigate their answers.

Finally, a topic that we have not mentioned yet but that is fundamental for statistical inference is **probability**, which is a framework for quantifying how likely various possible outcomes are. We'll study probability because it will help us answer questions such as, "If Brown were actually going to lose the election (that is, if he were supported by less than half of all voters), what's the chance that an exit poll of 3889 voters would show support by 53.1% of the voters?" If the chance were extremely small, we'd feel comfortable making the inference that his reelection was supported by the majority of all 9.5 million voters.

In Words

Variable refers to the characteristic being measured, such as number of hours per day that you watch TV.

▶ Activity 1

Downloading Data from the Internet

It is simple to get descriptive summaries of data from the General Social Survey (GSS). We'll demonstrate, using one question asked in recent surveys, "On a typical day, about how many hours do you personally watch television?"

- Go to the website sda.berkeley.edu/GSS.
- Click GSS—with NO WEIGHT as the default weight selection (SDA 4.0).
- The GSS name for the number of hours of TV watching is TVHOURS. Type TVHOURS as the row variable name. (See the output below on the left.)
- In the Weight menu, make sure that *No Weight* is selected. Click *Run the Table.*

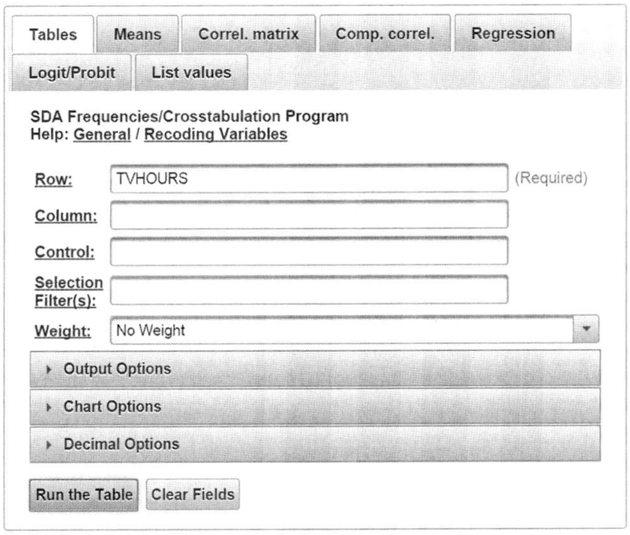

Tables | Means | Correl. matrix | Comp. correl. | Regression | Logit/Probit | List values

SDA Frequencies/Crosstabulation Program
Help: General / Recoding Variables

Row: TVHOURS (Required)
Column:
Control:
Selection Filter(s):
Weight: No Weight

▸ Output Options
▸ Chart Options
▸ Decimal Options

Run the Table | Clear Fields

Now you'll see a table that shows the number of people and, in bold, the percentage who made each of the possible responses. For all the years combined in which this question was asked, the most common response was 2 hours of TV a day (about 27% made this response as shown in the output on the right.).

What percentage of the people surveyed reported watching 0 hours of TV a day? How many people reported watching TV 24 hours a day?

Another question asked in the GSS is, "Taken all together, would you say that you are very happy, pretty happy, or not too happy?" The GSS name for this item is HAPPY. What percentage of people reported being very happy?

You might use the GSS to investigate what sorts of people are more likely to be very happy. Those who are happily married? Those who are in good health? Those who have lots of friends? We'll see how to find out in this book.

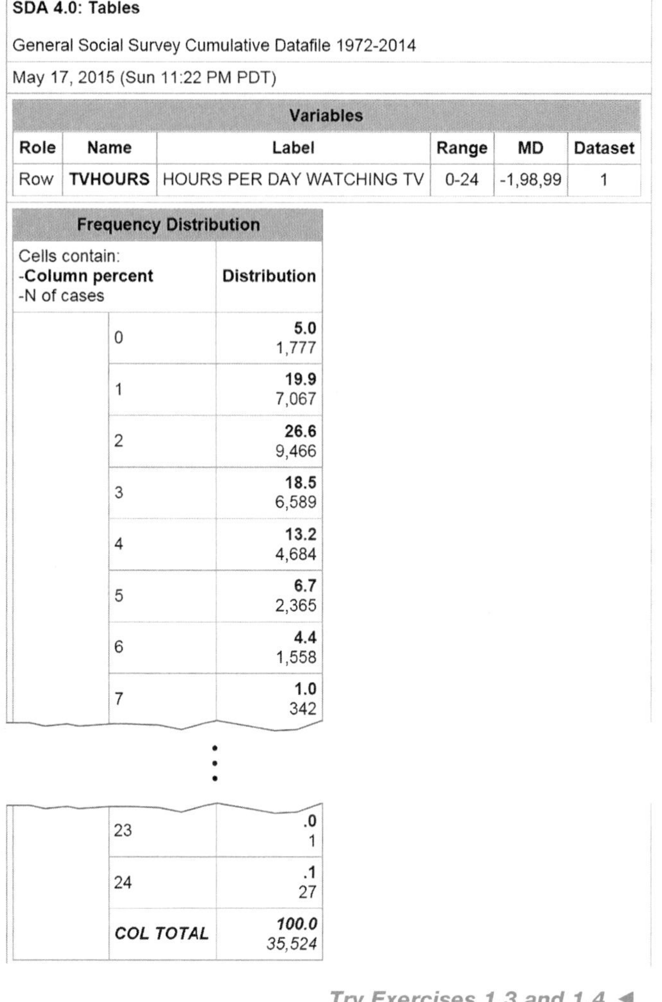

SDA 4.0: Tables

General Social Survey Cumulative Datafile 1972-2014

May 17, 2015 (Sun 11:22 PM PDT)

Variables					
Role	**Name**	**Label**	**Range**	**MD**	**Dataset**
Row	**TVHOURS**	HOURS PER DAY WATCHING TV	0-24	-1,98,99	1

Frequency Distribution

Cells contain: -**Column percent** -N of cases	**Distribution**
0	**5.0** 1,777
1	**19.9** 7,067
2	**26.6** 9,466
3	**18.5** 6,589
4	**13.2** 4,684
5	**6.7** 2,365
6	**4.4** 1,558
7	**1.0** 342
⋮	
23	**.0** 1
24	**.1** 27
COL TOTAL	***100.0*** *35,524*

Try Exercises 1.3 and 1.4 ◄

1.1 Practicing the Basics

1.1 Aspirin and heart attacks The Harvard Medical School study mentioned in Scenario 2 included about 22,000 male physicians. Whether a given individual would be assigned to take aspirin or the placebo was determined by flipping a coin. As a result, about 11,000 physicians were assigned to take aspirin and about 11,000 to take the placebo. The researchers summarized the results of the experiment by using percentages. Of the physicians taking aspirin, 0.9% had a heart attack, compared to 1.7% of those taking the placebo. Based on the observed results, the study authors concluded that taking aspirin reduces the risk of having a heart attack. Specify the aspect of this study that pertains to (a) design, (b) description, and (c) inference.

1.2 Poverty and race The Current Population Survey (CPS) is a survey conducted by the U.S. Bureau of the Census for the Bureau of Labor Statistics. It provides a comprehensive body of data on the labor force, unemployment, wealth, poverty, and so on. The data can be found online at www.census.gov/cps/. Data from the 2012 CPS examined about 68,000 households, each consisting of at least one related person under the age of 18. The report indicated that 18% of white households, 37.5% of black households, and 13.4% of Asian households had annual incomes below the poverty line. Based on these results, the study authors concluded that the percentage of *all* such black households with annual incomes below the poverty line is between 35.6% and 39.4%. Specify the aspect of this study that pertains to (a) description and (b) inference.

1.3 GSS and heaven Go to the General Social Survey website, http://sda.berkeley.edu/GSS. Enter HEAVEN as the row variable and then click *Run the Table*. When asked whether they believed in heaven, what percentage of those surveyed said yes, definitely; yes, probably; no, probably not; and no, definitely not?

TRY TECH

1.4 GSS and heaven and hell Refer to the previous exercise. You can obtain data for a particular survey year such as 2008 by entering YEAR(2008) in the Selection Filter option box before you click *Run the Table*.

TRY TECH

a. Do this for HEAVEN in 2008, giving the percentages for the four possible outcomes. Note that HEAVEN is not available for the 2014 data because the question wasn't asked that year.

b. Summarize opinions in 2008 about belief in hell (row variable HELL). Was the percentage of "yes, definitely" responses higher for belief in heaven or in hell?

1.5 GSS for subject you pick At the GSS website, click *Standard Codebook* under Codebooks and then click *Sequential Variable List*. Find a subject that interests you and look up a relevant GSS code name to enter as the row variable. Summarize the results that you obtain.

TECH

1.2 Sample Versus Population

We've seen that statistics consists of methods for **designing** investigative studies, **describing** (summarizing) data obtained for those studies, and making **inferences** (decisions and predictions) based on those data to answer a statistical question of interest.

We Observe Samples But Are Interested in Populations

The entities that we measure in a study are called the **subjects**. Usually subjects are people, such as the individuals interviewed in a General Social Survey. But they need not be. For instance, subjects could be schools, countries, or days. We might measure characteristics such as the following:

- For each school: the per-student expenditure, the average class size, the average score of students on an achievement test
- For each country: the percentage of residents living in poverty, the birth rate, the percentage unemployed, the percentage who are computer literate
- For each day in an Internet café: the amount spent on coffee, the amount spent on food, the amount spent on Internet access

The **population** is the set of all the subjects of interest. In practice, we usually have data for only *some* of the subjects who belong to that population. These subjects are called a **sample**.

Population and Sample

The **population** is the total set of subjects in which we are interested. A **sample** is the subset of the population for whom we have (or plan to have) data, often randomly selected.

In Practice

Sometimes the population is well-defined, but sometimes it is a hypothetical set of people that is not enumerated. For example, in a clinical trial to examine the impact of a new drug on lowering cholesterol, the population would be all people with high cholesterol who might have signed up for such a trial. This set of people is not specifically listed.

In the 2014 General Social Survey (GSS), the sample was the 2538 people who participated in this survey. The population was the set of all adult Americans at that time—more than 318 million people.

Sample and population ◀

Example 2

An Exit Poll

Picture the Scenario

Scenario 1 in the previous section discussed an exit poll. The purpose was to predict the outcome of the 2010 gubernatorial election in California. The exit poll sampled 3889 of the 9.5 million people who voted.

Question to Explore

For this exit poll, what was the population and what was the sample?

Think It Through

The population was the total set of subjects of interest, namely, the 9.5 million people who voted in this election. The sample was the 3889 voters who were interviewed in the exit poll. These are the people from whom the poll obtained data about their votes.

Insight

The ultimate goal of most studies is to learn about the *population*. For example, the sponsors of this exit poll wanted to make an inference (prediction) about *all* voters, not just the 3889 voters sampled by the poll.

▶ ***Try Exercises 1.9 and 1.10***

Did You Know?

Examples in this book use the five parts shown in this example: **Picture the Scenario** introduces the context. **Question to Explore** states the question addressed. **Think It Through** shows the reasoning used to answer that question. **Insight** gives follow-up comments related to the example. TRY **Try Exercises** direct you to a similar "Practicing the Basics" exercise at the end of the section. Also, each example title is preceded by a label highlighting the example's **concept**. In this example, the concept label is "Sample and population."◀

Occasionally data are available from an entire population. For instance, every ten years the U.S. Bureau of the Census gathers data from the entire U.S. population (or nearly all). But the census is an exception. Usually, it is too costly and time-consuming to obtain data from an entire population. It is more practical to get data for a sample. The General Social Survey and polling organizations such as the Gallup poll usually select samples of about 1000 to 2500 Americans to learn about opinions and beliefs of the population of *all* Americans. The same is true for surveys in other parts of the world, such as the Eurobarometer in Europe.

Descriptive Statistics and Inferential Statistics

Using the distinction between samples and populations, we can now tell you more about the use of **description** and **inference** in statistical analyses.

Description in Statistical Analyses

Descriptive statistics refers to methods for summarizing the collected data (where the data constitutes either a sample or a population). The summaries usually consist of graphs and numbers such as averages and percentages.

A descriptive statistical analysis usually combines graphical and numerical summaries. For instance, Figure 1.1 is a **bar graph** that shows the percentages of educational attainment in the United States in 2013. It summarizes a survey of 78,000 households by the U.S. Bureau of the Census. The main purpose of descriptive statistics is to reduce the data to simple summaries without distorting or losing much information. Graphs and numbers such as percentages and averages are easier to comprehend than the entire set of data. It's much easier to get a sense of the data by looking at Figure 1.1 than by reading through the

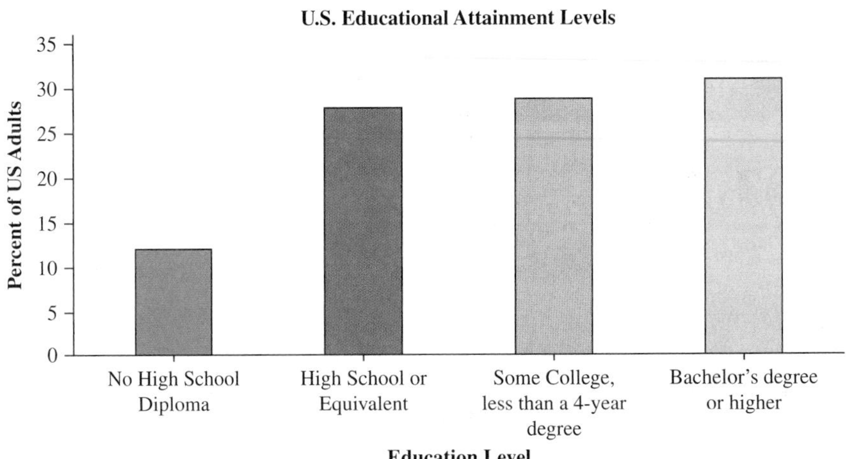

▲ **Figure 1.1** Educational Attainment, Based on a Sample of 78,000 Households in the 2013 Current Population Survey. (*Source:* Data from United States Census Bureau.)

questionnaires filled out by the 78,000 sampled households. From this graph, it's readily apparent that about a third of people have at least a bachelor's degree, whereas about 11% do not have a high school diploma.

Descriptive statistics are also useful when data are available for the entire population, such as in a census. By contrast, inferential statistics are used when data are available for a sample only, but we want to make a decision or prediction about the entire population.

Inference in Statistical Analyses

Inferential statistics refers to methods of making decisions or predictions about a population, based on data obtained from a sample of that population.

In most surveys, we have data for a sample, not for the entire population. We use descriptive statistics to summarize the sample data and inferential statistics to make predictions about the population.

Example 3

Descriptive and inferential statistics ◄

Polling Opinions on Handgun Control

Picture the Scenario

Suppose we'd like to know what people think about controls over the sales of handguns. Let's consider how people feel in Florida, a state with a relatively high violent-crime rate. The population of interest is the set of more than 10 million adult residents of Florida.

Because it is impossible to discuss the issue with all these people, we can study results from a recent poll of 834 Florida residents conducted by the Institute for Public Opinion Research at Florida International University. In that poll, 54.0% of the sampled subjects said they favored controls over the sales of handguns. A newspaper article about the poll reports that the margin of error for how close this number falls to the population percentage is 3.4%. We'll see (later in the textbook) that this means we can predict with high confidence (about 95% certainty) that the percentage of *all* adult Floridians favoring control over sales of handguns falls within 3.4% of the survey's value of 54.0%, that is, between 50.6% and 57.4%.

Question to Explore

In this analysis, what is the descriptive statistical analysis and what is the inferential statistical analysis?

Think It Through

The results for the sample of 834 Florida residents are summarized by the percentage, 54.0%, who favored handgun control. This is a descriptive statistical analysis. We're interested, however, not just in those 834 people but in the *population of all* adult Florida residents. The prediction that the percentage of *all* adult Floridians who favor handgun control falls between 50.6% and 57.4% is an inferential statistical analysis. In summary, we *describe* the *sample*, and we make *inferences* about the *population*.

Insight

The sample size of 834 was small compared to the population size of more than 10 million. However, because the values between 50.6% and 57.4% are all above 50%, the study concluded that a slim majority of Florida residents favored handgun control.

▶ ***Try Exercises 1.11, part a, and 1.12, parts a–c***

An important aspect of statistical inference involves reporting the likely *precision* of a prediction. How close is the *sample* value of 54% likely to be to the true (unknown) percentage of the *population* favoring gun control? We'll see (in Chapters 4 and 6) why a well-designed sample of 834 people yields a sample percentage value that is very likely to fall within about 3–4% (the so-called *margin of error*) of the population value. In fact, we'll see that inferential statistical analyses can predict characteristics of entire populations quite well by selecting samples that are small relative to the population size. Surprisingly, the absolute size of the sample matters much more than the size relative to the population total. For example, the population of China is about four times that of the United States, but a random sample of 1000 people from the Chinese population and a random sample of 1000 people from the U.S. population would achieve similar levels of accuracy. That's why most polls take samples of only about a thousand people, even if the population has millions of people. In this book, we'll see why this works.

Sample Statistics and Population Parameters

In Example 3, the percentage of the sample favoring handgun control is an example of a **sample statistic**. It is crucial to distinguish between sample statistics and the corresponding values for the population. The term **parameter** is used for a numerical summary of the population.

Recall

A **population** is the total group of individuals about whom you want to make conclusions. A **sample** is a subset of the population for whom you actually have data. ◀

Parameter and Statistic

A **parameter** is a numerical summary of the population. A **statistic** is a numerical summary of a sample taken from the population.

For example, the percentage of the population of all adult Florida residents favoring handgun control is a parameter. We hope to learn about parameters so that we can better understand the population, but the true parameter values are almost always unknown. Thus, we use sample statistics to estimate the parameter values.

Randomness and Variability

Random is often thought to mean chaotic or haphazard, but randomness is an extremely powerful tool for obtaining good samples and conducting experiments. A sample tends to be a good reflection of a population when each subject in the population has the same chance of being included in that sample. That's the basis of **random sampling**, which is designed to make the sample representative of the population. A simple example of random sampling is when a teacher puts each student's name on a slip of paper, places it in a hat, and then draws names from the hat without looking.

- Random sampling allows us to make powerful inferences about populations.
- Randomness is also crucial to performing experiments well.

If, as in Scenario 2 on page 4, we want to compare aspirin to a placebo in terms of the percentage of people who later have a heart attack, it's best to randomly select those in the sample who use aspirin and those who use the placebo. This approach tends to keep the groups balanced on other factors that could affect the results. For example, suppose we allowed people to choose whether to use aspirin (instead of randomizing whether the person receives aspirin or the placebo). Then, the people who decided to use aspirin might have tended to be healthier than those who didn't, which could produce misleading results.

People are different from each other, so, not surprisingly, the measurements we make on them *vary* from person to person. For the GSS question about TV watching in Activity 1 on page 6, different people reported different amounts of TV watching. In the exit poll of Example 2, not all people voted the same way. If subjects did not vary, we'd need to sample only one of them. We learn more about this variability by sampling more people. If we want to predict the outcome of an election, we're better off sampling 100 voters than one voter, and our prediction will be even more reliable if we sample 1000 voters.

- Just as people vary, so do samples vary.

Suppose you take an exit poll of 1000 voters to predict the outcome of an election. Suppose the Gallup organization also takes an exit poll of 1000 voters. Your sample will have different people than Gallup's. Consequently, the predictions will also differ. Perhaps your exit poll of 1000 voters has 480 voting for the Republican candidate, so you predict that 48% of all voters voted for that person. Perhaps Gallup's exit poll of 1000 voters has 440 voting for the Republican candidate, so they predict that 44% of all voters voted for that person. Activity 2 at the end of the chapter shows that with random sampling, the amount of variability from sample to sample is actually quite predictable. Both of your predictions are likely to fall within 5% of the actual population percentage who voted Republican, assuming the samples are random. If, on the other hand, Republicans are more likely than Democrats to refuse to participate in the exit poll, then we would need to account for this. In the 2004 U.S. presidential election, much controversy arose when George W. Bush won several states in which exit polling predicted that John Kerry had won. Is it likely that the way the exit polls were conducted led to these incorrect predictions?

One of the main goals of statistical inference is to make statements about large populations based on a small sample. We will see more on this in Chapters 8 and 9.

Estimation from Surveys with Random Sampling

Sample surveys are a common method of gathering data (see Chapter 4). Data from sample surveys are frequently used to estimate population percentages.

For instance, a Gallup poll recently reported that 30% of Americans worried that they might not be able to pay health care costs during the next 12 months. How close is a sample estimate to the true, unknown population percentage? When you read results of surveys, you'll often see a statement such as, "The **margin of error** is plus or minus 3 percentage points." The margin of error is a measure of the expected variability from one random sample to the next random sample. As we will see in Activity 2, there is variability in samples. A second sample of the same size could yield a proportion of 29%, whereas a third might yield 32%. A margin of error of plus or minus 3 percentage points means it is very likely that the population percentage is no more than 3% lower or 3% higher than the reported sample percentage. So if Gallup reports that 30% worry about health care costs, it's very likely that in the entire population, the percentage that worry about health care costs is between about 27% and 33% (that is, within 3% of 30%). "Very likely" typically means that about 95 times out of 100, such statements are correct. We refer to this as a 95% confidence interval. Chapter 8 will show details about margin of error and how to calculate it. For now, we'll use a rough approximation. In statistics, we let n denote the number of subjects in the sample. When creating a 95% confidence interval using a simple random sample of n subjects, and finding the margin of error for the estimation of a population proportion,

$$\text{approximate margin of error} = \frac{1}{\sqrt{n}} \times 100\%$$

Example 4

Margin of error ◀

Gallup Poll

Picture the Scenario

On April 20, 2010, one of the worst environmental disasters took place in the Gulf of Mexico, the Deepwater Horizon oil spill. As a result of an explosion on an oil drilling platform, oil flowed freely into the Gulf of Mexico for nearly three months until it was finally capped on July 15, 2010. It is estimated that more than 200 million gallons of crude oil spilled, causing extensive damage to marine and wildlife habitats and crippling the Gulf's fishing and tourism industries. In response to the spill, many activists called for an end to deepwater drilling off the U.S. coast and for increased efforts to eliminate our dependence on oil. Meanwhile, approximately nine months after the Gulf disaster, political turbulence gripped the Middle East, causing the price of gasoline in the United States to approach an all-time high. Between March 3 and 6, 2011, Gallup's annual environmental survey[2] reported that 60% of Americans favored offshore drilling as a means to reduce U.S. dependence on foreign oil, 37% opposed offshore drilling, and the remaining 3% had no opinion. The poll was based on interviews conducted with a random sample of 1021 adults, aged 18 and older, living in the continental United States, selected using random digit dialing.

Questions to Explore

a. Find an approximate margin of error for these results reported in the environmental survey report.

b. How is the margin of error interpreted?

[2] www.gallup.com/poll/146615/Oil-Drilling-Gains-Favor-Americans.aspx

Think It Through

a. The sample size was $n = 1021$ U.S. adults. The Gallup poll was a random sample but not a simple random sample. It used random digit dialing, which can give results nearly as accurate as with a simple random sample. We estimate the margin of error as approximately

$$\frac{1}{\sqrt{n}} \times 100\% = \frac{1}{\sqrt{1021}} \times 100\% = 0.03 \times 100\% = 3\%$$

b. Gallup reported that 60% of Americans support offshore drilling. This percentage refers to the sample of 1021 U.S. adults. The reported margin of error of 3% suggests that in the population of adult Americans, it's likely that between about 57% and 63% support offshore drilling.

Insight

You may be surprised or skeptical that a sample of only 1021 people out of a huge population (such as 200 million adult Americans) can provide such a precise inference. That's the power of random sampling. We'll see why this works in Chapter 7. The more precise formula shown there will give a somewhat smaller margin of error value when the sample percentage is far from 50%.

▶ ***Try Exercises 1.17 and 1.18***

Testing and Statistical Significance

Now suppose you've conducted an experiment to determine whether a new form of chemotherapy is effective at keeping cancer in remission for at least five years, compared to the standard chemotherapy, which we will call the control group. You find that the cancer remission rate (the rate at which the cancer is no longer observed in the patient) is 55% in subjects taking a new form of chemotherapy, whereas the cancer remission rate is 44% in the control group. Can you conclude that the new chemotherapy was effective?

Not quite yet. You must convince yourself that this difference between 44% and 55% cannot be explained by the variation that occurs naturally just by chance. Even if the effect of the chemotherapy is no different from the effect of control, the sample remission rates would not be *exactly* the same for the two groups. Just by ordinary chance, even if there is no effect of the treatment, the remission rate in the treatment group could be higher than the rate in the control group. In a randomized experiment, the variation that could be expected to occur just by chance alone is roughly like the margin of error with simple random sampling. So if a treatment has $n = 215$ observations, this is about $(1/\sqrt{215}) \times 100\%$, or about 7%. If the population percentage of people in remission is 50%, the sample percentage of 215 subjects in remission is very likely to fall between 43% and 57% (that is, within 7% of 50%). The difference in a study between 44% relapsing and 55% relapsing could be explained by the ordinary variation expected for this size of sample.

By contrast, if each treatment had $n = 1000$ observations, the ordinary variation we'd expect due to chance is only about $(1/\sqrt{1000}) \times 100\%$ or 3% for each percentage. Then, the difference between 44% and 55% could not be explained by ordinary variation: There is no plausible common population percentage for the two treatments such that 44% and 55% are both within 3% of its value. The new chemotherapy would truly seem to be better than standard chemotherapy. The difference expected due to ordinary variation is smaller with larger samples. You can be more confident that sample results reflect a true effect when the sample size is large than when it is small. Obviously, we cannot learn much by using only $n = 1$ subject for each treatment. When the difference between the results for the two treatments is so large that it would be rare to see such a difference by ordinary random variation, we say that the results are **statistically significant**. For example, the difference between 55% remission and 44% remission when $n = 1000$ for each group is statistically significant. We can then conclude that the observed difference is likely due to the effect of the treatments rather than merely due to ordinary random variation. Thus, in the population, we infer that the response truly depends on the treatment. How to determine this and how it depends on the sample size are topics we'll study in later chapters. For now, suffice it to say the larger the sample size, the better.

The Basic Ideas of Statistics

Here is a summary of the key concepts of statistics that you'll learn about in this book:

Chapter 2: Exploring Data with Graphs and Numerical Summaries How can you present simple summaries of data? You replace lots of numbers with simple graphs and numerical summaries.

Chapter 3: Association: Contingency, Correlation, and Regression How does annual income ten years after graduation correlate with college GPA? You can find out by studying the association between those characteristics.

Chapter 4: Gathering Data How can you design an experiment or conduct a survey to get data that will help you answer questions? You'll see why results may be misleading if you don't use randomization.

Chapter 5: Probability in Our Daily Lives How can you determine the chance of some outcome, such as winning a lottery? Probability, the basic tool for evaluating chances, is also a key foundation for inference.

Chapter 6: Probability Distributions You've probably heard of the normal distribution or bell-shaped curve that describes people's heights or IQs or test scores. What is the normal distribution, and how can we use it to find probabilities?

Chapter 7: Sampling Distributions Why is the normal distribution so important? You'll see why, and you'll learn its key role in statistical inference.

Chapter 8: Statistical Inference: Confidence Intervals How can an exit poll of 3889 voters possibly predict the results for millions of voters? You'll find out by applying the probability concepts of Chapters 5, 6, and 7 to make statistical inferences that show how closely you can predict summaries such as population percentages.

Chapter 9: Statistical Inference: Significance Tests About Hypotheses How can a medical study make a decision about whether a new drug is better than a placebo? You'll see how you can control the chance that a statistical inference makes a correct decision about what works best.

Chapters 10–15: Applying Descriptive and Inferential Statistics to Many Kinds of Data After Chapters 2 to 9 introduce you to the key concepts of statistics, the rest of the book shows you how to apply them in lots of situations. For instance, Chapter 10 shows how to compare two groups, such as using a sample of students from your university to make an inference about whether male and female students exhibit different rates of binge drinking.

1.2 Practicing the Basics

1.6 Description and inference

a. Distinguish between *description* and *inference* as reasons for using statistics. Illustrate the distinction using an example.

b. You have data for a population, such as obtained in a census. Explain why descriptive statistics are helpful but inferential statistics are not needed.

1.7 Censorship The General Social Survey in 2012 asked whether we should allow antireligious books in the library. Of the 3077 people who responded, 23% said they should be removed. Identify (a) the sample, (b) the population, and (c) the sample statistic reported.

1.8 Concerned about global warming? The Institute for Public Opinion Research at Florida International University has conducted the FIU/Florida Poll (www2.fiu.edu/orgs/ipor/globwarm2.htm) of about 1200 Floridians annually since 1988 to track opinions on a wide variety of issues. In 2006 the poll asked, "How concerned are you about the problem of global warming?" The possible responses were very concerned, somewhat concerned, not very concerned, and haven't heard about it. The poll reported percentages (44, 30, 21, 6) in these categories.

a. Identify the sample and the population.

b. Are the percentages quoted statistics or parameters? Why?

1.9 Graduate school information TRY Suppose a liberal arts student is interested in exploring graduate school in his or her field. The student identifies a program in which he or she is interested and finds the name of a few students from that program to interview. In this context, identify what is meant by the (a) subject, (b) sample, and (c) population.

1.10 Is globalization good? TRY The Voice of the People poll asks a random sample of citizens from different countries around the world their opinion about global issues. Included in the list of questions is whether they feel that globalization helps their country. The reported results were combined by regions. In the most recent poll, 74% of Africans felt globalization helps their country, whereas 38% of North Americans believe it helps their country. (a) Identify the samples and the populations. (b) Are these percentages sample statistics or population parameters? Explain your answer.

1.11 Graduating seniors' salaries TRY The job placement center at your school surveys *all* graduating seniors at the school. Their report about the survey provides numerical summaries such as the average starting salary and the percentage of students earning more than $30,000 a year.

a. Are these statistical analyses descriptive or inferential? Explain.

b. Are these numerical summaries better characterized as statistics or as parameters?

1.12 At what age did women marry? TRY A historian wants to estimate the average age at marriage of women in New England in the early 19th century. Within her state archives she finds marriage records for the years 1800–1820, which she treats as a sample of all marriage records from the early 19th century. The average age of the women in the records is 24.1 years. Using the appropriate statistical method, she estimates that the average age of brides in early 19th-century New England was between 23.5 and 24.7.

a. Which part of this example gives a descriptive summary of the data?

b. Which part of this example draws an inference about a population?

c. To what population does the inference in part b refer?

d. The average age of the sample was 24.1 years. Is 24.1 a statistic or a parameter?

1.13 Age pyramids as descriptive statistics The figure shown is a graph published by Statistics Sweden. It compares Swedish society in 1750 and in 2010 on the numbers of men and women of various ages, using age pyramids. Explain how this indicates that

a. In 1750, few Swedish people were old.

b. In 2010, Sweden had many more people than in 1750.

c. In 2010, of those who were very old, more were female than male.

d. In 2010, the largest five-year group included people born during the era of first manned space flight.

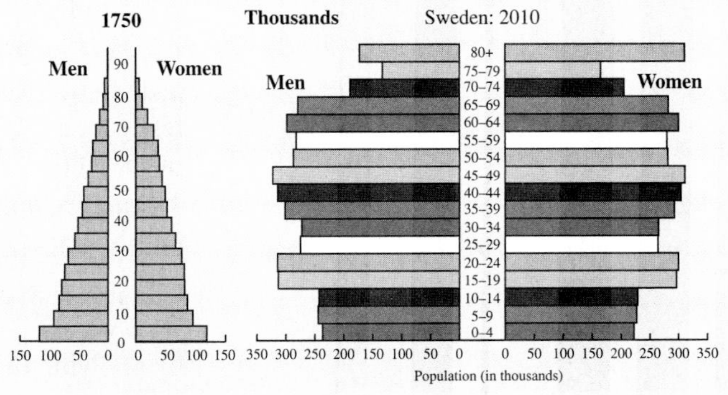

Graphs of number of men and women of various ages, in 1750 and in 2010. (*Source:* From Statistics Sweden.)

1.14 Gallup polls TECH Go to the website www.galluppoll.com for the Gallup poll. From reports listed on its home page, give an example of (a) a descriptive statistical analysis and (b) an inferential statistical analysis.

1.15 National service Consider the population of all students at your school. A certain proportion support mandatory national service (MNS) following high school. Your friend randomly samples 20 students from the school and uses the sample proportion who support MNS to predict the population proportion at the school. You take your own, separate random sample of 20 students and find the sample proportion that supports MNS. For the two studies,

a. Are the populations the same?

b. How likely is it that the samples are the same? Explain.

c. How likely is it that the sample proportions are the same? Explain.

1.16 Samples vary less with more data We'll see that the amount by which statistics vary from sample to sample always depends on the sample size. This important fact can be illustrated by thinking about what would happen in repeated flips of a fair coin.

a. Which case would you find more surprising—flipping the coin five times and observing all heads or flipping the coin 500 times and observing all heads?

b. Imagine flipping the coin 500 times, recording the proportion of heads observed, and repeating this experiment many times to get an idea of how much the proportion tends to vary from one sequence to another. Different sequences of 500 flips tend to result in proportions of heads observed which are less variable than the proportion of heads observed in sequences of only five flips each. Using part a, explain why you would expect this to be true.

1.17 Comparing polls TRY The following table shows the result of the 2012 presidential election along with the vote predicted by several organizations in the days before the election. The sample sizes were typically about 1000 to 2000 people. The percentages for each poll do not sum to 100 because of voters who indicated they were undecided or preferred another candidate.

	Predicted Vote	
Poll	**Obama**	**Romney**
Rasmussen	48	49
CNN	49	49
Gallup	48	49
Pew Research	50	47
Rand	54	43
Fox	46	46
Actual Vote	50.6	47.8

Source: http://ncpp.org/files/Presidential%20National%20Polls%202012%200103%20Full.pdf

a. Treating the sample sizes as 1000 each, find the approximate margin of error.

b. Do most of the predictions fall within the margin of error of the actual vote percentages? Considering the relative sizes of the sample, the population, and the undecided factor, would you say that these polls had good accuracy?

1.18 Margin of error and *n* TRY The Gallup Organization reported that during March 2011, 60% of Americans favored offshore drilling as a means of reducing U.S. dependence on foreign oil. The poll was based on the responses of $n = 1021$ individuals and resulted in a margin of error of approximately 3%. Find the approximate margin of error if the poll had been based on a sample of size (a) $n = 100$, (b) $n = 400$, and (c) $n = 1600$. Explain how the margin of error changes as n increases.

1.19 Smoking cessation A study published in 2010 in *The New England Journal of Medicine* investigated the effect of financial incentives on smoking cessation. As part of the study, 878 employees of a company, all of whom were smokers, were randomly assigned to one of two treatment groups. One group (442 employees) was to receive information about smoking cessation programs; the other (436 employees) was to receive that same information as well as a financial incentive to quit smoking. The outcome of interest of the study was smoking cessation status six months after the initial cessation was reported. After implementation of the program, 14.7% of individuals in the financial incentive group reported cessation six months after the initial report, compared to 5.0% of the information-only group. Assume that the observed difference in cessation rates between the groups (14.7% − 5.0% = 9.7%) is statistically significant.

a. What does it mean to be statistically significant? (choose the best option from (i)–(iv))

i. The financial option was offered to 9.7% more smokers in the study than the nonsmokers who were employees of the company.

ii. 9.7% was calculated using statistical techniques.

iii. If there were no true impact of the financial incentive, the observed difference of 9.7% is unlikely to have occurred by chance alone.

iv. We know that if the financial incentive were given to all smokers, 9.7% would quit smoking.

b. Is the difference between the groups attributable to the financial incentive?

1.3 Using Calculators and Computers

Today's researchers (and students) are lucky: Unlike those in the previous generation, they don't have to do complex statistical calculations by hand. Powerful user-friendly computing software and calculators are now readily available for statistical analyses. This makes it possible to do calculations that would be extremely tedious or even impossible by hand, and it frees time for interpreting and communicating the results.

Using (and Misusing) Statistics Software and Calculators

MINITAB, JMP (from SAS), StatCrunch (from Pearson), SPSS (from IBM), and R are popular statistical software packages on college campuses. The TI-83+, TI-84, TI-89, and TI-Inspire family calculators, which we will refer to as simply TI, are portable tools for generating simple statistics and graphs. The Microsoft Excel software can conduct some statistical methods, sorting and analyzing data with its spreadsheet program, but its capabilities are limited. Throughout this text, we'll show examples of these different software options. The emphasis in this book is on how to interpret the output, not on the details of using such software.

In Practice Selecting Valid Analyses

Given the current software capabilities, why do you still have to learn about statistical methods? Can't computers do all this analysis for you? The problem is that a computer will perform the statistical analysis you request whether or not its use is valid for the given situation. Just knowing how to use software does not guarantee a proper analysis. You'll need a good background in statistics to understand which statistical method to use, which options to choose with that method, and how to interpret and make valid conclusions from the computer output. This text helps give you this background.

Data Files

To make statistical analysis easier, large sets of data are organized in a **data file**. This file usually has the form of a spreadsheet. It is the way statistical software receives the data.

Figure 1.2 is an example of part of a data file. It shows how a data file looks in MINITAB. The file shows data for eight students on the following characteristics:

- Gender (f = female, m = male)
- Racial–ethnic group (b = black, h = Hispanic, w = white)
- Age (in years)
- College GPA (scale 0 to 4)
- Average number of hours per week watching TV
- Whether a vegetarian (yes, no)
- Political party (dem = Democrat, rep = Republican, ind = independent)
- Marital status (1 = married, 0 = unmarried)

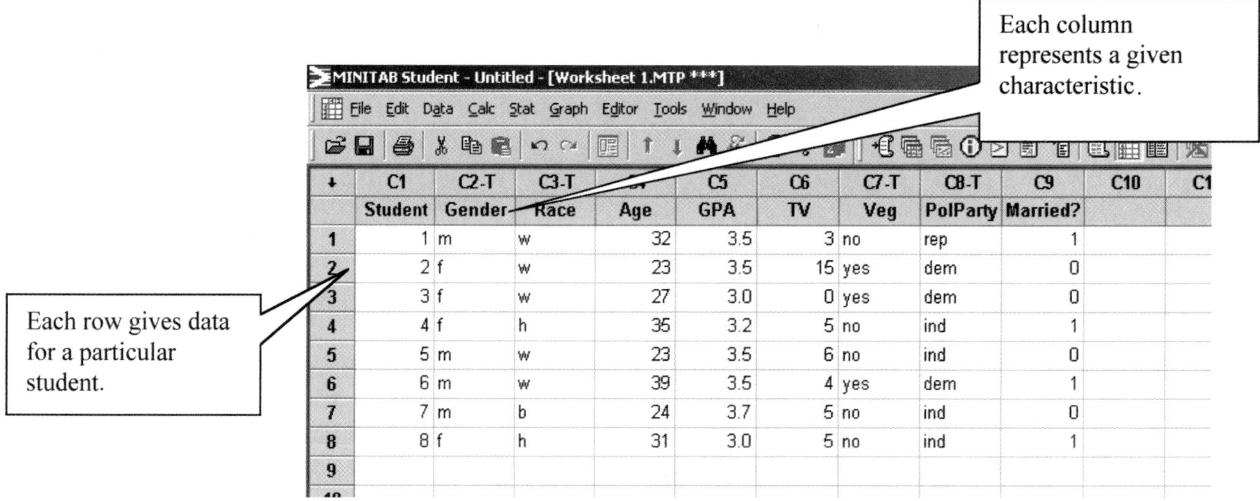

	C1	C2-T	C3-T		C5	C6	C7-T	C8-T	C9	C10
	Student	Gender	Race	Age	GPA	TV	Veg	PolParty	Married?	
1	1	m	w	32	3.5	3	no	rep	1	
2	2	f	w	23	3.5	15	yes	dem	0	
3	3	f	w	27	3.0	0	yes	dem	0	
4	4	f	h	35	3.2	5	no	ind	1	
5	5	m	w	23	3.5	6	no	ind	0	
6	6	m	w	39	3.5	4	yes	dem	1	
7	7	m	b	24	3.7	5	no	ind	0	
8	8	f	h	31	3.0	5	no	ind	1	
9										

▲ **Figure 1.2** Part of a MINITAB Data File.

Figure 1.2 shows the two basic rules for constructing a data file:

- Any one row contains measurements for a particular subject (for instance, person).
- Any one column contains measurements for a particular characteristic.

Some characteristics have numerical data, such as the values for hours of TV watching. Some characteristics have data that consist of categories or labels, such as the categories (yes, no) for vegetarians or the labels (dem, rep, ind) for political affiliation.

Figure 1.2 resembles a larger data file from a questionnaire administered to a sample of students at the University of Florida. That data file, which includes other characteristics as well, is called "FL student survey" and is available for download from the book's website (pearsonhighered.com/AFK).

To construct a similar data file for your class, try Activity 3 in the Student Activities at the end of the chapter.

Example 5

Data files

Ads on Facebook

Picture the Scenario

You are the manager of a digital media store (e.g., DVDs, video games). Your sales have been shrinking because of Internet competition such as Amazon, so you decide to try advertising and selling your products online. After launching your new website, you enter an advertising agreement with Facebook, the terms of which include your ad being displayed to 1000 Facebook users.

Anyone who clicks the ad will go to your website and a display of 10 featured items. For Facebook advertising to be profitable, the 1000 users to whom your ad is shown need to spend, on average, \$0.75 or more on the 10 featured items. The first person shown your ad doesn't click it and orders nothing. The second person visits your site but does not purchase anything. The third person orders one copy of item 3 at a cost of \$8 and two copies of item 5 at a cost of \$6 each. At the end of the advertising period, you create a data file containing the orders (in dollars) of the 10 featured items for each of the 1000 potential customers.

Questions to Explore

a. How do you record the responses from the first three people in the data file for the 10 featured items?

b. How many rows of data will your file contain?

Think It Through

a. Each row refers to a particular person to whom your ad was shown. Each column refers to one of the featured items. Each entry of data is the dollar amount spent on a given featured item by a particular person. So, the first three rows of the data file are

Person	item1	item2	item3	item4	item5	item6	item7	item8	item9	item10
1	0	0	0	0	0	0	0	0	0	0
2	0	0	0	0	0	0	0	0	0	0
3	0	0	8	0	12	0	0	0	0	0

b. The entire data file would consist of 1000 lines of data, one line for each potential customer.

Insight

From the entire data file, suppose you calculate that the average sales per person equals \$0.90. What could you conclude about the average sales if you decide to enter a new agreement to display your ad to 100,000 Facebook users? Is it likely to be at least \$0.75? Activity 2, later in this chapter, demonstrates the variability that exists in samples. As we'll see (in Chapters 4 and 9), you can use additional information about the customers and about the method of sampling to help answer this question. If you decide to advertise online, consider how statistics can help you use information gathered about customers' demographics and past purchases to develop and maintain a promising list of potential customers.

► ***Try Exercise 1.21***

Databases

Most studies design experiments or surveys to collect data to answer the questions of interest. Often, though, it is adequate to take advantage of existing archived collections of data files, called **databases**. Many Internet databases are available. By browsing various websites, you can obtain information about many topics.

The General Social Survey, discussed in Scenario 3 and Activity 1, is one such database that is accessed from the Internet. The website for this book contains several data files that you'll use in some exercises. Here are some other databases that can be fun and informative to browse:

- Are you interested in pro baseball, basketball, or football? Click the statistics links at www.mlb.com, www.nba.com, or www.nfl.com or see special sports data sites such as www.baseball-reference.com/.
- Are you interested in what people believe around the world? Check out www.globalbarometer.net or www.europa.eu.int/comm/public_opinion or www.latinobarometro.org.
- Are you interested in results of Gallup polls about people's beliefs? See www.gallup.com.
- Are you interested in population growth, unemployment rates, or the spread of sexually transmitted diseases? See www.google.com/publicdata for these and many other data sets, along with visualization tools.

Also very useful are search engines such as Google. Type in "U.S. Census data" in the search window at www.google.com, and it lists databases such as those maintained by the U.S. Bureau of the Census. Type in "Statistics Canada data" for census databases from Canada. A search engine also is helpful for finding data or descriptive statistics on a particular topic. For instance, if you want to find summaries of Canadians' opinions about the legalization of marijuana for medical treatment, try typing

poll legalize marijuana Canada medicine

in the search window. And if you would like to limit your searches to academic journals, search for them on Google Scholar (scholar.google.com).

In Practice Always Check Sources

Not all databases or reported data summaries give reliable information. Before you give credence to such data, verify that the data are from a trustworthy source and that the source provides information about the way the data were gathered.

For example, many news organizations and search websites (such as cnn.com) ask you to participate in a "topic of the day" poll on their home page. Their summaries of how people responded are not reliable indications of how the entire population feels. They are biased because it is unlikely that the people who respond are representative of the population. We'll explain why in Chapter 4.

Web Apps

Just like riding a bike, it's easier to learn statistics if you are actively involved, learning by doing. One way is to practice by using software or calculators with data files or data summaries that we'll provide. Another way is to perform activities that illustrate the ideas of statistics by using interactive **web apps**. We'll use them throughout the text. You can find these apps online at the book's website pearsonhighered.com/AFK. Because they simply run in your browser (no installation necessary), we call them web apps. For example, you can use a web app to take samples from artificial populations and analyze them to discover properties of statistical methods applied to those samples. This is a type of **simulation**—using a computer to mimic what would actually happen if you selected a sample and used statistics in real life. So, let's get started with your active involvement.

▶ Activity 2

Simulating Randomness and Variability

To get a feel for randomness and variability, let's simulate taking an exit poll of voters using the Sampling Distribution for the Sample Proportion web app available from the book's website pearsonhighered.com/AFK. When accessing this app, a graph will appear with two bars labeled "Failure (0)" and "Success (1)". This refers to a population where each observation of an individual has just two possible outcomes, as in a population where each subject votes for one of only two candidates. For the purpose of this activity, let's assume "Failure" denotes a vote for the Republican candidate and "success" means a vote for the Democratic candidate.

Let's see what would happen with exit polling when 50% of the entire population (a proportion of 0.50) voted for each candidate. We'll use a small poll, only 10 voters. First, represent this by flipping a coin ten times. Let the number of heads represent the number who voted for the Democrat. What proportion in your sample of size 10 voted for the Democrat?

Now let's do this with the app. To reflect that 50% are going to vote for each candidate, in the first menu set the population proportion to 0.5. Note how this updates the graph for the population, setting the bars over "Failure" and "Success" to the same height. To take a sample of size 10, in the second menu choose 10 as the sample size. Next, click on [Draw Sample(s)] and you will see two more graphs appearing. The first will show you exactly how many Failures and Successes occurred in the sample of size 10 that you just generated. The screenshot in Figure 1.3 shows the results we got when running the app: 7 Failures and 3 Successes. This simulates sampling 10 voters from a population where 50% prefer Republican and the other 50% prefer Democrat and obtaining 7 subjects who voted Republican and 3 who voted Democrat. The result from this one sample corresponds to a sample proportion of 0.30 voting for the Democrat.

When you do this, you might get a proportion different than 0.30 voting for the Democrat because the process is random. Now generate another sample of size 10 and find the sample proportion by clicking on [Draw Sample(s)] a second time. What did you get? Repeat taking samples of size 10 at least 15 times by repeatedly clicking on the button. Observe how the sample proportion for each sample (indicated by the blue triangle in the middle plot) "jumps around" the population proportion of 0.50 (indicated by the orange half-circle). Are they always close?

Now repeat this for a larger exit poll, taking a sample of 1000 voters instead of 10 (set the sample size to 1000 in the app). What proportion voted for the Democrat? Repeat taking samples of size 1000 at least 15 times. Do the sample proportions voting for Democrat tend to be close to 0.50? We predict that all of your sample proportions will fall between 0.45 and 0.55. Are we correct?

We would expect that some sample proportions generated using a sample size of 10 fell much farther from 0.50 than the sample proportions generated using a sample size of 1000. This illustrates that sample proportions tend to be closer to the population proportion when the sample size is larger. In fact, as we move forward we will discover that we do much better in making inferences about the population with larger sample sizes. To learn exactly how much better, you need to get to Chapter 7.

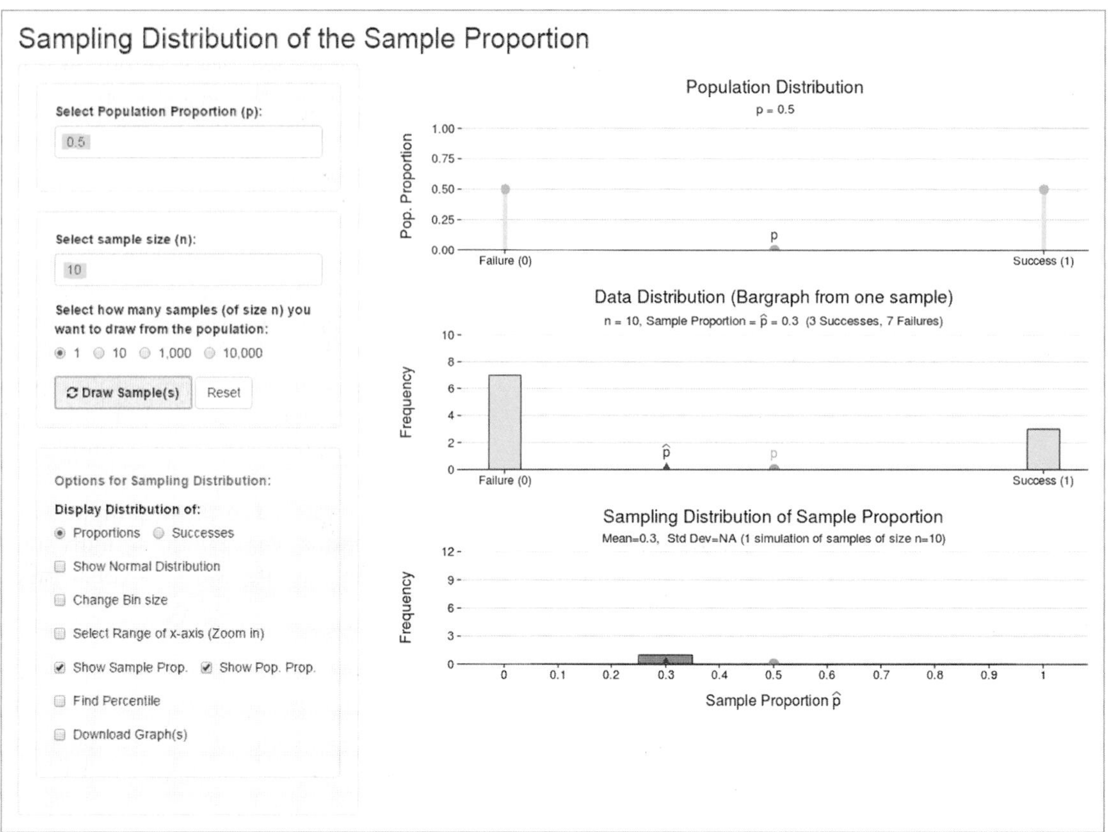

▲ **Figure 1.3 Using the Sampling Distribution for the Sample Proportion Web App.** This app, accessible from the book's website, simulates taking samples from a population with population proportion 0.50 (set in first menu, see highlighted portion). The first plot shows that a proportion of 0.5 of the subjects in the entire population vote Republican (generically labeled as "Failure") and 0.5 vote Democrat ("Success"). The second plot shows the result from taking a sample of size 10 (set in the second menu, see highlighted portion) taken from this population. Of the 10 subjects sampled, we see that 7 voted Republican and 3 voted Democrat, for a sample proportion of 0.3 voting Democrat (indicated by the blue triangle in the second plot). Other features of this app will be explained in Chapter 7.

Try Exercises 1.25 and 1.26 ◄

1.3 Practicing the Basics

1.20 Data file for friends Construct (by hand) a data file of the form of Figure 1.2, for two characteristics with a sample of four of your friends. One characteristic should take numerical values, and the other should take values that are categories.

1.21 Shopping sales data file Construct a data file describing the purchasing behavior of the five people, described below, who visit a shopping mall. Enter purchase amounts each spent on clothes, sporting goods, books, and music CDs as the data. Customer 1 spent $49 on clothes and $16 on music CDs, customer 4 spent $92 on books, and the other three customers did not buy anything.
TRY

1.22 Sample with caution Individuals with children who read the Ann Landers column were asked, if they had it to do all over again, whether they would want to have children. Of the nearly 10,000 readers who responded, only 30% responded by saying yes. Why is it not safe to infer anything from this survey about the proportion of the general population who would still want to have children if given the opportunity to do things over?

1.23 Create a data file with software Your instructor will show you how to create data files by using the software for your course. Use it to create the data file you constructed by hand in Exercise 1.20 or 1.21.
TECH

1.24 Use a data file with software You may need to learn how to open a data file from the book's website or download one from the Web for use with the software for your course. Do this for the "FL student survey" data file on the book's website, from the survey mentioned following Figure 1.2.

TECH

1.25 Simulate with the Sampling Distribution for the Sample Proportion web app Refer to Activity 2 on page 21.

TRY TECH

a. Repeat the activity using a population proportion of 0.60: Take at least five samples of size 10 each; observe how the sample proportions of successes vary around 0.60 and then do the same thing with at least five samples of size 1000 each.

b. In part a, what seems to be the effect of the sample size on the amount by which sample proportions tend to vary around the population proportion, 0.60?

c. What is the practical implication of the effect of the sample size summarized in part b with respect to making inferences about the population proportion when you collect data and observe only the sample proportion?

1.26 Margin of error Refer to the Sampling Distribution of the Sample Proportion web app used in Activity 2.

TRY

a. For a population proportion of 0.50, simulate a random sample of size 1000. What is the sample proportion of successes? Do this 10 times, keeping track of the 10 sample proportions.

b. Find the approximate margin of error for a sample proportion based on 1000 observations.

c. Using the margin of error found in part b and the 10 sample proportions found in part a, form 10 intervals of believable values for the true proportion. How many of these intervals captured the actual population proportion, 0.50?

d. Collect the 10 intervals from each member of the class. (If there are 20 students, 200 intervals will be collected.) What percentage of these intervals captured the actual population proportion, 0.50?

1.27 Ebola outbreaks Ebola virus disease outbreaks have a case fatality rate of 90% (meaning 90% of people who get it die). In a hospital that is treating 20 patients with ebola, 14 died. Is this result surprising? To reason an answer, use the web app (or other software) as described in Activity 2 to conduct at least 10 simulations of taking samples of size 20 from a population with a proportion 0.90. Note the sample proportions. Do you observe any sample proportions equal to or less than 14/20, or 0.70?

Chapter Review

CHAPTER SUMMARY

- Statistics consists of methods for conducting research studies and for analyzing and interpreting the data produced by those studies. **Statistics is the art and science of learning from data.**

- The first part of the statistical process for answering a statistical question involves **design**—planning an investigative study to obtain relevant data for answering the statistical question. The design often involves taking a **sample** from a **population** where the population contains *all* the **subjects** (usually, people) of interest. Summary measures of samples are called **statistics**; summary measures of populations are called **parameters**. After we've collected the data, there are two types of statistical analyses:

  Descriptive statistics summarize the sample data with numbers and graphs.

  Inferential statistics make decisions and predictions about the entire population, based on the information in the sample data.

- With **random sampling**, each subject in the population has the same chance of being in the sample. This is desirable because then the sample tends to be a good reflection of the population. Randomization is also important for good experimental design, for example, randomly assigning who gets the medicine and who gets the placebo in a medical study.

- The measurements we make of a characteristic **vary** from individual to individual. Likewise, results of descriptive and inferential statistics **vary**, depending on the sample chosen. We'll see that the study of **variability** is a key part of statistics. **Simulation** investigations generate many samples randomly, often using an **app**. They provide a way of learning about the impact of randomness and variability from sample to sample.

- The **margin of error** is a measure of variability of a statistic from one random sample to the next. For proportions, the margin of error is approximated by $1/\sqrt{(n)} \times 100\%$, where n is the sample size.

- Results of a study are considered **statistically significant** if they would rarely be observed with only ordinary random variation.

- The calculations for data analysis can use computer software. The data are organized in a **data file**. This file has a separate row of data for each subject and a separate column for each characteristic. However, you'll need a good background in statistics to understand which statistical method to use and how to interpret and make valid conclusions from the computer output.

CHAPTER PROBLEMS

Practicing the Basics

1.28 UW Student survey In a University of Wisconsin (UW) study about alcohol abuse among students, 100 of the 40,858 members of the student body in Madison were sampled and asked to complete a questionnaire. One question asked was, "On how many days in the past week did you consume at least one alcoholic drink?"

a. Identify the population and the sample.

b. For the 40,858 students at UW, one characteristic of interest was the percentage who would respond "zero" to this question. For the 100 students sampled, suppose 29% gave this response. Does this mean that 29% of the entire population of UW students would make this response? Explain.

c. Is the numerical summary of 29% a sample statistic or a population parameter?

1.29 Euthanasia The General Social Survey asked, in 2012, whether you would commit suicide if you had an incurable disease. Of the 3112 people who had an opinion about this, 1862, or 59.8%, would commit suicide.

a. Describe the population of interest.

b. Explain how the sample data are summarized using descriptive statistics.

c. For what population parameter might we want to make an inference?

1.30 Sleep disorders among college students An article in the *Journal of American College Health* reports that, in a survey of 1845 college students from a large, southeastern public university, 27% were at risk for at least one sleep disorder, with a margin of error of 2%. Explain how this margin of error provides an *inferential* statistical analysis.

1.31 Breaking down Brown versus Whitman Example 2 of this chapter discusses an exit poll taken during the 2010 California gubernatorial election. The administrators of the poll also collected demographic data, which allows for further breakdown of the 3889 voters from whom information was collected. Of the 1633 voters registered as Democrats, 91% voted for Brown, with a margin of error of 1.4%. Of the 1206 voters registered as Republicans, 10% voted for Brown, with a margin of error of 1.7%. And of the 1050 Independent voters, 42% voted for Brown, with a margin of error of 3.0%.

a. Do these results summarize sample data or population data?

b. Identify a descriptive aspect of the results.

c. Identify an inferential aspect of the results.

1.32 Online learning Your university is interested in determining the proportion of students who would be interested in completing summer courses online, compared to on campus. A survey is taken of 100 students who intend to take summer courses.

a. Identify the sample and the population.

b. For the study, explain the purpose of using (i) descriptive statistics and (ii) inferential statistics.

1.33 Marketing study For the marketing study about sales in Example 5, identify the (a) sample and population and (b) descriptive and inferential aspects.

1.34 Support of labor unions The Gallup organization has asked opinions about support of labor unions since its first poll in 1936, when 72% of the American population approved of them. In its 2014 poll, it found that support of labor unions had fallen to 53% of Americans, based on a sample of 1,540 adults.

a. Calculate an estimated margin of error for these data.

b. What is the range of likely values for Americans who support labor unions in 2014?

c. This analysis is an example of

i. descriptive statistics

ii. inferential statistics

iii. a data file

iv. designing a study

1.35 Multiple choice: Use of inferential statistics? Inferential statistics are used

a. to describe whether a sample has more females or males.

b. to reduce a data file to easily understood summaries.

c. to make predictions about populations by using sample data.

d. when we can't use statistical software to analyze data.

e. to predict the sample data we will get when we know the population.

1.36 True or false? In a particular study, you could use descriptive statistics, or you could use inferential statistics, but you would rarely need to use both.

Concepts and Investigations

1.37 Statistics in the news Pick up a recent issue of a national newspaper, such as *The New York Times* or *USA Today,* or consult a news website, such as msnbc.com or cnn.com. Identify an article that used statistical methods. Did it use descriptive statistics, inferential statistics, or both? Explain.

1.38 What is statistics? On a final exam that one of us recently gave, students were asked, "How would you define 'statistics' to someone who has never taken a statistics course?" One student wrote, "You want to know the answer to some question. There's no answer in the back of a book. You collect some data. Statistics is the body of procedures that helps you analyze the data to figure out the answer and how sure you can be about it." Pick a question that interests you and explain how you might be able to use statistics to investigate the answer.

1.39 Surprising suicide data? TECH In Exercise 1.29, of 3112 people who responded, 59.8% or 1862 people, said they would commit suicide if they had an incurable disease. Suppose that 50% of the entire population shares this view about suicide. If the sample of 3112 people were a random sample, would this sample proportion of 0.598 be surprising? Investigate, using the web app described in Activity 2, setting the samples size to 3112 and the population proportion to 0.5.

1.40 **Create a data file** Using the statistical software that your instructor has assigned for the course, find out how to enter a data file. Create a data file by using the data in Figure 1.2.
TECH

Student Activities

1.41 **Getting to know the class** Your instructor will help the class create a data file consisting of the values for class members of characteristics based on responses to a questionnaire like the one that follows. Alternatively, your instructor may ask you to use a data file of this type already prepared with a class of students at the University of Florida, the "FL student survey" data file on the book's website. Using a spreadsheet program or the statistical software the instructor has chosen for your course, create a data file containing this information. What are some questions you might ask about these data? Homework exercises in each chapter will use these data.
TECH

GETTING TO KNOW THE CLASS

Please answer the following questions. Do not put your name on this sheet. Skip any question that you feel uncomfortable answering. These data are being collected to learn more about you and your classmates and to form a database for the class to analyze.

1. What is your height (recorded in inches)? _____
2. What is your gender (M = Male, F = Female)? _____
3. How much did you spend on your last haircut? _____
4. Do you have a paying job during the school year at which you work on average at least 10 hours a week (y = yes, n = no)? _____
5. Aside from class time, how many hours a week, on average, do you expect to spend studying and completing assignments for this course? _____
6. Do you smoke cigarettes (y = yes, n = no)? _____
7. How many people have you dated in the past 30 days? _____
8. What was (is) your high school GPA (based on a 4.0 scale)? _____
9. What is your current college GPA? _____
10. What is the distance (in miles) between your current residence and this class? _____
11. How many minutes each day, on average, do you spend browsing the Internet? _____
12. How many minutes each day, on average, do you watch TV? _____
13. How many hours each week, on average, do you participate in sports or have other physical exercise? _____
14. How many times a week, on average, do you read a daily newspaper? _____
15. Do you consider yourself a vegetarian (y = yes, n = no)? _____
16. How would you rate yourself politically (1 = very liberal, 2 = liberal, 3 = slightly liberal, 4 = moderate, 5 = slightly conservative, 6 = conservative, 7 = very conservative)? _____
17. What is your political affiliation (D = Democrat, R = Republican, I = Independent)? _____

CHAPTER

2

We learned in Chapter 1 that every statistical analysis starts with describing the available data. This chapter presents ways of visualizing and summarizing data with appropriate graphs and numbers (i.e., statistics). Both will help us accurately describe key features of the data.

Exploring Data with Graphs and Numerical Summaries

Example 1

Statistics Informs About Threats to Our Environment

Picture the Scenario

Air pollution concerns many people, and the consumption of energy from fossil fuels affects air pollution. Most technologically advanced nations, such as the United States, use vast quantities of a diminishing supply of nonrenewable fossil fuels. Countries fast becoming technologically advanced, such as China and India, are greatly increasing their energy use. The result is increased emissions of carbon dioxide and other pollutants into the atmosphere. Emissions of carbon dioxide may also contribute to global warming. Scientists use descriptive statistics to explore energy use, to learn whether air pollution has an effect on climate, to compare different countries in how they contribute to the worldwide problems of air pollution and climate change, and to measure the impact of global warming on the environment.

Questions to Explore

- How can we investigate which countries emit the highest amounts of carbon dioxide or use the most nonrenewable energy?
- Is climate change occurring, and how serious is it?

Thinking Ahead

Chapter 1 distinguished between the ideas of **descriptive statistics** (summarizing data) and **inferential statistics** (making a prediction or decision about a population using sample data). In this chapter, we discuss both graphical and numerical summaries that are the key elements of descriptive statistics. And, we will use these summaries to investigate questions like the ones asked above. Several exercises (2.10, 2.31, 2.75, 2.82) and Examples 11 and 17 explore data on CO_2 emission and energy consumption for the United States and other nations. Example 9 uses descriptive statistics to analyze data about temperature change over time.

Before we begin our journey into the art and science of analyzing data by using descriptive statistics, we need to learn a few new terms. We'll then study ways of using graphs to describe data, followed by ways of summarizing the data numerically.

2.1 Different Types of Data

Life would be uninteresting if everyone looked the same, ate the same food, and had the same thoughts. Fortunately, **variability** is everywhere, and statistical methods provide ways to measure and understand it. For some characteristics in a study, we often see variation among the subjects. For example, there's variability among your classmates in weight, major, GPA, favorite sport, and religious affiliation. Other characteristics may vary both by subject and across time. For instance, the amount of time spent studying in a day can vary both by student and by day.

Variables

Variables are the characteristics observed in a study. In the previous paragraph, weight and major are two variables we might want to study.

Variable

A **variable** is any characteristic observed in a study.

In Practice

Variables are typically listed in the columns of a data set, with the rows referring to different observations on a variable.

The term *variable* highlights that data values *vary*. For example, to investigate whether global warming has occurred where you live, you could gather data on the high temperature each day over the past century at the nearest weather station. The variable is the high temperature. Examples of other variables for each day are the low temperature, the cloud cover, whether it rained that day, and the number of centimeters of precipitation.

Variables Can Be Quantitative (Numerical) or Categorical (in Categories)

The data values that we observe for a variable are called **observations**. Each observation can be a **number** such as the number of centimeters of precipitation in a day. Or each observation belongs to a **category**, such as "yes" or "no" for whether it rained.

In Words

Consider your classmates. From person to person, there is variability in age, GPA, major, and whether he or she is dating someone. These are **variables**. Age and GPA are **quantitative**—their values are numerical. Major and dating status are **categorical** because observations fall into distinct categories, such as "psychology," "business," or "history" for major and "yes" or "no" for dating status.

Categorical and Quantitative Variables

A variable is called **categorical** if each observation belongs to one of a set of distinct categories.

A variable is called **quantitative** if observations on it take numerical values that represent different magnitudes of the variable.

The daily high temperature and the amount of precipitation are quantitative variables. Other examples of quantitative variables are age, number of siblings, annual income, and number of years of education completed. The cloud cover (with categories cloudy, partly cloudy, sunny) or whether it rained on a given day (with categories yes and no) are categorical variables. For human subjects, examples of categorical variables include sex (with categories male and female), religious affiliation (with categories such as Catholic, Jewish, Muslim, Protestant, Other, None), type of residence (house, condominium, apartment, dormitory, other), and belief in life after death (yes, no).

In the definition of a quantitative variable, why do we say that numerical values must *represent different magnitudes*? Quantitative variables measure "how much" of something (that is, *quantity* or *magnitude*). With quantitative variables, we can find arithmetic summaries such as averages. However, some numerical variables, such as area codes or bank account numbers, are not considered quantitative variables because they do not vary in quantity. For example, a bank might be interested in the average of the sizes of loans made to its customers, but an "average" bank account number for its loan accounts does not make sense.

Caution

A variable using numbers as labels for its categories is still a categorical variable and is not quantitative.

Graphs and numerical summaries describe the main features of a variable:

- For **quantitative** variables, key features to describe are the **center** and the **variability** (sometimes referred to as **spread**) of the data. For instance, what's a typical annual amount of precipitation? Is there much variation from year to year?
- For **categorical** variables, a key feature to describe is the relative number of observations in the various categories. For example, what percentage of days were sunny in a given year?

Quantitative Variables Are Discrete or Continuous

For a quantitative variable, each value it can take is a number, and we classify quantitative variables as either **discrete** or **continuous**.

In Words

A **discrete** variable is usually a count ("the number of ..."). A **continuous** variable has a continuum of infinitely many possible values (such as time, distance, or physical measurements such as weight and height).

Discrete and Continuous Variables

A quantitative variable is **discrete** if its possible values form a set of separate numbers, such as 0, 1, 2, 3,... A quantitative variable is **continuous** if its possible values form an interval.

Examples of discrete variables are the number of pets in a household, the number of children in a family, and the number of foreign languages in which a person is fluent. Any variable phrased as "the number of..." is discrete. The possible values are separate numbers such as $\{0, 1, 2, 3, 4, \ldots\}$. The outcome of the variable is a count. *Any variable with a finite number of possible values is discrete.*

Examples of continuous variables are height, weight, age, and the amount of time it takes to complete an assignment. The collection of all the possible values of a continuous variable does not consist of a set of separate numbers but, rather, an infinite region of values. The amount of time needed to complete an assignment, for example, could take the value 2.496631... hours. *Continuous variables have an infinite continuum of possible values.*

In Practice Data Analysis Depends on Type of Variable

Why do we care whether a variable is *quantitative* or *categorical*, or whether a quantitative variable is *discrete* or *continuous*? We'll see that the method used to analyze a data set will depend on the type of variable the data represent.

Distribution of a Variable

The first step in analyzing data collected on a variable is to look at the observed values by using graphs and numerical summaries. The goal is to describe key features of the **distribution** of a variable.

Distribution

The **distribution** of a variable describes how the observations fall (are distributed) across the range of possible values.

For a categorical variable, the possible values are the different categories, and each observation falls in one of the categories. The distribution for a categorical variable then simply shows all possible categories and the number (or proportion) of observations falling into each category. For a quantitative variable, the entire range of possible values is split up into separate intervals, and the number (or proportion) of observations falling in each interval is given.

The distribution can be displayed by a graph (see next section) or a table. Features to look for in the distribution of a categorical variable are the category with the largest frequency, called the **modal category**, and more generally how frequently each category was observed. Features to look for in the distribution of a quantitative variable are its **shape** (do observations cluster in certain intervals and/or are they spread thin in others?), **center** (where does a typical observation fall?), and **variability** (how tightly are the observations clustering around a center?). We will learn more about these features and how to visualize them in the next section.

Frequency Table

A frequency table displays the distribution of a variable numerically.

Frequency Table

A **frequency table** is a listing of possible values for a variable, together with the number of observations for each value.

For a categorical variable, a frequency table lists the categories and the number of times each category was observed. A frequency table can also display the proportions or percentages of the number of observations falling in each category.

Proportion and Percentage (Relative Frequencies)

The **proportion** of observations falling in a certain category is the number of observations in that category divided by the total number of observations. The **percentage** is the proportion multiplied by 100. Proportions and percentages are also called **relative frequencies** and serve as a way to summarize the distribution of a categorical variable numerically.

Example 2

Shark Attacks

Picture the Scenario

The International Shark Attack File (ISAF) collects data on unprovoked shark attacks worldwide. When a shark attack is reported, the region where it took place is recorded. For the ten-year span from 2004 to 2013, a total of 689 unprovoked shark attacks have been reported, with most of them, 203, occurring in Florida. The **frequency table** in Table 2.1 shows the count for Florida and counts for other regions of the world (other U.S. states and some other countries with frequent shark attacks). For each region, the table lists the number (or **frequency**) of reported shark attacks in that region. The proportion is found by dividing the frequency by the total count of 689. The percentage equals the proportion multiplied by 100.

Table 2.1 Frequency of Shark Attacks in Various Regions for 2004–2013*

Region	Frequency	Proportion	Percentage
Florida	203	0.295	29.5
Hawaii	51	0.074	7.4
South Carolina	34	0.049	4.9
California	33	0.048	4.8
North Carolina	23	0.033	3.3
Australia	125	0.181	18.1
South Africa	43	0.062	6.2
Réunion Island	17	0.025	2.5
Brazil	16	0.023	2.3
Bahamas	6	0.009	0.9
Other	138	0.200	20.0
Total	**689**	**1.000**	**100.0**

**Source:* Data from www.flmnh.ufl.edu/fish/sharks/statistics/statsw.htm. Current as of March 2013.

Questions to Explore

a. What is the variable that was observed? Is it categorical or quantitative?

b. How many observations were there? Show how to find the proportion and percentage for Florida.

c. Identify the modal category for this variable.

d. Describe the distribution of shark attacks.

Think It Through

a. For each observation (a reported shark attack), the **region** was recorded where the attack occurred. Each time a shark attack was reported, this created a new data point for the variable. **Region of attack is the variable**. It is categorical, with the categories being the regions shown in the first column of Table 2.1.

b. There were a total of 689 observations (shark attack reports) for this variable, with 203 reported in Florida, giving a proportion of $203/689 = 0.295$. This tells us that roughly 3 out of 10 shark attacks were reported in Florida. The percentage is $100(0.295) = 29.5\%$.

c. For the regions listed, the greatest number of attacks occurred in Florida, with three-tenths of all reported attacks. Florida is the modal category because it shows the greatest frequency of attacks.

d. The relative frequencies displayed in Table 2.1 are numerical summaries of the variable region. They describe how shark attacks are distributed across the various regions: Most of the attacks (29%) reported in the International Shark Attack File occurred in Florida, followed by Australia (18%), Hawaii (7%), and South Africa (6%). The remaining 40% of attacks are distributed across several other U.S. states and international regions, with no single region having more than 5% of all attacks.

Insight

Don't mistake the frequencies or counts as values for the variable. They are merely a summary of how many times the observation (a reported shark attack) occurred in each category (the various regions). The variable summarized here is the region in which the attack took place. For tables that summarize frequencies, *the total proportion is 1.0, and the total percentage is 100%*, such as Table 2.1 shows in the last row. In practice, the separate numerical summaries may sum to a slightly different number (such as 99.9% or 100.1%) because of rounding.

▶ ***Try Exercises 2.8 and 2.9***

Frequency Table: Waiting Time Between Two Consecutive Eruptions of the Old Faithful Geyser

Minutes	Frequency	Percentage
< 50	21	7.7
50–60	56	20.6
60–70	26	9.6
70–80	77	28.3
80–90	80	29.4
> 90	12	4.4
Total	**272**	**100.0**

Table 2.1 showed the distribution (as a frequency table) for a categorical variable. To show the **distribution** for a **discrete quantitative variable**, we would similarly list the distinct values and the frequency of each one occurring. (The table in the margin next to Example 6 on page 39 shows such a frequency table.) For a **continuous quantitative variable** (or when the number of possible outcomes is very large for a discrete variable), we divide the numeric scale on which the variable is measured into a set of nonoverlapping intervals and count the number of observations falling in each interval. The frequency table then shows these intervals together with the corresponding count. For example, in Section 2.5, we show the distribution of the waiting time (measured in minutes) between eruptions of the Old Faithful geyser in Yellowstone National Park. A frequency table for this variable is shown in the margin and uses six non-overlapping intervals.

2.1 Practicing the Basics

2.1 Categorical/quantitative difference

a. Explain the difference between categorical and quantitative variables.

b. Give an example of each.

2.2 U.S. married-couple households According to a recent Current Population Survey of U.S. married-couple households, 13% are traditional (with children and with only the husband in the labor force), 31% are dual-income with children, 25% are dual-income with no children, and 31% are other (such as older married couples whose children no longer reside in the household). Is the variable "household type" categorical or quantitative? Explain.

2.3 Identify the variable type Identify each of the following variables as categorical or quantitative.

a. Number of pets in family

b. County of residence

c. Choice of auto to buy (domestic or import)

d. Distance (in kilometers) of commute to work

2.4 Categorical or quantitative? Identify each of the following variables as either categorical or quantitative.

a. Choice of diet (vegan, vegetarian, neither)

b. Time spent shopping online per week

c. Ownership of a tablet (yes, no)

d. Number of siblings

2.5 Discrete/continuous

a. Explain the difference between a discrete variable and a continuous variable.

b. Give an example of each type.

2.6 Discrete or continuous? Identify each of the following variables as continuous or discrete.

a. The length of time to run a marathon

b. The number of people in line at a box office to purchase theater tickets

c. The weight of a dog

d. The number of people you have dated in the past month

2.7 Discrete or continuous 2 Repeat the previous exercise for the following:

a. The total playing time of a CD

b. The number of courses for which a student has received credit

c. The amount of money in your pocket (*Hint:* You could regard a number such as $12.75 as 1275 in terms of "the number of cents.")

d. The distance between where you live and your statistics classroom, when you measure it precisely with values such as 0.5 miles, 2.4 miles, 5.38 miles

2.8 Number of children In the 2008 General Social Survey
 (GSS), 2020 respondents answered the question, "How many children have you ever had?" The results were

No. children	0	1	2	3	4	5	6	7	8+	Total
Count	521	323	524	344	160	77	30	19	22	2020

a. Is the variable, number of children, categorical or quantitative?

b. Is the variable, number of children, discrete or continuous?

c. Add proportions and percentages to this frequency table.

2.9 Fatal Shark Attacks Few of the shark attacks listed in
 Table 2.1 are fatal. Overall, 63 fatal shark attacks were recorded in the ISAF from 2004 to 2013, with 2 reported in Florida, 2 in Hawaii, 4 in California, 15 in Australia, 13 in South Africa, 6 in Réunion Island, 4 in Brazil, and 6 in the Bahamas. The rest occurred in other regions.

a. Construct the frequency table for the regions of the reported fatal shark attacks.

b. Identify the modal category.

c. Describe the distribution of fatal shark attacks across the regions.

2.2 Graphical Summaries of Data

Looking at a graph often gives you more of a feel for a variable and its distribution than looking at the raw data or a frequency table. In this section, we'll learn about graphs for categorical variables and then graphs for quantitative variables. We'll find out what we should look for in a graph to help us understand the distribution better.

Graphs for Categorical Variables

The two primary graphical displays for summarizing a categorical variable are the **pie chart** and the **bar graph**.

- A **pie chart** is a circle having a slice of the pie for each category. The size of a slice corresponds to the percentage of observations in the category.
- A **bar graph** displays a vertical bar for each category. The height of the bar is the percentage of observations in the category. Typically, the vertical bars for each category are apart, not side by side.

Example 3

Pie Charts and Bar Graphs

Shark Attacks in the United States

Picture the Scenario

For the United States alone, a total of 387 unprovoked shark attacks were reported between 2004 and 2013. Table 2.2 shows the breakdown by state; states such as Oregon, Alabama, or Georgia with only a few attacks are summarized in the Other category.

Questions to Explore

a. Display the distribution of shark attacks across U.S. states in a pie chart and a bar graph.

b. What percentage of attacks occurred in Florida and the Carolinas?

c. Describe the distribution of shark attacks across U.S. states.

Think It Through

a. The state where the attack occurred is a categorical variable. Each reported attack for the United States falls in one of the categories listed in

Table 2.2 Unprovoked Shark Attacks in the U.S. Between 2004 and 2013*

U.S. State	Frequency	Proportion	Percentage
Florida	203	0.525	52.5
Hawaii	51	0.132	13.2
South Carolina	34	0.088	8.8
California	33	0.085	8.5
North Carolina	23	0.059	5.9
Texas	16	0.041	4.1
Other	27	0.070	7.0
Total	**387**	**1.000**	**100.0**

**Source:* http://www.flmnh.ufl.edu/fish/sharks/statistics/statsus.htm

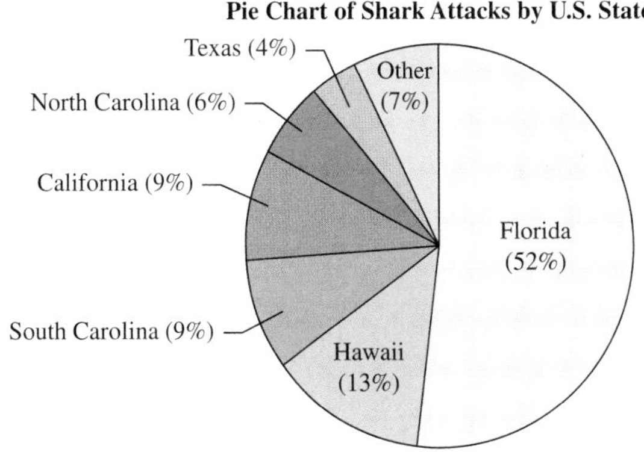

▲ **Figure 2.1** Pie Chart of Shark Attacks Across U.S. States. The label for each slice of the pie gives the category and the percentage of attacks in a state. The slice that represents the percentage of attacks reported in Hawaii is 13% of the total area of the pie. **Question** Why is it beneficial to label the pie wedges with the percent? (Hint: Is it always clear which of two slices is larger and what percent a slice represents?)

Table 2.2. Figure 2.1 shows the pie chart based on the frequencies listed in Table 2.2. States with more frequent attacks have larger slices of the pie. The percentages are included in the labels for each slice of the pie. Figure 2.2 shows the bar graph. The states with larger percentages have higher bars. The scale for the percentages is shown on the vertical axis. The width is the same for each bar.

b. Of all U.S. attacks, 67% (52.5 + 8.8 + 5.9) occurred in Florida and the Carolinas.

c. As the bar graph (or pie chart) shows, 52% of all shark attacks reported for the United States occurred in Florida. Florida is the modal category. Far fewer attacks were reported for Hawaii (13%), South Carolina (9%), California (9%), North Carolina (6%), and Texas (4%). The remaining 7% of attacks occurred in other U.S. states.

Insight

The pie chart and bar graph are both simple to construct using software. The bar graph is generally easier to read and more flexible. With a pie chart, when two slices are about the same size, it's often unclear which value is

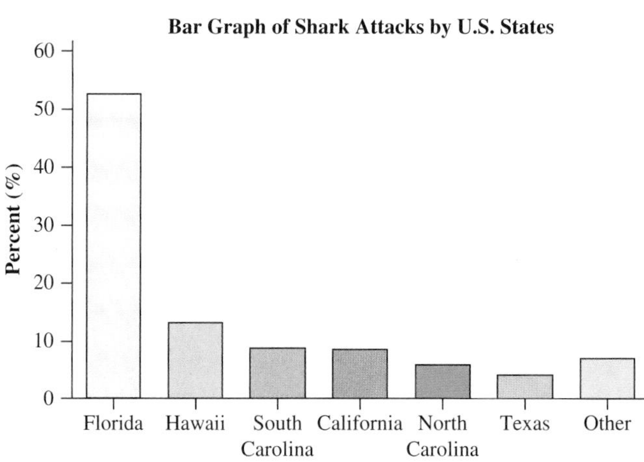

▲ **Figure 2.2** Bar Graph of Shark Attacks Across U.S. States. Except for the Other category, which is shown last, the bars are ordered from largest to smallest based on the frequency of shark attacks. **Question** What is the advantage of ordering the bars this way rather than alphabetically?

larger. This distinction is clearer when comparing heights of bars in a bar graph. We'll see that the bar graph can easily summarize how results compare for different groups (for instance, if we wanted to compare fatal and nonfatal attacks in the United States). Also, the bar graph is a better visual display when there are many categories.

▶ ***Try Exercise 2.10***

The bar graph in Figure 2.2 displays the categories in decreasing order of the category percentages except for the Other category. This order makes it easy to separate the categories with high percentages visually. In some applications, it is more natural to display them according to their alphabetical order or some other criterion. For instance, if the categories have a natural order, such as summarizing the percentages of grades (A, B, C, D, F) for students in a course, we'd use that order in listing the categories on the graph.

Market Share of Operating Systems for Smartphones Shipped in 2013

Percent Market Share: 80, 60, 40, 20, 0

Android, iOS, Windows, Black-Berry, Others

Smartphone Operating System

Source: idc.com

Pareto Charts

A bar graph with categories ordered by their frequency is called a **Pareto chart**, named after Italian economist Vilfredo Pareto (1848–1923), who advocated its use. The Pareto chart is often used in business applications to identify the most common outcomes, such as identifying products with the highest sales or identifying the most common types of complaints that a customer service center receives. The chart helps to portray the **Pareto principle**, which states that a small subset of categories often contains most of the observations. For example, the Pareto chart in the margin shows that of all the smartphones shipped in 2013 (about 1 billion), the two most common operating systems for these smartphones captured almost all (94%) of the market, with the remaining ones only contributing a tiny fraction.

Graphs for Quantitative Variables

Now let's explore how to summarize *quantitative* variables graphically and visualize their distribution. We'll look at three types of displays—the dot plot, stem-and-leaf plot, and histogram—and illustrate the graphs by analyzing data for a common daily food (cereal).

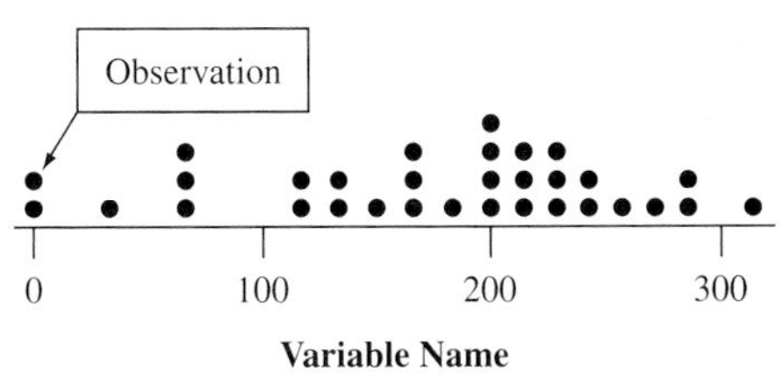

Dot Plots

A **dot plot** shows a dot for each observation, placed just above the value on the number line for that observation. To construct a dot plot,

- Draw a horizontal line. Label it with the name of the variable and mark regular values of the variable on it.
- For each observation, place a dot above its value on the number line.

Dot plot ◀

Example 4

Health Value of Cereals

Picture the Scenario

Let's investigate the amount of sugar and salt (sodium) in breakfast cereals. Table 2.3 lists 20 popular cereals and the amounts of sodium and sugar contained in a single serving. The sodium and sugar amounts are both quantitative variables. The variables are continuous because they measure amounts that can take any positive real number value. In this table, the amounts are rounded to the nearest number of grams for sugar and milligrams for sodium.

Table 2.3 Sodium and Sugar Amounts in 20 Breakfast Cereals

The amounts refer to one National Labeling and Education Act (NLEA) serving. A third variable, Type, classifies the cereal as being popular for adults (Type A) or children (Type C).

Cereal	Sodium (mg)	Sugar (g)	Type
Frosted Mini Wheats	0	11	A
Raisin Bran	340	18	A
All Bran	70	5	A
Apple Jacks	140	14	C
Cap'n Crunch	200	12	C
Cheerios	180	1	C
Cinnamon Toast Crunch	210	10	C
Crackling Oat Bran	150	16	A
Fiber One	100	0	A
Frosted Flakes	130	12	C
Froot Loops	140	14	C
Honey Bunches of Oats	180	7	A
Honey Nut Cheerios	190	9	C
Life	160	6	C
Rice Krispies	290	3	C
Honey Smacks	50	15	A
Special K	220	4	A
Wheaties	180	4	A
Corn Flakes	200	3	A
Honeycomb	210	11	C

Source: www.weightchart.com (click Nutrition).

Did You Know?

Nutritionists recommend that daily consumption should not exceed 2400 milligrams (mg) for sodium and 50 grams for sugar (on a 2000-calorie-a-day diet). ◀

Caution

Continuous data is often recorded to the nearest whole number. Although the data may now appear as discrete, the data are still analyzed and interpreted as continuous data. ◀

Questions to Explore

a. Construct a dot plot for the sodium values of the 20 breakfast cereals. (We'll consider sugar amounts in the exercises.)

b. What does the dot plot tell us about the distribution of sodium values?

Think It Through

a. Figure 2.3 shows a dot plot. Each cereal sodium value is represented with a dot above the number line. For instance, the labeled dot above 0 represents the sodium value of 0 mg for Frosted Mini Wheats.

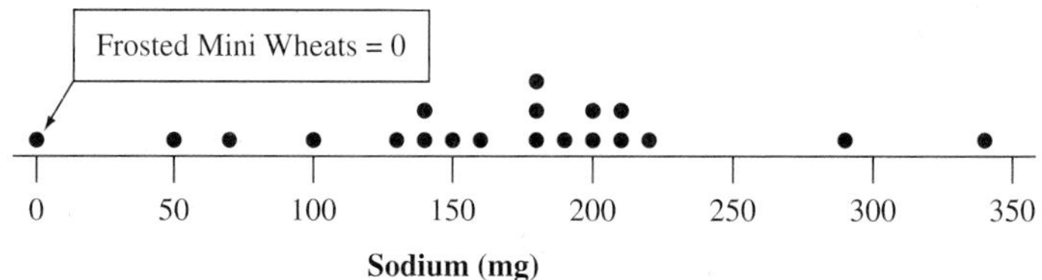

▲ **Figure 2.3 Dot Plot for Sodium Content of 20 Breakfast Cereals.** The sodium value for each cereal is represented with a dot above the number line. **Question** What does it mean when more than one dot appears above a value?

b. The dot plot gives us an overview of all the data. We see clearly that the sodium values fall between 0 and 340 mg, with most cereals falling between 125 mg and 225mg.

Insight

The dot plot displays the individual observations. The number of dots above a value on the number line represents the frequency of occurrence of that value. From a dot plot, we can reconstruct (at least approximately) all the data in the sample.

▶ ***Try Exercises 2.15 and 2.17, part b***

Stem-and-Leaf Plots

Another type of graph, called a **stem-and-leaf plot**, is similar to the dot plot in that it displays individual observations.

- Each observation is represented by a **stem** and a **leaf**. Usually the stem consists of all the digits except for the final one, which is the leaf.
- Sort the data in order from smallest to largest. Place the stems in a column, starting with the smallest. Place a vertical line to their right. On the right side of the vertical line, indicate each leaf (final digit) that has a particular stem. List the leaves in increasing order.

Stems	Leaves
7	69
8	00125699
9	12446

Observation = 92, in a sample of 15 test scores

Stem-and-leaf plot ◀

Cereal	Sodium
Frosted Mini Wheats	0
Raisin Bran	340
All Bran	70
Apple Jacks	140
Cap'n Crunch	200
Cheerios	180
Cinnamon Toast Crunch	210
Crackling Oat Bran	150
Fiber One	100
Frosted Flakes	130
Froot Loops	140
Honey Bunches of Oats	180
Honey Nut Cheerios	190
Life	160
Rice Krispies	290
Honey Smacks	50
Special K	220
Wheaties	180
Corn Flakes	200
Honeycomb	210

Example 5

Health Value of Cereals

Picture the Scenario

Let's reexamine the sodium values for the 20 breakfast cereals, shown again in the margin.

Questions to Explore

a. Construct a stem-and-leaf plot of the 20 sodium values.

b. How does the stem-and-leaf plot compare to the dot plot?

Think It Through

a. In the stem-and-leaf plot, we'll let the final digit of a sodium value form the leaf and the other digits form the stem. For instance, the sodium value for Honey Smacks is 50. The stem is 5, and the leaf is 0. Each stem is placed to the left of a vertical bar. Each leaf is placed to the right of the bar. Figure 2.4 shows the plot. Notice that a leaf has only one digit, but a stem can have one or more digits.

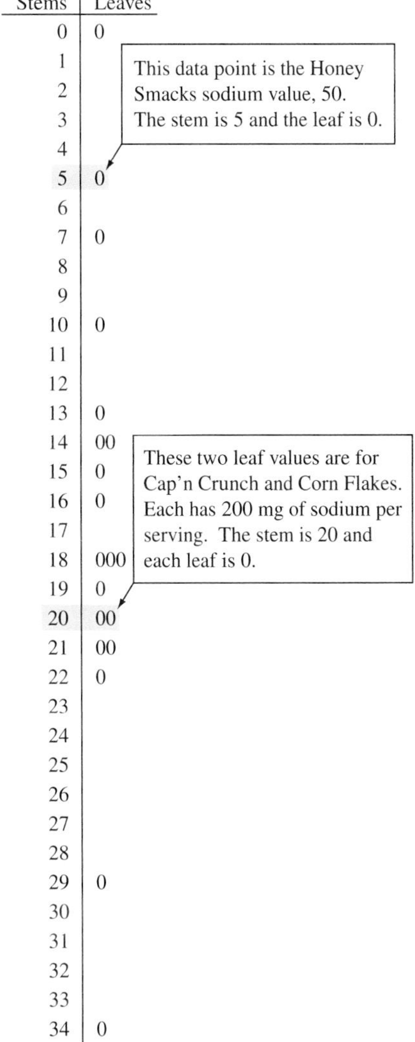

▲ **Figure 2.4** Stem-and-Leaf Plot for Cereal Sodium Values. The final digit of a sodium value forms the leaf, and the other digits form the stem. **Question** Why do some stems not have a leaf?

Truncated Data	
Frosted Mini Wheats	0
Raisin Bran	34
All Bran	7
Apple Jacks	14
Cap'n Crunch	20
Cheerios	18
Cinnamon Toast Crunch	21
Crackling Oat Bran	15
Fiber One	10
Frosted Flakes	13
Froot Loops	14
Honey Bunches of Oats	18
Honey Nut Cheerios	19
Life	16
Rice Krispies	29
Honey Smacks	5
Special K	22
Wheaties	18
Corn Flakes	20
Honeycomb	21

The Honey Smacks observation of 50 is labeled on the graph. Two observations have a stem of 20 and a leaf of 0. These are the sodium values of 200 for Cap'n Crunch and Corn Flakes.

b. The stem-and-leaf plot looks like the dot plot turned on its side, with the leaves taking the place of the dots. Often, with a stem-and-leaf plot, it is easier to read the actual observation value. In summary, we generally get the same information from a stem-and-leaf plot as from a dot plot.

Insight

A stem is shown for each possible value between the minimum and maximum even if no observation occurs for that stem. A stem has no leaf if there is no observation at that value. These are the values at which the dot plot has no dots.

▶ ***Try Exercise 2.16***

To make a stem-and-leaf plot more compact, we can **truncate** these data values: Cut off the final digit (it's not necessary to round it), as shown in the margin, and plot the data as 0, 34, 7, 14, 20, and so on, instead of 0, 340, 70, 140, 200,.... Arranging the leaves in increasing order on each line, we then get the stem-and-leaf plot

```
0 | 057
1 | 0344568889
2 | 001129
3 | 4
```

This is a bit *too* compact because it does not portray where the data fall as clearly as Figure 2.4 or the dot plot. We could instead list each stem twice, putting leaves from 0 to 4 on the first stem and from 5 to 9 on the second stem. We then get

```
0 | 0
0 | 57
1 | 0344
1 | 568889
2 | 00112
2 | 9
3 | 4
```

Like the dot plot, this gives us the sense that most sodium values are relatively high, with a couple of cereals being considerably lower than the others.

Histograms

With a dot plot or a stem-and-leaf plot, it's easy to reconstruct the original data set because the plot shows the individual observations. This becomes unwieldy for large data sets. In that case, a histogram is a more versatile way to graph the data and picture the distribution. It uses bars to display and summarize frequencies of different outcomes.

Histogram

A **histogram** is a graph that uses bars to portray the frequencies or the relative frequencies of the possible outcomes for a quantitative variable.

Example 6

Histogram

TV Watching

Picture the Scenario

The 2012 General Social Survey asked, "On an average day, about how many hours do you personally watch television?" Figure 2.5 shows the histogram of the 1298 responses.

Frequency Table for Histogram in Figure 2.5

Hours	Count	Hours	Count
0	90	13	2
1	255	14	4
2	325	15	3
3	238	16	1
4	171	17	0
5	61	18	1
6	58	19	0
7	19	20	2
8	31	21	0
9	3	22	1
10	17	23	0
11	0	24	5
12	11		

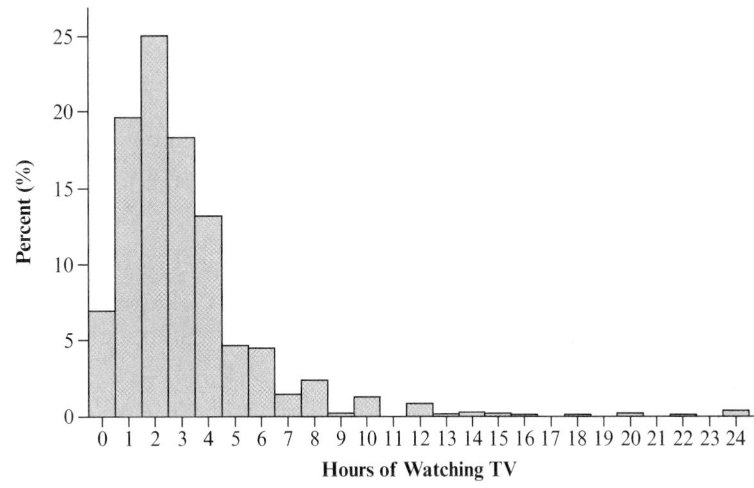

▲ **Figure 2.5** Histogram of GSS Responses about Number of Hours Spent Watching TV on an Average Day. *Source:* Data from CSM, UC Berkeley.

Questions to Explore

a. What was the most common outcome?

b. What does the histogram reveal about the distribution of TV watching?

c. What percentage of people reported watching TV no more than 2 hours per day?

Think It Through

a. The most common outcome is the value with the highest bar. This is 2 hours of TV watching. We call the most common value of a quantitative variable the **mode**. The distribution of TV watching has a mode at 2 hours.

b. We see that most people watch between 1 and 4 hours of TV per day. Very few watch more than 8 hours.

c. To find the percentage for "no more than 2 hours per day," we need to look at the percentages for 0, 1, and 2 hours per day. They seem to be about 7, 20, and 25. Adding these percentages together tells us that about 52% of the respondents reported watching no more than 2 hours of TV per day.

Insight

In theory, TV watching is a continuous variable. However, the possible responses subjects were able to make here were 0, 1, 2,…, 24, so it was measured as a discrete variable. Figure 2.5 is an example of a histogram of

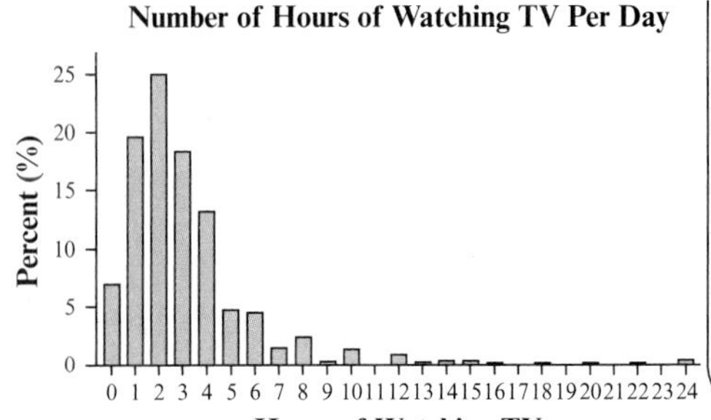

a discrete variable. Note that since the variable is treated as discrete, the histogram in Figure 2.5 could have been constructed with the bars apart instead of beside each other as shown in the margin. Also, although it is easy to calculate the mode, we usually use a different statistic to describe a typical value for a quantitative variable.(Here, we would use the median, which also equals 2; see Section 2.3.).

▶ ***Try Exercise 2.24, parts a and b***

Caution

The term *histogram* is used for a graph with bars representing a quantitative variable. The term *bar graph* is used for a graph with bars representing a categorical variable. ◀

For a discrete variable, a histogram usually has a separate bar for each possible value. For a continuous variable, we need to divide the range of possible values into smaller intervals of equal width, just as we have discussed when forming the frequency table for a continuous response. We can also do this when a discrete variable, such as the score on an exam, has a large number of possible values. We then count the number of observations falling in each interval. The height of the bars in the histogram represent the frequency (or relative frequency) of observations falling in the intervals.

SUMMARY: Steps for Constructing a Histogram

- Divide the range of the data into intervals of equal width. For a discrete variable with few values, use the actual possible values.
- Count the number of observations (the frequency) in each interval, forming a frequency table.
- On the horizontal axis, label the values or the endpoints of the intervals. Draw a bar over each value or interval with height equal to its frequency (or percentage), values of which are marked on the vertical axis.

Example 7

Histogram ◀

Health Value of Cereals

Picture the Scenario

Let's reexamine the sodium values of the 20 breakfast cereals. Those values are shown again in the margin of the next page.

Questions to Explore

a. Construct a frequency table.

b. Construct a corresponding histogram to visualize the distribution.

c. What information does the histogram not show that you can get from a dot plot or a stem-and-leaf plot?

Think It Through

a. To construct a frequency table, we divide the range of possible sodium values into separate intervals and count the number of cereals in each. The sodium values range from 0 to 340. We created Table 2.4 using nine intervals, each with a width of 40. With the interval labels shown in the table, 0 to 39 actually represents 0 to 39.999999…, that is, 0 up to every number *below* 40. So, 0 to 39 is then shorthand for "0 to less than 40."

Cereal	Sodium
Frosted Mini Wheats	0
Raisin Bran	340
All Bran	70
Apple Jacks	140
Cap'n Crunch	200
Cheerios	180
Cinnamon Toast Crunch	210
Crackling Oat Bran	150
Fiber One	100
Frosted Flakes	130
Froot Loops	140
Honey Bunches of Oats	180
Honey Nut Cheerios	190
Life	160
Rice Krispies	290
Honey Smacks	50
Special K	220
Wheaties	180
Corn Flakes	200
Honeycomb	210

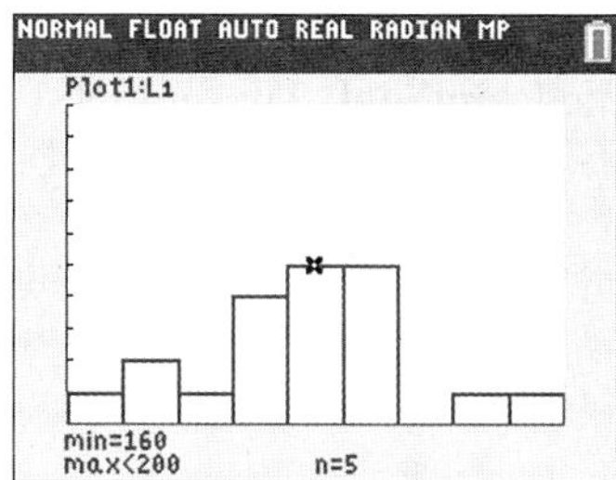

TI output of histogram

Table 2.4 Frequency Table for Sodium in 20 Breakfast Cereals

The table summarizes the sodium values using nine intervals and lists the number of observations in each as well as the corresponding proportions and percentages.

Interval	Frequency	Proportion	Percentage
0 to 39	1	0.05	5%
40 to 79	2	0.10	10%
80 to 119	1	0.05	5%
120 to 159	4	0.20	20%
160 to 199	5	0.25	25%
200 to 239	5	0.25	25%
240 to 279	0	0.00	0%
280 to 319	1	0.05	5%
320 to 359	1	0.05	5%

Sometimes you will see the intervals written as 0 to 40, 40 to 80, 80 to 120, and so on. However, for an observation that falls at an interval endpoint, then it's not clear in which interval it goes. When reading the histogram, we generally use a left endpoint convention where if an observation falls on an endpoint, it belongs to the interval with the observation as the left endpoint.

b. Figure 2.6 shows the histogram for this frequency table. A bar is drawn over each interval of values, with the height of each bar equal to its corresponding frequency. The histogram created using a TI calculator is in the margin.

c. The histogram does not show the actual numerical values. For instance, we know that one observation falls below 40, but we do not know its actual value. In summary, with a histogram, we may lose the actual numerical values of individual observations, unlike with a dot plot or a stem-and-leaf plot.

Insight

The bars in the histogram in Figure 2.6 display the frequencies in each interval (or bin), and the vertical axis shows the counts. If we had used relative

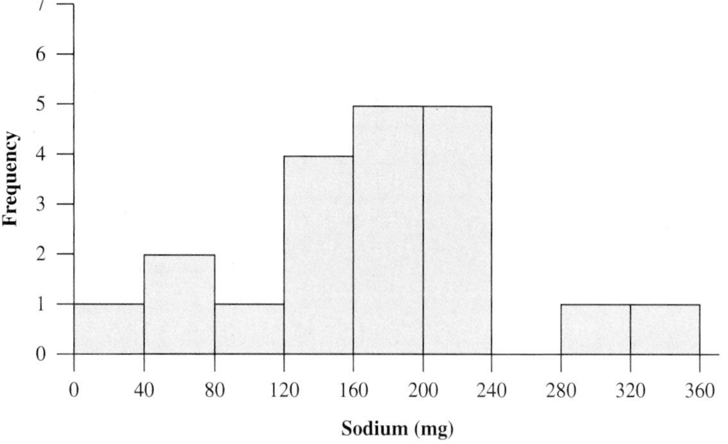

▲ **Figure 2.6 Histogram of Breakfast Cereal Sodium Values.** The rectangular bar over an interval has height equal to the number of observations in the interval.

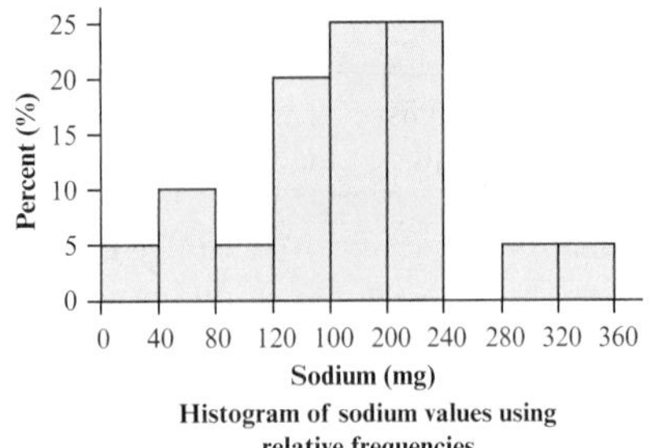

Histogram of sodium values using relative frequencies

frequencies (proportions or percentages) on the vertical axis instead, the appearance of the histogram would be identical (see margin). Only the label on the vertical axis would change. Each of these histograms shows that most cereals have a sodium value between 120 mg and 240 mg, with few having smaller or larger amounts.

▶ *Try Exercise 2.20*

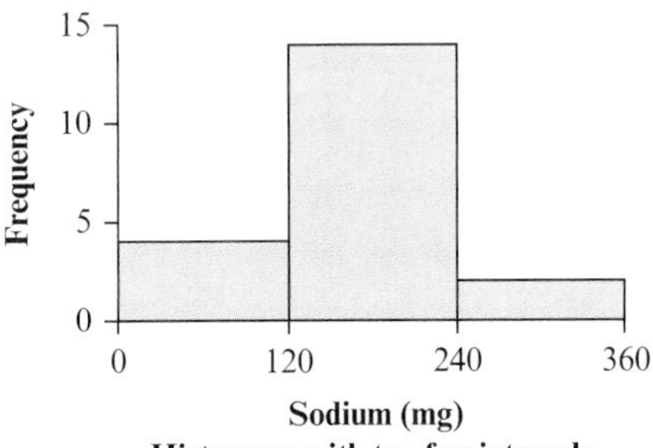

Histogram with too few intervals

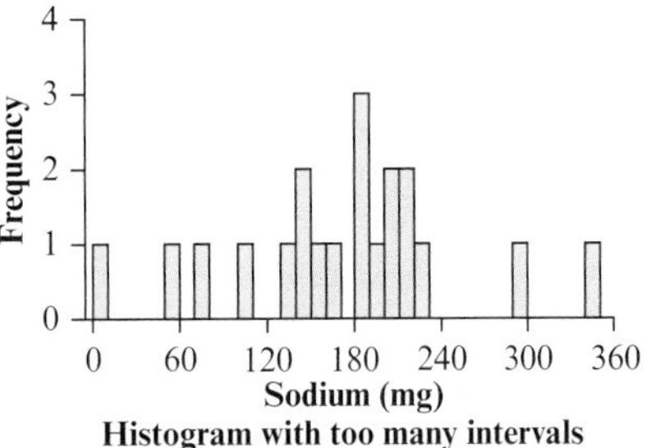

Histogram with too many intervals

How do you select the intervals? If you use too few intervals, the graph is usually too crude (see margin). It may consist mainly of a couple of tall bars. If you use too many intervals, the graph may be irregular, with many very short bars and/or gaps between bars (see margin). You can then lose information about the shape of the distribution. Usually about 5 to 10 intervals are adequate, with perhaps additional intervals when the sample size is quite large. There is no one right way to select the intervals. Software can select them for you, find the counts and percentages, and construct the histogram but it is always a good idea to override the default and look at a few options.

Choosing a Graph Type

We've now studied three graphs for quantitative variables—the dot plot, stem-and-leaf plot, and histogram. How do we decide which to use? With software for constructing histograms widely available, we suggest **always plotting the histogram** to get an idea about the distribution. If the number of observations is small (e.g., less than 50), supplement the histogram with a stem-and-leaf plot or a dot plot to show the numerical values of the observations.

In Practice Technology Can Construct Graphical Displays

Graphical displays are easily constructed using statistical software or graphing calculators. They choose the intervals for you when they construct histograms. In practice, you won't have to draw graphs yourself. But it is important to understand *how* they are drawn and *how to interpret* them.

The Shape of a Distribution

A histogram (or a stem-and-leaf or dot plot) visualizes the distribution of a quantitative variable. Here are important questions to ask when describing this distribution:

- Does the distribution have a single mound or peak? If so, the distribution is called **unimodal**, and the value that occurs most often is called the **mode**. A distribution with *two* distinct mounds is called **bimodal**. The graphs below illustrate both a unimodal and a bimodal distribution. A bimodal distribution can result, for example, when a population is polarized on a controversial issue. Suppose each subject is presented with ten scenarios in which a person found guilty of murder may be given the death penalty. If we count the number of those scenarios in which subjects feel the death penalty would be

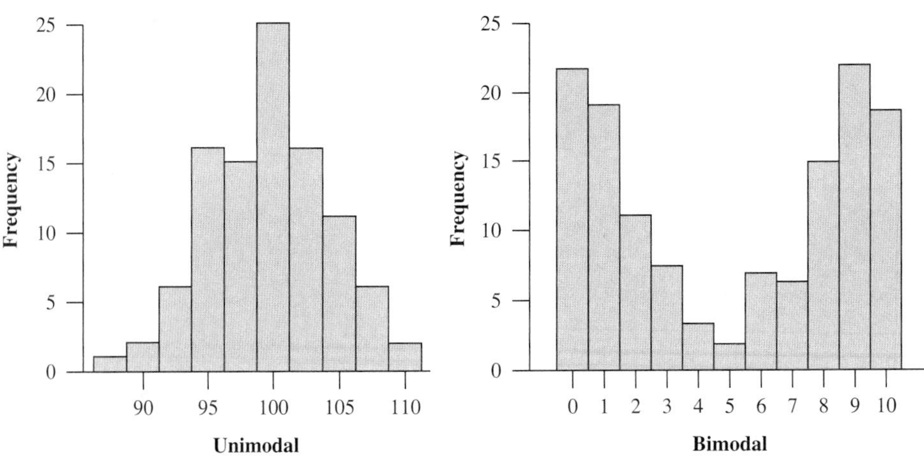

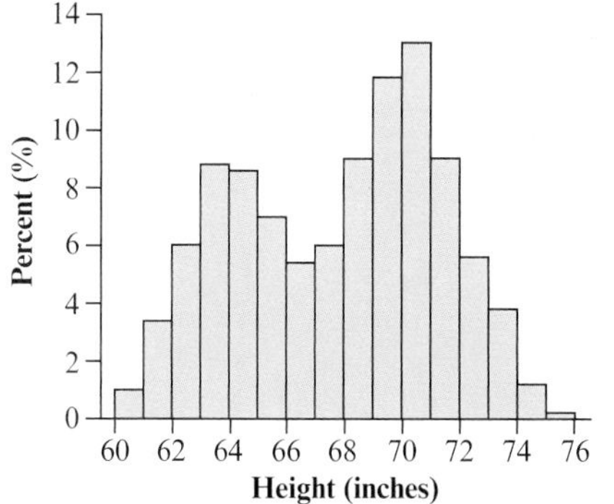

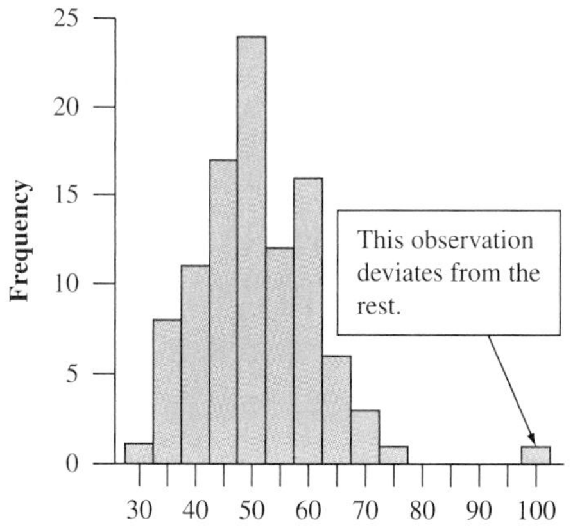

just, many responses would be close to 0 (for subjects who oppose the death penalty generally) and many would be close to 10 (for subjects who think it's always or usually warranted for murder).

A bimodal distribution can also result when the observations come from two different groups. For instance, a histogram of the height of students in your school might show two peaks, one for females and one for males (see plot in the margin).

- What is the **shape** of the distribution? The shape of a unimodal distribution is often described as **symmetric**, or **skewed**. A distribution is *symmetric* if the side of the distribution below a central value is a mirror image of the side above that central value. The distribution is *skewed* if one side of the distribution stretches out longer than the other side.
- Do the data cluster together, or is there a **gap** such that one or more observations noticeably deviate from the rest, as in the histogram in the margin? We'll discuss such "outlier" observations later in the chapter.

In picturing features such as symmetry and skew, it's common to use smooth curves as in Figure 2.7 to summarize the shape of a histogram. You can think of this as what can happen when you choose more and more intervals (making each interval narrower) and collect more data, so the histogram gets smoother. The parts of the curve for the lowest values and for the highest values are called the **tails** of the distribution.

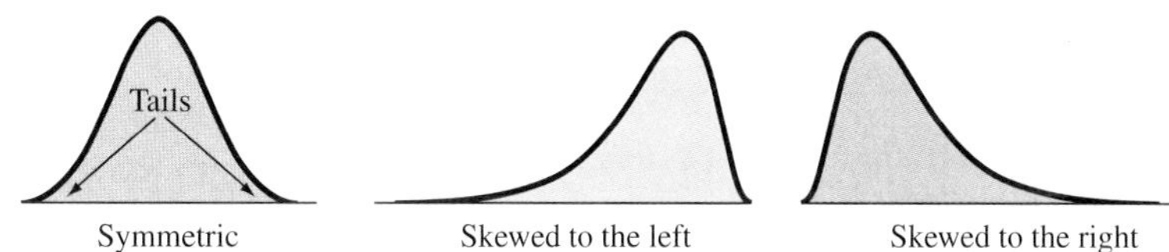

▲ **Figure 2.7** Curves for Distributions Illustrating Symmetry and Skew. **Question** What does the longer tail indicate about the direction of skew?

Skewed Distribution

To **skew** means to stretch in one direction.

A distribution is **skewed to the left** if the left tail is longer than the right tail.

A distribution is **skewed to the right** if the right tail is longer than the left tail.

A left-skewed distribution stretches to the left, a right-skewed to the right.

Identifying Skew

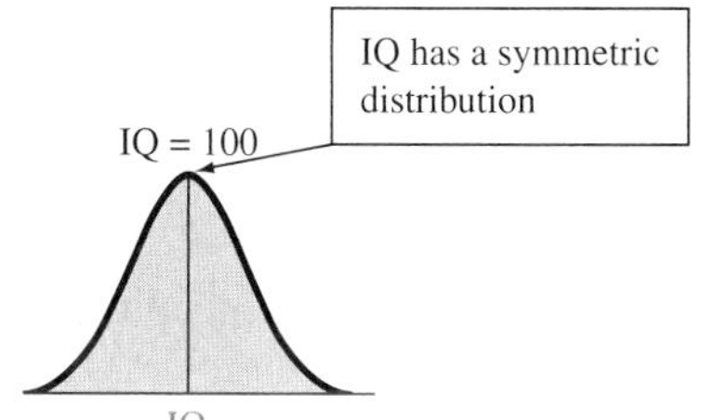

Let's consider some variables and think about what shape their distributions would have. How about IQ? Values cluster around 100 and tail off in a similar fashion in both directions. The appearance of the distribution on one side of 100 is roughly a mirror image of the other side, with tails of similar length. The distribution is approximately symmetric (see the green shaded graph in the margin).

How about life span for humans? Most people in advanced societies live to be at least about 70 years old, but some die at a very young age, so the distribution of life span would probably be skewed to the left (see the tan shaded graph on the next page).

What shape would we expect for the distribution of annual incomes of adults? There would probably be a long right tail, with some people having incomes much higher than the overwhelming majority of people. This suggests that the distribution would be skewed to the right (see the purple shaded graph on the next page).

In Practice

Sometimes, especially with small data sets, the shape of the distribution might not be so obvious.

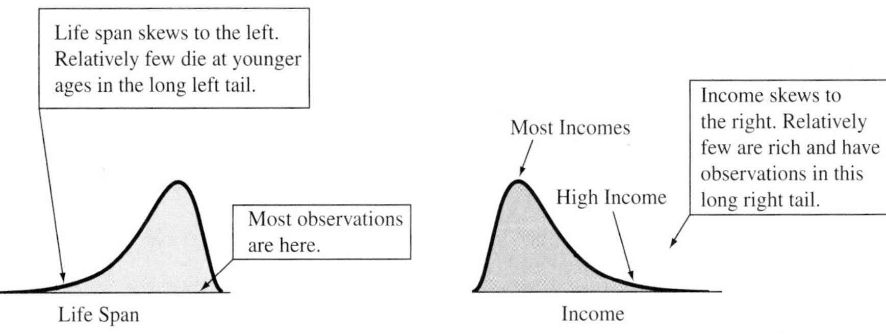

Shape of the distribution

Number of Hours of Watching TV Per Day

Percent (%)

Hours of Watching TV

Example 8

TV Watching

Picture the Scenario

In Example 6, we constructed a histogram of the number of hours of TV watching reported in the GSS. It is shown again in the margin.

Question to Explore

How would you describe the shape of the distribution?

Think It Through

There appears to be a single mound of data clustering around the mode of 2. The distribution is unimodal. There also appears to be a long right tail, so the distribution is skewed to the right.

Insight

In surveys, the observation that a subject reports is not necessarily the precise value. Often they either round or don't remember exactly and just guess. In this distribution, the percentage is quite a bit higher for 8 hours than for 7 or 9. Perhaps subjects reporting high values tend to pick even numbers.

▶ ***Try Exercises 2.21 and 2.24, part c***

Time Plots: Displaying Data over Time

For some variables, observations occur over time. Examples include the daily closing price of a stock and the population of a country measured every decade in a census. A data set collected over time is called a **time series**.

We can display time-series data graphically using a **time plot**. This charts each observation, on the vertical scale, against the time it was measured, on the horizontal scale. A common pattern to look for is a **trend** over time, indicating a tendency of the data to either rise or fall. To see a trend more clearly, it is beneficial to connect the data points in their time sequence.

Another way time series data is displayed is with a type of bar graph. The figure in the margin is such a graph displaying the number of people in the United Kingdom between 2006 and 2010 who used the Internet[1] (in millions). In 2006, it is estimated 16.5 million were using the Internet. By 2010, nearly

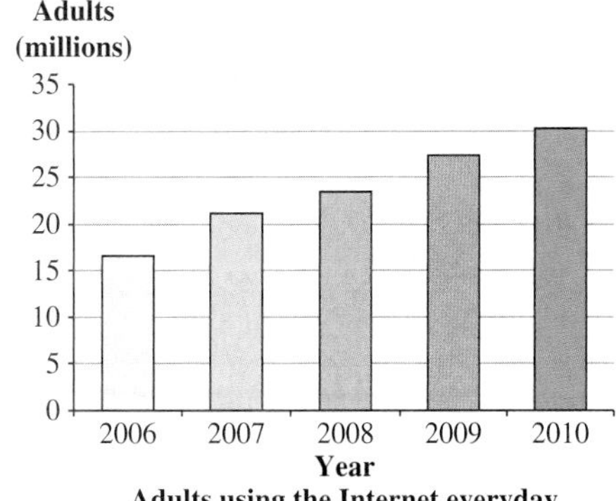

[1] *Source:* www.statistics.gov.uk/cci/nugget.asp?id=8. Copyright © 2000–2011, Miniwatts Marketing Group. All rights reserved.

double (30 million) were doing so. There is a clear increasing trend over time. In practice, there's often not such a clear trend, as the next example using a time plot illustrates.

With a computer, it is also possible to make animated plots, unleashing time from the horizontal axis. The site www.gapminder.org/ has many examples and tools for dynamic time plots.

Example 9

Time plot

Warming Trend in New York City

Picture the Scenario

In a given year, the annual average temperature is the average of the daily average temperatures for that year. Let's analyze data on annual average temperature (in degrees Fahrenheit) in Central Park, New York City, from 1869 to 2012. This is a continuous, quantitative variable. The data are in the Central Park Yearly Temps data file on the book's website.

Question to Explore

What do we learn from a time plot of these annual average temperatures? Is there a trend toward warming in New York City?

Think It Through

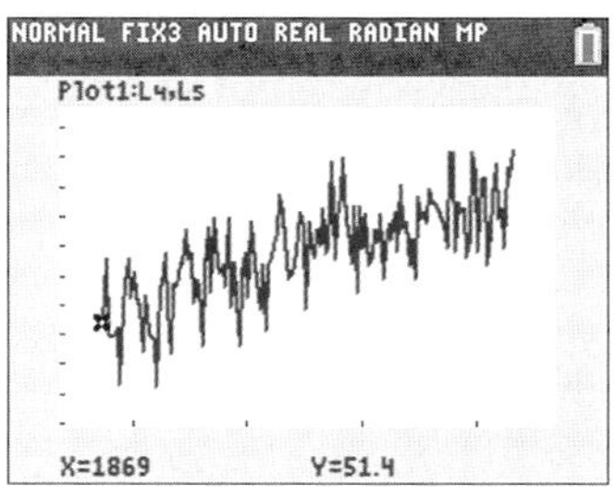

TI output of time plot

Figure 2.8 shows a time plot, constructed using MINITAB software. The time plot constructed using the TI calculator is in the margin. The observations fluctuate considerably, but the figure does suggest an increasing trend in the annual average temperatures in New York City.

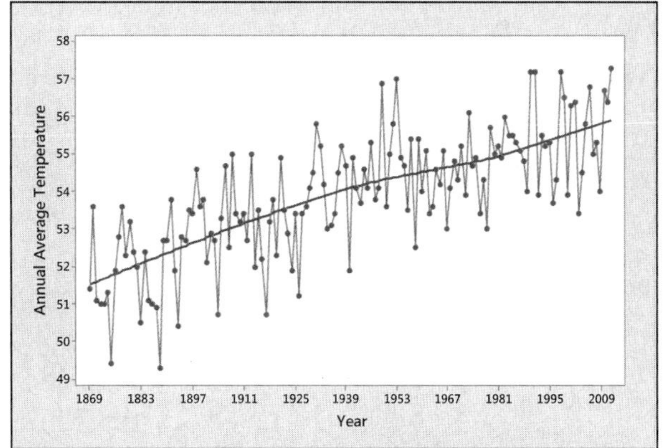

▲ **Figure 2.8** MINITAB Output for a Time Plot of Central Park, New York City, Average Annual Temperatures. The annual average temperatures are plotted against the year from 1869 to 2012. A smoothing curve is superimposed. **Question:** Are the annual average temperatures tending to increase, decrease, or stay the same over time?

Insight

The short-term fluctuations in a time plot can mask an overall trend. It's possible to get a clearer picture by smoothing the data. This is beyond our scope here. MINITAB presents the option of smoothing the data to portray a general trend (click *data view* and choose the Lowess option under Smoother). This is the smooth curve passing through the data points in

Figure 2.8. This curve goes from a level of 51.4 degrees in 1869 to 56.7 degrees in 2012.

The data reported in Figure 2.8 refer to one location in the United States. In a study of climate change, it would be important to explore other locations around the world to see whether similar trends are evident.

▶ *Try Exercises 2.27 and 2.28*

Florence Nightingale

On the Shoulders of...Florence Nightingale

Graphical Displays Showing Deaths From Disease Versus Military Combat

During the Crimean War in 1854, the British nurse Florence Nightingale (1820–1910) gathered data on the number of soldiers who died from various causes. She prepared graphical displays such as time plots and pie charts for policy makers. The graphs showed that more soldiers were dying from contagious diseases than from war-related wounds. The plots were revolutionary for her time. They helped promote her national cause of improving hospital conditions.

After implementing sanitary methods, Nightingale showed with time plots that the relative frequency of soldiers' deaths from contagious disease decreased sharply and no longer exceeded that of deaths from wounds.

Throughout the rest of her life, Nightingale promoted the use of data for making informed decisions about public health policy. For example, she used statistical arguments to campaign for improved medical conditions in the United States during the Civil War in the 1860s (Franklin, 2002).

2.2 Practicing the Basics

2.10 Generating Electricity In 2012 in the United States, most electricity was generated from coal (37%), natural gas (30%), or nuclear power plants (19%). Hydropower accounted for 7% of the total electricity produced; other renewable sources such as wind or solar power accounted for 5%. Other nonrenewable sources (such as petroleum) made up the remaining 2%. (*Source:* http://www.eia.gov/electricity/annual/html/epa_01_01.html)

TRY

- **a.** Display this information in a bar graph.
- **b.** Which is easier to sketch relatively accurately, a pie chart or a bar chart?
- **c.** What is the advantage of using a graph to summarize the results instead of merely stating the percentages for each source?
- **d.** What is the modal category?

2.11 What do alligators eat? The bar chart is from a study[2] investigating the factors that influence alligators' choice of food. For 219 alligators captured in four Florida lakes, researchers classified the primary food choice (in volume) found in the alligator's stomach in one of the categories—fish, invertebrate (snails, insects, crayfish), reptile (turtles, baby alligators), bird, or other (amphibian, mammal, plants). (Data available on the book's website.)

- **a.** Is primary food choice categorical or quantitative?
- **b.** Which is the modal category for primary food choice?
- **c.** About what percentage of alligators had fish as the primary food choice?
- **d.** This type of bar chart, with categories listed in order of frequency, has a special name. What is it?

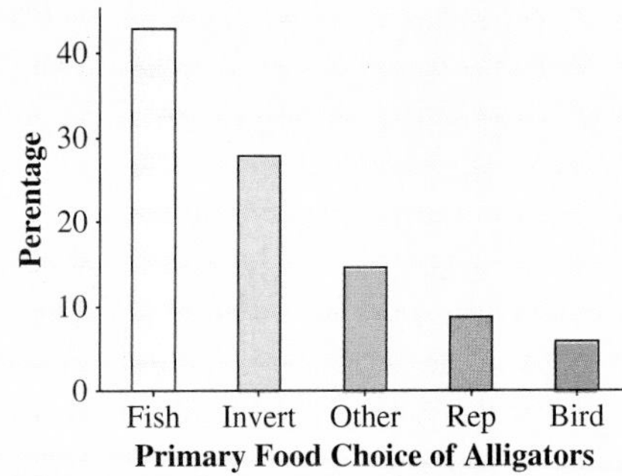

[2]Data courtesy of Clint Moore.

2.12 Weather stations The pie chart (constructed using EXCEL) shown portrays the regional distribution of weather stations in the United States.

a. Do the slices of the pie portray (i) variables or (ii) categories of a variable?

b. Identify what the two numbers mean that are shown for each slice of the pie.

c. Without inspecting the numbers, would it be easier to identify the modal category by using this graph or the corresponding bar graph? Why?

Regional Distribution of Weather Stations

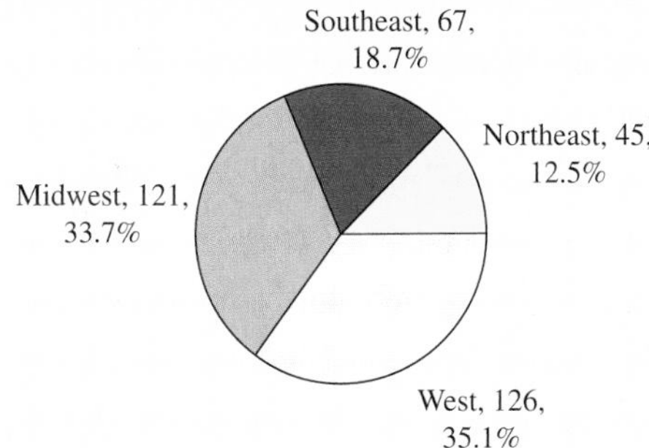

2.13 France is most popular holiday spot Which countries are most frequently visited by tourists from other countries? The table shows results according to *Travel and Leisure* magazine (2005).

a. Is country visited a categorical or a quantitative variable?

b. In creating a bar graph of these data, would it be most sensible to list the countries alphabetically or in the form of a Pareto chart? Explain.

c. Does either a dot plot or stem-and-leaf plot make sense for these data? Explain.

Most Visited Countries, 2005

Country	Number of Visits (millions)
France	77.0
China	53.4
Spain	51.8
United States	41.9
Italy	39.8
United Kingdom	24.2
Canada	20.1
Mexico	19.7

Source: Data from *Travel and Leisure* magazine, 2005.

2.14 Pareto chart for fatal shark attacks The data shown in Exercise 2.9 give frequencies of fatal shark attacks for different regions. Using software or sketching, construct a bar graph, ordering the regions (i) alphabetically and (ii) as in a Pareto chart. Which do you prefer? Why?

2.15 Sugar dot plot For the breakfast cereal data given in Table 2.3, a dot plot for the sugar values (in grams) is shown:

a. Identify the minimum and maximum sugar values.

b. Which sugar outcomes occur most frequently? What are these values called?

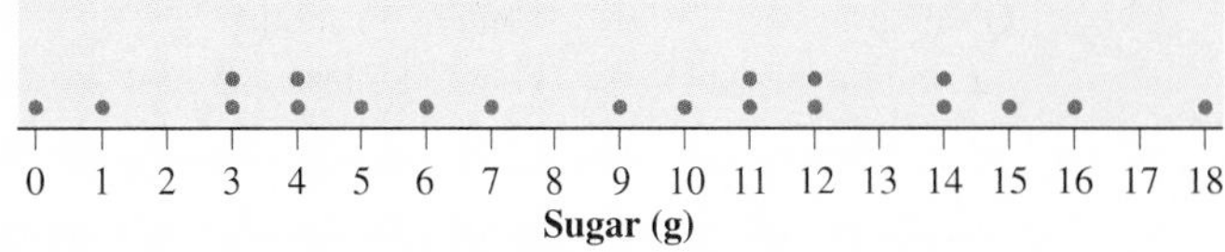

2.16 Spring break hotel prices For a trip to Miami, Florida, over spring break in 2014, the data below (obtained from travelocity.com) show the price per night (in U.S. dollars) for various hotel rooms.

239	237	245	310	218	175	330	196	178
245	255	190	330	124	162	190	386	145

a. Construct a stem-and-leaf plot. Truncate the data to the first two digits for purposes of constructing the plot. For example, 239 becomes 23.

b. Reconstruct the stem-and-leaf plot in part a by using split stems; that is, two stems of 1, two stems of 2, and so on. Compare the two stem-and-leaf plots. Explain how one may be more informative than the other.

c. Sketch a histogram by hand (or use software), using 6 intervals of length 50, starting at 100 and ending at 400. What does the plot tell about the distribution of hotel prices? (Mention where most prices tend to fall and comment about the shape of the distribution.)

2.17 Graphing exam scores A teacher shows her class the scores on the midterm exam in the stem-and-leaf plot shown:

6	588
7	01136779
8	1223334677789
9	011234458

a. Identify the number of students and their minimum and maximum scores.

b. Sketch how the data could be displayed in a dot plot.

c. Sketch how the data could be displayed in a histogram with four intervals.

2.18 Fertility rates The fertility rate for a nation is the average number of children per adult woman. The table below part c shows results for western European nations, the United States, Canada, and Mexico, as reported by the United Nations in 2005.

a. Construct a stem-and-leaf plot using stems 1 and 2 and the decimal parts of the numbers for the leaves. What is a disadvantage of this plot?

b. Construct a stem-and-leaf plot using split stems. (Take the first stem for 1 to have leaves 0 through 4, the second stem for 1 to have leaves 5 through 9, and the stem 2 to have leaves 0 through 4.)

c. Construct a histogram by using the intervals 1.1–1.3, 1.4–1.6, 1.7–1.9, 2.0–2.2, 2.3–2.5.

Country	Fertility	Country	Fertility
Austria	1.4	Netherlands	1.7
Belgium	1.7	Norway	1.8
Denmark	1.8	Spain	1.3
Finland	1.7	Sweden	1.6
France	1.9	Switzerland	1.4

Germany	1.3	United Kingdom	1.7
Greece	1.3	United States	2.0
Ireland	1.9	Canada	1.5
Italy	1.3	Mexico	2.4

2.19 Split Stems The figure below shows the stem-and-leaf plot for the cereal sugar values from Example 5, using *split stems.*

Stem and Leaf Plot for Cereal Sugar Values
with Leaf Unit = 1000

Stem	Leaf
0	01
0	33
0	445
0	67
0	9
1	011
1	22
1	445
1	6
1	8

a. What was the smallest and largest amount of sugar found in the 20 cereals?

b. What sugar values are represented on the 6th line of the plot?

c. How many cereals have a sugar content less than 5 g?

2.20 Histogram for sugar For the breakfast cereal data, TRY the figure below shows a histogram for the sugar values in grams.

a. Identify the intervals of sugar values used for the plot.

b. Describe the shape of the distribution. What do you think might account for this unusual shape? (*Hint:* How else are the cereals classified in Table 2.3?)

c. What information can you get from the dot plot or stem-and-leaf plot of these data shown in Exercises 2.15 and 2.19 that you cannot get from this plot?

d. This histogram shows frequencies. If you were to construct a histogram by using the *percentages* for each interval, how (if at all) would the shape of this histogram change?

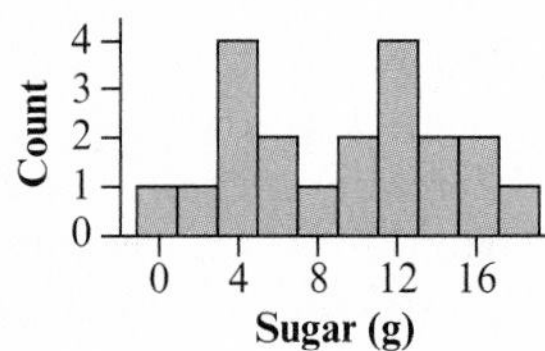

2.21 Shape of the histogram For each of the following vari- TRY ables, indicate whether you would expect its histogram to be symmetric, skewed to the right, or skewed to the left. Explain why.

a. Assessed value of houses in a large city (*Hint:* Would the relatively few homes with extremely high assessed value result in a long right tail or a long left tail?)

b. Number of times checking account overdrawn in the past year for the faculty in your school

c. IQ for the general population

d. The height of female college students

2.22 More shapes of histograms Repeat the preceding exercise for

a. The scores of students (out of 100 points) on a very easy exam in which most score perfectly or nearly so, but a few score very poorly

b. The weekly church contribution for all members of a congregation, in which the three wealthiest members contribute generously each week

c. Time needed to complete a difficult exam (maximum time is 1 hour)

d. Number of music CDs (compact discs) owned, for each student in your school.

2.23 Gestational Period The Animals data set at the TECH book's website contains data on the length of the gestational period (in days) of 21 animals. (*Source:* Wildlife Conservation Society)

a. Using software, plot a histogram of the gestational period.

b. Do you see any observation that is unusual? Which animal is it?

c. Is the distribution right-skewed or left-skewed?

d. Try to override the default setting and plot a histogram with only very few (e.g., 3 or 4) intervals and one with many (e.g., 30) intervals. Would you prefer either one to the histogram created in part a? Why or why not?

2.24 How often do students read the newspaper? Question TRY 14 on the class survey (Activity 3 in Chapter 1) asked, "Estimate the number of times a week, on average, that you read a daily newspaper."

a. Is this variable continuous or discrete? Explain.

b. The histogram shown gives results of this variable when this survey was administered to a class of 36 University of Georgia students. Report the (i) minimum response, (ii) maximum response, (iii) number of students who did not read the newspaper at all, and (iv) mode.

c. Describe the shape of the distribution.

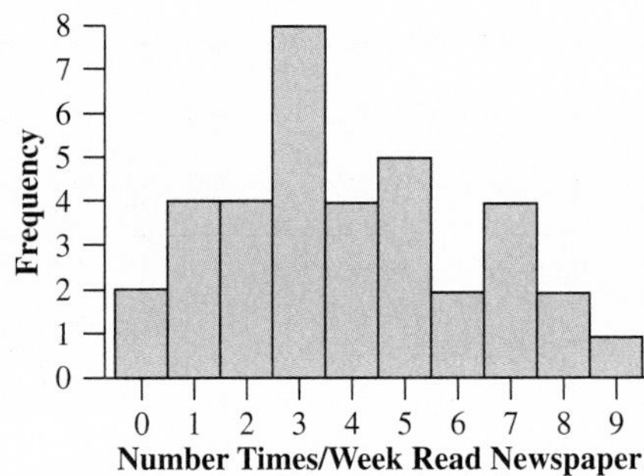

2.25 Blossom widths A data set (available at the book's website) analyzed by the famous statistician R. A. Fisher consisted of measurements of different varieties of iris blossoms. Histograms representing the widths of the petals of the two species, *Iris setosa* and *Iris versicolor*, are on the next page.

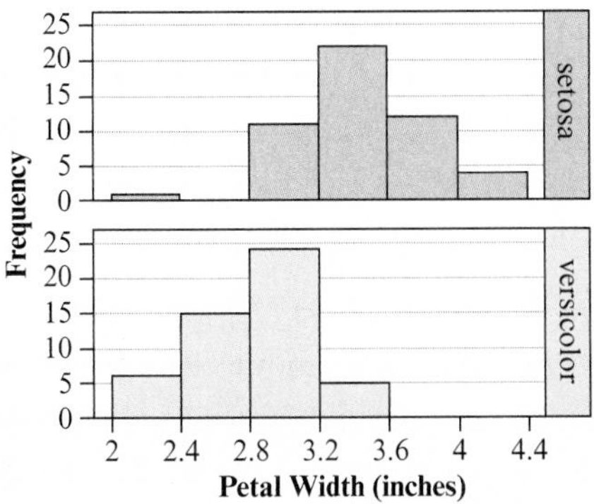

a. Describe the shape of the distribution of *setosa* petal widths.
b. Describe the shape of the distribution of *versicolor* petal widths.
c. Of the 50 *versicolor* blossoms in the data set, approximately what percentage has a petal width less than 3.2 inches?
d. Is it possible to determine accurately the percentage of *versicolor* blossoms with a width of more than 3 inches? Why or why not?

2.26 Central Park temperatures The first figure shows a histogram of the Central Park, New York, annual average temperatures from 1869 to 2012.

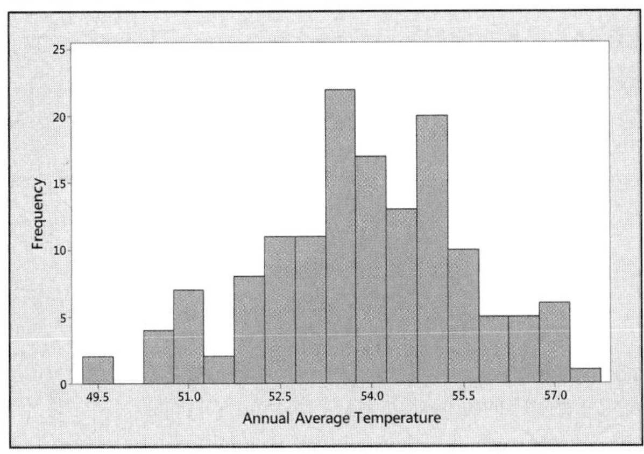

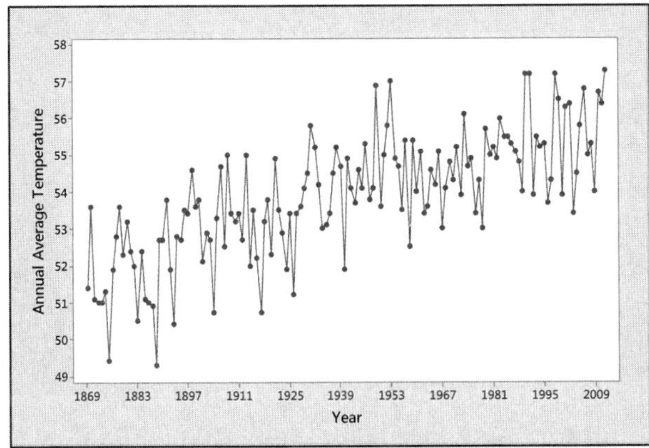

a. Describe the shape of the distribution.
b. What information can the time plot above show that a histogram cannot provide?
c. What information does the histogram show that a time plot does not provide?

2.27 Is whooping cough close to being eradicated?  In the first half of the 20th century, whooping cough was a frequently occurring bacterial infection that often resulted in death, especially among young children. A vaccination for whooping cough was developed in the 1940s. How effective has the vaccination been in eradicating whooping cough? One measure to consider is the **incidence rate** (number of infected individuals per 100,000 population) in the United States. The table shows incidence rates from 1925 to 1970.

Incidence Rates for Whooping Cough, 1925–1970

Year	Rate per 100,000
1925	131.2
1930	135.6
1935	141.9
1940	139.6
1945	101.0
1950	80.1
1955	38.2
1960	8.3
1965	3.5
1970	2.1

Source: Data from Historical Statistics of the United States, Colonial Times to 1970, U.S. Department of Commerce, p. 77.

a. Sketch a time plot. What type of trend do you observe? Based on the trend from 1945 to 1970, was the whooping cough vaccination proving effective in reducing the incidence of whooping cough?
b. The figure shown is a time plot of the incidence rate from 1980 to 2012, based on numbers reported by the Center for Disease Control and Prevention.[3] Describe the time series. Is the United States close to eradicating whooping cough? What do you think contributes to the recent trend? (Data available on the book's website in the pertussis.csv file.)
c. Would a histogram of the incidence rates since 1935 address the question about the success of the vaccination for whooping cough? Why or why not?

Time Plot of Whooping Cough Incidence Rates (per 100,000), 1980–2012

Incidence Rate

Year

2.28 Warming in Newnan, Georgia?   Access the Newnan, GA Temps file on the book's website, which reports the average annual temperatures during the 20th century for Newnan, Georgia. Construct a time plot to investigate a possible trend over time. Is there evidence of climate change?

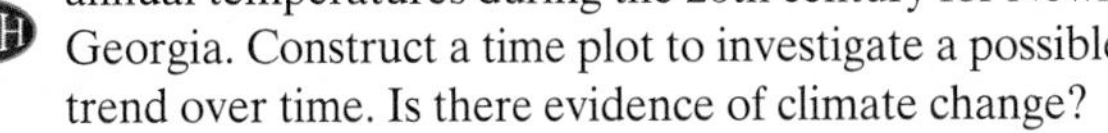

[3]*Source:* www.cdc.gov/pertussis

2.3 Measuring the Center of Quantitative Data

Section 2.2 introduced **graphs for displaying the distribution** of categorical and quantitative variables. For a categorical variable, a bar graph shows the proportion of observations in each category and the modal category. For a quantitative variable, a histogram shows the important feature of the **shape** of the distribution. It's always a good idea to look first at a variable with the appropriate graph to get a feel for the data. You can then consider computing **numerical summaries (statistics)** for the data to describe several other important features of a distribution. For instance, when describing a quantitative variable, we would like to know "What is a typical value for the observations?" and "Do the observations take similar values, or do they vary quite a bit?" Statistics that answer the first question describe the **center** of the distribution. Statistics that answer the second question describe the **variability (or spread)** of the distribution. We'll also study how the shape of the distribution influences our choice of which statistics are appropriate to describe center and variability.

Recall

A statistic is a numerical summary of a sample (i.e., the data observed for a variable). A parameter is a numerical summary of the population. ◀

Describing the Center: The Mean and the Median

The best-known and most frequently used measure of the center of a distribution of a quantitative variable is the **mean**. It is found by averaging the observations.

In Words

The **mean** refers to averaging, that is, adding up the data points and dividing by how many there are. The **median** is the point that splits the data in two, half the data below it and half above it (much like the median on a highway splits a road into two equal parts).

Mean

The **mean** is the sum of the observations divided by the number of observations. It is interpreted as the balance point of the distribution.

Another popular measure is the **median**. Half the observations are smaller than it, and half are larger.

Median

The **median** is the middle value of the observations when the observations are ordered from the smallest to the largest (or from the largest to the smallest).

Example 10

Mean and median ◀

Center of the Cereal Sodium Data

Picture the Scenario

In Examples 4, 5, and 7 in Section 2.2, we investigated the sodium level in 20 breakfast cereals and saw various ways to graph the data. Let's return to those data and learn how to describe their center. The observations (in mg) are

0	340	70	140	200	180	210	150	100	130
140	180	190	160	290	50	220	180	200	210

Questions to Explore

a. Find the mean.

b. Find the median.

Think It Through

a. We find the mean by adding all the observations and then dividing this sum by the number of observations, which is 20:

$$\text{Mean} = (0 + 340 + 70 + \ldots + 210)/20 = 3340/20 = 167.$$

b. To find the median, we arrange the data from the smallest to the largest observation.

0	50	70	100	130	140	140	150	160	180
180	180	190	200	200	210	210	220	290	340

For the 20 observations, the smaller 10 (on the first line) range from 0 to 180, and the larger 10 (on the second line) range from 180 to 340. The median is 180, which is the average of the two middle values, the tenth and eleventh observations, $(180 + 180)/2$.

Insight

The mean and median take different values. Why? The median measures the center by dividing the data into two equal parts, regardless of the actual numerical values above that point or below that point. The mean takes into account the actual numerical values of all the observations.

► ***Try Exercise 2.31***

In this example, what if the smaller 10 observations go from 0 to 180, and the larger ten go from 190 to 340? Then, the median is the average of the two middle observations, which is $(180 + 190)/2 = 185$.

SUMMARY: How to Determine the Median

- Put the n observations in order of their size.
- When the number of observations n is odd, the median is the middle observation in the ordered sample.
- When the number of observations n is even, two observations from the ordered sample fall in the middle, and the median is their average.

A Closer Look at the Mean and the Median

Notation for the mean is used both in formulas and as a shorthand in text.

In Words

The formula

$$\bar{x} = \frac{\Sigma x}{n}$$

is short for "sum the values on the variable x and divide by the sample size."

Notation for a Variable and Its Mean

Variables are symbolized by letters near the end of the alphabet, most commonly x and y. The sample size is denoted by n. For a sample of n observations on a variable x, the mean is denoted by $\bar{x}$ (pronounced "x bar"). Using the mathematical symbol Σ for "sum," the mean has the formula

$$\bar{x} = \frac{\Sigma x}{n}.$$

Did You Know?

The mean is also interpreted as the "fair share" value; for example, when considering these 20 cereals, the mean of 167 mg can be interpreted as the amount of sodium each cereal serving contains if all 20 cereals have the same amount. ◀

For instance, the cereal data set has $n = 20$ observations. As we saw in Example 10,

$$\bar{x} = (\Sigma x)/n = (0 + 340 + 70 + \ldots + 210)/20 = 3340/20 = 167.$$

Here are some basic **properties of the mean**:

- The mean is the *balance point* of the data: If we were to place identical weights on a line representing where the observations occur, then the line would balance by placing a fulcrum at the mean.

The Fulcrum Shows the Mean of the Cereal Sodium Data

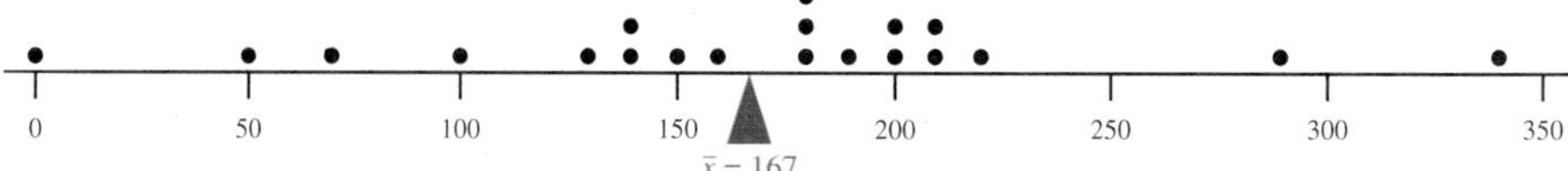

- Usually, the mean is not equal to any value that was observed in the sample. (For n odd, the median is always equal to an observed value.)
- For a skewed distribution, the mean is pulled in the direction of the longer tail, relative to the median. The next example illustrates this idea.
- The mean can be highly influenced by an **outlier**, which is an unusually small or unusually large observation.

Outlier

An **outlier** is an observation that falls well above or well below the overall bulk of the data.

Outliers typically call for further investigation to see, for example, whether they resulted from an error in data entry or from some surprising or unusual occurence.

Example 11

Mean, median, and outliers ◀

CO_2 Pollution

Picture the Scenario

The Pew Center on Global Climate Change[4] reports that global warming is largely a result of human activity that produces carbon dioxide (CO_2) emissions and other greenhouse gases. The CO_2 emissions from fossil fuel combustion are the result of electricity, heating, industrial processes, and gas consumption in automobiles. The International Energy Agency[5] reported the per capita CO_2 emissions by country (that is, the total CO_2 emissions for the country divided by the population size of that country) for 2011. For the nine largest countries in population size (which make up more than half the world's population), the values were, in metric tons per person:

China 5.9	Indonesia 1.8	Nigeria 0.3
India 1.4	Brazil 2.1	Bangladesh 0.4
United States 16.9	Pakistan 0.8	Russian Federation 11.6

[4]*Source:* www.pewclimate.org/global-warming-basics/facts_and_figures/.
[5]*Source:* www.iea.org/.

Questions to Explore

a. For these nine values, the mean is 4.6. What is the median?

b. Is any observation a potential outlier? Discuss its impact on how the mean compares to the median.

c. Using this data set, explain the effect an outlier can have on the mean.

Think It Through

a. The CO_2 values have $n = 9$ observations. The ordered values are

0.3, 0.4, 0.8, 1.4, 1.8, 2.1, 5.9, 11.6, 16.9

Because n is odd, the median is the middle value, which is 1.8.

Did You Know?

A metric ton is 1000 kilograms, which is about 2200 pounds. ◀

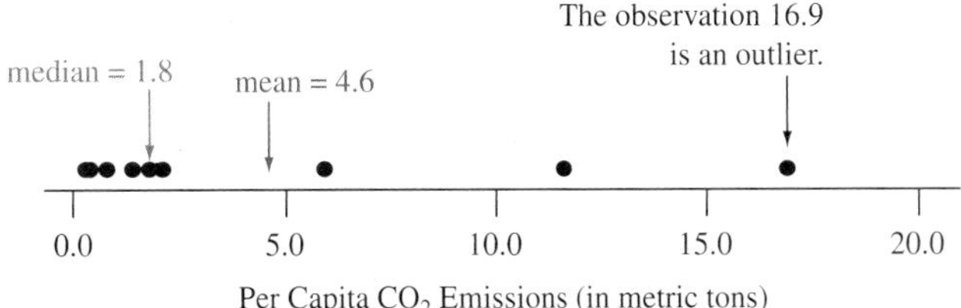

b. Let's consider a dot plot, as shown. The relatively high value of 16.9 falls well above the rest of the data. It is an outlier. This value, as well as the value at 11.6, causes the mean, which is 4.6, to fall well above the median, which is 1.8.

c. The size of the outlier affects the calculation of the mean but not the median. If the observation of 16.9 for the United States had been the same as for China (5.9), the nine observations would have had a mean of 3.4 instead of 4.6. The median would still have been 1.8. In summary, a single outlier can have a large impact on the value of the mean.

Insight

The mean may not be representative of where the bulk of the observations fall. This is fairly common with small samples when one observation is much larger or much smaller than the others. It's not surprising that the United States is an outlier because the other nations are not nearly as economically advanced. Later in the chapter (Example 17), we'll compare carbon dioxide emissions for the United States with those of European nations.

▶ ***Try Exercise 2.32***

Comparing the Mean and Median

The shape of a distribution influences whether the mean is larger or smaller than the median. For instance, an extremely large value out in the right-hand tail pulls the mean to the right. The mean then usually falls above the median, as we observed with the CO_2 data in Example 11.

Generally, if the shape is

- perfectly symmetric, the mean equals the median.
- skewed to the left, the mean is smaller than the median.
- skewed to the right, the mean is larger than the median.

As Figure 2.9 illustrates, the mean is drawn in the direction of the longer tail.

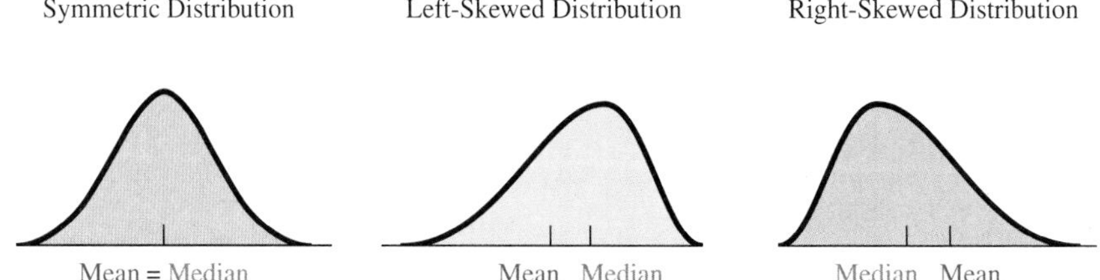

▲ **Figure 2.9** Relationship Between the Mean and Median. **Question** For skewed distributions, what causes the mean and median to differ?

When a distribution is close to symmetric, the tails will be of similar length, and therefore the median and mean are similar. For skewed distributions, the mean lies toward the direction of skew (the longer tail) relative to the median, as Figure 2.9 shows. This is because extreme observations in a tail affect the balance point for the distribution, which is the mean. The more highly skewed the distribution, the more the mean and median tend to differ.

Example 11 illustrated this property. The dot plot of CO_2 emissions shown there is skewed to the right. As expected, the mean of 4.6 falls in the direction of the skew, above the median of 1.8. Another example is given by mean household income in the United States. From a 2012 survey by the U.S. Bureau of the Census, the mean income was $71,274, and the median was $51,017. This suggests that the distribution of household incomes in the United States is skewed to the right.

Why is the median not affected by an outlier? How far an outlier falls from the middle of the distribution does not influence the median. The median is determined solely by having an equal number of observations above it and below it.

For the CO_2 data, for instance, if the value 16.9 for the United States were changed to 90, as shown below, the median would still equal 1.8. However, the calculation of the mean uses *all* the numerical values. So, unlike the median, it depends on how far observations fall from the middle. Because the mean is the balance point, an extreme value on the right side pulls the mean toward the right tail. Because the median is not affected, it is said to be **resistant** to the effect of extreme observations.

Resistant

A numerical summary of the observations is called **resistant** if extreme observations have little, if any, influence on its value.

The Median Is Resistant to Outliers

1. Change 16.9 to 90 for United States.

   0.3, 0.4, 0.8, 1.4, 1.8, 2.1, 5.9, 11.6, 90
   median = 1.8 (as before)

2. Find the mean using the value of 90.

   0.3, 0.4, 0.8, 1.4, 1.8, 2.1, 5.9, 11.6, 90
   mean = 12.7 (before: 4.6)

The median is resistant. The mean is not.

From these properties, you might think that it's always better to use the median rather than the mean. That's not true. The mean has other useful properties that we'll learn about and take advantage of in later chapters.

In practice, it is a good idea to report *both* the mean and the median when describing the center of a distribution. For the CO_2 emission data in Example 11, the median is the more relevant statistic because of the skew resulting from the extremely large value for the United States. However, knowing the mean for all the observations and then for the observations excluding the United States (in which case, the mean is 3.0) provides additional information.

In Practice Effect of Shape on Choice of Mean or Median

- If a distribution is highly skewed, the median is usually preferred over the mean because it better represents what is typical.
- If the distribution is close to symmetric or only mildly skewed, the mean is usually preferred because it uses the numerical values of all the observations.

The Mode

We've seen that the **mode** is the value that occurs most frequently. It describes a typical observation in terms of the most common outcome. The concept of the mode is most often used to describe the category of a categorical variable that has the highest frequency (the modal category). With quantitative variables, the mode is most useful with discrete variables taking a small number of possible values. For instance, for the TV-watching data of Example 6, the mode is 2 hours of daily watching. For continuous observations, it is usually not meaningful to look for a mode because there can be multiple modes or no mode at all. For the CO_2 data, for example, there is no mode. All values just occurred once.

Caution

The mode need not be near the center of the distribution. It may be the largest or the smallest value. Thus, it is somewhat inaccurate to call the mode a measure of center, but often it is useful to report the most common outcome. ◀

▶ Activity 1

Using an App to Explore the Relationship Between the Mean and Median*

The "Mean Versus Median" web app accessible via the book's website allows you to add and delete data points from a sample. When you access the app, select Skewed from the drop-down menu for the initial distribution. A dotplot with 20 observations from a skewed distribution is shown.

- Observe the location of the mean and median as you change the skewness from "right" to "symmetric " to "left".
- Click in the gray area to add points or click on a point to delete it, each time observing how the mean and median changes. Try this for different initial distributions or create your own dotplot by choosing the Create Own option from the drop-down menu.
- Under a skewed initial distribution and 100 points (i.e., a large sample size), does deleting one or two outliers have much of an effect on the mean or median?
- You can also supply your own data points. Select this option from the first drop-down menu. By default, the per capita CO_2 emissions for the 9 countries mentioned in Example 11 are shown. Investigate what happens when you change the largest observation from 16.9 to 90? (In the textbox showing the numerical value, replace 16.9 by 90) Does the median change much from its original value of 1.8? What about the mean?

*For more information about the apps see pages vii–viii and the back endpapers of this book.

Try Exercises 2.38 and 2.148 ◀

2.3 Practicing the Basics

2.29 Median versus mean For each of the following variables, would you use the median or mean for describing the center of the distribution? Why? (Think about the likely shape of the distribution.)

a. Salary of employees of a university

b. Time spent on a difficult exam

c. Scores on a standardized test

2.30 More median versus mean For each of the following variables, would you use the median or mean for describing the center of the distribution? Why? (Think about the likely shape of the distribution.)

a. Charges on a credit card

b. Weight of male students in your class this semester

c. Life expectancy of females in developed nations

2.31 More on CO_2 emissions The Energy Information Agency reported the CO_2 emissions (measured in gigatons, Gt) from fossil fuel combustion for the top 10 emitting countries in 2011. These are China (8 Gt), the United States (5.3 Gt), India (1.8 Gt), Russia (1.7 Gt), Japan (1.2 Gt), Germany (0.8 Gt), Korea (0.6 Gt), Canada(0.5 Gt), Iran (0.4 Gt), and Saudi Arabia (0.4 Gt).

TRY

a. Find the mean and median CO_2 emission.

b. The totals reported here do not take into account a nation's population size. Explain why it may be more sensible to analyze *per capita* values, as was done in Example 11.

2.32 Resistance to an outlier Consider the following three sets of observations:

TRY

Set 1: 8, 9, 10, 11, 12

Set 2: 8, 9, 10, 11, 100

Set 3: 8, 9, 10, 11, 1000

a. Find the median for each data set.

b. Find the mean for each data set.

c. What do these data sets illustrate about the resistance of the median and mean?

2.33 Income and health insurance According to the U.S. Bureau of the Census, *Current Population Reports 2013*, the mean and median income for households with health insurance was \$86,431 and \$66,000, respectively. For households without health insurance, the mean and median income was \$53,373 and \$39,000, respectively. Does this suggest that the distribution of income for households with health insurance is symmetric, skewed to the right, or skewed to the left? What about for households without health insurance? Explain.

2.34 Labor dispute The workers and the management of a company are having a labor dispute. Explain why the workers might use the median income of all the employees to justify a raise but management might use the mean income to argue that a raise is not needed.

2.35 Cereal sodium The dot plot shows the cereal sodium values from Example 4. What aspect of the distribution causes the mean to be less than the median?

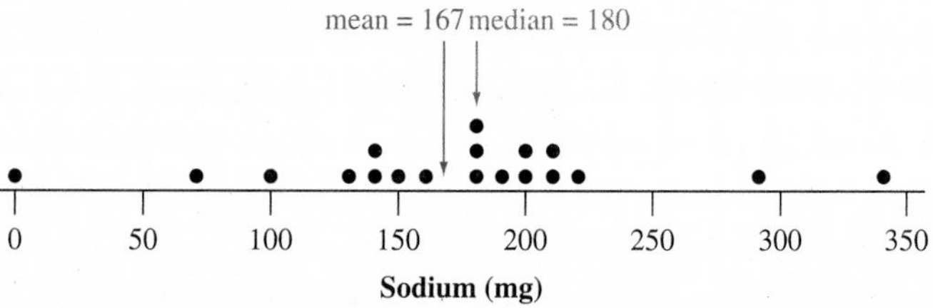

2.36 Center of plots The figure shows dot plots for three sample data sets.

a. For which, if any, data sets would you expect the mean and the median to be the same? Explain why.

b. For which, if any, data sets would you expect the mean and the median to differ? Which would be larger, the mean or the median? Why?

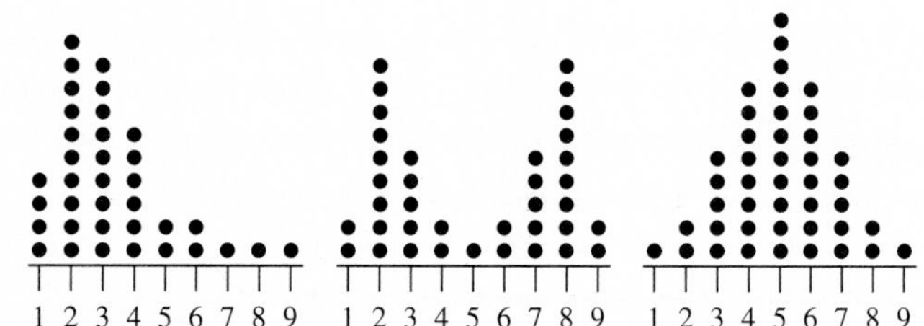

2.37 Public transportation—center The owner of a company in downtown Atlanta is concerned about the large use of gasoline by her employees due to urban sprawl, traffic congestion, and the use of energy-inefficient vehicles such as SUVs. She'd like to promote the use of public transportation. She decides to investigate how many miles her employees travel on public transportation during a typical day. The values for her 10 employees (recorded to the closest mile) are

0 0 4 0 0 0 10 0 6 0

a. Find and interpret the mean, median, and mode.

b. She has just hired an additional employee. He lives in a different city and travels 90 miles a day on public transport. Recompute the mean and median. Describe the effect of this outlier.

2.38 Public transportation—outlier Refer to the previous exercise.

TRY

a. Use the Mean Versus Median app (see Activity 1) to investigate what effect adding the outlier of 90 to the data set has on the mean and median. (In the app, select "Supply own sample" and type the data plus the value 90 into the textbox.)

b. Now add 10 more data values that are near the mean of 2 for the original 10 observations. Does the outlier of 90 still have such a strong effect on the mean?

2.39 Baseball salaries The players on the New York Yankees baseball team in 2014 had a mean salary of $7,387,498 and a median salary of $5,500,000.[6] What do you think causes these two values to be so different (data in NYYsalary file on book's website.)?

2.40 More baseball salaries Go to espn.go.com/mlb/teams and select a (or your favorite) team. Click Roster and then Salary. Copy the salary figures for the players into a software program and create a histogram. Describe the shape of the distribution for salary and comment on its center by quoting appropriate statistics.

TRY TECH

2.41 European fertility The European fertility rates (mean number of children per adult woman) from Exercise 2.18 are shown again in the table.

a. Find the median of the fertility rates. Interpret.

b. Find the mean of the fertility rates. Interpret.

c. For each woman, the number of children is a whole number, such as 2 or 3. Explain why it makes sense to measure a *mean* number of children per adult woman (which is not a whole number) to compare fertility levels, such as the fertility levels of 1.5 in Canada and 2.4 in Mexico.

Country	Fertility	Country	Fertility
Austria	1.4	Netherlands	1.7
Belgium	1.7	Norway	1.8
Denmark	1.8	Spain	1.3
Finland	1.7	Sweden	1.6
France	1.9	Switzerland	1.4
Germany	1.3	United Kingdom	1.7
Greece	1.3	United States	2.0
Ireland	1.9	Canada	1.5
Italy	1.3	Mexico	2.4

2.42 Sex partners A recent General Social Survey asked female respondents, "How many sex partners have you had in the last 12 months?" Of the 365 respondents, 102 said 0 partners, 233 said 1 partner, 18 said 2 partners, 9 said 3 partners, 2 said 4 partners, and 1 said 5 partners. (*Source:* Data from CSM, UC Berkeley.)

a. Display the data in a table. Explain why the median is 1.

b. Show that the mean is 0.85.

c. Suppose the 102 women who answered 0 instead had answered 5 partners. Show that the median would still be 1. (The mean would increase to 2.2. The mean uses the numerical values of the observations, not just their ordering.)

2.43 Marriage statistics for 20–24-year-olds The table in the next column shows the number of times 20–24-year-old U.S. residents have been married, based on a Bureau of the Census report from 2004. The frequencies are actually *thousands* of people. For instance, 8,418,000 men never married, but this does not affect calculations about the mean or median.

Number of Times Married, for Subjects of Age 20–24

Number Times Married	Frequency: Women	Frequency: Men
0	7350	8418
1	2587	1594
2	80	10
Total	**10,017**	**10,022**

a. Find the median and mean for each gender.

b. On average, have women or men been married more often? Which statistic do you prefer to answer this question? (The mean, as opposed to the median, uses the numerical values of all the observations, not just the ordering. For discrete data with only a few values such as the number of times married, it can be more informative.)

2.44 Knowing homicide victims The table summarizes responses of 4383 subjects in a recent General Social Survey to the question, "Within the past 12 months, how many people have you known personally that were victims of homicide?"

TRY

Number of People You Have Known Who Were Victims of Homicide

Number of Victims	Frequency
0	3944
1	279
2	97
3	40
4 or more	23
Total	**4383**

(*Source:* Data from CSM, UC Berkeley.)

a. To find the mean, it is necessary to give a score to the "4 or more" category. Find it, using the score 4.5. (In practice, you might try a few different scores, such as 4, 4.5, 5, 6, to make sure the resulting mean is not highly sensitive to that choice.)

b. Find the median. Note that the "4 or more" category is not problematic for it.

c. If 1744 observations shift from 0 to 4 or more, how do the mean and median change?

d. Why is the median the same for parts b and c, even though the data are so different?

2.45 Accidents One variable in a study measures how many serious motor vehicle accidents a subject has had in the past year. Explain why the mean would likely be more useful than the median for summarizing the responses of the 60 subjects.

[6] espn.go.com/mlb/team/salaries/_/name/nyy/new-york-yankees.

2.4 Measuring the Variability of Quantitative Data

A measure of the center is not enough to describe a distribution for a quantitative variable adequately. It tells us nothing about the variability of the data. With the cereal sodium data, if we report the mean of 167 mg to describe the center, would the value of 210 mg for Honeycomb be considered quite high, or are most of the data even farther from the mean? To answer this question, we need numerical summaries of the variability of the distribution.

Measuring Variability: The Range

To see why a measure of the center is not enough, let's consider Figure 2.10. This figure compares hypothetical income distributions of music teachers in public schools in Denmark and in the United States. Both distributions are symmetric and have a mean of about $40,000. However, the annual incomes in Denmark (converted to U.S. dollars) go from $35,000 to $45,000, whereas those in the United States go from $20,000 to $60,000. Incomes are more similar in Denmark and vary more in the United States. A simple way to describe this is with the **range**.

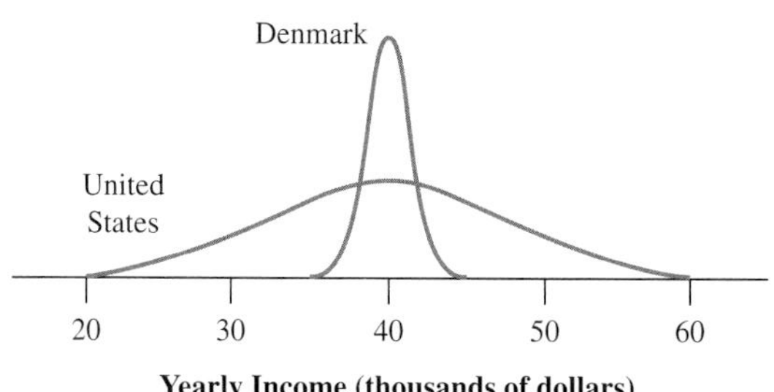

▲ **Figure 2.10** Income Distributions for Music Teachers in Denmark and in the United States. The distributions have the same mean, but the one for the United States shows more variability around the mean. **Question** How would the range for Denmark change if one teacher earned $100,000?

Range

The **range** is the difference between the largest and the smallest observations.

In Denmark the range is $45,000 − $35,000 = $10,000. In the United States the range is $60,000 − $20,000 = $40,000. The range is a larger value when the data vary more in the distribution.

The range is simple to compute and easy to understand, but it uses only the extreme values and ignores the other values. Therefore, it's affected severely by outliers. For example, if one teacher in Denmark made $100,000, the range would change from $45,000 − $35,000 = $10,000 to $100,000 − $35,000 = $65,000. The range is not a resistant statistic. It shares the worst property of the mean, not being resistant, and the worst property of the median, ignoring the numerical values of nearly all the data.

Measuring Variability: The Standard Deviation

Although it is good practice to mention the smallest and largest value when describing the distribution of a variable, we usually don't use the range to measure variability. A much better numerical summary of variability uses *all* the data, and it describes a typical distance of how far the data falls from the mean. It does this by summarizing **deviations** from the mean.

- The **deviation** of an observation x from the mean $\bar{x}$ is $(x - \bar{x})$, the difference between the observation and the sample mean.

For the cereal sodium values, the mean is $\bar{x} = 167$. The observation of 210 for Honeycomb has a deviation of $210 - 167 = 43$. The observation of 50 for Honey Smacks has a deviation of $50 - 167 = -117$. Figure 2.11 shows these deviations.

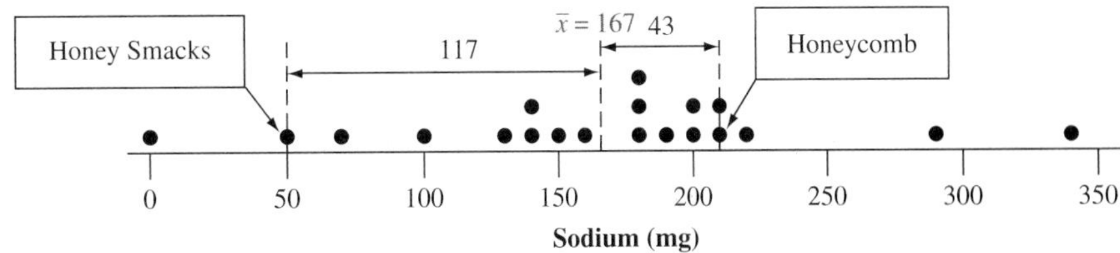

▲ **Figure 2.11** Dot Plot for Cereal Sodium Data, Showing Deviations for Two Observations. **Question** When is a deviation positive and when is it negative?

- Each observation has a deviation from the mean.
- A deviation $x - \bar{x}$ is *positive* when the observation falls *above* the mean. A deviation is *negative* when the observation falls *below* the mean.
- The interpretation of the mean as the balance point implies that the positive deviations counterbalance the negative deviations. Because of this, *the sum (and therefore the mean) of the deviations always equals zero*, regardless of the actual data values. Hence, summary measures of variability from the mean use either the **squared deviations** or their absolute values.
- The **average** of the squared deviations is called the **variance**. Because the variance uses the *square* of the units of measurement for the original data, its square root is easier to interpret. This is called the **standard deviation**.
- The symbol $\Sigma(x - \bar{x})^2$ is called a **sum of squares**. It represents finding the deviation for each observation, squaring each deviation, and then adding them.

Did You Know?

Another measure of the typical or average distance of observations from the mean is the Mean Absolute Deviation (MAD). The absolute value of the deviation is found instead of the square. Exercise 2.145 explores the MAD. ◀

The Standard Deviation *s*

The **standard deviation s** of n observations is

$$s = \sqrt{\frac{\Sigma(x - \bar{x})^2}{n - 1}} = \sqrt{\frac{\text{sum of squared deviations}}{\text{sample size} - 1}}.$$

This is the square root of the **variance s^2**, which is an average of the squares of the deviations from their mean,

$$s^2 = \frac{\Sigma(x - \bar{x})^2}{n - 1}.$$

A calculator can compute the standard deviation s easily. Its interpretation is quite simple: *Roughly, the standard deviation s represents a typical distance or a type of average distance of an observation from the mean.* The most basic property of the standard deviation is this:

- The larger the standard deviation s, the greater the variability of the data.

A small technical point: You may wonder why the denominators of the variance and the standard deviation use $n - 1$ instead of n. We said that the variance was an *average* of the n squared deviations, so should we not divide by n? Basically it is because the deviations provide only $n - 1$ pieces of information about variability: That is, $n - 1$ of the deviations determine the last one, because the deviations sum to 0. For example, suppose we have $n = 2$ observations and the first observation has deviation $(x - \bar{x}) = 5$. Then the second observation must have deviation $(x - \bar{x}) = -5$ because the deviations must add to 0. With $n = 2$, there's only $n - 1 = 1$ nonredundant piece of information about variability. And with $n = 1$, the standard deviation is undefined because with only one observation, it's impossible to get a sense of how much the data vary.

Example 12

Standard deviation

Women's and Men's Ideal Number of Children

Picture the Scenario

Students in a class were asked on a questionnaire at the beginning of the course, "How many children do you think is ideal for a family?" The observations, classified by student's gender, were

Men: 0, 0, 0, 2, 4, 4, 4

Women: 0, 2, 2, 2, 2, 2, 4

Question to Explore

Both men and women have a mean of 2 and a range of 4. Do the distributions of data have the same amount of variability around the mean? If not, which distribution has more variability?

Think It Through

Let's check dot plots for the data.

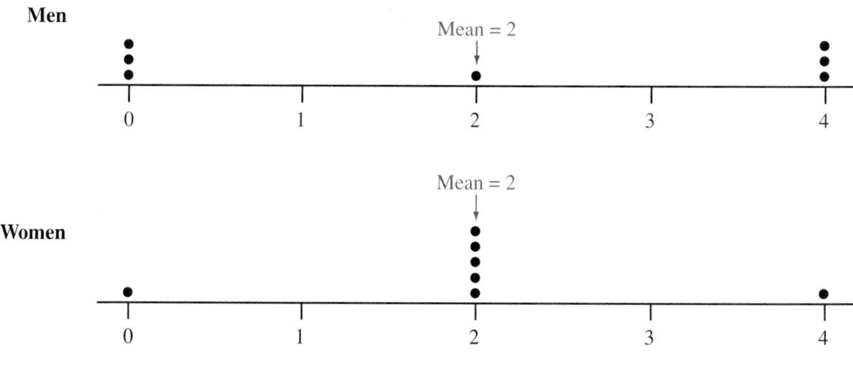

The typical deviation from the mean for the male observations appears to be about 2. The observations for females mostly fall right at the mean, so their typical deviation is smaller.

Let's calculate the standard deviation for men. Their observations are 0, 0, 0, 2, 4, 4, 4. The deviations and squared deviations about their mean of 2 are

Value	Deviation	Squared Deviation
0	$(0 - 2) = -2$	4
0	$(0 - 2) = -2$	4
0	$(0 - 2) = -2$	4
2	$(2 - 2) = 0$	0
4	$(4 - 2) = 2$	4
4	$(4 - 2) = 2$	4
4	$(4 - 2) = 2$	4

In Practice Rounding

Statistical software and calculators can find the standard deviation *s* for you. Try calculating *s* for a couple of small data sets to help you understand what it represents. After that, rely on software or a calculator. To ensure accurate results, don't round off while doing a calculation. (For example, use a calculator's memory to store intermediate results.) When presenting the solution, however, round off to two or three significant digits. In calculating *s* for women, you get $s = \sqrt{1.3333\ldots} = 1.1547005\ldots$. Present the value $s = 1.2$ or $s = 1.15$ to make it easier for a reader to comprehend.

The sum of squared deviations equals

$$\Sigma(x - \bar{x})^2 = 4 + 4 + 4 + 0 + 4 + 4 + 4 = 24.$$

The standard deviation of these $n = 7$ observations equals

$$s = \sqrt{\frac{\Sigma(x - \bar{x})^2}{n - 1}} = \sqrt{\frac{24}{6}} = \sqrt{4} = 2.0.$$

This indicates that for men a typical distance of an observation from the mean is 2.0. By contrast, you can check that the standard deviation for women is $s = 1.2$. The observations for males tended to be farther from the mean than those for females, as indicated by $s = 2.0 > s = 1.2$. In summary, the men's observations varied more around the mean.

Insight

The standard deviation is more informative than the range. For these data, the standard deviation detects that the women were more consistent than the men in their viewpoints about the ideal number of children. The range does not detect the difference because it equals 4 for each gender.

► ***Try Exercise 2.46***

Standard deviation ◄

Example 13

Exam Scores

Picture the Scenario

The first exam in your statistics course is graded on a scale of 0 to 100. Suppose that the mean score in your class is 80.

Question to Explore

Which value is most plausible for the standard deviation *s*: 0, 0.5, 10, or 50?

Think It Through

The standard deviation *s* is a *typical distance* of an observation from the mean. A value of $s = 0$ seems unlikely. For that to happen, every deviation would have to be 0. This implies that every student must have scored 80, the mean. A value of $s = 0.5$ is implausibly small because 0.5 would not be a typical distance above or below the mean score of 80. Similarly, a value of $s = 50$ is implausibly large because 50 would also not be a typical distance of a student's score from the mean of 80. (For instance, it is impossible to score 130.) We would instead expect to see a value of *s* such as 10. With $s = 10$, a typical distance is 10, as occurs with the scores of 70 and 90.

Insight

In summary, we've learned that *s* is a typical distance of observations from the mean, larger values of *s* represent greater variability, and $s = 0$ means that all observations take the same value.

► ***Try Exercises 2.49 and 2.50***

Caution

The size of the standard deviation also depends on the units of measurement. For instance, a value of $s = 1{,}000$ might not be considered large when the unit of measurement is millimeters instead of meters. $s = 1{,}000$ computed on the millimeter scale corresponds to $s = 1$ on the meter scale. ◄

SUMMARY: Properties of the Standard Deviation, s

- The greater the variability from the mean of the data, the larger is the value of s.
- $s = 0$ only when all observations take the same value. For instance, if the reported ideal number of children for seven people is 2, 2, 2, 2, 2, 2, 2, then the mean equals 2, each of the seven deviations equals 0, and $s = 0$. This is the smallest possible variability for a sample.
- s can be influenced by outliers. It uses the mean, which we know can be influenced by outliers. Also, outliers have large deviations, so they tend to have *extremely* large squared deviations. We'll see (for example, in Exercise 2.46 and the beginning of Section 2.6) that these can inflate the value of s and make it sensitive to outliers.

Bell-shaped Distribution

Interpreting the Magnitude of s: The Empirical Rule

Suppose that a distribution is unimodal and approximately symmetric with a **bell shape**, as in the margin figure. The value of s then has a more precise interpretation. Using the mean and standard deviation alone, we can form intervals that contain certain percentages (approximately) of the data.

In Words

- $\bar{x} - s$ denotes the value 1 standard deviation below the mean.
- $\bar{x} + s$ denotes the value 1 standard deviation above the mean.
- $\bar{x} \pm s$ denotes the values that are 1 standard deviation from the mean in either direction.

Empirical Rule

If a distribution of data is bell shaped, then approximately

- 68% of the observations fall within 1 standard deviation of the mean, that is, between the values of $\bar{x} - s$ and $\bar{x} + s$ (denoted $\bar{x} \pm s$).
- 95% of the observations fall within 2 standard deviations of the mean ($\bar{x} \pm 2s$).
- All or nearly all observations fall within 3 standard deviations of the mean ($\bar{x} \pm 3s$).

Figure 2.12 is a graphical portrayal of the empirical rule.

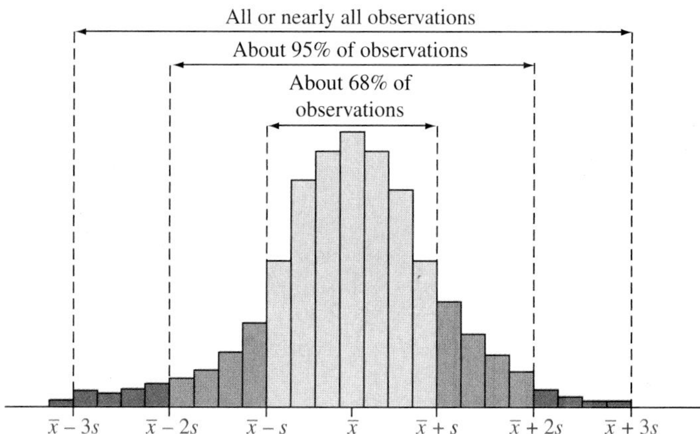

▲ **Figure 2.12 The Empirical Rule.** For bell-shaped distributions, this tells us approximately how much of the data fall within 1, 2, and 3 standard deviations of the mean. **Question** About what percentage would fall *more than* 2 standard deviations from the mean?

Did You Know?

The **empirical rule** has this name because many distributions of data observed in practice (*empirically*) are approximately bell shaped. ◀

Example 14

Empirical rule ◄

Female Student Heights

Picture the Scenario

Many human physical characteristics have bell-shaped distributions. Let's explore height. Question 1 on the student survey in Activity 3 of Chapter 1 asked for the student's height. Figure 2.13 shows a histogram of the heights from responses to this survey by 261 female students at the University of Georgia. (The data are in the Heights data file on the book's website. Note that the height of 92 inches was omitted from the analysis.) Table 2.5 presents some descriptive statistics, using MINITAB.

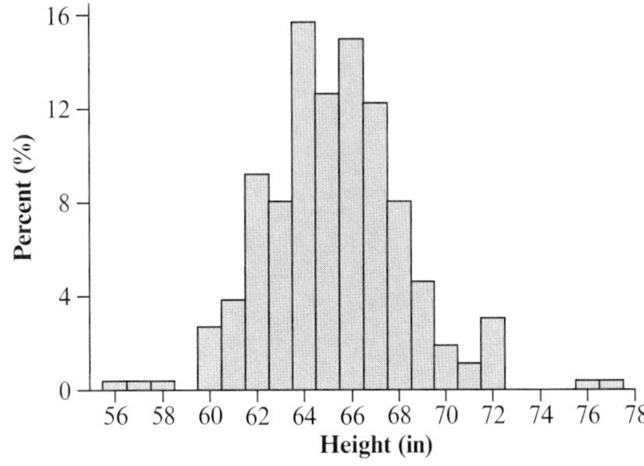

▲ **Figure 2.13** Histogram of Female Student Height Data. This summarizes heights, in inches, of 261 female college students. **Question** How would you describe the shape, center, and variability of the distribution?

Question to Explore

Can we use the empirical rule to describe the variability from the mean of these data? If so, how?

Table 2.5 MINITAB Output for Descriptive Statistics of Student Height Data

Variable	N	Mean	Median	StDev	Minimum	Maximum
HEIGHT	261	65.284	65.000	2.953	56.000	77.000

Think It Through

Figure 2.13 has approximately a bell shape. The figure in the margin shows a bell-shaped curve that approximates the histogram. From Table 2.5, the mean and median are close, about 65 inches, which reflects an approximately symmetric distribution. The empirical rule is applicable.

From Table 2.5, the mean is 65.3 inches and the standard deviation (labeled StDev) is 3.0 inches (rounded). By the empirical rule, approximately

- 68% of the observations fall between

$$\bar{x} - s = 65.3 - 3.0 = 62.3 \text{ and } \bar{x} + s = 65.3 + 3.0 = 68.3,$$

that is, within the interval (62.3, 68.3), about 62 to 68 inches.

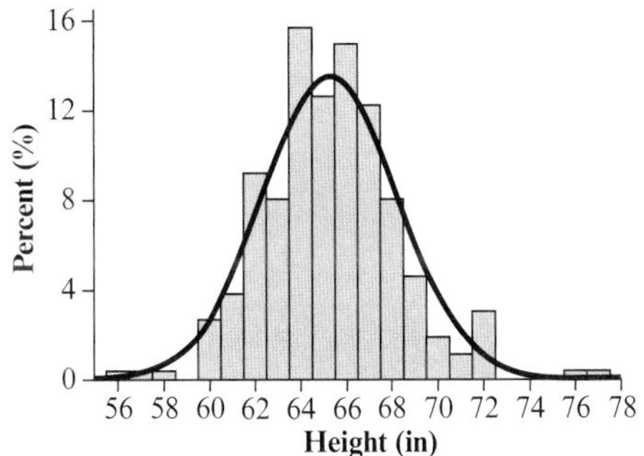

Caution

The empirical rule (which applies only to bell-shaped distributions) is not a general interpretation for what the standard deviation measures. The general interpretation is that the standard deviation measures the typical distance of observations from mean (this is for all distributions). ◀

- 95% of the observations fall within

  $\bar{x} \pm 2s$, which is $65.3 \pm 2(3.0)$, or (59.3, 71.3), about 59 to 71 inches.

- Almost all observations fall within $\bar{x} \pm 3s$, or (56.3, 74.3).

Of the 261 observations, by actually counting, we find that

- 187 observations, 72%, fall within (62.3, 68.3).
- 248 observations, 95%, fall within (59.3, 71.3).
- 258 observations, 99%, fall within (56.3, 74.3).

In summary, the percentages predicted by the empirical rule are near the actual ones.

Caution: Using the Empirical Rule

The empirical rule may approximate the actual percentages falling within 1, 2, and 3 standard deviations of the mean poorly if the data are highly skewed or highly discrete (the variable taking relatively few values). See Exercise 2.56. ◀

Insight

Because the distribution is close to bell shaped, we can predict simple summaries effectively using only two numbers—the mean and the standard deviation. We can do the same if we look at the data only for the 117 males, who had a mean of 70.9 and standard deviation of 2.9.

▶ ***Try Exercise 2.51***

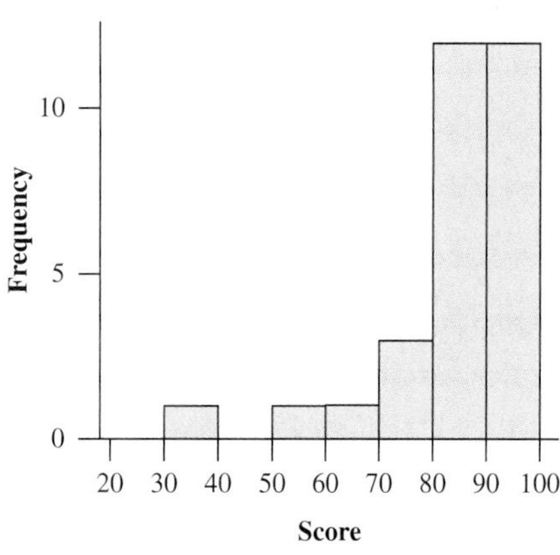

With a bell-shaped distribution for a large data set, the observations usually extend about 3 standard deviations below the mean and about 3 standard deviations above the mean.

When the distribution is highly skewed, the most extreme observation in one direction may not be nearly that far from the mean. For instance, on a recent exam, the scores ranged between 30 and 100, with median = 88, $\bar{x} = 84$, and $s = 16$. The maximum score of 100 was only 1 standard deviation above the mean (that is, $100 = \bar{x} + s = 84 + 16$). By contrast, the minimum score of 30 was more than 3 standard deviations below the mean. This happened because the distribution of scores was highly skewed to the left. (See the margin figure.)

Remember that the empirical rule is only for bell-shaped distributions. In Chapter 6, we'll see why the empirical rule works. For a special family of smooth, bell-shaped curves (called the **normal distribution**), we'll see how to find the percentage of the distribution in *any* particular region by knowing only the mean and the standard deviation.

Sample Statistics and Population Parameters

Of the numerical summaries introduced so far, the mean $\bar{x}$ and the standard deviation s are the most commonly used in practice. We'll use them frequently in the rest of the text. The formulas that define $\bar{x}$ and s refer to *sample* data. They are *sample statistics.*

We will distinguish between sample statistics and the corresponding *parameter* values for the population. The population mean is the average of all observations in the population. The population standard deviation describes the variability of the population observations about the population mean. Both of these population parameters are usually unknown. Inferential statistical methods help us make decisions and predictions about the population parameters based on the sample statistics.

Recall

From Section 1.2, a **population** is the total group about whom you want to make conclusions. A **sample** is a subset of the population for whom you actually have data. A **parameter** is a numerical summary of the population, and a **statistic** is a numerical summary of a sample. ◀

In later chapters, to help distinguish between sample statistics and population parameters, we'll use different notation for the parameter values. Often, Greek letters are used to denote the parameters. For instance, we'll use μ (the Greek letter, mu) to denote the population mean and σ (the Greek letter lowercase sigma) to denote the population standard deviation.

2.4 Practicing the Basics

2.46 Sick leave A company decides to investigate the amount of sick leave taken by its employees. A sample of eight employees yields the following numbers of days of sick leave taken in the past year:

TRY

0 0 4 0 0 0 6 0

a. Find and interpret the range.

b. Find and interpret the standard deviation s.

c. Suppose the 6 was incorrectly recorded and is supposed to be 60. Redo parts a and b with the corrected data and describe the effect of this outlier.

2.47 Life expectancy The *Human Development Report 2013*, published by the United Nations, showed life expectancies by country. For Western Europe, some values reported were

Austria 81, Belgium 80, Denmark 80, Finland 81, France 83, Germany 81, Greece 81, Ireland 81, Italy 83, Netherlands 81, Norway 81, Portugal 80, Spain 82, Sweden 82, Switzerland 83.

For Africa, some values reported were

Botswana 47, Dem. Rep. Congo 50, Angola 51, Zambia 57, Zimbabwe 58, Malawi 55, Nigeria 52, Rwanda 63, Uganda 59, Kenya 61, Mali 55, South Africa 56, Madagascar 64, Senegal 63, Sudan 62, Ghana 61.

a. Which group (Western Europe or Africa) of life expectancies do you think has the larger standard deviation? Why?

TECH **b.** Find the standard deviation for each group. Compare them to illustrate that s is larger for the group that shows more variability from the mean.

2.48 Life expectancy including Russia For Russia, the United Nations reported a life expectancy of 70. Suppose we add this observation to the data set for Western Europe in the previous exercise. Would you expect the standard deviation to be larger, or smaller, than the value for the Western European countries alone? Why?

2.49 Shape of home prices? According to the National Association of Home Builders, the median selling price of new homes in the United States in February 2014 was \$261,400. Which of the following is the most plausible value for the standard deviation: −\$15,000, \$1000, \$60,000, or \$1,000,000? Why? Explain what's unrealistic about each of the other values.

TRY

2.50 Exam standard deviation For an exam given to a class, the students' scores ranged from 35 to 98, with a mean of 74. Which of the following is the most realistic value for the standard deviation: −10, 0, 3, 12, 63? Clearly explain what's unrealistic about each of the other values.

TRY

2.51 Heights For the sample heights of Georgia college students in Example 14, the males had $\bar{x} = 71$ and $s = 3$, and the females had $\bar{x} = 65$ and $s = 3$.

TRY

a. Use the empirical rule to describe the distribution of heights for males.

b. The standard deviation for the overall distribution (combining females and males) was 4. Why would you expect it to be larger than the standard deviations for the separate male and female height distributions? Would you expect the overall distribution still to be unimodal?

2.52 Histograms and standard deviation The figure shows histograms for three samples, each with sample size $n = 100$.

a. Which sample has the (i) largest and (ii) smallest standard deviation?

b. To which sample(s) is the empirical rule relevant? Why?

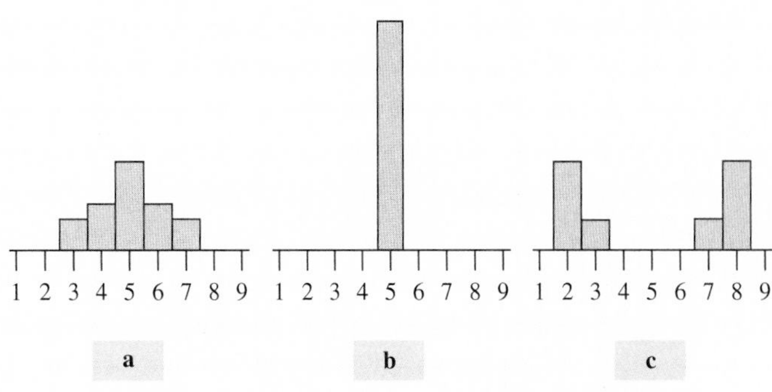

Histograms and relative sizes of standard deviations

2.53 Female strength The High School Female Athletes data file on the book's website has data for 57 female high school athletes on the maximum number of pounds they were able to bench press. The data are roughly bell shaped, with $\bar{x} = 79.9$ and $s = 13.3$. Use the empirical rule to describe the distribution.

2.54 Female body weight The College Athletes data file on the book's website has data for 64 female college athletes. The data on weight (in pounds) are roughly bell shaped, with $\bar{x} = 133$ and $s = 17$.

a. Give an interval within which about 95% of the weights fall.

b. Identify the weight of an athlete who is three standard deviations above the mean in this sample. Would this be a rather unusual observation? Why?

2.55 Shape of cigarette taxes A recent summary for the distribution of cigarette taxes (in cents) among the 50 states and Washington, D.C., in the United States reported $\bar{x} = 73$ and $s = 48$. Based on these values, do you think that this distribution is bell shaped? If so, why? If not, why not, and what shape would you expect?

2.56 Empirical rule and skewed, highly discrete distribution The table below shows data (from a 2004 Bureau of the Census report) on the number of times 20- to 24-year-old men have been married.

No. Times	Count	Percentage
0	8418	84.0
1	1594	15.9
2	10	0.1
Total	**10022**	**100.0**

a. Verify that the mean number of times men have been married is 0.16 and that the standard deviation is 0.37.

b. Find the actual percentages of observations within 1, 2, and 3 standard deviations of the mean. How do these compare to the percentages predicted by the empirical rule?

c. How do you explain the results in part b?

2.57 How much TV? The 2012 General Social Survey asked, "On the average day, about how many hours do you personally watch television?" Of 1298 responses, the mode was 2, the median was 2, the mean was 3.09, and the standard deviation was 2.87. Based on these statistics, what would you surmise about the shape of the distribution? Why? (*Source:* Data from CSM, UC Berkeley.)

2.58 How many friends? A recent General Social Survey asked respondents how many close friends they had. For a sample of 1467 people, the mean was 7.4 and the standard deviation was 11.0. The distribution had a median of 5 and a mode of 4. (*Source:* Data from CSM, UC Berkeley.)

a. Based on these statistics, what would you surmise about the shape of the distribution? Why?

b. Does the empirical rule apply to these data? Why or why not?

2.59 Judging skew using $\bar{x}$ and s If the largest observation is less than 1 standard deviation above the mean, then the distribution tends to be skewed to the left. If the smallest observation is less than 1 standard deviation below the mean, then the distribution tends to be skewed to the right. A professor examined the results of the first exam given in her statistics class. The scores were

35 59 70 73 75 81 84 86

The mean and standard deviation are 70.4 and 16.7. Using these, determine whether the distribution is either left or right skewed. Construct a dot plot to check.

2.60 Youth unemployment in the EU The Youth Unemployment data file on the book's website contains 2013 unemployment rates in the 28 EU countries for people between 15 and 24 years of age. (The data are also shown in Exercise 2.63). Using software,

a. Construct a graph to visualize the distribution of the unemployment rate.

b. Find the mean, median, and standard deviation.

c. Write a short paragraph summarizing the distribution of the youth unemployment rate, interpreting some of the above statistics in context.

2.61 Create data with a given standard deviation Use the Mean versus Median web app on the book's website to investigate how the standard deviation changes as the data change. When you start the app, you have a blank graph. Under "Options", you can request to show the standard deviation of the points you create by clicking in the graph.

a. Create 3 observations (by clicking in the graph) that have a mean of about 50 and a standard deviation of about 20. (Clicking on an existing point deletes it.)

b. Create 3 observations (click Refresh to clear the previous points) that have a mean of about 50 and a standard deviation of about 40.

c. Placing 4 values between 0 and 100, what is the largest standard deviation you can get? What are the values that have that standard deviation?

2.5 Using Measures of Position to Describe Variability

The mean and median describe the center of a distribution. The range and the standard deviation describe the variability of the distribution. We'll now learn about some other ways of describing a distribution using measures of **position**.

One type of measure of position tells us the point where a certain percentage of the data fall above or fall below that point. The median is an example. It specifies a location such that half the data fall below it and half fall above it. The range uses two other measures of position, the maximum value and the minimum value. Another type of measure of position tells us *how far* an observation falls from a particular point, such as the number of standard deviations an observation falls from the mean.

Measures of Position: The Quartiles and Other Percentiles

The median is a special case of a more general set of measures of position called **percentiles**.

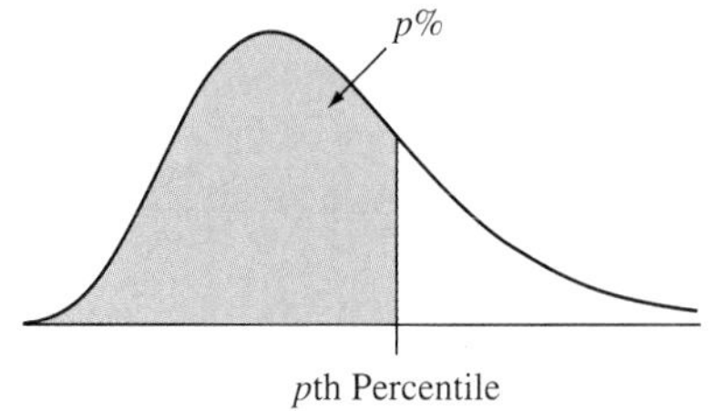

> **Percentile**
>
> The ***pth percentile*** is a value such that *p* percent of the observations fall below or at that value.

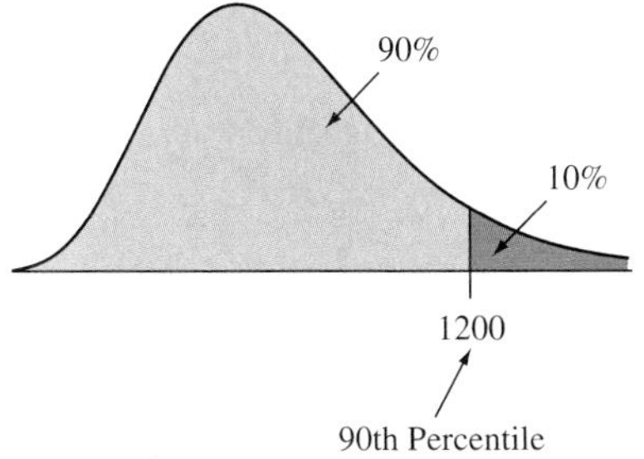

Suppose you're informed that your score of 1200 (out of 1600) on the SAT college entrance exam falls at the 90th percentile. Set $p = 90$ in this definition. Then, 90% of those who took the exam scored between the minimum score and 1200. Only 10% of the scores were higher than yours.

Substituting $p = 50$ in this definition gives the 50th percentile. For it, 50% of the observations fall below or at it and 50% above it. But this is simply the median. *The 50th percentile is usually referred to as the median.*

Three useful percentiles are the **quartiles**. The **first quartile** has $p = 25$, so it is the 25th percentile. Twenty-five percent of the data fall below it, 75% above it. The **second quartile** has $p = 50$, so it is the 50th percentile, which is the median. The **third quartile** has $p = 75$, so it is the 75th percentile. The highest 25% of the data fall above it. *The quartiles split the distribution into four parts, each containing one quarter (25%) of the observations.* See Figure 2.14.

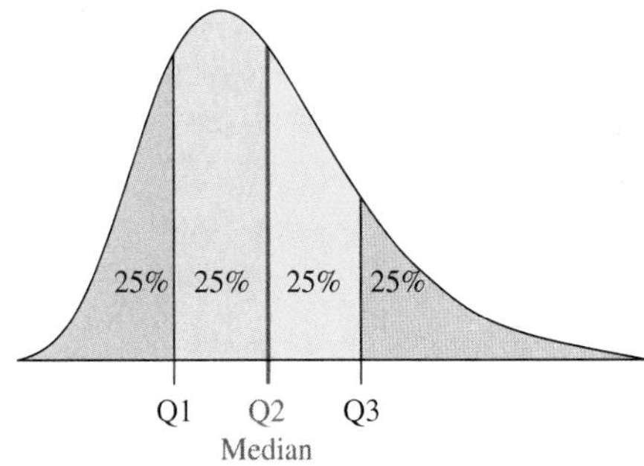

▲ **Figure 2.14 The Quartiles Split the Distribution Into Four Parts.** Twenty-five percent is below the first quartile (Q1), 25% is between the first quartile and the second quartile (the median, Q2), 25% is between the second quartile and the third quartile (Q3), and 25% is above the third quartile. **Question** Why is the second quartile also the median?

The quartiles are denoted by Q1 for the first quartile, Q2 for the second quartile, and Q3 for the third quartile. Notice that one quarter of the observations fall below Q1, two quarters (one half) fall below Q2 (the median), and three quarters fall below Q3.

SUMMARY: Finding Quartiles

- Arrange the data in order.
- Consider the median. This is the **second quartile, Q2**.
- Consider the lower half of the observations (excluding the median itself if *n* is odd). The median of these observations is the **first quartile, Q1**.
- Consider the upper half of the observations (excluding the median itself if *n* is odd). Their median is the **third quartile, Q3**.

Example 15

The quartiles ◄

Cereal Sodium Data

Picture the Scenario

Let's again consider the sodium values for the 20 breakfast cereals.

Questions to Explore

a. What are the quartiles for the 20 cereal sodium values?

b. Interpret the quartiles in the context of the cereal data.

Think it Through

a. From Table 2.3 the sodium values, arranged in ascending order, are

Q1 = 135									
0	50	70	100	**130**	**140**	140	150	160	**180**
180	180	190	200	**200**	**210**	210	220	290	340
Q3 = 205									

- The median of the 20 values is the average of the 10th and 11th observations, 180 and 180, which is **Q2** = **180 mg**.
- The first quartile Q1 is the median of the 10 smallest observations (in the top row), which is the average of 130 and 140, **Q1** = **135 mg**.
- The third quartile Q3 is the median of the 10 largest observations (in the bottom row), which is the average of 200 and 210, **Q3** = **205 mg**.

b. The quartiles tell you how the data split into four parts. The sodium values range from 0 mg to 135 mg for the first quarter, 135 mg to 180 mg for the second quarter, 180 mg to 205 mg for the third quarter, and 205 mg to 340 mg for the fourth quarter. So the smallest 25% of sodium values observed in our data are between 0 mg and 135 mg, and the largest 25% are between 205 mg and 340 mg. By dividing the distribution into four quarters, we see that some quarters of the distribution are more spread out than others.

Insight

The quartiles also give information about shape. The distance of 45 from the first quartile to the median exceeds the distance of 25 from the median to the third quartile. This commonly happens when the distribution is skewed to the left, as shown in the margin figure. Although each quarter of a distribution may span different lengths (indicating different amounts of variability within the quarters of the distribution), each quarter contains the same number (25%) of observations.

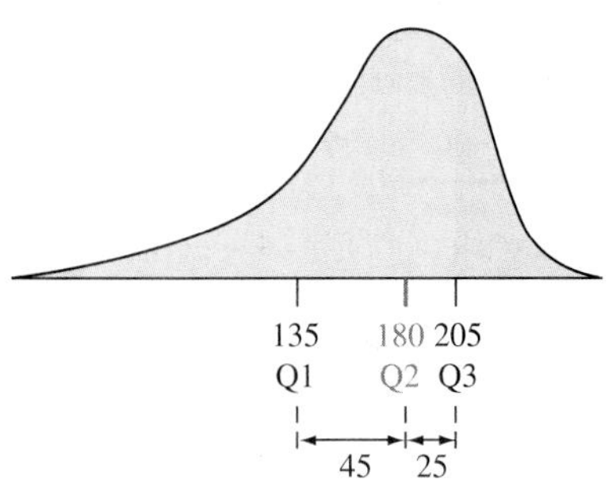

► ***Try Exercise 2.62***

In Practice Finding Percentiles Using Technology

Percentiles other than the quartiles are reported only for large data sets. Software can do the computational work for you, and we won't go through the details. Precise algorithms for the calculations use interpolations, and different software often uses slightly different rules. This is true even for the quartiles Q1 and Q3: Most software, but not all, does not use the median observation itself in the calculation when the number of observations *n* is odd.

Measuring Variability: The Interquartile Range

The quartiles are also used to define a measure of variability that is more resistant than the range and the standard deviation. This measure summarizes the range for the *middle half* of the data. The middle 50% of the observations fall between the first quartile and the third quartile—25% from Q1 to Q2 and 25% from Q2 to Q3. The distance from Q1 to Q3 is called the **interquartile range**, denoted by **IQR**.

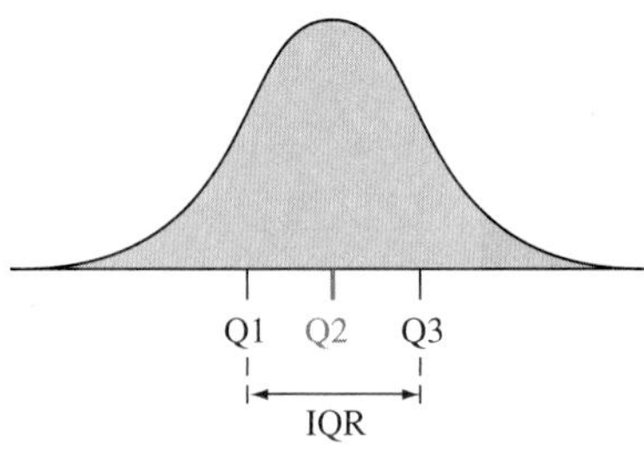

In Words

If the **interquartile range** of U.S. music teacher salaries equals $16,000, this tells us that the middle 50% of the distribution stretches over a distance of $16,000.

Interquartile Range (IQR)

The **interquartile range** is the distance between the third and first quartiles,

$$\text{IQR} = \text{Q3} - \text{Q1}$$

For instance, for the breakfast cereal sodium data, we just saw in Example 15 that

- Minimum value = 0
- First quartile Q1 = 135
- Median = 180
- Third quartile Q3 = 205
- Maximum value = 340

The range is 340 − 0 = 340. The interquartile range is Q3 − Q1 = 205 − 135 = 70. The middle 50% of sodium values stretches over a range of 70 mg.

As with the range and standard deviation s, the more variability in the observations, the larger the IQR tends to be. But unlike those measures, the IQR is not affected by any observations below the first quartile or above the third quartile. In other words, it is not affected by outliers. In contrast, the range depends solely on the minimum and the maximum values, the most extreme values, so the range changes as either extreme value changes. For example, if the highest sodium value were 1000 instead of 340, the range would change dramatically from 340 to 1000, but the IQR would not change at all. So, it's often better to use the IQR instead of the range or standard deviation to compare the variability for distributions that are very highly skewed or that have severe outliers.

Detecting Potential Outliers

Examining the data for unusual observations, such as outliers, is important in any statistical analysis. Is there a formula for flagging an observation as potentially being an outlier? One way uses the interquartile range.

The 1.5 × IQR Criterion for Identifying Potential Outliers

An observation is a potential outlier if it falls a distance of more than 1.5 × IQR below the first quartile or a distance of more than 1.5 × IQR above the third quartile.

Recall

Ordered Sodium Values

0 50...340

From Example 15, the breakfast cereal sodium data has Q1 = 135 and Q3 = 205. So, IQR = Q3 − Q1 = 205 − 135 = 70. For those data

1.5 × IQR = 1.5 × 70 = 105.

Q1 − 1.5 × IQR = 135 − 105 = 30 (lower boundary, potential outliers below),

and

Q3 + 1.5 × IQR = 205 + 105 = 310 (upper boundary, potential outliers above).

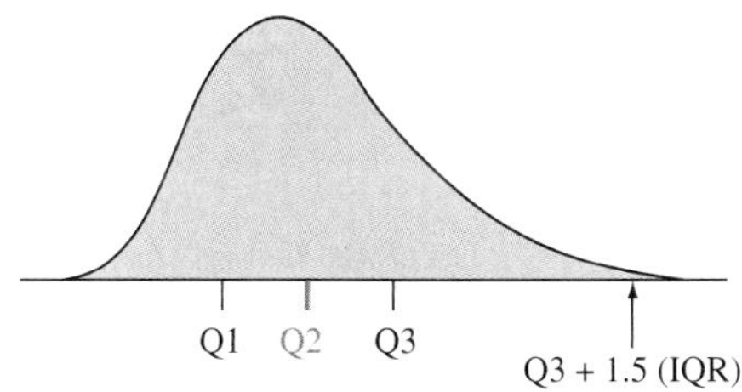

By the 1.5 × IQR criterion, observations below 30 or above 310 are potential outliers. The only observations below 30 or above 310 are the sodium values of 0 mg for Frosted Mini Wheats and 340 mg for Raisin Bran. These are the only potential outliers.

Why do we identify an observation as a *potential* outlier rather than calling it a *definite* outlier? When a distribution has a long tail, some observations may be more than 1.5 × IQR below the first quartile or above the third quartile even if they are not outliers, in the sense that they are not separated far from the bulk of the data. For instance, for a distribution with a long right tail, the largest observation may not be that far away from the remaining observations, and there isn't enough of a gap to call it an outlier.

The Box Plot: Graphing a Five-Number Summary of Positions

The quartiles and the maximum and minimum values are five numbers often used as a set to summarize positions that help describe center and variability of a distribution.

> **The Five-Number Summary of Positions**
>
> The five-number summary of a data set consists of the minimum value, first quartile Q1, median, third quartile Q3, and the maximum value.

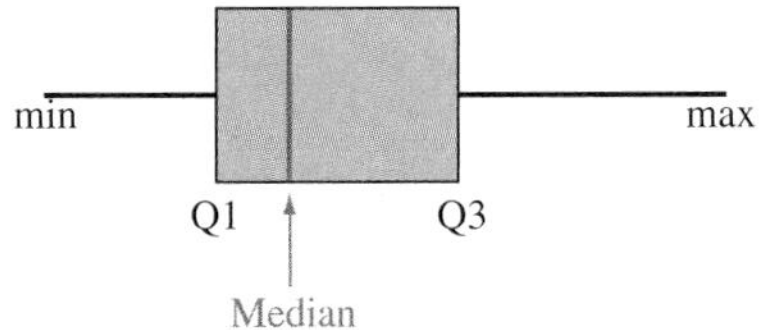

The **five-number summary** is the basis of a graphical display called the **box plot**. The **box** of a box plot contains the central 50% of the distribution, from the first quartile to the third quartile (see the margin figure). A line inside the box marks the median. The lines extending from each side of the box are called **whiskers**. These extend to show the stretch of the rest of the data, except for potential outliers, which are shown separately.

> **SUMMARY: Constructing a Box Plot**
>
> - A **box** goes from the lower quartile Q1 to the upper quartile Q3.
> - A line is drawn inside the box at the median.
> - A line goes from the lower end of the box to the smallest observation that is not a potential outlier. A separate line goes from the upper end of the box to the largest observation that is not a potential outlier. These lines are called **whiskers**. The potential outliers (more than 1.5 IQR below the first quartile or above the third quartile) are shown separately with special symbols (such as a dot or a star).

Example 16

Box plot

Cereal Sodium Data

Picture the Scenario

Example 7 constructed a histogram for the cereal sodium values. That figure is shown again in the margin. Figure 2.15 shows a box plot for the sodium values. Labels are also given for the five-number summary of positions.

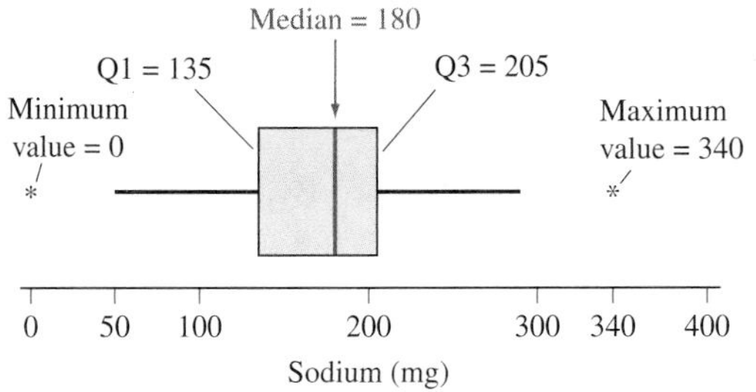

▲ **Figure 2.15 Box Plot and Five-Number Summary for 20 Breakfast Cereal Sodium Values.** The central box contains the middle 50% of the data. The line in the box marks the median. Whiskers extend from the box to the smallest and largest observations, which are not identified as potential outliers. Potential outliers are marked separately. The box plot can also be drawn vertically (see margin on the next page). **Question** Why is the left whisker drawn down only to 50 rather than to 0?

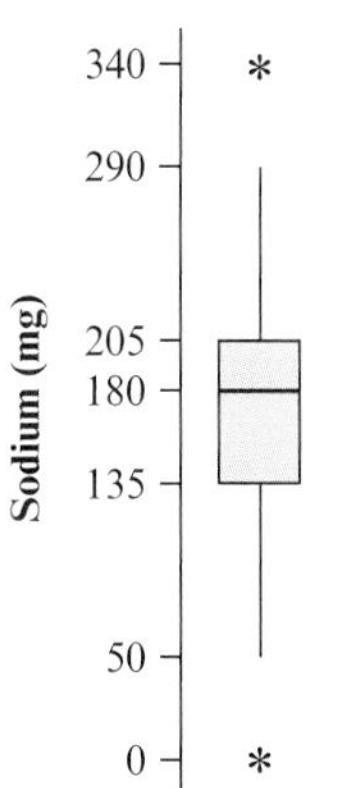

Vertically Drawn Box Plot of Sodium Data

Questions to Explore

a. Which, if any, values are considered outliers?

b. Explain how the box plot in Figure 2.15 was constructed and how to interpret it.

Think It Through

a. We can identify outliers using the 1.5 * IQR criterion. We know that Q1 = 135 mg and Q3 = 205 mg. Thus IQR = 205 − 135 = 70 mg, and the lower and upper boundaries are 135 − 1.5 * 70 = 30 mg and 205 + 1.5 * 70 = 310 mg, respectively. The sodium value of 0 mg for Frosted Mini Wheats is less than 30 mg, and the value of 340 mg for Raisin Bran is greater than 310 mg, so each of these values is considered an outlier.

b. The five-number summary of sodium values shown on the box plot (see the margin figure) is minimum = 0, Q1 = 135, median = 180, Q3 = 205, and maximum = 340. The middle 50% of the distribution of sodium values range from Q1 = 135 mg to Q3 = 205 mg, which are the two outer lines of the box. The median of 180 mg is indicated by the center line through the box. As we saw in part a, the 1.5 * IQR criterion flags the sodium values of 0 mg for Frosted Mini Wheats and 340 mg for Raisin Bran as outliers. These values are represented on the box plot as asterisks. The whisker extending from Q1 is drawn down to 50, which is the smallest observation that is not below the lower boundary of 30. The whisker extending from Q3 is drawn up to 290, which is the largest observation that is not above the upper boundary of 310.

Insight

Most software identifies observations that are more than 1.5 IQR from the quartiles by a symbol, such as *. (Some software uses a second symbol for observations more than 3 IQR from the quartiles.) The TI output for the box plot is shown in the margin. Why show potential outliers separately? One reason is to identify them for further study. Was the observation incorrectly recorded? Was that subject fundamentally different from the others in some way? Often it makes sense to repeat a statistical analysis without an outlier, to make sure the results are not overly sensitive to a single observation. For the cereal data, the sodium value of 0 (for Frosted Mini Wheats) was not incorrectly recorded. It is merely an unusually small value, relative to sodium levels for the other cereals. The sodium value of 340 for Raisin Bran was merely an unusually high value.

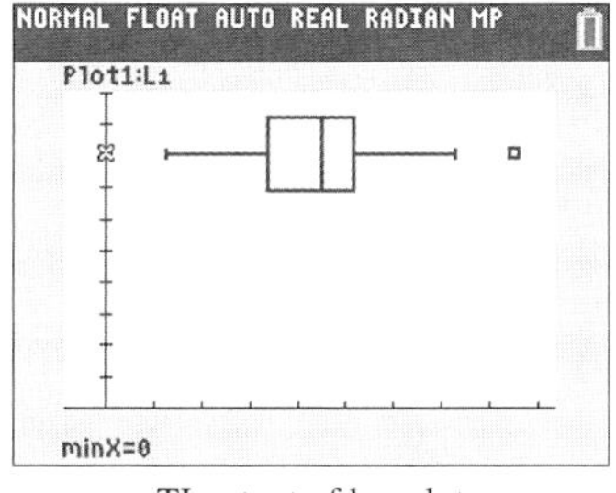

TI output of boxplot

▶ *Try Exercises 2.71 and 2.73*

Another reason for keeping outliers separate in a box plot is that they do not provide much information about the shape of the distribution, especially for large data sets. Some software can also provide a box plot that extends the whiskers to the minimum and maximum, even if outliers exist. However, an extreme value can then cause the box plot to give the impression of severe skew when actually the remaining observations are not at all skewed.

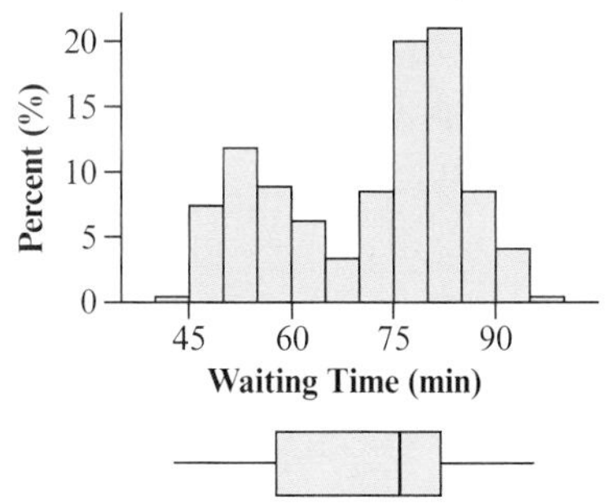

The Box Plot Compared with the Histogram

A box plot does not portray certain features of a distribution, such as distinct mounds and possible gaps, as clearly as a histogram. For example, the histogram and box plot in the margin refer to the same data, the waiting time between eruptions of the Old Faithful geyser in Yellowstone National Park. The histogram suggests that the distribution is bimodal (two distinct mounds), but we could not learn this from the box plot. This comparison shows that more than one type of graph may be needed to summarize a data set well.

A box plot does indicate skew from the relative lengths of the whiskers and the two parts of the box. The side with the larger part of the box and the longer whisker usually has skew in that direction. However, the box plot will not show us whether there is a large gap in the distribution contributing to the skew. But, as we've seen, **box plots are useful for identifying potential outliers.** We'll see next that they're also very useful for graphical comparisons of distributions.

In Practice

The histogram works best for larger data sets. For smaller data sets (those easily constructed by hand), the dot plot is a useful graph of the actual data to construct along with the box plot.

Side-by-Side Box Plots Help to Compare Groups

In Example 14, we looked at female college student heights from the Heights data file on the book's website. To compare heights for females and males, we could look at side-by-side box plots, as shown in Figure 2.16.

The side-by-side comparison immediately shows that generally males are taller than females. The median (the center line in a box) is approximately 71 inches for the males and 65 inches for the females. Although the centers differ, the variability of the middle 50% of the distribution is similar, as indicated by the width of the boxes (which is the IQR) being similar. Both samples have heights that are unusually short or tall, flagged as potential outliers. The upper 75% of the male heights are higher than the lower 75% of female heights. That is, 75% of the female heights fall below their third quartile, about 67 inches, whereas 75% of the male heights fall above their first quartile, about 69 inches. Although the histograms for the two genders more clearly show the shape (see margin figure), it is easier to describe key differences and similarities (such as the difference in center and the similarity in variability) between the distributions from the side-by-side box plots.

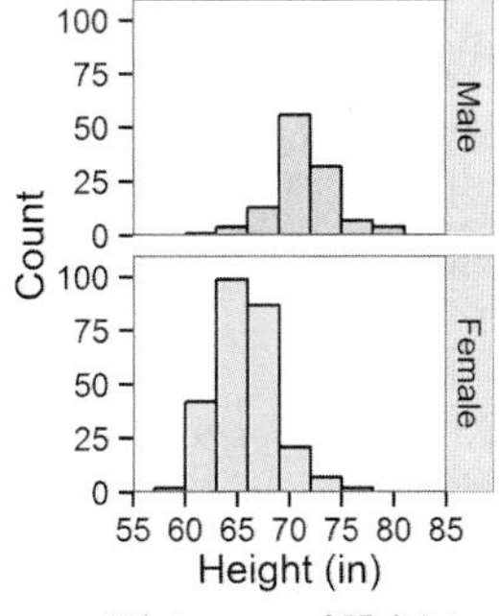

Histogram of Height for Males and Females

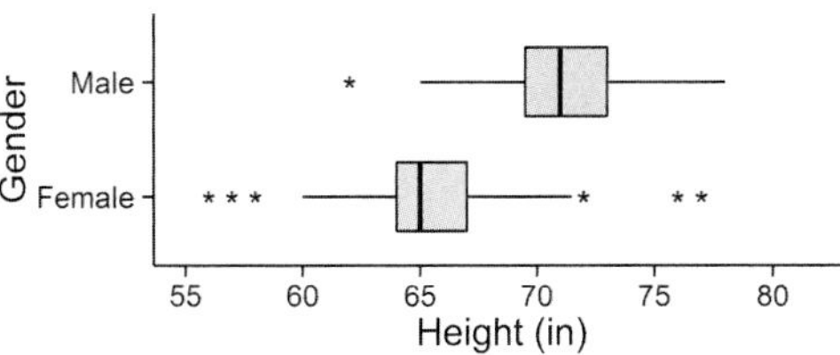

▲ **Figure 2.16 Box Plots of Male and Female College Student Heights.** The box plots use the same scale for height. **Question** What are approximate values of the quartiles for the two groups?

The *z*-Score Also Identifies Position and Potential Outliers

The empirical rule tells us that for a bell-shaped distribution, it is unusual for an observation to fall more than 3 standard deviations from the mean. An alternative criterion for identifying potential outliers uses the standard deviation.

- An observation in a bell-shaped distribution is regarded as a potential outlier if it falls more than 3 standard deviations from the mean.

Recall

For bell-shaped distributions, the interval $\bar{x} \pm 3s$ contains (almost) all observations. ◀

How do we know the number of standard deviations that an observation falls from the mean? When $\bar{x} = 84$ and $s = 16$, a value of 100 is 1 standard deviation above the mean because $(100 - 84) = 16$. Alternatively, $(100 - 84)/16 = 1$.

Taking the difference between an observation and the mean and dividing by the standard deviation tells us the number of standard deviations that the observation falls from the mean. This number is called the ***z*-score**.

z-Score for an Observation

The ***z*-score** for an observation is the number of standard deviations that it falls from the mean. A positive *z*-score indicates the observation is above the mean. A negative *z*-score indicates the observation is below the mean. For sample data, the *z*-score is calculated as

$$z = \frac{\text{observation} - \text{mean}}{\text{standard deviation}}.$$

The *z*-score allows us to tell quickly how surprising or extreme an observation is. The *z*-score converts an observation (regardless of the observation's unit of measurement) to a common scale of measurement, which allows comparisons.

Example 17

Pollution Outliers

Picture the Scenario

Let's consider air pollution data for the European Union (EU). The Energy-EU data file[7] on the book's website contains data on per capita carbon-dioxide (CO_2) emissions, in metric tons, for the 28 nations in the EU. The mean was 7.9 and the standard deviation was 3.6. Figure 2.17 shows a box plot of the data; the histogram is shown in the margin. The maximum of 21.4, representing Luxembourg, is highlighted as a potential outlier.

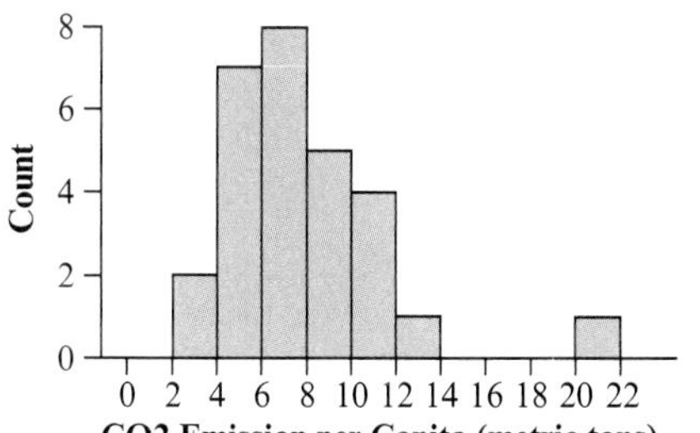

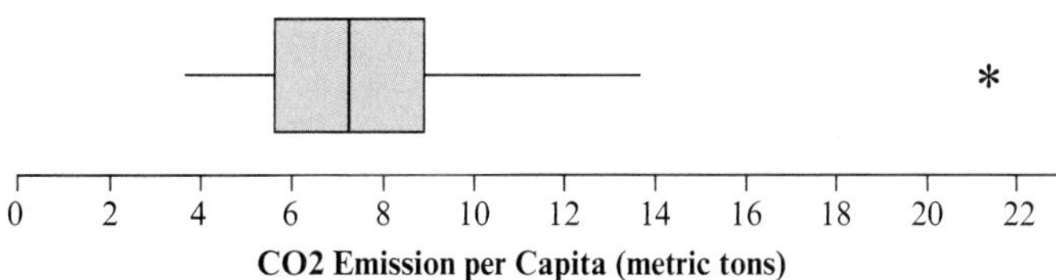

▲ **Figure 2.17** Box Plot of Carbon Dioxide Emissions for European Union Nations. **Question** Can you use this plot to approximate the five-number summary?

Questions to Explore

a. How many standard deviations from the mean was the CO_2 value of 21.4 for Luxembourg?

b. The CO_2 value for the United States was 16.9. According to the three standard deviation criterion, is the United States an outlier on carbon dioxide emissions relative to the EU?

Think It Through

a. Since $\bar{x} = 7.9$ and $s = 3.6$, the *z*-score for the observation of 21.4 is

$$z = \frac{\text{observation} - \text{mean}}{\text{standard deviation}} = \frac{21.4 - 7.9}{3.6} = \frac{13.5}{3.6} = 3.75$$

The carbon dioxide emission (per capita) for Luxembourg is 3.75 standard deviations above the mean. By the 3 standard deviation criterion,

[7] *Source:* www.iea.org/stats/index.asp.

this is a potential outlier. Because it's well removed from the rest of the data, we'd regard it as an actual outlier. However, Luxembourg has only about 500,000 people, so in terms of the *amount* of pollution, it is not a major polluter in the EU.

b. The z-score for the CO_2 value of the United States is $z = (16.9 - 7.9)/3.6 = 2.5$. This value does not flag the United States as an oulier relative to EU nations in terms of per-capita emission. (If we considered total emission, the situation would be different.)

Insight

The z-scores of 3.75 and 2.5 are positive. This indicates that the observations are *above* the mean, because an observation above the mean has a positive z-score. In fact, these large positive z-scores tell us that Luxembourg and the United States have very high per capita CO_2 emissions compared to the other nations. The z-score is negative when the observation is *below* the mean. For instance, France has a CO_2 value of 5.6, which is below the mean of 7.9 and has a z-score of -0.64.

▶ ***Try Exercises 2.75 and 2.76***

2.5 Practicing the Basics

2.62 Vacation days *National Geographic Traveler* magazine recently presented data on the annual number of vacation days averaged by residents of eight countries. They reported 42 days for Italy, 37 for France, 35 for Germany, 34 for Brazil, 28 for Britain, 26 for Canada, 25 for Japan, and 13 for the United States.

TRY

a. Report the median.

b. By finding the median of the four values below the median, report the first quartile.

c. Find the third quartile.

d. Interpret the values found in parts a–c in the context of these data.

2.63 Youth unemployment In recent years, many European nations have suffered from relatively high youth unemployment. For the 28 EU nations, the table below shows the unemployment rate among 15- to 24-year-olds in 2013, also available as a file on the book's website. (*Source:* World Bank). If you are computing the statistics below by hand, it may be easier to arrange the data in increasing order and write them in 4 rows of 7 values each.

TECH

a. Find and interpret the second quartile (=median).

b. Find and interpret the first quartile (Q1).

c. Find and interpret the third quartile (Q3).

d. Will the 10th percentile be around the value of 6 or 16? Explain.

Belgium 8.4	Germany 5.3	Spain 26.4	Cyprus 15.9	Netherlands 6.7	Slovakia 14.2
Bulgaria 13.0	Estonia 8.6	France 10.3	Latvia 11.9	Austria 4.9	Finland 8.2
Czech Republic 7.0	Ireland 13.1	Croatia 17.2	Lithuania 11.8	Poland 10.3	Sweden 8.0
Denmark 7.0	Greece 27.3	Italy 12.2	Luxembourg 5.8	Portugal 16.5	United Kingdom 7.5
			Hungary 10.2	Romania 7.3	
			Malta 6.5	Slovenia 10.1	

2.64 Female strength The High School Female Athletes data file on the book's website has data for 57 high school female athletes on the maximum number of pounds they were able to bench press, which is a measure of strength. For these data, $\bar{x} = 79.9$, Q1 = 70, median = 80, Q3 = 90.

a. Interpret the quartiles.

b. Would you guess that the distribution is skewed or roughly symmetric? Why?

2.65 Female body weight The College Athletes data file on the book's website has data for 64 college female athletes. The data on weight (in pounds) has $\bar{x} = 133$, Q1 = 119, median = 131.5, Q3 = 144.

a. Interpret the quartiles.

b. Would you guess that the distribution is skewed or roughly symmetric? Why?

2.66 Ways to measure variability The standard deviation, the range, and the interquartile range (IQR) summarize the variability of the data.

a. Why is the standard deviation s usually preferred over the range?

b. Why is the IQR sometimes preferred to s?

c. What is an advantage of s over the IQR?

2.67 Variability of cigarette taxes Here's the five-number summary for the distribution of cigarette taxes (in cents) among the 50 states and Washington, D.C., in the United States.

$$\text{Minimum} = 2.5, \text{Q1} = 36, \text{Median} = 60,$$
$$\text{Q3} = 100, \text{Maximum} = 205$$

a. About what proportion of the states have cigarette taxes (i) greater than 36 cents and (ii) greater than $1?

b. Between which two values are the middle 50% of the observations found?

c. Find the interquartile range. Interpret it.

d. Based on the summary, do you think that this distribution was bell shaped? If so, why? If not, why not, and what shape would you expect?

2.68 Sick leave Exercise 2.46 showed data for a company that investigated the annual number of days of sick leave taken by its employees. The data are

0 0 4 0 0 0 6 0

a. The standard deviation is 2.4. Find and interpret the range.

b. The quartiles are Q1 = 0, median = 0, Q3 = 2. Find the interquartile range.

c. Suppose the 6 was incorrectly recorded and is supposed to be 60. The standard deviation is then 21.1 but the quartiles do not change. Redo parts a–c with the correct data and describe the effect of this outlier. Which measure of variability, the range, IQR, or standard deviation is least affected by the outlier? Why?

2.69 Infant mortality Africa The *Human Development Report 2006,* published by the United Nations, showed infant mortality rates (number of infant deaths per 1000 live births) by country. For Africa, some of the values reported were:

South Africa 54, Sudan 63, Ghana 68, Madagascar 76, Senegal 78, Zimbabwe 79, Uganda 80, Congo 81, Botswana 84, Kenya 96, Nigeria 101, Malawi 110, Mali 121, Angola 154.

a. Find the first quartile (Q1) and the third quartile (Q3).

b. Find the interquartile range (IQR). Interpret it.

2.70 Infant mortality Europe For Western Europe, the infant mortality rates reported by the *Human Development Report 2006* were:

Sweden 3, Finland 3, Spain 3, Belgium 4, Denmark 4, France 4, Germany 4, Greece 4, Italy 4, Norway 4, Portugal 4, Netherlands 5, Switzerland 5, UK 5.

Show that Q1 = Q2 = Q3 = 4. (The quartiles, like the median, are less useful when the data are highly discrete.)

2.71 TRY **Computer use** During a recent semester at the University of Florida, students having accounts on a mainframe computer had storage space use (in kilobytes) described by the five-number summary, minimum = 4, Q1 = 256, median = 530, Q3 = 1105, and maximum = 320,000.

a. Would you expect this distribution to be symmetric, skewed to the right, or skewed to the left? Explain.

b. Use the $1.5 \times \text{IQR}$ criterion to determine whether any potential outliers are present.

2.72 Central Park temperature distribution revisited Exercise 2.26 showed a histogram for the distribution of Central Park annual average temperatures. The box plot for these data is shown here.

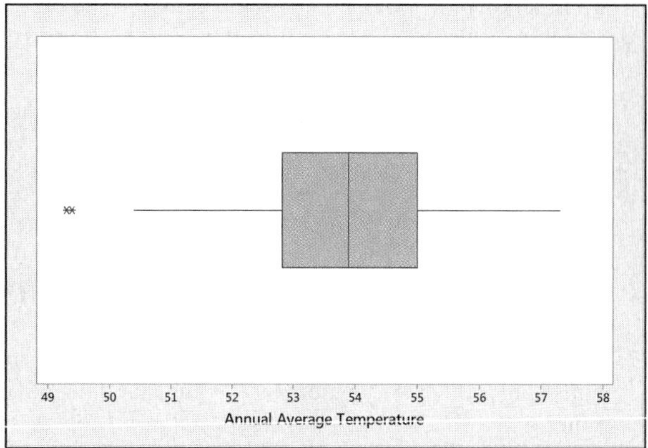

a. If this distribution is skewed, would you expect it to be skewed to the right or to the left? Explain.

b. Approximate each component of the five-number summary and interpret.

2.73 TRY **Box plot for exam** The scores on an exam have mean = 88, standard deviation = 10, minimum = 65, Q1 = 77, median = 85, Q3 = 91, maximum = 100. Sketch a box plot, labeling which of these values are used in the plot.

2.74 Public transportation Exercise 2.37 described a survey about how many miles per day employees of a company use public transportation. The sample values were:

0 0 4 0 0 0 10 0 6 0

a. Identify the five-number summary and sketch a box plot.

b. Explain why Q1 and the median share the same line in the box.

c. Why does the box plot not have a left whisker?

2.75 TRY **Energy statistics** The Energy Information Administration records per capita consumption of energy by country. The box plot below shows 2011 per capita energy consumption (in millions of BTUs) for 36 OECD countries, with a mean of 195 and a standard deviation of 120. Iceland had the largest per capita consumption at 665 million BTU.

a. Use the box plot to give approximate values for the five-number summary of energy consumption.

b. Italy had a per capita consumption of 139 million BTU. How many standard deviations from the mean was its consumption?

c. The United States was not included in the data, but its per capita consumption was 334 million BTU. Relative to the distribution for the included OECD nations, the United States is how many standard deviations from the mean?

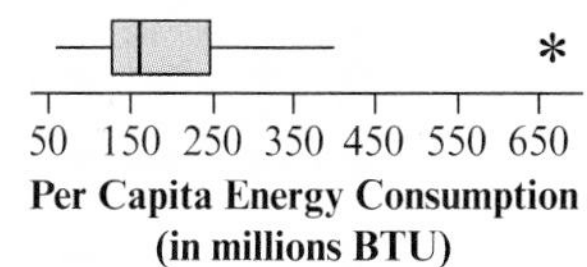

2.76 European Union youth unemployment rates The 2013 unemployment rates of countries in the European Union shown in Exercise 2.63 ranged from 4.9 to 27.3, with Q1 = 7.15, median = 10.15, Q3 = 13.05, a mean of 11.1, and a standard deviation of 5.6.

TRY

a. In a box plot, what would be the values at the outer edges of the box, and what would be the values to which the whiskers extend?

b. Which two countries will show up as outliers in the box plot? Why?

c. Greece had the highest unemployment rate of 27.3. Is it an outlier according to the 3 standard deviation criterion? Explain.

d. What unemployment value for a country would have a z-score equal to 0?

2.77 Air pollution Example 17 discussed EU carbon dioxide emissions, which had a mean of 7.9 and standard deviation of 3.6.

a. Finland's observation was 11.5. Find its z-score and interpret.

b. Sweden's observation was 5.6. Find its z-score, and interpret.

c. The UK's observation was 7.9. Find the z-score and interpret.

2.78 Female heights For the 261 female heights shown in the box plot in Figure 2.16, the mean was 65.3 inches and the standard deviation was 3.0 inches. The shortest person in this sample had a height of 56 inches.

a. Find the z-score for the height of 56 inches.

b. What does the negative sign for the z-score represent?

c. Is this observation a potential outlier according to the 3 standard deviation distance criterion? Explain.

2.79 Hamburger sales The manager of a fast-food restaurant records each day for a year the amount of money received from sales of food that day. Using software, he finds a bell-shaped histogram with a mean of \$1165 and a standard deviation of \$220. Today the sales equaled \$2000. Is this an unusually good day? Answer by providing statistical justification.

2.80 Florida students again Refer to the FL Student Survey data set on the book's website and the data on weekly hours of TV watching.

TECH

a. Use software to construct a box plot. Interpret the information on the plot and use it to describe the shape of the distribution.

b. Using a criterion for outliers, investigate whether there are any potential outliers.

2.81 Females or males watch more TV? Refer to the previous exercise. Suppose you wanted to compare TV watching by males and females. Construct a side-by-side box plot to do this. Interpret.

TECH

2.82 CO_2 comparison The vertical side-by-side box plots shown below compare per capita carbon dioxide emissions in 2011 for many Central and South American and European nations. (Data available on the book's website. *Source:* www.eia.gov)

a. Give the approximate value of carbon dioxide emissions for the outliers shown. (There are actually two outliers.)

b. What shape would you predict for the distribution in Central and South America? Why?

c. Summarize how the carbon dioxide emissions compare between the two regions.

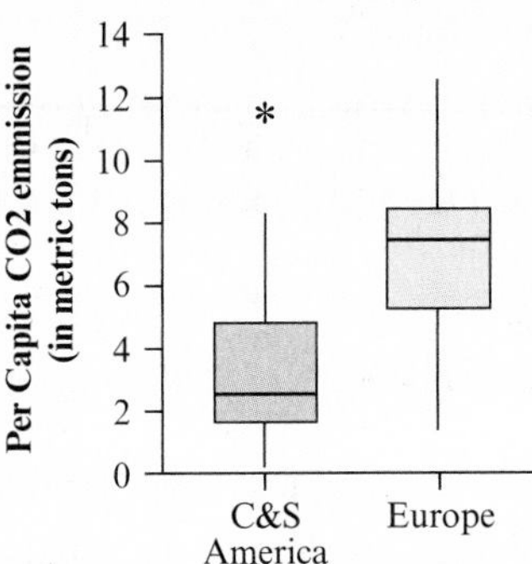

2.6 Recognizing and Avoiding Misuses of Graphical Summaries

In this chapter, we've learned how to describe data. We've learned that the nature of the data affects how we can effectively describe them. For example, if a distribution is very highly skewed or has extreme outliers, we've seen that some numerical summaries, such as the mean, can be misleading.

To illustrate, during a recent semester at the University of Florida, students with accounts on a mainframe computer had storage space usage (in kilobytes) described by the five-number summary:

$$\text{minimum} = 4, \text{Q1} = 256, \text{median} = 530, \text{Q3} = 1105, \text{maximum} = 320{,}000$$

and by the mean of 1921 and standard deviation of 11,495. The maximum value was an extreme outlier. You can see what a strong effect that outlier had on the mean and standard deviation. For these data, it's misleading to use these two values to summarize the distribution. To finish this chapter, let's look at how we also need to be on the lookout for misleading graphical summaries.

Beware of Poor Graphs

With modern computer-graphic capabilities, web sites, newspapers, and other periodicals use graphs in an increasing variety of ways to portray information. The graphs are not always well designed, however, and you should look at them skeptically.

Example 18

Misleading graphical summaries

Recruiting STEM Majors

Picture the Scenario

Look at Figure 2.18. According to the title and the two-sentence caption, the graph is intended to display how total enrollment has risen at a United States (U.S.) university in recent years while the number of STEM (science, technology, engineering, and mathematics) students has "dipped just about every year." A graphic designer used a software program to construct a graph for use in a local newspaper. The Sunday headline story was about the decline of STEM majors. The graph is a time plot showing the enrollment between 2004 and 2012, using outlined human figures to portray total enrollment and blue human figures to portray STEM enrollment.

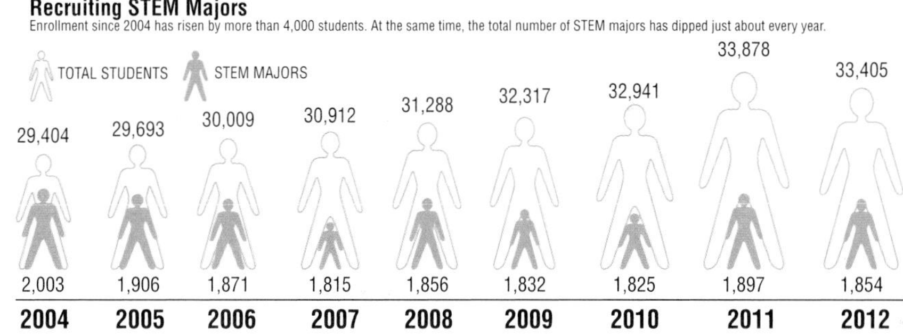

▲ **Figure 2.18** An Example of a Poor Graph. **Question** What's misleading about the way the data are presented?

Questions to Explore

a. Do the heights of the human figures accurately represent the counts? Are the areas of the figures in accurate proportions to each other? Answer by first comparing the two observations for 2004 and then by comparing those for 2004 to those for 2012.

b. Is an axis shown and labeled as a reference line for the enrollments displayed?

c. What other design problems do you see?

Think It Through

a. In the year 2004, the number of STEM majors (2003) is about 7% of the total of 29,404. However, the height of the number of STEM majors figure is about 2/3 the height of the total enrollment figure. The graphs also mislead by using different widths for the figures. Compare, for instance, the figures for total enrollment in 2004 and 2012. The total enrollments are not nearly as different as the areas taken up by the figures make them appear.

b. Figure 2.18 does not provide a vertical axis, much less a labeling of that axis. It is not clear whether the counts are supposed to be represented by the heights or by the areas of the human figures.

c. It is better to put the figures next to each other rather than to overlay the two sets of figures as was done here. The use of solid blue figures and outlined figures can easily distort your perception of the graph. Although it might not have been deliberate, the design obscures the data.

Insight

The intent of Figure 2.18 was to provide an intriguing visual display that quickly tells the story of the newspaper article. However, deviating from standard graphs gave a misleading representation of the data.

▶ *Try Exercise 2.86*

SUMMARY: Guidelines For Constructing Effective Graphs

- Label both axes and provide a heading to make clear what the graph is intended to portray. (Figure 2.18 does not even provide a vertical axis.)
- To help our eyes visually compare relative sizes accurately, the vertical axis should usually start at 0.
- Be cautious in using figures, such as people, in place of the usual bars or points. It can make a graph more attractive, but it is easy to get the relative percentages that the figures represent incorrect.
- It can be difficult to portray more than one group on a single graph when the variable values differ greatly. (In Figure 2.18, one frequency is very small compared to the other.) Consider instead using separate graphs or plotting relative sizes such as ratios or percentages.

Example 19

Improving graphical summaries

Recruiting STEM Majors

Picture the Scenario

Let's look at Figure 2.18 again—because it's such a good example of how things can go wrong. Suppose the newspaper asks you to repair the graph, providing an accurate representation of the data.

Questions to Explore

a. Show a better way to graphically portray the same information about the enrollment counts in Figure 2.18.

b. Describe two alternative ways to portray the data that more clearly show the number of STEM majors relative to the size of the student body over time.

Think It Through

a. Because the caption of Figure 2.18 indicates that counts are the desired data display, we can construct a time plot showing total and STEM major enrollments on the same scale. Figure 2.19 shows this revised graph. This time plot clearly labels the horizontal and vertical axes. There is the natural reference starting point of 0 for the vertical axis, allowing for better relative comparison of the two groups. We can see that the STEM major enrollment is a small part of the total enrollment. Between 2004 and 2012, there's been some tendency upward in the total enrollment, with relatively little change in the STEM major enrollment.

b. Figure 2.19 is better than Figure 2.18 but is not ideal. Any trend that may be there for STEM majors is not clear because their counts are small compared to the total enrollment counts. Given that both the total and the STEM major counts vary from year to year, it's more meaningful to look at the STEM major *percentage* of the student body and plot that over time. See Exercise 2.85, which shows that this percentage went down from 2004 to 2012.

Even if we plot the counts, as in Figure 2.19, it may be better to show a separate plot on its own scale for the STEM major counts. Or, in a single graph, rather than comparing the STEM major counts to the *total* enrollment (which contains the STEM majors group), it may be more meaningful to compare them to the *rest* of the enrollment, that is, the total enrollment minus the number of STEM majors.

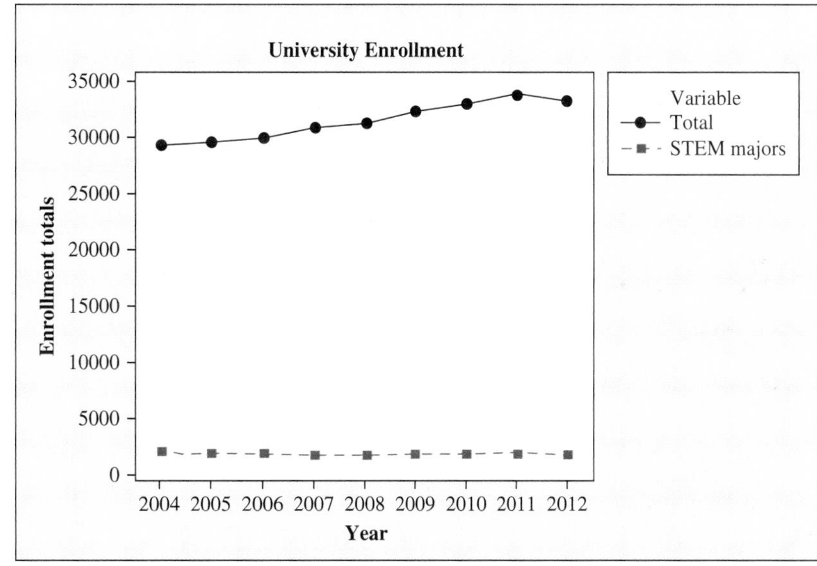

▲ **Figure 2.19** A Better Graph for the Data in Figure 2.18. **Question** What trends do you see in the enrollments from 2004 to 2012?

Insight

In constructing graphs, strive for clarity and simplicity. Many books have been written in recent years, showing innovative ways to portray information clearly in graphs. Examples are *The Visual Display of Quantitative Information* and *Envisioning Information*, by Edward Tufte (Graphics Press).

► ***Try Exercise 2.85***

When you plan to summarize data by graphical and numerical descriptive statistics, think about questions such as the following: What story are you attempting to convey with the data? Which graphical display and numerical summaries will most clearly and accurately convey this story?

John Tukey

On the Shoulders of...John Tukey

"The best thing about being a statistician is that you get to play in everyone's backyard."

—John Tukey (1915–2000)

In the 1960s, John Tukey of Princeton University was concerned that statisticians were putting too much emphasis on complex data analyses and ignoring simpler ways to examine and learn from the data. Tukey developed new descriptive methods, under the title of **exploratory data analysis (EDA)**. These methods make few assumptions about the structure of the data and emphasize data display and ways of searching for patterns and deviations from those patterns. Two graphical tools that Tukey invented were the stem-and-leaf plot and the box plot.

Initially, few statisticians promoted EDA. However, in recent years, some EDA methods have become common tools for data analysis. Part of this acceptance has been inspired by the availability of computer software and calculators that can implement some of Tukey's methods more easily.

Tukey's work illustrates that statistics is an evolving discipline. Almost all of the statistical methods used today were developed in the past century, and new methods continue to be created, largely because of increasing computer power.

2.6 Practicing the Basics

2.83 Great pay (on the average) The six full-time employees of Linda's Tanning Salon near campus had annual incomes last year of \$8900, \$9200, \$9200, \$9300, \$9500, \$9800. Linda herself made \$250,000.

a. For the seven annual incomes at Linda's Salon, report the mean and median.

b. Why is it misleading for Linda to boast to her friends that the average salary at her business is more than \$40,000?

2.84 Market share for food sales The pie chart shown was displayed in an article in *The Scotsman* newspaper (January 15, 2005) to show the market share of different supermarkets in Scotland.

a. Pie charts can be tricky to draw correctly. Identify two problems with this chart.

b. From looking at the graph without inspecting the percentages, would it be easier to identify the mode using this graph or using a bar graph? Why?

Market Share of Scottish Supermarket Chain

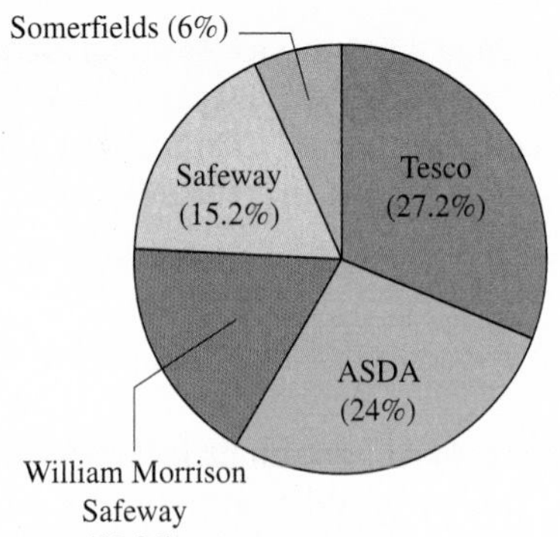

Source: Copyright The Scotsman Publications, Ltd.

2.85 Enrollment trends TRY TECH Examples 18 and 19 presented graphs showing the total student enrollment at a U.S. university between 2004 and 2012 and the data for STEM major enrollment during that same time period. The data are repeated here.

Enrollment at the U.S. University		
Year	**Total Students**	**STEM Majors**
2004	29,404	2,003
2005	29,693	1,906
2006	30,009	1,871
2007	30,912	1,815
2008	31,288	1,856
2009	32,317	1,832
2010	32,941	1,825
2011	33,878	1,897
2012	33,405	1,854

a. Construct a graph for only STEM major enrollments over this period. Describe the trend in these enrollment counts.

b. Find the percentage of enrolled students each year who are STEM majors and construct a time plot of the percentages.

c. Summarize what the graphs constructed in parts a and b tell you that you could not learn from Figures 2.18 and 2.19 in Examples 18 and 19.

2.86 Terrorism and war in Iraq TRY In 2004, a college newspaper reported results of a survey of students taken on campus. One question asked was, "Do you think going to war with Iraq has made Americans safer from terrorism, or not?" The figure shows the way the magazine reported results.

a. Explain what's wrong with the way this bar chart was constructed.

b. Explain why you would not see this error made with a pie chart.

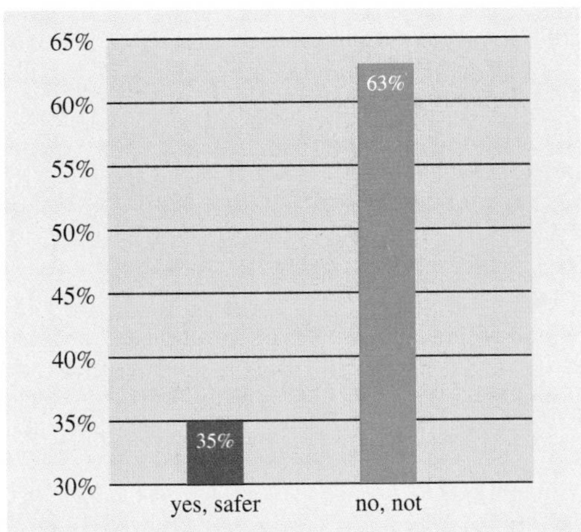

2.87 BBC license fee Explain what is wrong with the time plot shown of the annual license fee paid by British subjects for watching BBC programs. *(Source: Evening Standard*, November 29, 2006.)

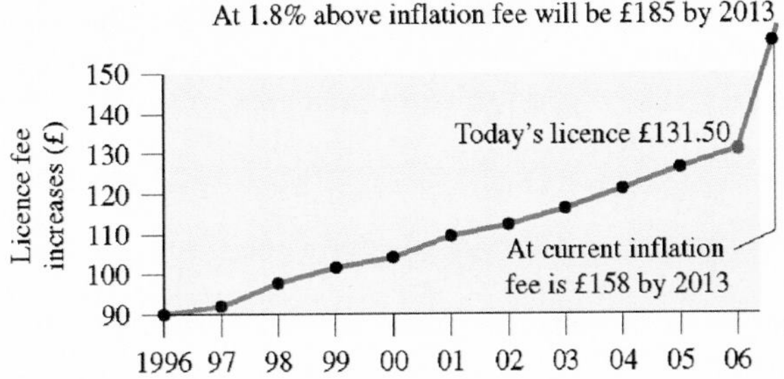

2.88 Federal government spending Explain what is wrong with the following pie chart, which depicts the federal government breakdown by category for 2010.

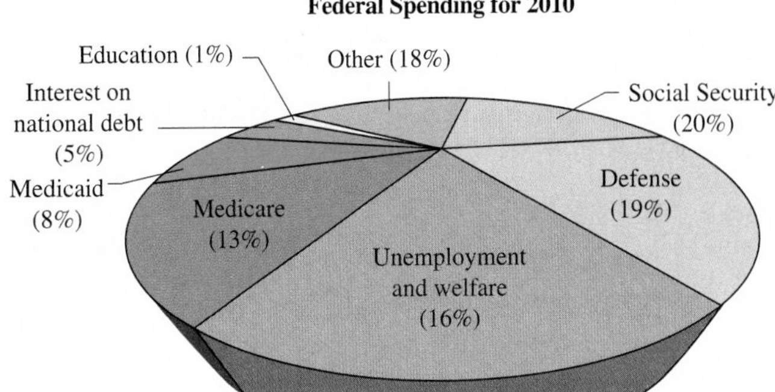

Source: www.gpoaccess.gov/usbudget/fy10.

2.89 Bad graph Search some publications and find an example of a graph that violates at least one of the principles for constructing good graphs. Summarize what's wrong with the graph and explain how it could be improved.

Chapter Review

ANSWERS TO THE CHAPTER FIGURE QUESTIONS

Figure 2.1 It is not always clear exactly what portion or percentage of a circle the slice represents, especially when a pie has many slices. Also, some slices may be representing close to the same percentage of the circle; thus, it is not clear which is larger or smaller.

Figure 2.2 Ordering the bars from largest to smallest immediately shows the (few) categories that are the most frequent. It also shows how rapid the heights of the bars decrease.

Figure 2.3 The number of dots above a value on the number line represents the frequency of occurrence of that value.

Figure 2.4 There's no leaf if there's no observation having that stem.

Figure 2.7 The direction of the longer tail indicates the direction of the skew.

Figure 2.8 The annual average temperatures are tending to increase over time.

Figure 2.9 The mean is pulled in the direction of the longer tail since extreme observations affect the balance point of the distribution. The median is not affected by the size of the observation.

Figure 2.10 The range would change from \$10,000 to \$65,000.

Figure 2.11 A deviation is positive when the observation falls above the mean and negative when the observation falls below the mean.

Figure 2.12 Since about 95% of the data fall within 2 standard deviations of the mean, about 100% − 95% = 5% fall more than 2 standard deviations from the mean.

Figure 2.13 The shape is approximately bell shaped. The center appears to be around 66 inches. The heights range from 56 to 77 inches.

Figure 2.14 The second quartile has two quarters (25% and 25%) of the data below it. Therefore, Q2 is the median since 50% of the data falls below the median.

Figure 2.15 The left whisker is drawn only to 50 because the next lowest sodium value, which is 0, is identified as a potential outlier.

Figure 2.16 The quartiles are about Q1 = 69, Q2 = 71, and Q3 = 73 for males and Q1 = 64, Q2 = 65, and Q3 = 67 for females.

Figure 2.17 Yes. The left whisker extends to the minimum (about 3.5), the left side of the box is at Q1 (about 5.5), the line inside the box is at the median (about 7), the right side of the box is at Q3 (about 9), and the outlier identified with a star is at the maximum (about 21).

Figure 2.18 Neither the height nor the area of the human figures accurately represents the frequencies reported.

Figure 2.19 The total enrollment increases until 2011. The STEM enrollment seems to be constant, but it would be better to plot STEM enrollments separately on a smaller scale.

CHAPTER SUMMARY

This chapter introduced **descriptive statistics**—graphical and numerical ways of **describing** data. The characteristics of interest that we measure are called **variables**, because values on them vary from subject to subject.

- A **categorical variable** has observations that fall into one of a set of categories.
- A **quantitative variable** takes numerical values that represent different magnitudes of the variable.
- A quantitative variable is **discrete** if it has separate possible values, such as the integers 0, 1, 2,... for a variable expressed as "the number of..." It is **continuous** if its possible values form an interval.

When we explore a variable, we are interested in its **distribution** (i.e., how the observations are distributed across the range of possible values). Distributions are described through graphs and tables. For categorical variables, we construct a **frequency table** showing the (relative) frequencies of observations in each category and mention the categories with the highest frequencies. For quantitative variables, frequency tables are obtained by partitioning the range into intervals. Key features to describe for quantitative variables are the **shape** (number of distinct mounds, symmetry or skew, outliers), **center**, and **variability**. *No description of a variable is complete without showing a graphical representation of its distribution through an appropriate* ***graph.***

Overview of Graphical Methods

- For categorical variables, data are displayed using **pie charts** and **bar graphs**. Bar graphs provide more flexibility and make it easier to compare categories having similar percentages.
- For quantitative variables, a **histogram** is a graph of a frequency table. It displays bars that specify frequencies or relative frequencies (percentages) for possible values or intervals of possible values. The **stem-and-leaf plot** (a vertical line dividing the final digit, the leaf, from the stem) and **dot plot** (dots above the number line) show the individual observations. They are useful for small data sets. These three graphs all show shape, such as whether the distribution is approximately bell shaped, skewed to the right (longer tail pointing to the right), or skewed to the left.
- The **box plot** has a box drawn between the first quartile and third quartile, with a line drawn in the box at the median. It has whiskers that extend to the minimum and maximum values, except for potential **outliers**. An **outlier** is an extreme value falling far below or above the bulk of the data.
- A **time plot** graphically displays observations for a variable measured over time. This plot can visually show **trends** over time.

Overview of Measures of the Center and of Position

Measures of the center attempt to describe a typical or representative observation.

- The **mean** is the sum of the observations divided by the number of observations. It is the balance point of the data.
- The **median** divides the ordered data set into two parts of equal numbers of observations, half below and half above that point. The median is the 50th percentile (second quartile). It is a more representative summary than the mean when the data are highly skewed and is resistant against outliers.
- The lower quarter of the observations fall below the **first quartile (Q1)**, and the upper quarter fall above the **third quartile (Q3)**. These are the 25th percentile and 75th percentile. These quartiles and the median split the data into four equal parts.

Overview of Measures of Variability

Measures of variability describe the variability of the observations.

- The **range** is the difference between the largest and smallest observations.
- The **deviation** of an observation x from the mean is $x - \bar{x}$. The **variance** is an average of the squared deviations. Its square root, the **standard deviation**, is more useful, describing a typical distance from the mean.
- The **empirical rule** states that for a bell-shaped distribution:

  About 68% of the data fall within 1 standard deviation of the mean, $\bar{x} \pm s$.

  About 95% of the data fall within 2 standard deviations, $\bar{x} \pm 2s$.

  Nearly all the data fall within 3 standard deviations, $\bar{x} \pm 3s$.
- The **interquartile range (IQR)** is the difference between the third and first quartiles, which span the middle 50% of the data in a distribution. It is more **resistant** than the range and standard deviation, being unaffected by extreme observations.
- An observation is a potential outlier if it falls (a) more than 1.5 × IQR below Q1 or more than 1.5 × IQR above Q3, or (b) more than 3 standard deviations from the mean. The ***z*-score** is the number of standard deviations that an observation falls from the mean.

SUMMARY OF NOTATION

Mean $\bar{x} = \frac{\Sigma x}{n}$ where x denotes the variable, n is the sample size, and Σ indicates to sum

Standard deviation $s = \sqrt{\frac{\Sigma(x - \bar{x})^2}{n - 1}}$

$z\text{-score} = \frac{\text{observed value} - \text{mean}}{\text{standard deviation}}$

CHAPTER PROBLEMS

Practicing the Basics

2.90 Categorical or quantitative? Identify each of the following variables as categorical or quantitative.

- **a.** Number of children in family
- **b.** Amount of time in football game before first points scored
- **c.** College major (English, history, chemistry,...)
- **d.** Type of music (rock, jazz, classical, folk, other)

2.91 Continuous or discrete? Which of the following variables are continuous, when the measurements are as precise as possible?

- **a.** Age of mother
- **b.** Number of children in a family
- **c.** Cooking time for preparing dinner
- **d.** Latitude and longitude of a city
- **e.** Population size of a city

2.92 Young non-citizens in the U.S. The table shows the number of 18- to 24-year-old noncitizens living in the United States between 2010 and 2012.

Noncitizens aged 18 to 24 in the United States

Region of Birth	Number (in Thousands)
Africa	115
Asia	590
Europe	148
Latin America & Caribbean	1,666
Other	49
Total	**2,568**

Source: www.census.gov

- **a.** Is Region of Birth quantitative or categorical? Show how to summarize results by adding a column of percentages to the table.
- **b.** Which of the following is a sensible numerical summary for these data: Mode (or modal category), mean, median? Explain, and report whichever is/are sensible.
- **c.** How would you order the Region of Birth categories for a Pareto chart? What's its advantage over the ordinary bar graph?

2.93 Cool in China A recent survey[8] asked 1200 university students in China to pick the personality trait that most defines a person as "cool." The possible responses allowed, and the percentage making each, were individualistic and innovative (47%), stylish (13.5%), dynamic and capable (9.5%), easygoing and relaxed (7.5%), other (22.5%).

- **a.** Identify the variable being measured.
- **b.** Classify the variable as categorical or quantitative.
- **c.** Which of the following methods could you use to describe these data: (i) bar chart, (ii) dot plot, (iii) box plot, (iv) median, (v) mean, (vi) mode (or modal category), (vii) IQR, (viii) standard deviation?

2.94 Chad voting problems The 2000 U.S. presidential election had various problems in Florida. One was overvotes—people mistakenly voting for more than one presidential candidate. (There were multiple minor-party candidates.) There were 110,000 overvote ballots, with Al Gore marked on 84,197 and George W. Bush on 37,731. These ballots were disqualified. Was overvoting related to the design of the ballot? The figure shows MINITAB dot plots of the overvote percentages for 65 Florida counties organized by the type of voting machine—optical scanning, Votomatic (voters manually punch out chads), and Datavote (voter presses a lever that punches out the chad mechanically)—and the number of columns on the ballot (1 or 2).

- **a.** The overvote was highest (11.6%) in Gadsden County. Identify the number of columns and the method of registering the vote for that county.
- **b.** Of the six ballot type and method combinations, which two seemed to perform best in terms of having relatively low percentages of overvotes?
- **c.** How might these data be summarized further by a bar graph with six bars?

Overvote Percentages by Number of Columns on Ballot and Method of Voting

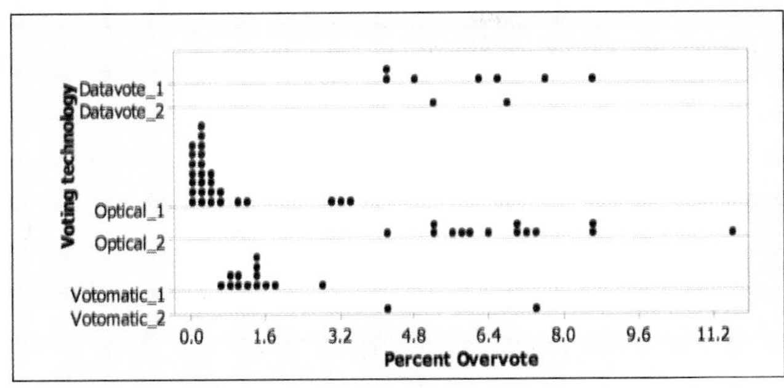

Source: A. Agresti and B. Presnell, *Statistical Science*, vol. 17, pp. 1–5, 2002.

[8]*Source:* Public relations firm Hill & Knowlton, as reported by *Time magazine.*

2.95 Number of children For the question "How many children have you ever had?" in the 2010 General Social Survey, the results were

No. children	0	1	2	3	4	5	6	7	8+
Count	562	332	528	329	144	61	35	18	32

a. Which is the most appropriate graph to display the data—dot plot, stem-and-leaf plot, or histogram? Why?

b. Based on sketching or using software to construct the graph, characterize this distribution as skewed to the left, skewed to the right, or symmetric. Explain.

2.96 Longevity The Animals data set on the book's website has data on the average longevity (measured in years) for 21 animals.

TECH

a. Construct a stem-and-leaf plot of longevity

b. Construct a histogram of longevity.

c. Summarize what you see in the histogram or stem-and-leaf plot. (Most animals live to be how old? Is the distribution skewed?)

2.97 Newspaper reading Exercise 2.24 gave results for the number of times a week a person reads a daily newspaper for a sample of 36 students at the University of Georgia. The frequency table is shown below.

a. Construct a dot plot of the data.

b. Construct a stem-and-leaf plot of the data. Identify the stems and the leaves.

c. The mean is 3.94. Find the median.

d. Is the distribution skewed to the left, skewed to the right, or symmetric? Explain.

No. Times	Frequency
0	2
1	4
2	4
3	8
4	4
5	5
6	2
7	4
8	2
9	1

2.98 Match the histogram Match each lettered histogram with one of the following descriptions: Skewed to the left, bimodal, symmetric, skewed to the right.

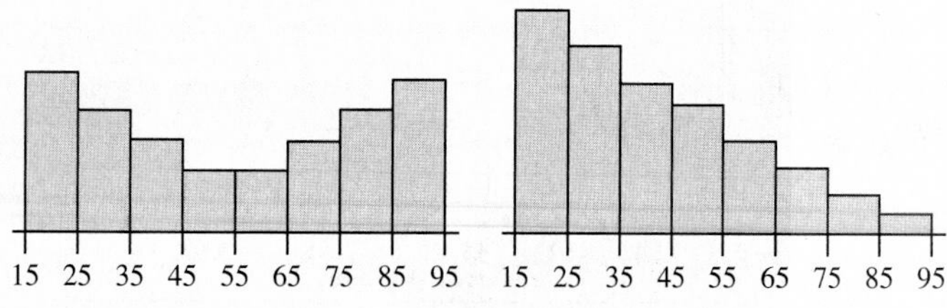

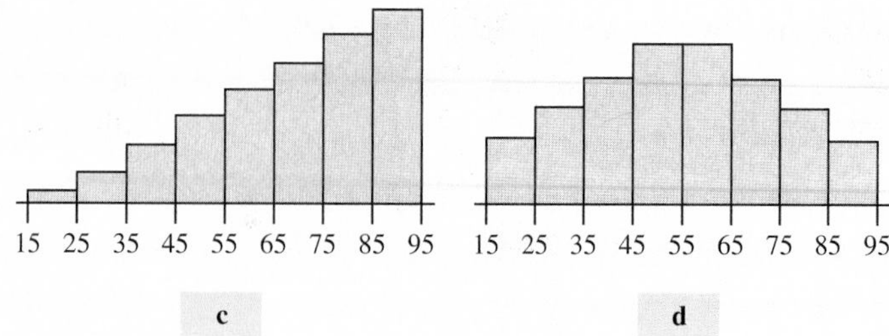

2.99 Sandwiches and protein Listed in the table below are the prices of six-inch Subway sandwiches at a particular franchise and the number of grams of protein contained in each sandwich.

Sandwich	Cost($)	Protein(g)
BLT	$2.99	17
Ham (Black Forest, without cheese)	$2.99	18
Oven Roasted Chicken	$3.49	23
Roast Beef	$3.69	26
Subway Club®	$3.89	26
Sweet Onion Chicken Teriyaki	$3.89	26
Turkey Breast	$3.49	18
Turkey Breast & Ham	$3.49	19
Veggie Delite®	$2.49	8
Cold Cut Combo	$2.99	21
Tuna	$3.10	21

a. Construct a stem-and-leaf plot of the protein amounts in the various sandwiches.

b. What is the advantage(s) of using the stem-and-leaf plot instead of a histogram?

c. Summarize your findings from these graphs.

2.100 Sandwiches and cost Refer to the previous exercise. Repeat parts a–c for the cost of the sandwiches. Summarize your findings.

2.101 What shape do you expect? For the following variables, indicate whether you would expect its histogram to be bell shaped, skewed to the right, or skewed to the left. Explain why.

a. Number of times arrested in past year

b. Time needed to complete difficult exam (maximum time is 1 hour)

c. Assessed value of house

d. Age at death

2.102 Sketch plots For each of the following, sketch roughly what you expect a histogram to look like and explain whether the mean or the median would be greater.

a. The selling price of new homes 2015.

b. The number of children ever born per woman age 40 or over

c. The score on an easy exam (mean $= 88$, standard deviation $= 10$, maximum $= 100$, minimum $= 50$)

d. Number of months in which subject drove a car last year

2.103 Median versus mean sales price of new homes The U.S. Bureau of the Census reported a median sales price of new houses sold in March 2014 of $290,000. Would you expect the mean sales price to have been higher or lower? Explain.

2.104 Household net worth A study reported that in 2007 the mean and median net worth of American families were $556,300 and $120,300, respectively.

a. Is the distribution of net worth for these families likely to be symmetric, skewed to the right, or skewed to the left? Explain.

b. During the Great Recession of 2008, many Americans lost wealth due to the large decline in values of assets such as homes and retirement savings. In 2009, mean and median net worth were reported as $434,782 and $91,304. Why do you think the difference in decline from 2007 to 2009 was larger for the mean than the median?

2.105 Golfers' gains During the 2010 Professional Golfers Association (PGA) season, 90 golfers earned at least $1 million in tournament prize money. Of those, 5 earned at least $4 million, 11 earned between $3 million and $4 million, 21 earned between $2 million and $3 million, and 53 earned between $1 million and $2 million.

a. Would the data for all 90 golfers be symmetric, skewed to the left, or skewed to the right?

b. Two measures of central tendency of the golfers' winnings were $2,090,012 and $1,646,853. Which do you think is the mean and which is the median?

2.106 Hiking In a guidebook about interesting hikes to take in national parks, each hike is classified as easy, medium, or hard and by the length of the hike (in miles). Which classification is quantitative and which is categorical?

2.107 Lengths of hikes Refer to the previous exercise.

a. Give an example of five hike lengths such that the mean and median are equal.

b. Give an example of five hike lengths such that the mode is 2, the median is 3, and the mean is larger than the median.

2.108 Central Park monthly temperatures The MINITAB graph below uses dot plots to compare the distributions of the Central Park temperatures from 1869–2010 for the months of January and July.

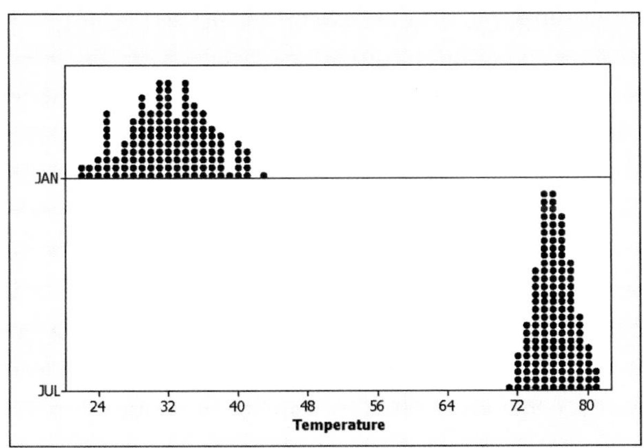

a. Describe the shape of each of the two distributions.

b. Estimate the balance point for each of the two distributions and compare.

c. Compare the variability of the two distributions. Estimate from the dot plots how the range and standard deviation for the January temperature distribution compare to the July temperature distribution. Are you surprised by your results for these two months?

2.109 What does s equal?

a. For an exam given to a class, the students' scores ranged from 35 to 98, with a mean of 74. Which of the following is the most realistic value for the standard deviation: -10, 1, 12, 60? Clearly explain what is unrealistic about the other values.

b. The sample mean for a data set equals 80. Which of the following is an impossible value for the standard deviation? 200, 0, -20? Why?

2.110 Female heights According to a recent report from the U.S. National Center for Health Statistics, females between 25 and 34 years of age have a bell-shaped distribution for height, with mean of 65 inches and standard deviation of 3.5 inches.

a. Give an interval within which about 95% of the heights fall.

b. What is the height for a female who is 3 standard deviations below the mean? Would this be a rather unusual height? Why?

2.111 Energy and water consumption In parts a and b, what shape do you expect for the distributions of electricity use and water use in a recent month in Gainesville, Florida? Why? (Data supplied by N. T. Kamhoot, Gainesville Regional Utilities.)

a. Residential electricity used had mean = 780 and standard deviation = 506 kilowatt hours (Kwh). The minimum usage was 3 Kwh and the maximum was 9390 Kwh.

b. Water consumption had mean = 7100 and standard deviation = 6200 (gallons).

2.112 Hurricane damage The histogram shows the distribution of the damage (in billion dollars) of the 30 most costly hurricanes hitting the U.S. mainland between 1900 and 2010. (Numbers are inflation adjusted and in 2010 dollars). The data are available in the Hurricane file on the book's website.

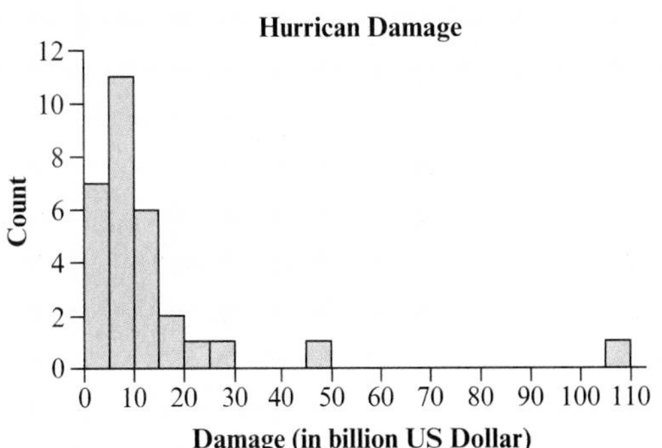

a. Describe the shape of the distribution.

b. Would you use the mean or median to describe the center? Why?

c. Verify with technology that the mean is 13.6, Q1 = 5.7, median = 7.9, and Q3 = 11.8. (Note that different software uses slightly different definitions for the quartiles.)

d. Write a short paragraph describing the distribution of hurricane damage.

2.113 More hurricane damage Refer to the previous exercise about hurricane damage and the histogram shown there.

a. For this data, 93% of damages (i.e., all but the two most expensive) fall within one standard deviation of the mean. Why is this so different from the 68% the empirical rule suggests?

b. How would removing the costliest hurricane (Katrina in 2005, shown on the far right in the histogram) from the data set affect the (i) mean, (ii) median, (iii) standard deviation, (iv) IQR, and (v) 10th percentile?

2.114 Student heights The Heights data file on the book's website has heights for female and male students (in inches). For males, the mean is 70.9 and the standard deviation is 2.9. For females, the mean is 65.3 and the standard deviation is 3.0.

a. Interpret the male heights by using the empirical rule.

b. Compare the center and variability of the height distributions for females and males.

c. The lowest observation for males was 62. How many standard deviations below the mean is it?

2.115 Cigarette tax TECH How do cigarette taxes per pack vary from one state to the next? The data set of 2003 cigarette taxes for all 50 states and Washington, D.C., is in the Cigarette Tax data file on the book's website.

a. Use software to construct a histogram. Write a short description of the distribution, noting shape and possible outliers.

b. Find the mean and median for the cigarette taxes. Which is larger, and why would you have expected that from the histogram?

c. Find the standard deviation and interpret it.

2.116 Cereal sugar values Revisit the sugar data for breakfast cereals that are given in Example 4.

a. Interpret the box plot in the figure (MINITAB output) by giving approximate values for the five-number summary.

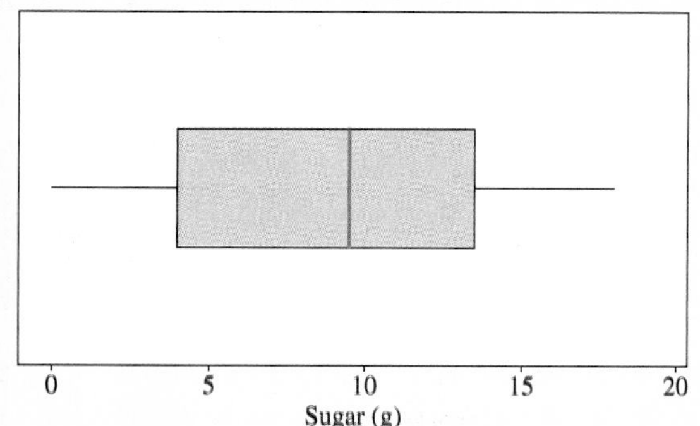

b. What does the box of the box plot suggest about possible skew?

c. The mean is 8.75 and the standard deviation is 5.32. Find the z-score associated with the minimum sugar value of 0. Interpret.

2.117 NASDAQ stock prices The data values below represent the closing prices of the 20 most actively traded stocks on the NASDAQ Stock Exchange (rounded to the nearest dollar) on May 2, 2014.

3	60	40	87	26	9	37	23	26	9
4	78	4	7	26	7	52	8	52	13

a. Sketch a dot plot or construct a stem-and-leaf plot.

b. Find the median, the first quartile, and the third quartile.

c. Sketch a box plot. What feature of the distribution displayed in the plot in part a is not obvious in the box plot? (Hint: Are there any gaps in the data?)

2.118 Temperatures in Central Park TECH Access the Central Park temps data file on the book's website.

a. Using software, construct a histogram of average March temperatures and interpret, noting shape, center, and variability.

b. Find and interpret the mean and standard deviation of March temperatures.

c. Construct a histogram of average November temperatures. Using the two histograms, make comparative statements regarding the March and November temperatures.

d. Make a side-by-side box plot of March and November temperatures. Again make some comparative statements regarding the two. How is the side-by-side box plot more useful than multiple histograms for comparing the two months?

2.119 Teachers' salaries According to *Statistical Abstract of the United States, 2012,* average salary (in dollars) of primary and secondary school classroom teachers in 2009 in the United States varied among states with a five-number summary of: minimum = 35,070, Q1 = 45,840, median = 48,630, Q3 = 55,820, maximum = 69,119. (Data available in the teacher_salary file.)

a. Find and interpret the range and interquartile range.

b. Sketch a box plot, marking the five-number summary on it.

c. Predict the direction of skew for this distribution. Explain.

d. If the distribution, although skewed, is approximately bell shaped, which of the following would be the most realistic value for the standard deviation: (i) 100, (ii) 1000, (iii) 7000, or (iv) 25,000? Explain your reasoning.

2.120 Health insurance In 2009, the five-number summary statistics for the distribution of statewide percentage of people without health insurance had a minimum of 4.4% (Massachusetts), Q1 = 12.35%, median = 14.8%,

Q3 = 17.3%, and maximum of 26.1% (Texas) (*Statistical Abstract of the United States,* data available on book's website as health_coverage.).

a. Do you think the distribution is symmetric, skewed right, or skewed left? Why?

b. Which is most plausible for the standard deviation: −16, 0, 4, 20, or 25? Why? Explain what is unrealistic about the other values.

2.121 What box plot do you expect? For each of the following variables, sketch a box plot that would be plausible.

a. Exam score (min = 0, max = 100, mean = 87, standard deviation = 10)

b. IQ (mean = 100 and standard deviation = 16)

c. Weekly religious contribution (median = $10 and mean = $17)

2.122 High school graduation rates The distribution of high school graduation rates in the United States in 2009 had a minimum value of 79.9 (Texas), first quartile of 84.0, median of 87.4, third quartile of 89.8, and maximum value of 91.8 (Wyoming) (*Statistical Abstract of the United States,* data available on book's website.)

a. Report the range and the interquartile range.

b. Would a box plot show any potential outliers? Explain.

c. The mean graduation rate is 86.9, and the standard deviation is 3.4. For these data, does any state have a z-score that is larger than 3 in absolute value? Explain.

2.123 SAT scores The U.S. statewide average total SAT scores math + reading + writing for 2010 are summarized in the box plot. These SAT scores are out of a possible 2400. (Data available on the book's website.)

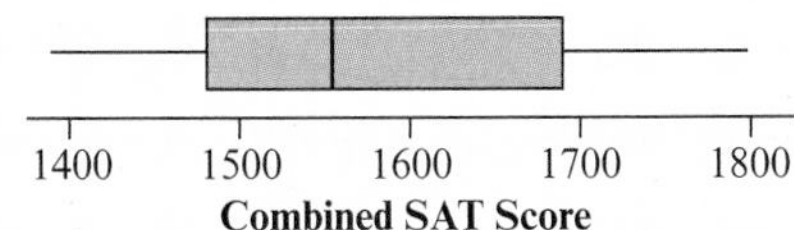

a. Explain how the box plot gives you information about the distribution shape.

b. Using the box plot, give the approximate value for each component of the five-number summary. Interpret each.

c. A histogram for these data is also shown. What feature of the distribution would be missed by using only the box plot?

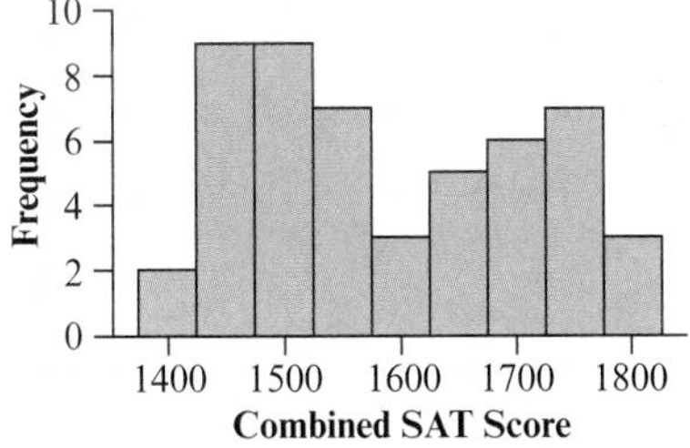

2.124 Blood pressure A World Health Organization study (the MONICA project) of health in various countries reported that in Canada, systolic blood pressure readings have a mean of 121 and a standard deviation of 16. A reading above 140 is considered to be high blood pressure.

a. What is the z-score for a blood pressure reading of 140? How is this z-score interpreted?

b. The systolic blood pressure values have a bell-shaped distribution. Report an interval within which about 95% of the systolic blood pressure values fall.

2.125 No cereal sodium The cereal sodium values have a mean of 167 and a standard deviation of 77.3. Find the z-score for the cereal that has a sodium value of 0. Interpret.

2.126 Who was Roger Maris? Roger Maris, who spent most of his professional baseball career with the New York Yankees, held the record for the most home runs in one season (61) from 1961 until 1998, when the record was broken by Mark McGwire. Maris played in the major leagues from 1957 to 1968. The number of home runs he hit in each year that he played is summarized in MINITAB output as shown.

```
Variable  N        Mean     Median  StDev
RMHR      12       22.92    19.50   15.98
Variable  Minimum  Maximum  Q1      Q3
RMHR      5.00     61.00    10.00   31.75
```

a. Use the 3 standard deviation criterion to determine whether any potential outliers are present.

b. The criterion in (part a) requires the distribution to be approximately bell-shaped. Is there any evidence here to contradict this? Explain.

c. A sports writer commented that Roger Maris hit *only* 13 home runs in 1966. Was this unusual for Maris? Comment, using statistical justification.

Concepts and Investigations

2.127 Baseball's great home run hitters TECH The Baseball's HR Hitters file on the book's website contains data on the number of home runs hit each season by some of baseball's great home run hitters. Analyze these data by using techniques introduced in this chapter to help judge statistically which player might be considered the best. Specify the criterion you use to compare the players.

2.128 How much spent on haircuts? TECH Is there a difference in how much males and females spend on haircuts? Access the Georgia Student Survey data file on the book's website or use your class data to explore this question, using appropriate graphical and numerical methods. Write a brief report describing your analyses and conclusions.

2.129 Controlling asthma TECH A study of 13 children suffering from asthma (*Clinical and Experimental Allergy,* vol. 20, pp. 429–432, 1990) compared single inhaled doses of formoterol (F) and salbutamol (S). Each child was evaluated using both medications. The outcome measured was the child's peak expiratory flow (PEF) eight hours following treament. Is there a difference in the PEF level for the two medications? The data on PEF follow:

Child	F	S
1	310	270
2	385	370
3	400	310
4	310	260
5	410	380
6	370	300
7	410	390
8	320	290
9	330	365
10	250	210
11	380	350
12	340	260
13	220	90

a. Construct plots to compare formoterol and salbutamol. Write a short summary comparing the two distributions of the peak expiratory flow.

b. Consider the distribution of differences between the PEF levels of the two medications. Find the 13 differences and construct and interpret a plot of the differences. If on the average there is no difference between the PEF level for the two brands, where would you expect the differences to be centered?

2.130 Google trend Go to www.google.com/trends and click Explore in Depth. Look up a subject of interest to you and try to create a time plot that shows interest in the subject over time. Interpret the plot and suggest ways the graph could be improved.

TECH

2.131 Youth unemployment by gender The side-by-side box plots below show the unemployment rate among 15- to 24-year-olds in 28 European nations for each gender. The two outliers shown for each box plot refer to the same countries, Greece and Spain. Write a short paragraph comparing the distribution for the males to the one for the females. (Data in youth_unemployment on book's website.)

TECH

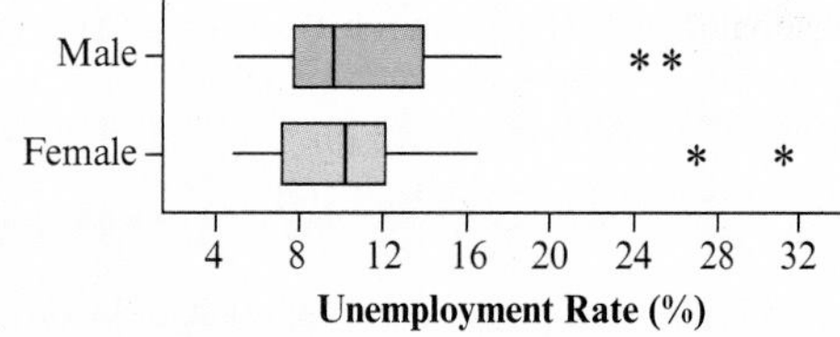

2.132 You give examples Give an example of a variable that you'd expect to have a distribution that is

a. Approximately symmetric

b. Skewed to the right

c. Skewed to the left

d. Bimodal

e. Skewed to the right, with a mode and median of 0 but a positive mean

2.133 Political conservatism and liberalism Where do Americans tend to fall on the conservative–liberal political spectrum? The General Social Survey asks, "I'm going to show you a seven-point scale on which the political views that people might hold are arranged from extremely liberal, point 1, to extremely conservative, point 7. Where would you place yourself on this scale?" The table shows the seven-point scale and the distribution of 1933 responses for a survey conducted in 2008.

Score	Category	Frequency
1.	Extremely liberal	69
2.	Liberal	240
3.	Slightly liberal	221
4.	Moderate	740
5.	Slightly conservative	268
6.	Conservative	327
7.	Extremely conservative	68

(*Source:* Data from CSM, UC Berkeley.)

This is a categorical scale with ordered categories, called an **ordinal scale**. Ordinal scales are often treated in a quantitative manner by assigning scores to the categories and then using numerical summaries such as the mean and standard deviation.

a. Using the scores shown in the table, the mean for these data equals 4.11. Show that you get the mean by multiplying each score by the frequency it occurred, summing up these values and then dividing the sum by the total number of observations.

b. Identify the mode (or modal category).

c. In which category does the median fall? Why?

2.134 Mode but not median and mean The previous exercise showed how to find the mean and median when a categorical variable has ordered categories. A categorical scale that does *not* have ordered categories (such as choice of religious affiliation or choice of major in college) is called a **nominal scale**. For such a variable, the mode (or modal category) applies, but not the mean or median. Explain why.

2.135 Multiple choice: GRE scores In a study of graduate students who took the Graduate Record Exam (GRE), the Educational Testing Service reported that for the quantitative exam, U.S. citizens had a mean of 529 and standard deviation of 127, whereas the non-U.S. citizens had a mean of 649 and standard deviation of 129. Which of the following is true?

a. Both groups had about the same amount of variability in their scores, but non-U.S. citizens performed better, on the average, than U.S. citizens.

b. If the distribution of scores was approximately bell shaped, then almost no U.S. citizens scored below 400.

c. If the scores range between 200 and 800, then probably the scores for non-U.S. citizens were symmetric and bell shaped.

d. A non-U.S. citizen who scored 3 standard deviations below the mean had a score of 200.

2.136 Multiple choice: Fact about s Which statement about the standard deviation s is false?

a. s can never be negative.

b. s can never be zero.

c. For bell-shaped distributions, about 95% of the data fall within $\bar{x} \pm 2s$.

d. s is a nonresistant (sensitive to outliers) measure of variability, as is the range.

2.137 Multiple choice: Relative GPA The mean GPA for all students at a community college in the fall semester was 2.77. A student with a GPA of 2.0 wants to know her relative standing in relation to the mean GPA. A numerical summary that would be useful for this purpose is the

a. standard deviation

b. median

c. interquartile range

d. number of students at the community college

2.138 True or false:

a. The mean, median, and mode can never all be the same.

b. The mean is always one of the data points.

c. When n is odd, the median is one of the data points.

d. The median is the same as the second quartile and the 50th percentile.

2.139 Bad statistic A teacher summarizes grades on an exam by Min = 26, Q1 = 67, Q2 = 80, Q3 = 87, Max = 100, Mean = 76, Mode = 100, Standard deviation = 76, IQR = 20.

She incorrectly recorded one of these. Which one do you think it was? Why?

2.140 True or false: Soccer According to a story in the *Guardian* newspaper (football.guardian.co.uk), in the United Kingdom the mean wage for a Premiership player in 2006 was £676,000. True or false: If the income distribution is skewed to the right, then the median salary was even larger than £676,000.

2.141 Mean for grouped data ◆◆ Refer to the calculation of the mean in Exercises 2.43 or 2.133. Explain why the mean for grouped data can be expressed as a sum, taking each possible outcome times the *proportion* of times it occurred.

2.142 Male heights ◆◆ According to a recent report from the U.S. National Center for Health Statistics, for males aged 25–34 years, 2% of their heights are 64 inches or less, 8% are 66 inches or less, 27% are 68 inches or less, 39% are 69 inches or less, 54% are 70 inches or less, 68% are 71 inches or less, 80% are 72 inches or less, 93% are 74 inches or less, and 98% are 76 inches or less. These are called **cumulative percentages**.

a. Which category has the median height? Explain why.

b. Nearly all the heights fall between 60 and 80 inches, with fewer than 1% falling outside that range. If the heights are approximately bell-shaped, give a rough approximation for the standard deviation of the heights. Explain your reasoning.

2.143 Range and standard deviation approximation ◆◆ Use the empirical rule to explain why the standard deviation of a bell-shaped distribution for a large data set is often roughly related to the range by evaluating Range $\approx 6s$. (For small data sets, one may not get any extremely large or small observations, and the range may be smaller, for instance about 4 standard deviations.)

2.144 Range the least resistant ◆◆ We've seen that measures such as the mean, the range, and the standard deviation can be highly influenced by outliers. Explain why the range is worst in this sense. (*Hint:* As the sample size increases, explain how a single extreme outlier has less effect on the mean and standard deviation but can still have a large effect on the range.)

2.145 Using MAD to measure variability ◆◆ The standard deviation is the most popular measure of variability from the mean. It uses squared deviations because the ordinary deviations sum to zero. An alternative measure is the **mean absolute deviation**, $\Sigma|x - \bar{x}|/n$.

a. Explain why greater variability tends to result in larger values of this measure.

b. Would the MAD be more, or less, resistant than the standard deviation? Explain.

2.146 Rescale the data ◆◆ The mean and standard deviation of a sample may change if data are rescaled (for instance, temperature changed from Fahrenheit to Celsius). For a sample with mean $\bar{x}$, adding a constant c to each observation changes the mean to $\bar{x} + c$, and the standard deviation s is unchanged. Multiplying each observation by $c > 0$ changes the mean to $c\,\bar{x}$ and the standard deviation to cs.

a. Scores on a difficult exam have a mean of 57 and a standard deviation of 20. The teacher boosts all the scores by 20 points before awarding grades. Report the mean and standard deviation of the boosted scores. Explain which rule you used and identify c.

b. Suppose that annual income for some group has a mean of \$39,000 and a standard deviation of \$15,000. Values are converted to British pounds for presentation to a British audience. If one British pound equals \$2.00, report the mean and standard deviation in British currency. Explain which rule above you used and identify c.

c. Adding a constant and/or multiplying by a constant is called a **linear transformation** of the data. Do linear transformations change the *shape* of the distribution? Explain your reasoning.

Student Activities

2.147 The average student TECH Refer to the data file you created in Activity 3 in Chapter 1. For variables chosen by your instructor, describe the "average student" in your class. Prepare a one-page summary report. In class, students will compare their analyses of what makes up an average student.

2.148 Create own data For the Mean Versus Median web app, using the option "Supply own sample" from the drop down menu, your instructor will give you a data set to illustrate the effect of extreme observations on the mean and median. Write a short summary of your observations.

TRY TECH

2.149 GSS Access the General Social Survey at sda.berkeley.edu/GSS.

TECH

a. Find the frequency table and histogram for Example 6 on TV watching. (*Hint:* Enter TVHOURS as the row variable, YEAR(2012) as the selection filter, choose bar chart for Type of Chart, and click *Run the Table.*)

b. Your instructor will have you obtain graphical and numerical summaries for another variable from the GSS. Students will compare results in class.

BIBLIOGRAPHY

Franklin, Christine A. (2002). "The Other Life of Florence Nightingale," *Mathematics Teaching in the Middle School* 7(6): 337–339.

Tukey, J. W. (1977). *Exploratory Data Analysis*. Reading, MA: Addison-Wesley.

CHAPTER

3

In Chapter 2, we distinguished between two major types of variables and explored ways of describing their distribution by using graphs and numerical summaries. However, we rarely look at a single variable in isolation and would miss important connections if we did. Many interesting questions revolve around the **relationship** between two variables and how they interact. This chapter presents methods of exploring and describing the nature of such relationships.

Association: Contingency, Correlation, and Regression

Example 1

Smoking and Your Health

Picture the Scenario

Although numerous studies have concluded that cigarette smoking is harmful to your health in many ways, one study found conflicting evidence. As part of the study, 1314 women in the United Kingdom were asked whether they smoked.[1] Twenty years later, a follow-up survey observed whether each woman was deceased or still alive. The researchers studied the possible link between whether a woman smoked and whether she survived the 20-year study period. During that period, 24% of the smokers died and 31% of the nonsmokers died. The higher death rate for the nonsmokers is surprising.

Questions to Explore

- How can we describe the relationship between smoking and survival with numbers (descriptive statistics)?
- Is smoking actually beneficial to your health, considering that a smaller percentage of smokers died?
- If we observe a link between smoking status and survival status, is there something that could explain how this happened?

Thinking Ahead

In this study, we can identify two categorical variables. One is smoking status—whether a woman was a smoker (yes or no). The other is survival status—whether a woman survived the 20-year study period (yes or no). In practice, research investigations almost always analyze more than one variable. The relationship between two variables is often the primary focus.

This chapter presents descriptive statistics for examining data on two variables. We'll analyze what these data suggest about the link between smoking and survival and learn that a third variable can influence the results. In this case, we'll see that the age of the woman is important. We'll revisit this example in Example 16 and analyze the data while taking age into account as well.

[1]Described by D. R. Appleton et al., *American Statistician*, vol. 50, pp. 340–341 (1996).

Example 1 has two categorical variables, but we'll also learn how to examine links between pairs of quantitative variables. For instance, we might want to answer questions such as, "What's the relationship between the daily amount of gasoline use by automobiles and the amount of air pollution?" or "Do high schools with higher per-student funding tend to have higher mean SAT scores for their students?"

Response Variables and Explanatory Variables

When we analyze data on two variables, our first step is to distinguish between the **response variable** and the **explanatory variable**.

In Words

The data analysis examines how the outcome on the **response** variable *depends on* or is *explained by* the value of the **explanatory** variable.

Response Variable and Explanatory Variable

The **response variable** is the outcome variable on which comparisons are made for different values of the **explanatory variable**.

When the **explanatory variable** is categorical, it defines the groups to be compared with respect to the response variable. When the explanatory variable is quantitative, we examine how different values of the explanatory variable relate to changes in the response variable.

In Example 1, survival status (whether a woman is alive after 20 years) is the response variable. Smoking status (whether the woman was a smoker) is the explanatory variable. We are interested in how survival (the response) compares across the two groups (smokers/nonsmokers) defined by the explanatory variable. In a study of air pollution in several countries, the carbon dioxide (CO_2) level in a country's atmosphere might be a response variable, and the explanatory variable could be the country's amount of gasoline use for automobiles. We would then investigate how more or less gasoline usage relates to changes in CO_2 levels. In a study of achievement for a sample of college students, college GPA might be a response variable, and the explanatory variable could be the number of hours a week spent studying. In each of these studies, there is a natural explanatory/response relationship between these quantitative variables.

In Words

We often use the words *association* and *relationship* interchangeably.

Some studies regard *either* or *both* variables as response variables. For example, this might be the case if we were analyzing data on smoking status and on alcohol status (whether the subject has at least one alcoholic drink per week) or data on the relationship between height and weight. There is no clear distinction as to which variable would be explanatory for the other.

The main purpose of a data analysis with two variables is to investigate whether there is an **association** and to describe the nature of that association.

In Words

When there's an **association**, the likelihood of particular values for one variable depends on the values of the other variable. It is more likely that students with a high school GPA near 4 will have a college GPA above 3.5 than students whose high school GPA is near 3. So high school GPA and college GPA have an association.

Association Between Two Variables

An **association** exists between two variables if particular values for one variable are more likely to occur with certain values of the other variable.

In Example 1, surviving the study period was more likely for smokers than for nonsmokers. So, there is an association between survival status and smoking status. For higher levels of gasoline use, does the CO_2 level in the atmosphere tend to be higher? If so, then there is an association between gasoline use and CO_2 level.

This chapter presents methods for studying whether associations exist and for describing how strong they are. We explore associations between categorical variables in Section 3.1 and between quantitative variables in Sections 3.2 and 3.3.

3.1 The Association Between Two Categorical Variables

How would you respond to the question, "Taken all together, would you say that you are very happy, pretty happy, or not too happy?" We could summarize the percentage of people who have each of the three possible outcomes for this categorical variable using a table, a bar graph, or a pie chart. However, we'd probably want to know how the percentages depend on the values for other variables, such as a person's marital status (married, unmarried). Is the percentage who report being very happy higher for married people than for unmarried people?

We'll now look at ways to summarize the association between two categorical variables. You can practice these concepts with data on personal happiness in Exercises 3.3, 3.10, and 3.64.

Example 2

Categorical explanatory and response variables

Pesticides in Organic Foods

Picture the Scenario

One appeal of eating organic foods is the belief that they are pesticide-free and thus healthier. However, little fruit and vegetable acreage is organic (only 2% in the United States), and consumers pay a premium for organic food.

How can we investigate how the percentage of foods carrying pesticide residues compares for organic and conventionally grown foods? The Consumers Union led a study based on sampling carried out by the U.S. Department of Agriculture (USDA) and the state of California.[2] The sampling was part of regulatory monitoring of foods for pesticide residues. For this study, Table 3.1 displays the frequencies of foods for all possible category combinations of the two variables, food type and pesticide status.

Table 3.1 Frequencies for Food Type and Pesticide Status

The row totals and the column totals are the frequencies for the categories of each variable. The counts inside the table give information about the association.

	Pesticide Status		
Food Type	**Present**	**Not Present**	**Total**
Organic	29	98	127
Conventional	19,485	7,086	26,571
Total	**19,514**	**7,184**	**26,698**

Questions to Explore

a. What is the response variable, and what is the explanatory variable?

b. Only 127 organic food types were sampled compared to 26,571 conventional ones. Despite this huge imbalance, can we still make a fair comparison?

c. How does the proportion of foods with pesticides present compare for the two food types?

d. What proportion of all sampled produce contained pesticide residues?

[2] *Source: Food Additives and Contaminants* 2002, vol. 19 no. 5, 427–446.

Think It Through

a. Pesticide status, namely whether pesticide residues are present, is the outcome of interest. The food type, organic or conventionally grown, is the variable that defines two groups to be compared on their pesticide status. So, pesticide status is the response variable and food type is the explanatory variable.

b. We can't compare the absolute numbers for each food type in Table 3.1 directly. However, by looking at relative frequencies, i.e., the proportions, a fair comparison can be made.

c. From Table 3.1, 29 out of 127 organic foods contained pesticide residues. The proportion with pesticides is $29/127 = 0.228$. Likewise, 19,485 out of 26,571 conventionally grown foods contained pesticide residues. The proportion is $19{,}485/26{,}571 = 0.733$, much higher than for organic foods. Since $0.733/0.228 = 3.2$, the relative occurrence of pesticide residues for conventionally grown produce is approximately three times that for organically grown produce.

d. The overall proportion of sampled produce with pesticide residues is the total number with pesticide residues out of the total number of food items, or

$$(29 + 19{,}485)/(127 + 26{,}571) = 19{,}514/26{,}698 = 0.731.$$

We can find this result using the column totals of Table 3.1.

Insight

The value of 0.731 for the overall proportion with pesticide residues is close to the proportion for conventionally grown foods alone, which we found to be 0.733. This is because conventionally grown foods make up a high percentage of the sample. (From the row totals, the proportion of the sampled items that were conventionally grown was $26{,}571/26{,}698 = 0.995$.) In summary, pesticide residues occurred in more than 73% of the sampled items, and they were much more common (about three times as common) for conventionally grown than organic foods.

▶ ***Try Exercise 3.3***

Did You Know?

Should we be alarmed that about 73% of the food tested contained pesticide residues? The study stated that the level is usually far below the limits set by the Environmental Protection Agency. Scientists did find that the pesticide residues on organic produce were generally less toxic. ◀

Contingency Tables

Table 3.1 has two categorical variables: food type and pesticide status. We can analyze the categorical variables separately, through the column totals for pesticide status and the row totals for food type. These totals are the category counts for the separate variables, for instance (19,514, 7,184) for the (present, not present) categories of pesticide status. We can also study the association between them, as we did by using the counts for the category combinations to find proportions, in Example 2, part c. Table 3.1 is an example of a **contingency table**.

Contingency Table

A **contingency table** is a display for **two categorical variables**. Its rows list the categories of one variable and its columns list the categories of the other variable. Each entry in the table is the number of observations in the sample at a particular combination of categories of the two categorical variables.

Each row and column combination in a contingency table is called a **cell**. For instance, the first cell in the second row of Table 3.1 (shown again in the margin)

Food Type	Pesticides: Yes	No
Organic	29	98
Conventional	19,485	7,086
	cell ↑	

has the frequency 19,485, the number of observations in the conventional category of food type with pesticides present. The process of taking a data file and finding the frequencies for the cells of a contingency table is referred to as **cross-tabulation** of the data. Table 3.1 is formed by cross-tabulation of food type and pesticide status for the 26,698 sampled food items.

Conditional Proportions

Consider the question, "Do organic and conventionally grown foods differ in the proportion of food items with pesticide residues?" To answer, we find the proportions on pesticide status within each category of food type and compare them. From Example 2, the proportions are $29/127 = 0.228$ for organic foods and $19{,}485/26{,}571 = 0.733$ for conventionally grown foods.

These proportions are called **conditional proportions** because their formation is **conditional** on (in this example) food type. Restricting our attention to organic foods, the proportion of food items with pesticides present equals 0.23. Table 3.2 shows the conditional proportions.

Recall

Using Table 3.1, shown again below, we obtain 0.23 from 29/127 and 0.77 from 98/127, the cell counts divided by the first row total. ◀

Food Type	Pesticide Status: Present	Not Present	Total
Organic	29	98	**127**
Conven.	19,485	7,086	**26,571**
Total	**19,514**	**7,184**	**26,698**

Table 3.2 Conditional Proportions on Pesticide Status for Two Food Types

These conditional proportions (using two decimal places) treat pesticide status as the response variable. The sample size n in a row shows the total on which the conditional proportions in that row were based.

Food Type	Pesticide Status: Present	Not Present	Total	n
Organic	0.23	0.77	**1.00**	127
Conventional	0.73	0.27	**1.00**	26,571

The conditional proportions in each row sum to 1.0. The sample size n for each set of conditional proportions is listed so you can determine the frequencies on which the conditional proportions were based. *Whenever we distinguish between a response variable and an explanatory variable, it is natural to form conditional proportions (based on the explanatory variable) for categories of the response variable.*

By contrast, the proportion of *all* sampled produce items with pesticide residues, which we found in part c of Example 2, is not a conditional proportion. It is not found for a particular food type. We ignored the information on food type and used the counts in the bottom margin of the table to form the proportion $19{,}514/26{,}698 = 0.731$. Such a proportion is called a **marginal proportion**. It is found using counts in the *margin* of the table.

Caution

Conditional proportions refer to a particular row (or a particular column) of the contingency table. **Marginal proportions** refer to the row (or column) sum of the contingency table. ◀

Example 3

Graphing the data ◀

Comparing Pesticide Residues for the Food Types

Picture the Scenario

For the food type and pesticide status, we've now seen two ways to display the data in a table. Table 3.1 showed cell frequencies in a contingency table, and Table 3.2 showed conditional proportions.

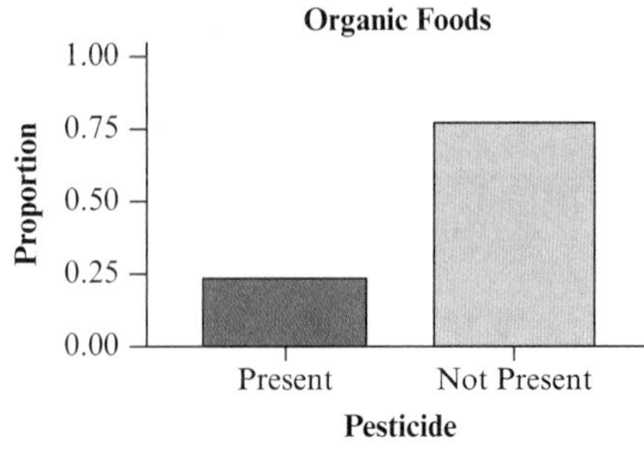

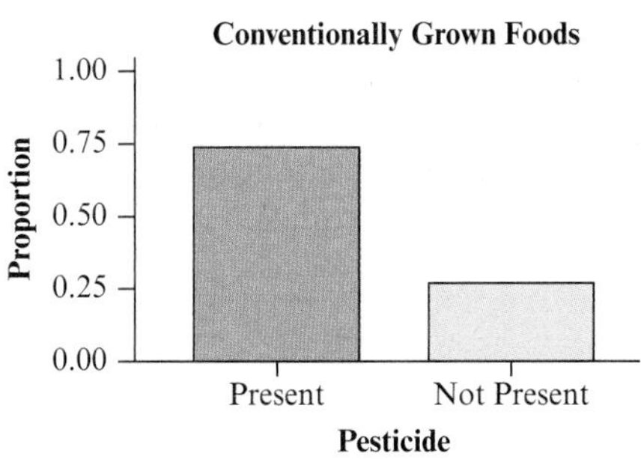

▲ **Figure 3.1 Bar Graphs of Conditional Proportions on Pesticide Status.** In these graphs, the conditional proportions are shown separately for each food type. **Question** Can you think of a way to construct a single graph that makes it easier to compare the food types on the pesticide status?

Questions to Explore

a. How can we use a single graph to show the relationship?

b. What does the graph tell us?

Think It Through

a. We've seen that to compare the two food types on pesticide status, the response variable, we can find conditional proportions for the pesticide status categories (shown in Table 3.2). Figure 3.1 in the margin shows bar graphs of the conditional proportions, one graph for organic foods and another for conventionally grown foods. More efficiently, we can construct a single bar graph that shows the bars for the conditional proportions **side by side**, as in Figure 3.2. This is called a side-by-side bar chart. Because pesticides are either present or not present, one of these two categories is redundant, and we only show the conditional proportions for pesticides present for the two food types. An alternative display, shown in the margin next to Figure 3.2, compares the conditional proportions for each food type by **stacking** the proportion present and not present on top of each other. This chart is referred to as a stacked bar chart. The advantage of either graph is that it allows an easy comparison of the conditional proportions across the two food types.

b. Figure 3.2 clearly shows that the proportion of foods with pesticides present is much higher for conventionally grown food than for organically grown food.

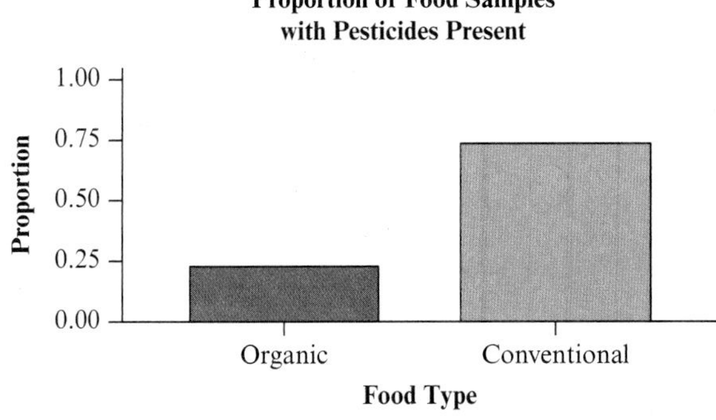

▲ **Figure 3.2 Conditional Proportions for Pesticide Status, Given the Food Type.** The graph shows the proportion of food samples with pesticides present for both organically and conventionally grown food. It is called a side-by-side bar graph and allows an easy and direct comparison of the conditional proportions. **Question** Using the information displayed in the chart, how would you describe the difference between organic and conventionally grown foods with regard to pesticide status?

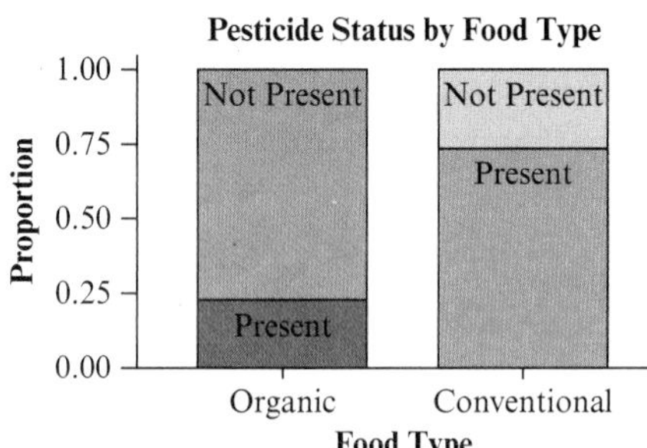

Stacked Bar Graph This type of graph stacks the proportions for pesticides present and not present on top of each other. It is called a stacked bar chart.

Insight

Chapter 2 used bar graphs to display proportions for a single variable. With two variables, bar graphs usually display conditional proportions, as in Figure 3.2. This display is useful for making comparisons, such as the way Figure 3.2 compares organic and conventionally grown foods in terms of the proportion of samples with pesticide residues present.

▶ ***Try Exercise 3.4***

Looking for an Association

When forming a contingency table, determine whether one variable should be the response variable. If there is a clear explanatory/response distinction, that dictates which way we compute the conditional proportions. In some cases, either variable could be the response variable, such as in cross-tabulating belief in heaven (yes, no) with belief in hell (yes, no). Then you can form conditional proportions in either or both directions. Studying the conditional proportions helps you judge whether there is an *association* between the variables.

Table 3.2 suggests that there is a reasonably strong association between food type and pesticide status because the proportion of food items with pesticides present differs considerably (0.23 versus 0.73) between the two food types. There would be *no association* if, instead, the proportion with pesticides present had been the same for each food type. For instance, *suppose* that for each food type, 40% had pesticides present and 60% did not have pesticides present, as shown in Table 3.3; the food types would have the same pesticide status distribution. We then say that pesticide status is **independent** of food type.

Table 3.3 Hypothetical Conditional Proportions on Pesticide Status for Each Food Type, Showing No Association

The conditional proportions for the response variable (pesticide status) categories are the same for each food type.

	Pesticide Status		
Food Type	**Present**	**Not Present**	**Total**
Organic	0.40	0.60	**127**
Conventional	0.40	0.60	**26,571**

Figure 3.3 shows a side-by-side bar graph for the hypothetical conditional proportions from Table 3.3. The figure in the margin shows the corresponding stacked bar chart. Compare Figure 3.3, no association, with Figure 3.2, which shows an association. In Figure 3.3, for both food types, 40% of the samples had pesticides present. This indicates **no association** between food type and pesticide status. The distribution of pesticide status is **the same** (40% present, 60% not present), whether the food type is organic or conventional. By contrast, the distribution of pesticide status looks quite different for the two food types in Figure 3.2 (23% present, 77% not present for organic food and 73% present, 27% not present for conventional food), indicating an association.

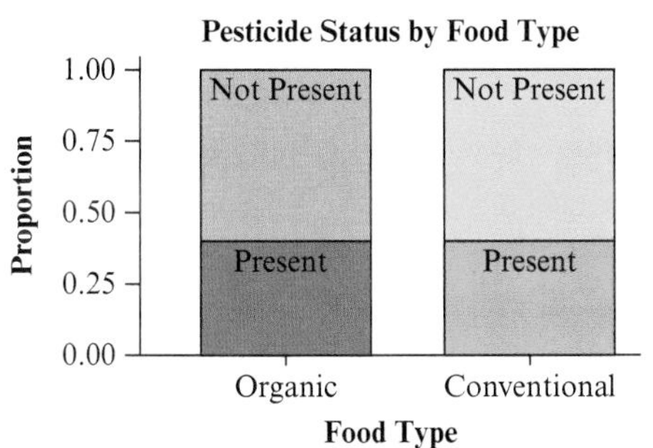

Stacked Bar Graph showing identical distributions.

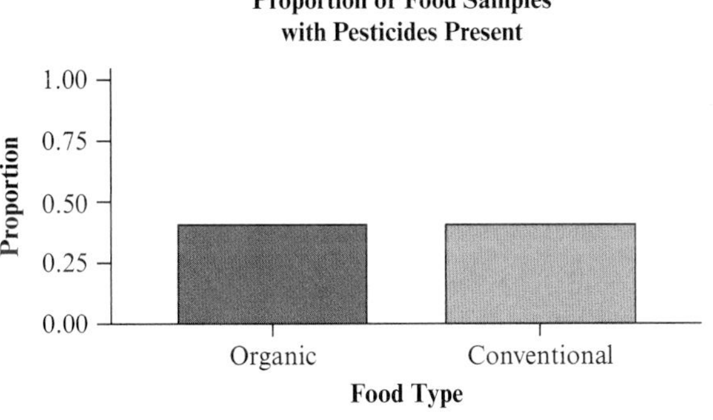

▲ **Figure 3.3** Hypothetical Conditional Proportions on Pesticide Status, Given Food Type, Showing No Association. **Question** What's the difference between Figures 3.2 and 3.3 in the pattern shown by the bars in the graph?

In Chapter 5, we will discuss the connection between marginal and conditional proportions when two variables are independent (not associated).

In Practice Comparing Population and Sample Conditional Proportions

When sampling from a population, even if there is *no* association between the two variables in the *population*, you can't expect the *sample* conditional proportions to be *exactly* the same because of ordinary random variation from sample to sample. Later in the text, we'll present inferential methods to determine if observed sample differences between conditional proportions are large enough to indicate that the variables are associated in the population.

Measuring the Strength of an Association Between Two Categorical Variables

For tables such as Table 3.2 that have two categories for the response and explanatory variables, there are several ways of describing the nature and strength of the association numerically.

Caution

Don't say the percentage of food samples with residues present is 50% higher for conventionally grown food. Say it is 50 **percentage points** higher. When comparing two percentages through their difference, we express the units of that difference as **percentage points**.

Difference of Proportions We have seen from Table 3.2 and Figure 3.2 that 73% of conventionally grown food samples had pesticide residues present, compared to only 23% for organic food samples. The difference between the two percentages is 73% − 23% = 50%. The percentage of conventionally grown food samples with residues present is 50 percentage points higher than the one for organic food samples. This is a substantial difference and indicates a rather strong association between the two variables. When there is no association, as in hypothetical Table 3.3 and Figure 3.3, this difference would be 0. The measure comparing two proportions (or percentages) through their difference is known as the **difference of proportions** and will be discussed in Chapter 10, Section 10.1, and Chapter 11, Section 11.3.

Ratio of Proportions Another way to measure and describe the strength of the association in Table 3.2 is through the ratio of the two conditional proportions, given by $0.73/0.23 = 3.2$. The proportion of food with pesticide residues present is 3.2 times larger for conventionally grown food than for organic food. Again, this indicates a rather strong association. What would that ratio be if the variables were not associated? In that case, the two proportions would be identical (or, in practice, nearly identical), as in Table 3.3. The ratio would then be close to or equal to 1, e.g., $0.4/0.4 = 1$ for the hypothetical conditional proportions in Table 3.3. This ratio is often referred to as the **risk ratio** or the **relative risk**. It is a popular measure for describing the association between a drug and a control treatment in medical studies.

Caution

It is easy to confuse the relative risk and the odds ratio. See Chapter 11.3 for more details.

Odds Ratio A third common measure describes the association by using a ratio of odds. For some types of studies, especially medical ones, it is the only measure that can be computed from the available data. We will discuss odds and the odds ratio, along with the relative risk, in Chapter 11, Section 11.3.

3.1 Practicing the Basics

3.1 Which is the response/explanatory variable? For the following pairs of variables, which more naturally is the response variable and which is the explanatory variable?

a. Carat (= weight) and price of a diamond

b. Dosage (low/medium/high) and severity of adverse event (mild/moderate/strong/serious) of a drug

c. Top speed and construction type (wood or steel) of a roller coaster

d. Type of college (private/public) and graduation rate

3.2 Sales and advertising Each month, the owner of Fay's Tanning Salon records in a data file the monthly total sales receipts and the amount spent that month on advertising.

a. Identify the two variables.

b. For each variable, indicate whether it is quantitative or categorical.

c. Identify the response variable and the explanatory variable.

3.3 Does higher income make you happy? Every General Social Survey (GSS) includes the question, "Taken all together, would you say that you are very happy, pretty happy, or not too happy?" The table below uses the 2010 survey to cross-tabulate happiness with family income, measured as the response to the question, "Compared with American families in general, would you say that your family income is below average, average, or above average?"

TRY

Happiness and Family Income, from General Social Survey

	Happiness			
Income	**Not Too Happy**	**Pretty Happy**	**Very Happy**	**Total**
Above average	21	213	126	**360**
Average	96	506	248	**850**
Below average	143	347	114	**604**
Total	**260**	**1066**	**488**	**1814**

a. Identify the response variable and the explanatory variable.

b. Construct the conditional proportions on happiness at each level of income. Interpret and summarize the association between these variables.

c. Overall, what proportion of people reported being very happy?

3.4 Diamonds The clarity and cut of a diamond are two of the four C's of diamond grading. (The other two are color and carat.) For a sample of diamonds, the following table lists the clarity (rated as internally flawless, IF, very very slightly included, VVS, very slightly included, VS, slightly included, SI and included, I) for the two lowest ratings for cut, which are "good" and "fair." The data for this exercise are in the Diamonds file on the book's website.

TRY TECH

Clarity by Cut

	Clarity					
Cut	**IF**	**VVS**	**VS**	**SI**	**I**	**Total**
Good	2	4	16	55	3	**80**
Fair	1	3	8	30	2	**44**

a. Find the conditional proportions for the five categories of clarity, given cut.

b. Sketch (or create using software) a side-by-side (or stacked) bar graph that compares the two cuts on clarity. Summarize findings in a paragraph.

c. Based on these data, is there an association between the cuts and clarity? Explain.

3.5 Alcohol and college students The Harvard School of Public Health, in its College Alcohol Study Survey, surveyed college students in about 200 colleges in 1993, 1997, 1999, and 2001. The survey asked students questions about their drinking habits. Binge drinking was defined as five drinks in a row for males and four drinks in a row for females. The table shows results from the 2001 study, cross-tabulating subjects' gender by whether they have participated in binge drinking.

Binge Drinking by Gender

	Binge Drinking Status		
Gender	**Binge Drinker**	**Non-Binge Drinker**	**Total**
Male	1,908	2,017	**3,925**
Female	2,854	4,125	**6,979**
Total	**4,762**	**6,142**	**10,904**

a. Identify the response variable and the explanatory variable.

b. Report the cell counts of subjects who were (i) male and a binge drinker, (ii) female and a binge drinker.

c. Can you compare the counts in part b to answer the question, "Is there a difference between male and female students who binge drink?" Explain.

d. Construct a contingency table that shows the conditional proportions of sampled students who do or do not binge drink, given gender. Interpret.

e. Based on part d, does it seem that there is an association between binge drinking and gender? Explain.

3.6 How to fight terrorism? A survey of 1000 adult Americans (*Rasmussen Reports*, April 15, 2004) asked each whether the best way to fight terrorism is to let the terrorists know we will fight back aggressively or to work with other nations to find an international solution. The first option was picked by 53% of the men but by only 36% of the women in the sample. Assume there were 600 men and 400 women in the sample.

a. Identify the response variable and the explanatory variable and their categories.

b. Construct a contingency table (similar to Table 3.1) that shows the counts for the different combination of categories.

c. Use a contingency table to display the percentages for the two options, separately for females and for males.

d. Explain why the percentages reported here are *conditional* percentages.

e. Sketch a graph similar to Figure 3.2 that compares the responses for men and women.

f. Compute the difference of proportions and the ratio of proportions and interpret each.

g. Give an example of how results would have to differ from these for you to conclude that there's *no* evidence of association between these variables.

3.7 Heaven and hell Two questions on the General Social Survey read, "Do you believe in heaven?" and "Do you believe in hell?" 955 subjects answered "yes" to both questions, 188 answered "no" to both, 162 answered "yes" to heaven but "no" to hell, and 9 answered "no" to heaven but "yes" to hell.

a. Explain how we could regard either variable (opinion about heaven, opinion about hell) as a response variable.

b. Display the data as a contingency table, labeling the variables and the categories.

c. Find the conditional proportions that treat opinion about heaven as the response variable and opinion about hell as the explanatory variable. Interpret.

d. Find the conditional proportions that treat opinion about hell as the response variable and opinion about heaven as the explanatory variable. Interpret.

e. Find the marginal proportion who (i) believe in heaven, (ii) believe in hell.

3.8 Surviving the *Titanic* Was the motto "Women and Children First" followed on the fateful journey of the *Titanic*? Refer to the following table on surviving the sinking of the *Titanic*.

	Survived	
Passenger	**Yes**	**No**
Children & Female Adult	373	161
Male Adult	338	1329

a. What's the percentage of children and female adult passengers who survived? What's the percentage of male adults who survived?

b. Compute the difference in the proportion of children and female adult passengers who survived and male adult passengers who survived. Interpret.

c. Compute the ratio of the proportion between children and female adult passengers and male adult passengers who survived. Interpret.

3.9 Gender gap in party ID In recent election years, political scientists have analyzed whether a gender gap exists in political beliefs and party identification. The table shows data collected from the 2010 General Social Survey on gender and party identification (ID).

Party ID by Gender

	Party Identification			
Gender	**Democrat**	**Independent**	**Republican**	**Total**
Male	111	155	89	**355**
Female	237	205	95	**537**
Total	**348**	**360**	**184**	**892**

a. Identify the response and explanatory variables.

b. What proportion of sampled individuals is (i) male and Republican, (ii) female and Republican?

c. What proportion of the overall sample is (i) male, (ii) Republican?

d. Are the proportions you computed in part c conditional or marginal proportions?

e. The two bar graphs, one for each gender, display the proportion of individuals identifying with each political party. What are these proportions called? Is there a difference between males and females in the proportions that identify with a particular party? Summarize whatever gender gap you observe.

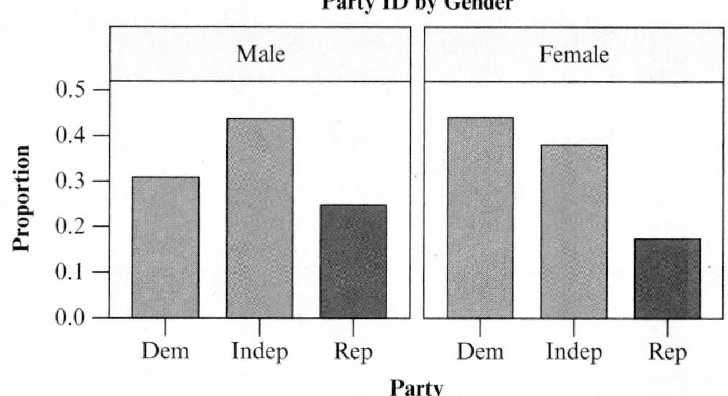

3.10 Use the GSS Go to the GSS website sda.berkeley.edu/GSS, click GSS, with *No Weight Variables* predefined (SDA 4.0), type SEX for the row variable and HAPPY for the column variable, put a check in the row box only for percentaging in the output options, and click *Run the Table.*

TECH

a. Report the contingency table of counts.

b. Report the conditional proportions to compare the genders on reported happiness.

c. Are females and males similar, or quite different, in their reported happiness? Compute and interpret the difference and ratio of the proportion of being not too happy between the two sexes.

3.2 The Association Between Two Quantitative Variables

In practice, when we investigate the association between two variables, there are three types of cases:

- The variables could be *categorical* as food type and pesticide status are. In this case, as we have already seen, the data are displayed in a contingency table, and we can explore the association by comparing conditional proportions.
- One variable could be *quantitative* and one could be *categorical* such as analyzing height and gender or income and race. As we saw in Chapter 2, we can compare the categories (such as females and males) using summaries of center and variability for the quantitative variable (such as the mean and standard deviation of height) and graphics such as side-by-side box plots.
- Both variables could be *quantitative*. In this case, we analyze how the outcome on the response variable tends to change as the value of the explanatory variable changes. The rest of the chapter considers this case.

Recall

Figure 2.16 in Chapter 2 used **side-by-side box plots** to compare heights for females and males. ◀

In exploring the relationship between two quantitative variables, we'll use the principles introduced in Chapter 2 for exploring the data of a single variable. We first use graphics to look for an overall pattern. We follow up with numerical summaries and check also for unusual observations that deviate from the overall pattern and may affect results.

Example 4

Numerical and graphical summaries ◀

Worldwide Internet and Facebook Use

Picture the Scenario

The number of worldwide Internet users and the number of users of social networking sites such as Facebook have grown significantly over the past decade. This growth though has not been distributed evenly throughout the world. Countries such as Australia, Sweden, and the Netherlands have achieved an Internet penetration of more than 85%, whereas only 13% of India's population uses the Internet. The story with Facebook is similar. More than 50% of the populations of countries such as the United States and Australia use Facebook, compared to fewer than 6% of the populations of countries such as China, India, and Russia.

The Internet Use data file on the book's website contains recent data for 32 countries on Internet penetration, Facebook penetration, broadband subscription percentage, and other variables related to Internet use. In this example, we'll investigate the relationship between Internet penetration and Facebook penetration. Note that we will often say "use" instead of "penetration" in these two variable names. Table 3.4 displays the values of these two variables for each of the 32 countries.

Table 3.4 Internet and Facebook Penetration Rates For 32 Countries

Country	Internet Penetration	Facebook Penetration
Argentina	55.8%	48.8%
Australia	82.4%	51.5%
Belgium	82.0%	44.2%

(Continued)

Country	Internet Penetration	Facebook Penetration
Brazil	49.9%	29.5%
Canada	86.8%	51.9%
Chile	61.4%	55.5%
China	42.3%	0.1%
Colombia	49.0%	36.3%
Egypt	44.1%	15.1%
France	83.0%	39.0%
Germany	84.0%	30.9%
Hong Kong	72.8%	56.4%
India	12.6%	5.1%
Indonesia	15.4%	20.7%
Italy	58.0%	38.1%
Japan	79.1%	13.5%
Malaysia	65.8%	46.5%
Mexico	38.4%	31.8%
Netherlands	93.0%	45.1%
Peru	38.2%	31.2%
Philippines	36.2%	30.9%
Poland	65.0%	25.6%
Russia	53.3%	5.6%
Saudi Arabia	54.0%	20.7%
South Africa	41.0%	12.3%
Spain	72.0%	38.1%
Sweden	94.0%	52.0%
Thailand	26.5%	26.5%
Turkey	45.1%	43.4%
United Kingdom	87.0%	52.1%
United States	81.0%	52.9%
Venezuela	44.1%	32.6%

Source: Data from the World Bank (data.worldbank.org) and www.internetworldstats.com for the year 2012.

Question to Explore

Use numerical and graphical summaries to describe the shape, center, and variability of the distributions of Internet penetration and Facebook penetration.

Think It Through

Using many of the statistics from Chapter 2, we obtain the following numerical summaries to describe center and variability for each variable:

Variable	N	Mean	StDev	Minimum	Q1	Median	Q3	Maximum	IQR
Internet Use	32	59.2	22.4	12.6	43.6	56.9	81.3	94.0	37.7
Facebook Use	32	33.9	16.0	0.0	24.4	34.5	47.1	56.4	22.7

Figure 3.4 portrays the distributions using histograms. We observe that the shape for Internet use is bimodal, with one mode around 45% and the other around 85%. We also see that Internet use has a wide range, from a minimum of just over 10% to a maximum of just under 95%. Facebook use ranges between 0% and about 55%, with most nations above 20%.

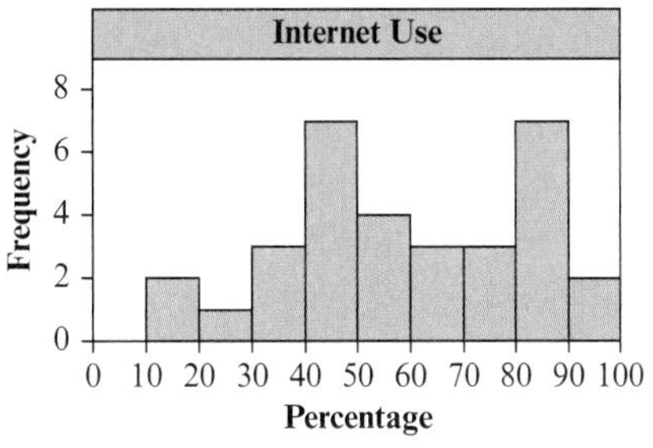

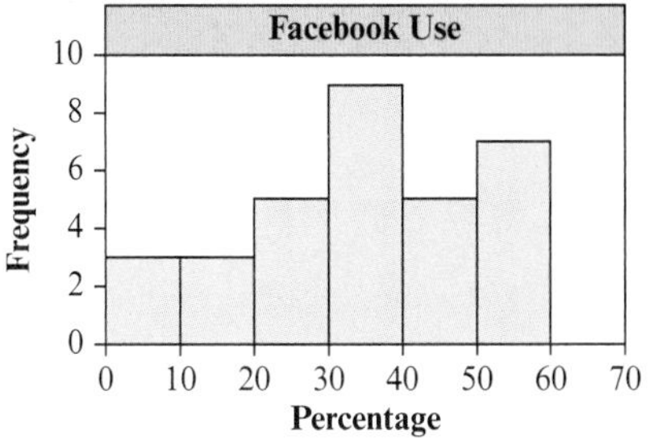

▲ **Figure 3.4** Histograms of Internet Use and Facebook Use for the 32 Countries. **Question** Which nations, if any, might be outliers in terms of Internet use? Facebook use? Which graphical display would more clearly identify potential outliers?

Insight

The histograms portray each variable separately but give no clue about their relationship. Is it true that countries with higher Internet use tend to have higher Facebook use? How can we picture the association between the two variables on a single display? We'll study how to do that next.

▶ ***Try Exercise 3.13, part a***

Looking for a Trend: The Scatterplot

With two quantitative variables, it is common to denote the response variable *y* and the explanatory variable *x*. We use this notation because graphical plots for examining the association use the *y*-axis for values of the response variable and the *x*-axis for values of the explanatory variable. This graphical plot is called a ***scatterplot***.

Scatterplot

A ***scatterplot*** is a graphical display for **two quantitative variables** using the horizontal (*x*) axis for the explanatory variable *x* and the vertical (*y*) axis for the response variable *y*. The values of *x* and *y* for a subject are represented by a point relative to the two axes. The observations for the *n* subjects are *n* points on the scatterplot.

Example 5

Scatterplots ◀

Internet and Facebook Use

Picture the Scenario

We return to the data from Example 4 for 32 countries on Internet and Facebook use.

Questions to Explore

a. Display the relationship between Internet use and Facebook use with a scatterplot.

b. What can we learn about the association by inspecting the scatterplot?

Think It Through

a. The first step is to identify the response variable and the explanatory variable. We'll study how Facebook use depends on Internet use. A temporal relationship exists between when individuals become Internet users and when they become Facebook users; the former precedes the latter. We will treat Internet use as the explanatory variable and Facebook use as the response variable. Thus, we use x to denote Internet use and y to denote Facebook use. We plot Internet use on the horizontal axis and Facebook use on the vertical axis. Any statistical software package can create a scatterplot. Using data such as those in Table 3.4, place Internet use in one column and Facebook use in another. Select the variable that plays the role of x and the variable that plays the role of y. Figure 3.5 shows the scatterplot for the data in Table 3.4.

Can you find the observation (dot) representing the United States on the scatterplot? It has Internet use $x = 81\%$ and Facebook use $y = 52.9\%$.

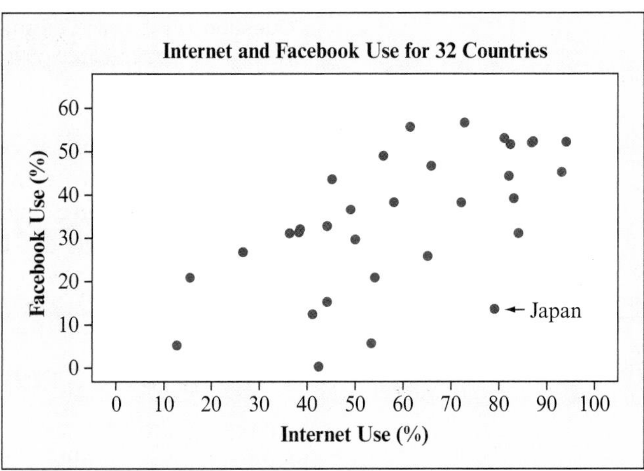

▲ **Figure 3.5** Scatterplot for Internet and Facebook Use (in % of the total population) The point for Japan is labeled and has coordinates $x = 79\%$ and $y = 13\%$. **Question** Is there any point that you would identify as standing out in some way? Which country does it represent, and how is it unusual in the context of these variables?

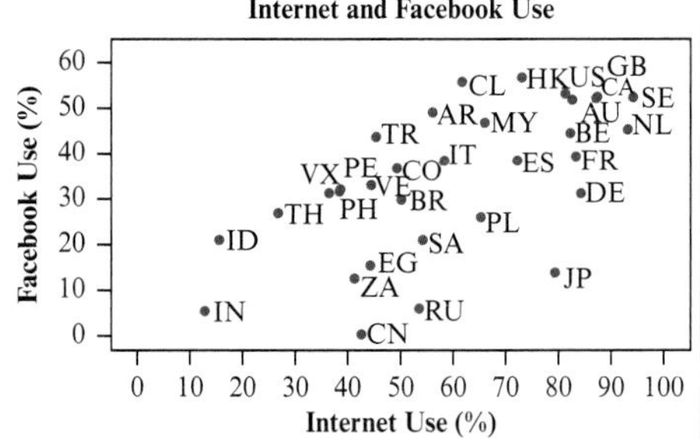

Scatterplot with two-letter country code

b. Here are some things we learn by inspecting the scatterplot:

- There is a clear trend. Nations with larger percentages of Internet use generally have larger percentages of Facebook use.
- The point for Japan seems unusual. Its Internet use is among the highest of all countries (79%), but its Facebook use is among the lowest (13%). Based on values for other countries with similarly high Internet use, we might expect Facebook use to be between 30% and 50% rather than 13%. Although not as unusual as Japan, Facebook use for Russia (6%) and China (0.1%) are much lower than we'd expect, based on what we see for other countries with similar Internet use of around 50%.
- Setting these three countries aside, the variability in Facebook use is similar across the whole range of Internet use. For countries with Internet use below about 50%, Facebook use varies from about 5% to 40%. For countries with Internet use larger than about 50%, it varies from about 20% to 60%.

Insight

Although the points for Japan and, to less extent, Russia and China, can be considered atypical, there is a clear overall association. The countries with lower Internet use tend to have lower Facebook use, and the countries with higher Internet use tend to have higher Facebook use.

▶ *Try Exercise 3.12, parts a and b*

How to Examine a Scatterplot

We examine a scatterplot to study the **association** (or the **relationship**) between two quantitative variables. How do values on the response variable change as values of the explanatory variable change? As Internet use rises, for instance, we see that Facebook use rises. When there's a trend in a scatterplot, what's the direction? Is the association **positive** or **negative?**

Positive Association and Negative Association

Two quantitative variables x and y are said to have a positive association when high values of x tend to occur with high values of y, and when low values of x tend to occur with low values of y. **Positive association:** As x goes up, y tends to go up.

Two quantitative variables have a negative association when high values of one variable tend to pair with low values of the other variable, and low values of one pair with high values of the other. **Negative association:** As x goes up, y tends to go down.

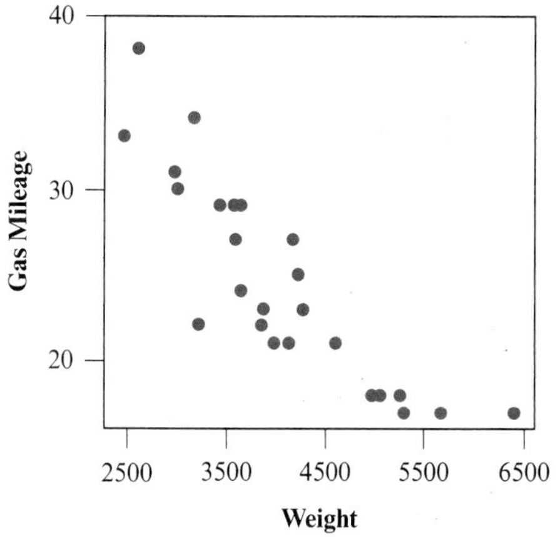

Figure 3.5 displays a positive association, because high (low) values of Internet use tend to occur with high (low) values of Facebook use. If we were to study the association between x = weight of car and y = gas mileage (in miles per gallon), we'd expect a negative association: Heavier cars would tend to get poorer gas mileage, i.e., drive fewer miles per gallon of gas. The figure in the margin illustrates this idea, using data from the Car Weight and Mileage data file on the book's website.

Here are some questions to explore when you examine a scatterplot:

- Does there seem to be a positive association, a negative association, or no association?
- Can the trend in the data points be approximated reasonably well by a straight line? In that case, do the data points fall close to the line, or do they tend to scatter quite a bit?
- Are some observations unusual, falling well apart from the overall trend of the data points? What do the unusual points tell us?

Examining scatterplots

Example 6

The Butterfly Ballot and the 2000 U.S. Presidential Election

Picture the Scenario

Al Gore and George W. Bush were the Democatric and Republican candidates in the 2000 U.S. presidential election. In Palm Beach County, Florida, initial election returns reported 3407 votes for the Reform party candidate, Pat Buchanan. Political analysts thought this total seemed surprisingly large. They felt that most of these votes may have actually been intended for

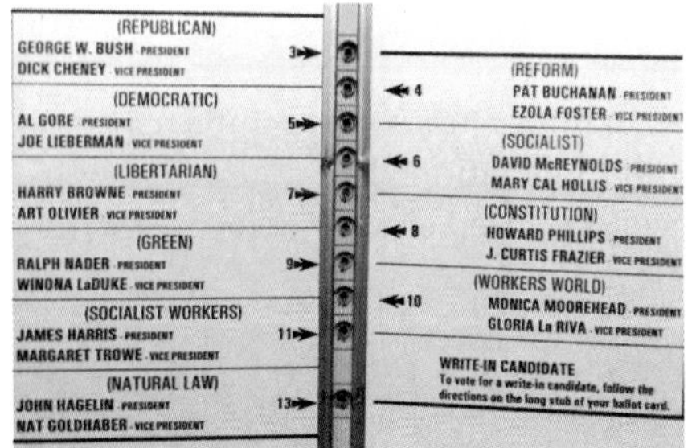

Gore (whose name was next to Buchanan's on the ballot) but were wrongly cast for Buchanan because of the design of the butterfly ballot used in that county, which some voters found confusing. On the butterfly ballot, Bush appeared first in the left column, followed by Buchanan in the right column, and Gore in the left column (see the photo in the margin).

Question to Explore

For each of the 67 counties in Florida, the Buchanan and the Butterfly Ballot data file on the book's website includes the Buchanan vote and the vote for the Reform party candidate in 1996 (Ross Perot). How can we explore graphically whether the Buchanan vote in Palm Beach County in 2000 was in fact surprisingly high, given the Reform party voting totals in 1996?

Think It Through

Figure 3.6 is a scatterplot of the countywide vote for the Reform party candidates in 2000 (Buchanan) and in 1996 (Perot). Each point represents a county. This figure shows a strong positive association statewide: Counties with a high Perot vote in 1996 tended to have a high Buchanan vote in 2000, and counties with a low Perot vote in 1996 tended to have a low Buchanan vote in 2000. Overall, the total number of votes for Buchanan in 2000 was only 3% of the total number of votes for Perot in 1996.

In Figure 3.6, one point falls well above the others. This severe outlier is the observation for Palm Beach County, the county that had the butterfly ballot. It is far removed from the overall trend for the other 66 data points, which follow an approximately straight-line trend.

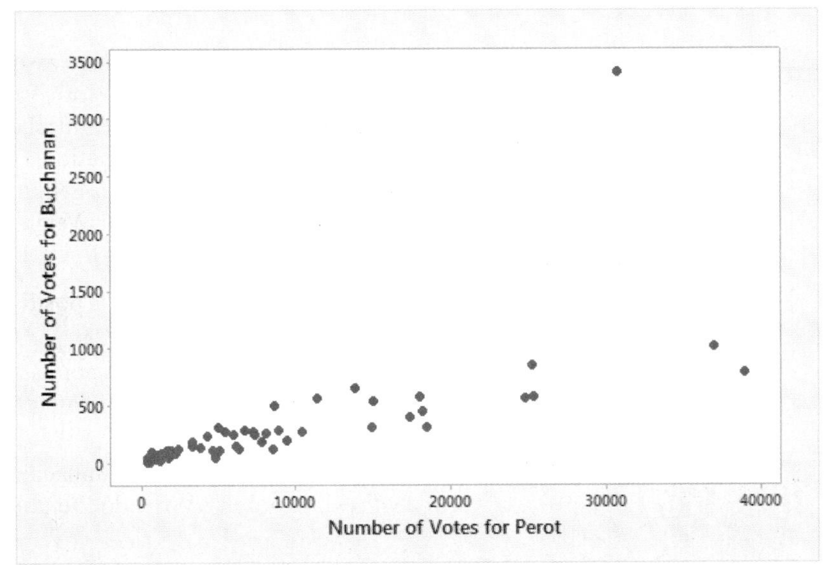

▲ **Figure 3.6** MINITAB Scatterplot of Florida Countywide Vote for Reform Party Candidates Pat Buchanan in 2000 and Ross Perot in 1996. **Question** Why is the top point, but not each of the two rightmost points, considered an outlier relative to the overall trend of the data points?

Insight

Alternatively, you could plot the Buchanan vote against the Gore vote or against the Bush vote (Exercise 3.23). These and other analyses conducted by statisticians[3] predicted that fewer than 900 votes were truly intended for

[3]For further discussion of these and related data, see Exercise 2.95 and the article by A. Agresti and B. Presnell, *Statistical Science*, vol. 17, pp. 1–5, 2002.

Buchanan in Palm Beach County, compared to the 3407 votes he actually received. Bush won the state by 537 votes and, with it, the Electoral College and the election. So, this vote may have been a pivotal factor in determining the outcome of that election. Other factors that played a role were 110,000 disqualified overvote ballots in which people mistakenly voted for more than one presidential candidate (with Gore marked on 84,197 ballots and Bush on 37,731), often because of confusion from names being listed on more than one page of the ballot, and 61,000 undervotes caused by factors such as hanging chads from manual punch-card machines in some counties.

► ***Try Exercise 3.23***

In practice, data points in a scatterplot sometimes fall close to a straight-line trend, as we saw for all data except Palm Beach County in Figure 3.6. This pattern represents a strong association in the sense that we can predict the y-value quite well from knowing the x-value. The next step in analyzing a relationship is summarizing the strength of the association.

Summarizing the Strength of Association: The Correlation

When the data points follow a roughly straight-line trend, the variables are said to have an approximately **linear** relationship. In some cases, the data points fall close to a straight line, but more often there is quite a bit of variability of the points around the straight-line trend. A summary measure called the **correlation** describes the strength of the linear association.

Correlation

The **correlation** summarizes the strength and direction of the **linear** (straight-line) association between two quantitative variables. Denoted by r, it takes values between -1 and $+1$.

- A positive value for r indicates a positive association, and a negative value for r indicates a negative association.
- The closer r is to ± 1 the closer the data points fall to a straight line, and the stronger the linear association is. The closer r is to 0, the weaker the linear association is.

Let's get a feel for the correlation r by looking at its values for the scatterplots shown in Figure 3.7:

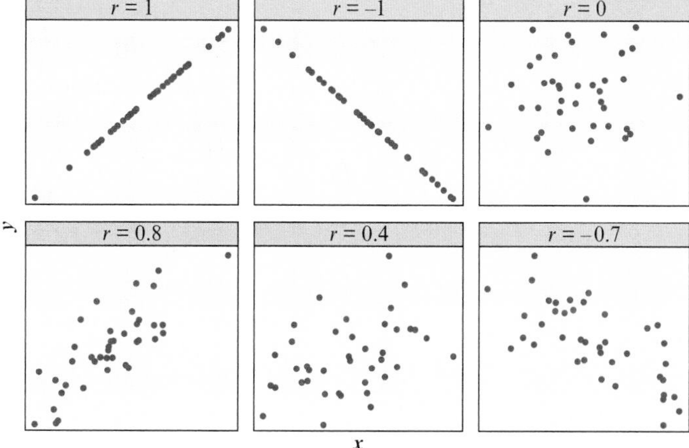

▲ **Figure 3.7** Some Scatterplots and Their Correlations. The correlation gets closer to ± 1 when the data points fall closer to a straight line. **Question** Why are the cases in which the data points are closer to a straight line considered to represent stronger association?

The correlation r takes the extreme values of $+1$ and -1 only when the data points follow a straight-line pattern *perfectly* as seen in the first two graphs in Figure 3.7. When $r = +1$ occurs, the line slopes upward. The association is positive because higher values of x tend to occur with higher values of y. The value $r = -1$ occurs when the line slopes downward, corresponding to a negative association.

In practice, don't expect the data points to fall perfectly on a straight line. However, the closer they come to that ideal, the closer the correlation is to 1 or -1. For instance, the scatterplot in Figure 3.7 with correlation $r = 0.8$ shows a stronger association than the one with correlation $r = 0.4$, for which the data points fall farther from a straight line.

Properties of the Correlation

Recall

The **absolute value** of a number gives the distance the number falls from zero on the number line. The correlation values of -0.9 and 0.9 both have an absolute value of 0.9. They both represent a stronger association than correlation values of -0.6 and 0.6, for example. ◀

- The correlation r always **falls between -1 and $+1$**. The closer the value to 1 in absolute value (see the margin comments), the stronger the **linear (straight-line) association** as the data points fall nearer to a straight line.
- A **positive correlation** indicates a **positive association**, and a **negative correlation** indicates a **negative association**.
- The value of the correlation **does not depend on the variables' units**. For example, suppose one variable is the income of a subject, in dollars. If we change the observations to units of euros or to units of thousands of dollars, we'll get the same correlation.
- The correlation **does not depend on** which variable is treated as the response and which as the explanatory variable.

Example 7

Finding and interpreting the correlation value ◀

Internet Use and Facebook Use

Picture the Scenario

Example 5 displayed a scatterplot for Internet use and Facebook use for 32 countries, shown again in the margin. We observed a positive association.

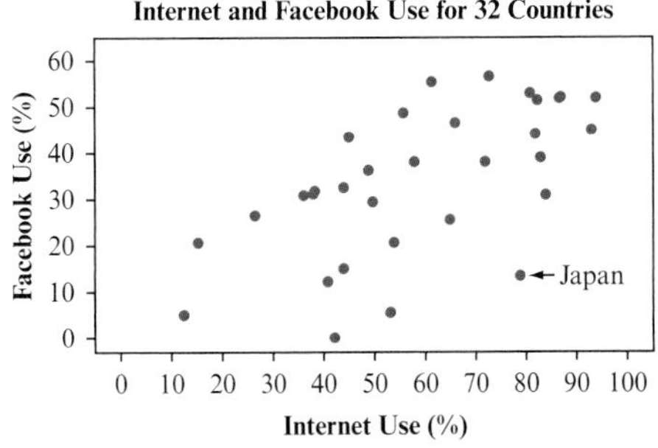

Questions to Explore

a. What value does software give for the correlation?
b. How can we interpret the correlation value?

Think It Through

Because the association is positive, we expect to find $r > 0$. If we input the columns of Internet use and Facebook use into, e.g., MINITAB and request the correlation from the Basic Statistics menu, we get

Correlations: Internet Use, Facebook Use
Pearson correlation of Internet Use and Facebook Use = 0.614.

The correlation of $r = 0.614$ is positive. This result confirms the positive linear association we observed in the scatterplot. In summary, a country's extent of Facebook use is moderately associated with its Internet use, with higher Internet use tending to correspond to higher Facebook use.

Insight

We get exactly the same correlation if we treat Facebook use as the explanatory variable and Internet use as the response variable. Also, it doesn't matter whether we use the proportions or the percentages when computing the correlation. Both sets of units result in $r = 0.614$.

The identifier *Pearson* for the correlation in the MINITAB output refers to the British statistician, Karl Pearson. In 1896 he provided the formula used to compute the correlation value from sample data. This formula is shown next.

► ***Try Exercises 3.14 and 3.15***

Formula for the Correlation Value

Recall

From Section 2.5 the ***z*-score** for an observation indicates the number of standard deviations and the direction (above or below) that the observation falls from the overall mean. ◄

Although software can compute the correlation for us, it helps to understand it if you see its formula. Let z_x denote the z-score for an observation x on the explanatory variable. Remember that z_x represents the number of standard deviations that x falls above or below the overall mean. That is,

$$z_x = \frac{\text{observed value} - \text{mean of all } x}{\text{standard deviation of all } x} = \frac{(x - \bar{x})}{s_x},$$

where s_x denotes the standard deviation of the x-values. Similarly, let z_y denote the number of standard deviations that an observation y on the response variable falls above or below the mean of all y. To obtain r, you calculate the product $z_x z_y$ for each observation and then find a typical value (a type of average) of those products.

In Practice Using Technology to Calculate r

Hand **calculation of the correlation** r is tedious. You should rely on software or a calculator. It's more important to understand how the correlation describes association in terms of how it reflects the relative numbers of points in the four quadrants.

Calculating the Correlation r

$$r = \frac{1}{n-1}\Sigma z_x z_y = \frac{1}{n-1}\Sigma\left(\frac{x-\bar{x}}{s_x}\right)\left(\frac{y-\bar{y}}{s_y}\right)$$

where n is the number of observations (points in the scatterplot), $\bar{x}$ and $\bar{y}$ are means, and s_x and s_y are standard deviations for x and y. The sum is taken over all n observations.

For x = Internet use and y = Facebook use, Example 7 found the correlation $r = 0.614$, using statistical software. To visualize how the formula works, let's revisit the scatterplot, reproduced in Figure 3.8, with a vertical line at the mean

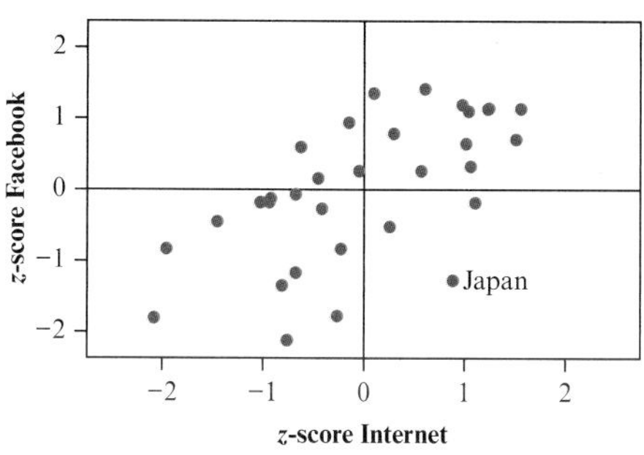

Plotting the z-scores of the variables on the axes, the relative position of the points doesn't change from Figure 3.8. We have merely relabeled the axis with different units. The points in this plot give exactly the same correlation as the points in Figure 3.8.

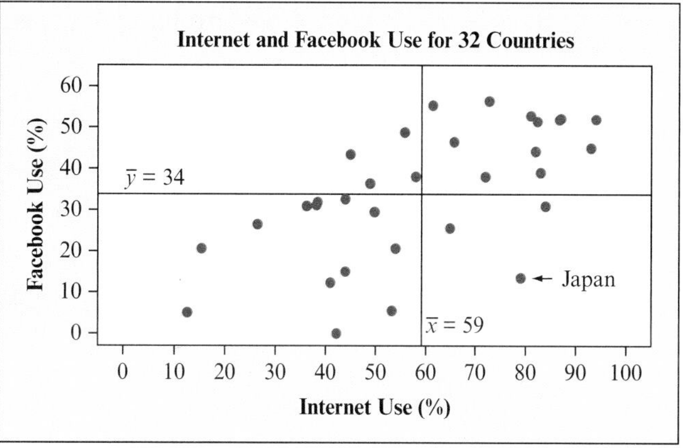

▲ **Figure 3.8** Scatterplot of Internet Use and Facebook Use Divided Into Quadrants at $(\bar{x}, \bar{y})$. Of the 32 data points, 25 lie in the upper-right quadrant (above the mean on each variable) or the lower-left quadrant (below the mean on each variable). **Question** Do the points in these two quadrants make a positive or a negative contribution to the correlation value? (*Hint:* Is the product of z-scores for these points positive or negative?)

In Words

A **quadrant** is any of the four regions created when a plane is divided by a horizontal line and a vertical line.

of x and a horizontal line at the mean of y. These lines divide the scatterplot into four **quadrants**. The summary statistics are

$$\bar{x} = 59.2 \qquad \bar{y} = 33.9$$
$$s_x = 22.4 \qquad s_y = 16.0.$$

The point for Japan ($x = 79, y = 13$) has as its z-scores $z_x = 0.89$, $z_y = -1.27$. This point is labeled in Figure 3.8. Since $x = 79$ is to the right of the mean for x and $y = 13$ is below the mean of y, it falls in the lower-right quadrant. This makes Japan somewhat atypical in the sense that all but 7 of the 32 countries have points that fall in the upper-right and lower-left quadrants. The product of the z-scores for Japan equals $0.89(-1.27) = -1.13$, indicating its negative contribution to r.

SUMMARY: Product of z-scores and correlation

- The product of the z-scores for any point in the upper-right quadrant is positive. The product is also positive for each point in the lower-left quadrant. Such points make a positive contribution to the correlation.
- The product of the z-scores for any point in the upper-left and lower-right quadrants is negative. Such points make a negative contribution to the correlation.

The overall correlation reflects the number of points in the various quadrants and how far they fall from the means. For example, if all points fall in the upper-right and lower-left quadrants, the correlation must be positive.

Graph Data to See If the Correlation Is Appropriate

▲ **Figure 3.9 The Correlation Poorly Describes the Association When the Relationship Is Curved.** For this U-shaped relationship, the correlation is 0 (or close to 0), even though the variables are strongly associated. **Question** Can you use the formula for r, in terms of how points fall in the quadrants, to reason why the correlation would be close to 0?

The correlation r is an efficient way to summarize the association shown by lots of data points with a single number. But be careful to use it only when it is appropriate. Figure 3.9 illustrates why. It shows a scatterplot in which the data points follow a U-shaped curve. There is an association because as x increases, y first tends to decrease and then tends to increase. For example, this might happen if x = age of person and y = annual medical expenses. Medical expenses tend to be high for newly born and young children, then they tend to be low until the person gets old, when they become high again. However, $r = 0$ for the data in Figure 3.9.

The correlation is designed for straight-line relationships. For Figure 3.9, $r = 0$, and it fails to detect the association. The correlation is not valid for describing association when the points cluster around a curve rather than around a straight line.

This figure highlights an important point to remember about *any* data analysis:

- **Always plot the data.**

If we merely used software to calculate the correlation for the data in Figure 3.9 without looking at the scatterplot, we might mistakenly conclude that the variables have no association. They *do* have one (and a fairly strong one), but it is not a straight-line association.

In Practice Always Construct a Scatterplot

Always **construct a scatterplot** to display a relationship between two quantitative variables. The correlation is only meaningful for describing the direction and strength of an approximate *straight-line* relationship.

3.2 Practicing the Basics

3.11 Used cars and direction of association For the 100 cars on the lot of a used-car dealership, would you expect a positive association, negative association, or no association between each of the following pairs of variables? Explain why.

a. The age of the car and the number of miles on the odometer

b. The age of the car and the resale value

c. The age of the car and the total amount that has been spent on repairs

d. The weight of the car and the number of miles it travels on a gallon of gas

e. The weight of the car and the number of liters it uses per 100 km.*

3.12 Broadband and GDP TRY TECH The Internet Use data file on the book's website contains data on the number of individuals with broadband access and Gross Domestic Product (GDP) for 32 nations. Let x represent GDP (in billions of U.S. dollars) and y = number of broadband users (in millions).

a. The figure below shows a scatterplot. Describe this plot in terms of the association between broadband subscribers and GDP.

b. Give the approximate x- and y-coordinates for the nation that has the highest number of broadband subscribers.

c. Use software to calculate the correlation coefficient between the two variables. What is the sign of the coefficient? Explain what the sign means in the context of the problem.

d. Identify one nation that appears to have fewer broadband subscribers than you might expect, based on that nation's GDP, and one that appears to have more.

e. If you recalculated the correlation coefficient after changing GDP from U.S. dollar to euro, would the correlation coefficient change? Explain.

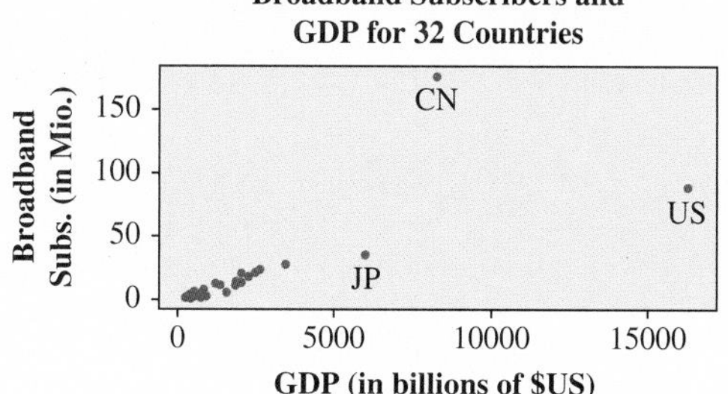

3.13 Economic development based on GDP TRY TECH The previous problem discusses GDP, which is a commonly used measure of the overall economic activity of a nation. For this group of nations, the GDP data have a mean of 1909 and a standard deviation of 3136 (in billions of U.S. dollars).

a. The five-number summary of GDP is minimum = 204, Q1 = 378, median = 780, Q3 = 2015, and maximum = 16,245. Sketch a box plot.

b. Based on these statistics and the graph in part a, describe the shape of the distribution of GDP values.

c. The data set also contains per capita GDP, or the overall GDP divided by the nation's population size. Construct a scatterplot of per capita GDP and GDP and explain why no clear trend emerges.

d. Your friend, Joe, argues that the correlation between the two variables must be 1 since they are both measuring the same thing. In reality, the actual correlation between per capita GDP and GDP is only 0.32. Identify the flaw in Joe's reasoning.

3.14 Politics and newspaper reading TRY For the FL Student Survey data file on the book's website, the correlation between y = political ideology (scored 1 = very liberal to 7 = very conservative) and x = number of times a week reading a newspaper is -0.07.

a. Would you call this association strong or weak? Explain.

b. The correlation between political ideology and religiosity (how often attend religious services) is 0.58. For this sample, which explanatory variable, newspaper reading or religiosity, seems to have a stronger association with y? Explain.

3.15 Internet use correlations TRY For the 32 nations in the Internet Use data file on the book's website, consider the following correlations:

Variable 1	Variable 2	Correlation
Internet users	Facebook users	0.293
Internet users	Broadband subscribers	0.974
Internet users	Population	0.834
Facebook users	Broadband subscribers	0.281
Facebook users	Population	0.234
Broadband subscribers	Population	0.704

a. Which pair of variables exhibits the *strongest* linear relationship?

b. Which pair of variables exhibits the *weakest* linear relationship?

c. In Example 7, we found the correlation between Internet use and Facebook use (measured in percentages of the population) to be 0.614. Why does the correlation between total number of Internet users and Facebook users differ from that of Internet use and Facebook use?

3.16 Match the scatterplot with r Match the following scatterplots with the correlation values.

1. $r = -0.9$

2. $r = -0.5$

3. $r = 0$

4. $r = 0.6$

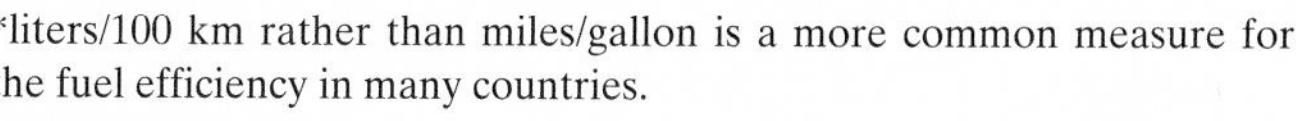

*liters/100 km rather than miles/gallon is a more common measure for the fuel efficiency in many countries.

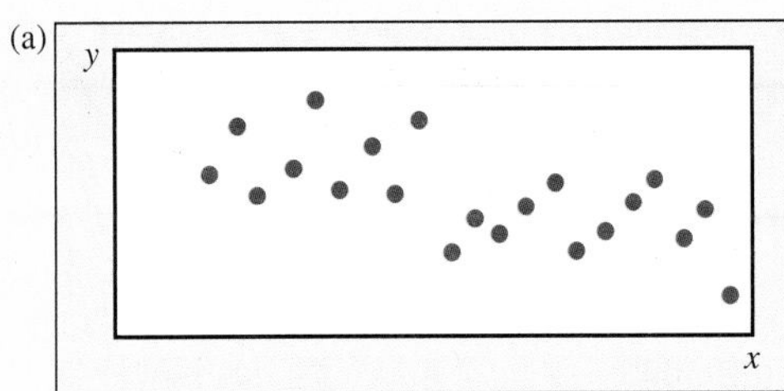
(a)

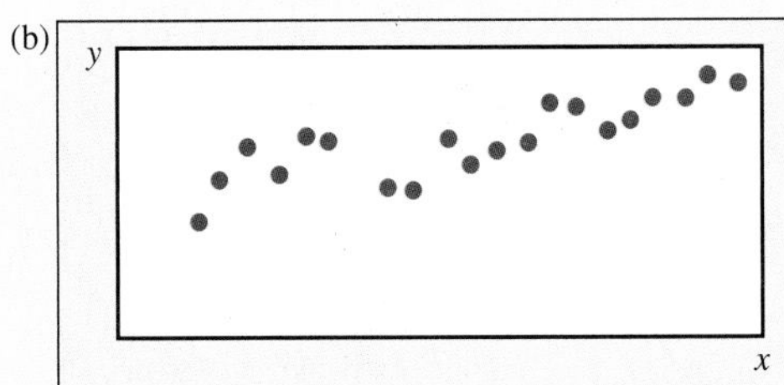
(b)

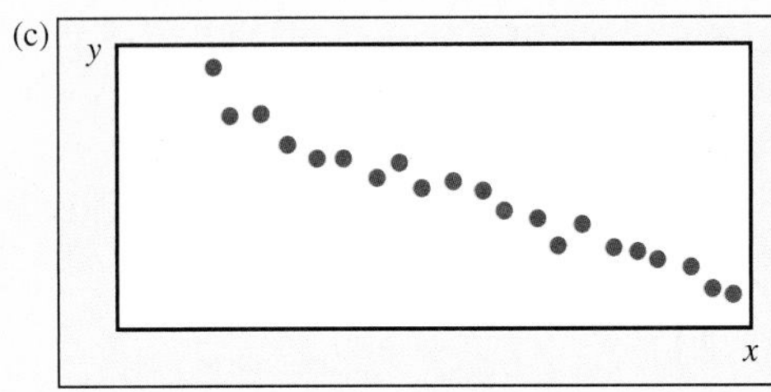
(c)

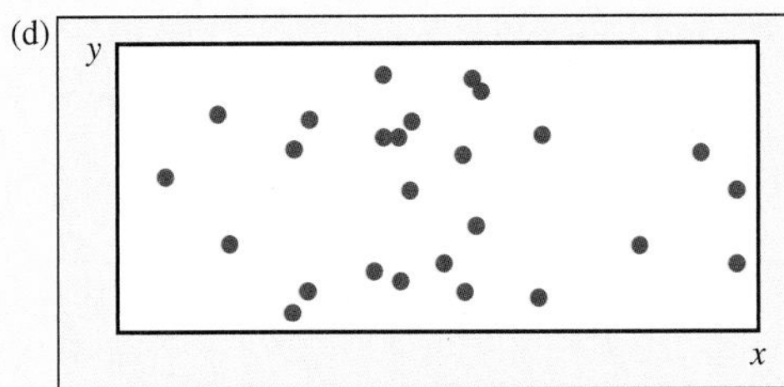
(d)

3.17 What makes $r = 1$? Consider the data:

x	3	4	5	6	7
y	8	13	12	14	16

a. Sketch a scatterplot.

b. If one pair of (x, y) values is removed, the correlation for the remaining four pairs equals 1. Which pair is it?

c. If one y value is changed, the correlation for the five pairs equals 1. Identify the y value and how it must be changed for this to happen.

3.18 Gender and Chocolate Preference The following table shows data on gender (coded as 1 = female, 2 = male) and preferred type of chocolate (coded as 1 = white, 2 = milk, 3 = dark) for a sample of 10 students.

Preferred Chocolate Type

Name	Gender	Type	Name	Gender	Type
Anna	1	2	Josef	2	3
Franz	2	3	Eva	1	3
Hans	2	2	Doris	1	2
Lisl	1	1	Sophie	1	1
Michael	2	3	Kathi	1	1

The students' teacher enters the data into software and reports a correlation of 0.640 between gender and type of preferred chocolate. He concludes that there is a moderately strong positive correlation between someone's gender and chocolate preference. What's wrong with this analysis?

3.19 $r = 0$ Sketch a scatterplot for which $r > 0$, but $r = 0$ after one of the points is deleted.

3.20 Correlation inappropriate Describe a situation in which it is inappropriate to use the correlation to measure the association between two quantitative variables.

3.21 Which mountain bike to buy? Is there a relationship between the weight of a mountain bike and its price? A lighter bike is often preferred, but do lighter bikes tend to be more expensive? The following table, from the Mountain Bike data file on the book's website, gives data on price, weight, and type of suspension (FU = full, FE = front end) for 12 brands.

TECH

Mountain Bikes

Brand and Model	Price($)	Weight(LB)	Type
Trek VRX 200	1000	32	FU
Cannondale Super V400	1100	31	FU
GT XCR-4000	940	34	FU
Specialized FSR	1100	30	FU
Trek 6500	700	29	FE
Specialized Rockhop	600	28	FE
Haro Escape A7.1	440	29	FE
Giant Yukon SE	450	29	FE
Mongoose SX 6.5	550	30	FE
Diamondback Sorrento	340	33	FE
Motiv Rockridge	180	34	FE
Huffy Anorak 36789	140	37	FE

Source: Data from *Consumer Reports,* June 1999.

a. You are shopping for a new bike. You are interested in whether and how weight affects the price. Which variable is the logical choice for the (i) explanatory variable, (ii) response variable?

b. Construct a scatterplot of price and weight. Does the relationship seem to be approximately linear? In what way does it deviate from linearity?

c. Use your software to verify that the correlation equals −0.32. Interpret it in context. Does weight appear to affect the price strongly in a linear manner?

3.22 Prices and protein revisited Is there a relationship between the protein content and the cost of Subway sandwiches? Use software to analyze the data in the following table:

TECH

Sandwich	Cost ($)	Protein (g)
BLT	$2.99	17
Ham (Black Forest, without cheese)	$2.99	18
Oven Roasted Chicken	$3.49	23
Roast Beef	$3.69	26
Subway Club®	$3.89	26
Sweet Onion Chicken Teriyaki	$3.89	26

Turkey Breast	$3.49	18
Turkey Breast & Ham	$3.49	19
Veggie Delite®	$2.49	8
Cold Cut Combo	$2.99	21
Tuna	$3.10	21

a. Construct a scatterplot to show how protein depends on cost. Is the association positive or negative? Do you notice any unusual observations?

b. What might explain the gap observed in the scatterplot? (Hint: Are vegetables generally high or low in protein relative to meat and poultry products?)

c. Obtain the correlation between cost and protein, r. Interpret this value in context.

3.23 Buchanan vote Refer to Example 6 and the Buchanan and the Butterfly Ballot data file on the book's website. Let y = Buchanan vote and x = Gore vote.

a. Construct a box plot for each variable. Summarize what you learn.

b. Construct a scatterplot. Identify any unusual points. What can you learn from a scatterplot that you cannot learn from box plots?

c. For the county represented by the most outlying observation, about how many votes would you have expected Buchanan to get if the point followed the same pattern as the rest of the data?

d. Repeat parts a and b using y = Buchanan vote and x = Bush vote.

3.3 Predicting the Outcome of a Variable

Recall

The correlation does not require one variable to be designated as response and the other as explanatory. ◄

We've seen how to explore the relationship between two quantitative variables graphically with a scatterplot. When the relationship has a straight-line pattern, the correlation coefficient describes its strength numerically. We can analyze the data further by finding an equation for the straight line that best describes that pattern. This equation can be used to predict the value of the variable designated as the response variable from the value of the variable designated as the explanatory variable.

In Words

The **symbol $\hat{y}$**, which denotes the predicted value of y, is pronounced *y-hat.*

Regression Line: An Equation for Predicting the Response Outcome

The **regression line** predicts the value for the response variable y as a straight-line function of the value x of the explanatory variable. Let $\hat{y}$ denote the **predicted value** of y. The equation for the regression line has the form

$$\hat{y} = a + bx.$$

In this formula, a denotes the ***y*-intercept** and b denotes the **slope**.

Example 8

Predict an outcome ◄

Height Based on Human Remains

Picture the Scenario

Anthropologists can reconstruct information using partial human remains at burial sites. For instance, after finding a femur (thighbone), they can predict how tall an individual was. They use the regression line, $\hat{y} = 61.4 + 2.4x$, where $\hat{y}$ is the predicted height and x is the length of the femur, both in centimeters.

Questions to Explore

What is the response and what is the explanatory variable? How can we graph the line that depicts how the predicted height depends on the femur length? A femur found at a particular site has a length of 50 cm. What is the predicted height of the person who had that femur?

Think It Through

It is natural here to treat the length of the femur as the explanatory variable to predict the height of a person, the response variable. The formula

In Practice Notation for the Regression Line

The formula $\hat{y} = a + bx$ uses slightly different notation from the traditional formula, which is $y = mx + b$. In that equation, m = *the slope* (the coefficient of x) and b = y-intercept. Regardless of the notation, the interpretation of the y-intercept and slope are the same.

$\hat{y} = 61.4 + 2.4x$ has y-intercept 61.4 and slope 2.4. It has the straight-line form $\hat{y} = a + bx$ with $a = 61.4$ and $b = 2.4$.

Each number x, when substituted into the formula $\hat{y} = 61.4 + 2.4x$, yields a value for $\hat{y}$. For simplicity in plotting the line, we start with $x = 0$, although in practice this would not be an observed femur length. The value $x = 0$ has $\hat{y} = 61.4 + 2.4(0) = 61.4$. This is called the **y-intercept** and is located 61.4 units up the y-axis at $x = 0$, at coordinates (0, 61.4). The value $x = 50$ has $\hat{y} = 61.4 + 2.4(50) = 181.4$. When the femur length is 50 cm, the predicted height of the person is 181.4 cm. The coordinates for this point are (50, 181.4). We can plot the line by connecting the points (0, 61.4) and (50, 181.4). Figure 3.10 plots the straight line for x between 0 and 50. In summary, the predicted height $\hat{y}$ increases from 61.4 to 181.4 as x increases from 0 to 50.

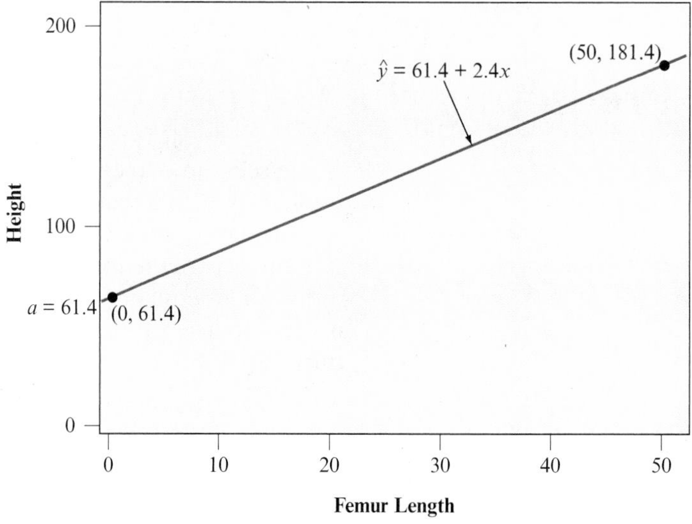

▲ **Figure 3.10** Graph of the Regression Line for x = Femur Length and y = Height of Person. **Question** At what point does the line cross the y-axis? How can you interpret the slope of 2.4?

Insight

A regression line is often called a **prediction equation** since it predicts the value of the response variable y at any value of x. Sadly, this particular prediction equation had to be applied to bones found in mass graves in Kosovo, to help identify Albanians who had been executed by Serbians in 1998.[4]

▶ ***Try Exercises 3.25, part a, and 3.26, part a***

Interpreting the *y*-Intercept and Slope

Recall

Math facts:

***y*-intercept** is the value of the line in the y direction when $x = 0$.

Slope = rise/run = change in y/change in x ◀

The **y-intercept** is the predicted value of y when $x = 0$. This fact helps us plot the line, but it may not have any interpretative value if no observations had x values near 0. It does not make sense for femur length to be 0 cm, so the y-intercept for the equation $\hat{y} = 61.4 + 2.4x$ is not a relevant predicted height.

The **slope** b in the equation $\hat{y} = a + bx$ equals the amount that $\hat{y}$ changes when x increases by one unit. For two x values that differ by 1.0, the $\hat{y}$ values differ by b. For the line $\hat{y} = 61.4 + 2.4x$, we've seen that $\hat{y} = 181.4$ at $x = 50$.

[4] "The Forensics of War," by Sebastian Junger in *Vanity Fair*, October 1999.

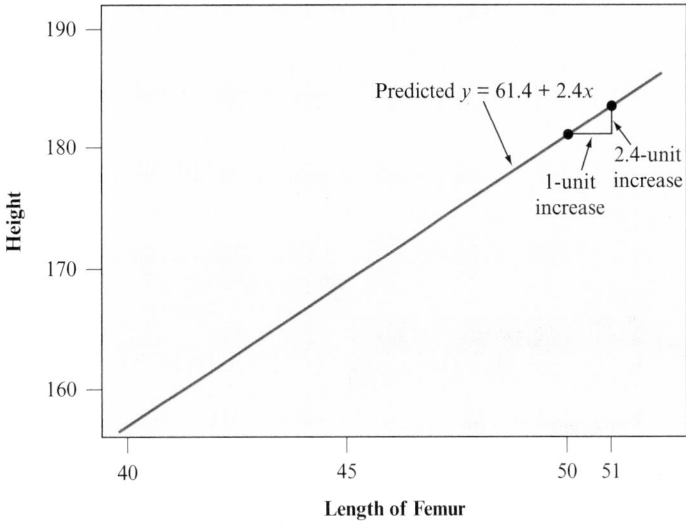

▲ **Figure 3.11 The Slope of a Straight Line.** The slope is the change in the predicted value $\hat{y}$ of the response variable for a 1-unit increase in the explanatory variable x. For an increase in femur length from 50 cm to 51 cm, the predicted height increases by 2.4 cm. **Question** What does it signify if the slope equals 0?

If x increases by 1.0 to $x = 51$, we get $\hat{y} = 61.4 + 2.4(51) = 183.8$. The increase in $\hat{y}$ is from 181.4 to 183.8, which is 2.4, the slope value. For each 1-cm increase in femur length, height is predicted to increase by 2.4 cm. Figure 3.11 portrays this interpretation.

When the slope is negative, the predicted value $\hat{y}$ *decreases* as x increases. The straight line then goes downward, and the association is *negative.*

When the slope = 0, the regression line is horizontal (parallel to the x-axis). The predicted value $\hat{y}$ of y stays constant at the y-intercept for any value of x. Then the predicted value $\hat{y}$ does not change as x changes, and the variables do not exhibit an association. Figure 3.12 illustrates the three possibilities for the sign of the slope.

The absolute value of the slope describes the *magnitude* of the change in $\hat{y}$ for a 1-unit change in x. The larger the absolute value, the steeper the regression line. A line with $b = 4.8$, such as $\hat{y} = 61.4 + 4.8x$, is steeper than one with $b = 2.4$. A line with $b = -0.07$ is steeper than one with $b = -0.04$.

Depending on the units of measurement, a 1-unit increase in a predictor x could be a trivial amount, or it could be huge. We will gain a better feel for how the slope works in context as we explore upcoming examples.

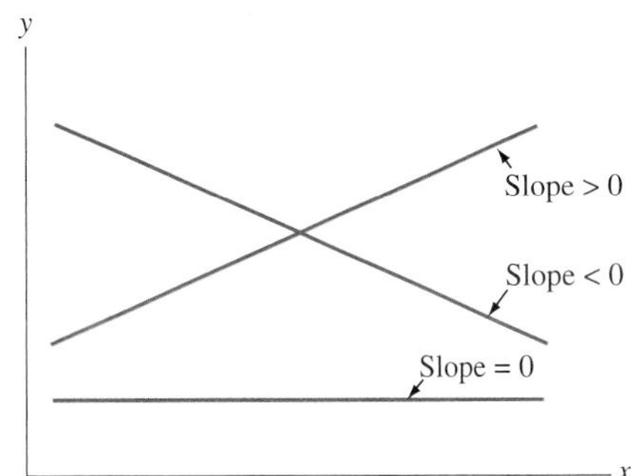

▲ **Figure 3.12 Three Regression Lines Showing Positive Association (slope > 0), Negative Association (slope < 0) and No Association (slope = 0). Question** Would you expect a positive or negative slope when y = annual income and x = number of years of education?

Finding a Regression Equation

How can we use the data to find the equation for the regression line? We should first construct a scatterplot to make sure that the relationship has a roughly straight line trend. If so, then software or calculators can easily find the straight line that best fits the data.

Example 9

Regression equation ◀

Predicting Baseball Scoring Using Batting Average

Picture the Scenario

In baseball, two summaries of a team's offensive ability are the team batting average (the proportion of times the team's players get a hit, out of the times they are officially at bat) and team scoring (the team's mean number of runs scored per game). Table 3.5 shows the 2010 statistics for the American League teams, from the AL Team Statistics data file on the book's website.

Scoring runs is a result of hitting, so team scoring is the response variable y and team batting average is the explanatory variable x. Figure 3.13 shows the scatterplot. There is a trend summarized by a positive correlation, $r = 0.568$.

Table 3.5 Team Batting Average and Team Scoring (Mean Number of Runs per Game) for American League Teams in 2010[5]

Team	Batting Average	Team Scoring
NY Yankees	0.267	5.30
Boston	0.268	5.05
Tampa Bay	0.247	4.95
Texas	0.276	4.86
Minnesota	0.273	4.82
Toronto	0.248	4.66
Chicago Sox	0.268	4.64
Detroit	0.268	4.64
LA Angels	0.248	4.20
Kansas City	0.274	4.17
Oakland	0.256	4.09
Cleveland	0.248	3.99
Baltimore	0.259	3.78
Seattle	0.236	3.17

[5] *Source:* Data from espn.go.com/mlb/stats.

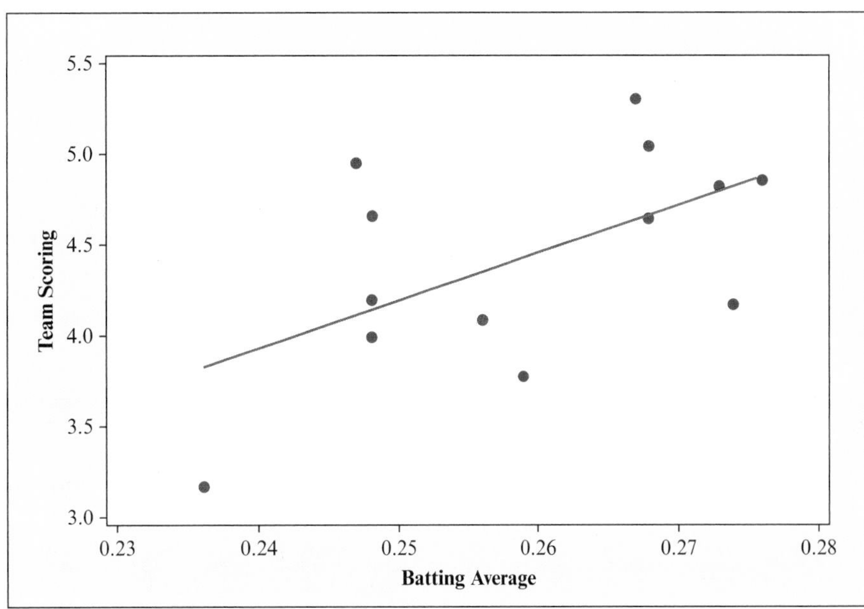

▲ **Figure 3.13** Scatterplot of Team Batting Average and Team Scoring, with Regression Line Superimposed. **Question** How can you find the prediction error that results when you use the regression line to predict team scoring for a team?

Questions to Explore

a. According to software, what is the regression equation?

b. If a team has a batting average of 0.275 next year, what is its predicted mean number of runs per game?

c. How do you interpret the slope in this context?

Think It Through

a. With the software package MINITAB, when we choose the regression option in the Regression part of the Statistics menu, part of the output tells us:

The regression equation is

Team Scoring = −2.32 + 26.1 Batting Average

The y-intercept is $a = -2.32$. The slope is the coefficient of the explanatory variable, denoted in the data file by batting. It equals $b = 26.1$. The regression equation is

$$\hat{y} = a + bx = -2.32 + 26.1x.$$

The TI calculator provides the output shown in the margin.

b. We predict that an American League team with a team batting average of 0.275 will score an average of $\hat{y} = -2.32 + 26.1(0.275) = 4.86$ runs per game.

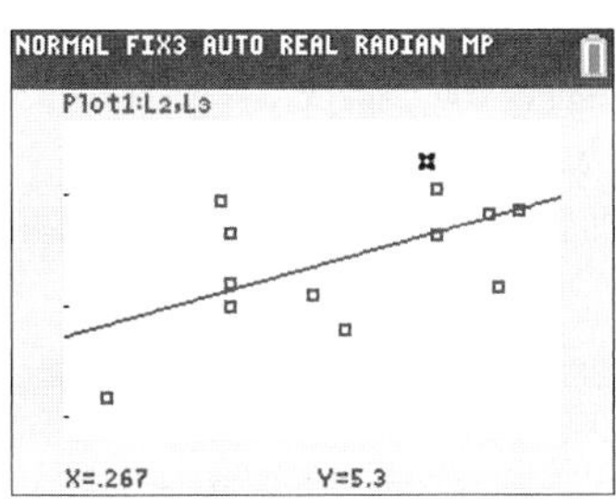

TI output of scatterplot

c. Because the slope $b = 26.1$ is positive, the association is positive: The predicted team scoring increases as team batting average increases. The slope refers to the change in $\hat{y}$ for a 1-unit change in x. However, x = team batting average is a proportion. In Table 3.5, the team batting averages fall between about 0.23 and 0.28, a range of 0.05. An increase of 0.05 in x corresponds to an increase of $(0.05)26.1 = 1.3$ in predicted team scoring. The mean number of runs scored per game is predicted to be about 1.3 higher for the best hitting teams than for the worst hitting teams.

Insight

Figure 3.13 shows the regression line superimposed over the scatterplot. It applies only over the range of observed batting averages. For instance, it's not sensible to predict that a team with batting average of 0.0 will average −2.32 runs per game.

▶ ***Try Exercises 3.25, part b, and 3.32 to get a feel for fitting a regression line; use the Explore Linear Regression web app discussed in Exercise 3.115***

Residuals Measure the Size of Prediction Errors

The regression equation $\hat{y} = -2.32 + 26.1x$ predicts team scoring for a given level of x = team batting average. Once we have used the regression equation, we can compare the predicted values to the actual team scoring to check the accuracy of those predictions.

For example, New York had $y = 5.3$ and $x = 0.267$. The prediction for y = mean number of runs per game at 0.267 is $-2.32 + 26.1x = -2.32 + 2.61(0.267) = 4.65$. The prediction error is the difference between the actual y value of 5.3 and the predicted value of 4.65, which is $y - \hat{y} = 5.3 - 4.65 = 0.65$. For New York, the regression equation under predicts y by 0.65 runs per game. For Seattle, $x = 0.236$ and $y = 3.17$. The regression line yields a predicted value of $-2.32 + 26.1(0.236) = 3.84$, so the prediction is too high. The prediction error is $3.17 - 3.84 = -0.67$. These prediction errors are called **residuals**.

Each observation has a residual. As we just saw, some are positive and some are negative. A positive residual occurs when the actual y is larger than the predicted value $\hat{y}$, so that $y - \hat{y} > 0$. A negative residual results when the actual y is smaller than the predicted value $\hat{y}$. The smaller the absolute value of a residual, the closer the predicted value is to the actual value, so the better is the prediction. If the predicted value is the same as the actual value, the residual is zero.

Graphically in the scatterplot, *for an observation, the vertical distance between the point and the regression line is the absolute value of the residual.* Figure 3.14 illustrates this fact for the positive residual for New York and the negative residual

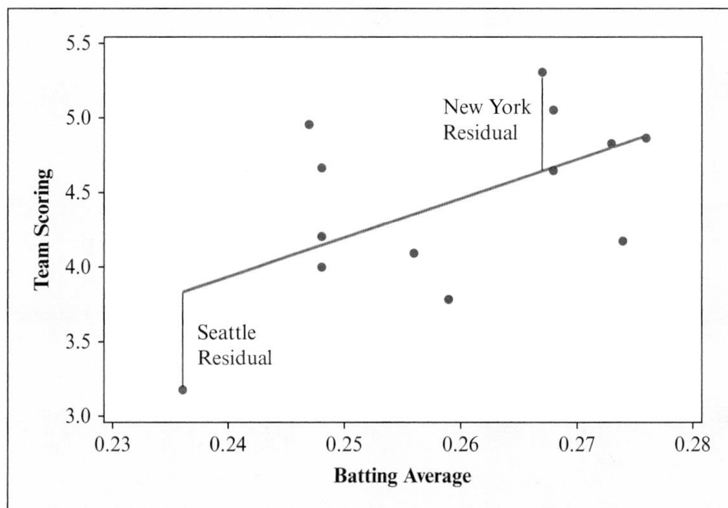

▲ **Figure 3.14** Scatterplot of Team Batting Average and Team Scoring, with the Residual for New York at the Point ($x = 0.267, y = 5.3$) and the Residual for Seattle at ($x = 0.236, y = 3.84$). The residual is the prediction error, which is represented by the vertical distance of the point from the regression line. **Question** Why is a residual represented by a *vertical* distance from the regression line?

for Seattle. The residuals are vertical distances because the regression equation predicts y, the variable on the vertical axis, at a given value of x. Notice the parallel with analyzing contingency tables by studying values of the response variable, *conditional* on (given) values of the explanatory variable.

Residual

In a scatterplot, the vertical distance between the point and the regression line is the absolute value of the residual. The residual is denoted as the difference $y - \hat{y}$ between the actual value and the predicted value of the response variable.

Example 10

Residuals

Detecting an Unusual Vote Total

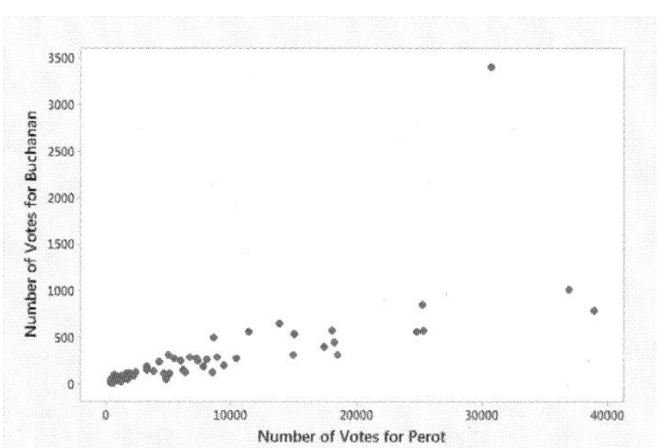

Picture the Scenario

Example 6 investigated whether the vote total in Palm Beach County, Florida, in the 2000 presidential election was unusually high for Pat Buchanan, the Reform party candidate. We did this by plotting, for all 67 counties in Florida, Buchanan's vote against the Reform party candidate (Ross Perot) vote in the 1996 election.

Question to Explore

If we fit a regression line to y = Buchanan vote and x = Perot vote for the 67 counties, would the residuals help us detect any unusual vote totals for Buchanan?

Think It Through

For a county with a large residual, the predicted vote is far from the actual vote, which would indicate an unusual vote total. We can easily have software find the regression line and the residual for each of the 67 counties. Then we can quickly see whether some residuals are particularly large by constructing a histogram of the residuals. Figure 3.15 shows this histogram

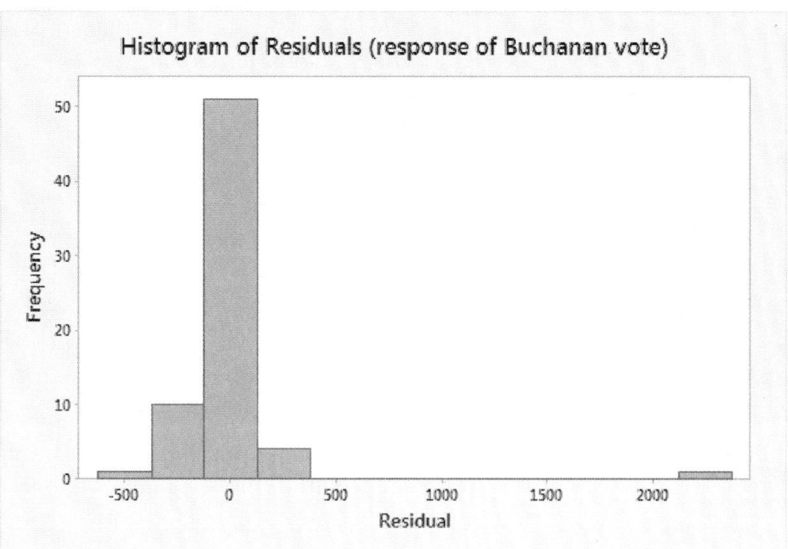

▲ **Figure 3.15** MINITAB Output of Residuals for Predicting 2000 Buchanan Presidential Vote in Florida Counties Using 1996 Perot Vote. **Question** What does the rightmost bar represent?

for the vote data. The residuals cluster around 0, but one is very large, greater than 2000. Inspection of the results shows that this residual applies to Palm Beach County, for which the actual Buchanan vote was $y = 3407$ and the predicted vote was $\hat{y} = 1100$. Its residual is $y - \hat{y} = 3407 - 1100 = 2307$. In summary, in Palm Beach County Buchanan's vote was much higher than predicted.[6]

Insight

As we'll discuss in the next section, an extreme outlier can pull the regression line toward it. Because of this, it's a good idea to fit the data *without* the Palm Beach County observation and see how well that line predicts results for Palm Beach County. We'd then get the regression equation $\hat{y} = 45.7 + 0.02414x$. Since the Perot vote in Palm Beach County was 30,739, this line would predict a Buchanan vote there of $\hat{y} = 45.7 + 0.02414(30.739) = 788$. This compares to the actual Buchanan vote of 3407 in Palm Beach County, for a residual of $3407 - 788 = 2619$. Again, the actual Buchanan vote seems surprisingly high.

► ***Try Exercises 3.26, part d and 3.33, part c***

The Method of Least Squares Yields the Regression Line

We've used software to find the equation for the regression line. But how is it done? The software chooses the optimal line to fit through the data points by making the residuals as small as possible. This process involves compromise because a line can perfectly predict one point (resulting in a residual of 0) but poorly predict many other points (resulting in larger residuals). The actual summary measure used to evaluate regression lines is called the

$$\text{Residual sum of squares} = \Sigma(\text{residual})^2 = \Sigma(y - \hat{y})^2.$$

This formula squares each vertical distance between a point and the line and then adds up these squared values. The better the line, the smaller the residuals tend to be, and the smaller the residual sum of squares tends to be. For each potential line, we have a set of predicted values, a set of residuals, and a residual sum of squares. The line that software reports is the one having the *smallest* residual sum of squares. This way of selecting a line is called the **least squares method**.

Least Squares Method

Among the many possible lines that could be drawn through data points in a scatterplot, the **least squares method** gives what we call the regression line. This method produces the line that has the smallest value for the residual sum of squares using $\hat{y} = a + bx$ to predict y.

In Practice

It's simple for software to use the least squares method to find the regression line for us.

Besides making the errors as small as possible, this regression line

- Has some positive residuals and some negative residuals, and the sum (and mean) of the residuals equals 0.
- Passes through the point $(\bar{x}, \bar{y})$.

---

[6] A more complex analysis accounts for larger counts tending to vary more. However, our analysis is adequate for highlighting data points that fall far from the linear trend.

The first property tells us that the too-low predictions are balanced by the too-high predictions. The second property tells us that the line passes through the center of the data.

Even though we usually rely on software to compute the regression line, the method of least squares does provide explicit formulas for the y-intercept and slope, based on summary statistics for the sample data. Let $\bar{x}$ denote the mean of x, $\bar{y}$ the mean of y, s_x the standard deviation of the x values, and s_y the standard deviation of the y values.

Regression Formulas for y-Intercept and Slope

The **slope** equals $b = r\left(\frac{s_y}{s_x}\right)$.

The **y-intercept** equals $a = \bar{y} - b(\bar{x})$.

Notice that the slope b is directly related to the correlation r, and the y-intercept depends on the slope. Let's return to the baseball data in Example 9 to illustrate the calculations. For that data set, we have $\bar{x} = 0.2597$ for batting average, $\bar{y} = 4.45$ for team scoring, $s_x = 0.01257$, and $s_y = 0.577$. The correlation is $r = 0.568$, so

$$b = r\left(\frac{s_y}{s_x}\right) = 0.568(0.577/0.01257) = 26.07$$

$$\text{and } a = \bar{y} - b(\bar{x}) = 4.45 - 26.07(0.2597) = -2.32$$

The regression line to predict team scoring from batting average is $\hat{y} = -2.32 + 26.1x$.

In Practice

The formulas for a and b help us interpret the regression line $\hat{y} = a + bx$ (for example, see Exercises 3.111 and 3.112), but you should rely on software[7] for calculations. Software doesn't round during the different steps of the calculation, so it will give more accurate results.

The Slope, the Correlation, and the Units of the Variables

We've used the correlation to describe the strength of the association. Why can't we use the *slope* to do this, with bigger slopes representing stronger associations? The reason is that the numerical value of the slope depends on the units for the variables.

For example, consider the 32 countries described in Table 3.4 with data for these countries found in the Internet Use file. The regression line between y = Internet penetration (in %) and x = GDP is $\hat{y} = 34.8 + 1.02x$. GDP was measured in *thousands* of U.S. dollars (per capita). A one-unit increase is therefore a thousand-dollar increase. For every thousand-dollar increase in a nation's GDP we predict Internet penetration to increase by 1.02%. Suppose we instead measure GDP in dollars, such as $x = 68{,}000$ for Australia instead of $x = 68$. A one-unit increase in GDP then refers to a single dollar (per capita) increase. This is only 1/1000 as much as a one-thousand dollar increase, so the change in the predicted value of y would be 1/1000 as much, or $(1/1000)1.02 = 0.00102$. Thus,

[7]In fact, software finds the slope without first finding the correlation, using the equivalent formula

$$b = \frac{1}{(n-1)s_x^2}\Sigma(x - \bar{x})(y - \bar{y}).$$

if x = GDP in dollars, the slope of the regression equation is 0.00102 instead of 1.02. (You can verify this with software by getting the new regression line with GDP in dollars.) Although we get two different slopes depending on what units we use, the strength of the association is the same in each case.

So the slope b doesn't tell us whether the association is strong or weak since we can make b as large or as small as we want by changing the units. By contrast, *the correlation does not change when the units of measurement change.* It is 0.879 between Internet penetration and GDP, whether we measure GDP in dollars or in thousands of dollars.

In summary, we've learned that the correlation describes the strength of the linear association. We've also seen how the regression line predicts the response variable y by using the explanatory variable x. Although correlation and regression methods serve different purposes, there are strong connections between them:

- They are both appropriate when the relationship between two quantitative variables can be approximated by a straight line.
- The correlation and the slope of the regression line have the same sign. If one is positive, so is the other one. If one is negative, so is the other one. If one is zero, the other is also zero.

However, there are some differences between correlation and regression methods. With regression, we must identify response and explanatory variables. We get a different line if we use x to predict y than if we use y to predict x. By contrast, correlation does not make this distinction. We get the same correlation either way. Also, the values for the y-intercept and slope of the regression line depend on the units, whereas the correlation does not. Finally, the correlation falls between −1 and +1, whereas the regression slope can equal any real number.

r-Squared (r^2)

Recall

Using the baseball data, following Example 9 we noted that the prediction error using the regression equation is $y - \hat{y}$, called the residual. ◀

When we predict a value of y, why should we use the regression line? We could instead predict y using the center of its distribution, such as the sample mean, $\bar{y}$. The reason for using the regression line is that if x and y have an association, then we can predict most y values more accurately by substituting x values into the regression equation, $\hat{y} = a + bx$, than by using the sample mean $\bar{y}$ for prediction. The stronger the correlation, the more accurate the regression equation becomes.

Recall

The regression equation results from making the residual sum of squares as small as possible. ◀

To judge how much better we are doing, we can compare the residual sum of squares resulting from either type of prediction. The smaller the residual sum of squares $\Sigma(y - \hat{y})^2$ from the regression equation is relative to $\Sigma(y - \bar{y})^2$, (the residual sum of squares when predicting y with $\bar{y}$), the more precise are, in an overall sense, our predictions. For the quantitative variables Internet use and Facebook use in Example 5, $\Sigma(y - \hat{y})^2$ is 37.7% smaller than $\Sigma(y - \bar{y})^2$. This means that the prediction error using the regression line to predict y is 37.7% smaller than when using the sample mean $\bar{y}$ to predict y.

In Practice

r^2 is interpreted as the percent of the variability in the response variable that can be explained by the linear relationship between x and y.

Because $\Sigma(y - \bar{y})^2$ also measures the variability in the values of the response variable (remember the derivation of the standard deviation in Chapter 2.4), we can interpret the 37.7% as the percent reduction in the variability of the response variable that is due to the linear relationship between y and x. That is 37.7% *of the variability* we observe in Facebook use (the response variable) is due to the linear relationship between Internet and Facebook use.

How did we get 37.7%? We will give details in Chapter 12, but a simple way to compute it is just to take the square of the correlation coefficient. In Example 7, we found $r = 0.614$, and squaring it gives $r^2 = (0.614)^2 = 0.377 = 37.7\%$.

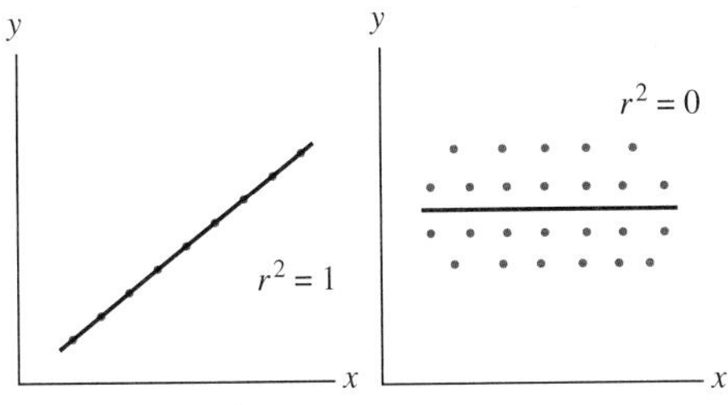

Caution

r^2 is a percentage of the *variability* in the response variable, not a percentage of the response variable. For instance, an r^2 value of 70% in a regression equation with y = rent of an apartment and x = square footage doesn't mean that 70% of the rent of an apartment can be explained by its square footage, but rather that 70% *of the variability* in the rent of apartments (i.e., that some have higher rents and some have lower rents) can be explained by their square footage. ◀

This means we can use the square of the correlation to judge how accurate the regression equation is. The larger r^2, the more accurate our predictions resulting from the regression equation.

When the data points fall exactly in a straight-line pattern, as in the scatterplot in the margin, y and $\hat{y}$ are identical for all points, which results in $r = 1$. Then, $r^2 = 1$ and all (100%) of the variability in the y-values can be explained by the linear relationship between x and y. When $r = 0$, there is no linear association between x and y, as in the scatterplot in the margin. Then r^2 is also equal to 0, and none (0%) of the variability we see in the response variable y can be explained by the linear relationship between x and y (because there is no linear relationship). In practice, r^2 falls somewhere between these two extremes. In Example 4, we have seen that 37.7% of the variability in Facebook use can be attributed to the linear relationship between Internet use and Facebook use.

We'll give further explanation of r^2 and related measures in Chapter 12. We mention r^2 here because you'll see it listed on regression software output or quoted together with the regression equation, so we want you to have a rough idea of what it represents.

Associations with Quantitative and Categorical Variables

In this chapter, we've learned how to explore an association between categorical variables and between quantitative variables. It's also possible to mix the variable types or add other variables. For example, with two quantitative variables, we can identify points in the scatterplot according to their values on a relevant categorical variable. This is done by using different symbols or colors on the scatterplot to portray the different categories.

Example 11

Comparing fitted lines ◀

The Gender Difference in Winning Olympic High Jumps

Picture the Scenario

The summer Olympic Games occur every four years, and one of the track and field events is the high jump. Men have competed in the high jump since 1896 and women since 1928. The High Jump data file on the book's website contains the winning heights (in meters) for each year.[8]

Questions to Explore

a. How can we display the data on these two quantitative variables (winning height, year) and the categorical variable (gender) graphically?

b. How have the winning heights changed over time? How different are the winning heights for men and women in a typical year?

Think It Through

a. Figure 3.16 shows a scatterplot with x = year and y = winning height. The data points are displayed with a red circle for men and a blue triangle for women. There were no Olympic Games during World War II, so no observations appear for 1940 or 1944.

[8]From www.olympic.org/medallists-results.

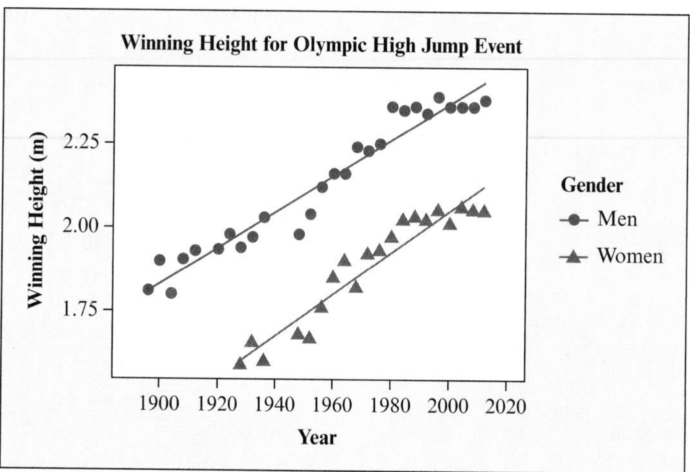

▲ **Figure 3.16** Scatterplot for the Winning High Jumps (in Meters) in the Olympics. The red dots represent men and the blue triangles represent women. **Question** In a typical year, what is the approximate difference between the winning heights for men and for women?

b. The scatterplot shows that for each gender the winning heights have an increasing trend over time. Men have consistently jumped higher than women, between about 0.3 and 0.4 meters in a given year. The women's winning heights are similar to those for the men about 60 years earlier—for instance, about 2.0 meters in 1990–2012 for women and in 1930–1940 for men.

Insight

We could describe these trends by fitting a regression line to the points for men and a separate regression line to the points for women. Figure 3.16 indicates these lines. The slopes are nearly identical, indicating a similar rate of improvement over the years for both genders. However, note that in recent Olympics the winning heights have leveled off somewhat. We should be cautious in using regression lines to predict future winning heights.

▶ ***Try Exercise 3.42***

3.3 Practicing the Basics

3.24 Sketch plots of lines Identify the values of the y-intercept a and the slope b, and sketch the following regression lines, for values of x between 0 and 10.

a. $\hat{y} = 7 + 0.5x$

b. $\hat{y} = 7 + x$

c. $\hat{y} = 7 - x$

d. $\hat{y} = 7$

3.25 Sit-ups and the 40-yard dash Is there a relationship between how many sit-ups you can do and how fast you can run 40 yards? The EXCEL output shows the relationship between these variables for a study of female athletes to be discussed in Chapter 12.

TRY

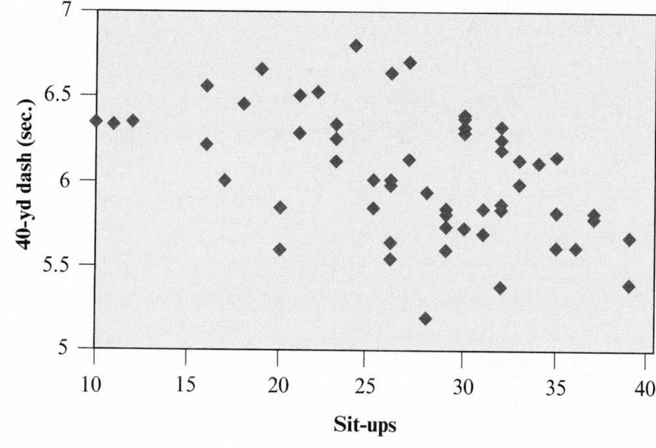

Excel scatterplot of time to run 40-yard dash by number of sit-ups.

a. The regression equation is $\hat{y} = 6.71 - 0.024x$. Find the predicted time in the 40-yard dash for a subject who can do (i) 10 sit-ups, (ii) 40 sit-ups. Based on these times, explain how to sketch the regression line over this scatterplot.

b. Interpret the y-intercept and slope of the equation in part a, in the context of the number of sit-ups and time for the 40-yard dash.

c. Based on the slope in part a, is the correlation positive or negative? Explain.

3.26 Home selling prices The House Selling Prices FL data file on the book's website lists selling prices of homes in Gainesville, Florida, in 2003 and some predictors for the selling price. For the response variable y = selling price in thousands of dollars and the explanatory variable x = size of house in thousands of square feet, $\hat{y} = 9.2 + 77.0x$.

TRY

a. How much do you predict a house would sell for if it has (i) 2,000 square feet, (ii) 3,000 square feet?

b. Using results in part a, explain how to interpret the slope.

c. Is the correlation between these variables positive or negative? Why?

d. One home that is 3000 square feet sold for $300,000. Find the residual, and interpret.

3.27 Rating restaurants Zagat restaurant guides publish ratings of restaurants for many large cities around the world (see www.zagat.com). The review for each restaurant gives a verbal summary as well as a 0- to 30-point rating of the quality of food, décor, service, and the cost of a dinner with one drink and tip. For 31 French restaurants in Boston in 2014, the food quality ratings had a mean of 24.55 and standard deviation of 2.08 points. The cost of a dinner (in U.S. dollars) had a mean of $50.35 and standard deviation of $14.92. The equation that predicts the cost of a dinner using the rating for the quality of food is $\hat{y} = -70 + 4.9x$. The correlation between these two variables is 0.68. (Data available in the Zagat_Boston file.)

a. Predict the cost of a dinner in a restaurant that gets the (i) lowest observed food quality rating of 21, (ii) highest observed food quality rating of 28.

b. Interpret the slope in context.

c. Interpret the correlation.

d. Show how the slope can be obtained from the correlation and other information given.

3.28 Predicting cost of meal from rating Refer to the previous exercise. The correlation with the cost of a dinner is 0.68 for food quality rating, 0.69 for service rating, and 0.56 for décor rating. According to the definition of r^2 as a measure for the reduction in the prediction error, which of these three ratings can be used to make the most accurate predictions for the cost of a dinner: quality of food, service, or décor? Why?

3.29 Internet in Indonesia For the 32 nations in Example 7, we found a correlation of 0.614 between Internet use and Facebook use (both as percentages of population). The regression equation is predicted Facebook use = 7.90 + 0.439 Internet use

a. Based on the correlation value, the slope had to be positive. Why?

b. Indonesia had an Internet use of 15.4% and Facebook use of 20.7%. Find its predicted Facebook use based on the regression equation.

c. Find the residual for Indonesia. Interpret.

3.30 Broadband subscribers and population The Internet Use data file on the book's website contains data on the number of individuals in a country with broadband access and the population size for each of 32 nations. When using population size as the explanatory variable, x, and broadband subscribers as the response variable, y, the regression equation is predicted broadband subscribers = 5,530,203 + 0.0761 population.

a. Interpret the slope of the regression equation. (Make sure to use a meaningful increase.) Is the association positive or negative? Explain what this means.

b. Predict broadband subscribers at the (i) minimum population size x value of 7,154,600, (ii) at the maximum population size x value of 1,350,695,000.

c. For the United States, broadband subscribers = 88,520,000, and population = 313,914,040. Find the predicted broadband use and the residual for the United States. Interpret the value of this residual.

3.31 SAT reading and math scores The SAT2010 data file on the book's website contains average reading and math SAT scores for each of the 50 states and Washington D.C. Let the explanatory variable x = reading and the response variable y = math. The regression equation is $\hat{y} = 18.1 + 0.975x$.

a. California had an average reading score of 501. Use the regression equation to predict the average math score for California.

b. Calculate the residual associated with California and comment on its value in the context of the problem.

c. Does it appear that a state's average reading score is a reliable predictor of its average math score?

3.32 How much do seat belts help? A study in 2000 by the National Highway Traffic Safety Administration estimated that failure to wear seat belts led to 9200 deaths in the previous year, and that the number of deaths would decrease by 270 for every 1 percentage point gain in seat belt usage. Let $\hat{y}$ = predicted number of deaths in a year and x = percentage of people who wear seat belts.

TRY

a. Report the slope b for the equation $\hat{y} = a + bx$.

b. If the y-intercept equals 28,910, then predict the number of deaths in a year if (i) no one wears seat belts, (ii) 73% of people wear seat belts (the value in 2000), (iii) 100% of people wear seat belts.

3.33 Regression between cereal sodium and sugar The following figure shows the result of a regression analysis of the explanatory variable x = sugar and the response variable y = sodium for the breakfast cereal data set discussed in Chapter 2 (the Cereal data file on the book's website).

TRY

a. What criterion is used in finding the line?

b. Can you draw a line that will result in a smaller sum of the squared residuals?

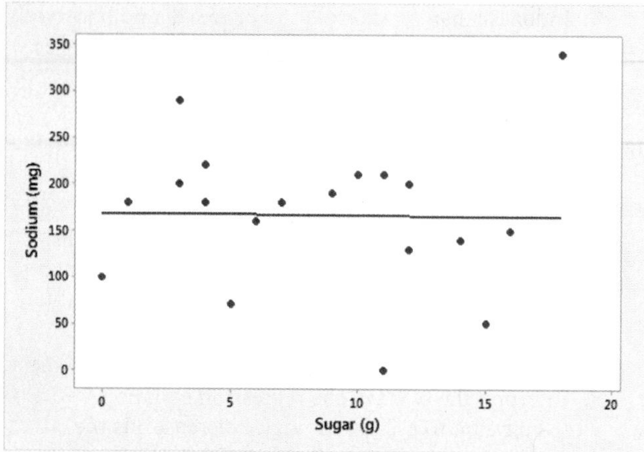

c. Now let's look at a histogram of the residuals. Explain what the two short bars on the far right of the histogram mean in the context of the problem. Which two brands of cereal do they represent? Can you find them on the scatterplot?

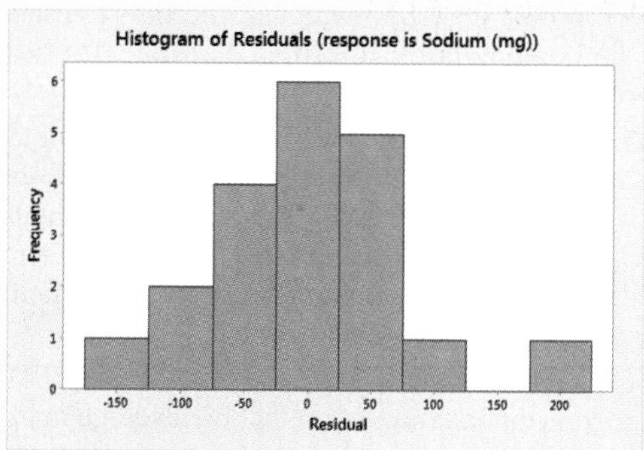

d. In general, how reliable would you say amount of sugar is as a predictor of the amount of sodium?

3.34 Regression and correlation between cereal sodium and sugar Refer to the previous exercise.

a. For this example, it seems that the average sodium content is as good a predictor as the one resulting from the regression equation. Do you expect r^2 to be large or small? Why?

b. For this data, $r = -0.017$. Interpret r^2.

c. Show the algebraic relationship between the correlation of -0.017 and the slope of the regression equation $b = -0.25$, using the fact that the standard deviations are 5.32 g for sugar and 77.3 mg for sodium. (Hint: Recall that $b = r\left(\frac{s_y}{s_x}\right)$.)

3.35 Advertising and sales Each month, the owner of Fay's Tanning Salon records in a data file y = monthly total sales receipts and x = amount spent that month on advertising, both in thousands of dollars. For the first three months of operation, the observations are as shown in the table.

Advertising	Sales
0	4
1	6
2	8

a. Sketch a scatterplot.

b. From inspection of the scatterplot, state the correlation and the regression line. (*Note*: You should be able to figure them out without using software or formulas.)

c. Find the mean and standard deviation for each variable.

d. Using part c, find the regression line, using the formulas for the slope and the y-intercept. Interpret the y-intercept and the slope.

3.36 Midterm–final correlation For students who take Statistics 101 at Lake Wobegon College in Minnesota, both the midterm and final exams have mean = 75 and standard deviation = 10. The professor explores using the midterm exam score to predict the final exam score. The regression equation relating y = final exam score to x = midterm exam score is $\hat{y} = 30 + 0.60x$.

a. Find the predicted final exam score for a student who has (i) midterm score = 100, (ii) midterm score = 50. Note that in each case the predicted final exam score *regresses toward the mean* of 75. (This is a property of the regression equation that is the origin of its name, as Chapter 12 will explain.)

b. Show that the correlation equals 0.60 and interpret it. (*Hint:* Use the relation between the slope and correlation.)

3.37 Predict final exam from midterm In an introductory statistics course, x = midterm exam score and y = final exam score. Both have mean = 80 and standard deviation = 10. The correlation between the exam scores is 0.70.

a. Find the regression equation.

b. Find the predicted final exam score for a student with midterm exam score = 80 and another with midterm exam score = 90.

3.38 NL baseball Example 9 related y = team scoring (per game) and x = team batting average for American League teams. For National League teams in 2010, $\hat{y} = -6.25 + 41.5x$. (Data available on the book's website in the NL team statistics file.)

a. The team batting averages fell between 0.242 and 0.272. Explain how to interpret the slope in context.

b. The standard deviations were 0.00782 for team batting average and 0.3604 for team scoring. The correlation between these variables was 0.900. Show how the correlation and slope of 41.5 relate in terms of these standard deviations.

c. Software reports $r^2 = 0.81$. Explain how to interpret this measure.

3.39 Study time and college GPA A graduate teaching assistant (Euijung Ryu) for Introduction to Statistics (STA 2023) at the University of Florida collected data from one of her classes in spring 2007 to investigate the relationship between using the explanatory variable x = study time per week (average number of hours) to predict the response variable y = college GPA. For the 21 females in her class, the correlation was 0.42. For the eight males in her class, the data were as shown in the following table.

TECH

a. Create a data file and use it to construct a scatterplot. Interpret.

b. Find and interpret the correlation.

c. Find and interpret the prediction equation by reporting the predicted GPA for a student who studies (i) 5 hours per week, (ii) 25 hours per week.

Student	Study Time	GPA
1	14	2.8
2	25	3.6
3	15	3.4
4	5	3.0
5	10	3.1
6	12	3.3
7	5	2.7
8	21	3.8

3.40 Oil and GDP An article in the September 16, 2006, issue of *The Economist* showed a scatterplot for many nations relating the response variable y = annual oil consumption per person (in barrels) and the explanatory variable x = gross domestic product (GDP, per person, in thousands of dollars). The values shown on the plot were approximately as shown in the table.

TECH

a. Create a data file and use it to construct a scatterplot. Interpret.

b. Find and interpret the prediction equation.

c. Find and interpret the correlation.

d. Find and interpret the residual for Canada.

Nation	GDP	Oil Consumption
India	3	1
China	8	2
Brazil	9	4
Mexico	10	7
Russia	11	8
S. Korea	20	18
Italy	29	12
France	30	13
Britain	31	11
Germany	31	12
Japan	31	16
Canada	34	26
U.S.	41	26

3.41 Mountain bikes revisited Is there a relationship between the weight and price of a mountain bike? This question was considered in Exercise 3.21. We will analyze the Mountain Bike data file on the book's website. (The data also were shown in Exercise 3.21.)

TECH

a. Construct a scatterplot. Interpret.

b. Find the regression equation. Interpret the slope in context. Does the y-intercept have contextual meaning?

c. You decide to purchase a mountain bike that weighs 30 pounds. What is the predicted price for the bike?

3.42 Mountain bike and suspension type Refer to the previous exercise. The data file contains price, weight, and type of suspension system (FU = full, FE = front-end in the scatterplot shown).

TRY TECH

a. Do you observe a linear relationship? Is the single regression line, which is $\hat{y} = 1896 - 40.45x$, the best way to fit the data? How would you suggest fitting the data?

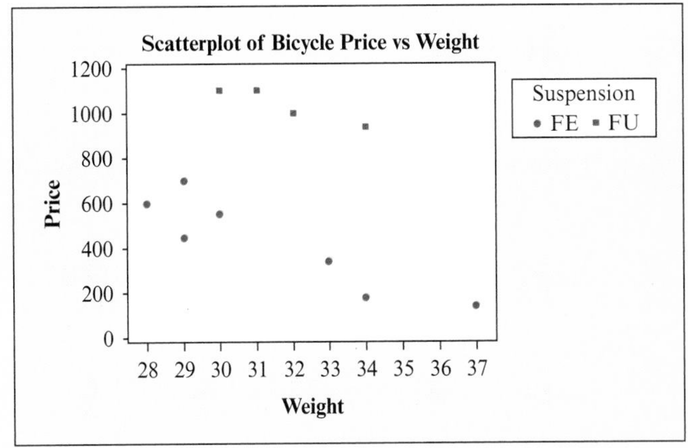

b. Find separate regression equations for the two suspension types. Summarize your findings.

c. The correlation for all 12 data points is $r = -0.32$. If the correlations for the full and front-end suspension bikes are found separately, how do you believe the correlations will compare to $r = -0.32$? Find them and interpret.

d. You see a mountain bike advertised for \$700 that weighs 28.5 lb. The type of suspension is not given. Would you predict that this bike has a full or a front-end suspension? Statistically justify your answer.

3.43 Fuel Consumption Most cars are fuel efficient when running at a steady speed of around 40 to 50 mph. A scatterplot relating fuel consumption (measured in mpg) and steady driving speed (measured in mph) for a mid-sized car is shown below. The data are available in the Fuel file on the book's Web site. (Source: Berry, I. M. (2010). *The Effects of Driving Style and Vehicle Performance on the Real-World Fuel Consumption of U.S. Light-Duty Vehicles.* Masters thesis, Massachusetts Institute of Technology, Cambridge, MA.)

a. The correlation equals 0.106. Comment on the use of the correlation coefficient as a measure for the association between fuel consumption and steady driving speed.

b. Comment on the use of the regression equation as a tool for predicting fuel consumption from the velocity of the car.

c. Over what subrange of steady driving speed might fitting a regression equation be appropriate? Why?

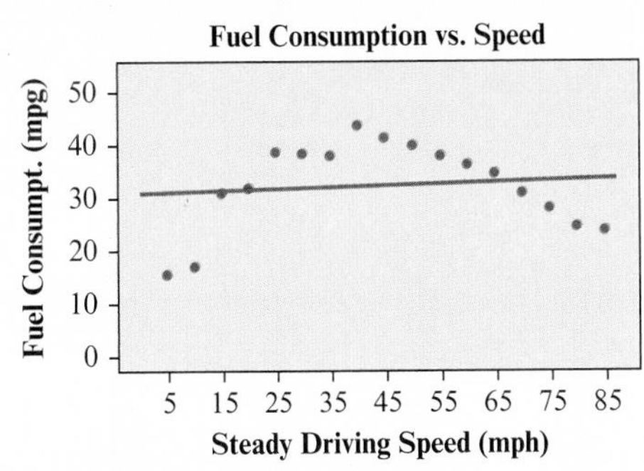

3.4 Cautions in Analyzing Associations

This chapter has introduced ways to explore **associations** between variables. When using these methods, you need to be cautious about certain potential pitfalls.

Extrapolation Is Dangerous

Extrapolation refers to using a regression line to predict y values for x values outside the observed range of data. This is riskier as we move farther from that range. If the trend changes, extrapolation gives poor predictions. For example, regression analysis is often applied to observations of a quantitative response variable over time. The regression line describes the time trend. But it is dangerous to use the line to make predictions far into the future.

Example 12

Extrapolation

Forecasting Future Global Warming

Picture the Scenario

In Chapter 2, we explored trends in temperatures over time using time plots. Let's use regression with the Central Park Yearly Temps data file on the book's website to describe the trend over time of the annual mean temperatures from 1869–2012 for Central Park, New York City.[9]

Questions to Explore

a. What does a regression line tell us about the trend over the 20th century?

b. What does it predict about the annual mean temperature in the year (i) 2015, (ii) 3000? Are these extrapolations sensible?

Think It Through

a. Figure 3.17 shows a time plot of the Central Park annual mean temperatures. For a regression analysis, the mean annual temperature is the response variable. Time (the year) is the explanatory variable. Software tells us that the regression line is $\hat{y} = -2.6894 + 0.0291x$. Figure 3.17 superimposes the regression trend line over the time plot.

The positive slope reflects an increasing trend: The annual mean temperature tended upward over the century. *The slope $b = 0.0291$ indicates that for each one-year increase, the predicted annual mean temperature increases by 0.0291 degrees Fahrenheit.* The slope value of 0.0291 seems close to 0, indicating little warming. However, 0.0291 is the predicted change *per year.* Over a century, the predicted change is $100(0.0291) = 2.91$ degrees, which is quite significant.

b. Using the trend line, the predicted annual mean temperature for the year 2015 is

$$\hat{y} = -2.6894 + 0.0291(2015) = 55.9 \text{ degrees Fahrenheit.}$$

Further into the future we see more dramatic increases. At the next millennium, for the year 3000, the forecast is $\hat{y} = -2.6894 + 0.0291(3000) = 84.6$. If this is accurate, it would be exceedingly uncomfortable to live in New York!

[9] *Source:* www.erh.noaa.gov/okx/climate/records/monthannualtemp.html.

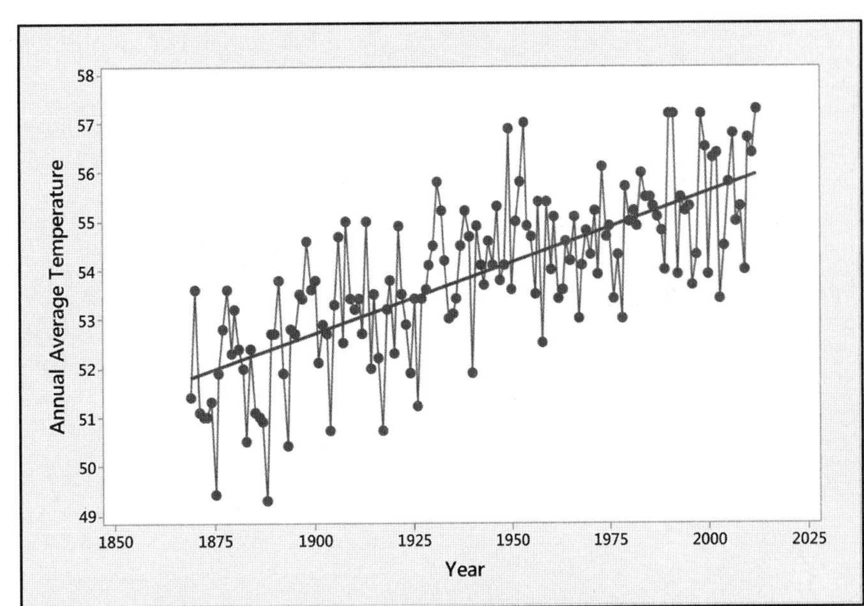

▲ **Figure 3.17** MINITAB Time Plot of Central Park Annual Mean Temperature Versus Time, Showing Fitted Regression Line. **Question** If the present trend continues, what would you predict for the annual mean temperature for 2015?

Insight

It is dangerous to extrapolate far outside the range of observed x values. There's no guarantee that the relationship will have the same trend outside that range. It seems reasonable to predict for 2015. That's not looking too far into the future from the last observation in 2012. However, it is foolhardy to predict for 3000. It's not sensible to assume that the same straight-line trend will continue for the next 988 years. As time moves forward, the annual mean temperatures may increase even faster or level off or even decrease.

► ***Try Exercise 3.45***

Predictions about the future using time series data are called **forecasts**. When we use a regression line to forecast a trend for future years, we must make the assumption that the past trend will remain the same in the future. This is risky.

Be Cautious of Influential Outliers

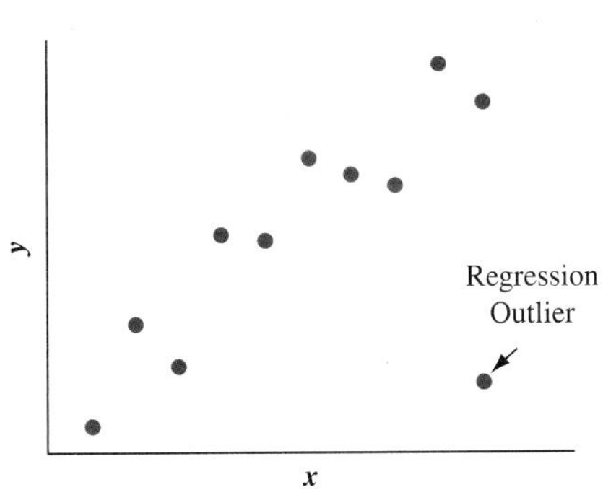

One reason to plot the data before you do a correlation or regression analysis is to check for unusual observations. Such an observation can tell you something interesting, as in Examples 6 and 10 about the Buchanan vote in the 2000 U.S. presidential election. Furthermore, a data point that is an outlier on a scatterplot can have a substantial effect on the regression line and correlation, especially with small data sets.

What's relevant here is not whether an observation is an outlier in its x value, relative to the other x values, or in its y value, relative to the other y values. Instead, we search for observations that are **regression outliers**, being well removed from the trend that the rest of the data follow. The margin figure shows an observation that is a regression outlier, although it is not an outlier on x alone or on y alone.

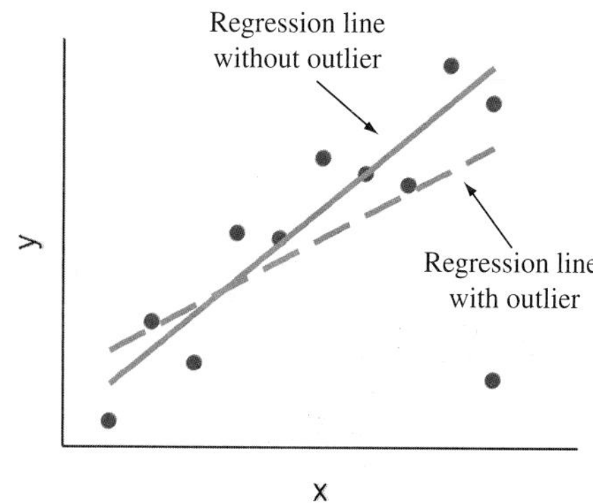

When an observation has a large effect on results of a regression analysis, it is said to be **influential**. For an observation to be influential, two conditions must hold:

- Its x value is relatively low or high compared to the rest of the data.
- The observation is a regression outlier, falling quite far from the trend that the rest of the data follow.

When both of these happen, the line tends to be pulled toward that data point and away from the trend of the rest of the points as the margin figure illustrates.

Figure 3.18 shows two regression outliers. The correlation without these two points equals 0.00. The first regression outlier is near the middle of the range of x. It does not have much potential for tilting the line up or down. It has little influence on the slope or the correlation. The correlation changes only to 0.03 when we add it to the data set. The second regression outlier is at the high end of the range of x-values. It is influential. The correlation changes to 0.47 when we add it to the data set.

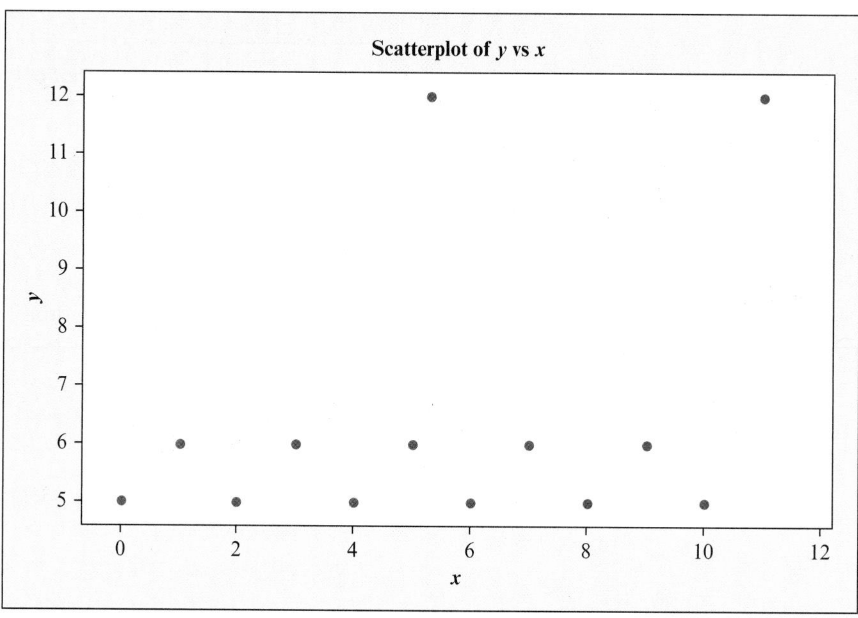

▲ **Figure 3.18 An Observation Is a Regression Outlier If It Is Far Removed from the Trend That the Rest of the Data Follow.** The top two points are regression outliers. Not all regression outliers are influential in affecting the correlation or slope. **Question** Which regression outlier in this figure is influential?

Example 13

Influential outliers ◄

Higher Education and Higher Murder Rates

Picture the Scenario

Table 3.6 shows data[10] for the 50 states and the District of Columbia on

Violent crime rate: The annual number of murders, forcible rapes, robberies, and aggravated assaults per 100,000 people in the population.

Murder rate: The annual number of murders per 100,000 people in the population.

[10]From *Statistical Abstract of the United States, 2003.*

Poverty: Percentage of the residents with income below the poverty level.

High school: Percentage of the adult residents who have at least a high school education.

College: Percentage of the adult residents who have a college education.

Single parent: Percentage of families headed by a single parent.

The data are in the U.S. Statewide Crime data file on the book's website. Let's look at the relationship between y = murder rate and x = college. We'll look at other variables in the exercises.

Table 3.6 Statewide Data on Several Variables

State	Violent Crime	Murder Rate	Poverty	High School	College	Single Parent
Alabama	486	7.4	14.7	77.5	20.4	26.0
Alaska	567	4.3	8.4	90.4	28.1	23.2
Arizona	532	7.0	13.5	85.1	24.6	23.5
Arkansas	445	6.3	15.8	81.7	18.4	24.7
California	622	6.1	14.0	81.2	27.5	21.8
Colorado	334	3.1	8.5	89.7	34.6	20.8
Connecticut	325	2.9	7.7	88.2	31.6	22.9
Delaware	684	3.2	9.9	86.1	24.0	25.6
District of Columbia	1508	41.8	17.4	83.2	38.3	44.7
Florida	812	5.6	12.0	84.0	22.8	26.5
Georgia	505	8.0	12.5	82.6	23.1	25.5
Hawaii	244	2.9	10.6	87.4	26.3	19.1
Idaho	253	1.2	13.3	86.2	20.0	17.7
Illinois	657	7.2	10.5	85.5	27.1	21.9
Indiana	349	5.8	8.3	84.6	17.1	22.8
Iowa	266	1.6	7.9	89.7	25.5	19.8
Kansas	389	6.3	10.5	88.1	27.3	20.2
Kentucky	295	4.8	12.5	78.7	20.5	23.2
Louisiana	681	12.5	18.5	80.8	22.5	29.3
Maine	110	1.2	9.8	89.3	24.1	23.7
Maryland	787	8.1	7.3	85.7	32.3	24.5
Massachusetts	476	2.0	10.2	85.1	32.7	22.8
Michigan	555	6.7	10.2	86.2	23.0	24.5
Minnesota	281	3.1	7.9	90.8	31.2	19.6
Mississippi	361	9.0	15.5	80.3	18.7	30.0
Missouri	490	6.2	9.8	86.6	26.2	24.3
Montana	241	1.8	16.0	89.6	23.8	21.4

(Continued)

State	Violent Crime	Murder Rate	Poverty	High School	College	Single Parent
Nebraska	328	3.7	10.7	90.4	24.6	19.6
Nevada	524	6.5	10.1	82.8	19.3	24.2
New Hampshire	175	1.8	7.6	88.1	30.1	20.0
New Jersey	384	3.4	8.1	87.3	30.1	20.2
New Mexico	758	7.4	19.3	82.2	23.6	26.6
New York	554	5.0	14.7	82.5	28.7	26.0
North Carolina	498	7.0	13.2	79.2	23.2	24.3
North Dakota	81	0.6	12.8	85.5	22.6	19.1
Ohio	334	3.7	11.1	87.0	24.6	24.6
Oklahoma	496	5.3	14.1	86.1	22.5	23.5
Oregon	351	2.0	12.9	88.1	27.2	22.5
Pennsylvania	420	4.9	9.8	85.7	24.3	22.8
Rhode Island	298	4.3	10.2	81.3	26.4	27.4
South Carolina	805	5.8	12.0	83.0	19.0	27.1
South Dakota	167	0.9	9.4	91.8	25.7	20.7
Tennessee	707	7.2	13.4	79.9	22.0	27.9
Texas	545	5.9	14.9	79.2	23.9	21.5
Utah	256	1.9	8.1	90.7	26.4	13.6
Vermont	114	1.5	10.3	90.0	28.8	22.5
Virginia	282	5.7	8.1	86.6	31.9	22.2
Washington	370	3.3	9.5	91.8	28.6	22.1
West Virginia	317	2.5	15.8	77.1	15.3	22.3
Wisconsin	237	3.2	9.0	86.7	23.8	21.7
Wyoming	267	2.4	11.1	90.0	20.6	20.8

Questions to Explore

a. Construct the scatterplot between y = murder rate and x = college. Does any observation look like it could be influential in its effect on the regression line?

b. Use software to find the regression line. Check whether the observation identified in part a actually is influential by finding the line again without that observation.

Think It Through

a. Figure 3.19 shows the scatterplot. The observation out by itself is D.C. with $x = 38.3$ and $y = 41.8$, which is the largest observation on both these variables. It satisfies both conditions for an observation to be influential: It has a relatively extreme value on the explanatory variable (college), and it is a regression outlier, falling well away from the linear trend of the other points.

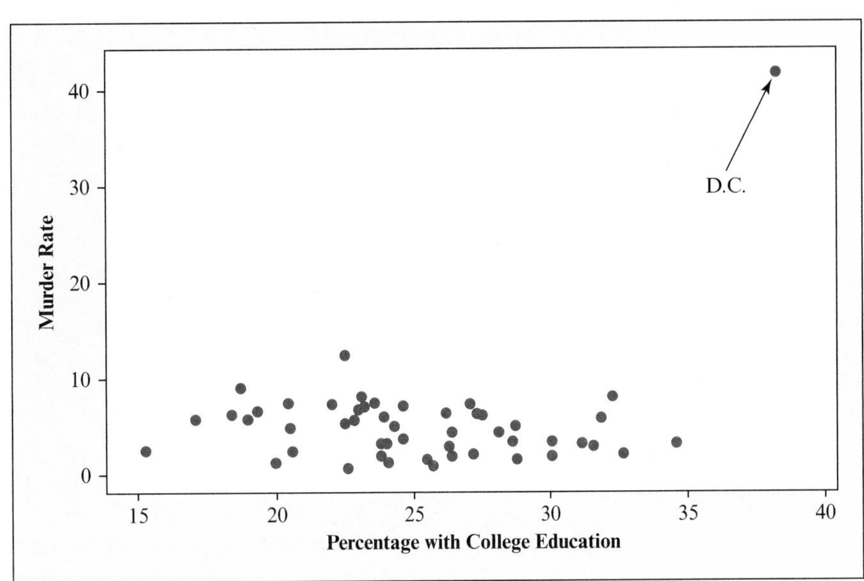

▲ **Figure 3.19** Scatterplot Relating Murder Rate to Percentage with College Education. **Question** How would you expect the slope to change if D.C. is excluded from the regression analysis?

b. Using software, the regression line fitted to all 51 observations, including D.C., equals $\hat{y} = -3.1 + 0.33x$. The slope is *positive*, as shown in the first plot in Figure 3.20. You can check that the predicted murder rates *increase* from 1.9 to 10.1 as the percentage with a college education increases from $x = 15\%$ to $x = 40\%$, roughly the range of observed x values. By contrast, when we fit the regression line only to the 50 states, excluding the observation for D.C., $\hat{y} = 8.0 - 0.14x$. The slope of -0.14 reflects a *negative* trend, as shown in the second plot in Figure 3.20. Now, the predicted murder rate *decreases* from 5.9 to 2.4 as the percentage with a college education increases from 15% to 40%.

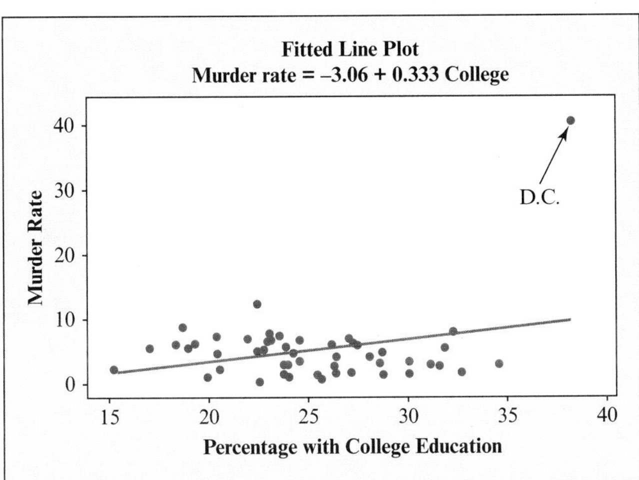

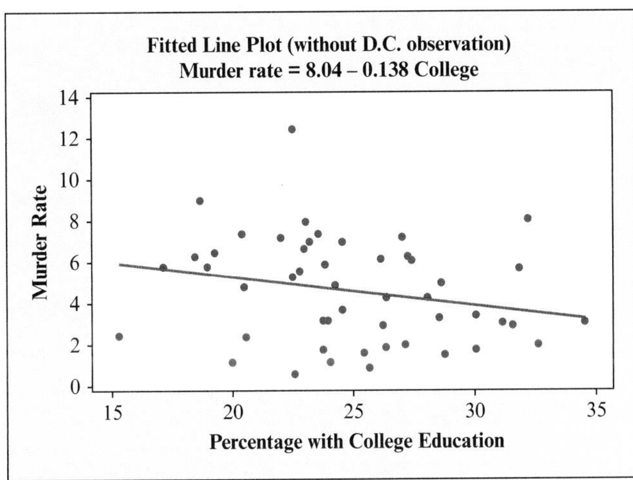

▲ **Figure 3.20** Scatterplots Relating Murder Rate to Percentage with College Education, With and Without Observation for D.C. **Question** Which line better describes the trend for the 50 states?

Insight

Including D.C. in the regression analysis has the effect of pulling the slope of the regression line upward. The regression line then makes it seem, misleadingly, as if the murder rate *increases* when the percentage with a college education increases. In fact, for the rest of the data, the predicted murder rate *decreases.* The regression line including D.C. distorts the relationship for the other 50 states. In summary, the D.C. data point is highly influential. The regression line for the 50 states alone better represents the overall negative trend. In reporting these results, we should show this line and then note that D.C. is a regression outlier that falls well outside this trend.

▶ ***Try Exercise 3.47***

Caution

Always construct a scatterplot before finding a correlation coefficient or fitting a regression line. ◀

This example shows the correlation and the regression line are **nonresistant**: They are prone to distortion by outliers. *Investigate any regression outlier.* Was the observation recorded incorrectly, or is it merely different from the rest of the data in some way? It is often a good idea to refit the regression line without it to see if it has a large effect, as we did in this last example.

Correlation Does Not Imply Causation

In a regression analysis, suppose that as x goes up, y also tends to go up (or go down). Can we conclude that there's a *causal* connection, with changes in x causing changes in y?

The concept of causality is central to science. We are all familiar with it, at least in an informal sense. We know, for example, that exposure to a virus can cause the flu or heating air will cause air to rise. But just observing an association between two variables is not enough to imply a causal connection. There may be some alternative explanation for the association.

Correlation and causation ◀

Example 14

Education and Crime

Picture the Scenario

Figure 3.21 shows recent data on y = crime rate and x = education for Florida counties, from the FL Crime data file on the book's website. Education was measured as the percentage of residents aged at least 25 in the county who had at least a high school degree. Crime rate was measured as the number of crimes in that county in the past year per 1000 residents.

As the figure shows, these variables have a positive association. The correlation is $r = 0.47$. Unlike the previous example, there is no obviously influential observation causing the positive correlation between education and higher crime rate. However, another variable measured for these counties is urbanization, measured as the percentage of the residents who live in metropolitan areas. It has a correlation of 0.68 with crime rate and 0.79 with education.

Question to Explore

From the positive correlation between crime rate and education, can we conclude that having a more highly educated populace causes the crime rate to go up?

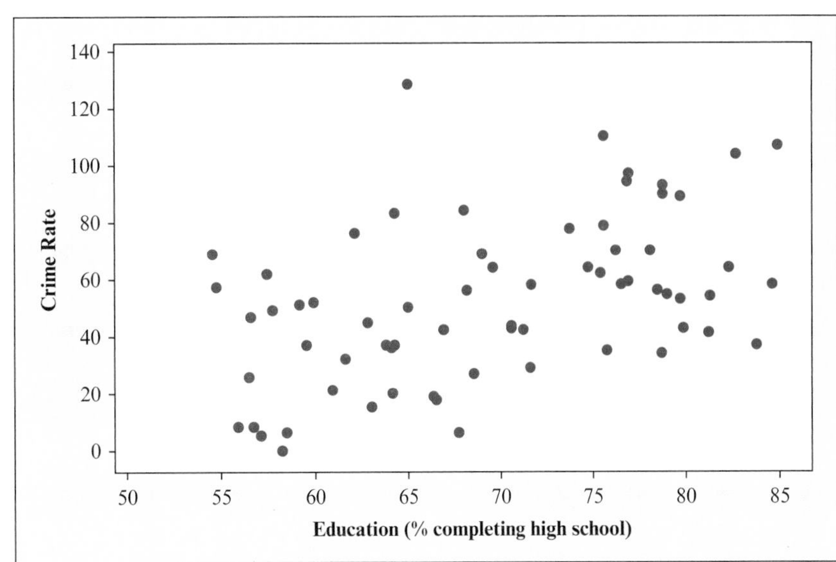

▲ **Figure 3.21** Scatterplot of Crime Rate and Percentage With at Least a High School Education. There is a moderate positive association ($r = 0.47$). **Question** Does more education cause more crime, or does more crime cause more education, or possibly neither?

Think It Through

The strong correlation of 0.79 between urbanization and education tells us that highly urban counties tend to have higher education levels. The moderately strong correlation of 0.68 between urbanization and crime rate tells us that highly urban counties also tend to have higher crime. So, perhaps the reason for the positive correlation between education and crime rate is that education tends to be greater in more highly urbanized counties, but crime rates also tend to be higher in such counties. In summary, a correlation could occur without any causal connection.

Insight

For counties with similar levels of urbanization, the association between crime rate and education may look quite different. You may then see a *negative* correlation. Figure 3.22 portrays how this could happen. It shows a negative trend between crime rate and education for counties having urbanization = 0 (none of the residents living in a metropolitan area), a separate negative trend

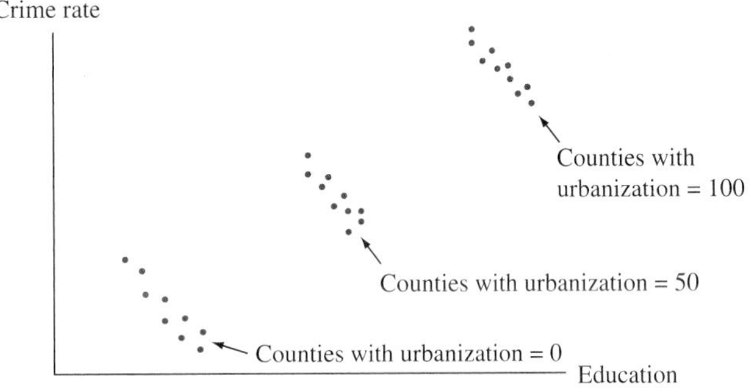

▲ **Figure 3.22** Hypothetical Scatter Diagram Relating Crime Rate and Education. The points are also labeled by whether urbanization = 0.50, or 100. **Question** Sketch lines that represent (a) the overall positive relationship between crime rate and education, and (b) the negative relationship between crime rate and education for counties having urbanization = 0.

for counties having urbanization = 50, and a separate negative trend for counties having urbanization = 100. If we ignore the urbanization values and look at all the points, however, we see a positive trend—higher crime rate tending to occur with higher education levels, as reflected by the overall positive correlation.

▶ ***Try Exercises 3.53 and 3.57***

Whenever two variables are associated, other variables may have influenced that association. In Example 14, urbanization influenced the association between crime rate and education. This illustrates an important point: **Correlation does not imply causation**.

In Example 14, crime rate and education were positively correlated, but that does not mean that having a high level of education causes a county's crime rate to be high. Whenever we observe a correlation between variables x and y, there may be a third variable correlated with both x and y that is responsible for their association. Let's look at another example to illustrate this point.

Example 15

Lurking variable ◀

Ice Cream and Drowning

Picture the Scenario

The Gold Coast of Australia, south of Brisbane, is famous for its beaches. Because of strong rip tides, however, each year many people drown. Data collected monthly show a positive correlation between y = number of people who drowned in that month and x = number of gallons of ice cream sold in refreshment stands along the beach in that month.

Question to Explore

Clearly, the high sales of ice cream don't cause more people to drown. Identify another variable that could be responsible for this association.

Think It Through

In the summer in Australia (especially January and February), the weather is hot. People tend to buy more ice cream in those months. They also tend to go to the beach and swim more in those months, and more people drown. In the winter, it is cooler. People buy less ice cream, fewer people go to the beach, and fewer people drown. So, the mean temperature in the month is a variable that could be responsible for the correlation. As mean temperature goes up, so does ice cream sales and so does the number of people who drown.

Insight

If we looked only at months having similar mean temperatures, probably we would not observe any association between ice cream sales and the number of people who drown.

▶ ***Try Exercise 3.54***

A third variable that is not measured in a study (or perhaps even known about to the researchers) but that influences the association between the response variable and the explanatory variable is referred to as a **lurking variable**.

Lurking Variable

A **lurking variable** is a variable, usually unobserved, that influences the association between the variables of primary interest.

In interpreting the positive correlation between crime rate and education for Florida counties, we'd be remiss if we failed to recognize that the correlation could be due to a lurking variable. This could happen if we observed those two variables but not urbanization, which would then be a lurking variable. Likewise, if we got excited by the positive correlation between ice cream sales and the number drowned in a month, we'd fail to recognize that the monthly mean temperature is a lurking variable. The difficulty in practice is that often we have no clue what the lurking variables may be.

Simpson's Paradox

We can express the statement that *correlation does not imply causation* more generally as **association does not imply causation**. This warning holds whether we analyze associations between quantitative variables or between categorical variables.

The direction of an association between two variables can change after we include a third variable and analyze the data at separate levels of that variable; this is known as **Simpson's paradox**.[11] We observed Simpson's paradox in Figure 3.22 in Example 14, in which a positive correlation between crime rate and education changed to a negative correlation when data were considered at separate levels of urbanization. This example serves as a warning: *Be cautious about interpreting an association.* Always be wary of lurking variables that may influence the association.

Let's illustrate by revisiting Example 1, which presented a study indicating that smoking could apparently be beneficial to your health. Could a lurking variable be responsible for this association?

Example 16

Reversal in direction of association

Smoking and Health

Picture the Scenario

Example 1 mentioned a survey[12] of 1,314 women in the United Kingdom that asked each woman whether she was a smoker. Twenty years later, a follow-up survey observed whether each woman was dead or still alive. Table 3.7 is a contingency table of the results. The response variable is

Table 3.7 Smoking Status and 20-Year Survival in Women

	Survival Status		
Smoker	**Dead**	**Alive**	**Total**
Yes	139	443	582
No	230	502	732
Total	**369**	**945**	**1,314**

[11]The paradox is named after a British statistician who in 1951 investigated conditions under which this flip-flopping of association can happen.

[12]Described by D. R. Appleton et al., *American Statistician,* vol. 50, pp. 340–341 (1996).

survival status after 20 years. We find that 139/582, which is 24%, of the smokers died, and 230/732, or 31%, of the nonsmokers died. There was a greater survival rate for the smokers.

Could the age of the woman at the beginning of the study explain the association? Presumably it could if the smokers tended to be younger than the nonsmokers. For this reason, Table 3.8 shows four contingency tables relating smoking status and survival status for these 1,314 women separated into four age groups.

Table 3.8 Smoking Status and 20-Year Survival for Four Age Groups

	Age Group							
	18–34 Survival?		35–54 Survival?		55–64 Survival?		65+ Survival?	
Smoker	**Dead**	**Alive**	**Dead**	**Alive**	**Dead**	**Alive**	**Dead**	**Alive**
Yes	5	174	41	198	51	64	42	7
No	6	213	19	180	40	81	165	28

Questions to Explore

a. Show that the counts in Table 3.8 are consistent with those in Table 3.7.

b. For each age group, find the (marginal) percentage of women who smoked.

c. For each age group, find the (marginal) percentage of women who died.

d. For each age group, compute the conditional percentage of dying for smokers and nonsmokers. To describe the association between smoking and survival status for each age group, find the difference in the percentages.

e. How can you explain the association in Table 3.7, whereby smoking seems to help women live a longer life? How can this association be so different from the one shown in the partial tables of Table 3.8?

Think It Through

a. If you add the counts in the four separate parts of Table 3.8, you'll get the counts in Table 3.7. For instance, from Table 3.7, we see that 139 of the women who smoked died. From Table 3.8, we get this from $5 + 41 + 51 + 42 = 139$, taking the number of smokers who died from each age group. Doing this for each cell, we see that the counts in the two tables are consistent with each other.

b. Of the 398 women in age group 1, 179 (= 45%) were smokers. In age group 2, 55% were smokers. In age group 3, 49%. But in age group 4, only 20% were smokers. So the oldest age group had the fewest smokers among them.

c. Of the 398 women in age group 1, 11 (= 3%) died. In age group 2, 14% died and in age group 3, 39%. As we would expect, the most women, 86%, died in age group 4 after a period of 20 years.

d. Table 3.9 shows the conditional percentages who died, for smokers and nonsmokers in each age group. Figure 3.23 plots them. The difference (in percentage points) is shown in the last row. For each age group, a higher percentage of smokers than nonsmokers died.

e. Could age explain the association? The proportion of smokers is higher in the younger age group (e.g., 45% and 55% for age groups 1 and 2,

Table 3.9 Conditional Percentages of Deaths for Smokers and Nonsmokers, by Age.

For instance, for smokers of age 18–34, from Table 3.8 the proportion who died was $5/(5 + 174) = 0.028$, or 2.8%.

	Age Group			
Smoker	**18–34**	**35–54**	**55–64**	**65+**
Yes	2.8%	17.2%	44.3%	85.7%
No	2.7%	9.5%	33.1%	85.5%
Difference	0.1%	7.7%	11.2%	0.2%

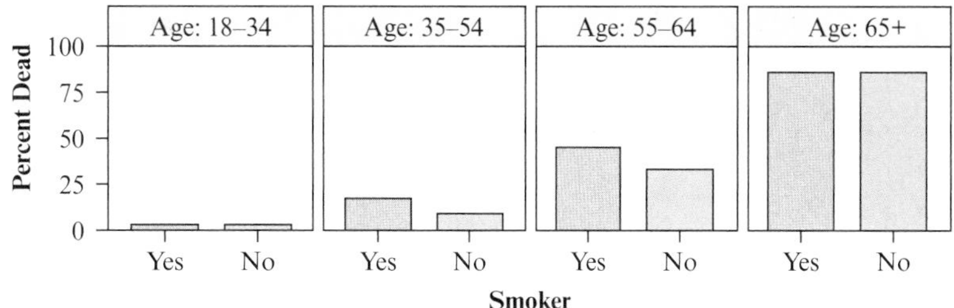

▲ **Figure 3.23** Bar Graph Comparing Percentage of Deaths for Smokers and Nonsmokers, by Age. This side-by-side bar graph shows the conditional percentages from Table 3.9.

20% in age group 4). Naturally, these younger women are less likely to die after 20 years (3% and 14% in age groups 1 and 2, 85% in age group 4). Overall, when ignoring age, this leads to fewer smokers dying compared to nonsmokers, as observed in Table 3.7. Although the overall association for this table indicates that smokers had *higher* survival rates than nonsmokers, it merely reflects the fact that younger women were more likely to be smokers and hence less likely to die during the study time frame compared to the nonsmokers, who were predominately older.

When we looked at the data separately for each age group in Table 3.8, we saw the reverse: Smokers had *lower* survival rates than nonsmokers. The analysis using Table 3.7 did not account for age, which strongly influences the association.

Insight

Because of the reversal in the association after taking age into account, the researchers did *not* conclude that smoking is beneficial to your health. This example illustrates the dramatic influence that a lurking variable can have, which would be unknown to researchers if they fail to include a certain variable in their study. An association can look quite different after adjusting for the effect of a third variable by grouping the data according to its values.

► ***Try Exercise 3.58***

The Effect of Lurking Variables on Associations

Lurking variables can affect associations in many ways. For instance, a lurking variable may be a **common cause** of both the explanatory and response variable. In Example 15, the mean temperature in the month is a common cause of both ice cream sales and the number of people who drown.

In practice, there's usually not a single variable that causally explains a response variable or the association between two variables. More commonly, there are **multiple causes**. When there are multiple causes, the association among them makes it difficult to study the effect of any single variable. For example, suppose someone claims that growing up in poverty causes crime. Realistically, probably lots of things contribute to crime. Many variables that you might think of as possible causes, such as a person's educational level, whether the person grew up in a stable family, and the quality of the neighborhood in which the person lives, are themselves likely to be associated with whether a person grew up in poverty. Perhaps people growing up in poverty tend to have poorly educated parents, grow up in high-crime neighborhoods, and achieve low levels of education. Perhaps all these factors make a person more likely to become a criminal. Growing up in poverty may have a direct effect on crime but also an indirect effect through these other variables.

It's especially tricky to study cause and effect when two variables are measured over time. The variables may be associated merely because they both have a *time trend.* Suppose that both the divorce rate and the crime rate have an increasing trend over a 10-year period. They will then have a positive correlation: Higher crime rates occur in years that have higher divorce rates. Does this imply that an increasing divorce rate *causes* the crime rate to increase? Absolutely not. They would also be positively correlated with all other variables that have a positive time trend, such as annual average house price and the annual use of cell phones. There are likely to be other variables that are themselves changing over time and have causal influences on the divorce rate and the crime rate.

Confounding

When two explanatory variables are both associated with a response variable but are also associated with each other, **confounding** occurs. It is difficult to determine whether either of them truly causes the response because a variable's effect could be at least partly due to its association with the other variable. Example 16 illustrates a study with confounding. Over the 20-year study period, smokers had a greater survival rate than nonsmokers. However, age was a confounding variable. Older subjects were less likely to be smokers, and older subjects were more likely to die. Within each age group, smokers had a *lower* survival rate than nonsmokers. Age had a dramatic influence on the association between smoking and survival status.

What's the difference between a confounding variable and a lurking variable? A lurking variable is not measured in the study. It has the *potential* for confounding. If it were included in the study and if it were associated both with the response variable and the explanatory variable, it would become a confounding variable. It would affect the relationship between the response and explanatory variables.

The potential for lurking variables to affect associations is the main reason it is difficult to study many issues of importance, whether for medical issues such as the effect of smoking on cancer or social issues such as what causes crime, what causes the economy to improve, or what causes students to succeed in school. It's not impossible—statistical methods can analyze the effect of an explanatory variable after adjusting for confounding variables (as we adjusted for age in Example 16)—but there's always the chance that an important variable was not included in the study.

3.4 Practicing the Basics

3.44 Extrapolating murder The SPSS figure shows the data and regression line for the 50 states in Table 3.6 relating

x = percentage of single-parent families to

y = annual murder rate (number of murders per 100,000 people in the population).

a. The lowest x value was for Utah and the highest was for Mississippi. Using the figure, approximate those x values.

b. Using the regression equation stated above the figure, find the predicted murder rate at $x = 0$. Why is it not sensible to make a prediction at $x = 0$ based on these data?

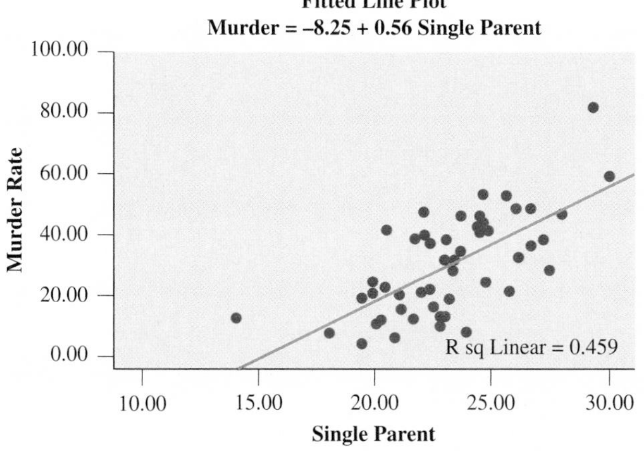

3.45 Men's Olympic long jumps TRY The Olympic winning men's long jump distances (in meters) from 1896 to 2012 and the fitted regression line for predicting them using x = year are displayed in the graph below (data on website).

a. Identify an observation that may influence the fit of the regression line. Why did you identify this observation?

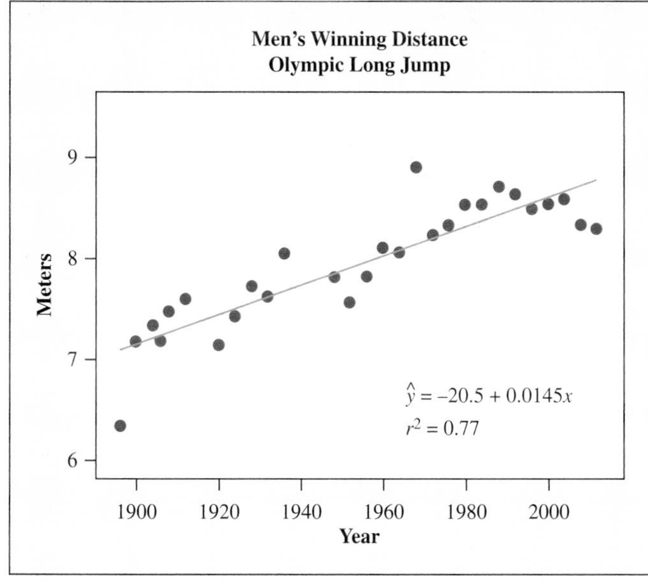

b. Which do you think is a better prediction for the year 2016—the sample mean of the y values in this plot or the value obtained by plugging 2016 into the fitted regression equation?

c. Would you feel comfortable using the regression line shown to predict the winning long jump for men in the year 2100? Why or why not?

3.46 U.S. average annual temperatures TECH Use the U.S. Temperatures data file on the book's website. (Source: National Climatic Data Center).

a. Construct a scatterplot, fit a trend line, and interpret the slope.

b. Predict the annual mean U.S. temperature for the year (i) 2016 and (ii) 2500.

c. In which prediction in part b do you have more faith? Why?

3.47 Murder and education TRY Example 13 found the regression line $\hat{y} = -3.1 + 0.33x$ for all 51 observations on y = murder rate and x = percent with a college education.

a. Show that the predicted murder rates increase from 1.85 to 10.1 as percent with a college education increases from $x = 15\%$ to $x = 40\%$, roughly the range of observed x values.

b. When the regression line is fitted only to the 50 states, $\hat{y} = 8.0 - 0.14x$. Show that the predicted murder rate decreases from 5.9 to 2.4 as percent with a college education increases from 15% to 40%.

c. D.C. has the highest value for x (38.3) and is an extreme outlier on y (41.8). Is it a regression outlier? Why?

d. What causes results to differ numerically according to whether D.C. is in the data set? Which line is more appropriate as a summary of the relationship? Why?

3.48 Murder and poverty For Table 3.6, the regression equation for the 50 states and D.C. relating y = murder rate and x = percent of people who live below the poverty level is $\hat{y} = -4.1 + 0.81x$. For D.C., $x = 17.4$ and $y = 41.8$.

a. When the observation for D.C. is removed from the data set, $\hat{y} = 0.4 + 0.36x$. Does D.C. have much influence on this regression analysis? Explain.

b. If you were to look at a scatterplot, based on the information given, do you think that the poverty value for D.C. would be relatively large or relatively small? Explain.

3.49 TV watching and the birth rate The figure shows recent data on x = the number of televisions per 100 people and y = the birth rate (number of births per 1000 people) for six African and Asian nations. The regression line, $\hat{y} = 29.8 - 0.024x$, applies to the data for these six countries. For illustration, another point is added at (81, 15.2), which is the observation for the United States. The regression line for all seven points is $\hat{y} = 31.2 - 0.195x$. The figure shows this line and the one without the U.S. observation.

a. Does the U.S. observation appear to be (i) an outlier on x, (ii) an outlier on y, or (iii) a regression outlier relative to the regression line for the other six observations?

b. State the two conditions under which a single point can have a dramatic effect on the slope and show that they apply here.

c. This one point also drastically affects the correlation, which is $r = -0.051$ without the United States but $r = -0.935$ with the United States. Explain why you would conclude that the association between birth rate and number of televisions is (i) very weak without the U.S. point and (ii) very strong with the U.S. point.

d. Explain why the U.S. residual for the line fitted using that point is very small. This shows that a point can be influential even if its residual is not large.

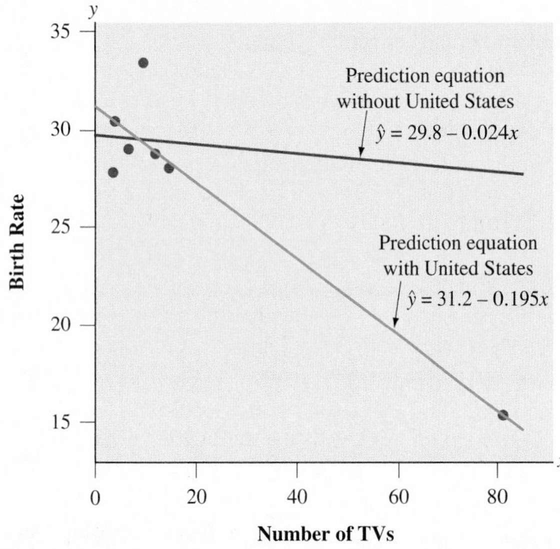

3.50 Looking for outliers Using software, analyze the relationship between x = college education and y = percentage single-parent families, for the data in Table 3.6, which are in the U.S. Statewide Crime data file on the book's website.

a. Construct a scatterplot. Based on your plot, identify two observations that seem quite different from the others, having a y value relatively large in one case and somewhat small in the other case.

b. Find the regression equation (i) for the entire data set, (ii) deleting only the first of the two outlying observations, and (iii) deleting only the second of the two outlying observations.

c. Is either deleted observation influential on the slope? Summarize the influence.

d. Including D.C., $\hat{y} = 21.2 + 0.089x$, whereas deleting that observation, $\hat{y} = 28.1 - 0.206x$. Find $\hat{y}$ for D.C. in the two cases. Does the predicted value for D.C. depend much on which regression equation is used?

3.51 Regression between cereal sodium and sugar Let x = sodium and y = sugar for the breakfast cereal data in the Cereal data file on the book's website and in Table 2.3 in Chapter 2.

a. Construct a scatterplot. Do any points satisfy the two criteria for a point to be potentially influential on the regression? Explain.

b. Find the regression line and correlation, using all the data points, and then using all except a potentially influential observation. Summarize the influence of that point.

3.52 Gestational period and life expectancy Does the life expectancy of animals depend on the length of their gestational period? The data in the Animals file on the book's website show observations on the average longevity (in years) and average gestational period (in days) for 21 animals. (Source: Wildlife Conservation Society)

a. Use the scatterplot below to describe the association. Are there any unusual observations?

b. Using software, verify the given numbers for the correlation and slope of the regression line shown on the plot.

c. Are there any outliers? If so, what makes the observations unusual? Would you expect any of them to be influential observations? Why or why not?

d. Find the regression line and the correlation without one of the observations identified in part c. Compare your results to those in part b. Was the observation influential? Explain.

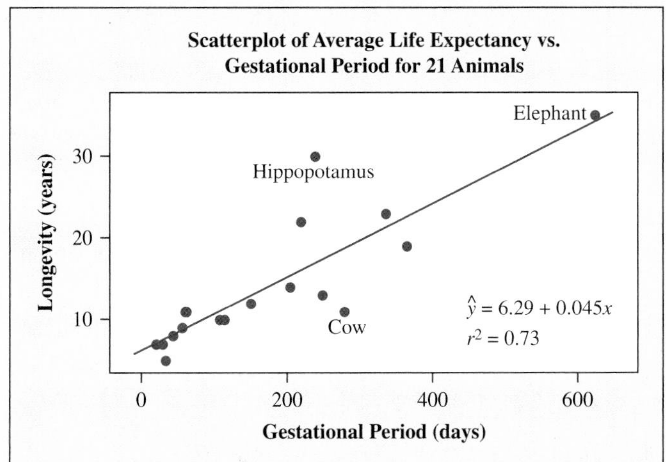

3.53 Height and vocabulary Do tall students tend to have better vocabulary skills than short students? We might think so looking at a sample of students from grades 1, 6, and 12 of Lake Wobegon school district. The correlation was 0.81 between their height and their vocabulary test score: Taller students tended to have higher vocabulary test scores.

a. Is there a causal relationship, whereby being taller gives you a better vocabulary?

b. Explain how a student's age could be a lurking variable that might be responsible for this association, being a common cause of both height and vocabulary test score.

c. Sketch a hypothetical scatterplot (as we did in Figure 3.22 for the example on crime and education), labeling points by the child's grade (1, 6, and 12), such that overall there is a positive trend, but the slope would be about 0 when we consider only children in a given grade. How does the child's age play a role in the association between height and test score?

3.54 More firefighters cause worse fires? Data are available for all fires in Chicago last year on x = number of firefighters at the fire and y = cost of damages due to the fire.

TRY

a. If the correlation is positive, does this mean that having more firefighters at a fire causes the damage to be worse? Explain.

b. Identify a third variable that could be a common cause of x and y. Construct a hypothetical scatterplot (like Figure 3.22 for crime and education), identifying points according to their value on the third variable, to illustrate your argument.

3.55 Antidrug campaigns An Associated Press story (June 13, 2002) reported, "A survey of teens conducted for the Partnership for a Drug Free America found kids who see or hear antidrug ads at least once a day are less likely to do drugs than youngsters who don't see or hear ads frequently. When asked about marijuana, kids who said they saw the ads regularly were nearly 15 percent less likely to smoke pot."

a. Discuss at least one lurking variable that could affect these results.

b. Explain how multiple causes could affect whether a teenager smokes pot.

3.56 What's wrong with regression? Explain what's wrong with the way regression is used in each of the following examples:

a. Winning times in the Boston marathon (at www.bostonmarathon.org) have followed a straight-line decreasing trend from 160 minutes in 1927 (when the race was first run at the Olympic distance of about 26 miles) to 128 minutes in 2014. After fitting a regression line to the winning times, you use the equation to predict that the winning time in the year 2300 will be about 13 minutes.

b. Using data for several cities on x = % of residents with a college education and y = median price of home, you get a strong positive correlation. You conclude that having a college education causes you to be more likely to buy an expensive house.

c. A regression between x = number of years of education and y = annual income for 100 people shows a modest positive trend, except for one person who dropped out after 10th grade but is now a multimillionaire. It's wrong to ignore any of the data, so we should report all results including this point. For this data, the correlation $r = -0.28$.

3.57 Education causes crime? The table shows a small data set that has a pattern somewhat like that in Figure 3.22 in Example 14. As in that example, education is measured as the percentage of adult residents who have at least a high school degree. Using software,

TRY TECH

a. Construct a data file with columns for education, crime rate, and a rural/urban label.

b. Construct a scatterplot between y = crime rate and x = education, labeling each point as rural or urban.

c. Find the overall correlation between crime rate and education for all eight data points. Interpret.

d. Find the correlation between crime rate and education for the (i) urban counties alone and (ii) rural counties alone. Why are these correlations so different from the correlation in part c?

Urban Counties		Rural Counties	
Education	**Crime Rate**	**Education**	**Crime Rate**
70	140	55	50
75	120	58	40
80	110	60	30
85	105	65	25

3.58 Death penalty and race The table shows results of whether the death penalty was imposed in murder trials in Florida between 1976 and 1987. For instance, the death penalty was given in 53 out of 467 cases in which a white defendant had a white victim.

TRY

Death Penalty, by Defendant's Race and Victim's Race

Victim's Race	Defendant's Race	Death Penalty		Total
		Yes	No	
White	White	53	414	**467**
	Black	11	37	**48**
Black	White	0	16	**16**
	Black	4	139	**143**

Source: Originally published in *Florida Law Review*. Michael Radelet and Glenn L. Pierce, Choosing Those Who Will Die: Race and the Death Penalty in Florida, vol. 43, *Florida Law Review* 1 (1991).

a. First, consider only those cases in which the victim was white. Find the conditional proportions that got the death penalty when the defendant was white and when the defendant was black. Describe the association.

b. Repeat part a for cases in which the victim was black. Interpret.

c. Now add these two tables together to get a summary contingency table that describes the association between the death penalty verdict and defendant's race, ignoring the information about the victim's race. Find the conditional proportions. Describe the association and compare to parts a and b.

d. Explain how these data satisfy Simpson's paradox. How would you explain what is responsible for this result to someone who has not taken a statistics course?

e. In studying the effect of defendant's race on the death penalty verdict, would you call victim's race a confounding variable? What does this mean?

3.59 NAEP scores Eighth-grade math scores on the National Assessment of Educational Progress had a mean of 277 in Nebraska compared to a mean of 271 in New Jersey (H. Wainer and L. Brown, *American Statistician*, vol. 58, 2004, p. 119).

a. Identify the response variable and the explanatory variable.

b. For white students, the means were 281 in Nebraska and 283 in New Jersey. For black students, the means were 236 in Nebraska and 242 in New Jersey. For other nonwhite students, the means were 259 in Nebraska and 260 in New Jersey. Identify the third variable given here. Explain how it is possible for New Jersey to have the higher mean for each race, yet for Nebraska to have the higher mean when the data are combined. (This is a case of Simpson's paradox for a quantitative response.)

3.60 Age a confounder? A study observes that the subjects in the study who say they exercise regularly reported only half as many serious illnesses per year, on the average, as those who say they do not exercise regularly. One paragraph in the results section of an article about the study starts out, "We next analyzed whether age was a confounding variable in studying this association."

a. Explain what this sentence means and how age could potentially explain the association between exercising and illnesses.

b. If age was not actually measured in the study and the researchers failed to consider its effects, could it be a confounding variable or a lurking variable? Explain the difference between a lurking variable and a confounding variable.

Chapter Review

ANSWERS TO THE CHAPTER FIGURE QUESTIONS

Figure 3.1 Construct a single graph with side-by-side bars (as in Figure 3.2) to compare the conditional proportions of pesticide residues in the two types of food.

Figure 3.2 The proportion of foods having pesticides present is much higher for conventionally grown food than for organically grown food.

Figure 3.3 The bars in Figure 3.2 have different heights, in contrast to Figure 3.3 for which the bars have the same height. For Figure 3.3, the proportion of foods having pesticides present is the same for both types of food.

Figure 3.4 There are no apparent outliers for either variable. A box plot would more clearly identify potential outliers.

Figure 3.5 The point for Japan appears atypical. All of the other countries with comparable Internet use have at least 25% Facebook use, whereas Japan has 13% Facebook use.

Figure 3.6 The top point is far above the overall straight-line trend of the other 66 points on the graph. The two rightmost points fall in the overall increasing trend.

Figure 3.7 If data points are closer to a straight line, there is a smaller amount of variability around the line; thus, we can more accurately predict one variable knowing the other variable, indicating a stronger association.

Figure 3.8 These 25 points make a positive contribution to the correlation because the product of their z-scores will be positive.

Figure 3.9 Yes, the points fall in a balanced way in the quadrants. The positive cross products in the upper-right quadrant are roughly counterbalanced by the negative cross products in the upper-left quadrant. The positive cross products in the lower-left quadrant are roughly counterbalanced by the negative cross products in the lower-right quadrant.

Figure 3.10 The line crosses the y-axis at 61.4. For each femur length increase of 1 cm, the height is predicted to increase 2.4 cm.

Figure 3.11 The height is predicted to be the same for each femur length.

Figure 3.12 We would expect a positive slope.

Figure 3.13 The error from predicting with the regression line is represented by a vertical line from the regression line to the observation. The distance between the point and line is the prediction error.

Figure 3.14 The absolute values of the residuals are vertical distances because the regression equation predicts y, the variable on the vertical axis.

Figure 3.15 The rightmost bar represents a county with a large positive residual. For it, the actual vote for Buchanan was much higher than what was predicted.

Figure 3.16 The difference in winning heights for men and women is typically about 0.3 to 0.4 meters.

Figure 3.17 $\hat{y} = a + bx = -2.689 + 0.029(2015) = 55.7$

Figure 3.18 The observation in the upper-right corner will influence the tilt of the straight-line fit.

Figure 3.19 The slope will decrease if D.C. is excluded from the regression analysis.

Figure 3.20 The fitted line to the data that does not include D.C.

Figure 3.21 Possibly neither. There may be another variable influencing the positive association between crime rate and amount of education.

Figure 3.22 Line (a) will pass through all the points, with a positive slope. In case (b), the lines pass only through the left set of points with *urbanization* = 0. It has the same negative slope that those points show.

CHAPTER SUMMARY

This chapter introduced descriptive statistics for studying the **association** between two variables. We explored how the value of a **response variable** (the outcome of interest) is related to the value of an **explanatory variable**.

- For two *categorical variables*, **contingency tables** summarize the counts of observations at the various combinations of categories of the two variables. Bar graphs can plot **conditional proportions** or percentages for the response variable, at different given values of the explanatory variable. For contingency tables with two rows and columns, various numerical measures (difference or ratio of proportions, odds ratio) describe the strength of the association.
- For two *quantitative variables*, **scatterplots** display the relationship and show whether there is a **positive association** (upward trend) or a **negative association** (downward trend). The **correlation**, r, describes this direction and the strength of linear (straight-line) association. It satisfies $-1 \le r \le 1$. The closer r is to -1 or 1, the stronger the linear association.

- When a relationship between two quantitative variables approximately follows a straight line, it can be described by a **regression line**, $\hat{y} = a + bx$. The slope b describes the direction of the association (positive or negative, like the correlation) and gives the effect on $\hat{y}$ of a one-unit increase in x. The regression line can be used to predict a value of the response variable y for a given value of the explanatory variable x. The square of the correlation is used to judge the overall accuracy of predictions.
- The correlation and the regression equation can be strongly affected by an **influential observation**. This observation takes a relatively small or large value on x and is a **regression outlier**, falling away from the straight-line trend of the rest of the data points. Be cautious of **extrapolating** a regression line to predict y at values of x that are far above or below the observed x-values.
- **Association does not imply causation**. A **lurking variable** may influence the association. It is even possible for the association to reverse in direction after we adjust for a third variable. This phenomenon is called **Simpson's paradox**.

SUMMARY OF NOTATION

Correlation $r = \frac{1}{n-1}\Sigma z_x z_y = \frac{1}{n-1}\Sigma\left(\frac{x-\bar{x}}{s_x}\right)\left(\frac{y-\bar{y}}{s_y}\right)$

where n is the number of points, $\bar{x}$ and $\bar{y}$ are means, s_x and s_y are standard deviations for x and y.

Regression equation: $\hat{y} = a + bx$, for predicted response $\hat{y}$, y-intercept a, slope b.

Formulas for the slope and y-intercept are

$$b = r\left(\frac{s_y}{s_x}\right) \text{ and } a = \bar{y} - b(\bar{x}).$$

CHAPTER PROBLEMS

Practicing the Basics

3.61 Choose explanatory and response For the following pairs of variables, identify the response variable and the explanatory variable.

a. Number of square feet in a house and assessed value of the house.

b. Political party preference (Democrat, Independent, Republican) and gender.

c. Annual income and number of years of education.

d. Number of pounds lost on a diet and type of diet (low-fat, low-carbohydrate).

3.62 Graphing data For each case in the previous exercise,

a. Indicate whether each variable is quantitative or categorical.

b. Describe the type of graph that could best be used to portray the results.

3.63 Life after death for males and females In a recent General Social Survey, respondents answered the question, "Do you believe in a life after death?" The table shows the responses cross-tabulated with gender.

Opinion About Life After Death by Gender

	Opinion About Life After Death	
Gender	**Yes**	**No**
Male	621	187
Female	834	145

a. Construct a table of conditional proportions.

b. Summarize results. Is there much difference between responses of males and females? Compute the difference and ratio of proportions and interpret each.

3.64 God and happiness TECH Go to the GSS website sda.berkeley.edu/GSS; click GSS, with *No Weight* as the default weight selection; type GOD for the row variable, HAPPY for the column variable; and YEAR(2014) for the Selection Filter, then click *Run the Table.*

a. Report the contingency table of counts.

b. Treating reported happiness as the response variable, find the conditional proportions. For which opinion about God are subjects most likely to be very happy?

c. To analyze the association, is it more informative to view the proportions in part b or the frequencies in part a? Why?

3.65 Degrees and income The mean annual salaries earned in 2005 by year-round workers with various educational degrees are given in the table:

Degree	Mean Salary
No diploma	$19,964
High school diploma	$29,448
Bachelor's degree	$54,689
Master's degree	$67,898
Doctoral degree	$92,863
Professional degree	$119,009

Source: U.S. Bureau of the Census.

a. Identify the response variable. Is it quantitative or categorical?

b. Identify the explanatory variable. Is it quantitative or categorical?

c. Explain how a bar graph could summarize the data.

3.66 Bacteria in ground turkey *Consumer Reports* magazine (June 2013) reported purchasing samples of ground turkey from different brands to test for the presence of bacteria.

The table below shows the number of samples that tested positive for Enterococcus bacteria for packages that claimed no use of antibiotics in the processing of the meat and for packages in which no such claim was made.

Bacteria in Ground Turkey

	Test result for Enterococcus	
Package Claim	**Positive**	**Negative**
No claim	26	20
No antibiotics	23	5

a. Find the difference in the proportion of packages that tested positive and interpret.

b. Find the ratio of the proportion of packages that tested positive and interpret.

3.67 **Women managers in the work force** The following side-by-side bar graph appeared in a 2003 issue of the *Monthly Labor Review* about women as managers in the work force. The graph summarized the percentage of managers in different occupations who were women, for the years 1972 and 2002.

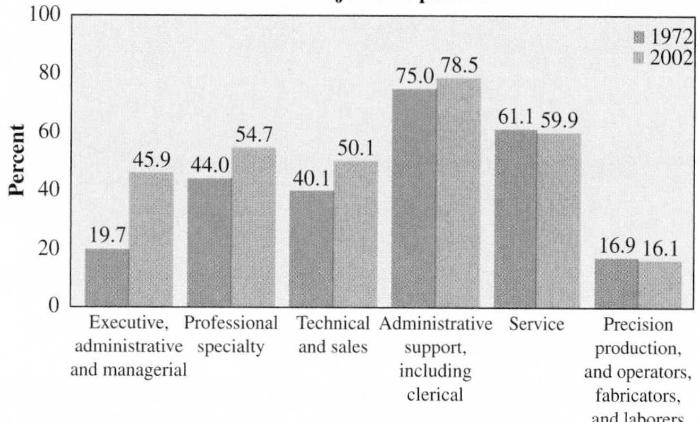

Source: Monthly Labor Review, vol. 126, no. 10, 2003, p. 48. Bureau of Labor Statistics.

a. Consider the first two bars in this graph. Identify the response variable and explanatory variable.

b. Express the information from the first two bars in the form of conditional proportions in a contingency table for two categorical variables.

c. Based on part b, does it seem as if there's an association between these variables? Explain.

d. The entire graph shows two explanatory variables. What are they?

3.68 **RateMyProfessor.com** The website RateMyProfessors.com[13] reported a correlation of 0.62 between the quality rating of the professor (on a simple 1 to 5 scale with higher values representing higher quality) and the rating of how easy a grader the professor is. This correlation is based on ratings of nearly 7000 professors.

a. How would you interpret this correlation?

b. What would you expect this correlation to equal if the quality rating did not tend to depend on the easiness rating of the professor?

3.69 TECH **Women in government and economic life** The OECD (Organization for Economic Cooperation and Development) consists of advanced, industrialized countries that accept the principles of representative democracy and a free market economy. For the nations outside of Europe that are in the OECD, the table shows UN data from 2007 on the percentage of seats in parliament held by women and female economic activity as a percentage of the male rate.

a. Treating women in parliament as the response variable, prepare a scatterplot and find the correlation. Explain how the correlation relates to the trend shown in the scatterplot.

b. Use software or a calculator to find the regression equation. Explain why the y-intercept is not meaningful.

c. Find the predicted value and residual for the United States. Interpret the residual.

d. With UN data for all 23 OECD nations, the correlation between these variables is 0.56. For women in parliament, the mean is 26.5% and the standard deviation is 9.8%. For female economic activity, the mean is 76.8 and the standard deviation is 7.7. Find the prediction equation, treating women in parliament as the response variable.

Nation	Women in Parliament (%)	Female Economic Activity
Iceland	33.3	87
Australia	28.3	79
Canada	24.3	83
Japan	10.7	65
United States	15.0	81
New Zealand	32.2	81

3.70 **African droughts and dust** Is there a relationship between the amount of dust carried over large areas of the Atlantic and the Caribbean and the amount of rainfall in African regions? In an article (by J. M. Prospero and P. J. Lamb, *Science*, vol. 302, 2003, pp. 1024–1027) the following scatterplots were given along with corresponding regression equations and correlations. The precipitation index is a measure of rainfall.

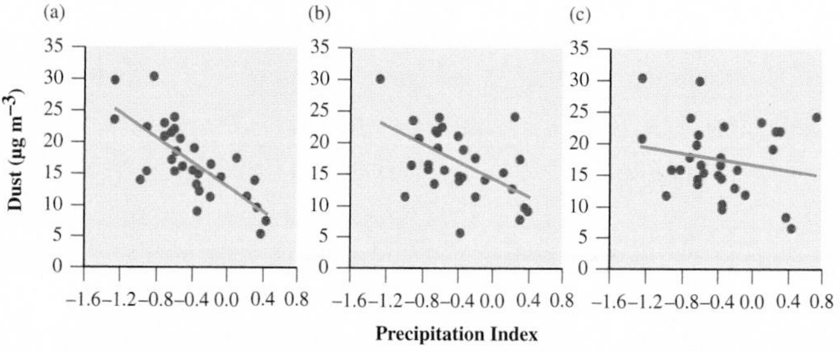

Source: J. M. Prospero and P. J. Lamb, *Science*, vol. 302, 2003, pp. 1024–1027.

[13]See insidehighered.com/news/2006/05/08/rateprof.

a. Match the following regression equations and correlations with the appropriate graph.

(i) $\hat{y} = 14.05 - 7.18x;\quad r = -0.75$

(ii) $\hat{y} = 16.00 - 2.36x;\quad r = -0.44$

(iii) $\hat{y} = 12.80 - 9.77x;\quad r = -0.87$

b. Based on the scatterplots and information in part a, what would you conclude about the relationship between dust amount and rainfall amounts?

3.71 Crime rate and urbanization For the data in Example 14 on crime in Florida, the regression line between y = crime rate (number of crimes per 1000 people) and x = percentage living in an urban environment is $\hat{y} = 24.5 + 0.56x$.

a. Using the slope, find the difference in predicted crime rates between counties that are 100% urban and counties that are 0% urban. Interpret.

b. Interpret the correlation of 0.67 between these variables.

c. Show the connection between the correlation and the slope, using the standard deviations of 28.3 for crime rate and 34.0 for percentage urban.

3.72 Gestational period and life expectancy revisited The data in the Animals file on the book's website holds observations on the average longevity (in years) and gestational period (in days) for a variety of animals. Exercise 3.52 showed the scatterplot together with the regression equation with intercept 6.29 and slope 0.045 and an r^2 value of 0.73.

a. Interpret the slope.

b. A leopard has a gestational period of about 98 days. What is its predicted average longevity?

c. Interpret the value of r^2.

d. Show that extrapolating from animals to humans (with gestational period of about 40 weeks) grossly underestimates average human longevity.

3.73 Height and paycheck The headline of an article in the *Gainesville Sun* (October 17, 2003) stated, "Height can yield a taller paycheck." It described an analysis of four large studies in the United States and Britain by a University of Florida professor on subjects' height and salaries. The article reported that for each gender, "an inch is worth about \$789 a year in salary. So, a person who is 6 feet tall will earn about \$5,523 more a year than a person who is 5 foot 5."

a. For the interpretation in quotes, identify the response variable and explanatory variable.

b. State the slope of the regression equation, when height is measured in inches and income in dollars.

c. Explain how the value \$5,523 relates to the slope.

3.74 Predicting college GPA An admissions officer claims that at his college the regression equation $\hat{y} = 0.5 + 7x$ approximates the relationship between y = college GPA and x = high school GPA, both measured on a four-point scale.

a. Sketch this equation between $x = 0$ and 4, labeling the x- and y-axes. Is this equation realistic? Why or why not?

b. Suppose that actually $\hat{y} = 0.5 + 0.7x$. Predict the GPA for two students having GPAs of 3.0 and 4.0. Interpret and explain how the difference between these two predictions relates to the slope.

3.75 College GPA = high school GPA Refer to the previous exercise. Suppose the regression equation is $\hat{y} = x$. Identify the y-intercept and slope. Interpret the line in context.

3.76 What's a college degree worth? In 2002, a census bureau survey reported that the mean total earnings that a full-time worker in the United States can expect to earn between ages 25 and 64 is \$1.2 million for those with only a high-school education and \$2.1 million for those with a college degree but no advanced degree.

a. Assuming four years for a college degree and a straight-line regression of y = total earnings on x = number years of education, what is the slope? Interpret it.

b. If y instead measures earnings per year (rather than for 40 years), then what is the slope? Interpret.

3.77 Car weight and gas hogs: The table shows a short excerpt from the Car Weight and Mileage data file on the book's website. That file lists several 2004 model cars with automatic transmission and their x = weight (in pounds) and y = mileage (miles per gallon of gas). The prediction equation is $\hat{y} = 47.32 - 0.0052x$.

Automobile Brand	Weight	Mileage
Honda Accord Sedan LX	3,164	34
Toyota Corolla	2,590	38
Dodge Dakota Club Cab	3,838	22
Jeep Grand Cherokee Laredo	3,970	21
Hummer H2	6,400	17

Sources: auto.consumerguide.com, honda.com, toyota.com, landrover.com, ford.com.

a. Interpret the slope in terms of a 1000 pound increase in the vehicle weight.

b. Find the predicted mileage and residual for a Hummer H2. Interpret.

3.78 Predicting Internet use from cell phone use We now use data from the Human Development data file on cell phone use and Internet use for 39 countries.

a. The MINITAB output below shows a scatterplot. Describe it in terms of (i) identifying the response variable and the explanatory variable, (ii) indicating whether it shows a positive or a negative association, and (iii) describing the variability of Internet use values for nations that have cellular use below 30% and for those that have cellular use above 30%.

b. Identify the approximate x- and y-coordinates for a nation that has less Internet use than you would expect, given its level of cell phone use.

c. The prediction equation is $\hat{y} = 1.27 + 0.475x$. Describe the relationship by noting how $\hat{y}$ changes as x increases from 0 to 90, which are roughly its minimum and maximum.

d. For the United States, $x = 45.1$ and $y = 50.15$. Find its predicted Internet use and residual. Interpret the large positive residual.

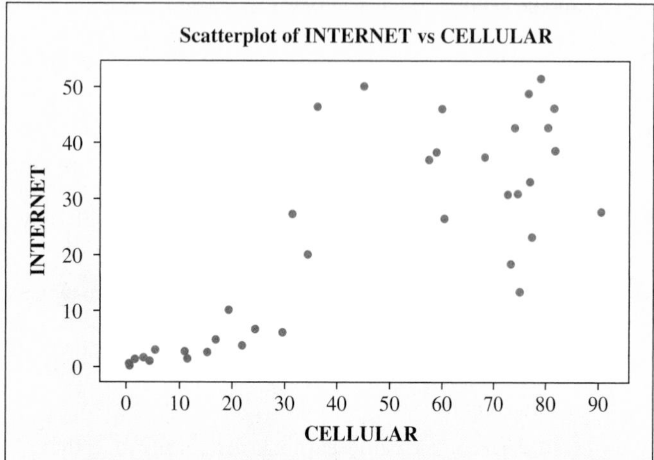

3.79 Income depends on education? For a study of counties in Florida, the table shows part of a printout for the regression analysis relating y = median income (thousands of dollars) to x = percent of residents with at least a high school education.

a. County A has 10% more of its residents than County B with at least a high school education. Find their difference in predicted median incomes.

b. Find the correlation. (*Hint:* Use the relation between the correlation and the slope of the regression line.) Interpret the (i) sign and (ii) strength of association.

Variable	Mean	Std Dev
Income	24.51	4.69
Education	69.49	8.86

The regression equation is income = −4.63 + 0.42 education

3.80 Fertility and GDP TECH Refer to the Human Development data file on the book's website. Use x = GDP and y = fertility (mean number of children per adult woman).

a. Construct a scatterplot and indicate whether regression seems appropriate.

b. Find the correlation and the regression equation.

c. With x = percent using contraception, $\hat{y} = 6.7 - 0.065x$. Can you compare the slope of this regression equation with the slope of the equation with GDP as a predictor to determine which has the stronger association with y? Explain.

d. Contraception has a correlation of −0.887 with fertility. Which variable has a stronger association with fertility: GDP or contraception?

3.81 Women working and birth rate Using data from several nations, a regression analysis of y = crude birth rate (number of births per 1000 population size) on women's economic activity (female labor force as a percentage of the male labor force) yielded the equation $\hat{y} = 36.3 - 0.30x$ and a correlation of −0.55.

a. Describe the effect by comparing the predicted birth rate for countries with $x = 0$ and countries with $x = 100$.

b. Suppose that the correlation between the crude birth rate and the nation's GNP equals −0.35. Which variable, GNP or women's economic activity, seems to have the stronger association with birth rate? Explain.

3.82 Education and income The regression equation for a sample of 100 people relating x = years of education and y = annual income (in dollars) is $\hat{y} = -20{,}000 + 4000x$, and the correlation equals 0.50. The standard deviations were 2.0 for education and 16,000 for annual income.

a. Show how to find the slope in the regression equation from the correlation.

b. Suppose that now we let x = annual income and y = years of education. Will the correlation or the slope change in value? If so, show how.

3.83 Income in euros Refer to the previous exercise. Results in the regression equation $\hat{y} = -20{,}000 + 4000x$ for y = annual income were translated to units of euros at a time when the exchange rate was \$1.25 per euro.

a. Find the intercept of the regression equation. (*Hint*: What does 20,000 dollars equal in euros?)

b. Find the slope of the regression equation.

c. What is the correlation when annual income is measured in euros? Why?

3.84 Changing units for cereal data TECH Refer to the Cereal data file on the book's website, with x = sugar (g) and y = sodium (mg), for which $\hat{y} = 169 - 0.25x$.

a. Convert the sugar measurements to mg and calculate the line obtained from regressing sodium (mg) on sugar (mg). Which statistics change and which remain the same? Clearly interpret the slope coefficient.

b. Suppose we instead convert the sugar measurements to ounces. How would this effect the slope of the regression line? Can you determine the new slope just from knowing that 1 ounce equals roughly 28.35 grams?

3.85 Murder and single-parent families For Table 3.6 on the 50 states and D.C., the figure below shows the relationship between the murder rate and the percentage of single-parent families.

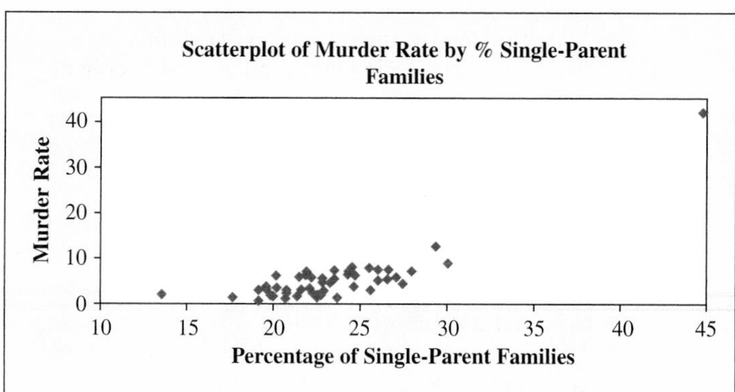

a. For D.C., the percentage of single-parent families = 44.7 and the murder rate = 41.8. Identify D.C. on the scatterplot and explain the effect you would expect it to have on a regression analysis.

b. The regression line fitted to all 51 observations is $\hat{y} = -21.4 + 1.14x$. The regression line fitted only to the 50 states is $\hat{y} = -8.2 + 0.56x$. Summarize the effect of including D.C. in the analysis.

3.86 TECH **Violent crime and college education** For the U.S. Statewide Crime data file on the book's website, let y = violent crime rate and x = percent with a college education.

a. Construct a scatterplot. Identify any points that you think may be influential in a regression analysis.

b. Fit the regression line, using all 51 observations. Interpret the slope.

c. Fit the regression line after deleting the observation identified in part a. Interpret the slope and compare results to part b.

3.87 TECH **Violent crime and high school education** Repeat the previous exercise using x = percent with at least a high school education. This shows that an outlier is not especially influential if its x-value is not relatively large or small.

3.88 TECH **Crime and urbanization** For the U.S. Statewide Crime data file on the book's website, using MINITAB to analyze y = violent crime rate and x = urbanization (percentage of the residents living in metropolitan areas) gives the results shown:

Variable	N	Mean	StDev	Minimum	Q1	Median	Q3	Maximum
violent	51	441.6	241.4	81.0	281.0	384.0	554.0	1508.0
urban	51	68.36	20.85	27.90	49.00	70.30	84.50	100.00

The regression equation is violent = 36.0 + 5.93 urban

a. Using the five-number summary of positions, sketch a box plot for y. What does your graph and the reported mean and standard deviation of y tell you about the shape of the distribution of violent crime rate?

b. Construct a scatterplot. Does it show any potentially influential observations? Would you predict that the slope would be larger, or smaller, if you delete that observation? Why?

c. Fit the regression without the observation highlighted in part b. Describe the effect on the slope.

3.89 TECH **High school graduation rates and health insurance** Access the HS Graduation Rates file on the book's website, which contains statewide data on x = high school graduation rate and y = percentage of individuals without health insurance.

a. Construct a scatterplot. Describe the relationship.

b. Find the correlation. Interpret.

c. Find the regression equation for the data. Interpret the slope, and summarize the relationship.

3.90 **Women's Olympic high jumps** Example 11 discussed how the winning height in the Olympic high jump changed over time. Using the High Jump data file on the book's website, we get (see also Figure 3.16)

Women_Meters = −10.94 + 0.0065 (Year_Women)

for predicting the women's winning height (in meters) using the year number.

a. Predict the winning Olympic high jump distance for women in (i) 2016 and (ii) 3000.

b. Do you feel comfortable making either prediction in part a? Explain.

3.91 **Income and height** A survey of adults revealed a positive correlation between the height of the subjects and their income in the previous year.

a. Explain how gender could be a potential lurking variable that could be responsible for this association.

b. If gender had actually been one of the variables measured in the study, would it be a lurking variable or a confounding variable? Explain.

3.92 **More TV watching goes with fewer babies?** For United Nations data from several countries, there is a strong negative correlation between the birth rate and the per capita television ownership.

a. Does this imply that having higher television ownership causes a country to have a lower birth rate?

b. Identify a lurking variable that could provide an explanation for this association.

3.93 **More sleep causes death?** An Associated Press story (February 15, 2002) quoted a study at the University of California at San Diego that reported, based on a nationwide survey, that those who averaged at least 8 hours sleep a night were 12% more likely to die within six years than those who averaged 6.5 to 7.5 hours of sleep a night.

a. Explain how the subject's age could be positively associated both with time spent sleeping and with an increased death rate and, hence, could be a lurking variable responsible for the observed association between sleeping and the death rate.

b. Explain how the subject's age could be a common cause of both variables.

3.94 **Ask Marilyn** Marilyn vos Savant writes a column for *Parade* magazine to which readers send questions, often puzzlers or questions with a twist. In the April 28, 1996, column, a reader asked, "A company decided to expand, so it opened a factory generating 455 jobs. For the 70 white-collar positions, 200 males and 200 females applied. Of the people who applied, 20% of the females and only 15% of the males were hired. Of the 400 males applying for the blue-collar positions, 75% were hired. Of the 100 females applying, 85% of were hired. A federal Equal Employment Opportunity Commission (EEOC) enforcement official noted that many more males were hired than females and decided to investigate. Responding to charges of irregularities in hiring, the company president denied any discrimination, pointing out that in both the white-collar and blue-collar fields, the percentage of female applicants hired was greater than it was for males. But the government official produced his own statistics, which showed that a female applying for a job had a 58% chance of being denied employment whereas male applicants had only a 45% denial rate. As the current law is written, this constituted a violation.... Can you explain how two opposing statistical outcomes are reached from the same raw data?" (Copyright 1996 Marilyn vos Savant. Initially published in *Parade* Magazine. All rights reserved.)

a. Construct two contingency tables giving counts relating gender to whether hired (yes or no), one table for white-collar jobs and one table for blue-collar jobs.

b. Construct a single contingency table for gender and whether hired, combining all 900 applicants into one table. Verify that the percentages not hired are as quoted above by the government official.

c. Comparing the data in the tables constructed in parts a and b, explain why this is an example of Simpson's paradox.

Concepts and Investigations

3.95 NL baseball team ERA and number of wins TECH Is a baseball team's earned run average (ERA = the average number of earned runs they give up per game) a good predictor of the number of wins that a team has for a season? The data for the National League teams in 2010 are available in the NL Team Statistics file on the book's website. Conduct a correlation and regression analysis, including graphical and numerical descriptive statistics. Summarize results in a two-page report.

3.96 Time studying and GPA TECH Is there a relationship between the amount of time a student studies and a student's GPA? Access the Georgia Student Survey file on the book's website or use your class data to explore this question using appropriate graphical and numerical methods. Write a brief report summarizing results.

3.97 Warming in Newnan, Georgia TECH Access the Newnan GA Temp's file on the book's website, which contains data on average annual temperatures for Newnan, Georgia, during the 20th century. Fit a regression line to these temperatures and interpret the trend. Compare the trend to the trend found in Example 12 for Central Park, New York, temperatures.

3.98 Regression for dummies You have done a regression analysis for the catalog sales company you work for, using monthly data for the last year on y = total sales in the month and x = number of catalogs mailed in preceding month. You are asked to prepare a 200-word summary of what regression does under the heading "Regression for Dummies," to give to fellow employees who have never taken a statistics course. Write the summary, being careful not to use any technical jargon with which the employees may not be familiar.

3.99 Fluoride and AIDS An Associated Press story (August 25, 1998) about the lack of fluoride in most of the water supply in Utah quoted antifluoride activist Norma Sommer as claiming that fluoride may be responsible for AIDS, since the water supply in San Francisco is heavily fluoridated and that city has an unusually high incidence of AIDS. Describe how you could use this story to explain to someone who has never studied statistics that association need not imply causation.

3.100 Fish fights Alzheimer's An AP story (July 22, 2003) described a study conducted over four years by Dr. Martha Morris and others from Chicago's Rush-Presbyterian-St. Luke's Medical Center involving 815 Chicago residents aged 65 and older (*Archives of Neurology*, July 21, 2003). Those who reported eating fish at least once a week had a 60% lower risk of Alzheimer's than those who never or rarely ate fish. However, the story also quoted Dr. Rachelle Doody of Baylor College of Medicine as warning, "Articles like this raise expectations and confuse people. Researchers can show an association, but they can't show cause and effect." She said it is not known whether those people who had a reduced risk had eaten fish most of their lives, and whether other dietary habits had an influence. Using this example, describe how you would explain to someone who has never taken statistics (a) what a lurking variable is, (b) how there can be multiple causes for any particular response variable, and (c) why they need to be skeptical when they read new research results.

3.101 Dogs make you healthier A study published in the *British Journal of Health Psychology* (D. Wells, vol.12, 2007, pp. 145–156) found that dog owners are physically healthier than cat owners. The author of the study was quoted as saying, "It is possible that dogs can directly promote our well being by buffering us from stress. The ownership of a dog can also lead to increases in physical activity and facilitate the development of social contacts, which may enhance physiological and psychological human health in a more indirect manner." Identify lurking variables in this explanation and use this quote to explain how lurking variables can be responsible for an association.

3.102 Multiple choice: Correlate GPA and GRE In a study of graduate students who took the Graduate Record Exam (GRE), the Educational Testing Service reported a correlation of 0.37 between undergraduate grade point average (GPA) and the graduate first year GPA.[14] This means that

a. As undergraduate GPA increases by one unit, graduate first-year GPA increases by 0.37 unit.

b. Because the correlation is not 0, we can predict a person's graduate first-year GPA perfectly if we know their undergraduate GPA.

c. The relationship between undergraduate GPA and graduate first-year GPA follows a curve rather than a straight line.

d. As one of these variables increases, there is a weak tendency for the other variable to increase also.

3.103 Multiple choice: Properties of r Which of the following is *not* a property of r?

a. r is always between -1 and 1.

b. r depends on which of the two variables is designated as the response variable.

[14]*Source:* GRE Guide to the Use of Scores, 1998–1999, www.gre.org.

c. r measures the strength of the linear relationship between x and y.

d. r does not depend on the units of y or x.

e. r has the same sign as the slope of the regression equation.

3.104 Multiple choice: Interpreting r One can interpret $r = 0.30$ as

a. a weak, positive association

b. 30% of the time $\hat{y} = y$

c. $\hat{y}$ changes 0.30 units for every one-unit increase in x

d. a stronger association than two variables with $r = -0.70$

3.105 Multiple choice: Correct statement about r Which one of the following statements is correct?

a. The correlation is always the same as the slope of the regression line.

b. The mean of the residuals from the least-squares regression line is 0 only when $r = 0$.

c. The correlation is the percentage of points that lie in the quadrants where x and y are both above the mean or both below the mean.

d. The correlation is inappropriate if a U-shaped relationship exists between x and y.

3.106 Multiple choice: Describing association between categorical variables You can summarize the data for two categorical variables x and y by

a. drawing a scatterplot of the x- and y-values.

b. constructing a contingency table for the x- and y-values.

c. calculating the correlation between x and y.

d. constructing a box plot for each variable.

3.107 Multiple choice: Slope and correlation The slope of the regression equation and the correlation are similar in the sense that

a. they do not depend on the units of measurement.

b. they both must fall between -1 and $+1$.

c. they both have the same sign.

d. neither can be affected by severe regression outliers.

3.108 Multiple choice: Interpretation of r^2 An r^2 measure of 0.85 implies that

a. the correlation between x and y equals 0.85.

b. for a one-unit increase in x, we predict y to increase by 85%.

c. 85% of the response variable y can be explained by the linear relationship between x and y.

d. 85% of the variability we observe in the response variable y can be explained by its linear relationship with x.

3.109 True or false The variables y = annual income (thousands of dollars), x_1 = number of years of education, and x_2 = number of years experience in job are measured for all the employees having city-funded jobs in Knoxville, Tennessee. Suppose that the following regression equations and correlations apply:

(i) $\hat{y} = 10 + 1.0x_1$, $r = 0.30$.

(ii) $\hat{y} = 14 + 0.4x_2$, $r = 0.60$.

The correlation is -0.40 between x_1 and x_2. Which of the following statements are true?

a. The weakest association is between x_1 and x_2.

b. The regression equation using x_2 to predict x_1 has negative slope.

c. Each additional year on the job corresponds to a $400 increase in predicted income.

d. The predicted mean income for employees having 20 years of experience is $4000 higher than the predicted mean income for employees having 10 years of experience.

3.110 Correlation doesn't depend on units ◆◆ Suppose you convert y = income from British pounds to dollars, and suppose a pound equals 2.00 dollars.

a. Explain why the y values double, the mean of y doubles, the deviations $(y - \bar{y})$ double, and the standard deviation s_y doubles.

b. Using the formula for calculating the correlation, explain why the correlation would not change value.

3.111 When correlation = slope ◆◆ Consider the formula $b = r(s_y/s_x)$ that expresses the slope in terms of the correlation. Suppose the data are equally spread out for each variable. That is, suppose the data satisfy $s_x = s_y$. Show that the correlation and the slope are the same. (In practice, the standard deviations are not usually identical. However, this provides an interpretation for the correlation as representing what we would get for the slope of the regression line if the two variables were equally spread out.)

3.112 Center of the data ◆◆ Consider the formula $a = \bar{y} - b\bar{x}$ for the y-intercept.

a. Show that $\bar{y} = a + b\bar{x}$. Explain why this means that the predicted value of the response variable is $\hat{y} = \bar{y}$ when $x = \bar{x}$.

b. Show that an alternative way of expressing the regression model is as $(\hat{y} - \bar{y}) = b(x - \bar{x})$. Interpret this formula.

3.113 Final exam "regresses toward mean" of midterm ◆◆ Let y = final exam score and x = midterm exam score. Suppose that the correlation is 0.70 and that the standard deviation is the same for each set of scores.

a. Using part b of the previous exercise and the relation between the slope and correlation, show that $(\hat{y} - \bar{y}) = 0.70(x - \bar{x})$.

b. Explain why this indicates that the predicted difference between your final exam grade and the class mean is 70% of the difference between your midterm exam score and the class mean. Your score is predicted to "regress toward the mean." (The concept of *regression toward the mean*, which is responsible for the name of regression analysis, will be discussed in Section 12.2.)

Student Activities

3.114 Analyze your data Refer to the data file the class created in Activity 3 in Chapter 1. For variables chosen by your instructor, conduct a regression and correlation analysis. Prepare a one-page report summarizing your analyses, interpreting your findings.

TECH

3.115 Activity: Effect of moving a point The Explore Linear Regression web app accessible at the book's website lets you add and delete points on a scatterplot. The regression line is automatically calculated for the points you provide.

TECH TRY

a. Select the option "Draw Own" and add 5 points to the empty scatterplot that have an approximate linear relationship between x and y but a slope near 0.

b. Add a sixth observation that is influential. What did you have to do to get the slope to change noticeably from 0?

c. Now consider the effect of sample size on the existence of influential points. Start by creating 50 points with a similar pattern as in part a. You can create this from scratch, point by point, or simply select "Random Scatter" from the drop down menu for the initial relationship and select 50 for the number of points. Is it now harder to add a single point that makes the slope change noticeably from 0? Why?

d. Try this activity, now exploring the effect of adding or deleting points on the correlation coefficient r. (Check the box to display r.) Repeat parts a–c in terms of the correlation instead of the slope.

3.116 Activity: Guess the correlation The Guess the Correlation web app accessible at the book's website allows you to guess the correlation r with randomly generated data points. How close are your guesses to the actual correlation of the points? Find the correlation between your guesses and the actual value after 10 guesses.

TECH

Quality study design and collecting quality data are crucial elements of statistical practice. Previous chapters have explored describing data. Future chapters explore making inferences using data from samples to larger populations. However, poor data quality compromises these conclusions. This chapter discusses ways of obtaining the data needed for such descriptions and inferences to be useful and valid. As it is said, "Garbage in, garbage out!"

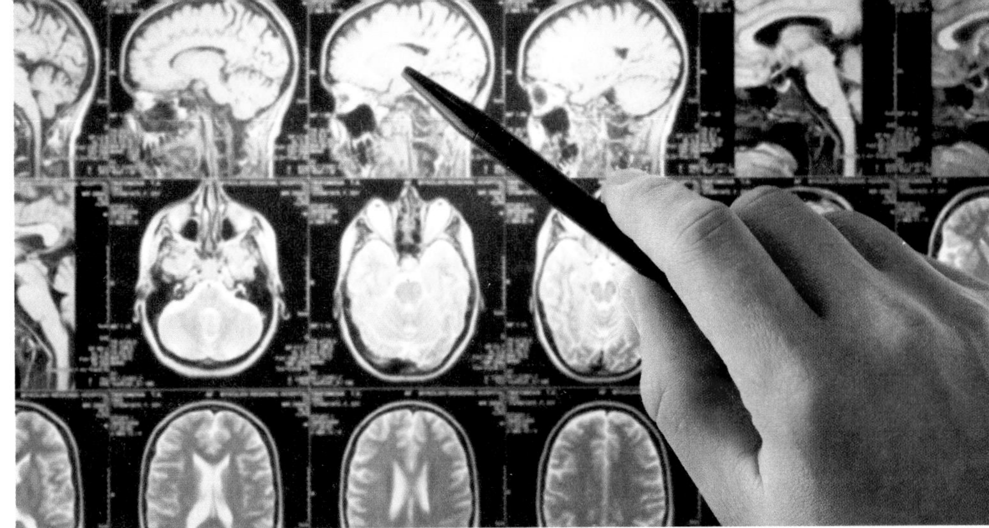

Gathering Data

Example 1

Cell Phones and Your Health

Picture the Scenario

How safe are cell phones to use? Cell phones emit electromagnetic radiation, and a cell phone's antenna is the main source of this energy. The closer the antenna is to the user's head, the greater the exposure to radiation. With the increased use of cell phones, there has been a growing concern over the potential health risks. Several studies have explored the possibility of such risks:

Study 1 A German study (Stang et al., 2001) compared 118 patients with a rare form of eye cancer called uveal melanoma to 475 healthy patients who did not have this eye cancer. The patients' cell phone use was measured using a questionnaire. On average, the eye cancer patients used cell phones more often.

Study 2 A British study (Hepworth et al., 2006) compared 966 patients with brain cancer to 1716 patients without brain cancer. The patients' cell phone use was measured using a questionnaire. Cell phone use for the two groups was similar.

Study 3 A study published in *The Journal of the American Medical Association* (Volkow et. al., 2011) indicates that cell phone use speeds up activity in the brain. As part of a randomized crossover study, 47 participants were fitted with a cell phone device on each ear and then underwent two positron emission topography, or PET, scans to measure brain glucose metabolism. During one scan, the cell phones were both turned off. During the other scan, an automated 50-minute muted call was made to the phone on the right ear. The order of when the call was received (for the first or second scan) was randomized. Comparison of the PET scans showed a significant increase in activity in the part of the brain closest to the antenna during the transmission of the automated call.

Studies 1 and 3 found potential physiological responses to cell phone use. Study 2 did not.

Question to Explore

- Why do results of different medical studies sometimes disagree?
- Consider the different study designs to explore whether cell phone use is associated with various types of physiological activities in our bodies. For each study,

1. Does the study design establish a causal link between cell phone use and potential health risks?

2. Is the study ethically feasible?
3. How can you design the study to be efficient?
4. What types of biases or lurking variables might exist?

Thinking Ahead

A knowledge of different **study designs for gathering data** helps us understand how contradictory results can happen in scientific research studies and determine which studies deserve our trust. In this chapter, we'll learn that the study design can have a major impact on its results. Unless the study is well designed and implemented, the results may be meaningless or, worse yet, misleading. Throughout Chapter 4, we will return to the cell phone studies introduced in Example 1 to ask more questions and understand how study design can affect what are appropriate conclusions to infer from an analysis of the data.

Chapters 2 and 3 introduced graphical and numerical ways of describing data. We described shape, center, and variability, looked for patterns and unusual observations, and explored associations between variables. For these and other statistical analyses to be useful, we must have "good data." But what's the best way to gather data to ensure they are "good"? The studies described in Example 1 used two methods. The first two studies merely *observed* subjects, whereas the third study *conducted an experiment* with them. We'll now learn about such methods, study their pros and cons, and see both good and bad ways to use them. This will help us understand when we can trust the conclusions of a study and when we need to be skeptical.

4.1 Experimental and Observational Studies

Recall

From Section 1.2, the **population** consists of *all* the subjects of interest. We collect data on a subset of the population, which we call the **sample**.

From the beginning of Chapter 3, the **response variable** measures the outcome of interest. Studies investigate how that outcome depends on the **explanatory variable**. ◀

We use statistics to learn about a **population**. The German and British studies in Example 1 examined subjects' cell phone use and whether the subjects had brain or eye cancer. Since it would be too costly and time-consuming to seek out *all* individuals in the populations of Germany or Great Britain, the researchers used **samples** to gather data. These studies, like many, have two variables of primary interest—a **response variable** and an **explanatory variable**. The response variable is whether a subject has cancer (eye or brain). The explanatory variable is the amount of cell phone use.

Types of Studies: Experimental and Observational

Some studies, such as Study 3 in Example 1, perform an **experiment**. Subjects are assigned to experimental conditions, such as when both cell phones are deactivated ("off" condition) or the right cell phone is activated ("on" condition), that we want to compare on the response outcome. These experimental conditions are called **treatments**. They correspond to different values of the explanatory variable.

Experimental Study

A researcher conducts an experimental study, or more simply, an **experiment**, by assigning subjects to certain experimental conditions and then observing outcomes on the response variable (or variables). The experimental conditions, which correspond to assigned values of the explanatory variable, are called **treatments**.

For example, Study 3 used 47 participants as the subjects. In this experimental study, each participant was assigned to both treatments. These are the categories of the explanatory variable, whether the cell phone is off or on. The purpose of the experiment was to examine the association between this variable and the response variable—the amount of brain activity changes—to determine whether it increased.

An experiment assigns each subject to a treatment (or to both treatments as in the cross-over design employed in Study 3) and then observes the response. By contrast, many studies merely *observe* the values on the response variable and the explanatory variable for the sampled subjects without doing anything to them. Such studies are called **observational studies**. They are **nonexperimental**.

Observational Study

In an **observational study**, the researcher observes values of the response variable and explanatory variables for the sampled subjects, without anything being done to the subjects (such as imposing a treatment).

In short, an **observational study** merely *observes* rather than *experiments* with the study subjects. An **experimental study** assigns each subject to one or more treatments and then observes the outcome on the response variable.

Identifying experimental versus observational studies

Example 2

Cell Phone Use

Picture the Scenario

Example 1 described three studies about whether relationships might exist between cell phone use and physiological activity in the human body. We've seen that Study 3 was an experiment. Studies 1 and 2 both examined the amount of cell phone use for cancer patients and for noncancer patients using a questionnaire.

Questions to Explore

a. Were Studies 1 and 2 experimental or observational studies?

b. How were Studies 1 and 2 fundamentally different from Study 3 in terms of how the treatments were determined for each subject?

Think It Through

a. In Studies 1 and 2, information on the amount of cell phone use was gathered by giving a questionnaire to the sampled subjects. The subjects (people) decided how much they would use a cell phone and thus determined their amount of radiation exposure. The studies merely observed this exposure. No experiment was performed. So, Studies 1 and 2 were *observational* studies.

b. In Study 3, each subject was given both treatments (the "off" condition and the "on" condition). The researchers did not merely observe the subjects for the amount of brain activity but exposed the subjects to both treatments and determined which treatment each would receive first: Some received the call during the first PET scan and some during the second scan. The researchers imposed the treatments on the subjects. So, Study 3 was an *experimental* study.*

*The researchers noted that "Results of this study provide evidence that acute cell phone exposure affects brain metabolic activity. However, these results provide no information about their relevance to potential carcinogenic effects (or lack thereof) from chronic cell phone use."

Insight

One reason that results of different medical studies sometimes disagree is that they are not the same *type* of study. Experimental studies allow direct causal inference to be made, whereas observational studies do not allow causal inference. As we'll see, there are different types of both observational and experimental studies, and some are more trustworthy than others.

▶ ***Try Exercises 4.1 and 4.3***

Let's consider another study. From its description, we'll try to determine whether it is an experiment or an observational study.

Example 3

Experiment or observational study ◀

Drug Testing and Student Drug Use

Picture the Scenario

"Student Drug Testing Not Effective in Reducing Drug Use" was the headline in a news release from the University of Michigan. It reported results from a study of 76,000 students in 497 high schools and 225 middle schools nationwide.[1] Each student in the study filled out a questionnaire. One question asked whether the student used drugs. The study found that drug use was similar in schools that tested for drugs and in schools that did not test for drugs. For instance, the table in the margin shows the frequency of drug use for sampled twelfth graders from the two types of schools. In addition, the figure in the margin shows the conditional proportions of drug use for these students.

	Drug Use		
Drug Tests?	**Yes**	**No**	**Total**
Yes	2,092	3,561	5,653
No	6,452	10,985	17,437

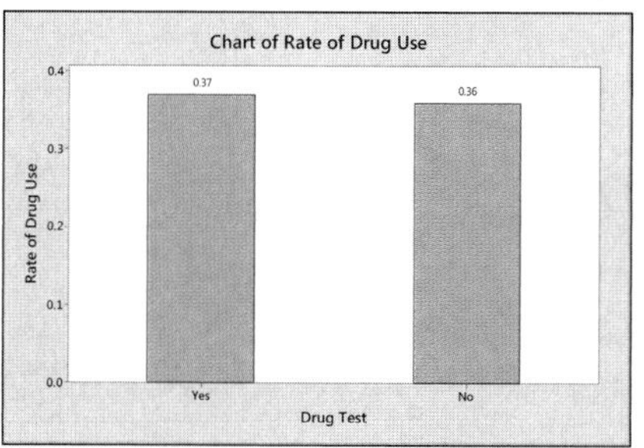

Questions to Explore

a. What were the response and explanatory variables?
b. Was this an observational study or an experiment?

Think It Through

a. The study compared the percentage of students who used drugs in schools that tested for drugs and in schools that did not test for drugs. Whether the student used drugs was the response variable. The explanatory variable was whether the student's school tested for drugs. Both variables were categorical, with categories "yes" and "no." For each grade, the data were summarized in a contingency table, as shown in the margin for twelfth graders.

b. For each student, the study merely observed whether his or her school tested for drugs and whether he or she used drugs. So this was an observational study.

Insight

An experiment would have assigned schools to use or not use drug testing rather than leaving the decision to the schools. For instance, the study could have randomly selected half the schools to perform drug testing and half not to perform it and then, a year later, measured the student drug use in each school.

▶ ***Try Exercise 4.7***

[1]Study by R. Yamaguchi et al., reported in *Journal of School Health*, vol. 73, pp. 159–164, 2003.

As we will soon discuss, an experimental study gives the researcher more control over outside influences. This control can allow more accuracy in studying the association.

Recall

From Section 3.4, a **lurking variable** is a variable not observed in the study that influences the association between the response and explanatory variables due to its own association with each of those variables. ◀

Advantage of Experiments Over Observational Studies

In an observational study, lurking variables can affect the results. Study 1 in Example 1 found an association between cell phone use and eye cancer. However, there could be lifestyle, genetic, or health differences between the subjects with eye cancer and those without it, and between those who use cell phones a lot and those who do not. A lurking variable could affect the observed association. For example, a possible lifestyle lurking variable is computer use. Perhaps those who use cell phones often also use computers frequently. Perhaps high exposure to computer screens increases the chance of eye cancer. In that case, the higher prevalence of eye cancer for heavier users of cell phones could be due to their higher use of computers, not their higher use of cell phones.

By contrast, an experiment reduces the potential for lurking variables to affect the results. Why? We'll see that with a type of "random" selection to determine which subjects receive each treatment, we are attempting to form and balance groups of subjects receiving the different treatments; that is, the groups have similar distributions on other variables, such as lifestyle, genetic, or health characteristics. For instance, suppose the researchers in cell phone Study 3 decided to have 24 subjects receive the "on" condition and 23 subjects receive the "off" condition instead of having each subject receive both treatments. The health of the subjects could be a factor in how the brain responds to the treatments and the amount of brain activity that appears on the scans. If we randomly determine which subjects receive the "on" condition and which do not, the two groups of subjects are expected to have similar distributions on health. One group will not be much healthier, on average, than the other group. When the groups are balanced on a lurking variable, there is no association between the lurking variable and the explanatory variable (for instance, between health of the subject and whether the subject receives the "on" condition). Then, the lurking variable will not affect how the explanatory variable is associated with the response variable. One treatment group will not tend to have more brain activity because of health differences, on the average.

In Study 3, described in Example 1, by using the same subjects for both treatments, the researchers were attempting to further control the variability from the subject's health. In this experimental study, it was important to randomize the order in which the subject received the treatment.

Caution

In Example 3, the problem with the conclusion they made is that schools with high rates of drug use might be more inclined to employ drug tests to address the problem. It is conceivable that drug tests reduced the rate of drug use from 0.74 to 0.37, cutting the rate in half. It is also conceivable that drug use rates started at 0.37 and didn't change at all due to the drug test program. The problem with this observational study is that we don't know which of the previous conceivable scenarios, or plethora of other ones, occurred. ◀

Establishing **cause and effect** is central to science. But it's not possible to establish cause and effect definitively with observational studies. There's always the possibility that some lurking variable could be responsible for the association. If people who make greater use of cell phones have a higher rate of eye cancer, it may be because of some variable that we failed to measure in our study, such as computer use. As we learned in Section 3.4, **association does not imply causation**.

Because it's easier to address the potential impact of lurking variables in an experiment than in an observational study, *we can study the effect of an explanatory variable on a response variable more accurately with an experiment than with an observational study*. With an experiment, the researcher has control over which treatment each subject receives. If we find an association between the explanatory variable and the response variable, we can be more sure that we've discovered a causal relationship than if we merely find an association in an observational study. Consequently, the best method for determining causality is to conduct an experiment.

Determining Which Type of Study Is Possible

If experiments are preferable, why ever conduct an observational study? Why bother to measure whether cell phone usage was greater for those with cancer than for those not having it? Why not instead conduct an experiment, such as the following: Pick half the students from your school at random and tell them to use a cell phone each day for the next 50 years. Tell the other half of the student body never to use cell phones. Fifty years from now, analyze whether cancer was more common for those who used cell phones.

There are obvious difficulties with such an experiment:

- It's not ethical for a study to expose over a long period of time some of the subjects to something (such as cell phone radiation) that we suspect may be harmful.
- It's difficult in practice to make sure that the subjects behave as told. How can you monitor them to ensure that they adhere to their treatment assignment over the 50-year experimental period?
- Who wants to wait 50 years to get an answer?

For these reasons, medical experiments are often performed over a short time period or often with exposure to treatments that would not be out of the ordinary (such as a one-time exposure to cell phone activity). To measure the effects on people of longer exposure to potentially harmful treatments, often the experiment uses animals such as mice instead of people. Because inferences about human populations are more trustworthy when we use samples of human subjects than when we use samples of animal subjects, scientists often resort to observational studies. Then we are not deliberately placing people in harm's way, but observing people who have chosen on their own to take part in the activity of interest. In today's information age, a lot of data is readily available to assist (or impede) people from making decisions about the relationship between variables. These data provide only observational comparisons. We'll study methods for designing a good observational study in Section 4.4. This can yield useful information when an experiment is not practical.

Finally, another reason nonexperimental studies are common is that many questions of interest do not involve trying to assess causality. For instance, if we want to gauge the public's opinion on some issue, or if we want to conduct a marketing study to see how people rate a new product, it's completely adequate to use a study that samples (appropriately) the population of interest.

Using Data Already Available

Of course, you will not conduct a study every time you want to answer some question, such as whether cell phone use is dangerous. It's human nature to rely instead on already available data. The most readily available data come from your personal observations. Perhaps a friend recently diagnosed with brain cancer was a frequent user of cell phones. Is this strong evidence that frequent cell phone use increases the likelihood of getting brain cancer?

Informal observations of this type are called **anecdotal evidence**. Unfortunately, there is no way to tell whether they are representative of what happens for an entire population. Sometimes you hear people give anecdotal evidence to attempt to disprove causal relationships. "My Uncle Geoffrey is 85 years old and he's smoked a pack of cigarettes a day for his entire adult life, yet he's as healthy as a horse." An association does not need to be perfect, however, to be causal. Not all people who smoke a pack of cigarettes each day will get lung cancer, but a much higher proportion of them will do so than people who are nonsmokers. Perhaps Uncle Geoffrey is lucky to be in good health, but that should not encourage you to smoke regularly.

A famous saying is, "The plural of anecdote is not data." Instead of using anecdotal evidence to draw conclusions, you should rely on data from reputable

Did You Know?

Examples of sources for available data:

- General Social Survey (GSS)
- http://fedstats.sites.usa.gov/
- www.statcan.ca (for Canada)
- www.inegi.gob.mx (for Mexico)
- www.statistics.gov.uk (for United Kingdom)
- www.abs.gov.au (for Australia)

research studies. You can find research results on topics of interest by entering keywords in Internet search engines. This search directs you to published results, such as in medical journals for medical studies.[2] Results from well-designed studies are more trustworthy than anecdotal evidence. Excellent sources of available data are listed in the margin on the previous page.

The Census and Other Sample Surveys

The General Social Survey (GSS) is an example of a **sample survey**. It gathers information by interviewing a sample of subjects from the U.S. adult population to provide a snapshot of that population. The study in Example 3 on student drug use in schools also used a sample survey.

Sample Survey

A **sample survey** selects a sample of subjects from a population and collects data from them. In the field of statistics a survey does not just indicate an opinion poll or a questionnaire; it includes any information gathered from or about the subject.

A sample survey is a type of nonexperimental study. The subjects provide data on the variable or variables measured. There is no assignment of subjects to different treatments.

Most countries conduct a regular **census**. A census attempts to count the number of people in the population and to measure certain characteristics about them. It is different from a sample survey, which selects only a small part of the entire population.

In Article 1, Section 2, the U.S. Constitution states that a complete counting of the U.S. population is to be done every 10 years. The first census was taken in 1790. It counted 3.9 million people; today the U.S. population is estimated to be more than 300 million (308,745,538 by the 2010 U.S. census). Other than counting the population size, here are three key reasons for conducting the U.S. census:

- The Constitution mandates that seats in the House of Representatives be apportioned to states based on their portion of the population measured by the census. When the 1910 census was completed, Congress fixed the number of seats at 435. With each new census, states may gain or lose seats, depending on how their population size compares with other states.
- Census data are used in the drawing of boundaries for electoral districts.
- Census data are used to determine the distribution of federal dollars to states and local communities.

Although it's the intention of a census to sample *everyone* in a population, in practice this is not possible. Some people do not have known addresses for the census bureau to send a census form. Some people are homeless or transient. Because data are needed regularly on economic variables, such as the unemployment rate, the U.S. Bureau of the Census continually takes samples of the population rather than relying solely on the complete census. An example is the monthly Current Population Survey, which surveys about 50,000 U.S. households and is the primary source of labor force statistics for the population of the United States, including the unemployment rate. It is usually more practical, in terms of time and money, to take a sample rather than to try to measure everyone in a population.

---

[2]Most surveys of research about cell phones suggest that there is no convincing evidence yet of adverse radiation effects (e.g., D. R. Cox, *J. Roy. Statist. Soc., Ser. A*, vol. 166, pp. 241–246, 2003). The primary danger appears to be people using cell phones while driving!

U.S. Commerce Secretary Gary Locke stands beside a screen showing the country's resident population during the 2010 Census presentation at the National Press Club in Washington.

For a sample survey to be informative, it is important for the sample to reflect the population well. As we'll discuss next, random selection—letting chance determine which subjects are in the sample—is the key to getting a good sample.

4.1 Practicing the Basics

4.1 Cell phones Consider the cell phone Study 3 described in Example 1.
TRY

a. Identify the response variable and the explanatory variable.

b. Was this an observational study or an experiment? Explain why.

4.2 High blood pressure and binge drinking Many studies have demonstrated that high blood pressure increases the risk of developing heart disease or having a stroke. It is also safe to say that the health risks associated with binge drinking far outweigh any benefits. A study published in *Heath Magazine* in 2010 suggested that a combination of the two could be a lethal mix. As part of the study that followed 6100 South Korean men aged 55 and over for two decades, men with high blood pressure who binge drank even occasionally had double the risk of dying from a stroke or heart attack when compared to teetotalers with normal blood pressure.

a. Is this an observational or experimental study?

b. Identify the explanatory and response variable(s).

c. Does the study prove that a combination of high blood pressure and binge drinking causes an increased risk of death by heart attack or stroke? Why or why not?

4.3 Low-fat versus low-carb diet? One hundred forty-eight men and women without heart disease or diabetes enrolled in a study. Half of the subjects were randomly assigned to a low-carb diet (<40 g/d), and the others were given a low-fat diet ($<30\%$ of daily energy intake from total fat). Subjects on the low-carb diet lost more weight after one year compared with those on the low-fat diet (an average of 8 pounds more). (L. A. Bazzano et al., *Ann Intern Med* 2014; 161(5): 309–318. doi: 10.7326/M14-0180)
TRY

a. Identify the response variable and the explanatory variable.

b. Was this study an observational study or an experimental study? Explain.

c. Based on this study, is it appropriate to recommend that everyone who wishes to lose weight should prefer a low-carb diet over a low-fat diet? Explain your answer.

4.4 Experiments versus observational studies When either type of study is feasible, an experiment is usually preferred over an observational study. Explain why, using an example to illustrate. Also explain why it is not always possible for researchers to carry out a study in an experimental framework. Give an example of such a situation.

4.5 School testing for drugs Example 3 discussed a study comparing high schools that tested for drugs with high schools that did not test for drugs, finding similar levels of student drug use in each. State a potential lurking variable that could affect the results of such a study. Describe what the effect could be.

4.6 Hormone therapy and heart disease Since 1976 the Nurses' Health Study has followed more than 100,000 nurses. Every two years, the nurses fill out a questionnaire about their habits and their health. Results from this study indicated that postmenopausal women have a reduced risk of heart disease if they take a hormone replacement drug.

a. Suppose the hormone-replacement drug actually has no effect. Identify a potential lurking variable that could explain the results of the observational study. (*Hint*: Suppose that the women who took the drug tended to be more conscientious about their personal health than those who did not take it.)

b. Recently a randomized experiment called the Women's Health Initiative was conducted by the National Institutes of Health to see whether hormone therapy is truly helpful. The study, planned to last for eight years, was stopped after five years when analyses showed that women who took hormones had 30% more heart attacks. This study suggested that rather than reducing the risk of heart attacks, hormone replacement drugs actually increase the risk.[3] How is it that two studies could reach such different conclusions? (For attempts to reconcile the studies, see a story by Gina Kolata in *The New York Times*, April 21, 2003.)

c. Explain why randomized experiments, when feasible, are preferable to observational studies.

4.7 **Speaking foreign languages** A 2014 study (http://www.futurity.org/foreign-languages-make-us-less-moral/) examined the relationship between using a foreign language and acting for the common good. They examined two groups of people, one that used their native language and one that used a foreign language. Each group was presented with a moral dilemma that required the subject to make a choice about saving himself or herself versus sacrificing his or her life for the sake of saving others. Those using a foreign language chose saving others at a higher rate than those using their native language.

TRY

a. Identify the response variable and the explanatory variable.

b. Is this study an observational study or an experiment? Explain.

c. Can we conclude that speaking a foreign language causes one to act morally? Explain.

4.8 **Breast-cancer screening** A study published in 2010 in the *New England Journal of Medicine* discusses a breast-cancer screening program that began in Norway in 1996 and was expanded geographically through 2005. Women in the study were offered mammography screening every two years. The goal of the study was to compare incidence-based rates of death from breast cancer across four groups:

1. Women who from 1996 through 2005 were living in countries with screening.
2. Women who from 1996 through 2005 were living in countries without screening.
3. A historical-comparison group who lived in screening countries from 1986 through 1995.
4. A historical-comparison group who lived in nonscreening countries from 1986 through 1995.

Data were analyzed for 40,075 women. Rates of death were reduced in the screening group as compared to the historical screening group and in the nonscreening group as compared to the historical nonscreening group.

a. Is this an observational or experimental study?

b. Identify the explanatory and response variable(s).

c. Does the study prove that being offered mammography screening causes a reduction in death rates associated with breast cancer? Why or why not?

4.9 **Experiment or observe?** Explain whether an experiment or an observational study would be more appropriate to investigate the following:

a. Whether smoking has an effect on coronary heart disease

b. Whether higher SAT scores tend to be positively associated with higher college GPAs

c. Whether a special coupon attached to the outside of a catalog makes recipients more likely to order products from a mail-order company

4.10 **Baseball under a full moon** During a baseball game between the Boston Brouhahas and the Minnesota Meddlers, the broadcaster mentions that the away team has won "13 consecutive meetings between the two teams played on nights with a full moon."

a. Is the broadcaster's comment based on observational or experimental data?

b. The current game is being played in Boston. Should the Boston Brouhahas be concerned about the recent full moon trend?

4.11 **Seat belt anecdote** Andy once heard about a car crash victim who died because he was pinned in the wreckage by a seat belt he could not undo. As a result, Andy refuses to wear a seat belt when he rides in a car. How would you explain to Andy the fallacy behind relying on this anecdotal evidence?

4.12 **Poker as a profession?** Tony's mother is extremely proud that her son will graduate college in a few months. She expresses concern, however, when Tony tells her that following graduation, he plans to move to Las Vegas to become a professional poker player. He mentions that his friend Nick did so and is now earning more than a million dollars per year. Should Tony's anecdotal evidence about Nick soothe his mother's concern?

4.13 **What's more to blame for obesity?** In a study published in the July 7, 2014, edition of the *American Journal of Medicine*, it was suggested that lack of exercise contributed more to weight gain than eating too much. The study examined the current exercise habits and caloric intake of a sample of both males and females. (Source: http://www.cbsnews.com/news/whats-more-to-blame-for-obesity-lack-of-exercise-or-eating-too-much/)

a. Was this an observational study or an experimental study? Explain why.

b. Identify the response variable and the explanatory variable(s).

c. Does this study prove that lack of exercise causes weight gain more often than eating too much?

d. It was reported that women younger than 40 are quite vulnerable to the risks of a sedentary lifestyle. Name

---

[3]See article by H. N. Hodis et al., *New England Journal of Medicine*, August 7, 2003.

a lurking variable that might explain this risk of a sedentary lifestyle for these younger women that in turn leads to little exercise and/or eating more.

4.14 Census every 10 years? A nationwide census is conducted in the United States every 10 years.

TECH

a. Give at least two reasons the United States takes a census only every 10 years.

b. What are reasons for taking the census at all?

c. The most commonly discussed characteristic learned from a census is the size of the population. However, other characteristics of the population are measured during each census. Using the Internet, report two such characteristics recorded during the 2010 U.S. census. (*Hint:* Visit the following website: www.census.gov/2010.census.)

4.2 Good and Poor Ways to Sample

The sample survey is a common type of nonexperimental study. The first step of a sample survey is to define the population targeted by the study. For instance, the Gallup organization (www.gallup.com) conducts a monthly survey of about 1000 adult Americans. Gallup then reports the percentage of those sampled who respond "approve" when asked, "Do you approve or disapprove of the way [the current president of the United States] is handling his job as president?" If the sampling is conducted properly, this provides a good estimate of the approval rate within the entire population. The population consists of all adults living in the United States.

Sampling Frame and Sampling Design

Once you've identified the population, the second step is to compile a list of subjects so you can sample from it. This list is called the **sampling frame**.

Sampling Frame

The **sampling frame** is the list of subjects in the population from which the sample is taken.

Ideally, the sampling frame lists the entire population of interest. In practice, as in a census, it's usually hard to identify every subject in the population.

Suppose you plan to sample students at your school, asking students to complete a questionnaire about various issues. The population is all students at the school. One possible sampling frame is the student directory. Another one is a list of registered students.

Once you have a sampling frame, you need to specify a method for selecting subjects from it. The method used is called the **sampling design**. Here's one possible sampling design for sampling students at your school: You select all students in your statistics class. Do you think your class is necessarily reflective of the entire student body? Do you have a representative mixture of freshmen through seniors, males and females, athletes and nonathletes, working and nonworking students, political party affiliations, and so on? With this sampling design, it's doubtful.

When you pick a sample merely by convenience, the results may not be representative of the population. Some response outcomes may occur much more frequently than in the population, and some may occur much less. Consider a survey question about the number of hours a week that you work at an outside job. If your class is primarily juniors and seniors, they may be more likely to work than freshmen or sophomores. The mean response in the sample may be much larger than in the overall student population. Information from the sample may be misleading.

Simple Random Sampling

You're more likely to obtain a representative sample if you let *chance*, rather than *convenience*, determine the sample. The sampling design should give each student an equal chance to be in the sample. It should also enable the data analyst to figure out how likely it is that descriptive statistics (such as sample means) fall close to corresponding values you'd like to make inferences about for the entire population (such as population means). These are reasons for using **random sampling**.

You may have been part of a selection process in which your name was put in a box or hat along with many other names, and someone blindly picked a name for a prize. If the names were thoroughly mixed before the selection, this emulates a *random* type of sampling called a **simple random sample**.

Recall

As in Chapters 2 and 3, n denotes the *number* of observations in the sample, called the **sample size**. ◀

Simple Random Sample

A **simple random sample** of n subjects from a population is one in which each possible sample of that size has the same chance of being selected.

A *simple random sample* is often just called a **random sample**. The "simple" adjective distinguishes this type of sampling from more complex random sampling designs presented in Section 4.4.

Example 4

Simple random samples ◀

Drawing Prize Winners

Picture the Scenario

A campus club decides to raise money for a local charity by selling tickets to a dinner banquet and raffle. The Athletic Department has donated two pairs of football season tickets as prizes. The winners will be drawn randomly from everyone who purchased a ticket, and each ticket can win only once. (This is called sampling without replacement.) To select the two winners, the organizers choose a simple random sample of size $n = 2$ from the 60 ticket holders. Each individual at the banquet receives an entry with a number between 1 and 60. Duplicate tickets numbered 1 to 60 are placed in a container and mixed, after which the two winning entries are chosen at random. Whoever holds the tickets containing the same numbers as those drawn at random wins the football tickets.

Questions to Explore

a. What are the possible samples?

b. What is the chance that a particular sample of size 2 will be drawn?

c. Professor Shaffer is in attendance at the banquet and holds entry number 1. What is the chance that her entry will be chosen? Mr. Chatterjee holds entry number 55. What is the chance that his entry will be chosen?

Think It Through

a. The entire collection of possible samples is too long to list, but we can visualize the possibilities by listing certain pairs:

(1,2), (1,3), (1,4),..., (1,58), (1,59), (1,60)
(2,3), (2,4),..., (2,58), (2,59), (2,60)

.
.
.

(57,58), (57,59), (57,60)
(58,59), (58,60)
(59,60)

b. The first row above contains 59 possible samples, the second row contains 58, and so forth. There are thus 59 + 58 + . . . + 2 + 1, which equals 1770 possible samples. The process of randomly selecting two unique entries ensures that each possible sample of size 2 has an equal chance of occurring. Since there are 1770 possible samples, the chance of any one sample being selected is 1 out of 1770.

c. Looking at the top row in part a, we see that 1 shows up in 59 of the samples (all of the samples listed in the top row). So the chance that Professor Shaffer wins season tickets is 59 out of 1770.

Insight

The chance of 59/1770 for Professor Shaffer is the same as that of Mr. Chatterjee and everyone else in attendance. In practice, especially with large populations, it is difficult to mix the entrants' numbers in a container so that each sample truly has an equal chance of selection. There are better ways of selecting simple random samples, as we'll learn next.

▶ ***Try Exercise 4.16***

Did You Know?

The Random Numbers web app from the book's website can also be used to generate random numbers. The screenshot in the margin next to Example 5 on the next page illustrates. ◀

Selecting a Simple Random Sample

What's a better way to take a simple random sample than blindly drawing slips of paper out of a hat? You first number the subjects in the sampling frame. You then generate a set of those numbers randomly. Finally, you sample the subjects whose numbers were generated. One method of generating numbers randomly is to use a random number table. In practice, technology is used to generate the sample. This could be an app or a statistical program. The following example demonstrates how a random sample is generated in MINITAB (left column).

Taking a Random Sample Consider taking a random sample of three students from a class in which the following students are enrolled: Aisha, Benedict, Chung, Diego, Emily, Francisco, Girish, Hank, Isabella, and Jing.

It can be done in MINITAB, as shown below.

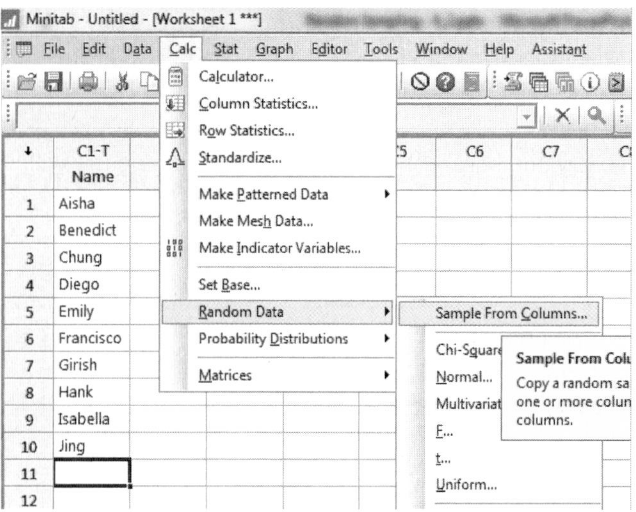

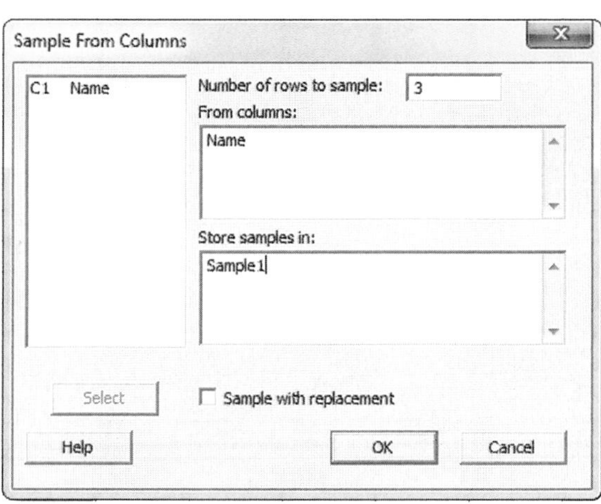

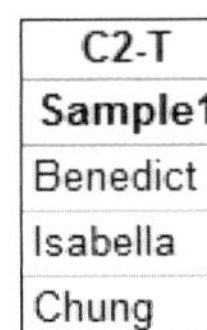

C2-T
Sample1
Benedict
Isabella
Chung

When we executed this command in MINITAB, the following random sample was obtained. This would be your sample of size 3.

Note that if you select a random sample, you will not necessarily get the same three people.

Example 5

Selecting a Simple Random Sample

Auditing a School District

Picture the Scenario

Local school districts must be prepared for annual visits from state auditors whose job is to verify the dollar amount of the accounts within the school district and determine whether the money is being spent appropriately. It is too time-consuming and expensive for auditors to review all accounts, so they typically review only some of them. So that a school district cannot anticipate which accounts will be reviewed, the auditors often take a simple random sample of the accounts.

Questions to Explore

a. How can the auditors use random numbers to select 10 accounts to audit in a school district that has 60 accounts?

b. Why is it important for the auditors not to use personal judgment in selecting the accounts to audit?

Think It Through

a. The sampling frame consists of the 60 accounts. We first number the accounts 1 through 60. Alternatively, they could list the names of the accounts. The accounts MINITAB selected (see below for details of the process) were 56, 43, 35, 47, 15, 8, 31, 9, 33, and 36. We cannot verify that these numbers are randomly selected, but we know that the process used to generate them employs random selection.

b. By using simple random sampling, the auditors hold the school district responsible for all accounts. If the auditors personally chose the accounts to audit, they might select certain accounts each year. A school district would soon learn which accounts they need to have in order and which accounts can be given less attention.

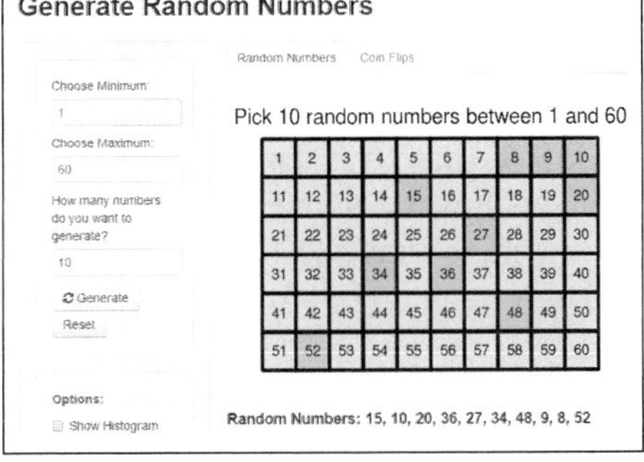

Screenshot of Random Numbers web app, selecting 10 numbers at random from 60 numbers.

Insight

Likewise, the Internal Revenue Service (IRS) randomly selects some tax returns for audit, so taxpayers cannot predict ahead of time whether they will be audited. For efficiency, the IRS samples a small proportion of tax returns with small amounts owed and a larger proportion of tax returns with high amounts owed. It does this because it cares about the total amount of tax revenue brought in.

▶ *Try Exercise 4.17*

Methods of Collecting Data in Sample Surveys

In Example 5, the subjects sampled were accounts. More commonly, they are people. For any survey, it is difficult to get a good sampling frame since a list of all adults in a population typically does not exist. So, it's necessary to pick a place where almost all people can be found—a person's place of residence.

Once we identify the desired sample for a survey, how do we contact the people to collect the data? The three most common methods are personal

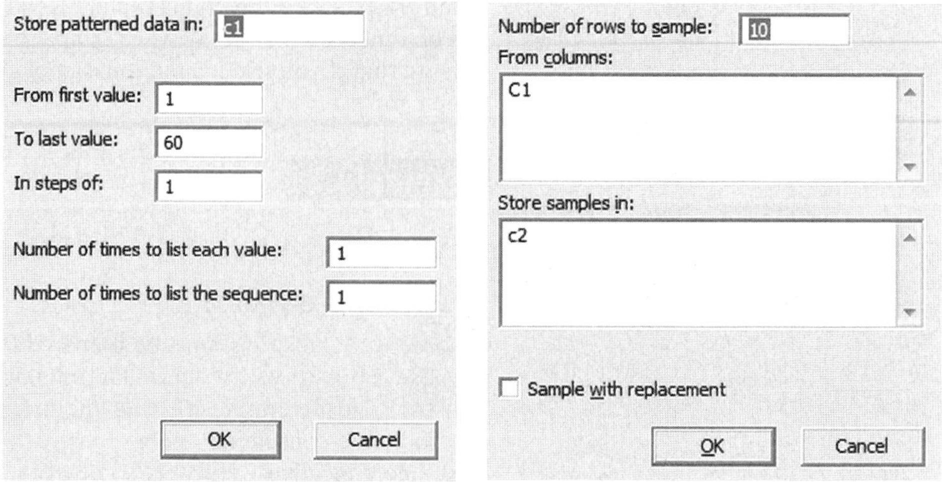

Store patterned data in: c1
From first value: 1
To last value: 60
In steps of: 1
Number of times to list each value: 1
Number of times to list the sequence: 1
OK Cancel

Number of rows to sample: 10
From columns:
C1
Store samples in:
c2
Sample with replacement
OK Cancel

▲ **Figure 4.1 This MINITAB screen is used to generate 10 integers randomly between 1 and 60, inclusively.** The 60 random numbers will be stored in Column 1 of the MINITAB spreadsheet (left screenshot). Then 10 accounts are selected and stored in Column 2 (right screenshot).

interview, telephone interview, and self-administered questionnaire (either in person or online).

Personal interview In a personal (face-to-face) interview, an interviewer asks prepared questions and records the subject's responses. An advantage is that subjects are more likely to participate. A disadvantage is the cost. Also, some subjects may not answer sensitive questions pertaining to opinions or lifestyle, such as alcohol and drug use, whether they have been victims of sexual abuse, or their HIV status that they might answer on a printed questionnaire.

Telephone interview A telephone interview is like a personal interview but conducted over the phone. A main advantage is lower cost because no travel is involved. A disadvantage is that the interview might have to be short. Subjects generally aren't as patient on the phone and may hang up before starting or completing the interview.

Self-administered questionnaire Subjects are requested to fill out a questionnaire mailed, e-mailed, or otherwise available online. An advantage is that it is cheaper than a personal interview. A disadvantage is that fewer people tend to participate.

So which method is most used? Most major national polls that survey regularly to measure public opinion use the telephone interview. An example is the polls conducted by the Gallup organization. The General Social Survey is an exception, using personal interviews for its questionnaire, which is quite long.

For telephone interviews, since the mid-1980s, many sample surveys have used **random digit dialing** to select households. The survey can then obtain a sample without having a sampling frame. In the United States, typically the area code and the 3-digit exchange are randomly selected from the list of all such codes and exchanges. Then, the last four digits are dialed randomly, and an adult is selected randomly within the household. Although this sampling design incorporates randomness, it is not a simple random sample because each sample is not equally likely to be chosen. (Do you see why not? Does everyone have a telephone, or exactly one telephone?)

Did You Know?

Besides Gallup, there are other polling groups that conduct national surveys, such as the Pew Research Center (www.people-press.org) and Zogby International (www.zogby.com). TV stations and newspapers commonly use such polling organizations to conduct polls. ◀

Sources of Potential Bias in Sample Surveys

A variety of problems can cause responses from a sample to favor some parts of the population over others. Then, results from the sample are not representative of the population and are said to exhibit **bias**.

In Words

There is **bias** if the way in which the study was designed or the data were gathered made certain outcomes occur more or less often in the sample than they do in the population. For example, consider the population of adults in your home town. The results of an opinion survey asking about raising the sales tax to support public schools may be biased in the direction of raising taxes if you sample only educators or biased in the direction of lowering taxes if you sample only business owners. Alternatively, the results could be biased toward raising taxes if a higher proportion of educators responded than business owners.

Sampling bias Bias may result from the sampling method. The main way this occurs is if the sample is not random. Another way it can occur is due to **undercoverage**—having a sampling frame that lacks representation from parts of the population. A phone survey using landlines will not reach homeless people, prison inmates, or people who don't have landline phones. If its sampling frame consists of the names in a phone directory, it will not reach those who don't have landlines. Most major polling agencies use randomized dialing. Responses by those who are not in the sampling frame might be quite different from those who are in the frame. Bias resulting from the sampling method, such as nonrandom sampling or undercoverage, is called **sampling bias**.

Nonresponse bias A second type of bias occurs when some sampled subjects cannot be reached or refuse to participate. This is called **nonresponse bias**. The subjects who are willing to participate may be different from the overall sample in some systematic way, perhaps having strong emotional convictions about the issues being surveyed. Even those who do participate may not respond to some questions, resulting in nonresponse bias due to **missing data**. All major surveys suffer from some nonresponse bias. The General Social Survey has a nonresponse rate of about 20–30%. The nonresponse rate is much higher for many telephone surveys. By contrast, government-conducted surveys often have lower nonresponse rates. The Current Population Survey has a nonresponse rate of only about 7%. To reduce nonresponse bias, investigators try to make follow-up contact with the subjects who do not return questionnaires.

Results have dubious worth when there is substantial nonresponse. For instance, in her best-selling and controversial book *Women and Love* (1987), author and feminist Shere Hite presented results of a survey of adult women in the United States. One of her conclusions was that 70% of women who had been married at least five years have extramarital affairs. She based this conclusion on responses to questionnaires returned from a sample of 4500 women. This sounds impressively large. However, the questionnaire was mailed to about 100,000 women. We cannot know whether this sample of 4.5% of the women who responded is representative of the 100,000 who received the questionnaire, much less the entire population of adult American women. In fact, Hite was criticized for her research methodology of using a nonrandom sample and the large nonresponse rate.

Response bias A third type of potential bias is in the actual responses made. This is called **response bias**. An interviewer might ask the questions in a leading way, such that subjects are more likely to respond a certain way. Or, subjects may lie because they think their response is socially unacceptable, or they may give the response that they think the interviewer prefers.

In Practice Be Alert for Potential Bias

With any sample survey, carefully scrutinize the results. Look for information about how the sample was selected, how large the sample size was, the nonresponse rate, how the questions were worded, and who sponsored the study. The less you know about these details, the less you should trust the results.

If you design an interview or questionnaire, you should strive to construct questions that are clear and understandable. *Avoid questions that are confusing, long, or leading*. The wording of a question can greatly affect the responses. A Roper poll was designed to determine the percentage of Americans who express some doubt that the Holocaust occurred in World War II. In response to the question, "Does it seem possible or does it seem impossible to you that the Nazi extermination of the Jews *never* happened?" 22% said it was possible the Holocaust never happened. The Roper organization later admitted that the question was worded in a confusing manner. When it asked, "Does it seem possible to you that the Nazi extermination of the Jews never happened, or do you feel certain that it happened?" only 1% said it was possible it never happened.[4]

Even the order in which questions are asked can dramatically influence results. One study[5] asked, during the Cold War, "Do you think the U.S. should let

[4]*Newsweek*, July 25, 1994.

[5]Described in Crossen (1994).

Russian newspaper reporters come here and send back whatever they want?" and "Do you think Russia should let American newspaper reporters come in and send back whatever they want?" For the first question, the percentage of yes responses was 36% when it was asked first and 73% when it was asked second.

SUMMARY: Types of Bias in Sample Surveys

- **Sampling bias** occurs from using nonrandom samples or having undercoverage.
- **Nonresponse bias** occurs when some sampled subjects cannot be reached or refuse to participate or fail to answer some questions.
- **Response bias** occurs when the subject gives an incorrect response (perhaps lying) or the way the interviewer asks the questions (or wording of a question in print) is confusing or misleading.

Poor Ways to Sample

How the sample is obtained can also result in bias. Two sampling methods that may be necessary but are not ideal are a convenience sample and a volunteer sample.

Convenience samples Have you ever been stopped on the street or at a shopping mall to participate in a survey? Such a survey is likely not a random sample but rather a **convenience sample**. It is easy for the interviewer to obtain data relatively cheaply. But the sample may poorly represent the population. Biases may result because of the time and location of the interview and the judgment of the interviewer about whom to interview. For example, working people might be underrepresented if the interviews are conducted on workdays between 9 A.M. and 5 P.M. Poor people may be underrepresented if the interviewer conducts interviews at an upscale shopping mall. Homosexuals might not be selected in a study about romantic relationships if the interviewer is homophobic.

Volunteer samples Have you ever answered a survey you've seen posted on the Internet, such as at the home page for a news organization? A sample of this type, called a **volunteer sample**, is the most common type of convenience sample. As the name implies, subjects *volunteer* to be in the sample. One segment of the population may be more likely to volunteer than other segments because they have stronger opinions about the issue or are more likely to visit that Internet site. This results in sampling bias. For instance, a survey by the Pew Research Center (January 6, 2003) estimated that 46% of Republicans said they like to register their opinions in online surveys, compared with only 28% of Democrats. (Why? One possible lurking variable is time spent on the Internet. Perhaps Republicans spend more time on the Internet than Democrats do.) Thus, results of online surveys may be more weighted in the direction of Republicans' beliefs than the general population.

Convenience samples are not ideal. Sometimes, however, they are necessary, both in observational studies and in experiments. This is often true in medical studies. Suppose we want to investigate how well a new drug performs compared to a standard drug for subjects who suffer from high blood pressure. We won't find a sampling frame of all who suffer from high blood pressure and take a simple random sample of them. We may, however, be able to sample such subjects at medical centers or by using volunteers. Even then, randomization should be used wherever possible. For the study patients, we can randomly select who is given the new drug and who is given the standard one.

Some samples are poor not only because of their convenience but also because they use a sampling frame that does not reflect the population. An example of this was a poll in 1936 to predict the result of a presidential election.

Example 6

A poor sample

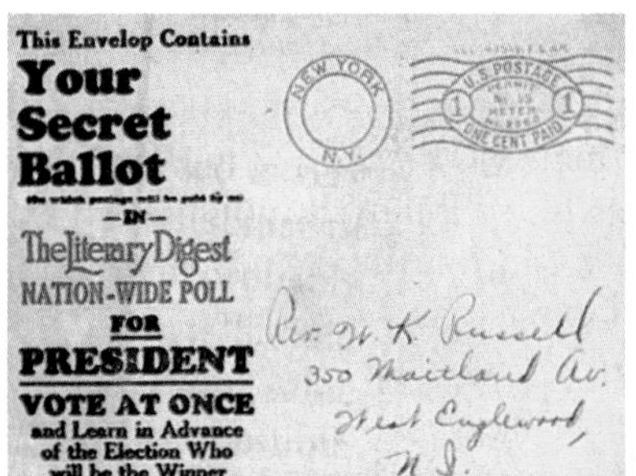

The *Literary Digest* Poll

Picture the Scenario

The *Literary Digest* magazine conducted a poll to predict the result of the 1936 presidential election between Franklin Roosevelt (Democrat and incumbent) and Alf Landon (Republican). At the time, the magazine's polls were famous because they had correctly predicted three successive elections. In 1936, *Literary Digest* mailed questionnaires to 10 million people and asked how they planned to vote. The sampling frame was constructed from telephone directories, country club memberships, and automobile registrations. Approximately 2.3 million people returned the questionnaire. The *Digest* predicted that Landon would win, getting 57% of the vote. Instead, Landon actually got only 36%, and Roosevelt won in a landslide.

Questions to Explore

a. What was the population?

b. How could the *Literary Digest* poll make such a large error, especially with such a huge sample size? What type of bias occurred in this poll?

Think It Through

a. The population was all registered voters in the United States in 1936.

b. This survey had two severe problems:

- Sampling bias due to undercoverage of the sampling frame and a nonrandom sample: In 1936, the United States was in the Great Depression. Those who had cars and country club memberships and thus received questionnaires tended to be wealthy. The wealthy tended to be primarily Republican, the political party of Landon. Many potential voters were not on the lists used for the sampling frame. There was also no guarantee that a subject in the sampling frame was a registered voter.
- Nonresponse bias: Of the 10 million people who received questionnaires, 7.7 million did not respond. As might be expected, those individuals who were unhappy with the incumbent (Roosevelt) were more likely to respond.

Insight

For this same election, a pollster who was getting his new polling agency off the ground surveyed 50,000 people and predicted that Roosevelt would win. Who was this pollster? George Gallup. The Gallup organization is still with us today. However, the *Literary Digest* went out of business soon after the 1936 election.[6]

▶ *Try Exercise 4.24*

A Large Sample Size Does Not Guarantee an Unbiased Sample

Many people think that as long as the sample size is large, it doesn't matter how the sample was selected. This is incorrect, as illustrated by the *Literary Digest* poll. A sample size of 2.3 million did not prevent poor results. The sample was

[6]Bryson, M. C. (1976), *American Statistician*, vol. 30, pp. 184–185.

not representative of the population, and the sample percentage of 57% who said they would vote for Landon was far from the actual population percentage of 36% who voted for him. As another example, consider trying to estimate the average grade point average (GPA) on your campus. If you select 10 students from the library, you can produce an estimate that is biased toward higher GPAs (assuming those students who go to the library are studying more than those who don't). If you, instead, gather a larger sample of 30 students from the library, you still have an estimate that is biased toward higher GPAs. The larger sample size did not fix the problem of sampling in the library. Many Internet surveys have thousands of respondents, but a volunteer sample of thousands is not as good as a random sample, even if that random sample is much smaller. *We're almost always better off with a simple random sample of 100 people than with a volunteer sample of thousands of people.*

SUMMARY: Key Parts of a Sample Survey

- Identify the **population** of all the subjects of interest.
- Define a **sampling frame**, which attempts to list all the subjects in the population.
- Use a **random sampling design**, implemented using random numbers, to select n subjects from the sampling frame.
- Be cautious about **sampling bias** due to nonrandom samples (such as volunteer samples) and sample undercoverage, **response bias** from subjects not giving their true response or from poorly worded questions, and **nonresponse bias** from refusal of subjects to participate.

In Section 4.1 we learned that *experimental* studies are preferable to *nonexperimental* studies but are not always possible. Some types of nonexperimental studies have fewer potential pitfalls than others. For a sample survey with random sampling, we can make inferences about the population of interest. By contrast, with a study using a convenience sample, results apply only to those subjects actually observed. For this reason, some researchers use the term *observational study* to refer only to studies that use available subjects (such as a convenience sample) and not to sample surveys that randomly select their sample.

4.2 Practicing the Basics

4.15 Choosing officers TRY A campus club consists of five officers: president (P), vice president (V), secretary (S), treasurer (T), and activity coordinator (A). The club can select two officers to travel to New Orleans for a conference; for fairness, they decide to make the selection at random. In essence, they are choosing a simple random sample of size $n = 2$.

a. What are the possible samples of two officers?

b. What is the chance that a particular sample of size 2 will be drawn?

c. What is the chance that the activity coordinator will be chosen?

4.16 Simple random sample of students TRY TECH In Example 4, a random drawing was held to select the winners of the football tickets. Organizers randomly chose numbers, using the computer to generate the sample randomly. Choose another sample by using either the Random Numbers web app from the book's website, the website random.org, or statistical software such as StatCrunch, MINITAB, JMP, SPSS or others. (*Note:* In practice, a statistician would include a seed number, which allows the computer to replicate the same sample.)

4.17 Auditing accounts—app TECH Use an app or computer program to select 10 of the 60 school district accounts described in Example 5. Explain how you did this and identify the accounts to be sampled.

4.18 Sampling from a directory TECH A local telephone directory has 50,000 names, 100 per page for 500 pages. Explaining how you found and used random numbers, select 10 numbers to identify subjects for a simple random sample of 10 names.

4.19 Bias due to perceived race A political scientist at the University of Chicago studied the effect of the race of the interviewer.[7] Following a phone interview, respondents were asked whether they thought the interviewer was black or white (all were actually black). Perceiving a white interviewer resulted in more conservative opinions. For example, 14% agreed that "American society is fair to everyone" when they thought the interviewer was black, but 31% agreed to this statement when posed by an interviewer that the respondent thought was white. Which type of bias does this illustrate: Sampling bias, nonresponse bias, or response bias? Explain.

4.20 Confederates Some southern states in the United States have wrestled with the issue of a state flag that is sensitive to African Americans and not divisive. Suppose a survey asks, "Do you oppose the present state flag that contains the Confederate symbol, a symbol of past slavery in the South and a flag supported by extremist groups?"

a. Explain why this is an example of a leading question.

b. Explain why a better way to ask this question would be, "Do you favor or oppose the current state flag containing the Confederate symbol?"

4.21 Instructor ratings The website www.ratemyprofessors.com provides students an opportunity to view ratings for instructors at their universities. A group of students planning to register for a statistics course in the upcoming semester are trying to identify the instructors who receive the highest ratings on the site. One student decides to register for Professor Smith's course because she has the best ratings of all statistics instructors. Another student comments:

a. The website ratings are unreliable because the ratings are from students who voluntarily visit the site to rate their instructors.

b. To obtain reliable information about Professor Smith, they would need to take a simple random sample of the 78 ratings left by students on the site and compile new overall ratings based on those in the random sample.

Which, if either, of the student's comments are valid?

4.22 Job trends The 2013–2014 Recruiting Trends report, produced each year by Michigan State University, reports that hiring over the past year of people with a bachelor's degree increased 7%, for people with a PhD increased 26%, and for people with an MBA decreased 25%. This was based on a voluntary poll of all employers who interacted with at least one of 300 career service centers on college campuses. The survey was answered by 6,500 employers.

a. What is the population for this survey?

b. We cannot calculate the nonresponse rate. Explain what other information is needed to calculate this rate.

c. Describe two potential sources of bias with this survey.

4.23 Gun control More than 75% of Americans answer yes when asked, "Do you favor cracking down against illegal gun sales?" but more than 75% say no when asked, "Would you favor a law giving police the power to decide who may own a firearm?"

a. Which statistic would someone who opposes gun control prefer to quote?

b. Explain what is wrong with the wording of each of these statements.

4.24 Violent video games and family closeness A recent study (*J Child Fam Stud*, DOI 10.1007/s10826-014-9949-9) found that children in Singapore who had a closer relationship with their parents played fewer hours of video games per week and had fewer pathological symptoms of video-gaming.

TRY

a. What is the population of interest for this survey?

b. Describe why this is an observational study.

c. Identify a lurking variable in this study.

4.25 Fracking The journal *Energy Policy* (2014, 65: 57–67) presents a survey of opinions about fracking. Hydraulic fracturing, or fracking, is the process of drilling through rock and injecting a pressurized mixture of sand, water, and chemicals that fractures the rock and releases oil and gas. There has been much debate in the media about its impact on the environment, on land owners, and on the economy. The survey involved contacting a nationally representative sample of 1960 adults in 2012. Of the 1960 people contacted, 1061 adults responded to the survey. The study reported that those more familiar with fracking, women, and those holding egalitarian worldviews were more likely to oppose fracking.

a. Describe the population of interest for this study.

b. Explain why a census is not practical for this study. What advantages does sampling offer?

c. Explain how nonresponse bias might be an issue in this study.

4.26 Teens buying alcohol over Internet In August 2006, a trade group for liquor retailers put out a press release with the headline, "Millions of Kids Buy Internet Alcohol, Landmark Survey Reveals." Further details revealed that in an Internet survey of 1001 teenagers, 2.1% reported that they had bought alcohol online. In such a study, explain how there could be

a. Sampling bias. (*Hint:* Are all teenagers equally likely to respond to the survey?)

b. Nonresponse bias, if some teenagers refuse to participate.

c. Response bias, if some teenagers who participate are not truthful.

4.27 Cheating spouses and bias In a survey conducted by vouchercloud.net and reported in the *Palm Beach Post*, it was found that of 2645 people who had participated in an extramarital affair, the average amount spent per month on the affair was $444. (*Source*: http://www.palmbeachpost.com/news/news/cheating-spouses-spend-444-month-affair-survey-fin/ngbgy/?_federated=1)

a. No information was given on how the surveyed individuals were selected. What type of bias could result if the 2645 individuals were not randomly selected? How would this type of bias potentially affect the responses and the sample mean amount spent per month on the affair?

b. The concern was raised in the article that the individuals' answers could not be validated. What type of bias could

---

[7]Study by Lynn Sanders, as reported by the *Washington Post*, June 26, 1995.

result from untruthful answers? How would this type of bias affect the responses and the sample mean amount spent per month on the affair?

4.28 Online dating A story titled "Personals, Sex Sites Changing the Rules of Love" reported results of a study about online dating by the MSNBC network. The study used online responses of 15,246 people. Of those who responded, three fourths were men and about two thirds had at least a bachelor's degree. One reported finding was that "29% of men go online intending to cheat." Identify the potential bias in this study that results from

a. Sampling bias due to undercoverage.

b. Sampling bias due to the sampling design.

c. Response bias.

4.29 Identify the bias A newspaper designs a survey to estimate the proportion of the population willing to invest in the stock market. It takes a list of the 1000 people who have subscribed to the paper the longest and sends each of them a questionnaire that asks, "Given the extremely volatile performance of the stock market as of late, are you willing to invest in stocks to save for retirement?" After analyzing result from the 50 people who reply, they report that only 10% of the local citizens are willing to invest in stocks for retirement. Identify the bias that results from the following:

a. Sampling bias due to undercoverage

b. Sampling bias due to the sampling design

c. Nonresponse bias

d. Response bias due to the way the question was asked

4.30 Types of bias Give an example of a survey that would suffer from

a. Sampling bias due to the sampling design

b. Sampling bias due to undercoverage

c. Response bias

d. Nonresponse bias

4.3 Good and Poor Ways to Experiment

Just as there are good and poor ways to gather a sample in an observational survey, there are good and poor ways to conduct an experiment. First, let's recall the definition of an experimental study from Section 4.1: We assign each subject to an experimental condition, called a **treatment**. We then observe the outcome on the response variable. The goal of the experiment is to investigate the association—how the treatment affects the response. An advantage of an experimental study over a nonexperimental study is that it provides stronger evidence for causation.

In an experiment, subjects are often referred to as **experimental units**. This name emphasizes that the objects measured need not be human beings. They could, for example, be schools, stores, mice, or computer chips.

The Elements of a Good Experiment

Let's consider another example to help us learn what makes a good experiment. It is common knowledge that smoking is a difficult habit to break. Studies have reported that regardless of what smokers do to quit, most relapse within a year. Some scientists have suggested that smokers are less likely to relapse if they take an antidepressant regularly after they quit. How can you design an experiment to study whether antidepressants help smokers to quit?

For this type of study, as in most medical experiments, it is not feasible to randomly sample the population (all smokers who would like to quit) because they cannot be readily identified. We need to use a convenience sample. For instance, a medical center might advertise to attract volunteers from the smokers who would like to quit.

Control comparison group Suppose you have 400 volunteers who would like to quit smoking. You could ask them to quit, starting today. You could have each start taking an antidepressant and then a year from now check how many have relapsed. Perhaps 42% of them would relapse. But this is not enough information.[8] You need to be able to compare this result to the percentage who would relapse if they were *not* taking the antidepressant.

---

[8]Chapter 12 explains another reason a control group is needed. The regression effect implies that, over time, poor subjects tend to improve and good subjects tend to get worse, in relative terms.

An experiment normally has a primary treatment of interest, such as receiving an antidepressant. But it should also have a second treatment for comparison to help you analyze the effectiveness of the primary treatment. So the volunteers should be split into two groups: One group receives the antidepressant, and the other group does not. You could give the second group a pill that looks like the antidepressant but that does not have any active ingredient—a placebo. This second group, using the placebo treatment, is called the **control group**. After subjects are assigned to the treatments and observed for a certain period of time, the relapse rates are compared. Because the only distinction between the groups, at least by design, is taking the antidepressant, the difference between the relapse rate of two groups is attributed to the treatment.

Why bother to give the placebo to the control group if the pill doesn't contain any active ingredient? This is partly so that the two treatments appear identical to the subjects. (As we'll discuss, subjects should not know which treatment they are receiving.) This is also because people who take a placebo tend to respond better than those who receive nothing, perhaps for psychological reasons. This is called the **placebo effect**. For instance, of the subjects not receiving the antidepressant, perhaps 75% would relapse within a year, but if they received a placebo pill perhaps 55% of them would relapse. If the relapse rate was 42% for subjects who received antidepressants, then in comparing relapse rates for the antidepressant and control groups, it makes a big difference how you define the control group. Using these numbers, you would say the reduction in relapse was 33% (75% − 42%) when comparing it to nothing, but 13% (55% − 42%) when compared to the placebo group.

In some experiments, *a control group may receive an existing treatment rather than a placebo.* For instance, a smoking cessation study might analyze whether an antidepressant works better than a nicotine patch in helping smokers to quit. It may be unethical not to provide the standard of care, in this case a nicotine patch, if it has already been shown in previous studies to be more effective than a placebo. Or the experiment could compare all three treatments: antidepressant, nicotine patch, and a placebo.

Randomization In the smoking cessation experiment, how should the 400 study subjects be assigned to the treatment groups? Should you personally decide which treatment each subject receives? This could result in bias. If you are conducting the study to show that the antidepressant is effective, you might consciously or subconsciously place smokers you believe will be more likely to succeed into the group that receives the antidepressant.

It is better to use **randomization** to assign the subjects: Randomly assign 200 of the 400 subjects to receive the antidepressant and the other 200 subjects to form the control group. Randomization helps to prevent bias from one treatment group tending to be different from the other in some way, such as having better health or being younger. In using randomization, we attempt to *balance the treatment groups* by making them similar with respect to their distribution on potential lurking variables. This enables us to attribute any difference in their relapse rates to the treatments they are using, not to lurking variables or to researcher bias.

You might think you can do better than randomization by using your own judgment to assign subjects to the treatment groups. For instance, when you identify a potential lurking variable, you could try to balance the groups according to its values. If age is that variable, every time you put someone of a particular age in one treatment group, you could put someone of the same age in the other treatment group. There are two problems with this: (1) *many* variables are likely to be important, and it is difficult to balance groups on *all* of them at once, and (2) you may not have thought of other relevant lurking variables. Even if you can balance the groups on the variables you identified, the groups could be unbalanced on these other variables, causing the overall results to be biased in favor of one treatment.

You can feel more confident about the worthiness of new research findings if they come from a randomized experiment with a control group rather than from an experiment without a control group, from an experiment that did not use randomization to assign subjects to the treatments, or from an observational study. An analysis[9] of published medical studies about treatments for heart attacks indicated that the new therapy provided improved treatment 58% of the time in studies without randomization and control groups but only 9% of the time in studies having randomization and control groups. This suggests that studies conducted without randomization or without other ways to reduce bias may produce results that tend to be overly optimistic.

SUMMARY: The Role of Randomization in Experiments

Use randomization for assigning subjects to the treatments

- To eliminate bias that may result if you (the researchers) assign the subjects
- To balance the groups on variables that you know affect the response
- To balance the groups on lurking variables that may be unknown to you

Blinding the study It is important that the treatment groups be treated as equally as possible. Ideally, the subjects are **blind** to the treatment to which they are assigned. In the smoking cessation study, the subjects should not know whether they are taking the antidepressant or a placebo. Whoever has contact with the subjects during the experiment, including the data collectors who record the subjects' response outcomes, should also be blind to the treatment information. Otherwise they could intentionally or unintentionally provide extra support to one group or make different decisions for subjects, depending on which treatment they received, including whether they have relapsed. (Does just one cigarette count? What about two? etc.) When neither the subject nor those having contact with the subject know the treatment assignment, the study is called **double-blind**. That's ideal.

Example 7

Study design

Antidepressants for Quitting Smoking

Picture the Scenario

To investigate whether antidepressants help people quit smoking, one study[10] used 429 men and women who were 18 or older and had smoked 15 cigarettes or more per day for the previous year. The subjects were highly motivated to quit and in good health. They were assigned to one of two groups: One group took 300 mg daily of an antidepressant that has the brand name bupropion. The other group did not take an antidepressant. At the end of a year, the study observed whether each subject had successfully abstained from smoking or had relapsed.

Questions to Explore

a. Identify the response and explanatory variables, the treatments, and the experimental units.

[9] See Crossen (1994), p. 168.

[10] *Annals of Internal Medicine* 2001; 135:423–433.

b. How should the researchers assign the subjects to the two treatment groups?

c. Without knowing more about this study, what would you identify as a potential problem with the study design?

Think It Through

a. This experiment has

Response variable: Whether the subject abstains from smoking for one year (yes or no)

Explanatory variable: Whether the subject received bupropion (yes or no)

Treatments: bupropion, no bupropion

Experimental units: The 429 volunteers who are the study subjects

b. The researchers should randomize to assign subjects to the two treatments. They could use random numbers to randomly assign half (215) of the subjects to form the group that uses bupropion and 214 subjects to the group that does not receive bupropion (the control group). The procedure would be as follows:

- Number the study subjects from 001 to 429.
- Pick a three-digit random number between 001 and 429. If the number is 392, for example, then the subject numbered 392 is put in the bupropion group.
- Continue to pick three-digit numbers until you've picked 215 distinct values between 001 and 429. This determines the 215 subjects who will receive bupropion. The remaining 214 subjects will form the control group.

c. The description of the experiment in Picture the Scenario did not say whether the subjects who did *not* receive bupropion were given a placebo or whether the study was blinded. If not, these would be potential sources of bias. In addition, the definition of what it means to relapse or abstain from smoking needs to be clearly defined.

Insight

In the actual reported study, the subjects were randomized to receive bupropion or a placebo for 45 weeks. The study *was* double-blinded. This experimental study was well designed. The study results showed that at the end of one year, 55% of the subjects receiving bupropion were not smoking, compared with 42% in the placebo group. After 18 months, 48% of the bupropion subjects were not smoking compared to 38% for the placebo subjects. However, after two years, the percentage of nonsmokers was similar for the two groups, 42% versus 40%.

▶ ***Try Exercise 4.32***

In Practice The Randomized Experiment in Medicine

In medicine, the randomized experiment (clinical trial) has become the gold standard for evaluating new medical treatments. The Cochrane Collaboration (www.cochrane.org) is an organization devoted to synthesizing evidence from medical studies all over the world. According to this organization, there have been hundreds of thousands of randomized experiments comparing medical treatments. In most countries, a company cannot get a new drug approved for sale unless it has been tested in a randomized experiment.

Source: Background information from S. Senn (2003), *Dicing with Death*. Cambridge University Press, p. 68.

Generalizing Results to Broader Populations

We've seen that random samples are preferable to convenience samples, yet convenience samples are more feasible than many experiments. When an experiment uses a convenience sample, be cautious about the extent to which results generalize to a larger population. Look carefully at the characteristics of the sample. Do they seem representative of the overall population? If not, the results have dubious worth.

Many medical studies use volunteers at *several* medical centers to try to obtain a broad cross section of subjects. But some studies mistakenly try to generalize to a broader population than the one from which the sample was taken. A psychologist may conduct an experiment using a sample of students from an introductory psychology course. For the results to be of wider interest, however, the psychologist might claim that the conclusions generalize to *all* college students, to all young adults, or even to all adults. Such generalizations may be wrong since the sample may differ from those populations in fundamental ways such as in average socioeconomic status, race, or gender, or attitudes.

SUMMARY: Key Parts of a Good Experiment

- A good experiment has a **control comparison group**, **randomization** in assigning experimental units to treatments, and **blinding**.
- The **experimental units** are the subjects—the people, animals, or other objects to which the treatments are applied.
- The **treatments** are the experimental conditions imposed on the experimental units. One of these may be a **control** (for instance, either a placebo or an existing treatment) that provides a basis for determining whether a particular treatment is effective. The treatments correspond to values of an explanatory variable.
- Randomly assign the experimental units to the treatments. This tends to balance the comparison groups with respect to lurking variables.
- Replication of studies increases confidence in the conclusions.

Carefully assess the scope of conclusions in research articles, mass media, and advertisements. Evaluate critically the basis for the conclusions by noting the experimental design or the sampling design upon which the conclusions are based.

4.3 Practicing the Basics

4.31 Smoking affects lung cancer? You would like to investigate whether smokers are more likely than nonsmokers to get lung cancer. From the students in your class, you pick half at random to smoke a pack of cigarettes each day and half not ever to smoke. Fifty years from now, you will analyze whether more smokers than nonsmokers got lung cancer.

a. Is this an experiment or an observational study? Why?

b. Summarize at least three practical difficulties with this planned study.

4.32 Never leave home without duct tape TRY There have been anecdotal reports of the ability of duct tape to remove warts. In an experiment conducted at the Madigan Army Medical Center in the state of Washington (*Archives of Pediatric and Adolescent Medicine* 2002; 156: 971–974), 51 patients between the ages of 3 and 22 were randomly assigned to receive either duct-tape therapy (covering the wart with a piece of duct tape) or cryotherapy (freezing a wart by applying a quick, narrow blast of liquid nitrogen). After two months, the percentage successfully treated was 85% in the duct tape group and 60% in the cryotherapy group.

a. Identify the response variable, the explanatory variable, the experimental units, and the treatments.

b. Describe the steps of how you could randomize in assigning the 51 patients to the treatment groups.

4.33 More duct tape In a follow-up study, 103 patients in the Netherlands having warts were randomly assigned to use duct tape or a placebo, which was a ring covered by tape so that the wart itself was kept clear (*Arch. Pediat. Adoles. Med.* 2006; 160: 1121–1125).

a. Identify the response variable, the explanatory variable, the experimental units, and the treatments.

b. After six weeks, the warts had disappeared for 16% of the duct tape group and 6% of the placebo group. However, the difference was declared to be "not statistically significant." Explain what this means.

4.34 Vitamin B A *New York Times* article (March 13, 2006) described two studies in which subjects who had recently had a heart attack were randomly assigned to one of four treatments: placebo and three different doses of vitamin B. In each study, after years of study, the differences among the proportions having a heart attack were judged to be not statistically significant. Identify the (a) response variable, (b) explanatory variable, (c) experimental units, and (d) treatments and (e) explain what it means to say that differences "were judged to be not statistically significant."

4.35 Facebook study During the one-week period of January 11–18, 2012, Facebook conducted an experiment to research whether emotional states can be transferred to others via emotional contagion. Facebook users were randomly selected to be part of two parallel studies in which Facebook manipulated the exposure to emotional expressions in the user's news feed. Two parallel experiments were conducted. In one study, it reduced the positive emotional content; in the other study, the negative emotional content was reduced. For each study, there was a control group (the users' news feed was not manipulated), and an experimental group (the users' news feed was manipulated—either positively or negatively). Two variables were measured in each study after the manipulation by Facebook: the percentage of all words produced by a person that was positive and the percentage of all words produced by a person that was negative. There were 689,003 Facebook users in the study. (Source: *PNAS,* June 17, 2014, vol. 111, no. 24, www.pnas.org/cgi/doi/10.1073/pnas.1320040111)

a. Explain why this study is an experiment.

b. Identity the experimental units.

c. For the study in which exposure to friends' positive emotional content was reduced, identity the explanatory variable and the two response variables.

d. The Facebook users randomly selected for the study were unaware they were part of this experiment. Provide a reason Facebook elected not to inform the selected users that they were part of an experiment. Provide a reason the users selected for the study may have felt not informing them about the study was unethical.

4.36 Science faculty selection of grad students In an experimental study, science faculty $(n = 127)$ from research universities rated application materials of a student. The 127 application folders were identical except that some were labeled male and some were labeled female. A folder was randomly assigned to each faculty member. The application was for a laboratory manager position. The science faculty rated their application folder on the competency of the applicant, how employable the applicant was, and the recommended starting salary of the applicant. It was found that the faculty rated the male application folders significantly higher on competency, being employable, and starting salary. (Source: www.pnas.org/cgi/doi/10.1073/pnas.1211286109)

a. What is a reasonable statistical question for this experiment?

b. Identify the explanatory variable, treatments, response variables (there are more than one), and experimental units.

c. Explain why it was important to assign the folders randomly.

4.37 Pain reduction medication Consider an experiment being designed to study the effectiveness of an experimental pain reduction medication. The plan includes recruiting 100 individuals suffering from moderate to severe pain to participate. One half of the group will be assigned to take the actual experimental drug, and the other half will be assigned a placebo. The study will be blind in the sense that the individuals will not know which treatment they are receiving. At the end of the study, individuals will be asked to record, using a standardized scale, how much pain relief they experienced. Why is it important to use a placebo in such a study?

4.38 Pain reduction medication, continued Consider the same setting as that of Exercise 4.37. Of the 100 participants, 45 are male and 55 are female. During the design of the study, one member of the research team suggests that all males be given the active drug and all females be given the placebo. Another member of the team wants to randomly assign each of the total group of 100 participants to one of the two treatments.

a. Which researcher's plan is the best experimental design for measuring the effectiveness of the medication if the results of the experiment are to be generalized to the entire population, which consists of both females and males?

b. Does the fact that the participants of the study were recruited rather than selected at random prohibit generalization of the results?

4.39 Pain reduction medication, yet again Revisit the setting of Exercise 4.37. Suppose that in addition to the participants being blinded, the researchers responsible for recording the results of the study are also blinded. Why does it matter whether the researchers know which participants receive which treatment?

4.40 Colds and vitamin C For some time there has been debate about whether regular large doses of vitamin C reduce the chance of getting a common cold.

a. Explain how you could design an experiment to test this. Describe all parts of the experiment, including (i) what the treatments are, (ii) how you assign subjects to the treatments, and (iii) how you could make the study double-blind.

b. An observational study indicates that people who take vitamin C regularly get fewer colds, on the average. Explain why these results could be misleading.

4.41 Reducing high blood pressure A pharmaceutical company has developed a new drug for treating high blood pressure. The company would like to compare the drug's effects to those of the most popular drug currently on the market. Two hundred volunteers with a history of high blood pressure and who are currently not on medication are recruited to participate in a study.

a. Explain how the researchers could conduct a randomized experiment. Indicate the experimental units, the response and explanatory variables, and the treatments.

b. Explain what would have to be done to make this study double-blind.

4.4 Other Ways to Conduct Experimental and Nonexperimental Studies

In this chapter, we've learned the basics of ways to conduct nonexperimental and experimental studies. This final section shows ways these methods are often extended in practice so they are even more powerful. We'll first learn about alternatives to simple random sampling in sample surveys and then about types of observational studies that enable us to study questions for which experiments with humans are not feasible. Finally, we'll learn how to study the effects of two or more explanatory variables with a single experiment.

Sample Surveys: Other Random Sampling Designs Useful in Practice

Simple random sampling gives every possible sample the same chance of selection. In practice, more complex random sampling designs are often easier to implement or are more efficient, requiring a smaller sampling size for the same precision. Sometimes they are even preferable to simple random sampling.

Cluster random sampling To use simple random sampling, we need a sampling frame—the list of all, or nearly all, subjects in the population. In some cases, this information is not available. It may be easier to identify **clusters** of subjects. A study of residents of a country can identify counties or census tracts. A study of students can identify schools. A study of the elderly living in institutions can identify nursing homes. We can obtain a sample by randomly selecting the clusters and observing each subject in the clusters chosen.

For instance, suppose you would like to sample about 1% of the families in your city. You could use city blocks as clusters. Using a map to label and number city blocks, you could select a simple random sample of 1% of the blocks and then select every family on each of those blocks for your observations.

Cluster Random Sample

Divide the population into a large number of **clusters**, such as city blocks. Select a simple random sample of the clusters. Use the subjects in those clusters as the sample. This is a **cluster random sample**.

For personal interviews, when the subjects within a cluster are close geographically, cluster sampling is less expensive per observation than simple random sampling. By interviewing every family in a particular city block, you can obtain many observations quickly and with little travel.

SUMMARY: Advantages and Disadvantages of a Cluster Random Sample

Cluster random sampling is a preferable sampling design if

- A reliable sampling frame is not available, or
- The cost of selecting a simple random sample is excessive.

The disadvantages are:

- We usually require a larger sample size with cluster sampling for the same level of precision.
- Selecting a small number of clusters might result in a sample that is more homogeneous than the population.

Stratified random sampling Suppose we are interested in estimating the mean number of hours a week that students in your school work on outside employment. The plan is to use the student directory to take a simple random sample of $n = 40$ students and analyze how the mean compares for freshmen, sophomores, juniors, and seniors. Merely by chance, you may get only a few observations from one of the classes, making it hard to estimate the mean well for that class. If the student directory also identifies students by their class, you could amend the sampling scheme to take a simple random sample of 10 students from each class, still having an overall $n = 40$. The four classes are called **strata** of the population. This type of sample is called a **stratified random sample**.

Stratified Random Sample

A **stratified random sample** divides the population into separate groups, called **strata**, based on some attribute or characteristic about the subjects, and then selects a simple random sample from each stratum.

Stratified sampling is particularly useful when the typical values of the response variable differ substantially across the strata. A limitation of stratification is that you must have a sampling frame and know the stratum into which each subject in the sampling frame belongs. You might want to stratify students in your school by whether the student has a job, to make sure you get enough students who work and who don't work. However, this information may not be available for each student.

SUMMARY: Advantages and Disadvantages of a Stratified Random Sample

Stratified random sampling has the

- Advantage that you can include in your sample enough subjects in each group (stratum) you want to evaluate.
- Disadvantage that you must have a sampling frame and know the stratum into which each subject belongs.

What's the difference between a stratified sample and a cluster sample? A stratified sample *uses every stratum.* By contrast, a cluster sample *uses a sample of the clusters* rather than all of them. Figure 4.2 illustrates the distinction among sampling subjects (simple random sample), sampling clusters of subjects (cluster random sample), and sampling subjects from within strata (stratified random sample).

In addition, a cluster sample uses predetermined groups to create a single sampling frame, whereas a stratified sample creates multiple sampling frames by strata based on a subject characteristic. In the previous examples, city blocks already exist and can be listed as the sampling frame. The sampling frames for class year have to be defined separately before random selection is performed.

Comparison of different random sampling methods A good sampling design ensures that each subject in a population has an opportunity to be selected. The design should incorporate randomness. Table 4.1 summarizes the random sampling methods we've presented.

In practice, sampling designs often have two or more stages. When carrying out a large survey for predicting national elections, the Gallup organization often (1) identifies election districts as clusters and takes a simple random sample of

Random Sampling

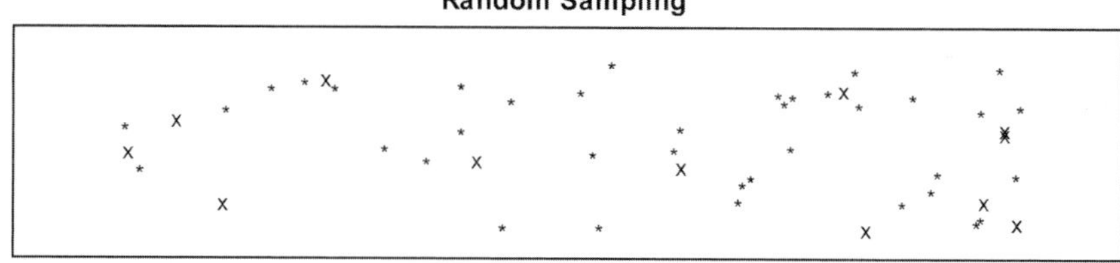

12 observations chosen randomly

Stratified Sampling

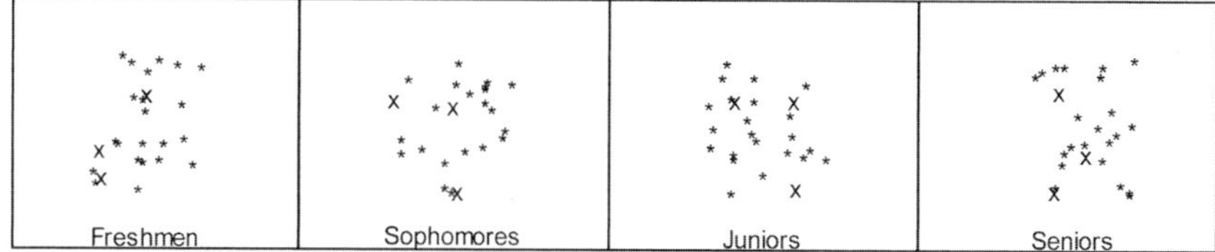

3 observations chosen randomly from each stratum

Cluster Sampling

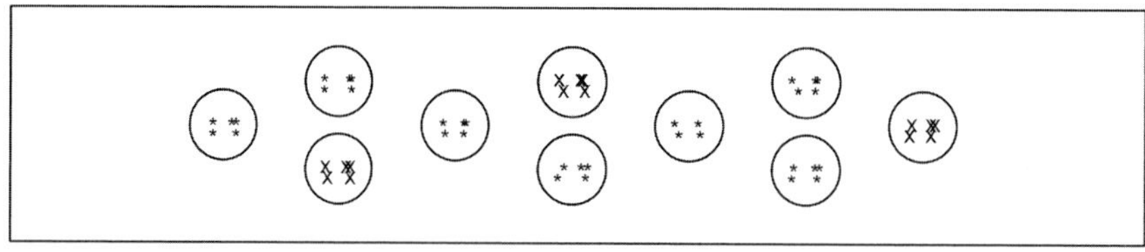

3 clusters chosen randomly

▲ **Figure 4.2** **Ways of Randomly Sampling 40 Students.** The figure is a schematic for a simple random sample of 16 students, a cluster random sample of 4 clusters of 4 students who live together, and a stratified random sample of 4 students from each class (Fresh., Soph., Jnr., Snr.). **Question** What's the difference between clustering and stratifying? The Xs represent an observation selected, whereas the *s represent observations that were not selected as part of the sample.

them, and (2) takes a simple random sample of households within each selected election district rather than sampling every household in a district, which might be infeasible.

Marketing companies also commonly use *two-stage cluster sampling*, first randomly selecting test market cities (the clusters) and then randomly selecting consumers within each test market city. Many major surveys, such as the General Social Survey, Gallup polls, and the Current Population Survey, incorporate both stratification and clustering.

In future chapters, when we use the term *random sampling*, we'll mean *simple random sampling*. The formulas for most statistical methods assume simple random sampling. Similar formulas exist for other types of random sampling, but they are complex and beyond the scope of this text.

Table 4.1 Summary of Random Sampling Methods

Method	Description	Advantages
Simple random sample	Each possible sample is equally likely	Sample tends to be a good reflection of the population
Cluster random sample	Identify clusters of subjects, take simple random sample of the clusters	Do not need a sampling frame of subjects, less expensive to implement
Stratified random sample	Divide population into groups (strata), take simple random sample from each stratum	Ensures enough subjects in each group that you want to compare

Retrospective and Prospective Observational Studies

We've seen that an experiment can investigate cause and effect better than an observational study. With an observational study, it's possible that an association is due to some lurking variable. However, observational studies do have advantages. It's often not practical to conduct an experiment. For instance, with human subjects it's not ethical to design an experiment to study the long-term effect of cell phone use on getting cancer. Nevertheless, it is possible to design an observational study that controls for identified lurking variables.

Rather than taking a cross section of a population at some time, such as with a sample survey, some studies are *backward looking* **(retrospective)** or *forward looking* **(prospective)**. Observational studies in medicine are often retrospective. How can we study whether there is an association between long-term cell phone use and brain cancer if we cannot perform an experiment? We can form a sample of subjects who have brain cancer and a similar sample of subjects who do not and then compare the past use of cell phones for the two groups. This approach was first applied to study smoking and lung cancer.

Example 8

Retrospective studies

Lung Cancer and Smoking

Picture the Scenario

In 1950 in London, England, medical statisticians Austin Bradford Hill and Richard Doll conducted one of the first studies linking smoking and lung cancer. In 20 hospitals, they matched 709 patients admitted with lung cancer in the preceding year with 709 noncancer patients at the same hospital of the same gender and within the same five-year grouping on age. All patients were queried about their smoking behavior. A smoker was defined as a person who had smoked at least one cigarette a day for at least a year. The study used a *retrospective* design to look into the past in measuring the patients' smoking behavior.

Table 4.2 shows the results. The 709 *cases* in the first column of the table were the patients with lung cancer. The 709 *controls* in the second column were the matched patients without lung cancer.

Table 4.2 Results of Retrospective Study of Smoking and Lung Cancer

The cases had lung cancer. The controls did not. The *retrospective* aspect refers to studying whether subjects had been smokers in the past.

	Lung Cancer	
Smoker	**Yes (case)**	**No (control)**
Yes	688	650
No	21	59
Total	**709**	**709**

Question to Explore

Compare the proportions of smokers for the lung cancer cases and the controls. Interpret.

Think It Through

For the lung cancer cases, the proportion who were smokers was $688/709 = 0.970$, or 97%. For the controls (not having lung cancer), the proportion who were smokers was $650/709 = 0.917$, or about 92%. The lung cancer cases were more likely than the controls to have been smokers.

Insight

An inferential analysis showed that these results were statistically significant. This suggested that an association exists between smoking and lung cancer.

▶ ***Try Exercise 4.46***

Case-control studies The type of retrospective study used in Example 8 to study smoking and lung cancer is called a **case-control study**.

In Words

In Example 8, the response outcome of interest was having lung cancer. The cases had lung cancer, the controls did not have lung cancer, and they were compared on the explanatory variable—whether the subject had been a smoker (yes or no).

Case-Control Study

A **case-control study** is a retrospective observational study in which subjects who have a response outcome of interest (the cases) and subjects who have the other response outcome (the controls) are compared on an explanatory variable.

This is a popular design for medical studies in which it is not practical or ethical to perform an experiment. We can't randomly assign subjects into a smoking group and a nonsmoking group—this would involve asking some subjects to start smoking. Since we can't use randomization to balance effects of potential lurking variables, usually the cases and controls are matched on such variables. In Example 8, cases and controls were matched on their age, gender, and hospital.

In a case-control study, the number of cases and the number of controls is fixed. The random part is observing the outcome for the explanatory variable. For instance, in Example 8, for the 709 patients of each type, we looked back in time to see whether they smoked. We found percentages for the categories of the explanatory variable (smoker, nonsmoker) given lung cancer status (cases or control). It is not meaningful to form a percentage for a category of the response variable. For example, we cannot estimate the population percentage of subjects who have lung cancer, for smokers or nonsmokers. By the study design, *half* the subjects had lung cancer. This does not mean that half the population had lung cancer.

Example 9

Cell Phone Use

Picture the Scenario

Studies 1 and 2 about cell phone use in Example 1 were both case-control studies. In Study 2, the cases were brain cancer patients. The controls were randomly sampled from general practitioner lists and were matched with the cases on age, sex, and place of residence. In Study 1, the cases had a type of eye cancer. In forming a sample of controls, Study 1 did not attempt to match subjects with the cases.

Question to Explore

Why might researchers decide to match cases and controls on characteristics such as age?

Think It Through

We've seen that one way to balance groups on potential lurking variables such as age is to randomize in assigning subjects to groups. However, these were observational studies, not experiments. So it was not possible for the researchers to use randomization to balance treatments on potential lurking variables. Matching is an attempt to achieve the balance that randomization provides.

When researchers fail to use relevant variables to match cases with controls, those variables could influence the results. They could mask the true relationship. The results could suggest an association when actually there is not one, or the reverse. Without matching, results are more susceptible to effects of lurking variables.

Insight

The lack of matching in Study 1 may be one reason that the results from the two studies differed, with Study 2 not finding an association and Study 1 finding one. For example, in Study 1 suppose the eye cancer patients tended to be older than the controls, and suppose older people tend to be heavier users of cell phones. Then, age could be responsible for the observed association between cell phone use and eye cancer.

► *Try Exercise 4.47*

Prospective studies A *retrospective* study, such as a case-control study, looks into the past. By contrast, a *prospective* study follows its subjects into the future.

Example 10

Prospective studies ◄

Nurses' Health

Picture the Scenario

The Nurses' Health Study, conducted by researchers at Harvard University,[11] began in 1976 with 121,700 female nurses age 30 to 55 years. The purpose of the study was to explore relationships among diet, hormonal factors, smoking habits, and exercise habits, and the risk of coronary heart disease, pulmonary disease, and stroke. Since the initial survey in 1976, the nurses have filled out a questionnaire every two years.

Question to Explore

What does it mean for this observational study to be called *prospective*?

Think It Through

The retrospective smoking study in Example 8 looked to the past to learn whether its lung cancer subjects had been smokers. By contrast, at the start of the Nurses' Health Study, it was not known whether a particular nurse would eventually have an outcome such as lung cancer. The study followed each nurse into the future to see whether she developed that outcome and to analyze whether certain explanatory variables (such as smoking) were associated with it.

---

[11]More information on this study can be found at clinicaltrials.gov/show/NCT00005152 and at www.channing.harvard.edu/nhs.

Insight

Over the years, several analyses have been conducted using data from the Nurses' Health Study. One finding (reported in *The New York Times*, February 11, 2003) was that nurses in this study who were highly overweight 18-year-olds were five times as likely as young women of normal weight to need hip replacement later in life.

▶ ***Try Exercise 4.48***

SUMMARY: Types of Nonexperimental Studies

- A **retrospective** study looks into the past.
- A **prospective** study identifies a group (cohort) of people and observes them in the future. In research literature, prospective studies are often referred to as cohort studies.
- A **sample survey** takes a **cross section** of a population at the current time. Sample surveys are sometimes called cross-sectional studies.

Observational Studies and Causation

Can we ever *definitively* establish causation with an observational study? No, we cannot. For example, because the smoking and lung cancer study in Example 8 was observational, cigarette companies argued that a lurking variable could have caused this association. So why are doctors so confident in declaring that smoking causes lung cancer? For a combination of reasons: (1) Experiments conducted using animals have shown an association, (2) in many countries, over time, female smoking has increased relative to male smoking, and the incidence of lung cancer has increased in women compared to men. Other studies, both retrospective and prospective, have added more evidence. For example, when a prospective study begun in 1951 with 35,000 doctors ended in 2001, researchers[12] estimated that cigarettes took an average of 10 years off the lives of smokers who never quit. This study estimated that at least half the people who smoke from youth are eventually killed by their habit.

Most important, studies carried out on different populations of people have *consistently* concluded that smoking is associated with lung cancer, even after adjusting for all potentially confounding variables that researchers have suggested. As more studies are done that adjust for confounding variables, the chance that a lurking variable remains that can explain the association is reduced. As a consequence, although we cannot definitively conclude that smoking causes lung cancer, physicians will not hesitate to tell you that they believe it does. As do most statisticians, including the four authors of this text!

Multifactor Experiments

In Words

A **factor** is a categorical explanatory variable (such as whether the subject takes an antidepressant) having as categories the experimental conditions (the **treatments**, such as bupropion or no bupropion).

Now let's learn about other ways of performing experiments. First, we'll learn how a single experiment can help us analyze the effects of two explanatory variables at once.

Categorical explanatory variables in an experiment are often referred to as **factors**. For example, consider the experiment described in Example 7 to study whether taking an antidepressant can help a smoker stop smoking. The factor

[12]See article by R. Doll et al., *British Med. J.*, June 26, 2004, p. 1519.

measured whether a subject used the antidepressant bupropion (yes or no). Suppose the researchers also wanted to study a second factor, using a nicotine patch versus not using one. The experiment could then have four treatment groups that result from cross-classifying the two factors. See Figure 4.3. The four treatments are bupropion alone, nicotine patch alone, bupropion and nicotine patch, neither bupropion nor nicotine patch.

Bupropion (Factor 2)		Nicotine Patch (Factor 1): Yes	Nicotine Patch (Factor 1): No
	Yes	Treatment 1 Nicotine Patch Bupropion	Treatment 2 No Nicotine Patch Bupropion
	No	Treatment 3 Nicotine Patch Placebo	Treatment 4 No Nicotine Patch Placebo

▲ **Figure 4.3 An Experiment Can Use Two (or More) Factors at Once.** The treatments are the combinations of categories of the factors, as numbered in the boxes.

Why use both factors at once in an experiment? Why not do one experiment about bupropion and a separate experiment about the nicotine patch? The reason is that we can learn more from a two-factor experiment. For instance, the combination of using both a nicotine patch and bupropion may be more effective than using either method alone.

Multifactor experiments ◄

Example 11

Antidepressants and/or Nicotine Patches

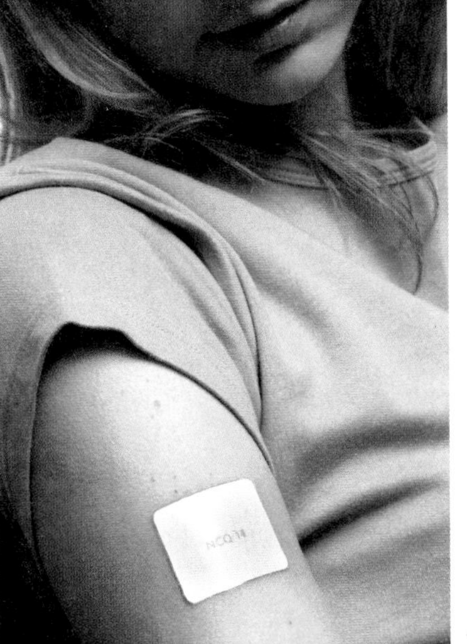

Picture the Scenario

Example 7 analyzed a study about whether bupropion helps a smoker quit cigarettes. Let's now also consider nicotine patches as another possible cessation aid.

Question to Explore

How can you design a single study to investigate the effects of nicotine patches and bupropion on whether a subject relapses into smoking?

Think It Through

You could use the two factors with four treatment groups shown in Figure 4.3. Figure 4.4 portrays the design of a randomized experiment, with placebo alternatives to bupropion and to the nicotine patch.

The study should be double-blind. After a fixed length of time, you compare the four treatments for the percentages who have relapsed.

Insight

In fact, a two-factor experiment *has* been conducted to study both these factors.[13] The most effective treatments were bupropion alone or in combination

[13] Jorenby, D. et al. (1999), *New England Journal of Medicine*, 340(9): 685–691.

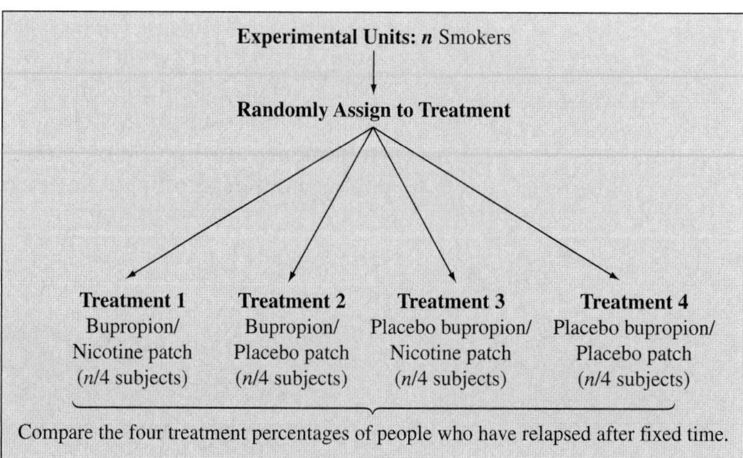

▲ **Figure 4.4** Diagram of a Randomized Experiment with Two Factors (Whether Use Bupropion and Whether Use a Nicotine Patch). **Question** A three-factor design could also incorporate whether a subject receives counseling to discourage smoking. What would such a diagram look like?

Recall

This study is double-blind if both the subjects and the evaluator(s) of the subjects do not know whether the pill is active and whether the patch is active. ◀

with a nicotine patch. We'll explore the results in Exercise 4.72. If we included a third factor of whether the subject receives counseling, we would have three factors with $2 \times 2 \times 2 = 8$ treatments to compare.

▶ ***Try Exercise 4.50***

Matched Pairs Designs

The experiments described in Examples 7 and 11 used **completely randomized designs:** The subjects were randomly assigned to one of the treatments. Sometimes we can use an alternative experimental design in which *each treatment is observed for each subject.* Medical experiments often do this to compare treatments for chronic conditions that do not have a permanent cure.

To illustrate, suppose a study plans to compare an oral drug and a placebo for treating migraine headaches. The subjects could take one treatment the first time they get a migraine headache and the other treatment the second time they get a migraine headache. The response is whether the subject's pain is relieved. The first three subjects might contribute the results that follow to the data file.

Subject	Drug	Placebo	
1	Relief	No relief	← first *matched pair*
2	Relief	Relief	
3	No relief	No relief	

For the entire sample, we would compare the percentage of subjects who have pain relief with the drug to the percentage who have pain relief with the placebo. The two observations for a particular subject are called a **matched pair** because they both come from the same person.

A matched-pairs design in which subjects cross over during the experiment from using one treatment to using another treatment is called a **crossover design**. Crossover design helps remove certain sources of potential bias. Using the same subjects for each treatment keeps potential lurking variables from affecting the results because those variables take the same values for each treatment. For instance, any difference observed between the drug and the placebo responses is not because subjects taking the drug had better overall health. Another example of a matched pair, crossover design is Study 3 discussed in Example 1.

An additional application of a matched-pairs design occurs in agricultural experiments that compare the crop yield for two fertilizer types. In each field, two plots are marked, one for each fertilizer. Two plots in the same field are likely to be more similar in soil quality and moisture than two plots from different fields. If we instead used a completely randomized design to assign entire fields to each fertilizer treatment, there's the possibility that by chance one fertilizer will be applied to fields that have better soil. This is especially true when the experiment can't use many fields.

Blocking in an Experiment

The matched-pairs design extends to the comparison of more than two treatments. The migraine headache crossover study could investigate relief for subjects who take a low dose of an oral drug, a high dose of that drug, and a placebo. The crop yield study could have several fertilizer types.

In experiments with matching, a set of matched experimental units is referred to as a **block**. A block design with random assignment of treatments to units within blocks is called a **randomized block** design. In the migraine headache study, each person is a block. In the crop yield study, each field is a block. A purpose of using blocks is to provide similar experimental units for the treatments, so they're on an equal footing in any subsequent comparisons.

To reduce possible bias, treatments are usually randomly assigned within a block. In the migraine headache study, the order in which the treatments are taken would be randomized. Bias could occur if all subjects received one treatment before another. An example of potential bias in a crossover study is a positive carry-over effect if the first drug taken has lingering effects that can help improve results for the second drug taken. Likewise, in a crop yield study, the fertilizers are randomly assigned to the plots in a field.

On the Shoulders of...Austin Bradford Hill (1897–1991) and Richard Doll (1912–2005)

How did statisticians become pioneers in examining the effects of smoking on lung cancer?

In the mid-20th century, Austin Bradford Hill was Britain's leading medical statistician. In 1946, to assess the effect of streptomycin in treating pulmonary tuberculosis, he designed what is now regarded as the first controlled randomized medical experiment. About that time, doctors noticed the alarming increase in the number of lung cancer cases. The cause was unknown but suspected to be atmospheric pollution, particularly coal smoke. In 1950, Bradford Hill and medical doctor and epidemiologist Richard Doll published results of the case-control study (Example 8) that identified smoking as a potentially important culprit. They were also pioneers in developing a sound theoretical basis for the case-control method. They followed their initial study with other case-control studies and with a long-term prospective study that showed that smoking was not only the predominant risk factor for lung cancer but also correlated with other diseases.

At first, Bradford Hill was cautious about claiming that smoking causes lung cancer. As the evidence mounted from various studies, he accepted the causal link as being overwhelmingly the most likely explanation. An influential article written by Bradford Hill in 1965 proposed criteria that should be satisfied before you conclude that an association reflects a causal link. For his work, in 1961 Austin Bradford Hill was knighted by Queen Elizabeth. Richard Doll was knighted in 1971.

4.4 Practicing the Basics

4.42 Student loan debt A researcher wants to compare student loan debt for students who attend four-year public universities with those who attend four-year private universities. She plans to take a random sample of 100 recent graduates of public universities and 100 recent graduates of private universities. Which type of random sampling is used in her study design?

4.43 Club officers again In Exercise 4.15, two officers were to be selected to attend a conference in New Orleans. Three of the officers are female and two are male. It is decided to send one female and one male to the convention.

a. Labeling the officers as 1, 2, 3, 4, 5, where 4 and 5 are male, draw a stratified random sample using random numbers. Explain how you did this.

b. Explain why this sampling design is not a simple random sample.

c. If the activity coordinator is female, what are her chances of being chosen? If male?

4.44 Security awareness training Of 400 employees at a company, 25% work in production, 40% work in sales and marketing, and 35% work in new product development. As part of a security awareness training program, the group overseeing implementation of the program will randomly choose a sample of 20 employees to begin the training; the percentages of workers from each department in the sample are to align with the percentages throughout the company.

a. What type of sampling could be used to achieve this goal?

b. Using this sampling method, determine a sample of 20 employees to be chosen.

4.45 Teaching and learning model A school district comprises 24 schools. The numbers of students in each of the schools are as follows:

TECH

455 423 399 388 348 344 308 299 297 272 266 260
252 244 222 209 175 161 151 148 128 109 101 98

The district wants to implement an experimental teaching and learning model for approximately 20% of the 6057 students in the district. Administrators want to choose the 20% randomly, but they will not be able to use simple random sampling throughout the entire district because the new model can be implemented only at an entire school, not just for a select group of students at each school. The schools not selected will continue to use the current teaching and learning model.

a. Explain how one could use cluster random sampling to achieve the goal of choosing approximately 20% of the students in the district for the experimental model.

b. Use cluster random sampling and an app or software to determine which schools will be randomly selected to use the new model. How many schools are in your sample? How many students are in your sample?

c. Repeat part b, drawing a new sample. Did you obtain the same number of schools?

d. Would it be possible for the school district to implement stratified random sampling? Explain.

4.46 German mobile study The contingency table shows results from the German study about whether there was an association between mobile phone use and eye cancer (Stang et al., 2001).

TRY

a. The study was retrospective. Explain what this means.

b. Explain what is meant by cases and controls in the headings of the table.

c. What proportion had used mobile phones, of those in the study who (i) had eye cancer and (ii) did not have eye cancer?

Eye Cancer and Use of Mobile Phones

Mobile Phones	Cases	Controls
Yes	16	46
No	102	429
Total	**118**	**475**

4.47 Smoking and lung cancer Refer to the smoking case-control study in Example 8. Since subjects were not matched according to *all* possible lurking variables, a cigarette company can argue that this study does not prove a causal link between smoking and lung cancer. Explain this logic, using diet as the lurking variable.

TRY

4.48 Smoking and death Example 1 in Chapter 3 described a survey of 1314 women during 1972–1974, in which each woman was asked whether she was a smoker. Twenty years later, a follow-up survey observed whether each woman was deceased or still alive. Was this study a retrospective study or a prospective study? Explain.

TRY

4.49 Baseball under a full moon Exercise 4.10 mentioned that the away team has won 13 consecutive games played between the Boston Brouhahas and Minnesota Meddlers during full moons. This is a statement based on retrospective observational data.

a. Many databases are huge, including those containing sports statistics. If you had access to the database, do you think you could uncover more surprising trends?

b. Would you be more convinced that the phase of the moon has predictive power if the away team were to win the *next* 13 games played under a full moon between Boston and Minnesota?

c. The results of which type of observational study are generally more reliable, retrospective or prospective?

4.50 Two factors helpful? A two-factor experiment designed to compare two diets and to analyze whether results depend on gender randomly assigns 20 men and 20 women to the two diets, 10 of each to each diet. After three months, the sample mean weight losses are as shown in the table.

TRY

Sample Mean Weight Loss by Diet Type and Gender			
	Gender		
Diet	**Female**	**Male**	**Overall**
Low-carb	12	0	6
Low-fat	0	12	6
Overall	6	6	6

a. Identify the two factors (explanatory variables) and the response variable.

b. What would the study have concluded if it did only a one-factor analysis on diet, looking at the overall results and not having the information about gender?

c. What could the study learn from the two-factor study that it would have missed by doing a one-factor study on diet alone or a one-factor study on gender alone?

4.51 Growth Mindset Carol Dweck is a noted psychologist from Stanford who believes that we should praise students' effort and not their intelligence. In her seminal study (2006), she gave students a test and then randomly divided the students into two groups. She praised the effort of one group and praised the intelligence of the other group. For their next exercise, the groups were given a choice of a challenging task or an easy task. Of those who were praised for their effort, 90% chose the challenging task, whereas fewer than half of the students who were praised for their intelligence chose the challenging task, fearful of losing their smart status.

a. Identify the response variable(s), explanatory variable, experimental units, and treatments.

b. What type of experimental design does this employ? Explain.

4.52 Allergy relief An experiment is being designed to compare relief from hay fever symptoms given by a low dose of a drug, a high dose of the drug, and a placebo. Each subject who suffers from hay fever and volunteers for the study is observed on three days, with a different treatment used each day. There are two days between treatments, so that a treatment does not have a carry-over effect for the next treatment assigned.

a. What are the blocks in this block design? What is this type of block design called?

b. Suppose the study is conducted as a double-blind study. Explain what this means.

c. Explain how randomization within blocks could be incorporated into the study.

4.53 Effect of partner smoking in smoking cessation study Smokers may have a more difficult time quitting smoking if they live with a smoker. How can an experiment explore this possibility in a study to compare bupropion with placebo? Suppose the researchers split the subjects into two groups: those who live with a smoker and those who do not live with smokers. Within each group, the subjects are randomly assigned to take bupropion or a placebo. The figure shows a flow chart of this design, when 250 of the 429 study subjects live with nonsmokers and 179 live with a smoker.

a. Is this design a *completely* randomized design? Why or why not? (*Hint*: Is the smoking status of the person a subject lives with randomly determined?)

b. Does this experiment have blocks? If so, identify them.

c. Is this design a randomized block design? Explain why or why not.

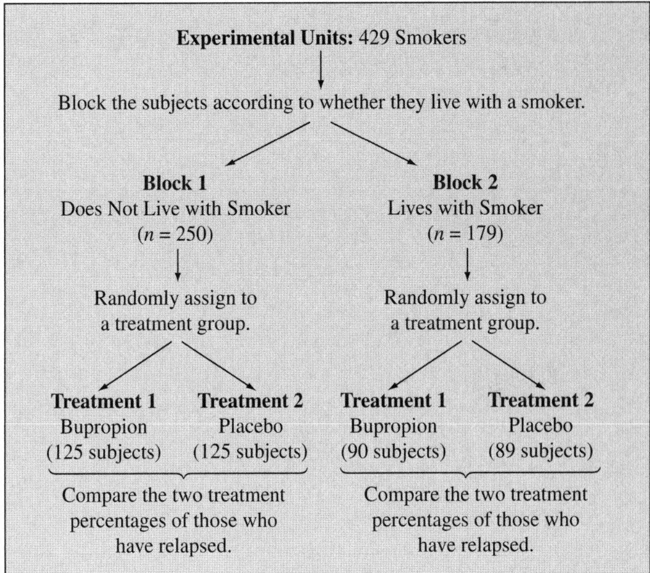

Diagram of an experiment to account for smoking status of partner

Chapter Review

ANSWERS TO THE CHAPTER FIGURE QUESTIONS

Figure 4.2 In a stratified sample, every stratum is used. A simple random sample is taken within each stratum. A cluster sample takes a simple random sample of the clusters. All the clusters are *not* used.

Figure 4.4 The diagram would look the same but have $2 \times 2 \times 2 = 8$ treatments.

CHAPTER SUMMARY

This chapter introduced methods for gathering data.

- An **experiment** assigns subjects to experimental conditions (such as drug or placebo) called **treatments**. These are categories of the explanatory variable. The outcome on the response variable is then observed for each subject.
- An **observational study** is a type of nonexperimental study that observes subjects on the response and explanatory variables. The study samples the population of interest, but merely observes rather than applies treatments to those subjects.

Since association does not imply causation, with observational studies we must be aware of potential **lurking variables** that influence the association. In an experiment, a researcher uses **randomization** in assigning experimental units (the subjects) to the treatments. This helps balance the treatments on lurking variables. A randomized experiment can provide support for causation. To reduce bias, experiments should be **double-blind**, with neither the subject nor the data collector knowing to which treatment a subject was assigned.

A **sample survey** is a type of nonexperimental study that takes a sample from a population. Good methods for selecting samples incorporate random sampling.

- A **simple random sample** of n subjects from a population is one in which each possible sample of size n has the same chance of being selected.
- A **cluster random sample** takes a simple random sample of clusters (such as city blocks) and uses subjects in those clusters as the sample.
- A **stratified random sample** divides the population into separate groups, called **strata**, and then selects a simple random sample from each stratum.

Be cautious of results from studies that use a convenience sample, such as a **volunteer sample**, which Internet polls use. Even with random sampling, **biases** can occur due to **sample undercoverage, nonresponse** by many subjects in the sample, and **responses that are biased** because of question wording or subjects' lying.

Most **sample surveys** take a cross section of subjects at a particular time. A **census** is a complete enumeration of an entire population. **Prospective** studies follow subjects into the future, as is true with many experiments. Medical studies often use **retrospective** observational studies, which look at subjects' behavior in the past.

- A **case-control study** is an example of a retrospective study. Subjects who have a response outcome of interest, such as cancer, serve as cases. Other subjects not having that outcome serve as controls. The cases and controls are compared on an explanatory variable, such as whether they had been smokers.

A categorical explanatory variable in an experiment is also called a **factor**. **Multifactor experiments** have at least two explanatory variables. With a **completely randomized design**, subjects are assigned randomly to categories of each explanatory variable. Some designs instead use **blocks**—sets of experimental units that are matched. **Matched-pairs designs** have two observations in each block. Often this is the same subject observed for each of two treatments, such as in a crossover study.

Data are only as good as the method used to obtain them. Unless we use a good study design, conclusions may be faulty.

CHAPTER PROBLEMS

Practicing the Basics

4.54 Cell phones If you want to conduct a study with humans to see whether cell phone use makes brain cancer more likely, explain why an observational study is more realistic than an experiment.

4.55 Observational versus experimental study Without using technical language, explain the difference between observational and experimental studies to someone who has not studied statistics. Illustrate with an example, using it also to explain the possible weaknesses of an observational study.

4.56 Unethical experimentation Give an example of a scientific question of interest for which it would be unethical to conduct an experiment. Explain how you could instead conduct an observational study.

4.57 Spinal fluid proteins and Alzheimer's A research study published in 2010 in the *Archives of Neurology* investigated the relationship between the results of a spinal fluid test and the presence of Alzheimer's disease. The study included 114 patients with normal memories, 200 with memory problems, and 102 with Alzheimer's disease. Each individual's spinal fluid was analyzed to detect the presence of two types of proteins. Almost everyone with Alzheimer's had the proteins in their spinal fluid. Nearly three quarters of the group with memory problems had the proteins, and each such member developed Alzheimer's within five years. About one third of those with normal memories had the proteins, and the researchers suspect that those individuals will develop memory problems and eventually Alzheimer's.

a. Identify the explanatory and response variable(s).

b. Was this an experimental or nonexperimental study? Why?

c. Would it be possible to design this study as an experiment? Explain why or why not.

4.58 Fear of asbestos Your friend reads about a study in an epidemiology journal that estimates that the chance is 15 out of 1 million that a teacher who works for 30 years in a school with typical asbestos levels gets cancer from asbestos. However, she also knows about a teacher who died recently who may have had asbestos exposure. In deciding whether to leave teaching, should she give more weight to the study or to the story she heard about the teacher who died? Why?

4.59 NCAA men's basketball poll The last four teams of the Southeast region of the 2011 NCAA Men's Basketball Tournament were Butler (located in Indiana), Brigham Young University (located in Utah), Florida, and Wisconsin. The sports website ESPN.com asked visitors of the site which team would win the Southeast region.

Nationwide results are depicted on the map that follows. It was reported that 44% of the more than 3300 Indiana resident respondents believed Butler would win the regional, and 78% of the more than 5600 Wisconsin resident respondents believed Wisconsin would win.

a. What are the estimated margins of error associated with the Indiana and Wisconsin polls?

b. Explain why the percentages within Indiana and Wisconsin vary so drastically from the nationwide percentages displayed in the figure.

c. It was reported that between 42.3% and 45.7% of Indiana residents believed Butler was likely to win. What type of potential bias prevented these results from being representative of the entire population of Indiana residents?

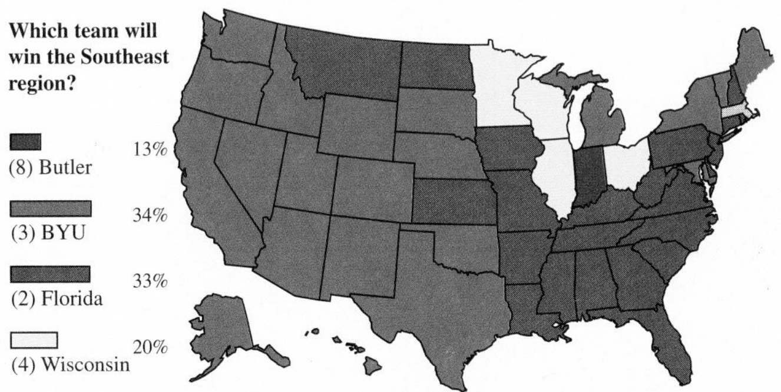

© ESPN.com (2012). Graphic feature used with permission.

4.60 Sampling your fellow students You are assigned to direct a study on your campus to discover factors that are associated with strong academic performance. You decide to identify 20 students who have perfect GPAs of 4.0 and then measure explanatory variables for them that you think may be important, such as high school GPA and average amount of time spent studying per day.

a. Explain what is wrong with this study design.

b. Describe a study design that would provide more useful information.

4.61 Beware of Internet polling An Internet survey at a newspaper website reports that only 14% of respondents believe in gun control. Mention a lurking variable that could bias the results of such an online survey, and explain how it could affect the results.

4.62 Comparing female and male students You plan to sample from the 3500 undergraduate students who are enrolled at the University of Rochester to compare the proportions of female and male students who would like to see the United States elect a female president.

a. Describe the steps for how you would proceed if you plan a simple random sample of 80 students. Illustrate by picking the first three students for the sample.

b. Suppose that you use random numbers to select students but stop selecting females as soon as you have 40, and you stop selecting males as soon as you have 40. Is the resulting sample a simple random sample? Why or why not?

c. What type of sample is the sample in part b? What advantage might it have over a simple random sample?

4.63 Football discipline A large southern university had problems with 17 football players being disciplined for team rule violations, arrest charges, and possible NCAA violations. The online *Atlanta Journal Constitution* ran a poll with the question, "Has the football coach lost control over his players?" having possible responses, "Yes, he's been too lenient," and "No, he can't control everything teenagers do."

a. Was there potential for bias in this study? If so, what types of bias?

b. The poll results after two days were

Yes	6012	93%
No	487	7%

Does this large sample size guarantee that the results are unbiased? Explain.

4.64 Obesity in metro areas A Gallup poll tracks obesity in the United States for the most and least obese metro areas in the United States. The poll, based on more than 200,000 responses between January and December 2010, reported that certain chronic conditions are more prevalent in the most obese metro areas. The table that follows presents a summary of the findings.

	10 Most Obese Metro Areas	**10 Least Obese Metro Areas**
Diabetes	14.6%	8.5%
High blood pressure	35.8%	25.6%
High cholesterol	28.5%	24.1%
Heart attack	5.9%	3.4%

Source: www.gallup.com/poll/146669/Adults-Obese-Metro-Areas-Nationwide.aspx

a. Are we able to conclude from the Gallup poll that obesity causes a higher incidence of these conditions?

b. What is a possible variable other than obesity that may be associated with these chronic conditions?

4.65 Voluntary sports polls In 2014, the Pittsburgh Penguins were ahead of the New York Rangers three games to one in the first round of the National Hockey League playoffs. ESPN.com conducted a voluntary, online poll that asked respondents to predict the outcomes of the rest of the series. Of all 1,094 respondents, 52% said Penguins in 5 games, 34% said Penguins in 6 games, 5% said Penguins in 7 games, and 9% said Rangers in 7 games.

a. Was this a simple random sample? Explain.

b. If ESPN.com wanted to determine the true proportions for all sports fans, how could it do so more reliably?

Source: http://espn.go.com/sportsnation/polls/_/category/5239/your-nhl-playoff-predictions

4.66 Video games mindless? "Playing video games not so mindless." This was the headline of a news report[14] about a study that concluded that young adults who regularly play video games demonstrated better visual skills than young adults who do not play regularly. Sixteen young men volunteered to take a series of tests that measured their visual skills; those who had played video games in the previous six months performed better on the tests than those who hadn't played.

a. What are the explanatory and response variables?

b. Was this an observational study or an experiment? Explain.

c. Specify a potential lurking variable. Explain your reasoning.

4.67 Physicians' health study Read about the first Physicians' Health Study at phs.bwh.harvard.edu.

a. Explain whether it was (i) an experiment or an observational study and (ii) a retrospective or prospective study.

b. Identify the response variable and the explanatory variable(s) and summarize results.

4.68 Aspirin prevents heart attacks? During the 1980s approximately 22,000 physicians over the age of 40 agreed to participate in a long-term study called the Physicians' Health Study. One question investigated was whether aspirin helps lower the rate of heart attacks. The physicians were randomly assigned to take aspirin or take a placebo.

a. Identify the response variable and the explanatory variable.

b. Explain why this is an experiment and identify the treatments.

c. There are other explanatory variables, such as the amount of exercise a physician got, that we would expect to be associated with the response variable. Explain how such a variable is dealt with by the randomized nature of the experiment.

4.69 Exercise and heart attacks Refer to Exercise 4.68. One potential confounding variable was the amount of exercise the physicians got. The randomization should have balanced the treatment groups on exercise. The contingency table shows the relationship between whether the physician exercised vigorously and the treatments.

	Exercise Vigorously?		
Treatment	**Yes**	**No**	**Total**
Aspirin	7,910	2,997	**10,907**
Placebo	7,861	3,060	**10,921**

a. Find the conditional proportions (recall Section 3.1) in the categories of this potential confounder (amount of exercise) for each treatment group. Are they similar?

b. Do you think that the randomization process did a good job of achieving balanced treatment groups in terms of this potential confounder? Explain.

4.70 Smoking and heart attacks Repeat the previous exercise, considering another potential confounding variable—whether the physicians smoked. The contingency table cross-classifies treatment group by smoking status.

	Smoking Status			
Treatment	**Never**	**Past**	**Current**	**Total**
Aspirin	5,431	4,373	1,213	**11,017**
Placebo	5,488	4,301	1,225	**11,014**

4.71 Aspirin, beta-carotene, and heart attacks In the study discussed in the previous three exercises, this completely randomized study actually used two factors: whether received aspirin or placebo and whether received beta-carotene or placebo. Draw a table or a flow chart to portray the four treatments for this study.

4.72 Bupropion and nicotine patch study results The subjects for the study described in Example 11 were evaluated for abstinence from cigarette smoking at the end of 12 months. The table shows the percentage in each group that were abstaining. Recall that margin of error and statistical significance are discussed in Chapter 1.

Group	Abstinence Percentage	Sample Size
Nicotine patch only	16.4	244
Bupropion only	30.3	244
Nicotine patch with bupropion	35.5	245
Placebo only	15.6	160

a. Find the approximate margin of error for the abstinence percentage in each group. Explain what a margin of error means.

b. Based on the results in part a, does it seem as if the difference between the bupropion-only and placebo-only treatments is statistically significant? Explain.

c. Based on the results in part a, does it seem as if the difference between the bupropion-only and nicotine patch with bupropion treatments is statistically significant? Explain.

d. Based on the results in parts a, b, and c, how would you summarize the results of this experiment?

4.73 Prefer Coke or Pepsi? You want to conduct an experiment with your class to see whether students prefer Coke or Pepsi.

a. Explain how you could do this, incorporating ideas of blinding and randomization, (i) with a completely randomized design and (ii) with a matched pairs design.

b. Which design would you prefer? Why?

4.74 Comparing gas brands The marketing department of a major oil company wants to investigate whether cars get better mileage using its gas (Brand A) than from an independent one (Brand B) that has cheaper prices. The department has 20 cars available for the study.

[14]See www.freerepublic.com/focus/f-news/919978/posts.

a. Identify the response variable, the explanatory variable, and the treatments.

b. Explain how to use a completely randomized design to conduct the study.

c. Explain how to use a matched-pairs design to conduct the study. What are the blocks for the study?

d. Give an advantage of using a matched-pairs design.

4.75 **Samples not equally likely in a cluster sample?** In a cluster random sample with equal-sized clusters, every subject has the same chance of selection. However, the sample is not a simple random sample. Explain why not.

4.76 **Nursing homes** You plan to sample residents of registered nursing homes in your county. You obtain a list of all 97 nursing homes in the county, and randomly select five of them. You obtain lists of residents from those five homes and interview all the residents in each home.

a. Are the nursing homes clusters or strata?

b. Explain why the sample chosen is not a simple random sample of the population of interest to you.

4.77 **Multistage health survey** A researcher wants to study regional differences in dental care. He takes a multistage sample by dividing the United States into four regions, taking a simple random sample of ten schools in each region, randomly sampling three classrooms in each school, and interviewing all students in those classrooms about whether they've been to a dentist in the previous year. Identify each stage of this sampling design, indicating whether it involves stratification or clustering.

4.78 **Hazing** Hazing within college fraternities is a continuing concern. Before a national meeting of college presidents, a polling organization is retained to conduct a survey among fraternities on college campuses, gathering information on hazing for the meeting. The investigators from the polling organization realize that it is not possible to find a reliable sampling frame of all fraternities. Using a list of all college institutions, they randomly sample 30 of them and then interview the officers of each fraternity at each of these institutions that has fraternities. Would you describe this as a simple random sample, cluster random sample, or stratified random sample of the fraternities? Explain.

4.79 **Marijuana and schizophrenia** Many research studies focus on a link between marijuana use and psychotic disorders such as schizophrenia. Studies have found that people with schizophrenia are twice as likely to smoke marijuana as those without the disorder. Data also suggest that individuals who smoke marijuana are twice as likely to develop schizophrenia as those who do not use the drug. Contributing to the apparent relationship, a comprehensive review done in 2007 of the existing research reported that individuals who merely try marijuana increase their risk of developing schizophrenia by 40%. Meanwhile, the percentage of the population who has tried marijuana has increased dramatically in the United States over the past 50 years, whereas the percentage of the population affected by schizophrenia has remained constant at about 1%. What might explain this puzzling result?

4.80 **Twins and breast cancer** Excessive cumulative exposure to ovarian hormones is believed to cause breast cancer. A study (*New England J. Medic.* 2003; 348: 2313–2322) used information from 1811 pairs of female twins, one or both of whom had breast cancer. Paired twins were compared with respect to age at puberty, when breast cancer was first diagnosed, and other factors. Their survey did not show an association between hereditary breast cancer and hormone exposure.

a. What type of observational study was used by the researchers?

b. Why do you think the researchers used this design instead of a randomized experiment?

Concepts and Investigations

4.81 **Cell phone use** Using the Internet, find a study about cell phone use and its potential risk when used by drivers of automobiles.

TECH

a. Was the study an experiment or an observational study?

b. Identify the response and explanatory variables.

c. Describe any randomization or control conducted in the study as well as attempts to take into account lurking variables.

d. Summarize conclusions of the study. Do you see any limitations of the study?

4.82 **Read a medical journal** Go to a website for an online medical journal, such as *British Medical Journal* (www.bmj.com). Pick an article in a recent issue.

TECH

a. Was the study an experiment or an observational study?

b. Identify the response variable and the primary explanatory variable(s).

c. Describe any randomization or control conducted in the study as well as attempts to take into account lurking variables.

d. Summarize conclusions of the study. Do you see any limitations of the study?

4.83 **Internet poll** Find an example of results of an Internet poll. Do you trust the results of the poll? If not, explain why not.

TECH

4.84 **Search for an observational study** Find an example of an observational study from a newspaper, journal, the Internet, or some other medium.

a. Identify the explanatory and response variables and the population of interest.

b. What type of observational study was conducted? Describe how the data were gathered.

c. Were lurking variables considered? If so, discuss how. If not, can you think of potential lurking variables? Explain how they could affect the association.

d. Can you identify any potential sources of bias? Explain.

4.85 **Search for an experimental study** Find an example of a randomized experiment from a newspaper, journal, the Internet, or some other media.

a. Identify the explanatory and response variables.

b. What were the treatments? What were the experimental units?

c. How were the experimental units assigned to the treatments?

d. Can you identify any potential sources of bias? Explain.

4.86 **Judging sampling design** In each of the following situations, summarize negative aspects of the sample design.

a. A newspaper asks readers to vote at its Internet site to determine whether they believe government expenditures should be reduced by cutting social programs. Based on 1434 votes, the newspaper reports that 93% of the city's residents believe that social programs should be reduced.

b. A congresswoman reports that letters to her office are running 3 to 1 in opposition to the passage of stricter gun control laws. She concludes that approximately 75% of her constituents oppose stricter gun control laws.

c. An anthropology professor wants to compare attitudes toward premarital sex of physical science majors and social science majors. She administers a questionnaire to her Anthropology 437, Comparative Human Sexuality class. She finds no appreciable difference in attitudes between the two majors, so she concludes that the two student groups are about the same in their views about premarital sex.

d. A questionnaire is mailed to a simple random sample of 500 household addresses in a city. Ten are returned as bad addresses, 63 are returned completed, and the rest are not returned. The researcher analyzes the 63 cases and reports that they represent a "simple random sample of city households."

4.87 **More poor sampling designs** Repeat the previous exercise for the following scenarios:

a. A principal in a large high school wants to sample student attitudes toward a proposal that seniors must pass a general achievement test to graduate. She lists all of the first-period classes. Then, using a random number table, she chooses a class at random and interviews every student in that class about the proposed test.

b. A new restaurant opened in January. In June, after six months of operation, the owner applied for a loan to improve the building. The loan application asked for the annual gross income of the business. The owner's record book contains receipts for each day of operation since opening. She decides to calculate the average daily receipt based on a sample of the daily records and multiply that by the number of days of operation in a year. She samples every Friday's record. The average daily receipt for this sample was then used to estimate the yearly receipts.

4.88 **Age for legal alcohol** You want to investigate the opinions students at your school have about whether the age for legal drinking of alcohol should be 18.

a. Write a question to ask about this in a sample survey in such a way that results would be biased. Explain why it would be biased.

b. Now write an alternative question that should result in unbiased responses.

4.89 **Quota sampling** An interviewer stands at a street corner and conducts interviews until obtaining a quota in various groups representing the relative sizes of the groups in the population. For instance, the quota might be 50 factory workers, 100 housewives, 60 elderly people, 30 Hispanics, and so forth. This is called **quota sampling**. Is this a random sampling method? Explain and discuss potential advantages or disadvantages of this method. (The Gallup organization used quota sampling until it predicted, incorrectly, that Dewey would easily defeat Truman in the 1948 presidential election.)

4.90 **Smoking and heart attacks** A Reuters story (April 2, 2003) reported that "The number of heart attack victims fell by almost 60% at one hospital six months after a smoke-free ordinance went into effect in the area (Helena, Montana), a study showed, reinforcing concerns about second-hand smoke." The number of hospital admissions for heart attack dropped from just under seven per month to four a month during the six months after the smoking ban.

a. Did this story describe an experiment or an observational study?

b. In the context of this study, describe how you could explain to someone who has never studied statistics that association does not imply causation. For instance, give a potential reason that could explain this association.

4.91 **Issues in clinical trials** A randomized clinical trial is planned for AIDS patients to investigate whether a new treatment provides improved survival over the current standard treatment. It is not known whether it will be better or worse.

a. Why do researchers use randomization in such experiments rather than letting the subjects choose which treatment they will receive?

b. When patients enrolling in the study are told the purpose of the study, explain why they may be reluctant to be randomly assigned to one of the treatments.

c. If a researcher planning the study thinks the new treatment is likely to be better, explain why he or she may have an ethical dilemma in proceeding with the study.

4.92 **Compare smokers with nonsmokers** Example 8 and Table 4.2 described a case-control study on smoking and lung cancer. Explain carefully why it is not sensible to use the study's proportion of smokers who had lung cancer (that is, $688/(688 + 650)$) and proportion of nonsmokers who had lung cancer $(21/(21 + 59))$ to estimate corresponding proportions of smokers and nonsmokers who have lung cancer in the overall population.

4.93 **Is a vaccine effective?** A vaccine is claimed to be effective in preventing a rare disease that occurs in about one of every 100,000 people. Explain why a randomized clinical trial comparing 100 people who get the vaccine to 100 people who do not get it is unlikely to be worth doing. Explain how you could use a case-control study to investigate the efficacy of the vaccine.

4.94 **Distinguish helping and hindering among infants** Researchers at Yale University's Infant Cognition Center were interested in determining whether infants had the ability to distinguish between the actions of helping and hindering. Each infant in the study was shown two videos. One video included a figure performing a helping action and the other included a figure performing a hindering action. Infants were presented with two toys resembling the helping and hindering figures from the videos and allowed to choose one of the toys to play with. The researchers conjectured that, even at a very young age, the infants would tend to choose the helpful object.

a. How might the results of this study been biased had each infant been shown the video with the helpful figure before being shown the video with the hindering figure?

b. How could such a potential bias be eliminated?

4.95 Distinguish helping and hindering among infants, continued In the previous exercise, we considered how showing each baby in the study the two videos in the same order might create a bias. In fact, of the 16 babies in the study, half were shown the videos in one order while the other half was shown the videos in the opposite order. Explain how to use the Random Numbers web app to randomly divide the 16 infants into two groups of 8.

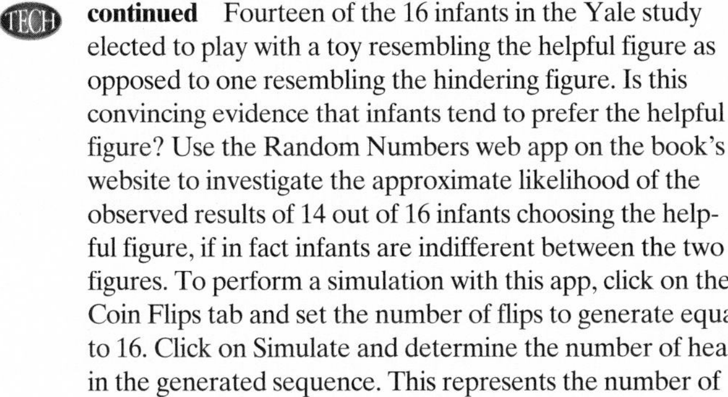

4.96 Distinguish helping and hindering among infants, continued Fourteen of the 16 infants in the Yale study elected to play with a toy resembling the helpful figure as opposed to one resembling the hindering figure. Is this convincing evidence that infants tend to prefer the helpful figure? Use the Random Numbers web app on the book's website to investigate the approximate likelihood of the observed results of 14 out of 16 infants choosing the helpful figure, if in fact infants are indifferent between the two figures. To perform a simulation with this app, click on the Coin Flips tab and set the number of flips to generate equal to 16. Click on Simulate and determine the number of heads in the generated sequence. This represents the number of times the child selects the helpful toy if they choose at random. Repeat this simulation for a total of 10 simulations. Out of the 10 simulations, how often did you obtain 14 or more heads out of 16 tosses? Are your results convincing evidence that infants actually tend to exhibit a preference?

For Exercises 4.97–4.103, select the best response.

4.97 Multiple choice: What's a simple random sample? A simple random sample of size n is one in which

a. Every nth member is selected from the population.

b. Each possible sample of size n has the same chance of being selected.

c. There is *exactly* the same proportion of women in the sample as is in the population.

d. You keep sampling until you have a fixed number of people having various characteristics (e.g., males, females).

4.98 Multiple choice: Be skeptical of medical studies? An analysis of published medical studies about heart attacks (Crossen, 1994, p. 168) noted that in the studies having randomization and strong controls for bias, the new therapy provided improved treatment 9% of the time. In studies without randomization or other controls for bias, the new therapy provided improved treatment 58% of the time.

a. This result suggests it is better not to use randomization in medical studies because it is harder to show that new ideas are beneficial.

b. Some newspaper articles that suggest a particular food, drug, or environmental agent is harmful or beneficial should be viewed skeptically unless we learn more about the statistical design and analysis for the study.

c. This result shows the value of case-control studies over randomized studies.

d. The randomized studies were poorly conducted, or they would have found the new treatment to be better much more than 9% of the time.

4.99 Multiple choice: Opinion and question wording A recent General Social Survey asked subjects whether they supported legalized abortion in each of seven circumstances. The percentage who supported legalization varied between 44.6% (if the woman is not married) to 88.6% (if the woman's health is seriously endangered by the pregnancy). This indicates that

a. Responses can depend greatly on the question wording.

b. Nonexperimental studies can never be trusted.

c. The sample must not have been randomly selected.

d. The sample must have had problems with response bias.

4.100 Multiple choice: Campaign funding When the Yankelovich polling organization asked, "Should laws be passed to eliminate all possibilities of special interests giving huge sums of money to candidates?" 80% of the sample answered yes. When they posed the question, "Should laws be passed to prohibit interest groups from contributing to campaigns, or do groups have a right to contribute to the candidate they support?" only 40% said yes (*Source: A Mathematician Reads the Newspaper,* by J. A. Paulos, New York: Basic Books, 1995, p. 15). This example illustrates problems that can be caused by

a. Nonresponse

b. Bias in the way a question is worded

c. Sampling bias

d. Undercoverage

4.101 Multiple choice: Emotional health survey An Internet poll conducted in the United Kingdom by Netdoctor.co.uk asked individuals to respond to an "emotional health survey" (see www.hfienberg.com/clips/pollspiked.htm). There were 400 volunteer respondents. Based on the results, the British Broadcasting Corporation (BBC) reported that "Britons are miserable—it's official." This conclusion reflected the poll responses, of which one quarter feared a "hopeless future," one in three felt "downright miserable," and nearly one in ten thought "their death would make things better for others." Which of the following is *not* correct about why these results may be misleading?

a. Many people who access a medical website and are willing to take the time to answer this questionnaire may be having emotional health problems.

b. Some respondents may not have been truthful or may have been Internet surfers who take pleasure in filling out a questionnaire multiple times with extreme answers.

c. The sample is a volunteer sample rather than a random sample.

d. It's impossible to learn useful results about a population from a sample of only 400 people.

4.102 Multiple choice: Sexual harassment In 1995 in the United Kingdom, the Equality Code used by the legal profession added a section to make members more aware of sexual harassment. It states that "research for the Bar found that over 40 percent of female junior tenants said they had encountered sexual harassment during their time at the Bar." This was based on a study conducted at the University of Sheffield that sent a questionnaire to 334 junior tenants at the Bar, of whom 159 responded. Of the 159, 67 were female. Of those females, 3 said they had experienced sexual harassment as a major problem, and 24 had experienced it as a slight problem.

a. The quoted statement might be misleading because the nonresponse was large.

b. No one was forced to respond, so everyone had a chance to be in the sample, which implies it was a simple random sample.

c. This was an example of a completely randomized experiment, with whether a female junior tenant experienced sexual harassment as the response variable.

d. This was a retrospective case-control study, with those who received sexual harassment as the cases.

4.103 Multiple choice: Effect of response categories A study (N. Schwarz et al., *Public Opinion Quarterly*, vol. 49, 1985, p. 388) asked German adults how many hours a day they spend watching TV on a typical day. When the possible responses were the six categories (up to $\frac{1}{2}$ hour, $\frac{1}{2}$ to 1 hour, 1 to $1\frac{1}{2}$ hours,..., more than $2\frac{1}{2}$ hours), 16% of respondents said they watched more than $2\frac{1}{2}$ hours per day. When the six categories were (up to $2\frac{1}{2}$ hours, $2\frac{1}{2}$ to 3 hours,..., more than 4 hours), 38% said they watched more than $2\frac{1}{2}$ hours per day.

a. The samples could not have been random, or this would not have happened.

b. This shows the importance of question design, especially when people may be uncertain what the answer to the question really is.

c. This study was an experiment, not an observational study.

4.104 ◆◆ **Systematic sampling** A researcher wants to select 1% of the 10,000 subjects from the sampling frame. She selects subjects by picking one of the first 100 on the list at random, skipping 100 names to get the next subject, skipping another 100 names to get the next subject, and so on. This is called a **systematic random sample**.

a. With simple random sampling, (i) every subject is equally likely to be chosen, and (ii) every possible sample of size n is equally likely. Indicate which, if any, of (i) and (ii) are true for systematic random samples. Explain.

b. An assembly-line process in a manufacturing company is checked by using systematic random sampling to inspect 2% of the items. Explain how this sampling process would be implemented.

4.105 ◆◆ TECH **Complex multistage GSS sample** Go to the website for the GSS, on *Documentation* and then click *Sampling Design and Weighting*. There you will see described the complex multistage design of the GSS. Explain how the GSS uses (a) clustering, (b) stratification, and (c) simple random sampling.

4.106 ◆◆ **Mean family size** You'd like to estimate the mean size of families in your community. Explain why you'll tend to get a smaller sample mean if you sample n families than if you sample n individuals (asking them to report their family size). (*Hint*: When you sample individuals, explain why you are more likely to sample a large family than a small family. To think of this, it may help to consider the case $n = 1$ with a population of two families, one with 10 people and one with only 2 people.)

4.107 ◆◆ **Capture–recapture** Biologists and naturalists often use sampling to estimate sizes of populations, such as deer or fish, for which a census is impossible. Capture–recapture is one method for doing this. A biologist wants to count the deer population in a certain region. She captures 50 deer, tags each, and then releases them. Several weeks later, she captures 125 deer and finds that 12 of them were tagged. Let N = population size, M = size of first sample, n = size of second sample, R = number tagged in second sample. The table shows how results can be summarized.

		In First Sample?		
		Yes (tagged)	**No (not tagged)**	**Total**
In Second Sample?	**Yes**	R		n
	No			
	Total	M		N

a. Identify the values of M, n, and R for the biologist's experiment.

b. One way to estimate N lets the sample proportion of tagged deer equal the population proportion of tagged deer. Explain why this means that

$$\frac{R}{n} = \frac{M}{N}$$

and, hence, that the estimated population size is $N = (M \times n)/R$

c. Estimate the number of deer in the deer population using the numbers given.

d. The U.S. Bureau of the Census uses capture–recapture to make adjustments to the census by estimating the undercount. The capture phase is the census itself (persons are "tagged" by having returned their census form and being recorded as counted), and the recapture phase (the second sample) is the postenumerative survey (PES) conducted after the census. Label the table in terms of the census application.

Student Activities

4.108 Munchie capture–recapture Your class can use the capture–recapture method described in the previous exercise to estimate the number of goldfish in a bag of Cheddar Goldfish. Pour the Cheddar Goldfish into a paper bag, which represents the pond. Sample 10 of them. For this initial sample, use Pretzel Goldfish to replace them, to represent the tagged fish. Then select a second sample and derive an estimate for N, the number of Cheddar Goldfish in the original bag. See how close your estimate comes to the actual number of fish in the bag. (Your teacher will count the population of Cheddar Goldfish in the bag before beginning the sampling.) If the estimate is not close, what could be responsible, and what would this reflect as difficulties in a real-life application such as sampling a wildlife population?

4.109 Activity: Sampling the states This activity illustrates how sampling bias can result when you use a nonrandom sample, even if you attempt to make it representative: You are in a geography class, discussing center and variability for several characteristics of the states in the contiguous United States. A particular value of center is the mean area of the states. A map and a list of the states with their areas (in square miles) are shown in the figure and table that follow. Area for a state includes dry land and permanent inland water surface.

TECH

Although we could use these data to calculate the actual mean area, let's explore *how well sampling performs in estimating the mean area* by sampling five states and finding the sample mean.

a. The most convenient sampling design is to use our eyes to pick five states from the map that we think have areas representative of all the states. Do this, picking five states that you believe have areas representative of the actual mean area of the states. Compute their sample mean area.

b. Collect the sample means for all class members. Construct a dot plot of these means. Describe the distribution of sample means. Note the shape, center, and variability of the distribution.

c. Another possible sampling design is simple random sampling. Randomly select five states (using an app or computer program) and compute the sample mean area.

d. Collect the sample means from part c of all class members. Construct a dot plot of the sample means using the same horizontal scale as in part b. Describe this distribution of sample means. Note the shape, center, and variability of the distribution.

e. The true mean total land area for the 48 states can be calculated from the accompanying table by dividing the total at the bottom of the table by 48. Which sampling method, using your eyes or using random selection, tended to be better at estimating the true population mean? Which method seems to be less biased? Explain.

f. Write a short summary comparing the two distributions of sample means.

Map of the continental United States.

Areas of the 48 States in the Continental U.S.

State	Area (square miles)
Alabama	52,419
Arizona	113,998
Arkansas	53,179
California	163,696
Colorado	104,094
Connecticut	5,543
Delaware	2,489
Florida	65,755
Georgia	59,425
Idaho	83,570
Illinois	57,914
Indiana	36,418
Iowa	56,272
Kansas	82,277
Kentucky	40,409
Louisiana	51,840
Maine	35,385
Maryland	12,407
Massachusetts	10,555
Michigan	96,716
Minnesota	86,939
Mississippi	48,430
Missouri	69,704
Montana	147,042
Nebraska	77,354
Nevada	110,561
New Hampshire	9,350
New Jersey	8,721
New Mexico	121,589
New York	54,556
North Carolina	53,819
North Dakota	70,700
Ohio	44,825
Oklahoma	69,898
Oregon	98,381
Pennsylvania	46,055
Rhode Island	1,545
South Carolina	32,020
South Dakota	77,116
Tennessee	42,143
Texas	268,581
Utah	84,899
Vermont	9,614
Virginia	42,774
Washington	71,300
West Virginia	24,230
Wisconsin	65,498
Wyoming	97,814
U.S. TOTAL	**3,119,819**

BIBLIOGRAPHY

Burrill, G., C. Franklin, L. Godbold, and L. Young (2003). *Navigating through Data Analysis in Grades 9–12*, NCTM

Crossen, C. (1994). *Tainted Truth: The Manipulation of Fact in America*. New York: Simon & Schuster.

Dweck, C. (2006). *Mindset: The New Psychology of Success*. New York: Random House Publishing Group.

Hepworth, S. J., et al. (2006). "Mobile phone use and risk of glioma in adults: case control study." *BMJ* 332: 883–887

Leake, J. (2001) "Scientists Link Eye Cancer to Mobile Phones," *The London Times*, Jan. 14. www.emf-health.com/reports-eyecancer.htm.

Stang, A., et al. (2001). "The possible role of radio frequency radiation in the development of uveal melanoma." *Epidemiology* 12(1): 7–12.

Volkow, N. (2011). "Effects of Cell Phone Radiofrequency Signal Exposure on Brain Flucose Metabolism." *JAMA* 305(8): 808–813.

PART

2

Probability, Probability Distributions, and Sampling Distributions

CHAPTER

5

With the concept of probability, we can quantify uncertainty and randomness that we experience in our daily lives. In this chapter we will define what we mean by probability and show how we can compute probabilities by following certain rules. Understanding probability and uncertainty is also necessary for understanding the inferential procedures (based on data) that we will discuss in later chapters.

Probability in Our Daily Lives

Example 1

Failing a Test for Illegal Drug Use

Picture the Scenario

Many employers require potential employees to take a diagnostic test for illegal drug use. Such tests are also used to detect drugs used by athletes. For example, at the 2008 Summer Olympic Games in Beijing, 6 out of 4500 sampled specimens tested positive for a banned substance.

But diagnostic tests have a broader use. They can be used to detect certain medical conditions. For example, one test for detecting HIV is the ELISA screening test.

Questions to Explore

- Given that a person recently used drugs, how can we estimate the likelihood that a diagnostic test will correctly predict drug use?
- Suppose a diagnostic test says that a person has recently used drugs. How likely is it that the person truly did use drugs?

Thinking Ahead

We'll learn how to answer the preceding questions by using probability methods. The answers might be quite different from what you might expect. In Example 8, we'll look at data on the performance of a diagnostic test for detecting Down syndrome in pregnant women. In Example 15, we'll analyze results of random drug tests for air traffic controllers.

Learning how to find probabilities and how to interpret them will help you, as a consumer of information, understand how to assess probabilities in many uncertain aspects of your life.

In everyday life, often you must make decisions when you are uncertain about the outcome. Should you invest money in the stock market? Should you get extra collision insurance on your car? Should you start a new business, such as opening a pizza place across from campus? Daily, you face even mundane decisions, such as whether to carry an umbrella with you in case it rains.

This chapter introduces **probability**—the way we quantify uncertainty. You'll learn how to measure the chances of the possible outcomes for **random phenomena**—everyday situations for which the outcome is uncertain. Using probability, for instance, you can find the chance of winning the lottery. You can find the likelihood that an employer's drug test correctly detects whether you've used drugs. You can measure the uncertainty that comes with randomized experiments and with random sampling in surveys. The ideas in this chapter set the foundation for how we'll use probability in the rest of the book to make inferences based on data.

5.1 How Probability Quantifies Randomness

As we discovered in Chapter 4, statisticians rely on an essential component to avoid bias in gathering data. This is **randomness**—randomly assigning subjects to treatments or randomly selecting people for a sample. Randomness also applies to the outcomes of a response variable. The possible outcomes are known, but it's uncertain which outcome will occur for any given observation.

We've all employed randomization in games. Some popular randomizers are rolling dice, spinning a wheel, and flipping a coin. Randomization helps to make a game fair, each player having the same chances for the possible outcomes. Rolls of dice and flips of coins are simple ways to represent the randomness of randomized experiments and sample surveys. For instance, the head and tail outcomes of a coin flip can represent drug and placebo when a medical study randomly assigns a subject to receive one of two treatments.

With a *small* number of observations, outcomes of *random phenomena* may look quite different from what you expect. For instance, you may expect to see a random pattern with different outcomes; instead, exactly the same outcome may happen a few times in a row. That's not necessarily a surprise; unpredictability for any given observation is the essence of randomness. We'll discover, however, that with a *large* number of observations, summary statistics settle down and get increasingly closer to particular numbers. For example, with 4 tosses of a coin, we wouldn't be surprised to find all 4 tosses resulting in heads. However, with 100 tosses, we would be surprised to see all 100 tosses resulting in heads. As we make more observations, the proportion of times that a particular outcome occurs gets closer and closer to a certain number we would expect. This long-run proportion provides the basis for the definition of *probability*.

In Words

Phenomena are any observable occurrences.

Example 2

Randomness

The Fairness of Rolling Dice

Picture the Scenario

The board game you've been playing has a die that determines the number of spaces moved on the board. After you've rolled the die 100 times, the number 6 has appeared 23 times, more frequently than each of the other 5 numbers, 1 through 5. At one point, it turns up three times in a row, resulting in you winning a game. Your opponent then complains that the die favors the number 6 and is not a fair die.

Did You Know?

The singular of *dice* is *die*. For a proper die, numbers on opposite sides add to 7, and when 4 faces up, the die can be turned so that 2 faces the player, 1 is at the player's right, and 6 is at the player's left. (*Ainslie's Complete Hoyle,* New York: Simon & Schuster, 2003) ◀

Questions to Explore

a. If a fair die is rolled 100 times, how many 6s do you expect?

b. Would it be unusual for a 6 to be rolled 23 times in 100 rolls? Would it be surprising to roll three 6s in a row at some point?

Think It Through

a. With many rolls of a fair die, each of the six numbers would appear about equally often. A 6 should occur about one sixth of the time. In 100 rolls, we expect a 6 to come up about $(1/6)100 = 16.7 \approx 17$ times.

b. How can we determine whether it is unusual for 6 to come up 23 times out of 100 rolls or three times in a row at some point? One way uses simulation. We could roll the die 100 times and see what happens, roll it another 100 times and see what happens that time, and so on. Does a 6 appear 23 (or more) times in many of the simulations? Does a 6 occur three times in a row in many simulations?

This simulation using a die would be tedious. Fortunately, we can use an app or other software to simulate rolling a fair die. Each simulated roll of a die is called a **trial**. After each trial, we record whether a 6 occurred. We will keep a running record of the proportion of times that a 6 has occurred. At each value for the number of trials, this is called a **cumulative proportion**. Table 5.1 shows partial results of one simulation

Table 5.1 Simulation Results of Rolling a Fair Die 100 Times

Each trial is a simulated roll of the die, with chance 1/6 of a 6. At each trial, we record whether a 6 occurred as well as the cumulative proportion of 6s by that trial.

Trial	Die Result	6 Occurs?	Cumulative Proportion of 6s	
1	6	yes	1/1	= 1.0
2	2	no	1/2	= 0.500
3	6	yes	2/3	= 0.667
4	5	no	2/4	= 0.500
5	6	yes	3/5	= 0.600
6	2	no	3/6	= 0.500
7	2	no	3/7	= 0.429
8	3	no	3/8	= 0.375
⋮	⋮	⋮	⋮	⋮
30	1	no	9/30	= 0.300
31	1	no	9/31	= 0.290
32	6	yes	10/32	= 0.313
33	6	yes	11/33	= 0.333
34	6	yes	12/34	= 0.353
35	2	no	12/35	= 0.343
⋮	⋮	⋮	⋮	⋮
99	5	no	22/99	= 0.220
100	6	yes	23/100	= 0.230

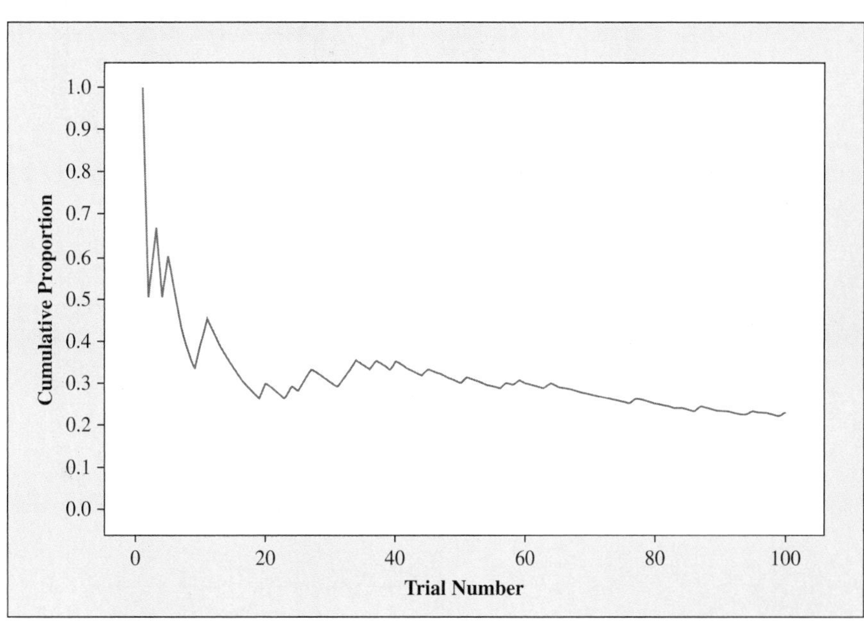

▲ **Figure 5.1 The Cumulative Proportion of Times a 6 Occurs, for a Simulation of 100 Rolls of a Fair Die.** The horizontal axis of this figure reports the number of the trial, and the vertical axis reports the cumulative proportion of 6s observed by then. **Question** The first four rolls of the die were 6, 2, 6, and 5. How can you find the cumulative proportion of 6s after each of the first four trials?

of 100 rolls. To find the cumulative proportion after a certain number of trials, divide the number of 6s at that stage by the number of trials. For example, by the eighth roll (trial), there had been three 6s in eight trials, so the cumulative proportion is $3/8 = 0.375$. Figure 5.1 plots the cumulative proportions against the trial number.

In this simulation of 100 rolls of a die, a 6 occurred 23 times, different from the expected value of about 17. From Table 5.1, a 6 appeared three times in a row for trials 32 through 34.

Insight

One simulation does not prove anything. It suggests, however, that rolling three 6s in a row out of 100 rolls may not be highly unusual. It also shows that 23 rolls with a 6 out of 100 trials can occur. To find out whether 23 rolls with a 6 is unusual, we need to repeat this simulation many times. In Chapter 6, we will learn about the binomial distribution, which allows us to compute the likelihood for observing 23 (or more) 6s out of 100 trials.

▶ ***Try Exercise 5.10***

▶ Activity

You can try this yourself using the website random.org and selecting the Dice Roller under Games (or see Activity 1).

Long-Run Behavior of Random Outcomes

The number of 6s in 100 rolls of a die can vary. One time we might get 19 rolls with 6s, another time we might get 22, another time 13, and so on. So what do we mean when we say that there's a one-in-six chance of a 6 on any given roll?

Let's continue the simulation from Example 2 and Table 5.1. In that example we stopped after only 100 rolls, but now let's continue simulating for a very large number of rolls. Figure 5.2 shows the cumulative proportion of 6s plotted against the trial number for a total of 10,000 rolls, beginning where we left off with the 100th trial. As the simulation progresses, with the trial number

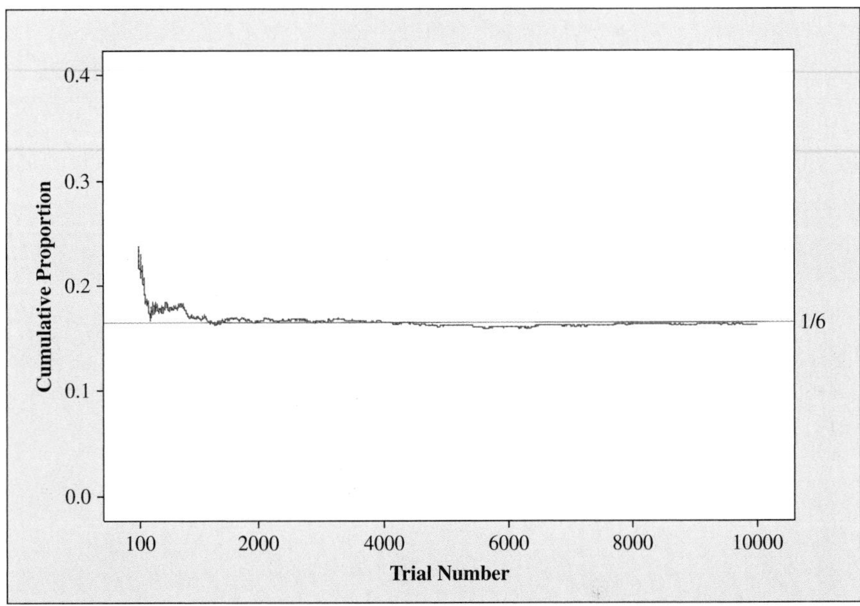

▲ **Figure 5.2 The Cumulative Proportion of Times That a 6 Occurs for a Simulation of 10,000 Rolls of a Fair Die.** Figure 5.1 showed the first 100 trials, and this figure shows results of trials 100 through 10,000. As the trial number gets larger, the cumulative proportion gets closer to 1/6. The probability of a 6 on any single roll is defined to be this *long-run* value. **Question** What would you expect for the cumulative proportion of heads after you flipped a balanced coin 10,000 times?

increasing, the cumulative proportion of 6s gradually settles down. After 10,000 simulated rolls, Figure 5.2 shows that the cumulative proportion is *very* close to the value of 1/6.

With a relatively short run, such as 10 rolls of a die, the cumulative proportion of 6s can fluctuate a lot. It need not be close to 1/6 after the final trial. However, as the number of trials keeps increasing, the proportion of times the number 6 occurs becomes more predictable and less random: It gets closer and closer to 1/6. *With random phenomena, the proportion of times that something happens is highly random and variable in the short run but very predictable in the long run.*

▶ Activity 1

Simulate Many Rolls of a Die

Since one simulation is insufficient to tell us what is typical, go to the Random Numbers web app at the book's website. Set the minimum to be 1, maximum to be 6, and the numbers to generate to be 100, then click on Generate. How many 6s did you observe out of the 100 simulated rolls? It may help to click on the "Show Frequency Table" if you want to see the exact number of each. After simulating 100 rolls, how close was the cumulative proportion of 6s to the expected value of 1/6?

Do the same simulation 25 times (hit the Reset button after each simulation) to get a feeling for how the sample cumulative proportion at 100 simulated rolls compares to the expected value of 1/6 (that is, 16.7%). You've probably seen that it's possible for 23 or more of the 100 rolls (that is, at least 23%) to result in 6s. If you keep doing this simulation over and over again, about 6.3% of the time you will get 23 or more 6s out of the 100 rolls. Also, about 30% of the time, you will see at least three 6s in a row somewhere out of the 100 rolls.

Now, click the Reset button but then click on the Generate button 10 times, without hitting Reset in between. This will generate a total of $10 \times 100 = 1000$ rolls. Here's a prediction: After each click, the cumulative proportion of 6s will tend to fall *closer and closer* to it's expected value of 1/6. At the end, we would be very surprised if at least 23% of the 1000 rolls resulted in 6s. This proportion should be close to 1/6 (or 16.7%).

Probability Quantifies Long-Run Randomness

Did You Know?

The **law of large numbers** is what helps keep casinos in business. For a short time, a gambler may be lucky and make money, but the casino knows that, in the long run, it's going to come out ahead. ◀

In 1689, the Swiss mathematician Jacob Bernoulli proved that as the number of trials increases, the proportion of occurrences of any given outcome approaches a particular number (such as 1/6) in the long run. To show this, he assumed that the outcome of any one trial does not depend on the outcome of any other trial. Bernoulli's result is known as the **law of large numbers**.

We will interpret the **probability** of an outcome to represent long-run results. Imagine a randomized experiment or a random sampling of subjects that provides a very long sequence of observations. Each observation does or does not have that outcome. The probability of the outcome is the proportion of times that it occurs in the long run.

> **Probability**
>
> With any random phenomenon, the **probability** of a particular outcome is the proportion of times that the outcome would occur in a long run of observations.

When we say that a roll of a fair die has outcome 6 with probability 1/6, this means that the proportion of times that a 6 would occur in a long run of observations is 1/6. The probability would also be 1/6 for each of the other possible outcomes: 1, 2, 3, 4, or 5.

A weather forecaster might say that the probability of rain today is 0.70. This means that in a large number of days with atmospheric conditions like those today, the proportion of days in which rain occurs is 0.70. Since a probability is a *proportion*, it takes a value between 0 and 1. Sometimes probabilities are expressed as percentages, such as when the weather forecaster reports the probability of rain as 70%. Probabilities then fall between 0 and 100, but we'll mainly use the proportion scale.

Why does probability refer to the *long run*? Because we can't accurately assess a probability with a small number of trials. If you sample 10 people and they are all right-handed, you can't conclude that the probability of being right-handed equals 1.0. As we've seen, there can be a lot of variability in the cumulative proportion for small samples. It takes a much larger sample of people to predict accurately the proportion of people in the population who are right-handed.

Independent Trials

With random phenomena, many believe that when some outcome has not happened in a while, it is *due* to happen: Its probability goes up until it happens. In many rolls of a fair die, if a particular value (say, 5) has not occurred in a long time, some think it's due and that the chance of a 5 on the next roll is greater than 1/6. If a family has four girls in a row and is expecting another child, are they due to get a boy? Does the next child have a different probability of being a boy than each of the first four children did?

Example 2 showed that over a short run, observations may deviate from what is expected. (Remember three 6s in a row?) But with many random phenomena, such as outcomes of rolling a die or having children, what happens on previous trials does not affect the trial that's about to occur. The trials are **independent** of each other.

> **Independent Trials**
>
> Different trials of a random phenomenon are **independent** if the outcome of any one trial is not affected by the outcome of any other trial.

With independent trials, whether you get a 5 on one roll of a fair die does not affect whether you get a 5 on the following roll. It doesn't matter if you had 20 rolls in a row that are not 5s, the next roll still has probability 1/6 of being a 5. The die has no memory. If you have lost many bets in a row, don't assume that you are due to win if you continue to gamble. The *law of large numbers*, which gamblers invoke as the *law of averages*, only guarantees *long-run* performance. In the short run, the variability may well exceed what you expect, which is why some people win at the casino and some people lose. However, the house (casino) can rely on the law of large numbers to win in the long run.

Finding Probabilities

In practice, we sometimes can find probabilities by making assumptions about the nature of the random phenomenon. For instance, by symmetry, it may be reasonable to assume that the possible outcomes of that phenomenon are *equally likely*. In rolling a die, we might assume that based on the physical makeup of the die, each of the six sides has an equal chance. Then the probability of rolling any particular number equals 1/6. If we flip a coin and assume that the coin is balanced, then the probability of flipping a tail (or a head) equals 1/2. Notice that, like proportions, *the total of the probabilities for all the possible outcomes equals 1.*

In Practice The Sample Proportion Estimates the Actual Probability

In theory, we could observe several trials of a random phenomenon and use the proportion of times an outcome occurs as its probability. In practice, this is imperfect. The sample proportion merely *estimates* the actual probability, and only for a *very large* number of trials is it necessarily close. In Chapters 7 and 8, we'll see how the sample size determines just how accurate that estimate is.

Types of Probability: Relative Frequency and Subjective Probability

We've defined the probability of an outcome as a long-run proportion (relative frequency) of times that the outcome occurs in a very large number of trials. However, this definition is not always helpful. Before the launch of the first space shuttle, how could NASA scientists assess the probability of success? No data were available about long-run observations of past flights. If you decide to start a new type of business when you graduate, you won't have a long run of trials with which to estimate the probability that the business is successful.

In such situations, you must rely on **subjective** information rather than solely on **objective** information such as data. You assess the probability of an outcome by taking into account all the information you have. Such probabilities are not based on a long run of trials. In this **subjective definition of probability**, the probability of an outcome is defined to be a *personal probability*—your degree of belief that the outcome will occur, based on the available information. A branch of statistics uses subjective probability as its foundation. It is called **Bayesian statistics**, in honor of Thomas Bayes, a British clergyman who discovered a probability rule on which it is based. The subjective approach is less common than the approach we discuss in this text. We'll merely warn you to be wary of anyone who gives a subjective probability of 1 (certain occurrence) or of 0 (certain nonoccurrence) for some outcome. As Benjamin Franklin said, nothing in life is certain but death and taxes!

5.1 Practicing the Basics

5.1 **Probability** Explain what is meant by the long-run relative frequency definition of probability.

5.2 **Testing a coin** Your friend decides to flip a coin repeatedly to analyze whether the probability of a head on each flip is 1/2. He flips the coin 10 times and observes a head 7 times. He concludes that the probability of a head for this coin is $7/10 = 0.70$.

a. Your friend claims that the coin is not balanced, since the probability is not 0.50. What's wrong with your friend's claim?

b. If the probability of flipping a head is actually 1/2, what would you have to do to ensure that the cumulative proportion of heads falls very close to 1/2?

5.3 **Vegetarianism** You randomly sample 10 people in your school, and none of them is a vegetarian. Does this mean that the probability of being a vegetarian for students at your school equals 0? Explain.

5.4 **Airline accident deaths** Airplane safety has been improving over the years. From 2000 to 2010, the average number of global airline deaths per year was over 1000, even when excluding the nearly 3000 deaths in the United States on September 11, 2001. The number of global airline deaths declined in 2011, again in 2012, and then hit a low of only 265 in 2013. In 2013, there were a total of 825 million passengers globally. *Sources:* en.wikipedia.org and www.transtats.bts.gov1.

a. Can you consider the 2013 data as a long run or short run of trials? Explain.

b. Estimate the probability of dying on a flight in 2013. (Note, the probability of dying from a 1000-mile automobile trip is about 1 in 42,000 by contrast.)

c. Raul is considering flying on an airplane. He noticed that over the past two months, there have been no fatal airplane crashes around the world. This raises his concern about flying because the airlines are "due for an accident." Comment on his reasoning.

5.5 **World Cup 2014** The powerrank.com website (http://thepowerrank.com/2014/06/06/world-cup-2014-win-probabilities-from-the-power-rank/) listed the probability of each team to win the 2014 World Cup in soccer as follows:

1. Brazil, 35.9%.
2. Argentina, 10.0%.
3. Spain, 8.9%.
4. Germany, 7.4%.
5. Netherlands, 5.7%.
6. Portugal, 3.9%.
7. France, 3.4%.
8. England, 2.8%.
9. Uruguay, 2.5%.
10. Mexico, 2.5%.
11. Italy, 2.3%.
12. Ivory Coast, 2.0%.
13. Colombia, 1.5%.
14. Russia, 1.5%.
15. United States, 1.1%.
16. Chile, 1.0%.
17. Croatia, 0.9%.
18. Ecuador, 0.8%.
19. Nigeria, 0.8%.
20. Switzerland, 0.7%.
21. Greece, 0.6%.
22. Iran, 0.6%.
23. Japan, 0.6%.
24. Ghana, 0.6%.
25. Belgium, 0.4%.
26. Honduras, 0.3%.
27. South Korea, 0.3%.
28. Bosnia-Herzegovina, 0.3%.
29. Costa Rica, 0.3%.
30. Cameroon, 0.2%.
31. Australia, 0.2%.
32. Algeria, 0.1%.

a. Interpret Brazil's probability of 35.9%, which was based on computer simulations of the tournament. Is it a relative frequency or a subjective interpretation of probability?

b. Germany would emerge as the actual winner of the 2014 World Cup. Does this indicate that the 7.4% chance of Germany winning, which was calculated before the tournament, should have been 100% instead?

5.6 **Random digits** Consider a random number generator designed for equally likely outcomes. Which of the following is *not* correct, and why?

a. For each random digit generated, each integer between 0 and 9 has probability 0.10 of being selected.

b. If you generate 10 random digits, each integer between 0 and 9 must occur exactly once.

c. If you generated a very large number of random digits, then each integer between 0 and 9 would occur close to 10% of the time.

d. The cumulative proportion of times that a 0 is generated tends to get closer to 0.10 as the number of random digits generated gets larger and larger.

5.7 **Polls and sample size** A pollster agency wants to estimate the proportion of citizens of the European Union who support same-sex unions. She claims that if the sample size is large enough, she does not need to worry about the method of selecting the sample. Do you agree with the pollster's comments? Explain.

5.8 **Heart transplant** Before the first human heart transplant, Dr. Christiaan Barnard of South Africa was asked to assess the probability that the operation would be successful. Did he need to rely on the relative frequency definition or the subjective definition of probability? Explain.

5.9 **Nuclear war** You are asked to use your best judgment to estimate the probability that there will be a nuclear war within the next 10 years. Is this an example of relative frequency or subjective definition of probability? Explain.

5.10 **Simulate coin flips** Use the web app Random Numbers (go to the tab that says Coin Flips) on the book's website or other software (such as random.org/coin) to illustrate the long-run definition of probability by simulating short-term and long-term results of flipping a balanced coin.

TRY TECH

a. Keep the probability of a head at the default value of 50% and set the number of flips to generate in a simulation to 10. Click on Simulate and record the proportion of heads for this simulation. Do this a total of 10 times by repeatedly clicking Simulate.

b. Now set the number of flips to 100. Click Simulate 10 times, and record the 10 proportions of heads for each simulation. Do they vary much?

c. Now set the number of flips to 1000. Click Simulate 10 times, and record the 10 proportions of heads for each simulation. Do they vary more, or less, than the proportions in part b based on 100 flips?

d. Summarize the effect of the number of flips on the variability of the proportion. How does this reflect what's implied by the law of large numbers?

5.11 Unannounced pop quiz A teacher announces a pop quiz for which the student is completely unprepared. The quiz consists of 100 true-false questions. The student has no choice but to guess the answer randomly for all 100 questions.

a. Simulate taking this quiz by random guessing. Number a sheet of paper 1 to 100 to represent the 100 questions. Write a T (true) or F (false) for each question, by predicting what you think would happen if you repeatedly flipped a coin and let a tail represent a T guess and a head represent an F guess. (Don't actually flip a coin; merely write down what you think a random series of guesses would look like.)

b. How many questions would you expect to answer correctly simply by guessing?

c. The table shows the 100 correct answers. The answers should be read across rows. How many questions did you answer correctly?

Pop Quiz Correct Answers																			
T	F	T	T	F	F	T	T	T	T	T	F	T	F	F	T	T	F	T	F
F	F	F	F	F	F	F	T	F	F	T	F	T	F	F	T	F	T	T	F
T	F	F	F	F	F	T	F	T	T	F	T	T	T	F	F	F	F	F	T
T	F	F	T	F	F	T	T	T	T	F	F	F	F	F	F	F	T	F	F
F	F	T	F	F	T	T	F	F	T	F	T	F	T	T	T	T	F	F	F

d. The preceding answers were actually randomly generated by an app. What percentage were true, and what percentage would you expect? Why are they not necessarily identical?

e. Are there groups of answers within the sequence of 100 answers that appear nonrandom? For instance, what is the longest run of Ts or Fs? By comparison, which is the longest run of Ts or Fs within your sequence of 100 answers? (There is a tendency in guessing what randomness looks like to identify too few long runs in which the same outcome occurs several times in a row.)

5.12 Stock market randomness An interview in an investment magazine (*In the Vanguard*, Autumn 2003) asked mathematician John Allen Paulos, "What common errors do investors make?" He answered, "People tend not to believe that markets move in random ways. Randomness is difficult to recognize. If you have people write down 100 Hs and Ts to simulate 100 flips of a coin, you will always be able to tell a sequence generated by a human from one generated by real coin flips. When humans make up the sequence, they don't put in enough consecutive Hs and Ts, and they don't make the lengths of those runs long enough or frequent enough. And that is one of the reasons people look at patterns in the stock market and ascribe significance to them." (© The Vanguard Group, Inc., used with permission.)

a. Suppose that on each of the next 100 business days the stock market has a 1/2 chance of going up and a 1/2 chance of going down, and its behavior one day is independent of its behavior on another day. Use software, such as the web app mentioned in exercise 5.10 or random.org/coin to simulate whether the market goes up or goes down for each of the next 100 days. What is the longest sequence of consecutive moves up or consecutive moves down that you observe?

b. Run the simulation nine more times, with 100 observations for each run, and each time record the longest sequence of consecutive moves up or consecutive moves down that you observe. For the 10 runs, summarize the proportion of times that the longest sequence was 1, 2, 3, 4, 5, 6, 7, 8, or more. (Your class may combine results to estimate this more precisely.)

c. Based on your findings, explain why if you are a serious investor you should not get too excited if sometime in the next few months you see the stock market go up for five days in a row or go down for five days in a row.

5.2 Finding Probabilities

We've learned that probability enables us to quantify uncertainty and randomness. Now, let's explore some basic rules that help us find probabilities.

Sample Spaces

The first step is to list all the possible outcomes. The set of possible outcomes for a random phenomenon is called the **sample space**.

Sample Space

For a random phenomenon, the **sample space** is the set of all possible outcomes.

For example, when you roll a die once, the sample space consists of the six possible outcomes, $\{1,2,3,4,5,6\}$. When you flip a coin twice, the sample space consists of the four possible outcomes, $\{HH, HT, TH, TT\}$, where, for instance, TH represents a tail on the first flip and a head on the second flip.

Example 3

Sample space ◀

Multiple-Choice Pop Quiz

Picture the Scenario

Your statistics instructor decides to give an unannounced pop quiz with three multiple-choice questions. Each question has five options, and the student's answer is either correct (C) or incorrect (I). If a student answered the first two questions correctly and the last question incorrectly, the student's outcome on the quiz can be symbolized by CCI.

Question to Explore

What is the sample space for the possible answers on this pop quiz?

Think It Through

One technique for listing the outcomes in a sample space is to draw a **tree diagram**, with branches showing what can happen on subsequent trials. For a student's performance on three questions, the tree has three sets of branches, as Figure 5.3 shows.

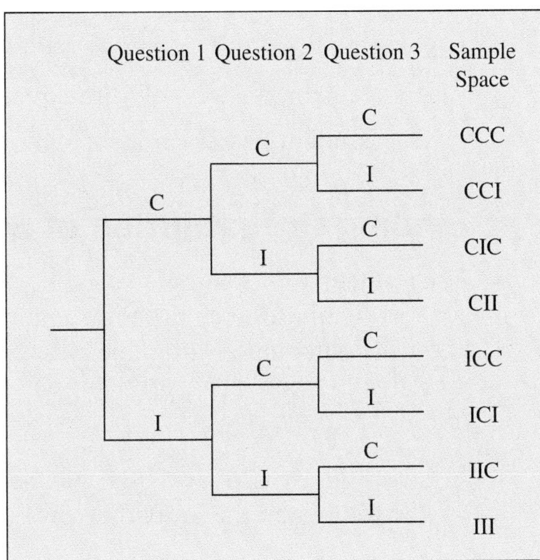

◀ **Figure 5.3** Tree Diagram for Student Performance on a Three-Question Pop Quiz. Each path from the first set of two branches to the third set of eight branches determines an outcome in the sample space. **Question** How many possible outcomes would there be if the quiz had four questions?

From the tree diagram, a student's performance has eight possible outcomes:

$$\{CCC, CCI, CIC, CII, ICC, ICI, IIC, III\}.$$

Insight

The number of branches doubles at each stage. There are 2 branches for question 1, $2 \times 2 = 4$ branches at question 2, and $2 \times 2 \times 2 = 8$ branches at question 3.

► ***Try Exercise 5.13***

How many possible outcomes are in a sample space when there are repeated trials? To determine this, multiply the number of possible outcomes for each trial. A pop quiz with three questions has $2 \times 2 \times 2 = 8$ possible outcomes when denoting each answer as correct or incorrect. With four questions, there are $2 \times 2 \times 2 \times 2 = 16$ possible outcomes.

What if we want to consider the actual responses made? With four multiple-choice questions and five possible responses on each, there are

$5 \times 5 \times 5 \times 5 = 625$ possible response sequences. The tree diagram is ideal for visualizing a small number of outcomes. As the number of trials or the number of possible outcomes on each trial increases, it becomes impractical to construct a tree diagram, so we'll also learn about methods for finding probabilities without having to list entire sample spaces.

Events

We'll sometimes need to specify a particular group of the outcomes in a sample space, that is, a *subset* of the outcomes. An example is the subset of outcomes for which a student passes the pop quiz by answering at least two of the three questions correctly. A subset of a sample space is called an **event**.

Event

An **event** is a subset of the sample space. An **event** corresponds to a particular outcome or a group of possible outcomes.

Events are usually denoted by letters from the beginning of the alphabet, such as A and B, or by a letter or string of letters that describes the event. For a student taking the three-question pop quiz, some possible events are

$$\text{A} = \text{student answers all three questions correctly} = \{\text{CCC}\}$$

$$\text{B} = \text{student passes (at least two correct)} = \{\text{CCI, CIC, ICC, CCC}\}.$$

Finding Probabilities of Events

Each outcome in a sample space has a probability. So does each event. To find such probabilities, we list the sample space and specify plausible assumptions about its outcomes. Sometimes, for instance, we can assume that the outcomes are equally likely. The probabilities for the outcomes in a sample space must follow two basic rules:

- The probability of each individual outcome is between 0 and 1.
- The total of all the individual probabilities equals 1.

Example 4

Probability for a sample space with equally likely outcomes ◄

Treating Colds

Picture the Scenario

The University of Wisconsin is conducting a randomized experiment[1] to compare an herbal remedy (echinacea) to a placebo for treating the common cold. The response variables are the cold's severity and its duration. Suppose a particular clinic in Madison, Wisconsin, has four volunteers, of whom two are men (Jamal and Ken) and two are women (Linda and Mei). Two of these volunteers will be randomly chosen to receive the herbal remedy, and the other two will receive the placebo.

Questions to Explore

a. Identify the possible samples to receive the herbal remedy. For each possible sample, what is the probability that it is the one chosen?

[1]See www.fammed.wisc.edu/research/news0503d.html.

b. What's the probability of the event that the sample chosen to receive the herbal remedy consists of one man and one woman?

Think It Through

a. The six possible samples to assign to the herbal remedy are {(Jamal, Ken), (Jamal, Linda), (Jamal, Mei), (Ken, Linda), (Ken, Mei), (Linda, Mei)}. This is the sample space for randomly choosing two of the four people. For a simple random sample, every sample is equally likely. Since there are six possible samples, each one has probability 1/6. These probabilities fall between 0 and 1, and their total equals 1, as is necessary for probabilities for a sample space.

b. The event in which the sample chosen has one man and one woman consists of the outcomes {(Jamal, Linda), (Jamal, Mei), (Ken, Linda), (Ken, Mei)}. These are the possible pairings of one man with one woman. Each outcome has probability 1/6, so the probability of this event is $4(1/6) = 4/6 = 2/3$.

Insight

When each outcome is equally likely, the probability of a single outcome is simply 1/(number of possible outcomes), such as 1/6 in part a of Think It Through. The probability of an event is then (number of outcomes in the event)/(number of possible outcomes), such as 4/6 in part b of Think It Through.

▶ ***Try Exercise 5.19***

This example shows that to find the probability for an event, we can (1) find the probability for each outcome in the sample space and (2) add the probabilities of each outcome that the event contains.

SUMMARY: Probability of an Event

The probability of an event A, denoted by P(A), is obtained by adding the probabilities of the individual outcomes in the event.

- When all the possible outcomes are equally likely,

$$P(A) = \frac{\text{number of outcomes in event A}}{\text{number of outcomes in the sample space}}$$

In Example 4, to find the probability of choosing one man and one woman, we first determined the probability of each of the six possible outcomes. Because the probability is the same for each, 1/6, and because the event contains four of those outcomes, the probability is 1/6 added four times. The answer equals 4/6, the number of outcomes in the event divided by the number of outcomes in the sample space.

In Practice Equally Likely Outcomes Are Unusual

Except for simplistic situations such as random sampling or flipping balanced coins or rolling fair dice, different outcomes are not usually equally likely. Then, probabilities are often estimated, using sample proportions from simulations or from large samples of data.

Probabilities for a sample space with outcomes that are not equally likely ◀

Recall

Section 3.1 introduced **contingency tables** to summarize the relationship between two categorical variables. ◀

Did You Know?

Most people find it easier to interpret probabilities, especially very small ones, by using their reciprocal. Thus, "there is a one in 1.9 million chance of being struck by lightning in the United States" is more accessible to most people than "the probably is 0.00000053," which is 1/1,900,000. (*Source:* http://www.lightningsafety.noaa.gov/odds.htm) ◀

Example 5

Tax Audit

Picture the Scenario

April 15 is tax day in the United States—the deadline for filing federal income tax forms. The main factor in the amount of tax owed is a taxpayer's income level. Each year, the IRS audits a sample of tax forms to verify their accuracy. Table 5.2 is a contingency table that cross-tabulates the 145.8 million long-form federal returns received in 2013 by the taxpayer's income level and whether the tax form was audited.

Table 5.2 Contingency Table Cross-Tabulating Tax Forms by Income Level and Whether Audited

There were 145.8 million returns filed. The frequencies in the table are reported in thousands. For example, 1,233 represents approximately 1,233,000 tax forms that reported income under $200,000 and were audited.

	Audited		
Income Level	**Yes**	**No**	**Total**
Under $200,000	1,233	139,305	**140,538**
$200,000–$1,000,000	133	4,747	**4,880**
More than $1,000,000	39	324	**363**
Total	**1,405**	**144,376**	**145,781**

Source: http://www.irs.gov/uac/Newsroom/FY-2013-Enforcement-and-Service-Results

Questions to Explore

a. Consider, for each return, the income level and whether it was audited. If we draw a return at random, what are the possible outcomes that define the sample space?

b. What is the probability of each outcome?

c. For a randomly selected return in 2013, what is the probability of (i) an audit, (ii) the return showing an income of more than $1,000,000?

Think It Through

a. The sample space is the set of possible outcomes. These are the six possible combinations of income level and audit status, such as (Under $200,000, Yes), (Under $200,000, No), ($200,000–$1,000,000, Yes), and so forth.

b. The probability of each outcome is the number of returns that fall in the corresponding cell of Table 5.2, divided by the total number of returns. E.g., the probability of the outcome (Under $200,000, Yes) equals $1233/145781 = 0.008458$ and the probability of the outcome (Over $1,000,000, No) equals $324/145781 = 0.002222$.

c. **(i)** The event of being audited consists of the three outcomes (Under $200,000, Yes), ($200,000 − $1,000,000, Yes) and (Over $1,000,000, Yes), with estimated probabilities of $1233/145781$, $133/145781$ and $39/145781$, for a total of $(1233 + 133 + 39)/145781 = 1405/145781 = 0.0096$, or about a 1 in 100 chance.

(ii) The event of a return showing an income of more than $1,000,000 consists of the outcomes (Over $1,000,000, No) and (Over $1,000,000, Yes), with probability $(39 + 324)/145781 = 0.0025$, or about a 1 in 400 chance.

Insight

The event of a randomly selected return being audited consists of three of the possible six outcomes. If we wrongly assumed each of the six possible outcomes as equally likely, than the probability for this event would be calculated as 3/6 = 0.5, vastly different from 0.0096.

▶ ***Try Exercise 5.23, parts a and b***

Basic Rules for Finding Probabilities About a Pair of Events

Some events are expressed as the outcomes that (a) are *not* in some other event, or (b) are in one event *and* in another event, or (c) are in one event *or* in another event. We'll next learn how to calculate probabilities for these three cases.

The Complement of an Event For an event A, the rest of the sample space that is *not* in that event is called the **complement** of A.

In Words

A^c reads as "**A-complement**." The *c* in the superscript denotes the term complement. You can think of A^c as meaning "not A."

Complement of an Event

The **complement** of an event A consists of all outcomes in the sample space that are *not* in A. It is denoted by A^c. The probabilities of A and of A^c add to 1, so

$$P(A^c) = 1 - P(A).$$

In Example 5, for instance, the event of having an income *less than* \$200,000 is the complement of the event of having an income of \$200,000 or more. Because the probability that a randomly selected taxpayer had an income of under \$200,000 is $140538/145781 = 0.964$, the probability of income at least \$200,000 is $1 - 0.964 = 0.036$.

Figure 5.4 illustrates the complement of an event. The box represents the entire sample space. The event A is the oval in the box. The complement of A, which is shaded, is everything else in the box that is not in A. Together, A and A^c cover the sample space. Because an event and its complement contain all possible outcomes, their total probability is 1, and the probability of either one of them is 1 minus the probability of the other. A diagram like Figure 5.4 that uses areas inside a box to represent events is called a **Venn diagram**.

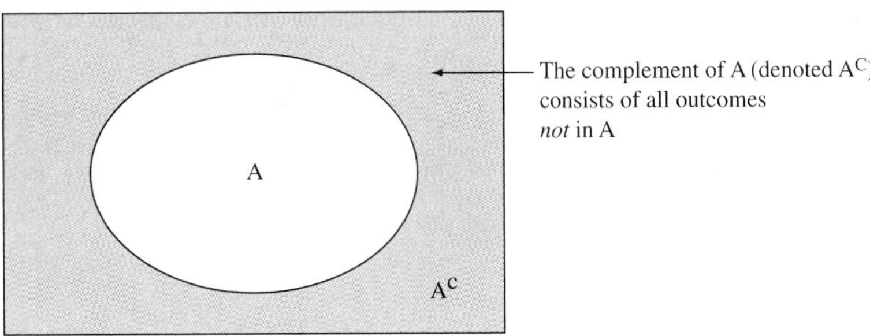

▲ **Figure 5.4** Venn Diagram Illustrating an Event A and Its Complement A^C. **Question** Can you sketch a Venn diagram of two events A and B such that they share some common outcomes, but some outcomes are only in A or only in B?

To find the probability of an event, it's sometimes easier to find the probability of its complement and then subtract that probability from 1. An example is when we need to find the probability that *at least one* of several events will occur. It's usually easier to find the probability of its complement, that *none* of these events will occur.

Complement of an event

Example 6

Women on a Jury

Picture the Scenario

A jury of 12 people is chosen for a trial. The defense attorney claims it must have been chosen in a biased manner because 50% of the city's adult residents are female, yet the jury contains no women.

Questions to Explore

If the jury were randomly chosen from the population, what is the probability that the jury would have (a) no females, (b) at least one female?

Think It Through

Let's use 12 letters, with F for female and M for male, to represent a possible jury selection. For instance, MFMMMMMMMMMM denotes the jury in which only the second person selected is female. The number of possible outcomes is $2 \times 2 \times 2 \times \ldots \times 2$, that is, 2 multiplied 12 times, which is $2^{12} = 4096$. This is a case in which listing the entire sample space is not practical. Since the population is 50% male and 50% female, these 4096 possible outcomes are equally likely.

a. Only 1 of the 4096 possible outcomes corresponds to a no-female jury, namely, MMMMMMMMMMMM. So the probability of this outcome is 1/4096, or 0.00024. This is extremely unlikely, if a jury is truly chosen by random sampling.

b. As noted previously, it would be tedious to list all possible outcomes in which at least one female is on the jury. But this is not necessary. The event that the jury contains *at least one* female is the complement of the event that it contains *no* females. Thus,

$$P(\text{at least one female}) = 1 - P(\text{no females}) = 1 - 0.00024 = 0.99976.$$

Insight

You might instead let the sample space be the possible values for the *number* of females on the jury, namely $0, 1, 2, \ldots 12$. But these outcomes are not equally likely. For instance, only one of the 4096 possible samples has 0 females, but 12 of them have 1 female: The female could be the first person chosen, or the second (as in MFMMMMMMMMMM), or the third, and so on. Chapter 6 will show a formula (binomial) that gives probabilities for this alternative sample space and will allow for cases when the outcomes are not equally likely.

▶ ***Try Exercise 5.16***

Disjoint Events Events that do not share any outcomes in common are said to be **disjoint**.

Disjoint Events

Two events, A and B, are **disjoint** if they do not have any common outcomes.

Example 3 discussed a pop quiz with three questions. The event that the student answers exactly one question correctly is {CII, ICI, IIC}. The event that the student answers exactly two questions correctly is {CCI, CIC, ICC}. These two events have no outcomes in common, so they are disjoint. In a Venn diagram, they have no overlap. (Figure 5.5). By contrast, neither is disjoint from the event that the student answers the first question correctly, which is {CCC, CCI, CIC, CII}, because this event has outcomes in common with each of the other two events.

Did You Know?

Disjoint events are also referred to as **mutually exclusive** events. We will use only the term "disjoint." ◀

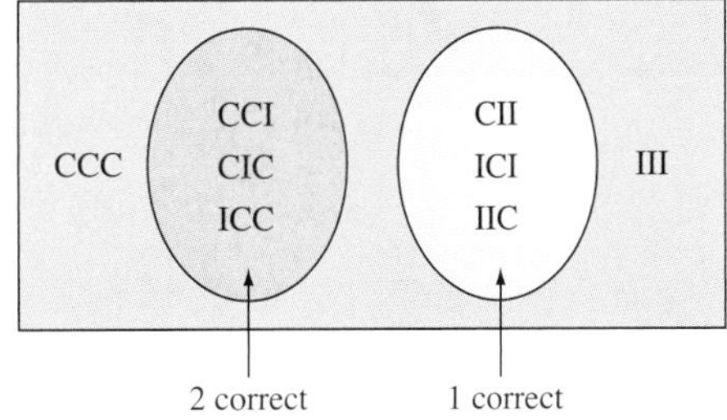

▲ **Figure 5.5 Venn Diagram Illustrating Disjoint Events.** The event of a student answering exactly one question correctly is disjoint from the event of answering exactly two questions correctly. **Question** Identify on this figure the event that the student answers the first question correctly. Is this event disjoint from either of the two events identified in the Venn diagram?

Consider an event A and its complement, A^c. They share no common outcomes, so they are disjoint events.

Intersection and Union of Events Some events are composed from other events. For instance, for two events A and B, the event that *both* occur is also an event. Called the **intersection** of A and B, it consists of the outcomes that are in both A and B. By contrast, the event that the outcome is in A *or* B or both is the **union** of A and B. It is a larger set, containing the intersection as well as outcomes that are in A but not in B and outcomes that are in B but not in A. Figure 5.6 shows Venn diagrams illustrating the intersection and union of two events.

In Words

Intersection means A *and* B (the "overlap" of the events). **Union** means A *or* B or both.

Intersection and Union of Two Events

The **intersection** of A and B consists of outcomes that are in both A *and* B.

The **union** of A and B consists of outcomes that are in A *or* B or both. In probability, "A *or* B" denotes that A occurs or B occurs or both occur.

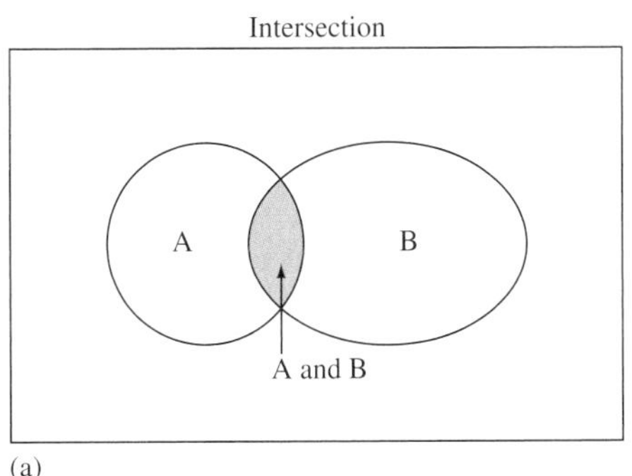

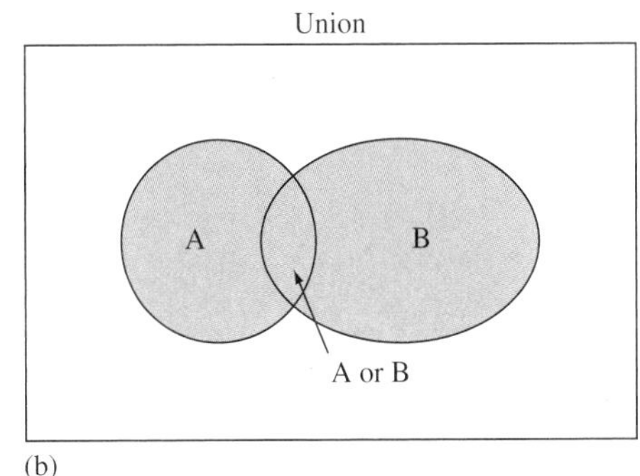

▲ **Figure 5.6 The Intersection and the Union of Two Events.** Intersection means A occurs *and* B occurs, denoted "A and B." The intersection consists of the shaded "overlap" part in Figure 5.6 (a). Union means A occurs *or* B occurs *or* both occur, denoted "A or B." It consists of all the shaded parts in Figure 5.6 (b). **Question** How could you find P(A or B) if you know P(A), P(B), and P(A and B)?

For instance, for the three-question pop quiz, consider the events:

A = student answers first question correctly = {CCC, CCI, CIC, CII}

B = student answers two questions correctly = {CCI, CIC, ICC}.

Then the intersection, A *and* B, is {CCI, CIC}, the two outcomes common to A and B. The union, A *or* B, is {CCC, CCI, CIC, CII, ICC}, the outcomes that are in A or in B or in both A and B.

Income	Audited: Yes	Audited: No
Under \$200,000	1,233	139,305
\$200,000–\$1,000,000	133	4,747
More than \$1,000,000	39	324

Counts refer to thousands of taxpayers

How do we find probabilities of intersections and unions of events? Once we identify the possible outcomes, we can use their probabilities. For instance, for Table 5.2 (shown in the margin) for 145.8 million tax forms, let

A denote {audited = yes}

B denote {income ≥ \$1,000,000}

The intersection A and B is the event that a taxpayer is audited *and* has income ≥ \$1,000,000. This probability is simply the proportion for the cell in which these two events occurred, namely P(A and B) = 39/145,781 = 0.00027. The union of A and B consists of all those who either were audited or had income greater than \$1,000,000 or both. From the table, these were (1,233 + 133 + 39 + 324) thousand people, so the probability is 1729/145781 = 0.012. We can formalize rules for finding the union and intersection of two events, as we'll see in the next two subsections.

Addition Rule: Finding the Probability That Event A or Event B Occurs

Since the union A or B contains outcomes from A and from B, we can add P(A) to P(B). However, this sum counts the outcomes that are in *both* A and B (their intersection) twice (Figure 5.7). We need to subtract the probability of the intersection from P(A) + P(B) so that it is only counted once. If there is no overlap, that is, if the events are disjoint, no outcomes are common to A and B. Then we can simply add the probabilities.

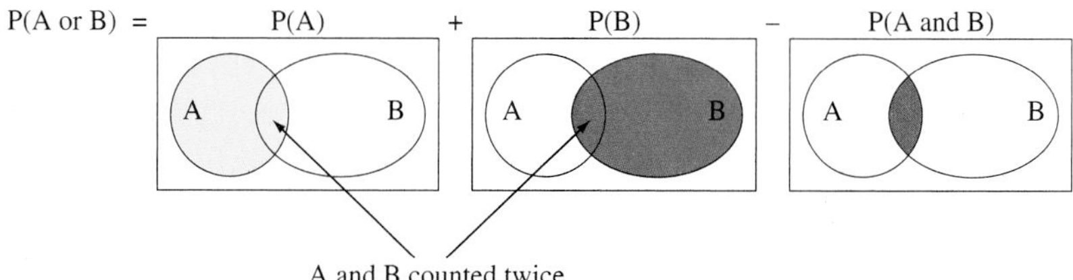

▲ **Figure 5.7 The Probability of the Union, Outcomes in A or B or Both.** Add P(A) to P(B) and subtract P(A and B) to adjust for outcomes counted twice. **Question** When does P(A or B) = P(A) + P(B)?

Addition Rule: Probability of the Union of Two Events

For the **union** of two events, P(A or B) = P(A) + P(B) − P(A and B).

If the events are **disjoint**, then P(A and B) = 0, so P(A or B) = P(A) + P(B).

For example, consider a family with two children. The sample space possibilities for the genders of the two children are {FF, FM, MF, MM}, where the first letter in a symbol is the first child's gender and the second letter is the second child's gender (F = female, M = male). Let A = {first child a girl} and B = {second child a girl}. Then, assuming the four possible outcomes in the sample space are equally likely, P(A) = P({FF, FM}) = 0.50, P(B) = P({FF, MF}) = 0.50, and P(A and B) = P({FF}) = 0.25. The event A or B is the event that the first child is a girl, or the second child is a girl, or both, that is, *at least* one child is a girl. Its probability is

P(A or B) = P(A) + P(B) − P(A and B) = 0.50 + 0.50 − 0.25 = 0.75.

Multiplication Rule: Finding the Probability That Events A and B Both Occur

The probability of the intersection of events A and B has a formula to be introduced in Section 5.3. In the special case discussed next, it equals P(A) × P(B).

Consider a basketball player who shoots two free throws. Let M1 denote making free throw 1, and let M2 denote making free throw 2. For any given free throw, suppose he has an 80% chance of making it, so P(M1) = P(M2) = 0.80. What is the probability of M1 and M2, making free throw 1 *and* free throw 2? In the long run of many pairs of free throws, suppose that for 80% of the cases in which he made the first free throw, he also made the second. Then the percentage of times he made both is the 80% of the 80% of times he made the first one, for a probability of $0.80 \times 0.80 = 0.64$ (that is, 64%).

This multiplication calculation is valid only under the assumption of **independent trials**. In this context, independent trials means the chance that the player makes the second free throw is independent of whether he makes the first. The chance of making the second is 80%, regardless of whether he made the first. For pro basketball players, independence is approximately true: Whether a player makes his first shot has almost no influence on whether he makes the second one. See Exercise 5.34 for data.

Recall

Independent trials means that what happens on one trial is not influenced by what happens on any other trial. ◀

To find the probability of the intersection of two events, we can multiply probabilities whenever the events are independent. We'll see a formal definition of independent events in the next section, but it essentially means that whether one event occurs does not affect the probability that the other event occurs.

Multiplication Rule: Probability of the Intersection of Independent Events

For the **intersection** of two **independent** events, A and B,

$$P(A \text{ and } B) = P(A) \times P(B).$$

The paradigm for independent events is repeatedly flipping a coin or rolling a die, where what happens on one trial does not affect what happens on another. For instance, for two rolls of a die,

$$P(6 \text{ on roll 1 } \textit{and } 6 \text{ on roll 2}) = P(6 \text{ on roll 1}) \times P(6 \text{ on roll 2}) = \frac{1}{6} \times \frac{1}{6} = \frac{1}{36}.$$

This multiplication rule extends to more than two independent events.

Example 7

Multiplication rule ◀

Guessing Yet Passing a Pop Quiz

Picture the Scenario

For a three-question multiple-choice pop quiz, a student is totally unprepared and randomly guesses the answer to each question. If each question has five options, then the probability of selecting the correct answer for any given question is 1/5, or 0.20. With guessing, the response on one question is not influenced by the response on another question. Thus, whether one question is answered correctly is independent of whether another question is answered correctly.

Questions to Explore

a. Find the probabilities of the possible student outcomes for the quiz, in terms of whether each response is correct (C) or incorrect (I).

b. Find the probability that the student passes, answering *at least two* questions correctly.

Think It Through

a. For each question P(C) = 0.20 and P(I) = 1 − 0.20 = 0.80. The probability that the student answers all three questions correctly is

$$P(CCC) = P(C) \times P(C) \times P(C) = 0.20 \times 0.20 \times 0.20 = 0.008.$$

This would be unusual. Similarly, the probability of answering the first two questions correctly and the third question incorrectly is

$$P(CCI) = P(C) \times P(C) \times P(I) = 0.20 \times 0.20 \times 0.80 = 0.032.$$

This is the same as P(CIC) and P(ICC), the other possible ways of getting two correct. Figure 5.8 is a tree diagram showing how to multiply probabilities to find the probabilities for all eight possible outcomes.

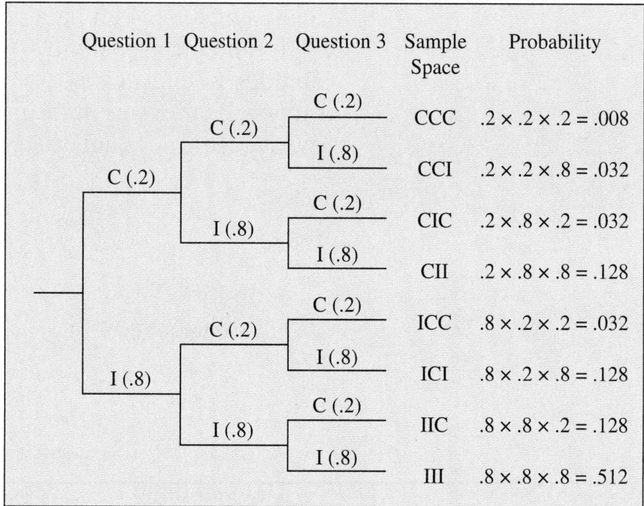

▲ **Figure 5.8 Tree Diagram for Guessing on a Three-Question Pop Quiz.** Each path from the first set of branches to the third set determines one sample space outcome. Multiplication of the probabilities along that path gives its probability, when trials are independent. **Question** Would you expect trials to be independent if a student is *not* merely guessing on every question? Why or why not?

b. The probability of *at least* two correct responses is

$$P(CCC) + P(CCI) + P(CIC) + P(ICC) = 0.008 + 3(0.032) = 0.104.$$

In summary, there is only about a 10% chance of passing when a student randomly guesses the answers.

Insight

As a check, you can see that the probabilities of the eight possible outcomes sum to 1.0. The probabilities indicate that it is in a student's best interests not to rely on random guessing.

▶ ***Try Exercise 5.15***

Events Often Are Not Independent

In practice, events need not be independent. For instance, on a quiz with only two questions, the instructor found the following proportions for the actual responses of her students (I = incorrect, C = correct):

Outcome:	II	IC	CI	CC
Probability:	0.26	0.11	0.05	0.58

Recall

From Section 3.1, the proportions expressed in contingency table form

	2nd Question	
1st Question	C	I
C	0.58	0.05
I	0.11	0.26

A and B (pointing to 0.58)

Let A denote {first question correct} and let B denote {second question correct}. Based on these probabilities,

$$P(A) = P(\{CI, CC\}) = 0.05 + 0.58 = 0.63$$

$$P(B) = P(\{IC, CC\}) = 0.11 + 0.58 = 0.69$$

and

$$P(A \text{ and } B) = P(\{CC\}) = 0.58.$$

If A and B were independent, then

$$P(A \text{ and } B) = P(A) \times P(B) = 0.63 \times 0.69 = 0.43.$$

Since P(A and B) actually equaled 0.58, A and B were not independent.

Responses to different questions on a quiz are typically not independent. Most students do not guess randomly. Students who get the first question correct may have studied more than students who do not get the first question correct, and thus they may also be more likely to get the second question correct.

In Practice Make Sure that Assuming Independence Is Realistic

Don't assume that events are independent unless you have given this assumption careful thought and it seems plausible. In Section 5.3, you will learn more about how to find probabilities when events are not independent.

Probability Rules

In this section, we have developed several rules for finding probabilities. Let's summarize them.

SUMMARY: Rules for Finding Probabilities

- The probability of each individual outcome is between 0 and 1, and the total of all the individual probabilities equals 1. The **probability of an event** is the sum of the probabilities of the individual outcomes in that event.
- For an event A and its **complement** A^c (not in A), $P(A^c) = 1 - P(A)$.
- The **union** of two events (that is, A occurs or B occurs or both) has

$$P(A \text{ or } B) = P(A) + P(B) - P(A \text{ and } B).$$

- When A and B are **independent**, the **intersection** of two events has

$$P(A \text{ and } B) = P(A) \times P(B).$$

- Two events A and B are **disjoint** when they have no common elements. Then

$$P(A \text{ and } B) = 0, \text{and thus } P(A \text{ or } B) = P(A) + P(B).$$

5.2 Practicing the Basics

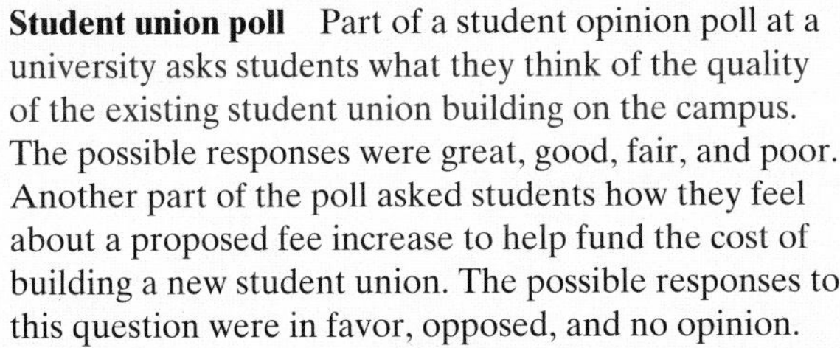

5.13 Student union poll Part of a student opinion poll at a university asks students what they think of the quality of the existing student union building on the campus. The possible responses were great, good, fair, and poor. Another part of the poll asked students how they feel about a proposed fee increase to help fund the cost of building a new student union. The possible responses to this question were in favor, opposed, and no opinion.

TRY

a. List all potential outcomes in the sample space for someone who is responding to both questions.

b. Show how a tree diagram can be used to display the outcomes listed in part a.

5.14 Random digit A single random digit (from 0–9) is selected using software or a random number table.

a. State the sample space for the possible outcomes.

b. State the probability for each possible outcome, based on what you know about the way random numbers are generated.

c. Each outcome in a sample space must have probability between 0 and 1, and the total of the probabilities must equal 1. Show that your assignment of probabilities in part b satisfies this rule.

5.15 Pop quiz A teacher gives a four-question unannounced true-false pop quiz, with two possible answers to each question.
TRY

a. Use a tree diagram to show the possible response patterns in terms of whether any given response is correct or incorrect. How many outcomes are in the sample space?

b. An unprepared student guesses all the answers randomly. Find the probabilities of the possible outcomes on the tree diagram.

c. Refer to part b. Using the tree diagram, evaluate the probability of passing the quiz, which the teacher defines as answering *at least* three questions correctly.

5.16 More true-false questions Your teacher gives a true-false pop quiz with 10 questions.
TRY

a. Show that the number of possible outcomes for the sample space of possible sequences of 10 answers is 1024.

b. What is the complement of the event of getting *at least* one of the questions wrong?

c. With random guessing, show that the probability of getting *at least* one question wrong is approximately 0.999.

5.17 Rolling two dice Some friends are playing a game in which two six-sided dice are rolled (craps, Settlers of Catan, etc.). One of them exclaims, "Since the sum of the dice is between 2 and 12, there is a one in eleven chance that each result will occur." Do you agree or disagree with his assessment of the probabilities? Explain.

5.18 Two girls A couple plans to have two children. Each child is equally likely to be a girl or boy, with gender independent of that of the other child.

a. Construct a sample space for the genders of the two children.

b. Find the probability that both children are girls.

c. Answer part b if in reality, for a given child, the chance of a girl is 0.49.

5.19 Three children A couple plans to have three children. Suppose that the probability of any given child being female is 0.5, and suppose that the genders of each child are independent events.
TRY

a. Write out all outcomes in the sample space for the genders of the three children.

b. What should be the probability associated with each outcome?

Using the sample space constructed in part a, find the probability that the couple will have

c. two girls and one boy.

d. at least one child of each gender.

5.20 Wrong sample space A couple plans to have four children. The father notes that the sample space for the number of girls the couple can have is 0, 1, 2, 3, and 4. He goes on to say that since there are five outcomes in the sample space, and since each child is equally likely to be a boy or girl, all five outcomes must be equally likely. Therefore, the probability of all four children being girls is 1/5. Explain the flaw in his reasoning.

5.21 Insurance Every year the insurance industry spends considerable resources assessing risk probabilities. To accumulate a risk of about one in a million of death, you can drive 100 miles, take a cross country plane flight, work as a police officer for 10 hours, work in a coal mine for 12 hours, smoke two cigarettes, be a nonsmoker but live with a smoker for two weeks, or drink 70 pints of beer in a year (Wilson and Crouch, 2001, pp. 208–209). Show that a risk of about one in a million of death is also approximately the probability of flipping 20 heads in a row with a balanced coin.

5.22 Cell phone and case At the local cell phone store, the probability that a customer who walks in will purchase a new cell phone is 0.2. The probability that the customer will purchase a new cell phone protective case is 0.25. Is this information sufficient to determine the probability that a customer will purchase a new cell phone and a new cell phone protective case? If so, find the probability. If not, explain why not. (*Hint:* Considering the buying practices of consumers in this context, is it reasonable to assume these events are independent?)

5.23 Seat belt use and auto accidents Based on records of automobile accidents in a recent year, the Department of Highway Safety and Motor Vehicles in Florida reported the counts who survived (S) and died (D), according to whether they wore a seat belt (Y = yes, N = no). The data are presented in the contingency table shown.
TRY

Outcome of auto accident by whether subject wore seat belt

Wore Seat Belt	Survived (S)	Died (D)	Total
Yes (Y)	412,368	510	**412,878**
No (N)	162,527	1,601	**164,128**
Total	**574,895**	**2,111**	**577,006**

a. What is the sample space of possible outcomes for a randomly selected individual involved in an auto accident? Use a tree diagram to illustrate the possible outcomes. (*Hint:* One possible outcome is YS.)

b. Using these data, estimate (i) P(D), (ii) P(N).

c. Estimate the probability that an individual did not wear a seat belt and died.

d. Based on part a, what would the answer to part c have been if the events N and D were independent? So, are N and D independent, and if not, what does that mean in the context of these data?

5.24 Protecting the environment When the General Social Survey most recently asked subjects whether they are a member of an environmental group (variable GRNGROUP) and whether they would be willing to pay higher prices to protect the environment (variable GRNPRICE), the results were as shown in the table.

		Pay Higher Prices (GRNPRICE)		
		Yes	**Not Sure**	**No**
Environmental Group Member (GRNGROUP)	Yes	293	71	66
	No	2,211	1,184	1,386

For a randomly selected American adult:

a. Estimate the probability of being (i) a member of an environmental group and (ii) willing to pay higher prices to protect the environment.

b. Estimate the probability of being both a member of an environmental group *and* willing to pay higher prices to protect the environment.

c. Given the probabilities in part a, show that the probability in part b is larger than it would be if the variables were independent. Interpret.

d. Estimate the probability that a person is a member of an environmental group *or* willing to pay higher prices to protect the environment. Do this (i) directly using the counts in the table and (ii) by applying the appropriate probability rule to the estimated probabilities found in parts a and b.

5.25 Global warming and trees A survey asks subjects whether they believe that global warming is happening (yes or no) and how much fuel they plan to use annually for automobile driving in the future, compared to their past use (less, about the same, more).

a. Show the sample space of possible outcomes by drawing a tree diagram that first gives the response on global warming and then the response on fuel use.

b. Let A be the event of a "yes" response on global warming and let B be the event of a "less" response on future fuel use. Suppose $P(A \text{ and } B) > P(A)P(B)$. Indicate whether A and B are independent events and explain what this means in nontechnical terms.

5.26 Newspaper sales You are the director of newspaper sales for the local paper. Each customer has signed up for either weekday delivery or weekend delivery. You record whether he or she received the delivery as Y for yes and N for no. The probabilities of the customer receiving the newspaper are as follows.

Outcome (Weekday, Weekend)	YY	YN	NY	NN
Probability	0.25	0.05	0.20	0.5

a. Display the outcomes in a contingency table, using the rows as the weekend event and the columns as the weekday event.

b. Let W denote the event that the customer bought a newspaper during the week and S be the event that he or she got it on the weekend (S for Saturday/Sunday). Find P(W) and P(S).

c. Explain what the event W and S means and find P(W and S).

d. Are W and S independent events? Explain why you would not normally expect customer choices to be independent.

5.27 Arts and crafts sales A local downtown arts and crafts shop found from past observation that 20% of the people who enter the shop actually buy something. Three potential customers enter the shop.

a. How many outcomes are possible for whether the clerk makes a sale to each customer? Construct a tree diagram to show the possible outcomes. (Let $Y = $ sale, $N = $ no sale.)

b. Find the probability of at least one sale to the three customers.

c. What did your calculations assume in part b? Describe a situation in which that assumption would be unrealistic.

5.3 Conditional Probability

As Example 1 explained, many employers require potential employees to take a diagnostic test for drug use. The diagnostic test has two categorical variables of interest: (1) whether the person has recently used drugs (yes or no), and (2) whether the diagnostic test shows that the person has used them (yes or no). Suppose the diagnostic test predicts that the person has recently used drugs. What's the probability that the person truly did use drugs?

This section introduces **conditional probability**, which deals with finding the probability of an event when you know that the outcome was in some particular part of the sample space. Most commonly, it is used to find a probability about a category for one variable (for instance, a person being a drug user), when we know the outcome on another variable (for instance, a test result showing drug use).

Finding the Conditional Probability of an Event

Example 5 showed a contingency table on income and whether a taxpayer is audited by the Internal Revenue Service. The table is shown again in the margin. We found that the probability that a randomly selected taxpayer was audited equaled $1405/145781 = 0.0096$. Were the chances higher if a taxpayer was at the highest income level? From the margin table, the number having income $\geq \$1,000,000$ was 363 (all numbers refer to thousands of taxpayers). Of them, 39 were audited, for a probability of $39/363 = 0.1074$. This is substantially higher than 0.0096, indicating that those earning the most are the most likely to be audited.

Income Level	**Audited**		
	Yes	**No**	**Total**
Under $200,000	1,233	139,305	**140,538**
$200,000–$1,000,000	133	4,747	**4,880**
More than $1,000,000	39	324	**363**
Total	**1,405**	**144,376**	**145,781**

Counts refer to thousands of taxpayers

In practice, tables often provide probabilities rather than counts for the outcomes in the sample space. Table 5.3 shows probabilities for the cells, based on the cell frequencies in the contingency table, for the six possible outcomes. For example, the probability of having income $\geq$ \$1,000,000 *and* being audited was $39/145781 = 0.00027$. The probability of income $\geq$ \$1,000,000 was $363/145781 = 0.00249$. So, of those at the highest income category, the proportion $0.00027/0.00249 = 0.1084$ were audited. This is the same answer we obtained earlier using the cell frequencies, apart from a small rounding error.

Table 5.3 Probabilities of Taxpayers at the Six Possible Combinations of Income Level and Audited

Each frequency in Table 5.2 was divided by 145,781 to obtain the cell probabilities shown here, such as $1{,}233/145{,}781 = 0.008$.

Income Level	Audited: Yes	Audited: No	Total
	These 6 probabilities sum to 1.0		
Under \$200,000	0.00846	0.95558	**0.96494**
\$200,000–\$1,000,000	0.00091	0.03256	**0.03347**
More than \$1,000,000	0.00027	0.00222	**0.00222**
Total	**0.00964**	**0.99036**	**1.00000**

Let event A denote {audited = yes} and let event B denote {income $\geq$ \$1,000,000}. The people in the highest income group and who are also audited make up the intersection event A and B (that is, audited = yes *and* income $\geq$ \$1,000,000). So, given B, the probability of A is the proportion of the cases in the intersection of A and B out of the cases in B. This is P(A and B)/P(B). This ratio is the **conditional probability** of the event A given the event B.

Conditional Probability

For events A and B, the **conditional probability** of event A, given that event B has occurred, is

$$P(A|B) = \frac{P(A \text{ and } B)}{P(B)}.$$

P(A|B) is read as "the probability of event A given event B." The vertical slash represents the word "given." Of the times that B occurs, **P(A|B)** is the proportion of times that A also occurs.

From Table 5.3 with events A (audited = yes) and B (income $\geq$ \$1,000,000),

$$P(A|B) = \frac{P(A \text{ and } B)}{P(B)} = \frac{0.00027}{0.00249} = 0.1084.$$

Given that a taxpayer has income $\geq$ \$1,000,000, the chances of being audited are 0.1084, or about 11%.

In Section 3.1, in learning about contingency tables, we saw that we could find **conditional proportions** for a categorical variable at any particular category of a second categorical variable. These enable us to study how the outcome of a response variable depends on the outcome of an explanatory variable. The conditional probabilities just found are merely conditional proportions. They refer to the population of taxpayers, treating audit status as a response variable and income level as an explanatory variable.

We could find similar conditional probabilities on audit status at each given level of income. We'd then get the results shown in Table 5.4. Using the cell probabilities in Table 5.3 (which refer to intersections of income events and audit events) we get each conditional probability by dividing a cell frequency for a particular audit status by the row total that is the frequency of income at that level. In each row of Table 5.4, the conditional probabilities sum to 1.0. Note that you can use the cell probabilities instead of the cell frequencies (1233/140538 is the same as 0.00846/0.96494).

Table 5.4 Conditional Probabilities on Audited Given the Income Level

Each cell probability in Table 5.3 was divided by the row marginal total probability to obtain the conditional probabilities shown here, such as 0.00878 = 0.00846/0.96494.

	Audited		
Income Level	**Yes**	**No**	**Total**
Under $200,000	0.00878	0.99122	**1.00000**
$200,000–$1,000,000	0.02719	0.97281	**1.00000**
More than $1,000,000	0.10843	0.89157	**1.00000**

Figure 5.9 is a graphical illustration of the definition of conditional probability. "Given event B" means that we restrict our attention to the outcomes in that event. This is the set of outcomes in the denominator. The proportion of those cases in which A occurred are those outcomes that are in event A as well as B. So the intersection of A and B is in the numerator.

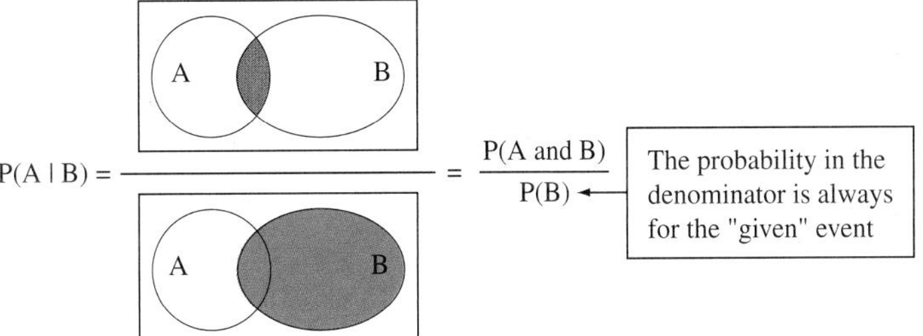

▲ **Figure 5.9** Venn Diagram of Conditional Probability of Event A Given Event B. Of the cases in which B occurred, $P(A|B)$ is the proportion in which A also occurred. **Question** Sketch a representation of $P(B|A)$. Is $P(A|B)$ necessarily equal to $P(B|A)$?

Example 8

Conditional probability

The Triple Blood Test for Down Syndrome

Picture the Scenario

A diagnostic test for a condition is said to be **positive** if it states that the condition is present and **negative** if it states that the condition is absent. How accurate are diagnostic tests? One way to assess accuracy is to measure the probabilities of the two types of possible error:

False positive: Test states the condition is present, but it is actually absent.

False negative: Test states the condition is absent, but it is actually present.

The Triple Blood Test screens a pregnant woman and provides an estimated risk of her baby being born with the genetic disorder Down syndrome. This syndrome, which occurs in about 1 in 800 live births, arises from an error in cell division that results in a fetus having an extra copy of chromosome 21. It is the most common genetic cause of mental impairment. The chance of having a baby with Down syndrome increases after a woman is 35 years old.

A study[2] of 5282 women aged 35 or over analyzed the Triple Blood Test to test its accuracy. It was reported that of the 5282 women, "48 of the 54 cases

[2]J. Haddow et al., *New England Journal of Medicine*, vol. 330, pp. 1114–1118, 1994.

of Down syndrome would have been identified using the test and 25 percent of the unaffected pregnancies would have been identified as being at high risk for Down syndrome (these are false positives)."

Questions to Explore

a. Construct the contingency table that shows the counts for the possible outcomes of the blood test and whether the fetus has Down syndrome.

b. Assuming the sample is representative of the population, estimate the probability of a positive test for a randomly chosen pregnant woman 35 years or older.

c. Given that the diagnostic test result is positive, estimate the probability that Down syndrome truly is present.

Think It Through

a. We'll use the following notation for the possible outcomes of the two variables:

Down syndrome status: D = Down syndrome present, D^c = unaffected

Blood test result: POS = positive, NEG = negative.

Table 5.5 shows the four possible combinations of outcomes. From the article quote, there were 54 cases of Down syndrome. This is the first row total. Of them, 48 tested positive, so $54 - 48 = 6$ tested negative. These are the counts in the first row. There were 54 Down cases out of $n = 5282$, so $5282 - 54 = 5228$ cases were unaffected, event D^c. That's the second row total. Now, 25% of those 5228, or $0.25 \times 5228 = 1307$, would have a positive test. The remaining $5228 - 1307 = 3921$ would have a negative test. These are the counts for the two cells in the second row.

Table 5.5 Contingency Table for Triple Blood Test of Down Syndrome

	Blood Test		
Down Syndrome Status	**POS**	**NEG**	**Total**
D (Down)	48	6	**54**
D^c (unaffected)	1307	3921	**5228**
Total	**1355**	**3927**	**5282**

b. From Table 5.5, the estimated probability of a positive test is $P(\text{POS}) = 1355/5282 = 0.257$.

c. The probability of Down syndrome, given that the test is positive, is the conditional probability, $P(\text{D}|\text{POS})$. Conditioning on a positive test means we consider only the cases in the first column of Table 5.5. Of the 1355 who tested positive, 48 cases actually had Down syndrome, so $P(\text{D}|\text{POS}) = 48/1355 = 0.035$. Let's see how to get this from the definition of conditional probability,

$$P(\text{D}|\text{POS}) = \frac{P(\text{D and POS})}{P(\text{POS})}.$$

Since $P(\text{POS}) = 0.257$ from part b and $P(\text{D and POS}) = 48/5282 = 0.0091$, we estimate $P(\text{D}|\text{POS}) = 0.0091/0.257 = 0.035$. In summary,

Caution

The $P(D|NEG)$ is not the same as the false negative rate. We found in Example 8 that the $P(D|NEG) = 0.0015$. The false negative rate is found by evaluating $P(NEG|D) = 6/54 = 0.11$. Be careful to watch the event being conditioned upon.

of the women who tested positive, fewer than 4% actually had fetuses with Down syndrome. This is somewhat comforting news to a woman who has a positive test result.

Insight

So why should a woman undergo this test, as most positives are false positives? From Table 5.5, $P(D) = 54/5282 = 0.0102$, so we estimate about a 1% chance of Down syndrome for women aged 35 or over. Also from Table 5.5, $P(D|NEG) = 6/3927 = 0.0015$, a bit more than 1 in 1000. A woman can have much less worry about Down syndrome if she has a negative test result because the chance of Down is then a bit more than 1 in 1000, compared to 1 in 100 overall.

▶ ***Try Exercises 5.34 and 5.37***

In Practice Conditional Probabilities in the Media

When you read or hear a news report that uses a probability statement, be careful to distinguish whether it is reporting a conditional probability. Most statements are conditional on some event and must be interpreted in that context. For instance, probabilities reported by opinion polls are often conditional on a person's gender, race, or age group.

Multiplication Rule for Finding P(A and B)

From Section 5.2, when A and B are independent events, $P(A \text{ and } B) = P(A) \times P(B)$. The definition of conditional probability provides a more general formula for P(A and B) that holds regardless of whether A and B are independent. We can rewrite the definition $P(A|B) = P(A \text{ and } B)/P(B)$, multiplying both sides of the formula by $P(B)$, to get $P(B) \times P(A|B) = P(B) \times [P(A \text{ and } B)/P(B)] = P(A \text{ and } B)$, so that

$$P(A \text{ and } B) = P(B) \times P(A|B).$$

Multiplication Rule for Evaluating P(A and B)

For events A and B, the probability that A and B both occur equals

$$P(A \text{ and } B) = P(B) \times P(A|B).$$

Applying the conditional probability formula to $P(B|A)$, we also see that

$$P(A \text{ and } B) = P(A) \times P(B|A).$$

Example 9

Multiplication rule

Double Faults in Tennis

Picture the Scenario

In a tennis match, on a given point, the player who is serving has two chances to hit the ball in play. The ball must fall in the correct marked box area on the opposite side of the net. A serve that misses that box is called a *fault.* Most players hit the first serve very hard, resulting in a fair chance of making a fault. If they do make a fault, they hit the second serve less hard and with some spin, making it more likely to be successful. Otherwise, with two misses—a *double fault*—they lose the point.

Question to Explore

The 2014 men's champion in the Wimbledon tournament was Novak Djokovic of Serbia. During the final match versus Roger Federer, he made 62% of his first serves. He faulted on the first serve 38% of the time (100% − 62% = 38%). Given that he made a fault with his first serve, he made a fault on his second serve only 4.5% of the time. Assuming these are typical of his serving performance, what is the probability that he makes a double fault when he serves?

Think It Through

Let F1 be the event that Djokovic makes a fault with the first serve, and let F2 be the event that he makes a fault with the second serve. We know $P(F1) = 0.38$ and $P(F2|F1) = 0.045$, as shown in the margin figure. The event that Djokovic makes a double fault is "F1 and F2." From the multiplication rule, its probability is

$$P(F1\,\text{and}\,F2) = P(F_1) \times P(F_2|F_1) = 0.38 \times 0.045 = 0.017.$$

Insight

Djokovic makes a fault on his first serve 38% of the time, and in 4.5% of those cases, he makes a fault on his second serve. He makes a double fault in 4.5% of the 38% of points in which he faults on the first serve, which is 0.017 (or 1.7%) of all his service points.

► *Try Exercise 5.40*

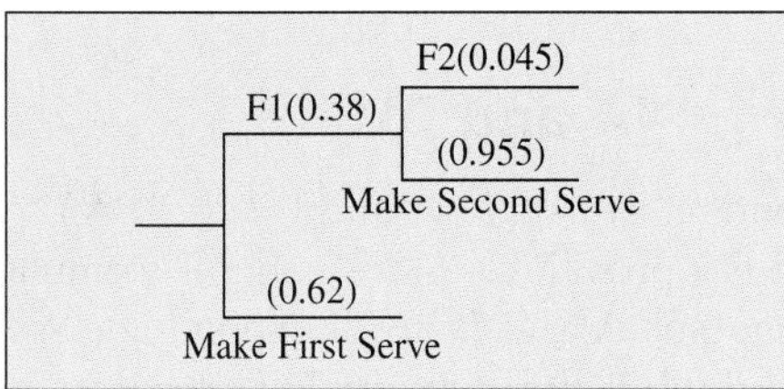

Sampling With or Without Replacement

In many sampling processes, once subjects are selected from a population, they are not eligible to be selected again. This is called *sampling without replacement.* At any stage of such a sampling process, probabilities of potential outcomes depend on the previous outcomes. Conditional probabilities are then used in finding probabilities of the possible samples.

Did You Know?

In tennis, you only serve a second time if you fault on the first serve. ◄

Example 10

Winning Lotto

Conditional probability ◄

Picture the Scenario

The biggest jackpot in state lotteries, typically millions of dollars, comes from the Lotto game. In Lotto South, available in Georgia, Kentucky, and Virginia, six numbers are randomly sampled without replacement from the integers 1 to 49. For example, a possible sample is (4, 9, 23, 26, 40, 46). Their order of selection is not important.

Question to Explore

You buy a Lotto South ticket. What is the probability that it is a winning ticket, having the six numbers chosen?

Think It Through

The probability of winning is the probability that the six numbers chosen are the six that you have on your ticket. Since your ticket has 6 of the 49 numbers that can be selected for the first number, P(you have 1st number) = 6/49. Given that you have the first number, for the second trial there are 5 numbers left that you hold out of 48 possible, so P(have 2nd number | have 1st number) = 5/48. Given that you have the first two, for the third trial there are 4 numbers left that you hold out of 47 possible, so P(have 3rd number | have 1st and 2nd numbers) = 4/47. Continuing with this logic, using an extension of the multiplication rule with conditional probabilities,

P(have all 6 numbers) = P(have 1st and 2nd and 3rd and 4th and 5th and 6th)

= P(have 1st) P(have 2nd | have 1st) P(have 3rd | have 1st and 2nd) . . .

. . . P(have 6th | have 1st and 2nd and 3rd and 4th and 5th)

$= (6/49) \times (5/48) \times (4/47) \times (3/46) \times (2/45) \times (1/44)$

$= 720/10{,}068{,}347{,}520 = 0.00000007.$

This is about 1 chance in 14 million.

► ***Try Exercise 5.44***

Did You Know?

Comparable to the probability of 0.00000007 (1 in 14 million) of winning Lotto South are the annual probabilities of about 0.0000004 (1 in 2.5 million) of being hit by a meteorite, 0.0000002 (1 in 5 million) of dying in a tornado, and 0.00000053 (1 in 1.9 million) of dying by a lightning strike (Wilson and Crouch 2001, p. 200). It's also roughly the probability that a person of average mortality will die in the next three minutes. ◄

Lotto South uses *sampling without replacement.* Once a number is chosen, it cannot be chosen again. If, by contrast, Lotto South allowed numbers to be picked more than once, the sampling scheme would be *sampling with replacement.*

After each observation without replacement, the population remaining is reduced by one and the conditional probability of a particular outcome changes. It can change considerably when the population size is small, as we saw in the Lotto example. However, with large population sizes, reducing the population by one does not much affect the probability from one trial to the next. In practice, when selecting random samples, we usually sample without replacement. With populations that are large compared to the sample size, the probability at any given observation depends little on the previous observations. Probabilities of possible samples are then quite similar for sampling without replacement and sampling with replacement.

Independent Events Defined Using Conditional Probability

Two events A and B are **independent** if the probability that one occurs is not affected by whether the other event occurs. This is expressed more formally using conditional probabilities.

Recall

Two events A and B are also independent if P(A and B) = P(A) × P(B). ◄

Independent Events, in Terms of Conditional Probabilities

Events A and B are **independent** if P(A|B) = P(A), or equivalently, if P(B | A) = P(B). If either holds, then the other does too.

For instance, let's consider the genders of two children in a family (F = female, M = male). The sample space is {FF, FM, MF, MM}. Suppose these four outcomes are equally likely, which is approximately true in practice. Let A denote {first child is female} and let B denote {second child is female}.

Then P(A) = 1/2, since two of the four possible outcomes have a female for the first child. Likewise, P(B) = 1/2. Also, P(A and B) = 1/4, since this corresponds to the single outcome, FF. So, from the definition of conditional probability,

$$P(B|A) = P(A \text{ and } B)/P(A) = (1/4)/(1/2) = 1/2.$$

Thus, P(B|A) = 1/2 = P(B), so A and B are independent events. Given A (that the first child is female), the probability that the second child was female is 1/2 since one outcome (FF) has this out of the two possibilities (FF, FM). Intuitively, the gender of the second child does not depend on the gender of the first child.

In sampling without replacement, outcomes of different trials are dependent. For instance, in the Lotto game described in Example 10, let A denote {your first number is chosen} and B denote {your second number is chosen}. Then P(A) = 6/49, but P(A|B) = 5/48 (since there are 5 possibilities out of 48 numbers), which differs slightly from P(A).

Example 11

Checking for independence

Two Events from Diagnostic Testing

Picture the Scenario

Table 5.5 showed a contingency table relating the result of a diagnostic blood test (POS = positive, NEG = negative) to whether a woman's fetus has Down syndrome (D = Down syndrome, D^c = unaffected). The estimated cell probabilities based on the frequencies in that table are shown in the marginal table.

	Blood Test		
Status	**POS**	**NEG**	**Total**
D	0.009	0.001	**0.010**
D^c	0.247	0.742	**0.990**
Total	**0.257**	**0.743**	**1.00**

Questions to Explore

a. Are the events POS and D independent or dependent?

b. Are the events POS and D^c independent or dependent?

Think It Through

a. The probability of a positive test result is 0.257. However, the probability of a positive result, given Down syndrome, is

$$P(POS|D) = P(POS \text{ and } D)/P(D) = 0.009/0.010 = 0.90.$$

Since P(POS|D) = 0.90 differs from P(POS) = 0.257, the events POS and D are dependent.

b. Likewise,

$$P(POS|D^c) = P(POS \text{ and } D^c)/P(D^c) = 0.247/0.990 = 0.250.$$

This differs slightly from P(POS) = 0.257, so POS and D^c are also dependent events.

Insight

As we'd expect, the probability of a positive result depends on whether the fetus has Down syndrome, and it's much higher if the fetus does. The diagnostic test would be worthless if the disease status and the test result were independent.

Generally, if A and B are dependent events, then so are A and B^c, and so are A^c and B, and so are A^c and B^c. For instance, if A depends on whether B occurs, then A also depends on whether B does not occur. So, once we find that POS and D are dependent events, we know that POS and D^c are dependent events also.

▶ ***Try Exercise 5.45***

We can now justify the formula given in Section 5.2 for the probability of the intersection of two independent events, namely P(A and B) = P(A) × P(B). This is a special case of the multiplication rule for finding P(A and B),

$$P(\text{A and B}) = P(\text{A}) \times P(\text{B} \mid \text{A}).$$

If A and B are independent, then P(B | A) = P(B), so the multiplication rule simplifies to

$$P(\text{A and B}) = P(\text{A}) \times P(\text{B}).$$

SUMMARY: Checking for Independence

Here are three ways to determine if events A and B are independent:

- Is P(A | B) = P(A)?
- Is P(B | A) = P(B)?
- Is P(A and B) = P(A) × P(B)?

If any of these is true, then the others are also true and the events A and B are independent.

Students often struggle to distinguish between the concepts of disjoint events and independent events. This is because the words seem to have a similar connotation. In fact, their precise meanings when referring to events of a sample space are very different, as illustrated in the following example.

Example 12

Checking for independence

Distinguishing Between Disjoint and Independent Events

Picture the Scenario

Consider three events: walking, chewing gum, and tying one's shoe. Let W = walking, C = chewing gum, and T = tying one's shoe. Suppose that while Joe works at his job in the campus cafeteria, the probability that he is walking at any given time is 0.1, the probability he is chewing gum is 0.3, and the probability he is tying his shoe is 0.001. Suppose also that for Joe, events W and C are independent.

Question to Explore

a. What does it mean contextually for events W and C to be independent?

b. What is the probability of the intersection of W and C? Are W and C disjoint events?

c. Of the events W, C, and T, which pair of events is Joe least likely to be doing at the same time? What is the probability of the intersection of those two events? Are they disjoint events?

Think It Through

a. Independence of W and C means that whether Joe is chewing gum does not depend on whether he is walking. For example, Joe is just as likely to be chewing gum while walking as chewing gum while not walking.

b. Since W and C are independent, P(W and C) = P(W) × P(C) = 0.1 × 0.3 = 0.03. Since P(W and C) ≠ 0, events W and C, although independent, are not disjoint.

c. We already know it is possible for Joe to walk and chew gum at the same time. It is also conceivable for him to be tying his shoe and chewing gum at the same time, so that P(T and C) is likely to be greater than zero. Meanwhile, it is simply not possible for him to walk and tie his shoe at the same time. (If you don't believe this, give it a try!) Therefore, P(W and T) = 0. The events walking and tying one's shoe are disjoint.

Insight

It is quite possible that for a different individual, the events W and C are not independent. Suppose for example that Jennifer only chews gum while she is walking back and forth to class. Whether she is chewing gum depends on whether she is walking. In fact, if she is not walking, then she is not chewing gum. For Joe (or anyone else), whether he is walking strongly depends on whether he is tying his shoe. If he is tying his shoe, then we know he is not walking. Likewise, if he is walking, then we know he is not tying his shoe. These two disjoint events, or any other pair of disjoint events, cannot be independent.

► *Try Exercise 5.45*

5.3 Practicing the Basics

5.28 Recidivism rates A 2014 article from *Business Insider* (http://www.businessinsider.com/department-of-justice-report-shows-high-recidivism-rate-2014-4) discusses recidivism rates in the United States. Recidivism is defined as being reincarcerated within five years of being sent to jail initially. Among the data reported, *Business Insider* cites that the recidivism rate for blacks is 81% compared to 73% among whites. Using notation, express each of these as a conditional probability.

5.29 Spam Because of the increasing nuisance of spam e-mail messages, many start-up companies have emerged to develop e-mail filters. One such filter was recently advertised as being 95% accurate. The way the advertisement is worded, 95% accurate could mean that (a) 95% of spam is blocked, (b) 95% of valid e-mail is allowed through, (c) 95% of the e-mail allowed through is valid, or (d) 95% of the blocked e-mail is spam. Let S denote {message is spam}, and let B denote {filter blocks message}. Using these events and their complements, identify each of these four possibilities as a conditional probability.

5.30 Audit and low income Table 5.3 on audit status and income follows. Show how to find the probability of:

a. Being audited, given that the taxpayer is in the lowest income category.

b. Being in the lowest income category, given that the taxpayer is audited.

	Audited	
Income	**No**	**Yes**
<\$200,000	0.9556	0.0085
\$200,000 − \$1mil	0.0326	0.0009
>\$1mil	0.0022	0.0003

5.31 Religious affiliation The 2012 Statistical Abstract of the United States[3] provides information on individuals' self-described religious affiliations. The information for 2008 is summarized in the following table (all numbers are in thousands).

Christian	
Catholic	57,199
Baptist	36,148
Christian (no denomination specified)	16,834
Methodist/Wesleyan	11,366
Other Christian	51,855
Jewish	2,680
Muslim	1,349
Buddhist	1,189
Other non-Christian	3,578
No Religion	34,169
Refused to Answer	11,815
Total Adult Population in 2008	228,182

a. Find the probability that a randomly selected individual is identified as Christian.

b. Given that an individual identifies as Christian, find the probability that the person is Catholic.

c. Given that an individual answered, find the probability the individual is identified as following no religion.

[3]*Source:* Data from www.census.gov/compendia/statab/2012/tables/12s0075.xls.

5.32 Cancer deaths Current estimates are that about 25% of all deaths are due to cancer, and of the deaths that are due to cancer, 30% are attributed to tobacco, 40% to diet, and 30% to other causes.

a. Define events and identify which of these four probabilities refer to conditional probabilities.

b. Find the probability that a death is due to cancer and tobacco.

5.33 Revisiting seat belts and auto accidents The following table is from Exercise 5.23 classifying auto accidents by survival status (S = survived, D = died) and seat belt status of the individual involved in the accident.

	Outcome		
Belt	**S**	**D**	**Total**
Yes	412,368	510	**412,878**
No	162,527	1,601	**164,128**
Total	**574,895**	**2,111**	**577,006**

a. Estimate the probability that the individual died (D) in the auto accident.

b. Estimate the probability that the individual died, given that the person (i) wore and (ii) did not wear a seat belt. Interpret results.

c. Are the events of dying and wearing a seat belt independent? Justify your answer.

5.34 Go Celtics! TRY Larry Bird, who played pro basketball for the Boston Celtics, was known for being a good shooter. In games during 1980–1982, when he missed his first free throw, 48 out of 53 times he made the second one, and when he made his first free throw, 251 out of 285 times he made the second one.

a. Form a contingency table that cross tabulates the outcome of the first free throw (made or missed) in the rows and the outcome of the second free throw (made or missed) in the columns.

b. For a given pair of free throws, estimate the probability that Bird (i) made the first free throw and (ii) made the second free throw. (*Hint*: Use counts in the (i) row margin and (ii) column margin.)

c. Estimate the probability that Bird made the second free throw, given that he made the first one. Does it seem as if his success on the second shot depends strongly, or hardly at all, on whether he made the first?

5.35 Identifying spam An article[4] on www.networkworld.com about evaluating e-mail filters that are designed to detect spam described a test of MailFrontier's Anti-Spam Gateway (ASG). In the test, there were 7840 spam messages, of which ASG caught 7005. Of the 7053 messages that ASG identified as spam, they were correct in all but 48 cases.

a. Set up a contingency table that cross classifies the actual spam status (with the rows "spam" and "not spam") by the ASG filter prediction (with the columns "predict message is spam" and "predict message is not spam"). Using the information given, enter counts in three of the four cells.

b. For this test, given that a message is truly spam, estimate the probability that ASG correctly detects it.

c. Given that ASG identifies a message as spam, estimate the probability that the message truly was spam.

5.36 Homeland security According to an article in *The New Yorker* (March 12, 2007), the Department of Homeland Security in the United States is experimenting with installing devices for detecting radiation at bridges, tunnels, roadways, and waterways leading into Manhattan. The New York Police Department (NYPD) has expressed concerns that the system would generate too many false alarms.

a. Form a contingency table that cross classifies whether a vehicle entering Manhattan contains radioactive material and whether the device detects radiation. Identify the cell that corresponds to the false alarms the NYPD fears.

b. Let A be the event that a vehicle entering Manhattan contains radioactive material. Let B be the event that the device detects radiation. Sketch a Venn diagram for which each event has similar (not the same) probability but the probability of a false alarm equals 0.

c. For the diagram you sketched in part b, explain why $P(A|B) = 1$, but $P(B|A) < 1$.

5.37 Down syndrome again TRY Example 8 discussed the Triple Blood Test for Down syndrome, using data summarized in a table shown again below.

	Blood Test		
Down	**POS**	**NEG**	**Total**
D	48	6	**54**
D^c	1307	3921	**5228**
Total	**1355**	**3927**	**5282**

a. Given that a test result is negative, show that the probability the fetus actually has Down syndrome is $P(D|NEG) = 0.0015$.

b. Is $P(D|NEG)$ equal to $P(NEG|D)$? If so, explain why. If not, find $P(NEG|D)$.

5.38 Obesity in America A 2014 Gallup poll reported that 27% of people in the United States are obese (having a body mass index score of 30 or more). Blacks have the highest obesity rate at 35%, whereas Asians have the lowest, at 9%.

a. Of the three percentages (estimated probabilities) reported, which are conditional? Explain.

b. These results are based on telephone interviews of 272,347 adults, aged 18 or older. Of these adults, 24,131 were black, and 5,752 were Asian. Create a contingency table showing estimated counts for race (Black, Asian, Other) and obesity (Yes, No).

c. Create a tree diagram with the first branching representing race and the second branching representing obesity. Be sure to include the appropriate percentages on each branch.

5.39 Happiness in relationship Are people happy in their romantic relationships? The table shows results from the 2012 General Social Survey for adults classified by gender and happiness.

[4] www.networkworld.com/reviews/2003/0915spamstats.html.

	Level of Happiness			
Gender	Very Happy	Pretty Happy	Not Too Happy	Total
Male	69	73	4	**146**
Female	78	80	13	**171**
Total	**147**	**153**	**17**	**317**

a. Estimate the probability that an adult is very happy in his or her romantic relationship.

b. Estimate the probability that an adult is very happy (i) given that he is male and (ii) given that she is female.

c. For these subjects, are the events being very happy and being a male independent? (Your answer will apply merely to this sample. Chapter 11 will show how to answer this for the population of all adults.)

5.40 Petra Kvitova serves Petra Kvitova of the Czech Republic won the 2014 Wimbledon Ladies' Singles Championship. In the final game against Eugenie Bouchard of Canada she had 41 first serves, of which 28 were good, and three double faults.

TRY

a. Find the probability that her first serve is good.

b. Find the conditional probability of double faulting, given that her first serve resulted in a fault.

c. On what percentage of her service points does she double fault?

5.41 Shooting free throws Pro basketball player Shaquille O'Neal is a poor free-throw shooter. Consider situations in which he shoots a pair of free throws. The probability that he makes the first free throw is 0.50. Given that he makes the first, suppose the probability that he makes the second is 0.60. Given that he misses the first, suppose the probability that he makes the second one is 0.40.

a. What is the probability that he makes both free throws?

b. Find the probability that he makes *one* of the two free throws (i) using the multiplicative rule with the two possible ways he can do this and (ii) by defining this as the complement of making neither or both of the free throws.

c. Are the results of the free throws independent? Explain.

5.42 Drawing cards A standard card deck has 52 cards consisting of 26 black and 26 red cards. Three cards are dealt from a shuffled deck, *without replacement.*

a. True or false: The probability of being dealt three black cards is $(1/2) \times (1/2) \times (1/2) = 1/8$. If true, explain why. If false, show how to get the correct probability.

b. Let A = first card red and B = second card red. Are A and B independent? Explain why or why not.

c. Answer parts a and b if each card is replaced in the deck after being dealt.

5.43 Drawing more cards A standard deck of poker playing cards contains four suits (clubs, diamonds, hearts, and spades) and 13 different cards of each suit. During a hand of poker, 5 of the 52 cards have been exposed. Of the exposed cards, 3 were diamonds. Tony will have the opportunity to draw two more cards, and he has surmised that to win the hand, each of those two cards will need to be diamonds. What is Tony's probability of winning the hand? (Assume the two unexposed cards are not diamonds.)

5.44 Big loser in Lotto Example 10 showed that the probability of having the winning ticket in Lotto South was 0.00000007. Find the probability of holding a ticket that has zero winning numbers out of the 6 numbers selected (without replacement) for the winning ticket out of the 49 possible numbers.

TRY

5.45 Family with two children For a family with two children, let A denote {first child is female}, let B denote (at least one child is female}, and let C denote {both children are female}.

TRY

a. Show that $P(C \mid A) = 1/2$.

b. Are A and C independent events? Why or why not?

c. Find $P(C \mid B)$.

d. Describe what makes $P(C \mid A)$ different than $P(C \mid B)$.

5.46 Checking independence In three independent flips of a balanced coin, let A denote $\{$first flip is a head$\}$, B denote $\{$second flip is a head$\}$, C denote $\{$first two flips are heads$\}$, and D denote $\{$three heads on the three flips$\}$.

a. Find the probabilities of A, B, C, and D.

b. Which, if any, pairs of these events are independent? Explain.

5.4 Applying the Probability Rules

Probability relates to many aspects of your daily life—for instance, when you make decisions that affect your financial well being and when you evaluate risks due to lifestyle decisions. Objectively or subjectively, you need to consider questions such as: What's the chance that the business you're thinking of starting will succeed? What's the chance that the extra collision insurance you're thinking of getting for your car will be needed?

We'll now apply the basics of probability to coincidence in our lives.

Is a Coincidence Truly an Unusual Event?

Some events in our lives seem to be coincidental. One of the authors, who lives in Georgia, once spent a summer vacation in Newfoundland, Canada. One day during that trip, she made an unplanned stop at a rest area and observed a camper with a Georgia license tag from a neighboring county to her hometown. She discovered that the camper's owner was a patient of her physician husband. Was this meeting as coincidental as it seemed?

Events that seem coincidental are often not so unusual when viewed in the context of *all* the possible random occurrences at all times. Lots of topics can trigger an apparent coincidence—the person you meet having the same last name as yours, the same birth place, the same high school or college, the same profession, the same birthday, and so on. It's really not so surprising that in your travels you will sometime have a coincidence, such as seeing a friend or meeting someone who knows somebody you know.

With a large enough sample of people or times or topics, seemingly surprising things are actually quite sure to happen. Events that are rare per person occur rather commonly with large numbers of people. If a particular event happens to one person in a million each day, then in the United States, we expect about 300 such events a day and more than 100,000 every year. The one in a million chance regularly occurs, however surprised we may be if it should happen to us.

If you take a coin now and flip it 10 times, you would probably be surprised to get 10 heads. But if you flipped the coin for a long time, would you be surprised to get 10 heads in a row at some point? Perhaps you would, but you should not be. For instance, if you flip a balanced coin 2000 times, then you can expect the longest run of heads during those flips to be about 10. When a seemingly unusual event happens to you, think about whether it is like seeing 10 heads on the next 10 flips of a coin, or more like seeing 10 heads in a row sometime in a long series of flips. If the latter, it's really not such an unusual occurrence.

Did You Know?

If something has a very large number of opportunities to happen, occasionally it will happen, even if it's highly unlikely at any one observation. This is a consequence of the **law of large numbers**. ◄

Coincidence and Seemingly Unusual Patterns

Once we have data, it's easy to find patterns: 10 heads in a row, 10 tails in a row, 5 tails followed by 5 heads, and so forth. Our minds are programmed to look for patterns. Out of the huge number of things that can happen to us and to others over time, it's not surprising to occasionally see patterns that seem unusual.

To illustrate that an event you may perceive as a coincidence is actually not that surprising, let's answer the question, "What is the chance that at least two people in your class have the same birthday?"

► Activity 2

Matching Birthdays

If your class is small to moderate in size (say, fewer than about 60 students), the instructor may ask you to state your birth dates. Does a pair of students in the class share the same birthday?

Example 13

Matching Birthdays

Picture the Scenario

Suppose a class has 25 students. Since there are 365 possible birth dates (without counting February 29), our intuition tells us that the probability is small that there will be any birthday matches. Assume that the birth date of a student is equally likely to be any one of the 365 days in a year and that students' birth dates are independent (for example, there are no twins in the class).

Question to Explore

What is the probability that *at least* two of the 25 students have the same birthday? Is our intuition correct that the probability of a match is small?

Think It Through

The event of *at least one* birthday match includes one match, two matches, or more. To find the probability of *at least one* match, it is simpler to find the complement probability of *no* matches. Then

$$P(\text{at least one match}) = 1 - P(\text{no matches}).$$

To begin, suppose a class has only two students. The first student's birthday could be any of 365 days. Given that student's birthday, the chance that the second student's birthday is different is 364/365 because 364 of the possible 365 birthdays are different. The probability is $1 - 364/365 = 1/365$ that the two students share the same birthday.

Now suppose a class has three students. The probability that all three have different birthdays is

$$P(\text{no matches}) = P(\text{students 1 and 2 and 3 have different birthdays}) = P(\text{students 1 and 2 different}) \times P(\text{student 3 different} \mid \text{students 1 and 2 different}) = (364/365) \times (363/365).$$

The second probability in this product equals 363/365 because there are 363 days left for the third student that differ from the different birthdays of the first two students.

For 25 students, similar logic applies. By the time we get to the 25th student, for that student's birthday to differ from the other 24, there are 341 choices left out of 365 possible birthdays. So

$$P(\text{no matches}) = P(\text{students 1 and 2 and 3} \ldots \text{and 25 have different birthdays})$$

$$= \underset{\substack{\text{student 2,} \\ \text{given 1}}}{\underset{\uparrow}{(364/365)}} \times \underset{\substack{\text{student 3,} \\ \text{given 1,2}}}{\underset{\uparrow}{(363/365)}} \times \underset{\substack{\text{student 4,} \\ \text{given 1,2,3}}}{\underset{\uparrow}{(362/365)}} \times \underset{\text{next 20 students}}{\underset{\uparrow}{\ldots \ldots \ldots}} \times \underset{\substack{\text{student 25,} \\ \text{given 1,...,24}}}{\underset{\uparrow}{(341/365)}}.$$

This product equals 0.43. Using the probability for the complement of an event,

$$P(\text{at least one match}) = 1 - P(\text{no matches}) = 1 - 0.43 = 0.57.$$

The probability exceeds 1/2 of at least one birthday match in a class of 25 students.

Insight

Is this probability higher than you expected? It should not be once you realize that with 25 students, there are 300 *pairs* of students who can share the same birthday (see Exercise 5.49). Remember that with lots of opportunities for something to happen, coincidences are really not so surprising.

Did you have a birthday match in your class? Was it coincidence? If the number of students in your class is at least 23, the probability of at least one match is greater than 1/2. For a class of 50 students, the probability of at least one match is 0.97. For 100 students, it is 0.9999997 (there are then 4950 different *pairs* of students). Here are a couple of other facts about matching birthdays that may surprise you:

- With 88 people, there's a 1/2 chance that at least three people have the same birthday.
- With 14 people, there's a 1/2 chance that at least two people have a birthday within a day of each other in the calendar year.

► ***Try Exercise 5.47***

Sometimes a cluster of occurrences of some disease, like cancer, in a neighborhood will cause worry in residents that there is some environmental cause. But *some* disease clusters will appear around a nation just by chance. If we look at a large number of places and times, we should expect some disease clusters.

By themselves, they seem unusual, but viewed in a broader context, they may not be. Epidemiologists are statistically trained scientists who face the difficult task of determining which events can be explained by ordinary random variation and which cannot.

In Practice, Probability Models Approximate Reality

We've now found probabilities in many idealized situations. In practice, it's often not obvious when different outcomes are equally likely or different events are independent. When calculating probabilities, it is advisable to specify a **probability model** that spells out all the assumptions made.

Probability Model

A **probability model** specifies the possible outcomes for a sample space and provides assumptions on which the probability calculations for events composed of those outcomes are based.

The next example illustrates a probability model used together with the rules for finding probabilities.

Example 14

Probability model ◄

Safety of the Space Shuttle

Picture the Scenario

Out of the 135 space shuttle missions, there were two catastrophic failures, the *Challenger* disaster on the 25th flight (January 28, 1986) and the *Columbia* disaster on the 113th flight (February 1, 2003). Since then, much attention has focused on estimating probabilities of success or failure (disaster) for a mission. But before the first flight, there were no trials to provide data for estimating probabilities.

Question to Explore

Based on all the information available, a scientist is willing to predict the probability of success for any particular mission. Consider flying 100 new missions. How can you use this to find the probability of *at least one* failure in a total of 100 new missions?

Think It Through

Let S1 denote the event that the first new mission is successful, S2 the event that the second new mission is successful, and so on up to S100, the event that new mission 100 is successful. If all these events occur, there is no failure in the 100 flights. The event of *at least one* failure in 100 flights is the complement of the event that they are all successful (0 failures). By the probability for complementary events,

$$P(\text{at least 1 failure}) = 1 - P(\text{0 failures})$$
$$= 1 - P(\text{S1 and S2 and S3} \ldots \text{and S100}).$$

The intersection of events S1 through S100 is the event that *all* 100 new missions are successful.

We now need a probability model to evaluate P(S1 and S2 and S3... and S100). If our probability model assumes that the 100 shuttle flights

Did You Know?

The space shuttle missions have served an important role in space exploration during the years 1981–2011 with 135 flights. ◀

are *independent*, then the multiplication rule for independent events implies that

$$P(S1 \text{ and } S2 \text{ and } S3 \ \ldots \text{ and } S100) =$$
$$P(S1) \times P(S2) \times P(S3) \times \ldots \times P(S100).$$

If our probability model assumes that each flight has the *same probability* of success, say P(S), then this product equals $[P(S)]^{100}$. To proceed further, we need a value for P(S). According to a discussion of this issue in the PBS series *Against All Odds: Inside Statistics*, a risk assessment study by the Air Force used the estimate $P(S) = 0.971$. With it,

$$P(\text{at least 1 failure}) = 1 - [P(S)]^{100} = 1 - [0.971]^{100} = 1 - 0.053 = 0.947.$$

Different estimates of P(S) can result in very different answers. For instance, the *Against All Odds* episode mentioned that a NASA study estimated that $P(S) = 0.9999833$. Using this,

$$P(\text{at least 1 failure}) = 1 - [P(S)]^{100} = 1 - [0.9999833]^{100}$$
$$= 1 - 0.998 = 0.002.$$

This was undoubtedly overly optimistic. We see that different probability models can result in drastically different probability assessments.

Insight

The preceding answer depended strongly on the assumed probability of success for each mission. Since there were two failures in the original 135 flights, an estimate of P(S) was $133/135 = 0.985$. But the assumptions of independence and of the same probability for each flight may also be suspect. For instance, other variables (e.g., temperature at launch, experience of crew, age of craft used, quality of O-ring seals) could affect that probability.

▶ ***Try Exercise 5.56***

In practice, probability models merely *approximate* reality. They are rarely *exactly* satisfied. For instance, in the matching birthday example, our probability model ignored February 29, assumed each of the other 365 birthdays are equally likely, and assumed that students' birth dates are independent. So, the answer found is only approximate. Whether probability calculations using a particular probability model are accurate depends on whether assumptions in that model are close to the truth or unrealistic.

Probabilities and Diagnostic Testing

We've seen the important role that probability plays in diagnostic testing, illustrated in Section 5.3 (Example 8) with the pregnancy test for Down syndrome. Table 5.6 summarizes conditional probabilities about the result of a diagnostic test, given whether some condition or state (such as Down syndrome) is present. We let S denote that the state is present and S^c denote that it is not present.

Recall

The vertical slash means "given." **P(POS|S)** denotes the conditional probability of a positive test result, given that the state is present. ◀

In Table 5.6, **sensitivity** and **specificity** refer to correct test results, given the actual state. For instance, given that the state tested for is present, sensitivity is the probability the test detects it by giving a positive result, that is, $P(POS \mid S)$.

Medical journal articles that discuss diagnostic tests commonly report the sensitivity and specificity. However, what's more relevant to you once you take a diagnostic test are the conditional probabilities that condition on the test result. If a diagnostic test for Down syndrome is positive, you want to know the probability that Down syndrome is truly present. If you know the sensitivity

Table 5.6 Probabilities of Correct and Incorrect Results in Diagnostic Testing

The probabilities in the body of the table refer to the test result, conditional on whether the state (S) is truly present. The sensitivity and specificity are the probabilities of the two types of correct diagnoses.

	Diagnostic Test Result		
State Present?	**Positive (POS)**	**Negative (NEG)**	**Total Probability**
Yes (S)	Sensitivity P(POS | S)	False negative rate P(NEG | S)	**1.0**
No (S^c)	False positive rate P(POS | S^c)	Specificity P(NEG | S^c)	**1.0**

and specificity and how often the state occurs, can you find P(S | POS) by using the rules of probability?

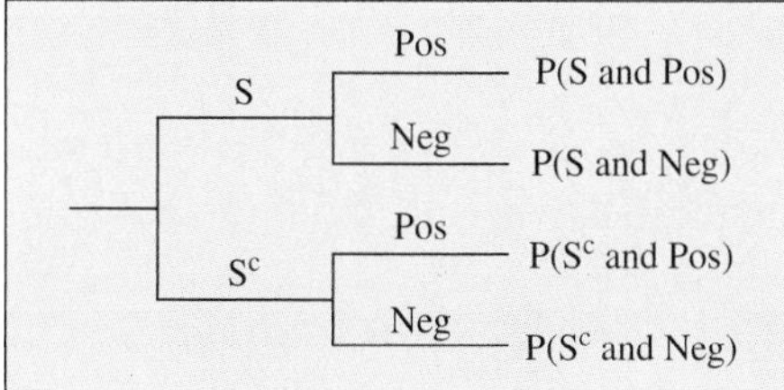
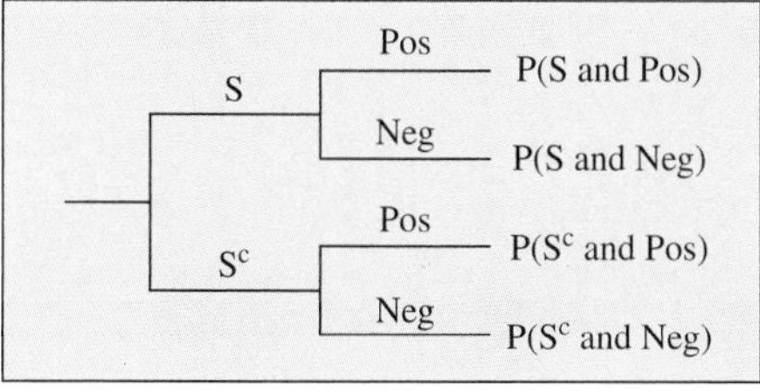

The easiest way to do this is with a tree diagram, as shown in the margin. The first branches show the probabilities of the two possible states, P(S) and P(S^c). The next set of branches show the known conditional probabilities, such as P(POS | S), for which we are given the true state. Then the products P(S)P(POS | S) and P(S^c)P(POS | S^c) give intersection probabilities P(S and POS) and P(S^c and POS), which can be used to get probabilities such as

$$P(POS) = P(S \text{ and } POS) + P(S^c \text{ and } POS).$$

Then you can find P(S | POS) = P(S and POS) / P(POS).

Example 15

Diagnostic tests

Random Drug Testing of Air Traffic Controllers

Picture the Scenario

Air traffic controllers monitor the flights of aircraft and help to ensure safe takeoffs and landings. In the United States, air traffic controllers are required to undergo periodic random drug testing. A urine test is used as an initial screening due to its low cost and ease of implementation. One such urine test, the *Triage Panel for Drugs of Abuse plus TCA*,[5] detects the presence of drugs. Its sensitivity and specificity have been reported[6] as 0.96 and 0.93. Based on past drug testing of air traffic controllers, the FAA reports that the probability of drug use at a given time is approximately 0.007 (less than 1%). This is called the **prevalence** of drug use.

Questions to Explore

a. A positive test result puts the air traffic controller's job in jeopardy. What is the probability of a positive test result?

b. Find the probability an air traffic controller truly used drugs, given that the test is positive.

Think It Through

a. We've been given the probability of drug use, P(S) = 0.007, the sensitivity P(POS | S) = 0.96, and the specificity P(NEG | S^c) = 0.93. Figure 5.10 shows a tree diagram that is useful for visualizing these probabilities and for finding P(POS).

[5]Screening assay from Biosite Diagnostics, San Diego, California.

[6]M. Peace et al., *Journal of Analytical Toxicology*, vol. 24 (2000).

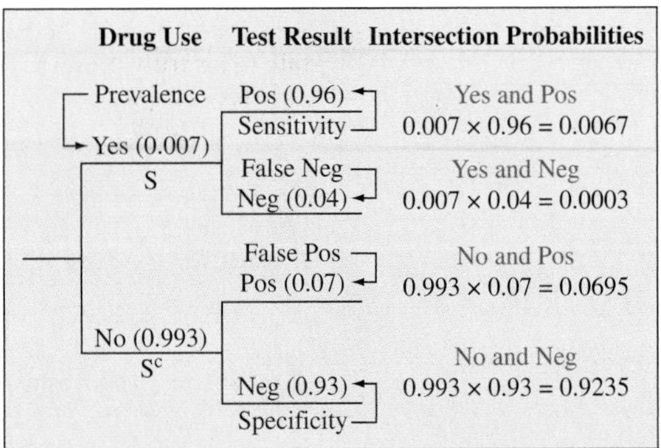

▲ **Figure 5.10** Tree Diagram for Random Drug Testing of Air Traffic Controllers. The first set of branches shows the probabilities for drug use. The second set of branches shows the conditional probabilities for the test result, given whether the person used drugs or not. Multiplication of the probabilities along each path gives the probabilities of intersections of the events.

From the tree diagram and the multiplicative rule for intersection probabilities,

$$P(S \text{ and } POS) = P(S)P(POS|S) = 0.007 \times 0.96 = 0.0067.$$

The other path with a positive test result has probability

$$P(S^c \text{and } POS) = P(S^c)P(POS|S^c) = 0.993 \times 0.07 = 0.0695.$$

To find P(POS), we add the probabilities of these two possible positive test paths. Thus,

$$P(POS) =$$

$$P(S \text{ and } POS) + P(S^c \text{ and } POS) = 0.0067 + 0.0695 = 0.0762.$$

There's nearly an 8% chance of the test suggesting that the person used drugs.

b. The probability of drug use, given a positive test, is $P(S|POS)$. From the definition of conditional probability,

$$P(S|POS) = P(S \text{ and } POS)/P(POS) = 0.0067/0.0762 = 0.09.$$

When the test is positive, only 9% of the time had the person actually used drugs.

If you're uncertain about how to answer part a and part b with a tree diagram, you can construct a contingency table, as shown in Table 5.7. The table shows the summary value of $P(S) = 0.007$ in the right margin, the other right-margin value $P(S^c) = 1 - 0.007 = 0.993$ determined by it, and the intersection probabilities $P(S \text{ and } POS) = 0.0067$ and $P(S^c \text{and} POS) = 0.0695$ found in part a. From that table, of the proportion 0.0762 of positive cases, 0.0067 truly had used drugs, so the conditional probability is $P(S|POS) = P(S \text{ and } POS)P(POS) = 0.0067/0.0762 = 0.09$.

Table 5.7 Contingency Table-Cell Probabilities for Air Controller Drug Test

	Drug Test Result		
State Present?	**POS**	**NEG**	**Total**
Yes (S)	0.0067	0.0003	0.007
NO (S^c)	0.0695	0.9235	0.993
Total	0.0762	**0.9238**	**1.000**

Insight

If the prevalence rate is truly near 0.007, the chances are low that an individual who tests positive is actually a drug user. Does a positive test mean the individual will automatically lose his or her job? No, if the urine test comes back positive, the individual is given a second test that is more accurate but more expensive than the urine test.

▶ ***Try Exercise 5.57***

Are you surprised that $P(S|POS)$ is so small (only 0.09) for the air controllers? To help understand the logic behind this, it's a good idea to show on a tree diagram what you'd expect to happen with a typical group of air controllers. Figure 5.11 shows a tree diagram for what we'd expect to happen for 1000 of them.

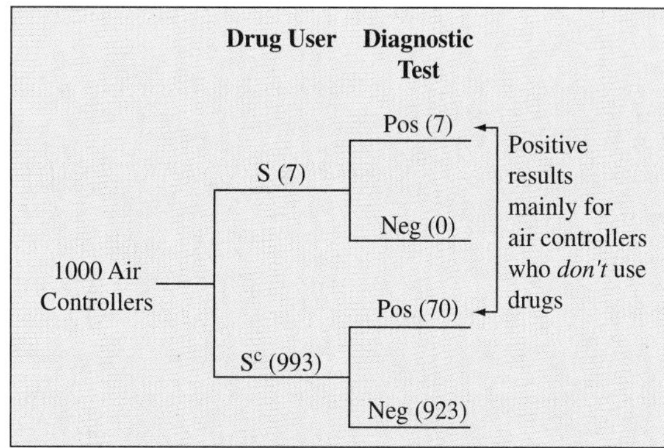

▲ **Figure 5.11 Expected Results of Drug Tests for 1000 Air Controllers.** This diagram shows typical results when the proportion 0.007 (7 in 1000) are drug users (event S), a positive result has probability 0.96 for those who use drugs, and a negative result has probability 0.93 for those who do not use drugs. Most positive results occur with individuals who are *not* using drugs because there are so many such individuals (more than 99% of the population). **Question** How would results change if a higher percentage of the population were using drugs?

Since the proportion 0.007 (which is 7 in 1000) of the target population uses drugs, the tree diagram shows 7 drug users and 993 nondrug users out of the 1000 air controllers. For the 7 drug users, there's a 0.96 chance the test detects the drug use. So we'd expect all 7 or perhaps 6 of the 7 to be detected with the test (Figure 5.11 shows 7). For the 993 nondrug users, there's a 0.93 chance the test is negative. So we'd expect about $0.93 \times 993 = 923$ individuals to have a negative result and the other $993 - 923 = 70$ nondrug users to have a positive result, as shown on Figure 5.11.

In summary, Figure 5.11 shows $7 + 70 = 77$ individuals having a positive test result, but only 7 were actually drug users. Of those with a positive test result, the proportion who truly were drug users is $7/77 = 0.09$. What's happening is that the 7% of errors for the large majority of individuals who *do not* use drugs is much larger than the 96% of correct decisions for the small number of individuals who *do* use drugs.

If the prevalence rate were $P(S) = 0.15$ (let's hope it's not really this high!) instead of 0.007, you can verify that $P(S|POS) = 0.71$ rather than 0.09. The probability that the person truly used drugs is then much higher, 0.71. In fact, the chance that a positive test result is truly correct depends very much on the prevalence rate. The lower the prevalence rate, the lower the chance. The more drug-free the population, the less likely an individual who tests positive for drugs truly used them.

In Example 15, we started with probabilities of the form P(POS | S) and used them to find a conditional probability P(S | POS) that reverses what is given and what is to be found. The method used to find this reverse conditional probability can be summarized in a single formula (see Exercise 5.116), known as **Bayes's rule**. We have not shown that formula here because it is easier to understand the logic behind evaluating this conditional probability using tree diagrams or contingency tables.

Probability Answers to Questions Can Be Surprising

The results in Example 15 on drug testing of air traffic controllers may seem surprising, but actually they are not uncommon. For instance, consider the mammogram for detecting breast cancer in women. One recent study[7] estimated sensitivity = 0.86 and specificity = 0.88. Of the women who receive a positive mammogram result, what proportion actually have breast cancer? In Exercise 5.57 you can work out that it may be only about 0.07.

These diagnostic testing examples point out that when probability is involved, answers to questions about our daily lives are sometimes not as obvious as you may think. Consider the question, "Should a woman have an annual mammogram?" Medical choices are rarely between certainty and risk but, rather, between different risks. If a woman fails to have a mammogram, this is risky—she may truly have breast cancer. If she has a mammogram, there's the risk of a false positive or false negative, such as the risk of needless worry and additional invasive procedures (often biopsy and other treatments) due to a false positive.

Likewise, with the Triple Blood Test for Down syndrome, most positive results are false, yet the recommendation after receiving a positive test may be to follow up the test with an amniocentesis, a procedure that gives a more definitive diagnosis but has the risk of causing a miscarriage. With some diagnostic tests (such as the PSA test for prostate cancer), testing can detect the disease, but the evidence is unclear about whether early detection has much, if any, effect on life expectancy.

Simulation to Estimate a Probability

Some probabilities are very difficult to find with ordinary reasoning. In such cases, one way to approximate an answer is to simulate. We have carried out simulations in previous chapters, in chapter exercises, and in Activity 1 in this chapter. The steps for a simulation are as follows:

- Identify the random phenomenon to be simulated.
- Describe how to simulate observations of the random phenomenon.
- Carry out the simulation many times.
- Summarize results and state the conclusion.

Example 16

Using the table of random digits

Estimating Probabilities

Picture the Scenario

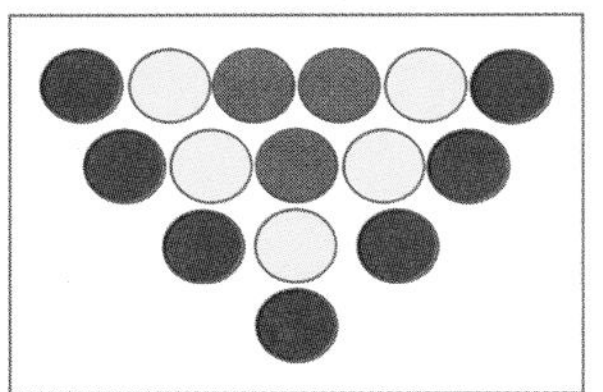

At carnivals and entertainment parks, there is a popular game of horseracing. Each player has a movable horse on the display whose number corresponds to his or her alley number. The game consists of rolling a ball up an alley, where it can land in one of 15 holes. The holes are colored according to the graphic in the margin.

If your ball lands in a red hole, your horse advances one space. If it lands in yellow, your horse advances two spaces, and if it lands in green, your horse

[7] W. Barlow et al., *J. Natl. Cancer Inst.*, 2002, vol. 94, p. 1151.

gallops ahead three spaces. After your ball goes in the hole, it returns to you for your next roll. The first horse that moves 12 spaces is the winner, and the jockey, the person rolling the ball, receives a stuffed animal as a prize.

One customer is at the game, bragging that he always wins after eight rolls.

You look over the game and estimate that you have a 40% chance of getting the ball in a red hole, a 30% chance of getting it in a yellow hole, and a 20% chance of getting it in a green hole. There is also a 10% chance that you miss the holes, and your ball returns to you without advancing the horse.

Question to Explore

Based on your estimates of the probabilities, is it worthwhile to play the game against the bragging customer? What is the chance you will win by the eighth roll?

Think It Through

We proceed according to the following steps:

Step 1: *Identify the random phenomenon to be simulated.* We want to simulate each roll of the ball to determine how far your horse advances. We then want to determine the number of rolls it takes you to win the game.

Step 2: *Describe how to simulate observations of the random phenomenon.* There are a number of ways to simulate. For this example, we will use MINITAB to do the simulation for us. You can use a number of other software programs or apps that will accomplish the same task. Recall that because this is a simulation, the results presented here will likely not match the ones that you get because this process is random.

Start by entering the possible outcomes of the roll of a single ball according to the probability of it occurring. In this example, we could enter 40 rows of Red, 30 of Yellow, 20 of Green, and 10 of Miss. These numbers correspond to the likelihood of each event. However, it will be easier to reduce these numbers to 4 Red, 3 Yellow, 2 Green, and 1 Miss. These numbers of each type also correspond to 40% red, 30% yellow, 20% green, and 10% miss and are easier to enter into MINITAB. You should have a column that looks like the one in the margin.

When you have these values, select one at random. Use the Sample From Columns command in MINITAB to select one

Did You Know?

You can also simulate the rolls by using random numbers from 1 to 10 from *random.org* or the Random Numbers web app. A generated number between 1 and 4 corresponds to red, numbers 5 and 6 to yellow, 8 and 9 to green and a 10 means a miss. ◀

↓	C1-T
	Results
1	Red
2	Red
3	Red
4	Red
5	Yellow
6	Yellow
7	Yellow
8	Green
9	Green
10	Miss

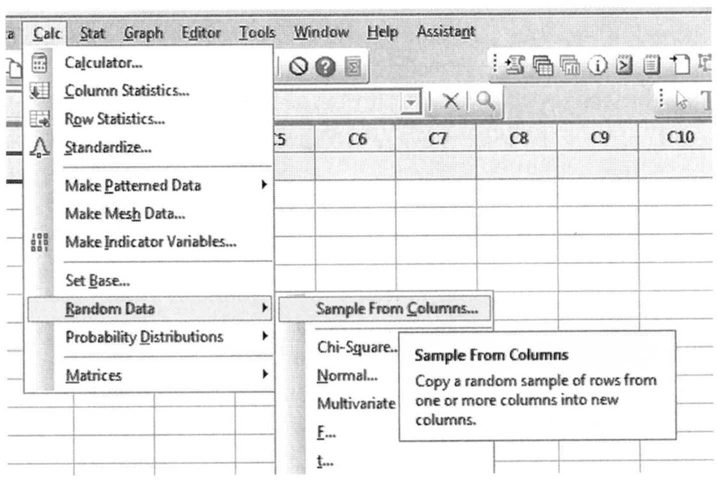

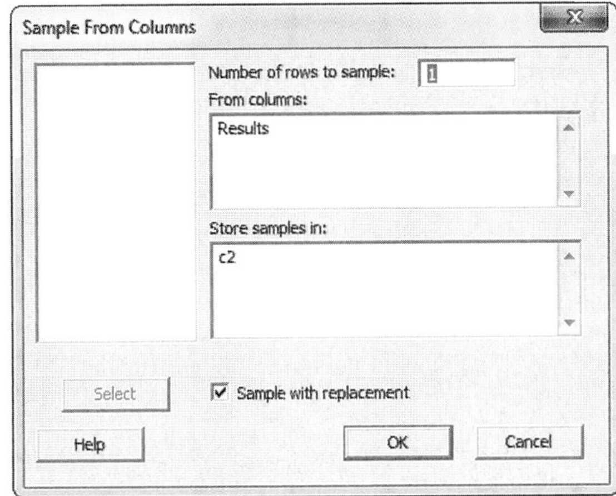

▲ **Figure 5.12** Minitab Screenshots for Sampling.

value at random. Figure 5.12 on the previous page the screens that you should see. The checked Sample With Replacement box is not necessary with only one row to sample. However, if you sample more than one observation at a time, you need to make sure it's selected.

The result of our first simulated roll, which is stored in column C2, was Red. This means that the horse advances one space. Simulate the next roll by using the same procedure. In our simulation, the next result was Yellow, so the horse advances two spaces. It has now moved three spaces. Because this is not yet 12 spaces, the program continues running the race. Continue this process until you have moved at least 12 spaces. The following table demonstrates the results that we obtained by continuing this process.

Roll #	Result	Horse Advances	Horse on Space #
1	Red	1	1
2	Yellow	2	$1 + 2 = 3$
3	Red	1	$3 + 1 = 4$
4	Red	1	$4 + 1 = 5$
5	Miss	0	$5 + 0 = 5$
6	Green	3	$5 + 3 = 8$
7	Red	1	$8 + 1 = 9$
8	Red	1	$9 + 1 = 10$
9	Green	3	$10 + 3 = 13$

Therefore, it took the jockey nine rolls for his horse to win. That is the roll that reached space 12. Unfortunately, you would have lost to the bragging customer, who finished the race after eight rolls, as he stated.

Note: To do this simulation using random.org or the Random Numbers web app, set the maximum to 10 (leave the minimum at the default value of 1) and generate a random number between 1 and 10 by clicking on Generate. If the number is 1, 2, 3, or 4, then the ball lands in a red hole, if it is 5, 6, or 7, then it lands in a yellow hole, if it is 8 or 9, it lands in a green hole, if it is 10, it misses.

Step 3: *Carry out the simulation many times.* In general, the more times you repeat the simulation, the more reliable the estimated result will be. In practice, we can program a computer to assist with the simulation and may want to simulate the random phenomenon thousands, or even hundreds of thousands of times. While learning the underlying ideas of simulation, we will repeat the random phenomenon 20 times to obtain the estimated probability.

If we perform the simulation again, the rolls are, in order, Green, Red, Green, Green, Red, Green. This moves the horse 14 spaces after only six rolls. This is much faster than the nine rolls it took the first time. Notice that you would have lost to the bragging customer the first time but beaten him the second time. You are interested in knowing which of these results are more likely to occur. To accomplish that task, continue the simulation. The following table summarizes these two results as well as 18 more simulations of the horse racing game.

Simulated Game #	# rolls to finish game	Beat 8 rolls?	Simulated Game #	# rolls to finish game	Beat 8 rolls?
1	9	No	11	9	No
2	6	Yes	12	7	Yes
3	6	Yes	13	7	Yes
4	7	Yes	14	7	Yes
5	6	Yes	15	6	Yes
6	7	Yes	16	10	No
7	8	Tie	17	7	Yes
8	7	Yes	18	6	Yes
9	8	Tie	19	7	Yes
10	8	Tie	20	8	Tie

Step 4: *Summarize results and state conclusion.* In 13 of the 20 simulated games, you beat the bragging customer. An estimated probability of beating him is $13/20 = 65\%$. Note, that you tied him 4/20 or 20% of the time and only lost to him $3/20 = 15\%$ of the time.

Insight

Simulation is a powerful tool in that we can estimate probabilities without having to use and understand more complex mathematical probability rules. In fact, many probabilities that are calculated these days in science and business are quite complex and are done using simulations.

If you are not satisfied with the precision of your estimate, you can increase the number of repetitions. Exercise 5.64 explores adding more repetitions. Exercise 5.65 extends this problem by thinking about alternative strategies for playing the game.

▶ ***Try Exercises 5.63 and 5.64***

Probability Is the Key to Statistical Inference

The concepts of probability hold the key to methods for conducting statistical inference–making conclusions about populations by using sample data. To help preview this connection, let's consider an opinion poll. Suppose a poll indicates that 45% of those sampled favor legalized gambling. What's the probability that this sample percentage falls within a certain margin of error, say plus or minus 3%, of the true population percentage? The next two chapters will build on the probability foundation of this chapter and enable us to answer such a question. We will study how to evaluate the probabilities of all the possible outcomes in a survey sample or an experiment. This will then be the basis of the statistical inference methods we'll learn about in Chapters 8–10.

5.4 Practicing the Basics

5.47 Birthdays of presidents Of the first 44 presidents of
TRY the United States (George Washington through Barack Obama), two had the same birthday (Polk and Harding). Is this highly coincidental? Answer by finding the probability of at least one birthday match among 44 people.

5.48 Matching your birthday You consider your birth date to be special since it falls on January 1. Suppose your class has 25 students.

a. Is the probability of finding at least one student with a birthday that matches yours greater, the same, or less than the probability found in Example 13 of a match for at least two students? Explain.

b. Find that probability.

5.49 Lots of pairs Show that with 25 students, there are 300 *pairs* of students who can have the same birthday. So it's really not so surprising if at least two students have the same birthday. (*Hint*: You can pair 24 other students with each student, but how can you make sure you don't count each pair twice?)

5.50 Holes in one at Masters The Augusta National Golf Course in Augusta, Georgia, hosts the Masters Tournament each April. The course consists of four par 3s, ten par 4s, and four par 5s. The par 4s and par 5s are long enough so that no golfer has a realistic chance of getting a hole in one, but the par 3s are each short enough so that the possibility of a hole in one does exist. Over the 75-year history of the tournament, golfers have teed off on par 3s approximately 70,000 times, and a total of 73 holes in one have been recorded. For a given golfer, suppose the probability of getting a hole in one on each of the par 3s at Augusta are as follows:

Hole Number	P(hole in one)
4	0.0005
6	0.0015
12	0.0005
16	0.0025

a. For a randomly selected golfer, find the probability of no holes in one during a round of golf. Assume independence from one hole to the next.

b. For a randomly selected golfer, find the probability of no holes in one during the next 20 rounds of golf. Assume independence from one round to the next.

c. Use your answer in part b to find the probability of making at least one hole in one during the next 20 rounds of golf.

5.51 Corporate bonds A simple way for a company to raise money to fund its operations is by selling corporate bonds. Suppose an investor buys a bond from a company for \$7500. As part of the terms of the bond, the company will repay the investor \$2000 at the end of each of the next five years. It seems like a good deal for the investor; the problem, however, lies in the fact that the company may not be able to afford to make the bond payments. In such a case, the company is said to default on the issue of the bond. Suppose that the probabilities of default in each of the next one-year periods are 0.05, 0.07, 0.07, 0.07, and 0.09 and that defaulting is independent from one year to the next. What is the probability the company does not default during the five-year term of the bond?

5.52 Horrible 11 on 9/11 The digits in 9/11 add up to 11 $(9 + 1 + 1)$, American Airlines flight 11 was the first to hit the World Trade Towers (which took the form of the number 11), there were 92 people on board $(9 + 2 = 11)$, September 11 is the 254th day of the year $(2 + 5 + 4 = 11)$, and there are 11 letters in Afghanistan, New York City, the Pentagon, and George W. Bush (see article by L. Belkin, *New York Times*, August 11, 2002). How could you explain to someone who has not studied probability that, because of the way we look for patterns out of the huge number of things that happen, this is not necessarily an amazing coincidence?

5.53 Coincidence in your life State an event that has happened to you or to someone you know that seems highly coincidental (such as seeing a friend while on vacation). Explain why that event may not be especially surprising, once you think of all the similar types of events that could have happened to you or someone that you know, over the course of several years.

5.54 Monkeys typing Shakespeare Since events of low probability eventually happen if you observe enough trials, a monkey randomly pecking on a typewriter could eventually write a Shakespeare play just by chance. Let's see how hard it would be to type the title of *Macbeth* properly. Assume 50 keys for letters and numbers and punctuation. Find the probability that the first seven letters that a monkey types are macbeth. (Even if the monkey can type 60 strokes a minute and never sleeps, if we consider each sequence of seven keystrokes as a trial, we would wait on the average over 100,000 years before seeing this happen!)

5.55 A *true* coincidence at DisneyWorld Wisconsin has 5.4 million residents. On any given day, the probability is 1/5000 that a randomly selected Wisconsin resident decides to visit DisneyWorld in Florida.

a. Find the probability that they all will decide to go tomorrow, in which case DisneyWorld has more than 5.4 million people in line when it opens in the morning.

b. What assumptions did your solution in part a make? Are they realistic? Explain.

5.56 Rosencrantz and Guildenstern TRY In the opening scene of Tom Stoppard's play *Rosencrantz and Guildenstern Are Dead*, about two Elizabethan contemporaries of Hamlet, Guildenstern flips a coin 91 times and gets a head each time. Suppose the coin was balanced.

a. Specify the sample space for 91 coin flips, such that each outcome in the sample space is equally likely. How many outcomes are in the sample space?

b. Show Guildenstern's outcome for this sample space. Show the outcome in which only the second flip is a tail.

c. What's the probability of the event of getting a head 91 times in a row?

d. What's the probability of at least one tail in the 91 flips?

e. State the probability model on which your solutions in parts c and d are based.

5.57 Mammogram diagnostics TRY Breast cancer is the most common form of cancer in women, affecting about 10% of women at some time in their lives. There is about a 1% chance of having breast cancer at a given time (that is, $P(S) = 0.01$ for the state of having breast cancer at a given time). The chance of breast cancer increases as a woman ages, and the American Cancer Society recommends an annual mammogram after age 40 to test for its presence. Of the women who undergo mammograms at any given time, about 1% are typically estimated to actually have breast cancer. The likelihood of a false test result varies according to the breast density and the radiologist's level of experience. For use of the mammogram to detect breast cancer, typical values reported are sensitivity $= 0.86$ and specificity $= 0.88$.

a. Construct a tree diagram in which the first set of branches shows whether a woman has breast cancer and the second set of branches shows the mammogram result. At the end of the final set of branches, show that $P(S \text{ and } POS) = 0.01 \times 0.86 = 0.0086$ and report the other intersection probabilities also.

b. Restricting your attention to the two paths that have a positive test result, show that $P(POS) = 0.1274$.

c. Of the women who receive a positive mammogram result, what proportion actually have breast cancer?

d. The following tree diagram illustrates how $P(S \mid POS)$ can be so small, using a typical group of 100 women who have a mammogram. Explain how to get the frequencies shown on the branches and why this suggests that $P(S \mid POS)$ is only about 0.08.

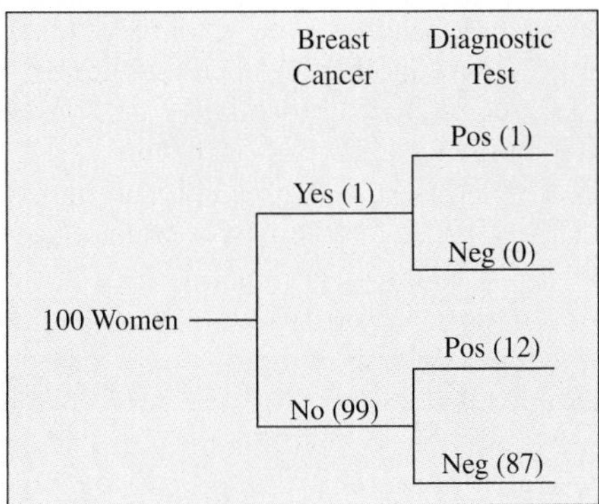

Typical results of mammograms for 100 women

5.58 More screening for breast cancer Refer to the previous exercise. For young women, the prevalence of breast cancer is lower. Suppose the sensitivity is 0.86 and the specificity is 0.88, but the prevalence is only 0.001.

a. Given that a test comes out positive, find the probability that the woman truly has breast cancer.

b. Show how to use a tree diagram with frequencies for a typical sample of 1000 women to explain to someone who has not studied statistics why the probability found in part a is so low.

c. Of the cases that are positive, explain why the proportion in error is likely to be larger for a young population than for an older population.

5.59 Was OJ actually guilty? Former pro football star O. J. Simpson was accused of murdering his wife. In the trial, a defense attorney pointed out that although Simpson had been guilty of earlier spousal abuse, annually only about 40 women are murdered per 100,000 incidents of partner abuse. This means that $P(\text{murdered by partner} \mid \text{partner abuse}) = 40/100{,}000$. More relevant, however, is $P(\text{murdered by partner} \mid \text{partner abuse and women murdered})$. Every year it is estimated that 5 of every 100,000 women in the United States who suffer partner abuse are killed by someone other than their partner (Gigerenzer, 2002, p. 144). Part of a tree diagram is shown starting with 100,000 women who suffer partner abuse.

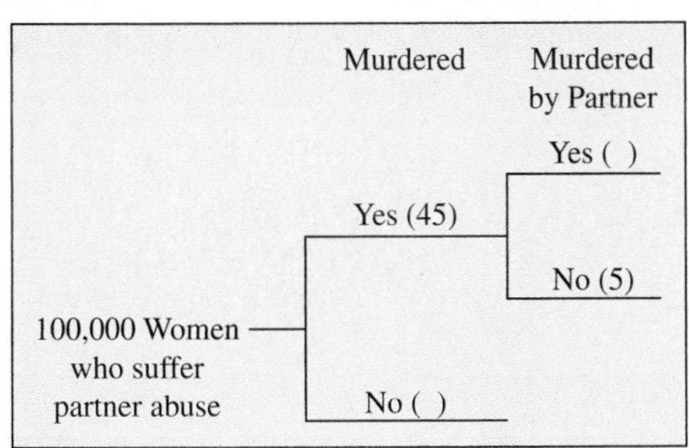

a. Based on the results stated, explain why the numbers 45 and 5 are entered as shown on two of the branches.

b. Fill in the two blanks shown in the tree diagram.

c. Conditional on partner abuse and the woman being murdered (by someone), explain why the probability the woman was murdered by her partner is 40/45. Why is this so dramatically different from $P(\text{murdered by partner} \mid \text{partner abuse}) = 40/100{,}000$?

5.60 Convicted by mistake In criminal trials (e.g., murder, robbery, driving while impaired, etc.) in the United States, it must be proven that a defendant is guilty beyond a reasonable doubt. This can be thought of as a very strong unwillingness to convict defendants who are actually innocent. In civil trials (e.g., breach of contract, divorce hearings for alimony, etc.), it must only be proven by a preponderance of the evidence that a defendant is guilty. This makes it easier to prove a defendant guilty in a civil case than in a murder case. In a high-profile pair of cases in the mid 1990s, O. J. Simpson was found to be not guilty of murder in a criminal case against him. Shortly thereafter, however, he was found guilty in a civil case and ordered to pay damages to the families of the victims.

a. In a criminal trial by jury, suppose the probability the defendant is convicted, given guilt, is 0.95, and the probability the defendant is acquitted, given innocence, is 0.95. Suppose that 90% of all defendants truly are guilty. Given that a defendant is convicted, find the probability he or she was actually innocent. Draw a tree diagram or construct a contingency table to help you answer.

b. Repeat part a, but under the assumption that 50% of all defendants truly are guilty.

c. In a civil trial, suppose the probability the defendant is convicted, given guilt is 0.99, and the probability the defendant is acquitted, given innocence, is 0.75. Suppose that 90% of all defendants truly are guilty. Given that a defendant is convicted, find the probability he or she was actually innocent. Draw a tree diagram or construct a contingency table to help you answer.

5.61 DNA evidence compelling? DNA evidence can be extracted from biological traces such as blood, hair, and saliva. "DNA fingerprinting" is increasingly used in the courtroom as well as in paternity testing. Given that a person is innocent, suppose that the probability of his or her DNA matching that found at the crime scene is only 0.000001, one in a million. Further, given that a person is guilty, suppose that the probability of his or her DNA matching that found at the crime scene is 0.99. Jane Doe's DNA matches that found at the crime scene.

a. Find the probability that Jane Doe is actually innocent, if absolutely her probability of innocence is 0.50. Interpret this probability. Show your solution by introducing notation for events, specifying probabilities that are given, and using a tree diagram to find your answer.

b. Repeat part a if the unconditional probability of innocence is 0.99. Compare results.

c. Explain why it is very important for a defense lawyer to explain the difference between $P(\text{DNA match} \mid \text{person innocent})$ and $P(\text{person innocent} \mid \text{DNA match})$.

5.62 Triple Blood Test Example 8 about the Triple Blood Test for Down syndrome found the results shown in the table on next column.

	Blood Test		
Down	**POS**	**NEG**	**Total**
Yes	48	6	**54**
No	1307	3921	**5228**
Total	**1355**	**3927**	**5282**

a. Estimate the probability that Down syndrome occurs (Down = Yes).

b. Find the estimated (i) sensitivity and (ii) specificity.

c. Find the estimated (i) $P(\text{Yes} \mid \text{POS})$ and (ii) $P(\text{No} \mid \text{NEG})$. (Note: These probabilities are the predictive values.)

d. Explain how the probabilities in parts b and c give four ways of describing the probability that a diagnostic test makes a correct decision.

5.63 Simulating donations to local blood bank The director of a local blood bank is in need of a donor with type AB blood. The distribution of blood types for Americans is estimated by the American Red Cross to be

Type	A	B	O	AB
Probability	40%	10%	45%	5%

The director decides that if more than 20 donors are required before the first donor with AB blood appears, she will need to issue a special appeal for AB blood.

a. Conduct a simulation 10 times, using the Random Numbers web app accessible on the book's website or a calculator or software, to estimate the probability this will happen. Show all steps of the simulation, including any assumptions that you make. Refer to Example 16 as a model for carrying out this simulation.

b. In practice, you would do at least 1000 simulations to estimate this probability well. You'd then find that the probability of exceeding 20 donors before finding a type AB donor is 0.36. Actually, simulation is not needed. Show how to find this probability by using the methods of this chapter.

5.64 Probability of winning In Example 16, we estimated the probability of winning the game was 0.65.

a. If you conducted another 20 simulations of this game, what probability of winning would you expect to get?

b. The simulation in the example consisted of 20 repetitions. Conduct another 80 repetitions, for a total of 100. What is the estimated probability based on these 100 repetitions? (We know that as the number of repetitions increases, the estimated probability of winning will get closer to the actual probability of winning.)

5.65 Probability of winning In Example 16, we explored the number of rolls it takes to win the game. In reality, it's not the number of rolls but rather the time it takes to move 12 spaces that dictates who wins the game. Consider two alternative strategies for playing the game. The first strategy, let's call it the aiming strategy, uses the probabilities given in Example 16 and takes 4 seconds to roll each ball. A second strategy is to roll the ball in rapid succession. The rapid-succession strategy takes only 3 seconds to roll each ball; however, the probabilities of landing in the holes become 50% for red, 20% for yellow, 10% for green, and 20% for no holes.

a. Using the results of the simulations from Example 16, calculate the time to finish each game, using the aiming strategy. Assuming that your competitor also takes 4 seconds per roll, determine whether you beat him for each race. Estimate the probability of beating him.

b. Using the rapid-succession strategy, simulate another 20 games. For each one, calculate the time to finish the race and determine whether you would beat the competitor. (The competitor continues to use the aiming strategy, taking 4 seconds per roll.) Estimate the probability of beating him by using this strategy.

c. Which strategy should you choose to maximize your chance of beating the competitor?

Chapter Review

ANSWERS TO THE CHAPTER FIGURE QUESTIONS

Figure 5.1 The cumulative proportion after each roll is evaluated as the frequency of 6s rolled through that trial (roll) divided by the total number of trials (rolls). The cumulative proportions are $1/1 = 1$ for roll 1, $1/2 = 0.50$ for roll 2, $2/3 = 0.67$ for roll 3, and $2/4 = 0.50$ for roll 4.

Figure 5.2 It should be very, very close to 1/2.

Figure 5.3 $2 \times 2 \times 2 \times 2 = 16$ branches.

Figure 5.4 Venn diagrams will vary. One possible Venn diagram follows.

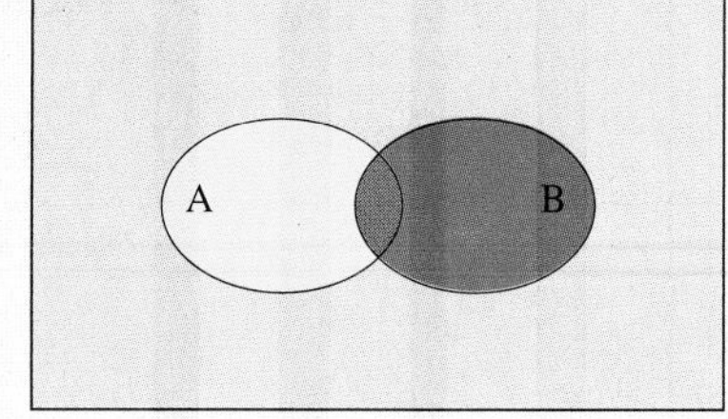

Figure 5.5 The favorable outcomes to the event that the student answers the first question correctly are {CCC,CCI,CIC,CII} This event is not disjoint from either of the two labeled events in the Venn diagram.

Figure 5.6 $P(A \text{ or } B) = P(A) + P(B) - P(A \text{ and } B)$

Figure 5.7 $P(A \text{ or } B) = P(A) + P(B)$ when the events A and B are disjoint.

Figure 5.8 We would not expect the trials to be independent if the student is not guessing. If the student is using prior knowledge, the probability of getting a correct answer on a question, such as question 3, may be more likely if the student answers questions 1 and 2 correctly.

Figure 5.9 $P(A|B)$ is not necessarily equal to $P(B|A)$. They have the same numerator, P(A and B), but different denominators, P(B) and P(A) respectively, which may not be equal.

Figure 5.11 As the prevalence rate increases, of the individuals that test positive, a higher percentage of positive test results will occur with individuals that actually use drugs. For example, if 5% of the population uses drugs, of the 115 individuals out of 1000 that would be expected to test positive, 48 would be actual drug users whereas 67 would not be drug users.

CHAPTER SUMMARY

In this chapter, we've seen how to quantify uncertainty and randomness. With many independent trials of random phenomena, outcomes do show certain regularities. The proportion of times an outcome occurs, in the long run, is its **probability**.

The **sample space** is the set of all possible outcomes of a random phenomenon. An **event** is a subset of the sample space. Two events A and B are **disjoint** if they have no common elements.

We find probabilities by using basic rules:

- The **probability** of each individual outcome falls between 0 and 1, and the total of all the individual probabilities equals 1.
- The **probability of an event** is the sum of the probabilities of individual outcomes in that event.
- For an event A and its **complement** $\mathbf{A^c}$ (the outcomes not in A),
$$P(A^c) = 1 - P(A).$$
- $P(A \text{ or } B) = P(A) + P(B) - P(A \text{ and } B)$. This simplifies to $P(A \text{ or } B) = P(A) + P(B)$ when the events are disjoint.
- $P(A \text{ and } B) = P(A) \times P(B|A)$, where $P(B|A)$ denotes the **conditional probability** of event B, given that event A occurs. Equivalently, the conditional probability satisfies
$$P(B|A) = \frac{P(A \text{ and } B)}{P(A)}.$$
- Likewise, $P(A \text{ and } B) = P(B)P(A|B)$, and $P(A|B) = P(A \text{ and } B)/P(B)$.
- When A and B are **independent**, $P(A|B) = P(A)$ and $P(B|A) = P(B)$. Then, also $P(A \text{ and } B) = P(A) \times P(B)$.

A **probability model** states certain assumptions and, based on them, finds the probabilities of events of interest.

Understanding probability helps us to make informed decisions in our lives. In the next four chapters, we'll see how an understanding of probability gives us the basis for making statistical inferences about a population.

SUMMARY OF NEW NOTATION IN CHAPTER 5

A, B, C	Events
A^c	Complement of event A (the outcomes *not* in A)
P(A)	Probability of event A
$P(A\|B)$	Conditional probability of event A, given event B (| denotes "given")

CHAPTER PROBLEMS

Practicing the Basics

5.66 Peyton Manning completions As of the end of the 2010 NFL season, Indianapolis Colts quarterback Peyton Manning, throughout his 13-year career, completed 65% of all of his pass attempts. Suppose the probability each pass attempted in the next season has probability 0.65 of being completed.

a. Does this mean that if we watch Manning throw 100 times in the upcoming season, he would complete exactly 65 passes? Explain.

b. Explain what this probability means in terms of observing him over a longer period, say for 1000 passes over the course of the next two seasons, assuming Manning is still at his typical playing level. Would it be surprising if his completion percentage over a large number of passes differed significantly from 65%?

5.67 Due for a boy? A couple has five children, all girls. They are expecting a sixth child. The father tells a friend that by the law of large numbers the chance of a boy is now much greater than 1/2. Comment on the father's statement.

5.68 P(life after death) Explain the difference between the relative frequency and subjective definitions of probability. Illustrate by explaining how it is possible to give a value for (a) the probability of life after death, (b) the probability that in the morning you remember at least one dream that you had in the previous night's sleep, based on what you observe every morning for the next year.

5.69 Choices for lunch For the set lunch at Amelia's Restaurant, customers can select one meat dish, one vegetable, one beverage, and one dessert. The menu offers two meats (beef and chicken), three vegetables (corn, green beans, or potatoes), three beverages (cola, ice tea, or coffee), and one dessert (Amelia's apple pie).

a. Use a tree diagram to list the possible meals and to determine how many there are.

b. In practice, would it be sensible to treat all the outcomes in the sample space as equally likely for the customer selections we'd observe? Why or why not?

5.70 Caught doctoring the books After the major accounting scandals with Enron, a large energy company, the question may be posed, "Was there any way to examine Enron's accounting books to determine if they had been doctored?" One way uses Benford's law, which states that in a variety of circumstances, numbers as varied as populations of small towns, figures in a newspaper or magazine, and tax returns and other business records begin with the digit 1 more often than other digits. This law states that the probabilities for the digits 1 through 9 are approximately:

Digit	1	2	3	4	5	6	7	8	9
Probability	0.30	0.18	0.12	0.10	0.08	0.07	0.06	0.05	0.04

a. If we were to randomly pick one of the digits between 1 and 9 using a random number table or software, what is the probability for each digit?

b. When people attempt to fake numbers, there's a tendency to use 5 or 6 as the initial digit more often than predicted by Benford's law. What is the probability of 5 or 6 as the first digit by (i) Benford's law and (ii) random selection?

5.71 Life after death In a General Social Survey, in response to the question "Do you believe in life after death?" 1455 answered yes and 332 answered no.

a. Based on this survey, estimate the probability that a randomly selected adult in the United States believes in life after death.

b. A married couple is randomly selected. Estimate the probability that both subjects believe in life after death.

c. What assumption did you make in answering part b? Explain why that assumption is probably unrealistic, making this estimate unreliable.

5.72 Death penalty jury In arguing against the death penalty, Amnesty International has pointed out supposed inequities, such as the many times a black person has been given the death penalty by an all-white jury. If jurors are selected randomly from an adult population, find the probability that all 12 jurors are white when the population is (a) 90% white and (b) 50% white.

5.73 Driver's exam Three 15-year-old friends with no particular background in driver's education decide to take the written part of the Georgia Driver's Exam. Each exam was graded as a pass (P) or a failure (F).

a. How many outcomes are possible for the grades received by the three friends together? Using a tree diagram, list the sample space.

b. If the outcomes in the sample space in part a are equally likely, find the probability that all three pass the exam.

c. In practice, the outcomes in part a are not equally likely. Suppose that statewide 70% of 15-year-olds pass the exam. If these three friends were a random sample of their age group, find the probability that all three pass.

d. In practice, explain why probabilities that apply to a random sample are not likely to be valid for a sample of three friends.

5.74 Independent on coffee? Students in a geography class are asked whether they've visited Europe in the past 12 months and whether they've flown on a plane in the past 12 months.

a. For a randomly selected student, would you expect these events to be independent or dependent? Explain.

b. How would you explain to someone who has never studied statistics what it means for these events to be either independent or dependent?

c. Students in a different class were asked whether they've visited Italy in the past 12 months and whether they've visited France in the past 12 months. For a randomly selected student, would you expect these events to be independent or dependent? Explain.

d. Students in yet another class were asked whether they've been to a zoo in the past 12 months and whether they drink coffee. For a randomly selected student, would you expect these events to be independent or dependent? Explain.

e. If you had to rank the pairs of events in parts a, c, and d in terms of the strength of any dependence, which pair of events is most dependent? Least dependent?

5.75 Health insurance According to a 2006 census bureau report, 59% of Americans have private health insurance, 25% have government health insurance (Medicare or Medicaid or military health care), and 16% have no health insurance.

a. Estimate the probability that a patient has health insurance.

b. Given that a subject has health insurance, estimate the probability it is private.

5.76 Teens and drugs In August 2006 the Center on Addiction and Substance Abuse (CASA) at Columbia University reported results of a survey of 1297 teenagers about their views on the use of illegal substances. Twenty percent of the teens surveyed reported going to clubs for music or dancing at least once a month. Of them, 26% said drugs were usually available at these club events. Which of these percentages estimates a conditional probability? For each that does, identify the event conditioned on and the event to which the probability refers.

5.77 Teens and parents In the CASA teen survey described in the previous exercise, 33% of teens reported that parents are never present at parties they attend. Thirty-one percent of teens who say parents are never present during parties report that marijuana is available at the parties they attend, compared to only 1% of teens who say parents are present at parties reporting that marijuana is available at the parties they attend.

a. Which of these percentages estimates a conditional probability? For each that does, identify the event conditioned on and the event to which the probability refers.

b. For the variables parents present (yes or no) and marijuana available (yes or no), construct a contingency table showing counts for the 1297 teenagers surveyed.

c. Using the contingency table, given that marijuana is not available at the party, estimate the probability that parents are present.

5.78 **Laundry detergent** A manufacturer of laundry detergent has introduced a new product that it claims to be more environmentally sound. An extensive survey gives the percentages shown in the table.

Result of Advertising for New Laundry Product

	Tried the New Product	
Advertising Status	**Yes**	**No**
Seen the ad	10%	25%
Have not seen ad	5%	60%

a. Estimate the probability that a randomly chosen consumer would have seen advertising for the new product and tried the product.

b. Given that a randomly chosen consumer has seen the product advertised, estimate the probability that the person has tried the product.

c. Let A be the event that a consumer has tried the product. Let B be the event that a consumer has seen the product advertised. Express the probabilities found in parts a and b in terms of A and B.

d. Are A and B independent? Justify your answer.

5.79 **Board games and dice** A board game requires players to roll a pair of balanced dice for each player's turn. Denote the outcomes by (die 1, die 2), such as (5, 3) for a 5 on die 1 and a 3 on die 2.

a. List the sample space of the 36 possible outcomes for the two dice.

b. Let A be the event that you roll doubles (that is, each die has the same outcome). List the outcomes in A and find its probability.

c. Let B be the event that the sum on the pair of dice is 7. Find P(B).

d. Find the probability of (i) A and B, (ii) A or B, and (iii) B given A.

e. Are events A and B independent, disjoint, or neither? Explain.

5.80 **Roll two more dice** Refer to the previous exercise. Define event D as rolling an odd sum with two dice.

a. B denotes a sum of 7 on the two dice. Find P(B and D). When an event B is contained within an event D, as here, explain why P(B and D) = P(B).

b. Find P(B or D). When an event B is contained within an event D, explain why P(B or D) = P(D).

5.81 **Conference dinner** Of the participants at a conference, 50% attended breakfast, 90% attended dinner, and 40% attended both breakfast and dinner. Given that a participant attended breakfast, find the probability that she also attended dinner.

5.82 **Waste dump sites** A federal agency is deciding which of two waste dump projects to investigate. A top administrator estimates that the probability of federal law violations is 0.30 at the first project and 0.25 at the second project. Also, he believes the occurrences of violations in these two projects are disjoint.

a. What is the probability of federal law violations in the first project or in the second project?

b. Given that there is not a federal law violation in the first project, find the probability that there is a federal law violation in the second project.

c. In reality, the administrator confused disjoint and independent, and the events are actually independent. Answer parts a and b with this correct information.

5.83 **A dice game** Consider a game in which you roll two dice, and you win if the total is 7 or 11 and you lose if the total is 2, 3, or 12. You keep rolling until one of these totals occurs. Using conditional probability, find the probability that you win.

5.84 **No coincidences** Over time, you have many conversations with a friend about your favorite actress, favorite musician, favorite book, favorite TV show, and so forth for 100 topics. On any given topic, there's only a 0.02 probability that you agree. If you did agree on a topic, you would consider it to be coincidental.

a. If whether you agree on any two topics are independent events, find the probability that you and your friend *never* have a coincidence on these 100 topics.

b. Find the probability that you have a coincidence on at least one topic.

5.85 **Amazing roulette run?** A roulette wheel in Monte Carlo has 18 even-numbered slots, 18 odd-numbered slots, a slot numbered zero, and a double zero slot. On August 18, 1913, it came up even 26 times in a row.[8] As more and more evens occurred, the proportion of people betting on an odd outcome increased because they figured it was due.

a. Comment on this strategy.

b. Find the probability of 26 evens in a row if each slot is equally likely.

c. Suppose that over the past 100 years there have been 1000 roulette wheels, each being used hundreds of times a day. Is it surprising if sometime in the previous 100 years one of these wheels had 26 evens in a row? Explain.

5.86 **Death penalty and false positives** For the decision about whether to convict someone charged with murder and give the death penalty, consider the variables reality (defendant innocent, defendant guilty) and decision (convict, acquit).

a. Explain what the two types of errors are in this context.

b. Jurors are asked to convict a defendant if they feel the defendant is guilty beyond a reasonable doubt. Suppose this means that given the defendant is executed, the probability that he or she truly was guilty is 0.99. For

[8] *What Are the Chances?* by B. K. Holland (Johns Hopkins University Press, 2002, p. 10).

the 1234 people put to death from the time the death penalty was reinstated in 1977 until December 2010, find the probability that (i) they were all truly guilty, and (ii) at least one of them was actually innocent.

c. How do the answers in part b change if the probability of true guilt is actually 0.95?

5.87 **Screening smokers for lung cancer** An article about using a diagnostic test (helical computed tomography) to screen adult smokers for lung cancer warned that a negative test may cause harm by providing smokers with false reassurance, and a false-positive test results in an unnecessary operation opening the smoker's chest (Mahadevia et al., *JAMA*, vol. 289, pp. 313–322, 2003). Explain what false negatives and false positives mean in the context of this diagnostic test.

5.88 **Screening for heart attacks** Biochemical markers are used by emergency room physicians to aid in diagnosing patients who have suffered acute myocardial infarction (AMI), or what's commonly referred to as a heart attack. One type of biochemical marker used is creatine kinase (CK). Based on a review of published studies on the effectiveness of these markers (by E. M. Balk et al., *Annals of Emergency Medicine*, vol. 37, pp. 478–494, 2001), CK had an estimated sensitivity of 37% and specificity of 87%. Consider a population having a prevalence rate of 25%.

a. Explain in context what is meant by the sensitivity equaling 37%.

b. Explain in context what is meant by the specificity equaling 87%.

c. Construct a tree diagram for this diagnostic test. Label the branches with the appropriate probabilities.

5.89 **Screening for colorectal cancer** Gigerenzer (2002, p. 105) reported that on the average, "Thirty out of every 10,000 people have colorectal cancer. Of these 30 people with colorectal cancer, 15 will have a positive hemoccult test. Of the remaining 9,970 people without colorectal cancer, 300 will still have a positive hemoccult test."

a. Sketch a tree diagram or construct a contingency table to display the counts.

b. Of the 315 people mentioned who have a positive hemoccult test, what proportion actually have colorectal cancer? Interpret.

5.90 **Color blindness** For genetic reasons, color blindness is more common in men than women: 5 in 100 men and 25 in 10,000 women suffer from color blindness.

a. Define events and identify in words these proportions as conditional probabilities.

b. If the population is half male and half female, what proportion of the population is color blind? Use a tree diagram or contingency table with frequencies to portray your solution, showing what you would expect to happen with 20,000 people.

c. Given that a randomly chosen person is color blind, what's the probability that person is female? Use the tree diagram or table from part b to find the answer.

5.91 **HIV testing** For a combined ELISA-Western blot blood test for HIV positive status, the sensitivity is about 0.999 and the specificity is about 0.9999 (Gigerenzer 2002, pp. 124, 126).

a. Consider a high-risk group in which 10% are truly HIV positive. Construct a tree diagram to summarize this diagnostic test.

b. Display the intersection probabilities from part a in a contingency table.

c. A person from this high-risk group has a positive test result. Using the tree diagram or the contingency table, find the probability that this person is truly HIV positive.

d. Explain why a positive test result is more likely to be in error when the prevalence is lower. Use tree diagrams or contingency tables with frequencies for 10,000 people with 10% and 1% prevalence rates to illustrate your arguments.

5.92 **Prostate cancer** A study of the PSA blood test for diagnosing prostate cancer in men (by R. M. Hoffman et al., *BMC Family Practice*, vol. 3, p. 19, 2002) used a sample of 2620 men who were 40 years and older. When a positive diagnostic test result was defined as a PSA reading of at least 4, the sensitivity was estimated to be 0.86 but the specificity only 0.33.

a. Suppose that 10% of those who took the PSA test truly had prostate cancer. Given that the PSA was positive, use a tree diagram and/or contingency table to estimate the probability that the man truly had prostate cancer.

b. Illustrate your answer in part a by using a tree diagram or contingency table with frequencies showing what you would expect for a typical sample of 1000 men.

c. Lowering the PSA boundary to 2 for a positive result changed the sensitivity to 0.95 and the specificity to 0.20. Explain why, intuitively, if the cases increase for which a test is positive, the sensitivity will go up but the specificity will go down.

5.93 **U Win** A fast-food chain is running a promotion to try to increase sales. Each customer who purchases a meal combo receives a game piece that contains one of the letters U, W, I, or N. If a player collects one of all four letters, that player is the lucky winner of a free milkshake. Suppose that of all game pieces, 10% contain the letter U, 30% contain W, 30% contain I, and 30% contain N. Use the table of random digits to estimate the probability that you will collect enough game pieces with your next five combo meal purchases to receive the free shake. Clearly describe the steps of your simulation. Your simulation should consist of at least 20 repetitions.

5.94 **Win again** Exercise 5.65 discussed how to use simulation and the table of random digits to estimate an *expected* value. Referring to the previous exercise, conduct a simulation consisting of at least 20 repetitions to estimate the expected number of combo meals one would need to purchase to win the free shake. Clearly describe the steps of your simulation.

Concepts and Investigations

5.95 Simulate law of large numbers Using the Random Numbers web app (or other software), simulate the flipping of balanced and biased coins.

TECH

a. Report the proportion of heads after (i) 10 flips, (ii) 100 flips, (iii) 1000 flips, and (iv) 10,000 flips. (Select the Coin Flips tab in the app. You can read off the proportions from the graph that appears after you press Simulate in each case.) Explain how the results illustrate the law of large numbers and the long-run relative frequency definition of probability.

b. Use the Random Numbers web app to simulate the roll of 3 or 4 with a die, using (i) 10 rolls, (ii) 100 rolls, (iii) 1000 rolls, and (iv) 10,000 rolls. (Hint: What is the probability of rolling a 3 or 4? Use this to set up a biased coin, where you identify rolling a 3 or 4 as flipping a head.) Summarize results.

5.96 Illustrate probability terms with scenarios

a. What is a sample space? Give an example of a sample space for a scenario involving (i) a designed experiment and (ii) an observational study.

b. What are disjoint events? Give an example of two events that are disjoint.

c. What is a conditional probability? Give an example of two events in your everyday life that you would expect to be (i) independent and (ii) dependent.

5.97 Short term versus long run Short-term aberrations do not affect the long run. To illustrate, suppose that you flip a coin 10 times and you get 10 heads. Find the cumulative proportion of heads, including these first 10 flips, if (a) in the 100 flips after those 10 you get 50 heads (so there are now 60 heads in 110 flips), (b) in the 1000 flips after those 10 you get 500 heads, and (c) in the 10,000 flips after those 10 you get 5000 heads. What number is the cumulative proportion tending toward as n increases?

5.98 Risk of space shuttle After the Columbia space shuttle disaster, a former NASA official who faulted the way the agency dealt with safety risk warned (in an AP story, March 7, 2003) that NASA workers believed, "If I've flown 20 times, the risk is less than if I've flown just once."

a. Explain why it would be reasonable for someone to form this belief from the way we use empirical evidence and margins of error to estimate an unknown probability.

b. Explain a criticism of this belief, using coin flipping as an analogy.

5.99 Mrs. Test Mrs. Test (see www.mrstest.com) sells diagnostic tests for various conditions. Its website gives only imprecise information about the accuracy of the tests. The test for pregnancy is said to be "over 99% accurate." Describe at least four probabilities to which this could refer.

5.100 Marijuana leads to heroin? Nearly all heroin addicts have used marijuana sometime in their lives. So, some argue that marijuana should be illegal because marijuana users are likely to become heroin addicts. Use a Venn diagram to illustrate the fallacy of this argument by sketching sets for M = marijuana use and H = heroin use such that $P(M|H)$ is close to 1 but $P(H|M)$ is close to 0.

5.101 Stay in school Suppose 80% of students finish high school. Of them, 50% finish college. Of them, 20% get a masters' degree. Of them, 30% get a Ph.D.

a. What percentage of students get a Ph.D.?

b. Explain how your reasoning in part a used a multiplication rule with conditional probabilities.

c. Given that a student finishes college, find the probability of getting a Ph.D.

5.102 How good is a probability estimate? In Example 8 about Down syndrome, we estimated the probability of a positive test result (predicting that Down syndrome is present) to be $P(POS) = 0.257$, based on observing 1355 positive results in 5282 observations. How good is such an estimate? From Section 4.2, $1/\sqrt{n}$ is an approximate margin of error in estimating a proportion with n observations.

a. Find the approximate margin of error to describe how well this proportion estimates the true probability, P(POS).

b. The *long run* in the definition of probability refers to letting n get very large. What happens to this margin of error formula as n keeps growing, eventually toward infinity? What's the implication of this?

5.103 Protective bomb Before the days of high security at airports, there was a legendary person who was afraid of traveling by plane because someone on the plane might have a bomb. He always brought a bomb himself on any plane flight he took, believing that the chance would be astronomically small that two people on the same flight would both have a bomb. Explain the fallacy in his logic, using ideas of independent events and conditional probability.

5.104 Streak shooter Sportscaster Maria Coselli claims that players on the New York Knicks professional basketball team are streak shooters. To make her case, she looks at the statistics for all the team's players over the past three games and points out that one of them (Joe Smith) made six shots in a row at one stage. Coselli argues, "Over a season, Smith makes only 45% of his shots. The probability that he would make six in a row if the shots were independent is $(0.45)^6 = 0.008$, less than one in a hundred. This would be such an unusual occurrence that we can conclude that Smith is a streak shooter."

a. Explain the flaws in Coselli's logic.

b. Use this example to explain how some things that look highly coincidental may not be so when viewed in a wider context.

Problems 5.105–5.109 may have more than one correct answer.

5.105 Multiple choice Choose ALL correct responses. For two events A and B, $P(A) = 0.5$ and $P(B) = 0.2$. Then P(A or B) equals

a. 0.10, if A and B are independent

b. 0.70, if A and B are independent

c. 0.60, if A and B are independent

d. 0.70, if A and B are disjoint

5.106 Multiple choice Which of the following is always true?

a. If A and B are independent, then they are also disjoint.

b. $P(A|B) + P(A|B^c) = 1$

c. If $P(A|B) = P(B|A)$, then A and B are independent.

d. If A and B are disjoint, then A and B cannot occur at the same time.

5.107 Multiple choice: Coin flip A balanced coin is flipped 100 times. By the law of large numbers:

a. There will almost certainly be *exactly* 50 heads and 50 tails.

b. If we got 100 heads in a row, almost certainly the next flip will be a tail.

c. For the 100 flips, the probability of getting 100 heads equals the probability of getting 50 heads.

d. It is absolutely impossible to get a head every time.

e. None of the above.

5.108 Multiple choice: Dream come true You have a dream in which you see your favorite movie star in person. The very next day, you are visiting Manhattan and you see her walking down Fifth Avenue.

a. This is such an incredibly unlikely coincidence that you should report it to your local newspaper.

b. This is somewhat unusual, but given the many dreams you could have in your lifetime about people you know or know of, it is not an incredibly unlikely event.

c. If you had not had the dream, you would definitely not have seen the film star the next day.

d. This proves the existence of ESP.

5.109 Multiple choice: Comparable risks Mammography is estimated to save about 1 life in every 1000 women. "Participating in annual mammography screening ... has roughly the same effect on life expectancy as reducing the distance one drives each year by 300 miles" (Gigerenzer 2002, pp. 60, 73). Which of the following do you think has the closest effect on life expectancy as that of smoking throughout your entire life?

a. Taking a commercial airline flight once a year

b. Driving about ten times as far every year as the average motorist

c. Drinking a cup of coffee every day

d. Eating a fast-food hamburger once a month

e. Never having a mammogram (if you are a woman)

5.110 True or false Answer true of false for each part.

a. When you flip a coin ten times, you are more likely to get *the* sequence HHHHHTTTTT than the sequence HHHHHHHHHH.

b. When you flip a coin ten times, you are more likely to get *a* sequence that contains five heads than a sequence that contains ten heads.

5.111 True or false When you flip a balanced coin twice, three things can happen: 0 heads, 1 head, or 2 heads. Since there are three possible outcomes, they each have probability 1/3. (This was claimed by the French mathematician, Jean le Rond d' Alembert, in 1754. To reason this, write down the sample space for the possible sequence of results for the two flips.)

5.112 Driving versus flying In the United States in 2002, about 43,000 people died in auto crashes and 0 people died in commercial airline accidents. G. Gigerenzer (2002, p. 31) states, "The terrorist attack on September 11, 2001, cost the lives of some 3,000 people. The subsequent decision of millions to drive rather than fly may have cost the lives of many more." Explain the reasoning behind this statement.

5.113 Prosecutor's fallacy An eyewitness to the crime says that the person who committed it was male, between 15 and 20 years old, Hispanic, and drove a blue Honda. The prosecutor points out that a proportion of only 0.001 people living in that city match all those characteristics, and one of them is the defendant. Thus, the prosecutor argues that the probability that the defendant is not guilty is only 0.001. Explain what is wrong with this logic. (*Hint:* Is $P(\text{match}) = P(\text{not guilty}|\text{match})$?)

5.114 ◆◆ **Generalizing the addition rule** For events A, B, and C such that each pair of events is disjoint, use a Venn diagram to explain why

$$P(A \text{ or } B \text{ or } C) = P(A) + P(B) + P(C).$$

5.115 ◆◆ **Generalizing the multiplication rule** For events A, B, and C, explain why $P(A \text{ and } B \text{ and } C) =$

$$P(A) \times P(B|A) \times P(C|A \text{ and } B).$$

5.116 ◆◆ **Bayes' rule** Suppose we know $P(A), P(B|A)$, and $P(B^c|A^c)$, but we want to find $P(A|B)$.

a. Using the definition of conditional probability for $P(A|B)$ and for $P(B|A)$, explain why $P(A|B) = P(A \text{ and } B)/P(B) = [P(A)P(B|A)]/P(B)$.

b. Splitting the event that B occurs into two parts, according to whether A occurs, explain why

$$P(B) = P(B \text{ and } A) + P(B \text{ and } A^c).$$

c. Using part b and the definition of conditional probability, explain why

$$P(B) = P(A)P(B|A) + P(A^c)P(B|A^c).$$

d. Combining what you have shown in parts a–c, reason that

$$P(A|B) = \frac{P(A)P(B|A)}{P(A)P(B|A) + P(A^c)P(B|A^c)}.$$

This formula is called **Bayes' rule**. It is named after a British clergyman who discovered the formula in 1763.

Student Activities

5.117 Simulating matching birthdays (TECH) Do you find it hard to believe that the probability of at least one birthday match in a class of 25 students is 0.57? Let's simulate the answer. Using the Random Numbers web app accessible from the book's website, each student in the class should simulate

25 numbers between 1 and 365. Observe whether there is at least one match of two numbers out of the 25 simulated numbers.

a. Combine class results. What proportion of the simulations had at least one birthday match?

b. Repeat part a for a birthday match in a class of 50 students. Again, combine class results. What is the simulated probability of at least one match?

5.118 Simulate table tennis In table tennis, the first person to get at least 21 points while being ahead of the opponent by at least two points wins the game. In games between you and an opponent, suppose successive points are independent and that the probability of your winning any given point is 0.40.

TECH

a. Do you have any reasonable chance to win a game? Showing all steps, simulate two games by generating random numbers between 1 and 10 using the Random Numbers web app accessible from the book's website or other software; let numbers 1–4 represent winning a point and 5–10 losing a point.

b. Combining results for all students in the class, estimate the probability of winning.

5.119 Which tennis strategy is better? A tennis match can consist of the best of three sets (that is, the winner is the first to win two sets) or the best of five sets (the winner is the first to win three sets). Which would you be better off playing if you are the weaker player and have probability 0.40 of winning any particular set?

TECH

a. Simulate 10 matches of each type, using the Random Numbers web app accessible from the book's website or other software. Show the steps of your simulation and specify any assumptions.

b. Combining results for all students in the class, estimate the probability of the weaker player winning the match under each type of match.

5.120 Saving a business The business you started last year has only $5000 left in capital. A week from now, you need to repay a $10,000 loan or you will go bankrupt. You see two possible ways to raise the money you need. You can ask a large company to invest the $10,000, wooing it with the $5000 you have left. You guess your probability of success is 0.20. Or you could ask, in sequence, several small companies each to invest $2000, spending $1000 on each to woo it. You guess your probability of success is 0.20 for each appeal. What's the probability you will raise enough money to repay the loan with each strategy? Which is the better strategy, to be bold with one large bet or to be cautious and use several smaller bets? With the bold strategy, the probability of success is simply 0.20. With the cautious strategy, we need to use simulation to find the probability of success.

TECH

a. Simulate the cautious strategy 10 times using the Random Numbers web app accessible from the book's website or other software. Show the steps of the simulations and specify any assumptions.

b. Combining simulation results for all students in the class, estimate the probability of the cautious strategy being successful.

c. Which strategy would you choose? The bolder strategy or the cautious strategy? Explain.

BIBLIOGRAPHY

Against All Odds: Inside Statistics (1989). Produced by Consortium for Mathematics and Its Applications for PBS. See www.learner.org.

Gigerenzer, G. (2002). *Calculated Risks.* New York: Simon & Schuster.

Wilson, R., and E. A. C. Crouch (2001). *Risk-Benefit Analysis.* Cambridge, MA: Harvard Univ. Press.

CHAPTER

6

In Chapter 2, we introduced variables and studied how to describe their distribution using data from a sample or experiment. In this chapter, we learn how to describe the distribution of a variable in probabilistic terms and introduce two important special cases, the normal and the binomial distribution.

Probability Distributions

Example 1

Gender Discrimination

Picture the Scenario

A 2001 lawsuit by seven female employees claimed that Wal-Mart Stores, Inc. promoted female workers less frequently than male workers. This lawsuit grew into the largest sex-discrimination class-action lawsuit in U.S. history, representing more than 1.5 million current and former female Wal-Mart employees, before it was eventually decided, in 2011, in favor of Wal-Mart by the Supreme Court.[1,2]

Question to Explore

Suppose that 10 individuals are chosen from a large pool of qualifying employees for a promotion program, and the pool has an equal number of female and male employees. When all 10 individuals chosen for promotion are male, the female employees claim that the program is gender-biased. How can we investigate statistically the validity of the women's claim?

Thinking Ahead

Other factors being equal, the probability of selecting a female for promotion is 0.50, as is the probability of selecting a male. If the employees are selected randomly in terms of gender, about half of the employees picked should be females and about half should be male. Due to ordinary sampling variation, however, it need not happen that exactly 50% of those selected are female. A simple analogy is in flipping a coin 10 times. We won't necessarily see exactly 5 heads.

Because none of the 10 employees chosen for promotion is female, we might be inclined to support the women's claim. The question we need to consider is, would these results be unlikely if there were no gender bias? An equivalent question is, if we flip a coin 10 times, would it be very surprising if we got 0 heads?

In this chapter, we'll apply the probability tools of the previous chapter to answer such questions. In Examples 13 and 14, we'll revisit this gender discrimination question. In Example 15, we'll use probability arguments to analyze whether racial profiling may have occurred when police officers make traffic stops.

[1] *Source:* Background information taken from www.reuters.com/article/2010/12/06/us-walmart-lawsuit-discrimination-idUSTRE6B531W20101206.

[2] www.cnn.com/2011/US/06/20/scotus.wal.mart.discrimination/index.html?hpt=hp_t1.

We learned the basics of probability in Chapter 5. We'll next study tables, graphs, and formulas for finding probabilities that will be useful to us for the rest of the book. We'll see how possible outcomes and their probabilities are summarized in a **probability distribution**. Then, we'll study two commonly used probability distributions—the **normal** and the **binomial**. The normal distribution, which has a bell-shaped graph, plays a key role in statistical inference.

6.1 Summarizing Possible Outcomes and Their Probabilities

With proper methods of gathering data, the numerical values that a variable assumes should be the result of some random phenomenon. For example, the randomness may stem from selecting a random sample from a population or performing a randomized experiment. In such cases, we call the variable a **random variable**.

Recall

The characteristics we measure are called **variables** because their values vary from subject to subject. If the possible outcomes are a set of separate numbers, the variable is **discrete** (for example, a variable expressed as "the number of..." with possible values 0, 1, 2,...). If the variable can take any value in an interval, such as the proportion of a tree leaf that shows a fungus (any number between 0 and 1), it is **continuous**. ◀

Random Variable

A **random variable** is a numerical measurement of the outcome of a random phenomenon. Often, the randomness results from the use of random sampling or a randomized experiment to gather the data.

We've used letters near the end of the alphabet, such as x, to symbolize variables. We'll also use letters such as x for the possible value of a random variable. When we refer to the random variable itself, rather than a particular value, we'll use a capital letter, such as X. For instance, X = number of heads in three flips of a coin denotes the random variable, whereas $x = 2$ is one of its possible values as is $x = 3$ or $x = 0$.

Because a random variable refers to the outcome of a random phenomenon, each possible outcome has a specific probability of occurring. The **probability distribution** of a random variable specifies its possible values and their probabilities. An advantage of a variable being a random variable is that it's possible to specify such probabilities. Without randomness, we would not be able to predict the probabilities of the possible outcomes in the long run.

Probability Distributions of Discrete Random Variables

When a random variable has separate possible values, such as 0, 1, 2, 3 for the number of heads in three flips of a coin, it is called **discrete**. The **probability distribution** of a discrete random variable assigns a probability to each possible value. Each probability falls between 0 and 1, and the sum of the probabilities of all possible values equals 1. We let $P(x)$ denote the probability of a possible value x, such as $P(2)$ for the probability that the random variable takes the value 2.

Recall

From Chapter 5, a **probability** is a long-run **proportion**. So, it can take any value in the interval from 0 up to 1. The probabilities for all the possible outcomes add up to 1.0, so that's the sum of the probabilities in a probability distribution. ◀

Probability Distribution of a Discrete Random Variable

A **discrete** random variable X takes a set of separate values (such as 0, 1, 2,...). Its **probability distribution** assigns a probability $P(x)$ to each possible value x.

- For each x, the probability $P(x)$ falls between 0 and 1.
- The sum of the probabilities for all the possible x values equals 1.

For instance, let X be a random number between 1 and 10, selected using software (such as random.org) as part of the process of identifying subjects to include in a random sample. The possible values for X are $x = 1, 2, \ldots, 8, 9, 10$. Each number is equally likely, so the probability distribution is

$$P(1) = P(2) = P(3) = P(4) = P(5) =$$
$$P(6) = P(7) = P(8) = P(9) = P(10) = 0.10.$$

Each probability falls between 0 and 1, and the probabilities add up to 1.0. If X is the outcome of rolling a balanced die, then the possible values for X are $x = 1, 2, 3, 4, 5, 6,$ and $P(1) = P(2) = P(3) = P(4) = P(5) = P(6) = 1/6$ again summing to 1.0.

Random variables can also be **continuous**, having possible values that form an interval rather than a set of separate numbers. We'll learn about continuous random variables and their probability distributions later in this section.

Probability Distribution

Example 2

Best of Seven

Picture the Scenario

Many playoff and championship games in professional sports such as basketball, baseball, or hockey are decided by a best of seven series, in which the team that is the first to get four victories wins the series. This often adds drama because the number of games that actually need to be played is not fixed in advance. Let X represent the number of games needed to determine a winner in a best of 7 series, with possible outcomes 4 (when one teams wins the first four games, called a sweep), 5, 6, or 7. Table 6.1 shows the probability distribution of X when we assume that the chances for either team to win a game are 50% for all games played.

Table 6.1 Probability Distribution of Number of Games Needed to Determine a Winner in a Best of Seven Series

Number of Games x	Probability $P(x)$
4	$1/8 = 0.125$
5	$1/4 = 0.25$
6	$5/16 = 0.3125$
7	$5/16 = 0.3125$

Questions to Explore

a. Why is X a random variable?

b. Show how Table 6.1 satisfies the two properties needed for a probability distribution.

c. What is the probability that a best of seven series will be decided by at least six games?

Think It Through

a. Before the start of the series, we are uncertain just how many games will be necessary to determine a winner. This number will be determined by a random phenomenon, making $X =$ number of games a random variable whose values are determined by chance.

Recall

P(6) denotes the probability that the random variable takes the value 6; that is, the probability that the number of games needed to be played to determine a winner is 6. ◀

b. In Table 6.1, the two conditions in the definition of a probability distribution are satisfied:

(i) For each x, the probability $P(x)$ falls between 0 and 1.

(ii) The sum of the probabilities for all the possible x values equals 1.

c. The probability of at least six games in a best of seven series is

$$P(6) + P(7) = 5/16 + 5/16 = 10/16 = 0.625.$$

Insight

We can display the probability distribution of a discrete random variable with a *graph* and sometimes with a *formula*. Figure 6.1 displays a graph for the probability distribution in Table 6.1.

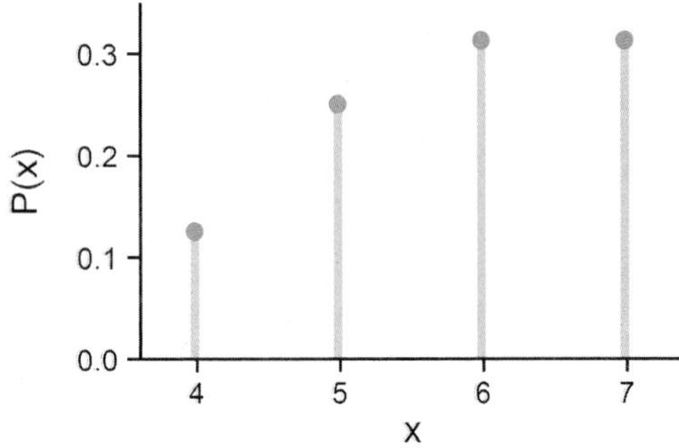

▲ **Figure 6.1 Graph of Probability Distribution of Number of Games Needed to Determine a Winner in a Best of Seven Series.** The line for each possible value of X has a height equal to its probability. **Question** How would you describe the shape of the distribution?

▶ ***Try Exercises 6.1 and 6.2***

In Chapter 2, we used graphs and numerical summaries to describe the three key components, shape, center, and variability, for the distribution of a quantitative variable. These summaries were calculated from observations on the variable obtained from a sample or experiment. For a probability distribution, a graph as in Figure 6.1 shows the shape, but how do we find corresponding summary measures for the center and variability of a probability distribution?

The Mean of a Probability Distribution

To describe characteristics of a probability distribution, we can use any of the numerical summaries defined in Chapter 2. These include mean, median, quartiles, and standard deviation. It is most common to use the *mean* to describe the center and the *standard deviation* to describe the variability.

Recall

Section 1.2 defined a **parameter** to be a numerical summary of the population, such as a population mean or a population proportion. ◀

Recall that numerical summaries of populations are called **parameters**. You can think of a **population distribution** as merely being a type of probability distribution—one that applies for selecting a subject at random from a population. Like numerical summaries of populations, numerical summaries of probability distributions are referred to as **parameters**. Typically, parameters are denoted by Greek letters. The mean of a probability distribution is denoted by μ, and the standard deviation is denoted by σ.

In Words

μ is the Greek letter mu, pronounced "mew." σ is the lowercase Greek letter sigma. The corresponding Roman letter s is used for the standard deviation of *sample* data. Recall that the sample mean is denoted by $\bar{x}$.

Suppose we repeatedly observe values of a random variable, such as repeatedly noting the outcome when we roll a die. The mean μ of the probability distribution for that random variable is the value we would get, in the long run, for the average of those values. This long-run interpretation parallels the interpretation (in Section 5.1) of probability itself as a summary of the long-run behavior of a random phenomenon.

Mean of Probability Distribution

Recall

Table 6.1 shows

Number of Games x	Probability $P(x)$
4	$1/8 = 0.125$
5	$1/4 = 0.25$
6	$5/16 = 0.3125$
7	$5/16 = 0.3125$

Example 3

The Expected Number of Games Played in a Best of Seven Series

Picture the Scenario

Let's refer back to the probability distribution for X = number of games needed to determine a winner in a best of seven series, when we assume the chance for either team to win a game is 50% for all games played. The probability distribution for X is shown again in the margin.

Question to Explore

Find the mean of this probability distribution and interpret it.

Think It Through

Because $P(4) = 1/8$, over the long run we expect $x = 4$ (that is, a sweep) to occur in one-eighth (or 12.5%) of all series played. Likewise, we expect $x = 5$ games are needed to determine a winner in one-fourth (25%) of all series played, $x = 6$ games in 31.25% and $x = 7$ games also in 31.25% of all series played. Over 10,000 series played (i.e., in the long run), we would observe the number 4 about 1,250 times $(10{,}000 \times (1/8) = 1{,}250)$, the number 5 about 2,500 times, and the numbers 6 and 7 each about 3,125 times. Because the mean equals the sum of all observations divided by the total number of observations, we can calculate the mean as

$$\mu = \frac{\overbrace{(4 + 4 + \ldots + 4)}^{\text{1250 terms}} + \overbrace{(5 + 5 + \ldots + 5)}^{\text{2500 terms}} + \overbrace{(6 + 6 + \ldots + 6)}^{\text{3125 terms}} + \overbrace{(7 + 7 + \ldots + 7)}^{\text{3125 terms}}}{10000}$$

$$= \frac{(1250 \times 4) + (2500 \times 5) + (3125 \times 6) + (3125 \times 7)}{10000} = \frac{58125}{10000} = 5.8125$$

The mean of the probability distribution is 5.8125. Under the assumption above (50% chance of winning each game), we'd expect that on average about 5.8 games are needed to determine a winner in a best of seven series.

Insight

Because $1{,}250/10{,}000 = 0.125$, $2{,}500/10{,}000 = 0.25$ and $3{,}125/10{,}000 = 0.3125$, the calculation for the mean has the form

$$\mu = 4 \times \frac{1{,}250}{10{,}000} + 5 \times \frac{2{,}500}{10{,}000} + 6 \times \frac{3{,}125}{10{,}000} + 7 \times \frac{3{,}125}{10{,}000}$$

$$= 4 \times 0.125 + 5 \times 0.25 + 6 \times 0.3125 + 7 \times 0.3125$$

$$= 4 \times P(4) + 5 \times P(5) + 6 \times P(6) + 7 \times P(7).$$

Each possible value x is multiplied by its probability $P(x)$. In fact, for any discrete random variable, the mean of its probability distribution results from multiplying each possible value x by its probability $P(x)$ and then adding up these values.

► ***Try Exercise 6.3***

Did You Know?

In baseball, for the 68 World Series played between 1945 and 2013, 13 ended after 4 games, 12 after 5 games, 15 after 6 games, and 28 needed to go all the way to 7 games. (See Exercise 6.101.) ◄

In Words

To get the **mean** of a probability distribution, multiply each possible value of the random variable by its probability and then add all these products.

Mean of a Discrete Probability Distribution

The **mean of a probability distribution** for a discrete random variable is

$$\mu = \Sigma x\,P(x),$$

where the sum is taken over all possible values of x.

For the number of games played in a best of seven series as we saw in the example,

$$\mu = \Sigma x P(x) = 4P(4) + 5P(5) + 6P(6) + 7P(7)$$
$$= 4(0.125) + 5(0.25) + 6(0.3125) + 7(0.3125) = 5.8125.$$

In Words

A **weighted average** is used when each x value is not equally likely. If a particular x value is more likely to occur, it has a larger influence on the mean, which is the balance point of the distribution.

The mean $\mu = \Sigma x P(x)$ is called a **weighted average**: Values of x that are more likely receive greater weight $P(x)$. It does not make sense to take a simple average of the possible values of x, $(4 + 5 + 6 + 7)/4 = 5.5$, because some outcomes are more likely than others and need to receive more weight.

Consider the special case in which the outcomes are *equally likely* such as the 6 possible outcomes for rolling a die, each occurring with probability 1/6. Then $\mu = \Sigma x P(x) = \Sigma x(1/6) = (1 + 2 + 3 + 4 + 5 + 6)/6 = 3.5$. Here, the formula $\Sigma x P(x)$ reduces to the ordinary mean of the 6 numbers, but this only happens for *equally likely* outcomes, such as the 6 faces of a die. The formula $\mu = \Sigma x P(x)$ for the mean of a probability distribution generalizes the ordinary formula for the mean to allow for outcomes that are not equally likely, such as the number of games played in a best of seven series.

The long-run average of observing some series with 4 games, some with 5 games, some with 6 games and some with 7 games is 5.8125. This can be rounded to 5.8, but rounding it to 6, the closest integer, would be too crude and, as we said, the mean doesn't need to equal any of the possible values.

There is also a general formula for the mean of a *continuous* probability distribution. It involves advanced material from calculus (an integral) so we will not present it here. However, we will discuss the mean for certain special and important continuous probability distributions, such as the normal distribution introduced in Section 6.2 (see also Exercise 6.14).

Recall

Section 2.3 showed how to find the **sample mean** to describe the center of quantitative data. ◀

The mean μ of the probability distribution of a random variable X is also called the **expected value of X**. The expected value reflects not what we'll observe in a *single* observation, but rather what we expect for the *average* in a long run of observations. In the preceding example, the expected value of the number of games played in a best of seven series is $\mu = 5.8125$. As with means of sample data, the mean of a probability distribution doesn't have to be one of the possible values for the random variable.

Example 4

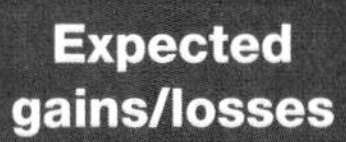

Responding to Risk

Picture the Scenario

Are you a risk-averse person who prefers the sure thing to a risky action that could give you a better or a worse outcome? Or are you a risk taker, willing to gamble in hopes of achieving the better outcome?

Questions to Explore

a. You are given \$1000 to invest. You must choose between (i) a sure gain of \$500, and (ii) a 0.50 chance of a gain of \$1000 and a 0.50 chance to gain nothing. What is the expected gain with each strategy? Which do you prefer?

b. You are given \$2000 to invest. You must choose between (i) a sure loss of \$500, and (ii) a 0.50 chance of losing \$1000 and a 0.50 chance to lose nothing. What is the expected loss with each strategy? Which do you prefer?

Think It Through

a. The expected gain is \$500 with the sure strategy (i), since that strategy has gain \$500 with probability 1.0. With the risk-taking strategy (ii), the probability distribution is shown in the margin. The expected gain is $\mu = \Sigma x P(x) = \$0(0.50) + \$1000(0.50) = \$500$.

Risk-Taking Probability Distribution

Gain x	P(x)
0	0.50
1000	0.50

b. The expected loss is \$500 with the sure strategy (i). With the risk-taking strategy (ii), the expected loss is $\mu = \Sigma x P(x) = \$0(0.50) + \$1000(0.50) = \$500$.

Insight

In each scenario, the expected values are the same with each strategy. Yet most people prefer the sure-gain strategy (i) in scenario a but the risk-taking strategy (ii) in scenario b. They are risk averse in scenario a but risk taking in scenario b. This preference was explored in research by Daniel Kahneman and Amos Tversky, for which Kahneman won the Nobel Prize in 2002.

▶ ***Try Exercise 6.8***

Summarizing the Variability of a Probability Distribution

As with distributions of sample data, it's useful to summarize both the *center* and the *variability* of a probability distribution. For instance, suppose two investment strategies have the same expected payout. Does one strategy have more variability in its payoffs?

The **standard deviation** of a probability distribution, denoted by σ, measures the variability from the mean. Larger values for σ correspond to greater variability. The margin figures show two distributions that have the same mean but different standard deviations. Roughly, σ describes how far values of the random variable fall, on the average, from the expected value of the distribution. We won't deal with the formula for calculating σ until we study particular types of probability distributions in Sections 6.2 and 6.3. (See Exercise 6.95 for the mathematical definition and formula for discrete random variables.)

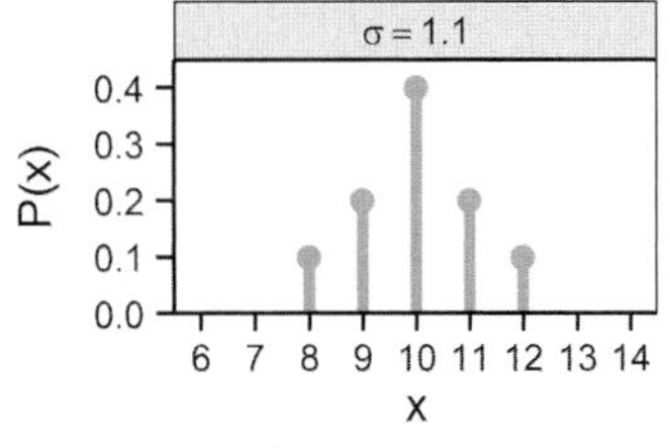

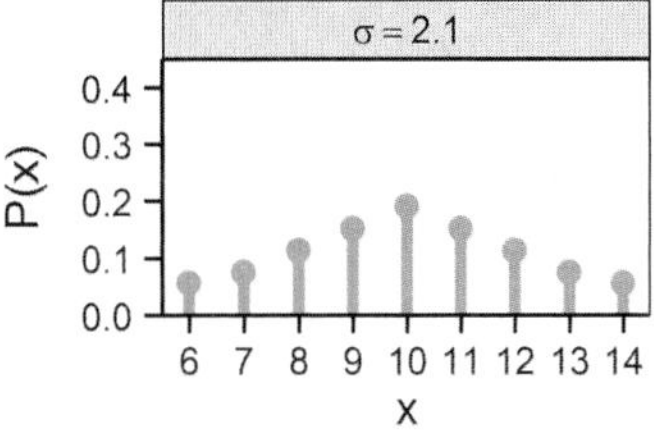

Two probability distributions with the same mean (10) but different standard deviations of 1.1 and 2.1.

Variability of a probability distribution ◀

Example 5

Risk Taking Entails More Variability

Picture the Scenario

Let's revisit the first scenario in Example 4. You are given \$1000 to invest and must choose between (i) a sure gain of \$500 and (ii) a 0.50 chance of a gain of \$1000 and a 0.50 chance to gain nothing. Table 6.2 shows the probability distribution of the gain X for the two strategies.

Table 6.2 Probability Distribution of X = Gain

Sure Strategy		Risk Taking	
x	P(x)	x	P(x)
500	1.0	0	0.50
		1000	0.50

Questions to Explore

Example 4 showed that both strategies have the same expected value, namely \$500. Which of the two probability distributions would have the larger standard deviation?

Think It Through

There is *no* variability for the sure strategy because the gain is always \$500, with no deviation. The standard deviation of this probability distribution is 0, the smallest possible value. With the risk-taking strategy, no matter what the outcome (either \$0 or \$1000), the result will be a distance of \$500 away from the expected value of \$500. In fact, the standard deviation of the probability distribution for the risk-taking strategy is \$500. With that strategy, there's much more variability in what can happen.

Insight

In practice, different investment strategies are often compared by their variability. Not only is an investor interested in the expected return of an investment but also the consistency of the yield in the investment from year to year as measured by the standard deviation.

► ***Try Exercises 6.9 and 6.10***

Did You Know?

In finance, the symbol *sigma* is used to describe the volatility (= variability in the price) of financial instruments like stocks. It is one of the standard indicators printed in stock quotes. ◄

Probability Distributions of Categorical Variables

In examples so far, variables have been quantitative rather than categorical. Partly this is because a random variable is defined to be a *numerical* measurement of the outcome of a random phenomenon. However, we'll see that for categorical variables having only two categories, it's often useful to represent the two possible outcomes by the numerical values 0 and 1.

For example, suppose you've conducted a marketing survey of many potential customers to estimate the probability a customer would buy a new product you are developing. Your study estimates that the probability is 0.20. If you denote the possible outcomes (success, failure) for whether a customer buys the product by (1, 0), then the probability distribution of X for the outcome is

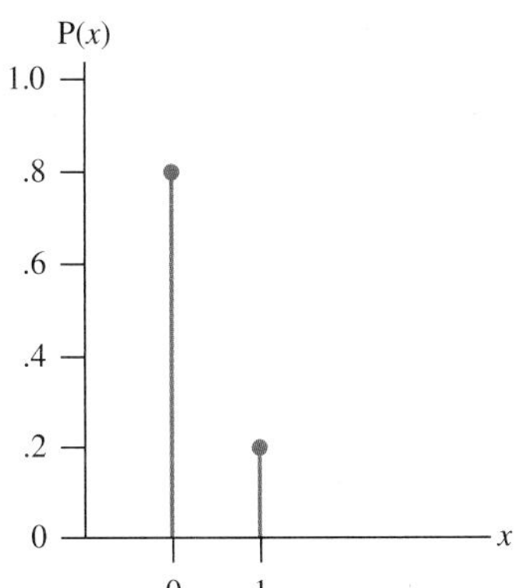

x	P(x)
0	0.80
1	0.20

The graph for this probability distribution is shown in the margin.

The mean of this probability distribution is

$$\mu = \Sigma x P(x) = 0(0.80) + 1(0.20) = 0.20.$$

The mean is equal to the probability of success. This is not a coincidence: *For random variables that have possible values 0 and 1, the mean is the probability of the outcome coded as 1.* We'll find this result to be quite useful in the next chapter.

Probability Distributions of Continuous Random Variables

A random variable is called **continuous** when its possible values form an interval. For instance, a recent study by the U.S. Bureau of the Census analyzed the time that people take to commute to work. Commuting time can be measured with real number values, such as between 0 and 150 minutes.

Probability distributions of continuous random variables assign probabilities to any interval of the possible values. For instance, a probability distribution for commuting time provides the probability that the travel time is less than 15 minutes or that the travel time is between 30 and 60 minutes. The probability that a random variable falls in any particular interval is between 0 and 1, and the probability of the interval that contains all the possible values equals 1.

When a random variable is continuous, the intervals that define the bars of a histogram can be chosen as desired. For instance, one possibility for commuting time is {0 to 30, 30 to 60, 60 to 90, 90 to 120, 120 to 150}, quite wide intervals. By contrast, using $\{0 \text{ to } 1, 1 \text{ to } 2, 2 \text{ to } 3, \ldots, 149 \text{ to } 150\}$ gives lots of very narrow intervals. As the number of intervals increases, with their width narrowing, the shape of the histogram gradually approaches a smooth curve. We'll use such curves to portray probability distributions of continuous random variables. See the graphs in the margin.

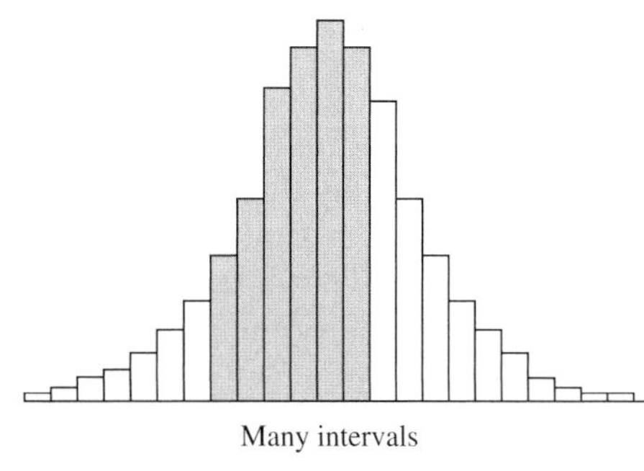

Many intervals

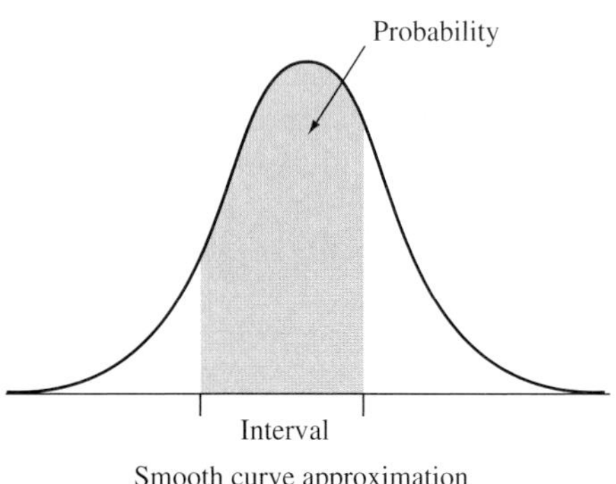

Smooth curve approximation

Probability Distribution of a Continuous Random Variable

A **continuous** random variable has possible values that form an interval. Its **probability distribution** is specified by a curve that determines the probability that the random variable falls in any particular interval of values.

- Each interval has probability between 0 and 1. The probability for the interval is given by the area under the curve, above that interval.
- The interval containing all possible values has probability equal to 1, so the total area under the curve equals 1.

Figure 6.2 shows the curve for the probability distribution of X = commuting time to work for workers in the United States, based on information from the 2009 American Community Survey. This survey implied that the distribution of the commuting time is skewed to the right, with a mean of around 25 minutes,[3] and the shape of the curves reflects this. Historically, in surveys about travel to work, a commute of 45 minutes has been the maximum time that people would be willing to spend. The shaded area in Figure 6.2 refers to the interval of a

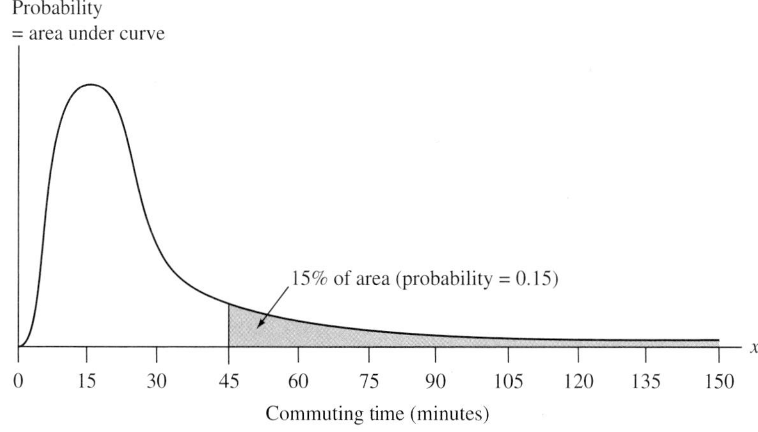

▲ **Figure 6.2 Probability Distribution of Commuting Time.** The area under the curve for values higher than 45 is 0.15. **Question** Identify the area under the curve representing the probability of a commute less than 15 minutes, which equals 0.27.

[3] *Source:* McKenzie and Rapino, 2011. *Commuting in the United States: 2009,* American Community Survey Reports, ACS-15. U.S. Bureau of the Census, Washington, D.C. (www.census.gov/hhes/commuting/data/commuting.html)

How many minutes did it usually take this person to get from home to work LAST WEEK?

Minutes

Snapshot of question from 2009 American Community Survey

commute longer than 45 minutes and the area above it to the probability of commuting longer than 45 minutes. This area equals 15% of the total area under the curve. So the probability of commuting longer than 45 minutes to work is 0.15, or 15%.

For continuous random variables, we need to round off our measurements. Probabilities are given for *intervals* of values rather than individual values. In measuring commuting time, the American Community Survey asked, "How many minutes did it usually take to get from home to work last week?" and respondents filled in a whole minute amount. Then, for instance, a commuting time of 24 minutes actually means the interval of real numbers that round to the integer value 24, which is the interval from 23.50 to 24.50. The corresponding probability is the area under the curve for this interval. *In practice, the probability that the commuting time falls in some given interval, such as above 45 minutes, less than 15 minutes, or between 30 and 60 minutes, is of greater interest than the probability it equals some particular single value.*

Did You Know?

For continuous random variables, the area above a single value equals 0. For example, the probability that the commuting time equals 23.7693611045 ... minutes is 0, but the probability that commuting time is between 23.5 and 24.5 minutes is positive. ◀

In Practice Continuous Variables Are Measured in a Discrete Manner

In practice, **continuous** variables are measured in a **discrete** manner because of rounding. With rounding, a continuous random variable can take on a large number of separate values. A probability distribution for a continuous random variable is used to approximate the probability distribution for the possible rounded values.

Example 6

Probability distribution ◀

Height

Picture the Scenario

Figure 6.3 shows a histogram of heights for a sample of females at the University of Georgia, with a smooth curve superimposed. (*Source:* Data from University of Georgia.)

Question to Explore

What does the smooth curve represent?

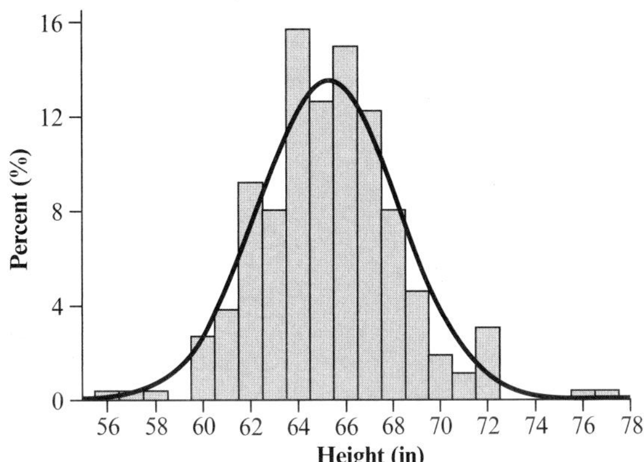

▲ **Figure 6.3** Histogram of Female Student Heights with Probability Distribution Curve Superimposed. Height is continuous but is measured as discrete by rounding to the nearest inch. The smooth curve approximates the probability distribution for height, treating it as a continuous random variable. **Questions** How would you describe the shape of the probability distribution? The probability for a female to be taller than 65 inches is approximately how much?

Think It Through

In theory, height is a continuous random variable. In practice, it is measured here by rounding to the nearest inch. For instance, the bar of the histogram above 64 represents heights between 63.5 and 64.5 inches, which were rounded to 64 inches. The histogram gives the data distribution for the discrete way height is actually measured in a sample. The smooth curve uses the data distribution to approximate the shape of the probability distribution (the population distribution) that height would have if we could actually measure all female heights precisely as a continuous random variable. The area under this curve between two points approximates the probability that height falls between those points. For instance, the area under the curve for the interval from 66 to 70 inches is 35% of the total area, so the probability of observing a height in this interval is 0.35, or 35%.

Insight

The histogram is a graphical representation of the distribution of the continuous variable in the sample. The smooth curve is a graphical representation of the distribution in the population. We observe the smooth curve has a bell shape. In the next section we'll study a probability distribution that has this shape and we'll learn how to find probabilities for it.

► ***Try Exercise 6.15***

Sometimes we can use a sample space to help us find a probability distribution, as you'll see in Exercises 6.1, 6.4, 6.11, and examples later in the chapter. Sometimes the probability distribution is available with a *formula*, a *table*, or a *graph*, as we'll see in the next two sections. Sometimes, though, it's helpful to use computer simulation to approximate the distribution, as shown in Activity 1 at the end of the chapter.

6.1 Practicing the Basics

6.1 Rolling dice

a. State in a table the probability distribution for the outcome of rolling a balanced die. (This is called the **uniform distribution** on the integers 1, 2, . . . ,6.)

b. Two balanced dice are rolled. Show that the probability distribution for X = total on the two dice is as shown in the figure. (*Hint*: First construct the sample space of the 36 equally likely outcomes you could get. For example, you could denote the six outcomes where you get a 1 on the first die by (1, 1), (1, 2), (1, 3), (1, 4), (1, 5), (1, 6), where the second number in a pair is the number you get on the second die.)

c. Show that the probabilities in part b satisfy the two conditions for a probability distribution.

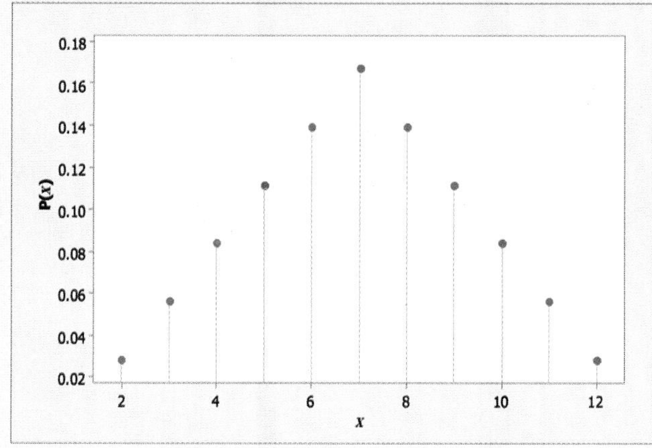

6.2 TRY **Dental Insurance** You plan to purchase dental insurance for your three remaining years in school. The insurance makes a one-time payment of \$1,000 in case of a major dental repair (such as an implant) or \$100 in case of a minor repair (such as a cavity). If you don't need dental repair over the next 3 years, the insurance expires and you receive no payout. You estimate the chances of requiring a major repair over the next 3 years as 5%, a minor repair as 60% and no repair as 35%.

a. Why is $X =$ payout of dental insurance a random variable?

b. Is X discrete or continuous? What are its possible values?

c. Give the probability distribution of X.

6.3 TRY **San Francisco Giants hitting** The table shows the probability distribution of the number of bases for a randomly selected time at bat for a San Francisco Giants player in 2010 (excluding times when the player got on base because of a walk or being hit by a pitch). In 74.29% of the at-bats the player was out, 17.04% of the time the player got a single (one base), 5.17% of the time the player got a double (two bases), 0.55% of the time the player got a triple, and 2.95% of the time the player got a home run.

a. Verify that the probabilities give a legitimate probability distribution.

b. Find the mean of this probability distribution.

c. Interpret the mean, explaining why it does not have to be a whole number, even though each possible value for the number of bases is a whole number.

San Francisco Giants Hitting

Number of Bases	Probability
0	0.7429
1	0.1704
2	0.0517
3	0.0055
4	0.0295

6.4 **Best of three** In a best out of three series played between teams A and B, the team that gets two wins first wins the entire series. Assuming that team A has a 70% chance of winning a game and that outcome of games are independent events, the probability that the series ends after two games is 58%.

a. Find the probability distribution of $X =$ number of games played in the series.

b. Find the expected number of games to be played in the series.

c. Verify that the probability that the series ends after two games is 58% by writing out the sample space of all possible sequences of wins and losses for team A in a best of three series. (A tree diagram may help.) Find the probability for each sequence and then add up those for which the series ends after two games. (Use what you learned in Section 5.2 about probabilities for intersections of independent events.)

6.5 **Grade distribution** An instructor always assigns final grades such that 20% are A, 40% are B, 30% are C, and 10% are D. The grade point scores are 4 for A, 3 for B, 2 for C, and 1 for D.

a. Specify the probability distribution for the grade point score of a randomly selected student of this instructor.

b. Find the mean of this probability distribution. Interpret it.

6.6 **Selling houses** Let X represent the number of homes a real estate agent sells during a given month. Based on previous sales records, she estimates that $P(0) = 0.68$, $P(1) = 0.19$, $P(2) = 0.09$, $P(3) = 0.03$, $P(4) = 0.01$, with negligible probability for higher values of x.

a. Explain why it does not make sense to compute the mean of this probability distribution as $(0 + 1 + 2 + 3 + 4)/5 = 2.0$ and claim that, on average, she expects to sell 2 homes.

b. Find the correct mean and interpret.

6.7 **Playing the lottery** The state of Ohio has several statewide lottery options. One is the Pick 3 game in which you pick one of the 1000 three-digit numbers between 000 and 999. The lottery selects a three-digit number at random. With a bet of \$1, you win \$500 if your number is selected and nothing (\$0) otherwise. (Many states have a very similar type of lottery.) (*Source:* Background information from www.ohiolottery.com.)

a. With a single \$1 bet, what is the probability that you win \$500?

b. Let X denote your winnings for a \$1 bet, so $x = \$0$ or $x = \$500$. Construct the probability distribution for X.

c. Show that the mean of the distribution equals 0.50, corresponding to an expected return of 50 cents for the dollar paid to play. Interpret the mean.

d. In Ohio's Pick 4 lottery, you pick one of the 10,000 four-digit numbers between 0000 and 9999 and (with a \$1 bet) win \$5000 if you get it correct. In terms of your expected winnings, with which game are you better off—playing Pick 4, or playing Pick 3? Justify your answer.

6.8 TRY **Roulette** A roulette wheel consists of 38 numbers, 0 through 36 and 00. Of these, 18 numbers are red, 18 are black, and 2 are green (0 and 00). You are given \$10 and told that you must pick one of two wagers, for an outcome based on a spin of the wheel: (1) Bet \$10 on number 23. If the spin results in 23, you win \$350 and also get back your \$10 bet. If any other number comes up, you lose your \$10, or (2) Bet \$10 on black. If the spin results in any one of the black numbers, you win \$10 and also get back your \$10 bet. If any other color comes up, you lose your \$10.

a. Without doing any calculation, which wager would you prefer? Explain why. (There is no correct answer. Peoples' choices are based on their individual preferences and risk tolerances.)

b. Find the expected outcome for each wager. Which wager is better in this sense?

6.9 TRY **More Roulette** The previous exercise on roulette described two bets: one bet on the single number 23 with winnings of either \$350 or $-\$10$ and a different bet on black with winnings of either \$10 or $-\$10$. For both types of bets, the expected winning is $-\$0.53$. Which of the two bets has the larger standard deviation? (*Hint:* Which bet has outcomes that are, on average, further from the mean?) Which bet would you prefer? Explain.

6.10 Ideal number of children Let X denote the response of a randomly selected person to the question, "What is the ideal number of children for a family to have?" The probability distribution of X in the United States is approximately as shown in the table, according to the gender of the person asked the question.

TRY

Probability Distribution of X = Ideal Number of Children

x	P(x) Females	P(x) Males
0	0.01	0.02
1	0.03	0.03
2	0.55	0.60
3	0.31	0.28
4	0.11	0.08

Note that the probabilities do not sum to exactly 1 due to rounding error.

a. Show that the means are similar, 2.50 for females and 2.39 for males.

b. The standard deviation for the females is 0.770 and 0.758 for the males. Explain why a practical implication of the values for the standard deviations is that males hold slightly more consistent views than females about the ideal family size.

6.11 Profit and the weather From past experience, a wheat farmer living in Manitoba, Canada, finds that his annual profit (in Canadian dollars) is \$80,000 if the summer weather is typical, \$50,000 if the weather is unusually dry, and \$20,000 if there is a severe storm that destroys much of his crop. Weather bureau records indicate that the probability is 0.70 of typical weather, 0.20 of unusually dry weather, and 0.10 of a severe storm. Let X denote the farmer's profit next year.

a. Construct a table with the probability distribution of X.

b. What is the probability that the profit is \$50,000 or less?

c. Find the mean of the probability distribution of X. Interpret.

d. Suppose the farmer buys insurance for \$3000 that pays him \$20,000 in the event of a severe storm that destroys much of the crop and pays nothing otherwise. Find the probability distribution of his profit. Find the mean and summarize the effect of buying this insurance.

6.12 Buying on eBay You are watching two items posted for sale on eBay and bid \$30 for the first and \$20 for the second item. You estimate that you are going to win the first bid with probability 0.1 and the second bid with probability 0.2, and you assume that winning the two bids are independent events. Let X denote the random variable denoting the total amount of money you will spend on the two items.

a. List the sample space of all possible outcomes of winning or losing the two bids. (Draw a tree diagram.)

b. Find the probability of each outcome in the sample space. (Use the tree diagram.)

c. Find the probability distribution of X.

d. Find the mean of X.

6.13 Selling at the right price Some companies, such as DemandTec, have developed software to help retail chains set prices that optimize their profits. An Associated Press story (April 28, 2007) about this software described a case in which a retail chain sold three similar power drills: one for \$90, a better one for \$120, and a top-tier one for \$130. Software predicted that by selling the middle-priced drill for only \$110, the cheaper drill would seem less a bargain and more people would buy the middle-price drill.

a. For the original pricing, suppose 50% of sales were for the \$90 drill, 20% for the \$120 drill, and 30% for the \$130 drill. Construct the probability distribution of X = selling price for the sale of a drill, find its mean, and interpret,

b. For the new pricing, suppose 30% of sales were for the \$90 drill, 40% for the \$110 drill, and 30% for the \$130 drill. Is the mean of the probability distribution of selling price higher with this new pricing strategy? Explain.

6.14 Uniform distribution A random number generator is used to generate a real number between 0 and 1, equally likely to fall anywhere in this interval of values. (For instance, 0.3794259832 . . . is a possible outcome.)

a. Sketch a curve of the probability distribution of this random variable, which is the continuous version of the **uniform distribution** (see Exercise 6.1).

b. The probability that the number falls in the interval from 0 to the mean is 50%. Find the mean. (Remember that the total area under the probability curve is 1.)

c. Find the probability that the random number falls between 0.35 and 0.75.

d. Find the probability that the random number is less than 0.8?

6.15 TV watching A social scientist uses the General Social Survey (GSS) to study how much time per day people spend watching TV. The variable denoted by TVHOURS at the GSS Web site measures this using the discrete values 0, 1, 2, . . . , 24.

TRY

a. Explain how, in theory, TV watching is a continuous random variable.

b. An article about the study shows two histograms, both skewed to the right, to summarize TV watching for females and males. Since TV watching is in theory continuous, why were histograms used instead of curves?

c. If the article instead showed two curves, explain what they would represent.

6.2 Probabilities for Bell-Shaped Distributions

The German-born Carl Friedrich Gauss (1777–1855), shown here on a former German 10-Mark bill, was one of the first to use the normal distribution, with curve shown to his right.

Some probability distributions merit special attention because they are useful for many applications. They have formulas or tables that provide probabilities of the possible outcomes. We next learn about a probability distribution, called the **normal distribution**, that is commonly used for continuous random variables. It is characterized by a particular symmetric, bell-shaped curve with two parameters—the mean μ and the standard deviation σ.[4]

The Normal Distribution: A Probability Distribution with a Bell-Shaped Curve

Figure 6.3 at the end of the previous section showed that heights of female students at the University of Georgia have approximately a bell-shaped distribution. The approximating curve describes a probability distribution with a mean of 65.0 inches and a standard deviation of 3.5 inches. In fact, adult female heights in North America have approximately a normal distribution with $\mu = 65.0$ inches and $\sigma = 3.5$ inches. Adult male heights have approximately a normal distribution with $\mu = 70.0$ inches and $\sigma = 4.0$ inches. Adult males tend to be a bit taller (since $70 > 65$) with heights varying from the mean a bit more (since $4.0 > 3.5$). Figure 6.4 shows the normal distribution for female heights and the one for male heights.

Did You Know?

The color blue is used throughout the text for graphs of normal distributions. For more information, refer to "A Guide to Learning From the Art in This Text" located at the very front of the text. ◀

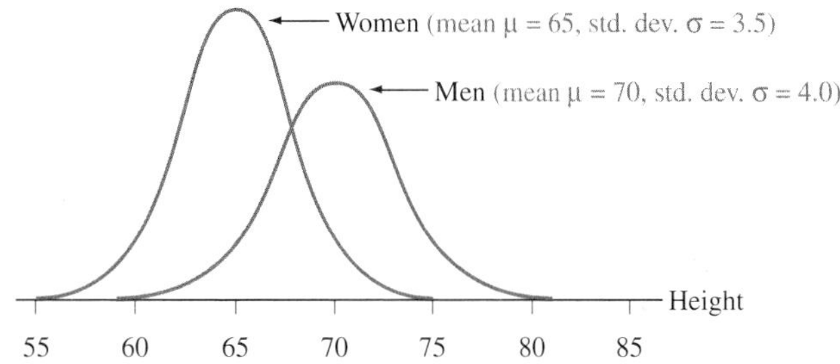

▲ **Figure 6.4 Normal Distributions for Women's Height and Men's Height.** For each different combination of μ and σ values, there is a normal distribution with mean μ and standard deviation σ. **Questions** Why is the normal curve for women more peaked than the one for men? Given that $\mu = 70$ and $\sigma = 4$, within what interval do almost all of the men's heights fall?

For any real number for the mean μ and any positive number for the standard deviation σ, there is a normal distribution with that mean and standard deviation.

> **Normal Distribution**
>
> The **normal distribution** is symmetric, bell-shaped, and characterized by its mean μ (expressing the center) and standard deviation σ (expressing the variability). The probability of observing values within any given number of standard deviations from the mean μ is the same for all normal distributions (i.e., for any μ and any $\sigma > 0$). This probability equals 0.68 for the interval within 1 standard deviation of the mean, 0.95 for the interval within 2 standard deviations of the mean, and 0.997 for the interval within 3 standard deviations of the mean. See Figure 6.5.

[4]A mathematical formula specifies *which* bell-shaped curve is the normal distribution, but it is complex and we'll not use it in this text. In Chapter 8, we'll learn about another bell-shaped distribution, one with thicker tails than the normal has.

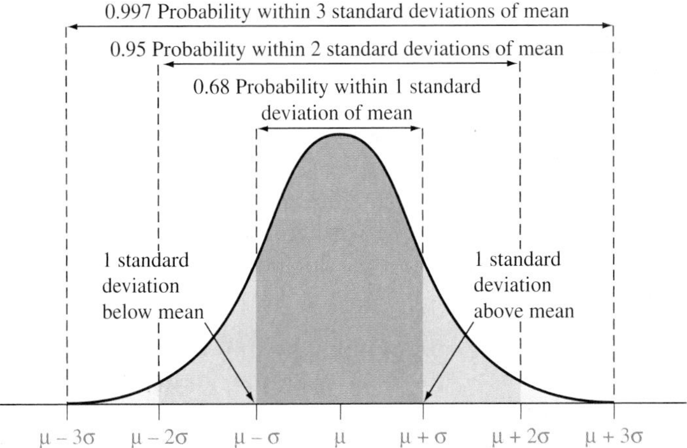

▲ **Figure 6.5 The Normal Distribution.** The probability equals 0.68 for the interval within 1 standard deviation of the mean, 0.95 for the interval within 2 standard deviations, and 0.997 for the interval within 3 standard deviations. **Question** How do these probabilities relate to the empirical rule?

To illustrate, for adult female heights, $\mu = 65.0$ and $\sigma = 3.5$ inches. Since

$$\mu - 2\sigma = 65.0 - 2(3.5) = 58.0 \text{ and } \mu + 2\sigma = 65.0 + 2(3.5) = 72.0,$$

about 95% of the female heights fall between 58 inches and 72 inches i.e., within two standard deviations from the mean. The probability of observing a female height between 58 inches and 72 inches is 0.95, or 95%. For adult male heights, $\mu = 70.0$ and $\sigma = 4.0$ inches. About 95% fall between $\mu - 2\sigma = 70.0 - 2(4.0) = 62$ inches and $\mu + 2\sigma = 70.0 + 2(4.0) = 78$ inches.

The property of the normal distribution in the definition tells us about probabilities within 1, 2, and 3 standard deviations of the mean. The multiples 1, 2, and 3 of the number of standard deviations from the mean are denoted by the symbol z in general. For instance, $z = 2$ for 2 standard deviations. For each fixed number z, the probability within z standard deviations of the mean is the area under the normal curve between $\mu - z\sigma$ and $\mu + z\sigma$ as shown in Figure 6.6. This probability is 0.68 for $z = 1$, so 68% of the area (probability) of a normal distribution falls between $\mu - \sigma$ and $\mu + \sigma$. Similarly, this probability is 0.95 for $z = 2$, and 0.997 (i.e., nearly 1.0) for $z = 3$. The entire area under the curve (i.e., from all the way to the left to all the way to the right) equals 1, or 100%.

Caution

From Section 2.5, the ***z*-score** for an observation is the number of standard deviations that it falls from the mean. The *z*-score can be used with any distribution for a quantitative variable. This includes both normal and nonnormal distributions. ◀

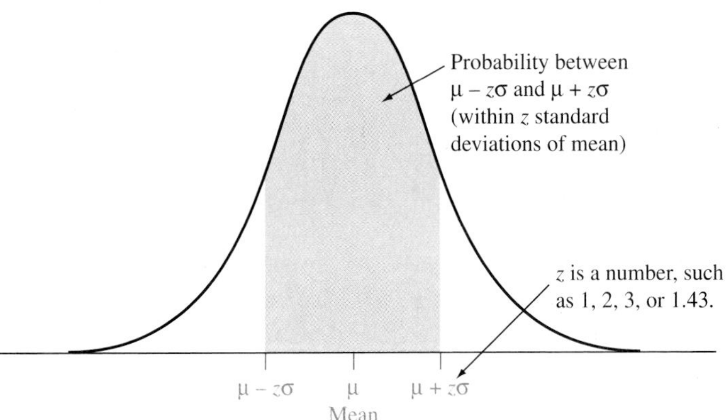

▲ **Figure 6.6 The Probability Between $\mu - z\sigma$ and $\mu + z\sigma$.** This is the area highlighted under the curve. It is the same for every normal distribution and depends only on the value of *z*. Figure 6.5 showed this for $z = 1$, 2, and 3, but z does not have to be an integer—it can be any number.

The normal distribution is the most important distribution in statistics, partly because many variables have approximately normal distributions. The normal distribution is also important because it approximates many discrete distributions well when there are a large number of possible outcomes. However, the main reason for the prominence of the normal distribution is that many statistical methods use it even when the data are not bell shaped. We'll see why in the next chapter.

Finding Probabilities for the Normal Distribution

Recall

A cumulative proportion (probability) was defined in Section 5.1

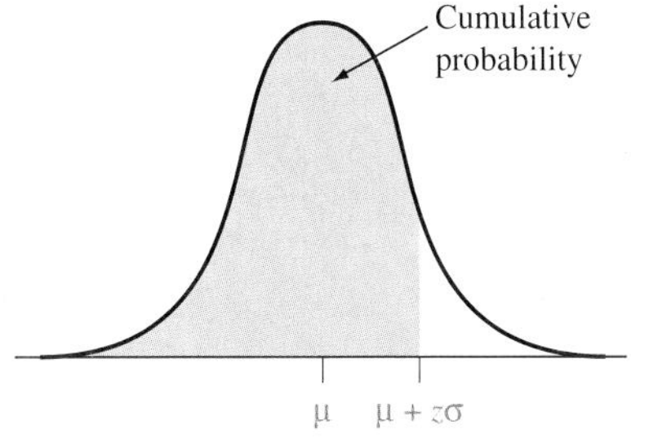

As we'll discuss, the probabilities 0.68, 0.95, and 0.997 within 1, 2, and 3 standard deviations of the mean are no surprise, because of the empirical rule. But what if we wanted to find the probability within, say, 1.43 standard deviations?

Table A at the end of the text enables us to find normal probabilities. It tabulates the normal **cumulative probability**, the probability of falling *below* the point $\mu + z\sigma$ (see the margin figure). The leftmost column of Table A lists the values for z to one decimal point, with the second decimal place listed above the columns. Table 6.3 shows a small excerpt from Table A. The tabulated probability for $z = 1.43$ falls in the row labeled 1.4 and in the column labeled 0.03. It equals 0.9236. For every normal distribution, the probability of falling below $\mu + 1.43\sigma$ equals 0.9236. Figure 6.7 illustrates.

Table 6.3 Part of Table A for Normal Cumulative (Left-Tail) Probabilities

The top of the table gives the second digit for z. The table entry is the probability of falling below $\mu + z\sigma$, for instance, 0.9236 below $\mu + 1.43\sigma$ for $z = 1.43$.

Second Decimal Place of z										
z	.00	.01	.02	.03	.04	.05	.06	.07	.08	.09
0.0	.5000	.5040	.5080	.5120	.5160	.5199	.5239	.5279	.5319	.5359
...										
1.3	.9032	.9049	.9066	.9082	.9099	.9115	.9139	.9147	.9162	.9177
1.4	.9192	.9207	.9222	.9236	.9251	.9265	.9278	.9292	.9306	.9319
1.5	.9332	.9345	.9357	.9370	.9382	.9394	.9406	.9418	.9429	.9441

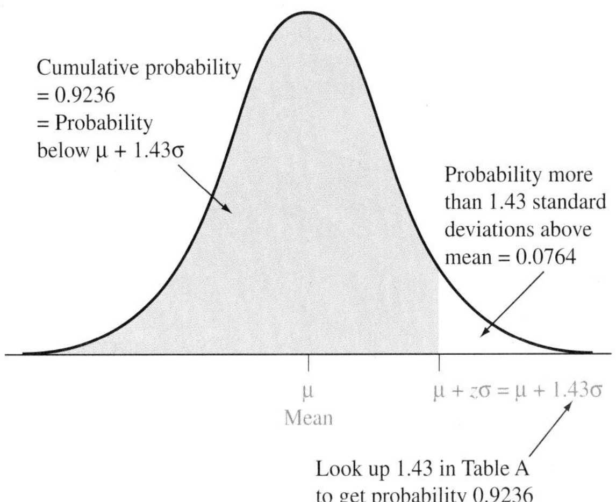

▲ **Figure 6.7 The Normal Cumulative Probability, Less Than z Standard Deviations above the Mean.** Table A lists a cumulative probability of 0.9236 for $z = 1.43$, so 0.9236 is the probability of falling less than 1.43 standard deviations above the mean for any normal distribution (that is, below $\mu + 1.43\sigma$). The complement probability of 0.0764 is the probability of falling *above* $\mu + 1.43\sigma$ in the right tail.

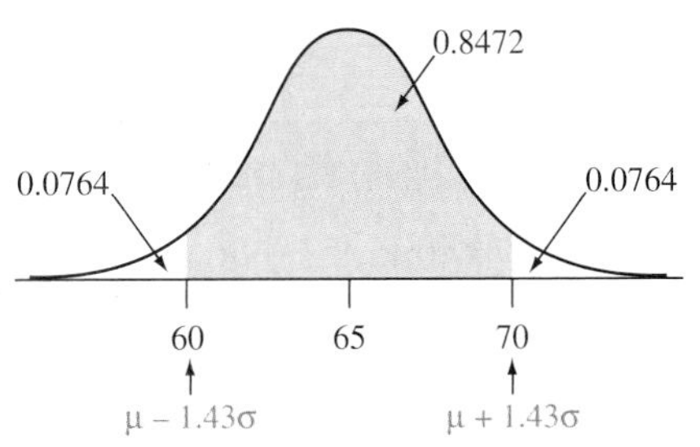

Since an entry in Table A is a probability *below* $\mu + z\sigma$, one minus that probability is the probability *above* $\mu + z\sigma$. For example, the right-tail probability above $\mu + 1.43\sigma$ equals $1 - 0.9236 = 0.0764$. By the symmetry of the normal curve, this probability also refers to the left tail below $\mu - 1.43\sigma$, which you'll find in Table A by looking up $z = -1.43$. The negative z-scores in the table refer to cumulative probabilities for random variable values *below* the mean.

Since the probability is 0.0764 in each tail, the probability of falling *more than* 1.43 standard deviations from the mean equals $2(0.0764) = 0.1528$. The total probability equals 1, so the probability falling *within* 1.43 standard deviations of the mean equals $1 - 0.1528 = 0.8472$, about 85%. For instance, 85% of women in North America have height between $\mu - 1.43\sigma = 65.0 - 1.43(3.5) = 60$ inches and $\mu + 1.43\sigma = 65 + 1.43(3.5) = 70$ inches (that is, between 5 feet and 5 feet, 10 inches).

Finding Normal Probabilities

Example 7

Standby Time of Smartphones

Picture the Scenario

One of the defining features of a smartphone is how long it can stay in standby mode on a single charge of the battery. Based on data from smartphones available from major cell phone carriers in the United States in 2014 (and relying on the fact that a manufacturer's claim of the standby time is accurate), the distribution of the standby time approximately follows a normal distribution with a mean of $\mu = 330$ minutes and a standard deviation of $\sigma = 80$ minutes.

Questions to Explore

a. What percentage of smartphones have a standby time 1.25 standard deviations *below* the mean?

b. What percentage of smartphones have a standby time 1.25 standard deviations *above* the mean?

c. Find the probability of observing a standby time that is within 1.25 standard deviations of the mean.

Think It Through

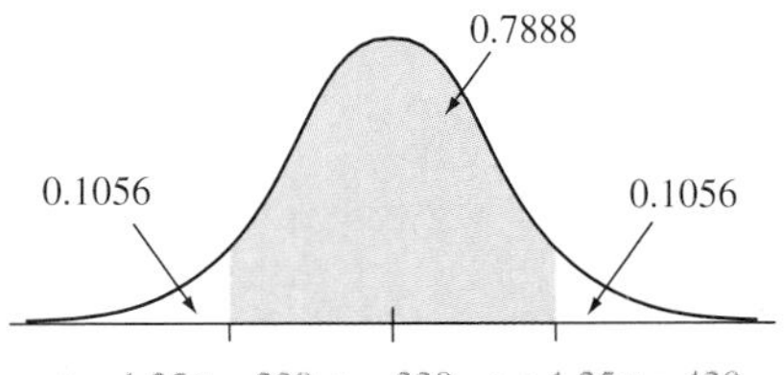

a. Because $\mu - 1.25\sigma = 330 - 1.25(80) = 230$, we are looking at the area under the normal curve (with mean 330 and standard deviation 80) that falls below 230 minutes. The figure in the margin illustrates. We can determine that area by finding the value in Table A for $z = -1.25$, which is 0.1056. So, 10.56% of smartphones have a standby time less than 1.25 standard deviations below the mean, i.e., shorter than 230 minutes.

b. By the symmetry of the normal distribution, the area above $\mu + 1.25\sigma = 330 + 1.25(80) = 430$ is also 0.1056. (If you want, you can look up the value for $z = 1.25$ in Table A, which is 0.8944, and subtract it from 1, which gives 0.1056 for the area in the upper tail, as expected.) So, 10.56% of smartphones have a standby time larger than 1.25 standard deviations above the mean, i.e., longer than 430 minutes.

c. Because the area below and above 1.25 standard deviations of the mean equals 0.1056 each, the area *outside* 1.25 standard deviations is $2(0.1056) = 0.2112$. Because the total area equals 1, the area *within* 1.25 standard deviations of the mean equals $1 - 0.2112 = 0.7888$. Hence, the probability of observing a standby time that is within 1.25 standard deviations of the mean (i.e., between 230 and 430 minutes) equals about 79%.

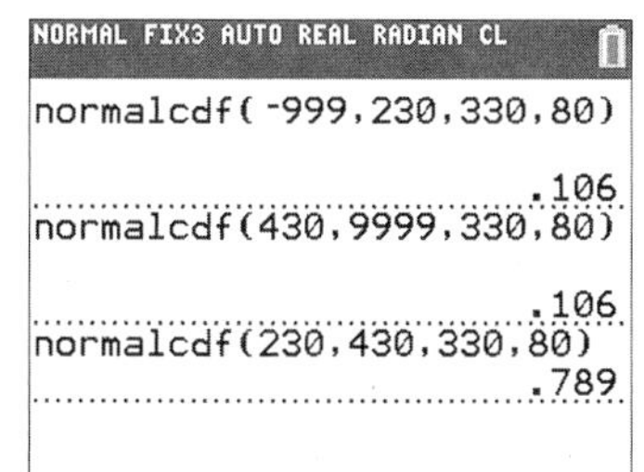

TI output for probabilities in parts a, b, and c.

Insight

Many (online) calculators or apps can compute the normal probabilities above without you having to use Table A. (Search for "normal distribution calculator" on the Internet or in an app store, or access the "Normal Distribution" web app available from the book's website.) The margin illustrates how to use the TI calculator for the computations in this example. No matter how you obtain the answer, drawing a quick **sketch** of the normal distribution and marking the area that you are looking for helps tremendously in avoiding mistakes.

▶ ***Try Exercises 6.16 and 6.17***

Normal Probabilities and the Empirical Rule

The empirical rule states that for an approximately bell-shaped distribution, about 68% of observations fall within 1 standard deviation of the mean, 95% within 2 standard deviations, and nearly all within 3. In fact, those percentages came from probabilities calculated for the normal distribution.

Recall

The empirical rule was introduced in Section 2.4. ◀

For instance, a value that is 2 standard deviations below the mean has $z = -2.00$. The cumulative probability below $\mu - 2\sigma$ listed in Table A opposite $z = -2.00$ is 0.0228. The right-tail probability above $\mu + 2\sigma$ also equals 0.0228, by symmetry. See Figure 6.8. The probability falling more than 2 standard deviations from the mean in either tail is $2(0.0228) = 0.0456$. Thus, the probability that falls *within* 2 standard deviations of the mean equals $1 - 0.0456 = 0.9544$. When a variable has a normal distribution, 95.44% of the distribution (95%, rounded) falls within 2 standard deviations of the mean.

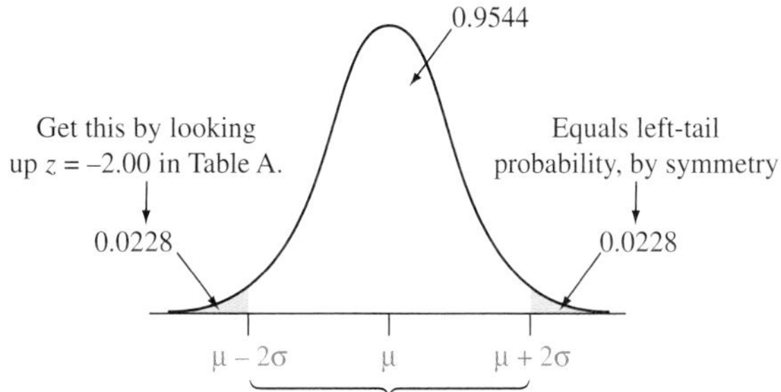

▲ **Figure 6.8 Normal Probability Within 2 Standard Deviations of the Mean.** Probabilities in one tail determine probabilities in the other tail by symmetry. Subtracting the total two-tail probability from 1.0 gives probabilities within a certain distance of the mean. **Question** Can you do the analogous calculation for 3 standard deviations?

The approximate percentages that the empirical rule lists are the percentages for the normal distribution, rounded. For instance, you can verify that the probability within 1 standard deviation of the mean of a normal distribution equals 0.68 (see Exercise 6.18). The probability within 3 standard deviations of the mean equals 0.997, or 1.00 rounded off. The empirical rule stated the probabilities as being *approximate* rather than *exact* because that rule referred to *all approximately* bell-shaped distributions, not just the normal.

How Can We Find the Value of *z* for a Certain Cumulative Probability?

In practice, we'll sometimes need to find the value of z that corresponds to a certain normal cumulative probability. How can we do this? To illustrate, let's find the value of z for a cumulative probability of 0.025. We look up the

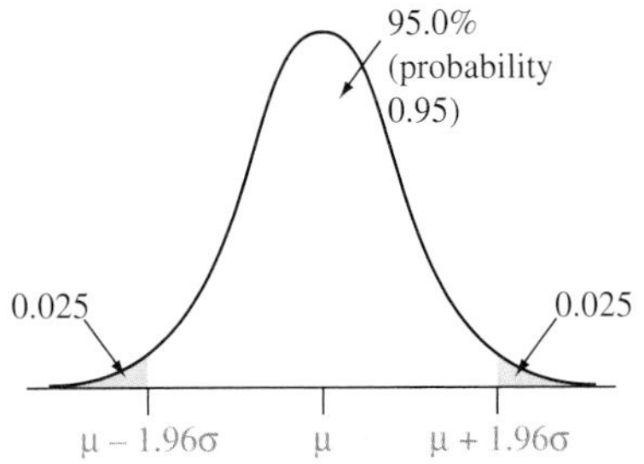

cumulative probability of 0.025 in the body of Table A. It corresponds to $z = -1.96$, since it is in the row labeled −1.9 and in the column labeled 0.06. So a probability of 0.025 lies below $\mu - 1.96\sigma$. Likewise, a probability of 0.025 lies above $\mu + 1.96\sigma$. A total probability of 0.050 lies more than 1.96σ from μ. Precisely 95.0% of a normal distribution falls within 1.96 standard deviations of the mean. (See figure in margin.) We've seen previously that 95.44% falls within 2.00 standard deviations, and we now see that precisely 95.0% falls within 1.96 standard deviations.

Cumulative probability and a percentile value ◀

Example 8

Mensa IQ Scores

Picture the Scenario

Mensa[5] is a society of high-IQ people whose members have IQ scores at the 98th percentile or higher. The Stanford-Binet IQ scores that are used as the basis for admission into Mensa are approximately normally distributed with a mean of 100 and a standard deviation of 16.

Questions to Explore

a. How many standard deviations above the mean is the 98th percentile?

b. What is the IQ score for that percentile?

Think It Through

a. For a value to represent the 98th percentile, its cumulative probability must equal 0.98, by the definition of a percentile. See Figure 6.9.

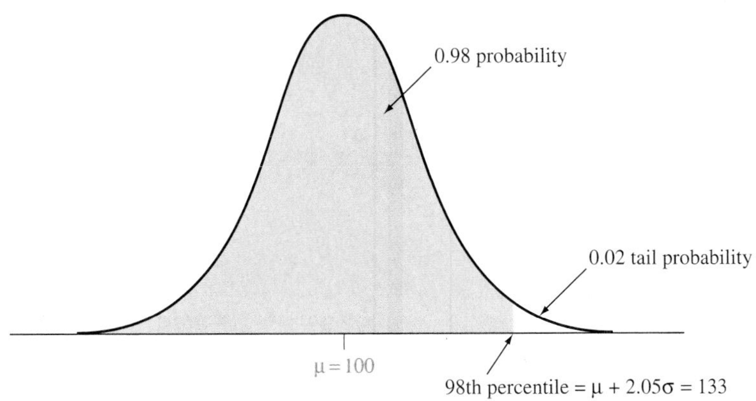

▲ **Figure 6.9 The 98th Percentile for a Normal Distribution.** This is the value such that 98% of the distribution falls below it and 2% falls above. **Question** Where is the second percentile located?

Recall

The **percentile** was defined in Section 2.5. For the 98th percentile, 98% of the distribution falls below that point. ◀

When looking up the cumulative probability of 0.980 in the body of Table A, we see it corresponds to $z = 2.05$. The 98th percentile is 2.05 standard deviations above the mean, at $\mu + 2.05\sigma$.

b. Since $\mu = 100$ and $\sigma = 16$, the 98th percentile of IQ scores equals

$$\mu + 2.05\sigma = 100 + 2.05(16) = 133.$$

In summary, 98% of the IQ scores fall below 133, and an IQ score of at least 133 is required to join Mensa.

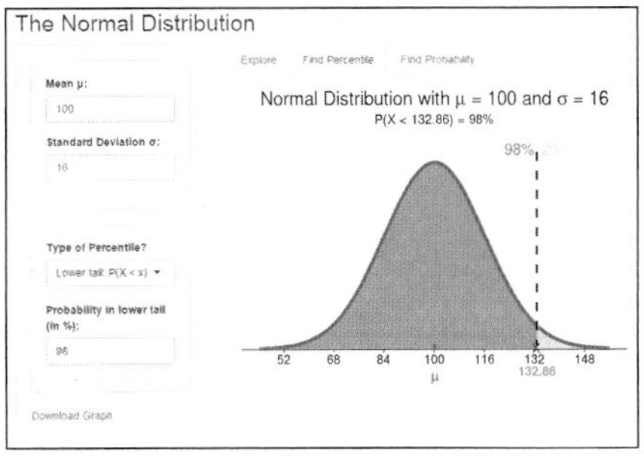

Screenshot from the Normal Distribution web app.

[5] See www.mensa.org.

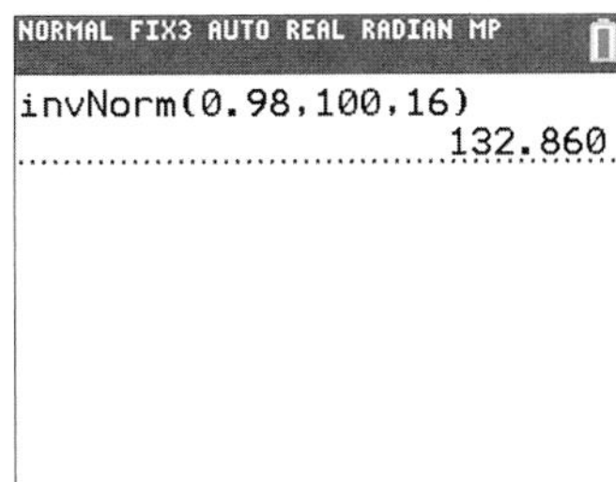

TI output to get 98th percentile

Insight

About 2% of IQ scores are higher than 133. By symmetry, about 2% of IQ scores are lower than $\mu - 2.05\sigma = 100 - 2.05(16) = 67$. This is the second percentile. The remaining 96% of the IQ scores fall between 67 and 133, which is the region within 2.05 standard deviations of the mean.

It's also possible to use software to find normal percentiles. The margin on the previous page shows a screen shot from the Normal Distribution web app accessible via the book's website and the margin to the left shows TI output for finding the 98th percentile.

▶ ***Try Exercises 6.20 and 6.29, part b***

Using z = Number of Standard Deviations to Find Probabilities

We've used the symbol z to represent the *number of standard deviations* a value falls from the mean. If we have a value x of a random variable, how can we figure out the number of standard deviations it falls from the mean μ of its probability distribution? The difference between x and μ equals $x - \mu$. The **z-score** expresses this difference as a number of standard deviations, using $z = (x - \mu)/\sigma$.

Recall

Section 2.5 defined the z-score for an **observation:** For sample data with mean $\bar{x}$ and standard deviation s, the number of standard deviations that an observation x falls from the sample mean is

$$z = \frac{x - \text{mean}}{\text{standard deviation}} = \frac{x - \bar{x}}{s}.$$

For example, if $z = 1.8$, then the observation falls 1.8 standard deviations *above* the sample mean, and if $z = -1.8$, then it falls 1.8 standard deviations *below* the sample mean. ◀

z-Score for a Value of a Random Variable

The **z-score** for a value x of a random variable is the number of standard deviations that x falls from the mean μ. It is calculated as

$$z = \frac{x - \mu}{\sigma}.$$

Caution

We use the notion of a z-score both to express how far an observation is from the sample mean and how far a value of a random variable is from the mean of the probability distribution. ◀

The formula for the z-score is useful when we are given the value of x for some normal random variable and need to find a probability relating to that value. We convert x to a z-score and then use a normal table to find the appropriate probability. The next two examples illustrate.

Using z-scores to find probabilities ◀

Example 9

Your Relative Standing on the SAT

Picture the Scenario

The Scholastic Aptitude Test (SAT), a college entrance examination, has three components: critical reading, mathematics, and writing. The scores on each component are approximately normally distributed with mean $\mu = 500$ and standard deviation $\sigma = 100$. The scores range from 200 to 800 on each component.

Questions to Explore

a. If your SAT score from one of the three components was $x = 650$, how many standard deviations from the mean was it?

b. What percentage of SAT scores was higher than yours?

Think It Through

a. The SAT score of 650 has a z-score of $z = 1.50$ because 650 is 1.50 standard deviations above the mean. In other words,

$x = 650 = \mu + z\sigma = 500 + z(100)$, where $z = 1.50$. We can find this directly using the formula

$$z = \frac{x - \mu}{\sigma} = \frac{650 - 500}{100} = 1.50.$$

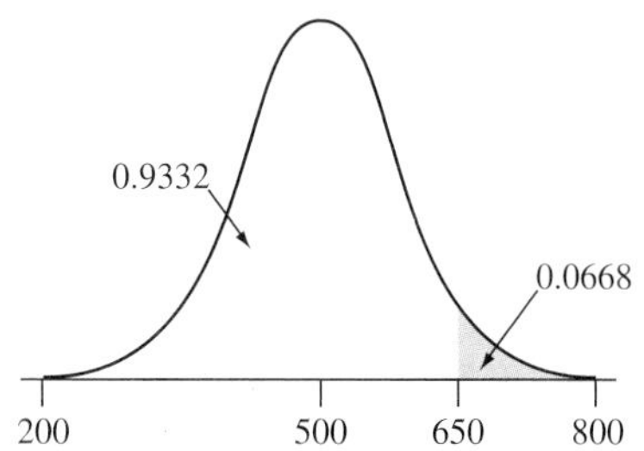

b. The percentage of SAT scores higher than 650 is the right-tail probability above 650, for a normal random variable with mean $\mu = 500$ and standard deviation $\sigma = 100$. From Table A, the z-score of 1.50 has cumulative probability 0.9332. That's the probability *below* 650, so the right-tail probability above it is $1 - 0.9332 = 0.0668$. (See figure in margin.) Only about 7% of SAT test scores fall above 650. In summary, a score of 650 was well above average, in the sense that relatively few students scored higher.

Insight

Positive z-scores occur when the value x falls *above* the mean μ. Negative z-scores occur when x falls *below* the mean. For instance, an SAT score of 350 has a z-score of

$$z = \frac{x - \mu}{\sigma} = \frac{350 - 500}{100} = -1.50.$$

The SAT score of 350 is 1.50 standard deviations *below* the mean. The probability that an SAT score falls below 350 is also 0.0668. Figure 6.10 illustrates.

As mentioned in Example 7, there are many normal calculators (search online for this term) or apps (such as the web app available at the book's website) that don't require you to convert to z-scores. These calculators can find the desired probability directly when you supply the mean and the standard deviation of the normal distribution and the endpoint(s) of the interval. The margin illustrates how to do this with the Normal Distribution web app from the book's website or with a TI calculator. When using a calculator, just don't forget to draw a rough sketch to check whether the answer is plausible!

► ***Try Exercise 6.25***

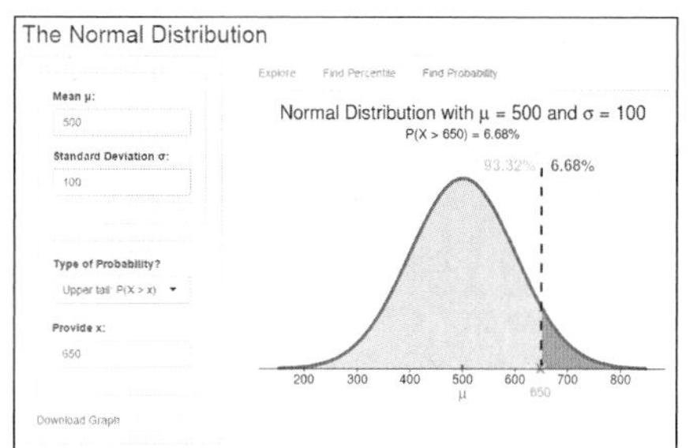

Screenshot from the Normal Distribution web app.

```
NORMAL FIX3 AUTO REAL RADIAN CL
normalcdf(-99,350,500,100)
                          .067
normalcdf(650,9999,500,100
)
                          .067
normalcdf(350,650,500,100)
                          .866
```

TI output for normal calculations

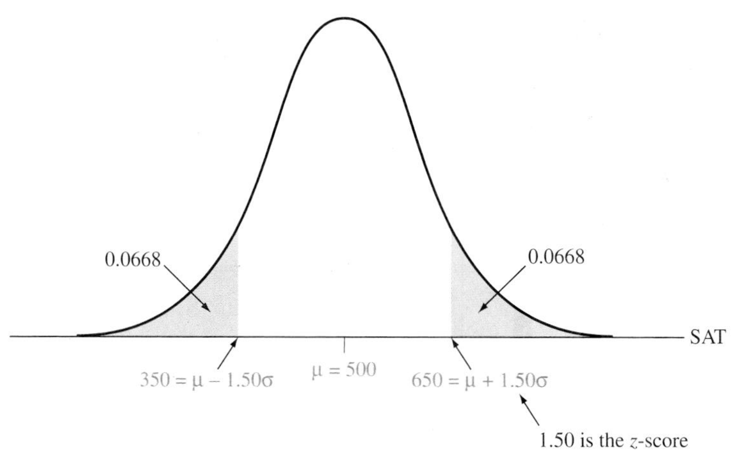

▲ **Figure 6.10 Normal Distribution for SAT.** The SAT scores of 650 and 350 have z-scores of 1.50 and −1.50 because they fall 1.50 standard deviations above and below the mean. **Question** Which SAT scores have $z = 3.0$ and $z = -3.0$?

Example 10

Using z-scores to find probabilities

The Proportion of Students Who Get a B

Picture the Scenario

On the midterm exam in introductory statistics, an instructor always gives a grade of B to students who score between 80 and 90.

Question to Explore

One year, the scores on the exam have approximately a normal distribution with mean 83 and standard deviation 5. About what proportion of students earn a B?

Think It Through

A midterm exam score of 90 has a *z*-score of

$$z = \frac{x - \mu}{\sigma} = \frac{90 - 83}{5} = 1.40.$$

Its cumulative probability of 0.9192 (from Table A) means that about 92% of the exam scores were below 90. Similarly, an exam score of 80 has a *z*-score of

$$z = \frac{x - \mu}{\sigma} = \frac{80 - 83}{5} = -0.60.$$

Its cumulative probability of 0.2743 means that about 27% of the exam scores were below 80. See the normal curves that follow. Therefore about $0.9192 - 0.2743 = 0.6449$, or about 64%, of the exam scores were in the B range.

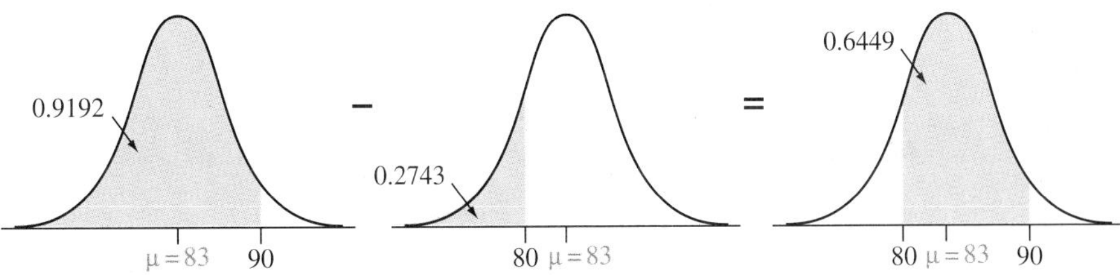

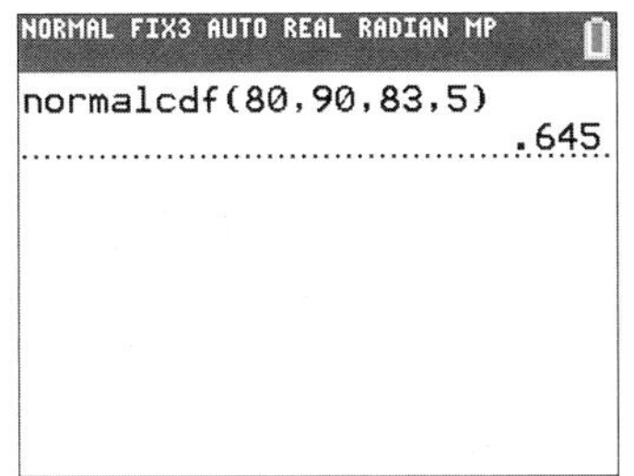

Screenshot from the Normal Distribution web app.

```
NORMAL FIX3 AUTO REAL RADIAN MP
normalcdf(80,90,83,5)
                              .645
```

TI output to compute probability between 80 and 90

Insight

Here, we took the difference between two cumulative probabilities to find a probability between two points.

► ***Try Exercise 6.32***

Here's a summary of how we've used *z*-scores so far:

Summary: Using *z*-Scores to Find Normal Probabilities or Random Variable *x* Values:

- If we're given a value *x* and need to find a probability, convert *x* to a *z*-score using $z = (x - \mu)/\sigma$, use a table of normal probabilities (or software, or a calculator) to get a cumulative probability, and then convert it to the probability of interest.
- If we're given a probability and need to find the value of *x*, convert the probability to the related cumulative probability, find the *z*-score using a normal table (or software or a calculator), and then evaluate $x = \mu + z\sigma$.

In Example 8, we used the equation $x = \mu + z\sigma$ to find a percentile score (namely, 98th percentile $= \mu + 2.05\sigma = 100 + 2.05(16) = 133$). In Examples 9 and 10, we used the equation $z = (x - \mu)/\sigma$ to determine how many standard deviations certain scores fell from the mean, which enabled us to find probabilities (and hence percentiles) relating to those scores.

Another use of z-scores is for comparing observations from different normal distributions in terms of their relative distances from the mean.

Example 11

Comparing z-scores ◀

Comparing Test Scores That Use Different Scales

Picture the Scenario

There are two primary standardized tests used by college admissions, the SAT and the ACT.[6]

Question to Explore

When you applied to college, you scored 650 on an SAT exam, which had mean $\mu = 500$ and standard deviation $\sigma = 100$. Your friend took the comparable ACT, scoring 30. For that year, the ACT had $\mu = 21.0$ and $\sigma = 4.7$. How can we compare these scores to tell who performed better?

Think It Through

The test scores of 650 and 30 are not directly comparable because the SAT and ACT are evaluated on different scales with different means and different standard deviations. But we can convert them to z-scores and analyze how many standard deviations each falls from the mean.

With $\mu = 500$ and $\sigma = 100$, we saw in Example 9 that an SAT test score of $x = 650$ converts to a z-score of $z = (x - \mu)/\sigma = (650 - 500)/100 = 1.50$. With $\mu = 21.0$ and $\sigma = 4.7$, an ACT score of 30 converts to a z-score of

$$z = \frac{x - \mu}{\sigma} = \frac{30 - 21}{4.7} = 1.91.$$

The ACT score of 30 is a bit higher than the SAT score of 650, since ACT = 30 falls 1.91 standard deviations above its mean, whereas SAT = 650 falls 1.50 standard deviations above its mean. In this sense, the ACT score is better even though its numerical value is smaller.

Insight

The SAT and ACT test scores both have approximately normal distributions. From Table A, $z = 1.91$ (for the ACT score of 30) has a cumulative probability of 0.97. Of all students who took the ACT, only about 3% scored above 30. From Table A, $z = 1.50$ (for the SAT score of 650) has a cumulative probability of 0.93. Of all students who took the SAT, about 7% scored above 650.

▶ *Try Exercise 6.33*

[6]See www.sat.org and www.act.org.

The Standard Normal Distribution Has Mean = 0 and Standard Deviation = 1

Many statistical methods refer to a particular normal distribution called the **standard normal distribution**.

Standard Normal Distribution

The **standard normal distribution** is the normal distribution with mean $\mu = 0$ and standard deviation $\sigma = 1$. It is the distribution of normal z-scores.

For the standard normal distribution, the number falling z standard deviations above the mean is $\mu + z\sigma = 0 + z(1) = z$, simply the z-score itself. For instance, the value of 2.0 is two standard deviations above the mean, and the value of -1.3 is 1.3 standard deviations below the mean. As Figure 6.11 shows, the original values are the same as the z-scores, since

$$z = \frac{x - \mu}{\sigma} = \frac{x - 0}{1} = x.$$

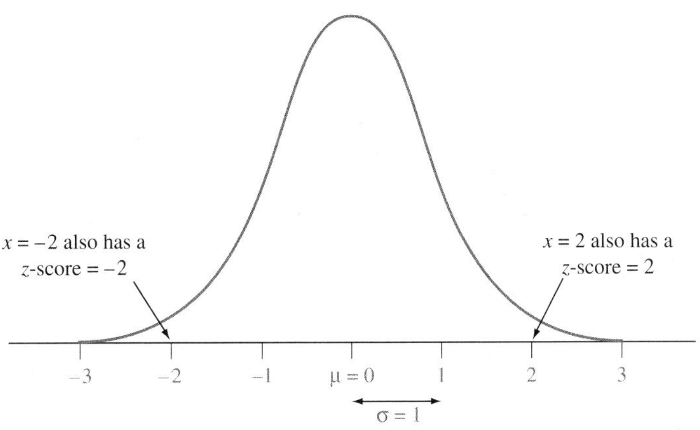

▲ **Figure 6.11 The Standard Normal Distribution.** It has mean = 0 and standard deviation = 1. The random variable value x is the same as its z-score. **Question** What are the limits within which almost all z-scores fall?

Examples 9 and 11 dealt with SAT scores, having $\mu = 500$ and $\sigma = 100$. Suppose we convert each SAT score x to a z-score by using $z = (x - \mu)/\sigma = (x - 500)/100$. Then $x = 650$ converts to $z = 1.50$, and $x = 350$ converts to $z = -1.50$. When the values for a normal distribution are converted to z-scores, those z-scores have a mean of 0 and have a standard deviation of 1. That is, the entire set of z-scores has the standard normal distribution.

z-Scores and the Standard Normal Distribution

When a random variable has a normal distribution and its values are converted to z-scores by subtracting the mean and dividing by the standard deviation, the z-scores have the **standard normal** distribution (mean = 0, standard deviation = 1).

This result will be useful for statistical inference in upcoming chapters.

6.2 Practicing the Basics

6.16 Probabilities in tails For a normal distribution, use Table A, software, or a calculator to find the probability that an observation is

TRY TECH

a. at least 1 standard deviation above the mean.

b. at least 1 standard deviation below the mean.

c. within 1 standard deviation of the mean.

For each part, sketch the normal curve and indicate the area corresponding to the probability.

6.17 Probability in graph For the normal distributions shown below, use Table A, software, or a calculator to find the probability that an observation falls in the shaded region.

TRY TECH

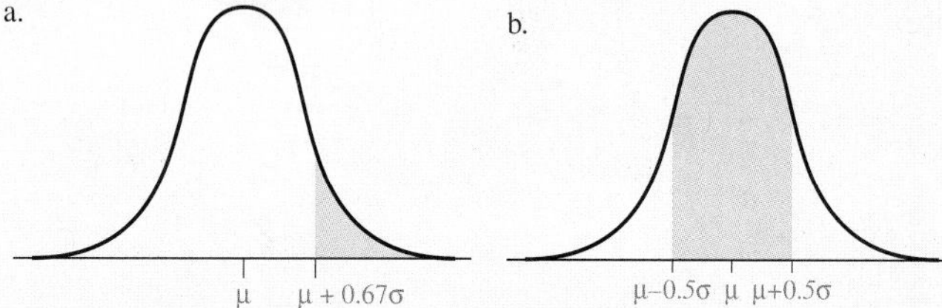

6.18 Empirical rule Verify the empirical rule by using Table A, software, or a calculator to show that for a normal distribution, the probability (rounded to two decimal places) within

TECH

a. 1 standard deviation of the mean equals 0.68.

b. 2 standard deviations of the mean equals 0.95.

c. 3 standard deviations of the mean is very close to 1.00.

In each case, sketch a normal distribution, identifying on the sketch the probabilities you used to show the result.

6.19 Central probabilities For a normal distribution, use Table A to verify that the probability (rounded to two decimal places) within

a. 1.64 standard deviations of the mean equals 0.90.

b. 2.58 standard deviations of the mean equals 0.99.

c. Find the probability that falls within 0.67 standard deviations of the mean.

d. Sketch these three cases on a single graph.

6.20 *z*-score for given probability in tails For a normal distribution,

TRY

a. Find the z-score for which a total probability of 0.02 falls more than z standard deviations (in either direction) from the mean, that is, below $\mu - z\sigma$ or above $\mu + z\sigma$.

b. For this z, explain why the probability more than z standard deviations above the mean equals 0.01.

c. Explain why $\mu + 2.33\sigma$ is the 99th percentile.

6.21 Probability in tails for given *z*-score For a normal distribution,

a. Show that a total probability of 0.01 falls more than $z = 2.58$ standard deviations from the mean.

b. Find the z-score for which the two-tail probability that falls more than that many standard deviations from the mean in either direction equals (a) 0.05, (b) 0.10. Sketch the two cases on a single graph.

6.22 *z*-score for right-tail probability

a. For the normal distribution shown below, find the z-score.

b. Find the value of z (rounding to two decimal places) for right-tail probabilities of (i) 0.05 and (ii) 0.005.

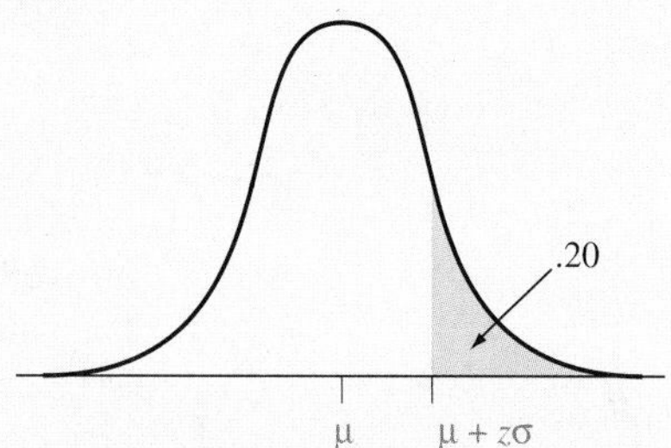

6.23 *z*-score and central probability Find the z-score such that the interval within z standard deviations of the mean (between $\mu - z\sigma$ and $\mu + z\sigma$) for a normal distribution contains

a. 50% of the probability.

b. 90% of the probability.

c. Sketch the two cases on a single graph.

6.24 Female heights The normal distribution for women's height in North America has $\mu = 65$ inches, $\sigma = 3.5$ inches. Most major airlines have height requirements for flight attendants (www.cabincrewjobs.com). Although exceptions are made, the minimum height requirement is 62 inches. What proportion of adult females in North America are not tall enough to be a flight attendant?

6.25 Blood pressure A World Health Organization study (the MONICA project) of health in various countries reported that in Canada, systolic blood pressure readings have a mean of 121 and a standard deviation of 16. A reading above 140 is considered high blood pressure.

TRY

a. What is the z-score for a blood pressure reading of 140?

b. If systolic blood pressure in Canada has a normal distribution, what proportion of Canadians suffers from high blood pressure?

c. What proportion of Canadians has systolic blood pressures in the range from 100 to 140?

d. Find the 90th percentile of blood pressure readings.

6.26 Coffee Machine Suppose your favorite coffee machine offers 12 ounce cups of coffee. The actual amount of coffee put in the cup by the machine varies according to a normal distribution, with mean equal to 13 ounces and standard deviation equal to 0.6 ounces. For each question below, sketch a graph, mark the mean, shade the area to which the answer refers and compute the percentage.

a. What percentage of cups will be filled with less than 12 ounces?

b. What percentage of cups will be filled with more than 12.5 ounces?

c. What percentage of cups will have in between 12 and 13 ounces of coffee?

6.27 Energy use An energy study in Gainesville, Florida, found that in March 2006, household use of electricity had a mean of 673 and a standard deviation of 556 kilowatt-hours. (*Source:* Data from Todd Kamhoot, Gainesville Regional Utilities.)

TECH

a. Suppose the distribution of energy use was normal. Using a table, calculator, or software that can give normal probabilities, find the proportion of households with electricity use greater than 1000 kilowatt-hours.

b. Based on the mean and standard deviation given, do you think that the distribution of energy use actually is normal? Why or why not?

6.28 Birth weight for boys In the United States, the mean birth weight for boys is 3.41 kg, with a standard deviation of 0.55 kg. (Source: cdc.com.) Assuming that the distribution of birth weight is approximately normal, find the following using a table, calculator, or software.

TECH

a. A baby is considered of low birth weight if it weighs less than 2.5 kg. What proportion of baby boys in the United States are born with low birth weight?

b. What is the z-score for a baby boy that weighs 1.5 kg (defined as extremely low birth weight)?

c. Typically, birth weight is between 2.5 kg and 4.0 kg. Find the probability a baby boy is born with typical birth weight.

d. Matteo weighs 3.6 kg at birth. He falls at what percentile?

e. Max's parents are told that their newborn son falls at the 96th percentile. How much does Max weigh?

6.29 MDI The Mental Development Index (MDI) of the Bayley Scales of Infant Development is a standardized measure used in observing infants over time. It is approximately normal with a mean of 100 and a standard deviation of 16.

TRY

a. What proportion of children has an MDI of (i) at least 120? (ii) at least 80?

b. Find the MDI score that is the 99th percentile.

c. Find the MDI score such that only 1% of the population has MDI below it.

6.30 Quartiles and outliers Refer to the previous exercise.

a. Find the z-score corresponding to the lower quartile (Q1) of a normal distribution.

b. Find and interpret the lower quartile and upper quartile of the MDI.

c. Find the interquartile range (IQR) of MDI scores.

d. Section 2.5 defined an observation to be a potential outlier if it is more than $1.5 \times$ IQR below Q1 or above Q3. Find the intervals of MDI scores that would be considered potential outliers.

6.31 April precipitation Over roughly the past 100 years, the mean monthly April precipitation in Williamstown, Massachusetts, equaled 3.6 inches with a standard deviation of 1.6 inches. (Source: http://web.williams.edu/weather/)

a. In April 1983, the wettest April on record, the precipitation equaled 8.4 inches. Find its z-score. If the distribution of precipitation were roughly normal, would this be unusually high? Explain.

b. Assuming a normal distribution, an April precipitation of 4.5 inches corresponds to what percentile?

c. Of the 119 measurements of April precipitation on record (reaching as far back as 1892), 66.5% fell within one, 97.5% within two, and 99.1% within three standard deviations of the mean. Do you think that the distribution of April precipitation is approximately normal? Why or why not?

6.32 Tall enough to ride? A new roller coaster at an amusement park requires individuals to be at least 4′ 8″ (56 inches) tall to ride. It is estimated that the heights of 10-year-old boys are normally distributed with $\mu = 54.5$ inches and $\sigma = 4.5$ inches.

TRY

a. What proportion of 10-year-old boys is tall enough to ride the coaster?

b. A smaller coaster has a height requirement of 50 inches to ride. What proportion of 10 year-old-boys is tall enough to ride this coaster?

c. What proportion of 10-year-old boys is tall enough to ride the coaster in part b but not tall enough to ride the coaster in part a?

6.33 SAT versus ACT SAT math scores follow a normal distribution with an approximate $\mu = 500$ and $\sigma = 100$. Also ACT math scores follow a normal distrubution with an approximate $\mu = 21$ and $\sigma = 4.7$. You are an admissions officer at a university and have room to admit one more student for the upcoming year. Joe scored 600 on the SAT math exam, and Kate scored 25 on the ACT math exam. If you were going to base your decision solely on their performances on the exams, which student should you admit? Explain.

TRY

6.34 Relative height Refer to the normal distributions for women's height ($\mu = 65$, $\sigma = 3.5$) and men's height ($\mu = 70, \sigma = 4.0$). A man's height of 75 inches and a woman's height of 70 inches are both 5 inches above their means. Which is relatively taller? Explain why.

6.3 Probabilities When Each Observation Has Two Possible Outcomes

We next study the most important probability distribution for discrete random variables. Learning about it helps us answer the questions we asked at the beginning of the chapter—for instance, whether there is strong evidence of discrimination against women in the selection of employees for management training.

The Binomial Distribution: Probabilities for Counts with Binary Data

In many applications, each observation is **binary:** It has one of two possible outcomes. For instance, a person may

- accept, or decline, an offer from a bank for a credit card,
- have, or not have, health insurance,
- vote yes or no in a referendum, such as whether to provide additional funds to the school district.

With a sample, we summarize such variables by counting the *number* or the *proportion* of cases with an outcome of interest. For instance, with a sample of size $n = 5$, let the random variable X denote the number of people who vote yes about some issue in a referendum. The possible values for X are 0, 1, 2, 3, 4, and 5. Under certain conditions, a random variable X that counts the number of observations of a particular type has a probability distribution called the **binomial distribution**.

Consider n cases, called **trials**, in which we observe a binary random variable. This is a *fixed number*, such as the $n = 5$ observations from a sample of five voters. The number X (trials in which the outcome of interest occurs) can take any one of the integer values $0, 1, 2, \ldots, n$. The binomial distribution specifies probabilities for these possible values of X when the following three conditions hold:

Conditions for Binomial Distribution

- Each of n trials has two possible outcomes. The outcome of interest is called a success and the other outcome is called a failure.
- Each trial has the same probability of a success. This is denoted by p, so the probability of a success is p and the probability of a failure is $1 - p$.
- The n trials are independent. That is, the result for one trial does not depend on the results of other trials.

The **binomial random variable** X is the **number of successes** in the n trials.

Flipping a coin n times, where n is determined in advance, is a prototype for the binomial distribution:

- Each trial is a flip of the coin. There are two possible outcomes for each flip, head or tail. Let's identify (arbitrarily) head as a success.
- If head or tail are equally likely, the probability of head (a success) equals $p = 0.50$. This success probability is the same for each flip.
- The flips are independent, since the result for any specific flip does not depend on the outcomes of previous flips.

The binomial random variable X counts the number of heads (the outcome of interest) in the n flips. With $n = 3$ coin flips, X = number of heads could equal 0, 1, 2, or 3.

Example 12

Binomial Probabilities ◄

Speed Dating

Picture the Scenario

You are planning to attend a local speed dating event where you will meet three randomly selected candidates. The rules dictate that you talk to each one for two minutes before moving on to the next. After meeting all three,

you reveal to the organizers the names of the candidates you liked, if any. For each candidate, a match is established if he or she liked you back. Going into the event, you assume your chances of establishing a match with any given candidate are 20% and that outcomes of meetings with different candidates are independent events.

Question to Explore

What is the probability that you will match with two of the three candidates you meet?

Think It Through

Each of your three meetings with a candidate is a trial, with binary outcome whether it results in a match or not. Let the random variable X = number of matches when meeting $n = 3$ candidates. Then $X = 0, 1, 2$, or 3. Let p denote the probability of a match, which you assume is 0.2. $1 - p = 0.8$ is the probability of not establishing a match. Denote the outcome of a trial (= meeting) by S or F, representing success or failure based on you matching with the candidate or not. Table 6.4 shows the eight possible outcomes when meeting 3 candidates. For instance, FSS represents no match with the first but successful matches with the second and third candidate. Table 6.4 also shows the probabilities for each outcome by using the multiplication rule for independent events. We can use it because we assume that outcomes of meetings with different candidates are independent events. The three ways in which we can get two matches are SSF, SFS, and FSS. Each of these has probability equal to $(0.2)^2(0.8) = 0.032$. The total probability of two matches is $3(0.2)^2(0.8) = 3(0.032) = 0.096$.

Recall

From Section 5.2, for independent events, P(A and B) = P(A)P(B). Thus, P(FSS) = P(F)P(S)P(S) = 0.8 × 0.2 × 0.2. ◀

Table 6.4 Sample Space and Probabilities in Three Meetings

For each of the three meetings, the probability of a match is 0.2.

Outcome	Probability	Outcome	Probability
SSS	$0.2 \times 0.2 \times 0.2 = (0.2)^3$	SFF	$0.2 \times 0.8 \times 0.8 = (0.2)^1(0.8)^2$
SSF	$0.2 \times 0.2 \times 0.8 = (0.2)^2(0.8)^1$	FSF	$0.8 \times 0.2 \times 0.8 = (0.2)^1(0.8)^2$
SFS	$0.2 \times 0.8 \times 0.2 = (0.2)^2(0.8)^1$	FFS	$0.8 \times 0.8 \times 0.2 = (0.2)^1(0.8)^2$
FSS	$0.8 \times 0.2 \times 0.2 = (0.2)^2(0.8)^1$	FFF	$0.8 \times 0.8 \times 0.8 = (0.8)^3$

Insight

With general probability of a match p, the solution for $x = 2$ matches in $n = 3$ trials equals $3(p)^2(1 - p)^1 = 3(p)^x(1 - p)^{n-x}$. The multiple of 3 represents the number of ways that two successes can occur in three trials (SSF or SFS or FSS). You can use similar logic to evaluate the probability that $x = 0$, or 1, or 3. Try $x = 1$, for which you should get P(1) = 0.384.

▶ ***Try Exercise 6.35, part a***

The formula for binomial probabilities When the number of trials n is large, it's tedious to write out all the possible outcomes in the sample space. But there's a formula you can use to find binomial probabilities for *any* n and p.

Did You Know?

For probability calculations with the normal distribution, we needed to specify two parameters, μ and σ. With the binomial distribution, we also need to specify two parameters, n and p. ◀

Probabilities for a Binomial Distribution

Denote the probability of success on a trial by p. For n independent trials, the probability of x successes equals

$$P(x) = \frac{n!}{x!(n-x)!}p^x(1-p)^{n-x},\ x = 0, 1, 2, \ldots, n.$$

Did You Know?

The term with factorials at the start of the binomial formula is

$$\binom{n}{x} = \frac{n!}{x!(n-x)!},$$

which is also called the **binomial coefficient**. It is the number of outcomes that have x successes in n trials, such as the

$$\binom{n}{x} = \binom{3}{2} = \frac{3!}{2!1!} = 3$$

outcomes (SSF, SFS, and FSS) that have $x = 2$ successes in $n = 3$ trials in Example 12. Another symbol used for the binomial coefficient, often shown on calculators, is nCx. ◀

The symbol $n!$ is called ***n* factorial**. It represents $n! = 1 \times 2 \times 3 \times \ldots \times n$, the product of all integers from 1 to n. That is, $1! = 1, 2! = 1 \times 2 = 2$, $3! = 1 \times 2 \times 3 = 6$, $4! = 1 \times 2 \times 3 \times 4 = 24$, and so forth. Also, 0! is defined to be 1. For given values for p and n, you can find the probabilities of the possible outcomes by substituting values for x into the binomial formula.

Let's use this formula to find the answer for Example 12 about speed dating:

- The random variable X represents the number of matches (successes) in $n = 3$ meetings (trials).
- The probability of a match in a particular trial is $p = 0.2$.
- The probability of exactly two matches in three meetings is the binomial probability with $n = 3, x = 2$ and success probability $p = 0.2$,

$$P(2) = \frac{n!}{x!(n-x)!}p^x(1-p)^{n-x} = \frac{3!}{2!1!}(0.2)^2(0.8)^1 = 3(0.04)(0.8) = 0.096.$$

What's the role of the different terms in this binomial formula?

- The factorial term tells us the number of possible outcomes that have $x = 2$ successes. Here, $3!/(2!1!) = (3 \times 2 \times 1)/[(2 \times 1)(1)] = 3$ tells us there were three possible outcomes with two successful matches, namely SSF, SFS, and FSS.
- The term $(0.2)^2(0.8)^1$ with the exponents gives the probability for each such sequence. Here, the probability is $(0.2)^2(0.8) = 0.032$ for each of the three sequences having $x = 2$ successful matches, for a total probability of $3(0.032) = 0.096$.

Try to calculate P(1) by letting $x = 1$ in the binomial formula with $n = 3$ and $p = 0.2$. You should get 0.384. You'll see that there are again three possible sequences, now each with probability $(0.2)^1(0.8)^2 = 0.128$. Table 6.5 summarizes the calculations for all four possible x values. You can also find binomial probabilities using statistical software, such as MINITAB, the Binomial Distribution web app (see screenshot in the margin) or a calculator with statistical functions.

Screenshot from the Binomial Distribution web app

Table 6.5 The Binomial Distribution for $n = 3, p = 0.20$

When $n = 3$, the binomial random variable X can take any integer value between 0 and 3. As always, the total probability equals 1.0.

x	$P(x) = [n!/(x!(n-x)!)]p^x(1-p)^{n-x}$
0	$0.512 = [3!/(0!3!)](0.2)^0(0.8)^3$
1	$0.384 = [3!/(1!2!)](0.2)^1(0.8)^2$
2	$0.096 = [3!/(2!1!)](0.2)^2(0.8)^1$
3	$0.008 = [3!/(3!0!)](0.2)^3(0.8)^0$

Binomial distribution ◀

Binomial Probability Distribution for $n = 10$ and $p = 0.5$

x	P(x)	x	P(x)
0	0.001	6	0.205
1	0.010	7	0.117
2	0.044	8	0.044
3	0.117	9	0.010
4	0.205	10	0.001
5	0.246		

Example 13

Testing for Gender Bias in Promotions

Picture the Scenario

Example 1 introduced a case involving possible discrimination against female employees. A group of women employees has claimed that female employees are less likely than male employees of similar qualifications to be promoted.

Question to Explore

Suppose the large employee pool that can be tapped for management training is half female and half male. In a group recently selected for promotion, none of the 10 individuals chosen were female. What would be the probability of 0 females in 10 selections, if there truly were no gender bias?

Think It Through

If there is no gender bias, other factors being equal, at each choice the probability of selecting a female equals 0.50 and the probability of selecting a male equals 0.50. Let X denote the number of females selected for promotion in a random sample of 10 employees. Then, the possible values for X are $0, 1, \ldots, 10$, and X has the binomial distribution with $n = 10$ and $p = 0.50$. For each x between 0 and 10, we can find the probability that x of the 10 people selected are female using the binomial formula

$$P(x) = \frac{n!}{x!(n-x)!}p^x(1-p)^{n-x} = \frac{10!}{x!(10-x)!}(0.50)^x(0.50)^{10-x}, x = 0, 1, 2, \ldots, 10.$$

The probability that no females are chosen $(x = 0)$ equals

$$P(0) = \frac{10!}{0!10!}(0.50)^0(0.50)^{10} = (0.50)^{10} = 0.001.$$

Any number raised to the power of 0 equals 1. Also, $0! = 1$, and the 10! terms in the numerator and denominator divide out, leaving $P(0) = (0.50)^{10}$. If the employees were chosen randomly, it is very unlikely (one chance in a thousand) that none of the 10 selected for promotion would have been female.

Insight

In summary, because this probability is so small, seeing no women chosen would make us highly skeptical that the choices were random with respect to gender.

▶ ***Try Exercise 6.46***

In this example, we found the probability that $x = 0$ female employees would be chosen for promotion. To get a more complete understanding of just which outcomes are likely, you can find the probabilities of *all* the possible x values. The table in the margin lists the entire binomial distribution for $n = 10$, $p = 0.50$. In the table, the least likely values for x are 0 and 10. If the employees were randomly selected, it is highly unlikely that 0 females or 10 females would be selected. If your statistical software provides binomial probabilities, see if

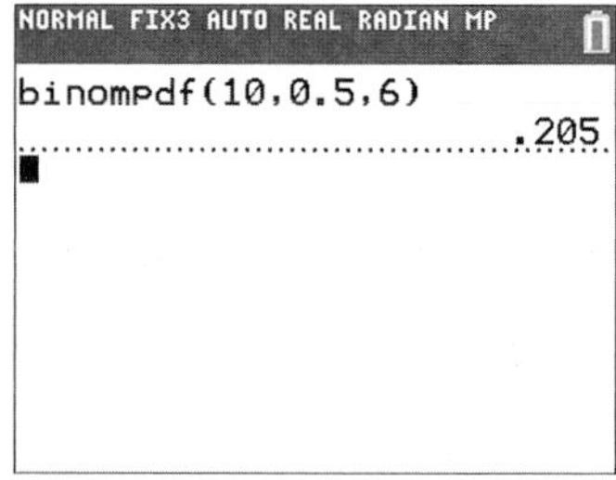

TI output for computing $P(X = 6)$

you can verify that $P(0) = 0.001$, $P(1) = 0.010$ and any of the other probabilities. The margin shows a screen shot of the TI calculator providing the binomial probability of $x = 6$.

The left graph in Figure 6.12 shows the binomial distribution with $n = 10$ and $p = 0.50$. It has a symmetric appearance around $x = 5$. For instance, $x = 10$ has the same probability as $x = 0$. The binomial distribution is perfectly symmetric only when $p = 0.50$. When $p \neq 0.50$, the binomial distribution has a skewed appearance. The degree of skew increases as p gets closer to 0 or 1. To illustrate, the graph on the right in Figure 6.12 shows the binomial distribution for $n = 10$ when $p = 0.15$. If 15% of the people who might be promoted were female, it would not be especially surprising to observe 3, 2, 1, or even 0 females in the sample, but the probabilities drop sharply for larger x-values.

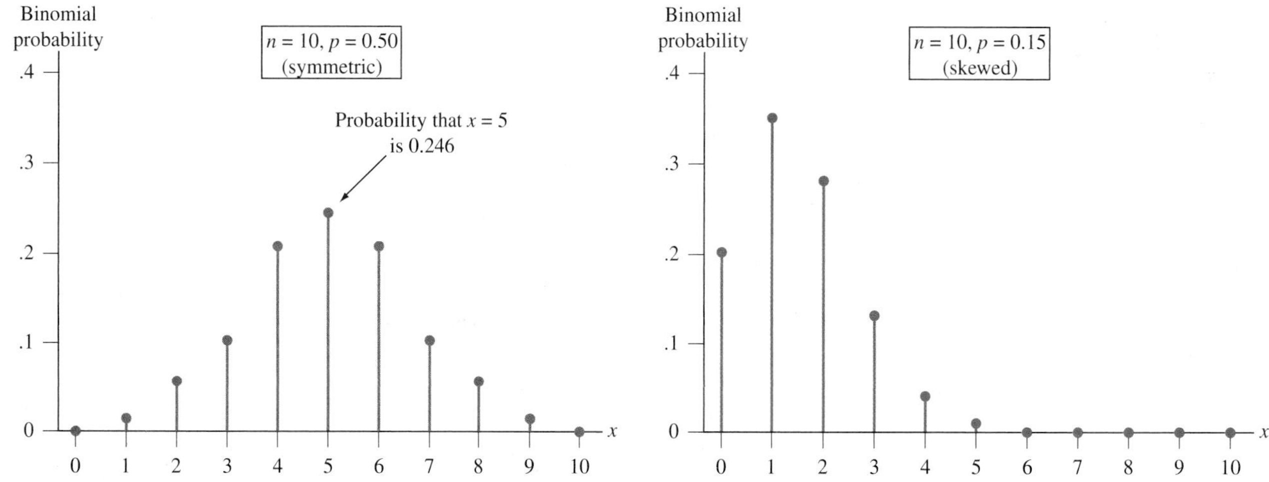

▲ **Figure 6.12** Binomial Distributions When $n = 10$ for $p = 0.5$ and for $p = 0.15$. The binomial probability distribution is symmetric when $p = 0.5$, but it can be quite skewed for p near 0 or near 1. **Question** How do you think the distribution would look if $p = 0.85$?

Check to See If Binomial Conditions Apply

Before you use the binomial distribution, check that its three conditions apply. These are (1) binary data (success or failure), (2) the same probability of success for each trial (denoted by p), and (3) a fixed number n of independent trials. To judge this, ask yourself whether the observations resemble coin flipping, the simple prototype for the binomial. For instance, it seems plausible to use the binomial distribution for Example 13 on gender bias in selecting employees for promotion. In this instance,

- The data are binary because (female, male) plays the role of (head, tail).
- If employees are randomly selected, the probability p of selecting a female on any given trial is 0.50.
- With random sampling of 10 employees, the outcome for one trial does not depend on the outcome of another trial.

Caution

A binomial random variable counts the **number of successes out of *n* trials**. Its possible values are 0 to n. In Example 2, where X was equal to the number of games played in a best out of seven series, X is **not** binomial. There, we didn't count successes but rather how many games are played, with possible values ranging from 4 to 7. ◄

Example 14

Binomial sampling ◄

Gender Bias in Promotions

Picture the Scenario

Consider the gender bias investigation in Example 13. Suppose the population of individuals to choose for promotion contained only four people, two men and two women (instead of the very large pool of employees), and the number chosen was $n = 2$.

Question to Explore

Do the binomial conditions apply for calculating the probability, under random sampling, of selecting 0 women in the two choices for promotion?

Think It Through

If zero women are selected, the two persons selected must be male. The probability that the first person selected is male is $1/2$. Given that the first person selected was male, the conditional probability that the second person selected is male equals $1/3$, since the pool of individuals now has one man and two women. So, the outcome of the second selection *depends* on that of the first. The trials are *not* independent, which the binomial requires. In summary, the binomial conditions do not apply.

Insight

This example suggests a caution when applying the binomial to a random sample from a population. For trials to be sufficiently close to independent with common probability p of success, the population size must be large relative to the sample size.

► ***Try Exercise 6.49***

Recall

As Section 5.3 discussed, if once subjects are selected from a population they are not eligible to be selected again, this is called *sampling without replacement.* Example 10 in Section 5.3 showed the effect on sampling from a small population versus a large population. ◀

In Practice Population and Sample Sizes to Use the Binomial

For sampling n separate subjects from a population (that is, sampling without replacement), the exact probability distribution of the number of successes is too complex to discuss in this text, but the binomial distribution approximates it well when n is less than 10% of the population size. In practice, sample sizes are usually small compared to population sizes, and this guideline is satisfied.

The margin shows a guideline about the relative sizes of the sample and population for which the binomial formula works well. For example, suppose your school has 4000 students. Then the binomial formula is adequate as long as the sample size is less than 10% of 4000, which is 400. Why? Because the probability of success for any one observation will be similar regardless of what happens on other observations. Likewise, Example 13 dealt with the selection of 10 employees for promotion when the employee pool for promotion was very large. Again, the sample size was less than 10% of the population size, so using the binomial is valid.

Mean and Standard Deviation of the Binomial Distribution

As with any discrete probability distribution, we can use the formula $\mu = \Sigma x P(x)$ to find the mean. However, finding the mean μ and standard deviation σ is actually simpler for the binomial distribution. There are special formulas based on the number of trials n and the probability p of success on each trial.

Binomial Mean and Standard Deviation

The binomial probability distribution for n trials with probability p of success on each trial has mean μ and standard deviation σ given by

$$\mu = np, \quad \sigma = \sqrt{np(1 - p)}.$$

The formula for the mean makes sense intuitively. If the probability of success is p for a given trial, then we expect about a proportion p of the n trials to be successes, or about np total. If we flipped a fair coin ($p = 0.50$) 100 times, we expect that about $np = 100(0.50) = 50$ flips come up heads.

When the number of trials n is large, it can be tedious to calculate binomial probabilities of all the possible outcomes. Often, it's adequate merely to use the mean and standard deviation to describe where most of the probability falls. The binomial distribution has a bell shape when n is large (as explained in a guideline at the end of this section), so in that case, we can use the normal distribution to approximate the binomial distribution and conclude that nearly all the probability falls between $\mu - 3\sigma$ and $\mu + 3\sigma$.

Example 15

Binomial distributions ◀

Checking for Racial Profiling

Picture the Scenario

In 2006, the New York City Police Department (NYPD) confronted approximately 500,000 pedestrians for suspected criminal violations. Of those confronted, 88.9% were non-white. Meanwhile, according to the 2006 American Community Survey conducted by the U.S. Bureau of the Census, of the more than 8 million individuals living in New York City, 44.6% were white.

Question to Explore

Are the data presented above evidence of racial profiling in police officers' decisions to confront particular individuals?

Think It Through

We'll treat the 500,000 confrontations as $n = 500{,}000$ trials. From the fact that 44.6% of the population was white, we can deduce that the other 55.4% was non-white. Then, if there is no racial profiling, the probability that any given confrontation should involve a non-white suspect is $p = 0.554$ (other things being equal, such as the rate of engaging in criminal activity). Suppose also that successive confrontations are independent. (They would not be, for example, if once an individual were stopped, the police followed that individual and repeatedly stopped her or him.) Under these assumptions, for the 500,000 police confrontations, the number of non-whites confronted has a binomial distribution with $n = 500{,}000$ and $p = 0.554$.

Recall

From Section 6.2, when a distribution has a normal distribution, nearly 100% of the observations fall within 3 standard deviations of the mean. ◀

The binomial distribution with $n = 500{,}000$ and $p = 0.554$ has

$$\mu = np = 500{,}000(0.554) = 277{,}000,$$
$$\text{and } \sigma = \sqrt{np(1-p)} = \sqrt{500{,}000(0.554)(0.446)} = 351.$$

Below we see that this binomial distribution is approximated reasonably well by the normal distribution because the number of trials is so large. Then, the probability of falling within 3 standard deviations of the mean is close to 1.0. This is the interval between

$$\mu - 3\sigma = 277{,}000 - 3(351) = 275{,}947$$
$$\text{and } \mu + 3\sigma = 277{,}000 + 3(351) = 278{,}053.$$

If no racial profiling is taking place, we would not be surprised if between about 275,947 and 278,053 of the 500,000 people stopped were non-white. See the smooth curve approximation for the binomial in the margin. However, 88.9% of all stops, or $500{,}000(0.889) = 444{,}500$, involved non-whites. This suggests that the number of non-whites stopped is much higher than we would expect if the probability of confronting a pedestrian were the same for each resident, regardless of his or her race.

275,947 277,000 278,053 444,500

Insight

By this approximate analysis, we would not expect to see so many non-whites stopped if there were truly a 0.554 chance that each confrontation involved a non-white. If we were to use software to do a more precise analysis by calculating the binomial probabilities of *all* possible values 0, 1, 2, ... 500,000 when $n = 500{,}000$ and $p = 0.544$, we'd find that the probability of getting 444,500 or a larger value out in the right tail of the distribution is 0 to the precision of many decimal places (that is, 0.00000000...).

The controversial subject of racial profiling continues to receive nationwide attention. A 2013 report by the Bureau of Justice Statistics[7] based on 2011 survey data found that relatively more black drivers (13%) than white (10%) and Hispanic (10%) drivers were pulled over in a traffic stop and that white drivers were both ticketed and searched at lower rates than black and Hispanic drivers.

▶ ***Try Exercise 6.45***

In Practice When the Binomial Distribution Is Approximately Normal

The binomial distribution can be approximated well by the normal distribution when n is large enough that the expected number of successes, np, and the expected number of failures, $n(1 - p)$, are both at least 15.

The solution in Example 15 treated the binomial distribution as having approximately a normal distribution. This holds when n is sufficiently large. The margin shows a guideline.[8]

In Example 15, of those stopped, the expected number who were non-white was $np = 500{,}000(0.554) = 277{,}000$. The expected number who were white was $n(1 - p) = 500{,}000(0.446) = 223{,}000$. Both exceed 15, so this binomial distribution has approximately a normal distribution which we can use to find the probability for any given interval. (See figure in margin.).

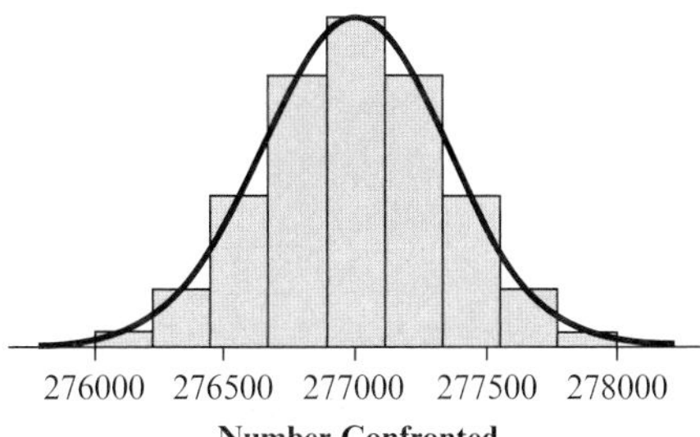

[7] *Source:* The report with accompanying statistics is available at http://www.bjs.gov and searching for "Police Behavior During Traffic And Street Stops, 2011."

[8] A lower bound of 15 is actually a bit higher than needed. The binomial is bell shaped even when both np and $n(1 - p)$ are about 10. We use 15 here because it ties in better with a guideline in coming chapters for using the normal distribution for inference about proportions.

6.3 Practicing the Basics

6.35 Kidney transplants In kidney transplantations, compatibility between donor and receiver depends on such factors as blood type and antigens. Suppose that for a randomly selected donor from a large national kidney registry, there is a 10% chance that he or she is compatible with a specific receiver. Three donors are randomly selected from this registry. Find the probability that 0, 1, 2, or all 3 selected donors are compatible.
TRY

a. Do this by constructing the sample space and finding the probability for each possible outcome of choosing three donors. Use these probabilities to construct the probability distribution.

b. Do this using the formula for the binomial distribution.

6.36 Compatible donors Refer to the previous exercise. Let the random variable X = number of compatible donors. Check the conditions for X to be binomial by answering parts a–c.

a. What constitutes a trial, how many trials are there, and how many outcomes does each trial have?

b. Does each trial have the same probability of success? Explain

c. Are the trials independent?

6.37 Symmetric binomial Construct a graph similar to that in Figure 6.1 for each of the following binomial distributions:

a. $n = 4$ and $p = 0.50$.

b. $n = 4$ and $p = 0.30$.

c. $n = 4$ and $p = 0.10$.

d. Which if any of the graphs in parts a–c are symmetric? Without actually constructing the graph, would the case $n = 20$ and $p = 0.50$ be symmetric or skewed?

e. Which of the graphs in parts a–c is the most heavily skewed? Without actually constructing the graph, would the case $n = 4$ and $p = 0.01$ exhibit more or less skewness than the graph in part c?

6.38 Number of girls in a family Each newborn baby has a probability of approximately 0.49 of being female and 0.51 of being male. For a family with four children, let X = number of children who are girls.

a. Explain why the three conditions are satisfied for X to have the binomial distribution.

b. Identify n and p for the binomial distribution.

c. Find the probability that the family has two girls and two boys.

6.39 Bidding on eBay You are bidding on four items available on eBay. You think that for each bid, you have a 25% chance of winning it, and the outcomes of the four bids are independent events. Let X denote the number of winning bids out of the four items you bid on.

a. Explain why the distribution of X can be modeled by the binomial distribution.

b. Find the probability that you win exactly 2 bids.

c. Find the probability that you win 2 bids or fewer.

d. Find the probability that you win more than 2 bids.

6.40 More eBay bidding For each of the following situations, explain whether the binomial distribution applies for X.

a. You are bidding on four items available on eBay. You think that you will win the first bid with probability 25% and the second through fourth bids with probability 30%. Let X denote the number of winning bids out of the four items you bid on.

b. You are bidding on four items available on eBay. Each bid is for $70, and you think there is a 25% chance of winning a bid, with bids being independent events. Let X be the total amount of money you pay for your winning bids.

6.41 Passing by guessing A quiz in a statistics course has four multiple-choice questions, each with five possible answers. A passing grade is three or more correct answers to the four questions. Allison has not studied for the quiz. She has no idea of the correct answer to any of the questions and decides to guess at random for each.

a. Find the probability she lucks out and answers all four questions correctly.

b. Find the probability that she passes the quiz.

6.42 NBA shooting In the National Basketball Association, the top free throw shooters usually have probability of about 0.90 of making any given free throw.

a. During a game, one such player (Dirk Nowitzki) shot 10 free throws. Let X = number of free throws made. What must you assume for X to have a binomial distribution? (Studies have shown that such assumptions are well satisfied for this sport.)

b. Specify the values of n and p for the binomial distribution of X in part a.

c. Find the probability that he made (i) all 10 free throws (ii) 9 free throws and (iii) more than 7 free throws.

6.43 Season performance Refer to the previous exercise. Over the course of a season, this player shoots 400 free throws.

a. Find the mean and standard deviation of the probability distribution of the number of free throws he makes.

b. By the normal distribution approximation, within what range would you expect the number made almost certainly to fall? Why?

c. Within what range would you expect the *proportion* made to fall?

6.44 Is the die balanced? A balanced die with six sides is rolled 60 times.

a. For the binomial distribution of X = number of 6s, what is n and what is p?

b. Find the mean and the standard deviation of the distribution of X. Interpret.

c. If you observe $x = 0$, would you be skeptical that the die is balanced? Explain why, based on the mean and standard deviation of X.

d. Show that the probability that $x = 0$ is 0.0000177.

6.45 Exit poll TRY An exit poll is taken of 3000 voters in a statewide election. Let X denote the number who voted in favor of a special proposition designed to lower property taxes and raise the sales tax. Suppose that in the population, exactly 50% voted for it.

a. Explain why this scenario would seem to satisfy the three conditions needed to use the binomial distribution. Identify n and p for the binomial.

b. Find the mean and standard deviation of the probability distribution of X.

c. Using the normal distribution approximation, give an interval in which you would expect X almost certainly to fall, if truly $p = 0.50$. (*Hint*: You can follow the reasoning of Example 15 on racial profiling.)

d. Now, suppose that the exit poll had $x = 1706$. What would this suggest to you about the actual value of p?

6.46 Jury duty TRY The juror pool for the upcoming murder trial of a celebrity actor contains the names of 100,000 individuals in the population who may be called for jury duty. The proportion of the available jurors on the population list who are Hispanic is 0.40. A jury of size 12 is selected at random from the population list of available jurors. Let X = the number of Hispanics selected to be jurors for this jury.

a. Is it reasonable to assume that X has a binomial distribution? If so, identify the values of n and p. If not, explain why not.

b. Find the probability that no Hispanic is selected.

c. If no Hispanic is selected out of a sample of size 12, does this cast doubt on whether the sampling was truly random? Explain.

6.47 Poor, poor, Pirates TECH On September 7, 2008, the Pittsburgh Pirates lost their 82nd game of the 2008 season and tied the 1933–1948 Philadelphia Phillies major sport record (baseball, football, basketball, and hockey) for most consecutive losing seasons at 16. In fact, their losing streak continued until 2012 with 20 consecutive losing seasons. A Major League Baseball season consists of 162 games, so for the Pirates to end their streak, they need to win at least 81 games in a season (which they did in 2013).

a. Over the course of the streak, the Pirates have won approximately 42% of their games. For simplicity, assume the number of games they win in a given season follows a binomial distribution with $n = 162$ and $p = 0.42$. What is their expected number of wins in a season?

b. What is the probability that the Pirates will win at least 81 games in a given season? (You may use technology to find the exact binomial probability or use the normal distribution to approximate the probability by finding a z-score for 81 and then evaluating the appropriate area under the normal curve.)

c. Can you think of any factors that might make the binomial distribution an inappropriate model for the number of games won in a season?

6.48 Checking guidelines For Example 13 on the gender distribution of promotions, the population size was more than one thousand, half of whom were female. The sample size was 10.

a. Check whether the guideline was satisfied about the relative sizes of the population and the sample, thus allowing you to use the binomial for the probability distribution for the number of females selected.

b. Check whether the guideline was satisfied for this binomial distribution to be approximated well by a normal distribution.

6.49 Class sample TRY Four of the 20 students (20%) in a class are fraternity or sorority members. Five students are picked at random. Does $X =$ the number of students in the sample who are fraternity or sorority members have the binomial distribution with $n = 5$ and $p = 0.20$? Explain why or why not.

6.50 Binomial needs fixed *n* For the binomial distribution, the number of trials n is a fixed number. Let X denote the number of girls in a randomly selected family in Canada that has three children. Let Y denote the number of girls in a randomly selected family in Canada (that is, the number of children could be any number). A binomial distribution approximates well the probability distribution for one of X and Y, but not for the other.

a. Explain why.

b. Identify the case for which the binomial applies and identify n and p.

6.51 Binomial assumptions For the following random variables, explain why at least one condition needed to use the binomial distribution is unlikely to be satisfied.

a. $X =$ number of people in a family of size 4 who go to church on a given Sunday, when any one of them goes 50% of the time in the long run (binomial, $n = 4$, $p = 0.50$). (*Hint:* Is the independence assumption plausible?)

b. $X =$ number voting for the Democratic candidate out of the 100 votes in the first precinct that reports results, when 60% of the population voted for the Democrat in that state (binomial, $n = 100$, $p = 0.60$). (*Hint:* Is the probability of voting for the Democratic candidate the same in each precinct?)

c. $X =$ number of females in a random sample of four students from a class of size 20, when half the class is female (binomial, $n = 4$, $p = 0.50$).

Chapter Review

ANSWERS TO THE CHAPTER FIGURE QUESTIONS

Figure 6.1 The shape of the distribution is skewed to the left.

Figure 6.2 The area under the curve from 0 to 15 should be shaded.

Figure 6.3 The shape of the distribution is bell shaped. The probability for a female to be taller than 65 inches is about 50%.

Figure 6.4 The distribution for women has a smaller standard deviation. It is more peaked (and its curve is higher) because it extends over a smaller range. We evaluate $70 \pm 3(4)$, which gives an interval for the men's heights from 58 inches to 82 inches.

Figure 6.5 These probabilities are similar to the percentages stated for the empirical rule. The empirical rule states that for an approximately bell-shaped distribution, approximately 68% of the observations fall within 1 standard deviation of the mean, 95% within 2 standard deviations of the mean, and nearly all within 3 standard deviations of the mean.

Figure 6.8 For 3 standard deviations, the probability in one tail is 0.0013. By symmetry, this is also the probability in the other tail. The total tail area is 0.0026, which subtracted from 1 gives an answer of 0.997.

Figure 6.9 The second percentile is the value located on the left side of the curve such that 2% of the distribution falls below it and 98% falls above.

Figure 6.10 The SAT score with $z = -3$ is $500 - 3(100) = 200$. The SAT score with $z = 3$ is $500 + 3(100) = 800$.

Figure 6.11 The values of -3 and 3.

Figure 6.12 The distribution with $p = 0.85$ is skewed to the left.

CHAPTER SUMMARY

- A **random variable** is a numerical measurement of the outcome of a random phenomenon. As with ordinary variables, random variables can be **discrete** (taking separate values) or **continuous** (taking an interval of values).

- A **probability distribution** specifies probabilities for the possible values of a random variable. Probability distributions have summary measures of the center and the variability, such as the mean μ and standard deviation σ. The mean (also called **expected value**) for a discrete random variable is

$$\mu = \Sigma x P(x),$$

where $P(x)$ is the probability of the outcome x and the sum is taken over all possible outcomes.

- The **normal distribution** is the probability distribution of a continuous random variable that has a symmetric bell-shaped graph specified by the parameters mean (μ) and standard deviation (σ). For any z, the probability of falling within z standard deviations of μ is the same for every normal distribution. For $z = 1, 2$, and 3, these probabilities are 68%, 95%, and almost 100%.

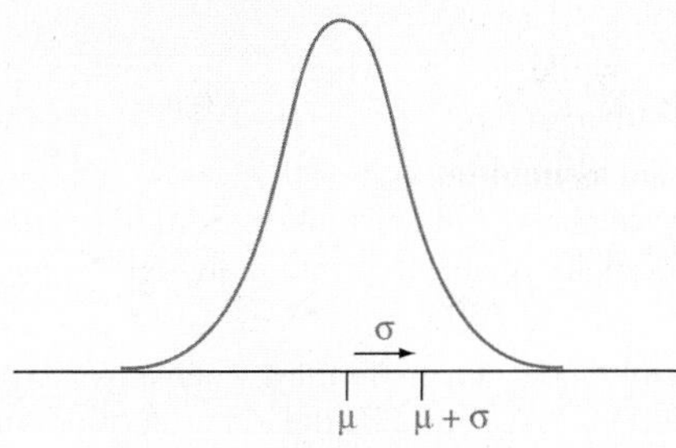

- The **z-score** for a value x of a random variable with mean μ and standard deviation σ equals

$$z = (x - \mu)/\sigma.$$

It measures the number of standard deviations that x falls from the mean μ. For a normal distribution, the z-scores have the **standard normal distribution**, which has mean = 0 and standard deviation = 1.

- The **binomial distribution** is the probability distribution of the discrete random variable that measures the number of successes X in n independent trials, with probability p of a success on a given trial. It has

$$P(x) = \frac{n!}{x!(n-x)!} p^x (1-p)^{n-x}, x = 0, 1, 2, \ldots, n.$$

The mean is $\mu = np$, and the standard deviation is

$$\sigma = \sqrt{np(1-p)}.$$

SUMMARY OF NEW NOTATION IN CHAPTER 6

$P(x)$	Probability that a random variable takes value x
σ	Standard deviation of the probability distribution or population distribution
μ	Mean of the probability distribution or population distribution
$p, 1 - p$	Probabilities of the two possible outcomes of a binary variable

CHAPTER PROBLEMS

Practicing the Basics

6.52 **Grandparents** Let X = the number of living grandparents that a randomly selected adult American has. According to recent General Social Surveys, its probability distribution is approximately $P(0) = 0.71$, $P(1) = 0.15$, $P(2) = 0.09$, $P(3) = 0.03$, $P(4) = 0.02$.

a. Does this refer to a discrete or a continuous random variable? Why?

b. Show that the probabilities satisfy the two conditions for a probability distribution.

c. Find the mean of this probability distribution.

6.53 **Straight or boxed?** Consider a Pick-3 lottery such as the one described in Exercise 6.7. Suppose your birthday is May 14, and like many people, you decide to bet $1 on your birthday number (i.e., 514) on your birthday. There are two options to play, straight or boxed. If you choose to play straight, you win $500 if and only if the number chosen is 514. If you choose to play boxed, you win $80 if the number chosen contains the digits 5, 1, and 4 in any order. Which option would you prefer to play and why?

6.54 **Auctioning paintings** A collector is interested in two paintings by the same artist available at an auction. She plans to bid $3,000 for the first painting auctioned off and $2,000 for the second. She estimates that the probability she will win the bid for the first painting (and spend $3,000) is 30%. If she gets that first painting, she thinks there is an 80% chance she will also win the bid for the second painting (and spend another $2,000). If she does not win the bid for the first painting, she thinks there is only a 10% chance she will win the bid for the second painting. Let X denote the random variable denoting the amount of money the collector will spend at the auction.

a. List the sample space of all possible outcomes of winning or losing the bids for the two paintings. (Draw a tree diagram.)

b. Are the events of winning the bid for the first painting and winning the bid for the second painting independent events? Explain.

c. Find the probability of each outcome in the sample space. (Use the tree diagram.)

d. Find the probability distribution of X.

e. Find the mean of X.

6.55 **NJ Lottery** New Jersey has a six-way combination lottery game in which you pick three digits (each can be any of 0, 1, 2, ..., 9) and you win if the digits the lottery picks are the same as yours in any of the six possible orders. For a dollar bet, a winner receives $45.50. Two possible strategies are (a) to pick three different digits, or (b) to pick the same digit three times. Let X = winnings for a single bet.

a. Find the probability distribution of X and its mean for strategy a.

b. Find the probability distribution of X and its mean for strategy b.

c. Which is the better strategy? Why?

6.56 Are you risk averse? You need to choose between two alternative programs for dealing with the outbreak of a deadly disease. In program 1, 200 people are saved. In program 2, there is a 2/3 chance that no one is saved and a 1/3 chance that 600 people are saved.

a. Find the expected number of lives saved with each program.

b. Now you need to choose between program 3, in which 400 people will die, and program 4, in which there is a 1/3 chance that no one will die and a 2/3 chance that 600 people will die. Find the expected number of deaths with each program.

c. Explain why programs 1 and 3 are similar and why 2 and 4 are similar. (If you had to choose, would you be like most people and be risk averse in part a, choosing program 1, and risk taking in part b, choosing program 4?)

6.57 Flyers' insurance An insurance company sells a policy to airline passengers for \$1. If a flyer dies on a given flight (from a plane crash), the policy gives \$100,000 to the chosen beneficiary. Otherwise, there is no return. Records show that a passenger has about a one in a million chance of dying on any given flight. You buy a policy for your next flight.

a. Specify the probability distribution of the amount of money the beneficiary makes from your policy.

b. Find the mean of the probability distribution in part a. Interpret.

c. Explain why the company is very likely to make money in the long run.

6.58 Normal probabilities For a normal distribution, find the probability that an observation is

a. Within 1.96 standard deviations of the mean.

b. More than 2.33 standard deviations from the mean.

6.59 z-scores Find the z-score such that the interval within z standard deviations of the mean contains probability (a) 0.95 and (b) 0.99 for a normal distribution. Sketch the two cases on a single graph.

6.60 z-score and tail probability

a. Find the z-score for the number that is less than only 1% of the values of a normal distribution. Sketch a graph to show where this value is.

b. Find the z-scores corresponding to the (i) 90th and (ii) 99th percentiles of a normal distribution.

6.61 Quartiles If z is the positive number such that the interval within z standard deviations of the mean contains 50% of a normal distribution, then

a. Explain why this value of z is about 0.67.

b. Explain why for any normal distribution the first and third quartiles equal $\mu - 0.67\sigma$ and $\mu + 0.67\sigma$.

c. The interquartile range, IQR, relates to σ by $\text{IQR} = 2 \times 0.67\sigma$. Explain why.

6.62 Boys and girls birth weight Exercise 6.28 mentioned that in the United States, birth weight of boys is approximately normal, with mean 3.41 kg and standard deviation 0.55 kg. For girls, the birth weight is also approximately normal with mean 3.29 kg and standard deviation 0.52 kg.

a. A weight below 2.5 kg is considered low birth weight. 2.5 kg corresponds to which percentile for boys and to which percentile for girls?

b. Is a birth weight of 2.5 kg more extreme for boys or girls? Why?

6.63 Cholesterol The American Heart Association reports that a total cholesterol score of 240 or higher represents high risk of heart disease. A study of postmenopausal women reported a mean of 220 and standard deviation of 40. If the total cholesterol scores have a normal distribution, what proportion of the women fall in the high-risk category? (*Source:* Data from *Clin. Drug. Invest.*, 2000, vol. 20, pp. 207–214. The American Heart Association.)

6.64 Female heights Female heights in North America follow a normal distribution with $\mu = 65$ inches and $\sigma = 3.5$ inches. Find the proportion of females who are

a. under five feet.

b. over six feet.

c. between 60 and 70 inches.

d. Repeat parts a–c for North American males, the heights of whom are normally distributed with $\mu = 70$ inches and $\sigma = 4$ inches.

6.65 Cloning butterflies The wingspans of recently cloned monarch butterflies follow a normal distribution with mean 9 cm and standard deviation 0.75 cm. What proportion of the butterflies has a wingspan

a. less than 8 cm?

b. wider than 10 cm?

c. between 8 and 10 cm?

d. Ten percent of the butterflies have a wingspan wider than how many cm?

6.66 Gestation times For 5459 pregnant women using Aarhus University Hospital in Denmark in a two-year period who reported information on length of gestation until birth, the mean was 281.9 days, with standard deviation 11.4 days. A baby is classified as premature if the gestation time is 258 days or fewer. (Data from *British Medical Journal*, July 24, 1993, p. 234.) If gestation times are normally distributed, what's the proportion of babies born in that hospital prematurely?

6.67 Used car prices Data from the Web site carmax.com compiled in July 2014 show that prices for used Audi A4 cars advertised on the Web site have a mean of \$23,800 and a standard deviation of \$4,380. Assume a normal distribution for the price.

a. What percent of used Audi A4s cost more than \$25,000?

b. What percent of used Audi A4s cost between \$18,000 and \$22,000?

c. The least expensive 10% of used Audi A4s offered on the Web site cost at most how much?

6.68 Used car deals Refer to the previous exercise. Suppose carmax.com decides to highlight any used car that is priced 1.5 standard deviations below the mean price as a special deal on its Web site.

a. If the distribution of used-car prices is normal, what percentage of used Audi A4s will be highlighted?

b. If the distribution of used-car prices is normal, what percentage of used Honda Civics will be highlighted? (Do you need to know the mean and standard deviation for used Honda Civics?)

c. If the distribution of used-car prices is in fact skewed to the right, will the percentage of used Audi A4s that are highlighted most likely be smaller or larger than the one from part a? Explain.

6.69 Global warming Suppose that weekly use of gasoline for motor vehicle travel by adults in North America has approximately a normal distribution with a mean of 20 gallons and a standard deviation of 6 gallons. Many people who worry about global warming believe that Americans should pay more attention to energy conservation. Assuming that the standard deviation and the normal shape are unchanged, to what level must the mean reduce so that 20 gallons per week is the third quartile rather than the mean?

6.70 Fast-food profits Mac's fast-food restaurant finds that its daily profits have a normal distribution with mean $140 and standard deviation $80.

a. Find the probability that the restaurant loses money on a given day (that is, daily profit less than 0).

b. Find the probability that the restaurant makes money for the next seven days in a row. What assumptions must you make for this calculation to be valid? (*Hint:* Use the binomial distribution.)

6.71 Metric height A Dutch researcher reads that male height in the Netherlands has a normal distribution with $\mu = 72.0$ inches and $\sigma = 4.0$ inches. She prefers to convert this to the metric scale (1 inch = 2.54 centimeters). The mean and standard deviation then have the same conversion factor.

a. In centimeters, would you expect the distribution still to be normal? Explain.

b. Find the mean and standard deviation in centimeters. (*Hint:* What does 72.0 inches equal in centimeters?)

c. Find the probability that height exceeds 200 centimeters.

6.72 Manufacturing tennis balls According to the rules of tennis, a tennis ball is supposed to weigh between 56.7 grams (2 ounces) and 58.5 grams (2 1/16 ounces). A machine for manufacturing tennis balls produces balls with a mean of 57.6 grams and a standard deviation of 0.3 grams when it is operating correctly. Suppose that the distribution of the weights is normal.

a. If the machine is operating properly, find the probability that a ball manufactured with this machine satisfies the rules.

b. After the machine has been used for a year, the process still has a mean of 57.6, but because of wear on certain parts, the standard deviation increases to 0.6 grams. Find the probability that a manufactured ball satisfies the rules.

6.73 Bride's choice of surname According to a study done by the *Lucy Stone League* and reported by *ABC News*[9] in February 2011, 90% of brides take the surname of their new husband. Ann notes that of her four best friends who recently married, none kept her own name. If they had been a random sample of brides, how likely would this have been to happen?

6.74 ESP Jane Doe claims to possess extrasensory perception (ESP). She says she can guess more often than not the outcome of a flip of a balanced coin in another room. In an experiment, a coin is flipped three times. If she does not actually have ESP, find the probability distribution of the number of her correct guesses.

a. Do this by constructing a sample space, finding the probability for each point, and using it to construct the probability distribution.

b. Do this using the formula for the binomial distribution.

6.75 More ESP In another experiment with Jane Doe from the previous exercise, she had to predict which of five numbers was chosen in each of three trials. Jane Doe does not actually have ESP and is just randomly guessing. Explain why this experiment satisfies the three conditions for the binomial distribution by answering parts a–c.

a. For the analogy with coin flipping, what plays the role of (head, tail)?

b. Explain why it is sensible to assume the same probability of a correct guess on each trial. What is this probability?

c. Explain why it is sensible to assume independent trials.

6.76 Yale babies In a study carried out at the Infant Cognition Center at Yale University, researchers showed 16 infants two videos: one featured a character that could be perceived as helpful, and the other featured a character that could be perceived as hindering. After the infants viewed the videos, the researchers presented the infants with two objects that resembled the figures from the videos and allowed the infants to choose one to play with. The researchers assumed that the infants would not exhibit a preference and would make their choices by randomly choosing one of the objects. Fourteen of the 16 infants chose the helpful object. If the assumption that infants choose objects randomly were true, what is the probability that 14 or more of the infants would have chosen the helpful object? Could this be considered evidence that the infants must actually be exhibiting a preference for the helpful object? (*Hint:* Use the binomial distribution.)

6.77 Weather A weather forecaster states, "The chance of rain is 50% on Saturday and 50% again on Sunday. So there's a 100% chance of rain sometime over the weekend." If whether it rains on Saturday is independent of

[9]*Source:* Background information from abcnews.go.com/Health/change-bride-marriage-uproar-judgment/story?id=12860570&page=1.

whether it rains on Sunday, find the actual probability of rain *at least once* during the weekend as follows:

a. Answer using methods from Chapter 5, such as by listing equally likely sample points or using the formula for the probability of a union of two events.

b. Answer using the binomial distribution.

6.78 **Dating success** Based on past experience, Julio believes he has a 60% chance of success when he calls a woman and asks for a date.

a. State assumptions needed for the binomial distribution to apply to the number of times he is successful on his next five requests.

b. If he asks the same woman each of the five times, is it sensible to treat these requests as independent trials?

c. Under the binomial assumptions, state n and p and the mean of the distribution.

6.79 **Canadian lottery** In one Canadian lottery option, you bet on one of the million six-digit numbers between 000000 and 999999. For a \$1 bet, you win \$100,000 if you are correct. In playing n times, let X be the number of times you win.

a. Find the mean of the distribution of X in terms of n.

b. How large an n is needed for you to expect to win once (that is, $np = 1$)?

c. If you play the number of times n that you determined in part b, show that your expected winnings is \$100,000, but your expected profit is −\$900,000.

6.80 **Likes on Facebook** A large retail chain sends out an ad about a new product to 15 million users on Facebook and asks them to like the message. Assume the probability that a user will like the message (instead of ignoring it) is 0.00001.

a. State assumptions for a binomial distribution to apply for $X =$ the number of likes the message will receive. Identify n and p for that distribution.

b. Suppose the assumptions are met. Find the mean and standard deviation of X.

c. Is it reasonable to approximate the binomial distribution with the normal one? Why? (Assume the assumptions are met.)

d. Based on the normal approximation of the binomial distribution, find the interval for the possible numbers of likes that are within three standard deviations of the mean.

e. Refer to the assumptions for the analysis in part a. Explain at least one way they may be violated.

6.81 **Likes with online credit** The retail chain from the previous exercise decides to follow up its first ad with a second one, again to 15 million Facebook users. This time it gives away a \$1 online credit for every user who likes the ad. Now, assume the probability is 0.0005 that a user will like it.

a. Find the mean and standard deviation for the number of likes this second ad will receive.

b. Find the interval for the possible number of likes that covers almost all possible values, using the normal approximation.

c. How much money would you advise the retail company to set aside for covering these \$1 online credits? Why?

6.82 **Which distribution for sales?** A salesperson uses random digit dialing to call people and try to interest them in applying for a charge card for a large department store chain. From past experience, she is successful on 2% of her calls. In a typical working day, she makes 200 calls. Let X be the number of calls on which she is successful.

a. What type of distribution does X have: normal, binomial, discrete probability distribution but not binomial, or continuous probability distribution but not normal?

b. Find the mean and standard deviation of X. Interpret the mean.

c. Find the probability that on a given day she has 0 successful calls.

Concepts and Investigations

6.83 **Best of five** Example 2 gave the probability distribution for the number of games played in a best out of seven series between teams A and B. Let's derive the probability distribution for a best of five series, in which the team that gets 3 wins first wins the entire series.

a. Write out the sample space of all possible sequences of wins and losses. (There are 20 such sequences. Constructing a [partial] tree diagram and stopping as soon as either 3 wins or 3 losses are observed may help in finding all 20.)

b. For each sequence in part a, determine its length. These are the distinct values of the random variable $X =$ number of games played.

c. Find the probability of each sequence in part a when team A has a 50% chance of winning each game.

d. For each value x of the random variable X, find $P(x)$ by adding up the probabilities for those sequences that end after x games.

6.84 **More best of five** Refer to the previous exercise which asked for the distribution of the number of games played in a best of 5 series when team A wins with probability 50%.

a. Find the expected number of games played in a best of five series.

b. Find the expected number of games played when team A has an 80% chance of winning each game.

6.85 **Family size in Gaza** The Palestinian Central Bureau of Statistics (www.pcbs.gov.ps) asked mothers of age 20–24 about the ideal number of children. For those living on the Gaza Strip, the probability distribution is approximately $P(1) = 0.01$, $P(2) = 0.10$, $P(3) = 0.09$, $P(4) = 0.31$, $P(5) = 0.19$, and $P(6 \text{ or more}) = 0.29$. Because the last category is open-ended, it is not possible to calculate the mean exactly. Explain why you can find the *median* of the distribution, and find it. (*Source:* Data from www.pcbs.gov.ps.)

6.86 **Longest streak made** In basketball, when the probability of making a free throw is 0.50 and successive shots are independent, the probability distribution of the longest streak of shots made has $\mu = 4$ for 25 shots, $\mu = 5$ for 50 shots, $\mu = 6$ for 100 shots, and $\mu = 7$ for 200 shots.

a. How does the mean change for each doubling of the number of shots taken? Interpret.

b. What would you expect for the mean of the longest number of consecutive shots made in a sequence of (i) 400 shots and (ii) 3200 shots?

c. For a long sequence of shots, the probability distribution of the longest streak is approximately bell shaped and σ equals approximately 1.9, no matter how long the sequence (Schilling, 1990). Explain why the longest number of consecutive shots made has more than a 95% chance of falling within about 4 of its mean, whether we consider 400 shots, 3200 shots, or 1 million shots.

6.87 Stock market randomness Based on the previous exercise and what you have learned in this and the previous chapter (for example, Exercise 5.12), if you are a serious investor, explain why you should not get too excited if sometime in the next year the stock market goes up for seven days in a row.

6.88 Airline overbooking For the Boston to Chicago route, an airline flies a Boeing 737–800 with 170 seats. Based on past experience, the airline finds that people who purchase a ticket for this flight have 0.80 probability of showing up for the flight. They routinely sell 190 tickets for the flight, claiming it is unlikely that more than 170 people show up to fly.

a. Provide statistical reasoning they could use for this decision.

b. Describe a situation in which the assumptions on which their reasoning is based may not be satisfied.

6.89 Babies in China The sex distribution of new babies is close to 50% each, with the percentage of males usually being just slightly higher. In China in recent years, the percentage of female births seems to have dropped, a combination of policy limiting family size, the desire of most families to have at least one male child, the possibility of determining sex well before birth, and the availability of abortion. Suppose that historically 49% of births in China were female but birth records in a particular town for the past year show 800 females born and 1200 males. Conduct an investigation to determine whether the current probability of a female birth in this town is less than 0.49, by using the mean and standard deviation of the probability distribution of what you would observe with 2000 births if it were still 0.49.

6.90 TRUE or FALSE? IQR for normal distribution For a normally distributed random variable, the IQR is larger than the length of the interval $\mu \pm \sigma$.

6.91 Multiple choice: Guess answers A question has four possible answers, only one of which is correct. You randomly guess the correct response. With 20 such questions, the distribution of the number of incorrect answers

a. is binomial with $n = 20$ and $p = 0.25$.

b. is binomial with $n = 20$ and $p = 0.50$.

c. has mean equal to 10.

d. has probability $(.75)^{20}$ that all 20 guesses are incorrect.

6.92 Multiple choice: Terrorist coincidence? On 9/11/2002, the first anniversary of the terrorist destruction of the World Trade Center in New York City, the winning three-digit New York State Lottery number came up 9-1-1. The probability of this happening was

a. $1/1000$.

b. $(1/1000)^2 = 0.000001$.

c. 1 in a billion.

d. $3/10$.

6.93 ◆◆ **SAT and ethnic groups** Lake Wobegon Junior College admits students only if they score above 1200 on the sum of their critical reading, mathematics, and writing scores. Applicants from ethnic group A have a mean of 1500 and a standard deviation of 300 on this test, and applicants from ethnic group B have a mean of 1350 and a standard deviation of 200. Both distributions are approximately normal.

a. Find the proportion not admitted for each ethnic group.

b. Both ethnic groups have the same size. Of the students who are not admitted, what proportion is from group B?

c. A state legislator proposes that the college lower the cutoff point for admission to 600, thinking that of the students who are not admitted, the proportion from ethnic group B would decrease. If this policy is implemented, determine the effect on the answer to part b, and comment.

6.94 ◆◆ **College acceptance** The National Center for Educational Statistics reported that in 2012 the ACT college placement and admission examination had a mean of 21.1 and standard deviation of 5.3. (*Source:* Data from nces.ed.gov/programs/digest/d12/tables/dt12_147.asp.)

a. Which probability distribution would you expect to be more appropriate for describing the scores: the normal or the binomial? Why?

b. A college requires applicants to have an ACT score in the top 20% of all scores. Using the distribution you chose in part a, find the lowest ACT score a student could get to meet this requirement.

c. Of five students picked at random from those taking the ACT, find the probability that *none* score high enough to satisfy the admission standard you found in part b.

6.95 ◆◆ **Standard deviation of a discrete probability distribution** The **variance** of a probability distribution of a random variable is a weighted average of its squared distances from the mean μ. For discrete random variables, it equals

$$\sigma^2 = \Sigma(x - \mu)^2 P(x).$$

Multiply each possible squared deviation $(x - \mu)^2$ by its probability $P(x)$ and then add. The **standard deviation** σ is the positive square root of the variance. The table below shows the probability distribution for the number of games played in a best of seven series when each team has a 50% (taken from Example 2) or 99% chance of winning a game.

# games	50% chance	99% chance
4	0.1250	0.9606
5	0.2500	0.0384
6	0.3125	0.0001
7	0.3125	$2(10^{-5})$
	1	1

a. Find the standard deviation of X = number of games played to determine a winner when each team has a 50% chance of winning a game. (In Example 3, the mean was found to be equal to 5.8125.)

b. The table also shows the probability distribution when one team has a 99% chance of winning each game. Would you expect the standard deviation for this distribution to be smaller or larger than the one in part a? (*Hint*: Note how almost all the time the game will end after 4 games.)

6.96 Mean and standard deviation for a binary random variable The previous exercise gave the formula for the standard deviation of a discrete random variable X. Let's look at a simple case. Suppose X is a binary random variable where $X = 1$ with probability p and $X = 0$ with probability $(1 - p)$.

a. Show that the mean of X is equal to p.

b. Since $(x - \mu)^2$ equals $(0 - p)^2 = p^2$ when $x = 0$ and $(1 - p)^2$ when $x = 1$, derive that $\sigma^2 = p(1 - p)$ and $\sigma = \sqrt{p(1 - p)}$, the special case of the binomial σ with $n = 1$.

6.97 ◆◆ **Linear transformations: Taxes and fees** Assume prices for used Audi A4s available on carmax.com follow a normal distribution with mean $23,800 and standard deviation $4,380.

a. Prices quoted on carmax.com are without sales tax. To account for a 6% sales tax, you multiply each price by 1.06. What is the distribution of these new prices that include tax? (*Hint*: When multiplying values of a random variable by a constant [such as multiplying all prices by 1.06], the mean and the standard deviation of this new random variable are simply the mean and the standard deviation of the original variable multiplied by that same constant. The shape of the distribution is not affected by multiplying.)

b. Carmax.com adds a $199 processing fee when a vehicle is sold through its Web page. What is the distribution of the prices when this fee is added to all prices? (*Hint*: When adding a constant to values of a random variable [such as adding 199 to all prices], the mean of this new random variable is obtained by simply adding the same constant to the original mean. The standard deviation, however, is unaffected by the addition, so the standard deviation of the new variable is the same as the standard deviation of the old variable, regardless of how much is added [or subtracted]. The shape of the distribution is also not affected by adding a constant to all values.)

6.98 ◆◆ **Binomial probabilities** Justify the $p^x(1 - p)^{n-x}$ part of the binomial formula for the probability P(x) of a particular sequence with x successes, using what you learned in Section 5.2 about probabilities for intersections of independent events.

6.99 ◆◆ **Waiting time for doubles** Most discrete random variables can take on a finite number of values. Let X = the number of rolls of two dice necessary until doubles (the same number on each die) first appears. The possible values for this discrete random variable (called the **geometric**) are 1, 2, 3, 4, 5, 6, 7, and so on, still separate values (and discrete) but now an infinite number of them.

a. Using intersections of independent events, explain why $P(1) = 1/6$, $P(2) = (5/6)(1/6)$, and $P(3) = (5/6)^2(1/6)$.

b. Find P(4) and explain how to find P(x) for an arbitrary positive integer x.

6.100 Geometric mean Exercise 6.47 discussed the record losing streak of the Pittsburgh Pirates. In particular, if the Pirates' chance of winning any single game is 0.42, then at the beginning of a new season, the probability of them winning at least 81 games, and hence not adding another losing season to the streak, is about 0.024. The previous exercise mentions a type of random variable called the *geometric random variable*. A simple formula exists for calculating the mean of a geometric variable; if the probability of success on any given trial is p, then the expected number of trials required for the first success to occur is $1/p$. If the first such trial is taken to be the 2000 Major League Baseball season (i.e., 5 years into their losing streak), during what year would we expect the Pirates to break their streak?

6.101 World Series in baseball For the 68 World Series played between 1945 and 2013, 13 (19%) ended after 4 games, 12 (18%) after 5 games, 15 (22%) after 6 games, and 28 (41%) needed to go all the way to 7 games.

a. Find the average number of games played based on these data. (Remember from Section 6.1 that the mean for the theoretical distribution given in Example 1 is 5.8125.)

b. Draw a histogram for these observations and compare it to the theoretical distribution in Table 6.1. What could be responsible for the differences?

c. A 2003 *New York Times* article mentioned that series going to seven games are unusually common. Is this true? Of 68 series, if the theoretical distribution given in Table 6.1 holds true, how many series do we expect to be decided in seven games? Compare this to the observed relative frequency.

Student Activities

6.102 TECH **Best of seven games** In professional baseball, basketball, and hockey in North America, the final two teams in the playoffs play a best of seven series of games. The first team to win four games is the champion. Use simulation with the Random Numbers app on the text's Web site to approximate the probability distribution of the number of games needed to declare a champion when (a) the teams are evenly matched and (b) the better team has probability 0.90 of winning any particular game. In each case, conduct 10 simulations. Then combine results with other students in your class and estimate the mean number of games needed in each case. In which case does the series tend to be shorter? (Hint: For part a, generate random numbers between 1 and 10, where 1–5 represents a win for team A and 6–10 a win for team B. With the app, keep on generating a single random number until one team reaches 4 wins. For part b, again generate random numbers between 1 and 10, but now let 1–9 represent a win for team A and 10 a win for team B. Keep on generating a single random number until one team reaches 4 wins. Then repeat the entire process 9 more times to get a total of 10 simulations.

The exact probabilities for part a are given in Example 2; the exact probabilities for part b are $P(4) = 0.6562$, $P(5) = 0.2628$, $P(6) = 0.0664$ and $P(7) = 0.0146$, resulting in a mean of 4.4. Your approximations should be close to these.)

▶ Activity 1

What Hot Streaks Should We Expect in Basketball?

In basketball games, TV commentators and media reporters often describe a player as being hot if he or she makes several shots in a row. Yet statisticians have shown that for players at the professional level, the frequency and length of streaks of good (or poor) shooting are similar to what we'd expect if the success of the shots were random, with the outcome of a particular shot being independent of previous shots.[10]

Shaquille O'Neal was one of the top players in the National Basketball Association, but he was a poor free-throw shooter. He made about 50% of his free-throw attempts over the course of a season. Let's suppose that he had probability 0.50 of making any particular free throw that he took in a game. Suppose also whether or not he made any particular free throw was independent of his previous ones. He took 20 free throws during the game. Let X denote the longest streak he made in a row during the game. This is a discrete random variable, taking the possible values $x = 0, 1, 2, 3, \ldots, 20$. Here, $x = 0$ if he made none of the 20, $x = 1$ if he never made more than 1 in a row, $x = 2$ if his longest streak was 2 in a row, and so forth.

What is the probability distribution of X? This is difficult to find using probability rules, so let's approximate it by simulating 10 games with $n = 20$ free throws in each, using either coin flipping, random.org or the Random Numbers web app accessible via the book's website. Representing each of O'Neal's shots by the flip of a coin, we treat a head as making a shot and a tail as missing it. We simulate O'Neal's 20 free throws by flipping a coin 20 times. We did this and got

TTHHHTHTTTHTHHTHTTHT

This corresponds to missing shots 1 and 2, then making shots 3, 4, and 5, missing shot 6, and so forth. The simulated value of X = the longest streak of shots made is the longest sequence of heads in a row. In the sequence just shown, the longest streak made is $x = 3$, corresponding to the heads on flips 3, 4, and 5.

You would do the 20 coin flips 10 times to simulate what would happen in 10 games with 20 free throws in each. This would be a bit tedious. Instead, we suggest that you use your own judgment to write down quickly 10 sets of 20 H and T symbols (as shown above for one set) on a sheet of paper to reflect the sort of results you would expect for 10 games with 20 free throws in each. After doing this, find the 10 values of X = longest streak of Hs, using each set of 20 symbols. Do you think your instructor would be able to look at your 200 Hs and Ts and figure out that you did not actually flip the coin?

A more valid way to do the simulation uses software, such as the Random Numbers app on the book's website. With it, generate 20 random number that are either 1 or 2, where 1 represents making a shot and 2 missing it. The screen shot shows one such simulation, which resulted in a longest streak of 4.

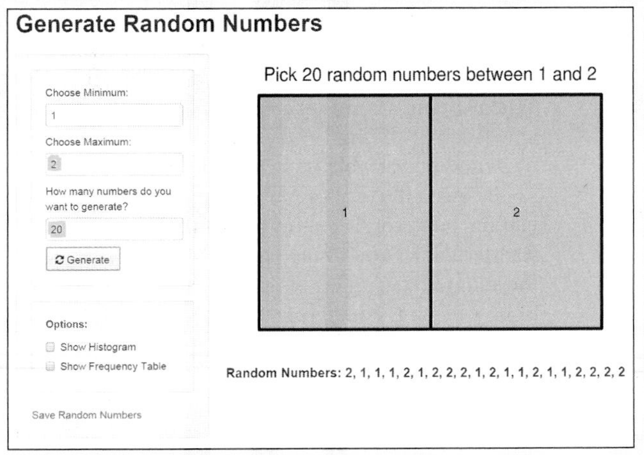

[10]For instance, see articles by A. Tversky and T. Gilovich, *Chance*, vol. 2 (1989), pp. 16–21 and 31–34.

Use this to simulate 10 games with $n = 20$ free throws in each. When we did this, we got the following results for the first three simulations:

Random numbers	**longest streak**
2, 1, 1, 1, 2, 1, 2, 2, 2, 1, 2, 1, 1, 2, 1, 1, 2, 2, 2, 2	4
2, 2, 2, 1, 2, 2, 1, 2, 2, 2, 2, 1, 2, 2, 1, 2, 1, 2, 1, 1	4
2, 2, 2, 2, 2, 1, 2, 2, 2, 2, 1, 1, 1, 2, 2, 2, 1, 1, 1, 1	5

In practice, to get accurate results you have to simulate a *huge* number of games (at least a thousand), for each set of 20 free throws observing the longest streak of successes in a row. Your results for the probability distribution would then approximate those shown in the table[11].

Probability Distribution of X = Longest Streak of Successful Free Throws

The distribution refers to 20 free throws with a 0.50 chance of success for each. All potential x values higher than 9 had a probability of 0.00 to two decimal places and a total probability of only 0.006.

x	P(x)	x	P(x)
0	0.00	5	0.13
1	0.02	6	0.06
2	0.20	7	0.03
3	0.31	8	0.01
4	0.23	9	0.01

The probability that O'Neal never made more than four free throws in a row equals $P(0) + P(1) + P(2) + P(3) + P(4) = 0.76$. This would usually be the case. The mean of the probability distribution is $\mu = 3.7$.

The longest streak of successful shots tends to be longer, however, with a larger number of total shots. With 200 shots, the distribution of the longest streak has a mean of $\mu = 7$. Although it would have been a bit unusual for O'Neal to make his next seven free throws in a row, it would not have been at all unusual if he made seven in a row sometime in his next 200 free throws. Making seven in a row was then not really a hot streak but merely what we expect by random variation. Sports announcers often get excited by streaks that they think represent a hot hand but merely represent random variation.

With 200 shots, the probability is only 0.03 that the longest streak equals four or fewer. Look at the 10 sets of 20 H and T symbols that you wrote on a sheet of paper to reflect the results you expected for 10 games of 20 free throws each. Find the longest streak of Hs out of the string of 200 symbols. Was your longest streak four or fewer? If so, your instructor could predict that you faked the results rather than used random numbers, because there's only a 3% chance of this if they were truly generated randomly. Most students underestimate the likelihood of a relatively long streak.

This concept relates to the discussion in Section 5.4 about coincidences. By itself, an event may seem unusual. But when you think of all the possible coincidences and all the possible times they could happen, it is probably not so unusual.

[11]*Source:* Background material from M. F. Schilling, "The longest run of heads," *The College Mathematics Journal,* vol. 21, 1990, pp. 196–207.

CHAPTER

7

We rely on statistics computed from random samples for inference about populations. In this chapter, we use what we learned about probability distributions to investigate the behavior of two important statistics, the sample proportion and the sample mean.

Sampling Distributions

Example 1

Predicting Election Results Using Exit Polls

Picture the Scenario

An exit poll is an opinion poll in which voters are randomly sampled after leaving the voting booth. Using exit polls, polling organizations predict winners after learning how a small number of people voted, often only a few thousand out of possibly millions of voters. What amazes many people is that these predictions almost always turn out to be correct.

In California in November 2010, the gubernatorial race pitted the Republican candidate Meg Whitman against the Democratic candidate, Jerry Brown. The exit poll on which TV networks relied for their projections found that, after sampling 3889 voters, 53.1% said they voted for Brown, 42.4% for Whitman, and 4.5% for other/no answer (www.cnn.com/ELECTION/2010). At the time of the exit poll, the percentage of the entire voting population (nearly 9.5 million people) that voted for Brown was unknown. In determining whether they could predict a winner, the TV networks had to decide whether the exit polls gave enough evidence to predict that the population percentage voting in favor of Brown was enough to win the election.

Questions to Explore

- How close can we expect a sample percentage to be to the population percentage? For instance, if 53.1% of 3889 sampled voters supported Brown, how close to 53.1% is the percentage of the entire population of 9.5 million voters who voted for him?
- How does the sample size influence our analyses? For instance, could we sample 100 voters instead of 3889 voters and make an accurate inference about the population percentage voting for Brown? On the other hand, are 3889 voters enough, or do we need tens of thousands of voters in our sample?

Thinking Ahead

In this chapter, we apply the probability tools of the previous two chapters to analyze how likely it is that sample results will be close to population values. You'll see why the results for 3889 voters allow us to make a reasonable prediction about the outcome for the entire population of nearly 9.5 million voters. This prediction will be an example of the use of inferential statistics.

Recall

From Section 1.2, a **statistic** is a numerical summary of sample data, such as the proportion in an exit poll who voted for Brown. A **parameter** is a numerical summary of a population, such as the proportion of all California voters who voted for Brown. ◀

We learned about probability in Chapter 5 and about probability distributions such as the normal distribution in Chapter 6. We'll next study how probability, and in particular the normal probability distribution, provides the basis for making statistical inferences. As Chapter 1 explained, inferential methods use statistics computed from sample data to make decisions and predictions about a population. The population summaries are called parameters. Inferential methods are the main focus of the rest of this book.

7.1 How Sample Proportions Vary Around the Population Proportion

In Chapter 6, we used probability distributions with known parameter values to find probabilities of possible outcomes of a random variable. In practice, we seldom know the values of parameters. They are estimated using sample data from surveys, observational studies, or experiments. However, elections provide a context in which we eventually know the population parameter (after election day). Before election day, candidates are interested in gauging where they stand with voters, so they rely on surveys (polls) to help predict whether they will receive the necessary percentage to win. On election day, TV networks rely on exit polls to assist in making early evening predictions before all the votes are counted.

Let's consider the California gubernatorial election mentioned in Example 1. Before all the votes were counted, the proportion of the population of voters who voted for Jerry Brown was an unknown parameter. An exit poll of 3889 voters reported that the sample proportion who voted for him was 0.531. This statistic *estimates* the unknown parameter in this scenario, the population proportion that voted for Jerry Brown. How do we know whether the sample proportion from the California exit poll is a good estimate, falling close to the population proportion? The total number of voters was over nine million, and the poll sampled a minuscule portion of them. This section introduces a type of probability distribution called the **sampling distribution** that helps us determine how close to the population parameter a sample statistic is likely to fall.

A Sampling Distribution Shows How Sample Statistics Vary

Recall

Section 6.1 introduced the term **random variable.** An uppercase letter, such as X, refers to the random variable. A lowercase letter, such as x, refers to particular values of the random variable. ◀

For an exit poll of randomly selected voters, a person's vote is a categorical random variable because the outcome (the vote) varies from voter to voter and falls into one out of several categories (the candidate voted for). Let X = vote outcome, with $x = 1$ for Jerry Brown and $x = 0$ for all other responses (Meg Whitman, other candidates, no response). In this case, we say that the outcome is **binary** and we are only interested in whether someone voted for Brown. The sample proportion (or percentage) of votes for Brown is a numerical summary of the binary outcomes and is a statistic. It can also be regarded as a random variable because a sample proportion varies from sample to sample. For example, before the exit poll sample was selected, the value of the sample proportion who voted for Brown was unknown. It was a random variable. The sample proportion from one exit poll likely differs from the one of another exit poll, which is based on different voters. You see this in practice when various news outlets predict (slightly) different proportions for the same candidate, each based on their own poll. (Exercise 1.17 in chapter 1 shows several exit poll results from the 2012 presidential election.)

For the exit poll in Example 1, the possible values of the random variable X (0 and 1) and the proportion of times these values occurred (0.469 and 0.531) give the **data distribution** for this one sample. For each random sample of voters taken, a different data distribution will result.

For all the voters in this election, final results showed that Brown officially received a proportion of 0.538 of the votes. So, for the population of voters on election day, the possible values of the random variable X (0 and 1) and the proportion of times these values occurred (0.462 and 0.538) form the **population distribution**. Note that $x = 0$ includes Whitman, all other candidates, and no response. We graphically represent the population distribution and the specific data distribution from this exit poll in Figure 7.1.

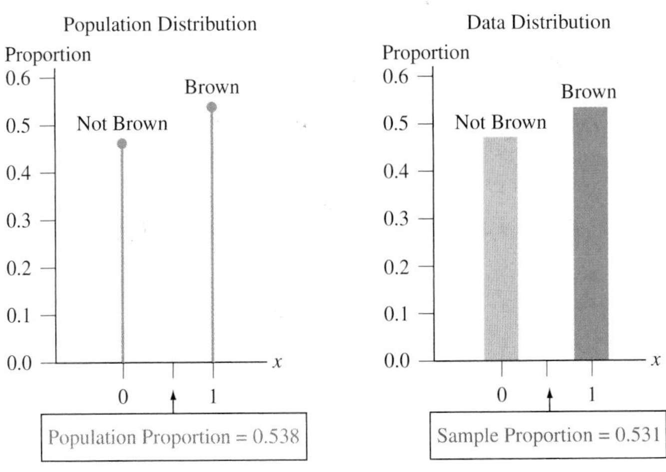

▲ **Figure 7.1** The Population (9.5 Million Voters) and Data ($n = 3889$) Distributions of Candidate Preference (0 = Not Brown, 1 = Brown). **Question** Why do these look so similar?

In Words

Individual polls ask different people and therefore use distinct samples. It makes sense then that specific samples have their own sample proportion values. The **sampling distribution** shows all possible values of the sample proportion and how often these sample proportions are expected to occur in random sampling.

We have considered one exit poll that gave a sample proportion for Brown (0.531) that was similar to the actual population proportion (0.538). What about other exit polls? Would they provide sample proportions similarly close to the true proportion, such as 0.54 in one poll, 0.56 in another, and 0.52 in a third? Or, might they tend to be quite different, such as 0.40 in one, 0.65 in another, and 0.59 in a third? To answer, we need to learn about a distribution that provides probabilities for the possible values of the sample proportion, called the **sampling distribution**.

Sampling Distribution

The **sampling distribution** of a statistic is the probability distribution that specifies probabilities for the possible values the statistic can take.

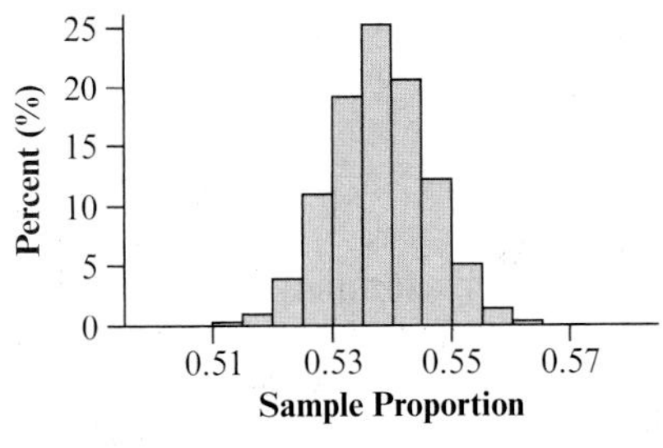

For sampling 3889 voters in an exit poll, imagine *all* the distinct samples of 3889 voters you could possibly get. Each such sample has a value for the sample proportion voting for Brown. Suppose you could look at each possible sample, find the sample proportion for each one, and then construct the frequency distribution of those sample proportion values (graphically, construct a histogram since sample proportions are numerical values). This would be the sampling distribution of the sample proportion. The figure in the margin shows a likely shape for this distribution.

A sampling distribution is merely a type of probability distribution. Rather than giving probabilities for the outcome of the vote of an individual subject (as in a population distribution), it gives probabilities for the value of a statistic computed from a sample. The concept that is sometimes hard to understand is that a statistic is a random variable, too. When we compute a statistic (such as the sample proportion) from a sample we have collected, we just happen to observe one of its possible values. Other samples will give different values, resulting in a whole distribution of values for the statistic, called the sampling distribution. The next activity shows how to use simulation to figure out what a sampling distribution looks like.

In Words

Statistics are random variables whose distribution is called the sampling distribution.

▶ Activity 1

Simulating the Sampling Distribution for a Sample Proportion

How much might a sample proportion vary from sample to sample? How would you describe the shape, center, and variability of the possible sample proportion values?

To answer these questions, we can simulate random samples of a given size. In this activity, we'll simulate samples, first using random numbers and then using web apps accessible from the book's website.

Simulating Using Random Numbers

We'll carry out this simulation by using the actual population proportion (rounded to two decimal places), $p = 0.54$, that voted for Jerry Brown in the 2010 California gubernatorial election. To simulate random sampling from a population in which exactly 54% of all voters voted for Brown, we randomly generate 100 integers between 1 and 100, using software such as the Random Numbers web app or the website random.org. We identify any number between 1 and 54 as voting for Brown and any number between 55 and 100 as voting for another candidate. That is,

1 2 3 4 . . . 53 54	55 56 . . . 99 100
Vote for Brown	**Vote for another candidate**

Then, for each number generated, Brown has a 54% chance of being voted for, because 54 of the 100 numbers (i.e., 54%) are less than or equal to 54, and all numbers are equally likely to show up.

In Practice Using Technology to Generate Random Numbers

Random numbers between 1 and 100 can be generated with random.org, the Random Numbers web app accessible from the book's website, other software, or calculators. For instance, the command *randInt(1,100,6)* on a TI will generate 6 random integers between 1 and 100.

Let's simulate taking a random sample of size $n = 6$. We will use a small sample size since sampling by hand is time-intensive. The six numbers generated with random.org were 65, 39, 8, 12, 40, and 47. (Your results will differ.) The first number, 65, falls above 54, so in this simulation, the first person sampled did not vote for Brown. The second number of 8 is below 54, indicating a vote for Brown. Overall, for the six votes simulated, five voted for Brown, for a sample proportion of 5/6.

Let's take another random sample of size 6 using random.org. This time, we got the numbers 54, 78, 69, 29, 49, and 80. Of these six votes, three—numbers 54, 29, and 49—voted for Brown, a sample proportion of 3/6. We could do this many

Screenshot from the webpage random.org.

more times to simulate how much sample proportions for sample of size $n = 6$ tend to vary from sample to sample. We already suspect that with a small sample size, there will be much variability in the sample proportions from one sample to the next. If possible, combine your simulation results with the results of classmates to gauge better the amount of variability occurring from sample to sample with a small sample size.

Typically exit polls interview more than six people. In the second part of the activity, we'll simulate polls with $n = 40$ and then with the actual sample size of $n = 3889$ used in the exit poll of the California governor's race. Rather then laboriously using random numbers, it is easier to use the Sampling Distribution of the Sample Proportion web app accessible via the book's website to generate a sample of voters randomly. Access that app now to follow our explanation here.

Simulating with the Web App

In the web app, "Sampling Distribution of the Sample Proportion," available on the book's website:

- Set the population proportion to $p = 0.538$, the actual proportion of voters who voted for Brown. The graph to the right will show the corresponding population distribution and mark the population proportion by an orange half-circle.
- In the box for the sample size n, type 40.
- Leave the default setting where we take 1 sample of this size.
- Click the Draw Sample(s) button once.

Figure 7.2 shows what the screen looks like after you make these selections and draw one sample. Note that your screen may look somewhat different because you will have a different random sample than shown here.

Just below the graph showing the population distribution, a bar chart appears that shows the data distribution, giving frequencies of the number of voters in the sample of size 40 voting (and not voting) for Brown. When we conducted this simulation, we had 26 people voting for Brown (and 14 not voting for him), as indicated in the title of that plot. (*Note*: This is the outcome of a *binomial* random variable with $n = 40$ and $p = 0.538$.) For this simulation, the sample proportion voting for Brown is 0.65, indicated by the blue triangle in that plot. This particular estimate seems pretty good because it is relatively close to the actual population

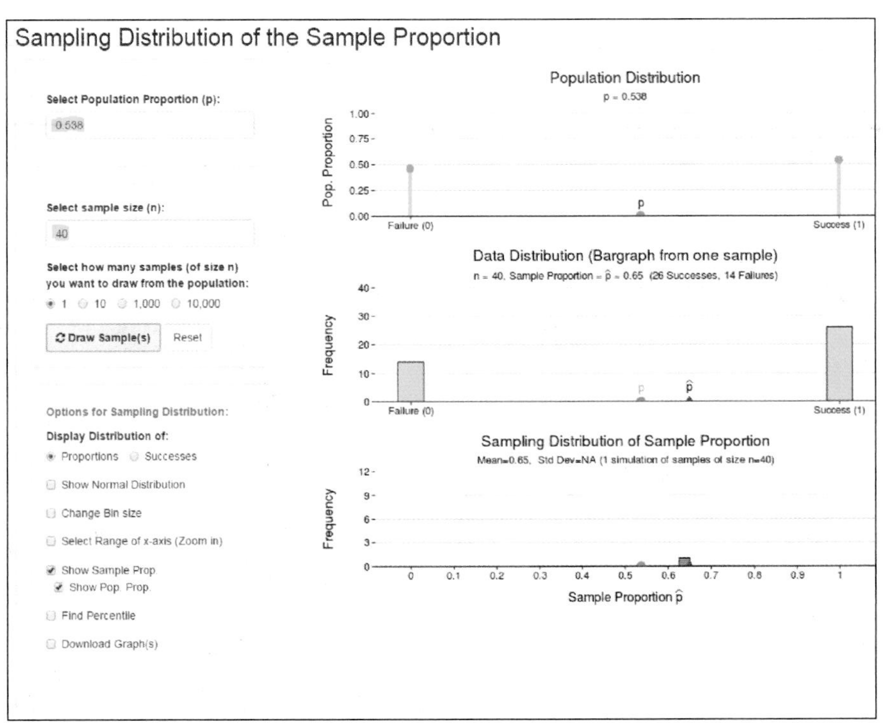

▶ Figure 7.2 **The Result of Taking One Sample of Size $n = 40$ Using the Sampling Distribution Web App.** The population proportion has been set at $p = 0.538$, and the sample size has been set at $n = 40$ (see highlighted portions). The first plot shows the **population distribution**. The second plot shows the **data distribution** for the one sample drawn, which resulted in a proportion of 0.65 $(= 26/40)$ successes and 0.35 $(= 14/40)$ failures. The third plot marks the location of the obtained sample proportion of successes, putting a bar above 0.65.

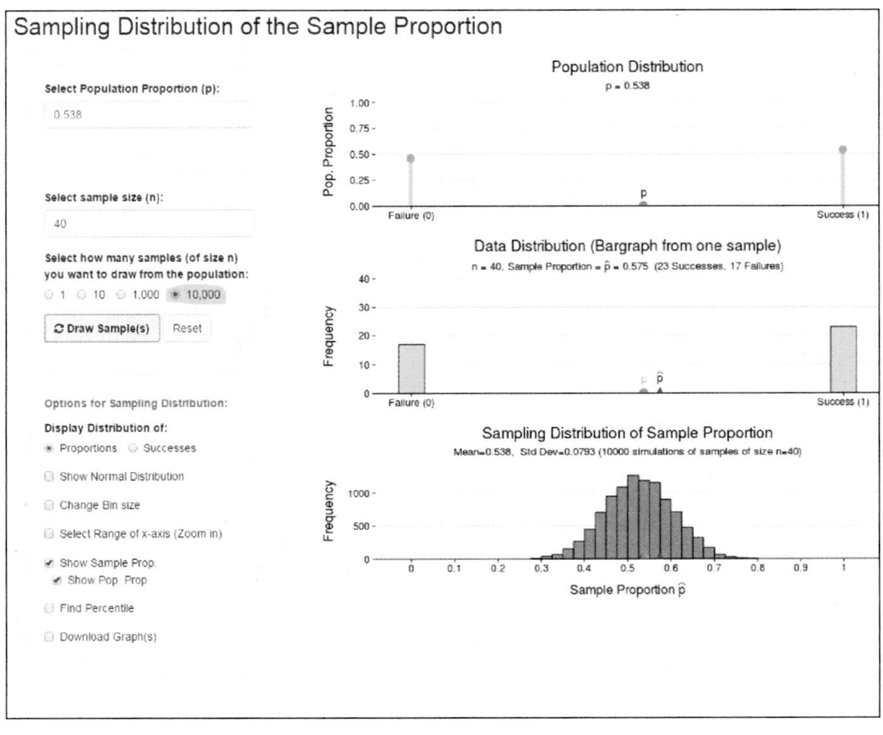

▶ Figure 7.3 **The Result of Taking 10,000 Samples of Size $n = 40$ Using the Sampling Distribution Web App.** This screen shot shows the same population proportion $(p = 0.538)$ and sample size $(n = 40)$ as the previous one, but now 10,000 random samples (see highlighted portion) are drawn from the population. The data distribution in the middle plot displays the number of successes and failures from the last of the 10,000 samples drawn (which differs from the one in Figure 7.2). The blue histogram at the bottom shows the simulated sampling distribution of the 10,000 generated sample proportions. **Question** With a mean of 0.538 and standard deviation of 0.079 for these 10,000 sample proportions and the bell-shaped distribution, find an interval within almost all sample proportions will fall.

proportion of 0.538 (the orange half-circle). Were we simply lucky to be this close? You can repeat the process of drawing one sample of size n from the population distribution by repeatedly clicking the Draw Sample(s) button. As you do this, the data distribution updates, showing the results of the current sample, and you can observe how close the sample proportion falls to the population proportion each time.

The third graph, titled "Sampling Distribution of Sample Proportion," keeps track of the sample proportions you generated in each draw and updates with each click. For the second sample generated, we obtained a sample proportion of 0.475, different but also pretty close to 0.538. Keep clicking Draw Sample(s) and observe how the histogram displaying the different sample proportions you generate keeps building and obtaining a particular shape.

To get a true feeling for the shape of the sampling distribution, we have to generate not only a few but several thousands of sample proportions. Rather than clicking the Draw Sample(s) button thousands of times, simply select 10,000 for the number of samples to draw. This way, we generate 10,000 samples of size $n = 40$ at once, compute the sample proportion for each, and summarize the resulting sample proportions visually in the histogram at the bottom. Figure 7.3 shows the screen under these settings. The histogram depicting the simulated sampling distribution for the sample proportion appears bell-shaped and centered at the population proportion of $p = 0.538$.

With $n = 40$, apparently almost all sample proportions fall between about 0.30 and 0.75. For an exit poll trying to predict who will win, this is too much variability. Let's find the sampling distribution when $n = 3889$, the actual size of the exit poll. In the web app, change n to this number (see below). The resulting histogram of sample proportions (again based on 10,000 samples) is shown in Figure 7.4. We see that the variability is greatly reduced when sampling 3889 instead of 40 voters. To get a feel for the sampling distribution, play around with the web app, such as changing the population proportion or the sample size while monitoring the shape of the blue histogram.

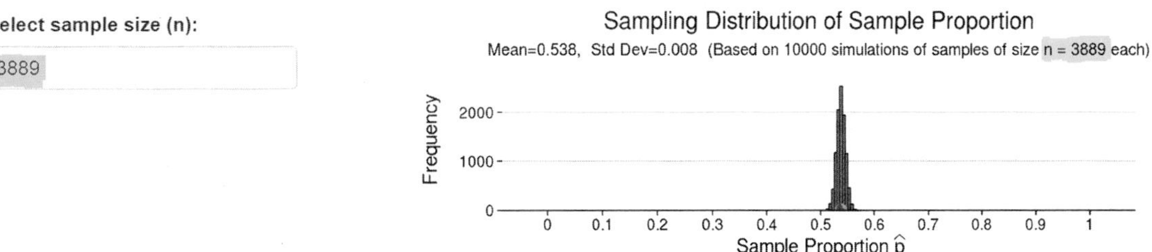

▲ **Figure 7.4** Simulated Sampling Distribution When Taking 10,000 Samples of Size $n = 3889$. **Question** With a mean of 0.538 and standard deviation of 0.008, find an interval within which almost all sample proportions will fall when sampling $n = 3889$ voters.

Try Exercises 7.1, 7.11, and 7.13 ◄

SUMMARY: Population Distribution, Data Distribution, Sampling Distribution

- **Population distribution:** This is the distribution from which we take the sample. Values of its parameters, such as the population proportion p for a categorical variable, are fixed (i.e., not random) but usually unknown. By taking a sample from the population distribution, we hope to learn and make predictions about the unknown population parameter(s).
- **Data distribution:** This is the distribution of the data obtained from the sample and is the one we actually see in practice. Its properties are described by statistics such as the sample proportion or the sample mean. With random sampling, the larger the sample size n, the more closely the data distribution resembles the population distribution.
- **Sampling distribution:** This is the distribution of a statistic such as a sample proportion or a sample mean. Because the numerical value of a statistic varies from sample to sample, we get an entire distribution of possible values for it. With random sampling, the sampling distribution provides probabilities (likelihood of occurrence) for all the possible values of the statistic. The sampling distribution holds the key for telling us how close a sample statistic, such as the sample proportion, falls to the corresponding unknown parameter such as the actual population proportion.

A Sampling Distribution Informs How Close a Statistic Falls to a Parameter

Sampling distributions describe the variability in a sample statistic that occurs from sample to sample (or study to study). If different polling organizations each take a sample and estimate the population proportion that voted a certain way, they will get varying estimates because their samples have different people. Figures 7.3 and 7.4 portrayed the variability of the sample proportion when taking samples of size $n = 40$ and $n = 3889$, respectively.

Sampling distributions help us to predict how close a statistic falls to the parameter it estimates. For instance, for a random sample of size 3889, the simulation with the web app showed that the probability is high that a sample proportion falls within a tiny interval of the (usually unknown) population proportion. In practice, **we usually don't have to perform simulations to figure out the sampling distribution of a statistic**. We'll learn in the rest of this section and in the next section about results that tell us the expected shape of the sampling distribution and its mean and standard deviation. These results will also show us how much the precision of estimation improves with larger samples.

In Practice We Generally Use Only One Sample From a Population

Typically we would observe only *one* sample of the given size n, not many. But we'll learn about results that tell us how much a statistic *would* vary from sample to sample if we had many samples each of size n.

Every sample statistic is a random variable and, hence, has a sampling distribution. Besides the sample proportion, there is a sampling distribution of a sample mean, a sampling distribution of a sample median, a sampling distribution of a sample standard deviation, and so forth. We'll focus in this section on the sample proportion and in the next section on the sample mean.

Describing the Sampling Distribution of a Sample Proportion

Caution

We typically use Greek letters for unknown population parameters. For the population proportion, we make an exception and denote it by p instead of π. (Because π is already reserved for the constant 3.1415... in mathematics.) ◀

We can describe the sampling distribution of a sample proportion by focusing on the key features of shape, center, and variability. We typically use the mean to describe center and the standard deviation to describe variability. For the sampling distribution of a sample proportion, the mean and standard deviation depend on the sample size n and the population proportion p.

Recall

You can regard the n observations as n trials for a binomial distribution. The population proportion p is then the probability of success on any given trial. ◀

Mean and Standard Deviation of the Sampling Distribution of the Sample Proportion

For a random sample of size n from a population with proportion p of outcomes in a particular category, the sampling distribution of the sample *proportion* in that category has

$$\text{mean} = p, \text{ standard deviation} = \sqrt{\frac{p(1-p)}{n}}.$$

Mean and standard deviation of sampling distribution ◀

Example 2

Exit Poll of California Voters Revisited

Picture the Scenario

Example 1 discussed an exit poll of 3889 voters for the 2010 California gubernatorial election.

Question to Explore

Election results showed that 53.8% of the population of all voters voted for Brown. What was the mean and standard deviation of the sampling distribution of the sample proportion who voted for him? Interpret these two measures.

Think It Through

For the sample of 3889 voters, the sample proportion who voted for Brown could be any of the following values: 0, 1/3889, 2/3889, 3/3889…, 3888/3889, 1. But some of these values are more likely to occur than others, and the sampling distribution describes the frequency of these values. Now, if we know the population proportion, then we can describe the sampling distribution of the sample proportion more specifically by finding its mean and standard deviation. In this case, the population proportion is $p = 0.538$ so the sampling distribution of the sample proportion has mean $= p = 0.538$ and standard deviation =

$$\sqrt{\frac{(0.538)(0.462)}{3889}} = 0.008 \text{ or approximately } 0.01.$$

On average, over many polls of the same size, we would observe a sample proportion of 0.538 (i.e., the population proportion), but there is variability around this mean. For example, we might observe a sample proportion of 0.53 or 0.55, both values falling approximately a standard deviation from the mean. In many exit polls of 3889 voters each, the sample proportion voting for Brown would vary from poll to poll, and the standard deviation of those sample proportion values would be approximately 0.01. Figure 7.4 showed this graphically.

Insight

Why would we care about finding a sampling distribution? Because it shows us how close the sample proportion is likely to fall to the population proportion, which is the parameter that we are really interested in. Here, the standard deviation of the sampling distribution is very small (0.008). This small value tells us that with $n = 3889$, the sample proportion will probably fall quite close to the population proportion.

► ***Try Exercises 7.3 and 7.5***

Recall

The number of successes in n independent trials, where each trial (vote) can result in two outcomes (Brown, not Brown) and the probability of success is constant ($p = 0.538$) follows a binomial distribution. See Section 6.3. ◄

Recall

For large n, the binomial distribution is approximately normal when the expected number of successes and failures, np and $n(1 - p)$, are both at least 15. Here, $np = 3889(0.538) = 2092$, and $n(1 - p) = 3889(0.462) = 1797$ are both much larger than 15. ◄

Now that we know the mean and standard deviation of the sampling distribution, what can we say about its shape? Our simulations in Activity 1 show that the possible sample proportions pile up in a bell shape around the population proportion, suggesting a normal distribution. This is not surprising. As the margin note recalls, the number of people (out of n randomly sampled) who vote for Brown follows a binomial distribution. And in Section 6.3, we mentioned that for a large sample size n, the binomial distribution can be well approximated by a normal distribution (see second margin note). Because for large n the *number of people* voting for Brown approximately follows a normal distribution, the *proportion of people* (i.e., the number divided by the sample size n) also approximately follows a normal distribution. The two histograms in Figure 7.5 illustrate this fact.

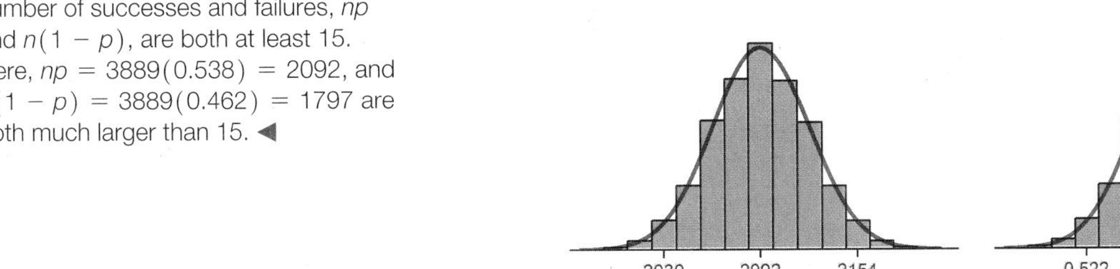

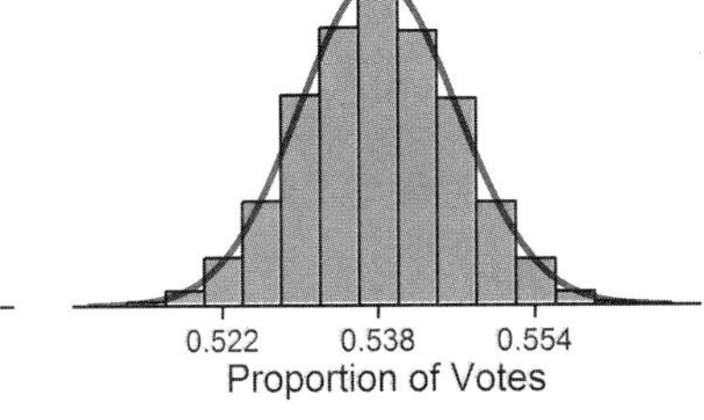

▲ **Figure 7.5 Histogram of the Sampling Distribution for the Number and Proportion of Votes for Brown in Samples of Size $n = 3889$, Assuming a Population Proportion of $p = 0.538$.** Note the identical shape, which is approximately normal as indicated by the superimposed normal curve.

The histogram on the left summarizes the sampling distribution of the *number of people* voting for Brown in samples of size $n = 3889$ when the population proportion is $p = 0.538$. It has an approximately normal shape. From Section 6.3, we know that the expected number of successes (here: votes for Brown) for a binomial distribution is $np = 3889(0.538) = 2092$, so it is no wonder that the distribution is centered at that value. When dividing each possible number of votes for Brown by the sample size 3889, we obtain all possible proportions of votes. The histogram on the right summarizes the sampling distribution of these sample proportions. We see that the two distributions (one for the number, the other for the proportion of votes) are identical in shape. Note that the sampling distribution for the proportion of votes is centered at $2092/3889 = 0.538$, i.e., the population proportion. Summing up, for large n, **the sampling distribution of the sample proportion is approximately normal** and centered at the population proportion.

Example 3

Normal shape for the sampling distribution

Predicting the Election Outcome

Picture the Scenario

Let's now conduct an analysis that uses the actual exit poll of 3889 voters for the 2010 California gubernatorial election. In that exit poll, 53.1% of the 3889 voters sampled said they voted for Jerry Brown.

Questions to Explore

a. Is it reasonable to assume a normal shape for the sampling distribution of the sample proportion resulting from exit polls such as this one?

b. Given that the actual population proportion supporting Brown was 0.538, what are the values of the sample proportion we would expect to observe from exit polls such as this one?

c. Based on the results of this exit poll, would you have been willing to predict Brown as the winner on election night while the votes were still being counted?

Think It Through

a. Yes. As mentioned in the margin note, both np and $n(1 - p)$ are larger than 15. Then, the sampling distribution of the sample proportion is approximately normal.

b. When $p = 0.538$, the normal distribution has, as noted in Example 2, a mean of 0.538 and a standard deviation of 0.008. Figure 7.6 shows the graph for the sampling distribution. Nearly all possible sample proportions will fall within 3 standard deviations of the mean, or within about $3(0.008) = 0.024$ of the mean of 0.538.

c. On election night, the polling agency does not know the actual population proportion. However, we know that the expected variability in the sampling distribution of the sample proportion is given by $\sqrt{p(1 - p)/n}$. Our best estimate of the population proportion on election day is the sample proportion from the exit poll. Therefore, we could estimate the expected standard deviation in the sampling distribution by substituting 0.531 for p and evaluating $\sqrt{(0.531)(0.469)/3889}$, resulting in 0.008. We know that in a

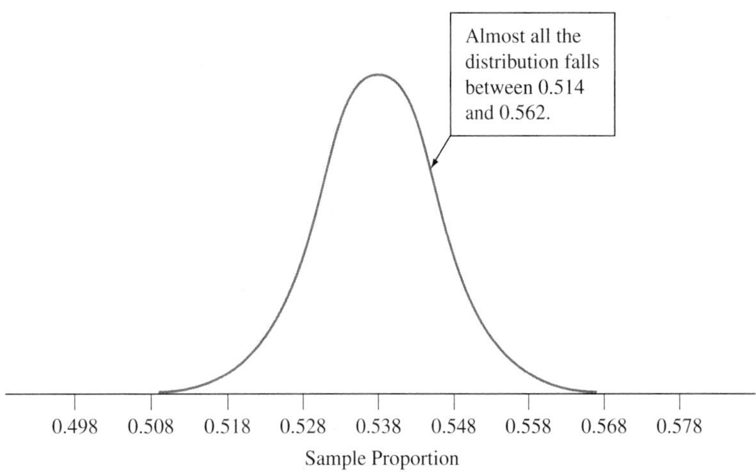

▲ **Figure 7.6 Sampling Distribution of Sample Proportion Voting for Brown in 2010 California Gubernatorial Election.** This graph shows where we expect sample proportions to fall for random samples of size $n = 3889$, when the population proportion that voted for Brown is $p = 0.538$. Nearly all the distribution falls between 0.514 and 0.562. The observed sample proportion of 0.531 is within this expected range of values for the sample proportion. We also observe that the likely range of values for the sample proportion lies completely above 0.5, indicating a majority of the votes. **Question** What would the sampling distribution look like if instead $p = 0.60$? Within what range would the sample proportion then be likely to fall?

bell-shaped distribution, we expect to find nearly 100% of our values within 3 standard deviations of the mean (in this case, the population proportion). If we take the sample proportion 0.531 from the exit poll, then add and subtract 3 standard deviations, we can find a range of plausible values for the actual population proportion as $0.531 \pm 3(0.008)$, which gives 0.507 to 0.555. We observe that all the plausible values estimated for the population proportion of voters who will vote for Brown are above the value of 0.50 and give Brown a majority over any other candidate. Therefore, we would expect the polling agency to tell the TV network it can feel confident in predicting Brown as the winner.

Insight

In this election, when all 9.5 million votes were tallied, 53.8% voted for Brown. The exit poll prediction that he would win was correct. Jerry Brown was elected as California governor.

If the sample proportion favoring Brown had been closer to 0.50, we would have been unwilling to make a prediction. For instance, when truly $p = 0.50$ or slightly less, obtaining a sample proportion of 0.51 (wrongly indicating a Brown majority) for a sample of size 3889 is not unlikely. However, in such cases, TV networks declare the election "too close to call." Also, if the polling agency used a smaller sample size, let's say $n = 800$ instead of $n = 3889$, then a sample proportion of 0.531 would not have been unlikely if $p = 0.50$ or slightly less than 0.50. *A smaller sample size creates more variability in the sampling distribution and therefore creates less precision in making a prediction about the actual population proportion.*

▶ ***Try Exercise 7.6***

SUMMARY: Sampling Distribution of a Sample Proportion

For a random sample of size n from a population with proportion p, the sampling distribution of the sample proportion has

$$\text{mean} = p, \text{ and standard deviation} = \sqrt{\frac{p(1-p)}{n}}.$$

If n is sufficiently large so that the expected numbers of outcomes of the two types, np in the category of interest and $n(1-p)$ not in that category, are both at least 15, then the sampling distribution of a sample proportion is approximately normal.

When we simulated a sampling distribution in Activity 1 for a sample size of 3889, we found that almost certainly the sample proportion falls within 0.024 of the population proportion $p = 0.538$. We now can see why this happens. We know that the standard deviation of this simulated sampling distribution is

$$\text{Standard deviation} = \sqrt{p(1-p)/n} = \sqrt{(0.538)(0.462)/3889} = 0.008.$$

Because the simulated sampling distribution is approximately normal, the probability is very close to 1.0 that the sample proportions would fall within 3 standard deviations of 0.538, that is, within $3(0.008) = 0.024$.

In practice, we seldom know the population parameter. An election is an exception in that we eventually know the population parameter. This allows the luxury of being able to compare the actual population proportion to the estimated proportions from surveys before the votes were counted.

In Practice Exit Polls Use a Multistage Type of Random Sampling

Exit polls use a multistage type of random sampling, not simple random sampling. The standard deviation formulas in this chapter technically apply only to simple random samples. However, they provide good approximations for the standard deviations with many multistage samples and are often used for such sampling schemes.

In the beginning of this section, we explored the shape of the sampling distribution and its mean and standard deviation by simulating thousands of potential samples and computing the statistic of interest. In practice, typically only **one sample** is taken from the population, not repeated samples. With the results for the sampling distribution developed in this section, this is all we require. The formulas for the mean and standard deviation of the sampling distribution only depend on the (unknown) population proportion p, and all we need to estimate p is the information contained in this one sample. We will explore exactly how to use the sampling distribution for making predictions about p in Chapters 8 and 9. Finally, it is important to remember that the results on the sampling distribution are only appropriate for a *randomly* selected sample.

7.1 Practicing the Basics

7.1 **Simulating the exit poll** Simulate an exit poll of 100 voters, using the Sampling Distribution web app accessible from the book's website, assuming that the population proportion is 0.53. Refer to Activity 1 for guidance on using the app.

TRY 

a. Simulate drawing one random sample of size 100. What sample proportion did you get? Why do you not expect to get exactly 0.53?

b. Keep the sample size n as 100 and p as 0.53, but now simulate drawing 10,000 samples of that size. Use the histogram of the 10,000 sample proportions you generated to describe the simulated sampling distribution (shape, center, spread). (*Note:* The app allows you to save the graph to file.)

c. Use a formula from this section to predict the value of the standard deviation of the sample proportions that you generated in part b. Compare it to the standard deviation of the 10,000 simulated sample proportions stated in the title of the graph.

d. Now change the population proportion to 0.7, keeping the sample size n at 100. Simulate the exit poll 10,000 times. How would you say the results differ from those in part b?

7.2 Simulate condo solicitations A company that is selling condos in Florida plans to send out an advertisement for the condos to 500 potential customers, in which they promise a free weekend at a resort on the Florida coast in exchange for agreeing to attend a four-hour sales presentation. The company would like to know how many people will accept this invitation. Its best guess is that there is a 10% chance that any particular customer will accept the offer. The company decides to simulate about what proportion could actually accept the offer, if this is the case. Simulate this scenario for the company, using the Sampling Distribution web app accessible from the book's website. Refer to Activity 1 for guidance on using the app.

TECH

a. Perform one simulation for a sample of size 500. What sample proportion did you get? Why do you not expect to get exactly 0.10?

b. Now simulate 10,000 times. Keep the sample size at $n = 500$ and $p = 0.10$. Describe the graph representing the simulated sampling distribution of the 10,000 sample proportion values. Does it seem likely that the sample proportion will fall close to 10%, say within 5 percentage points of 10%? (*Note:* An option in the app allows you to zoom in on the x-axis.)

7.3 Condo sample distribution Consider the sampling distribution you were simulating in parts a and b of the previous exercise, assuming $p = 0.10$ with samples of size 500 each. Using the appropriate formulas from this section, find the mean and the standard deviation of the sampling distribution of the sample proportion:

TRY

a. For a random sample of size $n = 500$, as in that exercise.

b. For a random sample of size $n = 2000$.

c. For a random sample of size $n = 125$. Summarize the effect of the sample size on the size of the standard deviation.

7.4 iPhone apps Let $p = 0.25$ be the proportion of iPhone owners who have a given app. For a particular iPhone owner, let $x = 1$ if they have the app and $x = 0$ otherwise. For a random sample of 50 owners:

a. State the population distribution (that is, the probability distribution of X for each observation).

b. State the data distribution if 30 of the 50 owners sampled have the app. (That is, give the sample proportions of observed 0s and 1s in the sample.)

c. Find the mean of the sampling distribution of the sample proportion who have the app among the 50 people.

d. Find the standard deviation of the sampling distribution of the sample proportion who have the app among the 50 people.

e. Explain what the standard deviation in part d describes.

7.5 Other scenario for exit poll Refer to Examples 1 and 2 about the exit poll, for which the sample size was 3889. In that election, 40.9% voted for Whitman.

TRY

a. Define a binary random variable X taking values 0 and 1 that represents the vote for a particular voter ($1 =$ vote for Whitman and $0 =$ another candidate). State its probability distribution, which is the same as the population distribution for X.

b. Find the mean and standard deviation of the sampling distribution of the proportion of the 3889 people in the sample who voted for Whitman.

7.6 Exit poll and n Refer to the previous exercise.

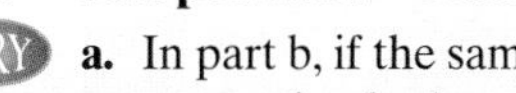

a. In part b, if the sampling distribution of the sample proportion had mean 0.409 and the standard deviation 0.008, give an interval of values within which the sample proportion will almost certainly fall. (*Hint*: You can use the approximate normality of the sampling distribution.)

b. The sample proportion for Whitman from the exit poll was 0.424. Using part a, was this one of the plausible values expected in an exit poll? Why?

7.7 Random variability in baseball A baseball player in the major leagues who plays regularly will have about 500 at-bats (that is, about 500 times he can be the hitter in a game) during a season. Suppose a player has a 0.300 probability of getting a hit in an at-bat. His batting average at the end of the season is the number of hits divided by the number of at-bats. When we consider the 500 at-bats as a random sample of all possible at-bats for this player, this batting average is a sample proportion, so it has a sampling distribution describing where it is likely to fall.

a. Describe the shape, mean, and standard deviation of the sampling distribution of the player's batting average.

b. Explain why a batting average of 0.320 or of 0.280 would not be especially unusual for this player's year-end batting average. (That is, you should not conclude that someone with a batting average of 0.320 is necessarily a better hitter than a player with a batting average of 0.280. Both players could have a probability of 0.300 of getting a hit.)

7.8 Relative frequency of heads Construct the sampling distribution of the sample proportion of heads obtained in the experiment of flipping a balanced coin:

a. Once. (*Hint*: The possible sample proportion values are 0, if the flip is a tail, and 1 if the flip is a head. What are their probabilities?)

b. Twice. (*Hint*: The possible samples are {HH, HT, TH, TT}, so the possible sample proportion values are 0, 0.50, and 1.0, corresponding to 0, 1, or 2 heads. What are their probabilities?)

c. Three times. (*Hint*: There are 8 possible samples.)

d. Refer to parts a–c. Sketch the sampling distributions and describe how the shape is changing as the number of flips n increases.

7.9 Experimental medication As part of a drug research study, individuals suffering from arthritis take an experimental pain relief medication. Suppose that 25% of all individuals who take the new drug experience a certain side effect. For a given individual, let X be either 1 or 0, depending on whether he or she experienced the side effect, respectively.

a. If $n = 3$ people take the drug, find the probability distribution of the proportion who will experience the side effect. (*Hint:* List all possible values for the sample proportion and their chances of occurring.)

b. Referring to part a, what are the mean and standard deviation of the sample proportion?

c. Repeat part b for a group of $n = 10$ individuals and $n = 100$ individuals. What happens to the mean and standard deviation of the sample proportion as n increases?

7.10 Effect of *n* on sample proportion The figure illustrates two sampling distributions for sample proportions when the population proportion $p = 0.50$.

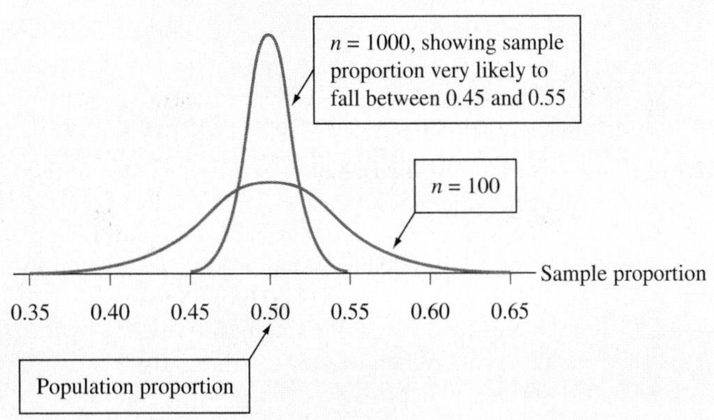

a. Find the standard deviation for the sampling distribution of the sample proportion with (i) $n = 100$ and (ii) $n = 1000$.

b. Explain why the sample proportion would be very likely (as the figure suggests) to fall (i) between 0.35 and 0.65 when $n = 100$, and (ii) between 0.45 and 0.55 when $n = 1000$. (*Hint:* Recall that for an approximately normal distribution, nearly the entire distribution is within 3 standard deviations of the mean.)

c. Explain how the results in part b indicate that the sample proportion tends to estimate the population proportion more precisely when the sample size is larger.

7.11 Syracuse full-time students You'd like to estimate the proportion of the 14,201 undergraduate students at Syracuse University who are full-time students. You poll a random sample of 350 students, of whom 330 are full-time. Unknown to you, the proportion of all undergraduate students who are full-time students is 0.951. Let X denote a random variable for which $x = 1$ denotes full-time student and for which $x = 0$ denotes part-time student. (For recent enrollment numbers, go to www.syr.edu/about/facts.html.)

TRY TECH

a. Describe the population distribution. Sketch a graph representing the population distribution.

b. Describe the data distribution. Sketch a graph representing the data distribution.

c. Find the mean and standard deviation of the sampling distribution of the sample proportion for a sample of size 350. Explain what this sampling distribution represents. Sketch a graph representing this sampling distribution.

d. Use the Sampling Distribution app accessible from the book's website to check your answers from parts a through c. Set the population proportion equal to $p = 0.951$ and $n = 350$. Compare the population, data, and sampling distribution graph from the app with your graphs from parts a through c.

7.12 Gender distributions At a university, 60% of the 7,400 students are female. The student newspaper reports results of a survey of a random sample of 50 students about various topics involving alcohol abuse, such as participation in binge drinking. They report that their sample contained 26 females.

TECH

a. Explain how you can set up a binary random variable X to represent gender.

b. Identify the population distribution of gender at this university. Sketch a graph.

c. Identify the data distribution of gender for this sample. Sketch a graph.

d. Identify the sampling distribution of the sample proportion of females in the sample. State its mean and standard deviation for a random sample of size 50. Sketch a graph.

e. Use the Sampling Distribution app accessible from the book's website to check your answers from parts b through d. Set the population proportion equal to $p = 0.60$ and $n = 50$. Compare the population, data, and sampling distribution graph from the app with your graphs from parts b through d.

7.13 Shapes of distributions

a. With random sampling, does the shape of the data distribution tend to resemble more closely the sampling distribution or the population distribution? Explain.

b. Is the sampling distribution of the sample proportion always bell shaped? Investigate with the Sampling Distribution app by setting $n = 30$ and increasing the population proportion p from 0.5 to 0.95. (You can do this by clicking the box for p.) What do you observe?

c. Why is it inappropriate to assume a bell shape for the sampling distribution of the sample proportion when $p = 0.95$ and $n = 30$?

7.14 Student government election A student running for a position in student government believes that 55% of the student body will vote for her. However, she is worried about low voter turnout.

a. Assuming she truly has 55% support in the entire student body, find the mean and standard deviation of the sampling distribution for the proportion of votes she will receive if only $n = 200$ students show up for voting.

b. Is it reasonable to assume a normal shape for this sampling distribution? Explain.

c. How likely is it that she will not get the majority of the vote, i.e., a sample proportion of 50% or lower from the 200 votes cast?

d. If instead $n = 1000$ students show up for voting, how likely is it then that she will not win the majority?

7.2 How Sample Means Vary Around the Population Mean

Recall

Population Distribution: The distribution of the random variable for the population from which we sample.

Data Distribution: The distribution of the sample data from one sample and the distribution we see in practice.

Sampling Distribution: The distribution of the sample statistic (sample proportion or sample mean) from repeated random samples.

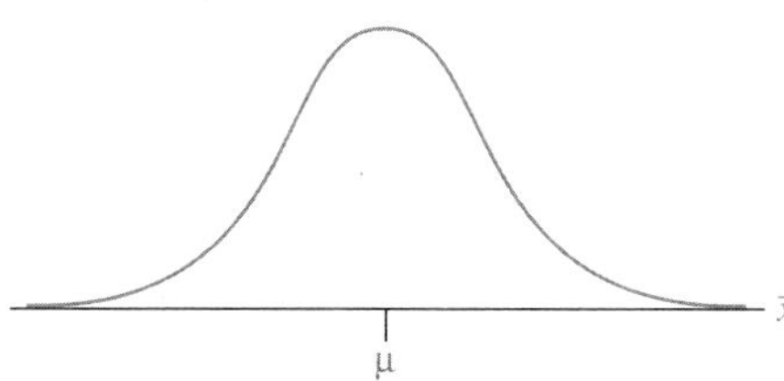

The sampling distribution of $\bar{x}$: The sample mean $\bar{x}$ fluctuates from sample to sample around the population mean μ.

The previous section discussed three types of distributions: the population distribution, the data distribution, and the sampling distribution (see Recall in margin). The sampling distribution is a probability distribution for the possible values of a statistic. We learned how much a sample proportion can vary among different random samples. Because the sample mean is so commonly used as a statistic to summarize sample numerical (quantitative) data, we'll now pay special attention to the sampling distribution of the sample mean. We'll discover results allowing us to predict how close a particular sample mean $\bar{x}$ falls to the population mean μ.

As with the sampling distribution of the sample proportion, there are two main results about the sampling distribution of the sample mean:

- One result provides formulas for the mean and standard deviation of the sampling distribution.
- The other indicates that its shape is often approximately a normal distribution, as we observed in the previous section for the sample proportion.

Let's use the Sampling Distribution for the Sample Mean web app to investigate with simulation how the sampling distribution for the sample mean might look with repeated random sampling from a population represented by a quantitative random variable.

Simulating the Sampling Distribution of the Sample Mean

How much might a sample mean vary from sample to sample? How would you describe the shape, center, and variability of the possible sample mean values? To answer these questions, we can use an app similar to the one in Activity 1.

▶ Activity 2

Simulating the Sampling Distribution of the Sample Mean from a Bell-Shaped Population Distribution

We use the Sampling Distribution of the Sample Mean web app from the book's website to simulate selecting random samples of a given size from a population represented by a quantitative random variable. Because we want to simulate from a bell-shaped population distribution, select Bell-Shaped in the first menu for the shape of the population distribution. Let's keep the default values of 50 for the population mean μ and 10 for the population standard deviation σ for that distribution. We will first generate random samples with a sample size of 10, so we set the sample size $n = 10$ in the app. Again, we begin with selecting just one random sample of that size. After you click on Draw Sample(s), you will get a screen that looks similar to Figure 7.7.

Did you also get a sample mean close to 50? Perform this simulation of drawing one sample of size 10 several times by repeatedly clicking the Draw Sample(s) button. Each time, the data distribution will update showing the last sample generated, and you can observe how close the sample mean (indicated by the blue triangle) falls to the population mean (indicated by the orange half-circle). The third plot on the bottom keeps track of all the sample means you have generated, and you can watch how a histogram for the generated sample means is building piece by piece, which will eventually approximate the sampling distribution.

To get a better idea of the shape of the sampling distribution via simulation, we need to repeat this process several thousands of times, which we do by selecting 10,000 in the second menu. Figure 7.8 shows the result of this simulation.

Judging from the histogram, the simulated sampling distribution for the 10,000 generated sample means is bell shaped and centered at the population mean of 50. In fact, the average of the 10,000 sample means is also 50. The standard deviation of the sample means is noticeably smaller

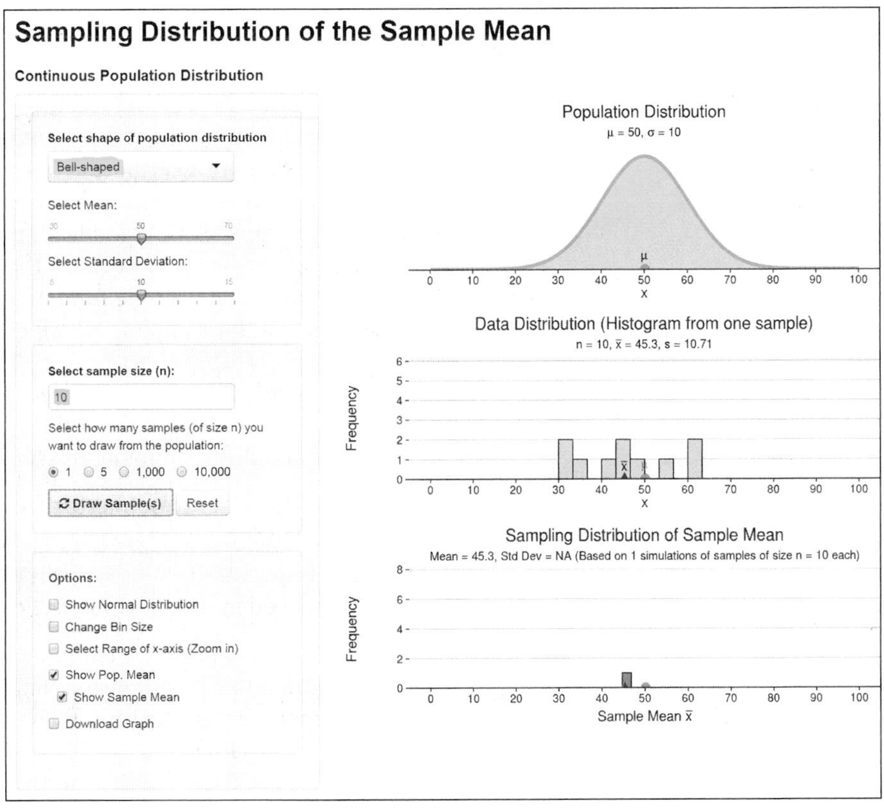

▶ Figure 7.7 The Result of Taking One Sample of Size $n = 10$ from a Bell-Shaped Population Distribution by Using the Web App. The population has been set to bell shaped (see highlighted portion) with a mean of 50 and a standard deviation of 10 (the default settings). The first plot shows the **population distribution** with these parameters. In the second menu, we set the sample size to $n = 10$ (see highlighted portion). After clicking Draw Sample(s), the second plot shows a histogram displaying the **data distribution** for one random sample of 10 observations drawn from the population distribution. These 10 observations have a sample mean of $\bar{x} = 45.3$ and a sample standard deviation of $s = 10.71$. The third plot at the bottom keeps track of the sample means generated.

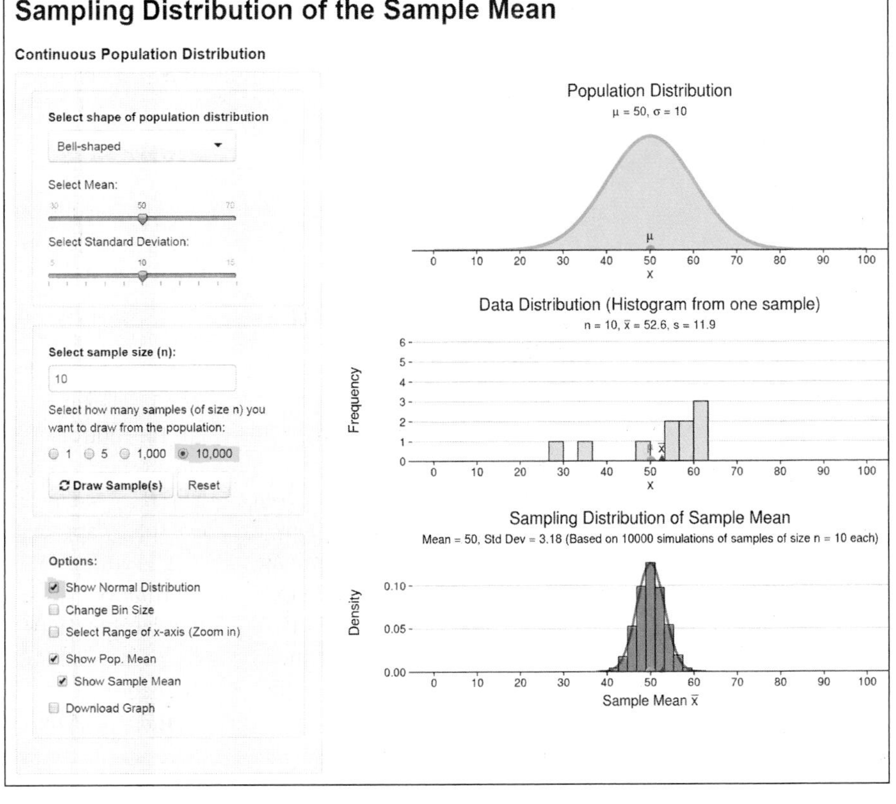

▶ Figure 7.8 Simulation Results of Repeated Random Sampling From a Bell-Shaped Population Distribution. 10,000 random samples (see highlighted part) of 10 observations each were simulated from the population distribution with $\mu = 50$ and $\sigma = 10$ (top plot). The middle plot shows the histogram for the last of these 10,000 samples (which is a different sample than the one from Figure 7.7). The sampling distribution of the resulting 10,000 sample means is summarized in the blue histogram at the bottom, where for better comparability a normal curve is superimposed. These 10,000 sample means have a mean of 50 and a standard deviation of 3.18.

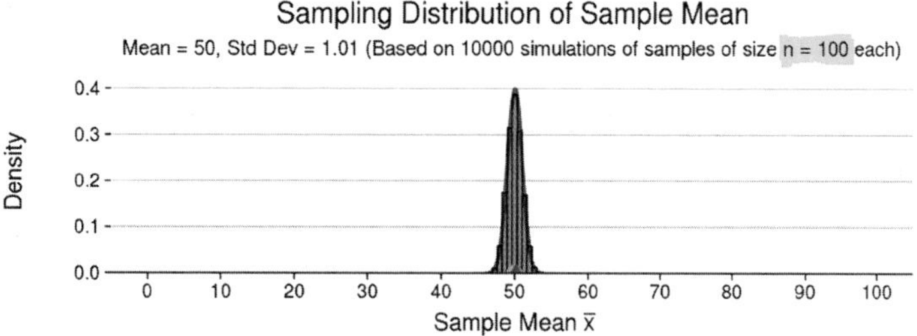

▲ **Figure 7.9** Simulated Sampling Distribution of the Sample Mean When Repeatedly Sampling From a Bell-Shaped Distribution. **Questions** With a mean of 50 and a standard deviation of 1.01, find an interval within which almost all sample means will fall when drawing samples of size $n = 100$. When increasing the sample size ten-fold (from 10 to 100), did the standard deviation of the sample means decrease by 10? Judge by comparing the quoted standard deviation in the title of the sampling distribution plots in Figures 7.8 and 7.9.

than the standard deviation of the population, with almost all sample means falling between 40 and 60. The superimposed normal curve shows good agreement with the histogram, indicating that the simulated sampling distribution follows a normal shape.

You should next simulate drawing 10,000 random samples from the same population distribution (bell shaped with $\mu = 50$ and $\sigma = 10$), but now with a sample size of $n = 100$ each. Figure 7.9 shows the results, and we see that this simulated sampling distribution with $n = 100$ is bell shaped (in fact, normal), centered at the population mean and with much smaller standard deviation compared to the $n = 10$ case. Feel free to play around with the many knobs of the web app, such as changing the standard deviation of the population distribution to the smallest and largest value or increasing or decreasing the sample size n.

Try Exercises 7.15 and 7.30 ◀

We observe from our simulation in Activity 2 that when we repeatedly sample from a population that is bell shaped, even with a small sample size of $n = 10$, the shape of the simulated sampling distribution is also bell shaped with a mean close to the population mean of 50 and a standard deviation close to 3.16. Mathematically, this is the population standard deviation of 10 divided by $\sqrt{n}$; that is, $10/\sqrt{10} = 3.16$. Under the assumption that the bell-shaped distribution is normal, we can state the following result in the next summary box.

SUMMARY: The Sampling Distribution of the Sample Mean When the Population Distribution is Normally Distributed

For a random sample of size n from a normally distributed population having mean μ and standard deviation σ, then regardless of the sample size n, the sampling distribution of the sample mean $\bar{x}$ is also normally distributed with its center described by the **population mean** μ and the variability described by the standard deviation of the sampling distribution, which equals **the population standard deviation divided by the square root of the sample size,** $\sigma/\sqrt{n}$.

In reality, the population distribution of a variable is rarely normal. What does this mean for the sampling distribution? Will it still have a bell shape?

Simulating the Sampling Distribution for a Sample Mean from a Non-Bell-Shaped Distribution

The simulation in Activity 2 for the sample mean with $n = 10$ showed a bell shape for the sampling distribution. This was not surprising since we were sampling from a population distribution with a bell shape. Is it typical for sampling distributions of a sample mean to have bell shapes even if the population distribution is not bell shaped?

Population, data, and sampling distributions

Customer Reviews

(47)

4.5 out of 5 stars

5 star

4 star

3 star

2 star

1 star

Example 4

Five-star Ratings

Picture the Scenario

Let's consider a scenario in which the probability distribution of the random variable X is highly skewed. Let X = customer rating of a popular TV model on an internet shopping website with possible values ranging from 1 to 5 stars.[1] Suppose the probability distribution for X is given by $P(1) = 0.10$, $P(2) = 0.05$, $P(3) = 0.10$, $P(4) = 0.20$ and $P(5) = 0.55$, where $P(x)$ stands for the probability of a randomly selected customer to rate the product with x stars. The top plot in Figure 7.10 displays this probability distribution of X, which is the population distribution. The picture in the margin, taken from the shopping website for this TV model, shows the data distribution for the ratings based on a sample of 47 customers, which resulted in an average rating of 4.5.

Now, suppose we reach out to 47 other customers and ask them for their rating. This will result in a different set of observations and a

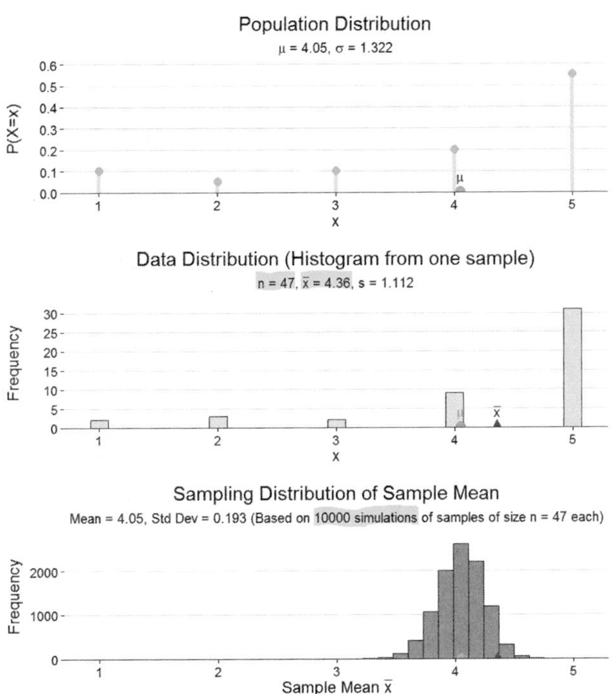

▲ **Figure 7.10 Simulation Results of Repeated Random Sampling From a Skewed Population Distribution.** 10,000 random samples of size 47 each were simulated from the population distribution with $\mu = 4.05$ (orange semicircle) and $\sigma = 1.32$ (top plot). The data distribution (middle plot) shows the result of the last of the 10,000 samples generated, which has a sample mean of 4.36 (blue triangle). The blue histogram at the bottom shows the shape of the simulated sampling distribution of all 10,000 sample means. These 10,000 sample means have a mean of 4.05 and a standard deviation of 0.19.

[1] Customer ratings are an example of an ordinal variable. These are categorical variables where the categories follow a natural ordering, such as from 1 star to 5 stars. Often, we can assign scores to the categories of an ordinal variable as we did here from 1 to 5, and treat it as quantitative. By assigning equally spaced scores, we implicitly assume that the difference between a 1 and 2 star rating is the same as between a 4 and 5 star rating, which may not be realistic.

different sample mean. The second plot in Figure 7.10 displays the data distribution of one such possible sample, which resulted in a sample mean of 4.36.

To get a feel for how the sample mean varies in samples of size 47, we repeat this process of drawing a sample of size 47 and computing the sample mean a very large number of times (such as 10,000 times). The bottom plot in Figure 7.10 shows the results of 10,000 such simulations. It displays the histogram representing the simulated sampling distribution for the 10,000 sample means, each based on a simulated sample of size 47 from the skewed population distribution. The simulated sampling distribution serves as a good approximation of the actual sampling distribution of the sample mean. In theory, the sampling distribution refers to an infinite number of samples of size 47, not just 10,000, but for almost all practical purposes, this suffices. You can simulate all these results yourself and explore more scenarios with the Sampling Distribution of the Sample Mean (discrete) web app from which we took the screen shot in Figure 7.10, available on the book's website.

Questions to Explore

a. Identify the population distribution and describe its shape, mean, and standard deviation.

b. Identify the data distribution and describe its shape, mean, and standard deviation.

c. Identify the sampling distribution of $\bar{x}$ and describe its shape, mean, and standard deviation.

Think It Through

a. The *population distribution* is given by the probability distribution of the random variable X = customer rating (see first plot of Figure 7.10). It is skewed to the left and described by the population mean $\mu = 4.05$ (indicated by the orange semicircle) and population standard deviation $\sigma = 1.32$.

b. The *data distribution* shows the distribution of the 47 values in one of the samples generated (here, the last sample) and looks similar to the population distribution, being skewed to the left. The data distribution is described by a sample mean of 4.36 (indicated by the blue triangle in Figure 7.10) and a sample standard deviation of 1.11. These values are shown in the subtitle of the data distribution plot.

c. The sampling distribution is the distribution of the sample mean when repeatedly taking samples of size 47 from the population. From the simulation, we see that it is roughly bell shaped, despite that the population and data distributions are left skewed. The histogram is centered at 4.05, which is the population mean (indicated by the orange semicircle in all three plots of Figure 7.10). It displays much less variability compared to the population distribution. The standard deviation in the population is $\sigma = 1.32$, whereas the standard deviation of the 10,000 simulated sample means is 0.19, which is $\sigma/\sqrt{n} = 1.32/\sqrt{47} = 0.19$. All this suggests that the theoretical sampling distribution of the sample mean has (i) mean equal to the population mean, (ii) standard deviation equal to the population standard deviation divided by $\sqrt{n}$, and (iii) a bell shape.

▶ ***Try Exercise 7.26 and conduct the simulation in Exercise 7.19***

Describing the Behavior of the Sampling Distribution for the Sample Mean for Any Population

Here we've seen a surprising result: Even when a population distribution is not bell shaped but rather skewed, the *sampling distribution* of the sample mean $\bar{x}$ can have a bell shape. We also observe that the mean of the sampling distribution of the sample mean appears to be the same as the population mean μ, and the standard deviation of the sampling distribution for the sample mean appears to be $\frac{\sigma}{\sqrt{n}}$. The bell shape is a consequence of the **central limit theorem (CLT)**. It states that the sampling distribution of the sample mean $\bar{x}$ often has approximately a normal distribution. This result applies no matter what the shape of the population distribution from which the samples are taken. For relatively large sample sizes, the sampling distribution is bell shaped even if the population distribution is highly discrete or highly skewed. We observed this in Example 4 (see also the figure in the margin) with a skewed, highly discrete population, using $n = 47$, which is not all that large but is the size of sample we sometimes see in practice.

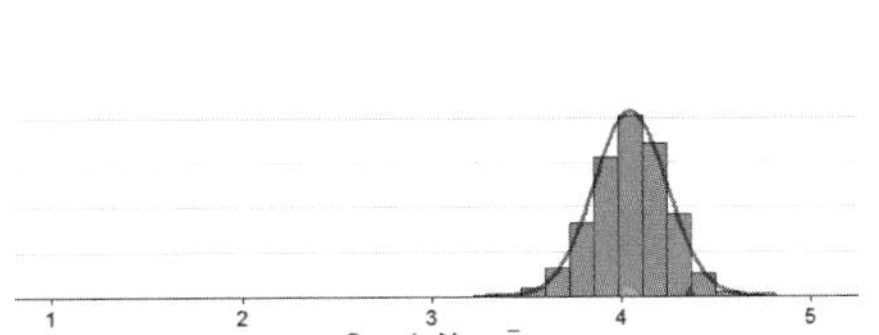

Mean and Standard Deviation of the Sampling Distribution of the Sample Mean $\bar{x}$

For a random sample of size n from a population having mean μ and standard deviation σ, the sampling distribution of the sample mean $\bar{x}$ has mean equal to the **population mean** μ and standard deviation equal to the **standard deviation of the population divided by the square root of the sample size,** i.e., $\frac{\sigma}{\sqrt{n}}$.

In Words

As the sample size increases, the sampling distribution of the sample mean has a more bell-shaped appearance.

The Central Limit Theorem (CLT): Describes the Expected Shape of the Sampling Distribution for a Sample Mean $\bar{x}$

For a random sample of size n from a population having mean μ and standard deviation σ, then as the sample size n increases, the sampling distribution of the sample mean $\bar{x}$ approaches an approximately normal distribution.

In Practice Expect Bell Shape When Sample Size at Least 30

The sampling distribution of $\bar{x}$ takes more of a bell shape as the random sample size n increases. The more skewed the population distribution, the larger n must be before the shape is close to normal (bell shape). In practice, the sampling distribution is usually close to bell shape when the sample size n is at least 30.

What is amazing about the central limit theorem is that no matter what the shape of the population distribution, the sampling distribution of the sample mean approaches an approximately normal distribution. In fact, for most population distributions, the bell shape is approached very quickly as the sample size n increases. Thus, if our sample size is sufficiently large, we don't need to worry or know about the shape of the population distribution in order to work with the sampling distribution of the sample mean.

Figure 7.11 displays sampling distributions of the sample mean $\bar{x}$ for five different shapes for the population distribution from which samples are taken. The population shapes are shown at the top of the figure; below them are portrayed the sampling distributions of $\bar{x}$ for random samples of sizes $n = 2, 5$, and 30. Even if the population distribution itself is uniform (column 1 of the figure) or U-shaped (column 2) or skewed (column 3) or bimodal (column 4), the sampling distribution of the sample mean has approximately a bell shape when n is at least 30 and sometimes for n as small as 5. In addition, the variability of the sampling distribution noticeably decreases as n increases, because the standard deviation of the sampling distribution decreases.

If the population distribution is normally distributed, then the sampling distribution is normally distributed no matter what the sample size. The rightmost column of Figure 7.11 shows this case.

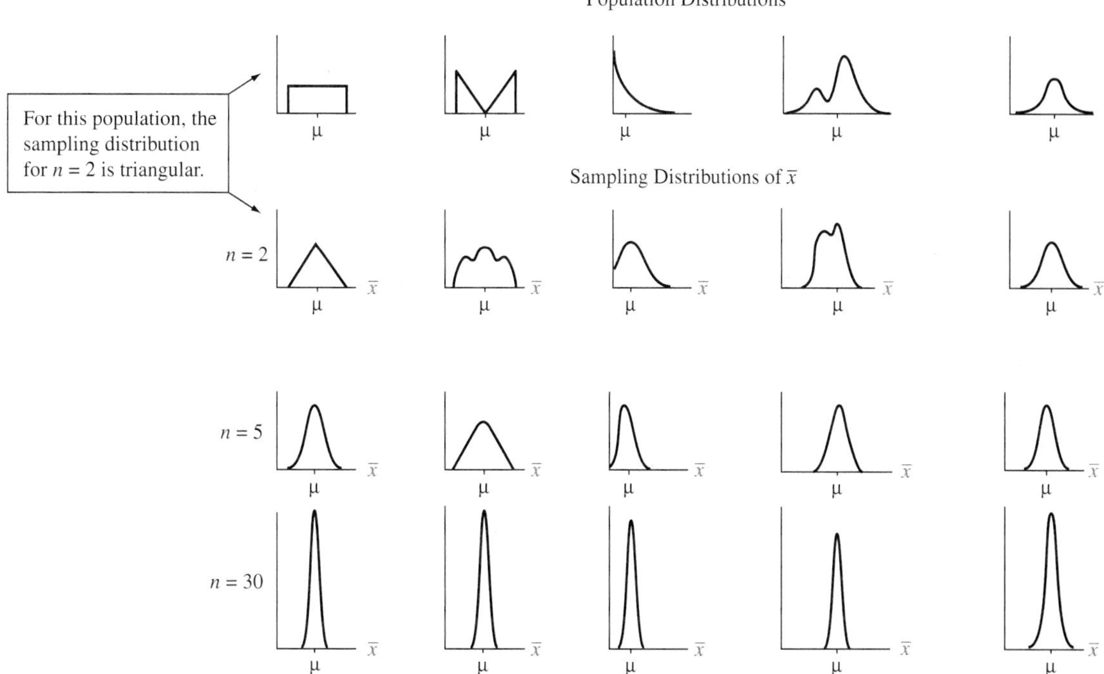

▲ **Figure 7.11** Five Population Distributions and the Corresponding Sampling Distributions of $\bar{x}$. Regardless of the shape of the population distribution, the sampling distribution becomes more bell shaped as the random sample size n increases. You can use the Sampling Distribution web app on the book's website to simulate how a population distribution shown has a sampling distribution for the sample mean that becomes more nearly normal as n increases. See Activity 3 and Exercises 7.28, 7.29, and 7.30.

▶ Activity 3

Exploring the Central Limit Theorem via Simulation

We can use the Sampling Distribution for the Sample Mean web app that we used in Activity 2 for bell-shaped population distributions to explore the sampling distribution when the population distribution is skewed, bimodal, or irregular. When accessing the web app, the default is a population distribution skewed to the right. You can explore the behavior of the sampling distribution when sampling from this population distribution and observe what happens as you change the skewness. For a sample size large enough (you can repeatedly click in the sample size box to increase or decrease the sample size by 1, and the plots will update interactively), the sampling distribution will look approximately normal, centered at the population mean.

Here, we illustrate the central limit theorem (CLT) under a population distribution that is rather irregular, with no specific shape. In the app, select Built Own for the shape of the population distribution. Let's use the default population values that are listed there and that define the shape of the population distribution, with population mean $\mu = 5.6$ and population standard deviation $\sigma = 1.7$, as shown in Figure 7.12. We simulated 10,000 samples of size $n = 30$ from this distribution. The middle plot for the data distribution shows the result for the last of these 10,000 samples. The blue histogram at the bottom shows the simulated sampling distribution of the 10,000 sample means from the 10,000 samples. Judging from the histogram, the simulated sampling distribution has an approximately normal shape and overlaps very well with the theoretical curve for the normal distribution with mean 5.6 and standard deviation $1.7/\sqrt{30} = 0.31$, also shown in the plot. This illustrates the CLT: Despite the ragged shape of the population distribution, for a sample of size 30, the sampling distribution of the sample mean is approximately normal. With the app, you can investigate several other population shapes to see the CLT in action.

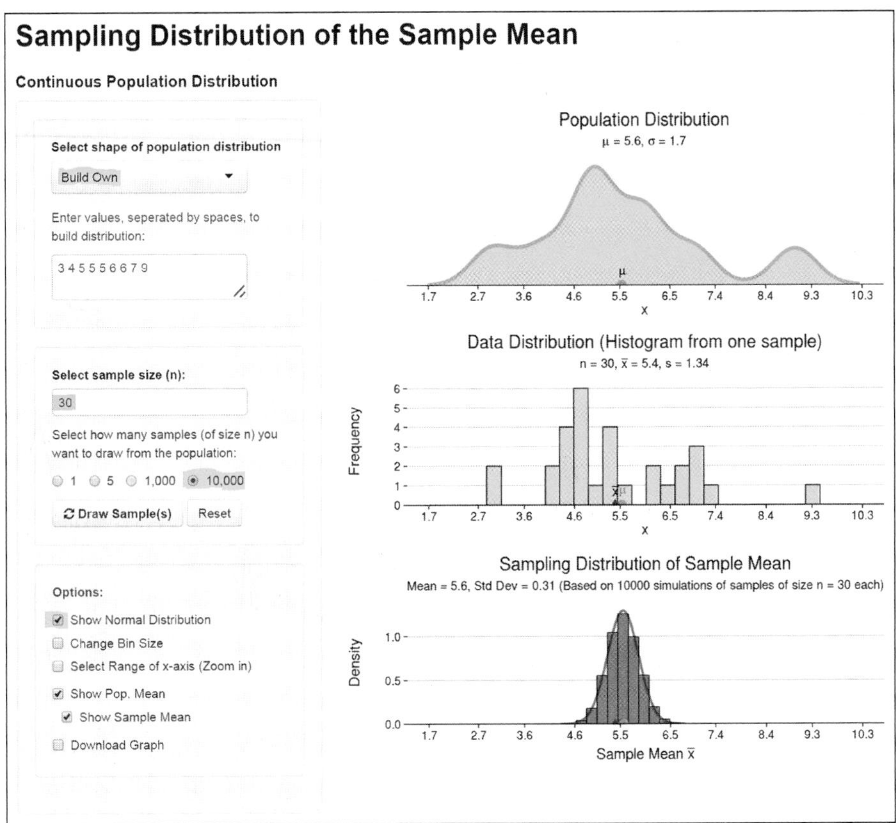

▲ **Figure 7.12** **Simulation Results of Repeated Random Sampling From an Irregular Population Distribution.** 10,000 random samples of size 30 were simulated from a population distribution with $\mu = 5.6$ and $\sigma = 1.7$. The distribution of the resulting 10,000 sample means is shown with the blue histogram at the bottom. The agreement with the normal distribution, also shown, is astonishing and illustrates the CLT.

Try Exercises 7.28, 7.29, 7.45, and 7.63 ◄

Distribution of the sample mean ◄

Example 5

Average Salary

Picture the Scenario

Each winter, Peter works numerous shifts as a seasonal waiter in a mountain ski resort in Austria. His salary (including tips) varies from shift to shift depending on the time (e.g., breakfast, lunch, dinner) or whether the shift falls on a weekday or weekend. However, experience from past seasons indicates that the salary for a shift follows a probability (population) distribution with a mean of μ = €150 and a standard deviation of σ = €60.

At the end of each winter, Peter randomly selects the pay stubs from 32 shifts he worked that season. To check how much he earned on average per shift, he computes the mean salary per shift from the information on these pay stubs.

Questions to Explore

a. Around which euro value would you expect his mean salary per shift to fluctuate?

b. How much variability would you expect in the mean salaries from one season to the next? Find the standard deviation of the sampling distribution of the sample mean and interpret it.

c. Between what values do you expect about 95% of his mean salaries per shift to fall?

d. What is the probability that there is a season when his mean salary per shift falls below €130?

Think It Through

a. The mean salary per shift computed from the 32 pay stubs is a sample mean (a statistic) from a sample of size $n = 32$. We would expect these sample means (one for each season) to fluctuate around the mean (a parameter) of the assumed population distribution, which is $\mu = €150$.

b. The sampling distribution of the sample mean has mean €150. Its standard deviation equals

$$\frac{\sigma}{\sqrt{n}} = \frac{60}{\sqrt{32}} = 10.6.$$

From one season to the next, Peter's mean salary per shift would vary around the value of €150, with variability described by the standard deviation of €10.6.

c. For a sample of size 32, we expect the sampling distribution of a sample mean to be approximately bell shaped, regardless of the actual shape of the population distribution. Then, around 95% of the mean salaries will fall within two standard deviations of the mean of that distribution, that is, within $2(€10.6) = €21$ of €150. So, we can expect his mean salary per shift to fall between $€150 \pm €21$, that is, between €129 and €171.

d. By the CLT, because 32 is a fairly large sample size, we may assume that the sampling distribution is approximately normal, with mean €150 and standard deviation €10.6. Then, the probability is the area below €130 under this normal distribution. As demonstrated in Chapter 6, we can use technology (such as the Normal Distribution web app from the book's website) or Table A in the appendix (with a z-score of $z = (130 - 150)/10.6 = -1.89$) to find that this area is equal to 2.96%. Note that we need to use the standard deviation of the sampling distribution (€10.6) and not the standard deviation of the population distribution (€60) for this calculation.

Insight

Figure 7.13 portrays a possible population distribution for Peter's salary per shift that is slightly right-skewed and unimodal, centered at €150. The figure also indicates the sampling distribution of the mean salary per shift over many seasons. Clearly, there is less variability in the mean salary per shift

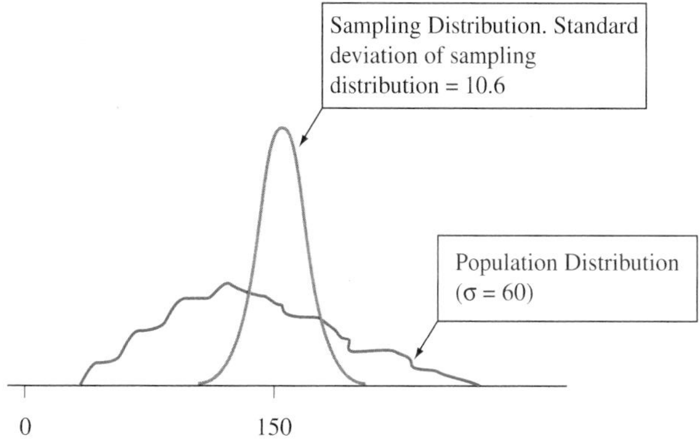

▲ **Figure 7.13 Salaries per Shift and the Sampling Distribution of Mean Salaries Over 32 Shifts in a Season.** There is more variability in the salaries from shift to shift than in the mean salaries from season to season.

from season to season than there is in the salary from shift to shift (as portrayed by the population distribution).

The assumptions for the probability (population) model in this example may be a bit unrealistic. Some shifts (such as weekends and holidays) may be much busier than others, bringing in more salary and tips. But the results would hold even if we assumed a more skewed or even bimodal distribution because 32 is a fairly large sample size. With the CLT, we actually don't need to know the shape of the population distribution.

Finally, knowing how to find a standard deviation for the sampling distribution gives us a mechanism for understanding how much variability to expect in sample statistics (such as sample means or proportions) that we observe in our jobs or in our daily lives.

▶ ***Try Exercises 7.16 and 7.22***

Effect of *n* on the Standard Deviation of the Sampling Distribution

Let's consider again the formula $\frac{\sigma}{\sqrt{n}}$ for the standard deviation of the sample mean. Notice that as the sample size n increases, the denominator increases, so the standard deviation of the sample mean decreases. This relationship has an important practical implication: **With larger samples, the sample mean tends to fall closer to the population mean.**

Example 6

Expected winnings ◀

Long-Run Consequence of Playing Roulette

Picture the Scenario

During an episode of the 2011 MTV series, *The Real World*, filmed in Las Vegas, one of the roommates (Adam) decided to play roulette. He had the option to bet smaller amounts of money on multiple spins but decided to bet his entire bankroll of \$400 on a single spin, placing the entire amount on red. As luck would have it, he won.

In Exercise 8 of Chapter 6, we learned that 18 of the 38 numbers on a roulette wheel are red. Let X denote the possible winnings associated with a single \$400 bet on red. If the ball lands on red, Adam wins \$400; otherwise, he loses \$400. Thus the possible values of x are \$400 and −\$400. This probability distribution has a mean of

$$\Sigma x\text{P}(x) = \frac{18}{38}(400) + \frac{20}{38}(-400) = -\$21.05.$$

So he can expect to lose an average of \$21.05 on a single spin.

Questions to Explore

Suppose rather than betting \$400 on a single spin, Adam decides to bet \$10 on red on each of the next 40 spins.

a. Find the mean and standard deviation of the sampling distribution of his sample mean winnings for 40 spins.

What would change if, instead of playing 40 spins, Adam plays 400 spins, betting \$10 on each?

b. Find the mean and standard deviation of the sampling distribution of his sample mean winnings for 400 spins.

Think It Through

a. As before, let X denote the possible winnings associated with a single bet on red. This time, the possible values of x are \$10 and $-$\$10, and the expected winnings of a single spin is

$$\mu = \Sigma x P(x) = \frac{18}{38}(10) + \frac{20}{38}(-10) = -\$0.53.$$

Additionally, the standard deviation, σ, of the winnings on a single \$10 bet equals approximately \$10.05.

The sampling distribution of the sample mean winnings, $\bar{x}$, has the same mean as the probability distribution of X for a single spin. When placing bets on 40 spins, the standard deviation of the sampling distribution of $\bar{x}$ is $\sigma/\sqrt{n}$. Thus the mean and standard deviation of the sampling distribution of $\bar{x}$ for 40 spins are $-$\$0.53 and $\$10.05/\sqrt{40} = \$1.59$.

b. The mean of this sampling distribution is still $-$\$0.53. The standard deviation of this sampling distribution is $\frac{\sigma}{\sqrt{n}} = \frac{10.05}{\sqrt{400}} = 0.503$. (approximately 50 cents).

Insight

As n increases, the standard deviation of the sampling distribution of $\bar{x}$ becomes smaller. Thus, as the number of spins played increases, the winnings per spin tend to get closer and closer to the mean of the probability distribution for each spin, namely $-$\$0.53. This phenomenon stems from the *law of large numbers* and is generally bad news for roulette players and good news for casino owners.

▶ ***Try Exercise 7.18, part b***

Recall

The sampling distribution of $\bar{x}$ has mean equal to the population mean μ and standard deviation equal to $\frac{\sigma}{\sqrt{n}}$, where σ is the population standard deviation. For large n by the central limit theorem, this sampling distribution is approximately a normal distribution. ◀

This example reinforces what we observed in the previous section about the effect of increased sample size on the precision of a sample proportion in estimating a population proportion. The larger the sample size, the smaller the standard deviation of the sampling distribution.

Example 7

Probability ◀

Coming Out Ahead When Playing Roulette

Picture the Scenario

In Example 6, we considered two options for playing roulette. You could place a \$400 bet for the ball to land on red during a single spin. In this case, you either win \$400 or lose \$400, and the outcome is based on the outcome of a single spin. The second option was to bet \$10 on red for each of 40 different spins. In this case, your overall winnings depend on the outcomes of each of the 40 spins.

Questions to Explore

Let's see how your probability of coming out ahead (winning more than you pay to play) depends on how often you play. What's the probability that you come out ahead if (a) you bet \$400 on red on a single spin; (b) you bet \$10 on red on each of 40 different spins.

Think It Through

You come out ahead if the sum of all your winnings is larger than zero, or, equivalently, if your mean winnings per spin $\bar{x}$ (the sum of all winnings divided by the number of spins played) is greater than zero.

a. In playing $n = 1$ time, you come out ahead only if you win. Since 18 of the 38 numbers on the wheel are red, your probability of winning and thus coming out ahead is simply 18/38.

b. When playing $n = 40$ spins, to determine the probability of coming out ahead, we must find the probability that $\bar{x}$ is greater than zero. To do so, we rely on the central limit theorem to determine the sampling distribution of $\bar{x}$. Since n is large, the sampling distribution of $\bar{x}$ is approximately normal. In Example 6, we found the mean and standard deviation of the distribution to be $-\$0.53$ and $\$1.59$, respectively. Figure 7.14 shows this distribution.

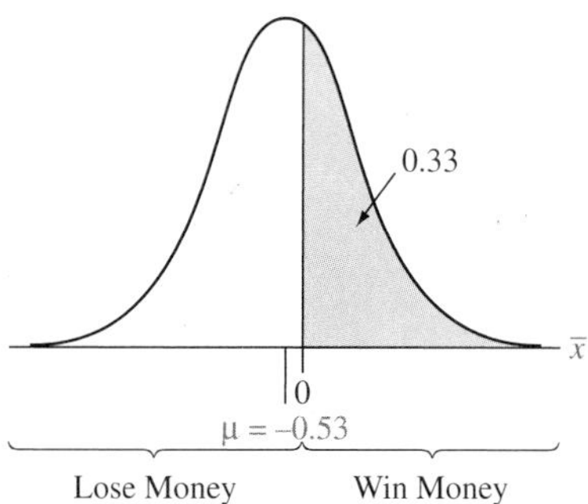

▲ **Figure 7.14 Approximate Sampling Distribution of the Sample Mean $\bar{x}$ when $\mu = -0.53$ and Standard Deviation of Sampling Distribution $= 1.59$.** We use this distribution to approximate the probability that $\bar{x}$ falls above \$0 when you play 40 spins. **Question** Does this distribution have the same shape as the probability distribution for each game? Explain.

The probability that, on average, you come out ahead after 40 spins (the sample mean exceeds \$0) is approximately the area (called probability) above 0 in the right tail of this figure. So we need to find the probability that a normal random variable with mean -0.53 and standard deviation 1.59 takes a value above 0. The value 0 has a z-score of

$$z = (\text{value} - \text{mean})/(\text{standard deviation of sampling distribution})$$
$$= [0 - (-0.53)]/1.59 = 0.33.$$

From Table A, the cumulative probability, or the area under the standard normal curve to the left of $z = 0.33$, is 0.6293. Thus, the right-tail probability is $1 - 0.6293 = 0.3707$. The probability you will come out ahead after 40 spins is 0.37.

Insight

The probability $(18/38 = 0.474)$ of coming out ahead in winnings is larger if we just make the single bet in part a. However, the probability is 0.526 of losing \$400. Meanwhile, the larger the value of n, the less likely you will come out ahead, but it also becomes less likely that you will lose a relatively large sum of money. We can see using the normal distribution that the probability is 0.95 that the average winnings per spin is within 2 standard deviations from the mean, or between $-0.53 - 2(1.59) = -\$3.71$ and $-0.53 + 2(1.59) = \$2.65$. Over the course of 40 spins, this translates to overall winnings between $-\$3.71(40) = -\$148.40$ and $\$2.65(40) = \$106.00$. Because the potential loss associated with part b will be smaller in magnitude than that of part a, we can think of this approach as more risk averse in terms of long-run winnings.

▶ ***Try Exercises 7.18, part c, and 7.20***

In Practice We Rarely Know the Exact Characteristics of the Population Distribution

Rarely does a researcher know the exact characteristics of the population distribution (shape, mean, and standard deviation). With random sampling, we hope that the data distribution will look similar to the population distribution. In the next chapter, we show how in practice the statistician uses the data distribution to estimate the mean and standard deviation of the population distribution. In turn, we can use the sample standard deviation from the data distribution to estimate the standard deviation of the sampling distribution of the sample mean. This standard deviation helps us predict how close the sample mean falls to the population mean.

The Central Limit Theorem Helps Us Make Inferences

Sampling distributions are fundamental to statistical inference for making decisions and predictions about populations based on sample data. The central limit theorem and the formula for the standard deviation of the sample mean $\bar{x}$ have many implications. These include the following:

- When the sampling distribution of the sample mean $\bar{x}$ is approximately normal, $\bar{x}$ falls within 2 standard deviations of the population mean μ with probability close to 0.95, and $\bar{x}$ almost certainly falls within 3 standard deviations of μ. Results of this type are vital to inferential methods that predict how close sample statistics fall to unknown population parameters.
- For large n, the sampling distribution is approximately normal even if the population distribution is not. This enables us to make inferences about population means regardless of the shape of the population distribution. This is helpful in practice because usually we don't know the shape of the population distribution. Often, it is quite skewed or irregular, as in Activity 3.

Using the fundamental concepts we have learned in this chapter for the sampling distribution of a sample proportion and for the sampling distribution of a sample mean will allow us to develop inference procedures for population proportions and population means in the upcoming chapters.

7.2 Practicing the Basics

7.15 Simulate taking midterms Assume that the distribution of the score on a recent midterm is bell shaped with population mean $\mu = 70$ and population standard deviation $\sigma = 10$. You randomly sample $n = 12$ students who took the midterm. Using the Sampling Distribution of the Sample Mean web app accessible on the book's website,

TRY TECH

a. Simulate drawing one random sample of size 12. What sample mean score did you get? Why do you not expect to get exactly 70?

b. Now, simulate drawing 10,000 samples of size 12. Describe the simulated sampling distribution by using the histogram of the 10,000 sample means you generated. (*Note*: The app allows you to save the graph to a file.)

c. Suppose the population standard deviation is 5 rather than 10. Change to this setting in the app. How does the simulated sampling distribution of the sample mean change?

7.16 Education of the self-employed According to a recent Current Population Reports, the population distribution of number of years of education for self-employed individuals in the United States has a mean of 13.6 and a standard deviation of 3.0.

TRY

a. Identify the random variable X whose population distribution is described here.

b. Find the mean and standard deviation of the sampling distribution of $\bar{x}$ for a random sample of size 100. Interpret the results.

c. Repeat part b for $n = 400$. Describe the effect of increasing n.

7.17 Rolling one die Let X denote the outcome of rolling a die.

a. Construct a graph of the (i) probability distribution of X and (ii) sampling distribution of the sample mean for $n = 2$. (You can think of (i) as the population distribution you would get if you could roll the die an infinite number of times.

b. The probability distribution of X has mean 3.50 and standard deviation 1.71. Find the mean and standard deviation of the sampling distribution of the sample mean for (i) $n = 2$, (ii) $n = 30$. What is the effect of n on the sampling distribution?

7.18 Playing roulette A roulette wheel in Las Vegas has 38 slots. If you bet a dollar on a particular number, you'll win $35 if the ball ends up in that slot and $0 otherwise. Roulette wheels are calibrated so that each outcome is equally likely.

TRY

a. Let X denote your winnings when you play once. State the probability distribution of X. (This also represents the population distribution you would get if you could play roulette an infinite number of times.) It has mean 0.921 and standard deviation 5.603.

b. You decide to play once a minute for 12 hours a day for the next week, a total of 5040 times. Show that the sampling distribution of your sample mean winnings has mean = 0.921 and standard deviation = 0.079.

c. Refer to part b. Using the central limit theorem, find the probability that with this amount of roulette playing, your mean winnings is at least $1, so that you have not lost money after this week of playing. (*Hint*: Find the probability that a normal random variable with mean 0.921 and standard deviation 0.079 exceeds 1.0.)

7.19 Simulate rolling dice Access the Sampling Distribution of the Sample Mean (discrete variable) web app on the book's website. Enter the probabilities $P(X = x)$ of 0.1667 for the numbers 1 through 6 to specify the probability distribution of a fair die. (This is a discrete version of the uniform distribution shown in the first column of Figure 7.11.) The resulting population distribution has $\mu = 3.5$ and $\sigma = 1.71$.

TRY TECH

a. In the box for the sample size n, enter 2 to simulate rolling two dice. Then, press the Draw Sample(s) button several times and observe how the histogram for the simulated sampling distribution for the mean number shown on two rolls is building up. Finally, simulate rolling two dice and finding their average 10,000 times by selecting the corresponding option. Describe (shape, center, spread) the resulting simulated sampling distribution of the sample mean, using the histogram of the 10,000 generated sample means. (*Note:* Statistics for the simulated sampling distribution are reported in the tile of its plot.)

b. Are the reported mean and standard deviation of the simulated sampling distribution close to the theoretical mean and standard deviation for this sampling distribution? Compute the theoretical values and compare.

c. Repeat part a, but now simulate rolling $n = 30$ dice an finding their average face value. What are the major changes you observe in the simulated sampling distribution?

7.20 Canada lottery In one lottery option in Canada (*Source:* Lottery Canada), you bet on a six-digit number between 000000 and 999999. For a $1 bet, you win $100,000 if you are correct. The mean and standard deviation of the probability distribution for the lottery winnings are $\mu = 0.10$ (that is, 10 cents) and $\sigma = 100.00$. Joe figures that if he plays enough times every day, eventually he will strike it rich, by the law of large numbers. Over the course of several years, he plays 1 million times. Let $\bar{x}$ denote his average winnings.

TRY

a. Find the mean and standard deviation of the sampling distribution of $\bar{x}$.

b. About how likely is it that Joe's average winnings exceed $1, the amount he paid to play each time? Use the central limit theorem to find an approximate answer.

7.21 Shared family phone plan A recent personalized information sheet from your wireless phone carrier claims that the mean duration of all your phone calls was $\mu = 2.8$ minutes with a standard deviation of $\sigma = 2.1$ minutes.

a. Is the population distribution of the duration of your phone calls likely to be bell shaped, right-, or left-skewed?

b. You are on a shared wireless plan with your parents, who are statisticians. They look at some of your recent monthly statements that list each call and its duration and randomly sample 45 calls from the thousands listed there. They construct a histogram of the duration to look at the data distribution. Is this distribution likely to be bell shaped, right-, or left-skewed?

c. From the sample of $n = 45$ calls, your parents compute the mean duration. Is the sampling distribution of the sample mean likely to be bell shaped, right-, or left-skewed, or is it impossible to tell? Explain.

7.22 Dropped from plan The previous exercise mentions that the duration of your phone calls follows a distribution with mean $\mu = 2.8$ minutes and standard deviation $\sigma = 2.1$ minutes. From a random sample of $n = 45$ calls, your parents computed a sample mean of $\bar{x} = 3.4$ minutes and a sample standard deviation of $s = 2.9$ minutes.

TRY

a. Sketch the population distribution for the duration of your phone calls. What are its mean and standard deviation?

b. What are the mean and standard deviation of the data distribution?

c. Find the mean and standard deviation of the sampling distribution of the sample mean.

d. Is the sample mean of 3.4 minutes unusually high? Find its z-score and comment.

e. Your parents told you that they will kick you off the plan when they find a sample mean larger than 3.5 minutes. How likely is this to happen?

7.23 Restaurant profit? Jan's All You Can Eat Restaurant charges $8.95 per customer to eat at the restaurant. Restaurant management finds that its expense per customer, based on how much the customer eats and the expense of labor, has a distribution that is skewed to the right with a mean of $8.20 and a standard deviation of $3.

a. If the 100 customers on a particular day have the characteristics of a random sample from their customer base, find the mean and standard deviation of the sampling distribution of the restaurant's sample mean expense per customer.

b. Find the probability that the restaurant makes a profit that day, with the sample mean expense being less than $8.95. (*Hint:* Apply the central limit theorem to the sampling distribution in part a.)

7.24 Survey accuracy A study investigating the relationship between age and annual medical expenses randomly samples 100 individuals in Davis, California. It is hoped that the sample will have a similar mean age as the entire population.

a. If the standard deviation of the ages of all individuals in Davis is $\sigma = 15$, find the probability that the mean age of the individuals sampled is within two years of the mean age for all individuals in Davis. (*Hint*: Find the sampling distribution of the sample mean age and use the central limit theorem. You don't have to know the population mean to answer this, but if it makes it easier, use a value such as $\mu = 30$.)

b. Would the probability be larger, or smaller, if $\sigma = 10$? Why?

7.25 Blood pressure Vincenzo Baranello was diagnosed with high blood pressure. He was able to keep his blood pressure in control for several months by taking blood pressure medicine (amlodipine besylate). Baranello's blood pressure is monitored by taking three readings a day, in early morning, at midday, and in the evening.

a. During this period, the probability distribution of his systolic blood pressure reading had a mean of 130 and a standard deviation of 6. If the successive observations behave like a random sample from this distribution, find the mean and standard deviation of the sampling distribution of the sample mean for the three observations each day.

b. Suppose that the probability distribution of his blood pressure reading is normal. What is the shape of the sampling distribution? Why?

c. Refer to part b. Find the probability that the sample mean exceeds 140, which is considered problematically high. (*Hint*: Use the sampling distribution, not the probability distribution for each observation.)

7.26 Household size According to the 2010 U.S. census
TRY bureau Current Population Survey (www.census.gov/population/www/socdemo/hh-fam/cps2010.html), the average number of people in family households that contain both family and non-family members is 4.43 with a standard deviation of 2.02. This is based on census information for the population. Suppose the Bureau of the Census instead had estimated this mean using a random sample of 225 homes. Suppose the sample had a sample mean of 4.2 and standard deviation of 1.9.

a. Identify the random variable X. Indicate whether it is quantitative or categorical.

b. Describe the center and variability of the population distribution. What would you predict as the shape of the population distribution? Explain.

c. Describe the center and variability of the data distribution. What would you predict as the shape of the data distribution? Explain.

d. Describe the center and variability of the sampling distribution of the sample mean for 225 homes. What would you predict as the shape of the sampling distribution? Explain.

7.27 Average monthly sales A large corporation employs 27,251 individuals. The average income in 2008 for all employees was \$74,550 with a standard deviation of \$19,872. You are interested in comparing the incomes of today's employees with those of 2008. A random sample of 100 employees of the corporation yields $\bar{x} = \$75{,}207$ and $s = \$18{,}901$.

a. Describe the center and variability of the population distribution. What shape does it probably have? Explain.

b. Describe the center and variability of the data distribution. What shape does it probably have? Explain.

c. Describe the center and variability of the sampling distribution of the sample mean for $n = 100$. What shape does it have? Explain.

d. Explain why it would not be unusual to observe an individual who earns more than \$100,000, but it would be highly unusual to observe a sample mean income of more than \$100,000 for a random sample size of 100 people.

7.28 Central limit theorem for uniform population Let's use
TRY the Sampling Distribution of the Sample Mean web app
TECH accessible from the book's website to show that the first population distribution shown in Figure 7.11 has a more nearly normal sampling distribution for the mean as n increases. Select uniform for the population distribution and keep the default settings of 0 and 1 for the lower and upper bound.

a. Use the app to simulate the sampling distribution when the sample size $n = 2$. Run 10,000 simulations and look at the resulting histogram of the sample means. (You may want to decrease the binsize a bit to get a clearer picture.) What shape does the simulated sampling distribution have?

b. Repeat part a, but now use a sample size of $n = 5$. Explain how the variability and the shape of the simulated sampling distribution changes as n increases from 2 to 5.

c. Repeat part a, but now use a sample size of $n = 30$. Explain how the variability and the shape of the simulated sampling distribution changes as n increases from 2 to 30. Compare results from parts a-c to the first column of Figure 7.11.

d. Explain how the central limit theorem describes what you have observed.

7.29 CLT for skewed population Access the Sampling
TRY Distribution of the Sample Mean web app and position
TECH the slider for the skewness of the default population distribution to the smallest value. The population distribution now looks similar to the one in the third column of Figure 7.11. Repeat parts a–c of the previous exercise and explain how the variability and shape of the simulated sampling distribution of the sample mean changes as n changes from 2 to 5 to 30. Explain how the central limit theorem describes what you have observed.

7.30 Sampling distribution for normal population Access the
TRY Sampling Distribution of the Sample Mean web app and
TECH select Bell-Shaped for the shape of the population distribution, which looks similar to the fourth column in Figure 7.11. Select a value for the population mean and standard deviation. Is the sampling distribution normal even for $n = 2$? What does this tell you?

Chapter Review

ANSWERS TO FIGURE QUESTIONS

Figure 7.1 The larger the sample size, the more we expect the data distribution to resemble the population distribution.

Figure 7.3 Using the empirical rule, almost all sample proportions will fall within 3 standard deviations, so within $3(0.079) = 0.2376$ of the mean of 0.538, which is the interval $[0.301, 0.775]$.

Figure 7.4 Using the empirical rule, almost all sample proportions will fall within 3 standard deviations, so within $3(0.008) = 0.024$ of the mean of 0.538, which is the interval $[0.514, 0.562]$.

Figure 7.6 With $p = 0.6$, the mean of the sampling distribution is 0.6 and the standard deviation is $\sqrt{0.6(0.4)/3889} = 0.008$, so that almost all sample proportions will fall between $0.6 \pm 3(0.008)$, or in the interval [0.592, 0.608]

Figure 7.9 Using the empirical rule, almost all sample means will fall within 3 standard deviations, so within $3(1.01) = 3.03$ of the mean of 50, which is the interval [47, 53]. No, the standard deviation of the 10,000 generated sample means when $n = 10$ was 3.18 (from Figure 7.8), and it was 1.01 when $n = 100$, so the standard deviation decreased by a factor of only about 3, not 10! As we will learn, the standard deviation decreases precisely by a factor of $\sqrt{n} = \sqrt{10} = 3.16$. The square root of the sample size determines how the standard deviation changes.

Figure 7.14 The probability distribution and the sampling distribution do not have the same shape. The sampling distribution is bell shaped. The probability distribution is discrete, concentrated at two values, −\$10 with height of 20/38 and \$10 with height of 18/38.

SUMMARY OF NEW NOTATION IN CHAPTER 7

μ Mean of population distribution
σ Standard deviation of population distribution
p Population proportion

CHAPTER SUMMARY

- The **sampling distribution** is the probability distribution of a sample statistic, such as a sample proportion or sample mean. With random sampling, it provides probabilities for all the possible values of the statistic.
- The **population distribution** is the probability distribution from which we take the sample. It is described by *parameters* (p or μ and σ), the values of which are usually unknown. The **data distribution** describes the sample data. It's the distribution we actually see in practice and is described by sample *statistics*, such as a sample proportion or a sample mean. The **sampling distribution** provides the key for telling us how close a sample statistic falls to the unknown parameter we'd like to make an inference about.

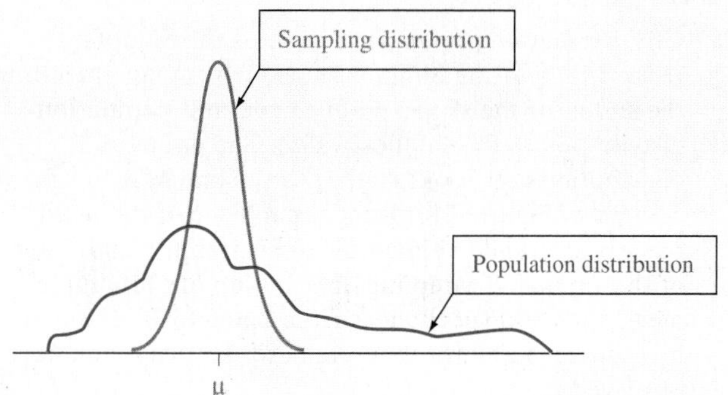

- The **sampling distribution of the sample proportion** has mean equal to the population proportion p and standard deviation equal to $\sqrt{p(1-p)/n}$.
- The **sampling distribution of the sample mean** $\bar{x}$ has mean equal to the population mean μ and standard deviation equal to $\sigma/\sqrt{n}$.
- The **central limit theorem** states that for random samples of sufficiently large size (at least about 30 is usually enough), the **sampling distribution of the sample mean is approximately normal**. This theorem holds *no matter what the shape of the population distribution.* It applies to sample proportions as well, because the sample proportion is a sample mean when the possible values are 0 and 1. In that case, the sampling distribution of the sample proportion is approximately normal whenever n is large enough that both np and $n(1-p)$ are at least 15. The bell-shaped appearance of the sampling distributions for most statistics is the main reason for the importance of the normal distribution.

CHAPTER PROBLEMS

Practicing the Basics

7.31 Exam performance An exam consists of 50 multiple-choice questions. Based on how much you studied, for any given question you think you have a probability of $p = 0.70$ of getting the correct answer. Consider the sampling distribution of the sample proportion of the 50 questions on which you get the correct answer.

a. Find the mean and standard deviation of the sampling distribution of this proportion.

b. What do you expect for the shape of the sampling distribution? Why?

c. If truly $p = 0.70$, would it be very surprising if you got correct answers on only 60% of the questions? Justify your answer by using the normal distribution to approximate the probability of a sample proportion of 0.60 or less.

7.32 Blue eyes According to a *Boston Globe* story, only about 1 in 6 Americans have blue eyes, whereas in 1900 about half had blue eyes. (*Source:* Data from *The Boston Globe*, October 17, 2006.)

a. For a random sample of 100 living Americans, find the mean and standard deviation of the proportion that have blue eyes.

b. In a course you are taking with 100 students, half of the students have blue eyes. Would this have been a surprising result if the sample were a random sample of Americans? Answer by finding how many standard deviations that sample result falls from the mean of the sampling distribution of the proportion of 100 students who have blue eyes.

c. In part b, identify the population distribution, the data distribution, and the sampling distribution of the sample proportion.

7.33 Alzheimer's According to the Alzheimer's Association,[2] as of 2014 Alzheimer's disease affects 1 in 9 Americans over the age of 65. A study is planned of health problems the elderly face. For a random sample of Americans over the age of 65, report the shape, mean, and standard deviation of the sampling distribution of the proportion who suffer from Alzheimer's disease, if the sample size is (a) 200 and (b) 800.

7.34 Basketball shooting In college basketball, a shot made from beyond a designated arc radiating about 20 feet from the basket is worth three points instead of the usual two points given for shots made inside that arc. Over his career, University of Florida basketball player Lee Humphrey made 45% of his three-point attempts. In one game in his final season, he made only 3 of 12 three-point shots, leading a TV basketball analyst to announce that Humphrey was in a shooting slump.

a. Assuming Humphrey has a 45% chance of making any particular three-point shot, find the mean and standard deviation of the sampling distribution of the proportion of three-point shots he will make out of 12 shots.

b. How many standard deviations from the mean is this game's result of making 3 of 12 three-point shots?

c. If Humphrey was actually not in a slump but still had a 45% chance of making any particular three-point shot, explain why it would not be especially surprising for him to make only 3 of 12 shots. Thus, this is not really evidence of a shooting slump.

7.35 Defective chips A supplier of electronic chips for tablets claims that only 4% of his chips are defective. A manufacturer tests 500 randomly selected chips from a large shipment from the supplier for potential defects.

a. Find the mean and standard deviation for the distribution of the sample proportion of defective chips in the sample of 500.

b. Is it reasonable to assume a normal shape for the sampling distribution? Explain.

c. The manufacturer will return the entire shipment if he finds more than 5% of the 500 sampled chips to be defective. Find the probability that the shipment will be returned.

7.36 Returning shipment Refer to the previous exercise, in which the manufacturer will return the entire shipment if more than 5% defective chips are found in the sample.

a. Find the probability that the shipment will be returned if the manufacturer decides to test only 380 randomly selected chips (instead of 500).

b. Suppose that despite the claim by the supplier, the shipment actually contains 6% defective chips. Find the probability that the shipment will be returned if the manufacturer randomly samples 380 chips from the shipment.

7.37 Aunt Erma's restaurant In Aunt Erma's Restaurant, the daily sales follow a probability distribution that has a mean of $\mu = \$900$ and a standard deviation of $\sigma = \$300$. This past week the daily sales for the seven days had a mean of \$980 and a standard deviation of \$276. Consider these seven days as a random sample from all days.

a. Identify the mean and standard deviation of the population distribution.

b. Identify the mean and standard deviation of the data distribution. What does the standard deviation describe?

c. Identify the mean and the standard deviation of the sampling distribution of the sample mean for samples of seven daily sales. What does this standard deviation describe?

7.38 Home runs Based on data from the 2010 Major League Baseball season, X = number of home runs the San Francisco Giants hit in a game has a mean of 1.0 and a standard deviation of 1.0.

a. Do you think X has a normal distribution? Why or why not?

b. Suppose that this year X has the same distribution. Report the shape, mean, and standard deviation of the sampling distribution of the mean number of home runs the team will hit in its 162 games.

c. Based on the answer to part b, find the probability that the mean number of home runs per game in this coming season will exceed 1.50.

7.39 Physicians' assistants The 2006 AAPA survey of the population of physicians' assistants who were working full time reported a mean annual income of \$84,396 and standard deviation of \$21,975. (*Source:* Data from 2006 AAPA survey [www.aapa.org].)

a. Suppose the AAPA had randomly sampled 100 physicians' assistants instead of collecting data for all of them. Describe the mean, standard deviation, and shape of the sampling distribution of the sample mean.

b. Using this sampling distribution, find the z-score for a sample mean of \$80,000.

c. Using parts a and b, find the probability that the sample mean would fall within approximately \$4000 of the population mean.

7.40 Bank machine withdrawals An executive in an Australian savings bank decides to estimate the mean amount of money withdrawn in bank machine transactions. From past experience, she believes that \$50 (Australian) is a reasonable guess for the standard deviation of the distribution of withdrawals. She would like her sample mean to be within \$10 of the population mean. Estimate the probability that this happens if she randomly samples 100 withdrawals. (*Hint:* Find the standard deviation of the sample mean. How many standard deviations does \$10 equal?)

7.41 PDI The scores on the Psychomotor Development Index (PDI), a scale of infant development, have a normal population distribution with mean 100 and standard deviation 15. An infant is selected at random.

a. Find the z-score for a PDI value of 90.

b. A study uses a random sample of 225 infants. Using the sampling distribution of the sample mean PDI, find the z-score corresponding to a sample mean of 90.

[2] www.alz.org/documents_custom/2014_Facts_Figures_Fact_Sheet.pdf.

c. Explain why a PDI value of 90 is not surprising, but a sample mean PDI score of 90 for 225 infants would be surprising.

7.42 Number of sex partners According to recent General Social Surveys, in the United States the population distribution for adults of X = number of sex partners in the past 12 months has a mean of about 1.0 and a standard deviation of about 1.0.

a. Does X have a normal distribution? Explain.

b. For a random sample of 100 adults, describe the sampling distribution of $\bar{x}$ and give its mean and standard deviation. What is the effect of X not having a normal distribution?

7.43 ◆◆ **Using control charts to assess quality** In many industrial production processes, measurements are made periodically on critical characteristics to ensure that the process is operating properly. Observations vary from item to item being produced, perhaps reflecting variability in material used in the process and/or variability in the way a person operates machinery used in the process. There is usually a target mean for the observations, which represents the long-run mean of the observations when the process is operating properly. There is also a target standard deviation for how observations should vary around that mean if the process is operating properly. A **control chart** is a method for plotting data collected over time to monitor whether the process is operating within the limits of expected variation. A control chart that plots *sample means* over time is called an **$\bar{x}$-chart**. As shown in the following, the horizontal axis is the time scale, and the vertical axis shows possible sample mean values. The horizontal line in the middle of the chart shows the target for the true mean. The upper and lower lines are called the **upper control limit** and **lower control limit**, denoted by **UCL** and **LCL**. These are usually drawn 3 standard deviations above and below the target value. The region between the LCL and UCL contains the values that theory predicts for the sample mean when the process is in control. When a sample mean falls above the UCL or below the LCL, it indicates that something may have gone wrong in the production process.

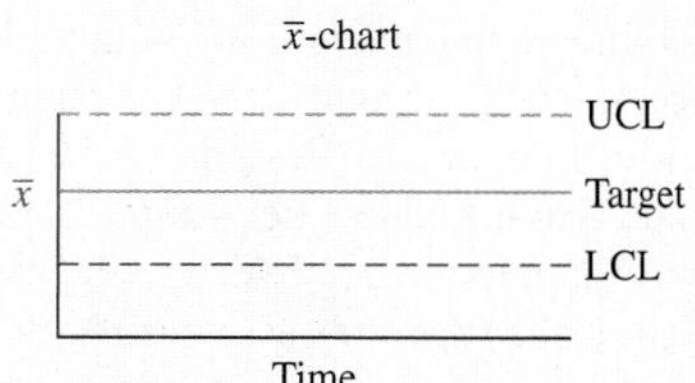

a. Walter Shewhart invented this method in 1924 at Bell Labs. He suggested using 3 standard deviations in setting the UCL and LCL to achieve a balance between having the chart fail to diagnose a problem and having it indicate a problem when none actually existed. If the process is working properly ("in statistical control") and if n is large enough that $\bar{x}$ has approximately a normal distribution, what is the probability that it indicates a problem when none exists? (That is, what's the probability a sample mean will be at least 3 standard deviations from the target, when that target is the true mean?)

b. What would the probability of falsely indicating a problem be if we used 2 standard deviations instead for the UCL and LCL?

c. When about nine sample means in a row fall on the same side of the target for the mean in a control chart, this is an indication of a potential problem, such as a shift up or a shift down in the true mean relative to the target value. If the process is actually in control and has a normal distribution around that mean, what is the probability that the next nine sample means in a row would (i) all fall above the mean and (ii) all fall above or all fall below the mean? (*Hint:* Use the binomial distribution, treating the successive observations as independent.)

7.44 Too little or too much cola? Refer to the previous exercise. When a machine for dispensing a cola drink into bottles is in statistical control, the amount dispensed has a mean of 500 ml (milliliters) and a standard deviation of 4 ml.

a. In constructing a control chart to monitor this process with periodic samples of size 4, how would you select the target line and the upper and lower control limits?

b. If the process actually deteriorates and operates with a mean of 491 ml and a standard deviation of 6 ml, what is the probability that the next value plotted on the control chart indicates a problem with the process, falling more than 3 standard deviations from the target? What do you assume in making this calculation?

Concepts and Investigations

7.45 TRY TECH **CLT for custom population** Access the Sampling Distribution for a Sample Mean web app and select Build Own as the shape for the population distribution. By typing numbers into the text field, you can create your own population distribution. Repeating a number several times will make the population distribution more peaked around that number. Create a population that is very far from bell-shaped. With it, simulate the sampling distribution of the sample mean by using 10,000 simulations. Explain how the shape and variability of the simulated sampling distribution changes as n changes from 2 to 5 to 30 to 100. Explain how the central limit theorem describes what you have observed. (Note that the app allows you to download the graphs for the population, data, and simulated sampling distribution.)

7.46 What is a sampling distribution? How would you explain to someone who has never studied statistics what a sampling distribution is? Explain by using the example of polls of 1000 Canadians for estimating the proportion who think the prime minister is doing a good job.

7.47 What good is a standard deviation? Explain how the standard deviation of the sampling distribution of a sample proportion gives you useful information to help gauge how close a sample proportion falls to the unknown population proportion.

7.48 Purpose of sampling distribution You'd like to estimate the proportion of all students in your school who are fluent in more than one language. You poll a random sample of 50 students and get a sample proportion of 0.12. Explain why the standard deviation of the sampling distribution of the sample proportion gives you useful information to help gauge how close this sample proportion is to the unknown population proportion.

7.49 Sampling distribution for small and large n The owners of Aunt Erma's Restaurant in Boston plan an advertising campaign with the claim that more people prefer the taste of their pizza (which we'll denote by A) than the current leading fast-food chain selling pizza (which we'll denote by D). To support their claim, they plan to sample three people in Boston randomly. Each person is asked to taste a slice of pizza A and a slice of pizza D. Subjects are blindfolded so they cannot see the pizza when they taste it, and the order of giving them the two slices is randomized. They are then asked which pizza tastes better. Use a symbol with three letters to represent the responses for each possible sample. For instance, ADD represents a sample in which the first subject sampled preferred pizza A and the second and third subjects preferred pizza D.

a. List the eight possible samples of size 3, and for each sample report the proportion that preferred pizza A.

b. In the entire Boston population, suppose that exactly half would prefer pizza A and half would prefer pizza D. Then, each of the eight possible samples is equally likely to be observed. Explain why the sampling distribution of the sample proportion who prefer Aunt Erma's pizza, when $n = 3$, is

Sample Proportion	Probability
0	1/8
1/3	3/8
2/3	3/8
1	1/8

c. In theory, you could use the same principle as in part b to find the sampling distribution for any n, but it is tedious to list all elements of the sample space. For instance, for $n = 50$, there are more than 10_{15} elements to list. Despite this, what is the mean, standard deviation, and approximate shape of the *sampling distribution* of the sample proportion when $n = 50$ (still assuming that the population proportion preferring pizza A is 0.5)?

7.50 Sampling distribution via the binomial Refer to the previous exercise, in which the proportion of people preferring pizza A is $p = 0.5$ and a sample of size $n = 3$ is taken. The sampling distribution of the sample proportion of people preferring pizza A as shown in part b of that exercise can also be derived using the binomial distribution with $n = 3$ and $p = 0.5$.

a. A sample proportion of 1/3 corresponds to 1 out of 3 randomly sampled persons preferring pizza A. Show that this occurs with probability 3/8. (*Hint:* Use the binomial formula with $p = 0.5$ and $x = 1$ person out of $n = 3$ preferring pizza A.)

b. Find the probabilities for the remaining sample proportions by using the binomial distribution with $x = 0, 2$, or 3.

c. Find the sampling distribution of the sample proportion when $n = 4$ people (instead of $n = 3$) are sampled and draw its graph.

7.51 Pizza preference with $p = 0.6$ Refer to the previous two exercises but now suppose the population proportion in Boston preferring pizza A is $p = 0.6$ instead of $p = 0.5$. (Then, the eight possible outcomes (AAA, AAD,..., DDA, DDD) of a sample of size $n = 3$ are *not* equally likely, as in part b of Exercise 7.49)

a. Use the binomial distribution to verify that the sampling distribution of the sample proportion in a sample of size $n = 3$ is given by

Number Preferring A	Proportion Preferring A	Probability
0	0	0.064
1	1/3	0.288
2	2/3	0.432
3	1	0.216

(*Note:* Using the binomial distribution, you can, in principle, find the sampling distribution for the sample proportion for any n and p.)

b. When $n = 100$, what is the mean number of persons that prefer pizza A in a sample of size $n = 100$? (*Hint:* Use the formula for the mean of a binomial distribution.)

c. Part b found the mean number (or expected value) of persons preferring pizza A in a sample of size 100. What then is the expected *proportion* of persons preferring pizza A in a sample of size 100? This is the mean of the sampling distribution of the sample proportion.

7.52 Simulating pizza preference with $p = 0.5$ Access the Sampling Distribution of the Sample Proportion web app.

TRY TECH

a. For $p = 0.5$ and a sample of size $n = 3$, the graph of the sampling distribution is given below. (This is the graph corresponding to the table in Exercise 7.49, part b.) Compute the mean of the sampling distribution from first principles, i.e., using the formula $\Sigma x P(X = x)$. The standard deviation of the sampling distribution is equal to 0.289.

b. Now, using the app, simulate the sampling distribution for a population proportion when $p = 0.5$ and $n = 3$, using 10,000 simulations. Do the graph and the results from the simulations agree? Compare the shapes, means, and standard deviations from the two graphs. (The mean and standard deviation of the 10,000 generated sample proportions are displayed in the title of the graph for the sampling distribution in the app.)

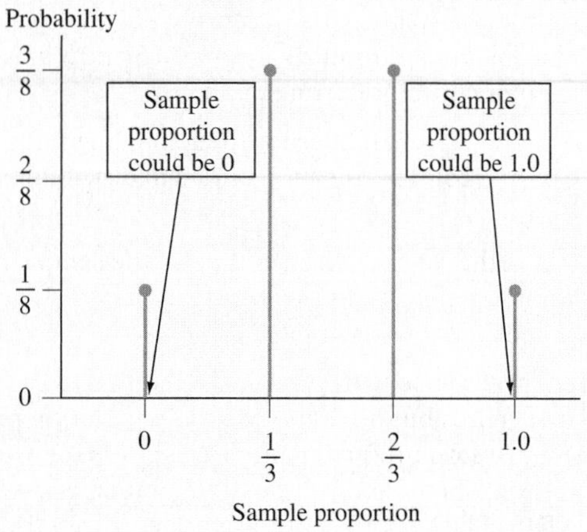

Probability

$\frac{3}{8}$, $\frac{2}{8}$, $\frac{1}{8}$, 0

Sample proportion could be 0

Sample proportion could be 1.0

0, $\frac{1}{3}$, $\frac{2}{3}$, 1.0

Sample proportion

7.53 Simulating pizza preference with $p = 0.6$ Access the Sampling Distribution of the Sample Proportion web app. When $p = 0.6$ and the sample size n = 3, the mean and standard deviation of the sampling distribution (given in the table in part a of Exercise 7.51) are equal to 0.6 and 0.283. With the app, simulate the sampling distribution by generating 10,000 samples. Are the mean and standard deviation of the 10,000 simulated sample proportions close to the true mean and standard deviation stated above? (The mean and standard deviation of the 10,000 generated sample proportions are displayed in the title of the graph for the sampling distribution in the app.)

TECH

7.54 Winning at roulette Part b of Example 7 used the central limit theorem to approximate the probability of coming out ahead if you bet $10 on red on each of 40 roulette wheel spins. For each spin, the winnings are $10 with probability 18/38 and −$10 with probability 20/38. You are interested in the probability of winning at least $100 over the course of the 40 spins.

a. The average winnings per spin need to be at least how much to win at least $100?

b. Use the central limit theorem to determine the approximate probability of winning at least $100.

c. You must win at least how many of the spins to win at least $100?

d. Using the binomial distribution, calculate the exact probability of winning at least $100 in the 40 spins. How does your answer compare with that of part b?

7.55 True or false As the sample size increases, the standard deviation of the sampling distribution of $\bar{x}$ increases. Explain your answer.

7.56 Multiple choice: Standard deviation Which of the following is *not* correct? The standard deviation of a statistic describes

a. The standard deviation of the sampling distribution of that statistic.

b. The standard deviation of the sample data measurements.

c. How close that statistic falls to the parameter that it estimates.

d. The variability in the values of the statistic for repeated random samples of size *n*.

7.57 Multiple choice: CLT The central limit theorem implies

a. All variables have approximately bell-shaped data distributions if a random sample contains at least about 30 observations.

b. Population distributions are normal whenever the population size is large.

c. For sufficiently large random samples, the sampling distribution of $\bar{x}$ is approximately normal, regardless of the shape of the population distribution.

d. The sampling distribution of the sample mean looks more like the population distribution as the sample size increases.

7.58 Multiple choice: Sampling distribution of sample proportion In a class of 150 students, the professor has each person toss a fair coin 50 times and calculate the proportion of times the tosses come up heads. Roughly 95% of students should have proportions between which two numbers?

a. 0.49 and 0.51

b. 0.05 and 0.95

c. 0.42 and 0.58

d. 0.36 and 0.64

e. 0.25 and 0.75

Explain your answer.

7.59 Multiple choice: Sampling distribution The sampling distribution of a sample mean for a random sample size of 100 describes

a. How sample means tend to vary from random sample to random sample of size 100.

b. How observations tend to vary from person to person in a random sample of size 100.

c. How the data distribution looks like the population distribution when the sample size is larger than 30.

d. How the standard deviation varies among samples of size 100.

7.60 ◆◆ **Sample = population** Let X = GPA for students in your school.

a. What would the sampling distribution of the sample mean look like if you sampled *every* student in the school, so the sample size equals the population size? (*Hint:* The sample mean then equals the population mean.)

b. How does the sampling distribution compare to the population distribution if we take a sample of size $n = 1$?

7.61 ◆◆ **Standard deviation of a proportion** Suppose $x = 1$ with probability p, and $x = 0$ with probability $(1 - p)$. Then, x is the special case of a binomial random variable with $n = 1$, so that $\sigma = \sqrt{np(1-p)} = \sqrt{p(1-p)}$. With n trials, using the formula $\sigma/\sqrt{n}$ for a standard deviation of a sample mean, explain why the standard deviation of a sample proportion equals $\sqrt{p(1-p)/n}$.

7.62 ◆◆ **Finite populations** The formula $\sigma/\sqrt{n}$ for the standard deviation of $\bar{x}$ actually is an approximation that treats the population size as *infinitely* large relative to the sample size n. The exact formula for a *finite* population size N is

$$\text{Standard deviation} = \sqrt{\frac{N-n}{N-1}}\frac{\sigma}{\sqrt{n}}.$$

The term $\sqrt{(N-n)/(N-1)}$ is called the **finite population correction.**

a. When $n = 300$ students are selected from a college student body of size $N = 30{,}000$, show that the standard deviation equals $0.995\,\sigma/\sqrt{n}$. (When n is small compared to the population size N, the approximate formula works very well.)

b. If $n = N$ (that is, we sample the entire population), show that the standard deviation equals 0. In other words, no sampling error occurs, since $\bar{x} = \mu$ in that case.

Student Activities

7.63 **Simulate a sampling distribution** The table (data are available on the book's website) provides prices per night for all 51 available hotel rooms (as of December 2014) in Panama City Beach, Florida, for a week in March 2015 (spring break). The distribution of these prices is characterized by $\mu = \$196$ and $\sigma = \$57.4$.

TRY TECH

Hotel	Price
St. Thomas Square	75
American Quality Lodge	92
Hathaway Inn	105
Top Of The Gulf	129
Palm Grove	134
Shores of Panama	139
Sleep Inn	140
La Quinta	155
Beachside Resort	156
Hawthorn Suites	159
Origin Beach	159
The Reef	159
Casa Loma	163
Sunbird Beach	165
...	

a. Each student or the class should construct a graphical display (stem-and-leaf plot, dotplot, or histogram) of the population distribution of the prices. (Alternatively, access the Sampling Distribution for the Sample Mean web app available on the book's website. Select Build Own for the shape and copy and paste the prices in the text field. This provides a smoothed graph for the population distribution of hotel prices, with $\mu = 196$ and $\sigma = 60$.)

b. Each student should select nine random numbers between 1 and 51, with replacement (e.g., using *random.org*). Using these numbers, each student should sample nine hotels and find the mean price for these hotels. Collect all sample mean prices. Using technology, construct a graph (using the same graphical display as in part a) of the simulated sampling distribution of the $\bar{x}$-values for all the student samples. Compare it to the distribution in part a. (Alternatively, you can simulate taking random samples of size 9 with the sampling distribution web app under the setting mentioned in part a.)

c. Find the mean of the $\bar{x}$-values in part b. How does it compare to the value you would expect in a long run of repeated samples of size 9?

d. Find the standard deviation of the $\bar{x}$-values in part b. How does it compare to the value you would expect in a long run of repeated samples of size 9?

7.64 **Coin-tossing distributions** For a single toss of a balanced coin, let $x = 1$ for a head and $x = 0$ for a tail.

a. Construct the probability distribution for x and calculate its mean. (You can think of this as the population distribution corresponding to a very long sequence of tosses.)

b. The coin is flipped 10 times, yielding 6 heads and 4 tails. Construct the data distribution.

c. Each student in the class should flip a coin 10 times and find the proportion of heads. Collect the sample proportion of heads from each student. Summarize the simulated sampling distribution by constructing a plot of all the proportions obtained by the students. Describe the shape and variability of the sampling distribution compared to the distributions in parts a and b.

d. If you performed the experiment in part c a huge number of times, what would you expect to get for the (i) mean and (ii) standard deviation of the sample proportions?

7.65 **Sample versus sampling** Each student should bring 10 coins to class. For each coin, observe its age, the difference between the current year and the year on the coin.

a. Using all the students' observations, the class should construct a histogram of the sample ages. What is its shape?

b. Now each student should find the mean for that student's 10 coins, and the class should plot the means of all the students. What type of distribution is this, and how does it compare to the one in part a? What concepts does this exercise illustrate?

PART

Inferential Statistics

CHAPTER 8

The tools from previous chapters, in particular the idea of the normal distribution as a sampling distribution, are used in this chapter to turn information from a sample into an interval of plausible values for an unknown population proportion or population mean.

Statistical Inference: Confidence Intervals

Example 1

Analyzing Data from the General Social Survey

Picture the Scenario

For more than 30 years, the National Opinion Research Center at the University of Chicago (www.norc.uchicago.edu) has conducted an opinion survey called the General Social Survey (GSS). The survey randomly samples about 2000 adult Americans. In a 90-minute in-person interview, the interviewer asks a long list of questions about opinions and behavior for a wide variety of issues. Other nations have similar surveys. For instance, every five years Statistics Canada conducts its own General Social Survey. *Eurobarometer* regularly samples about 1000 people in each country in the European Union and a host of other polling institutions, such as Gallup (gallup.com), the Pew Research Center (pewresearch.org), or Nielsen (nielsen.com), feature results from all sorts of polls on their websites.

Analyzing such data helps researchers learn about how people think and behave at a given time and track opinions over time. Activity 1 in Chapter 1 showed how to access the GSS data at sda.berkeley.edu/GSS.

Questions to Explore

Based on data from a recent GSS, how can you make an inference about

- The proportion of Americans who are willing to pay higher prices to protect the environment?
- The proportion of Americans who agree that it is better for everyone involved if the man is the achiever outside the home and the woman takes care of the home and family?
- The mean number of hours that Americans watch TV per day?

Thinking Ahead

We will analyze data from the GSS in examples and exercises throughout this chapter. For instance, in Example 3 we'll see how to estimate the proportion of Americans who are willing to pay higher prices to protect the environment.

We'll answer the other two questions in Examples 2 and 5, and in exercises we'll explore opinions about issues such as whether it should or should not be the government's responsibility to reduce income differences between the rich and poor, whether a preschool child is likely to suffer if his or her mother works, and how politically conservative or liberal Americans are.

A sample of about 2000 people (as the GSS takes) is relatively small. For instance, in the United States, a survey of this size gathers data for less than 1 of every 100,000 people. How can we possibly make reliable predictions about the entire population with so few people?

We now have the tools to see how this is done. We're ready to learn about a powerful use of statistics: **statistical inference** about population parameters using sample data. Inference methods help us to predict how close a sample statistic falls to the population parameter. We can make decisions and predictions about populations even if we have data for relatively few subjects from that population. The previous chapter illustrated that it's often possible to predict the winner of an election in which millions of people voted, knowing only how a couple of thousand people voted.

Recall

A **statistic** describes a **sample**. Examples are the sample mean $\bar{x}$ and standard deviation *s*.

A **parameter** describes a **population**. Examples are the population mean μ and standard deviation σ. ◀

For statistical inference methods, you may wonder what the relevance of learning about the role of randomization is in gathering data (Chapter 4), concepts of probability (Chapter 5), and the normal distribution (Chapter 6) and its use as a sampling distribution (Chapter 7). They're important for two primary reasons:

- Statistical inference methods use probability calculations that assume that the data were gathered with a random sample or a randomized experiment.
- The probability calculations refer to a sampling distribution of a statistic, which is often approximately a normal distribution.

Recall

A **sampling distribution** specifies the possible values a statistic can take and their probabilities. ◀

In other words, statistical inference uses sampling distributions of statistics calculated from data gathered using randomization, and those sampling distributions are often approximately normal.

There are two types of statistical inference methods—**estimation** of population parameters and **testing hypotheses** about the parameter values. This chapter discusses the first type, estimating population parameters. We'll learn how to estimate population proportions for categorical variables and population means for quantitative variables. For instance, a study dealing with how college students pay for their education might estimate the proportion of college students who work part time and the mean annual income for those who work. The most informative estimation method constructs an interval of numbers, called a **confidence interval**, within which the unknown parameter value is believed to fall.

Recall

We use the **proportion** to summarize the *relative frequency* of observations in a category for a categorical variable. The proportion equals the number in the category divided by the sample size. We use the **mean** as one way to summarize the *center* of the observations for a quantitative variable. ◀

8.1 Point and Interval Estimates of Population Parameters

Population parameters have two types of estimates, a point estimate and an interval estimate.

Point Estimate and Interval Estimate

A **point estimate** is a *single number* that is our best guess for the parameter.

An **interval estimate** is an *interval of numbers* that is believed to contain the actual value of the parameter.

For example, one General Social Survey asked, "Do you believe in hell?" From the sample data, the point estimate for the proportion of adult Americans who would respond yes equals 0.73—more than 7 of 10. The adjective "point" in *point estimate* refers to using a single number or *point* as the parameter estimate.

An interval estimate, found with the method introduced in the next section, predicts that the proportion of adult Americans who believe in hell falls between 0.71 and 0.75. Figure 8.1 illustrates this idea.

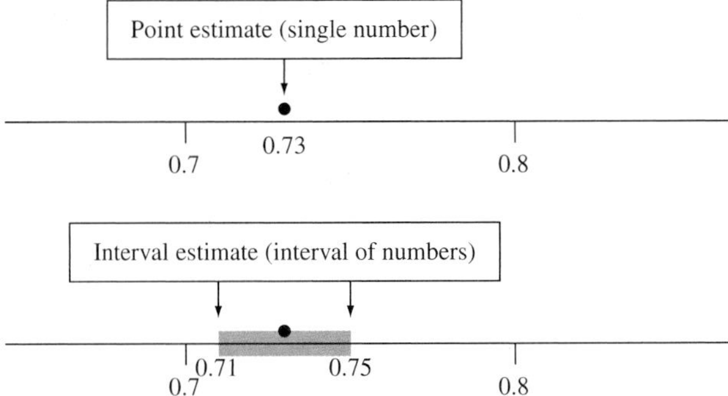

▲ **Figure 8.1** A Point Estimate Predicts a Parameter by a Single Number. An **interval estimate** is an interval of numbers that are believable values for the parameter. **Question** Why is a point estimate alone not sufficiently informative?

A point estimate by itself is not sufficient because it doesn't tell us *how close* the estimate is likely to be to the parameter. An interval estimate is more useful. It tells us that the point estimate of 0.73 falls within a *margin of error* of 0.02 of the actual population proportion. By incorporating a margin of error, the interval estimate helps us gauge the accuracy of the point estimate.

Point Estimation: Making a Best Guess for a Population Parameter

Once we've collected the data, how do we find a point estimate, representing our best guess for a parameter value? The answer is straightforward—we can use an appropriate sample statistic. For example, for a population mean μ, the sample mean $\bar{x}$ is a point estimate of μ. For the population proportion, the sample proportion is a point estimate.

Point estimates are the most common form of inference reported by the mass media. For example, the Gallup organization conducts a monthly survey to estimate the U.S. president's popularity, and the mass media report the results. In mid-July 2014, this survey reported that 42% of the American public approved of President Obama's performance in office. This percentage was a *point estimate* rather than a parameter because Gallup used a sample of about 1500 people rather than the entire population. For simplicity, we'll usually use the term *estimate* in place of point estimate when there is no risk of confusing it with an interval estimate.

Properties of Point Estimators For any particular parameter, there are several possible point estimates. Consider, for instance, estimating the parameter μ from a normal distribution, which describes the center. With sample data from a normal distribution, two possible estimates of μ are the sample mean but also the sample median because the distribution is symmetric. What makes one point estimator better than another? *A good estimator* of a parameter has two desirable properties:

Property 1: A good estimator has a sampling distribution that is centered at the parameter it tries to estimate. We define *center* in this case as the mean of that sampling distribution. An estimator with this property is said to be **unbiased**. From Section 7.2, we know that under random sampling the mean of the sampling distribution of the sample mean $\bar{x}$ equals the population mean μ. So, the sample mean $\bar{x}$ is an unbiased estimator of μ. Figure 8.2 recalls this result.

Similarly, from Section 7.1, we know that under random sampling the mean of the sampling distribution of the sample proportion equals the population proportion p. So, the sample proportion is an unbiased estimator of the population proportion p.

Recall

From Chapter 7, the standard deviation of the sampling distribution of the statistic describes the variability in the possible values of the statistic for the given sample size. It also tells us how much the statistic would vary from sample to sample of that size. ◀

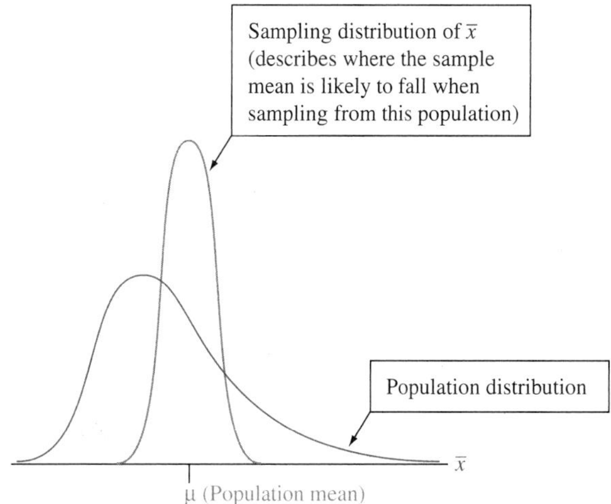

▲ **Figure 8.2 The Sample Mean $\bar{x}$ Is an Unbiased Estimator.** Its sampling distribution is centered at the parameter it estimates—the population mean μ. **Question** When is the sampling distribution bell shaped, as it is in this figure?

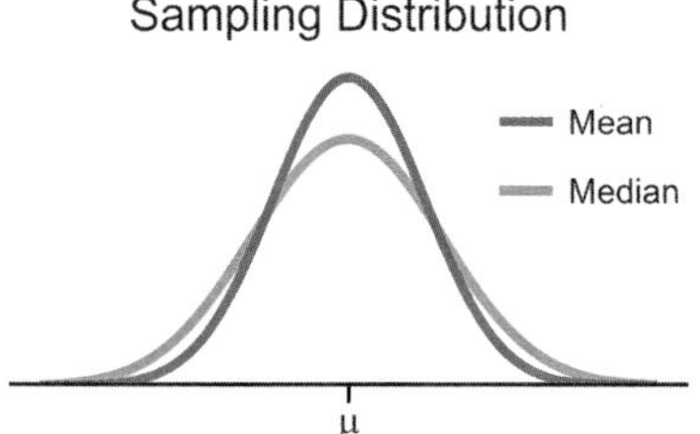

The sampling distribution of the sample mean has the smaller standard deviation.

Property 2: A good estimator has a *small standard deviation* compared to other estimators. This tells us the estimator tends to fall closer than other estimates to the parameter. For example, for estimating the center μ of a normal distribution, both the sample mean and the sample median are unbiased, but the sample mean has a smaller standard deviation (see margin figure and Exercise 8.123). Therefore, the sample mean is the better estimator for μ.

Interval Estimation: Constructing an Interval That Contains the Parameter (We Hope!)

A recent survey[1] on the starting salary of new college graduates estimated the mean starting salary equal to \$45,500. Does \$45,500 seem plausible to you? Too high? Too low? Any individual point estimate may or may not be close to the parameter it estimates. For the estimate to be useful, we need to know how close it is likely to fall to the actual parameter value. Is the estimate of \$45,500 likely to be within \$1000 of the actual population mean? Within \$5000? Within \$10,000? Inference about a parameter should provide not only a point estimate but should also indicate its likely precision.

An **interval estimate** indicates precision by giving an interval of numbers around the point estimate. The interval is made up of numbers that are the most believable values for the unknown parameter, based on the data observed. For instance, perhaps a survey of new college graduates predicts that the mean starting salary falls somewhere between \$43,500 and \$47,500, that is, within a *margin of error* of \$2000 of the point estimate of \$45,500. An interval estimate is designed to contain the parameter with some chosen probability, such as 0.95. Because interval estimates contain the parameter with a certain degree of confidence, they are referred to as **confidence intervals**.

Confidence Interval

A confidence interval is an interval containing the most believable values for a parameter. It is formed by a method that combines a point estimate with a margin of error. The probability that this method produces an interval that contains the parameter is called the confidence level. This is a number chosen to be close to 1, most commonly 0.95.

[1]By National Association of Colleges and Employers, www.naceweb.org.

The interval from \$48,500 to \$52,500 is an example of a confidence interval. It was constructed using a confidence level of 0.95. This is often expressed as a percentage, and we say that we have "95% confidence" that the interval contains the parameter. It is a **95% confidence interval**.

What method do we use to construct a confidence interval? The key is the *sampling distribution* of the point estimate. This distribution tells us the probability that the point estimate will fall within any certain distance of the parameter.

The Logic Behind Constructing a Confidence Interval

To construct a confidence interval, we'll put to work some results about sampling distributions that we learned in the previous chapter. Let's do this for estimating a proportion. We saw that the sampling distribution of a sample proportion:

- Gives the possible values for the sample proportion and their probabilities.
- Is approximately a normal distribution, for large random samples, where $np \geq 15$ and $n(1 - p) \geq 15$.
- Has mean equal to the population proportion, p.
- Has standard deviation equal to $\sqrt{\frac{p(1-p)}{n}}$.

Sampling Distribution of Sample Proportion

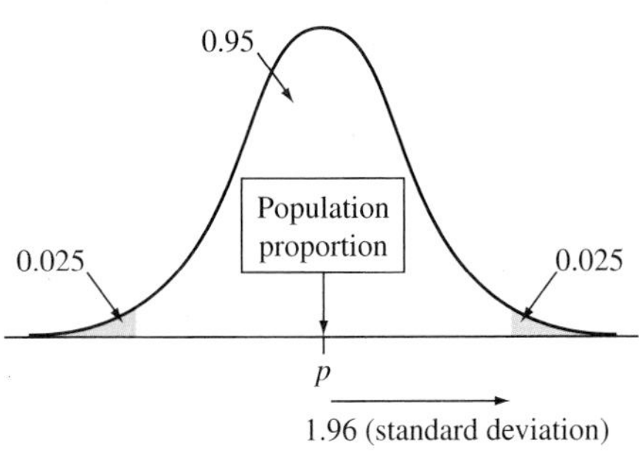

Let's use these results to construct a 95% confidence interval for a population proportion. From Chapter 6, approximately 95% of a normal distribution falls within 2 standard deviations of the mean. More precisely, we saw in Section 6.2 that the interval given by the mean plus and minus 1.96 standard deviations includes exactly 95% of a normal distribution. Since the sampling distribution of the sample proportion is approximately normal, with probability 0.95, the sample proportion falls within about 1.96 standard deviations of the population proportion (see the margin figure). The distance of 1.96 standard deviations is the **margin of error**. We've been using this term since Chapter 1. Let's take a closer look at how it's calculated.

Margin of Error

The **margin of error** measures how accurate the point estimate is likely to be in estimating a parameter. It is a multiple of the standard deviation of the sampling distribution of the point estimate, such as 1.96 × (standard deviation) when the sampling distribution is a normal distribution.

Recall

Example 5 in Chapter 1 showed how the **margin of error** is reported in practice for a sample proportion. We approximated it there by $1/\sqrt{n}$. This is a rough approximation for 1.96 × (standard deviation), as shown following Example 8 in Section 8.4. ◀

Once the sample is selected, if the sample proportion *does* fall within 1.96 standard deviations of the population proportion, which happens about 95% of the time, then the interval from

$$[\text{sample proportion} - 1.96(\text{standard deviation})] \text{ to}$$
$$[\text{sample proportion} + 1.96(\text{standard deviation})]$$

contains the population proportion. In other words, with probability about 0.95, a sample proportion value occurs such that the interval

$$\text{sample proportion} \pm 1.96(\text{standard deviation})$$

contains the unknown population proportion. This interval of numbers is a **95% confidence interval** for the population proportion.

In Words

"Sample proportion ± 1.96 (standard deviation)" represents taking the sample proportion and adding and subtracting 1.96 standard deviations.

Example 2

Margin of error ◀

A Wife's Career

Picture the Scenario

One question on the General Social Survey asks whether you agree or disagree with the following statement: "It is much better for everyone involved if the man is the achiever outside the home and the woman takes care of the home and family." In the 2012 GSS, 31% of 1285 respondents agreed. So the sample proportion agreeing was 0.31. From a formula in the next section, we'll see that this point estimate has an estimated standard deviation of 0.01.

Questions to Explore

a. Find and interpret the margin of error for a 95% confidence interval for the population proportion who agreed with the statement.

b. Construct the 95% confidence interval and interpret it in context.

Think It Through

a. The margin of error for a 95% confidence interval for a population proportion equals 1.96 × (standard deviation), or 1.96(0.01), approximately 0.02. This margin of error tells us that, with a probability of 95%, the point estimate of 0.31 for the proportion agreeing falls within a distance of 0.02 of the actual population proportion agreeing. In other words, the error we will make in predicting the proportion for the entire population using the point estimate of 0.31 from the GSS sample is no greater than 0.02.

b. The 95% confidence interval is

$$\text{Sample proportion} \pm 1.96(\text{standard deviation}),$$

$$\text{which is } 0.31 \pm 1.96\,(0.01), \text{ or } 0.31 \pm 0.02.$$

This gives the interval of proportions from 0.29 to 0.33, denoted by (0.29, 0.33). In summary, using this 95% confidence interval, we predict that the population proportion who believed it is much better for everyone involved if the man is the achiever outside the home, and the woman takes care of the home and family was somewhere between 0.29 and 0.33.

Insight

In 1977, when this question was first asked on the GSS, the point estimate was 0.66, and the 95% confidence interval was (0.64, 0.68). The proportion of Americans who agree with this statement has decreased considerably since then.

▶ *Try Exercise 8.8*

SUMMARY: A Confidence Interval

A confidence interval is constructed by taking a point estimate and adding and subtracting a margin of error. The margin of error is based on the standard deviation of the sampling distribution of that point estimate. When the sampling distribution is approximately normal, a 95% confidence interval has a margin of error equal to 1.96 standard deviations.

The sampling distribution of most point estimates is approximately normal when the random sample size is relatively large. Thus, this logic of taking the margin of error for a 95% confidence interval to be approximately 2 standard deviations applies with large random samples, such as those found in the General Social Survey. The next two sections show more details for estimating proportions and means.

▶ Activity 1

Download Data from the General Social Survey

We saw in Chapter 1 that it's easy to download data from the GSS. Let's recall how.

- Go to the sda.berkeley.edu/GSS website. Click the link there for GSS—with No Weight Variables predefined (SDA 4.0).
- The GSS name for the variable in Example 2 (whether the men should be the achiever) is FEFAM. Type FEFAM as the row variable name. Click Run the Table. Now you'll see category counts and the percentages for all the years combined in which this question was asked.
- To download results only for the year 2012 (the last year data are available), go back to the previous menu and enter YEAR(2012) in the Selection Filter space. When you click Run the Table again, you'll see that in 2012, 87 persons strongly agreed and 313 agreed, for a total of 87 + 313 = 400 agreeing (out of 1,285). This is a proportion of 0.31, or 31%.

Now, create other results. If you open the Standard Codebook, you will see indexes for the variables. Look up a subject that interests you and find the GSS code name for a variable. For example, to find the percentage who believe in hell, enter HELL as the code name.

Try Exercise 8.9 ◀

8.1 Practicing the Basics

8.1 Health care A study dealing with health care issues plans to take a sample survey of 1500 Americans to estimate the proportion who have health insurance and the mean dollar amount that Americans spent on health care this past year.

a. Identify two population parameters that this study will estimate.

b. Identify two statistics that can be used to estimate these parameters.

8.2 Video on demand A recent study from Nielsen (available from nielsen.com; search for "The Cross-Platform Report") took a sample to investigate how video on demand and other subscription-based services (such as Netflix, Amazon Prime, and Hulu) change TV viewing behavior of U.S. adults. Among others, the study recorded how many subscribers primarily watch content time-shifted (i.e., not live) and the weekly number of hours adults spend watching content over the Internet.

a. Mention two population parameters that this survey is trying to estimate.

b. Mention two corresponding statistics that will estimate these population parameters with the help of the survey.

c. The sample mean number of hours watched online is an unbiased estimator for what parameter? Explain what unbiased means.

8.3 Projecting winning candidate News coverage during a recent election projected that a certain candidate would receive 54.8% of all votes cast; the projection had a margin of error of ±3%.

a. Give a point estimate for the proportion of all votes the candidate will receive.

b. Give an interval estimate for the proportion of all votes the candidate will receive.

c. In your own words, state the difference between a point estimate and an interval estimate.

8.4 Believe in hell? TECH Using the General Social Survey website sda.berkeley.edu/GSS with YEAR(2008) as the filter, find the point estimate of the population proportion of Americans who would have answered "yes, definitely" in 2008 when asked whether they believe in hell (variable HELL).

8.5 Government spying In 2014, news reports worldwide alleged that the U.S. government had hacked German chancellor Angela Merkel's cell phone. A Pew Research Center survey of German citizens at about that time asked whether they find it acceptable or unacceptable for the U.S. government to monitor communications from their country's leaders. Results from the survey show that of 1000 citizens interviewed, 900 found it unacceptable. (*Source:* Pew Research Center, July 2014, "Global Opposition to U.S. Surveillance and Drones, But Limited Harm to America's Image")

a. Find the point estimate of the population proportion of German citizens who find spying unacceptable.

b. The Pew Research Center reports a margin of error at the 95% confidence level of 4.5% for this survey. Explain what this means.

8.6 Game apps The Google Play app store for smartphones offers hundreds of games to download for free or for a small fee. The ones for which a fee is charged are called paid games. For a random sample of five paid games taken in July 2014 on the Google platform, the following fees were charged: \$1.09, \$4.99, \$1.99, \$1.99, \$2.99.

a. Find a point estimate of the mean fee for paid games available on Google's platform.

b. The margin of error at the 95% confidence level for this point estimate is \$1.85. Explain what this means.

8.7 Nutrient effect on growth rate Researchers are interested in the effect of a certain nutrient on the growth rate of plant seedlings. Using a hydroponics growth procedure that used water containing the nutrient, they planted six tomato plants and recorded the heights of each plant 14 days after germination. Those heights, measured in millimeters, were as follows: 55.5, 60.3, 60.6, 62.1, 65.5, 69.2.

a. Find a point estimate of the population mean height of this variety of seedling 14 days after germination.

b. A method that we'll study in Section 8.3 provides a margin of error of 4.9 mm for a 95% confidence interval for the population mean height. Construct that interval.

c. Use this example to explain why a point estimate alone is usually insufficient for statistical inference.

8.8 Believe in heaven? When a GSS asked 1326 subjects, "Do you believe in heaven?" (coded HEAVEN), the  proportion who answered yes was 0.85. From results in the next section, the estimated standard deviation of this point estimate is 0.01.

a. Find and interpret the margin of error for a 95% confidence interval for the population proportion of Americans who believe in heaven.

b. Construct the 95% confidence interval. Interpret it in context.

8.9 Feel lonely often? TRY TECH The GSS has asked "On how many days in the past seven days have you felt lonely?" At sda.berkeley.edu/GSS, enter LONELY as the variable, select Summary Statistics in the menu of table options, and click Run the Table to see the responses.

a. Report the percentage making each response and the mean and standard deviation of the responses. Interpret.

b. The standard deviation of the sample mean can be estimated using this data as 0.06. Interpret the value of 0.06.

8.10 CI for loneliness Refer to the previous exercise. The margin of error for a 95% confidence interval for the population mean is 0.12. Construct that confidence interval and interpret it.

8.11 Newspaper article Conduct a search to find a newspaper or magazine article that reported a margin of error. If you prefer, use the Internet for the search.

a. Specify the population parameter, the value of the sample statistic, the point estimate, and the size of the margin of error.

b. Explain how to interpret the margin of error.

8.2 Constructing a Confidence Interval to Estimate a Population Proportion

Did You Know?

If a categorical variable has more than two categories, it can still be considered binary by classifying one or more categories as a success and the remaining categories as a failure. ◀

Let's now see how to construct a confidence interval for a population proportion. We'll apply the ideas discussed at the end of Section 8.1. In this case, the data are categorical, specifically *binary* (two categories), which means that each observation either falls or does not fall in the category of interest. We'll use the generic terminology "success" and "failure" for these two possible outcomes (as in the discussion of the binomial distribution in Section 6.3). We summarize the data by the sample proportion of successes and construct a confidence interval for the population proportion.

Finding the 95% Confidence Interval for a Population Proportion

One question on the 2012 General Social Survey asked whether it is true that the universe began with a big explosion. Of $n = 372$ respondents, 287 said it is true. The sample proportion of true responses was $287/372 = 0.77$, more than 75%. How can we construct a confidence interval for the population proportion who believe it is true?

In Words

It is traditional in statistics to use Greek letters for most parameters such as μ and σ for the population **m**ean and **s**tandard deviation. In a similar vein, we could use the Greek letter π (pi) for denoting the population **p**roportion. Because π already has its own meaning in math (3.14 ...), we use the symbol *p*. This is also the parameter for the probability of success in the binomial distribution (Section 6.3). The sample proportion $\hat{p}$ is read as "*p*-hat."

We symbolize the population proportion by *p*. The point estimate of the population proportion is the *sample proportion.*

We symbolize the sample proportion by $\hat{p}$, *called "p-hat."*

In statistics, the circumflex ("hat") symbol over a parameter symbol represents a point estimate of that parameter. Here, the sample proportion $\hat{p}$ is a point estimate, such as $\hat{p} = 0.77$ for the proportion who believe that the universe started with a big explosion.

For large random samples, the central limit theorem tells us that the sampling distribution of the sample proportion $\hat{p}$ is approximately normal. As discussed in the previous section, the *margin of error* for a 95% confidence interval with the normal sampling distribution is 1.96 (standard deviation). So there is about a 95% chance that $\hat{p}$ falls within 1.96 standard deviations of the population proportion *p* (the mean of the sampling distribution of $\hat{p}$). A 95% confidence interval is given by

[point estimate ± margin of error], which becomes $\hat{p} \pm 1.96$ (standard deviation).

The standard deviation of a sample proportion equals $\sqrt{p(1-p)/n}$. This formula depends on the unknown population proportion, *p*. In practice, we don't know *p*, and we need to estimate *p* to compute the standard deviation.

Did You Know?

The term *standard error* is often used for both the actual standard deviation of a statistic and the estimated standard deviation of a statistic. To help make the distinction of the actual versus the estimated, this textbook will use the term *standard error* only for the estimated standard deviation of a statistic. ◀

In Practice The Standard Deviation of a Sampling Distribution Is Estimated

The value of the standard deviation of a sampling distribution for a statistic depends on the parameter value. In practice, the parameter value is unknown, so we find the standard deviation of the sampling distribution by substituting an estimate of the parameter. The term *standard error* is commonly used for what is actually an "estimated standard deviation of a sampling distribution." Beginning here, we'll use **standard error** to refer to this estimated value because that's what we'll use in practice.

In Words

se = standard error
= estimated standard deviation of the sampling distribution

Standard Error

A standard error is an estimated standard deviation of a sampling distribution. We will use *se* as shorthand for standard error.

For example, the standard error for the sample proportion is given by

$$se = \sqrt{\hat{p}(1-\hat{p})/n}.$$

We will use it to compute the confidence interval for a population proportion *p*.

In Words

To find the **95% confidence interval**, you take the sample proportion and add and subtract 1.96 standard errors.

A 95% confidence interval for a population proportion *p* is

$$\hat{p} \pm 1.96(se), \text{ with } se = \sqrt{\frac{\hat{p}(1-\hat{p})}{n}},$$

where $\hat{p}$ denotes the sample proportion based on *n* observations.

Figure 8.3 shows the sampling distribution of $\hat{p}$ and how there's about a 95% chance that $\hat{p}$ falls within 1.96(*se*) of the population proportion *p*. This confidence interval is designed for large samples. We'll be more precise about what "large" means after the following example.

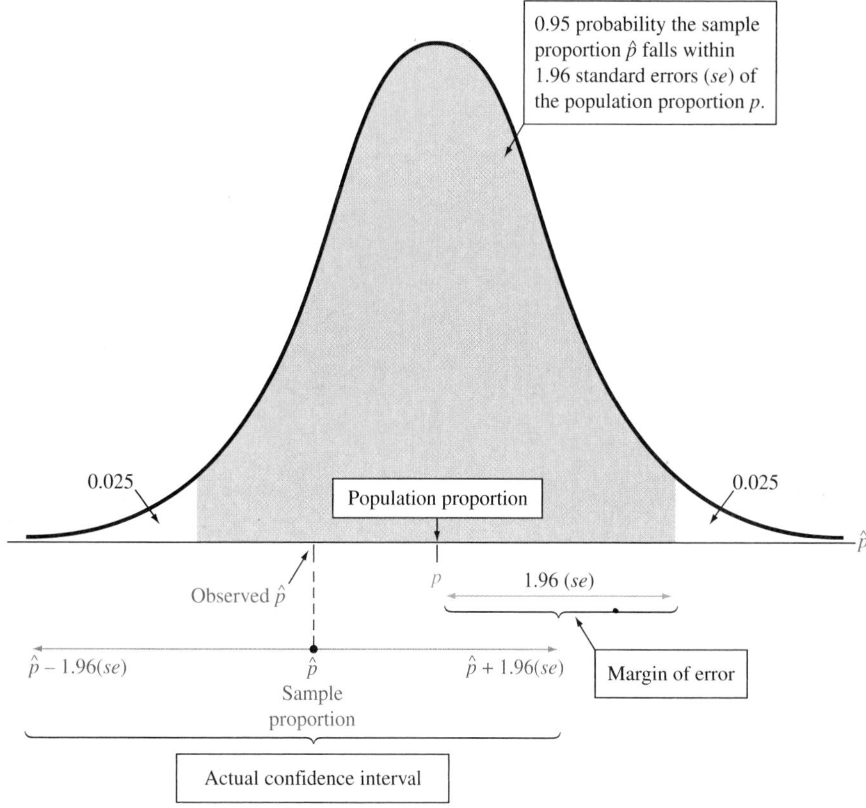

▲ **Figure 8.3** Sampling Distribution of Sample Proportion $\hat{p}$. For large random samples, the sampling distribution is normal around the population proportion p, so $\hat{p}$ has probability 0.95 of falling within 1.96(se) of p. As a consequence, $\hat{p} \pm 1.96(se)$ is a 95% confidence interval for p. **Question** Why is the confidence interval $\hat{p} \pm 1.96(se)$ instead of $p \pm 1.96(se)$?

Example 3

Constructing a confidence interval

Paying Higher Prices to Protect the Environment

Picture the Scenario

Many people consider themselves green, meaning that they support (in theory) environmental issues. But how do they act in practice? For instance, Americans' per capita use of energy is roughly double that of Western Europeans. If you live in North America, would you be willing to pay the same price for gas that Europeans do (often about $8 or more per gallon) if the government proposed a significant price hike as an incentive for conservation and for driving more fuel-efficient cars to reduce air pollution and its impact on global warming?

Questions to Explore

In 2010, the GSS asked subjects whether they would be willing to pay much higher prices to protect the environment. Of $n = 1{,}361$ respondents, 637 indicated a willingness to do so.

a. Find a 95% confidence interval for the population proportion of adult Americans willing to do so at the time of that survey.

b. Interpret that interval.

c. Is there evidence that fewer than half of the U.S. population is willing to pay higher prices?

▶ Activity

To obtain these data for yourself, go to the GSS sda.berkeley.edu/GSS website and download data on the variable GRNPRICE for the 2010 survey.

Recall

$se = 0.0135$ means that if many random samples of 1361 people each were taken to gauge their opinion about this issue, the standard deviation of the sample proportions would be about 0.0135. The sample proportions would vary relatively little from sample to sample. ◀

In Practice Standard Errors and Type of Sampling

The **standard errors** reported in this book and by most software assume **simple random sampling**. The GSS uses a multistage cluster random sample. In practice, the standard error based on the formula for a simple random sample should be adjusted slightly, as explained in Appendix A of the codebook at the GSS website. It's beyond our scope to show the details, but when you request an analysis at the GSS website, you can get the adjusted standard errors by selecting Complex rather than SRS (simple random sample) for the sample design.

Recall

From Section 6.3, the **binomial** random variable X counts the number of successes in n observations, and the sample proportion equals x/n, for instance, $637/1361 = 0.47$. ◀

Think It Through

a. The sample proportion that estimates the population proportion p is $\hat{p} = 637/1361 = 0.468$. The standard error of the sample proportion $\hat{p}$ equals

$$se = \sqrt{\hat{p}(1 - \hat{p})/n} = \sqrt{(0.468)(0.532)/1361} = 0.0135.$$

Using this se, a 95% confidence interval for the population proportion is

$$\hat{p} \pm 1.96(se), \text{ which is } 0.468 \pm 1.96(0.0135)$$
$$= 0.468 \pm 0.026, \text{ or } (0.442, 0.494).$$

b. At the 95% confidence level, we estimate that the population proportion of adult Americans willing to pay much higher prices to protect the environment was at least 0.44 but no more than 0.49, that is, between 44% and 49%. The point estimate of 0.47 has a margin of error of 0.026.

c. None of the numbers in the confidence interval (0.442, 0.494) fall above 0.50. So we infer that fewer than half the population was willing to pay much higher prices to protect the environment.

Insight

As usual, results depend on the question's wording. For instance, when asked whether the government should impose strict laws to make industry do less damage to the environment, a 95% confidence interval for the population proportion responding yes is (0.92, 0.95). (See Exercise 8.15.)

▶ ***Try Exercise 8.14***

Table 8.1 shows how MINITAB software reports the data summary and confidence interval. Here, X represents the number that *support* paying much higher prices. The notation reflects that this is the outcome of a random variable, specifically a binomial random variable. The heading "Sample p" stands for the sample proportion $\hat{p}$, "CI" stands for confidence interval, and "N" stands for the sample size (which we have denoted by n). In reporting results from such output, you should use only the first two or three significant digits. Report the confidence interval as (0.44, 0.49) or (0.442, 0.494) rather than (0.44153, 0.49455). Software's extra precision provides accurate calculations in finding se and the confidence interval. However, the extra digits are distracting when reported to others and do not tell them anything extra in a practical sense about the population proportion. *Likewise, if you do a calculation with a hand calculator, don't round off while doing the calculation or your answer may be affected, but do round off when you report the final answer.*

Table 8.1 MINITAB Output for 95% Confidence Interval for a Proportion for Example 3

(The italicized lines are added annotation to explain what's shown.)

X	N	Sample p	95.0% CI
637	1361	0.468038	(0.44153, 0.49455)
↑	↑	↑	↑
Category count	*Sample size*	*Sample proportion*	*Endpoints of confidence interval*

Above, we computed the confidence interval for the population proportion who *will* pay higher prices. What if instead you are interested in the proportion who *won't* pay higher prices? For a binary variable, inference about the second category (*won't* pay higher prices) follows directly from the one for the first category (*will* pay higher prices). Because the population parameter of interest is now $1 - p$, all we have to do is subtract each endpoint of the confidence interval for p from 1.0. So, since $1 - 0.49 = 0.51$ and $1 - 0.44 = 0.56$, the 95% confidence interval for the proportion who won't pay higher prices is given by (0.51, 0.56). With 95% confidence, the population proportion that won't pay higher prices to support the environment falls between 0.51 and 0.56.

Sample Size Needed for Validity of Confidence Interval for a Proportion

The confidence interval formula $\hat{p} \pm 1.96(se)$ applies with *large random samples.* This is because the sampling distribution of the sample proportion $\hat{p}$ is then approximately normal and the *se* also tends to be a good estimate of the standard deviation, allowing us to use the z-score of 1.96 from the normal distribution.

In practice, "large" means that *you should have at least 15 successes and at least 15 failures* for the binary outcome.[2] At the end of Section 8.4, we'll see how the large-sample method can fail when this guideline is not satisfied.

SUMMARY: Sample Size Needed for Large-Sample Confidence Interval for a Proportion

For the 95% confidence interval $\hat{p} \pm 1.96(se)$ for a proportion p to be valid, you should have at least 15 successes and 15 failures. This can also be expressed as

$$n\hat{p} \geq 15 \text{ and } n(1 - \hat{p}) \geq 15.$$

At the end of Section 8.4 we'll learn about a simple adjustment to this confidence interval formula that you should use when this guideline is violated.

Recall

From Section 6.3, the binomial distribution is bell shaped when the expected counts np and $n(1 - p)$ of successes and failures are both at least 15. Here, we don't know p, and we use the guideline with the observed counts of successes and failures. ◀

This guideline was easily satisfied in Example 3. The binary outcomes had counts 637 willing to pay much higher prices and 724 ($= 1361 - 637$) unwilling, both much larger than 15.

Recall

99% confidence interval: From Section 6.2, for central probability 0.99, you look up the cumulative probability of 0.005 or $1 - 0.005 = 0.995$ in Table A, or use software or a calculator, to find $z = 2.58$. ◀

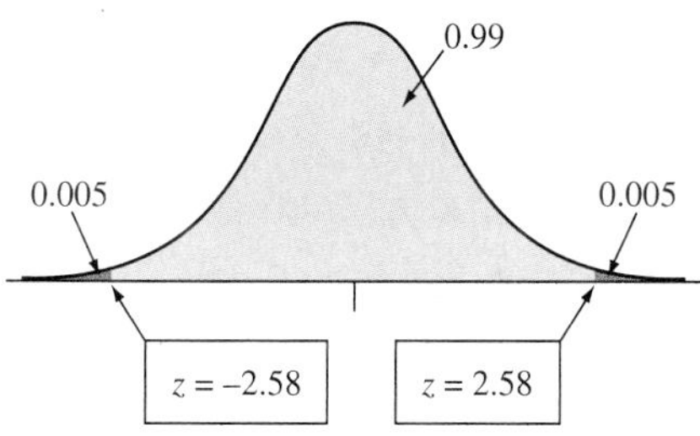

Using a Confidence Level Other Than 95%

So far we've used a confidence level of 0.95, that is, "95% confidence." This means that there's a 95% chance that a sample proportion value $\hat{p}$ occurs such that the confidence interval $\hat{p} \pm 1.96(se)$ contains the unknown value of the population proportion p. With probability 0.05, however, the method produces a confidence interval that misses p. The population proportion then does *not* fall in the interval, and the inference is incorrect.

In practice, the confidence level 0.95 is the most common choice. But some applications require greater confidence. This is often true in medical research, for example. For estimating the probability p that a new treatment for a deadly disease works better than the treatment currently used, we would want to be extremely confident about any inference we make. To increase the chance of a correct inference (that is, having the interval contain the parameter value), we use a larger confidence level, such as 0.99.

[2]Many statistics texts use 5 or 10 as the minimum instead of 15, but recent research suggests that those sizes are too small (e.g., L. Brown et al., *Statistical Science*, vol. 16, pp. 101–133, 2001).

Now, 99% of the normal sampling distribution for the sample proportion $\hat{p}$ occurs within 2.58 standard errors of the population proportion p. So, with probability 0.99, $\hat{p}$ falls within 2.58(se) of p. (See the margin figure on the previous page.) A 99% confidence interval for p is $\hat{p} \pm 2.58(se)$.

Example 4

Confidence Level ◄

Influenza Vaccine

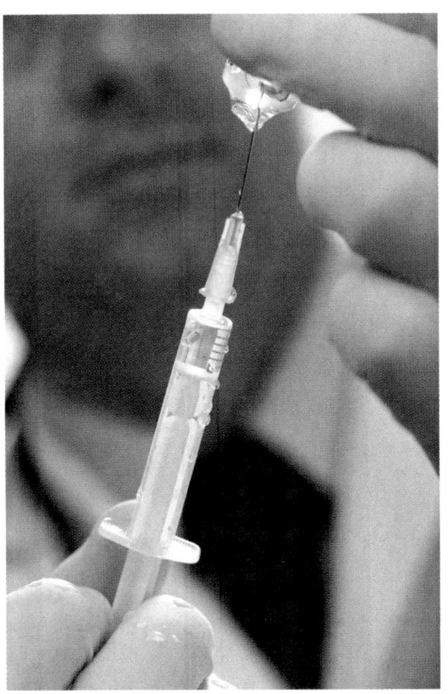

Picture the Scenario

According to the Centers for Disease Control and Prevention, the single best way to protect against the flu is to be vaccinated. Traditionally, flu vaccines are manufactured using viruses grown in chicken eggs. A new method allows growing viruses in cell cultures instead. To test the effectiveness of such vaccines, in a recent clinical trial $n = 3900$ randomly selected healthy subjects aged 18–49 received a cell-derived influenza vaccine by injection. During a follow-up period of approximately 28 weeks, each subject was assessed whether he or she developed influenza, which happened for 26 of the 3900 subjects.

Questions to Explore

a. Find a 99% confidence interval for the population proportion developing the flu over the follow-up period. (Here, the population is all 18- to 49-year-old people vaccinated with the cell-derived vaccine.)

b. How does it compare to the 95% confidence interval?

Think It Through

a. The assumptions for the method are satisfied in that the sample was randomly selected, and there were at least 15 successes and 15 failures (26 developing the flu, 3874 not developing it). The sample proportion developing the flu is $\hat{p} = 26/3900 = 0.0067$. Its standard error is

$$se = \sqrt{\hat{p}(1 - \hat{p})/n} = \sqrt{0.0067(1 - 0.0067/3900)} = 0.0013.$$

The 99% confidence interval is

$$\hat{p} \pm 2.58(se) \text{ or } 0.0067 \pm 2.58(0.0013),$$

which is 0.0067 ± 0.0034, or $(0.003, 0.010)$.

In summary, we can be 99% confident that between 0.3% and 1% of those vaccinated with the cell-derived flu vaccine will develop the flu. Note that statistical software or a statistical calculator can calculate this confidence interval. Screen shots from the TI are shown in the margin.

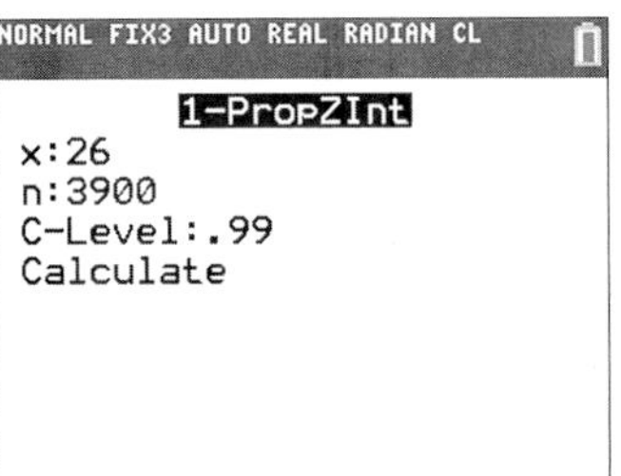

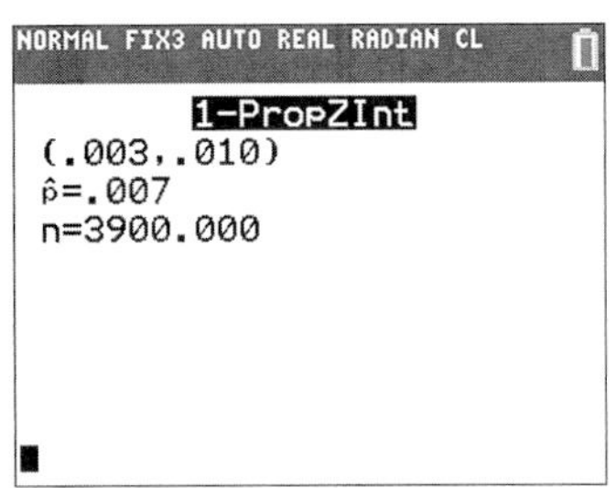

TI output of confidence interval for a proportion

b. The 95% confidence interval is $0.0067 \pm 1.96(0.0013)$ which is 0.0067 ± 0.0025, or $(0.004, 0.009)$. This is a bit narrower than the 99% confidence interval. Figure 8.4 illustrates.

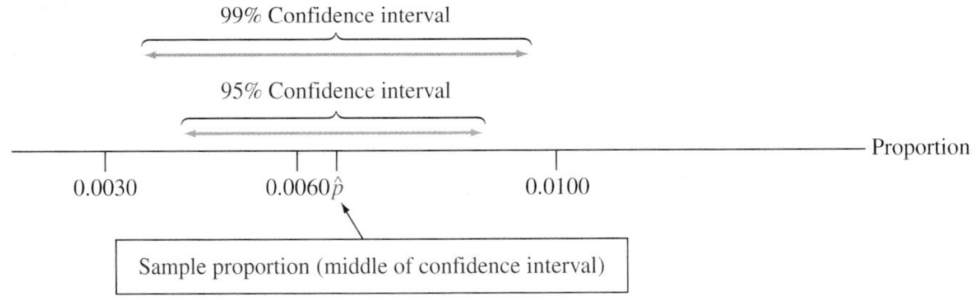

▲ **Figure 8.4** A 99% Confidence Interval Is Wider Than a 95% Confidence Interval. **Question** If you want greater confidence, why would you expect a wider interval?

Insight

The inference with a 99% confidence interval is less precise, with margin of error equal to 0.0034 instead of 0.0025. Having a greater margin of error is the sacrifice for gaining greater assurance (99% rather than 95%) of correctly inferring where p falls. A study that uses a higher confidence level will be less likely to make an incorrect inference, but it will not be able to narrow in as well on where the true parameter value falls.

► ***Try Exercise 8.23***

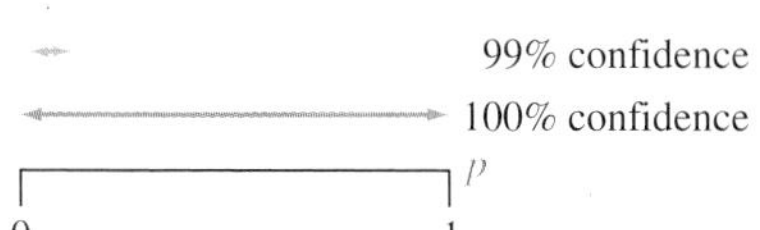

Why settle for anything less than 100% confidence? To be absolutely 100% certain of a correct inference (that is, of capturing the parameter value inside the confidence interval), the confidence interval must contain *all* possible values for the parameter. For example, a 100% confidence interval for the population proportion vaccinated but still developing the flu goes from 0.0 to 1.0. This inference would tell us only that some number between 0.0% and 100.0% of vaccinated people develop the flu. This obviously is not helpful and we wouldn't need to collect data to infer this. In practice, we settle for a little less than perfect confidence so we can estimate the parameter value more precisely (illustrated by the margin figure, showing 99% and 100% confidence intervals). It is far more informative to have 99% confidence that the population proportion is between 0.003 and 0.010 than to have 100% confidence that it is between 0.0 and 1.0.

In Practice Margin of Error Refers to 95% Confidence

When the news media report a **margin of error**, it is the margin of error for a 95% confidence interval.

In using confidence intervals, *we must compromise between the desired margin of error and the desired confidence of a correct inference.* As one gets better, the other gets worse. This is why you would probably not use a 99.9999% confidence interval. It would usually have too large a margin of error to tell you much about where the parameter falls (its z-score is 4.9). In practice, 95% confidence intervals are the most common.

Error Probability for the Confidence Interval Method

The general formula for the confidence interval for a population proportion is

$$\text{sample proportion} \pm (z\text{-score from normal table})(\text{standard error}),$$
$$\text{which in symbols is } \hat{p} \pm z(se).$$

The z-score depends on the confidence level. Table 8.2 shows the z-scores for the confidence levels usually used in practice. There is no need to memorize them. You can find them yourself, using Table A or a calculator or software.

Let's review how by finding the z-score for a 90% confidence interval. When 0.90 probability falls within z standard errors of the mean, then 0.10 probability falls in the two tails and $0.10/2 = 0.05$ falls in each tail. Looking up 0.05 in the body of Table A, we find $z = -1.64$, or we find $z = 1.64$ if we look up the

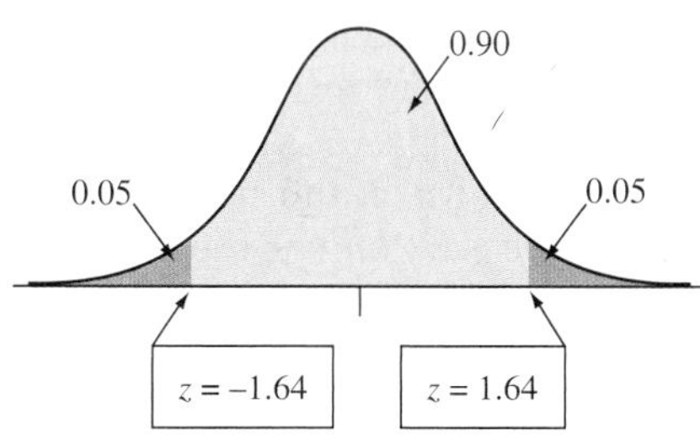

Table 8.2 z-Scores for the Most Common Confidence Levels

The large-sample confidence interval for the population proportion is $\hat{p} \pm z(se)$.

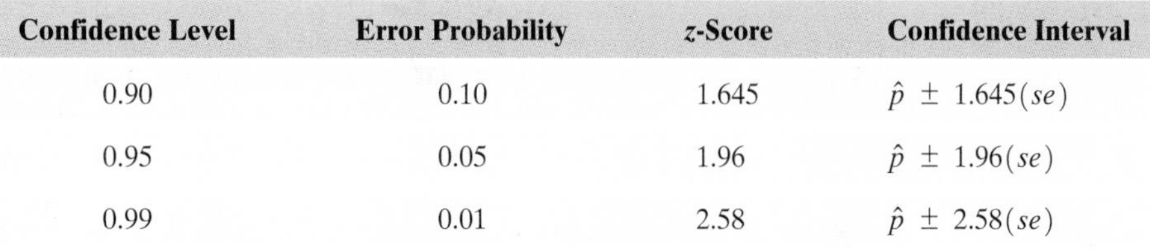

Confidence Level	Error Probability	z-Score	Confidence Interval
0.90	0.10	1.645	$\hat{p} \pm 1.645(se)$
0.95	0.05	1.96	$\hat{p} \pm 1.96(se)$
0.99	0.01	2.58	$\hat{p} \pm 2.58(se)$

cumulative probability $1 - 0.05 = 0.95$ corresponding to tail probability 0.05 in the right tail. (See margin figure on the previous page.) The 90% confidence interval equals $\hat{p} \pm 1.64(se)$. (More precise calculation using software or a calculator gives a z-score of 1.645.) Try this again for 99% confidence, using either the table or a calculator or software (you should get $z = 2.58$).

Table 8.2 contains a column labeled "Error Probability." This is the probability that the method results in an incorrect inference, namely, that the data generates a confidence interval that does *not* contain the population proportion. The error probability equals 1 minus the confidence level. For example, when the confidence level equals 0.95, the error probability equals 0.05. The error probability is the two-tail probability under the normal curve for the given z-score. Half the error probability falls in each tail. For 95% confidence with its error probability of 0.05, the z-score of 1.96 is the one with probability $0.05/2 = 0.025$ in each tail.

SUMMARY: Confidence Interval for a Population Proportion p

A confidence interval for a population proportion p, using the sample proportion $\hat{p}$ and the standard error $se = \sqrt{\hat{p}(1 - \hat{p})/n}$ for sample size n, is

$$\hat{p} \pm z(se), \text{ which is } \hat{p} \pm z\sqrt{\hat{p}(1 - \hat{p})/n}.$$

For 90%, 95%, and 99% confidence intervals, z equals 1.645, 1.96, and 2.58. This method assumes

- Data obtained by randomization (such as a random sample or a randomized experiment).
- A large enough sample size n so that the number of successes and the number of failures, that is, $n\hat{p}$ and $n(1 - \hat{p})$, are both at least 15.

Effect of the Sample Size

We'd expect that estimation should be more precise with larger sample sizes. With more data, we know more about the population. The margin of error is $z(se) = z\sqrt{\hat{p}(1 - \hat{p})/n}$. This margin decreases as the sample size n increases, for a given value of $\hat{p}$. The larger the value of n, the narrower the interval.

To illustrate, in Example 3, suppose the sample proportion $\hat{p} = 0.468$ of Americans willing to pay much higher prices to protect the environment had resulted from a sample of size $n = 340$, only *one-fourth* the actual sample size of $n = 1361$. Then the standard error would be

$$se = \sqrt{\hat{p}(1 - \hat{p})/n} = \sqrt{0.468\,(1 - 0.468)/340} = 0.0271,$$

twice as large as the $se = 0.0135$ we got for $n = 3900$ (up to rounding errors). With the se twice as large, the margin of error would also be twice as large. With 95% confidence, it would double from the $1.96(0.0135) = 0.026$ shown in Example 3 to $1.96(0.0271) = 0.053$, resulting in the interval $\hat{p} \pm 1.96(se)$ or $0.468 \pm 1.96(0.0271)$, which is 0.468 ± 0.053, or $(0.415, 0.521)$. The confidence interval (0.442, 0.494) obtained with the larger n in Example 3 is narrower (and falls entirely below 50%).

Because the standard error has the square root of n in the denominator, and because $\sqrt{4n} = 2\sqrt{n}$, *quadrupling* the sample size *halves* the standard error. That is, we must quadruple n, rather than double it, to halve the margin of error. By putting in 4 times as much information, we only cut the precision by half.

In summary, we've observed the following properties of a confidence interval:

SUMMARY: Effects of Confidence Level and Sample Size on Margin of Error

The **margin of error** for a confidence interval:

- Increases as the confidence level increases.
- Decreases as the sample size increases.

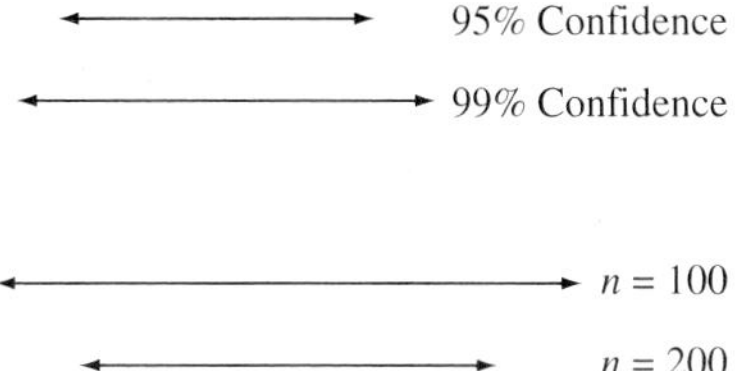

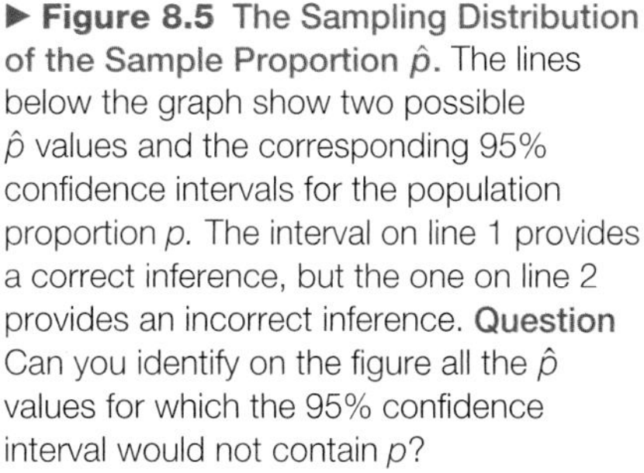

For instance, a 99% confidence interval is wider than a 95% confidence interval, and a confidence interval with 200 observations is narrower than one with 100 observations (see margin figure). These properties apply to *all* confidence intervals, not just the one for the population proportion.

Interpretation of the Confidence Level

In Example 3, the 95% confidence interval for the population proportion p willing to pay higher prices to protect the environment was (0.44, 0.49). The value of p is unknown to us, so we don't know that it actually falls in that interval. It may actually equal 0.42 or 0.51, for example.

So what does it mean to say that we have "95% confidence"? The meaning refers to a *long-run* interpretation—how the method performs when used over and over with many random samples. If we used the 95% confidence interval method over time to estimate many population proportions, then *in the long run about 95% of those intervals would give correct results, containing the population proportion.* This happens because 95% of the sample proportions would fall within 1.96(*se*) of the population proportion. A graphical example is the $\hat{p}$ in line 1 of Figure 8.5.

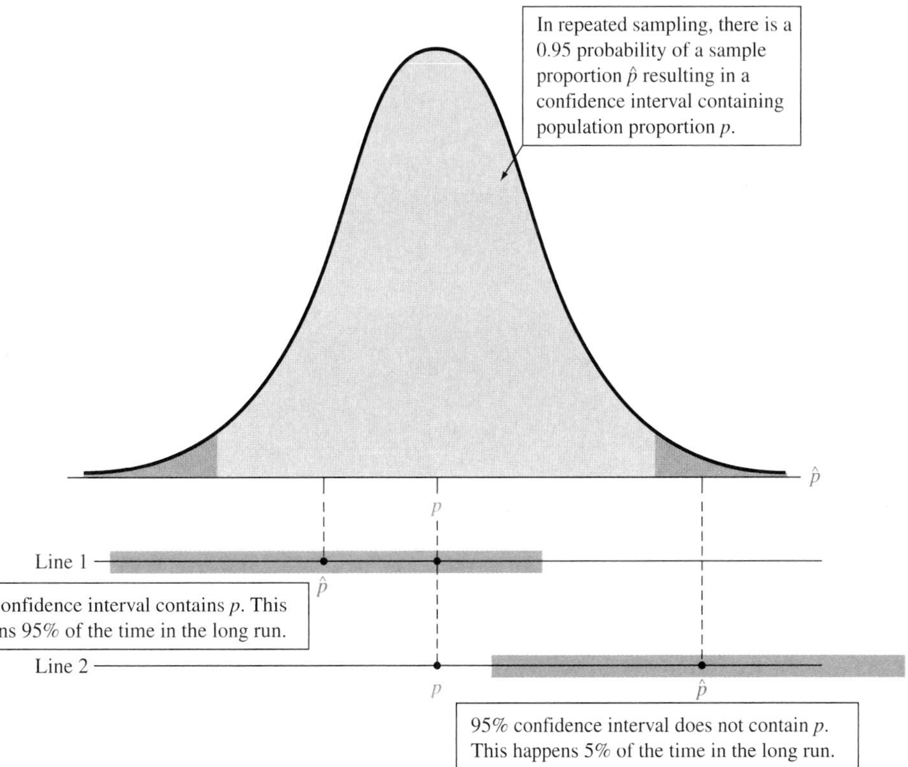

▶ **Figure 8.5 The Sampling Distribution of the Sample Proportion $\hat{p}$.** The lines below the graph show two possible $\hat{p}$ values and the corresponding 95% confidence intervals for the population proportion p. The interval on line 1 provides a correct inference, but the one on line 2 provides an incorrect inference. **Question** Can you identify on the figure all the $\hat{p}$ values for which the 95% confidence interval would not contain p?

Saying that a particular interval contains p with "95% confidence" signifies that in the long run, 95% of such intervals would provide a correct inference (containing the actual parameter value). On the other hand, in the long run, 5% of the time the sample proportion $\hat{p}$ *does not* fall within 1.96(se) of p. If that happens, then the confidence interval *does not* contain p, as is seen for $\hat{p}$ in line 2 of Figure 8.5.

By our choice of the confidence level, we can control the chance that we make a correct inference. If an error probability of 0.05 makes us too nervous, we can instead form a 99% confidence interval, which is in error only 1% of the time in the long run. But then we must settle for a wider confidence interval and less precision.

Long Run Versus Subjective Probability Interpretation of Confidence

You might be tempted to interpret a statement such as "We can be 95% confident that the population proportion p falls between 0.42 and 0.48" as meaning that the *probability* is 0.95 that p falls between 0.42 and 0.48. However, probabilities apply to statistics (such as the sample proportion), not to parameters (such as the population proportion). The estimate $\hat{p}$, not the parameter p, is the random variable having a sampling distribution and probabilities. The 95% confidence refers not to a probability for the population proportion p but rather to a probability that applies to the confidence interval *method* in its relative frequency sense: If we use it over and over for various samples, in the long run we make correct inferences (i.e., cover the true parameter) 95% of the time.

▶ Activity 2

Simulate the Performance of Confidence Intervals

Let's get a feel for how to interpret "95% confidence" by using simulation. Similar to Activity 1 in Chapter 7 (where we explored the sampling distribution of the sample proportion), we will simulate drawing a sample of a certain size n from a population with a prespecified population proportion p. From that sample, we compute $\hat{p}$ and use it to compute the 95% confidence interval for p. By repeating this several times, we can check how often the confidence interval constructed from each sample actually includes the population proportion p. If our theory is correct, this should be about 95% of the times in the long run.

To run and visualize the simulations, we will use the Inference for a Proportion web app accessible on the book's website. Click the Explore Coverage tab at the top. Let's use the default settings of $p = 0.3$ (a vertical line indicates this location), $n = 50$, and 95% confidence. When you press the Draw Sample(s) button, a random sample of size 50 will be drawn, and the 95% confidence interval is computed and displayed in the graph. The dot in the middle indicates the

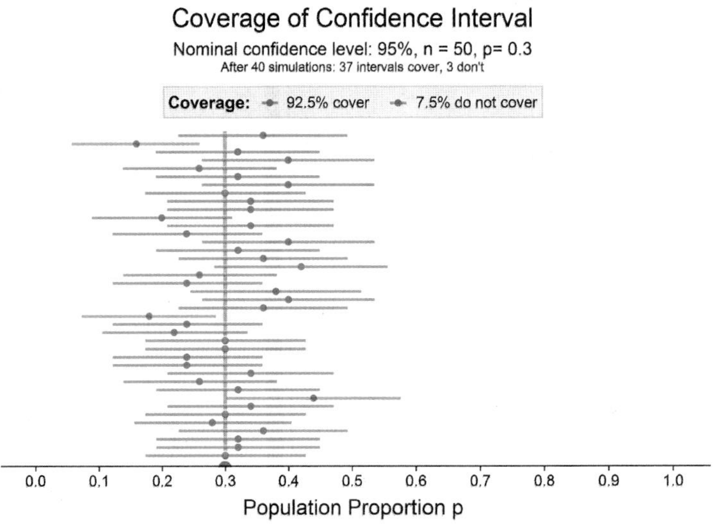

sample proportion. The interval is shown in green if the interval contains the population proportion and in red otherwise. Keep clicking the button to add new confidence intervals (each based on a new random sample) to the display. With 40 generated samples, we obtained the graph on the previous page, showing that 37 of the 40 intervals we generated (92.5%) covered and 3 (7.5%) did not cover the population proportion $p = 0.3$.

Use the app to see the effect of changing (i) the confidence level, (ii) the sample size, and (iii) the population proportion. The graph will update as you change each value. For instance, what happens as you change the confidence level from 95% to 99%? Are the intervals getting wider and are more of the intervals containing the population proportion? What about increasing the sample size: are intervals getting wider or narrower?

To get a feel for what happens in the long run, eventually you should simulate at least 1,000 samples and explore the percentage of intervals that cover the population parameter. Do this for various settings of the true population proportion and sample size.

Try Exercises 8.27,8.28, and 8.46 for the confidence interval for a mean ◀

Section 5.1 mentioned a *subjective* definition of probability that's an alternative to the relative frequency definition. This approach treats the *parameter* as a random variable. Statistical inferences based on the subjective definition of probability *do* make probability statements about parameters. For instance, with it you *can* say that the probability is 0.95 that p falls between 0.44 and 0.49. Statistical inference based on the subjective definition of probability is called *Bayesian statistics.*[3] It has gained in popularity in recent years, but it is beyond the scope of this text.

On the Shoulders of...Ronald A. Fisher

R. A. Fisher. Fisher was the statistician most responsible for the statistical methods used to analyze data today.

How do you conduct scientific inquiry, whether it be developing methods of experimental design, finding the best way to estimate a parameter, or answering specific questions such as which fertilizer works best?

Compared with other mathematical sciences, statistical science is a mere youth. The most important contributions were made between 1920 and 1940 by the British statistician Ronald A. Fisher (1890–1962). While working at an agricultural research station north of London, Fisher was the first statistician to show convincingly the importance of randomization in designing experiments. He also developed the theory behind point estimation and proposed several new statistical methods.

Fisher was involved in a wide variety of scientific questions, ranging from finding the best ways to plant crops to controversies (in his time) about whether smoking was harmful. He also did fundamental work in genetics and is regarded as a giant in that field as well.

Fisher had strong disagreements with others about the way statistical inference should be conducted. One of his main adversaries was Karl Pearson. Fisher corrected a major error Pearson made in proposing methods for contingency tables, and he criticized Pearson's son's work on developing the theory of confidence intervals in the 1930s. Although Fisher often disparaged the ideas of other statisticians, he reacted strongly if anyone criticized him in return. Writing about Pearson, Fisher once said, "If peevish intolerance of free opinion in others is a sign of senility, it is one which he had developed at an early age."

[3]The name refers to *Bayes's theorem,* which can generate probabilities of parameter values, given the data, from probabilities of the data, given the parameter values.

8.2 Practicing the Basics

8.12 Putin A Gallup poll of 2000 Russians taken between April and June 2014 (after the Olympic games in Russia and the annexation of the Crimean peninsula) showed that 83% approved of President Putin's performance. If random sampling were used for this survey, what is the margin of error for this estimate at the 95% confidence level? (In fact, Gallup uses weighted sampling and, based on it, reports a margin of error of 2.7%.) *Source:* gallup.com and search for "Russian Approval."

8.13 Flu shot In a clinical study (the same as mentioned in Example 4), 3900 subjects were vaccinated with a vaccine manufactured by growing cells in fertilized chicken eggs. Over a period of roughly 28 weeks, 24 of these subjects developed the flu.

a. Find the point estimate of the population proportion that were vaccinated with the vaccine but still developed the flu.

b. Find the standard error of this estimate.

c. Find the margin of error for a 95% confidence interval.

d. Construct the 95% confidence interval for the population proportion. Interpret the interval.

e. Can you conclude that fewer than 1% of all people vaccinated with the vaccine will develop the flu? Explain by using results from part d.

8.14 How green are you? TRY When the 2000 GSS asked subjects (variable GRNSOL) whether they would be willing to accept cuts in their standard of living to protect the environment, 344 of 1170 subjects said yes.

a. Estimate the population proportion who would answer yes.

b. Find the margin of error for a 95% confidence interval for this estimate.

c. Find a 95% confidence interval for that proportion and interpret.

d. State and check the assumptions needed for the interval in part c to be valid.

8.15 Make industry help environment? When the 2006 GSS asked subjects whether it should or should not be the government's responsibility to impose strict laws to make industry do less damage to the environment (variable GRNLAWS), 1403 of 1497 subjects said yes.

a. What assumptions are made to construct a 95% confidence interval for the population proportion who would say yes? Do they seem satisfied here?

b. Construct the 95% confidence interval. Interpret in context. Can you conclude whether a majority or minority of the population would answer yes?

8.16 Favor death penalty In the 2012 General Social Survey, respondents were asked whether they favored or opposed the death penalty for people convicted of murder. Software shows results

```
Sample   X     N     Sample p        95% CI
  1    1183  1824   0.648575   (0.626665, 0.670484)
```

Here, X refers to the number of the respondents who were in favor.

a. Show how to obtain the value reported under "Sample p."

b. Interpret the confidence interval reported, in context.

c. Explain what the "95% confidence" refers to, by describing the long-run interpretation.

d. Can you conclude that more than half of all American adults were in favor? Why?

8.17 Oppose death penalty TRY Refer to the previous exercise. Show how you can get a 95% confidence interval for the proportion of American adults who were *opposed* to the death penalty from the confidence interval stated in the previous exercise for the proportion in favor. (*Hint:* The proportion opposed is 1 minus the proportion in favor.)

8.18 Stem cell research A Harris poll of a random sample of 2113 adults in the United States in October 2010 reported that 72% of those polled believe that stem cell research has merit. (*Source:* www.harrisinteractive.com/vault/Harris-Interactive-Poll-HealthDay-2010-10.pdf.) The results, presented using MINITAB software, are

```
  X       N      Sample p          95% CI
1521    2113      0.7198      (0.7007, 0.7390)
```

Here, X denotes the number who believed that stem cell research has merit.

a. Explain how to interpret "Sample p" and "95% CI" on this printout.

b. What is the 95% margin of error associated with the poll?

8.19 *z*-score and confidence level Which *z*-score is used in a (a) 90%, (b) 98%, and (c) 99.9% confidence interval for a population proportion?

8.20 Believe in ghosts A Harris poll of a random sample of 2250 adults in the United States in 2013 reported that 74% believe in God, 68% believe in heaven, 58% believe in hell, and 42% believe in ghosts.[4] (Interestingly, except for the belief in ghosts, these numbers are all substantially smaller than the corresponding values in a similar poll taken by Harris in 2009.) The screen shot shows how the TI calculator reports results of interval estimation at the 95% confidence level for the proportion who believe in ghosts. Explain how to interpret the confidence interval shown.

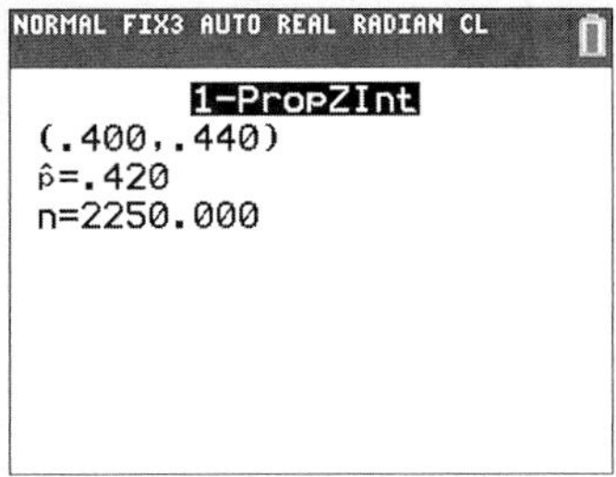

[4] www.harrisinteractive.com/vault/Harris%20Poll%2097%20-%20Beliefs_12.16.2013.pdf

8.21 Stem cell research and religion In Exercise 8.18, it was stated that 72% of the 2113 adults surveyed in a Harris poll believed that stem cell research has merit. In the same study, only 58% of those describing themselves as Republicans believed that it has merit. There were 1010 people who described themselves as Republican. The screen shot shows how the TI 83+/84 reports results of interval estimation at the 95% confidence level. Specify the population to which this inference applies and explain how to interpret the confidence interval.

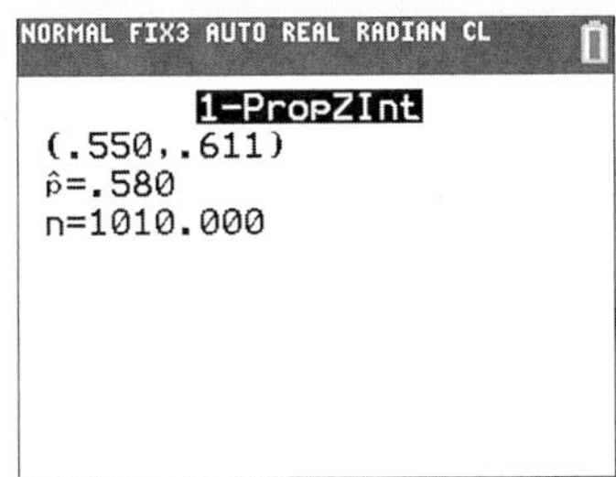

8.22 Fear of breast cancer A recent survey of 1000 American women between the ages of 45 and 64 asked them what medical condition they most feared. Of those sampled, 61% said breast cancer, 8% said heart disease, and the rest picked other conditions. By contrast, currently about 3% of female deaths are due to breast cancer, whereas 32% are due to heart disease.[5]

a. Construct a 90% confidence interval for the population proportion of women who most feared breast cancer. Interpret.

b. Indicate the assumptions you must make for the inference in part a to be valid.

8.23 Chicken breast In a 2014 *Consumer Reports* article titled, "The High Cost of Cheap Chicken," the magazine reported that out of 316 chicken breasts bought in retail stores throughout the United States, 207 contained E. coli bacteria.

a. Find and interpret a 99% confidence interval for the population proportion of chicken breasts that contain E. coli. Can you conclude that the proportion of chicken containing E. coli exceeds 50%? Why?

b. Without doing any calculation, explain whether the interval in part a would be wider or narrower than a 95% confidence interval for the population proportion.

8.24 Same-sex marriage A national survey by the Pew Research Center (www.people-press.org), conducted May 1-5, 2013, among 1,504 adults, finds that support for same-sex marriage continues to grow. It states, "For the first time in Pew Research Center polling, just over half (51%) of Americans favor allowing gays and lesbians to marry legally." Based on these data, can we conclude that more than half of Americans support same-sex marriage? Explain.

8.25 Exit poll predictions A national television network takes an exit poll of 1400 voters after each has cast a vote in a state gubernatorial election. Of them, 660 say they voted for the Democratic candidate and 740 say they voted for the Republican candidate.

a. Treating the sample as a random sample from the population of all voters, would you predict the winner? Base your decision on a 95% confidence interval.

b. Base your decision on a 99% confidence interval. Explain why you need stronger evidence to make a prediction when you want greater confidence.

8.26 Exit poll with smaller sample In the previous exercise, suppose the same proportions resulted from $n = 140$ (instead of 1400), with counts 66 and 74.

a. Now does a 95% confidence interval allow you to predict the winner? Explain.

b. Explain why the same proportions but with smaller samples provide less information. (*Hint:* What effect does n have on the standard error?)

8.27 Simulating confidence intervals Repeat the simulation from Activity 2, but this time simulate 1000 confidence intervals (repeatedly press the Draw Sample(s) button after selecting 100 as the number of samples to generate until you get 1000 simulations) with $p = 0.5$ instead of $p = 0.3$. Do this for a confidence level of 95% and then 99%. What percentage do you expect for each case?

8.28 Simulating confidence intervals with poor coverage Using the Inference for a Proportion web app, let's check that the large-sample confidence interval for a proportion may work poorly with small samples. Click on the Explore Coverage tab and set $p = 0.30$, $n = 10$ and leave the confidence level at 95%. Select to draw 100 random samples of size n and then click on Draw Sample(s).

a. How many of the intervals you generated with the app fail to contain the true value, $p = 0.30$?

b. How many would you expect not to contain the true value? What does this suggest?

c. To see that this is not a fluke, now take 1000 samples and see what percentage of 95% confidence intervals contain 0.30. (*Note:* For every interval formed, the number of successes is smaller than 15, so the large-sample formula is not adequate.)

d. Using the Sampling Distribution for a Sample Proportion web app, generate 10,000 random samples of size 10 when $p = 0.30$. The app will plot the simulated sampling distribution of the sample proportion values. Is it bell shaped? Use this to help you explain why the large-sample confidence interval performs poorly in this case. (This exercise illustrates that assumptions for statistical methods are important, because the methods may perform poorly if we use them when the assumptions are violated.)

[5]See B. Lomborg, *The Skeptical Environmentalist*, Cambridge University Press, 2001, p. 222.

8.3 Constructing a Confidence Interval to Estimate a Population Mean

We've learned how to construct a confidence interval for a population proportion—a parameter that summarizes a categorical variable. Next we'll learn how to construct a confidence interval for a population mean--a summary parameter for a quantitative variable. We'll analyze GSS data to estimate the mean number of hours per day that Americans watch television. The method resembles that for a proportion. The confidence interval again has the form

$$\text{point estimate} \pm \text{margin of error}.$$

The margin of error again equals a multiple of a standard error. What do you think plays the role of the point estimate and the role of the standard error (se) in this formula?

How to Construct a Confidence Interval for a Population Mean

The sample mean $\bar{x}$ is the point estimate of the population mean μ. In Section 7.2, we learned that the standard deviation of the sample mean equals $\sigma/\sqrt{n}$, where σ is the population standard deviation. Like the standard deviation of the sample proportion, the standard deviation of the sample mean depends on a parameter whose value is unknown, in this case σ. In practice, we need to estimate σ by the sample standard deviation s to be able to compute a margin of error and a confidence interval. So, the estimated standard deviation used in confidence intervals is the standard error,

$$se = s/\sqrt{n}.$$

Recall

Section 7.2 introduced the standard deviation of the sampling distribution of $\bar{x}$, which describes how much the sample mean varies from sample to sample for a given size n. ◀

We get a confidence interval by taking the sample mean and adding and subtracting the margin of error. We'll see the details following the next example.

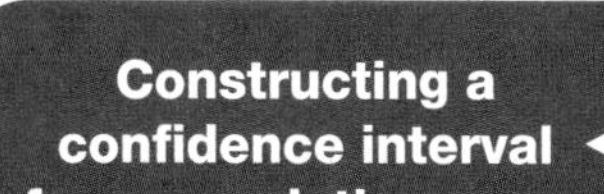

Example 5

Number of Hours Spent Watching Television

Picture the Scenario

How much of a typical person's day is spent in front of the TV? A recent General Social Survey asked respondents, "On the average day, about how many hours do you personally watch television?" A computer printout (from MINITAB) summarizes the results for the GSS variable, TV:

```
N       Mean     StDev    SE Mean   95% CI
1298    3.0886   2.8651   0.0795    (2.9326, 3.2446)
```

We see that the sample size was 1298, the sample mean was 3.09, the sample standard deviation was 2.87, the standard error of the sample mean was 0.08, and the 95% confidence interval for the population mean time μ spent watching TV goes from 2.93 to 3.24 hours per day.

Questions to Explore

a. What do the sample mean and standard deviation suggest about the likely shape of the population distribution?

b. How did the software get the standard error? What does it mean?

c. Interpret the 95% confidence interval reported by software.

▶ Activity

To reproduce these results you can download the dataset from the book's website and load them into a statistical software program or the web app Inference for the Population Mean. You can also get the data and summary statistics from the GSS directly: Access the GSS website and enter *TVHOURS* as the row variable and *YEAR(2012)* as the selection filter at the GSS website. You can get the sample size n, the mean, standard deviation, and *se* by clicking Summary Statistics in the Output Options menu. By clicking Confidence Interval there, you can also get the 95% confidence interval.

Think It Through

a. For the sample mean of $\bar{x} = 3.09$ and standard deviation of $s = 2.87$, the lowest possible value of 0 falls only a bit more than 1 standard deviation below the mean. This information suggests that the population distribution of TV watching may be skewed to the right. Figure 8.6 shows a histogram of the data, which confirms this. The median was 2, the lower and upper quartiles were 1 and 4, and the 95th percentile was 8, yet some subjects reported much higher values.

b. With sample standard deviation $s = 2.87$ and sample size $n = 1298$, the standard error of the sample mean is

$$se = s/\sqrt{n} = 2.87/\sqrt{1298} = 0.0797 \text{ hours.}$$

If many studies were conducted about TV watching, with $n = 1298$ for each, the sample mean would not vary much among those studies.

c. A 95% confidence interval for the population mean μ of TV watching in the United States is (2.93, 3.24) hours. We can be 95% confident that the mean amount of TV watched for Americans is between 2.9 to 3.2 hours of TV a day.

▲ **Figure 8.6** Histogram of Number of Hours a Day Watching Television. Question Does the skew affect the validity of a confidence interval for the population mean?

Insight

Because the sample size was relatively large, the estimation is precise and the confidence interval is quite narrow. The larger the sample size, the smaller the standard error and the subsequent margin of error.

▶ ***Try Exercise 8.29***

We have not yet seen how software found the margin of error for the confidence interval in Example 5. As with the proportion, the margin of error for a 95% confidence interval is roughly two standard errors. However, we need to introduce a new distribution similar to the normal distribution to give us a more precise margin of error. We'll find the margin of error by multiplying the *se* by a score that is a bit larger than the z-score when n is small but very close to it when n is large.

The *t* Distribution and Its Properties

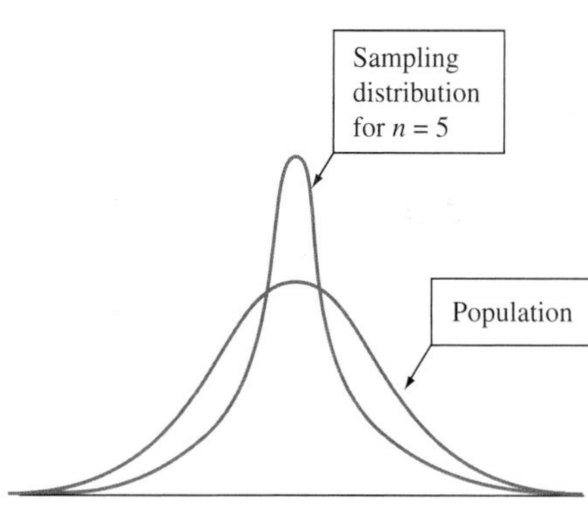

We'll now learn about a confidence interval that applies even for small sample sizes. A disadvantage is that it makes the assumption that the *population distribution of the variable is normal.* In that case, the sampling distribution of $\bar{x}$ is normal even for small sample sizes. (The right panel of Figure 7.11, which showed sampling distributions for various shapes of population distributions, illustrated this, as does the figure here in the margin.) When the population distribution is normal, the sampling distribution of $\bar{x}$ is normal for all n, not just large n.

Suppose we knew the standard deviation, $\sigma/\sqrt{n}$, of the sample mean. Then, with the additional assumption that the population is normal, with small n we could use the formula $\bar{x} \pm z(\sigma/\sqrt{n})$, for instance with $z = 1.96$ for 95% confidence. This interval would contain the population mean μ 95% of the time. In practice, we don't know the population standard deviation σ. Substituting the sample standard deviation s for σ to get $se = s/\sqrt{n}$ introduces extra error. This error can be sizeable when n is small. To account for this increased error, we must replace the z-score by a slightly larger score, called a ***t*-score**. The confidence interval is then a bit wider. *The t-score is like a z-score but it comes from a bell-shaped distribution that has slightly thicker tails (i.e., shows more variability) than a normal distribution.* This distribution is called the ***t* distribution**.

In Practice The *t* Distribution Adjusts for Estimating σ

In practice, we estimate the standard deviation of the sample mean by $se = s/\sqrt{n}$. Then we multiply *se* by a *t*-score from the ***t* distribution** to get the margin of error for a confidence interval for the population mean.

Recall

From Section 6.2, the **standard normal** distribution has mean 0 and standard deviation 1. ◀

The t distribution resembles the *standard normal* distribution, being bell shaped around a mean of 0. Its standard deviation is a bit larger than 1, the precise value depending on what is called the **degrees of freedom**, denoted by ***df***. For inference about a population mean, the degrees of freedom equal $df = n - 1$, one less than the sample size. Before presenting this confidence interval for a mean, we list the major properties of the t distribution.

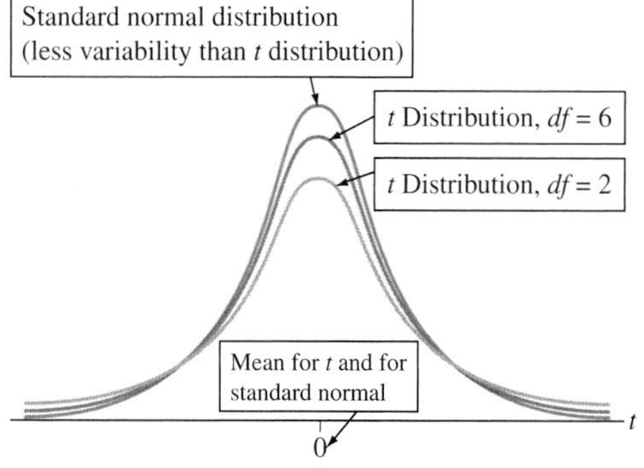

▲ **Figure 8.7 The *t* Distribution Relative to the Standard Normal Distribution.** The *t* distribution is more spread out than the standard normal but gets closer to it as the degrees of freedom (*df*) increase. The two are practically identical when $df \geq 30$.
Question Can you find *z*-scores (such as 1.96) for a normal distribution on the *t* table (Table B)?

SUMMARY: Properties of the *t* Distribution

- The *t* distribution is bell shaped and symmetric about 0.
- The *t* distribution has a slightly different shape for each distinct value for the degrees of freedom, *df*. Probabilities and *t*-scores computed from the *t* distribution depend on the value for the degrees of freedom.
- The *t* distribution has thicker tails and has more variability than the standard normal distribution. The larger the *df* value, however, the closer it gets to the standard normal. Figure 8.7 illustrates this point. When *df* is about 30 or more, the two distributions are nearly identical.
- A *t*-score multiplied by the standard error gives the margin of error for a confidence interval for the mean μ.

Table B at the end of the book lists *t*-scores from the *t* distribution for the right-tail probabilities of 0.100, 0.050, 0.025, 0.010, 0.005, and 0.001, for different values of *df*. The table labels these by $t_{.100}$, $t_{.050}$, $t_{.025}$, $t_{.010}$, $t_{.005}$, and $t_{.001}$. For instance, $t_{.025}$ is the *t*-score with probability 0.025 in the right tail and a two-tail probability of 0.05. It is used in 95% confidence intervals. Statistical software reports *t*-scores for any tail probability.

Table 8.3 Part of Table B Displaying *t*-Scores

The scores have right-tail probabilities of 0.100, 0.050, 0.025, 0.010, 0.005, and 0.001. When $n = 7$, $df = 6$, and $t_{.025} = 2.447$ is the *t*-score with right-tail probability = 0.025 and two-tail probability = 0.05. It is used in a 95% confidence interval, $\bar{x} \pm 2.447(se)$.

	Confidence Level					
	80%	**90%**	**95%**	**98%**	**99%**	**99.8%**
df	$t_{.100}$	$t_{.050}$	$t_{.025}$	$t_{.010}$	$t_{.005}$	$t_{.001}$
1	3.078	6.314	12.706	31.821	63.657	318.3
...						
6	1.440	1.943	2.447	3.143	3.707	5.208
7	1.415	1.895	2.365	2.998	3.499	4.785

Table 8.3 is an excerpt from the *t* table (Table B). To illustrate its use, suppose the sample size is 7. Then the degrees of freedom $df = n - 1 = 6$. Row 6 of the *t* table shows the *t*-scores for $df = 6$. The column labeled $t_{.025}$ contains *t*-scores with right-tail probability equal to 0.025. With $df = 6$, this *t*-score is $t_{.025} = 2.447$. This means that 2.5% of the *t* distribution falls in the right tail above 2.447. By symmetry, 2.5% also falls in the left tail below $-t_{.025} = -2.447$. Figure 8.8 illustrates. When $df = 6$, the probability equals 0.95 between −2.447 and 2.447. This is the *t*-score we use for constructing a 95% confidence interval for μ when $n = 7$. The confidence interval is $\bar{x} \pm 2.447(se)$. You can also use a web app, some calculators or software to find *t*-scores.

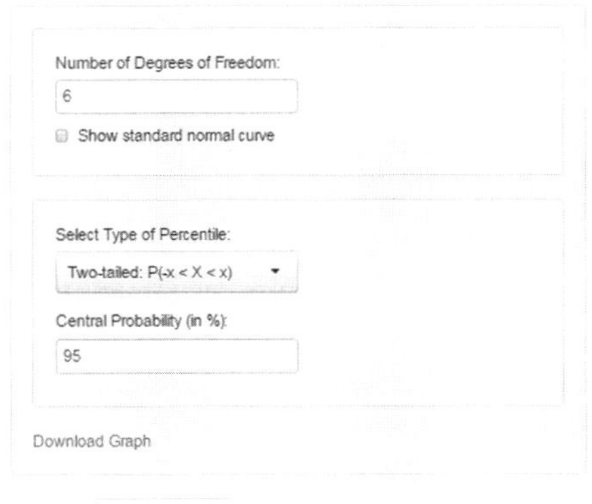

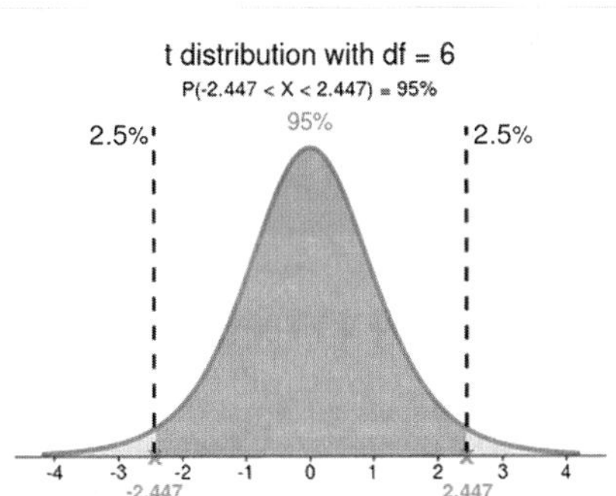

Screenshot of the *t* Distribution web app to find the *t*-score

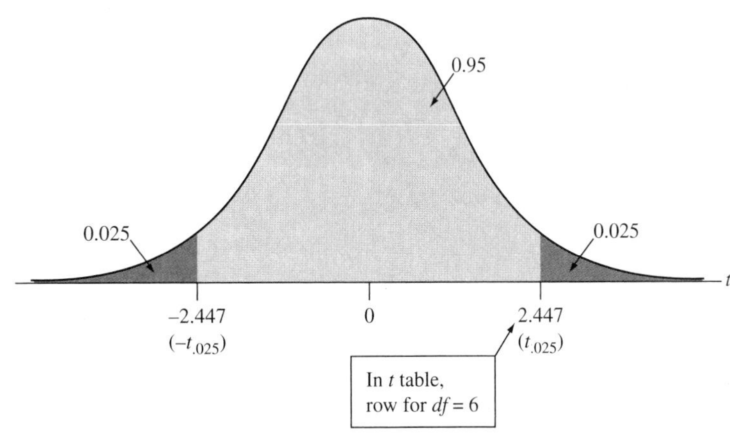

▲ **Figure 8.8** The *t* Distribution with $df = 6$. 95% of the distribution falls between −2.447 and 2.447. These *t*-scores are used with a 95% confidence interval when $n = 7$. **Questions** What are the values of the *z*-scores that contain the middle 95% of the standard normal distribution? Which *t*-scores with $df = 6$ contain the middle 99% of a *t* distribution (for a 99% confidence interval)?

Using the *t* Distribution to Construct a Confidence Interval for a Mean

The confidence interval for a mean has margin of error that equals a *t*-score times the standard error.

SUMMARY: 95% Confidence Interval for a Population Mean

A 95% confidence interval for the population mean μ is

$$\bar{x} \pm t_{.025}(se), \text{ where } se = s/\sqrt{n}.$$

Here, $df = n - 1$ for the t-score $t_{.025}$ that has right-tail probability 0.025 (total probability 0.05 in the two tails and 0.95 between $-t_{.025}$ and $t_{.025}$). To use this method, you need

- Data obtained by randomization (such as a random sample or a randomized experiment).
- An approximately normal population distribution.

Example 6

Using the *t* distribution for a confidence interval for the mean

Buying on eBay

Picture the Scenario

eBay is a popular Internet company for auctioning just about anything. How much can you save by buying items on eBay compared to their actual retail price? Following is a random sample of 11 completed auctions for an unlocked Apple iPhone 5s with 16GB storage in new condition (i.e., item not used, but original packaging might be missing), obtained from eBay in July 2014.

Closing Price (in \$): 570, 620, 610, 590, 540, 590, 565, 590, 580, 570, 595

Questions to Explore

a. Use numerical summaries and graphical displays to check the assumptions for using these data to find a 95% confidence interval for the mean closing price on eBay.

b. Find the 95% confidence interval and interpret it. Is there significant savings considering the \$649 retail price of the unlocked iPhone 5s in July 2014?

Think It Through

a. When we use MINITAB and request descriptive statistics, we get the mean, standard deviation, and five-number summary, using quartiles:

Variable	N	Mean	StDev	Minimum	Q1	Median	Q3	Maximum
Price	11	583.64	22.15	540.00	570.00	590.00	595.00	620.00

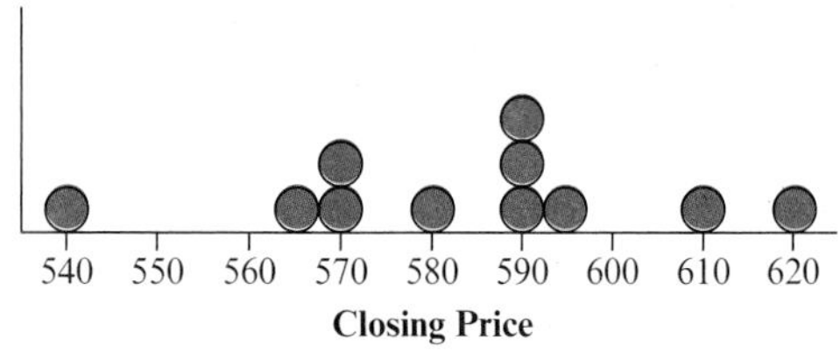

▲ **Figure 8.9** Dot Plot and Box Plot for closing prices of the 16GB iPhone 5s auctioned on eBay in July 2014. **Question** What other plot could you use to display the data?

Together with the dot plot and box plot shown in Figure 8.9 in the margin, we see that the shape of the distribution may be slightly skewed to the left but not too far from symmetric, although it is hard to tell much with only 11 observations. The mean closing price for these 11 auctions was \$584, close to the median of \$590. The lowest price was \$540 and is not shown as an outlier on the box plot. The z-score for this observation is -1.97, so it is within two standard deviations of the mean. The assumptions for using the t distribution are that the data come from a random sample and that the distribution of the final auction price is approximately normal. Although these 11 observations can be regarded as a random sample from the population of all possible closing prices for iPhones 5s posted for sale on eBay in the given time period, checking that they roughly follow a normal model is more difficult. With just 11 observations, dot plots, box plots, or histograms are not very informative about the true shape. However, the dot plot does not rule out a bell-shaped form for the distribution, and the box plot doesn't show an outlier, so we can proceed with the analysis. Later in this section, we discuss this assumption further.

b. Let μ denote the population mean for the closing price of the auction. The point estimate of μ is the sample mean of the 11 observations, which is $\bar{x} = 583.64$. This and the sample standard deviation of $s = 22.15$ are reported in part a. The standard error of the sample mean is

$$se = s/\sqrt{n} = 22.15/\sqrt{11} = 6.68$$

Because $n = 11$, the degrees of freedom to use for the t-score are $df = 11 - 1 = 10$. For a 95% confidence interval, from Table B in the appendix, we use $t_{.025} = 2.228$. The 95% confidence interval is

$$\bar{x} \pm t_{.025}(se) \text{ or } 583.64 \pm 2.228(6.68),$$
$$\text{which is } 583.64 \pm 14.88, \text{ or } (568.8, 598.5).$$

With 95% confidence, the range of believable values for the mean closing price of an unlocked 16 GB iPhones 5s posted for sale on eBay in new condition is \$569 to \$599. In the margin, a screen shot shows how TI reports this confidence interval, and Table 8.4 shows MINITAB output, with SE Mean standing for the standard error of the sample mean.

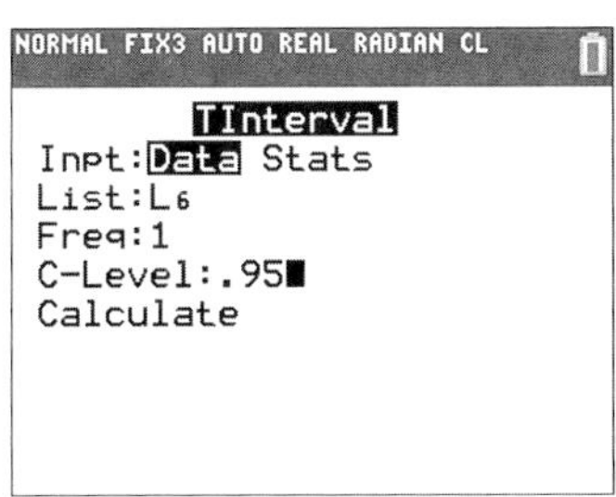

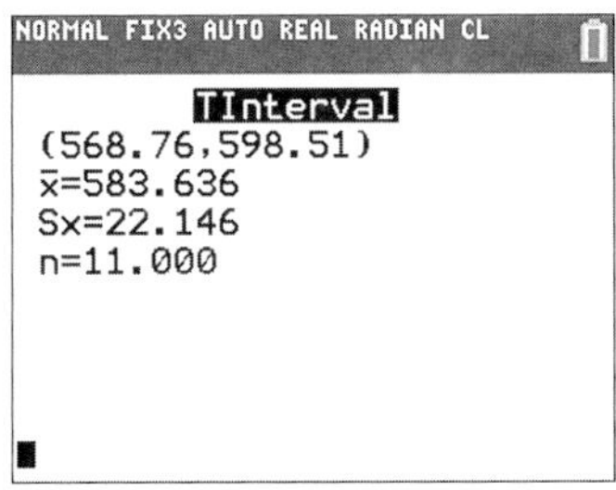

TI output of confidence interval for population mean

Table 8.4 MINITAB Output for 95% Confidence Interval for Mean

Variable	N	Mean	StDev	SE Mean	95% CI
Price	11	583.64	22.15	6.68	(568.76, 598.51)

We can be 95% confident that the mean closing price for an unlocked 16GB iPhone 5s in new condition is between \$569 and \$599. The upper bound is \$50 below the retail price of \$649, so some potential savings can be made when buying this phone from eBay.

Insight

The t-score of 2.228 for this confidence interval is larger than a corresponding z-score of 1.96, leading to a larger (i.e., less precise) interval. This is a consequence of having a small sample size and the need to estimate the standard deviation σ with s to compute the standard error.

▶ ***Try Exercise 8.35***

Finding a *t* Confidence Interval for Other Confidence Levels

The 95% confidence interval uses $t_{.025}$, the t-score for a right-tail probability of 0.025, since 95% of the probability falls between $-t_{.025}$ and $t_{.025}$. For 99% confidence, the error probability is 0.01, the probability is $0.01/2 = 0.005$ in each tail, and the appropriate t-score is $t_{.005}$. The top margin of Table B shows both the t subscript notation and the confidence level.

For instance, the eBay auction sample in the preceding example has $n = 11$, so $df = 10$ and from Table B, $t_{.005} = 3.169$. A 99% confidence interval for the mean closing price is

$$\bar{x} \pm t_{.005}(se) = 583.64 \pm 3.169(6.68),$$
$$\text{which is } 583.64 \pm 21.17, \text{ or } (562.47, 604.81).$$

As we saw with the confidence interval for a population proportion using a larger confidence level, this 99% confidence interval for a population mean is wider than the 95% confidence interval of (568.76, 598.52).

If the Population Is Not Normal, Is the Method Robust?

A basic assumption of the confidence interval using the t distribution is that the population distribution is normal. This is worrisome because many variables have distributions that are far from a bell shape. How problematic is it if we use the t confidence interval even if the population distribution is not normal? For large random samples, it's not problematic because of the central limit theorem. The sampling distribution is bell shaped even when the population distribution is not. But what about for small n?

For the confidence interval in Example 6 with $n = 11$ to be valid, we must assume that the probability distribution of closing prices is normal. Does this assumption seem plausible? Because there is an upper limit (no one would pay more than the retail price for a brand new phone), we would expect a distribution that is skewed to the left. A dot plot, histogram, or stem-and-leaf plot gives us some information about the population distribution, but it is not precise when n is small and it tells us little when $n = 11$. Fortunately, the confidence interval using the t distribution is a **robust** method in terms of the normality assumption.

Robust Statistical Method

A statistical method is said to be **robust** with respect to a particular assumption if it performs adequately even when that assumption is modestly violated.

Even if the population distribution is not normal, confidence intervals using t-scores usually work quite well. The actual probability that the 95% confidence interval method provides a correct inference (i.e., covers the true mean) is close to 0.95 and gets closer as n increases.

Recall

Section 2.5 identified an observation as a potential **outlier** if it falls more than 1.5 × *IQR* below the first quartile or above the third quartile, or if it falls more than 3 standard deviations from the mean. ◀

The most important case when the t confidence interval method does *not* work well is *when the data contain extreme outliers.* Partly this is because of the effect of outliers on summary statistics such as $\bar{x}$ and s. If we had observed an auction in Example 6 that resulted in a very low price of around $400, then this might call into question the validity of the confidence interval procedure. (One approach is to compute the confidence interval with and without the outlier[s] and see whether there are substantial changes.) Another issue with extreme outliers is that the mean itself might not be a representative summary of the center. Section 8.5 briefly mentions methods for constructing confidence intervals for other population parameters, such as the population median. Finally, the t distribution does not work with binary data and proportions, for which Section 8.2 presented a separate method for finding a confidence interval.

Caution

The t confidence interval method is not robust to violations of the random sampling assumption. The t method, like all inferential statistical methods, has questionable validity if the method for producing the data did not use randomization. ◀

In Practice Assumptions Are Rarely Perfectly Satisfied

Knowing that a statistical method is **robust** (that is, it still performs adequately) even when a particular assumption is violated is important because in practice assumptions are rarely perfectly satisfied. Confidence intervals for a mean using the ***t* distribution** are robust against most violations of the normal population assumption. However, you should check the data graphically to identify **outliers** that could affect the validity of the mean or its confidence interval. Also, unless the data production used **randomization**, statistical inference may be inappropriate.

The Standard Normal Distribution Is the *t* Distribution with *df* = ∞

Look at the table of *t*-scores (Table B in the appendix), part of which is shown in Table 8.5. As *df* increases, you move down the table. In each column, the *t*-score decreases toward the *z*-score for a standard normal distribution. For instance, when *df* increases from 1 to 100 in Table B, the *t*-score $t_{.025}$ that has right-tail probability equal to 0.025 decreases from 12.706 to 1.984. This reflects the *t* distribution having less variability and becoming more similar in appearance to the standard normal distribution as *df* increases. The *z*-score with right-tail probability of 0.025 for the standard normal distribution is $z = 1.96$. When *df* is above about 30, the *t*-score is similar to this *z*-score. For instance, they both round to 2.0. The *t*-score gets closer and closer to the *z*-score as *df* keeps increasing. *You can think of the standard normal distribution as a t distribution with df = infinity.*

Did You Know?

z-score = *t*-score with *df* = ∞ (infinity). ◀

Table 8.5 Part of Table B Displaying *t*-Scores for Large *df* Values

The *z*-score of 1.96 is the *t*-score $t_{.025}$ with right-tail probability of 0.025 and $df = \infty$.

	Confidence Level					
	80%	90%	95%	98%	99%	99.8%
	Right-Tail Probability					
df	$t_{.100}$	$t_{.050}$	$t_{.025}$	$t_{.010}$	$t_{.005}$	$t_{.001}$
1	3.078	6.314	12.706	31.821	63.657	318.3
30	1.310	1.697	2.042	2.457	2.750	3.385
40	1.303	1.684	2.021	2.423	2.704	3.307
50	1.299	1.676	2.009	2.403	2.678	3.261
60	1.296	1.671	2.000	2.390	2.660	3.232
80	1.292	1.664	1.990	2.374	2.639	3.195
100	1.290	1.660	1.984	2.364	2.626	3.174
∞	1.282	1.645	1.960	2.326	2.576	3.090

Table 8.5 shows the first row and the last several rows of Table B. The last row lists the *z*-scores for various confidence levels, opposite $df = \infty$ (infinity). The *t*-scores are not printed for $df > 100$, but they are close to the *z*-scores. For instance, to get the confidence interval about TV watching in Example 5, for which the GSS sample had $n = 1298$, software uses the $t_{.025}$ score for $df = 1298 - 1 = 1297$, which is 1.9618. This is nearly identical to the *z*-score of 1.960 from the standard normal distribution.

You can get *t*-scores for *any df* value using the web app, software and many calculators, so you are not restricted to Table B. (For instance, MINITAB provides percentile scores for various distributions under the *CALC* menu.) If you don't have access to software, you won't be far off if you use a *z*-score instead of a *t*-score for *df* values larger than shown in Table B (above 100). For a 95% confidence interval, you will then use

$$\bar{x} \pm 1.96(se) \text{ instead of } \bar{x} \pm t_{.025}(se).$$

You will not get *exactly* the same result that software would give, but it will be very, very close.

Recall

The reason we use a *t*-score instead of a *z*-score in the confidence interval for a mean is that it accounts for the extra error due to estimating σ by *s*. ◀

In Practice Use t for Inference About μ Whenever You Estimate

Statistical software and calculators use the t distribution for *all* cases when the sample standard deviation s is used to estimate the population standard deviation σ. The normal population assumption is mainly relevant for small n, but even then the t confidence interval is a robust method, working well unless there are extreme outliers or the data are binary.

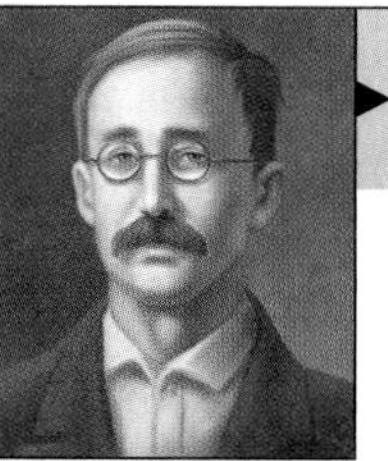

On the Shoulders of...William S. Gosset

W.S. Gosset: Discovered the t distribution allowing statistical methods for working with small sample sizes.

How do you find the best way to brew beer if you have only small samples?

The statistician and chemist William S. Gosset was a brewer in charge of the experimental unit of Guinness Breweries in Dublin, Ireland. The search for a better stout in 1908 led him to the discovery of the t distribution. Only small samples were available from his experiments pertaining to the selection, cultivation, and treatment of barley and hops. The established statistical methods at that time relied on large samples and the normal distribution. Because of company policy forbidding the publication of company work in one's own name, Gosset used the pseudonym "Student" in articles he wrote about his discoveries. The t distribution became known as *Student's t* distribution, a name still used today.

8.3 Practicing the Basics

8.29 Females' ideal number of children The 2012 General Social Survey asked, "What do you think is the ideal number of children for a family to have?" The 590 females who gave a numeric response from 0 to 6 had a median of 2, mean of 2.56, and standard deviation of 0.84. TRY

- **a.** What is the point estimate of the population mean?
- **b.** Find the standard error of the sample mean.
- **c.** The 95% confidence interval is (2.49, 2.62). Interpret.
- **d.** Is it plausible that the population mean $\mu = 2$? Explain.

8.30 Males' ideal number of children Refer to the previous exercise. For the 530 males in the sample who gave a numeric response from 0 to 6, the mean was 2.51 and the standard deviation was 0.87.

- **a.** Find the point estimate of the population mean and show that its standard error is 0.038.
- **b.** The 95% confidence interval is 2.43 to 2.59. Explain what "95% confidence" means for this interval.
- **c.** Compared to the interval for females, is there much evidence of a difference between the means? Explain.

8.31 Using t-table Using Table B, the web app, software or a calculator, report the t-score that you multiply by the standard error to form the margin of error for a TECH

- **a.** 95% confidence interval for a mean with 5 observations.
- **b.** 95% confidence interval for a mean with 15 observations.
- **c.** 99% confidence interval for a mean with 15 observations.

8.32 Anorexia in teenage girls A study[6] compared various therapies for teenage girls suffering from anorexia, an eating disorder. For each girl, weight was measured before and after a fixed period of treatment. The variable measured was the change in weight, X = weight at the end of the study minus weight at the beginning of the study. The therapies were designed to aid weight gain, corresponding to positive values of X. For the sample of 17 girls receiving the family therapy, the changes in weight during the study were 11, 11, 6, 9, 14, −3, 0, 7, 22, −5, −4, 13, 13, 9, 4, 6, 11. TECH

- **a.** Plot these with a dot plot or box plot and summarize.
- **b.** Using the web app, software or a calculator, show that the weight changes have $\bar{x} = 7.29$ and $s = 7.18$ pounds.
- **c.** Using the web app, software or a calculator, show that the standard error of the sample mean was $se = 1.74$.
- **d.** To use the t distribution, explain why the 95% confidence interval uses the t-score equal to 2.120.

[6]Data courtesy of Prof. Brian Everitt, Institute of Psychiatry, London.

e. Let μ denote the population mean change in weight for this therapy. Using results from parts b, c, and d, show that the 95% confidence interval for μ is (3.6, 11.0). Explain why this suggests that the true mean change in weight is positive but possibly quite small.

8.33 Talk time on smartphones One feature smartphone manufacturers use in advertising is the amount of time one can talk before recharging the battery. Below are 13 values from a random sample of the talk-time (in minutes) of smartphones running on lithium-ion batteries. The summary statistics are $\bar{x} = 553$, $s = 227$, Q1 = 420, median = 450, Q3 = 650. Talk time: 320, 360, 760, 580, 1050, 900, 360, 500, 420, 420, 650, 420, 450.

TECH

a. Construct an appropriate graph (dot plot, stem and leaf plot, histogram, box plot) to describe the shape of the distribution. What assumptions are needed to construct a 95% confidence interval for μ, the mean talk time? Point out any assumptions that seem questionable.

b. Check whether this data set has any potential outliers according to the criterion of (i) 1.5 * IQR below Q1 or above Q3 and (ii) 3 standard deviations from the mean.

c. Using the summary statistics, show that the 95% confidence interval is (416, 690). Interpret it in context.

d. The value 1050 is quite a bit larger than the others. Delete this observation, find the new mean and standard deviation, and construct the 95% confidence interval for μ without this observation. How does it compare to the 95% confidence interval, using all the data?

8.34 Heights of seedlings Exercise 8.7 reported heights (in mm) of 55.5, 60.3, 60.6, 62.1, 65.5, and 69.2 for six seedlings fourteen days after germination.

TECH

a. Using the web app, software or a calculator, verify that the 95% confidence interval for the population mean is (57.3, 67.1).

b. Name two things you could do to get a narrower interval than the one in part a.

c. Construct a 99% confidence interval. Why is it wider than the 95% interval?

d. On what assumptions is the interval in part a based? Explain how important each assumption is.

8.35 Buy it now Example 6 mentioned closing prices for listings of the iPhone 5s on eBay. If you don't feel comfortable bidding (or can't wait until a listing has ended), you can often purchase the item right away at the indicated Buy It Now price. A random sample of Buy It Now prices for an unlocked iPhone 5s, 16GB and in new condition in July 2014 showed the following prices (in $) with dot plot and box plot shown in the figure: 618, 650, 608, 634, 675, 618, 625, 619, 630.

TRY

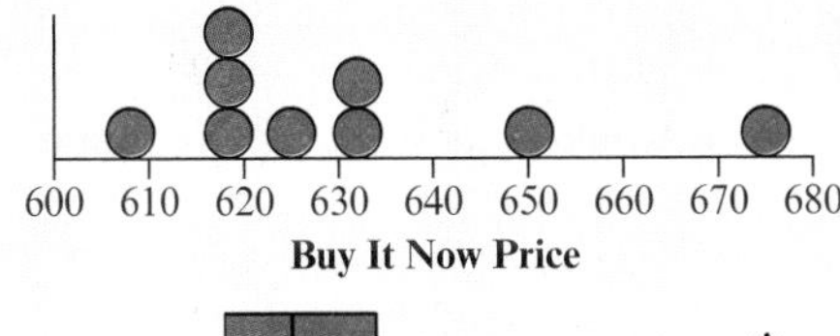

a. What must we assume to use these data to find a 95% confidence interval for the mean Buy It Now price on eBay? Do these assumptions seem plausible?

b. The table shows the way software reports results. How was the standard error of the mean (SE Mean) obtained?

Variable	N	Mean	StDev	SE Mean	95% CI
BuyItNow	9	630.78	20.47	6.82	(615.04 646.52)

c. Interpret the 95% confidence interval in context.

d. Compared to the confidence interval (569, 599) for prices from auctions obtained in Example 6, is there evidence that the mean price is higher when purchased through Buy It Now? Explain.

e. Excluding the observation of $675, the confidence interval equals (615, 636). Does this change your answer to part d?

8.36 Time spent on e-mail When the GSS asked $n = 1050$ people in 2012, "About how many hours per week do you spend sending and answering e-mail?" (EMAILHR), the summary statistics were $\bar{x} = 6.89$ and $s = 13.05$. TI output with these data (available on the book's website) is shown in the screen shot.

a. What is the margin of error at the 95% confidence level for the point estimate of the mean number of hours?

b. Interpret the 95% confidence interval shown in context.

c. The distribution of hours spent is right-skewed (e.g., the minimum of zero hours is only 0.5 standard deviations below the mean, but the largest value of 168 hours has a z-score larger than 12). Is this a concern for the validity of the confidence interval?

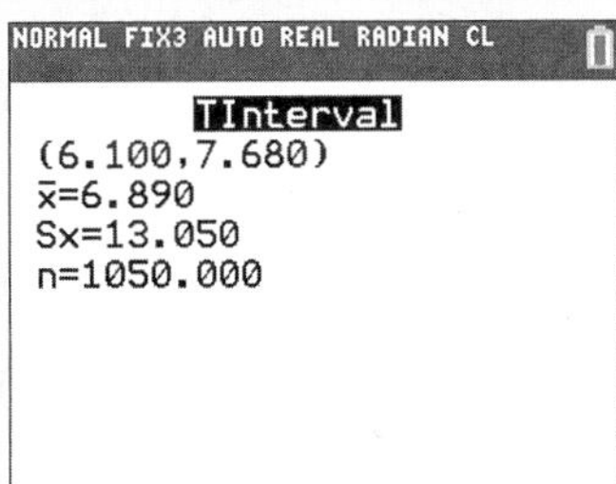

8.37 Grandmas using e-mail For the question about e-mail in the previous exercise, the 14 females in the GSS of age at least 80 had the responses

TECH

0, 0, 0, 0, 1, 1, 1, 2, 2, 6, 6, 7, 7, 10.

a. Using the web app, software or a calculator, find the sample mean and standard deviation and the standard error of the sample mean.

b. Find and interpret a 90% confidence interval for the population mean.

c. Explain why the population distribution may be skewed right. If this is the case, is the interval you obtained in part b useless, or is it still valid? Explain.

8.38 Wage discrimination? According to a union agreement, the mean income for all senior-level assembly-line workers in a large company equals $500 per week. A representative of a women's group decides to analyze whether the mean income for female employees matches this norm. For a random sample of nine female employees, using software, she obtains a 95% confidence interval of (371, 509). Explain what is wrong with each of the following interpretations of this interval.

a. We infer that 95% of the women in the population have income between $371 and $509 per week.

b. If random samples of nine women were repeatedly selected, then 95% of the time the sample mean income would be between \$371 and \$509.

c. We can be 95% confident that $\bar{x}$ is between \$371 and \$509.

d. If we repeatedly sampled the entire population, then 95% of the time the population mean would be between \$371 and \$509.

8.39 How often read a newspaper? For the FL Student Survey data file on the book's website, software reports the results for responses on the number of times a week the subject reads a newspaper:

```
Variable  N  Mean  Std Dev  SE Mean      95.0% CI
News     60  4.1     3.0     0.388   (3.307, 4.859)
```

a. Is it plausible that $\mu = 7$, where μ is the population mean for all Florida students? Explain.

b. Suppose that the sample size had been 240, with $\bar{x} = 4.1$ and $s = 3.0$. Find a 95% confidence interval and compare it to the one reported. Describe the effect of sample size on the margin of error.

c. Does it seem plausible that the population distribution of this variable is normal? Why?

d. Explain the implications of the term *robust* regarding the normality assumption made to conduct this analysis.

8.40 Political views The General Social Survey asks respondents to rate their political views on a seven-point scale, where 1 = extremely liberal, 4 = moderate, and 7 = extremely conservative. A researcher analyzing data from the 2012 GSS obtains MINITAB output:

```
Variable   N    Mean   StDev SE Mean        95% CI
POLVIEWS 1874 4.0624 1.4529 0.0336 (3.9965, 4.1283)
```

a. Show how to construct the confidence interval from the other information provided.

b. Can you conclude that the population mean is lower than the moderate score of 4.0? Explain.

c. Would the confidence interval be wider, or narrower, (i) if you constructed a 99% confidence interval and (ii) if $n = 500$ instead of 1874?

8.41 Length of hospital stays A hospital administrator wants to estimate the mean length of stay for all inpatients using that hospital. Using a random sample of 100 records of patients for the previous year, she reports that "The sample mean was 5.3 days. In repeated random samples of this size, the sample mean could be expected to fall within one day of the true mean about 95% of the time." Explain the meaning of this sentence from the report, showing what it suggests about the 95% confidence interval.

8.42 Effect of *n* Find the margin of error for a 95% confidence interval for estimating the population mean when the sample standard deviation equals 100, with a sample size of (i) 25 and (ii) 100. What is the effect of increasing the sample size? (You can use Table B in the back to find the appropriate *t*-scores.)

8.43 Effect of confidence level Find the margin of error for estimating the population mean when the sample standard deviation equals 100 for a sample size of 25, using confidence levels (i) 95% and (ii) 99%. What is the effect of the choice of confidence level? (You can use Table B in the back to find the appropriate *t*-scores.)

8.44 Catalog mail-order sales A company that sells its products through mail-order catalogs wants information about the success of its most recent catalog. The company decides to estimate the mean dollar amount of items ordered from those who received the catalog. For a random sample of 100 customers from their files, only 5 made an order, so 95 of the response values were \$0. The overall mean of all 100 orders was \$10, with a standard deviation of \$10.

a. Is it plausible that the population distribution is normal? Explain and discuss how much this affects the validity of a confidence interval for the mean.

b. Find a 95% confidence interval for the mean dollar order for the population of all customers who received this catalog. Normally, the mean of their sales per catalog is about \$15. Can we conclude that it declined with this catalog? Explain.

8.45 Number of children TECH For the question, "How many children have you ever had?" use the GSS website sda.berkeley.edu/GSS with the variable CHILDS to find the sample mean and standard deviation for the 2012 survey. (Use YEAR(2012) as filter and select Summary Statistics under Options.) (Treat the 23 respondents who answered "eight or more" as having eight children.)

a. Show how to obtain a standard error of 0.04 for a random sample of 1971 adults.

b. Construct a 95% confidence interval for the population mean. Can you conclude that the population mean is less than 2.0? Explain.

8.46 Simulating the confidence interval TRY TECH Go to the Inference for a Mean web app, accessible on the book's website. Select the Explore Coverage tab and keep the default skewed shape for the population distribution as well as the default confidence level of 95%. Set the sample size to 30 and generate 100 random samples by selecting 100 and clicking on Draw Sample(s). The graph will now show 100 confidence intervals for μ, based on 100 generated sample from the population distribution.

a. How many of the intervals you generated fail to contain the population mean $\mu = 14.3$?

b. How many would you expect not to contain the true value?

c. Now repeat the simulation using at least 1000 random samples of size 30. Why do close to 95% of the intervals contain μ, even though the population distribution is quite skewed?

8.4 Choosing the Sample Size for a Study

Have you ever wondered how sample sizes are determined for polls? How does a polling organization know whether it needs 10,000 people, 100 people, or some odd number such as 745 people? The simple answer is that this depends on how much precision is needed, as measured by the margin of error. The smaller the desired margin of error, the larger the sample size must be. We'll next learn how to find the sample size for a predetermined margin of error. For instance, we'll find out how large an exit poll must be so that a 95% confidence interval for the population proportion voting for a candidate has a margin of error of 0.04.

The key results for finding the sample size for a random sample are as follows:

- The *margin of error* depends on the *standard error* of the sampling distribution of the point estimate.
- The *standard error* itself depends on the *sample size.*

Once we specify a margin of error with a particular confidence level, we can determine the value of n that has a standard error giving that margin of error.

Choosing the Sample Size for Estimating a Population Proportion

How large should n be to estimate a population proportion? First we must decide on the desired *margin of error*—how close the sample proportion should be to the population proportion. Second, we must choose the *confidence level* for achieving that margin of error. In practice, 95% confidence intervals are most common. If we specify a margin of error of 0.04, this means that a 95% confidence interval should equal the sample proportion plus and minus 0.04.

Choosing a sample size ◀

Example 7

Exit Poll

Picture the Scenario

A TV network plans to predict the outcome of an election between Levin and Sanchez using an exit poll that randomly samples voters on election day. They want a reasonably accurate estimate of the population proportion that voted for Levin. The final poll a week before election day estimated her to be well ahead, 58% to 42%, so they do not expect the outcome to be close. Since their finances for this project are limited, they don't want to collect a large sample if they don't need it. They decide to use a sample size for which the margin of error is 0.04 rather than their usual margin of error of 0.03.

Recall

From Section 8.2, a 95% confidence interval for a population proportion p is

$$\hat{p} \pm 1.96(se),$$

where $\hat{p}$ denotes the sample proportion and the standard error (se) is

$$se = \sqrt{\hat{p}(1 - \hat{p})/n}.$$ ◀

Question to Explore

What is the sample size for which a 95% confidence interval for the population proportion has a margin of error equal to 0.04?

Think It Through

The 95% confidence interval for a population proportion p is $\hat{p} \pm 1.96(se)$. So, if the sample size is such that $1.96(se) = 0.04$, then the margin of error will be 0.04. See Figure 8.10.

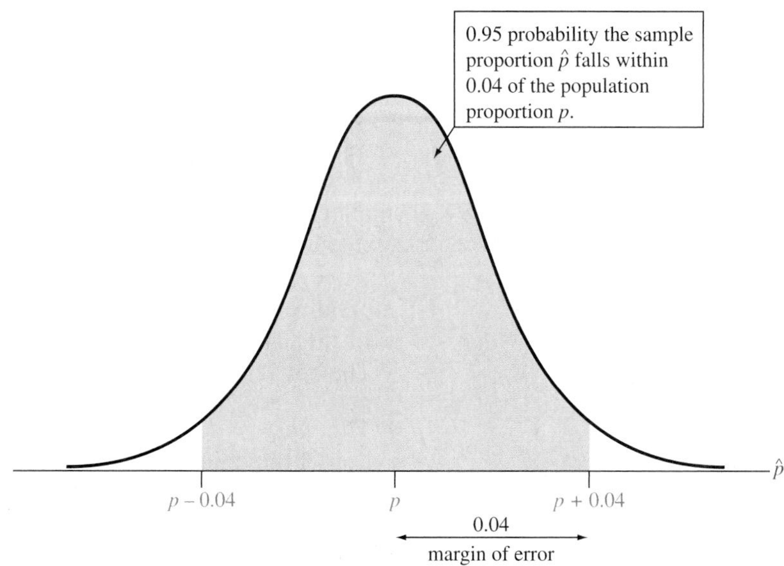

▲ **Figure 8.10 Sampling Distribution of Sample Proportion $\hat{p}$ Such That a 95% Confidence Interval Has Margin of Error 0.04.** We need to find the value of n that has this margin of error. **Question** What must we assume for this distribution to be approximately normal?

Let's find the value of the sample size n for which $0.04 = 1.96(se)$. For a confidence interval for a proportion, the standard error is $\sqrt{\hat{p}(1 - \hat{p})/n}$. So the equation $0.04 = 1.96(se)$ becomes

$$0.04 = 1.96\sqrt{\hat{p}(1 - \hat{p})/n}.$$

To find the answer, we solve algebraically for n:

$$n = (1.96)^2\hat{p}(1 - \hat{p})/(0.04)^2.$$

Now, we face a problem. We're doing this calculation *before* gathering the data, so we don't yet have a sample proportion $\hat{p}$. Since $\hat{p}$ is unknown, we must substitute an educated guess for what we'll get once we gather the sample and analyze the data.

Since the latest poll *before* election day predicted that 58% of the voters preferred Levin, it is sensible to substitute 0.58 for $\hat{p}$ in this equation. Then we find

$$n = (1.96)^2\hat{p}(1 - \hat{p})/(0.04)^2 = (1.96)^2(0.58)(0.42)/(0.04)^2 = 584.9.$$

In summary, a random sample of size about $n = 585$ should give a margin of error of about 0.04 for a 95% confidence interval for the population proportion.

Insight

Sometimes, we may have no idea what to expect for $\hat{p}$. We may prefer not to guess the value it will take, as we did in this example. We'll next learn what we can do in those situations.

▶ ***Try Exercise 8.48***

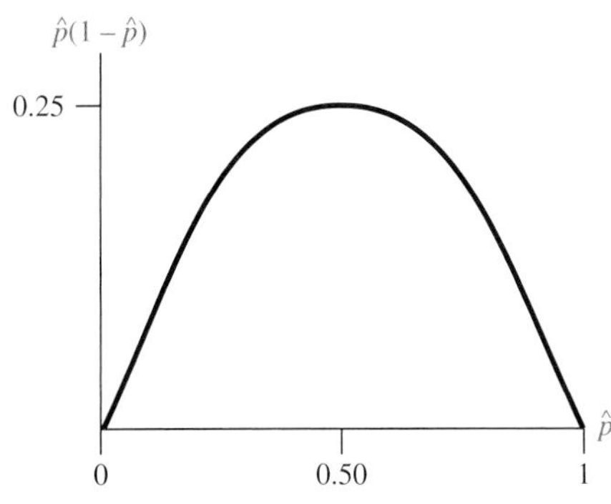

Selecting a Sample Size Without Guessing a Value for $\hat{p}$

In the previous example, the solution for n was proportional to $\hat{p}(1-\hat{p})$. The figure in the margin shows how that product depends on the value of $\hat{p}$. The largest possible value for $\hat{p}(1-\hat{p})$ is 0.25, which occurs when $\hat{p} = 0.50$. You can check by plugging values of $\hat{p}$ into $\hat{p}(1-\hat{p})$ that this product is near 0.25 unless $\hat{p}$ is quite far from 0.50. For example, $\hat{p}(1-\hat{p}) = 0.24$ when $\hat{p} = 0.40$ or $\hat{p} = 0.60$.

In the formula for determining n, setting $\hat{p} = 0.50$ out of all the possible values to substitute for $\hat{p}$ gives the largest value for n. This is the safe approach that guarantees we'll have a large enough sample. In the election exit poll example, for a margin of error of 0.04, we then get

$$n = (1.96)^2\hat{p}(1-\hat{p})/(0.04)^2$$
$$= (1.96)^2(0.50)(0.50)/(0.04)^2 = 600.25, \text{ rounded up to } 601.$$

This result compares to $n = 585$ from guessing that $\hat{p} = 0.58$. Using the slightly larger value of $n = 601$ ensures that the margin of error for a 95% confidence interval will not exceed 0.04, no matter what value $\hat{p}$ takes once we collect the data.

This safe approach is not always sensible, however. Substituting $\hat{p} = 0.50$ gives us an overly large solution for n if $\hat{p}$ actually falls far from 0.50. Suppose that based on other studies we expect $\hat{p}$ to be about 0.10. Then an adequate sample size to achieve a margin of error of 0.04 is

$$n = (1.96)^2\hat{p}(1-\hat{p})/(0.04)^2$$
$$= (1.96)^2(0.10)(0.90)/(0.04)^2 = 216.09, \text{ rounded up to } 217.$$

A sample size of 601 would be much larger and more costly than needed.

General Sample Size Formula for Estimating a Population Proportion A general formula exists for determining the sample size, based on solving algebraically for n by setting the margin of error formula equal to the desired value. Let m denote the desired margin of error such as $m = 0.04$ in the previous example. The general formula also uses the z-score for the desired confidence level.

SUMMARY: Sample Size for Estimating a Population Proportion

The random sample size n for which a confidence interval for a population proportion p has margin of error m (such as $m = 0.04$) is

$$n = \frac{\hat{p}(1-\hat{p})z^2}{m^2}.$$

The z-score is based on the confidence level, such as $z = 1.96$ for 95% confidence. You either guess the value you'd get for the sample proportion $\hat{p}$ based on other information or take the safe approach of setting $\hat{p} = 0.5$.

Example 8

Choosing sample size

Using an Exit Poll When a Race Is Close

Picture the Scenario

An election is expected to be close. Pollsters planning an exit poll decide that a margin of error of 0.04 is too large.

Question to Explore

How large should the sample size be for the margin of error of a 95% confidence interval to equal 0.02?

Think It Through

Since the election is expected to be close, we expect $\hat{p}$ to be near 0.50. In the formula, we set $\hat{p} = 0.50$ to be safe. We also set the margin of error $m = 0.02$ and use $z = 1.96$ for a 95% confidence interval. The required sample size is

$$n = \frac{\hat{p}(1 - \hat{p})z^2}{m^2} = \frac{(0.50)(0.50)(1.96)^2}{(0.02)^2} = 2401.$$

Insight

The sample size of about 2400 is four times the sample size of 600 necessary to guarantee a margin of error of $m = 0.04$. *Reducing the margin of error by a factor of one-half requires quadrupling n.*

▶ ***Try Exercise 8.49***

Samples taken by polling organizations typically contain 1000–2000 subjects. This is large enough to estimate a population proportion with a margin of error of about 0.02 or 0.03. At first glance, it seems astonishing that a sample of this size from a population of perhaps many millions is adequate for predicting outcomes of elections, summarizing opinions on controversial issues, showing relative sizes of television audiences, and so forth. The basis for this inferential power lies in the standard error formulas for the point estimates, with random sampling. Good estimates result no matter how large the population size.[7]

Revisiting the Approximation $1/\sqrt{n}$ for the Margin of Error Chapter 1 introduced a margin of error approximation of $1/\sqrt{n}$ for estimating a population proportion using random sampling. What's the connection between this approximation and the more exact margin of error we've just derived? Let's take the margin of error $1.96\sqrt{\hat{p}(1 - \hat{p})/n}$ for a 95% confidence interval, round the z-score to 2, and replace the sample proportion by the value of 0.50 that gives the maximum possible standard error. Then we get the margin of error

$$2\sqrt{0.50(0.50)/n} = 2(0.50)\sqrt{1/n} = 1/\sqrt{n}.$$

So for a 95% confidence interval, the margin of error is approximately $1/\sqrt{n}$ when $\hat{p}$ is near 0.50.

Choosing the Sample Size for Estimating a Population Mean

As with the population proportion, to derive the sample size for estimating a population mean, you set the margin of error equal to its desired value and solve for n. Recall that a 95% confidence interval for the population mean μ is

$$\bar{x} \pm t_{.025}(se),$$

where $se = s/\sqrt{n}$ and s is the sample standard deviation. If you don't know n, you also don't know the degrees of freedom and the t-score. However, we saw in Table B that when $df > 30$, the t-score is very similar to the z-score from a

[7] In fact, the mathematical derivations of these methods treat the population size as infinite. See Exercise 7.62.

In Words

The sample size n needed to estimate the population mean depends on how precisely you want to estimate it (by the choice of the margin of error m), how sure you want to be (by the confidence level, which determines the z-score), and how variable the data will be (by the guess for the population standard deviation σ).

normal distribution, such as 1.96 for 95% confidence. Also, before collecting the data, we do not know the sample standard deviation s, which we use to estimate the population standard deviation σ. When we use a z-score (in place of the t-score), supply an educated guess for the standard deviation of the sample mean $\sigma/\sqrt{n}$, and then set $z(\sigma/\sqrt{n})$ equal to a desired margin of error m and solve for n, we get the following result:

SUMMARY: Sample Size for Estimating a Population Mean

The random sample size n for which a confidence interval for a population mean μ has margin of error approximately equal to m is

$$n = \frac{\sigma^2 z^2}{m^2}.$$

The z-score is based on the confidence level, such as $z = 1.96$ for 95% confidence. To use this formula, you need to guess the value for the population standard deviation σ.

In practice, you don't know the population standard deviation. You must substitute an educated guess for σ. Sometimes you can guess it using the sample standard deviation from a similar study already conducted, or you can take a *pilot study*, which is a small study taken before the actual study. From the few observations in the pilot study, you can crudely estimate σ. The next example shows another sort of reasoning to form an educated guess.

Example 9

Finding n ◀

Estimating Mean Education in South Africa

Picture the Scenario

A social scientist studies adult South Africans living in townships on the outskirts of Cape Town, to investigate educational attainment in the black community. Educational attainment is the number of years of education completed. Many of the study's potential subjects were forced to leave Cape Town in 1966 when the government passed a law forbidding blacks to live in the inner cities. Under the apartheid system, black South African children were not required to attend school, so some residents had very little education.

Question to Explore

How large a sample size is needed so that a 95% confidence interval for the mean number of years of attained education has a margin of error equal to 1 year?

Recall

The Empirical Rule in Section 2.4 noted that for bell-shaped distributions, all or nearly all observations fall within 3 standard deviations of the mean. ◀

Think It Through

No prior information is stated about the standard deviation of educational attainment for the township residents. As a crude approximation, we might guess that the education values will fall within a range of about 18 years, such as between 0 and 18 years. If the distribution is bell shaped, the range from $\mu - 3\sigma$ to $\mu + 3\sigma$ will contain all or nearly all of the possible values. Since the distance from $\mu - 3\sigma$ to $\mu + 3\sigma$ equals 6σ, the range of 18 years would equal about 6σ. Then, solving $18 = 6\sigma$ for σ, $18/6 = 3$ is a crude guess for σ. So we'd expect a standard deviation value of about $\sigma = 3$.

The desired margin of error is $m = 1$ year. Then, the required sample size is

$$n = \frac{\sigma^2 z^2}{m^2} = \frac{3^2(1.96)^2}{1^2} = 35.$$

We need to sample randomly about 35 subjects for a 95% confidence interval for mean educational attainment to have a margin of error of 1 year.

Insight

A more cautious approach would select the *largest* value for the standard deviation that is plausible. This will give the largest sensible guess for how large n needs to be. For example, we could reasonably predict that σ will be no greater than 4, since a range of 6 standard deviations then extends over 24 years. Then we get $n = (1.96)^2(4^2)/(1^2) = 62$. If we collect the data and the sample standard deviation is actually less than 4, we will have more data than we need. The margin of error will be even less than 1.0.

▶ ***Try Exercise 8.53***

Other Factors That Affect the Choice of the Sample Size

We've looked at two factors that play a role in determining a study's sample size.

- The first is the desired *precision*, as measured by the *margin of error m.*
- The second is the *confidence level*, which determines the z-score in the sample size formulas.

Other factors also play a role.

- A third factor is the *variability* in the data.

Let's look at the formula $n = \sigma^2 z^2/m^2$ for the sample size for estimating a mean. The greater the value expected for the standard deviation σ, the larger the sample size needed. If subjects have little variation (that is, σ is small), we need fewer data than if they have substantial variation. Suppose a study plans to estimate the mean level of education in several countries. Western European countries have relatively little variation because students are required to attend school until the middle teen years. To estimate the mean to within a margin of error of $m = 1$, we need fewer observations than in South Africa.

- A fourth factor is *cost.*

Larger samples are more time consuming to collect. They may be more expensive than a study can afford. Cost is often a major constraint. You may need to ask, "Should we go ahead with the smaller sample that we can afford, even though the margin of error will be greater than we would like?"

Using a Small *n*

Sometimes, because of financial or ethical reasons, it's just not possible to take as large of a sample as we'd like. For example, each observation may result from an expensive experimental procedure. A consumer group that estimates the mean deceleration rate of the human body during an automobile collision by crashing cars with dummies into a concrete wall at 30 miles per hour would probably not want to crash a large sample of cars so they can get a narrow confidence interval!

If n must be small, how does that affect the validity of the confidence interval methods? The t methods for a mean are valid *for any n.* When n is small, though, you need to be extra cautious to look for extreme outliers or great departures from the normal population assumption (such as implied by highly skewed data). These can affect the results and the validity of using the mean as a summary of center.

For the confidence interval formula for a proportion, we've seen that we need at least 15 successes and at least 15 failures. Why? Otherwise, the central limit theorem no longer applies. The numbers of successes and failures must both be at least 15 for the normal distribution to approximate well the binomial distribution or the sampling distribution of a sample proportion (as discussed in Chapter 7). An even more serious difficulty is that the standard deviation of the sample proportion depends on the parameter we're trying to estimate. If the estimate $\hat{p}$ is far from the true p, as often happens for small n, then the estimate $se = \sqrt{\hat{p}(1-\hat{p})/n}$ of the standard deviation of the sample proportion may also be far off. As a result, the confidence interval formula works poorly, as we'll see in the next example.

Example 10

Small sample CI ◀

Proportion of University Students Who Own an MP3 Player

Picture the Scenario

For a statistics class project, a student randomly selected and interviewed 20 students at his university to estimate the proportion of students who own an MP3 player. Each of the 20 students interviewed owned one.

Question to Explore

What does a 95% confidence interval reveal about the proportion of students at the university who own an MP3 player?

Think It Through

Let p denote the proportion of students at the university who own an MP3 player. The sample proportion from the interviews was $\hat{p} = 20/20 = 1.0$. When $\hat{p} = 1.0$, then

$$se = \sqrt{\hat{p}(1-\hat{p})/n} = \sqrt{1.0(0.0)/20} = 0.0.$$

The 95% confidence interval for the proportion of students at the university who own an MP3 player is

$$\hat{p} \pm z(se) = 1.0 \pm 1.96(0.0),$$

which is 1.0 ± 0.0, or (1.0, 1.0). This investigation told the student that he can be 95% confident that p falls between 1 and 1, that is, that $p = 1$. He was surprised by this result. It seemed unrealistic to conclude that *every* student at the university owns an MP3 player.

Insight

Do you trust this inference? Just because everyone in a small sample owns an MP3 player, would you conclude that everyone in the much larger population owns one? We doubt it. Perhaps the population proportion p is close to 1, but it is almost surely not exactly equal to 1.

The confidence interval formula $\hat{p} \pm z\sqrt{\hat{p}(1-\hat{p})/n}$ is valid only if the sample contains at least 15 individuals who own an MP3 player and 15 individuals who don't. The sample did not contain at least 15 individuals who don't, so we have to use a different method. See the following section.

▶ ***Try Exercise 8.56, parts a–c***

Confidence Interval for a Proportion with Small Samples

Constructing a Small-Sample Confidence Interval for a Proportion p

Suppose a random sample does *not* have at least 15 successes and 15 failures. The confidence interval formula $\hat{p} \pm z\sqrt{\hat{p}(1-\hat{p})/n}$ still is valid if we use it after adding 2 to the original number of successes and 2 to the original number of failures. This results in adding 4 to the sample size n.

The sample of size $n = 20$ in Example 10 contained 20 individuals who owned an MP3 player and 0 who did not. We can apply the confidence interval formula with $20 + 2 = 22$ individuals who own an MP3 player and $0 + 2 = 2$ who do not. The value of the sample size for the formula is then $n = 24$. *Now we can use the formula, even though we don't have at least 15 individuals who do not own an MP3 player.* We get

$$\hat{p} = 22/24 = 0.917,\ se = \sqrt{\hat{p}(1-\hat{p})/n} = \sqrt{(0.917)(0.083)/24} = 0.056.$$

The resulting 95% confidence interval is

$$\hat{p} \pm 1.96(se), \text{ which is } 0.917 \pm 1.96(0.056), \text{ or } (0.807, 1.027).$$

A proportion cannot be greater than 1, so we report the interval as (0.807, 1.0). We can be 95% confident that the proportion of individuals at the university who own an MP3 player is at least 0.807.

This approach enables us to use a large-sample method even when the sample size is small. With it, the point estimate moves the sample proportion a bit toward 1/2 (e.g., from 1.0 to 0.917). This is particularly helpful when the ordinary sample proportion is 0 or 1, which we would not usually expect to be a believable estimate of a population proportion. Why do we add 2 to the counts of the two types? The reason is that the resulting confidence interval is then close to a confidence interval based on a more complex method (described in Exercise 8.125) that does not require estimating the standard deviation of a sample proportion.[8]

Finally, a word of caution: In the estimation of parameters, "margin of error" refers to the size of error resulting from having data from a random sample rather than the population—what's called *sampling error.* This is the error that the sampling distribution describes in showing how close the estimate is likely to fall to the parameter. But that's not the only source of potential error. Data may be missing for a lot of the target sample; some observations may be recorded incorrectly by the data collector; and some subjects may not tell the truth. When errors like these occur, the actual confidence level may be much lower than advertised. Be skeptical about a claimed margin of error and confidence level unless you know that the study was well conducted and these other sources of error are negligible.

[8]See article by A. Agresti and B. Coull (who proposed this small-sample confidence interval), *The American Statistician*, vol. 52, pp. 119–126, 1998.

8.4 Practicing the Basics

8.47 South Africa study The researcher planning the study in South Africa also will estimate the population proportion having at least a high school education. No information is available about its value. How large a sample size is needed to estimate it to within 0.07 with 95% confidence?

8.48 Binge drinkers TRY A study at the Harvard School of Public Health found that 44% of 10,000 sampled college students were binge drinkers. A student at the University of Minnesota plans to estimate the proportion of college students at that school who are binge drinkers. How large a random sample would she need to estimate it to within 0.05 with 95% confidence, if before conducting the study she uses the Harvard study results as a guideline?

8.49 Abstainers TRY The Harvard study mentioned in the previous exercise estimated that 19% of college students abstain from drinking alcohol. To estimate this proportion in your school, how large a random sample would you need to estimate it to within 0.05 with probability 0.95, if before conducting the study

a. You are unwilling to guess the proportion value at your school?

b. You use the Harvard study as a guideline?

c. Use the results from parts a and b to explain why strategy (a) is inefficient if you are quite sure you'll get a sample proportion that is far from 0.50.

8.50 How many businesses fail? A study is planned to estimate the proportion of businesses started in the year 2006 that had failed within five years of their start-up. How large a sample size is needed to guarantee estimating this proportion correct to within

a. 0.10 with probability 0.95?

b. 0.05 with probability 0.95?

c. 0.05 with probability 0.99?

d. Compare sample sizes for parts a and b, and b and c, and summarize the effects of decreasing the margin of error and increasing the confidence level.

8.51 Canada and the death penalty A poll in Canada in 1998 indicated that 48% of Canadians favor imposing the death penalty (Canada does not have it). A report by Amnesty International on this and related polls (www.amnesty.ca) did not report the sample size but stated, "Polls of this size are considered to be accurate within 2.5 percentage points 95% of the time." About how large was the sample size?

8.52 Farm size An estimate is needed of the mean acreage of farms in Ontario, Canada. A 95% confidence interval should have a margin of error of 25 acres. A study 10 years ago in this province had a sample standard deviation of 200 acres for farm size.

a. About how large a sample of farms is needed?

b. A sample is selected of the size found in part a. However, the sample has a standard deviation of 300 acres rather than 200. What is the margin of error for a 95% confidence interval for the mean acreage of farms?

8.53 Income of Native Americans TRY How large a sample size do we need to estimate the mean annual income of Native Americans in Onondaga County, New York, correct to within \$1000 with probability 0.99? No information is available to us about the standard deviation of their annual income. We guess that nearly all of the incomes fall between \$0 and \$120,000 and that this distribution is approximately bell shaped.

8.54 Population variability Explain the reasoning behind the following statement: "In studies about a very diverse population, large samples are often necessary, whereas for more homogeneous populations smaller samples are often adequate." Illustrate for the problem of estimating mean income for all medical doctors in the United States compared to estimating mean income for all entry-level employees at McDonald's restaurants in the United States.

8.55 Web survey to get large *n* A newspaper wants to gauge public opinion about legalization of marijuana. The sample size formula indicates that it need a random sample of 875 people to get the desired margin of error. But surveys cost money, and it can only afford to randomly sample 100 people. Here's a tempting alternative: If it places a question about that issue on its website, it will get more than 1000 responses within a day at little cost. Is it better off with the random sample of 100 responses or the website volunteer sample of more than 1000 responses? (*Hint:* Think about the issues discussed in Section 4.2 about proper sampling of populations.)

8.56 Do you like tofu? TRY You randomly sample five students at your school to estimate the proportion of students who like tofu. All five students say they like it.

a. Find the sample proportion who like it.

b. Find the standard error. Does its usual interpretation make sense?

c. Find a 95% confidence interval, using the large-sample formula. Is it sensible to conclude that *all* students at your school like tofu?

d. Why is it not appropriate to use the ordinary large-sample confidence interval in part c? Use a more appropriate approach and interpret the result.

8.57 Alleviate PMS? A pharmaceutical company proposes a new drug treatment for alleviating symptoms of PMS (premenstrual syndrome). In the first stages of a clinical trial, it was successful for 7 out of 10 women.

a. Construct an appropriate 95% confidence interval for the population proportion.

b. Is it plausible that it's successful for only half the population? Explain.

8.58 Google Glass TRY Google started selling Google Glass (a type of wearable technology that projects information onto the eye) in the United States in spring 2014 for

\$1500. A national poll reveals that out of 500 people sampled, nobody owned Google Glass.

a. Find the sample proportion who don't own Google Glass and its standard error.

b. Find a 95% confidence interval, using the large-sample formula. Is it sensible to conclude that no one in the United States owns Google Glass?

c. Why is it not appropriate to use the ordinary large-sample confidence interval in part b? Use a more appropriate approach and interpret the result.

d. Is it plausible to say that fewer than 1% of the population own Google Glass? Explain.

8.5 Using Computers to Make New Estimation Methods Possible

We've seen how to construct point and interval estimates of a population proportion and a population mean. Confidence intervals are relatively simple to construct for these parameters. For other parameters, it's not so easy because it's difficult to derive the sampling distribution or the standard error of a point estimate. We'll now introduce a relatively new simulation method for constructing a confidence interval that statisticians often use for such cases.

The Bootstrap: Using Simulation to Construct a Confidence Interval

When it is difficult to derive a standard error or a confidence interval formula that works well, you can "pull yourself up by your bootstraps" to attack the problem without using mathematical formulas. A recent computational invention, called the **bootstrap**, does just that.

The bootstrap is a simulation method that resamples from the observed data. It treats the data distribution as if it were the population distribution. You resample, *with replacement, n* observations from the data distribution. Each of the original n data points has probability $1/n$ for being selected as one of the "new" observations in the bootstrap sample. For this new sample of size n, you construct the point estimate of the parameter. You then resample another set of n observations from the original data distribution and construct another value of the point estimate. In the same way, you repeat this resampling process (using a computer) from the original data distribution a very large number of times, for instance, selecting 10,000 separate samples of size n and calculating 10,000 corresponding values of the point estimate.

The variability of the 10,000 resampled point estimates provides information about the accuracy of the original point estimate. For instance, a 95% confidence interval for the parameter is the 95% central set of the resampled point estimate values. These are the ones that fall between the 2.5th percentile and 97.5th percentile of those values.

Example 11

Bootstrap

How Variable Are Your Weight Readings on a Scale?

Picture the Scenario

Instruments used to measure physical characteristics such as weight and blood pressure do not give the same value every time they're used in a given situation. The measurements vary. One of the authors recently bought a scale

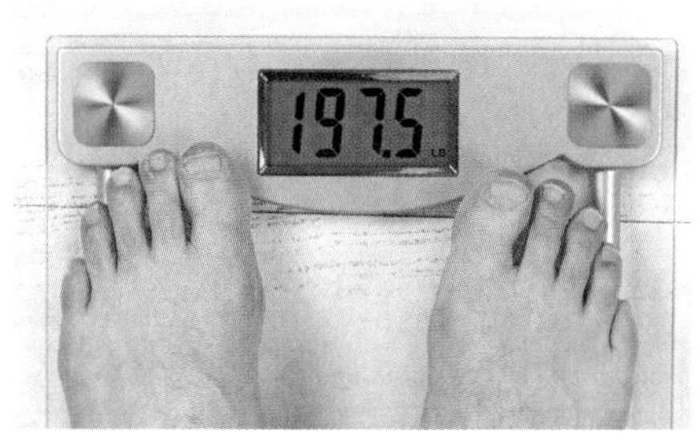

(called Thinner) that is supposed to give precise weight readings. To investigate how much the weight readings tend to vary, he weighed himself ten times, taking a 30-second break after each trial to allow the scale to reset. He got the following values (in pounds):

160.2, 160.8, 161.4, 162.0, 160.8, 162.0, 162.0, 161.8, 161.6, 161.8.

These 10 trials have a mean of 161.44 and standard deviation of 0.63.

Because weight varies from trial to trial, it has a probability distribution. You can regard this distribution as describing long-run population values that you would get if you could conduct a huge number of weight trials. The sample mean and standard deviation estimate the center and variability of the distribution. Ideally, you would like the scale to be precise and give the same value every time. Then the population standard deviation would be 0.0, but it's not that precise in practice.

How could we get a confidence interval for the population standard deviation? The sample standard deviation s has an approximate normal sampling distribution for very large n. However, its standard error is highly sensitive to any assumption we make about the shape of the population distribution. It is safer to use the bootstrap method to construct a confidence interval.

Question to Explore

Using the bootstrap method, find a 95% confidence interval for the population standard deviation.

Think It Through

We sample from a distribution that has probability 1/10 at each of the values in the sample. For each new observation in our bootstrap sample, this corresponds to selecting a random number between 1 and 10, and making the observation 160.2 if the random number is 1, 160.8 if it is 2, ..., and 161.8 if it is 10. This entire process of obtaining a bootstrap resample can be done with software or a web app. The bootstrap with 100,000 resamples of the data uses the following steps (as illustrated in the margin figure):

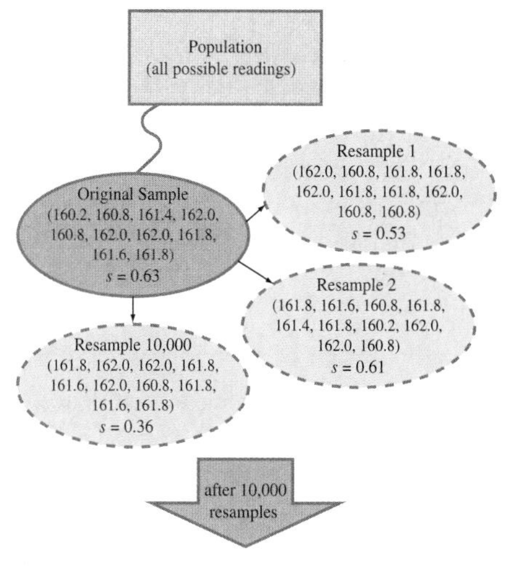

- Randomly sample 10 observations from this sample data distribution. This corresponds to randomly sampling with replacement 10 of the original 10 observations (see the bubble labeled Resample 1). We did this and got

  162.0, 160.8, 161.8, 161.8, 162.0, 161.8, 161.8, 162.0, 160.8, 160.8

  For these 10 observations, the sample standard deviation is $s = 0.53$.
- Repeat the preceding step 100,000 times, each time obtaining a resample of size 10 and computing s. This gives us 100,000 values of the sample standard deviation. Figure 8.11 shows a histogram of their values.
- Now identify the middle 95% of these 100,000 sample standard deviation values. For the 100,000 samples we took, the 2.5th percentile was 0.26 and the 97.5th percentile was 0.80. In other words, 95% of the resamples had sample standard deviation values between 0.26 and 0.80. This is our 95% bootstrap confidence interval for the population standard deviation.

In summary, the 95% confidence interval for σ is (0.26, 0.80). A typical deviation of a weight reading from the mean might be rather large, nearly a pound.

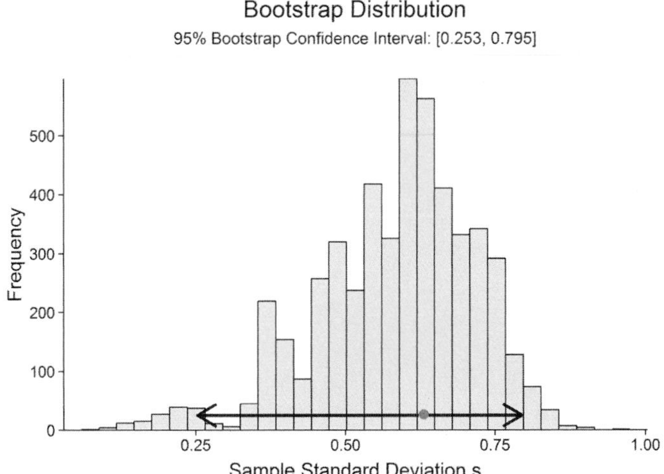

▲ Figure 8.11 A Bootstrap Frequency Distribution of Standard Deviation Values. These were obtained by taking 100,000 samples of size 10 each from the sample data distribution. **Questions** Does the sampling distribution of the sample standard deviation look approximately normal? What is the practical reason for using the bootstrap method?

Insight

Figure 8.11 is skewed and is quite irregular. This appearance is because of the small sample size ($n = 10$). Such simulated distributions take a more regular shape when n is large, usually becoming symmetric and bell shaped when n is sufficiently large.

▶ ***Try Exercise 8.60***

With modern computing power, methods such as the bootstrap (and others that will be introduced in Chapters 10 and 11) are now used to conduct inference when it is difficult to find a theoretical sampling distribution. Although a computer or specialized software is needed to implement these methods, they have the advantage of relying on fewer assumptions for their validity. For instance, the bootstrap can also be used to find a confidence interval for a population mean. When the assumption about approximate normality is in doubt, it presents an alternative method to the interval based on the t distribution.

▶ Activity 3

Bootstrap Confidence Interval for the Mean

The Bootstrap web app available on the book's website allows you to obtain bootstrap confidence intervals for selected parameters such as the mean, median or standard deviation. Access the app through the book's website and

- replicate the analysis of Example 11 finding a confidence interval for the standard deviation
- use the data from Example 11 to find a bootstrap confidence interval for the population mean. Does the simulated bootstrap distribution of $\bar{x}$ resemble the approximate normal shape of the sampling distribution of $\bar{x}$ for large samples?

Try Exercise 8.61 ◀

8.5 Practicing the Basics

8.59 Why bootstrap? Explain the purpose of using the bootstrap method.

8.60 Estimating variability Refer to Example 11 about weight readings of a scale. For 10 successive trials on the next day, the weight values were

TRY TECH

159.8, 159.8, 159.6, 159.0, 158.4
159.2, 158.8, 158.4, 158.8, 159.0.

a. Explain the steps of how you could use the bootstrap method to get a 95% confidence interval for the true standard deviation of weight measurements taken with this scale.

b. Use the Bootstrap web app accessible from the book's website to find the 95% bootstrap confidence interval. (See Activity 3.)

8.61 Bootstrap interval for the mean In 2014, the General Social Survey interviewed 1399 randomly selected U.S. residents about how much time per week they spent surfing the web. The responses revealed a very right-skewed distribution, with a sample mean of 12 hours and a standard deviation of 15 hours, indicating that the population distribution is very far from normal. Should we be worried that one of the assumptions for using the t confidence interval from Section 8.3 for the population mean is violated? Let's find the bootstrap confidence interval for the population mean. The data from the survey are available from the book's website under the name "wwwhours".

TRY TECH

a. Draw a histogram and find the sample mean and median time people spent surfing the web per week

b. Find a 95% confidence interval for the mean time using the t interval from Section 8.3.

c. Explain the steps of how you would obtain a 95% bootstrap confidence interval for the mean time.

d. Use the Bootstrap web app mentioned in Activity 3 or other software to find the 95% bootstrap confidence interval for the mean. (If you are using the web app, you can open the dataset in a spreadsheet and then copy and paste the values for the variable "hours" into the text field of the web app.)

e. The results from both approaches are virtually identical. Look at the bootstrap distribution of $\bar{x}$ displayed in the web app or other software. Is it surprising that it looks approximately normal? What theorem predicted this shape?

8.62 Bootstrap interval for the proportion We want a 90% confidence interval for the population proportion of students in a high school in Dallas, Texas, who can correctly find Iraq on an unlabeled globe. For a random sample of size 50, 5 get the correct answer.

TECH

a. Access the Sampling Distribution of the Sample Proportion web app from the book's website and set the population proportion to $p = 0.1$, pretending that the population proportion is equal to the sample proportion $(10/50 = 0.1)$. Generate one random sample of size $n = 50$ and find the sample proportion of correct answers.

b. Take 1,000 resamples like the one in part a (just click the 1,000 option) and find the 5th and 95th percentiles of the simulated sampling distribution. (*Note:* Click Find Percentile to find the percentiles.) This is the 90% bootstrap confidence interval for p.

c. Explain why the sample proportion does not fall exactly in the middle of the bootstrap confidence interval. (*Hint:* Is the sampling distribution symmetric or skewed?)

Chapter Review

ANSWERS TO THE CHAPTER FIGURE QUESTIONS

Figure 8.1 A point estimate alone will not tell us how close the estimate is likely to be to the parameter.

Figure 8.2 When the size of the random sample is relatively large, by the central limit theorem.

Figure 8.3 We don't know the value of p, the population proportion, to form the interval $p \pm 1.96(se)$. The population proportion p is what we're trying to estimate.

Figure 8.4 Having greater confidence means that we want to have greater assurance of a correct inference. Thus, it is natural that we would expect a wider interval of believable values for the population parameter.

Figure 8.5 The $\hat{p}$ values falling in the darker shaded left and right tails of the bell-shaped curve.

Figure 8.6 This skew should not affect the validity of the confidence interval for the mean because of the large sample size $(n = 1298)$, i.e., the CLT kicks in.

Figure 8.7 Using Table B or Table 8.5, $t = 1.96$ when $df = \infty$ with right-tail probability $= 0.025$.

Figure 8.8 $z = -1.96$ and $z = 1.96$, $t = -3.707$, and $t = 3.707$.

Figure 8.9 A stem and leaf plot or, probably less informative, a histogram.

Figure 8.10 The sample size n is sufficiently large that $np \geq 15$, and $n(1 - p) \geq 15$.

Figure 8.11 No, it is left skewed. The central limit theorem only applies for large sample sizes (here n is only 10) and for the distribution of the sample mean, not for the sample standard deviation. The bootstrap method is used when it is difficult to derive a standard deviation of a statistic or confidence interval formula by using mathematical techniques.

SUMMARY OF NOTATION

se = standard error

$\hat{p}$ = sample proportion

m = margin of error

$t_{.025}$ = *t*-score with right-tail probability 0.025 and two-tail probability 0.05

df = degrees of freedom ($= n - 1$ for inference about a mean)

CHAPTER SUMMARY

We've now learned how to **estimate** the population proportion p for categorical variables and the population mean μ for quantitative variables.

- An estimate of the population mean μ is the sample mean $\bar{x}$. An estimate of the population proportion p is the sample proportion $\hat{p}$. A **point estimate** (or **estimate**, for short) is our best guess for the unknown parameter value.
- A **confidence interval** contains the most plausible values for a parameter. Confidence intervals for most parameters have the form

$$\text{Estimate} \pm \text{margin of error},$$

$$\text{which is estimate} \pm (z\text{- or } t\text{-score}) \times (se),$$

  where *se* is the standard error of the estimate. The *se*, in turn, is the estimated standard deviation of the sampling distribution of the point estimate.
- For the proportion, the **score** is a *z*-score from the normal distribution. For the mean, the score is a *t*-score from the ***t* distribution** with degrees of freedom $\boldsymbol{df = n - 1}$. The *t*-score is similar to a *z*-score when $df >= 30$. Table 8.6 summarizes the point and interval estimation methods.
- The *z*- or *t*-score depends on the **confidence level**, the probability that the method produces a confidence interval that contains the population parameter value. For instance, the probability that the sample proportion $\hat{p}$ falls within 1.96 standard errors of the true proportion p is 0.95, so we use $z = 1.96$ for 95% confidence, we use $z = 1.96$ for 95% confidence. *To achieve greater confidence, we make the sacrifice of a larger margin of error and wider confidence interval.*
- For estimating a **proportion**, the formulas rely on the central limit theorem. For large random samples, this guarantees that the sample proportion has a normal sampling distribution. For estimating a proportion with small samples (fewer than 15 successes or fewer than 15 failures), the confidence interval formula $\hat{p} \pm z(se)$ still produces valid results if we use it after adding 2 successes and 2 failures (and add 4 to n).
- For estimating a **mean**, the ***t* distribution** accounts for the extra variability due to using the sample standard deviation s to estimate the population standard deviation in finding a standard error. The t method assumes that the population distribution is normal. This ensures that the sampling distribution of $\bar{x}$ is normal. This assumption is mainly important for small n, because when n is large the central limit theorem guarantees that the sampling distribution is normal. However, even for small n, the method is **robust** against departures from the normal assumption as long as there are no extreme outliers.
- Before conducting a study, we can **determine the sample size *n*** having a certain margin of error. Table 8.6 shows the sample size formulas. To use them, we must (1) select the margin of error m, (2) select the confidence level, which determines the *z*-score or *t*-score, and (3) guess the value the data will likely produce for the sample standard deviation s (to estimate a population mean) or the sample proportion $\hat{p}$ (to estimate a population proportion). In the latter case, substituting $\hat{p} = 0.50$ guarantees that the sample size is large enough regardless of the value the sample has for $\hat{p}$.

Table 8.6 Estimation Methods for Means and Proportions

Parameter	Point Estimate	Standard Error	Confidence Interval	Sample Size for Margin of Error m
Proportion p	$\hat{p}$	$se = \sqrt{\hat{p}(1-\hat{p})/n}$	$\hat{p} \pm z(se)$	$n = [\hat{p}(1-\hat{p})z^2]/m^2$
Mean μ	$\bar{x}$	$se = s/\sqrt{n}$	$\bar{x} \pm t(se)$	$n = (\sigma^2 z^2)/m^2$

Note: The *z*- or *t*-score depends on the confidence level. The *t*-score has $df = n - 1$.

CHAPTER PROBLEMS

Practicing the Basics

8.63 Unemployed college grads The U.S Bureau of the Census reports that based on data from the American Community Survey in 2012, 3.6 percent of all college graduates between the ages of 25 and 64 were unemployed. A larger percentage of men than women were unemployed: 3.7 percent and 3.5 percent, respectively.

a. Are these point estimates or interval estimates?

b. Is the information given here sufficient for you to construct confidence intervals for the unemployment rate of males and females? Why or why not?

8.64 Approval rating for president In July 2014, midway through his second term as president, Gallup estimated Obama's approval rate at 42%. According to gallup.com,

"... [R]esults are based on telephone interviews with approximately 1,500 national adults; margin of error is ±3 percentage points." How could you explain the meaning of this to someone who has not taken a statistics course?

8.65 British monarchy After the British monarchy celebrated its diamond jubilee in 2012, a July poll conducted by YouGov.com and the *Sunday Times* of 1,667 British residents showed that 86% think the Queen personally has done a good job during her time on the throne, and 73% think that Britain should continue to have a monarchy. If the sample was random, find the 95% margin of error for each of these estimated proportions.

8.66 Born again A poll of a random sample of $n = 2000$ Americans by the Pew Research Center (www.people-press.org) indicated that 36% considered themselves born-again or evangelical Christians. How would you explain to someone who has not studied statistics:

a. What it means to call this a *point estimate*?

b. Why this does not mean that *exactly* 36% of *all* Americans consider themselves to be born-again or evangelical Christians?

8.67 Life after death The variable POSTLIFE in the 2012 General Social Survey asked, "Do you believe in life after death?" A report based on these data stated that "81% of Americans believe in life after death. The margin of error for this result is plus or minus 1.8%." Explain how you could form a 95% confidence interval using this information and interpret that confidence interval in context.

8.68 Female belief in life after death Refer to the previous exercise. The following printout shows results for the females in the sample, where $X =$ the number answering yes. Explain how to interpret each item, in context.

```
Sample    X    N    Sample p         95% CI
1        822  977   0.841351   (0.818442, 0.864260)
```

8.69 Vegetarianism *Time* magazine (July 15, 2002) quoted a poll of 10,000 Americans in which only 4% said they were vegetarians.

a. What has to be assumed about this sample to construct a confidence interval for the population proportion of vegetarians?

b. Construct a 99% confidence interval for the population proportion. Explain why the interval is so narrow, even though the confidence level is high.

c. In interpreting this confidence interval, can you conclude that fewer than 10% of Americans are vegetarians? Explain your reasoning.

8.70 Alternative therapies The Department of Public Health at the University of Western Australia conducted a survey in which they randomly sampled general practitioners (GP) in Australia. One question asked whether the GP had ever studied alternative therapy, such as acupuncture, hypnosis, homeopathy, and yoga. Of 282 respondents, 132 said yes. Is the interpretation, "We are 95% confident that the percentage of all GPs in Australia who have ever studied alternative therapy equals 46.8%" correct or incorrect? Explain.

8.71 Population data You would like to find the proportion of bills passed by Congress that were vetoed by the president in the last congressional session. After checking congressional records, you see that for the population of all 40 bills passed, 15 were vetoed. Does it make sense to construct a confidence interval using these data? Explain. (*Hint:* Identify the sample and population.)

8.72 Wife supporting husband Consider the statement that it is better for the man to work and the woman to tend the home, from the GSS (variable denoted FEFAM).

TECH

a. Go to the sda.berkeley.edu/GSS website. Find the number who agreed or strongly agreed with that statement and the sample size for the year 2008.

b. Find the sample proportion and standard error.

c. Find a 99% confidence interval for the population proportion who would agree or strongly agree, and interpret it.

8.73 Legalize marijuana? The General Social Survey has asked respondents, "Do you think the use of marijuana should be made legal or not?" Go to the GSS website, sda.berkeley.edu/GSS. For the 2008 survey with variable GRASS:

TECH

a. Of the respondents, how many said "legal" and how many said "not legal"? Report the sample proportions.

b. Is there enough evidence to conclude whether a majority or a minority of the population support legalization? Explain your reasoning.

c. Now look at the data on this variable for all years by entering YEAR as the column variable. Describe any trend you see over time in the proportion favoring legalization.

8.74 Smoking A report in 2004 by the U.S. National Center for Health Statistics provided an estimate of 20.4% for the percentage of Americans over the age of 18 who were currently smokers. The sample size was 30,000. Assuming that this sample has the characteristics of a random sample, a 99.9% confidence interval for the proportion of the population who were smokers is (0.20, 0.21). When the sample size is extremely large, explain why even confidence intervals with large confidence levels are narrow.

8.75 Streaming A Harris Poll of 2300 U.S. adults surveyed online in April 2014 reports that 43% regularly watch television shows through streaming. (*Source:* "Cable Is King but Streaming Stands Strong When It Comes to Americans' TV Viewing Habits," available at harrisinteractive.com)

a. Find a 95% confidence interval and interpret it in context.

b. Would a 99% confidence interval result in a wider or narrower interval? Explain.

c. If the survey had found the 43% streaming based on a survey including 5000 adults (instead of 2300), would the interval be wider or narrower compared to the one in part a? Explain.

8.76 Edward Snowden A report from the Pew Research Center found that disclosures by former National Security Administration (NSA) contractor Edward Snowden about NSA spying have damaged one major element of America's global image: its reputation for protecting individual liberties. One question in the report asked, "Do you think the government of the U.S. respects the personal freedoms of its people?" (*Source:* Pew Research Center, July 2014, "Global Opposition to U.S. Surveillance and Drones, But Limited Harm to America's Image.")

a. Of 1000 adults surveyed in the United Kingdom, 65% said yes, resulting in a 99% confidence interval of (0.61, 0.69). **True or false:** The confidence interval means that we can be 99% confident that between 61% and 69% of the population of the United Kingdom believes that the U.S. government respects the personal freedoms of its people.

b. Of 1000 adults surveyed in Germany, 58% said yes, resulting in a 99% confidence interval of (0.54, 0.62). **True or false:** The confidence interval means that we can be 99% confident that of 1000 Germans sampled, between 540 and 620 of them think the U.S. government respects the personal freedom of its people.

8.77 More NSA spying Refer to the previous exercise.

a. Of the 1001 adults surveyed in Turkey, 49% said yes to the question from the Pew Research Center, resulting in a 95% confidence interval of (0.46, 0.52). **True or false:** We can be 95% confident that less than half of Turkey's population thinks the U.S. government respects the personal freedoms of its people.

b. In Brazil in 2013 (before the revelations by Ed Snowden), about 76% believed the U.S. government respects personal freedom, but of 1003 adults surveyed in Brazil in 2014, 51% do so, resulting in a 95% confidence interval of (0.48, 0.54). **True or false:** There is evidence that the opinion of Brazilians on the U.S. government respecting personal freedom has dropped from 2013 levels.

8.78 Grandpas using e-mail When the GSS asked in 2012, "About how many hours per week do you spend sending and answering e-mail?" the nine males in the sample of age at least 80 responded:

0, 0, 0, 1, 2, 3, 4, 4, 13

a. The TI-83+/84 screen shot shows results of a statistical analysis for finding a 90% confidence interval. Explain what each line represents.

b. Verify the computation of the interval and interpret it.

c. Explain why the population distribution may be skewed right. If this is the case, is the interval you obtained in part b useless, or is it still valid? Explain.

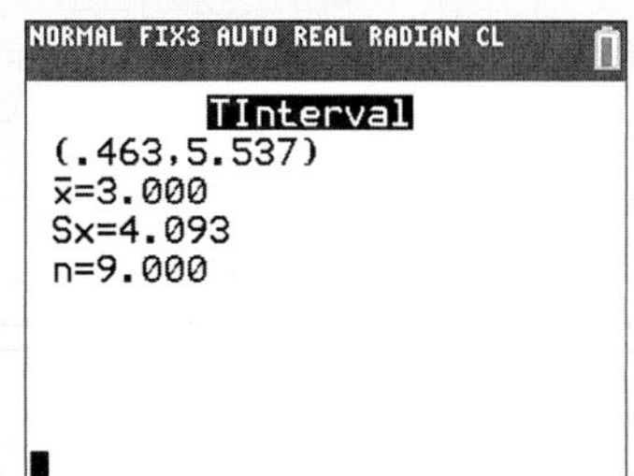

8.79 Travel to work As part of the 2000 census, the Bureau of the Census surveyed 700,000 households to study transportation to work. It reported that 76.3% drove alone to work, 11.2% carpooled, 5.1% took mass transit, 3.2% worked at home, 0.4% bicycled, and 3.8% took other means.

a. With such a large survey, explain why the margin of error for any of these values is extremely small.

b. The survey also reported that the mean travel time to work was 24.3 minutes, compared to 22.4 minutes in 1990. Explain why this is not sufficient information to construct a confidence interval for the population mean. What else would you need?

8.80 *t*-scores

a. Show how the *t*-score for a 95% confidence interval changes as the sample size increases from 10 to 20 to 30 to infinity.

b. What does the answer in part a suggest about how the *t* distribution compares to the standard normal distribution?

8.81 Fuel efficiency TECH The government website fueleconomy.gov has data on thousands of cars regarding their fuel efficiency. A random sample from this website of SUVs manufactured between 2012 and 2015 gives the following data on the combined (city and highway) miles per gallon (mpg):

26, 23, 21, 23, 19, 29, 15, 26, 19, 26.

a. Construct an appropriate plot (or plots) to check the distributional assumption for computing a *t* interval for the mean mpg for SUVs. Comment briefly.

b. Find and interpret a 95% confidence interval for the mean mpg for SUVs manufactured between 2012 and 2015.

8.82 Psychologists' income In 2003, the American Psychological Association conducted a survey (at research.apa.org) of a random sample of psychologists to estimate mean incomes for psychologists with various academic degrees and levels of experience. Of the 31 psychologists who received a masters degree in 2003, the mean income was $43,834 with a standard deviation of $16,870.

a. Construct a 95% confidence interval for the population mean. Interpret.

b. What assumption about the population distribution of psychologists' incomes does the confidence interval method make?

c. If the assumption about the shape of the population distribution is not valid, does this invalidate the results? Explain.

8.83 More psychologists Refer to the previous exercise. Interpret each item on the following printout that software reports for psychologists with a doctorate but with less than one year of experience.

```
Variable   N    Mean  StDev  SE Mean      95.0% CI
income   190  49411  15440   1120.1  (47204, 51618)
```

8.84 How long lived in town? The General Social Survey has asked subjects, "How long have you lived in the city, town, or community where you live now?" The responses of 1415 subjects in one survey had a mode of less than 1 year, a median of 16 years, a mean of 20.3, and a standard deviation of 18.2.

a. Do you think that the population distribution is normal? Why or why not?

b. Based on your answer in part a, can you construct a 95% confidence interval for the population mean? If not, explain why not. If so, do so and interpret.

8.85 How often do women feel sad? A recent GSS asked, "How many days in the past seven days have you felt sad?" The 816 women who responded had a median of 1, mean of 1.81, and standard deviation of 1.98. The 633 men who responded had a median of 1, mean of 1.42, and standard deviation of 1.83.

a. Find a 95% confidence interval for the population mean for women. Interpret.

b. Do you think that this variable has a normal distribution? Does this cause a problem with the confidence interval method in part a? Explain.

8.86 How often feel sad? Refer to the previous exercise. This question was asked of 10 students in a class at the University of Wisconsin recently. The responses were

0, 0, 1, 0, 7, 2, 1, 0, 0, 3.

Find and interpret a 90% confidence interval for the population mean and indicate what you would have to assume for this inference to apply to the population of all University of Wisconsin students.

8.87 TECH **Happy often?** The 1996 GSS asked, "How many days in the past seven days have you felt happy?" (This was the most recent year this question was posed.)

a. Using the GSS variable HAPFEEL, verify that the sample had a mean of 5.27 and a standard deviation of 2.05. What was the sample size?

b. Find the standard error for the sample mean.

c. Stating assumptions, construct and interpret a 95% confidence interval for the population mean. Can you conclude that the population mean is at least 5.0?

8.88 TECH **Revisiting mountain bikes** Use the Mountain Bike data file on the book's website, shown also below.

a. Form a 95% confidence interval for the population mean price of all mountain bikes. Interpret.

b. What assumptions are made in forming the interval in part a? State at least one important assumption that does not seem to be satisfied and indicate its impact on this inference.

Mountain Bikes

Brand and Model	Price($)
Trek VRX 200	1000
Cannondale SuperV400	1100
GT XCR-4000	940
Specialized FSR	1100
Trek 6500	700
Specialized Rockhop	600
Haro Escape A7.1	440
Giant Yukon SE	450
Mongoose SX 6.5	550
Diamondback Sorrento	340
Motiv Rockridge	180
Huffy Anorak 36789	140

8.89 TECH **eBay selling prices** For eBay auctions of the Samsung S5 16GB smartphone (unlocked and in new condition), a sample was taken in July 2014 where the Buy It Now prices were (in dollars):

549, 600, 560, 519, 535, 570, 600, 625, 640, 550, 575, 600

a. Explain what a parameter might represent that you could estimate with these data.

b. Find the point estimate of μ.

c. Find the standard deviation of the data and the standard error of the sample mean. Interpret each.

d. Find the 95% confidence interval for μ. Interpret the interval in context.

8.90 TECH **Income for families in public housing** A survey is taken to estimate the mean annual family income for families living in public housing in Chicago. For a random sample of 29 families, the annual incomes (in hundreds of dollars) are as follows:

90 77 100 83 64 78 92 73 122 96 60 85 86 108 70
139 56 94 84 111 93 120 70 92 100 124 59 112 79

a. Construct a box plot of the incomes. What do you predict about the shape of the population distribution? Does this affect the possible inferences?

b. Using software, find point estimates of the mean and standard deviation of the family incomes of all families living in public housing in Chicago.

c. Obtain and interpret a 95% confidence interval for the population mean.

8.91 Females watching TV The GSS asked in 2008, "On the average day about how many hours do you personally watch television?" Software reports the results for females,

```
Variable  N   Mean   St Dev  SE Mean      95% CI
TV       698 3.080  2.700   0.102   (2.879, 3.281)
```

a. Would you expect that TV watching has a normal distribution? Why or why not?

b. On what assumptions is the confidence interval shown based? Are any of them violated here? If so, is the reported confidence interval invalid? Explain.

c. What's wrong with the interpretation, "In the long run, 95% of the time females watched between 2.88 and 3.28 hours of TV a day."

8.92 Males watching TV Refer to the previous exercise. The 626 males had a mean of 2.87 and a standard deviation of 2.61. The 95% confidence interval for the population mean is (2.67, 3.08). Interpret in context.

8.93 Working mother In response to the statement on a recent General Social Survey, "A preschool child is likely to suffer if his or her mother works," suppose the response categories (strongly agree, agree, disagree, strongly disagree) had counts (104, 370, 665, 169). Scores $(2, 1, -1, -2)$ were assigned to the four categories to treat the variable as quantitative. Software reported

```
Variable    N    Mean  St Dev SE Mean        95% CI
Response 1308 -0.325  1.234   0.034  (-0.392, -0.258)
```

a. Explain what this choice of scoring assumes about relative distances between categories of the scale.

b. Based on this scoring, how would you interpret the sample mean of -0.325?

c. Explain how you could also make an inference about proportions for these data.

8.94 Miami spring break For a trip to Miami, Florida, over spring break 2014, the following data (obtained from travelocity.com) are a random sample of hotel prices per night (in $) for a double room:

TECH

239 237 245 310 218 175 330 196 178

245 255 190 330 124 162 190 386 145.

a. Construct a histogram and box plot and comment on the shape of the distribution.

b. Find a 95% confidence interval for the mean price and interpret.

c. Are you concerned that any assumptions about the interval in part b might be violated?

8.95 Sex partners in previous year The 2008 General Social Survey asked respondents how many sex partners they had in the previous 12 months (variable PARTNERS). Software summarizes the results of the responses by

```
Variable  N    Mean   StDev  SE Mean      95% CI
partners 1766 1.1100 1.2200 0.0290  (1.0531, 1.1669)
```

a. Based on the reported sample size and standard deviation, verify the reported value for the standard error.

b. Based on these results, explain why the distribution was probably skewed to the right.

c. Explain why the skew need not cause a problem with constructing a confidence interval for the population mean unless there are extreme outliers such as a reported value of 1000.

8.96 Men don't go to the doctor A survey of 1084 men age 18 and older in 1998 for the Commonwealth Fund (www.cmwf.org) indicated that more than half did not have a physical exam or a blood cholesterol test in the past year. A medical researcher plans to sample men in her community randomly to see whether similar results occur. How large a random sample would she need to estimate this proportion to within 0.05 with probability 0.95?

8.97 Driving after drinking In December 2004, a report based on the National Survey on Drug Use and Health estimated that 20% of all Americans of ages 16 to 20 drove under the influence of drugs or alcohol in the previous year (AP, December 30, 2004). A public health unit in Wellington, New Zealand, plans a similar survey for young people of that age in New Zealand. It wants a 95% confidence interval to have a margin of error of 0.04.

a. Find the necessary sample size if the New Zealand public health unit expects results similar to those in the United States.

b. Suppose that in determining the sample size, it uses the safe approach that sets $\hat{p} = 0.50$ in the formula for n. Then, how many records need to be sampled? Compare this to the answer in part a. Explain why it is better to make an educated guess about what to expect for $\hat{p}$ when possible.

8.98 Changing views of United States The June 2003 report on *Views of a Changing World*, conducted by the Pew Global Attitudes Project (www.people-press.org), discussed changes in views of the United States by other countries. In the largest Muslim nation, Indonesia, a poll conducted in May 2003 after the Iraq war began reported that 83% had an unfavorable view of America, compared to 36% a year earlier. The 2003 result was claimed to have a margin of error of 3 percentage points. How can you approximate the sample size the study was based on?

8.99 Mean property tax A tax assessor wants to estimate the mean property tax bill for all homeowners in Madison, Wisconsin. A survey 10 years ago got a sample mean and standard deviation of $1400 and $1000.

a. How many tax records should the tax assessor randomly sample for a 95% confidence interval for the mean to have a margin of error equal to $100? What assumption does your solution make?

b. In reality, suppose that it would now get a standard deviation equal to $1500. Using the sample size you derived in part a, without doing any calculation, explain whether the margin of error for a 95% confidence interval would be less than $100, equal to $100, or more than $100.

c. Refer to part b. Would the probability that the sample mean falls within $100 of the population mean be less than 0.95, equal to 0.95, or greater than 0.95? Explain.

8.100 Accept a credit card? A bank wants to estimate the proportion of people who would sign up for a credit card if it sends a particular mailing advertising it. For a trial mailing to a random sample of 100 potential customers, 0 people accept the offer. Can the bank conclude that fewer than 10% of their population of potential customers would take the credit card? Answer by finding an appropriate 95% confidence interval.

8.101 Kicking accuracy A football coach decides to estimate the kicking accuracy of a player who wants to join the team. Of 10 extra-point attempts, the player makes all 10.

a. Find an appropriate 95% confidence interval for the probability that the player makes any given extra point attempt.

b. What's the lowest value that you think is plausible for that probability?

c. How would you interpret the random sample assumption in this context? Describe a scenario in which it would not be sensible to treat these 10 kicks as a random sample.

Concepts and Investigations

8.102 Religious beliefs A column by *New York Times* columnist Nicholas Kristof (August 15, 2003) discussed results of polls indicating that religious beliefs in the United States tend to be quite different from those in other Western nations. He quoted recent Gallup and Harris polls of random samples of about 1000 Americans estimating that 83% believe using the Virgin Birth of Jesus but only 28% believe in evolution. A friend of yours is skeptical, claiming that it's impossible to predict beliefs of over 200 million adult Americans by interviewing only 1000 of them. Write a one-page report using this context to show how you could explain about random sampling, the margin of error, and how a margin of error depends on the sample size.

8.103 TV watching and race For the number of hours of TV watching, the 2008 GSS reported a mean of 2.98 for the 1324 white subjects, with a standard deviation of 2.66. The mean was 4.38 for the 188 black subjects, with a standard deviation of 3.58. Analyze these data, preparing a short report in which you mention the methods used and the assumptions on which they are based, and summarize and interpret your findings.

8.104 Housework and gender Using data from the National Survey of Families and Households, a study (from S. South and G. Spitze, *American Sociological Review*, vol. 59, 1994, pp. 327–347) reported the descriptive statistics in the following table for the hours spent on housework. Analyze these data. Summarize results in a short report, including assumptions you made to perform the inferential analyses.

Gender	Sample Size	Mean	Std Dev
Men	4252	18.1	12.9
Women	6764	32.6	18.2

8.105 Women's role opinions When subjects in a recent GSS were asked whether they agreed with the following statements, the (yes, no) counts under various conditions were as follows:

- Women should take care of running their homes and leave running the country up to men: (275, 1556).
- It is better for everyone involved if the man is the achiever outside the home and the woman takes care of the home and the family: (627, 1208).
- A preschool child is likely to suffer if his or her mother works: (776, 1054).

Analyze these data. Prepare a one-page report stating assumptions, showing results of description and inference, and summarizing conclusions.

8.106 Types of estimates An interval estimate for a mean is more informative than a point estimate, because with an interval estimate you can figure out the point estimate, but with the point estimate alone you have no idea how wide the interval estimate is. Explain why this statement is correct, illustrating using the reported 95% confidence interval of (4.0, 5.6) for the mean number of dates in the previous month based on a sample of women at a particular college.

8.107 Width of a confidence interval Why are confidence intervals wider when we use larger confidence levels but narrower when we use larger sample sizes, other things being equal?

8.108 99.9999% confidence Explain why confidence levels are usually large, such as 0.95 or 0.99, but not extremely large, such as 0.999999. (*Hint:* What impact does the extremely high confidence level have on the margin of error?)

8.109 Need 15 successes and 15 failures To use the large-sample confidence interval for p, you need at least 15 successes and 15 failures. Show that the smallest value of n for which the method can be used is (a) 30 when $\hat{p} = 0.50$, (b) 50 when $\hat{p} = 0.30$, (c) 150 when $\hat{p} = 0.10$. That is, the overall n must increase as $\hat{p}$ moves toward 0 or 1. (When the true proportion is near 0 or 1, the sampling distribution can be highly skewed unless n is quite large.)

8.110 Outliers and CI For the observations 618, 650, 608, 634, 675, 618, 625, 619, 630 on Buy It Now prices for the iPhone 5s on eBay considered in Exercise 8.35, a confidence interval for the population mean Buy It Now price on eBay is (615, 647). Suppose the 5th observation was actually 875 instead of 675. What would have been obtained for the 95% confidence interval? Compare to the original interval. How does this warn you about potential effects of outliers when you construct a confidence interval for a mean?

TECH

8.111 What affects n? Using the sample size formula $n = [\hat{p}(1 - \hat{p})z^2]/m^2$ for a proportion, explain the effect on n of (a) increasing the confidence level and (b) decreasing the margin of error.

8.112 Multiple choice: CI property Increasing the confidence level causes the margin of error of a confidence interval to **(a)** increase, **(b)** decrease, **(c)** stay the same.

8.113 Multiple choice: CI property 2 Other things being equal, increasing n causes the margin of error of a confidence interval to **(a)** increase, **(b)** decrease, **(c)** stay the same.

8.114 Multiple choice: Number of close friends Based on responses of 1467 subjects in a General Social Survey, a 95% confidence interval for the mean number of close friends equals (6.8, 8.0). Which *two* of the following interpretations are correct?

a. We can be 95% confident that $\bar{x}$ is between 6.8 and 8.0.

b. We can be 95% confident that μ is between 6.8 and 8.0.

c. Ninety-five percent of the values of X = number of close friends (for this sample) are between 6.8 and 8.0.

d. If random samples of size 1467 were repeatedly selected, then 95% of the time $\bar{x}$ would be between 6.8 and 8.0.

e. If random samples of size 1467 were repeatedly selected, then in the long run 95% of the confidence intervals formed would contain the true value of μ.

8.115 Multiple choice: Why z? The reason we use a z-score from a normal distribution in constructing a large-sample confidence interval for a proportion is that

a. For large random samples the sampling distribution of the sample proportion is approximately normal.

b. The population distribution is normal.

c. For large random samples the data distribution is approximately normal.

d. For any n we use the t distribution to get a confidence interval, and for large n the t distribution looks like the standard normal distribution.

8.116 Mean age at marriage A random sample of 50 records yields a 95% confidence interval of 21.5 to 23.0 years for the mean age at first marriage of women in a certain county. Explain what is wrong with each of the following interpretations of this interval.

a. If random samples of 50 records were repeatedly selected, then 95% of the time the sample mean age at first marriage for women would be between 21.5 and 23.0 years.

b. Ninety-five percent of the ages at first marriage for women in the county are between 21.5 and 23.0 years.

c. We can be 95% confident that $\bar{x}$ is between 21.5 and 23.0 years.

d. If we repeatedly sampled the entire population, then 95% of the time the population mean would be between 21.5 and 23.5 years.

8.117 Interpret CI For the previous exercise, provide the proper interpretation.

8.118 True or false Suppose a 95% confidence interval for the population proportion of students at your school who regularly drink alcohol is (0.61, 0.67). The inference is that you can be 95% confident that the sample proportion falls between 0.61 and 0.67.

8.119 True or false The confidence interval for a mean with a random sample of size $n = 2000$ is invalid if the population distribution is bimodal.

8.120 True or false If you have a volunteer sample instead of a random sample, then a confidence interval for a parameter is still completely reliable as long as the sample size is larger than about 30.

8.121 True or false Quadrupling the sample size n cuts the margin of error into half, other things being equal.

8.122 Women's satisfaction with appearance A special issue of *Newsweek* in March 1999 on women and their health reported results of a poll of 757 American women aged 18 or older. When asked, "How satisfied are you with your overall physical appearance?" 30% said very satisfied, 54% said somewhat satisfied, 13% said not too satisfied, and 3% said not at all satisfied. **True or false:** Since all these percentages are based on the same sample size, they all have the same margin of error.

8.123 Opinions over time about the death penalty ◆◆ For many years, the General Social Survey has asked respondents whether they favor the death penalty for persons convicted of murder. Support has been quite high in the United States, one of few Western nations that currently has the death penalty. The following figure uses the 26 General Social Surveys taken between 1975 and 2012 and plots the 95% confidence intervals for the population proportion in the United States who supported the death penalty in each of the 26 years of these surveys.

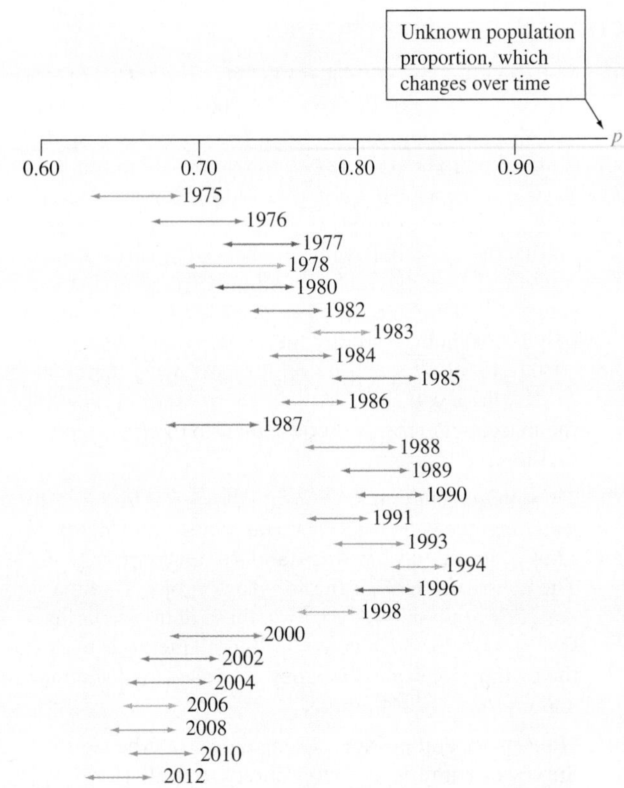

Twenty-six 95% confidence intervals for the population proportions supporting the death penalty.

a. When we say we have "95% confidence" in the interval for a particular year, what does this mean?

b. For 95% confidence intervals constructed using data for 26 years, let X = the number of the intervals that contain the true parameter values. Find the probability that $x = 26$, that is, all 26 inferences are correct. (*Hint:* You can use the binomial distribution to answer this.)

c. Refer to part b. Find the mean of the probability distribution of X.

d. What could you do differently so it is more likely that all 26 inferences are correct?

8.124 Why called "degrees of freedom"? ◆◆ You know the sample mean $\bar{x}$ of n observations. Once you know $(n - 1)$ of the observations, show that you can find the remaining one. In other words, for a given value of $\bar{x}$, the values of $(n - 1)$ observations determine the remaining one. In summarizing scores on a quantitative variable, having $(n - 1)$ *degrees of freedom* means that only that many observations are independent. (If you have trouble with this, try to show it for $n = 2$, for instance showing that if you know that $\bar{x} = 80$ and you know that one observation is 90, then you can figure out the other observation. The *df* value also refers to the divisor in $s^2 = \Sigma(x - \bar{x})^2/(n - 1)$.)

8.125 An alternative interval for the population proportion ◆◆ The large-sample confidence interval for a proportion substitutes $\hat{p}$ for the unknown value of p in the formula for the standard deviation of $\hat{p}$. An alternative method to form a 95% confidence interval determines the endpoints of the interval by finding the values for p that are 1.96 standard deviations from the sample proportion, without a need to estimate the standard deviation. To do this, you solve for p in the equation

$$|\hat{p} - p| = 1.96\sqrt{p(1 - p)/n}.$$

This interval is known as the (Wilson) score confidence interval for a proportion.

a. For Example 10 with no students without an MP3 player in a sample of size 20, substitute $\hat{p}$ and n in this equation and show that the equation is satisfied at $p = 0.83337$ and at $p = 1$. So the confidence interval is (0.83887,1), compared to (1, 1) with $\hat{p} \pm 1.96(se)$.

b. Which confidence interval seems more believable? Why?

8.126 ◆◆ ***m* and *n*** Consider the sample size formula $n = [\hat{p}(1 - \hat{p})z^2]/m^2$ for estimating a proportion. When $\hat{p}$ is close to 0.50, for 95% confidence explain why this formula gives roughly $n = 1/m^2$.

8.127 ◆◆ **Median as point estimate** When the population distribution is normal, the population mean equals the population median. How good is the sample median as a point estimate of this common value? For a random sample, the standard error of the sample median equals $1.25(s/\sqrt{n})$. If the population is normal, explain why the sample mean tends to be a better estimate than the sample median. (*Note:* Both estimators are unbiased.)

Student Activities

8.128 ◆◆ **Randomized response** To encourage subjects to make honest responses on sensitive questions, the method of *randomized response* is often used. Let's use your class to estimate the proportion who have had alcohol at a party. Before carrying out this method, the class should discuss what they would guess for the value of the proportion of students in the class who have had alcohol at a party. Come to a class consensus. Now each student should flip a coin in secret. If it is a head, toss the coin once more and report the outcome, head or tails. If the first flip is a tail, report instead the response to whether you have had alcohol, reporting the response *head* if the true response is yes and reporting the response *tail* if the true response is no. Let p denote the true probability of the *yes* response on the sensitive question.

a. Explain why the numbers in the following table are the probabilities of the four possible outcomes.

b. Let $\hat{q}$ denote the sample proportion of subjects who report *head* for the second response. Explain why we can set $\hat{q} = 0.25 + p/2$ and hence use $\hat{p} = 2\hat{q} - 0.5$ to estimate p.

c. Using this approach with your class, estimate the probability of having had alcohol at a party. Is it close to the class guess?

Table for Randomized Response

	Second Response	
First Coin	**Head**	**Tail**
Head	0.25	0.25
Tail	$p/2$	$(1 - p)/2$

8.129 TECH **GSS project** The instructor will assign the class a theme to study. Download recent results for variables relating to that theme from sda.berkeley.edu/GSS. Find and interpret confidence intervals for relevant parameters. Prepare a two-page report summarizing results.

CHAPTER

9

The confidence intervals introduced in the previous chapter estimate a range of plausible values for an unknown population parameter. To test the plausibility of statements, called hypotheses, about these parameters, this chapter introduces the second major tool of statistical inference: significance tests. The so-called P-value computed from such tests indicates whether the data support a certain hypothesis.

Statistical Inference: Significance Tests About Hypotheses

Example 1

Are Astrology Predictions Better than Guessing?

Picture the Scenario

Astrologers believe that the positions of the planets and the moon at the moment of your birth determine your personality traits. But have you ever seen any scientific evidence that astrology works? One scientific test of astrology used the following experiment: Each of 116 volunteers was asked to give his or her date and time of birth. From this information, an astrologer prepared each subject's horoscope based on the positions of the planets and the moon at the moment of birth. Each volunteer also filled out a California Personality Index survey. Then the birth data and horoscope for one subject, together with the results of the personality survey for that individual and for two other participants randomly selected from the experimental group, were given to an astrologer. The astrologer was asked to predict which of the three personality charts matched the birth data and horoscope for the subject.[1]

Let p denote the probability of a correct prediction by an astrologer. Suppose an astrologer actually has no special predictive powers, as would be expected by those who view astrology as "quack science." The predictions then merely correspond to random guessing, that is, picking one of the three personality charts at random, so $p = 1/3$. However, the participating astrologers claimed that $p > 1/3$. They felt they could predict better than with random guessing.

Questions to Explore

- How can we use data from such an experiment to summarize the evidence about the claim by the astrologers?
- How can we decide, based on the data, whether the claim is plausible?

[1]S. Carlson, *Nature*, vol. 318, pp. 419–425, 1985.

Thinking Ahead

In this chapter, we'll learn how to use inferential statistics to answer such questions. We will use an inferential method called a **significance test** to analyze evidence in favor of the astrologers' claim. We'll analyze data from the astrology experiment, referring to a population proportion in Examples 3, 5, and 12.

To illustrate a significance test about a population mean, we use data on weight gain in anorexic girls. In an experiment with a cognitive therapy, girls had an average weight gain of 3 pounds. Does this support the claim that the therapy is effective? We will analyze such a claim in Example 8.

The significance test is the second major method for conducting statistical inference about a population. Like a confidence interval for estimating a parameter (the first major method), the significance test uses probability to quantify how plausible a parameter value is while controlling the chance of an incorrect inference. With significance tests, we'll be able to use data to answer questions such as:

- Does a proposed diet truly result in weight loss, on average?
- Is there evidence of discrimination against women in promotion decisions?
- Does one advertising method result in better sales, on average, than another advertising method?

9.1 Steps for Performing a Significance Test

The main goal of many research studies is to check whether the data support certain statements or predictions. These statements are **hypotheses** about a population. They are usually expressed in terms of population parameters for variables measured in the study.

Hypothesis

In statistics, a **hypothesis** is a statement about a population, usually claiming that a population parameter takes a particular numerical value or falls in a certain range of values.

For instance, the parameter might be a population proportion or a probability. Here's an example of a hypothesis for the astrology experiment in Example 1:

Hypothesis: Using a person's horoscope, the probability p that an astrologer can correctly predict which of three personality charts applies to that person equals $1/3$. In other words, astrologers' predictions correspond to random guessing.

A *significance test* (or "test" for short) is a method for using data to summarize the evidence about a hypothesis. For instance, if a high proportion of the astrologers' predictions are correct, the data might provide strong evidence against the hypothesis that $p = 1/3$ and in favor of an alternative hypothesis representing the astrologers' claim that $p > 1/3$.

Before conducting a significance test, we identify the variable measured and the population parameter of interest. For a categorical variable, the parameter is typically a proportion, and for a quantitative variable the parameter is typically a mean. Section 9.2 shows the details for tests about proportions. Section 9.3 presents tests about means.

The Steps of a Significance Test

A significance test has five steps. In this section, we introduce the general ideas behind these steps.

Step 1: Assumptions

Each significance test makes certain assumptions or has certain conditions under which it applies. Foremost, a test assumes that the data production used randomization. Other assumptions may be about the sample size or about the shape of the population distribution.

Step 2: Hypotheses

Each significance test has two hypotheses about a population parameter: the null hypothesis and an alternative hypothesis.

In Words

H_0: null hypothesis (read as "H zero" or "H naught")
H_a: alternative hypothesis (read as "H a")
In everyday English, "null" is an adjective meaning "of no consequence or effect, amounting to nothing."

Null Hypothesis, Alternative Hypothesis

The **null hypothesis** is a statement that the parameter takes a particular value.
The **alternative hypothesis** states that the parameter falls in some alternative range of values.
The value in the null hypothesis usually represents *no effect.* The value in the alternative hypothesis then represents an effect of some type.
The symbol $\mathbf{H_0}$ denotes the **null hypothesis** and the symbol $\mathbf{H_a}$ denotes the **alternative hypothesis.**

For the experiment in Example 1, consider the hypothesis, "Based on any person's horoscope, the probability p that an astrologer can correctly predict which of three personality charts applies to that person equals $1/3$." This hypothesis states that there is *no effect* in the sense that an astrologer's predictive power is no better than random guessing. This is a *null hypothesis.* It is symbolized by H_0: $p = 1/3$. If it is true, any difference that we observe between the sample proportion of correct guesses and $1/3$ is due merely to ordinary sampling variability. The *alternative hypothesis* states that there *is* an effect—an astrologer's predictions are *better* than random guessing. It is symbolized by H_a: $p > 1/3$.

A null hypothesis has a *single* parameter value, such as H_0: $p = 1/3$. An alternative hypothesis has a *range* of values that are alternatives to the one in H_0, such as H_a: $p > 1/3$ or H_a: $p \neq 1/3$. You formulate the hypotheses for a significance test *before* viewing or analyzing the data.

Example 2

Null and alternative hypotheses

Fracking

Picture the Scenario

Through the use of fracking, a drilling method that uses high-pressure water and chemicals to extract oil and natural gas from underground rock formations, the United States has become the largest oil producer in the world. Despite its economic benefits, fracking is becoming more and more controversial due to its potential effects on the environment, and some U.S. states and other countries have already banned it. What does the public think about fracking? Let's investigate whether those who oppose the increased use of fracking in the United States are still in the minority. Let p denote the proportion of people in the United States who oppose the increased use of fracking.

Questions to Explore

Consider the claim, "In the United States, the proportion of people who oppose the increased use of fracking is less than 0.50; i.e., they are in the minority."

a. Is this a null or an alternative hypothesis?

b. How can we express the hypothesis that the population proportion opposed to fracking may actually be 0.50?

Think It Through

a. When those opposing the increased use of fracking are in the minority, $p < 0.50$. This is an *alternative* hypothesis—H_a: $p < 0.50$. It specifies a range of potential values for the population proportion, all less than 0.50.

b. The hypothesis stating that the population proportion of those supporting fracking is less than 0.50 is an alternative to the null hypothesis that it may be 0.50. This null hypothesis is formulated as H_0: $p = 0.50$. It specifies a single value for the parameter p. Here, "no effect" means an equal proportion of people are either in opposition to or in support of fracking.

► ***Try Exercises 9.1 and 9.2***

In a significance test, the null hypothesis is presumed to be true unless the data give strong evidence against it. The burden of proof falls on the researcher who claims the alternative hypothesis is true. In the astrology study, we assume that $p = 1/3$ (i.e., astrologers are just guessing) unless the data provide strong evidence against it and in favor of the astrologers' claim that $p > 1/3$. In the fracking study, we will assume that an equal proportion (i.e., 0.50) opposes or supports fracking until data provide enough evidence that, in fact, the proportion opposing it is less than 0.50. An analogy may be found in a courtroom trial, in which a jury must decide the guilt or innocence of a defendant. The null hypothesis, corresponding to no effect, is that the defendant is innocent. The alternative hypothesis is that the defendant is guilty. The jury presumes the defendant is innocent unless the prosecutor can provide strong evidence that the defendant is guilty beyond a reasonable doubt. The burden of proof is on the prosecutor to convince the jury that the defendant is guilty.

In Words

The courtroom provides an analogy for a significance test. H_0 is that the defendant is innocent. H_a is that the defendant is guilty. The jury presumes H_0 to be true unless the evidence (data) suggests otherwise.

Step 3: Test Statistic

The parameter to which the hypotheses refer has a point estimate. A **test statistic** describes how far that point estimate falls from the parameter value given in the null hypothesis. Usually this distance is measured by the number of standard errors between the point estimate and the parameter.

For instance, consider the null hypothesis H_0: $p = 1/3$ that, based on a person's horoscope, the probability p that an astrologer can correctly predict which of three personality charts belongs to that person equals $1/3$. For the experiment described in Example 1, 40 of 116 predictions were correct. The estimate of the probability p is the sample proportion, $\hat{p} = 40/116 = 0.345$. The test statistic compares this point estimate to the value in the null hypothesis $(p = 1/3)$, using a z-score that measures the number of standard errors that the estimate falls from the null hypothesis value of $1/3$.

Recall

The **standard error** of a point estimate is what we use in practice to describe the variability of the sampling distribution of that point estimate (Section 8.2). Denoted by *se*, it is used both in confidence intervals and in significance tests. ◄

Step 4: P-Value

To interpret a test statistic value, we use a probability summary of the evidence against the null hypothesis, H_0. Here's how we get it: We presume that H_0 is true, since the burden of proof is on the alternative, H_a. Then we consider the sorts of values we'd expect to get for the test statistic, according to its sampling distribution presuming H_0 is true. If the test statistic falls well out in a tail of the sampling distribution, it is far from what H_0 predicts. If H_0 were true, such a value would be unusual.

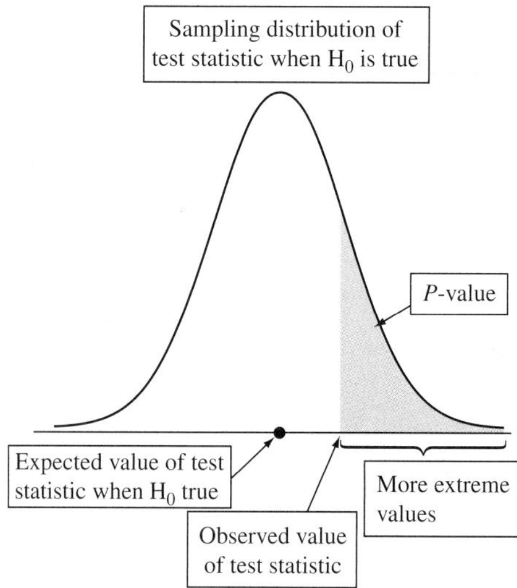

▲ **Figure 9.1 Suppose H_0 Were True. The P-value Is the Probability of a Test Statistic Value Like the Observed One or Even More Extreme.** This is the shaded area in the tail of the sampling distribution. **Question** Which gives stronger evidence against the null hypothesis, a P-value of 0.20 or of 0.01? Why?

When there are a large number of possible values for the test statistic, any single one may be unlikely, so we summarize how far out in the tail the test statistic falls by the tail probability of the observed value and values even more extreme (meaning, even farther from what H_0 predicts). See Figure 9.1. This probability is called a **P-value**. The smaller the P-value, the stronger the evidence is against H_0.

In Words

The **P-value** is a tail probability, beyond the observed test statistic value if we presume $\mathbf{H_0}$ is true. Smaller P-values provide stronger evidence against the null hypothesis.

P-value

The **P-value** is the probability that the test statistic equals the observed value or a value even more extreme. It is calculated by presuming that the null hypothesis H_0 is true.

In the astrology study, suppose the P-value is small, such as 0.01. This means that if H_0 were true (that an astrologer's predictions correspond to just random guessing), it would be unusual (rather unlikely) to get sample data such as we observed. Such a P-value provides strong evidence against the null hypothesis of random guessing and in support of the astrologers' claim. On the other hand, if the P-value is not near 0, the data are consistent with H_0. For instance, a P-value such as 0.26 or 0.63 indicates that if the astrologers were actually randomly guessing, the observed data would not be unusual and any difference from the hypothesized value of $p = 1/3$ could be attributed to just random variation.

Step 5: Conclusion

The conclusion of a significance test reports the P-value and *interprets* what it says about the question that motivated the test. Sometimes this includes a decision about the validity of the null hypothesis H_0. For instance, based on the P-value, can we reject H_0 and conclude that astrologers' predictions are better than random guessing? As we'll discuss in the next section, we can reject H_0 in favor of H_a only when the P-value is very small, such as 0.05 or less.

SUMMARY: The Five Steps of a Significance Test

1. **Assumptions**

   First, specify the variable and parameter. The assumptions commonly pertain to the method of data production (randomization), the sample size, and the shape of the population distribution.

2. **Hypotheses**
State the null hypothesis, H_0 (a single parameter value, usually describing no effect), and the alternative hypothesis, H_a (a set of alternative parameter values) that usually describes some sort of claim.
3. **Test statistic**
The test statistic measures the distance between the point estimate of the parameter and its null hypothesis value, usually by the number of standard errors between them.
4. **P-value**
The P-value is the probability that the test statistic takes the observed value or a value more extreme if we presume H_0 is true. Smaller P-values represent stronger evidence against H_0.
5. **Conclusion**
Report and interpret the P-value in the context of the study. Based on the P-value, make a decision about H_0 (either reject or do not reject H_0) if a decision is needed.

9.1 Practicing the Basics

9.1 **H_0 or H_a?** For parts a and b, is the statement a null hypothesis, or an alternative hypothesis?
TRY
- **a.** In Canada, the proportion of adults who favor legalized gambling equals 0.50.
- **b.** The proportion of all Canadian college students who are regular smokers is less than 0.24, the value it was 10 years ago.
- **c.** Introducing notation for a parameter, state the hypotheses in parts a and b in terms of the parameter values.

9.2 **H_0 or H_a?** For each of the following, is the statement a null hypothesis or an alternative hypothesis? Why?
TRY
- **a.** The mean IQ of all students at Lake Wobegon High School is higher than 100.
- **b.** The probability of rolling a 6 with a particular die equals 1/6.
- **c.** The proportion of all new business enterprises that remain in business for at least five years is less than 0.50.

9.3 **Burden of proof** For a new pesticide, should the Environmental Protection Agency (EPA) bear the burden of proof to show that it is harmful to the environment, or should the producer of the pesticide have to show that it is not harmful to the environment? The pesticide is considered harmful if its toxicity level exceeds a certain threshold and not harmful if its toxicity level is below the threshold. Consider the statements, "The mean toxicity level equals the threshold," "The mean toxicity level exceeds the threshold," and "The mean toxicity level is below the threshold."
- **a.** Which of these statements should be the null and which the alternative hypothesis when the burden of proof is on the EPA to show that the new pesticide is harmful?
- **b.** Which of these statements should be the null and which the alternative hypothesis when the burden of proof is on the producer to show that the new pesticide is not harmful?

9.4 **Financial aid** The average financial aid package for students admitted at Williams College in 2010 was $44,000. A student organization plans to investigate whether this average has changed for students admitted in 2016. Define the population parameter of interest and state the null and alternative hypotheses for this investigation.

9.5 **Low-carbohydrate diet** A study plans to have a sample of obese adults follow a proposed low-carbohydrate diet for three months. The diet imposes limited eating of starches (such as bread and pasta) and sweets, but otherwise no limit on calorie intake. Consider the hypothesis,

The population mean of the values of weight change (= weight at start of study − weight at end of study) is larger than zero.

- **a.** Is this a null or an alternative hypothesis? Explain your reasoning.
- **b.** Define a relevant parameter and express the hypothesis that the diet has no effect in terms of that parameter. Is it a null or an alternative hypothesis?

9.6 **Examples of hypotheses** Give an example of a null hypothesis and an alternative hypothesis about a (a) population proportion and (b) population mean.

9.7 **Proper hypotheses?** Explain what is wrong with each set of null and alternative hypotheses shown. Then, correct each to form a proper set of hypotheses.
- **a.** H_0: $\hat{p} = 0.50$, H_a: $\hat{p} > 0.50$
- **b.** H_0: $\mu = 100$, H_a: $\mu = 200$
- **c.** H_0: $p = 0.30$, H_a: $p > 0.10$

9.8 **z test statistic** To test H_0: $p = 0.50$ that a population proportion equals 0.50, the test statistic is a z-score that measures the number of standard errors between the sample proportion and the H_0 value of 0.50. If $z = 3.6$, do the data support the null hypothesis, or do they give strong evidence against it? Explain.

9.9 **P-value** Indicate whether each of the following P-values gives strong evidence or not especially strong evidence against the null hypothesis.
- **a.** 0.38
- **b.** 0.001

9.2 Significance Tests About Proportions

For categorical variables, the parameters of interest are the population proportions in the categories. We'll use the astrology study to illustrate a significance test for population proportions.

Example 3

Hypotheses for a significance test

Are Astrologers' Predictions Better than Guessing?

Picture the Scenario

Many people take astrological predictions seriously, but there has never been any scientific evidence that astrology works. One scientific test of astrology used the experiment mentioned in Example 1: For each of 116 adult volunteers, an astrologer prepared a horoscope based on the positions of the planets and the moon at the moment of the person's birth. Each adult subject also filled out a California Personality Index (CPI) survey. For a given adult, his or her birth data and horoscope were shown to one of the participating astrologers in the experiment, together with the results of the personality survey for that adult and for two other adults randomly selected from the experimental group. The astrologer was asked which personality chart of the three subjects was the correct one for that adult, based on the horoscope.

The 28 participating astrologers were randomly chosen from a list prepared by the National Council for Geocosmic Research (NCGR), an organization dealing with astrology and respected by astrologers worldwide. The NCGR sampling frame consisted of astrologers with some background in psychology who were familiar with the CPI and who were held in high esteem by their astrologer peers. The experiment was double-blind; each subject was identified by a random number, and neither the astrologers nor the experimenter knew which number corresponded to which subject. The chapter of the NCGR that recommended the participating astrologers claimed that the probability of a correct guess on any given trial in the experiment was larger than $1/3$, the value for random guessing. (In fact, they felt that it would exceed $1/2$.)

Question to Explore

Put this investigation in the context of a significance test by stating the parameter of interest and the null and alternative hypotheses.

Think It Through

The variable specifying the outcome of any given trial in the experiment is categorical. The categories are correct prediction and incorrect prediction. For each person, let p denote the probability of a correct prediction by the astrologer. We can regard this as the population proportion of correct guesses for the population of people and population of astrologers from which the study participants were sampled. Hypotheses refer to the probability p of a correct prediction. With random guessing, $p = 1/3$. If the astrologers can predict better than random guessing, then $p > 1/3$. To test the hypothesis of random guessing against the astrologers' claim that $p > 1/3$, we would test H_0: $p = 1/3$ against H_a: $p > 1/3$.

Insight

In the experiment, the astrologers were correct with 40 of their 116 predictions. We'll see how to use these data to test these hypotheses as we work through the five steps of a significance test for a proportion in the next subsection.

▶ *Try Exercises 9.10 and 9.11*

Steps of a Significance Test About a Population Proportion

This section presents a significance test about a population proportion that applies with relatively large samples. Here are the five steps of the test:

Step 1: Assumptions

- The variable is categorical.
- The data are obtained using randomization (such as a random sample or a randomized experiment).
- The sample size is sufficiently large that the sampling distribution of the sample proportion $\hat{p}$ is approximately normal. The approximate normality happens when the *expected numbers of successes and failures are both at least 15, using the null hypothesis value for p.*

Recall

Section 7.1 introduced the sampling distribution of a sample proportion. It has mean p and standard deviation

$$\sqrt{p(1-p)/n}$$

and is well approximated by the normal distribution when

$np \geq 15$ and $n(1-p) \geq 15$. ◀

The sample size guideline is the one we used in Chapter 6 for judging when the normal distribution approximates the binomial distribution well. For the astrology experiment with $n = 116$ trials, when H_0 is true that $p = 1/3$, we expect $116(1/3) = 38.7 \approx 39$ correct guesses and $116(2/3) = 77.3 \approx 77$ incorrect guesses. Both of these are above 15, so the sample size guideline is satisfied.

As with other statistical inference methods, if randomization is not used, the validity of the results is questionable. A survey should use random sampling. An experiment should use principles of randomization and blinding with the study subjects, as was done in the astrology study. In that study, the astrologers were randomly selected, but the subjects evaluated were people (mainly students) who volunteered for the study. Consequently, any inference applies to the population of astrologers but only to the particular subjects in the study. If the study could have chosen the subjects randomly as well, then the inference would extend more broadly to *all* people.

Step 2: Hypotheses

The null hypothesis of a test about a proportion has the form

$$H_0: p = p_0,$$

In Words

p_0 is read as "p-zero" (or as "p-naught") and is the hypothesized value of the population proportion under the null hypothesis

where p_0 represents a particular proportion value between 0 and 1. In Example 3, the null hypothesis of no effect states that the astrologers' predictions correspond to random guessing. This is H_0: $p = 1/3$. The null hypothesis value p_0 is $1/3$.

The alternative hypothesis refers to alternative parameter values from the number in the null hypothesis. One possible alternative hypothesis has the form

$$H_a: p > p_0.$$

One-sided $H_a: p > 1/3$

H_0 at 1/3; H_a from 1/3 to 1.0 on the p axis (0.0, 1/3, 1.0)

This is used when a test is designed to detect whether p is *larger* than the number in the null hypothesis. In the astrology experiment, the astrologers claimed they could predict *better* than by random guessing. Their claim corresponds to H_a: $p > 1/3$. This is called a **one-sided** alternative hypothesis because it has values falling only on one side of the null hypothesis value. (See margin figure.) We'll use this H_a below. The other possible one-sided alternative hypothesis is H_a: $p < p_0$, such as H_a: $p < 1/3$.

Two-sided $H_a: p \neq 1/3$

A **two-sided** alternative hypothesis has the form

$$H_a: p \neq p_0.$$

It includes *all* the other possible values, both below and above the value p_0 in H_0. It states that the population proportion *differs* from the number in the null hypothesis. An example is $H_a: p \neq 1/3$, which states that the population proportion equals some number other than $1/3$. (See margin figure.)

In summary, for Example 3 we used $H_0: p = 1/3$ and the one-sided $H_a: p > 1/3$.

Step 3: Test Statistic

The test statistic measures how far the sample proportion $\hat{p}$ falls from the null hypothesis value p_0, relative to what we'd expect if H_0 were true. The sampling distribution of the sample proportion has mean equal to the population proportion p and standard deviation equal to $\sqrt{p(1-p)/n}$. When H_0 is true, $p = p_0$, so the sampling distribution has mean p_0 and standard error $se_0 = \sqrt{p_0(1-p_0)/n}$. (We use the zero subscript here on *se* to reflect using the value p_0 rather than $\hat{p}$ for estimating p in the standard error because we're presuming H_0 to be true in conducting the test.) The test statistic is

$$z = \frac{\hat{p} - p_0}{se_0} = \frac{\hat{p} - p_0}{\sqrt{\dfrac{p_0(1-p_0)}{n}}} = \frac{\text{Sample proportion} - \text{Value of proportion under } H_0}{\text{Standard error when null hypothesis is true}}$$

Recall

The standard error estimates the standard deviation of the sampling distribution of $\hat{p}$. Here in the context of a significance test, we are estimating how much $\hat{p}$ would tend to vary from sample to sample of size n if the null hypothesis were true. ◀

This z-score measures the number of standard errors between the sample proportion $\hat{p}$ and the null hypothesis value p_0.

In testing $H_0: p = 1/3$ for the astrology experiment with $n = 116$ trials, the standard error is $\sqrt{p_0(1-p_0)/n} = \sqrt{[(1/3)(2/3)]/116} = 0.0438$. The astrologers were correct with 40 of their 116 predictions, a sample proportion of $\hat{p} = 0.345$. The test statistic is

$$z = \frac{\hat{p} - p_0}{se_0} = \frac{\hat{p} - p_0}{\sqrt{\dfrac{p_0(1-p_0)}{n}}} = \frac{0.345 - 1/3}{0.0438} = 0.26.$$

Recall

The numbers shown in formulas are rounded, such as 0.345 for $40/116 = 0.34482758\ldots$, but calculations are done without rounding. ◀

The sample proportion of 0.345 is only 0.26 standard errors above the null hypothesis value of $1/3$.

Step 4: P-value

Does $z = 0.26$ give much evidence against $H_0: p = 1/3$ and in support of $H_a: p > 1/3$? The P-value summarizes the evidence. It describes how unusual the data would be if H_0 were true, that is, if the probability of a correct prediction were $1/3$. The P-value is the probability that the test statistic takes a value like the observed test statistic or an even more extreme one, if actually $p = 1/3$.

Figure 9.2 shows the approximate sampling distribution of the z test statistic when H_0 is true. This is the **standard normal distribution**. For the astrology study, $z = 0.26$. Values even farther out in the right tail, above 0.26, are even more extreme, in that they provide even stronger evidence against H_0.

When a random variable has a large number of possible values, the probability of any single value is usually very small. (For the normal distribution, the probability of a single value, such as $z = 0.26$, is *zero,* because the area under the curve above a single point is 0.) So the P-value is taken to be the probability of a *region* of values, specifically the more extreme values, $z > 0.26$. From Table A or using software, the right-tail probability above 0.26 is 0.40. This P-value of 0.40 tells us that if H_0 were true, the probability would be 0.40 that the test statistic would be as or more extreme than the observed value.

Recall

The **standard normal** is the normal distribution with mean $= 0$ and standard deviation$= 1$. See the end of Section 6.2. ◀

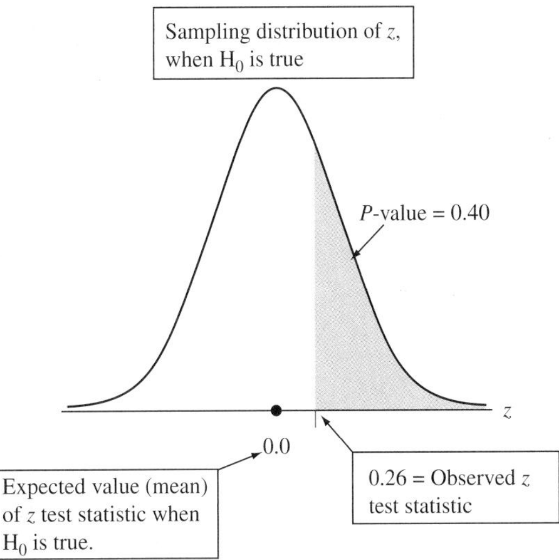

▲ **Figure 9.2 Calculation of P-value, When $z = 0.26$ for Testing H_0: $p = 1/3$ Against H_a: $p > 1/3$.** Presuming that H_0 is true, the P-value is the right-tail probability of a test statistic value even more extreme than observed. **Question** Logically, why are the *right-tail* z-scores considered the *more extreme* values for testing H_0 against H_a: $p > 1/3$?

Step 5: Conclusion
We summarize the test by reporting and interpreting the P-value. The P-value of 0.40 is not especially small. It does *not* provide strong evidence against H_0: $p = 1/3$ and in favor of the astrologers' claim that $p > 1/3$. The sample data are the sort we'd expect to see if $p = 1/3$ (that is, if astrologers were randomly guessing the personality type). Thus, it is plausible that $p = 1/3$. We would not conclude that astrologers have special predictive powers.

Interpreting the P-value

A significance test analyzes the strength of the evidence against the null hypothesis, H_0. We start by presuming that H_0 is true, putting the *burden of proof* on H_a. The approach taken is the indirect one of *proof by contradiction.* To convince ourselves that H_a is true, we must show the data contradict H_0, by showing they'd be unusual if H_0 were true. We analyze whether the data would be unusual if H_0 were true by finding the P-value. If the P-value is small, the data contradict H_0 and support H_a.

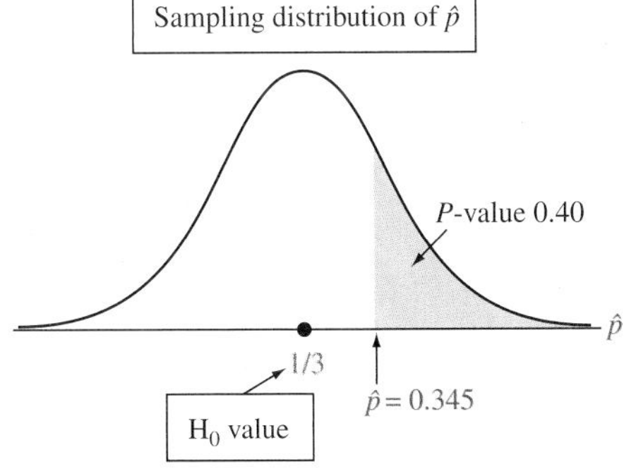

In the astrology study, the P-value for H_a: $p > 1/3$ is the right-tail probability of 0.40 from the sampling distribution of the z statistic. We can also see this P-value directly in the sampling distribution for the sample proportion. The P-value of 0.40 is the probability that the sample proportion $\hat{p}$ takes a value that is at least as far above the null hypothesis value of $1/3$ as the observed sample proportion of $\hat{p} = 0.345$. The margin figure illustrates this. Since the P-value is not small, if truly $p = 1/3$, it would not be unusual to observe $\hat{p} = 0.345$. Based on the data, it is plausible that the astrologers' predictions merely correspond to random guessing.

Why do we find the P-value (i.e., the probability) in the *right tail*? Because the alternative hypothesis H_a: $p > 1/3$ has values *above* (that is, to the right of) the null hypothesis value of $1/3$. It's the relatively *large* values of $\hat{p}$ that support this alternative hypothesis.

Why do smaller P-values indicate stronger evidence against H_0? Because the data would then be more unusual if H_0 were true. For instance, if we got a P-value of 0.01, then we might be more impressed by the astrologers' claims. With such a small P-value, the sample proportion must have fallen more than 2 standard deviations away from the hypothesized null value of $1/3$, out in the tails of the

Caution

When interpreting the P-value, always include the conditional statement that it is computed assuming that the value specified in the null hypothesis is the true parameter value. ◀

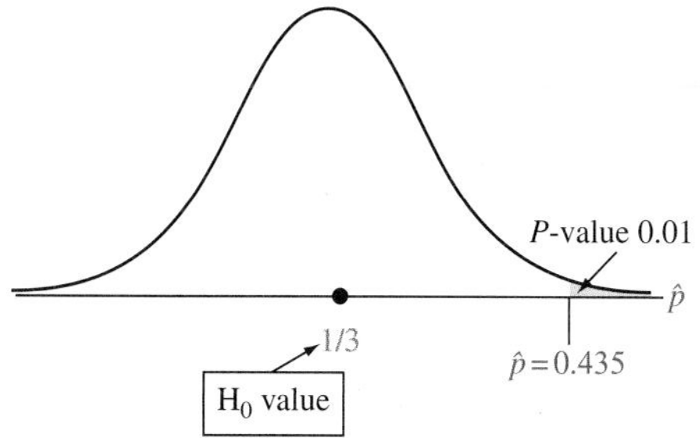

sampling distribution. It must be considered extreme and unusual, assuming the astrologers were just guessing. The fact that such an extreme sample proportion was observed calls into question (and contradicts) the main assumption we made when computing the P-value, namely that H_0 is true, i.e., that $p = 1/3$. So, a small P-value provides evidence against H_0. The margin figure illustrates that a P-value of 0.01 would result for a sample proportion of 0.435. This is far out in the right tail of the sampling distribution for the sample proportion.

Two-Sided Significance Tests

Sometimes we're interested in investigating whether a proportion falls above or below some point. For instance, can we conclude whether the population proportion who voted for a particular candidate is different from 1/2 (either above or below)? We then use a *two-sided* alternative hypothesis. This has the form H_a: $p \neq p_0$, such as H_a: $p \neq 1/2$.

For two-sided tests, the values that are more extreme than the observed test statistic value are ones that fall farther in the tail in *either* direction. The P-value is the *two-tail* probability under the standard normal curve because these are the test statistic values that provide even stronger evidence in favor of H_a: $p \neq p_0$ than the observed value. We calculate this by finding the tail probability in a single tail and then doubling it, since the distribution is symmetric. See Figure 9.3.

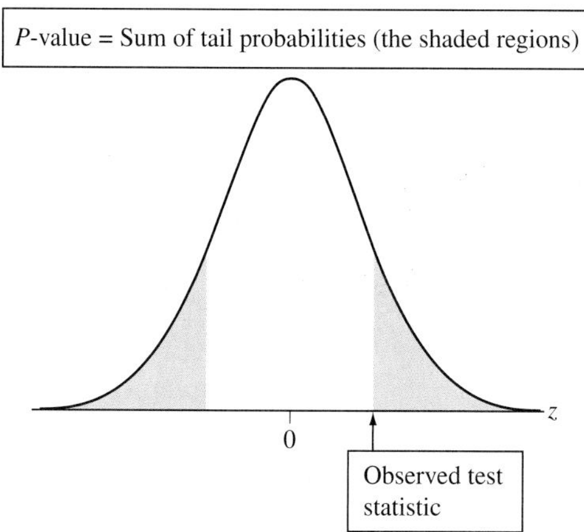

▲ **Figure 9.3 For the Two-Sided Alternative H_a: $p \neq p_0$, the P-value Is a Two-Tail Probability. Question** Logically, why are both the left-tail values and the right-tail values the more extreme values for H_a: $p \neq p_0$?

Two-sided significance test ◀

Example 4

Dogs Detecting Cancer by Smell

Picture the Scenario

Recent research suggests that dogs may be helpful in detecting when a person has cancer. In this example, we describe a study investigating whether dogs can be trained to distinguish a patient with bladder cancer by smelling certain compounds in the patient's urine.[2] Six dogs of varying breeds were trained to discriminate between urine from patients with bladder cancer and urine from control patients without it. The dogs were taught to indicate which among several specimens was from the bladder cancer patient by lying beside it.

[2]Article by C. M. Willis et al., *British Medical Journal,* vol. 329, September 25, 2004.

An experiment was conducted to analyze how the dogs' ability to detect the correct urine specimen compared to what would be expected with random guessing. Each of the six dogs was tested with nine trials. In each trial, one urine sample from a bladder cancer patient was randomly placed among six control urine samples. In the total of 54 trials with the six dogs, the dogs made the correct selection 22 times.

Let p denote the probability that a dog makes the correct selection on a given trial. Since the urine from the bladder cancer patient was one of seven specimens, with random guessing we have $p = 1/7$.

Question to Explore

Did this study provide strong evidence that the dogs' predictions were better or worse than with random guessing? Specifically, is there strong evidence that $p > 1/7$, with dogs able to select better than with random guessing, or that $p < 1/7$, with dogs' selections being poorer than random guessing?

Think It Through

The outcome of each trial is binary. The categories are correct selection and incorrect selection. Since we want to test whether the probability of a correct selection differs from random guessing, the hypotheses are

$$H_0: p = 1/7 \text{ and } H_a: p \neq 1/7.$$

The null hypothesis represents no effect, the selections being like random guessing. The alternative hypothesis says there is an effect, the selections differing from random guessing. You might instead use $H_a: p > 1/7$ if you expect the dogs' predictions to be better than random guessing. Most medical studies, however, use two-sided alternative hypotheses. This represents an open-minded research approach that recognizes that if an effect exists, it could be negative rather than positive.

The sample proportion of correct selections by the dogs was $\hat{p} = 22/54 = 0.407$, for the sample size $n = 54$. The null hypothesis value is $p_0 = 1/7$. When $H_0: p = 1/7$ is true, the expected counts are $np_0 = 54(1/7) = 7.7$ correct selections and $n(1-p_0) = 54(6/7) = 46.3$ incorrect selections. The first of these is not larger than 15, so according to the sample size guideline for step 1 of the test, n is not large enough to use the large-sample test. Later in this section, we'll see that the *two-sided* test is robust when this assumption is not satisfied. So we'll use the large-sample test, under the realization that the P-value is a good approximation for the P-value of a more appropriate small-sample test mentioned later.

Recall

From Section 8.3, a method is **robust** with respect to a particular assumption if it works well even when that assumption is violated. ◀

The standard error is $se_0 = \sqrt{p_0(1 - p_0)/n} = \sqrt{(1/7)(6/7)/54} = 0.0476$. The test statistic for $H_0: p = 1/7$ $(= 0.143)$ equals

$$z = \frac{\hat{p} - p_0}{se_0} = \frac{0.407 - (1/7)}{0.0476} = 5.6.$$

The sample proportion, 0.407, falls more than 5 standard errors above the null hypothesis value of $1/7$.

Figure 9.4 shows the approximate sampling distribution of the z test statistic when H_0 is true. The test statistic value of 5.6 is well out in the right tail. Values farther out in the tail, above 5.6, are even more extreme. The P-value is the total two-tail probability of the more extreme outcomes, above 5.6 or below -5.6. From software, the cumulative probability in the right tail above $z = 5.6$ is 0.00000001, and the probability in the two tails equals $2(0.00000001) = 0.00000002$. (Some software, such as MINITAB, rounds off and reports the P-value as 0.000.) This tiny P-value provides extremely strong evidence against $H_0: p = 1/7$, and we would conclude p is not equal to $1/7$.

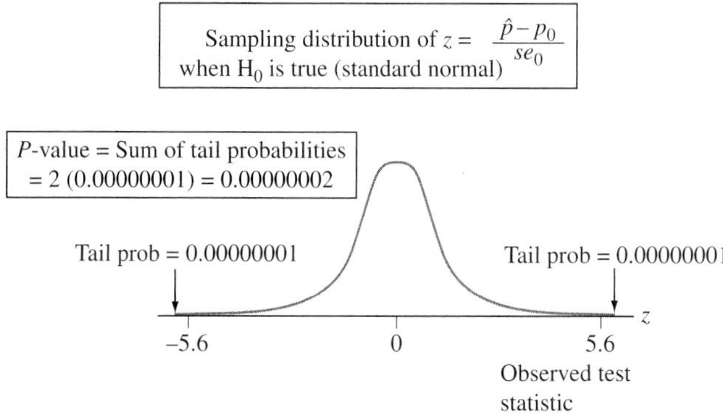

▲ **Figure 9.4 Calculation of P-value, When $z = 5.6$, for Testing H_0: $p = 1/7$ Against H_a: $p \neq 1/7$.** Presuming H_0 is true, the P-value is the two-tail probability of a test statistic value even more extreme than observed. **Question** Is the P-value of 0.00000002 strong evidence supporting H_0 or strong evidence against H_0?

When the P-value in a two-sided test is small, the point estimate tells us the direction in which the parameter appears to differ from the null hypothesis value. In summary, since the P-value is very small and $\hat{p} > 1/7$, the evidence strongly suggests that the dogs' selections are *better* than random guessing.

Recall

See Section 4.2 for potential difficulties with convenience samples, which use subjects who are conveniently available. ◀

Insight

Recall that one assumption for this significance test is randomization for obtaining the data. This study is like most medical studies in that its subjects were a *convenience sample* rather than a random sample from some population. It is not practical that a study can identify the population of all people who have bladder cancer and then randomly sample them for an experiment. Likewise, the dogs were not randomly sampled. As a result, any inferential predictions are tentative. They are valid only to the extent that the patients and the dogs in the experiment are representative of their populations. The predictions become more conclusive if similar results occur in other studies with other samples. In medical studies, even though the sample is not random, it is important to employ randomization in any experimentation, for instance in the placement of the bladder cancer patient's urine specimen among the six control urine specimens.

▶ ***Try Exercises 9.15 and 9.19***

Summing up, the P-value is the probability of values as extreme or more extreme than the observed test statistic value, computed under the assumption that the null hypothesis is true. What is "more extreme" and, hence, how the P-value is calculated depends on the alternative hypothesis. For a two-sided alternative, the P-value is the sum of the two tail probabilities, whereas for a one-sided hypothesis, the P-value is the probability in the corresponding tail. The following box summarizes the different scenarios.

SUMMARY: P-values for Different Alternative Hypotheses

Alternative Hypothesis	P-value
H_a: $p > p_0$	Right-tail probability
H_a: $p < p_0$	Left-tail probability
H_a: $p \neq p_0$	Two-tail probability

The Significance Level Tells Us How Strong the Evidence Must Be

Sometimes we need to make a decision about whether the data provide sufficient evidence to reject H_0. Before seeing the data, we decide how small the P-value would need to be to reject H_0. For example, we might decide that we will reject H_0 if the P-value ≤ 0.05. The cutoff point of 0.05 is called the **significance level**. It is shown in Figure 9.5.

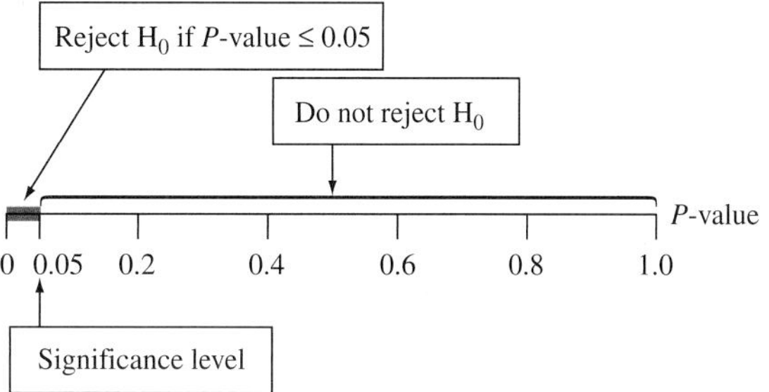

▲ **Figure 9.5** The Decision in a Significance Test. Reject H_0 if the P-value is less than or equal to a chosen **significance level**, usually 0.05.

Significance Level

The **significance level** is a number such that we reject H_0 if the P-value is less than or equal to that number. In practice, the most common significance level is 0.05.

Table 9.1 summarizes the two possible outcomes for a test decision when the significance level is 0.05. We either reject H_0 or do not reject H_0. If the P-value if larger than 0.05, the data do not contradict H_0 sufficiently for us to reject it. Then, H_0 is still plausible to us. If the P-value is ≤ 0.05, the data provide enough evidence to reject H_0. Recall that H_a had the burden of proof, and in this case we feel that the proof is sufficient. When we reject H_0, we say the results are **statistically significant**.

Table 9.1 Possible Decisions in a Test of Significance

P-value	Decision About H_0
≤ 0.05	Reject H_0
>0.05	Do not reject H_0

Statistical Significance

When the data provide sufficient evidence to reject H_0 and support H_a (i.e., when the P-value is less than the significance level), the results of the test are called statistically significant.

Example 5

Significance levels ◄

The Astrology Study

Picture the Scenario

Let's continue our analysis of the astrology study from Example 3. The parameter p is the probability that an astrologer picks the correct one of three personality charts, based on the horoscope and birth data provided. We tested H_0: $p = 1/3$ against H_a: $p > 1/3$ and got a P-value of 0.40.

Questions to Explore

What decision would we make for a significance level of (a) 0.05? (b) 0.50?

Think It Through

a. For a significance level of 0.05, the P-value of 0.40 is *not* less than 0.05. So we do not reject H_0. The evidence is not strong enough to conclude that the astrologers' predictions are better than random guessing. There is no statistical significance for such a claim.

b. For a significance level of 0.50, the P-value of 0.40 *is* less than 0.50. So we reject H_0 in favor of H_a. We conclude that this result provides sufficient evidence to support the astrologers' claim that the probability of correctly identifying a personality chart is larger than 1/3. The results are statistically significant at the 0.50 significance level.

Insight

In practice, significance levels are typically close to 0, such as 0.05 or 0.01. The reason is that the significance level is also a type of error probability. We'll see in Section 9.4 that when H_0 is true, the significance level is the probability of making an error by rejecting H_0. We used the significance level of 0.50 in part b for illustrative purposes, but the value of 0.05 used in part a is much more typical. The astrologers' predictions are consistent with random guessing, and we would not reject H_0 for these data.

► ***Try Exercise 9.20***

In Practice Report the P-value

Report the P-value rather than merely indicating whether the results are statistically significant. Learning the actual P-value is more informative than learning only whether the test is "statistically significant at the 0.05 level." The P-values of 0.001 and 0.049 are both statistically significant in this sense, but the first P-value provides much stronger evidence that the result is statistically significant than the second P-value.

Now that we've studied all five steps of a significance test about a proportion, let's use them in a new example, much like those you'll see in the exercises. In this example and in the exercises, it may help you to refer to the following summary box.

SUMMARY: Steps of a Significance Test for a Population Proportion p

1. Assumptions

- Categorical variable, with population proportion p defined in context.
- Randomization, such as a simple random sample or a randomized experiment, for gathering data.
- n large enough to expect at least 15 successes and 15 failures under H_0 (that is $np_0 \geq 15$ and $n(1 - p_0) \geq 15$). This is mainly important for one-sided tests.

2. Hypotheses

Null: H_0: $p = p_0$, where p_0 is the hypothesized value.
Alternative: H_a: $p \neq p_0$ (two-sided) or H_a: $p < p_0$ (one-sided) or H_a: $p > p_0$ (one-sided)

3. Test statistic

$$z = \frac{\hat{p} - p_0}{se_0} \text{ with } se_0 = \sqrt{p_0(1 - p_0)/n}$$

4. P-value

Alternative hypothesis	P-value
H_a: $p > p_0$	Right-tail probability
H_a: $p < p_0$	Left-tail probability
H_a: $p \neq p_0$	Two-tail probability

5. Conclusion

Smaller P-values give stronger evidence against H_0. If a decision is needed, reject H_0 if the P-value is less than or equal to the preselected significance level (such as 0.05). Relate the conclusion to the context of the study.

Example 6

Significance test about a proportion

Opinion on Fracking

Picture the Scenario

Let's revisit the question on the public opinion about the increasing use of fracking to extract oil and gas discussed in Example 2. Here, we will use data from a Pew Research survey (www.pewresearch.org) conducted in the United States in November 2014, which used a random sample of $n = 1353$ people. Of these, 47.1% (637 people) were opposed to the increased use of fracking; the rest either favored it or had no definite opinion.

Questions to Explore

How strong is the evidence to support the claim that those opposing the increased use of fracking in the United States are still in the minority? Does a sample proportion of 0.471 in a sample of size 1353 provide no, weak, or strong evidence? What decision would be made regarding this claim at a 0.05 significance level?

Think It Through

Let's follow the five steps of a significance test to organize our response to these questions:

1. Assumptions

- The response from each respondent in the survey is categorical, with outcomes "favor," "oppose," or "don't know." Let p denote the proportion that responded "oppose."
- The 1353 people in the survey were selected by random-digit dialing of both land lines and cell phones. The sample can be treated as a random sample representative of the adult population in the United States.
- The sample size requirement is met to use the large sample test is met. (See next step.)

2. Hypotheses

When those opposing the increased use of fracking in the United States are neither in the minority nor in the majority, $p = 0.50$. This is the null hypothesis—it represents no preference either way. The claim that those opposing the increased use of fracking are in the minority is formulated as the alternative

Recall

H_0 contains a single number, whereas H_a has a range of values. ◀

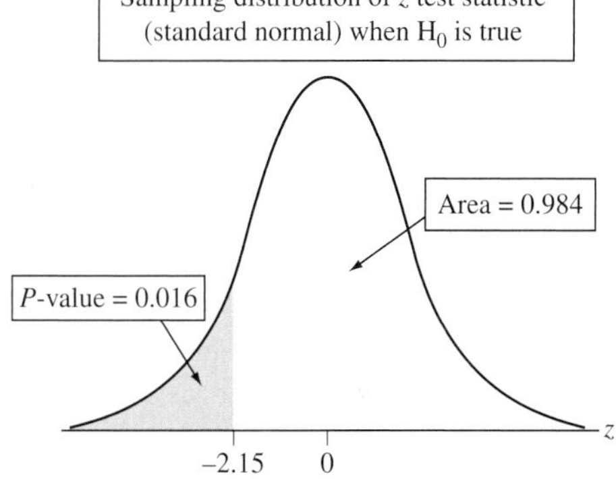

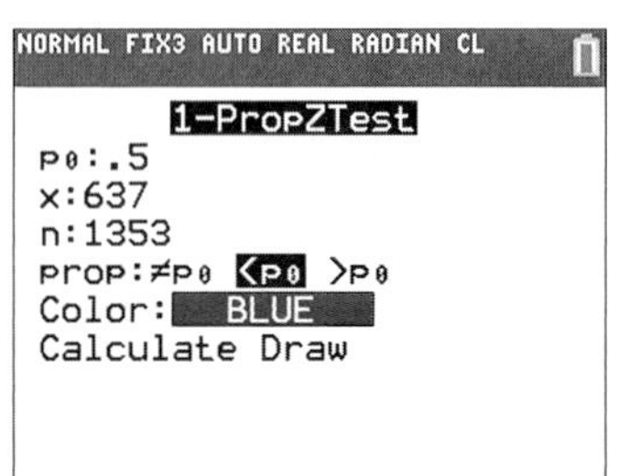

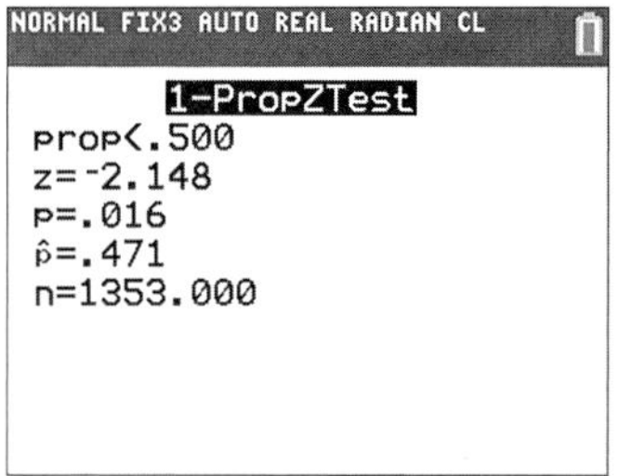

TI input and output for test about proportion

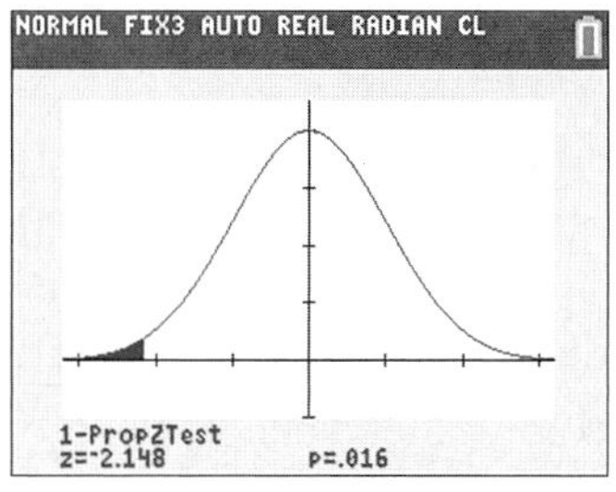

hypothesis, H_a: $p < 0.50$. Hence, we'll test H_0: $p = 0.50$ against H_a: $p < 0.50$, resulting in a one-sided test. The hypothesized null value for the proportion is $p_0 = 0.50$. Because we expect $1353(0.50) = 676.5$ successes and $1353(1 - 0.5) = 676.5$ failures under the null, both greater than 15, the sample size criterion from the assumptions is easily fulfilled. Therefore, it is appropriate to use the standard normal distribution as the sampling distribution for the test statistic, i.e., we can use the large-sample test.

3. Test statistic

The sample proportion opposing the increased use of fracking in the sample of size $n = 1353$ is $\hat{p} = 637/1353 = 0.471$. The standard error of $\hat{p}$ when H_0: $p = 0.50$ is true is

$$se_0 = \sqrt{p_0(1 - p_0)/n} = \sqrt{0.50(1 - 0.50)/1353} = 0.0136.$$

The value of the test statistic is

$$z = \frac{\hat{p} - p_0}{se_0} = \frac{0.471 - 0.50}{0.0136} = -2.15.$$

The sample proportion of 0.471 is 2.15 standard deviations below the null hypothesis value of 0.50, so it's rather extreme, assuming the null hypothesis is true.

4. P-value

For testing H_0: $p = 0.50$ against H_a: $p < 0.50$, the P-value is the *left-tail* probability below $z = -2.15$ in the standard normal distribution (see the margin figure). From software (such as the Normal Distribution web app) or a normal table, this is 0.016. TI output is also provided in the margin.

5. Conclusion

The P-value of 0.016 is pretty small. If the null hypothesis H_0: $p = 0.50$ were true, observing a test statistic (or, equivalently, a sample proportion) such as the one we observed or an even smaller one is quite unlikely (i.e., occurs with a probability of 0.016, or 1.6%). Because $0.016 < 0.05$, at a 0.05 significance level, the evidence is strong enough to reject H_0. Based on the survey, we do have strong evidence that those opposing the increased use of fracking are in the minority (i.e., that $p < 0.5$).

Insight

If we wanted to check more generally whether the proportion opposing is significantly *different* from 0.5 (i.e., if there is either a minority or majority), we need to use the two-sided alternative hypothesis H_a: $p \neq 0.50$. The P-value for this alternative hypothesis would be the sum of the two tail probabilities, $2(0.016) = 0.032$. With a 0.05 significance level, we have sufficient evidence (P-value $= 0.032 < 0.05$) to conclude that in the population, the proportion opposing the increased use of fracking is different from 0.50.

▶ ***Try Exercise 9.18***

In Practice Picking H_a and Using Software for Significance Tests

In practice, you should pick H_a before seeing the data. You can use software to do the test. For the one-sided test of Example 6 with H_a: $p < 0.50$, MINITAB reports the results shown in Table 9.2. Unless requested otherwise, by default, software reports the two-sided P-value.

Some software reports the P-value to several decimals, such as 0.015868. We recommend rounding it to two or three decimal places, for instance to 0.016, before reporting it. Reporting a P-value as 0.015868 suggests greater accuracy than actually exists, since the normal sampling distribution is only *approximate.*

Table 9.2 MINITAB Output for One-Sided Test in Example 6

```
Test of p = 0.5 vs p < 0.5

Sample      X       N       Sample p     Z-Value     P-Value

frack      637     1353     0.470806      -2.15       0.016
```

	↑	↑	↑	↑	
	Category Count	*Sample Size*	*Sample Proportion*	*Test Statistic*	

`Using the normal approximation` ← *Large sample test*

In calculating the standard error in the test statistic, we substituted the null hypothesis value p_0 for the population proportion p in the formula $\sqrt{p(1-p)/n}$ for the actual standard deviation of the sample proportion. This is correct because we compute the P-value *assuming that H_0 is true,* which just says that $p = p_0$. This practice differs from confidence intervals, in which the sample proportion $\hat{p}$ is substituted for p (which is unknown) in the actual standard deviation. When we estimate a confidence interval, we do not have a hypothesized value for p, so that method uses the point estimate $\hat{p}$ for p.[3] To differentiate between the two cases, we've denoted $se_0 = \sqrt{p_0(1-p_0)/n}$ and $se = \sqrt{\hat{p}(1-\hat{p})/n}$.

Caution

Use p_0 instead of $\hat{p}$ when computing the standard error for the significance test about a proportion ◀

"Do Not Reject H_0" Does Not Mean "Accept H_0"

Caution

When the P-value does not provide strong evidence to reject H_0, do not conclude that the hypothesized value is true. We can only conclude it is plausible. ◀

A small P-value means that the sample data would be unusual if H_0 were true. If the P-value is not small, such as 0.40 for the one-sided test in the astrology example, the null hypothesis is plausible. In this case, the conclusion is reported as do not reject H_0 because the data do not contradict H_0.

"*Do not reject* H_0" *is not the same as saying "accept* H_0." The population proportion has many plausible values besides the number in the null hypothesis. For instance, we did not reject H_0: $p = 1/3$ in the astrology study, where p was the probability of a correct prediction by an astrologer. Thus, p may equal $1/3$, but other values are also plausible. In fact, a 95% confidence interval for p is

$$\hat{p} \pm 1.96\sqrt{\hat{p}(1-\hat{p})/n}, \text{ or } 0.345 \pm 1.96\sqrt{(0.345)(0.655)/116},$$

which equals (0.26, 0.43). Even though insufficient evidence exists to reject H_0, it is improper to accept it and conclude that $p = 1/3$. It is plausible that p is as low as 0.26 or as high as 0.43.

An analogy here is again that of a courtroom trial. The null hypothesis is that the defendant is innocent. The alternative hypothesis is that the defendant is guilty. If the jury acquits the defendant, this does not mean that it *accepts* the defendant's claim of innocence. It merely means that innocence is plausible because guilt has not been established *beyond a reasonable doubt.*

The null hypothesis contains a single possible value for the parameter. Saying "Do not reject H_0" instead of "Accept H_0" emphasizes that that value is merely one of many plausible ones. However, saying "Accept H_a" **is permissible** for the alternative hypothesis when that is the conclusion of the test. When the P-value is sufficiently small (no greater than the significance level), the entire range of plausible values is contained in the values specified in H_a.

---

[3]If we instead conduct the test by substituting the sample proportion in the standard deviation of the sample proportion, the standard normal approximation for the sampling distribution of the test statistic z is much poorer.

Deciding Between a One-Sided and a Two-Sided Test?

In practice, two-sided tests are more common than one-sided tests. Even if we think we know the direction of an effect, two-sided tests can also detect an effect that falls in the opposite direction. For example, in a medical study, even if we think a drug will perform better than a placebo, using a two-sided alternative allows us to detect whether the drug is actually worse, perhaps because of bad side effects. However, as we saw with the astrology example, in some scenarios a one-sided test is natural.

Guidelines in Forming the Alternative Hypothesis

- In deciding between one-sided and two-sided alternative hypotheses in a particular exercise or in practice, *consider the context of the real problem.*

For instance, in the astrology experiment, to test whether someone can guess *better* than with random guessing, we used the values $p > 1/3$ in the alternative hypothesis corresponding to that possibility. An exercise that says "test whether the population proportion *differs* from 0.50" suggests a two-sided alternative, H_a: $p \neq 0.50$, to allow for p to be larger or smaller than 0.50. "Test whether the population proportion is *larger* than 0.50" suggests the one-sided alternative, H_a: $p > 0.50$.

- In most research articles, significance tests use two-sided P-values.

Partly this reflects an objective approach to research that recognizes that an effect could go in either direction. Using an alternative hypothesis in which an effect can go in either direction is regarded as the most even-handed way to perform the test. In using two-sided P-values, researchers avoid the suspicion that they chose H_a when they saw the direction in which the data occurred. That is not ethical and would be cheating, as we'll discuss in Section 9.5.

In Practice Tests Are Usually Two-Sided

For the reasons just discussed, two-sided tests are more common than one-sided tests. Most examples and exercises in this book reflect the way tests are most often used and employ two-sided alternatives. *In practice, you should use a two-sided test unless you have a well-justified reason for a one-sided test.*

- Confidence intervals are two-sided.

The practice of using a two-sided test coincides with the ordinary approach for confidence intervals, which are two-sided, obtained by adding and subtracting a margin of error from the point estimate. There is a way to construct one-sided confidence intervals, for instance, concluding that a population proportion is *at least* equal to 0.70. In practice, though, two-sided confidence intervals are much more common.

SUMMARY: Three Basic Facts When Specifying Hypotheses

- The null hypothesis has an equal sign (such as H_0: $p = 0.5$), but the alternative hypothesis does not.
- You shouldn't pick H_a based on looking at the data.
- The hypotheses always refer to population parameters, not sample statistics.

The last bullet point implies that you should *never* express a hypothesis by using sample statistic notation, such as H_0: $\hat{p} = 0.5$ (or H_0: $\bar{x} = 40$). There is no need to conduct inference about statistics such as the sample proportion $\hat{p}$ (or the sample mean $\bar{x}$), because you can find their values exactly from the data.

The Binomial Test for Small Samples

The test about a proportion uses normal sampling distributions for the sample proportion $\hat{p}$ and the z test statistic. Therefore, it is a *large-sample* test because the central limit theorem implies approximate normality of the sampling distribution for large random samples. The guideline is that the expected numbers of successes and failures should be at least 15 when H_0 is true; that is, $np_0 \geq 15$ and $n(1 - p_0) \geq 15$.

In practice, the large-sample z test performs well for *two-sided* alternatives even for small samples. When p_0 is below 0.3 or above 0.7 and n is small, the sampling distribution is quite skewed. However, a tail probability that is smaller than the normal probability in one tail is compensated by a tail probability that is larger than the normal probability in the other tail. Because of this, the P-value from the two-sided test using the normal table approximates well a P-value from a small-sample test.

For one-sided tests, when p_0 differs from 0.5, the large-sample test does not work well when the sample size guideline ($np_0 \geq 15$ and $n(1 - p_0) \geq 15$) is violated. In that case, you should use a small-sample test. This test uses the binomial distribution with parameter value p_0 to find the exact probability of the observed value and all the more extreme values, according to the direction in H_a. Since one-sided tests with small n are not common in practice, we will not study the binomial test here. Exercises 9.26 and 9.27 show how to do it.

9.2 Practicing the Basics

9.10 Psychic A person who claims to be psychic says he predicts the outcome of a flip of a fair coin more often right than wrong. If we want to test this claim, we could use the data from an experiment in which he predicts the outcome for n flips of the coin. State the parameter of interest and the hypotheses for a significance test for testing this claim, where the alternative hypothesis reflects the psychic's claim.

TRY

9.11 Believe in astrology? You plan to apply significance testing to your own experiment for testing astrology, in which astrologers have to guess which of four personality profiles is the correct one for someone who has a particular horoscope. Define the parameter of interest and state the hypotheses, letting one hypothesis reflect the possibility that the astrologers' predictions could be better than random guessing.

TRY

9.12 Get P-value from z For a test of H_0: $p = 0.50$, the z test statistic equals 1.04.

a. Find the P-value for H_a: $p > 0.50$.

b. Find the P-value for H_a: $p \neq 0.50$.

c. Find the P-value for H_a: $p < 0.50$. (*Hint:* The P-values for the two possible one-sided tests must sum to 1.)

d. Do any of the P-values in part a, part b, or part c give strong evidence against H_0? Explain.

9.13 Get more P-values from z Refer to the previous exercise. Suppose $z = 2.50$ instead of 1.04.

a. Find the P-value for (i) H_a: $p > 0.50$, (ii) H_a: $p \neq 0.50$, and (iii) H_a: $p < 0.50$.

b. Do any of the P-values in part a provide strong evidence against H_0? Explain.

9.14 Find test statistic and P-value For a test of H_0: $p = 0.50$, the sample proportion is 0.35 based on a sample size of 100.

a. Show that the test statistic is $z = -3.0$.

b. Find the P-value for H_a: $p < 0.50$.

c. Does the P-value in part b give much evidence against H_0? Explain.

9.15 Dogs and cancer A recent study[4] considered whether dogs could be trained to detect whether a person has lung cancer or breast cancer by smelling the subject's breath. The researchers trained five ordinary household dogs to distinguish, by scent alone, exhaled breath samples of 55 lung and 31 breast cancer patients from those of 83 healthy controls. A dog gave a correct indication of a cancer sample by sitting in front of that sample when it was randomly placed among four control samples. Once trained, the dogs' ability to distinguish cancer patients from controls was tested using breath samples from subjects not previously encountered by the dogs. (The researchers blinded both dog handlers and experimental observers to the identity of breath samples.) Let p denote the probability a dog correctly detects a cancer sample placed among five samples when the other four are controls.

TRY

a. Set up the null hypothesis that the dog's predictions correspond to random guessing.

b. Set up the alternative hypothesis to test whether the probability of a correct selection *differs* from random guessing.

c. Set up the alternative hypothesis to test whether the probability of a correct selection is *greater than* with random guessing.

d. In one test with 83 Stage I lung cancer samples, the dogs correctly identified the cancer sample 81 times. The test statistic for the alternative hypothesis in part c was $z = 17.7$. Report the P-value to three decimal

[4] M. McCulloch et al., *Integrative Cancer Therapies*, vol 5, p. 30, 2006.

places and interpret. (The success of dogs in this study made researchers wonder whether dogs can detect cancer at an earlier stage than conventional methods such as MRI scans.)

9.16 Religion important in your life? Americans ages 18 to 29 are considered to be less religious than older Americans. According to recent studies by the Pew Forum on Religion & Public Life, fewer young adults are affiliated with a specific religion than older people today. And, compared with their elders, fewer young people say that religion is very important in their lives. Yet, many young people still believe in traditional religious concepts and practices. Pew Research Center surveys show, for example, that "young adults' beliefs about life after death and the existence of heaven, hell and miracles closely resemble the beliefs of older people today." According to GSS (General Social Survey) results from a random sample of 1,679 subjects, 45% in the 18–29 age group pray daily whereas 55% pray less often.[5] The MINITAB output shows the results for a significance test for which the alternative hypothesis is that the percentage of 18–29-year-olds who pray daily differs from 50%. State and interpret the five steps of a significance test in this context, using information shown in the output to provide the particular values for the hypothesis, test statistic, and P-value.

Test and CI for One Proportion

```
Test of p = 0.5 vs p ≠ 0.5
 X    N   Sample p        95% CI       Z-Value  P-Value
756 1679  0.450268  (0.426, 0.474)    -4.08    0.000
Using the normal approximation.
```

9.17 Another test of astrology Examples 1, 3, and 5 referred to a study about astrology. Another part of the study used the following experiment: Professional astrologers prepared horoscopes for 83 adults. Each adult was shown three horoscopes, one of which was the one an astrologer prepared for him or her and the other two were randomly chosen from ones prepared for other subjects in the study. Each adult had to guess which of the three was his or hers. Of the 83 subjects, 28 guessed correctly.

a. Define the parameter of interest and set up the hypotheses to test that the probability of a correct prediction is 1/3 against the astrologers' claim that it exceeds 1/3.

b. Show that the sample proportion = 0.337, the standard error of the sample proportion for the test is 0.052, and the test statistic is $z = 0.08$.

c. Find the P-value. Would you conclude that people are more likely to select their horoscope than if they were randomly guessing, or are results consistent with random guessing?

9.18 Opinion on fracking a year earlier TRY The question about the opinion on the increased use of fracking from the November 2014 survey mentioned in Example 6 was also included in an earlier survey in September 2013. Using this earlier survey, let's again focus on those who oppose the increased use of fracking.

a. Define the parameter of interest and set up hypotheses to test that those who oppose fracking in 2013 are in the minority.

b. Of the 1506 respondents in the 2013 survey, 740 indicated that they oppose the increased use of fracking. Find and interpret the test statistic.

c. Report the P-value. Indicate your decision, in the context of this survey, using a 0.05 significance level.

d. Check whether the sample size was large enough to conduct the inference in part c. Indicate what the assumptions are for your inferences to apply to the entire U.S. population.

e. Find the P-value for the two-sided alternative that the proportion opposing is different from 0.50.

9.19 Testing a headache remedy TRY Studies that compare treatments for chronic medical conditions such as headaches can use the same subjects for each treatment. This type of study is commonly referred to as a crossover design. With a crossover design, each person crosses over from using one treatment to another during the study. One such study considered a drug (a pill called Sumatriptan) for treating migraine headaches in a convenience sample of children.[6] The study observed each of 30 children at two times when he or she had a migraine headache. The child received the drug at one time and a placebo at the other time. The order of treatment was randomized and the study was double-blind. For each child, the response was whether the drug or the placebo provided better pain relief. Let p denote the proportion of children having better pain relief with the drug in the population of children who suffer periodically from migraine headaches. Can you conclude that p is different from 0.5, that is, either more or less than half of the population is getting better pain relief with the drug? Of the 30 children, 22 had more pain relief with the drug and 8 had more pain relief with the placebo.

a. For testing $H_0: p = 0.50$ against $H_a: p \neq 0.50$, show that the test statistic $z = 2.56$.

b. Show that the P-value is 0.01. Interpret.

c. Check the assumptions needed for this test and discuss the limitations due to using a convenience sample rather than a random sample.

9.20 Gender bias in selecting managers TRY For a large supermarket chain in Florida, a women's group claimed that female employees were passed over for management training in favor of their male colleagues. The company denied this claim, saying it picked the employees from the eligible pool at random to receive this training. Statewide, the large pool of more than 1000 eligible employees who can be tapped for management training is 40% female and 60% male. Since this program began, 28 of the 40 employees chosen for management training were male and 12 were female.

a. The company claims that it selected employees for training according to their proportion in the pool of eligible employees. Define a parameter of interest and

[5]Accessed from pewforum.org/Age/Religion-Among-the-Millennials.aspx.

[6]Data based on those in a study by M. L. Hamalainen et al., reported in *Neurology*, vol. 48, pp. 1100–1103, 1997.

state this claim as a hypothesis. Explain why this hypothesis is a no-effect hypothesis.

b. State the null and alternative hypotheses for a test to investigate the strength of evidence to support the women's claim of gender bias. (*Hint:* Gender bias means that either males or females are disproportionately selected.)

c. The table shows results of using MINITAB to do a large-sample analysis. Explain why the large-sample analysis is justified and show how software obtained the test statistic value.

```
Test of p = 0.4 vs p ≠ 0.4
X`  N  Sample p       95% CI          Z-Value  P-Value
12  40  0.300000  (0.158, 0.442)   -1.29    0.197
Using the normal approximation.
```

d. To what alternative hypothesis does the P-value in the table refer? Use it to find the P-value for the significance test you specified in part b and interpret it.

e. What decision would you make for a 0.05 significance level? Interpret.

9.21 Gender discrimination Refer to the 95% confidence interval shown in the MINITAB output in the previous exercise. What are the plausible values for the probability of a female to be selected for training? Is this in accordance with our decision of the significance test from part e of the previous exercise? Explain.

9.22 Garlic to repel ticks A study (*J. Amer. Med. Assoc.*, vol. 284, p. 831, 2000) considered whether daily consumption of 1200 mg of garlic could reduce tick bites. The study used a crossover design with a sample of Swedish military conscripts, half of whom used placebo first and garlic second and half the reverse. The authors did not present the data, but the effect they described is consistent with garlic being more effective with 37 subjects and placebo being more effective with 29 subjects. Does this suggest a real difference between garlic and placebo, or are the results consistent with random variation? Answer by:

a. Identifying the relevant variable and parameter. (*Hint:* The variable is categorical with two categories. The parameter is a population proportion for one of the categories.)

b. Stating hypotheses for a large-sample two-sided test and checking that sample size guidelines are satisfied for that test.

c. Finding the test statistic value.

d. Finding and interpreting a P-value and stating the conclusion in context.

9.23 Exit-poll predictions According to an exit poll of the 2010 California gubernatorial election (see Chapter 7), 53.1% of the 3889 voters sampled reported voting for Brown. Is this enough evidence to predict who won? Test that the population proportion who voted for Brown was 0.50 against the alternative that it differed from 0.50. Answer by:

a. Identifying the variable and parameter of interest and defining notation.

b. Stating hypotheses and checking assumptions for a large-sample test.

c. Reporting the test statistic and P-value, interpreting the latter.

d. Explaining how to make a decision for the significance level of 0.05. Is the proportion voting for Brown significantly different from 50%?

9.24 Which cola? The 49 students in a class at the University of Florida made blinded evaluations of pairs of cola drinks. For the 49 comparisons of Coke and Pepsi, Coke was preferred 29 times. In the population that this sample represents, is this strong evidence that a majority prefers one of the drinks? Refer to the following MINITAB printout.

Test and CI for One Proportion

```
Test of p = 0.5 vs. p > 0.5
 X   N  Sample p  95% Lower Bound  Z-Value  P-Value
29  49  0.591837      0.476346        1.29    0.099
Using the normal approximation
```

Test and CI for One Proportion

```
Test of p = 0.5 vs. p ≠ 0.5
 X  N  Sample p          95% CI             Z-Value  P-Value
29 49 0.591837 (0.454221, 0.729452)    1.29    0.199
Using the normal approximation
```

a. Explain how to get the test statistic value that MINITAB reports.

b. Explain how to get the P-value. Interpret it.

c. Based on the result in part b, does it make sense to accept H_0? Explain.

d. What does the 95% confidence interval tell you that the test does not?

9.25 How to sell a burger A fast-food chain wants to compare two ways of promoting a new burger (a turkey burger). One way uses a coupon available in the store. The other way uses a poster display outside the store. Before the promotion, its marketing research group matches 50 pairs of stores. Each pair has two stores with similar sales volume and customer demographics. The store in a pair that uses coupons is randomly chosen, and after a month-long promotion, the increases in sales of the turkey burger are compared for the two stores. The increase was higher for 28 stores using coupons and higher for 22 stores using the poster. Is this strong evidence to support the coupon approach, or could this outcome be explained by chance? Answer by performing all five steps of a two-sided significance test about the population proportion of times the sales would be higher with the coupon promotion.

9.26 ◆◆ **A binomial headache** A null hypothesis states that the population proportion p of headache sufferers who have better pain relief with aspirin than with another pain reliever equals 0.50. For a crossover study with 10 subjects, all 10 have better relief with aspirin. If the null hypothesis were true, by the binomial distribution the probability of this sample result (which is the most extreme) equals $(0.50)^{10} = 0.001$. In fact, this is the small-sample P-value for testing H_0: $p = 0.50$ against H_a: $p > 0.50$. Does this P-value give (a) strong evidence in favor of H_0 or (b) strong evidence against H_0? Explain why.

9.27 ◆◆ **P-value for small samples** Example 4, on whether dogs can detect bladder cancer by selecting the correct urine specimen (out of seven), used the normal sampling distribution to find the P-value. The normal distribution P-value approximates a P-value using the binomial distribution. That binomial P-value is more appropriate when either expected count is less than 15. In Example 4, n was 54, and 22 of the 54 selections were correct.

a. If H_0: $p = 1/7$ is true, X = number of correct selections has the binomial distribution with $n = 54$ and $p = 1/7$. Why?

b. For H_a: $p > 1/7$, with $x = 22$, the small sample P-value using the binomial is $P(22)+P(23)+\cdots+P(54)$, where $P(x)$ denotes the binomial probability of outcome x with $p = 1/7$. (This equals 0.0000019.) Why would the P-value be this sum rather than just P(22)?

9.3 Significance Tests About Means

For quantitative variables, significance tests often refer to the population mean μ. We illustrate the significance test about means with the following example.

Example 7

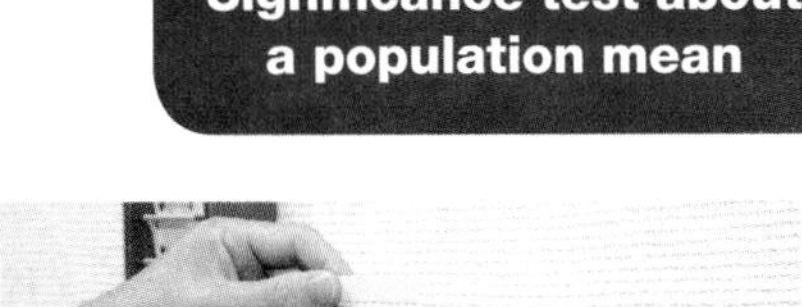

The 40-Hour Work Week

Picture the Scenario

Since the Fair Labor Standards Act was passed in 1938, the standard work week in the United States has been 40 hours. In recent years, the standard work week has fallen to less than 40 hours in most of Western Europe and in Australia. But many believe that the work-oriented culture in the United States has resulted in pressure among workers to put in longer hours than the 40-hour standard. In industries such as investment banking, a 40-hour work week is considered slacker behavior and may result in losing a job. Because the mean number of working hours may differ between males and females (perhaps due to females working more part-time jobs), here we will analyze a sample of working hours for males. Exercise 9.32 conducts a similar analysis for a sample of females.

Question to Explore

How could we frame a study of working hours using a significance test that can detect whether the mean work week for the male U.S. working population equals 40 hours or differs from 40 hours? State the null and alternative hypotheses for such a test.

Think It Through

The response variable, length of work week, is quantitative. Hypotheses refer to the mean work week μ for the male U.S. working population, whether it is 40 hours or differs from 40 hours. To use a significance test to analyze the strength of evidence about this question, we'll test H_0: $\mu = 40$ against H_a: $\mu \neq 40$.

Insight

For those who were working in 2012, the General Social Survey asked, "How many hours did you work last week?" For the 583 men included in the survey, the mean was 43.5 hours with a standard deviation of 15.3 hours. (For comparison, for the 583 females included in the survey, the mean was 37.0 hours, with a standard deviation of 15.1 hours.) The next subsection explains the five steps of a significance test about a population mean μ, such as H_0: $\mu = 40$ against H_a: $\mu \neq 40$, where μ is the mean number of hours men work per week. We'll analyze whether the difference between the sample mean work week and the historical standard of 40 hours can be explained by random variability. In Chapter 10, we will learn how to compare the two sexes directly in terms of the difference in the mean duration of the work week. The data for the example are available on the book's website.

▶ ***Try Exercise 9.32, parts a and b***

Steps of a Significance Test About a Population Mean

A significance test about a mean has the same five steps as a test about a proportion: Assumptions, hypotheses, test statistic, P-value, and conclusion. We will mention modifications as they relate to the test for a mean. However, the reasoning is the same as that for the significance test for a proportion.

Five Steps for a Significance Test About a Population Mean

Step 1: Assumptions

The three basic assumptions of a test about a mean are as follows:

- The variable is quantitative.
- The data production employed randomization.
- The *population distribution* is approximately normal. This assumption is most crucial when n is small and H_a is one-sided, as discussed later in the section.

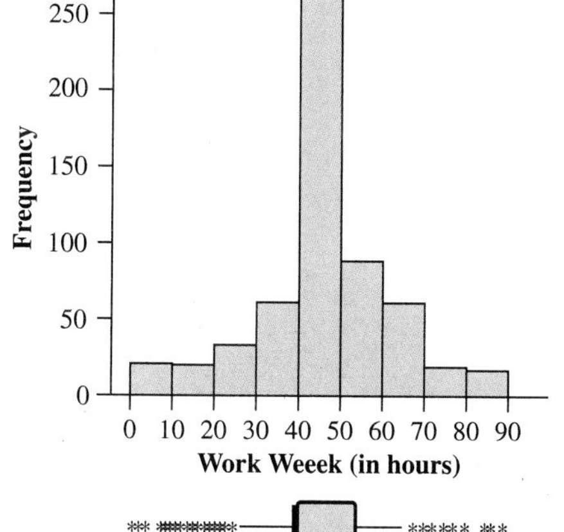

For our study about the length of the work week, the variable is the number of hours worked in the past week, which is quantitative. The GSS used random sampling. The figure in the margin shows a histogram and box plot for the data collected on the males. The histogram reveals a shape that is much more peaked than a normal distribution and a bit skewed to the right. (From the box plot, we see that the median equals the 1st quartile.) There are also many outliers on either side, but none that are dramatically removed from the rest of the observations. All in all, the histogram reveals that the population distribution may be decidedly different from normal but not in a dramatic way. As we will discuss, the sample size is large enough here ($n = 583$) that the assumption for the normality of the population distribution is less important.

Step 2: Hypotheses

The null hypothesis in a test about a population mean has the form

$$H_0\colon \mu = \mu_0,$$

where μ_0 denotes a particular value for the population mean. The two-sided alternative hypothesis

$$H_a\colon \mu \neq \mu_0$$

includes values both below and above the number μ_0 specified in H_0. Also possible are the one-sided alternative hypotheses,

$$H_a\colon \mu > \mu_0 \text{ or } H_a\colon \mu < \mu_0.$$

For instance, let μ denote the mean work week for the U.S. male working population. If the mean equals the historical standard, then $\mu = 40$. If today's working pressures have forced this above 40, then $\mu > 40$. To test that the population mean equals the historical standard against the alternative that it is greater than that, we would test $H_0\colon \mu = 40$ against $H_a\colon \mu > 40$. In practice, the two-sided alternative $H_a\colon \mu \neq 40$ is more common and lets us take an objective approach that can detect whether the mean is larger or smaller than the historical standard.

Recall

From Section 7.2, the standard deviation of the sample mean is $\sigma/\sqrt{n}$, where σ = population standard deviation. In practice, σ is unknown, so from Section 8.3 we estimate the standard deviation by the standard error

$$se = s/\sqrt{n}.$$ ◀

Step 3: Test Statistic

The test statistic is the distance between the sample mean $\bar{x}$ and the null hypothesis value μ_0, as measured by the number of standard errors between them. This is measured by

$$\frac{(\bar{x} - \mu_0)}{se} = \frac{\text{sample mean} - \text{null hypothesis mean}}{\text{standard error of sample mean}}.$$

In practice, as in forming a confidence interval for a mean (Section 8.3), the standard error is $se = s/\sqrt{n}$. The test statistic is

$$t = \frac{(\bar{x} - \mu_0)}{se} = \frac{(\bar{x} - \mu_0)}{s/\sqrt{n}}.$$

In the length of work week study, the sample mean for men was $\bar{x} = 43.5$ and the sample standard deviation $s = 15.3$. The standard error $se = s/\sqrt{n} = 15.3/\sqrt{583} = 0.636$. The test statistic equals

$$t = (x - \mu_0)/se = (43.5 - 40)/0.636 = 5.54.$$

Recall

You can review the ***t* distribution** in Section 8.3. ◀

Caution

Do not confuse the *t* statistic with the *t* score, which is a certain (e.g., 97.5th) percentile of the *t* distribution and was used to construct the confidence interval for μ. ◀

We use the symbol *t* rather than *z* for the test statistic because, as in forming a confidence interval, using *s* to estimate σ introduces additional error: The *t* sampling distribution has more variability than the standard normal. When H_0 is true, the *t* test statistic has approximately the *t distribution.* The *t* distribution is specified by its degrees of freedom, which equal $n-1$ for inference about a mean. This test statistic is called a ***t* statistic**.

Figure 9.6 shows the *t* sampling distribution. The farther $\bar{x}$ falls from the null hypothesis mean μ_0, the farther out in a tail the *t* test statistic falls, and the stronger the evidence is against H_0.

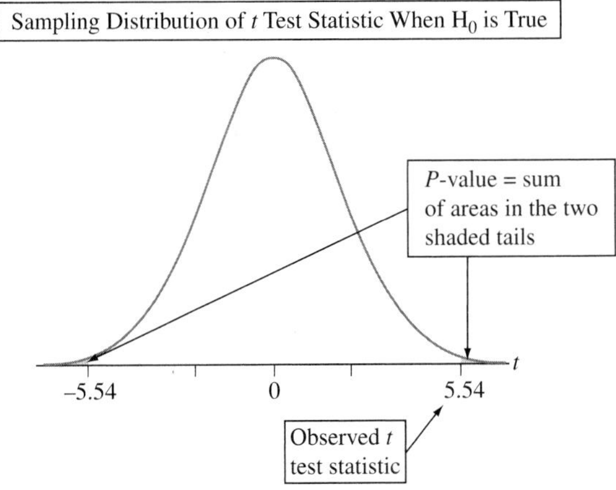

▲ **Figure 9.6 The *t* Distribution of the *t* Test Statistic.** The *t* distribution looks like the standard normal but has more variability, i.e., fatter tails. There is stronger evidence against H_0 when the *t* test statistic falls farther out in a tail. The P-value for a two-sided H_a is a two-tail probability (shaded in figure). **Question** Why is it that *t*-scores farther out in the tails provide stronger evidence against H_0?

Step 4: P-Value

The P-value is a single tail or a two-tail probability depending on whether the alternative hypothesis is one-sided or two-sided.

Alternative Hypothesis	P-value
H_a: $\mu \neq \mu_0$	Two-tail probability from t distribution
H_a: $\mu > \mu_0$	Right-tail probability from t distribution
H_a: $\mu < \mu_0$	Left-tail probability from t distribution

For the length of work week study for men with H_a: $\mu \neq 40$, the P-value is the two-tail probability of a test statistic value farther out in either tail than the observed value of 5.54. See Figure 9.6. This probability is double the single-tail probability. Table 9.3 shows the way MINITAB software reports results. Since $n = 583$, $df = n - 1 = 582$. The P-value is very small, less than 0.001. This is the two-tail probability of the t test statistic values below −5.54 and above +5.54 when $df = 582$.

Table 9.3 MINITAB Output for Analyzing Data From Study of Work Week

Test of μ = 40 vs ≠ 40

N	Mean	StDev	SE Mean	95% CI	T	P
583	43.520	15.349	0.6357	(42.271, 44.768)	5.537	0.000

Step 5: Conclusion

The conclusion of a significance test reports the P-value and *interprets* what it says about the question that motivated the test. Sometimes this includes a decision about the validity of H_0. We reject the null hypothesis when the P-value is less than or equal to the preselected significance level. In this study, the P-value of 0 provides strong evidence against the null hypothesis. If we had preselected a significance level of 0.05, this would be enough evidence to reject H_0: $\mu = 40$ in favor of H_a: $\mu \neq 40$. We can then say that the mean work week is different from 40 hours.

Table 9.3 also shows a 95% confidence interval for μ of (42.3, 44.8). This shows the plausible values for the population mean length of work week for working men. The interval does not contain 40. From this interval of values, we can infer that the population mean of 40 is not a plausible value for the mean number of hours in a work week for men, in accordance with the results of the significance test.

When research scientists conduct a significance test, their report would not show all results of a printout but would instead present a simple summary such as, "The evidence that the work week for men differs from 40 hours was statistically significant (sample mean = 43.5, standard deviation = 15.3, $n = 583$, $t = 5.52$, P-value < 0.001)." Often results are summarized even further, such as, "There was statistically significant evidence that the work week differs from 40 hours (P-value < 0.05)." This brief a summary is undesirable because it does not show the estimated mean or the actual P-value. It isn't even clear whether the mean (and not, for example, the median or the proportion working longer than 40 hours) was used as the parameter. Don't condense your conclusions this much.

The *t* Statistic and *z* Statistic Have the Same Form

As you read the examples in this section, notice the parallel between each step of the test for a mean and the test for a proportion. For instance, the t test statistic for a mean has the same form as the z test statistic for a proportion, namely,

Form of Test Statistic

$$\frac{\text{Estimate of parameter} - \text{Value of parameter under } H_0}{\text{Standard error of estimate}}$$

For the test about a mean, the estimate $\bar{x}$ of the population mean μ replaces the estimate $\hat{p}$ of the population proportion p, the H_0 mean μ_0 replaces the H_0 proportion p_0, and the standard error of the sample mean replaces the standard error of the sample proportion.

SUMMARY: Steps of a Significance Test for a Population Mean μ

1. Assumptions

- Quantitative variable, with population mean μ defined in context
- Data are obtained using randomization, such as a simple random sample or a randomized experiment
- Population distribution is approximately normal (mainly needed for one-sided tests with small n)

2. Hypotheses

Null: H_0: $\mu = \mu_0$, where μ_0 is the hypothesized value (such as H_0: $\mu = 40$)
Alternative: H_a: $\mu \neq \mu_0$ (two-sided) or H_a: $\mu < \mu_0$ (one-sided) or
H_a: $\mu > \mu_0$ (one-sided)

3. Test statistic

$$t = \frac{(\bar{x} - \mu_0)}{se}, \text{ where } se = s/\sqrt{n}$$

4. P-value Use t distribution with $df = n - 1$

Alternative Hypothesis	P-value
H_a: $\mu \neq \mu_0$	Two-tail probability
H_a: $\mu > \mu_0$	Right-tail probability
H_a: $\mu < \mu_0$	Left-tail probability

5. Conclusion

Smaller P-values give stronger evidence against H_0 and supporting H_a. If using a significance level to make a decision, reject H_0 if P-value is less than or equal to the significance level (such as 0.05). Relate the conclusion to the context of the study.

Performing a One-Sided Test About a Population Mean

One-sided alternative hypotheses apply for a prediction that μ differs from the null hypothesis value in a certain direction. For example, H_a: $\mu > 0$ predicts that the true mean is *larger* than the null hypothesis value of 0. Its P-value is the probability of a t value *larger* than the observed value, that is, in the *right* tail. Likewise, for H_a: $\mu < 0$ the P-value is the *left*-tail probability. In each case, again, $df = n - 1$.

Example 8

One-sided significance test about a mean

Weight Change in Anorexic Girls

Picture the Scenario

A recent study compared different psychological therapies for teenage girls suffering from anorexia, an eating disorder that causes them to become dangerously underweight.[7] Each girl's weight was measured before and after a period of therapy. The variable of interest was the weight change, defined as weight at the end of the study minus weight at the beginning of the study. The weight change was positive if the girl gained weight and negative if she lost weight.

In this study, 29 girls received cognitive behavioral therapy. This form of psychotherapy stresses identifying the thinking that causes the undesirable behavior and replacing it with thoughts designed to help improve this behavior. Table 9.4 shows the data. The weight changes for the 29 girls had a sample mean of $\bar{x} = 3.00$ pounds and standard deviation of $s = 7.32$ pounds.

[7]The data are courtesy of Prof. Brian Everitt, Institute of Psychiatry, London.

Table 9.4 Weights of Anorexic Girls (in Pounds) Before and After Treatment

This example uses the weight change as the variable of interest. The data are available on the book's website.

	Weight				Weight				Weight		
Girl	**Before**	**After**	**Change**	**Girl**	**Before**	**After**	**Change**	**Girl**	**Before**	**After**	**Change**
1	80.5	82.2	1.7	11	85.0	96.7	11.7	21	83.0	81.6	−1.4
2	84.9	85.6	0.7	12	89.2	95.3	6.1	22	76.5	75.7	−0.8
3	81.5	81.4	−0.1	13	81.3	82.4	1.1	23	80.2	82.6	2.4
4	82.6	81.9	−0.7	14	76.5	72.5	−4.0	24	87.8	100.4	12.6
5	79.9	76.4	−3.5	15	70.0	90.9	20.9	25	83.3	85.2	1.9
6	88.7	103.6	14.9	16	80.6	71.3	−9.3	26	79.7	83.6	3.9
7	94.9	98.4	3.5	17	83.3	85.4	2.1	27	84.5	84.6	0.1
8	76.3	93.4	17.1	18	87.7	89.1	1.4	28	80.8	96.2	15.4
9	81.0	73.4	−7.6	19	84.2	83.9	−0.3	29	87.4	86.7	−0.7
10	80.5	82.1	1.6	20	86.4	82.7	−3.7				

Question to Explore

Conduct a significance test for finding the strength of evidence supporting the effectiveness of the cognitive behavioral therapy, that is, to determine whether it results in a positive mean weight change.

Think It Through

The response variable, weight change, is quantitative. A significance test about the population mean weight change assumes that the population distribution of weight change is approximately normal. We'll learn how to check this assumption later in the section. The test also assumes randomization for the data production. The anorexia study is like the dogs detecting cancer study in Example 4 in that its subjects were a convenience sample. As a result, inferences are highly tentative. They are more convincing if researchers can argue that the girls in the sample are representative of the population of girls who suffer from anorexia. The study did employ randomization in assigning girls to one of three therapies, only one of which (cognitive behavioral) is considered in this example.

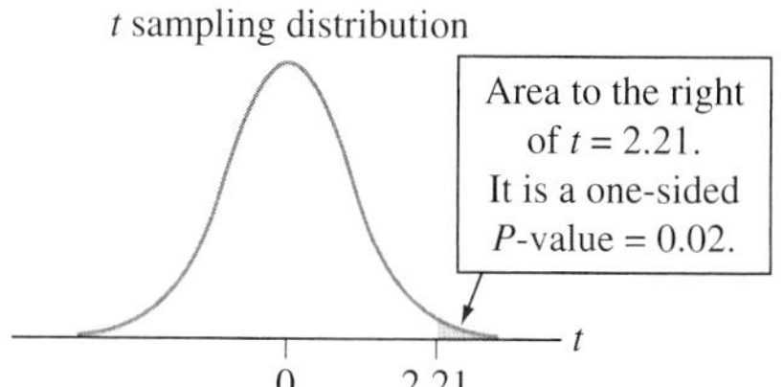

▲ **Figure 9.7** P-value for Testing H_0: $\mu = 0$ against H_0: $\mu > 0$. **Question** Why are large positive, rather than large negative, t test statistic values the ones that support H_0: $\mu > 0$?

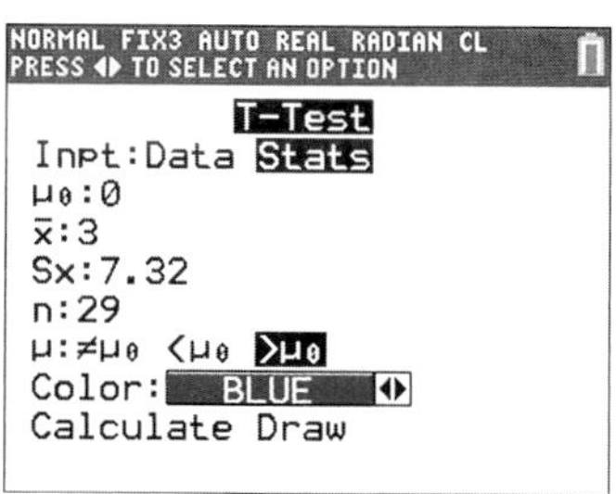

Hypotheses refer to the population mean weight change μ, namely whether it is 0 (the no effect value) or is positive. To use a significance test to analyze the strength of evidence about the therapy's effect, we'll test H_0: $\mu = 0$ against H_a: $\mu > 0$.

Now let's find the test statistic. Using the information from the start of this example, the standard error $se = s/\sqrt{n} = 7.32/\sqrt{29} = 1.36$. The test statistic equals

$$t = (\bar{x} - \mu_0)/se = (3.00 - 0)/1.36 = 2.21,$$

with $df = n - 1 = 28$. Because H_a predicts that the mean is *above* 0, the P-value is the right-tail probability *above* the test statistic value of 2.21. This is 0.018, or 0.02 rounded to two decimal places. See Figure 9.7 and the TI output in the margin on this and the next page. The P-value of 0.02 means that if H_0: $\mu = 0$ were true, it would be unusual (about a 2% chance) to observe a t statistic of 2.21 or even larger in the

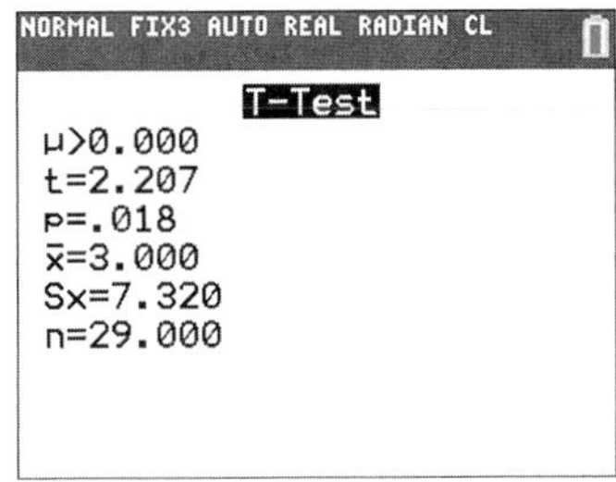

TI output for t test

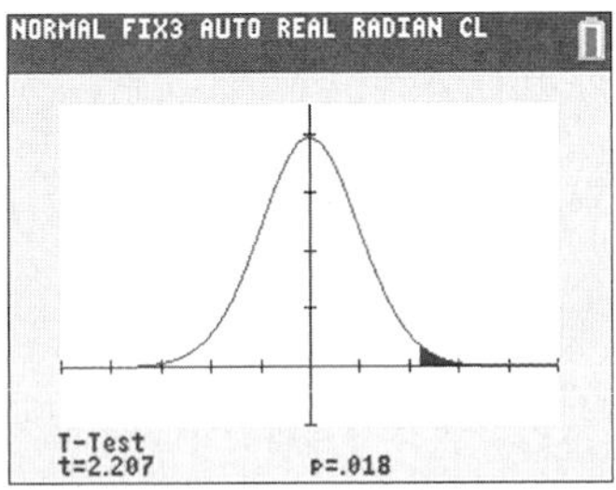

positive direction. A P-value of 0.02 provides substantial evidence against H_0: $\mu = 0$ and in favor of H_a: $\mu > 0$. If we needed to make a decision and had preselected a significance level of 0.05, we would reject H_0: $\mu = 0$ in favor of H_a: $\mu > 0$.

In summary, anorexic girls on this therapy appear to gain weight, on average. This conclusion is tentative, however, for two reasons. First, as with nearly all medical studies, this study used a convenience sample rather than a random sample. Second, we have not yet investigated the shape of the distribution of weight changes. We'll study this issue later in the section.

Insight

We used a one-sided alternative hypothesis in this test to detect a positive effect of the therapy. In practice, the two-sided alternative H_a: $\mu \neq 0$ is more common and lets us take an objective approach that can detect either a positive or a negative effect. For H_a: $\mu \neq 0$, the P-value is the two-tail probability, so $P = 2(0.02) = 0.04$. This two-sided test also provides relatively strong evidence against the no effect null hypothesis.

▶ ***Try Exercise 9.31***

For the one-sided H_a: $\mu > 0$ in this example, the P-value is the probability of t values above the observed t test statistic value of 2.21. Equivalently, it is the probability of a sample mean weight change $\bar{x}$ of 3 pounds or even more if the null hypothesis of no weight change is true. (See the figure in the margin.)

We've seen that if $\mu = 0$, it would be unusual to get a sample mean of 3.0. If in fact μ were a number *less than* 0, it would be even more unusual. For example, a sample value of $\bar{x} = 3.0$ is even more unusual when $\mu = -5$ than when $\mu = 0$, since 3.0 is farther out in the tail of the sampling distribution of $\bar{x}$ when $\mu = -5$ than when $\mu = 0$. (See the figure in the margin.)

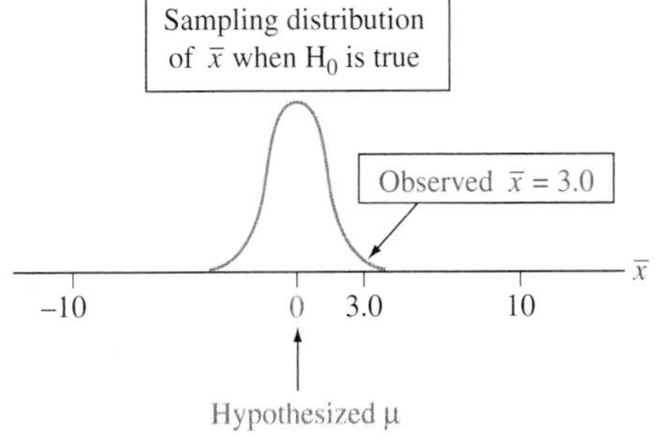

Thus, when we reject H_0: $\mu = 0$ in favor of H_a: $\mu > 0$, we can also reject the broader null hypothesis of H_0: $\mu \leq 0$. In other words, once we conclude that $\mu = 0$ is false, we automatically know that $\mu < 0$ is also false. This is why sometimes you see a one-sided significance test hypothesis written as H_0: $\mu \leq 0$ against H_a: $\mu > 0$. However, in computing the test statistic, we use the single number $\mu = 0$ because it presents the most extreme case. If we can reject the null hypothesis in favor of H_a: $\mu > 0$ when $\mu = 0$, we can reject it for any μ less than 0.

Results of Two-Sided Tests and Results of Confidence Intervals Agree

For the anorexia study, we got a P-value of 0.04 for testing H_0: $\mu = 0$ against H_a: $\mu \neq 0$ for the mean weight change with the cognitive behavioral therapy. With the 0.05 significance level, we would reject H_0. A 95% confidence interval for the population mean weight change μ is $\bar{x} \pm t_{.025}(se)$, which is $3.0 \pm 2.048(1.36)$, or (0.2, 5.8) pounds. The confidence interval shows just how different from 0 the population mean weight change is likely to be. It is estimated to fall between 0.2 and 5.8 pounds. We infer that the population mean weight change μ is positive because all the numbers in this interval are greater than 0, but the effect of the therapy may be very small, such as only a 0.2 pound weight gain.

Both the significance test and the confidence interval suggested that μ differs from 0. In fact, conclusions about means using two-sided significance tests are consistent with conclusions using confidence intervals. If a two-sided test says you can reject the hypothesis that $\mu = 0$, then 0 is not in the corresponding confidence interval for μ.

By contrast, suppose that the P-value > 0.05 in a two-sided test of H_0: $\mu = 0$, so we cannot reject H_0 at the 0.05 significance level. Then, a 95% confidence interval for μ will contain 0. Both methods will show that the value of 0 is a plausible one for μ.

Did You Know?

If the P-value ≤ 0.05 in a two-sided test, a 95% confidence interval does not contain the H_0 value. ◀

Confidence Intervals and Two-Sided Tests About Means Are Consistent Figure 9.8 illustrates why decisions from two-sided tests about means are consistent with confidence intervals.

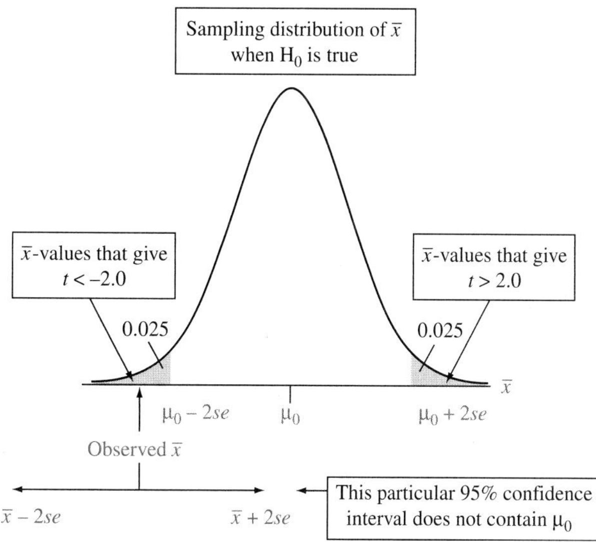

▲ **Figure 9.8 Relation Between Confidence Interval and Significance Test.** With large samples, if the sample mean falls more than about two standard errors from the null value μ_0, then μ_0 does not fall in the 95% confidence interval, and μ_0 is rejected in a test at the 0.05 significance level. **Question** Inference about proportions does not have an *exact* equivalence between confidence intervals and tests. Why? (*Hint:* Are the same standard error values used in the two methods?)

With large samples, the *t*-score for a 95% confidence interval is approximately 2, so the confidence interval is roughly $\bar{x} \pm 2(se)$. If this interval does not contain a particular value μ_0, then the sample mean $\bar{x}$ falls more than 2 standard errors from μ_0, which means that the test statistic $t = (\bar{x} - \mu_0)/se$ is larger than 2 in absolute value. Consequently, the two-tail P-value is less than 0.05, so we would reject the hypothesis that $\mu = \mu_0$.

When the Population Does Not Satisfy the Normality Assumption

For the test about a mean, the third assumption states that the population distribution should be approximately normal. This ensures that the sampling distribution of the sample mean $\bar{x}$ is normal and, after using s to estimate σ, the test statistic has the t distribution. For large samples (roughly about 30 or higher), this assumption is usually not important. Then, an approximate normal sampling distribution occurs for $\bar{x}$ regardless of the population distribution. (Remember the central limit theorem? See the Recall box in margin.)

Recall

From Section 7.2, with random sampling the **sampling distribution of the sample mean is approximately normal** for large *n*, by the central limit theorem. ◀

In Practice Two-Sided Inferences Are Robust

Two-sided inferences using the t distribution are *robust* against violations of the normal population assumption. They still usually work well if the actual population distribution is not normal. The test does not work well for a one-sided test with small n when the population distribution is highly skewed.

What do we mean by "may not work well"? For 95% confidence intervals, we said in Chapter 8 that when assumptions are grossly violated, we make incorrect inference (such as the confidence interval not containing the population mean μ) in much more than only 5% of the cases. Similarly, for significance tests, a violation of the assumptions may result in the actual sampling distribution being quite different from the t distribution. Then, the actual tail probabilities may be larger or smaller than the reported P-value, potentially leading to wrong conclusions about rejecting the null hypothesis.

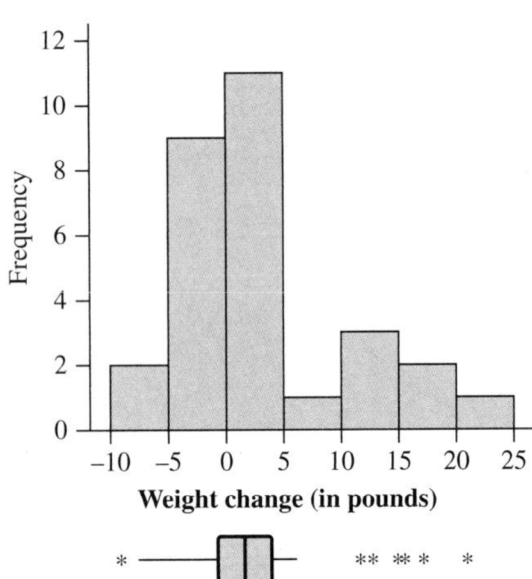

▲ **Figure 9.9** Histogram and Box Plot of Weight Change for Anorexia Sufferers. **Question** What do these plots suggest about the shape of the population distribution of weight change?

Checking for Normality in the Anorexia Study Figure 9.9 shows a histogram and a box plot of the data from the anorexia study. With small n, such plots are very rough estimates of the population distribution. It can be difficult to determine whether the population distribution is approximately normal. However, Figure 9.9 does suggest skew to the right, with a small proportion of girls having considerable weight gains.

A two-sided t test still works quite well even if the population distribution is skewed. So, we feel comfortable with the two-sided test summarized in the Insight step of Example 8. However, this plot makes us cautious about using a one-sided test for these data. The sample size is not large ($n = 29$), and the histogram in Figure 9.9 shows substantial skew, with the box plot highlighting six quite large weight change values.

Regardless of Robustness, Look at the Data Whether n is small or large, you should look at the data to check for severe skew or for outliers that occur primarily in one direction. They could cause the sample mean to be a misleading measure. For the anorexia data, the median weight change is only 1.4 pounds, less than the mean of 3.0 because of the skew to the right. Even though the significance test indicated that the population mean weight change was positive, the sample median is another indication that the size of the effect could be small. You also need to be cautious about any conclusion if it changes after removing an extreme outlier from the data set (see Exercise 9.41).

9.3 Practicing the Basics

9.28 Which t has P-value = 0.05? A t test for a mean uses a sample of 15 observations. Find the t test statistic value that has a P-value of 0.05 when the alternative hypothesis is (a) H_a: $\mu \neq 0$, (b) H_a: $\mu > 0$, and (c) H_a: $\mu < 0$. (Among others, you can use the t Distribution web app to find the answer.)

9.29 Practice mechanics of a t test A study has a random sample of 20 subjects. The test statistic for testing H_0: $\mu = 100$ is $t = 2.40$. Find the approximate P-value for the alternative, (a) H_a: $\mu \neq 100$, (b) H_a: $\mu > 100$, and (c) H_a: $\mu < 100$. (Among others, you can use the t Distribution web app to find the answer.)

9.30 Effect of n Refer to the previous exercise. If the same sample mean and standard deviation had been based on $n = 5$ instead of $n = 20$, the test statistic would have been $t = 1.20$. Would the P-value for H_a: $\mu \neq 100$ be larger, or smaller, than when $t = 2.40$? Why?

9.31 Low carbohydrate diet In a recent study,[8] 272 moderately obese subjects were randomly assigned to one of three diets: low-fat, restricted-calorie; Mediterranean, restricted-calorie; or low-carbohydrate,

TRY

[8] *Am. J. Med.*, vol. 359, 2008, pp. 229–44.

nonrestricted-calorie. The prediction was that subjects on a low-carbohydrate diet would lose weight, on the average. After two years, the mean weight loss was 5.5 kg for the 109 subjects in the low-carbohydrate group with a standard deviation of 7.0 kg. The MINITAB output shows results of a significance test for testing H_0: $\mu = 0$ against H_a: $\mu \neq 0$, where μ is the population mean weight change. Note that weight change is determined by calculating after weight − before weight.

```
                    SE
  N    Mean  StDev  Mean       95% CI          T       P
109 -5.500 7.000  0.670 (-6.829,-4.171) -8.20 0.000
```

a. Identify the P-value for this test.

b. How is the P-value interpreted?

c. Would the P-value and 95% confidence interval lead to the same conclusion about H_0? Explain.

9.32 Female work week When the 583 female workers in the 2012 GSS were asked how many hours they worked in the previous week, the mean was 37.0 hours, with a standard deviation of 15.1 hours. Does this suggest that the population mean work week for females is significantly different from 40 hours? Answer by:

a. Identifying the relevant variable and parameter.

b. Stating null and alternative hypotheses.

c. Reporting and interpreting the P-value for the test statistic value.

d. Explaining how to make a decision for the significance level of 0.01.

9.33 Facebook friends Many students brag that they have more than 100 friends on Facebook. For a class project in 2014, a group of students asked a random sample of 13 students at Williams College who used Facebook about their number of friends and got the following data:

55, 130, 210, 75, 80, 205, 20, 130, 150, 50, 270, 110, 110

Is there strong evidence that the mean number of friends for the student population at Williams who use Facebook is larger than 100? Answer by:

a. Identifying the relevant variable and parameter.

b. Stating null and alternative hypotheses.

c. Finding and interpreting the test statistic value.

d. Reporting and interpreting the P-value and stating the conclusion in context.

9.34 Lake pollution An industrial plant claims to discharge no more than 1000 gallons of wastewater per hour, on the average, into a neighboring lake. An environmental action group decides to monitor the plant in case this limit is being exceeded. Doing so is expensive, and only a small sample is possible. A random sample of four hours is selected over a period of a week. The observations (gallons of wastewater discharged per hour) are

2000, 1000, 3000, 2000.

a. Show that $\bar{x} = 2000$, $s = 816.5$, and standard error $= 408.25$.

b. To test H_0: $\mu = 1000$ vs. H_a: $\mu > 1000$, show that the test statistic equals 2.45.

c. Using Table B or software, show that the P-value is less than 0.05, so there is enough evidence to reject the null hypothesis at the 0.05 significance level.

d. Explain how your one-sided analysis in part b implicitly tests the broader null hypothesis that $\mu \leq 1000$.

9.35 Weight change for controls A disadvantage of the experimental design in Example 8 on weight change in anorexic girls is that girls could change weight merely from participating in a study. In fact, girls were randomly assigned to receive a therapy or to serve in a control group, so it was possible to compare weight change for the therapy group to the control group. For the 26 girls in the control group, the weight change had $\bar{x} = -0.5$ and $s = 8.0$. Repeat all five steps of the test of H_0: $\mu = 0$ against H_a: $\mu \neq 0$ for this group and interpret the P-value.

9.36 Crossover study A crossover study of 13 children suffering from asthma (*Clinical and Experimental Allergy,* vol. 20, pp. 429–432, 1990) compared single inhaled doses of formoterol (F) and salbutamol (S). The outcome measured was the child's peak expiratory flow (PEF) 8 hours following treatment. The data on PEF follow:

Child	F	S	Child	F	S	Child	F	S	Child	F	S
1	310	270	5	410	380	9	330	365	13	220	90
2	385	370	6	370	300	10	250	210			
3	400	310	7	410	390	11	380	350			
4	310	260	8	320	290	12	340	260			

Let μ denote the population mean of the difference between the PEF values for the F and S treatments. Use a calculator or software for the following analyses:

a. Form the 13 difference scores, for instance $310 - 270 = 40$ for child 1 and $330 - 365 = -35$ for child 9, always taking F − S. Construct a dot plot or a box plot. Describe the sample data distribution.

b. Carry out the five steps of the significance test for a mean of the difference scores, using H_0: $\mu = 0$ and H_a: $\mu \neq 0$.

c. Discuss whether the assumptions seem valid for this example. What is the impact of using a convenience sample?

9.37 Too little or too much wine? Wine-pouring vending machines, previously available in Europe and international airports, have become popular in the past few years in the United States. They are even approved to dispense wine in some Walmart stores. The available pouring options are a 5-ounce glass, a 2.5-ounce half-glass, and a 1-ounce taste. When the machine is in statistical control (see Exercise 7.43), the amount dispensed for a full glass is 5.1 ounces. Four observations are taken each day to plot a daily mean over time on a control chart to check for irregularities. The most recent day's observations were 5.05, 5.15, 4.95, and 5.11. Could the difference between the sample mean and the target value be due to random variation, or can you conclude that the true mean is now different from 5.1? Answer by showing the five steps of a significance test, making a decision using a 0.05 significance level.

9.38 Selling a burger In Exercise 9.25, a fast-food chain compared two ways of promoting a turkey burger. In a separate experiment with 10 pairs of stores, the difference in the month's increased sales between the store that used coupons and the store with the outside poster had a mean of $3000. Does this indicate a true difference between mean sales for the two advertising approaches? Answer by using the output shown to test that the population mean difference is 0, carrying out the five steps of a significance test. Make a decision using a 0.05 significance level.

One-Sample T

```
Test of μ = 0 vs ≠ 0
N   Mean   StDev  SE Mean     95% CI          T      P
10  3000   4000    1265    (139, 5861)   2.37  0.042
```

9.39 Assumptions important? Refer to the previous exercise.

a. Explain how the result of the 95% confidence interval shown in the table agrees with the test decision using the 0.05 significance level.

b. Suppose you instead wanted to perform a one-sided test because the study predicted that the increase in sales would be higher with coupons. Explain why the normal population assumption might be problematic.

9.40 Anorexia in teenage girls TECH Example 8 described a study about various therapies for teenage girls suffering from anorexia. For each of 17 girls who received the family therapy, the changes in weight were

11, 11, 6, 9, 14, −3, 0, 7, 22, −5, −4, 13, 13, 9, 4, 6, 11.

a. Plot these data with a dot plot or box plot and summarize.

b. Verify that the weight changes have $\bar{x} = 7.29$, $s = 7.18$, and $se = 1.74$ pounds.

c. Give all steps of a significance test about whether the population mean was 0 against an alternative designed to see whether there is any effect.

9.41 Sensitivity study TECH Ideally, results of a statistical analysis should not depend greatly on a single observation. To check this, it's a good idea to conduct a **sensitivity study.** This entails redoing the analysis after deleting an outlier from the data set or changing its value to a more typical value and checking whether results change much. If results change little, this gives us more faith in the conclusions that the statistical analysis reports. For the weight changes in Table 9.4 from the anorexia study (shown again here and available on the book's website), the greatest reported value of 20.9 pounds was a severe outlier. Suppose this observation was actually 2.9 pounds but was incorrectly recorded. Redo the two-sided test of that example and summarize how the results differ. Does the ultimate conclusion depend on that single observation?

Weight Changes in Anorexic Girls

1.7	11.7	−1.4
0.7	6.1	−0.8
−0.1	1.1	2.4
−0.7	−4.0	12.6
−3.5	20.9	1.9
14.9	−9.3	3.9
3.5	2.1	0.1
17.1	1.4	15.4
−7.6	−0.3	−0.7
1.6	−3.7	

9.42 Test and CI Results of 99% confidence intervals are consistent with results of two-sided tests with which significance level? Explain the connection.

9.4 Decisions and Types of Errors in Significance Tests

In significance tests, the P-value summarizes the evidence about H_0. A P-value such as 0.001 casts strong doubt on H_0 being true because if it were true the observed data would be very unusual.

When we need to decide if the evidence is strong enough to reject H_0, we've seen that the key is whether the P-value falls below a prespecified **significance level**. The significance level is usually denoted by the Greek letter α (alpha). In practice, $\alpha = 0.05$ is most common: We reject H_0 if the P-value ≤ 0.05. We do not reject H_0 if the P-value > 0.05. The smaller α is, the stronger the evidence must be to reject H_0. To avoid bias, we select α *before* looking at the data.

Two Potential Types of Errors in Test Decisions

Because of sampling variability, decisions in significance tests always have some uncertainty. A decision can be in error. For instance, in the anorexia study of Example 8, we got a P-value of 0.04 for testing H_0: $\mu = 0$ of no weight change, on average, against H_a: $\mu \neq 0$. With significance level $\alpha = 0.05$ we rejected H_0 and concluded that the mean was not equal to 0. The data indicated that anorexic girls have a positive mean weight change when undergoing the therapy. If the therapy truly has a positive effect, this is a correct decision. In reality, though, perhaps the therapy has no effect, and the population mean weight change (unknown to us) is actually 0.

Tests have two types of potential errors, called **Type I** and **Type II errors**.

Type I and Type II Errors

When H_0 is true, a **Type I error** occurs when H_0 is rejected.
When H_0 is false, a **Type II error** occurs when H_0 is not rejected.

If you have a hard time distinguishing the two, you can think of a Type I error as a **false positive.** (A positive decision is reached by rejecting H_0, yet the decision is false.) A Type II error is a **false negative.** (A negative decision is reached by not rejecting H_0, yet the decision is false.)

If the anorexia therapy actually has no effect (that is, if $\mu = 0$), we've made a Type I error. H_0 was actually true, but we rejected it. We have a positive result (claiming a significant weight change), yet it is false; there actually is no weight change. A consequence of committing this Type I error would be implementing a therapy that actually has no effect on helping with weight gain and thus gives patients false hope.

Consider the experiment about astrology in Example 5. In that study H_0: $p = 1/3$ corresponded to random guessing by the astrologers. We got a P-value of 0.40. With significance level $= 0.05$, we do not reject H_0. If truly $p = 1/3$, this is a correct decision. However, if astrologers actually can predict better than random guessing (so that $p > 1/3$), we've made a Type II error, failing to reject H_0 when it is false. We have a negative result (claiming astrologers can't make predictions), yet it is false because they actually can. A consequence of committing this Type II error would be calling these astrologers fakes when actually they have predictive powers.

When we make a decision, there are four possible results. These refer to the two possible decisions combined with the two possibilities for whether H_0 is true. Table 9.5 summarizes these four possibilities. In practice, when we plan to make a decision in a significance test, it's important to know the probability of an incorrect decision.

Table 9.5 The Four Possible Results of a Decision in a Significance Test

Type I and Type II errors are the two possible incorrect decisions. A Type I error (false positive) occurs if we reject H_0 when it is actually true. A Type II error (false negative) occurs if we do not reject H_0 when it is actually false. We make a correct decision if we do not reject H_0 when it is true or if we reject it when it is false.

	Decision	
Reality About H_0	**Do not reject H_0**	**Reject H_0**
H_0 true	Correct decision	Type I error
H_0 false	Type II error	Correct decision

An Analogy: Decision Errors in a Legal Trial The two types of errors can occur with any decision having two options, one of which is incorrect. For instance, consider a decision in a legal trial. The null hypothesis tested is the defendant's claim of innocence. The alternative hypothesis is that the defendant is guilty. The jury rejects H_0 if it decides that the evidence is sufficient to convict. The defendant is then judged guilty. A Type I error, rejecting a true null hypothesis, occurs in convicting a defendant who is actually innocent. Not rejecting H_0 means the defendant is acquitted (judged not guilty). A Type II error, not rejecting H_0 even though it is false, occurs in acquitting a defendant who is actually guilty. See Table 9.6.

A potential consequence of a Type I error is sending an innocent person to jail. A potential consequence of a Type II error is setting free a guilty person.

Table 9.6 Possible Results of a Legal Trial

	Legal Decision	
Defendant	**Acquit**	**Convict**
Innocent (H_0)	Correct decision	Type I error
Guilty (H_a)	Type II error	Correct decision

The Significance Level Is the Probability of a Type I Error

The probability of rejecting H_0 even though it is actually true is equal to the significance level. So when the significance level is 0.05, the probability of incorrectly rejecting H_0, i.e., committing a Type I error, is 5%. Let's look at a two-sided test about a proportion to see how we got this result.

With a significance level of $\alpha = 0.05$, we reject H_0 if the P-value ≤ 0.05. For two-sided tests about a proportion, the two-tail probability that forms the P-value is ≤ 0.05 whenever the test statistic z satisfies $|z| \geq 1.96$. The collection of test statistic values for which a test rejects H_0 is called the **rejection region**. These are the z test statistic values that occur when the sample proportion falls at least 1.96 standard errors from the null hypothesis value. They are the values we'd least expect to observe if H_0 were true. Figure 9.10 illustrates.

In Words

The expression $|z| \geq 1.96$ is the same as saying $z < -1.96$ or $z > 1.96$.

Now, if H_0 is actually true, the sampling distribution of the z test statistic is the standard normal. The probability of rejecting H_0 is the probability of observing a test statistic that falls in the rejection region. In our case, this would be a test statistic z that is less than -1.96 or larger than 1.96. The probability of observing such a z under the standard normal distribution is exactly 0.05, which is precisely the significance level.

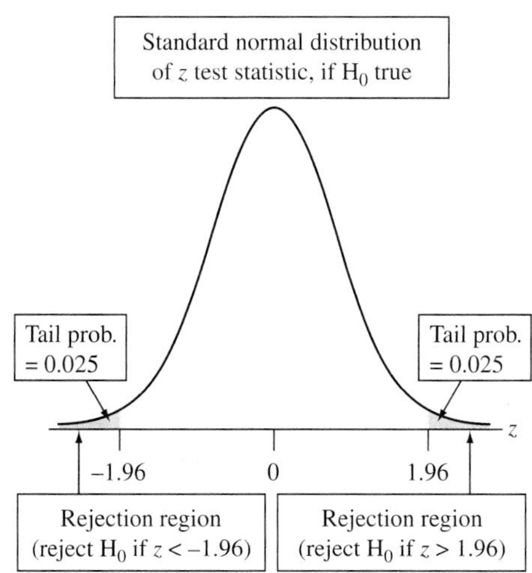

▲ **Figure 9.10** The Rejection Region Is the Set of Test Statistic Values That Reject H_0. For a two-sided test about a proportion with significance level 0.05, these are the z test statistic values that exceed 1.96 in absolute value. **Question** If instead we use a one-sided H_a: $p > p_0$, what is the rejection region?

P(Type I error) = Significance level α

Suppose H_0 is true. The probability of rejecting H_0, thereby making a Type I error, equals the significance level for the test.

In Practice We Don't Know If a Decision Is Correct

In practice, we don't know whether a decision in a significance test is correct, just as we don't know whether a particular confidence interval truly contains an unknown parameter value. However, we can control the *probability* of an incorrect decision for either type of inference.

The good news about this result is that we can control the probability of a Type I error by our choice of the significance level. The more serious the consequences of a Type I error, the smaller α should be. In practice, $\alpha = 0.05$ is most common, just as a probability of error of 0.05 in interval estimation is most common (that is, 95% confidence intervals). However, this number may be too high when a decision has serious implications. For example, suppose a convicted defendant gets the death penalty. Then, if a defendant is actually innocent, we would hope that the probability of conviction is smaller than 0.05.

Although we don't know if the decision in a particular test is correct, we justify the method in terms of the long-run proportions of Type I and Type II errors. If every time we conduct a test we reject H_0 when the P-value is less than 0.05, in the long run we will make a Type I error in no more than 5% of the cases. We'll learn how to calculate P(Type II error) later in the chapter.

Example 9

Probability of a Type I error

Type I Errors in Legal Verdicts

Picture the Scenario

In an ideal world, Type I or Type II errors would not occur. In practice, however, whether in significance tests or in applications such as courtroom trials or medical diagnoses, errors do happen. It can be surprising and disappointing how often they occur, as we saw in the diagnostic testing examples of Chapter 5. Likewise, we've all read about defendants who were given the death penalty but were later determined to be innocent, but we don't have reliable information about how often this occurs.

Question to Explore

When we make a decision, why don't we use an extremely small probability of Type I error such as $\alpha = 0.000001$? For instance, why don't we make it almost impossible to convict someone who is really innocent?

Think It Through

When we make α smaller in a significance test, we need a smaller P-value to reject H_0. It then becomes harder to reject H_0. But this means that it will also be harder to reject H_0 even if H_0 is false. The stronger the evidence that is required to convict someone, the more likely it becomes that we will fail to convict defendants who are actually guilty. In other words, the smaller we make the probability of Type I error, the *larger* the probability of Type II error becomes (that is, failing to reject H_0 even though it is false).

If we tolerate only an extremely small chance of a Type I error (such as $\alpha = 0.000001$), then the test may be unlikely to reject the null hypothesis even if it is false—for instance, unlikely to convict someone even if they are guilty. In fact, some of our laws are set up to make Type I errors very unlikely, and as a consequence some truly guilty individuals are not punished for their crimes.

Insight

This reasoning reflects a fundamental relation between the probabilities of the two types of errors for a given sample size n:

As P(Type I Error) Goes Down, P(Type II Error) Goes Up

The two probabilities are inversely related.

▶ ***Try Exercise 9.50, part c***

Except in the final section of this chapter, we will not calculate the probability of a Type II error. This calculation can be complex. In practice, to make a decision in a test, we only need to set the probability of Type I error, which is the significance level α.

These days, most research articles merely report the P-value rather than a decision about whether to reject H_0. From the P-value, readers can see the strength of evidence against H_0 and make their own decisions.

▶ Activity 1

Why Is 0.05 Commonly Used as a Significance Level?

Suppose someone tosses a coin you can't confirm ahead of time is fair. Based on a couple of tosses, you need to decide whether you can reject H_0: p = probability of head = 0.50 (fair coin) in favor of H_a: $p \neq 0.50$. Consider the following:

- On the first toss, the coin lands heads. Would you reject H_0 and conclude that the coin is not fair?
- On the second toss, the coin lands heads. Would you now reject H_0 and conclude that the coin is not fair?
- On the third toss, the coin also lands heads. Would you now reject H_0 and conclude that the coin is not fair?
- On the fourth toss, the coin lands heads again. Are you now starting to doubt that H_0 is true and willing to believe that H_a may be true?
- On the fifth toss, the coin lands heads again. Are you now ready to reject H_0 and conclude that the coin cannot be fair?

If you are like many people, by the time you see the fifth straight head, you are willing to predict that the coin is not fair. (By then, you may even visually inspect the coin to make sure it has different sides.) If the null hypothesis that $p = 0.50$ is actually true, then by the binomial distribution, the probability of five heads in a row is $(0.50)^5 = 1/32 = 0.03$. For a two-sided test, this result gives a P-value of $2(0.03) = 0.06$, close to 0.05. So, for many people, it takes a P-value near 0.05 before they feel there is enough evidence to reject a null hypothesis. (For comparison, many people would not get too suspicious of the null hypothesis after four straight heads, for which the P-value is 0.125.) This may be one reason the significance level of 0.05 has become common over the years in a wide variety of disciplines that use significance tests.

Exercise 9.129 presents this activity in the context of comparing a drug (for instance, against migraine) to a placebo to test which one is better. You start by assuming they are equally effective (the null hypothesis). One patient after another tries both the drug and the placebo (in random order) and reports which one is better. After the first five patients report better results with the placebo, are you willing to accept that the placebo works better?

Try Exercise 9.129 ◀

9.4 Practicing the Basics

9.43 Dr. Dog In the experiment in Example 4, we got a P-value < 0.001 for testing H_0: $p = 1/7$ about dogs' ability to diagnose urine from bladder cancer patients.

a. For the significance level 0.05, what decision would you make?

b. If you made an error in part a, what type of error was it? Explain what the error means in context of the dog experiment.

9.44 Error probability A significance test about a proportion is conducted using a significance level of 0.05. The test statistic equals 2.58. The P-value is 0.01.

a. If H_0 were true, for what probability of a Type I error was the test designed?

b. If this test resulted in a decision error, what type of error was it?

9.45 Fracking errors Example 6, in testing H_0: $p = 0.5$ against H_a: $p < 0.5$, analyzed whether those opposing increased use of fracking are in the minority. In the words of that example, what would be (a) a Type I error and (b) a Type II error?

9.46 Anorexia errors Example 8 tested a therapy for anorexia, using hypotheses H_0: $\mu = 0$ and H_a: $\mu \neq 0$ about the population mean weight change μ. In the words of that example, what would be (a) a Type I error and (b) a Type II error?

9.47 Anorexia decision Refer to the previous exercise. When we test H_0: $\mu = 0$ against H_a: $\mu > 0$, we get a P-value of 0.02.

a. What would the decision be for a significance level of 0.05? Interpret in context.

b. If the decision in part a is in error, what type of error is it?

c. Suppose the significance level were instead 0.01. What decision would you make, and if it is in error, what type of error is it?

9.48 Errors in the courtroom Consider the test of H_0: The defendant is not guilty against H_a: The defendant is guilty.

a. Explain, in context, the conclusion of the test if H_0 is rejected.

b. Describe, in context, a Type I error.

c. Explain, in context, the conclusion of the test if you fail to reject H_0.

d. Describe, in context, a Type II error.

9.49 Errors in medicine Consider the test of H_0: The new drug is safe against H_a: the new drug is not safe.

a. Explain, in context, the conclusion of the test if H_0 is rejected.

b. Describe, in context, a Type I error.

c. Explain, in context, the conclusion of the test if you fail to reject H_0.

d. Describe, in context, a Type II error.

9.50 Decision errors in medical diagnostic testing Consider medical diagnostic testing, such as using a mammogram to detect if a woman may have breast cancer. Define the null hypothesis of no effect as the patient does not have the disease. Define rejecting H_0 as concluding that the patient has the disease. See the table for a summary of the possible outcomes:

TRY

Medical Diagnostic Testing

	Medical Diagnosis	
Disease	**Negative**	**Positive**
No (H_0)	Correct	Type I error
Yes (H_a)	Type II error	Correct

a. When a radiologist interprets a mammogram, explain why a Type I error is a false positive, predicting that a woman has breast cancer when actually she does not.

b. A Type II error is a false negative. What does this mean, and what is the consequence of such an error to the woman?

c. A radiologist wants to decrease the chance of telling a woman that she may have breast cancer when actually she does not. Consequently, a positive test result will be reported only when there is *extremely* strong evidence that breast cancer is present. What is the disadvantage of this approach?

9.51 Detecting prostate cancer Refer to the previous exercise about medical diagnoses. A *New York Times* article (February 17, 1999) about the PSA blood test for detecting prostate cancer stated: "The test fails to detect prostate cancer in 1 in 4 men who have the disease."

a. For the PSA test, explain what a Type I error is and explain the consequence to a man of this type of error.

b. For the PSA test, what is a Type II error? What is the consequence to a man of this type of error?

c. To which type of error does the probability of 1 in 4 refer?

d. The article also stated that if you receive a positive result, the probability that you do not actually have prostate cancer is 2/3. Explain the difference between this and the conditional probability of a Type I error, given that you do not actually have prostate cancer.

9.52 Which error is worse? Which error, Type I or Type II, would usually be considered more serious for decisions in the following tests? Explain why.

a. A trial to test a murder defendant's claimed innocence, when conviction results in the death penalty.

b. A medical diagnostic procedure, such as a mammogram.

9.5 Limitations of Significance Tests

Chapters 8 and 9 have presented the two primary methods of statistical inference—confidence intervals and significance testing. We will use both of these methods throughout the rest of the book. Of the two methods, confidence intervals can be more useful for reasons we'll discuss in this section. Significance tests have more potential for misuse. We'll now summarize the major limitations of significance tests.

Statistical Significance Does Not Mean Practical Significance

When we conduct a significance test, its main relevance is studying whether the true parameter value is

- above, or below, the value in H_0, and
- sufficiently different from the value in H_0 to be of practical importance.

A significance test gives us information about whether the parameter differs from the H_0 value and its direction from that value, but we'll see now that it does not tell us about the practical significance (or importance) of the finding.

There is an important distinction between *statistical significance* and *practical significance.* A small P-value, such as 0.001, is highly statistically significant, giving strong evidence against H_0. It may not, however, imply an *important* finding in any practical sense. The small P-value means that if H_0 were true, the observed data would be unusual. It does not mean that the true value of the parameter is far from the null hypothesis value in practical terms. In particular, whenever the sample size is large, small P-values can occur when the point estimate is near the parameter value in H_0, as the following example shows.

Example 10

Statistical significance and practical significance ◄

Political Conservatism and Liberalism in America

Picture the Scenario

Where do Americans say they fall on the conservative–liberal political spectrum? The General Social Survey asks, "I'm going to show you a seven-point scale on which the political views that people might hold are arranged from extremely liberal, point 1, to extremely conservative, point 7. Where would you place yourself on this scale?" Table 9.7 shows the scale and the distribution of 2449 responses for the GSS in 2014.

Table 9.7 Responses of 2449 Subjects on a Seven-Point Scale of Political Views. Data are available from the book's website.

Category	Count
1. Extremely liberal	94
2. Liberal	304
3. Slightly liberal	263
4. Moderate, middle of road	989
5. Slightly conservative	334
6. Conservative	358
7. Extremely conservative	107

This categorical variable has seven categories that are ordered in terms of degree of liberalism or conservatism. Categorical variables that have *ordered* categories are called **ordinal variables.** Sometimes we treat an ordinal variable in a quantitative manner by assigning scores to the categories and summarizing the data by the mean. This summarizes whether observations gravitate toward the conservative or the liberal end of the scale. For the category scores of 1 to 7, as in Table 9.7, a mean of 4.0 corresponds to the moderate outcome. A mean below 4 shows a propensity toward liberalism, and a mean above 4 shows a propensity toward conservatism. The 2449 observations in Table 9.7 have a mean of 4.09 and a standard deviation of 1.43.

Questions to Explore

a. Do these data indicate that the population in 2014 has a propensity toward liberalism or toward conservatism? Answer by conducting a significance test that compares the population mean to the moderate value of 4.0 by testing H_0: $\mu = 4.0$ against H_a: $\mu \neq 4.0$.

b. Does this test show (i) statistical significance? (ii) practical significance?

In Words

An ordinal variable is a categorical variable for which the categories are ordered from low to high in some sense. Table 9.7 lists categories of political views from low to high in terms of conservatism.

Think It Through

a. For the sample data, the standard error $se = s/\sqrt{n} = 1.43/\sqrt{2449} = 0.0290$. The test statistic for H_0: $\mu = 4.0$ equals

$$t = (\bar{x} - \mu_0)/se = (4.09 - 4.00)/0.0290 = 3.1.$$

Its two-sided P-value is 0.002. There is strong evidence that the population mean differs from 4.0. The data indicates that true mean exceeds 4.0, with the true mean falling on the conservative side of moderate.

b. Although the P-value is small, on a scale of 1 to 7, the sample mean of 4.09 is close to the value of 4.0 in H_0. It is only 9% of the distance from the moderate score of 4.0 to the slightly conservative score of 5.0. Although the difference of 0.09 between the sample mean of 4.09 and the null hypothesis mean of 4.0 is highly significant statistically, this difference is small in practical terms. We'd regard a mean of 4.09 as moderate on this 1 to 7 scale. In summary, there's statistical significance but not practical significance.

Insight

With large samples, P-values can be small even when the sample estimate falls near the parameter value in H_0. The P-value measures the extent of evidence about H_0, not how far the true parameter value happens to be from H_0. Always inspect the difference between the sample estimate and the null hypothesis value to gauge the practical implications of a test result.

► ***Try Exercise 9.54***

Significance Tests Are Less Useful Than Confidence Intervals

Although significance tests are useful, most statisticians believe that this method has been overemphasized in research.

- A significance test merely indicates whether the particular parameter value in H_0 (such as $\mu = 0$) is plausible.

When a P-value is small, the significance test indicates that the hypothesized value is not plausible, but it tells us little about which potential parameter values *are* plausible.

- A confidence interval is more informative because it displays the entire set of plausible values.

A confidence interval shows if H_0 may be badly false by showing if the values in the interval are far from the H_0 value. It helps us to determine whether the difference between the true value and the H_0 value has practical importance.

Let's illustrate with Example 10 and the 1 to 7 scale for political beliefs. A 95% confidence interval for μ is $\bar{x} \pm 1.96(se) = 4.09 \pm 1.96(0.0290)$, or (4.03, 4.15). We can conclude that the difference between the population mean and the moderate score of 4.0 is small. Figure 9.11 illustrates. Although the P-value of 0.002 provided strong evidence against H_0: $\mu = 4.0$, in practical terms the confidence interval shows that H_0 is not wrong by much.

In contrast, if $\bar{x}$ had been 6.09 (instead of 4.09), the 95% confidence interval would equal (6.03, 6.15). This confidence interval indicates a substantial difference from 4.0, the mean response being near the conservative score rather than near the moderate score.

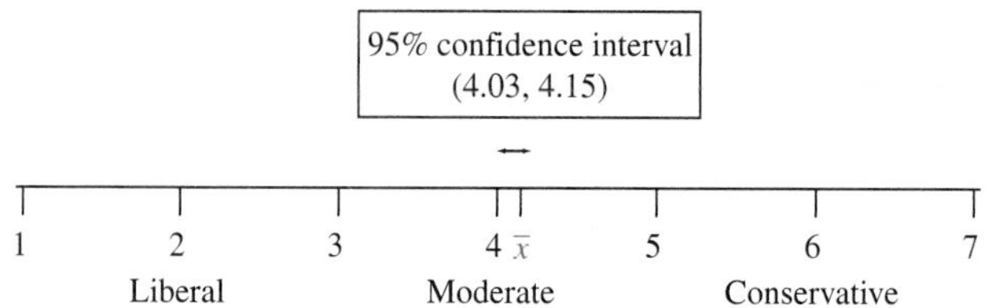

▲ **Figure 9.11 Statistical Significance But Not Practical Significance.** In testing H_0: $\mu = 4.0$, the P-value = 0.002, but the confidence interval of (4.03, 4.15) shows that μ is very close to the H_0 value of 4.0. **Question** For H_0: $\mu = 4.0$, does a sample mean of 6.09 and confidence interval of (6.03, 6.15) indicate (a) statistical significance? (b) practical significance?

Misinterpretations of Results of Significance Tests

Unfortunately, results of significance tests are often misinterpreted. Here are some important comments about significance tests, some of which we've already discussed:

- **"Do not reject H_0" does not mean "Accept H_0."** If you get a P-value above 0.05 when the significance level is 0.05, you cannot conclude that H_0 is correct. We can never accept a single value, which H_0 contains, such as $p = 0.50$ or $\mu = 0$. A test merely indicates whether a particular parameter value is plausible. A confidence interval shows that there is a *range* of plausible values, not just a single one.
- **Statistical significance does not mean practical significance.** A small P-value does not tell us if the parameter value differs by much in practical terms from the value in H_0. Even a small and practically unimportant difference between a sample mean or proportion and the null hypothesis value can lead to a statistically significant result if the sample size is large enough. A small P-value alone does not imply that the effect that the alternative hypothesis spells out is practically meaningful. By contrast, a confidence interval allows you to estimate the magnitude or effect size of the parameter. From it, you can immediately judge whether the effect is practically relevant.
- **The P-value cannot be interpreted as the probability that H_0 is true.** This is a common mistake. The P-value is

$$P(\text{test statistic takes observed value or beyond in tails} \mid H_0 \text{ true}),$$
$$\text{NOT } P(H_0 \text{ true} \mid \text{observed test statistic value}).$$

  We've been calculating probabilities about test statistic values, not about parameters. It makes sense to find the probability that a test statistic takes a value in the tail, but the probability that a population mean = 0 does not make sense because probabilities do not apply to parameters (since parameters are fixed numbers and not random variables). The null hypothesis H_0 is either true or not true, and we simply do not know which.[9]

Recall

$P(A|B)$ denotes the conditional probability of event A, given event B. To find a P-value, we condition on H_0 being true (that is, we presume it is true), rather than find the probability it is true. ◀

- **It is misleading to report results only if they are "statistically significant."** Some research journals have the policy of publishing results of a study only if the P-value ≤ 0.05. Here's a danger of this policy: If there truly is no effect, but 20 researchers independently conduct studies about it, we would expect about $20(0.05) = 1$ of them to obtain significance at the 0.05 level merely by chance. (When H_0 is true, about 5% of the time we get a P-value below 0.05 anyway.) If that researcher then submits results to a journal but the other 19 researchers do not, the article published will be a Type I error—reporting an effect when there really is not one. The popular media may then also report on this study, causing the general public to hear about an effect that does not actually exist.

[9]It is possible to find probabilities about parameter values by using an approach called *Bayesian statistics*, but this requires extra assumptions and is beyond the scope of this text.

- **Some tests may be statistically significant just by chance.** You should never scan pages and pages of computer output for results that are statistically significant and report only those. If you run 100 tests, even if all the null hypotheses are correct, you would expect to get P-values of 0.05 or less about $100(0.05) = 5$ times. Keep this in mind and be skeptical of reports of significance that might merely reflect ordinary random variability. For instance, suppose an article reports an unusually high rate of a rare type of cancer in your town. It could be due to some cause such as air or water pollution. However, if researchers found this by looking at data for *all* towns and cities nationwide, it could also be due to random variability. Determining which is true may not be easy.
- **True effects may not be as large as initial estimates reported by the media.** Even if a statistically significant result is a true effect, the true effect may be smaller than suggested in the first article about it. For instance, often several researchers perform similar studies, but the results that get attention are the most extreme ones. This sensationalism may come about because the researcher who is the first to publicize the result is the one who got the most impressive sample result, perhaps way out in the tail of the sampling distribution of all the possible results. Then the study's estimate of the effect may be greater than later research shows it to be.

Example 11

Type I errors

Medical "Discoveries"

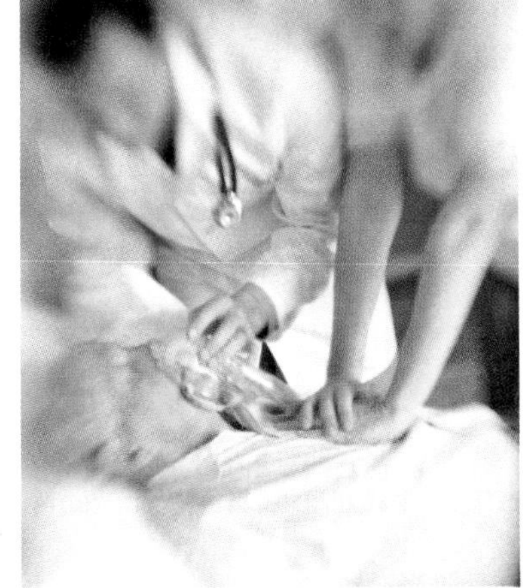

Picture the Scenario

What can be done with heart attack victims to increase their chance of survival? In the 1990s, trials of a clot-busting drug called anistreplase suggested that it doubled the chance of survival. Likewise, another study estimated that injections of magnesium could double the chance of survival. However, a much larger study of heart attack survival rates among 58,000 patients indicated that this optimism was premature. The actual effectiveness of anistreplase seemed to be barely half that estimated by the original trial, and magnesium injections seemed to have no effect at all.[10] The anistreplase finding is apparently an example of a true effect not being as large as the initial estimate, and the report from the original magnesium study may well have been a Type I error.

Question to Explore

In medical studies, suppose that a true effect exists only 10% of the time. Suppose also that when an effect truly exists, there's a 50% chance of making a Type II error and failing to detect it. These were the hypothetical percentages used in an article in a medical journal.[11] The authors noted that many medical studies have a high Type II error rate because they are not able to use a large sample size. Assuming these rates, could a substantial percentage of medical "discoveries" actually be Type I errors? Given that H_0 is rejected, approximate the P(Type I error) by considering a tree diagram of what you would expect to happen with 1000 medical studies that test various hypotheses.

[10] "The Great Health Hoax," by R. Matthews, in *The Sunday Telegraph*, September 13, 1998.
[11] By J. Sterne, G. Smith, and D.R. Cox, *BMJ*, vol. 322, pp. 226–231 (2001).

Think It Through

Figure 9.12 is a tree diagram of what's expected. A true effect exists 10% of the time, or in 100 of the 1000 studies. We do not get a small enough P-value to detect this true effect 50% of the time, that is, in 50 of these 100 studies. No effect will be reported for the other 50 of the 100 studies that do truly have an effect. Now, for the 900 cases in which there truly is no effect, with the usual significance level of 0.05, we expect 5% of the 900 studies (that is, 45 studies) to reject the null hypothesis incorrectly and predict that there is an effect. So, of the original 1000 studies, we expect 50 to report an effect that is truly there, but we also expect 45 to report an effect that does not really exist. If the assumptions are reasonable, then a proportion of $45/(45+50) = 0.47$ of medical studies that report effects (that is, reject H_0) are actually reporting Type I errors. In summary, nearly half the time when an effect is reported, there actually is no effect in the population!

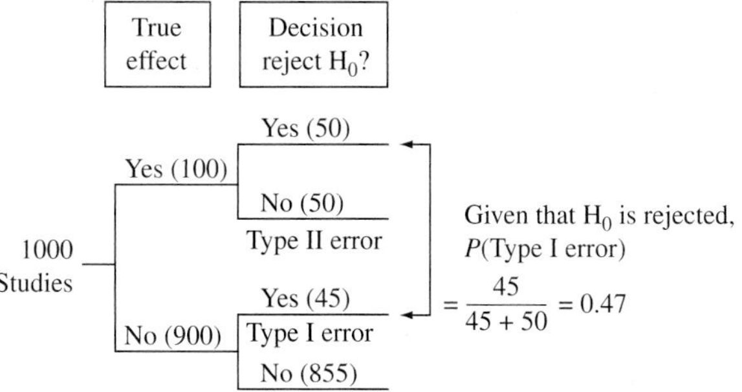

▲ **Figure 9.12 Tree Diagram of Results of 1000 Hypothetical Medical Studies.** This assumes that a true effect exists 10% of the time and that there's a 50% chance of a Type II error when an effect truly does exist.

Insight

Be skeptical when you hear reports of new medical advances. The true effect may be weaker than reported, or there may actually be no effect at all.

► ***Try Exercise 9.58***

Ethics in Data Analysis

Statistics, like any field, has standards for ethical behavior. The comments just made have implications about proper and improper use of significance tests. For example, when you conduct a study, it's not ethical to perform lots and lots of significance tests but only report results when the P-value is small. Even when *all* null hypotheses tested are true, just by chance small P-values occasionally occur. You should report *all* the analyses you have conducted. In fact, before you collect the data, you should formulate a research plan that sets out exactly what analyses you will conduct. (For instance, a protocol that has to be approved by authorities is required before the start of a clinical trial.)

The discussion in Section 9.2 about how to decide between a one-sided and a two-sided test mentioned that it is not ethical to choose a one-sided H_a after seeing the direction in which the data fall. This is because the sampling distribution used in a significance test presumes only that H_0 is true, and it allows sample data in each direction. If we first looked at the data, the valid sampling distribution would be one that is conditioned on the extra information about the direction of the sample data. For example, if the test statistic is positive, the proper sampling distribution would not include negative values. Again, before you collect the data, your research plan should set out the details of the hypotheses you plan to test.

Finally, remember that tests and confidence intervals use *sample* data to make inferences about *populations*. If you have data for an entire population, statistical inference is not necessary. For instance, if your college reports that the class of entering freshmen had a mean high school GPA of 3.60, there is no need to perform a test or construct a confidence interval. You already know the mean for that population.

On the Shoulders of... Jerzy Neyman and the Pearsons

Jerzy Neyman. Neyman, together with Egon Pearson, developed statistical theory for making decisions about hypotheses.

How can you build a framework for making decisions?

The methods of confidence intervals and hypothesis testing were introduced in a series of articles beginning in 1928 by Jerzy Neyman (1894–1981) and Egon Pearson (1895–1980). Neyman emigrated from Poland to England and then to the United States, where he established a top-notch statistics department at the University of California at Berkeley. He helped develop the theory of statistical inference, and he applied the theory to scientific questions in a variety of areas, such as agriculture, astronomy, biology, medicine, and weather modification. For instance, late in his career, Neyman's analysis of data from several randomized experiments showed that cloud-seeding can have a considerable effect on rainfall.

Much of Neyman's theoretical research was done with Egon Pearson, a professor at University College, London. Pearson's father, Karl Pearson, had developed one of the first statistical tests in 1900 to study various hypotheses, including whether the outcomes on a roulette wheel were equally likely. (We'll study his test, the *chi-squared test,* in Chapter 11.) Neyman and the younger Pearson developed the decision-making framework that introduced the two types of errors and the most powerful significance tests for various hypotheses.

9.5 Practicing the Basics

9.53 Misleading summaries? Two researchers conduct separate studies to test H_0: $p = 0.50$ against H_a: $p \neq 0.50$, each with $n = 400$.

- **a.** Researcher A gets 220 observations in the category of interest, and $\hat{p} = 220/400 = 0.550$ and test statistic $z = 2.00$. Show that the P-value $= 0.046$ for Researcher A's analysis.
- **b.** Researcher B gets 219 in the category of interest, and $\hat{p} = 219/400 = 0.5475$ and test statistic $z = 1.90$. Show that the P-value $= 0.057$ for Researcher B's analysis.
- **c.** Using $\alpha = 0.05$, indicate in each case from part a and part b whether the result is "statistically significant." Interpret.
- **d.** From part a, part b, and part c, explain why important information is lost by reporting the result of a test as "P-value ≤ 0.05" versus "P-value > 0.05," or as "reject H_0" versus "do not reject H_0," instead of reporting the actual P-value.
- **e.** Show that the 95% confidence interval for p is (0.501, 0.599) for Researcher A and (0.499, 0.596) for Researcher B. Explain how this method shows that, in practical terms, the two studies had very similar results.

9.54 Practical significance A study considers whether the mean score on a college entrance exam for students in 2010 is any different from the mean score of 500 for students who took the same exam in 1985. Let μ represent the mean score for all students who took the exam in 2010. For a random sample of 25,000 students who took the exam in 2010, $\bar{x} = 498$ and $s = 100$.

TRY

- **a.** Show that the test statistic is $t = -3.16$.
- **b.** Find the P-value for testing H_0: $\mu = 500$ against H_a: $\mu \neq 500$.
- **c.** Explain why the test result is statistically significant but not practically significant.

9.55 Effect of n Example 10 analyzed political conservatism and liberalism in the United States. Suppose that the sample mean of 4.09 and sample standard deviation of 1.43 were from a sample size of only 25, rather than 2449.

- **a.** Find the test statistic.
- **b.** Find the P-value for testing H_0: $\mu = 4.0$ against H_a: $\mu \neq 4.0$. Interpret.
- **c.** Show that a 95% confidence interval for μ is (3.5, 4.7).
- **d.** Together with the results of Example 10, explain what this illustrates about the effect of sample size on (i) the size of the P-value (for a given mean and standard deviation) and (ii) the width of the confidence interval.

9.56 Fishing for significance A marketing study conducts 60 significance tests about means and proportions for several groups. Of them, 3 tests are statistically significant at the 0.05 level. The study's final report stresses only the tests with significant results, not mentioning the other 57 tests. What is misleading about this?

9.57 Selective reporting In 2004, New York Attorney General Eliot Spitzer filed a lawsuit against GlaxoSmithKline pharmaceutical company, claiming that the company failed to publish results of one of its studies that showed that an antidepressant drug (Paxil) may make adolescents more likely to commit suicide. Partly as a consequence, editors of 11 medical journals agreed to a new policy to make researchers and companies register all clinical trials when they begin, so that negative results cannot later be covered up. The *International Journal of Medical Journal Editors* wrote, "Unfortunately, selective reporting of trials does occur, and it distorts the body of evidence available for clinical decision-making." Explain why this controversy relates to the argument that it is misleading to report results only if they are "statistically significant." (*Hint:* See the subsection of this chapter on misinterpretations of significance tests.)

9.58 How many medical discoveries are Type I errors? Refer to Example 11. Using a tree diagram, given that H_0 is rejected, approximate P(Type I error) under the assumption that a true effect exists 20% of the time and that there's a 30% chance of a Type II error.

TRY

9.59 Interpret medical research studies

a. An advertisement by Schering Corp. in 1999 for the allergy drug Claritin mentioned that in a clinical trial, the proportion who showed symptoms of nervousness was not significantly greater for patients taking Claritin than for patients taking placebo. Does this mean that the population proportion having nervous symptoms is exactly the same using Claritin and using placebo? How would you explain this to someone who has not studied statistics?

b. An article in the medical journal *BMJ* (by M. Petticrew et al., published November 2002) found no evidence to back the commonly held belief that a positive attitude can lengthen the lives of cancer patients. The authors noted that the studies that had indicated a benefit from some coping strategies tended to be smaller studies with weaker designs. Using this example and the text discussion, explain why you need to have some skepticism when you hear that new research suggests that some therapy or drug has an impact in treating a disease.

9.6 The Likelihood of a Type II Error and the Power of a Test

The probability of a Type I error is the significance level α of the test. Given that H_0 is true, when $\alpha = 0.05$, the probability of rejecting H_0 equals 0.05.

Given that H_0 is false, a Type II error results from *not* rejecting H_0. This probability is not constant but depends on factors such as the actual value of the parameter, the significance level α, and the sample size n. Let's see how to find the probability of a Type II error in a significance test about a proportion.

Example 12

Finding P (Type II error)

Part of a Study Design

Picture the Scenario

Examples 1, 3, and 5 discussed an experiment to test astrologers' predictions. For each person's horoscope, an astrologer must predict which of three personality charts is the actual one. Let p denote the probability of a correct prediction. Consider the test of H_0: $p = 1/3$ (astrologers' predictions are like random guessing) against H_a: $p > 1/3$ (better than random guessing), using the 0.05 significance level. Suppose an experiment plans to use $n = 116$ people, as this experiment did.

Questions to Explore

a. For what values of the sample proportion can we reject H_0?

b. The National Council for Geocosmic Research claimed that p would be 0.50 or higher. If truly $p = 0.50$, for what values of the sample proportion would we make a Type II error, failing to reject H_0 even though it's false?

c. If truly $p = 0.50$, what is the probability that a significance test based on this experiment will make a Type II error?

Think It Through

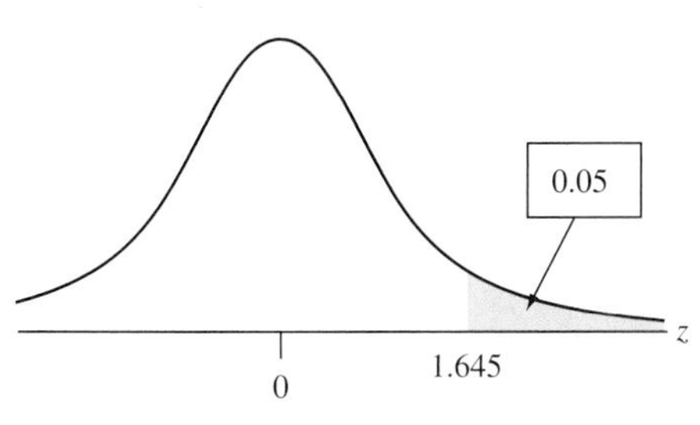

a. For testing H_0: $p = 1/3$ with $n = 116$, the standard error for the test statistic is

$$se_0 = \sqrt{p_0(1-p_0)/n} = \sqrt{[(1/3)(2/3)]/116} = 0.0438.$$

For H_a: $p > 1/3$, a test statistic of $z = 1.645$ has a P-value (right-tail probability) of 0.05. So, if $z \geq 1.645$, the P-value is ≤ 0.05 and we reject H_0. That is, we reject H_0 when $\hat{p}$ falls at least 1.645 standard errors above $p_0 = 1/3$,

$$\hat{p} \geq 1/3 + 1.645(se_0) = 1/3 + 1.645(0.0438) = 0.405.$$

So we reject H_0 when we get a sample proportion that is 0.405 or larger. Figure 9.13 shows the sampling distribution of $\hat{p}$ and this rejection region. The figure is centered at 1/3 because the test statistic is calculated, and the rejection region is formed presuming that H_0 is correct.

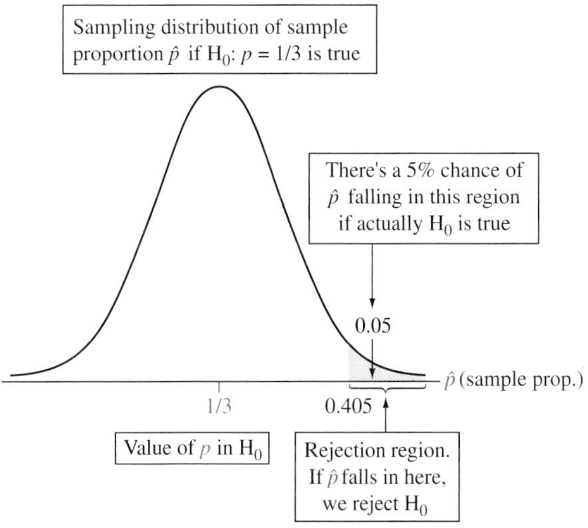

▲ **Figure 9.13 For Sample Proportion $\hat{p}$ Above 0.405, Reject H_0: $p = 1/3$ Against H_a: $p > 1/3$ at the 0.05 Significance Level.** When the true $p > 1/3$, a Type II error occurs if $\hat{p} < 0.405$, since then the P-value > 0.05 and we do not reject H_0. **Question** With a 0.10 significance level, does the blue area above become smaller or larger? Is the probability of a Type II error smaller or larger compared to a 0.05 significance level?

Recall

From Chapter 7.1, the sampling distribution of the sample proportion $\hat{p}$ is approximately normal with mean p and standard deviation $\sqrt{p(1-p)/n}$. ◀

b. When H_0 is false, a Type II error occurs when we fail to reject H_0. From part a and Figure 9.13, we do not reject H_0 if $\hat{p} < 0.405$.

c. If the true value of p is 0.50, then the true sampling distribution of $\hat{p}$ is centered at 0.50, as Figure 9.14 (on the next page) shows. The probability of a Type II error is the probability that $\hat{p} < 0.405$. When $p = 0.5$, the sampling distribution of $\hat{p}$ is approximately normal, with mean 0.5 and standard deviation $\sqrt{0.5(1-0.5)/116} = 0.0464$. So, to find the probability of a Type II error when $p = 0.5$, all we need to do is find the area to the left of 0.405 under this normal distribution. Using software for calculating normal probabilities (or Table A after converting to a z-score), this area equals 0.02. In summary, when $p = 0.50$, the probability of making a Type II error and failing to reject H_0: $p = 1/3$ is only 0.02.

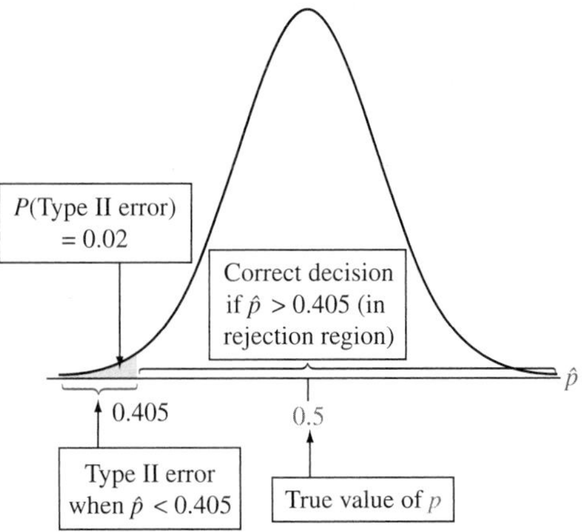

▲ Figure 9.14 Calculation of P(Type II Error) when True Parameter $p = 0.50$. A Type II error occurs if the sample proportion $\hat{p} < 0.405$. **Question** If the value of p decreases to 0.40, will the probability of Type II error decrease or increase?

Figure 9.15 shows the two figures together that we used in our reasoning. The normal distribution with mean $1/3$ was used to find the rejection region, based on what we expect for $\hat{p}$ when H_0: $p = 1/3$ is true. The normal distribution with mean 0.50 was used to find the probability that $\hat{p}$ does not fall in the rejection region even though $p = 0.50$ (that is, a Type II error occurs).

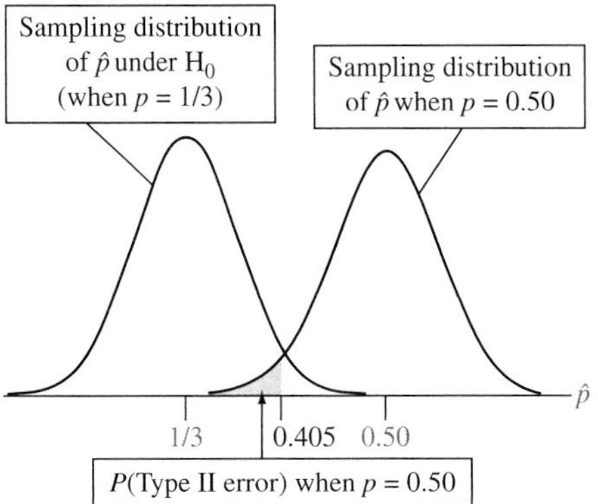

▲ Figure 9.15 Sampling Distributions of $\hat{p}$ When H_0: $p = 1/3$ Is True and When $p = 0.50$. Question Why does the shaded area under the left tail of the curve for the case $p = 0.50$ represent P(Type II error) for that value of p?

Insight

If astrologers truly had the predictive power claimed by the National Council for Geocosmic Research, the experiment would have been very likely to detect it (probability $1 - 0.02 = 0.98$).

► ***Try Exercise 9.61***

The probability of a Type II error increases when the true parameter value moves closer to H_0. To verify this, try to find the probability of a Type II error when $p = 0.40$ instead of 0.50. You should get P(Type II error) $= 0.54$. (Parts a and b of Example 12 are the same and, in part c, the sampling distribution of $\hat{p}$ now has mean 0.4 and standard deviation $\sqrt{0.4(1 - 0.4)/116} = 0.0455$.) If an astrologer can predict better than random guessing but not *much* better, we may not detect it with this experiment. Figure 9.16 plots P(Type II error) for various values of p

above 1/3. The farther the parameter value falls from the number in H_0, the less likely a Type II error.

SUMMARY: For a fixed significance level α, P(Type II error) decreases

- as the parameter value moves farther into the H_a values and away from the H_0 value
- as the sample size increases

Also, recall from the discussion in Example 9 about legal verdicts that P(Type II error) increases as α decreases. One reason that extremely small values, such as $\alpha = 0.001$, are not common is that P(Type II error) is then too high. We may be unlikely to reject H_0, even though it is false.

Before conducting a study, researchers should find P(Type II error) for the size of effect they want to be able to detect. If P(Type II error) is high, it may not be worth (or even ethical) conducting the study unless they can use a larger sample size and lower the probability. Graphs such as the one in Figure 9.16 are helpful for this purpose. To draw it, all we need to know is the sample size n and the null hypothesis value p_0. In fact, often several graphs are drawn for several possible sample sizes to see how the probability of a Type II error depends on n.

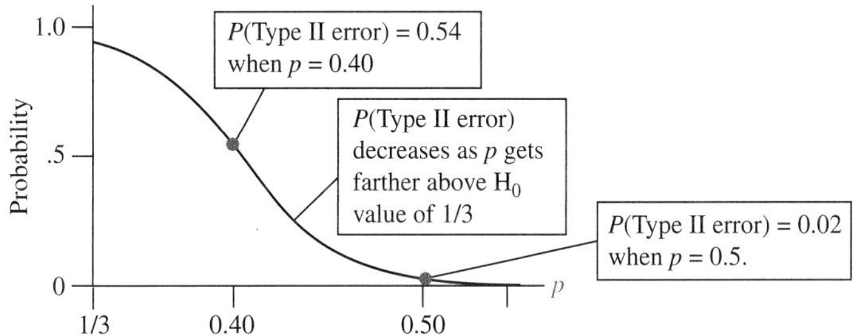

▲ **Figure 9.16** Probability of a Type II Error for Testing H_0: $p = 1/3$ Against H_a: $p > 1/3$. This is plotted for the values of p in H_a when the significance level $= 0.05$. **Question** If the sample size n increases, how do you think this curve would change?

The Power of a Test

When H_0 is false, you want the probability of rejecting it to be high. The probability of rejecting H_0 when it is false is called the **power** of the test. For a particular value of the parameter from the range of alternative hypothesis values,

$$\text{Power} = 1 - P(\text{Type II error})$$

In Example 12, for instance, $P(\text{Type II error}) = 0.02$ when $p = 0.50$. Therefore, the power of the test at $p = 0.50$ is $1 - 0.02 = 0.98$. The higher the power, the better, so a test power of 0.98 is quite good.

In practice, it is ideal for studies to have high power while using a relatively small significance level such as 0.05 or 0.01. For a fixed α, the power increases in the same cases that P(Type II error) decreases, namely as the sample size increases and as the parameter value moves farther into the H_a values away from the H_0 value.

Did You Know?

Before granting research support, many agencies (such as the National Institutes of Health) expect research scientists to show that for the planned study, reasonable power (usually, at least 0.80) exists at values of the parameter that are considered practically significant. ◀

Example 13

Treating Infertility in Women

Picture the Scenario

The most recent iteration of the National Survey of Family Growth estimated that 2.3 percent or about 1.4 million women aged 15–44 were infertile in the United States. Occlusions (blockages) in fallopian tubes are thought to be one of the major contributors for infertility, which are often treated with surgery. An alternative approach based on manual physical therapy is less invasive. A grant proposal to explore the effectiveness of this therapy plans to recruit women with blocked tubes and measure the rate at which at least one of the two tubes opens after therapy (called the patency rate). Without any intervention, the patency rate is about 10%. To test the effectiveness of the manual therapy, the null hypothesis H_0: $p = 0.1$ is tested against the alternative hypothesis H_a: $p > 0.1$, where p is the probability of at least one unblocked tube after therapy. Under "Statistical Considerations" in the grant proposal, the following sentence can be found regarding the power of the test: "At a 0.05 significance level, the proposed trial will have 82% power when the true patency rate is 25%."

Questions to Explore

a. How should "82% power" be interpreted?

b. In context, what is a Type II error for the proposed trial? What are the consequences of a Type II error?

c. If $p = 0.25$, what is the probability of committing a Type II error?

d. What can be done to lower the probability of a Type II error, i.e., to increase the power of the test?

Think It Through

a. A power of 82% means the probability of correctly rejecting H_0 when it is false is 0.82. If the actual probability of at least one unblocked tube after therapy is 0.25, there is an 82% chance that the significance test performed with the data of the proposed trial would reject H_0.

b. A Type II error occurs if we do not reject H_0 when in fact the probability of at least one unblocked tube after therapy is larger than 0.1. The consequence would be to dismiss a therapy that may actually result in a patency rate that is better than without any intervention.

c. If $p = 0.25$, the value of P(Type II error) is $1 - (\text{Power at } p = 0.25)$. This is $1 - 0.82 = 0.18$. A Type II error is not that unlikely to occur for the proposed trial.

d. One way to decrease the probability of a Type II error (and hence to increase the power of the test) is to increase the sample size, i.e., to recruit more patients. (Another option would be to increase the significance level, i.e., increase the probability of a Type I error.)

Insight

Those proposing the grant actually felt satisfied with a probability of a Type II error of 0.18. For cost considerations, they didn't want to recruit more patients. Also, preliminary studies showed that the patency rate may actually be larger than 25%, which would result in a smaller Type II error and, hence, greater than 82% power for the test.

▶ *Try Exercise 9.65*

► Activity 2

Explore Type I and Type II Errors and Power with an App

Let's get a feel for the two types of errors possible in hypothesis testing and what affects them. The web app Power, accessible on the book's website, visualizes these errors (and power) and lets you interactively change various parameters, such as the sample size, to observe how the errors are affected. Let's refer to the example about the astrologers' claim that they can correctly identify a person based on his or her horoscope with a probability greater than 1/3. For the null hypothesis value requested in the first box of the app, change the default of 0.5 to 0.33, the p_0 for the astrologers' study. To visualize the errors and power when astrologers correctly identify a person 50% of the time, set the slider for the true value of p to 0.5. Further, set the slider for the sample size to around 116, the sample size used in the study. Now click Show Type I Error and Type II Error to see the two errors in the displayed chart. (See the following screen shot, which is similar to Figure 9.15). Use the app to explore interactively how the Type II error changes when

- A larger or smaller sample is taken. Move the corresponding slider for n to explore. What is the probability of a Type II error if only about 50 (rather than 116) astrologers had taken part in the study?
- The true probability of correct identification is actually smaller than 0.5 but still larger than 0.33. Move the slider for p to explore this. What is the Type II error when $p = 0.33$? (Reset the sample size slider for n to 116.)
- A larger or smaller probability of a Type I error (i.e., the significance level) is selected. Move the corresponding slider for α. From Example 12, the probability of a Type II error was 0.02 when $\alpha = 0.05$, $n = 116$ and $p = 0.5$. What is the probability of a Type II error when $\alpha = 0.10$?

Click Show Power to explore how the power of a test changes as a function of the sample size or the true probability p. The second tab in the app, Population Mean, contains similar functionality to explore errors and power for a significance test about a population mean μ.

Errors and Power in Significance Testing

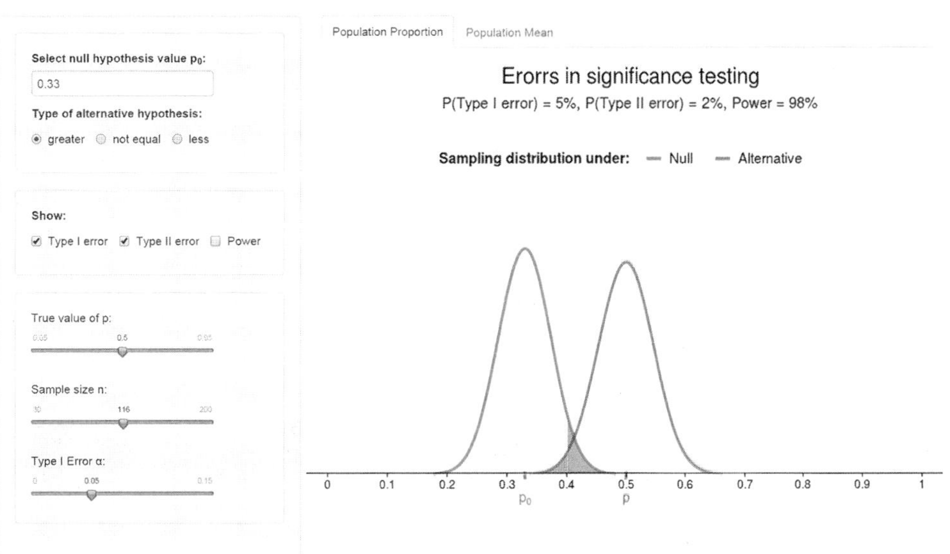

Try Exercise 9.66 ◄

9.6 Practicing the Basics

9.60 Find P(Type II error) A study is designed to test H_0: $p = 0.50$ against H_a: $p > 0.50$, taking a random sample of size $n = 100$, using significance level 0.05.

a. Show that the rejection region consists of values of $\hat{p} > 0.582$.

b. Sketch a single picture that shows (i) the sampling distribution of $\hat{p}$ when H_0 is true and (ii) the sampling distribution of $\hat{p}$ when $p = 0.60$. Label each sampling distribution with its mean and standard error and highlight the rejection region.

c. Find P(Type II error) when $p = 0.60$.

9.61 Gender bias in selecting managers Exercise 9.20 tested the claim that female employees were passed over for management training in favor of their male colleagues.

TRY

Statewide, the large pool of more than 1000 eligible employees who can be tapped for management training is 40% female and 60% male. Let p be the probability of selecting a female for any given selection. For testing H_0: $p = 0.40$ against H_a: $p < 0.40$ based on a random sample of 50 selections, using the 0.05 significance level, verify that:

a. A Type II error occurs if the sample proportion falls less than 1.645 standard errors below the null hypothesis value, which means that $\hat{p} > 0.286$.

b. When $p = 0.20$, a Type II error has probability 0.06.

9.62 Balancing Type I and Type II errors Recall that for the same sample size, the smaller the probability of a Type I error, α, the larger the P(Type II error). Let's check this for Example 12. There we found P(Type II error) for testing H_0: $p = 1/3$ (astrologers randomly guessing) against H_a: $p > 1/3$ when actually $p = 0.50$, with $n = 116$. If we use $\alpha = 0.01$, verify that:

a. A Type II error occurs if the sample proportion falls less than 2.326 standard errors above the null hypothesis value, which means $\hat{p} < 0.435$.

b. When $p = 0.50$, a Type II error has probability 0.08. (By comparison, Example 12 found P(Type II error) = 0.02 when $\alpha = 0.05$, so we see that P(Type II error) increased when P(Type I error) decreased.)

9.63 P(Type II error) large when p close to H_0 For testing H_0: $p = 1/3$ (astrologers randomly guessing) against H_a: $p > 1/3$ with $n = 116$, Example 12 showed that P(Type II error) = 0.02 when $p = 0.50$. Now suppose that $p = 0.35$. Recall that P(Type I error) = 0.05.

a. Show that P(Type II error) = 0.89.

b. Explain intuitively why P(Type II error) is large when the parameter value is close to the value in H_0 and decreases as it moves farther from that value.

9.64 Type II error with two-sided H_a In Example 12 for testing H_0: $p = 1/3$ (astrologers randomly guessing) with $n = 116$ when actually $p = 0.50$, suppose we used H_a: $p \neq 1/3$. Then show that:

a. A Type II error occurs if $0.248 < \hat{p} < 0.419$.

b. The probability is 0.00 that $\hat{p} < 0.248$ and 0.96 that $\hat{p} > 0.419$.

c. P(Type II error) = 0.04.

9.65 Power for infertility trial TRY Consider Example 13 about the power of the test of H_0: $p = 0.1$ against H_a: $p > 0.1$ used to test the effectiveness of a manual therapy in opening blocked tubes, where p is the probability of at least one unblocked tube after therapy. Another statement in that grant proposal read as follows: "However, if the patency rate is only 20%, the power of the test drops to 60%."

a. How should the power of 60% be interpreted?

b. In context, what is a Type II error for this trial?

c. What is the probability of committing a Type II error if $p = 0.2$?

9.66 Exploring Type II errors TRY TECH Refer to the web app from Activity 2 at the end of this section, now assuming that we are using the two-sided test H_0: $p = 0.33$ against H_a: $p \neq 0.33$. (Select "not equal" for the type of the alternative hypothesis in the web app.)

a. Explain the effect of increasing the sample size on the probability of a Type II error when the true $p = 0.50$.

b. Use the app to find the sample size needed to achieve a power of at least 90% when truly $p = 0.50$.

c. For a fixed sample size, do you think the probability of a Type II error will increase or decrease when the true p is 0.40 instead of 0.50? Check your answer with the app.

d. Does the power increase or decrease when the significance level is 0.10 instead of 0.05? Check your answer with the app.

Chapter Review

ANSWERS TO THE CHAPTER FIGURE QUESTIONS

Figure 9.1 A P-value of 0.01 gives stronger evidence against the null hypothesis. This smaller P-value (0.01 compared to 0.20) indicates it would be more unusual to get the observed sample data or a more extreme value if the null hypothesis is true.

Figure 9.2 It is the relatively large values of $\hat{p}$ (with their corresponding right-tail z-scores) that support the alternative hypothesis of $p > 1/3$.

Figure 9.3 Values more extreme than the observed test statistic value can be either relatively smaller or larger to support the alternative hypothesis $p \neq p_0$. These smaller or larger values are ones that fall farther in either the left or right tail.

Figure 9.4 A P-value = 0.00000002 is strong evidence against H_0.

Figure 9.6 The t-score indicates the number of standard errors $\bar{x}$ falls from the null hypothesis mean. The farther out a t-score falls in the tails, the farther the sample mean falls from the null hypothesis mean, providing stronger evidence against H_0.

Figure 9.7 For H_a: $\mu > 0$, the t test statistics providing stronger evidence against H_0 will be t statistics corresponding to the relatively large $\bar{x}$ values falling to the right of the hypothesized mean of 0. The t test statistics for these values of $\bar{x}$ are positive.

Figure 9.8 The standard error for the significance test is computed using p_0, the hypothesized proportion. The standard error for the confidence interval is computed using $\hat{p}$, the sample proportion. The values p_0 and $\hat{p}$ are not necessarily the same; therefore, there is not an exact equivalence.

Figure 9.9 The plots suggest that the population distribution of weight change is skewed to the right.

Figure 9.10 Using a significance level of 0.05, the rejection region consists of values of $z \geq 1.645$.

Figure 9.11 A sample mean of 6.09 indicates both statistical and practical significance.

Figure 9.13 The blue area becomes larger (i.e., the upper 10% instead of the upper 5%), and we are rejecting for even smaller values of $\hat{p}$. Then, the probability of making a Type II error is even larger because the probability is greater that the sample proportion $\hat{p}$ falls in the upper 10% when in fact $p > 1/3$.

Figure 9.14 The probability of a Type II error will increase.

Figure 9.15 A correct decision for the case $p = 0.50$ is to reject H_0: $p = 1/3$. The shaded area under the left tail of the curve for the case $p = 0.50$ represents the probability we would not reject H_0: $p = 1/3$, which is the probability of an incorrect decision for this situation. This shaded area is the probability of committing a Type II error.

Figure 9.16 By increasing the sample size n, the probability of a Type II error decreases. The curve would more quickly approach the horizontal axis, indicating that the Type II error probability more rapidly approaches a probability of 0 as p increases.

CHAPTER SUMMARY

A significance test helps us to judge whether or not a particular value for a parameter is plausible. Each significance test has five steps:

1. **Assumptions** The most important assumption for any significance test is that the data result from a *random sample* or *randomized experiment.* Specific significance tests make other assumptions, such as those summarized below for significance tests about means and proportions.
2. **Null and alternative hypotheses about the parameter** Null hypotheses have the form H_0: $p = p_0$ for a proportion and H_0: $\mu = \mu_0$ for a mean, where p_0 and μ_0 denote particular values, such as $p_0 = 0.4$ and $\mu_0 = 0$. The most common alternative hypothesis is **two-sided**, such as H_a: $p \neq 0.4$. **One-sided** hypotheses such as H_a: $p > 0.4$ and H_a: $p < 0.4$ are also possible.
3. **Test statistic** This measures how far the sample estimate of the parameter falls from the null hypothesis value. The z statistic for proportions and the t statistic for means have the form

$$\text{Test statistic} = \frac{\text{Parameter estimate} - \text{Null hypothesis value}}{\text{Standard error}}$$

   This measures the number of standard errors that the parameter estimate ($\hat{p}$ or $\bar{x}$) falls from the null hypothesis value (p_0 or μ_0).
4. **P-value** This is a probability summary of the evidence that the data provide about the null hypothesis. It equals the probability that the test statistic takes a value like the observed one or even more extreme if the hypothesized value in H_0 is true.
   - It is calculated by presuming that H_0 is true.
   - The test statistic values that are "more extreme" depend on the alternative hypothesis. When H_a is two-sided, the P-value is a two-tail probability. When H_a is one-sided, the P-value is a one-tail probability.
   - When the P-value is small, the observed data would be unusual if H_0 were true. The smaller the P-value, the stronger the evidence against H_0.
5. **Conclusion** A test concludes by interpreting the P-value in the context of the study. Sometimes a decision is needed, using a fixed **significance level** α, usually $\alpha = 0.05$. Then we reject H_0 if the P-value $\leq \alpha$. Two types of error can occur:
   - A **Type I error** results from rejecting H_0 when it is true. When H_0 is true, the significance level = P(Type I error).
   - When H_0 is false, a **Type II error** results from failing to reject H_0. The **power** of the test is the probability to reject H_0 correctly.

SUMMARY: Significance Tests for Population Proportions and Means

	Parameter	
	Proportion	**Mean**
1. Assumptions	Categorical variable Randomization Expected numbers of successes and failures ≥ 15	Quantitative variable Randomization Approximately normal population
2. Hypotheses	H_0: $p = p_0$ H_a: $p \neq p_0$ (two-sided) H_a: $p > p_0$ (one-sided) H_a: $p < p_0$ (one-sided)	H_0: $\mu = \mu_0$ H_a: $\mu \neq \mu_0$ (two-sided) H_a: $\mu > \mu_0$ (one-sided) H_a: $\mu < \mu_0$ (one-sided)
3. Test statistic	$z = \frac{\hat{p} - p_0}{se_0}$ $(se_0 = \sqrt{p_0(1 - p_0)/n})$	$t = \frac{\bar{x} - \mu_0}{se}$ $(se = s/\sqrt{n})$
4. P-value	Two-tail (H_a: $p \neq p_0$) or right tail (H_a: $p > p_0$) or left tail (H_a: $p < p_0$) probability from standard normal distribution	Two-tail (H_a: $\mu \neq \mu_0$) or right tail (H_a: $\mu > \mu_0$) or left tail (H_a: $\mu < \mu_0$) probability from t distribution ($df = n - 1$)
5. Conclusion	Interpret P-value in context Reject H_0 if P-value $\leq \alpha$	Interpret P-value in context Reject H_0 if P-value $\leq \alpha$

SUMMARY OF NOTATION

H_0 = null hypothesis, H_a = alternative hypothesis,
p_0 = null hypothesis value of proportion,
μ_0 = null hypothesis value of mean

α = significance level
= probability of Type I error
(usually 0.05; the P-value must be $\leq \alpha$ to reject H_0)

CHAPTER PROBLEMS

Practicing the Basics

9.67 H_0 or H_a? For each of the following hypotheses, explain whether it is a null hypothesis or an alternative hypothesis:

a. For females, the population mean on the political ideology scale is equal to 4.0.

b. For males, the population proportion who support the death penalty is larger than 0.50.

c. The diet has an effect, the population mean change in weight being less than 0.

d. For all Subway (submarine sandwich) stores worldwide, the difference between sales this month and in the corresponding month a year ago has a mean of 0.

9.68 Write H_0 and H_a For each of the following scenarios, define the parameter of interest and appropriate null and alternative hypotheses.

a. To motivate more fathers to take a parental leave, the government of Austria extended child care benefits for two more months if the father stays home for that time. Now, a study wants to investigate whether more fathers stayed home compared to the 15% before the incentive was available.

b. To curb CO_2 emissions, the government of Austria subsidized the purchase of green vehicles. Now, a study wants to investigate whether the average CO_2 emissions from cars purchased last year has dropped from the 160 g/km of 5 years ago.

c. The legal retirement age for female workers in Austria is 60. A study wants to assess whether the actual average retirement age of female workers is different from 60.

9.69 ESP A person who claims to possess extrasensory perception (ESP) says she can guess more often than not the outcome of a flip of a balanced coin. Out of 30 flips, she guesses correctly 18 times. Would you conclude that she truly has ESP? Answer by reporting all five steps of a significance test of the hypothesis that each of her guesses has probability 0.50 of being correct against the alternative that corresponds to her having ESP.

9.70 Free-throw accuracy Consider all cases in which a pro basketball player shoots two free throws and makes one and misses one. Which do you think is more common: making the first and missing the second, or missing the first and making the second? One of the best shooters was Larry Bird of the Boston Celtics. During 1980–1982 he made only the first free throw 34 times and made only the second 48 times (A. Tversky and T. Gilovich, *Chance*, vol. 2, pp. 16–21, 1989). Does this suggest that one sequence was truly more likely than the other sequence for Larry Bird? Answer by conducting a significance test (a) defining notation and specifying assumptions and hypotheses, (b) finding the test statistic, and (c) finding the P-value and interpreting in this context.

9.71 Brown or Whitman? California's governor election in 2010 had two major candidates, Brown and Whitman.

a. For a random sample of 650 voters in one exit poll, 360 voted for Brown, 240 for Whitman, and the rest for someone else. Conduct all five steps of a test of H_0: $p = 0.50$ against H_a: $p \neq 0.50$, where p denotes the probability that a randomly selected voter prefers Brown. Would you be willing to predict the outcome of the election? Explain how to make a decision, using a significance level of 0.05.

b. Suppose the sample size had been 50 voters, of whom 28 voted for Brown. Show that the sample proportion is similar to the sample proportion in part a, but the test statistic and P-value are very different. Are you now willing to predict the outcome of the election?

c. Using part a and part b, explain how results of a significance test can depend on the sample size.

9.72 Protecting the environment? When the 2010 General Social Survey asked, "Would you be willing to pay much higher taxes in order to protect the environment?" (variable GRNTAXES), 459 people answered yes and 626 answered no. (We exclude those who made other responses.) Let p denote the population proportion who would answer yes. MINITAB shows the following results to analyze whether a majority or minority of Americans would answer yes:

```
Test of p = 0.5 vs p ≠ 0.5
  X    N   Sample p         95% CI        Z-Value P-Value
459 1085 0.423041  (0.3936,0.4524)   -5.07   0.000
Using the normal approximation.
```

a. What are the assumptions for the significance test? Do they seem to be satisfied for this application? Explain.

b. For this printout, specify the null and alternative hypotheses that are tested and report the point estimate of p and the value of the test statistic.

c. Report and interpret the P-value in context.

d. According to the P-value, is it plausible that $p = 0.50$? Explain.

e. Explain an advantage of the confidence interval shown over the significance test.

9.73 Majority supports gay marriage An Associated Press article appearing in the *New York Times* in March 2015 mentioned that "In the late 1980s, support for gay marriage was essentially unheard of in America. Just a quarter century later, it's now favored by a clear majority of Americans." The article supports this conclusion by using data from the 2014 General Social Survey, which asked whether homosexuals should have the right to marry. Of the 1690 respondents, 955 agreed. Conduct all five steps of a significance test to see whether the proportion among Americans supporting gay marriage in 2014 is different from 0.5. Use a significance level of 0.05.

9.74 **Plant inheritance** In an experiment on chlorophyll inheritance in maize (corn), of the 1103 seedlings of self-fertilized green plants, 854 seedlings were green and 249 were yellow. Theory predicts the ratio of green to yellow is 3 to 1. Show all five steps of a test of the hypothesis that 3 to 1 is the true ratio. Interpret the P-value in context.

9.75 **Ellsberg paradox** You are told that a ball will be randomly drawn from one of two boxes (A and B), both of which contain black balls and red balls, and if a red ball is chosen, you will win $100. You are also told that Box A contains half black balls and half red balls, but you are not told the proportions in Box B. Which box would you pick?

a. Set up notation and specify hypotheses to test whether the population proportion who would pick Box A is 0.50.

b. For a random sample of 40 people, 36 pick Box A. Can you make a conclusion about whether the proportion for one option is higher in the population? Explain all steps of your reasoning. (Logically those who picked Box A would seem to think that Box B has greater chance of a black ball. However, a paradox first discussed by Daniel Ellsberg predicts that if they were now told that they would instead receive $100 if a black ball is chosen, they would overwhelmingly pick Box A again because they prefer definite information over ambiguity.)

9.76 **Start a hockey team** A fraternity at a university lobbies the administration to start a hockey team. To bolster its case, it reports that of a simple random sample of 100 students, 83% support starting the team. Upon further investigation, their sample has 80 males and 20 females. Should you be skeptical of whether the sample was random if you know that 55% of the student body population was male? Answer this by performing all steps of a two-sided significance test.

9.77 **Interest charges on credit card** A bank wants to evaluate which credit card would be more attractive to its customers, one with a high interest rate for unpaid balances but no annual cost or one with a low interest rate for unpaid balances but an annual cost of $40. For a random sample of 100 of its 52,000 customers, 40 say they prefer the one that has an annual cost. Software reports the following:

```
Test of p = 0.50 vs p not = 0.50
X    N    Sample p    95.0% CI         Z-Value   P-Value
40   100  0.40000     (0.304,0.496)    -2.00     0.04550
```

Explain how to interpret all results on the printout. What would you tell the company about what the majority of its customers prefer?

9.78 **Jurors and gender** A jury list contains the names of all individuals who may be called for jury duty. The proportion of the available jurors on the list who are women is 0.53. If 40 people are selected to serve as candidates to serve on the jury, show all steps of a significance test of the hypothesis that the selections are random with respect to gender.

a. Set up notation and hypotheses and specify assumptions.

b. Five of the 40 selected were women. Find the test statistic.

c. Report the P-value and interpret.

d. Explain how to make a decision using a significance level of 0.01.

9.79 **Type I and Type II errors** Refer to the previous exercise.

a. Explain what Type I and Type II errors mean in the context of that exercise.

b. If you made an error with the decision in part d, is it a Type I or a Type II error?

9.80 **Levine = author?** The authorship of an old document is in doubt. A historian hypothesizes that the author was a journalist named Jacalyn Levine. Upon a thorough investigation of Levine's known works, it is observed that one unusual feature of her writing was that she consistently began 10% of her sentences with the word "whereas." To test the historian's hypothesis, it is decided to count the number of sentences in the disputed document that begin with the word *whereas.* Out of the 300 sentences in the document, none begin with that word. Let p denote the probability that any one sentence written by the unknown author of the document begins with the word "whereas."

a. Conduct a test of the hypothesis H_0: $p = 0.10$ against H_a: $p \neq 0.10$. What conclusion can you make, using a significance level of 0.05?

b. What assumptions are needed for that conclusion to be valid? (F. Mosteller and D. Wallace conducted an investigation similar to this to determine whether Alexander Hamilton or James Madison was the author of 12 of the *Federalist Papers.* See *Inference and Disputed Authorship: The Federalist,* Addison-Wesley, 1964.)

9.81 **Practice steps of test for mean** For a quantitative variable, you want to test H_0: $\mu = 0$ against H_a: $\mu \neq 0$. The 10 observations are

TECH

3, 7, 3, 3, 0, 8, 1, 12, 5, 8.

a. Show that (i) $\bar{x} = 5.0$, (ii) $s = 3.71$, (iii) standard error $= 1.17$, (iv) test statistic $= 4.26$, and (v) $df = 9$.

b. The P-value is 0.002. Make a decision using a significance level of 0.05. Interpret.

c. If you had instead used H_a: $\mu > 0$, what would the P-value be? Interpret it.

d. If you had instead used H_a: $\mu < 0$, what would the P-value be? Interpret it. (*Hint:* Recall that the two one-sided P-values should sum to 1.)

9.82 **Two ideal children?** Is the ideal number of children equal or different from 2? For testing that the mean response from the 2014 GSS equals 2.0 for the question,

"What do you think is the ideal number of children to have?" software shows results:

```
Test of μ = 2 vs ≠ 2
   N   Mean  StDev SE Mean        95% CI          T     P
1417 2.518 0.875   0.023   (2.472, 2.564) 22.29 0.000
```

a. Report the test statistic value and show how it was obtained from other values reported in the table.

b. Explain what the P-value represents and interpret its value.

9.83 Hours at work When all subjects in the 2012 GSS who were working full- or part-time were asked how many hours they worked in the previous week at all jobs (variable HRS1), software produced the following analyses:

```
Test of μ = 40 vs ≠ 40
Variable  N    Mean   StDev SE Mean  95% CI     T    P
                                    (39.381,
Hours    1166 40.274 15.540  0.455  41.166) 0.60 0.548
```

For this printout,

a. State the hypotheses.

b. Explain how to interpret the values of (i) SE Mean, (ii) T, and (iii) P.

c. Show the correspondence between a decision in the test using a significance level of 0.05 and whether 40 falls in the confidence interval reported.

9.84 Females liberal or conservative? TECH Example 10 compared mean political beliefs (on a 1 to 7 point scale) to the moderate value of 4.0, using GSS data. Test whether the population mean equals 4.00 for females, for whom the sample mean was 4.06 and standard deviation was 1.37 for a sample of size 1345. Carry out the five steps of a significance test, reporting and interpreting the P-value in context.

9.85 Blood pressure TECH When Vincenzo Baranello's blood pressure is in control, his systolic blood pressure reading has a mean of 130. For the last six times he has monitored his blood pressure, he has obtained the values

140, 150, 155, 155, 160, 140.

a. Does this provide strong evidence that his true mean has changed? Carry out the five steps of the significance test, interpreting the P-value.

b. Review the assumptions that this method makes. For each assumption, discuss it in context.

9.86 Increasing blood pressure In the previous exercise, suppose you had predicted that if the mean changed, it would have increased above the control value. State the alternative hypothesis for this prediction and report and interpret the P-value.

9.87 Tennis balls in control? TECH When it is operating correctly, a machine for manufacturing tennis balls produces balls with a mean weight of 57.6 grams. The last eight balls manufactured had weights

57.3, 57.4, 57.2, 57.5, 57.4, 57.1, 57.3, 57.0

a. Using a calculator or software, find the test statistic and P-value for a test of whether the process is in control against the alternative that the true mean of the process now differs from 57.6.

b. For a significance level of 0.05, explain what you would conclude. Express your conclusion so it would be understood by someone who never studied statistics.

c. If your decision in part b is in error, what type of error have you made?

9.88 Catalog sales A company that sells products through mail-order catalogs wants to evaluate whether the mean sales for its most recent catalog were different from the mean of \$15 from past catalogs. For a random sample of 100 customers, the mean sales were \$10, with a standard deviation of \$10. Find a P-value to provide the extent of evidence that the mean differed with this catalog. Interpret.

9.89 Wage claim false? TECH Management claims that the mean income for all senior-level assembly-line workers in a large company equals \$500 per week. An employee decides to test this claim, believing that it is actually different from \$500. For a random sample of nine employees, the incomes are

430, 450, 450, 440, 460, 420, 430, 450, 440.

Conduct a significance test of whether the population mean income equals \$500 per week. Include all assumptions, the hypotheses, test statistic, and P-value and interpret the result in context.

9.90 CI and test Refer to the previous exercise.

a. For which significance levels can you reject H_0? (i) 0.10, (ii) 0.05, or (iii) 0.01.

b. Based on the answers in part a, for which confidence levels would the confidence interval contain 500? (i) 0.90, (ii) 0.95, or (iii) 0.99.

c. Use part a and part b to illustrate the correspondence between results of significance tests and results of confidence intervals.

d. In the context of this study, what is (i) a Type I error and (ii) a Type II error?

9.91 CI and test connection The P-value for testing H_0: $\mu = 100$ against H_a: $\mu \neq 100$ is 0.043.

a. What decision is made using a 0.05 significance level?

b. If the decision in part a is in error, what type of error is it?

c. Does a 95% confidence interval for μ contain 100? Explain.

9.92 Religious beliefs statistically significant? A journal article that deals with changes in religious beliefs over time states, "For these subjects, the difference in their responses on the scale of religiosity between age 16 and the current survey was statistically significant (P-value < 0.05)."

a. How would you explain to someone who has never taken a statistics course what it means for the result to be "statistically significant" with a P-value < 0.05?

b. Explain why it would have been more informative if the authors provided the actual P-value rather than merely indicating that it is below 0.05.

c. Can you conclude that a practically *important* change in religiosity has occurred between age 16 and the time of the current survey? Why or why not?

9.93 **How to reduce chance of error?** In making a decision in a significance test, a researcher worries about rejecting H_0 when it may actually be true.

a. Explain how the researcher can control the probability of this type of error.

b. Why should the researcher probably not set this probability equal to 0.00001?

9.94 **Legal trial errors** Consider the analogy discussed in Section 9.4 between making a decision about a null hypothesis in a significance test and making a decision about the innocence or guilt of a defendant in a criminal trial.

a. Explain the difference between Type I and Type II errors in the trial setting.

b. In this context, explain intuitively why decreasing the chance of Type I error increases the chance of Type II error.

9.95 **P(Type II error) with smaller *n*** Consider Example 12 about testing H_0: $p = 1/3$ against H_a: $p > 1/3$ for the astrology study, with $n = 116$. Find P(Type II error) for testing H_0: $p = 1/3$ against H_a: $p > 1/3$ when actually $p = 0.50$, if the sample size is 60 instead of 116. Do this by showing that

a. The standard error is 0.061 when H_0 is true.

b. The rejection region consists of $\hat{p}$ values above 0.433.

c. When $p = 0.50$, the probability that $\hat{p}$ falls below 0.433 is the left-tail probability below -1.03 under a standard normal curve. What is the answer? Why would you expect P(Type II error) to be larger when n is smaller?

Concepts and Investigations

9.96 **Student data** Refer to the FL Student Survey data file on the text's website. Test whether the (a) population mean political ideology (on a scale of 1 to 7, where 4 = moderate) equals or differs from 4.0 and (b) population proportion favoring affirmative action equals or differs from 0.50. For each part, write a one-page report showing all five steps of the test, including what you must assume for each inference to be valid.

TECH

9.97 **Class data** Refer to the data file your class created in Activity 3 at the end of Chapter 1. For a variable chosen by your instructor, conduct inferential statistical analyses. Prepare a report, summarizing and interpreting your findings. In this report, also use graphical and numerical methods presented earlier in this text to describe the data.

TECH

9.98 **Gender of best friend** A GSS question asked the gender of your best friend. Of 1381 people interviewed, 147 said their best friend had the opposite gender, and 1234 said their best friend had the same gender. Prepare a short report in which you analyze these data using a confidence interval and a significance test where you test whether half of the population has someone from the opposite sex as their best friend. Which do you think is more informative? Why?

TECH

9.99 **Baseball home team advantage** In Major League Baseball's 2010 season, the home team won 1359 games, and the away team won 1071 (www.mlb.com).

a. Although these games are not a random sample, explain how you could think of these data as giving you information about some long-run phenomenon.

b. Analyze these data using (i) a significance test and (ii) a confidence interval. Which method is more informative? Why?

9.100 **Statistics and scientific objectivity** The president of the American Statistical Association stated, "Statistics has become the modern-day enforcer of scientific objectivity. Terms like randomization, blinding, and 0.05 significance wield a no-doubt effective objectivity nightstick." He also discussed how learning what effects *aren't* in the data is as important as learning what effects *are* significant. In this vein, explain how statistics provides an objective framework for testing the claims of what many believe to be quack science, such as astrology and therapeutic touch where practitioners claim to improve medical conditions by using their hands to manipulate the human energy field. (*Source:* Bradley Efron, *Amstat News*, July 2004, p. 3.)

9.101 **Two-sided or one-sided?** A medical researcher gets a P-value of 0.056 for testing H_0: $\mu = 0$ against H_a: $\mu \neq 0$. Since he believes that the true mean is positive and is worried that his favorite journal will not publish the results because they are not "significant at the 0.05 level," he instead reports in his article the P-value of 0.028 for H_a: $\mu > 0$. Explain what is wrong with

a. Reporting the one-sided P-value after seeing the data.

b. The journal's policy to publish results only if they are statistically significant.

9.102 **No significant change and P-value** An article in a journal states that "no statistical significant change was found in the mean glucose level of the brain before and after making a cell phone call for 50 minutes (P-value = 0.63)." In practical terms, how would you explain to someone who has not studied statistics what this means?

9.103 **Subgroup lack of significance** A crossover study on comparing a magnetic device to placebo for reducing pain in 54 people suffering from low back or knee pain (neuromagnetics.mc.vanderbilt.edu/publications) reported a significant result overall, the magnetic device being preferred to placebo. However, when the analysis was done separately for the 27 people with shorter illness duration and the 27 people with longer illness duration, results were not significant. Explain how it might be possible that an analysis could give a P-value below 0.05 using an entire sample but not with subgroups, even if the subgroups have the same effects. (*Hint:* What is the impact of the smaller sample size for the subgroups?)

9.104 **Vitamin E and prostate cancer** A study in Finland in 1998 suggested that vitamin E pills reduced the risk of prostate cancer in a group of male smokers. This was only one effect in a series of reported successes for vitamin E and other health conditions. A more recent study reported that selenium or vitamin E, used alone or in combination, did not prevent prostate cancer in a population of relatively healthy men (*JAMA*, April 2009). Discuss the factors that can cause different medical studies to come to different conclusions.

9.105 Overestimated effect When medical stories in the mass media report dangers of certain agents (e.g., coffee drinking), later research often suggests that the effects may not exist or are weaker than first believed. Explain how this could happen if some journals tend to publish only statistically significant results.

9.106 Choosing α An alternative hypothesis states that a newly developed drug is better than the one currently used to treat a serious illness. If we reject H_0, the new drug will be prescribed instead of the current one.

a. Why might we prefer to use a smaller significance level than 0.05, such as 0.01?

b. What is a disadvantage of using $\alpha = 0.01$ instead of 0.05?

9.107 Why not accept H_0? Explain why the terminology "do not reject H_0" is preferable to "accept H_0."

9.108 Report P-value It is more informative and potentially less misleading to conclude a test by reporting and interpreting the P-value rather than by merely indicating whether you reject H_0 at the 0.05 significance level. One reason is that a reader can then tell whether the result is significant *at a significance level he or she thinks is acceptable,* which may be different from 0.05. Give another reason.

9.109 Significance Explain the difference between *statistical significance* and *practical significance.* Make up an example to illustrate your reasoning.

9.110 More doctors recommend An advertisement by Company A says that three of every four doctors recommend pain reliever A over all other brands combined.

a. If the company based this claim on interviewing a random sample of doctors, explain how it could use a significance test to back up the claim.

b. Explain why this claim would be more impressive if it is based on a (i) random sample of 40 doctors than if it is based on a random sample of 4 doctors and (ii) random sample of 40 doctors nationwide than the sample of all 40 doctors who work in a particular hospital.

9.111 Medical diagnosis error Consider the medical diagnosis of breast cancer with mammograms. An AP story (September 19, 2002) said that a woman has about a 50% chance of having a false-positive diagnosis over the course of 10 annual mammography tests. Relate this result to the chance of eventually making a Type I error if you do lots of significance tests.

9.112 Bad P-value interpretations A random sample of size 1000 has $\bar{x} = 104$. The significance level α is set at 0.05. The P-value for testing H_0: $\mu = 100$ against H_a: $\mu \neq 100$ is 0.057. Explain what is incorrect about each of the following interpretations of this P-value and provide a proper interpretation.

a. The probability that the null hypothesis is correct equals 0.057.

b. The probability that $\bar{x} = 104$ if H_0 is true equals 0.057.

c. If in fact $\mu \neq 100$ so H_0 is false, the probability equals 0.057 that the data would show at least as much evidence against H_0 as the observed data.

d. The probability of a Type I error equals 0.057.

e. We can accept H_0 at the $\alpha = 0.05$ level.

f. We can reject H_0 at the $\alpha = 0.05$ level.

9.113 Interpret P-value One interpretation for the P-value is that it is the smallest value for the significance level α for which we can reject H_0. Illustrate using the P-value of 0.057 from the previous exercise.

9.114 Incorrectly posed hypotheses What is wrong with expressing hypotheses about proportions and means in a form such as H_0: $\hat{p} = 0.50$ and H_0: $\bar{x} = 0$?

9.115 Multiple choice: Small P-value The P-value for testing H_0: $\mu = 100$ against H_a: $\mu \neq 100$ is 0.001. This indicates that

a. There is strong evidence that $\mu = 100$.

b. There is strong evidence that $\mu \neq 100$, since if μ were equal to 100, it would be unusual to obtain data such as those observed.

c. The probability that $\mu = 100$ is 0.001.

d. The probability that $\mu = 100$ is the significance level, usually taken to be 0.05.

9.116 Multiple choice: Probability of P-value When H_0 is true in a *t* test with significance level 0.05, the probability that the P-value falls ≤ 0.05

a. equals 0.05.

b. equals 0.95.

c. equals 0.05 for a one-sided test and 0.10 for a two-sided test.

d. can't be specified because it depends also on P(Type II error).

9.117 Multiple choice: Pollution Exercise 9.34 concerned an industrial plant that may be exceeding pollution limits. An environmental action group took four readings to analyze whether the true mean discharge of wastewater per hour exceeded the company claim of 1000 gallons. When we make a decision in the one-sided test by using $\alpha = 0.05$:

a. If the plant is not exceeding the limit, but actually $\mu = 1000$, there is only a 5% chance that we will conclude that it is exceeding the limit.

b. If the plant is exceeding the limit, there is only a 5% chance that we will conclude that it is not exceeding the limit.

c. The probability that the sample mean equals exactly the observed value would equal 0.05 if H_0 were true.

d. If we reject H_0, the probability that it is actually true is 0.05.

e. All of the above.

9.118 Multiple choice: Interpret P(Type II error) For a test of H_0: $\mu = 0$ against H_a: $\mu > 0$ based on $n = 30$ observations and using $\alpha = 0.05$ significance level, P(Type II error) $= 0.36$ at $\mu = 4$. Identify the response that is *incorrect.*

a. At $\mu = 5$, P(Type II error) < 0.36.

b. If $\alpha = 0.01$, then at $\mu = 4$, P(Type II error) > 0.36.

c. If $n = 50$, then at $\mu = 4$, P(Type II error) > 0.36.

d. The power of the test is 0.64 at $\mu = 4$.

9.119 True or false It is always the case that P(Type II error) = 1 − P(Type I error).

9.120 True or false If we reject H_0: $\mu = 0$ in a study about change in weight on a new diet using $\alpha = 0.01$, then we also reject it using $\alpha = 0.05$.

9.121 True or false A study about the change in weight on a new diet reports P-value = 0.043 for testing H_0: $\mu = 0$ against H_a: $\mu \neq 0$. If the authors had instead reported a 95% confidence interval for μ, then the interval would have contained 0.

9.122 True or false A 95% confidence interval for μ = population mean IQ is (96, 110). So, in the test of H_0: $\mu = 100$ against H_a: $\mu \neq 100$, the P-value > 0.05.

9.123 True or false For a fixed significance level α, the probability of a Type II error increases when the sample size increases.

9.124 True or false When testing H_0: $\mu = 100$ against H_a: $\mu \neq 100$, the probability of a Type II error decreases the further the true population mean μ is from 100.

9.125 True or false The P-value is the probability that H_0 is true.

9.126 True or false The power of a test = 1 − P(Type II error).

9.127 Standard error formulas ◆◆ Suppose you wanted to test H_0: $p = 0.50$, but you had 0 successes in n trials. If you had found the test statistic by using the $se = \sqrt{\hat{p}(1-\hat{p})/n}$ designed for confidence intervals, show what happens to the test statistic. Explain why $se_0 = \sqrt{p_0(1-p_0)/n}$ is a more appropriate se for tests.

9.128 Rejecting true H_0? ◆◆ A medical researcher conducts a significance test whenever she analyzes a new data set. Over time, she conducts 100 independent tests.

a. Suppose the null hypothesis is true in every case. What is the distribution of the number of times she rejects the null hypothesis at the 0.05 level?

b. Suppose she rejects the null hypothesis in five of the tests. Is it plausible that the null hypothesis is correct in every case? Explain.

Student Activities

9.129 TRY A study compares a new drug for pain relief in patients with chronic migraine against a placebo. Each patient is given both the drug and the placebo (in random order) and reports which one works better. Let p denote the probability that the pain relief is better with the drug. You have to decide whether you can reject H_0: $p = 0.50$ in favor of H_a: $p \neq 0.50$ based on seeing the results of one patient after another. Ahead of time, you have no idea whether the drug or placebo works better, and you assume they are equally effective (i.e., you assume the null hypothesis is true.) Each student should indicate

a. How many consecutive patients reporting better relief with the drug would be necessary before he or she would feel comfortable rejecting H_0: $p = 0.50$ in favor of H_a: $p \neq 0.50$ and concluding that the drug works better.

b. How many consecutive patients reporting better relief with the placebo would be necessary before he or she would feel comfortable rejecting H_0: $p = 0.50$ in favor of H_a: $p \neq 0.50$ and concluding that the placebo works better.

The instructor will compile a "distribution of significance levels" for the two cases. Are they the same? In principle, should they be?

9.130 Refer to Exercise 8.128, "Randomized response," in Chapter 8. Before carrying out the method described there, the class was asked to hypothesize or predict what they believe is the value for the population proportion of students who have had alcohol at a party. Use the class estimate for $\hat{p}$ to carry out the significance test for testing this hypothesized value. Discuss whether to use a one-sided or two-sided alternative hypothesis. Describe how the confidence interval formed in Exercise 8.128 relates to the significance test results.

CHAPTER

10

Chapter 9 focused on statistical inference based on a single sample, but often we want to compare parameters such as proportions or means across two different groups. This chapter presents confidence intervals and significance tests for this purpose.

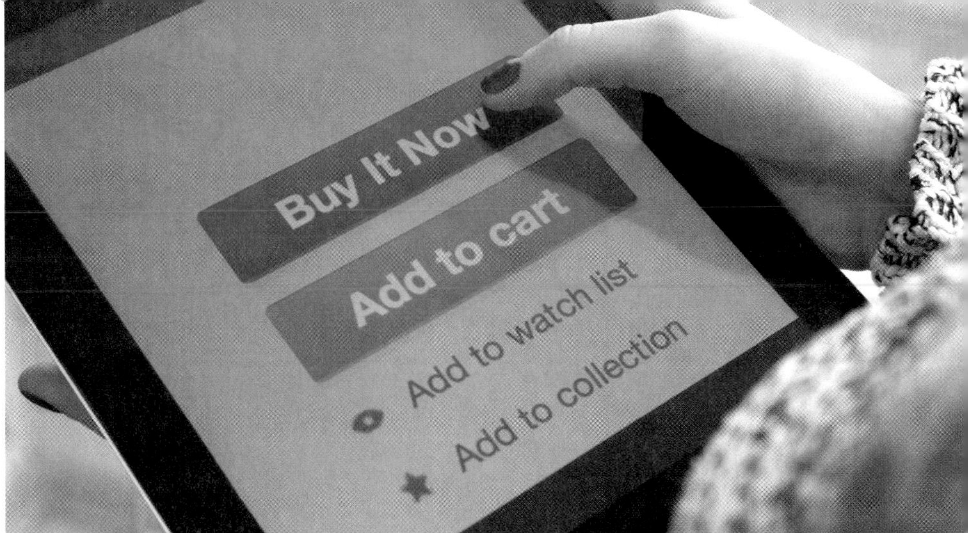

Comparing Two Groups

Example 1

Making Sense of Studies Comparing Two Groups

Picture the Scenario

When e-commerce or marketing companies design webpages, there are a lot of things to consider. For instance, Amazon researched extensively which color to use for the Add To Cart button and where to place it on the site. To improve on an existing website, web designers often use so-called A/B tests in which, over a few days, some visitors to the site are routed to the existing design and others to a test site with some new design feature (such as a redesigned button) but otherwise the same functionality. Then, various metrics, such as the proportion of people who signed up for a newsletter or the amount of sales generated from each version of the site, are compared.

Questions to Explore

- How can we use data from such experiments to compare two web designs in terms of number of clicks or amount of sales generated?
- How can we use the information in the data to make an inference about the larger population of all visitors to the website? What are the assumptions we need to make for our inference to be valid?

Thinking Ahead

This chapter shows how to compare two groups on a categorical outcome (e.g., whether a visitor signed up for a newsletter) or on a quantitative outcome (e.g., the dollar amount of products a visitor puts into the shopping cart). To do this, we'll use the inferential statistical methods that the previous two chapters introduced: confidence intervals and significance tests.

For categorical variables, we will compare proportions between two groups. In Examples 2 to 4, we'll look at aspirin and placebo treatments, studying the proportions of subjects getting cancer under each treatment. Exercise 10.12 presents the result of an A/B test comparing a button that reads Sign Up to a button that reads Learn More on the 2008 fundraising website of a then relatively unknown U.S. senator, Barack Obama.

For quantitative variables, we will compare means between two groups. In Examples 6 to 8, we will examine whether including a basic graph in the description of a product leads to a higher mean rating of the product's usefulness and, in Example 9, we will investigate how the mean reaction time differs between students using a cell phone and those just listening to the radio in a simulated car-driving environment.

In reading this book, you are becoming an educated consumer of information based on statistics. By now, you know to be skeptical of studies that do not or could not use randomization in the sampling procedure or the experimental design. By the end of this chapter, you'll know about other potential pitfalls. You'll be better able to judge how much credence to give to claims made in newspaper stories. Such stories nearly always report only "statistically significant" results. Occasionally such a report may be a Type I error, claiming an effect that actually does not exist in the population. Some may predict that effects are larger than they truly are in that population. Does drinking tea really help heart attack victims as much as reported? Or, as Figure 10.1 suggests, is this merely today's random medical news?

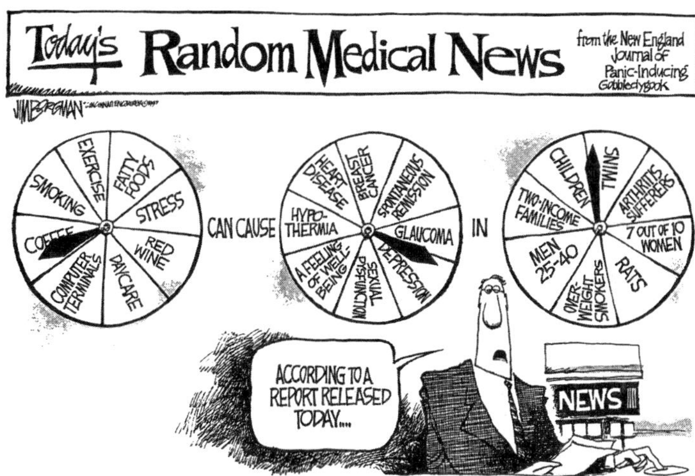

▲ **Figure 10.1** Today's Random Medical News

Bivariate Analyses: A Response Variable and a Binary Explanatory Variable

Consider a study that compares female and male college students on the proportion who say they have participated in binge drinking. Such a study involves two variables. The **response** variable, binge drinking, measures whether a student participated in binge drinking, with outcome categories yes and no. The response variable is the one on which comparisons are made. The **explanatory** variable, gender, measures the sex of each student with outcome categories female and male. The explanatory variable defines the two groups being compared.

Recall
Chapter 3 defined the **response variable** as the outcome variable on which comparisons are made for different values of the **explanatory variable**. ◀

An analysis that looks at any type of relationship between two variables is called a **bivariate** analysis. (Analyses with just one variable, such as the ones presented in Chapters 8 and 9, are called univariate.) One special case of a bivariate analysis occurs when the explanatory variable is binary (i.e., has only two possible outcomes, such as female and male). Then, we want to investigate how the outcomes of the response variable differ between the two groups defined by the explanatory variable. In our example, binge drinking is the response variable, and we want to study how it differs by gender.

Dependent and Independent Samples

Most comparisons of groups use **independent samples** from the groups. The observations in one sample are *independent* of those in the other sample. For instance, randomized experiments that randomly allocate subjects to two treatments have independent samples. An example is the A/B experiment mentioned in Example 1 in which visitors to a website are randomly shown two versions of that site. Whether a visitor directed to the first version of the site clicks a button is independent of whether another visitor directed to the second version of the site clicks a button. Another way independent samples occur is when an observational study separates subjects into groups according to their value for an explanatory variable, such as smoking status or gender. If the overall sample was randomly selected, then the groups (for instance, smokers and nonsmokers or females and males) can be treated as independent random samples.

When the two samples involve the same subjects, they are **dependent**. An example is a diet study in which subjects' weights are measured before and after the diet. For a given subject, the observation in the first (before the diet) and second (after the diet) sample are related because they refer to the same person. In general, any time we measure the same subject twice (e.g., before and after the diet or in the morning and in the afternoon) leads to dependent samples. Dependent samples also result when the data are **matched pairs**—each subject in one sample is matched with a subject in the other sample. An example is a set of married couples, the men being in one sample and the women in the other. Data from dependent samples need different statistical methods than data from independent samples. We'll study them in Section 10.4. Sections 10.1–10.3 show how to analyze independent samples, first for a categorical response variable and then for a quantitative response variable.

10.1 Categorical Response: Comparing Two Proportions

For a *categorical response variable*, inferences compare groups in terms of their population proportions in a particular category. Let p_1 represent the population proportion for the first group and p_2 the population proportion for the second group. We can compare the groups by their difference, $(p_1 - p_2)$. This is estimated by the difference of the sample proportions, $(\hat{p}_1 - \hat{p}_2)$. Let n_1 and n_2 denote the sample sizes for the two groups.

Example 2

Compare two proportions

Aspirin, the Wonder Drug

Picture the Scenario

Most of us think of aspirin as a simple pill that helps relieve pain. In recent years, though, researchers have been on the lookout for new ways that aspirin may be helpful. Increasing attention has focused on aspirin since a landmark five-year study (Physicians Health Study Research Group, Harvard Medical School) about whether regular aspirin intake reduces deaths from heart disease. Studies have shown that treatment with daily aspirin for five years or longer reduces risk of colorectal cancer. These studies suggest that aspirin might reduce the risk of other cancers as well. Results of a recent meta-analysis combined the results of eight related studies with a minimum duration of treatment of four years to determine the effects of aspirin on the risk of cancer death. A **meta-analysis** combines the results of several studies that address a set of related statistical questions. After analyzing the individual studies, the researchers assumed the different studies were measuring the same effect and pooled the results of the different studies.

Recall

Section 4.3 discussed the importance of **randomization** in experimental design and introduced **double blinding**. Exercises 4.68–4.70 in that chapter show other data from this study. ◀

All experimental trials used were randomized and double-blind. The combined results provided evidence that daily aspirin reduced deaths due to several common cancers during and after the trials. We will explore some of these results.

Table 10.1 shows the study results. This is a **contingency table**, a data summary for categorical variables introduced in Section 3.1. Of the 25,570 individuals studied, 347 of those in the control group died of cancer, whereas 327 in the aspirin treatment died of cancer within 20 years following the study.

Table 10.1 Whether Subject Died of Cancer, for Placebo and Aspirin Treatment Groups

	Death from Cancer		
Group	**Yes**	**No**	**Total**
Placebo	347	11,188	11,535
Aspirin	327	13,708	14,035

Questions to Explore

a. What is the response variable, and what are the groups to compare?

b. Construct an appropriate graph to visualize the data in the contingency table.

c. What are the two population parameters to compare? Estimate the difference between them using the data in Table 10.1. Interpret that difference.

Think It Through

a. In Table 10.1, the response variable is whether the subjects died of cancer, with categories yes and no. Group 1 consists of the subjects who took placebo and Group 2 consists of the subjects who took aspirin. Placebo and Aspirin are the categories of the explanatory variable measuring which treatment was received.

b. An appropriate graph compares the (conditional) proportions of subjects who died from cancer in the two groups through a bar chart (see Chapter 3, Section 3.1). The figure in the margin shows one based on the data in Table 10.1.

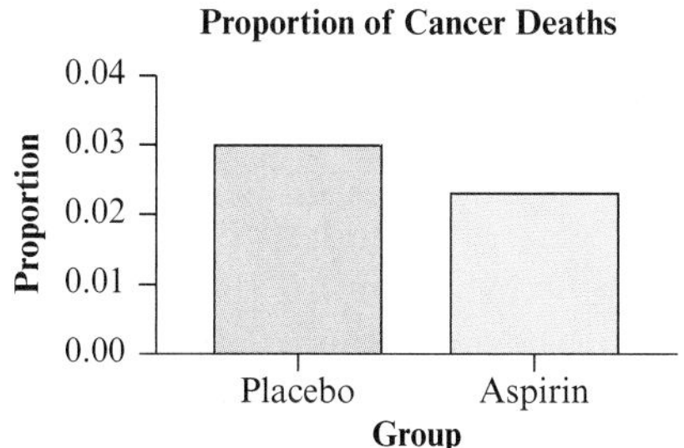

Bar Chart Comparing Proportions

c. For the population from which this sample was taken, the proportion who died of cancer is represented by p_1 for taking placebo and p_2 for taking aspirin. The sample proportions of death from cancer were

$$\hat{p}_1 = 347/11535 = 0.030$$

for the $n_1 = 11{,}535$ in the placebo group and

$$\hat{p}_2 = 327/14035 = 0.023$$

for the $n_2 = 14{,}035$ in the aspirin group. Since $(\hat{p}_1 - \hat{p}_2) = 0.030 - 0.023 = 0.007$, the proportion of those who died of cancer was 0.007 higher for those who took placebo. In percentage terms, the difference was 3.0% − 2.3% = 0.7%, less than 1 percent. For the combined studies, the percentage of cancer deaths in the placebo group was 0.7 percentage points higher than in the aspirin group.

Recall

Chapter 3.1 introduced the difference of proportion as one measure of the strength of the association between a categorical (binary) response and an explanatory variable. ◀

Insight

The sample proportion of subjects who died of cancer was smaller for the aspirin group. But we really want to know whether this result is true also for the population. To make an inference about the difference of population proportions, $(p_1 - p_2)$, we need to learn how much the difference $(\hat{p}_1 - \hat{p}_2)$ between the sample proportions would tend to vary from study to study. This is described by the standard error of the sampling distribution for the difference between the sample proportions.

▶ ***Try Exercises 10.2 and 10.3, part a***

Sampling Distribution of the Difference Between Two Sample Proportions

Just as a single sample proportion has a sampling distribution that describes its likely values, so does the difference $(\hat{p}_1 - \hat{p}_2)$ between two sample proportions. For large sample sizes n_1 and n_2, recall from Chapter 7 that each of the two sample proportions, $\hat{p}_1$ and $\hat{p}_2$, has an approximately normal distribution, centered at p_1 and p_2 and with standard deviations $\sqrt{\frac{p_1(1-p_1)}{n_1}}$ and $\sqrt{\frac{p_2(1-p_2)}{n_2}}$, respectively. Consequently, the sampling distribution of the difference $(\hat{p}_1 - \hat{p}_2)$ of the two sample proportions also has an approximately normal distribution, centered at the population difference $(p_1 - p_2)$ and with standard deviation as shown in the following formula.

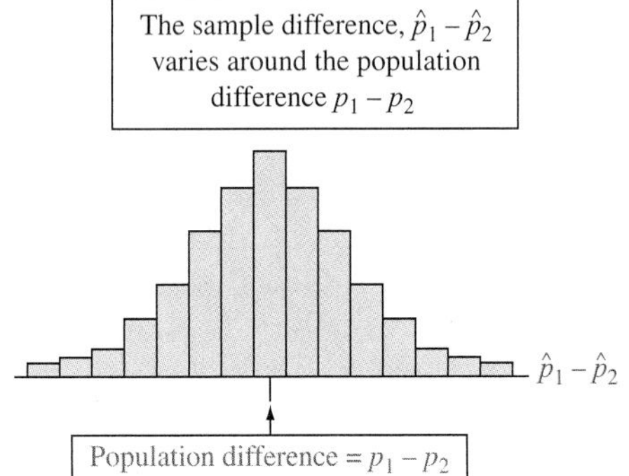

Mean and Standard Deviation of the Sampling Distribution for the Difference of Two Proportions

For two independent random samples of size n_1 and n_2 from two groups with population proportions p_1 and p_2, the sampling distribution of the difference in the sample proportions has

$$\text{mean} = p_1 - p_2 \text{ and standard deviation} = \sqrt{\frac{p_1(1-p_1)}{n_1} + \frac{p_2(1-p_2)}{n_2}}.$$

Recall

From Section 8.1, the standard error (*se*) is the estimated standard deviation of a sampling distribution. ◀

In practice, we will have to estimate the standard deviation because it depends on the unknown population proportions. This gives the **standard error** of the difference, which we will need to construct a confidence interval. It is obtained by replacing the unknown population proportions p_1 and p_2 in the formula for the standard deviation by the corresponding sample proportions. The standard error tells us how variable the estimate $(\hat{p}_1 - \hat{p}_2)$ is from one randomized experiment of the same size to another. It describes how far, in an average sense, the estimated differences from many such experiments fall from the actual difference $(p_1 - p_2)$ in the population. (See margin figure.)

The formula for the standard error of $(\hat{p}_1 - \hat{p}_2)$ is

Recall

From Section 8.2, for using a confidence interval to estimate a proportion p, the **standard error** of a sample **proportion** $\hat{p}$ is

$$\sqrt{\frac{\hat{p}(1-\hat{p})}{n}}. ◀$$

$$se = \sqrt{\frac{\hat{p}_1(1-\hat{p}_1)}{n_1} + \frac{\hat{p}_2(1-\hat{p}_2)}{n_2}}.$$

We'll take a closer look at this formula at the end of the section. For now, notice that if you ignore one of the two samples (and half of this formula), you get the usual standard error for a proportion, as shown in the second marginal Recall.

Example 3

Standard error ◀

Cancer Death Rates for Aspirin and Placebo

Picture the Scenario

In Example 2, the sample proportions of subjects who died of cancer were $\hat{p}_1 = 347/11535 = 0.030$ for placebo (Group 1) and $\hat{p}_2 = 327/14035 = 0.023$ for aspirin (Group 2). The estimated difference was $\hat{p}_1 - \hat{p}_2 = 0.030 - 0.023 = 0.007$.

Questions to Explore

a. What is the standard error of this estimate?

b. How should we interpret this standard error?

Think It Through

a. Using the standard error formula given, we have

$$se = \sqrt{\frac{\hat{p}_1(1-\hat{p}_1)}{n_1} + \frac{\hat{p}_2(1-\hat{p}_2)}{n_2}} = $$
$$= \sqrt{\frac{0.030(1-0.030)}{11535} + \frac{0.023(1-0.023)}{14035}} = 0.002.$$

b. Consider all the possible experiments with 11,535 participants in the placebo group and 14,035 participants in the aspirin group, just as in the contingency table shown in Table 10.1. From each experiment, compute the difference $(\hat{p}_1 - \hat{p}_2)$ in the sample proportions between these two groups. This difference will not always equal 0.007, the difference obtained from Table 10.1, but vary from one experiment to the next. The standard error of 0.002 describes how much these differences vary around the actual (unknown) difference in the population.

Insight

From the *se* formula, we see that *se* decreases as n_1 and n_2 increase. The standard error is very small for these data because the sample sizes were so large. This means that the $(\hat{p}_1 - \hat{p}_2)$ values would be very similar from study to study. It also implies that $(\hat{p}_1 - \hat{p}_2) = 0.007$ is quite precise as an estimate of the actual difference in the population proportions.

▶ ***Try Exercise 10.3, part b***

Confidence Interval for the Difference Between Two Population Proportions

The standard error helps us predict how close an estimate such as 0.007 is likely to be to the population difference $(p_1 - p_2)$. Figure 10.2 shows the approximate normal sampling distribution of $(\hat{p}_1 - \hat{p}_2)$ and highlights the range within which we expect the sample difference to fall about 95% of the time.

To obtain a confidence interval for $p_1 - p_2$, we take the estimated difference and add and subtract a margin of error based on the standard error. As in the single proportion case, to get the margin of error, we multiply the standard error by a *z*-score from the normal distribution. The confidence interval has the form

$$(\hat{p}_1 - \hat{p}_2) \pm z(se).$$

Recall

Review Section 8.2 for a discussion of the **confidence interval** for a single **proportion**. This has form

$$\hat{p} \pm z(se),$$

with $z = 1.96$ for 95% confidence. ◀

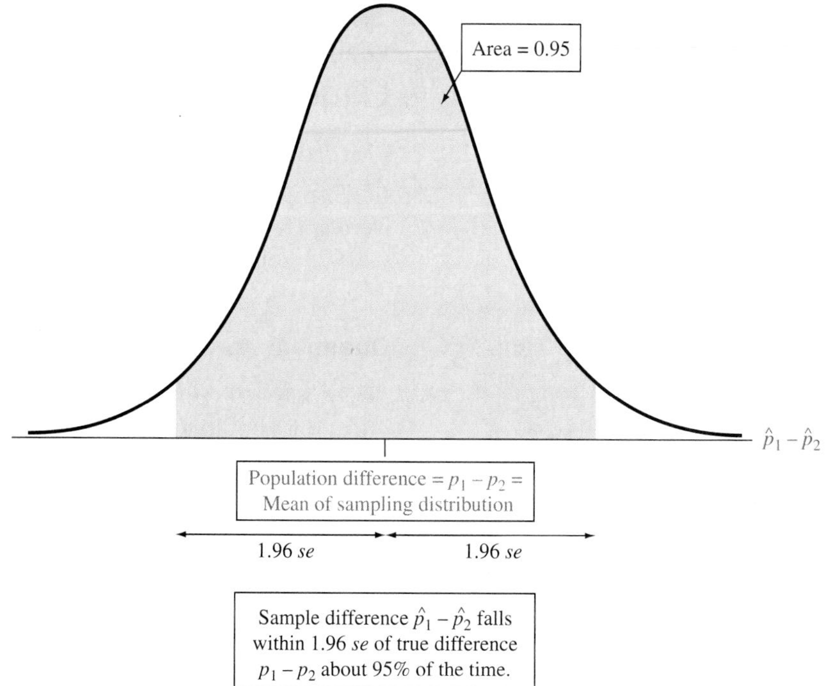

▲ **Figure 10.2 Sampling Distribution of the Difference ($\hat{p}_1 - \hat{p}_2$) Between Two Sample Proportions.** With large random samples, the sampling distribution is approximately normal, centered at the difference ($p_1 - p_2$) between the two population proportions. **Questions** For the aspirin and cancer death study (Examples 2 and 3), to what do ($\hat{p}_1 - \hat{p}_2$) and ($p_1 - p_2$) refer? What is the mean of this sampling distribution if cancer death rates are identical for aspirin and placebo?

SUMMARY: Confidence Interval for the Difference Between Two Population Proportions

A confidence interval for the difference ($p_1 - p_2$) between two population proportions is

$$(\hat{p}_1 - \hat{p}_2) \pm z(se), \text{ where } se = \sqrt{\frac{\hat{p}_1(1-\hat{p}_1)}{n_1} + \frac{\hat{p}_2(1-\hat{p}_2)}{n_2}}.$$

The *z*-score depends on the confidence level, such as $z = 1.96$ for 95% confidence. To use this method, you need

- A categorical response variable observed in each of two groups
- Independent random samples for the two groups, either from random sampling or a randomized experiment
- Large enough sample sizes n_1 and n_2 so that, in each sample, there are at least 10 successes and at least 10 failures. The confidence interval for a single proportion required at least 15 successes and 15 failures. Here, the method works well with slightly smaller samples, at least 10 of each type in each group.

Example 4

Confidence interval ◄

Comparing Cancer Death Rates for Aspirin and Placebo

Picture the Scenario

In the aspirin and cancer study, the estimated difference between placebo and aspirin in the proportions dying of cancer was $\hat{p}_1 - \hat{p}_2 =$

0.030 − 0.023= 0.007. In Example 3, we found that this estimate has a standard error of 0.002.

Question to Explore

What can we say about the difference of population proportions of cancer deaths for those taking placebo versus those taking aspirin? Construct a 95% confidence interval for $(p_1 - p_2)$ and interpret.

Think It Through

From Table 10.1, shown again in the margin, the four outcome counts (347, 327, 11188, and 13708) were at least 10 for each group, so the large-samples confidence interval method is valid. A 95% confidence interval for $(p_1 - p_2)$ is

$$(\hat{p}_1 - \hat{p}_2) \pm 1.96(se), \text{ or } 0.007 \pm 1.96(0.002),$$
$$\text{which is } 0.007 \pm 0.004, \text{ or } (0.003, 0.011).$$

Group	Death from Cancer: Yes	No
Placebo	347	11,188
Aspirin	327	13,708

In Words

The interval (0.003,0.011) for $(p_1 - p_2)$ predicts that the population proportion for the first group is between 0.003 and 0.011 larger than the population proportion for the second group.

The inference at the 95% confidence level that $(p_1 - p_2)$ is between 0.003 and 0.011 means that in experiments like this, the population proportion p_1 of cancer deaths for those taking placebo would be between 0.003 higher and 0.011 higher than the population proportion p_2 of cancer deaths for those taking aspirin. Since both endpoints of the confidence interval (0.003, 0.011) for $(p_1 - p_2)$ are positive, we infer that $(p_1 - p_2)$ is positive. This means that p_1 is larger than p_2: The population proportion of cancer deaths is larger when subjects take the placebo than when they take aspirin. Table 10.2 shows how MINITAB reports this result, and the margin shows screen shots from the TI. In terms of percentages, the 95% confidence interval means that the percentage of cancer deaths in the placebo group is at least 0.3 and at most 1.1 percentage points higher than in the aspirin group.

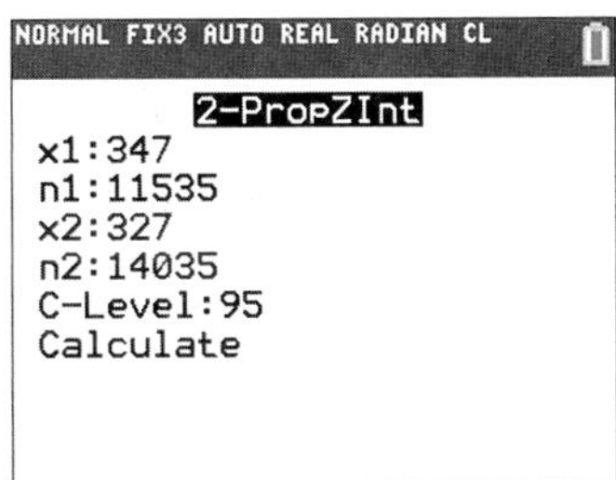

NORMAL FIX3 AUTO REAL RADIAN CL
2-PropZInt
(.003,.011)
$\hat{p}_1$=.030
$\hat{p}_2$=.023
n1=11535.000
n2=14035.000

TI output for confidence interval comparing two proportions

Table 10.2 MINITAB Output for Confidence Interval Comparing Proportions

```
         Number of Cancer Deaths      Observed p̂
                   ↓                       ↓
Sample             X          N       Sample p
   1             347      11535       0.030082
   2             327      14035       0.023299
Difference = p(1) − p(2)
Estimate for difference: 0.00678346 ←   [This is (p̂1 − p̂2)]
95% CI for difference: (0.00279030, 0.0107766)
```

Insight

All the numbers in the confidence interval fall near 0. This suggests that the population difference $(p_1 - p_2)$ is small. However, this difference, small as it is, may be important in public health terms. For instance, projected over a population of 200 million adults (as in the United States or in Western Europe), a decrease over a twenty-year period of 0.01 in the proportion of people dying from cancer would mean two million fewer people dying from cancer.

This cancer study provided some of the first evidence that aspirin reduces deaths from several common cancers. Benefit was consistent across the different trial populations from the different randomized studies, suggesting that the findings have broader scope of generalization. However, it is important to replicate the study to see whether results are similar or different for populations used in this study and other populations. Also, because there were fewer women than men in the study, findings about the effect of aspirin use and cancers related to women (such as breast cancer) were limited.

This example shows how the use of statistics can result in conclusions that benefit public health. An article[1] about proper and improper scientific methodology stated, "The most important discovery of modern medicine is not vaccines or antibiotics, it is the randomized double-blind study, by means of which we know what works and what doesn't."

▶ ***Try Exercise 10.6***

Recall

for **99% confidence** we use $z = 2.58$, because 99% of the standard normal distribution falls between -2.58 and 2.58. ◀

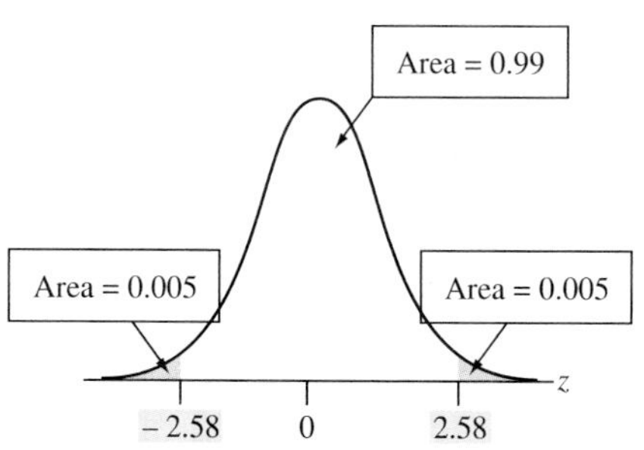

As in the one-sample case, we can use a higher confidence level, but the interval is then wider. For instance, a 99% confidence interval uses $z = 2.58$ (see margin figure) and equals

$$(\hat{p}_1 - \hat{p}_2) \pm 2.58(se), \text{ or } 0.007 \pm 2.58(0.002),$$
$$\text{which is } 0.007 \pm 0.005, \text{ or } (0.002, 0.012).$$

We can be 99% confident that the population proportion of cancer deaths is between 0.002 higher and 0.012 higher for the placebo treatment than for the aspirin treatment. For this example, the confidence interval is slightly wider than the 95% confidence interval of (0.003, 0.011). With very large sample sizes, it is often worth the slight widening to obtain greater confidence.

Interpreting a Confidence Interval That Compares Proportions

Example 4 illustrated how to interpret a confidence interval for $(p_1 - p_2)$ in context. Whether a particular group is called Group 1 or Group 2 is completely arbitrary. If we reverse the labels, each endpoint of the confidence interval reverses sign. For instance, if we instead call aspirin Group 1 and placebo Group 2, then $(\hat{p}_1 - \hat{p}_2) = 0.0023 - 0.0030 = -0.007$. The 95% confidence interval is then $(-0.011, -0.003)$ instead of (0.003, 0.011). Since this confidence interval contains entirely negative numbers, we infer that $(p_1 - p_2)$ is negative; that is, p_1 is smaller than p_2. Since Group 1 is now aspirin, the interval $(-0.011, -0.003)$ predicts that the population proportion of cancer deaths is between 0.011 less and 0.003 less for aspirin than for placebo. (The negative signs translate to the first proportion being *less* than the second.)

If a confidence interval for the difference between two proportions contains 0, then it is plausible that $(p_1 - p_2) = 0$, that is, $p_1 = p_2$. The population proportions might be equal. In such a case, insufficient evidence exists to infer which of p_1 or p_2 is larger. See Figure 10.3.

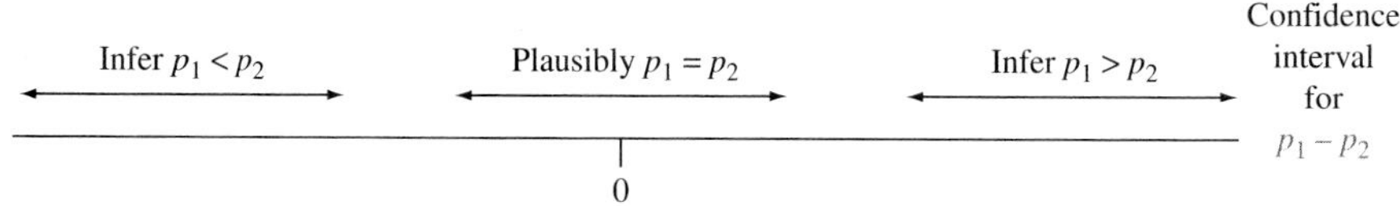

▲ **Figure 10.3** Three Confidence Intervals for the Difference Between Proportions, $p_1 - p_2$. When the confidence interval for $p_1 - p_2$ contains 0 (the middle interval above), the population proportions may be equal. When it does not contain 0, we can infer which population proportion is larger. **Question** For the two confidence intervals that do not contain 0, how can we tell which population proportion is predicted to be larger?

[1]By R. L. Park, *The Chronicle of Higher Education*, January 31, 2003.

For instance, Exercise 10.6 summarizes a study comparing population proportions for a placebo group and a treatment group. The study had a much smaller sample size than the aspirin and cancer study, so its standard error was larger. Its 95% confidence interval for $(p_1 - p_2)$ is $(-0.005, 0.034)$. Since the interval contains 0, the population proportions might well be equal. This interval infers that the population proportion p_1 for the placebo group is as much as 0.005 lower or as much as 0.034 higher than the population proportion p_2 for the treatment group. A *negative* value for $(p_1 - p_2)$, such as -0.005, means that p_1 could be *below* p_2, whereas a *positive* value for $(p_1 - p_2)$, such as $+0.034$, means that p_1 could be *above* p_2.

Caution

Although technology will report the endpoints of a confidence interval for a difference of proportions to several decimal places, it is simpler to report and interpret these confidence intervals using at most 3 decimal places for the endpoints. ◀

SUMMARY: Interpreting a Confidence Interval for a Difference of Proportions

- Check whether 0 falls in the confidence interval. If so, it is plausible (but not necessary) that the population proportions are equal.
- If all values in the confidence interval for $(p_1 - p_2)$ are positive, you can infer that $(p_1 - p_2) > 0$, or $p_1 > p_2$. The interval shows just how much larger p_1 might be. If all values in the confidence interval are negative, you can infer that $(p_1 - p_2) < 0$, or $p_1 < p_2$.
- The magnitude of values in the confidence interval tells you how *large* any true difference is. If all values in the confidence interval are near 0, the true difference may be relatively small in practical terms.

Significance Tests Comparing Population Proportions

Another way to compare two population proportions p_1 and p_2 is with a significance test. The null hypothesis is H_0: $p_1 = p_2$, the population proportion taking the same value for each group. In terms of the difference of proportions, this is H_0: $(p_1 - p_2) = 0$, *no difference*, or *no effect.*

Under the presumption for H_0 that $p_1 = p_2$, we estimate the common value of p_1 and p_2 by the proportion of the *total* sample in the category of interest. We denote this by $\hat{p}$. For example, if Group 1 had 7 successes in $n_1 = 20$ observations and Group 2 had 5 successes in $n_2 = 10$ observations, then $\hat{p}_1 = 7/20 = 0.35, \hat{p}_2 = 5/10 = 0.50$, and $\hat{p} = (7 + 5)/(20 + 10) = 12/30 = 0.40$. This makes sense because if $p_1 = p_2$, the two groups have identical proportions of successes, and we can merge them. All we need for estimating this common proportion are the total number of successes and the total sample size from the two groups combined, such as the 12 successes out of the 30 observations resulting in an overall proportion of 0.4.

The proportion $\hat{p}$ is called a **pooled estimate** because it pools the total number of successes and total number of observations from the two samples. Whenever the sample sizes n_1 and n_2 are roughly equal, it falls about halfway between $\hat{p}_1$ and $\hat{p}_2$. Otherwise, it falls closer to the sample proportion that has the larger sample size.

Recall

Section 9.2 presented the **significance test** for a single **proportion**. The *z* test statistic measures the number of standard errors that the sample proportion falls from the value in the null hypothesis. ◀

The test statistic measures the number of standard errors that the sample estimate $(\hat{p}_1 - \hat{p}_2)$ of $(p_1 - p_2)$ falls from its null hypothesis value of 0:

$$z = \frac{\text{Estimate} - \text{Null hypothesis value}}{\text{Standard error}} = \frac{(\hat{p}_1 - \hat{p}_2) - 0}{se_0}.$$

The standard error for the test, denoted by se_0, is based on the presumption stated in H_0 that $p_1 = p_2$. If this is the case, we can use the pooled estimate $\hat{p}$ to estimate each population proportion instead of estimating them separately.

This standard error is given by (replacing p_1 and p_2 in the standard deviation formula by $\hat{p}$)

$$se_0 = \sqrt{\frac{\hat{p}(1-\hat{p})}{n_1} + \frac{\hat{p}(1-\hat{p})}{n_2}} = \sqrt{\hat{p}(1-\hat{p})\left(\frac{1}{n_1} + \frac{1}{n_2}\right)}.$$

Similar to the one-sample case, we use the subscript 0 to indicate that this is the standard error when assuming that the null hypothesis is true. In practice, when the sample proportions are close, se_0 is very close to se used in a confidence interval, which does not presume equal proportions.

As usual, the P-value for $H_0: p_1 = p_2$ depends on whether the alternative hypothesis is two-sided, $H_a: p_1 \neq p_2$, or one-sided, $H_a: p_1 > p_2$ or $H_a: p_1 < p_2$. When it is two-sided, the P-value is the two-tail probability beyond the observed z test statistic value from the standard normal distribution. This is the probability, presuming H_0 to be true, of obtaining results more extreme than observed in either direction.

Recall

A **P-value** (introduced in Section 9.1) is the probability that the test statistic equals the observed value or a value even more extreme (in one tail for a one-sided H_a or both tails for a two-sided H_a) presuming that H_0 is true. Smaller P-values provide stronger evidence against H_0. ◀

In Practice Sample Size Guidelines for Significance Tests

Significance tests comparing proportions use the **sample size** guideline from confidence intervals: Each sample should have at least about 10 successes and 10 failures. Note that *two-sided tests* are robust against violations of this condition. In that case you can use the test with smaller samples. In practice, the two-sided test works well if there are at least five successes and five failures in each sample.

SUMMARY: Two-Sided Significance Test for Comparing Two Population Proportions

1. **Assumptions**
   - A categorical response variable observed in each of two groups
   - Independent random samples, either from random sampling or a randomized experiment
   - n_1 and n_2 are large enough that there are at least five successes and five failures in each group if using a two-sided alternative
2. **Hypotheses**
   Null $H_0: p_1 = p_2$ (that is, $p_1 - p_2 = 0$)
   Alternative $H_a: p_1 \neq p_2$ (one-sided H_a also possible; see after Example 5)
3. **Test Statistic**
   $$z = \frac{(\hat{p}_1 - \hat{p}_2) - 0}{se_0} \text{ with } se_0 = \sqrt{\hat{p}(1-\hat{p})\left(\frac{1}{n_1} + \frac{1}{n_2}\right)},$$
   where $\hat{p}$ is the pooled estimate.
4. **P-value**
   P-value = Two-tail probability from standard normal distribution (Table A) of values even more extreme than observed z test statistic presuming the null hypothesis is true
5. **Conclusion**
   Smaller P-values give stronger evidence against H_0 and supporting H_a. Interpret the P-value in context. If a decision is needed, reject H_0 if P-value ≤ significance level (such as 0.05).

Example 5

Compare two population proportions ◀

TV Watching and Aggressive Behavior

Picture the Scenario

A study[2] considered whether greater levels of television watching by teenagers were associated with a greater likelihood of aggressive behavior. The researchers randomly sampled 707 families in two counties in northern New

[2]By J.G. Johnson et al., *Science*, vol. 295, March 29, 2002, pp. 2468–2471.

Proportion Committing Violent Acts

Proportion: 0.3, 0.2, 0.1, 0.0

Less than 1h | More than 1h

Average daily TV consumption

York state and made follow-up observations over 17 years. Table 10.3 shows results about whether a sampled teenager later conducted any aggressive act against another person, according to a self-report by that person or by his or her parent. The bar chart in the margin figure summarizes the results.

Table 10.3 TV Watching by Teenagers and Later Aggressive Acts

	Aggressive Act		
TV Watching	**Yes**	**No**	**Total**
Less than 1 hour per day	5	83	88
At least 1 hour per day	154	465	619

We'll identify Group 1 as those who watched less than 1 hour of TV per day, on average, as teenagers. Group 2 consists of those who averaged at least 1 hour of TV per day, as teenagers. Denote the population proportion committing aggressive acts by p_1 for the lower level of TV watching and by p_2 for the higher level of TV watching.

Questions to Explore

a. Find and interpret the P-value for testing $H_0: p_1 = p_2$ against $H_a: p_1 \neq p_2$.

b. Make a decision about H_0 using the significance level of 0.05.

Think It Through

a. The study used a random sample of teenagers, who were classified into two groups by the level of TV watching (the explanatory variable); therefore, we can treat the sample of teenagers in each group as two independent samples. Each count in Table 10.3 is at least five, so we can use a large-sample test. The sample proportions of aggressive acts were $\hat{p}_1 = 5/88 = 0.057$ for the lower level of TV watching and $\hat{p}_2 = 154/619 = 0.249$ for the higher level. Under the null hypothesis presumption that $p_1 = p_2$, the pooled estimate of the common value p is $\hat{p} = (5 + 154)/(88 + 619) = 159/707 = 0.225$.

The standard error for the test is

$$se_0 = \sqrt{\hat{p}(1 - \hat{p})\left(\frac{1}{n_1} + \frac{1}{n_2}\right)} = \sqrt{(0.225)(0.775)\left(\frac{1}{88} + \frac{1}{619}\right)} = 0.0476.$$

The test statistic for $H_0: p_1 = p_2$ is

$$z = \frac{(\hat{p}_1 - \hat{p}_2) - 0}{se_0} = \frac{(0.057 - 0.249) - 0}{0.0476} = \frac{-0.192}{0.0476} = -4.04.$$

For the two-sided alternative hypothesis, the P-value is the two-tail probability from the standard normal distribution. A z-score of -4.04 is far out in the left tail. See the margin figure. From tables (such as Table A) or software, it has a P-value $= 2(0.000027) = 0.000054$, or 0.0001 rounded to four decimal places. Extremely strong evidence exists against the null hypothesis that the population proportions committing aggressive acts are the same for the two levels of TV watching. The study provides strong evidence in support of H_a.

b. Since the P-value is less than 0.05, we can reject H_0. We support $H_a: p_1 \neq p_2$ and conclude that the population proportions of

Recall

It was noted in the Chapter 10 introduction that if a sample is randomly selected and the selected subjects are separated into groups according to their value for an explanatory variable, then the groups can be treated as independent random samples. ◀

P-value is equal to sum of the shaded tail areas

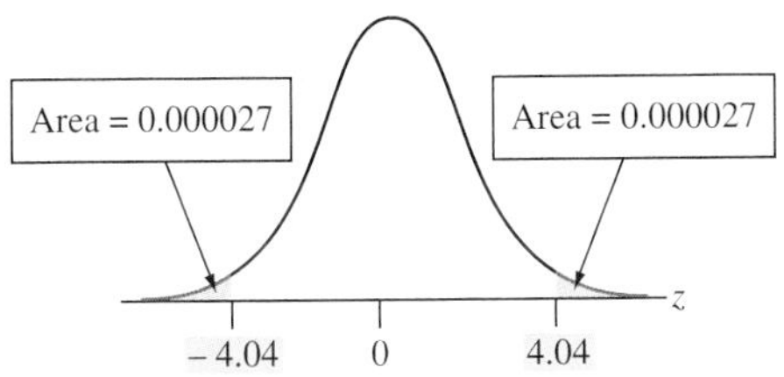

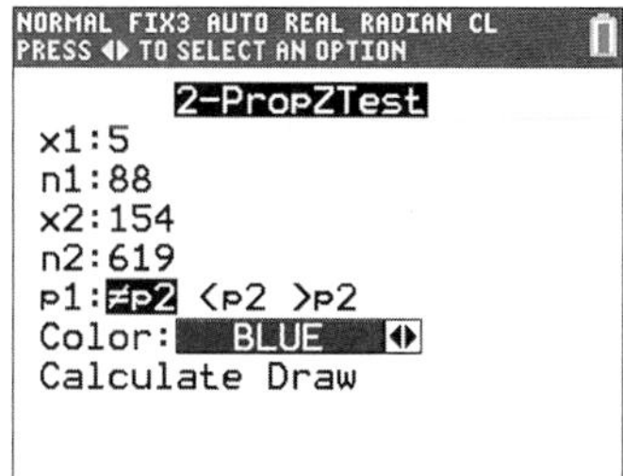

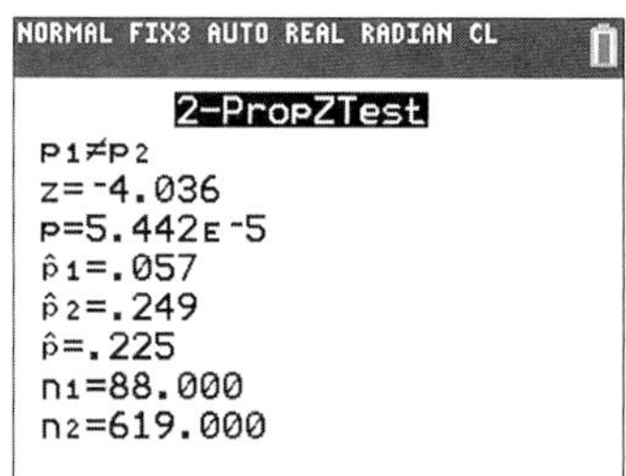

TI output for significance test comparing proportions

aggressive acts differ for the two groups. The sample values suggest that the population proportion is higher for the higher level of TV watching. The final row of Table 10.4 shows how MINITAB reports this result, and the margin next to Table 10.4 shows screen shots from TI calculators.

Table 10.4 MINITAB Output for Example 5 on TV Watching and Aggression

```
Sample      X      N     Sample p
   1        5     88     0.056818
   2      154    619     0.248788
Difference = p(1) - p(2)
Estimate for difference: -0.191970
95% CI for difference: (-0.251124, -0.132816)
Test for difference = 0 (vs ≠ 0): z = -4.04 P-value = 0.000
```

Insight

This was an observational study. In practice, it would be impossible to conduct an experimental study by randomly assigning teenagers to watch little TV or watch much TV over several years. Also, just because a person watches more TV does not imply that he or she watches more violence, which then leads to more aggressive behavior. We must be cautious of effects of lurking variables when we make conclusions. It is not proper to conclude that greater levels of TV watching *cause* later aggressive behavior. For instance, perhaps those who watched more TV had lower education levels, and perhaps lower education levels are associated with a greater likelihood of aggressive acts.

Recall

An **observational** study merely observes the explanatory variable, such as TV watching. An **experimental** study randomly allocates subjects to its levels. Sections 4.1 and 4.4 discussed limitations of observational studies, such as effects that lurking variables may have on the association. ◀

▶ ***Try Exercise 10.8***

When the test indicates rejection of H_0 (i.e., when the P-value $<$ significance level), we call the results of the test statistically significant. In the context of comparing two groups, we often speak of a significant difference.

Significant Difference

Two groups are called (statistically) significantly different if a test based on comparing the two population parameters results in a significant result, i.e., a small P-value.

For example, with regard to the proportion committing violent acts, the group with teenagers who watched less than 1 hour of TV per day differed significantly (P-value < 0.001) from the group that watched at least one hour of TV. However, the same caution as mentioned in Section 9.5 applies regarding statistical significance versus practical significance. Just because a difference is statistically significant doesn't mean it's practically relevant. The difference might be small in practical terms. The confidence interval tells you about the size of the effect. For the preceding example, the percentage of teenagers committing violent acts was at least 13 percentage points lower for those who watched less than one hour of TV per day. This is much more informative than just saying that a (statistically) significant difference was found between the two groups.

Caution

Considering a one-sided alternative would be questionable for this data since one of the counts is less than 10. ◀

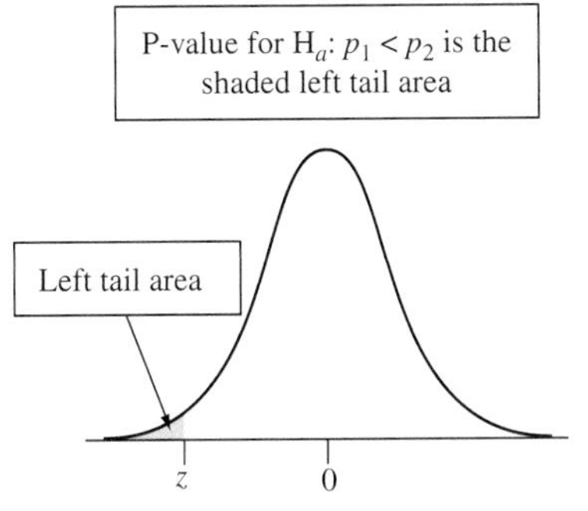

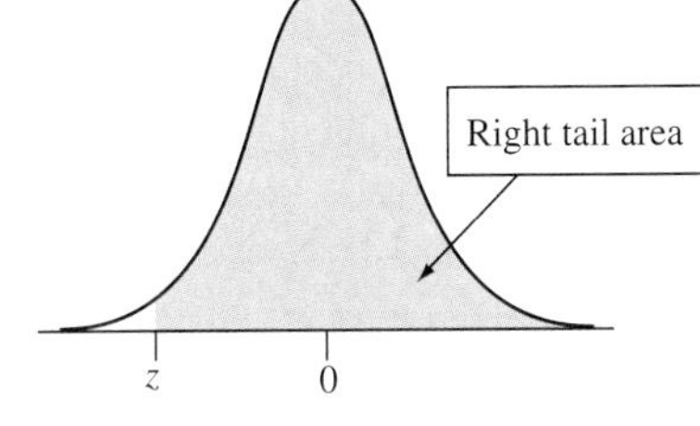

A One-Sided Alternative Hypothesis Example 5 requested a test for the two-sided alternative, H_a: $p_1 \neq p_2$. Two-sided P-values are typically reported in journals. However, suppose the researchers specifically predicted that greater levels of TV watching by teenagers were associated with greater likelihood of committing aggressive acts years later. Then they may have preferred to use the one-sided alternative, H_a: $p_1 < p_2$. This states that the population proportion of aggressive acts is higher at the higher level of TV watching. Equivalently, it is H_a: $(p_1 - p_2) < 0$.

The P-value is then a left-tail probability below the observed test statistic, $z = -4.04$. See the first margin figure. From Table A or software, this is about 0.00003. The conclusion is that there was significantly greater probability of aggression for those who had watched more TV.

On the other hand, suppose researchers wanted to show that the proportion of violent acts is larger in the group that watched less TV. Then they would have tested the one-sided hypothesis H_a: $p_1 > p_2$ when now the P-value would be the tail probability to the right of the observed test statistic. (See second margin figure.) However, this alternative was not relevant for this study.

The Standard Error for Comparing Two Statistics

Now that we've seen how to compare two proportions, let's learn where the *se* formula comes from. Whenever we estimate a difference between two population parameters, a general rule specifies the standard error.

Standard Error of the Difference Between Two Estimates

For two estimates from independent samples, the standard error is

$$se(\text{estimate 1} - \text{estimate 2}) = \sqrt{[se(\text{estimate 1})]^2 + [se(\text{estimate 2})]^2}.$$

Notice that we *add* squared standard errors under the square root sign, rather than subtract. For example, if we're comparing two proportions, then the standard error of the difference is *larger* than the standard error for either sample proportion alone. Why is this true? In practical terms, $(\hat{p}_1 - \hat{p}_2)$ is often farther from $(p_1 - p_2)$ than $\hat{p}_1$ is from p_1 or $\hat{p}_2$ is from p_2. For instance, in the aspirin and cancer study, *suppose that*

$$p_1 = p_2 = 0.0265 \text{ (unknown to us)},$$

but the sample proportions were

$$\hat{p}_1 = 0.030 \text{ and } \hat{p}_2 = 0.023,$$

as was actually observed for the sample data. Then the errors of estimation were

$$\hat{p}_1 - p_1 = 0.03 - 0.0265 = 0.0035 \text{ and } \hat{p}_2 - p_2 = 0.023 - 0.0265 = -0.0035,$$

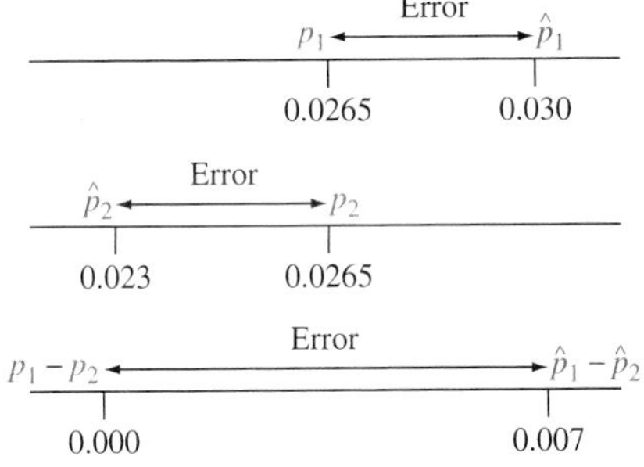

each estimate being off by a distance of 0.0035. But then $(\hat{p}_1 - \hat{p}_2) = 0.030 - 0.023 = 0.007$. That is, the estimate is 0.007 from $(p_1 - p_2) = 0$, larger than the error for either proportion individually. See the margin figure.

Let's apply the formula for the standard error of the difference between two estimates to the comparison of two proportions. The standard error of a single sample proportion $\hat{p}$ is $se = \sqrt{\hat{p}(1 - \hat{p})/n}$. Then, for two samples, the *se* of $(\hat{p}_1 - \hat{p}_2)$ is

$$se = \sqrt{[se(\text{estimate 1})]^2 + [se(\text{estimate 2})]^2} = \sqrt{\frac{\hat{p}_1(1 - \hat{p}_1)}{n_1} + \frac{\hat{p}_2(1 - \hat{p}_2)}{n_2}}.$$

We use this *se* formula to construct a confidence interval for the difference between two population proportions.

Small-Sample Inference for Comparing Proportions

The confidence interval for a difference of proportions specifies that each sample should have at least 10 outcomes of each type. For smaller sample sizes, the method may not work well: The sampling distribution of $(\hat{p}_1 - \hat{p}_2)$ may not be close to normal, and the estimate of the standard error may be poor. We won't cover this case here, but it is briefly discussed in Exercise 10.126. There are also small-sample significance tests for comparing proportions. We will discuss one, called *Fisher's exact test*, in the next chapter. Such tests have their own disadvantages, however, and for two-sided alternatives, the large-sample test usually performs quite well for small samples also.

10.1 Practicing the Basics

10.1 Unemployment rate According to the Bureau of Labor Statistics, the official unemployment rate was 10.4% among blacks and 4.7% among whites as of February 2015. (www.bls.gov/).

a. Identify the response variable and the explanatory variable.

b. Identify the two groups that are the categories of the explanatory variable.

c. The unemployment statistics are based on a sample of individuals. Were the samples of white individuals and black individuals independent samples or dependent samples? Explain.

10.2 Sampling sleep TRY The 2011 Bedroom Sleep poll of a random sample of 1500 adults reported that respondents slept an average of 6.5 hours on weekdays and 7.2 hours on weekends, and that 21% of respondents got eight or more hours of sleep on weekdays, whereas 44% got eight or more hours of sleep on weekends (www.sleepfoundation.org).

a. To compare the means or the percentages using inferential methods, should you treat the samples on weekdays and weekends as independent samples or as dependent samples? Explain.

b. To compare these results to polls of other people taken in previous years, should you treat the samples in the two years as independent samples or as dependent samples? Explain.

10.3 Binge drinking TRY The PACE project at the University of Wisconsin in Madison dealt with problems associated with high-risk drinking on college campuses. Based on random samples, the study stated that the percentage of UW students who reported bingeing at least three times within the past two weeks was 42.2% in 1999 ($n = 334$) and 21.2% in 2009 ($n = 843$).

a. Estimate the difference between the proportions in 1999 and 2009 and interpret.

b. Find the standard error for this difference. Interpret it.

c. Define the two relevant population parameters to compare in the context of this exercise.

d. Construct and interpret a 95% confidence interval for the difference in proportions, explaining how your interpretation reflects whether the interval contains 0.

e. State and check the assumptions for the confidence interval in part d to be valid.

10.4 Smoking and lung obstruction A National Center for Health Statistics data brief published in 2015 (Nr. 181) looked at the association between lung obstruction and smoking status in adults 40 to 79 years old. In a random sample of 6927 adults without any lung obstruction, 54.1% never smoked. In a random sample of 1146 adults with lung obstruction (such as asthma or COPD), 23.8% never smoked.

a. Find and interpret a point estimate of the difference between the proportion of adults without and with lung obstruction who never smoked.

b. A 99% confidence interval for the true difference is (0.267, 0.339). Interpret.

c. What assumptions must you make for the interval in part b to be valid?

10.5 Do you believe in miracles? TECH Let p_1 and p_2 denote the population proportions of males and females in the United States who answer, yes, definitely when asked whether they believe in miracles. Estimate these by visiting the General Social Survey website (sda.berkeley.edu/GSS), selecting GSS with No Weight as the default, and then entering the variable MIRACLES for the rows, SEX for the columns, and YEAR (2008) as the selection filter. (The table shows 277 males out of 603 and 461 females out of 730 answering "Yes, definitely.")

a. Report point estimates of p_1 and p_2.

b. Construct a 95% confidence interval for $(p_1 - p_2)$, specifying the assumptions you make to use this method. Interpret.

c. Based on the interval in part b, explain why the proportion believing in miracles may have been quite a bit larger for females, or it might have been only moderately larger.

10.6 Aspirin and heart attacks in Sweden TRY A Swedish study used 1360 patients who had suffered a stroke. The study randomly assigned each subject to an aspirin treatment or a placebo treatment.[3] The table shows MINITAB output,

[3]Based on results described in *Lancet*, vol. 338, pp. 1345–1349 (1991).

where X is the number of deaths due to heart attack during a follow-up period of about 3 years. Sample 1 received the placebo and sample 2 received aspirin.

a. Explain how to obtain the values labeled "Sample p."

b. Explain how to interpret the value given for "estimate for difference."

c. Explain how to interpret the confidence interval, indicating the relevance of 0 falling in the interval.

d. If we instead let sample 1 refer to the aspirin treatment and sample 2 the placebo treatment, explain how the estimate of the difference and the 95% confidence interval would change. Explain how then to interpret the confidence interval.

Deaths due to heart attacks in Swedish study

```
Sample    X     N     Sample p
  1      28    684    0.040936
  2      18    676    0.026627
Difference = p(1) - p(2)
Estimate for difference: 0.0143085
95% CI for difference: (-0.00486898, 0.0334859)
Test for differnce = 0 (vs ≠ 0):
z = 1.46 P-Value = 0.144
```

10.7 Swedish study test Refer to the previous exercise.

a. State the hypotheses that were tested.

b. Explain how to interpret the P-value for the test.

c. Even though the difference between the sample proportions was larger than in the Physicians Health Study (Examples 2–4), the P-value is larger (i.e., the test results are less statistically significant). Explain how this could be. (*Hint:* How do the sample sizes compare for the two studies? How does this affect the standard error and thus the test statistic and P-value?)

d. Report the P-value for the one-sided alternative hypothesis that the chance of death due to heart attack is lower for the aspirin group.

10.8 Significance test for aspirin and cancer deaths study

TRY In the study for cancer death rates, consider the null hypothesis that the population proportion of cancer deaths p_1 for placebo is the same as the population proportion p_2 for aspirin. The sample proportions were $\hat{p}_1 = 347/11535 = 0.0301$ and $\hat{p}_2 = 327/14035 = 0.0233$.

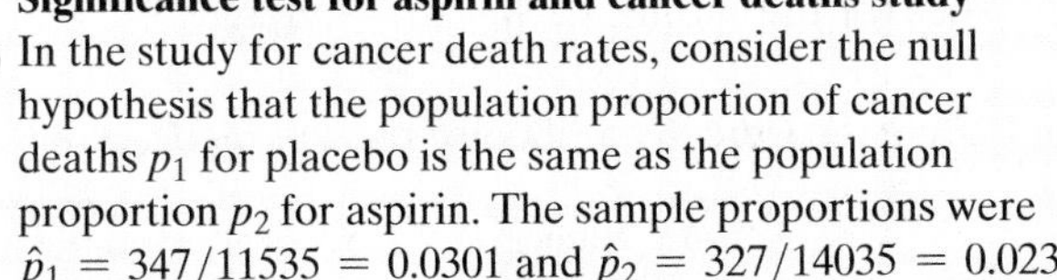

a. For testing H_0: $p_1 = p_2$ against H_a: $p_1 \neq p_2$, show that the pooled estimate of the common value p under H_0 is $\hat{p} = 0.026$ and the standard error is 0.002.

b. Show that the test statistic is $z = 3.4$.

c. Find and interpret the P-value in context.

10.9 Drinking and unplanned sex In the study of binge drinking mentioned in Exercise 10.3, the percent who said they had engaged in unplanned sexual activities because of drinking alcohol was 30.7% in 1999 and 23.0% in 2009. Is this change statistically significant at the 0.05 significance level?

a. Specify assumptions, notation, and hypotheses for a two-sided test.

b. Show how to find the pooled estimate of the proportion to use in a test. (*Hint:* You need the count in each year rather than the proportion. In 1999, note this is $(0.307)334 = 103$.) Interpret this estimate.

c. Find the test statistic and P-value. Make a decision using a significance level of 0.05.

10.10 Comparing marketing commercials Two TV commercials

TECH are developed for marketing a new product. A volunteer test sample of 200 people is randomly split into two groups of 100 each. In a controlled setting, Group A watches commercial A and Group B watches commercial B. In Group A, 25 say they would buy the product. In group B, 20 say they would buy the product. The marketing manager who devised this experiment concludes that commercial A is better. Is this conclusion justified? Analyze the data. If you prefer, use software (such as MINITAB or a web app) for which you can enter summary counts.

a. Show all steps of your analysis (perhaps including an appropriate graph) and check assumptions.

b. Comment on the manager's conclusion and indicate limitations of the experiment.

10.11 Hormone therapy for menopause The Women's Health

TECH Initiative conducted a randomized experiment to see whether hormone therapy was helpful for postmenopausal women. The women were randomly assigned to receive the estrogen plus progestin hormone therapy or a placebo. After five years, 107 of the 8506 on the hormone therapy developed cancer and 88 of the 8102 in the placebo group developed cancer. Is this a significant difference?

a. Set up notation and state assumptions and hypotheses.

b. Find the test statistic and P-value and interpret. (If you prefer, use software, such as MINITAB or a web app, for which you can conduct the analysis by entering summary counts.)

c. What is your conclusion for a significance level of 0.05? (The study was planned to be eight years long but was stopped after five years because of increased heart and cancer problems for the therapy group. This shows a benefit of doing two-sided tests, because results sometimes have the opposite direction from the expected one.)

10.12 Obama A/B testing To increase Barack Obama's visibility and to raise money for the campaign leading up to the 2008 presidential election, Obama's analytics team conducted an A/B test with his website. In the original version, the button to join the campaign read "Sign Up". In an alternative version, it read "Learn More". Of 77,858 visitors to the original version, 5851 clicked the button. Of 77,729 visitors to the alternative version, 6927 clicked the button. Is there evidence that one version was more successful than the other in recruiting campaign members?

```
Sample          X       N      Sample p
SignUp      77858    5851      0.075150
LearnMore   77729    6927      0.089117
Difference = p(SignUp) - p(LearnMore)
Estimate for difference: -0.013968
95% CI for difference: (-0.016695, -0.011239)
Test for difference = 0(vs ≠ 0):
Z = -10.03 P-Value = 0.000
```

a. Sketch an appropriate graph to compare the sample proportions visually.

b. Show all steps of a significance test, using the computer output. Define any parameters you are using when specifying the hypotheses. Mention whether there is a significant difference at the 0.05 significance level.

c. Interpret the confidence interval shown in the output. Why is this interval more informative than just reporting the P-value?

10.13 Believe in heaven and hell A recent survey asked each participant whether he or she believes in heaven and in hell. Of the 1314 participants, a proportion of 0.85 believed in heaven and a proportion of 0.73 believed in hell. Can we use the inferential methods (confidence interval, significance test) in this section to compare the two proportions? If yes, find a 95% confidence interval for the difference in the population proportions. If no, explain why.

10.2 Quantitative Response: Comparing Two Means

We can compare two groups on a *quantitative response variable* by comparing their means. What does the difference between the sample means tell us about the difference between the population means? We'll find out in this section.

Compare two groups on a quantitative variable ◄

Example 6

A Graph Is Worth a Thousand Words

Picture the Scenario

We learned in previous chapters that graphs provide a powerful way of conveying information. Public relations, media, or marketing companies all use graphs to draw attention to their services or products and ultimately boost sales. Are we giving more credence to a service or product if its description is accompanied by a graph, i.e., looks more scientific? To explore this, in a recent experiment participants were randomly split into two groups. One group just read a short generic text about the effectiveness of a drug. The other group read that same text but now accompanied by a basic bar graph that just mirrored the text and did not provide any new information.[4] After the experiment, participants rated the perceived effectiveness of the drug on a 9-point scale, with 1 representing "not at all effective" and 9 representing "very effective." Figure 10.4 shows side-by-side box plots, and Table 10.5 provides some summary statistics for the ratings in the two groups.

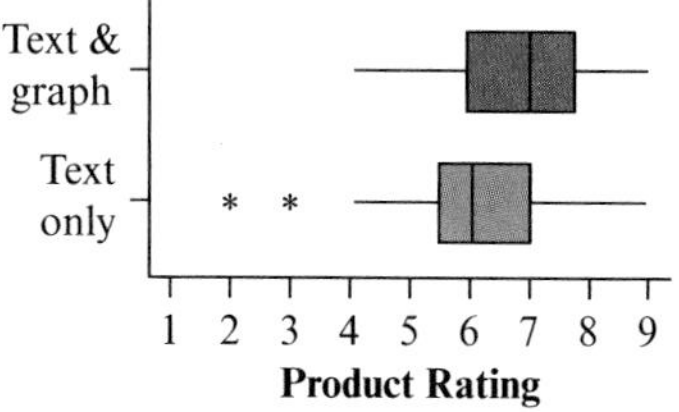

▲ **Figure 10.4** Side-by-Side Box Plots Showing the Distribution of Ratings in the Two Groups. **Question** What other graph would you like to see?

Table 10.5 Summary for Ratings on Perceived Effectiveness of Medication

		Ratings on perceived effectiveness	
Group	**Sample Size**	**Mean**	**Standard Deviation**
Text and graph	30	6.83	1.18
Text only	31	6.13	1.43

Question to Explore

How can we compare the ratings between the group that saw the text and the graph and the group that just saw the text?

Think It Through

One way to compare the two groups compares the mean ratings by looking at their difference. Let Group 1 be the one that read the text and saw the

[4] A. Tal and B. Wansink, *Public Understanding of Science*, published online October 2014 DOI: 10.1177/0963662514549688.

graph and Group 2 be the one that just read the text. The sample mean rating is $\bar{x}_1 = 6.83$ in Group 1 and $\bar{x}_2 = 6.13$ in Group 2 (see Table 10.5), resulting in a difference of $\bar{x}_1 - \bar{x}_2 = 6.83 - 6.13 = 0.7$. In this experiment, the mean rating on the perceived effectiveness of the medication is 0.7 points higher in the group that also saw the graph.

Insight

This analysis uses descriptive statistics only. We'll next see how to make inferences about the difference between two population means when the population refers to all people who might read the short description of the medication, one with and one without the graph.

▶ ***Try Exercise 10.16, part a***

Sampling Distribution of the Difference Between Two Sample Means

How well does the difference $(\bar{x}_1 - \bar{x}_2)$ between two sample means estimate the difference between the corresponding population means $\mu_1 - \mu_2$? This is described by the sampling distribution of $(\bar{x}_1 - \bar{x}_2)$ and, in particular, its estimated standard deviation, the standard error. For large sample sizes n_1 and n_2, recall from Chapter 7 that each of the two sample means $\bar{x}_1$ and $\bar{x}_2$ has an approximate normal distribution, centered at μ_1 and μ_2 and with standard deviations $\frac{\sigma_1}{\sqrt{n_1}}$ and $\frac{\sigma_2}{\sqrt{n_2}}$, respectively. Here, σ_1 is the population standard deviation in the first group, and σ_2 is the population standard deviation in the second group.

Mean and Standard Deviation of the Sampling Distribution for the Difference of Two Sample Means

For two independent random samples of size n_1 and n_2 from two groups with population means μ_1 and μ_2 and population standard deviations σ_1 and σ_2, the sampling distribution of the difference in the sample means has mean $= \mu_1 - \mu_2$ and standard deviation $= \sqrt{\frac{\sigma_1^2}{n_1} + \frac{\sigma_2^2}{n_2}}$.

In practice, we will have to estimate the standard deviation because it depends on the unknown population standard deviations. Replacing σ_1 and σ_2 by the sample standard deviations s_1 and s_2, we get the **standard error** of the difference

$$se = \sqrt{\frac{s_1^2}{n_1} + \frac{s_2^2}{n_2}}.$$

Recall

From the formula box at the end of Section 10.1, for two estimates from independent samples,

se(estimate 1 − estimate 2) =

$\sqrt{[se(\text{est. }1)]^2 + [se(\text{est. }2)]^2}$,

the square root of the sum of squared standard errors of the two estimates. ◀

Notice how the expression follows the general rule for the standard error of a difference, shown again in the margin. One adds the squared standard error for each estimate and then takes the square root:

$$se \text{ of } (\bar{x}_1 - \bar{x}_2) = \sqrt{[se(\bar{x}_1)]^2 + [se(\bar{x}_2)]^2} = \sqrt{\frac{s_1^2}{n_1} + \frac{s_2^2}{n_2}}.$$

Interpret *se* for difference between means

Example 7

Text with Graph

Picture the Scenario

In the experiment mentioned in Example 6, the group of $n_1 = 30$ participants that read the text and saw the graph had a sample mean of $\bar{x}_1 = 6.83$ and a sample standard deviation of $s_1 = 1.18$. For the $n_2 = 31$ participants in the group just reading the text, $\bar{x}_2 = 6.13$ and $s_2 = 1.43$. (See Table 10.5.) We mentioned in Example 6 that the group reading the text and seeing the graph rated the drug, on average, 0.7 points higher than the group just reading the text.

Question to Explore

What is the standard error of the difference in sample mean ratings about the effectiveness of the drug? How do you interpret that *se*?

Think it Through

Applying the formula for the *se* of $(\bar{x}_1 - \bar{x}_2)$ for these data,

$$se = \sqrt{\frac{s_1^2}{n_1} + \frac{s_2^2}{n_2}} = \sqrt{\frac{(1.18)^2}{30} + \frac{(1.43)^2}{31}} = 0.336.$$

This describes the variability of the sampling distribution of $(\bar{x}_1 - \bar{x}_2)$, as shown in the margin figure. Over many experiments of the same kind, randomly assigning 30 people to the group that reads the text and sees the graph and 31 people to the group that just reads the text, the difference in the sample mean ratings would vary. The standard error of 0.336 expresses how far from the mean of the sampling distribution we can expect these differences to fall. The margin figure illustrates the sampling distribution, which is approximately normal for large samples. It is centered at $\mu_1 - \mu_2$ (the value of which is unknown to us), and its standard deviation is estimated as 0.336.

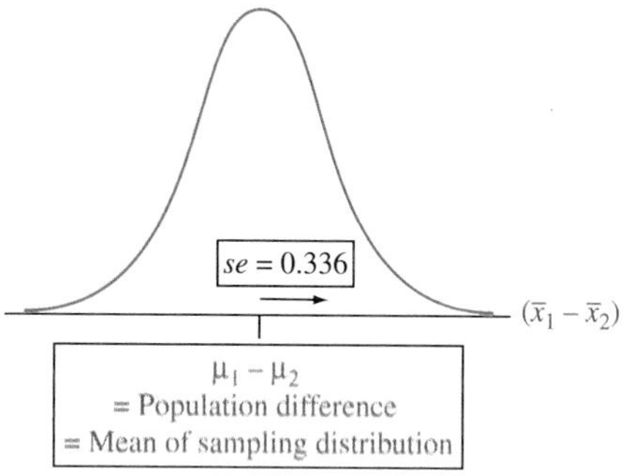

$se = 0.336$

$(\bar{x}_1 - \bar{x}_2)$

$\mu_1 - \mu_2$
= Population difference
= Mean of sampling distribution

Insight

This standard error will be used in confidence intervals and in significance tests for comparing means.

► ***Try Exercise 10.16, part b***

Confidence Interval for the Difference Between Two Population Means

As usual, a confidence interval takes the estimate and adds and subtracts a margin of error. For large random samples:

- The sampling distribution of a sample mean is approximately normal, by the central limit theorem.
- Likewise, $(\bar{x}_1 - \bar{x}_2)$ has a sampling distribution that is approximately normal.
- For 95% confidence, the margin of error is about two standard errors, so the confidence interval for the difference $(\mu_1 - \mu_2)$ between the population means is approximately

$$(\bar{x}_1 - \bar{x}_2) \pm 2(se).$$

More precisely, the multiple of *se* is a *t*-score (rather than a *z*-score) from a table of *t* distribution values. In estimating the standard deviation of the sampling distribution, we replaced the unknown population standard deviations

Recall

See Section 8.3 to review the **confidence interval** for a single **mean**, the ***t* distribution** and *t*-scores from it. The 95% confidence interval is

$$\bar{x} \pm t_{.025}(se),$$

where $se = s/\sqrt{n}$. Recall that $df = n - 1$ for inference about a single mean. ◄

σ_1 and σ_2 by s_1 and s_2. This creates additional uncertainty of how close the sample difference $\bar{x}_1 - \bar{x}_2$ falls to the actual population difference. To counteract, we have to make the confidence interval a bit wider, using a *t*-score instead of a *z*-score.

The degrees of freedom for the *t*-score depend on the sample standard deviations and the sample sizes. The formula is messy and does not give insight into the method, so we leave it as a footnote.[5] If $s_1 = s_2$ and $n_1 = n_2$, it simplifies to $df = (n_1 + n_2 - 2)$. This is the sum of the *df* values for single-sample inference about each group, or $df = (n_1 - 1) + (n_2 - 1) = n_1 + n_2 - 2$. *Generally, df falls somewhere between* $n_1 + n_2 - 2$ *and the minimum of* $(n_1 - 1)$ *and* $(n_2 - 1)$.

In Practice Software Finds *df* for Comparing Means

Software calculates the *df* value for comparing means for you. When s_1 and s_2 are similar and n_1 and n_2 are close, *df* is close to $n_1 + n_2 - 2$. Without software, you can take *df* to be the smaller of $(n_1 - 1)$ and $(n_2 - 1)$, and this will be safe because the *t*-score will be larger than you actually need.

Recall

From Section 8.3, a method is **robust** with respect to a particular assumption if it works well even when that assumption is violated. ◀

When either sample size is small (roughly $n_1 < 30$ or $n_2 < 30$), we cannot rely on the central limit theorem. In that instance, the method makes the assumption that the population distributions are normal, so $(\bar{x}_1 - \bar{x}_2)$ has a bell-shaped sampling distribution. In practice, the method is *robust*, and it works quite well even if the distributions are not normal. This is subject to the usual caveat: We need to be on the lookout for outliers that might affect the means or their usefulness as a summary measure.

SUMMARY: Confidence Interval for Difference Between Population Means

For two samples with sizes n_1 and n_2 and standard deviations s_1 and s_2, a 95% confidence interval for the difference $(\mu_1 - \mu_2)$ between the population means is

$$(\bar{x}_1 - \bar{x}_2) \pm t_{.025}(se), \text{ with } se = \sqrt{\frac{s_1^2}{n_1} + \frac{s_2^2}{n_2}}.$$

Software provides $t_{.025}$, the *t*-score with right-tail probability 0.025 (total probability $= 0.95$ between $-t_{.025}$ and $t_{.025}$).

This method assumes:

- A quantitative response variable observed in each of two groups
- Independent random samples from the two groups, either from random sampling or a randomized experiment.
- An approximately normal population distribution for each group. (This is mainly important for small sample sizes, and even then the method is robust to violations of this assumption.)

[5]It is $df = \dfrac{\left(\dfrac{s_1^2}{n_1} + \dfrac{s_2^2}{n_2}\right)^2}{\dfrac{1}{n_1 - 1}\left(\dfrac{s_1^2}{n_1}\right)^2 + \dfrac{1}{n_2 - 1}\left(\dfrac{s_2^2}{n_2}\right)^2}$, called the Welch-Satterthwaite formula.

Confidence Interval for difference between means

Example 8

Text with Graph

Picture the Scenario

When using software to analyze the data, a 95% confidence interval for the difference between the mean product rating of the effectiveness of a drug between people who read a short description of the drug accompanied by a graph and people who just read the short description but did not see the graph equals [0.03, 1.38]. Table 10.6 shows the MINITAB output.

Table 10.6 MINITAB Output for Comparing Two Means

```
Two-sample T for Text&Graph vs Text
                N      Mean      StDev      SE Mean
Text&Graph     30      6.83       1.18       0.21
Text           31      6.13       1.43       0.26
Difference = μ (Text&Graph) − μ (Text)
Estimate for difference: 0.704
95% CI for difference: (0.033, 1.375)
```

Questions to Explore

a. Is it reasonable to assume an approximate normal population distribution for product effectiveness ratings in the two groups? How does this affect inference?

b. Show how the confidence interval was obtained and interpret it. The *df* value for the *t*-score, not shown in the computer output in Table 10.6, equals $df = 57.5$. With it, the *t*-score $t_{0.025} = 2.002$.

Think It Through

a. Figure 10.4 showed side-by-side box plots for the ratings, based on the 30 and 31 observations in the two groups. To get a better picture of the shape, the figure in the margin shows histograms. These indicate a right skew for the Text and Graph group and a left skew for the Text only group. However, the shape of the histograms doesn't indicate any dramatic deviation from normality. Also, the sample size is large enough for the central limit theorem to apply. Then the assumption of approximate normality of the population distribution of ratings in each group is less important. Overall, we can proceed with any inference comparing the two means, using the methods developed in this section.

b. Let μ_1 be the mean rating of the population of people who read the text and see the graph. Let μ_2 be the mean rating of the population of people who just read the text. From Example 7, the difference in the sample means is $\bar{x}_1 - \bar{x}_2 = 0.7$, and the standard error $se = 0.336$. The 95% confidence interval for $\mu_1 - \mu_2$ is

$$(\bar{x}_1 - \bar{x}_2) \pm t_{0.025}\, se, \text{ or } 0.7 \pm 2.002(0.336),$$
$$\text{which equals } 0.7 \pm 0.67, \text{ or } (0.03, 1.38).$$

We can be 95% confident that the difference in the mean ratings between people reading the text and seeing the graph and people just reading the text falls between 0.03 points and 1.38 points. Since this

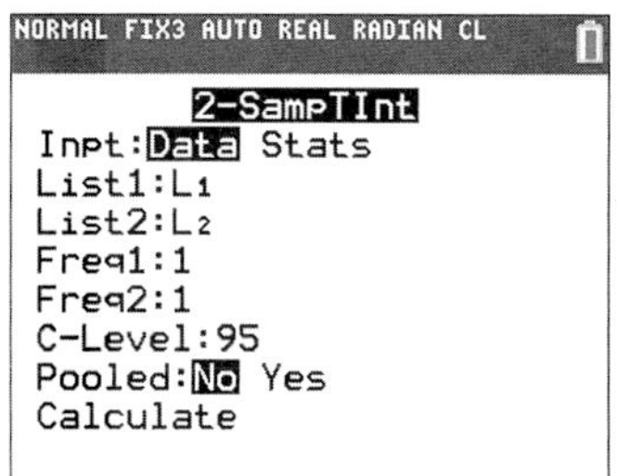

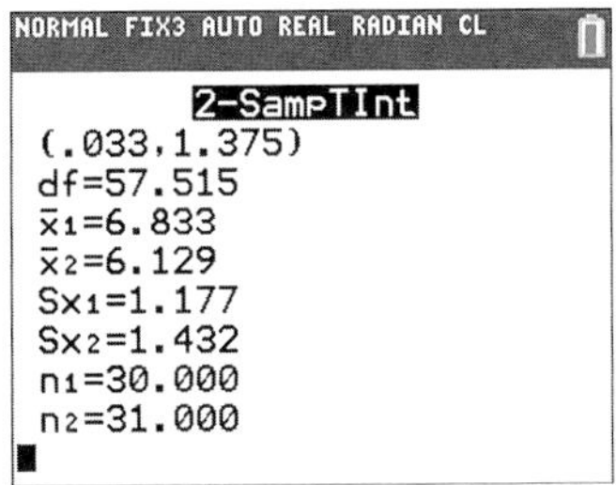

TI output for comparing two means. (Here, we entered the data and not the summary statistics.)

interval is completely above 0, we can infer that people who read the text and see the graph rate the drug's effectiveness, on average, by as little as 0.03 points and as much as 1.38 points higher (on a 9-point scale).

Insight

The lower bound of the confidence interval is close to 0, so the effect of including the graph with the text may be small.

▶ ***Try Exercise 10.16, parts c and d***

Interpret a Confidence Interval for a Difference of Means

Besides interpreting the confidence interval comparing two means in context, you can judge the implications using the same criteria as in comparing two proportions:

- *Check whether or not 0 falls in the interval.* When it does, 0 is a plausible value for $(\mu_1 - \mu_2)$, meaning that possibly $\mu_1 = \mu_2$. Figure 10.5 illustrates. For example, suppose the confidence interval for $(\mu_1 - \mu_2)$ equals $(-0.03, 1.38)$ Then, the mean rating for those reading the text and seeing the graph may be as much as 0.03 points lower or as much as 1.38 points larger compared to those that just read the text. This doesn't rule out that the population mean ratings are the same.

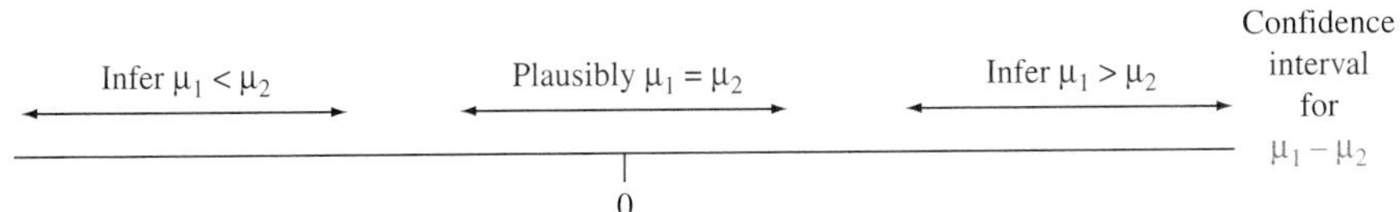

▲ **Figure 10.5 Three Confidence Intervals for the Difference Between Two Means.** When the interval contains 0, it is plausible that the population means may be equal. Otherwise, we can predict which is larger. **Question** Why do positive numbers in the confidence interval for $(\mu_1 - \mu_2)$ suggest that $\mu_1 > \mu_2$?

- *A confidence interval for $(\mu_1 - \mu_2)$ that contains only positive numbers suggests that $(\mu_1 - \mu_2)$ is positive.* We then infer that μ_1 is larger than μ_2. The 95% confidence interval in Example 8 is (0.03, 1.38). Since $(\mu_1 - \mu_2)$ is the difference between the mean ratings, we can infer that the mean rating is higher for those reading the text and seeing the graph.
- *A confidence interval for $(\mu_1 - \mu_2)$ that contains only negative numbers suggests that $(\mu_1 - \mu_2)$ is negative.* We then infer that μ_1 is smaller than μ_2.
- *Which group is labeled 1 and which is labeled 2 is arbitrary.* If you change this, the confidence interval has the same endpoints but with different sign. For instance, (0.03, 1.38) becomes $(-1.38, -0.03)$. We would then conclude that the mean rating for those just reading the text is by at least 0.03 points and at most 1.38 points *smaller*. This is the same conclusion as reached in Example 8.

Significance Tests Comparing Population Means

Another way to compare two population means is with a significance test of the null hypothesis H_0: $\mu_1 = \mu_2$ of equal means. The assumptions of the test are the same as for a confidence interval—independent random samples and approximately normal population distributions for each group. When n_1 and n_2 are at least about 30 each, the normality assumption is not important because of the central limit theorem. For two-sided alternatives, the test is robust against violations of the normal assumption even when sample sizes are small. However, one-sided t tests are not trustworthy if a sample size is below 30 and the population distribution is highly skewed.

Recall

Section 9.3 presented the **significance test** for a single **mean.** The t test statistic measures the number of standard errors that the sample mean falls from the value in the null hypothesis. ◀

The test uses the usual form for a test statistic,

$$\frac{\text{Estimate of parameter} - \text{Null hypothesis value of parameter}}{\text{Standard error of estimate}}.$$

The parameter of interest is the difference in the population means $(\mu_1 - \mu_2)$, which is estimated by the difference in the sample means $(\bar{x}_1 - \bar{x}_2)$. The null hypothesis H_0: $\mu_1 = \mu_2$ implies that $(\mu_1 - \mu_2) = 0$, so 0 is the null hypothesis value of the parameter. The standard error of $(\bar{x}_1 - \bar{x}_2)$ is the same as the one we used for constructing the confidence interval. With this, the test statistic is

$$t = \frac{(\bar{x}_1 - \bar{x}_2) - 0}{se}, \text{ where } se = \sqrt{\frac{s_1^2}{n_1} + \frac{s_2^2}{n_2}}.$$

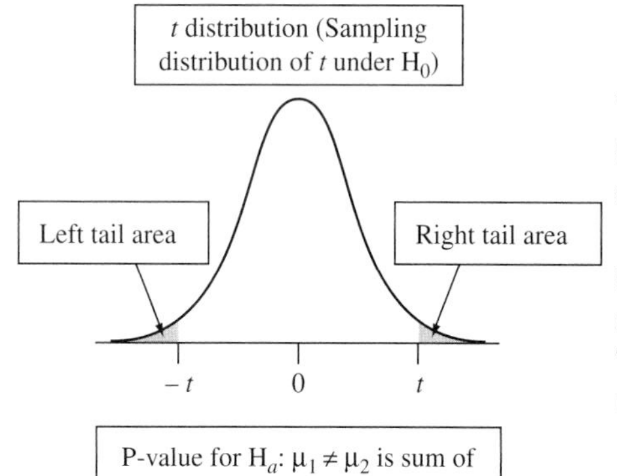

When H_0 is true, this statistic has approximately a t sampling distribution. Software can determine the df value, which is the same as the one used for constructing a confidence interval.

The P-value for the test depends on whether the alternative hypothesis is two-sided, H_a: $\mu_1 \neq \mu_2$, or one-sided, H_a: $\mu_1 > \mu_2$ or H_a: $\mu_1 < \mu_2$. For the two-sided alternative, the P-value is the two-tail probability beyond the observed t value. That is, we find the probability of results more extreme in either direction under the presumption that H_0 is true. See the margin figure.

SUMMARY: Two-Sided Significance Test for Comparing Two Population Means

1. **Assumptions**
   - A quantitative response variable observed in each of two groups
   - Independent random samples, either from random sampling or a randomized experiment
   - Approximately normal population distribution for each group. (This is mainly important for small sample sizes, and even then the two-sided test is robust to violations of this assumption.)

2. **Hypotheses**

   H_0: $\mu_1 = \mu_2$

   H_a: $\mu_1 \neq \mu_2$ (one-sided H_a: $\mu_1 > \mu_2$ or H_a: $\mu_1 < \mu_2$ also possible)

3. **Test Statistic**

   $$t = \frac{(\bar{x}_1 - \bar{x}_2) - 0}{se} \text{ where } se = \sqrt{\frac{s_1^2}{n_1} + \frac{s_2^2}{n_2}}$$

4. **P-value**

   P-value = Two-tail probability from t distribution of values even more extreme than observed t test statistic, presuming the null hypothesis is true with df given by software.

5. **Conclusion**

   Smaller P-values give stronger evidence against H_0 and supporting H_a. Interpret the P-value in context and, if a decision is needed, reject H_0 if P-value $\leq$ significance level (such as 0.05).

Example 9

Compare population means using significance test

Cell Phone Use While Driving Reaction Times

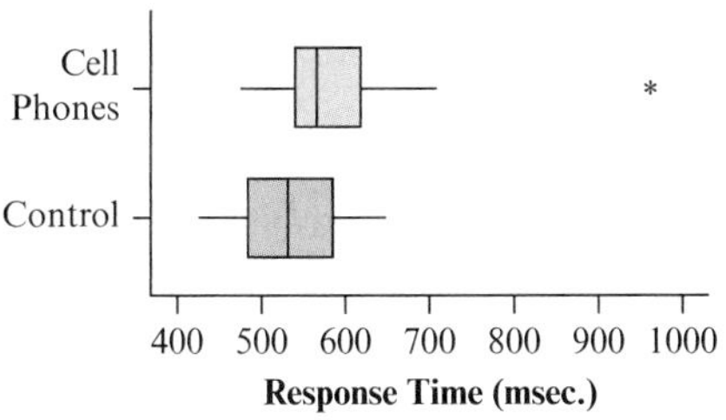

▲ **Figure 10.6** Box Plots of Response Times for Cell Phone Study. **Question** Does either box plot show any features that could affect the analysis?

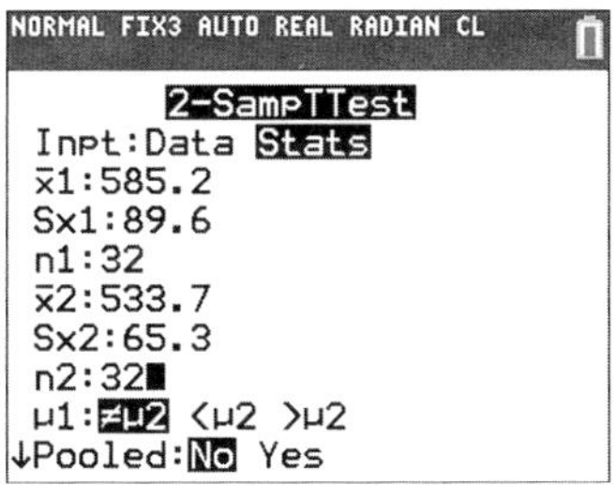


```
NORMAL FIX3 AUTO REAL RADIAN CL
2-SampTTest
μ1≠μ2
t=2.628
p=.011
df=56.685
x̄1=585.200
x̄2=533.700
Sx1=89.600
↓Sx2=65.300
```

TI output for two-sample t test when inputting summary statistics.

Picture the Scenario

An experiment[6] investigated whether cell phone use impairs drivers' reaction times, using a sample of 64 students from the University of Utah. Students were randomly assigned to a cell phone group or to a control group, 32 to each. On a simulation of driving situations, a target flashed red or green at irregular periods. Participants pressed a brake button as soon as they detected a red light. The control group listened to radio or books on tape while they performed the simulated driving. The cell phone group carried out a phone conversation about a political issue with someone in a separate room.

The experiment measured each subject's mean response time over many trials. Averaged over all trials and subjects, the mean response time was 585.2 milliseconds (a bit over half a second) for the cell phone group and 533.7 milliseconds for the control group. Figure 10.6 shows box plots of the responses for the two groups.

Denote the population mean response time by μ_1 for the cell phone group and by μ_2 for the control group. Table 10.7 shows how MINITAB reports inferential comparisons of those two means. The margin that follows contains screen shots from a TI calculator.

Table 10.7 MINITAB Output Comparing Mean Response Times for Cell Phone and Control Groups

```
Sample      N     Mean    StDev
Cell        32    585.2   89.6
Control     32    533.7   65.3
Difference = μ (Cell) − μ (Control)
Estimate for difference: 51.5
95% CI for difference: (12.2, 90.8)
T-Test of difference = 0 (vs ≠):
T-Value = 2.63 P-Value = 0.011 DF = 56
```

Questions to Explore

a. Show how MINITAB got the test statistic for testing H_0: $\mu_1 = \mu_2$ against H_a: $\mu_1 \neq \mu_2$.

b. Report and interpret the P-value and state the decision you would make about the population using a 0.05 significance level.

c. What do the box plots tell us about the suitability of these analyses? What effect does the outlier for the cell phone group have on the analysis?

Think It Through

a. We estimate the difference $\mu_1 - \mu_2$ by $(\bar{x}_1 - \bar{x}_2) = 585.2 - 533.7 = 51.5$, shown in Table 10.7. The standard error of this estimate is

$$se = \sqrt{\frac{s_1^2}{n_1} + \frac{s_2^2}{n_2}} = \sqrt{\frac{(89.6)^2}{32} + \frac{(65.3)^2}{32}} = 19.6.$$

[6]Data courtesy of David Strayer, University of Utah. Example based on Experiment 1a in article by D. Strayer and W. Johnston, *Psych. Science*, vol. 21, 2001, pp. 462–466.

The test statistic for H_0: $\mu_1 = \mu_2$ equals

$$t = \frac{(\bar{x}_1 - \bar{x}_2)}{se} = \frac{51.5}{19.6} = 2.63.$$

b. The P-value is the two-tail probability from a t distribution. Table 10.7 reports $df = 56$ and a P-value $= 0.01$. If H_0 were true, the probability would be 0.01 of getting a t test statistic this large or even larger in either tail. The P-value is less than 0.05, so we can reject H_0. We have enough evidence to conclude that in the setting of experiments like this, the population mean response time for those using a cell phone while driving differs from the population mean response time for those just listening to the radio. The sample means suggest that the population mean is higher for the cell phone group.

c. The t inferences assume normal population distributions. The box plots do not show any substantial skew, but there is an extreme outlier for the cell phone group. One subject in that group had a very slow mean reaction time. Because this observation is so far from the others in that group, it's a good idea to make sure the results of the analysis aren't affected too strongly by that single observation.

If we delete the extreme outlier for the cell phone group, software reports

```
Sample        N        Mean        StDev
Cell          31       573.1       58.9
Control       32       533.7       65.3
Difference = μ (Cell) − μ (Control)
Estimate for difference: 39.4
95% CI for difference: (8.1, 70.7)
T-Test of difference = 0 (vs ≠):
T-Value = 2.52 P-Value = 0.015 DF = 60
```

The mean and standard deviation for the cell phone group now decrease substantially. However, the t test statistic is not much different, and the P-value is still small, 0.015, leading to the same conclusion.

Insight

Even though the difference between the sample means decreased from 51.5 to 39.4 when we deleted the outlier, the standard error also got smaller (you can check that it equals 15.7) because of the smaller standard deviation for the cell phone group after removing the outlier. That's why the t test statistic did not change much. In practice, you should not delete outliers from a data set without sufficient cause (for example, if it seems the observation was incorrectly recorded). However, it's a good idea to check for *sensitivity* of an analysis to an outlier, as we did here, by repeating the analysis without it. If the results change much, it means that the inference including the outlier is on shaky ground.

▶ ***Try Exercise 10.25***

Example 9 used a two-sided alternative, which is the way that research results are usually reported in journal articles. But the researchers thought that the mean response time would be *greater* for the cell phone group than for the control. So, for their own purposes, they could find the P-value for the one-sided H_a: $\mu_1 > \mu_2$

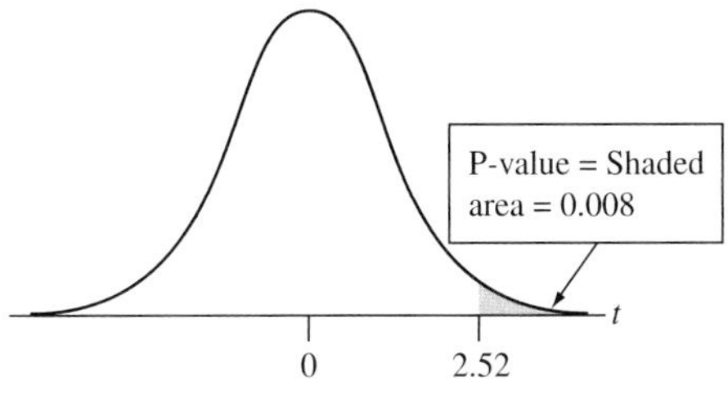

(that is, $\mu_1 - \mu_2 > 0$), which predicts a higher mean response time for the cell phone group. For the analysis without the outlier, the P-value is the probability to the *right* of $t = 2.52$. This is half the two-sided P-value, namely $0.015/2 = 0.008$. See margin figure. There is very strong evidence in favor of this alternative.

Connection Between Confidence Intervals and Tests

We learn even more by constructing a confidence interval for $(\mu_1 - \mu_2)$. Let's do this for the data set without the outlier, for which $df = 60$ and the difference of sample means of 39.4 had a standard error of 15.7. The *t*-score with $df = 60$ for a 95% confidence interval is $t_{.025} = 2.000$. The confidence interval is

$$(\bar{x}_1 - \bar{x}_2) \pm t_{.025}(se), \text{ which is } 39.4 \pm 2.000(15.7), \text{ or } (8.1, 70.8).$$

This result is more informative than the test because it shows the range of realistic values for the difference between the population means. The interval (8.1, 70.8) for $\mu_1 - \mu_2$ is quite wide. It tells us that the population means could be similar, or the mean response may be as much as about 71 milliseconds higher for the cell phone group. This is nearly a tenth of a second, which could be crucial in a practical driving situation.

The confidence interval (8.1, 70.8) does not contain 0. This inference agrees with the significance test that the population mean response times differ. Recall that Section 9.3 showed that the result of a two-sided significance test about a mean is consistent with a confidence interval for that mean. The same is true in comparing two means. If a test rejects H_0: $\mu_1 = \mu_2$, then the confidence interval for $(\mu_1 - \mu_2)$ having the same error probability does not contain 0.

In Example 9 without the outlier, the P-value = 0.015, so we rejected H_0: $\mu_1 = \mu_2$ at the 0.05 significance level. Likewise, the 95% confidence interval for $(\mu_1 - \mu_2)$ of (8.1, 70.8) does not contain 0, the null hypothesis value.

By contrast, when a 95% confidence interval for $(\mu_1 - \mu_2)$ *contains* 0, then 0 is a plausible value for $(\mu_1 - \mu_2)$. In a test of H_0: $\mu_1 = \mu_2$ against H_a: $\mu_1 \neq \mu_2$, the P-value would be > 0.05. The test would not reject H_0 at the 0.05 significance level and would conclude that the population means may be equal.

10.2 Practicing the Basics

10.14 Alcohol and Energy Drinks A 2013 article in the journal *Adolescent Health* stated that adding energy drinks to alcohol was associated with an elevated blood alcohol content compared to consuming alcohol without energy drinks in college students.

a. Suppose this conclusion was based on a significance test comparing means. Defining notation in context, identify the groups and the population means and state the null hypothesis for the test.

b. Suppose the study conclusion was based on a P-value of 0.01 obtained for the significance test mentioned in part a. Explain what you could learn from a confidence interval comparing the means that you are not able to learn from this P-value.

10.15 Address global warming You would like to determine what students at your school would be willing to do to help address global warming and the development of alternatively fueled vehicles. To do this, you take a random sample of 100 students. One question you ask them is, "How high of a tax would you be willing to add to gasoline (per gallon) to encourage drivers to drive less or to drive more fuel-efficient cars?" You also ask, "Do you believe (yes or no) that global warming is a serious issue that requires immediate action such as the development of alternatively fueled vehicles?" In your statistical analysis, use inferential methods to compare the mean response on gasoline taxes (the first question) for those who answer yes and for those who answer no to the second question. For this analysis,

a. Identify the response variable and the explanatory variable.

b. Are the two groups being compared independent samples or dependent samples? Why?

c. Identify a confidence interval you could form to compare the groups, specifying the parameters used in the comparison.

10.16 Housework for women and men Do women tend to spend more time on housework than men? If so, how much more? Based on data from the National Survey of Families and Households, one study reported the results in the table for the number of hours spent in housework per week. (*Source*: Data from A. Lincoln, *Journal of Marriage and Family,* vol. 70, 2008, pp. 806–814.)

Housework Hours			
Gender	**Sample Size**	**Mean**	**Standard Deviation**
Women	476	33.0	21.9
Men	496	19.9	14.6

a. Based on this study, calculate how many more hours, on the average, women spend on housework than men.

b. Find the standard error for comparing the means. What factor causes the standard error to be small compared to the sample standard deviations for the two groups?

c. Calculate the 95% confidence interval comparing the population means for women and men. Interpret the result including the relevance of 0 being within the interval or not. (*Hint:* For such large sample sizes, the t-score is practically identical to a z-score.)

d. State the assumptions upon which the interval in part c is based.

10.17 More confident about housework Refer to part c in the previous exercise.

a. Show that a 99% confidence interval is (10.0, 16.2).

b. Explain why this interval is wider than the 95% confidence interval.

10.18 Employment by gender The study described in Exercise 10.16 also evaluated the weekly time spent in employment. This sample comprises men and women with a high level of labor force attachment. Software shows the results.

```
Gender     N     Mean    StDev    SE Mean
Men       496   47.54    9.92      0.45
Women     476   42.01    6.53      0.30
Difference = mu (Men) - mu (Women)
95% CI for difference: (4.477, 6.583)
T-Test of difference = 0 (vs ≠):
T-Value = 10.30 P-Value = 0.000
```

a. Does it seem plausible that employment has a normal distribution for each gender? Explain.

b. What effect does the answer to part a have on inference comparing population means? What assumptions are made for the inferences in this table?

c. Explain how to interpret the confidence interval.

d. Refer to part c. Do you think that the population means are equal? Explain.

10.19 Ideal number of children In 2014, the GSS asked, "What is the ideal number of children for a family to have?" For those giving a numerical response (and treating the response "7 or more" as 7), the following table shows summary statistics. (You can reproduce these data by typing CHLDIDEL(0–7) as the row variable, SEX as the column variable, and YEAR(2014) as the selection filter on the GSS website sda.berkeley.edu/GSS.)

Ideal Number of Children			
Gender	**Sample Size**	**Mean**	**Standard Deviation**
Women	921	2.54	0.89
Men	754	2.50	0.85

a. Find the standard error for the difference in the sample means.

b. The sample size is large, resulting in degrees of freedom in excess of 100, so the t-score is essentially the same as the z-score. Using this, find and interpret the 95% confidence interval for the difference between the population means for females and males.

10.20 Pay by gender The study described in the Exercise 10.18 also evaluated personal income by gender. The average earnings per year was $35,800 for men with a standard deviation of $14,600. The average earnings for women was $23,900 with a standard deviation of $21,900. Software shows the following results:

Two-Sample T-Test and CI

```
Sample     N      Mean     StDev     SE Mean
  1       496    35800     14600       656
  2       476    23900     21900      1004
Difference = μ(1) - μ(2)
Estimate for difference: 11900
95% CI for difference: (9547, 14253)
T-Test of difference = 0 (vs ≠):
T-Value = 9.93 P-Value = 0.000 DF = 822
```

a. Does it seem plausible that income has a normal distribution for each gender? Explain.

b. What effect does the answer to part a have on inference comparing population means? What assumptions are made for the inferences in this table?

c. A 95% confidence interval for the difference in the population means for women and men is ($9,547, $14,253). Interpret, indicating the relevance of $0 not falling in the interval.

10.21 Bulimia CI A study of bulimia among college women (J. Kern and T. Hastings, *Journal of Clinical Psychology*, vol. 51, 1995, p. 499) studied the connection between childhood sexual abuse and a measure of family cohesion (the higher the score, the greater the cohesion). The sample mean on the family cohesion scale was 2.0 for 13 sexually abused students ($s = 2.1$) and 4.8 for 17 nonabused students ($s = 3.2$).

a. Find the standard error for comparing the means.

b. Construct a 95% confidence interval for the difference between the mean family cohesion for sexually abused students and non-abused students. Interpret.

10.22 Chelation useless? Chelation is an alternative therapy for heart disease that uses repeated intravenous administration of a human-made amino acid in combination with oral vitamins and minerals. Practitioners believe it removes calcium deposits from buildup in arteries. However, the evidence for a positive effect is anecdotal or comes from nonrandomized, uncontrolled studies.

A double-blind randomized clinical trial comparing chelation to placebo used a treadmill test in which the response was the length of time until a subject experienced ischemia (lack of blood flow and oxygen to the heart muscle).

a. After 27 weeks of treatment, the sample mean time for the chelation group was 652 seconds. A 95% confidence interval for the population mean for chelation minus the population mean for placebo was −53 to 36 seconds. Explain how to interpret the confidence interval.

b. A significance test comparing the means had P-value = 0.69. Specify the hypotheses for this test, which was two-sided.

c. The authors concluded from the test, "There is no evidence to support a beneficial effect of chelation therapy" (M. Knudtson et al., *JAMA*, vol. 287, p. 481, 2002). Explain how this conclusion agrees with inference based on the values in the confidence interval.

10.23 Nicotine dependence A study on nicotine dependence for teenage smokers obtained a random sample of seventh graders. The response variable was constructed from a questionnaire called the Hooked on Nicotine Checklist (HONC). This is a list of ten questions such as, "Have you ever tried to quit but couldn't?" and "Is it hard to keep from smoking in places where it is banned, like school?" The HONC score is the total number of questions to which a student answered yes, so each student's HONC score falls between 0 and 10. The higher the score, the more hooked that student is on nicotine. One explanatory variable considered in the study was whether a subject reported inhaling when smoking. The following table reports descriptive statistics.

		HONC Score	
Group	**Students**	**Mean**	**Standard Deviation**
Inhalers	237	2.9	3.6
Noninhalers	95	0.1	0.5

a. Explain why (i) the overwhelming majority of noninhalers must have had HONC scores of 0 and (ii) on average, those who reported inhaling answered yes to nearly three more questions than those who denied inhaling.

b. Might the HONC scores have been approximately normal for each group? Why or why not?

c. Find the standard error for the estimate $(\bar{x}_1 - \bar{x}_2) = 2.8$. Interpret.

d. The 95% confidence interval for $(\mu_1 - \mu_2)$ is (2.3, 3.3). What can you conclude about the population means for inhalers and noninhalers?

10.24 Inhaling affect HONC? Refer to the previous exercise.

a. Show that the test statistic for H_0: $\mu_1 = \mu_2$ equals $t = 11.7$. If the population means were equal, explain why it would be nearly impossible by random variation to observe this large a test statistic.

b. What decision would you make about H_0, at common significance levels? Can you conclude which group had higher mean nicotine dependence? How?

c. State the assumptions for the inference in this exercise.

10.25 Females or males more nicotine dependent? TRY TECH Refer to Exercise 10.23 about studying nicotine dependence using a random sample of teenagers. Of those seventh graders in the study who had tried tobacco, the mean HONC score was 2.8 ($s = 3.6$) for the 150 females and 1.6 ($s = 2.9$) for the 182 males.

a. Find a standard error for comparing the sample means. Interpret.

b. Find the test statistic and P-value for H_0: $\mu_1 = \mu_2$ against H_a: $\mu_1 \neq \mu_2$. Interpret and explain what (if any) effect gender has on the mean HONC score.

c. Do you think that the HONC scores were approximately normal for each gender? Why or why not? How does this affect the validity of the analysis in part b?

10.26 Female and male monthly smokers TECH Refer to the previous exercise. A subject was called a monthly smoker if he or she had smoked cigarettes over an extended period of time. The 74 female monthly smokers had a mean HONC score of 5.4 ($s = 3.5$), and the 71 male monthly smokers had a mean HONC score of 3.9 ($s = 3.6$). Using software (such as the Comparing Means web app or MINITAB) that can conduct analyses using summary statistics, repeat parts b and c of the previous exercise.

10.27 Body language TECH In an experiment investigating body language (M. Koppensteiner et al., *Personality and Individual Differences*, vol. 74, 2015, pp. 182–185), researchers turned short video clips of randomly selected speeches by male and female politicians into an animated, gender-neutral stick-figure clip. These clips showed the movements of the upper body parts during the speech. Each clip was rated (on a scale from −100 to 100) by a random sample of students in terms of personality traits. For one trait measuring the perceived dominance of a speaker, the following statistics on the scores were reported (a higher score means higher dominance):

Clips based on	n	Mean	SD
male speaker	30	10.7	26.3
female speaker	30	−1.1	27.8

a. Set up the hypotheses for a significance test to analyze whether the population mean score differs between clips based on a male or female speaker.

b. Using software in which you can use summary statistics (or access the data set at the book's website), find the P-value for the significance test. Interpret it and report the conclusion for a significance level of 0.05.

c. If you were to construct a 95% confidence interval for the difference in population means, would it contain 0? Answer based on the result of part b, without actually finding the interval.

10.28 Student survey TECH Refer to the FL Student Survey data file on the book's website. Use the number of times reading a newspaper as the response variable and gender as the explanatory variable. The observations are as follows:

Females: 5, 3, 6, 3, 7, 1, 1, 3, 0, 4, 7, 2, 2, 7, 3, 0, 5, 0, 4, 4, 5, 14, 3, 1, 2, 1, 7, 2, 5, 3, 7

Males: 0, 3, 7, 4, 3, 2, 1, 12, 1, 6, 2, 2, 7, 7, 5, 3, 14, 3, 7, 6, 5, 5, 2, 3, 5, 5, 2, 3, 3

Using software,

a. Construct and interpret a plot comparing responses by females and males.

b. Construct and interpret a 95% confidence interval comparing population means for females and males.

c. Show all five steps of a significance test comparing the population means.

d. State and check the assumptions for part b and part c.

10.29 Study time A graduate teaching assistant for Introduction to Statistics (STA 2023) at the University of Florida collected data from students in one of her classes in spring 2007 to investigate whether study time per week (average number of hours) differed between students in the class who planned to go to graduate school and those who did not. The data were as follows:

TECH

Graduate school: 15, 7, 15, 10, 5, 5, 2, 3, 12, 16, 15, 37, 8, 14, 10, 18, 3, 25, 15, 5, 5

No graduate school: 6, 8, 15, 6, 5, 14, 10, 10, 12, 5

Using software or a calculator,

a. Find the sample mean and standard deviation for each group. Interpret.

b. Find the standard error for the difference between the sample means. Interpret.

c. Find a 95% confidence interval comparing the population means. Interpret.

10.30 More on study time Refer to the data in the previous exercise.

TECH

a. Show all steps of a two-sided significance test of the null hypothesis that the population mean is equal for the two groups. Interpret results in context.

b. Based on the explanation given in the previous exercise, do you think that the sample was a random sample or a convenience sample? Why? (In practice, you should not place much faith in inferences using such samples!)

10.31 Time spent on social networks As part of a class exercise, an instructor at a major university asks her students how many hours per week they spend on social networks. She wants to investigate whether time spent on social networks differs for male and female students at this university. The results for those age 21 or under were:

TECH

Males: 5, 7, 9, 10, 12, 12, 12, 13, 13, 15, 15, 20

Females: 5, 7, 7, 8, 10, 10, 11, 12, 12, 14, 14, 14, 16, 18, 20, 20, 20, 22, 23, 25, 40

a. Using software or a calculator, find the sample mean and standard deviation for each group. Interpret.

b. Find the standard error for the difference between the sample means.

c. Find and interpret a 90% confidence interval comparing the population means.

10.32 More time on social networks In the previous exercise, plot the data. Do you see any outliers that could influence the results? Remove the most extreme observation from each group and redo the analyses. Compare results and summarize the influence of the extreme observations.

TECH

10.33 Normal assumption The methods of this section make the assumption of a normal population distribution. Why do you think this is more relevant for small samples than for large samples? (*Hint:* What shape does the sampling distribution of $\bar{x}_1 - \bar{x}_2$ have for large samples, regardless of the actual shape of the population distributions?)

10.34 Vital capacity One of the authors of this book has his lung function checked every other year. At each checkup, his lung volume (called the forced vital capacity, or FVC) is measured before and after using an inhaler that contains medication against asthma. The last five checkups provided the following results (in liters):

	Checkup				
	1	**2**	**3**	**4**	**5**
Before using inhaler:	5.08	5.99	5.32	6.03	5.44
After using inhaler:	5.36	5.98	5.62	6.26	5.68

Can we use the inferential methods (confidence interval, significance test) developed in this section to compare the mean FVC before and after using the inhaler? If yes, use software to find a 95% confidence interval for the difference in the population means before and after using the inhaler and interpret it. If no, explain why.

10.3 Other Ways of Comparing Means, Including a Permutation Test

We've now learned about the primary methods for comparing two proportions or two means. We'll next study an alternative method for comparing means that is useful when we can assume that two groups have similar variability on the response variable. This alternative method and all the previous methods for comparing means work well for large samples or when we can assume that the distribution of the response variable is normal. For small samples or when the population distribution may be very skewed, we will present an alternative method that does not rely on the normality assumption. It is based on creating, using software, thousands of permutations of the original data to approximate the sampling distribution and find a P-value for comparing two groups.

Comparing Means, Assuming Equal Population Standard Deviations

An alternative t method to the one described in Section 10.2 is sometimes used when, under the null hypothesis, it is reasonable to expect the *variability* as well as the mean to be the same. For example, consider a study comparing a drug to a placebo in terms of lowering blood pressure. If the drug has no effect, then we expect the entire distributions of the response variable (blood pressure) to be identical for the two groups, not just the mean. This method requires an extra assumption in addition to the usual ones of independent random samples and approximately normal population distributions:

The population standard deviations are equal, that is, $\sigma_1 = \sigma_2$ (see Figure 10.7).

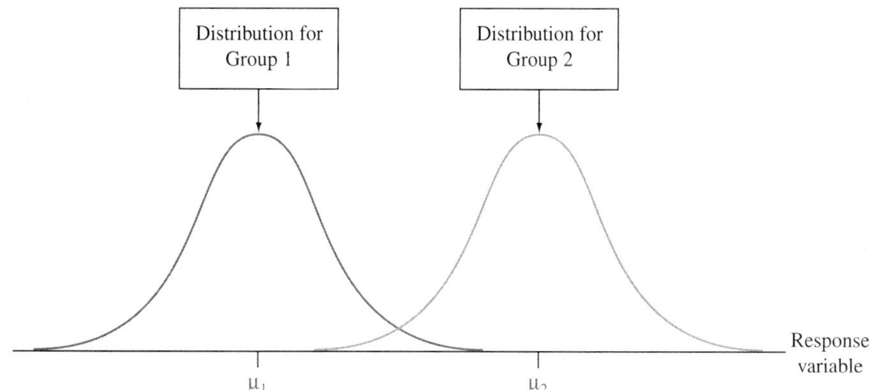

▲ **Figure 10.7** Two Groups With Equal Population Standard Deviations. **Question** What would a histogram of the sample data look like to make you doubt this assumption?

This alternative method estimates the common value σ of σ_1 and σ_2 by

$$s = \sqrt{\frac{(n_1 - 1)s_1^2 + (n_2 - 1)s_2^2}{n_1 + n_2 - 2}}.$$

The estimate s, called the **pooled standard deviation**, combines information from the two samples to provide a single estimate of variability and falls somewhere between s_1 and s_2. The degrees of freedom for this method are $df = n_1 + n_2 - 2$, which appears in the denominator of the formula for s.

In Practice Robustness of Two-Sided Inferences

Confidence intervals and two-sided tests using this alternative method are robust. They work well even when the population distributions are not normal and when the population standard deviations are not exactly equal. This is particularly true when the sample sizes are similar and not extremely small. In practice, however, these alternative methods are not usually used if one sample standard deviation is more than double the other one.

SUMMARY: Comparing Population Means, Assuming Equal Population Standard Deviations

Using the pooled standard deviation estimate s of $\sigma = \sigma_1 = \sigma_2$, the standard error of $(\bar{x}_1 - \bar{x}_2)$ simplifies to

$$se = \sqrt{\frac{s^2}{n_1} + \frac{s^2}{n_2}} = s\sqrt{\frac{1}{n_1} + \frac{1}{n_2}}.$$

Otherwise, inference formulas look the same as those that do not assume $\sigma_1 = \sigma_2$:

- A 95% confidence interval for $(\mu_1 - \mu_2)$ is $(\bar{x}_1 - \bar{x}_2) \pm t_{.025}(se)$.
- The test statistic for H_0: $\mu_1 = \mu_2$ is $t = (\bar{x}_1 - \bar{x}_2)/se$.

These methods have $df = n_1 + n_2 - 2$. To use them, you assume

- Independent random samples from the two groups, either from random sampling or a randomized experiment

- An approximately normal population distribution for each group (This is mainly important for small sample sizes, and even then the confidence interval and two-sided test are usually robust to violations of this assumption.)
- $\sigma_1 = \sigma_2$ (In practice, this type of inference is not usually relied on if one sample standard deviation is more than double the other one.)

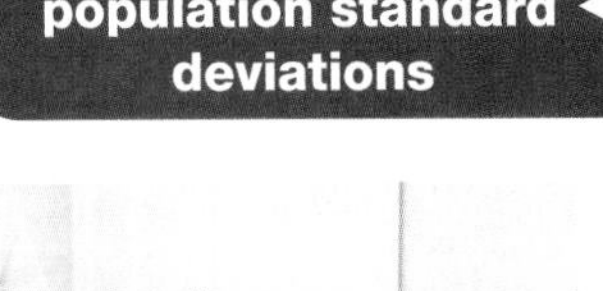

Example 10

Arthroscopic Surgery

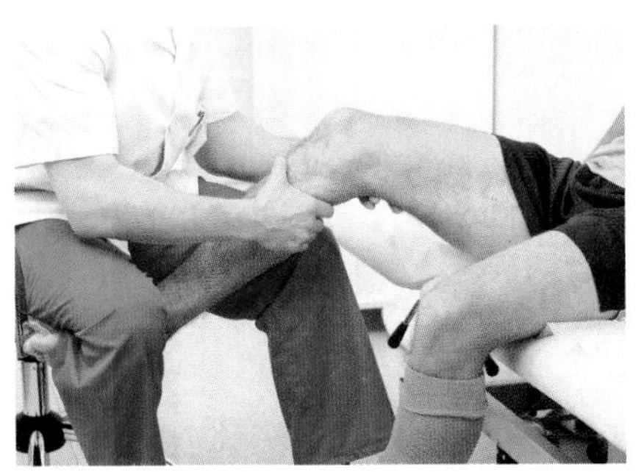

Picture the Scenario

A random trial study assessed the usefulness of arthroscopic surgery.[7] Over a three-year period, patients suffering from osteoarthritis who had at least moderate knee pain were recruited from a medical center in Houston. Patients were randomly assigned to one of three groups, to receive one of two types of arthroscopic surgeries or a surgery that was actually a placebo procedure. In the arthroscopic surgeries, the lavage group had the joint flushed with fluid, but instruments were not used to remove tissue, whereas the debridement group had tissue removal as well. In the placebo procedure, the same incisions were made in the knee as with surgery, and the surgeon manipulated the knee as if surgery was being performed, but none was actually done. The patients did not know which treatment they received.

A knee-specific pain scale was created for the study. Administered two years after the surgery, it ranged from 0 to 100, with higher scores indicating more severe pain. Table 10.8 shows summary statistics.

Table 10.8 Summary of Knee Pain Scores

The descriptive statistics compare lavage and debridement arthroscopic surgery to a placebo (fake surgery) treatment.

	Knee Pain Score		
Group	**Sample Size**	**Mean**	**Standard Deviation**
Placebo	60	51.6	23.7
Arthroscopic—lavage	61	53.7	23.7
Arthroscopic—debridement	59	51.4	23.2

Denote the population mean of the pain scores by μ_1 for the placebo group and by μ_2 for the debridement arthroscopic group. Most software gives you the option of assuming equal population standard deviations. Table 10.9 is the MINITAB output for the two-sample t inferences. (We'll consider the comparison between the lavage and placebo procedure in an exercise.)

Questions to Explore

a. Does the t test inference in Table 10.9 seem appropriate for these data?

b. Show how to find the pooled standard deviation estimate of σ, the standard error, the test statistic, and its *df*.

c. Identify the P-value for testing H_0: $\mu_1 = \mu_2$ against H_a: $\mu_1 \neq \mu_2$. With the 0.05 significance level, can you reject H_0? Interpret.

[7] By J. B. Moseley et al., *New England Journal of Medicine*, vol. 347, 2002, pp. 81–88.

Table 10.9 MINITAB Output for Comparing the Mean Knee Pain for Placebo and Arthroscopic Surgery Groups

This analysis assumes equal population standard deviations.

```
Sample      N      Mean      StDev      SE Mean
   1       60      51.6       23.7        3.1
   2       59      51.4       23.2        3.0
Difference = μ(1) − μ(2)
Estimate for difference: 0.20
95% CI for difference: (−8.32, 8.72)
T-Test of difference = 0(vs ≠):
T-Value = 0.047 P-Value = 0.963 DF = 117
Both use Pooled StDev = 23.4535
```

Think It Through

a. If the arthroscopic surgery has no real effect, its population distribution of pain score should be the same as for the placebo. Not only will the population means be equal, but so will the population standard deviations. So, in testing whether this surgery has no effect, we will use a method that assumes equal population standard deviations. Because the sample standard deviations are nearly the same in the two groups, this assumption is justified.

b. The pooled standard deviation estimate of the common value σ of $\sigma_1 = \sigma_2$ is

$$s = \sqrt{\frac{(n_1 - 1)s_1^2 + (n_2 - 1)s_2^2}{n_1 + n_2 - 2}} =$$

$$\sqrt{\frac{(60 - 1)23.7^2 + (59 - 1)23.2^2}{60 + 59 - 2}} = 23.45,$$

shown at the bottom of Table 10.9. We estimate the difference $\mu_1 - \mu_2$ by $(\bar{x}_1 - \bar{x}_2) = 51.6 - 51.4 = 0.2$. The standard error of $(\bar{x}_1 - \bar{x}_2)$ equals

$$se = s\sqrt{\frac{1}{n_1} + \frac{1}{n_2}} = 23.45\sqrt{\frac{1}{60} + \frac{1}{59}} = 4.30.$$

The test statistic for H_0: $\mu_1 = \mu_2$ equals

$$t = \frac{(\bar{x}_1 - \bar{x}_2)}{se} = \frac{51.6 - 51.4}{4.30} = 0.047.$$

Its $df = (n_1 + n_2 - 2) = (60 + 59 - 2) = 117$. When H_0 is true, the test statistic has the t distribution with $df = 117$.

c. The two-sided P-value equals 0.96. So, if the true population means were equal, by random variation, it would not at all be surprising to observe a test statistic of this size. The P-value is larger than 0.05, so we cannot reject H_0. Consider the population of people who suffer from osteoarthritis and could conceivably receive one of these treatments. For this population, we don't have enough evidence to conclude that the mean pain level differs for the placebo treatment and the arthroscopic surgery treatment.

Insight

Table 10.9 reports a 95% confidence interval for $(\mu_1 - \mu_2)$ of $(-8.3, 8.7)$. Because the interval contains 0, it is plausible that there is no difference between the population means. This is the same conclusion as that for the significance test. We infer that the population mean for the knee pain score could be as much as 8.3 lower or as much as 8.7 higher for the placebo treatment than for the arthroscopic surgery. On the pain scale with range 100, this is a relatively small difference in practical terms.

▶ *Try Exercise 10.37*

Suppose the researchers specifically predicted that the debridement surgery would give *better* pain relief than the placebo. Then they would find the P-value for the one-sided H_a: $\mu_1 > \mu_2$ (that is, $\mu_1 - \mu_2 > 0$), which predicts higher mean pain with the placebo. The P-value is the probability to the *right* of $t = 0.047$. Software reports this as 0.48. See margin figure. There is no evidence in favor of this alternative.

Comparing Population Standard Deviations

There is even a test to compare the population standard deviations to see whether it is reasonable to assume they are equal, with null hypothesis H_0: $\sigma_1 = \sigma_2$. The test statistic for this test is often denoted by F, and the test is called an F-test. It assumes that the population distributions are normal. Unfortunately, this F-test is *not* a robust method.

Recall

For large sample sizes, the normality assumption is less important because the t test is robust against violations of that assumption. ◀

In Practice *F* Test for Comparing Standard Deviations Is Not Robust

The ***F* test for comparing standard deviations** of two populations performs poorly if the populations are not close to normal. Consequently, statisticians do not recommend it for general use. If the data show evidence of a potentially large difference in standard deviations, with one of the sample standard deviations being at least double the other, it is better to use the two-sample t-inference methods (of Section 10.2) that do not have this extra assumption.

Permutation Test for Comparing Two Groups

For large sample sizes, we mentioned that the assumption of normality for the response variable in each group is less crucial in deriving the sampling distribution and P-value for a significance test comparing two means. However, for small sample sizes, we need approximate normality of the population distributions to ensure that the t test statistic for testing H_0: $\mu_1 = \mu_2$ has a t sampling distribution. If the normality assumption doesn't hold, the P-value and the conclusion based on the t test may be invalid. In this section we will explore an alternative method of comparing two groups, one that doesn't need to assume normality for the population distributions. It is called a permutation test because it derives the sampling distribution of the test statistic not by relying on normal population distributions (like the t test) but by considering permutations (rearrangements) of the originally observed data set.

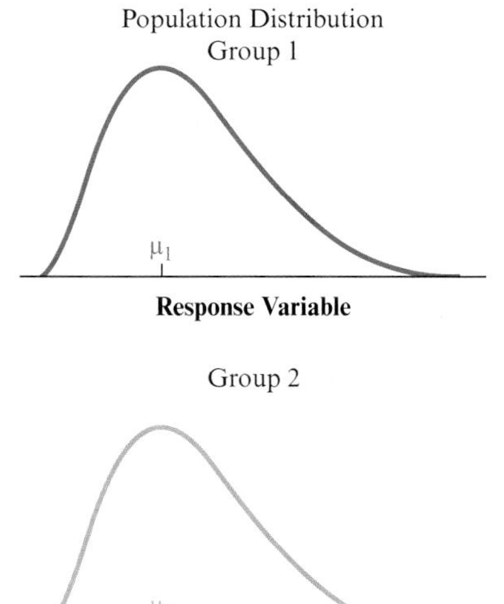

Equal population distributions in the two groups

A permutation test starts from a null hypothesis of equal population distributions (see the margin figure showing two identical skewed population distributions):

H_0: population distribution in Group 1 = population distribution in Group 2

This null hypothesis goes beyond just requiring the population means to be the same and is a stronger statement of "no effect." For instance, if the two groups to be compared refer to two different surgery procedures (such as in Example 10), then "no effect" means that the entire population distribution of the response variable (pain score) is identical under the two surgical procedures, not just that the population means are identical. The alternative hypothesis expresses one way in which the two population distributions differ, such as having different population means (H_a: $\mu_1 \neq \mu_2$).

Recall

From Section 7.1, the **sampling distribution** of a statistic is the probability distribution that specifies probabilities for the possible values the statistic can take. ◀

How can we obtain the sampling distribution of a test statistic under the null hypothesis of identical population distributions without assuming normality for them? Remember from Chapter 7 that the sampling distribution is the distribution of all the possible values the statistic can take (see margin Recall). A permutation test constructs this distribution by considering all possible samples that could have been observed with the given data if the null hypothesis were true.

Example 11

Permutations ◀

Comparing Dosages

Picture the Scenario

A new medication for patients suffering from allergies has just passed pre-clinical trials and is now ready to be tested on humans to determine an appropriate dosage. Because this is the first time the drug is evaluated on humans and not much is known about the dose–response profile, the drug is tested on only five allergy patients. Two of the five patients are randomly assigned to receive a high dose of the drug, and the remaining three receive a low dose. The response variable measured is the number of days a patient stays symptom-free. Table 10.10 in the margin and the dotplot below it show the data obtained from this small experiment.

Table 10.10 Symptom-Free Days of Allergy Patients on High and Low Doses of an Experimental Drug

Patient	Dose	Days without symptoms
1	High	12
2	High	13
3	Low	6
4	Low	6
5	Low	7

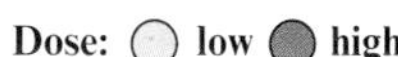

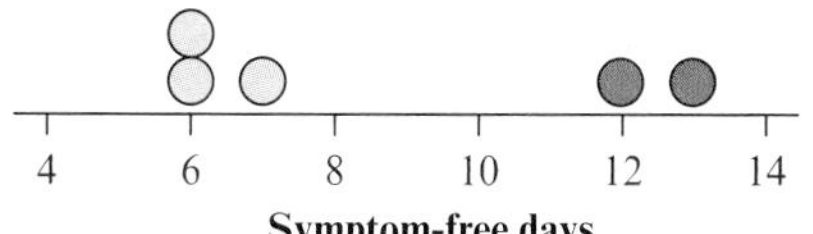

Questions to Explore

a. List all possible ways of assigning two of the five patients to the high-dose group and the remaining three to the low-dose group.

b. For each assignment, find the group means and their differences, using the responses of the patients (days without symptoms) shown in Table 10.10.

Think It Through

a. Each possible assignment divides the five patients into one group of size two and another of size three. You can think of it as writing High on two cards and Low on the other three cards in a five-card deck, shuffling the cards, and then dealing one to each patient. Table 10.11 shows all possible ways the cards could have been dealt to the patients. These are all possible ways (there are 10) of assigning two patients to the high-dose group and three to the low-dose group.

Table 10.11 All Ten Possible Ways of Assigning Five Patients to the High and Low Groups.

Each assignment has two patients in the high group and three patients in the low group.

	Assignment				
Patient	**1**	**2**	**3**	**4**	**5**
1	High	High	High	High	Low
2	High	Low	Low	Low	High
3	Low	High	Low	Low	High
4	Low	Low	High	Low	Low
5	Low	Low	Low	High	Low

Patient	Assignment 6	7	8	9	10
1	Low	Low	Low	Low	Low
2	High	High	Low	Low	Low
3	Low	Low	High	High	Low
4	High	Low	High	Low	High
5	Low	High	Low	High	High

The first possible assignment listed in Table 10.11 is the original one, with patients 1 and 2 in the high-dose group and patients 3, 4, and 5 in the low-dose group. The second possible assignment has patients 1 and 3 in the high-dose group and patients 2, 4, and 5 in the low-dose group. The third assignment has patients 1 and 4 in the high-dose group and so on. Overall, there are 10 possible assignments of the five patients into two groups of size two and three, respectively.

b. Table 10.12 lists, for each assignment, the means in the high- and low-dose groups. For instance, for the original assignment, the sample mean in the high-dose group was 12.50 and, in the low-dose group, 6.33, for a difference of 6.17. For the second possible assignment, which has patients 1 and 3 in the high-dose group, with responses 12 and 6, the sample mean in the high-dose group is $(12 + 6)/2 = 9$. For patients 2, 4, and 5, which are in the low-dose group under this assignment, the sample mean is $(13 + 6 + 7)/3 = 8.67$, yielding a difference of $9 - 8.67 = 0.33$.

Table 10.12 Group Means and Their Differences for All Possible Assignments.

For each assignment, the sample mean of the responses for patients in the high-($\bar{x}_1$) and low-dose ($\bar{x}_2$) groups were computed and their difference taken.

Patient	Response	Assignment 1	2	3	4	5
1	12	High	High	High	High	Low
2	13	High	Low	Low	Low	High
3	6	Low	High	Low	Low	High
4	6	Low	Low	High	Low	Low
5	7	Low	Low	Low	High	Low
Mean High: $\bar{x}_1$		12.50	9.00	9.00	9.50	9.50
Mean Low: $\bar{x}_2$		6.33	8.67	8.67	8.33	8.33
Difference: $\bar{x}_1 - \bar{x}_2$		6.17	0.33	0.33	1.17	1.17

Patient	Response	Assignment 6	7	8	9	10
1	12	Low	Low	Low	Low	Low
2	13	High	High	Low	Low	Low
3	6	Low	Low	High	High	Low
4	6	High	Low	High	Low	High
5	7	Low	High	Low	High	High
Mean High: $\bar{x}_1$		9.50	10.00	6.00	6.50	6.50
Mean Low: $\bar{x}_2$		8.33	8.00	10.67	10.33	10.33
Difference: $\bar{x}_1 - \bar{x}_2$		1.17	2.00	−4.67	−3.83	−3.83

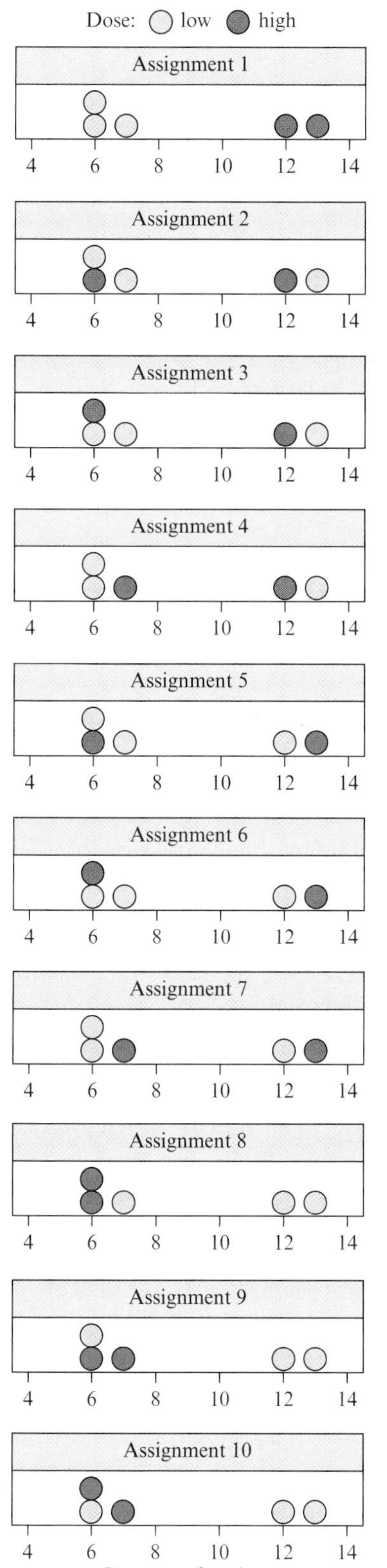

▲ Figure 10.8 All Possible Permutations Each dot plot shows the resulting data set under one of the 10 possible assignments. **Question** Which dot plot would provide the most evidence that the high dose has more symptom-free days?

The last row in Table 10.12 shows all differences that are possible with the observed responses from the five patients. Figure 10.8 in the margin shows the dot plots we would get under each assignment with the responses from the patients in Table 10.10.

Insight

Each of the 10 possible assignments represents one unique permutation (shuffling) of the five original group labels (High, High, Low, Low, Low). If the response distributions are identical in the two groups (the null hypothesis), each permutation (shuffle) of the group labels results in a data set that could have been observed. A permutation test either considers all or, if there are too many, a large random sample of all such permutations.

► ***Try Exercise 10.42***

If truly there is no difference in the response distributions (the null hypothesis), the response of a subject does not depend on the group they are in. For instance, if truly the population distribution of the number of symptom-free days is the same in both dose groups, a response of 7 days is equally likely to occur for a patient assigned to the high-dose group as it is for a patient assigned to the low-dose group. In fact, if the null hypothesis of identical population distributions is correct, the responses we observe on all five patients in the experiment are equally likely to occur under *any* of the 10 possible assignments we listed in Table 10.12.

If the responses are equally likely under any of the 10 assignments, so are the differences in sample means we computed for each assignment. Because there are 10 of them, each difference listed in the last row of Table 10.12 occurs with a probability of 1/10 under the null hypothesis of identical population distributions. This allows us to build the sampling distribution of the difference in the sample means. We simply list all possible differences and their probability of occurrence under the null hypothesis.

Table 10.13 and Figure 10.9 on the next page show the sampling distribution for the difference in the sample means $(\bar{x}_1 - \bar{x}_2)$ for the data in Example 11. We obtain the possible values for the difference from Table 10.12 and their probabilities by noting that each difference occurs with probability 1/10. Note that some assignments, such as the three assignments 4, 5, and 6, lead to the same difference of 1.17. Then, the probability of observing this difference is 3/10.

Table 10.13 Sampling Distribution of $\bar{x}_1 - \bar{x}_2$ Derived By Considering All Possible Permutations (Assignments).

The table shows each possible difference, how often it occurs among the 10 permutations, and the probability of observing this difference under the null hypothesis.

Difference $\bar{x}_1 - \bar{x}_2$	Permutations	Probability
−4.67	1	1/10
−3.83	2	2/10
0.33	2	2/10
1.17	3	3/10
2.00	1	1/10
6.17	1	1/10
Total	**10**	**1**

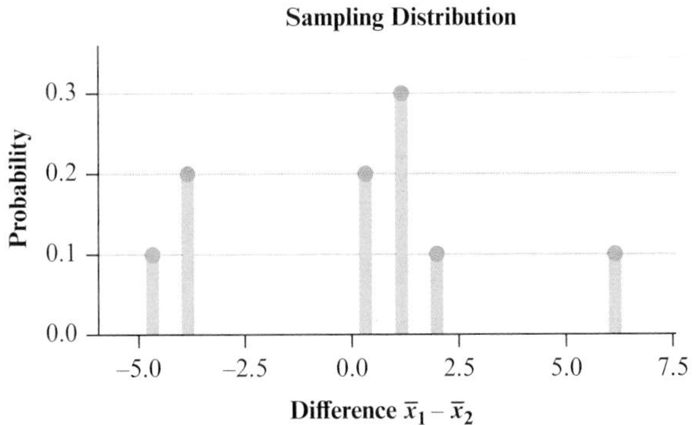

▲ **Figure 10.9** Graph of Sampling Distribution of $\bar{x}_1 - \bar{x}_2$ Derived By Considering All Possible Permutations. **Question** For large sample sizes, what would be the shape of the sampling distribution of $\bar{x}_1 - \bar{x}_2$?

Permutation P-value

We can use the sampling distribution generated from the permutations to judge how extreme the actually observed difference of 6.17 is when we assume that the null hypothesis of identical population distributions is true. If the alternative hypothesis is that the mean number of symptom-free days is larger in the population of all subjects receiving the high dose, i.e., H_a: $\mu_1 > \mu_2$, then all values of the test statistic that are as large or larger than the observed difference of 6.17 are more extreme. Of the 10 possible differences, only one, namely the observed one, is extreme. It occurs with a probability of $1/10 = 0.10$. This is the P-value for the permutation test of the null hypothesis of equal population distributions against the alternative H_a: $\mu_1 > \mu_2$. If truly there is no difference in the population distribution of the number of symptom-free days for patients assigned to the high- and low-dose group, we would see a difference of 6.17 in the sample means with a probability of 0.10. This is not that unusual. For instance, using a significance level of 0.05, we would fail to reject the null hypothesis.

If we assumed that the population distribution of symptom-free days followed a normal distribution in both dose groups, we could have used a t test to assess whether the mean is larger in the high-dose group. The t statistic for the data in Table 10.10 equals 10.3 $(df = 1.9)$, yielding a very small P-value of 0.006, quite different from the permutation P-value. Of course, with small samples such as these, there is no way of checking whether the normality assumption for the population distributions is appropriate, and it is safer to rely on the P-value from the permutation test. On the other hand, note that the smallest possible P-value for the permutation test is 1/10 (the one we actually observed, because the actual data yielded the most extreme difference possible), so the smallest significance level that allows us to reject the null hypothesis is 0.10. However, with just a few more observations, the number of possible permutations quickly increases, and this is no longer an issue.

Permutation Test for Larger Sample Sizes

In the preceding example with only five patients, we could list all possible permutations of the original data. When the sample size is larger, computing the test statistic (such as the difference in sample means) for all possible permutations can be too computationally demanding because there are simply too many to consider. For instance, for Example 10 comparing knee surgeries, with 60 subjects in the placebo group and 59 in the surgery group, there are almost 10^{32} possible permutations. For such cases, one generates a large number (such as 10,000 or 100,000) of random permutations. The proportion out of the generated permutations that yield a test statistic as or more extreme than the observed one is then a very accurate approximation of the exact permutation P-value.

▶ Activity

Exercise 10.90 gives step-by-step instructions on how to use the web app to build the permutation distribution and implement the test.

For implementing the permutation test, one needs a computer to (i) generate all possible permutations or a very large number of random permutations and (ii) compute the test statistic for each. The Permutation Test web app available on the book's website can run the permutation test and compute the permutation P-value for data you supply.

Permutation test for comparing two groups ◀

Example 12

Do Dogs Prefer Petting to Vocal Praise?

Picture the Scenario

In a study to explore whether dogs prefer petting to vocal praise, researchers set up the following experiment.[8] They randomly divided 14 dogs into two groups of seven dogs each. Each dog in the first group of seven dogs is placed in a room where his owner would provide petting and, some distance apart, an assistant (familiarized with the dog for 1 minute before the experiment began) would provide vocal praise (e.g., saying in a high tone of voice, "You are such a good doggie! What a sweet dog you are"). For the second group of 7 dogs, the roles were reversed, and the owner of the dog would provide vocal praise and an assistant would provide petting. The experiment lasted for 5 minutes, during which the dog could switch freely between interacting with the owner, the assistant, or neither. The response variable is the time the dog interacted with its owner.

Is there evidence based on experiments like this that the population mean time dogs interact with their owners is larger when the owners provide petting? Table 10.14 shows the data collected from this experiment, with sample mean $\bar{x}_1 = 232$ seconds in the first group and $\bar{x}_2 = 68$ seconds in the second group.

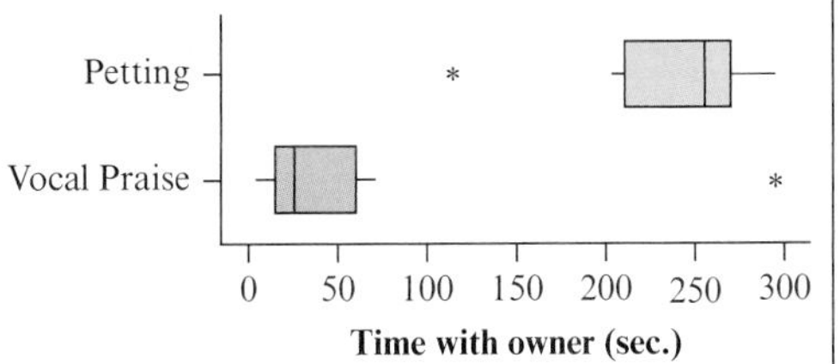

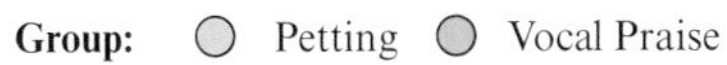

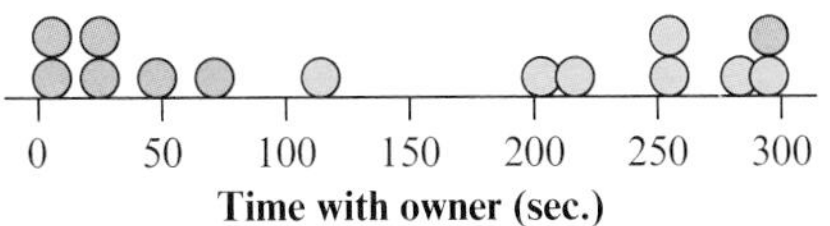

Box- and dotplots of time dogs spent with owners in the two groups

Table 10.14 The Time Dogs Interact with Their Owners.

For dogs in Group 1, owners provided petting. For dogs in Group 2, owners provided vocal praise. In each group, values are sorted in ascending order.

Group	Responses	Mean
1	114, 203, 217, 254, 256, 284, 296	232
2	4, 7, 24, 25, 48, 71, 294	68

The figures in the margin show box plots and dot plots, both revealing potentially skewed distributions. All but one dog in the second group spent less time with the owner compared to the dogs in Group 1. This one dog clearly is an outlier in Group 2 but might be typical for some dogs that choose to stay with their owner no matter what kind of interaction is offered. It shows that the distribution might be rather skewed to the right in this group.

Questions to Explore

a. Why might a t test comparing these two groups not be appropriate?

b. Conduct a permutation test. What are the hypotheses and how can you find the sampling distribution of the difference in sample means?

c. Obtain the permutation P-value and interpret.

Think It Through

a. The t test makes the assumption of a normal distribution for the population distribution of time dogs spent with owners, which we really

[8]E. Feuerbacher and C. Wynne, *Behavioural Processes*, vol. 110, 2015, pp. 47–59

```
Two-sample T for Group 1 vs
Group 2

Difference = μ(Group 1) −
μ(Group 2)

Estimate for difference: 164.4

T-Test of difference = 0(vs >):

T-Value = 3.64 P-Value = 0.0023
DF = 9.8
```

Software Output for *t* Test.

Note that software doesn't tell you whether the requested analysis is valid, i.e., whether the assumptions hold for the *t* test.

Did you know?

The number 3,432 is equal to the binomial coefficient $\binom{14}{7}$, which in Chapter 6.3 we defined as all possible ways of obtaining exactly $x = 7$ successes in $n = 14$ trials. Here, a trial is whether any of the 14 dogs is assigned to Group 1, with a "success" if it is. ◀

can't check with just seven observations in each group. From the context and the data observed, this assumption looks implausible. In addition, we are interested in a one-sided alternative hypothesis, and although the *t* test is robust for two-sided hypotheses, it might not be for one-sided hypotheses for small sample sizes. These are reasons we may not trust the result of the *t* test, which reports a P-value of 0.002 for these data, as shown in the margin.

b. A permutation test tests the null hypothesis that the distribution of the time dogs interact with their owners is the same in each group:

H_0: *Distribution of time that dogs spend with owner when owner provides petting* = *Distribution of time that dogs spend with owner when owner provides vocal praise.*

This null hypothesis in particular implies that the population means are the same. The alternative hypothesis captures some way the two population distributions differ. Here, we are interested in whether the population mean time dogs spend with their owners is larger when the owners provide petting instead of vocal praise, so the alternative hypothesis is H_a: $\mu_1 > \mu_2$.

Overall, there are 3,432 different permutations of the original data, which correspond to all possible ways of dividing 14 dogs into two groups of seven dogs each. Table 10.15 shows one such permutation, in which three dogs previously in Group 1 are now in Group 2, and three dogs from Group 2 are now in Group 1. For this particular permutation, the difference in the sample means is $165 - 135 = 30$, much smaller than the observed difference of $232 - 68 = 164$.

Table 10.15 One Permutation of the Original Dataset.

Color code shows original group membership (yellow = Group 1, green = Group 2).

Group	Responses	Mean
1	7, 25, 71, 217, 254, 284, 296	165
2	4, 24, 48, 114, 203, 256, 294	135

We need many more such permutations to construct the sampling distribution of $\bar{x}_1 - \bar{x}_2$. To obtain these, you need to enter the data from Table 10.14 into computer software that can run a permutation test, such as the Permutation Test web app. In Figure 10.10, we show a screenshot from this app, which includes the histogram for the sampling distribution. Here, because of the relatively small number of total possible permutations, the app could compute the difference in the sample means for each.

From Figure 10.10, we can see that the value for the observed difference of 164 is extreme because it is far out in the upper tail of the sampling distribution. Because the P-value for our one-sided hypothesis is the probability of obtaining a test statistic as large or larger than the observed one if the null hypothesis is true, we can find the P-value by the proportion of the 3,432 permutations that yielded a difference as large or larger than 164. As indicated in the subtitle of the plot in Figure 10.10, only 13 permutations yielded a difference as large or larger than 164 (including the observed one), for a proportion of $13/3432 = 0.004$. This is the permutation P-value for testing the null hypothesis of equal distributions against the alternative hypothesis H_a: $\mu_1 > \mu_2$. In experiments like this, the probability of observing a difference of 164 seconds or larger is only 0.004 if the time dogs interact with their owners is the same in the two groups. This is small, so we have strong

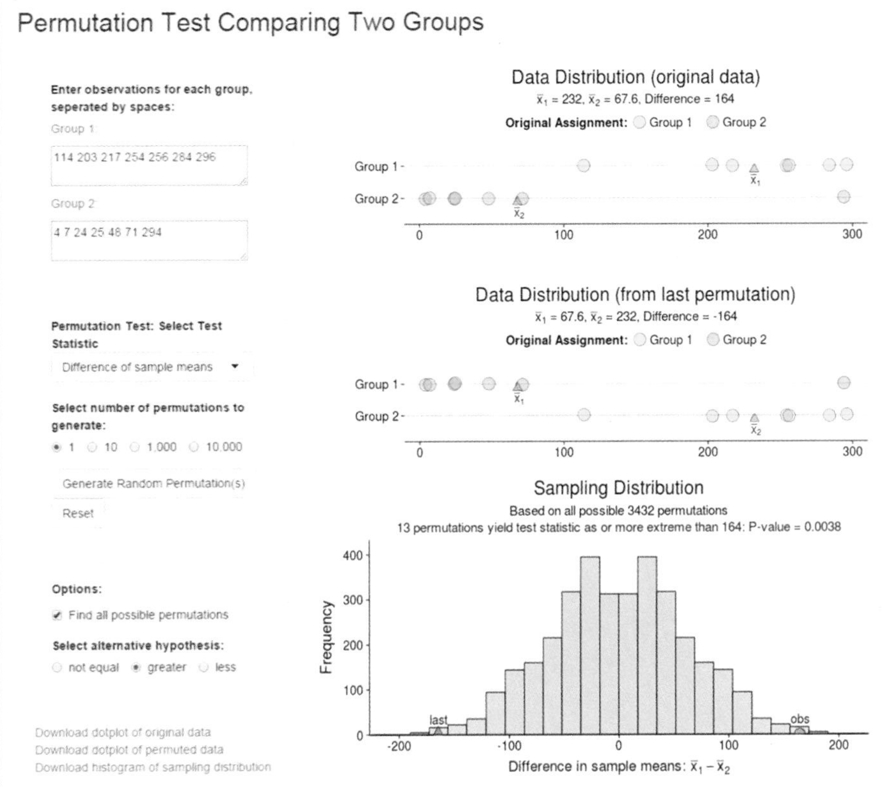

▲ **Figure 10.10 Screenshot from Permutation Web App.** The histogram shows the permutation sampling distribution of the difference between sample means. This sampling distribution is obtained by considering all possible ways of dividing the responses of the 14 dogs into two groups of size 7 and computing the difference in sample means for each. The semi-circle in the right tail indicates the actually observed difference. (The dot plots above the histogram show the original data and the data after a random permutation, in this case, the permutation when all dogs in Group 1 are switched with all dogs from Group 2) **Question** Is the observed difference extreme?

evidence to reject the null hypothesis of identical population distributions at any reasonable significance level and conclude that under the settings of this experiment, the mean time dogs interact with their owners is larger when the owners provide petting than when they provide vocal praise.

Insight

Although the P-value for the permutation test is twice as large as the one from the t test, both are very small, and the same conclusions are reached. This doesn't have to be the case (in Example 11, they differed considerably) and without running the permutation test, we wouldn't even know whether the two P-values are comparable.

▶ ***Try Exercise 10.45***

Another strength of the permutation test besides not requiring normality is that it is not restricted to comparing means. For example, if we want to see whether the *median time* that dogs interact with their owners is larger in the first group (which may be a more reasonable measure of the center of the distribution if it is skewed), all we have to change in Example 12 is the test statistic. Instead of computing the difference of sample means for each permutation, we compute the difference of sample medians. Without further simplifying assumptions on the population distribution, such as normality, it is difficult to derive the theoretical sampling distribution for the difference in sample medians, and we would be at a loss to judge how extreme the observed difference is.

SUMMARY: Comparing Two Groups with a Permutation Test

This test derives the sampling distribution by considering all possible (or a large sample of random) permutations of the original data. A permutation is one particular way of dividing the $(n_1 + n_2)$ observations into two groups of size n_1 and n_2, respectively. For each such permutation, the test statistic (e.g., the difference in the sample means) is computed from the resulting dataset.

1. **Assumptions**
   - A quantitative response variable observed in each of two groups
   - Independent random samples, either from random sampling or a randomized experiment. For an experiment, the assumption of a random sample of subjects is not necessary as long as the subjects are assigned to the two groups randomly.
2. **Hypotheses**
   H_0: Identical population distributions for the two groups (this implies equal population means, $\mu_1 = \mu_2$)
   H_a: $\mu_1 \neq \mu_2$ Population means differ between the two groups. One-sided versions are also possible, H_a: $\mu_1 < \mu_2$ or H_a: $\mu_1 > \mu_2$.
   H_a could also be in terms of other population parameters, such as population medians.
3. **Test Statistic**
   The difference $(\bar{x}_1 - \bar{x}_2)$ of the sample means. If the alternative hypothesis is in terms of medians, then the test statistic is the difference in the sample medians.
4. **P-value**
   The P-value is the proportion out of all possible permutations with a test statistic as extreme or even more extreme than the observed test statistic. When the number of all possible permutations is too large, a random sample of a large number of permutations (such as 10,000) is considered. Then, the P-value is the proportion out of these 10,000 random permutations that give a test statistic as extreme or even more extreme than the observed one.
5. **Conclusion**
   Smaller P-values give stronger evidence against H_0 and supporting H_a. Interpret the P-value in context and, if a decision is needed, reject H_0 if P-value $\leq$ significance level (such as 0.05).

Here, we looked at the permutation test for comparing the distribution of a quantitative response variable between two groups. Section 11.5 discusses a permutation test for comparing the distribution of a categorical response variable between two groups. Section 15.1 discusses an alternative permutation test that uses the ranks of the observations instead of the original observations.

The Ratio of Proportions or Means

Examples 2 through 4 discussed data from a study comparing the proportions of cancer deaths between a group who took placebo and a group that took aspirin. The difference in the sample proportion of $0.030 - 0.023 = 0.007$ seemed small. This effect of aspirin over placebo seems more substantial when viewed as the *ratio* $0.030/0.023 = 1.3$ of the two proportions, which is a statistic commonly reported in medical journals and called the **relative risk**. We first saw how to interpret it in Chapter 3, Section 3.2. The proportion of cancer deaths is estimated to be 30% larger in the placebo group compared to the aspirin group. Inference for the relative risk is discussed in Chapter 11.

You can also use the ratio to compare means. For example, the National Center for Health Statistics recently reported that the mean weight for adult American women was 140 pounds in 1962 and 164 pounds in 2002. Since $164/140 = 1.17$, the mean in 2002 was 1.17 times the mean in 1962. This can also be expressed by saying that the mean increased by 17% over this 40-year period.

10.3 Practicing the Basics

10.35 Body dissatisfaction Female college student participation in athletics has increased dramatically over the past few decades. Sports medicine providers are aware of some unique health concerns of athletic women, including disordered eating. A study (M. Reinking and L. Alexander, *Journal of Athletic Training,* vol. 40, 2005, pp. 47–51) compared disordered-eating symptoms and their causes for collegiate female athletes (in lean and nonlean sports) and nonathletes. The sample mean of the body dissatisfaction assessment score was 13.2 ($s = 8.0$) for 16 lean sport athletes (those sports that place value on leanness, including distance running, swimming, and gymnastics) and 7.3 ($s = 6.0$) for the 68 nonlean sport athletes. Assuming equal population standard deviations,

a. Find the standard error for comparing the means.

b. Construct a 95% confidence interval for the difference between the mean body dissatisfaction for lean sport athletes and nonlean sport athletes. Interpret.

10.36 Body dissatisfaction test Refer to the previous exercise.

a. Find the P-value for testing whether the population means are equal. Use a two-sided alternative.

b. Summarize assumptions for the analysis in part a. Do you think the normality assumption is justified? If not, what is the consequence of violating it?

10.37 Surgery versus placebo for knee pain Refer to Example 10, "Arthroscopic Surgery." Here we show MINITAB output comparing mean knee pain scores for the placebo (Group 1) to lavage arthroscopic surgery (Group 2) assuming equal population standard deviations.

TRY

a. State and interpret the result of the confidence interval.

b. Is it reasonable to assume equal population standard deviations?

c. State all steps and interpret the result of the significance test.

```
Sample   N    Mean   StDev   SE Mean
  1     60    51.6   23.7     3.1
  2     61    53.7   23.7     3.0
Difference = μ(1) − μ(2)
Estimate for difference: −2.10
95% CI for difference: (−10.63, 6.43)
T-Test of difference = 0 (vs ≠):
T-Value = −0.49 P-Value = 0.627 DF = 119
Both use Pooled StDev = 23.7000
```

10.38 Comparing clinical therapies A clinical psychologist wants to choose between two therapies for treating severe cases of mental depression. She selects six patients who are similar in their depressive symptoms and in their overall quality of health. She randomly selects three of the patients to receive Therapy 1, and the other three receive Therapy 2. She selects small samples for ethical reasons—if her experiment indicates that one therapy is superior, she will use that therapy on all her other depression patients. After one month of treatment, the improvement in each patient is measured by the change in a score for measuring severity of mental depression. The higher the score, the better. The improvement scores are

TECH

Therapy 1: 30, 45, 45
Therapy 2: 10, 20, 30

Analyze these data (you can use software if you wish), assuming equal population standard deviations.

a. Show that $\bar{x}_1 = 40, \bar{x}_2 = 20, s = 9.35, se = 7.64,$ $df = 4$, and a 95% confidence interval comparing the means is $(-1.2, 41.2)$.

b. Explain how to interpret what the confidence interval tells you about the therapies. Why do you think that it is so wide?

c. When the sample sizes are very small, it may be worth sacrificing some confidence to achieve more precision. Show that a 90% confidence interval is (3.7, 36.3). At this confidence level, can you conclude that Therapy 1 is better?

10.39 Clinical therapies 2 Refer to the previous exercise.

a. For the null hypothesis, H_0: $\mu_1 = \mu_2$, show that $t = 2.62$ and the two-sided P-value $= 0.059$. Interpret.

b. What decision would you make in the test, using a (i) 0.05 and (ii) 0.10 significance level? Explain what this means in the context of the study.

c. Suppose the researcher had predicted ahead of time that Therapy 1 would be better. To which H_a does this correspond? Report the P-value for it, and make a decision with significance level 0.05.

10.40 Vegetarians more liberal? When a sample of social science graduate students at the University of Florida gave their responses on political ideology (ranging from 1 = very liberal to 7 = very conservative), the mean was

3.18 ($s = 1.72$) for the 51 nonvegetarian students and 2.22 ($s = 0.67$) for the 9 vegetarian students. Software for comparing the means provides the printout, which shows results first for inferences that assume equal population standard deviations and then for inferences that allow them to be unequal.

```
Sample    N     Mean     StDev    SE Mean
  1      51     3.18     1.72      0.24
  2       9     2.220    0.670     0.22
Difference = μ(1) − μ(2)
Estimate for difference: 0.960
95% CI for difference: (−0.210, 2.130)
T-Test of difference = 0 (vs ≠): T-Value = 1.64
P-Value = 0.106 DF = 58
Both use Pooled StDev = 1.6162
95% CI for difference: (0.289, 1.631)
T-Test of difference = 0 (vs ≠):
T-Value = 2.92 P-Value = 0.007 DF = 30
```

a. Explain why the results of the two approaches differ so much. Which do you think is more reliable?

b. State your conclusion about whether the true means are plausibly equal.

10.41 Teeth whitening results One scientific "test of whiteness" tested the effect of a self applied tooth-whitening peroxide gel system in a randomized, controlled clinical trial.[9] The 58 adults assigned to the gel whitening group applied the gel after normal brushing according to the manufacturer's instructions. The fluoride toothpaste group was instructed to brush twice a day. The procedure was repeated for both groups twice a day for 14 days. An experienced examiner determined the tooth shades comparing each tooth to the shade tabs from an accepted shade scale (Vita shade guide) at the start of the experiment to create a baseline and then after one and two weeks of product application. Changes between the baseline score and the one- and two-week assessments were expressed as a difference of the respective Vita score, with a positive difference indicating an improvement in tooth whiteness. The results of the study are shown in the following table.

Mean Vita Shade Score Recorded at Two Weeks and Change from Baseline

Group	n	Two Weeks Mean Vita Shade (s.d.)	Change From Baseline (s.d.)	Treatment Difference
Xtra White whitening gel	58	6.80 (2.48)	1.02 (1.32)	0.67 ($p < 0.05$)
Toothpaste only	59	7.01 (2.19)	0.35 (1.29)	

a. State the hypotheses that were tested for the change from baseline means.

b. The P-value is reported as <0.05 for the test comparing the means. Explain how to interpret this value.

c. Calculate the pooled standard error, the t statistic, and the resulting P-value.

d. The ratio of the change from baseline sample means was 2.91. Interpret this ratio.

[9] *Source*: Data from L. Z. Collins et. al., *Journal of Dentistry*, vol. 32, 2004, pp. 13–17.

10.42 Permuting therapies TRY Refer to Exercise 10.38, which compared two therapies for depression patients. Suppose that in a different experiment, only four patients took part; two were randomly assigned to the group that received therapy 1 and the remaining two to the group that received therapy 2. The following table shows the improvement scores for these 4 patients.

Patient:	1	2	3	4
Therapy:	1	1	2	2
Score:	30	60	20	30

a. List all six possible ways these four patients could have been assigned to the two therapies. That is, give all six possible ways of dividing the four patients into two groups of two patients each.

b. Using the observed improvement scores shown in the table, find the sample means in each group and their difference under each possible assignment.

10.43 Permutations equally likely Refer to the previous exercise comparing improvement scores under two therapies for depression patients.

a. State the null hypothesis of equal population distributions in the context of this experiment.

b. Argue that if the null hypothesis is true, the sampling distribution for the difference in sample means is $P(-20) = 2/6$, $P(-10) = 1/6$, $P(10) = 1/6$, $P(20) = 2/6$.

c. Find the permutation P-value for testing the null hypothesis in part a (which implies the population mean scores are the same) against the alternative that the population mean improvement score is larger under therapy 1, using the difference in the sample means as a test statistic. Interpret it.

10.44 Two-sided permutation P-value Refer to the previous exercise and the sampling distribution mentioned there. What is the permutation P-value for the two-sided test with alternative hypothesis that the mean improvement scores are different under therapies 1 and 2? (*Hint:* As for any regular test, the two-sided P-value is the the sum of the tail probabilities of test statistic values as extreme as the observed one. Extreme differences are those with an absolute value as large as or larger than the absolute value of the observed difference.)

10.45 Time spent on social networks revisited TRY TECH Exercise 10.31 considered the following data on the number of hours students spent on social network sites per week:

Males: 5, 7, 9, 10, 12, 12, 12, 13, 13, 15, 15, 20

Females: 5, 7, 7, 8, 10, 10, 11, 12, 12, 14, 14, 14, 16, 18, 20, 20, 20, 22, 23, 25, 40

Enter the observations (separated by spaces) into the Permutation Test web app. Let males be Group 1 and females be Group 2. We are interested in testing whether the population mean number of hours spent on social networks differs between males and females, using as test statistic the difference in sample means.

a. What are the observed group means and their difference? (The subtitle of the dot plot shows this information.)

b. Press the Generate Random Permutation(s) button once to generate one permutation of the original data. What are the two group means and their difference under this permutation? (The subtitle of the dot plot shows this information.)

c. Did this one permutation lead to a difference that is less extreme, as extreme, or more extreme than the observed difference?

d. Select to generate 10,000 random permutations. How many of them resulted in a test statistic as or more extreme than the observed difference? (Remember, the alternative hypothesis is H_a: $\mu_1 \neq \mu_2$.)

e. Find and interpret the permutation P-value.

10.46 Compare permutation test to *t* test Refer to the previous exercise.

a. Run a *t* test and report the P-value for the two-sided alternative hypothesis.

b. Using a significance level of 0.10, are the decisions based on the *t* test and based on the permutation test comparable? Which one would you trust more?

c. Remove the largest observations (which could be outliers) in each of the two groups, as was done in Exercise 10.32. Does the conclusion of the permutation test change?

10.47 Dominance of politicians For a rating experiment, researchers translated short video clips of randomly selected speeches by 30 male and 30 female politicians into animated, gender-neutral stick-figures. These animated sequences were rated (on a scale from −100 to 100) by a panel of students on the perceived dominance of the speaker. A higher rating indicates higher dominance. The following data show the average rating each speech received. (The data are also in the stickfigures.csv file.)

TECH

Male politicians: −11, 37, 40, −14, 41, −43, 19, 35, 42, 18, 2, −1, −6, 49, −6, 20, 27, −24, 19, −33, 48, 21, 26, −21, 28, −11, −7, 15, 39, −29

Female politicians: 23, 32, 12, −45, 19, 21, −25, 2, −27, −32, −26, −14, −6, 22, −22, −18, 66, 22, 3, −9, −12, −43, −1, −36, 23, 44, 9, 32, −40, −7

a. State the null and alternative hypothesis and run a permutation test (e.g., using the web app) to see whether there is a difference in the ratings on competence between female and male speakers. What is the conclusion when the significance level is 0.05?

b. Run a *t* test. Are results comparable to the ones from the permutation test? Why or why not?

10.48 Sampling distribution of $\bar{x}_1 - \bar{x}_2$ Refer to Example 12, which compared two groups of seven dogs each in terms of their time interacting with their owners. The following graph shows a smoothed version of the sampling distribution of $\bar{x}_1 - \bar{x}_2$ derived from the permutation approach. Superimposed (in blue) is the theoretical sampling distribution of $\bar{x}_1 - \bar{x}_2$ if the sample sizes were large.

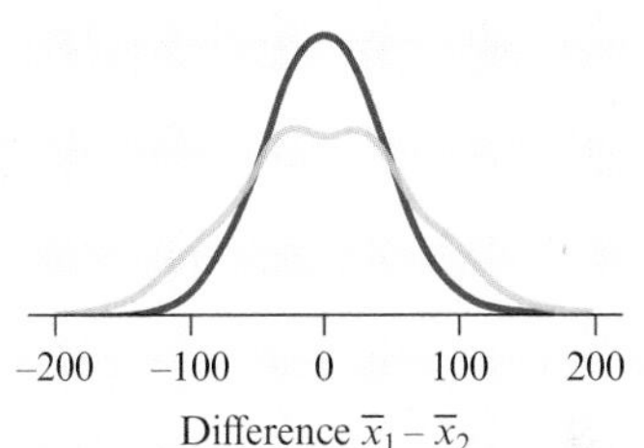

a. What would the mean, standard error, and approximate shape of the theoretical sampling distribution of $\bar{x}_1 - \bar{x}_2$ be if the sample sizes were large?

b. Comment on how the permutation sampling distribution of $\bar{x}_1 - \bar{x}_2$ differs from the theoretical, large-sample one.

c. Consider the one-sided alternative H_a: $\mu_1 > \mu_2$. If the actually observed difference in sample means were 100, would the P-values computed from each sampling distribution be the same or different? Explain.

10.4 Analyzing Dependent Samples

With **dependent samples**, each observation in one sample has a matched observation in the other sample. The observations are called **matched pairs**. We've already seen examples of matched-pairs data. In Example 8 of Chapter 9, each of a sample of anorexic girls had her weight measured before and after a treatment for anorexia. The weights before the treatment form one group of observations. The weights after the treatment form the other group. The same girls were in each sample, so the samples were dependent.

By contrast, in Examples 2, 5, and 6 of this chapter, the samples were *independent*. The two groups consisted of different people, and there was no matching of an observation in one sample with an observation in the other sample.

Example 13

Dependent samples ◀

Cell Phones and Driving

Picture the Scenario

Example 9 in this chapter analyzed whether the use of cell phones impairs reaction times in a driving skills test. The analysis used independent samples—one group used cell phones and a separate control group did not use them. An alternative design uses the same subjects for both groups. Reaction times are measured when subjects performed the driving task without using cell phones and then again while the same subjects used cell phones.

Table 10.16 shows the mean of the reaction times (in milliseconds) for each subject under each condition. Figure 10.11 in the margin shows box plots of the data for the two conditions.

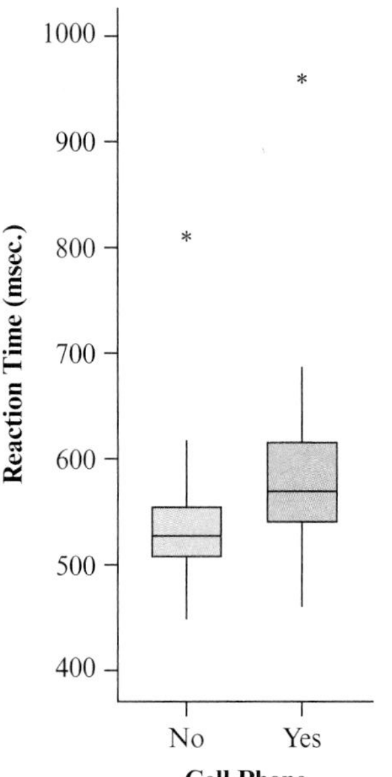

▲ **Figure 10.11** Box Plots of Observations on Reaction Times. **Question** From the data in Table 10.16, what do the outliers for the two distributions have in common?

Table 10.16 Reaction Times on Driving Skills Before and While Using Cell Phone

The difference score is the reaction time using the cell phone minus the reaction time not using it, such as 636 − 604 = 32 milliseconds.

	Using Cell Phone?				Using Cell Phone?		
Student	**No**	**Yes**	**Difference**	**Student**	**No**	**Yes**	**Difference**
1	604	636	32	17	525	626	101
2	556	623	67	18	508	501	−7
3	540	615	75	19	529	574	45
4	522	672	150	20	470	468	−2
5	459	601	142	21	512	578	66
6	544	600	56	22	487	560	73
7	513	542	29	23	515	525	10
8	470	554	84	24	499	647	148
9	556	543	−13	25	448	456	8
10	531	520	−11	26	558	688	130
11	599	609	10	27	589	679	90
12	537	559	22	28	814	960	146
13	619	595	−24	29	519	558	39
14	536	565	29	30	462	482	20
15	554	573	19	31	521	527	6
16	467	554	87	32	543	536	−7

Questions to Explore

a. Summarize the sample data distributions for the two conditions.

b. To compare the mean response times using statistical inference, should we treat the samples as independent or dependent?

Think It Through

a. The box plots show that the distribution of reaction times is fairly symmetric in each group, save for a very large outlier in each group. In general, reaction times tend to be larger for those using a cell phone.

b. The responses under the No and Yes columns in Table 10.16 were made by the same subject, so they are not independent. A subject who in general is slow to react will have a large reaction time under both experimental conditions. These are matched-pairs data because each control observation (Sample 1) pairs with a cell phone observation (Sample 2). Because this study used the same subjects for each sample, the samples are dependent.

Insight

Table 10.16 shows that subject number 28 had a large reaction time in each case. This one subject was slow to react, regardless of the condition.

▶ ***Try Exercise 10.49, part a***

Why would we use dependent instead of independent samples? A major benefit is that sources of potential bias are controlled so we can make a more accurate comparison. Using matched pairs keeps many other factors fixed that could affect the analysis. Often this results in the benefit of smaller standard errors.

From Figure 10.11, for instance, the sample mean was higher when subjects used cell phones. This did not happen because the subjects using cell phones tended to be older than the subjects not using them. Age was not a lurking variable, because each sample had the same subjects. When we used independent samples (different subjects) for the two conditions in Example 9, the two samples could differ somewhat on characteristics that might affect the results, such as physical fitness or gender or age. With independent samples, studies ideally use randomization to assign subjects to the two groups attempting to minimize the extent to which this happens. With observational studies, however, this is not an option.

Compare Means with Matched Pairs: *Use Paired Differences*

For each matched pair in Table 10.16, we construct a new variable consisting of a difference score (d for difference),

$$d = \text{reaction time using cell phone} - \text{reaction time without cell phone.}$$

For Subject 1, $d = 636 - 604 = 32$. Table 10.16 also shows these 32 difference scores. The sample mean of these difference scores, denoted by $\bar{x}_d$, is

$$\bar{x}_d = (32 + 67 + 75 + \cdots -7)/32 = 50.6.$$

The sample mean of the difference scores necessarily equals the difference between the means for the two samples. In Table 10.16, the mean reaction time without the cell phone is $(604 + 556 + 540 + \cdots + 543)/32 = 534.6$, the mean reaction time using the cell phone is $(636 + 623 + 615 + \cdots + 536)/32 = 585.2$, and the difference between these means is 50.6. This is also the mean of the differences, $\bar{x}_d$.

For Dependent Samples, Mean of Differences = Difference of Means

For dependent samples, the difference $(\bar{x}_1 - \bar{x}_2)$ between the means of the two samples equals the mean $\bar{x}_d$ of the difference scores for the matched pairs.

Likewise, the difference $(\mu_1 - \mu_2)$ between the population means is identical to the parameter μ_d that is the population mean of the difference scores. So the sample mean $\bar{x}_d$ of the differences not only estimates μ_d, the population

In Words

For **dependent** samples, we calculate the **difference** scores and then use the one-sample methods of Chapters 8 and 9.

mean difference, but also the difference $(\mu_1 - \mu_2)$. We can base inference about $(\mu_1 - \mu_2)$ on inference about the population mean of the difference scores. *This simplifies the analysis since it reduces a two-sample (bivariate) problem to a one-sample (univariate) analysis using the difference scores.*

Let n denote the number of observations in each sample. This equals the number of difference scores. The 95% confidence interval for the population mean difference is

$$\bar{x}_d \pm t_{.025}(se) \text{ with } se = s_d/\sqrt{n},$$

Recall

You can review **confidence intervals for a mean** in Section 8.3 and **significance tests for a mean** in Section 9.3. ◀

where $\bar{x}_d$ is the sample mean of the difference scores and s_d is their standard deviation. The t-score comes from the t table with $df = n - 1$.

Likewise, to test the hypothesis H_0: $\mu_1 = \mu_2$ of equal means, we can conduct the single-sample test of H_0: $\mu_d = 0$ with the difference scores. The test statistic is

$$t = \frac{\bar{x}_d - 0}{se} \text{ with } se = s_d/\sqrt{n}.$$

Caution

Although $\bar{x}_d = \bar{x}_1 - \bar{x}_2$, there is no way of obtaining s_d from the sample standard deviations s_1 and s_2 in the two groups. In particular, s_d is *not* equal to $s_1 - s_2$! You (or the software) have to compute all difference scores first and then find s_d. ◀

This compares the sample mean of the differences to the null hypothesis value of 0. The standard error is the same as for the confidence interval. The $df = n - 1$. Since this test uses the difference scores for the pairs of observations, it is called a **paired *t* test**. Software can do the computations for us.

Because these paired-difference inferences are special cases of single-sample inferences about a population mean, they make the same assumptions:

- The sample of difference scores is a random sample from a population of such difference scores.
- The difference scores have a population distribution that is approximately normal. This is mainly important for small samples (less than about 30) and for one-sided inferences.

For example, when checking assumptions for inference with the data in Example 13, we do not need approximate normality of the reaction times when using and when not using a cell phone. All we care about is the differences in reaction times, so we only need to check whether the differences follow approximately a normal distribution. The margin figure included with the next example shows that this is a plausible assumption.

Confidence intervals and two-sided tests are **robust**: They work quite well even if the normality assumption is violated. One-sided tests do not work well when the sample size is small and the distribution of differences is highly skewed.

Example 14

Matched-pairs analysis ◀

Cell Phones and Driver Reaction Time

Picture the Scenario

The matched-pairs data in Table 10.16 showed the reaction times for the sampled subjects using and not using cell phones. Figure 10.12 shows a histogram with box plot of the $n = 32$ difference scores. Table 10.17 shows MINITAB output for these data. The first part of Table 10.17 shows the mean, standard deviation, and standard error for each sample and for the differences. The second part shows inference about the mean of the differences.

Questions to Explore

a. How can you conduct and interpret the significance test reported in Table 10.17?

b. How can you construct and interpret the confidence interval reported in Table 10.17?

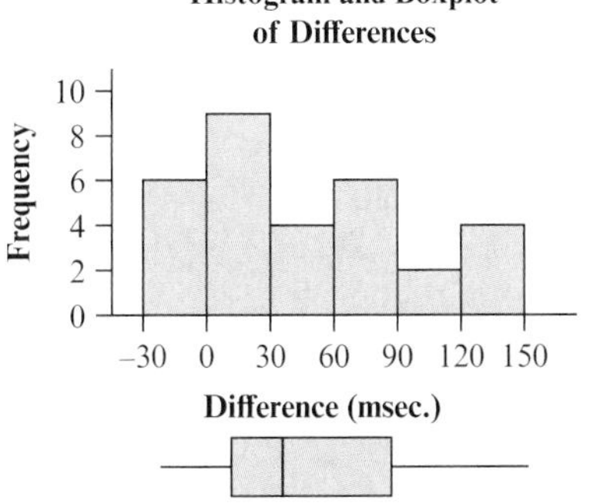

▲ **Figure 10.12** Histogram and Box Plot of Difference Scores from Table 10.16. **Question** The plot shows that some of the differences are negative. How can that be?

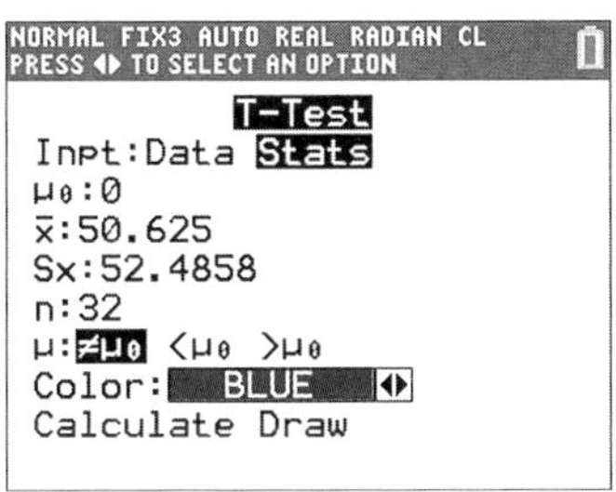

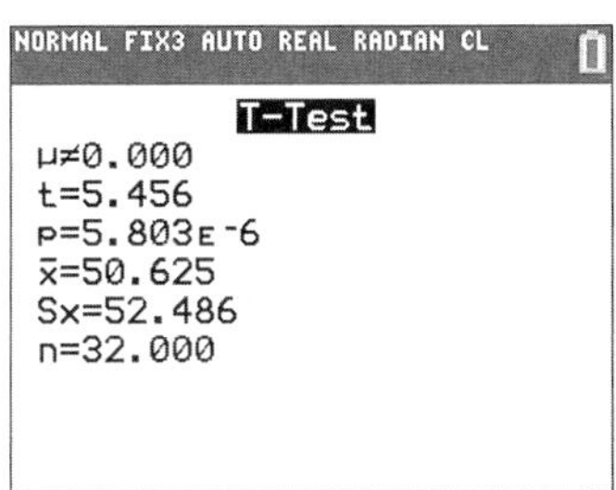

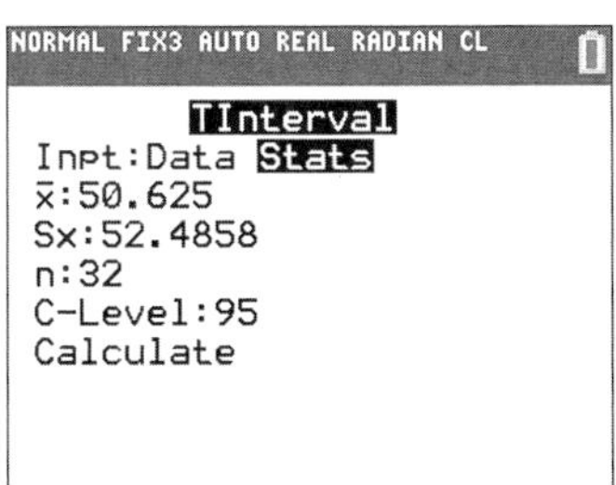

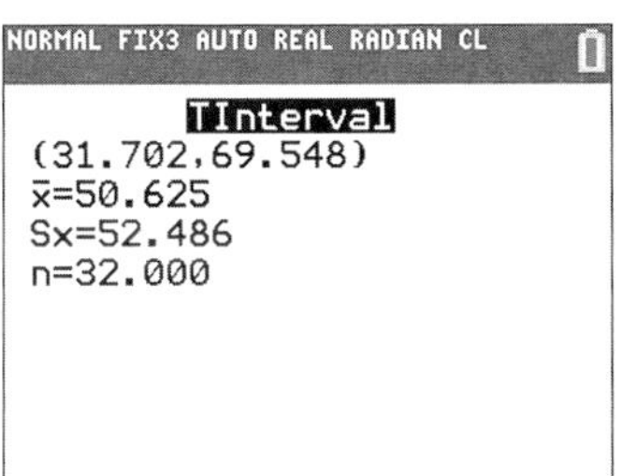

TI output for test and confidence interval based on difference scores

Table 10.17 Software Output for Matched-Pairs Analysis With Table 10.17

The margin shows screen shots from the TI.

Paired T for Cell phone – Pre-cell phone

	N	Mean	StDev	SE Mean
Cell	32	585.2	89.6	15.8
Pre-cell	32	534.6	66.4	11.7
Difference	32	50.63	52.49	9.28

95% CI for mean difference: (31.70, 69.55)

T-Test of mean difference = 0 (vs ≠ 0):

T-Value = 5.46 P-Value = 0.000

Think It Through

a. Figure 10.12 shows skew to the right for the difference scores. Two-sided inference is robust to violations of the assumption of a normal population distribution. The plots do not show any severe outliers that would raise questions about the validity of using the mean to summarize the difference scores.

The sample mean difference is $\bar{x}_d = 50.6$, and the standard deviation of the difference scores is $s_d = 52.5$. The standard error is $se = s_d/\sqrt{n} = 52.5/\sqrt{32} = 9.28$. The t test statistic for the significance test of H_0: $\mu_d = 0$ (hence equal population means for the two conditions) against H_a: $\mu_d \neq 0$ is

$$t = \bar{x}_d/se = 50.6/9.28 = 5.46.$$

With 32 difference scores, $df = n - 1 = 31$. Table 10.17 reports the two-sided P-value of 0.000. There is extremely strong evidence that the population mean reaction times are different.

b. For a 95% confidence interval for $\mu_d = \mu_1 - \mu_2$, with $df = 31$, $t_{.025} = 2.040$. We can use $se = 9.28$ from part a. The confidence interval equals

$$\bar{x}_d \pm t_{.025}(se), \text{ or } 50.6 \pm 2.040(9.28),$$

which equals 50.6 ± 18.9, or $(31.7, 69.5)$.

At the 95% confidence level, we infer that the population mean when using cell phones is between about 32 and 70 milliseconds higher than when not using cell phones. The confidence interval does not contain 0, so we can infer that the population mean reaction time is greater when using a cell phone. The confidence interval *is* more informative than the significance test because it predicts just how large the difference might be.

The article about the study did not indicate whether the subjects were randomly selected, so inferential conclusions are tentative.

Insight

The study also showed that reaction times were similar with hands-free versus hand-held cell phones. It also showed that the probability of missing a simulated traffic signal doubled when students used cell phones.

A later related study[10] showed that the mean reaction time of students using cell phones was similar to that of older drivers not using cell phones. The study concluded, "The net effect of having younger drivers converse on a cell phone was to make their average reactions equivalent to those of older drivers who were not using a cell phone."

▶ ***Try Exercises 10.49 and 10.50***

[10] D. L. Strayer and F. A. Drews, *Human Factors,* vol. 46, 2004, pp. 640–649.

In summary, comparing means with matched-pairs data is easy. We merely use methods we've already learned about in Chapters 8 and 9 for single samples.

SUMMARY: Comparing Means of Dependent Samples

To compare means with dependent samples, construct confidence intervals and significance tests using the single sample of difference scores,

$$d = \text{observation in Sample 1} - \text{observation in Sample 2}.$$

The 95% confidence interval $\bar{x}_d \pm t_{.025}(se)$ and the test statistic $t = (\bar{x}_d - 0)/se$ are the same as for a single sample. The assumptions are also the same: A random sample or a randomized experiment and a normal population distribution of difference scores.

Comparing Proportions with Dependent Samples

We next present methods for comparing proportions with dependent samples.

Example 15

Dependent proportions

Beliefs in Heaven and Hell

Picture the Scenario

A recent General Social Survey asked subjects whether they believed in heaven and whether they believed in hell. For the 1314 subjects who responded, Table 10.18 shows the data in contingency table form. The rows of Table 10.18 are the response categories for belief in heaven. The columns are the same categories for belief in hell. In the U.S. adult population, let p_1 denote the proportion who believe in heaven and let p_2 denote the proportion who believe in hell.

Table 10.18 Beliefs in Heaven and Hell

	Belief in Hell		
Belief in Heaven	**Yes**	**No**	**Total**
Yes	955	162	**1117**
No	9	188	**197**
Total	**964**	**350**	**1314**

Questions to Explore

a. How can we estimate p_1, p_2, and their difference?

b. Are the samples used to estimate p_1 and p_2 independent or dependent samples?

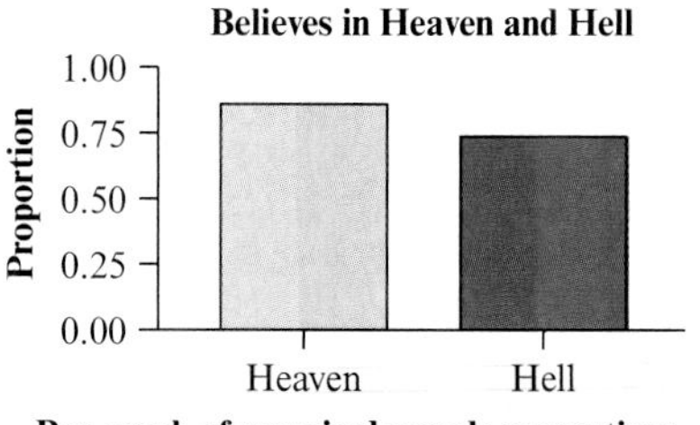

Bar graph of marginal sample proportions

Think It Through

a. The counts in the two margins of Table 10.18 summarize the responses. Of the 1,314 subjects, 1,117 said they believed in heaven, so $\hat{p}_1 = 1117/1314 = 0.85$. Of the same 1,314 subjects, 964 said they believed in hell, so $\hat{p}_2 = 964/1314 = 0.73$. Since $(\hat{p}_1 - \hat{p}_2) = .85 - .73 = 0.12$, we estimate that 12% more people believe in heaven than in hell.

b. Each sample of 1,314 responses refers to the same 1,314 subjects. Any given subject's response on belief in heaven can be matched with that subject's response on belief in hell. This falls under the general concept of measuring each subject twice. So the samples for these two proportions are dependent.

▶ ***Try Exercise 10.60, parts a and b***

Confidence Interval Comparing Proportions with Matched-Pairs Data

Recall

From Section 10.1, the sampling distribution of $\hat{p}_1 - \hat{p}_2$ for two *independent* random samples has standard deviation estimated by the standard error

$$se = \sqrt{\frac{\hat{p}_1(1-\hat{p}_1)}{n_1} + \frac{\hat{p}_2(1-\hat{p}_2)}{n_2}}.$$ ◀

To conduct inference about the difference $(p_1 - p_2)$ between the population proportions, we need a point estimate and a standard error. The point estimate is the difference $\hat{p}_1 - \hat{p}_2$ in the marginal sample proportions, 0.12 for the preceding example. To find the standard error of this point estimate, we *cannot* use the result about the sampling distribution of $\hat{p}_1 - \hat{p}_2$ mentioned in Section 10.1. As the margin note recalls, these results only apply for two independent samples, but here we have two dependent samples (matched pairs).

Instead, we need to use a formula that modifies the standard error from the independent sample case to account for the dependency. We will not give the formula here but rely on software (or the web app) to compute it. With the point estimate and its standard error, we get the usual confidence interval that applies when the sample size is large: Take the point estimate and add and subtract the margin of error, which is a z-score times the se: $(\hat{p}_1 - \hat{p}_2) \pm z(se)$. Usually, software reports this or a related confidence interval under the heading of McNemar's test.

What do we gain by using two dependent samples instead of two independent samples? Typically, the standard error for the difference is smaller when using two dependent samples. A smaller standard error results in more precise inference, such as shorter confidence intervals and smaller P-values. This implies that a matched-pairs design can reach the desired level of precision (e.g., a certain margin of error) with fewer subjects than a comparable design that uses two independent samples. If observations on subjects are expensive, this can result in substantial savings.

Confidence Interval for $p_1 - p_2$ with dependent samples ◀

Example 16

Beliefs in Heaven and Hell

Picture the Scenario

We continue our analysis of the data on belief in heaven and/or hell. When entering the data into software (or the Inference Comparing Two Proportions web app), we get output like the one shown in Table 10.19 in the margin.

Table 10.19 MINITAB Output for Analyzing the Difference of Proportions with Matched-Pairs Data

```
McNemar's Test
Estimated
Difference      95% CI          P
0.11644     (0.097, 0.136) 0.000
Difference = p(Heaven Yes)
           - p(Hell Yes)
```

Question to Explore

Interpret the reported 95% confidence interval.

Think It Through

We've already mentioned that 12% more people believe in heaven than in hell, which is also the point estimate (labeled "Estimated Difference") reported in the output. The output also shows a 95% confidence interval of (0.097, 0.136). With 95% confidence, the proportion of U.S. adults believing in heaven is between 0.10 and 0.14 higher than the proportion of those same adults who believe in hell. In absolute numbers, this means that we are 95% confident that between 10% and 14% more adults believe in heaven than in hell.

▶ ***Try Exercise 10.61, part b***

McNemar Test Comparing Proportions with Matched-Pairs Data

For testing $H_0: p_1 - p_2 = 0$ with two dependent samples, there's actually a simple way to calculate a test statistic. If the null hypothesis is true, that is, if an equal proportion believes in heaven and hell $(p_1 = p_2)$, we expect that the same number of people believe in heaven as believe in hell. Computing the standard error for the difference in the sample proportions under this assumption results in a simple formula. (See Exercise 10.127.) We can then use the usual way to find a test statistic for H_0, which reduces to (skipping the algebra):

a	b
c	d

The four cells of a 2 × 2 contingency table labeled as *a, b, c*, and *d*.

$$z = \frac{\text{estimate} - \text{null value}}{se_0} = \frac{(\hat{p}_1 - \hat{p}_2) - 0}{se_0} = \frac{b - c}{\sqrt{b + c}}$$

Here, b and c refer to the off-diagonal counts in the 2 × 2 contingency table, with b the count in the upper right cell and c the count in the lower left cell. For the contingency table in Example 15, $b = 162$, $c = 9$ and $z = (162 - 9)/\sqrt{162 + 9} = 11.7$.

We have called the test statistic z because it has an approximate standard normal distribution when H_0 is true, which we use for computing the P-value. With $z = 11.7$, the two-sided P-value is extremely small (P-value = 0.000, which is the P-value shown in the computer output of Table 10.19). There is very strong evidence that the proportion of U.S. adults believing in heaven differs from (in fact, is larger than) the proportion believing in hell. This conclusion agrees with the confidence interval for $(p_1 - p_2)$ that we found in Example 16. The advantage of the confidence interval is that it indicates *how different* the proportions are likely to be. In percentage terms, we infer that the belief in heaven is about 10% to 14% higher.

The z test comparing proportions with dependent samples is often called **McNemar's test** in honor of a psychologist (Quinn McNemar) who proposed it in 1947. It is a large-sample test. It applies when the sum, $b + c$, of the two counts used in the test is at least 30 (this sum is $162 + 9 = 171$ for the example above). For two-sided tests, however, the test is robust and works well even for small samples.

SUMMARY: McNemar Test Comparing Proportions from Dependent Samples

Assumption: Random sample of matched pairs

Hypotheses: $H_0: p_1 = p_2$, H_a can be two-sided or one-sided.

Test Statistic: $z = (b - c)/\sqrt{(b + c)}$, where b and c are the off-diagonal elements in the contingency table, with b the one in the first row and c the one in the second row. The sum of the two off-diagonal counts b and c should be at least 30, but in practice the two-sided test works well even if this is not true.

P-value: For $H_a: p_1 \neq p_2$, two-tail probability of z test statistic values more extreme than observed z, using standard normal distribution.

Example 17

McNemar's test

Speech Recognition Systems

Picture the Scenario

Research in comparing the quality of different speech recognition systems uses a series of isolated words as a benchmark test, finding for each system the proportion of words for which an error of recognition occurs. Table 10.20

shows data from one of the first articles[11] that showed how to conduct such a test. The article compared speech recognition systems called generalized minimal distortion segmentation (GMDS) and continuous density hidden Markov model (CDHMM). Table 10.20 shows the counts of the four possible sequences to test outcomes for the two systems with a given word, for a test using 2000 words.

Table 10.20 Results of Test Using 2000 Words to Compare Two Speech Recognition Systems (GMDS and CDHMM)

	CDHMM		
GMDS	**Correct**	**Incorrect**	**Total**
Correct	1921	58	**1979**
Incorrect	16	5	**21**
Total	**1937**	**63**	**2000**

Question to Explore

Conduct McNemar's test of the null hypothesis that the probability of a correct outcome is the same for each system.

Think It Through

The article about this test did not indicate how the words were chosen. Inferences are valid if the 2000 words were a random sample of the possible words on which the systems could have been tested. Let p_1 denote the population proportion of correct results for GMDS and let p_2 denote the population proportion correct for CDHMM. The test statistic for McNemar's test of H_0: $p_1 = p_2$ against H_a: $p_1 \neq p_2$ is

$$z = \frac{58 - 16}{\sqrt{58 + 16}} = 4.88.$$

The two-sided P-value is 0.000001. There is extremely strong evidence against the null hypothesis that the correct detection rates are the same for the two systems.

Insight

We learn more by estimating parameters. A confidence interval for $p_1 - p_2$ indicates that the GMDS system is better, but the difference in correct detection rates is small. See Exercise 10.60.

▶ ***Try Exercise 10.61, part c***

[11]From S. Chen and W. Chen, *IEEE Transactions on Speech and Audio Processing*, vol. 3, 1995, pp. 141–145.

10.4 Practicing the Basics

10.49 Does exercise help blood pressure? TRY Several recent studies have suggested that people who suffer from abnormally high blood pressure can benefit from regular exercise. A medical researcher decides to test her belief that walking briskly for at least half an hour a day has the effect of lowering blood pressure. She conducts a small pilot study. If results from it are supportive, she will apply for funding for a larger study. She randomly samples three of her patients who have high blood pressure. She measures their systolic blood pressure initially and then again a month later after they participate in her exercise program. The table shows the results.

Subject	Before	After
1	150	130
2	165	140
3	135	120

a. Explain why the three before observations and the three after observations are dependent samples.

b. Find the sample mean of the before scores, the sample mean of the after scores, and the sample mean of the difference scores d = before − after. How are they related?

c. Find a 95% confidence interval for the difference between the population means of subjects before and after going through such a study. Interpret.

10.50 Test for blood pressure Refer to the previous exercise. TRY The output shows some results of using software to analyze the data with a significance test.

```
Paired T for Before-After
              N     Mean    StDev    SE Mean
Before        3    150.0     15.0      8.660
After         3    130.0     10.0      5.774
Difference    3     20.0      5.0      2.887
T-Test of mean difference = 0 (vs ≠ 0):
T-Value = 6.93 P-Value = 0.020
```

a. State the hypotheses to which the reported P-value refers.

b. Explain how to interpret the P-value. Does the exercise program seem beneficial to lowering blood pressure?

c. What are the assumptions on which this analysis is based?

10.51 Social activities for students As part of her class project, a student at the University of Florida randomly sampled 10 fellow students to investigate their most common social activities. As part of the study, she asked the students to state how many times they had done each of the following activities during the previous year: going to a movie, going to a sporting event, or going to a party. The table shows the data.

Frequency of Attending Movies, Sports Events, and Parties

	Activity		
Student	Movies	Sports	Parties
1	10	5	25
2	4	0	10
3	12	20	6
4	2	6	52
5	12	2	12
6	7	8	30
7	45	12	52
8	1	25	2
9	25	0	25
10	12	12	4

a. To compare the mean movie attendance and mean sports attendance using statistical inference, should we treat the samples as independent or dependent? Why?

b. The figure is a dot plot of the $n = 10$ difference scores for movies and sports. Does this show any irregularities that would make statistical inference unreliable?

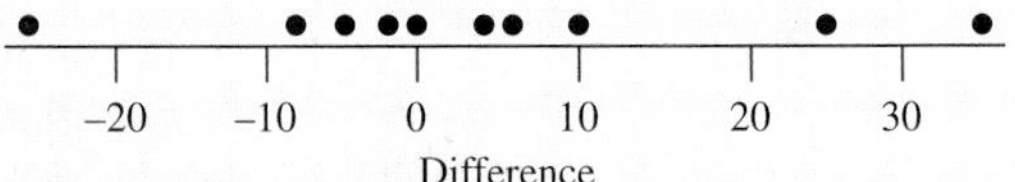

Dot plot of difference scores.

c. Using the MINITAB output shown for these data, show how the 95% confidence interval was obtained from the other information given in the printout. Interpret the interval.

d. Show how the test statistic shown on the printout was obtained from the other information given. Report the P-value and interpret in context.

MINITAB Output for Inferential Analyses:

```
Paired T for Movies - Sports
              N     Mean    StDev    SE Mean
Movies       10    13.00    13.17       4.17
Sports       10     9.00     8.38       2.65
Difference   10     4.00    16.17       5.11
95% CI for mean difference: (-7.56, 15.56)
T-Test of mean difference = 0 (vs ≠ 0):
T-Value = 0.78 P-Value = 0.454
```

10.52 More social activities Refer to the previous exercise. The output shows the result of comparing the mean responses on parties and sports.

```
Paired T for Parties - Sports
              N     Mean    StDev    SE Mean
Parties      10    21.80    18.58       5.87
Sports       10     9.00     8.38       2.65
Difference   10    12.80    22.55       7.13
95% CI for mean difference: (-3.33, 28.93)
T-Test of mean difference = 0 (vs ≠ 0):
T-Value = 1.80 P-Value = 0.106
```

a. Explain how to interpret the reported 95% confidence interval.

b. State the hypotheses to which the P-value refers and interpret its value.

c. Explain the connection between the results of the test and the confidence interval.

d. What assumptions are necessary for these inferences to be appropriate?

10.53 Movies versus parties Refer to the previous two exercises. TECH Using software, compare the responses on movies and parties using (a) all steps of a significance test and (b) a 95% confidence interval. Interpret results in context.

10.54 Freshman 15 a myth? The freshman 15 is the name of a common belief that college students, particularly women, gain an average of 15 pounds during their first year of college. A recent study (*Journal of American Health*, vol. 58, 2009, pp. 223–231) found that female students weighed an average of 133.0 pounds at the start of the school year and an average of 135.1 pounds at the end of the school year. The standard deviation of weights was about 30 pounds at each time. Other reports have been consistent with this finding.

a. Estimate the change in the mean weight.

b. Is this sufficient information to find a confidence interval or conduct a test about the change in the mean? If not, what else do you need to know?

10.55 Checking for freshman 15 Refer to the previous exercise. Suppose that the change in weight scores for the 132 freshmen had a standard deviation of 2.0 pounds.

a. Explain how this standard deviation could be so much less than the standard deviation of 30 for the weight scores at each time.

b. Is 15 pounds a plausible mean weight change in the population of freshman women? Answer by constructing a 95% confidence interval for the population mean change in weight or conducting a significance test of the hypothesis that the mean weight change in the population equals 15. Interpret.

c. What assumptions are necessary for the inference in part b?

10.56 Internet book prices TECH Anna's project for her introductory statistics course was to compare the selling prices of textbooks at two Internet bookstores. She first took a random sample of 10 textbooks used that term in courses at her college, based on the list of texts compiled by the college bookstore. The prices of those textbooks at the two Internet sites were

Site A: \$115, \$79, \$43, \$140, \$99, \$30, \$80, \$99, \$119, \$69
Site B: \$110, \$79, \$40, \$129, \$99, \$30, \$69, \$99, \$109, \$66

a. Are these independent samples or dependent samples? Justify your answer.

b. Find the mean for each sample. Find the mean of the difference scores. Compare and interpret.

c. Using software or a calculator, construct a 90% confidence interval comparing the population mean prices of all textbooks used that term at her college. Interpret.

10.57 Comparing book prices 2 TECH For the data in the previous exercise, use software or a calculator to perform a significance test comparing the population mean prices. Show all steps of the test and indicate whether you would conclude that the mean price is lower at one of the two Internet bookstores.

10.58 Lung capacity revisited TECH Refer to Exercise 10.34 about measuring the lung function (called the forced vital capacity, or FVC, measured in liters) before and after using an inhaler. The data are shown again in the following table.

	Checkup				
	1	2	3	4	5
Before using inhaler:	5.08	5.99	5.32	6.03	5.44
After using inhaler:	5.36	5.98	5.62	6.26	5.68

a. By how much, on average, did the FVC improve after using the inhaler?

b. Find a 95% confidence interval for the mean improvement and interpret.

c. Suppose you wrongly analyzed the data as two independent samples. Find the confidence interval for the difference in the population means and show how the conclusions would change substantially.

10.59 Comparing speech recognition systems Table 10.20 in Example 17, repeated here, showed results of an experiment comparing the results of two speech recognition systems, GMDS and CDHMM.

	CDHMM	
GMDS	**Correct**	**Incorrect**
Correct	1921	58
Incorrect	16	5

a. Estimate the population proportion p_1 of correct results for GMDS and p_2 of correct results for CDHMM.

b. Software reports a 95% interval for $p_1 - p_2$ of (0.013, 0.029). Interpret.

10.60 Treat juveniles as adults? TRY The table that follows refers to a sample of juveniles convicted of a felony in Florida. Matched pairs were formed using criteria such as age and the number of prior offenses. For each pair, one subject was handled in the juvenile court and the other was transferred to the adult court. The response of interest was whether the juvenile was rearrested within a year.

a. Are the outcomes for the courts independent samples or dependent samples? Explain.

b. Estimate the population proportions of rearrest for the adult and juvenile courts.

c. Test the hypothesis that the population proportions rearrested were identical for the adult and juvenile court assignments. Use a two-sided alternative, and interpret the P-value.

	Juvenile Court	
Adult Court	**Rearrest**	**No Rearrest**
Rearrest	158	515
No Rearrest	290	1134

Source: Data provided by Larry Winner.

10.61 Change coffee brand? TRY A study was conducted to see if an advertisement campaign would increase market share for Sanka instant decaffeinated coffee (R. Grover and V. Srinivasan, *J. Marketing Research*, vol. 24, 1987, pp. 139–153). Subjects who use instant decaffeinated coffee were asked which brand they bought last. They were asked this before the campaign and after it. The results are shown in the table, with computer output based on it below.

a. Estimate the population proportion choosing Sanka for the (i) first purchase and (ii) second purchase. Find the difference and interpret it.

b. Explain how to interpret the 95% confidence interval.

c. The software output also shows a P-value. State the hypotheses that this P-value refers to in the context of this exercise and give the conclusion of the test when using a significance level of 0.05.

Two Purchases of Coffee

	Second Purchase	
First Purchase	**Sanka**	**Other Brand**
Sanka	155	49
Other brand	76	261

```
McNemar's Test
Estimated
Difference           95% CI               P
 -0.0499      (-0.0920, -0.0078)      0.020
 Difference = p(First Purchase) - p(Second
 Purchase Sanka)
```

10.62 President's popularity Last month a random sample of 1000 subjects was interviewed and asked whether they thought the president was doing a good job. This month the same subjects were asked this again. The results are: 450 said yes each time, 450 said no each time, 60 said yes on the first survey and no on the second survey, and 40 said no on the first survey and yes on the second survey.

a. Form a contingency table showing these results.

b. Estimate the proportion giving a favorable rating (i) last month and (ii) this month.

c. Find the difference in the proportions and interpret.

d. Find the test statistic and P-value for applying McNemar's test that the population proportion was the same each month. Interpret.

10.63 Heaven and hell Results of polls about belief in heaven and hell depend strongly on question wording. For instance, a survey conducted by the International Social Science Program at the National Opinion Research Center (NORC) asked Americans whether they "definitely believe in heaven" or "definitely believe in hell." The percentage who answered yes was 63.1% for heaven and 49.6% for hell.

a. Estimate the difference between the population proportions believing in heaven and believing in hell.

b. In this survey, suppose that 65 subjects believed in heaven but not in hell, whereas 35 believed in hell but not in heaven. Report the (i) assumptions, (ii) hypotheses, (iii) test statistic, (iv) P-value, and (v) conclusion for testing that the probability of belief is the same for heaven and for hell.

10.64 Heaven and hell around the world Refer to the previous exercise. Results in this poll also depended strongly on the country in which the question was asked. For instance, the percentages believing in (heaven, hell) were (52%, 26%) in Ireland, (32%, 19%) in New Zealand, (28%, 22%) in Italy, (25%, 13%) in Great Britain, (21%, 11%) in the Netherlands, and (18%, 9%) in Germany. If for a given country you know the sample size was 1000, does this give you enough information to compare the two proportions inferentially for that country? Explain.

10.5 Adjusting for the Effects of Other Variables

When a practically significant difference exists between two groups, can we identify a reason for the difference? As Chapters 3 and 4 explained, an association may be due to a *lurking variable* not measured in the study. Example 5 in Section 10.1 indicated that teenagers who watch more TV have a tendency later in life to commit more aggressive acts. Why? Might education be a lurking variable? Perhaps teenagers who watch more TV tend to attain lower educational levels, and perhaps lower education tends to be associated with higher levels of aggression.

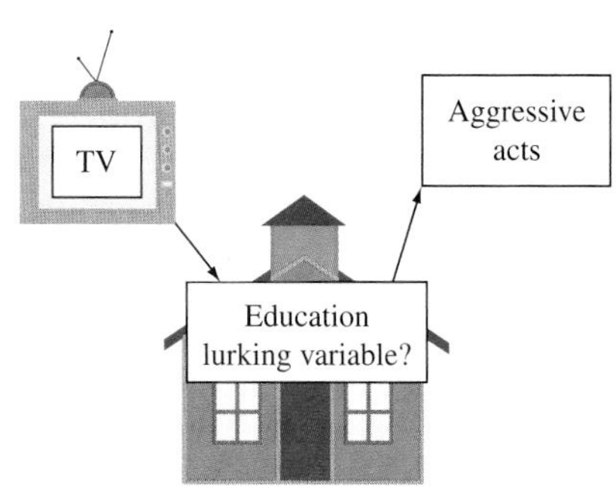

To investigate why differences occur between groups, we must measure potential lurking variables and use them in the statistical analysis. For instance, suppose we planned to study TV watching and aggression, and we thought that educational level was a potential lurking variable. Then, in the study we would want to measure educational level.

Let's examine the TV study again. Suppose we did so using categories (did not complete high school, did not attend college, attended college). We could then evaluate TV watching and aggressive behavior separately for subjects in these three educational levels and obtain the results in Table 10.21.

This analysis uses three variables—level of TV watching, committing of aggressive acts, and educational level. This takes us from a **bivariate** analysis (two variables) to a **multivariate** analysis (more than two variables): Whether the subject has committed aggressive acts is the response variable, the level of TV watching is the explanatory variable, and the educational level is called a **control variable.**

Recall

You can review Section 3.4 to see how **lurking variables** can influence an association. ◀

Table 10.21 Percentage Committing Aggressive Acts, According to Level of Teenage TV Watching, Controlling for Educational Level

For example, for those who attended college who watched TV less than 1 hour per day, 2% committed an aggressive act.

	Educational Level		
TV Watching	**Less than High School**	**High School**	**College**
Less than 1 hour per day	8%	4%	2%
At least 1 hour per day	30%	20%	10%

Control Variable

A **control variable** is a variable that is held constant in a multivariate analysis.

Table 10.21 treats educational level as a control variable. Within each of the three education groups, educational level is approximately constant.

Statistical Control

To analyze whether an association can be explained by a third variable, we treat that third variable as a control variable. We conduct the ordinary bivariate analysis, such as comparing two proportions, while holding that control variable constant at fixed values. Then, whatever association occurs cannot be due to effects of the control variable, because in each part of the analysis it is not allowed to vary.

In Table 10.21, at each educational level, the percentage committing an aggressive act is higher for those who watched more TV. If these were the actual results, then the association between TV watching and aggressive acts was not because of education. In each part of Table 10.21, educational level is approximately constant, so changes in aggression as TV watching varies are not due to changes in educational level. To conduct inference, we could use the methods of this chapter to compare the population proportions of aggression at each education level.

Conducting a statistical analysis while holding a control variable constant occurs in scientific laboratory experiments, too. Such experiments hold certain variables constant so they do not affect results. For instance, a chemistry experiment might control temperature by holding it constant throughout the experiment. Otherwise, a sudden increase or decrease in the temperature might cause a reaction that would not happen normally. Unlike experiments, observational studies cannot assign subjects to particular values of variables that we want to control, such as educational level. But we can approximate an experimental control by grouping observations with similar values on the control variable, as just described. This is a **statistical control** rather than an experimental control.

The next example shows that if we control for a variable, the results can look quite different than if we do not take that control variable into account.

Example 18

Control variables ◀

Death Penalty and Race

Picture the Scenario

The United States is one of only a few Western nations that still imposes the death penalty. Are those convicted of murder more likely to get the death penalty if they are black than if they are white?

Table 10.22 comes from one of the first studies on racial inequities of the death penalty.[12] The 326 subjects were defendants convicted of homicide in Florida murder trials. The variables are the defendant's race and whether the defendant received the death penalty. The contingency table shows that about 12% of white defendants and about 10% of black defendants received the death penalty.

Table 10.22 Defendant's Race and Death Penalty Verdict for Homicide Cases in Florida

	Death Penalty			
Defendant's Race	**Yes**	**No**	**Total**	**Percentage Yes**
White	19	141	160	11.9
Black	17	149	166	10.2

In this study, the difference between the percentages of white defendants and black defendants who received the death penalty is small (1.7%), but the percentage was lower for black defendants.

Is there some explanation for these results? Does a control variable lurk that explains why relatively fewer black defendants got the death penalty in Florida? Researchers who study the death penalty stress that the *victim's* race is often an important factor. So, let's control for victim's race. We'll construct a table like Table 10.22 *separately* for cases in which the victim was white and for cases in which the victim was black. Table 10.23 shows this three-variable table.

Table 10.23 shows the effect of a defendant's race on the death penalty verdict while controlling for victim's race, that is, when victim's race is kept constant at white or kept constant at black. Table 10.23 decomposes Table 10.22 into two contingency tables, one for each victim's race. You can recover Table 10.22 by summing corresponding entries, $19 + 0 = 19$, $132 + 9 = 141$, $11 + 6 = 17$, and $52 + 97 = 149$.

Table 10.23 Defendant's Race and Death Penalty Verdict, Controlling for Victim's Race

		Death Penalty			
Victim's Race	**Defendant's Race**	**Yes**	**No**	**Total**	**Percentage Yes**
White	White	19	132	151	12.6
	Black	11	52	63	17.5
Black	White	0	9	9	0.0
	Black	6	97	103	5.8

Questions to Explore

a. Summarize the association between a defendant's race and the death penalty verdict in Florida after controlling for victim's race.

b. Describe the difference in the results between ignoring and controlling victim's race.

c. Why does the control for victim's race make such a difference?

Think It Through

a. The top part of Table 10.23 lists cases in which the victim's race was white. Relatively more black defendants than white defendants got

[12] M. Radelet, *American Sociological Review*, vol. 46, 1981, pp. 918–927.

the death penalty in Florida. The difference between the percentages is 17.5 − 12.6 = 4.9. The bottom part of the table lists cases in which the victim's race was black. Again, relatively more black defendants got the death penalty. The difference between the percentages is 5.8 − 0.0 = 5.8. In summary, controlling for victim's race, more black defendants than white defendants received the death penalty in Florida.

b. Table 10.22 showed that a *larger* percentage of white defendants than black defendants got the death penalty. By contrast, controlling for victim's race, Table 10.23 showed that a *smaller* percentage of white defendants than black defendants got the death penalty. This was true for each victim's race category.

c. In Table 10.23, look at the percentages who got the death penalty. When the victim was white, they are quite a bit larger (12.6 and 17.5) than when the victim was black (0.0 and 5.8). That is, defendants who killed a white person were more likely to get the death penalty. Now look at the totals for the four combinations of victim's race and defendant's race. The most common cases are white defendants having white victims (151 times) and black defendants having black victims (103 times). In summary, white defendants usually had white victims and black defendants usually had black victims. Killing a white person was more likely to result in the death penalty than killing a black person. These two factors operating together produce an overall association that shows (in Table 10.22) that a higher percentage of white defendants than black defendants got the death penalty.

Insight

Overall, relatively more white defendants in Florida got the death penalty than black defendants. Controlling for victim's race, however, relatively more black defendants got the death penalty. The effect changes direction after we control for victim's race. This shows that the association at each level of a control variable can have a different direction than overall when that third variable is ignored instead of controlled. This phenomenon is called **Simpson's paradox**.

In Table 10.23, the death penalty was imposed most often when a black defendant had a white victim. By contrast, it was never imposed when a white defendant had a black victim. Similar results have occurred in other studies of the death penalty. See Exercises 10.66 and 3.58.

▶ ***Try Exercise 10.66***

Recall

Section 3.4 first introduced **Simpson's paradox.** It is named after a British statistician who wrote an article in 1951 about mathematical conditions under which the association can change direction when you control for a variable. ◀

With statistical control imposed for a variable, the results tend to change considerably when that control variable has a strong association both with the response variable and the explanatory variable. In Example 18, for instance, victim's race was the control variable. Victim's race had a noticeable association both with the death penalty response (the death penalty was given more often when the victim was white) and with defendant's race (defendants and victims usually had the same race).

Recall

From the end of Section 3.4, we say that defendant's race and victim's race are confounded in their effects on the death penalty verdict. ◀

In Practice Control for Variables Associated Both with the Response and Explanatory Variables

In determining which variables to control in observational studies, *researchers choose variables that they expect to have a practically significant association with both the response variable and the explanatory variable.* A statistical analysis that controls such variables can have quite different results than when those variables are ignored.

Statistical control is also relevant when the response variable is quantitative. The difference between means for two groups can change substantially after controlling for a third variable. See Exercise 10.68.

▶ Activity 1

Interpreting Newspaper Articles

This chapter began by stating that many newspaper articles describe research studies that use the statistical methods of this chapter. At this stage of your statistics course, you should be able to read and understand those articles much better than you could before you knew the basis of such terms as margin of error, statistical significance, and randomized clinical trial.

For the next three days, read a daily newspaper such as *The New York Times*. Make a copy of any article you see that refers to a study that used statistics to help make its conclusions. For one article, prepare a one-page report that answers the following questions:

- What was the purpose of the study?
- Was the study experimental or observational? Can you provide any details about the study design and sampling method?
- Identify explanatory and response variables.
- Can you tell whether the statistical analysis used (1) independent samples or dependent samples and (2) a comparison of proportions or a comparison of means?
- Can you think of any lurking variables that could have affected the results?
- Are there any limitations that would make you skeptical to put much faith in the conclusions of the study?

You might find additional information to answer these questions by browsing the Web or going to the research journal that published the results.

10.5 Practicing the Basics

10.65 Benefits of drinking A *USA Today* story (May 22, 2010) about the medical benefits of moderate drinking of alcohol stated that a major French study links those who drink moderately to a lower risk for cardiovascular disease but challenges the idea that moderate drinking is the cause. "Instead, the researchers say, people who drink moderately tend to have a higher social status, exercise more, suffer less depression and enjoy superior health overall compared to heavy drinkers and lifetime abstainers. A causal relationship between cardiovascular risk and moderate drinking is not at all established." The study looked at the health status and drinking habits of 149,773 French adults.

a. Explain how this story refers to an analysis of three types of variables. Identify those variables.

b. Suppose socioeconomic status is treated as a control variable when we compare moderate drinkers to abstainers in their heart attack rates. Explain how this analysis shows that an effect of an explanatory variable on a response variable can change at different values of a control variable.

10.66 Death penalty in Kentucky A study of the death penalty in Kentucky reported the results shown in the table. (*Source*: Data from T. Keil and G. Vito, *Amer. J. Criminal Justice*, vol. 20, 1995, pp. 17–36.)

TRY

a. Find and compare the percentage of white defendants with the percentage of black defendants who received the death penalty, when the victim was (i) white and (ii) black.

b. In the analysis in part a, identify the response variable, explanatory variable, and control variable.

c. Construct the summary 2 × 2 table that ignores, rather than controls, victim's race. Compare the overall percentages of white defendants and black defendants who got the death penalty (ignoring, rather than controlling, victim's race). Compare to part a.

d. Do these data satisfy Simpson's paradox? If not, explain why not. If so, explain what is responsible for Simpson's paradox occurring.

e. Explain, without doing the calculations, how you could inferentially compare the proportions of white and black defendants who get the death penalty (i) ignoring victim's race and (ii) controlling for victim's race.

Victim's Race	Defendant's Race	Death Penalty Yes	Death Penalty No	Total
White	White	31	360	391
	Black	7	50	57
Black	White	0	18	18
	Black	2	106	108

10.67 Basketball paradox The following list summarizes shooting percentage in the 2001–2002 season in the National Basketball Association by Brent Barry and Shaquille O'Neal.

2-point shots

- Brent Barry: 58.8% (237/403)
- Shaquille O'Neal: 58.0% (712/1228)

3-point shots

- Brent Barry: 42.4% (164/387)
- Shaquille O'Neal: 0% (0/1)

Overall

- Brent Barry: 50.8% (401/790)
- Shaquille O'Neal: 57.9% (712/1229)

(Data from www.nba.com and article by T. P. Ryan, *Chance,* vol. 16, 2003, p. 16.)

a. Treating the type of shot as a control variable, whether a shot is made as the response variable, and the player as the explanatory variable, explain how these results illustrate Simpson's paradox.

b. Explain how O'Neal could have the higher overall percentage, even though he made a lower percentage of each type of shot.

10.68 Teacher salary, gender, and academic rank The American Association of University Professors (AAUP) reports yearly on faculty salaries for all types of higher education institutions across the United States. The following table lists the mean salary, in thousands of dollars, of full-time instructional faculty on nine-month contracts at four-year public institutions of higher education in 2010, by gender and academic rank. Regard salary as the response variable, gender as the explanatory variable, and academic rank as the control variable.

Mean Salary (Thousands of Dollars) for Men and Women Faculty Members

	Academic Rank				
Gender	**Professor**	**Associate**	**Assistant**	**Instructor**	**Overall**
Men	109.2	77.8	66.1	46.0	84.4
Women	96.2	72.7	61.8	46.9	68.8

a. Find the difference between men and women faculty members on their mean salary (i) overall and (ii) after controlling for academic rank.

b. The overall difference between the mean salary of men and women faculty members was larger than the difference at each academic rank. What could be a reason for this? (Simpson's paradox does not hold here, but the gender effect does weaken when we control for academic rank.)

10.69 Family size in Canada The table shows the mean number of children in Canadian families, classified by whether the family was English speaking or French speaking and by whether the family lived in Quebec or in another province.

Mean Number of Children in Canada

Province	**English Speaking**	**French Speaking**
Quebec	1.64	1.80
Other	1.97	2.14
Overall	1.95	1.85

a. Overall, compare the mean number of children for English-speaking and French-speaking families.

b. Compare the means, controlling for province (Quebec, Other).

c. How is it possible that for each level of province the mean is higher for French-speaking families, yet overall the mean is higher for English-speaking families? Which paradox does this illustrate?

10.70 Heart disease and age In the United States, the median age of residents is lowest in Utah. At each age level, the death rate from heart disease is higher in Utah than in Colorado. Overall, the death rate from heart disease is lower in Utah than Colorado. Are there any contradictions here, or is this possible? Explain.

10.71 Breast cancer over time The percentage of women who get breast cancer sometime during their lifetime is higher now than in 1900. Suppose that breast cancer incidence tends to increase with age, and suppose that women tend to live longer now than in 1900. Explain why a comparison of breast cancer rates now with the rate in 1900 could show different results if we control for the age of the woman.

Chapter Review

ANSWERS TO THE CHAPTER FIGURE QUESTIONS

Figure 10.2 $\hat{p}_1 - \hat{p}_2$ represents the difference between the sample proportions suffering a cancer death with placebo and with aspirin. $p_1 - p_2$ represents the difference between the population proportions. The mean of this sampling distribution is zero if cancer death rates are identical for aspirin and placebo.

Figure 10.3 If the interval contains only negative values, $p_1 - p_2$ is predicted to be negative, so p_1 is predicted to be smaller than p_2. If the interval contains only positive values, p_1 is predicted to be larger than p_2.

Figure 10.4 A histogram of the ratings in each group to get a better idea about the possible shape of the population distribution in each group.

Figure 10.5 Positive numbers in the confidence interval for $(\mu_1 - \mu_2)$ suggest that $\mu_1 - \mu_2 > 0$ and, thus, that $\mu_1 > \mu_2$.

Figure 10.6 The box plot for the cell phone group indicates an extreme outlier. It's important to check that the results of the analysis aren't affected too strongly by that single observation.

Figure 10.7 One histogram will show more variability (a larger spread) than the other.

Figure 10.8 The top one, because it has the two largest observations in the high group and the three smallest observations in the low group, resulting in the largest possible separation (difference) in the sample means.

Figure 10.9 If n_1 and n_2 were large, the sampling distribution of $\bar{x}_1 - \bar{x}_2$ is approximately normal.

Figure 10.10 Yes, it is located far out in the upper tail of the sampling distribution.

Figure 10.11 The outliers for the two distributions are both from subject number 28.

Figure 10.12 This plot represents a student's difference score in reaction time using the cell phone minus the reaction time not using it. Some students had a slower reaction time when not using the cell phone, resulting in a negative difference.

CHAPTER SUMMARY

This chapter introduced inferential methods for comparing two groups.

- For categorical data, we compare the *proportions* of individuals in a particular category. Confidence intervals and significance tests apply to the difference between the population proportions, $(p_1 - p_2)$, for the two groups. The test of H_0: $p_1 = p_2$ analyzes whether the population proportions are equal. If the test has a small P-value, or if the confidence interval for $(p_1 - p_2)$ does not contain 0, we conclude that they differ.
- For quantitative data, we compare the *means* for the two groups. Confidence intervals and significance tests apply to $(\mu_1 - \mu_2)$.

Table 10.24 summarizes two-sided estimation and testing methods for large, **independent random samples**. This is the most common case in practice.

Table 10.24 Comparing Two Groups for Large, Independent Random Samples

	Type of Response Variable	
	Categorical	**Quantitative**
Estimation		
1. Parameter	$p_1 - p_2$	$\mu_1 - \mu_2$
2. Point estimate	$(\hat{p}_1 - \hat{p}_2)$	$(\bar{x}_1 - \bar{x}_2)$
3. Standard error (se)	$\sqrt{\frac{\hat{p}_1(1-\hat{p}_1)}{n_1} + \frac{\hat{p}_2(1-\hat{p}_2)}{n_2}}$	$\sqrt{\frac{s_1^2}{n_1} + \frac{s_2^2}{n_2}}$
4. 95% confidence int.	$(\hat{p}_1 - \hat{p}_2) \pm 1.96(se)$	$(\bar{x}_1 - \bar{x}_2) \pm t_{.025}(se)$
Significance Test		
1. Assumptions	Randomization with at least five of each type for each group if using a 2-sided alternative	Randomization from Normal population (test robust)
2. Hypotheses	H_0: $p_1 = p_2$ $(p_1 - p_2 = 0)$ H_a: $p_1 \neq p_2$	H_0: $\mu_1 = \mu_2$ $(\mu_1 - \mu_2 = 0)$ H_a: $\mu_1 \neq \mu_2$
3. Test statistic	$z = (\hat{p}_1 - \hat{p}_2)/se_0$ $se_0 = \sqrt{\hat{p}(1-\hat{p})\left(\frac{1}{n_1} + \frac{1}{n_2}\right)}$ with $\hat{p}$ = pooled proportion	$t = (\bar{x}_1 - \bar{x}_2)/se$ can also use se $= s\sqrt{\frac{1}{n_1} + \frac{1}{n_2}}$ with s = pooled standard deviation
4. P-value	Two-tail probability from standard normal distribution	Two-tail probability from t distribution
5. Conclusion	Interpret P-value in context. Reject H_0 if P-value $\leq \alpha$	Interpret P-value in context. Reject H_0 if P-value $\leq \alpha$

Both for differences of proportions and differences of means, confidence intervals have the form

$$\text{Estimate} \pm (z\text{- or } t\text{-score})(\text{standard error}),$$

such as for 95% confidence intervals,

$$(\hat{p}_1 - \hat{p}_2) \pm 1.96(se), \text{ and } (\bar{x}_1 - \bar{x}_2) \pm t_{.025}(se).$$

For significance tests, the test statistic equals the estimated difference divided by the standard error, $z = (\hat{p}_1 - \hat{p}_2)/se_0$ and $t = (\bar{x}_1 - \bar{x}_2)/se$.

When assumptions underlying the t test are in doubt, a **permutation test** looks at thousands of permutations of the original data to see whether the observed difference in sample means is extreme.

With **dependent samples**, each observation in one sample is matched with an observation in the other sample. This occurs, for instance, when the same subject is measured twice. We compare means by analyzing the mean of the differences between the paired observations. The confidence interval and test procedures apply one-sample methods to the difference scores. For comparing marginal proportions in 2×2 contingency tables, specialized methods (McNemar's test) are used.

At this stage, you may feel confused about which method to use for any given exercise. It may help if you use the following checklist. Ask yourself, do you have

- Means or proportions (a quantitative or categorical response variable)?
- Independent samples or dependent samples?
- Confidence interval or significance test?
- Large n_1 and n_2 or not?

In practice, most applications have large, independent samples, and confidence intervals are more useful than tests. So the following cases are especially important: confidence intervals comparing proportions with large independent samples, and confidence intervals comparing means with large independent samples.

SUMMARY OF NOTATION

A subscript index identifies the group number. For instance,

n_1 = sample size for Group 1; n_2 = sample size for Group 2.

Likewise for population means μ_1, μ_2, sample means $\bar{x}_1, \bar{x}_2$, sample standard deviations s_1, s_2, population proportions p_1, p_2, sample proportions $\hat{p}_1, \hat{p}_2$. For dependent samples, $\bar{x}_d$ and μ_d are sample mean and population mean of difference scores, and s_d is standard deviation of difference scores.

CHAPTER PROBLEMS

Practicing the Basics

10.72 Pick the method Steve Solomon, the owner of Leonardo's Italian restaurant, wonders whether a redesigned menu will increase, on the average, the amount that customers spend in the restaurant. For the following scenarios, pick a statistical method from this chapter that would be appropriate for analyzing the data, indicating whether the samples are independent or dependent, which parameter is relevant, and what inference method you would use:

a. Solomon records the mean sales the week before the change and the week after the change and then wonders whether the difference is "statistically significant."

b. Solomon randomly samples 100 people and shows them each both menus, asking them to give a rating between 0 and 10 for each menu.

c. Solomon randomly samples 100 people and shows them each both menus, asking them to give an overall rating of positive or negative to each menu.

d. Solomon randomly samples 100 people and randomly separates them into two groups of 50 each. He asks those in Group 1 to give a rating to the old menu and those in Group 2 to give a rating to the new menu, using a 0 to 10 rating scale.

10.73 Public versus scientists' opinions on fracking A Pew Research Center survey of 2002 U.S. adults in August 2014 and a survey of 3748 scientists connected to the American Association for the Advancement of Science (AAAS) in September 2014 both asked the following question: "Do you favor or oppose the increased use of fracking?" In the Pew Research Center survey, fracking was favored by 37%, whereas in the survey of scientists, it was favored by 31%. Both surveys used random samples.

a. Identify the response variable and the explanatory variable.

b. To conduct inference, should we treat the sample of U.S. adults and the sample of scientists from the AAAS as dependent or as independent? Explain.

c. The AAAS survey also asked each of the 3748 scientists whether they favor or oppose more offshore oil and gas drilling. Thirty-two percent responded that they favor it. To compare this to the percentage who favored fracking, should you treat the samples as dependent or as independent? Why?

10.74 BMI then and now The Centers for Disease Control (www.cdc.gov) periodically administers large randomized surveys to track health of Americans. In a survey of 4431 adults in 2003/2004, 66% were overweight (body mass index BMI ≥ 25). In the most recently available survey of 5181 adults in 2011/2012, 69% were overweight.

a. Estimate the change in the population proportion who are overweight and interpret.

b. The standard error for estimating this difference equals 0.0096. What is the main factor that causes *se* to be so small?

c. The 95% confidence interval comparing the population proportions in 2011/2012 to the one in 2003/2004 is (0.011, 0.049). Interpret, taking into account whether 0 is in this interval.

10.75 Marijuana and gender In a survey conducted by Wright State University, senior high school students were asked if they had ever used marijuana. The table shows results of one analysis, where X is the count who said yes. Assuming these observations can be treated as a random sample from a population of interest,

a. Interpret the reported estimate and the reported confidence interval. Explain how to interpret the fact that 0 is not in the confidence interval.

b. Explain how the confidence interval would change if males were Group 1 and females were Group 2. Express an interpretation for the interval in that case.

```
Sample          X       N       Sample p
1. Female      445     1120     0.3973
2. Male        515     1156     0.4455
estimate for p(1) - p(2):      -0.0482
95% CI for p(1) - p(2): (-0.0887, -0.0077)
```

10.76 Gender and belief in afterlife The table shows results from the 2014 General Social Survey on gender and whether one believes in an afterlife.

	Belief in Afterlife		
Gender	**Yes**	**No**	**Total**
Female	1026	207	1233
Male	757	252	1009

a. Denote the population proportion who believe in an afterlife by p_1 for females and by p_2 for males. Estimate p_1, p_2, and $(p_1 - p_2)$.

b. Find the standard error for the estimate of $(p_1 - p_2)$. Interpret.

c. Construct a 95% confidence interval for $(p_1 - p_2)$. Can you conclude which of p_1 and p_2 is larger? Explain.

d. Suppose that, unknown to us, $p_1 = 0.81$ and $p_2 = 0.72$. Does the confidence interval in part c contain the parameter it is designed to estimate? Explain.

10.77 Belief depend on gender? Refer to the previous exercise.

a. Find the standard error of $(\hat{p}_1 - \hat{p}_2)$ for a test of H_0: $p_1 = p_2$.

b. For a two-sided test, find the test statistic and P-value and make a decision using significance level 0.05. Interpret.

c. Suppose that actually $p_1 = 0.81$ and $p_2 = 0.72$. Was the decision in part b in error?

d. State the assumptions on which the methods in this exercise are based.

10.78 Females or males have more close friends? A recent GSS reported that the 486 surveyed females had a mean of 8.3 close friends $(s = 15.6)$ and the 354 surveyed males had a mean of 8.9 close friends $(s = 15.5)$.

a. Estimate the difference between the population means for males and females.

b. The 95% confidence interval for the difference between the population means is 0.6 ± 2.1. Interpret.

c. For each gender, does it seem like the distribution of number of close friends is normal? Why? How does this affect the validity of the confidence interval in part b?

10.79 Heavier horseshoe crabs more likely to mate? A study of a sample of horseshoe crabs on a Florida island (J. Brockmann, *Ethology*, vol. 102, 1996, pp. 1–21) investigated the factors that were associated with whether female crabs had a male crab mate. Basic statistics, including the five-number summary on weight (kg) for the 111 female crabs who had a male crab nearby and for the 62 female crabs who did not have a male crab nearby, are given in the table. Assume that these horseshoe crabs have the properties of a random sample of all such crabs.

Summary Statistics for Weights of Horseshoe Crabs

	n	Mean	Std. Dev.	Min	Q1	Med	Q3	Max
Mate	111	2.6	0.6	1.5	2.2	2.6	3.0	5.2
No Mate	62	2.1	0.4	1.2	1.8	2.1	2.4	3.2

a. Sketch box plots for the weight distributions of the two groups. Interpret by comparing the groups with respect to shape, center, and variability.

b. Estimate the difference between the mean weights of female crabs who have mates and female crabs who do not have mates.

c. Find the standard error for the estimate in part b.

d. Construct a 90% confidence interval for the difference between the population mean weights, and interpret.

10.80 TV watching and race The 2014 GSS asked about the number of hours you watch TV per day. An analysis that evaluates this by race shows the results (note the codes: 1 = Black and 2 = White):

```
Race        N       Mean     StDev     SE Mean
Black      260      3.97      3.54      0.22
White     1251      2.77      2.25      0.064
Difference = μ(black) − μ(white)
Estimate for difference: 1.198
95% CI for difference: (0.749, 1.648)
T-Test of difference = 0 (vs ≠):
T-Value = 5.25 P-Value = 0.000 DF = 303
```

a. Do you believe that TV watching has a normal distribution for each race? Why or why not? What effect does this have on inference comparing population means?

b. Explain how to interpret the reported confidence interval. Can you conclude that one population mean is higher? If so, which one? Explain.

c. On what assumptions is this inference based?

10.81 Test TV watching by race Refer to the previous exercise.

a. Specify the hypotheses that are tested in the output shown.

b. Report the value of the test statistic and the P-value. Interpret.

c. Make a decision, using the 0.05 significance level.

d. Explain the connection between the result of this significance test in part c and the result of the confidence interval in the previous exercise.

10.82 Ibuprofen and lifespan Geneticists hypothesized that one reason for a prolonged lifespan observed in yeast cells treated with the common drug ibuprofen stems from inhibiting the uptake of certain amino acids. In an experiment, they compared levels of amino acids in cells treated with ibuprofen to cells from an untreated control group. For the amino acid tryptophan, the six measurements in the treated group had a mean level of 0.0067 with a standard deviation of 0.0038. The six measurements in the control group had a mean level of 0.0080 with a standard deviation of 0.0050.

a. Identify the response variable and explanatory variable. Indicate whether each is quantitative or categorical.

b. Find the standard error of the sample mean in each group and the standard error of the difference in the sample means.

c. A 95% confidence interval for the difference between the mean level of tryptophan in the treated versus the control group is $(-0.007, 0.004)$. Interpret.

10.83 Time spent on Internet In 2014, the General Social Survey asked about the number of hours a week spent on the World Wide Web (variable denoted WWWHR). Some results are as follows:

TECH

Group	N	Mean	StDev	SE Mean
Male	621	12.1	16.6	0.027
Female	778	11.2	13.7	0.018

Difference = mu(Male) − mu (Female)
Estimate for difference: 1.3
95% CI for difference: (−0.8, 2.5)
T-Test of difference = 0 (vs ≠):
T-value = 1.03 P-value = 0.3044

a. Identify the response variable and explanatory variable. Indicate whether each variable is quantitative or categorical.

b. Report and interpret the 95% confidence interval shown for the difference between the population means for males and females.

c. Report and interpret the steps of the significance test comparing the two population means. Make a decision, using significance level 0.05.

d. Try to replicate the results by downloading the wwwhours data set from the book's website and using it with your favorite software.

10.84 Test—CI connection In the previous exercise, explain how the result of the 95% confidence interval in part b corresponds to the result of the decision using significance level 0.05 in part c.

10.85 Sex roles A study of the effect of the gender of the tester on sex-role differentiation scores[13] in Manhattan gave a random sample of preschool children the Occupational Preference Test. Children were asked to give three choices of what they wanted to be when they grew up. Each occupation was rated on a scale from 1 (traditionally feminine) to 5 (traditionally masculine), and a child's score was the mean of the three selections. When the tester was male, the 50 girls had $\bar{x} = 2.9$ and $s = 1.4$, whereas when the tester was female, the 90 girls had $\bar{x} = 3.2$ and $s = 1.2$. Show all steps of a test of the hypothesis that the population mean is the same for female and male testers, against the alternative that they differ. Report the P-value and interpret.

10.86 How often do you feel sad? A recent General Social Survey asked, "How many days in the past seven days have you felt sad?" Software comparing results for men and women who responded showed the following results.

```
Gender    N     Mean    StDev    SE Mean
Female    816   1.81    1.98     0.069
Male      633   1.42    1.83     0.073
Difference = μ(Female) − μ(Male)
Estimate for difference: 0.390
95% CI for difference: (0.193, 0.587)
T-Test of difference = 0 (vs ≠):
T-Value = 3.88 P-Value = 0.000 DF = 1403
```

a. Explain how to interpret the P-value. Do you think that the population means may be equal? Why?

b. Explain how to interpret the confidence interval for the difference between the population means. What do you learn from the confidence interval that you cannot learn from the test?

c. What assumptions are made for these inferences? Can you tell from the summary statistics shown whether any of the assumptions is seriously violated? What's the effect?

10.87 Parental support and household type A recent study interviewed youths with a battery of questions that provides a summary measure of perceived parental support. This measure had sample means of 46 ($s = 9$) for the single-mother households and 42 ($s = 10$) for the households with both biological parents. One conclusion in the study stated, "The mean parental support was 4 units higher for the single-mother households. If the true means were equal, a difference of at least this size could be expected only 2% of the time. For samples of this size, 95% of the time one would expect this difference to be within 3.4 of the true value." Explain how this conclusion refers to the results of (a) a confidence interval and (b) a significance test.

10.88 Car bumper damage An automobile company compares two types of front bumpers for its new model by driving sample cars into a concrete wall at 20 miles per hour. The response is the amount of damage to the car, as measured by the repair costs, in hundreds of dollars. Due to the costs, the study uses only six cars, obtaining results for three bumpers of each type. The results are in the table. Conduct statistical inference (95% confidence interval or significance test with significance level 0.05) about the difference between the population means, using software if you wish. Can you conclude that the mean is higher for one bumper type?

TECH

Bumper A	Bumper B
11	1
15	3
13	4

10.89 Teenage anorexia Example 8 in Section 9.3 described a study that used a cognitive behavioral therapy to treat a sample of teenage girls who suffered from anorexia. The study observed the mean weight change after a period of treatment. Studies of that type also usually have a control group that receives no treatment or a standard treatment. Then researchers can analyze how the change in weight compares for the treatment group to the control group. In fact, the anorexia study had a control group that received

[13]Obtained from Bonnie Seegmiller, a psychologist at Hunter College.

a standard treatment. Teenage girls in the study were randomly assigned to the cognitive behavioral treatment (Group 1) or to the control group (Group 2). The figure shows box plots of the weight changes for the two groups (displayed vertically). The output shows how MINITAB reports inferential comparisons of those two means.

MINITAB Output Comparing Mean Weight Changes

```
                 N     Mean      StDev    SE Mean
cogchange        29     3.01      7.31      1.4
controlchange    26    -0.45      7.99      1.6
Difference = μ(cogchange) - μ(controlchange)
Estimate for difference: 3.46
95% CI for difference: (-0.71, 7.62)
T-Test of difference = 0 (vs ≠):
T-Value = 1.67 P-Value = 0.102 DF = 50
```

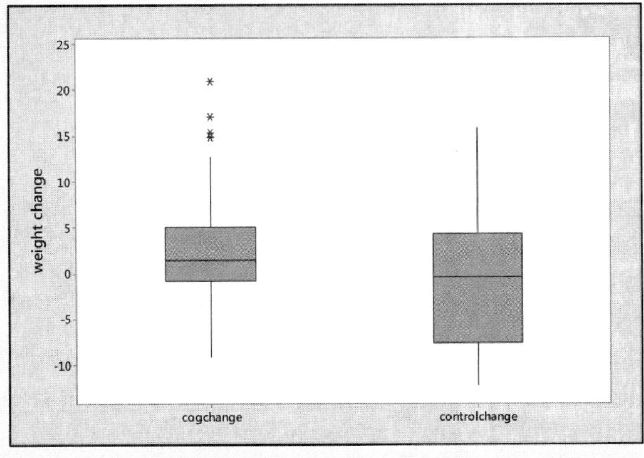

Box plots of weight change for anorexia study.

a. Report and interpret the P-value for testing H_0: $\mu_1 = \mu_2$ against H_a: $\mu_1 \neq \mu_2$.

b. Summarize the assumptions needed for the analysis in part a. Based on the box plots, would you be nervous if you had to perform a one-sided test instead? Why?

c. The reported 95% confidence interval tells us that if the population mean weight change is less for the cognitive behavioral group than for the control group, it is just barely less (less than 1 pound), but if the population mean change is greater, it could be nearly 8 pounds greater. Explain how to get this interpretation from the interval reported.

d. Explain the correspondence between the confidence interval and the decision in the significance test for a 0.05 significance level.

10.90 Equal pay in sports? The following data refer to a random sample of prize money earned by male and female skiers racing in the 2014/2015 FIS world cup season (in Swiss Franc).

Males: 89000, 179000, 8820, 12000, 10750, 66000, 6700, 3300, 74000, 56800

Females: 73000, 95000, 32400, 4000, 2000, 57100, 4500

Enter the observations (separated by spaces) into the Permutation Test web app. Let male skiers be Group 1 and female skiers be Group 2 and let the test statistic be the difference in sample means. Is there evidence that male skiers earn more, on average, than female skiers?

a. What are the observed group means and their difference? (The subtitle of the dot plot shows this information.)

b. Why would we prefer to run a permutation test over a *t* test?

c. Press the Generate Random Permutation(s) button once to generate one permutation of the original data. What are the two group means and their difference under this permutation?

d. Did this one permutation lead to a difference that is less extreme or more extreme than the observed difference?

e. Click Generate Random Permutation(s) nine more times, for a total of 10 permutations. How many of them resulted in a test statistic at least as extreme as the observed one?

f. Select to generate 10,000 random permutations. How many of them resulted in a test statistic as or more extreme?

g. Find and interpret the permutation P-value.

h. Select the option to generate all possible permutations. Do you notice a big difference in the histogram and P-value based on 10,000 randomly sampled permutations and on all possible permutations?

10.91 Surgery versus placebo for knee pain Refer to Example 10 on whether arthroscopic surgery is better than placebo. The following table shows the pain scores one year after surgery. Using software (such as MINITAB) that can conduct analyses using summary statistics, compare the placebo to the debridement group, using a 95% confidence interval. Use the method that assumes equal population standard deviations. Explain how to interpret the interval found by using software.

		Knee Pain Score	
Group	**Sample Size**	**Mean**	**Standard Deviation**
Placebo	60	48.9	21.9
Arthroscopic–lavage	61	54.8	19.8
Arthroscopic–debridement	59	51.7	22.4

10.92 More knee pain  Refer to the previous exercise. Compare the placebo to the debridement group using a significance test. State the assumptions and explain how to interpret the P-value.

10.93 Anorexia again Refer to Exercise 10.89, comparing mean weight changes in anorexic girls for cognitive behavioral therapy and a control group. The MINITAB output shows results of doing analyses while assuming equal population standard deviations.

MINITAB output for comparing mean weight changes

```
                  N     Mean    StDev    SE Mean
cogchange        29     3.01     7.31        1.4
controlchange    26    −0.45     7.99        1.6
Difference = μ(cogchange) − μ(controlchange)
Estimate for difference: 3.46
95% CI for difference:(−0.68, 7.59)
T-Test of difference = 0 (vs ≠):
T-Value = 1.68 P-Value = 0.100 DF = 53
Both use Pooled StDev = 7.6369
```

a. Interpret the reported confidence interval.

b. Interpret the reported P-value.

c. What would be the P-value for H_a: $\mu_1 > \mu_2$? Interpret it.

d. What assumptions do these inferences make?

10.94 Breast-feeding helps IQ? A Danish study of individuals born at a Copenhagen hospital between 1959 and 1961 reported higher mean IQ scores for adults who were breast-fed for longer lengths of time as babies (E. Mortensen et al., *JAMA*, vol. 287, 2002, pp. 2365–2371). The mean IQ score was 98.1 ($s = 15.9$) for the 272 subjects who had been breast-fed for no longer than a month and 108.2 ($s = 13.1$) for the 104 subjects who had been breast-fed for seven to nine months.

TECH

a. With software that can analyze summarized data, use an inferential method to analyze whether the corresponding population means differ, assuming the population standard deviations are equal. Interpret.

b. Was this an experimental or an observational study? Can you think of a potential lurking variable?

10.95 Australian cell phone use In Western Australia, handheld cell phone use while driving has been banned since 2001, but hands-free devices are legal. A study (published in the *British Medical Journal* in 2005) of 456 drivers in Perth who had been in a crash observed if they were using a cell phone before the crash and if they were using a cell phone during an earlier period when no accident occurred. Thus, each driver served as his or her own control group in the study.

a. In comparing rates of cell phone use before the crash and the earlier accident-free period, should we use methods for independent samples or for dependent samples? Explain.

b. Identify a test you can use to see whether the proportion of drivers using a cell phone differs between the period before the crash and the earlier accident-free period.

10.96 Improving employee evaluations Each of a random sample of 10 customer service representatives from a large department store chain answers a questionnaire about how they respond to various customer complaints. Based on the responses, a summary score measures how positively the employees react to complaints. This is measured both before and after employees undergo an intensive training course designed to improve such scores. A report about the study states, "The mean was significantly higher after taking the training course [$t = 3.40$ ($df = 9$), P-value < 0.05]." Explain how to interpret this to someone who has never studied statistics. What else should have been reported to make this more informative?

10.97 Which tire is better? A tire manufacturer believes that a new tire it is introducing (Brand A) will have longer wear than the comparable tire (Brand B) sold by its main competitor. To get evidence to back up its claim in planned advertising, the manufacturer conducts a study. On each of four cars it uses a tire of Brand A on the left front and a tire of Brand B on the right front. The response is the number of thousands of miles until a tire wears out, according to a tread marking on the tire. The sample mean response is 50 for Brand A and 40 for Brand B.

a. Show a pattern of four pairs of observations with these means for which you think Brand A would be judged better according to statistical inference. You do not need to actually conduct the inference. (*Hint:* What affects the value of the test statistic other than the sample means and n?)

b. How could the design of this study be improved?

10.98 Effect of alcoholic parents A study[14] compared personality characteristics between 49 children of alcoholics and a control group of 49 children of nonalcoholics who were matched on age and gender. On a measure of well-being, the 49 children of alcoholics had a mean of 26.1 ($s = 7.2$) and the 49 subjects in the control group had a mean of 28.8 ($s = 6.4$). The difference scores between the matched subjects from the two groups had a mean of 2.7 ($s = 9.7$).

a. Are the groups to be compared independent samples or dependent samples? Why?

b. Show all steps of a test of equality of the two population means for a two-sided alternative hypothesis. Report the P-value and interpret.

c. What assumptions must you make for the inference in part b to be valid?

10.99 CI versus test Consider the results from the previous exercise.

a. Construct a 95% confidence interval to compare the population means.

b. Explain what you learn from the confidence interval that you do not learn from the significance test.

10.100 Breast augmentation and self-esteem A researcher in the College of Nursing, University of Florida, hypothesized that women who undergo breast augmentation surgery would gain an increase in self-esteem. The article about the study[15] indicated that for the 84 subjects who volunteered for the study, the scores on the Rosenberg Self-Esteem Scale were 20.7 before the surgery (std. dev. = 6.3) and 24.9 after the surgery (std. dev = 4.6). The author reported that a paired difference significance test had $t = 9.8$ and a P-value below 0.0001.

---

[14] D. Baker and L. Stephenson, *Journal of Clinical Psychology*, vol. 51, 1995.

[15] By C. Figueroa-Haas, *Plastic Surgical Nursing*, vol. 27, 2007, p. 16.

a. Were the samples compared dependent samples, or independent samples? Explain.

b. Can you obtain the stated t statistic from the values reported for the means, standard deviation, and sample size? Why or why not?

10.101 Internet use As part of her class project in a statistics course, a student decided to study ways in which her fellow students use the Internet. She randomly sampled 5 of the 165 students in her course and asked them, "In the past week, how many days did you use the Internet to (a) read news stories, (b) communicate with friends using e-mail or text messaging?" The table shows the results. Using software, construct a confidence interval or conduct a significance test to analyze these data. Interpret, indicating the population to which the inferences extend.

TECH

Pair	News	Communicating
1	2	5
2	3	7
3	0	6
4	5	5
5	1	4

10.102 TV or rock music a worse influence? In a recent General Social Survey, subjects were asked to respond to the following: "Children are exposed to many influences in their daily lives. What kind of influence does each of the following have on children? 1. Programs on network television, 2. rock music." The possible responses were (very negative, negative, neutral, positive, very positive). The responses for 12 of the sampled subjects, using scores $(-2, -1, 0, 1, 2)$ for the possible responses are given in the table:

TECH

Subject	TV	Rock	Subject	TV	Rock	Subject	TV	Rock
1	0	−1	5	−1	−1	9	−1	−1
2	0	0	6	−2	−2	10	0	1
3	1	−2	7	−1	0	11	1	−1
4	0	1	8	1	−1	12	−1	−2

a. When you compare responses for TV and Rock, are the samples independent or dependent? Why?

b. Use software to construct a 95% confidence interval for the population difference in means. Interpret in the context of the variables studied.

c. Use software to conduct a significance test of equality of the population means for TV and Rock. Interpret the P-value.

10.103 Influence of TV and movies Refer to the previous exercise. The GSS also asked about the influence of movies. The responses for these 12 subjects were −1, 1, 0, 2, 0,−2, −1, 0,−1, 1, 1, −1. The results of using MINITAB to compare the influence of movies and TV are shown below. Explain how to interpret (a) the confidence interval and (b) the significance test results.

```
Paired T for movies - TV
              N      Mean     StDev    SE Mean
Movies       12    -0.083     1.165      0.336
TV           12    -0.250     0.965      0.279
Difference   12     0.167     0.937      0.271
95% CI for mean difference: (-0.429, 0.762)
T-Test of mean difference = 0 (vs ≠ 0):
T-Value = 0.62 P-Value = 0.551
```

10.104 Crossover study The table summarizes results of a crossover study to compare results of low-dose and high-dose analgesics for relief of menstrual bleeding (B. Jones and M. Kenward, *Statistics in Medicine*, vol. 6, 1987, pp. 555–564).

a. Find the sample proportion of successes for each dose of the analgesic.

b. Find the P-value for testing that the probability of success is the same with each dose, for a two-sided alternative. Interpret. What assumptions does this inference make?

	High Dose	
Low Dose	Success	Failure
Success	53	8
Failure	16	9

10.105 Belief in ghosts and in astrology A poll by Louis Harris and Associates of 1249 Americans indicated that 36% believe in ghosts and 37% believe in astrology.

a. Is it valid to compare the proportions using inferential methods for independent samples? Explain.

b. Do you have enough information to compare the proportions using methods for dependent samples? If yes, do so. If not, explain what else you would need to know.

10.106 Death penalty paradox Exercise 3.58 showed results of another study about the death penalty and race. The data are repeated here.

a. Treating victim's race as the control variable, show that Simpson's paradox occurs.

b. Explain what causes the paradox to happen.

		Death Penalty	
Vic Race	Def Race	Yes	No
W	W	53	414
	B	11	37
B	W	0	16
	B	4	139

10.107 Death rate paradoxes The crude death rate is the number of deaths in a year, per size of the population, multiplied by 1000.

a. According to the U.S. Bureau of the Census, in 1995 Mexico had a crude death rate of 4.6 (i.e., 4.6 deaths per 1000 population) while the United States had a crude death rate of 8.4. Explain how this overall death rate could be higher in the United States even if the United States had a lower death rate than Mexico for people of each specific age.

b. For each age level, the death rate is higher in South Carolina than in Maine. Overall, the death rate is higher in Maine (H. Wainer, *Chance*, vol. 12, 1999, p. 44). Explain how this could be possible.

10.108 Income and gender For a particular Big Ten university, the mean income for male faculty is $8000 higher than the mean income for female faculty. Explain how this difference could disappear:

a. Controlling for number of years since received highest degree. (*Hint:* What if relatively few female professors were hired until recent years?)

b. Controlling for college of employment.

Concepts and Investigations

10.109 Student survey Refer to the FL Student Survey data file on the book's website. Using software, prepare a short report summarizing the use of confidence intervals and significance tests (including checking assumptions) to compare males and females in terms of opinions about whether there is life after death.

TECH

10.110 Review the medical literature Your instructor will pick a medical topic of interest to the class. Find a recent article of a medical journal that reports results of a research study on that topic. Describe the statistical analyses that were used in that article. Did the article use (a) descriptive statistics, (b) confidence intervals, and (c) significance tests? If so, explain how these methods were used. Prepare a one-page summary of your findings that you will present to your class.

10.111 Attractiveness and getting dates The results in the table are from a study of physical attractiveness and subjective well-being (E. Diener et al., *Journal of Personality and Social Psychology*, vol. 69, 1995, pp. 120–129). As part of the study, college students in a sample were rated by a panel on their physical attractiveness. The table presents the number of dates in the past three months for students rated in the top or bottom quartile of attractiveness. Analyze these data. Write a short report that summarizes the analyses and makes interpretations.

TECH

	No. Dates, Men			No. Dates, Women		
Attractiveness	**Mean**	**StdDev**	***n***	**Mean**	**StdDev**	***n***
More	9.7	10.0	35	17.8	14.2	33
Less	9.9	12.6	36	10.4	16.6	27

10.112 Pay discrimination against women? A *Time Magazine* article titled "Wal-Mart's Gender Gap" (July 5, 2004) stated that in 2001 women managers at Wal-Mart earned $14,500 less than their male counterparts.

a. If these data are based on a random sample of managers at Wal-Mart, what more would you need to know about the sample to determine whether this is a "statistically significant" difference?

b. If these data referred to *all* the managers at Wal-Mart and if you can get the information specified in part a, is it relevant to conduct a significance test? Explain.

10.113 Mean of permutation distribution Refer to Example 11, which compared two doses of a medication in terms of the number of symptom-free days, using a permutation approach. Table 10.13 and Figure 10.9 showed the sampling distribution of the difference in sample means between the two doses. If truly the population distribution of the number of symptom-free days is identical for both doses (the null hypothesis), what value would you expect for the center of the sampling distribution of $\bar{x}_1 - \bar{x}_2$? Find the mean of the sampling distribution given in Table 10.13. (Hint: Recall the formula for the mean of a discrete probability distribution from Chapter 6.)

10.114 Treating math anxiety Two new programs were recently proposed at the University of Florida for treating students who suffer from math anxiety. Program A provides counseling sessions, one session a week for six weeks. Program B supplements the counseling sessions with short quizzes that are designed to improve student confidence. For ten students suffering from math anxiety, five were randomly assigned to each program. Before and after the program, math anxiety was measured by a questionnaire with 20 questions relating to different aspects of taking a math course that could cause anxiety. The study measured, for each student, the drop in the number of items that caused anxiety. The sample values were

TECH

Program A: 0, 4, 4, 6, 6

Program B: 6, 12, 12, 14, 16

Using software, analyze these data. Write a report, summarizing the analyses and interpretations.

10.115 Obesity and earnings An AP story (April 9, 2005) with headline Study: Attractive People Make More stated that "A study concerning weight showed that women who were obese earned 17 percent lower wages than women of average weight."

a. Identify the two variables stated to have an association.

b. Identify a control variable that might explain part or all of this association. If you had the original data including data on that control variable, how could you check whether the control variable does explain the association?

10.116 Multiple choice: Alcoholism and gender Suppose that a 99% confidence interval for the difference $p_1 - p_2$ between the proportions of men and women in California who are alcoholics equals (0.02, 0.09). Choose the best correct choice.

a. We are 99% confident that the proportion of alcoholics is between 0.02 and 0.09.

b. We are 99% confident that the proportion of men in California who are alcoholics is between 0.02 and 0.09 larger than the proportion of women in California who are.

c. We can conclude that the population proportions may be equal.

d. We are 99% confident that a minority of California residents are alcoholics.

e. Since the confidence interval does not contain 0, it is impossible that $p_1 = p_2$.

10.117 Multiple choice: Comparing mean incomes A study compares the population mean annual incomes for Hispanics (μ_1) and for whites (μ_2) having jobs in construction, using a 95% confidence interval for $\mu_1 - \mu_2$. Choose the best correct choice.

a. If the confidence interval is $(-6000, -3000)$, then at this confidence level we conclude that the mean income for whites is less than for Hispanics.

b. If the confidence interval is $(-3000, 1000)$, then the test of H_0: $\mu_1 = \mu_2$ against H_a: $\mu_1 \neq \mu_2$ with significance level 0.05 rejects H_0.

c. If the confidence interval is $(-3000, 1000)$, then we can conclude that $\mu_1 = \mu_2$.

d. If the confidence interval is $(-3000, 1000)$, then we are 95% confident that the population mean annual income for Hispanics is between 3000 less and 1000 more than the population mean annual income for whites.

10.118 Multiple choice: Sample size and significance If the sample proportions in Example 4 comparing cancer death rates for aspirin and placebo had sample sizes of only 1000 each, rather than about 11,000 each, then the 95% confidence interval for $(p_1 - p_2)$ would be $(-0.007, 0.021)$ rather than (0.003, 0.011). This reflects that

a. When an effect is small, it may take very large samples to have much power for establishing statistical significance.

b. Smaller sample sizes are preferable because there is more of a chance of capturing 0 in a confidence interval.

c. Confidence intervals get wider when sample sizes get larger.

d. The confidence interval based on small sample sizes must be in error because it is impossible for the parameter to take a negative value.

10.119 True or false: Positive values in CI If a 95% confidence interval for $(\mu_1 - \mu_2)$ contains only positive numbers, then we can conclude that both μ_1 and μ_2 are positive.

10.120 True or false: Afford food? A 2013 survey by the Pew Research Center asked whether there have been times in the past year the respondent has been unable to afford food. Of advanced economies, the country with the second highest response was the United States, 24%. Worldwide, the highest response was in Uganda, 70%. Because the same question was asked in both countries, the samples are dependent.

10.121 True or false: Control for clinic Suppose there is a higher percentage of successes with Treatment A than with Treatment B at a clinic in Rochester, and there is a higher percentage of successes with Treatment A than with Treatment B at a clinic in Syracuse. For the overall sample (combining results for the two cities), there must be a higher percentage of successes with Treatment A than with Treatment B.

10.122 Guessing on a test ◆◆ A test consists of 100 true-false questions. Joe did not study, and on each question he randomly guesses the correct response. Jane studied a little and has a 0.60 chance of a correct response for each question.

a. Approximate the probability that Jane's score is nonetheless lower that Joe's. (*Hint:* Use the sampling distribution of the difference of sample proportions.)

b. Intuitively, do you think that the probability answer to part a would decrease or increase if the test had only 50 questions? Explain.

10.123 Standard error of difference ◆◆ From the box formula for the standard error at the end of Section 10.1,

$$se(\text{estimate 1} - \text{estimate 2}) = \sqrt{[se(\text{estimate 1})]^2 + [se(\text{estimate 2})]^2},$$

if you know the *se* for each of two independent estimates, you can find the *se* of their difference. This is useful because often articles report an *se* for each sample mean or proportion, but not the *se* or a confidence interval for their difference. Many medical studies have used a large sample of subjects from Framingham, Massachusetts, who have been followed since 1948. A study (*Annual of Internal Medicine*, vol. 138, 2003, pp. 24–32) estimated the number of years of life lost by being obese and a smoker. For females of age 40, adjusting for other factors, the number of years of life left were estimated to have a mean of 46.3 ($se = 0.6$) for nonsmokers of normal weight and a mean of 33.0 ($se = 1.8$) for smokers who were obese. Construct a 95% confidence interval for the population mean number of years lost. Interpret.

10.124 Gap between rich and poor: $\sqrt{2/n}$ margin ◆◆

a. For comparisons of groups in which $n_1 = n_2$, with common value denoted by n, use the fact that the largest possible value of $\hat{p}(1 - \hat{p})$ occurs at $\hat{p} = 0.5$ to show that the margin of error for a large-sample 95% confidence interval for $(p_1 - p_2)$ can be no greater than $2\sqrt{0.5/n} = \sqrt{2/n}$.

b. A 2014 survey by the Pew Research Center reported that the percentage of people who think the gap between the rich and the poor is a very big problem in their country is 46% in the United States, 47% in the U.K., 39% in Germany, 74% in Turkey and 72% in Argentina. Assuming that each country had a random sample of 1000 people, use the $\sqrt{2/n}$ bound to identify any pairs of countries for which the true percentages might not be different.

10.125 Small-sample CI ◆◆ The small-sample confidence interval for comparing two proportions is a simple adjustment of the large-sample one. Recall that for a small-sample confidence interval for a single proportion, we used the ordinary formula after adding four observations, two of each type (see the end of Section 8.4). In the two-sample case we also add four observations, two of each type, and then use the ordinary formula by adding one observation of each type to each sample.[16] When the proportions are near 0 or near 1, results are more sensible than with the ordinary formula. Suppose there are no successes in either group, with $n_1 = n_2 = 10$.

---

[16]This is a new method. It was first proposed by A. Agresti and B. Caffo in the journal, *The American Statistician*, vol. 54, 2000, pp. 280–288.

a. With the ordinary formula, show that (i) $\hat{p}_1 = \hat{p}_2 = 0$, (ii) $se = 0$, and (iii) the 95% confidence interval for $p_1 - p_2$ is 0 ± 0, or (0, 0). Obviously, it is too optimistic to predict that the true difference is exactly equal to 0.

b. Find the 95% confidence interval, using the small-sample method described here. Are the results more plausible?

10.126 ◆◆ **Symmetry of permutation distribution** Refer to Example 12, which compared two groups of seven dogs each in terms of their time interacting with their owners. Figure 10.10 showed the sampling distribution by considering all possible permutations. When $n_1 = n_2$, as here, explain why the permutation distribution based on all possible permutations is symmetric. (*Hint:* Consider a particular permutation for which you compute the difference in sample means. How does this difference change when all dogs that were in Group 1 are switched to Group 2 and vice versa?)

10.127 Null standard error for matched pairs Under the null hypothesis H_0: $p_1 = p_2$ of equal population proportions, the standard error for the difference in the two sample proportions mentioned in the previous exercise reduces to se_0: $= \sqrt{(b + c)/n^2}$, where b and c are the off-diagonal elements and n is the number of subjects.

a. Show that the null standard error se_0 equals 0.010 for the contingency table in Table 10.18.

b. Compute the value of the test statistic

$$z = \frac{\text{estimate} - \text{null value}}{se_0} = \frac{(\hat{p}_1 - \hat{p}_2) - 0}{se_0}$$ and

verify that it equals $\frac{b - c}{\sqrt{b + c}}$. The P-value in the computer output of Table 10.19 refers to this test statistic.

10.128 ◆◆ **Graphing Simpson's paradox** The figure illustrates Simpson's paradox for Example 18 on the death penalty. For each defendant's race, the figure plots the percentage receiving the death penalty. Each percentage is labeled by a letter symbol giving the category of the victim's race. Surrounding each observation is a circle of an area representing the number of observations on which that percentage is based. For instance, the W in the largest circle represents a percentage of 12.6 receiving the death penalty for cases with white defendants and white victims. That circle is largest because the number of cases at that combination (151) is largest. When we add results across victim's race to get a summary result ignoring that variable, the largest circles, having the greater number of cases, have greater influence. Thus, the summary percentages for each defendant's race, marked on the figure by an ×, fall closer to the center of the larger circles than to the center of the smaller circles.

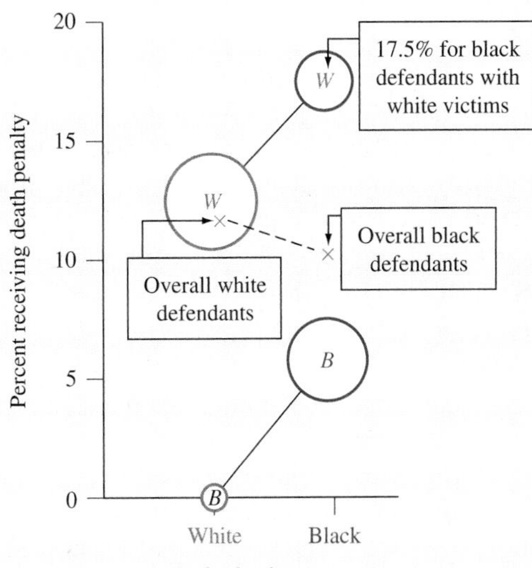

Percentage receiving death penalty by defendant's race, controlling victim's race (labels in center of circles) and ignoring victim's race (overall values marked by × for white defendants and black defendants).

a. Explain why a comparison of a pair of circles having the same letter in the middle indicates that the death penalty was more likely for black defendants, when we control for victim's race.

b. Explain why a comparison of the × marks shows that overall the death penalty was more likely for white defendants than black defendants.

c. For white defendants, why is the overall percentage who got the death penalty so close to the percentage for the case with white victims?

Student Activities

10.129 Reading the medical literature Refer to Activity 2, which follows, about reading an article in a medical journal. Your instructor will pick a recent article at the website for the *British Medical Journal.* Prepare a short report in which you summarize the main conclusions of the article and explain how those conclusions depended on statistical analyses. After you have done this, your entire class will discuss this article and the statistical analyses.

▶ **Activity 2**

Interpreting Statistics in a Medical Journal

Medical research makes frequent use of statistical methods shown in this chapter. At *British Medical Journal (BMJ)* bmj.com on the Internet, pull up the April 19, 2003, issue. Browse through the article titled "Behavioural counseling to increase consumption of fruit and vegetables in low income adults: randomized trial" by A. Steptoe et al. You will see a variety of statistical analyses used. See whether you can answer these questions:

- What was the objective of the study?
- Was the study experimental or observational? Summarize the design and the subjects used in the study.
- Identify response and explanatory variables.
- According to Table 2 in the article, the 135 subjects in the nutrition counseling group had a baseline mean of 3.67 and standard deviation of 2.00 for the number of portions per day they ate of fruits and vegetables. Over the 12 months of the study, the mean increased by 0.99. Report the 95% confidence interval for the change in the mean and interpret. Report the corresponding results for the behavioral counseling group. Were the groups in this analysis independent or dependent samples?
- Adjusted for confounding variables, the difference between the change in the mean for the behavioral counseling group and the nutrition counseling group was 0.62. Report and interpret the 95% confidence interval for the true difference and report the P-value for testing that the difference was 0. Were the groups in this analysis independent or dependent samples?
- According to Table 2, at the baseline for the nutrition counseling group, the proportion of subjects who ate at least five portions a day of fruits and vegetables was 0.267, and this increased by 0.287 over the 12 months. Report and interpret the 95% confidence interval for the change in the true proportion. Was this analysis for independent or dependent samples? Was this change in the proportion significantly larger, or smaller, than the change for the behavioral counseling group?
- What were the primary conclusions of the study?
- Describe two limitations of the study, as explained in the sections titled "Representativeness of the sample" and "Limitations of the study."

Analyzing Association and Extended Statistical Methods

PART

CHAPTER

11

Chapter 3 presented ways of explaining the association between two binary response variables, and in Chapter 10, we learned how to compare two groups inferentially when the response is binary. This chapter extends these ideas to categorical responses, with the overall goal to analyze the association for data summarized in contingency tables.

Analyzing the Association Between Categorical Variables

Example 1

Happiness

Picture the Scenario

What contributes to your overall happiness? Is it love? Your health? Your friendships? The amount of money you make?

To investigate which variables are associated with happiness, we can use data from the General Social Survey (GSS). In each survey, the GSS asks, "Taken all together, would you say that you are very happy, pretty happy, or not too happy?" Table 11.1 uses the 2012 survey to cross-tabulate happiness with family income, here measured as the response to the question, "Compared with American families in general, would you say that your family income is below average, average, or above average?"

Questions to Explore

- How can you determine if there is an association between happiness and family income in the population of all adult Americans?
- If there is an association, what is its nature? For example, do people with above-average family income tend to be happier than people with below-average family income?
- Can you think of a variable that might have a stronger association with happiness than family income?

Table 11.1 Happiness and Family Income, from 2012 General Social Survey

	Happiness			
Income	**Not Too Happy**	**Pretty Happy**	**Very Happy**	**Total**
Above average	29	178	135	342
Average	83	494	277	854
Below average	104	314	119	537

Thinking Ahead

Both variables in Table 11.1 are categorical. The focus of this chapter is learning how to describe associations between categorical variables to answer questions such as, "Do people with higher family incomes tend to be happier?" and "Are married people happier than unmarried people?" Using our standard tools of statistical inference, we'll analyze Table 11.1 in Examples 3 and 4 and other data on happiness in numerous exercises.

Association Between Variables

Let's recap where we are at this stage of our study. Chapter 7 introduced the fundamental concept of a *sampling distribution*. Chapter 8 showed how the sampling distribution is the basis of estimation, using *confidence intervals*, and Chapter 9 showed how it is the basis of *significance testing*. Those chapters focused on inference for a single proportion or a single mean.

Recall

In the Chapter 3 introduction, we stated that two variables have an **association** if particular values for one variable are more likely to occur with certain values of the other variable—for example, if being very happy is more likely to happen if a person has an above average income. Section 3.1 introduced the analysis of association for categorical variables. ◀

Chapter 10 introduced methods for comparing two means (when the response was quantitative) or two proportions (when the response was binary). This chapter presents methods for investigating, more generally, the association between two categorical variables. We'll refine what we mean by an association or lack of association in the context of contingency tables such as Table 11.1. The association between two quantitative variables is explored in Chapter 12.

11.1 Independence and Dependence (Association)

First, let's identify the response variable and the explanatory variable. In Table 11.1 it's more natural to study how happiness depends on income than how income depends on happiness. We'll treat happiness as the response variable and income as the explanatory variable.

Comparing Percentages

Table 11.1 is easier to digest if we convert the frequencies to percentages for the response categories. Within each category of income, Table 11.2 shows the percentages for the three categories of happiness. For example, of the 342 subjects who reported their family income as above average, 135 identified themselves as very happy. This is a proportion of $135/342 = 0.395$ or 39%. By contrast, 119 out of the 537 below-average income subjects said they were very happy, a percentage of only 22%. The row totals in Table 11.1 are the basis of these percentage calculations. Within each row, the percentages sum to 100%.

Table 11.2 Conditional Percentages for Happiness Categories, Given Each Category of Family Income

The percentages are computed by dividing the counts in Table 11.1 by their row totals and then multiplying by 100. If a particular row doesn't sum to 100%, it is due to rounding errors.

	Happiness			
Income	**Not Too Happy**	**Pretty Happy**	**Very Happy**	**Total**
Above average	8%	52%	39%	342 (100%)
Average	10%	58%	32%	854 (100%)
Below average	19%	58%	22%	537 (100%)

Recall

Section 3.1 introduced **conditional proportions**, which are proportions for the categories of a categorical response variable that are calculated **conditional** upon (i.e., "given") the value of another variable. ◀

The three percentages in a particular row are called **conditional percentages**. They refer to the distribution of happiness, *conditional* on the category for family income. This distribution is called the **conditional distribution** for happiness, given a particular income level. For those who reported above-average family income, the conditional distribution of happiness is the set of percentages (8%, 52%, 39%) for the responses (not too happy, pretty happy, very happy). The proportions (0.08, 0.52, 0.39) are the estimated **conditional probabilities** of happiness, given above-average family income. For instance, given that a subject reported above-average family income, the estimated probability of being very happy is 0.39.

Let's compare the happiness percentages for the subjects who reported above-average income to those who reported below-average income. From Table 11.2, the higher-income subjects were more likely to be very happy (39% versus 22%) and less likely to be not too happy (8% versus 19%). An about equal percentage (52% versus 58%) was pretty happy. Figure 11.1 uses a bar graph to portray the three conditional distributions.

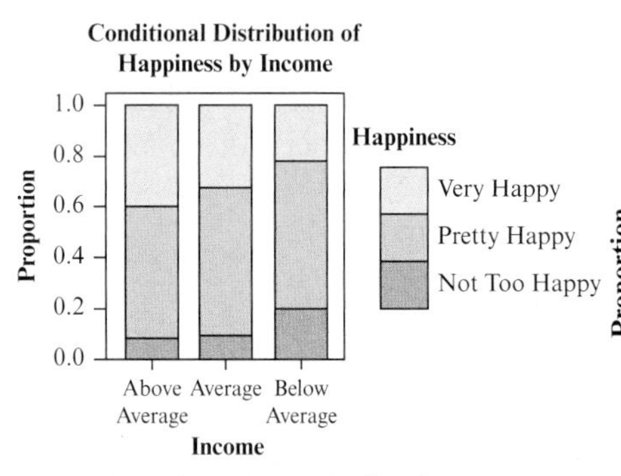

Stacked version of bar plot in Figure 11.1.

▲ **Figure 11.1** Bar Graph of Conditional Distributions of Happiness, Given Income, from Table 11.2. Each box shows the conditional distribution of happiness for that income category. You can compare how the proportion in a given happiness category (i.e., not too happy) changes across the income categories. **Question** Based on this graph, how would you say that happiness depends on income?

We'll use the following guidelines when constructing tables with conditional distributions:

- Make the response variable the column variable. The response categories are shown across the top of the table.
- Compute conditional proportions for the response variable within each row by dividing each cell frequency by the row total. Those proportions multiplied by 100 are the conditional percentages.
- Include the total sample sizes on which the percentages are based. That way, readers who want to can reconstruct the cell counts.

Independence Versus Dependence (Association)

Table 11.2 showed conditional distributions for a sample. We'll use these sample conditional distributions to make inferences about the corresponding population conditional distributions.

For instance, to investigate how happiness compares for females and males, we'd make inferences about the population conditional distributions of happiness for females and for males. Suppose that those population distributions are as shown in Table 11.3. (In fact, the percentages in Table 11.3 are consistent with actual data from the 2012 GSS. See Exercise 11.4.) We see that the percentage classified as very happy is the same for females and males, 30%. Similarly, the percentage classified as pretty happy (56%) and the percentage classified as not too happy (14%) are the same for females and for males. The probability that a person is classified in a particular happiness category is identical for females and males. The categorical variables happiness and gender are then said to be **independent**.

Table 11.3 Population Conditional Distributions Showing Independence

The conditional distribution of happiness is the same for each gender, namely (14%, 56%, 30%).

	Happiness			
Gender	**Not Too Happy**	**Pretty Happy**	**Very Happy**	**Total**
Female	14%	56%	30%	100%
Male	14%	56%	30%	100%
Overall	**14%**	**56%**	**30%**	**100%**

Source: Data from CSM, UC Berkeley.

In Words

Happiness and gender are **independent** if (as in Table 11.3) the probability of a particular response on happiness is the same for females and males.

Independence and Dependence (Association)

Two categorical variables are **independent** if the population conditional distributions for one of them are identical at each category of the other. The variables are **dependent** (or **associated**) if the conditional distributions are not identical.

For two variables to be independent, the population percentage in any category of one variable is the same for all categories of the other variable, as in Table 11.3. Figure 11.2 portrays this for Table 11.3.

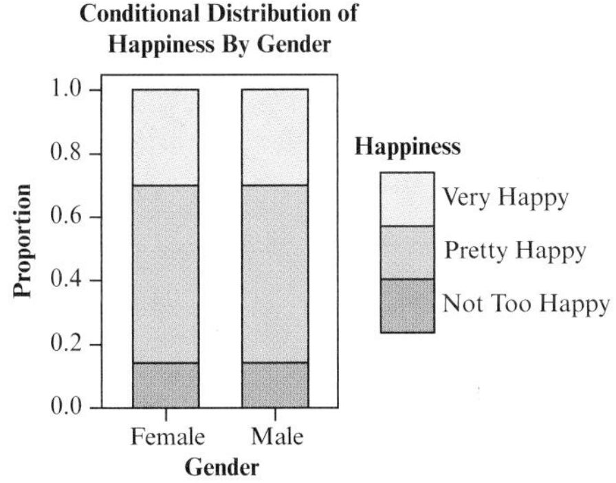

The stacked bar chart shows identical distributions of happiness for females and males, i.e., independence.

▲ Figure 11.2 Bar Graph of Population Conditional Distributions Showing Independence. **Question** What feature of the bar graph reflects the independence?

Recall

Section 5.3 in Chapter 5 defined A and B to be **independent events** if

$$P(A \mid B) = P(A).$$

Chapter 10 used **independent samples** to mean that observations in one sample are independent of those in the other sample. ◀

This definition extends independence of **events** to independence of **variables**. Recall that two *events* A and B are independent if P(A) is the same as the conditional probability of A, given B, denoted by $P(A \mid B)$. When two *variables* are independent, any event about one variable is independent of any event about the other variable. In Table 11.3, $P(A \mid B) = P(A)$ if A is an event about happiness and B is an event about gender. For example if A = very happy and B = female, then $P(A \mid B) = 0.30$. Notice in Table 11.3, this also equals P(A).

Independence and dependence

Conditional Distribution of Belief in Life After Death, by Race

Example 2

Belief in Life After Death and Race

Picture the Scenario

Table 11.4 cross-tabulates belief in life after death with race, using data from the 2012 GSS. The table also shows sample conditional distributions for life after death, given race, and the overall percentages for the life after death categories.

Table 11.4 Sample Conditional Distributions for Belief in Life After Death, Given Race. The margin figure shows the distributions graphically

	Postlife		
Race	**Yes**	**No**	**Total**
White	1043 (79.7%)	266 (20.3%)	1309 (100%)
Black	241 (86.7%)	37 (13.3%)	278 (100%)
Other	143 (79.4%)	37 (20.6%)	180 (100%)
Overall	**1427 (80.8%)**	**340 (19.2%)**	**1767 (100%)**

Source: Data from CSM, UC Berkeley.

Question to Explore

Are race and belief in life after death independent or dependent?

Think It Through

The three conditional distributions in Table 11.4 are similar but not exactly identical. So it is tempting to conclude that the variables are dependent. For example, if A = yes for belief in life after death, we estimate $P(A|\text{white}) = 1043/1309 = 0.797$, $P(A|\text{black}) = 0.867$ and $P(A|\text{other}) = 0.794$, whereas we estimate that $P(A) = 1427/1767 = 0.808$. However, the definition of independence between variables refers to the *population.* Since Table 11.4 refers to a *sample* rather than a population, it provides evidence but does not definitively tell us whether these variables are independent or dependent.

Even if the variables *were* independent, we would not expect the *sample* conditional distributions to be identical. Because of sampling variability, each sample percentage typically differs somewhat from the true population percentage. We would expect to observe *some* differences between sample conditional distributions such as we see in Table 11.4 even if *no* differences exist in the population.

Insight

If the observations in Table 11.4 were the entire population, the variables would be dependent. But the association would not necessarily be practically important, because the percentages are similar from one category to another of race. The next section presents a significance test of the hypothesis that the variables are independent.

► ***Try Exercise 11.2***

11.1 Practicing the Basics

11.1 Gender gap in politics? In the United States, is there a gender gap in political beliefs? That is, do women and men tend to differ in their political thinking and voting behavior? The table taken from the 2012 GSS relates gender and political party identification. Subjects indicated whether they identified more strongly with the Democratic or Republican party or as Independents.

	Political Party Identification			
Gender	Democrat	Independent	Republican	Total
Female	421	398	244	1063
Male	278	367	198	843

Source: Data from CSM, UC Berkeley.

a. Identify the response variable and the explanatory variable.

b. Construct a table that shows the conditional distributions of the response variable. Interpret.

c. Give a hypothetical example of population conditional distributions for which these variables would be independent.

d. Sketch bar graphs to portray the distributions in part b and in part c.

11.2 Beliefs of college freshmen TRY Every year, a large-scale poll of college freshmen conducted by the Higher Education Research Institute at UCLA asks their opinions about a variety of issues. In 2004, although women were more likely to rate their time management skills as "above average," they were also twice as likely as men to indicate that they frequently feel overwhelmed by all they have to do (36.4% versus 16.3%).

a. If results for the population of college freshmen were similar to these, would gender and feelings of being overwhelmed be independent or dependent?

b. Give an example of hypothetical population percentages for which these variables would be independent.

11.3 Williams College admission Data from 2013 posted on the Williams College website shows that of all 3,195 males applying, 18.2% were admitted, and of all 3,658 females applying, 16.9% were admitted. Let X denote gender of applicant and Y denote whether admitted.

a. Which conditional distributions do these percentages refer to, those of Y at given categories of X, or those of X at given categories of Y? Set up a table showing the two conditional distributions.

b. Are X and Y independent or dependent? Explain. (*Hint:* These percentages refer to the population of all applicants in 2013.)

11.4 Happiness and gender The contingency table shown relates happiness and gender for the 2012 GSS.

	Happiness			
Gender	Not Too Happy	Pretty Happy	Very Happy	Total
Female	154	592	336	1082
Male	123	502	257	882

Source: Data from CSM, UC Berkeley.

a. Identify the response variable and the explanatory variable.

b. Construct a table or graph showing the conditional distributions. Interpret.

c. Give an example of population conditional distributions (i.e., proportions or percentages) that would seem to be consistent with this sample and for which happiness and gender would be independent.

11.5 Marital happiness and income TECH In the GSS, subjects who were married were asked about the happiness of their marriage, the variable coded as HAPMAR.

a. Go to the GSS website sda.berkeley.edu/GSS/, click GSS with no weight as the default, and construct a contingency table for 2012 relating family income (measured as in Table 11.1) to marital happiness: Enter FINRELA(r:4;3;2) as the row variable (where 4 = "above average," 3 = "average," and 2 = "below average") and HAPMAR(r:3;2;1) as the column variable (3 = not too, 2 = pretty, and 1 = very happy). As the selection filter, enter YEAR(2012). Under Output Options, put a check in the row box (instead of in the column box) for the Percentaging option and put a check in the Summary Statistics box further below. Click on *Run the Table.*

b. Construct a table or graph that shows the conditional distributions of marital happiness, given family income. How would you describe the association?

c. Compare the conditional distributions to those in Table 11.2. For a given family income, what tends to be higher, general happiness or marital happiness for those who are married? Explain.

11.6 What is independent of happiness? Which one of the following variables would you think most likely to be independent of happiness: belief in an afterlife, family income, quality of health, region of the country in which you live, satisfaction with job? Explain the basis of your reasoning.

11.7 Sample evidence about independence TECH Refer to the previous exercise. Go to the GSS website and construct a table relating happiness (HAPPY) to the variable you chose (AFTERLIF, FINRELA, HEALTH, REGION, or JOBSAT). Inspect the conditional distributions and indicate whether independence seems plausible, with the sample conditional distributions all being quite similar.

11.2 Testing Categorical Variables for Independence

How can we judge whether two categorical variables are independent or dependent? The definition of independence refers to the *population*. Could the observed *sample* association be due to sampling variation? Or would the observed results be unusual if the variables were truly independent?

A significance test can answer these questions. The hypotheses for the test are

H_0: The two variables are independent.

H_a: The two variables are dependent (associated).

The test assumes randomization and a large sample size. The idea of the test is to compare the observed cell counts in the contingency table with counts we would expect to see if the null hypothesis of independence were true.

Expected Cell Counts If the Variables Are Independent

The count in any particular cell is a random variable: Different samples result in different values for the count. The mean of its distribution is called an **expected cell count**. This is found under the presumption that H_0 is true. That is, the expected cell counts are values that satisfy the null hypothesis of independence.

Table 11.5 shows the observed cell counts from Table 11.1, with the expected cell counts below them. How do we find expected cell counts? Recall that when two variables are independent, any event about one variable is independent of any event about the other variable. Consider the events A = not too happy and B = above-average income. From the Total column and the Total row (the table margins) of Table 11.5 we estimate P(A) by 216/1733 and P(B) by 342/1733. The event A and B (not too happy *and* above-average income) corresponds to the first cell in the table, with cell count of 29. Under the presumption of independence, the probability for this cell is

$$P(\text{A and B}) = P(\text{A}) \times P(\text{B}),$$

which we estimate by $(216/1733) \times (342/1733) = 2.46\%$. Under independence, we would expect 2.46% of the $n = 1733$ subjects included in the survey to fall in this cell. Of 1,733 subjects, 2.46% is 42.6 subjects. This is the **expected cell count**

Recall

From Section 5.2, two events A and B are **independent** if

$$P(\text{A and B}) = P(\text{A}) \times P(\text{B}).$$ ◄

Table 11.5 Happiness by Family Income, Showing Observed and Expected Cell Counts

We use the highlighted totals to get the expected count of $42.6 = (216 \times 342)/1733$ in the first cell.

	Happiness			
Income	**Not Too Happy**	**Pretty Happy**	**Very Happy**	**Total**
Above average	29	178	135	342
	42.6	194.6	104.8	
Average	83	494	277	854
	106.4	485.9	261.7	
Below average	104	314	119	537
	66.9	305.5	164.5	
Total	**216 (12.5%)**	**986 (56.9%)**	**531 (30.6%)**	**1733 (100%)**

for that first cell, assuming independence. To recap, we estimate the expected cell count under independence (i.e., presuming H_0 to be true) by

$$1733\left(\frac{216}{1733}\right)\left(\frac{342}{1733}\right) = \frac{216 \times 342}{1733} = 42.6.$$

Since the observed cell count of 29 is lower than the expected cell count of 42.6, fewer people had above-average income and were not too happy than we would expect if the variables were independent.

This discussion illustrates the general rule for calculating expected cell counts.

Expected Cell Count

For a particular cell, the **expected cell count** equals

$$\text{Expected cell count} = \frac{(\text{Row total}) \times (\text{Column total})}{\text{Total sample size}}.$$

For instance, the first cell in Table 11.5 has expected cell count $= (216 \times 342)/1733 = 42.6$, the product of the row total (342) for that cell by the column total (216) for that cell, divided by the overall sample size (1733).

Let's see more about why this rule makes sense. For A = not too happy, we estimated P(A) by $216/1733 = 0.125$ or 12.5%. If the variables were independent, we would expect this probability to be the same if we condition on any event about income. For instance, for B = above-average income, we expect $P(A|B) = P(A)$. Thus, 12.5% of the 342 who report above average income should be classified in the not too happy category. The expected cell count is then $0.125(342) = (216/1733)(342) = 42.6$. But this is the column total of 216 times the row total of 342 divided by the overall sample size of 1,733.

Table 11.5 shows that for the overall sample, the percentages in the three happiness categories are (12.5%, 56.9%, 30.6%). You can check that the expected cell counts have these percentages in each of the three rows. For instance, for the first cell in row one, $42.6/342 = 0.125$. In fact, the expected cell counts are values that have the same row and column totals as the observed counts, but for which the conditional distributions are identical.

Chi-Squared Test Statistic

The test statistic for the test of independence measures how close the observed cell counts fall to the expected cell counts. Symbolized by X^2, it is called the **chi-squared statistic**, taking the name of its (approximate) sampling distribution. It is the oldest test statistic in use today. Introduced by the British statistician Karl Pearson in 1900, it is sometimes also called Pearson's chi-squared statistic.

In Words

The Greek letter chi is written as χ and pronounced "ki" (k + eye). Later in this section, we'll see that chi-squared (χ^2) is the name of the approximate sampling distribution of the statistic denoted here by X^2. The Roman letter denotes the statistic, and the Greek letter denotes the sampling distribution.

Chi-Squared Statistic

The **chi-squared statistic** is an overall measure of how far the observed cell counts in a contingency table fall from the expected cell counts for a null hypothesis. Its formula is

$$X^2 = \Sigma\frac{(\text{observed count} - \text{expected count})^2}{\text{expected count}}.$$

For each cell, square the difference between the observed count and expected count and then divide that square by the expected count. After calculating this term for every cell, sum the terms over all cells to find X^2.

When H_0: independence is true, the observed and expected cell counts tend to be close for each cell. Then each part in the sum is small, leading to an overall X^2 value that is relatively small. If H_0 is false, at least some observed counts and expected counts tend to be far apart. For a cell where this happens, its value of $[(\text{observed count} - \text{expected count})^2/\text{expected count}]$ tends to be large. This and other cells where this happens make a sizable contribution to the overall sum, resulting in a value for X^2 that is relatively large.

Example 3

Chi-squared statistic ◀

Happiness and Family Income

Picture the Scenario

Table 11.5 showed the observed and expected cell counts for the data on family income and happiness. Table 11.6 shows MINITAB output for the chi-squared test. The margin shows screen shots from the TI calculator. The matrix [B] referred to with the word **Expected** in the second screen shot contains the expected cell counts, shown in the last screen shot.

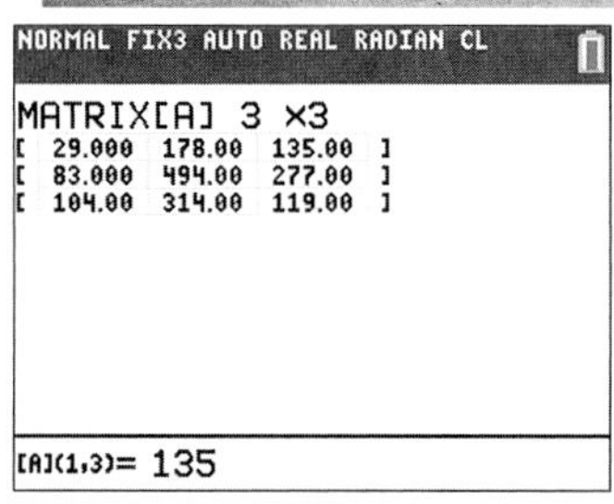

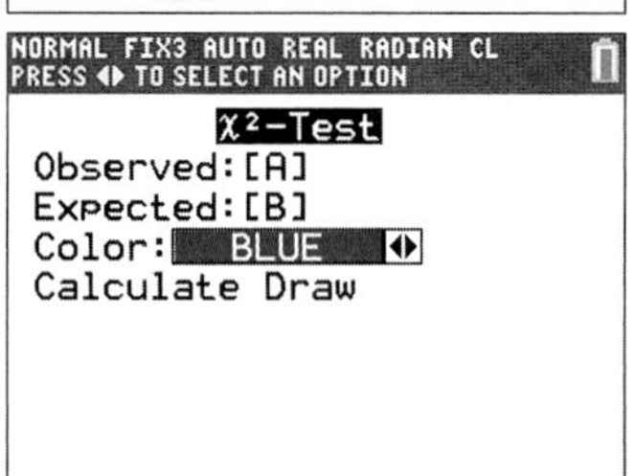

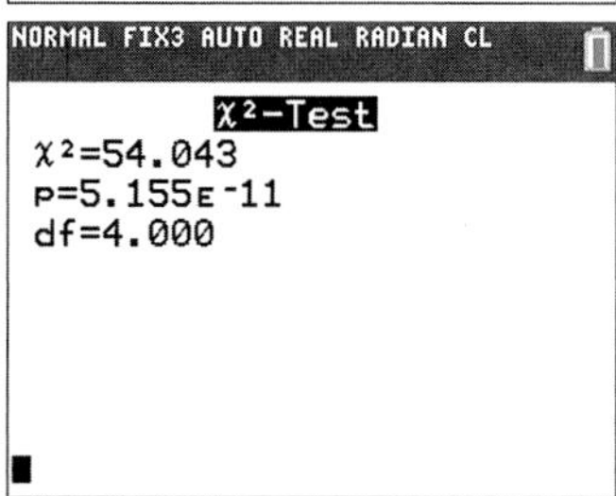

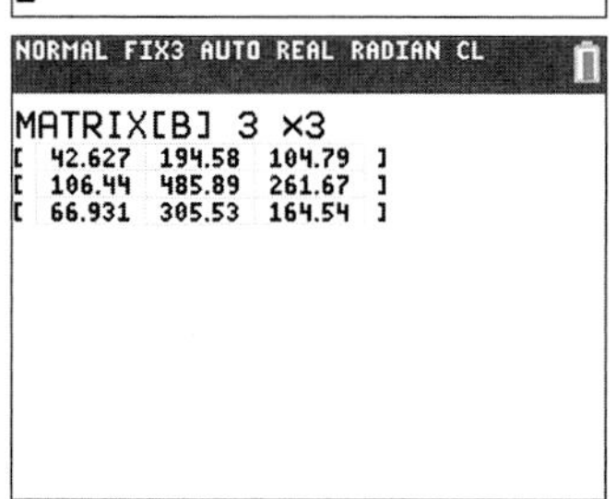

TI output for Chi-Squared test of independence

Table 11.6 Chi-Squared Test of Independence of Happiness and Family Income

This table shows how MINITAB reports, for each cell, the observed and expected cell counts and the contribution $[(\text{observed} - \text{expected})^2/\text{expected}]$ to X^2 as well as the overall X^2 value and its P-value for testing H_0: independence.

Rows: income Columns: happy

	not	pretty	very	All	
above	29	178	135	342	← Observed cell count
	42.6	194.6	104.8		← Expected cell count
	4.356	1.413	8.709		← Contribution to X^2
average	83	494	277	854	
	106.4	485.9	261.7		
	5.163	0.135	0.898		
below	104	314	119	537	
	66.9	305.5	164.5		
	20.530	0.235	12.604		
All	216	986	531	1733	

Cell Contents: Count
Expected count
Contribution to Chi-square

Pearson Chi-Square = 54.043, DF = 4, P-Value = 0.000

↑ X^2 statistic

Questions to Explore

a. State the null and alternative hypotheses for this test.

b. Report the X^2 statistic and explain how it was calculated.

Think It Through

a. The hypotheses for the chi-squared test are

H_0: Happiness and family income are independent.

H_a: Happiness and family income are dependent (associated).

The alternative hypothesis implies that there's an association between happiness and family income.

b. Finding X^2 involves a fair amount of computation, and it's best to let software do the work for us. Minitab reports a chi-squared statistic of $X^2 = 54.0$. Beneath the observed and expected cell counts in a cell, MINITAB reports the contribution of that cell to the X^2 statistic. For the first cell (above average income and not too happy), for instance,

$$(\text{observed count} - \text{expected count})^2/\text{expected count} =$$
$$(29 - 42.63)^2/42.63 = 4.36.$$

For all nine cells,

$$X^2 = \frac{(29-42.6)^2}{42.6} + \frac{(178-194.6)^2}{194.6} + \frac{(135-104.8)^2}{104.8} + \frac{(83-106.4)^2}{106.4} + \frac{(494-485.9)^2}{485.9} + \frac{(277-261.7)^2}{261.7} + \frac{(104-66.9)^2}{66.9} + \frac{(314-305.5)^2}{305.5} + \frac{(119-164.5)^2}{164.5}$$

$$= 4.356 + 1.413 + 8.709 + 5.163 + 0.135 + 0.898 + 20.530 + 0.235 + 12.604 = 54.0$$

Insight

Table 11.6 has a few large differences between observed and expected cell counts, so X^2 is large. The larger the X^2 value, the greater the evidence against H_0: independence and in support of the alternative hypothesis that happiness and income are associated. But is 54.0 large enough to support the conclusion of an association? We next learn how to interpret the magnitude of the X^2 test statistic, so we know what is a small and what is a large value and how to find the P-value.

▶ ***Try Exercise 11.8***

▶ Activity 1

Entering a Contingency Table into Software or a Web App

When using software, try to re-create a table like Table 11.6. First create a data file with nine rows, such as shown below, and then choose an option to create a contingency table and find appropriate statistics. When using the web app, you can either enter the original observations or the summary counts in a format such as the table below.

Income	Happy	Count
above	not	29
above	pretty	178
above	very	135
average	not	83
average	pretty	494
average	very	277
below	not	104
below	pretty	314
below	very	119

Chi-Squared Distribution

To find the P-value for the X^2 test statistic, we use the sampling distribution of the X^2 statistic. For large sample sizes, this sampling distribution is well approximated by the **chi-squared probability distribution**. (For small sample sizes, see Section 11.5.) Figure 11.3 on the next page shows several chi-squared distributions.

The main properties of the chi-squared distribution are as follows:

- **Always positive.** The chi-squared distribution falls on the positive part of the real number line. The X^2 test statistic cannot be negative since it sums squared differences divided by positive expected frequencies. The minimum possible value, $X^2 = 0$, would occur if the observed count equals the expected count in every single cell.
- **Degrees of freedom from row and column.** Similar to the t distribution, the precise shape of the chi-squared distribution depends on the **degrees of freedom** (df). For testing independence in a table with r rows and c columns (called an $r \times c$ table), the formula for the degrees of freedom is
$$df = (r - 1) \times (c - 1).$$
For example, Table 11.5 has $r = 3$ rows, and $c = 3$ columns, so $df = (3 - 1) \times (3 - 1) = 2 \times 2 = 4$. (Exercise 11.84 explains the reason behind this formula.)

Caution

For the t-distribution, the degrees of freedom depend on the sample size. This is not the case for the chi-squared distribution, where the df are obtained from the number of rows and columns of the contingency table. ◀

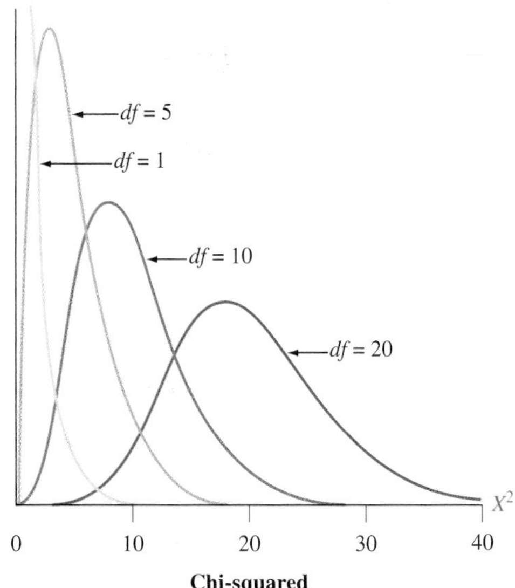

▲ **Figure 11.3 The Chi-Squared Distribution.** The curve has larger mean and standard deviation as the degrees of freedom increase. **Question** Why can't the chi-squared statistic be negative?

- **Mean equals *df*, Standard deviation equals $\sqrt{2df}$.** The mean (or expected value) of the chi-squared distribution equals the *df* value. The standard deviation of the chi-squared distribution equals $\sqrt{2df}$. Since $df = (r - 1) \times (c - 1)$, larger numbers of rows and columns produce larger *df* values. Since larger tables have more terms in the summation for the X^2 statistic, the X^2 values also tend to be larger and vary more in magnitude. Figure 11.3 shows how (i) the center of the chi-squared distribution gets larger for larger *df* and (ii) the variability of the chi-squared distribution gets larger for larger *df*.
- **As *df* increases, distribution goes to bell shaped.** The chi-squared distribution is skewed to the right. As *df* increases, the skew lessens and the chi-squared curve becomes more bell-shaped (see the curve for $df = 20$ in Figure 11.3).
- **Large X^2 provides evidence against independence.** The larger the X^2 value, the greater the evidence against H_0: independence. Thus, the P-value equals the right-tail probability above the observed X^2 statistic. It measures the probability that the X^2 statistic for a random sample would be larger than the observed value if the variables are truly independent. Figure 11.4 depicts the P-value.

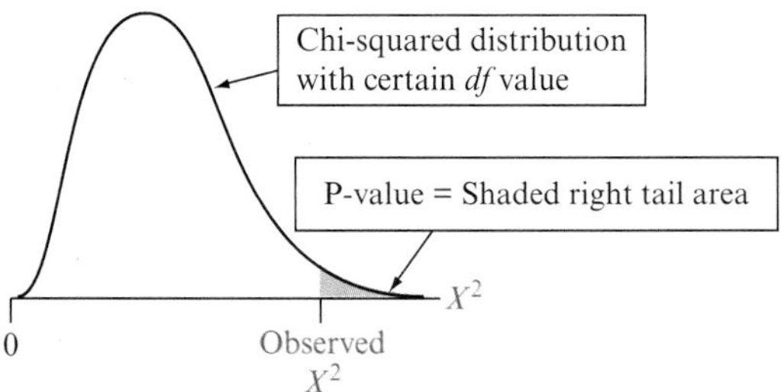

▲ **Figure 11.4 The P-value for the Chi-Squared Test of Independence.** This is the right-tail probability, above the observed value of the X^2 test statistic. **Question** Why do we not also use the left tail in finding the P-value?

Table C in the back of the book lists values from the chi-squared distribution for various right-tail probabilities. These are X^2 test statistic values that have P-values equal to those probabilities. Table 11.7 shows an excerpt from Table C for small *df* values. For example, a 3×3 table has $df = 4$, for which Table 11.7 reports that an X^2 value of 9.49 has P-value $= 0.05$. In practice, software provides the P-value or you can use the Chi-square web app.

Table 11.7 Rows of Table C Displaying Chi-Squared Values

The values have right-tail probabilities between 0.250 and 0.001. For a table with $r = 3$ rows and $c = 3$ columns, $df = (r - 1) \times (c - 1) = 4$, and 9.49 is the chi-squared value with a right-tail probability of 0.05.

	Right-Tail Probability						
df	.250	.100	.050	.025	.010	.005	.001
1	1.32	2.71	3.84	5.02	6.63	7.88	10.83
2	2.77	4.61	5.99	7.38	9.21	10.60	13.82
3	4.11	6.25	7.81	9.35	11.34	12.84	16.27
4	5.39	7.78	9.49	11.14	13.28	14.86	18.47

Example 4

Chi-squared distribution

Happiness and Income

Picture the Scenario

For testing the null hypothesis of independence of happiness and family income, Table 11.6 in Example 3 reported a test statistic value of $X^2 = 54.0$.

Questions to Explore

a. What is the P-value for the chi-squared test of independence for these data?

b. State your decision for a significance level of 0.05 and interpret in context.

Think It Through

a. Since the table has $r = 3$ rows and $c = 3$ columns, $df = (r - 1) \times (c - 1) = 4$. In Table 11.7, for $df = 4$ the largest chi-squared value shown is 18.47. It has tail probability = 0.001 (see the margin figure). Since $X^2 = 54.0$ falls well above this, it has a smaller right-tail probability. Thus, the P-value is < 0.001. The actual P-value would be 0 to many decimal places. MINITAB reports P-value = 0.000, as Table 11.6 showed.

b. Since the P-value is below 0.05, we can reject H_0. Based on this sample, we have evidence to support that an association exists between happiness and family income in the population.

Insight

The extremely small P-value provides very strong evidence against H_0: independence. If the variables were independent, it would be highly unusual for a random sample to have this large a chi-squared statistic. The small P-value is not surprising when considering the shape of the chi-squared distribution with $df = 4$. Remember that it has mean $= df = 4$ and standard deviation $= \sqrt{2df} = 2.8$. Then, the observed value of 54.0 is many standard deviations to the right of the mean, indicating an extreme value. Note, however, that both the mean and the standard deviation of the chi-squared distribution depend on the *df*. So, for instance, a X^2 value of 13 is extreme when $df = 4$, but it is not extreme when $df = 8$.

► ***Try Exercise 11.11, parts a to e***

Sample Size and the Chi-Squared Test

Presuming H_0 is true, the sampling distribution of the X^2 test statistic gets closer to the chi-squared distribution as the sample size increases. The approximation is good when each expected cell count exceeds about 5. Section 11.5 discusses the sample size issue further and presents a small-sample test.

The box summarizes the steps of the chi-squared test of independence.

SUMMARY: The Five Steps of the Chi-Squared Test of Independence

1. **Assumptions:** Two categorical variables
   Randomization, such as random sampling or a randomized experiment
   Expected count ≥ 5 in all cells (otherwise, use small-sample test in Section 11.5)
2. **Hypotheses:**
   H_0: The two variables are independent.
   H_a: The two variables are dependent (associated).
3. **Test statistic:**

$$X^2 = \sum \frac{(observed\ count - expected\ count)^2}{expected\ count},$$

   where expected count = (row total × column total)/total sample size
4. **P-value:** Right-tail probability above observed X^2 value, for the chi-squared distribution with $df = (r - 1) \times (c - 1)$
5. **Conclusion:** Report P-value and interpret in context. If a decision is needed, reject H_0 when P-value $\leq$ significance level (such as 0.05).

Caution

As with any hypotheses test, failing to reject the null hypothesis doesn't mean the variables are definitely independent. All that can be said is that independence is still plausible and can't be ruled out. ◀

As with other inferential methods, the chi-squared test assumes randomization, such as the simple random sampling that many surveys use. The General Social Survey uses a rather complex multistage random sampling design. Its characteristics are similar, however, to those of a simple random sample. Inferences that assume simple random sampling, such as the chi-squared test, are routinely used with GSS data. The chi-squared test is also valid with randomized experiments. In that case, subjects are randomly assigned to different treatments, and the contingency table summarizes the subjects' responses on a categorical response variable. If the table compares groups, the random samples from those groups must be independent random samples. The next example illustrates this.

Testing Homogeneity: Comparing Several Groups on a Categorical Response

The chi-squared test **for independence** does not differentiate between a response and explanatory variable. The steps of the test and the results are identical no matter which of the two categorical variables defines the rows or columns. When a response variable *is* identified and the population conditional distributions are identical across the levels of the explanatory variable, they are said to be **homogeneous**. The chi-squared test for this hypothesis is then often referred to as a **test of homogeneity**.

The test of homogeneity uses the same chi-squared test statistic and procedure as the test of independence. The only differences are in the nature of the hypotheses being tested (homogeneity of conditional distributions and independence of two variables, respectively) and the study design employed for collecting data. The independence test is used when each subject provides observations on two categorical variables (e.g., family income and opinion on happiness). A test of homogeneity is used when two or more groups are compared on a single categorical response variable (e.g., comparing a sample of smokers to a sample of nonsmokers in terms of their severity of asthma). In the latter case the data consist of several independent samples, one for each group. With two groups, this is the same setup as in Chapter 10 when we compared two means or two proportions, but now the response is categorical with possibly several categories. Such data arise when people from each group (say smokers and nonsmokers) complete the same survey, or they arise from an experiment in which subjects are randomly assigned to different treatment groups and a categorical response is measured.

Example 5

Testing Homogeneity ◄

Headache from Receiving a Flu Vaccine

Picture the Scenario

Many vaccines can lead to side effects such as soreness, a low fever, or headache. In a recent clinical trial, subjects were randomized to receive either the active ingredient of a flu shot (the active group) or a harmless sugar solution injection (the placebo group). The study was double blind, meaning neither the subject nor the one giving the shot knew what type was administered. Of all subjects reporting a headache after the shot, Table 11.8 shows the observed counts for the severity of the headache, which was rated as mild, moderate, or severe. The first row shows results for the active group and the second row for the placebo group. The sample conditional distribution for each group is shown in parentheses.

Table 11.8 Severity of Headache in the Active and Placebo Group.

Shown are the counts and conditional distributions (in parentheses) of those reporting a headache after receiving the shot.

	Severity of Headache			
Flu Shot	**Mild**	**Moderate**	**Severe**	**Total**
Active	486 (79%)	113 (18%)	16 (3%)	615 (100%)
Placebo	355 (81%)	80 (18%)	5 (1%)	440 (100%)
Total	**841 (80%)**	**193 (18%)**	**21 (2%)**	**1055 (100%)**

Questions to Explore

a. State the null and alternative hypotheses of interest.

b. Carry out the chi-squared test and interpret results.

Think It Through

a. The categorical response variable in this study is the severity of headache (with three categories), and the explanatory variable is whether a subject received the active or the placebo shot. The two groups are independent; subjects were randomly assigned to receive either the active or placebo treatment. We want to test whether the distribution of severity of headache is the same in the two groups (homogeneity) or if they differ, leading to the following hypotheses:

H_0: The conditional distribution of severity of headache is the same for patients randomized to the active or placebo group (homogeneity).

H_a: The conditional distributions differ.

b. For the homogeneity test, expected cell counts, the chi-squared statistic X^2, and its P-value are computed in exactly the same way as for the

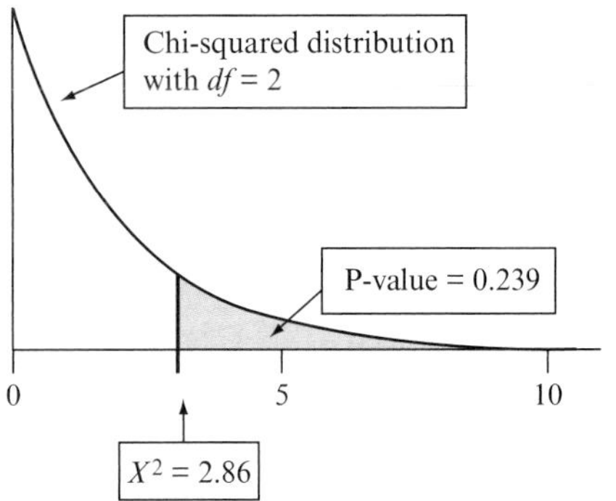

test of independence. Table 11.9 shows MINITAB output for the test of homogeneity. All expected cells counts are pretty close to the observed ones, resulting in $X^2 = 2.86$. Right away, this doesn't seem that large, given that the test has $df = (r - 1)(c - 1) = (2 - 1)(3 - 1) = 2$ and that the corresponding chi-squared distribution has mean 2 and standard deviation $\sqrt{2df} = \sqrt{4} = 2$. So, 2.86 is less than one standard deviation away from 2, the value we expect to get under homogeneity. Not surprisingly, the MINITAB output in Table 11.9 shows a large P-value of 0.239, which is illustrated in the margin figure. We thus fail to reject the hypothesis that the distribution of severity of headache is homogeneous for the two groups. There is no evidence of a difference in the distribution of the severity of headache in the active and placebo groups for those that report headache after receiving a shot.

Table 11.9 MINITAB Output for Chi-Squared Test of Homogeneity of Distribution of Severity of Headache Between Active and Placebo Group

```
Rows: Flu Shot          Columns: Severity

                   Mild   Moderate     Severe    All
Active              486        113         16    615
                 490.25     112.51      12.24
                0.03686    0.00216    1.15382

Placebo             355         80          5    440
                 350.75      80.49       8.76
                0.05153    0.00302    1.61273

All                 841        193         21   1055

Cell Contents:          Count
                        Expected count
                        Contribution to Chi-square

Pearson Chi-Square = 2.860, DF = 2, P-Value = 0.239
```

Insight

Whether you use a test of independence or homogeneity depends on the sampling design. If your sample consists of a single sample with two categorical observations on each subject, then you test whether these two variables are independent or associated. When you have a random sample from each of several groups, as in this example, you test for the homogeneity of the categorical response distribution across the groups. Computationally, the chi-squared test statistic and the P-value are identical for the two tests. For simplicity and in practice, both types of tests are often referred to as tests for independence. (For instance, the null hypothesis in the preceding example tests whether severity of headache is *independent* of which treatment group a subject was assigned to.)

▶ *Try Exercise 11.16*

Chi-Squared and the Test Comparing Proportions in 2 × 2 Tables

In practice, contingency tables of size 2×2 are very common. These occur in comparing two groups on a binary response variable, such as males and females on their belief in life after death (yes, no). For convenience, here, as in the discussion of the binomial distribution in Section 6.3, we label the two possible outcomes by the generic labels *success* and *failure.*

Denote the population proportion of success by p_1 in group 1 and p_2 in group 2, so that the population distribution is $(p_1, 1 - p_1)$ in group 1 and $(p_2, 1 - p_2)$ in group 2. Homogeneity of the population distributions simply means that $p_1 = p_2$, because, then, also $(1 - p_1) = (1 - p_2)$. Therefore, the test of homogeneity in a 2×2 table is the same as testing whether the success probabilities in the two groups are the same.

Section 10.1 presented a z test of H_0: $p_1 = p_2$. The test statistic is the difference between the sample proportions divided by its standard error; that is,

$$z = (\hat{p}_1 - \hat{p}_2)/se_0$$

where se_0 is the standard error estimated under the presumption that H_0 is true. In fact, using algebra, it can be shown that the chi-squared statistic for 2×2 tables is related to this z statistic by

$$X^2 = z^2.$$

In other words, square the z statistic, and you get the X^2 statistic. For H_a: $p_1 \neq p_2$, the z test has exactly the same P-value as the chi-squared test.

Example 6

Aspirin and Cancer Death Rates Revisited

Chi-squared test in 2×2 contingency tables

Group	Cancer Death Yes	No	Prop. Yes
Placebo	347	11,188	0.030
Aspirin	327	13,708	0.023

```
Pearson Chi-Square = 11.35,
DF = 1, P-Value = 0.001
```

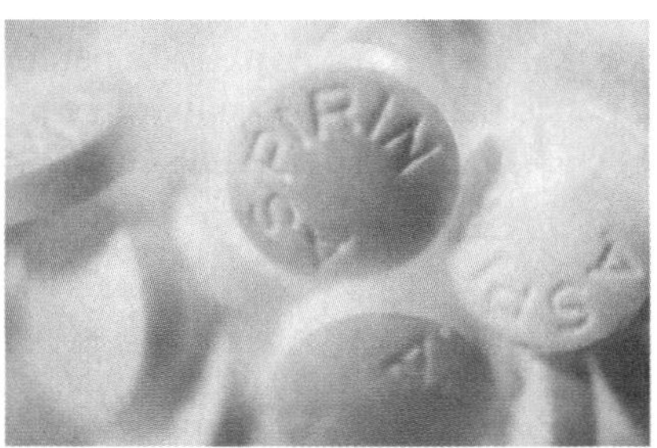

Picture the Scenario

Examples 2–4 in Chapter 10 discussed a meta-study on the effects of aspirin on cancer death rates, in which subjects were randomly assigned to take aspirin or placebo regularly. That example analyzed a 2×2 contingency table that compared the proportions of cancer deaths during a five-year period (shown again in the margin).

Denote the population proportion of cancer deaths by p_1 for the placebo treatment and by p_2 for the aspirin treatment. The corresponding sample proportions are $\hat{p}_1 = 0.030$ and $\hat{p}_2 = 0.023$. For H_0: $p_1 = p_2$, the z test of Section 10.1 has a test statistic value of $z = 3.369$ (Exercise 10.8). Its P-value is 0.001 for H_a: $p_1 \neq p_2$.

Questions to Explore

a. What are the hypotheses for the chi-squared test for these data?

b. Using the MINITAB output in the margin, report the test statistic and P-value for the chi-squared test. How do these relate to results from the z test comparing the proportions?

Think It Through

a. The null hypothesis is that the distributions of cancer deaths (i.e., whether someone dies of certain cancers) are the same in the placebo and aspirin group (homogeneity). As argued, this is equivalent to H_0: $p_1 = p_2$, the population proportion of cancer deaths being the same for each group. The alternative hypothesis is that they are not homogeneous. This is equivalent to H_a: $p_1 \neq p_2$.

b. From the MINITAB output, we get $X^2 = 11.35$. This equals the square of the z test statistic, $X^2 = z^2 = (3.369)^2 = 11.35$. The P-value of 0.001 provides strong evidence that the population proportions of cancer deaths differed for those taking aspirin and for those taking placebo. The sample proportions suggest that the aspirin group had a lower rate of cancer deaths than the placebo group.

Insight

Because of the relationship between the two test statistics, the chi-squared test and the two-sided z test necessarily have the same P-value and lead to the same conclusion. An advantage of the z test over the chi-squared test is that it also can be used with one-sided alternative hypotheses. The direction of the effect is lost in squaring z and using X^2, which only measures overall deviations from homogeneity (or independence).

► ***Try Exercise 11.18***

For 2×2 tables, we don't really need the chi-squared test because we can use the z test. Why can't we use a z statistic to test independence for larger tables, for which $df > 1$? The reason is that a z statistic can be used only to compare a *single* estimate to a *single* null hypothesis value. Examples are a z statistic for comparing a sample proportion to a null hypothesis proportion, or a difference of sample proportions to a null hypothesis value of 0 for $p_1 - p_2$.

When a table is larger than 2×2 and thus $df > 1$, we need more than one difference parameter to describe the association. For instance, suppose the aspirin trial had three groups: placebo, regular-dose aspirin, and low-dose (children's) aspirin. Then the null hypothesis of equal cancer deaths probabilities in the three groups (i.e., homogeneity) corresponds to $p_1 = p_2 = p_3$, where p_3 is the population proportion of cancer death rates for the low-dose aspirin group. (See margin for an example of a 3×2 table.) The comparison parameters are $(p_1 - p_2)$, $(p_1 - p_3)$, and $(p_2 - p_3)$. We could use a z statistic for each comparison, but not a single z statistic for the overall test of homogeneity. Only the chi-squared test can provide an overall statement about whether these three proportions are equal.

	Cancer Death	
Group	**Yes**	**No**
Placebo	p_1	$1 - p_1$
Regular dose	p_2	$1 - p_2$
Low dose	p_3	$1 - p_3$

Limitations of the Chi-Squared Test

The chi-squared test of independence, like other significance tests, provides limited information. If the P-value is very small, strong evidence exists against the null hypothesis of independence. We can infer that the variables are associated. The chi-squared statistic and the P-value tell us nothing, however, about the nature or the strength of the association. We know there is statistical significance, but the test alone does not indicate whether there is practical significance as well. A large X^2 (i.e., small P-value) means strong evidence of association but not necessarily a strong association. We'll see how to investigate the strength of association in the next section.

Recall

From Section 9.5, a small P-value does not imply an important result in practical terms. Statistical significance is not the same as *practical* significance. ◄

What about a large P-value? As with any significance test, a large P-value doesn't mean the null hypothesis is true, i.e., that the variables are independent. All we can say is that there is not enough evidence that the two variables are associated. Independence is still a plausible option, but the chi-squared test cannot be used to prove it.

SUMMARY: Misuses of the Chi-Squared Test

The chi-squared test is often misused. Some common misuses are interpreting

- a small P-value as automatically providing evidence for a strong and practically meaningful association.
- a large P-value as providing evidence for independence.

Other misuses are applying the chi-squared test.

- When some of the expected frequencies are too small (see Section 11.5).
- When separate rows or columns are dependent samples,[1] such as when each row of the table refers to the same subjects.

[1]With dependent samples, McNemar's test (Section 10.4) is the appropriate test with binary variables, and extensions of it handle categorical variables with more than two categories.

- To data that do not result from a random sample or randomized experiment.
- To data by classifying quantitative variables into categories. This results in a loss of information. It is usually more appropriate to analyze the data with methods for quantitative variables, like those the next chapter presents.

"Goodness of Fit" Chi-Squared Tests

So far we've used the chi-squared statistic to test the null hypothesis that two categorical variables are independent. In practice, the chi-squared statistic is used for a variety of hypotheses about categorical variables. For example, for three variables, the chi-squared statistic can test the hypothesis that two variables are independent at each fixed category of the third variable, such as happiness and income being independent both for women and for men (the two categories of the categorical variable, sex). What all of the various chi-squared tests have in common is that they all have a formula for finding the expected frequencies that satisfy that hypothesis and a formula for the *df* value for the test statistic.

The chi-squared statistic can be used even for a hypothesis involving a *single* categorical variable from a *single* sample.

Example 7

Testing "Goodness of Fit"

Mendelian Genetics

Picture the Scenario

In one of his experiments, the geneticist Gregor Mendel crossed pea plants of pure yellow strain with plants of pure green strain. He predicted that a second-generation hybrid seed would have probability 0.75 of being yellow and 0.25 of being green (yellow being the dominant strain). For the 8,023 hybrid seeds produced in the experiment, 6,022 were yellow and 2,001 were green.

Question to Explore

Are these results different enough from Mendel's predictions to give evidence against his theory?

Think It Through

If Mendel's theory is correct, we would expect 75% of the 8,023 seeds produced in the second generation to be yellow and 25% to be green; that is, $8023(0.75) = 6017.25$ yellow seeds and $8023(0.25) = 2005.75$ green seeds. The table in the margin shows these expected counts alongside the observed ones. To test Mendel's hypothesis, we formulate the null hypothesis as H_0: $P(\text{yellow}) = 0.75$, $P(\text{green}) = 0.25$ and the alternative hypothesis as H_a: the probabilities are different from those stated in H_0.

Applying the chi-squared statistic to test Mendel's theory, we obtain

$$X^2 = \sum \frac{(\text{observed count} - \text{expected count})^2}{\text{expected count}} =$$

$$\frac{(6022 - 6017.25)^2}{6017.25} + \frac{(2001 - 2005.75)^2}{2005.75} = 0.015$$

When a hypothesis predicts a population proportion value for each category of a variable that has c categories, the chi-squared statistic has $df = c - 1$. For this example with $c = 2$ categories (green and yellow), $df = 2 - 1 = 1$. The chi-squared statistic value of 0.015 (much lower than

Observed and expected counts for testing Mendel's theory that 75% of the seed will be yellow and 25% green.

Count	Yellow	Green	Total
observed	6022	2001	8023
expected	6017.25 (= 8023 × 0.75)	2005.75 (= 8023 × 0.25)	8023

its expected value of 1) has P-value = 0.90. There is no evidence that the data in Mendel's experiment contradicted his hypothesis.

Insight

When testing particular proportion values for a categorical variable, the chi-squared statistic is referred to as a **goodness-of-fit statistic.** The idea behind it is the same as before: to summarize how well the expected counts (computed from the hypothesized proportions) agree with the observed ones. With $c = 2$ categories, the chi-squared statistic equals the square of the z statistic used in Chapter 9 to test a hypothesis about the proportion value for one of the two categories. For example, to test Mendel's hypothesis back then, we would have formulated the null hypothesis as H_0: $p = 0.75$ that the probability p that a second-generation hybrid seed is yellow is 0.75. We find $\hat{p} = 6022/8023 = 0.7506$, $se_0 = \sqrt{p_0(1 - p_0)/n} = \sqrt{0.75(0.25)/8023} = 0.00483$, and

$$z = \frac{\hat{p} - p_0}{se_0} = \frac{0.7506 - 0.75}{0.00483} = 0.124. \text{ Note that } z^2 = 0.015.$$

The P-value using the chi-squared distribution with test statistic X^2 is identical to the two-sided P-value by using the standard normal distribution with test statistic z. An advantage of the X^2 test is that it applies even when there are more than two categories. See Exercise 11.22 for an example.

► ***Try Exercise 11.22***

A limitation of the goodness-of-fit test, like other significance tests, is that it does not tell you the ranges of plausible values for the proportion parameters. To do this, you can find confidence intervals for the individual population proportions (Section 8.2). For Mendel's experiment, a 95% confidence interval for the probability of a yellow hybrid seed is

$$0.7506 \pm 1.96(0.0048), \text{ which is } (0.74, 0.76).$$

► Activity 2

Analyzing Contingency Tables of GSS Data

It's easy to analyze associations between categorical variables measured by the General Social Survey. Let's see how.

- Go to the GSS website, sda.berkeley.edu/GSS/. Click *GSS*, with *No Weight* as the default.
- The GSS names for Table 11.1 are HAPPY (for general happiness) and FINRELA (for family income in relative terms). Enter HAPPY in the column space and FINRELA in the row space to construct a table with these as the column and row variables. Entering YEAR (2012) in the selection filter restricts the search to GSS data from the survey in 2012. By the time you read this, the 2014 GSS has been published. You can rerun the analysis with YEAR(2014) and compare results with the year 2012.
- Under Output Options, put a check in the row box (instead of in the column box) for the Percentaging option and put a check in the Summary Statistics box further below. Click on *Run the Table.*

You'll now get a contingency table relating happiness to family income for the 2012 survey. The table shows the cell counts and sample conditional distributions. It treats as the response variable the one you check for the Percentaging option. The output also shows some statistics (such as Chisq-P for the Pearson chi-squared statistic) that we're using in this chapter to analyze contingency tables.

The family income variable has five categories (far below average, below average, average, above average, far above average). Table 11.1 only used categories 2, 3 and 4. To create this table, type the family income variable as FINRELA(2, 3, 4) instead of FINRELA. (This is the same table as Table 11.1, but rows and columns are sorted differently.) Often, you may want to combine categories, such as categories 1 and 2, into a single category (for below average) and categories 4 and 5 into another single category (for above average). To create this collapsed table, type the family income variable as FINRELA(r: 1-2; 3; 4-5).

Now, create a table relating another variable to happiness. At the page on which you enter the variable names, click *Standard Codebook* and then Sequential Variable List, and you will see a range of topics covered by the GSS. Look up a topic that interests you and find the GSS code name for a variable. For the table you create,

- Find the chi-squared statistic and *df* value.
- Report the P-value and interpret the results in context.

11.2 Practicing the Basics

11.8 Life after death and gender In the 2012 GSS, 605 of 790 males and 822 of 977 females indicated a belief in life after death. (*Source*: Data from CSM, UC Berkeley.)

TRY

a. Construct a 2×2 contingency table relating gender of respondent (SEX, categories male and female) as the rows to belief about life after death (POSTLIFE, categories yes and no) as the columns.

b. Find the four expected cell counts when assuming independence. Compare them to the observed cell counts, identifying cells having more observations than expected.

c. For this data, $X^2 = 16.0$. Verify this value by plugging into the formula for X^2 and computing the sum.

11.9 Happiness and gender For the 2×3 table on gender and happiness in Exercise 11.4 (shown below), software tells us that $X^2 = 1.04$ and the P-value $= 0.59$.

	Happiness		
Gender	Not	Pretty	Very
Female	154	592	336
Male	123	502	257

a. State the null and alternative hypothesis, in context, to which these results apply.

b. Interpret the P-value.

11.10 What gives P-value = 0.05? How large an X^2 test statistic value provides a P-value of 0.05 for testing independence for the following table dimensions?

a. 2×2

b. 2×3

c. 2×5

d. 5×5

e. 3×9

11.11 Marital happiness and income In Exercise 11.5 when you used the GSS to download a 3×3 table for family income and marital happiness in 2012, you should have obtained results similar to the following table.

TRY

	Marital Happiness		
Income	Not	Pretty	Very
Above	6	62	139
Average	7	125	283
Below	6	69	115

a. State the null and alternative hypotheses for the test.

b. What is the number of degrees of freedom for the chi-squared test?

c. The chi-squared statistic for the table equals $X^2 = 4.58$. (i) What value do you expect for X^2 if the null hypothesis were true? (ii) How many standard deviations is 4.58 from this expected value? (*Hint:* The standard deviation of the chi-squared distribution equals $\sqrt{2 \times df}$). (iii) Is $X^2 = 4.58$ an extreme value? Explain.

d. How large an X^2 value would give a P-value of exactly 0.05?

e. Find (at least approximately, using Table C in the appendix) the P-value and give a conclusion for the test in context.

f. Verify that the expected cell count in the first cell equals 4.84. Could this be a problem? Explain.

11.12 First and second free throw independent? In pro basketball games during 1980–1982, when Larry Bird of the Boston Celtics made his first free throw, 251 out of 285 times he made the second one, and when he missed his first free throw, 48 out of 53 times he made the second one.

a. Form a 2×2 contingency table that cross-tabulates the outcome of the first free throw (with categories made and missed) and the outcome of the second free throw (made and missed).

b. When we use MINITAB to analyze the contingency table, we get the result

```
Pearson Chi-Square = 0.273, DF = 1,
        P-Value = 0.602
```

Does it seem as if his success on the second shot depends on whether he made the first? Explain how to interpret the result of the chi-squared test. (Here, for the chi-squared test to apply, we assume that each pair of free throws attempted is independent of any other pair during the same or other games. This is reasonable in professional sports.)

11.13 Cigarettes and marijuana The table on the following page refers to a survey[2] in which senior high school students in Dayton, Ohio, were randomly sampled. It cross-tabulates whether a student had ever smoked cigarettes and whether a student had ever used marijuana. Analyze these data by

TECH

[2]*Source*: Data from personal communication from Harry Khamis, Wright State University.

(a) finding and interpreting conditional distributions with marijuana use as the response variable and (b) reporting all five steps of the chi-squared test of independence.

	Marijuana	
Cigarettes	**Yes**	**No**
Yes	914	581
No	46	735

11.14 Smoking and alcohol Refer to the previous exercise. A similar table relates cigarette use to alcohol use. The MINITAB output for the chi-squared test follows.

a. True or false: If we use cigarette use as the column variable and alcohol use as the row variable, then we will get different values for the chi-squared statistic and the P-value shown in the output.

b. Explain what value you would get for the z statistic and P-value if you conducted a significance test of H_0: $p_1 = p_2$ against H_a: $p_1 \neq p_2$, where p_1 is the population proportion of non-cigarette users who have drunk alcohol and p_2 is the population proportion of cigarette users who have drunk alcohol.

Dayton student survey

```
Row: cigarette  Columns: alcohol
          no        yes
no        281       500
yes        46      1449

Pearson Chi-Square = 451.404,
DF = 1, P-Value = 0.000
```

11.15 Help the environment In 2010 the GSS asked whether a subject was willing to accept cuts in the standard of living to help the environment (GRNSOL), with categories (vw = very willing, fw = fairly willing, nwu = neither willing nor unwilling, nvw = not very willing, nw = not at all willing). When this was cross-tabulated with whether the respondent is currently in school or has retired (WORKSTAT), as shown below, $X^2 = 9.56$.

a. What are the hypotheses for the test to which X^2 refers?

b. Report r and c and the df value on which X^2 is based.

c. Is the P-value less than (i) 0.05? (ii) 0.025? Explain.

d. What conclusion would you make, using a significance level of (i) 0.05 and (ii) 0.025? State your conclusion in the context of this study.

	Help the Environment				
Status	**vw**	**fw**	**nwu**	**nvw**	**nw**
in school	14	47	41	43	27
retired	34	189	177	169	189

11.16 Primary food choice of alligators For alligators caught in two Florida lakes, the following table shows their primary food choice. The four food categories refer to fish, invertebrates (such as snails, insects, or crayfish), birds and reptiles (such as egrets or turtles), and others, including mammals or plants. Is there evidence that primary food choice differs between the two lakes?

	Primary Food				
Lake	**Fish**	**Invertebrates**	**Birds & Reptiles**	**Others**	***n***
Hancock	30	4	8	13	55
Trafford	13	18	12	10	53

a. Find the conditional sample distributions of primary food choice in lakes Hancock and Trafford.

b. Set up the hypotheses of interest.

c. The X^2 value for this table equals 16.79. Based on the df for the corresponding chi-squared distribution, can this be considered large? Why?

d. The P-value for the chi-squared test is less than 0.001. Write the conclusion of the test in context.

11.17 Aspirin and heart attacks A Swedish study used 1,360 patients who had suffered a stroke. The study randomly assigned each subject to an aspirin treatment or a placebo treatment. In this study, heart attacks were suffered by 28 of the 684 subjects taking placebo and 18 of the 676 subjects taking aspirin.

a. Report the data in the form of a 2×2 contingency table.

b. Show how to carry out all five steps of the null hypothesis that having a heart attack is not associated with whether one takes placebo or aspirin. (You should get a chi-squared statistic equal to 2.1.) Interpret.

11.18 z test for heart attack study Refer to the previous exercise. The printout from MINITAB reports

```
Test for difference = 0 (vs not = 0):
        Z = 1.46 P-Value = 0.144
```

a. Define population proportions p_1 and p_2 and state the hypotheses for that test.

b. Explain how the result of the chi-squared test in (b) in the previous exercise corresponds to this z test result.

11.19 Severity of fever after flu shot The study mentioned in Example 5 also looked at the severity of fever (rated as mild, moderate or severe) for all subjects who developed one after receiving a flu shot. The following table shows counts for subjects randomized to the group that received the active ingredient of the flu shot and the placebo group that received a sugar injection.

	Severity		
Group	**Mild**	**Moderate**	**Severe**
Active	39	12	12
Placebo	19	11	4

a. Researchers want to know whether the distribution of the severity of fever is the same in both groups. Formulate appropriate null and alternative hypotheses.

b. The X^2 value for these data equals 2.49. Based on the df for the chi-squared distribution, argue that this value is not extreme.

c. The P-value for the chi-squared test equals 0.287. Write the conclusion of the test in context.

11.20 What is independent of happiness? Refer to Exercises 11.6 and 11.7. For the variables that you thought might be independent,

TECH

a. At the GSS website, conduct all five steps of the chi-squared test.

b. Based on part a, which inference is most appropriate? (i) We accept the hypothesis that the variables are independent; (ii) the variables may be independent; (iii) the variables are associated.

11.21 Testing a genetic theory In an experiment on chlorophyll inheritance in corn, for 1,103 seedlings of self-fertilized heterozygous green plants, 854 seedlings were green and 249 were yellow. Theory predicts that 75% of the seedlings would be green.

TECH

a. Specify a null hypothesis for testing the theory.

b. Find the value of the chi-squared goodness-of-fit statistic and report its *df*.

c. Report the P-value and interpret.

11.22 Birthdays by quarters Based on a random sample of 84 students taken at Williams College, the table shows how many had their birthday in the first, second, third, or fourth quarter of the year. Is there evidence that the probabilities of having a birthday in a given quarter are not equal?

TRY TECH

Birthday				
Jan-Mar	**Apr-Jun**	**Jul-Sep**	**Oct-Dec**	n
19	21	31	13	84

a. Formulate the null and alternative hypotheses.

b. Find the expected values and compute the chi-squared statistic, either by hand or using software.

c. The test will be based on how many degrees of freedom?

d. Find the P-value and write a conclusion in context.

11.23 Checking a roulette wheel Karl Pearson devised the chi-squared goodness-of-fit test partly to analyze data from an experiment to analyze whether a particular roulette wheel in Monte Carlo was fair, in the sense that each outcome was equally likely in a spin of the wheel. For a given European roulette wheel with 37 pockets (with numbers 0, 1, 2, ..., 36), consider the null hypothesis that the wheel is fair.

a. For the null hypothesis, what is the probability for each pocket?

b. For an experiment with 3,700 spins of the roulette wheel, find the expected number of times each pocket is selected.

c. In the experiment, the 0 pocket occurred 110 times. Show the contribution to the X^2 statistic of the results for this pocket.

d. Comparing the observed and expected counts for all 37 pockets, we get $X^2 = 34.4$ Specify the *df* value and indicate whether there is strong evidence that the roulette wheel is not balanced. (*Hint:* Recall that the *df* value is the mean of the distribution.)

11.3 Determining the Strength of the Association

Three questions are normally addressed in analyzing contingency tables:

- **Is there an association?** The chi-squared test of independence addresses this. When the P-value is small, we infer that the variables are associated.
- **How do the cell counts differ from what independence predicts?** To answer this question, we compare each observed cell count to the corresponding expected cell count. We'll say more about this in Section 11.4.
- **How strong is the association?** Analyzing the *strength* of the association reveals whether the association is an important one or if it is statistically significant but weak and unimportant in practical terms. We now focus on this third question.

Measures of Association

For recent GSS data (2012), Table 11.10 shows associations between opinion about the death penalty and two explanatory variables—gender and race. Both sides of Table 11.10 have large chi-squared statistics and small P-values for the test of independence. We can conclude that both gender and race are associated with the death penalty opinion.

The X^2 test statistic is larger for the first table. Does this mean that opinion is more strongly associated with race than with gender? How can we quantify the strength of the association in a contingency table?

Table 11.10 GSS Data Showing Race and Gender as Explanatory Variables for Opinion About the Death Penalty

	Opinion				Opinion		
Race	Favor	Oppose	n	Gender	Favor	Oppose	n
White	70%	30%	1367	Male	69%	31%	830
Black	48%	52%	268	Female	61%	39%	994
Chi-squared = 56.4				Chi-squared = 12.3			
$df = 1$, P-value < 0.001				$df = 1$, P-value < 0.001			

Source: Data from CSM, UC Berkeley.

Recall

Section 3.1 introduced the difference and ratio of two proportions for measuring the strength of the association between two categorical variables. Section 3.2 discussed the correlation coefficient as a measure of association between two quantitative variables. ◀

Measure of Association

A **measure of association** is a statistic or a parameter that summarizes the strength of the dependence between two variables.

A measure of association takes a range of values from one extreme to another as data range from the weakest to the strongest association. It is useful for comparing associations to determine which is stronger. Later in this section we'll see that although the chi-squared test tells us how strong the evidence is that an association truly exists in the population, it does not describe the strength of that association.

Difference of Proportions

An easily interpretable measure of association is the difference between the proportions making a particular response. The population difference of proportions is 0 whenever the conditional distributions are identical, that is, when the variables are independent. The difference of proportions falls between -1 and $+1$, where 1 and -1 represent the strongest possible association. Whether you get a negative or a positive value merely reflects how the rows are ordered. Section 10.1 showed how to use a sample difference of proportions value to conduct inference (such as a confidence interval) about a population value.

Table 11.11 shows two hypothetical contingency tables relating a subject's income and whether the subject responds to a promotional mailing from a bank offering a special credit card. Case A exhibits the weakest possible association—no association. Both the high-income and the low-income subjects have 60% rejecting the credit card. The difference of proportions is $0.60 - 0.60 = 0$. By contrast, case B exhibits the strongest possible association. All those with high income accept the card, whereas all those with low income decline it. The difference of proportions is $0 - 1.0 = -1$.

Table 11.11 Decision About Accepting a Credit Card Cross-Tabulated by Income

In Case A, the conditional distributions are the same in each row (independence), so the difference of proportions is 0. In Case B the acceptance decision is completely dependent on income level, and the difference of proportions is -1.

	Case A Accept Credit Card			Case B Accept Credit Card		
Income	No	Yes	Total	No	Yes	Total
High	240 (60%)	160 (40%)	400 (100%)	0 (0%)	400 (100%)	400 (100%)
Low	360 (60%)	240 (40%)	600 (100%)	600 (100%)	0 (0%)	600 (100%)

Race	Opinion: Favor	Oppose
White	70%	30%
Black	48%	52%
Gender		
Male	69%	31%
Female	61%	39%

In practice, we don't expect data to follow either of these extremes, but the stronger the association, the larger the absolute value of the difference of proportions. For Table 11.10, shown again in the margin, the difference of proportions is 0.70 − 0.48 = 0.22 for whites and blacks and 0.69 − 0.61 = 0.08 for males and females. The difference of 0.22 between whites and blacks is much larger than the difference of 0.08 between males and females. The percentage favoring the death penalty is 22 percentage points higher for whites than for blacks but only 8 percentage points higher for males than females.

Example 8

Strength of an association

Student Stress, Depression, and Gender

Picture the Scenario

Every year, the Higher Education Research Institute at UCLA conducts a large-scale survey of college freshmen on a variety of issues. From the survey of more than 165,900 freshmen in 2013 (results available at www.heri.ucla.edu), Table 11.12 compares females and males on the percent who reported feeling frequently stressed (overwhelmed by all they have to do) and the percent who reported feeling frequently depressed during the past year. P-values for chi-squared tests of independence were less than 0.001 for each data set.

Table 11.12 Conditional Distributions of Stress and Depression, by Gender

	Stress				Depression		
Gender	Yes	No	Total	Gender	Yes	No	Total
Female	44%	56%	100%	Female	11%	89%	100%
Male	20%	80%	100%	Male	6%	94%	100%

Question to Explore

Which response variable, stress or depression, has the stronger sample association with gender?

Think It Through

The difference of proportions between females and males was 0.44 − 0.20 = 0.24 for feeling stressed and 0.11 − 0.06 = 0.05 for feeling depressed. Since 0.24 is much larger than 0.05, there is evidence of a greater difference between females and males on their feelings about stress than on depression. In the sample, stress has the stronger association with gender. The proportion feeling stressed was 24 percentage points higher for females, whereas the proportion feeling depressed was only 5 percentage points higher.

Insight

Although the difference of proportions can be as large as 1 or −1, in practice in comparisons of groups, it is rare to find differences near these limits.

In a next step, one would compute confidence intervals for each of these differences in the population, using the methods from Section 10.1. Because of the large sample size (93,824 females and 71,734 males), these are narrow: [0.237, 0.245] for the difference in stress and [0.043, 0.049] for the difference in depression, each at 95% confidence. Because the first one covers much larger values, the association is much stronger for stress.

▶ ***Try Exercise 11.24, part a***

Recall

Section 3.1 introduced the **ratio of two proportions** and showed how to interpret it. ◀

The Ratio of Proportions: Relative Risk

Another measure of association is the ratio of two proportions, p_1/p_2. In medical applications in which the proportion refers to an adverse outcome, it is called the **relative risk.**

Example 9

Relative Risk ◀

Vaccine Efficacy

Picture the Scenario

Example 4 in Chapter 8 mentioned a study in which 3,900 healthy subjects were given a flu shot manufactured with a new method that grows viruses in cell cultures. Twenty-six of the 3,900 subject still developed the flu. That same study also included a control arm of the same size, in which subjects instead receive a sugar solution. Of these 3,900 subjects, 70 developed the flu. Table 11.13 shows the data, for which $X^2 = 20.4$ $(df = 1)$, and the P-value is less than 0.0001.

Table 11.13 Results from a Vaccine Efficacy Study. Subjects are either vaccinated with a cell-derived flu vaccine or a placebo (Control Group)

	Developed Flu		
Group	**Yes**	**No**	**Total**
Vaccinated	26	3874	3900
Control	70	3830	3900

Question to Explore

Find and interpret the relative risk of developing the flu.

Think It Through

The sample proportion developing the flu is $\hat{p}_1 = 26/3900 = 0.0067$ in the vaccinated group and $\hat{p}_2 = 70/3900 = 0.0179$ in the control group. The sample relative risk is the ratio $0.0067/0.0179 = 0.374$. The proportion of subjects developing the flu in the vaccinated group is 0.374 times the proportion of subjects developing the flu in the control (unvaccinated) group. So the proportion in the vaccinated group is about a third of the proportion in the control group.

Equivalently, because $0.0179/0.0067 = 1/0.374 = 2.67$, the proportion in the control group is 2.67 times the proportion in the vaccinated group. This reciprocal value is the relative risk when the two rows are interchanged, with the control group in row 1. We see that the proportion developing the flu is 2.67 times higher in the control group compared to the vaccinated group. Commonly, this is interpreted as follows: Unvaccinated subjects are 2.67 times *more likely* to develop the flu, where 2.67 times more likely refers to the relative risk.

Insight

The ordering of rows is arbitrary. Many people find it easier to interpret the relative risk for the ordering for which its value is *above* 1.0. A sample relative risk of 2.67 represents a fairly strong association. To see whether the true relative risk is far from the value of 1.0, which represents independence (i.e., the proportion of developing the flu are the same in each group), we could construct a 95% confidence interval for it. Using methods not covered in this book, the confidence interval for the population relative risk equals [1.7, 4.2], so the proportion developing the flu can be as little as 70% and as much as 4 times larger in the control (unvaccinated) group.

▶ ***Try Exercises 11.24, part b, and 11.30, part a***

In Example 9, the proportion of interest was close to 0 for each group, but the relative risk was relatively far from 1. When this happens, an association may be practically important even though the difference of proportions is close to 0. (For the data in Example 9, the difference of proportion equals 0.0113, or 1.1 percentage points.) If the chance of getting the flu is only a bit higher in the unvaccinated group, but that chance is nearly three times higher, the association is practically significant. The relative risk is often more informative than the difference of proportions for comparing proportions that are both close to 0.

Properties of the Relative Risk

- The relative risk can equal any nonnegative number.
- When $p_1 = p_2$, the variables are independent, and the relative risk $= 1.0$.
- Values farther from 1.0 (in either direction) represent stronger associations. Two values for the relative risk represent the same strength of association, but in opposite directions, when one value is the reciprocal of the other. See Figure 11.5.

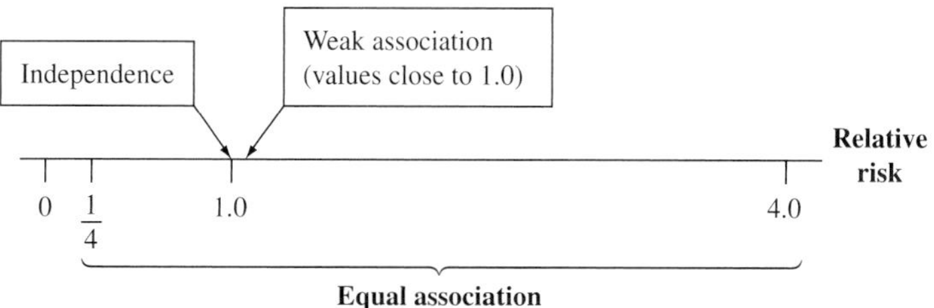

▲ **Figure 11.5** Values of the Relative Risk Farther from 1.0 Represent Stronger Association. **Question** Why do relative risks that take reciprocal values, such as 4 and $\frac{1}{4}$, represent the same strength of association?

A relative risk of 8 is farther from independence and represents a stronger association than a relative risk of 4, and a relative risk of $\frac{1}{8}$ is farther from independence than a relative risk of $\frac{1}{4}$. But relative risk $= 4.0$ and relative risk $= 1/4.0 = 0.25$ represent the same strength of association. When the relative risk $p_1/p_2 = 0.25$, then p_1 is 0.25 times p_2. Equivalently, p_2 is $1/0.25 = 4.0$ times p_1. Whether we get 4.0 or 0.25 for the relative risk depends merely on which group we call group 1 and which we call group 2.

Odds and Odds Ratio

A third measure for the association uses the concept of the **odds**. For contingency tables such as Table 11.13, the odds in a given row are defined as the ratio of the two conditional proportions in that row. This equals $p_1/(1 - p_1)$ in the first row and $p_2/(1 - p_2)$ in the second row. The **odds ratio** is then the ratio of these two odds, $\dfrac{p_1/(1 - p_1)}{p_2/(1 - p_2)}$.

For the vaccine efficacy study from Example 9, the table in the margin shows the conditional distribution for whether someone developed the flu.

Conditional Proportions for Table 11.13

	Developed Flu		
Group	**Yes**	**No**	**Total**
Vaccinated	0.0067	0.9933	1
Control	0.0179	0.9821	1

For the vaccinated group (row 1), the estimated odds of developing the flu are $\hat{p}_1/(1 - \hat{p}_1) = 0.0067/0.9933 = 0.0067$. For the control group (row 2), the estimated odds equal $\hat{p}_2/(1 - \hat{p}_2) = 0.0179/0.9821 = 0.0182$. How can these numbers be interpreted? The odds compare the proportion of subjects developing the flu to those who don't. For instance, in the control group, the proportion developing the flu is about 0.02 times the proportion not developing the flu. Writing an odds of 0.02 (or 1/50) as 1:50, we get the interpretation that, in the control group, for every one subject developing the flu, 50 are not developing it. In the vaccinated group, the odds of 0.0067, which is 1/150 or 1:150, means that for every one subject developing the flu, 150 do not.

Clearly, the odds of developing the flu are much lower in the vaccinated group, but how much lower? The odds *ratio* tells you. Because for every subject with the flu there are 150 without it in the vaccinated group, but only about 50 without it in the control group, the odds are about a third lower in the vaccinated group. We get the precise number by computing the sample odds ratio as $\frac{\hat{p}_1/(1 - \hat{p}_1)}{\hat{p}_2/(1 - \hat{p}_2)} = \frac{0.0067}{0.0182} = 0.368$. The odds of developing the flu in the vaccinated group are 0.368 times the odds in the control group, so about one-third of it. We could also say that the odds of developing the flu are two-thirds lower in the vaccinated group.

Similar to the relative risk, when flipping the rows so that the control group is row 1 and the vaccinated group is row 2, we get the reciprocal: The odds of developing the flu in the control group are about $1/(1/3) = 3$ times the odds in the vaccinated group. An odds ratio of 3 (or similarily 1/3) indicates a fairly strong association.

Properties of the Odds Ratio

The odds ratio has several properties in common with the relative risk:

- The odds ratio can equal any nonnegative number.
- Under independence $(p_1 = p_2)$, the odds ratio equals 1.
- Values farther from 1.0 (in either direction) represent stronger associations. Two values for the odds ratio represent the same strength of association, but in opposite directions, when one value is the reciprocal of the other. See Figure 11.6.

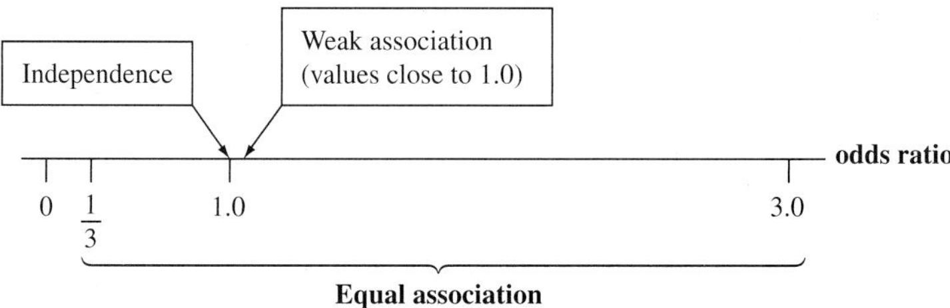

▲ **Figure 11.6 Values of the Odds Ratio Farther from 1.0 Represent Stronger Association.** An odds ratio of 1 implies independence.

Caution

Do not confuse the odds ratio with the relative risk. Any interpretation involving "times more likely" refers to the relative risk. ◀

Despite these similarities, the odds ratio is **not the same** as the relative risk! One is a ratio of odds, the other a ratio of proportions, and they have different interpretations. For instance, for the study on stress between female and male college freshmen in Table 11.12, you can check that the odds ratio equals 3.14 and the relative risk 2.20. A common mistake is to compute the odds ratio and interpret it like a relative risk, e.g., saying that females are *3.14 times more likely* to experience stress than males. In fact, females are only 2.2 times more likely to experience stress (the relative risk), but the *odds* of experiencing stress are 3.14 times greater.

Caution

Estimating the proportion of smokers (or nonsmokers) that develop lung cancer is not possible because the rows do not represent a random sample. ◀

	Lung Cancer		
Smoker	Cases (= Yes)	Controls (= No)	Total
Yes	688	650	**1338**
No	21	59	**70**
Total	**709**	**709**	

Not a random sample

You may wonder why statisticians bother with computing such a complicated measure that is prone to misinterpretations. There are two main reasons. One is that for case-control studies such as those discussed in Section 4.4, it is impossible to estimate the difference or ratio of proportions because the study design did not employ random sampling. However, the odds ratio can be estimated. So, the only way to measure the association in such studies is to compute the odds ratio. An example is the case-control study on the association between smoking and lung cancer discussed in Example 8 in Section 4.4 and shown again in the margin.

Because the study did not use a random sample of smokers and nonsmokers to see whether they developed lung cancer, it is impossible to estimate the difference (or ratio) of proportions developing lung cancer from it. However, one can compute the odds ratio, which is 2.97, indicating a rather strong association between smoking and lung cancer.

The second reason the odds (and the odds ratio) are so popular is that they naturally appear in regression models for a binary response variable, called logistic regression. This will be further discussed in Section 13.6.

Did you know?

The odds ratio approximately equals the relative risk if the outcome of interest is rare. Because developing lung cancer is rare in general (i.e., for both smokers and nonsmokers), and because the odds ratio was about 3, we can actually say that smokers are about 3 times *more likely* to develop lung cancer. ◀

Income and Happiness from Table 11.1. The percentages are the conditional distributions of happiness in each row.

	Happiness		
Income	Not Too	Pretty	Very
Above	29 (8%)	178 (52%)	135 (39%)
Average	83 (10%)	494 (58%)	277 (32%)
Below	104 (19%)	314 (58%)	119 (22%)

Association in $r \times c$ Tables

The difference and ratio of proportions and the odds ratio are all defined for 2×2 tables. How can we measure the association in larger tables? For general $r \times c$ (r = # of rows, c = # of columns) tables, one option is to pick out a particular response category and compare it across two rows. For instance, consider the 3×3 table from Section 11.1 on income and happiness, shown again in the margin. For it, we found a large X^2, i.e., a significant association, but how strong is it in practical terms and how can we describe it? Let's pick the two rows for above- and below-average income (rows 1 and 3) and compare them on the outcome, Very Happy. Using the ratio of proportions as the measure of association, the proportion reporting being very happy is $0.39/0.22 = 1.77$ times larger (or 77% larger) for those with above- rather than below-average income. For the Not Too Happy outcome, the ratio of proportions is $0.08/0.19 = 0.42$. So the proportion of subjects Not Too Happy is 58% lower for those with above-average income compared to those with below-average income. These numbers (and you can compute those for other comparisons) show an association, but with ratios of proportions around 2 (or 0.5), it is not that strong.

Chi-Squared and Association

You may be tempted to regard a large value of the X^2 statistic (or a very small P-value) in the test of independence as indicating a strong association. As mentioned before, this is a misuse of the statistic.

In Practice Large X^2 Does Not Mean There's a Strong Association

A large value for X^2 provides strong evidence that the variables are associated. It does not imply, however, that the variables have a strong association. This statistic merely indicates (through its P-value) how certain we can be that the variables are associated, not how strong that association is. The evidence can be strong, yet the association itself can be very weak. For a given strength of association, larger X^2 values occur for larger sample sizes. Large X^2 values can occur with weak associations if the sample size is sufficiently large.

For example, Cases A, B, and C in Table 11.14 are hypothetical tables relating gender and whether one attends religious services weekly. The association in each case is weak—the conditional distribution for females (51% yes, 49% no) is nearly identical to the conditional distribution for males (49% yes, 51% no). All three cases show the same weak strength of association: The difference between the proportions of females and males who say yes is $0.51 - 0.49 = 0.02$ in each, and the relative risk of $0.51/0.49 = 1.04$ is very close to 1.

Table 11.14 Response on Attending Religious Services Weekly by Gender, Showing Weak but Identical Associations

In each case the difference between proportions is small, only 0.02, and the relative risk (1.04) is close to 1.

	Case A			Case B			Case C		
	Yes	No	n	Yes	No	n	Yes	No	n
Female	51%	49%	100	51%	49%	200	51%	49%	10,000
Male	49%	51%	100	49%	51%	200	49%	51%	10,000
	Chi-squared = 0.08			Chi-squared = 0.16			Chi-squared = 8.0		
	P-value = 0.78			P-value = 0.69			P-value = 0.005		

Caution

If the sample size is sufficiently large, a X^2 value large enough to be considered statistically significant can occur even if the association between the two categorical variables is weak. ◀

For the sample of size 200 in Case A, $X^2 = 0.08$, which has a P-value of 0.78. Case B has twice as large a sample size, with the cell counts doubling. For its sample of size 400, $X^2 = 0.16$, for which the P-value = 0.69. So, when the cell counts double, X^2 doubles. Similarly, for the sample size of 20,000 (100 times as large as $n = 200$) in Case C, $X^2 = 8.0$ (100 times as large as $X^2 = 0.08$). Then the P-value = 0.005.

In summary, for fixed conditional distributions, the value of X^2 is directly proportional to the sample size—larger values occur with larger sample sizes. Like other test statistics, the larger the X^2 statistic, the smaller the P-value and the stronger the evidence against the null hypothesis. However, a small P-value results from even a weak association when the sample size is large, as Case C shows.

11.3 Practicing the Basics

11.24 Democrat, race, and gender The two tables show 2012 GSS data on whether someone is identified as Democrat, by race and by gender. TRY

	Democrat				Democrat		
race	Yes	No	Total	gender	Yes	No	Total
black	212	88	300	female	421	660	1081
white	422	1046	1468	male	278	601	879

a. Find the difference of proportions between blacks and whites and between females and males. Interpret each. Which variable has a stronger association with whether someone identifies as Democrat, race or gender? Explain.

b. Find the ratio of proportions between blacks and whites and between females and males. Interpret each. Which variable has a stronger association with whether someone identifies as Democrat, race or gender? Explain.

c. Find the odds of identifying as Democrat for blacks and whites and interpret each. Then find the odds ratio and interpret.

11.25 Death penalty associations Table 11.10, summarized again here, showed the associations between death penalty opinion and gender or race.

	Opinion			Opinion	
race	Favor	Oppose	gender	Favor	Oppose
black	70%	30%	female	69%	31%
white	48%	52%	male	61%	39%

a. True or false: The table with the larger X^2 statistic necessarily has the stronger association. Explain.

b. To make an inference about the strength of association in the population, you can construct confidence intervals around the sample differences of proportions. The 95% confidence intervals are (0.15, 0.28) comparing whites and blacks and (0.04, 0.12) comparing males and females. In the *population*, can you make a conclusion about which variable is more strongly associated with the death penalty opinion? Explain.

11.26 Smoking and alcohol The table refers to a survey of senior high school students in Dayton, Ohio. It cross-tabulates whether a student had ever smoked cigarettes and whether a student had ever drunk alcohol and shows counts and the conditional distributions of alcohol use.

	Alcohol		
Cigarettes	**Yes**	**No**	**Total**
Yes	1449 (97%)	46 (3%)	1495 (100%)
No	500 (64%)	281 (36%)	781 (100%)

a. Describe the strength of association by using the difference between users and nonusers of cigarettes in the proportions who have used alcohol. Interpret.

b. Describe the strength of association by using the relative risk of using alcohol, comparing those who have used or not used cigarettes. Interpret.

c. Find the odds of having used alcohol for users and nonusers of cigarettes. Interpret each. Then, describe the strength of association, using the odds ratio.

11.27 Sex of victim and offender For murders in the United States in 2012, the table cross-tabulates the sex of the victim by the sex of the offender. Find and interpret a measure of association, treating sex of victim as the response variable.

	Sex of Victim	
Sex of Offender	**Female**	**Male**
Female	124	421
Male	1609	3725

Source: Data from www.fbi.gov.

11.28 Smelling and mortality A recent study (Pinto et al., Olfactory Dysfunction Predicts 5-Year Mortality in Older Adults. PLoS ONE 9(10):e107541, 2014) mentions that anosmic (those with almost no sense of smell) older adults had more than three times the odds of death over a 5-year span compared to normosmic (those with normal smell) individuals. Does this imply that anosmic older adults were more than three times as likely to die over the next 5 years than normosmic ones? Explain.

11.29 Vioxx In September 2004, the pharmaceutical company Merck withdrew its blockbuster drug rofecoxib (a painkiller, better known under its brand name, Vioxx) from the worldwide market amid concerns about its safety. By that time, millions of people had used the drug. In a 2000 study comparing rofecoxib to a control group (naproxen), it was mentioned that "Myocardial infarctions were less common in the naproxen group than in the rofecoxib group (0.1 percent vs. 0.4 percent; 95 percent confidence interval for the difference, 0.1 to 0.6 percent; relative risk, 0.2; 95 percent confidence interval, 0.1 to 0.7)". (*Source:* Bombadier et al., *New England Journal of Medicine*, vol. 343, 2000, pp. 1520-8.)

a. Find and interpret the difference of proportions between the naproxen and rofecoxib groups.

b. Interpret the stated relative risk.

c. In this study, myocardial infarctions were how much more likely to occur in the rofecoxib group than in the naproxen group?

11.30 Egg and cell derived vaccine TRY When comparing the cell-derived flu vaccine mentioned in Example 9 to a more traditionally manufactured egg-derived vaccine, the following data were obtained.

	Developed Flu		
Group	**Yes**	**No**	**Total**
Cell-derived	26	3874	3900
Egg-derived	24	3876	3900

a. Find the relative risk of developing the flu and interpret.

b. Find the odds ratio and interpret.

c. Based on either measure, is it likely that the probability of developing the flu is similar in the two groups? Explain.

11.31 Risk of dying for teenagers According to summarized data from 1999 to 2006 accessed from the Centers of Disease Control and Prevention, the annual probability that a male teenager at age 19 is likely to die is about 0.00135 and 0.00046 for females age 19. (www.cdc.gov)

a. Compare these rates using the difference of proportions, and interpret.

b. Compare these rates using the relative risk, and interpret.

c. Which of the two measures seems more useful when both proportions are very close to 0? Explain.

11.32 Marital happiness The table shows 2012 GSS data on marital and general happiness for married respondents.

	General Happiness		
Marital Happiness	**Not Too Happy**	**Happy**	**Very Happy**
Not Too Happy	11	11	4
Happy	31	215	34
Very Happy	20	231	337

a. The chi-squared test of independence has $X^2 = 214$. What conclusion would you make using a significance level of 0.05? Interpret.

b. Does this large chi-squared value imply there is a strong association between marital and general happiness? Explain.

c. Find the difference in the proportion of being not too happy between those that are not too happy in their marriage and those that are very happy in their marriage. Interpret that difference.

d. Find and interpret the relative risk of being not too happy, comparing the lowest and highest marital happiness group. Interpret.

11.33 Party ID and gender The table shows the 2012 GSS data on gender and political party identification from Exercise 11.1. (The row totals are slightly different from the second table in Exercise 11.24 because selecting Independent is ignored.) The chi-squared test of independence has $X^2 = 10.04$ with a P-value of 0.0066, indicating a significant association. Let's describe this association:

	Political Party Identification			
Gender	Democrat	Independent	Republican	Total
Female	421	398	244	1063
Male	278	367	198	843

Source: Data from CSM, UC Berkeley.

a. Estimate the difference between females and males in the proportion who identify themselves as Republicans. Interpret.

b. Estimate the difference between females and males in the proportion who identify themselves as Democrat. Interpret.

c. Estimate the ratio between females and males in the proportion who identify themselves as Republican. Interpret.

d. Estimate the ratio between females and males in the proportion who identify themselves as Democrat. Interpret.

e. What can you say about the strength of the association between gender and whether identifying as Republican? What about gender and whether identifying as Democrat?

11.34 Chi-squared versus measuring association For the table on marital happiness in Exercise 11.32, the chi-squared statistic equals 214 ($df = 4$, P-value < 0.0001). Explain the difference between the purposes of the chi-squared test in part a and the descriptive analysis in parts c and d in that exercise, which compares conditional distributions by using measures of association. (*Hint:* Is a chi-squared test a descriptive or inferential analysis?)

11.4 Using Residuals to Reveal the Pattern of Association

The chi-squared test and measures of association such as the difference and ratio of proportions and the odds ratio are fundamental methods for analyzing contingency tables. The P-value for X^2 summarizes the strength of evidence against H_0: independence (or homogeneity). If the P-value is small, then we conclude that somewhere in the contingency table the population cell proportions differ from independence (or homogeneity). The chi-squared test does not indicate, however, for which cells this is the case.

Residual Analysis

Recall

Section 3.3 introduced a **residual** for quantitative variables as the difference between an observed response and a predicted response for a regression equation. For categorical variables, a residual compares an observed count to an expected count that represents what H_0 predicts. ◀

A cell-by-cell comparison of the observed counts with the counts that are expected when H_0 is true reveals the nature of the evidence. The difference between an observed and expected count in a particular cell is called a **residual**.

For example, Table 11.5 reported observed and expected cell counts for happiness and family income. The first column of this table is summarized in the margin, with the expected cell counts in parentheses. The first cell reports 29 subjects with above-average income who are not too happy. The expected count is 42.6. The residual is $29 - 42.6 = -13.6$. The residual is negative when, as in this cell, fewer subjects are in the cell than expected under H_0. The residual is positive when more subjects are in the cell than expected, as in the cell having observed count $= 104$ (below-average income subjects who are not too happy) and residual $104 - 66.9 = 37.1$.

Income	Not Too Happy
Above average	29 (42.6)
Average	83 (106.4)
Below average	104 (66.9)

How do we know whether a residual is large enough to indicate strong evidence of a deviation from independence in that cell? To answer this question, we use an adjusted form of the residual that behaves like a *z*-score. It is called the **standardized residual**.

Standardized Residual

The **standardized residual** for a cell equals

$$(\text{observed count} - \text{expected count})/se.$$

Here, *se* denotes a standard error for the sampling distribution of (observed count − expected count), when the variables are independent.

A standardized residual reports the number of standard errors that an observed count falls from its expected count. The *se* describes how much the (observed − expected) difference would tend to vary in repeated random sampling if the variables were independent. Its formula is complex, and we'll not give it here. Software can easily find standardized residuals for us.

When H_0: independence is true, the standardized residuals have approximately a standard normal distribution: They fluctuate around a mean of 0, with a standard deviation of 1. There is about a 5% chance that any particular standardized residual exceeds 2 in absolute value, and less than a 1% chance that it exceeds 3 in absolute value. See the margin figure. Therefore, a standardized residual larger than 3 in absolute value provides strong evidence against independence in that cell. If independence would hold, it would be highly unlikely (less than a 1% chance) to observe such a value in that cell. A value above +3 suggests that the population proportion for that cell is higher than what independence predicts. A value below −3 indicates that the population proportion for that cell is lower than what independence predicts.

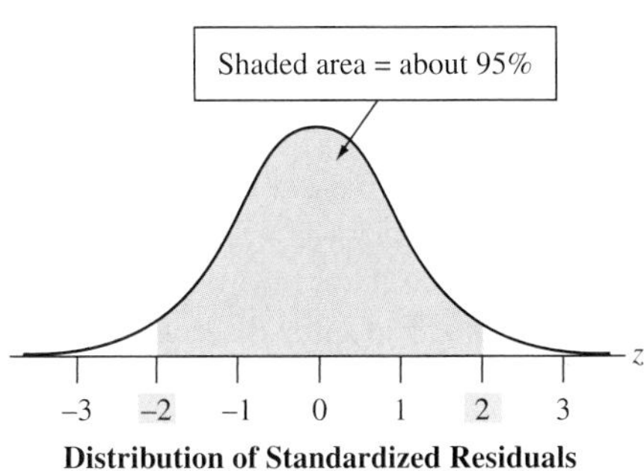

Distribution of Standardized Residuals

When we inspect many cells in a table, some standardized residuals could be large just by random variation. Values below −3 or above +3, however, are quite convincing evidence of a true effect in that cell.

Standardized residuals

Example 10

Religiosity and Gender

Picture the Scenario

Table 11.14 showed some artificial data comparing females and males on their religious attendance. Let's look at some actual data on religiosity. Table 11.15 displays observed and expected cell counts and the standardized residuals for the association between gender and response to the question, "To what extent do you consider yourself a religious person?" The possible responses were (very religious, moderately religious, slightly religious, not religious at all). The data are from the 2012 GSS. The table is in the form provided by MINITAB (which actually calls the standardized residuals "adjusted residuals").

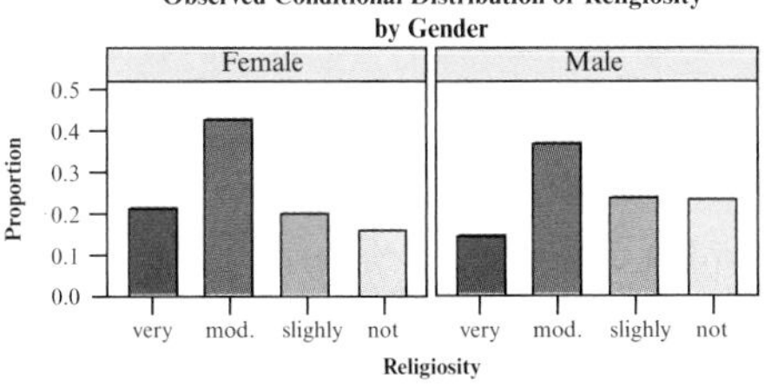

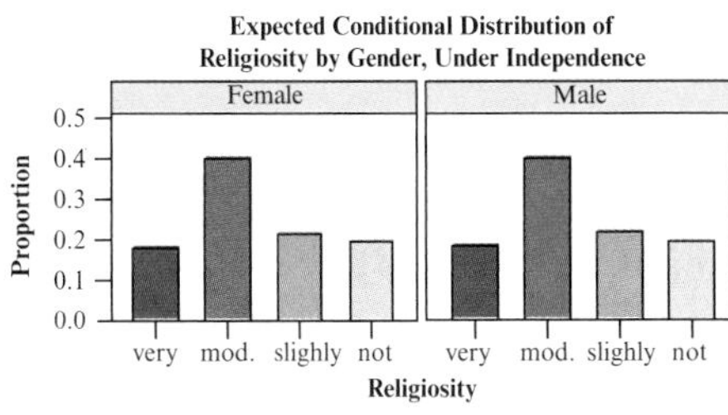

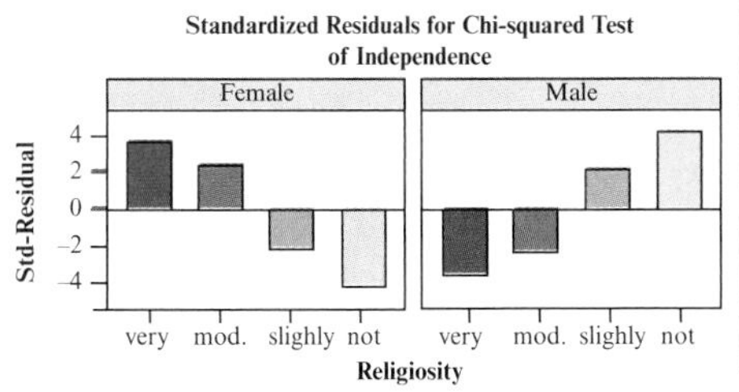

Table 11.15 Religiosity by Gender, with Expected Counts and Standardized Residuals

Large positive standardized residuals (in green) indicate strong evidence of a higher population cell proportion than expected under independence. Large negative standardized residuals (in red) indicate strong evidence of a lower population proportion than expected. The three margin figures show the observed proportion, the ones expected under independence and the standardized residuals.

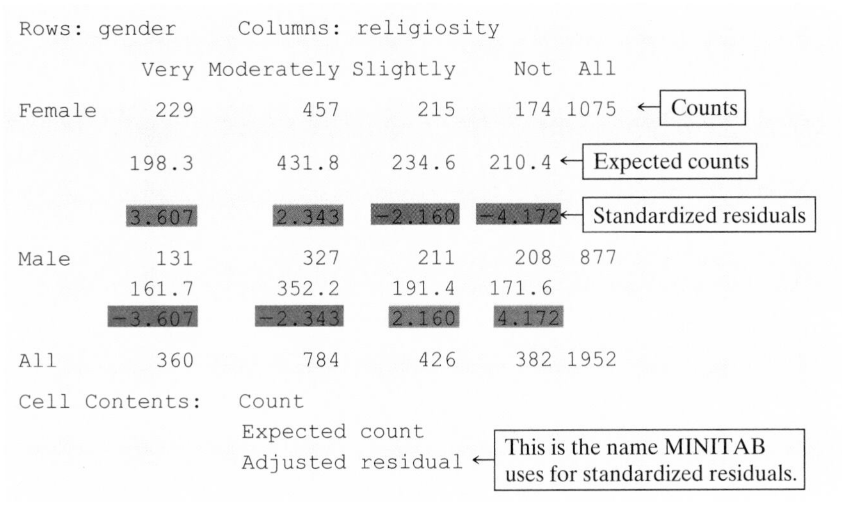

Rows: gender   Columns: religiosity

	Very	Moderately	Slightly	Not	All	
Female	229	457	215	174	1075	← Counts
	198.3	431.8	234.6	210.4		← Expected counts
	3.607	2.343	−2.160	−4.172		← Standardized residuals
Male	131	327	211	208	877	
	161.7	352.2	191.4	171.6		
	−3.607	−2.343	2.160	4.172		
All	360	784	426	382	1952	

Cell Contents: Count
Expected count
Adjusted residual ← This is the name MINITAB uses for standardized residuals.

Source: Data from CSM, UC Berkeley.

Questions to Explore

a. How would you interpret the standardized residual of 3.607 in the first cell?

b. Interpret the standardized residuals in the entire table.

Think It Through

a. The cell for females who are very religious has observed count = 229, expected count = 198.3, and standardized residual = 3.607. The difference between the observed and expected counts is more than 3 standard errors. This tells us this cell shows a much greater discrepancy than we'd expect if the variables were truly independent. There's strong evidence that the population proportion for that cell (female and very religious) is higher than independence predicts.

b. Table 11.15 exhibits standardized residuals larger than 3 in absolute value in 4 out of the 8 cells. These are the cells in which the observed count is very different from that expected under independence. For the two cells with standardized residual larger than 3, there is strong evidence of a more frequent occurrence than if religiosity and gender were independent. For the two cells with standardized residual less than −3, the observed count is much smaller than the expected count. There's strong evidence that the population proportion for these cells is much lower than what independence would imply.

Insight

The X^2 value for this table is 31.5 (P-value < 0.001), indicating strong evidence for an association. The standardized residuals help to describe the pattern of this association: Compared to what we'd expect if religiosity and gender were independent, there are more females who are very religious or moderately religious and more males who are slightly religious or not at all religious.

▶ ***Try Exercise 11.35***

In Practice Software Can Find Standardized Residuals

Most software has the option of reporting **standardized residuals.** For instance, they are available in MINITAB (where they are called *adjusted residuals*), in SPSS (where they are called *adjusted standardized residuals*), and at the GSS website (by checking *Z*-statistic under Output Options).

11.4 Practicing the Basics

11.35 Standardized residuals for happiness and income

TRY The table displays the observed and expected cell counts and the standardized residuals for testing independence of happiness and family income, for GSS data.

Rows: Income Columns: Happiness

	not	pretty	very	All
above	29	178	135	342
	42.6	194.6	104.8	
	-2.490	-2.021	3.955	
average	83	494	277	854
	106.4	485.9	261.7	
	-3.410	0.787	1.598	
below	104	314	119	537
	66.9	305.5	164.5	
	5.830	0.889	-5.131	
All	216	986	531	1733

a. How would you interpret the standardized residual of −2.49?

b. Interpret the standardized residuals highlighted in green.

c. Interpret the standardized residuals highlighted in red.

11.36 Happiness and religious attendance The table shows MINITAB output for data from the 2008 GSS on happiness and frequency of attending religious services (1 = at most several times a year, 2 = once a month to nearly every week, 3 = every week to several times a week).

```
Rows: religion      Columns:         happiness
Not too happy     Pretty happy      Very happy

1      201             609              268
     4.057           1.731           -5.107
2       46             224              132
    -2.566           0.456            1.541
3       66             265              196
    -2.263          -2.376            4.385
Cell Contents:      Count
                    Adjusted residual
Pearson Chi-Square = 36.445, DF = 4,
P-Value = 0.000
```

a. Based on the chi-squared statistic and P-value, give a conclusion about the association between the variables.

b. The numbers below the counts in the table are standardized residuals. Which cells have strong evidence that in the population there are more subjects than if the variables were independent?

c. Which cells have strong evidence that in the population there are fewer subjects than if the variables were independent?

11.37 Marital happiness and general happiness Exercise 11.32 showed the association between general happiness and marital happiness. The table shown here gives the standardized residuals for those data in parentheses.

a. Explain what a relatively small standardized residual such as −0.9 in the second cell represents.

b. Identify the cells in which you'd infer that the population has more cases than would occur if happiness and marital happiness were independent. Pick one of these cells and explain the association relative to independence.

Marital Happiness	Happiness		
	Not Too Happy	Pretty Happy	Very Happy
Not too happy	11 (7.2)	11 (−0.9)	4 (−2.8)
Pretty happy	31 (3.3)	215 (10.4)	34 (−12.2)
Very happy	20 (−5.8)	231 (−9.8)	337 (12.9)

11.38 Happiness and marital status The screen shot from the GSS website shows standardized residuals (called Z-statistics) and cell counts for 2012 GSS data on happiness (the column) and marital status (the row). The color coding is based on the magnitude of the Z-statistic (= standardized residual) and is explained in the legend. Summarize the association by indicating which marital statuses have strong evidence of (i) more and (ii) fewer people in the population in the Very Happy category than if the variables were independent.

Frequency Distribution

Cells contain: -Z-statistic -N of cases		HAPPY			
		1 VERY HAPPY	2 PRETTY HAPPY	3 NOT TOO HAPPY	ROW TOTAL
MARITAL	1: MARRIED	10.3 375	-3.8 458	-8.1 64	--- 897
	2: WIDOWED	-2.4 35	1.2 97	1.5 29	--- 161
	3: DIVORCED	-4.2 64	1.9 191	2.8 60	--- 315
	4: SEPARATED	-2.7 10	-1.2 32	5.3 24	--- 66
	5: NEVER MARRIED	-5.5 109	2.4 316	3.8 100	--- 525
	COL TOTAL	--- 593	--- 1,094	--- 277	--- 1,964

Color coding:	<-2.0	<-1.0	<0.0	>0.0	>1.0	>2.0	Z
N in each cell:	Smaller than expected			Larger than expected			

11.39 Gender gap? The table in Exercise 11.1 on gender and party identification is shown again. The largest standardized residuals in absolute value were +2.98 for females who identified as Democrats and −2.98 for males who identified as Democrats. Interpret.

Gender	Political Party Identification			Total
	Democrat	Independent	Republican	
Female	421	398	244	1063
Male	278	367	198	843

Source: Data from CSM, UC Berkeley.

11.40 Ideology and political party Go to the GSS website sda.berkeley.edu/GSS/. Construct the 7 × 8 contingency table relating political ideology (POLVIEWS) and party identification (PARTYID) for the year 2012. (Enter YEAR (2012) in the Selection filter.) Select Summary Statistics and Z-statistic under Output Options to get the value of the chi-squared statistic and standardized residuals.

TECH

a. Summarize the results of carrying out the chi-squared test.

b. What do you learn from the residuals that you did not learn from the chi-squared test?

11.5 Fisher's Exact and Permutation Tests

The chi-squared test of independence, like one- and two-sample z tests for proportions, is a large-sample test. When the expected cell counts are small, any of them less than about 5, the sampling distribution of X^2 may not follow a chi-squared distribution. Then, tests that do not rely on this assumption to find P-values are more appropriate. For 2×2 contingency tables, one such test is **Fisher's exact test** of independence. For larger tables, we present a related **permutation** test. These tests work for any sample size but are particularly useful when the sample size is small. They find the exact sampling distribution of the test statistic rather than using the approximation provided by the chi-squared distribution. This is why they are often called exact tests.

Fisher's Exact Test

Fisher's exact test of the null hypothesis that two variables are independent was proposed by the British statistician and geneticist, Sir Ronald Fisher. The test is called *exact* because it uses a sampling distribution that gives exact probability calculations rather than the approximate ones that use the chi-squared distribution.

The calculations for Fisher's exact test are complex and beyond the scope of this text. The principle behind the test is straightforward (see the next section and Exercise 11.87), however, and statistical software (or a web app) provides its P-value. The smaller the P-value, the stronger the evidence that the variables are associated.

Example 11

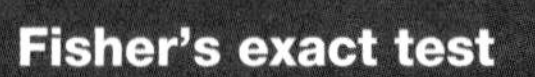

A Tea-Tasting Experiment

Picture the Scenario

In introducing his small-sample test of independence in 1935, Fisher described the following experiment: Fisher enjoyed taking a break in the afternoon for tea. One day, his colleague Dr. Muriel Bristol claimed that when drinking tea she could tell whether the milk or the tea had been added to the cup first (she preferred milk first). To test her claim, Fisher asked her to taste eight cups of tea, four of which had the milk added first and four of which had the tea added first. She was told there were four cups of each type and was asked to indicate which four had the milk added first. The order of presenting the cups to her was randomized.

Table 11.16 shows the result of the experiment. Dr. Bristol identified three of the four cups correctly that had milk poured first.

Table 11.16 Result of Tea-Tasting Experiment

The table cross-tabulates what was actually poured first (milk or tea) by what Dr. Bristol guessed was poured first. She had to indicate which four of the eight cups had the milk poured first. The first row refers to the four cups that had milk poured first, of which Dr. Bristol correctly identified three, and one (incorrectly) as having tea poured first.

	Dr. Bristol's Guess		
Actual	**Milk**	**Tea**	**Total**
Milk	3	1	4
Tea	1	3	4
Total	**4**	**4**	**8**

In Practice The hypotheses in Fisher's exact test are often formulated in terms of the odds ratio, a measure for the association discussed in the previous section. Here, we test whether the odds of guessing milk are the same for cups with milk or tea added first (H_0: odds ratio = 1, no association) against the alternative that the odds of guessing milk are higher for those cups with milk added first (H_a: odds ratio > 1, a positive association).

In Words

In statistics, **asymptotic** means "large sample." Mathematically, the theory behind large-sample statistical methods applies as the sample size grows toward infinity "asymptotically."

For those cases when milk was poured first (row 1), denote p_1 as the probability of guessing that milk was added first. For those cases when tea was poured first, denote p_2 as the probability of guessing that milk was added first. If Dr. Bristol has no ability to distinguish what was poured first, then her probability of guessing milk is the same, regardless what was poured first, so $p_1 = p_2$. If she has a higher probability of guessing milk for those cups that actually had milk first, then $p_1 > p_2$. So we shall test H_0: $p_1 = p_2$ (no ability) against H_a: $p_1 > p_2$. This tests the null hypothesis of no association between her guesses and the actual pouring order against the alternative that there is a *positive* association, i.e., that she more often gets it right when indeed milk was added first.

Questions to Explore

a. Show the five possible contingency tables that could have occurred for this experiment. (This is the sample space.)

b. Table 11.17 shows the result of using SPSS software to conduct the chi-squared test of the null hypothesis that her predictions were independent of the actual order of pouring. Is this test and its P-value appropriate for these data? Why or why not?

Table 11.17 Result of Fisher's Exact Test for Tea-Tasting Experiment

The chi-squared P-value is listed under Asymp. Sig., and the Fisher's exact test P-values are listed under Exact Sig. "Sig" is short for *significance* and "asymp." is short for *asymptotic*.

	Value	df	Asymp. Sig. (2-sided)	Exact Sig. (2-sided)	Exact Sig. (1-sided)
Pearson Chi-Square	2.000	1	.157		
Fisher's Exact Test				.486	.243

4 cells (100.0%) have expected count less than 5.

c. Table 11.17 also shows the result for Fisher's exact test of the same null hypothesis. The one-sided version of the test pertains to the alternative that she has a higher probability of guessing milk for those cups that actually had milk first (i.e., a positive association). What does this P-value suggest about Dr. Bristol's ability to distinguish what was poured first?

Think It Through

a. The possible sample tables have four observations in each row because there were four cups with milk poured first and four cups with tea poured first. The tables also have four observations in each column because Dr. Bristol was told there were four cups of each type and was asked to identify which four had the milk added first. Of the four cups in which milk was poured first (row 1 of the table), the number she could identify correctly is 4, 3, 2, 1, or 0. These outcomes correspond to the sample tables:

	Guess Poured First									
Poured First	Milk	Tea	Milk	Tea	Milk	Tea	Milk	Tea	Milk	Tea
Milk	4	0	3	1	2	2	1	3	0	4
Tea	0	4	1	3	2	2	3	1	4	0

These are the five possible tables with totals of 4 in each row and 4 in each column.

b. The cell counts in Table 11.16 are small. Each cell has expected count $(4 \times 4)/8 = 2$. Since they are less than 5, the chi-squared test is not appropriate. In fact, the last line of the SPSS output warns us that all four cells have expected counts less than 5. The output reports $X^2 = 2.0$ with P-value $= 0.157$, but software provides results whether or not they are valid, and it's up to us to know when we can use a method.

c. The one-sided P-value reported by SPSS is for the alternative $H_a: p_1 > p_2$. It equals 0.243. This is the probability, presuming H_0 to be true, of the observed table (Table 11.16) and the more extreme table giving even more evidence in favor of $p_1 > p_2$. That more extreme table is the one with counts (4, 0) in the first row and (0, 4) in the second row, corresponding to guessing all four cups correctly. The P-value of 0.243 does not give much evidence against the null hypothesis.

Recall
Expected cell count = (row total × column total) divided by total sample size. ◀

Insight

This experiment did not establish an association between the actual order of pouring and Dr. Bristol's predictions. If she had predicted all four cups correctly, the one-sided P-value would have been 0.014. We might then believe her claim. With a larger sample, we would not need such extreme results to get a small P-value. For instance, if 12 instead of 8 cups were used, she could afford to guess one incorrectly, and the P-value would still be less than 0.05.

► ***Try Exercise 11.43***

In Practice To get the P-value, one adds the probability (computed under H_0) of all those tables that are as extreme or even more extreme. For the tea-tasting example, these are the probabilities of 3 or 4 correct guesses.

In part a of Example 11, notice that for the given row and column marginal totals of four each, the count in the first cell determines the other three cell counts. For example, for the actual data (Table 11.16), knowing she guessed three of the four cups correctly that had milk poured first determines the other three cells (see the margin). Because the count in the first cell determines the others, that cell count is regarded as the test statistic for Fisher's exact test. The P-value sums the probability of that count and of the other possible counts for that cell that provide even more evidence in support of H_a.

	Guess		
Actual	**Milk**	**Tea**	**Total**
Milk	3	—	4
Tea	—	—	4
Total	4	4	8

For the two-sided alternative $H_a: p_1 \neq p_2$, Table 11.17 indicates a P-value of 0.486. This alternative hypothesis investigates whether her predictions are better or worse than with random guessing. The P-value of 0.486 also does not give much evidence against the null hypothesis of no association between her guesses and the actual pouring order.

SUMMARY: Fisher's Exact Test of Independence for 2 × 2 Tables

1. **Assumptions:**
   Two binary categorical variables
   Randomization, such as random sampling or a randomized experiment
2. **Hypotheses:**
   H_0: The two variables are independent ($H_0: p_1 = p_2$)
   H_a: The two variables are associated
   (Choose $H_a: p_1 \neq p_2$ or $H_a: p_1 > p_2$ or $H_a: p_1 < p_2$).
3. **Test statistic:** First cell count (this determines the others, given the margin totals).
4. **P-value:** Probability that the first cell count equals the observed value or a value even more extreme than observed in the direction predicted by H_a.
5. **Conclusion:** Report P-value and interpret in context. If a decision is needed, reject H_0 when P-value ≤ significance level (such as 0.05).

The main use of Fisher's exact test is for small sample sizes, when the chi-squared test is not valid. However, Fisher's exact test can be used with *any* sample sizes. It also extends to tables of arbitrary size $r \times c$. The computations are complex, and unfortunately most software currently can perform it only for 2×2 tables, but the next section shows how Fisher's exact test is a special case of a permutation test and how this can be used (together with a web app) to test independence in general $r \times c$ tables.

Setup of Tea Tasting Experiment
The last column shows one random permutation (shuffeling) of the original guesses.

Cup	Actual	Guess	Random Permutation
1	M	M	T
2	M	T	M
3	T	T	M
4	T	M	T
5	M	M	T
6	T	T	T
7	M	M	M
8	T	T	M

Contingency Table Based on Random Permutation

	Guess	
Actual	**Milk**	**Tea**
Milk	2	2
Tea	2	2

Fisher's Exact Test Is a Permutation Test

Suppose the random ordering of the eight cups presented to Dr. Bristol is as shown in the second column of the table in the margin, where M and T stand for milk or tea being poured first, respectively. The third column shows what Dr. Bristol thinks was poured first. We see that three of her guesses of those cups that had milk first are correct (cups 1, 5, and 7) and one is incorrect (cup 2).

Under the null hypothesis of no association, we believe Dr. Bristol is just randomly guessing, i.e., randomly picking a sequence of four Ms and four Ts for column three. Because she is randomly deciding which four have milk or tea first, any sequence of four Ms and four Ts is equally likely to occur. For instance, she could have picked the sequence T M M T T T M M as shown in the last column of the margin table, which would have yielded two incorrect guesses (cups 1 and 3) out of the ones with milk first. Overall, there are 70 different sequences (or **permutations**) of the four Ms and four Ts that could have been picked, all equally likely under the null hypothesis of no association. Using these, we can build the sampling distribution under the null hypothesis of no association. Because the test uses permutations of the original observations, it is called a **permutation test**.

For each of the 70 permutations, we form the contingency table as in Table 11.16 and find how many guesses are correct out of the ones when milk was poured first, i.e., we find the count in the first cell. For the random permutation mentioned above, this would be the count of 2 (see margin table). Table 11.18 shows the possible cell counts for the first cell and how often each one arises among the 70 permutations.

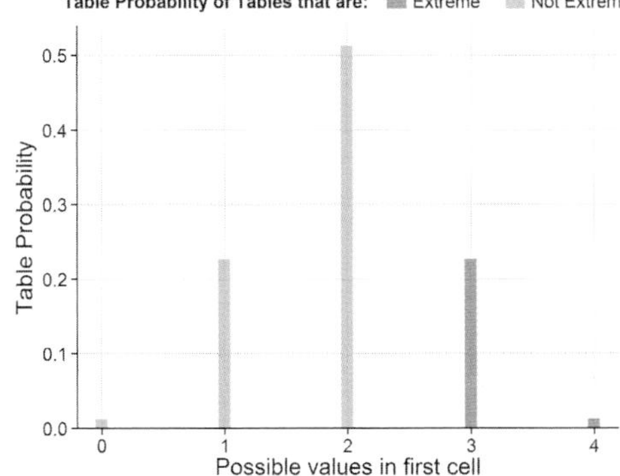

Sampling distribution of first cell count. (Screenshot taken from Fisher's Exact Test web app.)

Table 11.18 Sampling Distribution of the Number of Correct Guesses of Cups with Milk Poured First.

This distribution assumes that the null hypothesis of no association is true. The margin figure shows the distribution graphically.

	Correct Guesses (first cell count)					
	0	**1**	**2**	**3**	**4**	**Total**
Number of Permutations	1	16	36	16	1	**70**
Relative Frequency	1.4%	22.9%	51.4%	22.9%	1.4%	**100%**

There is exactly 1 permutation out of the 70 possible with 0 correct guesses (the sequence T T M M T M T M, the exact opposite of the actual pouring sequence), 16 permutations with exactly 1 incorrect guess (one of them the actually observed one from Dr. Bristol), 36 permutations with exactly 2 incorrect guesses (such as the one mentioned), another 16 with exactly 3 incorrect guesses, and exactly 1 permutation in which all 4 guesses are correct (the permutation that equals the actual pouring sequence). We already knew from part b of Example 11 that 0, 1, 2, 3 and 4 are the possible entries for the first cell, but now, by looking at the relative frequencies in Table 11.18, we also know how likely they occur under the null hypothesis of no association. For instance, if we repeated the experiment over and over again, in every 1 out of 70 repetitions (i.e., in 1.4% of all cases), Dr. Bristol would actually correctly identify all four cups with milk added first, simply by chance (i.e., sheer luck) and without having any ability.

Using the exact sampling distribution of the number of correct guesses, we can now judge how likely it is to get 3 or even all 4 (the more extreme outcomes under the alternative $H_a: p_1 > p_2$) correct when one is just guessing. Because $0.229 + 0.014 = 0.243$, there is a 24.3% chance of getting 3 or 4 correct, just by chance. This is precisely the P-value for Fisher's exact test for the one-sided alternative that we obtained in Example 11 and which led to the conclusion indicated there. The P-value is called an exact P-value because it uses the exact, not approximate, sampling distribution derived by considering all possible permutations.

Permutation Test for an Association in General $r \times c$ Tables

Recall

The larger X^2, the stronger the evidence for an association, but the chi-squared distribution is only appropriate to use as a reference when all expected cell counts are larger than 5. See Section 11.2. ◄

The same idea of constructing a sampling distribution by permutations can be extended to general $r \times c$ tables. The only difference to the 2×2 case is that we no longer can use the first cell (the number of correctly identified cups with milk added first) as a test statistic but need a more general measure summarizing the association. We will use one that we have used all along to test for an association, the chi-squared statistic X^2. However, finding the P-value under the chi-squared distribution with $df = (r - 1)(c - 1)$ may no longer be appropriate because of small cell counts. Instead, we will find its exact sampling distribution considering all possible permutations or, if there are too many, a very large number of randomly generated permutations. This will let us judge whether the observed value of X^2 is large. We used a similar idea when we compared two population means across two groups in Section 10.3. There, we found the permutation distribution of the difference in sample means to judge how extreme the observed difference is under the null hypothesis of equal distributions. Similarly, here we will find the permutation distribution of X^2 to judge how extreme the observed X^2 is under the null hypothesis of independence (i.e., identical conditional distributions). To carry out the permutation test in practice, we will need specialized software, such as the Permutation Test for Independence web app available on the book's website.

Example 12

Permutation test ◄

Edward Snowden—Hero or Criminal?

Picture the Scenario

In 2013, Edward Snowden revealed classified material about massive spying activities by the U.S National Security Agency (NSA), not only on U.S citizens but on citizens worldwide. Although the United States wants to try him in court for breaking several laws, many other countries point out that the activities of the NSA severely violated their privacy laws. In these countries, Snowden is often celebrated as a hero. In a 2014 survey at Williams College, 12 randomly selected U.S. students and 8 randomly selected international students were asked whether Edward Snowden should be considered a hero, a criminal, or neither. Table 11.19 shows the results, for which $X^2 = 6.9$. We want to test whether these data provide evidence that the opinion on Edward Snowden differs between U.S. and international students at Williams College. The null hypothesis is that there is no association, i.e., the conditional distribution of opinion is the same for U.S. and international students.

Table 11.19 Survey Conducted at Williams College on Whether Edward Snowden Should Be Considered a Hero, a Criminal, or Neither

$X^2 = 6.9$ for this table.

	Opinion on Edward Snowden			
Student Status	**Hero**	**Criminal**	**Neither**	**Total**
U.S.	1	9	2	12
International	5	2	1	8
Total	**6**	**11**	**3**	**20**

Questions to Explore

a. Can we use the chi-squared distribution with $df = (2 - 1)(3 - 1) = 2$ to find the P-value for $X^2 = 6.9$?

b. How can we construct the permutation distribution of X^2 under the null hypothesis of no association?

c. How can we judge whether the observed value of 6.9 is extreme and find the permutation P-value?

Table 11.20 Original Observations for Data Summarized in Table 11.19.

The last column shows one random permutation of the original status labels.

Student	Status	Response	Random Permutation
1	Int	Hero	US
2	US	Criminal	Int
3	US	Neither	US
4	US	Criminal	US
5	US	Hero	US
6	US	Criminal	US
7	US	Criminal	Int
8	US	Criminal	US
9	US	Criminal	US
10	Int	Criminal	Int
11	Int	Hero	Int
12	US	Neither	US
13	Int	Hero	US
14	Int	Hero	Int
15	Int	Hero	US
16	US	Criminal	US
17	Int	Criminal	Int
18	Int	Neither	US
19	US	Criminal	Int
20	US	Criminal	Int

Think It Through

a. Many counts in Table 11.19 are small, leading to expected values that are smaller than 5. For instance, the expected count is 3.6 in the first cell and 1.2 in the last cell. Using the chi-squared distribution may lead to questionable conclusions because it may not approximate the actual sampling distribution of X^2 well, especially in the upper tail.

b. The first three columns of Table 11.20 in the margin show the raw data from the survey before summarizing it in Table 11.19. (You can check that there are, for instance, 5 international students with response Hero.) Under the null hypothesis of no association, any given response is equally likely to have come from a U.S. student or an international student. For instance, under the null hypothesis, the probability of a student selecting Hero does not depend on whether he or she is a U.S. or international student. Then, the status of a student is merely a label that loses its relevance, and we get a data set that is equally likely to occur (under the null hypothesis) when we rearrange (permute) these labels.

This is similar to the tea-tasting experiment, in which, under the null hypothesis of no association, any of the 70 permutations of the four Ms and four Ts was equally likely to occur. Here, any permutation (or shuffling) of the status labels for the 12 U.S. and 8 international students yields a data set that is equally likely to occur.

The last column in the margin table shows one such random permutation. Taken together with the response column, it leads to the cell counts shown in Table 11.21. For instance, with the permuted status labels, we now have 4 U.S. students and 2 international students with response Hero.

Table 11.21 has the same row and column margins as the originally observed Table 11.19. (Permuting the labels doesn't change the fact that we have a total of 12 U.S. and 8 international students as well as a total of 6 students responding Hero, 11 responding Criminal, and 2 responding Neither, so the margins don't change.) However, the cell counts in the body of the table differ from the ones in Table 11.19, leading to a chi-squared statistic of $X^2 = 3.1$. If the null hypothesis

Table 11.21 Contingency Table Based on the Permuted Status Labels
$X^2 = 3.1$ for this table.

	Opinion on Edward Snowden			
Student	**Hero**	**Criminal**	**Neither**	**Total**
U.S.	4	5	3	12
International	2	6	0	8
Total	**6**	**11**	**3**	**20**

is true, this table (and hence this value for the chi-squared statistic) is equally likely to be observed as the originally observed table (and its chi-squared value).

A different permutation of the status labels results in yet another table with the same margins but different cell counts. For each table generated from a permutation, we compute the chi-squared statistic X^2. Note that several permutations can give rise to the same table and hence X^2 statistic. For instance, just switching the last two labels for students 19 and 20 (both U.S. students with response Criminal) results in the same table (hence X^2 statistic) as the one observed.

Tabulating all the unique values of X^2 that can arise and their frequency of occurrence yields the exact (as opposed to approximate) sampling distribution of X^2 under the null hypothesis of no association. When the cell counts are large, it will have the shape of a chi-squared distribution, but for small cell counts, it may look more irregular. The table in the margin shows an excerpt of the permutation distribution, whereas Figure 11.7, taken from the web app, represents it with a histogram. Both are based on 10,000 randomly generated permutations.

Excerpt of sampling distribution of X^2 based on 10,000 random permutations

X^2	# Perms	Freq. (%)	Cumulative Freq. (%)
0.3	1713	17.3	17.3
...	...	...	...
3.1	554	5.5	84.3
...	...	...	...
6.6	80	0.8	96.8
6.9	154	1.5	98.4
7.4	81	0.8	99.2
...	...	...	...
13.4	1	<0.0	100
	10,000	100%	

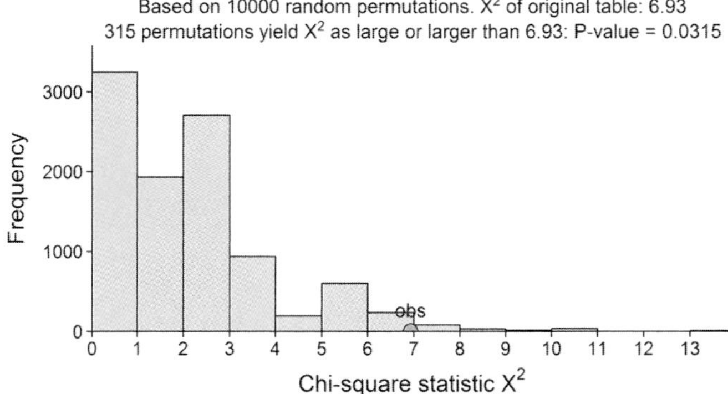

▲ **Figure 11.7** Permutation Distribution of X^2 Based on Data in Table 11.19. **(Screenshot from Permutation Test for Independence web app.)** The dot indicates the observed value of $X^2 = 6.9$. **Question** For tables with larger cell counts than Table 11.19, the shape of the permutation distribution is approximately equal to the shape of which distribution?

c. How extreme is the observed chi-squared statistic of 6.9? Figure 11.7 already gives us an idea. The observed value is indicated by the dot, which is in the upper tail of the sampling distribution. To find the permutation P-value, we need to find the proportion of the 10,000 randomly generated permutations that gave a chi-squared statistic as large or larger than the one observed. As the title of the plot in Figure 11.7 indicates, 315 of the 10,000 permutations had an X^2 as large or larger than 6.9, for a proportion of 0.0315. This is the

In Practice When the number of all possible permutations is too large, one takes a large random sample (such as 10,000) of them and computes X^2 for each. The proportion of permutations with X^2 as large or larger than the observed one is then a very good approximation of the exact permutation P-value.

permutation P-value for the chi-squared test. If there were no difference in the opinion of U.S. and international students, observing a test statistic of 6.9 or larger would be unlikely (estimated probability of 0.031). Because the P-value is small, there is evidence that the opinion on Edward Snowden differs between U.S. and international students.

► ***Try Exercises 11.46 and the Activity in Exercise 11.89***

Using the Ordering of Categories

Some categorical variables have a natural ordering of the categories. There is a low end and a high end of the categorical scale. Examples are education attained (less than high school, high school, some college, college degree, advanced degree), appraisal of a company's inventory level (too low, about right, too high), and the happiness and income variables used in this chapter. Such variables are called **ordinal** variables. The chi-squared test of independence treats the categories as unordered. It takes the same value regardless of the order the categories are listed in the table. This is because with any reordering of the categories, the set of row and column totals does not change, so the expected frequency that goes with a particular observed cell count does not change.

When there is only a weak association, tests that use the ordering information are often more powerful than the chi-squared, giving smaller P-values and stronger evidence against H_0. One way to do this treats the two categorical variables as quantitative: Assign scores to the rows and to the columns and then use the correlation to describe the strength of the association. A significance test can be based on the size of the correlation. This is beyond our scope here, but the next chapter presents inference methods for two quantitative variables.

11.5 Practicing the Basics

11.41 Keeping old dogs mentally sharp In an experiment with beagles ages 7–11, the dogs attempted to learn how to find a treat under a certain black-colored block and then relearn that task with a white-colored block. The control group of dogs received standard care and diet. The diet and exercise group were given dog food fortified with vegetables and citrus pulp and vitamin E and C supplements plus extra exercise and social play. All 12 dogs in the diet and exercise group were able to solve the entire task, but only 2 of the 8 dogs in the control group could do so. (Background material from N. W. Milgram et al., *Neurobiology of Aging*, vol. 26, 2005, pp. 77–90.)

TECH

a. Show how to summarize the results in a contingency table.

b. Conduct all steps of Fisher's exact test of the hypothesis that whether a dog can solve the task is independent of the treatment group. Use the two-sided alternative hypothesis. Interpret.

c. Why is it improper to conduct the chi-squared test for these data?

11.42 Tea-tasting results Consider the tea-tasting experiment of Example 11 and Table 11.16. Consider the possible sample table in which all four of her predictions about the cups that had milk poured first are correct. Using software, find the P-value for the one-sided alternative. Interpret the P-value.

TECH

11.43 Claritin and nervousness An advertisement by Schering Corporation for the allergy drug Claritin mentioned that in a pediatric randomized clinical trial, symptoms of nervousness were shown by 4 of 188 patients on Claritin and 2 of 262 patients taking placebo. Denote the population proportion who would show such symptoms by p_1 for Claritin and by p_2 for placebo. The computer printout shows results of significance tests for H_0: $p_1 = p_2$.

TRY

a. Report the P-value for the small-sample test with H_a: $p_1 \neq p_2$. Interpret in the context of this study.

b. Is it appropriate to conduct the chi-squared test for these data? Why or why not?

Analyses of Claritin data

```
Rows: treatment  Columns: nervousness

              yes     no

Claritin       4     184
Placebo        2     260

Statistic                          P-Value
Fisher's Exact Test (2-Tail)        0.24
Chi-squared = 1.55                  0.21
```

11.44 AIDS and condom use Chatterjee et al. (1995, p. 132) described a study about the effect of condoms in reducing the spread of AIDS. This two-year Italian study followed heterosexual couples where one partner was infected with the HIV virus. Of 171 couples who always used condoms, 3 partners became infected with HIV, whereas of 55 couples who did not always use condoms, 8 partners became infected. Test whether the rates are significantly different.

a. Define p_1 and p_2 in this context and specify the null and two-sided alternative hypotheses.

b. For these data, software reports

```
Pearson Chi-Square = 14.704, DF = 1,
P-Value = 0.0001
*Note* 1 cell with expected count
less than 5 Fisher's exact test:
P-Value = 0.0007
```

Report the result of the test that you feel is most appropriate for these data. For the test you chose, report the P-value and interpret in the context of this study.

11.45 Quizzes worthwhile? TECH To help students gauge their understanding of basic concepts, short online quizzes with immediate feedback were administered in an introductory statistics (STAT) and an unrelated computer science (CS) course in the first few weeks of the semester. For those students who realized they knew less than they thought after taking the quizzes, did this change their study habits? All 5 students in the STAT course said it did, whereas 6 of the 12 students in the CS course said it did. Is there evidence that students in the STAT course had a larger probability of changing their habits?

a. Write these results as a 2 × 2 contingency table.

b. The sampling distribution (derived from all possible 6188 permutations) for the possible counts in the first cell of the contingency table is

cell count:	0	1	2	3	4	5	Total
#perms:	6	165	1100	2475	1980	462	6188

Find the proportion of tables that have a cell count as large or larger than the one observed.

c. Find the permutation P-value and write a conclusion for the hypothesis when using a 5% significance level.

d. Check your results by entering the contingency table from part a into the Fisher's Exact Test web app accessible from the book's website.

11.46 Quizzes enhance learning? TRY TECH Refer to the previous exercise. After the semester, students were asked whether the quizzes were beneficial, with possible answers (i) Yes, I realized that I knew more than I thought, (ii)Yes, I realized that I knew less than I thought, (iii) No. Results of the survey are shown in the following table. Is there evidence that the distribution of the student responses differ between the two courses?

	Beneficial		
Group	**Yes, More**	**Yes, Less**	**No**
STAT	3	5	18
CS	9	12	20

a. Formulate the null and alternative hypotheses of interest.

b. Suggest a test statistic to use for this test.

c. If all expected cell counts were at least 5, what distribution would the test statistic from part b follow?

d. Of 10,000 random permutations, 2,660 resulted in an X^2 statistic as large or larger than the observed one of 3.2. Approximate the permutation P-value and write a conclusion for the test.

e. Use the Permutation Test of Independence web app accessible from the book's website to enter the contingency table and replicate the results from part d.

Chapter Review

ANSWERS TO THE CHAPTER FIGURE QUESTIONS

Figure 11.1 The proportion of those not too happy increases with lower income, whereas the proportion of those very happy decreases with lower income. The proportion of those pretty happy is roughly the same in each of the three income categories.

Figure 11.2 The height of the bars is the same for males and females at each level of happiness.

Figure 11.3 The chi-squared statistic can't be negative because it sums squared differences divided by positive expected frequencies.

Figure 11.4 We use only the right tail because larger chi-squared values provide greater evidence against H_0. Chi-squared values in the left tail represent small differences between observed and expected frequencies and do not provide evidence against H_0.

Figure 11.5 Whether we get $\frac{1}{4}$ or 4 for the relative risk depends merely on which group we call group 1 and which we call group 2.

Figure 11.7 For tables with large cell counts, the permutation (= sampling) distribution of X^2 looks like the chi-squared distribution.

CHAPTER SUMMARY

This chapter showed how to analyze the association between two categorical variables:

- By *describing the counts* in contingency tables using the **conditional distributions** across the categories of the response variable. If the population conditional distributions are identical, the two variables are **independent.**
- By using the **chi-squared** statistic to **test the null hypothesis of independence.** When comparing several groups in terms of a single categorical response variable, the test is also referred to as a test of **homogeneity.**
- By *describing the strength of association with a* **measure of association** such as the **difference of proportions**, the **ratio of proportions** (the **relative risk**) or the **ratio of odds** (the odds ratio). Under independence, the population difference of proportions equals 0 and the population relative risk and odds ratio equal 1. The stronger the association, the farther the measures fall on either side from these baseline values.
- By *describing the pattern of association* by comparing observed and expected cell counts using **standardized residuals.** A standardized residual reports the number of standard errors that an observed count falls from an expected count. A value larger than about 3 in absolute value indicates that the cell provides strong evidence of association.

The **expected cell counts** are values with the same margins as the observed cell counts but that satisfy the null hypothesis of independence. The **chi-squared test statistic** compares the observed cell counts to the expected cell counts, using

$$X^2 = \sum \frac{(\text{observed count} - \text{expected count})^2}{\text{expected count}}.$$

Under the null hypothesis, the X^2 test statistic has a large sample **chi-squared distribution.** The **degrees of freedom** depend on the number of rows r and the number of columns c through $df = (r - 1) \times (c - 1)$. The P-value is the right-tail probability above the observed value of X^2.

The expected cell counts for the chi-squared test should be at least 5. **Fisher's exact test** does not have a sample size restriction. It is used to test independence in 2×2 tables with samples that are too small for the chi-squared test to apply. Fisher's exact test is a special case of a **permutation test** in general $r \times c$ tables that use the exact rather than the approximate sampling distribution of the X^2 statistic.

The chi-squared statistic can also be used for a hypothesis involving a single categorical variable. For testing a hypothesis that predicts particular population proportion values for each category of the variable, the chi-squared statistic is referred to as a **goodness-of-fit** statistic.

SUMMARY OF NOTATION

X^2 = chi-squared statistic for testing independence of two categorical variables

CHAPTER PROBLEMS

Practicing the Basics

11.47 Female for president? When recent General Social Surveys have asked, "If your party nominated a woman for president, would you vote for her if she were qualified for the job?" about 94% of females and 94% of males answered yes, the rest answered no. (*Source*: Data from CSM, UC Berkeley.)

a. For males and for females, report the conditional distributions on this response variable in a 2×2 table, using outcome categories (yes, no).

b. If results for the entire population are similar to these, does it seem possible that gender and opinion about having a woman president are independent? Explain.

11.48 Down syndrome diagnostic test The table shown, from Example 8 in Chapter 5, cross-tabulates whether a fetus has Down syndrome by whether the triple blood diagnostic test for Down syndrome is positive (that is, indicates that the fetus has Down syndrome).

a. Tabulate the conditional distributions for the blood test result, given the true Down syndrome status.

b. For the Down cases, what percentage was diagnosed as positive by the diagnostic test? For the unaffected cases, what percentage got a negative test result? Does the diagnostic test appear to be a good one?

c. Construct the conditional distribution on Down syndrome status for those who have a positive test result. (*Hint:* You condition on the first column total and find proportions in that column.) Of those cases, what percentage truly have Down syndrome? Is the result surprising? Explain why this probability is small.

	Blood Test Result		
Down Syndrome Status	**Positive**	**Negative**	**Total**
D (Down)	48	6	54
D^c (unaffected)	1307	3921	5228
Total	1355	3927	5282

11.49 Down and chi-squared For the data in the previous exercise, $X^2 = 114.4$. Show all steps of the chi-squared test of independence.

11.50 Herbs and the common cold A recent randomized experiment of a multiherbal formula (Immumax) containing echinacea, garlic, ginseng, zinc, and vitamin C was found to improve cold symptoms in adults over a placebo group. "At the end of the study, eight (39%) of the placebo recipients and 18 (60%) of the Immumax recipients reported that the study medication had helped improve their cold symptoms (chi-squared P-value = 0.01)." (M. Yakoot et al., *International Journal of General Medicine*, vol. 4, 2011, pp. 45–51).

a. Identify the response variable and the explanatory variable and their categories for the 2×2 contingency table that provided this particular analysis.

b. How would you explain to someone who has never studied statistics how to interpret the parenthetical part of the quoted sentence?

11.51 Happiness and number of friends The table shows GSS data on happiness and the number of close friends, with expected cell counts given underneath the observed counts.

	Happiness			
Number of Close Friends	Not Too Happy	Pretty Happy	Very Happy	Total
0–1	34	92	43	169
	19.2	95.1	54.7	
2–5	83	418	200	701
	79.5	394.6	226.9	
6 or more	47	304	225	576
	65.3	324.3	186.4	
Total	164	814	468	1446

a. Suppose the variables were independent. Explain what this means in this context.

b. Explain what is meant by an expected cell count. Show how to get the expected cell count for the first cell, for which the observed count is 34.

c. Compare the expected cell frequencies to the observed counts. Based on this, what is a profile of subjects who tend to be (i) more happy than independence predicts and (ii) less happy than independence predicts.

11.52 Gender gap? Exercise 11.1 showed a 2×3 table relating gender and political party identification, shown again here. The chi-squared statistic for these data equals 10.04 with a P-value of 0.0066. Conduct all five steps of the chi-squared test.

	Political Party Identification			
Gender	Democrat	Independent	Republican	Total
Female	421	398	244	1063
Male	278	367	198	843

Source: Data from CSM, UC Berkeley.

11.53 Job satisfaction and income A recent GSS was used to cross-tabulate income (<\$15 thousand, \$15–25 thousand, \$25–40 thousand, >\$40 thousand) in dollars with job satisfaction (very dissatisfied, little dissatisfied, moderately satisfied, very satisfied) for 96 subjects.

a. For these data, $X^2 = 6.0$. What is its *df* value, and what is its approximate sampling distribution, if H_0 is true?

b. For this test, the P-value is 0.74. Interpret in the context of these variables.

c. What decision would you make with a 0.05 significance level? Can you accept H_0 and conclude that job satisfaction is independent of income?

11.54 Aspirin and heart attacks for women A study in the *New England Journal of Medicine* compared cardiovascular events for treatments of low-dose aspirin or placebo among 39, 876 healthy female health care providers for an average duration of about 10 years. Results indicated that women receiving aspirin and those receiving placebo did not differ for rates of a first major cardiovascular event, death from cardiovascular causes, or fatal or nonfatal heart attacks. However, women receiving aspirin had lower rates of stroke than those receiving placebo (data from *N. Engl. J. Med.*, vol. 352, 2005, pp. 1293–1304).

TECH

Women's Aspirin Study Data

	Cardiovascular Events		
Group	Mini-Stroke	Stroke	No Strokes
Placebo	240	259	19443
Aspirin	185	219	19530

a. Use software to test independence. Show (i) assumptions, (ii) hypotheses, (iii) test statistic, (iv) P-value, (v) conclusion in the context of this study.

b. Describe the association by finding and interpreting the relative risk for the stroke category.

11.55 Crossing peas When crossing round (R) and yellow (Y) peas with wrinkled (W) and green (G) peas, one can get any combination of color and appearance, denoted here as RY, RG, WY and WG, but traits round and yellow are dominant. In particular, Gregor Mendel postulated that these four possible combinations would appear in the ratio 9:3:3:1. From an experiment involving 556 such crossings, 315 were RY, 108 RG, 101 WY and 32 WG.

a. Construct a table showing these counts.

b. If Mendel's theory about the ratio 9:3:3:2 is correct, how likely is each combination to occur? (*Hint:* Of $9 + 3 + 3 + 1 = 16$ crossings, how many are of type RY?)

c. Find the expected values for the four combinations assuming Mendel's theory is correct.

d. A chi-squared test for testing Mendel's theory will be based on how many degrees of freedom?

e. The chi-squared statistic for these data equals 0.47. Will the P-value for the test be large or small? Why?

11.56 Women's role A recent GSS presented the statement, "Women should take care of running their homes and leave running the country up to men," and 14.8% of the male respondents agreed. Of the female respondents, 15.9% agreed. Of respondents having less than a high school education, 39.0% agreed. Of respondents having at least a high school education, 11.7% agreed.

a. Report the difference between the proportion of males and the proportion of females who agree.

b. Report the difference between the proportion at the low education level and the proportion at the high education level who agree.

c. Which variable, gender or educational level, seems to have the stronger association with opinion? Explain your reasoning.

11.57 Seat belt helps? The table refers to passengers in autos and light trucks involved in accidents in the state of Maine in a recent year.

a. Use the difference of proportions to describe the strength of association. Interpret.

b. Use the relative risk to describe the strength of association. Interpret.

Maine Accident Data

	Injury	
Seat Belt	**Yes**	**No**
No	3865	27,037
Yes	2409	35,383

Source: Dr. Cristanna Cook, Medical Care Development, Augusta, Maine.

11.58 Serious side effects In 2007, the FDA announced that the popular drug Zelnorm used to treat irritable bowel syndrome was withdrawn from the market, citing concerns about serious side effects. The analysis of several studies revealed that 13 of 11,614 patients receiving the drug had a serious side effect such as heart attack or stroke, compared to just 1 out of 7,031 on placebo.

a. Construct a 2×2 contingency table from these data.

b. Compute the relative risk and interpret.

c. Compute the odds ratio and interpret.

d. In a letter to health care professionals, the drug maker quoted a P-value of 0.024 for the comparison between the probability of a serious side effect in the drug and placebo group. By entering the data into the Fisher's Exact Test web app (or other software), show that this is the P-value for Fisher's exact test with a two-sided alternative hypothesis. What are the conclusions at a 0.05 significance level?

11.59 Pesticides The following table, on the presence of pesticide residues in samples of organic and conventional food, was analyzed in Examples 2 and 3 in Chapter 3.

	Pesticides	
Food Type	**Yes**	**No**
Organic	29	98
Conventional	19485	7086

a. Compute the relative risk and interpret.

b. Find the reciprocal of your answer to part a and interpret.

c. Compute the odds ratio and interpret.

d. Find the reciprocal of your answer to part c and interpret.

e. What's wrong with this statement: The proportion of conventional food samples with pesticide residues present is more than 9 times larger than the proportion of organic food samples with pesticide residues present.

11.60 Race and party ID The table shows data from an SPSS printout for some analyses of 2008 GSS data on race and party ID.

a. Interpret the expected count for the first cell.

b. Interpret the standardized residual of 12.5 for the first cell (SPSS calls it an adjusted residual).

c. How would you summarize to someone who has never studied statistics what you learn from the standardized residuals given in the four corner cells on this printout?

race * party_ID Crosstabulation

			party ID			
			democrat	**independent**	**republican**	**Total**
race	black	Count	192	75	8	275
		Expected Count	100.0	101.5	73.5	275.0
		Adjusted Residual	12.5	−3.6	−9.7	
	white	Count	459	586	471	1516
		Expected Count	551.0	559.5	405.5	1516.0
		Adjusted Residual	−12.5	3.6	9.7	
Total		Count	651	661	479	1791
		Expected Count	651.0	661.0	479.0	1791.0

Source: Data from CSM, UC Berkeley.

11.61 Happiness and sex A contingency table from the 2012 GSS relating happiness to number of sex partners in the previous year (0, 1, at least 2) had standardized residuals (called Z-statistic here) as shown in the screen shot. Interpret the standardized residuals in the last column.

Frequency Distribution

Cells contain: -Z-statistic -N of cases		HAPPY 1 Not	2 Pretty	3 Very	*ROW TOTAL*
PARTNERS	1: 0	4.60 81	1.10 238	-4.60 84	--- *403*
	2: 1	-5.42 105	-2.90 575	7.15 385	--- *1,065*
	3: 2 or more	1.93 40	2.72 150	-4.38 41	--- *231*
	COL TOTAL	--- *226*	--- *963*	--- *510*	--- *1,699*

Color coding:	<-2.0	<-1.0	<0.0	>0.0	>1.0	>2.0	Z
N in each cell:	Smaller than expected			Larger than expected			

11.62 Education and religious beliefs When data from a recent GSS were used to form a 3×3 table that cross-tabulates highest degree (1 = less than high school, 2 = high school or junior college, 3 = bachelor or graduate) with religious beliefs (F = fundamentalist, M = moderate, L = liberal), the three largest standardized residuals were: 6.8 for the cell (3, F), 6.3 for the cell (3, L), and 4.5 for the cell (1, F). Summarize how to interpret these three standardized residuals.

11.63 TV and aggression From a study described in Example 5 in the previous chapter, the proportion of males committing aggressive acts was 4 out of 45 for those who watched less than 1 hour of TV a day and 117 out of 315 for those who watched at least 1 hour per day. MINITAB reports the printout shown for conducting Fisher's exact test (two-sided) for these data.

a. State hypotheses for the test, defining the notation.

b. Report the P-value that software reports and interpret in the context of this study.

Data on TV watching and aggression

```
Rows: TV  Columns: aggression
              no     yes
high         198     117
low           41       4
Fisher's exact test:
P-Value = 0.0000751
```

11.64 Botox side effects TECH An advertisement for Botox Cosmetic by Allergan, Inc. for treating wrinkles appeared in several magazines. The back page of the ad showed the results of a randomized clinical trial to compare 405 people receiving Botox injections to 130 people receiving placebo in terms of the frequency of various side effects. The side effect of pain in the face was reported by 9 people receiving Botox and 0 people receiving placebo. Use software (or a web app) to conduct a two-sided test of the hypothesis that the probability of this side effect is the same for each group. Report all steps of the test and interpret results.

11.65 Clarity of diamonds TECH Does the clarity of a diamond depend on its cut? Exercise 3.4 showed data, reproduced below, on the clarity (rated as internally flawless, IF, very very slightly included, VVS, very slightly included, VS, slightly included, SI and included, I) for the two lowest ratings for cut, which are "good" and "fair."

	Clarity					
Cut	**IF**	**VVS**	**VS**	**SI**	**I**	**Total**
Good	2	4	16	55	3	80
Fair	1	3	8	30	2	44

a. Verify, using software, that $X^2 = 0.267$ for this table. The (raw) data are available on the book's website as Diamonds.csv.

b. Can you use the chi-squared distribution to find a P-value? Why or why not?

c. Of 10,000 random permutations, 9,908 resulted in an X^2 value as large or larger than the one observed. Find the (approximate) permutation P-value and interpret.

d. Use the Permutation Test of Independence web app accessible from the book's website to enter the contingency table and replicate the results from part c.

Concepts and Applications

11.66 Benford's Law TECH When looking at a collection of numbers, such as population sizes, the figures on tax returns or the charges on a credit card, one may think that the leading digit of the number is equally likely to be any of the numbers from 1 to 9. However, such data sets often show a distribution for the leading digit that is quite different from uniform and is described by Benford's Law. This law stipulates that the probability for the leading digit to be 1 is 30.1%, whereas the probability of the leading digit to be 9 is only 4.6% instead of a uniform 1/9 = 11.1% probability for each. The following table shows the distribution of the leading digit of the last 130 transactions on the credit card of one of the authors. The raw data file is available for download on the book's website.

Leading digit:	1	2	3	4	5	6	7	8	9	Total
Benford probabilities (%):	30.1	17.6	12.5	9.7	7.9	6.7	5.8	5.1	4.6	100
Observed counts:	39	24	20	7	6	10	11	6	7	130

a. Find the expected counts, assuming the leading digits for the transactions follow Benford's Law.

b. Is there evidence that the distribution of the leading digit does not follow Benford's Law? Write a conclusion based on an appropriate test. If available, use software to read in the raw data and compute the test statistic and P-value.

11.67 Student data TECH Refer to the FL Student Survey data file on the book's website. Using software, create and analyze descriptively and inferentially the contingency table relating religiosity and belief in life after death. Summarize your analyses in a short report.

11.68 Marital happiness decreasing? TECH At sda.berkeley.edu/GSS, cross-tabulate HAPMAR with YEAR so you can see how conditional distributions on marital happiness in the GSS have changed since 1973. Using conditional distributions and standardized residuals, explain how these results show a very slight trend over time for fewer people to report being very happy. (With HAPMAR as the column variable, you can get conditional proportions by selecting Row for Percentaging under Output options. There, you can also get the standardized residuals by selecting Show Z-statistic.)

11.69 Another predictor of happiness? TECH Go to sda.berkeley.edu/GSS and find a variable that is associated with happiness, other than variables used in this chapter. Use methods from this chapter to describe and make inferences about the association, in a one-page report.

11.70 Pregnancy associated with contraceptive use? Whether a young married woman becomes pregnant in the next year is a categorical variable with categories (yes, no). Another categorical variable to consider is whether she and her partner use contraceptives with categories (yes, no). Would you expect these variables to be independent or associated? Explain.

11.71 Babies and gray hair A young child wonders what causes women to have babies. For each woman who lives on her block, she observes whether her hair is gray and whether she has young children, with the results shown in the table that follows.

a. Construct the 2×2 contingency table that cross-tabulates gray hair (yes, no) with has young children (yes, no) for these nine women.

b. Treating has young children as the response variable, obtain the conditional distributions for those women who have gray hair and for those who do not. Does there seem to be an association?

c. Noticing this association, the child concludes that not having gray hair is what causes women to have children. Use this example to explain why association does not necessarily imply causation.

Woman	Gray Hair	Young Children
Andrea	No	Yes
Mary	Yes	No
Linda	No	Yes
Jane	No	Yes
Maureen	Yes	No
Judy	Yes	No
Margo	No	Yes
Carol	Yes	No
Donna	No	Yes

11.72 When is chi-squared not valid? Give an example of a contingency table for which the chi-squared test of independence should not be used.

11.73 Gun homicide in United States and Britain According to recent United Nations figures, the annual intentional homicide rate is 4.7 per 100,000 residents in the United States and 1.0 per 100,000 residents in Britain.

a. Compare the proportion of residents of the two countries killed intentionally using the difference of proportions. Show how the results differ according to whether the United States or Britain is identified as Group 1.

b. Compare the proportion of residents of the two countries by using the relative risk. Show how the results differ according to whether the United States or Britain is identified as Group 1.

c. When both proportions are very close to 0, as in this example, which measure do you think is more useful for describing the strength of association? Why?

11.74 Colon cancer and race The State Center for Health Statistics for the North Carolina Division of Public Health released a report in 2010 that indicates that there are racial disparities in colorectal cancer incidence and mortality rates. The report states, "African Americans are less likely to receive appropriate screenings that reduce the risk of developing or dying from colorectal cancer." During 2002–2006, the rate of incidence for African Americans was 57.3 per 100,000 versus 46.5 per 100,000 for white residents (www.schs.state.nc.us). African Americans were 19% more likely to have been diagnosed with colon cancer. Explain how to get this estimate.

11.75 True or false: $X^2 = 0$ The null hypothesis for the test of independence between two categorical variables is H_0: $X^2 = 0$ for the sample chi-squared statistic X^2. (*Hint:* Do hypotheses refer to a sample or the population?)

11.76 True or false: Group 1 becomes Group 2 Interchanging two rows or interchanging two columns in a contingency table has no effect on the value of the X^2 statistic.

11.77 True or false: Relative risk Interchanging the rows in a 2×2 contingency table has no effect on the value of the relative risk.

11.78 True or false: Relative risk versus odds ratio Refer to a contingency table that cross-classifies subjects in two rows and two columns (labeled Success and Failure) and for which the odds ratio equals 4. True or False: Subjects in row 1 are 4 times as likely to have a success as subjects in row 2.

11.79 True or false: Statistical but not practical significance Even when the sample conditional distributions in a contingency table are only slightly different, when the sample size is very large it is possible to have a large X^2 statistic and a very small P-value for testing H_0: independence.

11.80 Statistical versus practical significance In any significance test, when the sample size is very large, we have not necessarily established an important result when we obtain statistical significance. Explain what this means in the context of analyzing contingency tables with a chi-squared test.

11.81 Normal and chi-squared with $df = 1$ When $df = 1$, the P-value from the chi-squared test of independence is the same as the P-value for the two-sided test comparing two proportions with the z test statistic. This is because of a direct connection between the standard normal distribution and the chi-squared distribution with $df = 1$: Squaring a z-score yields a chi-squared value with $df = 1$ having chi-squared right-tail probability equal to the two-tail normal probability for the z-score.

a. Illustrate this with $z = 1.96$, the z-score with a two-tail probability of 0.05. Using the chi-squared table or software, show that the square of 1.96 is the chi-squared score for $df = 1$ with a P-value of 0.05.

b. Show the connection between the normal and chi-squared values with P-value = 0.01.

11.82 ◆◆ **Multiple response variables** Each subject in a sample of 100 men and 100 women is asked to indicate which of the following factors (one or more) are responsible for increases in crime committed by teenagers: A—the increasing gap in income between the rich and poor, B—the increase in the percentage of single-parent families, C—insufficient time that parents spend with their children. To analyze whether responses differ by gender of respondent, we cross-classify the responses by gender, as the table shows.

a. Is it valid to apply the chi-squared test of independence to these data? Explain.

b. Explain how this table actually provides information needed to cross-classify gender with each of three variables. Construct the contingency table relating gender to opinion about whether factor A is responsible for increases in teenage crime.

Three Factors for Explaining Teenage Crime

Gender	A	B	C
Men	60	81	75
Women	75	87	86

11.83 ◆◆ **Standardized residuals for 2×2 tables** The table that follows shows the standardized residuals in parentheses for GSS data about the statement, "Women should take care of running their homes and leave running the country up to men." The absolute value of the standardized residual is 13.2 in every cell. For chi-squared tests with 2×2 tables, since $df = 1$, only one nonredundant piece of information exists about whether an association exists. If observed count > expected count in one cell, observed count < expected count in the other cell in that row or column. Explain why this is true, using the fact that observed and expected counts have the same row and column totals. (In fact, in 2 × 2 tables, all four standardized residuals have absolute value equal to the square root of the X^2 test statistic.)

Year	Agree	Disagree
1974	509 (13.2)	924 (−13.2)
1998	280 (−13.2)	1534 (13.2)

11.84 Degrees of freedom explained For testing independence in a contingency table of size $r \times c$, the degrees of freedom (df) for the chi-squared distribution equal $df = (r - 1) \times (c - 1)$. They have the following interpretation: Given the row and column marginal totals in an $r \times c$ contingency table, the cell counts in a rectangular block of size $(r - 1) \times (c - 1)$ determine all the other cell counts. Consider the following table, which cross-classifies political views by whether the subject would ever vote for a female president, based on the 2010 GSS. For this 3 × 2 table, suppose we know the counts in the upper left-hand $(3 - 1) \times (2 - 1) = 2 \times 1$ block of the table, as shown.

	Vote for Female President		
Political Views	**Yes**	**No**	**Total**
Extremely Liberal	56		58
Moderate	490		509
Extremely Conservative			61
Total	**604**	**24**	**628**

a. Given the cell counts and the row and column totals, fill in the counts that must appear in the blank cells.

b. Now, suppose instead of the preceding table, you are shown the following table, this time only revealing a 2 × 1 block in the lower-right part. Find the counts in the remaining cells.

	Vote for Female President		
Political Views	**Yes**	**No**	**Total**
Extremely Liberal			58
Moderate		19	509
Extremely Conservative		3	61
Total	**604**	**24**	**628**

This example serves to show that once the marginal totals are fixed in a contingency table, a block of only $(r - 1) \times (c - 1)$ cell counts is free to vary. Once these are given (as in part a or b), the remaining cell counts follow automatically. The value for the degrees of freedom is exactly the number of cells in this block, or $df = (r - 1) \times (c - 1)$.

11.85 What is *df*? The contingency table that follows has $df = 4$. Show that you can reconstruct the entire table by filling in the remaining cell counts based on the 4 cell counts shown.

	A	B	C	D	E	Total
	24	21	12	10	—	100
	—	—	—	—	—	100
Total	**40**	**40**	**40**	**40**	**40**	**200**

11.86 Variability of chi-squared For the chi-squared distribution, the mean equals df and the standard deviation equals $\sqrt{2(df)}$.

a. Explain why, as a rough approximation, for a large df value, 95% of the chi-squared distribution falls within $df \pm 2\sqrt{2(df)}$.

b. With $df = 8$, show that $df \pm 2\sqrt{2(df)}$ gives the interval (0, 16) for *approximately* containing 95% of the distribution. Using the chi-squared table, show that *exactly* 95% of the distribution actually falls between 0 and 15.5.

11.87 ◆◆ **Explaining Fisher's exact test** A pool of six candidates for three managerial positions includes three females and three males. Denote the three females by F1, F2, F3 and the three males by M1, M2, M3. The result of choosing three individuals for the managerial positions is (F2, M1, M3).

a. Identify the 20 possible samples that could have been selected. Explain why the contingency table relating gender to whether chosen for the observed sample is

	Chosen For Position	
Gender	**Yes**	**No**
Male	2	1
Female	1	2

b. For each of the 20 samples, find the corresponding contingency table as in part a. Show that of these 20 tables, 1 has a cell count of 0, 9 have a cell count of 1, another 9 have a cell count of 2, and 1 has a cell count of 3 in the first cell. Hence, show that 10 of the 20 tables have a cell count in the first cell as large or larger than the observed table from part a. (Note that, if the managers were randomly selected, each of the 20 tables is equally likely to be observed. Then, the probability is $10/20 = 0.5$ of observing a table that shows equal or even stronger evidence that males are selected more often, and 0.5 is the P-value for Fisher's exact test with H_a: $p_1 > p_2$, where p_1 is the proportion of males and p_2 the proportion of females chosen for the position.)

11.88 ◆◆ **Likelihood-ratio chi-squared** For testing independence, most software also reports another chi-squared statistic, called **likelihood-ratio chi-squared.** It equals

$$G^2 = 2\sum\left[\text{observed count} \times \log\left(\frac{\text{observed count}}{\text{expected count}}\right)\right].$$

It has similar properties as the X^2 statistic, such as $df = (r - 1) \times (c - 1)$.

a. Show that $G^2 = X^2 = 0$ when each observed count = expected count.

b. Explain why in practice you would not expect to get *exactly* $G^2 = X^2 = 0$, even if the variables are truly independent.

Student Activities

11.89 Voting with 16 A recent survey of Austrian high school students asked whether it makes sense for 16-year-olds to be allowed to vote in the next parliamentary election. The following table shows results.

TRY TECH

	Voting with 16 Makes Sense			
Grade	**Definitely**	**Probably**	**Probably not**	**Definitely not**
Sophomores	9	12	5	3
Juniors	16	9	3	6
Seniors	20	5	2	0

a. Verify, using software, that $X^2 = 14.1$ for this table.

b. Can you use the chi-squared distribution to find a P-value for testing whether an association exists between the grade level and the opinion on voting with 16? Why or why not?

c. Enter the data in the Permutation Test for Independence web app. Press the Generate Random Permutation(s) button once to generate one random permutation of the data. Did this permutation lead to a chi-squared test statistic smaller, equal, or larger than the observed value?

d. Press the button 9 more times. How many of the 10 permutations you generated resulted in a X^2 value as large or large than the observed? (The subtitle of the plot shows this information.)

e. Generate 10,000 permutations and find the permutation P-value. Interpret it.

11.90 Conduct a research study using the GSS Go to the GSS codebook at sda.berkeley.edu/GSS. Your instructor will assign a categorical response variable. Conduct a research study in which you find at least two other categorical variables that have both a statistically significant and a practically significant association with that response variable, using data for the most recent year in which the response variable was surveyed. Analyze each association, using the methods of this chapter. Write a two-page report, describing your analyses and summarizing the results of your research study. Be prepared to discuss your results in a class discussion, because the class will discuss which variables seemed to be especially relevant.

BIBLIOGRAPHY

Alan Agresti (2007). *An Introduction to Categorical Data Analysis,* 2nd edition. Hoboken, New Jersey: Wiley.

Samprit Chatterjee, Mark S. Handcock, and Jeffrey S. Simonoff (1995). A Case Book for *A First Course in Statistics and Data Analysis.* Hoboken, New Jersey: Wiley.

CHAPTER

12

Chapter 11 analyzed the association between two categorical variables; this chapter introduces methods for describing and conducting inferences about the association between two *quantitative* variables. We'll learn more about the correlation and regression methods that we discussed in Chapter 3.

Analyzing the Association Between Quantitative Variables: Regression Analysis

Example 1

Estimate a Person's Strength

Picture the Scenario

How can you measure a person's strength? One way is to find the *maximum* number of pounds that the individual can bench press. However, this technique can be risky for people who are unfamiliar with proper lifting techniques or who are inexperienced in using a bench press. Is there a variable that is easier to measure yet is a good predictor of the maximum bench press?

There have been many studies about strength using males but relatively few using females. One exception was a recent study of 57 female athletes in a Georgia high school. Several variables were measured, including ones that are easier and safer to assess than maximum bench press but are thought to correlate highly with it. One such variable is the number of times that a female athlete can lift a bench press set at only 60 pounds (a relatively low weight) before she becomes too fatigued to lift it again. The data are in the High School Female Athletes data file on the book's website. Let x = number of 60-pound bench presses performed (before fatigue) and let y = maximum bench press (in lbs.).

Questions to Explore

- How well can we predict an athlete's maximum bench press from knowing the number of 60-pound bench presses that she can perform?
- What can we say about the association between these variables in the population?

Thinking Ahead

The bench press variables are quantitative. This chapter presents methods for analyzing the association between two quantitative variables. Like the methods presented in the previous chapter for categorical variables, these methods enable us to answer questions such as:

- Could the variables x and y realistically be independent (in the population), or can we conclude that there is an association between them?
- If the variables are associated, how strong is the association?
- How does the outcome for the response variable depend on the value of the explanatory variable, and which observations are unusual?

To address these questions, we will use what is known as a **regression analysis**. (We will even explain where this name comes from.) Several examples in this chapter will illustrate the use of regression analysis with data from the female strength study. A regression analysis that includes a single explanatory variable to study its linear association with a response variable is known as simple linear regression.

Recall

From Section 3.3, a **regression line** is a straight line that predicts the value of a response variable y from the value of an explanatory variable x. From Section 3.2, the **correlation r** is a summary measure of the association that falls between -1 and $+1$. ◀

Chapter 3 introduced regression analysis. Here we'll review and learn more about using a **regression line** to predict the response variable y and the **correlation** to describe the strength of association. We'll study how to make inferences about the regression line for a population and how the variability of data points around the regression line helps us predict how far from the line a value of y is likely to fall. Finally, we'll discuss an alternative regression analysis that is useful when two quantitative variables have a curved rather than a straight-line relationship.

12.1 Modeling How Two Variables Are Related

In Words

y = response variable
Graph on vertical (y) axis.

x = explanatory variable
Graph on horizontal (x) axis.
Regression uses x to predict y.

As in most statistical analyses, the first step of a regression analysis is to identify the response and explanatory variables. In Example 1 we want to know how well we can predict an athlete's maximum bench press, so that's the response variable. The predictor, the number of 60-pound bench presses that an athlete can manage, is the explanatory variable. As in Chapter 3, we use y to denote the response variable and x to denote the explanatory variable.

The Scatterplot: Evaluating Whether a Straight-Line Trend Exists

Is there an association between the number of 60-pound bench presses and the maximum bench press? The first step in answering this question is to look at the data. Recall that a **scatterplot** shows, for each observation, a point representing its value on the two variables. The points are shown relative to the x (horizontal) and y (vertical) axes. The scatterplot shows whether there is roughly a straight-line trend, in which case the relationship between x and y is said to be approximately **linear**.

Example 2

Scatterplot ◀

The Strength Study

Picture the Scenario

Let's look at the High School Female Athletes data file on the book's website. For each of the 57 female athletes in the study, the response variable y is the maximum weight that the athlete bench pressed (in 5-pound increments). The explanatory variable x is the number of times she could bench press 60 pounds. The first four entries of the data file (where x is coded as BP60 and y as maxBP) are:

Athlete	x	y
1	10	80
2	12	85
3	20	85
4	5	65

The sample mean of the x variable is 11.0 (standard deviation = 7.1), and the sample mean of the y variable is 79.9 pounds (standard deviation = 13.3 pounds).

Question to Explore

Using the entire data file for the 57 athletes, construct a scatterplot and interpret it.

Think It Through

With any statistical software, you can construct a scatterplot after identifying in the data file the variables that play the role of x and y. For the column names in the Bench Press data file, x = BP60 and y = maxBP. Figure 12.1 shows the scatterplot that MINITAB produces. It shows that female athletes with higher numbers of 60-pound bench presses also tended to have higher values for the maximum bench press. The data points follow roughly an increasing linear trend. The margin shows a screen shot of the scatterplot from a TI calculator.

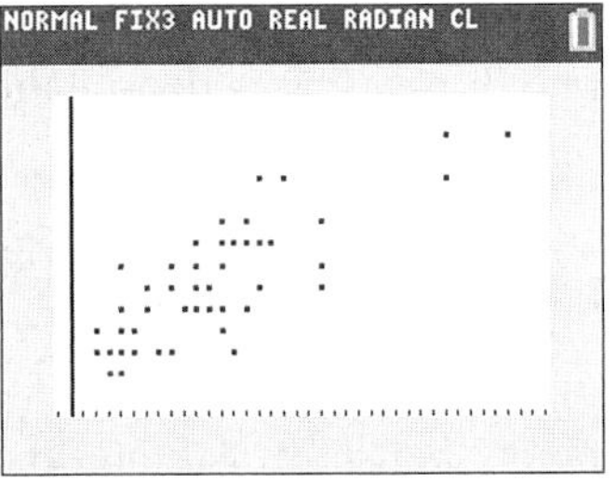

TI output of scatterplot

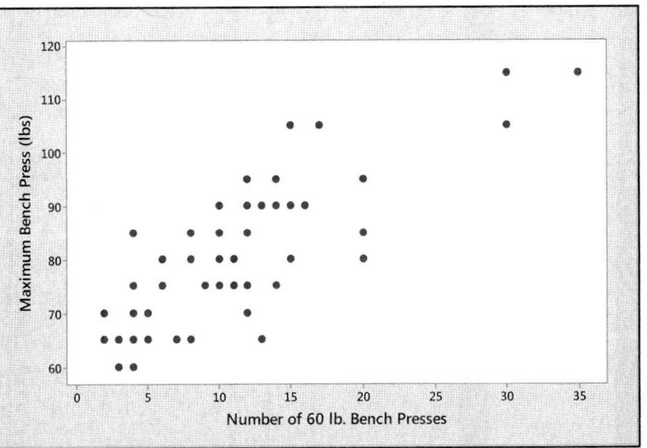

▲ **Figure 12.1** Scatterplot for y = Maximum Bench Press and x = Number of 60-Pound Bench Presses. **Question** How can you tell from this plot that (a) two athletes had a maximum bench press of only 60 pounds, and (b) 5-pound increments were used in determining maximum bench press—60, 65, 70, and so on?

Insight

The three data points at the upper right represent subjects who could do a large number of 60-pound bench presses. Their maximum bench presses were also high.

▶ ***Try Exercise 12.9, part a***

Describing the Association in the Scatterplot by the Correlation

In Chapter 3, we learned that if the scatterplot shows an approximate linear relationship, we can describe the strength of this association by computing the correlation r.

Did you know?

r is often referred to as **Pearson's correlation coefficient**, after the British scientist Karl Pearson who also developed the chi-squared test from Chapter 11. ◀

SUMMARY: Properties of the Correlation r

- The correlation r falls between -1 and $+1$ $(-1 \leq r \leq +1)$. The association is positive if $r > 0$, negative if $r < 0$.
- The larger the absolute value of r, the stronger the linear association. ($r = \pm 1$ when data points fall exactly on a straight line.)
- The value of r does not depend on the variables' units.
- r does not depend on which variable is the response and which the explanatory variable.

For example, because the scatterplot in Example 2 showed an approximate linear trend, it is reasonable to compute the correlation between the two variables number of 60-pound bench presses and maximum possible bench press to measure how strongly they are associated. Using software, $r = 0.80$, indicating a strong and positive linear association.

The Regression Line Equation Uses x to Predict y

When the scatterplot shows a linear trend, a straight line fitted through the data points describes that trend. As in Chapter 3, we use the notation

$$\hat{y} = a + bx$$

for this line, called the **regression line**. The symbol $\hat{y}$ represents the *predicted value* of the response variable y. In the formula, a is the **y-intercept** and b is the **slope**. The regression line allows us to describe further the nature of the linear relationship in a way that goes beyond just stating the strength of the association using the correlation r.

In Words

$\hat{y}$ ("y-hat") denotes the predicted value you get for the response variable y by plugging a value into the equation for the explanatory variable x.

Example 3

Regression line ◀

Regression Line Predicting Maximum Bench Press

Picture the Scenario

Let's continue our analysis of the Bench Press data.

Questions to Explore

a. Using software, find the regression line for y = maximum bench press and x = number of 60-pound bench presses.

b. Interpret the slope by comparing the predicted maximum bench press for subjects at the highest and lowest levels of x in the sample (35 and 2).

Think It Through

a. Let's denote the maximum bench press variable by maxBP and the number of 60-pound bench presses by BP60. Using software, we pick

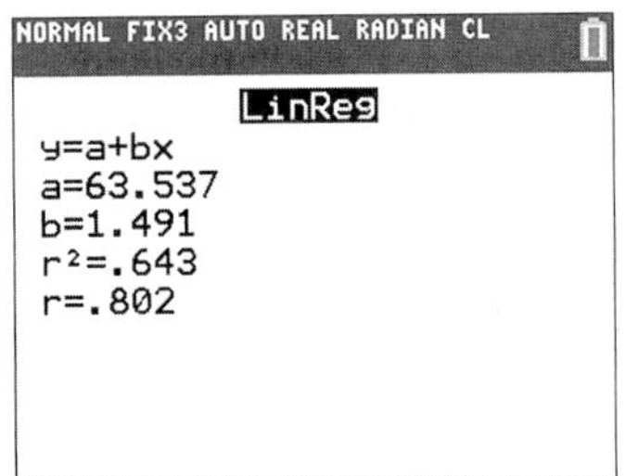

TI output for linear regression

the regression option with maxBP as the response variable and BP60 as the explanatory variable. Table 12.1 shows some output using MINITAB. We'll interpret some of this, such as standard errors and t statistics, later in the chapter. The margin shows TI output.

Table 12.1 MINITAB Printout for Regression Analysis of y = Maximum Bench Press (maxBP) and x = Number of 60-Pound Bench Presses (BP60)

```
The regression equation is maxBP = 63.54 + 1.491 BP60

Coefficients
```

Term	Coef	SE Coef	T-Value	P-Value
Constant	63.54	1.96	32.48	0.000
BP60	1.491	0.150	9.96	0.000

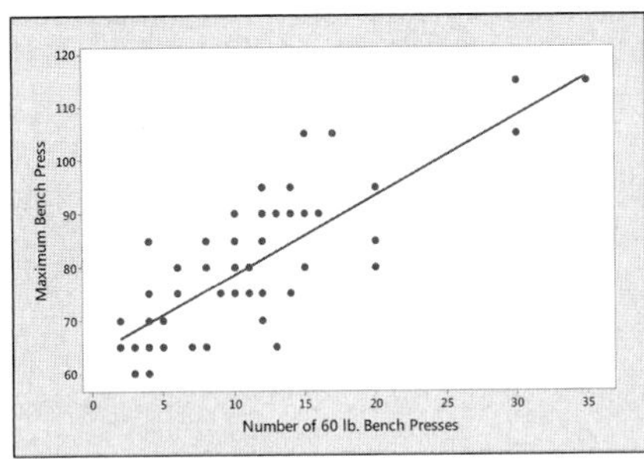

The output tells us that $\hat{y}$ = predicted maximum bench press (maxBP) relates to x = number of 60-pound bench presses (BP60) by

$$\text{maxBP} = 63.5 + 1.49\ \text{BP60}, \text{ that is, } \hat{y} = 63.5 + 1.49x.$$

The y-intercept is 63.5 and the slope is 1.49. These are also shown in the column labeled "Coef," an abbreviation for *coefficient.* The slope appears opposite the variable name for which it is the coefficient, "BP60." The term "Constant" refers to the y-intercept. The margin figure (Figure 12.1 reproduced) plots the regression line through the scatterplot.

b. The slope of 1.49 tells us that the predicted maximum bench press $\hat{y}$ increases by an average of $1\frac{1}{2}$ pounds for every additional 60-pound bench press an athlete can do. The impact on $\hat{y}$ of a 33-unit change in x, from the sample minimum of $x = 2$ to the maximum of $x = 35$, is $33(1.49) = 49.2$ pounds. An athlete who can do thirty-five 60-pound bench presses has a predicted maximum bench press nearly 50 pounds higher than an athlete who can do only two 60-pound bench presses. Those predicted values are $\hat{y} = 63.5 + 1.49(2) = 66.5$ pounds at $x = 2$ and $\hat{y} = 63.5 + 1.49(35) = 115.7$ pounds at $x = 35$.

Recall

The direction of the association (positive or negative) refers to the sign of the slope and whether the line slopes upward or downward. ◀

Insight

The slope of 1.49 is positive: As x increases, the predicted value $\hat{y}$ increases. The association is *positive.* When the association is *negative*, the predicted value $\hat{y}$ *decreases* as x increases. When the slope = 0, the regression line is horizontal.

▶ ***Try Exercise 12.1***

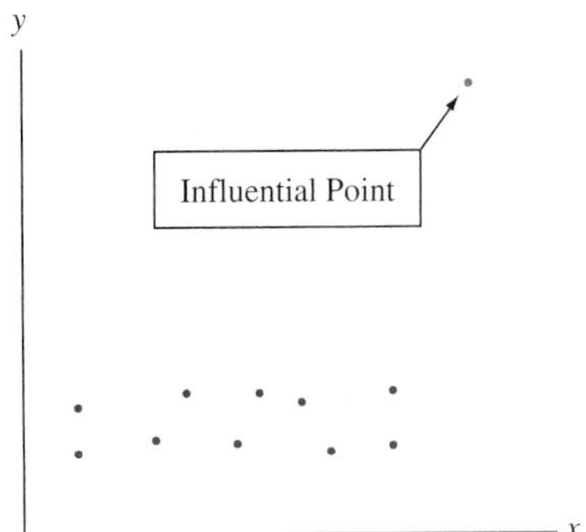

One reason for plotting the data before you do a regression analysis is to check for outliers. The regression line can be pulled toward an outlier and away from the general trend of points. We observed in Section 3.4 that an observation can be **influential** in affecting the regression line when two things happen (see margin figure):

- Its x value is low or high compared to the rest of the data.
- It does not fall in the straight-line pattern that the rest of the data have.

In Figure 12.1, three subjects had quite large values of x. However, their values of y fit in with the trend exhibited by the other data, so those points are not influential with respect to changing the equation of the regression line. However, as we will discuss later, the correlation may strengthen.

Finding the Correlation and the Prediction Equation

In Practice Check the Model Graphically; Use Software for Computations

Check whether it is sensible to do a regression analysis by looking at a scatterplot. If you see an approximately linear relationship, you can let technology do the computational work of finding the correlation, slope, and y-intercept.

Software uses the sample data to find the prediction equation $\hat{y} = a + bx$ and the correlation r. Sections 3.2 and 3.3 in Chapter 3 gave the formulas. We saw there that $r > 0$ and $b > 0$ when most observations are in the quadrants where x and y are both above their means or both below their means. See Figure 12.2. By contrast, $r < 0$ and $b < 0$ when subjects who are above the mean on one variable tend to be below the mean on the other variable.

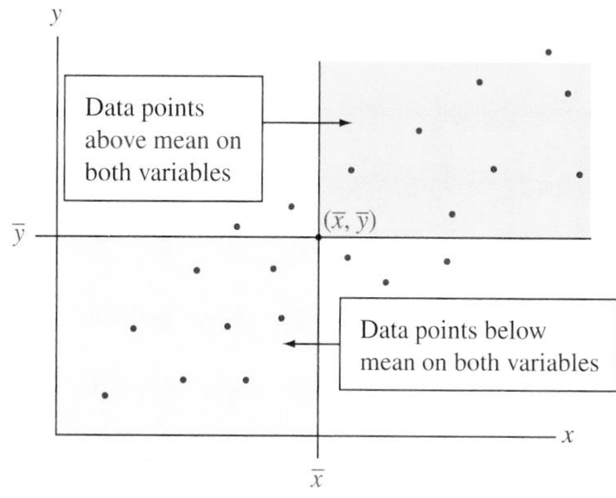

▲ **Figure 12.2 The Correlation r and the Slope b Are Positive When Most Data Points Are Above the Mean on Both Variables or Below the Mean on Both.** These are the areas shaded in this figure. **Question** Where do most data points usually fall when the slope and correlation are negative?

Recall

From Section 3.3,

$$b = r\left(\frac{s_y}{s_x}\right),$$

$$a = \bar{y} - b\bar{x}.$$ ◀

The formulas for the slope b and the y-intercept a (shown again in the margin) use the correlation r and the sample means $\bar{x}$ and $\bar{y}$ of the x values and the y values and the sample standard deviations s_x and s_y. The slope b is proportional to the correlation r, and we'll discuss their connection below. The formula $a = \bar{y} - b\bar{x}$ for the y-intercept can be rewritten as $\bar{y} = a + b\bar{x}$. This shows that if we substitute $x = \bar{x}$ into the regression equation $\hat{y} = a + bx$, then the predicted outcome is $\hat{y} = a + b\bar{x} = \bar{y}$. In words, *a subject who is average on x is predicted to be average on y.*

Residuals Are Prediction Errors for the Least Squares Line

The regression equation is often called a **prediction equation** because substituting a particular value of x into the equation provides a prediction for y at that value of x. For instance, the third athlete in the data file could do $x = 20$ bench presses of 60 pounds. Her predicted maximum bench press is

$$\hat{y} = 63.5 + 1.49x = 63.5 + 1.49(20) = 93.3 \text{ pounds.}$$

The difference $y - \hat{y}$ between an observed outcome y and its predicted value $\hat{y}$ is the *prediction error*, called a **residual**. For instance, the third athlete in the data file had a maximum bench press of $y = 85$ pounds. Since her $\hat{y} = 93.3$ pounds, the prediction error is $y - \hat{y} = 85 - 93.3 = -8.3$ pounds.

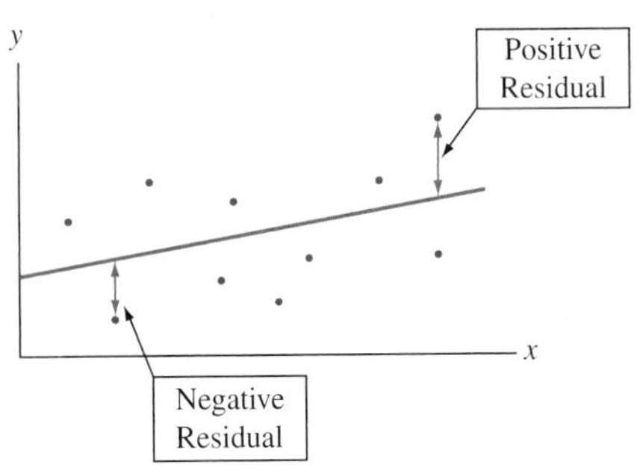

SUMMARY: Review of Residuals from Chapter 3

- Each observation has a residual. Some are positive, some are negative, some may be zero, and their average equals 0.
- In the scatterplot, a residual is the vertical distance between the data point and the regression line. The smaller the distance, the better the prediction. (See margin figure.)
- We can summarize how close to the regression line the data points fall by

$$\text{sum of squared residuals} = \Sigma(\text{residual})^2 = \Sigma(y - \hat{y})^2.$$

- The regression line has a smaller sum of squared residuals than any other line drawn through the scatterplot. Because of this property, it is called the least squares line.

Regression Model: A Line Describes How the Mean of *y* Depends on *x*

At a given value of x, the equation $\hat{y} = a + bx$ predicts a single value $\hat{y}$ of the response variable. However, we should not expect all subjects at that value of x to have the same value of y. Variability occurs in their y values.

For example, let x = number of years of education and y = annual income in dollars for the adult residents in the workforce of your hometown. For a random sample, suppose you find $\hat{y} = -20{,}000 + 4{,}000x$. Those workers with $x = 12$ years of education have predicted annual income

$$\hat{y} = -20{,}000 + 4{,}000(12) = 28{,}000.$$

It's not the case that every worker with 12 years of education would have an annual income of \$28,000. Income is not completely dependent upon education. One person may have an income of \$35,000, another \$15,000, and so forth. Instead, you can think of $\hat{y} = 28{,}000$ as estimating the mean annual income for all workers with $x = 12$ years of education.

In fact, there's a mean for the annual income at each separate education value. For those residents with 13 years of education, the estimated mean annual income is $-20{,}000 + 4{,}000(13) = 32{,}000$. The slope is 4,000, so the estimated mean goes up by \$4,000 (from \$28,000 to \$32,000) for this one-year increase in education (from 12 to 13 years).

SUMMARY: The Regression Line Connects the Estimated Means of *y* at the Various *x* Values

$\hat{y} = a + bx$ describes the relationship between x and the estimated means of y at the various values of x.

A similar equation describes the relationship between x and the means of y in the population. This **population regression equation** is denoted by

$$\mu_y = \alpha + \beta x.$$

Recall

Parameters describe the population. They are often denoted by Greek symbols. Here, α is *alpha*, β is *beta*, and μ_y is *mu-sub-y*. ◀

Here, α is a population y-intercept and β is a population slope. These are parameters, so in practice their values are unknown. The parameter μ_y denotes the population mean of y for all the subjects at a particular value of x. It takes a different value at each separate x value. In practice, we estimate the population regression equation using the prediction equation for the sample data. We use a to estimate α, b to estimate β and $a + bx$ to estimate μ_y. We'll see how to use these estimates to conduct inference about the unknown parameters in Sections 12.2 and 12.4.

A straight line is the simplest way to describe the relationship between two quantitative variables. In practice, most relationships are not *exactly* linear. The equation $\mu_y = \alpha + \beta x$ merely *approximates* the actual relationship between x and the population means of y. It is a **model**.

Model

A **model** is a simple approximation for how variables relate in a population.

Figure 12.3 shows how a regression model can approximate the true relationship between x and the mean of y. The true relationship is unlikely to be exactly a straight line. That's not a problem as long as a straight line provides a reasonably good approximation, as we expect of a model.

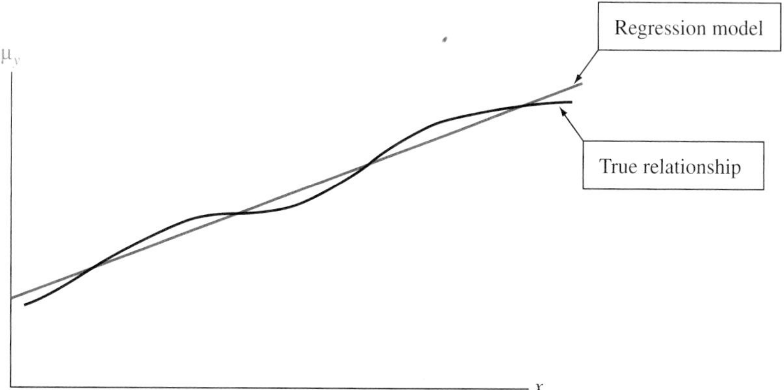

▲ **Figure 12.3** **The Regression Model $\mu_y = \alpha + \beta x$ for the Means of y Is a Simple Approximation for the True Relationship Between x and the Mean of y. Question** Can you sketch a true relationship for which this model is a very *poor* approximation?

If the true relationship is far from a straight line, this regression model may be a poor one. Figure 12.4 illustrates. In that case, the figure shows a U-shaped relationship. It requires a parabolic curve rather than a straight line to describe it well. To check the straight-line assumption, you should always construct a scatterplot.

How could you get into trouble by using a straight-line regression model even when the true relationship is U-shaped? First, predictions about y would be poor. Second, inference about the association could be misleading. The variables are associated, since the mean of y changes as x does. The slope (and correlation) might not detect this, however, since the prediction line would be close to horizontal (slope close to 0), even though a substantial association exists.

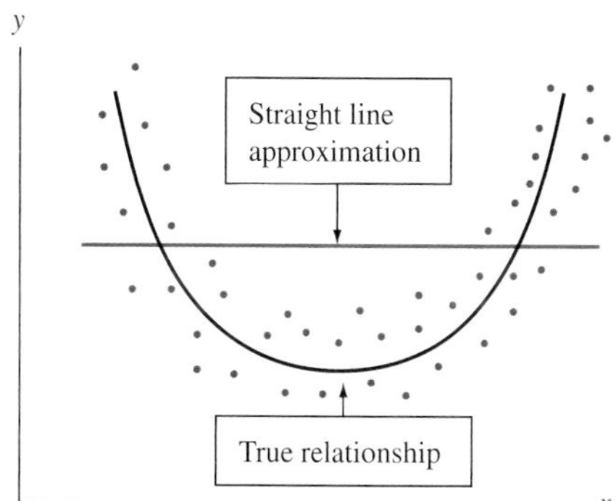

▲ **Figure 12.4** **The Straight-Line Regression Model Provides a Poor Approximation When the Actual Relationship Is Highly Nonlinear. Question** What type of mathematical function might you consider using for a regression model in this case?

Recall

Chapter 11 used a **conditional distribution** to describe percentages in categories of a categorical response variable, at each value of an explanatory variable. Each conditional distribution refers to possible values of the response variable at a fixed value of the explanatory variable. ◄

The Regression Model Also Allows Variability About the Line

At each fixed value of x, variability occurs in the y values around their mean μ_y. For instance, at education = 12 years, annual income varies around the mean annual income for all workers with 12 years of education. The probability distribution of y values at a fixed value of x is a **conditional distribution.** At each value of x, there is a conditional distribution of y values. The standard deviation of this conditional distribution (denoted by σ) tells you how much the response variable varies around the mean μ_y at the given x value. In practice, σ is unknown. It is another parameter that is part of the regression model specification.

In Words

A **regression model** uses a formula (usually a straight line) to approximate how the expected value (the mean) for y changes at different values of x. It also describes the variability of observations on y around the line.

SUMMARY: Regression Model

A **regression model** describes how the population mean μ_y of each conditional distribution for the response variable depends on the value x of the explanatory variable. A **straight-line regression model** uses the line $\mu_y = \alpha + \beta x$ to connect the means. The model also has a parameter σ that describes variability of observations around the mean of y at each x value.

Example 4

Regression model ◄

Income and Education

Picture the Scenario

As described previously, suppose the regression line $\mu_y = -20{,}000 + 4{,}000x$ models the relationship for the population of working adults in your hometown between x = number of years of education and the mean of y = annual income. This model tells us that income goes up as education does, on average, but how much variability is there? Suppose also that the conditional distribution of annual income at each value of x is modeled by a normal distribution, with standard deviation $\sigma = 13{,}000$.

Question to Explore

Use this regression model to describe the mean income and the variability around the mean income for workers with (i) 12 and (ii) 16 years of education.

Think It Through

This regression model states that for workers with x years of education, their annual incomes have a normal distribution with a mean of $\mu_y = -20{,}000 + 4{,}000x$ and a standard deviation of $\sigma = 13{,}000$. For those having a high school education ($x = 12$), the mean annual income is $\mu_y = -20{,}000 + 4{,}000(12) = 28{,}000$ and the standard deviation is 13,000. Those with a college education ($x = 16$) have a mean annual income of $\mu_y = -20{,}000 + 4{,}000(16) = 44{,}000$ and a standard deviation of 13,000.

Since the conditional distributions are modeled as normal, the model predicts that nearly all of the y values fall within 3 standard deviations of the mean. For instance, for those with 16 years of education, $\mu_y = 44{,}000$ and $\sigma = 13{,}000$. Since

$$44{,}000 - 3(13{,}000) = 5{,}000 \text{ and } 44{,}000 + 3(13{,}000) = 83{,}000$$

the model predicts that nearly all of their annual incomes fall between \$5,000 and \$83,000.

Insight

Figure 12.5 portrays this regression model. It plots the regression equation (in red) and the conditional distributions of y = income at x = 12 years and at x = 16 years of education (in blue). The value of σ determines the shape of the normal curves. In practice, σ is unknown, but we'll see how to estimate it using data later in the chapter.

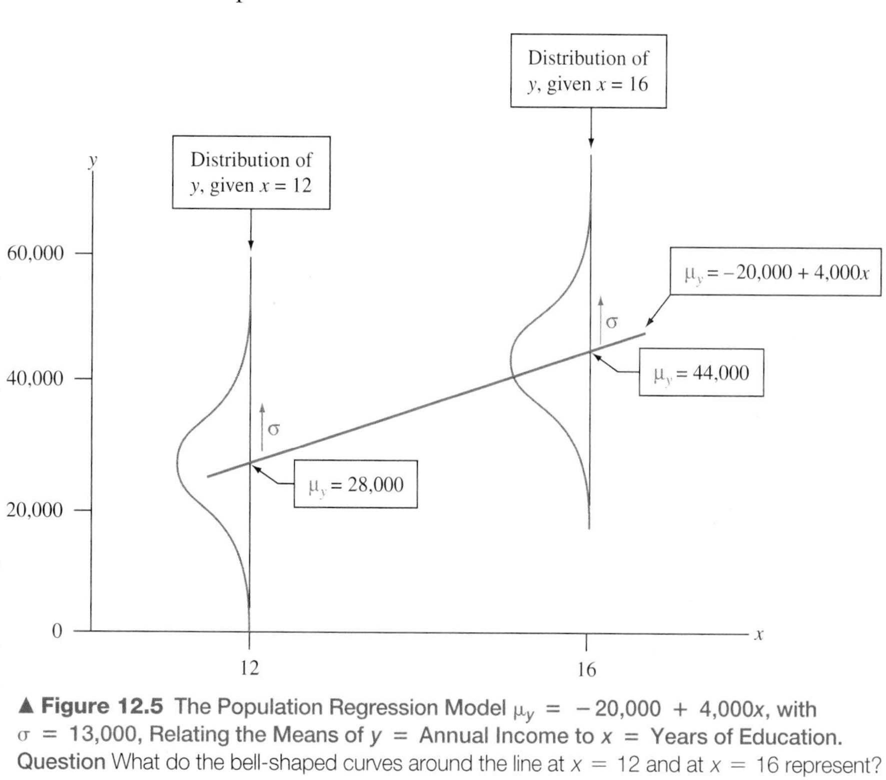

▲ **Figure 12.5** The Population Regression Model $\mu_y = -20{,}000 + 4{,}000x$, with $\sigma = 13{,}000$, Relating the Means of y = Annual Income to x = Years of Education.
Question What do the bell-shaped curves around the line at $x = 12$ and at $x = 16$ represent?

▶ ***Try Exercise 12.4***

In Figure 12.5, each conditional distribution is normal, and each has the same standard deviation, $\sigma = 13{,}000$. But a model merely approximates reality. In practice, the means of the conditional distributions would not perfectly follow a straight line. Those conditional distributions would not be exactly normal. The standard deviation would not be exactly the same for each conditional distribution. For instance, the conditional distributions might be somewhat skewed to the right, and incomes might vary more for college graduates than for high school graduates.

In Practice A Model Is a Simple *Approximation* of Reality

A statistical **model** never holds exactly in practice. It is merely a simple approximation of reality. But even though it does not describe reality exactly, a model is useful if the true relationship is close to what the model predicts.

12.1 Practicing the Basics

12.1 Car mileage and weight The Car Weight and Mileage data file on the book's website shows the weight (in pounds) and mileage (miles per gallon) of 25 different model autos.
TRY

a. Identify the natural response variable and explanatory variable.

b. The regression of mileage on weight has MINITAB regression output

```
Term          Coef     SE Coef   T-Value P-Value
Constant      45.65       2.60     17.54   0.000
weight    -0.005222  0.000627     -8.33   0.000
```

State the prediction equation and report the y-intercept and slope.

c. Interpret the slope in terms of a 1,000-pound increase in the vehicle weight.

d. Does the y-intercept have any contextual meaning for these data? (*Hint:* The weight values range between 2,460 and 6,400 pounds.)

12.2 Predicting car mileage Refer to the previous exercise.

a. Find the predicted mileage for the Toyota Corolla, which weighs 2,590 pounds.

b. Find the residual for the Toyota Corolla, which has observed mileage of 38.

c. Sketch a graphical representation of the residual in part b.

12.3 Predicting maximum bench strength in males For the Male Athlete Strength data file on the book's website, the prediction equation relating y = maximum bench press (maxBP) in kilograms to x = repetitions to fatigue bench press (repBP) is $\hat{y} = 117.5 + 5.86x$.

a. Find the predicted maxBP for a male athlete with a repBP of 35, which was one of the highest repBP values.

b. Find the predicted maxBP for a male athlete with a repBP of 0, which was the lowest repBP value.

c. Interpret the y-intercept. Use the slope to describe how predicted maxBP changes as repBP increases from 0 to 35.

12.4 Income higher with age TRY Suppose the regression line $\mu_y = -10{,}000 + 1{,}000x$ models the relationship for the population of working adults in Canada between x = age and the mean of y = annual income (in Canadian dollars). The conditional distribution of y at each value of x is modeled as normal, with $\sigma = 5{,}000$. Use this regression model to describe the mean and the variability around the mean for the conditional distribution at age (a) 20 years and (b) 50 years.

12.5 Mu, not y For a population regression equation, why is it more sensible to write $\mu_y = \alpha + \beta x$ instead of $y = \alpha + \beta x$? Explain with reference to the variables x = height and y = weight for the population of girls in elementary schools in your hometown.

12.6 Parties and dating Let y = number of parties attended in the past month and x = number of dates in the past month, measured for all single students at your school. Explain the mean and variability aspects of the regression model $\mu_y = \alpha + \beta x$ in the context of these variables. In your answer, explain why (a) it is more sensible to use a straight line to model the *means* of the conditional distributions rather than individual observations and (b) the model needs to allow variation around the mean.

12.7 Study time and college GPA TECH Exercise 3.39 in Chapter 3 showed data collected at the end of an introductory statistics course to investigate the relationship between x = study time per week (average number of hours) and y = college GPA. The table here shows the data for the eight males in the class on these variables and on the number of class lectures for the course that the student reported skipping during the term.

Student	Study Time	GPA	Skipped
1	14	2.8	9
2	25	3.6	0
3	15	3.4	2
4	5	3.0	5
5	10	3.1	3
6	12	3.3	2
7	5	2.7	12
8	21	3.8	1

a. Create a data file and use it to construct a scatterplot between x and y. Interpret.

b. Find the prediction equation and interpret the slope.

c. Find the predicted GPA for a student who studies 25 hours per week.

d. Find and interpret the residual for Student 2, who reported $x = 25$.

12.8 GPA and skipping class TECH Refer to the previous exercise. Now let x = number of classes skipped and y = college GPA.

a. Construct a scatterplot. Does the association seem to be positive or negative?

b. Find the prediction equation and interpret the y-intercept and slope.

c. Find the predicted GPA and residual for Student 1.

12.9 Cell phone specs TRY TECH Refer to the cell phone data set available on the book's website, which shows various specs of a random sample of cell phones. Engineers would like to analyze how the weight (measured in grams) of a phone depends on the size of the battery, the heaviest component of a cell phone. Here, the size is measured by the capacity of the battery, which is the amount of energy it can supply on a full charge (measured in milliampere-hours, mAh).

a. Identify the response and explanatory variables and then construct and interpret the scatterplot. Mention any outliers you see.

b. What effect will the outlier have on the fitted regression equation? Will its residual be positive or negative, and will it be small or large in absolute value?

c. Remove the outlier and find the prediction equation. Predict the weight of a cell phone when the battery capacity is (i) 1,000 mAh and (ii) 1,500 mAh.

d. Interpret the slope in context.

12.10 Exercise and watching TV TECH For the Georgia Student Survey file on the book's website, let y = exercise and x = watch TV (minutes per day).

a. Construct a scatterplot. Identify an outlier that could have an impact on the fit of the regression model. What would you expect its effect to be on the slope?

b. Fit the model with and without that observation. Summarize its impact.

12.2 Inference About Model Parameters and the Association

Section 12.1 showed how a regression line models a relationship between two quantitative variables, when the means of y at various values of x follow approximately a straight line. For the population that the sample refers to, we have learned that this relationship is given by $\mu_y = \alpha + \beta x$. Statistical inference is concerned with constructing confidence intervals and testing hypotheses about these parameters so that we can draw conclusions that apply to the larger population that is studied. For instance, we would like to use the data on the 57 female athletes analyzed in the previous section to learn (and predict) more broadly how various strength measures are related in the population of all female athletes.

Assumptions for Regression Analysis

We have already mentioned that we must inspect the scatterplot first to see whether there is an approximate linear trend before we can use a linear regression model. More formally, we need to assume that the model we use accurately represents the true relationship in the population.

SUMMARY: Basic Assumption for Using a Linear Regression Model

The population means of y at different values of x have a straight-line relationship with x, that is, $\mu_y = \alpha + \beta x$.

This assumption states that fitting the proposed linear regression model is valid. If it is violated, the model we use misrepresents the actual relationship between the response and the explanatory variable in the population. Any descriptions (such as interpreting the slope), conclusions, and inferences drawn from the model will be invalid. The foremost tool to check this assumption is the scatterplot. Section 13.4 will discuss additional plots using the residuals to check this assumption.

If the model we propose is valid and we want to use it not only for describing the relationship observed in the data but more generally to draw inferences about the underlying population, we need two more assumptions.

SUMMARY: Extra Assumptions When Using Linear Regression Model for Statistical Inference

- The data were gathered using **randomization**, such as random sampling or a randomized experiment.
- The population values of y at each value of x follow a **normal distribution**, with the same standard deviation (σ) at each x value.

Recall

By definition, **models** merely approximate the true relationship. A relationship will not be exactly linear, with exactly normal distributions for y at each x and with exactly the same standard deviation of y values at each x value. A model is useful as long as the approximation is reasonably good. ◀

The randomness assumption applies for any statistical inference. For inferences to be valid, the sample must be representative of the population.

As in the case of inference about a mean, the assumption about normality is what leads to t test statistics having t distributions. This assumption is never exactly satisfied in practice. However, the closer reality resembles this ideal, the more appropriate are the confidence interval and test procedures for the regression model. This assumption is less important than the other two, especially when the sample size is large. In that case, an extended central limit theorem implies that estimates from regression models have bell-shaped sampling distributions, no matter what shape the population distribution of y has at each value of x.

Testing Independence Between Quantitative Variables

Suppose that the slope β of the regression line $\mu_y = \alpha + \beta x$ equals 0, as Figure 12.6 shows. Then, the population mean of y is identical at each x value. In fact, the two quantitative variables are statistically independent: The outcome for y does not depend on the value of x. It does not help us to know the value of x when predicting the value of y.

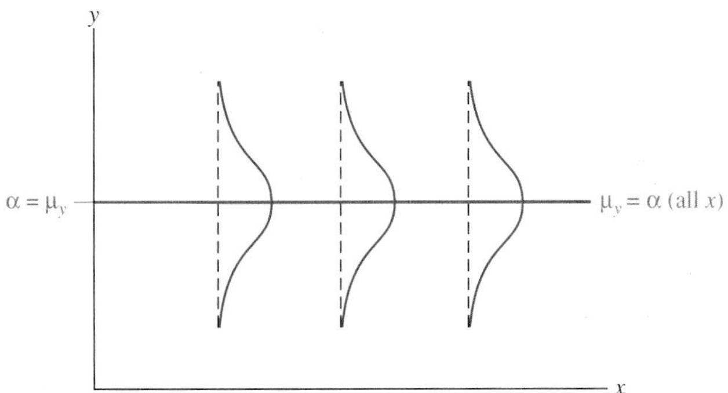

▲ **Figure 12.6 Quantitative Variables x and y Are Statistically Independent When the True Slope β = 0.** Each normal curve shown here represents the variability in y values at a particular value of x. When $\beta = 0$, the normal distribution of y is the same at each value of x. **Question** How can you express the null hypothesis of independence between x and y in terms of a parameter from the regression model?

Recall

Section 12.1 showed that a regression model allows **variability** around a line $\mu_y = \alpha + \beta x$ that describes how the mean of y changes as x changes. ◀

The null hypothesis that x and y are statistically independent is H_0: $\beta = 0$. Its significance test has the same purpose as the chi-squared test of independence for categorical variables (Chapter 11). It investigates how much evidence there is that the variables truly are linearly associated. The smaller the P-value, the greater the evidence.

Usually, the alternative hypothesis for the test of independence is two-sided, H_a: $\beta \neq 0$. Also possible is a one-sided alternative, H_a: $\beta > 0$ or H_a: $\beta < 0$, when you predict the direction of the association to be either positive or negative. The test statistic in each case equals

$$t = \frac{b - 0}{se},$$

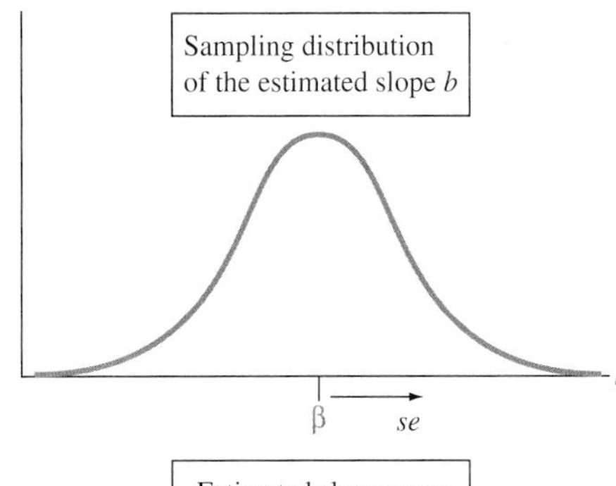

where b is the estimated slope computed from the sample and se denotes its standard error. Software supplies the slope b, the se, the t test statistic, and its P-value. The formula for se is rather complex, and we won't need it here (it's in Exercise 12.104). The form of the test statistic is the usual one for a t or z test. We take the estimate (b) of the parameter (β), subtract the null hypothesis value ($\beta = 0$), and divide by the standard error. The se describes the variability of the sampling distribution that measures how the estimated slope varies from sample to sample of size n (see the margin figure).

The symbol t is used for this test statistic because, under the assumptions stated, it has a t sampling distribution. The P-value for H_a: $\beta \neq 0$ is the two-tail probability from the t distribution (Table B). The degrees of freedom are $df = n - 2$. Software provides the P-value.

Recall

Sections 8.3 and 9.3 used $df = n - 1$ for inference using the t distribution, so why is $df = n - 2$ here? We'll see that in regression, $df = n -$ number of parameters in equation for mean, μ_y.

The equation $\mu_y = \alpha + \beta x$ has two parameters (α and β), so $df = n - 2$. The inferences in Chapters 8 and 9 had one parameter (μ), so $df = n - 1$. ◀

SUMMARY: Steps of Two-Sided Significance Test About a Population Slope β

1. **Assumptions:** (1) Relationship in population satisfies regression model $\mu_y = \alpha + \beta x$, (2) data gathered using randomization, (3) population y values at each x value have normal distribution, with same standard deviation at each x value.
2. **Hypotheses:** H_0: $\beta = 0$, H_a: $\beta \neq 0$
3. **Test statistic:** $t = (b - 0)/se$, where software supplies sample slope b and its se.
4. **P-value:** Two-tail probability of t test statistic value more extreme than observed, using t distribution with $df = n - 2$ (supplied by software).
5. **Conclusions:** Interpret P-value in context. If a decision is needed, reject H_0 if P-value $\leq$ significance level (such as 0.05).

Example 5

Inference about the slope ◀

60-Pound Strength and Bench Presses

Picture the Scenario

One purpose of the strength study introduced in Example 1 was to analyze whether x = number of times an athlete can lift a 60-pound bench press helps us predict y = maximum number of pounds the athlete can bench press. Table 12.2 shows the regression analysis for the 57 female athletes, with x denoted by BP60 and y denoted by maxBP. The margin shows screen shots from a TI calculator.

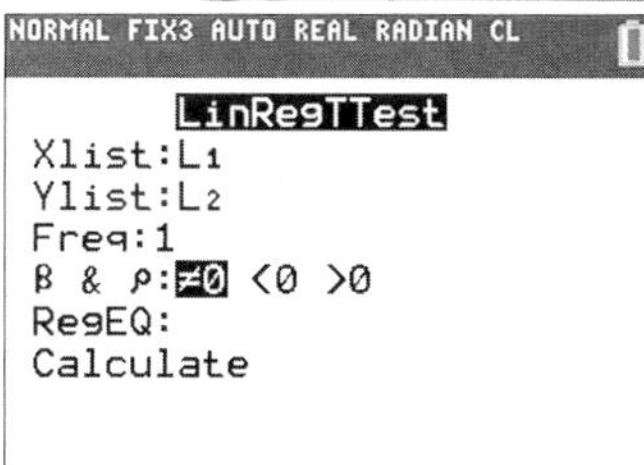

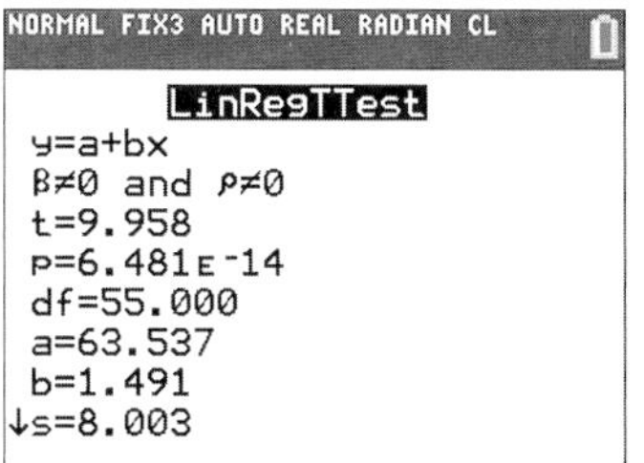

TI output of testing whether slope equals 0.

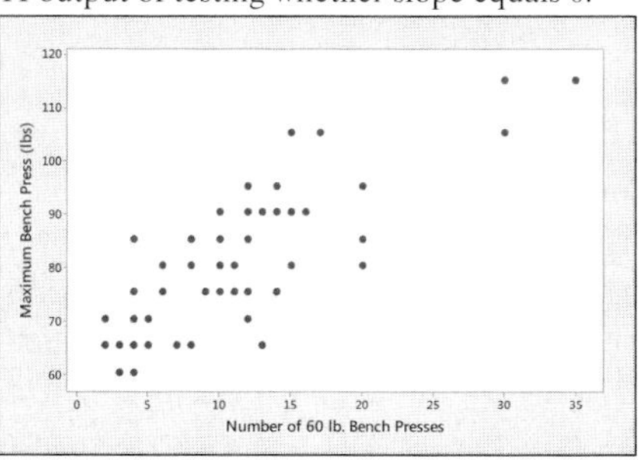

Table 12.2 MINITAB Printout for Regression Analysis of y = Maximum Bench Press (maxBP) and x = Number of 60-Pound Bench Presses (BP60)

```
The regression equation is maxBP = 63.54 + 1.491 BP60

Coefficients

Term        Coef   SE Coef   T-Value   P-Value
Constant   63.54      1.96     32.48     0.000
BP60       1.491     0.150      9.96     0.000
```

Questions to Explore

a. Conduct a two-sided significance test of the null hypothesis of independence.

b. Report the P-value for the alternative hypothesis of a positive association, which is a sensible one for these variables. Interpret the results in context.

Think It Through

a. From Table 12.2, the prediction equation is $\hat{y} = 63.5 + 1.49x$. Here are the steps of a significance test of the null hypothesis of independence.

1. **Assumptions:** The scatterplot in Figure 12.1, shown again in the margin, revealed a linear trend, with scatter of points having similar variability (or spread) at different x values. The straight-line regression model $\mu_y = \alpha + \beta x$ seems appropriate. The 57 female athletes were *all* the female athletes at a particular high school. This was a convenience sample rather than a random sample of the population of female high school athletes. Although the goal was

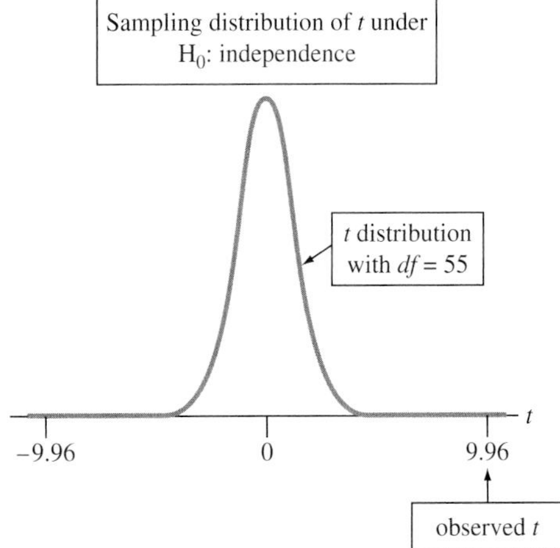

to make inferences about that population, inferences are tentative because the sample was not random.

2. **Hypotheses:** The null hypothesis that the variables are independent is H_0: $\beta = 0$. The two-sided alternative hypothesis of dependence is H_a: $\beta \neq 0$.
3. **Test statistic:** For the estimated slope $b = 1.49$, Table 12.2 reports a standard error of $se = 0.150$. This is listed under "SE Coef," in the row of the table for the term BP60. For testing H_0: $\beta = 0$, the t test statistic is

$$t = (b - 0)/se = 1.49/0.150 = 9.96.$$

This is extremely large. The sample slope falls nearly 10 standard errors above the null hypothesis value. The t test statistic appears in Table 12.2 under the column labeled "T-Value." The sample size equals $n = 57$, so $df = n - 2 = 55$.

4. **P-value:** The P-value listed in Table 12.2 right next to the t statistic of 9.96 is 0.000 rounded to three decimal places. Software reports the P-value for the two-sided alternative, H_a: $\beta \neq 0$. It is the two-tailed probability of "more extreme values" above 9.96 and below −9.96. See the margin figure.
5. **Conclusion:** If the population slope β were equal to 0 (i.e., the null hypothesis is true), it would be extremely unusual to get a sample slope as far from 0 as $b = 1.49$. The P-value gives very strong evidence against H_0. We conclude that an association exists between the number of 60-pound bench presses and maximum bench press.

b. The one-sided alternative H_a: $\beta > 0$ predicts a positive association. For it, the P-value is halved because it is then the right-tail probability of $t > 9.96$. This also equals 0.000, to three decimal places. On average, we infer that maximum bench press increases (because the slope is significantly larger than 0) as the number of 60-pound bench presses increases.

Insight

In practice, studies must often rely on convenience samples. Results may be biased if the study subjects differ in an important way from those in the population of interest. Here, inference is reliable only to the extent that the sample is representative of the population of female high school athletes. This is a common problem with studies of this type, in which it would be difficult to arrange for a random sample of all subjects but a sample is conveniently available locally. We can place more faith in the inference if similar results occur in other studies.

The printout in Table 12.2 also contains a standard error and t statistic for testing that the population y-intercept α equals 0. This information is usually not of interest. Rarely is there any reason to test the hypothesis that a y-intercept equals 0.

▶ ***Try Exercise 12.12, part a***

You probably did not expect maximum bench press and number of 60-pound bench presses to be independent. The test confirms that they are positively associated. As usual, a confidence interval is more informative. It will help us learn about the actual size of the slope.

A Confidence Interval Tells Us How Precisely We Can Estimate the Slope

A small P-value in the significance test of H_0: $\beta = 0$ suggests that the population regression line has a nonzero slope. To learn just how far the slope β for the population regression model falls from 0, we construct a confidence interval. A 95% confidence interval for β has the typical form of adding and subtracting a margin of error (a multiple of the *se*) from the point estimate:

Recall

For **95% confidence,** the error probability is 0.05, and the *t*-score with half this probability in the right tail is denoted $t_{.025}$ in the *t* table. ◀

$$b \pm t_{.025}(se).$$

The *t*-score is found by software, using the *t*-distribution web app, or in a *t* table (such as Table B) with $df = n - 2$. (Don't confuse it with the *t* statistic shown for the significance test, which is something different!) This inference is valid under the same assumptions as the significance test.

Example 6

A 95% confidence interval for the slope ◀

Estimating the Slope for Predicting Maximum Bench Press

Picture the Scenario

For the female athlete strength study, the sample regression equation is $\hat{y} = 63.5 + 1.49x$. From Table 12.2, the estimated slope $b = 1.49$ has standard error $se = 0.150$.

Questions to Explore

a. Construct a 95% confidence interval for the population slope β.
b. What are the plausible values for the increase in maximum bench press, on average, for each additional 60-pound bench press that a female athlete can do?

Think It Through

a. For a 95% confidence interval, the $t_{.025}$ value for $df = n - 2 = 55$ is $t_{.025} = 2.00$. (If your software does not supply the entire interval or even *t*-scores, you can use the *t*-distribution web app to find *t*-scores or you can approximate them from Table B.) The confidence interval is

$$b \pm t_{.025}(se) = 1.49 \pm 2.00(0.150),$$
$$\text{which is } 1.49 \pm 0.30$$
$$\text{or } (1.2, 1.8).$$

b. We can be 95% confident that the population slope β falls between 1.2 and 1.8. On average, the maximum bench press increases by between 1.2 and 1.8 pounds for each additional 60-pound bench press that an athlete can do.

Insight

Confidence intervals and two-sided significance tests about slopes are consistent: When a two-sided test has P-value below 0.05, providing evidence against $\beta = 0$, the 95% confidence interval for β does not contain 0.

► ***Try Exercise 12.12, part b***

A confidence interval for β may not have a useful interpretation if a one-unit increase in *x* is relatively small (or large) in practical terms. In that case, we can estimate the effect for an increase in x that is a more relevant portion of the actual range of x values. For instance, an increase of 10 units in x has change 10β in the mean of y. To find the confidence interval for 10β, multiply the endpoints of the confidence interval for β by 10.

In the strength study, $x =$ number of 60-pound bench presses varied between 2 and 35, with a standard deviation of 7.1. A change of 1 is very small. Let's estimate the effect of a 10-unit increase in x. Since the 95% confidence interval for β is (1.2, 1.8), the 95% confidence interval for 10β has endpoints $10(1.2) = 12$ and $10(1.8) = 18$. We infer that, on average, the maximum bench press increases by at least 12 pounds and at most 18 pounds, for every 10 additional 60-pound bench presses that an athlete can do more. The interval from 12 to 18 is also a 95% confidence interval for the difference between the mean maximum bench press for athletes who can do $x = 25$ bench presses and athletes who can do $x = 15$ bench presses (since $25 - 15 = 10$).

SUMMARY: Confidence interval for β

Assumptions: (1) Relationship in population satisfies regression model $\mu_y = \alpha + \beta x$, (2) data gathered using randomization, (3) population y values at each x value have normal distribution, with same standard deviation at each x value.

A 95% confidence interval for the slope β in the population regression model $\mu_y = \alpha + \beta x$ is

$$b \pm t_{.025}(se)$$

Software provides the estimated slope b, its standard error *se*, and the *t*-score with right tail probability 0.025.

Inferences Also Apply to the Correlation

When the slope $\beta = 0$ for the population regression model $\mu_y = \alpha + \beta x$, the value of x is irrelevant in determining μ_y. In that case, the conditional distribution of y at a particular x value does not depend on x, i.e., it is the same for all values of x. Then, the two variables x and y are independent, and their correlation in the population is zero. (Compare Figure 12.5, where the mean of y and, hence, the distribution of y depends on x, i.e., there is an association, and Figure 12.6, which shows identical distributions at each x value, i.e., independence.)

Because of this connection, the test of H_0: $\beta = 0$ is also automatically a test of H_0: the population correlation of x and y is zero. We do not need to come up with a new test statistic and sampling distribution to determine the P-value for this latter test; we just use the results from the test about the slope. For example, the sample correlation between the number of 60-pound bench presses and the maximum possible bench press is $r = 0.80$. To determine whether in the population the correlation between these two variables is different from zero (the value of the correlation under independence), we test the null hypothesis H_0: the population correlation between number of 60-pound bench presses and maximum bench press is zero (i.e., independence) against the two-sided alternative hypothesis H_a: the population correlation is different from zero (association).

The P-value for this test equals 0.000, which is the P-value we obtained when testing H_0: $\beta = 0$. We have sufficient evidence (P-value < 0.001) to reject the null hypothesis that the two variables are independent and can conclude that the correlation between the number of 60-pound bench presses and maximum possible bench press is different from zero, i.e., a significant association exists. Because $r = 0.80$, we can conclude that the association is, in fact, positive and relatively strong. The assumptions under which this test is valid are the same as those for the significance test of whether $\beta = 0$.

12.2 Practicing the Basics

12.11 *t*-score? A regression analysis is conducted with 25 observations.

a. What is the *df* value for inference about the slope β?

b. Which two *t* test statistic values would give a P-value of 0.05 for testing H_0: $\beta = 0$ against H_a: $\beta \neq 0$?

c. What is the value of the *t*-score that you multiply the standard error by to find the margin of error for a 95% confidence interval for β?

12.12 Predicting house prices TRY For the House Selling Prices FL data file on the book's website, MINITAB results of a regression analysis are shown for 100 homes relating y = selling price (in dollars) to x = the size of the house (in square feet).

a. Using this output, go through all steps of a significance test of independence (testing whether the population slope equals 0) by (i) mentioning the necessary assumptions for inferences to be valid, (ii) stating the hypotheses, (iii) giving the value of the test statistic, (iv) stating the P-value, and (v) writing a conclusion.

b. Show that a 95% confidence interval for the population slope is (64, 90). (*Hint:* The *t*-score with $df = 98$ equals 1.984.)

c. A builder had claimed that the selling price increases $100, on average, for every extra square foot. Based on part b, what would you conclude about this claim?

House selling prices and size of home

Term	Coef	SE Coef	T-Value	P-Value
Constant	9161	10760	0.85	0.397
size	77.01	6.63	11.62	0.000

12.13 Confidence interval for slope Refer to the previous exercise, which mentioned a confidence interval of (64, 90) for the slope. The 100 houses included in the data set had sizes ranging from 370 square feet to 4,050 square feet.

a. Interpret what the confidence interval implies for a one-unit increase in the size of the house.

b. Repeat part a, now using a more meaningful increase of 100 square feet in the size of a house.

12.14 House prices in bad part of town Refer to the previous exercise. Of the 100 homes, 25 were in a part of town considered less desirable. For a regression analysis using y = selling price and x = size of house for these 25 homes,

a. You plan to test H_0: $\beta = 0$ against H_a: $\beta > 0$. Explain what H_0 means and why a data analyst might choose a one-sided H_a for this test.

b. For this one-sided alternative hypothesis, how large would the *t* test statistic need to be to get a P-value equal to (i) 0.05 and (ii) 0.01?

12.15 Strength through leg press The high school female athlete strength study also considered prediction of y = maximum leg press (maxLP) using x = number of 200-pound leg presses (LP200). MINITAB results of a regression analysis are shown.

Regression Equation maxLP = 233.9 + 5.271 LP200

Term	Coef	SE Coef	T-Value	P-Value
Constant	233.9	13.1	17.90	0.000
LP200	5.271	0.547	9.64	0.000

a. Show all steps of a two-sided significance test of the hypothesis of independence.

b. Use the quoted *se* to find and then interpret a 95% confidence interval for the true slope. (*Hint:* $t_{0.025} = 2.00$.) What do you learn from the interval that you cannot learn from the significance test in part a?

12.16 More boys are bad? TECH A study of 375 women who lived in pre-industrial Finland (by S. Helle et al., *Science*, vol. 296, p. 1085, 2002), using Finnish church records from 1640 to 1870, found that there was roughly a linear relationship between y = life length (in years) and x = number of sons the woman had, with a slope estimate of -0.65 ($se = 0.29$).

a. Interpret the sign of the slope. Is the effect of having more boys good or bad?

b. Show all steps of the test of the hypothesis that life length is independent of number of sons for the two-sided alternative hypothesis. Interpret the P-value.

c. Construct a 95% confidence interval for the true slope. Interpret. Is it plausible that the effect is relatively weak, with true slope near 0?

12.17 More girls are good? TECH Repeat the previous exercise using x = number of daughters the woman had, for which the slope estimate was 0.44 ($se = 0.29$).

12.18 CI and two-sided tests correspond Refer to the previous two exercises. Using significance level 0.05, what decision would you make? Explain how that decision is in agreement with whether 0 falls in the confidence interval. Do this for the data for both the boys and the girls.

12.19 Advertising and sales TECH Each month, the owner of Café Gardens restaurant records y = monthly total sales receipts and x = amount spent that month on advertising, both in thousands of dollars. For the first four months of operation, the observations are as shown in the table. The correlation equals 0.857.

Advertising	Sales
0	4
1	7
2	8
5	9

a. Find the mean and standard deviation for each variable.

b. Using the formulas for the slope and the y-intercept or software, find the regression line.

c. The *se* of the slope estimate is 0.364. Test the null hypothesis that these variables are independent, using a significance level of 0.05.

12.20 GPA and study time—revisited Refer to the association you investigated in Exercise 12.7 between study time and college GPA. Using software with the data file you constructed, conduct a significance test of the hypothesis of independence for the one-sided alternative of a positive population slope. Report the hypotheses, appropriate assumptions, sample slope, its standard error, the test statistic, and the P-value and interpret.

12.21 GPA and skipping class—revisited Refer to the association you investigated in Exercise 12.8 between skipping class and college GPA. Using software with the data file you constructed, construct a 90% confidence interval for the slope in the population. Interpret.

12.22 Battery capacity Refer to the cell phone data set from Exercise 12.9 about various specs of cell phones. Treat the weight of the phone as the response and the capacity of the battery as the explanatory variable. Remove the outlier (phone no. 70).

a. Is there evidence for an association between these two variables? Show all steps of a relevant significance test with significance level 0.05 and interpret.

b. Confirm, using the output of the software, that the 95% confidence interval for the population slope equals (0.028, 0.060). Interpret the interval and explain the correspondence with the result of the significance test in part a.

12.3 Describing the Strength of Association

In the straight-line regression model, the slope indicates whether the association is positive or negative and describes the trend. The slope does not, however, describe the *strength* of the association. As always, a small P-value in a significance test for testing whether the slope (or correlation) equals 0 only implies that an association exists; it does not give any information about how strong that association is. For instance, the P-value for testing H_0: $\beta = 0$ (or, equivalently, H_0: population correlation $= 0$) can be less than 0.001, indicating strong evidence for a correlation, yet in practical terms that correlation can be very small and practically meaningless, such as $r = 0.1$. In this section, we will discuss ways of using the correlation and its squared value to interpret the strength of the association.

The Correlation Is a Standardized Slope

Why do we need the correlation? Why can't we use the slope to describe the strength of the association? The reason is that the slope's numerical value depends on the units of measurement. Example 3 found a slope of 1.49 pounds in predicting y = maximum bench press using x = number of 60-pound bench presses. Suppose we instead measure y in kilograms (kg). Since 1 kg = 2.2 pounds, a slope of 1.49 pounds is equivalent to a slope of $1.49/2.2 = 0.68$ kilograms. In grams, the slope would be 680. Whether a slope is a small number or a large number merely depends on the units of measurement.

The correlation is a *standardized* version of the slope. Unlike the slope b, the correlation does not depend on units of measurement. It takes the same value regardless of whether maximum bench press is measured in pounds, kilograms, or grams. Since the correlation r and slope b are related by $b = r(s_y/s_x)$, we can write,

Recall

From Section 3.3,

$$b = r\left(\frac{s_y}{s_x}\right),$$

$$a = \bar{y} - b\bar{x}.$$ ◀

$$r = b\left(\frac{s_x}{s_y}\right).$$

You can see from this formula that the correlation equals the slope when $s_x = s_y$. In practice, the standard deviations will never be identical. However, remember that the correlation does not depend on the units of measurements, which means we can look at the z-scores for x and y (i.e., standardize them) and still get the same correlation. (If you remember from Chapter 3, that's actually what we did when we discussed the formula for the correlation, which we expressed in terms of z-scores.) By construction, z-scores have standard deviation equal to 1. Let z_x and z_y denote the z-scores of x and y, respectively. Then, $s_{z_x} = s_{z_y} = 1$, and the slope estimated from the regression model using the z-scores instead of the original variables equals the correlation r.

This leads to an important interpretation of the correlation r as a standardized slope: Technically, for every one-unit change in the z-score of x, we predict the z-score of y to change by r units. Remember, however, that a z-score just expresses how many standard deviations an observation falls from its mean, so the technical interpretation implies more practically that if x changes by one standard deviation, we predict y to change by r standard deviations.

Example 7

Correlation

Predicting Strength

Picture the Scenario

For the female athlete strength study (Examples 1–3), with x = number of 60-pound bench presses and y = maximum bench press, we had:

x: mean = 11.0, standard deviation = 7.1

y: mean = 79.9, standard deviation = 13.3 (both in pounds)

regression equation: $\hat{y} = 63.5 + 1.49x$.

Questions to Explore

a. Find the correlation r between these two variables.

b. Show that r does not change value if you measure y in kilograms.

c. Predict the change in maximum bench press when the number of 60-pound presses increases by one standard deviation.

Think It Through

a. The slope of the regression equation is $b = 1.49$. Since $s_x = 7.1$ and $s_y = 13.3$,

$$r = b\left(\frac{s_x}{s_y}\right) = 1.49\left(\frac{7.1}{13.3}\right) = 0.80.$$

The variables have a strong, positive association.

b. If y had been measured in kilograms, the y values would have been divided by 2.2, since 1 kg = 2.2 pounds. For instance, Subject 1 had y = 80 pounds, which is $80/2.2 = 36.4$ kg. Likewise, the standard deviation s_y of 13.3 in pounds would have been divided by 2.2 to get $13.3/2.2 = 6.05$ in kg. The slope of 1.49 expressing the change in pounds for a unit change in x would have been divided by 2.2, giving 0.68, since a change of 1.49 pounds = a change of 0.68 kg. Then

$$r = b(s_x/s_y) = 0.68(7.1/6.05) = 0.80.$$

The correlation is the same (0.80) if we measure y in pounds or in kilograms. (Alternatively, we could have argued that the correlation is computed from the z-scores of x and y, and since the z-scores for y are the same when y is measured in pounds or in kilograms, the correlation is the same.)

c. As mentioned just before Example 7, when x changes by *one standard deviation*, we predict y to change by r standard deviation. So, for a one-standard deviation change in the number of 60-pound presses, we predict the maximum possible bench press to change by 0.80 standard deviations.

Insight

Now if we change units from kilograms to grams, s_y changes from 6.05 to 6,050, b changes from 0.68 to 680, but again $r = 0.80$ because r does not depend on the units. Similarly, the predicted change in y will always be 0.80 standard deviations of y, regardless of the units we use for y.

▶ ***Try Exercise 12.26***

Regression Toward the Mean

An important property of the correlation is that at any particular x value, the predicted value of y is relatively closer to its mean than x is to its mean. As we have just argued when discussing that the correlation is a standardized slope:

If an x value is a certain number of standard deviations from its mean, then the predicted y is r times that many standard deviations from its mean.

Let's illustrate for $r = 0.50$ and a subject who is 1 standard deviation above the mean of x, that is with x value, $x = \bar{x} + s_x$. The predicted value of y is 0.50 standard deviation above the mean, $\bar{y}$. That is, at $x = \bar{x} + s_x$, the predicted outcome is $\hat{y} = \bar{y} + 0.50s_y$. The predicted y is relatively closer to its mean. See Figure 12.7, which also recalls that for subjects at the mean $\bar{x}$ of x, their predicted value of y is $\bar{y}$.

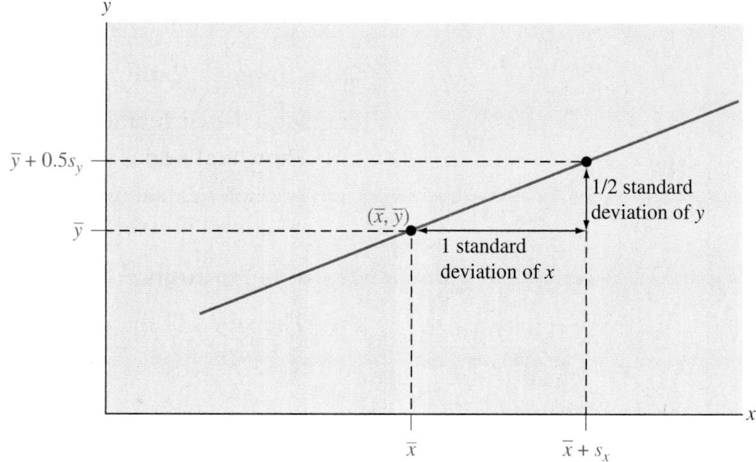

▲ **Figure 12.7 The Predicted Value of y Is Closer to Its Mean $\bar{y}$ Than x Is to Its Mean $\bar{x}$ (in Number of Standard Deviations).** When x is 1 standard deviaton above $\bar{x}$, the predicted y value is r standard deviations above $\bar{y}$ (shown in the figure for $r = 1/2$). **Question** When x is 2 standard deviations above $\bar{x}$, how many standard deviations does the predicted y value fall above $\bar{y}$ (if $r = 1/2$)?

Example 8

Regression toward the mean

Tall Parents and Tall Children

Picture the Scenario

British scientist Francis Galton discovered the basic ideas of regression and correlation in the 1880s. He observed that very tall parents tended to have tall children, but on average not quite so tall. For instance, for all fathers with height 7 feet, their sons averaged 6 feet 5 inches when fully grown—taller than average but not extremely tall. Likewise, for fathers with height 5 feet, perhaps their sons averaged 5 feet 5 inches—shorter than average, but not extremely short.

In his research, Galton accounted for gender height differences by multiplying each female height by 1.08, so heights of mothers and daughters had about the same mean as heights of fathers and sons. Then, for each son or daughter, he summarized their father's and mother's heights by parents' height $=$ (father's height $+$ mother's height)$/2$, the mean of their heights.

Question to Explore

Galton found a correlation of 0.5 between $x =$ parents' height and $y =$ child's height. How does his observation about very tall or very short

parents with children who are not so very tall or so very short relate to the property about the correlation that a predicted value of y is relatively closer to its mean than x is to its mean?

Think It Through

From the property of r with $r = 0.5$, when x = parents' height is a certain number of standard deviations from its mean, then y = child's predicted height is *half* as many standard deviations from its mean. For example, if the parents' height is 2 standard deviations above the mean, the child is predicted to be 1 standard deviation above the mean (half as far, in relative terms, when $r = 0.5$). At $x = \bar{x} + 3s_x$, we predict $\hat{y} = \bar{y} + 1.5s_y$. In each case, on average a child's height is above the mean but only half as far above the mean as his or her parent's height is above the parent's mean.

Insight

The correlation r is no greater than 1 in absolute value. So, a y value is predicted to be fewer standard deviations from its mean than x is from its mean.

► ***Try Exercise 12.35***

In Words

In English, "regression" means going back, or returning. Here, the predicted value of y is going back toward the mean.

In summary, the predicted y is relatively closer to its mean than x is to its mean. Because of this, there is said to be **regression toward the mean.** This is the origin of the name that Francis Galton chose for regression analysis.

For all cases in which parents' height is *extremely* tall, say 3 standard deviations above the mean (essentially at the upper limit of observed heights), it's no surprise that their children would tend to be shorter. For all cases in which parents' height is extremely short, say 3 standard deviations below the mean, it's no surprise that their children would tend to be taller. In both these cases, we'd expect regression toward the mean. What's interesting and perhaps surprising is that regression of y toward the mean happens not only at the very extreme values of x.

Example 9

Regression toward the mean

The Placebo Effect

Picture the Scenario

A clinical trial admits subjects suffering from high blood cholesterol (over 225 mg/dl). The subjects are randomly assigned to take either a placebo or a drug being tested for reducing cholesterol levels. After the three-month study, the mean cholesterol level for subjects taking the drug drops from 270 to 230. However, the researchers are surprised to see that the mean cholesterol level for the placebo group also drops, from 270 to 250.

Question to Explore

Explain how this placebo effect could merely reflect regression toward the mean.

Think It Through

For a group of people, a person's cholesterol reading at one time would likely be positively correlated with their reading three months later. So, for all people who are not taking the drug, a subject with relatively high cholesterol at one time would also tend to have relatively high cholesterol three months later. By regression toward the mean, however, subjects who are relatively high at one time will, on average, be lower at a later time. So, if a study gives placebo to people with relatively high cholesterol (that is, in the right-hand tail of the blood cholesterol distribution), on average we expect their values three months later to be lower.

Insight

Regression toward the mean is pervasive. In sports, excellent performance tends to be followed by good, but less outstanding, performance. A football team that wins all its games in the first half of its schedule will probably not win all its games in the second half. A baseball player who hits 0.400 in the first month will probably not be hitting that high at the end of the season.

By contrast, the good news about regression toward the mean is that very poor performance tends to be followed by improved performance. If you got the worst score in your statistics class on the first exam, you probably did not do so poorly on the second exam (but you were probably still below the mean).

► ***Try Exercise 12.32***

The Squared Correlation (r^2) Describes Predictive Power

If you know how many times a person can bench press 60 pounds, can you predict well their maximum bench press? Another way to describe the strength of association refers to how close predictions for y tend to be to observed y values. The variables are strongly associated if you can predict y much better by substituting x values into the prediction equation $\hat{y} = a + bx$ than by merely using the sample mean $\bar{y}$, ignoring x and its relationship with y.

For a given person, the prediction error is the difference between the observed and predicted values of y.

- The error using the regression line to make a prediction is $y - \hat{y}$.
- The error using $\bar{y}$ to make a prediction is $y - \bar{y}$.

For each potential predictor ($\hat{y}$ and $\bar{y}$), some errors are positive, some errors are negative, some errors may be zero, and the sum of the errors for the sample equals 0. You can summarize the sizes of the errors by the sum of their squared values,

$$\text{Error summary} = \Sigma(\text{observed } y \text{ value} - \text{predicted } y \text{ value})^2.$$

When we predict y using $\bar{y}$ (that is, ignoring x), the error summary equals

$$\Sigma(y - \bar{y})^2.$$

Recall

$\Sigma(y - \bar{y})^2$ is the numerator of the variance of the y values. $\Sigma(y - \hat{y})^2$ is what's minimized in finding the least squares estimates for the regression equation. ◄

This is called the **total sum of squares**. When we predict y using $\hat{y}$ (that is, using x with the regression equation), the error summary equals

$$\Sigma(y - \hat{y})^2.$$

This is called the **residual sum of squares** because it sums the squared residuals.

When a strong linear association exists, the regression equation predictions ($\hat{y}$) tend to be much better than $\bar{y}$. Then, $\Sigma(y - \hat{y})^2$ is much less than $\Sigma(y - \bar{y})^2$. The difference between the two error summaries depends on the units of measure: It's different, for instance, with weight measured in kilograms than in pounds. We can eliminate this dependence on units by converting the difference to a proportion, by dividing by $\Sigma(y - \bar{y})^2$. This gives the summary measure of association,

$$r^2 = \frac{\Sigma(y - \bar{y})^2 - \Sigma(y - \hat{y})^2}{\Sigma(y - \bar{y})^2}.$$

This measure falls on the same scale as a proportion, 0 to 1.

The measure r^2 is interpreted as the **proportional reduction in error**. If $r^2 = 0.40$, for instance, the error using $\hat{y}$ to predict y is 40% smaller than the error using $\bar{y}$ to predict y. We use the notation r^2 for this measure because, in fact, it can be shown that this measure equals the square of the correlation r.

In Practice Get r^2 by Squaring the Correlation

If you know the correlation r, it is simple to calculate r^2 by squaring the correlation. The formula shown previously for r^2 is useful for interpretation of r^2, but it's not needed for calculation.

The squared correlation r^2

Example 10

The Strength Study

Picture the Scenario

For the female athlete strength study, Example 7 showed that x = number of 60-pound bench presses, and y = maximum bench press had a correlation of 0.80.

Question to Explore

Find and interpret r^2.

Think It Through

Since the correlation $r = 0.80$, $r^2 = (0.80)^2 = 0.64$. For predicting maximum bench press, the regression equation has 64% less error than $\bar{y}$ has. "Error" here refers to the summary given by the sum of squared prediction errors. The overall prediction error when using the regression equation with number of 60-pound bench presses to predict the maximum bench press is 64% smaller compared to using the sample mean maximum bench press for predictions.

Insight

Since $r^2 = 0.64$ is quite far from 0, we can predict y much better using the regression equation than using $\bar{y}$. In this sense, the association is quite strong.

▶ ***Try Exercise 12.27, part b***

Typically, software provides r^2 as part of the standard output when fitting a regression model, but it's also possible to calculate r^2 directly from the definition. Software for regression also routinely provides tables of sums of squares. Table 12.3 (showing partial output from MINITAB) is an example. The heading SS stands for "sum of squares." From Table 12.3, the residual sum of squared errors is $\Sigma(y - \hat{y})^2 = 3522.8$, and the total sum of squares is $\Sigma(y - \bar{y})^2 = 9874.6$. Thus,

$$r^2 = \frac{\Sigma(y - \bar{y})^2 - \Sigma(y - \hat{y})^2}{\Sigma(y - \bar{y})^2} = \frac{9874.6 - 3522.8}{9874.6} = 0.643.$$

Normally, it is unnecessary to perform this computation, since most software reports r or r^2 or both.

A table that reports the sums of squares used in regression analysis is called an **analysis of variance table**, or **ANOVA table** for short. We'll discuss the ANOVA table further in Section 12.4.

Table 12.3 Annotated MINITAB Table Showing Sums of Squares and r^2 for Strength Study

Under the heading for Source, "Total" refers to $\Sigma(y - \bar{y})^2$ and "Error" refers to $\Sigma(y - \hat{y})^2$. The "Regression" sum of squares equals their difference, which is the numerator of r^2.

Source	SS		
		←	SS stands for "sum of squares"
Regression	6351.8	←	This is 9874.6 − 3522.8, the numerator of r^2
Error	3522.8	←	$\Sigma(y - \hat{y})^2$
Total	9874.6	←	$\Sigma(y - \bar{y})^2$
R-Sq = 64.3%		←	This is r^2, in percentage terms

Properties of r^2

The r^2 measure, like the correlation r, measures the strength of the *linear* association. We emphasize *linear* because r^2 compares predictive power of the *straight-line* regression equation to $\bar{y}$.

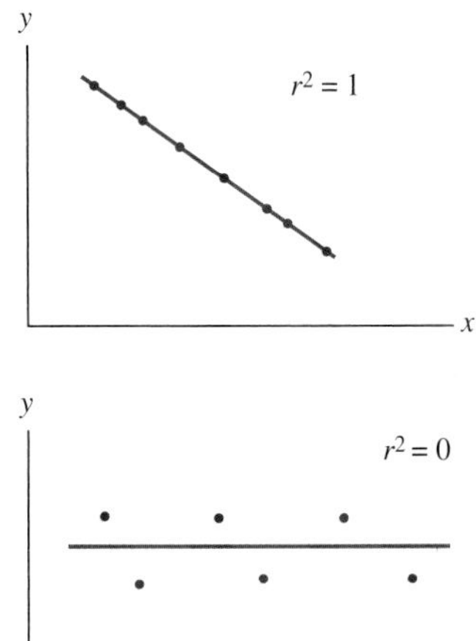

SUMMARY: Properties of r^2

- Since $-1 \leq r \leq 1$, r^2 falls between 0 and 1.
- $r^2 = 1$ when $\Sigma(y - \hat{y})^2 = 0$, which happens only when all the data points fall exactly on the regression line. There is then no prediction error using x to predict y (that is, $y = \hat{y}$ for each observation). This corresponds to $r = \pm 1$. (See top scatterplot in margin figure.)
- $r^2 = 0$ when $\Sigma(y - \hat{y})^2 = \Sigma(y - \bar{y})^2$. This happens when the slope $b = 0$, in which case each $\hat{y} = \bar{y}$. The regression line and $\bar{y}$ then give the same predictions. (See bottom scatterplot in margin figure.)
- The closer r^2 is to 1, the stronger the linear association: The more effective the regression equation $\hat{y} = a + bx$ then is compared to $\bar{y}$ in predicting y.

Next to the interpretation of r^2 as the proportional reduction in the prediction error, it has a second interpretation as the percentage of the variability in the response variable y that can be explained by its linear relationship with the explanatory variable x. For instance, the r^2 value of 0.64 from Example 10 indicates that 64% of the variability observed in maximum bench press can be explained by its linear relationship with the number of 60-pound bench presses. (We will show the reasoning behind this interpretation by using a graph in Section 12.4.) This interpretation has the weakness, however, that variability in this case is summarized by the variance. Some statisticians find r^2 to be less useful than r because (being based on sums of squares) it uses the square of the original scale of measurement. It's easier to interpret the original scale than a squared scale. This is a strong advantage of the standard deviation over the variance (i.e., r over r^2). Another disadvantage of r^2 is that the direction of the relationship is lost.

Caution

If finding the correlation r by evaluating $\sqrt{r^2}$, the sign (positive or negative) of the correlation r must be found by either looking at the scatterplot of the two variables or by knowing the slope of the corresponding least squares regression line. ◀

SUMMARY: Correlation r and Its Square r^2

Both the correlation r and its square r^2 describe the strength of association. They have different interpretations. The correlation falls between −1 and +1. It represents by how many standard deviations y is predicted to change when x changes by one standard deviation. Thereby, it governs the extent of "regression toward the mean." The r^2 measure falls between 0 and 1 (or 0% and 100% when reported by software in percentage terms). It summarizes the reduction in the prediction error when using the regression equation rather than $\bar{y}$ to predict y. It is also used to indicate how much of the variability in y can be explained by x.

Factors Affecting the Correlation

Section 3.4 showed that certain regression outliers can unduly influence the slope and the correlation. A single observation can have a large influence if its x value is unusually large or unusually small and if it falls quite far from the trend of the rest of the data.

Besides being influenced by outliers, the size of the correlation (and r^2) depends strongly on two other factors.

- First, if the subjects are grouped for the observations, such as when the data refer to county summaries instead of individual people, the correlation tends to increase in magnitude.

Suppose you want to find the correlation between number of years of education completed and annual income. You could measure these variables for a sample of individuals. Or you could use summary education and income measures such as means or medians for counties (or states or provinces). The scatterplot in Figure 12.8 shows that at the individual level, the correlation could be much weaker. Lots of variability in income exists for individuals, but not much variability in income (mean or median) exists for counties. The summary values for counties fall closer to a straight line.

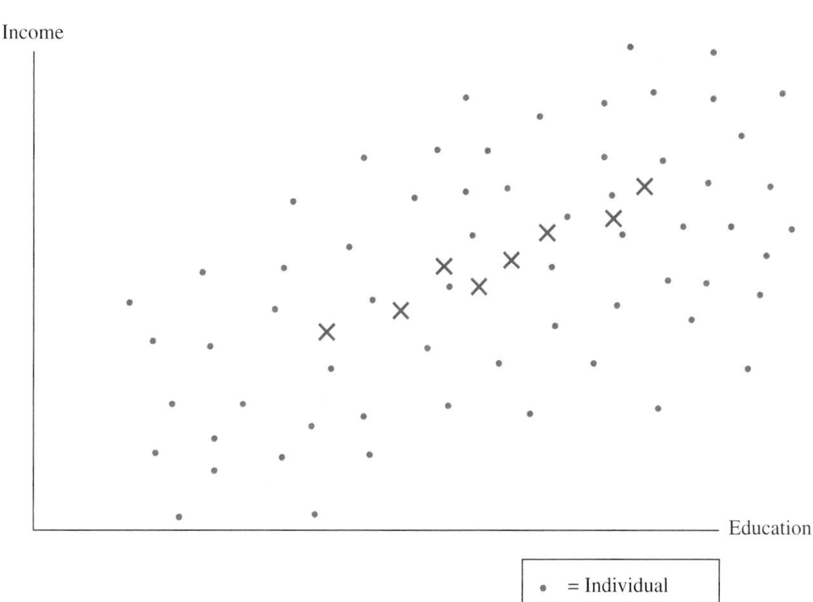

▲ **Figure 12.8 The Effect of Grouping of Subjects on the Correlation.** There is a stronger linear trend for the countywide data than for the data on individuals. **Question** Why would you expect much more variability for income of individuals than for mean income of counties?

Did You Know?

The **ecological fallacy** is a danger even with single variables. If the mean income in your town is $50,000, you'd be wrong to assume that each worker makes $50,000. Perhaps half are professionals making $90,000 and half are service workers making $10,000. ◀

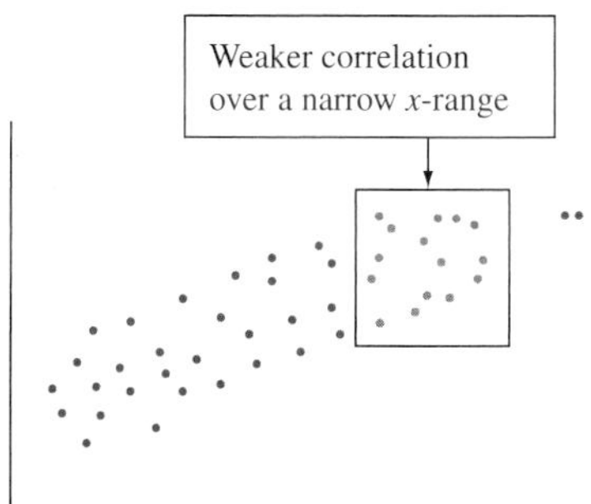

Because correlations can change dramatically when data are grouped, it is misleading to take results for groupings such as counties and extend them to individuals. If income and education are strongly correlated when we measure the summary means for each county, this does not imply they will be strongly correlated for measurements on individuals. Making predictions about individuals based on the summary results for groups is known as the **ecological fallacy** and should be avoided.

- Second, the size of the correlation depends on the range of x values sampled: The correlation tends to be smaller when we sample only a restricted range of x values than when we use the entire range. (See margin figure.)

By contrast, the prediction equation remains valid when we observe a restricted range of x values. The slope is usually not much affected by the range of x values, and we simply limit our predictions to that range. The correlation makes most sense, however, when x takes its full range of values. Otherwise, it can be misleading.

Factors affecting the correlation

Example 11

High School GPA Predicting College GPA

Picture the Scenario

Consider the correlation between high school GPA and later performance in college measured by college GPA.

Question to Explore

For which group would these variables have a stronger correlation: All students who graduate from Harvard University this year, or all students who graduate from college somewhere in the United States this year?

College GPA

Harvard sample

High school GPA

Think It Through

The magnitude of the correlation depends on the variability in high school GPA. For Harvard students, the high school GPAs will concentrate narrowly at the upper end of the scale. So, the correlation would probably be weak. By contrast, for all students who finish college, high school GPA values would range from very low to very high. We would likely see a stronger correlation for them.

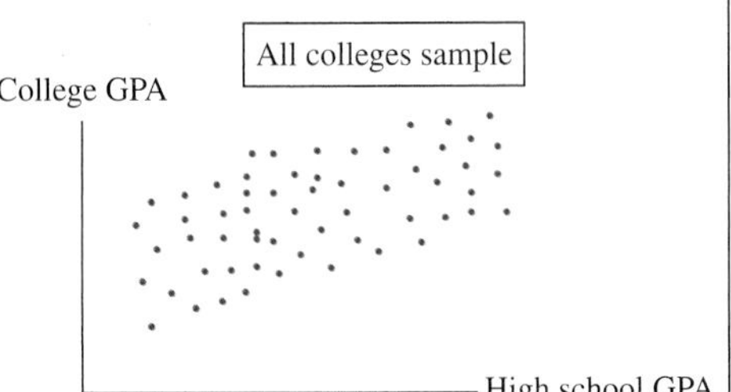

Insight

What reason explains this property of the correlation? Recall the formula, $r = b(s_x/s_y)$. When we use a much wider range of x values, s_x increases a lot. So, if the slope does not change much and if the variability of the y values is not much larger with the expanded sample, r will tend to increase because it is proportional in value to s_x.

▶ ***Try Exercise 12.38***

On the Shoulders of ... Francis Galton

Francis Galton

Heights and peas—what do they have in common?

—Francis Galton (1822–1911)

Francis Galton, like his cousin Charles Darwin, was interested in genetics. In his work on inheritance, he collected data on parents' and children's heights. He found that, on average, the heights of children were not as extreme as those of the parents and tended toward the mean height. There was regression toward the mean. This refers to this average, not to every observation. It does not imply that over the course of many generations, heights will all vary less from the mean height.

Galton also conducted experiments examining the weight of sweet peas. The mean weight of offspring peas was closer than the weight of the parent group to the mean for all peas. Again, Galton observed regression toward the mean.

Galton discovered a way to summarize linear associations numerically. He named this numerical summary the "coefficient of correlation." In 1896, the British statistician Karl Pearson (who proposed the chi-squared test for contingency tables in 1900) derived the current method for estimating the correlation using sample data.

12.3 Practicing the Basics

12.23 Dollars and thousands of dollars If a slope is 1.50 when x = income in thousands of dollars, then what is the slope when x = income in dollars? (*Hint:* A \$1 change has only 1/1000 of the impact of a \$1,000 change.)

12.24 When can you compare slopes? Although the slope does not measure association, it *is* useful for comparing effects for two variables that have the *same* units. For the Internet Use data file of 32 nations on the book's website, let x = GDP (thousands of dollars per capita). For predicting y = percentage of adults using the Internet, the prediction equation is $\hat{y} = 34.8 + 1.02x$. For predicting y = percentage of adults using Facebook, the prediction equation is $\hat{y} = 23.0 + 0.46x$.

a. Explain how to interpret the two slopes.

b. For these nations, explain why a one-unit increase in GDP has a slightly greater impact on the percentage using the Internet than on the percentage using Facebook.

12.25 Sketch scatterplot Sketch a scatterplot, identifying quadrants relative to the sample means as in Figure 12.2, for which (a) the slope and correlation would be negative and (b) the slope and correlation would be approximately zero.

12.26 Sit-ups and the 40-yard dash TRY Is there a relationship between x = how many sit-ups you can do and y = how fast you can run 40 yards (in seconds)? The MINITAB output of a regression analysis based on the female athlete strength study is shown here.

```
Coefficients
Term          Coef     SE Coef   T-Value   P-Value
Constant      6.707     0.178     37.70     0.000
SIT-UP    -0.02435   0.00635     -3.83     0.000
Model Summary
        S       R-sq
0.327208     21.10%
```

a. Find the predicted time in the 40-yard dash for a subject who can do (i) 10 sit-ups and (ii) 40 sit-ups. (The minimum and maximum in the study were 10 and 39.) Relate the difference in predicted times to the slope.

b. The correlation between these two variables equals −0.46 (the negative square root of the R-Sq value shown, because the estimated slope has a negative sign). Predict by how many standard deviations the time of the 40-yard dash decreases for a one standard deviation increase in the number of sit-ups the athlete can do.

c. The number of sit-ups had mean 27.175 and standard deviation 6.887. The time in the 40-yard dash had mean 6.045 and standard deviation 0.365. Show how the correlation relates to the slope and verify the value given in part b.

d. The time difference for the 40-yard run between two athletes that are one standard deviation apart in the number of sit-ups they can do is predicted to be how much? First, answer in terms of standard deviations of the time for the 40-yard dash. Then, using the standard deviation given in part c, answer in absolute terms (i.e., in seconds).

12.27 Body fat TRY For the Male Athlete Strength data file on the book's website, the correlation between weight (pounds) and percent body fat (BF%) equals 0.883.

a. Interpret the sign and the strength of the correlation.

b. Find and interpret r^2.

c. If weight were measured instead with metric units, would any results differ in parts a and b? Explain.

12.28 Verbal and math SAT All students who attend Lake Wobegon College must take the math and verbal SAT exams. Both exams have a mean of 500 and a standard deviation of 100. The regression equation relating y = math SAT score and x = verbal SAT score is $\hat{y} = 250 + 0.5x$.

a. Find the predicted math SAT score for a student who has the mean verbal SAT score of 500. (*Note*: At the x value equal to $\bar{x}$, the predicted value of y equals $\bar{y}$.)

b. Show how to find the correlation. Interpret its value as a standardized slope. (*Hint:* Both standard deviations are equal.)

c. Find r^2 and interpret its value.

12.29 SAT regression toward mean Refer to the previous exercise.

a. Predict the math SAT score for a student who has a verbal SAT = 800.

b. The correlation is 0.5. Interpret the prediction in part a in terms of regression toward the mean.

12.30 GPA and TV watching For the Georgia Student Survey data file on the book's website, the correlation between daily time spent watching TV and college GPA is −0.35.

a. Interpret r and r^2. Use the interpretation of r^2 that (i) refers to the prediction error and (ii) the percent of variability explained.

b. One student is 2 standard deviations above the mean on time watching TV. (i) Would you expect that student to be above or below the mean on college GPA? Explain (ii) How many standard deviations would you expect that student to be away from the mean on college GPA? Use your answer to explain "regression toward the mean."

12.31 GPA and study time TECH Refer to the association you investigated in Exercise 12.7 between study time and college GPA. Using software or a calculator with the data file you constructed for that exercise,

a. Find and interpret the correlation.

b. Find and interpret r^2. Use the interpretation of r^2 that (i) refers to the prediction error and (ii) the percent of variability explained.

12.32 Placebo helps cholesterol? TRY A clinical trial admits subjects suffering from high cholesterol, who are then randomly assigned to take a drug or a placebo for a 12-week study. For the population, without taking any drug, the correlation between the cholesterol readings at times 12 weeks apart is 0.70. The mean cholesterol reading at any given time is 200, with the same standard deviation at each time. Consider all the subjects with a cholesterol level of 300 at the start of the study, who take placebo.

a. What would you predict for their mean cholesterol level at the end of the study?

b. Does this suggest that placebo is effective for treating high cholesterol? Explain.

12.33 Does tutoring help? For a class of 100 students, the teacher enrolls the 10 students who performed poorest on the midterm exam in a special tutoring program. Both the midterm and final have a class mean of 70 with standard deviation 10, and the correlation is 0.50 between the two exam scores. The mean for the specially tutored students increases from 50 on the midterm to 60 on the final. Can we conclude that the tutoring program was successful? Explain, identifying the response and explanatory variables and the role of regression toward the mean.

12.34 What's wrong with your stock fund? Last year you looked at all the financial firms that had stock growth funds. You picked the growth fund that had the best performance last year (ranking at the 99th percentile on performance) and invested all your money in it this year. This year, with its new investments, it ranked only at the 65th percentile on performance. Your friend suggests that its stock picker became complacent or was burned out. Can you give another explanation?

12.35 Golf regression In the first round of a golf tournament, five players tied for the lowest round, at 65. The mean score of all players was 75. If the mean score of all players is also 75 in the second round, what does regression toward the mean suggest about how well we can expect the five leaders to do, on the average, in the second round? (*Hint:* Suppose the standard deviation is also the same in each round.)

TRY

12.36 Car weight and mileage The Car Weight and Mileage data file on the book's website shows the weight and the mileage per gallon of gas of 25 cars of various models. The regression of mileage on weight has $r^2 = 0.75$. Explain how to interpret this in terms of how well you can predict a car's mileage if you know its weight.

12.37 Food and drink sales The owner of Bertha's Restaurant is interested in whether an association exists between the amount spent on food and the amount spent on drinks for the restaurant's customers. She decides to measure each variable for every customer in the next month. Each day she also summarizes the mean amount spent on food and the mean amount spent on drinks. Which correlation between amounts spent on food and drink do you think would be higher, the one computed for the 2500 customers in the next month, or the one computed using the means for the 30 days of the month? Why? Sketch a sample scatterplot showing what you expect for each case as part of your answer.

12.38 Yale and UConn For which student body do you think the correlation between high school GPA and college GPA would be higher: Yale University or the University of Connecticut? Explain why.

TRY

12.39 Violent crime and single-parent families Use software to analyze the U.S. Statewide Crime data file on the book's website on y = violent crime rate and x = percentage of single parent families.

TECH

a. Construct a scatterplot. What does it show?

b. One point is quite far removed from the others, having a much higher value on both variables than the rest of the sample, but it fits in well with the linear trend exhibited by the rest of the points. Show that the correlation changes from 0.77 to 0.59 when you delete this observation. Why does it drop so dramatically?

12.40 Correlations for the strong and for the weak Refer to the High School Female Athlete and Male Athlete Strength data files on the book's website.

TECH

a. Find the correlation between number of 60-pound bench presses before fatigue and bench press maximum for females and between bench presses before fatigue and bench press maximum for males. Interpret.

b. Find the correlation using only the x values (i) below the median of 10 for females and below the median of 17 for males and (ii) above the median of 10 for females and above the median of 17 for males. Compare to the correlation in part a. Why are they so different?

12.4 How the Data Vary Around the Regression Line

We've used regression to describe and make inferences about the relationship between two quantitative variables. Now, we'll see what we can learn from the variability of the data around the regression line. We'll see that a type of residual helps us detect unusual observations. We'll also see that the sizes of the residuals affect how well we can predict y or the mean of y at any given value of x.

Standardized Residuals

The magnitude of the residuals depends on the units of measurement for y. If we measure the bench press in kilograms instead of pounds, we'll get different residuals. A *standardized* version of the residual does not depend on the units.

Recall

A **residual** is a prediction error—the difference $y - \hat{y}$ between an observed outcome y and its predicted value $\hat{y}$. For contingency tables, Section 11.4 constructed a **standardized residual** by dividing the difference between a cell count and its expected count by a standard error. In regression, an observation y takes the place of the cell count, and the predicted value $\hat{y}$ takes the place of the expected cell count. ◀

It equals the residual divided by a standard error that describes the sampling variability of the residuals. This ratio is called a **standardized residual**,

$$\text{Standardized residual} = \frac{y - \hat{y}}{se \text{ of } (y - \hat{y})}.$$

The *se* formula is complex, but we can rely on software to find this.

A standardized residual behaves like a z-score. It indicates how many standard errors a residual falls from the overall mean of all residuals, which is 0. If the relationship is truly linear and if the standardized residuals have approximately a bell-shaped distribution, absolute values larger than about 3 should be quite rare. Often, observations with standardized residuals larger than 3 in absolute value represent outliers—observations that are far from what the model predicts.

Standardized residual ◀

Example 12

Detecting an Underachieving College Student

Picture the Scenario

Two of the variables in the Georgia Student Survey data file on the book's website are college GPA and high school GPA (variables CGPA and HSGPA). These were measured for a sample of 59 students at the University of Georgia. Identifying y = CGPA and x = HSGPA, we find $\hat{y} = 1.19 + 0.64x$.

Question to Explore

MINITAB highlights observations that have standardized residuals with absolute value larger than 2 in a table of "unusual observations." Table 12.4 shows this data. Interpret the results for observation 59.

Table 12.4 Observations with Large Standardized Residuals in Student GPA Regression Analysis, as Reported by MINITAB

Fits and Diagnostics for Unusual Observations

Obs	CGPA	Fit	Resid	Std Resid ⟵ Standardized Residuals		
3	3.600	3.101	0.499	1.71		X
14	2.600	3.292	−0.692	−2.26	R	
27	3.140	2.814	0.326	1.27		X
28	2.980	3.610	−0.630	−2.01	R	
59	2.500	3.483	−0.983	−3.14	R	

R Large residual X Unusual X

Think It Through

Observation 59 is a student who had high school GPA $x = 3.60$ (not shown in the table), college GPA $y = 2.50$, predicted college GPA $\hat{y} = 3.48$ (the "fit"), and residual $= y - \hat{y} = -0.98$. The reported standardized residual of -3.14 indicates that the residual is 3.14 standard errors below 0. This student's actual college GPA is quite far below what the regression line predicts.

Insight

Based on his or her high school GPA and predicted college GPA, this student with an actual college GPA of 2.50 seems to be an underachiever in college.

▶ ***Try Exercise 12.41***

When a standardized residual is larger than about 3 in absolute value, check out if the observation is unusual in some way. Why does it fall away from the linear trend that the other points follow? Does it have too much influence on the results? As we've observed, a severe regression outlier can substantially affect the fit, especially when the value of the explanatory variable is relatively high or low and when the overall sample size is not very large.

Keep in mind that some large standardized residuals may occur just because of ordinary random variability. Table 12.4 reports three observations with standardized residuals having absolute value above 2 (labeled by R in the table). Even if the model is perfect we'd expect about 5% of the standardized residuals to have absolute value above 2 just by chance. So it's not at all surprising to find 3 such values out of 59 observations. This does not suggest that the model fits poorly.

Recall

About 5% of a normal distribution is more than 2 standard deviations from the mean. ◀

Checking the Response Distribution With a Histogram of Residuals

To detect unusual observations, it's helpful to construct a histogram of the residuals. This also helps us check the inference assumption that the conditional distribution of y is normal. If this assumption is true, the residuals should have approximately a bell-shaped histogram. To check this, software can construct a histogram of the residuals or the standardized residuals.

Example 13

Using residuals to check our model assumptions ◀

College GPA

Picture the Scenario

For the regression model of Example 12 predicting college GPA from high school GPA, Figure 12.9 on the next page is a MINITAB histogram of the standardized residuals. The margin next to it shows a MINITAB box plot of the standardized residuals.

Question to Explore

What does Figure 12.9 tell you?

Think It Through

The standardized residuals show some skew to the left. It may be that for a fixed value of high school GPA, college GPA tends to be skewed to the left, with some students doing much more poorly than the regression model would predict. The large negative standardized residual of -3.14 in Example 12, summarized by the left-most bar in Figure 12.9, may merely reflect skew in the distribution of college GPA. However, each of the three bars farthest to the left represents only a single observation, so this conclusion is tentative and requires a larger sample to check more thoroughly.

Insight

The sample size was 59. When n is not especially large, a graph like Figure 12.9 is an imprecise estimate of a corresponding graph for the population. Although this graph shows some evidence of skew, much of this evidence is based on only three observations. This is not strong evidence that the conditional distribution is highly non-normal. In viewing such graphs, we need to be careful not to let a few observations influence our judgment too much. We're mainly looking for dramatic departures from the assumptions.

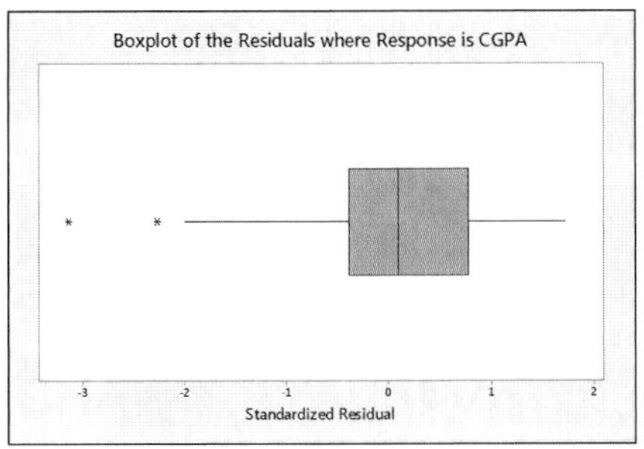

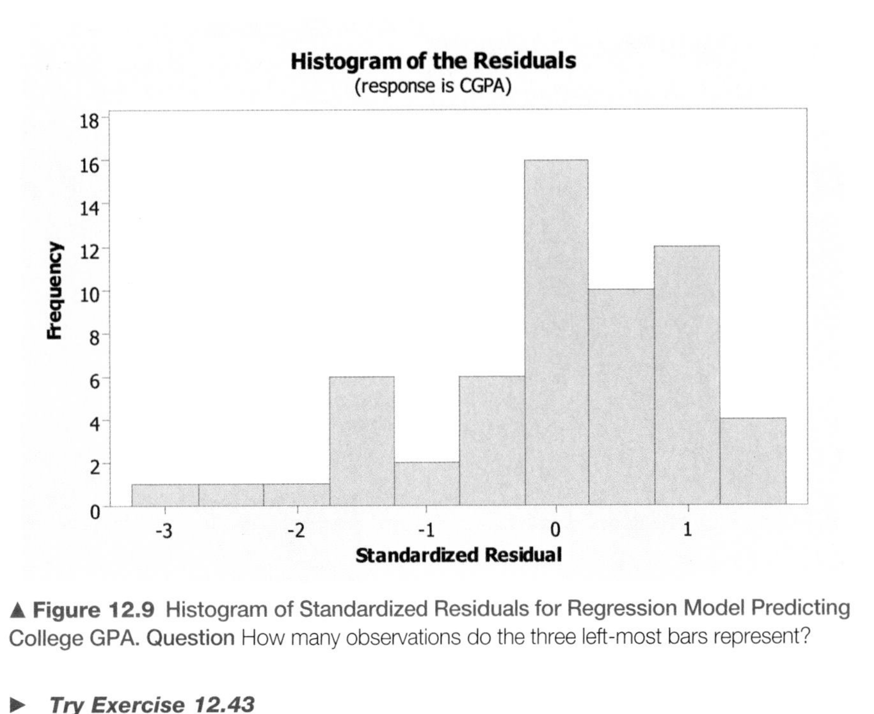

▲ **Figure 12.9** Histogram of Standardized Residuals for Regression Model Predicting College GPA. **Question** How many observations do the three left-most bars represent?

▶ ***Try Exercise 12.43***

If the distribution of the residuals is not normal, two-sided inferences about the slope parameter still work quite well. The t inferences are *robust*. The normality assumption is not as important as the assumption that the regression equation approximates well the true relationship between the explanatory variable and the mean of y. If the model assumes a linear effect but the effect is actually U-shaped, for instance, descriptive and inferential statistics will be seriously faulty.

We'll study residuals in more detail in the next chapter. We'll learn there how to plot them to check other model assumptions.

Recall

From Section 12.1, σ **describes the variability** of y values from the mean of y at each fixed x value, that is, the variability of a **conditional distribution** of y values. (See figure below.) ◀

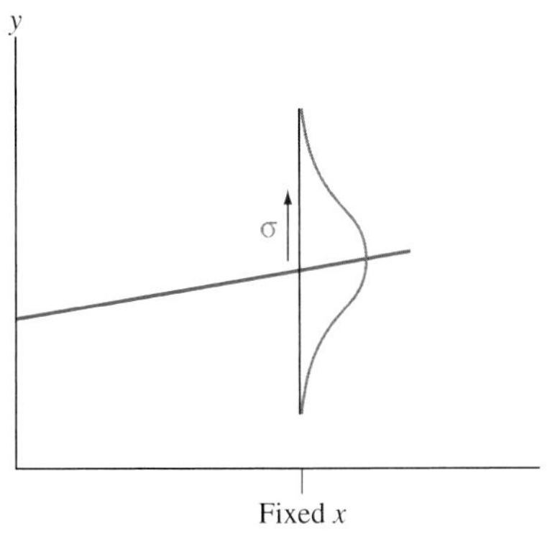

The Residual Standard Deviation

Recall that the sample prediction equation $\hat{y} = a + bx$ estimates a population regression equation, $\mu_y = \alpha + \beta x$. For statistical inference, the regression model also assumes that the conditional distribution of y at a fixed value of x is normal, with the same standard deviation at each x. This standard deviation, denoted by σ, refers to the variability of y values for all subjects with the same value of x. This is a parameter that also can be estimated from the data.

The estimate of σ uses $\Sigma(y - \hat{y})^2$, the *residual sum of squares*, which summarizes sample variability about the regression line. The estimate, called the **residual standard deviation**, is

$$s = \sqrt{\frac{\Sigma(y - \hat{y})^2}{n - 2}}.$$

It describes the typical size of the residuals. The $n - 2$ term in the denominator is the df value of the t distribution used for inference about β in the previous section.

Residual standard deviation

MINITAB output of regression analysis

```
Coefficients
Term      Coef SE Coef T-Value P-Value
Constant 63.54   1.96    32.48   0.000
BP60      1.49   0.15     9.96   0.000

Model Summary
      S     R-sq
8.00319  64.32%
```

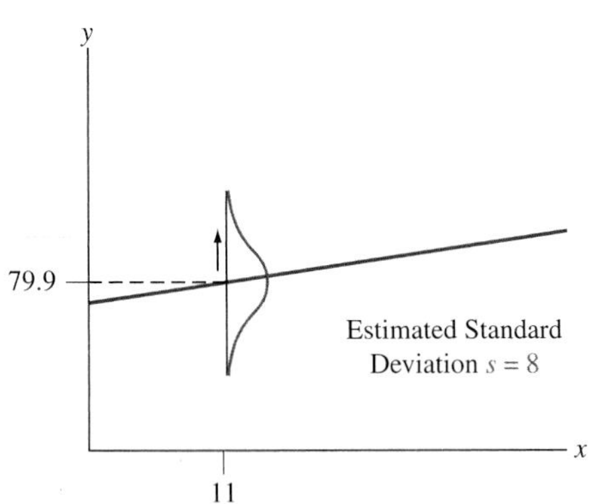

Recall

$$s_y = \sqrt{\frac{\Sigma(y - \bar{y})^2}{n - 1}}$$

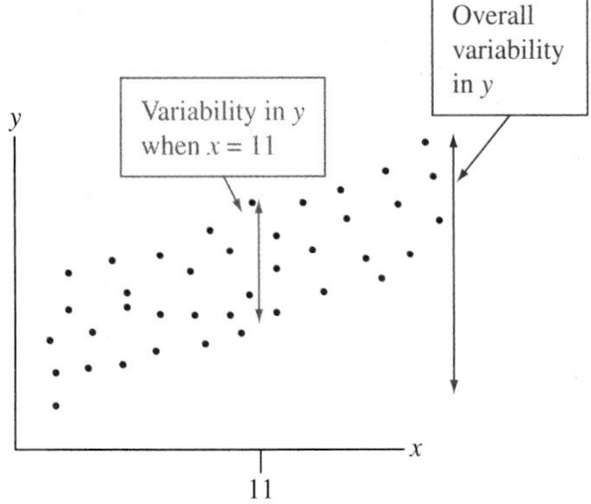

Example 14

Variability of the Athletes' Strengths

Picture the Scenario

Let's return to the analysis of y = maximum bench press and x = number of 60-pound bench presses for 57 female high school athletes. The prediction equation is $\hat{y} = 63.5 + 1.49x$. We'll see later in Table 12.6 that the residual sum of squares equals 3522.8.

Questions to Explore

a. Find the residual standard deviation of y.

b. Interpret the value you obtain in context when $x = 11$ (the mean of the x-values).

Think It Through

a. Since $n = 57$, $df = n - 2 = 55$. The residual standard deviation of the y values is

$$s = \sqrt{\frac{\Sigma(y - \hat{y})^2}{n - 2}} = \sqrt{\frac{3522.8}{55}} = \sqrt{64.1} = 8.0.$$

Often, the residual standard deviation s is part of the standard software output, such as in the MINITAB output shown in the margin under the heading Model Summary (denoted by S).

b. At any fixed value x of number of 60-pound bench presses, the model estimates that the maximum bench press values vary around a mean of $\hat{y} = 63.5 + 1.49x$ with a standard deviation of 8.0. See the figure in the margin.

At $x = 11$, the predicted maximum bench press is $\hat{y} = 63.5 + 1.49(11) = 79.9$. For female high school athletes who can do eleven 60-pound bench presses, we estimate that the maximum bench press values have a mean of about 80 pounds and a standard deviation of 8.0 pounds.

Insight

Why does the residual standard deviation $(s = 8.0)$ differ from the standard deviation $(s_y = 13.3)$ of the 57 y values in the sample? The reason is that s_y refers to the variability of *all* the y values around their mean, not just those at a fixed x value. That is, $s_y = 13.3$ describes variability around the overall mean of $\bar{y} = 80$ for *all* 57 high school female athletes, whereas $s = 8.0$ describes variability at a fixed x value such as $x = 11$. See the margin figure.

When the correlation is strong, at a fixed value of x we see less variability than the overall sample has. For instance, at the fixed value $x = 11$, we estimate the variability in maximum bench press values by $s = 8.0$, whereas overall we estimate the variability in maximum bench press values by $s_y = 13.3$.

▶ ***Try Exercise 12.47, part a***

r^2: Percentage of Overall Variability

The last figure in the margin sheds light on the interpretation of r^2 as the percentage of the overall variability observed in the response variable y that can be explained by the linear relationship with x. Here, variability refers to the sum of squares. $\Sigma(y - \bar{y})^2$ is a summary measure (a sum of squares) of the overall variability in the response variable (represented by the red arrow in the margin figure). $\Sigma(y - \hat{y})^2$ is a summary measure (a sum of squares) of the variability in the residuals (represented by the green arrow in the margin figure). The ratio $\Sigma(y - \hat{y})^2/\Sigma(y - \bar{y})^2$ expresses the proportion of the overall variability that is left unexplained after fitting the linear regression model. For instance, this proportion would be 0 if all points would fall on a straight line. Then, none of the variability in y is left unexplained and all (100%) of it can be explained by the (perfect) linear relationship with x.

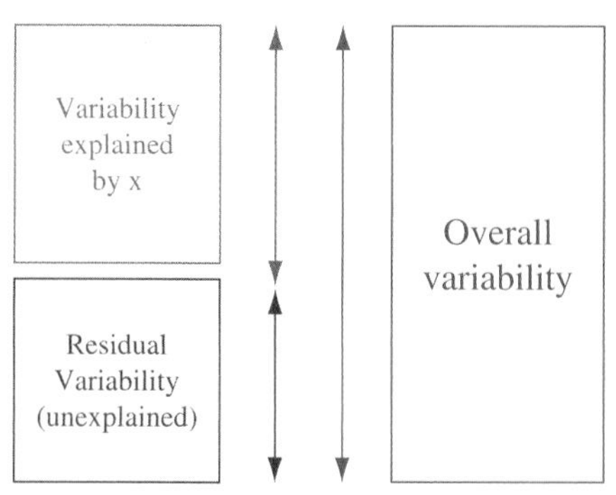

In practice, the ratio is larger than 0 because there is some variation around the line and therefore some variability of y is left unexplained. To get the proportion of the variability that *can be explained* by the linear regression model, we subtract this ratio from 1, as in $1 - \dfrac{\Sigma(y - \hat{y})^2}{\Sigma(y - \bar{y})^2}$. This is exactly the formula for r^2, just written slightly differently, so, r^2 gives the proportion of the overall variability in y that can be attributed to the linear regression model, i.e., that is due to the change in x.

Using Intervals to Predict *y* Values and Their Mean at a Given Value of *x*

Consider all female high school athletes who can manage x = eleven 60-pound bench presses before fatigue. Based on the results for the sample, which do you think you can estimate more precisely: The maximum bench press for a randomly chosen one of them or the mean of the maximum bench press values for all of them? We'll see that the estimate is the same in each case, but the margins of error are quite different for the two situations.

For the straight-line regression model, we estimate μ_y, the population mean of y at a given value of x, by $\hat{y} = a + bx$. How good is this estimate? We can use its *se* to construct a 95% **confidence interval for μ_y**. This interval is

$$\hat{y} \pm t_{.025}(se \text{ of } \hat{y}).$$

Again, the t-score has $df = n - 2$. The standard error formula is complex (we'll show a simple approximation later), and in practice we rely on software.

The estimate $\hat{y} = a + bx$ for the mean of y at a fixed value of x is also a prediction for the outcome on y for a particular subject at that value. With most regression software, you can form an interval within which an outcome y itself is likely to fall. This interval is called a **prediction interval for *y*.**

What's the difference between the prediction interval for y and the confidence interval for μ_y? The prediction interval for y is an inference about where individual observations fall, whereas the confidence interval for μ_y is an inference about where a population mean falls. Use a prediction interval for y if you want to predict where a single observation on y will fall. Use a confidence interval for μ_y if you want to estimate the mean of y for everyone having a particular x value. These inferences make the same assumptions as the regression inferences of Section 12.2.

Confidence and prediction intervals

Example 15

Maximum Bench Press and Its Mean

Picture the Scenario

We've seen that the equation $\hat{y} = 63.5 + 1.49x$ predicts y = maximum bench press using x = number of 60-pound bench presses. For $x = 11$, Table 12.5 shows how MINITAB reports a confidence interval (CI) for the population mean of y and a prediction interval (PI) for a single y value. The predicted value, $\hat{y}$, is reported under the heading "Fit."

Table 12.5 MINITAB Output for Confidence Interval (CI) and Prediction Interval (PI) on Maximum Bench Press for Athletes Who Do Eleven 60-Pound Bench Presses Before Fatigue

```
Variable    Setting
BP60          11

Fit         SE Fit            95% CI                 95% PI
79.9384     1.06005     (77.8140, 82.0628)    (63.7596, 96.1173)
```

Questions to Explore

a. Using $\hat{y}$ and its *se* reported in Table 12.5, find and interpret a 95% *confidence interval* for the population mean of the maximum bench press values for all female high school athletes who can do $x = 11$ 60-pound bench presses.

b. Report and interpret a 95% *prediction interval* for a single new observation on maximum bench press for a randomly chosen female high school athlete with $x = 11$.

Think It Through

a. At $x = 11$, the predicted maximum bench press is $\hat{y} = 63.5 + 1.49(11) = 79.94$ pounds. Table 12.5 reports a standard error for this estimate, $se = 1.06$, under the heading "SE Fit." With $n = 57$ we've seen that $df = n - 2 = 55$ and the *t*-score is $t_{.025} = 2.00$. So, the 95% confidence interval for the population mean of maximum bench press values at $x = 11$ is

$$\hat{y} \pm t_{.025}(se \text{ of } \hat{y}),$$
$$\text{which is } 79.94 \pm 2.00(1.06),$$
$$\text{or } 79.94 \pm 2.12,$$
$$\text{that is } (77.8, 82.1).$$

This is labeled "95% CI" on the MINITAB printout. For all female high school athletes who can do eleven 60-pound bench presses, we are 95% confident that the mean of their maximum bench press values falls between about 78 and 82 pounds.

b. MINITAB reports the 95% prediction interval (63.8, 96.1) under the heading "95% PI." This predicts where maximum bench press y will fall for a randomly chosen female high school athlete having $x = 11$. Equivalently, this refers to where 95% of the corresponding population values fall. For all female high school athletes who can do eleven 60-pound bench presses, we predict that 95% of them have maximum bench press between about 64 and 96 pounds. Look at the figure in the margin. Locate $x = 11$. Of all possible data points at that x value, we predict that 95% of them would fall between about 64 and 96.

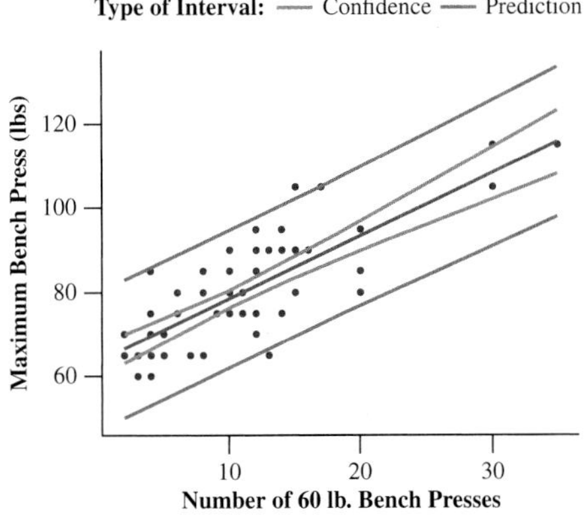

Lower and upper bounds of confidence (orange) and prediction (green) intervals for the entire range of x values.

Insight

The 95% prediction interval (63.8, 96.1) predicts the maximum bench press y for a randomly chosen female high school athlete having $x = 11$. The 95% confidence interval (77.8, 82.1) estimates the mean of such y values for all female high school athletes having $x = 11$. The prediction interval for a single observation y is much wider than the confidence interval for the mean of y. In other words, you can estimate a population mean more precisely than you can predict a single observation.

▶ ***Try Exercise 12.45***

The margins of error for these intervals use the residual standard deviation s. For an approximately normal conditional distribution for y, about 95% of the observations fall within about 2 standard deviations of the true mean μ_y at a particular value of x. For large n, $\hat{y}$ is close to μ_y, especially near the mean of the x values. Also, for large n the residual standard deviation s estimates the standard deviation σ well. So we could predict that about 95% of the y values would fall within $\hat{y} \pm 2s$. In fact, this is roughly what software does to form a prediction interval when n is large and x is at or near the mean. The margin of error is approximately a t-score times s for predicting an individual observation and a t-score times $s/\sqrt{n}$ for estimating a mean.

SUMMARY: Prediction Interval for y and Confidence Interval for μ_y at Fixed Value of x

For large samples with an x value equal to or close to the mean of x,

- The 95% **prediction interval** for y is approximately $\hat{y} \pm 2s$.
- The 95% **confidence interval** for μ_y is approximately

$$\hat{y} \pm 2(s/\sqrt{n}),$$

where s is the residual standard deviation. Software uses *exact* formulas. We show these *approximate* formulas here merely to give a sense of what these intervals do. *In practice, use software.*

For instance, for female student athletes, about 95% of the observations fall within about $2s = 2(8.0) = 16$ of the true mean at a particular value of x. At $x = 11$, which is the mean of x for the sample, $\hat{y} = 79.94 \approx 80$. So we predict that about 95% of the maximum bench press values would fall within $\hat{y} \pm 2s$, which is 80 ± 16, or between 64 and 96. This is the 95% PI result in Table 12.5. This formula is only an approximate one (because of using $\hat{y}$ as an approximation for μ_y and 2 as an approximation for the t-score), and you should rely on software for more precise results.

Use these confidence intervals and prediction intervals with caution. For these intervals to be valid, the true relationship must be close to linear, with about the same variability of y values at each fixed x value. You can get a rough visual check from the scatterplot. The variability of points around the regression line should be similar for the various possible x values. If it isn't, don't use these confidence and prediction intervals.

Because the model assumptions never hold exactly in practice, these inferences are sometimes inaccurate. For instance, suppose the variability in y values is smaller at small values of x and larger at large values of x. The prediction interval will have similar widths in each case. See Figure 12.10, which shows curves for the lower and upper endpoints of prediction intervals at all the possible x values. At a fixed x value, there should be a 95% chance a data point falls between the curves. In Case A, prediction intervals are justified. In Case B, they are not. At a large value of x in Case B, a 95% prediction interval for y actually has a much smaller than 95% chance (perhaps even less than 50%) of containing a value of y.

The Analysis of Variance (ANOVA) Table Summarizes Variability

Software reports the sums of squares (SS) used in estimating standard deviations and variances (their squares) in an **analysis of variance (ANOVA) table**. Table 12.6 shows the ANOVA table that MINITAB software reports for the strength study.

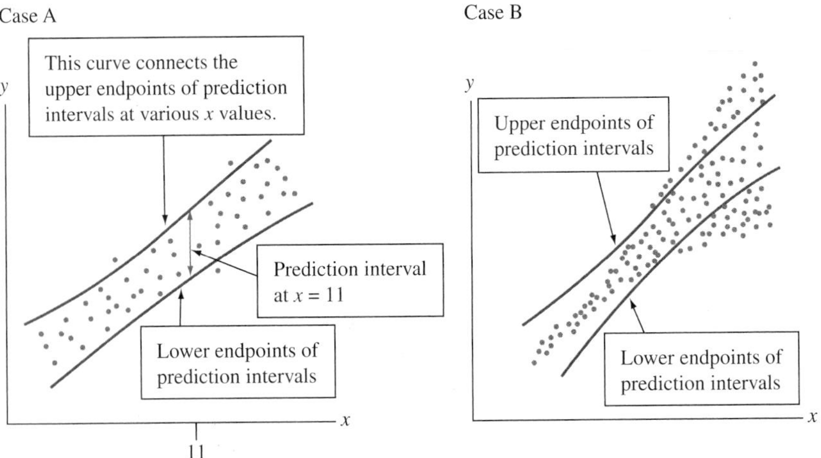

▲ **Figure 12.10 When a Regression Model Assumption Is Badly Violated, Prediction Intervals May Perform Poorly.** The curves plot how the endpoints of a 95% prediction interval change as *x* changes. For Case A, inferences are valid. For Case B, a 95% prediction interval has actual probability of containing *y* above 0.95 for small *x* and below 0.95 for large *x*. **Question** How can you tell from the figure that Case B will lead to inaccurate inferences?

Table 12.6 Analysis of Variance (ANOVA) Table for the Strength Study

Analysis of Variance

Source	DF	SS	MS	F	P
Regression	1	6351.8	6351.8	99.17	0.000
Error	55	3522.8	64.1		
Total	56	9874.6			

In the ANOVA table, the *total sum of squares* is $\Sigma(y - \bar{y})^2$. It summarizes the total variability of the *y* values and the overall error when using $\bar{y}$ to predict *y*. The ANOVA table breaks the total SS into two parts. One part is the *residual sum of squares*, $\Sigma(y - \hat{y})^2$. It represents the overall error when using the regression line to predict *y*. MINITAB labels this row Error, but other labels in common use are "Residuals" or "Residual Error." The other sum of squares is called the *regression sum of squares*. Its formula is

$$\text{regression SS} = \Sigma(\hat{y} - \bar{y})^2, \text{ and it equals } \Sigma(y - \bar{y})^2 - \Sigma(y - \hat{y})^2.$$

It summarizes how much less error there is in predicting *y* using the regression line compared to using $\bar{y}$. Recall that this difference is the numerator of r^2.

These three types of sums of squares are connected by the basic **ANOVA identity**

$$\text{Total SS} = \text{Regression SS} + \text{Residual SS}.$$

In Table 12.6, regression SS + residual SS = 6351.8 + 3522.8 = 9874.6, the total SS.

By itself, each sum of squares cannot be interpreted, but viewed relative to each other, we get statements about the reduction in the prediction error (e.g., through r^2, which equals Regression SS/Total SS). Each sum of squares in the ANOVA table has an associated degrees of freedom value. For instance, *df* for the residual sum of squares equals $n - 2 = 57 - 2 = 55$. For the *df*, it also holds that Total *df* = Regression *df* + Residual *df*. The ratio of a sum of squares to its *df* value is called a **mean square**. It is listed in the ANOVA table under the heading MS. In Table 12.6 the ratio of $\Sigma(y - \hat{y})^2 = 3522.8$ to its $df = 55$ gives 64.1. This ratio is the **mean square error,** often abbreviated as **MS error** or as **MSE.** It is roughly a mean of the squared errors in using the regression line to predict y. Equaling $s^2 = \Sigma(y - \hat{y})^2/(n - 2)$, it estimates the variance σ^2 of the conditional distribution of y at a given x value. In practice, it's easier to interpret its square root, s, the residual standard deviation of y.

Recall

We also used s to estimate the standard deviation σ of the conditional distribution of the y values at a given x value. ◀

Mean Square Error

The **mean square error** is the residual sum of squares divided by its *df* value (sample size −2). Its square root s (the residual standard deviation) is a typical size of a residual (that is, a prediction error).

The ANOVA *F* Statistic Also Tests for an Association

The ANOVA table contains values labeled F and P. The F value is the ratio of the mean squares,

$$F = \frac{\text{Mean square for regression}}{\text{Mean square error}}.$$

This is an alternative test statistic for testing H_0: $\beta = 0$ against H_a: $\beta \neq 0$. In fact, it can be shown that *F is the square of the t statistic* for this null hypothesis. Using the sampling distribution of F values, which we'll discuss in the next chapter, we get exactly the same P-value as with the t test for the two-sided alternative hypothesis.

In Table 12.6, the F statistic equals the ratio of MS values, $6351.8/64.1 = 99.17$. Table 12.2, which listed the parameter estimates and their standard errors, showed the t test:

Term	Coef	SE Coef	T-Value	P-Value
Constant	63.54	1.96	32.48	0.000
BP60	1.491	0.150	9.96	0.000

The F statistic of 99.17 here is the square of the t statistic value $t = 9.96$. The P-value, labeled as P on Table 12.6, is 0.000 to three decimal places, necessarily the same as the P-value for the two-sided t test.

Why do we need the F statistic if it does the same thing as a t statistic? In the next chapter, which generalizes regression to handle multiple explanatory variables, we'll see that the main use of an F statistic is for testing effects of several explanatory variables at once. The t test can only be used to test the effect of a single explanatory variable, one at a time.

12.4 Practicing the Basics

12.41 Poor predicted strengths The MINITAB output shows
TRY the large standardized residuals for the female athlete strength study.

Large standardized residuals for strength study:

Obs	maxBP (lbs)	Fit	Resid	Std Resid
10	105.00	85.90	19.10	2.41
25	105.00	88.88	16.12	2.04
37	65.00	82.92	−17.92	−2.26

a. Explain how to interpret all the entries in the row of the output for athlete 10, who had $x = \text{BP60} = 15$.

b. Out of 57 observations, is it surprising that 3 observations would have standardized residuals with absolute value above 2.0? Explain.

12.42 Loves TV and exercise For the Georgia Student Survey file on the book's website, let y = time exercising and x = time watching TV. One student reported watching TV an average of 180 minutes a day and exercising 60 minutes a day. This person's residual was 48.8 and the standardized residual was 6.41.

a. Interpret the residual, and use it to find the predicted value of exercise.

b. Interpret the standardized residual.

12.43 Bench press residuals The figure is a histogram of the standardized residuals for the regression of maximum bench press on number of 60-pound bench presses for the high school female athletes.

TRY

a. Which distribution does this figure provide information about?

b. What would you conclude based on this figure?

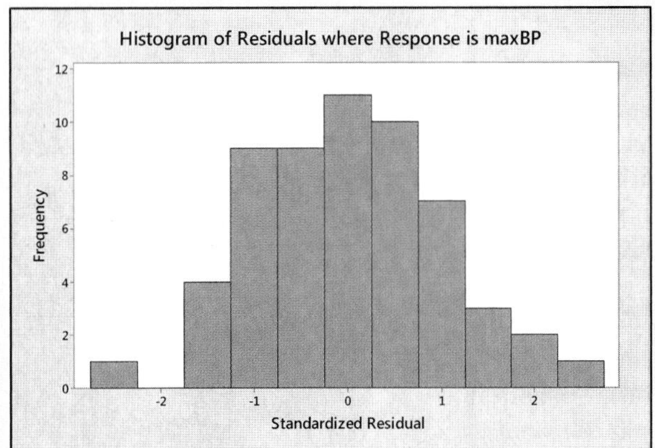

12.44 Predicting house prices The House Selling Prices FL data file on the book's website has several predictors of house selling prices. The table here shows the ANOVA table for a regression analysis of y = the selling price (in thousands of dollars) and x = the size of house (in thousands of square feet). The prediction equation is $\hat{y} = 9.2 + 77x$.

ANOVA table for selling price and size of house:

Source	DF	SS	MS	F	P
Regression	1	182220	182220	135.07	0.000
Error	98	132213	1349		
Total	99	314433			

a. What was the sample size? (*Hint:* You can figure it out from the residual *df*.)

b. The sample mean house size was 1.53 thousand square feet. What was the sample mean selling price? (*Hint:* What does $\hat{y}$ equal when $x = \bar{x}$?)

c. Estimate the standard deviation of the selling prices for homes that have $x = 1.53$. Interpret.

d. Report an approximate prediction interval within which you would expect about 95% of the selling prices to fall for homes of size $x = 1.53$.

12.45 Predicting clothes purchases For a random sample of children from a school district in South Carolina, a regression analysis is conducted of y = amount spent on clothes in the past year (dollars) and x = year in school. MINITAB reports the tabulated results for observations at $x = 12$.

TRY

```
Variable    Setting
year          12
Fit         SE Fit        95% CI        95% PI
448.0        10.6       (427, 469)    (101, 795)
```

a. Interpret the value listed under "Fit."

b. Interpret the interval listed under "95% CI."

c. Interpret the interval listed under "95% PI."

12.46 CI versus PI Using the context of the previous exercise, explain the difference between the purpose of a 95% prediction interval (PI) for an observation and a 95% confidence interval (CI) for the mean of y at a given value of x. Why would you expect the PI to be wider than the CI?

12.47 ANOVA table for leg press Exercise 12.15 referred to an analysis of leg strength for 57 female athletes, with y = maximum leg press and x = number of 200-pound leg presses until fatigue, for which $\hat{y} = 233.89 + 5.27x$. The table shows ANOVA results from SPSS for the regression analysis.

ANOVA[b]

Model		Sum of Squares	df	Mean Square	F	Sig.
1	Regression	121082.4	1	121082.400	92.875	.000[a]
	Residual	71704.442	55	1303.717		
	Total	192786.8	56			

a. Show that the residual standard deviation is 36.1. Interpret it.

b. For this sample, $\bar{x} = 22.2$. For female athletes with $x = 22$, what would you estimate the variability to be of their maximum leg press values? If the y values are approximately normal, find an interval within which about 95% of them would fall.

12.48 Predicting leg press Refer to the previous exercise. MINITAB reports the tabulated results for observations at $x = 25$.

```
Variable   Setting
LegPress     25
Fit        SE Fit         95% CI              95% PI
365.7       5.02      (355.6, 375.7)    (292.6, 438.7)
```

a. Show how MINITAB got the "Fit" of 365.7.

b. Using the predicted value and *se* value, explain how MINITAB got the interval listed under "95% CI." Interpret this interval.

c. Interpret the interval listed under "95% PI."

12.49 Variability and *F* Refer to the previous two exercises.

a. In the ANOVA table, show how the Total SS breaks into two parts and explain what each part represents.

b. From the ANOVA table, explain why the overall sample standard deviation of y values is $s_y = \sqrt{192787/56} = 58.7$. Explain the difference between the interpretation of this standard deviation and the residual standard deviation s of 36.1.

c. Exercise 12.15 reported a t statistic of 9.64 for testing independence of these variables. Report the F test statistic from the table here and explain how it relates to that t statistic.

12.50 Assumption violated For prediction intervals, an important inference assumption is a constant standard deviation σ of y values at different x values. In practice, the standard deviation often tends to be larger when μ_y is larger.

a. Sketch a hypothetical scatterplot for which this happens, using observations on x = family income and y = amount donated to charity.

b. Explain why a 95% prediction interval would not work well at very small or at very large x values.

12.51 Understanding an ANOVA table For a random sample of U.S. counties, the ANOVA table shown refers to hypothetical data on x = percentage of the population aged over 50 and y = per capita expenditure (dollars) on education.

a. Fill in the blanks in the table.

b. For what hypotheses can the F test statistic be used?

Source	DF	SS	MS	F
Regression	1	200000	____	____
Error	31	700000	____	
Total	32	900000		

12.52 Predicting cell phone weight Refer to the cell phone data file on the book's website. Regress y = weight on x = capacity of battery, excluding the outlier (phone no. 70).

TECH

a. Stating the necessary assumptions, find a 95% confidence interval for the mean weight of cell phones with a battery capacity of 1500mAh. Interpret the interval.

b. Find a 95% prediction interval for the weight of a cell phone with a battery capacity of 1500mAh. Interpret.

c. Explain the difference between the purposes of the intervals in part a and part b.

12.53 Cell phone ANOVA Report the ANOVA table for the previous exercise.

TECH

a. Verify that total SS = residual SS + regression SS. Explain what each of the three sums of squares represent.

b. Find the estimated residual standard deviation of y. Interpret it.

c. Find the sample standard deviation s_y of y values. Explain the difference between the interpretation of this standard deviation and the residual standard deviation in part b.

12.5 Exponential Regression: A Model for Nonlinearity

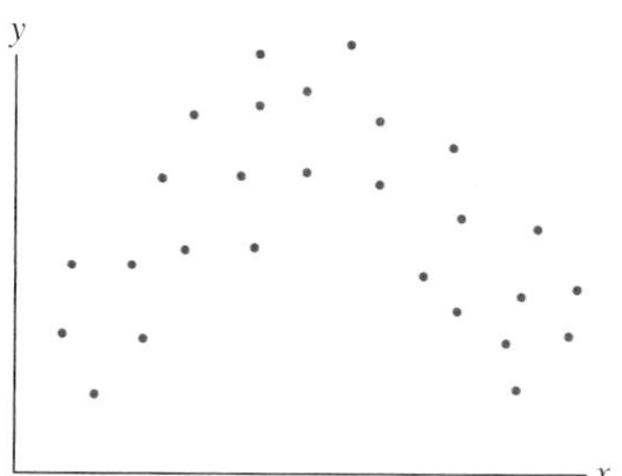

The straight line is by far the most common equation for a regression model. Sometimes, however, a scatterplot indicates substantial curvature in a relationship. In such cases, equations that provide curvature are more appropriate.

Occasionally a scatterplot has a parabolic appearance: As x increases, y tends to go up and then it goes back down (as shown in the margin figure), or the reverse. Then the regression model can use an equation giving the shape of a parabola. More often, y tends to continually increase or to continually decrease, but the trend shows curvature. Let's see a mechanism for how this can happen.

Example 16

Exponential regression ◀

Growth in Population Size

Picture the Scenario

The population size of the United States has been growing rapidly in recent years, much of it due to immigration. According to the 2010 census, the population size was about 309 million on April 1, 2010.

Questions to Explore

a. Suppose that the rate of growth after 2010 is 2% a year. That is, the population is 2% larger at the end of each year than it was at the beginning of the year. Find the population size after (i) 1 year, (ii) 2 years, and (iii) 10 years.

b. Give a formula for the population size in terms of x = number of years since 2010.

Think It Through

a. With a 2% growth rate, the population size one year after 2010 is $309 \times 1.02 = 315.2$ million. That is, increasing the population size by

2% corresponds to multiplying it by 1.02. The population size after 2 years is 2% higher than this, or

$$315.2 \times 1.02 = (309 \times 1.02) \times 1.02 = 309 \times (1.02)^2 = 321.5 \text{ million.}$$

After 10 years, the population size is $309 \times 1.02 \times 1.02 \times 1.02 \times \cdots \times 1.02 = 309 \times (1.02)^{10} = 376.7$ million.

b. Can you see the pattern? For each additional year, we mulitply by another factor of 1.02. After x years, the population size is 309×1.02^x million.

Population Size

2000 2100

Insight

The population size formula, 309×1.02^x, is called **exponential growth.** Plotted, the response goes up faster than a straight line. See the margin figure. The amount of change in y per unit change in x increases as x increases. After 100 years (that is, in the year 2110), taking $x = 100$, population size $= 309 \times (1.02)^{100} = 2238.6$ million, more than 2.2 billion people!

▶ ***Try Exercise 12.54***

A statistical analysis that uses a regression function with x in the *exponent* is called **exponential regression.**

SUMMARY: Exponential Regression Model

An **exponential regression model** has the formula

$$\mu_y = \alpha\beta^x$$

for the mean μ_y of y at a given value of x, where α and β are parameters.

The formula 309×1.02^x for U.S. population size in Example 16 has the form $\alpha\beta^x$, with $\alpha = 309$, $\beta = 1.02$, and $x =$ number of years since 2010. Exponential regression can model quantities that tend to increase by increasingly large amounts over time.

In the exponential regression equation, the explanatory variable x appears as the exponent of a parameter. Unlike with straight-line regression, the mean μ_y and the effect parameter β can take only positive values. As x increases, the mean μ_y continually increases when $\beta > 1$. It continually decreases when $0 < \beta < 1$. Figure 12.11 shows the shape for the two cases. We provide interpretations for the model parameters later in this section.

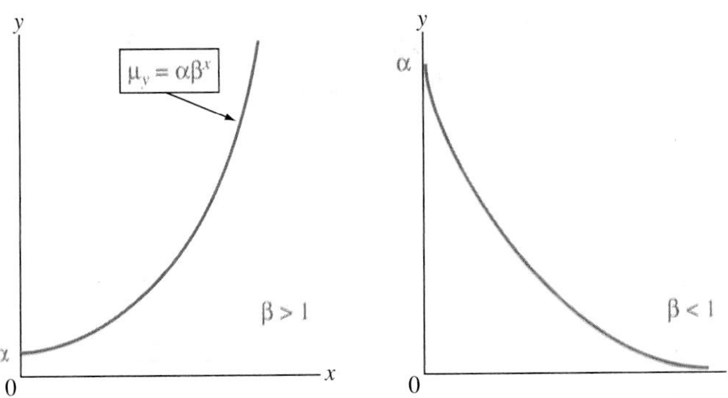

▲ **Figure 12.11** The Exponential Regression Curve for $\mu_y = \alpha\beta^x$. Question Why does μ_y decrease if $\beta = 0.5$, even though $\beta > 0$?

For exponential regression, the logarithm of the mean is a linear function of x. When the exponential regression model holds, a plot of the log of the y values versus x should show an approximate straight-line relation with x. Don't worry if you have forgotten logarithms. You will not need to use logarithms to understand how to fit the model. Software can do it. It's more important to know when it is appropriate and to be able to interpret the model fit.

Example 17

Exponential Regression◄

Moore's Law

Picture the Scenario

In 1965, Gordon Moore, who a couple of years later would go on to co-found the chip company Intel, had been asked by the journal *Electronics* to predict what would happen in the microchip industry over the next 10 years. In a graph (see margin figure, where the y axis is on the logarithmic scale), Moore showed that the number of components that could be packed on a microchip roughly doubled each year, and he predicted that this trend would continue. He speculated that by 1975, it was possible to squeeze as many as 65,000 components economically on a single chip. (In 1965, only 64 components fitted on a chip.) Based on the graph from Moore, we constructed Table 12.7, which shows the number of components on a chip for several years, beginning with the first microchip in 1959.

Logarithm of number of components on a microchip over time. (*Source:* G. Moore, 1965, "Cramming More Components onto Integrated Circuits," *Electronics*, pp. 114–117.)

The first graph in Figure 12.12 plots the number of components on a microchip over the years, based on the data in Table 12.7. The number of

Table 12.7 Number of Components Per Square Inch on Microchips Produced Between 1959 and 1965

Year	Years since 1959 (x)	Number of components (y)	Logarithm of number ($\log_2(y)$)	Predicted number ($\hat{y}$)
1959	0	1	0.00	1
1962	3	7	2.85	8
1963	4	19	4.25	16
1964	5	29	4.85	32
1965	6	64	6.00	63

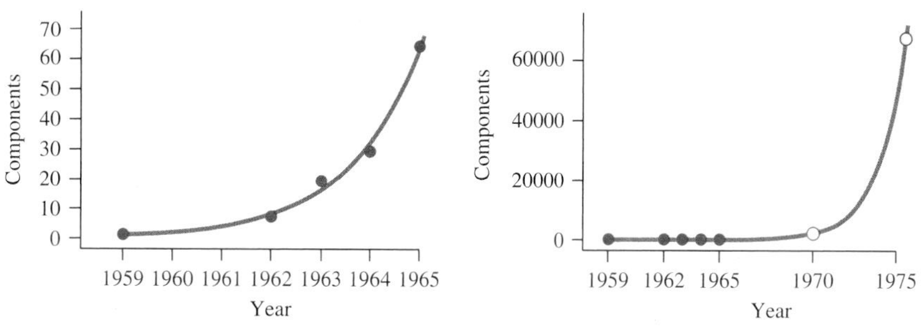

▲ **Figure 12.12** Plot of Number of Components on a Microchip Over the Years. The first graph shows the data from Table 12.7 for the years 1959 to 1965 and overlays the prediction curve from an exponential regression model. The second graph shows the same data but now displays what would happen if the exponential trend would continue for 10 years after 1965, to 1975. The circles for 1970 and 1975 shown in the plot are predictions beyond the observed range of the data.

components increases over time, and the amount of increase from one year to the next seems itself to increase over time. Moore's graph plotted the log values (base 2) of the number of components (shown in the third column of Table 12.7) over time. They appear to follow a linear trend. In fact, the correlation between the log of the number of components and the year is 0.997, indicating an extremely strong linear association. This suggests that the increase in the number of components was approximately exponential over those years.

Questions to Explore

Let x denote the years since the invention of the microchip in 1959 ($x = 0$ for 1959, $x = 3$ for 1962, $x = 4$ for 1964, etc.) and let y be the number of components on a chip x years after the invention of the first chip. Using software to fit the exponential regression model for the mean of y, we obtain

$$\hat{y} = 0.973 \times 2.006^x$$

What does this equation predict for the number of components on a chip in the year 1965 (i.e., $x = 6$), the year Moore published the graph? And what is the predicted number of components in 1975, $x = 16$ years after the invention of the first chip and the year for which Moore predicted 65,000 components?

Think It Through

By plugging $x = 6$ into the preceding prediction equation, we obtain $\hat{y} = 0.973 \times 2.006^6 = 63.4$. This is pretty close to the observed number of 64 for that year (1965). Ten years later, in 1975 and $x = 16$ years after the invention of the first chip, we obtain $\hat{y} = 0.973 \times 2.006^{16} = 66897$ as a prediction for the mean number of components that would fit on a microchip. Table 12.7 also shows the predicted numbers for each of the other years, and the right graph in Figure 12.12 shows how the trend would look if it were to continue into the year 1975.

Insight

Ten years after Moore's prediction, in 1975, a new chip that had almost 65,000 components was indeed introduced to the market. In subsequent years, the rate of packing ever more components on a chip slowed down a little, although it was still exponential. In an interview in March 2015 (celebrating the 50th anniversary of Moore's law, which now is used to describe trends in the entire computer industry), Moore once again made a prediction—the likely demise of Moore's law within the next decade or so. He indicated that technological advancement would inevitably slow down from the rate of progress we have seen in the 1990s through 2010s.[1] For the applicability of Moore's law to microchips used over the past 15 years, see Exercise 12.56.

▶ ***Try Exercise 12.56***

Interpreting Exponential Regression Models

From what we've just seen in the example, here's how to interpret the parameters in the exponential regression model, $\mu_y = \alpha\beta^x$. The parameter α represents the mean of y when $x = 0$ because $\beta^0 = 1$. The parameter β represents the

[1]IEEE Spectrum. Interview with Rachel Courtland. Special Report: 50 Years of Moore's Law, 2015. The entire interview is accessible at http://spectrum.ieee.org/computing/hardware/gordon-moore-the-man-whose-name-means-progress

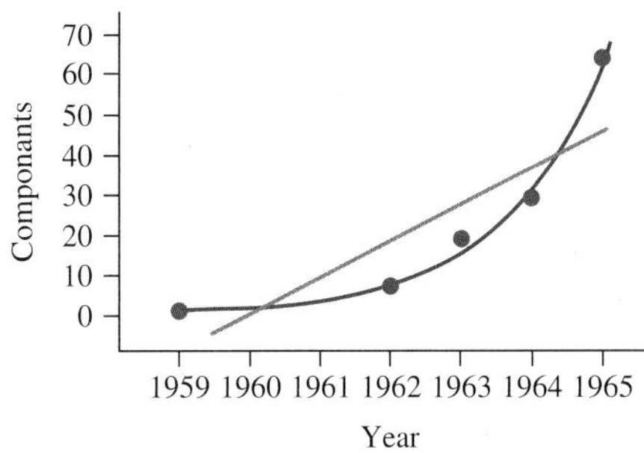

Exponential model (blue line) and linear model (green line) fit for Moore's data.

multiplicative effect on the mean of y for a one-unit increase in x. The mean of y at $x = 1$ equals the mean of y at $x = 0$ multiplied by β. For instance, for the equation $\hat{y} = 0.973 \times 2.006^x$ that uses the estimated β of 2.006, the predicted number of components is 0.973 (or roughly 1) in 1959, for which $x = 0$. One year later, the predicted number is $0.973(2.006) = 1.95$ (or roughly 2), larger by a factor of roughly 2. Another year later, the predicted number of components is $0.973(2.006)^2 = 1.95(2.006) = 3.9$ and increases by a factor of roughly 2 from the previous year's number of 1.95.

By contrast, the parameter β in the straight-line model $\mu_y = \alpha + \beta x$ represents an *additive* effect on the mean of y for a one-unit increase in x. The mean of y at $x = 1$ equals the mean of y at $x = 0$ plus β. The straight-line (i.e., the linear regression) model fitted to Moore's data is $\hat{y} = -8.9 + 9.1x$. (See the green line in the margin figure.) This model predicts that the number of components on a chip increases by 9.1 every year (as opposed to doubling every year as the exponential regression model suggests). The model may not be appropriate for these data, although this is difficult to judge with so few observations (and the insufficient knowledge of the industry in 1965). For example, the model predicts a negative number for the year 1959 and gives an inaccurate prediction for the year 1965: Plugging in $x = 6$, it predicts $\hat{y} = -8.9 + 9.1(6) = 46$ components, when the actual value was 65. (The standardized residual for this observation is 4.0.) Compare this to the prediction of 64 from the exponential regression model.

For the straight-line model, μ_y changes by the same amount (9.1) for each one-unit increase in x, whereas for the exponential model, μ_y changes by the same *factor* (or percentage) for each one-unit increase. For instance, by using the estimate of 2 for β in the exponential model for Moore's data, we predict that with every passing year since the invention of the microchip, the number of components the chip can hold increases by a factor of 2; that is, it doubles. (This corresponds to an increase of 100%.)

12.5 Practicing the Basics

12.54 Savings grow exponentially You invest $100 in a savings account with interest compounded annually at 10%.
TRY

- **a.** How much money does the account have after one year?
- **b.** How much money does the account have after five years?
- **c.** How much money does the account have after x years?
- **d.** How many years does it take until your savings more than double in size?

12.55 Growth by year versus decade You want your savings to double in a decade.

- **a.** Explain why 7.2% interest a year would do this. (*Hint:* What does $(1.072)^{10}$ equal?)
- **b.** You might think that 10% interest a year would give 100% interest (that is, double your savings) over a decade. Explain why interest of 10% a year would actually cause your savings to multiply by 2.59 over a decade.

12.56 Moore's law today The following data show the number of components (per square inch, in millions) being packed on a Pentium-type chip, for years 1994 to 2015. Let x be the number of years since 1994 (e.g., $x = 0$ for 1994, $x = 3$ for 1997, ..., $x = 21$ for 2015) and let y be the number of components on a chip. The prediction equation when fitting an exponential regression model to these data equals $\hat{y} = 151.61 \times 1.191^x$.
TRY

Chip	Year	Count	Chip	Year	Count
Pentium	1994	14	PentiumE	2008	1794
PentiumII	1997	24	PentiumG	2010	3043
PentiumIII	1999	48	PentiumG	2011	2482
Pentium4	2000	125	PentiumG	2013	5645
PentiumD	2005	720	PentiumG	2015	5103
PentiumE	2007	971			

- **a.** What is the predicted number of components per square inch in 2015?
- **b.** By how much does the predicted number of components increase per year over the time range that these data cover?
- **c.** The correlation between the logarithm of the count and x equals 0.985, and the scatterplot with the log counts shows a linear trend. What does this suggest about whether the exponential regression model is appropriate for these data?

12.57 U.S. population growth The table shows the approximate U.S. population size (in millions) at 10-year intervals beginning in 1900. Let x denote the number of decades since 1900. That is, 1900 is $x = 0$, 1910 is $x = 1$, and so forth. The exponential regression model fitted to y = population size and x gives $\hat{y} = 81.14 \times 1.1339^x$.

U.S. population sizes (in millions) from 1900 to 2010

Year	Population Size	Year	Population Size	Year	Population Size
1900	76.2	1940	132.1	1980	226.5
1910	92.2	1950	150.7	1990	248.7
1920	106.0	1960	179.3	2000	281.4
1930	122.8	1970	203.3	2010	308.7

Source: U.S. Bureau of the Census.

a. Show that the predicted population sizes are 81.14 million in 1900 and 323.3 million in 2010.

b. Explain how to interpret the value 1.1339 in the prediction equation.

c. The correlation equals 0.98 between the log of the population size and the year number. What does this suggest about whether the exponential regression model is appropriate for these data?

12.58 Future shock Refer to the previous exercise, for which predicted population growth was 14.18% per decade. Suppose the growth rate is now 15% per decade. Explain why the population size will (a) double after five decades, (b) quadruple after 100 years (10 decades), and (c) be 16 times its original size after 200 years. (The exponentially increasing function has the property that its doubling time is constant. This is a fast increase, even though the annual rate of growth seems small.)

12.59 Age and death rate Let x denote a person's age and let y be the death rate, measured as the number of deaths per thousand individuals of a fixed age within a period of a year. For men in the United States, these variables follow approximately the equation $\hat{y} = 0.32(1.078)^x$.

a. Interpret 0.32 and 1.078 in this equation.

b. Find the predicted death rate when age is (i) 20, (ii) 50, and (iii) 80.

c. In every how many years does the death rate double? (*Hint:* What is x such that $(1.078)^x = 2$?)

12.60 Leaf litter decay TECH Ecologists believe that organic material decays over time according to an *exponential decay* model. This is the case $0 < \beta < 1$ in the exponential regression model, for which μ_y decreases over time. The rate of decay is determined by a number of factors, including composition of material, temperature, and humidity. In an experiment carried out by researchers at the University of Georgia Ecology Institute, leaf litter was allowed to sit for a 20-week period in a bag in a moderately forested area. Initially, the total weight of the organic mass in the bag was 75.0 kg. Each week, the remaining amount (y) was measured. The table shows the weight y by x = number of weeks of time that have passed.

x	y	x	y	x	y	x	y	x	y	x	y
0	75.0	1	60.9	2	51.8	3	45.2	4	34.7	5	34.6
6	26.2	7	20.4	8	14.0	9	12.3	11	8.2	15	3.1
20	1.4										

a. Construct a scatterplot. Why is a straight-line model inappropriate?

b. Show that the ordinary regression model gives the fit $\hat{y} = 54.98 - 3.59x$. Find the predicted weight after $x = 20$ weeks. Does this prediction make sense? Explain.

c. Plot the log of y against x. Does a straight-line model now seem appropriate?

d. The exponential regression model has prediction equation $\hat{y} = 80.6(0.813)^x$. Find the predicted weight (i) initially and (ii) after 20 weeks.

e. Interpret the coefficient 0.813 in the prediction equation.

12.61 More leaf litter Refer to the previous exercise.

a. The correlation equals -0.890 between x and y and -0.997 between x and $\log(y)$. What does this tell you about which model is more appropriate?

b. The half-life is the time for the weight remaining to be one-half of the original weight. Use the equation $\hat{y} = 80.6(0.813)^x$ to predict the half-life of this organic material. (*Hint:* By trial and error, find the value of x for which $(0.813)^x$ is about $1/2$.)

Chapter Review

ANSWERS TO THE CHAPTER FIGURE QUESTIONS

Figure 12.1 (a) There are two dots at the value of 60 pounds on the vertical axis (representing maximum bench press); (b) all dots in the scatterplot are in rows corresponding to the values 60, 65, 70, etc., on the vertical axis.

Figure 12.2 This happens when most observations are in the quadrants where data points are above the mean on one variable and below the mean on the other variable, which are the upper-left and lower-right quadrants.

Figure 12.3 Answers will vary. One possible sketch is Figure 12.4.

Figure 12.4 A mathematical function that has a parabolic shape.

Figure 12.5 The bell-shaped curves represent the conditional distributions of income at $x = 12$ years and $x = 16$ years. Each conditional distribution is assumed to be normal and to have the same standard deviation, $\sigma = \$13{,}000$.

Figure 12.6 H_0: $\beta = 0$.

Figure 12.7 1 standard deviation.

Figure 12.8 The variability of the sampling distribution of a sample mean is much less than the variability of the distribution of individual observations.

Figure 12.9 Three observations, one for each bar.

Figure 12.10 The curves that represent the lower and upper endpoints of the prediction interval are too wide for the x values on the lower end (the 95% prediction interval for y has a greater than 95% chance of containing a value of y) and too narrow for the x values on the upper end (a 95% prediction interval for y has a much smaller than 95% chance of containing a value of y).

Figure 12.11 When x increases by 1, the mean μ_y is multiplied by β. When $0 < \beta < 1$, multiplying by β causes the mean to decrease.

CHAPTER SUMMARY

In Chapters 10–12 we've learned how to detect and describe *association between two variables.* Chapter 10 showed how to compare means or proportions for two groups. Chapter 11 dealt with *association between two categorical variables.* This chapter showed how to analyze linear *association between two quantitative variables.*

A regression analysis investigates the relationship between a quantitative explanatory variable x and a quantitative response variable y.

- At each value of x, a conditional distribution of y values summarizes how y varies at that value. We denote the population mean of the conditional distribution of y by μ_y. The simple linear **regression model** $\mu_y = \alpha + \beta x$, with y-intercept α and slope β, uses a straight line to approximate the relationship between x and the mean μ_y of the conditional distribution of y at the different possible values of x. The *sample* **prediction equation** $\hat{y} = a + bx$ predicts y and estimates the mean of y at the fixed value of x.

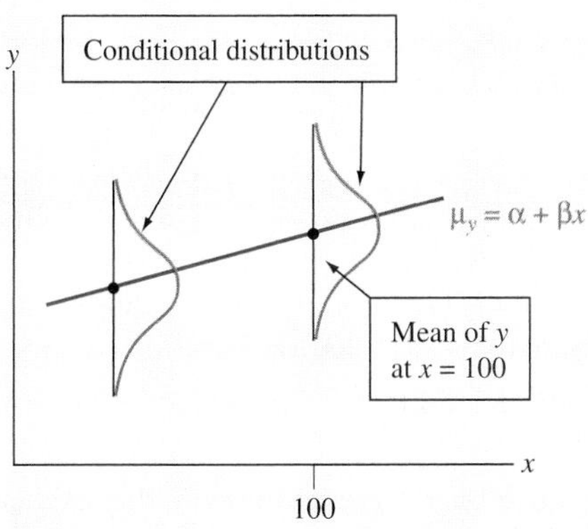

- The **correlation r** describes the strength of linear association. It has the same sign as the slope b but falls between -1 and $+1$. The weaker the correlation, the greater the *regression toward the mean*, with the y values tending to fall closer to their mean (in terms of the number of standard deviations) than the x values fall to their mean. The squared correlation, r^2, describes the proportional reduction in the sum of squared errors using the prediction equation $\hat{y} = a + bx$ to predict y compared to using the sample mean $\bar{y}$ to predict y.
- Inference: A significance test of $\mathbf{H_0}$: $\boldsymbol{\beta = 0}$ for the population slope β tests **statistical independence** of x and y. It has test statistic

$$t = (b - 0)/se,$$

for the sample slope b and its standard error. Interval estimation is also useful for:

- A confidence interval for β.
- A confidence interval for μ_y, the mean of y at a given value of x.
- A **prediction interval** for a value of y at a given value of x.

These inferences all use the t distribution with $\boldsymbol{df = n - 2}$. Their basic assumptions are:

1. The population mean of y has a straight-line relationship with x.
2. The data were gathered using randomization.
3. The distribution of y at each value of x is normal, with the same standard deviation at each x value.

- An **ANOVA table** displays sums of squares, their df values, and an **F statistic** (which equals the square of the t statistic) that also tests H_0: $\beta = 0$. In this table, the **residual sum of squares** $\Sigma (y - \hat{y})^2$ squares and adds each **residual** (prediction error) $y - \hat{y}$. The residual SS divided by its df value of $n - 2$ is the **mean square error**. Its square root is the **residual standard deviation** s, which estimates the parameter σ. The parameter σ describes the variability of the conditional distribution of y at each fixed x. A residual divided by its se is a **standardized residual**, which measures the number of standard errors that a residual falls from 0. It helps us identify unusual observations.
- The **exponential regression** model $\mu_y = \alpha\beta^x$ has an increasing or a decreasing curved shape. For it, a one-unit increase in x has a *multiplicative* effect of β on the mean rather than an *additive* effect as in the linear regression model $\mu_y = \alpha + \beta x$.

SUMMARY OF NOTATION

μ_y = population mean of conditional distribution of y values at fixed value of x

$\mu_y = \alpha + \beta x$ = population straight-line regression equation; (α and β are the population intercept and slope)

$\hat{y} = a + bx$ = prediction equation computed from the sample, it estimates the population regression equation; (a and b are the estimated intercept and slope)

σ = population standard deviation of conditional distribution of y values at fixed value of x

s = residual standard deviation. It estimates σ.

r^2 = proportional reduction in prediction error = square of correlation r

$\Sigma (y - \hat{y})^2$ = residual sum of squares, which summarizes how well $\hat{y}$ predicts y. This is used to compute the mean square error, s and r^2.

$\Sigma (y - \bar{y})^2$ = total sum of squares, which summarizes how well $\bar{y}$ predicts y. This is used in finding r^2.

$\mu_y = \alpha\beta^x$ = exponential regression model: mean = α when $x = 0$ and the mean multiplies by β for each one-unit increase in x.

CHAPTER PROBLEMS

Practicing the Basics

12.62 Parties and sports Let y = number of parties attended in the past month and x = number of sports events watched in the past month, measured for all students at your school. Explain the mean and variability about the mean aspects of the regression model $\mu_y = \alpha + \beta x$ in the context of these variables. In your answer, explain why (a) it is more sensible to let $\alpha + \beta x$ represent the *means* of the conditional distributions rather than individual observations, (b) the model allows variation around the mean with its σ parameter.

12.63 Verbal–math correlation A report summarizing scores for students on a verbal aptitude test x and a mathematics aptitude test y states that $\bar{x} = 480$, $\bar{y} = 500$, $s_x = 80$, $s_y = 120$, and $r = 0.60$.

a. Find the slope of the regression line, based on its connection with the correlation.

b. Find the y-intercept of the regression line (*Hint:* Use its formula in Section 12.1) and state the prediction equation.

c. Find the prediction equation for predicting verbal test result using math test result.

12.64 Stem cells In the article, "Variation in cancer risk among tissues can be explained by the number of stem cell divisions" (Tomasetti and Vogelstein, *Science*, vol. 47, 2015), the authors stated: "A linear correlation equal to 0.804 suggests that 65% of the differences in cancer risk among different tissues can be explained by the total number of stem cell divisions in those tissues."

a. How did they get 65%?

b. By how many percentage points does the overall prediction error (as measured by the sum of squares) decrease when using the prediction equation from a linear regression model to predict cancer risk rather than using the sample mean of the observed risks to predict it?

12.65 Short people Do very short parents tend to have children who are even shorter, or short but not as short as they are? Explain, identifying the response and explanatory variables and the role of regression toward the mean.

12.66 Income and education in Florida The FL Crime data file on the book's website contains data for all counties in Florida on y = median annual income (thousands of dollars) for residents of the county and x = percentage of residents with at least a high school education. The table shows some summary statistics and results of a regression analysis.

Income and Education for Florida Counties

Variable	Mean	Std Dev	Predictor	Parameter Estimate
INCOME	24.51	4.69	INTERCEPT	−4.60
EDUC	69.49	8.86	EDUC	0.42

a. Find the correlation r. Interpret (i) the sign and (ii) the magnitude.

b. Find the predicted median income for a county that is 1 standard deviation above the mean on x and use it to explain the concept of regression toward the mean.

12.67 Bedroom residuals For the House Selling Prices FL data set on the book's website, when we regress y = selling price (in dollars) on x = number of bedrooms, we get the results shown in the printout.

a. One home with three bedrooms sold for $338,000. Find the residual and interpret.

b. The home in part a had a standardized residual of 4.02. Interpret.

House selling prices and number of bedrooms

```
Variable   Mean   StDev  Minimum   Q1    Median    Q3    Maximum
price     126698  56357   21000   86625  123750  155625  338000
Bedrooms   2.990  0.659   1.000   3.000   3.000   3.000   5.000

Term        Coef    SE Coef    T-Value    P-Value
Constant    33778    24637      1.37       0.173
Bedrooms    31077     8049      3.86       0.000
S = 52771.5  R-Sq = 13.2%
```

12.68 Bedrooms affect price? Refer to the previous exercise.

a. Explain what the regression parameter β means in this context.

b. Construct and interpret a 95% confidence interval for β.

c. Use the result of part b to form a 95% confidence interval for the difference in the mean selling prices for homes with $x = 4$ bedrooms and with $x = 2$ bedrooms. (*Hint:* How does this difference in means relate to the slope?)

12.69 Types of variability Refer to the previous two exercises.

a. Explain the difference between the residual standard deviation of 52,771.5 and the standard deviation of 56,357 reported for the selling prices.

b. Since they're not much different, explain why this means that number of bedrooms is not strongly associated with selling price. Support this by reporting and interpreting the value of r^2.

12.70 Exercise and college GPA TECH For the Georgia Student Survey file on the book's website, let y = exercise and x = college GPA.

a. Construct a scatterplot. Identify an outlier that could influence the regression line. What would you expect its effect to be on the slope and the correlation?

b. Fit the model. Find the standardized residual for that observation. Interpret.

c. Fit the model without the outlying observation. Summarize its impact.

12.71 Bench press predicting leg press For the study of high school female athletes, when we use x = maximum bench press (maxBP) to predict

y = maximum leg press (maxLP), we get the results that follow. The sample mean of maxBP was 80.

```
Regression Equation
maxLP (lbs) = 174.0 + 2.216 maxBP (lbs)
Term            Coef    SE Coef    T-Value    P-Value
Constant       174.0      41.7       4.17      0.000
maxBP (lbs)    2.216     0.515       4.30      0.000
Variable       Setting
maxBP (lbs)       80
  Fit     SE Fit         95% CI              95% PI
351.25   6.7847   (337.65, 364.84)  (247.70, 454.79)
```

a. Interpret the confidence interval listed under "95% CI."

b. Interpret the interval listed under "95% PI." What's the difference between the purpose of the 95% PI and the 95% CI?

12.72 Leg press ANOVA The analysis in the previous exercise has the ANOVA table shown.

```
Analysis of Variance
Source       DF     SS       MS       F       P
Regression    1   48483   48483   18.48   0.000
Error        55  144304    2624
Total        56  192787
```

a. For those female athletes who had maximum bench press equal to the sample mean of 80 pounds, what is the estimated standard deviation of their maximum leg press values?

b. Assuming that maximum leg press has a normal distribution, show how to find an approximate 95% prediction interval for the y values at $x = 80$.

12.73 Savings grow You invest $1,000 in an account having interest such that your principal doubles every 10 years.

a. How much money would you have after 50 years?

b. If you were still alive in 100 years, show that you'd be a millionaire.

c. Give the equation that relates y = principal to x = number of decades for which your money has been invested.

12.74 Florida population The population size of Florida (in thousands) since 1830 has followed approximately the exponential regression $\hat{y} = 46(1.036)^x$. Here, x = year − 1830 (so, $x = 0$ for 1830 and $x = 170$ for the year 2000).

a. What has been the approximate rate of growth per year?

b. Find the predicted population size in (i) 1830 and (ii) 2000.

c. Find the predicted population size in 2100. Do you think that this same formula will continue to hold between 2000 and 2100? Why?

12.75 World population growth The table shows the world population size (in billions) since 1900.

World Population Sizes (in billions)

Year	Population	Year	Population
1900	1.65	1975	4.07
1910	1.75	1980	4.43
1920	1.86	1985	4.83
1930	2.07	1990	5.26
1940	2.30	1995	5.67
1950	2.52	2000	6.07
1960	3.02	2005	6.47
1970	3.69	2010	6.85

Source: U.S. Bureau of the Census.

a. Let x denote the number of years since 1900. The exponential regression model fitted to y = population size and x gives $\hat{y} = 1.424 \times 1.014^x$. Show that the predicted population sizes are 1.42 billion in 1900 and 6.57 billion in 2010.

b. Explain why the fit of the model corresponds to a rate of growth of 1.4% per year.

c. For this model fit, explain why the predicted population size (i) doubles after 50 years and (ii) quadruples after 100 years.

d. The correlation equals 0.961 between the population size and the year number, and it equals 0.991 between the log of the population size and the year number. What does this suggest about whether the straight-line regression model or the exponential regression model is more appropriate for these data?

12.76 Match the scatterplot Match each of the following scatterplots to the description of its regression and correlation. The plots are the same except for a single point. Justify your answer for each scatterplot. (*Hint:* Think about the possible effect of an outlier in the x-direction and an outlier in the y-direction relative to the regression line for the rest of the data.)

a. $r = -0.46$ $\hat{y} = 142 - 15.6x$

b. $r = -0.86$ $\hat{y} = 182 - 25.8x$

c. $r = -0.74$ $\hat{y} = 165 - 21.8x$

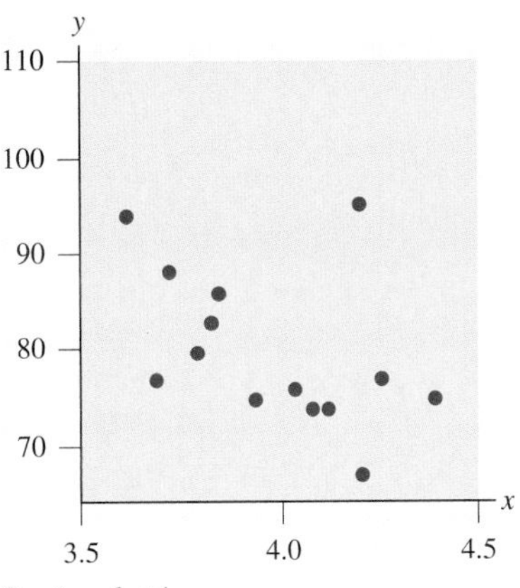

Scatterplot 1

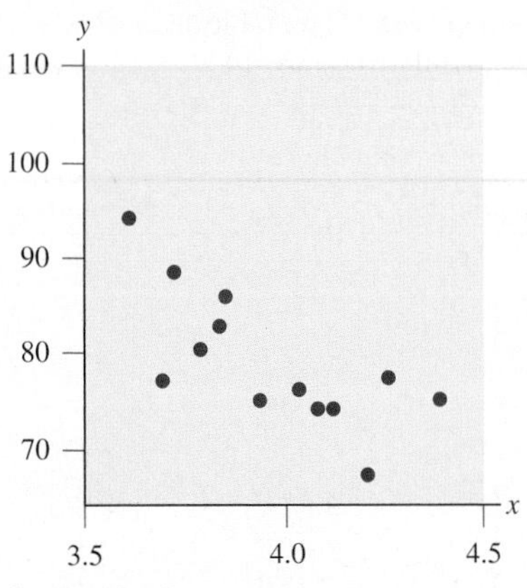

Scatterplot 2

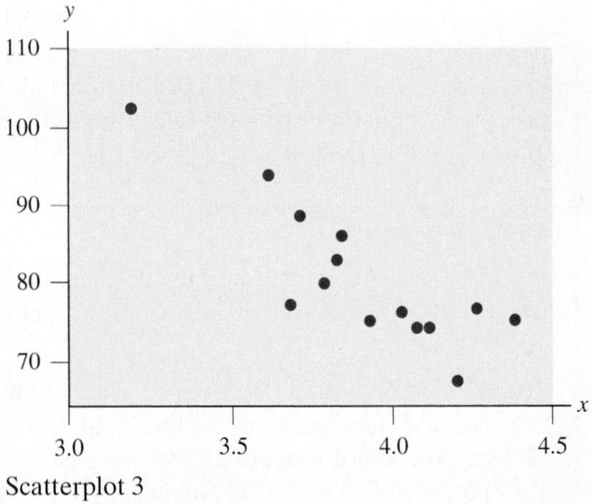

Scatterplot 3

Concepts and Investigations

12.77 Softball data The Softball data file on the book's website contains the records of a University of Georgia coed intramural softball team for 277 games over a 20-year period. (The players changed, but the team continued.) The variables include, for each game, the team's number of runs scored (RUNS), number of hits (HIT), number of errors (ERR), and the difference (DIFF) between the number of runs scored by the team and by the other team. Let DIFF be the response variable. Note that DIFF > 0 means the team won and DIFF < 0 means the team lost.

a. Construct a modified box plot of DIFF. What do the three outlying observations represent?

b. Find the prediction equation relating DIFF to RUNS. Show that the team is predicted to win when RUNS $= 8$ or more.

c. Construct the correlation matrix for RUNS, HIT, ERR, and DIFF and interpret.

d. Conduct statistical inference about the slope of the relationship between DIFF and RUNS.

12.78 Runs and hits Refer to the previous exercise. Conduct a regression analysis of $y =$ RUNS and $x =$ HIT. Does a straight-line regression model seem appropriate? Prepare a report

a. Using graphical ways of portraying the individual variables and their relationship.

b. Interpreting descriptive statistics for the individual variables and their relationship.

c. Viewing standardized residuals to find games with unusual results.

d. Conducting statistical inference about the slope of the relationship.

12.79 GPA and TV watching Using software with the FL Student Survey data file on the book's website, conduct regression analyses relating $y =$ high school GPA and $x =$ hours of TV watching. Prepare a two-page report, showing descriptive and inferential methods for analyzing the relationship.

12.80 Female athletes' speed For the High School Female Athletes data set on the book's website, conduct a regression analysis using the time for the 40-yard dash as the response variable and weight as the explanatory variable. Prepare a two-page report, indicating why you conducted each analysis and interpreting the results.

12.81 Football point spreads For a football game in the National Football League, let $y =$ difference between number of points scored by the home team and the away team (so, $y > 0$ if the home team wins). Let x be the predicted difference according to the Las Vegas betting spread. For the 768 NFL games played between 2003 and 2006, MINITAB results of a regression analysis follow.[2]

a. Explain why you would expect the true y-intercept to be 0 and the true slope to be 1 if there is no bias in the Las Vegas predictions.

b. Based on the results shown in the table, is there much evidence that the sample fit differs from the model $\mu_y = \alpha + \beta x$ with $\alpha = 0$ and $\beta = 1$? Explain.

Term	Coef	SE Coef	T-Value	P-Value
Constant	−0.4022	0.5233	−0.77	0.442
LasVegas	1.0251	0.0824	12.44	0.000

R - Sq = 16.8%

12.82 Iraq war and reading newspapers A study by the Readership Institute[3] at Northwestern University used survey data to analyze how newspaper reader behavior was influenced by the Iraq war. The response variable was a Reader Behavior Score (RBS), a combined measure summarizing newspaper use frequency, time spent with the newspaper, and how much was read. Comparing RBS scores pre-war and during the war, the study noted that there was a significant increase in reading by light readers (mean RBS changing from 2.05 to 2.32) but a significant decrease in reading by heavy readers (mean RBS changing from 5.87 to 5.66). Identify $x =$ pre-war RBS and $y =$ during-war RBS and explain how this finding could merely reflect regression toward the mean.

12.83 Sports and regression One of your relatives is a big sports fan but has never taken a statistics course. Explain how you could describe the concept of regression toward the mean in terms of a sports application, without using technical jargon.

[2] *Source:* Data from P. Everson, *Chance*, vol. 20, 2007, pp. 49–56.

[3] www.readership.org/consumers/data/FINAL_war_study.pdf.

12.84 Regression toward the mean paradox Does regression toward the mean imply that, over many generations, there are fewer and fewer very short people and very tall people? Explain your reasoning. (*Hint:* What happens if you look backward in time in doing the regressions?)

12.85 Height and weight Suppose the correlation between height and weight is 0.50 for a sample of males in elementary school and 0.50 for a sample of males in middle school. If we combine the samples, explain why the correlation will probably be larger than 0.50.

12.86 Income and education Explain why the correlation between x = number of years of education and y = annual income is likely to be smaller if we use a random sample of adults who have a Ph.D. than if we use a random sample of all adults.

12.87 Dollars and pounds Annual income, in dollars, was the response variable in a regression analysis. For a British version of a written report about the analysis, all responses were converted to British pounds sterling (£1 equaled $2.00 when this was done).

a. How, if at all, does the slope of the prediction equation change?

b. How, if at all, does the correlation change?

c. How, if at all, does the t statistic change for testing the effect of an explanatory variable?

12.88 All models are wrong The statistician George Box, who had an illustrious academic career at the University of Wisconsin, is often quoted as saying, "All models are wrong, but some models are useful." Why do you think that, in practice,

a. All models are wrong?

b. Some models are *not* useful?

12.89 *df* for *t* tests in regression In regression modeling, for t tests about regression parameters, $df = n -$ number of parameters in equation for the mean.

a. Explain why $df = n - 2$ for the model $\mu_y = \alpha + \beta x$.

b. Chapter 8 discussed how to estimate a single mean μ. Treating this as the parameter in a simpler regression model, $\mu_y = \mu$, with a single parameter, explain why $df = n - 1$ for inference about a single mean.

12.90 Assumptions What assumptions are needed to use the linear regression model to (a) obtain a meaningful fit that represents the true relationship well and (b) to make *inferences* about the relationship. For part b, which assumption is least critical?

12.91 Assumptions fail? Refer to the previous exercise. In view of these assumptions, indicate why such a model would or would not be good in the following situations:

a. x = year (from 1900 to 2005), y = percentage unemployed workers in the United States. (*Hint:* Does y continually tend to increase or decrease?)

b. x = age of subject, y = subject's annual medical expenses. (*Hint:* Suppose expenses tend to be relatively high for the newborn and for the elderly.)

c. x = per capita income, y = life expectancy, for nations. (*Hint:* The increasing trend eventually levels off.)

12.92 Lots of standard deviations Explain carefully the interpretations of the standard deviations (a) s_y, (b) s_x, (c) residual standard deviation s, and (d) se of slope estimate b.

12.93 Decrease in home values A Freddie Mac quarterly statement (May 2010) reported that U.S. home sales for one of the central regions (including Illinois, Indiana, Ohio, and Wisconsin) have shown that home values decreased by 3.4% in the last previous year. What if someone interprets this information by saying, "The decrease in home sales is of concern. The decreased rate of 3.4% amounts to a decrease of 17% over five years and 34% over ten years."

a. Explain what is incorrect about this statement.

b. If, in fact, the current median house price for this region is $175,000 and in each of the next 10 years the house values decrease in price by 3.4% relative to the previous year, then what is the estimated house value after a decade? What percentage decrease occurs for the decade?

12.94 Population growth Exercise 12.57 about U.S. population growth showed a predicted growth rate of 13% per decade.

a. Show that this is equivalent to a 1.23% predicted growth *per year.*

b. Explain why the predicted U.S. population size (in millions) x years after 1900 is $81.137(1.0123)^x$

12.95 Multiple choice: Interpret r One can interpret $r = 0.30$ or the corresponding $r^2 = 0.09$ as follows:

a. A 30% reduction in error occurs in using x to predict y.

b. A 9% reduction in error occurs in using x to predict y compared to using $\bar{y}$ to predict y.

c. 9% of the time $\hat{y} = y$.

d. y changes 0.3 unit for every one-unit increase in x.

e. x changes 0.3 standard deviations when y changes 1 standard deviation.

12.96 Multiple choice: Correlation invalid The correlation is appropriate for describing association between two quantitative variables

a. Even when different people measure the variables using different units (e.g., kilograms and pounds).

b. When the relationship is highly nonlinear.

c. When the slope of the regression equation is 0 using nearly all the data, but a couple of outliers are extremely high on y at the high end of the x-scale.

d. When the sample has a much narrower range of x values than does the population.

e. When the response variable and explanatory variable are both categorical.

12.97 Multiple choice: Slope and correlation The slope of the least squares regression equation and the correlation are similar in the sense that

a. They both must fall between −1 and +1.

b. They both describe the strength of association.

c. Their squares both have proportional reduction in error interpretations.

d. They have the same t statistic value for testing H_0: Independence.

e. They both are unaffected by severe outliers.

12.98 Multiple choice: Regress x on y The regression of y on x has a prediction equation of $\hat{y} = -2.0 + 5.0x$ and a correlation of 0.3. Then, the regression of x on y

a. also has a correlation of 0.3.

b. could have a negative slope.

c. has $r^2 = \sqrt{0.3}$.

d. $= 1/(-2.0 + 5.0y)$.

12.99 Multiple choice: Income and height University of Rochester economist Steven Landsburg surveyed economic studies in England and the United States that showed a positive correlation between height and income. The article stated that in the United States each one-inch increase in height was worth about \$1,500 extra earnings a year, on the average (*Toronto Globe and Mail*, 4/1/2002). The regression equation that links y = annual earnings (in thousands of dollars) to x = height (in inches)

a. has y-intercept = \$1,500.

b. has slope 1.5.

c. has slope 1/1500.

d. has slope 1,500.

e. has correlation 0.150.

12.100 True or false The variables y = annual income (thousands of dollars), x_1 = number of years of education, and x_2 = number of years experience in job are measured for all the employees having city-funded jobs in Knoxville, Tennessee. Suppose that the following regression equations and correlations apply:

i) $\hat{y} = 10 + 1.0x_1, \quad r = 0.30.$

ii) $\hat{y} = 14 + 0.4x_2, \quad r = 0.60.$

The correlation is -0.40 between x_1 and x_2. Which of the following statements are true and which are false?

a. The strongest sample association is between y and x_2.

b. A standard deviation increase in education corresponds to a predicted increase of 0.3 standard deviations in income.

c. There is a 30% reduction in error in using education, instead of $\bar{y}$, to predict y.

d. When x_1 is the predictor of y, the sum of squared residuals is larger than when x_2 is the predictor of y.

e. If $s = 8$ for the model using x_1 to predict y, then it is not unusual to observe an income of \$100,000 for an employee who has 10 years of education.

12.101 ◆◆ **Golf club velocity and distance** A study about the effect of the swing on putting in golf (by C. M. Craig et al., *Nature*, vol. 405, 2000, pp. 295–296) showed a very strong linear relationship between y = putting distance and the square of x = club's impact velocity (r^2 is in the range 0.985 to 0.999).

a. For the model $\mu_y = \alpha + \beta x^2$, explain why it is sensible to set $\alpha = 0$.

b. If the appropriate model is $\mu_y = \beta x^2$, explain why if you double the velocity of the swing, you can expect to quadruple the putting distance.

12.102 ◆◆ **Why is there regression toward the mean?** Refer to the relationship $r = (s_x/s_y)b$ between the slope and correlation, which is equivalently $s_x b = r s_y$.

a. Explain why an increase in x of s_x units relates to a change in the predicted value of y of $s_x b$ units. (For instance, if $s_x = 10$, it corresponds to a change in $\hat{y}$ of $10b$.)

b. Based on part a, explain why an increase of one standard deviation in x corresponds to a change of only r standard deviations in the predicted y-variable.

12.103 ◆◆ **r^2 and variances** Suppose $r^2 = 0.30$. Since $\Sigma(y - \bar{y})^2$ is used in estimating the overall variability of the y values and $\Sigma(y - \hat{y})^2$ is used in estimating the residual variability at any fixed value of x, explain why approximately the estimated variance of the conditional distribution of y for a given x is 30% smaller than the estimated variance of the marginal distribution of y.

12.104 ◆◆ **Standard error of slope** The formula for the standard error of the sample slope b is $se = s/\Sigma(x - \bar{x})^2$, where s is the residual standard deviation.

a. Show that the smaller the value of s, the more precisely b estimates β.

b. Explain why a small s occurs when the data points show little variability about the prediction equation.

c. Explain why the standard error of b decreases as the sample size increases and when the x values display more variability.

12.105 ◆◆ **Regression with an error term**[4] An alternative to the regression formula $\mu_y = \alpha + \beta x$ expresses each y value, rather than the mean of the y values, in terms of x. This approach models an observation on y as

$$y = \text{mean} + \text{error} = \alpha + \beta x + \epsilon,$$

where the mean $\mu_y = \alpha + \beta x$ and the error $= \epsilon$.

The **error term** denoted by ϵ (the Greek letter epsilon) represents the deviation of the observation from the mean, that is, ϵ = error = y − mean.

a. If an observation has $\epsilon > 0$, explain why the observation falls above the mean.

b. What does ϵ equal when the observation falls exactly at the mean? The ϵ term represents the error that results from using the mean value $(\alpha + \beta x)$ of y at a certain value of x for the prediction of the individual observation on y.

c. For the sample data and their prediction equation $\hat{y} = a + bx$, explain why an analogous equation to the population equation $y = \alpha + \beta x + \epsilon$ is $y = a + bx + e$, where e is the residual, $e = y - \hat{y}$. (The residual e estimates ϵ. We can interpret e as a sample residual and ϵ as a **population residual.**)

[4]This formula is less useful than the one for the mean because it does not apply to regression models when y is not assumed to be normal, such as logistic regression for binary data.

d. Explain why it does not make sense to use the simpler model, $y = \alpha + \beta x$, which does not have the error term.

12.106 Rule of 72 You invest \$1000 at 6% compound interest a year. How long does it take until your investment is worth \$2000?
◆◆

a. Based on what you know about exponential regression, explain why the answer is the value of x for which $1000(1.06)^x = 2000$.

b. Using the property of logarithms that $\log(a^x) = x \log(a)$, show that the answer x satisfies $x[\log(1.06)] = \log(2)$, or $x = \log(2)/\log(1.06) = 12$.

c. The rule of 72 says that if you divide 72 by the interest rate, you will find approximately how long it takes your money to double. According to this rule, about how long (in years) does it take your money to double at an interest rate of (i) 1% and (ii) 18%?

Student Activities

12.107 Analyze your data Refer to the data file you created in Activity 3 at the end of Chapter 1. For variables chosen by your instructor, conduct a regression and correlation analysis. Report both descriptive and inferential statistical analyses, interpreting and summarizing your findings and prepare to discuss the results in class.
TECH

▶ Activity 1

SAT French Exam and Years of Study

In 2003, high school students taking the SAT French II language exam after two to four years of study scored, on average, 35 points higher for each additional year of study (*Source*: www.collegeboard.com/). The scores of students with two years of study averaged 505. For each number of years of study, the standard deviation was approximately 100. Let y = French II exam score and x = number of years of study beyond two years (so $x = 0, 1,$ or 2 for 2, 3, and 4 years of study).

1. Explain why the regression equation $\mu_y = \alpha + \beta x$ is $\mu_y = 505 + 35x$.
2. Suppose y has a normal conditional distribution. Using software, randomly select a student who has two years of French study, a student who has three years, and a student who has four years, by simulating from the appropriate normal distributions. Record each exam score.
3. Perform Step 2 at least 100 times. Store your results in a data file. You now have 100 values of y at each value of x.
4. Construct parallel dot plots and/or box plots for the sample conditional distributions. Compare the mean of the simulated distribution at each x to the actual mean, based on $\mu_y = 505 + 35x$. Is the variability similar for the three sample conditional distributions?
5. Fit a regression line, $\hat{y} = a + bx$, to the simulated values. How does this line compare to the actual regression line, $\mu_y = 505 + 35x$?

The simulated results in Step 4 and Step 5 are not *exactly* equal to those for the model because they use a sample, whereas $\mu_y = 505 + 35x$ refers to a population.

CHAPTER

13

Chapter 12 used a regression model with a single explanatory variable to analyze the association and make predictions. In this chapter, we learn how we can extend the model to include several explanatory variables.

Multiple Regression

Example 1

Predicting the Selling Price of a House

Picture the Scenario

You are saving to buy a home, and you wonder how much it will cost. The House Selling Prices OR data file on the book's website has observations on 200 recent home sales in Corvallis, Oregon. Table 13.1 shows data for two homes.

Variables listed are the selling price (in dollars), house size (in square feet), number of bedrooms, number of bathrooms, the lot size (in square feet), the year built, and whether the house has a garage. Table 13.2 reports the mean and standard deviation of these variables for all 200 home sales. Note that in the descriptive summaries, the variable 'Year Built' is used to determine the variable 'Age'.

Questions to Explore

In your community, if you know the values of such variables,

- How can you predict a home's selling price?
- How can you describe the association between selling price and the other variables?
- How can you make inferences about the population of all houses in the community, based on the information in the sample?

Table 13.1 Selling Prices and Related Factors for a Sample of Home Sales

House	Selling Price	House Size (sq. ft)	Number of Bedrooms	Number of Bathrooms	Lot Size (sq. ft)	Year Built	Garage (Y/N)
1	\$232,500	1,679	3	1.5	10,019	1976	Y
2	\$158,000	1,292	1	1	217,800	1958	N

Table 13.2 Descriptive Statistics for Sales of 200 Homes

	Selling Price	House Size (sq. ft)	Number of Bedrooms	Number of Bathrooms	Lot Size (sq. ft)	Age
Mean	\$267,466	2,551	3.08	2.03	23,217	34.75
Standard deviation	\$115,808	1,238	1.10	0.77	47,637	24.44

Thinking Ahead

You can find a regression equation to predict selling price by treating one of the other variables as the explanatory variable. However, since there are *several* explanatory variables, you might make better predictions by using *all* of them at once. That's the idea behind **multiple regression**. It uses *more than one* explanatory variable to predict a response variable.

Recall

Review the concept of *lurking variables* in Section 3.4. ◀

Besides helping you to predict a response variable better, multiple regression can help you analyze the association between two variables while controlling (keeping fixed) values of other variables. Such adjustment is important because the effect of an explanatory variable can change considerably after you account for potential lurking variables. A multiple regression analysis provides information not available from simple regression analyses involving only two variables at a time.

Recall

This chapter builds strongly on the content in Chapter 12 on **regression** and **correlation** methods. You may want to review Sections 12.1 through 12.3 as you read through this chapter. ◀

Section 13.1 presents the basics of multiple regression. Section 13.2 extends the concepts of correlation and r^2 for describing strength of association to multiple predictors (explanatory variables). Section 13.3 presents inference methods, and Section 13.4 shows how to check the model. Section 13.5 extends the model further to incorporate categorical explanatory variables. The final section presents a regression model for a categorical response variable.

13.1 Using Several Variables to Predict a Response

Chapter 12 modeled the mean μ_y of a quantitative response variable y using a quantitative explanatory variable x by the straight-line equation $\mu_y = \alpha + \beta x$. We refer to this model with a *single* predictor as **the simple linear regression model** because it contains only one explanatory variable that is linearly related to the mean of y.

Now, suppose there are two explanatory variables, denoted by x_1 and x_2. The simple regression model generalizes to the **multiple regression** model,

$$\mu_y = \alpha + \beta_1 x_1 + \beta_2 x_2.$$

In Words

As in the simple linear regression model, we use the Greek letter β (beta) for parameters describing effects of explanatory variables, with β_1 and β_2 read as "beta one" and "beta two."

In this equation, α, β_1, and β_2 are parameters. When we substitute values for x_1 and x_2, the equation specifies the population mean of y for all subjects with those values of x_1 and x_2. When there are additional explanatory variables, each has a βx term.

Multiple Regression Model

The **multiple regression model** relates the mean μ_y of a quantitative response variable y to a set of explanatory variables $x_1, x_2, \ldots$. For three explanatory variables, for example, the multiple regression equation is

$$\mu_y = \alpha + \beta_1 x_1 + \beta_2 x_2 + \beta_3 x_3,$$

and the sample prediction equation is

$$\hat{y} = a + b_1 x_1 + b_2 x_2 + b_3 x_3.$$

With sample data, software estimates the multiple regression equation. As in the simple case, it uses the method of least squares to find the best prediction equation (the one with the smallest possible sum of squared residuals).

Example 2

Multiple regression ◄

Predicting Selling Price Using House Size and Number of Bedrooms

Picture the Scenario

For the house selling price data described in Example 1, MINITAB reports the results in Table 13.3 for a multiple regression analysis with selling price as the response variable and with house size and number of bedrooms as explanatory variables.

Table 13.3 Regression of Selling Price on House Size and Bedrooms

```
Regression Equation

Price = 60102 + 62.98 House Size + 15170 Bedrooms

Coefficients
```

Term	Coef	SE Coef	T-Value	P-Value
Constant	60102	18623	3.23	0.001
House Size	63.0	4.75	13.25	0.000
Bedrooms	15170	5330	2.85	0.005

Questions to Explore

a. State the prediction equation.

b. The first home listed in Table 13.1 has house size = 1,679 square feet, three bedrooms, and selling price \$232,500. Find its predicted selling price and the residual (prediction error). Interpret the residual.

Think It Through

a. The response variable is y = selling price. Let x_1 = house size and x_2 = the number of bedrooms. From Table 13.3, the prediction equation is

$$\hat{y} = 60{,}102 + 63.0x_1 + 15{,}170x_2,$$

where $\hat{y}$ is the predicted price.

b. For $x_1 = 1{,}679$ and $x_2 = 3$, the predicted selling price is

$$\hat{y} = 60{,}102 + 63.0(1{,}679) + 15{,}170(3) = 211{,}389, \text{ that is, } \$211{,}389.$$

The residual is the prediction error,

$$y - \hat{y} = \$232{,}500 - \$211{,}389 = \$21{,}111.$$

This result tells us that the actual selling price was \$21,111 higher than predicted.

Insight

The coefficients of house size and number of bedrooms are positive. As these variables increase, the predicted selling price increases, as we would expect.

► *Try Exercise 13.1*

In Practice **The Number of Explanatory Variables You Can Use Depends on the Amount of Data**

In practice, you should not use many explanatory variables in a multiple regression model unless you have lots of data. A rough guideline is that *the sample size n should be at least 10 times the number of explanatory variables.* For example, to use two explanatory variables, you should have at least $n = 20$ observations. (When the number of explanatory variables is very large, more recently developed guidelines and statistical methodologies apply, which are beyond the scope of this book.)

Plotting Relationships

Always look at the data before doing a multiple regression analysis. Most software has the option of constructing scatterplots on a single graph for each pair of variables. This type of plot is called a **scatterplot matrix.**

Figure 13.1 shows a MINITAB scatterplot matrix for selling price, house size, and number of bedrooms. It shows each pair of variables twice. For a given pair, in one plot a variable is on the y-axis and in another it is on the x-axis. For instance, selling price of house is on the y-axis for the plots in the first row, whereas it is on the x-axis for the plots in the first column. Since selling price is the response variable for this example, the plots in the first row (where selling price is on the y-axis) are the ones of primary interest. These graphs show positive linear relationships between selling price and both house size and number of bedrooms. Because a scatterplot matrix shows each pair of variables twice, you only need to look at the plots in the upper-right triangle.

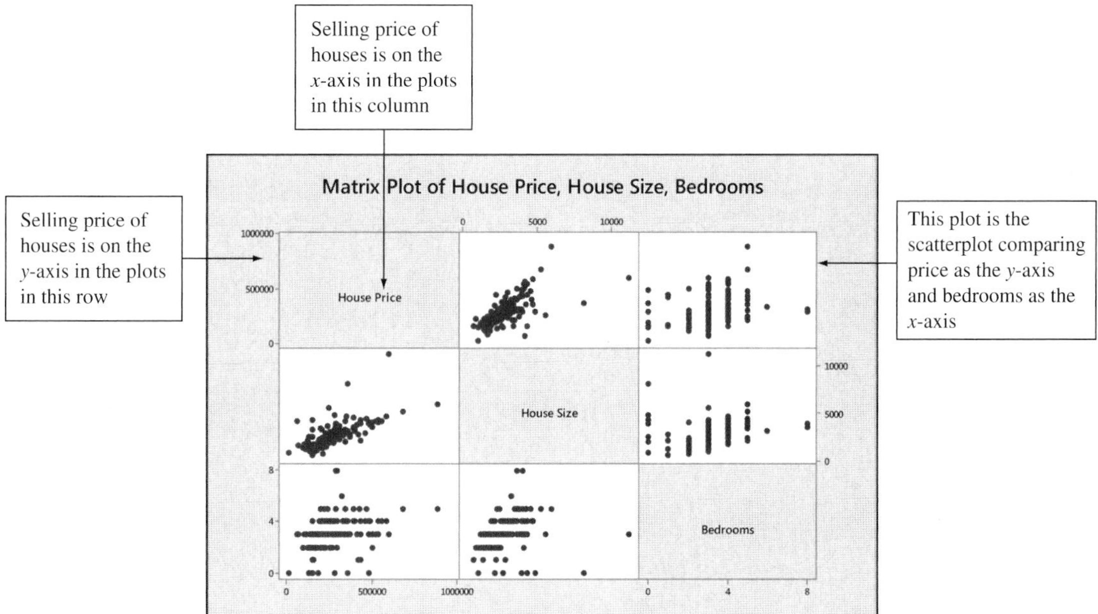

▲ **Figure 13.1 Scatterplot Matrix for Selling Price, House Size, and Number of Bedrooms.** The middle plot in the top row has house size on the x-axis and selling price on the y-axis. The first plot in the second row reverses this, with selling price on the x-axis and house size on the y-axis. **Question** Why are the plots of main interest the ones in the top row?

Each scatterplot portrays only *two* variables. It's a two-dimensional picture. A multiple regression equation, which has *several* variables, is more difficult to portray graphically. Note also that the scatterplot involving the variable Number of Bedrooms as an explanatory variable has an appearance of columns of points. This is due to the highly discrete nature of this quantitative variable.

Interpretation of Multiple Regression Coefficients

The simplest way to interpret a multiple regression equation is to look at it in *two dimensions* as a function of a *single* explanatory variable. We can do this by fixing values for the other explanatory variable(s). For instance, let's fix x_1 = house size at the value 2,000 square feet. Then the prediction equation simplifies to one with x_2 = number of bedrooms alone as the predictor,

$$\hat{y} = 60{,}102 + 63.0(2{,}000) + 15{,}170x_2 = 186{,}102 + 15{,}170x_2.$$

For 2,000-square-foot houses, the predicted selling price relates to number of bedrooms by $\hat{y} = 186{,}102 + 15{,}170x_2$. Since the slope coefficient of x_2 is 15,170, the predicted selling price increases by \$15,170 for every bedroom added.

Likewise, we could fix the number of bedrooms and then describe how the predicted selling price depends on the house size. Let's consider houses with number of bedrooms $x_2 = 3$. The prediction equation becomes

$$\hat{y} = 60{,}102 + 63.0x_1 + 15{,}170(3) = 105{,}612 + 63.0x_1.$$

For houses with three bedrooms, the predicted selling price increases by \$63 for every additional square foot in house size or \$6300 for every 100 square foot in size increase.

Can we say an increase of one bedroom has a larger impact on the selling price (\$15,170) than an increase of a square foot in house size (\$63 per square foot)? No, we cannot compare these slopes for these explanatory variables because their units of measurement are not the same. Slopes can't be compared when the units differ. We could compare house size and lot size directly if they had the same units of square feet.

Summarizing the Effect While Controlling for a Variable

The multiple regression model states that *each* explanatory variable has a straight-line relationship with the mean of y, given fixed values of the other explanatory variables. Specifically, *the model assumes that the slope for a particular explanatory variable is identical for all fixed values of the other explanatory variables.* For instance, the coefficient of x_1 in the prediction equation $\hat{y} = 60{,}102 + 63.0x_1 + 15{,}170x_2$ is 63.0 regardless of whether we plug in $x_2 = 1$ or $x_2 = 2$ or $x_2 = 3$ for the number of bedrooms. When you fix x_2 at each of these three levels, you can check that:

x_2	$\hat{y} = 60{,}102 + 63.0x_1 + 15{,}170x_2$
1	$\hat{y} = 75{,}272 + 63.0x_1$
2	$\hat{y} = 90{,}442 + 63.0x_1$
3	$\hat{y} = 105{,}612 + 63.0x_1$

The slope of house size (x_1) is 63.0 for each equation. Setting x_2 at a variety of values yields a collection of parallel lines, each having slope 63.0. See Figure 13.2.

When we fix the value of x_2 we are holding it constant: We are *controlling* for x_2. That's the major difference between the interpretation of slopes in multiple and simple regression:

- In multiple regression, a slope describes the effect of an explanatory variable while *controlling* effects of the other explanatory variables in the model.
- Simple regression has only a single explanatory variable. The slope in a simple regression model describes the effect of that variable while *ignoring* all other possible explanatory variables.

Recall

Section 10.5 showed that in multivariate analyses, we can **control** a variable statistically by keeping its value constant while we study the association between other variables. ◀

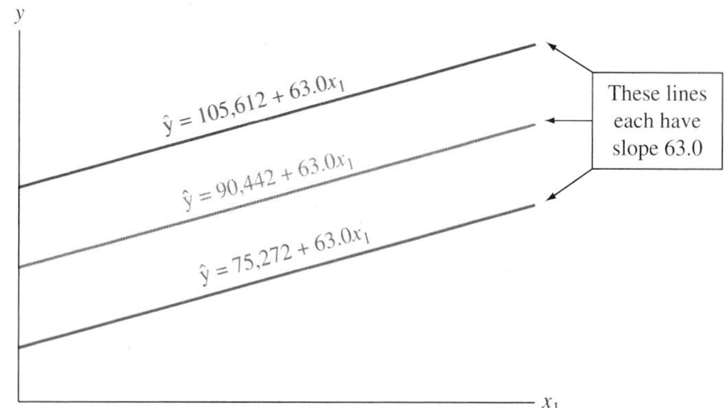

▲ **Figure 13.2** **The Relationship Between $\hat{y}$ and x_1 for the Multiple Regression Equation $\hat{y} = 60{,}102 + 63.0x_1 + 15{,}170x_2$.** This shows how the equation simplifies when number of bedrooms $x_2 = 1$ (red line), or $x_2 = 2$ (blue line), or $x_2 = 3$ (green line). **Question** The lines jump upward (to higher $\hat{y}$-values) as x_2 increases. How would you interpret this fact?

For example, the prediction equation for the simple regression between y = selling price and x_1 = house size is $\hat{y} = 97{,}997 + 66.4x_1$. In this equation, the number of bedrooms and other possible predictors are ignored, not controlled. The prediction equation describes the relationship for *all* the house sales in the data set regardless of how many bedrooms they have. On the other hand, the equation $\hat{y} = 90{,}442 + 63.0x_1$ we obtained above by substituting $x_2 = 2$ into the multiple regression equation applies only for houses that have two bedrooms. In this case, number of bedrooms is controlled. This is why the slopes are different, 66.4 for simple regression and 63.0 for multiple regression.

One of the main uses of multiple regression is to identify potential lurking variables and control for them by including them as explanatory variables in the model. Doing so can have a major impact on a variable's effect. When we control a variable, we keep that variable from influencing the associations among the other variables in the study. As we've seen before, the direction of the effect can change after we control for a variable. Exercise 13.5 illustrates this for multiple regression modeling.

13.1 Practicing the Basics

13.1 Predicting weight For a study of female college athletes, the prediction equation relating y = total body weight (in pounds) to x_1 = height (in inches) and x_2 = percent body fat is $\hat{y} = -121 + 3.50x_1 + 1.35x_2$.

TRY

a. Find the predicted total body weight for a female athlete at the mean values of 66 and 18 for x_1 and x_2.

b. An athlete with $x_1 = 66$ and $x_2 = 18$ has actual weight $y = 115$ pounds. Find the residual and interpret it.

13.2 Does study help GPA? For the Georgia Student Survey file on the book's website, the prediction equation relating y = college GPA to x_1 = high school GPA and x_2 = study time (hours per day), is $\hat{y} = 1.13 + 0.643x_1 + 0.0078x_2$.

a. Find the predicted college GPA of a student who has a high school GPA of 3.5 and who studies three hours a day.

b. For students with fixed study time, what is the change in predicted college GPA when high school GPA increases from 3.0 to 4.0?

13.3 Predicting college GPA For all students at Walden University, the prediction equation for y = college GPA (range 0–4.0) and x_1 = high school GPA (range 0–4.0) and x_2 = college board score (range 200–800) is $\hat{y} = 0.20 + 0.50x_1 + 0.002x_2$.

a. Find the predicted college GPA for students having (i) high school GPA = 4.0 and college board score = 800 and (ii) $x_1 = 2.0$ and $x_2 = 200$.

b. For those students with $x_2 = 500$, show that $\hat{y} = 1.20 + 0.50x_1$.

c. For those students with $x_2 = 600$, show that $\hat{y} = 1.40 + 0.50x_1$. Thus, compared to part b, the slope for x_1 is still 0.50, and increasing x_2 by 100 (from 500 to 600) shifts the intercept upward by $100 \times (\text{slope for } x_2) = 100(0.002) = 0.20$ units.

13.4 Interpreting slopes on GPA Refer to the previous exercise.

a. Explain why setting x_2 at a variety of values yields a collection of parallel lines relating $\hat{y}$ to x_1. What is the value of the slope for those parallel lines?

b. Since the slope 0.50 for x_1 is larger than the slope 0.002 for x_2, does this imply that x_1 has a larger effect than x_2 on y in this sample? Explain.

13.5 Does more education cause more crime? The FL Crime data file on the book's website has data for the 67 counties in Florida on

y = crime rate: Annual number of crimes in county per 1000 population

x_1 = education: Percentage of adults in county with at least a high school education

x_2 = urbanization: Percentage in county living in an urban environment.

The figure shows a scatterplot matrix. MINITAB multiple regression results are also displayed.

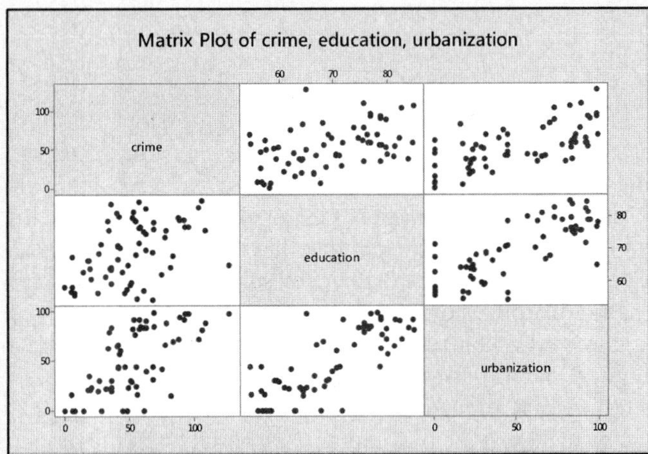

Scatterplot matrix for crime rate, education, and urbanization.

Multiple regression for y = crime rate, x_1 = education, and x_2 = urbanization.

Term	Coef	SE Coef	T-Value	P-Value
Constant	59.1	28.4	2.08	0.041
education	−0.583	0.472	−1.23	0.221
urbanization	0.683	0.123	5.54	0.000

a. Find the predicted crime rate for a county that has 0% in an urban environment and (i) 70% high school graduation rate and (ii) 80% high school graduation rate.

b. Use results from part a to explain how education affects the crime rate, controlling for urbanization, interpreting the slope coefficient −0.58 of education.

c. Using the prediction equation, show that the equation relating crime rate and education when urbanization is fixed at (i) 0, (ii) 50, and (iii) 100, is as follows:

x_2	$\hat{y} = 59.1 - 0.58x_1 + 0.68x_2$
0	$\hat{y} = 59.1 - 0.58x_1$
50	$\hat{y} = 93.2 - 0.58x_1$
100	$\hat{y} = 127.4 - 0.58x_1$

Sketch a plot with these lines and use it to interpret the effect of education on crime rate, controlling for urbanization.

d. The scatterplot matrix shows that education has a *positive* association with crime rate, but the multiple regression equation shows that the association is *negative* when we keep x_2 = urbanization fixed. Consider the hypothetical figure that follows. Sketch lines that represent (i) the prediction equation from a simple regression model using only education and ignoring the information on urbanization and (ii) the prediction equation from the multiple regression model for counties having urbanization = 50. Use these lines to explain the difference in the interpretation of the slope for education in simple and multiple regression models with regard to ignoring or controlling for urbanization. (*Note:* The reversal in the association between crime rate and education is an example of **Simpson's paradox**; see Example 16 in Sec. 3.4 and Example 18 in Sec. 10.5).

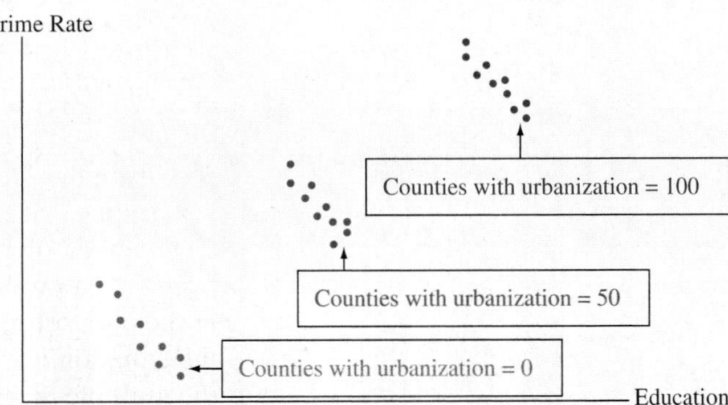

Hypothetical scatterplot for crime rate and education, labeling by urbanization.

13.6 Crime rate and income Refer to the previous exercise. MINITAB reports the following results for the multiple regression of y = crime rate on x_1 = median income (in thousands of dollars) and x_2 = urbanization.

Results of regression analysis

Term	Coef	SE Coef	T-Value	P-Value
Constant	40.0	16.4	2.44	0.017
income	−0.791	0.805	−0.98	0.330
urbanization	0.642	0.111	5.78	0.000

a. Report the prediction equations relating crime rate to income at urbanization levels of (i) 0 and (ii) 100. Interpret.

b. For the simple regression model relating y = crime rate to x = income, MINITAB reports

```
crime = −11.6 + 2.61 income
```

Interpret the effect of income, according to the sign of its slope. How does this effect differ from the effect of income in the multiple regression equation?

c. Use the estimated slope for income in the simple and multiple regression model to explain the difference in the interpretation of the slope when (i) ignoring urbanization (ii) controlling urbanization. (Note: The reversal in the association between income and education is an example of **Simpson's paradox**.)

13.7 The economics of golf The earnings of a PGA Tour golfer are determined by performance in tournaments. A study analyzed tour data to determine the financial return for certain skills of professional golfers. The sample consisted of 393 golfers competing in one or both of the 2002 and 2008 seasons. The most significant factors that contribute to earnings were the percent of attempts a player was able to hit the green in regulation (GIR), the number of times that a golfer made par or better after hitting a bunker divided by the number of bunkers that were hit (SS), the average of putts after reaching the green (AvePutt), and the number of PGA events entered (Events). The resulting coefficients from multiple regression to predict yearly earnings (in $) are:

Predictor	Coefficient
Constant	26,417,000
GIR	168,300
SS	33,859
AvePutt	−19,784,000
Events	−44,725

Source: Some data from K. Rinehart, *Major Themes in Economics*, 2009.

a. State the prediction equation for a PGA Tour golfer's yearly earnings.

b. Explain how to interpret the coefficient for AvePutt.

c. Find the predicted earnings for a golfer who had a GIR score of 60, SS score of 50, AvePutt of 1.5 and participated in 20 events.

13.8 Comparable number of bedrooms and house size effects In Example 2, the prediction equation between y = selling price and x_1 = house size and x_2 = number of bedrooms was $\hat{y} = 60{,}102 + 63.0x_1 + 15{,}170x_2$.

a. For fixed number of bedrooms, how much is the house selling price predicted to increase for each square foot increase in house size? Why?

b. For a fixed house size of 2000 square feet, how does the predicted selling price change for two, three, and four bedrooms?

13.9 Controlling can have no effect Suppose that the correlation between x_1 and x_2 equals 0. Then, for multiple regression with those predictors, it can be shown that the slope for x_1 is the same as in simple linear regression when x_1 is the only predictor. Explain why you would expect this to be true. (*Hint:* If you don't control x_2, would you expect it to have an impact on how x_1 affects y, if x_1 and x_2 have correlation of 0?)

13.10 House selling prices TECH Using software with the House Selling Prices OR data file on the book's website, analyze y = selling price, x_1 = house size, and x_2 = lot size.

a. Construct box plots for each variable and a scatterplot matrix or scatter plots between y and each of x_1 and x_2. Interpret.

b. Find the multiple regression prediction equation.

c. If house size remains constant, what, if any, is the effect of an increase in lot size? Why do you think this is?

13.11 Used cars TECH The following data (also available from the book's website) is from a random sample of campus newspaper ads on used cars for sale. Consider the age and horsepower (HP) of a car to predict its selling price. (The variable Type stands for whether the car is from the United States, coded as 1, or a foreign car, coded as 0. This variable will be considered in exercise 13.48.)

a. Construct a scatterplot matrix (or separate scatterplots) to investigate the relationship among price, age, and horsepower and interpret.

b. Find the multiple regression prediction equation for the selling price in terms of age and horsepower of a car. What is the predicted price for a car that has a horsepower of 80 and (i) is 8 years old, (ii) 10 years old, rounded to the nearest hundred?

c. Based on this multiple regression, can you predict the price difference between a car with 60 HP and a car with 80 HP without knowing the ages of the two cars? Explain.

Car	Price	Age	HP	Type	Car	Price	Age	HP	Type
1	8700	9	55	1	11	5050	10	44	1
2	11200	7	75	1	12	14800	7	75	0
3	9000	9	69	0	13	1800	12	55	1
4	10300	10	76	0	14	7200	10	82	1
5	10500	8	76	0	15	8600	9	73	1
6	5250	12	49	1	16	13000	9	130	0
7	12000	5	120	0	17	11790	8	95	0
8	2500	11	79	1	18	12350	7	124	0
9	8300	8	90	0	19	6100	10	74	1
10	9300	8	38	0					

13.2 Extending the Correlation and R^2 for Multiple Regression

The correlation r and its square r^2 describe the strength of the association in a simple linear regression analysis. These measures can also describe the association between y and a whole set of explanatory variables that predict y in a multiple regression model.

Correlation Matrix

After plotting the scatterplot matrix and checking whether the associations are roughly linear, software can compute a **correlation matrix**. This is a square table,

Correlation matrix of selling price (y), house size (x_1), number of bedrooms (x_2) and age (x_3)

	y	x_1	x_2	x_3
y	—	0.71	0.32	−0.17
x_1	0.71	—	0.26	−0.09
x_2	0.32	0.26	—	−0.19
x_3	−0.17	−0.09	−0.19	—

arranged in a fashion similar to the scatterplot matrix. It lists the variables in the rows and again in the columns and shows the correlation r between each pair. The table in the margin shows the correlation matrix for the three variables of selling price (y), house size (x_1) and number of bedrooms (x_2) for which Figure 13.1 displayed the scatterplot matrix. In addition, it includes a fourth variable, the age of the house (x_3). Remember that the correlation does not distinguish between response and explanatory variable and that the correlation between x and y is the same as the correlation between y and x. This is why you see identical values above and below the diagonal. It is a good idea to look at the scatterplot matrix and the corresponding correlation matrix before fitting a multiple regression model to get a feel for the strengths of the associations among the variables considered.

From the correlation matrix, we see that house size has a moderately strong correlation (0.71) with selling price. As the size increases, the price tends to increase. The strength of the linear association between price and number of bedrooms is much weaker, with $r = 0.32$. The correlation between price and age of the house is negative (−0.17), indicating that older houses tend to cost less. However, the correlation is very weak, and a scatterplot reveals no visible trend. Also, note that the correlation between the house size and the number of bedrooms is, perhaps surprisingly, relatively weak (0.26).

Multiple Correlation

To summarize how well a multiple regression model predicts y, we analyze how well the observed y values correlate with the predicted $\hat{y}$ values. As a set, the explanatory variables are strongly associated with y if the correlation between the y and $\hat{y}$ values is strong. Treating $\hat{y}$ as a variable gives us a way of summarizing several explanatory variables by *one* variable, for which we can use its ordinary correlation with the y values. The correlation between the observed y values and the predicted $\hat{y}$ values from the multiple regression model is called the **multiple correlation**.

In Words

The **correlation *r*** describes the association between the response variable y and a single explanatory variable x. The **multiple correlation** describes the association between y and a set of explanatory variables in a multiple regression model. It is denoted by R (uppercase).

Multiple Correlation, *R*

For a multiple regression model, the **multiple correlation** is the correlation between the observed y values and the predicted $\hat{y}$ values. It is denoted by R.

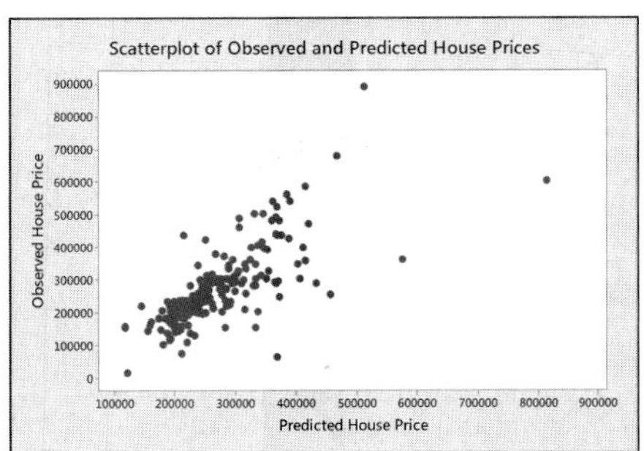

For each subject in the dataset, the regression equation provides a predicted value $\hat{y}$. So, each subject has a y value and a $\hat{y}$ value. For the two houses listed in Table 13.1, Table 13.4 shows the actual selling price y and the predicted selling price $\hat{y}$ from the equation $\hat{y} = 60{,}102 + 63.0x_1 + 15{,}170x_2$ with house size and number of bedrooms as predictors. The correlation computed between all 200 pairs of y and $\hat{y}$ values is the multiple correlation, R. Software tells us that this equals 0.72. The scatterplot in the margin displays these pairs of y and $\hat{y}$ values.

Table 13.4 Selling Prices and Their Predicted Values

These values refer to the two home sales listed in Table 13.1. The predictors are x_1 = house size and x_2 = number of bedrooms.

House	Selling Price	Predicted Selling Price
1	232,500	$\hat{y} = 60{,}102 + 63.0(1{,}679) + 15{,}170(3) = 211{,}389$
2	158,000	$\hat{y} = 60{,}102 + 63.0(1{,}292) + 15{,}170(1) = 156{,}668$

Recall

For the first home sale listed in Table 13.1, $y = 232{,}500$, $x_1 = 1679$ and $x_2 = 3$. ◀

The larger the multiple correlation, the better the predictions of y by the set of explanatory variables. For the housing data, $R = 0.72$ indicates a moderately strong association.

The predicted values $\hat{y}$ cannot correlate negatively with y. Otherwise, the predictions would be worse than merely using $\bar{y}$ to predict y. Therefore, *R falls between 0 and 1.* In this way, the multiple correlation R differs from the correlation r between y and a single variable x, which falls between -1 and $+1$.

R^2

Recall

Section 12.3 introduced r^2 **(r-squared)** as measuring the proportional reduction in prediction error from using $\hat{y}$ to predict y compared to using $\bar{y}$ to predict y. It falls between 0 and 1, with larger values representing stronger association. ◀

For predicting y, the statistic R^2 describes the relative improvement from using the prediction equation instead of using the sample mean $\bar{y}$. The error in using the prediction equation to predict y is summarized by the *residual sum of squares*, $\Sigma(y - \hat{y})^2$. The error in using $\bar{y}$ to predict y is summarized by the *total sum of squares*, $\Sigma(y - \bar{y})^2$. The *proportional reduction in error* is

$$R^2 = \frac{\Sigma(y - \bar{y})^2 - \Sigma(y - \hat{y})^2}{\Sigma(y - \bar{y})^2}.$$

The better the predictions are using the regression equation, the larger R^2 is. The measure r^2 we discussed in Section 12.3 is the special case of R^2 applied to regression with one explanatory variable. As the notation suggests, for multiple regression, R^2 is the square of the multiple correlation. Regression software reports R^2, and you can take the positive square root of it to get the multiple correlation, R.

Multiple correlation and R^2 ◀

Example 3

Predicting House Selling Prices

Picture the Scenario

For the 200 observations on y = selling price in thousands of dollars, using x_1 = house size in thousands of square feet and x_2 = number of bedrooms, Table 13.5 shows part of the ANOVA (analysis of variance) table that MINITAB reports for the multiple regression model.

Table 13.5 ANOVA Table and R^2 for Predicting House Selling Price (in thousands of dollars) Using House Size (in thousands of square feet) and Number of Bedrooms

R-Sq = 52.4%

Analysis of Variance

Source	DF	SS
Regression	2	1399524
Error	197	1269345
Total	199	2668870

Questions to Explore

a. Show how to use the sums of squares in the ANOVA table to find R^2 for this multiple regression model. Interpret.

b. Find and interpret the multiple correlation.

Think It Through

a. From the sum of squares (SS) column, the total sum of squares is $\Sigma(y - \bar{y})^2 = 2{,}668{,}870$. The residual sum of squares from using the multiple regression equation to predict y is $\Sigma(y - \hat{y})^2 = 1{,}269{,}345$. The value of R^2 is

$$R^2 = \frac{\Sigma(y - \bar{y})^2 - \Sigma(y - \hat{y})^2}{\Sigma(y - \bar{y})^2} = \frac{2{,}668{,}870 - 1{,}269{,}345}{2{,}668{,}870} = 0.524.$$

Using house size and number of bedrooms together to predict selling price reduces the prediction error by 52%, relative to using $\bar{y}$ alone to predict selling price. The R^2 statistic appears (in percentage form) in Table 13.5 under the heading "R-sq."

b. The multiple correlation between selling price and the two explanatory variables is $R = \sqrt{R^2} = \sqrt{0.524} = 0.72$. This equals the correlation for the 200 homes between the observed selling prices y and the predicted selling prices $\hat{y}$ from multiple regression that we mentioned before. There's a moderately strong association between the observed and the predicted selling prices. In summary, house size and number of bedrooms are very helpful in predicting selling prices.

Insight

From the correlation matrix, we saw that the correlation between price and size of a house is $r = 0.71$. In that case, the r^2 measure for the simple regression model with just size as a predictor equals $r^2 = (0.71)^2 = 0.50$. The multiple regression model has $R^2 = 0.52$, only a marginally larger value. We appear to be just as well off with the simple model using house size as the predictor as using the multiple model. An advantage of using the simple model is easier interpretation of the coefficients.

▶ ***Try Exercise 13.12***

Properties of R^2

The example showed that R^2 for the multiple regression model was larger than r^2 for a simple model using only one of the explanatory variables. In fact, *a key property of R^2 is that it cannot decrease when predictors are added to a model.*

The difference $\Sigma(y - \bar{y})^2 - \Sigma(y - \hat{y})^2$ that forms the numerator of R^2 also appears in the ANOVA table. It is called the *regression sum of squares.* A simpler formula for it is

$$\text{Regression SS} = \Sigma(\hat{y} - \bar{y})^2.$$

If each $\hat{y} = \bar{y}$, then the regression equation predicts no better than $\bar{y}$. Then regression SS $= 0$, and $R^2 = 0$.

The numerical values of the sums of squares reported in Table 13.5 result when y is measured in *thousands* of dollars (for instance, the first house y is 232.5 rather than 232,500, and $\hat{y}$ is 211.4 rather than 211,389). We truncated the numbers for convenience because the sums of squares would otherwise be enormous with each one having six more zeros on the end! It makes no difference to the result. Another property of R and R^2 is that, like the correlation, *their values don't depend on the units of measurement.*

In summary, the properties of R^2 are similar to those of r^2 for the simple linear regression model. Here's a list of the main properties:

SUMMARY: Properties of R^2

- R^2 falls between 0 and 1. The larger the value, the better the explanatory variables collectively predict y.

- $R^2 = 1$ only when all residuals are 0, that is, when all regression predictions are perfect (each $y = \hat{y}$), so residual $SS = \Sigma(y - \hat{y})^2 = 0$.
- $R^2 = 0$ when each $\hat{y} = \bar{y}$. In that case, the estimated slopes all equal 0, and the correlation between y and each explanatory variable equals 0.
- R^2 gets larger, or at worst stays the same, whenever an additional explanatory variable is added to the multiple regression model.
- The value of R^2 does not depend on the units of measurement.

Values of r^2 for the association between selling price and various explanatory variables

Explanatory variable	r^2
House Size	0.50
Bedrooms	0.10
Lot Size	0.05
Baths	0.33
Garage	0.01
Age	0.03

Table 13.6 shows how R^2 increases as we add explanatory variables to a multiple regression model to predict y = house selling price. As we saw from the correlation matrix, the single predictor in the data set that is most strongly associated with y is the house size ($r^2 = 0.50$). See the margin table. When we add number of bedrooms as a second predictor, R^2 goes up from 0.50 to 0.52. As other predictors are added, R^2 continues to go up, but not by much, except when adding number of bathrooms, for which there is a more noticeable jump in R^2. Predictive power is not much worse with only house size as a predictor than with all six predictors in the regression model.

Table 13.6 R^2 Value for Multiple Regression Models for y = House Selling Price

Explanatory Variables in Model	R^2
House size	0.50
House size, Number of bedrooms	0.52
House size, Number of bedrooms, Lot size	0.52
House size, Number of bedrooms, Lot size, Number of bathrooms	0.60
House size, Number of bedrooms, Lot size, Number of bathrooms, Garage	0.61
House size, Number of bedrooms, Lot size, Number of bathrooms, Garage, Age	0.61

Although R^2 goes up by only small amounts when we add other variables after house size is already in the model, this does not mean that the other predictors are only weakly correlated with selling price. Because the predictors are themselves highly correlated, once one or two of them are in the model, the remaining ones don't help much in adding to the predictive power. For instance, lot size is highly positively correlated with number of bedrooms and with the size of the house. So, once the size of the house and the number of bedrooms are included as predictors in the model, there's not much benefit to including lot size as an additional predictor.

In Practice R^2 **Often Does Not Increase Much After a Few Predictors Are in the Model**

When there are many explanatory variables but the correlations among them are strong, once you have included a few of them in the model, R^2 usually doesn't increase much more when you add additional ones. This does not mean that the additional variables are uncorrelated with the response variable but merely that they don't add much new information for predicting y, given the values of the predictors already in the model.

Similar to the simple regression model, we can also interpret R^2 as the percentage of the variability in the response variable y that can be explained by the regression model. The total sum of squares $\Sigma(y - \bar{y})^2$ measures the variability of y over the entire range of all predictor values, and the residual sum of squares $\Sigma(y - \hat{y})^2$ measures the variability of y at a fixed setting for all predictors (see the discussion in the next section). Their ratio $\frac{\Sigma(y - \hat{y})^2}{\Sigma(y - \bar{y})^2}$ is the proportion of the overall variability that occurs locally at a fixed setting for all predictors. For instance, from Table 13.5, this ratio equals $\frac{1,269,345}{2,668,870} = 0.476$, indicating that 47.6% of the overall variability we observe in house prices is due to the variability that occurs locally at any particular setting for the number of bedrooms and size of the house.

This is the variability that *cannot* be explained or accounted for by these predictors because they are fixed. So, for the OR house price data, about 48% of the variability we see in the selling price of a house cannot be explained by its number of bedrooms or its size. However, the other 52% of the overall variability in selling prices *can* be explained by the varying number of bedrooms and sizes of houses. This remaining percentage is R^2, expressed as a percentage. In a formula, $R^2 = 1 - \frac{\Sigma(y - \hat{y})^2}{\Sigma(y - \bar{y})^2} = 0.524$, which implies that 52.4% of the overall variability in selling prices can be explained by differences in number of bedrooms and house sizes. The remaining 47.6% of the variability must be due to other sources that we didn't or even couldn't measure, such as quality of school district.

13.2 Practicing the Basics

13.12 Predicting sports attendance Keeneland Racetrack in Lexington, Kentucky, has been a social gathering place since 1935. Every spring and fall thousands of people come to the racetrack to socialize, gamble, and enjoy the horse races that have become so popular in Kentucky. A study investigated the different factors that affect the attendance at Keeneland. To many people, the social aspect of Keeneland is just as important as watching the races, if not more. The study investigates which factors significantly contribute to attendance by Keeneland visitors. (*Source*: Data from Gatton School of Business and Economics publication, Gatton College, 2009.)

TRY

ANOVA table for y = attendance at Keeneland

Source	DF	SS	MS	F-Value	P-Value
Regression	6	2360879925	393479988	21.71	0.00
Error	110	1993805006	18125500		
Total	116	4354684931			

a. Show how R^2 is calculated from the SS values and report its value.

b. Interpret the R^2 value. Does the multiple regression equation help us predict the attendance much better than we could without knowing that equation?

c. Find the multiple correlation. Interpret.

13.13 Predicting weight Let's use multiple regression to predict total body weight (TBW, in pounds) using data from a study of female college athletes. Possible predictors are HGT = height (in inches), %BF = percent body fat, and age. The display shows the correlation matrix for these variables.

	TBW	HGT	%BF	AGE
TBW	-	0.74	0.39	−0.19
HGT	0.74	-	0.10	−0.12
%BF	0.39	0.10	-	0.02
AGE	−0.19	−0.12	0.02	-

a. Which explanatory variable gives by itself the best predictions of weight? Explain.

b. With height as the sole predictor, $\hat{y} = -106 + 3.65$ (HGT) and $r^2 = 0.55$. If you add %BF as a predictor, you know that R^2 will be at least 0.55. Explain why.

c. When you add % body fat to the model, $\hat{y} = -121 + 3.50(\text{HGT}) + 1.35(\%\text{BF})$ and $R^2 = 0.66$. When you add age to the model, $\hat{y} = -97.7 + 3.43(\text{HGT}) + 1.36(\%\text{BF}) - 0.960(\text{AGE})$ and $R^2 = 0.67$. Once you know height and % body fat, does age seem to help you in predicting weight? Explain, based on comparing the R^2 values.

13.14 When does controlling have little effect? Refer to the previous exercise. Height has a similar estimated slope for each of the three models. Why do you think that controlling for % body fat and then age does not change the effect of height much? (*Hint:* How strongly is height correlated with the other two variables?)

13.15 Price of used cars For the 19 used cars listed in the Used Cars data file on the book's website (see also Exercise 13.11), modeling the mean of y = used car price in terms of x_1 = age results in $r^2 = 0.66$.

Adding x_2 = horsepower (HP) to the model yields the results in the following display.

Regression Equation

Price = 19349 − 1406 Age + 25.5 HP

Coefficients

Term	Coef	SE Coef	T-Value	P-Value
Constant	19349	4053	4.77	0.000
Age	−1406	320	−4.40	0.000
HP	25.5	22.3	1.14	0.270

Model Summary

S	R-sq
2084.69	68.69%

Analysis of Variance

Source	DF	SS	MS	F-value	P-value
Regression	2	152567500	76283750	17.55	0.000
Error	16	69534753	4345922		
Total	18	222102253			

a. Report R^2 and show how it is determined by SS values in the ANOVA table.

b. Interpret its value as a proportional reduction in prediction error.

c. Interpret its value as the percentage of the variability in the response variable that can be explained.

13.16 Price, age, and horsepower In the previous exercise, $r^2 = 0.66$ when age is the predictor and $R^2 = 0.69$ when both age and HP are predictors. Why do you think that the predictions of price don't improve much when HP is added to the model? (The correlation between HP and price is $r = 0.56$, and the correlation between HP and age is $r = -0.51$.)

13.17 Softball data For the Softball data set on the book's website, for each game, the variables are a team's number of runs scored (RUNS), number of hits (HIT), number of errors (ERR), and the difference (DIFF) between the number of runs scored by that team and by the other team, which is the response variable. MINITAB reports

Difference = -4.03 + 0.0260 Hits
+ 1.04 Run - 1.22 Errors

a. If you know the team's number of runs and number of errors in a game, explain why it does not help much to know how many hits the team has.

b. Explain why the result in part a is also suggested by knowing that $R^2 = 0.7594$ for this model, whereas $R^2 = 0.7593$ when only runs and errors are the explanatory variables in the model.

13.18 Slopes, correlations, and units In Example 2 on y = house selling price, x_1 = house size, and x_2 = number of bedrooms, $\hat{y} = 60{,}102 + 63.0x_1 + 15{,}170x_2$, and $R = 0.72$.

a. Interpret the value of the multiple correlation.

b. Suppose house selling prices are changed from dollars to *thousands* of dollars. Explain why if each price in Table 13.1 is divided by 1000, the prediction equation changes to $\hat{y} = 60.102 + 0.063x_1 + 15.170x_2$.

c. In part b, does the multiple correlation change to 0.00072? Justify your answer.

13.19 Predicting college GPA Using software with the TECH Georgia Student Survey data file from the book's website, find and interpret the multiple correlation and R^2 for the relationship between y = college GPA, x_1 = high school GPA, and x_2 = study time. Use both interpretations of R^2 as the reduction in prediction error and the percentage of the variability explained.

13.3 Inferences Using Multiple Regression

We've seen that multiple regression uses more than one explanatory variable to predict a response variable y. With it, we can study an explanatory variable's effect on y while controlling other variables that could affect the results. Now, let's turn our attention to using multiple regression to make inferences about the population.

Inferences require the same assumptions as in simple regression:

- The regression equation truly holds for the population means.
- The data were gathered using randomization.
- The response variable y has a normal distribution at each combination of values of the explanatory variables, with the same standard deviation.

The first assumption implies that there is a straight-line relationship between the mean of y and each explanatory variable for given values for the other predictors. This straight line has the same slope, no matter what values are considered for these other predictors. (See Figure 13.2 for an illustration with two explanatory variables.) We will see how to check this assumption in Section 13.4.

Estimating Variability Around the Regression Equation

A check for normality is needed to validate the third assumption; this is discussed in the next section. In addition to normality, a constant standard deviation for each combination of explanatory variables is assumed. As in the simple linear regression model, the parameter σ describes the variability of the response variable at a fixed setting of predictor variables. Its sample estimate is

$$s = \sqrt{\frac{\text{Residual SS}}{df}} = \sqrt{\frac{\Sigma(y - \hat{y})^2}{n - (\text{number of parameters in regression equation})}}.$$

This *residual standard deviation* describes the variability of y at given predictor settings and equals the typical size of the residuals. Its degrees of freedom are df = sample size n – number of parameters in the regression equation. Software reports s and its square, the **mean square error.**

Example 4

Estimating residual standard deviation ◀

Female Athletes' Weight

Picture the Scenario

The College Athletes data set on the book's website comes from a study of 64 University of Georgia female athletes who participated in Division I sports. The study measured several physical characteristics, including total body weight in pounds (TBW), height in inches (HGT), the percent of body fat (%BF), and age. Table 13.7 shows the ANOVA table for the regression of weight on height, % body fat, and age.

Table 13.7 ANOVA Table for Multiple Regression Analysis of Athlete Weights

Analysis of Variance

Source	DF	SS	MS	F-Value	P-Value
Regression	3	12407.9	4136.0	40.48	0.000
Error	60	6131.0	102.2		
Total	63	18539.0			

S = 10.1086 R-Sq = 66.9%

Question to Explore

For female athletes at particular values of height, percent of body fat, and age, estimate the standard deviation of their weights.

Recall

Recall that the prediction equation was $\hat{y} = -97.7 + 3.43x_1 + 1.36x_2 - 0.96x_3$, so there were four parameters in the regression model. ◀

Think It Through

The SS column tells us that the residual sum of squares is 6,131.0. There were $n = 64$ observations and 4 parameters in the regression model, so the DF column reports $df = n - 4 = 60$ opposite the residual SS. The mean square error is

$$s^2 = (\text{residual SS})/df = 6131.0/60 = 102.2.$$

It appears in the mean square (MS) column, in the row labeled "Error." The residual standard deviation is $s = \sqrt{102.2} = 10.1$, identified as S. For athletes with certain fixed values of height, percent body fat, and age, the weights vary with a standard deviation of about 10 pounds.

Insight

If the conditional distributions of weight are approximately bell shaped, about 95% of the weight values fall within about $2s = 20$ pounds of the true mean, as determined by the regression equation. More precisely, software can report *prediction intervals* within which a response outcome has a certain chance of falling. For instance, at $x_1 = 66$, $x_2 = 18$, and $x_3 = 20$, which are close to the sample means for height, body fat, and age, software reports $\hat{y} = 133.9$ and a 95% prediction interval of 133.9 ± 20.4.

► ***Try Exercise 13.22***

Recall

For simple regression, Example 16 in Section 12.4 discussed confidence intervals for the mean and prediction intervals for *y* at a particular setting of *x*. These intervals can be formed with multiple regression as well. ◄

In the sample of athletes, weight has a standard deviation of 17 pounds, describing the variability around the mean weight of 133 pounds (see Table 13.9 on page 637). How is it that the *residual* standard deviation could be only 10 pounds? The residual standard deviation is smaller because it refers to variability at *fixed* values of the predictors. (Recall the margin figure next to Example 15 in Chapter 12.) Weight varies less at given values of the predictors than it does overall. If we could predict weight perfectly knowing height, percent body fat, and age, the residual standard deviation would be 0.

The ANOVA table also reports another mean square, called a *mean square for regression*, or *regression mean square* for short. We'll next see how to use the mean squares to conduct a significance test about all the slope parameters together.

The Collective Effect of Explanatory Variables

Do the explanatory variables collectively have a statistically significant effect on the response variable *y*? With three predictors in a model, we can check this by testing

$$H_0: \beta_1 = \beta_2 = \beta_3 = 0.$$

This hypothesis states that the mean of *y* does not depend on *any* of the predictors in the model. That is, *y is statistically independent of all the explanatory variables.* The alternative hypothesis is

$$H_a\text{: At least one } \beta \text{ parameter is not equal to } 0.$$

Caution

The opposite (alternative) of all betas being equal to zero is that at least one of them is different from zero and not that all of them are different from zero. ◄

This states that *at least one* explanatory variable is associated with *y*.

The null hypothesis that all the slope parameters equal 0 is equivalent to the hypothesis that the population values of the multiple correlation and R^2 equal 0. The equivalence occurs because the population values of R and R^2 equal 0 only in those situations in which all the β parameters equal 0.

The test statistic for H_0 is denoted by F. It equals the ratio of the mean squares from the ANOVA table,

$$F = \frac{\text{Mean square for regression}}{\text{Mean square error}}.$$

We won't need the formulas for the mean squares here, but the value of F is proportional to $R^2/(1 - R^2)$. As R^2 increases, the F test statistic increases.

When H_0 is true, the expected value of the F test statistic is approximately 1. When H_0 is false, F tends to be larger than 1. The larger the F test statistic, the stronger the evidence against H_0. The P-value is the right-tail probability from the sampling distribution of the F test statistic.

ANOVA Table from Table 13.7

```
Source DF     SS      MS     F     P
Reg.    3 12407.9 4136.0 40.5 0.000
Error  60  6131.0  102.2
Total  63 18539.0
```

From the ANOVA table in Table 13.7 (shown again in the margin) for the regression model predicting weight, the mean square for regression = 4,136.0 and the mean square error = 102.2. Then the test statistic

$$F = 4136.0/102.2 = 40.5.$$

Before conclusions can be made about this test, we must first understand the F distribution better.

The *F* Distribution and Its Properties

The sampling distribution of the F test statistic is called the ***F* distribution**. The symbol for the F statistic and its distribution honors the eminent British statistician R. A. Fisher, who derived the F distribution in 1922. Like the chi-squared distribution, the F distribution can assume only nonnegative values and is skewed to the right. See Figure 13.3. The mean is approximately 1.

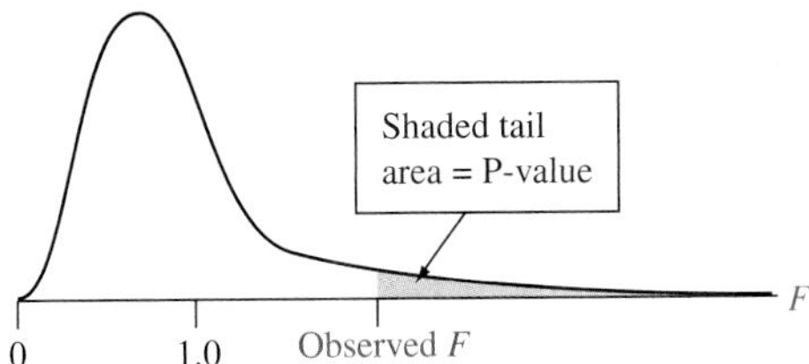

▲ **Figure 13.3** The *F* Distribution and the P-Value for *F* Tests. **Question** Why does the P-value use the right tail but not the left tail?

The precise shape of the F distribution is determined by two degrees of freedom terms, denoted by df_1 and df_2. These are the df values in the ANOVA table for the two mean squares whose ratio equals F. The first one is

$$df_1 = \text{number of explanatory variables in the model.}$$

The second,

$$df_2 = n - \text{number of parameters in regression equation,}$$

is the df for the residual sum of squares. Sometimes df_1 is called the **numerator *df*** because it is listed in the ANOVA table next to the mean square for regression, which goes in the numerator of the F test statistic. Likewise, df_2 is called the **denominator *df***, because it is listed in the ANOVA table next to the mean square error, which goes in the denominator of the F test statistic.

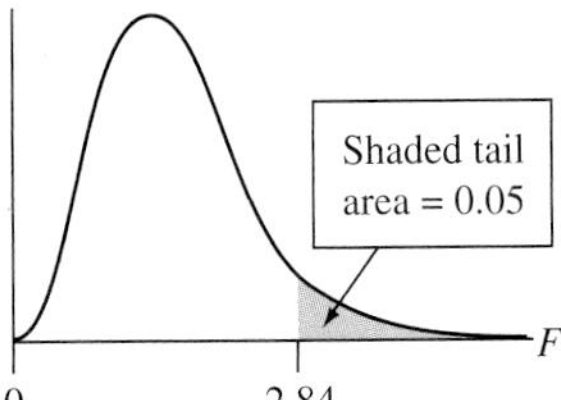

Table D in the Appendix lists the F values that have P-value = 0.05, for various df_1 and df_2 values. Table 13.8 shows a small excerpt. For instance, when $df_1 = 3$ and $df_2 = 40$, $F = 2.84$ has P-value = 0.05. When $F > 2.84$, the test statistic is farther out in the tail and the P-value < 0.05. (See margin figure.) Regression software reports the actual P-value. The F value for our example is extremely large ($F = 40.5$). See Table 13.7. With this large value of F, the ANOVA table reports P-value = 0.000.

Table 13.8 An Excerpt of Table D Displaying *F* Values

These are the values that have right-tail probability equal to 0.05.

	df_1				
df_2	1	2	3	4	5
30	4.17	3.32	2.92	2.69	2.69
40	4.10	3.23	2.84	2.61	2.45
60	4.00	3.15	2.76	2.52	2.37

SUMMARY: F Test That All the Multiple Regression β Parameters = 0

1. **Assumptions:**
   - Multiple regression model holds for population mean. This implies that there is a linear relationship between the mean of y and each explanatory variable, holding the others constant. The slope of this line is the same, no matter what the values for these other predictors.
   - Data gathered using randomization
   - Normal distribution for y with same standard deviation at each combination of predictors.
2. **Hypotheses:**

$$H_0: \beta_1 = \beta_2 = \ldots = 0 \text{ (all the } \beta \text{ parameters in the model} = 0)$$

$$H_a: \text{At least one } \beta \text{ parameter differs from 0.}$$

3. **Test statistic:** F = (mean square for regression)/(mean square error)
4. **P-value:** Right-tail probability above observed F test statistic value from F distribution with

$$df_1 = \text{number of explanatory variables, } (= \text{number of } \beta \text{ parameters})$$

$$df_2 = n - \text{(number of parameters in regression equation)}.$$

5. **Conclusion:** The smaller the P-value, the stronger the evidence that at least one explanatory variable has an effect on y. If a decision is needed, reject H_0 if P-value $\leq$ significance level, such as 0.05. Interpret in context.

Example 5

***F* test for predictors ◄**

Athletes' Weight

Picture the Scenario

For the 64 female college athletes, the ANOVA table for the multiple regression predicting y = weight using x_1 = height, x_2 = percent body fat, and x_3 = age shows:

Source	DF	SS	MS	F-Value	P-Value
Regression	3	12407.9	4136.0	40.48	0.000
Error	60	6131.0	102.2		

Questions to Explore

a. State and interpret the null hypothesis tested in this table.

b. From the F table, which F value would have a P-value of 0.05 for these data?

c. Report the observed test statistic and P-value. Interpret the P-value and make a decision for a 0.05 significance level.

Think It Through

a. Since there are three explanatory variables, the null hypothesis is H_0: $\beta_1 = \beta_2 = \beta_3 = 0$. It states that weight is independent of height, percent body fat, and age.

b. In the DF column, the ANOVA table shows $df_1 = 3$ and $df_2 = 60$. The F table or software indicates that the F value with right-tail probability of 0.05 is 2.76. (See also Table 13.8.)

c. From the ANOVA table, the observed F test statistic value is 40.48. Since this is well above 2.76, the P-value is less than 0.05. The ANOVA table reports P-value = 0.000. If H_0 were true, it would be extremely unusual to get such a large F test statistic. We can reject H_0 at the 0.05 significance level. In summary, we conclude that at least one predictor has an effect on weight.

Insight

The F test tells us that *at least one* explanatory variable has an effect. The following section discusses how to follow up from the F test to investigate which explanatory variables have a statistically significant effect on predicting y.

► ***Try Exercise 13.26***

Inferences About Individual Regression Parameters

Recall

Section 12.2 showed that the ***t* test** statistic for H_0: $\beta = 0$ in the simple model is

$$t = \frac{\text{(sample slope} - 0)}{\text{std. error of sample slope}} = (b - 0)/se,$$

with $df = n - 2$. ◄

For the simple linear regression model, $\mu_y = \alpha + \beta x$, we have used a t test for the null hypothesis H_0: $\beta = 0$ that x and y are statistically independent. Likewise, a t test applies to any slope parameter in multiple regression. Let's consider a particular parameter, say β_1 in the model $\mu_y = \alpha + \beta_1 x_1 + \beta_2 x_2 + \beta_3 x_3$.

If $\beta_1 = 0$, the mean μ_y of y is identical for all values of x_1, at fixed values for the other explanatory variables. So, H_0: $\beta_1 = 0$ states that *y and x_1 are statistically independent, controlling for the other variables.* This implies that once the other explanatory variables are in the model, it doesn't help to have x_1 in the model. The alternative hypothesis usually is two sided, H_a: $\beta_1 \neq 0$, but one-sided alternative hypotheses are also possible.

The test statistic for H_0: $\beta_1 = 0$ is

$$t = (b_1 - 0)/se,$$

where se is the standard error of the slope estimate b_1 of β_1. Software provides b_1, the se value, the t test statistic, and the P-value. If H_0 is true and the inference assumptions hold, the t test statistic has the t distribution. The degrees of freedom are

$$df = n - \text{number of parameters in the regression equation.}$$

The degrees of freedom are also equal to those used to calculate the residual standard deviation. The simple model $\mu_y = \alpha + \beta x$ has two parameters (α and β), so $df = n - 2$, as Section 12.2 used. The model with two predictors, $\mu_y = \alpha + \beta_1 x_1 + \beta_2 x_2$, has three parameters, so $df = n - 3$. Likewise, with three predictors, $df = n - 4$, and so on.

SUMMARY: Significance Test About a Multiple Regression Parameter (such as β_1)

1. Assumptions:

- Multiple regression model holds for population mean. This implies that there is a linear relationship between the mean of y and each explanatory variable, holding the others constant. The slope of this line is the same, no matter what the values for these other predictors.
- Data gathered using randomization
- Normal distribution for y with same standard deviation at each combination of predictors.

2. Hypotheses:

$$H_0: \beta_1 = 0$$

$$H_a: \beta_1 \neq 0$$

When H_0 is true, y is independent of x_1, controlling for the other predictors.

3. **Test statistic:** $t = (b_1 - 0)/se$. Software supplies the slope estimate b_1, its *se*, and the value of *t*.
4. **P-value:** Two-tail probability from *t* distribution of values larger than observed *t* test statistic (in absolute value). The *t* distribution has

$$df = n - \text{number of parameters in regression equation}$$

(such as $df = n - 3$ when $\mu_y = \alpha + \beta_1 x_1 + \beta_2 x_2$, which has three parameters).
5. **Conclusion:** Interpret P-value in context; compare to significance level if decision needed.

Example 6

Hypothesis test for multiple regression parameter β

What Helps Predict a Female Athlete's Weight?

Picture the Scenario

The College Athletes data set (Examples 4 and 5) measured several physical characteristics, including total body weight in pounds (TBW), height in inches (HGT), the percent of body fat (%BF), and age. Table 13.9 shows summary statistics for these variables.

Table 13.9 Summary Statistics for Study of Female College Athletes

Variables are TBW = total body weight, HGT = height, %BF = percent body fat, and AGE.

Variable	Mean	StDev	Minimum	Q1	Median	Q3	Maximum
TBW	133.0	17.2	96.0	119.2	131.5	143.8	185.0
HGT	65.6	3.5	56.0	63.0	65.0	68.2	75.0
%BF	18.4	4.1	11.2	15.2	18.5	21.5	27.6
AGE	20.0	1.98	17.0	18.0	20.0	22.0	23.0

Table 13.10 shows results of fitting a multiple regression model for predicting weight using the other variables. The predictive power is good, with $R^2 = 0.669$.

Table 13.10 Multiple Regression Analysis for Predicting Weight

Predictors are HGT = height, %BF = body fat, and age of subject.

Term	Coef	SE Coef	T-Value	P-Value
Constant	−97.7	28.8	−3.39	0.001
HGT	3.428	0.368	9.32	0.000
%BF	1.364	0.313	4.36	0.000
AGE	−0.960	0.648	−1.48	0.144

R-Sq = 66.9%

Questions to Explore

a. Interpret the effect of age on weight in the multiple regression equation.

b. In the population, does age help you to predict weight if you already know height and percent body fat? Show all steps of a significance test and interpret.

Think It Through

a. Let $\hat{y}$ = predicted weight, x_1 = height, x_2 = %body fat, and x_3 = age. Then

$$\hat{y} = -97.7 + 3.43x_1 + 1.36x_2 - 0.96x_3.$$

The slope coefficient of age is −0.96. The sample effect of age on weight is negative, which may seem surprising, but in practical terms it is small: For athletes having fixed values of x_1 and x_2, the predicted weight decreases by only 0.96 pounds for a one-year increase in age, and the ages vary only from 17 to 23.

b. If $\beta_3 = 0$, then x_3 = age has *no* effect on weight in the population of female college athletes, controlling for height and body fat. The hypothesis that age does *not* help us better predict weight, if we already know height and body fat, is H_0: $\beta_3 = 0$. Here are the steps:

1. **Assumptions:** The 64 female athletes were a convenience sample, not a random sample. Although the goal was to make inferences about all female college athletes, inferences are tentative. We'll discuss the other assumptions and learn how to check them in Section 13.4.
2. **Hypotheses:** The null hypothesis is H_0: $\beta_3 = 0$. Since there's no prior prediction about whether the effect of age is positive or negative (for fixed values of x_1 and x_2), we use the two-sided H_a: $\beta_3 \neq 0$.
3. **Test statistic:** Table 13.10 reports a slope estimate of −0.960 for age and a standard error of se = 0.648. It also reports the t test statistic of
$$t = (b_3 - 0)/se = -0.960/0.648 = -1.48.$$
Since the sample size equals $n = 64$ and the regression equation has four parameters, the degrees of freedom are $df = n - 4 = 60$.
4. **P-value:** Table 13.10 reports the P-value = 0.14. This is the two-tailed probability of a t statistic below −1.48 or above 1.48 if H_0 were true.
5. **Conclusion:** The P-value of 0.14 does not give much evidence against the null hypothesis that $\beta_3 = 0$. At common significance levels, such as 0.05, we cannot reject H_0. Age does not contribute significantly in predicting weight if we already know height and percentage of body fat. These conclusions are tentative because the sample of 64 female athletes was selected using a convenience sample rather than a random sample.

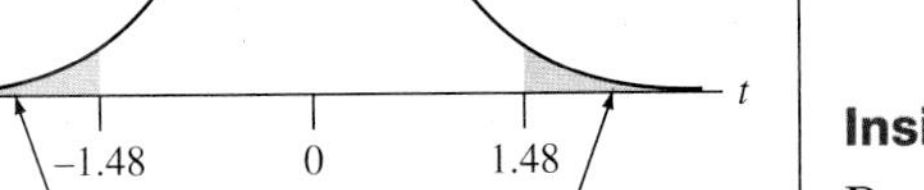

Insight

By contrast, Table 13.10 shows that $t = 9.3$ for testing the effect of height (H_0: $\beta_1 = 0$) and $t = 4.4$ for testing the effect of %BF (H_0: $\beta_2 = 0$). Both P-values are 0.000. It *does* help to have each of these variables in the model, given the other two.

▶ ***Try Exercise 13.20***

As usual, a test merely tells us whether the null hypothesis is plausible. In Example 6 we saw that β_3 may equal 0, but what are its other plausible values? A confidence interval answers this question.

Confidence Interval for a Multiple Regression β Parameter

A 95% confidence interval for a β slope parameter in multiple regression equals

$$\text{Estimated slope} \pm t_{.025}(se).$$

The t-score has $df = n$ − number of parameters in regression equation, as in the t test. The assumptions are also the same as for the t test.

Confidence interval for β

Example 7

What's Plausible for the Effect of Age on Weight?

Picture the Scenario

For the college athletes data, consider the multiple regression analysis of y = weight and predictors x_1 = height, x_2 = %body fat, and x_3 = age.

Question to Explore

Find and interpret a 95% confidence interval for β_3, the effect of age while controlling for height and percent of body fat.

Recall

From Table 13.10,

Term	Coef	SE Coef
Constant	−97.7	28.8
HGT	3.428	0.368
%BF	1.364	0.313
AGE	−0.960	0.648

Think It Through

From the previous example, $df = 60$. For $df = 60, t_{.025} = 2.00$. From Table 13.10 (shown partly in the margin), the estimate of β_3 is −0.96, with $se = 0.648$. The 95% confidence interval equals

$$b_3 \pm t_{.025}(se) = -0.96 \pm 2.00(0.648),$$

$$\text{or } -0.96 \pm 1.30, \text{ roughly } (-2.3, 0.3).$$

At fixed values of x_1 and x_2, we infer that for the population of female college athletes, the mean weight changes very little (and may not change at all) for a one-year increase in age.

Insight

The confidence interval contains 0. Age may have *no* effect on weight, once we control for height and percent body fat. This is in agreement with not rejecting H_0: $\beta_3 = 0$ in favor of H_a: $\beta_3 \neq 0$ at the $\alpha = 0.05$ level in the significance test.

► ***Try Exercise 13.21***

Model Building

Unless the sample size is small and the correlation is weak between y and each explanatory variable, the F test usually has a small P-value. If the explanatory variables are chosen sensibly, at least one should have *some* predictive power. When the P-value is small, we can conclude merely that *at least* one explanatory variable affects y. The more narrowly focused t inferences about individual slopes judge *which* effects are nonzero and estimate their sizes.

In Practice The Overall F Test is Done Before the Individual t Inferences

As illustrated in the previous examples, the F test is typically performed *first* before looking at the individual t inferences. The F test result tells us if there is sufficient evidence to make it worthwhile to consider the individual effects. When there are many explanatory variables, doing the F test first provides protection from doing lots of t tests and having one of them be significant merely by random variation when, in fact, there truly are no effects in the population.

After finding the highly significant F test result of Example 5, we would study the individual effects, as we did in Examples 6 and 7. When we look at an individual t inference, suppose we find that the plausible values for a parameter are all relatively near 0. This was the case for the effect of age on weight (controlling for the other variables) as shown by the confidence interval in Example 7.

Then, to simplify the model, you can remove that predictor, refitting the model with the other predictors. When we do this for y = weight, x_1 = height, and x_2 = percent body fat, we get

$$\hat{y} = -121.0 + 3.50x_1 + 1.35x_2.$$

Recall

The multiple regression equation using all three predictors was

$$\hat{y} = -97.7 + 3.43x_1 + 1.36x_2 - 0.96x_3.$$

The effects of height and percent body fat are similar in the equation without x_3 = age. ◀

For the simpler model, $R^2 = 0.66$. This is nearly as large as the value of $R^2 = 0.67$ with age also in the model. The predictions of weight are essentially as good without age in the model.

When you have several potential explanatory variables for a multiple regression model, how do you decide which ones to include? As just mentioned, the lack of statistical and practical significance is one criterion for deleting a term from the model. Many other possible criteria can also be considered. Most regression software has automatic procedures that successively add or delete predictor variables from models according to criteria such as statistical significance. Three of the most common procedures are **backward elimination**, **forward selection**, and **stepwise regression**. It is possible that all three procedures result in identical models; however, this is not always the case. In a situation where you must choose between models it is best to look at R^2 values and sensibility of model. These procedures must be used with great caution. There is no guarantee that the final model chosen is sensible. Model selection requires quite a bit of statistical sophistication, and for applications with many potential explanatory variables we recommend that you seek guidance from a statistician.

Caution

Procedures for regression model selection must be used with care. Consultation with a trained statistician is recommended. ◀

13.3 Practicing the Basics

13.20 Predicting GPA For the 59 observations in the Georgia Student Survey data file on the book's website, the result of regressing college GPA on high school GPA and study time follows.

TRY

```
Regression Equation
CGPA = 1.126 + 0.643 HSGPA + 0.0078 Studytime
Coefficients
```

Term	Coef	SE Coef	T-Value	P-Value
Constant	1.126	0.569	1.98	0.053
HSGPA	0.643	0.146	4.41	0.000
Studytime	0.0078	0.0161	0.48	0.633

Model Summary

S	R-sq
0.318824	25.82%

a. Explain in nontechnical terms what it means if the population slope coefficient for high school GPA equals 0.

b. Show all steps for testing the hypothesis that this slope equals 0.

13.21 Study time help GPA? Refer to the previous exercise.

a. Report and interpret the P-value for testing the hypothesis that the population slope coefficient for study time equals 0.

b. Find a 95% confidence interval for the true slope for study time. Explain how the result is in accord with the result of the test in part a.

c. Does the result in part a imply that in the corresponding population, study time has no association with college GPA? Explain. (*Hint:* What is the impact of also having HSGPA in the model?)

13.22 Variability in college GPA Refer to the previous two exercises.

TRY

a. Report the residual standard deviation. What does this describe?

b. Interpret the residual standard deviation by predicting where approximately 95% of the Georgia college GPAs fall when high school GPA = 3.80 and study time = 5.0 hours per day, which are the sample means.

13.23 Does leg press help predict body strength? Chapter 12 analyzed strength data for 57 female high school athletes. Upper body strength was summarized by the maximum number of pounds the athlete could bench press (denoted maxBP). This was predicted well by the number of times she could do a 60-pound bench press (denoted BP60). Can we predict maxBP even better if we also know how many times an athlete can perform a 200-pound leg press? The table shows results after adding this second predictor (denoted LP200) to the model.

Term	Coef	SE Coef	T-Value	P-Value
Constant	60.60	2.87	21.10	0.000
BP60	1.332	0.188	7.10	0.000
LP200	0.211	0.152	1.39	0.171

Analysis of Variance

Source	DF	Adj SS	Adj MS	F-Value	P-Value
Regression	2	6473.3	3236.65	51.39	0.000
Error	54	3401.3	62.99		
Total	56	9874.6			

a. Does LP200 have a significant effect on maxBP if BP60 is also in the model? Show all steps of a significance test to answer this.

b. Show that the 95% confidence interval for the slope for LP200 equals 0.21 $\pm$ 0.30, roughly $(-0.1, 0.5)$. Based on this interval, does LP200 seem to have a strong impact, or a weak impact, on predicting maxBP if BP60 is also in the model?

c. Given that LP200 is in the model, provide evidence from a significance test that shows why it *does* help to add BP60 to the model.

13.24 Leg press uncorrelated with strength? The P-value of 0.17 in part a of the previous exercise suggests that LP200 plausibly had no effect on maxBP once BP60 is in the model. Yet when LP200 is the sole predictor of BP, the correlation is 0.58 and the significance test for its effect has a P-value of 0.000, suggesting very strong evidence of an effect. Explain why this is not a contradiction.

13.25 Interpret strength variability Refer to the previous two exercises. The sample standard deviation of maxBP was 13.3. The residual standard deviation of maxBP when BP60 and LP200 are predictors in a multiple regression model is 7.9.

a. Explain the difference between the interpretations of these two standard deviations.

b. If the conditional distributions of maxBP are approximately bell shaped, explain why most maximum bench press values fall within about 16 pounds of the regression equation when the predictors BP60 and LP200 are near their sample mean values.

c. At BP60 = 11 and LP200 = 22, which are close to the sample mean values, software reports $\hat{y} = 80$ and a 95% prediction interval of 80 $\pm$ 16, or (64, 96). Is this interval an inference about where the population maxBP values fall or where the population *mean* of the maxBP values fall (for subjects having BP60 = 11 and LP200 = 22)? Explain.

d. Refer to part c. Would it be unusual for a female athlete with these predictor values to be able to bench press more than 100 pounds? Why?

13.26 Any predictive power? Refer to the previous three exercises.

TRY

a. State and interpret the null hypothesis tested with the *F* statistic in the ANOVA table given in Exercise 13.23.

b. From the *F* table (Table D), which *F* statistic value would have a P-value of 0.05 for these data?

c. Report the observed *F* test statistic and its P-value. Interpret the P-value, and make a decision for a 0.05 significance level. Explain in nontechnical terms what the result of the test means.

13.27 Predicting pizza revenue Aunt Erma's Pizza restaurant keeps monthly records of total revenue, amount spent on TV advertising, and amount spent on newspaper advertising.

a. Specify notation and formulate a multiple regression equation for predicting the monthly revenue. Explain how to interpret the parameters in the equation.

b. State the null hypothesis that you would test if you want to analyze whether TV advertising is helpful, for a given amount of newspaper advertising.

c. State the null hypothesis that you would test if you want to analyze whether *at least one* of the sources of advertising has some effect on monthly revenue.

13.28 Regression for mental health A study in Alachua County, Florida, investigated an index of mental health impairment, which had $\bar{y} = 27.3$ and $s = 5.5$. Two explanatory variables were x_1 = life events score (mean = 44.4, $s = 22.6$) and x_2 = SES (socioeconomic status, mean = 56.6, $s = 25.3$). Life events is a composite measure of the number and severity of major life events, such as death in the family, that the subject experienced within the past three years. SES is a composite index based on occupation, income, and education. The table shows data for 6 subjects. The complete data[1] for a random sample of 40 adults in the county is in the Mental Health data file on the book's website. Some regression results are also shown.

a. Find the 95% confidence interval for β_1.

b. Explain why the interval in part a means that an increase of 100 units in life events corresponds to anywhere from a 4- to 17-unit increase in mean mental impairment, controlling for SES. (This lack of precision reflects the small sample size.)

y = mental impairment, x_1 = life events index, and x_2 = socioeconomic status

y	x_1	x_2	y	x_1	x_2	y	x_1	x_2
17	46	84	26	50	40	30	44	53
19	39	97	26	48	52	31	35	38

```
Coefficients
Term          Coef      SE Coef    T-Value    P-Value
Constant      28.23     2.17       12.98      0.000
life          0.1033    0.0325     3.18       0.003
ses          -0.0975    0.0291    -3.35       0.002
Model Summary
      S         R-sq
4.55644     33.92%

Analysis of Variance
Source       DF    SS       MS       F-Value   P-Value
Regression    2    394.2    197.12   9.49      0.000
Error        37    768.2    20.76
Total        39   1162.4
```

13.29 Mental health again Refer to the previous exercise.

a. Report the test statistic and P-value for testing H_0: $\beta_1 = \beta_2 = 0$.

b. State the alternative hypothesis that is supported by the result in part a.

c. Does the result in part a imply that necessarily *both* life events and SES are needed in the model? Explain.

13.30 More predictors for selling price The MINITAB results are shown for predicting selling price using x_1 = size of home, x_2 = number of bedrooms, and x_3 = age.

[1] Based on a larger survey reported in a Ph.D. thesis by C. E. Holzer III at University of Florida.

```
Regression Equation

Price = 80489 + 62.65 House Size + 13543
Bedrooms - 418 Age

Coefficients

Term          Coef    SE Coef   T-Value   P-Value
Constant      80489   21810      3.69     0.000
House Size    62.65    4.73     13.24     0.000
Bedrooms      13543    5380      2.52     0.013
Age           -418      236     -1.77     0.078
```

a. State the null hypothesis for an F test, in the context of these variables.
b. The F statistic equals 74.23, with P-value = 0.000. Interpret.
c. Explain in nontechnical terms what you learn from the results of the t tests reported in the table for the three explanatory variables.

13.31 House prices Use software to do further analyses with the multiple regression model of y = selling price of home in thousands, x_1 = size of home, and x_2 = number of bedrooms, considered in Section 13.1. The data file House Selling Prices OR is on the book's website.

TECH

a. Report the F statistic and state the hypotheses to which it refers. Report its P-value and interpret. Why is it not surprising to get a small P-value for this test?
b. Report and interpret the t statistic and P-value for testing H_0: $\beta_2 = 0$ against H_a: $\beta_2 > 0$.
c. Construct a 95% confidence interval for β_2 and interpret. This inference is more informative than the test in part b. Explain why.

13.4 Checking a Regression Model Using Residual Plots

In capsule form, recall that the three assumptions for inference with a multiple regression model are that (1) the regression equation approximates the true relationship between the predictors and the mean of y (that is, straight-line relationships between the mean of y and each explanatory variable, at fixed values of the other explanatory variables), (2) the data were gathered randomly, and (3) y has a normal distribution with the same standard deviation at each combination of predictors. Now, let's see how to check the assumptions about the regression equation and the distribution of y.

For simple linear regression, the 2-dimensional scatterplot provides a simple visual check of whether the straight-line model is appropriate. For multiple regression, a plot of all the variables at once would require many dimensions. So instead, we study how the predicted values $\hat{y}$ from the multiple regression model compare to the observed values y. This is done using the residuals, $y - \hat{y}$.

Checking Shape and Detecting Unusual Observations

Recall

As discussed in Section 12.4, software can plot a histogram of the residuals or the *standardized residuals*, which are the residuals divided by their standard errors. ◀

Consider first the assumption that the conditional distribution of y is normal at any fixed values of the explanatory variables. If this is true, the residuals, which measure the deviations from the mean of y as predicted by the regression equation, should have approximately a bell-shaped histogram. When standardized, nearly all of them should fall between about -3 and $+3$. A standardized residual below -3 or above $+3$ indicates a potential regression outlier.

When some observations have large standardized residuals, you should think about whether there is an explanation. Often this merely reflects skew in the conditional distribution of y, with a long tail in one direction. Other times the observations differ from the others on a variable that was not included in the model. Once that variable is added, those observations cease to be so unusual. For instance, suppose the data file from the weight study of Examples 4–7 also contained observations for a few males. Then we might have observed a few y values considerably above the others and with very large positive standardized residuals. These residuals would probably diminish considerably once the model also included gender as a predictor.

Histogram of Residuals

Example 8

House Selling Price

Picture the Scenario

For the House Selling Price OR data set (Examples 1–3), Figure 13.4 is a MINITAB histogram of the standardized residuals for the multiple regression model predicting selling price by the house size and the number of bedrooms.

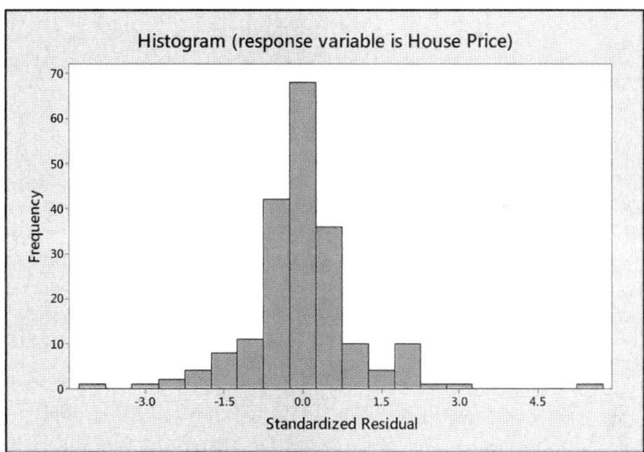

▲ **Figure 13.4** Histogram of Standardized Residuals for Multiple Regression Model Predicting Selling Price. **Question** Give an example of a shape for this histogram that would indicate that a few observations are highly unusual.

Question to Explore

What does Figure 13.4 tell you? Interpret.

Think It Through

The distribution of the standardized residuals looks roughly bell shaped, and almost all of them fall between −3 and 3. This indicates that the normal assumption for the distribution of the price of the house at given predictor settings is reasonable.

Insight

When n is small, don't make the mistake of reading too much into such plots. We're mainly looking for dramatic departures from normality and highly unusual observations that stand apart from the others.

► ***Try Exercise 13.32***

Two-sided inferences about slope parameters are *robust.* The normality assumption is not as important as the assumption that the regression equation approximates the true relationship between the predictors and the mean of y. We consider this assumption and the assumption that the standard deviation of y is constant next.

Plotting Residuals Against Each Explanatory Variable

Plots of the residuals against each explanatory variable help us check for potential problems with the regression model. We discuss this in terms of x_1, but you should view a plot for each predictor. Ideally, the residuals should fluctuate randomly about the horizontal line at 0, as in Figure 13.5a. There should be no obvious change in trend or change in variation as the values of x_1 increase.

By contrast, a pattern of the residuals as in Figure 13.5b suggests that y is actually *nonlinearly* related to x_1. It suggests that y tends to be *below* $\hat{y}$ for very small and very large x_1 values (giving negative residuals) and *above* $\hat{y}$ for medium-sized x_1 values (giving positive residuals).

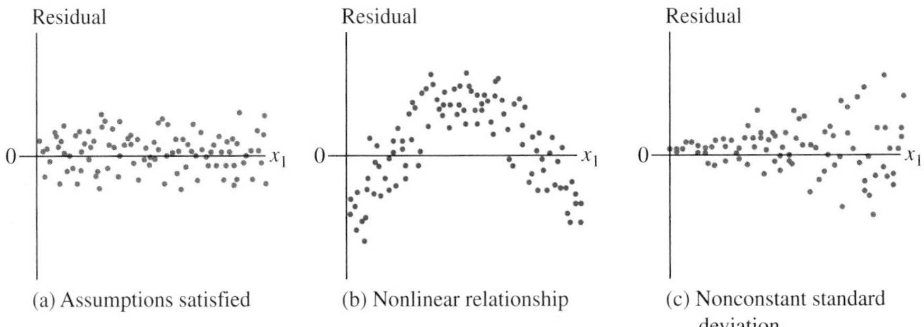

▲ **Figure 13.5** Possible Patterns for Residuals, Plotted Against an Explanatory Variable. **Question** Why does the pattern in (b) suggest that the effect of x_1 is not linear?

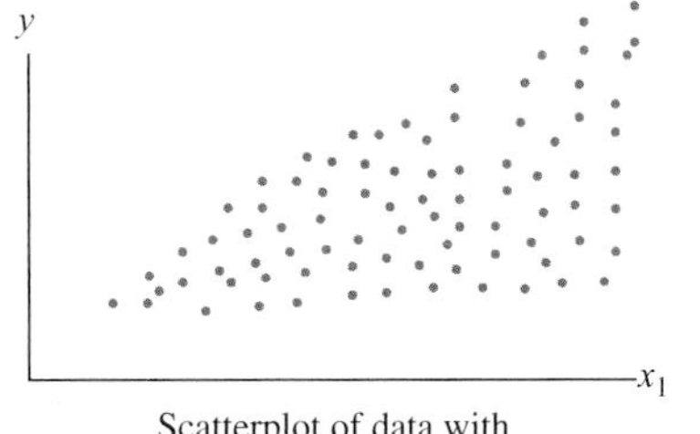

Scatterplot of data with nonconstant variance

Another common occurrence is that the variability in the residuals increases as x_1 increases, as seen in Figure 13.5c. A pattern like this indicates that the standard deviation of y is not constant—the response variable displays more variability at larger values of x_1 (see the margin figure). Two-sided inferences about slope parameters still perform well. However, ordinary prediction intervals are invalid. The width of such intervals is similar at relatively high and relatively low x_1 values, but in reality, observations on y are displaying more variability at high x_1 values than at low x_1 values.

Figure 13.5a suggests that y is linearly related to x_1. It also suggests that the variability in y stays constant across the entire range of x_1 values and doesn't increase or decrease as x_1 changes. Therefore, Assumption 1 and part of Assumption 3 are met.

In Practice Use Caution in Interpreting Residual Patterns

Residual patterns are often not as neat as the ones in Figure 13.5. Be careful not to let a single outlier or ordinary sampling variability overly influence your reading of a pattern from the plot.

Example 9

Plotting residuals

House Selling Price

Picture the Scenario

For the House Selling Price OR data set, Figure 13.6 is a residual plot for the multiple regression model relating selling price to house size and to number of bedrooms. It plots the standardized residuals against house size.

Question to Explore

Does this plot suggest any irregularities with the model?

Think It Through

The residual plot does not show any clear trend, so the assumption about a linear relationship between price and size of a house (for given number of bedrooms) seems reasonable. However, as house size increases, the variability of the standardized residuals seems to increase. This suggests more

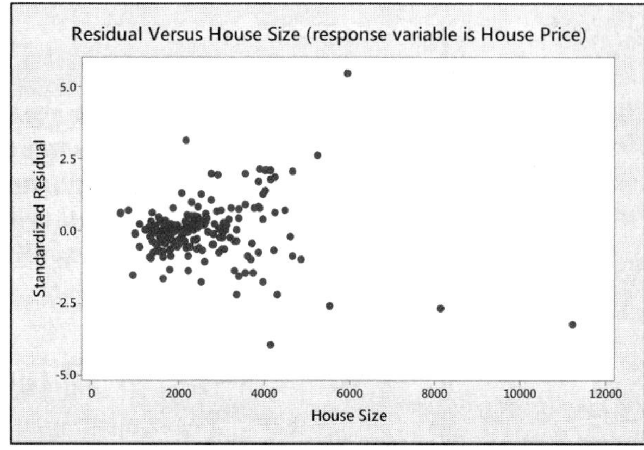

▲ **Figure 13.6** **Standardized Residuals of Selling Price Plotted Against House Size, for Model With House Size and Number of Bedrooms as Predictors. Questions** How does this plot suggest that selling price has more variability at higher house size values, for given number of bedrooms? You don't see number of bedrooms on the plot, so how do its values affect the analysis?

variability in selling prices when house size is larger, for a given number of bedrooms. We must be cautious, though, because the few points with large negative residuals for the largest houses and the one point with a large positive residual may catch our eyes more than the others. Generally, it's not a good idea to allow a few points to overly influence your judgment about the shape of a residual pattern, but here the variability of the residuals around a size of 4000 square feet seems to be a bit larger than at, say, 2000 square feet. A larger data set would provide more evidence about this.

Insight

Nonconstant variability does not invalidate the use of multiple regression. It would, however, make us cautious about using prediction intervals. We would expect predictions about selling price to have smaller prediction errors when house size is small than when house size is large.

▶ ***Try Exercise 13.33***

We have seen several examples illustrating the components of multiple regression analysis. A summary of the entire process of multiple regression follows.

SUMMARY: The Process of Multiple Regression

Steps should include:

1. Identify response and potential explanatory variables
2. Create a multiple regression model; perform appropriate tests (F and t) to see if and which explanatory variables have a statistically significant effect in predicting y
3. Plot y versus $\hat{y}$ for resulting models and find R and R^2 values
4. Check assumptions (residual plot, randomization, histogram of standardized residuals)
5. Choose appropriate model
6. Create confidence intervals for slope
7. Make predictions at specified levels of explanatory variables
8. Create prediction intervals

13.4 Practicing the Basics

13.32 Body weight residuals Examples 4–7 used multiple regression to predict total body weight of college athletes in terms of height, percent body fat, and age. The following figure shows a histogram of the standardized residuals resulting from fitting this model.

a. About which distribution do these give you information—the overall distribution of weight or the conditional distribution of weight at fixed values of the predictors?

b. What does the histogram suggest about the likely shape of this distribution? Why?

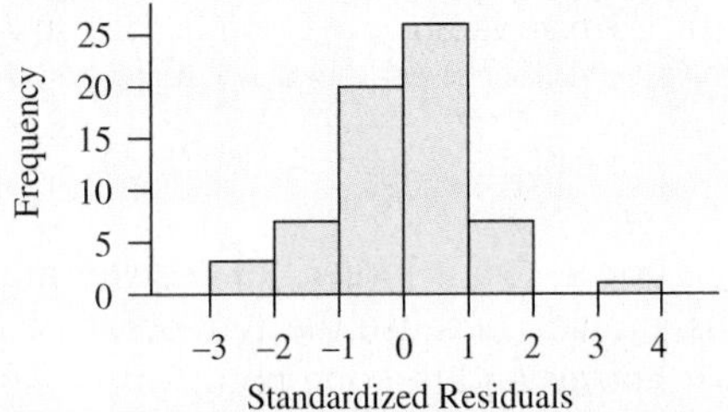

13.33 Strength residuals In Chapter 12, we analyzed strength data for a sample of female high school athletes. The following figure is a residual plot for the multiple regression model relating the maximum number of pounds the athlete could bench press (maxBP) to the number of 60-pound bench presses (BP60) and the number of 200-pound leg presses (LP200). It plots the standardized residuals against the values of LP200.

a. You don't see BP60 on the plot, so how do its values affect the analysis?

b. Explain how the plot might suggest less variability at the lower values of LP200.

c. Suppose you remove the three points with standardized residuals around −2. Then is the evidence about variability in part b so clear? What does this suggest about cautions in looking at residual plots?

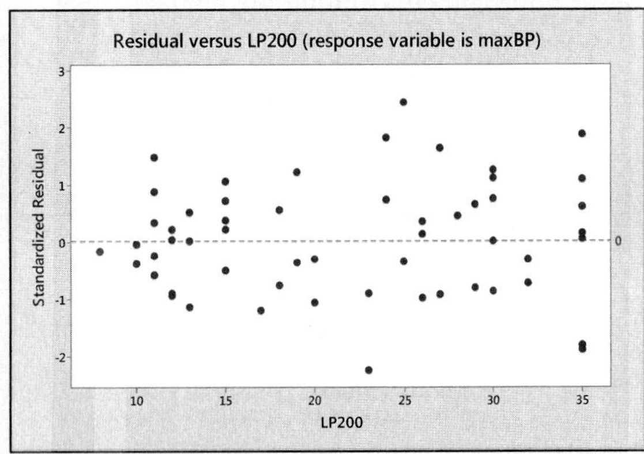

13.34 More residuals for strength Refer to the previous exercise. The following figure is a residual plot for the model relating maximum bench press to LP200 and BP60. It plots the standardized residuals against the values of BP60. Does this plot suggest any irregularities with the model? Explain.

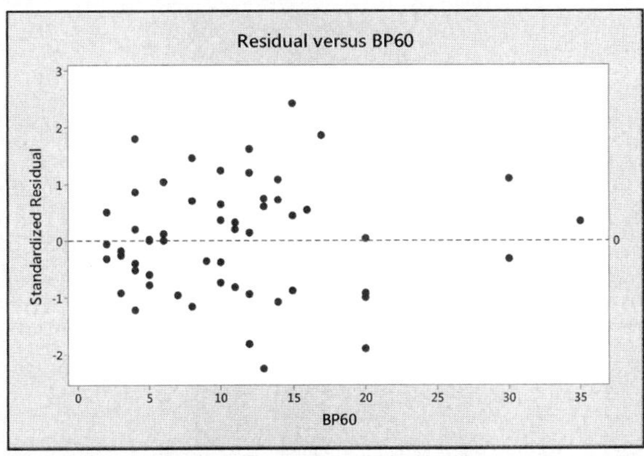

13.35 Nonlinear effects of age Suppose you fit a straight-line regression model to y = amount of time sleeping per day and x = age of subject. Values of y in the sample tend to be quite large for young children and for elderly people, and they tend to be lower for other people. Sketch what you would expect to observe for (a) the scatterplot of x and y and (b) a plot of the residuals against the values of age.

13.36 Driving accidents Suppose you fit a straight-line regression model to x = age of subjects and y = driving accident rate. Sketch what you would expect to observe for (a) the scatterplot of x and y and (b) a plot of the residuals against the values of age.

13.37 Why inspect residuals? When we use multiple regression, what's the purpose of doing a residual analysis? Why can't we just construct a single plot of the data for all the variables at once to tell whether the model is reasonable?

13.38 College athletes The College Athletes data set on the book's website comes from a study of University of Georgia female athletes. Using the column names from the data set, the response variable 1RM = maximum bench press has explanatory variables LBM = lean body mass (which is weight times 1 minus the proportion of body fat) and REPS70 = number of repetitions before fatigue with a 70-pound bench press. Let's look at all the steps of a regression analysis for these data.

a. The first figure shows a scatterplot matrix. Which two plots in the figure describe the associations with 1RM as a response variable? Describe those associations.

b. Results of a multiple regression analysis are shown. Write down the prediction equation and interpret the coefficient of REPS70.

c. Report R^2 and interpret its value in the context of these variables.

d. Based on the value of R^2, report and interpret the multiple correlation.

e. Interpret results of the F test that 1RM is independent of these two predictors. Show how to obtain the F statistic from the mean squares in the ANOVA table.

f. Once REPS70 is in the model, does it help to have LBM as a second predictor? Answer by showing all steps of a significance test for a regression parameter.

g. Examine the histogram shown of the residuals for the multiple regression model. What does this describe, and what does it suggest?

h. Examine the plot shown of the residuals plotted against values of REPS70. What does this describe, and what does it suggest?

i. From the plot in part h, can you identify a subject whose 1RM value was considerably lower than expected based on the predictor values? Identify by indicating the approximate values of REPS70 and the standardized residual for that subject.

```
Regression Equation
1RM = 55.01 + 0.1668 LBM + 1.658 REPS70
Coefficients
Term          Coef    SE Coef   T-Value   P-Value
Constant     55.01       7.74      7.11     0.000
LBM         0.1668     0.0752      2.22     0.030
REPS70       1.658      0.109     15.21     0.000
Model Summary
      S       R-sq
7.11957     83.17%
Analysis of Variance
Source        DF      SS       MS    F-Value   P-Value
Regression     2   15283   7641.5     150.75     0.000
Error         61    3092     50.7
Total         63   18375
```

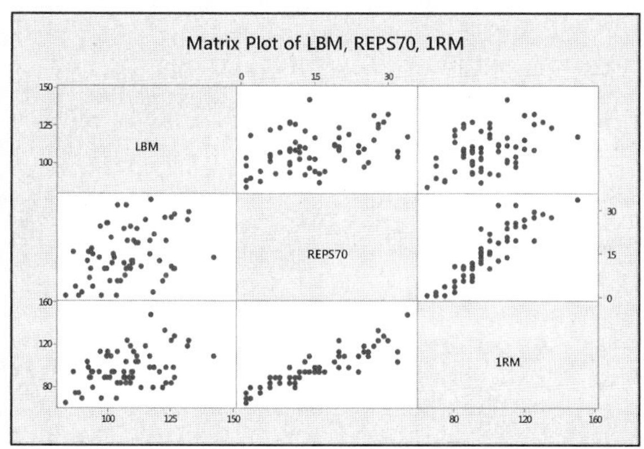

Scatterplot matrix for Exercise 13.38.

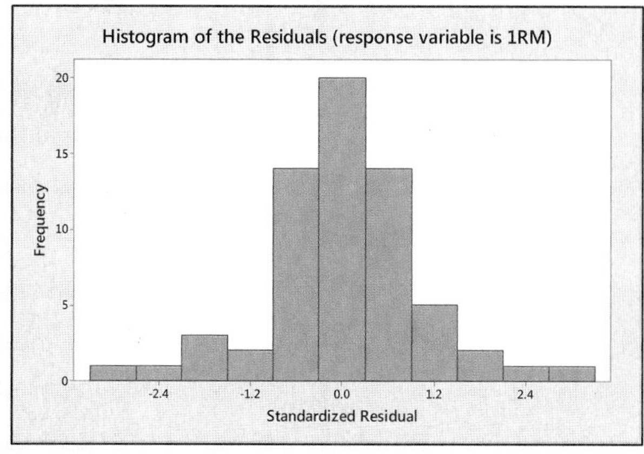

Residual plot for Exercise 13.38, part g.

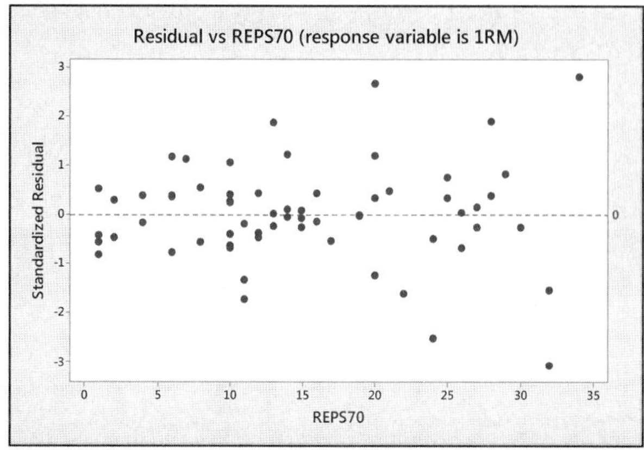

Residual plot for Exercise 13.38, part h.

13.39 House prices Use software with the House Selling Prices OR data file on the book's website to do residual analyses with the multiple regression model for y = house selling price (in thousands), x_1 = lot size, and x_2 = number of bathrooms.

a. Find a histogram of the standardized residuals. What assumption does this check? What do you conclude from the plot?

b. Plot the standardized residuals against the lot size. What does this check? What do you conclude from the plot?

13.40 Selling prices level off In the previous exercise, suppose house selling price tends to increase with a straight-line trend for small to medium size lots, but then levels off as lot size gets large, for a fixed value of number of bathrooms. Sketch the pattern you'd expect to get if you plotted the residuals against lot size. What assumption of the multiple regression model is violated?

13.5 Regression and Categorical Predictors

So far, we've studied regression models for quantitative variables. Next, we'll learn how to include a *categorical explanatory* variable. The final section shows how to perform regression for a *categorical response* variable.

Indicator Variables

Regression models specify categories of a categorical explanatory variable using artificial variables called **indicator variables.** The indicator variable for a particular category is binary. It equals 1 if the observation falls into that category, and it equals 0 otherwise.

In the house selling prices (Oregon) data set, the condition of the house is a categorical variable. It was measured with categories (good, not good). The indicator variable x for condition is

$$x = 1 \text{ if house in good condition}$$
$$x = 0 \text{ otherwise.}$$

This indicator variable indicates whether a home is in good condition. Let's see how an indicator variable works in a regression equation. To start, suppose condition is the only predictor of selling price. The simple regression model is then $\mu_y = \alpha + \beta x$, with x as just defined. Substituting the possible values 1 and 0 for x,

$$\mu_y = \alpha + \beta(1) = \alpha + \beta, \text{ if house is in good condition (so } x = 1)$$
$$\mu_y = \alpha + \beta(0) = \alpha, \quad \text{ if house is not in good condition (so } x = 0).$$

The difference between the mean selling price for houses in good condition and houses in not good condition is

$$(\mu_y \text{ when } x = 1) - (\mu_y \text{ when } x = 0) = (\alpha + \beta) - \alpha = \beta.$$

The coefficient β of the indicator variable x is the difference between the mean selling prices for houses in good condition and for houses in not good condition.

Example 10

Indicator variables ◄

Including House Condition in Multiple Regression for Selling Price

Picture the Scenario

Let's now fit a multiple regression model for y = selling price of house using x_1 = house size and x_2 = condition of the house. Table 13.11 shows MINITAB output when fitting the model $\mu_y = \alpha + \beta_1 x_1 + \beta_2 x_2$.

Table 13.11 Regression Analysis of y = Selling Price Using x_1 = House Size and x_2 = Indicator Variable for Condition (Good, Not Good)

The regression equation is

Price = 96271 + 66.5 House Size + 12927 Condition

Term	Coef	SE Coef	T-Value	P-Value
Constant	96271	13465	7.15	0.000
House Size	66.463	4.682	14.20	0.000
Condition	12927	17197	0.75	0.453

S = 81787.4 R-Sq = 50.6%

Questions to Explore

a. Find and plot the lines showing how the predicted selling price varies as a function of house size for houses in good condition and for houses in not good condition.

b. Interpret the coefficient of the indicator variable for condition.

Think It Through

a. Table 13.11 reports the prediction equation,

$$\hat{y} = 96{,}271 + 66.5x_1 + 12{,}927x_2.$$

For houses not in good condition, $x_2 = 0$. The prediction equation for y = selling price using x_1 = house size then simplifies to

$$\hat{y} = 96{,}271 + 66.5x_1 + 12{,}927(0) = 96{,}271 + 66.5x_1.$$

For houses in good condition, $x_2 = 1$. The prediction equation then simplifies to

$$\hat{y} = 96{,}271 + 66.5x_1 + 12{,}927(1) = 109{,}198 + 66.5x_1.$$

Both lines have the same slope, 66.5. For houses in either condition, the predicted selling price increases by \$66.5 for each square-foot increase in house size. Figure 13.7 plots the two prediction equations. The quantitative explanatory variable, house size, is on the x-axis. The figure portrays a separate line for each category of condition (good, not good).

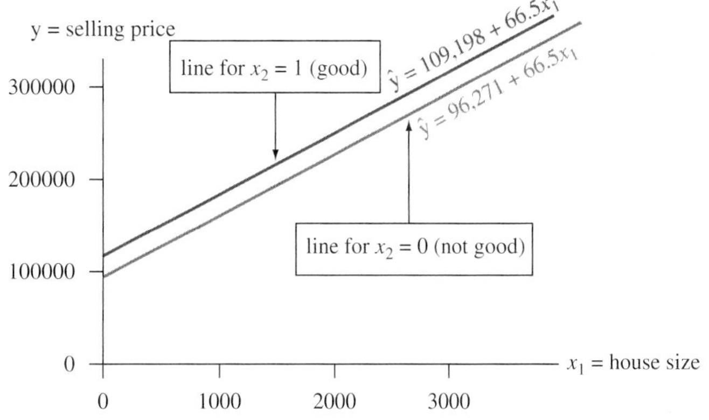

▲ **Figure 13.7 Plot of Equation Relating $\hat{y}$ = Predicted Selling Price to x_1 = House Size, According to x_2 = Condition (1 = Good, 0 = Not Good). Question** Why are the lines parallel?

b. At a fixed value of x_1 = house size, the difference between the predicted selling prices for houses in good ($x_2 = 1$) versus not good ($x_2 = 0$) condition is

$$(109{,}198 + 66.5x_1) - (96{,}271 + 66.5x_1) = 12{,}927.$$

This is precisely the coefficient of the indicator variable, x_2. For any fixed value of house size, we predict that the selling price is \$12,927 higher for houses that are in good condition compared to those that are in not good condition.

Insight

Since the two lines have the same slope, they are parallel. The line for houses in good condition is above the other line because its y-intercept is larger. This means that for any fixed value of house size, the predicted selling price is higher for houses in good condition. The P-value of 0.453 for the test H_0: $\beta_2 = 0$ for the coefficient of the indicator variable suggests that this difference is not statistically significant.

► ***Try Exercise 13.41***

A categorical variable having more than two categories uses an additional indicator variable for each category. For instance, assume that we measured condition with the three categories "good," "average," and "poor" instead of just using the two categories "good" and "not good." Then, instead of just including one indicator variable x_2 in the multiple regression model as in Example 10, we would need to include (in addition to x_1 for house size) two indicator variables, x_2 and x_3, with

$$x_2 = 1 \text{ for houses in good condition, and } x_2 = 0 \text{ otherwise,}$$
$$x_3 = 1 \text{ for houses in average condition, and } x_3 = 0 \text{ otherwise,}$$

If $x_2 = x_3 = 0$, the house is neither in good condition nor in average condition, so it must be in poor condition. Therefore, we don't need a third indicator variable for coding houses in poor condition because this is already determined by the settings of the first two indicator variables. That is, we can tell whether a house is in poor condition merely from seeing the values of x_2 and x_3. Generally, *a categorical explanatory variable in a regression model uses one fewer indicator variable than the number of categories.* For instance, with the two categories (good, not good) condition, we needed only a single indicator variable, whereas for the three categories (good, fair, poor) condition, we needed two indicator variables.

Why can't we specify the three categories merely by setting up a variable x that equals 1 for homes in good condition, 0 for homes in average condition, and say, −1 for poor condition? Because this would treat condition as *quantitative* rather than *categorical.* It would treat condition as if different categories corresponded to different *amounts* of the variable. But the variable measures *which* condition, not *how much* condition. Treating it as quantitative is inappropriate.

Determining Whether Interaction Exists

In Example 10, the regression equation simplified to two straight lines:

$$\hat{y} = 109{,}198 + 66.5x_1 \text{ for houses in good condition,}$$
$$\hat{y} = 96{,}271 + 66.5x_1 \text{ for houses in not good conditions.}$$

Both equations have the same slope. The model forces the effect of x_1 = house size on selling price to be the same for both conditions. For houses in either condition, the predicted selling price increases by \$66.5 for every additional square foot in size.

More generally, in a multiple regression model, *the slope of the relationship between the population mean of y and each explanatory variable is identical for all values of the other explanatory variables.* Such models are sometimes too simple. The effect of an explanatory variable may change considerably as the value of another explanatory variable in the model changes. The multiple regression models we've considered so far assume this does not happen. When it does happen, there is **interaction**.

Interaction

For two explanatory variables, **interaction** exists when the slope of the linear relationship between μ_y and one explanatory variable changes as the other explanatory variable changes.

Suppose the *actual* population relationship between x_1 = house size and the mean selling price is

$$\mu_y = 100{,}000 + 50x_1 \text{ for houses in good condition,}$$

and

$$\mu_y = 80{,}000 + 35x_1 \text{ for houses in not good condition.}$$

The slope of the regression line between the mean selling price μ_y and the size of the house x_1 changes (from 50 to 35) when x_2 changes from 1 to 0, that is, from considering houses in good condition to houses in not good condition. There is then interaction between house size and condition in their effects on selling price. The mean price increases by $50 for every one square foot increase in size for houses in good condition but only by $35 for houses in not good condition. Figure 13.8 illustrates the different slopes.

How can you allow for interaction when you do a regression analysis? With two explanatory variables, one quantitative and one categorical (as in Example 10), you can fit a separate line with a different slope for each category of the categorical variable.

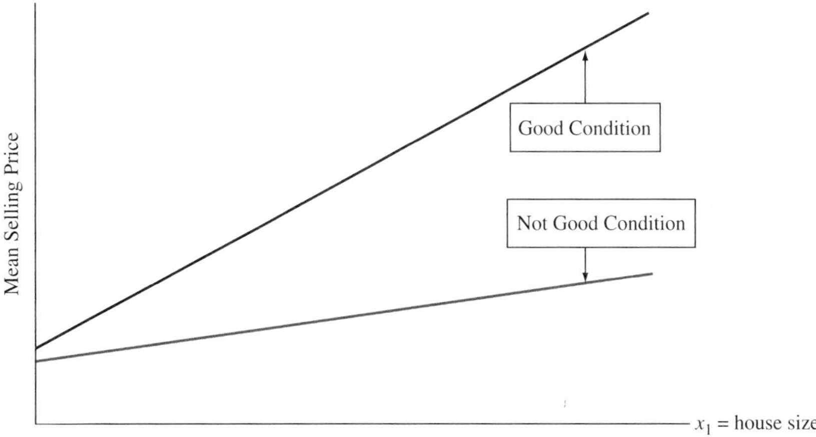

▲ **Figure 13.8 An Example of Interaction.** There's a larger slope between selling price and house size for houses in good condition than in not good conditions.

Example 11

Comparing Winning High Jumps for Men and Women

Picture the Scenario

Men have competed in the high jump in the Olympics since 1896 and women since 1928. Figure 13.9 shows how the winning high jump in the Olympics has changed over time for men and women. The High Jump data file on the book's website contains the winning heights for each year up to 2012. A multiple regression analysis of y = winning height (in meters) as a function of x_1 = number of years since 1928 (when women first participated in the high jump) and x_2 = gender (1 = male, 0 = female) gives $\hat{y} = 1.63 + 0.0056x_1 + 0.35x_2$.

Questions to Explore

a. Interpret the coefficient of year and the coefficient of gender in the equation.

b. To allow interaction, we can fit equations separately to the data for males and the data for females. We then get $\hat{y} = 1.98 + 0.0054x_1$ for males and $\hat{y} = 1.60 + 0.0062x_1$ for females. Describe the interaction by comparing slopes.

c. Describe the interaction allowed in part b by comparing predicted winning high jumps for males and females in 1928 and in 2012.

Recall

These data were first analyzed in Example 11 in Chapter 3. ◀

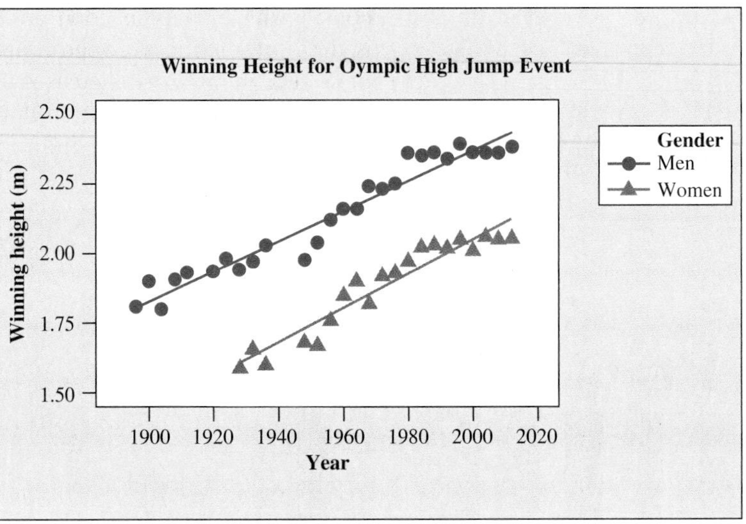

▲ **Figure 13.9** Scatterplot for the Winning High Jumps (in Meters) in the Olympic Games from 1896–2012.

Think It Through

a. For the prediction equation $\hat{y} = 1.63 + 0.0056x_1 + 0.35x_2$, the coefficient of year is 0.0056. For each gender, the predicted winning high jump increases by 0.0056 meters per year. This seems small, but over fifty years, it projects to an increase of $50(0.0056) = 0.28$ meters, about 11 inches. The model does not allow interaction because it assumes that the slope of 0.0056 is the same for each gender. The coefficient of gender is 0.35. In a given year, the predicted winning high jump for men is 0.35 meters higher than for women. Because this model does not allow interaction, the predicted difference between men and women is the same each year.

b. The slope of 0.0062 for females is higher than the slope of 0.0054 for males. So the predicted winning high jump increases a bit more for females than for males over this time period.

c. In 1928, $x_1 = 0$, and the predicted winning high jump was $\hat{y} = 1.98 + 0.0054(0) = 1.98$ for males and $\hat{y} = 1.60 + 0.0062(0) = 1.60$ for females, a difference of 0.38 meters. In 2012, $x_1 = 2012 - 1928 = 84$ and the predicted winning high jump was $1.98 + 0.0054(84) = 2.43$ for males and $1.60 + 0.0062(84) = 2.12$ for females, a difference of 0.31 meters. The predicted difference between the winning high jumps of males and females decreased a bit between 1928 and 2012.

Insight

When we allow interaction, the estimated slope is a bit higher for females than for males. This is what caused the difference in predicted winning high jumps to be less in 2012 than in 1928. However, the slopes were not dramatically different, as shown by the fitted regression lines for each gender superimposed in Figure 13.9. The observed degree of interaction was not strong.

▶ ***Try Exercises 13.47 and 13.48***

How do we know whether the interaction shown by the sample is sufficiently large to indicate that there is interaction in the population? There is a significance test for checking this, but it is beyond the scope of this book. In practice, it's usually adequate to investigate interaction informally by using graphics. For example, suppose there are two predictors, one quantitative and one categorical. Then you can plot y against the quantitative predictor, identifying the data points by the category of the categorical variable, as we did in Example 11. Do the points seem to go up or go down at quite different rates, taking into account sampling error? If so, it's safer to fit a separate regression line for each category, which then allows different slopes.

13.5 Practicing the Basics

13.41 U.S. and foreign used cars Refer to the used car data file from Exercise 13.11. The prediction equation relating y = selling price of used car (in \$) as a function of x_1 = age of car and x_2 = type of car (1 = US, 0 = Foreign) is $\hat{y} = 20{,}493 - 1{,}185x_1 - 2{,}379x_2$.

TRY

a. Using this equation, find the prediction equation relating selling price and age, separately for U.S. and foreign cars.

b. Predict by how much the price changes for a one year increase in the age of the car. Does this apply for both types of cars? Explain.

c. Find the predicted price of a (i) U.S. and (ii) foreign car that is eight years old. Show how the difference between them relates to a parameter estimate for the model.

13.42 Mountain bike prices The Mountain Bike data file on the book's website shows selling prices for mountains bikes. When y = mountain bike price (\$) is regressed on x_1 = weight of bike (lbs) and x_2 = the type of suspension (0 = full, 1 = front end), $\hat{y} = 2{,}741.62 - 53.752x_1 - 643.595x_2$.

a. Interpret the estimated effect of the weight of the bike.

b. Interpret the estimated effect of the type of suspension on the mountain bike.

13.43 Predict using house size and condition For the House Selling Prices OR data set, when we regress y = selling price (in thousands) on x_1 = house size and x_2 = condition (1 = Good, 0 = Not Good), we get the results shown.

Regression of selling price of house in thousands versus house size and condition

Term	Coef	SE Coef	T-Value	P-Value
Constant	96.27	13.46	7.15	0.000
House Size	0.066463	0.004682	14.20	0.000
Condition	12.93	17.20	0.75	0.453

S = 81.7874 R-Sq = 50.6%

a. Report the regression equation. Find and interpret the separate lines relating predicted selling price to house size for good condition homes and for homes in not good condition.

b. Sketch how selling price varies as a function of house size for homes in good condition and for homes in not good condition.

c. Estimate the difference between the mean selling price of homes in good and in not good condition, controlling for house size.

13.44 Quality and productivity The table shows data from 27 automotive plants on y = number of assembly defects per 100 cars and x = time (in hours) to assemble each vehicle. The data are in the Quality and Productivity file on the book's website.

Number of defects in assembling 100 cars and time to assemble each vehicle

Plant	Defects	Time	Plant	Defects	Time	Plant	Defects	Time
1	39	27	10	89	17	19	69	54
2	38	23	11	48	20	20	79	18
3	42	15	12	38	26	21	29	31
4	50	17	13	68	21	22	84	28
5	55	12	14	67	26	23	87	44
6	56	16	15	69	30	24	98	23
7	57	18	16	69	32	25	100	25
8	56	26	17	70	31	26	140	21
9	61	20	18	68	37	27	170	28

Source: Data from S. Chatterjee, M. Handcock, and J. Simonoff, *A Casebook for a First Course in Statistics and Data Analysis* (Wiley, 1995); based on graph in *The Machine That Changed the World*, by J. Womack, D. Jones, and D. Roos (Macmillan, 1990).

a. The prediction equation is $\hat{y} = 61.3 + 0.35x$. Find the predicted number of defects for a car having assembly time (i) 12 hours (the minimum) and (ii) 54 hours (the maximum).

b. The first 11 plants were Japanese facilities and the rest were not. Let x_1 = time to assemble vehicle and x_2 = whether facility is Japanese (1 = yes, 0 = no). The fit of the multiple regression model is $\hat{y} = 105.0 - 0.78x_1 - 36.0x_2$. Interpret the coefficients that estimate the effect of x_1 and the effect of x_2.

c. Explain why part a and part b indicate that Simpson's paradox has occurred.

d. Explain *how* Simpson's paradox occurred. To do this, construct a scatterplot between y and x_1 in which points are identified by whether the facility is Japanese. Note that the Japanese facilities tended to have low values for both x_1 and x_2.

13.45 Predicting hamburger sales A chain restaurant that specializes in selling hamburgers wants to analyze how y = sales for a customer (the total amount spent by a customer on food and drinks, in dollars) depends on the location of the restaurant, which is classified as inner city, suburbia, or at an interstate exit.

a. Construct indicator variables x_1 for inner city and x_2 for suburbia so you can include location in a regression equation for predicting the sales.

b. For part a, suppose $\hat{y} = 5.8 - 0.7x_1 + 1.2x_2$. Find the difference between the estimated mean sales in suburbia and at interstate exits.

13.46 Houses, size, and garage Use the House Selling Prices OR data file on the book's website to regress selling price in thousands on house size and whether the house has a garage.

TECH

a. Report the prediction equation. Find and interpret the equations predicting selling price using house size for homes with and without a garage.

b. How do you interpret the coefficient of the indicator variable for whether the home has a garage?

13.47 House size and garage interact? Refer to the previous exercise.

TRY

a. Explain what the no interaction assumption means for this model.

b. Sketch a hypothetical scatter diagram, showing points identified by garage or no garage, suggesting that there is actually a substantial degree of interaction.

13.48 Equal slopes for car prices? Refer to Exercise 13.41, with $\hat{y}$ = predicted selling price of used car and x_1 = age of car. When equations are fitted *separately* for U.S. and foreign cars, we get $\hat{y} = 23{,}417 - 1{,}715x_1$ for U.S. cars and $\hat{y} = 15{,}536 - 557x_1$ for foreign cars.

TRY

a. In allowing the lines to have different slopes, we allow for an ____________ between age and type of car in their effects on the price. (Fill in the correct word.)

b. Predict by how much the price changes for a one-year increase in the age of the car. Do you need to do this separately for each type of car? Explain.

c. Based on the separate prediction equations, find the predicted price of a (i) U.S. and (ii) foreign car that is eight years old.

13.49 Comparing sales You own a gift shop that has a campus location and a shopping mall location. You want to compare the regressions of y = daily total sales on x = number of people who enter the shop, for total sales listed by day at the campus location and at the mall location. Explain how you can do this using regression modeling

a. With a single model, having an indicator variable for location, that assumes the slopes are the same for each location.

b. With separate models for each location, permitting the slopes to be different.

13.6 Modeling a Categorical Response

The regression models studied so far are designed for a quantitative response variable y. When y is categorical, a different regression model applies, called **logistic regression.** Logistic regression can model

- A voter's choice in an election (Democrat or Republican), with explanatory variables of annual income, political ideology, religious affiliation, and race.
- Whether a credit card holder pays his or her bill on time (yes or no), with explanatory variables of family income and the number of months in the past year that the customer paid the bill on time.

We'll study logistic regression in this section for the special case of a **binary** response variable y.

The Logistic Regression Model

Recall

Section 2.3 (Example 12) showed that the **mean** for a binary variable coded as 0 and 1 is also equal to the **proportion** of 1s. So, if a 1 stands for "success," the mean of y equals the proportion of successes. ◀

Denote the possible outcomes for y by 0 and 1. We'll use the generic terms *failure* and *success* for these outcomes. The population mean of the 0 and 1 scores equals the population *proportion* of 1 outcomes (successes) for the response variable. That is, $\mu_y = p$, where p denotes the population proportion of successes. This proportion also represents the *probability* that a randomly selected subject has a success outcome. The model describes how p depends on the values of the explanatory variables.

For a single explanatory variable, x, Figure 13.10 shows the straight-line regression model

$$p = \alpha + \beta x.$$

This model has the disadvantage that p can be larger than 1 (or smaller than 0) for sufficiently large (small) x values. However, the probability p must fall between 0 and 1. Although the straight-line model may be valid over a restricted range of x-values, it is usually inadequate when there are multiple explanatory variables.

Figure 13.10 also shows a more realistic model. It has a curved, S-shape instead of a straight-line trend. The regression equation that best models this S-shaped curve is known as the **logistic regression equation**.

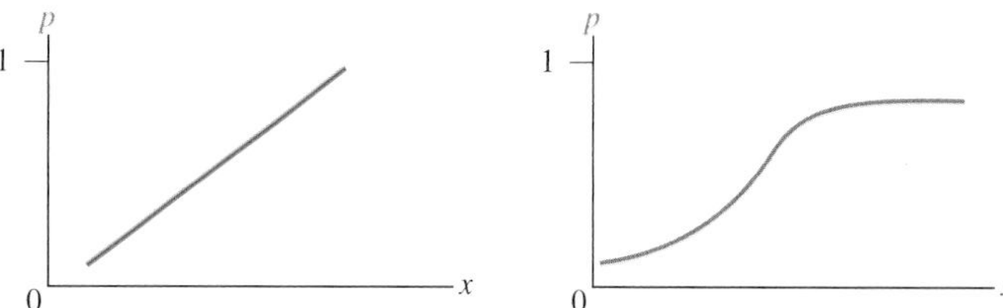

▲ **Figure 13.10** Two Possible Regression Models for a Probability p of a Binary Response Variable. A straight line is usually less appropriate than an S-shaped curve. **Question** Why is the straight-line regression model for a binary response variable often inadequate?

Logistic Regression

A regression equation for an S-shaped curve for the probability of success p is

$$p = \frac{e^{\alpha+\beta x}}{1 + e^{\alpha+\beta x}}.$$

This equation for p is called the **logistic regression** equation. Logistic regression is used when the response variable has only two possible outcomes (it's binary.)

Here, e raised to a power represents the *exponential function* evaluated at that number. Most calculators have an e^x key that provides values of e raised to a power. The model has two parameters, α and β. Since the numerator of the formula for p is smaller than the denominator, the model forces p to fall between 0 and 1. With a regression model having this S-shape, the probability p falls between 0 and 1 for all possible x values.

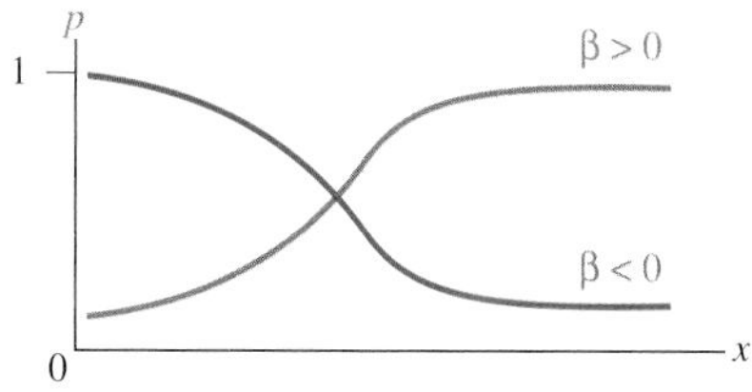

Like the slope of a straight line, the parameter β in this model refers to whether the mean of y increases or decreases as x increases. When $\beta > 0$, the probability p increases as x increases. When $\beta < 0$, the probability p decreases as x increases. See the margin figure. If $\beta = 0$, p does not change as x changes, so the curve flattens to a horizontal straight line. The steepness of the curve increases as the absolute value of β increases. However, unlike in the straight-line model, β is *not* a slope and therefore cannot be interpreted as the change in the mean per one-unit change in x. For this S-shaped curve, the rate at which the curve climbs or descends *changes* over the range of x values.

Software can estimate the parameters α and β in the logistic regression model and find estimated probabilities $\hat{p}$ based on the model fit.

Logistic regression model ◀

Example 12

Travel Credit Cards

Picture the Scenario

An Italian study with 100 randomly selected Italian adults considered factors associated with whether a person has at least one travel credit card. Table 13.12 shows results for the first 15 people on this response variable

and on the person's annual income, in thousands of euros.[2] The complete data set is in the Credit Card and Income data file on the book's website. Let x = annual income and let y = whether the person has a travel credit card $(1 = \text{yes}, 0 = \text{no})$.

Table 13.12 Annual Income (in thousands of euros) and Whether Person Has a Travel Credit Card

The response y equals 1 if a person has a travel credit card and equals 0 otherwise. The complete data set is on the book's website.

Adult	Income	y	Adult	Income	y	Adult	Income	y
1	12	0	6	14	1	11	15	0
2	13	0	7	14	0	12	15	1
3	14	1	8	14	0	13	15	0
4	14	0	9	14	0	14	15	0
5	14	0	10	14	0	15	15	0

Source: Data from R. Piccarreta, Bocconi University, Milan (personal communication).

Questions to Explore

Table 13.13 shows what software provides for conducting a logistic regression analysis.

Table 13.13 Results of Logistic Regression for Italian Credit Card Data

Term	Coef	SE Coef	Z-Value	P-Value
Constant	-3.5180	0.71034	-4.95	0.000
income	0.1054	0.02616	4.03	0.000

a. State the prediction equation for the probability of owning a travel credit card and explain whether annual income has a positive or a negative effect.

b. Find the estimated probability of having a travel credit card at the lowest and highest annual income levels in the sample, which were $x = 12$ and $x = 65$.

Think It Through

a. Substituting the α and β estimates from Table 13.13 into the logistic regression model formula, $p = e^{\alpha+\beta x}/(1 + e^{\alpha+\beta x})$, we get the equation for the estimated probability $\hat{p}$ of having a travel credit card,

$$\hat{p} = \frac{e^{-3.52+0.105x}}{1 + e^{-3.52+0.105x}}.$$

Because the estimate 0.105 of β (the coefficient of x) is positive, this sample suggests that annual income has a positive effect: The estimated probability of having a travel credit card is higher at higher levels of annual income. The margin figure shows a plot of the estimated probability.

Estimated probability of owning a travel credit card

Probability: 1.00, 0.75, 0.50, 0.25, 0.00

Income (in 1,000 Euro): 10, 20, 30, 40, 50, 60

[2]The data were originally recorded in Italian lira but have been changed to euros and adjusted for inflation.

b. For subjects with income $x = 12$ thousand euros, the estimated probability of having a travel credit card equals

$$\hat{p} = \frac{e^{-3.52+0.105(12)}}{1 + e^{-3.52+0.105(12)}} = \frac{e^{-2.26}}{1 + e^{-2.26}} = \frac{0.104}{1.104} = 0.09.$$

For $x = 65$, the highest income level in this sample, you can check that the estimated probability equals 0.97.

Insight

There is a strong effect. The estimated probability of having a travel credit card changes from 0.09 to 0.97 (nearly 1.0) as annual income changes over its range.

Using software, we could also fit the straight-line regression model. Its prediction equation is $\hat{p} = -0.159 + 0.0188x$. However, its $\hat{p}$ predictions are quite different at the low end and at the high end of the annual income scale. At $x = 65$, for instance, it provides the prediction $\hat{p} = 1.06$. This is an invalid prediction because we know that a probability must fall between 0 and 1.

▶ ***Try Exercise 13.51***

Ways to Interpret the Logistic Regression Model

The sign of β in the logistic regression model tells us whether the probability p increases or decreases as x increases. Besides looking at the graph for the estimated probability, how else can we interpret the model parameters and their estimates? Here, we'll describe three ways.

1. To describe the effect of x, you can compare estimates of p at two values of x. One possibility is to compare $\hat{p}$ found at the minimum and maximum values of x, as we did in Example 12. There we saw that the estimated probability changed from 0.09 to 0.97, a considerable change. An alternative is instead to use values of x to evaluate this probability that are not as affected by outliers, such as the first and third quartiles.
2. It's good to know the value of x at which $p = 0.50$, that is, that value of x for which each outcome is equally likely. This depends on the logistic regression parameters α and β. It can be shown that $x = -\alpha/\beta$ when $p = 0.50$. (Exercise 13.93).
3. The simplest way to use the logistic regression parameter β to interpret the *steepness* of the curve uses a straight-line approximation. Because the logistic regression formula is a curve rather than a straight line, β itself is no longer the ordinary slope. At the x-value where $p = 0.50$, the line drawn tangent to the logistic regression curve has slope $\beta/4$. See Figure 13.11. The value $\beta/4$ represents the approximate change in the probability p for a one-unit increase in x, when x is close to the value at which $p = 0.50$. Tangent lines at other points have weaker slopes (Exercise 13.92), close to 0 when p is near 0 or 1.

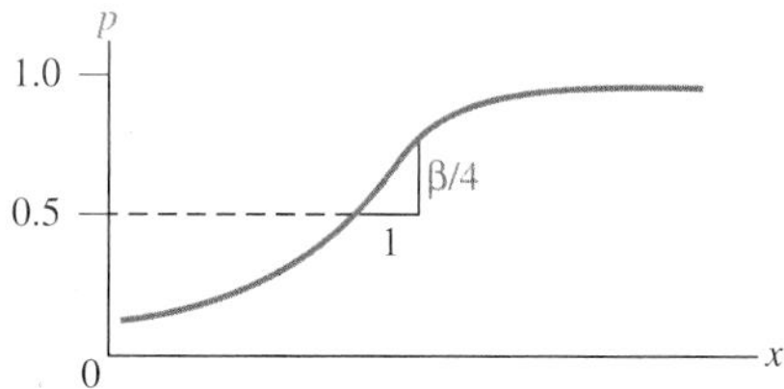

▲ **Figure 13.11** **When the Probability $p = 0.50$, for a One-Unit Change in x, p Changes by About $\beta/4$.** Here, β is the coefficient of x from the logistic regression model.

Interpreting a logistic regression model

Example 13

Effect of Income on Credit Card Use

Picture the Scenario

For the Italian travel credit card study, Example 12 found that the equation

$$\hat{p} = \frac{e^{-3.52+0.105x}}{1 + e^{-3.52+0.105x}}$$

estimates the probability p of having such a credit card as a function of annual income x.

Questions to Explore

Interpret this equation by (a) finding the income value at which the estimated probability of having a credit card equals 0.50 and (b) finding the approximate rate of change in the probability at that income value.

Think It Through

a. The estimate of α is -3.52 and the estimate of β is 0.105. Substituting the estimates into the expression $-\alpha/\beta$ for the value of x at $p = 0.50$, we get $x = (3.52)/(0.105) = 33.5$. The estimated probability of having a travel credit card equals 0.50 when annual income equals €33,500.

b. A line drawn tangent to the logistic regression curve at the point where $p = 0.50$ has slope equal to $\beta/4$. The estimate of this slope is $0.105/4 = 0.026$. For each increase of €1000 in annual income near the income value of €33,500, the estimated probability of having a travel credit card increases by approximately 0.026, or 2.6 percentage points.

Insight

Figure 13.12 shows the estimated logistic regression curve, highlighting what we've learned in Examples 12 and 13: The estimated probability increases from 0.09 to 0.97 between the minimum and maximum income values, and it equals 0.50 at an annual income of €33,500.

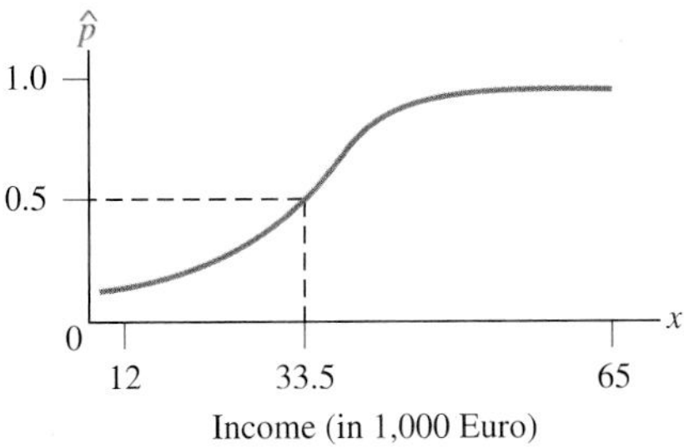

▲ **Figure 13.12** Logistic Regression Curve Relating Estimated Probability $\hat{p}$ of Having a Travel Credit Card to Annual Income x.

► ***Try Exercise 13.55***

Inference for Logistic Regression

Software also reports a z test statistic for the hypothesis H_0: $\beta = 0$. When $\beta = 0$, the probability of possessing a travel credit card is the same at all income levels. Then, the logistic curve in Figure 13.11 is a straight, horizontal line, indicating a constant probability of success p. The test statistic equals the ratio of the estimate b of β divided by its standard error. Sections 8.2 and 9.2 showed that

Table 13.13 was

Term	Coef	SE	Z-Value	P-Value
Constant	−3.518	0.710	−4.95	0.000
income	0.105	0.0262	4.03	0.000

inference about proportions uses z test statistics rather than t test statistics. From Table 13.13 (shown again in the margin), the z test statistic equals

$$z = (b - 0)/se = (0.105 - 0)/0.0262 = 4.0.$$

This has a P-value of 0.000 for H_a: $\beta \neq 0$. Since the sample slope is positive, for the population of adult Italians, there is strong evidence of a positive association between annual income and having a travel credit card.

The result of this test is no surprise. We would expect people with higher annual incomes to be more likely to have travel credit cards. Some software can construct a confidence interval for the probability p at various x levels. A 95% confidence interval for the probability of having a credit card equals (0.04, 0.20) at the lowest sample income level of €12,000 and (0.78, 0.996) at the highest sample income level of €65,000.

Multiple Logistic Regression

Just as ordinary regression extends to handle several explanatory variables, so does logistic regression. Also, logistic regression can include categorical explanatory variables using indicator variables.

Example 14

Multiple logistic regression

Estimating Proportion of Students Who've Used Marijuana

Picture the Scenario

Table 13.14 is a three-variable contingency table from a Wright State University survey asking senior high school students near Dayton, Ohio, whether they had ever used alcohol, cigarettes, or marijuana. We'll treat marijuana use as the response variable and cigarette use and alcohol use as explanatory variables.

Table 13.14 Alcohol, Cigarette, and Marijuana Use for High School Seniors

		Marijuana Use	
Alcohol Use	**Cigarette Use**	**Yes**	**No**
Yes	Yes	911	538
	No	44	456
No	Yes	3	43
	No	2	279

Source: Data from Professor Harry Khamis, Wright State University (personal communication).

Questions to Explore

Let y indicate marijuana use, coded 1 = yes, 0 = no. Let x_1 be an indicator variable for alcohol use (1 = yes, 0 = no), and let x_2 be an indicator variable for cigarette use (1 = yes, 0 = no). Table 13.15 shows MINITAB output for a logistic regression model.

Table 13.15 MINITAB Output for Estimating the Probability of Marijuana Use Based on Alcohol Use and Cigarette Use

Term	Coef	SE Coef	Z-Value	P-Value
Constant	−5.30904	0.475190	−11.17	0.000
alcohol	2.98601	0.464671	6.43	0.000
cigarettes	2.84789	0.163839	17.38	0.000

a. Report the prediction equation and interpret.

b. Find the estimated probability $\hat{p}$ of having used marijuana (i) for students who have not used alcohol or cigarettes and (ii) for students who have used both alcohol and cigarettes.

Think It Through

a. From Table 13.15, the logistic regression prediction equation is

$$\hat{p} = \frac{e^{-5.31 + 2.99x_1 + 2.85x_2}}{1 + e^{-5.31 + 2.99x_1 + 2.85x_2}}.$$

The coefficient of alcohol use (x_1) is positive (2.99). The indicator variable x_1 equals 1 for those who've used alcohol. Thus, the alcohol users have a higher estimated probability of using marijuana, controlling for whether they used cigarettes. Likewise, the coefficient of cigarette use (x_2) is positive (2.85), so the cigarette users have a higher estimated probability of using marijuana, controlling for whether they used alcohol. Table 13.15 tells us that for each predictor, the test statistic is large. In other words, the estimated effect is a large number of standard errors from 0. The P-values are both 0.000, so there is strong evidence that the corresponding population effects are positive also.

b. For those who have not used alcohol or cigarettes, $x_1 = x_2 = 0$. For them, the estimated probability of marijuana use is

$$\hat{p} = \frac{e^{-5.31+2.99(0)+2.85(0)}}{1 + e^{-5.31+2.99(0)+2.85(0)}} = \frac{e^{-5.31}}{1 + e^{-5.31}} = \frac{0.0049}{1.0049} = 0.005.$$

For those who have used alcohol and cigarettes, $x_1 = x_2 = 1$. For them, the estimated probability of marijuana use is

$$\hat{p} = \frac{e^{-5.31+2.99(1)+2.85(1)}}{1 + e^{-5.31+2.99(1)+2.85(1)}} = 0.629.$$

In summary, the probability that students have tried marijuana seems highly related to whether they've used alcohol and cigarettes.

Insight

Likewise, you can find the estimated probability of using marijuana for those who have used alcohol but not cigarettes (let $x_1 = 1$ and $x_2 = 0$) and for those who have not used alcohol but have used cigarettes. Table 13.16 summarizes results. We see that marijuana use is unlikely unless a student has used both alcohol and cigarettes.

Table 13.16 Estimated Probability of Marijuana Use, by Alcohol Use and Cigarette Use, Based on Logistic Regression Model

The sample proportions of marijuana use are shown in parentheses for the four cases.

	Cigarette Use	
Alcohol Use	**Yes**	**No**
Yes	0.629 (0.629)	0.089 (0.088)
No	0.079 (0.065)	0.005 (0.007)

► ***Try Exercises 13.57 and 13.58***

Checking the Logistic Regression Model

		Marijuana	
Alcohol	**Cigarette**	**Yes**	**No**
Yes	Yes	911	538
	No	44	456
No	Yes	3	43
	No	2	279

How can you check whether a logistic regression model fits the data well? When the explanatory variables are categorical, you can find the sample proportions for the outcome of interest. Table 13.16 also shows these for the marijuana use example. For instance, for those who had used alcohol and cigarettes, from Table 13.14 (shown again in the margin) the sample proportion who had used marijuana is $911/(911 + 538) = 0.629$. Table 13.16 shows that the sample proportions are close to the estimated proportions generated by the model. The model seems to fit well.

Table 13.16 may suggest the question, why bother to fit the model? Why not merely inspect a table of sample proportions? One important reason is that the model enables us to conduct inferences about the effects of explanatory variables easily while controlling for other variables. For instance, if we want to test the effect of alcohol use on marijuana use, controlling for cigarette use, we can test H_0: $\beta_1 = 0$ in the model with alcohol use and cigarette use as predictors.

13.6 Practicing the Basics

13.50 Income and credit cards Example 12 used logistic regression to estimate the probability of having a travel credit card when x = annual income (in thousands of euros). At the mean income of €25,000, show that the estimated probability of having a travel credit card equals 0.29.

13.51 Hall of Fame induction Baseball's highest honor is election to the Hall of Fame. The history of the election process, however, has been filled with controversy and accusations of favoritism. Most recently, there is also the discussion about players who used performance enhancement drugs. The Hall of Fame has failed to define what the criteria for entry should be. Several statistical models have attempted to describe the probability of a player being offered entry into the Hall of Fame. How does hitting 400 or 500 home runs affect a player's chances of being enshrined? What about having a .300 average or 1500 RBI? One factor, the number of home runs, is examined by using logistic regression as the probability of being elected:

$$P(\text{HOF}) = \frac{e^{-6.7+0.0175\text{HR}}}{1 + e^{-6.7+0.0175\,\text{HR}}}.$$

a. Compare the probability of election for two players who are 10 home runs apart—say, 369 home runs versus 359 home runs.

b. Compare the probability of election for a player with 475 home runs versus the probability for a player with 465 home runs. (These happen to be the figures for Willie Stargell and Dave Winfield.)

13.52 Horseshoe crabs A study of horseshoe crabs by zoologist Dr. Jane Brockmann at the University of Florida used logistic regression to predict the probability that a female crab had a male partner nesting nearby. One explanatory variable was x = weight of the female crab (in kilograms). The results were

```
Term        Coef
Constant   -3.695
Weight      1.815
```

The quartiles for weight were Q1 = 2.00, Q2 = 2.35, and Q3 = 2.85.

a. Find the estimated probability of a male partner at Q1 and at Q3.

b. Interpret the effect of weight by estimating how much the probability increases over the middle half of the sampled weights, between Q1 and Q3.

13.53 More crabs Refer to the previous exercise. For what weight values do you estimate that a female crab has probability (a) 0.50, (b) greater than 0.50, and (c) less than 0.50, of having a male partner nesting nearby?

13.54 Voting and income A logistic regression model describes how the probability of voting for the Republican candidate in a presidential election depends on x, the voter's total family income (in thousands of dollars) in the previous year. The prediction equation for a particular sample is

$$\hat{p} = \frac{e^{-1.00+0.02x}}{1 + e^{-1.00+0.02x}}.$$

Find the estimated probability of voting for the Republican candidate when (a) income = \$10,000, (b) income = \$100,000. Describe how the probability seems to depend on income.

13.55 Equally popular candidates Refer to the previous exercise.

a. At which income level is the estimated probability of voting for the Republican candidate equal to 0.50?

b. Over what region of income values is the estimated probability of voting for the Republican candidate (i) greater than 0.50 and (ii) less than 0.50?

c. At the income level for which $\hat{p} = 0.50$, give a linear approximation for the change in the probability for each \$1000 increase in income.

13.56 Many predictors of voting Refer to the previous two exercises. When the explanatory variables are x_1 = family income, x_2 = number of years of education, and x_3 = gender (1 = male, 0 = female), suppose a logistic regression reports

```
Term         Coef    SE Coef
Constant    -2.40    0.12
income       0.02    0.01
education    0.08    0.05
gender       0.20    0.06
```

For this sample, x_1 ranges from 6 to 157 with a standard deviation of 25, and x_2 ranges from 7 to 20 with a standard deviation of 3.

a. Interpret the effects by using the sign of the coefficient for each predictor.

b. Illustrate the gender effect by finding and comparing the estimated probability of voting Republican for (i) a man with 16 years of education and income \$40,000 and (ii) a woman with 16 years of education and income \$40,000.

13.57 Graduation, gender, and race The U.S. Bureau of the Census lists college graduation numbers by race and gender. The table shows the data for graduating 25-year-olds.

TRY

College graduation

Group	Sample Size	Graduates
White females	31,249	10,781
White males	39,583	10,727
Black females	13,194	2,309
Black males	17,707	2,054

Source: J. J. McArdle and F. Hamagami, *J. Amer. Statist. Assoc.*, vol. 89 (1994), pp. 1107–1123. Data from U.S. Bureau of the Census, American Community Survey 2005–2007.

a. Identify the response variable.

b. Express the data in the form of a three-variable contingency table that cross-classifies whether graduated (yes, no), race, and gender.

c. When we use indicator variables for race (1 = white, 0 = black) and for gender (1 = female, 0 = male), the coefficients of those predictors in the logistic regression model are 0.975 for race and 0.375 for gender. Based on these estimates, which race and gender combination has the highest estimated probability of graduation? Why?

13.58 Death penalty and race The three-dimensional contingency table shown is from a study of the effects of racial characteristics on whether individuals convicted of homicide receive the death penalty. The subjects classified were defendants in indictments involving cases with multiple murders in Florida between 1976 and 1987.

TRY

Death penalty verdict by defendant's race and victims' race

Defendant's Race	Victims' Race	Death Penalty Yes	Death Penalty No	Percent Yes
White	White	53	414	11.3
	Black	0	16	0.0
Black	White	11	37	22.9
	Black	4	139	2.8

Source: Data from M. L. Radelet and G. L. Pierce, *Florida Law Rev.*, vol. 43, 1991, pp. 1–34.

a. Based on the percentages shown, controlling for victims' race, for which defendant's race was the death penalty more likely?

b. Let y = death penalty verdict (1 = yes, 0 = no), let d be an indicator variable for defendant's race (1 = white, 0 = black), and let v be an indicator variable for victims' race (1 = white, 0 = black). The logistic regression prediction equation is

$$\hat{p} = \frac{e^{-3.596 - 0.868d + 2.404v}}{1 + e^{-3.596 - 0.868d + 2.404v}}.$$

According to this equation, for which of the four groups is the death penalty most likely? Explain your answer.

13.59 Death penalty probabilities Refer to the previous exercise.

a. Based on the prediction equation, when the defendant is black and the victims were white, show that the estimated death penalty probability is 0.233.

b. The model-estimated probabilities are 0.011 when the defendant is white and victims were black, 0.113 when the defendant and the victims were white, and 0.027 when the defendant and the victims were black. Construct a table cross-classifying defendant's race by victims' race and show the estimated probability of the death penalty for each cell. Use this to interpret the effect of defendant's race.

c. Collapse the contingency table over victims' race, and show that (ignoring victims' race) white defendants were more likely than black defendants to get the death penalty. Comparing this with what happens when you control for victims' race, explain how Simpson's paradox occurs.

Chapter Review

ANSWERS TO THE CHAPTER FIGURE QUESTIONS

Figure 13.1 Selling price is the response variable, and the graphs that show it as the response variable are in the first row.

Figure 13.2 The coefficient (15,170) of x_2 = number of bedrooms is positive, so increasing it has the effect of increasing the predicted selling price (for fixed house size).

Figure 13.3 We use only the right tail because larger F values provide greater evidence against H_0.

Figure 13.4 A histogram that shows a few observations that have extremely large or extremely small standardized residuals, well removed from the others.

Figure 13.5 The pattern suggests that y tends to be below $\hat{y}$ for very small and large x_1-values and above $\hat{y}$ for medium-sized x_1-values. The effect of x_1 appears to be better modeled by a mathematical function that has a parabolic shape.

Figure 13.6 As house size increases, the variability of the standardized residuals appears to increase, suggesting more variability in selling prices when house size is larger, for a given number of bedrooms. The number of bedrooms affects the analysis because it has an effect on the predicted values for the model, on which the residuals are based.

Figure 13.7 Each line has the same slope.

Figure 13.10 A straight line implies that p falls below 0 or above 1 for sufficiently small or large x-values. This is a problem because a proportion must always fall between 0 and 1.

CHAPTER SUMMARY

This chapter generalized regression to include more than one explanatory variable in the model. The **multiple regression model** relates the mean μ_y of a response variable y to several explanatory variables, for instance,

$$\mu_y = \alpha + \beta_1 x_1 + \beta_2 x_2$$

for two predictors. Advantages over simple linear regression include better predictions of y and being able to study the effect of an explanatory variable on y while *controlling* (keeping fixed) values of other explanatory variables in the model.

- The **regression parameters** (the betas) are slopes that represent effects of the explanatory variables while controlling for the other variables in the model. For instance, β_1 represents the change in the mean of y for a one-unit increase in x_1, at fixed values of the other explanatory variables.
- The **multiple correlation** R and its square (R^2) describe the predictability of the response variable y by the set of explanatory variables. The multiple correlation R equals the correlation between the observed and predicted y values. Its square, R^2, is the proportional reduction in error from predicting y using the prediction equation instead of using $\bar{y}$ (and ignoring all explanatory variables). Both R and R^2 fall between 0 and 1, with larger values representing stronger association.
- An ***F* statistic** tests H_0: $\beta_1 = \beta_2 = \ldots = 0$, which states that y is independent of all the explanatory variables in the model. The F test statistic equals a ratio of mean squares. A small P-value suggests that at least one explanatory variable affects the response.
- Individual ***t* tests** and **confidence intervals** for each β parameter analyze separate population effects of each explanatory variable, controlling for the other variables in the model.
- Categorical explanatory variables can be included in a regression model using **indicator variables.** With two categories, the indicator variable equals 1 when the observation is in the first category and 0 when it is in the second.
- For binary response variables, the **logistic regression model** describes how the probability of a particular category depends on the values of explanatory variables. An S-shaped curve describes how the probability changes as the value of a quantitative explanatory variable increases.

Table 13.17 summarizes the basic properties and inference methods for multiple regression and those that Chapter 12 introduced for simple linear regression, with quantitative variables.

Table 13.17 Summary of Simple and Multiple Regression

	Simple Regression	Multiple Regression	
Model formula	$\mu_y = \alpha + \beta x$	$\mu_y = \alpha + \beta_1 x_1 + \beta_2 x_2 + \ldots$	
		Simultaneous Effect	**Separate Effects**
Parameters for association	β = slope, r = sample correlation $(-1 \le r \le 1)$, r^2 is proportional reduction in error (PRE)	R = multiple correlation $(0 \le R \le 1)$, R^2 is PRE	$\beta_1, \beta_2, \ldots$ are slopes for each predictor at fixed values of others
Hypotheses of no effect	H_0: $\beta = 0$	H_0: $\beta_1 = \beta_2 = \ldots = 0$	H_0: $\beta_1 = 0$, H_0: $\beta_2 = 0, \ldots$
Test Statistic	$t = (b - 0)/se$	$F = \dfrac{\text{MS Regression}}{\text{MS Error}}$	$t = (\beta_1 - 0)/se$, $t = (\beta_2 - 0)/se, \ldots$
Degrees of Freedom	$df = n - 2$	df_1 = # predictors, $df_2 = n$ − # regression parameters.	$df = n$ − # regression parameters.

SUMMARY OF NOTATION

$x_1, x_2, \ldots$ = explanatory variables in multiple regression model
R = multiple correlation = correlation between observed y and predicted y values

R^2 = proportional reduction in prediction error, for multiple regression

F = test statistic for testing that all β parameters = 0 in regression model

$e^{\alpha+\beta x}$ = exponential function used in numerator and denominator of logistic regression equation, which models the probability p of a binary outcome by

$$p = e^{\alpha+\beta x}/(1 + e^{\alpha+\beta x}).$$

CHAPTER PROBLEMS

Practicing the Basics

13.60 House prices This chapter has considered many aspects of regression analysis. Let's consider several of them at once by using software with the House Selling Prices OR data file on the book's website to conduct a multiple regression analysis of y = selling price of home, x_1 = size of home, x_2 = number of bedrooms, x_3 = number of bathrooms.

a. Construct a scatterplot matrix. Identify the plots that pertain to selling price as a response variable. Interpret and explain how the highly discrete nature of x_2 and x_3 affects the plots.

b. Fit the model. Write down the prediction equation and interpret the coefficient of size of home by its effect when x_2 and x_3 are fixed.

c. Show how to calculate R^2 from SS values in the ANOVA table. Interpret its value in the context of these variables.

d. Find and interpret the multiple correlation.

e. Show all steps of the F test that selling price is independent of these predictors. Explain how to obtain the F statistic from the mean squares in the ANOVA table.

f. Report the t statistic for testing H_0: $\beta_2 = 0$. Report the P-value for H_a: $\beta_2 < 0$ and interpret. Why do you think this effect is not significant? Does this imply that the number of bedrooms is not associated with selling price?

g. Construct and examine the histogram of the residuals for the multiple regression model. What does this describe, and what does it suggest?

h. Construct and examine the plot of the residuals plotted against size of home. What does this describe, and what does it suggest?

13.61 Predicting body strength In Chapter 12, we analyzed strength data for a sample of female high school athletes. When we predict the maximum number of pounds the athlete can bench press using the number of times she can do a 60-pound bench press (BP60), we get $r^2 = 0.643$. When we add the number of times an athlete can perform a 200-pound leg press (LP200) to the model, we get $\hat{y} = 60.6 + 1.33(\text{BP60}) + 0.21(\text{LP200})$ and $R^2 = 0.656$.

a. Find the predicted value and residual for an athlete who has maxBP = 85, BP60 = 10, and LP200 = 20.

b. Find the prediction equation for athletes who have LP200 = 20, and explain how to interpret the slope for BP60.

c. Note that $R^2 = 0.656$ for the multiple regression model is not much larger than $r^2 = 0.643$ for the simple model with LP200 as the only explanatory variable. What does this suggest?

13.62 Softball data Refer to the Softball data set on the book's website. Regress the difference (DIFF) between the number of runs scored by that team and by the other team on the number of hits (HIT) and the number of errors (ERR).

a. Report the prediction equation, and interpret the slopes.

b. From part a, approximately how many hits does the team need so that the predicted value of DIFF is positive (corresponding to a predicted win) if they can play error-free ball (ERR = 0)?

13.63 Violent crime A MINITAB printout is provided from fitting the multiple regression model to U.S. crime data for the 50 states (excluding Washington, D.C.) on y = violent crime rate, x_1 = poverty rate, and x_2 = percent living in urban areas.

a. Predict the violent crime rate for Massachusetts, which has violent crime rate = 476, poverty rate = 10.2%, and urbanization = 92.1%. Find the residual and interpret.

b. Interpret the effects of the predictors by showing the prediction equation relating y and x_1 for states with (i) $x_2 = 0$ and (ii) $x_2 = 100$. Interpret.

Regression of violent crime rate on poverty rate and urbanization

Term	Coef	SE Coef	T-Value	P-Value
Constant	−270.7	121.1	−2.23	0.030
poverty	28.334	7.249	3.91	0.000
urbanization	5.416	1.035	5.23	0.000

13.64 Effect of poverty on crime Refer to the previous exercise. Now we add x_3 = percentage of single-parent families to the model. The SPSS table below shows results. Without x_3 in the model, poverty has slope 28.33, and when x_3 is added, poverty has slope 14.95. Explain the differences in the interpretations of these two slopes.

Violent crime predicted by poverty rate, urbanization, and single-parent family

Coefficients[a]

Model		Unstandardized Coefficients			
		B	Std. Errort	t	Sig.
1	(Constant)	−631.700	149.604	−4.222	.000
	poverty	14.953	7.540	1.983	.053
	urbanization	4.406	.973	4.528	.000
	singleparent	25.362	7.220	3.513	.001

[a] Dependent Variable: violent crime rate.

13.65 Modeling fertility For the World Data for Fertility and Literacy data file on the book's website, a MINITAB printout follows that shows fitting a multiple regression model for y = fertility, x_1 = adult literacy rate (both sexes), x_2 = combined educational enrollment (both sexes). Report the value of each of the following:

a. r between y and x_1

b. R^2

c. Total sum of squares

d. Residual sum of squares

e. Standard deviation of y

f. Residual standard deviation of y

g. Test statistic value for H_0: $\beta_1 = 0$

h. P-value for H_0: $\beta_1 = \beta_2 = 0$

Analysis of fertility, literacy, and combined educational enrollment:

Variable	N	Mean	SE Mean	StDev	Median
Adolescent fertility	142	60.42	3.73	44.50	49.55
Adult literacy rate (both sexes)	142	80.80	1.64	19.56	88.40
Combined educ enrol (both sexes)	142	68.59	1.32	15.79	71.20

Term	Coef	SE Coef	T-Value	P-Value
Constant	187.95	12.92	14.55	0.000
Adult literacy rate (both sexes)	-1.2590	0.2416	-5.21	0.000
Combined educ enrollment(both sexes)	-0.3762	0.2994	-1.26	0.211

S = 33.4554 R-Sq = 44.3%

Analysis of Variance

Source	DF	SS	MS	F-Value	P-Value
Regression	2	123582	61791	55.21	0.000
Error	139	155577	1119		
Total	141	279160			

Correlations:

	y	x_1	x_2
y	-	-0.661	-0.578
x_1	-0.661	-	0.803
x_2	-0.578	0.803	-

13.66 Significant fertility prediction? Refer to the previous exercise.

a. Show how to construct the F statistic for testing H_0: $\beta_1 = \beta_2 = 0$ from the reported mean squares, report its P-value, and interpret.

b. If these are the only nations of interest to us for this study, rather than a random sample of such nations, is this significance test relevant? Explain.

13.67 GDP, CO_2, and Internet Consider predicting the per capita GDP (gross domestic product, in thousands of dollars), of a country, using x_1 = carbon dioxide emissions per capita (in metric tons) and x_2 = percent of country population not using the Internet. Based on data for several countries, the following computer output was obtained:

Coefficients:

	Estimate	Std. Error	t	Pr(>|t|)
Intercept	39892	4474	8.9	0.0000
CO_2	798	254	3.1	0.0119
NoInternet	-399	51	-7.8	0.0000

a. Find the equation relating predicted GDP to the explanatory variables listed.

b. Interpret the coefficients in the equation for each of the explanatory variables.

13.68 Education and gender in modeling income Consider the relationship between $\hat{y}$ = annual income (in thousands of dollars) and x_1 = number of years of education by x_2 = gender. Many studies in the United States have found that the slope for a regression equation relating y to x_1 is larger for men than for women. Suppose that in the population, the regression equations are $\mu_y = -10 + 4x_1$ for men and $\mu_y = -5 + 2x_1$ for women. Explain why these equations imply that there is *interaction* between education and gender in their effects on income.

13.69 Horseshoe crabs and width A study of horseshoe crabs found a logistic regression equation for predicting the probability that a female crab had a male partner nesting nearby by using x = width of the carapace shell of the female crab (in centimeters). The results were

Term	Coef
Constant	-12.351
Width	0.497

a. For width, Q1 = 24.9 and Q3 = 27.7. Find the estimated probability of a male partner at Q1 and at Q3. Interpret the effect of width by estimating the increase in the probability over the middle half of the sampled widths.

b. At which carapace shell width level is the estimated probability of a male partner (i) equal to 0.50, (ii) greater than 0.50, and (iii) less than 0.50?

13.70 AIDS and AZT In a study (reported in the *New York Times*, February 15, 1991) on the effects of AZT in slowing the development of AIDS symptoms, 338 veterans whose immune systems were beginning to falter after infection with the AIDS virus were randomly assigned either to receive AZT immediately or to wait until their T cells showed severe immune weakness. The study classified the veterans' race, whether they received AZT immediately, and whether they developed AIDS symptoms during the three-year study. Let x_1 denote whether they used AZT (1 = yes, 0 = no) and let x_2 denote race (1 = white, 0 = black). A logistic regression analysis for the probability of developing AIDS symptoms gave the prediction equation

$$\hat{p} = \frac{e^{-1.074-0.720x_1+0.056x_2}}{1 + e^{-1.074-0.720x_1+0.056x_2}}.$$

a. Interpret the sign of the effect of AZT.

b. Show how to interpret the AZT effect for a particular race by comparing the estimated probability of AIDS symptoms for black veterans with and without immediate AZT use.

c. The *se* value was 0.279 for the AZT use effect. Does AZT use have a significant effect at the 0.05 significance level? Show all steps of a test to justify your answer.

13.71 Factors affecting first home purchase The table summarizes results of a logistic regression model for predictions about first home purchase by young married households. The response variable is whether the subject owns a home (1 = yes, 0 = no). The explanatory variables are husband's income, wife's income (each in ten-thousands of dollars), the number of years the respondent has been married, the number of children aged 0–17 in the household, and an indicator variable that equals 1 if the subject's parents owned a home in the last year the subject lived in the parental home.

a. Explain why, other things being fixed, the probability of home ownership increases with husband's earnings, wife's earnings, the number of children, and parents' home ownership.

b. From the table, explain why the number of years married seems to show little evidence of an effect, given the other variables in the model.

Results of logistic regression for probability of home ownership

Variable	Estimate	Std. Error
Husband earnings	0.569	0.088
Wife earnings	0.306	0.140
No. years married	−0.039	0.042
No. children	0.220	0.101
Parents' home ownership	0.387	0.176

Source: Data from J. Henretta, "Family Transitions, Housing Market Context, and First Home Purchase," *Social Forces,* vol. 66, 1987, pp. 520–536.

Concepts and Investigations

13.72 Student data Refer to the FL Student Survey data file on the book's website. Using software, conduct a regression analysis using y = college GPA and predictors high school GPA and sports (number of weekly hours of physical exercise). Prepare a report, summarizing your graphical analyses, simple regression models and interpretations, multiple regression models and interpretations, inferences, checks of effects of outliers, and overall summary of the relationships.

TECH

13.73 Why regression? In 100–200 words, explain to someone who has never studied statistics the purpose of multiple regression and when you would use it to analyze a data set or investigate an issue. Give an example of at least one application of multiple regression. Describe how multiple regression can be useful in analyzing complex relationships.

13.74 Unemployment and GDP Refer to Exercise 13.67. When unemployment rate of a country is added as an additional predictor to the model already containing CO_2 and percentage of population not using the Internet, we get the following output.

```
Coefficients:
              Estimate  Std. Error     t   Pr(>|t|)
(Intercept)     38923        7259    5.4    0.0007
CO2               813         282    2.9    0.0204
NoInternet       -395          58   -6.9    0.0001
Unemployed        107         606    0.2    0.8645
```

a. Interpret the sign of the coefficient for unemployment. Is this the direction of the effect you would expect?

b. Is the coefficient for unemployment significantly different from zero? Explain. Does this automatically mean unemployment is unrelated to GDP? (*Hint:* Does the effect of employment depend on other variables in the model?)

c. What measure would you use to investigate whether unemployment helps in predicting GDP?

d. R_2 increases from 94.26% to 94.28% when adding unemployment to the model with CO_2 and NoInternet. Explain what this means.

13.75 Multiple choice: Interpret parameter If $\hat{y} = 2 + 3x_1 + 5x_2 - 8x_3$, then controlling for x_2 and x_3, the change in the estimated mean of y when x_1 is increased from 10 to 20

a. equals 30.

b. equals 0.3.

c. Cannot be given—depends on specific values of x_2 and x_3.

d. Must be the same as when we ignore x_2 and x_3.

13.76 Multiple choice: Interpret indicator In the model $\mu_y = \alpha + \beta_1 x_1 + \beta_2 x_2$, suppose that x_2 is an indicator variable for gender, equaling 1 for females and 0 for males.

a. We set $x_2 = 0$ if we want a predicted mean without knowing gender.

b. The slope effect of x_1 is β_1 for males and β_2 for females.

c. β_2 is the difference between the population mean of y for females and for males.

d. β_2 is the difference between the population mean of y for females and males, for all those subjects having x_1 fixed, such as $x_1 = 10$.

13.77 Multiple choice: Regression effects Multiple regression is used to model y = annual income using x_1 = number of years of education and x_2 = number of years employed in current job.

a. It is possible that the coefficient of x_2 is positive in a simple regression but negative in multiple regression.

b. It is possible that the correlation between y and x_1 is 0.30 and the multiple correlation between y and x_1 and x_2 is 0.26.

c. If the F statistic for H_0: $\beta_1 = \beta_2 = 0$ has a P-value = 0.001, then we can conclude that *both* predictors have an effect on annual income.

d. If $\beta_2 = 0$, then annual income is independent of x_2 in simple regression.

13.78 True or false: R and R^2 For each of the following statements, indicate whether it is true or false. If false, explain why it is false.

a. The multiple correlation is always the same as the ordinary correlation computed between the values of the response variable and the values $\hat{y}$ predicted by the regression model.

b. The multiple correlation is like the ordinary correlation in that it falls between −1 and 1.

c. R^2 describes how well you can predict y using x_1 when you control for the other variables in the multiple regression model.

d. It's impossible for R^2 to go down when you add explanatory variables to a regression model.

13.79 True or false: Regression For each of the following statements, indicate whether it is true or false. If false, explain why it is false. In regression analysis:

a. The estimated coefficient of x_1 can be positive in the simple model but negative in a multiple regression model.

b. When a model is refitted after y = income is changed from dollars to euros, R^2, the correlation between y and x_1, the F statistics and t statistics will not change.

c. If $r^2 = 0.6$ between y and x_1 and if $r^2 = 0.6$ between y and x_2, then for the multiple regression model with both predictors, $R^2 = 1.2$.

d. The multiple correlation between y and $\hat{y}$ can equal -0.40.

13.80 True or false: Slopes For data on y = college GPA, x_1 = high school GPA, and x_2 = average of mathematics and verbal entrance exam score, we get $\hat{y} = 2.70 + 0.45x_1$ for simple regression and $\hat{y} = 0.3 + 0.40x_1 + 0.003x_2$ for multiple regression. For each of the following statements, indicate whether it is true or false. Give a reason for your answer.

a. The correlation between y and x_1 is positive.

b. A one-unit increase in x_1 corresponds to a change of 0.45 in the predicted value of y, controlling for x_2.

c. Controlling for x_1, a 100-unit increase in x_2 corresponds to a predicted increase of 0.30 in college GPA.

13.81 Scores for religion You want to include religious affiliation as a predictor in a regression model, using the categories Protestant, Catholic, Jewish, Other. You set up a variable x_1 that equals 1 for Protestants, 2 for Catholics, 3 for Jewish, and 4 for Other, using the model $\mu_y = \alpha + \beta x_1$. Explain why this is inappropriate.

13.82 Lurking variable Give an example of three variables for which you expect $\beta \neq 0$ in the model $\mu_y = \alpha + \beta x_1$ but $\beta_1 = 0$ in the model $\mu_y = \alpha + \beta_1 x_1 + \beta_2 x_2$. (*Hint*: The effect of x_1 could be completely due to a lurking variable, x_2.)

13.83 Properties of R^2 Using its definition in terms of SS values, explain why $R^2 = 1$ only when all the residuals are 0, and $R^2 = 0$ when each $\hat{y} = \bar{y}$. Explain what this means in practical terms.

13.84 Why an F test? When a model has a very large number of predictors, even when none of them truly have an effect in the population, one or two may look significant in t tests merely by random variation. Explain why performing the F test first can safeguard against getting such false information from t tests.

13.85 Multicollinearity For the high school female athletes data file, regress the maximum bench press on weight and percent body fat.

TECH

a. Show that the F test is statistically significant at the 0.05 significance level.

b. Show that the P-values are both larger than 0.35 for testing the individual effects with t tests. (It seems like a contradiction when the F test tells us that at least one predictor has an effect but the t tests indicate that neither predictor has a significant effect. This can happen when the predictor variables are highly correlated, so a predictor has little impact when the other predictors are in the model. Such a condition is referred to as **multicollinearity.** In this example, the correlation is 0.871 between weight and percent body fat.)

13.86 Logistic versus linear For binary response variables, one reason that logistic regression is usually preferred over straight-line regression is that a fixed change in x often has a smaller impact on a probability p when p is near 0 or near 1 than when p is near the middle of its range. Let y refer to the decision to rent or to buy a home, with p = the probability of buying, and let x = weekly family income. In which case do you think an increase of \$100 in x has greater effect: when $x = 50{,}000$ (for which p is near 1), when $x = 0$ (for which p is near 0), or when $x = 500$? Explain how your answer relates to the choice of a linear versus logistic regression model.

13.87 ◆◆ **Adjusted R^2** When we use R^2 for a random sample to estimate a population R^2, it's a bit biased. It tends to be a bit too large, especially when n is small. Some software also reports

$$\text{Adjusted } R^2 = R^2 - \{p/[n - (p + 1)]\}(1 - R^2),$$

where p = number of predictor variables in the model. This is slightly smaller than R^2 and is less biased. Suppose $R^2 = 0.500$ for a model with $p = 2$ predictors. Calculate adjusted R^2 for the following sample sizes: 10, 100, 1000. Show that the difference between adjusted R^2 and R^2 diminishes as n increases.

13.88 ◆◆ ***R* can't go down** The least squares prediction equation provides predicted values $\hat{y}$ with the strongest possible correlation with y out of all possible prediction equations of that form. Based on this property, explain why the multiple correlation R cannot decrease when you add a variable to a multiple regression model. (*Hint*: The prediction equation for the simpler model is a special case of a prediction equation for the full model that has coefficient 0 for the added variable.)

13.89 ◆◆ **Indicator for comparing two groups** Chapter 10 presented methods for comparing means for two groups. Explain how it's possible to perform a significance test of equality of two population means as a special case of a regression analysis. (*Hint*: The regression model then has a single explanatory variable—an indicator variable for the two groups being compared. What does $\mu_1 = \mu_2$ correspond to in terms of a value of a parameter in this model?)

13.90 ◆◆ **Simpson's paradox** Let y = death rate and x = average age of residents, measured for each county in Louisiana and in Florida. Draw a hypothetical scatterplot, identifying points for each state, such that the mean death rate is higher in Florida than in Louisiana when x is ignored, but lower when it is controlled. (*Hint*: When you fit a line for each state, the line should be higher for Louisiana, but the y-values for Florida should have an overall higher mean.)

13.91 ◆◆ **Parabolic regression** A regression formula that gives a parabolic shape instead of a straight line for the relationship between two variables is

$$\mu_y = \alpha + \beta_1 x + \beta_2 x^2.$$

a. Explain why this is a multiple regression model, with x playing the role of x_1 and x^2 (the square of x) playing the role of x_2.

b. For x between 0 and 5, sketch the prediction equation (i) $\hat{y} = 10 + 2x + 0.5x^2$ and (ii) $\hat{y} = 10 + 2x - 0.5x^2$. This shows how the shape of the parabolic regression equation changes, depending on whether the coefficient for x^2 is positive or negative.

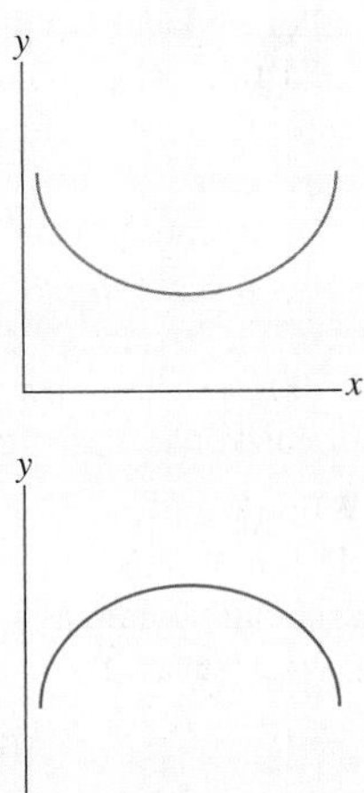

13.92 Logistic slope At the x value where the probability of success is some value p, the line drawn tangent to the logistic regression curve has slope $\beta p(1 - p)$.
◆◆

a. Explain why the slope is $\beta/4$ when $p = 0.5$.

b. Show that the slope is weaker at other p values by evaluating this at $p = 0.1, 0.3, 0.7$, and 0.9. What does the slope approach as p gets closer and closer to 0 or 1? Sketch a curve to illustrate.

13.93 When is $p = 0.50$? When $\alpha + \beta x = 0$, so that $x = -\alpha/\beta$, show that the logistic regression equation $p = e^{\alpha+\beta x}/(1 + e^{\alpha+\beta x})$ gives $p = 0.50$.
◆◆

Student Activities

13.94 Class data Refer to the data file your class created in Activity 3 in Chapter 1. For variables chosen by your instructor, fit a multiple regression model and conduct descriptive and inferential statistical analyses. Interpret and summarize your findings and prepare to discuss these in class.
TECH

CHAPTER

14

In Chapter 10, we learned how to compare two groups on a quantitative response variable by comparing their means, using a t test. In this chapter, we extend these ideas to compare several means at once and show how to follow up a significance test to learn about pairwise differences.

Comparing Groups: Analysis of Variance Methods

Example 1

Investigating Customer Satisfaction

Picture the Scenario

In recent years, many companies have increased the attention paid to measuring and analyzing customer satisfaction. Here are examples of two recent studies of customer satisfaction:

- A company that makes personal computers has provided a toll-free telephone number for owners of their PCs to call and seek technical support. For years the company had two service centers for these calls: San Jose, California, and Toronto, Canada. Recently the company outsourced many of the customer service jobs to a new center in Bangalore, India, because employee salaries are much lower there. The company wanted to compare customer satisfaction at the three centers.
- An airline has a toll-free telephone number that potential customers can call to make flight reservations. Usually the call volume is heavy and callers are placed on hold until an agent is free to answer. Researchers working for the airline recently conducted a randomized experiment to analyze whether callers would remain on hold longer if they heard (a) an advertisement about the airline and its current promotions, (b) recorded Muzak ("elevator music"), or (c) recorded classical music. Currently, recordings are five minutes long and then repeated; the researchers also wanted to find out whether it would make a difference if recordings were instead 10 minutes long before repeating.

Questions to Explore

In the second study, the company's CEO had some familiarity with statistical methods, based on a course he took in college. He asked the researchers:

- In this experiment, are the sample mean times that callers stayed on hold before hanging up significantly different for the three recording types?

- What conclusions can you make if you take into account both the type of recording and whether it was repeated every five minutes or every ten minutes?

Thinking Ahead

Chapter 10 showed how to compare two means. In practice, there may be *several* means to compare, such as in the first and second examples. This chapter shows how to use statistical inference to compare several means. We'll see how to determine whether a set of sample means is significantly different and how to estimate the differences among corresponding population means. To illustrate, we'll analyze data from the second study in Examples 2 to 4 and 7.

The methods introduced in this chapter apply when a quantitative response variable has a categorical explanatory variable. The categories of the explanatory variable identify the groups to be compared in terms of their means on the response variable. For example, the first study in Example 1 compared mean customer satisfaction for three groups—customers who call the service centers at the three locations. The response variable is customer satisfaction (on a scale of 0 to 10), and the explanatory variable is the service center location.

The inferential method for comparing means of several groups is called **analysis of variance**, denoted **ANOVA**. Section 14.1 shows that the name "analysis of variance" refers to the significance test's focus on two types of variability in the data. Section 14.2 shows how to construct confidence intervals comparing the means. It also shows that ANOVA methods are special cases of a multiple regression analysis.

Categorical explanatory variables in multiple regression and in ANOVA are often referred to as **factors**. ANOVA with a single factor, such as service center location, is called **one-way ANOVA**. Section 14.3 introduces ANOVA for two factors, called **two-way ANOVA**. The second study in Example 1 requires the use of two-way ANOVA to analyze how the mean telephone holding time (the response variable) varies across categories of recording type (factor 1) and categories defined by the length of time before repeating the recording (factor 2).

14.1 One-Way ANOVA: Comparing Several Means

The analysis of variance method compares means of *several* groups. Let g denote the number of groups. Each group has a corresponding population of subjects. The means of the response variable for the g populations are denoted by $\mu_1, \mu_2, \ldots, \mu_g$.

Hypotheses and Assumptions for the ANOVA Test Comparing Means

The analysis of variance is a significance test of the null hypothesis of equal population means,

$$H_0: \mu_1 = \mu_2 = \cdots = \mu_g.$$

An example is $H_0: \mu_1 = \mu_2 = \mu_3$ for testing population mean satisfaction at $g = 3$ service center locations. The null hypothesis says that the population mean satisfaction score is the same at all three service centers. The alternative hypothesis is

$$H_a: \text{at least two of the population means are unequal.}$$

If H_0 is false, perhaps all the population means differ, but perhaps merely one mean differs from the others. The test analyzes whether the differences observed among the *sample* means could have reasonably occurred by chance, if the null hypothesis of equal *population* means were true.

The assumptions for the ANOVA test comparing population means are as follows:

Recall

For $g = 2$ groups, the assumptions for the ANOVA test are the same as those used in Section 10.3 for the pooled t test to compare two population means. ◀

- The population distributions of the response variable for the g groups are normal, with the same standard deviation for each group.
- Randomization (depends on data collection method): In a survey sample, independent random samples are selected from each of the g populations. For an experiment, subjects are randomly assigned to the g groups.

Under the first assumption, when the population means are equal, the population distribution of the response variable is the same for each group. If that is the case, the population distribution does not depend on the group to which a subject belongs.

Example 2

ANOVA hypotheses ◀

Tolerance of Being on Hold?

Picture the Scenario

Let's refer back to the second scenario in Example 1. An airline has a toll-free telephone number for reservations. Often the call volume is heavy, and callers are placed on hold until a reservation agent is free to answer. The airline hopes a caller remains on hold until the call is answered, so as not to lose a potential customer.

The airline recently conducted a randomized experiment to analyze whether callers would remain on hold longer, on average, if they heard (a) an advertisement about the airline and its current promotions, (b) Muzak, or (c) classical music (Vivaldi's *Four Seasons*). The company randomly selected one out of every 1000 calls in a particular week. For each call, they randomly selected one of the three recordings to play and then measured the number of minutes that the caller remained on hold before hanging up (these calls were purposely not answered). The total sample size was 15. The company kept the study small, hoping it could make conclusions without alienating too many potential customers! Table 14.1 shows the data. It also shows the mean and standard deviation for each recording type.

Table 14.1 Telephone Holding Times by Type of Recorded Message

Each observation is the number of minutes a caller remained on hold before hanging up, rounded to the nearest minute.

Recording	Holding Time Observations	Sample Size	Mean	Standard Deviation
Advertisement	5, 1, 11, 2, 8	5	5.4	4.2
Muzak	0, 1, 4, 6, 3	5	2.8	2.4
Classical	13, 9, 8, 15, 7	5	10.4	3.4

Questions to Explore

a. What is the factor in this experiment and what are the hypotheses for the ANOVA test?

b. Figure 14.1 displays the sample means. Since these means are quite different, is there sufficient evidence to conclude that the population means differ?

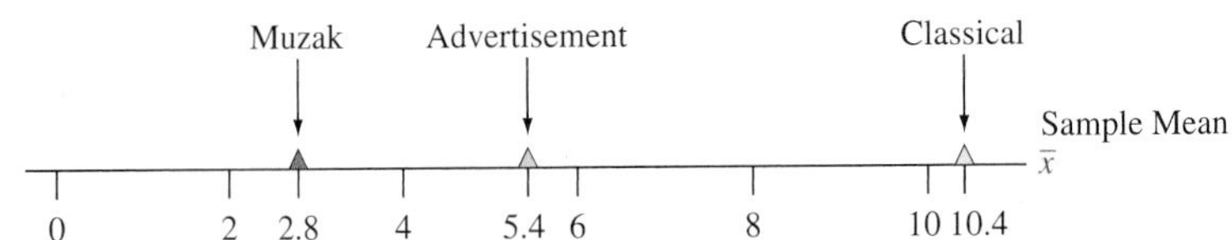

▲ **Figure 14.1** Sample Means of Telephone Holding Times for Callers Who Hear One of Three Recordings. **Question** Since the sample means are quite different, can we conclude that the population means differ?

Think It Through

a. The factor (= explanatory variable) is the type of recording (advertisement, Muzak, or classical music) that was played for a randomly selected caller. Let μ_1, μ_2, and μ_3 denote the mean holding time for the population of callers that were played an advertisement, Muzak, or classical music, respectively. ANOVA tests whether these three population means are equal. The null hypothesis is H_0: $\mu_1 = \mu_2 = \mu_3$. The alternative hypothesis is that at least two of the population means are different.

b. The sample means are quite different. But even if the population means are equal, we expect the sample means to differ because of sampling variability. So these differences alone are not sufficient evidence to enable us to reject H_0.

Insight

The strength of evidence against H_0 will also depend on the sample sizes and the variability of the observations. We'll next study how to test H_0.

▶ ***Try Exercise 14.1, parts a and b***

Variability Between Groups and Within Groups Is the Key to Significance

The ANOVA method is used to compare population *means*. So, why is it called analysis of *variance*? The reason is that the test statistic uses evidence about two types of variability. Rather than presenting a formula now for this test statistic, which is rather complex, we'll discuss the reasoning behind it, which is quite simple.

Table 14.1 listed data for three groups. Figure 14.2a shows dot plots of these data. Suppose the data were different, as shown in Figure 14.2b. The data in Figure 14.2b have the same means as the data in Figure 14.2a but have smaller standard deviations within each group. Which case do you think gives stronger evidence against H_0: $\mu_1 = \mu_2 = \mu_3$?

What's the difference between the data in these two cases? The variability *between* group means is the same in each case because the group means are identical. However, the variability *within* each group is much smaller in Figure 14.2b than in Figure 14.2a. The sample standard deviation is about 1.0 for each group in Figure 14.2b whereas it is between 2.4 and 4.2 for the groups in Figure 14.2a. We'll see that the evidence against H_0: $\mu_1 = \mu_2 = \mu_3$ is stronger when the variability *within* each group is smaller. Figure 14.2b shows less variability within each group than Figure 14.2a. Therefore, it gives stronger evidence against H_0. The evidence against H_0 is also stronger when the variability *between* group means increases (that is, when the group means are farther apart) and as the sample sizes increase. These considerations lead to the ANOVA test statistic that compares variability between and within groups.

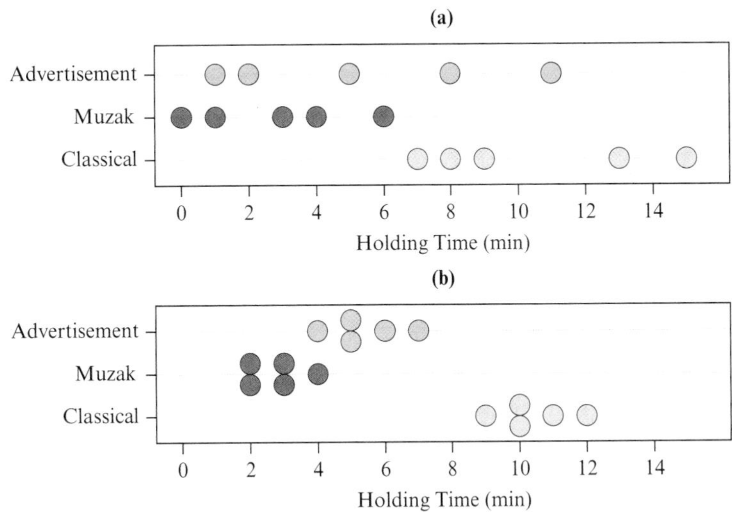

▲ **Figure 14.2 Dotplots Based on (a) Data in Table 14.1 and (b) Hypothetical Data With the Same Means but Less Variability Within Groups. Question** Do the data in Figure 14.2b give stronger or weaker evidence against H_0: $\mu_1 = \mu_2 = \mu_3$ than the data in Figure 14.2a. Why?

ANOVA *F* Test Statistic

The **analysis of variance (ANOVA) *F* test statistic** summarizes

$$F = \frac{\text{Between-groups variability}}{\text{Within-groups variability}}.$$

The larger the variability *between* groups relative to the variability *within* groups, the larger the F test statistic tends to be. For instance, $F = 6.4$ for the data in Figure 14.2a, whereas $F = 67.8$ for the data in Figure 14.2b. The between-groups variability is the same in each figure, but Figure 14.2b has much less within-groups variability and thus a larger test statistic value. Later in the section, we'll see that the two types of variability described in the F test statistic are measured by estimates of *variances.*

The Test Statistic for Comparing Means Has the *F* Distribution

When H_0 is true, the F test statistic has the F sampling distribution. The formula for the F test statistic is such that when H_0 is true, the F distribution has a mean of approximately 1. When H_0 is false, the F test statistic tends to be larger than 1, more so as the sample sizes increase. The larger the F test statistic value, the stronger the evidence against H_0.

Recall that we used the F distribution in the F test that the slope parameters of a multiple regression model are all zero (Section 13.3). As in that test, the P-value here is the probability (presuming that H_0 is true) that we obtain an F test statistic that is larger than the observed F value. That is, it is the right-hand tail probability, as shown in the margin figure, representing results even more extreme than observed. The larger the observed F test statistic, the smaller the P-value.

In Words

The P-value for an ANOVA *F* test statistic is the right-tail probability from the *F* distribution.

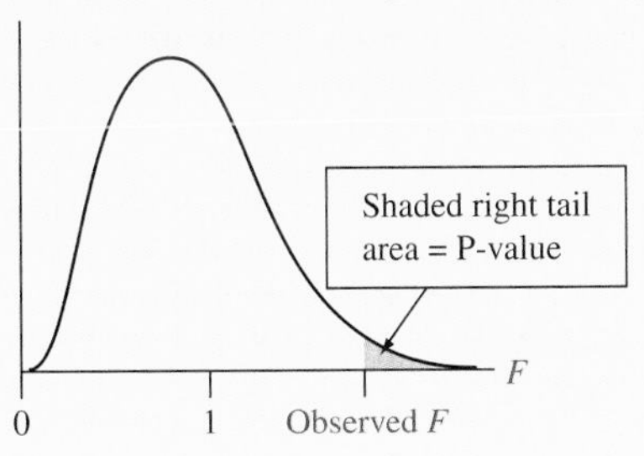

In Section 13.3, we learned that the F distribution has two df values. For ANOVA with g groups and total sample size for all groups combined of $N = n_1 + n_2 + \cdots + n_g$,

$$df_1 = g - 1 \text{ and } df_2 = N - g.$$

Table D in the appendix reports F values having P-value of 0.05 for various df_1 and df_2 values. For any given F value and df values, software (or a web app) provides the P-value. The following summarizes the steps of an ANOVA F test.

Recall

The **F distribution** was introduced in Section 13.3. It's used for tests about several parameters (rather than a single parameter or a difference between two parameters, for which we can use a t test). ◀

SUMMARY: Steps of ANOVA F Test for Comparing Population Means of Several Groups

1. **Assumptions:** Independent random samples (either from random sampling or a randomized experiment), normal population distributions with equal standard deviations.
2. **Hypotheses:** H_0: $\mu_1 = \mu_2 = \cdots = \mu_g$ (Equal population means for g groups), H_a: at least two of the population means are not equal.
3. **Test statistic:** $F = \frac{\text{Between-groups variability}}{\text{Within-groups variability}}$.

   F sampling distribution has $df_1 = g - 1$, $df_2 = N - g$ = total sample size − number of groups.
4. **P-value:** Right-tail probability above observed F value.
5. **Conclusion:** Interpret in context. If decision needed, reject H_0 if P-value ≤ significance level (such as 0.05).

Example 3

One-way ANOVA ◀

Telephone Holding Times

Picture the Scenario

Examples 1 and 2 discussed a study of the length of time that 15 callers to an airline's toll-free telephone number remain on hold before hanging up. The study compared three recordings: an advertisement about the airline, Muzak, and classical music. Let μ_1, μ_2, and μ_3 denote the population mean telephone holding times for the three recordings.

Questions to Explore

a. For testing H_0: $\mu_1 = \mu_2 = \mu_3$ based on this experiment, what value of the F test statistic would have a P-value of 0.05?

b. For the data in Table 14.1, we'll see that software reports $F = 6.4$. Based on the answer to part a, will the P-value be larger, or smaller, than 0.05?

c. Can you reject H_0, using a significance level of 0.05? What can you conclude from this?

Think It Through

a. With $g = 3$ groups and a total sample size of $N = 15$ (5 in each group), the test statistic has

$$df_1 = g - 1 = 2 \text{ and } df_2 = N - g = 15 - 3 = 12.$$

From Table D (see the excerpt in the margin) with these df values, an F test statistic value of 3.88 results in a P-value of 0.05.

b. Since the F test statistic of 6.4 is farther out in the tail than 3.88 (see figure in margin), the right-tail probability above 6.4 is less than 0.05. So, the P-value is less than 0.05.

c. Since P-value < 0.05, there is sufficient evidence to reject H_0: $\mu_1 = \mu_2 = \mu_3$. We conclude that the population mean time that customers are willing to remain on hold differs for at least two of the three types of recordings.

F values corresponding to a P-value of 0.05

	df_1		
df_2	1	2	3
6	5.99	5.14	4.76
12	4.75	3.88	3.49
18	4.41	3.55	3.16
24	4.26	3.40	3.01
30	4.17	3.32	2.92
120	3.92	3.07	2.68

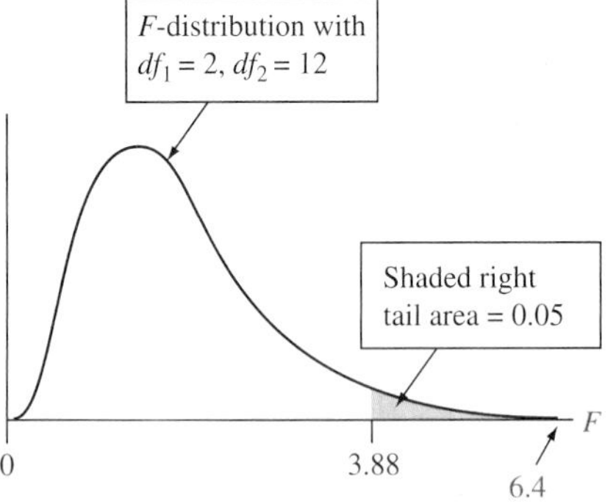

Insight

We'll see that software reports a P-value = 0.013. This is quite strong evidence against H_0. If H_0 were true, there'd be only about a 1% chance of getting an F test statistic value larger than the observed F value of 6.4.

▶ ***Try Exercise 14.2, parts a–c***

The Variance Estimates and the ANOVA Table

Now let's take a closer look at the *F* test statistic. Denote the group sample means by $\bar{y}_1, \bar{y}_2, \ldots, \bar{y}_g$. (We use *y* rather than *x* because the quantitative variable is the response variable when used in a corresponding regression analysis.) We'll see that the *F* test statistic depends on these sample means, the sample standard deviations $s_1, s_2, \ldots, s_g$ for the *g* groups, and the sample sizes.

One assumption for the ANOVA *F* test is that each population has the same standard deviation. Let σ denote the standard deviation for each of the *g* population distributions. The *F* test statistic for H_0: $\mu_1 = \mu_2 = \cdots = \mu_g$ is the ratio of two estimates of σ^2, the population *variance* for each group. Since we won't usually do computations by hand, we'll show formulas merely to give a better sense of what the *F* test statistic represents. The formulas are simplest when the group sample sizes are equal (as in Example 3), the case we'll show.

The estimate of σ^2 in the *denominator* of the *F* test statistic uses the variability *within* each group. The sample standard deviations $s_1, s_2, \ldots, s_g$ summarize the variation of the observations within the groups around their means.

Recall

With $g = 2$, s^2 is the square of the pooled standard deviation we used for the *t* test in Section 10.3. ◀

- With equal sample sizes, the **within-groups estimate** of the variance σ^2 is the average of the *g* sample variances for the *g* groups,

$$\text{Within-groups variance estimate } s^2 = \frac{s_1^2 + s_2^2 + \cdots + s_g^2}{g}.$$

When the sample sizes are not equal, the within-groups estimate is a *weighted average* of the sample variances, with greater weight given to samples with larger sample sizes. In either case, this estimate is unbiased: Its sampling distribution has σ^2 as its mean, regardless of whether H_0 is true.

The estimate of σ^2 in the *numerator* of the *F* test statistic uses the variability *between* each sample mean and the overall sample mean $\bar{y}$ for all the data.

Did You Know?

Without *n* in the formula, the between-groups estimate is the sample variance of the *g* sample means. That sample variance of $\{\bar{y}_1, \bar{y}_2, \ldots, \bar{y}_g\}$ estimates the variance of the sampling distribution of each sample mean, which is σ^2/n. Multiplying by *n* then gives an estimate of σ^2 itself. See Exercise 14.67. ◀

- With equal sample sizes, *n* in each group, the **between-groups estimate** of the variance σ^2 is

$$\begin{array}{c}\text{Between-groups}\\ \text{variance estimate}\end{array} = \frac{n[(\bar{y}_1 - \bar{y})^2 + (\bar{y}_2 - \bar{y})^2 + \cdots + (\bar{y}_g - \bar{y})^2]}{g - 1}.$$

If H_0 is true, this estimate is also unbiased. We expect this estimate to take a similar value as the within-groups estimate, apart from sampling error. If H_0 is false, however, the population means differ and the sample means tend to differ more greatly. Then, the between-groups estimate tends to overestimate σ^2.

The *F* test statistic is the ratio of these two estimates of the population variance,

$$F = \frac{\text{Between-groups estimate of } \sigma^2}{\text{Within-groups estimate of } \sigma^2}.$$

Computer software displays the two estimates in an ANOVA table similar to tables displayed in regression. Table 14.2 shows the basic format, illustrating the test in Example 3:

Recall

In Sections 12.4 and 13.3, we saw that a **mean square** (MS) is a ratio of a sum of squares (SS) to its *df* value. ◀

- The MS column contains the two estimates, which are called *mean squares*.
- The ratio of the two mean squares is the *F* test statistic, $F = 74.6/11.6 = 6.4$.

This *F* test statistic has P-value = 0.013, also shown in Table 14.2.

The mean square in the group row of the ANOVA table is based on variability *between* the groups. It is the *between-groups* estimate of the population variance σ^2. This is 74.6 in Table 14.2, listed under MS. The mean square error is the *within-groups* estimate s^2 of σ^2. This is 11.6 in Table 14.2. The "Error" label for this MS refers to the fact that it summarizes the error from not being able to predict subjects' responses exactly if we know only the group to which they belong.

Table 14.2 ANOVA Table for *F* Test Using Data From Table 14.1

Source	DF	SS	MS	F	P
Group	2	149.2	74.6	6.43	0.013
Error	12	139.2	11.6		
Total	14	288.4			

Between groups (→ Group); Within groups (→ Error); *F test statistic* = ratio of the MS values

```
NORMAL FIX3 AUTO REAL RADIAN CL
One-way ANOVA
F=6.431
p=.013
Factor
 df=2.000
 SS=149.200
 MS=74.600
Error
↓ df=12.000
```

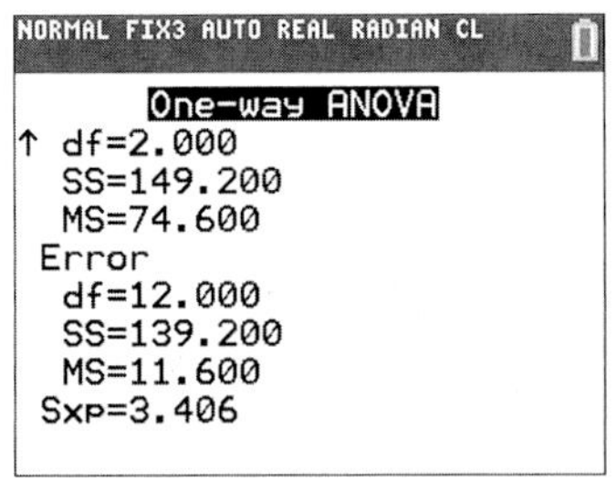

TI output for ANOVA

Each mean square equals a sum of squares (in the SS column) divided by a degrees of freedom value (in the DF column). The *df* values for Group and Error in Table 14.2 are the *df* values for the *F* distribution, $df_1 = g - 1 = 3 - 1 = 2$ and $df_2 = N - g = 15 - 3 = 12$.

The sum of the between-groups sum of squares and the within-groups (Error) sum of squares is the **total sum of squares**. This is the sum of squares of the combined sample of *N* observations around the overall sample mean. The analysis of variance partitions the total sum of squares into two independent parts, the between-groups SS and the within-groups SS. It can be shown that the total sum of squares equals

$$\text{Total SS} = \Sigma(y - \bar{y})^2 = \text{between-groups SS} + \text{within-groups SS}.$$

In Table 14.2, for example,

$$\text{Total SS} = 288.4 = 149.2 + 139.2.$$

The total SS divided by $N - 1$ (the *df* for the total SS) is the sample variance when the data for the *g* groups are combined and treated as a single sample. The margin shows the TI output for this one-way ANOVA.

Assumptions and the Effects of Violating Them

The assumptions for the ANOVA *F* test comparing population means are:

(1) The population distributions of the response variable for the *g* groups are normal,

(2) Those distributions have the same standard deviation σ, and

(3) The data resulted from randomization.

Figure 14.3 portrays the population distribution assumptions.

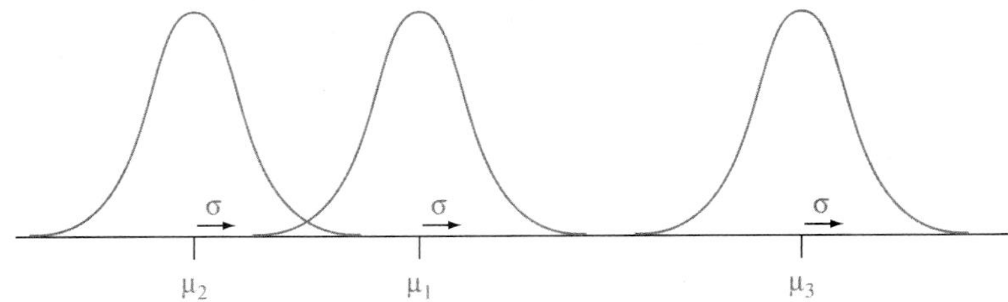

▲ **Figure 14.3** The Assumptions About the Population Distributions: Normal With Equal Standard Deviations. **Question** In practice, what types of evidence would suggest that these assumptions are badly violated?

The assumptions that the population distributions are normal with identical standard deviations seem stringent. They are never satisfied exactly in practice. Moderate violations of the normality assumption are not serious. The *F* sampling distribution still provides a reasonably good approximation to the actual sampling distribution of the F test statistic. This becomes even more the case as the sample sizes increase, because the sampling distribution then has weaker dependence on the form of the population distributions.

Moderate violations of the equal population standard deviation assumption are also not serious. When the sample sizes are identical for the groups, the F test still works well even with severe violations of this assumption. When the sample sizes are not equal, the F test works quite well as long as the largest group standard deviation is no more than about twice the smallest group standard deviation.

You can construct box plots or dot plots for the sample data distributions to check for extreme violations of normality. Misleading results may occur with the F test if the distributions are highly skewed and the sample size N is small, or if there are relatively large differences among the standard deviations (the largest sample standard deviation being more than double the smallest one) and the sample sizes are unequal. When the distributions are highly skewed, the mean may not even be a relevant summary measure.[1]

In Practice Robustness of ANOVA F test

Since the ANOVA F test is robust to moderate breakdowns in the population normality and equal standard deviation assumptions, in practice it is used unless (1) graphical methods show extreme skew for the response variable or (2) the largest group standard deviation is more than about double the smallest group standard deviation and the sample sizes are unequal.

Example 4

ANOVA assumptions ◄

Telephone Holding Time Study

Picture the Scenario

Let's check the assumptions for the F test on telephone holding times (Example 3).

Question to Explore

Is it appropriate to apply ANOVA to the data in Table 14.1 to compare mean telephone holding times for three recording types?

Think It Through

Subjects were selected randomly for the experiment and assigned randomly to the three recording types. From Table 14.1 (summarized in the margin), the largest sample standard deviation of 4.2 is less than twice the smallest standard deviation of 2.4. (In any case, the sample sizes are equal, so this assumption is not crucial.) The sample sizes in Table 14.1 are small, so it is difficult to make judgments about shapes of population distributions. However, the dot plots in Figure 14.2a did not show evidence of severe nonnormality, and the box plots in the margin show no outliers. Thus, ANOVA is suitable for these data.

Recall

Table 14.1 showed the following:

Recording	Sample Size	Mean	Std. Dev.
Advert.	5	5.4	4.2
Muzak	5	2.8	2.4
Classical	5	10.4	3.4

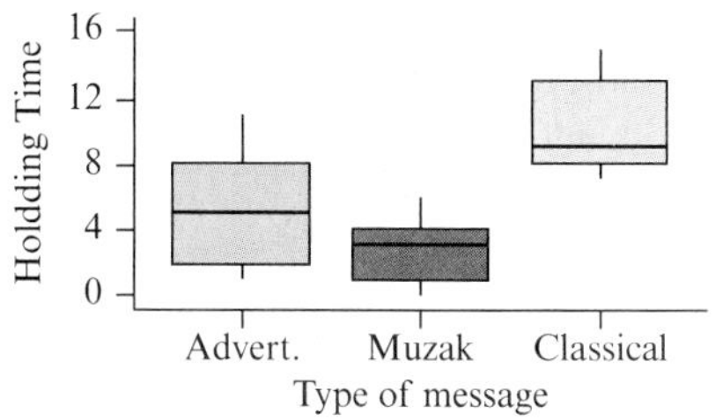

Insight

As in other statistical inferences, the method used to gather the data is the most crucial factor. Inferences have greater validity when the data are from an experimental study that randomly assigned subjects to groups or from a sample survey that used random sampling.

► ***Try Exercise 14.11, part c***

[1]Chapter 15 discusses methods that apply when these assumptions are badly violated.

Recall

See the beginning of Chapter 10 to review the distinction between **independent samples** and **dependent samples.** ◀

The ANOVA methods in this chapter are designed for *independent* samples. Recall that for independent samples, the subjects in one sample are distinct from those in other samples. Separate methods, beyond the scope of this text, handle *dependent* samples.

Using One *F* Test or Several *t* Tests to Compare the Means

Recall

To compare two means while assuming equal population standard deviations, Section 10.3 showed the test statistic is

$$t = \frac{\bar{y}_1 - \bar{y}_2}{s\sqrt{\frac{1}{n_1} + \frac{1}{n_2}}},$$

where the standard deviation s pools information from within both samples. It has $df = n_1 + n_2 - 2 = N - g$ for $N = n_1 + n_2$ and $g = 2$. ◀

With two groups, Section 10.3 showed how a t test can compare the means under the assumption of equal population standard deviations. That test also uses between-groups and within-groups variation. The t test statistic has the difference *between* the two group means in the numerator and a denominator based on pooling variability *within* the two groups. See the formula in the margin. In fact, if we apply the ANOVA F test to data from $g = 2$ groups, it can be shown that the F test statistic equals the square of this t test statistic. The P-value for the F test is exactly the same as the two-sided P-value for the t test. We can use either test to conduct the analysis.

When there are several groups, instead of using the F test why not use a t test to compare each pair of means? One reason for doing the F test is that using a *single* test rather than multiple tests enables us to control the probability of a Type I error. With a significance level of 0.05 in the F test, for instance, the probability of incorrectly rejecting a true H_0 is fixed at 0.05. When we do a separate t test for each pair of means, by contrast, a Type I error probability applies for *each* comparison. In that case, we are not controlling the *overall* Type I error rate for all the comparisons.

But the F test has its own disadvantages. With a small P-value, we can conclude that the population means are not identical. However, the result of the F test does not tell us *which* groups are different or *how* different they are. In Example 3, we have not concluded whether one recording works significantly better than the other two at keeping potential customers on the phone. We can address these issues using confidence intervals, as the next section shows.

14.1 Practicing the Basics

14.1 Hotel satisfaction The CEO of a company that owns five resort hotels wants to evaluate and compare satisfaction with the five hotels. The company's research department randomly sampled 125 people who had stayed at any of the hotels during the past month and asked them to rate their expectations of the hotel before their stay and to rate the quality of the actual stay at the hotel. Both observations used a rating scale of 0–10, with 0 = very poor and 10 = excellent. The researchers compared the hotels on the gap between prior expectation and actual quality, using the difference score, y = performance gap = (prior expectation score − actual quality score).

TRY

a. Identify the response variable, the factor, and the categories that form the groups.

b. State the null and alternative hypotheses for conducting an ANOVA.

c. Explain why the *df* values for this ANOVA are $df_1 = 4$ and $df_2 = 120$.

d. How large an F test statistic is needed to get a P-value = 0.05 in this ANOVA?

14.2 Satisfaction with banking A bank conducts a survey in which it randomly samples 400 of its customers. The survey asks the customers which way they use the bank the most: (1) interacting with a teller at the bank, (2) using ATMs, or (3) using the bank's online banking service. It also asks their level of satisfaction with the service they most often use (on a scale of 0 to 10 with 0 = very poor and 10 = excellent). Does mean satisfaction differ according to how they most use the bank?

TRY

a. Identifying notation, state the null and alternative hypotheses for conducting an ANOVA with data from the survey.

b. Report the *df* values for this ANOVA. Above what F test statistic values give a P-value below 0.05?

c. For the data, $F = 0.46$ and the P-value equals 0.63. What can you conclude?

d. What were the assumptions on which the ANOVA was based? Which assumption is the most important?

14.3 What's the best way to learn French? The following table shows scores on the first quiz (maximum score

10 points) for eighth-grade students in an introductory level French course. The instructor grouped the students in the course as follows:

Group 1: Never studied foreign language before but have good English skills

Group 2: Never studied foreign language before and have poor English skills

Group 3: Studied at least one other foreign language

French scores on the quiz

	Group 1	Group 2	Group 3
	4	1	9
	6	5	10
	8		5
Mean	6.0	3.0	8.0
Std. Dev.	2.000	2.828	2.646

Source	DF	SS	MS	F	P
Group	2	30.00	15.00	2.50	0.177
Error	5	30.00	6.00		
Total	7	60.00			

a. Defining notation and using results obtained with software, also shown in the table, report the five steps of the ANOVA test.

b. The sample means are quite different, but the P-value is not small. Name one important reason for this. (*Hint*: For given sample means, how do the results of the test depend on the sample sizes?)

c. Was this an experimental study, or an observational study? Explain how a lurking variable could be responsible for Group 3 having a larger mean than the others. (Thus, even if the P-value were small, it is inappropriate to assume that having studied at least one foreign language causes one to perform better on this quiz.)

14.4 What affects the *F* value? Refer to the previous exercise.

a. Suppose that the first observation in the second group was actually 9, not 1. Then the standard deviations are the same as reported in the table, but the sample means are 6, 7, and 8 rather than 6, 3, and 8. Do you think the *F* test statistic would be larger, the same, or smaller? Explain your reasoning, without doing any calculations.

b. Suppose you had the same means as shown in the table but the sample standard deviations were 1.0, 1.8, and 1.6, instead of 2.0, 2.8, and 2.6. Do you think the *F* test statistic would be larger, the same, or smaller? Explain your reasoning.

c. Suppose you had the same means and standard deviations as shown in the table but the sample sizes were 30, 20, and 30, instead of 3, 2, and 3. Do you think the *F* test statistic would be larger, the same, or smaller? Explain your reasoning.

d. In parts a, b, and c, would the P-value be larger, the same, or smaller? Why?

14.5 Outsourcing Example 1 at the beginning of this chapter mentioned a study to compare customer satisfaction at service centers in San Jose, California; Toronto, Canada; and Bangalore, India. Each center randomly sampled 100 people who called during a two-week period. Callers rated their satisfaction on a scale of 0 to 10, with higher scores representing greater satisfaction. The sample means were 7.6 for San Jose, 7.8 for Toronto, and 7.1 for Bangalore. The table shows the results of conducting an ANOVA.

a. Define notation and specify the null hypothesis tested in this table.

b. Explain how to obtain the *F* test statistic value reported in the table from the MS values shown and report the values of df_1 and df_2 for the *F* distribution.

c. Interpret the P-value reported for this test. What conclusion would you make using a 0.05 significance level?

Customer satisfaction with outsourcing

Source	DF	SS	MS	F	P
Group	2	26.00	13.00	27.6	0.000
Error	297	140.00	0.47		
Total	299	60.00			

14.6 ANOVA and box plots For two studies, each comparing three groups, the box plots below show results. (Each box plot is based on a random sample of size 40.)

a. Judging from the box plots, which study will more likely lead to a rejection of the ANOVA null hypothesis of equal population means? Explain.

b. Which study will have the large value for the *F* test statistic? Why?

c. The P-value for the ANOVA *F* test for the second study equals 0.001. Does this necessarily imply that all three population means are different from each other?

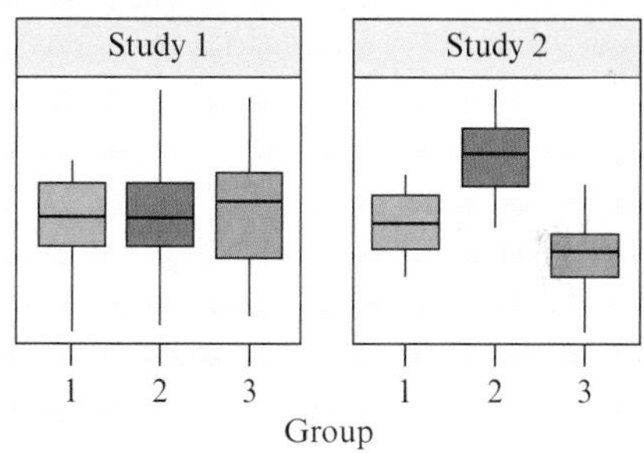

14.7 How many kids to have? A recent General Social Survey asked subjects, "What is the ideal number of kids for a family?" Do responses tend to depend on the subjects' religious affiliation? Results of an ANOVA are shown in the printout, for religion categories (Protestant, Catholic, Jewish, or Other).

a. Define notation and specify the null hypothesis tested in this printout.

b. Summarize the assumptions made to conduct this test.

c. Report the *F* test statistic value and the P-value for this test. Interpret the P-value.

d. Based on part c, can you conclude that *every* pair of religious affiliations has different population means for ideal family size? Explain.

Ideal number of kids in a family by religious affiliation

Source	DF	SS	MS	F	P
Religion	3	11.72	3.91	5.48	0.001
Error	1295	922.82	0.71		
Total	1298	934.54			

14.8 Smoking and personality A study about smoking and personality (by A. Terracciano and P. Costa, *Addiction*, vol. 99, 2004, pp. 472–481) used a sample of 1638 adults in the Baltimore Longitudinal Study on Aging. The subjects formed three groups according to smoking status (never, former, current). Each subject completed a personality questionnaire that provided scores on various personality scales designed to have overall means of about 50 and standard deviations of about 10. The table shows some results for three traits, giving the means with standard deviations in parentheses.

	Never smokers (n = 828)	Former smokers (n = 694)	Current smokers (n = 116)	F
Neuroticism	46.7 (9.6)	48.5 (9.2)	51.9 (9.9)	17.77
Extraversion	50.4 (10.3)	50.2 (10.0)	50.9 (9.4)	0.24
Conscientiousness	51.8 (10.1)	48.9 (9.7)	45.6 (10.3)	29.42

a. For the F test for the extraversion scale, using the 0.05 significance level, what conclusion would you make?

b. Refer to part a. Does this mean that the population means are necessarily equal?

14.9 French cuisine The restaurant guide Zagat compiles customer ratings on the quality of food on a 30-point scale. The data set French Cuisine on the book's website contains a random sample of ratings of French cuisine restaurants in New York, London, and Paris, compiled in June 2015 from the zagat.com website.

TECH

a. Using software, construct dot plots or side-by-side box plots that show the data and find the mean and standard deviation of the ratings in each city.

b. Conduct an ANOVA. Report the hypotheses, F test statistic value, P-value, and interpret results. Use a significance level of 0.05.

14.10 Software and French ANOVA Refer to Exercise 14.3. Using software,

TECH

a. Create the data file and find the sample means and standard deviations.

b. Find and report the ANOVA table. Interpret the P-value.

c. Change an observation in Group 2 so that the P-value will be smaller. Specify the value you changed and report the resulting F test statistic and the P-value. Explain why the value you changed would have this effect.

14.11 Comparing therapies for anorexia The Anorexia data file on the book's website shows weight change for 72 anorexic teenage girls who were randomly assigned to one of three psychological treatments (cognitive or family therapy and a control treatment). Use software to analyze these data. (The change scores are in the last three columns of the data set. Alternatively, the website also contains a dataset that shows the data in "long" format, with the treatment in one column and the change score in another column.)

TRY TECH

a. Construct box plots for the three groups. Use these and sample summary means and standard deviations to describe the three samples.

b. For the one-way ANOVA comparing the three mean weight changes, report the test statistic and P-value. Explain how to interpret.

c. State and check the assumptions for the test in part b.

14.2 Estimating Differences in Groups for a Single Factor

When an analysis of variance F test has a small P-value, the test does not specify *which* means are different or *how* different they are. In practice, we can estimate differences between population means with confidence intervals.

Confidence Intervals Comparing Pairs of Means

Remember that one of the assumptions in ANOVA is a common standard deviation σ for the distribution of the response variable in each group. We can estimate this common standard deviation by s, the square root of the within-groups variance s^2 that we used in the denominator of the F test statistic. It is the square root of the mean square error that software reports (the MS in the row for "Error" of any ANOVA table).

Recall

s^2 is an unbiased estimator of σ^2, regardless of whether H_0 is true in the ANOVA F test. ◀

SUMMARY: Confidence Interval Comparing Means

For two groups i and j, with sample means $\bar{y}_i$ and $\bar{y}_j$ having sample sizes n_i and n_j, the 95% confidence interval for $\mu_i - \mu_j$ is

$$\bar{y}_i - \bar{y}_j \pm t_{.025}\, s\sqrt{\frac{1}{n_i} + \frac{1}{n_j}}.$$

The t-score from the t table has $df = N - g$ = total sample size − # groups.

The df value of $N - g$ for the t-score is also df_2 for the F test. This is the df for the MS error. For $g = 2$ groups, $N = n_1 + n_2$ and $df = N - g = (n_1 + n_2 - 2)$. This confidence interval is then identical to the one introduced in Section 10.3 for $(\mu_1 - \mu_2)$ based on a pooled standard deviation. In the context of follow-up analyses after the ANOVA F test where we form this confidence interval to compare a pair of means, some software (such as MINITAB) refers to this method of comparing means as the **Fisher method**.

When the confidence interval does not contain 0, we can infer that the population means are different. The interval shows just how different they may be.

Example 5

Fisher method

Number of Good Friends and Happiness

Picture the Scenario

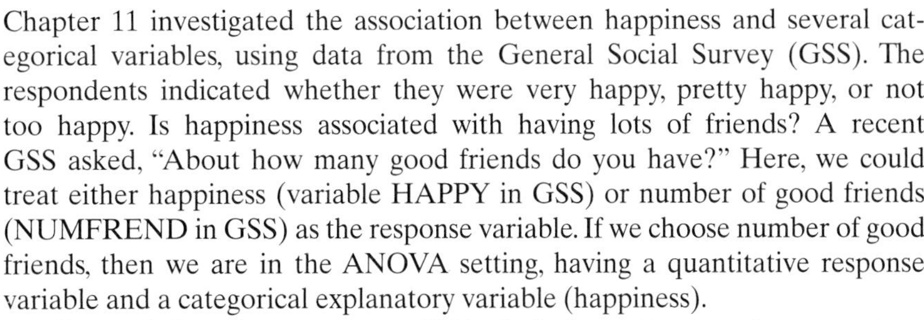

Chapter 11 investigated the association between happiness and several categorical variables, using data from the General Social Survey (GSS). The respondents indicated whether they were very happy, pretty happy, or not too happy. Is happiness associated with having lots of friends? A recent GSS asked, "About how many good friends do you have?" Here, we could treat either happiness (variable HAPPY in GSS) or number of good friends (NUMFREND in GSS) as the response variable. If we choose number of good friends, then we are in the ANOVA setting, having a quantitative response variable and a categorical explanatory variable (happiness).

For each happiness category, Table 14.3 shows the sample mean, standard deviation, and sample size for the number of good friends. It also shows the ANOVA table for the F test comparing the population means. The small P-value of 0.0025 suggests that at least two of the three population means are different.

Table 14.3 Summary of ANOVA for Comparing Mean Number of Good Friends for Three Happiness Categories

The analysis is based on GSS data.

	Very happy	Pretty happy	Not too happy
Mean	7.6	5.7	6.3
Standard deviation	8.7	5.9	8.0
Sample size	267	459	85

Source	DF	SS	MS	F	P
Group	2	617	308.32	6.023	0.0025
Error	808	41362	51.19		
Total	810	41979			

Question to Explore

Use 95% confidence intervals to compare the population mean number of good friends for the three pairs of happiness categories—very happy with pretty happy, very happy with not too happy, and pretty happy with not too happy.

Think It Through

From Table 14.3, the MS error equals 51.19. The estimated standard deviation of the number of friends at each category of happiness is $s = \sqrt{51.19} = 7.15$.

For a 95% confidence interval with $df = 808$ (listed in the same row as MS error), the t score is $t_{0.025} = 1.963$. (Because the df are so large, this is essentially the same as the corresponding z-score.) For comparing the very happy and pretty happy categories, the confidence interval for $\mu_1 - \mu_2$ is

$$(\bar{y}_1 - \bar{y}_2) \pm t_{.025}\, s\sqrt{\frac{1}{n_1} + \frac{1}{n_2}} = (7.6 - 5.7) \pm 1.963(7.15)\sqrt{\frac{1}{267} + \frac{1}{459}}$$

which is 1.9 ± 1.1, or $(0.8, 3.0)$.

We infer that the population mean number of good friends is between about 1 and 3 higher for those who are very happy than for those who are pretty happy. Since the confidence interval contains only positive numbers, this suggests that $\mu_1 - \mu_2 > 0$; that is, μ_1 exceeds μ_2. On the average, people who are very happy have more good friends than people who are pretty happy.

For the other comparisons, you can find

Very happy, not too happy: 95% CI for $\mu_1 - \mu_3$ is
$(7.6 - 6.3) \pm 1.7$, or $(-0.4, 3.0)$.
Pretty happy, not too happy: 95% CI for $\mu_2 - \mu_3$ is
$(5.7 - 6.3) \pm 1.7$, or $(-2.3, 1.1)$.

These two confidence intervals contain 0. So there's not enough evidence to conclude that a difference exists between μ_1 and μ_3 or between μ_2 and μ_3.

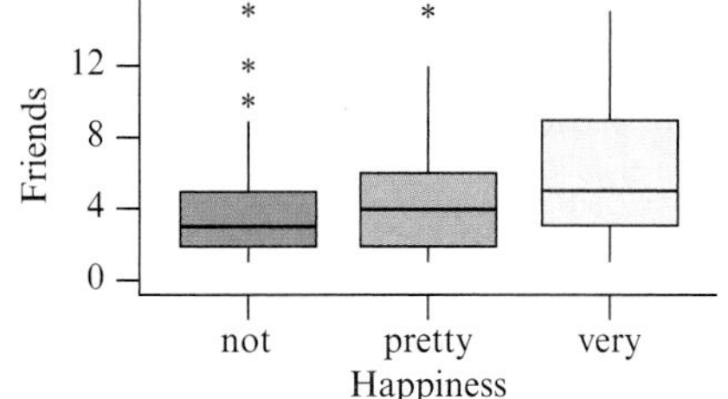

Insight

The confidence intervals are quite wide, even though the sample sizes are fairly large. This is because the sample standard deviations (and hence s) are large. Table 14.3 reports that the sample standard deviations are larger than the sample means, suggesting that the three distributions are skewed to the right. The margin figure shows box plots of the distribution of number of good friends in each group, except for many large outliers (as large as 75). Do non-normal population distributions invalidate this inferential analysis? We'll discuss this next.

▶ ***Try Exercise 14.12***

The Effects of Violating Assumptions

Recall

From Section 10.2, a 95% confidence interval for $\mu_2 - \mu_1$ using separate standard deviations s_1 and s_2 is

$$\bar{y}_1 - \bar{y}_2 \pm t_{.025}\sqrt{\frac{s_1^2}{n_1} + \frac{s_2^2}{n_2}}.$$

Software supplies the *df* value and the confidence interval. ◀

The t confidence intervals have the same assumptions as the ANOVA F test: (1) normal population distributions, (2) identical standard deviations, and (3) data that resulted from randomization. These inferences also are not highly dependent on the normality assumption, especially when the sample sizes are large, such as in Example 5. When the standard deviations are quite different, with the ratio of the largest to smallest exceeding about 2, it is preferable to use the confidence interval formula from Section 10.2 (see the margin Recall) that uses *separate* standard deviations for the groups rather than a single pooled value s. That approach does not assume equal standard deviations.

In Example 5, the sample standard deviations are not very different (ranging from 5.9 to 8.7), and the GSS is a multistage random sample with properties similar to a simple random sample. Thus, Assumptions 2 and 3 are reasonably well satisfied. The sample sizes are fairly large, so Assumption 1 of normality is not crucial. It's justifiable to use ANOVA and follow-up confidence intervals with these data.

Controlling Overall Confidence With Many Confidence Intervals

With g groups, there are $g(g - 1)/2$ pairs of groups to compare. With $g = 3$, for instance, there are $g(g - 1)/2 = 3(2)/2 = 3$ comparisons: Group 1 with Group 2, Group 1 with Group 3, and Group 2 with Group 3.

The confidence interval method just discussed is mainly used when g is small or when only a few comparisons are of main interest. When there are many groups, the number of comparisons can be large. For example, when $g = 10$, there are $g(g - 1)/2 = 45$ pairs of means to compare. If we plan to construct 95% confidence intervals for these comparisons, an error probability of 0.05 applies to *each* comparison. On average, $45(0.05) = 2.25$ of the confidence intervals would *not* contain the true differences of means.

For 95% confidence intervals, the confidence level of 0.95 is the probability that *any particular* confidence interval that we plan to construct will contain the parameter. The probability that *all* the confidence intervals will contain the parameters is considerably smaller than the confidence level for any particular interval. How can we construct the intervals so that the 95% confidence extends to the *entire set* of intervals rather than to *each single* interval? Methods that control the probability that *all* confidence intervals will contain the true differences in means are called **multiple comparison methods**. For these methods, *all* intervals are designed to contain the true parameters *simultaneously* with an overall fixed probability.

Multiple Comparisons for Comparing All Pairs of Means

Multiple comparison methods compare pairs of means with a confidence level that applies simultaneously to the entire set of comparisons rather than to each separate comparison.

To ensure that the overall confidence level is met, we need to make each interval wider. One simple way to achieve this is to construct each confidence interval with a higher confidence level, that is, using a t-score that is larger than $t_{0.025}$. To find the exact confidence level at which to construct each interval, the desired overall error probability is split into equal parts for each comparison. Suppose we want a confidence level of 0.95 that *all* confidence intervals will be simultaneously correct. If we plan to construct five confidence intervals comparing means, then the method uses error probability $0.05/5 = 0.01$ for each one; that is, a 99% confidence level for each separate interval. This approach ensures that the overall confidence level is *at least* 0.95. (It is actually slightly larger.) Called the **Bonferroni** method, it is based on a special case of a probability theorem shown by Italian probabilist, Carlo Bonferroni, in 1936 (Exercise 14.68).

We shall instead use the **Tukey method**. It is designed to give an overall confidence level *very close* to the desired value (such as 0.95), and it has the advantage that its confidence intervals are slightly narrower than the Bonferroni intervals. The Tukey method is more complex, using a sampling distribution pertaining to the difference between the largest and smallest of the g sample means. We do not present its formula, but it is easy to obtain with software.

Recall

John Tukey was responsible for many statistical innovations, including box plots and other methods of exploratory data analysis (EDA). See On the Shoulders of... John Tukey in Section 2.6 to read more about Tukey and EDA. ◀

Example 6

Tukey method ◀

Number of Good Friends

Picture the Scenario

Example 5 compared the population mean numbers of good friends, for three levels of reported happiness. There, we constructed a *separate* 95% confidence interval for the difference between each pair of means. Table 14.4

displays these three intervals. The probability that at least one of them will not contain the true parameter value is larger than 0.05 because these intervals are not constructed using a multiple comparison method. Table 14.4 also displays the confidence intervals that software reports for the Tukey multiple comparison method. The probability that one of these will not contain the true difference is about 0.05.

Table 14.4 Multiple Comparisons of Mean Number of Good Friends for Three Happiness Categories

Groups	Difference of means	Separate 95% CIs	Tukey 95% Multiple Comparison CIs
(Very happy, Pretty happy)	$\mu_1 - \mu_2$	(0.8, 3.0)	(0.6, 3.2)
(Very happy, Not too happy)	$\mu_1 - \mu_3$	(−0.4, 3.0)	(−0.8, 3.4)
(Pretty happy, Not too happy)	$\mu_2 - \mu_3$	(−2.3, 1.1)	(−2.6, 1.4)

Question to Explore

a. Explain how the Tukey multiple comparison confidence intervals differ from the separate confidence intervals in Table 14.4.

b. Summarize results shown for the Tukey multiple comparisons.

Think It Through

a. The Tukey confidence intervals hold with an *overall* confidence level of about 95%. This confidence applies to the entire set of three intervals. The Tukey confidence intervals are wider than the separate 95% confidence intervals because the multiple comparison approach uses a higher confidence level for each separate interval to ensure achieving the overall confidence level of 95% for the entire set of intervals.

b. The Tukey confidence interval for $\mu_1 - \mu_2$ contains only positive values, so we infer that $\mu_1 > \mu_2$. The mean number of good friends is higher, although perhaps barely so, for those who are very happy than for those who are pretty happy. The other two Tukey intervals contain 0, so we cannot infer that those pairs of means differ.

Insight

Figure 14.4 summarizes the three Tukey comparisons from Table 14.4. The intervals have different lengths because the group sample sizes are different.

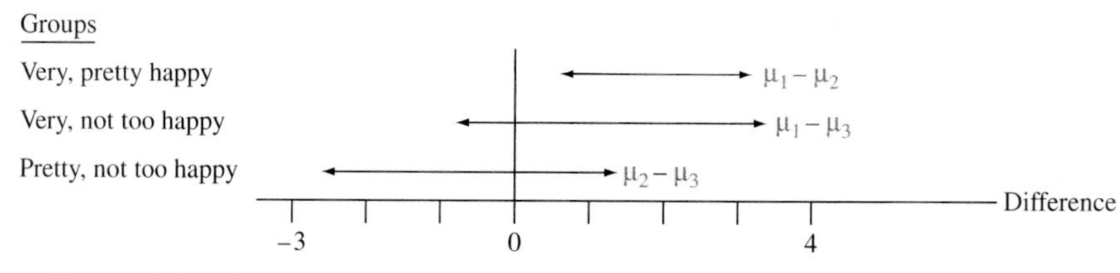

▲ **Figure 14.4** Summary of Tukey Comparisons of Pairs of Means.

► ***Try Exercise 14.15***

ANOVA and Regression

ANOVA can be presented as a special case of multiple regression. The factor defining the groups enters the regression model using *indicator variables.* Each indicator

Recall

You can review **indicator variables** in Section 13.5. We used them there to include a categorical explanatory variable in a regression model. ◀

variable takes only two values, 0 and 1, and indicates whether an observation falls in a particular group.

With three groups, we need two indicator variables to indicate the group membership. The first indicator variable is

$$x_1 = 1 \text{ for observations from the first group}$$
$$= 0 \text{ otherwise.}$$

The second indicator variable is

$$x_2 = 1 \text{ for observations from the second group}$$
$$= 0 \text{ otherwise.}$$

The indicator variables identify the group to which an observation belongs as follows:

$$\text{Group 1: } x_1 = 1 \text{ and } x_2 = 0$$
$$\text{Group 2: } x_1 = 0 \text{ and } x_2 = 1$$
$$\text{Group 3: } x_1 = 0 \text{ and } x_2 = 0.$$

We don't need a separate indicator variable for the third group. We know an observation is in that group if $x_1 = 0$ and $x_2 = 0$.

With these indicator variables, the multiple regression equation for the mean of y is

$$\mu_y = \alpha + \beta_1 x_1 + \beta_2 x_2.$$

For observations from the third group, $x_1 = x_2 = 0$, and the equation reduces to

$$\mu_y = \alpha + \beta_1(0) + \beta_2(0) = \alpha.$$

So the parameter α represents the population mean of the response variable y for the last group. For observations from the first group, $x_1 = 1$ and $x_2 = 0$, so

$$\mu_y = \alpha + \beta_1(1) + \beta_2(0) = \alpha + \beta_1$$

equals the population mean μ_1 for that group. Similarly, $\alpha + \beta_2$ equals the population mean μ_2 for the second group (for which $x_1 = 0$ and $x_2 = 1$).

Since $\alpha + \beta_1 = \mu_1$ and $\alpha = \mu_3$, the difference between the means

$$\mu_1 - \mu_3 = (\alpha + \beta_1) - \alpha = \beta_1.$$

That is, the coefficient β_1 of the first indicator variable represents the difference between the first mean and the last mean. Likewise, $\beta_2 = \mu_2 - \mu_3$. In other words, the beta coefficients of the indicator variables represent differences between the mean of each group and the mean of the last group. Table 14.5 summarizes the parameters of the regression model and their correspondence with the three population means.

Table 14.5 Interpretation of Coefficients of Indicator Variables in Regression Model

The indicator variables represent a categorical predictor with three categories specifying three groups.

	Indicator			
Group	x_1	x_2	**Mean of y**	**Interpretation of β**
1	1	0	$\mu_1 = \alpha + \beta_1$	$\beta_1 = \mu_1 - \mu_3$
2	0	1	$\mu_2 = \alpha + \beta_2$	$\beta_2 = \mu_2 - \mu_3$
3	0	0	$\mu_3 = \alpha$	

Using Regression for the ANOVA Comparison of Means

Recall

Section 13.3 introduced the ***F* test** that all the beta parameters in a multiple regression model equal 0. ◀

For three groups, the null hypothesis for the ANOVA F test is H_0: $\mu_1 = \mu_2 = \mu_3$. If H_0 is true, then $\mu_1 - \mu_3 = 0$ and $\mu_2 - \mu_3 = 0$. In the multiple regression model

$$\mu_y = \alpha + \beta_1 x_1 + \beta_2 x_2$$

with indicator variables, recall that $\mu_1 - \mu_3 = \beta_1$ and $\mu_2 - \mu_3 = \beta_2$. Therefore, the ANOVA null hypothesis H_0: $\mu_1 = \mu_2 = \mu_3$ is equivalent to H_0: $\beta_1 = \beta_2 = 0$ in the regression model. If the beta parameters in the regression model all equal 0, then the mean of the response variable equals α for each group. We can perform the ANOVA test comparing means using the F test of H_0: $\beta_1 = \beta_2 = 0$ for this regression model.

Example 7

Regression analysis ◀

Telephone Holding Times

Picture the Scenario

Let's return to the data we analyzed in Examples 1 to 4 on telephone holding times for callers to an airline for which the recording that they hear is an advertisement, Muzak, or classical music.

Questions to Explore

a. Set up indicator variables to use regression to model the mean holding times with the type of recorded message as explanatory variable.

b. Table 14.6 shows a portion of a MINITAB printout for fitting this model. Use it to find the estimated mean holding time for the advertisement recording.

c. Use Table 14.6 to conduct the ANOVA F test (note that the table is the same as the one presented in Example 3).

Table 14.6 Printout for Regression Model $\mu_y = \alpha + \beta_1 x_1 + \beta_2 x_2$ for Telephone Holding Times and Type of Recording

The indicator variables are x_1 for the advertisement and x_2 for Muzak.

Term	Coef	SE Coef	T-Value	P-Value
Constant	10.400	1.523	6.83	0.000
x_1	−5.000	2.154	−2.32	0.039
x_2	−7.600	2.154	−3.53	0.004

Analysis of Variance

Source	DF	SS	MS	F-Value	P-Value
Regression	2	149.20	74.60	6.43	0.013
Error	12	139.20	11.60		
Total	14	288.40			

Think It Through

a. The factor (type of recording) has three categories—advertisement, Muzak, and classical music. With three groups, we need to set up two indicator variables x_1 and x_2 with

$$x_1 = 1 \text{ for the advertisement (and 0 otherwise)},$$
$$x_2 = 1 \text{ for Muzak (and 0 otherwise)}.$$

When $x_1 = x_2 = 0$, this indicates that the recording played was classical music, and no separate indicator variable for this group is needed.

The regression model for the mean of y = telephone holding time is then

$$\mu_y = \alpha + \beta_1 x_1 + \beta_2 x_2.$$

b. From Table 14.6, the prediction equation is

$$\hat{y} = 10.4 - 5.0x_1 - 7.6x_2.$$

For the advertisement, $x_1 = 1$ and $x_2 = 0$, so the estimated mean is $\hat{y} = 10.4 - 5.0(1) - 7.6(0) = 5.4$. This just equals the sample mean for the five subjects in that group.

c. From Table 14.6, the F test statistic for testing

$$H_0: \beta_1 = \beta_2 = 0$$

is $F = 6.43$, with $df_1 = 2$ and $df_2 = 12$. This null hypothesis is equivalent to

$$H_0: \mu_1 = \mu_2 = \mu_3.$$

Table 14.6 reports a P-value of 0.013. The regression approach provides the same F test statistic and P-value as the ANOVA did in Table 14.2.

Insight

Testing that the beta coefficients equal zero is equivalent to testing that the population means are equal. Because each beta coefficient refers to a particular difference in population means, confidence intervals for those coefficients give us confidence intervals for the difference between two population means. For instance, since $\beta_1 = \mu_1 - \mu_3$, a confidence interval for β_1 is also a confidence interval comparing μ_1 and μ_3. From Table 14.6, the estimate -5.0 of β_1 has $se = 2.154$. Since $df = 12$ ($= 15 - 3$, see margin recall), $t_{.025} = 2.179$, and a 95% confidence interval for β_1 (equivalently $\mu_1 - \mu_3$) is

$$-5.0 \pm 2.179(2.154), \text{ or } -5.0 \pm 4.7, \text{ which is } (-9.7, -0.3).$$

This agrees with the 95% confidence interval you would obtain using the formula presented at the beginning of this section (see summary box on page 680). Note that it is not straightforward to find the confidence interval for $\mu_1 - \mu_2$ using the multiple regression model, so for this interval you use the formula on page 681.

▶ ***Try Exercise 14.17***

Recall

Section 13.3 showed how to find a confidence interval for a multiple regression parameter beta as

estimated slope $\pm\, t_{0.025}(se)$,

where the *df* for the *t*-score is n − number of parameters in the regression equation. ◀

Table 14.2: ANOVA Table for Comparing Means

Source	DF	SS	MS	F	P
Group	2	149.2	74.6	6.4	0.013
Error	12	139.2	11.6		
Total	14	288.4			

Table 14.6: ANOVA Table for Regression Model

Source	DF	SS	MS	F	P
Regression	2	149.2	74.6	6.4	.013
Error	12	139.2	11.6		
Total	14	288.4			

Notice the similarity between the ANOVA table for comparing means (Table 14.2) and the ANOVA table for regression (Table 14.6), both shown again in the margin. The "between-groups sum of squares" for ordinary ANOVA is the "regression sum of squares" for the regression model. This is the variability explained by the indicator variables for the groups. The "error sum of squares" for ordinary ANOVA is the residual error sum of squares for the regression model. This represents the variability within the groups. This sum of squares divided by its degrees of freedom is the mean square error = 11.6 (MS in the error row), which is also the within-groups estimate of the variance of the observations within the groups. The regression mean square is the between-groups estimate = 74.6. The ratio of the regression mean square to the mean square error is the F test statistic ($F = 6.4$).

So far, this chapter has shown how to compare groups for a single factor. This is **one-way ANOVA**. Sometimes the groups to compare are the cells of a cross-classification of two or more factors. For example, the four groups (employed men, employed women, unemployed men, unemployed women) result from cross classifying employment status and gender. The next section presents **two-way ANOVA**, the procedure for comparing the mean of a quantitative response variable across categories of each of two factors.

14.2 Practicing the Basics

14.12 House prices and age For the House Selling Prices OR data file on the book's website, the output shows the result of conducting an ANOVA comparing mean house selling prices (in \$1000) by Age Category (New = 0 to 24 years old, Medium = 25 to 50 years old, Old = 51 to 74 years old, Very Old = 75 + years old). It also shows a summary table of means and standard deviations of the selling prices, by age group.

TRY

a. Using information given in the tables, show how to construct a 95% confidence interval comparing the population means of new and medium-aged houses.

b. Interpret the confidence interval.

Age	N	Mean	StDev
New	78	305.8	125.9
Medium	72	242.8	79.3
Old	37	217.5	85.4
Very Old	13	316.3	195.4

Source	DF	SS	MS	F	P
Age Condition	3	281852	93951	7.70	0.000
Error	196	2387017	12179		
Total	199	2668870			

14.13 Time on Facebook Do freshmen spent significantly more time on Facebook than other class ranks? A recent study (R. Junco, *Journal of Applied Developmental Psychology*, 2015, vol. 36, p. 18–29) investigated the amount of time per day freshman, sophomores, juniors, and seniors spent on Facebook while doing schoolwork. The students surveyed were U.S. residents from a 4-year, public, primarily residential institution in the Northeastern United States. The data from the survey are available on the book's website, with time measured in minutes. The following computer output shows the mean time each cohort spent on Facebook and an ANOVA table. Construct a 95% confidence interval to compare the population mean time spent per day on Facebook between freshmen and seniors.

Summary statistics for time spent on Facebook by class year and ANOVA table

	FR	SO	JU	SE
n	440	347	403	407
Mean	63.7	56.5	70.4	49.0
s	71.5	67.7	79.0	63.7

Source	DF	SS	MS	F	P
Class	3	102903	34301	6.84	0.000
Error	1593	7988051	5014		
Total	1596	8090954			

14.14 Comparing telephone holding times Examples 2 and 3 analyzed whether telephone callers to an airline would stay on hold different lengths of time, on average, if they heard (a) an advertisement about the airline, (b) Muzak, or (c) classical music. The sample means were 5.4, 2.8, and 10.4, with $n_1 = n_2 = n_3 = 5$. The ANOVA test had $F = 74.6/11.6 = 6.4$ and a P-value of 0.013.

a. A 95% confidence interval comparing the population mean times that callers are willing to remain on hold for classical music and Muzak is (2.9, 12.3). Interpret this interval.

b. The margin of error was 4.7 for this comparison. Without doing a calculation, explain why the margin of error is 4.7 for comparing *each* pair of means.

c. The 95% confidence intervals are (0.3, 9.7) for $\mu_3 - \mu_1$ and $(-2.1, 7.3)$ for $\mu_1 - \mu_2$. Interpret these two confidence intervals. Using these two intervals and the interval from part a, summarize what the airline company learned from this study.

d. The confidence intervals are wide. In the design of this experiment, what could you change to estimate the differences in means more precisely?

14.15 Tukey holding time comparisons Refer to the previous exercise. We could instead use the Tukey method to construct multiple comparison confidence intervals. The Tukey confidence intervals having *overall* confidence level 95% have margins of error of 5.7, compared to 4.7 for the separate 95% confidence intervals in the previous exercise.

TRY

a. According to this method, which groups are significantly different?

b. Why are the margins of error larger than with the separate 95% intervals?

14.16 REM sleep A psychologist compares the mean amount of time of rapid-eye movement (REM) sleep for subjects under three conditions. She randomly assigns 12 subjects to the three groups, four per group. The sample means for the three groups were 18, 15, and 12. The table shows the ANOVA table from SPSS.

REM sleep

Source	DF	SS	MS	F	P
Group	2	72.00	36.00	0.79	0.481
Error	9	408.00	45.33		
Total	11	480.00			

a. Report and interpret the P-value for the ANOVA *F* test.

b. For the Tukey 95% multiple comparison confidence intervals comparing each pair of means, the margin of error for each interval is 13.3. Is it true or false that since all the confidence intervals contain 0, it is plausible that all three population means equal 0.

c. Would the margin of error for each separate 95% confidence interval be less than 13.3, equal to 13.3, or larger than 13.3? Explain why.

14.17 REM regression Refer to the previous exercise.

TRY a. Set up indicator variables for a regression model so that an *F* test for the regression parameters is equivalent to the ANOVA test comparing the three means.

b. Express the null hypothesis both in terms of population means and in terms of regression parameters for the model in part a.

c. The prediction equation from fitting the multiple regression model equals $\hat{y} = 12 + 6x_1 + 3x_2$. Use this equation to find the predicted population means for each group.

14.18 Outsourcing satisfaction Exercise 14.5 showed an ANOVA for comparing mean customer satisfaction scores for three service centers. The sample means on a scale of 0 to 10 were 7.60 in San Jose, 7.80 in Toronto, and 7.10 in Bangalore. Each sample size = 100, MS error = 0.47, and the *F* test statistic = 27.6 has P-value < 0.001.

a. Explain why the margin of error for separate 95% confidence intervals is the same for comparing the population means for each pair of cities. Show that this margin of error is 0.19.

b. Find the 95% confidence interval for the difference in population means for each pair of service centers. Interpret.

c. The margin of error for Tukey 95% multiple comparison confidence intervals for comparing the service centers is 0.23. Construct the intervals. Interpret.

d. Why are the confidence intervals different in part b and in part c? What is an advantage of using the Tukey intervals?

14.19 Regression for outsourcing Refer to the previous exercise.

a. Set up indicator variables to represent the three service centers.

b. The prediction equation is $\hat{y} = 7.1 + 0.5x_1 + 0.7x_2$, where x_1 is an indicator variable for San Jose and x_2 an indicator variable for Toronto. Find the estimate for the difference in population means (i) between San Jose and Bangalore and (ii) between Toronto and Bangalore.

14.20 Advertising effect on sales Each of 100 restaurants in a fast-food chain is randomly assigned one of four media for an advertising campaign: A = radio, B = TV, C = newspaper, D = mailing. For each restaurant, the observation is the change in sales, defined as the difference between the sales for the month during which the advertising campaign took place and the sales in the same month a year ago (in thousands of dollars).

a. By creating indicator variables, write a regression equation for the analysis to compare mean change in sales for the four media.

b. Explain how you could use the regression model to test the null hypothesis of equal population mean change in sales for the four media.

c. The prediction equation is $\hat{y} = 35 + 5x_1 - 10x_2 + 2x_3$ where x_1, x_2, and x_3 are indicator variables for media A, B, and C, respectively. Estimate the difference in mean change in sales for media (i) A and D, (ii) A and B. (*Hint:* For part (ii), write the prediction equation for the mean for media A, then for media B, and then subtract.)

14.21 French ANOVA Refer to Exercise 14.3 about studying French, with data shown again below. Using software,

TECH a. Compare the three pairs of means with separate 95% confidence intervals. Interpret.

b. Compare the three pairs of means with Tukey 95% multiple comparison confidence intervals. Interpret and explain why the intervals are different than in part a.

Group 1	Group 2	Group 3
4	1	9
6	5	10
8		5

14.22 Multiple comparison for time on Facebook Refer to Exercise 14.13, which investigated the amount of time freshman, sophomores, juniors, and seniors spent on Facebook while doing schoolwork. The data from the study are available on the book's website, where time is measured in minutes.

TECH

a. If you want to construct confidence intervals between all possible pairs of means for the four classes, how many intervals do you need to construct?

b. Using software (such as the web app ANOVA accessible from the book's website), find the confidence intervals for all possible pairs of population means such that the overall error rate of all intervals is 0.05 (use Tukey's method). Visualize the confidence intervals in a figure similar to Figure 14.4. (The web app can construct such a plot, which you can download.)

c. Is it true that seniors spent significantly less time than all other classes? Explain.

14.3 Two-Way ANOVA

Recall

A **factor** is a categorical explanatory variable. **One-way ANOVA** has a single factor. ◀

One-way ANOVA is a *bivariate* (two-variable) method. It analyzes the relationship between the mean of a quantitative response variable and the groups that are categories of a factor. ANOVA extends to handle two or more factors. With multiple factors, the analysis is *multivariate*. We'll illustrate for the case of two factors. This extension is a **two-way ANOVA**. It enables us to study the effect of one factor at a fixed level of a second factor.

The great British statistician R. A. Fisher (see *On the Shoulders of R. A. Fisher* at the end of Section 8.5) developed ANOVA methods in the 1920s. Agricultural experiments were the source of many of the early ANOVA applications. For instance, ANOVA has often been used to compare the mean yield of a crop for different fertilizers.

Two factors ◀

Did You Know?

A **metric ton** is 1000 kilograms, which is about 2200 pounds. A **hectare** is 10,000 square meters (e.g., 100 meters by 100 meters), which is about 2.5 acres. ◀

Example 8

Amounts of Fertilizer and Manure

Picture the Scenario

This example presents a typical ANOVA application, based on a study at Iowa State University.[2] A large field was portioned into 20 equal-size plots. Each plot was planted with the same amount of corn seed, using a fixed spacing pattern between the seeds. The goal was to study how the yield of corn later harvested from the plots (in metric tons) depended on the levels of use of nitrogen-based fertilizer and manure. Each factor was measured in a binary manner. The fertilizer level was low (45 kg per hectare) or high (135 kg per hectare). The manure level was low (84 kg per hectare) or high (168 kg per hectare).

Questions to Explore

a. What are four treatments you can compare with this experiment?

b. What comparisons are relevant when you control for (keep fixed) manure level?

Think It Through

a. Four treatments result from cross-classifying the two binary factors: fertilizer level and manure level. You can compare corn yield at (i) low levels of both fertilizer and manure, at (ii) low levels of fertilizer and high levels of manure, at (iii) high levels of fertilizer and low levels of manure, and at (iv) high levels for both fertilizer and manure. Table 14.7 shows the four treatments, defined for the $2 \times 2 = 4$ combinations of categories of the two factors (fertilizer level and manure level).

Table 14.7 Four Groups for Comparing Mean Corn Yield

These result from the two-way cross classification of fertilizer level with manure level.

	Fertilizer	
Manure	**Low**	**High**
Low	(Low, Low)	(Low, High)
High	(High, Low)	(High, High)

[2]Thanks to Dan Nettleton, Iowa State University, for data on which this example is based.

b. We can compare the mean corn yield for the two levels of fertilizer, controlling for manure level (that is, at a fixed level of manure use). For fields in which manure level was *low*, we can compare the mean yields for the two levels of fertilizer use. These refer to the first row of Table 14.7. Likewise, for fields in which manure level was *high*, we can compare the mean yields for the two levels of fertilizer use. These refer to the second row of Table 14.7.

Insight

Among the questions we'll learn how to answer in this section are: Does the mean corn yield depend significantly on the fertilizer level? Does it depend on the manure level? Does the effect of fertilizer depend on the manure level, such as the fertilizer having no effect when the manure level is low but having an effect when the manure level is high?

▶ ***Try Exercise 14.23***

Inference About Effects in Two-Way ANOVA

In two-way ANOVA, a null hypothesis states that the population means are the same in each category of one factor, at each fixed level of the other factor. For example, we could test

H_0: Mean corn yield is equal for plots at the low and high levels of fertilizer, for each fixed level of manure.

Table 14.8a displays a set of population means satisfying this null hypothesis of "no effect of fertilizer level."

Table 14.8 Population Mean Corn Yield Satisfying Null Hypotheses: (a) No Effect of Fertilizer Level, (b) No Effect of Manure Level

(a)	Fertilizer		(b)	Fertilizer	
Manure	Low	High	Manure	Low	High
Low	10	10	Low	10	20
High	20	20	High	10	20

We could also test

H_0: Mean corn yield is equal for plots at the low and high levels of manure, for each fixed level of fertilizer.

Table 14.8b displays a set of population means satisfying this null hypothesis of "no effect of manure level." The effects of individual factors tested with these two null hypotheses are called **main effects**. We'll discuss a third null hypothesis that needs to be tested before these main effects hypotheses later in the section.

As in one-way ANOVA, the F tests of hypotheses in two-way ANOVA assume that

- The population distribution for each group is normal.
- The population standard deviations are identical.
- The data result from random sampling or a randomized experiment.

Here, each group refers to a cell in the two-way classification of the two factors. ANOVA procedures still usually work quite well if the population distributions are not normal with identical standard deviations. As in other ANOVA inferences, the randomization assumption is the most important assumption.

The test statistics have complex formula so we'll rely on software. As in one-way ANOVA, the test for a factor uses two estimates of the variance for each group. These estimates appear in the mean square (MS) column of the ANOVA table.

SUMMARY: *F* Test Statistics in Two-Way ANOVA

For testing the main effect for a factor, the test statistic is the ratio of mean squares,

$$F = \frac{\text{MS for the factor}}{\text{MS error}}.$$

The MS for the factor is a variance estimate based on between-groups variation for that factor. The MS error is a within-groups variance estimate that is always unbiased.

When the null hypothesis of equal population means for the factor (controlling for the other factor) is true, the F test statistic values tend to fluctuate around 1. When it is false, they tend to be larger. As before, the P-value is the right-tail probability above the observed F value. That is, it is the probability (presuming H_0 is true) of even more extreme results than we observed in the sample.

Example 9

Testing the main effects

Corn Yield

Picture the Scenario

Let's analyze the relationship between corn yield and the two factors, fertilizer level and manure level. Table 14.9 shows the data and the sample mean and standard deviation for each group.

Table 14.9 Corn Yield by Fertilizer Level and Manure Level

Fertilizer Level	Manure Level	Plot					Sample Size	Mean	Std. Dev.
		1	2	3	4	5			
High	High	13.7	15.8	13.9	16.6	15.5	5	15.1	1.3
High	Low	16.4	12.5	14.1	14.4	12.2	5	13.9	1.7
Low	High	15.0	15.1	12.0	15.7	12.2	5	14.0	1.8
Low	Low	12.4	10.6	13.7	8.7	10.9	5	11.3	1.9

Means from Table 14.9

Manure	Fertilizer Low	Fertilizer High
Low	11.3	13.9
High	14.0	15.1

Questions to Explore

a. Summarize the factor effects as shown by the sample means.

b. Table 14.10 is typical software output of an ANOVA table for two-way ANOVA. Specify the two hypotheses tested, give the test statistics and P-values, and interpret.

Think It Through

a. Table 14.9 (with means summarized in the margin) shows that for each manure level, the sample mean yield is higher for the plots using

Table 14.10 Two-Way ANOVA for Corn Yield Data in Table 14.9

Source	DF	SS	MS	F	P
Fertilizer	1	17.67	17.67	6.33	0.022
Manure	1	19.21	19.21	6.88	0.018
Error	17	47.44	2.79		
Total	19	84.32			

MS values for numerator of F statistics

MS error is denominator of each F statistic

more fertilizer. Also, for a given fertilizer level, the sample mean yield is higher for the plots using more manure.

b. First, consider the hypothesis

H_0: Mean corn yield is equal for plots at the low and high levels of fertilizer, for each fixed level of manure.

For the fertilizer main effect, Table 14.10 reports a mean square (MS) of 17.67. This is the between-groups estimate for the variance of the yield. The within-groups estimate is the MS error, or 2.79. The F test statistic is the ratio,

$$F = 17.67/2.79 = 6.33.$$

From Table 14.10, the *df* values are 1 and 17 for the two estimates. From the F distribution with $df_1 = 1$ and $df_2 = 17$, the P-value is 0.022, also reported in Table 14.10. If the population means were equal at the two levels of fertilizer (at a given manure level), the probability of an F test statistic value larger than 6.33 would be only 0.022. With such a small P-value, there is strong evidence that the mean corn yield depends on fertilizer level.

Next, consider the hypothesis

H_0: Mean corn yield is equal for plots at the low and high levels of manure, for each fixed level of fertilizer.

For the manure main effect, the F test statistic is $F = 19.21/2.79 = 6.88$. From Table 14.10, $df_1 = 1$ and $df_2 = 17$, and the P-value is 0.018. There is strong evidence that the mean corn yield also depends on the manure level.

Insight

As with any significance test, the information gain is limited. We do not learn *how large* the fertilizer and manure effects are on the corn yield. We can use confidence intervals to investigate the sizes of the main effects. We'll now learn how to do this by using regression modeling with indicator variables.

▶ ***Try Exercise 14.28***

Regression Model With Indicator Variables for Two-Way ANOVA

Let f denote an indicator variable for fertilizer level and let m denote an indicator variable for manure level. (We could have called the indicator variables

x_1 and x_2, but f and m reminds us that these indicators stand for fertilizer and manure use, respectively.) Specifically,

$$f = 1 \text{ for plots with high fertilizer level}$$
$$= 0 \text{ for plots with low fertilizer level}$$
$$m = 1 \text{ for plots with high manure level}$$
$$= 0 \text{ for plots with low manure level.}$$

The multiple regression model for the mean corn yield with these two indicator variables is

$$\mu_y = \alpha + \beta_1 f + \beta_2 m.$$

To find the population means for the four groups, we substitute the possible combinations of values for the indicator variables. For example, for plots that have high fertilizer level ($f = 1$) and low manure level ($m = 0$), the mean corn yield is

$$\mu_y = \alpha + \beta_1(1) + \beta_2(0) = \alpha + \beta_1.$$

Table 14.11 shows the four means. The difference between the means at the high and low levels of fertilizer equals β_1 for each manure level. That is, the coefficient β_1 of the indicator variable f for fertilizer level equals the difference between the means at its high and low levels, controlling for manure level. The null hypothesis of no fertilizer effect is H_0: $\beta_1 = 0$. Likewise, β_2 is the difference between the means at the high and low levels of manure, for each fertilizer level.

Table 14.11 Population Mean Corn Yield for Fertilizer and Manure Levels

		Indicator Variables		
Fertilizer	**Manure**	f	m	**Mean of y**
High	High	1	1	$\alpha + \beta_1 + \beta_2$
High	Low	1	0	$\alpha + \beta_1$
Low	High	0	1	$\alpha + \beta_2$
Low	Low	0	0	α

We do not need to use regression modeling to conduct the ANOVA F tests. They're easy to do using software. But the modeling approach helps us to focus on estimating the means and the differences among them. We can compare means using an ordinary confidence interval for the regression parameter that equals the difference between those means. The 95% confidence interval has the usual form of

$$\text{parameter estimate} \pm t_{0.025}(se).$$

The *df* for the *t*-score is the *df* value for the MS error.

Example 10

Regression modeling

Estimate and Compare Mean Corn Yields

Picture the Scenario

Table 14.12 shows the result of fitting the regression model for predicting corn yield with indicator variables for fertilizer level and manure level.

Questions to Explore

a. Find and use the prediction equation to estimate the mean corn yield for each group.

Table 14.12 Estimates of Regression Parameters for Two-Way ANOVA of the Mean Corn Yield by Fertilizer Level and Manure Level

Term	Coef	SE Coef	T-Value	P-Value
Constant	11.6500	0.6470	18.01	0.000
fertilizer	1.8800	0.7471	2.52	0.022
manure	1.9600	0.7471	2.62	0.018

b. Use a parameter estimate from the prediction equation to estimate the difference between mean corn yields for the high and low levels of fertilizer, at each manure level.

c. Find a 95% confidence interval comparing the mean corn yield at the high and low levels of fertilizer, controlling for manure level. Interpret it.

Think It Through

a. From Table 14.12, the prediction equation is (rounding to one decimal place)

$$\hat{y} = 11.6 + 1.9f + 2.0m.$$

The y-intercept equals 11.6. This is the estimated mean yield (in metric tons per hectare) when both indicator variables equal 0, that is, with fertilizer and manure at their low level. The estimated means for the other cases result from substituting values for the indicator variables. For instance, at fertilizer level = high and manure level = low, $f = 1$ and $m = 0$, so the estimated mean yield is $\hat{y} = 11.6 + 1.9(1) + 2.0(0) = 13.5$. Doing this for all four groups, we get

	Fertilizer	
Manure	**Low**	**High**
Low	11.6	11.6 + 1.9 = 13.5
High	11.6 + 2.0 = 13.6	11.6 + 1.9 + 2.0 = 15.5

b. The coefficient of the fertilizer indicator variable f is 1.9. This is the estimate for β_1 and is the estimated difference in mean corn yield between the high and low levels of fertilizer, for each level of manure (for instance, $13.5 - 11.6 = 1.9$ when manure level = low).

c. As shown, β_1 represents the difference in the mean corn yield at the high and low levels of fertilizer. To find a confidence interval for this difference, we simply need to find a confidence interval for β_1. The point estimate of β_1 is 1.9. Its standard error, reported in Table 14.12, is 0.747. From Table 14.10 (see page 693), the df for the MS error is 17. The t-score, $t_{.025} = 2.11$ when $df = 17$. The 95% confidence interval is

$$1.9 \pm 2.11(0.747), \text{ which is } (0.3, 3.5).$$

At each manure level, we estimate that the mean corn yield is between 0.3 and 3.5 metric tons per hectare higher at the high fertilizer level than at the low fertilizer level. The confidence interval contains only positive values (does not contain 0), reflecting the conclusion that the mean yield is significantly higher at the higher level of fertilizer. This agrees with the P-value falling below 0.05 in the test for the fertilizer effect.

Estimated Means

	Fertilizer	
Manure	**Low**	**High**
Low	11.6	13.5
High	13.6	15.5

Table 14.9: Sample Means

	Fertilizer	
Manure	**Low**	**High**
Low	11.3	13.9
High	14.0	15.1

Insight

The *estimated* means are not the same as the *sample* means in Table 14.9. (Both sets are shown again in the margin.) The model *smooths* the sample means so that the difference between the estimated means for two categories of a factor is *exactly* the same at each category of the other factor. For example, the increase in the mean yield when switching from a low level of the fertilizer to a high level of the fertilizer is the same (namely 1.9 tons) for low manure levels ($13.5 - 11.6 = 1.9$) and high manure levels ($15.5 - 13.6 = 1.9$).

► ***Try Exercise 14.29***

The regression model assumes that the difference between means for the two categories for one factor is the same in each category of the other factor. The next section shows how to check this assumption. When it is reasonable, we can use a single comparison rather than a separate one at each category of the other variable. In Example 10, we estimated that the difference in mean corn yield between high- and low-level use of fertilizer equals 1.9 tons, regardless of the level of manure use.

Recall

Section 13.5 introduced the concept of **interaction** between two explanatory variables in their effects on a response variable. In a regression context, **no interaction** implied parallel lines (common slopes). ◄

Exploring Interaction Between Factors in Two-Way ANOVA

Investigating whether **interaction** occurs is important whenever we analyze multivariate relationships. *No interaction* between two factors means that the effect of either factor on the response variable is the same at each category of the other factor. The regression model in Example 10 and the ANOVA tests of main effects assume there is no interaction between the factors. What does this mean in this context?

From Example 10, the estimated mean corn yields from the regression model having an indicator variable for fertilizer level and an indicator variable for manure level are shown in the table in the margin.

	Fertilizer	
Manure	**Low**	**High**
Low	11.6	13.5
High	13.6	15.5

What pattern do these show? Let's plot the means for the two fertilizer levels, within each level of manure. Figure 14.5 shows a plot in which the y-axis gives estimated mean corn yields, and points are shown for the four fertilizer–manure combinations. The horizontal axis is not a numerical scale but merely lists the two fertilizer levels. The drawn lines connect the means for the two fertilizer levels, for a given manure level. The absence of interaction is indicated by the *parallel lines.*

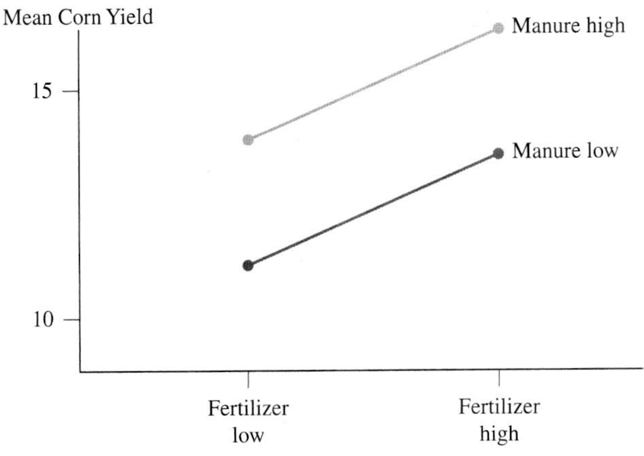

▲ **Figure 14.5 Mean Corn Yield, by Fertilizer and Manure Levels, Showing No Interaction.** The parallel lines reflect an absence of interaction. This implies that the difference in estimated means between the two fertilizer levels is the same for each manure level. **Question** Is it also true that the difference in estimated means between the two manure levels is the same for each fertilizer level?

The parallel lines occurs because the difference in the estimated mean corn yield between the high and low levels of fertilizer is the same for each manure level. The difference equals 1.9. Also, the difference between the high and low levels of manure in the estimated mean corn yield is 2.0 for each fertilizer level.

By contrast, Table 14.13 and Figure 14.6 show a set of means for which there is interaction. The difference between the high and low levels of fertilizer in the mean corn yield is $14 - 10 = 4$ for low manure and $12 - 16 = -4$ for high manure. Here, the difference in means depends on the manure level: According to these means, it's better to use a high level of fertilizer when the manure level is low, but it's better to use a low level of fertilizer when the manure level is high. Similarly, the manure effect differs at the two fertilizer levels; for the low level, it is $16 - 10 = 6$ whereas at the high level, it is $12 - 14 = -2$. The lines in Figure 14.6 are not parallel.

Table 14.13 Means that Show Interaction Between the Factors in Their Effects on the Response

The effect of fertilizer differs according to whether manure level is low or high. See Figure 14.6.

	Fertilizer	
Manure	**Low**	**High**
Low	10	14
High	16	12

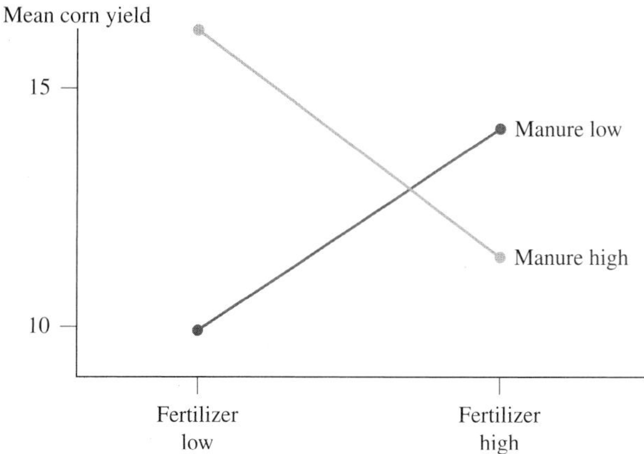

▲ **Figure 14.6** Mean Corn Yield, by Fertilizer and Manure Levels, Displaying Interaction.
Question What aspect of the plot reflects the interaction?

In Table 14.13, suppose the numbers of observations are the same for each group. Then the overall mean corn yield, ignoring manure level, is 13 for each fertilizer level (the average of 10 and 16, and the average of 14 and 12). The overall difference in means between the two fertilizer levels then equals 0. A one-way analysis of mean corn yield by fertilizer level would wrongly conclude that fertilizer level has no effect. However, a two-way analysis that allows for interaction would detect that fertilizer has an effect, but that effect differs according to the manure level. This demonstrates the advantage of a two-way analysis, which can consider the joint effects of two factors over a one-way analysis that has to ignore the effect of one factor.

Testing for Interaction

In conducting a two-way ANOVA, before testing the main effects, it is customary to test a third null hypothesis stating that there is no interaction between the factors in their effects on the response. The test statistic providing the sample evidence of interaction is

$$F = \frac{\text{MS for interaction}}{\text{MS error}}.$$

When H_0 is false, the F statistic tends to be large. Therefore, as usual, the P-value is the right-tail probability.

Testing for interaction

Corn Yields

Fertilizer Level	Manure Level	Mean	Std. Dev.
High	High	15.1	1.3
High	Low	13.9	1.7
Low	High	14.0	1.8
Low	Low	11.3	1.9

Example 11

Corn Yield Data

Picture the Scenario

Let's return to our analysis of the corn yield data, summarized in the margin table. In Example 10 we analyzed these data assuming no interaction. Let's see if that analysis is valid. Table 14.14 shows typical output for an ANOVA table for a model that allows interaction in assessing the effects of fertilizer level and manure level on the mean corn yield.

Table 14.14 Two-Way ANOVA of Mean Corn Yield by Fertilizer Level and Manure Level, Allowing Interaction

Source	DF	SS	MS	F	P
Fertilizer	1	17.67	17.67	6.37	0.023
Manure	1	19.21	19.21	6.92	0.018
Interaction	1	3.04	3.04	1.10	0.311
Error	16	44.40	2.78		
Total	19	84.32			

F statistic for test of no interaction

Question to Explore

Give the result of the test of H_0: no interaction and interpret.

Think It Through

The test statistic for H_0: no interaction is

$$F = (\text{MS for interaction})/(\text{MS error}) = 3.04/2.78 = 1.10.$$

Based on the F distribution with $df_1 = 1$ and $df_2 = 16$ for these two mean squares, the ANOVA table reports P-value = 0.31. This is not much evidence of interaction. We would not reject H_0 at the usual significance levels, such as 0.05.

Insight

Because there is not much evidence of interaction, we are justified in conducting the simpler two-way ANOVA about main effects. The tests presented previously in Table 14.10 for effects of fertilizer and manure on mean corn yield, as well as the confidence interval we constructed in Example 10, are valid.

▶ ***Try Exercise 14.30***

It is not meaningful to test the main effects hypotheses when there is interaction. A small P-value in the test of H_0: no interaction suggests that each factor has an effect, but the size of effect for one factor varies according to the category of the other factor. Then, you should investigate the nature of the interaction by plotting the sample cell means, using a plot like Figure 14.6. You should compare categories of one factor separately at different levels of the other factor.

In Practice Check Interaction Before Main Effects

In practice, in two-way ANOVA you should *first test the hypothesis of no interaction.* If the evidence of interaction is not strong (that is, if the P-value is not small), then test the main effects hypotheses and/or construct confidence intervals for those effects. But if important evidence of interaction exists, plot and compare the cell means for a factor separately at each category of the other factor.

Recall

From the box at the beginning of Section 14.2, the 95% confidence interval comparing two means is

$(\bar{y}_i - \bar{y}_j) \pm t_{.025}\, se$, where $se = s\sqrt{\frac{1}{n_i} + \frac{1}{n_j}}$,

s is the square root of the MS error, and df for the t distribution is df for MS error. ◀

For comparing means in two cells using a confidence interval, use the formula from the box at the beginning of Section 14.2, shown again in the margin. Substitute the cell sample sizes for n_i and n_j and use the MS error for the two-way ANOVA that allows interaction.

Interactions and confidence interval ◀

Example 12

Political Ideology by Gender and Race

Picture the Scenario

In most years, the General Social Survey asks subjects to report their political ideology, measured with seven categories in which 1 = extremely liberal, 4 = moderate, 7 = extremely conservative. Table 14.15 shows results from the 2008 General Social Survey on mean political ideology classified by gender and by race.

Caution

When conducting a two-way ANOVA for samples of different sizes, the analysis (using software) will often have to be performed as a General Linear Model. Notice that the Analysis of Variance table here shows both a Seq SS and an Adj SS column. You should use the Adjusted SS and Adjusted MS for the tests. ◀

Table 14.15 Mean Political Ideology by Gender and by Race

	Race	
Gender	**Black**	**White**
Female	4.164 (n = 165)	4.268 (n = 840)
Male	3.819 (n = 116)	4.444 (n = 719)

For the test of H_0: no interaction, software reports an F test statistic of 6.19 with $df_1 = 1$ and $df_2 = 1836$, for a P-value of 0.013. So, in comparing females and males on their mean political ideology, we should do it separately by race. The MS error for the model allowing interaction equals 2.534, so $s = \sqrt{2.534} = 1.592$.

```
Analysis of Variance for POLVIEWS, using Adjusted SS for Tests
Source       DF      Seq SS     Adj SS     Adj MS       F        P
SEX           1       5.138      1.652      1.652     0.65    0.420
RACE          1      24.786     30.780     30.780    12.15    0.001
SEX*RACE      1      15.693     15.693     15.693     6.19    0.013
Error      1836    4651.981   4651.981      2.534
Total      1839    4697.598
```

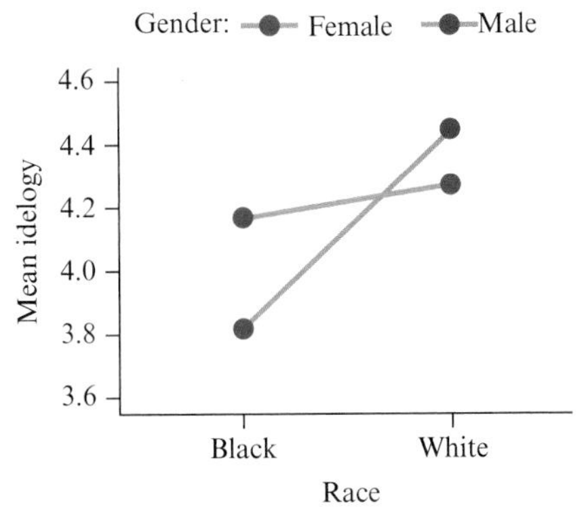

Questions to Explore

a. Interpret the significant interaction by comparing sample mean political ideology of females and males for each race descriptively and using 95% confidence intervals.

b. Interpret the confidence intervals derived in part a.

Think It Through

a. The sample means show that for black subjects, females are more conservative (have the higher mean). By contrast, for white subjects, males are more conservative. The margin figure shows the means and the interaction. For a confidence interval comparing mean political ideology for females and males who are black, the standard error (using the sample sizes reported in the table) is

$$se = s\sqrt{\frac{1}{n \text{ for black females}} + \frac{1}{n \text{ for black males}}} =$$

$$1.592\sqrt{\frac{1}{165} + \frac{1}{116}} = 0.193.$$

The 95% confidence interval is

$$(4.164 - 3.819) \pm 1.96(0.193), \text{ which is } 0.345 \pm 0.378, \text{ or } (-0.03, 0.72).$$

Likewise, you can find that the 95% confidence interval comparing mean political ideology for females and males who are white is -0.179 ± 0.159, or $(-0.34, -0.02)$.

b. Since the confidence interval for black subjects contains zero, we cannot infer that there is a difference in the populations. For white subjects, however, all values in the interval are negative. We infer that white females are *less* conservative than white males in the population.

Insight

The confidence interval for white subjects has an endpoint that is close to 0. So, the true gender effect in the population could be small. In fact, for 2014 GSS data, the interaction is not significant, and the gender main effect is also not significant; see Exercises 14.54 and 14.25.

▶ ***Try Exercise 14.34***

Why Not Instead Perform Two One-Way ANOVAs?

When you have two factors, rather than performing a two-way ANOVA, why not instead perform two one-way ANOVAs? For instance, in Example 12 you could compare the mean political ideology for females and males using a one-way ANOVA, ignoring the information about race. Likewise, you could perform a separate one-way ANOVA to compare the means for blacks and whites, ignoring the information about gender.

The main reason is that you learn more from a two-way ANOVA. The two-way ANOVA indicates whether there is interaction. When there is, as in Example 12, it is more informative to compare levels of one factor *separately* at each level of the other factor. This enables us to investigate how the effect depends on that other factor. For instance, a one-way ANOVA of mean political ideology by gender might show *no* gender effect, whereas the two-way ANOVA has shown that there *is* a gender effect, but it varies by race.

Similarly, in experimental studies, rather than carrying out one experiment to investigate the effect of one factor and a separate experiment to investigate the effect of a second factor, it is better to carry out a *single* experiment and study both factors at the same time. Besides the advantage of being able to check for interaction, this is more cost effective. If we have funds to experiment with 100 subjects, we can use a sample size of 100 for studying each factor with a two-way ANOVA rather than use 50 subjects in one experiment about one factor and 50 subjects in a separate experiment about the other factor.

Yet another benefit of a two-way ANOVA is that the residual variability (the estimated standard deviation of the response variable in each group), which affects the MS error and the denominators of the F test statistics, tends to decrease. When we use two factors to predict a response variable, we usually tend to get better predictions (that is, less residual variability) than when we use one factor. With less residual (within-groups) variability, we get larger test statistics and, hence, greater power for rejecting false null hypotheses.

Factorial ANOVA

The methods of two-way ANOVA extend to the analysis of several factors. A multifactor ANOVA with observations from all combinations of the factors is called **factorial ANOVA**. For example, with three factors, **three-way ANOVA** considers main effects for those factors as well as possible interactions.

In Practice Use Regression With Categorical and Quantitative Predictors

With several explanatory variables, usually some are categorical and some are quantitative. Then, it is sensible to build a multiple regression model containing both types of predictors. That's what we did in Example 10 in the previous chapter when we modeled house selling prices in terms of house size and condition of the house.

14.3 Practicing the Basics

14.23 Reducing cholesterol An experiment randomly assigns 100 subjects suffering from high cholesterol to one of four groups: low-dose Lipitor, high-dose Lipitor, low-dose Zocor, high-dose Zocor. After three months of treatment, the change in cholesterol level is measured.

TRY

- **a.** Identify the response variable and the two factors.
- **b.** What are four treatments that can be compared with this experiment?
- **c.** What comparisons are relevant when we control for dose level?

14.24 Drug main effects For the previous exercise, show a hypothetical set of population means for the four groups that would have

- **a.** A dose effect but no drug effect.
- **b.** A drug effect but no dose effect.
- **c.** A drug effect and a dose effect.
- **d.** No drug effect and no dose effect.

14.25 Political ideology in 2014 The GSS measures political ideology on a seven-point scale, starting with 1 = extremely liberal, to 4 = moderate, to 7 = extremely conservative. The following table shows results from an ANOVA analysis about political ideology, with sex (female, male) and race (black, white) as two factors, using 2014 GSS data.

- **a.** State the null hypothesis to which the F test statistic in the race row refers.
- **b.** Show how to use mean squares to construct the F test statistic for the race main effect, report its P-value, and interpret.
- **c.** Is there evidence that the mean political ideology in the United States differs between females and males, for either blacks or whites? Explain.

Source	DF	SS	MS	F	P
Sex	24	3.0	3.0	1.4	0.229
Race	1	36.5	36.5	17.4	0.000
Error	2203	4524.3	2.1		
Total	2205	4563.8			

14.26 House prices, age, and bedrooms For the House Selling Prices OR data file on the book's website, the output shows the result of conducting a two-way ANOVA of house selling prices (in thousands) by the number of bedrooms in the house and the age (New, Medium, Old, Very Old—see exercise 14.12) of the houses in Corvallis, Oregon.

- **a.** For testing the main effect of age, report the F test statistic value and show how it was formed from other values reported in the ANOVA table.

b. Report the P-value for the main effect test for age and interpret.

Source	DF	SS	MS	F	P
Bedrooms	7	517868	73981	7.325	0.000
Age Condition	3	242042	80681	7.988	0.000
Error	189	1908959	10100		
Total	199	2668870			

14.27 Corn and manure In Example 10, the coefficient of the manure-level indicator variable m is 1.96.

a. Explain why this coefficient is the estimated difference in mean corn yield between the high and low levels of manure, for each level of fertilizer.

b. Explain why the 95% confidence interval for the difference in mean corn yield between the high and low levels of manure is $1.96 \pm 2.11(0.747)$.

14.28 Hang up if recording repeated? Example 2 described an experiment in which telephone callers to an airline were put on hold with an advertisement, Muzak, or classical music in the background. Each caller who was chosen was also randomly assigned to a category of a second factor: whether the recording played was five minutes long or ten minutes long. (In each case, it was repeated at the end.) The table shows the data classified by both factors and the results of a two-way ANOVA.

TRY

Telephone holding times by type of recording and repeat time

	Repeat Time	
Recording	**Ten Minutes**	**Five Minutes**
Advertisement	8, 11, 2	5, 1
Muzak	1, 4, 3	0, 6
Classical	13, 8, 15	7, 9

Source	DF	SS	MS	F	P
Recording	2	149.20	74.60	7.09	0.011
Repeat	1	23.51	23.51	2.24	0.163
Error	11	115.69	10.52		
Total	14	288.40			

a. State the null hypothesis to which the F test statistic in the Recording row refers.

b. Show how to use mean squares to construct the F test statistic for the Recording main effect, report its P-value, and interpret.

c. On what assumptions is this analysis based?

14.29 Regression for telephone holding times Refer to the previous exercise. Let $x_1 = 1$ for the advertisement and 0 otherwise, $x_2 = 1$ for Muzak and 0 otherwise, and $x_1 = x_2 = 0$ for classical music. Likewise, let $x_3 = 1$ for repeating in 10-minute cycles and $x_3 = 0$ for repeating in 5-minute cycles. The display shows results of a regression of the telephone holding times on these indicator variables.

TRY

Regression for telephone holding times

Term	Coef	SE Coef	T-Value	P-Value
Constant	8.867	1.776	4.99	0.000
x1	-5.000	2.051	-2.44	0.033
x2	-7.600	2.051	-3.71	0.003
x3	2.556	1.709	1.50	0.163

a. Give the corresponding regression model for the population mean and show the equation for the population mean at each setting of the two factor levels. (Create a table similar to Table 14.11.)

b. State the prediction equation. Interpret the parameter estimates.

c. Find the estimated means for the six groups in the two-way cross-classification of type of recording and repeat time.

d. Find the estimated difference between the mean holding times for 10-minute repeats and 5-minute repeats, for a fixed recording type. How can you get this estimate from a coefficient of an indicator variable in the prediction equation?

e. Find a 95% confidence interval for the difference between the mean holding times for 10-minute repeats and 5-minute repeats.

14.30 Interaction between message and repeat time? Refer to the previous two exercises. When we allow interaction, two of the rows in the new ANOVA table are

TRY

Source	DF	SS	MS	F	P
Group*Repeat	2	15.02	7.51	0.67	0.535
Error	9	100.67	11.19		

where Group*Repeat denotes the interaction effect.

a. Show the hypotheses, test statistic, and P-value for the test of H_0: no interaction.

b. What is the implication of the result of this test? For instance, the analyses in previous exercises assumed a lack of interaction. Was it valid to do so?

14.31 Income by gender and degree In 2012, the population mean hourly wage for males was $17 for high school graduates, $33 for college graduates and $43 for males with more advanced degrees. For females, the means were $14 for high school graduates, $24 for college graduates, and $32 for females with more advanced degrees.[3]

a. Identify the response variable and the two factors.

b. Show these means in a two-way classification of the two factors, similar to the table in the margin of Example 9.

c. Compare the differences between males and females for (i) high school graduates and (ii) college graduates. Explain why there is interaction and describe it.

d. Show a set of six population mean wages that would satisfy H_0: no interaction.

14.32 Ideology by gender and race Refer to Example 12, the sample means from which are shown again below (for 2008 data).

Mean political Ideology

	Race	
Gender	**Black**	**White**
Female	4.164	4.2675
Male	3.819	4.4443

[3] *Source*: Data from *The State of Working America*, 12th edition, Economic Policy Institute.

a. Explain how to obtain the following interpretation for the interaction from the sample means: "For females there is no race effect on ideology. For males, whites are more conservative by about half an ideology category, on the average."

b. Suppose that instead of the two-way ANOVA, you performed a one-way ANOVA with gender as the predictor and a separate one-way ANOVA with race as the predictor. Suppose the ANOVA for gender does not show a significant effect. Explain how this could happen, even though the two-way ANOVA showed a gender effect for each race. (*Hint:* Will the overall sample means for females and males be more similar than they are for each race?)

c. Refer to part b. Summarize what you would learn about the gender effect from a two-way ANOVA that you would fail to learn from a one-way ANOVA.

14.33 Attractiveness and getting dates The results in the table are from a study of physical attractiveness and subjective well-being (E. Diener et al., *Journal of Personality and Social Psychology*, vol. 69, 1995, pp. 120–129). A panel rated a sample of college students on their physical attractiveness. The table presents the number of dates in the past three months for students rated in the top or bottom quartile of attractiveness.

a. Identify the response variable and the factors.

b. Do these data appear to show interaction? Explain.

c. Based on the results in the table, specify one of the ANOVA assumptions that these data violate. Is this the most important assumption?

Dates and attractiveness

	Number of DATES, MEN			Number of DATES, WOMEN		
ATTRACTIVENESS	**Mean**	**Std. Dev**	***n***	**Mean**	**Std. Dev**	***n***
More	9.7	10.0	35	17.8	14.2	33
Less	9.9	12.6	36	10.4	16.6	27

14.34 Diet and weight gain A randomized experiment[4] measured weight gain (in grams) of male rats under six diets varying by source of protein (beef, cereal, pork) and level of protein (high, low). Ten rats were assigned to each diet. The data are shown in the table that follows and are also available in the Protein and Weight Gain data file on the book's website.

TRY TECH

a. Conduct a two-way ANOVA that assumes a lack of interaction. Report the *F* test statistic and the P-value for testing the effect of the protein level. Interpret.

b. Now conduct a two-way ANOVA that also considers potential interaction. Report the hypotheses, test statistic, and P-value for a test of no interaction. What do you conclude at the 0.05 significance level? Explain.

c. Refer to part b. Allowing interaction, construct a 95% confidence interval to compare the mean weight gain for the two protein levels, for the beef source of protein.

Weight gain by source of protein and by level of protein

	High Protein	Low Protein
Beef	73, 102, 118, 104, 81, 107, 100, 87, 117, 111	90, 76, 90, 64, 86, 51, 72, 90, 95, 78
Cereal	98, 74, 56, 111, 95, 88, 82, 77, 86, 92	107, 95, 97, 80, 98, 74, 74, 67, 89, 58
Pork	94, 79, 96, 98, 102, 102, 108, 91, 120, 105	49, 82, 73, 86, 81, 97, 106, 70, 61, 82

14.35 Regression of weight gain on diet Refer to the previous exercise.

a. Set up indicator variables for protein source and for protein level and specify a regression model with the effects both of protein level and protein source on weight gain.

b. Fit the model in part a and explain how to interpret the parameter estimate for the protein level indicator variable.

c. Show how you could test a hypothesis about beta parameters in the model in part a to analyze the effect of protein source on weight gain.

d. Using the fit of the model, find the estimated mean for each of the six diets. Explain what it means when we say that these estimated means do not allow for interaction between protein level and source in their effects on weight loss.

[4]*Source:* Data from G. Snedecor and W. Cochran, *Statistical Methods*, 6th ed. (Iowa State University Press, 1967), p. 347.

Chapter Review

ANSWERS TO THE CHAPTER FIGURE QUESTIONS

Figure 14.1 No, even if the population means are equal, we would expect the sample means to vary due to sample-to-sample variability. Differences among the sample means is not sufficient evidence to conclude that the population means differ.

Figure 14.2 The data in Figure 14.2b give stronger evidence against H_0 because Figure 14.2b has less variability within each sample than Figure 14.2a.

Figure 14.3 Evidence suggesting the normal with equal standard deviation assumptions are violated would be (1) graphical methods showing extreme skew for the response variable, or (2) the largest group standard deviation is more than about double the smallest group standard deviation when the sample sizes are unequal.

Figure 14.5 Yes. The parallelism of lines implies that no interaction holds no matter which factor we choose for making comparisons of means.

Figure 14.6 The lines are not parallel.

CHAPTER SUMMARY

Analysis of variance (ANOVA) methods compare several groups according to their means on a quantitative response variable. The groups are categories of categorical explanatory variables. A categorical explanatory variable is also called a **factor**.

- The **one-way ANOVA** *F* test compares means for a single factor. The groups are specified by categories of a single categorical explanatory variable. The larger the *F* test statistic, the smaller the P-value and the more evidence that the population means are different, although the *F* test doesn't tell which ones are different.
- **Two-way ANOVA** methods compare means across categories of one factor, at fixed levels of another factor. When there is **interaction** between the two factors, the effect on the mean of one factor differs depending on the particular level of the other factor.
- **Multiple comparison methods** such as the **Tukey method** compare means for each pair of groups while controlling the overall confidence level.
- Analysis of variance methods can be conducted by using multiple regression models. The regression model uses **indicator variables** as explanatory variables to represent the factors. Each indicator variable equals 1 for observations from a particular category and 0 otherwise.
- The ANOVA methods assume randomization and that the population distribution for each group is normal, with the same standard deviation for each group. In practice, *the randomness assumption is the most important*, and ANOVA methods are *robust* to moderate violations of the other assumptions.

CHAPTER PROBLEMS

Practicing the Basics

14.36 Good friends and marital status Is the number of good friends associated with marital status? For GSS data with marital status measured with the categories (married, widowed, divorced, separated, never married), an ANOVA table reports $F = 0.80$ based on $df_1 = 4, df_2 = 612$.

a. Introduce notation and specify the null hypothesis and the alternative hypothesis for the ANOVA *F* test.

b. Based on what you know about the *F* distribution, would you guess that the test statistic value of 0.80 provides strong evidence against the null hypothesis? Explain.

c. Software reports a P-value of 0.53. Explain how to interpret it.

14.37 Going to bars and having friends Do people who go to bars and pubs a lot tend to have more friends? A recent GSS asked, "How often do you go to a bar or tavern?" The table shows results of ANOVA for comparing the mean number of good friends at three levels of this variable. The very often group reported going to a bar at least several times a week. The occasional group reported going occasionally, but not as often as several times a week.

Summary of ANOVA for mean number of good friends and going to bars

	Very often	Occasional	Never
Mean	12.1	6.4	6.2
Standard dev.	21.3	10.2	14.0
Sample size	41	166	215

Source	DF	SS	MS	F	P
Group	2	1116.8	558.4	3.03	0.049
Error	419	77171.8	184.2		
Total	421	78288.5			

a. State the (i) hypotheses, (ii) test statistic value, and (iii) P-value for the significance test displayed in this table. Interpret the P-value.

b. Based on the assumptions needed to use the method in part a, is there any aspect of the data summarized here that suggests that the ANOVA test and follow-up confidence intervals may not be appropriate? Explain.

14.38 Singles watch more TV The 2014 General Social Survey asked 1475 subjects how many hours per day they watched TV, on average. Are there differences in population means according to the marital status of the subject (single, married, divorced)? The sample means were 3.27 for singles ($n = 459$), 2.64 for married subjects ($n = 731$), and 2.85 for divorced subjects ($n = 285$). In a one-way ANOVA, the between-groups estimate of the variance is 54.8 and the within-groups estimate is 6.0. (The dataset is available online as TV Hours 2014.)

a. Conduct the ANOVA test and make a decision using a 0.05 significance level.

b. The 95% confidence interval comparing the population means is (0.3, 0.9) for single and married subjects, (0.06, 0.8) for single and divorced subjects, and (−0.5, 0.1) for married and divorced subjects. Based on the three confidence intervals, indicate which pairs of means are significantly different. Interpret.

c. Based on the information given, show how to construct the confidence interval that compares the population mean TV watching for single and married subjects.

d. Refer to part c. Would the corresponding interval formed with the Tukey method be wider or narrower? Explain why.

14.39 Comparing auto bumpers A consumer organization compares the sturdiness of three types of front bumpers. In the study, a particular brand of car is driven into a concrete wall at 15 miles per hour. The response is the amount of damage, as measured by the repair costs, in hundreds of dollars. Due to the potentially large costs, the study conducts only two tests with each bumper type, using six cars. The table shows the data and some ANOVA results. Show the (a) assumptions,

(b) hypotheses, (c) test statistic and *df* values, (d) P-value, and (e) interpretation for testing the hypothesis that the true mean repair costs are the same for the three bumper types.

Bumper A	Bumper B	Bumper C
1	2	11
3	4	15

```
Source    DF      SS        MS       F        P
Bumper     2   148.00    74.00   18.50    0.021
Error      3    12.00     4.00
Total      5   160.00
```

14.40 Compare bumpers Refer to the previous exercise.

a. Find the margin of error for constructing a 95% confidence interval for the difference between any pair of the true means. Interpret by showing which pairs of bumpers (if any) are significantly different in their true mean repair costs.

b. For Tukey 95% multiple comparison confidence intervals, the margin of error is 8.4. Explain the difference between confidence intervals formed with this method and separate confidence intervals formed with the method in part a.

c. Set up indicator variables for a multiple regression model, including bumper type.

d. The prediction equation for part c is $\hat{y} = 13 - 11x_1 - 10x_2$. Explain how to interpret the three parameter estimates in this model and show how these estimates relate to the sample means for the three bumpers.

14.41 Segregation by region Studies of the degree of residential racial segregation often use the *segregation index*. This is the percentage of nonwhites who would have to change the block on which they live to produce a fully nonsegregated city—one in which the percentage of nonwhites living in each block is the same for all blocks in the city. This index can assume values ranging from 0 to 100, with higher values indicating greater segregation. (The national average for large U.S. metropolitan areas in 2009 was 27, down from 33 in 2000.) The table shows the index for a sample of cities for 2005–2009, classified by region.

TECH

Segregation index

Northeast	North Central	South	West
Boston: 67	Minneapolis-St. Paul: 56	New Orleans: 64	San Francisco-Oakland: 64
NY, Long Island, Northern NJ: 79	Detroit: 80	Tampa: 58	Dallas-Ft Worth: 57
Philadelphia: 69	Chicago: 78	Miami: 66	Los Angeles: 70
Pittsburgh: 68	Milwaukee: 81	Atlanta: 60	Seattle: 54

Source: Racial and Ethnic Residential Segregation in the United States, 1980–2000, U.S. Bureau of the Census Series CENSR-3, 2002. www.psc.isr.umich.edu/dis/census/segregation.html.

a. Report the mean and standard deviation for each of the four regions.

b. Define notation and state the hypotheses for one-way ANOVA.

c. Report the *F* test statistic and its P-value. What do you conclude about the mean segregation indices for the four regions?

d. Suppose we took these data from the census bureau report by choosing only the cities in which we know people. Is the ANOVA valid? Explain.

14.42 Compare segregation means Refer to the previous exercise.

TECH

a. Using software, find the margin of error that pertains to each comparison, using the Tukey method for 95% multiple comparison confidence intervals.

b. Using part a, determine which pairs of means, if any, are significantly different.

14.43 Georgia political ideology The Georgia Student Survey file on the book's website asked students their political party affiliation (1 = Democrat, 2 = Republican, 3 = Independent) and their political ideology (on a scale from 1 = very liberal to 7 = very conservative). The table shows results of an ANOVA, with political ideology as the response variable.

Georgia political ideology and party affiliation

	Political ideology		
Affiliation	N	Mean	StDev
Democrat	8	2.6250	1.0607
Republican	36	5.5000	1.0000
Independent	15	3.4667	0.9155

```
Source        DF      SS       MS       F       P
PoliticalAff   2   79.629   39.814   40.83   0.000
Error         56   54.608    0.975
Total         58  134.237
```

a. Does the ANOVA assumption of equal population standard deviations seem plausible, or is it so badly violated that ANOVA is inappropriate?

b. Dotplots reveal skewed distributions for the response variable (and an outlier). Which is more important, the normality assumption or the assumption that the groups are random samples from the population of interest?

c. The next table shows 95% confidence intervals comparing pairs of means. Interpret the confidence interval comparing Republicans and Democrats.

Affiliations

	95% CI		
	Lower	Center	Upper
Republican–Democrat	2.10	2.87	3.65
Independent–Democrat	−0.02	0.84	1.71
Republican–Independent	1.43	2.03	2.64

d. Explain how you would summarize the results of the ANOVA *F* test and the confidence intervals to someone who has not studied statistics.

14.44 Comparing therapies for anorexia The Anorexia data file on the book's website shows weight change for 72 anorexic teenage girls who were randomly assigned to one of three psychological treatments.

TECH

a. Show how to construct 95% confidence intervals to investigate how the population means differ. Interpret them.

b. Report the Tukey 95% multiple comparison confidence intervals. Interpret and explain why they are wider than the confidence intervals in part a.

14.45 Lot size varies by region? A geographer compares residential lot sizes in four quadrants of a city. To do this, she randomly samples 300 records from a city file on home residences and records the lot sizes (in thousands of square feet) by quadrant. The ANOVA table, shown in the table that follows, refers to a comparison of mean lot sizes for the northeast (NE), northwest (NW), southwest (SW), and southeast (SE) quadrants of the city. Fill in all the blanks in the table.

Lot sizes by quadrant of city

Source	DF	SS	MS	F	P-value
Quadrant	_____	_____	_____	_____	0.000
Error	296	1480	_____		
Total	_____	4180			

14.46 House with garage Refer to the House Selling Price OR data file on the book's website.

TECH

a. The variable "Garage" included in the dataset is an indicator variable for whether a house has a garage (with 1 indicating that it does have one). Using software, put this as the sole predictor of house selling price (in thousands) in a regression model. Report the prediction equation and interpret the intercept and slope estimates.

b. For the model fitted in part a, conduct the t test for the effect of the indicator variable in the regression analysis (that is, test H_0: $\beta = 0$). Interpret.

c. Use software to conduct the F test for the analysis of variance comparing the mean selling prices of homes with and without a garage. Interpret.

d. Explain the connection between the value of t in part b and the value of F in part c.

14.47 Ideal number of kids by gender and race The GSS asks, "What is the ideal number of kids for a family?" When we use a recent GSS to evaluate how the mean response depends on gender and race (black or white), we get the results shown in the ANOVA table.

a. Identify the response variable and the factors.

b. Explain what it would mean if there were no interaction between gender and race in their effects. Show a hypothetical set of population means that would show a strong race effect and a weak gender effect and no interaction.

c. Using the table, specify the null and alternative hypotheses, test statistic, and P-value for the test of no interaction. Interpret the result.

ANOVA of ideal number of kids by gender and race

Source	DF	SS	MS	F	P
Gender	1	0.25	0.25	0.36	0.546
Race	1	16.98	16.98	24.36	0.000
Interaction	1	0.95	0.95	1.36	0.244
Error	1245	867.72	0.70		
Total	1248	886.12			

14.48 Regress kids on gender and race Refer to the previous exercise. Let $f = 1$ for females and 0 for males and let $r = 1$ for blacks and 0 for whites. The regression model for predicting y = ideal number of kids is $\hat{y} = 2.42 + 0.04f + 0.37r$.

a. Interpret the coefficient of f. What is the practical implication of this estimate being so close to 0?

b. Find the estimated mean for each of the four combinations of gender and race.

c. Summarize what you learn about the effects based on the analyses in this and the previous exercise.

14.49 Energy drink In a class experiment at Williams College, students were randomly assigned either to drink or abstain from drinking an energy drink before attempting a straightforward but tedious mathematical task. They were also randomly assigned to start the task at 11 P.M. at night or at 8 A.M. in the morning. (The resulting data set is available on the book's website.) When we regress y = time it took to complete task (in minutes) on e = energy drink (1 = yes, 0 = no) and d = daytime (1 = 11P.M., 0 = 8A.M.) we get the prediction equation $\hat{y} = 9.8 - 0.39e - 2.0d$.

TECH

a. Interpret the effect of the energy drink.

b. Interpret the coefficient of d.

c. State a corresponding model for the population and indicate which parameters would need to equal zero for the response variable to be independent of whether one drinks an energy drink, for given time of the day.

d. Fit the regression model with software and comment on whether the mean times differ significantly between consuming and not consuming an energy drink, for a given time of day.

14.50 Income, gender, and education According to the U.S. Bureau of the Census, as of March 2009, the average earnings of full-time workers was estimated to be $31,666 for females with high school education, $43,493 for males with high school education, $60,293 for white females with a bachelor's degree, and $94,206 for males with a bachelor's degree.

a. Identify the response variable and the two factors.

b. Show these means in a two-way classification of the factors.

c. Compare the differences between males and females for (i) high school graduates and (ii) college graduates. If these are close estimates of the population means, explain why there is interaction. Describe its nature.

14.51 Birth weight, age of mother, and smoking A study on the effects of prenatal exposure to smoke (by J. Nigg and N. Breslau, *Journal of the American Academy of Child & Adolescent Psychiatry*, vol. 46, 2009, pp. 362–369) indicated that mean birth weight was significantly lower for babies born to mothers who smoked during pregnancy. It also suggested that increasing age of the mother resulted in increased effects. Explain how this suggests interaction between smoking status and age of mother in their effects on birth weight of the child.

14.52 TV watching by gender and race When we use the 2008 GSS to evaluate how the mean number of hours a day watching TV depends on gender and race, we get the results shown in the ANOVA table that follows.

a. Identify the response variable and the factors.

b. From the table, specify the test statistic and P-value for the test of no interaction. Interpret the result.

c. Is there a significant (i) gender effect and (ii) race effect? Explain.

d. The sample means were 2.82 for white females, 2.68 for white males, 4.52 for black females, and 4.19 for black males. Explain how these results are compatible with the results of the tests discussed in part c.

Analysis of Variance for TVHOURS, using Adjusted SS for Tests

Source	DF	Seq SS	Adj SS	Adj MS	F	P
RACE	1	419.60	399.12	399.12	58.32	0.000
SEX	1	8.74	8.74	8.74	1.28	0.259
RACE*SEX	1	1.42	1.42	1.42	0.21	0.649
Error	1198	8199.10	8199.10	6.84		
Total	1201	8628.86				

S = 2.61610 R-Sq = 4.98% R-Sq(adj) = 4.74%

14.53 Salary and gender The American Association of University Professors (AAUP) reports yearly on faculty salaries for all types of higher education institutions across the United States. Regard *Salary* as the response variable, *Gender* as the explanatory variable, and *Academic Rank* as the control variable. A regression analysis using these data could include an indicator variable for *Gender* and an indicator variable for *Rank*. The estimated coefficients are −13 (thousands of dollars) for *Gender* ($x_1 = 1$ for female and $x_1 = 0$ for male) and −40 (thousands of dollars) for a lower assistant *Rank* ($x_2 = 1$ for assistant professor and $x_2 = 0$ for professor).

a. Interpret the coefficient for gender.

b. At particular settings of the other predictors, the estimated mean salary for female professors was 96.2 thousand dollars. Using the estimated coefficients, find the estimated means for (i) male professors and (ii) female assistant professors.

14.54 Political ideology interaction The first table shown summarizes responses on political ideology (where 1 = extremely liberal and 7 = extremely conservative) from the 2014 GSS by gender and race.

a. From these sample means, is there evidence of a significant interaction? Explain what this means in the context of this example. (*Hint:* Is the difference between males and females in sample mean ideology about the same for blacks and whites?)

b. From the ANOVA table shown, write a conclusion for testing the null hypothesis of no interaction.

Sample means for political ideology by sex and race

	Black	White
Female	3.82	4.13
Male	3.81	4.22

ANOVA for political ideology by sex and race

Source	DF	SS	MS	F	P
Sex	1	3.0	3.0	1.4	0.229
Race	1	36.5	36.5	17.8	0.000
Interaction	1	0.8	0.8	0.4	0.539
Error	2202	4521.4	2.1		
Total	2205	4563.8			

Concepts and Applications

14.55 Regress TV watching on gender and marital status When we use the 2014 GSS and regress y = number of hours per day watching TV on g = gender (1 = male, 0 = female) and marital status ($m_1 = 1$ for singles, 0 otherwise, $m_2 = 1$ for married subjects, 0 otherwise), we get the following output

Term	Coef	SE Coef	T-Value	P-value
Constant	2.78	0.155	17.95	0.000
g	0.16	0.127	1.29	0.197
m_1	0.41	0.184	2.21	0.027
m_2	−0.21	0.170	−1.26	0.209

a. Write down the corresponding regression model for the population mean and give the equation for the population mean at each combination of the two factor levels. (Create a table similar to Table 14.11.)

b. Write down the prediction equation and interpret the estimated gender effect.

c. From the expression for the population means in part a, find the difference in means between single and divorced subjects, separately for each gender. This difference is equal to what regression coefficient?

d. Find and interpret a 95% confidence interval for the difference in means between single and divorced subjects, for given gender. (*Note:* The *df* for the *t*-score equals 1471.)

14.56 Number of friends and degree TECH Using the GSS website sda.berkeley.edu/GSS, analyze whether the number of good friends (the variable NUMFREND) depends on the subject's highest degree (the variable DEGREE). To do so, click the MEANS tab (next to the default TABLES tab) and enter the variable names. Under Output Options, deselect "Complex std errs" and select "ANOVA stats". Prepare a short report summarizing your analysis and its interpretation.

14.57 Sketch within- and between-groups variability Sketch a dot plot of data for 10 observations in each of three groups such that

a. You believe the P-value would be very small for a one-way ANOVA. (You do not need to do the ANOVA; merely show points for which you think this would happen.)

b. The P-value in one-way ANOVA would not be especially small.

14.58 A = B and B = C, but A ≠ C? In multiple comparisons following a one-way ANOVA with equal sample sizes, the margin of error with a 95% confidence interval for comparing each pair of means equals 10. Give three sample means illustrating that it is possible that Group A is not significantly different from Group B and Group B is not significantly different from Group C, yet Group A is significantly different from Group C.

14.59 Multiple comparison confidence For four groups, explain carefully the difference between a confidence level of 0.95 for a single comparison of two means and a confidence level of 0.95 for a multiple comparison of all six pairs of means.

14.60 Another Simpson paradox The 25 women faculty members in the humanities division of a college have a mean salary of $65,000, whereas the five women faculty in the science division have a mean salary of $72,000. The 20 men in the humanities division have a mean salary of $64,000, and the 30 men in the science division have a mean salary of $71,000.

a. Construct a 2×2 table of sample mean incomes for the table of gender and division of college. Use weighted averages to find the overall means for men and women.

b. Discuss how the results of a one-way comparison of mean incomes by gender would differ from the results of a two-way comparison of mean incomes by gender, controlling for division of college. (*Note*: This reversal of which gender has the higher mean salary, according to whether one controls division of college, illustrates *Simpson's paradox.*)

14.61 Multiple choice: ANOVA/regression similarities Analysis of variance and multiple regression have many similarities. Which of the following is *not* true?

a. The response variable is quantitative for each.

b. They both have F tests for testing that the response variable is statistically independent of the explanatory variable(s).

c. For inferential purposes, they both assume that the response variable y is normally distributed with the same standard deviation at all combinations of levels of the explanatory variable(s).

d. They are both appropriate when the main focus is on describing straight-line effects of quantitative explanatory variables.

14.62 Multiple choice: ANOVA variability One-way ANOVA provides relatively more evidence that H_0: $\mu_1 = \cdots = \mu_g$ is false:

a. The smaller the between-groups variation and the larger the within-groups variation.

b. The smaller the between-groups variation and the smaller the within-groups variation.

c. The larger the between-groups variation and the smaller the within-groups variation.

d. The larger the between-groups variation and the larger the within-groups variation.

14.63 Multiple choice: Multiple comparisons For four means, it is planned to construct Tukey 95% multiple comparison confidence intervals for the differences between the six pairs.

a. For each confidence interval, there is a 0.95 chance that the interval will contain the true difference.

b. The probability that all six confidence intervals will contain the true differences is 0.70.

c. The probability that all six confidence intervals will contain the true differences is about 0.95.

d. The probability that all six confidence intervals will contain the true differences is $(0.95)^6$.

14.64 Multiple choice: Interaction There is interaction in a two-way ANOVA model when

a. The two factors are associated.

b. Both factors have significant effects in the model without interaction terms.

c. The difference in true means between two categories of one factor varies among the categories of the other factor.

d. The mean square for interaction is about the same size as the mean square error.

14.65 True or false: Interaction For subjects aged under 50, there is little difference in mean annual medical expenses for smokers and nonsmokers. For subjects aged over 50, there is a large difference. Is it true or false that there is interaction between smoking status and age in their effects on annual medical expenses?

14.66 ◆◆ **What causes large or small *F*?** An experiment used four groups of five individuals each. The overall sample mean was 60.

a. What did the sample means look like if the one-way ANOVA for comparing the means had test statistic $F = 0$? (Hint: What would have to happen for the between-groups variability to be 0?)

b. What did the data look like in each group if $F =$ infinity? (*Hint*: What would have to happen for the within-groups variability to be 0?)

14.67 ◆◆ **Between-subjects estimate** This exercise motivates the formula for the between-subjects estimate of the variance in one-way ANOVA. Suppose each population mean equals μ (that is, H_0 is true) and each sample size equals n. Then the sampling distribution of each $\bar{y}_i$ has mean μ and variance σ^2/n, and the sample mean of the $\bar{y}_i$ values is the overall sample mean, $\{\bar{y}\}$.

a. Treating the g sample means as g observations having sample mean $\bar{y}$, explain why $\Sigma(\bar{y}_i - \bar{y})^2/(g - 1)$ estimates the variance σ^2/n of the distribution of the $\{\bar{y}_i\}$ values.

b. Using part a, explain why the between-groups estimate $\Sigma n(\bar{y}_i - \bar{y})^2/(g - 1)$ estimates σ^2. (For the unequal sample size case, the formula replaces n by n_i.)

14.68 ◆◆ **Bonferroni multiple comparisons** The Bonferroni theorem states that the probability that *at least* one of a set of events occurs can be no greater than the sum of the separate probabilities of the events. For instance, if the probability of an error for each of five separate confidence intervals equals 0.01, then the probability that *at least* one confidence interval will be in error is no greater than $(0.01 + 0.01 + 0.01 + 0.01 + 0.01) = 0.05$.

a. Following Example 10, construct a confidence interval for each factor and guarantee that they both hold with overall confidence level at least 95%. [*Hint*: Each interval should use $t_{.0125} = 2.46$.]

b. Exercise 14.8 referred to a study comparing three groups (smoking status never, former, or current) on various personality scales. The study measured 35 personality scales and reported an F test comparing the three smoking groups for each scale. The researchers mentioned doing a Bonferroni correction for the 35 F tests. If the nominal *overall* probability of Type I error was 0.05 for the 35 tests, how small did the P-value have to be for a particular test to be significant? (*Hint*: What should the Type I error probability be for each of 35 tests for the overall Type I error probability to be no more than 0.05?)

14.69 Independent confidence intervals You plan to construct
◆◆ a 95% confidence interval in five situations with independent data sets.

a. Assuming that the results of the confidence intervals are statistically independent, find the probability that *all* five confidence intervals will contain the parameters they are designed to estimate. (*Hint*: Use the binomial distribution.)

b. Which confidence level should you use for each confidence interval so that the probability that all five intervals contain the parameters equals *exactly* 0.95?

14.70 Regression or ANOVA? You want to analyze
◆◆ y = house selling price and x = number of bathrooms (1, 2, or 3) by testing whether x and y are independent.

a. You could conduct a test of independence using (i) the ANOVA F test for a multiple regression model with two indicator variables or (ii) a regression t test for the coefficient of the number of bathrooms when it is treated as a quantitative predictor in a straight-line regression model. Explain the difference between these two ways of treating the number of bathrooms in the analysis.

b. What do you think are the advantages and disadvantages of the straight-line regression approach to conducting the test?

c. Give an example of three population means for which the straight-line regression model would be less appropriate than the model with indicator variables.

14.71 Three factors An experiment analyzed how the
◆◆ mean corn yield depends on three different fertilizers: Nitrogen (applied at low and high levels), phosphate (applied at low and high levels), and potash (applied at low and high levels). In the experiment, each plot of land received a combination of levels from these three fertilizers.

a. How many groups result from the different combinations of the three factors?

b. Defining indicator variables, state the regression model that corresponds to an ANOVA assuming a lack of interaction.

c. Give possible estimates of the model parameters in part b for which the estimated corn yield would be highest at the high level of nitrogen fertilizer and phosphate fertilizer and the low level of potash.

Student Activities

14.72 Student survey data Refer to the student survey data
TECH file that your class created with Activity 3 in Chapter 1. For variables chosen by your instructor, use ANOVA methods and related inferential statistical analyses. Interpret and summarize your findings in a short report and prepare to discuss your findings in class.

CHAPTER

15

The various t tests introduced in Chapter 10 and the ANOVA F test from Chapter 14 compare population means under the assumption of approximately normal population distributions. When such assumptions are in doubt, this chapter presents alternative methods to compare two or more groups based on ranking the observations.

Nonparametric Statistics

Example 1

How to Get a Better Tan

Picture the Scenario

Statistics students were asked to design an experiment about a topic of choice, conduct the experiment, and then analyze the data. One student, Allison, decided to compare tanning methods without exposure to the sun to avoid skin cancer risk. She investigated two treatments—a bronze tanning lotion applied twice over a two-day period, or a tanning studio where the person is exposed to ultraviolet (UV) light. We'll refer to these treatments as "tanning lotion" and "tanning studio."

The tanning lotion is much less expensive, but Allison predicted that the tanning studio would give a better tan. To investigate this hypothesis, she recruited five untanned female friends to participate in an experiment. Another student in the class used a random number generator to pick three of the friends to use the tanning lotion. The other two friends used the tanning studio. After three days, Allison evaluated the tans produced. She was blinded to the treatment allocation, not knowing which participants used which tanning method. Allison ranked the friends in terms of the quality of their tans. The ranks went from 1 to 5, with 1 = most natural looking and 5 = least natural-looking

Questions to Explore

- Once Allison ranked the five tanned participants, how could she summarize the evidence in favor of one treatment over the other?
- How can Allison find a P-value to determine whether one treatment is significantly better than the other?

Thinking Ahead

You learned in Sections 10.2 and 10.3 how to compare means for two treatments using t tests. The tests assume a *normal* distribution for a quantitative response variable. The t tests are *robust*, usually working well even when population distributions are *not* normal. An exception is when the distribution is skewed, the sample sizes are small, and the alternative hypothesis is one-sided.

To use the t test, suppose Allison created a quantitative variable by assigning a score between 0 and 10 for each girl to describe the quality of tan. With such small sample sizes (only 2 and 3 in each group), she would not be able to assess whether quality of tan is approximately normal. Moreover, her prediction that the studio gives a better tan than the lotion was one-sided. In any case, Allison found it easier to rank the participants than to create a quantitative variable. For these reasons, then, it's not appropriate for her to use a t test to compare the tanning methods.

We'll now learn about an alternative way to compare treatments (or, more generally, two groups) without having to assume a normal distribution for the response variable. **Nonparametric statistical methods** provide statistical inference without this assumption. They use solely the *ranking* of the subjects on the response variable.

Nonparametric Statistical Methods

Nonparametric statistical methods are inferential methods that do not assume a particular form of distribution, such as the normal distribution, for the population distribution.

In Example 2, we'll use the best known nonparametric method, the Wilcoxon test, to analyze the ranking of the tans from Allison's experiment.

Nonparametric methods are especially useful in two cases:

- When the data are ranks for the subjects (as in Example 1) rather than quantitative measurements.
- When it's inappropriate to assume normality, and when the ordinary statistical method is not robust to violations of the normality assumption. For instance, we might prefer not to assume normality because we think the distribution will be skewed. Or, perhaps we have no idea about the distribution shape, and the sample size is too small to give us much information about it.

Statisticians developed the primary nonparametric statistical methods starting in the late 1940s, long after most other methods described in this text. Since then, many nonparametric methods have been devised to handle a wide variety of scenarios. This final chapter is designed to show you the idea behind nonparametric methods. In Section 15.1, we'll learn about the most popular nonparametric test, the Wilcoxon test for comparing two groups. Section 15.2 briefly describes other popular nonparametric methods.

We have already seen a nonparametric method in the form of the permutation test of comparing two means that we presented in Section 10.3. The nonparametric methods introduced in this chapter are special cases of permutation tests when applied to the ranks of the observations instead of using the original values.

Recall

The permutation tests from Sections 10.3 and 11.5 construct the sampling distribution of a test statistic from all possible (or a large random sample of all possible) permutations of the responses between the two groups, finding the value of the test statistic for each permutation. ◀

15.1 Compare Two Groups by Ranking

Of the five participants in Example 1, three were randomly assigned to use the tanning lotion and two to use a tanning studio. The tans were then ranked from 1 to 5, with 1 representing the most natural-looking tan. Let's consider all the possible outcomes for this experiment. Each possible outcome divides the ranks of 1, 2, 3, 4, 5 into two groups—three ranks for the tanning lotion group and two ranks for the tanning studio group. Table 15.1 shows the possible rankings. For instance, in the first case, the three using the tanning lotion got the three best ranks, (1, 2, 3).

Table 15.1 Possible Rankings of Tanning Quality

Each case shows the three ranks for those using the tanning lotion and the two ranks for those using the tanning studio. It also shows the sample mean ranks and their difference.

Treatment	Ranks				
Lotion	(1, 2, 3)	(1, 2, 4)	(1, 2, 5)	(1, 3, 4)	(1, 3, 5)
Studio	(4, 5)	(3, 5)	(3, 4)	(2, 5)	(2, 4)
Lotion mean rank	2	2.3	2.7	2.7	3
Studio mean rank	4.5	4	3.5	3.5	3
Difference of mean ranks	−2.5	−1.7	−0.8	−0.8	0
Lotion	(1, 4, 5)	(2, 3, 4)	(2, 3, 5)	(2, 4, 5)	(3, 4, 5)
Studio	(2, 3)	(1, 5)	(1, 4)	(1, 3)	(1, 2)
Lotion mean rank	3.3	3	3.3	3.7	4
Studio mean rank	2.5	3	2.5	2	1.5
Difference of mean ranks	0.8	0	0.8	1.7	2.5

We summarize the outcome of the experiment by finding the mean rank for each group and taking its difference. Table 15.1 shows the mean ranks and their differences. For example, in the first case the mean is $(1 + 2 + 3)/3 = 2$ for the tanning lotion and $(4 + 5)/2 = 4.5$ for the tanning studio. The difference is $2 - 4.5 = -2.5$. In other words, for the first case the rank for the lotion tanned participants is on average 2.5 less than the rank for the studio tanned participants.

Allison predicted that the tanning studio would tend to give better tans. When this happens in the sample, the ranks for the tanning studio are smaller than those for the tanning lotion. Then the mean rank is larger for the tanning lotion, and the difference between the mean ranks is positive, as in the last case in the table.

Comparing Mean Ranks: The Wilcoxon Test

For this experiment, the samples were independent random samples—the responses for the participants using the tanning lotion were independent of the responses for the participants using the tanning studio. Suppose that the two treatments have identical effects, in the sense that the quality of tan would be the same regardless of which treatment a participant uses. Then, each of the ten possible outcomes shown in Table 15.1 is equally likely. Each has probability 1/10. Using the ten possible outcomes, we can construct a sampling distribution for the difference between the mean ranks. Table 15.2 shows this sampling distribution. For instance, the difference between the sample mean ranks is 0 for two of the ten samples in Table 15.1, so the probability of this outcome is 2/10.

Figure 15.1 displays this sampling distribution. It is symmetric around 0. This is the expected value for the difference between the sample mean ranks if the two treatments truly have identical effects.

Allison hypothesized that the tanning studio would give a better tan than the tanning lotion. She wanted to test the null hypothesis,

Recall

Section 10.3 discussed the null hypothesis of identical population distributions for the *t* test, assuming equal standard deviations and the permutation test. ◀

H_0: The treatments are identical in tanning quality,

against the alternative hypothesis

H_a: Better tanning quality results with the tanning studio.

This alternative hypothesis is one-sided. It implies that the mean rank in the population of subjects assigned to the tanning studio is smaller than in the population of subjects assigned to the tanning lotion. (Remember, a smaller rank indicates a

Table 15.2 Sampling Distribution of Difference Between Sample Mean Ranks

These probabilities apply when the treatments have identical effects. For example, only one of the ten possible samples in Table 15.1 has a difference between the mean ranks equal to −2.5, so this value has probability 1/10.

Difference Between Mean Ranks	Probability
−2.5	1/10
−1.7	1/10
−0.8	2/10
0	2/10
0.8	2/10
1.7	1/10
2.5	1/10

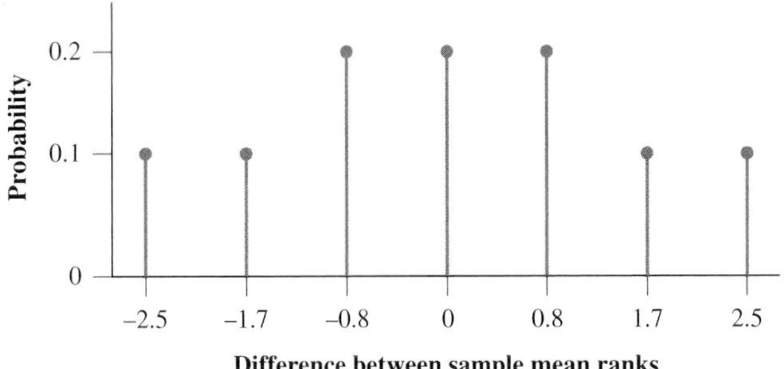

▲ **Figure 15.1** Sampling Distribution of Difference Between Sample Mean Ranks. This sampling distribution, which is symmetric around 0, applies when the treatments have identical effects. It is used for the significance test of the null hypothesis that the treatments are identical in their tanning quality.

better tanning quality.) If this were true, we would expect that the difference in the sample mean ranks between the tanning lotion and the tanning studio is positive, whereas under the null hypothesis, we would expect this difference to be around 0.

To find the P-value, we presume that H_0 is true. Then, all samples in Table 15.1 are equally likely, and the sampling distribution is the one shown in Table 15.2. The P-value is the probability of a difference between the sample mean rankings like the observed difference or even more extreme, in terms of giving even more evidence in favor of H_a. The test comparing two groups based on the sampling distribution of the difference between the sample mean ranks is called the **Wilcoxon test**. It is named after the chemist-turned-statistician, Frank Wilcoxon, who devised it in 1945.

SUMMARY: Wilcoxon Nonparametric Test for Comparing Two Groups

1. **Assumptions:** Independent random samples from two groups, either from random sampling or a randomized experiment.
2. **Hypotheses:**
   H_0: Identical population distributions for the two groups (this implies equal population mean ranks)
   H_a: Different population mean ranks (two-sided), or
   H_a: Higher population mean rank for a specified group (one-sided)

3. **Test statistic:** Difference between sample mean ranks for the two groups (equivalently, can use sum of ranks for one sample, as discussed after Example 2).
4. **P-value:** One-tail or two-tail probability, depending on H_a, that the difference between the sample mean ranks is as extreme or more extreme than observed.
5. **Conclusion:** Report the P-value and interpret in context. If a decision is needed, reject H_0 if the P-value $\leq$ significance level, such as 0.05.

Example 2

P-value for Wilcoxon test

Tanning Studio Versus Tanning Lotion

Picture the Scenario

Example 1 describes Allison's experiment to determine whether a tanning lotion or a tanning studio produced a better tan. Table 15.1 showed the possible rankings for five tans. Table 15.2 showed the sampling distribution of the difference between the sample mean ranks, presuming the null hypothesis is true that the tanning treatments have identical effects. For Allison's actual experiment, the ranks were (2, 4, 5) for the three participants using the tanning lotion and (1, 3) for the two participants using the tanning studio.

Questions to Explore

a. Find and interpret the P-value for comparing the treatments, using the one-sided alternative hypothesis that the tanning studio gives a better tan than the tanning lotion.

b. What's the smallest possible P-value you could get for this experiment?

Think It Through

a. For the observed sample, the mean ranks are $(2 + 4 + 5)/3 = 3.7$ for the tanning lotion and $(1 + 3)/2 = 2$ for the tanning studio. The test statistic is the difference between the sample mean ranks, $3.7 - 2 = 1.7$. Differences as or more extreme than this, for which the ranks tended to be better (lower) with the tanning studio, are in the right tail of the sampling distribution in Figure 15.1. For the one-sided H_a, the P-value is the probability,

$$\text{P-value} = P(\text{difference between sample mean ranks at least as large as observed}).$$

That is, under the presumption that H_0 is true,

$$\text{P-value} = P(\text{difference between sample mean ranks} \geq 1.7).$$

From Table 15.2 (shown again in the margin) or Figure 15.1 (reproduced on the next page), the probability of a sample mean difference of 1.7 or even larger is $1/10 + 1/10 = 2/10 = 0.20$. This is the P-value. It is not very close to 0. Although there is some evidence that the tanning studio gives a better tan (it *did* have a lower sample mean rank), the evidence is not strong enough. If the treatments had identical effects, the probability would be 0.20 of getting a sample like we observed or one even more extreme.

b. In this experiment, suppose the tanning studio gave the two most natural-looking tans. The ranks would then be (1, 2) for the tanning studio and (3, 4, 5) for the tanning lotion. The difference of sample means then equals $4 - 1.5 = 2.5$. It is the most extreme possible sample, and (from Table 15.2 or Figure 15.1) its tail probability is 0.10. This is the smallest possible one-sided P-value.

Recall

Sampling distribution of the difference between mean ranks:

Difference	Probability
−2.5	1/10
−1.7	1/10
−0.8	2/10
0	2/10
0.8	2/10
1.7	1/10
2.5	1/10

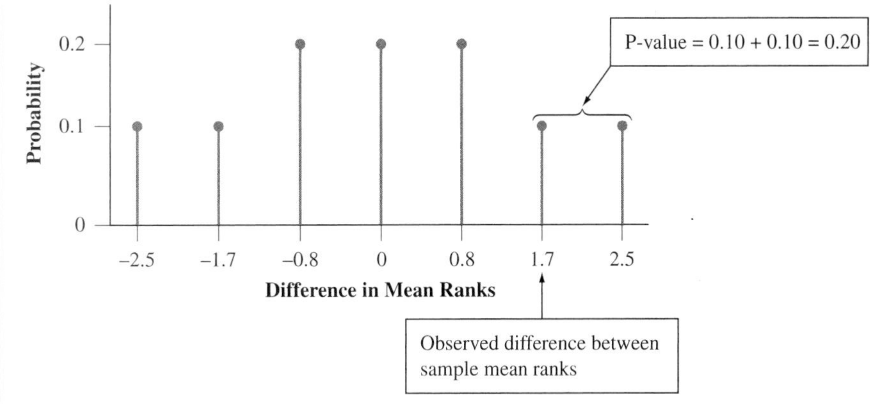

Insight

With sample sizes of only 2 for one treatment and 3 for the other treatment, it's not possible to get a very small P-value. If Allison wanted to make a decision using a 0.05 significance level, she would never be able to get strong enough evidence to reject the null hypothesis. To get informative results, she'd need to conduct an experiment with larger sample sizes.

▶ ***Try Exercises 15.1 and 15.2***

Suppose Allison instead used a two-sided H_a, namely that there is a treatment difference without specifying which is better. Then the P-value is a two-tail probability. In Example 2, we would get P-value $= 2(0.20) = 0.40$.

The Wilcoxon Rank Sum Statistic The Wilcoxon test can, equivalently, use as the test statistic the sum of the ranks in just one of the samples. For example, Table 15.3 shows the possible sum of ranks for the tanning lotion. They have the same probabilities as the differences between the sample mean ranks because the ranks in one sample determine the ranks in the other sample (since the ranks must be the integers 1 through 5). For example, the ranks were (2, 4, 5) for the participants using the tanning lotion, for which the sum of ranks is 11. This implies that the ranks were (1, 3) for those using the tanning studio, and it implies that the difference between the mean ranks was $(2 + 4 + 5)/3 - (1 + 3)/2 = 3.7 - 2 = 1.7$. The right-tail probability of the observed rank sum of 11 or a more extreme value is again $1/10 + 1/10 = 0.20$, as seen in the following figure. Some software reports the sum of ranks as the *Wilcoxon rank sum statistic*, sometimes denoted by *W*.

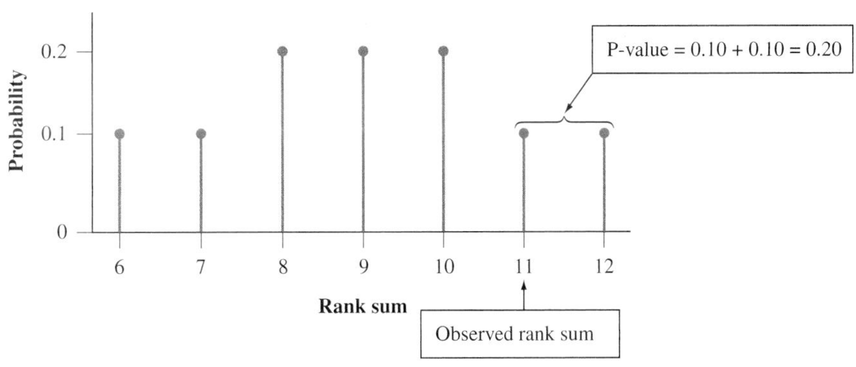

Table 15.3 Sampling Distribution of Sum of Ranks

The observed tanning lotion ranks of (2, 4, 5) have a rank sum of 11. These ranks imply that the tanning studio ranks were (1, 3) and that the difference between the sample mean ranks was 1.7.

Tanning Lotion Ranks	Sum of Tanning Lotion Ranks	Probability
(1, 2, 3)	6	1/10
(1, 2, 4)	7	1/10
(1, 2, 5), (1, 3, 4)	8	2/10
(2, 3, 4), (1, 3, 5)	9	2/10
(2, 3, 5), (1, 4, 5)	10	2/10
(2, 4, 5)	11	1/10
(3, 4, 5)	12	1/10

Large-Sample P-Values Use a Normal Sampling Distribution

With sample sizes of 3 and 2, it was simple to enumerate all the possible outcomes and construct a sampling distribution for the sum of ranks for a sample or for the difference between the mean ranks. With the sample sizes usually used in practice, it is tedious to do this. It's best to use software to get the results. Table 15.4 shows the way SPSS reports results for the Wilcoxon test conducted in Example 2. It shows the P-value of 0.20 for the one-sided and the P-value of 0.40 for the two-sided alternative hypothesis.

Table 15.4 SPSS Output for Wilcoxon Test with Example 2

SPSS uses the sum of the two ranks (1, 3) for the tanning studio as the Wilcoxon test statistic W. The P-value for the one-sided test is listed next to "Exact Sig. (1-tailed)," where "Sig." is short for significance. When W is the sum of the ranks for the tanning studio, values of W as *small or smaller* are in favor of the alternative hypothesis. (By contrast, if W is the sum of the ranks for the lotion, values of W as large or larger are in favor of the alternative hypothesis.) The two-sided P-value is listed next to "Exact Sig. [2*(1-tailed Sig.)]." This output was obtained using the Legacy Dialog option under Nonparametrics in the Analyze menu of SPSS 21.

Ranks

	Treatment	N	Mean Rank	Sum of Ranks
Tanning	Lotion	3	3.67	11.00
	Studio	2	2.00	4.00
	Total	5		

Test Statistics

	Tanning
Mann-Whitney U	1.000
Wilcoxon W	4.000
Z	−1.155
Asymp. Sig. (2-tailed)	.248
Exact Sig. [2*(1-tailed Sig.)]	.400
Exact Sig. (1-tailed)	.200

▶ Activity

You can also get the exact P-value for the Wilcoxon test by using the Permutation Test for Means web app from the book's website by (i) entering the ranks for the two groups, (ii) selecting Wilcoxon rank sum statistic as the test statistic, and (iii) checking the option for all possible permutations.

In Example 2, we found the P-value with an exact probability calculation using the actual sampling distribution. With large samples, an alternative approach finds a z test statistic and a P-value based on a normal distribution approximation to the actual sampling distribution. (Some software, such as MINITAB, *only* provides results for the large-sample z test analysis.) For example, in Table 15.4, SPSS reports $z = -1.155$ and Asymp. Sig. (2-tailed) $= 0.248$.

In Words

"Asymp." is short for **asymptotic,** which in statistics means "large-sample" or "as the sample size grows" (mathematically, as it grows toward infinity).

These are the results of the large-sample approximate analysis. This analysis is not appropriate for Example 2 because the sample sizes are only 2 and 3 for the two groups.

The large-sample test has a z test statistic because the difference between the sample mean ranks (or the sum of ranks for one sample) has an approximate normal sampling distribution. The z test statistic has the form

$$z = (\text{difference between sample mean ranks})/se.$$

The standard error formula is complex but easily calculated by software. The P-value is then the right-tail, left-tail, or two-tail probability, depending on H_a. Using the normal distribution for the large-sample test does not mean we are assuming that the response variable has a normal distribution. We are merely using the fact that the sampling distribution for the test statistic is approximately normal.

Ties Often Occur When We Rank Observations

Often in ranking the observations, some pairs of subjects are tied. They are judged to perform equally well. We then *average the ranks* in assigning them to those subjects. For example, suppose a participant using the tanning studio got the most natural-looking tan (rank 1), two participants using the tanning lotion got the two least natural-looking tans (ranks 4 and 5), but the other participant using the tanning studio and the other participant using the tanning lotion were judged to have equally good tans. Then, those two participants share ranks 2 and 3, and each gets the average rank of 2.5. The ranks are then

Tanning studio: 1, 2.5

Tanning lotion: 2.5, 4, 5

In Practice Software and Implementing the Wilcoxon Test

Software can find tied ranks and then calculate the P-value for the Wilcoxon test. Most software reports only the large-sample approximate P-value when either sample size is larger than some value, typically 20. For example, SPSS reports the small-sample exact P-value only when each sample size is 20 or less.

Using the Wilcoxon Test with a Quantitative Response

In Examples 1 and 2, the response was a rank. When the response variable is quantitative, the Wilcoxon test is applied by converting the observations to ranks. For the combined sample, the observations are ordered from smallest to largest. The smallest observation gets rank 1, the second smallest gets rank 2, and so forth. The test compares the mean ranks for the two samples. Software can implement the test.

Example 3

Wilcoxon test: finding ranks (large sample)

Driving Reaction Times

Picture the Scenario

Example 9 in Chapter 10 discussed an experiment investigating whether cell phone use impairs drivers' reaction times. A sample of 64 college students was randomly assigned to a cell phone group or a control group, 32 to each.

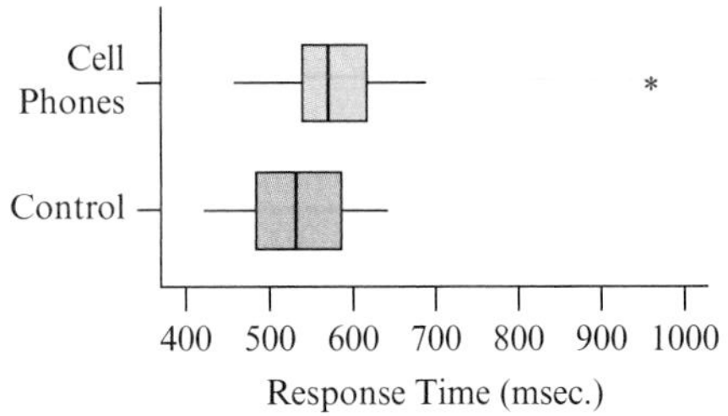

▲ Figure 15.2 Box Plots of Response Times for Cell Phone Study. **Question** Does either box plot show any irregularities that suggest it's safer to use a nonparametric test than a two-sample *t* test?

On a machine that simulated driving situations, participants were instructed to press a brake button as soon as possible when they detected a red light. The control group listened to a radio broadcast or to books-on-tape while they performed the simulated driving. The cell phone group carried out a conversation on a cell phone with someone in a separate room.

A subject's reaction time observation is defined to be his or her response time to the red lights (in milliseconds), averaged over all the trials. Figure 15.2 shows box plots of the data for the two groups. Here's some of the data showing the four smallest observations and the four largest observations for each treatment.

Cell phone:	456	468	482	501	....	672	679	688	960
Control:	426	436	444	449	....	626	626	642	648

The *t* inferences for comparing the treatment means assume normal population distributions. The box plots do not show any substantial skew, but there is an extreme outlier for the cell phone group. One subject in that group had a very slow mean reaction time, 960 milliseconds.

Questions to Explore

a. Explain how to find the ranks for the Wilcoxon test by showing which of the 64 observations get ranks 1, 2, 63, and 64.

b. Table 15.5 shows the SPSS output for conducting the Wilcoxon test. Report and interpret the mean ranks.

Table 15.5 SPSS Output for Wilcoxon Test with Data from Cell Phone Study

Ranks

	group	N	Mean Rank	Sum of Ranks
Reactime	Cell Phone	32	38.00	1216.00
	Control	32	27.00	864.00
	Total	64		

Test Statistics

	Reactime
Mann-Whitney U	336.000
Wilcoxon W	864.000
Z	−2.363
Asymp. Sig. (2-tailed)	.018

c. Report the test statistic and the P-value for the two-sided Wilcoxon test. Interpret.

Think It Through

a. Let's look at the smallest and largest observations for each group that were shown above:

Cell phone:	456	468	482	501	....	672	679	688	960
Control:	426	436	444	449	....	626	626	642	648

We give rank 1 to the *smallest* reaction time, so the value 426 gets rank 1. The second smallest observation is 436, which gets rank 2. The largest of the 64 reaction times, which was 960, gets rank 64. The next largest observation, 688, gets rank 63.

b. Table 15.5 reports mean ranks of 38 for the cell phone group and 27 for the control group. The smaller mean for the control group

▶ Activity

You can get an accurate approximation of the exact P-value by copying and pasting the data for the two groups into the Permutation Test for Means web app, selecting Wilcoxon rank sum statistic as the test statistic and generating 10,0000 random permutations. When you do this, notice how the sampling distribution of W looks approximately normal, giving credence to using the asymptotic P-value, which is nearly identical to the exact one.

suggests that that group tends to have smaller ranks and, thus, faster reaction times.

c. The z test statistic divides the difference between the sample mean ranks by a standard error. Table 15.5 reports $z = -2.363$. The P-value of 0.018, reported as "Asymp. Sig. (2-tailed)," is the two-tail probability for the two-sided H_a. It shows strong evidence against the null hypothesis that the distribution of reaction time is identical for the two treatments. Specifically, the sample mean ranks suggest that reaction times tend to be slower for those using cell phones.

Insight

The observation of 960 would get rank 64 if it were *any* number larger than 688 (the second largest value). So, *the Wilcoxon test is not affected by an outlier.* No matter how far the largest observation falls from the next largest, it still gets the same rank. Likewise, no matter how far the smallest observation is below the next smallest, it still gets the rank of 1.

▶ ***Try Exercise 15.4***

Nonparametric Estimation Comparing Two Groups

Throughout this text, we've seen the importance of *estimating* parameters. We learn more from a confidence interval for a parameter than from a significance test about the value of that parameter. Nonparametric estimation methods, like nonparametric tests, do not require the assumption of normal population distributions.

When the response is quantitative, we can compare a measure of center for the two groups. Chapter 10 did this for the mean. Nonparametric methods are often used when the response distribution may be skewed. Then, it can be more informative to summarize each group by the *median.* We then estimate the difference between the population medians for the two groups.

Most software for the Wilcoxon test reports point and interval estimates comparing medians. (Some software, such as MINITAB, refers to the equivalent Mann-Whitney test instead. See Exercise 15.35.) Although this inference does not require a normal population assumption, it *does* require an extra assumption, namely that *the population distributions for the two groups have the same shape.*

Under the extra assumption, here's how software estimates the difference between the population medians. For every possible pair of subjects, one from each group, it takes the difference between the response from the first group and the response from the second group. The point estimate is the median of all those differences. Software also reports a confidence interval for the difference between the population medians. The mechanics of this are beyond the scope of this text.

Example 4

Wilcoxon test ◀

Difference Between Median Reaction Times

Picture the Scenario

Example 3 used the Wilcoxon test to compare reaction time distributions in a simulated driving experiment for subjects using cell phones and for a control group. The MINITAB output in Table 15.6 shows results of comparing the

distributions using medians. (It uses the Greek letter name *eta*, which is η, to denote the population median.)

Table 15.6 MINITAB Output for Comparing Medians for Cell Phone Group and Control Group

	N	Median
Cell Phone	32	569.00
Control	32	530.00

Point estimate for $\eta 1 - \eta 2$ is 44.50 ← η (the Greek eta) is MINITAB notation for the median

95.1 Percent CI for $\eta 1 - \eta 2$ is (8.99, 79.01)

W = 1216.0

Test of $\eta 1 = \eta 2$ vs $\eta 1 \neq \eta 2$ is significant at 0.0184 ← P-value

Questions to Explore

a. Report the sample medians and the point estimate of the difference between the population medians.

b. Report and interpret the 95% confidence interval for the difference between the population medians.

Recall

From the discussion before the example, the **point estimate** of the difference between the population medians equals the median of the differences between responses from the two groups. ◀

Think It Through

a. The median reaction times were 569 milliseconds for the cell phone group and 530 milliseconds for the control group. For the cell phone group, for example, half of the reaction times were smaller than 569 milliseconds and half were larger than 569. Table 15.6 reports a point estimate of the difference between the population medians for the two groups of 44.5 milliseconds. (*Note*: This is not the same as the difference between the two sample medians, which is an alternative estimate.)

b. Table 15.6 reports that a 95.1% confidence interval for the difference between the population medians is (8.99, 79.01). (For these types of intervals, achieving the exact confidence level is often impossible, so software uses a confidence level that is close to 95%.) Since zero is not contained in the 95.1% interval, this interval supports that the median reaction times are not the same for the cell phone and control groups. We infer from the interval that the population median reaction time for the cell phone group is between 9 milliseconds and 79 milliseconds larger than for the control group. This inference agrees with the conclusion of the Wilcoxon test that the reaction time distributions differ for the two groups (P-value = 0.018).

Insight

Example 9 in Chapter 10 estimated the difference between the population *means* to be 51.5, with a 95% confidence interval of (12, 91). However, those results were influenced by the outlier of 960 for the cell phone group. When estimation focuses on medians rather than means, outliers do not influence the analysis. *The lack of an influence of outliers is an advantage of the analysis reported here for the medians.*

▶ ***Try Exercise 15.5***

15.1 Practicing the Basics

15.1 Tanning experiment Suppose the tanning experiment described in Examples 1 and 2 used only four participants, two for each treatment.
TRY

a. Show the six possible ways the four ranks could be allocated, two to each treatment, with no ties.

b. For each possible sample, find the mean rank for each treatment and the difference between the mean ranks.

c. Presuming H_0 is true of identical treatment effects, construct the sampling distribution of the difference between the sample mean ranks for the two treatments.

15.2 Test for tanning experiment Refer to the previous exercise. For the actual experiment, suppose the participants using the tanning studio got ranks 1 and 2 and the participants using the tanning lotion got ranks 3 and 4.
TRY

a. Find and interpret the P-value for the alternative hypothesis that the tanning studio tends to give better tans than the tanning lotion.

b. Find and interpret the P-value for the alternative hypothesis that the treatments have different effects.

c. Explain why it is a waste of time to conduct this experiment if you plan to use a 0.05 significance level to make a decision.

15.3 Comparing clinical therapies A clinical psychologist wants to choose between two therapies for treating severe mental depression. She selects six patients who are similar in their depressive symptoms and overall quality of health. She randomly selects three patients to receive Therapy 1. The other three receive Therapy 2. After one month of treatment, the improvement in each patient is measured by the change in a score for measuring severity of mental depression—the higher the change score, the better. The improvement scores are

Therapy 1: 25, 40, 45

Therapy 2: 10, 20, 30

a. Show all possible ways the ranks from 1 to 6 could be distributed between the two treatments. (*Hint:* There are 20 allocations.)

b. For each possible allocation of ranks, find the mean rank for each treatment and the difference between the mean ranks.

c. Consider the null hypothesis of identical response distributions for the two treatments. Presuming H_0 is true, construct the sampling distribution of the difference between the sample mean ranks for the two treatments.

d. For the actual data shown above, find and interpret the P-value for the alternative hypothesis that the two treatments have different effects. (You can check your answers by entering the data in the Permutation Test for Means web app, selecting Wilcoxon rank sum as the test statistic, and selecting the option for generating all possible permutations.)

15.4 Baby weight and smoking Smoking during pregnancy is a known cause of reduced infant birth weight and other issues that can affect the delivery and mortality. Despite this strong evidence, women who smoke find it difficult to quit even when they are pregnant. Suppose a study is done measuring the birth weight of babies of mothers who smoked during pregnancy and those who did not smoke. The birth weight data in pounds are:
TRY

Smokers: 3.1, 4.2, 4.5, 5.0, 6.4, 4.7, 6.0

Nonsmokers: 5.5, 6.5, 7.1, 8.0, 6.8, 7.5, 6.2

a. State the hypotheses for conducting a one-sided (right tailed) Wilcoxon test.

b. Find the ranks for the two groups and their sum and mean of ranks.

c. Software reports a small-sample one-sided P-value of 0.002. Interpret. (You can reproduce these results by entering the data in the Permutation Test for Means web app, selecting Wilcoxon rank sum as the test statistic, and selecting the option for generating all possible permutations.)

15.5 Estimating smoking effect Refer to the previous exercise. For these data, MINITAB reports
TRY

```
Point estimate for η1 − η2 is −2.00
95.9 Percent CI for η1 − η2 is (−3.30,−0.70)
W = 31.0
Test of η1 = η2 vs η1 ≠ η2 is significant at 0.006
```

Explain how to interpret the reported (a) point estimate and (b) confidence interval.

15.6 Trading volumes The following data show the number of shares of General Electric stock traded on Mondays and on Fridays from February through April of 2011. The trading volumes (rounded to the nearest million) are as follows:
TECH

Mondays: 45, 43, 43, 66, 91, 53, 35, 45, 29, 64, 56

Fridays: 43, 41, 45, 46, 61, 56, 80, 40, 48, 49, 50, 41

Using software,

a. Plot the data. Summarize what the plot shows.

b. State the hypotheses and give the P-value for the Wilcoxon test for comparing the two groups with a two-sided alternative hypothesis. (As one option, you can find an accurate approximation of the exact P-value by using the Permutation Test for Means web app.)

c. A 95.5% confidence interval for comparing the population medians equals (−11, 13). Interpret and explain what (if any) effect the day of the week (Monday versus Friday) has on the median number of shares traded.

d. State the assumptions for the methods in parts b and c.

15.7 Teenage anorexia Previous chapters described a study that used therapy to treat teenage girls who suffered from anorexia. The girls were randomly assigned to the cognitive behavioral treatment (Group 1) or to the control group (Group 2). The study observed the weight change after a period of time. The following output shows results of a nonparametric comparison. (The data set is available online.)

a. Interpret the reported point estimate of the difference between the population medians for the weight changes for the two groups.

b. Interpret the reported confidence interval and summarize the assumptions on which it is based.

c. Report a P-value for testing the null hypothesis of identical population distributions of weight change. Specify the alternative hypothesis, and interpret the P-value.

MINITAB output comparing weight changes

```
                     N      Median
Cognitive_change    29       1.400
Control_change      26      -0.350
Point estimate for η1 − η2 is 3.05
95.0 Percent CI for η1 − η2 is (−0.60,8.10)
W = 907.0
Test of η1 = η2 vs η1 ≠ η2 is significant at 0.1111
```

15.2 Nonparametric Methods for Several Groups and for Matched Pairs

This final section describes a few other nonparametric methods. We'll first learn about a method that extends the Wilcoxon test to comparisons of mean ranks for *several* groups. We then study two methods for comparing *dependent* samples in the form of *matched pairs* data that Section 10.4 studied.

Comparing Mean Ranks of Several Groups: The Kruskal-Wallis Test

Chapter 14 showed that comparisons of means for two groups extend to comparisons for many groups, using the **analysis of variance (ANOVA) *F* test**. Likewise, the Wilcoxon test for comparing mean ranks of two groups extends to a comparison of mean ranks for several groups. This rank test is called the **Kruskal-Wallis test**, named after the statisticians who proposed it in 1952.

As in the Wilcoxon test, the Kruskal-Wallis test assumes that the samples are independent random samples, and the null hypothesis states that the groups have identical population distributions for the response variable. The test determines the ranks for the entire sample and then finds the sample mean rank for each group. The test statistic is based on the between-groups variability in the sample mean ranks. To calculate this test statistic, denote the sample mean rank by $\overline{R}_i$ for group i and by $\overline{R}$ for the combined sample of g groups. The Kruskal-Wallis test statistic is

$$\left(\frac{12}{n(n+1)}\right)\Sigma n_i(\overline{R}_i - \overline{R})^2.$$

Recall

Section 11.2 introduced the chi-squared distribution as a right-skewed distribution on the positive real line and with mean equal to the degrees of freedom. ◀

The constant $12/(n(n+1))$ is there so that the test statistic values have approximately a chi-squared sampling distribution. Software easily calculates it for us.

The sampling distribution of the test statistic indicates whether the variability among the sample mean ranks is large compared to what's expected under the null hypothesis that the groups have identical population distributions. With g groups, the test statistic has an approximate chi-squared distribution with $g - 1$ degrees of freedom. (Recall that for the chi-squared distribution, the *df* is the mean.) The approximation improves as the sample sizes increase. The larger the differences among the sample mean ranks, the larger the test statistic and the stronger the evidence against H_0. The P-value is the right-tail probability above the observed test statistic value.

When would we use this test? The ANOVA *F* test assumes normal population distributions. The Kruskal-Wallis test does not have this assumption. It's a safer method to use with small samples when not much information is available about the shape of the distributions. It's also useful when the data are merely ranks and we don't have a quantitative measurement of the response variable. Here's a basic summary of the test:

Summary: Kruskal-Wallis Nonparametric Test for Comparing Several Groups

1. **Assumptions:** Independent random samples from several (g) groups, either from random sampling or a randomized experiment
2. **Hypotheses:**
   H_0: Identical population distributions for the g groups
   H_a: Population distributions not all identical
3. **Test statistic:** Uses between-groups variability of sample mean ranks
4. **P-value:** Right-tail probability above observed test statistic value from chi-squared distribution with $df = g - 1$
5. **Conclusion:** Report the P-value and interpret in context.

Example 5

Kruskal-Wallis test ◀

Frequent Dating and College GPA

Picture the Scenario

Tim decided to study whether dating was associated with college GPA. He wondered whether students who date a lot tend to have poorer GPAs. He asked the 17 students in the class to anonymously fill out a short questionnaire in which they were asked to give their college GPA (0 to 4 scale) and to indicate whether during their college careers they had dated regularly, occasionally, or rarely.

Figure 15.3 shows the dot plots that Tim constructed of the GPA data for the three dating groups. Since the dot plots showed evidence of severe skew to the left and since the sample size was small in each group, he felt safer analyzing the data with the Kruskal-Wallis test than with the ordinary ANOVA F test.

Finding ranks for data in Table 15.7

GPA	Rank
1.75	1
2.00	2
2.40	3
2.95	4
3.15	5
3.20	6
3.40	7
3.44	8
3.50	9.5 ← average of 9 and 10
3.50	9.5
3.60	11
3.67	12
3.68	13
3.70	14
3.71	15
3.80	16
4.00	17

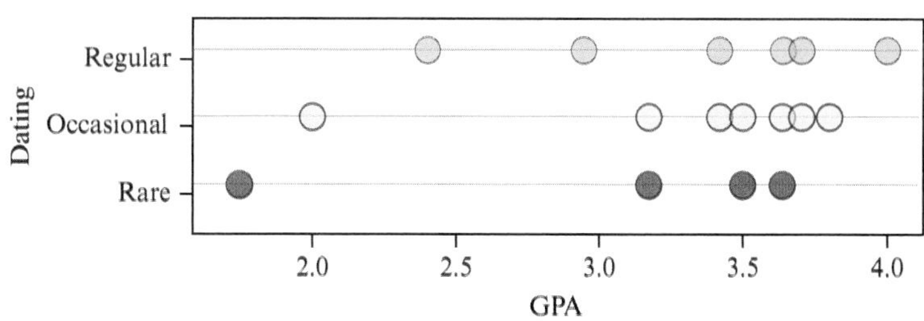

▲ **Figure 15.3** Dot Plots of GPA by Dating Group. **Question** Why might it not be appropriate to use the ordinary ANOVA F test to compare mean GPA for the three dating groups?

Table 15.7 shows the data, with the college GPA values ordered from smallest to largest for each dating group. The table in the margin shows the combined and sorted sample of 17 observations from the three groups and their ranks. Table 15.7 also shows these ranks as well as the mean rank for each group.

Table 15.7 College GPA by Dating Group

Dating Group	GPA Observations	Ranks	Mean Rank
Rare	1.75, 3.15, 3.50, 3.68	1, 5, 9.5, 13	7.1
Occasional	2.00, 3.20, 3.44, 3.50, 3.60, 3.71, 3.80	2, 6, 8, 9.5, 11, 15, 16	9.6
Regular	2.40, 2.95, 3.40, 3.67, 3.70, 4.00	3, 4, 7, 12, 14, 17	9.5

Question to Explore

Table 15.8 shows MINITAB output for the Kruskal-Wallis test. MINITAB denotes the chi-squared test statistic by H. Interpret these results.

Table 15.8 Results of Kruskal-Wallis Test for Data in Table 15.7

```
Kruskal-Wallis Test on GPA
Date Group      N      Median      Ave Rank        Z
Rare            4      3.325         7.1         -0.85
Occasional      7      3.500         9.6          0.44
Regular         6      3.535         9.5          0.30
H = 0.72     DF = 2  P = 0.696 (adjusted for ties)
```

Think It Through

If H_0: identical population distributions for the three groups were true, the Kruskal-Wallis test statistic would have an approximate chi-squared distribution with $df = 2$. Table 15.8 reports that the test statistic is H = 0.72. The P-value is the right-tail probability above 0.72. Table 15.8 reports this as 0.696, about 0.7. It is plausible that GPA is independent of dating group. Table 15.8 shows that the sample median GPAs are not very different, and since the sample sizes are small, these sample medians do not give much evidence against H_0.

Insight

If the P-value had been small, to find out which pairs of groups significantly differ, we could follow up the Kruskal-Wallis test by a Wilcoxon test to compare each pair of dating groups. Or, we could find a confidence interval for the difference between the population medians for each pair.

► ***Try Exercise 15.8***

Comparing Matched Pairs: The Sign Test

Chapter 10 showed that it's possible to compare groups using either *independent* or *dependent* samples. So far in this chapter, the samples have been independent. When the subjects in the two samples are matched, such as when each treatment in an experiment uses the same subjects, the samples are dependent. Then we must use different methods.

For example, the tanning experiment from Examples 1 and 2 could have used a crossover design instead: The participants get a tan using one treatment, and after it wears off they get a tan using the other treatment. The order of using the two treatments is random. For each participant, we observe which treatment gives the better tan. That is, we make comparisons by pairing the two observations for the same participant.

For such a matched pairs experiment, let p denote the population proportion of cases for which a particular treatment does better than the other treatment. Under the null hypothesis of identical treatment effects, $p = 0.50$. That is, each treatment should have the better response outcome about half the time. (We ignore those cases in which each treatment gives the *same* response.) Let n denote the sample number of pairs of observations for which the two responses differ. For large n, we can use the z test statistic to compare the sample proportion $\hat{p}$ to the null hypothesis value of 0.50. (See the margin Recall box.) The P-value is based on the approximate standard normal sampling distribution.

Recall

From Section 9.2, to test H_0: $p = 0.50$ with sample proportion $\hat{p}$ when $n \geq 30$, the test statistic is

$$z = (\hat{p} - 0.50)/se,$$

with $se = \sqrt{(0.50)(0.50)/n}$. ◄

A test that compares matched pairs in this way is called a **sign test**. The name refers to how the method evaluates for each matched pair whether the difference between the first and second response is *positive* or *negative.*

SUMMARY: Sign Test for Matched Pairs

1. **Assumptions:** Random sample of matched pairs for which we can evaluate which observation in a pair has the better response.
2. **Hypotheses:** H_0: Population proportion $p = 0.50$ who have better response for a particular group

   H_a: $p \neq 0.50$ (two-sided) or H_a: $p > 0.50$ or H_a: $p < 0.50$ (one-sided)
3. **Test statistic:** $z = (\hat{p} - 0.50)/se$, as shown in margin recall box.
4. **P-value:** For large samples ($n \geq 30$), use tail probabilities from standard normal. For smaller n, use binomial distribution (discussed in Example 7).
5. **Conclusion:** Report the P-value and interpret in context.

Example 6

Sign test for matched pairs

Time Browsing the Internet or Watching TV

Picture the Scenario

Which do most students spend more time doing—browsing the Internet or watching TV? Let's consider the students surveyed at the University of Georgia whose responses are in the Georgia Student Survey data file. The results for the first three students in the data file (in minutes per day) were

Student	Internet	TV
1	60	120
2	20	120
3	60	90

All three spent more time watching TV. For the entire sample, 35 students spent more time watching TV and 19 students spent more time browsing the Internet. (The analysis ignores the 5 students who reported the same time for each.)

Question to Explore

Let p denote the population proportion who spent more time watching TV. Find the test statistic and P-value for the sign test of H_0: $p = 0.50$ against H_a: $p \neq 0.50$. Interpret.

Think It Through

Here, $n = 35 + 19 = 54$. The sample proportion who spent more time watching TV was $35/54 = 0.648$. For testing that $p = 0.50$, the se of the sample proportion is

$$se = \sqrt{(0.50)(0.50)/n} = \sqrt{(0.50)(0.50)/54} = 0.068.$$

The test statistic is

$$z = (\hat{p} - 0.50)/se = (0.648 - 0.50)/0.068 = 2.18.$$

From the normal distribution table (Table A or software), the two-sided P-value is 0.03. This provides considerable evidence that most students spend more time watching TV than browsing the Internet. The conclusion must be tempered by the fact that the data resulted from a convenience sample (students in a class for a statistics course) rather than a random sample of all college students.

Insight

The sign test uses merely the information about *which* response is higher and *how many* responses are higher, not the quantitative information about *how much* higher. This is a disadvantage compared to the corresponding parametric test, the matched pairs t test of Section 10.4, which analyzes the mean of the differences between the two responses. The sign test is most appropriate when we can order the responses but do not have quantitative information, such as in the next example.

► ***Try Exercise 15.10***

For small n, we can conduct the sign test by using the *binomial* distribution. The next example illustrates this case as well as a situation in which we can order responses for each pair but do not have quantitative information about how different the responses are.

Example 7

Sign test for matched pairs (small sample) ◄

Crossover Experiment Comparing Tanning Methods

Picture the Scenario

When Allison told another student in the class (Megan) about her planned experiment to compare tanning methods, Megan decided to do a separate tanning experiment. She used a crossover design for a different sample of five untanned female friends. The results of her experiment were that the tanning studio gave a better tan than the tanning lotion for four of the five participants.

Question to Explore

Find and interpret the P-value for testing that the population proportion p of participants for whom the tanning studio gives a better tan than the tanning lotion equals 0.50. Use the alternative hypothesis that this population proportion is larger than 0.50, because Megan predicted that the tanning studio would give better tans.

Recall

Section 6.3 presented the **binomial** distribution. With probability p of success on a trial, out of n independent trials the probability of x successes is

$$P(x) = \frac{n!}{x!(n-x)!}p^x(1-p)^{n-x}. \blacktriangleleft$$

Think It Through

The null hypothesis is H_0: $p = 0.50$. For H_a: $p > 0.50$, the P-value is the probability of the observed sample outcome or an even larger one. The sample size ($n = 5$) was small, so we use the binomial distribution rather than its normal approximation to find the P-value.

If $p = 0.50$, from the margin Recall box the binomial probability that $x = 4$ of the $n = 5$ participants would get better tans with the tanning studio is

$$P(4) = \frac{5!}{4!(5-4)!}(0.50)^4(0.50)^1 = 0.156.$$

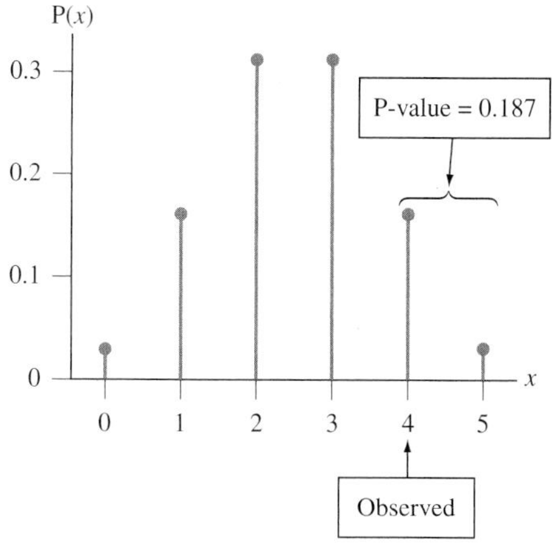

The more extreme result that all five participants would get better tans with the tanning studio has probability $P(5) = (0.50)^5 = 0.031$. The P-value is the right-tail probability of the observed result and the more extreme one, that is, $0.156 + 0.031 = 0.187$. See the margin figure. In summary, the evidence is not strong that more participants get a better tan from the tanning studio than the tanning lotion.

Insight

Megan would instead use the two-sided alternative, H_a: $p \neq 0.50$, if she did not make a prior prediction about which tanning method would be better. The P-value would then be $2(0.19) = 0.38$. With only $n = 5$ observations, the smallest possible two-sided P-value would be $2(0.031) = 0.06$, which occurs when $x = 0$ or when $x = 5$.

▶ ***Try Exercise 15.11***

Ranking Matched Pairs: The Wilcoxon Signed-Rank Test

With matched pairs data, for each pair the sign test merely observes which treatment does better, but not *how much* better. The **Wilcoxon signed-rank test** is a nonparametric test designed for cases in which the comparisons of the paired observations can themselves be ranked. For each matched pair of responses, it measures the difference between the responses. It tests the hypothesis,

H_0: population median of difference scores is 0.

The test uses the quantitative information provided by the n difference scores by ranking their magnitudes, in absolute value. (Like the sign test, it ignores observation pairs for which the difference equals 0.) The test statistic is the sum of the ranks for those differences that are positive.

SUMMARY: Wilcoxon Signed-Rank Test for Matched Pairs

1. **Assumptions:** Random sample of matched pairs for which the differences of observations have a symmetric population distribution and can be ranked.
2. **Hypotheses:**
   H_0: Population median of difference scores is 0.
   H_a: Population median of difference scores is not 0 (one-sided also possible).
3. **Test statistic:** Rank the absolute values of the difference scores for the matched pairs and then find the sum of ranks for those differences that were positive.
4. **P-value:** Software can find a P-value based on all the possible samples with the given absolute differences. (For large samples, it uses an approximate normal sampling distribution, as discussed following.)
5. **Conclusion:** Report the P-value and interpret in context.

Example 8

Wilcoxon signed-rank test ◀

GRE Test Scores

Picture the Scenario

If you want to attend graduate school, taking the Graduate Record Examination (GRE) is usually a requirement. Many graduate schools consider GRE scores for admittance, to qualify for financial aid, to determine fellowships and grants, and for other program research or teaching assignments. The GRE includes three sections designed to test verbal, quantitative, and writing skills.

The verbal and quantitative sections are each scored between 130 and 170. The analytical writing portion of the GRE is given a score between 0 and 6 in half point increments.

In our example, three students volunteered for a study to determine whether taking a two-day workshop on GRE preparation improved their GRE analytical writing score from a previous score. Note: The original data was larger ($n = 12$), but a small sample is used in this example to make it easier to explain. The results are shown in the following table:

	Subject		
	1	2	3
Before	2.5	4	1.5
After	3	3.5	3

A negative difference (after – before) represents a lower score. A positive difference represents an improved score. Let's test the null hypothesis that the two-day GRE workshop has no effect, in the sense that the population median gained score is 0, against the alternative hypothesis that the population median gained score is positive.

Questions to Explore

a. Find the absolute values of the differences, rank them, and then find the sum of the ranks for those differences that were positive.

b. Consider each of the possible ways that positive and negative signs could be assigned to these three differences. For each case, find the rank sum for the positive differences. Create the sampling distribution of this rank sum that applies if the workshop truly has no effect.

c. Find the P-value for the Wilcoxon signed-rank test, using the sampling distribution of the rank sum created in part b.

Think It Through

a. The Wilcoxon test begins by calculating the difference and then the absolute value for each paired observation. In most applications of the Wilcoxon procedure, the pairs for which the difference is zero are eliminated from consideration because they provide no useful information; the remaining absolute differences are then ranked from lowest to highest, with tied ranks included where appropriate.

Recall

How to handle ties is discussed on page 717. ◀

After sorting the GRE data, the differences have absolute values and ranks as follows:

Subject	Before	After	Difference	Absolute Value	Rank of Absolute Value
1	2.5	3	0.5	0.5	1.5
2	4	3.5	–0.5	0.5	1.5
3	1.5	3	1.5	1.5	3

The rank sum for the positive differences is $1.5 + 3 = 4.5$.

b. For the difference values of the three subjects, 0.5, −0.5, and 1.5, Table 15.9 shows all the possible ways the differences could have been positive or negative. For each sample, this table also shows the sum of ranks for the positive differences. The observed data are Sample 1, which had a rank sum of 4.5.

Table 15.9 Possible Samples with Absolute Difference Values of Sample

	Sample								
Subject	**1**	**2**	**3**	**4**	**5**	**6**	**7**	**8**	**Rank of Absolute Value**
1	0.5	0.5	−0.5	0.5	−0.5	0.5	−0.5	−0.5	1.5
2	−0.5	−0.5	−0.5	0.5	−0.5	0.5	0.5	0.5	1.5
3	1.5	−1.5	1.5	1.5	−1.5	−1.5	1.5	−1.5	3
	Sum of Ranks for Positive Differences								
	4.5	1.5	3	6	0	3	4.5	1.5	

If the workshop has no effect, then the eight possible samples in Table 15.9 are equally likely. The table that follows summarizes the sampling distribution of the rank sum for the positive differences, presuming no effect of the workshop. For example, the rank sum was 4.5 for two of the eight samples, so its probability is 2/8.

Sampling Distribution of Rank Sum for the Positive Differences

Rank Sum	Probability
0	$1/8$
1.5	$2/8$
3	$2/8$
4.5	$2/8$
6	$1/8$

c. The larger the sum of ranks for the positive differences, the greater the evidence that the workshop has a positive effect. So, the P-value is the probability that this sum of ranks is at least as large as observed. Since three of the eight possible samples had a rank sum for the positive differences of at least 4.5 (the observed value), the P-value is $3/8 = 0.375$.

Insight

Suppose we instead used the sign test. We then observe that two of the three differences are positive. For the alternative hypothesis that the workshop has a positive effect, the P-value is the probability that at least two of the three differences are positive, when the chance is 0.50 that any particular difference is positive. Using the binomial distribution, you can find that the P-value is 0.50 (Exercise 15.12).

The sign test ignores the fact that the two positive differences are larger than the negative difference. The Wilcoxon signed-rank test uses this information. By taking this extra information into account, its P-value of 0.375 is smaller than the P-value of 0.50 from the sign test. However, the P-value is still not small. With only three observations, the one-sided P-value can be no smaller than one-eighth, which is the P-value for the largest possible value (which is 6) for the rank sum of positive differences.

The MINITAB output for the complete data set with all 12 students is shown below. The Wilcoxon signed-rank test between the two groups results in a statistically significant P-value of 0.018.

Wilcoxon Signed Rank Test: Difference

Test of median = 0.000000 versus median not = 0.000000

	N	N for Test	Wilcoxon Statistic	P	Estimated Median
Diff	12	11	60.0	0.018	1.000

One difference was zero, so there are 11 differences to rank

Sum of ranks for positive differences

▶ *Try Exercise 15.12*

Caution

For **independent** samples, rank all of the data combined and then compare the sum (or mean) of the ranks of the two groups. (See Wilcoxon test in Section 15.1) For **dependent** samples, find the difference between the two groups and then rank the differences. These methods often are confused—especially if the independent samples have equal sample sizes. ◀

Although the Wilcoxon signed-rank test has the advantage compared to the sign test that it can take into account the *sizes* of the differences and not merely their *sign*, it also has a disadvantage. For the possible samples (such as the eight samples shown in Table 15.9) to be equally likely, it must make an additional assumption: The population distribution of the difference scores must be *symmetric*.

The symmetry assumption for the Wilcoxon signed-rank test is a bit weaker than the assumption of a normal population distribution for the differences that the matched pairs t test of Section 10.4 makes. However, with small samples, there's not much evidence to check this symmetry assumption. Also, recall that the t test is *robust* for violations of the assumption of normality, especially for two-sided inference. The extra assumption of symmetry for the Wilcoxon signed-ranks test weakens the advantage of using a nonparametric method. Because of this, many statisticians prefer to use the matched pairs t test for such data.

Like the Wilcoxon test for comparing mean ranks for two independent samples, the Wilcoxon signed-rank test can allow for ties, and it has a large-sample z test statistic that has an approximate standard normal sampling distribution. For instance, Example 6 used the sign test to compare times spent on Internet browsing and watching TV for 54 students. If we create difference scores

$$\text{Difference} = \text{TV watching time} - \text{Internet browsing time}$$

for the students and analyze them with the Wilcoxon signed-rank test, MINITAB reports the results shown in Table 15.10.

Table 15.10 Results of Wilcoxon Signed-Rank Test for Time Differences Between TV Watching and Internet Browsing (from Example 6)

Wilcoxon Signed Rank Test: Difference

Test of median = 0.000000 versus median not = 0.000000

	N	N for Test	Wilcoxon Statistic	P	Estimated Median
difference	59	54	1012.5	0.020	22.50

The Wilcoxon test statistic is the sum of ranks for the positive differences. The two-sided P-value of 0.020 provides strong evidence that the population median of the differences is not 0. There were 59 subjects, but only 54 were used in the test, because five difference scores were equal to 0. MINITAB also estimates that the population median difference between the time watching TV and the time browsing the Internet was 22.5 minutes. Separately, it provides a 95% confidence interval for the population median of the differences of 2.5 to 40.0 minutes (not shown).

Advantages and Limitations of Nonparametric Statistics

Nonparametric methods make weaker assumptions than the parametric methods we've studied in the rest of the text. For comparing two groups, for instance, it's not necessary to assume that the response distribution is normal. This is especially appealing for small samples because then the normality assumption is more important than it is for larger samples, for which the central limit theorem applies.

Statisticians have shown that nonparametric tests are often very nearly as good as parametric tests even in the exact case for which the parametric tests are designed. To illustrate, suppose two population distributions are normal in shape and have the same standard deviation but different means. Then, the Wilcoxon test is very nearly as powerful in detecting this difference as the *t* test, even though it uses only the ranks of the observations.

Nonetheless, nonparametric methods have some disadvantages. For example, confidence interval methods have not been as thoroughly developed as significance tests. Also, methods have not yet been well developed for multivariate procedures, such as multiple regression. Finally, recall that in many cases (especially two-sided tests and confidence intervals), most parametric methods are *robust*, working well even if assumptions are somewhat violated.

15.2 Practicing the Basics

15.8 How long do you tolerate being put on hold?

TRY Examples 1–4 and 7 in Chapter 14 referred to the following randomized experiment: An airline analyzed whether telephone callers to their reservations office would remain on hold longer, on average, if they heard (a) an advertisement about the airline, (b) Muzak, or (c) classical music. For 15 callers randomly assigned to these three conditions, the table shows the data. It also shows the ranks for the 15 observations as well as the mean rank for each group and some results from using MINITAB to conduct the Kruskal-Wallis test.

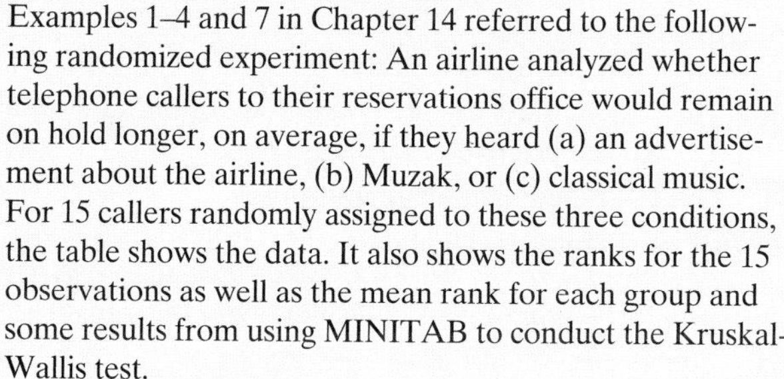

a. State the null and alternative hypotheses for the Kruskal-Wallis test.

b. Identify the value of the test statistic for the Kruskal-Wallis test and state its approximate sampling distribution, presuming H_0 is true.

c. Report and interpret the P-value shown for the Kruskal-Wallis test.

d. To find out which pairs of groups significantly differ, how could you follow up the Kruskal-Wallis test?

Telephone holding times by type of recorded message

Recorded Message	Holding Time Observations	Ranks	Mean Rank
Muzak	0, 1, 3, 4, 6	1, 2.5, 5, 6, 8	4.5
Advertisement	1, 2, 5, 8, 11	2.5, 4, 7, 10.5, 13	7.4
Classical	7, 8, 9, 13, 15	9, 10.5, 12, 14, 15	12.1

Kruskal-Wallis Test: Holding Time Versus Group

```
Group        N    Median    Ave Rank
Muzak        5    3.000        4.5
advert       5    5.000        7.4
classical    5    9.000       12.1
H = 7.38  DF = 2  P = 0.025  (adjusted for ties)
```

15.9 What's the best way to learn French? Exercise 14.3 gave the data in the table for scores on the first quiz for ninth-grade students in an introductory-level French course. The instructor grouped the students in the course as follows:

Group 1: Never studied foreign language before, but have good English skills

Group 2: Never studied foreign language before; have poor English skills

Group 3: Studied at least one other foreign language

The table also shows results of using MINITAB to perform the Kruskal-Wallis test.

a. Find the rank associated with each observation and show how to find the mean rank for Group 1.

b. Report and interpret the P-value for the test.

Scores on the quiz

Group 1	Group 2	Group 3
4	1	9
6	5	10
8		5

```
Kruskal-Wallis Test on response
 Group   N    Median    Ave Rank
   1     3    6.000       4.3
   2     2    3.000       2.3
   3     3    9.000       6.2
H = 3.13 DF = 2 P = 0.209 (adjusted for ties)
```

15.10 Sports versus TV Which do students spend more time doing—playing sports or watching TV? For the students surveyed at the University of Florida whose responses are in the FL Student Survey data file, 24 students spent more time playing sports and 30 students spent more time watching TV. Let p denote the corresponding population proportion who spend more time watching TV.

TRY TECH

a. Find the test statistic for the sign test of H_0: $p = 0.50$ against H_a: $p \neq 0.50$.

b. Refer to part a. Find and interpret the P-value.

15.11 Cell phones and reaction times Example 13 in Chapter 10 compared reaction times in a simulated driving test for the same students when they were using a cell phone and when they were not. The table shows data for the first four students. For all 32 students, 26 had faster reaction times when not using the cell phone and 6 had faster reaction times when using it.

TRY

a. Are the observations for the two treatments independent samples or dependent samples? Explain.

b. Let p denote the population proportion who would have a faster reaction time when not using a cell phone. Estimate p based on this experiment.

c. Using all 32 observations, find the test statistic and the P-value for the sign test of H_0: $p = 1/2$ against H_a: $p > 1/2$. Interpret.

d. What is the parametric method for comparing the scores? What is an advantage of it over the sign test? (*Hint:* Does the sign test use the magnitude of the difference between the two scores or just its direction?)

Reaction times in cell phone study

	Using Cell Phone?		
Student	**No**	**Yes**	**Difference**
1	604	636	32
2	556	623	67
3	540	615	75
4	522	672	150

15.12 Sign test for GRE scores Consider Example 8, for which the changes in the writing portion GRE scores for the first three people who attended a training workshop were 0.5, −0.5, and 1.5. Show how to use the sign test to test that the probability that the difference is positive equals 0.50 against the alternative hypothesis that it is greater than 0.50.

TRY

15.13 Does exercise help blood pressure? Exercise 10.50 in Chapter 10 discussed a pilot study of people who suffer from abnormally high blood pressure. A medical researcher decides to test her belief that walking briskly for at least half an hour a day has the effect of lowering blood pressure. She randomly samples three of her patients who have high blood pressure. She measures their systolic blood pressure initially and then again a month later after they participate in her exercise program. The table shows the results. Show how to analyze the data with the sign test. State the hypotheses, find the P-value, and interpret.

Subject	Before	After
1	150	130
2	165	140
3	135	120

15.14 More on blood pressure Refer to the previous exercise. The analysis there did not take into account the *size* of the change in blood pressure. Show how to do this with the Wilcoxon signed-ranks test.

a. State the hypotheses for that test, for the relevant one-sided alternative hypothesis.

b. Construct the sampling distribution for the rank sum of the positive differences when you consider the possible samples that have absolute differences in blood pressure of 20, 25, and 15.

c. Using the sampling distribution from part b, find and interpret the P-value. (When every difference is positive, or when every difference is negative, this test and the sign test give the same P-value for a given alternative hypothesis.)

15.15 More on cell phones Refer to Exercise 15.11. That analysis did not take into account the magnitudes of the differences in reaction times. Show how to do this with the Wilcoxon signed-ranks test, illustrating by using only the four observations shown in the table there.

a. State the hypotheses for the relevant one-sided test.

b. Create the sampling distribution of the sum of ranks for the positive differences.

c. Find the P-value and interpret.

15.16 Use all data on cell phones Refer to the previous exercise. When we use the data for all 32 subjects, MINITAB reports result in the following for the Wilcoxon signed-ranks test.

Wilcoxon signed-ranks test results

```
Test of median = 0.000000 versus median
not = 0.000000
              N for   Wilcoxon                 Estimated
         N    Test    Statistic      P          Median
diff    32     32       490.0      0.000        47.25
```

a. State the null and alternative hypotheses for this test.

b. Explain how MINITAB found the value reported for the Wilcoxon test statistic.

c. Report and interpret the P-value.

d. Report and interpret the estimated median.

Chapter Review

ANSWERS TO THE CHAPTER FIGURE QUESTIONS

Figure 15.2 Yes, there is an extreme outlier for the cell phone group. This may have a large effect on the mean for that group but will not affect the nonparametric test.

Figure 15.3 The dot plots show evidence of severe skew to the left. Because the sample sizes are very small, severe violation of the normality assumption could invalidate the ANOVA *F* test.

CHAPTER SUMMARY

Nonparametric statistical methods provide statistical inference without an assumption of normality about the probability distribution of the response variable.

- The **Wilcoxon test** is a nonparametric test for the null hypothesis of identical population distributions for two groups. It assumes independent random samples and uses the ranks for the combined sample of observations. The P-value is a one- or two-tail probability for the sampling distribution of the difference between the sample mean ranks.
- Nonparametric methods can also estimate differences between groups, for example to construct a confidence interval for the difference between two population **medians**.
- Other popular nonparametric methods include
  - The **Kruskal-Wallis test** for comparing mean ranks of *several* groups with independent random samples.
  - The **sign test** for comparing two groups with *matched pairs* data (dependent samples rather than independent samples) in terms of the proportion of times the response is better for a particular group.
  - The **Wilcoxon signed-ranks test** for comparing two groups with *matched pairs data* when the differences can be ranked.

CHAPTER PROBLEMS

Practicing the Basics

15.17 Car bumper damage An automobile company compares two types of front bumper for its new model by driving sample cars into a concrete wall at 15 miles per hour. The response is the amount of damage to the car, as measured by the repair costs, in dollars. Due to the costs, the study uses only six cars, obtaining results for three bumpers of each type. The results are in the table.

a. Find the ranks and the mean rank for each bumper type.

b. Show that there are 20 possible allocations of ranks to the two bumper types.

c. Explain why the observed ranks for the two groups are one of the two most extreme ways the two groups can differ, for the 20 possible allocations of the ranks.

d. Explain why the P-value for the two-sided test equals 0.10.

Bumper A	Bumper B
2100	1100
2500	1300
2300	1400

15.18 Comparing more bumpers Refer to the previous exercise.

a. Would the results of your analysis change if for the second Bumper A the repair cost was \$9000 instead of \$2500? What does this illustrate about the analysis?

b. Suppose the company actually wanted to compare *three* bumper types. Which significance test could it use to do this if it did not want to assume that the repair costs have a normal distribution for each bumper type?

15.19 Telephone holding times In Exercise 15.8, the telephone holding times for Muzak and classical music were

Muzak 0, 1, 4, 6, 3

Classical 13, 9, 8, 15, 7

a. For comparing these two groups with the Wilcoxon test, report the ranks and the mean rank for each group.

b. Two groups of size 5 each have 252 possible allocations of rankings. For a two-sided test of H_0: identical distributions with these data, explain why the P-value is $2/252 = 0.008$. Interpret the P-value.

15.20 Treating alcoholics The nonparametric statistics textbook by Hollander and Wolfe (1999) discussed a study on a social skills training program for alcoholics. A sample of male alcoholics was randomly split into two groups. The control group received traditional treatment. The treatment group received the traditional treatment plus a class in social skills training. Every two weeks for a year after the treatment, subjects indicated the quantity of alcohol they consumed during that period. The summary response was the total alcohol intake for the year (in centiliters).

a. Suppose the researchers planned to conduct a one-sided test and believed that the response variable could be highly skewed to the right. Why might they prefer to use the Wilcoxon test rather than a two-sample *t* test to compare the groups?

b. The data were

Controls: 1042, 1617, 1180, 973, 1552, 1251, 1151, 1511, 728, 1079, 951, 1319

Treated: 874, 389, 612, 798, 1152, 893, 541, 741, 1064, 862, 213

Show how to find the ranks and the mean ranks for the two groups.

c. MINITAB reports the results shown in the output below. Report and interpret the P-value.

d. Report and interpret the confidence interval shown in the output.

MINITAB output

```
          N              Median
control   12             1165.5
treated   11              798.0
Point estimate for η1 − η2 is 435.5
95.5 Percent CI for η1 − η2 is (186.0, 713.0)
Test of η1 = η2 vs η1 ≠ η2 is significant
at 0.0009
```

15.21 Comparing tans Examples 1 and 2 compared two methods of getting a tan. Suppose Allison conducted an expanded experiment in which nine participants were randomly assigned to one of two brands of tanning lotion or to the tanning studio, three participants to each treatment. The nine were ranked on the quality of tan.

a. Which nonparametric test could be used to compare the three treatments?

b. Give an example of ranks for the three treatments that would have the largest possible test statistic value and the smallest possible P-value for this experiment. (*Hint:* What allocation of ranks would have the greatest between-groups variation in the mean ranks?)

15.22 Comparing therapies for anorexia TECH The Anorexia data file on the book's website shows weight change for 72 anorexic teenage girls who were randomly assigned to one of three psychological treatments. Using software, analyze these data with a nonparametric Kruskal Wallis test to compare the three weight change distributions.

a. State the hypotheses.

b. Report the test statistic and its sampling distribution.

c. Report the P-value and explain how to interpret it.

15.23 Internet versus cell phones TECH For the countries in the Human Development data file on the book's website, in 4 countries a higher percentage of people used the Internet than used cell phones, whereas in 35 countries a higher percentage of people used cell phones than the Internet.

a. Show how you could use a nonparametric test to compare Internet use and cell phone use in the population of all countries. State the (i) hypotheses, (ii) test statistic value, and (iii) find and interpret the P-value.

b. Is the analysis in part a relevant if the 39 countries in the data file are all the countries of interest to you rather than a random sample of countries? Explain.

15.24 Browsing the Internet TECH Refer to the Georgia Student Survey data file on the book's website. Use a method from this chapter to test whether the amount of time spent browsing the Internet is independent of one's political affiliation. State the (a) hypotheses, (b) test statistic, and (c) P-value and interpret the result.

15.25 GPAs TECH The Georgia Student Survey data file has data on college GPA and high school GPA for 59 University of Georgia students.

a. If you wanted to use a nonparametric test to check your friend's prediction that high school GPAs tend to be higher than college GPAs, which would you use?

b. What would be a reason for using the nonparametric method to do this?

c. Use the test in part a to do this analysis and interpret the result.

15.26 Sign test about the GRE workshop In Exercise 15.12 on the effect of a GRE training workshop on the writing, you used the sign test to evaluate the test differences of 0.5, −0.5, and 1.5. Suppose the test differences were 5.5, −0.5, and 1.5 instead of 0.5, −0.5., and 1.5.

a. State the hypotheses and find the P-value for the one-sided sign test for evaluating the effect of the workshop. Interpret.

b. Compare results to those in Exercise 15.12 and indicate what this tells you about the effect that outliers have on this nonparametric statistical method.

15.27 Wilcoxon signed-rank test about the GRE workshop Example 8 on the GRE workshop used the Wilcoxon signed-rank test to evaluate the score differences of 0.5, −0.5, and 1.5. Suppose the test differences were 5.5, −0.5, and 1.5 instead of 0.5 −0.5, and 1.5.

a. State the hypotheses and find the P-value for the one-sided Wilcoxon signed-ranks test for evaluating the effect of the workshop. Interpret.

b. Compare results to those in Example 8 and indicate what this tells you about the effect that outliers have on this nonparametric statistical method.

Concepts and Investigations

15.28 Student survey TECH For the FL Student Survey data file on the book's website, we identify the number of times reading a newspaper as the response variable and gender as the explanatory variable. The observations are as follows:

Females: 5, 3, 6, 3, 7, 1, 1, 3, 0, 4, 7, 2, 2, 7, 3, 0, 5, 0, 4, 4, 5, 14, 3, 1, 2, 1, 7, 2, 5, 3, 7

Males: 0, 3, 7, 4, 3, 2, 1, 12, 1, 6, 2, 2, 7, 7, 5, 3, 14, 3, 7, 6, 5, 5, 2, 3, 5, 5, 2, 3, 3

Using software, analyze these data using methods of this chapter. Write a one-page report summarizing your analyses and conclusions.

15.29 Why nonparametrics? Present a situation for which it's preferable to use a nonparametric method instead of a parametric method and explain why.

15.30 Why matched pairs? Refer to Example 7. Describe the advantages of an experiment using a crossover design instead of independent samples to compare the tanning methods.

15.31 Complete the analogy The t test for comparing two means is to the one-way ANOVA F test as the Wilcoxon test is to the __________ test.

15.32 Complete the analogy The t test for comparing two means is to the Wilcoxon test (for independent samples) as the matched pairs t test is to the __________ (for dependent samples in matched pairs).

15.33 True or false For a one-sided significance test comparing two means with small samples from highly skewed population distributions, it's safer to use a t test than a Wilcoxon test. This is because the Wilcoxon test assumes normal population distributions and is not robust if that assumption is violated.

15.34 Multiple choice Nonparametric statistical methods are used

a. Whenever the response variable is known to have a normal distribution.

b. Whenever the assumptions for a parametric method are not *perfectly* satisfied.

c. When the data are ranks for the subjects rather than quantitative measurements or when it's inappropriate to assume normality and the ordinary statistical method is not robust when the normal assumption is violated.

d. Whenever we want to compare two methods for getting a good tan.

15.35 ◆◆ **Mann-Whitney statistic** For the tanning experiment, Table 15.2 showed the sampling distribution of the difference between the sample mean ranks. Suppose you instead use as a test statistic the sample proportion of pairs of participants for which the tanning studio gave a better tan than the tanning lotion. This is the basis of the **Mann-Whitney** test, devised by two statisticians about the same time as Wilcoxon devised his test.

a. The table shows the proportion of pairs for which the tanning studio gave a better tan, for the possible sample results. Explain how to find these proportions.

b. Using this table, construct the sampling distribution that applies under the null hypothesis for this proportion.

c. For the one-sided alternative hypothesis of a better tan with the tanning studio, find the P-value for the observed sample proportion of 5/6. (*Note*: P-values based on this sample proportion are identical to P-values for the Wilcoxon test based on the mean ranks.)

Sample Proportion of Pairs, One from Each Treatment, for Which Tanning Studio Gave Better Tan Than Tanning Lotion

Treatments	Ranks				
Tanning lotion ranks	(1, 2, 3)	(1, 2, 4)	(1, 2, 5)	(1, 3, 4)	(1, 3, 5)
Tanning studio ranks	(4, 5)	(3, 5)	(3, 4)	(2, 5)	(2, 4)
Proportion	0/6	1/6	2/6	2/6	3/6
Tanning lotion ranks	(2, 3, 4)	(1, 4, 5)	(2, 3, 5)	(2, 4, 5)	(3, 4, 5)
Tanning studio ranks	(1, 5)	(2, 3)	(1, 4)	(1, 3)	(1, 2)
Proportion	3/6	4/6	4/6	5/6	6/6

15.36 ◆◆ **Rank-based correlation** For data on two quantitative variables, x and y, an alternative correlation uses the *rankings* of the data. Let n denote the number of observations on the two variables. You rank the values of the x-variable from 1 to n according to their magnitudes, and you separately rank the values of the y-variable from 1 to n. The correlation computed between the two sets of ranks is called the **Spearman rank correlation**. Like the ordinary correlation, it falls between -1 and $+1$, with values farther from 0 representing stronger association.

a. The ordinary correlation can be strongly affected by a regression outlier. Is this true also for the Spearman rank correlation? Why or why not?

b. If you want to test the null hypothesis of no association, what value for the Spearman rank correlation would go in the null hypothesis?

15.37 ◆◆ **Nonparametric regression** Nonparametric methods have also been devised for regression. Here's a simple way to estimate the slope: For each pair of subjects, the slope of the line connecting their two points is the difference between their y values divided by the difference between their x values. (See the figure.) With n subjects, we can find this slope for each pair of points. (There are $n(n-1)/2$ pairs of points.) A nonparametric estimate of the slope is the median of all these slopes for the various pairs of points. The ordinary slope (least squares, minimizing the sum of squared residuals) can be strongly affected by a regression outlier. Is this true also for the nonparametric estimate of the slope? Why or why not?

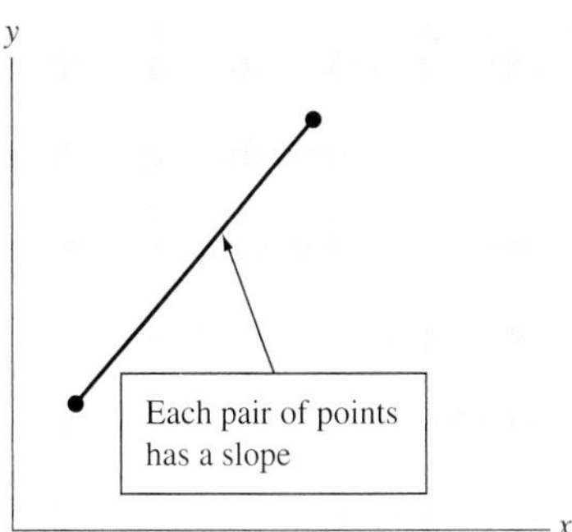

BIBLIOGRAPHY

Hollander, M., and Wolfe, D. (1999). *Nonparametric Statistical Methods*, 2nd edition. Wiley.

Lehmann, E. L. (1975). *Nonparametrics: Statistical Methods Based on Ranks.* Holden-Day.

Appendix A

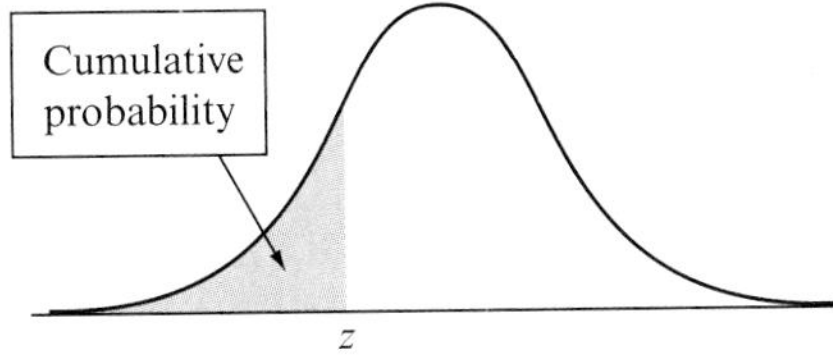

Cumulative probability for z is the area under the standard normal curve to the left of z

z	.00
−5.0	.000000287
−4.5	.00000340
−4.0	.0000317
−3.5	.000233

Table A Standard Normal Cumulative Probabilities

z	.00	.01	.02	.03	.04	.05	.06	.07	.08	.09
−3.4	.0003	.0003	.0003	.0003	.0003	.0003	.0003	.0003	.0003	.0002
−3.3	.0005	.0005	.0005	.0004	.0004	.0004	.0004	.0004	.0004	.0003
−3.2	.0007	.0007	.0006	.0006	.0006	.0006	.0006	.0005	.0005	.0005
−3.1	.0010	.0009	.0009	.0009	.0008	.0008	.0008	.0008	.0007	.0007
−3.0	.0013	.0013	.0013	.0012	.0012	.0011	.0011	.0011	.0010	.0010
−2.9	.0019	.0018	.0018	.0017	.0016	.0016	.0015	.0015	.0014	.0014
−2.8	.0026	.0025	.0024	.0023	.0023	.0022	.0021	.0021	.0020	.0019
−2.7	.0035	.0034	.0033	.0032	.0031	.0030	.0029	.0028	.0027	.0026
−2.6	.0047	.0045	.0044	.0043	.0041	.0040	.0039	.0038	.0037	.0036
−2.5	.0062	.0060	.0059	.0057	.0055	.0054	.0052	.0051	.0049	.0048
−2.4	.0082	.0080	.0078	.0075	.0073	.0071	.0069	.0068	.0066	.0064
−2.3	.0107	.0104	.0102	.0099	.0096	.0094	.0091	.0089	.0087	.0084
−2.2	.0139	.0136	.0132	.0129	.0125	.0122	.0119	.0116	.0113	.0110
−2.1	.0179	.0174	.0170	.0166	.0162	.0158	.0154	.0150	.0146	.0143
−2.0	.0228	.0222	.0217	.0212	.0207	.0202	.0197	.0192	.0188	.0183
−1.9	.0287	.0281	.0274	.0268	.0262	.0256	.0250	.0244	.0239	.0233
−1.8	.0359	.0351	.0344	.0336	.0329	.0322	.0314	.0307	.0301	.0294
−1.7	.0446	.0436	.0427	.0418	.0409	.0401	.0392	.0384	.0375	.0367
−1.6	.0548	.0537	.0526	.0516	.0505	.0495	.0485	.0475	.0465	.0455
−1.5	.0668	.0655	.0643	.0630	.0618	.0606	.0594	.0582	.0571	.0559
−1.4	.0808	.0793	.0778	.0764	.0749	.0735	.0721	.0708	.0694	.0681
−1.3	.0968	.0951	.0934	.0918	.0901	.0885	.0869	.0853	.0838	.0823
−1.2	.1151	.1131	.1112	.1093	.1075	.1056	.1038	.1020	.1003	.0985
−1.1	.1357	.1335	.1314	.1292	.1271	.1251	.1230	.1210	.1190	.1170
−1.0	.1587	.1562	.1539	.1515	.1492	.1469	.1446	.1423	.1401	.1379
−0.9	.1841	.1814	.1788	.1762	.1736	.1711	.1685	.1660	.1635	.1611
−0.8	.2119	.2090	.2061	.2033	.2005	.1977	.1949	.1922	.1894	.1867
−0.7	.2420	.2389	.2358	.2327	.2296	.2266	.2236	.2206	.2177	.2148
−0.6	.2743	.2709	.2676	.2643	.2611	.2578	.2546	.2514	.2483	.2451
−0.5	.3085	.3050	.3015	.2981	.2946	.2912	.2877	.2843	.2810	.2776
−0.4	.3446	.3409	.3372	.3336	.3300	.3264	.3228	.3192	.3156	.3121
−0.3	.3821	.3783	.3745	.3707	.3669	.3632	.3594	.3557	.3520	.3483
−0.2	.4207	.4168	.4129	.4090	.4052	.4013	.3974	.3936	.3897	.3859
−0.1	.4602	.4562	.4522	.4483	.4443	.4404	.4364	.4325	.4286	.4247
−0.0	.5000	.4960	.4920	.4880	.4840	.4801	.4761	.4721	.4681	.4641

Did You Know?

The web app Normal Distribution from the book's website www.pearsonhighered.com/AFK let's you find any cumulative probabilities or quantiles (z-scores) from any normal distribution interactively, including a visualization for checking results. ◀

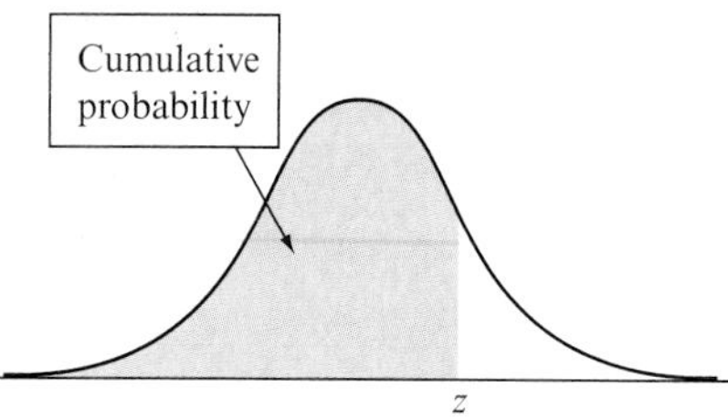

Cumulative probability for z is the area under the standard normal curve to the left of z

Table A Standard Normal Cumulative Probabilities (*continued*)

z	.00	.01	.02	.03	.04	.05	.06	.07	.08	.09
0.0	.5000	.5040	.5080	.5120	.5160	.5199	.5239	.5279	.5319	.5359
0.1	.5398	.5438	.5478	.5517	.5557	.5596	.5636	.5675	.5714	.5753
0.2	.5793	.5832	.5871	.5910	.5948	.5987	.6026	.6064	.6103	.6141
0.3	.6179	.6217	.6255	.6293	.6331	.6368	.6406	.6443	.6480	.6517
0.4	.6554	.6591	.6628	.6664	.6700	.6736	.6772	.6808	.6844	.6879
0.5	.6915	.6950	.6985	.7019	.7054	.7088	.7123	.7157	.7190	.7224
0.6	.7257	.7291	.7324	.7357	.7389	.7422	.7454	.7486	.7517	.7549
0.7	.7580	.7611	.7642	.7673	.7704	.7734	.7764	.7794	.7823	.7852
0.8	.7881	.7910	.7939	.7967	.7995	.8023	.8051	.8078	.8106	.8133
0.9	.8159	.8186	.8212	.8238	.8264	.8289	.8315	.8340	.8365	.8389
1.0	.8413	.8438	.8461	.8485	.8508	.8531	.8554	.8577	.8599	.8621
1.1	.8643	.8665	.8686	.8708	.8729	.8749	.8770	.8790	.8810	.8830
1.2	.8849	.8869	.8888	.8907	.8925	.8944	.8962	.8980	.8997	.9015
1.3	.9032	.9049	.9066	.9082	.9099	.9115	.9131	.9147	.9162	.9177
1.4	.9192	.9207	.9222	.9236	.9251	.9265	.9279	.9292	.9306	.9319
1.5	.9332	.9345	.9357	.9370	.9382	.9394	.9406	.9418	.9429	.9441
1.6	.9452	.9463	.9474	.9484	.9495	.9505	.9515	.9525	.9535	.9545
1.7	.9554	.9564	.9573	.9582	.9591	.9599	.9608	.9616	.9625	.9633
1.8	.9641	.9649	.9656	.9664	.9671	.9678	.9686	.9693	.9699	.9706
1.9	.9713	.9719	.9726	.9732	.9738	.9744	.9750	.9756	.9761	.9767
2.0	.9772	.9778	.9783	.9788	.9793	.9798	.9803	.9808	.9812	.9817
2.1	.9821	.9826	.9830	.9834	.9838	.9842	.9846	.9850	.9854	.9857
2.2	.9861	.9864	.9868	.9871	.9875	.9878	.9881	.9884	.9887	.9890
2.3	.9893	.9896	.9898	.9901	.9904	.9906	.9909	.9911	.9913	.9916
2.4	.9918	.9920	.9922	.9925	.9927	.9929	.9931	.9932	.9934	.9936
2.5	.9938	.9940	.9941	.9943	.9945	.9946	.9948	.9949	.9951	.9952
2.6	.9953	.9955	.9956	.9957	.9959	.9960	.9961	.9962	.9963	.9964
2.7	.9965	.9966	.9967	.9968	.9969	.9970	.9971	.9972	.9973	.9974
2.8	.9974	.9975	.9976	.9977	.9977	.9978	.9979	.9979	.9980	.9981
2.9	.9981	.9982	.9982	.9983	.9984	.9984	.9985	.9985	.9986	.9986
3.0	.9987	.9987	.9987	.9988	.9988	.9989	.9989	.9989	.9990	.9990
3.1	.9990	.9991	.9991	.9991	.9992	.9992	.9992	.9992	.9993	.9993
3.2	.9993	.9993	.9994	.9994	.9994	.9994	.9994	.9995	.9995	.9995
3.3	.9995	.9995	.9995	.9996	.9996	.9996	.9996	.9996	.9996	.9997
3.4	.9997	.9997	.9997	.9997	.9997	.9997	.9997	.9997	.9997	.9998

z	.00
3.5	.999767
4.0	.9999683
4.5	.9999966
5.0	.999999713

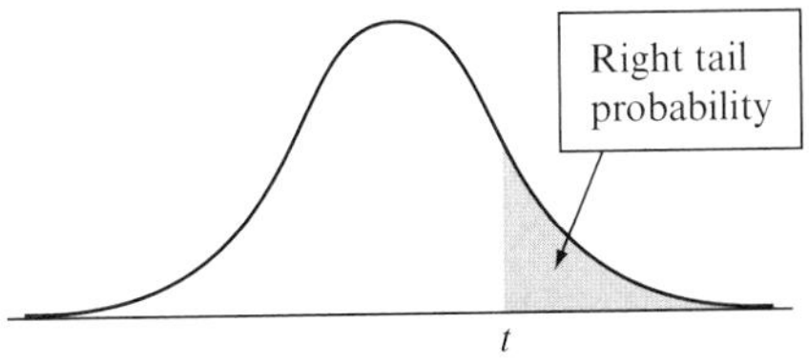

Table B *t* Distribution Critical Values

	Confidence Level					
	80%	90%	95%	98%	99%	99.8%
	Right-Tail Probability					
df	$t_{.100}$	$t_{.050}$	$t_{.025}$	$t_{.010}$	$t_{.005}$	$t_{.001}$
1	3.078	6.314	12.706	31.821	63.656	318.289
2	1.886	2.920	4.303	6.965	9.925	22.328
3	1.638	2.353	3.182	4.541	5.841	10.214
4	1.533	2.132	2.776	3.747	4.604	7.173
5	1.476	2.015	2.571	3.365	4.032	5.894
6	1.440	1.943	2.447	3.143	3.707	5.208
7	1.415	1.895	2.365	2.998	3.499	4.785
8	1.397	1.860	2.306	2.896	3.355	4.501
9	1.383	1.833	2.262	2.821	3.250	4.297
10	1.372	1.812	2.228	2.764	3.169	4.144
11	1.363	1.796	2.201	2.718	3.106	4.025
12	1.356	1.782	2.179	2.681	3.055	3.930
13	1.350	1.771	2.160	2.650	3.012	3.852
14	1.345	1.761	2.145	2.624	2.977	3.787
15	1.341	1.753	2.131	2.602	2.947	3.733
16	1.337	1.746	2.120	2.583	2.921	3.686
17	1.333	1.740	2.110	2.567	2.898	3.646
18	1.330	1.734	2.101	2.552	2.878	3.611
19	1.328	1.729	2.093	2.539	2.861	3.579
20	1.325	1.725	2.086	2.528	2.845	3.552
21	1.323	1.721	2.080	2.518	2.831	3.527
22	1.321	1.717	2.074	2.508	2.819	3.505
23	1.319	1.714	2.069	2.500	2.807	3.485
24	1.318	1.711	2.064	2.492	2.797	3.467
25	1.316	1.708	2.060	2.485	2.787	3.450
26	1.315	1.706	2.056	2.479	2.779	3.435
27	1.314	1.703	2.052	2.473	2.771	3.421
28	1.313	1.701	2.048	2.467	2.763	3.408
29	1.311	1.699	2.045	2.462	2.756	3.396
30	1.310	1.697	2.042	2.457	2.750	3.385
40	1.303	1.684	2.021	2.423	2.704	3.307
50	1.299	1.676	2.009	2.403	2.678	3.261
60	1.296	1.671	2.000	2.390	2.660	3.232
80	1.292	1.664	1.990	2.374	2.639	3.195
100	1.290	1.660	1.984	2.364	2.626	3.174
∞	1.282	1.645	1.960	2.326	2.576	3.091

Did You Know?

The web app *t* Distribution from the book's website www.pearsonhighered.com/AFK let's you find any probabilities or quantiles (critical values) for Student's *t* distribution interactively, including a visualization for checking results. ◀

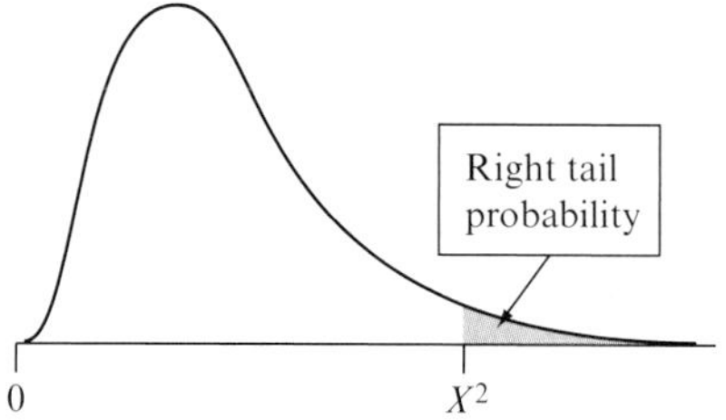

Table C Chi-Squared Distribution for Values of Various Right Tail Probabilities

	Right-Tail Probability						
df	**0.250**	**0.100**	**0.050**	**0.025**	**0.010**	**0.005**	**0.001**
1	1.32	2.71	3.84	5.02	6.63	7.88	10.83
2	2.77	4.61	5.99	7.38	9.21	10.60	13.82
3	4.11	6.25	7.81	9.35	11.34	12.84	16.27
4	5.39	7.78	9.49	11.14	13.28	14.86	18.47
5	6.63	9.24	11.07	12.83	15.09	16.75	20.52
6	7.84	10.64	12.59	14.45	16.81	18.55	22.46
7	9.04	12.02	14.07	16.01	18.48	20.28	24.32
8	10.22	13.36	15.51	17.53	20.09	21.96	26.12
9	11.39	14.68	16.92	19.02	21.67	23.59	27.88
10	12.55	15.99	18.31	20.48	23.21	25.19	29.59
11	13.70	17.28	19.68	21.92	24.72	26.76	31.26
12	14.85	18.55	21.03	23.34	26.22	28.30	32.91
13	15.98	19.81	22.36	24.74	27.69	29.82	34.53
14	17.12	21.06	23.68	26.12	29.14	31.32	36.12
15	18.25	22.31	25.00	27.49	30.58	32.80	37.70
16	19.37	23.54	26.30	28.85	32.00	34.27	39.25
17	20.49	24.77	27.59	30.19	33.41	35.72	40.79
18	21.60	25.99	28.87	31.53	34.81	37.16	42.31
19	22.72	27.20	30.14	32.85	36.19	38.58	43.82
20	23.83	28.41	31.41	34.17	37.57	40.00	45.32
25	29.34	34.38	37.65	40.65	44.31	46.93	52.62
30	34.80	40.26	43.77	46.98	50.89	53.67	59.70
40	45.62	51.80	55.76	59.34	63.69	66.77	73.40
50	56.33	63.17	67.50	71.42	76.15	79.49	86.66
60	66.98	74.40	79.08	83.30	88.38	91.95	99.61
70	77.58	85.53	90.53	95.02	100.4	104.2	112.3
80	88.13	96.58	101.8	106.6	112.3	116.3	124.8
90	98.65	107.6	113.1	118.1	124.1	128.3	137.2
100	109.1	118.5	124.3	129.6	135.8	140.2	149.5

Did You Know?

The web app Chi-Square Distribution from the book's website www.pearsonhighered.com/AFK let's you find any probabilities or quantiles (critical values) for the Chi-square distribution interactively, including a visualization for checking results. ◀

Right tail probability = 0.05

0 F

Table D *F* Distribution for Values of Right-Tail Probability = 0.05

	df_1									
df_2	1	2	3	4	5	6	8	12	24	∞
1	161.45	199.50	215.71	224.58	230.16	233.99	238.88	243.91	249.05	254.31
2	18.51	19.00	19.16	19.25	19.30	19.33	19.37	19.41	19.45	19.50
3	10.13	9.55	9.28	9.12	9.01	8.94	8.85	8.74	8.64	8.53
4	7.71	6.94	6.59	6.39	6.26	6.16	6.04	5.91	5.77	5.63
5	6.61	5.79	5.41	5.19	5.05	4.95	4.82	4.68	4.53	4.37
6	5.99	5.14	4.76	4.53	4.39	4.28	4.15	4.00	3.84	3.67
7	5.59	4.74	4.35	4.12	3.97	3.87	3.73	3.57	3.41	3.23
8	5.32	4.46	4.07	3.84	3.69	3.58	3.44	3.28	3.12	2.93
9	5.12	4.26	3.86	3.63	3.48	3.37	3.23	3.07	2.90	2.71
10	4.96	4.10	3.71	3.48	3.33	3.22	3.07	2.91	2.74	2.54
11	4.84	3.98	3.59	3.36	3.20	3.09	2.95	2.79	2.61	2.40
12	4.75	3.89	3.49	3.26	3.11	3.00	2.85	2.69	2.51	2.30
13	4.67	3.81	3.41	3.18	3.03	2.92	2.77	2.60	2.42	2.21
14	4.60	3.74	3.34	3.11	2.96	2.85	2.70	2.53	2.35	2.13
15	4.54	3.68	3.29	3.06	2.90	2.79	2.64	2.48	2.29	2.07
16	4.49	3.63	3.24	3.01	2.85	2.74	2.59	2.42	2.24	2.01
17	4.45	3.59	3.20	2.96	2.81	2.70	2.55	2.38	2.19	1.96
18	4.41	3.55	3.16	2.93	2.77	2.66	2.51	2.34	2.15	1.92
19	4.38	3.52	3.13	2.90	2.74	2.63	2.48	2.31	2.11	1.88
20	4.35	3.49	3.10	2.87	2.71	2.60	2.45	2.28	2.08	1.84
21	4.32	3.47	3.07	2.84	2.68	2.57	2.42	2.25	2.05	1.81
22	4.30	3.44	3.05	2.82	2.66	2.55	2.40	2.23	2.03	1.78
23	4.28	3.42	3.03	2.80	2.64	2.53	2.37	2.20	2.01	1.76
24	4.26	3.40	3.01	2.78	2.62	2.51	2.36	2.18	1.98	1.73
25	4.24	3.39	2.99	2.76	2.60	2.49	2.34	2.16	1.96	1.71
26	4.23	3.37	2.98	2.74	2.59	2.47	2.32	2.15	1.95	1.69
27	4.21	3.35	2.96	2.73	2.57	2.46	2.31	2.13	1.93	1.67
28	4.20	3.34	2.95	2.71	2.56	2.45	2.29	2.12	1.91	1.65
29	4.18	3.33	2.93	2.70	2.55	2.43	2.28	2.10	1.90	1.64
30	4.17	3.32	2.92	2.69	2.53	2.42	2.27	2.09	1.89	1.62
40	4.08	3.23	2.84	2.61	2.45	2.34	2.18	2.00	1.79	1.51
60	4.00	3.15	2.76	2.53	2.37	2.25	2.10	1.92	1.70	1.39
120	3.92	3.07	2.68	2.45	2.29	2.18	2.02	1.83	1.61	1.25
∞	3.84	3.00	2.60	2.37	2.21	2.10	1.94	1.75	1.52	1.00

Did You Know?

The web app *F* Distribution from the book's website www.pearsonhighered.com/AFK let's you find any probabilities or quantiles (critical values) for the *F* distribution interactively, including a visualization for checking results. ◀

Did You Know?

We show Table E for legacy reasons only, but we do not emphasize it in the book. Rather, we generate random numbers using online tools, such as the Random Numbers web app from the book's website www.pearsonhighered.com/AFK or websites such as random.org. ◀

Table E Table of Random Numbers

Line/Col.	(1)	(2)	(3)	(4)	(5)	(6)	(7)	(8)
1	10480	15011	01536	02011	81647	91646	69179	14194
2	22368	46573	25595	85393	30995	89198	27982	53402
3	24130	48360	22527	97265	76393	64809	15179	24830
4	42167	93093	06243	61680	07856	16376	39440	53537
5	37570	39975	81837	16656	06121	91782	60468	81305
6	77921	06907	11008	42751	27756	53498	18602	70659
7	99562	72905	56420	69994	98872	31016	71194	18738
8	96301	91977	05463	07972	18876	20922	94595	56869
9	89579	14342	63661	10281	17453	18103	57740	84378
10	85475	36857	53342	53988	53060	59533	38867	62300
11	28918	69578	88231	33276	70997	79936	56865	05859
12	63553	40961	48235	03427	49626	69445	18663	72695
13	09429	93969	52636	92737	88974	33488	36320	17617
14	10365	61129	87529	85689	48237	52267	67689	93394
15	07119	97336	71048	08178	77233	13916	47564	81056
16	51085	12765	51821	51259	77452	16308	60756	92144
17	02368	21382	52404	60268	89368	19885	55322	44819
18	01011	54092	33362	94904	31273	04146	18594	29852
19	52162	53916	46369	58586	23216	14513	83149	98736
20	07056	97628	33787	09998	42698	06691	76988	13602

only just saw them, and scuttled away as quickly as possible. I should have been more considerate; but small boyhood is rather ruthless in dealing with what seems topsy-turvy according to its own conventions. Parents do not always sense the true situation. Do you remember "Entertaining Alice," a chapter in that delightful account of boy-life, "The Believing Years," by Edmund L. Pearson?

"It was sprung on me," he writes, "without any pretense of a fair warning. Rob Currier, Ed Mason, and I had just rounded up a herd of buffaloes in the back of my garden, and we were busily engaged in lassoing separate members of the herd before they should slip through the fence into Mr. Jilton's vegetable patch. Once let them get there and it would be well-nigh impossible, among the lettuce and tomatoes, ever to reduce them to submission. Your buffalo is tractable and decent on even turf, but when he gets all mixed up with vegetables he becomes a perfect nuisance.

"At the most exciting moment came a voice which had to be obeyed:

"'Sam!'"

Then Sam had to drop "that old rope," and wash up, without knowing why, and was shoved downstairs. He continues:

"Here I was dragged—a whited sepulchre—into a front room where sat a lady—a perfect stranger to me, and a *little girl.*

"Toward the smaller and the younger of these beings I was propelled.

"'Here, Alice, this is Sam. Sam, this is little Alice Remick, who is going to be your neighbor. I want you to be nice to her, and play with her this afternoon, and entertain her.'

"The concentrated perfidy of it! The unmitigated baseness! What more could Lucretia Borgia have contrived?

"Entertain her! Entertain this spindle-legged pig-tailed creature who was sucking her thumb in lively embarrassment! Was I a dancing bear, or a mountebank, that I should be called upon to furnish amusement to *this?*

"But there was no escape for Sam. 'Perhaps Alice would like to see some of the things in your playroom. Sam—why don't you take her out there?' was the parental suggestion.

"I had expected it. There only remained this final blow, and I knew it would fall. Admit this girl to my inner sanctum—oh, well, the world was turned upside down this afternoon. What had to be, had to be, and there was an end to it.

"'Come on,' I said, in a tone that mingled resignation and gruffness."

Then the painful tale goes on, through Alice's unvarying lack of interest in polliwogs, small snakes, dog, rabbit, guinea pigs, marbles, a real conductor's railroad ticket punch, and best of all Sam's white mice, from which Alice ran screaming. Then Sam was through.

"Well, I gave it up. I had made every effort —there was no pleasing the creature. My conscience was clear at all events—and that was the principal thing."

How far was Sam wrong in his reluctance to entertain Alice? How far was Sam's mother right in expecting him to do the honors? Can we cultivate in the small boy such a sense of obligation to hospitality that even Alice can be taken on gracefully, and the "buffaloes" allowed to wander unhindered by that "old rope"?

In the impulsive days of small boyhood, and later, the boy will always invite to his home the fellows with whom he happens to be "thick" at the time. If he is hampered in this, he will feel that you do not like his friends well enough to know them. If he has no help from you in selecting the fellows who are to have a guest's share in your home life, then he may easily choose the wrong guests, and also acquire the feeling that you really care little about his place as one of the hosts at home. Great wisdom and genuine interest on the part of father and mother are needed, as in so many other phases of boy-life. One thing is certain, you as a father can help the boy at this point very definitely if you will be observant and cordial.

The father can do much to bring into the home, even as the mother can, older guests whom the children ought to know. That growing boy of yours is keen to observe the kind of guests you do bring; and who they are and what they are matter to him perhaps more than you think. If you entertain too lavishly, make "company" too obviously of the guest, put a best foot forward that never is seen when guests are not present, the boy reacts uncomfortably from the unreality of it all. He likes little touches of special courtesy, but he dislikes the idea of cleaning up the house, and straightening out the rooms, and stuffing odds and ends into closet shelves in. disorder—all because "somebody" is coming. He asks, naturally, why the house cannot be kept in just as good order for "us" as when a guest comes? He is not sorry to see guests come, if not much fuss is made about them, and if he doesn't have to "show off," or be too large a factor in entertaining them. But he looks, and listens—absorbs a visitor as he would a picture or a short story, and gets his impression quickly.

A wise father will think twice before he will bring home with him, even for a single meal, an acquaintance whom he would not wish his son to know personally, and about whom his boy could ask questions that the father wouldn't exactly like to answer. In the miscellaneous relationships of business and professional life men have contacts that may never go beyond buying and selling in an impersonal way, while even there the drawing of certain lines of separation is not by any means unknown. But around the home the right-minded father will draw careful lines of separation from contamination by cheap, sordid, or vile personalities, who would perhaps not be instantly discerned as such by the family, but known in their true character by the father. Many a boy looks in wonderment at some who claim to be his father's friends, and suffers under a sense of shame when he learns what they are, from some chance phrase or unexpected showing of their real character. For the sake of business, men sometimes bring home other men who could not possibly be brought there for the sake of the boy. Many men think themselves "diplomatic" about this in the name of business, and sometimes to their own chagrin by their wrongly applied hospitality they leave a sediment of low ideals in the curious, but troubled and puzzled, soul of the boy. What is a fellow to think of his father when the father introduces to the family a business acquaintance, who the boy later learns is crooked in business and unfaithful in his family life a gentleman outwardly, a low character in reality—and the father knew, but evidently thought these things wouldn't show in just one visit—a "business" visit?

On the other hand, a father may create for his boy an education by guests quite as truly influential as any education he can provide by books. It does not take wealth or social prominence to do this. It does not take superlative effrontery in "head-hunting" to secure notable guests—or any effrontery whatever. Simple, unaffected hospitality is high courtesy at any time and in any home. If you in any case have reasonable and proper cause for supposing that an invitation from you to a visiting minister, missionary, lecturer, or any one of useful life, worthy character, and desirable personality, would not be looked upon as an intrusion, offer that invitation in the spirit of hospitality, and in order to enlarge not the fame but the outlook of your family. For the children in your home are often more attentive and impressed than you think, when a guest is present.

Two small boys in a home in a college town were sitting with the family in the library during the evening visit of a speaker who had addressed the college students. He was a friend of the boys' father, but had never before met the family. He was a man of friendly ways, fascinating conversation, earnest Christian spirit, and with a quaint and frequent glint of humor in his way of saying things.

The boys sat in unwonted silence while the visitor told of experiences in his travels, in his Christian work, and among men that he knew. At length the father reluctantly nodded to the boys, pointed to the clock, and upward to their bedroom. With slow muscles, like old men, the two small boys rose up, said a solemn good-night, and left the room. A half hour later, the father, stepping across the hall to the dining-room, found to his surprise the two boys seated there, listening with all their ears.

"Why, how's this, boys!" exclaimed the father. "Didn't I tell you to go to bed? You know it's long past your bedtime."

The boys looked really hurt. "Aw, father," protested the older one, "you don't want us to go to bed, do you, while talk like *that is* going on?"

The father didn't hesitate an instant. "You're right!" he said, emphatically. "Come in again. It will do you more good than going to bed." And in they went, to a never-to-be-forgotten evening with a well-remembered guest. Was that father "spoiling" his boys? Or was he helping to educate them?

In any event, their wise mother was present, and *she* thought there was no "spoiling" about it.

It is not always the personage of prominence who has a lasting influence upon the boy. He is keen to sense character, and he is not much impressed by big names. But he likes to meet those who are true, and who have been doing interesting things, and who are not egotistical about their doings. Egotism seems to "queer" any one, no matter how notable. When that quality begins to be noticeable to the boy, he will completely lose sight of a man's great deeds if the man who has done them cannot lose sight of himself.

No one is more worth while as a guest than the missionary. His—or her—qualities are those that have survived the refiner's fire. His objectives are usually selfless, his spirit humble, and his experiences adventurous and informing and strengthening to faith. His reality and the very fact of his presence in the home are likely to be the most direct and personal reminders that a boy can have concerning the call of the world-field. To see the need through the eyes of a real missionary is often the initial vision that grows into a personal conviction of a personal call. As I write, I turn to a little book in which the names of many guests appear, and as I find therein the names of missionaries in Paraguay, Bolivia, China, India, West Africa, Belgium, and other lands, I ask myself by what measure one could possibly assess the value of these fireside friendships in the education and life decisions of the children in that home? Is it nothing that the children can see for themselves what manner of men and women are these ambassadors of Christ, and learn of their work at first hand? The missionaries themselves are the most vivid missionary biographies that a boy can read. One little fellow of seven, after a summer in a conference center where he came to know intimately one missionary and heard and met many others, said very earnestly, "I'm going to be a missionary some day." And now, seventeen years later, he is in the final stages of his preparation for the foreign field.

Henry Clay Trumbull lived until young manhood in Stonington, Connecticut, the place of his birth. It was an important transfer point in travel in those days, and always a place of historic interest. There he saw, or met personally, Andrew Jackson, John Tyler, Commodore Hull, of the frigate *Constitution,* Colonel John Trumbull, of Washington's staff, John Quincy Adams, Adoniram Judson, Albert Bushnell, "the patriarch of West African missions," and others of distinction in their fields of service. Of his boyhood memory of Judson he wrote, some fifty years later: "The sight of that countenance was an inspiration and a blessing to me. I have never forgotten it. I never can forget it. In appearance Dr. Judson was tall, spare, wiry, of firmly compacted nerves. In his face were the signs of the many battles through which he had passed, and of the spirit in which he had been a victor through all. And under all, and in all, there was a spiritual uplook showing that he had endured as seeing Him who is invisible. It was the look of Michelangelo's David, with his sling across his shoulder, ready to meet the grim giant of Gath, and doubting not that he would overcome in the combat in the name of Him for whom he stood a champion."

But you don't live in Stonington, and perhaps your family hasn't a colonial history that will open doors to distinguished acquaintances for you. That may be what you are saying, with a shake of the head. And that would be, if true, about the thinnest excuse imaginable for neglecting to bring that boy of yours into fellowship with guests of great soul. It is not a question of public distinction. The real question is: Are you doing all you can—really paying attention to the matter—to give your home the best you know? Perhaps you are moving right out in the current of a life of activity among men who are eminently worth while. Does your boy know them? Perhaps you have come to know a great soul who is not known to many others. Have you let your boy, and the others in the family, know him? Has he really discovered his teachers in school, for instance, as real human beings, as he might very profitably if you invited them to the homes one by one? Try it!

VII

THE BOY'S RELIGION

THE little chap was trudging along with his father on the way home from church. "How did you like what the minister said today?" asked the man—not to start a critical discussion, but to discover how the sermon had impressed the boy.

"Oh," exclaimed the six-year-old, "I liked it very much when he was telling about the Crucifixion, but then just when I was most interested, he stopped—and went on with his sermon!" And the boy seemed so disappointed.

He stopped—and went on with his sermon! Yes; and what was it that minister had stopped? The telling of the story of the Cross—the narrative that gripped the interest of the child, and held him in unconscious attention, which is the strongest attention always. And when the minister "went on," it was to the boy then no more than a "sermon," a type of utterance that the little fellow perhaps could seldom understand, because so little designed for him.

"What did Dr. B.—talk about today?" a father asked his small boy after the morning service.

"I don't know, father," was the quiet reply. "But don't you remember anything he said?" urged the father encouragingly. "No, father, 'cause you know ministers don't talk so little boys can understand," came the answer, with a note in it of childlike tolerance of the father's ignorance.

But are certain ministers any more obscure in their preaching in the presence of children than are most of us fathers in our utterances on religion, as we give information and counsel to our boys? Why is it we are so often puzzled by the boy's queries on matters of fact, or by his eager rush into the history and the mystery of man's relation to God? What would you have said to the keenly watchful and enquiring boy in his early teens who asked, "Father, how do we know we are right in our beliefs, when so many others believe differently? And you think our Church is the right one, but how do you know that others are not right when they think their Church is the best?" *Are we, as fathers, forgetting that any fog that clouds our minds on life's greatest issues will weave its trailing streamers about the mind of the boy who comes to us for light?*

Theoretically, it may have been rather too early, by all the rules, to have told that small boy in church the story of the Crucifixion. Some would think so. But his quiet interest, his wish that the "sermon" need not have broken in upon the narrative, throw light upon the oft-times inaptness and unwisdom of general rules, in too rigid application to the individual case. To be sure, there is need, as between father and son, for wise reserves in the father's teaching; but it is also true that the boy's questing and questioning mind swiftly and far outruns the father's estimate of what it is, in character and in scope, that interests the boy. So a father makes no mistake in speaking with his boy, not in smooth or evasive platitudes, but in the direct, and even rugged presentation of the facts of religion. For boys have no liking for anything evasive—in others—and they want the facts. It is unexplored country to them at first, this whole question of religion, and they want a look at your road map, if you have a good one, that is, one you would follow confidently. But if you are not sure of your own road map, they wonder a bit, and must simply ask somebody else. For they must find out somehow.

A group of college students recently attended a meeting where a distinguished preacher unfolded to them his ideas of modern Christian service. When he had set forth his views, a voice called out, "Doctor, do you believe in the Trinity?"

The doctor hesitated. "I'm surprised," he said, "at a question like that from a young man like yourself. I could expect that from an older man, but you, I should think, would be asking about problems of service in these days."

"But, Doctor," came the student's voice again, "do you believe in the Trinity?"

"Oh, of course," returned the doctor somewhat impatiently, "I believe in a Trinity, but perhaps not in what you mean by the word." And he went on to explain so confusedly what he meant that the students went away wholly unsatisfied, especially with the spirit of evasiveness, which so took away their confidence in the speaker that only a few came to hear him in later addresses.

In our grown-up forgetfulness we do not take sufficiently into account the impetuousness, the clarity, the frank directness of the boy mind, nor the childlikeness to which our Lord Jesus invited, and which he enjoined upon His followers. *The questionings of the small boy are not commonly those of the doubter, but of the hopeful and teachable explorer* Hence, the father must take seriously the expression of the boy's interest in religious questions.

At a university psychological clinic a bright-eyed boy

was under examination, who had been troubled with disagreeable and sometimes terrifying visions at night. This was disclosed by the questionings of the teacher, in the presence of a keenly attentive class of young men and young women. "And what do you do when these visions trouble you?" asked the psychologist. "I say, 'the Lord is my Shepherd,' and then they go away," answered the boy, unaffectedly. For a moment there was a silence in that room not to be forgotten. "What did you think of him?" the teacher was asked after the class period was over. "Oh, probably lying, all through," he responded.

Do *you* think the boy was lying? Are you incredulous, or if not incredulous, perhaps not wholly sympathetic, and at least quite surprised when your own boy discloses a spiritual interest of such a very definite and practical sort?

It was doubtless a surprise to certain fathers in a large city church when their boys banded themselves together, under an older boy's leadership, for individual soul-winning. But could boys in their early teens do such work as that? They did. They met once in two weeks to study how to lead other boys to Christ, and meanwhile they did, in His name, what they had learned how to do in their study of the problem. One boy after another was led to Christ, and united with the church in which the other boys were members. And then the son of the pastor of the church was approached on this subject by one of the older boys. (The son's purposes had probably been taken for granted up to that moment.) He quietly thanked his boy friend, told him he had never really faced the question before, and promised to consider it, with the result that he did unite with the church a few weeks later. Who can measure the heart of a boy—especially if no one tries to!

In applied religion the boy is much more sensitive and logical than some of us fathers have quite realized. In the border-line questions of social practises, and in those that are really not of the border-line sort at all, the boy who would be a loyal follower of Christ—I mean the true born-again, whole-hearted Christian boy—is seeing many things level-eyed. In a town where dancing is very popular, a boy was explaining to his father why he did not dance. "The fellows may talk as they please to their parents about dancing's being all right," he exclaimed, "but I hear what the boys say among themselves about it, and why they dance. I tell you, I wouldn't want them to talk about my sister as they talk about the other girls. No, I'm not going in for it." And another boy in his teens, when he heard a community leader in good works say publicly that he did not object to dancing and card playing if they were done in the right way, said earnestly to some other boys: "I wish he hadn't said that. The trouble is, they can't be done in the right way." Would you agree with the boy, or would you, if he were your son, encourage him to dance and play cards "in the right way"?

But, after all, what religion do you mean when you talk about religion with your boy of any age? Whatever has been written here is in the light of an acceptance of the "old-fashioned faith"—the boy's need of a Saviour from sin, a Saviour who died in his stead, a Bible you are wholly safe in teaching him to trust, a call to tell others of his Lord and Saviour. It must be a puzzling task for a father who has his doubts about the Atonement, or about the deity of Christ, to lead his son to a Saviour. It must be a puzzling task for one who selects what he chooses to believe in the Bible, to give his son even a free working confidence in the Book; or for one who has no real sense of mission, to explain away the dynamic of the Gospel. In such a case the boy will become as abnormally sub-Christian as others who see only the need for work "at home."

Many a father is unaware of the fact that some of the most highly prized findings of those who question the accuracy of the Bible are today hopelessly out of date and entirely abandoned by scholars of the first rank. Still others do not know that the monumental evidences from ancient days, now coming to light, have increasingly corroborated the Scriptures.

But the boy is now facing not only ignorant comment on the Word of God, but also the current materialism—and he needs father-guidance in pointing him to the Light and Life in Christ Jesus. Come, man, let's not talk mere patter about "following the principles of Jesus," and about "accepting the ideals of Christ"! You know how futile that is, if you have ever tried it, apart from an acceptance of Christ *himself* as Saviour and Lord—not as a mere leader. Let us give the boy the heart of it all, and not an empty bit of advice that he cannot follow!

I shall never forget a service down by the lake at Camp Becket, in Massachusetts, when the leader gave the boys a talk on "chums." It was dark under the trees before he finished. Those boys of the camp knew well enough what Mr. Gibson meant when he gave them the invitation to come forward and accept Christ, and he actually had to warn them not to come unless they really meant it. Up from among the bowed heads, one boy, and then another, and another, would rise, and walk quickly to the rustic pulpit where Mr. Gibson was, have a quiet word with him, and then join the others on the front seats, to await a word from the leader, when the rest of us had made our way back into the camp.

Perhaps your boy was there. Did the leader's word to him that night supplement what you had already made plain to him, or was it something rather new to the boy as a definite call? Is it "up to you"?

VIII

THE GIRL PROBLEM

WHEN he is just a little fellow there seems to be almost no "girl problem" at all. He and his small sister, and other boys' sisters play very much the same games, enjoy the same stories and pictures; and while there are differences in interests as between boy and girl, yet you know that the old rag doll that you kept close by you was just as real to you as was the flossy-looking doll of bisque, real hair, and flounces to your small sister.

It was a wondrously long time before little Bill ceased to care with a watchful fatherly love for Jacky, the sailor-doll who for some years had been his inseparable companion. It was an epoch in Bill's life when he first showed signs of a waning interest in Jacky, because just there, possibly, the diverging lines of interest separating the boy-life from the girl-life, were beginning to have their influence on Bill. And it was some years after that before he would condescend to recognize the existence of girls—especially if he thought that you knew he was aware of their presence in his world. No, sir, no girls for *him.* It was during that contemptuous period that his little sister wondered what brothers were good for, anyway. And perhaps that was why she was so insistent that the next child in the family must be a girl, because as she frankly declared, "I have had enough of brothers!"

It is just after the era of contempt that the pendulum

of interest swings far in the opposite direction and possibly gets caught there. Some day the awakening comes. Perhaps a youthful visitor is in the home for a brief hour. Bill seems entirely different. His mother and father are a bit disappointed in his lack of cordiality. But after Eleanor has gone Bill sidles up to his father, shifts about from one foot to the other, and then blurts out, "Gee, father, did you notice that girl's face? Why, I think she has the most wonderful face I ever saw in my life!" Then Bill's father knows that the awakening has come. He is glad that Bill likes the kind of face that Eleanor has, because it is the right kind. But he knows that the contempt period is over,—and there are new problems just ahead.

And where does the father come in on the girl problem? What can he do to help toward right relationships in this tremendously vital issue in the life of the growing boy?

The father must be himself wholesome and considerate, and a gentleman in every way, in his own attitude toward the boy's mother and sister, and toward other women. Boys are keen to sense the exact nature of a father's attitude toward the women and the girls of the household. If he is careless as to the little amenities of life in their presence; if he ignores their opinions, scouts their convictions as hardly worth mentioning, treats them with a somewhat amused tolerance, and expects them to wait upon him with unwearying enthusiasm, then who can wonder if the boy shouts from the front door when he is in a hurry, "Ma! Gimme my cap! I'm going out." And when with the cap comes the motherly query, "Where are you going, Billy?" the only answer is "Oh, just out!" as he dashes away. Mother's ideas about his doings count for just as little as her ideas about "dad's" doings—dad's ways and manners constituting the example and the proof.

And is it strange that the well-bred girls in the neighborhood say among themselves that they would like Billy well enough if he were not such a "roughneck" (Yes, even they will sometimes use that term!). One man says that he cannot to this day dismiss from his boyhood memories the picture of the old farm kitchen with his grandfather literally "pitching into" the food on the table, while the gentle-hearted and hard-working grandmother sat on the edge of her chair, eating when she could, but ever ready to move constantly to serve the slightest wish of her husband. That is not exactly a picture of the queen of the household rightly enthroned.

Yes, man, what the boy believes you think of women greatly matters to him. And much more subtly than we realize, the respect, or the contempt, or the mere tolerance that you show enters into his attitude in ways that affect the deep moral issues of the sex relationship. For the boy who is not trained in true respect for women may lack in an hour of temptation an element of reserve and consideration which would otherwise have been among the safeguards within his own soul.

When the sex-awakening comes and you have earlier prepared the boy for this—he likes to be trusted. Given a right relationship to Jesus Christ, with the consequent moral awareness and sustaining grace, and an intimacy in everyday problems with a father upon whom he can count for an understanding sympathy, the boy responds to trust by honoring it. His life is enriched by your confidence, and impoverished by your suspicions. Don't you remember what it meant to you when more than once in the electric teens father put his hands on your shoulders, and looking deep into your eyes said heartily, "My boy, mother and I are counting upon you!" And you may be humbled and ashamed some day when you are probing into things a little, to find a young soldier of pure and courageous heart where you feared you might discover a potential deserter.

A father who thought he knew his boys well says that he was walking with one of them under the trees in an intimate evening hour, when the boy told of some of the sex temptations of the neighborhood. One or two names were mentioned, and then, in an effort to help, the father says that he asked the boy a direct question about the real character of one or two other girls. Instantly came back the answer, "I don't know, father, and I don't want to know." He hesitated and then said, emphatically, "It wouldn't be good for me to know. The less I know about that the better." Did that father probe too far? Or did he rightly attempt to warn his boy of the traps that might be spread for him?

That there are many girls of frivolous spirit, of shallow brain, and even of evil habits cannot be denied in these days of frank exposure of a deteriorated soul revealed in the immodest dress and ways of so many girls and women. But on the other hand, such a disclosure of a decadent soul as is shown by individual exhibits cannot truthfully interpret for the boy the girlhood of the hour, for there is a girlhood that is gloriously existent, and that has not lost "the fine velvet of the soul." It will matter much to the boy whether his father is chiefly interested in warning him against the "vamp" of lesser or greater skill, or in promoting an interest in the girl who will be a true friend.

Some men have chosen to forewarn their boys of the dangers of sex depravity by taking them to see what goes on in resorts where evil flourishes, but in doing this they have, to say the least, taken fearful risks. "I know a man," said Robert E. Speer, to a group of college students, "who was urged once to go down and see the seamy side of life in New York. He went. A friend who was a newspaper man showed him what there was to see. I asked him when he came back if it had been a good experience, It had been such an experience, he told me, as he would gladly give a hand to obliterate. But the knowledge was his now, and he could not rid himself of it. That is the mischief about memory. . . . Ignorance is freedom from all this. Men, young and old, do not need to know the worst, or to feel the slavery which the knowledge of the worst brings. . . . I believe in the attitude of ignorance (of evil) because it alone holds the secret of life's freshness and joy."

It is utterly Cruel and vastly misleading to allow a boy to become suspicious of almost every girl he meets, because of his father's quiet cynicism about girls in general. How far do you as a father want to be responsible for your boy's possible experience of Kipling's "Gentlemen Rankers"?

"We have done with Hope and Honor, we are lost to
Love and Truth,
We are dropping down the ladder rung by rung,
And the measure of our torment is the measure of our
youth,
God help us, for we knew the worst too young!"

It is exactly the opposite side of life that the boy needs to know. Perhaps your neighborhood is shot through and through with the ideals that have let the best blood of spiritual vitality run out, until the social and religious life is anemic and withered. What can you do to let the boy know that not all young people are like this? For one thing, there is the summer conference, where selected young people gather for Bible and mission study, and for healthy recreation. One boy who attended for the first time such a conference said afterwards, when asked what he had learned there: "I learned, for one thing, what fine Christian fellows there are. Why, I didn't really know there were such fellows." And the same discovery as to girls may be made by many a boy who is sent to a young people's conference. Such was the experience of a boy who writes in his straightforward way about a girl who influenced him greatly:

"I got to know Louise up at Northfield three years ago last July. I just saw her for an afternoon and evening, but even in that time I had a more serious talk with her than I'd had with most girls in all my life. I never wrote her, or saw her for a year, and still I didn't forget her, as the talk we'd had left so deep an impression on my mind. The next year I saw her at Northfield again. . . . Everything that has counted most in my life seems to have come more in the last two years than in all previous years put together. . . . The help that Louise gave me I can never estimate . . . her ideal of purity brought me to realize where I was, and how unworthy I was of her friendship. I can't tell you how much she helped me there. She always trusted her friends so absolutely it seemed to demand the very best you had to give, and it helped me more than any earthly means I know of to keep me nearer to the ideals I wanted to live up to."

And the girl who had so helped him wrote somewhere

in her journals in one of the prayers that, among other glimpses of her life, are given in "One Girl's Influence," Mr. Speer's story of Louise Andrews' life: "And, Father, I ask that the boys whom I love as friends may be absolutely pure. God, may they never do anything that will make them ashamed. In 'let down' times be there to help them. May they always be able to look me in the eyes with wonderful frankness. Help them to remember 'I would be pure, for there are those who care.' I thank thee for my trust in my friends. Thou will let me help. Wilt thou not? When they think of me may it always be, of some strong, pure, true friend, who although she does not know how hard their struggles, still trusts them to win with Thy help. Hear my prayer, dear Heavenly Father, for the sake of Him who is our Saviour from sin, Jesus Christ. Amen."

What can such a friendship mean to the boy you know best! One of Louise Andrews' friends has called her "a perfectly possible girl"—she was so hearty and fun loving, and genuine in her gloriously happy life, even when a lingering and fatal illness had laid its hand upon her. It is the type that she represents which, thank God, is not smothered by the eruption of worldliness in this volcanic hour. By all the trend and religious training and sound discipline of your home life, by all your own trustful expectancy and earnest prayer, and wholesome outlook, and careful help in the selection of welcome friends for the boy—by all these are you making it the normal thing for your boy to want to know the right girls? They are "perfectly possible"—never doubt that for a moment!

IX

HIS SCHOOLING

WHAT school for my boy?" That's a question, indeed. It is not so hard to decide when there is a good public school in the neighborhood, for the question then for most of us almost settles itself. The boy likes to get his schooling with fellows he knows best in his own neighborhood, and it is not to his discredit that he feels so about it.

But one trouble with us as fathers is this: we allow others to "run" our schools, and we take far too little interest in seeing to it that the local school where our children go is rightly conducted. Some fathers are more watchful than others. One young father in a suburban town has established a prize in the public school for good work in certain directions, and that was a good move. However, he did better. He is often at the school, helpfully. He attends the school games. He knows the teachers. He is a busy man, with a fairly large and young family; but that school is a great center of interest to him.

Another father, just in the crowded hours of preparation for a vacation, said to a friend: "I meant to go away today, but I decided to stay over tonight, so that I could attend a meeting at the school, where some questions about the school are to be discussed. I'm interested; my boys are in that school."

And it is needful for fathers to be interested, keenly so. For what vital influences are inherent in the boy's school life! When the parents can choose the school, ought the choice to be made on mere casual hearsay, or for social preferment, or for eminence in athletics? Should we not look into the Christian life of the school, the atmosphere, the character of the personnel, and the kind of product turned out by that school?

For an out-of-doors boy of years ago, study was irksome in his teens. The crisis came when he insisted on leaving school, a private school at this period, to enter business. But just on the threshold of that alluring career, a real teacher asked the boy, while waiting for a business opening, to come temporarily to his school. So the trap was set with kindly guile, and the diversion once accomplished, the snare held fast. For that teacher taught the boy something more than the textbooks. He gave horizons. He showed by word and deed how expectant he was that the boy would have a great time as he followed his teacher into the unfolding mysteries of why such things as the classics and mathematics, and history, and much English, were worth while. Moreover, he put the boy in charge of the athletics of the school as trainer. How responsibility makes a youngster grow! Then one golden afternoon, far out in the country, the teacher sat with the boy on a log by the roadside and just talked. That was the intellectual turning point. Nor did the teacher stop there. One day the boy received at his home a very personal letter from his teacher friend, urging him to accept Christ. It was the first letter of the kind he had ever seen. It went to the heart of the whole matter and to the boy's heart. Not at once, but later, he united with the church, and so moved on into Christian service.

Many years afterwards when attending, as an alumnus, a celebration at his college, he grew enthusiastic over an address that exalted the place of the religious in education, and turning to an old classmate, now a teacher in the college, he exclaimed, "That's great, isn't it?" "Good speech," was the reply, "but I have no use for what he is saying just now. Religion has no place in education."

Who was right? The little chap in the New England town, the teacher of "prep" school days, or the classmate-instructor in the big college?

It is not a superfluous question for anyone who has the choosing of a school today for boy or girl, for none too many schools are educationally efficient in the fostering of that without which mere so-called education is a menace. Some teachers who give keen attention to the curriculum are highly superficial, or worse, in dealing with character, and the soul's relation to the Life that is the Light of men. The principal of a famous private schools for boys, when asked if he had any real difficulty in securing the right teachers, replied, "Oh, I can get plenty of men who know their subjects, but the trouble is to find a man who knows boys"; and he might have added, "and who knows Christ." One teacher in a public school, in referring to a bit of Bible history, remarked, "Of course no one nowadays believes this sort of thing," whereupon a young girl in the class rose in her place and exclaimed, "Why, Miss ——, I believe that, and so do lots of people I know." "That will do," said the teacher, "we won't discuss that," and the subject was dropped.

But the principle involved cannot be dropped. The Christian family is necessarily dissatisfied with any school that denies Christ His rightful pre-eminence, and gives the pupil no protection against the disparaging of sacred things. More than one educator has pointed out the far-reaching importance of "education by atmosphere"; and the mental and religious atmosphere of the classroom and of the whole school life ought to be carefully considered by parents. "What do you suppose one of our professors did today?" exclaimed a mature and much-disturbed college upperclassman. "Why, he took about fifteen minutes of the hour to enlarge upon the advantages of swearing!" And the principle of education by atmosphere was illustrated in the approving delight of the class.

On the other hand, there are schools where this type of miseducation is rendered impossible. A certain college president, when asked about his method of choosing teachers, replied that he first inquired as to their fundamental Christian beliefs, and then as to their personal habits. While never abating his requirements as to scholarship and pedagogical skill, he never accepts a teacher, no matter how expert in his specialty, who does not qualify on the other points. One result of this is a free and genuine and whole-hearted religious atmosphere in a school where severely taxing mental and physical standards are also steadily maintained. It would be idle to suppose that there are no fires of temptation smouldering or burning in that institution. Young life is a favorite mark for Satan everywhere. But at least it can be said that the authorities in that school are not giving him their approval.

And why should Christians not encourage by their gifts, their influence, their direct management, and especially by the presence of their children, the schools and colleges that do recognize the pre-eminence of Christ, not only as the Master Teacher, but as the Saviour who alone makes us into the new creations that are capable then of the guidance of the Spirit into "all the truth"?

Two fathers were discussing the comparative merits of two available schools for the daughter of one of these Christian men. One school was nearer, less expensive, and more convenient. Both schools stood well in scholarship, but the nearby institution dealt with the Bible in the most destructive fashion, while the other strongly upheld the old faith. The father was puzzled. He thought his daughter might be strengthened through having to encounter the spiritual disadvantages of the more convenient school. "But here is the question as I see it," said his friend. "If we are free to choose, ought we to commit our children to the care of a school where the beliefs that we count essential are directly denied by the fixed policy of that school? Is it even educationally correct to put your adolescent child into an atmosphere which is directly contrary to the life purposes you cherish for your children?" The questions needed only to be asked to make the point clear.

No, the Christian who squarely considers the facts cannot be satisfied with a school where his son or daughter must constantly struggle for breath in an atmosphere spiritually suffocating. Nor does he willingly choose, if he gives Christ the pre-eminence, a school where sheer worldliness is the ever-present ideal, where, in miniature, the materialistic nonreligious elements of a gainful, selfish and Christ-forgetting society are strongly influential.

The aroused Christian will prefer, and will go far if need be, to find the school that is frankly Christian, and not hostile, or even cautiously non-committal on that question. That school at its best will provide an equipment of able Christian teachers first of all, and in support of their work, simple, healthy housing, carefully supervised physical work, not always competitive, but always constructive in building strength at weak points. The Bible will be prominent in the curriculum, and taught by one who *believes* it. And Christ will walk the halls of that school, frequent the classrooms and living rooms and athletic field, in the life and ways and spirit of the faculty, so that the students may see Him exalted in the common tasks that spell school life to them.

The students in that school will know that the masters are interested personally in their boys, with the same genuineness of interest that the Master showed in His "boys" when He called them by that familiar name.

And would it sound strange to you, if a boy, when asked how things were going in his school (and this did occur), should reply with genuine boyish enthusiasm, "Fine! Why, we have had lots of new students come lately," and when asked how he accounted for this, should answer frankly, "Why, I guess it's just an answer to prayer"?

Have we not, as Christians, too carelessly committed our boys and girls to a school life (even when we could choose as among several schools) the atmosphere of which is taken for granted as satisfactory, because of purely worldly tests of popularity and efficiency? Have we taken seriously enough the sacred trust of fatherhood as counselor in selecting the group that is to have such abiding influence over our children in their most impressionable years?

X

HIS LIFE WORK

YOU have been praying and planning and working for that boy of yours ever since he was a little chap, and now he is in the later teens—a living, vigorous, alert and outlooking young fellow who has a big question in his mind, It will not be denied an answer. For as surely as the sun rises and sets, as surely must the boy come to a decision concerning the work that shall be his own.

A college student had invited two or three of his college chums to dine in his home, just as their course was drawing to a close. They were soon comparing notes as to what they were to do when college was over. "How about you?" asked one of the fellows, turning to the student in whose home they were. "I have decided to study law," he said.

"Why, I thought you were going in for engineering," said one, in surprise.

"No," was the reply, "I had thought of that, but now I've decided to study law."

His father glanced at him with a smile, and asked: "Harry, is that a strictly correct statement?"

Harry hesitated, looked puzzled, and then catching his father's meaning, laughingly, but somewhat ruefully, replied, "Perhaps not, father, for it wasn't really my decision, it was yours!" The father, who was a skilled corporation lawyer, nodded and with a gleam of amusement in his eyes, he said, "That is better. That is correct, it was my decision."

Then the subject was changed; but at least one of the guests has never forgotten the impression made upon him by the nature of that decision. Was the father right to take the matter into his own hands, and dictate to his very able son, whose interests were not in the direction of a study of law, but in the direction of mathematics and mechanics? To be sure, the son did turn out to be a highly competent lawyer; but how was the father to know in advance how to guide him in the choice of a life work, to say nothing of actually deciding for him? What are the factors that may rightly be taken into account in reaching the vocational decision?

It is a noteworthy fact that very many men of forty or fifty are not doing today what they once planned to do. Check up what you know of your intimate friends, and see how far this is true. It would seem that by no means a majority of men in middle life are in the work that they had chosen during high school and college years. Many are not now doing what they then seemed either inclined, or best fitted to do. Some are restless and unhappy misfits today, while others, who have made a success of their tasks, secretly would much prefer something else. Here is a young diplomat of great distinction in many lands who was a light-hearted, apparently heedless, aimless, and inattentive student. Here is a confectioner, trained in college as an engineer; there, a promoter of business enterprises, who passed through untold hardships in his days of preparation for the practise of medicine, and was a physician in active service for years. What is a father to say and to do in counseling his teen age boy concerning the intricate cross currents of the vocational choice?

That which has gone before in these Studies progressively developed through the unfolding years of the boy's life, has had a direct bearing upon the nature of his later life choices. He will be likely to choose in accordance with the emphasis that you have placed, and are placing, upon what you regard as the purpose of life. If a son is fathered into a conception of life that makes the ingathering of money the great objective, or even the distinctive mark of success, then the boy is pretty sure to cast about in his mind for the field, and the opening, that seem to promise the most cash.

A man who had been spending a Sunday of addresses and conferences in an eastern college, was walking in the evening with the Christian Association Secretary, who led him to a place on the campus from which they could look down a long valley over miles of busy steel works. Pillars of fire flung their wild flare against the sky; the clank of machinery came up from the great mills; the vastness, the fascination of modern industry gripped the imagination. "There's our problem," said the secretary, "I mean our problem in Christian service. The works down there stand out before our fellows as the greatest thing they know, and most of them hope that some day they can run, or own, mills like those. It's hard to get them interested in specific Christian work as a life calling." And the overwhelming appeal such as the great mills sent up to the campus day and night by their existence and their material success is reflected, for example, in the appalling dearth of ministerial students and recruits for the foreign mission field.

More intimate, more subtle, far more impressive than the big mill is the vision that a son may have of his rightful life work in the steady influence of a wise Christian father who has been the boy's chum since babyhood. It may well be true that in the plan of God that boy is to become a mill owner who will conduct his majestic enterprise for God. There are those who do precisely that. But the pull of the sheer materialism of it all, the glitter of the world's prizes, the challenge to the normal boy's competitive spirit—all are so powerful that many a father will need to discriminate in his talks with his son between business success as the world visions it, and a successful, worthwhile life. A father need not be afraid that he will deter his boy from a noble business career by keeping prominently before him the claim; of specific Christian work as such, for the urgent influences of school and college, and the glamour of lucrative business life need precisely such an offsetting influence to give anything like a balanced prospect of usefulness. Who is to help the boy to discern the deeper elements that make up a life of God-led service, if his father cannot throw his own study and experience and loving counsel into the solution of the problem and on the side of the higher values?

On the other hand, it would be contrary to the evident plan of God to lead any son to suppose that business or professional life is necessarily a secondary calling. The highest possible place for any one is the precise place where God would have that one live and serve. It would be a calamity to be in the ministry when one ought to be in the merchant marine. The central question for the father is this: "Am I helping my son to discover, not his bent or inclination merely, and not even what I may just now assume are his abilities, but am I encouraging him in every way to find what God wants him to do?" How can one discover the will of God for himself or in behalf of a loved son, when so many complex factors seem to press for consideration? To many a man, younger or older, George Mueller's simple suggestions as to his own way of finding the will of God have been a definite blessing. And they can readily have their place in the critical question of the steps that lead to a choice of a life work. Mr. Mueller thus wrote:

1. An obedient heart. I seek at the beginning to get my heart into such a state that it has no will of its own in regard to a given matter. Nine-tenths of the difficulties are overcome when our hearts are ready to do the Lord's will, whatever it may be. When one is truly in this state it is usually but a little way to the knowledge of what His will is.

2. Feelings not enough. Having done this, I do not leave the result to feeling, or simple impression. If I do so, I make myself liable to great delusions.

3. The will of God revealed through His Word. I seek the Spirit of God, through, or in connection with, the Word of God. The Spirit and the Word must be combined. If I look to the Spirit alone, without the Word, I lay myself open to great delusions also. If the Holy Spirit guides us at all, He will do it according to the Scriptures and never contrary to them.

4. Providential circumstances. Next I take into account providential circumstances. These often plainly indicate God's will in connection with his Word and Spirit.

5. Prayer. I ask God in prayer to reveal His will to me aright.

6. Deliberate judgment, and a mind "at peace." Thus, through prayer to God, the study of the Word, and reflection, I come to a deliberate judgment according to the best of my ability and knowledge, and if my mind is thus at peace, and continues so after two or three more petitions, I proceed accordingly. In trivial matters, and in transactions involving most important issues, I have found the method always effective.

Many of us have already tried at least several of Mr. Mueller's suggestions; but how many can say, with him, "I proceed accordingly!"

God has not bestowed certain gifts upon a boy, and a degree of intelligent perception upon his father, just to have such factors ignored or discontinued. What are your boy's gifts? Note them well. In what field could they be used? In what has he already shown an inherent, though perhaps embryonic ability? Are these gifts finding expression in the right spirit, unfolding under the touch of the Master himself in outgoing service? Some of the interests into which your boy has been led may not have taken just the shape you would have chosen, or that he will choose later on. Yet they may be pointing to something in which they are yet to be a factor.

A boy who loved the woods decided in his middle teens that he would become a forester. It was not a mere impulse. He studied the subject, considered it, came to understand its bearings. But his life was increasingly exposed, through a yielded will, and a personal acquaintance with many missionaries, to the claims of foreign missions. When he became a student volunteer he did so in prayer and in quiet waiting upon God. He "proceeded accordingly." But it has been noticed that in his considering of a specific field, his whole heart turns to pioneer work among hitherto unreached tribes. It is the forest that still calls him, though now with a voice of different meaning. Who can say that his boyhood experiences, his love of the woods, have no true bearing upon his proper choice of a field?

Is it not a privilege of fatherhood to note such signs as this, and to conserve and deepen the desires that may contribute to the successful application of such desires to highest ends? After all, it is not so important for the father to visualize the precise limitations of his son's rightful life work in order to be helpful to him in choosing wisely, as it is to make sure of the next step in the direction of serviceable, God-led life. When we have put aside our own will; when feelings stand aside in favor of judgment; when the Word speaks to us, and circumstances point in the same direction, and prayer leads to a deliberate judgment and peace of mind as to how we shall counsel the boy concerning his life—then why not "proceed accordingly"?

XI

BREAKING HOME TIES

IT is such a little while that the boy is with us in the home! When the brief years have fled during which your home is his home, you look back over the road you and he have traveled together, and you wonder how time and opportunity could have slipped away so swiftly.

But that home, in proportion to its faithfulness and worthiness, is still the boy's home, and you are his father, even after he goes forth into his life work and lays the foundation of a home of his own.

There are tragedies sometimes in the breaking of home ties. The boy may even be glad to get away from the tyranny, the irksomeness, the smothering atmosphere of a home that is only a house, and a house of troubled memories, at that. "I never can speak of my father without getting angry," said one poor young fellow whose deadly home-life was a dark memory. Home ties of mere binding obligation that are without the constraints and golden cords of love are broken by many a young man as early as possible, and with tragic eagerness to be away, "on his own." That break did not originate in the strain of the last days at home, but somewhere in the neglect, the hardness, the blindness of a fatherhood—or motherhood—that did not guard and wisely use the golden hours of the beginning-years. And such breaks need never come, need never disturb the wholesomeness and glad unity of the family life, if parenthood has been true.

To be sure, there are restless, forthfaring young fellows who talk, and even sometimes act, as though home had no longer any real hold upon their affections. But let the day come when the trunk is packed, the ticket bought, and the good-byes impending—then you needn't be surprised if the boy lingers in his old room awhile, and says good-bye over and over again at the threshold of the home. Here is no tragedy. Here is the out-working of law and of love, and the boy's eager look forward toward the new experiences is simply a part of that transition from your shelter and guidance to the open road under the wide sky for which you have been helping to prepare him.

It is right that the boy should lift his eyes to the horizons that await him. And it is wrong for the father to harness the boy with bit and bridle. Fatherhood has done its part thus far in fostering the boy's growth into young manhood, and now, while interest and loving counsel and constant readiness to help are not to cease, there is to be nevertheless a lifting of the detaining hand, a release from parental control in an unanxious willingness to encourage the boy in his pioneering.

No young man will thrive and grow in his life-work if he has no free opportunity to learn his own lessons. One young business man confessed that in the large business in which his father and his brother were engaged, there was nothing he could do without feeling that his father might veto it. And the nervous strain of the minute and constant supervision and reversals to which his intense energy was subjected by his father's arbitrary will led to a complete breakdown in health from which the young man never recovered.

He had a home of his own, and several children, but there were "home ties" that should have been gladly released by that young man's father, which proved to be heavy fetters. Such ties are not fastened upon a faithful, energetic, cleanly ambitious son by a wise father.

One father, fearing lest his eager interest in his grown-up son might be a hindrance to independent action, relates that he asked the son upon one occasion whether his fatherly counsel was now a bother or an intrusion.

"Oh, no!" said the younger man, "not at all. I like to swim out into the deep water, but I like to know that the wharf is right there!"

It is that consciousness of having a father "right there" that has strengthened many a young man for his task. A father surely need not be an intruder.

It is the extension of the proper functions of fatherhood that may well have the careful thought of the man whose son has broken home ties. For not all ought to be "broken," or even strained.

An able lawyer, in his sixties, whose father had just died at the age of ninety said to a friend; "I miss him! For the first time in my life I feel that I am now right out on the firing line." And that from a son more than sixty years old! Were his home ties broken? How he used to delight in the visits to the old home neighborhood! How proud he was of that father of his when the venerable man used to visit the son in his city home! There was a bond between them that time had not strained. It was the son who helped the father in the later years, but the son never seemed to think of that. When the aged man was called Home, then the son for the first time realized that he himself was to receive, with no intervening human fatherhood, the full impact of life.

It may be that you as a father will watch the departure of your boy as he sets forth on his first long absence from home, with a poignant sense of separation from him in the dear fellowship of the years in which he has companioned with you.

It may seem to you at first that you will now be of little further service to him, and that he will not be especially conscious of any need of you.

But the relationship you have begun and established is not so easily set aside. Home is Sanctuary to him. It is the place of return. Yes, he will have his own home, his little family around him, and yet there is a sense in which the soul of any true son turns with a peculiarly eager affection to a gladly remembered boyhood home. Let it be so with your boy! Let it be true that whether the house is the same or not, in these changeful days, the home is always there, because you and the mother, as long as God spares you, are steadily, surely there. Even as at the first you prepared for fatherhood and cherished that little son of yours in the first few years, and on through the course of his development, so now your fatherhood may none the less lovingly and effectually be available in accordance with the grown-up needs of that son. He will like to take to deep water, yet he is glad to know that not far away is the familiar landing where you await him.

He is your boy still.

who has the power of death, that is, the
devil,[t] 15 and free those who through fear
of death had been subject to slavery all
their life. 16 Surely he did not help angels
but rather the descendants of Abraham;
17 therefore, he had to become like his
brothers in every way, that he might be a
merciful and faithful high priest before
God to expiate the sins of the people.[u]
18 Because he himself was tested through
what he suffered, he is able to help those
who are being tested.

III. JESUS, FAITHFUL AND COMPASSIONATE HIGH PRIEST

CHAPTER 3

Jesus, Superior to Moses.* 1 Therefore,
holy "brothers," sharing in a heavenly calling, reflect on Jesus, the apostle and high
priest of our confession, 2 who was faithful
to the one who appointed him, just as
Moses was "faithful in [all] his house."[v]
3 But he is worthy of more "glory" than
Moses, as the founder of a house has more
"honor" than the house itself.[w] 4 Every
house is founded by someone, but the
founder of all is God. 5 Moses was "faithful
in all his house" as a "servant" to testify to
what would be spoken, 6 [x] but Christ was
faithful as a son placed over his house. We
are his house, if [only] we hold fast to our
confidence and pride in our hope.*

Israel's Infidelity a Warning. 7 * Therefore,
as the holy Spirit says:

"Oh, that today you would hear his
voice,[y]
8 'Harden not your hearts as at the
rebellion
in the day of testing in the desert,
9 where your ancestors tested and tried
me
and saw my works[z] 10 for forty
years.
Because of this I was provoked with
that generation
and I said, "They have always been
of erring heart,
and they do not know my ways."
11 As I swore in my wrath,
"They shall not enter into my
rest." ' "

12 Take care, brothers, that none of you
may have an evil and unfaithful heart, so as
to forsake the living God. 13 Encourage
yourselves daily while it is still "today," so
that none of you may grow hardened by
the deceit of sin. 14 We have become partners of Christ if only we hold the beginning
of the reality firm until the end,[a] 15 for it is
said:

"Oh, that today you would hear his
voice:
'Harden not your hearts as at the rebellion.' "[b]

16 [c] Who were those who rebelled when
they heard? Was it not all those who came

t Is 25, 8; Hos 13, 14; Jn 12, 31; Rom 6, 9; 1 Cor 15, 54-55; 2 Tm 1, 10; Rv 12, 10.—u Heb 4, 15; 5, 1-3.—v Nm 12, 7.—w 2 Cor 3, 7-8.—x Heb 10, 21; Eph 2, 19; 1 Tm 3, 15; 1 Pt 4, 17.—y 7-11 Ps 95, 7-11.—z Ex 17, 7; Nm 20, 2-5.—a Rom 8, 17.—b Ps 95, 7-8.—c 16-19: Nm 14, 1-38; Dt 1, 19-40.

3, 1-6: The author now takes up the two qualities of Jesus mentioned in Heb 2, 17, but in inverse order: faithfulness (Heb 3, 1—4, 13) and mercy (Heb 4, 14—5, 10). Christians are called *holy "brothers"* because of their common relation to him (Heb 2, 11), the *apostle*, a designation for Jesus used only here in the New Testament (cf Jn 13, 16; 17, 3), meaning one sent as God's final word to us (Heb 1, 2). He is compared with Moses probably because he is seen as mediator of the new covenant (Heb 9, 15) just as Moses was of the old (Heb 9, 19-22, including his sacrifice). But when the author of Heb speaks of Jesus' sacrifice, he does not consider Moses as the Old Testament antitype, but rather the high priest on the Day of Atonement (Heb 9, 6-15). Moses' faithfulness *"in [all] his house"* refers back to Nm 12, 7, on which this section is a midrashic commentary. In vv 3-6, the author does not indicate that he thinks of either Moses or Christ as the founder of the household. *His house* (2.5.6) means God's house, not that of Moses or Christ; in the case of Christ, compare v 6 with Heb 10, 21. The *house* of v 6 is the Christian community; the author suggests its continuity with Israel by speaking not of two houses but of only one. Verse 6 brings out the reason why Jesus is superior to Moses: the latter was the faithful *servant* laboring *in* the house founded by God, but Jesus is God's *son*, placed *over* the house.

3, 6: The majority of manuscripts add "firm to the end," but these words are not found in the three earliest and best witnesses and are probably an interpolation derived from v 14.

3, 7—4, 13: The author appeals for steadfastness of faith in Jesus, basing his warning on the experience of Israel during the Exodus. In the Old Testament the Exodus had been invoked as a symbol of the return of Israel from the Babylonian exile (Is 42, 9; 43, 16-21; 51, 9-11). In the New Testament the redemption was similarly understood as a new exodus, both in the experience of Jesus himself (Lk 9, 31) and in that of his followers (1 Cor 10, 1-4). The author cites Ps 95, 7-11, a salutary example of hardness of heart, as a warning against the danger of growing weary and giving up the journey. To call God *living* (12) means that he reveals himself in his works (cf Jos 3, 10; Jer 10, 10). The *rest* (11) into which Israel was to enter was only a foreshadowing of that rest to which Christians are called. They are to remember the example of Israel's revolt in the desert that cost a whole generation the loss of the promised land (15-19; cf Nm 14, 20-29). In Heb 4, 1-11, the symbol of *rest* is seen in deeper dimension: because the promise to the ancient Hebrews foreshadowed that given to Christians, it is *good news;* and because the promised land was the place of rest that God provided for his people, it was a share in his own rest, which he enjoyed after he had finished his creative work (3-4; cf Gn 2, 2). The author attempts to read this meaning of God's rest into Ps 95, 7-11 (6-9). The Greek form of the name of Joshua, who led Israel into the promised land, is Jesus (8). The author plays upon the name but stresses the superiority of Jesus, who leads his followers into heavenly rest. Verses 12 and 13 are meant as a continuation of the warning, for the word of God brings judgment as well as salvation. Some would capitalize *the word of God* and see it as a personal title of Jesus, comparable to that of Jn 1, 1-18.

out of Egypt under Moses? [17]With whom
was he "provoked for forty years"? Was it
not those who had sinned, whose corpses
fell in the desert?[d] [18]And to whom did he
"swear that they should not enter into his
rest," if not to those who were disobedient?[e] [19]And we see that they could not
enter for lack of faith.

CHAPTER 4

The Sabbath Rest. [1]Therefore, let us be
on our guard while the promise of entering
into his rest remains, that none of you
seem to have failed. [2]For in fact we have
received the good news just as they did.
But the word that they heard did not profit
them, for they were not united in faith
with those who listened. [3]For we who believed enter into [that] rest, just as he has
said:[f]

"As I swore in my wrath,
'They shall not enter into my rest,' "

and yet his works were accomplished at the
foundation of the world. [4]For he has spoken somewhere about the seventh day in
this manner, "And God rested on the
seventh day from all his works";[g] [5]and
again, in the previously mentioned place,
"They shall not enter into my rest."[h]
[6]Therefore, since it remains that some will
enter into it, and those who formerly received the good news did not enter because
of disobedience, [7]he once more set a day,
"today," when long afterwards he spoke
through David, as already quoted:[i]

"Oh, that today you would hear his
voice:
'Harden not your hearts.' "

[8]Now if Joshua had given them rest, he
would not have spoken afterwards of another day.[j] [9]Therefore, a sabbath rest still
remains for the people of God. [10]And whoever enters into God's rest, rests from his
own works as God did from his. [11]There-
fore, let us strive to enter into that rest, so
that no one may fall after the same example
of disobedience.

[12]Indeed, the word of God is living and
effective, sharper than any two-edged
sword, penetrating even between soul and
spirit, joints and marrow, and able to discern reflections and thoughts of the heart.[k]
[13]No creature is concealed from him, but
everything is naked and exposed to the
eyes of him to whom we must render an account.[l]

Jesus, Compassionate High Priest. [14] *
Therefore, since we have a great high
priest who has passed through the heavens,
Jesus, the Son of God, let us hold fast to
our confession.[m] [15]For we do not have a
high priest who is unable to sympathize
with our weaknesses, but one who has
similarly been tested in every way, yet
without sin.[n] [16]So let us confidently approach the throne of grace to receive mercy
and to find grace for timely help.[o]

CHAPTER 5

[1] * Every high priest is taken from among
men and made their representative before
God, to offer gifts and sacrifices for sins.*
[2]He is able to deal patiently* with the ignorant and erring, for he himself is beset
by weakness [3]and so, for this reason, must
make sin offerings for himself as well as for
the people.[p] [4]No one takes this honor

d Nm 14, 29.—e Nm 14, 22-23; Dt 1, 35.—f Heb 3, 11; Ps 95, 11.—g Gn 2, 2.—h Ps 95, 11.—i Heb 3, 7-8.15; Ps 95, 7-8.—j Dt 31, 7; Jos 22, 4.—k Wis 18, 15-16; Is 49, 2; Eph 6, 17; Rv 1, 16; 2, 12.—l Jb 34, 21-22; Pss 90, 8; 139, 2-4.—m Heb 9, 11.24.—n Heb 2, 17-18; 5, 2.—o Heb 8, 1; 10, 19.22.35; 12, 2; Eph 3, 12.—p Lv 9, 7; 16, 15-17.30.34.

4, 14-16: These verses, which return to the theme first sounded in Heb 2, 16—3, 1, serve as an introduction to the section that follows. The author here alone calls Jesus *a great high priest* (14), a designation used by Philo for the Logos; perhaps he does so in order to emphasize Jesus' superiority over the Jewish high priest. He has *been tested in every way, yet without sin* (15); this indicates an acquaintance with the tradition of Jesus' temptations, not only at the beginning (as in Mk 1, 13) but throughout his public life (cf Lk 22, 28). Although the reign of the exalted Jesus is a theme that occurs elsewhere in Heb, and Jesus' throne is mentioned in Heb 1, 8, *the throne of grace* (16) refers to the throne of God. The similarity of v 16 to Heb 10, 19-22 indicates that the author is thinking of our confident access to God, made possible by the priestly work of Jesus.

5, 1-10: The true humanity of Jesus (see the note on Heb 2, 5-18) makes him a more rather than a less effective high priest to the Christian community. In Old Testament tradition, the high priest was identified with the people, guilty of personal sin just as they were (1-3). Even so, the office was of divine appointment (4), as was also the case with the sinless Christ (5). For v 6, see the note on Ps 110, 4. Although Jesus was Son of God, he was destined as a human being to learn obedience by accepting the suffering he had to endure (8). Because of his perfection through this experience of human suffering, he is the cause of salvation for all (9), a *high priest according to the order of Melchizedek* (10; cf Heb 5, 6 and Heb 7, 3).

5, 1: *To offer gifts and sacrifices for sins:* the author is thinking principally of the Day of Atonement rite, as is clear from Heb 9, 7. This ritual was celebrated to atone for "all the sins of the Israelites" (Lv 16, 34).

5, 2: *Deal patiently:* the Greek word *metriopathein* occurs only here in the Bible; this term was used by the Stoics to designate the golden mean between excess and defect of passion. Here it means rather the ability to sympathize.

upon himself but only when called by God, just as Aaron was.[q] 5 In the same way, it was not Christ who glorified himself in becoming high priest, but rather the one who said to him:

"You are my son;
this day I have begotten you";[r]

6 just as he says in another place:*

"You are a priest forever
according to the order of Melchizedek."[s]

7 In the days when he was in the flesh, he offered prayers and supplications with loud cries and tears to the one who was able to save him from death,* and he was heard because of his reverence.[t] 8 Son though he was,* he learned obedience from what he suffered;[u] 9 and when he was made perfect, he became the source of eternal salvation for all who obey him,[v] 10 declared by God high priest according to the order of Melchizedek.[w]

IV. JESUS' ETERNAL PRIESTHOOD AND ETERNAL SACRIFICE

Exhortation to Spiritual Renewal. 11 * About this we have much to say, and it is difficult to explain, for you have become sluggish in hearing. 12 Although you should be teachers by this time, you need to have someone teach you again the basic elements of the utterances of God. You need milk, [and] not solid food.[x] 13 Everyone who lives on milk lacks experience of the word of righteousness, for he is a child. 14 But solid food is for the mature, for those whose faculties are trained by practice to discern good and evil.

CHAPTER 6

1 Therefore, let us leave behind the basic teaching about Christ and advance to maturity, without laying the foundation all over again: repentance from dead works and faith in God,[y] 2 instruction about baptisms* and laying on of hands, resurrection of the dead and eternal judgment.[z] 3 And we shall do this, if only God permits. 4 For it is impossible in the case of those who have once been enlightened and tasted the heavenly gift* and shared in the holy Spirit[a] 5 and tasted the good word of God and the powers of the age to come,* 6 and then have fallen away, to bring them to repentance again, since they are recrucifying the Son of God for themselves* and holding him up to contempt.[b] 7 Ground that has absorbed the rain falling upon it repeatedly and brings forth crops useful to those for whom it is cultivated receives a blessing from God.[c] 8 But if it produces thorns and thistles, it is rejected; it will soon be cursed and finally burned.[d]

---

q Ex 28, 1.—r Ps 2, 7.—s Ps 110, 4.—t Mt 26, 38-44; Mk 14, 34-40; Lk 22, 41-46; Jn 12, 27.—u Rom 5, 19; Phil 2, 8.—v Heb 7, 24-25.28.—w Heb 6, 20; Ps 110, 4.—x 1 Cor 3, 1-3.—y Heb 9, 14.—z Heb 9, 10; Mk 7, 4 / Acts 6, 6; 8, 17; 13, 3; 19, 6; 1 Tm 4, 14; 5, 22; 2 Tm 1, 6.—a Heb 10, 26.32; Ps 34, 6; 2 Cor 4, 6.—b 2 Pt 2, 21.—c Gn 1, 11-12; Dt 11, 11.—d Gn 3, 17-18; Mt 7, 16; 13, 7; Mk 4, 7; Lk 8, 7.

5, 6-8: The author of Heb is the only New Testament writer to cite v 4 of Ps 110, here and in Heb 7, 17.21, to show that Jesus has been called by God to his role as priest. Verses 7-8 deal with his ability to sympathize with sinners, because of his own experience of the trials and weakness of human nature, especially fear of death. In his present exalted state, weakness is foreign to him, but he understands what we suffer because of his previous earthly experience.

5, 7: *He offered prayers . . . to the one who was able to save him from death:* at Gethsemane (cf Mk 14, 35), though some see a broader reference (see the note on Jn 12, 27).

5, 8: *Son though he was:* two different though not incompatible views of Jesus' sonship coexist in Heb, one associating it with his exaltation, the other with his preexistence. The former view is the older one (cf Rom 1, 4).

5, 11—6, 20: The central section of Heb (5, 11—10, 39) opens with a reprimand and an appeal. Those to whom the author directs his teaching about Jesus' priesthood, which is *difficult to explain,* have become *sluggish in hearing* and forgetful of even *the basic elements* (Heb 5, 12). But rather than treating of basic teachings, the author apparently believes that the challenge of more advanced ones may shake them out of their inertia (*therefore,* Heb 6, 1). The six examples of *basic teaching* in Heb 6, 1-3 are probably derived from a traditional catechetical list. No effort is made to address apostates, for their very hostility to the Christian message cuts them off completely from Christ (Heb 6, 4-8). This harsh statement seems to rule out repentance after apostasy, but perhaps the author deliberately uses hyperbole in order to stress the seriousness of abandoning Christ. With Heb 6, 9 a milder tone is introduced, and the criticism of the community (Heb 6, 1-3.9) is now balanced by an expression of confidence that its members are living truly Christian lives, and that God will justly reward their efforts (10). The author is concerned especially about their persevering (11-12), citing in this regard the achievement of Abraham, who relied on God's promise and on God's oath (13-18; cf Gn 22, 16), and proposes to them as a firm anchor of Christian hope the high priesthood of Christ, who is now living with God (19-20).

6, 2: *Instruction about baptisms:* not simply about Christian baptism but about the difference between it and similar Jewish rites, such as proselyte baptism, John's baptism, and the washings of the Qumran sectaries. *Laying on of hands:* in Acts 8, 17; 19, 6 this rite effects the infusion of the holy Spirit; in Acts 6, 6; 13, 3; 1 Tm 4, 14; 5, 22; 2 Tm 1, 6 it is a means of conferring some ministry or mission in the early Christian community.

6, 4: *Enlightened and tasted the heavenly gift:* this may refer to baptism and the Eucharist, respectively, but more probably means the neophytes' enlightenment by faith and their experience of salvation.

6, 5: *Tasted the good word of God and the powers of the age to come:* the proclamation of the *word of God* was accompanied by signs of the Spirit's power (1 Thes 1, 5; 1 Cor 2, 4).

6, 6: *They are recrucifying the Son of God for themselves:* a colorful description of the malice of apostasy, which is portrayed as again crucifying and deriding the Son of God.

9 But we are sure in your regard, beloved, of better things related to salvation, even though we speak in this way. 10 For God is not unjust so as to overlook your work and the love you have demonstrated for his name by having served and continuing to serve the holy ones. 11 We earnestly desire each of you to demonstrate the same eagerness for the fulfillment of hope until the end,[e] 12 so that you may not become sluggish, but imitators of those who, through faith and patience,[f] are inheriting the promises.*

God's Promise Immutable. 13 [g] When God made the promise to Abraham, since he had no one greater by whom to swear, "he swore by himself,"* 14 and said, "I will indeed bless you and multiply" you.[h] 15 And so, after patient waiting,[i] he obtained the promise.* 16 Human beings swear by someone greater than themselves; for them an oath serves as a guarantee and puts an end to all argument. 17 So when God wanted to give the heirs of his promise an even clearer demonstration of the immutability of his purpose, he intervened with an oath,[j] 18 so that by two immutable things,* in which it was impossible for God to lie, we who have taken refuge might be strongly encouraged to hold fast to the hope that lies before us.[k] 19 This we have as an anchor of the soul,[l] sure and firm, which reaches into the interior behind the veil,* 20 where Jesus has entered on our behalf as forerunner, becoming high priest forever according to the order of Melchizedek.[m]

CHAPTER 7

Melchizedek, a Type of Christ. 1 * This "Melchizedek, king of Salem and priest of God Most High,"* "met Abraham as he returned from his defeat of the kings" and "blessed him."[n] 2 And Abraham apportioned to him "a tenth of everything." His name first means righteous king, and he was also "king of Salem," that is, king of peace.* 3 Without father, mother, or ancestry, without beginning of days or end of life,* thus made to resemble the Son of God, he remains a priest forever.[o]

4 * See how great he is to whom the patriarch "Abraham [indeed] gave a tenth" of his spoils.[p] 5 The descendants of Levi who receive the office of priesthood have a commandment according to the law to exact tithes from the people, that is, from their brothers, although they also have come from the loins of Abraham.[q] 6 But he who was not of their ancestry received tithes from Abraham and blessed him who had received the promises. 7 Unquestionably, a lesser person is blessed by a greater.* 8 In

e Heb 3, 14.—f Heb 5, 11; Gal 3, 14; Eph 1, 13-14.—g Gn 22, 16.—h Gn 22, 17.—i Heb 6, 12; Rom 4, 20.—j Heb 6, 12.—k Nm 23, 19; 1 Sm 15, 29; Jn 8, 17; 2 Tm 2, 13.—l Heb 10, 20; Ex 26, 31-33; Lv 16, 2.—m Heb 5, 10; Ps 110, 4.—n Gn 14, 17-20.—o Heb 4, 14; 6, 6; 10, 29.—p Gn 14, 20.—q Nm 18, 21 / Gn 35, 11.

6, 12: *Imitators of those . . . inheriting the promises:* the author urges the addressees to imitate the faith of the holy people of the Old Testament, who now possess the promised goods of which they lived in hope. This theme will be treated fully in ch 11.

6, 13: *He swore by himself:* God's promise to Abraham, which he confirmed by an oath ("I swear by myself," Gn 22, 16), was the basis for the hope of all Abraham's descendants.

6, 15: *He obtained the promise:* this probably refers not to Abraham's temporary possession of the land but to the eschatological blessings that Abraham and the other patriarchs have now come to possess.

6, 18: *Two immutable things:* the promise and the oath, both made by God.

6, 19: *Anchor . . . into the interior behind the veil:* a mixed metaphor. The Holy of Holies, beyond the veil that separates it from the Holy Place (Ex 26, 31-33), is seen as the earthly counterpart of the heavenly abode of God. This theme will be developed in ch 9.

7, 1-3: Recalling the meeting between Melchizedek and Abraham described in Gn 14, 17-20, the author enhances the significance of this priest by providing the popular etymological meaning of his name and that of the city over which he ruled (2). Since Genesis gives no information on the parentage or the death of Melchizedek, he is seen here as a type of Christ, representing a priesthood that is unique and eternal (3).

7, 1: The author here assumes that Melchizedek was a priest of the God of Israel (cf Gn 14, 22 and the note there).

7, 2: In Gn 14, the Hebrew text does not state explicitly who gave tithes to whom. The author of Heb supplies Abraham as the subject, according to a contemporary interpretation of the passage. This supports the argument of the midrash and makes it possible to see in Melchizedek a type of Jesus. The messianic blessings of righteousness and peace are foreshadowed in the names "Melchizedek" and "Salem."

7, 3: *Without father, mother, or ancestry, without beginning of days or end of life:* this is perhaps a quotation from a hymn about Melchizedek. The rabbis maintained that anything not mentioned in the Torah does not exist. Consequently, since the Old Testament nowhere mentions Melchizedek's ancestry, birth, or death, the conclusion can be drawn that he *remains . . . forever.*

7, 4-10: The tithe that Abraham gave to Melchizedek (4), a practice later followed by the levitical priesthood (5), was a gift (6) acknowledging a certain superiority in Melchizedek, the foreign priest (7). This is further indicated by the fact that the institution of the levitical priesthood was sustained by hereditary succession in the tribe of Levi, whereas the absence of any mention of Melchizedek's death in Gn implies that his personal priesthood is permanent (8). The levitical priesthood itself, through Abraham, its ancestor, paid tithes to Melchizedek, thus acknowledging the superiority of his priesthood over its own (9-10).

7, 7: *A lesser person is blessed by a greater:* though this sounds like a principle, there are some examples in the Old Testament that do not support it (cf 2 Sm 14, 22; Jb 31, 20). The author may intend it as a statement of a liturgical rule.

the one case, mortal men receive tithes; in
the other, a man of whom it is testified that
he lives on. 9 One might even say that
Levi* himself, who receives tithes, was
tithed through Abraham, 10 for he was still
in his father's loins when Melchizedek met
him.

11 * If, then, perfection came through
the levitical priesthood, on the basis of
which the people received the law, what
need would there still have been for another priest to arise according to the order
of Melchizedek, and not reckoned according to the order of Aaron?[r] 12 When there is
a change of priesthood, there is necessarily
a change of law as well. 13 Now he of whom
these things are said* belonged to a different tribe, of which no member ever officiated at the altar. 14 It is clear that our
Lord arose from Judah,* and in regard to
that tribe Moses said nothing about
priests.[s] 15 * It is even more obvious if another priest is raised up after the likeness
of Melchizedek, 16 who has become so, not
by a law expressed in a commandment concerning physical descent but by the power
of a life that cannot be destroyed.* 17 For it
is testified:

"You are a priest forever
according to the order of Melchizedek."[t]

18 On the one hand, a former commandment is annulled because of its weakness
and uselessness,[u] 19 for the law brought
nothing to perfection; on the other hand, a
better hope* is introduced, through which
we draw near to God. 20 * And to the degree that this happened not without the
taking of an oath*—for others became
priests without an oath, 21 but he with an
oath, through the one who said to him:

"The Lord has sworn, and he will not
repent:[v]
'You are a priest forever' "—

22 [w] to that same degree has Jesus [also]
become the guarantee of an [even] better
covenant.* 23 Those priests were many because they were prevented by death from
remaining in office, 24 but he, because he
remains forever, has a priesthood that does
not pass away.[x] 25 Therefore, he is always
able to save those who approach God
through him, since he lives forever to make
intercession* for them.[y]

26 [z] It was fitting that we should have
such a high priest:* holy, innocent, undefiled, separated from sinners, higher than
the heavens.* 27 He has no need, as did the

r Heb 5, 6; Ps 110, 4.—s Gn 49, 10; Is 11, 1; Mt 1, 1-2.16.20; 2, 6; Lk 1, 27; 2, 4; Rom 1, 3; Rv 5, 5.—t Heb 5, 6; Ps 110, 4.—u Heb 10, 1.—v Ps 110, 4.—w Heb 8, 6-10; 9, 15-20; 10, 29; 12, 24; 13, 20.—x Heb 5, 6; 13, 8.—y Rom 8, 34; 1 Jn 2, 1; Rv 1, 18.—z Heb 4, 14.15.

7, 9: *Levi:* for the author this name designates not only the son of Jacob mentioned in Genesis but the priestly tribe that was thought to be descended from him.

7, 11-14: The levitical priesthood was not typified by the priesthood of Melchizedek, for Ps 110, 4 speaks of a priesthood of a new order, the order of Melchizedek, to arise in messianic times (11). Since the levitical priesthood served the Mosaic law, a new priesthood (12) would not come into being without a change in the law itself. Thus Jesus was not associated with the Old Testament priesthood, for he was a descendant of the tribe of Judah, which had never exercised the priesthood (13-14).

7, 13: *He of whom these things are said:* Jesus, the priest "according to the order of Melchizedek." According to the author's interpretation, Ps 110 spoke prophetically of Jesus.

7, 14: *Judah:* the author accepts the early Christian tradition that Jesus was descended from the family of David (cf Mt 1, 1-2.16.20; Lk 1, 27; 2, 4; Rom 1, 3). The Qumran community expected two Messiahs, one descended from Aaron and one from David; Heb shows no awareness of this view or at least does not accept it. Our author's view is not attested in contemporaneous Judaism.

7, 15-19: Jesus does not exercise a priesthood through family lineage but through his immortal existence (15-16), fulfilling Ps 110, 4 (17; cf Heb 7, 3). Thus he abolishes forever both the levitical priesthood and the law it serves, because neither could effectively sanctify people (18) by leading them into direct communication with God (19).

7, 16: *A life that cannot be destroyed:* the life to which Jesus has attained by virtue of his resurrection; it is his exaltation rather than his divine nature that makes him priest. The Old Testament speaks of the Aaronic priesthood as eternal (see Ex 40, 15); our author does not explicitly consider this possible objection to his argument but implicitly refutes it in vv 23-24.

7, 19: *A better hope:* this hope depends upon the sacrifice of the Son of God; through it we "approach the throne of grace" (Heb 4, 16); cf Heb 6, 19.20.

7, 20-25: As was the case with the promise to Abraham (Heb 6, 13), though not with the levitical priesthood, the eternal priesthood of the order of Melchizedek was confirmed by God's oath (20-21); cf Ps 110, 4. Thus Jesus becomes the guarantee of a permanent covenant (22) that does not require a succession of priests as did the levitical priesthood (23) because his high priesthood is eternal and unchangeable (24). Consequently, Jesus is able to save all who draw near to God through him since he is their ever-living intercessor (25).

7, 20: *An oath:* God's oath in Ps 110, 4.

7, 22: *An [even] better covenant:* better than the Mosaic covenant because it will be eternal, like the priesthood of Jesus upon which it is based. Verse 12 argued that a change of priesthood involves a change of law; since "law" and "covenant" are used correlatively, a new covenant is likewise instituted.

7, 25: *To make intercession:* the intercession of the exalted Jesus, not the sequel to his completed sacrifice but its eternal presence in heaven; cf Rom 8, 34.

7, 26-28: Jesus is precisely the high priest whom the human race requires, holy and sinless, installed far above humanity (26); one having no need to offer sacrifice daily for sins but making a single offering of himself (27) once for all. The law could only appoint high priests with human limitations, but the fulfillment of God's oath regarding the priesthood of Melchizedek (Ps 110, 4) makes the Son of God the perfect priest forever (28).

7, 26: This verse with its list of attributes is reminiscent of v 3 and is perhaps a hymnic counterpart to it, contrasting the exalted Jesus with Melchizedek.

high priests, to offer sacrifice day after
day,[a] first for his own sins and then for
those of the people; he did that once for all
when he offered himself.* 28 For the law
appoints men subject to weakness to be
high priests, but the word of the oath,
which was taken after the law, appoints a
son, who has been made perfect forever.[b]

CHAPTER 8

Heavenly Priesthood of Jesus.* 1 The
main point of what has been said is this: we
have such a high priest, who has taken his
seat at the right hand of the throne of the
Majesty in heaven,[c] 2 a minister of the
sanctuary* and of the true tabernacle that
the Lord, not man, set up.[d] 3 Now every
high priest is appointed to offer gifts and
sacrifices; thus the necessity for this one
also to have something to offer.[e] 4 If then
he were on earth, he would not be a priest,
since there are those who offer gifts according to the law.[f] 5 They worship in a copy
and shadow of the heavenly sanctuary, as
Moses was warned when he was about to
erect the tabernacle. For he says, "See that
you make everything according to the pattern shown you on the mountain."[g] 6 Now
he has obtained so much more excellent a
ministry as he is mediator of a better covenant, enacted on better promises.[h]

Old and New Covenants.* 7 For if that
first covenant had been faultless, no place
would have been sought for a second one.
8 But he finds fault with them and says:*
"Behold, the days are coming, says the Lord,[i]
when I will conclude a new covenant with the house of Israel and the house of Judah.
9 It will not be like the covenant I made with their fathers
the day I took them by the hand to lead them forth from the land of Egypt;
for they did not stand by my covenant
and I ignored them, says the Lord.
10 But this is the covenant I will establish with the house of Israel
after those days, says the Lord:
I will put my laws in their minds
and I will write them upon their hearts.
I will be their God,
and they shall be my people.[j]
11 And they shall not teach, each one his fellow citizen
and kinsman, saying, 'Know the Lord,'
for all shall know me,
from least to greatest.
12 For I will forgive their evildoing
and remember their sins no more."
13 [k] When he speaks of a "new" covenant,
he declares the first one obsolete. And
what has become obsolete and has grown
old is close to disappearing.*

a Heb 5, 3; 9, 12.25-28; 10, 11-14; Ex 29, 38-39; Lv 16, 6.11.15-17; Nm 28, 3-4; Is 53, 10; Rom 6, 10.—b Heb 5, 1.2.9.—c Heb 1, 3; 4, 14; 7, 26-28.—d Heb 9, 11; Ex 33, 7; Nm 24, 6 LXX.—e Heb 5, 1.—f Heb 7, 13.—g Heb 9, 23; Ex 25, 40; Acts 7, 44; Col 2, 17.—h Heb 7, 22; 9, 15.—i Jer 31, 31-34.—j Heb 10, 16-17.—k Rom 10, 4.

7, 27: Such daily sacrifice is nowhere mentioned in the Mosaic law; only on the Day of Atonement is it prescribed that the high priest must *offer sacrifice . . . for his own sins and then for those of the people* (Lv 16, 11-19). *Once for all:* this translates the Greek words *ephapax/hapax* that occur eleven times in Heb.

8, 1-6: The Christian community has in Jesus the kind of high priest described in Heb 7, 26-28. In virtue of his ascension Jesus has taken his place at God's right hand in accordance with Ps 110, 1 (1), where he presides over the heavenly sanctuary established by God himself (2). Like every high priest, he has his offering to make (3; cf Heb 9, 12.14), but it differs from that of the levitical priesthood in which he had no share (4) and which was in any case but a shadowy reflection of the true offering in the heavenly sanctuary (5). But Jesus' ministry in the heavenly sanctuary is that of mediator of a superior covenant that accomplishes what it signifies (6).

8, 2: *The sanctuary:* the Greek term could also mean "holy things" but bears the meaning "sanctuary" elsewhere in Heb (Heb 9, 8.12.24.25; 10, 19; 13, 11). *The true tabernacle:* the heavenly tabernacle *that the Lord . . . set up* is contrasted with the earthly tabernacle that Moses set up in the desert. *True* means "real" in contradistinction to a mere "copy and shadow" (5); compare the Johannine usage (e.g., Jn 1, 9; 6, 32; 15, 1). The idea that the earthly sanctuary is a reflection of a heavenly model may be based upon Ex 25, 9, but probably also derives from the Platonic concept of a real world of which our observable world is merely a shadow.

8, 7-13: Since the first covenant was deficient in accomplishing what it signified, it had to be replaced (7), as Jeremiah (Jer 31, 31-34) had prophesied (8-12). Even in the time of Jeremiah, the first covenant was antiquated (13). In Heb 7, 22-24, the superiority of the new covenant was seen in the permanence of its priesthood; here the superiority is based on better promises, made explicit in the citation of Jer 31 (LXX: 38), 31-34, namely, in the immediacy of the people's knowledge of God (11) and in the forgiveness of sin (12).

8, 8-12: In citing Jer the author follows the Septuagint; some apparent departures from it may be the result of a different Septuagintal text rather than changes deliberately introduced.

8, 13: *Close to disappearing:* from the prophet's perspective, not that of the author of Heb.

CHAPTER 9

The Worship of the First Covenant.* 1 Now [even] the first covenant had regulations for worship and an earthly sanctuary. 2 For a tabernacle was constructed, the outer one,* in which were the lampstand, the table, and the bread of offering; this is called the Holy Place.[l] 3 Behind the second veil* was the tabernacle called the Holy of Holies,[m] 4 in which were the gold altar of incense* and the ark of the covenant entirely covered with gold. In it were the gold jar containing the manna, the staff of Aaron that had sprouted, and the tablets of the covenant.[n] 5 Above it were the cherubim of glory overshadowing the place of expiation.* Now is not the time to speak of these in detail.[o]

6 With these arrangements for worship, the priests, in performing their service,* go into the outer tabernacle repeatedly,[p] 7 but the high priest alone goes into the inner one once a year, not without blood* that he offers for himself and for the sins of the people.[q] 8 In this way the holy Spirit shows that the way into the sanctuary had not yet been revealed while the outer tabernacle still had its place. 9 This is a symbol of the present time,* in which gifts and sacrifices are offered that cannot perfect the worshiper in conscience 10 but only in matters of food and drink and various ritual washings: regulations concerning the flesh, imposed until the time of the new order.[r]

Sacrifice of Jesus. 11 * But when Christ came as high priest of the good things that have come to be,* passing through the greater and more perfect tabernacle not made by hands, that is, not belonging to this creation,[s] 12 he entered once for all into the sanctuary, not with the blood of goats and calves but with his own blood, thus obtaining eternal redemption.[t] 13 For if the blood of goats and bulls and the sprinkling of a heifer's ashes* can sanctify those who are defiled so that their flesh is cleansed,[u] 14 how much more will the blood of Christ, who through the eternal spirit* offered himself unblemished to God, cleanse our consciences from dead works to worship the living God.[v]

---

l Ex 25, 23-30.—m Ex 26, 31-34.—n Ex 16, 32-34; 25, 10.16.21; 30, 1-10; Lv 16, 12-13; Nm 17, 2-7.16-26.—o Ex 25, 16-22; 26, 34; Lv 16, 14-15.—p Ex 27, 21; 30, 7; Lv 24, 8.—q Ex 30, 10; Lv 16, 1-14.—r Heb 13, 9; Lv 11; 14, 8; Nm 19, 11-21; Col 2, 16.—s Heb 4, 14; 10, 1.20.—t Heb 7, 27; Mt 26, 28.—u Heb 10, 4; Lv 16, 6-16; Nm, 19, 9.14-21.—v Heb 10, 10; Rom 5, 9; 1 Tm 3, 9; Ti 2, 14; 1 Pt 1, 18-19; 1 Jn 1, 7; Rv 1, 5.

9, 1-10: The regulations for worship under the old covenant permitted all the priests to enter the Holy Place (Heb 2, 6), but only the high priest to enter the Holy of Holies and then only once a year (3-5.7). The description of the sanctuary and its furnishings is taken essentially from Ex 25—26. This exclusion of the people from the Holy of Holies signified that they were not allowed to stand in God's presence (8) because their offerings and sacrifices, which were merely symbols of their need of spiritual renewal (10), could not obtain forgiveness of sins (9).

9, 2: *The outer one:* the author speaks of *the outer tabernacle* (6) and *the inner one* (7) rather than of one Mosaic tabernacle divided into two parts or sections.

9, 3: *The second veil:* what is meant is the veil that divided the Holy Place from the Holy of Holies. It is here called *the second,* because there was another veil at the entrance to the Holy Place, or "outer tabernacle" (Ex 26, 36).

9, 4: *The gold altar of incense:* Ex 30, 6 locates this altar in the Holy Place, i.e., the first tabernacle, rather than in the Holy of Holies. Neither is there any Old Testament support for the assertion that the jar of manna and the staff of Aaron were in the ark of the covenant. For the tablets of the covenant, see Ex 25, 16.

9, 5: *The place of expiation:* the gold "mercy seat" (Greek *hilastērion,* as in Rom 3, 25), where the blood of the sacrificial animals was sprinkled on the Day of Atonement (Lv 16, 14-15). This rite achieved "expiation" or atonement for the sins of the preceding year.

9, 6: *In performing their service:* the priestly services that had to be performed regularly in the Holy Place or *outer tabernacle* included burning incense on the incense altar twice each day (Ex 30, 7), replacing the loaves on the table of the bread of offering once each week (Lv 24, 8), and constantly caring for the lamps on the lampstand (Ex 27, 21).

9, 7: *Not without blood:* blood was essential to Old Testament sacrifice because it was believed that life was located in the blood. Hence blood was especially sacred, and its outpouring functioned as a meaningful symbol of cleansing from sin and reconciliation with God. Unlike Heb, the Old Testament never says that the blood is "offered." The author is perhaps retrojecting into his description of Mosaic ritual a concept that belongs to the New Testament antitype, as Paul does when he speaks of the Israelites' passage through the sea as a "baptism" (1 Cor 10, 2).

9, 9: *The present time:* this expression is equivalent to the "present age," used in contradistinction to the "age to come."

9, 11-14: Christ, the high priest of the spiritual blessings foreshadowed in the Old Testament sanctuary, has actually entered the true sanctuary of heaven that is not of human making (11). His place there is permanent, and his offering is his own blood that won eternal redemption (12). If the sacrifice of animals could bestow legal purification (13), how much more effective is the blood of the sinless, divine Christ who spontaneously offered himself to purge the human race of sin and render it fit for the service of God (14).

9, 11: *The good things that have come to be:* the majority of later manuscripts here read "the good things to come"; cf Heb 10, 1.

9, 13: *A heifer's ashes:* ashes from a red heifer that had been burned were mixed with water and used for the cleansing of those who had become ritually defiled by touching a corpse; see Nm 19, 9.14-21.

9, 14: *Through the eternal spirit:* this expression does not refer either to the holy Spirit or to the divine nature of Jesus but to the life of the risen Christ, "a life that cannot be destroyed" (Heb 7, 16).

15 * For this reason he is mediator of a
new covenant: since a death has taken
place for deliverance from transgressions
under the first covenant, those who are
called may receive the promised eternal inheritance.[w] 16 * Now where there is a will,
the death of the testator must be established. 17 For a will takes effect only at
death; it has no force while the testator is
alive. 18 Thus not even the first covenant
was inaugurated without blood. 19 * When
every commandment had been proclaimed
by Moses to all the people according to the
law, he took the blood of calves [and
goats], together with water and crimson
wool and hyssop, and sprinkled both the
book itself and all the people,[x] 20 saying,
"This is 'the blood of the covenant which
God has enjoined upon you.' "[y] 21 In the
same way, he sprinkled also the tabernacle* and all the vessels of worship with
blood.[z] 22 According to the law almost
everything is purified by blood,[a] and without the shedding of blood there is no forgiveness.*

23 * Therefore, it was necessary for the
copies of the heavenly things to be purified
by these rites, but the heavenly things
themselves by better sacrifices than these.[b]
24 For Christ did not enter into a sanctuary
made by hands, a copy of the true one, but
heaven itself, that he might now appear before God on our behalf.[c] 25 Not that he
might offer himself repeatedly, as the high
priest enters each year into the sanctuary
with blood that is not his own; 26 if that
were so, he would have had to suffer repeatedly from the foundation of the world.
But now once for all he has appeared at the
end of the ages* to take away sin by his sacrifice.[d] 27 Just as it is appointed that human
beings die once, and after this the judgment,[e] 28 so also Christ, offered once to
take away the sins of many,* will appear a
second time, not to take away sin but to
bring salvation to those who eagerly await
him.[f]

w 1 Tm 2, 5.—x Heb 9, 12-13.—y Ex 24, 3-8; Mt 26, 28; Mk 14, 24.—z Ex 40, 9; Lv 8, 15.19.—a Lv 17, 11.—b Jb 15, 15.—c Heb 7, 25; Rom 8, 34; 1 Jn 2, 1-2.—d Heb 7, 27; Jn 1, 29; Gal 4, 4.—e Gn 3, 19.—f Heb 10, 10; Is 53, 12.

9, 15-22: Jesus' role as *mediator of the new covenant* is based upon his sacrificial *death* (cf Heb 8, 6). His death has effected *deliverance from transgressions*, i.e., deliverance from sins committed under the old covenant, which the Mosaic sacrifices were incapable of effacing. Until this happened, the *eternal inheritance* promised by God could not be obtained (15). This effect of his work follows the human pattern by which a last will and testament becomes effective only with the death of the testator (16-17). The Mosaic covenant was also associated with death, for Moses made use of blood to seal the pact between God and the people (18-21). In Old Testament tradition, guilt could normally not be remitted without the use of blood (22; cf Lv 17, 11).

9, 16-17: *A will . . . death of the testator:* the same Greek word *diathēkē*, meaning "covenant" in vv 15 and 18, is used here with the meaning *will*. The new covenant, unlike the old, is at the same time a will that requires *the death of the testator*. Jesus as eternal Son is the one who established the new covenant together with his Father, author of both covenants; at the same time he is the testator whose death puts his *will* into effect.

9, 19-20: A number of details here are different from the description of this covenant rite in Ex 24, 5-8. Exodus mentions only calves ("young bulls," NAB), not goats (but this addition in Heb is of doubtful authenticity), says nothing of the use of *water and crimson wool and hyssop* (these features probably came from a different rite; cf Lv 14, 3-7; Nm 19, 6-18), and describes Moses as splashing blood on the altar, whereas Heb says he sprinkled it on the book (but both book and altar are meant to symbolize the agreement of God). The words of Moses are also slightly different from those in Exodus and are closer to the words of Jesus at the Last Supper in Mk 14, 24 // Mt 26, 28.

9, 21: According to Ex, the tabernacle did not yet exist at the time of the covenant rite. Moreover, nothing is said of sprinkling it with blood at its subsequent dedication (Ex 40, 9-11).

9, 22: *Without the shedding of blood there is no forgiveness:* in fact, ancient Israel did envisage other means of obtaining forgiveness; the Old Testament mentions contrition of heart (Ps 51, 19), fasting (Jl 2, 12), and almsgiving (Sir 3, 29). The author is limiting his horizon to the sacrificial cult, which did always involve the shedding of blood for its expiatory and unitive value.

9, 23-28: Since the blood of animals became a cleansing symbol among Old Testament prefigurements, it was necessary that the realities foreshadowed be brought into being by a shedding of blood that was infinitely more effective by reason of its worth (23). Christ did not simply prefigure the heavenly realities (24) by performing an annual sacrifice with a blood not his own (25); he offered the single sacrifice of himself as the final annulment of sin (26). Just as death is the unrepeatable act that ends a person's life, so Christ's offering of himself for all is the unrepeatable sacrifice that has once for all achieved redemption (27-28).

9, 26: *At the end of the ages:* the use of expressions such as this shows that the author of Heb, despite his interest in the Platonic concept of an eternal world above superior to temporal reality here below, nevertheless still clings to the Jewish Christian eschatology with its sequence of "the present age" and "the age to come."

9, 28: *To take away the sins of many:* the reference is to Is 53, 12. Since the Greek verb *anapherō* can mean both "to take away" and "to bear," the author no doubt intended to play upon both senses: Jesus took away sin by bearing it himself. See the similar wordplay in Jn 1, 29. *Many* is used in the Semitic meaning of "all" in the inclusive sense, as in Mk 14, 24. *To those who eagerly await him:* Jesus will appear *a second time* at the parousia, as the high priest reappeared on the Day of Atonement, emerging from the Holy of Holies, which he had entered *to take away sin*. This dramatic scene is described in Sir 50, 5-11.

CHAPTER 10

One Sacrifice instead of Many. 1 * Since
the law has only a shadow of the good
things to come,* and not the very image of
them, it can never make perfect those who
come to worship by the same sacrifices that
they offer continually each year.[g] 2 Otherwise, would not the sacrifices have ceased
to be offered, since the worshipers, once
cleansed, would no longer have had any
consciousness of sins? 3 But in those sacrifices there is only a yearly remembrance
of sins,[h] 4 for it is impossible that the blood
of bulls and goats take away sins.[i] 5 For
this reason, when he came into the world,
he said:*

"Sacrifice and offering you did not desire,[j]
but a body you prepared for me;
6 holocausts and sin offerings you took no delight in.
7 Then I said, 'As is written of me in the scroll,
Behold, I come to do your will, O God.' "

8 First he says, "Sacrifices and offerings,
holocausts and sin offerings,* you neither
desired nor delighted in." These are offered according to the law.[k] 9 Then he
says, "Behold, I come to do your will." He
takes away the first to establish the second.[l] 10 By this "will," we have been consecrated through the offering of the body
of Jesus Christ once for all.[m]

11 * Every priest stands daily at his
ministry, offering frequently those same
sacrifices that can never take away sins.[n]
12 But this one offered one sacrifice for
sins, and took his seat forever at the right
hand of God;[o] 13 now he waits until his
enemies are made his footstool.* 14 For by
one offering he has made perfect forever
those who are being consecrated.[p] 15 The
holy Spirit also testifies to us, for after saying:*

16 "This is the covenant I will establish with them after those days, says the Lord:
'I will put my laws in their hearts,
and I will write them upon their minds,' "[q]

17 he also says:*

"Their sins and their evildoing
I will remember no more."[r]

18 Where there is forgiveness of these, there
is no longer offering for sin.

---

g Heb 8, 5; Col 2, 17.—h Lv 16, 21; Nm 5, 15 LXX.—i Is 1, 11; Mi 6, 6-8.—j 5-7: Ps 40, 7-9.—k Heb 10, 5-6; Ps 40, 7.—l Heb 10, 7; Ps 40, 8; Mt 26, 39; Mk 14, 36; Lk 22, 42; Jn 6, 38.—m Heb 9, 12.14.—n Heb 7, 27; Dt 10, 8; 18, 7.—o 12-13: Ps 110, 1.—p Heb 9, 28.—q Heb 8, 10; Jer 31, 33.—r Heb 8, 12; Jer 31, 34.

10, 1-10: Christian faith now realizes that the Old Testament sacrifices did not effect the spiritual benefits to come but only prefigured them (1). For if the sacrifices had actually effected the forgiveness of sin, there would have been no reason for their constant repetition (2). They were rather a continual reminder of the people's sins (3). It is not reasonable to suppose that human sins could be removed by the blood of animal sacrifices (4). Christ, therefore, is here shown to understand his mission in terms of Ps 40, 6-8, cited according to the Septuagint (5-7). Jesus acknowledged that the Old Testament sacrifices did not remit the sins of the people and so, perceiving the will of God, offered his own body for this purpose (8-10).

10, 1: *A shadow of the good things to come:* the term *shadow* was used in Heb 8, 5 to signify the earthly counterpart of the Platonic heavenly reality. But here it means a prefiguration of what is to come in Christ, as it is used in the Pauline literature; cf Col 2, 17.

10, 5-7: A passage from Ps 40, 7-9a is placed in the mouth of the Son at his incarnation. As usual, the author follows the Septuagint text.There is a notable difference in v 5 (= Ps 40, 7b), where the Masoretic text reads "ears you have dug for me" ("ears open to obedience you gave me," NAB), but most Septuagint manuscripts have "a body you prepared for me," a reading obviously more suited to the interpretation of Heb.

10, 8: *Sacrifices and offerings, holocausts and sin offerings:* these four terms taken from the preceding passage of Ps 40 (with the first two changed to plural forms) are probably intended as equivalents to the four principal types of Old Testament sacrifices: peace offerings (Lv 3, here called *sacrifices*); cereal offerings (Lv 2, here called *offerings*); *holocausts* (Lv 1); and *sin offerings* (Lv 4—5). This last category includes the guilt offerings of Lv 5, 14-26.

10, 11-18: Whereas the levitical priesthood offered daily sacrifices that were ineffectual in remitting sin (11), Jesus offered a single sacrifice that won him a permanent place at God's right hand. There he has only to await the final outcome of his work (12-13; cf Ps 110, 1). Thus he has brought into being in his own person the new covenant prophesied by Jeremiah (Jer 31, 33-34) that has rendered meaningless all other offerings for sin (14-18).

10, 13: *Until his enemies are made his footstool:* Ps 110, 1 is again used; the reference here is to the period of time between the enthronement of Jesus and his second coming. The identity of the *enemies* is not specified; cf 1 Cor 15, 25-27.

10, 15-17: The testimony of the scriptures is now invoked to support what has just preceded. The passage cited is a portion of the new covenant prophecy of Jer 31, 31-34, which the author previously used in Heb 8, 8-12.

10, 17: *He also says:* these words are not in the Greek text, which has only *kai,* "also," but the expression *after saying* in v 15 seems to require such a phrase to divide the Jeremiah text into two sayings. Others understand "the Lord says" of v 16 (here rendered *says the Lord*) as outside the quotation and consider v 16b as part of the second saying. Two ancient versions and a number of minuscules introduce the words "then he said" or a similar expression at the beginning of v 17.

Recalling the Past.* [19]Therefore,
brothers, since through the blood of Jesus
we have confidence of entrance into the
sanctuary[s] [20]by the new and living way he
opened for us through the veil,[t] that is, his
flesh,* [21] [u] and since we have "a great
priest over the house of God,"* [22]let us approach with a sincere heart and in absolute
trust, with our hearts sprinkled clean from
an evil conscience* and our bodies washed
in pure water.[v] [23]Let us hold unwaver-
ingly to our confession that gives us hope,
for he who made the promise is trustworthy.[w] [24]We must consider how to rouse
one another to love and good works. [25]We
should not stay away from our assembly,*
as is the custom of some, but encourage
one another, and this all the more as you
see the day drawing near.[x]

[26] [y] If we sin deliberately* after receiving knowledge of the truth, there no longer
remains sacrifice for sins [27]but a fearful
prospect of judgment and a flaming fire
that is going to consume the adversaries.[z]
[28]Anyone who rejects the law of Moses* is
put to death without pity on the testimony
of two or three witnesses.[a] [29]Do you not
think that a much worse punishment is due
the one who has contempt for the Son of
God, considers unclean the covenant-blood
by which he was consecrated, and insults
the spirit of grace?[b] [30]We know the one
who said:

"Vengeance is mine; I will repay,"

and again:

"The Lord will judge his people."[c]

[31]It is a fearful thing to fall into the hands
of the living God.[d]

[32]Remember the days past when, after
you had been enlightened,* you endured a
great contest of suffering.[e] [33]At times you
were publicly exposed to abuse and affliction; at other times you associated yourselves with those so treated.[f] [34]You even
joined in the sufferings of those in prison
and joyfully accepted the confiscation of
your property, knowing that you had a better and lasting possession.[g] [35]Therefore,
do not throw away your confidence; it will
have great recompense.[h] [36]You need endurance to do the will of God and receive
what he has promised.[i]

37 "For, after just a brief moment,*
he who is to come shall come;
he shall not delay.[j]

38 But my just one shall live by faith,
and if he draws back I take no pleasure in him."[k]

[39]We are not among those who draw back
and perish, but among those who have
faith and will possess life.

s Heb 3, 6; 4, 16; 6, 19-20; Eph 1, 7; 3, 12.—t Jn 14, 6 / Heb 6, 19-20; 9, 8.11-12; Mt 27, 51; Mk 15, 38; Lk 23, 45.—u Heb 3, 6.—v Heb 9, 13-14; Ez 36, 25; 1 Cor 6, 11; Ti 3, 5; 1 Pt 3, 21.—w Heb 3, 1.6; 4, 14; 1 Cor 10, 13.—x Rom 13, 12; 1 Cor 3, 13.—y Heb 3, 12; 6, 4-8.—z Heb 10, 31; 9, 27; Is 26, 11 LXX; Zep 1, 18.—a Dt 17, 6.—b Heb 6, 6.—c Dt 32, 35.36; Rom 12, 19.—d Heb 10, 27; Mt 10, 28; Lk 12, 4-5.—e Heb 6, 4.—f 1 Cor 4, 9.—g Heb 13, 3; Mt 6, 19-20; Lk 12, 33-34.—h Heb 4, 16.—i Lk 21, 19.—j Is 26, 20; Hb 2, 3.—k Hb 2, 4; Rom 1, 17; Gal 3, 11.

10, 19-39: Practical consequences from these reflections on the priesthood and the sacrifice of Christ should make it clear that Christians may now have direct and confident access to God through the person of Jesus (19-20), who rules God's house as high priest (21). They should approach God with sincerity and faith, in the knowledge that through baptism their sins have been remitted (22), reminding themselves of the hope they expressed in Christ at that event (23). They are to encourage one another to Christian love and activity (24), not refusing, no matter what the reason, to participate in the community's assembly, especially in view of the parousia (25; cf 1 Thes 4, 13-18). If refusal to participate in the assembly indicates rejection of Christ, no sacrifice exists to obtain forgiveness for so great a sin (26); only the dreadful judgment of God remains (27). For if violation of the Mosaic law could be punished by death, how much worse will be the punishment of those who have turned their backs on Christ by despising his sacrifice and disregarding the gifts of the holy Spirit (28-29). Judgment belongs to the Lord, and he enacts it by his living presence (30-31). There was a time when the spirit of their community caused them to welcome and share their sufferings (32-34). To revitalize that spirit is to share in the courage of the Old Testament prophets (cf Is 26, 20; Hb 2, 3-4), the kind of courage that must distinguish the faith of the Christian (35-39).

10, 20: *Through the veil, that is, his flesh:* the term *flesh* is used pejoratively. As the temple veil kept people from entering the Holy of Holies (it was rent at Christ's death, Mk 15, 38), so the flesh of Jesus constituted an obstacle to approaching God.

10, 21: *The house of God:* this refers back to Heb 3, 6, "we are his house."

10, 22: *With our hearts sprinkled clean from an evil conscience:* as in Heb 9, 13 (see the note there), the sprinkling motif refers to the Mosaic rite of cleansing from ritual impurity. This could produce only an external purification, whereas sprinkling with the blood of Christ (Heb 9, 14) cleanses the *conscience. Washed in pure water:* baptism is elsewhere referred to as a washing; cf 1 Cor 6, 11; Eph 5, 26.

10, 25: *Our assembly:* the liturgical *assembly* of the Christian community, probably for the celebration of the Eucharist. *The day:* this designation for the parousia also occurs in the Pauline letters, e.g., Rom 2, 16; 1 Cor 3, 13; 1 Thes 5, 2.

10, 26: *If we sin deliberately:* verse 29 indicates that the author is here thinking of apostasy; cf Heb 3, 12; 6, 4-8.

10, 28: *Rejects the law of Moses:* evidently not any sin against the law, but idolatry. Dt 17, 2-7 prescribed capital punishment for idolaters who were convicted on the testimony of two or three witnesses.

10, 32: *After you had been enlightened:* "enlightenment" is an ancient metaphor for baptism (cf Eph 5, 14; Jn 9, 11), but see Heb 6, 4 and the note there.

10, 37-38: In support of his argument, the author uses Hb 2, 3-4 in a wording almost identical with the text of the Codex Alexandrinus of the Septuagint but with the first and second lines of v 4 inverted. He introduces it with a few words from Is 26, 20: *after just a brief moment.* Note the Pauline usage of Hb 2, 4 in Rom 1, 17; Gal 3, 11.

V. EXAMPLES, DISCIPLINE, DISOBEDIENCE

CHAPTER 11*

Faith of the Ancients. 1 Faith is the realization of what is hoped for and evidence* of things not seen.[l] 2 Because of it the ancients were well attested. 3 [m] By faith we understand that the universe was ordered by the word of God,* so that what is visible came into being through the invisible. 4 * By faith Abel offered to God a sacrifice greater than Cain's. Through this he was attested to be righteous, God bearing witness to his gifts, and through this, though dead, he still speaks.[n] 5 By faith Enoch was taken up so that he should not see death, and "he was found no more because God had taken him." Before he was taken up, he was attested to have pleased God.[o] 6 But without faith it is impossible to please him,[p] for anyone who approaches God must believe that he exists and that he rewards those who seek him.* 7 By faith Noah, warned about what was not yet seen, with reverence built an ark for the salvation of his household. Through this he condemned the world and inherited the righteousness that comes through faith.[q]

8 By faith Abraham obeyed when he was called to go out to a place that he was to receive as an inheritance; he went out, not knowing where he was to go.[r] 9 By faith he sojourned in the promised land as in a foreign country, dwelling in tents with Isaac and Jacob, heirs of the same promise;[s] 10 for he was looking forward to the city with foundations, whose architect and maker is God.[t] 11 By faith he received power to generate, even though he was past the normal age—and Sarah herself was sterile—for he thought that the one who had made the promise was trustworthy.[u] 12 So it was that there came forth from one man, himself as good as dead, descendants as numerous as the stars in the sky and as countless as the sands on the seashore.[v]

13 All these died in faith. They did not receive what had been promised but saw it and greeted it from afar and acknowledged themselves to be strangers and aliens on earth,[w] 14 for those who speak thus show that they are seeking a homeland. 15 If they had been thinking of the land from which they had come, they would have had opportunity to return. 16 But now they desire a better homeland, a heavenly one. Therefore, God is not ashamed to be called their God, for he has prepared a city for them.[x]

17 By faith Abraham, when put to the test, offered up Isaac, and he who had received the promises was ready to offer his only son,[y] 18 of whom it was said, "Through Isaac descendants shall bear

l Heb 1, 3; 3, 14; Rom 8, 24; 2 Cor 4, 18.—m Gn 1, 3; Ps 33, 6; Wis 9, 1; Jn 1, 3.—n Heb 12, 24; Gn 4, 4.10.—o Gn 5, 24; Sir 44, 16.—p Wis 4, 10.—q Gn 6, 8-22; Sir 44, 17-18; Mt 24, 37-39; Lk 17, 26-27; 1 Pt 3, 20; 2, Pt 2, 5.—r Gn 12, 1-4; 15, 7-21; Sir 44, 19-22; Acts 7, 2-8; Rom 4, 16-22.—s Gn 12, 8; 13, 12; 23, 4; 26, 3; 35, 27.—t Heb 12, 22; 13, 14; Rv 21, 10-22.—u Gn 17, 19; 21, 2; Rom 4, 19-21 / 1 Cor 10, 13.—v Gn 15, 5; 22, 17; 32, 13; Ex 32, 13; Dt 10, 22; Dn 3, 36 LXX.—w Gn 23, 4; Ps 39, 13.—x Heb 13, 14; Ex 3, 6.—y Gn 22, 1-10; Sir 44, 20; 1 Mc 2, 52; Jas 2, 21.

11, 1-40: This chapter draws upon the people and events of the Old Testament to paint an inspiring portrait of religious faith, firm and unyielding in the face of any obstacles that confront it. These pages rank among the most eloquent and lofty to be found in the Bible. They expand the theme announced in Heb 6, 12, to which the author now returns (Heb 10, 39). The material of this chapter is developed chronologically. Verses 3-7 draw upon the first nine chapters of Gn; vv 8-22, upon the period of the patriarchs; vv 23-31, upon the time of Moses; vv 32-38, upon the history of the judges, the prophets, and the Maccabean martyrs. The author gives the most extensive description of faith provided in the New Testament, though his interest does not lie in a technical, theological definition. In view of the needs of his audience he describes what authentic faith does, not what it is in itself. Through faith God guarantees the blessings to be hoped for from him, providing evidence in the gift of faith that what he promises will eventually come to pass (1). Because they accepted in faith God's guarantee of the future, the biblical personages discussed in vv 3-38 were themselves commended by God (2). Christians have even greater reason to remain firm in faith since they, unlike the Old Testament men and women of faith, have perceived the beginning of God's fulfillment of his messianic promises (39-40).

11, 1: *Faith is the realization . . . evidence:* the author is not attempting a precise definition. There is dispute about the meaning of the Greek words *hypostasis* and *elenchos,* here translated *realization* and *evidence,* respectively. *Hypostasis* usually means "substance," "being" (as translated in Heb 1, 3), or "reality" (as translated in Heb 3, 14); here it connotes something more subjective, and so *realization* has been chosen rather than "assurance" (RSV). *Elenchos,* usually "proof," is used here in an objective sense and so translated *evidence* rather than the transferred sense of "(inner) conviction" (RSV).

11, 3: *By faith . . . God:* this verse does not speak of the faith of the Old Testament men and women but is in the first person plural. Hence it seems out of place in the sequence of thought.

11, 4: The "Praise of the Ancestors" in Sir 44, 1—50, 21 gives a similar list of heroes. The Cain and Abel narrative in Gn 4, 1-16 does not mention Abel's faith. It says, however, that God "looked with favor on Abel and his offering" (Gn 4, 4); in view of v 6 the author probably understood God's favor to have been activated by Abel's faith. *Though dead, he still speaks:* possibly because his blood "cries out to me from the soil" (Gn 4, 10), but more probably a way of saying that the repeated story of Abel provides ongoing witness to faith.

11, 6: One must believe not only that God *exists* but that he is concerned about human conduct; the Old Testament defines folly as the denial of this truth; cf Ps 52, 2.

your name."[z] 19 He reasoned that God was
able to raise even from the dead,[a] and he
received Isaac back as a symbol.* 20 By
faith regarding things still to come Isaac*
blessed Jacob and Esau.[b] 21 By faith Jacob,
when dying, blessed each of the sons of
Joseph and "bowed in worship, leaning on
the top of his staff."[c] 22 By faith Joseph,
near the end of his life, spoke of the
Exodus of the Israelites and gave instructions about his bones.[d]

23 [e] By faith Moses was hidden by his
parents for three months after his birth,
because they saw that he was a beautiful
child, and they were not afraid of the
king's edict. 24 * By faith Moses, when he
had grown up, refused to be known as the
son of Pharaoh's daughter;[f] 25 he chose to
be ill-treated along with the people of God
rather than enjoy the fleeting pleasure of
sin. 26 He considered the reproach of the
Anointed greater wealth than the treasures
of Egypt, for he was looking to the recompense. 27 By faith he left Egypt, not fearing
the king's fury, for he persevered as if seeing the one who is invisible.[g] 28 By faith he
kept the Passover and sprinkled the blood,
that the Destroyer of the firstborn might
not touch them.[h] 29 By faith they crossed
the Red Sea as if it were dry land, but
when the Egyptians attempted it they were
drowned.[i] 30 By faith the walls of Jericho
fell after being encircled for seven days.[j]
31 By faith Rahab the harlot did not perish
with the disobedient, for she had received
the spies in peace.[k]

32 What more shall I say? I have not time
to tell of Gideon, Barak, Samson,
Jephthah, of David and Samuel and the
prophets,[l] 33 who by faith conquered kingdoms, did what was righteous, obtained
the promises; they closed the mouths of
lions,[m] 34 put out raging fires, escaped the
devouring sword; out of weakness they
were made powerful, became strong in battle, and turned back foreign invaders.[n]
35 Women received back their dead
through resurrection. Some were tortured
and would not accept deliverance, in order
to obtain a better resurrection.[o] 36 Others
endured mockery, scourging, even chains
and imprisonment.[p] 37 They were stoned,
sawed in two, put to death at sword's
point; they went about in skins of sheep or
goats, needy, afflicted, tormented.[q] 38 The
world was not worthy of them. They wan-
dered about in deserts and on mountains,
in caves and in crevices in the earth.[r]

39 Yet all these, though approved because of their faith, did not receive what
had been promised. 40 God had foreseen
something better for us, so that without us
they should not be made perfect.*

CHAPTER 12

God our Father.* 1 Therefore, since we
are surrounded by so great a cloud of witnesses, let us rid ourselves of every burden
and sin that clings to us* and persevere in
running the race that lies before us 2 while
keeping our eyes fixed on Jesus, the leader
and perfecter of faith. For the sake of the
joy that lay before him he endured the
cross, despising its shame, and has taken
his seat at the right of the throne of God.[s]
3 Consider how he endured such opposition
from sinners, in order that you may not
grow weary and lose heart. 4 In your struggle against sin you have not yet resisted to

z Gn 21, 12 LXX; Rom 9, 7.—a Rom 4, 16-22.—b Gn 27, 27-40.—c Gn 27, 38-40; 47, 31 LXX; 48, 15-16.—d Gn 50, 24-25.—e Ex 2, 2; Acts 7, 20.—f 24-25: Ex 2, 10-15; Acts 7, 23-29.—g Ex 2, 15; Acts 7, 29.—h Ex 12, 21-23; Wis 18, 25; 1 Cor 10, 10.—i Ex 14, 22-28.—j Jos 6, 12-21.—k Jos 2, 1-21; 6, 22-25; Jas 2, 25.—l Jgs 4, 6-22; 6, 11—8, 32; 11, 1—12, 7.—m Dn 6, 23.—n Dn 3, 22-25.49-50.—o 1 Kgs 17, 17-24; 2 Kgs 4, 18-37; 2 Mc 6, 18—7, 42.—p 2 Chr 36, 16; Jer 20, 2; 37, 15.—q 2 Chr 24, 21.—r 1 Mc 2, 28-30.—s Heb 2, 10; Ps 110, 1; Phil 2, 6-8.

11, 19: *As a symbol:* Isaac's "return from death" is seen as a *symbol* of Christ's resurrection. Others understand the words *en parabolē* to mean "in figure," i.e., the word *dead* is used figuratively of Isaac, since he did not really die. But in the one other place that *parabolē* occurs in Heb, it means symbol (Heb 9, 9).

11, 20-22: Each of these three patriarchs, Isaac, Jacob, and Joseph, had faith in the future fulfillment of God's promise and renewed this faith when near death.

11, 24-27: The reason given for Moses' departure from Egypt differs from the account in Ex 2, 11-15. The author also gives a christological interpretation of his decision to share the trials of his people.

11, 40: *So that without us they should not be made perfect:* the heroes of the Old Testament obtained their recompense only after the saving work of Christ had been accomplished. Thus they already enjoy what Christians who are still struggling do not yet possess in its fullness.

12, 1-13: Christian life is to be inspired not only by the Old Testament men and women of faith (1) but above all by Jesus. As the architect of Christian faith, he had himself to endure the cross before receiving the glory of his triumph (2). Reflection on his sufferings should give his followers courage to continue the struggle, if necessary even to the shedding of blood (3-4). Christians should regard their own sufferings as the affectionate correction of the Lord, who loves them as a father loves his children.

12, 1: *That clings to us:* the meaning is uncertain, since the Greek word *euperistatos,* translated *cling,* occurs only here. The papyrus P[46] and one minuscule read *euperispastos,* "easily distracting," which also makes good sense.

the point of shedding blood. 5 You have
also forgotten the exhortation addressed to
you as sons:

"My son, do not disdain the discipline
of the Lord[t]
or lose heart when reproved by him;
6 for whom the Lord loves, he disciplines;
he scourges every son he acknowledges."

7 Endure your trials as "discipline"; God
treats you as sons. For what "son" is there
whom his father does not discipline?[u] 8 If
you are without discipline, in which all
have shared, you are not sons but bastards.
9 Besides this, we have had our earthly
fathers to discipline us, and we respected
them. Should we not [then] submit all the
more to the Father of spirits and live?[v]
10 They disciplined us for a short time as
seemed right to them, but he does so for
our benefit, in order that we may share his
holiness. 11 At the time, all discipline seems
a cause not for joy but for pain, yet later it
brings the peaceful fruit of righteousness
to those who are trained by it.[w]

12 So strengthen your drooping hands
and your weak knees.[x] 13 Make straight
paths for your feet, that what is lame may
not be dislocated but healed.[y]

Penalties of Disobedience. 14 [z] Strive for
peace with everyone, and for that holiness
without which no one will see the Lord. 15
* See to it that no one be deprived of the
grace of God, that no bitter root spring up
and cause trouble, through which many
may become defiled,[a] 16 that no one be an
immoral or profane person like Esau, who
sold his birthright for a single meal.[b] 17 For
you know that later, when he wanted to inherit his father's blessing, he was rejected
because he found no opportunity to change
his mind, even though he sought the blessing with tears.[c]

18 * You have not approached that
which could be touched[d] and a blazing fire
and gloomy darkness and storm* 19 and a
trumpet blast and a voice speaking words
such that those who heard begged that no
message be further addressed to them,[e]
20 for they could not bear to hear the command: "If even an animal touches the
mountain, it shall be stoned."[f] 21 Indeed,
so fearful was the spectacle that Moses
said, "I am terrified and trembling."[g]
22 No, you have approached Mount Zion
and the city of the living God, the heavenly
Jerusalem, and countless angels in festal
gathering,[h] 23 and the assembly of the
firstborn enrolled in heaven,* and God the
judge of all, and the spirits of the just made
perfect,[i] 24 and Jesus, the mediator of a
new covenant, and the sprinkled blood
that speaks more eloquently* than that of
Abel.[j]

25 See that you do not reject the one who
speaks. For if they did not escape when
they refused the one who warned them on
earth, how much more in our case if we
turn away from the one who warns from
heaven.[k] 26 His voice shook the earth at
that time, but now he has promised, "I will
once more shake not only earth but
heaven."[l] 27 That phrase, "once more,"
points to [the] removal of shaken, created
things, so that what is unshaken may remain.[m] 28 Therefore, we who are receiving
the unshakable kingdom should have

t 5-6: Prv 3, 11-12 / Dt 8, 5; 1 Cor 11, 32.—u Prv 13, 24; Sir 30, 1.—v Nm 16, 22; 27, 16 LXX.—w 2 Cor 4, 17; Phil 1, 11; Jas 3, 18.—x Is 35, 3; Sir 25, 23; Jb 4, 3-4.—y Prv 4, 26 LXX.—z Rom 12, 18; 14, 19.—a Dt 29, 18 (17 LXX).—b Gn 25, 33.—c Gn 27, 34-38.—d Ex 19, 12-14; Dt 4, 11; 5, 22-23.—e Ex 19, 16.19; 20, 18-19.—f Ex 19, 12-13.—g Dt 9, 19.—h Gal 4, 26; Rv 21, 2.—i Lk 10, 20; Rv 5, 11.—j Heb 7, 22; 8, 6; 9, 15 / Heb 11, 4; Gn 4, 10.—k Ex 20, 19.—l Ex 19, 18; Jgs 5, 4-5; Ps 68, 9; Hg 2, 6.—m Is 66, 22; Mt 24, 35; Mk 13, 31; Lk 21, 33.

12, 15-17: Esau serves as an example in two ways: his *profane* attitude illustrates the danger of apostasy, and his inability to secure a blessing afterward illustrates the impossibility of repenting after falling away (see Heb 6, 4-6).

12, 18-29: As a final appeal for adherence to Christian teaching, the two covenants, of Moses and of Christ, are compared. The Mosaic covenant, the author argues, is shown to have originated in fear of God and threats of divine punishment (18-21). The covenant in Christ gives us direct access to God (22), makes us members of the Christian community, God's children, a sanctified people (23), who have Jesus as mediator to speak for us (24). Not to heed the voice of the risen Christ is a graver sin than the rejection of the word of Moses (25-26). Though Christians fall away, God's kingdom in Christ will remain and his justice will punish those guilty of deserting it (28-29).

12, 18-24: This remarkably beautiful passage contrasts two great assemblies of people: that of the Israelites gathered at Mount Sinai for the sealing of the old covenant and the promulgation of the Mosaic law, and that of the followers of Jesus gathered at *Mount Zion, the heavenly Jerusalem,* the assembly of the *new covenant.* This latter scene, marked by the presence of *countless angels* and of *Jesus* with his redeeming *blood,* is reminiscent of the celestial liturgies of the Book of Revelation.

12, 23: *The assembly of the firstborn enrolled in heaven:* this expression may refer to the angels of v 22, or to the heroes of the Old Testament (see ch 11), or to the entire assembly of the new covenant.

12, 24: *Speaks more eloquently:* the blood of Abel, the first human blood to be shed, is contrasted with that of Jesus. Abel's blood cried out from the earth for vengeance, but the blood of Jesus has opened the way for everyone, providing cleansing and access to God (Heb 10, 19).

gratitude, with which we should offer worship pleasing to God in reverence and
awe.[n] 29 For our God is a consuming fire.[o]

VI. FINAL EXHORTATION, BLESSING, GREETINGS

CHAPTER 13

1 * Let mutual love continue. 2 Do not
neglect hospitality, for through it some
have unknowingly entertained angels.[p]
3 Be mindful of prisoners as if sharing their
imprisonment, and of the ill-treated as of
yourselves, for you also are in the body.[q]
4 Let marriage be honored among all and
the marriage bed be kept undefiled, for
God will judge the immoral and adulterers.[r] 5 Let your life be free from love of
money but be content with what you have,
for he has said, "I will never forsake you or
abandon you."[s] 6 Thus we may say with
confidence:

"The Lord is my helper,
[and] I will not be afraid.
What can anyone do to me?"[t]

7 Remember your leaders who spoke the
word of God to you. Consider the outcome
of their way of life and imitate their faith.
8 Jesus Christ is the same yesterday, today,
and forever.[u]

9 Do not be carried away by all kinds of
strange teaching.* It is good to have our
hearts strengthened by grace and not by
foods, which do not benefit those who live
by them.[v] 10 We have an altar* from which
those who serve the tabernacle have no
right to eat. 11 The bodies of the animals
whose blood the high priest brings into the
sanctuary as a sin offering are burned outside the camp.[w] 12 Therefore, Jesus also
suffered outside the gate, to consecrate the
people by his own blood.[x] 13 Let us then go
to him outside the camp, bearing the reproach that he bore. 14 For here we have no
lasting city, but we seek the one that is to
come.[y] 15 Through him [then] let us continually offer God a sacrifice of praise, that
is, the fruit of lips that confess his name.[z]
16 Do not neglect to do good and to share
what you have; God is pleased by sacrifices
of that kind.[a]

17 * Obey your leaders and defer to
them, for they keep watch over you and
will have to give an account, that they may
fulfill their task with joy and not with sorrow, for that would be of no advantage to
you.

18 Pray for us, for we are confident that
we have a clear conscience, wishing to act
rightly in every respect. 19 I especially ask
for your prayers that I may be restored to
you very soon.

20 * May the God of peace, who brought
up from the dead the great shepherd of the
sheep by the blood of the eternal covenant,
Jesus our Lord,[b] 21 furnish you with all
that is good, that you may do his will. May
he carry out in you what is pleasing to him
through Jesus Christ, to whom be glory
forever [and ever]. Amen.

22 Brothers, I ask you to bear with this
message of encouragement, for I have written to you rather briefly. 23 I must let you
know that our brother Timothy has been
set free. If he comes soon, I shall see you
together with him.[c] 24 Greetings to all your
leaders and to all the holy ones. Those
from Italy send you greetings. 25 Grace be
with all of you.[d]

n Dn 7, 14.18 / Rom 1, 9.—o Dt 4, 24; Is 33, 14.—p Gn 18, 3; 19, 2-3; Jgs 6, 11-22; Tb 5, 4.—q Mt 25, 36.—r 1 Cor 5, 13; Eph 5, 5.—s Dt 31, 6.8; Jos 1, 5.—t Pss 27, 1-3; 118, 6.—u Heb 1, 12; 7, 24; Rv 1, 17.—v Rom 14, 17; 1 Cor 8, 8; Eph 4, 14; Col 2, 16.—w Ex 29, 14; Lv 16, 27.—x Mt 21, 39; Mk 12, 8; Lk 20, 15; Jn 19, 17.—y Heb 11, 10.14.—z Hos 14, 3.—a Phil 4, 18.—b Is 63, 11; Zec 9, 11; Jn 10, 11; Acts 2, 24; Rom 15, 33.—c Acts 16, 1.—d Ti 3, 15.

13, 1-16: After recommendations on social and moral matters (1-6), the letter turns to doctrinal issues. The fact that the original leaders are dead should not cause the recipients of this letter to lose their faith (7), for Christ still lives and he remains always the same (8). They must not rely for their personal sanctification on regulations concerning foods (9), nor should they entertain the notion that Judaism and Christianity can be intermingled (10; cf the notes on Gal 2, 11-14 and Gal 2, 15-21). As Jesus died separated from his own people, so must the Christian community remain apart from the religious doctrines of Judaism (11-14). Christ must be the heart and center of the community (15-16).

13, 9: *Strange teaching:* this doctrine about *foods* probably refers to the Jewish food laws; in view of v 10, however, the author may be thinking of the Mosaic sacrificial banquets.

13, 10: *We have an altar:* this does not refer to the Eucharist, which is never clearly mentioned in Heb, but to the sacrifice of Christ.

13, 17-25: Recommending obedience to the leaders of the community, the author asks for prayers (17-19). The letter concludes with a blessing (20-21), a final request for the acceptance of its message (22), information regarding Timothy (23), and general greetings (24-25).

13, 20-21: These verses constitute one of the most beautiful blessings in the New Testament. The resurrection of Jesus is presupposed throughout Heb, since it is included in the author's frequently expressed idea of his exaltation, but this is the only place where it is explicitly mentioned.

THE CATHOLIC LETTERS

In addition to the thirteen letters attributed to Paul and the Letter to the Hebrews, the New Testament contains seven other letters. Three of these are attributed to John, two to Peter, and one each to James and Jude, all personages of the apostolic age. The term "catholic letter" first appears, with reference only to 1 John, in the writings of Apollonius of Ephesus, a second-century apologist, known only from a citation in Eusebius' *Ecclesiastical History*. Eusebius himself (A.D. 260-340) used the term to refer to all seven letters.

The reason for the term "catholic," which means "universal," was the perception that these letters, unlike those of Paul, which were directed to a particular local church, were apparently addressed more generally to the universal church. This designation is not entirely accurate, however. On the one hand, Hebrews has no specifically identified addressees, and originally this was probably true of Ephesians as well. On the other hand, 3 John is addressed to a named individual, 2 John to a specific, though unnamed, community, and 1 Peter to a number of churches that are specified as being located in Asia Minor.

While all seven of these writings begin with an epistolary formula, several of them do not appear to be real letters in the modern sense of the term. In the ancient world it was not unusual to cast an exhortation in the form of a letter for literary effect, a phenomenon comparable to the "open letter" that is sometimes used today.

With the exception of 1 Peter and 1 John, the ancient church showed reluctance to include the catholic letters in the New Testament canon. The reason for this was widespread doubt whether they had actually been written by the apostolic figures to whom they are attributed. The early Christians saw the New Testament as the depository of apostolic faith; therefore, they wished to include only the testimony of apostles. Today we distinguish more clearly between the authorship of a work and its canonicity: even though written by other, later witnesses than those whose names they bear, these writings nevertheless testify to the apostolic faith and constitute canonical scripture. By the late fourth or early fifth centuries, most objections had been overcome in both the Greek and the Latin churches (though not in the Syriac), and all seven of the catholic letters have since been acknowledged as canonical.

THE LETTER OF JAMES

INTRODUCTION

The person to whom this letter is ascribed can scarcely be one of the two members of the Twelve who bore the name James (see Mt 10, 2-3; Mk 3, 17-18; Lk 6, 14-15), for he is not identified as an apostle but only as "slave of God and of the Lord Jesus Christ" (1, 1). This designation most probably refers to the third New Testament personage named James, a relative of Jesus who is usually called "brother of the Lord" (see Mt 13, 55; Mk 6, 3). He was the leader of the Jewish Christian community in Jerusalem whom Paul acknowledged as one of the "pillars" (Gal 2, 9). In Acts he appears as the authorized spokesman for the Jewish Christian position in the early Church (Acts 12, 17; 15, 13-21). According to the Jewish historian Josephus (Antiquities *20, 9, 1 §§200-203), he was stoned to death by the Jews under the high priest Ananus II in A.D. 62.*

The letter is addressed to "the twelve tribes in the dispersion." In Old Testament terminology the term "twelve tribes" designates the people of Israel; the "dispersion" or "diaspora" refers to the non-Palestinian Jews who had settled throughout the Greco-Roman world (see Jn 7, 35). Since in Christian thought the church is the new Israel, the address probably designates the Jewish Christian churches located in Palestine, Syria, and elsewhere. Or perhaps the letter is meant more generally for all Christian communities, and the "dispersion" has the symbolic meaning of exile from our true home, as it has in the address of 1 Peter (1, 1). The letter is so markedly Jewish in character that some scholars have regarded it as a Jewish document subsequently "baptized" by a few Christian insertions, but such an origin is scarcely tenable in view of the numerous contacts discernible between the Letter of James and other New Testament literature.

From the viewpoint of its literary form, James is a letter only in the most conventional sense; it has none of the characteristic features of a real letter except the address. It belongs rather to the genre of parenesis *or exhortation and is concerned almost exclusively with ethical conduct. It therefore falls within the tradition of Jewish wisdom literature, such as can be found in the Old Testament (Proverbs, Sirach) and in the extracanonical Jewish literature* (Testaments of the Twelve Patriarchs, *the* Books of Enoch, *the* Manual of Discipline *found at Qumran). More specifically, it consists of sequences of didactic proverbs, comparable to Tb 4, 5-19, to many passages in Sirach, and to sequences of sayings in the synoptic gospels. Numerous passages in James treat of subjects that also appear in the synoptic sayings of Jesus, especially in Matthew's Sermon on the Mount, but the correspondences are too general to establish any literary dependence. James represents a type of early Christianity that emphasized sound teaching and responsible moral behavior. Ethical norms are derived not primarily from christology, as in Paul, but from a concept of salvation that involves conversion, baptism, forgiveness of sin, and expectation of judgment (1, 17; 4, 12).*

Paradoxically, this very Jewish work is written in an excellent Greek style, which ranks among the best in the New Testament and appears to be the work of a trained Hellenistic writer. Those who continue to regard James of Jerusalem as its author are therefore obliged to suppose that a secretary must have put the letter into its present literary form. This assumption is not implausible in the light of ancient practice. Some regard the letter as one of the earliest writings in the New Testament and feel that its content accurately reflects what we would expect of the leader of Jewish Christianity. Moreover, they argue that the type of Jewish Christianity reflected in the letter cannot be situated historically after the fall of Jerusalem in A.D. 70.

Others, however, believe it more likely that James is a pseudonymous work of a later period. In addition to its Greek style, they observe further that (a) the prestige that the

greed. Accursed children! 15 Abandoning
the straight road, they have gone astray,
following the road of Balaam, the son of
Bosor,* who loved payment for wrongdoing,[t] 16 but he received a rebuke for his
own crime: a mute beast spoke with a
human voice and restrained the prophet's
madness.[u]

17 These people are waterless springs and
mists driven by a gale; for them the gloom
of darkness has been reserved.[v] 18 For,
talking empty bombast, they seduce with
licentious desires of the flesh those who
have barely escaped* from people who live
in error.[w] 19 They promise them freedom,
though they themselves are slaves of corruption, for a person is a slave of whatever
overcomes him.[x] 20 For if they, having escaped the defilements of the world through
the knowledge of [our] Lord and savior
Jesus Christ, again become entangled and
overcome by them, their last condition is
worse than their first.[y] 21 For it would have
been better for them not to have known the
way of righteousness than after knowing it
to turn back from the holy commandment
handed down* to them.[z] 22 What is expressed in the true proverb has happened
to them,[a] "The dog returns to its own
vomit," and "A bathed sow returns to wal-
lowing in the mire."*

IV. THE DELAY OF THE SECOND COMING

CHAPTER 3

Denial of the Parousia. 1 * This is now,
beloved, the second letter I am writing to
you; through them by way of reminder I
am trying to stir up your sincere disposition, 2 to recall the words previously spoken by the holy prophets and the commandment of the Lord and savior through
your apostles.[b] 3 Know this first of all, that
in the last days scoffers* will come [to]
scoff, living according to their own desires[c]
4 and saying, "Where is the promise of his
coming?* From the time when our ancestors fell asleep, everything has remained as
it was from the beginning of creation."[d]
5 They deliberately ignore the fact that the
heavens existed of old and earth was
formed out of water and through water* by
the word of God;[e] 6 through these the
world that then existed was destroyed,[f]
deluged with water.* 7 The present
heavens and earth have been reserved by
the same word for fire, kept for the day of
judgment and of destruction of the godless.[g]

8 * But do not ignore this one fact, beloved, that with the Lord one day is like a
thousand years* and a thousand years like
one day.[h] 9 The Lord does not delay his
promise, as some regard "delay," but he is
patient with you, not wishing that any
should perish but that all should come to

t Nm 31, 16; Jude 11.—u Nm 22, 28-33.—v Jude 12-13.—w Jude 16.—x Jn 8, 34; Rom 6, 16-17.—y Mt 12, 45.—z Ez 3, 20.—a Prv 26, 11.—b Jude 17.—c 1 Tm 4, 1; 2 Tm 3, 1; Jude 18.—d Is 5, 19.—e Gn 1, 2.6.8; Ps 24, 2.—f Gn 7, 21.—g Is 51, 6; Mt 3, 12.—h Ps 90, 4.

2, 15: *Balaam, the son of Bosor:* in Nm 22, 5, Balaam is said to be the son of Beor, and it is this name that turns up in a few ancient Greek manuscripts by way of "correction" of the text. Balaam is not portrayed in such a bad light in Nm 22. His evil reputation and his *madness* (16), and possibly his surname Bosor, may have come from a Jewish tradition about him in the first/second century, of which we no longer have any knowledge.

2, 18: *Barely escaped:* some manuscripts read "really escaped."

2, 21: *Commandment handed down:* cf 2 Pt 3, 2 and Jude 3.

2, 22: The second proverb is of unknown origin, while the first appears in Prv 26, 11.

3, 1-4: The false teachers not only flout Christian morality (cf Jude 8-19); they also deny the second coming of Christ and the judgment (4; cf 2 Pt 3, 7). They seek to justify their licentiousness by arguing that the promised return of Christ has not been realized and the world is the same, no better than it was before (3-4). The author wishes to strengthen the faithful against such errors by reminding them in this *second letter* of the instruction in 1 Pt and of the teaching of the *prophets* and of Christ, conveyed through the *apostles* (1-2; cf Jude 17); cf 1 Pt 1, 10-12.16-21, especially 16-21; Eph 2, 20.

3, 3: *Scoffers:* cf Jude 18, where, however, only the passions of the scoffers are mentioned, not a denial on their part of Jesus' parousia.

3, 4-7: The false teachers tried to justify their immorality by pointing out that the promised *coming (parousia)* of the Lord has not yet occurred, even though early Christians expected it in their day. They thus insinuate that God is not guiding the world's history anymore, since nothing has changed and the first generation of Christians, *our ancestors* (4), has all died by this time. The author replies that, just as God destroyed the earth by water in the flood (5-6, cf 2 Pt 2, 5), so he will destroy it along with the false teachers on judgment day (7). *The word of God,* which called the world into being (Gn 1; Ps 33, 6) and *destroyed* it by the waters of a flood, will destroy it again by fire on *the day of judgment* (5-7).

3, 5: *Formed out of water and through water:* Gn 1, 2.6-8 is reflected as well as Greek views that water was the basic element from which all is derived.

3, 6: *Destroyed, deluged with water:* cf 2 Pt 2, 5; Gn 7, 11—8, 2.

3, 8-10: The scoffers' objection (4) is refuted also by showing that *delay* of the Lord's second coming is not a failure to fulfill his word but rather a sign of his patience: God is giving time for repentance before the final judgment (cf Wis 11, 23-26; Ez 18, 23; 33, 11).

3, 8: Cf Ps 90, 4.

writer is assumed to enjoy points to the later legendary reputation of James; (b) the discussion of the importance of good works seems to presuppose a debate subsequent to that in Paul's own day; (c) the author does not rely upon prescriptions of the Mosaic law, as we would expect from the historical James; (d) the letter contains no allusions to James's own history and to his relationship with Jesus or to the early Christian community of Jerusalem. For these reasons, many recent interpreters assign James to the period A.D. 90-100.

The principal divisions of the Letter of James are the following:

I. Address (1, 1)
II. The Value of Trials and Temptation (1, 2-18)
III. Exhortations and Warnings (1, 19—5, 12)
IV. The Power of Prayer (5, 13-20)

I. ADDRESS

CHAPTER 1

1 James, a slave of God and of the Lord
Jesus Christ,* to the twelve tribes in the
dispersion, greetings. [a]

II. THE VALUE OF TRIALS AND TEMPTATION

Perseverance in Trial. 2 [b] Consider it all
joy, my brothers, when you encounter various trials,* 3 for you know that the testing* of your faith produces perseverance.
4 And let perseverance be perfect, so that
you may be perfect and complete, lacking
in nothing. 5 But if any of you lacks wisdom,* he should ask God who gives to all
generously and ungrudgingly, and he will
be given it. [c] 6 But he should ask in faith,
not doubting, for the one who doubts is
like a wave of the sea that is driven and
tossed about by the wind. [d] 7 For that person must not suppose that he will receive
anything from the Lord, 8 since he is a man
of two minds, unstable in all his ways.
9 The brother in lowly circumstances*
should take pride in his high standing, [e]
10 and the rich one in his lowliness, for he
will pass away "like the flower of the
field." [f] 11 For the sun comes up with its
scorching heat and dries up the grass, its
flower droops, and the beauty of its appearance vanishes. So will the rich person
fade away in the midst of his pursuits.
Temptation. 12 [g] Blessed is the man who
perseveres in temptation,* for when he has
been proved he will receive the crown of
life that he promised to those who love
him. 13 * No one experiencing temptation
should say, "I am being tempted by God";
for God is not subject to temptation to evil,
and he himself tempts no one. [h] 14 Rather,
each person is tempted when he is lured
and enticed by his own desire. 15 Then desire conceives and brings forth sin, and
when sin reaches maturity it gives birth to
death.

a Jn 7, 35; 1 Pt 1, 1.—b Rom 5, 3-5; 1 Pt 1, 6; 4, 13-16.—c Prv 2, 2-6; Wis 9, 4.9-12.—d Mt 7, 7; Mk 11, 24.—e Jas 2, 5.—f Is 40, 6-7.—g 1 Cor 9, 25; 2 Tm 4, 8; 1 Pt 5, 4; Rv 2, 10.—h Sir 15, 11-20; 1 Cor 10, 13.

1, 1: *James, a slave of God and of the Lord Jesus Christ:* a declaration of the writer's authority for instructing the Christian communities; cf Rom 1, 1. Regarding the identity of the author, see Introduction. *Dispersion:* see Introduction.

1, 2: *Consider it all joy . . . various trials:* a frequent teaching of the New Testament derived from the words and sufferings of Jesus (Mt 5, 10-12; Jn 10, 11; Acts 5, 41).

1, 3-8: The sequence of testing, perseverance, and being perfect and complete indicates the manner of attaining spiritual maturity and full preparedness for the coming of Christ (Jas 5, 7-12; cf 1 Pt 1, 6-7; Rom 5, 3-5). These steps require wisdom (5).

1, 5: *Wisdom:* a gift that God readily grants to all who ask in faith and that sustains the Christian in times of trial. It is a kind of knowledge or understanding not accessible to the unbeliever or those who doubt, which gives the recipient an understanding of the real importance of events. In this way a Christian can deal with adversity with great calm and hope (cf 1 Cor 2, 6-12).

1, 9-11: Throughout his letter (see Jas 2, 5; 4, 10.13-16; 5, 1-6), the author reaffirms the teaching of Jesus that worldly prosperity is not necessarily a sign of God's favor but can even be a hindrance to proper humility before God (cf Lk 6, 20-25; 12, 16-21; 16, 19-31).

1, 12: *Temptation:* the Greek word used here is the same one used for "trials" in v 2. *The crown of life:* in ancient Palestine, crowns or wreaths of flowers were worn at festive occasions as signs of joy and honor. In the Hellenistic world, wreaths were given as a reward to great statesmen, soldiers, athletes. *Life:* here means eternal life. *He promised:* some manuscripts read "God" or "the Lord," while the best witnesses do not specify the subject of "promised."

1, 13-15: It is contrary to what we know of God for God to be the author of human temptation (13). In the commission of a sinful act, one is first beguiled by passion (14), then consent is given, which in turn causes the sinful act. When sin permeates the entire person, it incurs the ultimate penalty of death (15).

16 * Do not be deceived, my beloved brothers: 17 all good giving and every perfect gift* is from above, coming down from the Father of lights, with whom there is no alteration or shadow caused by change. 18 [i] He willed to give us birth by the word of truth that we may be a kind of firstfruits of his creatures.*

III. EXHORTATIONS AND WARNINGS

Doers of the Word. 19 Know this, my dear brothers: everyone should be quick to hear,* slow to speak, slow to wrath,[j] 20 for the wrath of a man does not accomplish the righteousness of God.[k] 21 Therefore, put away all filth and evil excess and humbly welcome the word that has been planted in you and is able to save your souls.[l]

22 Be doers of the word and not hearers only, deluding yourselves.[m] 23 For if anyone is a hearer of the word and not a doer, he is like a man who looks at his own face in a mirror. 24 He sees himself, then goes off and promptly forgets what he looked like. 25 But the one who peers into the perfect law* of freedom and perseveres, and is not a hearer who forgets but a doer who acts, such a one shall be blessed in what he does.[n]

26 * If anyone thinks he is religious and does not bridle his tongue* but deceives his heart, his religion is vain.[o] 27 Religion that is pure and undefiled before God and the Father is this: to care for orphans and widows* in their affliction and to keep oneself unstained by the world.[p]

CHAPTER 2

Sin of Partiality.* 1 My brothers, show no partiality as you adhere to the faith in our glorious Lord Jesus Christ. 2 For if a man with gold rings on his fingers and in fine clothes comes into your assembly, and a poor person in shabby clothes also comes in, 3 and you pay attention to the one wearing the fine clothes and say, "Sit here, please," while you say to the poor one, "Stand there," or "Sit at my feet," 4 have you not made distinctions among yourselves and become judges with evil designs?*

5 Listen, my beloved brothers. Did not God choose those who are poor* in the world to be rich in faith and heirs of the kingdom that he promised to those who love him?[q] 6 But you dishonored the poor person. Are not the rich oppressing you? And do they themselves not haul you off to court? 7 Is it not they who blaspheme the noble name that was invoked over you?[r] 8 However, if you fulfill the royal* law according to the scripture, "You shall love your neighbor as yourself," you are doing well.[s] 9 But if you show partiality, you commit sin, and are convicted by the law as transgressors.[t] 10 For whoever keeps the whole law, but falls short in one particular, has become guilty in respect to all of it.[u] 11 For he who said, "You shall not commit

i Jn 1, 12-13; 1 Pt 1, 23.—j Prv 14, 17; Sir 5, 11.—k Eph 4, 26.—l Col 3, 8.—m Mt 7, 26; Rom 2, 13.—n Jas 2, 12; Ps 19, 8; Rom 8, 2.—o Jas 3, 2; Ps 34, 14.—p Ex 22, 21.—q 1 Cor 1, 26-28; Rv 2, 9.—r 1 Pt 4, 4.—s Lv 19, 18; Mt 22, 39; Rom 13, 9.—t Dt 1, 17.—u Gal 3, 10.

1, 16-18: The author here stresses that God is the source of all good and of good alone, and the evil of temptation does not come from him.

1, 17: *All good giving and every perfect gift* may be a proverb written in hexameter. *Father of lights:* God is here called the Father of the heavenly luminaries, i.e., the stars, sun, and moon that he created (Gn 1, 14-18). Unlike orbs moving from nadir to zenith, he never changes or diminishes in brightness.

1, 18: Acceptance of the gospel message, *the word of truth,* constitutes new birth (Jn 3, 5-6) and makes the recipient the *firstfruits* (i.e., the cultic offering of the earliest grains, symbolizing the beginning of an abundant harvest) of a new creation; cf 1 Cor 15, 20; Rom 8, 23.

1, 19-25: To *be quick to hear* the gospel is to accept it readily and to act in conformity with it, removing from one's soul whatever is opposed to it, so that it may take root and effect salvation (19-21). To listen to the gospel message but not practice it is failure to improve oneself (22-24). Only conformity of life to the perfect law of true freedom brings happiness (25).

1, 25: *Peers into the perfect law:* the image of a person doing this is paralleled to that of hearing God's word. The *perfect law* applies the Old Testament description of the Mosaic law to the gospel of Jesus Christ that brings freedom.

1, 26-27: A practical application of v 22 is now made.

1, 26: For control of the tongue, see the note on Jas 3, 1-12.

1, 27: In the Old Testament, orphans and widows are classical examples of the defenseless and oppressed.

2, 1-13: In the Christian community there must be no discrimination or favoritism based on status or wealth (2-4; cf Mt 5, 3; 11, 5; 23, 6; 1 Cor 1, 27-29). Divine favor rather consists in God's election and promises (5). The rich who oppress the poor blaspheme the name of Christ (6-7). By violating one law of love of neighbor, they offend against the whole law (8-11). On the other hand, conscious awareness of the final judgment helps the faithful to fulfill the whole law (12).

2, 4: When Christians show favoritism to the rich they are guilty of the worst kind of prejudice and discrimination. The author says that such Christians set themselves up as judges who judge not by divine law but by the basest, self-serving motives.

2, 5: The poor, "God's poor" of the Old Testament, were seen by Jesus as particularly open to God for belief in and reliance on him alone (Lk 6, 20). God's law cannot tolerate their oppression in any way (9).

2, 8: *Royal:* literally, "kingly"; because the Mosaic law came from God, the universal king. There may be an allusion to Jesus' uses of this commandment in his preaching of the kingdom of God (Mt 22, 39; Mk 12, 31; Lk 10, 27).

adultery," also said, "You shall not kill."[v]
Even if you do not commit adultery but
kill, you have become a transgressor of the
law. 12 [w] So speak and so act as people who
will be judged by the law of freedom.*
13 For the judgment is merciless to one who
has not shown mercy; mercy triumphs
over judgment.[x]

Faith and Works.* 14 What good is it, my
brothers, if someone says he has faith but
does not have works? Can that faith save
him?[y] 15 If a brother or sister has nothing
to wear and has no food for the day, 16 and
one of you says to them, "Go in peace,
keep warm, and eat well," but you do not
give them the necessities of the body, what
good is it?[z] 17 So also faith of itself, if it
does not have works, is dead.

18 Indeed someone might say, "You have
faith and I have works." Demonstrate your
faith to me without works, and I will demonstrate my faith to you from my works.
19 You believe that God is one. You do
well. Even the demons believe that and
tremble. 20 Do you want proof, you igno-
ramus, that faith without works is useless?
21 Was not Abraham our father justified by
works when he offered his son Isaac upon
the altar?[a] 22 You see that faith was active
along with his works, and faith was completed by the works. 23 Thus the scripture
was fulfilled that says, "Abraham believed
God, and it was credited to him as righteousness," and he was called "the friend
of God."[b] 24 See how a person is justified
by works and not by faith alone. 25 And in
the same way, was not Rahab the harlot
also justified by works when she welcomed
the messengers and sent them out by a different route?[c] 26 For just as a body without
a spirit is dead, so also faith without works
is dead.

CHAPTER 3

Power of the Tongue.* 1 Not many of you
should become teachers, my brothers, for
you realize that we will be judged more
strictly, 2 for we all fall short in many respects. If anyone does not fall short in
speech, he is a perfect man, able to bridle
his whole body also.[d] 3 If we put bits into
the mouths of horses to make them obey
us, we also guide their whole bodies. 4 It is
the same with ships: even though they are
so large and driven by fierce winds, they
are steered by a very small rudder wherever the pilot's inclination wishes. 5 In the
same way the tongue is a small member
and yet has great pretensions.

Consider how small a fire can set a huge
forest ablaze. 6 The tongue is also a fire. It
exists among our members as a world of
malice, defiling the whole body and setting
the entire course of our lives on fire, itself
set on fire by Gehenna. 7 For every kind of
beast and bird, of reptile and sea creature,
can be tamed and has been tamed by the
human species, 8 but no human being can
tame the tongue. It is a restless evil, full of
deadly poison.[e] 9 With it we bless the Lord
and Father, and with it we curse human
beings who are made in the likeness of
God. 10 From the same mouth come blessing and cursing. This need not be so, my
brothers. 11 Does a spring gush forth from
the same opening both pure and brackish
water? 12 Can a fig tree, my brothers, produce olives, or a grapevine figs? Neither
can salt water yield fresh.[f]

True Wisdom.* 13 Who among you is wise
and understanding? Let him show his
works by a good life in the humility that
comes from wisdom.[g] 14 But if you have
bitter jealousy and selfish ambition in your
hearts, do not boast and be false to the
truth. 15 Wisdom of this kind does not
come down from above but is earthly, un-

Jas

---

v Ex 20, 13-14; Dt 5, 17-18.—w Jas 1, 25; Rom 8, 2.—x Mt 5, 7; 6, 14-15; 18, 32-33.—y Mt 25, 31-46; Gal 5, 6.—z 1 Jn 3, 17.—a Gn 22, 9-12; Heb 11, 17.—b Gn 15, 6; Rom 4, 3; Gal 3, 6 / 2 Chr 20, 7; Is 41, 8.—c Jos 2, 1-21.—d Jas 1, 26; Prv 13, 3; Sir 28, 12-26.—e Ps 140, 4.—f Mt 7, 16-17.—g Eph 4, 1-2.

2, 12-13: The law upon which the last judgment will be based is the law of freedom. As Jesus taught, mercy (which participates in God's own loving mercy) includes forgiveness of those who wrong us (see Mt 6, 12.14-15).

2, 14-26: The theme of these verses is the relationship of faith and works (deeds). It has been argued that the teaching here contradicts that of Paul (see especially Rom 4, 5-6). The problem can only be understood if the different viewpoints of the two authors are seen. Paul argues against those who claim to participate in God's salvation because of their good deeds as well as because they have committed themselves to trust in God through Jesus Christ (Paul's concept of faith). Paul certainly understands, however, the implications of true faith for a life of love and generosity (see Gal 5, 6.13-15). The author of James is well aware that proper conduct can only come about with an authentic commitment to God in faith (18.26). Many think he was seeking to correct a misunderstanding of Paul's view.

3, 1-12: The use and abuse of the important role of teaching in the church (1) are here related to the good and bad use of the tongue (9-12), the instrument through which teaching was chiefly conveyed (see Sir 5, 11—6, 1; 28, 12-26).

3, 13-18: This discussion of true wisdom is related to the previous reflection on the role of the teacher as one who is in control of his speech. The qualities of the wise man endowed from above are detailed (17-18; cf Gal 5, 22-23), in contrast to the qualities of earthbound wisdom (14-16; cf 2 Cor 12, 20).

spiritual, demonic. 16 For where jealousy
and selfish ambition exist, there is disorder
and every foul practice. 17 But the wisdom
from above is first of all pure, then peace-
able, gentle, compliant, full of mercy and
good fruits, without inconstancy or insincerity.[h] 18 And the fruit of righteousness is
sown in peace for those who cultivate
peace.[i]

CHAPTER 4

Causes of Division.* 1 Where do the wars
and where do the conflicts among you
come from? Is it not from your passions*
that make war within your members?[j]
2 You covet but do not possess. You kill
and envy but you cannot obtain; you fight
and wage war. You do not possess because
you do not ask. 3 You ask but do not receive, because you ask wrongly, to spend it
on your passions. 4 Adulterers!* Do you
not know that to be a lover of the world
means enmity with God? Therefore, whoever wants to be a lover of the world makes
himself an enemy of God.[k] 5 Or do you
suppose that the scripture speaks without
meaning when it says, "The spirit that he
has made to dwell in us tends toward
jealousy"?* 6 But he bestows a greater
grace; therefore, it says:[l]

"God resists the proud,
but gives grace to the humble."*

7 So submit yourselves to God. Resist the
devil, and he will flee from you.[m] 8 Draw
near to God, and he will draw near to you.
Cleanse your hands, you sinners, and pur-
ify your hearts, you of two minds.[n] 9 Begin
to lament, to mourn, to weep. Let your
laughter be turned into mourning and your
joy into dejection. 10 Humble yourselves
before the Lord and he will exalt you.[o]

11 Do not speak evil of one another,
brothers. Whoever speaks evil of a brother
or judges his brother speaks evil of the law
and judges the law.* If you judge the law,
you are not a doer of the law but a judge.
12 There is one lawgiver and judge who is
able to save or to destroy. Who then are
you to judge your neighbor?[p]

Warning against Presumption.* 13 Come
now, you who say, "Today or tomorrow
we shall go into such and such a town,
spend a year there doing business, and
make a profit"—14 you have no idea what
your life will be like tomorrow.* You are a
puff of smoke that appears briefly and then
disappears.[q] 15 Instead you should say, "If
the Lord wills it,* we shall live to do this or
that." 16 But now you are boasting in your
arrogance. All such boasting is evil. 17 [r] So
for one who knows the right thing to do
and does not do it, it is a sin.*

h Jas 1, 17; Wis 7, 22-23.—i Mt 5, 9.—j Rom 7, 23; 1 Pt 2, 11.—k Mt 6, 24; Lk 16, 13; Rom 8, 7; 1 Jn 2, 15-16.—l Jb 22, 29; Prv 3, 34; Mt 23, 12; 1 Pt 5, 5.—m 1 Pt 5, 8-9.—n Zec 1, 3; Mal 3, 7.—o Jb 5, 11; Mt 23, 12; Lk 14, 11; 18, 14; 1 Pt 5, 6.—p Mt 7, 1; Rom 2, 1; 14, 4.—q Prv 27, 1 / Ps 39, 6-7.—r Lk 12, 47.

4, 1-12: The concern here is with the origin of conflicts in the Christian community. These are occasioned by love *of the world,* which *means enmity with God* (4). Further, the conflicts are bound up with failure to pray properly (cf Mt 7, 7-11; Jn 14, 13; 15, 7; 16, 23), that is, not asking God at all or using God's kindness only for one's pleasure (2-3). In contrast, the proper dispositions are submission to God, repentance, humility, and resistance to evil (7-10).

4,1: *Passions:* the Greek word here (literally, "pleasures") does not indicate that pleasure is evil. Rather, as the text points out (2-3), it is the manner in which one deals with needs and desires that determines good or bad. The motivation for any action can be wrong, especially if one does not pray properly but seeks only selfish enjoyment (3).

4, 4: *Adulterers:* a common biblical image for the covenant between God and his people is the marriage bond. In this image, breaking the covenant with God is likened to the unfaithfulness of adultery.

4, 5: The meaning of this saying is difficult because the author of Jas cites, probably from memory, a passage that is not in any extant manuscript of the Bible. Other translations of the text with a completely different meaning are possible: "The Spirit that he (God) made to dwell in us yearns (for us) jealously," or, "He (God) yearns jealously for the spirit that he has made to dwell in us." If this last translation is correct, the author perhaps had in mind an apocryphal religious text that echoes the idea that God is zealous for his creatures; cf Ex 20, 5; Dt 4, 24; Zec 8, 2.

4, 6: The point of this whole argument is that God wants the happiness of all, but that selfishness and pride can make that impossible. We must work with him in humility (10).

4, 11: Slander of a fellow Christian does not break just one commandment but makes mockery of the authority of law in general and therefore of God.

4, 13-17: The uncertainty of life (14), its complete dependence on God, and the necessity of submitting to God's will (15) all help one know and do what is right (17). To disregard this is to live in pride and arrogance (16); failure to do what is right is a sin (17).

4, 14: Some important Greek manuscripts here have, "You who have no idea what tomorrow will bring. Why, what is your life?"

4, 15: *If the Lord wills it:* often in piety referred to as the *"conditio Jacobaea,"* the condition James says we should employ to qualify all our plans.

4, 17: *It is a sin:* those who live arrogantly, forgetting the contingency of life and our dependence on God (13-16), are guilty of sin.

CHAPTER 5

Warning to the Rich.* 1 Come now, you rich, weep and wail over your impending miseries.[s] 2 Your wealth has rotted away, your clothes have become moth-eaten,[t] 3 your gold and silver have corroded, and that corrosion will be a testimony against you; it will devour your flesh like a fire. You have stored up treasure for the last days.[u] 4 Behold, the wages you withheld from the workers who harvested your fields are crying aloud, and the cries of the harvesters have reached the ears of the Lord of hosts.[v] 5 You have lived on earth in luxury and pleasure; you have fattened your hearts for the day of slaughter.[w] 6 You have condemned; you have murdered the righteous one;[x] he offers you no resistance.*

Patience and Oaths. 7 * Be patient, therefore, brothers, until the coming of the Lord. See how the farmer waits for the precious fruit of the earth, being patient with it until it receives the early and the late rains.* 8 You too must be patient. Make your hearts firm, because the coming of the Lord is at hand.[y] 9 Do not complain, brothers, about one another, that you may not be judged. Behold, the Judge is standing before the gates. 10 Take as an example of hardship and patience, brothers, the prophets who spoke in the name of the Lord. 11 Indeed we call blessed those who have persevered. You have heard of the perseverance of Job, and you have seen the purpose of the Lord, because "the Lord is compassionate and merciful."[z]

12 [a] But above all, my brothers, do not swear, either by heaven or by earth or with any other oath, but let your "Yes" mean "Yes" and your "No" mean "No," that you may not incur condemnation.*

IV. THE POWER OF PRAYER

Anointing of the Sick. 13 Is anyone among you suffering? He should pray. Is anyone in good spirits? He should sing praise. 14 Is anyone among you sick?* He should summon the presbyters of the church, and they should pray over him and anoint [him] with oil in the name of the Lord,[b] 15 and the prayer of faith will save the sick person, and the Lord will raise him up. If he has committed any sins, he will be forgiven.*

Confession and Intercession. 16 Therefore, confess your sins to one another and pray for one another, that you may be healed. The fervent prayer of a righteous person is very powerful. 17 Elijah was a human being like us; yet he prayed earnestly that it might not rain, and for three years and six months it did not rain upon the land.[c] 18 Then he prayed again, and the sky gave rain and the earth produced its fruit.[d]

Conversion of Sinners. 19 [e] My brothers, if anyone among you should stray from the truth and someone bring him back, 20 [f] he should know that whoever brings back a sinner from the error of his way will save his soul from death and will cover a multitude of sins.*

s Lk 6, 24.—t Mt 6, 19.—u Ps 21, 10; Prv 11, 4; Jdt 16, 17.—v Lv 19, 13; Dt 24, 14-15; Mal 3, 5.—w Jer 12, 3; Lk 16, 19-25.—x Wis 2, 10-20.—y Lk 21, 19; Heb 10, 36 / Heb 10, 25; 1 Pt 4, 7.—z Ex 34, 6; Ps 103, 8.—a Mt 5, 34-37.—b Mk 6, 13.—c 1 Kgs 17, 1; Lk 4, 25.—d 1 Kgs 18, 45.—e Mt 18, 15; Gal 6, 1.—f Prv 10, 12; 1 Pt 4, 8.

5, 1-6: Continuing with the theme of the transitory character of life on earth, the author points out the impending ruin of the godless. He denounces the unjust rich, whose victims cry to heaven for judgment on their exploiters (4-6). The decay and corrosion of the costly garments and metals, which symbolize wealth, prove them worthless and portend the destruction of their possessors (2-3).

5, 6: The author does not have in mind any specific crime in his readers' communities but rather echoes the Old Testament theme of the harsh oppression of the righteous poor (see Prv 1, 11; Wis 2, 10.12.20).

5, 7-11: Those oppressed by the unjust rich are reminded of the need for patience, both in bearing the sufferings of human life (9) and in their expectation of the coming of the Lord. It is then that they will receive their reward (7-8.10-11; cf Heb 10, 25; 1 Jn 2, 18).

5, 7: *The early and the late rains:* an expression related to the agricultural season in ancient Palestine (see Dt 11, 14; Jer 5, 24; Jl 2, 23).

5, 12: This is the threat of condemnation for the abuse of swearing oaths (cf Mt 5, 33-37). *By heaven or by earth:* these words were substitutes for the original form of an oath, to circumvent its binding force and to avoid pronouncing the holy name of God (see Ex 22, 10).

5, 14: In case of sickness a Christian should ask for the presbyters of the church, i.e., those who have authority in the church (cf Acts 15, 2.22-23; 1 Tm 5, 17; Ti 1, 5). They are to pray over the person and anoint with oil; oil was used for medicinal purposes in the ancient world (see Is 1, 6; Lk 10, 34). In Mk 6, 13, the Twelve anoint the sick with oil on their missionary journey. *In the name of the Lord:* by the power of Jesus Christ.

5, 15: The results of the prayer and anointing are physical health and forgiveness of sins. The Roman Catholic Church (Council of Trent, Session 14) declared that this anointing of the sick is a sacrament "instituted by Christ and promulgated by blessed James the apostle."

5, 20: When a Christian is instrumental in the conversion of a sinner, the result is forgiveness of sins and a reinstatement of the sinner to the life of grace.

THE FIRST LETTER OF PETER

INTRODUCTION

This letter begins with an address by Peter to Christian communities located in five provinces of Asia Minor (1, 1), including areas evangelized by Paul (Acts 16, 6-7; 18, 23). Christians there are encouraged to remain faithful to their standards of belief and conduct in spite of threats of persecution. Numerous allusions in the letter suggest that the churches addressed were largely of Gentile composition (1, 14.18; 2, 9-10; 4, 3-4), though considerable use is made of the Old Testament (1, 24; 2, 6-7.9-10.22; 3, 10-12).

The contents following the address both inspire and admonish these "chosen sojourners" (1, 1) who, in seeking to live as God's people, feel an alienation from their previous religious roots and the society around them. Appeal is made to Christ's resurrection and the future hope it provides (1, 3-5) and to the experience of baptism as new birth (1, 3.23-25; 3, 21). The suffering and death of Christ serve as both source of salvation and example (1, 19; 2, 21-25; 3, 18). What Christians are in Christ, as a people who have received mercy and are to proclaim and live according to God's call (2, 9-10), is repeatedly spelled out for all sorts of situations in society (2, 11-17), work (even as slaves, 2, 18-20), the home (3, 1-7), and general conduct (3, 8-12; 4, 1-11). But over all hangs the possibility of suffering as a Christian (3, 13-17). In 4, 12-19 persecution is described as already occurring, so that some have supposed the letter was addressed both to places where such a "trial by fire" was already present and to places where it might break out.

The letter constantly mingles moral exhortation (paraklēsis) *with its catechetical summaries of mercies in Christ. Encouragement to fidelity in spite of suffering is based upon a vision of the meaning of Christian existence. The emphasis on baptism and allusions to various features of the baptismal liturgy suggest that the author has incorporated into his exposition numerous homiletic, credal, hymnic, and sacramental elements of the baptismal rite that had become traditional at an early date.*

From Irenaeus in the late second century until modern times, Christian tradition regarded Peter the apostle as author of this document. Since he was martyred at Rome during the persecution of Nero between A.D. 64 and 67, it was supposed that the letter was written from Rome shortly before his death. This is supported by its reference to "Babylon" (5, 13), a code name for Rome in the early church.

Some modern scholars, however, on the basis of a number of features that they consider incompatible with Petrine authenticity, regard the letter as the work of a later Christian writer. Such features include the cultivated Greek in which it is written, difficult to attribute to a Galilean fisherman, together with its use of the Greek Septuagint translation when citing the Old Testament; the similarity in both thought and expression to the Pauline literature; and the allusions to widespread persecution of Christians, which did not occur until at least the reign of Domitian (A.D. 81-96). In this view the letter would date from the end of the first century or even the beginning of the second, when there is evidence for persecution of Christians in Asia Minor (the letter of Pliny the Younger to Trajan, A.D. 111-12).

Other scholars believe, however, that these objections can be met by appeal to use of a secretary, Silvanus, mentioned in 5, 12. Such secretaries often gave literary expression to the author's thoughts in their own style and language. The persecutions may refer to local harassment rather than to systematic repression by the state. Hence there is nothing in the document incompatible with Petrine authorship in the 60s.

Still other scholars take a middle position. The many literary contacts with the Pauline literature, James, and 1 John suggest a common fund of traditional formulations rather than direct dependence upon Paul. Such liturgical and catechetical traditions must have been very ancient and in some cases of Palestinian origin.

Yet it is unlikely that Peter addressed a letter to the Gentile churches of Asia Minor while Paul was still alive. This suggests a period after the death of the two apostles, perhaps A.D. 70-90. The author would be a disciple of Peter in Rome, representing a Petrine group that served as a bridge between the Palestinian origins of Christianity and its flowering in the Gentile world. The problem addressed would not be official persecution but the difficulty of living the Christian life in a hostile, secular environment that espoused different values and subjected the Christian minority to ridicule and oppression.

The principal divisions of the First Letter of Peter are the following:

I. Address (1, 1-2)
II. The Gift and Call of God in Baptism (1, 3—2, 10)
III. The Christian in a Hostile World (2, 11—4, 11)
IV. Advice to the Persecuted (4, 12—5, 11)
V. Conclusion (5, 12-14)

I. ADDRESS

CHAPTER 1

Greeting.* [1]Peter, an apostle of Jesus Christ, to the chosen sojourners of the dispersion* in Pontus, Galatia, Cappadocia, Asia, and Bithynia,[a] [2]in the foreknowledge of God the Father, through sanctification by the Spirit, for obedience and sprinkling with the blood of Jesus Christ: may grace and peace be yours in abundance.[b]

II. THE GIFT AND CALL OF GOD IN BAPTISM

Blessing. [3] * Blessed be the God and Father of our Lord Jesus Christ, who in his great mercy gave us a new birth to a living hope through the resurrection of Jesus Christ from the dead,[c] [4]to an inheritance that is imperishable, undefiled, and unfading, kept in heaven for you[d] [5]who by the power of God are safeguarded through faith, to a salvation that is ready to be revealed in the final time. [6] * In this you rejoice, although now for a little while you may have to suffer through various trials,[e] [7]so that the genuineness of your faith, more precious than gold that is perishable even though tested by fire, may prove to be for praise, glory, and honor at the revelation of Jesus Christ.[f] [8]Although you have not seen him you love him; even though you do not see him now yet believe in him, you rejoice with an indescribable and glorious joy,[g] [9]as you attain the goal of [your] faith, the salvation of your souls.

[10] * Concerning this salvation, prophets who prophesied about the grace that was to be yours searched and investigated it, [11]investigating the time and circumstances that the Spirit of Christ within them indicated when it testified in advance to the sufferings destined for Christ and the glories to follow them.[h] [12]It was revealed to them that they were serving not themselves but you with regard to the things that have now been announced to you by those who preached the good news to you [through] the holy Spirit sent from heaven, things into which angels longed to look.

a Jas 1, 1.—b Rom 8, 29.—c Ti 3, 5.—d Mt 6, 19-20.—e Jas 1, 2-3.—f 1 Cor 3, 13.—g 2 Cor 5, 6-7.—h Is 52, 13—53, 12; Dn 9, 24.

1, 1-2: The introductory formula names *Peter* as the writer (but see Introduction). In his comments to the presbyters (1 Pt 5, 1), the author calls himself a "fellow presbyter." He addresses himself to the Gentile converts of Asia Minor. Their privileged status as a *chosen* and sanctified people makes them worthy of God's *grace* and *peace.* In contrast is their actual existence as aliens and *sojourners,* scattered among pagans, far from their true country.

1, 1: *Dispersion:* literally, diaspora; see Jas 1, 1 and Introduction to that letter. *Pontus . . . Bithynia:* five provinces in Asia Minor, listed in clockwise order from the north, perhaps in the sequence in which a messenger might deliver the letter.

1, 3-5: A prayer of praise and thanksgiving to God who bestows the gift of new life and hope in baptism *(new birth,* 3) *through the resurrection of Jesus Christ from the dead.* The new birth is a sign of an *imperishable inheritance* (4), of *salvation* that is still in the future *(to be revealed in the final time,* 5).

1, 6-9: As the glory of Christ's resurrection was preceded by his sufferings and death, the new life of faith that it bestows is to be subjected to many *trials* (6) while achieving its goal: the glory of the fullness of *salvation* (9) at the coming of Christ (7).

1, 10-12: The *Spirit of Christ* (11) is here shown to have been present in the prophets, moving them to search, investigate, and prophesy about the *grace* of *salvation* that was to come (10), and in the apostles impelling them to preach the fulfillment of salvation in the message of Christ's sufferings and glory (12).

Obedience. 13 * Therefore, gird up the
loins of your mind,* live soberly, and set
your hopes completely on the grace to be
brought to you at the revelation of Jesus
Christ. 14 Like obedient children, do not
act in compliance with the desires of your
former ignorance* 15 but, as he who called
you is holy, be holy yourselves in every aspect of your conduct,[i] 16 for it is written,
"Be holy because I [am] holy."[j]

Reverence. 17 Now if you invoke as
Father him who judges impartially according to each one's works, conduct yourselves with reverence during the time of
your sojourning,[k] 18 realizing that you were
ransomed from your futile conduct, handed on by your ancestors, not with perishable things like silver or gold[l] 19 but with
the precious blood of Christ[m] as of a spotless unblemished lamb.* 20 He was known
before the foundation of the world but revealed in the final time for you, 21 who
through him believe in God who raised
him from the dead and gave him glory, so
that your faith and hope are in God.

Mutual Love.* 22 Since you have purified
yourselves by obedience to the truth for
sincere mutual love, love one another in-
tensely from a [pure] heart.[n] 23 You have
been born anew,[o] not from perishable but
from imperishable seed, through the living
and abiding word of God,* 24 for:

"All flesh is like grass,
and all its glory like the flower of the
field;
the grass withers,
and the flower wilts;[p]
25 but the word of the Lord remains
forever."
This is the word that has been proclaimed
to you.

CHAPTER 2

God's House and People. 1 * Rid yourselves of all malice and all deceit, insincerity, envy, and all slander;[q] 2 like newborn
infants, long for pure spiritual milk so that
through it you may grow into salvation, 3 [r]
for you have tasted that the Lord is good.*
4 Come to him, a living stone,* rejected by
human beings but chosen and precious in
the sight of God,[s] 5 and, like living stones,
let yourselves be built* into a spiritual
house to be a holy priesthood to offer
spiritual sacrifices acceptable to God
through Jesus Christ.[t] 6 For it says in scripture:
"Behold, I am laying a stone in Zion,
a cornerstone, chosen and precious,
and whoever believes in it shall not be
put to shame."[u]
7 Therefore, its value is for you who have
faith, but for those without faith:
"The stone which the builders rejected
has become the cornerstone,"[v]
8 and
"A stone that will make people stumble,
and a rock that will make them fall."
They stumble by disobeying the word, as
is their destiny.[w]

---

i Mt 5, 48; 1 Jn 3, 3.—j Lv 11, 44; 19, 2.—k 1 Pt 2, 11.—l Is 52, 3; 1 Cor 6, 20.—m Ex 12, 5; Jn 1, 29; Heb 9, 14.—n Rom 12, 10.—o 1 Jn 3, 9.—p Is 40, 6-8.—q 1-2: Jas 1, 21.—r Ps 34, 9.—s Ps 118, 22; Mt 21, 42; Acts 4, 11.—t Eph 2, 21-22.—u Is 28, 16.—v Ps 118, 22; Mt 21, 42; Lk 20, 17; Acts 4, 11.—w Is 8, 14; Rom 9, 33.

1, 13-25: These verses are concerned with the call of God's people to holiness and to mutual love by reason of their redemption through the blood of Christ (18-21).

1, 13: *Gird up the loins of your mind:* a figure reminiscent of the rite of Passover when the Israelites were in flight from their oppressors (Ex 12, 11), and also suggesting the vigilance of the Christian people in expectation of the parousia of Christ (Lk 12, 35).

1, 14-16: The *ignorance* here referred to (14) was their former lack of knowledge of God, leading inevitably to godless conduct. Holiness (15-16), on the contrary, is the result of their call to the knowledge and love of God.

1, 19: Christians have received the redemption prophesied by Isaiah (Is 52, 3), through the blood (Jewish symbol of life) of the spotless lamb (Is 53, 7.10; Jn 1, 29; Rom 3, 24-25; cf 1 Cor 6, 20).

1, 22-25: The new birth of Christians (23) derives from Christ, the *imperishable seed* or sowing that produces a new and lasting existence in those who accept the gospel (24-25), with the consequent duty of loving *one another* (22).

1, 23: *The living and abiding word of God:* or, "the word of the living and abiding God."

2, 1-3: Growth toward salvation is seen here as two steps: first, stripping away all that is contrary to the new life in Christ; second, the nourishment (*pure spiritual milk*) that the newly baptized have received.

2, 3: *Tasted that the Lord is good:* cf Ps 34, 9.

2, 4-8: Christ is the cornerstone (cf Is 28, 16) that is the foundation of the spiritual edifice of the Christian community (5). To unbelievers, Christ is an obstacle and a stumbling block on which they are destined to fall (8); cf Rom 11, 11.

2, 5: *Let yourselves be built:* the form of the Greek word could also be indicative passive, "you are being built" (cf 9).

[9] * But you are "a chosen race, a royal priesthood, a holy nation, a people of his own, so that you may announce the praises" of him who called you out of darkness into his wonderful light.[x]

[10] Once you were "no people"
but now you are God's people;
you "had not received mercy"
but now you have received mercy.[y]

III. THE CHRISTIAN IN A HOSTILE WORLD

Christian Examples. [11] * Beloved, I urge you as aliens and sojourners* to keep away from worldly desires that wage war against the soul.[z] [12] Maintain good conduct among the Gentiles, so that if they speak of you as evildoers, they may observe your good works and glorify God on the day of visitation.

Christian Citizens.* [13] Be subject to every human institution for the Lord's sake, whether it be to the king as supreme[a] [14] or to governors as sent by him for the punishment of evildoers and the approval of those who do good. [15] For it is the will of God that by doing good you may silence the ignorance of foolish people. [16] Be free, yet without using freedom as a pretext for evil, but as slaves of God.[b] [17] Give honor to all, love the community, fear God, honor the king.[c]

Christian Slaves. [18] * Slaves, be subject to your masters with all reverence, not only to those who are good and equitable but also to those who are perverse.[d] [19] For whenever anyone bears the pain of unjust suffering because of consciousness of God, that is a grace. [20] But what credit is there if you are patient when beaten for doing wrong? But if you are patient when you suffer for doing what is good, this is a grace before God. [21] For to this you have been called, because Christ also suffered* for you, leaving you an example that you should follow in his footsteps.[e]

[22] "He committed no sin,[f]
and no deceit was found in his mouth."*

[23] When he was insulted, he returned no insult; when he suffered, he did not threaten; instead, he handed himself over to the one who judges justly.[g] [24] He himself bore our sins in his body upon the cross, so that, free from sin, we might live for righteousness. By his wounds you have been healed.[h] [25] For you had gone astray like sheep,[i] but you have now returned to the shepherd and guardian of your souls.*

x Ex 19, 6; Is 61, 6; Rv 1, 6; 20, 6.—y Hos 1, 9; 2, 25 / Hos 1, 6.—z Gal 5, 24.—a Rom 13, 1-7.—b Gal 5, 13.—c Prv 24, 21; Mt 22, 21.—d Eph 6, 5.—e Mt 16, 24.—f Is 53, 9.—g Mt 5, 39.—h Is 53, 4.12 / Is 53, 5.—i Is 53, 6.

2, 9-10: The prerogatives of ancient Israel mentioned here are now more fully and fittingly applied to the Christian people: "a chosen race" (cf Is 43, 20-21) indicates their divine election (Eph 1, 4-6); "a royal priesthood" (cf Ex 19, 6) to serve and worship God in Christ, thus continuing the priestly functions of his life, passion, and resurrection; "a holy nation" (Ex 19, 6) reserved for God, a people he claims for his own (cf Mal 3, 17) in virtue of their baptism into his death and resurrection. This transcends all natural and national divisions and unites the people into one community to glorify the one who led them from the darkness of paganism to the light of faith in Christ. From being "no people" deprived of all mercy, they have become the very people of God, the chosen recipients of his mercy (cf Hos 1, 9; 2, 25).

2, 11—3, 12: After explaining the doctrinal basis for the Christian community, the author makes practical applications in terms of the virtues that should prevail in all the social relationships of the members of the community: good example to Gentile neighbors (1 Pt 2, 11-12); respect for human authority (1 Pt 2, 13-17); obedience, patience, and endurance of hardship in domestic relations (1 Pt 2, 18-25); Christian behavior of husbands and wives (1 Pt 3, 1-7); mutual charity (1 Pt 3, 8-12).

2, 11: *Aliens and sojourners:* no longer signifying absence from one's native land (Gn 23, 4), this image denotes rather their estrangement from the world during their earthly pilgrimage (see also 1 Pt 1, 1.17).

2, 13-17: True Christian freedom is the result of being servants of God (16; see the note on 1 Pt 2, 18-23). It includes reverence for God, esteem for every individual, and committed love for fellow Christians (17). Although persecution may threaten, subjection to human government is urged (13.17) and concern for the impact of Christians' conduct on those who are not Christians (12.15).

2, 18-21: Most of the labor in the commercial cities of first-century Asia Minor was performed by a working class of slaves. The sense of freedom contained in the gospel undoubtedly caused great tension among Christian slaves: witness the special advice given concerning them here and in 1 Cor 7, 21-24; Eph 6, 5-8; Col 3, 22-25; Phlm. The point made here does not have so much to do with the institution of slavery, which the author does not challenge, but with the nonviolent reaction (20) of slaves to unjust treatment. Their patient suffering is compared to that of Jesus (21), which won righteousness for all humanity.

2, 21: *Suffered:* some ancient manuscripts and versions read "died" (cf 1 Pt 3, 18).

2, 22-25: After the quotation of Is 53, 9b, the passage describes Jesus' passion with phrases concerning the Suffering Servant from Is 53, 4-12, perhaps as employed in an early Christian confession of faith; cf 1 Pt 1, 18-21 and 1 Pt 3, 18-22.

2, 25: *The shepherd and guardian of your souls:* the familiar shepherd and flock figures express the care, vigilance, and love of God for his people in the Old Testament (Ps 23; Is 40, 11; Jer 23, 4-5; Ez 34, 11-16) and of Jesus for all humanity in the New Testament (Mt 18, 10-14; Lk 15, 4-7; Jn 10, 1-16; Heb 13, 20).

CHAPTER 3

Christian Spouses. 1 * Likewise, you
wives should be subordinate to your husbands so that, even if some disobey the
word, they may be won over without a
word by their wives' conduct 2 when they
observe your reverent and chaste behavior.[j] 3 Your adornment should not be
an external one: braiding the hair, wearing
gold jewelry, or dressing in fine clothes,[k]
4 but rather the hidden character of the
heart, expressed in the imperishable
beauty of a gentle and calm disposition,
which is precious in the sight of God. 5 For
this is also how the holy women who hoped
in God once used to adorn themselves and
were subordinate to their husbands; 6 thus
Sarah obeyed Abraham, calling him
"lord." You are her children when you do
what is good and fear no intimidation.

7 [l] Likewise, you husbands should live
with your wives in understanding, showing
honor to the weaker female sex, since we
are joint heirs of the gift of life, so that
your prayers may not be hindered.*

Christian Conduct.* 8 Finally, all of you,
be of one mind, sympathetic, loving toward one another, compassionate, humble.
9 Do not return evil for evil, or insult for insult; but, on the contrary, a blessing, because to this you were called, that you
might inherit a blessing.[m] 10 For:

"Whoever would love life[n]
and see good days
must keep the tongue from evil
and the lips from speaking deceit,
11 must turn from evil and do good,
seek peace and follow after it.
12 For the eyes of the Lord are on the
righteous
and his ears turned to their prayer,
but the face of the Lord is against evildoers."

Christian Suffering.* 13 Now who is going
to harm you if you are enthusiastic for
what is good? 14 But even if you should suffer because of righteousness, blessed are
you. Do not be afraid or terrified with fear
of them, 15 but sanctify Christ as Lord in
your hearts. Always be ready to give an explanation to anyone who asks you for a
reason for your hope,[o] 16 but do it with
gentleness and reverence, keeping your
conscience clear, so that, when you are
maligned, those who defame your good
conduct in Christ may themselves be put to
shame. 17 For it is better to suffer for doing
good, if that be the will of God, than for
doing evil.

18 For Christ also suffered* for sins once,
the righteous for the sake of the unrighteous, that he might lead you to God. Put
to death in the flesh, he was brought to life
in the spirit.[p] 19 In it he also went to preach
to the spirits in prison,* 20 who had once
been disobedient while God patiently
waited in the days of Noah during the
building of the ark, in which a few persons, eight in all, were saved through
water.[q] 21 This prefigured baptism, which
saves you now. It is not a removal of dirt
from the body but an appeal to God* for a
clear conscience, through the resurrection

j 1 Cor 7, 12-16; Eph 5, 22-24; Col 3, 18; 1 Tm 2, 9-15.—k 1 Tm 2, 9-10.—l Eph 5, 25-33; Col 3, 19.—m Mt 5, 44; Lk 6, 28; Rom 12, 14.—n 10-12: Ps 34, 13-17.—o Is 8, 12.—p 1 Cor 15, 45.—q Gn 7, 7.17; 2 Pt 2, 5.

3, 1-6: The typical marital virtues of women of the ancient world, obedience, reverence, and chastity (1-2), are outlined here by the author, who gives them an entirely new motivation: Christian wives are to be virtuous so that they may be instrumental in the conversion of their husbands. In imitation of *holy women* in the past (5) they are to cultivate the interior life (4) instead of excessive concern with their appearance (3).

3, 7: Husbands who do not respect their wives will have as little success in prayer as those who, according to Paul, have no love: their prayers will be "a resounding gong or a clashing cymbal" (1 Cor 13, 1). Consideration for others is shown as a prerequisite for effective prayer also in Mt 5, 23-24; 1 Cor 11, 20-22; Jas 4, 3. After all, whatever the social position of women in the world and in the family, they are equal recipients of the gift of God's salvation. Paul is very clear on this point, too (see 1 Cor 11, 11-12; Gal 3, 28).

3, 8-12: For the proper ordering of Christian life in its various aspects as described in 1 Pt 2, 11—3, 9, there is promised the blessing expressed in Ps 34, 13-17. In the Old Testament this refers to longevity and prosperity; here, it also refers to eternal life.

3, 13-22: This exposition, centering on v 17, runs as follows: by his suffering and death Christ the righteous one saved the unrighteous (18); by his resurrection he received new life in the spirit, which he communicates to believers through the baptismal bath that cleanses their consciences from sin. As Noah's family was saved *through water,* so Christians are saved through the waters of baptism (19-22). Hence they need not share the fear of sinners; they should rather rejoice in suffering because of their hope in Christ. Thus their innocence disappoints their accusers (13-16; cf Mt 10, 28; Rom 8, 35-39).

3, 18: *Suffered:* very many ancient manuscripts and versions read "died." *Put to death in the flesh:* affirms that Jesus truly died as a human being. *Brought to life in the spirit:* that is, in the new and transformed existence freed from the limitations and weaknesses of natural human life (cf 1 Cor 15, 45).

3, 19: *The spirits in prison:* it is not clear just who these spirits are. They may be the spirits of the sinners who died in the flood, or angelic powers, hostile to God, who have been overcome by Christ (cf 1 Pt 3, 22; Gn 6, 4; Enoch 6-36, especially 21, 6; 2 Enoch 7, 1-5).

3, 21: *Appeal to God:* this could also be translated "pledge," that is, a promise on the part of Christians to live with a good conscience before God, or a pledge from God of forgiveness and therefore a good conscience for us.

of Jesus Christ,[r] 22 who has gone into heaven and is at the right hand of God, with angels, authorities, and powers subject to him.[s]

CHAPTER 4

Christian Restraint.* 1 Therefore, since Christ suffered in the flesh, arm yourselves also with the same attitude (for whoever suffers in the flesh has broken with sin), 2 so as not to spend what remains of one's life in the flesh on human desires, but on the will of God. 3 For the time that has passed is sufficient for doing what the Gentiles like to do: living in debauchery, evil desires, drunkenness, orgies, carousing, and wanton idolatry.[t] 4 They are surprised that you do not plunge into the same swamp of profligacy, and they vilify you; 5 but they will give an account to him who stands ready to judge the living and the dead.[u] 6 For this is why the gospel was preached even to the dead* that, though condemned in the flesh in human estimation, they might live in the spirit in the estimation of God.

Christian Charity.* 7 The end of all things is at hand. Therefore, be serious and sober for prayers. 8 [v] Above all, let your love for one another be intense, because love covers a multitude of sins.* 9 Be hospitable to one another without complaining.[w] 10 As each one has received a gift, use it to serve one another as good stewards of God's varied grace.[x] 11 Whoever preaches, let it be with the words of God; whoever serves, let it be with the strength that God supplies, so that in all things God may be glorified through Jesus Christ,[y] to whom belong glory and dominion forever and ever. Amen.*

IV. ADVICE TO THE PERSECUTED

Trial of Persecution.* 12 Beloved, do not be surprised that a trial by fire is occurring among you, as if something strange were happening to you.[z] 13 But rejoice to the extent that you share in the sufferings of Christ, so that when his glory is revealed you may also rejoice exultantly.[a] 14 If you are insulted for the name of Christ, blessed are you, for the Spirit of glory and of God rests upon you.[b] 15 But let no one among you be made to suffer as a murderer, a thief, an evildoer, or as an intriguer. 16 But whoever is made to suffer as a Christian should not be ashamed but glorify God because of the name. 17 For it is time for the judgment to begin with the household of God; if it begins with us, how will it end for those who fail to obey the gospel of God?[c]

18 "And if the righteous one is barely
saved,
where will the godless and the sinner
appear?"[d]

19 As a result, those who suffer in accord with God's will hand their souls over to a faithful creator as they do good.

CHAPTER 5

Advice to Presbyters.* 1 So I exhort the presbyters* among you, as a fellow presbyter and witness to the sufferings of Christ and one who has a share in the glory to be revealed. 2 Tend the flock of God in your midst, [overseeing] not by constraint but willingly, as God would have it, not for

r Eph 5, 26; Heb 10, 22.—s Eph 1, 20-21.—t Eph 2, 2-3; 4, 17-19; Col 3, 7; Ti 3, 3.—u Acts 10, 42; 2 Tm 4, 1.—v Prv 10, 12; Jas 5, 20.—w Heb 13, 2.—x Rom 12, 6-8; 1 Cor 12, 4-11.—y 1 Cor 10, 31.—z 1 Pt 1, 6-7; 3, 14.17.—a Rom 5, 3-5; 8, 17; 2 Tm 2, 12.—b Acts 5, 41 / Is 11, 2.—c Lk 23, 31; 2 Thes 1, 8.—d Prv 11, 31 LXX.

4, 1-6: Willingness to suffer with Christ equips the Christian with the power to conquer sin (1). Christ is here portrayed as the judge to whom those guilty of pagan vices must render an account (5; cf Jn 5, 22-27; Acts 10, 42; 2 Tm 4, 1).

4, 6: *The dead:* these may be the sinners of the flood generation who are possibly referred to in 1 Pt 3, 19. But many scholars think that there is no connection between these two verses, and that *the dead* here are Christians who have died since hearing the preaching of the gospel.

4, 7-11: The inner life of the eschatological community is outlined as *the end* (the parousia of Christ) and the judgment draws near in terms of seriousness, sobriety, prayer, and love expressed through hospitality and the use of one's gifts for the glory of God and of Christ.

4, 8: *Love covers a multitude of sins:* a maxim based on Prv 10, 12; see also Ps 32, 1; Jas 5, 20.

4, 11: Some scholars feel that this doxology concludes the part of the homily addressed specifically to the newly baptized, begun in 1 Pt 1, 3; others that it concludes a baptismal liturgy. Such doxologies do occur within a New Testament letter, e.g., Rom 9, 5. Some propose that v 11 was an alternate ending, with 1 Pt 4, 12—5, 14 being read in places where persecution was more pressing. But such doxologies usually do not occur at the end of letters (the only examples are 2 Pt 3, 18, Jude 25, and Rom 16, 27, the last probably a liturgical insertion).

4, 12-19: The suffering to which the author has already frequently referred is presented in more severe terms. This has led some scholars to see these verses as referring to an actual persecution. Others see the heightening of the language as only a rhetorical device used at the end of the letter to emphasize the suffering motif.

5, 1-4: In imitation of Christ, the chief shepherd, those entrusted with a pastoral office are to tend the flock by their care and example.

5, 1: *Presbyters:* the officially appointed leaders and teachers of the Christian community (cf 1 Tm 5, 17-18; Ti 1, 5-8; Jas 5, 14).

shameful profit but eagerly.[e] [3]Do not lord it over those assigned to you, but be examples to the flock. [4] [f] And when the chief Shepherd is revealed, you will receive the unfading crown of glory.*

Advice to the Community.* [5]Likewise, you younger members,* be subject to the presbyters. And all of you, clothe yourselves with humility in your dealings with one another, for:

"God opposes the proud
but bestows favor on the humble."[g]

[6]So humble yourselves under the mighty hand of God, that he may exalt you in due time.[h] [7]Cast all your worries upon him because he cares for you.[i] [8]Be sober and vigilant. Your opponent the devil is prowling around like a roaring lion looking for [someone] to devour.[j] [9]Resist him, steadfast in faith, knowing that your fellow believers throughout the world undergo the same sufferings. [10]The God of all grace who called you to his eternal glory through Christ [Jesus] will himself restore, confirm, strengthen, and establish you after you have suffered a little.[k] [11]To him be dominion forever. Amen.

V. CONCLUSION

[12]I write you this briefly through Silvanus,* whom I consider a faithful brother, exhorting you and testifying that this is the true grace of God. Remain firm in it. [13]The chosen one* at Babylon sends you greeting, as does Mark, my son. [14]Greet one another with a loving kiss. Peace to all of you who are in Christ.[l]

e Acts 20, 28; Ti 1, 7.—f Wis 5, 15-16; 1 Cor 9, 25; 2 Tm 4, 8; Jas 1, 12.—g Prv 3, 34.—h Jb 22, 29; Jas 4, 10.—i Ps 55, 23; Mt 6, 25-33; Lk 12, 22-31; Phil 4, 6.—j 1 Thes 5, 6.—k Rom 8, 18; 2 Cor 4, 17.—l Rom 16, 16; 1 Cor 16, 20; 2 Cor 13, 12.

5, 4: See the note on 1 Pt 2, 25.

5, 5-11: The community is to be subject to the presbyters and to show humility toward one another and trust in God's love and care (5-7). With sobriety, alertness, and steadfast faith they must resist the evil one; their sufferings are shared with Christians everywhere (8-9). They will be strengthened and called to eternal glory (10-11).

5, 5: *Younger members:* this may be a designation for office-holders of lesser rank.

5, 12: *Silvanus:* the companion of Paul (see 2 Cor 1, 19; 1 Thes 1, 1; 2 Thes 1, 1). Jews and Jewish Christians, like Paul, often had a Hebrew name (Saoul, Silas) and a Greek or Latin name (Paul, Silvanus). On Silvanus's possible role as amanuensis, see Introduction.

5, 13: *The chosen one:* feminine, referring to the Christian community *(ekklēsia)* at *Babylon,* the code name for Rome in Rv 14, 8; 17, 5; 18, 2. *Mark, my son:* traditionally a prominent disciple of Peter and co-worker at the church in Rome, perhaps the John Mark referred to in Acts 12, 12.25; 13, 5.13; and in Acts 15, 37-39, a companion of Barnabas. Perhaps this is the same Mark mentioned as Barnabas's cousin in Col 4, 10, a co-worker with Paul in Phlm 24 (see also 2 Tm 4, 11).

THE SECOND LETTER OF PETER

INTRODUCTION

This letter can be appreciated both for its positive teachings and for its earnest warnings. It seeks to strengthen readers in faith (1, 1), hope for the future (3, 1-10), knowledge (1, 2.6.8), love (1, 7), and other virtues (1, 5-6). This aim is carried out especially by warning against false teachers, the condemnation of whom occupies the long central section of the letter (2, 1-22). A particular crisis is the claim by "scoffers" that there will be no second coming of Jesus, a doctrine that the author vigorously affirms (3, 1-10). The concept of God's "promises" is particularly precious in the theology of 2 Peter (1, 4; 3, 4.9.13). Closing comments at 3, 17-18 well sum up the twin concerns: that you not "be led into" error and "fall" but instead "grow in grace" and "knowledge" of Jesus Christ.

Second Peter is clearly structured in its presentation of these points. It reminds its readers of the divine authenticity of Christ's teaching (1, 3-4), continues with reflections on Christian conduct (1, 5-15), then returns to the exalted dignity of Jesus by incorporating into the text the apostolic witness to his transfiguration (1, 16-18). It takes up the ques-

tion of the interpretation of scripture by pointing out that it is possible to misunderstand the sacred writings (1, 19-21) and that divine punishment will overtake false teachers (2, 1-22). It proclaims that the parousia is the teaching of the Lord and of the apostles and is therefore an eventual certainty (3, 1-13). At the same time, it warns that the meaning of Paul's writings on this question should not be distorted (3, 14-18).

In both content and style this letter is very different from 1 Peter, which immediately precedes it in the canon. The opening verse attributes it to "Symeon Peter, a slave and apostle of Jesus Christ." Moreover, the author in 3, 1 calls his work a "second letter," referring probably to 1 Peter as his first, and in 1, 18 counts himself among those present at the transfiguration of Jesus.

Nevertheless, acceptance of 2 Peter into the New Testament canon met with great resistance in the early church. The oldest certain reference to it comes from Origen in the early third century. While he himself accepted both Petrine letters as canonical, he testifies that others rejected 2 Peter. As late as the fifth century some local churches still excluded it from the canon, but eventually it was universally adopted. The principal reason for the long delay was the persistent doubt that the letter stemmed from the apostle Peter.

Among modern scholars there is wide agreement that 2 Peter is a pseudonymous work, i.e., one written by a later author who attributed it to Peter according to a literary convention popular at the time. It gives the impression of being more remote in time from the apostolic period than 1 Peter; indeed, many think it is the latest work in the New Testament and assign it to the first or even the second quarter of the second century.

The principal reasons for this view are the following. The author refers to the apostles and "our ancestors" as belonging to a previous generation, now dead (3, 2-4). A collection of Paul's letters exists and appears to be well known, but disputes have arisen about the interpretation of them (3, 14-16). The passage about false teachers (2, 1-18) contains a number of literary contacts with Jude 4-16, and it is generally agreed that 2 Peter depends upon Jude, not vice versa. Finally, the principal problem exercising the author is the false teaching of "scoffers" who have concluded from the delay of the parousia that the Lord is not going to return. This could scarcely have been an issue during the lifetime of Simon Peter.

The Christians to whom the letter is addressed are not identified, though it may be the intent of 3, 1 to identify them with the churches of Asia Minor to which 1 Peter was sent. Except for the epistolary greeting in 1, 1-2, 2 Peter does not have the features of a genuine letter at all, but is rather a general exhortation cast in the form of a letter. The author must have been a Jewish Christian of the dispersion for, while his Jewish heritage is evident in various features of his thought and style, he writes in the rather stilted literary Greek of the Hellenistic period. He appeals to tradition against the twin threat of doctrinal error and moral laxity, which appear to reflect an early stage of what later developed into full-blown gnosticism. Thus he forms a link between the apostolic period and the church of subsequent ages.

The principal divisions of the Second Letter of Peter are the following:

2Pt

I. Address (1, 1-2)
II. Exhortation to Christian Virtue (1, 3-21)
III. Condemnation of the False Teachers (2, 1-22)
IV. The Delay of the Second Coming (3, 1-16)
V. Final Exhortation and Doxology (3, 17-18)

I. ADDRESS

CHAPTER 1

Greeting. 1 Symeon Peter,* a slave and
apostle of Jesus Christ, to those who have
received a faith of equal value to ours
through the righteousness of our God and
savior Jesus Christ: 2 may grace and peace
be yours in abundance through knowledge* of God and of Jesus our Lord.

II. EXHORTATION TO CHRISTIAN VIRTUE

The Power of God's Promise. 3 * His divine power has bestowed on us everything
that makes for life and devotion, through
the knowledge of him[a] who called us by
his own glory and power.* 4 Through
these, he has bestowed on us the precious
and very great promises, so that through
them you may come to share in the divine
nature, after escaping from the corruption
that is in the world because of evil desire.[b]
5 * For this very reason, make every effort
to supplement your faith with virtue, virtue with knowledge,[c] 6 knowledge with
self-control, self-control with endurance,
endurance with devotion, 7 devotion with
mutual affection, mutual affection with
love. 8 If these are yours and increase in
abundance, they will keep you from being
idle or unfruitful in the knowledge of our
Lord Jesus Christ. 9 [d] Anyone who lacks
them is blind and shortsighted, forgetful of
the cleansing of his past sins. 10 * Therefore, brothers, be all the more eager to
make your call and election firm, for, in
doing so, you will never stumble. 11 For, in
this way, entry into the eternal kingdom of
our Lord and savior Jesus Christ will be
richly provided for you.

Apostolic Witness. 12 * Therefore, I will
always remind you of these things, even
though you already know them and are established in the truth you have. 13 I think it
right, as long as I am in this "tent,"* to stir
you up by a reminder, 14 since I know that
I will soon have to put it aside, as indeed
our Lord Jesus Christ has shown me.[e] 15 I
shall also make every effort to enable you
always to remember these things after my
departure.

16 We did not follow cleverly devised
myths when we made known to you the
power and coming* of our Lord Jesus
Christ, but we had been eyewitnesses of his
majesty.[f] 17 For he received honor and
glory from God the Father* when that
unique declaration came to him from the
majestic glory, "This is my Son, my beloved, with whom I am well pleased."[g]
18 We* ourselves heard this voice come
from heaven while we were with him on
the holy mountain. 19 [h] Moreover, we pos-

---

a 2 Cor 4, 6; 1 Pt 2, 9.—b 2 Cor 7, 1; 1 Jn 2, 15.—c 5-7: Gal 5, 22-23.—d 1 Jn 2, 9.11.—e Is 38, 12; Jn 21, 18-19.—f Lk 9, 28-36; Jn 1, 14.—g Ps 2, 7; Mt 17, 4-6.—h Lk 1, 78-79; Rv 2, 28.

1, 1: *Symeon Peter:* on the authorship of 2 Peter, see Introduction; on the spelling here of the Hebrew name *Šim'ôn,* cf Acts 15, 14. The greeting is especially similar to those in 1 Peter and Jude. The words translated *our God and savior Jesus Christ* could also be rendered "our God and the savior Jesus Christ"; cf 2 Pt 1, 11; 2, 20; 3, 2.18.

1, 2: *Knowledge:* a key term in the letter (2 Pt 1, 3.8; 2, 20; 3, 18), perhaps used as a Christian emphasis against gnostic claims.

1, 3-4: Christian life in its fullness is a gift of divine power effecting a knowledge of Christ and the bestowal of divine promises (2 Pt 3, 4.9). *To share in the divine nature,* escaping from a corrupt world, is a thought found elsewhere in the Bible but expressed only here in such Hellenistic terms, since it is said to be accomplished through *knowledge* (3); cf 2 Pt 1, 2; 2, 20; but see also Jn 15, 4; 17, 22-23; Rom 8, 14-17; Heb 3, 14; 1 Jn 1, 3; 3, 2.

1, 3: *By his own glory and power:* the most ancient papyrus and the best codex read "through glory and power."

1, 5-9: Note the climactic gradation of qualities (5-7), beginning with faith and leading to the fullness of Christian life, which is love; cf Rom 5, 3-4; Gal 5, 6.22 for a similar series of "virtues," though the program and sense here are different than in Paul. The fruit of these is knowledge of Christ (8) referred to in v 3; their absence is spiritual blindness (9).

1, 10-11: Perseverance in the Christian vocation is the best preventative against losing it and the safest provision for attaining its goal, the kingdom. *Kingdom of . . . Christ,* instead of "God," is unusual; cf Col 1, 13 and Mt 13, 41, as well as the *righteousness of . . . Christ* (1).

1, 12-19: The purpose in writing is to call to mind the apostle's witness to the truth, even as he faces the end of his life (12-15), his eyewitness testimony to Christ (16-18), and the true prophetic message (19) through the Spirit in scripture (20-21), in contrast to what false teachers are setting forth (ch 2).

1, 13: *Tent:* a biblical image for transitory human life (Is 38, 12), here combined with a verb that suggests not folding or packing up a tent but its being discarded in death (cf 2 Cor 5, 1-4).

1, 16: *Coming:* in Greek *parousia,* used at 2 Pt 3, 4.12 of the second coming of Christ. The word was used in the extrabiblical writings for the visitation of someone in authority; in Greek cult and Hellenistic Judaism it was used for the manifestation of the divine presence. What the apostles *made known* has been interpreted to refer to Jesus' transfiguration (17) or to his entire first coming or to his future coming in power (ch 3).

1, 17: The author assures the readers of the reliability of the apostolic message (including Jesus' power, glory, and coming; cf the note on 2 Pt 1, 16) by appeal to the transfiguration of Jesus in glory (cf Mt 17, 1-8 and parallels) and by appeal to the prophetic message (2 Pt 1, 19; perhaps Nm 24, 17). Here, as elsewhere, the New Testament insists on continued reminders as necessary to preserve the historical facts about Jesus and the truths of the faith; cf 2 Pt 3, 1-2; 1 Cor 11, 2; 15, 1-3. *My Son, my beloved:* or, "my beloved Son."

1, 18: *We:* at Jesus' transfiguration, referring to Peter, James, and John (Mt 17, 1).

sess the prophetic message that is altogether reliable. You will do well to be attentive to it, as to a lamp shining in a dark place, until day dawns and the morning star rises in your hearts.
20 * Know this first of all, that there is no prophecy of scripture that is a matter of personal interpretation,
21 for no prophecy ever came through human will; but rather human beings moved by the holy Spirit spoke under the influence of God.

III. CONDEMNATION OF THE FALSE TEACHERS

CHAPTER 2

False Teachers.* 1 There were also false prophets among the people, just as there will be false teachers among you, who will introduce destructive heresies and even deny the Master who ransomed them, bringing swift destruction on themselves.[i]
2 Many will follow their licentious ways, and because of them the way of truth will be reviled.[j]
3 In their greed they will exploit you with fabrications, but from of old their condemnation has not been idle and their destruction does not sleep.[k]

Lessons from the Past.
4 * For if God did not spare the angels when they sinned, but condemned them to the chains of Tartarus* and handed them over to be kept for judgment;[l]
5 * and if he did not spare the ancient world, even though he preserved Noah, a herald of righteousness, together with seven others, when he brought a flood upon the godless world;[m]
6 and if he condemned the cities of Sodom and Gomorrah [to destruction], reducing them to ashes, making them an example for the godless [people] of what is coming;[n]
7 and if he rescued Lot, a righteous man oppressed by the licentious conduct of unprincipled people
8 (for day after day that righteous man living among them was tormented in his righteous soul at the lawless deeds that he saw and heard),
9 then the Lord knows how to rescue the devout from trial and to keep the unrighteous under punishment for the day of judgment,[o]
10 and especially those who follow the flesh with its depraved desire and show contempt for lordship.[p]

False Teachers Denounced.* Bold and arrogant, they are not afraid to revile glorious beings,*
11 whereas angels,[q] despite their superior strength and power, do not bring a reviling judgment against them from the Lord.*
12 But these people, like irrational animals born by nature for capture and destruction, revile things that they do not understand, and in their destruction they will also be destroyed,[r]
13 suffering wrong* as payment for wrongdoing. Thinking daytime revelry a delight, they are stains and defilements as they revel in their deceits while carousing with you.[s]
14 Their eyes are full of adultery and insatiable for sin. They seduce unstable people, and their hearts are trained in

i Mt 24, 11.24; 1 Tm 4, 1; Jude 4.—j Is 52, 5.—k Rom 16, 18.—l Jude 6.—m Gn 8, 15-19; Heb 11, 7.—n Gn 19, 24-25; Jude 7.—o 1 Cor 10, 13; Rv 3, 10.—p Jude 8.—q Jude 9.—r Ps 49, 13-15; Jude 10.—s Jude 12.

1, 20-21: Often cited, along with 2 Tm 3, 16, on the "inspiration" of scripture or against private interpretation, these verses in context are directed against the false teachers of ch 2 and clever tales (16). The prophetic word in scripture comes admittedly through *human beings* (21), but *moved by the holy Spirit,* not from their own interpretation, and is a matter of what the author and Spirit intended, not the *personal interpretation* of false teachers. Instead of *under the influence of God,* some manuscripts read "holy ones of God."

2, 1-3: The pattern of *false prophets* among the Old Testament people of God will recur through *false teachers* in the church. Such destructive opinions of heretical sects bring loss of faith in Christ, contempt for the way of salvation (cf 2 Pt 2, 21), and immorality.

2, 4-6: The false teachers will be punished just as surely and as severely as were the fallen *angels* (4; cf Jude 6; Gn 6, 1-4), the sinners of Noah's day (5; Gn 7, 21-23), and the inhabitants of the cities of the Plain (6; Jude 7; Gn 19, 25). Whereas there are three examples in Jude 5-7 (Exodus and wilderness; rebellious angels; Sodom and Gomorrah), 2 Peter omitted the first of these, has inserted a new illustration about Noah (5) between Jude's second and third examples, and listed the resulting three examples in their Old Testament order (Gn 6; 7; 19).

2, 4: *Chains of Tartarus:* cf Jude 6; other manuscripts in 2 Peter read "pits of Tartarus." *Tartarus:* a term borrowed from Greek mythology to indicate the infernal regions.

2, 5-10a: Although God did not spare the sinful, he kept and saved the righteous, such as *Noah* (5) and *Lot* (7), and he *knows how to rescue the devout* (9), who are contrasted with the false teachers of the author's day. On Noah, cf Gn 5, 32—9, 29, especially 7, 1. On Lot, cf Gn 13 and 19.

2, 10b-22: Some take 10b and 11 with the preceding paragraph. Others begin the new paragraph with 10a, supplying from v 9 *The Lord knows how . . . to keep . . . under punishment,* with reference to God and probably specifically Christ (1). The conduct of the false teachers is described and condemned in language similar to that of Jude 8-16. This arrogance knows no bounds; animal-like, they are due to be caught and destroyed. They seduce even those who have knowledge of Christ (20).

2, 10b: *Glorious beings:* literally, "glories"; cf Jude 8. While some think that illustrious personages are meant or even political officials behind whom (fallen) angels stand, it is more likely that the reference is to glorious angelic beings (cf Jude 9).

2, 11: *From the Lord:* some manuscripts read "before the Lord"; cf Jude 9.

2, 13: *Suffering wrong:* some manuscripts read "receiving a reward." *In their deceits:* some manuscripts read "in their love feasts" (Jude 12).

repentance.[i] 10 But the day of the Lord will
come like a thief,* and then the heavens
will pass away with a mighty roar and the
elements will be dissolved by fire, and the
earth and everything done on it will be
found out.[j]

Exhortation to Preparedness.* 11 Since
everything is to be dissolved in this way,
what sort of persons ought [you] to be,
conducting yourselves in holiness and devotion,[k] 12 waiting for and hastening the
coming of the day of God,[l] because of
which the heavens will be dissolved in
flames and the elements melted by fire.*
13 But according to his promise we await
new heavens and a new earth* in which
righteousness dwells.[m]

14 Therefore, beloved, since you await
these things, be eager to be found without
spot or blemish before him, at peace.
15 And consider the patience of our Lord as
salvation, as our beloved brother Paul, according to the wisdom given to him, also
wrote to you,[n] 16 speaking of these things*
as he does in all his letters. In them there
are some things hard to understand that
the ignorant and unstable distort to their
own destruction, just as they do the other
scriptures.

V. FINAL EXHORTATION AND DOXOLOGY*

17 Therefore, beloved, since you are
forewarned, be on your guard not to be led
into the error of the unprincipled and to
fall from your own stability.[o] 18 But grow
in grace and in the knowledge of our Lord
and savior Jesus Christ. To him be glory
now and to the day of eternity. [Amen.][p]

i Ez 18, 23; 1 Tm 2, 4.—j Is 66, 15-16; Mt 24, 29.—k Acts 3, 19-21.—l Is 34, 4; Heb 10, 27.—m Is 65, 17; 66, 22; Rom 8, 21; Rv 21, 1.27.—n Rom 8, 19; Jude 24.—o Mk 13, 5; Heb 2, 1.—p Rom 16, 27.

3, 10: *Like a thief:* Mt 24, 43; 1 Thes 5, 2; Rv 3, 3. *Will be found out:* cf 1 Cor 3, 13-15. Some few versions read, as the sense may demand, "will not be found out"; many manuscripts read "will be burned up"; there are further variants in other manuscripts, versions, and Fathers. Total destruction is assumed (11).

3, 11-16: The second coming of Christ and the judgment of the world are the doctrinal bases for the moral exhortation to readiness through vigilance and a virtuous life; cf Mt 24, 42.50-51; Lk 12, 40; 1 Thes 5, 1-11; Jude 20-21.

3, 12: *Flames . . . fire:* although this is the only New Testament passage about a final conflagration, the idea was common in apocalyptic and Greco-Roman thought. *Hastening:* eschatology is here used to motivate ethics (11), as elsewhere in the New Testament. Jewish sources and Acts 3, 19-20 assume that proper ethical conduct can help bring the promised day of the Lord; cf 2 Pt 3, 9. Some render the phrase, however, "desiring it earnestly."

3, 13: *New heavens and a new earth:* cf Is 65, 17; 66, 22. The divine promises will be fulfilled after the day of judgment will have passed. The universe will be transformed by the reign of God's *righteousness* or justice; cf Is 65, 17-18; Acts 3, 21; Rom 8, 18-25; Rv 21, 1.

3, 16: *These things:* the teachings of this letter find parallels in Paul, e.g., God's will to save (Rom 2, 4; 9, 22-23; 1 Cor 1, 7-8), the coming of Christ (1 Thes 4, 16-17; 1 Cor 15, 23-52), and preparedness for the judgment (Col 1, 22-23; Eph 1, 4-14; 4, 30; 5, 5-14). *Other scriptures:* used to guide the faith and life of the Christian community. The letters of Paul are thus here placed on the same level as books of the Old Testament. Possibly other New Testament writings could also be included.

3, 17-18: To avoid the dangers of *error* and loss of *stability,* Christians are *forewarned* to be *on guard* and to *grow in grace and knowledge* (2 Pt 1, 2) of Christ. The doxology (18) recalls 1 Pt 4, 11. Some manuscripts add *Amen.*

THE FIRST LETTER OF JOHN

INTRODUCTION

Early Christian tradition identified this work as a letter of John the apostle. Because of its resemblance to the fourth gospel in style, vocabulary, and ideas, it is generally agreed that both works are the product of the same school of Johannine Christianity. The terminology and the presence or absence of certain theological ideas in 1 John suggest that it was written after the gospel; it may have been composed as a short treatise on ideas that were developed more fully in the fourth gospel. To others, the evidence suggests that 1 John was written after the fourth gospel as part of a debate on the proper interpretation of that gospel. Whatever its relation to the gospel, 1 John may be dated toward the end of the first century. Unlike 2 and 3 John, it lacks in form the salutation and epistolary conclusion of a letter. These features, its prologue, and its emphasis on doctrinal teaching make it more akin to a theological treatise than to most other New Testament letters.

The purpose of the letter is to combat certain false ideas, especially about Jesus, and to deepen the spiritual and social awareness of the Christian community (3, 17). Some former members (2, 19) of the community refused to acknowledge Jesus as the Christ (2,

22) and denied that he was a true man (4, 2). The specific heresy described in this letter cannot be identified exactly, but it is a form of docetism or gnosticism; the former doctrine denied the humanity of Christ to insure that his divinity was untainted, and the latter viewed the appearance of Christ as a mere stepping-stone to higher knowledge of God. These theological errors are rejected by an appeal to the reality and continuity of the apostolic witness to Jesus. The author affirms that authentic Christian love, ethics, and faith take place only within the historical revelation and sacrifice of Jesus Christ. The fullness of Christian life as fellowship with the Father must be based on true belief and result in charitable living; knowledge of God and love for one another are inseparable, and error in one area inevitably affects the other. Although the author recognizes that Christian doctrine presents intangible mysteries of faith about Christ, he insists that the concrete Christian life brings to light the deeper realities of the gospel.

The structure and language of the letter are straightforward yet repetitious. The author sets forth the striking contrasts between light and darkness, Christians and the world, and truth and error to illustrate the threats and responsibilities of Christian life. The result is not one of theological argument but one of intense religious conviction expressed in simple truths. The letter is of particular value for its declaration of the humanity and divinity of Christ as an apostolic teaching and for its development of the intrinsic connection between Christian moral conduct and Christian doctrine.

The principal divisions of the First Letter of John are the following:

I. Prologue (1, 1-4)
II. God as Light (1, 5—3, 10)
III. Love for One Another (3, 11—5, 12)
IV. Epilogue (5, 13-21)

I. PROLOGUE

CHAPTER 1

The Word of Life*

1 What was from the beginning,
what we have heard,
what we have seen with our eyes,
what we looked upon
and touched with our hands
concerns the Word of life—[a]
2 for the life was made visible;
we have seen it and testify to it
and proclaim to you the eternal life
that was with the Father and was made visible to us—[b]
3 what we have seen and heard
we proclaim now to you,
so that you too may have fellowship with us;
for our fellowship is with the Father
and with his Son, Jesus Christ.[c]
4 We are writing this so that our joy may be complete.[d]

II. GOD AS LIGHT

God is Light. [5]Now this is the message
that we have heard from him and proclaim
to you: God is light,* and in him there is
no darkness at all. [6]If we say, "We have
fellowship with him," while we continue to
walk in darkness, we lie and do not act in
truth.[e] [7]But if we walk in the light as he is
in the light, then we have fellowship with
one another, and the blood of his Son Jesus
cleanses us from all sin.[f] [8]If we say, "We
are without sin," we deceive ourselves,*

a 1 Jn 2, 13; Jn 1, 1.14; 20, 20.25.27.—b Jn 15, 27; 17, 5.—c Jn 17, 21; Acts 4, 20.—d Jn 15, 11; 2 Jn 12.—e Jn 12, 35.—f Mt 26, 28; Rom 3, 24-25; Heb 9, 14; 1 Pt 1, 19; Rv 1, 5.

1, 1-4: There is a striking parallel to the prologue of the gospel of John (Jn 1, 1-18), but the emphasis here is not on the preexistent Word but rather on the apostles' witness to the incarnation of *life* by their experience of the historical Jesus. He is *the Word of life* (1; cf Jn 1, 4), *the eternal life that was with the Father and was made visible* (2; cf Jn 1, 14), and was *heard, seen, looked upon,* and *touched* by the apostles. The purpose of their teaching is to share that *life,* called *fellowship . . . with the Father and with his Son, Jesus Christ,* with those who receive their witness (3; Jn 1, 14.16).

1, 5-7: *Light* is to be understood here as truth and goodness; *darkness* here is error and depravity (cf Jn 3, 19-21; 17, 17; Eph 5, 8). To *walk* in light or darkness is to live according to truth or error, not merely intellectual but moral as well. Fellowship with God and with one another consists in a life according to the truth as found in God and in Christ.

1, 8-10: Denial of the condition of sin is self-deception and even contradictory of divine revelation; there is also the continual possibility of sin's recurrence. Forgiveness and deliverance from sin through Christ are assured through acknowledgment of them and repentance.

and the truth is not in us.[g] 9 If we acknowledge our sins, he is faithful and just and will forgive our sins and cleanse us from every wrongdoing.[h] 10 If we say, "We have not sinned," we make him a liar, and his word is not in us.[i]

CHAPTER 2

Christ and His Commandments. 1 My children,* I am writing this to you so that you may not commit sin. But if anyone does sin, we have an Advocate with the Father, Jesus Christ the righteous one.[j] 2 He is expiation for our sins, and not for our sins only but for those of the whole world.[k] 3 The way we may be sure* that we know him is to keep his commandments.[l] 4 Whoever says, "I know him," but does not keep his commandments is a liar, and the truth is not in him.[m] 5 But whoever keeps his word, the love of God is truly perfected in him. This is the way we may know that we are in union with him:[n] 6 whoever claims to abide in him ought to live [just] as he lived.

The New Commandment.* 7 Beloved, I am writing no new commandment to you but an old commandment that you had from the beginning. The old commandment is the word that you have heard.[o] 8 And yet I do write a new commandment to you, which holds true in him and among you,* for the darkness is passing away, and the true light is already shining.[p] 9 Whoever says he is in the light, yet hates his brother, is still in the darkness.[q] 10 Whoever loves his brother remains in the light, and there is nothing in him to cause a fall.[r] 11 Whoever hates his brother is in darkness; he walks in darkness and does not know where he is going because the darkness has blinded his eyes.

Members of the Community.* 12 I am writing to you, children, because your sins have been forgiven[s] for his name's sake.*

13 I am writing to you, fathers, because you know him who is from the beginning.

I am writing to you, young men, because you have conquered the evil one.[t]

14 I write to you, children, because you know the Father.

I write to you, fathers, because you know him who is from the beginning.

I write to you, young men, because you are strong and the word of God remains in you, and you have conquered the evil one.

15 Do not love the world or the things of the world.* If anyone loves the world, the love of the Father is not in him.[u] 16 For all that is in the world, sensual lust,* enticement for the eyes, and a pretentious life, is not from the Father but is from the world. 17 Yet the world and its enticement are passing away. But whoever does the will of God remains forever.[v]

Antichrists. 18 Children, it is the last hour;* and just as you heard that the antichrist was coming, so now many antichrists have appeared. Thus we know this is the last hour.[w] 19 They went out from us, but they were not really of our number;* if

g 2 Chr 6, 36; Prv 20, 9.—h Prv 28, 13; Jas 5, 16.—i 1 Jn 5, 10.—j Jn 14, 16; Heb 7, 25.—k 1 Jn 4, 10.—l Jn 14, 15; 15, 10.—m 1 Jn 4, 20.—n Jn 14, 23.—o 1 Jn 3, 11; Dt 6, 5; Mt 22, 37-40.—p Jn 13, 34 / Jn 1, 5; Rom 13, 12.—q Jn 8, 12.—r Eccl 2, 14; Jn 11, 10.—s 1 Cor 6, 11.—t 1 Jn 1, 1; Jn 1, 1.—u Rom 8, 7-8; Jas 4, 4; 2 Pt 1, 4.—v Is 40, 8; Mt 7, 21; 1 Cor 7, 31; 1 Pt 4, 2.—w 1 Tim 4, 1.

2, 1: *Children:* like the term "beloved," this is an expression of pastoral love (cf Jn 13, 33; 21, 5; 1 Cor 4, 14). *Advocate:* for the use of the term, see Jn 14, 16. Forgiveness of sin is assured through Christ's intercession and expiation or "offering"; the death of Christ effected the removal of sin.

2, 3-6: *The way we may be sure:* to those who claim, "I have known Christ and therefore I know him," our author insists on not mere intellectual knowledge but obedience to God's commandments in a life conformed to the example of Christ; this confirms our knowledge of him and is *the love of God . . . perfected.* Disparity between moral life and the commandments proves improper belief.

2, 7-11: The author expresses the continuity and freshness of mutual charity in Christian experience. Through Christ the commandment of love has become the *light* defeating the *darkness* of evil in a new age. All hatred as darkness is incompatible with the light and Christian life. Note also the characteristic Johannine polemic in which a positive assertion is emphasized by the negative statement of its opposite.

2, 8: *Which holds true in him and among you:* literally, "a thing that holds true in him and in you."

2, 12-17: The Christian community that has experienced the grace of God through forgiveness of sin and knowledge of Christ is armed against the evil one.

2, 12: *For his name's sake:* because of Christ our sins are forgiven.

2, 15: *The world:* all that is hostile toward God and alienated from him. Love of the *world* and love of God are thus mutually exclusive; cf Jas 4, 4.

2, 16: *Sensual lust:* literally, "the lust of the flesh," inordinate desire for physical gratification. *Enticement for the eyes:* literally, "the lust of the eyes," avarice or covetousness; the eyes are regarded as the windows of the soul. *Pretentious life:* literally, "pride of life," arrogance or ostentation in one's earthly style of life that reflects a willful independence from God and others.

2, 18: *It is the last hour:* literally, "a last hour," the period between the death and resurrection of Christ and his second coming. *The antichrist:* opponent or adversary of Christ; the term appears only in 1-2 John, but "pseudochrists" (translated "false messiahs") in Mt 24, 24 and Mk 13, 22, and Paul's "lawless one" in 2 Thes 2, 3, are similar figures. *Many antichrists:* Mt, Mk, and Rv seem to indicate a collectivity of persons, here related to the false teachers.

2, 19: *Not really of our number:* the apostate teachers only proved their lack of faith by leaving the community.

they had been, they would have remained with us. Their desertion shows that none of them was of our number. 20 But you have the anointing that comes from the holy one,* and you all have knowledge.[x]
21 I write to you not because you do not know the truth but because you do, and because every lie is alien to the truth.[y] 22 *
Who is the liar? Whoever denies that Jesus is the Christ. Whoever denies the Father and the Son, this is the antichrist.[z] 23 No
one who denies the Son has the Father, but whoever confesses the Son has the Father as well.[a]

Life from God's Anointing. 24 [b] Let what you heard from the beginning remain in you. If what you heard from the beginning remains in you, then you will remain in the Son and in the Father.* 25 And this is the
promise that he made us: eternal life.[c] 26 I
write you these things about those who would deceive you. 27 As for you, the anointing that you received from him remains in you, so that you do not need anyone to teach you. But his anointing teaches you about everything and is true and not false; just as it taught you, remain in him.

Children of God. 28 * And now, children, remain in him, so that when he appears we may have confidence and not be put to
shame by him at his coming. 29 If you consider that he is righteous, you also know that everyone who acts in righteousness is begotten by him.

CHAPTER 3

1 * See what love the Father has bestowed on us that we may be called the children of God. Yet so we are. The reason the world does not know us is that it did
not know him.[d] 2 Beloved, we are God's children now; what we shall be has not yet been revealed. We do know that when it is revealed* we shall be like him, for we shall
see him as he is.[e] 3 Everyone who has this hope based on him makes himself pure, as he is pure.[f]

Avoiding Sin. 4 Everyone who commits sin commits lawlessness, for sin is lawlessness.* 5 You know that he was revealed to take away sins, and in him there is no sin.[g]
6 No one who remains in him sins; no one who sins has seen him or known him.
7 Children, let no one deceive you. The person who acts in righteousness is righteous, just as he is righteous. 8 Whoever sins belongs to the devil, because the devil has sinned from the beginning. Indeed, the Son of God was revealed to destroy the
works of the devil.[h] 9 No one who is begotten by God commits sin, because God's seed remains in him; he cannot sin because
he is begotten by God.* 10 In this way, the children of God and the children of the devil are made plain; no one who fails to act in righteousness belongs to God, nor anyone who does not love his brother.

III. LOVE FOR ONE ANOTHER

11 * For this is the message you have heard from the beginning: we should love
one another,[i] 12 unlike Cain who belonged to the evil one and slaughtered his brother. Why did he slaughter him? Because his own works were evil, and those of his

x Jn 14, 26.—y 1 Jn 3, 19; 2 Pt 1, 12.—z 2 Thes 2, 4.—a Jn 14, 7-9.—b Jn 14, 23.—c Jn 5, 24; 10, 28; 17, 2.—d Jn 1, 12; Eph 1, 5 / Jn 15, 21; 17, 25.—e Phil 3, 21.—f 1 Jn 2, 6.—g Is 53, 9; Jn 1, 29; 8, 46; 1 Pt 2, 22.—h Jn 8, 44; 12, 31-32.—i 1 Jn 2, 7; Jn 13, 34; 15, 12.17.

2, 20: *The anointing that comes from the holy one:* this anointing is in the Old Testament sense of receiving the Spirit of God. The *Holy One* probably refers to Christ. True knowledge is the gift of the Spirit (cf Is 11, 2), and the function of the Spirit is to lead Christians to the truth (Jn 14, 17.26; 16, 13).

2, 22-23: Certain gnostics denied that the earthly Jesus was the Christ; to deny knowledge of the Son is to deny the Father, since only through the Son has God been fully revealed (Jn 1, 18; 14, 8-9).

2, 24: Continuity with the apostolic witness as proclaimed in the prologue is the safeguard of right belief.

2, 28-29: Our confidence at his judgment is based on the daily assurance of salvation. Our actions reflect our true relation to him.

3, 1-3: The greatest sign of God's love is the gift of his Son (Jn 3, 16) that has made Christians true children of God. This relationship is a present reality and also part of the life to come; true knowledge of God will ultimately be gained, and Christians prepare themselves now by virtuous lives in imitation of the Son.

3, 2: *When it is revealed:* or "when he is revealed" (the subject of the verb could be Christ).

3, 4: *Lawlessness:* a reference to the activity of the antichrist, so it is expressed as hostility toward God and a rejection of Christ. The author goes on to contrast the states of sin and righteousness. Christians do not escape sin but realize that when they sin they cease to have fellowship with God. Virtue and sin distinguish the children of God from the children of the devil.

3, 9: A habitual sinner is a child of the devil, while a child of God, who by definition is in fellowship with God, cannot sin. *Seed:* Christ or the Spirit who shares the nature of God with the Christian.

3, 11-18: Love, even to the point of self-sacrifice, is the point of the commandment. The story of Cain and Abel (12-15; Gn 4, 1-16) presents the rivalry of two brothers, in a contrast of evil and righteousness, where envy led to murder. For Christians, proof of deliverance is love toward others, after the example of Christ. This includes concrete acts of charity, out of our material abundance.

brother righteous.[j] 13 Do not be amazed, [then,] brothers, if the world hates you.[k] 14 We know that we have passed from death to life because we love our brothers. Whoever does not love remains in death.[l] 15 Everyone who hates his brother is a murderer, and you know that no murderer has eternal life remaining in him.[m] 16 The way we came to know love was that he laid down his life for us; so we ought to lay down our lives for our brothers.[n] 17 If someone who has worldly means sees a brother in need and refuses him compassion, how can the love of God remain in him?[o] 18 Children, let us love not in word or speech but in deed and truth.[p]

Confidence before God.* 19 [Now] this is how we shall know that we* belong to the truth and reassure our hearts before him 20 in whatever our hearts condemn, for God is greater than our hearts and knows everything. 21 Beloved, if [our] hearts do not condemn us, we have confidence in God 22 and receive from him whatever we ask, because we keep his commandments and do what pleases him.[q] 23 And his commandment is this: we should believe in the name of his Son, Jesus Christ, and love one another just as he commanded us.[r] 24 Those who keep his commandments remain in him, and he in them, and the way we know that he remains in us is from the Spirit that he gave us.[s]

CHAPTER 4

Testing the Spirits.* 1 Beloved, do not trust every spirit but test the spirits to see whether they belong to God, because many false prophets have gone out into the world.[t] 2 This is how you can know the Spirit of God: every spirit that acknowledges Jesus Christ come in the flesh belongs to God,[u] 3 and every spirit that does not acknowledge Jesus* does not belong to God. This is the spirit of the antichrist that, as you heard, is to come, but in fact is already in the world.[v] 4 You belong to God, children, and you have conquered them, for the one who is in you is greater than the one who is in the world. 5 They belong to the world; accordingly, their teaching belongs to the world, and the world listens to them.[w] 6 We belong to God, and anyone who knows God listens to us, while anyone who does not belong to God refuses to hear us. This is how we know the spirit of truth and the spirit of deceit.[x]

God's Love and Christian Life. 7 * Beloved, let us love one another, because love is of God; everyone who loves is begotten by God and knows God. 8 Whoever is without love does not know God, for God is love. 9 In this way the love of God was revealed to us: God sent his only Son into the world so that we might have life through him.[y] 10 In this is love: not that we have loved God, but that he loved us and sent his Son as expiation for our sins.[z] 11 Beloved, if God so loved us, we also must love one another. 12 No one has ever seen God. Yet, if we love one another, God remains in us, and his love is brought to perfection in us.[a]

13 * This is how we know that we remain in him and he in us, that he has given us of his Spirit. 14 Moreover, we have seen and

j Gn 4, 8; Jude 11.—k Mt 24, 9; Jn 15, 18; 17, 14.—l Lv 19, 17; Jn 5, 24.—m Jn 8, 44.—n Mt 20, 28; Jn 10, 11; 15, 13.—o Dt 15, 7.11; Jas 2, 15-16.—p Jas 1, 22.—q 1 Jn 5, 15; Mt 7, 7-11; 21, 22; Jn 14, 13-14.—r Jn 13, 34; 15, 17.—s 1 Jn 4, 13; Jn 14, 21-23.—t 1 Jn 2, 18; Mt 24, 24.—u 1 Cor 12, 3; 1 Thes 5, 21.—v 1 Jn 1, 22.—w Jn 15, 19.—x Jn 8, 47; 10, 16.—y Jn 3, 16.—z Rom 5, 8.—a Jn 1, 18; 1 Tm 6, 16.

3, 19-24: Living a life of faith in Jesus and of Christian love assures us of abiding in God no matter what our feelings may at times tell us. Our obedience gives us confidence in prayer and trust in God's judgment. This obedience includes our belief in Christ and love for one another.

3, 19b-20: This difficult passage may also be translated "we shall be at peace before him in whatever our hearts condemn, for . . ." or "and before God we shall convince our hearts, if our hearts condemn us, that God is greater than our hearts."

4, 1-6: Deception is possible in spiritual phenomena and may be tested by its relation to Christian doctrine (cf 1 Cor 12, 3): those who fail to acknowledge Jesus Christ in the flesh are false prophets and belong to the antichrist. Even though these false prophets are well received in the world, the Christian who belongs to God has a greater power in the truth.

4, 3: *Does not acknowledge Jesus:* some ancient manuscripts add "Christ" and/or "to have come in the flesh" (cf 1 Jn 4, 2), and others read "every spirit that annuls (or severs) Jesus."

4, 7-12: Love as we share in it testifies to the nature of God and to his presence in our lives. One who loves shows that one is a child of God and knows God, for God's very being is love; one without love is without God. The revelation of the nature of God's love is found in the free gift of his Son to us, so that we may share life with God and be delivered from our sins. The love we have for one another must be of the same sort: authentic, merciful; this unique Christian love is our proof that we know God and can "see" the invisible God.

4, 13-21: The testimony of the Spirit and that of faith join the testimony of love to confirm our knowledge of God. Our love is grounded in the confession of Jesus as the Son of God and the example of God's love for us. Christian life is founded on the knowledge of God as love and on his continuing presence that relieves us from fear of judgment (16-18). What Christ is gives us confidence, even as we live and love in this world. Yet Christian love is not abstract but lived in the concrete manner of love for one another.

testify that the Father sent his Son as
savior of the world. 15 Whoever acknowledges that Jesus is the Son of God, God remains in him and he in God. 16 We have
come to know and to believe in the love
God has for us.

God is love, and whoever remains in love
remains in God and God in him. 17 In this
is love brought to perfection among us,
that we have confidence on the day of judgment because as he is, so are we in this
world.[b] 18 There is no fear in love, but perfect love drives out fear because fear has to
do with punishment, and so one who fears
is not yet perfect in love. 19 We love because he first loved us. 20 If anyone says, "I
love God," but hates his brother, he is a
liar; for whoever does not love a brother
whom he has seen cannot love God* whom
he has not seen.[c] 21 This is the commandment we have from him: whoever loves
God must also love his brother.[d]

CHAPTER 5

Faith is Victory over the World. 1 * Everyone who believes that Jesus is the Christ is
begotten by God, and everyone who loves
the father loves [also] the one begotten by
him.[e] 2 In this way we know that we love
the children of God when we love God and
obey his commandments. 3 For the love of
God is this, that we keep his commandments. And his commandments are not
burdensome,[f] 4 for whoever is begotten by
God conquers the world. And the victory
that conquers the world is our faith.[g]
5 Who [indeed] is the victor over the world
but the one who believes that Jesus is the
Son of God?[h]

6 This is the one who came through
water and blood,* Jesus Christ, not by
water alone, but by water and blood. The
Spirit is the one that testifies, and the
Spirit is truth.[i] 7 So there are three that testify, 8 the Spirit, the water, and the blood,
and the three are of one accord.[j] 9 If we accept human testimony, the testimony of
God is surely greater. Now the testimony
of God is this, that he has testified on behalf of his Son.[k] 10 Whoever believes in the
Son of God has this testimony within himself. Whoever does not believe God has
made him a liar by not believing the testimony God has given about his Son.[l]
11 And this is the testimony: God gave us
eternal life, and this life is in his Son.[m]
12 Whoever possesses the Son has life; whoever does not possess the Son of God does
not have life.

IV. EPILOGUE*

Prayer for Sinners. 13 I write these things
to you so that you may know that you have
eternal life, you who believe in the name of
the Son of God.[n] 14 And we have this confidence in him, that if we ask anything according to his will, he hears us.[o] 15 And if
we know that he hears us in regard to
whatever we ask, we know that what we
have asked him for is ours. 16 If anyone sees
his brother sinning, if the sin is not deadly,
he should pray to God and he will give him
life. This is only for those whose sin is not
deadly. There is such a thing as deadly sin,
about which I do not say that you should
pray.[p] 17 All wrongdoing is sin, but there is
sin that is not deadly.

18 We know that no one begotten by God
sins; but the one begotten by God he protects, and the evil one cannot touch him.

b 1 Jn 2, 28.—c 1 Jn 2, 4.—d Jn 13, 34; 14, 15.21; 15, 17.—e Jn 8, 42; 1 Pt 1, 23.—f Jn 14, 15.—g Jn 16, 33.—h 1 Cor 15, 57.—i Jn 15, 26; 19, 34.—j Jn 5, 32.36; 15, 26.—k Jn 5, 32.37.—l 1 Jn 3, 33.—m 1 Jn 1, 2; Jn 1, 4; 5, 21.26; 17, 3.—n Jn 1, 12; 20, 31.—o 1 Jn 3, 21-22; Mt 7, 7; Jn 14, 13-14.—p Mt 12, 31.

4, 20: *Cannot love God:* some ancient manuscripts read "how can he love . . . ?"

5, 1-5: Children of God are identified not only by their love for others (1 Jn 4, 7-9) and for God (1 Jn 5, 1-2) but by their belief in the divine sonship of Jesus Christ. Faith, the acceptance of Jesus in his true character and the obedience in love to God's commands (3), is the source of the Christian's power in the world and conquers the world of evil (4-5), even as Christ overcame the world (Jn 16, 33).

5, 6-12: *Water and blood* (6) refers to Christ's baptism (Mt 3, 16-17) and to the shedding of his blood on the cross (Jn 19, 34). *The Spirit* was present at the baptism (Mt 3, 16; Mk 1, 10; Lk 3, 22; Jn 1, 32.34). *The testimony* to Christ as the Son of God is confirmed by divine witness (7-9), greater by far than the two legally required human witnesses (Dt 17, 6). To deny this is to deny God's truth; cf Jn 8, 17-18. The gist of the divine witness or *testimony* is that *eternal life* (11-12) is given in Christ and nowhere else. To *possess the Son* is not acceptance of a doctrine but of a person who lives now and provides life.

5, 13-21: As children of God we have confidence in prayer because of our intimate relationship with him (14-15). In love, we pray (16-17) for those who are in *sin,* but not in *deadly sin* (literally, "sin unto death"), probably referring to apostasy or activities brought on under the antichrist; cf Mk 3, 29; Heb 6, 4-6; 10, 26-31. Even in the latter case, however, prayer, while not enjoined, is not forbidden. The letter concludes with a summary of the themes of the letter (18-20). There is a sharp antithesis between the children of God and those belonging to the world and to the evil one. The Son reveals the God of truth; Christians dwell in the true God, *in his Son,* and have eternal life. The final verse (21) voices a perennial warning about *idols,* any type of rival to God.

[19]We know that we belong to God, and the
whole world is under the power of the evil
one. [20]We also know that the Son of God
has come and has given us discernment to
know the one who is true. And we are in
the one who is true, in his Son Jesus
Christ. He is the true God and eternal life.[q]
[21]Children, be on your guard against idols.

q Jer 24, 7; Jn 17, 3; Eph 1, 17.

THE SECOND LETTER OF JOHN

INTRODUCTION

Written in response to similar problems, the Second and Third Letters of John are of the same length, perhaps determined by the practical consideration of the writing space on one piece of papyrus. In each letter the writer calls himself "the Presbyter," and their common authorship is further evidenced by internal similarities in style and wording, especially in the introductions and conclusions. The literary considerations that link 2 and 3 John also link them with the First Letter and the Gospel of John. The concern with "truth," christology, mutual love, the new commandment, antichrist, and the integrity of witness to the earthly Jesus mark these works as products of the Johannine school. The identity of the Presbyter is problematic. The use of the title implies more than age, and refers to his position of leadership in the early church. The absence of a proper name indicates that he was well known and acknowledged in authority by the communities to which he writes. Although traditionally attributed to John the apostle, these letters were probably written by a disciple or scribe of an apostle. The traditional place and date of composition, Ephesus at the end of the first century, are plausible for both letters.

The Second Letter is addressed to "the chosen Lady" and "to her children." This literary image of a particular Christian community reflects the specific destination and purpose of the letter. Unlike 1 John, this brief letter is not a theological treatise but a reply to problems within the church. The Johannine themes of love and truth are used to support practical advice on Christian living. The Presbyter encourages community members to show their Christianity by adhering to the great commandment of mutual love and to the historical truth about Jesus. The false teaching present among them is a spiritualizing christology that may tempt some members to discount teachings about the incarnation and death of Jesus the Christ; cf 1 Jn 4, 2. For their protection the Presbyter forbids hospitality toward unknown or "progressive" Christians to prevent their infiltration of the community. The Second Letter preserves the Johannine concerns of doctrinal purity and active love in the form of pastoral advice to a threatened community.

1 [a] The Presbyter to the chosen Lady*
and to her children whom I love in truth—
and not only I but also all who know the
truth—[2]because of the truth that dwells in
us and will be with us forever. [3]Grace,
mercy, and peace* will be with us from
God the Father and from Jesus Christ the
Father's Son in truth and love.

a Jn 8, 32; 3 Jn 1.

1: *The chosen Lady:* literally "elected"; this could also be translated "Kyria (a woman's name) chosen (by God)" or "the lady Electa" or "Electa Kyria." The adjective "chosen" is applied to all Christians at the beginning of other New Testament letters (1 Pt 1, 1; Ti 1, 1). The description is of a specific community with "children" who are its members. *The truth:* the affirmation of Jesus in the flesh and in contrast to false teaching (7).

3: *Grace, mercy, and peace:* like 1 and 2 Tm this letter adds *mercy* to the terms used frequently in a salutation to describe Christian blessing; it appears only here in the Johannine writings. The author also puts the blessing in relation to *truth* and *love,* the watchwords of the Johannine teaching. *The Father's Son:* the title that affirms the close relationship of Christ to God; similar variations of this title occur elsewhere (Jn 1, 14; 3, 35), but the precise wording is not found elsewhere in the New Testament.

4 I rejoiced greatly to find some of your
children* walking in the truth just as we
were commanded by the Father.[b] 5 But
now, Lady, I ask you, not as though I were
writing a new commandment but the one
we have had from the beginning: let us
love one another.[c] 6 For this is love, that
we walk according to his commandments;*
this is the commandment, as you heard
from the beginning, in which you should
walk.[d]

7 [e] Many deceivers have gone out into
the world, those who do not acknowledge
Jesus Christ as coming in the flesh; such is
the deceitful one and the antichrist.*
8 Look to yourselves that you* do not lose
what we worked for but may receive a full
recompense. 9 [f] Anyone who is so "progressive"* as not to remain in the teaching
of the Christ does not have God; whoever
remains in the teaching has the Father and
the Son. 10 * If anyone comes to you and
does not bring this doctrine, do not receive
him in your house or even greet him;[g]
11 for whoever greets him shares in his evil
works.

12 Although I have much to write to you,
I do not intend to use paper and ink. Instead, I hope to visit you and to speak face
to face so that our joy* may be complete.[h]
13 The children of your chosen sister* send
you greetings.

b 3 Jn 3.—c Jn 13, 34; 15, 12; 1 Jn 4, 7.—d Jn 13, 34; 14, 15; 1 Jn 5, 3.—e 1 Jn 2, 22; 4, 2.—f Jn 8, 31; 1 Jn 2, 23; 4, 15.—g Rom 16, 17; 2 Thes 3, 6.—h Jn 15, 11; 1 Jn 1, 4; 3 Jn 13.

4: *Some of your children:* this refers to those whom the Presbyter has recently encountered, but it may also indicate the presence of false doctrine in the community: the Presbyter encourages those who have remained faithful. *Walking in the truth:* an expression used in the Johannine writings to describe a way of living in which the Christian faith is visibly expressed; cf 1 Jn 1, 6-7; 2, 6.11; 3 Jn 3.

6: *His commandments:* cf 1 Jn 3, 23; 2, 7-8; 4, 21; obedience to the commandment of faith and love includes all others.

7: *The antichrist:* see 1 Jn 2, 18-19.22; 4, 3.

8: *You* (plural): it is not certain whether this means the Christians addressed or includes the Presbyter, since some of the ancient Greek manuscripts and Greek Fathers have "we."

9: *Anyone who is so "progressive":* literally, "Anyone who goes ahead." Some gnostic groups held the doctrine of the Christ come in the flesh to be a first step in belief, which the more advanced and spiritual believer surpassed and abandoned in his knowledge of the spiritual Christ. The author affirms that fellowship with God may be gained only by holding to the complete doctrine of Jesus Christ (1 Jn 2, 22-23; 4, 2; 5, 5-6).

10-11: At this time false teachers were considered so dangerous and divisive as to be shunned completely. From this description they seem to be wandering preachers. We see here a natural suspicion of early Christians concerning such itinerants and can envisage the problems faced by missionaries such as those mentioned in 3 Jn 10.

12: *Our joy:* a number of other Greek manuscripts read "your joy."

13: *Chosen sister:* the community of which the Presbyter is now a part greets you (singular), the community of the Lady addressed.

THE THIRD LETTER OF JOHN

INTRODUCTION

The Third Letter of John preserves a brief glimpse into the problems of missionary activity and local autonomy in the early church. In contrast to the other two letters of John, this work was addressed to a specific individual, Gaius. This letter is less theological in content and purpose. The author's goal was to secure hospitality and material support for his missionaries, and the Presbyter is writing to another member of the church who has welcomed missionaries in the past. The Presbyter commends Gaius for his hospitality and encourages his future help. He indicates he may come to challenge the policy of Diotrephes that is based on evil gossip.

The problems of the Presbyter in this short letter provide us with valuable evidence of the flexible and personal nature of authority in the early church. The Presbyter writes to Gaius, whom perhaps he had converted or instructed, on the basis of their personal links. The brothers have also confirmed him as a loyal Christian in action and belief. Gaius accepted the missionaries from the Presbyter and presumably will accept Demetrius on the Presbyter's recommendation. In contrast, Diotrephes refuses to receive either letters or friends of the Presbyter. Although he is portrayed as ambitious and hostile, he perhaps exemplifies the cautious and sectarian nature of early Christianity; for its own protection the local community mistrusted missionaries as false teachers. Most interestingly, Diotrephes seems comfortable in ignoring the requests of the Presbyter. The Pres-

byter seems to acknowledge that only a personal confrontation with Diotrephes will remedy the situation (10). The division, however, may also rest on doctrinal disagreement in which Gaius and the other "friends" accept the teaching of the Presbyter, and Diotrephes does not; the missionaries are not received for suspicion of theological error. Diotrephes has thus been viewed by some as an overly ambitious local upstart trying to thwart the advance of orthodox Christianity, by others as an orthodox church official suspicious of the teachings of the Presbyter and those in the Johannine school who think as he does, or by still others as a local leader anxious to keep the debates in the Johannine community out of his own congregation.

This brief letter and the situation that it mirrors show us how little we know about some details of early development in the church: schools of opinion existed around which questions of faith and life were discussed, and personal ties as well as doctrine and authority played a role in what happened amid divisions and unity.

1 The Presbyter to the beloved Gaius*
whom I love in truth.[a]

2 Beloved, I hope you are prospering in
every respect and are in good health, just
as your soul is prospering. 3 I rejoiced
greatly when some of the brothers* came
and testified to how truly you walk in the
truth.[b] 4 Nothing gives me greater joy than
to hear that my children are walking in the
truth.[c]

5 Beloved, you are faithful in all you do*
for the brothers, especially for strangers;[d]
6 they have testified to your love before the
church.[e] Please help them in a way worthy
of God to continue their journey.* 7 For
they have set out for the sake of the Name*
and are accepting nothing from the pagans.
8 Therefore, we ought to support such persons, so that we may be co-workers in the
truth.

9 I wrote to the church, but Diotrephes,
who loves to dominate,* does not acknowledge us. 10 Therefore, if I come,* I will
draw attention to what he is doing, spreading evil nonsense about us. And not content with that, he will not receive the
brothers, hindering those who wish to do
so and expelling them from the church.

11 Beloved, do not imitate evil* but imitate good. Whoever does what is good is of
God; whoever does what is evil has never
seen God.[f] 12 Demetrius* receives a good
report from all, even from the truth itself.
We give our testimonial as well, and you
know our testimony is true.[g]

13 I have much to write to you, but I do
not wish to write with pen and ink.[h] 14 Instead, I hope to see you soon, when we can
talk face to face. 15 Peace be with you. The
friends greet you; greet the friends* there
each by name.[i]

a 2 Jn 1.—b 3 Jn 5; Gal 6, 10; 2 Jn 4.—c 1 Thes 2, 11-12; 1 Tm 1, 2; 2 Tm 1, 2; 1 Jn 2, 1; 2 Jn 4.—d Rom 12, 13; Gal 6, 10; Heb 13, 2.—e Acts 15, 3; Col 1, 10; 1 Thes 2, 12.—f 1 Jn 2, 29; 3, 6.10.—g Jn 19, 35; 21, 24; 1 Tm 3, 7.—h 2 Jn 12.—i Jn 20, 19.21.26; Eph 6, 23; 1 Pt 5, 14.

1: *Beloved Gaius:* a frequent form of address for fellow Christians in New Testament epistolary literature.

3: *The brothers:* in this letter, the term may refer to Christians who have been missionaries and received hospitality from Gaius (5-6). *Walk in the truth:* the common Johannine term to describe Christian living; this description presents Gaius as following the teachings of the Presbyter in contrast to Diotrephes.

5: *You are faithful in all you do:* Gaius's aid to the missionaries is a manifestation of his true Christian faith.

6: *Help them . . . to continue their journey:* the Presbyter asks Gaius not only to continue to welcome the missionaries to his community but also to equip them for further travels.

7: *The Name:* of Jesus Christ (cf Acts 5, 41; 1 Jn 2, 12; 3, 23; 5, 13). *Accepting nothing:* not expecting support from the pagans to whom they preach the gospel, so that they will not be considered as beggars; they required support from other Christians; cf Paul's complaints to the Corinthians (1 Cor 9, 3-12).

9: *Who loves to dominate:* the Presbyter does not deny Diotrephes' place as leader but indicates that his ambition may have caused him to disregard his letter and his influence.

10: *If I come:* the Presbyter may visit the community to challenge the actions of Diotrephes toward himself and the missionaries. *Will not receive the brothers:* Diotrephes may have been critical of the teachings of the Presbyter and sought to maintain doctrinal purity; cf 1 Jn 2, 19 and 2 Jn 10-11.

11: *Do not imitate evil:* Gaius should not be influenced by the behavior of Diotrephes.

12: *Demetrius:* because of the fear of false teachers, Demetrius, perhaps the bearer of the letter, is provided with a recommendation from the Presbyter; cf 2 Cor 3, 1; Rom 16, 1. *Even from the truth itself:* this refers probably to the manner of Demetrius's life that testifies to his true belief; cf Gaius above (v 3).

15: *Friends:* although a Johannine term for Christians (Jn 15, 15), the word here may refer to those in the community loyal to the Presbyter and to Gaius.

THE LETTER OF JUDE

INTRODUCTION

This letter is by its address attributed to "Jude, a slave of Jesus Christ and brother of James" (1). Since he is not identified as an apostle, this designation can hardly be meant to refer to the Jude or Judas who is listed as one of the Twelve (Lk 6, 16; Acts 1, 13; cf Jn 14, 22). The person intended is almost certainly the other Jude, named in the gospels among the relatives of Jesus (Mt 13, 55; Mk 6, 3), and the James who is listed there as his brother is the one to whom the Letter of James is attributed (see the Introduction to James). Nothing else is known of this Jude, and the apparent need to identify him by reference to his better-known brother indicates that he was a rather obscure personage in the early church.

The letter is addressed in the most general terms to "those who are called, beloved in God the Father and kept safe for Jesus Christ" (1), hence apparently to all Christians. But since its purpose is to warn the addressees against false teachers, the author must have had in mind one or more specific Christian communities located in the unidentified region where the errors in question constituted a danger. While the letter contains some Semitic features, there is nothing to identify the addressees specifically as Jewish Christians; indeed, the errors envisaged seem to reflect an early form of gnosticism, opposed to law, that points rather to the cultural context of the Gentile world. Like James and 2 Peter, the Letter of Jude manifests none of the typical features of the letter form except the address.

There is so much similarity between Jude and 2 Peter, especially Jude 4-16 and 2 Peter 2, 1-18, that there must be a literary relationship between them. Since there is no evidence for the view that both authors borrowed from the same source, it is usually supposed that one of them borrowed from the other. Most scholars believe that Jude is the earlier of the two, principally because he quotes two apocryphal Jewish works, the Assumption of Moses (9) and the Book of Enoch (14-15), as part of his structured argument, whereas 2 Peter omits both references. Since there was controversy in the early church about the propriety of citing noncanonical literature that included legendary material, it is more probable that a later writer would omit such references than that he would add them.

Many interpreters today consider Jude a pseudonymous work dating from the end of the first century or even later. In support of this view they adduce the following arguments: (a) the apostles are referred to as belonging to an age that has receded into the past (17-18); (b) faith is understood as a body of doctrine handed down by a process of tradition (3); (c) the author's competent Greek style shows that he must have had a Hellenistic cultural formation; (d) the gnostic character of the errors envisaged fits better into the early second century than into a period several decades earlier. While impressive, these arguments are not entirely compelling and do not completely rule out the possibility of composition around the year A.D. 80, when the historical Jude may still have been alive.

This little letter is an urgent note by an author who intended to write more fully about salvation to an unknown group of readers, but who was forced by dangers from false teachers worming their way into the community (3-4) to dash off a warning against them (5-16) and to deliver some pressing Christian admonitions (17-23). The letter is justly famous for its majestic closing doxology (24-25).

Address and Greeting. 1 Jude, a slave of
Jesus Christ and brother of James,* to
those who are called, beloved in God the
Father and kept safe for Jesus Christ:[a]
2 may mercy, peace, and love be yours in
abundance.[b]

Occasion for Writing. 3 Beloved, although
I was making every effort to write to you
about our common salvation,* I now feel a
need to write to encourage you to contend
for the faith that was once for all handed
down to the holy ones.[c] 4 For there have
been some intruders, who long ago were
designated for this condemnation, godless
persons, who pervert the grace of our God
into licentiousness and who deny our only
Master and Lord, Jesus Christ.[d]

The False Teachers. 5 [e] I wish to remind
you, although you know all things, that
[the] Lord who once saved a people from
the land of Egypt later destroyed those
who did not believe.* 6 [f] The angels too,
who did not keep to their own domain but
deserted their proper dwelling, he has kept
in eternal chains, in gloom, for the judgment of the great day.* 7 Likewise, Sodom,
Gomorrah, and the surrounding towns,
which, in the same manner as they, indulged in sexual promiscuity and practiced
unnatural vice,* serve as an example by
undergoing a punishment of eternal fire.[g]

8 Similarly, these dreamers* nevertheless
also defile the flesh, scorn lordship, and revile glorious beings. 9 Yet the archangel
Michael, when he argued with the devil in
a dispute over the body of Moses, did not
venture to pronounce a reviling judgment*
upon him but said, "May the Lord rebuke
you!"[h] 10 But these people revile what they
do not understand and are destroyed by
what they know by nature like irrational
animals.[i] 11 Woe to them![j] They followed
the way of Cain, abandoned themselves to
Balaam's error for the sake of gain, and
perished in the rebellion of Korah.*
12 These are blemishes on your love feasts,*
as they carouse fearlessly and look after
themselves. They are waterless clouds
blown about by winds, fruitless trees in
late autumn, twice dead and uprooted.[k]
13 They are like wild waves of the sea,
foaming up their shameless deeds, wandering stars for whom the gloom of darkness
has been reserved forever.

14 * Enoch, of the seventh generation
from Adam, prophesied also about them
when he said,[l] "Behold, the Lord has
come with his countless holy ones 15 to ex-
ecute judgment on all and to convict everyone for all the godless deeds that they committed and for all the harsh words godless
sinners have uttered against him." 16 These

a Mt 13, 55; Mk 6, 3; Acts 12, 17; Rom 1, 7.—b Gal 6, 16; 1 Tm 1, 2; 2 Pt 1, 2.—c Jude 17.20; 1 Tm 6, 12.—d Gal 2, 4; 2 Tm 3, 6; 2 Pt 2, 1.—e Nm 14, 35; 1 Cor 10, 5; Heb 3, 16.17.—f 2 Pt 2, 4.9.—g Dt 29, 22-24; Mt 25, 41; 2 Thes 1, 8-9; 2 Pt 2, 6; 3, 7.—h Dn 10, 21; 12, 1.—i 2 Pt 2, 12.—j Gn 4, 8-16; 1 Jn 3, 12 / Nm 31, 15-16; 2 Pt 2, 15; Rv 2, 14 / Nm 16, 19-35.—k 2 Pt 2, 13.17.—l 14-15: Mt 16, 27; Heb 12, 22-23.

1: *Jude . . . brother of James:* for the identity of the author of this letter, see Introduction. *To those who are called:* the vocation to the Christian faith is God's free gift to those whom he loves and whom he safely protects in Christ until the Lord's second coming.

3-4: *Our common salvation:* the teachings of the Christian faith derived from the apostolic preaching and to be kept by the Christian community.

5: For this first example of divine punishment on those who had been saved but did not then keep faith, see Nm 14, 28-29 and the note there. Some manuscripts have the word "once" (*hapax* as at Jude 3) after "you know"; some commentators have suggested that it means "knowing one thing" or "you know all things once for all." Instead of "[the] Lord" manuscripts vary, having "Jesus," "God," or no subject stated.

6: This second example draws on Gn 6, 1-4 as elaborated in the apocryphal Book of Enoch (cf Jude 14): heavenly beings came to earth and had sexual intercourse with women. God punished them by casting them out of heaven into darkness and bondage.

7: *Practiced unnatural vice:* literally, "went after alien flesh." This example derives from Gn 19, 1-25, especially 4-11, when the townsmen of Sodom violated both hospitality and morality by demanding that Lot's two visitors (really messengers of Yahweh) be handed over to them so that they could abuse them sexually. *Unnatural vice:* this refers to the desire for intimacies by human beings with angels (the reverse of the example in Jude 6). Sodom (whence "sodomy") and Gomorrah became proverbial as object lessons for God's punishment on sin (Is 1, 9; Jer 50, 40; Am 4, 11; Mt 10, 15; 2 Pt 2, 6).

8: *Dreamers:* the writer returns to the false teachers of v 4, applying charges from the three examples in vv 5, 6, 7. This may apply to claims they make for revelations they have received by night (to the author, hallucinations). *Defile the flesh:* this may mean bodily pollutions from the erotic dreams of sexual license (7). *Lordship . . . glorious beings:* these may reflect the Lord (5; Jesus, 4) whom they spurn and the angels (6; cf the note on 2 Pt 2, 10, here, as there, literally, "glories").

9: *The archangel Michael . . . judgment:* a reference to an incident in the apocryphal Assumption of Moses. Dt 34, 6 had said of Moses, literally in Greek, "they buried him" or "he (God?) buried him" (taken to mean "he was buried"). The later account tells how Michael, who was sent to bury him, was challenged by the devil's interest in the body. Our author draws out the point that if an archangel refrained from reviling even the devil, how wrong it is for mere human beings to revile glorious beings (angels).

11: *Cain . . . Balaam . . . Korah:* examples of rebellious men and of the punishment their conduct incurred; cf Gn 4, 8-16; Nm 16, 1-35; 31, 16. See the note on 2 Pt 2, 15.

12: *Blemishes on your love feasts:* or "hidden rocks" or "submerged reefs" (cf Jude 13). The opponents engaged in scandalous conduct in connection with community gatherings called *love feasts* (agape meals), which were associated with eucharistic celebrations at certain stages of early Christian practice; cf 1 Cor 11, 18-34 and the note on 2 Pt 2, 13.

14-15: Cited from the apocryphal Book of Enoch 1, 9.

people are complainers, disgruntled ones
who live by their desires; their mouths
utter bombast as they fawn over people to
gain advantage.[m]

Exhortations. 17 But you, beloved, remember the words spoken beforehand by
the apostles of our Lord Jesus Christ,[n]
18 for they told you,[o] "In [the] last time
there will be scoffers who will live according to their own godless desires."* 19 These
are the ones who cause divisions; they live
on the natural plane, devoid of the Spirit.[p]
20 But you, beloved, build yourselves up in
your most holy faith; pray in the holy
Spirit.[q] 21 Keep yourselves in the love of
God and wait for the mercy of our Lord
Jesus Christ that leads to eternal life.[r]
22 On those who waver, have mercy;*
23 save others by snatching them out of the
fire; on others have mercy with fear,*
abhorring even the outer garment stained
by the flesh.

Doxology.* 24 To the one who is able to
keep you from stumbling and to present
you unblemished and exultant, in the presence of his glory,[s] 25 to the only God, our
savior, through Jesus Christ our Lord be
glory, majesty, power, and authority from
ages past, now, and for ages to come.
Amen.[t]

m Jude 18; 1 Cor 10, 10; 2 Pt 2, 10.18.—n Heb 2, 3; 2 Pt 3, 2.—o 1 Tm 4, 1; 2 Tm 3, 1-5; 2 Pt 3, 3.—p 1 Cor 2, 14; Jas 3, 15.—q Jude 2; Eph 6, 18; Col 2, 7.—r Ti 2, 13.—s 2 Cor 4, 14; 1 Pt 4, 13.—t Rom 11, 36; 1 Tm 1, 17.

18: This is the substance of much early Christian preaching rather than a direct quotation of any of the various New Testament passages on this theme (see Mk 13, 22; Acts 20, 30; 1 Tm 4, 1-3; 2 Pt 3, 3).

22: *Have mercy:* some manuscripts read "convince," "confute," or "reprove." Others have "even though you waver" or "doubt" instead of *who waver.*

23: *With fear:* some manuscripts connect the phrase "with fear" with the imperative "save" or with the participle "snatching." Other manuscripts omit the phrase "on others have mercy," so that only two groups are envisioned. Rescue of those led astray and caution in the endeavor are both enjoined. *Outer garment stained by the flesh:* the imagery may come from Zec 3, 3-5, just as that of *snatching. . . out of the fire* comes from Zec 3, 2; the very garments of the godless are to be abhorred because of their contagion.

24-25: With this liturgical statement about the power of God to keep the faithful from stumbling, and praise to him through Jesus Christ, the letter reaches its conclusion by returning to the themes with which it began (1-2).

THE BOOK OF REVELATION

INTRODUCTION

The Apocalypse, or Revelation to John, the last book of the Bible, is one of the most difficult to understand because it abounds in unfamiliar and extravagant symbolism, which at best appears unusual to the modern reader. Symbolic language, however, is one of the chief characteristics of apocalyptic literature, of which this book is an outstanding example. Such literature enjoyed wide popularity in both Jewish and Christian circles from ca. 200 B.C. to A.D. 200.

This book contains an account of visions in symbolic and allegorical language borrowed extensively from the Old Testament, especially Ezekiel, Zechariah, and Daniel. Whether or not these visions were real experiences of the author or simply literary conventions employed by him is an open question.

This much, however, is certain: symbolic descriptions are not to be taken as literal descriptions, nor is the symbolism meant to be pictured realistically. One would find it difficult and repulsive to visualize a lamb with seven horns and seven eyes; yet Jesus Christ is described in precisely such words (5, 6). The author used these images to suggest Christ's universal (seven) power (horns) and knowledge (eyes). A significant feature of apocalyptic writing is the use of symbolic colors, metals, garments (1, 13-16; 3, 18; 4, 4; 6, 1-8; 17, 4; 19, 8), and numbers (four *signifies the world,* six *imperfection,* seven *totality of perfection,* twelve *Israel's tribes or the apostles,* one thousand *immensity). Finally the vindictive language in the book (6, 9-10; 18, 1—19, 4) is also to be understood symbolically and not literally. The cries for vengeance on the lips of Christian martyrs that sound so harsh are in fact literary devices the author employed to evoke in the reader and hearer a feeling of horror for apostasy and rebellion that will be severely punished by God.*

The lurid descriptions of the punishment of Jezebel (2, 22) and of the destruction of the great harlot, Babylon (16, 9—19, 2), are likewise literary devices. The metaphor of Babylon as harlot would be wrongly construed if interpreted literally. On the other hand, the stylized figure of the woman clothed with the sun (12, 1-6), depicting the New Israel, may seem to be a negative stereotype. It is necessary to look beyond the literal meaning to see that these images mean to convey a sense of God's wrath at sin in the former case and trust in God's providential care over the church in the latter.

The Book of Revelation cannot be adequately understood except against the historical background that occasioned its writing. Like Daniel and other apocalypses, it was composed as resistance literature to meet a crisis. The book itself suggests that the crisis was ruthless persecution of the early church by the Roman authorities; the harlot Babylon symbolizes pagan Rome, the city on seven hills (17, 9). The book is, then, an exhortation and admonition to Christians of the first century to stand firm in the faith and to avoid compromise with paganism, despite the threat of adversity and martyrdom; they are to await patiently the fulfillment of God's mighty promises. The triumph of God in the world of men and women remains a mystery, to be accepted in faith and longed for in hope. It is a triumph that unfolded in the history of Jesus of Nazareth and continues to unfold in the history of the individual Christian who follows the way of the cross, even, if necessary, to a martyr's death.

Though the perspective is eschatological—ultimate salvation and victory are said to take place at the end of the present age when Christ will come in glory at the parousia—the book presents the decisive struggle of Christ and his followers against Satan and his cohorts as already over. Christ's overwhelming defeat of the kingdom of Satan ushered in the everlasting reign of God (11, 15; 12, 10). Even the forces of evil unwittingly carry out the divine plan (17, 17), for God is the sovereign Lord of history.

The Book of Revelation had its origin in a time of crisis, but it remains valid and meaningful for Christians of all time. In the face of apparently insuperable evil, either from within or from without, all Christians are called to trust in Jesus' promise, "Behold, I am with you always, until the end of the age" (Mt 28, 20). Those who remain steadfast in their faith and confidence in the risen Lord need have no fear. Suffering, persecution, even death by martyrdom, though remaining impenetrable mysteries of evil, do not comprise an absurd dead end. No matter what adversity or sacrifice Christians may endure, they will in the end triumph over Satan and his forces because of their fidelity to Christ the victor. This is the enduring message of the book; it is a message of hope and consolation and challenge for all who dare to believe.

The author of the book calls himself John (1, 1.4.9; 22, 8), who because of his Christian faith has been exiled to the rocky island of Patmos, a Roman penal colony. Although he never claims to be John the apostle, whose name is attached to the fourth gospel, he was so identified by several of the early church Fathers, including Justin, Irenaeus, Clement of Alexandria, Tertullian, Cyprian, and Hippolytus. This identification, however, was denied by other Fathers, including Denis of Alexandria, Eusebius of Caesarea, Cyril of Jerusalem, Gregory Nazianzen, and John Chrysostom. Indeed, vocabulary, grammar, and style make it doubtful that the book could have been put into its present form by the same person(s) responsible for the fourth gospel. Nevertheless, there are definite linguistic and theological affinities between the two books. The tone of the letters to the seven churches (1, 4—3, 22) is indicative of the great authority the author enjoyed over the Christian communities in Asia. It is possible, therefore, that he was a disciple of John the apostle, who is traditionally associated with that part of the world. The date of the book in its present form is probably near the end of the reign of Domitian (A.D. 81-96), a fierce persecutor of the Christians.

The principal divisions of the Book of Revelation are the following:

I. Prologue (1, 1-3)
II. Letters to the Churches of Asia (1, 4—3, 22)
III. God and the Lamb in Heaven (4, 1—5, 14)
IV. The Seven Seals, Trumpets, and Plagues, with Interludes (6, 1—16, 21)
V. The Punishment of Babylon and the Destruction of Pagan Nations (17, 1—20, 15)
VI. The New Creation (21, 1—22, 5)
VII. Epilogue (22, 6-21)

I. PROLOGUE*

CHAPTER 1

1The revelation of Jesus Christ, which God gave to him, to show his servants what must happen soon. He made it known by sending his angel to his servant John,[a]
2who gives witness to the word of God and to the testimony of Jesus Christ by reporting what he saw.
3Blessed is the one* who reads aloud and blessed are those who listen to this prophetic message and heed what is written in it, for the appointed time is near.[b]

a Rv 22, 6-8.20; Dn 2, 28 / Rv 19, 10.—b Rv 22, 7 / Lk 11, 28.

1, 1-3: This prologue describes the source, contents, and audience of the book and forms an inclusion with the epilogue (Rv 22, 6-21), with its similar themes and expressions.

1, 3: ***Blessed is the one:*** this is the first of seven beatitudes in this book; the others are in Rv 14, 13; 16, 15; 19, 9; 20, 6; 22, 7.14. ***This prophetic message:*** literally, "the words of the prophecy"; so Rv 22, 7.10.18.19 by inclusion. ***The appointed time:*** when Jesus will return in glory; cf Rv 1, 7; 3, 11; 22, 7.10.12.20.

II. LETTERS TO THE CHURCHES OF ASIA

Greeting.* [4]John, to the seven churches
in Asia:* grace to you and peace from him
who is and who was and who is to come,
and from the seven spirits before his
throne,[c] [5]and from Jesus Christ, the faithful witness, the firstborn of the dead and
ruler of the kings of the earth. To him who
loves us and has freed us* from our sins by
his blood,[d] [6]who has made us into a kingdom, priests for his God and Father, to
him be glory and power forever [and ever].
Amen.[e]

7 Behold, he is coming amid the clouds,
and every eye will see him,
even those who pierced him.
All the peoples of the earth will lament
him.
Yes. Amen.[f]

[8]"I am the Alpha and the Omega,"* says
the Lord God, "the one who is and who
was and who is to come, the almighty."[g]

The First Vision.* [9]I, John, your brother,
who share with you the distress, the kingdom, and the endurance we have in Jesus,
found myself on the island called Patmos*
because I proclaimed God's word and gave
testimony to Jesus. [10]I was caught up in
spirit on the Lord's day* and heard behind
me a voice as loud as a trumpet, [11]which
said, "Write on a scroll* what you see and
send it to the seven churches: to Ephesus,
Smyrna, Pergamum, Thyatira, Sardis,
Philadelphia, and Laodicea." [12] * Then I
turned to see whose voice it was that spoke
to me, and when I turned, I saw seven gold
lampstands [13]and in the midst of the
lampstands one like a son of man,* wearing an ankle-length robe, with a gold sash
around his chest.[h] [14]The hair of his head
was as white as white wool or as snow,*
and his eyes were like a fiery flame. [15]His
feet were like polished brass refined in a
furnace,* and his voice was like the sound
of rushing water. [16]In his right hand he
held seven stars.* A sharp two-edged
sword came out of his mouth, and his face
shone like the sun at its brightest.[i]

[17]When I caught sight of him, I fell
down at his feet as though dead.* He
touched me with his right hand and said,
"Do not be afraid. I am the first and the
last,[j] [18]the one who lives. Once I was
dead, but now I am alive forever and ever.
I hold the keys to death and the netherworld.* [19]Write down, therefore, what

c Rv 1, 8; 4, 8; 11, 17; 16, 5; Ex 3, 14.—d Rv 3, 14; 1 Cor 15, 20; Col 1, 18 / Heb 9, 14; 1 Pt 1, 19; 1 Jn 1, 7.—e Ex 19, 6; 1 Pt 2, 9.—f Dn 7, 13 / Zec 12, 10; Mt 24, 30; Jn 19, 37.—g Rv 1, 17; 21, 6; 22, 13; Is 41, 4; 44, 6; 48, 12.—h Dn 7, 13; 10, 5.—i Heb 4, 12.—j Dn 8, 18 / Rv 1, 8.

1, 4-8: Although Revelation begins and ends (Rv 22, 21) with Christian epistolary formulae, there is nothing between chs 4 and 22 resembling a letter. The author here employs the standard word order for greetings in Greek letter writing: "N. to N., greetings . . ."; see the note on Rom 1, 1.

1, 4: *Seven churches in Asia:* Asia refers to the Roman province of that name in western Asia Minor (modern Turkey); these representative churches are mentioned by name in v 11, and each is the recipient of a message (Rv 2, 1—3, 22). *Seven* is the biblical number suggesting fullness and completeness; thus the seer is writing for the whole church.

1, 5: *Freed us:* the majority of Greek manuscripts and several early versions read "washed us"; but "freed us" is supported by the best manuscripts and fits well with Old Testament imagery, e.g., Is 40, 2.

1, 8: *The Alpha and the Omega:* the first and last letters of the Greek alphabet. In Rv 22, 13 the same words occur together with the expressions "the First and the Last, the Beginning and the End"; cf Rv 1, 17; 2, 8; 21, 6; Is 41, 4; 44, 6.

1, 9-20: In this first vision, the seer is commanded to write what he sees to the seven churches (9-11). He sees Christ in glory, whom he depicts in stock apocalyptic imagery (12-16), and hears him describe himself in terms meant to encourage Christians by emphasizing his victory over death (17-20).

1, 9: *Island called Patmos:* one of the Sporades islands in the Aegean Sea, some fifty miles south of Ephesus, used by the Romans as a penal colony. *Because I proclaimed God's word:* literally, "on account of God's word."

1, 10: *The Lord's day:* Sunday. *As loud as a trumpet:* the imagery is derived from the theophany at Sinai (Ex 19, 16.19; cf Heb 12, 19 and the trumpet in other eschatological settings in Is 27, 13; Jl 2, 1; Mt 24, 31; 1 Cor 15, 52; 1 Thes 4, 16).

1, 11: *Scroll:* a papyrus roll.

1, 12-16: A symbolic description of Christ in glory. The metaphorical language is not to be understood literally; cf Introduction.

1, 13: *Son of man:* see the note on Mk 8, 31. *Ankle-length robe:* Christ is priest; cf Ex 28, 4; 29, 5; Wis 18, 24; Zec 3, 4. *Gold sash:* Christ is king; cf Ex 28, 4; 1 Mc 10, 89; 11, 58; Dn 10, 5.

1, 14: *Hair . . . as white as white wool or as snow:* Christ is eternal, clothed with the dignity that belonged to the "Ancient of Days"; cf Rv 1, 18; Dn 7, 9. *His eyes were like a fiery flame:* Christ is portrayed as all-knowing; cf Rv 2, 23; Ps 7, 10; Jer 17, 10; and similar expressions in Rv 2, 18; 19, 12; cf Dn 10, 6.

1, 15: *His feet . . . furnace:* Christ is depicted as unchangeable; cf Ez 1, 27; Dn 10, 6. The Greek word translated "refined" is unconnected grammatically with any other word in the sentence. *His voice . . . water:* Christ speaks with divine authority; cf Ez 1, 24.

1, 16: *Seven stars:* in the pagan world, Mithras and the Caesars were represented with seven stars in their right hand, symbolizing their universal dominion. *A sharp two-edged sword:* this refers to the word of God (cf Eph 6, 17; Heb 4, 12) that will destroy unrepentant sinners; cf Rv 2, 16; 19, 15; Wis 18, 15; Is 11, 4; 49, 2. *His face . . . brightest:* this symbolizes the divine majesty of Christ; cf Rv 10, 1; 21, 23; Jgs 5, 31; Is 60, 19; Mt 17, 2.

1, 17: It was an Old Testament belief that for sinful human beings to see God was to die; cf Ex 19, 21; 33, 20; Jgs 6, 22-23; Is 6, 5.

1, 18: *Netherworld:* Greek Hades, Hebrew Sheol, the abode of the dead; cf Rv 20, 13-14; Nm 16, 33.

you have seen, and what is happening, and
what will happen afterwards.* 20 This is
the secret meaning* of the seven stars you
saw in my right hand, and of the seven
gold lampstands: the seven stars are the
angels of the seven churches, and the seven
lampstands are the seven churches.

CHAPTER 2

To Ephesus. 1 * "To the angel of the
church* in Ephesus,* write this:

" 'The one who holds the seven stars in
his right hand and walks in the midst of the
seven gold lampstands says this: 2 "I know
your works, your labor, and your endurance, and that you cannot tolerate the
wicked; you have tested those who call
themselves apostles but are not, and discovered that they are impostors.* 3 Moreover, you have endurance and have suffered for my name, and you have not
grown weary. 4 Yet I hold this against you:
you have lost the love you had at first.
5 Realize how far you have fallen. Repent,
and do the works you did at first. Otherwise, I will come to you and remove your
lampstand from its place, unless you repent. 6 But you have this in your favor: you
hate the works of the Nicolaitans,* which I
also hate.

7 " ' "Whoever has ears ought to hear
what the Spirit says to the churches. To
the victor* I will give the right to eat from
the tree of life that is in the garden of
God." '[k]

To Smyrna.* 8 "To the angel of the church
in Smyrna,* write this:

" 'The first and the last, who once died
but came to life, says this: 9 "I know your
tribulation and poverty, but you are rich.*
I know the slander of those who claim to be
Jews and are not, but rather are members
of the assembly of Satan.[l] 10 Do not be
afraid of anything that you are going to suffer. Indeed, the devil will throw some of
you into prison, that you may be tested,
and you will face an ordeal for ten days.
Remain faithful until death, and I will give
you the crown of life.

11 " ' "Whoever has ears ought to hear
what the Spirit says to the churches.[m] The
victor shall not be harmed by the second
death." '*

To Pergamum.* 12 "To the angel of the
church in Pergamum,* write this:

k Rv 2, 11.17.29; 3, 6.13.22; 13, 9; Mt 11, 15.—l Jas 2, 5.—m Rv 20, 6.14; 21, 8.

1, 19: *What you have seen, and what is happening, and what will happen afterwards:* the three parts of the Book of Revelation, the vision (10-20), the situation in the seven churches (chs 2-3), and the events of chs 6-22.

1, 20: *Secret meaning:* literally, "mystery." *Angels:* these are the presiding spirits of the seven churches. Angels were thought to be in charge of the physical world (cf Rv 7, 1; 14, 18; 16, 5) and of nations (Dn 10, 13; 12, 1), communities (the seven churches), and individuals (Mt 18, 10; Acts 12, 15). Some have seen in the "angel" of each of the seven churches its pastor or a personification of the spirit of the congregation.

2, 1—3, 22: Each of the seven letters follows the same pattern: address; description of the exalted Christ; blame and/or praise for the church addressed; threat and/or admonition; final exhortation and promise to all Christians.

2, 1-7: The letter to Ephesus praises the members of the church there for their works and virtues, including discerning false teachers (2-3), but admonishes them to repent and return to their former devotion (4-5). It concludes with a reference to the Nicolaitans (see the note on 6) and a promise that the victor will have access to eternal life (7).

2, 1: *Ephesus:* this great ancient city had a population of ca. 250,000; it was the capital of the Roman province of Asia and the commercial, cultural, and religious center of Asia. The other six churches were located in the same province, situated roughly in a circle; they were selected for geographical reasons rather than for the size of their Christian communities. *Walks in the midst of the seven gold lampstands:* this signifies that Christ is always present in the church; see the note on Rv 1, 4.

2, 2: *Who call themselves . . . impostors:* this refers to unauthorized and perverse missionaries; cf Acts 20, 29-30.

2, 6: *Nicolaitans:* these are perhaps the impostors of v 2; see the note on vv 14-15. There is little evidence for connecting this group with Nicolaus, the proselyte from Antioch, mentioned in Acts 6, 5.

2, 7: *Victor:* referring to any Christian individual who holds fast to the faith and does God's will in the face of persecution. *The tree of life that is in the garden of God:* this is a reference to the tree in the primeval paradise (Gn 2, 9); cf Rv 22, 2.14.19. The decree excluding humanity from the tree of life has been revoked by Christ.

2, 8-11: The letter to Smyrna encourages the Christians in this important commercial center by telling them that although they are impoverished, they are nevertheless rich, and calls those Jews who are slandering them members of the assembly of Satan (9). There is no admonition; rather, the Christians are told that they will suffer much, even death, but the time of tribulation will be short compared to their eternal reward (10), and they will thus escape final damnation (11).

2, 8: *Smyrna:* modern Izmir, ca. thirty miles north of Ephesus, and the chief city of Lydia, with a temple to the goddess Roma. It was renowned for its loyalty to Rome, and it also had a large Jewish community very hostile toward Christians.

2, 9-10: The church in Smyrna was materially poor but spiritually rich. Accusations made by Jewish brethren there occasioned the persecution of Christians; cf Acts 14, 2.19; 17, 5.13.

2, 11: *The second death:* this refers to the eternal death, when sinners will receive their final punishment; cf Rv 20, 6.14-15; 21, 8.

2, 12-17: The letter to Pergamum praises the members of the church for persevering in their faith in Christ even in the midst of a pagan setting and in face of persecution and martyrdom (13). But it admonishes them about members who advocate an unprincipled morality (14; cf 2 Pt 2, 15; Jude 11) and others who follow the teaching of the Nicolaitans (15; see the note there). It urges them to repent (16) and promises them the hidden manna and Christ's amulet (17).

2, 12: *Pergamum:* modern Bergama, ca. forty-five miles northeast of Smyrna, a center for various kinds of pagan worship. It also had an outstanding library (the word *parchment* is derived from its name).

“ ‘The one with the sharp two-edged
sword says this: 13“I know that you live
where Satan’s throne* is, and yet you hold
fast to my name and have not denied your
faith in me, not even in the days of Antipas, my faithful witness, who was martyred among you, where Satan lives. 14 *
Yet I have a few things against you. You
have some people there who hold to the
teaching of Balaam, who instructed Balak
to put a stumbling block before the Israelites: to eat food sacrificed to idols and to
play the harlot.[n] 15 Likewise, you also have
some people who hold to the teaching of
[the] Nicolaitans. 16 Therefore, repent.
Otherwise, I will come to you quickly and
wage war against them with the sword of
my mouth.

17“ ‘ “Whoever has ears ought to hear
what the Spirit says to the churches. To
the victor I shall give some of the hidden
manna;* I shall also give a white amulet
upon which is inscribed a new name,
which no one knows except the one who
receives it.” ’[o]

To Thyatira.* 18“To the angel of the
church in Thyatira,* write this:

“ ‘The Son of God, whose eyes are like a
fiery flame and whose feet are like polished
brass, says this: 19“I know your works,
your love, faith, service, and endurance,
and that your last works are greater than
the first. 20 Yet I hold this against you, that
you tolerate the woman Jezebel, who calls
herself a prophetess, who teaches and mis-
leads my servants to play the harlot and to
eat food sacrificed to idols.* 21 I have given
her time to repent, but she refuses to repent of her harlotry. 22 So I will cast her on
a sickbed and plunge those who commit
adultery with her into intense suffering unless they repent of her works. 23 I will also
put her children* to death. Thus shall all
the churches come to know that I am the
searcher of hearts and minds and that I will
give each of you what your works deserve.[p] 24 But I say to the rest of you in
Thyatira, who do not uphold this teaching
and know nothing of the so-called deep
secrets of Satan:* on you I will place no
further burden, 25 except that you must
hold fast to what you have until I come.

26 “ ‘ “To the victor,* who keeps to my
ways* until the end,
I will give authority over the nations.[q]
27 He will rule them with an iron rod.
Like clay vessels will they be
smashed,
28 just as I received authority from my
Father. And to him I will give the morning
star.

29“ ‘ “Whoever has ears ought to hear
what the Spirit says to the churches.” ’

CHAPTER 3

To Sardis.* 1“To the angel of the church
in Sardis,* write this:

n Nm 22—24; 25, 1-3; 31, 16; 2 Pt 2, 15; Jude 11.—o Is 62, 2; 65, 15.—p 1 Sm 16, 7; Jer 11, 20; 17, 10.—q Rv 12, 5; Ps 2, 8-9.

2, 13: *Satan’s throne:* the reference is to emperor worship and other pagan practices that flourished in Pergamum, perhaps specifically to the white marble altar erected and dedicated to Zeus by Eumenes II (197-160 B.C.).

2, 14-15: Like Balaam, the biblical prototype of the religious compromiser (cf Nm 25, 1-3; 31, 16; 2 Pt 2, 15; Jude 11), the Nicolaitans in Pergamum and Ephesus (6) accommodated their Christian faith to paganism. They abused the principle of liberty enunciated by Paul (1 Cor 9, 19-23).

2, 17: *The hidden manna:* this is the food of life; cf Ps 78, 24-25. *White amulet:* literally, “white stone,” on which was written a magical name, whose power could be tapped by one who knew the secret name. It is used here as a symbol of victory and joy; cf Rv 3, 4-5. *New name:* this is a reference to the Christian’s rebirth in Christ; cf Rv 3, 12; 19, 12; Is 62, 2; 65, 15.

2, 18-29: The letter to Thyatira praises the progress in virtue of this small Christian community (19) but admonishes them for tolerating a false prophet who leads them astray (20). Her fate is sealed, but there is hope of repentance for her followers (21-22). Otherwise, they too shall die (23). They are warned against Satanic power or knowledge (24-25). Those who remain faithful will share in the messianic reign, having authority over nations (26-27), and will in fact possess Christ himself (28).

2, 18: *Thyatira:* modern Akhisar, ca. forty miles southeast of Pergamum, a frontier town famous for its workers’ guilds (cf Acts 16, 14), membership in which may have involved festal meals in pagan temples.

2, 20: The scheming and treacherous Jezebel of old (cf 1 Kgs 19, 1-2; 21, 1-14; 2 Kgs 9, 22.30-34) introduced pagan customs into the religion of Israel; this new Jezebel was doing the same to Christianity.

2, 23: *Children:* spiritual descendants.

2, 24: *The so-called deep secrets of Satan:* literally, “the deep things of Satan,” a scathing reference to the perverse teaching of the Nicolaitans (15).

2, 26-28: The Christian who perseveres in faith will share in Christ’s messianic authority (cf Ps 2, 8-9) and resurrection victory over death, symbolized by the morning star; cf Rv 22, 16.

2, 26: *Who keeps to my ways:* literally, “who keeps my works.”

3, 1-6: The letter to Sardis does not praise the community but admonishes its members to watchfulness, mutual support, and repentance (2-3). The few who have remained pure and faithful will share Christ’s victory and will be inscribed in the book of life (4-5).

3, 1: *Sardis:* this city, located ca. thirty miles southeast of Thyatira, was once the capital of Lydia, known for its wealth at the time of Croesus (6th century B.C.). Its citadel, reputed to be unassailable, was captured by surprise, first by Cyrus and later by Antiochus. The church is therefore warned to be on guard.

" 'The one who has the seven spirits of God and the seven stars says this: "I know your works, that you have the reputation of being alive, but you are dead. 2 Be watchful and strengthen what is left, which is going to die, for I have not found your works complete in the sight of my God. 3 Remember then how you accepted and heard; keep it, and repent. If you are not watchful, I will come like a thief, and you will never know at what hour I will come upon you.[r] 4 However, you have a few people in Sardis who have not soiled their garments; they will walk with me dressed in white, because they are worthy.[s]

5" ' "The victor will thus be dressed in white,* and I will never erase his name from the book of life but will acknowledge his name in the presence of my Father and of his angels.[t]

6" ' "Whoever has ears ought to hear what the Spirit says to the churches." '

To Philadelphia.* 7"To the angel of the church in Philadelphia,* write this:

" 'The holy one, the true,
who holds the key of David,
who opens and no one shall close,
who closes and no one shall open,[u]

says this:

8" ' "I know your works (behold, I have left an open door* before you, which no one can close). You have limited strength, and yet you have kept my word and have not denied my name. 9 Behold, I will make those of the assembly of Satan who claim to be Jews and are not, but are lying, behold I will make them come and fall prostrate at your feet, and they will realize that I love you.[v] 10 Because you have kept my message of endurance,* I will keep you safe in the time of trial that is going to come to the whole world to test the inhabitants of the earth. 11 I am coming quickly. Hold fast to what you have, so that no one may take your crown.[w]

12" ' "The victor I will make into a pillar* in the temple of my God, and he will never leave it again. On him I will inscribe the name of my God and the name of the city of my God, the new Jerusalem, which comes down out of heaven from my God, as well as my new name.[x]

13" ' "Whoever has ears ought to hear what the Spirit says to the churches." '

To Laodicea.* 14"To the angel of the church in Laodicea,* write this:

" 'The Amen, the faithful and true witness, the source of God's creation, says this:[y] 15"I know your works; I know that you are neither cold nor hot.* I wish you were either cold or hot. 16 * So, because you are lukewarm, neither hot nor cold, I

---

r Mt 24, 42-44; Mk 13, 33; 1 Thes 5, 2; 2 Pt 3, 10.—s Rv 7, 13-14.—t Ps 69, 29; Dn 12, 1 / Mt 10, 32.—u Is 22, 22; Mt 16, 19.—v Rv 2, 9 / Is 45, 14; 60, 14.—w Rv 2, 25; 22, 7.20.—x Rv 21, 2-3; Ez 48, 35 / Rv 19, 13.—y Rv 1, 5.

3, 5: *In white:* white is a sign of victory and joy as well as resurrection; see the note on Rv 2, 17. *The book of life:* the roll in which the names of the redeemed are kept; cf Rv 13, 8; 17, 8; 20, 12.15; 21, 27; Phil 4, 3; Dn 12, 1. They will be acknowledged by Christ in heaven; cf Mt 10, 32.

3, 7-13: The letter to Philadelphia praises the Christians there for remaining faithful even with their limited strength (8). Members of the assembly of Satan are again singled out (9; see Rv 2, 9 above). There is no admonition; rather, the letter promises that they will be kept safe at the great trial (10-11) and that the victors will become pillars of the heavenly temple, upon which three names will be inscribed: God, Jerusalem, and Christ (12).

3, 7: *Philadelphia:* modern Alasehir, ca. thirty miles southeast of Sardis, founded by Attalus II Philadelphus of Pergamum to be an "open door" (8) for Greek culture; it was destroyed by an earthquake in A.D. 17. Rebuilt by money from the Emperor Tiberius, the city was renamed Neo-Caesarea; this may explain the allusions to "name" in v 12. *Key of David:* to the heavenly city of David (cf Is 22, 22), "the new Jerusalem" (12), over which Christ has supreme authority.

3, 8: *An open door:* opportunities for sharing and proclaiming the faith; cf Acts 14, 27; 1 Cor 16, 9; 2 Cor 2, 12.

3, 10: *My message of endurance:* this does not refer to a saying of Jesus about patience but to the example of Christ's patient endurance. *The inhabitants of the earth:* literally, "those who live on the earth." This expression, which also occurs in Rv 6, 10; 8, 13; 11, 10; 13, 8.12.14; 17, 2.8, always refers to the pagan world.

3, 12: *Pillar:* this may be an allusion to the rebuilding of the city; see the note on v 7. *New Jerusalem:* it is described in Rv 21, 10—22, 5.

3, 14-22: The letter to Laodicea reprimands the community for being lukewarm (15-16), but no particular faults are singled out. Their material prosperity is contrasted with their spiritual poverty, the violet tunics that were the source of their wealth with the white robe of baptism, and their famous eye ointment with true spiritual perception (17-18). But Christ's chastisement is inspired by love and a desire to be allowed to share the messianic banquet with his followers in the heavenly kingdom (19-21).

3, 14: *Laodicea:* ca. forty miles southeast of Philadelphia and ca. eighty miles east of Ephesus, a wealthy industrial and commercial center, with a renowned medical school. It exported fine woolen garments and was famous for its eye salves. It was so wealthy that it was proudly rebuilt without outside aid after the devastating earthquake of A.D. 60/61. *The Amen:* this is a divine title (cf Hebrew text of Is 65, 16) applied to Christ; cf 2 Cor 1, 20. *Source of God's creation:* literally, "the beginning of God's creation," a concept found also in Jn 1, 3; Col 1, 16-17; Heb 1, 2; cf Prv 8, 22-31; Wis 9, 1-2.

3, 15-16: Halfhearted commitment to the faith is nauseating to Christ; cf Rom 12, 11.

3, 16: *Spit:* literally, "vomit." The image is that of a beverage that should be either hot or cold. Perhaps there is an allusion to the hot springs of Hierapolis across the Lycus river from Laodicea, which would have been lukewarm by the time they reached Laodicea.

will spit you out of my mouth. 17 [z] For you
say, 'I am rich and affluent and have no
need of anything,' and yet do not realize
that you are wretched, pitiable, poor,
blind, and naked.* 18 I advise you to buy
from me gold refined by fire* so that you
may be rich, and white garments to put on
so that your shameful nakedness may not
be exposed, and buy ointment to smear on
your eyes so that you may see. 19 Those
whom I love, I reprove and chastise. Be
earnest, therefore, and repent.[a]

20 " ' "Behold, I stand at the door and
knock. If anyone hears my voice and opens
the door, [then] I will enter his house and
dine with him, and he with me.* 21 I will
give the victor the right to sit with me on
my throne, as I myself first won the victory
and sit with my Father on his throne.[b]

22 " ' "Whoever has ears ought to hear
what the Spirit says to the churches." ' "

III. GOD AND THE LAMB IN HEAVEN

CHAPTER 4

Vision of Heavenly Worship.* 1 After this I
had a vision of an open door* to heaven,
and I heard the trumpetlike voice that had
spoken to me before, saying, "Come up
here and I will show you what must happen afterwards." 2 * At once I was caught
up in spirit.[c] A throne was there in heaven,
and on the throne sat 3 one whose appearance sparkled like jasper and carnelian.
Around the throne was a halo as brilliant as
an emerald. 4 Surrounding the throne I saw
twenty-four other thrones on which
twenty-four elders* sat, dressed in white
garments and with gold crowns on their
heads.[d] 5 From the throne came flashes of
lightning, rumblings, and peals of thunder.* Seven flaming torches burned in
front of the throne, which are the seven
spirits of God. 6 [e] In front of the throne
was something that resembled a sea of glass
like crystal.*

In the center and around the throne,
there were four living creatures covered
with eyes in front and in back. 7 The first
creature resembled a lion, the second was
like a calf, the third had a face like that of
a human being, and the fourth looked like
an eagle* in flight. 8 The four living creatures, each of them with six wings,* were
covered with eyes inside and out. Day and
night they do not stop exclaiming:

"Holy, holy, holy is the Lord God almighty,
who was, and who is, and who is to
come."[f]

9 Whenever the living creatures give glory
and honor and thanks to the one who sits
on the throne, who lives forever and ever,
10 the twenty-four elders fall down before
the one who sits on the throne and worship
him, who lives forever and ever. They
throw down their crowns before the
throne, exclaiming:

11 "Worthy are you, Lord our God,
to receive glory and honor and
power,
for you created all things;
because of your will they came to be
and were created."[g]

z Prv 13, 7; Lk 12, 21.—a Prv 3, 11-12; 1 Cor 11, 32; Heb 12, 5-11.—b Lk 22, 28-30; Mt 19, 28.—c 2-3: Is 6, 1 / Ez 1, 26-28.—d Is 24, 23.—e Ex 24, 10.—f Is 6, 2-3 / Rv 1, 4.8; 11, 17; 16, 5.—g Rom 4, 17; 16, 27.

3, 17: Economic prosperity occasioned spiritual bankruptcy.

3, 18: *Gold . . . fire:* God's grace. *White garments:* symbol of an upright life; the city was noted for its violet/purple cloth. *Ointment . . . eyes:* to remove spiritual blindness; one of the city's exports was eye ointment (see the note on Rv 3, 14).

3, 20: Christ invites all to the messianic banquet in heaven; cf Is 25, 6; Lk 14, 15; 22, 30.

4, 1-11: The seer now describes a vision of the heavenly court in worship of God enthroned. He reverently avoids naming or describing God but pictures twenty-four elders in priestly and regal attire (4) and God's throne and its surroundings made of precious gems and other symbols that traditionally express the majesty of God (5-6). Universal creation is represented by the four living creatures (6-7). Along with the twenty-four elders, they praise God unceasingly in humble adoration (8-11).

4, 1: The ancients viewed heaven as a solid vault, entered by way of actual doors.

4, 2-8: Much of the imagery here is taken from Ez 1 and 10.

4, 4: *Twenty-four elders:* these represent the twelve tribes of Israel and the twelve apostles; cf Rv 21, 12-14.

4, 5: *Flashes of lightning, rumblings, and peals of thunder:* as in other descriptions of God's appearance or activity; cf Rv 8, 5; 11, 19; 16, 18; Ex 19, 16; Ez 1, 4.13. *The seven spirits of God:* the seven "angels of the presence" as in Rv 8, 2 and Tb 12, 15.

4, 6: *A sea of glass like crystal:* an image adapted from Ez 1, 22-26. *Four living creatures:* these are symbols taken from Ez 1, 5-21; they are identified as cherubim in Ez 10, 20. *Covered with eyes:* these suggest God's knowledge and concern.

4, 7: *Lion . . . calf . . . human being . . . eagle:* these symbolize, respectively, what is noblest, strongest, wisest, and swiftest in creation. *Calf:* traditionally translated "ox," the Greek word refers to a heifer or young bull. Since the second century, these four creatures have been used as symbols of the evangelists Mark, Luke, Matthew, and John, respectively.

4, 8: *Six wings:* like the seraphim of Is 6, 2.

CHAPTER 5

The Scroll and the Lamb.* 1 I saw a scroll*
in the right hand of the one who sat on the
throne. It had writing on both sides and
was sealed with seven seals.[h] 2 Then I saw
a mighty angel who proclaimed in a loud
voice, "Who is worthy to open the scroll
and break its seals?" 3 But no one in heaven
or on earth or under the earth was able to
open the scroll or to examine it. 4 I shed
many tears because no one was found
worthy to open the scroll or to examine it.
5 One of the elders said to me, "Do not
weep. The lion of the tribe of Judah, the
root of David,* has triumphed, enabling
him to open the scroll with its seven
seals."[i]

6 Then I saw standing in the midst of the
throne and the four living creatures and
the elders a Lamb* that seemed to have
been slain. He had seven horns and seven
eyes; these are the [seven] spirits of God
sent out into the whole world.[j] 7 He came
and received the scroll from the right hand
of the one who sat on the throne. 8 When
he took it, the four living creatures and the
twenty-four elders fell down before the
Lamb. Each of the elders held a harp and
gold bowls filled with incense, which are
the prayers of the holy ones. 9 They sang a
new hymn:

"Worthy are you to receive the scroll
and to break open its seals,
for you were slain and with your
blood you purchased for God
those from every tribe and tongue,
people and nation.
10 You made them a kingdom and priests
for our God,
and they will reign on earth."[k]

11 I looked again and heard the voices of
many angels who surrounded the throne
and the living creatures and the elders.
They were countless* in number,[l] 12 and
they cried out in a loud voice:

"Worthy is the Lamb that was slain
to receive power and riches, wisdom
and strength,
honor and glory and blessing."

13 Then I heard every creature in heaven
and on earth and under the earth and in the
sea, everything in the universe, cry out:

"To the one who sits on the throne and
to the Lamb
be blessing and honor, glory and
might,
forever and ever."

14 The four living creatures answered,
"Amen," and the elders fell down and worshiped.

IV. THE SEVEN SEALS, TRUMPETS, AND PLAGUES, WITH INTERLUDES*

CHAPTER 6*

The First Six Seals. 1 * Then I watched
while the Lamb broke open the first of the
seven seals, and I heard one of the four living creatures cry out in a voice like thunder, "Come forward." 2 I looked, and there
was a white horse, and its rider had a

h Is 29, 11.—i Is 11, 1.10; Rom 15, 12.—j Jn 1, 29.—k Rv 1, 6; Ex 19, 6; Is 61, 6.—l Dn 7, 10; Jude 14-15.

5, 1-14: The seer now describes a papyrus roll in God's right hand (1) with seven seals indicating the importance of the message. A mighty angel asks who is worthy to open the scroll, i.e., who can accomplish God's salvific plan (2). There is despair at first when no one in creation can do it (3-4). But the seer is comforted by an elder who tells him that Christ, called the lion of the tribe of Judah, has won the right to open it (5). Christ then appears as a Lamb, coming to receive the scroll from God (6-7), for which he is acclaimed as at a coronation (8-10). This is followed by a doxology of the angels (11-12) and then finally by the heavenly church united with all of creation (13-14).

5, 1: *A scroll:* a papyrus roll possibly containing a list of afflictions for sinners (cf Ez 2, 9-10) or God's plan for the world. *Sealed with seven seals:* it is totally hidden from all but God. Only the Lamb (7-9) has the right to carry out the divine plan.

5, 5: *The lion of the tribe of Judah, the root of David:* these are the messianic titles applied to Christ to symbolize his victory; cf Rv 22, 16; Gn 49, 9; Is 11, 1.10; Mt 1, 1.

5, 6: Christ is the Paschal Lamb without blemish, whose blood saved the new Israel from sin and death; cf Ex 12; Is 53, 7; Jn 1, 29.36; Acts 8, 32; 1 Pt 1, 18-19. This is the main title for Christ in Rv, used twenty-eight times. *Seven horns and seven eyes:* Christ has the fullness (see the note on Rv 1, 4) of power (horns) and knowledge (eyes); cf Zec 4, 10. *[Seven] spirits:* as in Rv 1, 4; 3, 1; and 4, 5.

5, 11: *Countless:* literally, "100,000,000 plus 1,000,000," used by the author to express infinity.

6, 1—16, 21: A series of seven disasters now begins as each seal is broken (Rv 6, 1—8, 1), followed by a similar series as seven trumpets sound (Rv 8, 2—11, 19) and as seven angels pour bowls on the earth causing plagues (Rv 15, 1—16, 21). These gloomy sequences are interrupted by longer or shorter scenes suggesting the triumph of God and his witnesses (e.g., chs 7, 10, 11, 12, 13, 14).

6, 1-17: This chapter provides a symbolic description of the contents of the sealed scroll. The breaking of the first four seals reveals four riders. The first rider (of a white horse) is a conquering power (1-2), the second (red horse) a symbol of bloody war (3-4), the third (black horse) a symbol of famine (5-6), the fourth (pale green horse) a symbol of Death himself, accompanied by Hades (the netherworld) as his page (7-8). Verse 8b summarizes the role of all four riders. The breaking of the fifth seal reveals Christian martyrs in an attitude of sacrifice as blood poured out at the foot of an altar begging God for vindication, which will come only when their quota is filled; but they are given a white robe symbolic of victory (9-11). The breaking of the sixth seal reveals typical apocalyptic signs in the sky and the sheer terror of all people at the imminent divine judgment (12-17).

6, 1-8: The imagery is adapted from Zec 1, 8-10; 6, 1-8.

bow.* He was given a crown, and he rode
forth victorious to further his victories.[m]

3 When he broke open the second seal, I
heard the second living creature cry out,
"Come forward." 4 [n] Another horse came
out, a red one. Its rider was given power to
take peace away from the earth, so that
people would slaughter one another. And
he was given a huge sword.*

5 When he broke open the third seal, I
heard the third living creature cry out,
"Come forward." I looked, and there was a
black horse,* and its rider held a scale in
his hand. 6 I heard what seemed to be a
voice in the midst of the four living creatures. It said, "A ration of wheat costs a
day's pay,* and three rations of barley cost
a day's pay. But do not damage the olive oil
or the wine."[o]

7 When he broke open the fourth seal, I
heard the voice of the fourth living creature cry out, "Come forward." 8 I looked,
and there was a pale green* horse. Its rider
was named Death, and Hades accompanied him. They were given authority
over a quarter of the earth, to kill with
sword, famine, and plague, and by means
of the beasts of the earth.[p]

9 When he broke open the fifth seal, I
saw underneath the altar* the souls of
those who had been slaughtered because of
the witness they bore to the word of God.
10 They cried out in a loud voice, "How
long will it be, holy and true master,* before you sit in judgment and avenge our
blood on the inhabitants of the earth?"
11 Each of them was given a white robe,
and they were told to be patient a little
while longer until the number was filled of
their fellow servants and brothers who
were going to be killed as they had been.

12 * Then I watched while he broke open
the sixth seal, and there was a great earthquake; the sun turned as black as dark sackcloth* and the whole moon became like
blood.[q] 13 The stars in the sky fell to the
earth like unripe figs* shaken loose from
the tree in a strong wind. 14 Then the sky
was divided* like a torn scroll curling up,
and every mountain and island was moved
from its place.[r] 15 The kings of the earth,
the nobles,* the military officers, the rich,
the powerful, and every slave and free person hid themselves in caves and among
mountain crags. 16 They cried out to the
mountains and the rocks, "Fall on us and
hide us from the face of the one who sits on
the throne and from the wrath of the
Lamb,[s] 17 because the great day of their*
wrath has come and who can withstand it?"

CHAPTER 7*

The 144,000 Sealed. 1 After this I saw
four angels standing at the four corners of
the earth,* holding back the four winds of

m Zec 1, 8-10; 6, 1-3.—n Ez 21, 14-16.—o Lv 26, 26; Ez 4, 16-17.—p Ez 14, 21.—q Jl 3, 4; Mt 24, 29.—r Is 34, 4 / Rv 16, 20.—s Is 2, 19; Hos 10, 8; Lk 23, 30.

6, 2: *White horse . . . bow:* this may perhaps allude specifically to the Parthians on the eastern border of the Roman empire. Expert in the use of the bow, they constantly harassed the Romans and won a major victory in A.D. 62; see the note on Rv 9, 13-21. But the Old Testament imagery typifies the history of oppression of God's people at all times.

6, 4: *Huge sword:* this is a symbol of war and violence; cf Ez 21, 14-17.

6, 5: *Black horse:* this is a symbol of famine, the usual accompaniment of war in antiquity; cf Lv 26, 26; Ez 4, 16-17. The *scale* is a symbol of shortage of food with a corresponding rise in price.

6, 6: *A day's pay:* literally, "a denarius," a Roman silver coin that constitutes a day's wage in Mt 20, 2. Because of the famine, food was rationed and sold at an exorbitant price. A liter of flour was considered a day's ration in the Greek historians Herodotus and Diogenes Laertius. *Barley:* food of the poor (Jn 6, 9.13; cf 2 Kgs 7, 1.16.18); it was also used to feed animals; cf 1 Kgs 5, 8. *Do not damage:* the olive and the vine are to be used more sparingly in time of famine.

6, 8: *Pale green:* symbol of death and decay; cf Ez 14, 21.

6, 9: *The altar:* this altar corresponds to the altar of holocausts in the temple in Jerusalem; see also Rv 11, 1. *Because of the witness . . . word of God:* literally, "because of the word of God and the witness they had borne."

6, 10: *Holy and true master:* Old Testament usage as well as the context indicates that this is addressed to God rather than to Christ.

6, 12-14: Symbolic rather than literal description of the cosmic upheavals attending the day of the Lord when the martyrs' prayer for vindication (10) would be answered; cf Am 8, 8-9; Is 34, 4; 50, 3; Jl 2, 10; 3, 3-4; Mt 24, 4-36; Mk 13, 5-37; Lk 21, 8-36.

6, 12: *Dark sackcloth:* for mourning, sackcloth was made from the skin of a black goat.

6, 13: *Unripe figs:* literally, "summer (or winter) fruit."

6, 14: *Was divided:* literally, "was split," like a broken papyrus roll torn in two, each half then curling up to form a roll on either side.

6, 15: *Nobles:* literally, "courtiers," "grandees." *Military officers:* literally, "commanders of 1,000 men," used in Josephus and other Greek authors as the equivalent of the Roman *tribunus militum.* The listing of various ranks of society represents the universality of terror at the impending doom.

6, 17: *Their:* this reading is attested in the best manuscripts, but the vast majority read "his" in reference to the wrath of the Lamb in the preceding verse.

7, 1-17: An interlude of two visions precedes the breaking of the seventh seal, just as two more will separate the sixth and seventh trumpets (ch 10). In the first vision (1-8), the elect receive the seal of the living God as protection against the coming cataclysm; cf Rv 14, 1; Ez 9, 4-6; 2 Cor 1, 22; Eph 1, 13; 4, 30. The second vision (9-17) portrays the faithful Christians before God's throne to encourage those on earth to persevere to the end, even to death.

7, 1: *The four corners of the earth:* the earth is seen as a table or rectangular surface.

the earth so that no wind could blow on
land or sea or against any tree.[t] 2 Then I
saw another angel come up from the East,*
holding the seal of the living God. He cried
out in a loud voice to the four angels who
were given power to damage the land and
the sea, 3 "Do not damage the land or the
sea or the trees until we put the seal on the
foreheads of the servants of our God."[u] 4 I
heard the number of those who had been
marked with the seal, one hundred and
forty-four thousand marked* from every
tribe of the Israelites:[v] 5 twelve thousand
were marked from the tribe of Judah,*
twelve thousand from the tribe of Reuben,
twelve thousand from the tribe of Gad,
6 twelve thousand from the tribe of Asher,
twelve thousand from the tribe of Naph-
tali, twelve thousand from the tribe of
Manasseh, 7 twelve thousand from the tribe
of Simeon, twelve thousand from the tribe
of Levi, twelve thousand from the tribe of
Issachar, 8 twelve thousand from the tribe
of Zebulun, twelve thousand from the
tribe of Joseph, and twelve thousand were
marked from the tribe of Benjamin.

Triumph of the Elect. 9 After this I had a
vision of a great multitude, which no one
could count, from every nation, race, people, and tongue. They stood before the
throne and before the Lamb, wearing
white robes and holding palm branches* in
their hands. 10 They cried out in a loud
voice:

"Salvation comes from* our God, who
is seated on the throne,
and from the Lamb."

11 All the angels stood around the throne
and around the elders and the four living
creatures. They prostrated themselves before the throne, worshiped God, 12 and
exclaimed:

"Amen. Blessing and glory, wisdom
and thanksgiving,
honor, power, and might
be to our God forever and ever.
Amen."

13 Then one of the elders spoke up and said
to me, "Who are these wearing white
robes, and where did they come from?" 14 I
said to him, "My lord, you are the one who
knows." He said to me, "These are the
ones who have survived the time of great
distress;* they have washed their robes and
made them white in the blood of the
Lamb.[w]

15 "For this reason they stand before
God's throne
and worship him day and night in his
temple.
The one who sits on the throne will
shelter them.
16 They will not hunger or thirst anymore,
nor will the sun or any heat strike
them.[x]
17 For the Lamb who is in the center of
the throne will shepherd them
and lead them to springs of life-giving water,*
and God will wipe away every tear
from their eyes."[y]

CHAPTER 8*

The Seven Trumpets. 1 When he broke
open the seventh seal, there was silence in
heaven* for about half an hour.[z] 2 And I
saw that the seven angels who stood before
God were given seven trumpets.[a]

t Jer 49, 36; Zec 6, 5.—u Ex 12, 7-14; Ez 9, 4; 2 Cor 1, 22; Eph 1, 13; 4, 30.—v Rv 14, 1.—w Mt 24, 21.—x Is 49, 10.—y Rv 21, 4; Is 25, 8.—z Hb 2, 20; Zep 1, 7; Zec 2, 17.—a Rv 4, 5; Tb 12, 15.

7, 2: *East:* literally, "rising of the sun." The east was considered the source of light and the place of paradise (Gn 2, 8). *Seal:* whatever was marked by the impression of one's signet ring belonged to that person and was under his protection.

7, 4-9: *One hundred and forty-four thousand:* the square of twelve (the number of Israel's tribes) multiplied by a thousand, symbolic of the new Israel (cf Rv 14, 1-5; Gal 6, 16; Jas 1, 1) that embraces people *from every nation, race, people, and tongue* (9).

7, 5-8: Judah is placed first because of Christ; cf "the Lion of the tribe of Judah" (Rv 5, 5). Dan is omitted because of a later tradition that the antichrist would arise from it.

7, 9: *White robes . . . palm branches:* symbols of joy and victory; see the note on Rv 3, 5.

7, 10: *Salvation comes from:* literally, "(let) salvation (be ascribed) to." A similar hymn of praise is found at the fall of the dragon (Rv 12, 10) and of Babylon (Rv 19, 1).

7, 14: *Time of great distress:* fierce persecution by the Romans; cf Introduction.

7, 17: *Life-giving water:* literally, "the water of life," God's grace, which flows from Christ; cf Rv 21, 6; 22, 1.17; Jn 4, 10.14.

8, 1-13: The breaking of the seventh seal produces at first silence and then seven symbolic disasters, each announced by a trumpet blast, of which the first four form a unit as did the first four seals. A minor liturgy (3-5) is enclosed by a vision of seven angels (2.6). Then follow the first four trumpet blasts, each heralding catastrophes modeled on the plagues of Egypt affecting the traditional prophetic third (cf Ez 5, 12) of the earth, sea, fresh water, and stars (7-12). Finally, there is a vision of an eagle warning of the last three trumpet blasts (13).

8, 1: *Silence in heaven:* as in Zep 1, 7, a prelude to the eschatological woes that are to follow; cf Introduction.

The Gold Censer. 3 Another angel came and stood at the altar,* holding a gold censer. He was given a great quantity of incense to offer, along with the prayers of all the holy ones, on the gold altar that was before the throne.[b] 4 The smoke of the incense along with the prayers of the holy ones went up before God from the hand of the angel. 5 Then the angel took the censer, filled it with burning coals from the altar, and hurled it down to the earth. There were peals of thunder, rumblings, flashes of lightning, and an earthquake.[c]

The First Four Trumpets. 6 The seven angels who were holding the seven trumpets prepared to blow them.[d]

7 When the first one blew his trumpet, there came hail and fire mixed with blood, which was hurled down to the earth. A third of the land was burned up, along with a third of the trees and all green grass.*

8 * When the second angel blew his trumpet, something like a large burning mountain was hurled into the sea. A third of the sea turned to blood,[e] 9 a third of the creatures living in the sea* died, and a third of the ships were wrecked.

10 When the third angel blew his trumpet, a large star burning like a torch fell from the sky. It fell on a third of the rivers and on the springs of water.[f] 11 The star was called "Wormwood,"* and a third of all the water turned to wormwood. Many people died from this water, because it was made bitter.[g]

12 When the fourth angel blew his trumpet, a third of the sun, a third of the moon, and a third of the stars were struck, so that a third of them became dark. The day lost its light for a third of the time, as did the night.[h]

13 Then I looked again and heard an eagle flying high overhead cry out in a loud voice, "Woe! Woe! Woe* to the inhabitants of the earth from the rest of the trumpet blasts that the three angels are about to blow!"

CHAPTER 9

The Fifth Trumpet.* 1 Then the fifth angel blew his trumpet, and I saw a star* that had fallen from the sky to the earth. It was given the key for the passage to the abyss. 2 It opened the passage to the abyss,[i] and smoke came up out of the passage like smoke from a huge furnace. The sun and the air were darkened by the smoke from the passage.[j] 3 Locusts came out of the smoke onto the land, and they were given the same power as scorpions* of the earth.[k] 4 They were told not to harm the grass of the earth or any plant or any tree, but only those people who did not have the seal of God on their foreheads. 5 They were not allowed to kill them but only to torment them for five months;* the torment they inflicted was like that of a scorpion when it stings a person. 6 During that time these people will seek death but will not find it, and they will long to die but death will escape them.[l]

7 * The appearance of the locusts was like that of horses ready for battle. On their heads they wore what looked like crowns of gold; their faces were like human faces,[m] 8 and they had hair like women's hair. Their teeth were like lions' teeth,[n] 9 and they had chests like iron breastplates. The

b Ps 141, 2; Tb 12, 12.—c Ez 10, 2; Ps 11, 6 / Rv 4, 5; 11, 19; 16, 18.—d Rv 16, 1-21.—e Ex 7, 20.—f Is 14, 12.—g Jer 9, 14.—h Ex 10, 21-23.—i Rv 20, 1.—j Gn 19, 28.—k Ex 10, 12-15; Wis 16, 9.—l Jb 3, 21.—m Jl 2, 4.—n Jl 1, 6.

8, 3: *Altar:* there seems to be only one altar in the heavenly temple, corresponding to the altar of holocausts in Rv 6, 9, and here to the altar of incense in Jerusalem; cf also Rv 9, 13; 11, 1; 14, 18; 16, 7.

8, 7: This woe resembles the seventh plague of Egypt (Ex 9, 23-24); cf Jl 3, 3.

8, 8-11: The background of these two woes is the first plague of Egypt (Ex 7, 20-21).

8, 9: *Creatures living in the sea:* literally, "creatures in the sea that had souls."

8, 11: *Wormwood:* an extremely bitter and malignant plant symbolizing the punishment God inflicts on the ungodly; cf Jer 9, 12-14; 23, 15.

8, 13: *Woe! Woe! Woe:* each of the three woes pronounced by the angel represents a separate disaster; cf Rv 9, 12; 11, 14. The final woe, released by the seventh trumpet blast, includes the plagues of ch 16.

9, 1-12: The fifth trumpet heralds a woe containing elements from the eighth and ninth plagues of Egypt (Ex 10, 12-15.21-23) but specifically reminiscent of the invasion of locusts in Jl 1, 4—2, 10.

9, 1: *A star:* late Judaism represented fallen powers as stars (Is 14, 12-15; Lk 10, 18; Jude 13), but a comparison with Rv 1, 20 and Rv 20, 1 suggests that here it means an angel. *The passage to the abyss:* referring to Sheol, the netherworld, where Satan and the fallen angels are kept for a thousand years, to be cast afterwards into the pool of fire; cf Rv 20, 7-10. The abyss was conceived of as a vast subterranean cavern full of fire. Its only link with the earth was a kind of passage or mine shaft, which was kept locked.

9, 3: *Scorpions:* their poisonous sting was proverbial; Ez 2, 6; Lk 11, 12.

9, 5: *For five months:* more or less corresponding to the life-span of locusts.

9, 7-10: Eight characteristics are listed to show the eschatological and diabolical nature of these locusts.

sound of their wings was like the sound of many horse-drawn chariots racing into battle. 10 They had tails like scorpions, with stingers; with their tails they had power to harm people for five months. 11 They had as their king the angel of the abyss, whose name in Hebrew is Abaddon* and in Greek Apollyon.

12 The first woe has passed, but there are two more to come.

The Sixth Trumpet.* 13 Then the sixth angel blew his trumpet, and I heard a voice coming from the [four]* horns of the gold altar before God,[o] 14 telling the sixth angel who held the trumpet, "Release the four angels* who are bound at the banks of the great river Euphrates." 15 So the four angels were released, who were prepared for this hour, day, month, and year to kill a third of the human race. 16 The number of cavalry troops was two hundred million; I heard their number. 17 Now in my vision this is how I saw the horses and their riders. They wore red, blue,* and yellow breastplates, and the horses' heads were like heads of lions, and out of their mouths came fire, smoke, and sulfur.[p] 18 By these three plagues of fire, smoke, and sulfur that came out of their mouths a third of the human race was killed. 19 For the power of the horses is in their mouths and in their tails; for their tails are like snakes, with heads that inflict harm.

20 The rest of the human race, who were not killed by these plagues, did not repent of the works of their hands,* to give up the worship of demons and idols made from gold, silver, bronze, stone, and wood, which cannot see or hear or walk.[q] 21 Nor did they repent of their murders, their magic potions, their unchastity, or their robberies.

CHAPTER 10

The Angel with the Small Scroll. 1 * Then I saw another mighty angel come down from heaven wrapped in a cloud, with a halo around his head; his face was like the sun and his feet were like pillars of fire. 2 In his hand he held a small scroll that had been opened. He placed his right foot on the sea and his left foot on the land,* 3 and then he cried out in a loud voice as a lion roars. When he cried out, the seven thunders* raised their voices, too.[r] 4 When the seven thunders had spoken, I was about to write it down; but I heard a voice from heaven say, "Seal up what the seven thunders have spoken, but do not write it down." 5 Then the angel I saw standing on the sea and on the land raised his right hand to heaven 6 and swore by the one who lives forever and ever, who created heaven and earth and sea* and all that is in them, "There shall be no more delay.[s] 7 At the time when you hear the seventh angel blow his trumpet, the mysterious plan of God* shall be fulfilled, as he promised to his servants the prophets."[t]

8 Then the voice that I had heard from heaven spoke to me again and said, "Go, take the scroll that lies open in the hand of the angel who is standing on the sea and on the land." 9 So I went up to the angel and told him to give me the small scroll. He

o Ex 30, 1-3.—p Jb 41, 10-13.—q Ps 135, 15-17; Is 17, 8; Dn 5, 4.—r Ps 29, 3-9; Jer 25, 30; Am 3, 8.—s Dt 32, 40; Dn 12, 7 / Ez 12, 28.—t Am 3, 7.

9, 11: *Abaddon:* Hebrew (more precisely, Aramaic) for destruction or ruin. *Apollyon:* Greek for the "Destroyer."

9, 13-21: The sixth trumpet heralds a woe representing another diabolical attack symbolized by an invasion by the Parthians living east of the Euphrates; see the note on Rv 6, 2. At the appointed time (15), the frightful horses act as God's agents of judgment. The imaginative details are not to be taken literally; see Introduction and the note on Rv 6, 12-14.

9, 13: *[Four]:* many Greek manuscripts and versions omit the word. The horns were situated at the four corners of the altar (Ex 27, 2; 30, 2-3); see the note on Rv 8, 3.

9, 14-15: *The four angels:* they are symbolic of the destructive activity that will be extended throughout the universe.

9, 17: *Blue:* literally, "hyacinth-colored." *Yellow:* literally, "sulfurous."

9, 20: *The works of their hands:* i.e., the gods their hands had made.

10, 1—11, 14: An interlude in two scenes (Rv 10, 1-11 and Rv 11, 1-14) precedes the sounding of the seventh trumpet; cf Rv 7, 1-17. The first vision describes an angel astride sea and land like a colossus, with a small scroll open, the contents of which indicate that the end is imminent (ch 10). The second vision is of the measuring of the temple and of two witnesses, whose martyrdom means that the kingdom of God is about to be inaugurated.

10, 1-4: *The seven thunders:* God's voice announcing judgment and doom; cf Ps 29, 3-9, where thunder, as the voice of Yahweh, is praised seven times.

10, 2: *He placed . . . on the land:* this symbolizes the universality of the angel's message, as does the figure of the small scroll open to be read.

10, 6: *Heaven and earth and sea:* the three parts of the universe. *No more delay:* cf Dn 12, 7; Hb 2, 3.

10, 7: *The mysterious plan of God:* literally, "the mystery of God," the end of the present age when the forces of evil will be put down (Rv 17, 1—19, 4.11-21; 20, 7-10; cf 2 Thes 2, 6-12; Rom 16, 25-26), and the establishment of the reign of God when all creation will be made new (Rv 21, 1—22, 5).

10, 9-10: The small scroll was sweet because it predicted the final victory of God's people; it was sour because it also announced their sufferings. Cf Ez 3, 1-3.

said to me, "Take and swallow it. It will
turn your stomach sour, but in your mouth
it will taste as sweet* as honey." 10 I took
the small scroll from the angel's hand and
swallowed it. In my mouth it was like
sweet honey, but when I had eaten it, my
stomach turned sour.[u] 11 Then someone
said to me, "You must prophesy again
about many peoples, nations, tongues, and
kings."*

CHAPTER 11

The Two Witnesses. 1 [v] Then I was given
a measuring rod like a staff and I was told,
"Come and measure the temple of God and
the altar, and count those who are worship-
ing in it.* 2 But exclude the outer court* of
the temple; do not measure it, for it has
been handed over to the Gentiles, who will
trample the holy city for forty-two months.
3 I will commission my two witnesses* to
prophesy for those twelve hundred and
sixty days, wearing sackcloth." 4 [w] These
are the two olive trees and the two
lampstands* that stand before the Lord of
the earth. 5 * If anyone wants to harm
them, fire comes out of their mouths and
devours their enemies. In this way, anyone
wanting to harm them is sure to be slain.
6 They have the power to close up the sky
so that no rain can fall during the time of
their prophesying. They also have power
to turn water into blood and to afflict the
earth with any plague as often as they
wish.[x]
7 When they have finished their testimony, the beast that comes up from the
abyss* will wage war against them and conquer them and kill them.[y] 8 Their corpses
will lie in the main street of the great city,*
which has the symbolic names "Sodom"
and "Egypt," where indeed their Lord was
crucified. 9 * Those from every people,
tribe, tongue, and nation will gaze on their
corpses for three and a half days, and they
will not allow their corpses to be buried.
10 The inhabitants of the earth will gloat
over them and be glad and exchange gifts
because these two prophets tormented the
inhabitants of the earth. 11 But after the
three and a half days, a breath of life from
God entered them. When they stood on
their feet, great fear fell on those who saw
them.[z] 12 Then they heard a loud voice
from heaven say to them, "Come up here."
So they went up to heaven in a cloud as
their enemies looked on.[a] 13 At that moment there was a great earthquake, and a
tenth of the city fell in ruins. Seven
thousand people* were killed during the
earthquake; the rest were terrified and
gave glory to the God of heaven.

14 The second woe has passed, but the
third is coming soon.

The Seventh Trumpet.* 15 Then the
seventh angel blew his trumpet. There
were loud voices in heaven, saying, "The
kingdom of the world now belongs to our
Lord and to his Anointed, and he will
reign forever and ever." 16 The twenty-four
elders who sat on their thrones before God

u Ez 3, 1-3.—v Ez 40, 3-5 / Zec 2, 5-9.—w Zec 4, 3.14.—x Ex 7, 17.—y Dn 7, 21.—z Ez 37, 5.10.—a 2 Kgs 2, 11.

10, 11: This further prophecy is contained in chs 12-22.

11, 1: The temple and altar symbolize the new Israel; see the note on Rv 7, 4-9. The worshipers represent Christians. The measuring of the temple (cf Ez 40, 3—42, 20; 47, 1-12; Zec 2, 5-6) suggests that God will preserve the faithful remnant (cf Is 4, 2-3) who remain true to Christ (Rv 14, 1-5).

11, 2: *The outer court:* the Court of the Gentiles. *Trample . . . forty-two months:* the duration of the vicious persecution of the Jews by Antiochus IV Epiphanes (Dn 7, 25; 12, 7); this persecution of three and a half years (half of seven, counted as 1260 days in Rv 11, 3; 12, 6) became the prototype of periods of trial for God's people; cf Lk 4, 25; Jas 5, 17. The reference here is to the persecution by the Romans; cf Introduction.

11, 3: The two witnesses, wearing sackcloth symbolizing lamentation and repentance, cannot readily be identified. Do they represent Moses and Elijah, or the Law and the Prophets, or Peter and Paul? Most probably they refer to the universal church, especially the Christian martyrs, fulfilling the office of witness (two because of Dt 19, 15; cf Mk 6, 7; Jn 8, 17).

11, 4: *The two olive trees and the two lampstands:* the martyrs who stand in the presence of the Lord; the imagery is taken from Zec 4, 1-3.11-14, where the olive trees refer to Zerubbabel and Joshua.

11, 5-6: These details are derived from stories of Moses, who turned *water into blood* (Ex 7, 17-20), and of Elijah, who called down fire from heaven (1 Kgs 18, 36-40; 2 Kgs 1, 10) and closed up the sky for three years (1 Kgs 17, 1; cf 1 Kgs 18, 1).

11, 7: *The beast . . . from the abyss:* the Roman emperor Nero, who symbolizes the forces of evil, or the antichrist (Rv 13, 1.8; 17, 8); cf Dn 7, 2-8.11-12.19-22 and Introduction.

11, 8: *The great city:* this expression is used constantly in Rv for Babylon, i.e., Rome; cf Rv 14, 8; 16, 19; 17, 18; 18, 2.10.21. *"Sodom" and "Egypt":* symbols of immorality (cf Is 1, 10) and oppression of God's people (cf Ex 1, 11-14). *Where indeed their Lord was crucified:* not the geographical but the symbolic Jerusalem that rejects God and his witnesses, i.e., Rome, called Babylon in chs 16-18; see the note on Rv 17, 9 and Introduction.

11, 9-12: Over the martyrdom (7) of the two witnesses, now called prophets, the ungodly rejoice *for three and a half days,* a symbolic period of time; see the note on v 2. Afterwards they go in triumph to heaven, as did Elijah (2 Kgs 2, 11).

11, 13: *Seven thousand people:* a symbolic sum to represent all social classes (seven) and large numbers (thousands); cf Introduction.

11, 15-19: The seventh trumpet proclaims the coming of God's reign after the victory over diabolical powers; see the note on Rv 10, 7.

prostrated themselves and worshiped God
17 and said:

"We give thanks to you, Lord God almighty,
who are and who were.
For you have assumed your great power
and have established your reign.
18 The nations raged,
but your wrath has come,
and the time for the dead to be judged,
and to recompense your servants, the prophets,
and the holy ones and those who fear your name,
the small and the great alike,
and to destroy those who destroy the earth."[b]

19 Then God's temple in heaven was
opened, and the ark of his covenant could
be seen in the temple. There were flashes
of lightning, rumblings, and peals of thunder,
an earthquake, and a violent
hailstorm.

CHAPTER 12

The Woman and the Dragon. 1 * A great
sign appeared in the sky, a woman*
clothed with the sun, with the moon under
her feet, and on her head a crown of twelve
stars.[c] 2 She was with child and wailed
aloud in pain as she labored to give birth.*
3 Then another sign appeared in the sky; it
was a huge red dragon,* with seven heads
and ten horns, and on its heads were seven
diadems.[d] 4 Its tail swept away a third of
the stars in the sky and hurled them down
to the earth. Then the dragon stood before
the woman about to give birth, to devour
her child when she gave birth.[e] 5 She gave
birth to a son, a male child, destined to
rule all the nations with an iron rod.* Her
child was caught up to God and his
throne.[f] 6 The woman herself fled into the
desert where she had a place prepared by
God, that there she might be taken care of
for twelve hundred and sixty days.*

7 * Then war broke out in heaven;
Michael* and his angels battled against the
dragon. The dragon and its angels fought
back, 8 but they did not prevail and there
was no longer any place for them in
heaven. 9 The huge dragon, the ancient serpent,*
who is called the Devil and Satan,
who deceived the whole world, was thrown
down to earth, and its angels were thrown
down with it.[g]

10 Then I heard a loud voice in heaven
say:

"Now have salvation and power come,
and the kingdom of our God
and the authority of his Anointed.
For the accuser* of our brothers is cast out,
who accuses them before our God
day and night.
11 They conquered him by the blood of the Lamb
and by the word of their testimony;

---

b Ps 2, 1.5 / Am 3, 7.—c Gn 37, 9.—d Dn 7, 7.—e Dn 8, 10.—f Is 66, 7 / Ps 2, 9.—g Gn 3, 1-4 / Lk 10, 18.

12, 1—14, 20: This central section of Rv portrays the power of evil, represented by a dragon, in opposition to God and his people. First, the dragon pursues the woman about to give birth, but her son is saved and "caught up to God and his throne" (Rv 12, 5). Then Michael and his angels cast the dragon and his angels out of heaven (Rv 12, 7-9). After this, the dragon tries to attack the boy indirectly by attacking members of his church (Rv 12, 13-18). A beast, symbolizing the Roman empire, then becomes the dragon's agent, mortally wounded but restored to life and worshiped by all the world (Rv 13, 1-10). A second beast arises from the land, symbolizing the antichrist, which leads people astray by its prodigies to idolize the first beast (Rv 13, 11-18). This is followed by a vision of the Lamb and his faithful ones, and the proclamation of imminent judgment upon the world in terms of the wine of God's wrath (Rv 14, 1-20).

12, 1-6: The woman adorned with the sun, the moon, and the stars (images taken from Gn 37, 9-10) symbolizes God's people in the Old and the New Testament. The Israel of old gave birth to the Messiah (5) and then became the new Israel, the church, which suffers persecution by the dragon (6.13-17); cf Is 50, 1; 66, 7; Jer 50, 12. This corresponds to a widespread myth throughout the ancient world that a goddess pregnant with a savior was pursued by a horrible monster; by miraculous intervention, she bore a son who then killed the monster.

12, 2: Because of Eve's sin, the woman gives birth in distress and pain (Gn 3, 16; cf Is 66, 7-14).

12, 3: *Huge red dragon:* the Devil or Satan (cf Rv 12, 9; 20, 2), symbol of the forces of evil, a mythical monster known also as Leviathan (Ps 74, 13-14) or Rahab (Jb 26, 12-13; Ps 89, 11). *Seven diadems:* these are symbolic of the fullness of the dragon's sovereignty over the kingdoms of this world; cf Christ with many diadems (Rv 19, 12).

12, 5: *Rule . . . iron rod:* fulfilled in Rv 19, 15; cf Ps 2, 9. *Was caught up to God:* reference to Christ's ascension.

12, 6: God protects the persecuted church in the desert, the traditional Old Testament place of refuge for the afflicted, according to the typology of the Exodus; see the note on Rv 11, 2.

12, 7-12: Michael, mentioned only here in Rv, wins a victory over the dragon. A hymn of praise follows.

12, 7: *Michael:* the archangel, guardian and champion of Israel; cf Dn 10, 13.21; 12, 1; Jude 9. In Hebrew, the name Michael means "Who can compare with God?"; cf Rv 13, 4.

12, 9: *The ancient serpent:* who seduced Eve (Gn 3, 1-6), mother of the human race; cf Rv 20, 2; Eph 6, 11-12. *Was thrown down:* allusion to the expulsion of Satan from heaven; cf Lk 10, 18.

12, 10: *The accuser:* the meaning of the Hebrew word "Satan," found in v 9; Jb 1—2; Zec 3, 1; 1 Chr 21, 1; he continues to accuse Christ's disciples.

love for life did not deter them from
death.
12 Therefore, rejoice, you heavens,
and you who dwell in them.
But woe to you, earth and sea,
for the Devil has come down to you
in great fury,
for he knows he has but a short
time."

13 When the dragon saw that it had been
thrown down to the earth, it pursued the
woman who had given birth to the male
child.[h] 14 But the woman was given the two
wings of the great eagle,* so that she could
fly to her place in the desert, where, far
from the serpent, she was taken care of for
a year, two years, and a half-year.[i] 15 The
serpent,* however, spewed a torrent of
water out of his mouth after the woman to
sweep her away with the current. 16 But the
earth helped the woman and opened its
mouth and swallowed the flood that the
dragon spewed out of its mouth. 17 Then
the dragon became angry with the woman
and went off to wage war against the rest of
her offspring, those who keep God's commandments and bear witness to Jesus.*
18 It took its position* on the sand of the
sea.[j]

CHAPTER 13

The First Beast.* 1 Then I saw a beast
come out of the sea with ten horns and
seven heads; on its horns were ten
diadems, and on its heads blasphemous
name[s].[k] 2 The beast I saw was like a
leopard, but it had feet like a bear's, and its
mouth was like the mouth of a lion.[l] To it
the dragon gave its own power and throne,
along with great authority.* 3 I saw that
one of its heads seemed to have been mortally wounded, but this mortal wound was
healed.* Fascinated, the whole world followed after the beast. 4 They worshiped the
dragon because it gave its authority to the
beast; they also worshiped the beast* and
said, "Who can compare with the beast or
who can fight against it?"

5 * The beast was given a mouth uttering
proud boasts and blasphemies,[m] and it was
given authority to act for forty-two
months.* 6 It opened its mouth to utter
blasphemies against God, blaspheming his
name and his dwelling and those who dwell
in heaven. 7 It was also allowed to wage war
against the holy ones and conquer them,
and it was granted authority over every
tribe, people, tongue, and nation.[n] 8 All
the inhabitants of the earth will worship it,
all whose names were not written from the
foundation of the world in the book of life,
which belongs to the Lamb who was
slain.[o]

9 Whoever has ears ought to hear these
words.[p]
10 Anyone destined for captivity goes into
captivity.
Anyone destined to be slain by the
sword shall be slain by the sword.[q]

Such is the faithful endurance of the holy
ones.

The Second Beast.* 11 Then I saw another beast come up out of the earth; it had
two horns like a lamb's but spoke like a
dragon. 12 It wielded all the authority of the
first beast in its sight and made the earth
and its inhabitants worship the first beast,
whose mortal wound had been healed. 13 It

h Gn 3, 15.—i Ex 19, 4; Dn 7, 25; 12, 7.—j Gn 3, 15.—k 2 Thes 2, 3-12.—l Dn 7, 3-6.—m Dn 7, 8.11.25; 8, 14; 9, 27; 11, 36; 12, 7.—n Dn 7, 21.—o Rv 3, 5; 17, 8; 20, 12.—p Mt 13, 9.—q Jer 15, 2.

12, 14: *Great eagle:* symbol of the power and swiftness of divine help; cf Ex 19, 4; Dt 32, 11; Is 40, 31.

12, 15: The serpent is depicted as the sea monster; cf Rv 13, 1; Is 27, 1; Ez 32, 2; Ps 74, 13-14.

12, 17: Although the church is protected by God's special providence (16), the individual Christian is to expect persecution and suffering.

12, 18: *It took its position:* many later manuscripts and versions read "I took my position," thus connecting the sentence to the following paragraph.

13, 1-10: This wild beast, combining features of the four beasts in Dn 7, 2-28, symbolizes the Roman empire; the seven heads represent the emperors; see the notes on Rv 17, 10 and Rv 17, 12-14. The blasphemous names are the divine titles assumed by the emperors.

13, 2: Satan (Rv 12, 9), the prince of this world (Jn 12, 31), commissioned the beast to persecute the church (5-7).

13, 3: This may be a reference to the popular legend that Nero would come back to life and rule again after his death (which occurred in A.D. 68 from a self-inflicted stab wound in the throat); cf Rv 13, 14; 17, 8. Domitian (A.D. 81-96) embodied all the cruelty and impiety of Nero. Cf Introduction.

13, 4: *Worshiped the beast:* allusion to emperor worship, which Domitian insisted upon and ruthlessly enforced. *Who can compare with the beast:* perhaps a deliberate parody of the name Michael; see the note on Rv 12, 7.

13, 5-6: Domitian, like Antiochus IV Epiphanes (Dn 7, 8.11.25), demanded that he be called by divine titles such as "our lord and god" and "Jupiter." See the note on Rv 11, 2.

13, 5: *Forty-two months:* this is the same duration as the profanation of the holy city (Rv 11, 2), the prophetic mission of the two witnesses (Rv 11, 3), and the retreat of the woman into the desert (Rv 12, 6.14).

13, 11-18: The second beast is described in terms of the false prophets (cf Rv 16, 13; 19, 20; 20, 10) who accompany the false messiahs (the first beast); cf Mt 24, 24; Mk 13, 22; 2 Thes 2, 9; cf also Dt 13, 2-4. Christians had either to worship the emperor and his image or to suffer martyrdom.

performed great signs, even making fire
come down from heaven to earth in the
sight of everyone.[r] 14 It deceived the inhabitants of the earth with the signs it was
allowed to perform in the sight of the first
beast, telling them to make an image for
the beast who had been wounded by the
sword and revived. 15 It was then permitted
to breathe life into the beast's image, so
that the beast's image could speak and
[could] have anyone who did not worship it
put to death.[s] 16 It forced all the people,
small and great, rich and poor, free and
slave, to be given a stamped image on their
right hands or their foreheads,[t] 17 so that
no one could buy or sell except one who
had the stamped image of the beast's name
or the number that stood for its name.

18 [u] Wisdom is needed here; one who
understands can calculate the number of
the beast, for it is a number that stands for
a person. His number is six hundred and
sixty-six.*

CHAPTER 14

The Lamb's Companions.* 1 Then I
looked and there was the Lamb standing
on Mount Zion,* and with him a hundred
and forty-four thousand who had his name
and his Father's name written on their
foreheads.[v] 2 I heard a sound from heaven
like the sound of rushing water or a loud
peal of thunder. The sound I heard was
like that of harpists playing their harps.
3 They were singing [what seemed to be] a
new hymn before the throne, before the
four living creatures and the elders. No
one could learn this hymn except the
hundred and forty-four thousand who had
been ransomed from the earth.[w] 4 These
are they who were not defiled with women;
they are virgins* and these are the ones
who follow the Lamb wherever he goes.
They have been ransomed as the firstfruits
of the human race for God and the Lamb.[x]
5 On their lips no deceit* has been found;
they are unblemished.[y]

The Three Angels.* 6 Then I saw another
angel flying high overhead, with everlasting good news* to announce to those who
dwell on earth, to every nation, tribe,
tongue, and people. 7 He said in a loud
voice, "Fear God and give him glory, for
his time has come to sit in judgment. Worship him who made heaven and earth and
sea and springs of water."[z]

8 A second angel followed, saying:

"Fallen, fallen is Babylon the great,[a]
that made all the nations drink
the wine of her licentious passion."*

9 A third angel followed them and said in a
loud voice, "Anyone who worships the
beast or its image, or accepts its mark on
forehead or hand, 10 will also drink the
wine of God's fury,* poured full strength
into the cup of his wrath, and will be tormented in burning sulfur before the holy
angels and before the Lamb. 11 The smoke
of the fire that torments them will rise
forever and ever, and there will be no relief
day or night for those who worship the

r Dt 13, 2-4; Mt 24, 24; 2 Thes 2, 9-10.—s Dn 3, 5-7.15.—t Rv 14, 9; 16, 2; 19, 20; 20, 4.—u Rv 17, 9.—v Jl 3, 5; Ob 17; Acts 2, 21.—w Pss 33, 3; 96, 1; 98, 1; Is 42, 10.—x Jer 2, 2; Jas 1, 18.—y Zep 3, 13.—z Rv 2, 10; Mt 10, 28.—a Rv 18, 2-3; Is 21, 9; Jer 51, 8 / Is 51, 17; Jer 25, 15-17.

13, 18: Each of the letters of the alphabet in Hebrew as well as in Greek has a numerical value. Many possible combinations of letters will add up to 666, and many candidates have been nominated for this infamous number. The most likely is the emperor Caesar Nero (see the note on Rv 13, 3), the Greek form of whose name in Hebrew letters gives the required sum. (The Latin form of this name equals 616, which is the reading of a few manuscripts.) Nero personifies the emperors who viciously persecuted the church. It has also been observed that "6" represents imperfection, falling short of the perfect number "7," and is represented here in a triple or superlative form.

14, 1-5: Now follows a tender and consoling vision of the Lamb and his companions.

14, 1: *Mount Zion:* in Jerusalem, the traditional place where the true remnant, the Israel of faith, is to be gathered in the messianic reign; cf 2 Kgs 19, 30-31; Jl 3, 5; Ob 17; Mi 4, 6-8; Zep 3, 12-20. *A hundred and forty-four thousand:* see the note on Rv 7, 4-9. *His Father's name . . . foreheads:* in contrast to the pagans who were marked with the name or number of the beast (Rv 13, 16-17).

14, 4: *Virgins:* metaphorically, because they never indulged in any idolatrous practices, which are considered in the Old Testament to be adultery and fornication (Rv 2, 14-15.20-22; 17, 1-6; cf Ez 16, 1-58; 23, 1-49). The parallel passages (Rv 7, 3; 22, 4) indicate that the 144,000 whose foreheads are sealed represent all Christian people.

14, 5: *No deceit:* because they did not deny Christ or do homage to the beast. Lying is characteristic of the opponents of Christ (Jn 8, 44), but the Suffering Servant spoke no falsehood (Is 53, 9; 1 Pt 2, 22). *Unblemished:* a cultic term taken from the vocabulary of sacrificial ritual.

14, 6-13: Three angels proclaim imminent judgment on the pagan world, calling all peoples to worship God the creator. Babylon (Rome) will fall, and its supporters will be tormented forever.

14, 6: *Everlasting good news:* that God's eternal reign is about to begin; see the note on Rv 10, 7.

14, 8: This verse anticipates the lengthy dirge over Babylon (Rome) in Rv 18, 1—19, 4. The oracle of Is 21, 9 to Babylon is applied here.

14, 10-11: *The wine of God's fury:* image taken from Is 51, 17; Jer 25, 15-16; 49, 12; 51, 7; Ez 23, 31-34. Eternal punishment in the fiery pool of burning sulfur (or "fire and brimstone"; cf Gn 19, 24) is also reserved for the Devil, the beast, and the false prophet (Rv 19, 20; 20, 10; 21, 8).

beast or its image or accept the mark of its
name."[b] 12 Here is what sustains the holy
ones who keep God's commandments[c] and
their faith in Jesus.*

13 [d] I heard a voice from heaven say,
"Write this: Blessed are the dead who die
in the Lord from now on." "Yes," said the
Spirit, "let them find rest from their
labors, for their works accompany them."*

The Harvest of the Earth.* 14 Then I
looked and there was a white cloud, and
sitting on the cloud one who looked like a
son of man, with a gold crown on his head
and a sharp sickle in his hand.[e] 15 Another
angel came out of the temple, crying out in
a loud voice to the one sitting on the cloud,
"Use your sickle and reap the harvest, for
the time to reap has come, because the
earth's harvest is fully ripe."[f] 16 So the one
who was sitting on the cloud swung his
sickle over the earth, and the earth was
harvested.

17 Then another angel came out of the
temple in heaven who also had a sharp
sickle. 18 Then another angel [came] from
the altar,* [who] was in charge of the fire,
and cried out in a loud voice to the one who
had the sharp sickle, "Use your sharp
sickle and cut the clusters from the earth's
vines, for its grapes are ripe." 19 So the
angel swung his sickle over the earth and
cut the earth's vintage. He threw it into the
great wine press of God's fury.[g] 20 The
wine press was trodden outside the city
and blood poured out of the wine press to
the height of a horse's bridle for two
hundred miles.*

b Rv 19, 3.—c Rv 12, 17.—d Mt 11, 28-29; 2 Thes 1, 7; Heb 4, 10.—e Rv 1, 7; Dn 7, 13.—f Jl 4, 13; Mt 13, 36-43.—g Rv 19, 15; Is 63, 1-6.—h Rv 7, 9.14; 13, 15-18.—i Pss 92, 6; 98, 1 / Dt 32, 4; Ps 145, 17.—j Ps 86, 9-10; Jer 10, 7.—k Rv 19, 8.—l 1 Kgs 8, 10; Is 6, 4.

14, 12: In addition to *faith in Jesus*, the seer insists upon the necessity and value of works, as in Rv 2, 23; 20, 12-13; 22, 12; cf Mt 16, 27; Rom 2, 6.

14, 13: See the note on Rv 1, 3. According to Jewish thought, people's actions followed them as witnesses before the court of God.

14, 14-20: The reaping of the harvest symbolizes the gathering of the elect in the final judgment, while the reaping and treading of the grapes symbolizes the doom of the ungodly (cf Jl 4, 12-13; Is 63, 1-6) that will come in Rv 19, 11-21.

14, 18: *Altar:* there was only one altar in the heavenly temple; see the notes above on Rv 6, 9; 8, 3; 11, 1.

14, 20: *Two hundred miles:* literally sixteen hundred stades. The *stadion*, a Greek unit of measurement, was about 607 feet in length, approximately the length of a furlong.

CHAPTER 15

The Seven Last Plagues. 1 * Then I saw
in heaven another sign,* great and awe-in-
spiring: seven angels with the seven last
plagues, for through them God's fury is
accomplished.

2 Then I saw something like a sea of glass
mingled with fire.* On the sea of glass
were standing those who had won the victory over the beast and its image and the
number that signified its name. They were
holding God's harps,[h] 3 and they sang the
song of Moses,* the servant of God, and
the song of the Lamb:

"Great and wonderful are your works,
Lord God almighty.
Just and true are your ways,
O king of the nations.[i]
4 Who will not fear you, Lord,
or glorify your name?
For you alone are holy.
All the nations will come
and worship before you,
for your righteous acts have been revealed."[j]

5 * After this I had another vision. The
temple that is the heavenly tent of testimony* opened, 6 and the seven angels
with the seven plagues came out of the
temple. They were dressed in clean white
linen, with a gold sash around their
chests.[k] 7 One of the four living creatures
gave the seven angels seven gold bowls
filled with the fury of God, who lives
forever and ever. 8 Then the temple became so filled with the smoke from God's
glory and might that no one could enter it
until the seven plagues of the seven angels
had been accomplished.[l]

15, 1—16, 21: The seven bowls, the third and last group of seven after the seven seals and the seven trumpets, foreshadow the final cataclysm. Again, the series is introduced by a heavenly prelude, in which the victors over the beast sing the canticle of Moses (15, 2-4).

15, 1-4: A vision of the victorious martyrs precedes the vision of woe in Rv 15, 5—16, 21; cf Rv 7, 9-12.

15, 2: *Mingled with fire:* fire symbolizes the sanctity involved in facing God, reflected in the trials that have prepared the victorious Christians or in God's wrath.

15, 3: *The song of Moses:* the song that Moses and the Israelites sang after their escape from the oppression of Egypt (Ex 15, 1-18). The martyrs have escaped from the oppression of the Devil. *Nations:* many other Greek manuscripts and versions read "ages."

15, 5-8: Seven angels receive the bowls of God's wrath.

15, 5: *Tent of testimony:* the name of the meeting tent in the Greek text of Ex 40. Cf 2 Mc 2, 4-7.

CHAPTER 16

The Seven Bowls.* 1 I heard a loud voice
speaking from the temple to the seven
angels, "Go and pour out the seven bowls
of God's fury upon the earth."

2 The first angel went and poured out his
bowl on the earth. Festering and ugly sores
broke out on those who had the mark of
the beast or worshiped its image.*

3 * The second angel poured out his
bowl on the sea. The sea turned to blood
like that from a corpse; every creature living in the sea died.

4 The third angel poured out his bowl on
the rivers and springs of water. These also
turned to blood.[m] 5 Then I heard the angel
in charge of the waters say:

"You are just, O Holy One,
who are and who were,
in passing this sentence.[n]
6 For they have shed the blood of the
holy ones and the prophets,
and you [have] given them blood to
drink;
it is what they deserve."[o]
7 Then I heard the altar cry out,
"Yes, Lord God almighty,
your judgments are true and
just."[p]

8 The fourth angel poured out his bowl on
the sun. It was given the power to burn
people with fire. 9 People were burned by
the scorching heat and blasphemed the
name of God who had power over these
plagues, but they did not repent or give
him glory.[q]

10 [r] The fifth angel poured out his bowl
on the throne of the beast.* Its kingdom
was plunged into darkness, and people bit
their tongues in pain 11 and blasphemed the
God of heaven because of their pains and
sores. But they did not repent of their
works.[s]

12 The sixth angel emptied his bowl on
the great river Euphrates. Its water was
dried up to prepare the way for the kings of
the East.* 13 I saw three unclean spirits like
frogs* come from the mouth of the dragon,
from the mouth of the beast, and from the
mouth of the false prophet.[t] 14 These were
demonic spirits who performed signs.
They went out to the kings of the whole
world to assemble them for the battle on
the great day of God the almighty.[u]
15 ("Behold, I am coming like a thief."*
Blessed is the one who watches and keeps
his clothes ready, so that he may not go
naked and people see him exposed.)[v]
16 They then assembled the kings in the
place that is named Armageddon* in Hebrew.

17 The seventh angel poured out his bowl
into the air. A loud voice came out of the
temple from the throne, saying, "It is
done."[w] 18 Then there were lightning
flashes, rumblings, and peals of thunder,
and a great earthquake. It was such a violent earthquake that there has never been
one like it since the human race began on
earth.[x] 19 The great city* was split into
three parts, and the gentile cities fell. But
God remembered great Babylon, giving it
the cup filled with the wine of his fury and
wrath. 20 * Every island fled, and mountains disappeared. 21 Large hailstones like
huge weights came down from the sky on
people, and they blasphemed God for the
plague of hail because this plague was so
severe.[y]

---

m Ex 7, 14-24.—n Rv 1, 4.—o Ez 35, 6; Mt 23, 34-35.—p Dn 3, 27; Tb 3, 2.—q Am 4, 6.—r Ex 10, 21-23.—s Ex 9, 8-11 / Jer 5, 3.—t Ex 8, 2-3.—u 1 Cor 1, 8.—v Mt 24, 42-44 / Rv 3, 17.—w Is 66, 6.—x Mk 13, 19.—y Ex 9, 22-26.

16, 1-21: These seven bowls, like the seven seals (Rv 6, 1-17; 8, 1) and the seven trumpets (Rv 8, 2—9, 21; 11, 15-19), bring on a succession of disasters modeled in part on the plagues of Egypt (Ex 7—12). See the note on Rv 6, 12-14.

16, 2: Like the sixth Egyptian plague (Ex 9, 8-11).

16, 3-4: Like the first Egyptian plague (Ex 7, 20-21). The same woe followed the blowing of the second trumpet (Rv 8, 8-9).

16, 10: *The throne of the beast:* symbol of the forces of evil. *Darkness:* like the ninth Egyptian plague (Ex 10, 21-23); cf Rv 9, 2.

16, 12: *The kings of the East:* Parthians; see the notes on Rv 6, 2 and Rv 17, 12-13. *East:* literally, "rising of the sun," as in Rv 7, 2.

16, 13: *Frogs:* possibly an allusion to the second Egyptian plague (Ex 7, 26—8, 11). *The false prophet:* identified with the two-horned second beast (Rv 13, 11-18 and the note there).

16, 15: *Like a thief:* as in Rv 3, 3 (cf Mt 24, 42-44; 1 Thes 5, 2). *Blessed:* see the note on Rv 1, 3.

16, 16: *Armageddon:* in Hebrew, this means "Mountain of Megiddo." Since Megiddo was the scene of many decisive battles in antiquity (Jgs 5, 19-20; 2 Kgs 9, 27; 2 Chr 35, 20-24), the town became the symbol of the final disastrous rout of the forces of evil.

16, 19: *The great city:* Rome and the empire.

16, 20-21: See the note on Rv 6, 12-14. *Hailstones:* as in the seventh Egyptian plague (Ex 9, 23-24); cf Rv 8, 7. *Like huge weights:* literally, "weighing a talent," about one hundred pounds.

V. THE PUNISHMENT OF BABYLON AND THE DESTRUCTION OF PAGAN NATIONS

CHAPTER 17

Babylon the Great. 1 * Then one of the seven angels who were holding the seven bowls came and said to me, "Come here. I will show you the judgment on the great harlot* who lives near the many waters.[z] 2 The kings of the earth have had intercourse with her,[a] and the inhabitants of the earth became drunk on the wine of her harlotry."* 3 Then he carried me away in spirit to a deserted place where I saw a woman seated on a scarlet beast* that was covered with blasphemous names, with seven heads and ten horns.[b] 4 The woman was wearing purple and scarlet and adorned with gold, precious stones, and pearls.[c] She held in her hand a gold cup that was filled with the abominable and sordid deeds of her harlotry.* 5 On her forehead was written a name, which is a mystery, "Babylon the great, the mother of harlots and of the abominations of the earth." 6 I saw that the woman was drunk on the blood of the holy ones and on the blood of the witnesses to Jesus.

Meaning of the Beast and Harlot.* When I saw her I was greatly amazed. 7 The angel said to me, "Why are you amazed? I will explain to you the mystery of the woman and of the beast that carries her, the beast with the seven heads and the ten horns. 8 [d] The beast that you saw existed once but now exists no longer. It will come up from the abyss and is headed for destruction. The inhabitants of the earth whose names have not been written in the book of life from the foundation of the world shall be amazed when they see the beast, because it existed once but exists no longer, and yet it will come again.* 9 Here is a clue* for one who has wisdom. The seven heads represent seven hills upon which the woman sits. They also represent seven kings:[e] 10 five have already fallen, one still lives, and the last has not yet come,* and when he comes he must remain only a short while. 11 The beast* that existed once but exists no longer is an eighth king, but really belongs to the seven and is headed for destruction. 12 The ten horns that you saw represent ten kings who have not yet been crowned;* they will receive royal authority along with the beast for one hour.[f] 13 They are of one mind and will give their power and authority to the beast. 14 They will fight with the Lamb, but the Lamb will conquer them, for he is Lord of lords and king of kings, and those with him are called, chosen, and faithful."[g]

15 Then he said to me, "The waters that you saw where the harlot lives represent large numbers of peoples, nations, and tongues. 16 The ten horns* that you saw and the beast will hate the harlot; they will leave her desolate and naked; they will eat her flesh and consume her with fire.[h] 17 For God has put it into their minds to carry out his purpose and to make them come to an agreement to give their kingdom to the beast until the words of God are accomplished. 18 The woman whom you saw represents the great city that has sovereignty over the kings of the earth."

z Jer 50, 38; 51, 13.—a Jer 51, 7.—b Rv 13, 1.—c Rv 18, 16.—d Rv 13, 3-4 / Rv 3, 5; 13, 8; 20, 12.—e Rv 13, 18.—f Dn 7, 24.—g Rv 19, 11-21; 2 Mc 13, 4; 1 Tm 6, 15 / Rom 1, 6; 1 Pt 2, 9; Jude 1.—h Ez 16, 37-41; 23, 25-29.

17, 1—19, 10: The punishment of Babylon is now described as a past event and, metaphorically, under the image of the great harlot who leads people astray into idolatry.

17, 1-6: Babylon, the symbolic name (5) of Rome, is graphically described as "the great harlot."

17, 2: *Intercourse . . . harlotry:* see the note on Rv 14, 4. The pagan kings subject to Rome adopted the cult of the emperor.

17, 3: *Scarlet beast:* see the note on Rv 13, 1-10. *Blasphemous names:* divine titles assumed by the Roman emperors; see the note on Rv 13, 5-6.

17, 4: Reference to the great wealth and idolatrous cults of Rome.

17, 6b-18: An interpretation of the vision is here given.

17, 8: Allusion to the belief that the dead Nero would return to power (11); see the note on Rv 13, 3.

17, 9: *Here is a clue:* literally, "Here a mind that has wisdom." *Seven hills:* of Rome.

17, 10: There is little agreement as to the identity of the Roman emperors alluded to here. The number seven (9) suggests that all the emperors are meant; see the note on Rv 1, 4.

17, 11: *The beast:* Nero; see the note on Rv 17, 8.

17, 12-13: *Ten kings who have not yet been crowned:* perhaps Parthian satraps who are to accompany the revived Nero (the beast) in his march on Rome to regain power; see the note on Rv 13, 3. In Rv 19, 11-21, the Lamb and his companions will conquer them.

17, 16-18: *The ten horns:* the ten pagan kings (12) who unwittingly fulfill God's will against harlot Rome, the great city; cf Ez 16, 37.

CHAPTER 18

The Fall of Babylon.* 1 After this I saw another angel coming down from heaven,
having great authority, and the earth became illumined by his splendor.[i] 2 He cried
out in a mighty voice:

"Fallen, fallen is Babylon the great.[j]
She has become a haunt for demons.
She is a cage for every unclean spirit,
a cage for every unclean bird,
[a cage for every unclean] and dis-
gusting [beast].*
3 For all the nations have drunk*
the wine of her licentious passion.
The kings of the earth had intercourse
with her,
and the merchants of the earth grew
rich from her drive for luxury."[k]

4 Then I heard another voice from heaven
say:

"Depart from her,* my people,
so as not to take part in her sins
and receive a share in her plagues,[l]
5 for her sins are piled up to the sky,
and God remembers her crimes.[m]
6 Pay her back as she has paid others.
Pay her back double for her deeds.
Into her cup pour double what she
poured.[n]
7 To the measure of her boasting and
wantonness
repay her in torment and grief;
for she said to herself,
'I sit enthroned as queen;
I am no widow,
and I will never know grief.'[o]
8 Therefore, her plagues will come in one
day,
pestilence, grief, and famine;
she will be consumed by fire.
For mighty is the Lord God who judges
her."

9 The kings of the earth who had intercourse with her in their wantonness will
weep and mourn over her when they see
the smoke of her pyre. 10 They will keep
their distance for fear of the torment inflicted on her, and they will say:

"Alas, alas, great city,
Babylon, mighty city.
In one hour your judgment has
come."

11 The merchants of the earth will weep
and mourn for her, because there will be
no more markets* for their cargo: 12 their
cargo of gold, silver, precious stones, and
pearls; fine linen, purple silk, and scarlet
cloth; fragrant wood of every kind, all articles of ivory and all articles of the most expensive wood, bronze, iron, and marble;
13 cinnamon, spice,* incense, myrrh, and
frankincense; wine, olive oil, fine flour,
and wheat; cattle and sheep, horses and
chariots, and slaves, that is, human beings.

14 "The fruit you craved
has left you.
All your luxury and splendor are gone,
never again will one find them."[p]

15 The merchants who deal in these goods,
who grew rich from her, will keep their
distance for fear of the torment inflicted on
her. Weeping and mourning, 16 they cry
out:

"Alas, alas, great city,
wearing fine linen, purple and scarlet,
adorned [in] gold, precious stones,
and pearls.[q]
17 In one hour this great wealth has been
ruined."

Every captain of a ship, every traveler at
sea, sailors, and seafaring merchants stood
at a distance 18 and cried out when they saw
the smoke of her pyre, "What city could
compare with the great city?" 19 [r] They
threw dust on their heads and cried out,
weeping and mourning:

---

i Ez 43, 2.—j Rv 14, 8; Is 21, 9; Jer 50, 2-3; 51, 8.—k Rv 17, 2; Jer 51, 7.—l Is 48, 20; Jer 50, 8.—m Jer 51, 9.—n Jer 50, 15 / Jer 16, 18.—o Is 47, 8-9.—p Hos 10, 5 / Am 6, 7.—q Rv 17, 4.—r Ez 27, 27-32.

18, 1—19, 4: A stirring dirge over the fall of Babylon-Rome. The perspective is prophetic, as if the fall of Rome had already taken place. The imagery here, as elsewhere in this book, is not to be taken literally. The vindictiveness of some of the language, borrowed from the scathing Old Testament prophecies against Babylon, Tyre, and Nineveh (Is 23; 24; 27; Jer 50—51; Ez 26—27), is meant to portray symbolically the inexorable demands of God's holiness and justice; cf Introduction. The section concludes with a joyous canticle on the future glory of heaven.

18, 2: Many Greek manuscripts and versions omit *a cage for every unclean . . . beast.*

18, 3-24: Rome is condemned for her immorality, symbol of idolatry (see the note on Rv 14, 4), and for persecuting the church; cf Rv 19, 2.

18, 4: *Depart from her:* not evacuation of the city but separation from sinners, as always in apocalyptic literature.

18, 11: Ironically, the merchants weep not so much for Babylon-Rome, but for their lost markets; cf Ez 27, 36.

18, 13: *Spice:* an unidentified spice plant called in Greek *amōmon.*

"Alas, alas, great city,
in which all who had ships at sea
grew rich from her wealth.
In one hour she has been ruined.
20 Rejoice over her, heaven,
you holy ones, apostles, and prophets.
For God has judged your case against her."[s]

21 A mighty angel picked up a stone like a
huge millstone and threw it into the sea
and said:

"With such force will Babylon the great city be thrown down,
and will never be found again.[t]
22 No melodies of harpists and musicians,
flutists and trumpeters,
will ever be heard in you again.
No craftsmen in any trade
will ever be found in you again.
No sound of the millstone
will ever be heard in you again.[u]
23 No light from a lamp
will ever be seen in you again.
No voices of bride and groom
will ever be heard in you again.
Because your merchants were the great ones of the world,
all nations were led astray by your magic potion.[v]
24 In her was found the blood of prophets and holy ones
and all who have been slain on the earth."[w]

CHAPTER 19

1 After this I heard what sounded like the
loud voice of a great multitude in heaven,
saying:

"Alleluia!*
Salvation, glory, and might belong to our God,
2 for true and just are his judgments.
He has condemned the great harlot
who corrupted the earth with her harlotry.
He has avenged on her the blood of his servants."[x]

3 They said a second time:

"Alleluia! Smoke will rise from her forever and ever."[y]

4 The twenty-four elders and the four living
creatures fell down and worshiped God
who sat on the throne, saying, "Amen. Alleluia."

The Victory Song.* 5 A voice coming from
the throne said:

"Praise our God, all you his servants,
[and] you who revere him, small and great."[z]

6 Then I heard something like the sound of
a great multitude or the sound of rushing
water or mighty peals of thunder, as they
said:

"Alleluia!
The Lord has established his reign,
[our] God, the almighty.
7 Let us rejoice and be glad
and give him glory.
For the wedding day of the Lamb* has come,
his bride has made herself ready.[a]
8 She was allowed to wear
a bright, clean linen garment."[b]

(The linen represents the righteous deeds
of the holy ones.)*

9 Then the angel said to me, "Write this:
Blessed* are those who have been called to
the wedding feast of the Lamb." And he
said to me, "These words are true; they
come from God."[c] 10 I fell at his feet to
worship him. But he said to me, "Don't! I
am a fellow servant of yours and of your
brothers who bear witness to Jesus. Worship God.[d] Witness to Jesus is the spirit of
prophecy."*

The King of Kings. 11 * Then I saw the
heavens opened, and there was a white
horse; its rider was [called] "Faithful and

s Rv 19, 1-2; Dt 32, 43.—t Jer 51, 63-64; Ez 26, 21.—u Is 24, 8; Ez 26, 13.—v Jer 7, 34; 16, 9; 25, 10.—w Rv 16, 6.—x Dn 3, 27 / Jer 51, 48-49.—y Rv 14, 11; Is 34, 10.—z Rv 11, 18; Ps 115, 13.—a Mt 22, 9; Eph 5, 27.—b Rv 15, 6; Is 61, 10; Mt 22, 11-12.—c Mt 8, 11; Lk 14, 15.—d Rv 22, 8-9.

19, 1.3.4.6: *Alleluia:* found only here in the New Testament, this frequent exclamation of praise in the Hebrew psalms was important in Jewish liturgy.

19, 5-10: A victory song follows, sung by the entire church, celebrating the marriage of the Lamb, the union of the Messiah with the community of the elect.

19, 7: *The wedding day of the Lamb:* symbol of God's reign about to begin (Rv 21, 1—22, 5); see the note on Rv 10, 7. *His bride:* the church; cf 2 Cor 11, 2; Eph 5, 22-27. Marriage is one of the biblical metaphors used to describe the covenant relationship between God and his people; cf Hos 2, 16-22; Is 54, 5-6; 62, 5; Ez 16, 6-14. Hence, idolatry and apostasy are viewed as adultery and harlotry (Hos 2, 4-15; Ez 16, 15-63); see the note on Rv 14, 4.

19, 8: See the note on Rv 14, 12.

19, 9: *Blessed:* see the note on Rv 1, 3.

19, 10: *The spirit of prophecy:* as the prophets were inspired to proclaim God's word, so the Christian is called to give witness to the Word of God (13) made flesh; cf Rv 1, 2; 6, 9; 12, 17.

19, 11-16: Symbolic description of the exalted Christ (cf Rv 1, 13-16) who together with the armies of heaven overcomes the beast and its followers; cf Rv 17, 14.

True." He judges and wages war in righteousness.[e] 12 His eyes were [like] a fiery
flame, and on his head were many
diadems. He had a name* inscribed that no
one knows except himself.[f] 13 He wore a
cloak that had been dipped in* blood, and
his name was called the Word of God.[g]
14 The armies of heaven followed him,
mounted on white horses and wearing
clean white linen.[h] 15 Out of his mouth
came a sharp sword to strike the nations.
He will rule them with an iron rod, and he
himself will tread out in the wine press*
the wine of the fury and wrath of God the
almighty.[i] 16 He has a name written on his
cloak and on his thigh, "King of kings and
Lord of lords."[j]

17 * Then I saw an angel standing on the
sun. He cried out [in] a loud voice to all the
birds flying high overhead, "Come here.
Gather for God's great feast, 18 to eat the
flesh of kings, the flesh of military officers,
and the flesh of warriors, the flesh of
horses and of their riders, and the flesh of
all, free and slave, small and great."[k]
19 Then I saw the beast and the kings of the
earth and their armies gathered to fight
against the one riding the horse and against
his army. 20 The beast was caught and with
it the false prophet* who had performed in
its sight the signs by which he led astray
those who had accepted the mark of the
beast and those who had worshiped its
image. The two were thrown alive into the
fiery pool burning with sulfur.[l] 21 The rest
were killed by the sword that came out of
the mouth of the one riding the horse, and
all the birds gorged themselves on their
flesh.

CHAPTER 20

The Thousand-year Reign. 1 * Then I saw
an angel come down from heaven, holding
in his hand the key to the abyss* and a
heavy chain.[m] 2 He seized the dragon, the
ancient serpent, which is the Devil or
Satan,* and tied it up for a thousand years[n]
3 and threw it into the abyss, which he
locked over it and sealed, so that it could
no longer lead the nations astray until the
thousand years are completed. After this,
it is to be released for a short time.

4 Then I saw thrones; those who sat on
them were entrusted with judgment. I also
saw the souls of those who had been
beheaded for their witness to Jesus and for
the word of God, and who had not worshiped the beast or its image nor had accepted its mark* on their foreheads or
hands. They came to life and they reigned
with Christ for a thousand years.[o] 5 The
rest of the dead did not come to life until
the thousand years were over. This is the
first resurrection. 6 Blessed* and holy is the
one who shares in the first resurrection.
The second death has no power over these;
they will be priests of God and of Christ,
and they will reign with him for [the]
thousand years.

7 * When the thousand years are completed, Satan will be released from his
prison. 8 He will go out to deceive the nations at the four corners of the earth, Gog
and Magog,* to gather them for battle;
their number is like the sand of the sea.[p]
9 They invaded the breadth of the earth*
and surrounded the camp of the holy ones

e Is 11, 4.—f Rv 1, 14-16; 2, 18 / Lk 10, 22.—g Is 63, 1 / Jn 1, 1.—h Rv 15, 6; 19, 8.—i Rv 14, 20; Is 63, 3.—j Rv 17, 14; 2 Mc 13, 4.—k Ez 39, 17-20.—l Rv 14, 10.—m Rv 9, 1.—n Gn 3, 1.—o Mt 19, 28.—p Ez 38, 2.9.16.

19, 12: *A name:* in Semitic thought, the name conveyed the reality of the person; cf Mt 11, 27; Lk 10, 22.

19, 13: *Had been dipped in:* other Greek manuscripts and versions read "had been sprinkled with"; cf Rv 19, 15. *The Word of God:* Christ is the revelation of the Father; cf Jn 1, 1.14; 1 Jn 2, 14.

19, 15: The treading of the wine press is a prophetic symbol used to describe the destruction of God's enemies; cf Is 63, 1-6; Jl 4, 13.

19, 17-21: The certainty of Christ's victory is proclaimed by an angel, followed by a reference to the mustering of enemy forces and a fearsome description of their annihilation. The gruesome imagery is borrowed from Ez 39, 4.17-20.

19, 20: *Beast . . . false prophet:* see the notes on ch 13. *The fiery pool . . . sulfur:* symbol of God's punishment (Rv 14, 10; 20, 10.14-15), different from the abyss; see the note on Rv 9, 1.

20, 1-6: Like the other numerical values in this book, the thousand years are not to be taken literally; they symbolize the long period of time between the chaining up of Satan (a symbol for Christ's resurrection-victory over death and the forces of evil) and the end of the world. During this time God's people share in the glorious reign of God that is present to them by virtue of their baptismal victory over death and sin; cf Rom 6, 1-8; Jn 5, 24-25; 16, 33; 1 Jn 3, 14; Eph 2, 1.

20, 1: *Abyss:* see the note on Rv 9, 1.

20, 2: *Dragon . . . serpent . . . Satan:* see the notes on Rv 12, 3.9.10.15.

20, 4: *Beast . . . mark:* see ch 13 and its notes.

20, 6: *Blessed:* see the note on Rv 1, 3. *Second death:* see the note on Rv 2, 11. *Priests:* as in Rv 1, 6; 5, 10; cf 1 Pt 2, 9.

20, 7-10: A description of the symbolic battle to take place when Satan is released at the end of time, when the thousand years are over; see the note on Rv 20, 1-6.

20, 8: *Gog and Magog:* symbols of all pagan nations; the names are taken from Ez 38, 1—39, 20.

20, 9: *The breadth of the earth:* Palestine. *The beloved city:* Jerusalem; see the note on Rv 14, 1.

and the beloved city. But fire came down from heaven and consumed them.[q] 10 The Devil who had led them astray was thrown into the pool of fire and sulfur, where the beast and the false prophet were. There they will be tormented day and night forever and ever.

The Large White Throne.* 11 Next I saw a large white throne and the one who was sitting on it. The earth and the sky fled from his presence and there was no place for them.[r] 12 I saw the dead, the great and the lowly, standing before the throne, and scrolls were opened. Then another scroll was opened, the book of life.* The dead were judged according to their deeds, by what was written in the scrolls.[s] 13 The sea gave up its dead; then Death and Hades* gave up their dead. All the dead were judged according to their deeds. 14 [t] Then Death and Hades were thrown into the pool of fire. (This pool of fire is the second death.*) 15 Anyone whose name was not found written in the book of life was thrown into the pool of fire.

VI. THE NEW CREATION*

CHAPTER 21

The New Heaven and the New Earth. 1 [u] Then I saw a new heaven and a new earth. The former heaven and the former earth had passed away, and the sea was no more.* 2 I also saw the holy city, a new Jerusalem,* coming down out of heaven from God, prepared as a bride adorned for her husband.[v] 3 I heard a loud voice from the throne saying, "Behold, God's dwelling is with the human race.[w] He will dwell with them and they will be his people* and God himself will always be with them [as their God].* 4 He will wipe every tear from their eyes, and there shall be no more death or mourning, wailing or pain, [for] the old order has passed away."[x]

5 The one who sat on the throne* said, "Behold, I make all things new." Then he said, "Write these words down, for they are trustworthy and true."[y] 6 He said to me, "They are accomplished.* I [am] the Alpha and the Omega, the beginning and the end. To the thirsty I will give a gift from the spring of life-giving water.[z] 7 The victor* will inherit these gifts, and I shall be his God, and he will be my son.[a] 8 But as for cowards,* the unfaithful, the depraved, murderers, the unchaste, sorcerers, idol-worshipers, and deceivers of every sort, their lot is in the burning pool of fire and sulfur, which is the second death."[b]

The New Jerusalem.* 9 One of the seven angels who held the seven bowls filled with the seven last plagues came and said to me, "Come here. I will show you the bride, the wife of the Lamb."* 10 He took me in spirit to a great, high mountain and showed me the holy city Jerusalem coming down out of heaven from God.[c] 11 It gleamed with the splendor of God. Its radiance was like that of a precious stone, like jasper, clear as crystal.[d] 12 It had a massive, high wall, with twelve gates where twelve angels were stationed and on which names were inscribed, [the names] of the twelve tribes of the Israelites. 13 There were three gates facing east, three north, three south, and three west.[e] 14 The wall of the city had

q Ez 38, 22.—r 2 Pt 3, 7.10.12.—s Rom 2, 6.—t 1 Cor 15, 26.54-55.—u Is 65, 17; 66, 22; Rom 8, 19-23; 2 Pt 3, 13.—v Rv 19, 7-9.—w Ez 37, 27.—x Rv 7, 17; Is 25, 8; 35, 10.—y Is 43, 19; 2 Cor 5, 17.—z Rv 22, 17; Ps 36, 8-9; Is 55, 1.—a 2 Sm 7, 14.—b Rv 22, 15; Rom 1, 29-32.—c Ez 40, 2.—d Heb 11, 10.—e Ez 48, 31-35.

20, 11-15: A description of the final judgment. After the intermediate reign of Christ, all the dead are raised and judged, thus inaugurating the new age.

20, 12: *The book of life:* see the note on Rv 3, 5. *Judged . . . scrolls:* see the note on Rv 14, 12.

20, 13: *Hades:* the netherworld; see the note on Rv 1, 18.

20, 14: *Second death:* see the note on Rv 2, 11.

21, 1—22, 5: A description of God's eternal kingdom in heaven under the symbols of a new heaven and a new earth; cf Is 65, 17-25; 66, 22; Mt 19, 28.

21, 1: *Sea . . . no more:* because as home of the dragon it was doomed to disappear; cf Jb 7, 12.

21, 2: *New Jerusalem . . . bride:* symbol of the church (Gal 4, 26); see the note on Rv 19, 7.

21, 3: *People:* other ancient manuscripts read a plural, "peoples."

21, 3-4: Language taken from Ez 37, 27; Is 25, 8; 35, 10; cf Rv 7, 17.

21, 5: *The one . . . on the throne:* God himself; cf Rv 4, 1-11.

21, 6: *They are accomplished:* God's reign has already begun; see the note on Rv 20, 1-6. *Alpha . . . Omega:* see the note on Rv 1, 8. *Life-giving water:* see the note on Rv 7, 17.

21, 7: *The victor:* over the forces of evil; see the conclusions of the seven letters (Rv 2, 7.11.17.26; 3, 5.12.21). *He will be my son:* the victorious Christian enjoys divine affiliation by adoption (Gal 4, 4-7; Rom 8, 14-17); see the note on Rv 2, 26-28.

21, 8: *Cowards:* their conviction is so weak that they deny Christ in time of trial and become traitors. *Second death:* see the note on Rv 2, 11.

21, 9—22, 5: Symbolic descriptions of the new Jerusalem, the church. Most of the images are borrowed from Ez 40—48.

21, 9: *The bride, the wife of the Lamb:* the church (2), the new Jerusalem (10); cf 2 Cor 11, 2.

twelve courses of stones as its foundation,
on which were inscribed the twelve names
of the twelve apostles* of the Lamb.[f]

15 * The one who spoke to me held a
gold measuring rod to measure the city, its
gates, and its wall. 16 The city was square,
its length the same as [also] its width. He
measured the city with the rod and found it
fifteen hundred miles* in length and width
and height. 17 He also measured its wall:
one hundred and forty-four cubits* according to the standard unit of measurement the angel used. 18 * The wall was
constructed of jasper, while the city was
pure gold, clear as glass. 19 The foundations of the city wall were decorated with
every precious stone; the first course of
stones was jasper, the second sapphire, the
third chalcedony, the fourth emerald,[g]
20 the fifth sardonyx, the sixth carnelian,
the seventh chrysolite, the eighth beryl,
the ninth topaz, the tenth chrysoprase, the
eleventh hyacinth, and the twelfth ame-
thyst. 21 The twelve gates were twelve
pearls, each of the gates made from a single
pearl; and the street of the city was of pure
gold, transparent as glass.

22 [h] I saw no temple in the city, for its
temple is the Lord God almighty and the
Lamb.* 23 The city had no need of sun or
moon to shine on it,[i] for the glory of God
gave it light, and its lamp was the Lamb.*
24 The nations will walk by its light,* and
to it the kings of the earth will bring their
treasure.[j] 25 During the day its gates will
never be shut, and there will be no night
there. 26 The treasure and wealth of the nations will be brought there, 27 but nothing
unclean will enter it, nor any[one] who
does abominable things or tells lies. Only
those will enter whose names are written in
the Lamb's book of life.[k]

CHAPTER 22

1 Then the angel showed me the river of
life-giving water,* sparkling like crystal,
flowing from the throne of God and of the
Lamb[l] 2 down the middle of its street. On
either side of the river grew the tree of life*
that produces fruit twelve times a year,
once each month; the leaves of the trees
serve as medicine for the nations. 3 Nothing accursed will be found there anymore.
The throne of God and of the Lamb will be
in it, and his servants will worship him.
4 They will look upon his face,* and his
name will be on their foreheads. 5 Night
will be no more, nor will they need light
from lamp or sun, for the Lord God shall
give them light, and they shall reign
forever and ever.[m]

VII. EPILOGUE*

6 And he said to me, "These words are
trustworthy and true, and the Lord, the
God of prophetic spirits, sent his angel to
show his servants what must happen
soon."[n] 7 "Behold, I am coming soon."*
Blessed* is the one who keeps the prophetic message of this book.[o]

8 It is I, John, who heard and saw these
things, and when I heard and saw them I
fell down to worship at the feet of the angel
who showed them to me. 9 But he said to
me, "Don't! I am a fellow servant of yours
and of your brothers the prophets and of

f Eph 2, 20.—g Is 54, 11-12.—h Jn 2, 19-20.—i Is 60, 1-2.19-20.—j Is 60, 11.—k Is 35, 8; 52, 1; Zec 13, 2 / Rv 3, 5; 20, 12.—l Ez 47, 1-12.—m Is 60, 20.—n Rv 1, 1.—o Rv 22, 12.20 / Rv 1, 3.

21, 14: *Courses of stones . . . apostles:* literally, "twelve foundations"; cf Eph 2, 19-20.

21, 15-17: The city is shaped like a gigantic cube, a symbol of perfection (cf 1 Kgs 6, 19-20). The measurements of the city and its wall are multiples of the symbolic number twelve; see the note on Rv 7, 4-9.

21, 16: *Fifteen hundred miles:* literally, twelve thousand stades, about 12,000 furlongs (see the note on Rv 14, 20); the number is symbolic: twelve (the apostles as leaders of the new Israel) multiplied by 1,000 (the immensity of Christians); cf Introduction. *In length and width and height:* literally, "its length and width and height are the same."

21, 17: *One hundred and forty-four cubits:* the cubit was about eighteen inches in length. *Standard unit of measurement the angel used:* literally, "by a human measure, i.e., an angel's."

21, 18-21: The gold and precious gems symbolize the beauty and excellence of the church; cf Ex 28, 15-21; Tb 13, 16-17; Is 54, 11-12.

21, 22: Christ is present throughout the church; hence, no temple is needed as an earthly dwelling for God; cf Mt 18, 20; 28, 20; Jn 4, 21.

21, 23: *Lamp . . . Lamb:* cf Jn 8, 12.

21, 24-27: All men and women of good will are welcome in the church; cf Is 60, 1.3.5.11. *The . . . book of life:* see the note on Rv 3, 5.

22, 1.17: *Life-giving water:* see the note on Rv 7, 17.

22, 2: *The tree of life:* cf Rv 22, 14; see the note on Rv 2, 7. *Fruit . . . medicine:* cf Ez 47, 12.

22, 4: *Look upon his face:* cf Mt 5, 8; 1 Cor 13, 12; 1 Jn 3, 2.

22, 6-21: The book ends with an epilogue consisting of a series of warnings and exhortations and forming an inclusion with the prologue by resuming its themes and expressions; see the note on Rv 1, 1-3.

22, 7.12.20: *I am coming soon:* Christ is the speaker; see the note on Rv 1, 3.

22, 7.14: *Blessed:* see the note on Rv 1, 3.

those who keep the message of this book. Worship God."[p]

10 Then he said to me, "Do not seal up the prophetic words of this book, for the appointed time* is near.
11 Let the wicked still act wickedly, and the filthy still be filthy. The righteous must still do right, and the holy still be holy."

12 "Behold, I am coming soon. I bring with me the recompense I will give to each according to his deeds.[q]
13 I am the Alpha and the Omega,[r] the first and the last, the beginning and the end."*

14 Blessed are they who wash their robes so as to have the right to the tree of life and enter the city* through its gates.[s]
15 Outside are the dogs, the sorcerers, the unchaste, the murderers, the idol-worshipers, and all who love and practice deceit.[t]

16 "I, Jesus, sent my angel to give you this testimony for the churches. I am the root and offspring of David,* the bright morning star."[u]

17 The Spirit and the bride* say, "Come." Let the hearer say, "Come." Let the one who thirsts come forward, and the one who wants it receive the gift of life-giving water.[v]

18 I warn everyone who hears the prophetic words in this book: if anyone adds to them, God will add to him the plagues described in this book,
19 and if anyone takes away from the words in this prophetic book, God will take away his share in the tree of life and in the holy city described in this book.[w]

20 [x] The one who gives this testimony says, "Yes, I am coming soon." Amen! Come, Lord Jesus!*

21 The grace of the Lord Jesus be with all.

p Rv 19, 10.—q Rv 22, 7.20 / Ps 62, 12; 2 Tm 4, 14.—r Rv 1, 8; 21, 6; Is 41, 4; 44, 6.—s Rv 7, 14-15; 22, 2.—t Rv 21, 8; Rom 1, 29-32.—u Rv 1, 1.11-12; 22, 6 / Rv 2, 28.—v Rv 21, 6; Is 55, 1.—w Dt 4, 2.—x Rv 22, 7.12 / Acts 3, 20-21; 1 Cor 15, 23; 16, 22.

22, 10: *The appointed time:* see the note on Rv 1, 3.

22, 13: Christ applies to himself words used by God in Rv 1, 8.

22, 14: *The city:* heavenly Jerusalem; see the note on Rv 21, 2.

22, 16: *The root . . . of David:* see the note on Rv 5, 5. *Morning star:* see the note on Rv 2, 26-28.

22, 17: *Bride:* the church; see the note on Rv 21, 2.

22, 20: *Come, Lord Jesus:* a liturgical refrain, similar to the Aramaic expression *Marana tha*—"Our Lord, come!"—in 1 Cor 16, 22; cf the note there. It was a prayer for the coming of Christ in glory at the parousia; see the note on Rv 1, 3.

COLLABORATORS ON THE OLD TESTAMENT OF THE NEW AMERICAN BIBLE

BISHOPS' COMMITTEE OF THE CONFRATERNITY OF CHRISTIAN DOCTRINE

Most Rev. Charles P. Greco, D.D., *Chairman*
Most Rev. Joseph T. McGucken, S.T.D.
Most Rev. Vincent S. Waters, D.D.
Most Rev. Romeo Blanchette, D.D.
Most Rev. Christopher J. Weldon, D.D.

EDITORS IN CHIEF

Rev. Louis F. Hartman, C.SS.R., S.S.L., Ling. Or. L., *Chairman*
Rev. Msgr. Patrick W. Skehan, S.T.D., LL.D., *Vice-Chairman*
Rev. Stephen J. Hartdegen, O.F.M., S.S.L., *Secretary*

ASSOCIATE EDITORS AND TRANSLATORS

Rev. Edward P. Arbez, S.S., S.T.D.
Rev. Msgr. Edward J. Byrne, Ph.D., S.T.D.
Rev. Edward A. Cerny, S.S., S.T.D.
Rev. James E. Coleran, S.J., S.T.L., S.S.L.
Rev. John J. Collins, S.J., M.A., S.S.L.
Sr. M. Emmanuel Collins, O.S.F., Ph.D.
Prof. Frank M. Cross, Jr., Ph.D.
Rev. Patrick Cummins, O.S.B., S.T.D.
Rev. Antonine A. De Guglielmo, O.F.M., S.T.D., S.S.L., S.S. Lect. Gen.
Rev. Alexander A. DiLella, O.F.M., S.T.L., S.S.L., Ph.D.
Most Rev. John J. Dougherty, S.T.L., S.S.D.
William A. Dowd, S.J., S.T.D., S.S.L.
Prof. David Noel Freedman, Ph.D.
Rev. Michael J. Gruenthaner, S.J., S.T.D., S.S.D.
Rev. Msgr. Maurice A. Hofer, S.S.L.
Rev. Justin Krellner, O.S.B., S.T.D.
Rev. Joseph L. Lilly, C.M., S.T.D., S.S.L.
Rev. Roderick F. MacKenzie, S.J., M.A., S.S.D.
Rev. Edward A. Mangan, C.SS.R., S.S.L.
Rev. Daniel W. Martin, C.M., S.T.L., S.S.L.
Rev. William H. McClellan, S.J.
Rev. James McGlinchey, C.M., S.T.D.
Rev. Frederick Moriarty, S.J., S.S.L., S.T.D.
Rev. Richard T. Murphy, O.P., S.T.D., S.S.D.
Rev. Roland E. Murphy, O. Carm., M.A., S.T.D., S.S.L.
Rev. Msgr. William R. Newton, M.S., S.S.D.
Rev. Eberhard Olinger, O.S.B.
Rev. Charles H. Pickar, O.S.A., S.T.L., S.S.L.
Rev. Christopher Rehwinkel, O.F.M., S.T.D., S.S. Lect. Gen.
Rev. Msgr. John R. Rowan, S.T.D., S.S.L.
Prof. J. A. Sanders, Ph.D.
Rev. Edward F. Siegman, C.PP.S., S.T.D., S.S.L.
Rev. Msgr. Matthew P. Stapleton, S.T.D., S.S.L.
Rev. Msgr. John E. Steinmueller, S.T.D., S.S.L.
Rev. John Ujlaki, O.S.B., Litt.D.
Rev. Bruce Vawter, C.M., S.T.L., S.S.D.
Rev. John B. Weisengoff, S.T.D., S.S.L.

COLLABORATORS ON THE REVISED PSALMS OF THE NEW AMERICAN BIBLE

BISHOPS' AD HOC COMMITTEE
Most Rev. Enrique San Pedro, S.J.
Most Rev. Richard Sklba, D.D.
Most Rev. Donald W. Troutman, S.T.D., S.S.L.
Most Rev. Emil A. Wcela
Most Rev. John F. Whealon, S.S.L., *Chairman*

BOARD OF EDITORS
Rev. Richard Clifford, S.J.
Brother Aloysius Fitzgerald, F.S.C.
Rev. Joseph Jensen, O.S.B. *(Chair)*
Rev. Roland Murphy, O. CARM.
Sr. Irene Nowell, O.S.B.
Dr. Judith Sanderson

REVISERS
Prof. Gary Anderson
Rev. Michael L. Barré
Rev. Christopher T. Begg
Dr. Joseph Blenkinsopp
Rev. Anthony R. Ceresko, O.S.F.S.
Rev. Richard J. Clifford, S.J.
Rev. Aelred Cody, O.S.B.
Prof. Michael D. Coogan
Rev. Alexander A. Di Lella, O.F.M.
Dr. Robert A. Di Vito
Br. Aloysius Fitzgerald, F.S.C.
Rev. Michael D. Guinan, O.F.M.
Rev. William L. Holladay
Rev. William Irwin, C.S.B.
Rev. Joseph Jensen, O.S.B.
Rev. John S. Kselman
Dr. Conrad E. L'Heureux
Rev. Leo Laberge, O.M.I.
Dr. Paul G. Mosca
Rev. Dr. Roland E. Murphy, O. CARM.
Dr. Michael Patrick O'Connor
Rev. Brian J. Peckham, S.J.
Prof. Jimmy J. Roberts
Sr. Eileen M. Schuller, O.S.U.
Dr. Byron E. Shafer
Prof. Mark S. Smith
Prof. Matitiahu Tsevat
Dr. Eugene C. Ulrich
Prof. James C. VanderKam
Rev. Jerome T. Walsh

ENGLISH CONSULTANTS
Dr. Catherine Dunn
Brother Daniel Burke, F.S.C.

BUSINESS MANAGER
Charles A. Buggé

COLLABORATORS ON THE REVISED NEW TESTAMENT OF THE NEW AMERICAN BIBLE

BISHOPS' AD HOC COMMITTEE
Most Rev. Theodore E. McCarrick, D.D.
Most Rev. Richard J. Sklba, D.D.
Most Rev. J. Francis Stafford, D.D.
Most Rev. John F. Whealon, D.D., *Chairman*

BOARD OF EDITORS
Rev. Msgr. Myles M. Bourke
Rev. Francis T. Gignac, S.J., *Chairman*
Rev. Stephen J. Hartdegen, O.F.M., *Secretary*
Rev. Claude J. Peifer, O.S.B.
Rev. John H. Reumann

REVISERS
Rev. Msgr. Myles M. Bourke
Rev. Frederick W. Danker
Rev. Alexander A. Di Lella, O.F.M.
Rev. Charles H. Giblin, S.J.
Rev. Francis T. Gignac, S.J.
Rev. Stephen J. Hartdegen, O.F.M.
Dr. Maurya P. Horgan
Rev. John R. Keating, S.J.
Rev. John Knox
Dr. Paul J. Kobelski
Dr. J. Rebecca Lyman
Bro. Elliott C. Maloney, O.S.B.
Dr. Janet A. Timbie

CONSULTANTS
Rev. Joseph Jensen, O.S.B.
Rev. Aidan Kavanagh, O.S.B.
Dr. Marianne Sawicki

BUSINESS MANAGER
Charles A. Buggé

WORD PROCESSOR
Suzanna Jordan

BIBLE DICTIONARY

ABEL. The religious and just son of Adam and Eve whose sacrifice pleased God, yet aroused the murderous envy of his brother Cain. He was a shepherd and offered the firstlings of his flock to the Lord (Gn 4, 2-8).

ABRAHAM. "Father of believers." At God's command he left his home in Ur of the Chaldees about 2000 B.C. and settled in Palestine. God made a covenant with him and promised him a great posterity. In his old age his wife Sarah bore him a son (Isaac) in fulfillment of God's promise (Gn 11—25).

ABYSS. In the Old Testament this word refers to the primordial ocean of the ancient Semitic cosmogony. After God's creative activity this vast body forms the salt-water seas (Gn 1, 9f); part of it is the fresh water under the earth (Ps 33, 7), which wells forth on the earth as springs and fountains (Gn 7, 11). Part of it, "the upper water" (Ps 148, 4), is held up by the dome of the sky (Gn 1, 6f), from which rain descends on the earth (Gn 7, 11). In the New Testament this word is used to describe the depths of the earth, variously considered the abode of the dead (Rom 10, 7) or of the demons (Lk 8, 3; Rv 9, 1ff; 11, 7; 17, 8; 20, 1.3). Sheol, Pool of Fire, Gehenna and the nether world are similar conceptions.

ADONAI. One of the names of God. It is a plural of majesty and signifies "my lord." In Jewish tradition, it is the word which designates God and replaces the "ineffable Name" (YHWH), which no one was permitted to pronounce. *See* **LORD. NAME. YAHWEH.**

ALLELUIA. Triumphal acclamation signifying: "Praise God," which is often found at the beginning or the end of certain psalms (105-107; 135; Rv 19, 1). It has passed over, untranslated, into the Catholic liturgy.

ALPHA AND OMEGA. The first and last letters of the Greek alphabet. The Hebrews used these two letters to symbolize the fulness, the eternity of God. The Christians inherited this tradition and used alpha and omega to express their belief that in Jesus, the Son of God, is to be found all grace and truth (Rv 1, 8; 21, 6; 22, 13).

ALTAR. A stone or pile of stones, or any structure or place on which sacrifices were burned or incense was offered to God. In the temple at Jerusalem there was an altar of bronze. Solomon had a special altar constructed for burning incense (2 Chr 4, 1).

AMEN. A Hebrew word meaning, "certainly, truly," used to give assent to a statement, a curse, a blessing, a prayer, or the like; in this sense of "so be it," the term came to be employed in Jewish worship and as such the Christian liturgy also uses it after prayers and blessings. In the Gospels, Jesus uses it to give force to his statements (Mt 5, 18. 26). However, the present translation does not reproduce "Amen" but translates it according to the sense of the context.

ANANIAS. Three persons bear this name in the New Testament: (1) the husband of Sapphira (Acts 5); (2) a Christian who received Paul after his conversion (Acts 9 and 22); (3) a high priest who ordered St. Paul to be slapped (Acts 23) and was later assassinated (66 A.D.).

ANATHEMA (DOOMED). In Hebrew: *herem*, which originally signified some thing (or person) set aside from profane use and made sacred to the Lord (Dt 12, 12ff; Jos 11, 11. 14). Hence, it could not be appropriated by anyone; in a good number of cases, the obligation existed to destroy it. This often barbaric custom expressed God's absolute rights over every creature. In the course of time, the term was softened and came to refer to nothing more than objects offered to God (Lv 27, 28; Ez 44, 27; Mk 7, 11). The Greek term *anathema* in the New Testament is used in the sense of "cursed," "separated from God." Later Christianity used this word in the sense of "excommunication" (1 Cor 12, 3: "let a curse be upon him").

ANCIENTS. The forebears of Israel, whose traditions were supposed to be the authority for the unwritten law (Mt 5, 27-33; 15, 2). *See* **ELDERS.**

ANGEL OF THE LORD. Someone who has received a divine delegation, through whom God reveals himself, says, or does something (Jgs 6, 11ff). In numerous biblical texts, the word designates the visible manifestation of God (Gn 16, 7-13; Zec 3, 1ff). In the New Testament, *angels* are heavenly spirits (Heb 1, 7).

ANGER (WRATH) OF GOD. This expression is to be compared with other similar expressions: repentance, jealousy, hand and arm of God. It is an "anthropomorphism," a figure of speech, an image. Seeking to explain the external phenomena supposedly produced by God (storms, floods, earthquakes, catastrophes), we attribute to him sentiments or attitudes which would be found in similar circumstances among men (Ps 78; Dt 32, 15ff; Is 1, 18-20; Lk 13, 3-5).

ANTICHRIST. This word, which is found only in the Epistles of St. John (1 Jn 2, 18-22; 4, 3; 2 Jn 7), designates a personage who is at once both an enemy of Christ and his evildoing imitator. The idea stems from the Jewish writers of the age preceding Christianity. These described the Messiah as having to appear at the end of times to renew all things, but as having to take part in a very violent struggle against a mysterious Adversary. This idea is found throughout the New Testament. Paul calls him "the man of lawlessness," "the son of perdition and adversity" (2 Thes 2, 3. 8; 2 Cor 6, 15). Matthew, Mark and Revelation seem to refer to a collectivity of persons (Mt 24, 23f; Mk 13, 14-20; Rv 13, 17; 17, 7-14).

ANTIOCH. Capital of the Roman province of Syria, it was the most active center of early Christianity (Acts 11, 26).

APOCRYPHA. Religious books used by both Jews and Christians which were not included in the collection of inspired writings. In the Protestant Church, this term designates the books of Tobit, Judith, Maccabees, Wisdom, Baruch, and Ecclesiasticus, which were introduced rather late into the collection of the Bible. Catholics call them "deuterocanonical" books.

APOSTLES. Twelve men chosen by Christ to enjoy special jurisdiction and to teach. They are: Peter, Andrew, James, John, Philip, Bartholomew, Thomas, Matthew, James the Less, Jude, Simon the Zealot and Judas, who was replaced by Matthias. Within the circle of Jesus' disciples, the Twelve were given a privileged position. They alone were present with him at the Last Supper (Mk 14, 17). Later they exercised leadership over the primitive community in Jerusalem (Acts 1, 26; 2, 14; 5, 20f), and were responsible for the information about Jesus that developed into the gospel tradition (Acts 6, 2. 4). Paul and Barnabas are also called Apostles (Gal 2, 7ff), which means literally "one who is sent" (Lk 24, 35. 48; Mt 28, 19-20).

ARK OF THE COVENANT. Wooden chest, overlaid with gold, fashioned by Moses, which contained the two tablets of the law (Ex 25, 10-16; 37, 1-5). It was the symbol of the covenant and God's presence among his people. God was pictured as resting his feet on its golden lid (called "propitiatory"). The ark was placed in the sanctuary of the temple (1 Kgs 8, 1-9) in Jerusalem and disappeared in its ruin at the destruction of the city by the Chaldeans in 586 B.C. (2 Kgs 25, 1-21).

ARMOR. Leather or metal covering which was worn by warriors. It included a helmet, breastplate and shield (Eph 6, 13-17).

ASIA. In the New Testament, used of the Roman Province of Asia, which included only the western third of what is now Asia Minor. Ephesus was its capital, and of its other important cities and districts many are mentioned in the New Testament. The evangelization of the province was accomplished by St. Paul on his third missionary journey (Acts 18—21), St. Peter addressed the churches of Asia (1 Pt 1, 7), and the Book of Revelation conveys messages to each of its most important cities, the "seven churches" (Rv 1, 4ff).

ASSYRIA. A country occupying the northern and middle part of Mesopotamia, including Babylonia and Chaldea. The Assyrians were probably of Semitic origin, descendants of Asshur, one of the sons of Shem (Gn 10, 22). An independent kingdom began about the seventeenth century B.C. In 605 B.C. Nineveh was destroyed by the Medes and Babylonians, and Assyria became a province of these countries.

ASTARTE. Phoenician goddess of fertility, often associated with Baal. Her cult experienced great success in Palestine and her attraction frequently led the Hebrews into idolatry (Jgs 2, 13; 10, 6; 2 Kgs 17, 16).

AZYMES. Unleavened bread which was the only kind permitted during the week of the Jewish Passover. They recalled at the same time the agricultural feast of the barley harvest and the exodus from Egypt, when the Hebrews in their haste were unable to have their dough leavened (Ex 34, 25; 23, 18).

BAAL. This Hebrew word is translated as master, lord. It designates the chief god of the Canaanites and the Phoenicians. His cult was preserved by the Hebrews in Palestine, in spite of the efforts of the prophets (1 Kgs 16, 31-33). The word Baal also designates small local gods (Jgs 2, 11).

BABYLON. Capital of Babylonia, to which many Jewish captives were deported after the fall of Jerusalem in 586 B.C.; this is known as the Babylonian Captivity (2 Kgs 25, 7ff). The name was then applied to any nation hostile to God (Rv 14; 17; etc.).

BALANCES. Scales for weighing money and other items. The moral necessity of a just balance and true weights and the iniquity of false ones are frequently emphasized by the prophets (Am 8, 5; Mi 6, 11).

BAPTISM. The baptism of John the Baptist (Mt 3, 1) is thought to stem from the rabbinical custom of baptizing proselytes who had converted to the faith of Israel (Mt 21, 25). This seems to be a remembrance of the baptism the Jewish people received in crossing the sea (1 Cor 10, 1-2) to acquire the law at Sinai and to attain the promised land. The events of the Exodus foreshadowed the imminent coming of the Lord. Jesus himself underwent baptism to inaugurate his mission (Mt 3, 13ff; Jn 1, 32). He thus became one with the Jewish people and took personal charge of them (Is 53). In this sense, baptism was a preparation for the cross (Mk 10, 38; Lk 12, 50). After the Redemption, baptism became a sacrament for entering a new state of grace (Mt 28, 19; Acts 2, 38-41), the way of regeneration to the divine life.

BEELZEBUL (BAALZEBUB). Name of the god of the nation of Canaan. In the Old Testament it appears under the form *Baalzebub*, "Baal (Lord) of Flies." Later association with the Aramaic *beeldebaba*, "enemy," gave the ancient name its connotation of "devil," and the New Testament uses Beelzebul to refer to the prince of demons (Mt 10, 25; 12, 24; Lk 11, 15).

BETHEL. In Hebrew: house of God. This town was originally called Luz. It is there that Abraham established one of the first sanctuaries and that Jacob had the famous vision of the ladder (Gn 12, 8; 13, 3 and 28, 10). King Jeroboam established the idol of the golden calf here after the schism of the northern tribes (1 Kgs 12, 26-30). The prophets saw therein the symbol of idolatry and gave it the surname of *Bethaven*, house of iniquity (Hos 4, 15).

BISHOP. Greek word signifying "overseer." From the beginning, it has designated the heads of the Christian communities, also called "presbyters" or "elders" (1 Tm 3, 1-7).

BLESSING. The word *bless* changes its meaning according to whether its subject is God or man. Man blesses God by his acts of adoration and thanksgiving (Ps 103, 1. 2); men bless other men by wishing them well or happiness (Mt 5, 44). The ancient Hebrews believed that such wishes were always efficacious (belief in magic) just as they did in the case of maledictions which are the opposite of blessings.

God blesses men by giving them material or spiritual benefits (Gn 24, 1).

Finally, man pronounces blessings on objects, on nourishment, to consecrate them to God (1 Cor 10, 16) or on persons, to sanctify them (Gn 49).

BLOOD. According to the ancients, blood is the seat and sign of life over which only God has power and so must be respected (Gn 9, 4). It is forbidden to consume it in the various offerings (Lv 1-7). This abstention was extended to the consummation of all fleshly nourishment. In the solemn sacrifice of the Day of Atonement, the blood of the victim was spilled over the ark of the convenant. Hence, the blood of Christ, who died for men, has in the eyes of Christians taken on an expiatory value (Heb 9, 28).

BREAD. In an extended sense, this often designates all that is necessary for subsistence. In the Gospels, we find the expression "bread of life," and "living bread" (Jn 6, 31-35), an image by which Jesus affirms that he is the principle of eternal life; at the same time it suggests the use of the Eucharist. Bread of heaven refers first of all to manna and secondly to the sacrament of the Eucharist.

In the Acts of the Apostles, the rite of breaking bread designates the Eucharist (Acts 2, 42).

BREAK BREAD. Among the Jews, the person who presided at the repast would break bread and distribute it to those at table. This is what Jesus did at the multiplication of the loaves (Mt 14, 19) and the Last Supper (Mt 26, 26).

BROTHERS OF THE LORD. Persons who formed part of Jesus' entourage. Among them are James, Joseph, Jude, and Simon. They are "relatives" of Jesus. For Greek-speaking Semites used the terms *adelphos* and *adelphe* not only in the ordinary sense of blood brother and sister but also for nephew, niece, half-brother, half-sister and cousin. Since, according to tradition, Jesus was Mary's only child, this expression is understood in the sense of "cousin," as belonging to the same blood (Mk 6, 1-6).

CAIAPHAS. High priest functioning at Jerusalem from the year 18 to 36 A.D. He was the son-in-law of the former high priest Annas and involved in the conspiracy to destroy Jesus (Jn 11, 49; Mt 26, 57). He was deposed by the legate of Syria, Vitellius, after the recall of Pontius Pilate in 36 A.D.

CALENDAR. (1) The civil *day* was reckoned from sunset to sunset, and hence Jewish Sabbaths and feasts began with the setting of the sun. (2) The *hours* of the day were twelve, beginning at about our 6:00 A.M. and ending at 6:00 P.M. The third, sixth, ninth and twelfth hours were specially sacred to prayer. The night was divided into four watches, the evening watch beginning at 6:00 P.M., the midnight watch at 9:00, "cockcrow" at 12:00, the morning watch at 3:00 A.M. (3) The *week* contained seven days ending in the sabbath, or "Rest." The "first day of the week" became sacred for Christians because of Christ's Resurrection (Jn 20, 19; Acts 20, 7). (4) The *year* consisted of twelve lunar months of twenty-nine or thirty days — i.e., 354 days. The month began with the new moon, and this first day was observed as a holy day. To preserve the proper relation between the lunar and solar calendars, an extra lunar month was intercalated every two or three years. The first month, Nisan, always began on the new moon nearest to and preceding the vernal equinox, March 21.

CANAANITE. Inhabitant of the country of Canaan situated east of the Jordan River (Mt 15, 22). At the time of Jesus, a variant of this word ("Canaanean," translated from the Greek as "Zealot") signified a political party which laid claim to national independence. The apostle Simon was a member of this movement (Mt 10, 4).

CAPTIVITY. This word denotes the exile and deportation of the northern kingdom into Babylonia in 721 (2 Kgs 17—18) and more especially of the southern kingdom in 586 (2 Kgs 25). After the latter date, Israel continually asks God for deliverance from her slavery, the return of the exiles, and the restoration of the chosen people. In 539 Cyrus the Great conquered Babylonia and allowed the Israelites to return home (Ezr 1, 1-4). From then on the Babylonian captivity became a symbol of man's state after Adam's sin from which Jesus has delivered him (Heb 2, 14-15).

CENTURION. Officer in charge of a century (originally 100 men), sixtieth part of the Roman legion. Legionnaires in Palestine were recruited locally, but officers were Roman (Mt 8, 5-13).

CHALICE-CUP. These words are often taken in a figurative sense. For a cup contains either a bitter beverage, symbol of trial (the cup of the divine wrath, for example) (Rv 15, 7) or a sweet beverage, symbol of divine blessing (Rv 5, 8). Since the Last Supper, in which it contained Christ's blood, it has become the expression for the eucharistic mystery (1 Cor 10, 21). In another sense, the word signifies man's destiny, fixed by God. Indeed, in an apportionment the lots to be drawn were in a cup (Ps 16, 5-6).

CHARISM. Word copied from the Greek. It designates, in the Epistles of St. Paul, certain extraordinary spiritual gifts, enabling Christians to collaborate fruitfully in the building up of the mystical body of Christ. For example, the gifts of healing, preaching, and teaching (1 Cor 13).

CHARITY. Word taken from the Latin *caritas* but translating the Greek term *agape*. It designates a very elevated and pure love similar to the love of God for men and the love of Christians for God and their brothers. This word is not to be confused with the sense of almsgiving, or charitable work. The fraternal meals of the first Christians often followed by the Eucharist received the name *agape* (Jude 12; 2 Pt 2, 13) translated by "feast" in this Bible.

CHRIST. This word, derived from the Greek, signifies "anointed" and translates the Hebrew word for *Messiah*. The Hebrew king was anointed with holy oil: so was the high priest (2 Sm 12, 7; Ex 29, 21). In the Bible, it is the title given to the one who, in the future, will come to restore Israel (Dn 9, 25-26). Jesus presents himself as the expected Messiah (Mk 14, 62). St. Paul and the first Christians gave him the name *Christos* (past participle of the verb) which quickly became a proper name: Jesus Christ, Christ Jesus, or simply Christ (Acts 17, 3). *See* **JESUS**.

CHRISTIAN. This word is derived from *Christ*. It was used for the first time at Antioch around 35 A.D. to designate the disciples of Jesus Christ who until then had been called *Nazoreans* (Acts 11, 26).

CHURCH. (1) Among the Hebrews, this word designates the sacred assembly of the Israelites (cf Jgs 21, 8 where it is translated "assembly"). (2) In the New Testament, it refers first to the assembly of the Christians of Jerusalem (Acts 5, 11). Later, the word was applied to each of the communities founded by St. Paul (1 Cor 1, 2). Finally, it designates the totality of Christians and that ideal church which will be fully realized only at the end of times. In this sense, the church is the body of Christ (Mt 16, 18).

CIRCUMCISION. Removal of the prepuce. It is a very ancient ethical practice which the Hebrews converted into a religious rite. Abraham received it as a sign of the covenant (Gn 17, 10ff). Later, the prophets stressed the fact that this bodily mark has no value unless it is accompanied by an "internal circumcision" signifying moral purity (Jer 9, 25f).

COMING. Translation of the Greek word *parousia*. This word designates the second coming of Christ for the last judgment (Mt 24, 3; 1 Thes 4, 15). The belief in a twofold messianic coming distinguishes the Christian mentality from Jewish messianism.

COMMUNION. State in which the faithful is united to God, is close to God, and enjoys his intimacy. Christianity has as its object to place us in communion with the Father and the Son through the action of the Holy Spirit, that is, to give us a share in the divine life (Jn 15). In the Bible, the word never signifies sacramental communion in the Eucharist.

CONSECRATE. Withdrawal of an object or person from secular use so as to transfer it into the domain of God and keep it there (Ex 13, 1; 30, 29).

CONVERSION. This word is frequently associated with other terms of repentance and penitence. It signifies changing one's life. In their preaching, the apostles ask that their hearers be converted (repent) and be baptized (Acts 2, 38). In the Bible, the word conversion is never used in the sense of "changing one's religion."

COVENANT. Man has always sought to place himself in contact with the divinity. In sacred history, this contact has taken the form of a kind of contract between God and the people of Israel. But there had already been a personal covenant between God and Noah (Gn 6, 18-22), and between God and Abraham (with the sign of circumcision: Gn 17, 10-14). This covenant is made by God without the opinion of the other party being asked. It is therefore gratuitous. But it is bilateral by reason of the promises of the contracting parties: the people promise to observe the law, and God promises to reward fidelity (Ex 19, 4-8; Dt 5, 1-21).

Unfortunately, the people were often unfaithful. It is then that the prophets promise (for the messianic times) a new covenant in which the union between God and man will no longer be solely in a national religion but in an interior and spiritual piety (Jer 31, 31-34; 11, 1-17).

This hope is realized by the Gospel in Jesus Christ, in whom Christians receive the grace promised (Mt 26, 28; Heb 10, 9-18).

Hence, the two parts of the Bible were designated by the first Christians with the terms Old Covenant, New Covenant. However, since the Greek word *diatheke* (covenant) also signifies testament, the custom arose (we do not know why) in Latin and the modern languages of using this latter word, even though the meaning is almost incomprehensible.

CREATION. This notion is at the basis of the faith of Israel. It is presented not only as an abstract notion (2 Mc 7, 28), but also as the corollary to the existence of an active Creator, present in the world (Ps 104; Jb 38). It expresses itself in popular cosmological descriptions of the time (Gn 1—3) and establishes the fundamental relation between man and God in the Judaeo-Christian religion. The revelation and redemption of the Messiah sometimes appears as a re-creation: "new world," "new heaven" (Is 45, 8), reestablishing the order and first destiny of things and of men, lost through sin.

CROSS. This instrument of Roman torture reserved for slaves was particularly infamous. It was known to Jesus who preached a type of detachment to his disciples which would go as far as this humiliation of the cross (Mt 10, 38). He himself followed this way of self-denial out of love and obedience (Phil 2, 8). The death on the cross of the Messiah, Son of God, is a scandal, the paradox which will become the most incontestable historical and spiritual center of the work of salvation accomplished by Jesus (1 Cor 1, 18-23). By his abasement on the cross which paid men's debt to sin and crushed the devil (1 Cor 2, 8; Col 2, 14) Jesus is elevated (2 Cor 13, 4) and the wood of infamy has become a tree of life (Rv 2, 7). Crucified with Christ through baptism and the life of faith (Gal 2, 19; Rom 6, 6), the Christian must glory only in the cross of Jesus (Gal 6, 12-15).

DAGON. Word derived from the root *dag:* fish. It is the name originally of a Mesopotamian deity who became the principal god of the Philistines. His body was half-man and half-fish (Jgs 16, 23).

DAMASCUS. Capital of Syria, destroyed in 732 B.C. (2 Kgs 16, 9), which had a large Jewish population. It was the scene of Paul's conversion (Acts 9, 1-27).

DARKNESS. Absence of light. In the Bible God, who is eternal truth, is considered the true light and the source of all light (Is 10, 17); therefore darkness becomes a symbol of estrangement from God. Jesus said that those who followed him would not walk in darkness (John 8, 12), i.e., he would show them clearly the truth.

DAY OF THE LORD (JUDGMENT). This is the day on which God will judge. The judgment is often conceived of as a punishment. The "day of the Lord" was announced by the prophets as affecting chiefly the pagan nations, who were guilty of attacking and enslaving the people of God (Is 2, 12-22). Later, the same prophets will affirm that the judgment will also touch Israel (Zep 1, 7. 14-18) and, at the end of times, all mankind (Zec 14, 1-7). In the New Testament, this idea persists, and it is toward this glorious manifestation of Christ that the whole of Christian hope tends (1 Cor 1, 8; 1 Thes 5, 2. 4).

DEACON. This word signifies: server, assistant. It has taken on a particular meaning with the institution of the deacons in the early church to serve the poor and assist the apostles (Acts 6, 1-6).

DEMON. The Jews recognized the existence of destructive evil spirits, wicked powers dedicated to doing harm. These are the demons, enslaved by Satan, who dwell within and stir up those who are possessed (Mt 8, 28-32).

DESERT. This word holds a major place in biblical thought: it is in the desert that the people has experienced divine intimacy (Ex 19). The desert symbolizes the desolate sojourn of the times of trial. Jesus withdraws to the desert before beginning his ministry (Mt 4, 1).

DIASPORA (DISPERSION). This word designates the Jews scattered throughout the pagan regions of the Roman Empire (Jn 7, 35).

DIVORCE. The Bible presents marriage as a union of the natural order, indissoluble and allowable once for each couple, in order to assure the mutual complement of man and woman (Gn 2, 24). Moses, for reasons of "hardness of heart" and in order to limit the abuses of polygamy, codified the custom of repudiation then in use, exacting a tribute, that is, a written piece of paper which the married man had to give his wife signifying that her freedom was restored. He was not allowed to take her back again (Dt 24, 1-4). Our Lord, in bringing the law of charity and a higher moral order, renewed the natural precept of Gn 2, 24, and gave marriage its original unity and indissolubility (Mt 19, 3; 5, 32; Mk 10, 2; Lk 16, 18).

ELDER. In the Old Testament the word refers to an official class having both civil and religious jurisdiction (Ex 3, 16; 24, 1). In the New Testament it refers to an official of the early Christian church, such as a bishop or priest (Acts 20, 17. 28; Jas 5, 14).

ELECT, ELECTION. This refers to the divine choice. (1) Abraham is chosen and taken from his family and country. This election culminates in the election of Israel (Gn 12, 1-7; Ex 19, 1-9). (2) Certain persons are said to be chosen (David, the Messiah) (2 Sm 7, 14ff). (3) Jesus is called the elect ("chosen one") of God (Lk 23, 35). (4) Christ chooses his apostles (Mt 10, 2-4). (5) All Christians are the object of a divine election (Rom 1, 6).

ELOHIM. Ordinary Hebrew word for God. It is the plural of majesty. Elohim ordinarily designates God in his action on the world in contrast to Yahweh which is used of the God of the covenant (Ex 3, 14).

ESSENES. The Dead Sea Scrolls have indicated that the Essenes ranked in importance with the Pharisees and Sadducees. There were about 4000 Essenes although only 200 lived in Qumran, their most important center. A member had to undergo a one-year "postulancy" and a three-year "novitiate." He then vowed to be reverent, just, hate sinners, help the just, obey his superiors, tell the truth, share his property, and keep Essene teaching secret. Meals and ritual baths were of great importance. Some think that John the Baptist was a member of this sect (Lk 1, 80; 3, 1-21).

ETERNAL. This corresponds to the Hebrew word *olam*, signifying a long period of time; these terms indicate primarily something that perdures throughout the centuries (Gn 17, 8); then something that has neither beginning nor end, like God (Gn 21, 33); and, finally, something outside of time (1 Jn 5, 11-12).

EXPIATION-PROPITIATION. Translation of the Hebrew *Kippur* signifying pardon or suppression of sin. Jesus is called "expiation" because he assures pardon of all sins (Rom 3, 25).

FAITH. In the Old Testament, faith is rarely mentioned. Its essential component is trust in God. Thus, Abraham's trust becomes the type of true faith (Gal 3, 6). In the New Testament, faith holds a predominant place: Jesus requires faith in himself which presupposes the acceptance of his message and trust in the person of the Master (Jn 6, 29-40) In St. Paul, faith is the chief element of his teaching and the key to salvation (Rom 1, 16).

FASTS. The chief Jewish fast was that of the Day of Atonement known as "the (autumn) fast" (Acts 27, 9). The especially devout customarily fasted on the second and fifth days of the week (Mt 9, 14; Lk 18, 12). Our Lord's great fast (Mt 4, 2) was foreshadowed by those of Moses (Ex 24, 18) and Elijah (1 Kgs 19, 8).

FEAR OF GOD. (1) Feeling experienced before any kind of divine manifestation: dread, fear, dismay (Ex 20, 18ff). (2) The same word also serves to denote the service of God, religion (Dt 4, 10). (3) The term "God-fearer" was used of a pagan who had adopted Jewish religious practices, without however belonging completely to the religion of Israel (Acts 10, 1).

FEASTS. In memory of the rest of God after the work of creation, the Jews kept as sacred the seventh day, or sabbath, the seventh month, the seventh or sabbatical year, and the fiftieth or jubilee year (Gn 2, 1-3; Lv 25, 1-22).

The weekly sabbath was observed by special sacrifices, by rest from servile work, and by attendance at religious instruction (Ex 20, 8-11; Lv 23, 2f).

The first day of the month, the New Moon, was a holy day on which special offerings were made (Nm 28, 11-15; Col 2, 16).

The three major feasts of the year, on which male Israelites were required to go to the temple, were Passover, in March or April, Pentecost, fifty days later, and Tabernacles, toward the end of September.

Passover began on the evening of the fourteenth Nisan with the eating of the lamb. On the fourteenth, after all leaven had been removed from the house, the lamb was sacrificed at the temple, and then brought home for cooking. It was eaten with herbs and unleavened bread in memory of the going out of Israel from Egypt (Lv 23, 5f; Heb 11, 27-29). The following week was known as the days of the Unleavened Bread (Lv 23, 6-8). The eve of the sabbath within this week was the Preparation Day (Mt 27, 62). During this week the first-fruits of the barley harvest were presented as the opening of the seven weeks of harvest.

Pentecost recalled the giving of the law, and it offered in thanks the first-fruits of the wheat harvest (Lv 23, 15-11). At Pentecost the Holy Spirit came upon the apostles and the others gathered in the Upper Room (Acts 2, 1ff).

Tabernacles was celebrated in the month of Tishri. The first day of that month was the feast of Trumpets, the civil New Year. On the tenth fell the Day of Atonement, a day of fast and of expiatory sacrifices, when the high priest entered the holy of holies to sprinkle blood (Lv 16; 23, 23-36; Nm 29, 7-11). From the fifteenth to the twenty-first of the month the feast of Tabernacles (Booths) was celebrated. It recalled the wanderings of the Israelites in the desert. This week marked the end of the harvest of fruit, wine and oil (Lv 23, 39-43). The last day of the feast was a day of rest on which were observed the ceremonies of water libation and the lighting of the four great golden candelabra (Jn 7, 37; 8, 12).

Two minor feasts were kept during the winter, Dedication and Purim (Lots). The former was held in our December, and was a joyous commemoration of the rededication of the temple by Judas Maccabeus (1 Mc 4, 56-59). It was also known as the feast of Lights, since during it the temple was illuminated (Jn 10, 22). Purim, held at the close of winter, recalled the rescue of the Jews by Esther when Haman cast lots to determine the day on which they should be destroyed (Est 9, 20-32; 2 Mc 15, 36).

FIGURE (TYPE). A person, event, or object which in God's intention signifies or foreshadows something else. Many realities of the Old Testament foreshadowed those of the New (Heb 7, 1-22).

FIRE. This is used as a symbol to express the divinity which radiates and consumes at the same time, with a joyous or terrifying aspect: God present in the fire on Mt. Sinai, in a storm (Ex 19, 18). On the altar of the temple, there was a perpetual fire (Lv 6, 5; 2 Chr 4, 1). God, a devouring fire, consumes Sodom and Gomorrah (Gn 19, 24-25). Jesus is said to baptize "with fire," that is, with the Holy Spirit (Mt 3, 11).

FIRST-BORN. By right, every first-born male must be reserved for God. He must be either immolated or (since infant-sacrifice was abolished by the Hebrews) redeemed (Ex 13, 2; Nm 3, 11-13). The title "first-born" could be given to the boy even if he had no brother or sister. And it entailed the privilege of "birthright," entitling him to a position of honor in the family and to a double share in the possessions inherited from the father (Ex 25, 31). Jesus is called the first-born of creation because of his position as the head of mankind (Heb 1, 6).

FIRST-FRUITS. The first fruits of the season which out of obligation were offered to God (Ex 23, 19). Paul calls Jesus "the first fruits" of the dead, showing that his resurrection will be followed by theirs (1 Cor 15, 20. 23).

FLESH. (1) First meaning: the flesh of an animal in contrast to the blood and bones (Gn 9, 3ff). (2) Everything that has life (Gn 6, 13). (3) Man in contrast to God by reason of his weakness; hence, the person, human nature (Mt 26, 41). (4) Especially in St. Paul's Epistles, natural man, without grace, witn his weaknesses and tendencies toward sin, in contrast to the "spirit" which designates the faculty that enables man to share in the Holy Spirit through the new birth of baptism (Rom 7, 14).

FOREIGNERS. Term reserved for those who were not of Hebrew stock, the Gentiles (Ex 12, 44).

GALILEE. The most northerly region of Palestine and the most favored by nature. Among its flourishing towns were Cana, Chorazin, Nazareth, Capernaum, Bethsaida, Tiberias. The population was predominantly Jewish, but there was a noticeable Galilean dialect (Mt 26, 73). The Galileans were very loyal to their religion and nation, though regarded by the Judeans as ignorant and lawless (Jn 7, 41; Mk 14, 70). Our Lord was reared in Galilee, he spent most of his time preaching there, and all but one of his apostles were from Galilee.

GALILEE, SEA OF. A lake which formed the eastern boundary of Galilee. It was also called the Lake of Gennesaret, from the plain on its northwest corner (Lk 5, 1), and the Sea of Tiberias, from the city of this name, the residence of Herod Antipas (Jn 6, 1). The lake is about thirteen miles long and six broad.

GEHENNA. This comes from the Hebrew "Valley of Hinnom," a place near Jerusalem where ritual infant-sacrifices had been practiced (2 Chr 28, 3). This place was later used as a depot for refuse. The word became synonymous with place of malediction (Jer 7, 31) and then in the New Testament with the abode of the damned, a place of torment, unquenchable fire and the consuming worm (Mt 5, 29; 10, 28; 18, 8f; Mk 9, 44ff). *See* **SHEOL.**

GETHSEMANI. This word, which signifies "oil press," became the name for a plantation of olive trees located opposite the temple of Jerusalem, east of the torrent of Kidron. This is the "mount of Olives," scene of Christ's agony and betrayal (Mt 26, 36-56).

GLORY. A very important notion in biblical theology. In Hebrew *(kabod)*, the word designates "to be heavy," "to be illustrious." It often denotes the radiant manifestation of God in his grandeur (Ez 1, 28). This divine glory is possessed by Jesus (Jn 1, 14). According to St. Paul, every Christian shares in this divine glory already here below (Phil 3, 21).

GOEL. *See* **KIN, NEXT OF.**

GOLGOTHA. Aramaic word signifying "skull place." It was the name of a little hill located northwest of the city of Jerusalem. Those condemned were executed there, and it was here that Jesus suffered crucifixion (Mt 27, 33). The Latin rendering of this word is *Calvaria* which is the origin of our "Calvary."

GOOD NEWS. *See* **GOSPEL.**

GOSPEL. In Greek, this word signifies good news, and specifically the good news of the Kingdom of God (Heb 4, 2; Mt 4, 23). St. Paul uses the word to indicate his preaching; later, the same word will be applied to the accounts of Christ's life (1 Cor 9, 16; Rom 1, 3).

GRACE. This word (in Greek: *doxa)* has a great variety of meanings: favor, benevolence, benefit. Hence, it signifies God's gratuitous love which makes the creature its acceptable beneficiary (Rom 11, 5. 6). The grace par excellence is salvation, justification (Eph 2, 5). In the plural—graces—it signifies the supernatural gifts and helps given to each one by the Holy Spirit.

HASIDEANS. This word is derived from the Hebrew word *hasidim*, "pious ones," and designates the faithful servants of God. They are mentioned in the book of Proverbs (2, 8) and in the Psalms (40, 5; 50, 5; 148, 14). They played a leading part during the resistance directed by Judas Maccabeus (1 Mc 2, 42 and 7, 6; 2 Mc 14, 6). They are undoubtedly at the origin of the Essenes, the brotherhood established in the monastery of Qumran which left us the famous Dead Sea Scrolls.

HEART. The Hebrews regarded the heart as the seat not only of emotions but also of thoughts and voluntary acts. Thus, the heart represents the whole man (Jl, 2, 13; 1 Pt 3, 4).

HEAVEN. This word has several meanings: (1) the firmament in which the stars are perceived (Gn 1, 14-17); (2) the region of the atmosphere where the birds fly (Dt 4, 17); (3) the place of God's residence, the throne-room where the Everlasting One is seated surrounded by the angels (Mt 5, 12; 24, 36). Jewish tradition had imagined several heavens or firmaments superimposed on one another, populated with various kinds of angels. It is in this sense that they spoke of the "heavenly host" and that St. Paul spoke of having been caught up in ecstasy "to the third heaven" (2 Cor 12, 2).

HELL. The place of eternal punishment, also called Gehenna. *See* **GEHENNA. SHEOL.**

HELLENIST. A Jew, or a Jew turned Christian, living in a foreign land and speaking Greek (Acts 6, 1).

HERITAGE. *See* **INHERITANCE.**

HEROD. The Herodian family, though Jewish in religion, was Idumean in origin. Herod "the Great" (B.C. 62 to 4) was appointed by Rome as king of Judea in B.C. 40, to the exclusion of the native Hasmonean line. He rebuilt the temple, and was in general an efficient ruler, but his cruelties made him odious. He slaughtered the infants at Bethlehem (Mt 2, 16-18). Four of his children are mentioned in the New Testament: Archelaus, Antipas and two named Philip.

Archelaus, ethnarch of Judea (4 B.C.-6 A.D.), was deposed on account of his cruelty and exiled to Vienne in Gaul.

Antipas, tetrach of Galilee and Perea, was deposed in 39 A.D. He divorced his wife, the daughter of King Aretas, and married Herodias, the wife of his brother Philip, who resided in Rome. He imprisoned and later beheaded John the Baptizer (Mt 14, 1ff). He was present in Jerusalem at the time of our Lord's trial (Lk 23, 7-12).

Philip, tetrarch of Trachonitis (4 B.C.—34 A.D.) unlike his brothers, was a moderate and peaceful ruler.

Two other descendants of Herod are also mentioned in the New Testament. Herod Agrippa I, grandson of Herod the Great, was king of all Palestine from 41 to 44 A.D. He was a strict observer of Judaism, and a persecutor of Christianity (Acts 12, 1ff). His death is mentioned in Acts 12, 23. His son, Agrippa II, ruled in Trachonitis until his death in 100 A.D. This Agrippa and his sister Bernice heard St. Paul's defense (Acts 25—26). Another sister, Drusilla, was married to the procurator Felix (Acts 24, 24).

HERODIANS. These were partisans and courtiers of the reigning dynasty of the Herods. Though they were Jews in religion, their spirit was Gentile. They conspired with their enemies the Pharisees against Christ (Mt 22, 16).

HERODIAS. Daughter of Aristobulus and granddaughter of Herod the Great and Mariamme. She was the wife of Philip but left him to marry Antipas. Her daughter Salome (who has unfortunately achieved some notoriety) resulted from the first marriage (Mt 14, 6-10).

HIGH PLACES. In Hebrew *bamoth* designates the sanctuaries ordinarily built on the heights by the inhabitants of Canaan (Nm 33, 52) as well as the Hebrews before the temple was built (1 Kgs 3, 2). However, later they became the symbol of idolatry for Israel, a symbol to which the ancient Jewish people constantly returned, in spite of the prohibition of Deuteronomy (12, 4ff), and the constant condemnations of the prophets (Ez 6, 3-6).

HIGH PRIEST. The chief of the sacred ministers among the Jews. He was supreme in religious matters, and to him was reserved the exclusive right of offering the great sacrifice of expiation and of entering the holy of holies (Heb 9, 7). Through him at times God announced things to come (Jn 11, 51). He was a member of the Sanhedrin and ordinarily presided over its deliberations (Mt 26, 57; Acts 4, 5f; 5, 27; etc.). Induction into this high priesthood was by anointing or by investiture in the precious robes of the office. The dignity descended at first by primogeniture from Aaron and the elder branch of Aaron's family and was held for life. But in the days of Christ the high priests were appointed and removed at will by the Herods and the Roman procurators. During the lifetime of our Lord some fifteen different individuals held the office, the most noted of whom were Annas (6-5 A.D.) and his son-in-law Caiaphas (18-36 A.D.). Annas and Caiaphas, often named together, judged Christ (Jn 18, 13. 24), Peter and John (Acts 4, 6), then all the Apostles (Acts 5, 17ff) and St. Stephen (Acts 6, 12ff), while Ananias acted against Paul (Acts 23, 2; 24, 1).

HOLOCAUST. In the ancient sacrifices only the blood and certain parts of the victim were offered to God; the rest was divided among the priest and faithful who had offered it (Lv 7, 11-21). A holocaust (from the Greek "wholly burned") was a sacrifice in which an entire animal except its hide was consumed in the fire on the altar, with the primary purpose of rendering glory to God (Lv 1, 1ff).

HOLY (SANCTIFY). The term "holy" is applied to anything that is consecrated to God, and hence withdrawn from all (secular) human use. In this sense, holy or sacred implies that no one can touch the object, for such contact would entail an "impurity" (1 Kgs 8, 4). God is "holy," because he is completely apart from any contact with the universe; but also because he possesses moral perfection. The people of Israel was to be "holy" in order to resemble God (Lv 20, 7. 26). Christians are "holy" because they have been consecrated to God by baptism. They are thus called to achieve moral perfection (Rom 6, 3ff). To *sanctify* means to consecrate something or someone to the service of God (Heb 13, 12). God shows himself to be holy by manifesting his justice (Is 5, 16).

HOPE. The messianic hope is at the center of the life of Israel, the source of all its unity, its action, and influence on others. The Hebrew terms which designate it express the tension of a bow ready to shoot its arrow to infinity (Zec 9, 13-14); this hope thus represents a search, an absolute confidence and a concentration of all one's energy flowing from God's covenant with Israel. It does not rest on human resources and initiative, but on the all-powerful Presence of God (Ps 18; 7). It is unshakable in spite of all the vicissitudes of the history of Israel (Mi 7, 7-9; Ps 22, 5-6; Jer 30, 7). It is the constant on which many of the words of the prophets are predicated (Mi 4—5; Is 40ff; Jer 30—33; Ez 40ff). This hope was confirmed and reinforced by the coming of the Messiah, the incarnation and redemption of Christ. Christian hope takes its character from this absolute witness of love and God's fidelity to his promises. It brings the gospel to the far corners of the world as well as souls to a more complete assurance of salvation (Rom 5, 1-11; Heb 6, 18-20) until the end of time (1 Pt 1, 3-5).

HORNS. These are the symbol of power and strength (1 Sm 2, 1). The Bible often speaks of the horns of the altar, ornaments jutting out over the four corners of the altar of the temple of Jerusalem (1 Kgs 1, 50).

HOSANNA Hebrew expression signifying: "may God save," used in the course of Jewish feasts (Ps 118, 25f). It served as an acclamation during Christ's entrance into Jerusalem, in the sense of "Long live," and it is always chanted during the course of the Catholic liturgy (Mt 21, 9).

HOSTS. Translation of the Hebrew word *sabaoth* which signifies armies. These armies are either a warrior grouping (material sense) (Ex 14, 17) or the multitude (such as an army) of stars (Ps 33, 6) or angelic beings that express God's glory (Jb 25, 3).

IMPOSITION OF HANDS. The customary Jewish way of designating a person for a task and invoking upon him the divine blessing and power to perform it (Nm 8, 10-11). Jesus used it when healing (Mk 6, 5). By the imposition of hands, the apostles conferred the Holy Spirit (Acts 8, 17), the diaconate (Acts 6, 6), and the priesthood (1 Tm 4, 14).

INHERITANCE. The corresponding Greek indicates a portion (of a share) as the result of drawing lots. This word designates the various parts of the promised land chosen for each Israelite tribe (Jos 15, 1). The word is retained in the New Testament in reference to Jesus who has been constituted by God as the heir of all things (Heb 1, 2); and in reference to Christians, sons and heirs of God, through Jesus Christ (Rom 4, 13-16; 8, 17).

ISRAEL. Proper name signifying "one who struggles with God." The popular explanation of this glorious surname recalling Jacob's struggle (Gn 32, 29) then passes on to his posterity and designates the People of the Promise (Ex 3, 16).

JEALOUS (GOD). This is the translation used for a Hebrew verb which contains the concept of ardor; it can characterize the divine justice as ardent, zealous, and prompt to chastise sinners (Ex 20, 5). God is also termed jealous because since he is unique he cannot allow man not to render single-minded worship to him (Ex 34, 14).

JERUSALEM. In Hebrew, *Yerushalaim*, vision of peace. But the origin of the name seems to be *Ursalim* which signifies "foundation of Salem," a Canaanite divinity. The city was a citadel of the Jebusites (Jgs 1, 8). It was conquered by David who made it his capital (2 Sm 5; 6). Destroyed in 586 B.C., it was rebuilt by the Jews who returned from the exile, in the fifth century before the Christian era (2 Kgs 25, 1-21; Ezr 3—6). It was besieged and destroyed for the second time by the emperor Titus in 70 A.D. At the time of Christ, Jerusalem was the chief city of Palestine and the religious center of Judaism. Situated on a plateau, its walls looked down into deep ravines, the Kidron on the east and the Valley of Hinnom on the south and west. Within the walls the city was divided by the Valley of the Tyropoean, and sloped gradually toward the southeast.

The northeastern part of the city rested on Mount Moriah and was occupied chiefly by the temple and the fortress Antonia. North of the temple were the Sheep Gate and the Pool of Bethesda (Jn 5, 2). The Golden Gate, in the eastern wall of the city, opened on the road to Gethsemani, Mount Olivet, Bethany and Jericho. On its western side the temple had a bridge that led over the Tyropoean to the Upper City. The southeastern section of the city was the ancient city of David, whose walls contained the tower of Siloam (Lk 13, 4) and the various gates that led to the fountains outside the walls. This part of the city was inhabitated largely by priests. The southwestern section of the city contained the business districts, the palaces of Annas and Caiaphas, of Herod and of the Hasmoneans. To the east of it was the Pool of Siloam (Jn 9, 7), and to the south the Valley of Hinnom (a place for refuse) and Akeldama ("Blood Field") (Mt 27, 8; Acts 1, 19).

Another section of the city lay to the northwest, across from the temple. Beyond its walls were fields, gardens and places of burial. The Ephraim Gate which opened here on the highway to Jaffa was not far from the place of the Crucifixion, which lay just outside the city (Jn 19, 17-20; Heb 13, 12).

JESUS. This name, which was common in Israel, signifies "God saves." It was bestowed by God (Lk 1, 31) on the son of the Virgin Mary—who was truly man (Acts 2, 22. 32) and later recognized as Lord (Phil 2, 11) and Savior (2 Tm 1, 10)—in consequence of his mission (Mt 1, 21).

But before being recognized as the Messiah and Son of God, Jesus of Nazareth is taken for the son of Joseph and Mary, and he appears in history at the moment when John the Baptizer is preaching repentance in Judea (Lk 3, 1ff). Jesus wins the admiration of the crowds by his preaching and healing, proclaiming the good news of the kingdom of God and doing good. He is soon followed by numerous disciples and like John his precursor becomes a sign of contradiction for the Judaism of his time (Mt 10, 34; Lk 4, 15; 11, 27). He speaks with authority in the synagogues and is called Teacher and Rabbi. He criticizes the formalism of certain religious practices (the sabbath, ablutions), questions the worship tied down to the perdurance of the temple, and overturns social barriers (publicans and sinners draw near to him). He allows himself to be called Messiah and Son of David by the enthusiastic crowds. However, Jesus knows that this is an ambiguous messianism and so he reveals his true identity to a few of those chosen for their faith (Mt 16, 16; Jn 6, 67-70).

Jesus is condemned as a blasphemer by those who hand him over to the Roman authority to be crucified (Mt 26, 65). Under the Roman procurator Pontius Pilate (26-36 A.D.) he is put to death for the crime of having made himself "King of the Jews."

All the direct testimonies about Jesus and his work (the New Testament) concern firstly his resurrection and the divine character of his person. Foretold by the prophets and all the Scriptures (Lk 18, 31; 24, 25-27; Heb 1, 1ff), Jesus can be known only in the light of the Spirit of God. He will be understood only after his resurrection when he has sent forth this Spirit to the witnesses of his work, chosen by him. They will then recognize him as the Suffering Servant (Mt 3, 17; Phil 2, 7), the Son of David (Jn 7, 41-42), the High Priest and Mediator of the new Covenant (Jn 16, 26; Heb 3, 1; 8, 6), the Son of Man manifested as the savior at the time willed by God (1 Tm 1, 1-5), the Lord, image and Son of God, and God himself (Acts 2, 36; 11, 20; Rom 8, 29; 9, 5; Phil 2, 11; Heb 1, 3); the one who has come from God in the humility of the flesh (Jn 1; 7, 15-16. 27; 8, 14; Phil 2, 6-7) and, after his death, has been exalted by the Father whom he has revealed (Jn 3, 14; 12, 32).

All these titles—Word, Elect or Holy One of God, Lamb of God, Rabbi, Messiah, Son of God, Son of Man, King of Israel—are gathered together by John in the introduction accorded Jesus in the first chapter of his Gospel. But his name Jesus is henceforth above every name (Phil 2, 9). Lord of the universe and head of the church, he is the salvation which he brings to us (Lk 1, 71); thus the one who believes in him will desire to be worthy to die for his name (Acts 15, 26; 21, 13).

JORDAN. The foremost river of Palestine. From the Lebanons to the Dead Sea it covers a distance of 125 miles, though with its meanderings the stream itself is more than double that. The width varies from 80 to 150 feet, and the depth in summer from 4 to 12 feet. The river is generally hidden by a thick growth of willow. There are many fords which allow passage from the one bank to the other (Jos 2, 7; Mt 3, 13).

JUBILEE. Year of joy and amnesty, celebrated at the end of each 49 year period, in the course of which one's debts must be remitted and slaves set free (Lv 25, 8-55).

JUDGMENT. In the Old Testament, judgment is related to the covenant. Judges and kings were established to maintain or reestablish the faithfulness to the covenant in the midst of national difficulties and in matters concerning the observation of the law (1 Kgs 3, 6). They represented the supreme Judge (Is 11, 3-5). Referring to God, judgment designates divine intervention, sometimes to assure his people victory or deliverance and at other times to condemn and punish them after an infidelity (Dt 32, 36; Jer 30, 11ff).

In the Psalms Yahweh appears as the supreme Judge above all in the great deeds of the "Day of the Lord" *(see this term)* and his power extends over all the earth. Among the prophets this perspective becomes more and more connected with the eschatological plane (Zec 14; Dn 7, 12).

In the New Testament, judgment is connected with the work of Christ, accepted by the faithful or rejected by the unbelievers. It is already present and marks a difference between groups of people (Jn 3, 17-21; 8, 15; 12, 31). Hence, it is necessary to be on one's guard, because judgment is coming. It will be made evident at the last day, which will be marked by the definitive triumph of Christ (Mt 25, 31; 1 Thes 4, 16; 2 Thes 2, 3-10).

JUST (JUSTICE). The just man is one who is virtuous, faithful to God and to the law of Moses (Mt 19, 17-20). In the New Testament the "just" man is one who does the will of God (Mt 7, 21). In the teachings of St. Paul, the terms justice and justification appear often: God makes man "just," free from sin and pleasing to God through grace (grace attested by faith) (Rom 3, 20-30).

KINGDOM (REIGN) OF GOD. The Kingdom will be established by the Messiah, over Israel first (Zep 3, 14-15), and then over all the nations of the earth (Zec 14, 9). "Kingdom" signifies a state of things in which God is recognized as King to whom everything must be submitted: Kingdom of God and Kingdom of heaven are equivalent. The Kingdom is proclaimed by John the Baptizer (Mt 3, 2), inaugurated by Jesus (Mt 12, 25-28), continued in the church (Mt 10, 7; 16, 19), and will be definitively accomplished in the glory of Christ's return (Mt 24, 26-31). The members of the Kingdom are children of God and even in this life enjoy that eternal life which will be completely expanded in the future world (Jn 3, 15-16; Rv 22, 2).

KIN (NEXT OF), AVENGER OF BLOOD, GOEL. *See* **LEVIRATE.**

KISHON. Name of a brook flowing at the foot of Mt. Tabor. It witnessed several violent scenes and battles (Jgs 4, 13, 1 Kgs 18, 40).

KITTIM. This name referred originally to inhabitants of Kiti, capital of the isle of Cyprus, then to any Cypriots (Gn 10, 4; Is 23, 1; Jer 2, 10), later to Greeks in general (Nm 24, 24), and finally even to Romans (Dn 11, 30).

KNOW. God knows everything, since he is the Creator (Jb 37, 16). He knows his people, since he has chosen it (Gn 18, 19). On his part, man seeks to know God in faith (Dt 29, 3; Jer 31, 31-34). The word "know" has a third meaning in the Bible: man "knows" his wife; he has carnal relations with her (Gn 4, 1).

LAW OF MOSES. The law, respected by all Jews as from God, consisted of the five books of Moses. These formed the basis of the Scripture reading and instruction in the synagogue services. In addition the Pharisees observed a traditional law, the *Mishna*, which they taught also had its author in Moses. Our Lord observed the Mosaic law and promulgated for his followers its essential element, the Ten Commandments (Mt 5, 17). He criticized the Pharisees for their neglect of it in favor of their traditions (Mt 15, 2-9).

LEBANON. Mountainous chain north of Palestine. Its name, derived from *laban* which signifies "to be white," alludes to its tops covered with permanent snows (Jer 18, 14).

LEVIATHAN. A mythological sea monster symbolizing the chaos that existed in the beginning of creation. Also used for a crocodile or a whale (Ps 74, 14).

LEVIRATE. This word, derived from the Latin *levir* (brother-in-law) designates an ancient Israelite custom (Gn 38, 8ff), codified in the Bible: when a man dies without leaving a male child, the closest relative of the deceased—generally, his brother—must marry the widow who is his sister-in-law and thus perpetuate the line. The first son born of this union would be considered the son and heir of the dead man (Dt 25, 5-10).

LEVITES. Sacred ministers of lowest rank among the Jews. Unlike the priests, they were members of the tribe of Levi who did not belong to the house of Aaron. While on duty they wore a distinctive linen dress, but they entered only the inner court and not the holy place of the temple. The higher levites assisted the officiating priests, others had charge of the music during the services, and still others acted as doorkeepers and overseers of the temple (1 Chr 23, 4-6).

LIGHT. Has various meanings in Scripture: (1) material sense of outward light or daybreak (Gn 1, 3); (2) symbol of God (showing his incorporeal, pure and holy nature) (1 Jn 1, 5); (3) symbol of Christ (Jn 8, 12); (4) Christians are children of light because they have received the spiritual light of truth and grace, and are to radiate it in the world by their good example (Mt 5, 14; Eph 5, 8).

LORD. Originally, this title signified nothing more than "sir." From the 3rd century B.C. onward, the Jews replaced the ineffable name *Yahweh* with *Adonai* (Lord) in reading the Bible. Applied to Jesus by the first Christians, the name "Lord" was thus equivalent to an affirmation of his divinity (Acts 2, 36). *See* **ADONAI. NAME. YAHWEH.**

LOVE. In the Old Testament, the love of God expresses itself in his many interventions of creation (Gn 1, 3; Jb 38ff) and the history of Israel (Dt 4, 37; Ps 41, 12). It is a freely-given elective love (Dt 7, 7) working for the salvation of mankind, ever merciful in the face of human infidelity (Hos 11, 1-4).

The New Testament explores these first glimmerings more fully. The love of God is historical because God has not spared his own Son and has delivered him to death in order to save us (Jn 3, 16). It is also freely-given and elective by the work of Christ, which was in perfect correspondence with the will of the Father and which made the faithful the beloved ones of God (Jn 5, 20-25; Col 3, 12). Finally, this love in action is merciful, as shown above all by the cross and explained in the parables (Jn 15, 13; Lk 15, 11-32).

The love of man for God is thus a love which is returned. It must be sealed by a total obedience to the Commandements, a fidelity to the covenant. In the New Testament it must respond without limit to the prior love of God and Christ (1 Jn 3, 1-16; 4, 10-19).

MAGI. In the texts of the Old Testament, they are often associated with sorcerers and diviners. They seem to have been a Persian religious caste of royal advisers (Jer 39, 2: "princes"), and were regarded as wise men, astrologers. In the Gospel of Matthew, many think it refers to learned men from Babylon who had contact with Jewish Messianism (cf Dn 2, 2). In the Acts of the Apostles, the word is taken in the pejorative sense in the case of a magician who sets himself up as an adversary of Paul the Apostle (Acts 8, 9).

MEDIATOR. In its primary sense, the word signifies an intermediary, a third person who intervenes between other parties to bring them together or reconcile them. Moses was thus a mediator between God and the people (Nm 14, 13-20). Applied to Jesus, the term takes on an even more profound meaning, for Jesus is at the same time God and man; he belongs, at once, to the two parties. Through Christ we have access to the Father, and through Christ the Father gives himself to mankind (Heb 9, 11-25; 12, 24).

MERCY. This word is found in both Testaments, but retains all the primitive value of the Hebrew word *hesed*, which suggests love more than pity (Jas 2, 1-13).

MESSIAH. Hebrew word signifying "one who has been anointed." The kings of Israel were anointed in the name of God (1 Sm 9, 16). The term Messiah later was used to designate a "future king" who would make all things new (Dn 9, 25-26). This son of David, expected by the Jewish nation, was the Messiah par exellence (Mk 10, 47-48), a term that has been rendered in Greek by *Christos*. This was a common name that ultimately became a title for Jesus the Savior (Rom 1, 1). *See* **CHRIST. JESUS.**

MIRACLES. This word corresponds to two biblical words: sign and wonder. In the sense of "sign," a miracle is an unaccustomed and unexpected event which serves as a motive for credibility by manifesting the power of Christ, and leads the spectator to believe in his person (Jn 2, 11).

MISSION. Out of love the Father sends his only Son into the world. Jesus speaks in this way of his "mission" which is to save men by giving them Life (Jn 16, 27-28). Then, just as the Father has sent the Son into the world, so Jesus sends the apostles into the world (Jn 20, 21). This second mission is a prolongation of the former one.

MONEY. In the time of our Lord the coins current in Palestine were Roman, Greek, Syrian and Jewish. The Jews might issue coins only in bronze.

1) Large sums were expressed in *talents* and *mnas*. The talent equalled about $1920.00 in United States currency. The mna was one-sixtieth of a talent, or about $32.00. The units of Luke 19, 13ff were mnas.

2) Silver coins mentioned in the New Testament are: the Syrian *stater* (51 cents), the Roman *denarius* (about 17 cents), the Greek *drachme*, equivalent to the denarius. The stater was accepted as equal to the Jewish *shekel*, one-fiftieth of a mna (about 64 cents), the temple tax for two persons (Mt 17, 26). The denarius was the usual day's wage for a laborer in the field, and it was the coin of the tax to the Emperor (Mt 20, 2; 22, 19).

3) Bronze coins referred to are the Roman *assarion* (one cent) and *quadrans* (one-fourth of a cent), the Jewish *perutah* or *lepton* (one-eighth of a cent), the coin of the "widow's mite" (Mt 10, 29; 5, 26; Mk 12, 42).

It should be remembered that the coin values here given are only approximate, and that the purchasing power of money was much greater in ancient times than today.

MOUNTAIN (MOUNT). A mountain is regarded as the dwelling place of divinity. Sanctuaries were set up on a good many mounts. It was on mountains that God chose to give his revelations (Sinai, Tabor) (Dt 33, 2; Mt 17, 1ff). Zion is called the "mountain God has chosen" (Ps 68, 17).

MUSICAL INSTRUMENTS. The Hebrews were devoted to music and used it for both secular and religious purposes. Various types of instruments are mentioned in the Bible — stringed, wind and percussive instruments (Ps 150, 3-5).

MYSTERY. The origin of this word is Greek. It signified first of all the place where religious ceremonies took place which were reserved only to those who had been "initiated." In the plural, it signified the rites themselves. In a derived sense, the word is synonymous with divine secret. St. Paul uses it in the sense of divine plan (inaccessible to man, secret, but revealed by Jesus Christ), having the salvation of men as its object (Rom 16, 25-26). In Scripture it must never be taken in the sense (to which the catechism has accustomed us) of revealed truth incomprehensible to the human intelligence (for example, the mystery of the Blessed Trinity).

NAME. According to the conception of the ancients, the *Name* designates more than the external person; it tends to express his basic character, his personality (Gn 21, 3ff). We might say it is an emanation of the person himself. Change of vocation entailed changing one's name (Mt 16, 16-19). In the ancient texts of the Bible, to name or give a name can signify "to have power over" (Gn 2, 19-21). The "name of God" thus signifies God himself. Hence, we find the expressions: God acting for his name's sake — to glorify and sanctify his name (Ez 20, 14; Is 29, 23). In the same way sin profanes the name of God (Lv 18, 21). Among the Israelites, the veneration which came to be accorded to the name of God approached superstition. The Israelites did not dare pronounce this name and forbade even the use of the name *Yahweh*. In place of this word whose consonants were written out, the reader had to read *Adonai* (Lord). This custom continues to exist in present-day Judaism. Hence, the first Christians surrounded the name of Jesus with great veneration and the expressions: "in the name of Jesus" and "for the name of Jesus" occur frequently in the sense of: "acting in such an intention in dependence on Jesus" and "by authority of Jesus" (Col 3, 17). In John's Gospel, we are urged to pray "in the name of Jesus" (Jn 14, 13). Moreover, this manner of speaking has been retained until our own day; for example, we say: "In the name of the Father, and of the Son, and of the Holy Spirit." In the Our Father, the expression: "Hallowed be thy name," signifies that we pray for God's holiness to be acknowledged and adored by all men.

NATIONS. The Israelites distinguished themselves from foreign peoples. They designated the latter by the Hebrew term *goiim;* this word, which includes a certain nuance of scorn, is often translated in our modern languages as "nations" or "Gentiles" (Is 49, 6). *See* **FOREIGNERS.**

NAZIRITE. This term stems from the Hebrew word *nazir,* meaning "set apart as sacred, dedicated, vowed." The nazirite vow could be either for a limited period or for life. Those bound by this vow had to abstain from all the products of the grapevine, from cutting or shaving their hair, and from contact with a corpse. They were regarded as men of God like the prophets; cf Am 2, 11f. Examples of lifelong nazirites were Samson (Jgs 13, 4f. 7; 16, 17), Samuel (1 Sm 1, 11), and John the Baptizer (Lk 1, 15). At the time of Christ the practice of taking the nazirite vow for a limited period seems to have been quite common, even among the early Christians; cf Acts 18, 18; 21, 23f. 26.

NAZOREAN. A title of Jesus which the Gospel derives from the name of the town of Nazareth (Mt 2, 23). The Christians were called Nazoreans for a long time (Acts 24, 5). In Hebrew this word has a certain resemblance with the word *nezer* which signifies "shoot." Primitive Christian tradition thus saw in this an allusion to a passage of Isaiah (11, 11) in which the Messiah is presented as the shoot par excellence of David, son of Jesse.

NUMBERS. In the Bible, numbers often have a symbolic value. For example 7 (seven days, seven angels, seven lights ...); 12 (tribes, apostles); 40 (days of rain, days of prayer on Sinai, days of fast, period before the Ascension); 144,000 (the elect, in the Book of Revelation). It must also be noted that in the ancient accounts numbers must be regarded in accord with Oriental custom and they are subject to poetic approximation: *thousand* can signify a group or family. In the military accounts, most numbers are considerably exaggerated (Dt 32, 30).

PARACLETE (COUNSELLOR). Word derived from the Greek. It is used only in John's Gospel and signifies "advocate or defender." This word is applied either to Christ, who fulfilled this role toward his disciples, or to the Holy Spirit, who continues to exercise it with Christ himself (Jn 14, 16).

PARADISE. Word of Persian origin, which passed over into Hebrew and then Greek, used to designate a garden; in particular, the garden of Eden (Gn 2, 15). Later, it signified the eternal abode of the just (Lk 23, 43).

PASSOVER. *See* **FEASTS.**

PASTOR. *See* **SHEPHERD.**

PEACE. This word is used in the Bible to express two ideas: (1) peace with God, reestablished by the covenant, often a synonym for reconciliation, and (2) peace between individuals and peoples.

The promises of the messianic covenant are often accompanied by the announcement of peace. Thus the Messiah will be called the "Prince of Peace" (Is 9, 5). The word "peace" is contained in the literal translation of the word Jerusalem (Salem) (Heb 7, 2). Peace demands faithfulness to the covenant and justice among men (Ps 72, 3-7) so often invoked by the prophets. Christ came to bring peace (Lk 2, 14) and to render it effective by a reconciliation of mankind to God (Jn 14, 27; Eph 2, 14-17). The extension of the peaceful reign of Christ is thus for the true Christian the condition and source of true peace and true justice between individuals and between nations.

PEOPLE OF GOD. This is how Israel is designated throughout the Bible. God has gratuitously chosen her and she is his own possession (Dt 7, 6). God dwells in her midst (Ex 25, 8). The people is thus holy and set apart from other peoples (Lv 20, 24). In its turn, Christianity is also called the People "[God] claims for his own," but it rejects any kind of national particularism (1 Pt 2, 9).

PERFECT. In the ancient text, this word indicates someone who avoids sin and practices the law. The passage in which Jesus says: "Be perfected as your heavenly Father is perfect" (Mt 5, 48) signifies — according to its context — that one must imitate the divine mercy and impartiality. In a single passage (Mt 19, 21) Jesus speaks of the perfection of the disciple who goes beyond his ordinary duties. St. Paul uses the term perfect of the "spiritually mature" Christians who know true wisdom and want all men to be perfect in Christ (1 Cor 2, 6ff).

PHARISEES. A religious sect of the Jews that numbered about 6000 in the time of Christ. Originating in the days of the Greek conquest of Palestine, they sought above all to preserve the Jews from the contamination of foreign religion, and to this end insisted upon strict separation from the Gentiles. They insisted also on strict loyalty to the Scriptures and to the traditions of the rabbis. Among many Pharisaic hedges about the law, ceremonial purity and payment of religious dues were emphasized. In doctrine the Pharisees were inclined to fatalism, but on the other hand they strongly upheld the resurrection and the future life. By the time of Christ their primitive zeal had degenerated into fanaticism and hypocrisy. They took a leading part in the opposition to Christ, and he scathingly rebuked their insincerity (Mt 23, 25; Lk 11, 39; 18, 9-14). That they were not all bad is evidenced by such men as Gamaliel (Acts 5, 34).

PHILADELPHIA. A city of Lydia in Asia Minor, founded by Attalus II Philadelphus, king of Pergamum. The book of Revelation alludes to it twice (1, 11 and 3, 7).

PHILISTINES. Non-Semitic invaders who gave their name to all of Palestine although they occupied only its southwestern plains. They were subdued by David (2 Sm 5, 17-25), but became practically independent under the separated kingdom and disappeared as a people after the time of the Maccabees.

PIETY. In Hebrew as in English, account must be taken of the relationship between this word *piety* and *pity* (in the sense of goodness). God is called pious, that is, good (Is 1, 4). Men are termed pious, that is, faithful, just and devoted to God (Acts 10, 7).

POOR. Originally, this word had merely an economic and social meaning. Gradually, it took on the meaning of humble, modest, small, the little people often oppressed by the rich and powerful but who remained faithful to God (Am 2, 6-7). It was in this sense that Jesus said: "Blest are the poor in spirit" (Mt 5, 3).

PRESBYTER. *See* **ELDER.**

PRIESTS, JEWISH. Sacred ministers, whose duty it was to offer sacrifice at the altar of holocausts, and to enter morning and evening into the holy place to burn incense at the golden altar (Heb 7, 27; 10, 11). They also had care of the loaves of proposition (Mt 12, 4) and certified the cure of lepers (Lk 17, 13f). They were divided into twenty-four classes, each of which in turn officiated for a week at the temple (Lk 1, 5). During the three great feasts all the classes ministered together. Their dress comprised a long linen tunic, ornamented sash and turban. The priesthood was hereditary, by descent from the tribe of Levi through the younger branch of Aaron's family (Heb 7, 5). For their support the priests received tithes and other offerings.

PROMISE. This term of Greek origin is employed only in the New Testament. It designates and interprets the meaning of all the previous prophetic history of the chosen people in their messianic mission. The Old Testament gave promise of Christ. But it is in Christ that all this preparatory and figurative history finds its perfect fulfillment (Mt 5, 17; Acts 13, 32-33; Rom 15, 8; 2 Cor 1, 20; Gal 3, 14). An analogous relationship exists between Christ's work of the Redemption and his second coming which, at the end of time, will asssure the glorious consummation of all things (Acts 1, 4-5; 2, 16-21) and fulfill the promise of Christ's work.

PROPHET. One who speaks to another on the part of God (Dt 18, 18). Prophets are also called "seers" by reason of their gift of reading thoughts. Prophet does not necessarily signify that one foretells the future and there were prophets in the first Christian communities (1 Cor 12, 28ff).

PUBLICANS. Management of imperial taxation was farmed by the Roman government to the highest bidders, who in turn entrusted the collection in the provinces to native agents by whom the privilege had been purchased with advance payments. These agents are the "publicans." They were often guilty of merciless extortion, and were universally hated as plunderers of their own people. Among the Jews they were also considered as disloyal to their religion, since they cooperated with Gentiles and exacted tribute from the race that God had made free (Jn 8, 33; Mt 22, 17). Like the Baptizer, our Lord condemned the injustice of the publicans, but did not reject those who were sincerely repentant (Mt 5, 46; 21, 31f). Two publicans are distinguished in the Gospels, Zacchaeus (Lk 19, 2) and Matthew (Mt 10, 3), who became an apostle and evangelist.

PURITY (RITUAL). State of the man who fulfills the conditions imposed by the Mosaic law on every one of the faithful who appeared for worship (Lv 7, 19-21). Certain bodily functions, contact with forbidden animals, and with corpses forbade participation in worship; anyone who was guilty of such things was "impure" or "unclean" (Nm 19, 1-10). "Purity" could be recovered by various rites: sacrifices, washings, aspersions, etc. (Nm 19, 19). There is no relation between this term and what we call "purity" in the sense of chastity.

REDEMPTION. This word comes from the Latin *redimere* which signifies to buy back or redeem. The corresponding Hebrew term was used in the Bible for the first time with reference to the exodus from Egypt (Ex 15, 13). God has redeemed his people from the bondage of Egypt, gratuitously, just as a master sets free his slave (Lv 19, 20). In the New Testament, it signifies that God, through Jesus Christ (gratuitously), redeems his people in order to establish his kingdom (Rom 3, 24).

REMNANT. An expression often used by the prophets. It designates the survivors of great catastrophes: the flood, the exile (Gn 7, 1f; Is 6, 13). God reserves this remnant for himself to help in the restoration (Is 37, 31). It is they who are and will remain the depositaries of the promise (Mi 4, 6-7). In the New Testament, the church is presented as fulfilling the function of the faithful Remnant and the "Israel after the flesh" is contrasted with the "Israel of God" which is the church (Rom 9, 27; 1 Cor 10, 18; Gal 6, 16); and this interpretation follows the teaching of the Old Testament.

RESURRECTION. The Bible does not have this unique and specific term. It uses the verbs to awake, to raise up, to cure, or the intransitive verbs, to get up, to appear, to show (one's self) sometimes as an act showing the power of God, sometimes as a manifestation of the victory of life over death. In the Old Testament, the idea is made known little by little at first in the perspective of the entire people (Ez 37, 1, 14), then for the Servant of Yahweh (Is 53) but always in a very limited fashion (Pss 16, 10ff; 49, 16; 73, 26; 17, 15). In the New Testament, this idea takes on an elemental importance through the resurrection of Jesus, which became the fundamental historical fact, the principal witness of his divinity (1 Cor 15, 4. 12). The Resurrection is also the divine judgment which has ordered the defeat of death and pledges salvation and resurrection to all the faithful (Rom 4, 25; Col 2, 12ff; Eph 2, 1-7). This resurrection in grace is the prelude to the final and glorious resurrection (1 Cor 15, 2ff; 1 Thes 4, 14ff).

SACRED. The same Hebrew word has both the active meaning of "holy," that is, keeping oneself free from profane impurities, and the passive meaning of "sacred," that is, set apart from what is profane and therefore treated with religious reverence (Lv 21, 6).

SACRIFICE. The supreme form of divine worship, by which some creature is offered to God and used in adoration as an acknowledgment of his majesty and the creature's subjection. True sacrifices were offered in the Old Law (Heb 9, 1ff), but they were only preparations for the perfect sacrifice of Christ on the cross (Heb 9, 11).

SADDUCEES. A religious sect of the Jews, less numerous than their rivals the Pharisees, but very influential on account of the many noble and wealthy persons who belonged to their ranks (Acts 4, 1; 5, 17). They set aside traditions and even rejected truths taught in the Sacred Books themselves. They insisted upon human free will, but denied immortality, the resurrection and the existence of angels (Mt 22, 23; Mk 12, 18; Lk 20, 27; Acts 23, 8). They were denounced by John the Baptizer (Mt 3, 7) and by our Lord (Mt 16, 6). Though less prominent in their opposition to Christ than the Pharisees, they nevertheless sought to entrap him (Mt 16, 1; 22, 23), and through their representatives joined in his condemnation by the Sanhedrin. They also strongly opposed the early church because the apostles proclaimed our Lord's Resurrection (Acts 4, 1f; etc.).

SALVATION, SAVIOR. Inasmuch as the terms express redemption (cf. **REDEMPTION**) and appear as a cause of salvation, the Hebrew uses one word: *Yacha*, which means to be generous, to deliver from slavery or from distress. This term in the Old Testament expresses the Work of God, assuring the deliverance of his people as a whole (Hos 5, 13; Is 31, 1; Ps 33, 16-17) and then personal salvation (Ps 51, 14) — the whole bound up in the messianic and eschatological perspective. This term provides the substantive "machia," translated as Savior (Is 45, 21). In the New Testament, the term is employed very frequently for a cure, the health of the body, but often, in connection with faith, of the soul (Mk 5, 34; Lk 8, 48; 18, 42). Thus, the work of the New Testament even in its temporal action is entirely oriented toward the work of spiritual salvation, of remission of sins (Lk 17, 19) and the liberation from the servitude that sin brings to man (Mt 1, 21; Lk 1, 77; Acts 5, 31, etc.) and leading the Christian to his highest destiny (Rom 1, 16; 5, 9-10; 1 Cor 15, 2; Jas 1, 21). This work will be definitively manifested at the last judgment (Rom 8, 22-25).

SAMARITANS. The inhabitants of Samaria were a mixed race, descended from intermarriage of Israelites and Assyrian colonists. The enmity between the Jews and the Samaritans was so great that travelers between Galilee and Judea often had to cross the Jordan into Perea for safety. In various uprisings this race was almost exterminated, and only a small remnant survives today.

In religion the Samaritans acknowledged the Pentateuch, Joshua and Judges, but not the additional revelation or Jewish traditional doctrine. They looked for the Messiah who would teach all truth (Jn 4, 25f). In practice they worshiped the same God as the Jews, and in such matters as sabbaths and feasts, circumcision and worship, they did not dissent. But through vying with the Jews in the strict observance of Mosaic regulations, they disowned the Jerusalem temple and priesthood. The rival sanctuary of Gerizim they revered as their holy place (Jn 4, 20). Our Lord passed through their country more than once, and preached and worked miracles among the people. He also spoke well of them (Lk 10, 30-37), defended them (Lk 9, 51-56), and commanded that the gospel be preached to them. This was done with success, and a Christian community was early formed among the Samaritans (Acts 8, 4-17; 9, 31; 15, 3).

SANHEDRIN. Literally *session*, a council, national or local, endowed with authority to pass on cases ecclesiastical or civil.

1) The national Sanhedrin, or Great Council, of the Jews met at Jerusalem. The high priest himself seems to have presided as a rule. The full membership was seventy-two, representing equally the three groups of priests, scribes and elders. This council took cognizance of grave matters of a doctrinal, judicial or administrative character affecting the Jewish religion and nation. The Romans acknowledged the decrees of the Sanhedrin, and guards attended the meetings to fulfill the orders of the judges (Mt 26, 58). Sentence of death, however, was reserved to the Roman authority (Jn 18, 31).

2) Local tribunals, subordinate to the supreme Sanhedrin, were found in the towns of Palestine. Their membership varied from three to twenty-three, according to the size of the male population of the place. The "Sanhedrin" of Mt 5, 22 probably refers to one of these lower tribunals.

SAVIOR. Exact translation of the word *Yehoshua* which has become "Jesus" (Lk 1, 31ff). *See* **SALVATION**.

SCRIBES. Literally this title means a writer, but in the New Testament the reference is to the learned class among the Jews, the official authorities on the written law and oral traditions. One who had made successful studies became a scribe at the age of thirty by receiving imposition of hands with the delivery of a tablet and key.

As the function of the priests was ritualistic, that of the scribes was doctrinal. These latter were interpreters of the Scriptures (Mt 2, 4; 17, 10; Mk 12, 35), but our Lord condemned them for their burdensome additions to the divine law (Mt 23). They taught by quoting the celebrated doctors of the past (Mk 1, 22). In our Lord's day the chief rival schools among the scribes were those of the liberal Hillel and the severe Shammai. Generally the scribes opposed the Sadducees (Lk 20, 39) and upheld the Pharisees. Like the Pharisees, the scribes were noted for hypocrisy, pride, and contradiction of Christ (Mt 23, 2ff; Mk 12, 28-30; Lk 20, 46; Mt 9, 3). But there were noble and sincere characters among them (Mt 8, 19), especially Nicodemus and Gamaliel (Jn 3; Acts 5, 34).

SCRIPTURES. (1) The inspired books, the work of the Holy Spirit. They were customarily divided into three series: the Law, the Prophets, and the Writings. (2) Christianity added its own writings: the Gospels and the Letters of the Apostles.

SEPTUAGINT. Translation into Greek of the Hebrew and Aramaic Old Testament (including the deuterocanonical books) made in Egypt by various authors during the period between 250 B.C. and 100 B.C. Its name comes from the fact that legend ascribes the work to a group of seventy-two scholars and it is designated by the Roman numerals LXX. It is by far the most important ancient version of the Old Testament and until recently was our sole witness for the state of the original text of the Hebrew Old Testament before the Christian era. The Septuagint was the version used by the Hebrews in Christ's time, by the apostles and New Testament writers, and by the Greek Fathers of the Church; it is still the official text of the Greek Church.

SHEOL. The ancient concept of the abode of the dead (*the nether world*, in Hebrew, *Sheol*) supposed no activity or lofty emotion among the deceased, who were pictured as surrounded by the darkness of oblivion (Nm 16, 30ff; Ps 6, 6). The Hebrews shared in this common idea almost to the time of Christ, when God revealed a clearer notion of the hearafter (Wis 3). It is at this time that belief in the resurrection of the dead was introduced (Dn 12, 2). Some (for example, the Sadducees) refused to believe it; but the people embraced it like some great revelation. In the New Testament, the whole concept is transfigured in the light of Christ's resurrection. His body did not see corruption in Hades; he has the keys of death and the nether world (Rv 1, 18). The word "Gehenna" (hell) is used of the nether world when punishment is involved (Mt 5, 29; 10, 28). *See* **GEHENNA.**

SIN. In the Old Testament sin is not so much a wrong action in one's conscience as something which disrupts the order of the world wished by God, and particularly the covenant fixed by the law. Thus the Israelite did not search himself for deep causes or establish its relationship with original sin; it is necessary to wait for the book of Wisdom to find such an allusion (2,24). The New Testament describes sin as relating to original sin and tells of the universal sorrow because of sin (Rom 1—5) erased by the Redemption (Rom 5—8). It describes responsibility for it. This conception of sin thus became linked with the ideas of faith and love which gave life to Christians (Rom 13, 8ff; 1 Cor 5, 9; 13, 4ff).

SON. In Hebrew, this word is used to designate diverse relations or dependencies: (1) relations of direct descendence (Ex 1, 1-5); (2) relations of disciples to their master (Prv 1, 8); (3) relations of origin or analogy (Jb 1, 3; 42, 13); (4) moral relations (Jos 7, 19).

SON OF MAN. An enigmatic title. Jewish apocryphal tradition (1 Henoch, 2 Esdras, 2 Baruch) uses it to describe a unique religious personage, a messiah with extraordinary spiritual endowments. Jesus' use of it seems to derive from Ez 2, where it is a title of humility, and Dn 7, 13f, where it indicates a clearly messianic figure. It expresses for him his twofold destiny, of suffering (Mk 8, 31; 9, 11. 31; 10, 33; 12, 31; 14, 21) and of glory (Mk 8, 38; 12, 36; 14, 62). Peter, along with the other disciples, fails (despite his confession) to grasp the association of suffering and death with the office of Messiah. Only after the resurrection does the Christian community endow it with its messianic meaning (Acts 7, 56; Rv 1, 3).

SOUL. In its first sense, the Hebrew word *nephesh* signifies breath, life, the principle of animal life (Gn 1, 20). It was only much later (toward the beginning of the Christian era) that the Hebrews adopted the distinction (of Greek philosophy) of soul and body (Rv 6, 9; 20, 4).

SPIRIT. Literally, breath. It is an element with as little materiality as possible; it is the innermost part of man, more subtle than his soul. The Old Testament attributes to the Spirit of God both external and internal actions that surpass human powers (Nm 11, 24-29). The Spirit is a person distinct from the Father and the Son (Jn 14, 26). Each Christian possesses the Spirit. He is the principle of life and a pledge of resurrection (Rom 8, 2. 11).

SYNAGOGUES. Minor places of religious assembly among the Jews, used also as schools, libraries and halls of judgment. The central place of worship was the temple, the one national sanctuary and the only place of sacrifice. The synagogue served local communities or separate congregations for less solemn religious functions. Every considerable Jewish community, whether in or out of Palestine, had at least one synagogue. The building, commonly rectangular, was erected on the plan of the temple. There was a gallery reserved for women, another space for men, and the worshipers faced toward Jerusalem and the holy of holies. In front was a platform on which stood the holy ark containing the Scriptures and an eight-branch candlestick burning before it. Nearest the platform were the chief seats, where sat the leading men facing the congregation (Mt 23, 6; Mk 12, 39; Lk 11, 43; 20, 46). Among these leading men were the ruler of the synagogue and the elders, and various functionaries whom they appointed.

TEMPLE. The sacred place of worship on Mount Moriah, including all buildings and courts. The first temple was built by Solomon, in 967 to 964 B.C., but was destroyed by the Chaldeans in 586 B.C. The second was erected by Zerubbabel in 515 B.C., but was profaned in 167 B.C. by the Syrians. Herod the Great began a magnificent restoration of this temple. It is his structure that is the temple referred to in the time of our Lord. In a more restricted sense, the term applies only to the "House" in which were the holy place and the holy of holies, or to the immediate precincts of this "House." The space covered by the temple and its courts was about 585 by 6100 feet.

The temple proper (Naos) measured 30 feet north to south, and 90 feet east to west. The innermost part of this building was the holy of holies, set apart from the outer room, the holy place, by a double curtain (Mt 27, 51). The holy of holies contained the stone on which once rested the ark of the covenant. It was entered once a year by the high priest (Heb 9, 3-5). The holy place had within it the golden altar of incense (Lk 1, 11), and the table of loaves (Mt 12, 4). About the Naos ran an uncovered court reserved to the priests. In front of the entrance to the holy place stood the altar of holocausts (Ex 27, 1-8). The lay Israelite might approach this altar only to bring his sacrifice to the priests (Mt 5, 23).

Outside this court of the priests, toward the east, was the court of the Israelites, where the laity could assist at the services. Beyond this was an outer court known as the court of the women, since to it women were admitted. This court was surrounded by rooms, one of which was the treasury with thirteen boxes for contributions (Lk 21, 1ff). To these courts only Jews were admitted, inscriptions warning non-Jews not to enter under pain of death (Acts 21, 28). By a staircase of fifteen steps one descended to the outer court which was known as that of the Gentiles. This outside court was surrounded by walls with high towers. The court of the Gentiles was open to all, and it was used for buying and selling (Mk 11, 15). Against the walls of this court on the interior were porches or colonnades where the people listened to religious teachers (Lk 2, 46; Mt 26, 55). The porch attached to the eastern wall was known as Solomon's (Jn 10, 23; Acts 3, 11; 5, 12). At its northwestern corner this court was adjacent to the fortress Antonia, whose garrison was ready to keep order among the crowds (Acts 21, 30ff). But the Jews had also their own temple police, with captains and officers, who patrolled the whole area day and night (Lk 22, 52; Acts 4, 1).

TIME. In Hebrew, *olam* designates a very long and indefinite period. In Greek, this word has been translated by two terms: "world" and "age" which are often taken for one another. Hence, one says: this world, the next world or the ages to come. In the plural, ages is practically equivalent to eternity (Mt 12, 32; Eph 2, 7).

TONGUES (SPEAK IN). Two passages of the New Testament speak of the *gift of tongues* (Acts 2 and 1 Cor 14). In the first, we find the mention of the miracle by which the apostles suddenly began to speak in tongues foreign to them — or by which their auditors each understand in their own language what the apostles said to them in the apostles' tongue. In the second, it is a case of a phenomenon that is difficult to describe and analyze: this was a manner of expressing oneself in inarticulate sounds or cries, proper to certain states of mystical exaltation.

TRUTH. This word, in Hebrew *emeth*, designates something firm and solid, hence something faithful. The adjective "true" signifies not only what is true and authentic but also what is the principle of this truth and this authenticity (Gn 32, 10; Ps 12, 1-2).

VULGATE. The official Latin translation of the Bible which was prepared almost entirely by St. Jerome from 382 to 405 A.D. Jerome borrowed heavily from Origen in translating the Psalter and took Ecclesiasticus, Baruch and both books of Maccabees from Old Latin texts. He translated everything else from the existing Hebrew, Aramaic or Greek manuscripts. The Council of Trent declared the Vulgate to be "authentic in public readings, disputations, preachings and exposition" because it conforms to the original texts and contains no errors in faith or morals. Since 1907 the Benedictine Order has, at the request of St. Pius X, been working on a revised edition of the modern Vulgate text to make it conform as closely as possible to the text of St. Jerome, and several parts have already been published.

YAHWEH. The proper personal name of the God of Israel, signifying, "I am who am" (Ex 3, 14-15). It is commonly explained in reference to God as the absolute and necessary Being. It may be understood of God as the Source of all created beings. Out of reverence for this name, the term *Adonai*, "my Lord," was later used as a substitute. The word Lord in the present version represents this traditional usage. The word "Jehovah" arose from a false reading of this name as it is written in the current Hebrew text. *See* **ADONAI. NAME.**

THE NEW 3 - YEAR CYCLE OF READINGS FOR SUNDAY MASS

Year A

1987 1993 1999 2005 2011
1990 1996 2002 2008 2014

GUIDE—
1- refers to Reading I
2- refers to Reading II
3- refers to Gospel

	Old Test.	New Test.
ADVENT SEASON		
1st Sunday of Advent		
1- Is 2, 1-5	826	
2- Rom 13, 11-14		238
3- Mt 24, 37-44		56
2nd Sunday of Advent		
1- Is 11, 1-10	836	
2- Rom 15, 4-9		239
3- Mt 3, 1-12		13
3rd Sunday of Advent		
1- Is 35, 1-6a. 10	858	
2- Jas 5, 7-10		361
3- Mt 11, 2-11		29
4th Sunday of Advent		
1- Is 7, 10-14	831	
2- Rom 1, 1-7		233
3- Mt 1, 18-24		11
CHRISTMAS SEASON		
Christmas Vigil		
1- Is 62, 1-5	887	
2- Acts 13, 16-17. 22-25		198
3- Mt 1, 1-25		11
Christmas (At Midnight)		
1- Is 9, 1-6	833	
2- Ti 2, 11-14		334
3- Lk 2, 1-14		100
Christmas (At Dawn)		
1- Is 62, 11-12	888	
2- Ti 3, 4-7		334
3- Lk 2, 15-20		101
Christmas (During the Day)		
1- Is 52, 7-10	878	
2- Heb 1, 1-6		339
3- Jn 1, 1-18		145
Sunday After Christmas (Holy Family)		
1- Sir 3, 2-6. 12-14	773	
2- Col 3, 12-21		312
3- Mt 13-15. 19-23		13
January 1 (Solemnity of Mary, Mother of God)		
1- Nm 6, 22-27	139	
2- Gal 4, 4-7		289
3- Lk 2, 16-21		101

	Old Test.	New Test.
2nd Sunday After Christmas		
1- Sir 24, 1-2. 8-12	793	
2- Eph 1, 3-6. 15-18		293
3- Jn 1, 1-18		145
Epiphany		
1- Is 60, 1-6	885	
2- Eph 3, 2-3a. 5-6		195
3- Mt 2, 1-12		14
Sunday After Epiphany (Baptism of the Lord)		
1- Is 42, 1-4. 6-7	886	
2- Acts 10, 34-38		195
3- Mt 3, 13-17		14
LENTEN SEASON		
Ash Wednesday		
1- Jl 2, 12-18	1055	
2- 2 Cor 5, 20—6, 2		272
3- Mt 6, 1-6. 16-18		18
1st Sunday of Lent		
1- Gn 2, 7-9; 3, 1-7	5	
2- Rom 5, 12-19		229
3- Mt 4, 1-11		14
2nd Sunday of Lent		
1- Gn 12, 1-4a	14	
2- 2 Tm 1, 8b-10		329
3- Mt 17, 1-9		39
3rd Sunday of Lent		
1- Ex 17, 3-7	75	
2- Rom 5, 1-2. 5-8		228
3- Jn 4, 5-42		150
4th Sunday of Lent		
1- 1 Sm 16, 1b. 6-7 10-13a	280	
2- Eph 5, 8-14		298
3- Jn 9, 1-41		160
5th Sunday of Lent		
1- Ez 37, 12-14	1008	
2- Rom 8, 8-11		231
3- Jn 11, 1-45		162
Passion Sunday (Palm Sunday)		
Procession: Mt 21, 1-11		46
1- Is 50, 4-7	876	
2- Phil 2, 6-11		303
3- Mt 26, 14—27, 66		59
EASTER TRIDUUM AND EASTER SEASON		
Holy Thursday		
Chrism Mass		
1- Is 61, 1-3a. 6a, 8b-9	886	
2- Rv 1, 5-8		387
3- Lk 4, 16-21		105

	Old Test.	New Test.
Mass of Lord's Supper		
1- Ex 12, 1-8. 11-14	69	
2- 1 Cor 11, 23-26		257
3- Jn 13, 1-15		166
Good Friday		
1- Is 52, 13—53, 12	879	
2- Heb 4, 14-16; 5, 7-9		342
3- Jn 18, 1—19, 42		172
Easter Vigil		
1- Gn 1, 1—2, 2	4	
Gn 22, 1-18	24	
Ex 14, 15—15, 1	72	
Is 54, 5-14	880	
Is 55, 1-11	880	
Bar 3, 9-15. 32—4, 4	966	
Ez 36, 16-28	1007	
2- Rom 6, 3-11		229
3- Mt 28, 1-10		65
Easter Sunday		
1- Acts 10, 34a. 37-43		195
2- Col 3, 1-4		311
or 1 Cor 5, 6b-8		248
3- Jn 20, 1-9		176
or Mt 28, 1-10		65
Evening: 3- Lk 24, 13-35		141
2nd Sunday of Easter		
1- Acts 2, 42-47		183
2- 1 Pt 1, 3-9		363
3- Jn 20, 19-31		177
3rd Sunday of Easter		
1- Acts 2, 14. 22-28		182
2- 1 Pt 1, 17-21		364
3- Lk 24, 13-35		124
4th Sunday of Easter		
1- Acts 2, 14a. 36-41		182
2- 1 Pt 2, 20b-25		365
3- Jn 10, 1-10		161
5th Sunday of Easter		
1- Acts 6, 1-7		188
2- 1 Pt 2, 4-9		364
3- Jn 14, 1-12		168
6th Sunday of Easter		
1- Acts 8, 5-8, 14-17		191
2- 1 Pt 3, 15-18		366
3- Jn 14, 15-21		168
Ascension of Our Lord		
1- Acts 1, 1-11		180
2- Eph 1, 17-23		294
3- Mt 28, 16-20		66

	Old Test.	New Test.
7th Sunday of Easter		
1- Acts 1, 12-14		181
2- 1 Pt 4, 13-16		367
3- Jn 17, 1-11a		171
Pentecost		
Vigil		
1- Gn 11, 1-9	13	
or Ex 19, 3-8a. 16-20b	77	
or Ex 37, 1-14	1007	
or Jl 3, 1-5	1056	
2- Rom 8, 22-27		232
3- Jn 7, 37-39		157
Mass of the Day		
1- Acts 2, 1-11		181
2- 1 Cor 12, 3b-7. 12-13		257
3- Jn 20, 19-23		177
SOLEMNITIES OF THE LORD DURING ORDINARY TIME		
Trinity Sunday (Sunday after Pentecost)		
1- Ex 34, 4b-6. 8-9	93	
2- 2 Cor 13, 11-13		282
3- Jn 3, 16-18		149
Corpus Christi		
1- Dt 8, 2-3. 14b-16a	183	
2- 1 Cor 10, 16-17		255
3- Jn 6, 51-58		155
Sacred Heart of Jesus		
1- Dt 7, 6-11	182	
2- 1 Jn 4, 7-16		377
3- Mt 11, 25-30		28
ORDINARY TIME		
1st Sunday		
(See Baptism of the Lord, above)		
2nd Sunday		
1- Is 49, 3. 5-6	874	
2- 1 Cor 1, 1-3		244
3- Jn 1, 29-34		146
3rd Sunday		
1- Is 8, 23b—9, 3	833	
2- 1 Cor 1, 10-13. 17		244
3- Mt 4, 12-23		15
4th Sunday		
1- Zep 2, 3; 3, 12-13	1085	
2- 1 Cor 1, 26-31		245
3- Mt 5, 1-12a		16
5th Sunday		
1- Is 58, 7-10	883	
2- 1 Cor 2, 1-5		245
3- Mt 5, 13-16		16
6th Sunday		
1- Sir 15, 15-20	784	
2- 1 Cor 2, 6-10		245
3- Mt 5, 17-37		17
7th Sunday		
1- Lv 19, 1-2. 17-18	119	
2- 1 Cor 3, 16-23		247
3- Mt 5, 38-48		18

	Old Test.	New Test.
8th Sunday		
1- Is 49, 14-15	875	
2- 1 Cor 4, 1-5		247
3- Mt 6, 24-34		20
9th Sunday		
1- Dt 11, 18. 26-28	186	
2- Rom 3, 21-25a. 28		226
3- Mt 7, 21-27		24
10th Sunday		
1- Hos 6, 3-6	1047	
2- Rom 4, 18-25		228
3- Mt 9, 9-13		24
11th Sunday		
1- Ex 19, 2-6a	77	
2- Rom 5, 6-11		228
3- Mt 9, 36—10, 8		25
12th Sunday		
1- Jer 20, 10-13	917	
2- Rom 5, 12-15		229
3- Mt 10, 26-33		26
13th Sunday		
1- 2 Kgs 4, 8-11. 14-16a	354	
2- Rom 6, 3-4. 8-11		229
3- Mt 10, 37-42		27
14th Sunday		
1- Zec 9, 9-10	1095	
2- Rom 8, 9. 11-13		231
3- Mt 11, 25-30		28
15th Sunday		
1- Is 55, 10-11	881	
2- Rom 8, 18-23		231
3- Mt 13, 1-23		31
16th Sunday		
1- Wis 12, 13. 16-19	761	
2- Rom 8, 26-27		232
3- Mt 13, 24-43		32
17th Sunday		
1- 1 Kgs 3, 5. 7-12	326	
2- Rom 8, 28-30		232
3- Mt 13, 44-52		33
18th Sunday		
1- Is 55, 1-3	880	
2- Rom 8, 35. 37-39		232
3- Mt 14, 13-21		34
19th Sunday		
1- 1 Kgs 19, 9a. 11-13a	345	
2- Rom 9, 1-5		233
3- Mt 14, 22-33		35
20th Sunday		
1- Is 56, 1. 6-7	881	
2- Rom 11, 13-14. 29-32		236
3- Mt 15, 21-28		36
21st Sunday		
1- Is 22, 19-23	845	
2- Rom 11, 33-36		237
3- Mt 16, 13-20		37

	Old Test.	New Test.
22nd Sunday		
1- Jer 20, 7-9	916	
2- Rom 12, 1-2		237
3- Mt 16, 21-27		38
23rd Sunday		
1- Ez 33, 7-9	1003	
2- Rom 13, 8-10		238
3- Mt 18, 15-20		42
24th Sunday		
1- Sir 27, 30—28, 7	797	
2- Rom 14, 7-8		239
3- Mt 18, 21-35		42
25th Sunday		
1- Is 55, 6-9	881	
2- Phil 1, 20c-24. 27a		303
3- Mt 20, 1-16a		45
26th Sunday		
1- Ez 18, 25-28	987	
2- Phil 2, 1-11		303
3- Mt 21, 28-32		48
27th Sunday		
1- Is 5, 1-7	829	
2- Phil 4, 6-9		306
3- Mt 21, 33-43		49
28th Sunday		
1- Is 25, 6-10a	848	
2- Phil 4, 12-14. 19-20		307
3- Mt 22, 1-14		49
29th Sunday		
1- Is 45, 1. 4-6	870	
2- 1 Thes 1, 1-5b		314
3- Mt 22, 15-21		50
30th Sunday		
1- Ex 22, 20-26	81	
2- 1 Thes 1, 5c-10		314
3- Mt 22, 34-40		51
31st Sunday		
1- Mal 1, 14b—2, 2b. 8-10	1100	
2- 1 Thes 2, 7b-9, 13		314
3- Mt 23; 1-12		52
32nd Sunday		
1- Wis 6, 12-16	754	
2- 1 Thes 4, 13-18		316
3- Mt 25, 1-13		57
33rd Sunday		
1- Prv 31, 10-13. 19-20. 30-31	733	
2- 1 Thes 5, 1-6		316
3- Mt 25, 14-30		57
34th Sunday (Christ the King)		
1- Ez 34, 11-12. 15-17	1005	
2- 1 Cor 15, 20-26. 28		261
3- Mt 25, 31-46		58

Year B

1988 1994 2000 2006 2012
1991 1997 2003 2009 2015

GUIDE—
1- refers to Reading I
2- refers to Reading II
3- refers to Gospel

	Old Test.	New Test.
ADVENT SEASON		
1st Sunday of Advent		
1- Is 63, 16b-17. 19b; 64, 2b-7	889	
2- 1 Cor 1, 3-9		244
3- Mk 13, 33-37		89
2nd Sunday of Advent		
1- Is 40, 1-5. 9-11	863	
2- 2 Pt 3, 8-14		372
3- Mk 1, 1-8		69
3rd Sunday of Advent		
1- Is 61, 1-2a. 10-11	886	
2- 1 Thes 5, 16-24		317
3- Jn 1, 6-8. 19-28		145
4th Sunday of Advent		
1- 2 Sm 7, 1-5. 8b-11. 16	301	
2- Rom 16, 25-27		242
3- Lk 1, 26-38		98
CHRISTMAS SEASON		
Christmas Vigil		
1- Is 62, 1-5	887	
2- Acts 13, 16-17. 22-25		198
3- Mt 1, 1-25		11
Christmas (At Midnight)		
1- Is 9, 1-6	833	
2- Ti 2, 11-14		334
3- Lk 2, 1-14		100
Christmas (At Dawn)		
1- Is 62, 11-12	888	
2- Ti 3, 4-7		334
3- Lk 2, 15-20		101
Christmas (During the Day)		
1- Is 52, 7-10	878	
2- Heb 1, 1-6		339
3- Jn 1, 1-18		145
Sunday After Christmas (Holy Family)		
1- Sir 3, 2-6. 12-14	773	
2- Col 3, 12-21		312
3- Lk 2, 22-40		101
January 1 (Solemnity of Mary, Mother of God)		
1- Nm 6, 22-27	139	
2- Gal 4, 4-7		289
3- Lk 2, 16-21		101
2nd Sunday After Christmas		
1- Sir 24, 1-2. 8-12	793	
2- Eph 1, 3-6. 15-18		293
3- Jn 1, 1-18		145

	Old Test.	New Test.
Epiphany		
1- Is 60, 1-6	885	
2- Eph 3, 2-3a. 5-6		295
3- Mt 2, 1-12		12
Sunday After Epiphany (Baptism of the Lord)		
1- Is 42, 1-4. 6-7	866	
2- Acts 10, 34-38		195
3- Mk 1, 6b-11		69
LENTEN SEASON		
Ash Wednesday		
1- Jl 2, 12-18	1055	
2- 2 Cor 5, 20—6, 2		272
3- Mt 6, 1-6. 16-18		18
1st Sunday of Lent		
1- Gn 9, 8-15	11	
2- 1 Pt 3, 18-22		366
3- Mk 1, 12-15		70
2nd Sunday of Lent		
1- Gn 22, 1-2. 9a. 10-13. 15-18	24	
2- Rom 8, 31b-34		232
3- Mk 9, 2-10		82
3rd Sunday of Lent		
1- Ex 20, 1-17	78	
2- 1 Cor 1, 22-25		245
3- Jn 2, 13-25		148
4th Sunday of Lent		
1- 2 Chr 36, 14-16. 19-23	443	
2- Eph 2, 4-10		295
3- Jn 3, 14-21		149
5th Sunday of Lent		
1- Jer 31, 31-34	930	
2- Heb 5, 7-9		343
3- Jn 12, 20-33		165
Passion Sunday (Palm Sunday)		
Procession: Mk 11, 1-10		85
or Jn 12, 12-16		165
1- Is 50, 4-7	876	
2- Phil 2, 6-11		303
3- Mk 14, 1—15, 47		89
EASTER TRIDUUM AND EASTER SEASON		
Holy Thursday Chrism Mass		
1- Is 61, 1-3a. 6a. 8b-9	886	
2- Rv 1, 5-8		387
3- Lk 4, 16-21		105
Mass of Lord's Supper		
1- Ex 12, 1-8. 11-14	69	
2- 1 Cor 11, 23-26		257
3- Jn 13, 1-15		166

	Old Test.	New Test.
Good Friday		
1- Is 52, 13—53, 12	879	
2- Heb 4, 14-16. 5, 7-9		342
3- Jn 18, 1—19, 42		172
Easter Vigil		
1- Gn 1, 1—2, 2	4	
Gn 22, 1-18	24	
Ex 14, 15—15, 1	72	
Is 54, 5-14	880	
Is 55, 1-11	880	
Bar 3, 9-15. 32—4, 4	966	
Ez 36, 16-28	1007	
2- Rom 6, 3-11		229
3- Mk 16, 1-8		64
Easter Sunday		
1- Acts 10, 34a. 37-43		195
2- Col 3, 1-4		311
or 1 Col 5, 6b-8		248
3- Jn 20, 1-9		176
or Mk 16, 1-8		93
Evening: 3- Lk 24, 13-35		141
2nd Sunday of Easter		
1- Acts 4, 32-35		186
2- 1 Jn 5, 1-6		378
3- Jn 20, 19-31		177
3rd Sunday of Easter		
1- Acts 3, 13-15. 17-19		184
2- 1 Jn 2, 1-5a		375
3- Lk 24, 35-48		142
4th Sunday of Easter		
1- Acts 4, 8-12		185
2- 1 Jn 3, 1-2		376
3- Jn 10, 11-18		161
5th Sunday of Easter		
1- Acts 9, 26-31		193
2- 1 Jn 3, 18-24		377
3- Jn 15, 1-8		169
6th Sunday of Easter		
1- Acts 10, 25-26. 34-35. 44-48		195
2- 1 Jn 4, 7-10		377
3- Jn 15, 9-17		169
Ascension of Our Lord		
1- Acts 1, 1-11		180
2- Eph 1, 17-23		294
3- Mk 16, 15-20		94
7th Sunday of Easter		
1- Acts 1, 15-17. 20a. 20c-26		181
2- 1 Jn 4, 11-16		377
3- Jn 17, 11b-19		172

	Old Test.	New Test.
Pentecost		
Vigil		
1- Gn 11, 1-9	13	
or Ex 19, 3-a. 16-20b	77	
or Ez 37, 1-14	1007	
or Jl 3, 1-5	1056	
2- Rom 8, 22-27		232
3- Jn 7, 37-39		157
Mass of the Day		
1- Acts 2, 1-11		181
2- 1 Cor 12, 3b-7. 12-13		257
3- Jn 20, 19-23		177
SOLEMNITIES OF THE LORD DURING ORDINARY TIME		
Trinity Sunday (Sunday after Pentecost)		
1- Dt 4, 32-34. 39-40	179	
2- Rom 8, 14-17		232
3- Mt 28, 16-20		66
Corpus Christi		
1- Ex 24, 3-8	82	
2- Heb 9, 11-15		347
3- Mk 14, 12-16. 22-26		90
Sacred Heart of Jesus		
1- Hos 11, 1. 3-4. 8c-9	1051	
2- Eph 3, 8-12. 14-19		296
3- Jn 19, 31-37		175
ORDINARY TIME		
1st Sunday		
(See Baptism of the Lord, above)		
2nd Sunday		
1- 1 Sm 3, 3b-10. 19	267	
2- 1 Cor 6, 13c-15a. 17-20		249
3- Jn 1, 35-42		146
3rd Sunday		
1- Jon 3, 1-5. 10	1070	
2- 1 Cor 7, 29-31		251
3- Mk 1, 14-20		70
4th Sunday		
1- Dt 18, 15-20	193	
2- 1 Cor 7, 32-35		251
3- Mk 1, 21-28		70
5th Sunday		
1- Jb 7, 1-4. 6-7	575	
2- 1 Cor 9, 16-19. 22-23		253
3- Mk 1, 29-39		70
6th Sunday		
1- Lv 13, 1-2. 45-46	111	
2- 1 Cor 10, 31—11, 1		255
3- Mk 1, 40-45		71
7th Sunday		
1- Is 43, 18-19. 21-22. 24b-25	868	
2- 2 Cor 1, 18-22		267
3- Mk 2, 1-12		71
8th Sunday		
1- Hos 2, 16b. 17b. 21-22	1043	
2- 2 Cor 3, 1b-6		267
3- Mk 2, 18-22		72
9th Sunday		
1- Dt 5, 12-15	180	
2- 2 Cor 4, 6-11		270
3- Mk 2, 23—3, 6		72
10th Sunday		
1- Gn 3, 9-15	6	
2- 2 Cor 4, 13—5, 1		271
3- Mk 3, 20-35		73
11th Sunday		
1- Ez 17, 22-24	986	
2- 2 Cor 5, 6-10		272
3- Mk 4, 26-34		74
12th Sunday		
1- Jb 38, 1. 8-11	598	
2- 2 Cor 5, 14-17		272
3- Mk 4, 35-41		75
13th Sunday		
1- Wis 1, 13-15; 2, 23-24	751	
2- 2 Cor 8, 7. 9. 13-15		275
3- Mk 5, 21-43		76
14th Sunday		
1- Ez 2, 2-5	973	
2- 2 Cor 12, 7-10		280
3- Mk 6, 1-6		76
15th Sunday		
1- Am 7, 12-15	1064	
2- Eph 1, 3-14		293
3- Mk 6, 7-13		77
16th Sunday		
1- Jer 23, 1-6	919	
2- Eph 2, 13-18		295
3- Mk 6, 30-34		78
17th Sunday		
1- 2 Kgs 4, 42-44	355	
2- Eph 4, 1-6		296
3- Jn 6, 1-15		153
18th Sunday		
1- Ex 16, 2-4. 12-15	74	
2- Eph 4, 17. 20-24		297
3- Jn 6, 24-35		154
19th Sunday		
1- 1 Kgs 19, 4-8	345	
2- Eph 4, 30—5, 2		297
3- Jn 6, 41-45		155
20th Sunday		
1- Prv 9, 1-6	709	
2- Eph 5, 15-20		298
3- Jn 6, 51-58		155
21st Sunday		
1- Jos 24, 1-2a. 15-17. 18b	234	
2- Eph 5, 21-32		298
3- Jn 6, 60-69		155
22nd Sunday		
1- Dt 4, 1-2. 6-8	178	
2- Jas 1, 17-18. 21b-22. 27		358
3- Mk 7, 1-8. 14-15. 21-23		79
23rd Sunday		
1- Is 35, 4-7a	857	
2- Jas 2, 1-5		358
3- Mk 7, 31-37		80
24th Sunday		
1- Is 50, 5-9a	876	
2- Jas 2, 14-18		359
3- Mk 8, 27-35		81
25th Sunday		
1- Wis 2, 12. 17-20	751	
2- Jas 3, 16—4, 3		360
3- Mk 9, 30-37		83
26th Sunday		
1- Nm 11, 25-29	145	
2- Jas 5, 1-6		361
3- Mk 9, 38-43. 45. 47-48		83
27th Sunday		
1- Gn 2, 18-24	5	
2- Heb 2, 9-11		340
3- Mk 10, 2-16		84
28th Sunday		
1- Wis 7, 7-11	756	
2- Heb 4, 12-13		342
3- Mk 10, 17-30		84
29th Sunday		
1- Is 53, 10-11	879	
2- Heb 4, 14-16		342
3- Mk 10, 35-43		85
30th Sunday		
1- Jer 31, 7-9	929	
2- Heb 5, 1-6		342
3- Mk 10, 46-53		85
31st Sunday		
1- Dt 6, 2-6	181	
2- Heb 7, 23-28		345
3- Mk 12, 28b-34		87
32nd Sunday		
1- 1 Kgs 17, 10-16	343	
2- Heb 9, 24-28		348
3- Mk 12, 38-44		88
33rd Sunday		
1- Dn 12, 1-3	1038	
2- Heb 10, 11-14. 18		349
3- Mk 13, 24-32		89
34th Sunday (Christ the King)		
1- Dn 7, 13-14	1032	
2- Rv 1, 5-8		387
3- Jn 18, 33b-37		173

Year C

1989 1995 2001 2007 2013
1992 1998 2004 2010 2016

GUIDE—
1- refers to Reading I
2- refers to Reading II
3- refers to Gospel

	Old Test.	New Test.
ADVENT SEASON		
1st Sunday of Advent		
1- Jer 33, 14-16	933	
2- 1 Thes 3, 12—4, 2		315
3- Lk 21, 25-28. 34-36		136
2nd Sunday of Advent		
1- Bar 5, 1-9	969	
2- Phil 1, 4-6. 8-11		302
3- Lk 3, 1-6		102
3rd Sunday of Advent		
1- Zep 3, 14-18a	1087	
2- Phil 4, 4-7		306
3- Lk 3, 10-18		103
4th Sunday of Advent		
1- Mi 5, 1-4a	1074	
2- Heb 10, 5-10		349
3- Lk 1, 39-45		98
CHRISTMAS SEASON		
Christmas Vigil		
1- Is 62, 1-6	887	
2- Acts 13, 16-17. 22-25		198
3- Mt 1, 1-25		11
Christmas (At Midnight)		
1- Is 9, 1-6	833	
2- Ti 2, 11-14		334
3- Lk 2, 1-14		100
Christmas (At Dawn)		
1- Is 62, 11-12	888	
2- Ti 3, 4-7		334
3- Lk 2, 15-20		101
Christmas (During the Day)		
1- Is 57, 7-10	878	
2- Heb 1, 1-6		339
3- Jn 1, 1-18		145
Sunday After Christmas (Holy Family)		
1- Sir 3, 2-6. 12-14	773	
2- Col 3, 12-21		312
3- Lk 2, 41-52		102
January 1 (Solemnity of Mary, Mother of God)		
1- Nm 6, 22-27	139	
2- Gal 4, 4-7		289
3- Lk 2, 16-21		101
2nd Sunday After Christmas		
1- Sir 24, 1-2. 8-12	793	
2- Eph 1, 3-6. 15-18		293
3- Jn 1, 1-18		145
Epiphany		
1- Is 60, 1-6	885	
2- Eph 3, 2-3a. 5-6		295
3- Mt 2, 1-12		12
Sunday After Epiphany (Baptism of the Lord)		
1- Is 42, 1-4. 6-7	866	
2- Acts 10, 34-38		195
3- Lk 3, 15-16. 21-22		103
LENTEN SEASON		
Ash Wednesday		
1- Jl 2, 12-18	1055	
2- 2 Cor 5, 20—6, 2		272
3- Mt 6, 1-6. 16-18		18
1st Sunday of Lent		
1- Dt 26, 4-10	200	
2- Rom 10, 8-13		235
3- Lk 4, 1-13		104
2nd Sunday of Lent		
1- Gn 15, 5-12. 17-18	17	
2- Phil 3, 17—4, 1		306
3- Lk 9, 28b-36		116
3rd Sunday of Lent		
1- Ex 3, 1-8a. 13-15	60	
2- 1 Cor 10, 1-6. 10-12		254
3- Lk 13, 1-9		123
4th Sunday of Lent		
1- Jos 5, 9a. 10-12	216	
2- 2 Cor 5, 17-21		272
3- Lk 15, 1-3. 11-32		126
5th Sunday of Lent		
1- Is 43, 16-21	868	
2- Phil 3, 8-14		305
3- Jn 8, 1-11		157
Passion Sunday (Palm Sunday)		
Procession: Lk 19, 28-40		132
1- Is 50, 4-7	876	
2- Phil 2, 6-11		303
3- Lk 22, 14—23, 56		137
EASTER TRIDUUM AND EASTER SEASON		
Holy Thursday		
Chrism Mass		
1- Is 61, 1-3a. 6a. 8b-9	886	
2- Rv 1, 5-8		387
3- Lk 4, 16-21		105
Mass of Lord's Supper		
1- Ex 12, 1-8. 11-14	69	
2- 1 Cor 11, 23-26		257
3- Jn 13, 1-15		166
Good Friday		
1- Is 52, 13—53, 12	879	
2- Heb 4, 14-16; 5, 7-9		342
3- Jn 18, 1—19, 42		172
Easter Vigil		
1- Gn 1, 1—2, 2	4	
Gn 22, 1-18	24	
Ex 14, 15—15, 1	72	
Is 54, 5-14	880	
Is 55, 1-11	880	
Bar 3, 9-15. 32—4, 4	966	
Ez 36, 16-28	1007	
2- Rom 6, 3-11		229
3- Lk 24, 1-12		140
Easter Sunday		
1- Acts 10, 34a. 37-43		195
2- Col 3, 1-4		311
or 1 Cor 5, 6b-8		248
3- Jn 20, 1-9		176
or Lk 24, 1-12		140
Evening: 3- Lk 24, 13-35		141
2nd Sunday of Easter		
1- Acts 5, 12-16		186
2- Rv 1, 9-11a. 12-13. 17-19		387
3- Jn 20, 19-31		177
3rd Sunday of Easter		
1- Acts 5, 27b-32. 40b-41		187
2- Rv 5, 11-14		392
3- Jn 21, 1-19		177
4th Sunday of Easter		
1- Acts 13, 14. 43-52		198
2- Rv 7, 9. 14b-17		394
3- Jn 10, 27-30		162
5th Sunday of Easter		
1- Acts 14, 21-27		198
2- Rv 21, 1-5a		407
3- Jn 13, 31-33a. 34-35		167
6th Sunday of Easter		
1- Acts 15, 1-2. 22-29		201
2- Rv 21, 10-14. 22-23		407
3- Jn 14, 23-29		169
Ascension of the Lord		
1- Acts 1, 1-11		180
2- Eph 1, 17-23		294
3- Lk 24, 46-53		142
7th Sunday of Easter		
1- Acts 7, 55-60		190
2- Rv 22, 12-14. 16-17. 20		409
3- Jn 17, 20-26		172
Pentecost		
Vigil		
1- Gn 11, 1-9	13	
or Ex 19, 3-8a. 16-20b	77	
or Ez 37, 1-14	1007	
or Jl 3, 1-5	1056	
2- Rom 8, 22-27		232
3- Jn 7, 37-39		157
Mass of the Day		
1- Acts 2, 1-11		181
2- 1 Cor 12, 3b-7. 12-13		257
3- Jn 20, 19-23		177

	Old Test.	New Test.
SOLEMNITIES OF THE LORD DURING ORDINARY TIME		
Trinity Sunday (Sunday After Pentecost)		
1- Prv 8, 22-31	709	
2- Rom 5, 1-5		228
3- Jn 16, 12-15		170
Corpus Christi		
1- Gn 14, 18-20	17	
2- 1 Cor 11, 23-26		257
3- Lk 9, 11b-17		115
Sacred Heart of Jesus		
1- Ez 34, 11-16	1005	
2- Rom 5, 5-11		228
3- Lk 15, 3-7		126
ORDINARY TIME		
1st Sunday		
(See Baptism of the Lord, above)		
2nd Sunday		
1- Is 62, 1-5	887	
2- 1 Cor 12, 4-11		257
3- Jn 2, 1-12		147
3rd Sunday		
1- Neh 8, 1-4a. 5-6. 8-10	462	
2- 1 Cor 12, 12-30		258
3- Lk 1, 1-4; 4, 14-21		97
4th Sunday		
1- Jer 1, 4-5. 17-19	893	
2- 1 Cor 12. 31—13, 13		258
3- Lk 4, 21-30		105
5th Sunday		
1- Is 6, 1-2a. 3-8	830	
2- 1 Cor 15, 1-11		261
3- Lk 5, 1-11		106
6th Sunday		
1- Jer 17, 5-8	913	
2- 1 Cor 15, 12. 16-20		261
3- Lk 6, 17. 20-26		109
7th Sunday		
1- 1 Sm 26, 2. 7-9. 12-13. 22-23	291	
2- 1 Cor 15, 45-49		263
3- Lk 6, 27-38		109
8th Sunday		
1- Sir 27, 4-7	796	
2- 1 Cor 15, 54-58		263
3- Lk 6, 39-45		110
9th Sunday		
1- 1 Kgs 8, 41-43	333	
2- Gal 1, 1-2. 6-10		284
3- Lk 7, 1-10		110
10th Sunday		
1- 1 Kgs 17, 17-24	344	
2- Gal 1, 11-19		285
3- Lk 7, 11-17		110
11th Sunday		
1- 2 Sm 12, 7-10. 13	305	
2- Gal 2, 16. 19-21		286
3- Lk 7, 36—8, 3		111
12th Sunday		
1- Zec 12, 10-11	1097	
2- Gal 3, 26-29		288
3- Lk 9, 18-24		115
13th Sunday		
1- 1 Kgs 19, 16b. 19-21	346	
2- Gal 5, 1. 13-18		290
3- Lk 9, 51-62		117
14th Sunday		
1- Is 66, 10-14c	891	
2- Gal 6, 14-18		292
3- Lk 10, 1-12. 17-20		117
15th Sunday		
1- Dt 30, 10-14	205	
2- Col 1, 15-20		309
3- Lk 10, 25-37		118
16th Sunday		
1- Gn 18, 1-10a.	19	
2- Col 1, 24-28		310
3- Lk 10, 38-42		119
17th Sunday		
1- Gn 18, 20-32	20	
2- Col 2, 12-14		311
3- Lk 11, 1-13		119
18th Sunday		
1- Eccl 1, 2; 2, 21-23	734	
2- Col 3, 1-5. 9-11		311
3- Lk 12, 13-31		122
19th Sunday		
1- Wis 18, 6-9	768	
2- Heb 11, 1-2. 8-19		351
3- Lk 12, 32-48		122
20th Sunday		
1- Jer 38, 4-6. 8-10	938	
2- Heb 12, 1-4		352
3- Lk 12, 49-53		123
21st Sunday		
1 Is 66, 18-21	892	
2- Heb 12, 5-7. 11-13		353
3- Lk 13, 22-30		124
22nd Sunday		
1- Sir 3, 17-18. 20. 28-29	794	
2- Heb 12, 18-19. 22-24a		353
3- Lk 14, 1. 7-14		125
23rd Sunday		
1- Wis 9, 13-18b	758	
2- Phlm 9b-10. 12-17		336
3- Lk 14, 25-33		126
24th Sunday		
1- Ex 32, 7-11. 13-14	91	
2- 1 Tm 1, 12-17		323
3- Lk 15, 1-32		126
25th Sunday		
1- Am 8, 4-7	1065	
2- 1 Tm 2, 1-8		323
3- Lk 16, 1-13		127
26th Sunday		
1- Am 6, 1a. 4-7	1063	
2- 1 Tm 6, 11-16		327
3- Lk 16, 19-31		128
27th Sunday		
1- Hb 1, 2-3; 2, 2-4	1081	
2- 2 Tm 1, 6-8. 13-14		329
3- Lk 17, 5-10		129
28th Sunday		
1- 2 Kgs 5, 14-17	356	
2- 2 Tm 2, 8-13		330
3- Lk 17, 11-19		129
29th Sunday		
1- Ex 17, 8-13	76	
2- 2 Tm 3, 14—4, 2		331
3- Lk 18, 1-8		130
30th Sunday		
1- Sir 35, 12-14. 16-18	805	
2- 2 Tm 4, 6-8. 16-18		331
3- Lk 18, 9-14		130
31st Sunday		
1- Wis 11, 23—12, 2	761	
2- 2 Thes 1, 11—2, 2		319
3- Lk 19, 1-10		131
32nd Sunday		
1- 2 Mc 7, 1-2. 9-14	555	
2- 2 Thes 2, 16—3, 5		320
3- Lk 20, 27-38		134
33rd Sunday		
1- Mal 3, 19-20a	1103	
2- 2 Thes 3, 7-12		320
3- Lk 21, 5-19		135
34th Sunday (Christ the King)		
1- 2 Sm 5, 1-3	300	
2- Col 1, 12-20		309
3- Lk 23, 35-43		140

DOCTRINAL BIBLE INDEX

Other subjects will be found in the Bible Dictionary, pp. 412ff. The cross references to the passages cited below should also be consulted.

— D —

— E —

— Q —

— R —

— S —

Answers

Chapter 1

1.1 (a) The 22,000 physicians, the randomization, and the plan to obtain percentages of each group that have heart attacks **(b)** The actual percentages of each group who have heart attacks **(c)** The generalization that aspirin reduces the risk of having a heart attack **1.3** 64.6%; 20.8%; 8.7%; 5.9% **1.5** Responses will differ for each student **1.7 (a)** The 3,077 people who responded **(b)** All adults in the United States **(c)** 23% said antireligious books should be removed. **1.9 (a)** Each student in the program **(b)** The students identified **(c)** All students in the program **1.11 (a)** Descriptive statistics; they summarize data from a population. **(b)** Parameter, since they refer to a population. **1.13 (a)** Very short bars toward the top indicate very few old men and women in 1750. **(b)** Bars are much longer for both men and women in 2010 than in 1750. **(c)** The bars for women in their 70s and 80s in 2010 are longer than those for men. **(d)** From the graph, the longest bars are associated with the 45–49 age group. **1.15 (a)** Yes, the populations are the same in the two studies. For both, it's all students at your school. **(b)** It is *very* unlikely that you will choose the same 20 students. **(c)** Although it is most likely that the sample proportions will not be the same, they should be close to each other. **1.17 (a)** $1/\sqrt{n} \times 100\% = 1/\sqrt{1000} \times 100\% = 1/32 \times 100\% = 0.032 \times 100\% = 3.2\%$ **(b)** The first four polls are all within the margin of error; however, Rand favored Obama slightly, and Fox underestimated Obama's margin. Generally, the polls are fairly accurate. **1.19 (a)** iii **(b)** Yes. Because the employees were assigned to treatments randomly, the study provides us with convincing evidence that the difference was due to the effect of the financial incentive.

1.21

Customer	Clothes	Sporting Goods	Books	Music
1	$49	$0	$0	$16
2	$0	$0	$0	$0
3	$0	$0	$0	$0
4	$0	$0	$92	$0
5	$0	$0	$0	$0

1.23 For example, MINITAB data (from Exercise 1.21) will be in the following format, although it will reside in the cells of the MINITAB worksheet.

Customers	Clothes	Sporting Goods	Books	Music
1	49	0	0	16
2	0	0	0	0
3	0	0	0	0
4	0	0	92	0
5	0	0	0	0

1.25 (a) Answers will vary. **(b)** The amounts by which sample percentages tend to vary get smaller as the sample size n gets larger. **(c)** Larger sample sizes tend to provide more accurate estimates of the true population percentage value. **1.27** The answer to this problem is based on a random process. This leads to potentially different answers each time it is performed. The binomial distribution (see Section 6.3) says that 14 or fewer people who died should occur in only about 1 in 100 simulations, so most students will likely not see any of these situations. **1.29 (a)** All American adults **(b)** The sample data are summarized by a proportion, 0.598. **(c)** The population proportion who would commit suicide. **1.31 (a)** sample data; **(b)** percentages reported; **(c)** reporting margin of error for sample percentage **1.33 (a)** Population: all customers; Sample: 1000 customers **(b)** Descriptive: average sales per person in sample; Inferential: estimate of average sales per person in population. **1.35** (c) **1.37** Will be different for each student. **1.39** The likelihood of getting this result is extremely small.

Chapter 2

2.1 (a) Categorical: observations belong to one of a set of categories. Quantitative: observations are numerical. **(b)** Examples will differ for each student. **2.3 (a)** Quantitative. **(b)** Categorical. **(c)** Categorical. **(d)** Quantitative. **2.5 (a)** Discrete: possible values are separate numbers, such as 0, 1, 2,.... Continuous: possible values form an interval. **(b)** Examples will differ for each student. **2.7 (a)** Continuous. **(b)** Discrete. **(c)** Discrete. **(d)** Continuous. **2.9 (a)** The percentages for each of the categories are 3.2, 3.2, 6.3, 23.8, 20.6, 9.5, 6.3, 9.5, and 17.5. **(b)** Australia **(c)** Regions with most frequent fatal shark attacks are Australia and South Africa **2.11 (a)** Categorical. **(b)** "Fish." **(c)** Approximately 43%. **(d)** Pareto chart. **2.13 (a)** Categorical. **(b)** Pareto chart. **(c)** Neither. These graphs are not for categorical data. **2.15 (a)** Minimum 0 g, maximum = 18 g. **(b)** 3, 4, 11, 12, and 14 each occur twice; these values are modes. **2.17 (a)** 33; minimum = 65; maximum = 98. **2.19 (a)** smallest 0 g, largest 18 g **(b)** 10 g, 11 g, 11 g **(c)** 6 **2.21 (a)** Skewed to the right because of some very expensive homes. **(b)** Skewed to the right because of the few faculty who overdraw frequently. **(c)** Symmetric because most would be in the middle, with some higher and some lower. **(d)** Symmetric because most would fall in the middle, with some higher and some lower. **2.23 (b)** elephant with a gestational period of 624 days **(c)** right-skewed **(d)** Neither of the two histograms accurately summarizes the distribution. One is too coarse, the other too fine. **2.25 (a)** The distribution is slightly right-skewed (or roughly symmetric). Most blossoms have a width between 3.2 and 3.6 in. There is one blossom with an unusually small width for that species of less than 2.4 in. **(b)** Left-skewed. Most blossoms have a width between 2.8 and 3.2 in. **(c)** 90% **(d)** No. We don't know how many blossoms in the interval from 2.8 to 3.2 in. are actually wider than 3 in. **2.27 (a)** After an initial slight increase, there was a sharp and steady decrease in incidence of whooping cough starting around 1940. The decrease leveled off starting around 1960. Yes. **(b)** Incidence rate stayed low until about 2000, after which a sharp increase can be observed. No. Potential reasons: Fewer people decide to get vaccinated, less efficient vaccination. **(c)** No. **2.29 (a)** Median (right-skewed) **(b)** Median (left-skewed) **(c)** Mean (symmetric) **2.31 (a)** mean = 2.07, median = 1 **(b)** Comparing absolute emission values for nations with different population sizes might be misleading because nations with larger populations tend to have larger total emissions. When viewed per capita, a different picture might emerge. **2.33** Skewed to the right (for both) because mean is much larger than median **2.35** The moderate skewness to the left causes the mean to be lower than the median. **2.37 (a)** Mean: 2; median: 0; and mode: 0 **(b)** Mean: 10; median: 0. Outlier affects mean but not median. **2.39** The high salaries for a few top players **2.41 (a)** 1.7. **(b)** 1.65. **(c)** The mean need not take one of the possible values for the variable. Although the number of children born to each adult woman is a whole number, the mean number of children born per adult woman need not be a whole number. **2.43 (a)** Women: median = 0, mean = $(7350 \times 0 + 2587 \times 1 + 80 \times 2)/10017 = 0.274$, Men: median = 0, mean = 0.161 **(b)** Using the medians, it seems that there is no difference. Using the mean, in this age group, women have, on average, been married more often. **2.45** Because so many people would report 0 motor accidents, the median is not very useful. **2.47 (a)** Africa, since life expectancies vary much more than for Europe, where all values are very similar. **(b)** Western Europe: $s = 1.05$; Africa: $s = 5.18$ **2.49** $60,000. Not −$15,000 because a standard deviation cannot be negative, $1,000 is too small for a typical deviation and $1,000,000 is too large. **2.51 (a)** 68% of men would be between 68 and 74 inches, 95% of men would be between 65 and 77 inches, all or nearly all men would be between 62 and 80 inches. **(b)** The mean for women is lower than the mean for men. Because each gender's heights would tend to be closer to that gender's mean than to the overall mean, the standard deviation would be smaller when we compared them with the appropriate gender group than when we compared them to the overall group. Would not expect unimodal but more bimodal. **2.53** 68% of women would be able to lift between 66.6 and 93.2 pounds, 95% of women would be able to lift between 53.3 and 106.5 pounds, all or nearly all women would be able to lift between 40.0 and 119.8 pounds. **2.55** Since the lowest possible value is only 1.52 standard deviations below the mean, the distribution likely is skewed to the right. **2.57** Skewed to the right because mean is larger than median. The standard deviation is almost as large as the mean, which indicates right skewness here because the lowest possible value of 0 is only just over one standard deviation below mean. **2.59** Skewed to the left. **2.61 (a)** One possibility: 30, 50, 80. **(b)** One possibility: 10, 50, 90. **(c)** two 0s and two 100s, with s = 57.74. **2.63 (a)** In 2013, half of the European Union nations had an unemployment rate less than 10.15%. **(b)** In 2013, 75% of the European Union nations had an unemployment rate larger than 7.15% (or 25% had rate less than 7.15%). **(c)** In 2013, the unemployment rate was larger than 13.05% for 25% of the European Union nations. **(d)** Around 6% because Q1 = 7.15% **2.65 (a)** One quarter had weight below 119 and one quarter had weight above 144. **(b)** Mean ≈ median and the first and third quartiles are approximately equidistant from the median. Roughly symmetric distribution. **2.67 (a) (i)** 75%; **(ii)** 25%. **(b)** 36 cents and 100 cents (i.e., one dollar). **(c)** IQR = 64 cents. **(d)** No. Q1 and Q3 are not roughly equidistant from the median and the maximum value is also quite far from Q3. Distribution is skewed to the right. **2.69 (a)** Q1 = 76; Q3 = 101. **(b)** IQR = 25. **2.71 (a)** Skewed to the right because of the distance between the minimum and the median. **(b)** Outliers would be those values more than 1273.5 kilobytes from the first and third quartiles; 320,000 is a potential outlier. **2.73** The minimum, Q1, median, Q3, and maximum are used in the box plot. **2.75 (a)** Min = 50, Q1 = 130, median = 160, Q3 = 250, Max = 665 **(b)** $z = -0.47$. Italy's consumption is 0.47 standard deviations below the mean of 195. **(c)** $z = 1.16$. The United States' consumption is 1.16 standard deviation above the mean of 195. **2.77 (a)** $z = 1$. Finland's pollution is exactly one standard deviation above the mean pollution of all countries in the EU. **(b)** $z = -0.64$. Sweden's pollution is 0.64 standard deviation below the mean pollution of all countries in the EU. **(c)** $z = 0$. The United Kingdom's pollution is exactly equal to the mean pollution of all countries in the EU. **2.79** Yes, the sales for this day are more than three standard deviations above the mean. **2.81** TV watching tends to be higher for females (median, Q1 and Q3 higher than for males). **2.83 (a)** Mean = $43,700; Median = $9300. **(b)** Misleading because the mean is heavily influenced by the outlier. **2.85 (a)** Overall decrease in enrollment of STEM students followed by an apparent plateau. **(b)** This graph shows a gradual decrease over time in percentages. **(c)** There is a steady decrease in the percentages of enrolling students who are STEM majors. **2.87** The 2013 projection is shown where the observation would be plotted for the year 2007, not 2013. **2.89** Answers will vary. **2.91 (a)**, **(c)** and **(d)** are continuous. **(b)** and **(e)** are discrete. **2.93 (a)** Personality trait that defines "cool." **(b)** Categorical. **(c)** Bar chart and the mode. **2.95 (a)** Histogram. **(b)** Skewed to right. **2.97 (c)** 3.5. **(d)** Slightly skewed to the right. **2.99 (b)** Allows one to see the individual scores. **(c)** The distribution is skewed to the left with one low outlier. **2.101 (a)** Skewed to the right, since most values at 0 but some large values. **(b)** Skewed to the left, since most values at 1 hour or slightly less but some could be quite a bit less. **(c)** Skewed to the right, since some extremely large values. **(d)** Skewed to the left, since most values are high but some very young people die. **2.103** Larger; right skew (some very large values) would pull the mean higher. **2.105 (a)** Skewed to the right. **(b)** 2,090,012 is the mean and $1,646,853 is the median. **2.107 (a)** 1, 2, 4, 6, 7. **(b)** 2, 2, 3, 5, 6. **2.109 (a)** 12 is best; −10 is negative (not possible); 1 indicates almost no variability; 60 is almost as large as the whole range. **(b)** −20. standard deviations must be nonnegative. **2.111 (a)** Skewed to the right; maximum is much farther from the mean than the minimum is, and the lowest possible value of 0 is only 780/506 = 1.54 standard deviations below the mean. **(b)** Skewed to the right; the standard deviation is almost as large as the mean and the smallest possible value is 0. **2.113 (a)** Because of the extreme right skew **(b)** Mean and standard deviation would get much smaller, median, IQR, and 10th percentile would not change much. **2.115 (a)** Unimodal distribution, skewed to the right, possible outliers around 200. **(b)** Mean = 72.85, median = 60; skewed to the right. **(c)** $s = 48.00$. **2.117 (b)** Median = 24.5, Q1 = 7.5, Q3 = 46 **(c)** The gaps from 40 to 50 and 60 to 70 **2.119 (a)** Range = $34,048, IQR = $9,980 **(b)** lower whisker = 35070, upper whisker = 69118 **(c)** skewed to the right because there is a lower limit but no hard upper limit **(d)** 7000. 100 and 1000 are too small, and 25000 is too large given a range of roughly 34000. 7000 is most reasonable for the average distance of observations from the mean. **2.123 (a)** Line through rectangle is left of center, indicating skewness to the right. **(b)** Minimum ≈ 1400; Q1 ≈ 1475; Median ≈ 1550; Q3 ≈ 1700; Maximum ≈ 1800. **(c)** We would not see that the distribution is bimodal. **2.125** −2.16; this sodium value falls 2.16 standard deviations below the mean. **2.127** Responses will vary. **2.129 (a)** Both distributions skewed to the left, S more so; smallest observation in S data set is a possible outlier; children on F do better, on average, than those on S. **(b)** If no difference, distribution will be centered around 0. **2.131** Median unemployment rate similar (at about 10%) for males and females. Also, for both genders, unemployment rate varies among countries (except Greece and Spain) from roughly 6% to 16%. The middle 50% of the distribution for females (IQR about 5%) has less variability than the distribution for males (IQR about 7%). For the two countries with highest unemployment rate (Greece and Spain, with rate larger than 20%), unemployment rate for females is even higher than for males. Including the outliers, both the male and female distributions are right skewed. **2.133 (a)**

$$\bar{x} = \frac{69(1) + 240(2) + 221(3) + 740(4) + 268(5) + 327(6) + 68(7)}{1933} = \frac{7950}{1933} = 4.11.$$

(b) 4. **(c)** The median, 4 (representing the Moderate category), is found from the middle score being the 967th score. **2.135** (a). **2.137** (a). **2.139** Standard deviation, much too large. **2.141** When computing the mean, we take each score, multiply it by the (absolute) frequency, and then divide the result by the total number of observations. Because the proportion for a score is equal to the (absolute) frequency divided by the total number of observations, this is the same as multiplying the score times the proportion. **2.143** $\bar{x} \pm 3s$ would encompass all or nearly all scores. A range of $3s + 3s = 6s$ contains all or nearly all scores, so approximates the range. **2.145 (a)** With greater variability, numbers tend to be further from the mean. Thus, the absolute values of their deviations from the mean would be larger. When we take the average of all these values, the overall MAD is larger than with distributions with less variability. **(b)** The MAD is more resistant than the standard deviation because by squaring the deviations using the standard deviation formula, a large deviation has greater effect.

Chapter 3

3.1 (a) Response: Price; Explanatory: Carat **(b)** Response: Severity of adverse event; Explanatory: Dosage **(c)** Response: Top speed; Explanatory: Construction type **(d)** Response: Graduation rate; Explanatory: Type of college **3.3 (a)** The response variable is happiness and the explanatory variable is income. **(b)** Using 2010 data,

Income	Not Too Happy	Pretty Happy	Very Happy	Total	n
Above average	0.06	0.59	0.35	1.00	360
Average	0.11	0.60	0.29	1.00	850
Below average	0.24	0.57	0.19	1.00	604

The proportion of people who are very happy is larger for those with above-average income (35%) compared to those with below-average income (19%), showing an association between these two variables. Also, the proportion of people who are not too happy is much larger (24%) for people with below-average income compared to people with average (11%) or above-average (6%) income. **(c)** 0.269 **3.5 (a)** Response: binge drinking; explanatory: gender. **(b) (i)** 1908; **(ii)** 2854. **(c)** No; these are not proportions of male and female students; these are counts and there are far more females than males in this study. **(d)**

Gender	Binge Drinker	Non-Binge Drinker	Total	n
Male	0.49	0.51	1.00	3925
Female	0.41	0.59	1.00	6979

(e) It appears that men are more likely than are women to be binge drinkers. **3.7 (a)** Each one could be the outcome of interest, and how it depends on the other could be studied. **(b)** Using 2008 data,

	Do you believe in hell?		
Do you believe in heaven?	**Yes**	**No**	**Total**
Yes	955	162	1117
No	9	188	197
Totals	964	350	1314

(c)

	Do you believe in heaven?			
Do you believe in hell?	**Yes**	**No**	**Total**	n
Yes	0.991	0.009	1.00	964
No	0.463	0.537	1.00	350

(d)

	Do you believe in hell?			
Do you believe in heaven?	**Yes**	**No**	**Total**	n
Yes	0.855	0.145	1.00	1117
No	0.046	0.954	1.00	197

(e) (i) 85.01%; **(ii)** 73.4%. **3.9 (a)** Response: party identification; Explanatory: gender **(b) (i)** $89/892 = 0.10$; **(ii)** $95/892 = 0.11$ **(c) (i)** $355/892 = 0.40$; **(ii)** $184/892 = 0.21$ **(d)** Marginal because they are proportions referring to the entire sample **(e)** These *conditional* proportions suggest that more females (about 43%) identify as Democrat than males (about 30%), whereas a higher proportion of males identifies as Independent or Republican than females. **3.11 (a)** Positive; as cars age, they tend to have covered more miles. **(b)** Negative; as cars age, they tend to be worth less. **(c)** Positive; older cars tend to have needed more repairs. **(d)** Negative; heavier cars tend to travel fewer miles on a gallon of gas. **(e)** Positive; the heavier the car, the more fuel it will burn to move forward **3.13 (b)** Skewed to the right with two clear outliers (China and United States) **(c)** Nations with small GDP can have both large and small population sizes, resulting in both small and large per capita GDP and revealing no overall trend. **(d)** These two variables are not measuring the same thing. If the GDP were divided by the same value for all nations (such as in standardizing when dividing by the standard deviation of GDP), the correlation between GDP and standardized GDP would be 1. Here, each nation's GDP value is divided by a different value (the nation's population size). **3.15 (a)** Internet users and Broadband subscribers. **(b)** Facebook users and Population. **(c)** Because each pair of observations for Internet users and Facebook users are divided by the corresponding nation's population size to obtain the percentages. **3.17 (a)** (answer is scatterplot). **(b)** (4, 13). **(c)** The value of 13 would have to be changed to 10. **3.19** Answer is scatterplot. **3.21 (a) (i)** weight; **(ii)** price. **(b)** Bikes with weights in the middle tend to cost the most (scatterplot is part of answer). **(c)** Negative and fairly small; weight does not appear to affect price strongly in a linear manner. **3.23 (a)** Both box plots indicate that the counts are skewed to the right with few counties in the high ranges of vote counts (two box plots are part of the answer). **(b)** The point close to 3500 on the variable Buchanan is a regression outlier; we were unable to make this comparison from the box plots because there were two separate depictions, one for each candidate (scatterplot is part of the answer). **(c)** About 1000 **(d)** The point close to 3500 on the variable Buchanan is still an outlier (two box plots and a scatterplot are part of the answer). **3.25 (a) (i)** 6.47; **(ii)** 5.75. Connect the points $(x = 10, y = 6.47)$ and $(x = 40, y = 5.75)$. **(b)** The y-intercept indicates that when a person cannot do any sit-ups, she/he would be predicted to run the 40-yard dash in 6.71 seconds. The slope indicates that every increase of one sit-up leads to a decrease in running time of 0.024 seconds. **(c)** The slope indicates a negative correlation (the slope and correlation have the same sign). **3.27 (a) (i)** \$32.9; **(ii)** \$67.2 **(b)** For every point increase in the quality rating of the food, the cost is predicted to increase by \$4.90. **(c)** There is a moderately strong linear relationship $(r = 0.68)$ between the rating and cost of a meal. Higher ratings tend to correspond with higher prices. **(d)** $b = r\left(\frac{s_y}{s_x}\right) = (0.68)\left(\frac{14.92}{2.08}\right) = 4.9$. **3.29 (a)** The positive correlation means a positive association, i.e., nations with higher Internet use tend to have higher Facebook use, which results in a positive slope for the regression line. Also, mathematically, because $b = r\left(\frac{s_y}{s_x}\right)$ and r, s_y and s_x are all > 0, b must be positive. **(b)** 14.7% **(c)** residual $= 20.7\% - 14.7\% = 6\%$. The predicted Facebook use for Indonesia based on the regression equation is 6% below its actual use. **3.31 (a)** 506.6. **(b)** 9.5; this means Californians scored about 9.5 points higher on math than what might have been expected based on the reading scores. **(c)** $r^2 = 95.5\%$, so reading is a very good predictor of math. **3.33 (a)** The line minimizes the sum of the squared residuals. **(b)** No **(c)** Two cereals had more sodium than we would expect based on their sugar contents. These were Raisin Bran and Rice Krispies. **(d)** Not reliable at all; r^2 is close to zero (0.2%). **3.35 (a)** answer is a scatterplot **(b)** 1.0; $\hat{y} = 4 + 2x$. **(c)** Advertising: 1, 1; Sales: 6, 2. **(d)** $\hat{y} = 4 + 2x$; when there is no advertising, it is predicted that sales will be about \$4,000. For each increase of \$1000 in advertising, predicted sales increase by \$2000. **3.37 (a)** $\hat{y} = 24 + 0.70x$. **(b)** 80 and 87 **3.39 (b)** 0.81; strong positive association, with longer study times associated with higher GPAs. **(c)** $\hat{y} = 2.63 + 0.044x$. **(i)** 2.84, **(ii)** 3.72 **3.41 (b)** From MINITAB: price $= 1896 - 40.5$ weight. Predicted price decreases by \$40.5 for each pound increase in weight. No, because there were no weights around 0. **(c)** \$681. **3.43 (a)** The scatterplot reveals a nonlinear (curved) pattern. The correlation coefficient measuring the strength of a linear relationship is meaningless for nonlinear relationships. **(b)** Due to the nonlinear relationship, the regression equation is not appropriate to model the relationship between driving speed and mpg and cannot be used for making predictions. **(c)** For the range from about 40 mph to 85 mph (or from 5 mph to 40 mph). Over each of these ranges, the relationship is approximately linear. **3.45 (a)** The observation for 1896 is well below the general trend. **(b)** Value obtained from regression equation because there is a strong linear trend. **(c)** No. Extrapolating predictions well beyond the range of the observed x values is unreliable. No one knows whether the linear trend continues so many years out. **3.47 (a)** $\hat{y} = -3.1 + 0.33(15) = 1.85$; $\hat{y} = -3.1 + 0.33(40) = 10.1$. **(b)** $\hat{y} = 8.0 - 0.14(15) = 5.9$; $\hat{y} = 8.0 - 0.14(40) = 2.4$. **(c)** D.C. is a regression outlier because it is well removed from the trend of the rest of the data. **(d)** Because D.C. is so high on both variables, it pulls the line upward on the right and suggests a positive correlation, when the rest of the data (without D.C.) are negatively correlated. The relationship is best summarized after removing D.C. **3.49 (a)** Yes on all three counts. **(b) (1)** the x value (the United States in this case) is relatively low or high compared to the rest of the data; **(2)** the observation (the United States) is a regression outlier, falling quite far from the trend that the rest of the data follow. TV watching in the United States is very high despite the very low birth rate. **(c)** The association is **(i)** very weak without the United States because the six countries, although they vary in birth rates, all have very few televisions, and is; **(ii)** very strong with the United States because the United States is so much higher in number of televisions and so much lower on birth rate that it makes the two variables seem related. **(d)** Because that point has a large effect on pulling the line downward. **3.51 (a)** Perhaps Raisin Bran. **(b)** With Raisin Bran removed, r changed from -0.017 to -0.300, which is a substantial increase. **3.53 (a)** Not likely. **(b)** Values would be higher on both variables as age increases. **(c)** There is an overall positive correlation between height (in inches) and vocabulary (assessed on a scale of 1–10) if we ignore grade; if we look within each grade, we see roughly a horizontal trend and no particular association (scatterplot part of answer). **3.55 (a)** Several possible responses to this exercise (e.g., students who watch TV more may be more likely to see the ads and less likely to spend time with peers who smoke pot). **(b)** Pot smoking (or the lack thereof) might be caused by many variables (e.g., antidrug ads, television watching, regular school attendance, parental influence, neighborhood type). **3.57 (c)** 0.73, **(d) (i)** -0.96, **(ii)** -0.95. **3.59 (a)** Response: eighth grade math scores; explanatory: state **(b)** The third variable is race. Nebraska has the overall higher mean because there is a higher percentage of whites and a lower percentage of blacks in Nebraska than in New Jersey, and overall, whites tended to have higher math scores than blacks. **3.61 (a)** Response: assessed value; explanatory: square feet. **(b)** Response: political party; explanatory: gender. **(c)** Response: income; explanatory: education. **(d)** Response: pounds lost; explanatory: type of diet. **3.63 (a)** Opinion about life after death and using 2008 data,

Gender	Yes	No	Total
Male	76.9	23.1	808
Female	85.2	14.8	979

(b) 76.9% of males believe in life after death as opposed to 85.2% of females. Difference in proportion between females and males = 0.852 − 0.769 = 0.083. The proportion of females believing in life after death is about 8 percentage points higher than the one for males. Ratio of proportions = 0.852/0.769 = 1.108. The proportion of females believing in life after death is about 11% higher (or 1.1 times higher) than the one for males. **(c)** Proportions in (b). **3.65 (a)** Income; quantitative **(b)** Degree; categorical. **(c)** A bar graph could have a separate bar for each degree type. **3.67 (a)** Response: gender; explanatory: year. **(b)** For executive, administrative, and managerial

Year	Female	Male	Total
1972	0.197	0.803	1.00
2002	0.459	0.541	1.00

(c) Yes; women made up a larger proportion of the executive work force in 2002 than in 1972. **(d)** Year and type of occupation. **3.69 (a)** Correlation = 0.745 **(b)** $\hat{y} = -48.91 + 0.919x$. Since the y-intercept would correspond to female economic activity = 0, which is well outside of the range of data. **(c)** The predicted value for the United States is $-48.91 + 0.919(81) = 25.5$ with $15.0 - 25.5 = -10.5$ as the corresponding residual. The regression equation overestimates the percentage of women in parliament by 10.5% for the United States. **(d)** $b = 0.56(9.8/7.7) = 0.713$ and $a = 26.5 - 0.713(76.8) = -28.2$. Thus, the prediction equation is given by $\hat{y} = -28.2 + 0.713x$. **3.71 (a)** Slope: 0.56; as urban goes from 0 to 100, predicted crime rate increases by 56. **(b)** Relatively strong, positive relationship. **(c)** $b = r\left(\frac{s_y}{s_x}\right)$; $0.56 = 0.67(28.3/34.0)$. **3.73 (a)** Response: salary; explanatory: height. **(b)** Slope: \$789 per inch. **(c)** An increase of seven inches (from 5 foot 5 to 6 feet) is worth \$789 per inch, or \$5523. **3.75** y-intercept: 0; slope: 1; this means that your predicted college GPA equals your high school GPA. **3.77 (a)** A 1000 increase in x would mean a predicted change in y of -5.2 (poorer mileage). **(b)** 14.04; 2.96. The Hummer gets 2.96 more miles/gallon than one would predict. **3.79 (a)** \$4200. **(b)** $r = 0.79$; **(i)** positive; **(ii)** strong. **3.81 (a)** When economic activity is 0%, predicted birth rate is much higher (36.3) than when economic activity is 100% (6.3). **(b)** women's economic activity; the correlation between birth rate and women's economic activity is larger in magnitude than the correlation between birth rate and GNP. **3.83 (a)** $-16{,}000$. **(b)** 3200; **(c)** same (0.50); correlation does not depend on the units used **3.85 (a)** D.C. is the outlier to the far, upper right. This would have an effect on the regression analysis because it is a regression outlier. **(b)** When D.C. is included, the y-intercept decreases and the slope increases. **3.87 (a)** The point with a y value of around 1500 (scatterplot is part of answer). **(b)** Violent crime rate = 2545 − 24.6 high school; for each increase of 1% of people with a high school education, the predicted violent crime rate decreases by 24.6. **(c)** Violent crime rate = 2268 − 21.6 high school; for each increase of 1% of people with a high school education, predicted violent crime rate decreases by 21.6, similar to the slope in part b. **3.89 (a)** Negative relationship (scatterplot is part of answer). **(b)** -0.45; negative association. **(c)** Predicted percentage without health ins = 49.2 − 0.42 HS Grad Rate; for each increase of one percent in the high school graduation rate, the predicted percentage of individuals without health insurance goes down by 0.42; negative relationship. **3.91 (a)** Men tend to be taller and make more money than women. **(b)** When measured, a lurking variable becomes a confounding variable. **3.93 (a)** As people age, they might both sleep more and be more likely to die. **(b)** Subject's age might actually cause people to sleep more and be more likely to die. **3.95** Responses will vary. **3.97** Temp = 119 − 0.029 Year; the regression line indicates a very slight decrease over time, the opposite of what is indicated by the Central Park data. **3.99** San Francisco could be higher than other cities on lots of variables, but that does not mean those variables cause AIDS, as association does not imply correlation. Alternative explanations are that San Francisco has a relatively high gay population or relatively high intravenous drug use, and AIDS is more common among gays and IV drug users. **3.101** Stress level, physical activity, wealth, and social contacts are all possible lurking variables. Any one of these variables may contribute to one's physiological and psychological human health as well as be associated with whether or not a person owns a dog. For example, it may be that people who are more active are more likely to own a dog as well as being physically healthier. **3.103** (b). **3.105** (d). **3.107** (c) **3.109 (a)** False. **(b)** True. **(c)** True. **(d)** True. **3.111** The ratio of standard deviations equals 1, so $b = r(1) = r$. **3.113 (a)** When standard deviations are equal, the slope equals the correlation. If we use the equation from part b in the previous exercise and substitute 0.70 for b, we get $(\hat{y} - \bar{y}) = 0.70(x - \bar{x})$. **(b)** For example, if the midterm class mean were 80 and your score were 90, you'd be 10 points above the mean. If you multiplied that by 0.70, you'd predict that you'd deviate from the mean on y by seven points. If the mean on y also were 80, your predicted score would be 87. Thus, your predicted score is closer to the mean.

Chapter 4

4.1 (a) Explanatory is whether or not the automated call was placed to the phone on the right ear; response is a specific type of brain activity while the call is being received. **(b)** Experimental; the researchers controlled via randomization to determine whether the call to a given participant would be received during the first PET scan or the second. **4.3 (a)** Response variable – weight loss (weight after 1 year minus weight before experiment). Explanatory variable – low-fat vs. low-carb diet. **(b)** An experimental study. The subjects were randomized by the researchers into one of the two groups. **(c)** No. This is an issue of generalizability. Because patients with heart disease or diabetes were excluded from the study, it is inappropriate to say that this applied to *everyone*. **4.5** For example, it is possible that schools that institute drug testing are those in higher crime areas than are those that did not choose to use drug testing. **4.7 (a)** Explanatory variable – language used (native vs. foreign). Response variable – saving self vs. sacrificing self. **(b)** Observational – no assignment of treatments was made by the researchers; the researchers simply observed the language choice made by the subjects and the response. **(c)** No, the reason someone chooses to speak a foreign language (i.e., his or her global awareness or higher education level) might be the true cause of the choice they made. **4.9 (a)** Observational study; **(b)** Observational study; **(c)** Experiment **4.11** The seat belt incident might be the exception, rather than what is typical. Death rates are in fact higher for those who do not wear seat belts. **4.13 (a)** An observational study – no assignment of treatments was made by the researchers; the researchers simply observed current habits of the subjects. **(b)** Response variable – weight gain.

Explanatory variables – Exercise habits and caloric intake. **(c)** No, it demonstrates a correlation, but an experiment would be needed to show causation. **(d)** Motherhood leads to less exercise, eating more, and a more sedentary lifestyle. **4.15 (a)** PV, PS, PT, PA, VS, VT, VA, ST, SA, TA. **(b)** 1/10 **(c)** 4/10 **4.17** With e.g., the Random Numbers web app, select 1 as the minimum, 60 as the maximum and set the numbers to generate as 10. Pressing 'Generate' will show ten numbers (accounts) selected at random from the 60 numbers (accounts). **4.19** Response bias. **4.21** The first comment is valid; the second comment is not. If the information in the entire collection of ratings is unreliable, no type of sampling will make it reliable. **4.23 (a)** More than 75% of Americans say no when asked, "Would you favor a law giving police the power to decide who may own a firearm?" **(b)** Both statements are leading. **4.25 (a)** All adults in the United States. **(b)** It is almost impossible to ask all adults in the United States their opinions. A random sample gives a reliable estimate of this value with a much smaller set of people. **(c)** Those who chose to respond might feel more strongly than those who did not respond. **4.27 (a)** Those who don't admit to being in an extramarital affair might spend more money to hide the fact. Therefore this estimate would be too low. **(b)** If people lied about how much money they spent on an affair, it seems likely that they would underestimate the amount spent, to assuage their guilt. **4.29 (a)** Not all parts of the population have representation (because they may not have read the paper a long time) **(b)** Instead of random sampling, the newspaper used the 1000 people who subscribed the longest, who were probably the oldest and most conservative in terms of retirement planning. **(c)** Those who take the time to respond might not be representative. A large percentage of people did not respond. **(d)** The question seems to go out of the way to remind readers of volatility of stocks as of late. **4.31 (a)** Experiment; subjects are randomly assigned to treatments **(b)** Among the possible answers: unethical, impossible to ensure that subjects do as assigned and smoke or not smoke according to the assignment, too long to wait for answer **4.33 (a)** Response variable: whether the wart was successfully removed; explanatory variable: type of treatment for removing the wart (duct tape or the placebo). Experimental units: The 103 patients; treatments: duct-tape therapy and the placebo. **(b)** The difference between the number of patients whose warts were successfully removed using the duct-tape method and those using the placebo was not large enough to attribute to the treatment type. The difference in the success rates could be due to random variation. **4.35 (a)** Because there was a control group and an experimental group and the researchers assigned the Facebook users to each group. **(b)** The experimental units are Facebook users. **(c)** Explanatory variable – positively manipulated vs. not manipulated. Response variables – percentages of all words that were positive and percentage of all words that were negative. **(d)** If the participants were informed, they would not have acted authentically. They were likely upset that they were not informed because that violates the requirement of informed consent. **4.37** Without a placebo or a control comparison group, there is no way to separate the placebo effect from the actual effect of the medication. **4.39** The researchers being blinded prohibits them from deliberately biasing the results, for example by intentionally or unintentionally providing extra support to one of the treatment groups. **4.41 (a)** Recruit volunteers (the experimental units) with a history of high blood pressure; randomly assign to one of two treatments: the new drug or the current drug; explanatory: treatment type; response: blood pressure after experimental period. **(b)** To make the study double-blind, the two drugs would have to look identical so that neither the subjects nor the experimenters know what drug the subjects are taking. **4.43 (a)** Number the students from 1 to 5. Pick one-digit numbers randomly. Select the first female student to have her number picked (1 to 3) and the first male student to have his number picked (4 or 5). Ignore duplicates and digit 0, and digits 6-9. **(b)** Because every sample of size 2 does not have an equal chance of being selected (e.g., samples with two males have probability 0 of being selected.) **(c)** 1 in 3; 1 in 2. **4.45 (b)** The answer to this problem is based on a random process. This leads to potentially different answers each time it is performed. **4.47** It is possible that people with lung cancer had a different diet than did those without. These people might have eaten out at restaurants quite a bit, consuming more fat, and smoking socially. It could have been the fat and not the smoking that caused lung cancer. **4.49 (a)** Yes; if we look at enough data, some coincidental relationships are bound to be encountered. **(b)** Anticipated results stated in advance are usually more convincing than results that have already occurred. **(c)** Prospective. **4.51 (a)** Explanatory variable – Type of praise. Treatments – praised for effort vs. praised for intelligence. Response variable – whether they chose a challenging task on the subsequent task. Experimental units – study participants. **(b)** A randomized experiment. **4.53 (a)** No; the researchers are not randomly assigning subjects to living situation. **(b)** Yes; those living with smokers and those not living with smokers. **(c)** Yes; randomization of units to treatments occurs within blocks. **4.55** In an observational study, we observe people in the groups they already are in. In an experiment, we actually assign people to the groups of interest. The major weakness of an observational study is that we can't control (such as by balancing through randomization) other possible factors that might influence the outcome variable. **4.57 (a)** Explanatory is status of protein presence; response is memory status. **(b)** Nonexperimental because the researchers are not assigning any treatments. **(c)** No; either the proteins are present or not; its presence is not something the researchers can control for each patient. **4.59 (a)** Indiana: 1.7%; Wisconsin: 1.3%. **(b)** State results vary so vastly from nationwide results because fans want their favorite teams to win, which often translates into fans thinking their teams will win. **(c)** Sampling bias. The ESPN poll was a sample of volunteers who chose to visit the Web site and respond. **4.61** Gun ownership. **4.63 (a)** Yes; sampling bias. **(b)** If the sample is biased due to undercoverage and lack of random sampling, it doesn't matter how big the sample. **4.65 (a)** No, it was done by voluntary response. **(b)** They could send out a survey to all sports fans (perhaps using a cluster sampling method by choosing to sample from each sports stadium). **4.67 (a) (i)** Experiment; **(ii)** Prospective. **(b)** Response variable: presence/absence of myocardial infarction; explanatory variable: treatment group. **4.69 (a)** 72.5% of physicians in the aspirin group exercised vigorously, 72.0% of physicians in the placebo group exercised vigorously; yes. **(b)** Yes.
4.71

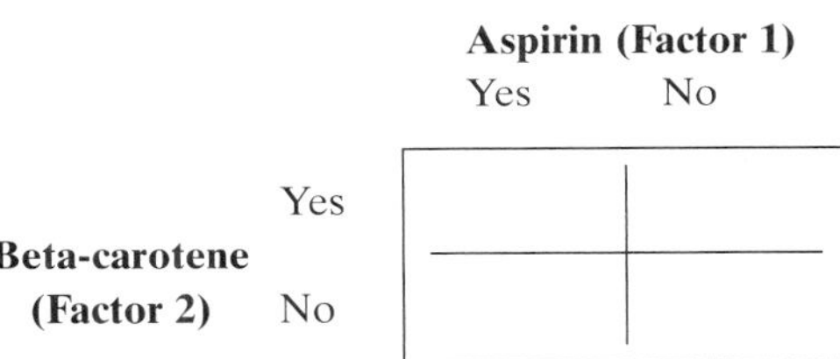

4.73 (a) (i) Randomly assign subjects to one of the two treatments, Coke or Pepsi, and have them rate it on a scale such as 0 to 10. Neither the subject nor the experimenter would know which cola the subject was drinking. (For example, an experimenter with no contact with the subjects could put both types of colas into identical cups; a code could be used to later identify the type of cola.) **(ii)** Randomly assign each subject to drink either Coke or Pepsi first, then to drink the other one, and then to indicate which they prefer. Neither the subject nor the experimenter administering the cola would know which type of cola the subject was drinking. **(b)** The completely randomized design eliminates the possibility that drinking one cola would alter one's preference for the second cola. The matched-pairs design decreases the possible effects of lurking variables because the two groups are made up of the same people. **4.75** Every possible *sample* of a given size does not have an equal chance of being selected. **4.77** Region: stratification; 10 schools: clustering; classrooms: clustering. **4.79** Perhaps any relationship is coincidental, not causal. For example, perhaps those genetically susceptible to acquiring schizophrenia are the same group who especially enjoy marijuana. **4.81** Answers will vary, depending on the study. **4.83** No; due to the volunteer nature of the sample. **4.85** Answers will vary. **4.87 (a)** The sample includes only one cluster. **(b)** Sampling just Fridays is an example of sampling bias (values might be higher than usual because days sampled are at start of weekend). **4.89** This is not a random sampling method. People who approach the street corner are interviewed as they arrive (and as they agree to the interview!), and may not be representative. **4.91 (a)** Such a study would measure how well a treatment works if patients believe in it, rather than how much a treatment works independent of subjects' beliefs about its efficacy. **(b)** Patients might be reluctant to be randomly assigned to one of the treatments because they might perceive it as inferior to another treatment. **(c)** He or she might feel that all patients should get the new treatment. **4.93** Since the disease is rare, this proposed study might not sample anyone that gets it. With the case-control study, one would find a certain number of people who already have the rare disease (the cases), and compare the proportion of these people who had received the vaccine to the proportion in a group of controls who did not have the disease. **4.95** Using the Generate Random Numbers web app, set the minimum to 1, the maximum to 16 and select to generate 8 random numbers. Press 'Generate. The highlighted numbers (also printed below the table) identify the group of 8 babies to show the videos in one order. The remaining babies are shown the videos in the other order. **4.97** (b) **4.99** (a) **4.101** (d) **4.103** (b) **4.105 (a)** The researchers randomly selected among all possible Standard Metropolitan Statistical Areas (SMSAs) or nonmetropolitan counties. **(b)** The researchers stratified participants based on region, age, and race. **(c)** The GSS Web site notes: "The full-probability GSS samples used since 1975 are designed to give each household an equal probability of inclusion in the sample." **4.107 (a)** $M = 50, n = 125, R = 12$ **(c)** 520.8. **(d)** Column headings: In the census?: Yes (returned form), No (did not return form); Row headings: In the PES?: Yes, No. **4.109** Answers will vary.

Chapter 5

5.1 The long-run relative frequency definition of probability refers to the probability of a particular outcome as the proportion of times that the outcome would occur in a long run of observations. **5.3** No. In the short run, the proportion of a given outcome can fluctuate a lot. **5.5 (a)** 35.9% is the subjective probability that Brazil will win the World Cup. It is not based on a frequency of events. **(b)** No. Any event with nonzero probability could occur. Even Algeria could have won the World Cup. **5.7** Disagree. A large sample size could still be biased. **5.9** Subjective; it's not based on previous nuclear wars because none have occurred. **5.11 (b)** About 50. **(c)** The results will depend on the answer to part a. **(d)** 42% of the answers were true. We would expect 50%. They are not necessarily identical, because observed percentage of a given outcome fluctuates in the short run. **(e)** There are some groups of answers that appear nonrandom. For example, there are strings of five trues and eight falses, but this can happen by random variation. **5.13 (a)** Great/in favor, great/opposed, great/no opinion, good/in favor, good/opposed, good/no opinion, fair/in favor, fair/opposed, fair/no opinion, poor/in favor, poor/opposed, poor/no opinion.
(b)

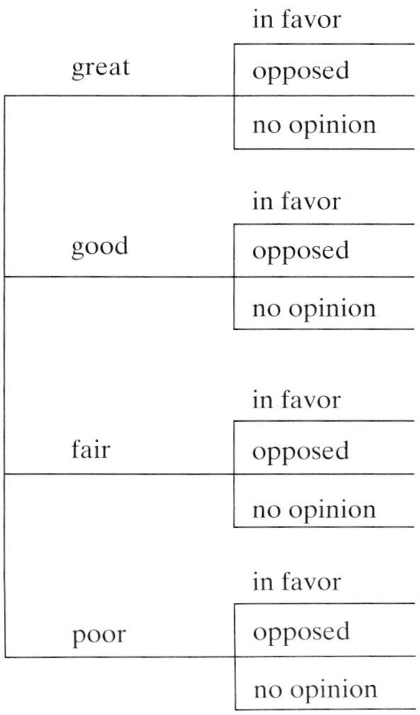

- great
  - in favor
  - opposed
  - no opinion
- good
  - in favor
  - opposed
  - no opinion
- fair
  - in favor
  - opposed
  - no opinion
- poor
  - in favor
  - opposed
  - no opinion

5.15 (a) Answer is tree diagram with 16 possible outcomes. **(b)** The probability of each possible individual outcome is $1/16 = 0.0625$. **(c)** 0.3125. **5.17** Disagree. Not all events from the sample space are equally likely. Specifically, there are six ways of getting a 7 (1 on the first die and 6 on the second, 2 and 5, etc.) whereas there is only one way of getting a 2 (1 on both dice). **5.19 (a)** BBB, BBG, BGB, GBB, BGG, GBG, GGB, GGG. **(b)** 1/8. **(c)** 3/8. **(d)** 6/8 or 3/4. **5.21** 20 heads has probability (1/2) to the 20th power, which is $1/1{,}048{,}576 = 0.000001$. Risk of a one in a million death: $1/1{,}000{,}000 = 0.000001$. **5.23 (a)** YS; YD; NS; and ND. **(b) (i)** 0.004; **(ii)** 0.284. **(c)** 0.003. **(d)** Answer would have been $P(\text{N and D}) = P(\text{N}) \times P(\text{D}) = (0.004)(0.284) = 0.001$. This indicates that chance of death depends on seat belt use since 0.001 is not equal to 0.003. **5.25 (b)** If A and B were independent events, $P(\text{A and B}) = P(\text{A}) \times P(\text{B})$. Since $P(\text{A and B}) > P(\text{A})P(\text{B})$, A and B are not independent. The probability of responding yes on global warming and less on future fuel use is higher than what is predicted by independence. **5.27 (a)** There are eight possible outcomes. Answer is tree diagram. **(b)** 0.488. **(c)** They assumed independence, but that might not be so (e.g., three customers are friends, or three members of the same family). **5.29 (a)** $P(B|S)$. **(b)** $P(B^C|S^C)$. **(c)** $P(S^C \mid B^C)$. **(d)** $P(S \mid B)$. **5.31 (a)** 0.7599. **(b)** 0.3299. **(c)** 0.1579. **5.33 (a)** 0.004. **(b) (i)** 0.001. **(ii)** 0.010. **(c)** Neither $P(\text{D}|\text{wore seat belt})$ nor $P(\text{D}|\text{didn't wear seat belt})$ equals $P(\text{D})$; specifically, 0.001 and 0.010 are different from 0.004. Thus, the events are not independent.
5.35

	Identified as Spam by ASG	
Spam	**Yes**	**No**
Yes	7005	835
No	48	

(b) $7005/(7005 + 835) = 0.8935$. **(c)** $7005/(7005 + 48) = 0.9932$. **5.37 (a)** $P(\text{D}|\text{NEG}) = 6/3927 = 0.0015$. **(b)** No; $P(\text{NEG}|\text{D}) = 6/54 = 0.111$. **5.39 (a)** $147/317 = 46\%$ **(b) (i)** $69/146 = 47\%$ **(ii)** $78/171 = 46\%$ **(c)** Because $46\%\,(\text{from a}) = 46\%\,(\text{from b})$, we can say that the events of being very happy and being male are independent. **5.41 (a)** 0.30. **(b) (i)** 0.40; **(ii)** 0.40. **(c)** No; the probability that he will make the second shot depends on whether he made the first. **5.43** 0.0416. **5.45 (a)** $P(\text{C and A})/P(\text{A}) = (1/4)/(1/2) = (1/2)$. **(b)** No; C implies A. **(c)** $P(\text{C and B})/P(\text{B}) = (1/4)/(3/4) = (1/3)$. **(d)** The event "at least one child is female" includes more outcomes than the event "first child is female." **5.47** 0.9329. **5.49** Each student can be matched with 24 other students, for a total of 25(24) pairs. But this considers each pair twice (e.g., student 1 with student 2, and student 2 with student 1), so the answer is $25(24)/2 = 300$. **5.51** 0.6954. **5.53** The explanation should discuss the context of the huge number of possible random occurrences that happen in one's life, and the likelihood that at least some will happen (and appear coincidental) just by chance. **5.55 (a)** The probability that the first will go, multiplied by the probability that the second will go, and so on for all 5.4 million, that is $(1/5000)$ taken to the 5.4 millionth power, which is zero to a huge number of decimal places. **(b)** This solution assumes that each person decides independently of all others. This is not realistic because families and friends often make vacation plans together. **5.57 (a)** The first answer is a tree diagram. **(b)** $P(\text{POS}) = P(\text{S and POS}) + P(\text{S}^c \text{ and POS}) = 0.0086 + 0.1188 = 0.1274$. **(c)** 0.068. **(d)** They are calculated by multiplying the proportion for each branch by the total number. The proportion of positive tests with breast cancer is $1/(1 + 12) = 0.08$. **5.59 (a)** Of the 100,000 who suffer abuse, $40 + 5 = 45$ are killed; 5 of those 45 are killed by someone other than the partner. **(b)** 99,955 and 40. **(c)** They differ because the number who are abused is much larger than the number killed, whereas of all those killed, most are killed by the partner. **5.61 (a)** Tree diagram is part of answer. $P(\text{Innocent}|\text{Match}) = P(\text{Innocent and Match})/P(\text{Match}) = 0.0000005/0.4950005 = 0.000001$. **(b)** Tree diagram is part of answer. $P(\text{Innocent}|\text{Match}) = P(\text{Innocent and Match})/P(\text{Match}) = 0.00000099/0.00990099 = 0.0001$. When the probability of being innocent is higher, there's a larger probability of being innocent given a match. **(c)** $P(\text{Innocent}|\text{Match})$ can be much different from $P(\text{Match}|\text{Innocent})$. **5.63 (b)** $(0.95) \times (0.95) \times (0.95) \ldots \times (0.95)$

– a grand total of twenty 0.95s (or 0.95^{20}) = 0.36. **5.65 (a)** Multiply the table results by 4 seconds to get the answers. **(b)** Answers will vary. Depends on simulation, but likely the rapid succession. **5.67** The gender of a child is independent of the previous children's genders; the chance is still 1/2. **5.69 (a)** There are 18 possible meals [$(2 \times 3 \times 3 \times 1) = 18$]. Tree diagram is part of answer. **(b)** No; some menu options would be more popular than are others. **5.71 (a)** 0.8142. **(b)** 0.6629. **(c)** That the responses of the two subjects are independent; married couples share many beliefs. **5.73 (a)** 8; tree diagram is part of answer. **(b)** 0.125. **(c)** 0.343. **(d)** Three friends are likely to be similar on many characteristics that might affect performance. **5.75 (a)** 0.84. **(b)** 0.70. **5.77 (a)** The percentages 31% and 1% are conditional probabilities. The 31% is conditioned on the event that the teen says that parents are never present at the parties attend. The 1% is conditioned on the event that the teen says that parents are present at the parties. For both percentages, the event to which the probability refers is a teen reporting that marijuana is available at the parties.
(b)

	Parents Present	
Marijuana available	**Yes**	**No**
Yes	9	133
No	860	295

(c) 860/(860 + 295) = 0.74. **5.79 (a)** (1,1); (1,2); (1,3); (1,4); (1,5); (1,6); (2,1); (2,2); (2,3); (2,4); (2,5); (2,6); (3,1); (3,2); (3,3); (3,4); (3,5); (3,6); (4,1); (4,2); (4,3); (4,4); (4,5); (4,6); (5,1); (5,2); (5,3); (5,4); (5,5); (5,6); (6,1); (6,2); (6,3); (6,4); (6,5); (6,6). **(b)** (1,1); (2,2); (3,3); (4,4); (5,5); and (6,6); 0.167. **(c)** (1,6); (2,5); (3,4); (4,3); (5,2); and (6,1); 0.167. **(d) (i)** 0; **(ii)** 0.333; **(iii)** 0. **(e)** A and B are disjoint. You cannot roll doubles that add up to seven. **5.81** 0.80. **5.83** 0.67. **5.85 (a)** This strategy is a poor one; the chance of an even slot is the same on each spin of the wheel. **(b)** (18/38) to the 26th power, which is essentially 0. **(c)** No; events that seem highly coincidental are often not so unusual when viewed in the context of *all* the possible random occurrences at all times. **5.87** False negatives: test indicates that an adult smoker does not have lung cancer when he or she does have lung cancer. False positives: test indicates the presence of lung cancer when there is none. **5.89 (b)** 0.048; because so few people have this cancer, most of the positive tests will be false. **5.91 (c)** 0.999. **(d)** A positive result is more likely to be in error when the prevalence is lower, as relatively more of the positive results are for people who do not have the condition. Tree diagrams or contingency tables are part of the answer. **5.93** Will vary. **5.95 (a)** The cumulative proportion of heads approaches 0.50 with larger numbers of flips, illustrating the law of large numbers and the long-run relative frequency definition of probability. **(b)** The outcome will be similar to that in part a, with the cumulative proportion of 3 or 4 approaching one third with larger numbers of rolls. **5.97 (a)** 0.545. **(b)** 0.505. **(c)** 0.500; as n increases, the cumulative proportion tends toward 0.50. **5.99 (1)** Specificity: if pregnant, 99% chance of a positive test. **(2)** Sensitivity: if not pregnant, 99% chance of a negative test. **(3)** 99% chance of pregnancy given a positive test. **(4)** 99% chance of not pregnant given a negative test. **5.101 (a)** 2.4%. **(b)** Multiply (1) probability of getting a high school degree by (2) probability of getting a college degree once you had a high school degree by (3) probability of getting a masters' once you had the earlier degrees by (4) probability of getting a Ph.D. once you had the earlier degrees. **(c)** 0.06. **5.103** The event of a person bringing a bomb is independent of the event of any other person bringing a bomb. **5.105** (c) and (d). **5.107** (e). **5.109** (b). **5.111** False. **5.113** Being not guilty is a separate event from the event of matching all the characteristics listed. Suppose there are 100,000 people in the population. Since the probability of a match is 0.001, out of the 100,000 people, 100 people would match all the characteristics. Suppose that in the population, 5% of the people are guilty of such a crime, 95% are not guilty. The contingency table is

	Guilty	Not Guilty	Total
Match		???	100
No Match			99,900
Total	5000	95,000	100,000

Thus, P(not guilty | match) = ???/100. **5.115** When two events are not independent, P(A and B) = P(A) × P(B|A). If we think about (A and B), as one event, then P[C and (A and B)] = P(A and B) × P(C|A and B). If we replace P(A and B) with its equivalent, P(A) × P(B|A), we see that: P(A and B and C) = P(A) × P(B|A) × P(C|A and B). **5.117 (b)** The simulated probability should be close to 1. **5.119** Answers will vary.

Chapter 6

6.1 (a) Uniform distribution; P(1) = P(2) = P(3) = P(4) = P(5) = P(6) = 1/6. **(b)** There will be a probability for each x from 2 through 12; for example, there are three rolls that add up to four [(1,3), (2,2) (3,1)]; thus, the probability of four is 3/36 = 0.083. **(c)** $0 \le P(x) \le 1$; and $\Sigma P(x) = 1$. **6.3 (a)** All are between 0 and 1 and they sum to 1. **(b)** 0.4083. **(c)** Over the course of many at-bats, the average number of bases per at-bat is 0.4083. **6.5 (a)** P(4) = 0.20, P(3) = 0.40, P(2) = 0.30, P(1) = 0.10. **(b)** 2.7. **6.7 (a)** 0.001. **(b)** P(0) = 0.999, P(500) = 0.001. **(c)** 0.999(0) + 0.001(500) = 0.50. **(d)** The expected winnings in each game is 0.50; thus in terms of expected values we are indifferent between Pick 3 and Pick 4. **6.9** The one on 23; winnings are, on average, further from the mean for this bet. **6.11 (a)** P($80,000) = 0.70, P($50,000) = 0.20, P($20,000) = 0.10. **(b)** 0.30. **(c)** $68,000. **(d)** P($77,000) = 0.70, P($47,000) = 0.20, P($37,000) = 0.10; μ = $67,000.
6.13 (a)

x	P(x)
$90	0.50
$120	0.20
$130	0.30

μ = 108. The expected selling price for the sale of a drill is $108. **(b)** μ = 110. The new strategy gives higher mean profit, in the long run. **6.15 (a)** The response could fall anywhere within an interval, i.e., exactly 1 hour or 1.835 hours or 2.07 hours. **(b)** Because TV watching was measured to the nearest integer. The histograms then display the frequencies of the rounded (to the nearest integer) values obtained in the sample. **(c)** The two smooth curves would represent the approximate (based on the histograms) shape of the probability distribution for TV watching in the population if we could measure it in a continuous manner. Then, the area under the curve above an interval would represent the probability of an observation falling in that interval. **6.17 (a)** 0.251 **(b)** 0.383. **6.19 (a)** 0.9495 – 0.0505 = 0.899, which rounds to 0.90. **(b)** 0.9951 – 0.0049 = 0.9902, which rounds to 0.99. **(c)** 0.7486 – 0.2514 = 0.4972, which rounds to 0.50. **6.21 (a)** Divide by two for amount in each tail, 0.005. Subtract from 1.0 for cumulative probability, 0.995. Look up this probability on Table A to find the z-score of 2.58. **(b)** (a) 1.96. (b) 1.645; graph is part of answer. **6.23 (a)** 0.67. **(b)** 1.645. **6.25 (a)** 1.19. **(b)** 0.12. **(c)** 0.79. **(d)** 141.5. **6.27 (a)** $z = (1000 - 673)/556 = 0.59$ has a cumulative probability of 0.72. The probability that household electricity use was greater than 1000 kilowatt-hours is 1 – 0.72 or 0.28. **(b)** No, because electricity use = 0 gives a minimum possible z-score of $(0 - 673)/556 = -1.21$. **6.29 (a) (i)** 0.106; **(ii)** 0.894; **(b)** 137.3. **(c)** 62.7. **6.31 (a)** $z = 3$, which is unusually high (99.9% of observations fall below that level) **(b)** 71.3 percentile **(c)** These are similar to the percentages within 1, 2, or 3 standard deviations for the normal distribution. **6.33** $Z_{\text{joe}} = 1$, $Z_{\text{kate}} = 0.851$; in terms of math scores, Joe is better. **6.35 (a)** S = successful match, F = no match. Sample space: SSS, SSF, SFS, SFF, FSS, FSF, FFS, FFF, with probabilities $(0.1)^3$, $(0.1)^2(0.9)^1$, $(0.1)^2(0.9)^1$, $(0.1)^1(0.9)^2$, $(0.1)^2(0.9)^1$, $(0.1)^1(0.9)^2$, $(0.1)^1(0.9)^2$, $(0.9)^3$. Probabilities for $x = 0, 1, 2, 3$ are $P(0) = (0.9)^3$, $P(1) = (2)(0.1)^1(0.9)^2$, $P(2) = (2)(0.1)^2(0.9)^1$, $P(3) = (0.1)^3$. **(b)** Same as part a, e.g., $P(1) = (3!/[1!2!])\,(0.1)^1(0.9)^{3-1} = (2)(0.1)^1(0.9)^2$. **6.37 (d)** The graph in part a is symmetric, as is the case anytime p = 0.50. **(e)** The graph in part c is most heavily skewed; the graph with p = 0.01 would be even more skewed. **6.39 (a)** Each trial (= bid) can result in two outcomes (win/lose), trials are independent, and on each trial there is a constant probability of 25% of winning. The number of winning bids is binomial. **(b)** $P(2) = (4!/[2!2!])\,(0.25)^2(0.75)^{4-2} = 0.211$. **(c)** 0.949 **(d)** 0.051. **6.41 (a)** 0.002. **(b)** 0.027. **6.43 (a)** μ = 360, σ = 6.

(b) (342, 378) or within 3 standard deviations of the mean. **(c)** (0.855, 0.945). **6.45 (a)** Binary data (voted for proposition or not), probability of success for each trial = 0.50 is constant from trial to trial, and the trials are independent (one individual's vote unlikely to affect another's vote); $n = 3000$; $p = 0.50$. **(b)** $\mu = 1500$, $\sigma = 27.4$. **(c)** (1418, 1582). **(d)** p is actually higher than 0.50. **6.47 (a)** 68.04. **(b)** 0.0242. **(c)** Different players, especially the pitchers; different stadiums, weather, etc. **6.49** No; the trials are not independent, and n is greater than 10% of the population size. **6.51 (a)** The independence assumption is not plausible since families tend to make decisions about church attendance together. **(b)** The 100 votes are not randomly selected from the population and do not constitute a random sample. **(c)** Independence cannot be assumed since 4 is not less than 10% of the population size of 20. **6.53** Taking into account the \$1 bet, the expected winnings of straight is about−\$0.50; expected winnings for boxed is about−\$0.52; in terms of expected return, straight is better; however, you have a better chance of winning by playing boxed. **6.55 (a)** Probability distribution: P(0) = 0.994, P(45.50) = 0.006. **(b)** Probability distribution: P(0) = 0.999, P(45.50) = 0.001. **(c)** The first; because you have a higher chance of winning. **6.57 (a)** Probability distribution: P(0) = 0.999999, P(100,000) = 0.000001. **(b)** 0.10. **(c)** Because the flyer's return on each \$1 spent averages to only \$0.10. **6.59 (a)** 1.96. **(b)** 2.58; answer includes graph. **6.61 (a)** 25% between the mean and the positive z-score. Added to 50% below mean, 75% of the normal distribution is below the positive z-score, corresponding to a z-score of 0.67. **(b)** First quartile: 25th percentile; third quartile: 75th percentile. The 75th percentile has a z-score of 0.67. The z-score at the 25th percentile is $z = -0.67$. **(c)** The interquartile range is $Q3 - Q1 = (\mu + 0.67\sigma) - (\mu - 0.67\sigma) = 2(0.67)\sigma$. **6.63** 0.31. **6.65 (a)** 0.0912, 0.092 with table. **(b)** 0.0912, 0.092 with table. **(c)** 0.82. **(d)** 9.96 inches. **6.67 (a)** 39.2% **(b)** 24.8% **(c)** \$18,187. **6.69** 16.0. **6.71 (a)** Yes, changing scale does not change the distribution. **(b)** Mean = 182.9, standard deviation = 10.2. **(c)** 0.05. **6.73** 0.6561. **6.75 (a)** Head (success) = a correct guess [on any trial]; tail (failure) = an incorrect guess [on any trial]. **(b)** Because with random guessing, she has a constant probability of 0.2 of guessing the right number, for each of the three trials **(c)** Trials are not affected by the outcomes of previous trials. **6.77 (a)** 0.75 since it rains at least once in 3 out of the 4 equally likely outcomes: RR, RD, DR, DD. **(b)** $1 - P(0) = 1 - \frac{2!}{0!(2-0)!}0.5^0(1-0.5)^{2-0} = 1 - 0.25 = 0.75$. **6.79 (a)** $n(0.000001)$. **(b)** 1,000,000. **(c)** Winnings: 1(100,000) = \$100,000; Profit: 100,000 − 1,000,000 =−\$900,000. **6.81 (a)** $\mu = np = 7500$, $\sigma = 86.6$ **(b)** Almost all values will fall within 3 standard deviations of the mean, i.e., in the interval [7240, 7760]. **(c)** Since with high probability at most 7760 users will like the message, the company should set aside \$7760. (Answers may vary.) **6.83 (d)** P(3) = 0.25 P(4) = 0.375 P(5) = 0.375. **6.85** The median would be the score that falls at 50%; median = 4. **6.87** A streak of seven is likely to occur just by chance given enough trials. **6.89** Mean = 980, standard deviation = 22; since 800 is more than 3 standard deviations below the expected mean, the probability of a female birth in this town is probably less than 0.49. **6.91** (d). **6.93 (a)** For group A, 0.16 and for group B, 0.23. **(b)** 0.59. **(c)** The proportion of those not admitted belonging to group B decreases to 0.061; the legislator was correct. **6.95 (a)** 1.01 **(b)** smaller. **6.97 (a)** Normal (shape not affected) with mean 23800(1.06) = 25228 and standard deviation 4380(1.06) = 4643 **(b)** Normal (shape not affected) with mean 23800 + 199 = 23999 and standard deviation 4380. **6.99 (a)** The probability of rolling doubles is 1/6. The outcome on the second die has a 1/6 chance of matching the first. To have doubles occur first on the second roll, you'd have to have no match on the first, a 5/6 chance. You'd then have to have a match on the second roll, a 1/6 chance. The probability of both occurring is (5/6)(1/6). For no doubles until the third roll, the first and the second roll would not match, a 5/6 chance for each, followed by doubles on the third, a 1/6 chance. The probability of all of three events is $(5/6)^2(1/6)$. **(b)** By the logic in part a, $P(4) = (5/6)(5/6)(5/6)(1/6)$ or $(5/6)^3(1/6)$. By extension, we could calculate $P(x)$ for any x by $(5/6)^{x-1}(1/6)$. **6.101 (a)** 5.853 **(b)** among others: non-constant win probability (home-field advantage) **(c)** $68 \times 0.3125 = 21.25$.

Chapter 7

7.1 (a) Although the population proportion is 0.53, by random variability it is unlikely that exactly 53 out of 100 polled voters will vote yes. Sample proportions close to 0.53 will be more likely than those further from 0.53. **(b)** The graph of the sample proportions should be bell shaped and centered around 0.53.

(c) Predicted standard deviation $= \sqrt{\frac{0.53(1-0.53)}{100}} = 0.05$.

(d) The graph should look similar as in part b but shifted so that it is centered around 0.70. Also, standard deviation changes to 0.046. **7.3 (a)** Mean $= p = 0.10$, standard deviation $= \sqrt{0.10(1-0.10)/500} = 0.0134$. **(b)** Mean $= p = 0.10$, standard deviation $= \sqrt{0.10(1-0.10)/2000} = 0.0067$. **(c)** Mean $= p = 0.10$, standard deviation $= \sqrt{0.10(1-0.10)/125} = 0.0268$. As the sample size gets larger (i.e., from 500 to 2000), the standard deviation decreases (in fact, it is only half as large). As the sample size gets smaller (i.e., from 500 to 125), the standard deviation increases (in fact, it becomes twice as large). **7.5 (a)** P(1) = 0.409 and P(0) = 0.591. **(b)** Mean = 0.409, standard deviation = 0.008. **7.7 (a)** Bell shaped, mean = 0.300, standard deviation = 0.020 **(b)** These values are only about a standard deviation from the mean, which is not unusual. **7.9 (a)** P(0 out of 3) = 27/64, P(1 out of 3) = 27/64, P(2 out of 3) = 9/64, P(3 out of 3) = 1/64. **(b)** Mean = 0.25, standard deviation = 0.25. **(c)** For $n = 10$, mean = 0.25, standard deviation = 0.137; for $n = 100$, mean = 0.25, standard deviation = 0.0433; the mean stays the same and the standard deviation gets smaller as n gets larger. **7.11 (a)** The population distribution is based on the x values of the 14,201 students, 95.1% of which are 1 and 4.9% of which are 0, so P(0) = 0.049, P(1) = 0.951. **(b)** The data distribution is based on the x values in the sample of size 350, 330 of which are 1 and 20 of which are 0, so the data distribution has P(0) = 20/350 = 0.0571 and P(1) = 330/350 = 0.9429. **(c)** Mean = 0.951, standard deviation $= \sqrt{0.951(1-0.951)/350} = 0.0115$. It represents the probability distribution of the sample proportion of the number of full-time students in a random sample of 350 students. Graph is bell shaped and centered at 0.951. **(d)** Population and sampling distribution graph look the same. Data distribution may look different, since based on a different sample. **7.13 (a)** population distribution. **(b)** For a population proportion of 0.9 or 0.95, with $n = 30$, the sampling distribution does not look bell shaped but rather skewed to the left. **(c)** Because we expect the bell shape to occur only when $n(p)$ is larger than 15, which is not the case here. **7.15 (a)** Although the mean of the population distribution is 70, by random variability (as expressed by the population standard deviation), the sample mean of a sample of size 12 will sometimes be smaller or larger than 70. **(b)** The simulated sampling distribution is bell shaped and centered at 70. Almost all sample means fall between a score of about 60 to 80. **(c)** It is still bell shaped and centered at 70 but now has smaller variability. Now, almost all sample means fall within about 65 to 75. **7.17 (b) (i)** Mean = 3.50, standard deviation = 1.21. **(ii)** Mean = 3.50, standard deviation = 0.31; As n increases, the sampling distribution becomes more normal in shape and has less variability around the mean. **7.19 (a)** Judging by the histogram, the simulated sampling distribution is not bell shaped but, rather, has a triangular shape. **(b)** When we ran the simulation, we got a mean of 3.49 and a standard deviation of 1.21 for the simulated sampling distribution of the 10,000 sample means. These are very close to the theoretical mean and standard deviation of the sampling distribution, which are 3.5 and $\sigma/\sqrt{n} = 1.71/\sqrt{2} = 1.21$. **(c)** With $n = 30$, the histogram representing the sampling distribution is now bell shaped and shows a much smaller standard deviation compared to the case with $n = 2$. **7.21 (a)** Since σ is almost as large as μ and 0 is a lower bound only 1.33 standard deviations below the mean, the distribution is right skewed. **(b)** With a random sample, the data distribution picks up the characteristics from the population distribution, so we anticipate it as right skewed. **(c)** With $n = 45$, sampling distribution of sample mean is bell shaped by the central limit theorem. **7.23 (a)** Mean = 8.20. Standard deviation = 0.30. **(b)** 0.994. **7.25 (a)** Mean = 130, standard deviation = 3.46. **(b)** Normal. If the population distribution is approximately normal, then the sampling distribution is approximately normal for any sample size. **(c)** 0.002. **7.27 (a)** Mean is \$74,550 and standard deviation is \$19,872; likely skewed right because of a few large salaries. **(b)** \$75,207 and \$18,901; shape similar to population distribution. **(c)** \$74,550 and \$1987; approximately normal distribution due to Central Limit Theorem. **(d)** \$100,000 is barely one standard deviation above the population mean, but it is more than 12 standard deviations above the mean of the sampling distribution of the sample mean. **7.29 (a)** The shape is decisively right skewed. **(b)** The shape is still right skewed but begins to resemble a bell shape. Compared to $n = 2$, the variability is a bit smaller because the right tail's extend is smaller. **(c)** The shape is bell shaped, and the variability is much smaller compared to $n = 2$. Most sample means fall between about 5 and 10. Results are similar to the ones indicated in Figure 7.11. **(d)** As the sample size increases, the sampling distribution increasingly resembles a normal distribution. **7.31 (a)** Mean = 0.70, standard deviation = 0.065. **(b)** Bell shaped, by central limit theorem. **(c)** Probability = 0.06. **7.33 (a)** $np = 200(1/9) = 22.2$, $n(1-p) = 200(8/9) = 177.8$; number of successes and number of failures both larger than 15; shape is approximately normal with mean $= p = 1/9$ and standard deviation $= \sqrt{p(1-p)/n} = \sqrt{(1/9)(8/9)/200} = 0.022$. **(b)** Shape is approximately normal (number of successes and numbers of failures both larger than 15), with mean $= p = 1/9$ and standard deviation $= \sqrt{(1/9)(8/9)/800} = 0.011$. **7.35 (a)** Mean = 0.04, standard deviation = 0.0088 **(b)** Yes: $np = 500(0.04) = 20$ and $n(1-p) = 500(0.96) = 480$, both the number of successes and the number of failures are larger than 15. **(c)** Probability of observing a sample proportion of 0.05 or larger under a normal distribution with mean = 0.04 and standard deviation = 0.0088: 12.8% (from technology or Table A in appendix after converting to z-score) **7.37 (a)** Mean = \$900, standard deviation = \$300. **(b)** Mean = \$980, standard deviation = \$276 describes the variability of the daily sales values for this past week. **(c)** Mean = \$900, standard deviation = \$113.4 describes the variability of sample means based on samples of seven daily sales. **7.39 (a)** Bell shape with mean = \$84,396, standard deviation = \$2197.5. **(b)** $z = -2.00$. **(c)** 0.93. **7.41 (a)** $z = -0.67$. **(b)** $z = -10$. **(c)** For an individual PDI value, 90 is only 0.67 standard deviations below the mean and is not surprising. However, it would be unusual for the mean of a sample of size 225 to be 10 standard deviations below the mean of its sampling distribution. **7.43 (a)** 0.003. **(b)** 0.05. **(c) (i)** 0.002; **(ii)** 0.004. **7.45** As n increases, the sampling distribution becomes more bell shaped and has less variability around the mean **7.47** The standard deviation of the sampling distribution describes how closely a sample statistic will be to the parameter it is designed to estimate, in this case how close the sample proportion will be to the unknown population proportion. **7.49 (a)**

Sample	Number Who Prefer Pizza A	Proportion Who Prefer Pizza A
AAA	3	1
AAD	2	2/3
ADA	2	2/3
DAA	2	2/3
ADD	1	1/3
DAD	1	1/3
DDA	1	1/3
DDD	0	0

(b) If the proportion of the population that favors Aunt Erma's pizza is 0.50, each of the eight outcomes listed in part a are equally likely. Thus, the probability of obtaining a sample proportion of 0 is 1/8, a sample proportion of 1/3 has a $(1 + 1 + 1)/8 = 3/8$ chance, a sample proportion of 2/3 has a $(1 + 1 + 1)/8 = 3/8$ chance and a sample proportion of 1 has a 1/8 chance. This describes the sampling distribution of the sample proportion for $n = 3$ with $p = 0.50$. **(c)** For $p = 0.5$ and $n = 50$, the mean and standard deviation of the sampling distribution are 0.5 and $\sqrt{(0.5)(0.5)/50} = 0.0707$. **7.51 (a)** For example, P(sample proportion $= 2/3) = P(X = 2) = 3(0.6)^2(0.4)^1 = 0.432$. **(b)** Mean number of persons preferring A: $n(p) = 100(0.6) = 60$. **(c)** Expected proportion $= 60/100 = 0.6$. **7.53** When we ran the simulations, we got a mean of 0.60 and a standard deviation of 0.282 for the 10,000 simulated sample proportions. These are almost identical to the theoretical mean and standard deviation of the sampling distribution, which are 0.60 and 0.283. **7.55** False. **7.57** (c). **7.59** (a) **7.61** Standard deviation $= \sigma/\sqrt{n} = \sqrt{p(1-p)}/\sqrt{n} = \sqrt{p(1-p)/n}$. **7.63** **(c)** You expect the mean to be close to the population mean of 196. **(d)** You expect the standard deviation to be close to $57.4/\sqrt{9} = 19.1$, which is the standard deviation of the sampling distribution when $n = 9$. **7.65** **(b)** This is a sampling distribution, and with ten coins in each sample, the distribution should be closer to a normal distribution than that in part a. It should also have less variability around the mean than the distribution in part a.

Chapter 8

8.1 (a) Proportion with health insurance in population; mean amount spent on insurance by population. **(b)** Sample proportion and sample mean. **8.3 (a)** 0.548. **(b)** (0.518, 0.578). **(c)** A point estimate gives one specific number, such as a mean. An interval estimate gives a range of numbers. **8.5 (a)** 0.90 or 90% **(b)** With a probability of 95%, the point estimate of 0.9 falls within a distance of 0.045 of the actual proportion of German citizens who find it unacceptable. **8.7 (a)** 62.2. **(b)** (57.3, 67.1). **(c)** An interval estimate gives us a sense of the accuracy of the point estimate whereas a point estimate alone does not. **8.9 (a)**

Response	Percentage
0	54.0
1	13.9
2	8.6
3	6.6
4	4.1
5	3.0
6	1.4
7	8.4

Mean = 1.5, standard deviation = 2.2. **(b)** This is the standard deviation of the sampling distribution for samples of size 1450. **8.11** Answers will vary. **8.13 (a)** 0.00615 **(b)** 0.00125 **(c)** 0.00245 **(d)** $0.00615 \pm 0.00245 = [0.00370, 0.00861]$. We are 95% confident that the proportion of people receiving the flu shot but still developing the flu is between 0.37% and 0.86%. **(e)** Yes. The upper limit of the confidence interval is 0.86%, which is less than 1%. **8.15 (a)** Random sample, number of successes and failures both greater than 15; yes. **(b)** (0.925, 0.949); yes, a majority. **8.17** 1 − [0.63, 0.67]; 95% confidence interval for proportion opposing: [0.33, 37] **8.19 (a)** 1.645. **(b)** 2.33. **(c)** 3.29. **8.21** The population is all Republicans; we can be 95% confident that the population proportion of Republicans who believe stem cell research has merit is between 0.55 and 0.61. **8.23 (a)** $0.655 + -2.58\sqrt{(0.655 \times 0.345/316)} = -.655 + -0.069 = (0.586, 0.724)$. At the 99% confidence level, a range of plausible values for the population proportion of chicken breast that contain E.coli is 0.586 to 0.724. Yes, I can conclude the proportion of chicken containing E.coli exceeds 50% because all plausible values are above 0.50. **(b)** The 95% confidence interval would be narrower because the margin of error will decrease. The z-score will be 1.96 compared to 2.58 for the 99% confidence interval. **8.25 (a)** Yes; because 0.50 falls outside of the confidence interval of 0.445 to 0.498. **(b)** No; because 0.50 falls in the confidence interval of 0.437 to 0.506. The more confident we want to be, the wider the confidence interval must be. **8.27** The percentage we'd expect would be 95% and 99%, but the actual values may differ a bit because of sampling variability. **8.29 (a)** The sample mean 2.56 **(b)** $0.84/\sqrt{590} = 0.035$ **(c)** We are 95% confident that the mean ideal number of children for females is between 2.49 and 2.62. **(d)** No, because 2 falls outside the interval. **8.31 (a)** 2.776. **(b)** 2.145. **(c)** 2.977. **8.33 (a)** Shape is right-skewed. Assumptions are a random sample (fulfilled) and approximately normal distribution (questionable because of right-skew, but the t-interval is robust to deviation from normal). Outlier at 1050 might make validity of results questionable. **(b)** $553 \pm 2.179 \times 227/\sqrt{13} = (416, 690)$. We are 95% confident that the mean talk time of smartphones is at least 416 minutes and at most 690 minutes. **(c)** i.) $Q3 + 1.5 \times IQR = 650 + 1.5 \times (650 - 420) = 995$, so value of 1050 is outlier; $Q1 - 1.5 \times IQR = 75$, no outliers on lower end. ii.) $z = (1050 - 553)/227 = 2.19$, so 1050 not an outlier using 3*s*. **(d)** New interval: (399, 624) using $df = 11$; interval is narrower and centered at a smaller value (512 instead of 553). **8.35 (a)** Assumptions are a random sample (fulfilled) and approximately normal distribution of Buy It Now price. The dotplot and box plot suggest a bell-shaped distribution except for an outlier indicated by the box plot that might make results questionable. However, its *z*-score = 2.2, so it is within 3*s*. **(b)** $20.47/\sqrt{9} = 6.82$ **(c)** We are 95% confident that the mean Buy It Now price of the iPhone 5s on eBay is between \$615 and \$647. **(d)** Yes, all plausible values for the mean Buy It Now price are larger than the plausible values for mean closing price of auctions. **(e)** No, the interval computed without \$675 still lies above (569, 599). **8.37 (a)** $\bar{x} = 3.07$, $s = 3.38$, $se = 3.38/\sqrt{14} = 0.90$ **(b)** (1.47, 4.67). We have 90% confidence that the mean amount of time 80 years and older females spent on e-mail per week is between 1.5 and 4.7 hours. **(c)** Many women of age 80 or older will spend 0 or 1 hour per week on e-mail, with only a few spending more time. This leads to a right-skewed distribution. However, the *t*-interval is robust against departures from the normal distribution assumption. Also, there are no outliers in the preceding sample, so the inference should still be valid. **8.39 (a)** No, 7 is outside of the interval. **(b)** (3.7, 4.5), margin of error decreases as sample size increases. **(c)** No, standard deviation is large relative to the mean. **(d)** Robust method, so analysis is still valid even if the assumption is not fully met. **8.41** Confidence interval is (4.3, 6.3). **8.43 (i)** 41.3 **(ii)** 55.9 Margin of error increases as confidence level increases. **8.45 (a)** $\bar{x} = 1.89$, $s = 1.67$, $se = \frac{1.67}{\sqrt{1971}} = 0.04$ **(b)** $1.89 \pm 1.96(0.04) = (1.81, 1.97)$; Yes, because entire interval is below 2. **8.47** 196. **8.49 (a)** 385. **(b)** 237. **(c)** Larger sample is unnecessary resulting in greater time/cost. **8.51** 1535. **8.53** 2663. **8.55** Random sample of 100 because website does not provide random sample. **8.57 (a)** (0.39, 0.89). **(b)** Yes, 0.50 is in the interval. **8.59** Allows us to calculate confidence intervals for various parameters when the usual formulas do not apply. **8.61 (a)** Mean = 11.6, Median = 6 **(b)** (10.8, 12.4) **(c)** Sample, with replacement, 1399 values from the sample (where each value has a 1 in 1399 chance of being selected). Compute the mean for each such resample. Do this 10,000 times. The 2.5th and 97.5th percentile of these 10,000 values are the lower and upper bounds for a confidence interval for the mean. **(d)** (10.8, 12.4) , using 10,000 resamples **(e)** The bootstrap distribution of looks approximately normal. This is not surprising. The central limit theorem predicts that for large sample sizes (here 1399), the sampling distribution of the mean will have this shape, regardless of the shape of the population distribution. **8.63 (a)** Point estimates **(b)** Not sufficient. Need to know sample size for females and males. **8.65** $1.96\sqrt{0.86(1 - 0.86)/1667} = 0.017$ and $1.96\sqrt{0.73(1 - 0.73)/1667} = 0.021$ **8.67** $0.81 \pm 0.018 = (0.792, 0.828)$; with 95% confidence, we predict the proportion of Americans believing in life after death to be between 79.2% and 82.8%. **8.69 (a)** Data were obtained randomly. **(b)** (0.035, 0.045); mainly because of the very large sample size. **(c)** Yes; 10% falls above the highest plausible value in the confidence interval. **8.71** No; because you have data for the entire population; you don't have to estimate it. **8.73 (a)** 496 said "legal." 751 said "not legal." 0.398 and 0.602. **(b)** Minority; 0.50 is above the highest believable value for the percentage who think it should be made legal in the 95% confidence interval of 0.37 to 0.43. **(c)** It appears that the proportion favoring legalization is increasing over time. **8.75 (a)** We are 95% confident that the percentage of U.S. adults regularly watching television shows via streaming is between 41% and 45%. **(b)** Wider. To have more confidence, we need a wider interval. Technically, the *z*-score changes from 1.96 to 2.58, resulting in a wider interval. **(c)** Narrower. With 5000 adults, we have more information, resulting in a smaller standard error for the sample proportion. A smaller standard error leads to a narrower margin of error and thus narrower interval. **8.77 (a)** FALSE (true percentage may be as large as 52%) **(b)** TRUE, because 76% is no longer a plausible value and is outside the confidence interval **8.79 (a)** Because the standard error is very small. **(b)** We need the standard deviation. **8.81 (a)** With only 10 observations, hard to determine shape, but distribution may be bell shaped or skewed right. There are no outliers in the sample. **(b)** (19.7, 25.7). We have 95% confidence that the mean combined mpg for SUVs manufactured from 2012 to 2015 is between 19.7 and 25.7 mpg. **8.83** Sample size = N = 190, sample mean income = \$49,411, standard deviation = \$15,440, standard error = \$1120.1, we can be 95% confident that the population mean income is between \$47,204 and \$51,618. **8.85 (a)** (1.67, 1.95). We can be 95% confident that the population mean number of days women have felt sad over the past seven days is between 1.68 and 1.95. **(b)** Not likely normal; not a problem since random sample size is large. **8.87 (a)** $n = 1451$. **(b)** 0.05. **(c)** Random sample, population distribution approximately normal; CI = (5.2, 5.4); yes since the values in the interval are greater than 5. **8.89 (a)** Mean Buy It Now selling price of all Samsung phones of this type posted on sale on eBay in July 2014. **(b)** $\bar{x} = 557$ **(c)** $s = 37$, $se = 10.6$. The average deviation of prices from the sample mean of \$557 is \$37. The average deviation of the sample mean $\bar{x}$ to the population mean μ is \$10.6. **(d)** (554, 600). We are 95% confident that the average Buy It Now price for this type of smartphone on eBay is between \$554 and \$600. **8.91 (a)** No, because the standard deviation is large relative to the mean. **(b)** Random sample and approximately normal population distribution; distribution is not normal, but method is valid since sample size is large. **(c)** The interval refers to the mean number of hours of TV watched in a typical day for adult females. It does not refer to the range of possible hours of TV watched by a typical female 95% of the time. **8.93 (a)** Assumes that strongly agree and agree are the same distance apart as strongly disagree and disagree but there is a larger difference between agree and disagree. **(b)** The sample mean is close to neutral, but slightly closer to disagree. **(c)** Consider the proportion who responded in each way. **8.95 (a)** $se = 0.029$. **(b)** The lowest possible value of 0 is less than one standard deviation below the mean. **(c)** Because the method is robust with respect to the normal distribution assumption. **8.97 (a)** 385. **(b)** 601; if we can make an educated guess, we can use a smaller sample size. **8.99 (a)** 385; the solution makes the assumption that the standard deviation will be similar now. **(b)** More than \$100 because the standard error will be larger than predicted. **(c)** With a larger margin of error, the 95% confidence interval is wider; thus, the probability that the sample mean is within \$100 of the population mean is less than 0.95. **8.101 (a)** (0.67, 1.00). **(b)** 0.67. **(c)** The random sample assumption might not be met, the player might react well to a first success, increasing his or her chances of future successes. **8.103** The assumptions on which the confidence intervals are based are that the data were randomly produced and that the population distributions are approximately normal. The confidence interval for white subjects is (2.837, 3.123) and for black subjects it is (3.865, 4.895). It seems that blacks watch more TV than do whites, on the average. **8.105** Running the house: CI = (0.134, 0.166); because 0.50 does not fall in this range, we can conclude that fewer than half of the population agrees with the statement that women should take care of running their homes and leave running the country up to the men. Man as the achiever: CI = (0.320, 0.364); because 0.50 does not fall in this range, we can conclude that fewer than half of the population agrees with the statement that it is better for everyone involved if the man is the achiever outside the home and the woman takes care of the home and the family. Preschool child: CI = (0.401, 0.447); because 0.50 does not fall in this range and all plausible values are less than 0.50, we can conclude that fewer than half of the population agrees with the statement that a preschool child is likely to suffer if her mother works. **8.107** When we have more confidence that our parameter falls within the interval, the interval will be wider; when the sample size is larger, we have greater accuracy in our interval estimate (i.e., the standard error is smaller) so the interval will be narrower. **8.109 (a)** $(0.5)(30) = 15$. **(b)** $(0.3)(50) = 15$. **(c)** $(0.1)(150) = 15$. **8.111 (a)** Increasing the confidence level increases *z* which increases *n*. **(b)** Decreasing *m* increases *n* since *m* is in the denominator. **8.113** (b). **8.115** (a). **8.117** If we repeatedly took samples of 50 records from the population, approximately 95% of those intervals would contain the population mean age. **8.119** False. **8.121** True **8.123 (a)** If we took many samples of the same size from the population in that year and computed the confidence interval for each, 95% of the time the interval captures the true proportion supporting the death penalty. **(b)** $n = 26, p =$ probability of capturing true proportion $= 0.95$. $P(X = 26) = (0.95)^{26} = 0.2635$ **(c)** $26(0.95) = 24.7$ **(d)** Increase the confidence level, e.g., to 99.5%. **8.125 (a)** $|\hat{p} - p| = 1.96\sqrt{p(1-p)/n}$; $|1 - p| = 1.96\sqrt{p(1-p)/20}$; If we substitute 0.83887 for p, we get $1 - 0.83887 = 0.16113$ on both sides of the equation. If we substitute 1 for p, we get 0 on the left and on the right. **(b)** This confidence interval seems more believable because it forms an actual interval and contains more than just the value of 1. **8.127** If the population is normal, the standard error of the median is 1.25 times the standard error of the mean. This means a larger margin of error, and therefore, a wider confidence interval. **8.129** Answers will vary.

Chapter 9

9.1 (a) Null. **(b)** Alternative. **(c)** (a) H_0: $p = 0.50$; H_a: $p \neq 0.50$. **(b)** H_0: $p = 0.24$; H_a: $p < 0.24$. **9.3 (a)** H_0: The mean toxicity level equals the threshold ("no effect," H_0 specifies a single value, the threshold, for the parameter); H_a: The mean toxicity level exceeds the threshold. **(b)** H_0: The mean toxicity level equals the threshold; H_a: The mean toxicity level is below the threshold. **9.5 (a)** Alternative; it has a range of parameter values. **(b)** The relevant parameter is the mean weight change, μ. H_0: $\mu = 0$; this is a null hypothesis. **9.7 (a)** Null and alternative hypothesis are always about population parameters (e.g., p or μ) and never about sample statistics such as $\hat{p}$ or $\bar{x}$. Correct: H_0: $p = 0.5$, H_a: $p > 0.5$ **(b)** The alternative hypothesis needs to specify a range of parameters. Correct: H_0: $\mu = 100$, H_a: $\mu > 100$ **(c)** The range of values in the alternative hypothesis needs to be an "alternative" to the value specified in the null, so it cannot include the null value. ($p > 0.10$ includes the null value 0.30.) Correct: H_0: $p = 0.30$, H_a: $p > 0.30$ or H_0: $p = 0.10$, H_a: $p > 0.10$. **9.9 (a)** Not strong evidence against null hypothesis. **(b)** Strong evidence against null. **9.11** H_0: $p = 1/4$ and H_a: $p > 1/4$; p is the true probability of a correct prediction. **9.13 (a) (i)** 0.006; **(ii)** 0.012; **(iii)** 0.994. **(b)** Yes, those in **(i)** and **(ii)** are very small. **9.15 (a)** H_0: $p = 1/5$. **(b)** H_a: $p \neq 1/5$. **(c)** H_a: $p > 1/5$. **(d)** P-value ≈ 0. The probability of obtaining a sample proportion of 81 or more successes in 83 trials is essentially 0. **9.17 (a)** $p =$ proportion of adults who guess correctly; H_0: $p = 1/3$ and H_a: $p > 1/3$. **(b)** $\hat{p} = 28/83 = 0.337$; $se = \sqrt{p_0(1 - p_0)/n} = \sqrt{0.333(1 - 0.333)/83} = 0.052$; $z = (0.337 - 0.333)/0.052 = 0.08$. **(c)** The P-value is 0.47. If the null hypothesis were true, the probability would be 0.47 of getting a test statistic at least as extreme as the value observed. We would not conclude that people are more likely to select their correct horoscope than if they were randomly guessing. **9.19 (a)** $\hat{p} = 22/30 = 0.733$; $se = \sqrt{p_0(1 - p_0)/n} = \sqrt{0.50(1 - 0.50)/30} = 0.091$; $z = (0.733 - 0.5)/0.091 = 2.56$. **(b)** Area beyond $z = 2.56$ is 0.005, doubling to include both tails gives a P-value of 0.01. If the null hypothesis were true, the probability would be 0.01 of getting a test statistic at least as extreme as the value observed. **(c)** The data must be categorical and obtained using randomization, and the sample size must be large enough that the sampling distribution is approximately normal. Sample size was large enough for normality assumption. In this case, the data were obtained from a convenience sample which might not be representative of the population. **9.21** Plausible values for probability of a female to be selected range from 0.16 to 0.44. This is in accordance with the decision reached in part e of the previous exercise not to reject the null hypothesis H_0: $p = 0.4$ in favor of the alternative hypothesis H_a: $p \neq 0.4$ because 0.4 is a plausible value for that probability. **9.23 (a)** The variable is whether someone voted for Brown. The parameter of interest is the proportion among all California voters who voted for Brown. **(b)** H_0: $p = 0.5$ against H_a: $p \neq 0.5$. Assumption: The variable of whether someone votes for Brown is categorical. The 3889 voters in the exit poll need to be a random sample from all eligible voters, which they are. We expect $3889(0.5) = 1944.5$ successes and failures, which is more than 15, so we can use the normal sampling distribution of the large sample test. **(c)** Test statistic $z = 3.87$. P-value < 0.001. Assuming $p = 0.5$, the probability of observing a sample percentage of 53.1% or higher (or 46.9% or smaller, since two-sided) is highly unlikely, i.e., less than 0.1%. We thus have strong evidence that the proportion voting for Brown in the population is different from 50%. **(d)** Because the P-value is less than 5%, we can reject the null hypothesis. There is very strong evidence that the proportion of voters voting for Brown is different from 50%. Our sample percentage of 53.1% indicated it is higher. We predict that Brown will win the election. **9.25 (1)** Assumptions: The data are categorical, assume the data are obtained randomly, the expected successes and failures are both at least 15 under H_0; $np = (50)(0.5) \geq 15$, and $np \geq (50)(0.5) \geq 15$. **(2)** Hypotheses: H_0: $p = 0.50$; H_a: $p \neq 0.50$. **(3)** Test statistic: $z = 0.85$. **(4)** P-value $= 0.40$. **(5)** Conclusion: There is weak evidence against H_0. We would not reject H_0. **9.27 (a)** There are two possible outcomes, each trial holds the same probability of success, and the n trials are independent. **(b)** The P-value represents the probability of observing the test statistic $x = 22$ or a value even more extreme (larger) if the population proportion is 1/7. **9.29 (a)** 0.026 or 0.03. **(b)** 0.013. **(c)** 0.987. **9.31 (a)** P-value $= 0.00$. **(b)** This is the probability of observing a test statistic of -8.2 or even more extreme (in either direction) if the null hypothesis of no weight change is true. Equivalently, this is the probability of observing a sample mean weight change (loss or gain) of 5.5 kg or more if the null hypothesis is true. **(c)** Yes, we would reject H_0. The P-value $= 0$ is less than a significance level of 0.05. The 95% confidence interval contains all negative differences and does not contain the hypothesized value of 0. **9.33 (a)** Variable: Number of friends on Facebook. Parameter: Mean number μ of friends for students at Williams that use Facebook **(b)** H_0: $\mu = 100$, H_a: $\mu > 100$. **(c)** $t = (122.7 - 100)/(71.8/\sqrt{13}) = 1.14$. The observed sample mean of 122.7 falls 1.14 standard errors above the null hypothesis value of 100. **(d)** P-value $=$ probability in upper tail $= 0.138$. The probability of observing a test statistic this large or larger (equivalently a sample mean that is this high or even higher) when the null hypothesis is true is not that small (about 14%). This does not provide evidence to reject the null hypothesis. There is insufficient evidence to conclude that the mean number of Facebook friends is larger than 100. **9.35 (1)** Assumptions: Random sample on a quantitative variable having a normal population distribution. Here, the data are not likely produced using randomization. Population distribution may be skewed, but the test is two-sided so is robust to a violation of the normal population assumption. **(2)** Hypotheses: H_0: $\mu = 0$; H_a: $\mu \neq 0$. **(3)** Test statistic: $t = -0.32$. **(4)** P-value: 0.75. **(5)** Conclusion: Since the P-value is large, it is plausible that the null hypothesis is correct, and that there was no change in mean weight in the control group. **9.37 (1)** Assumptions: The data are produced using randomization, from a normal population distribution. **(2)** Hypotheses: H_0: $\mu = 5.1$; H_a: $\mu \neq 5.1$. **(3)** Test statistic: $t = \dfrac{(5.065 - 5.1)}{0.087/\sqrt{4}} = -0.80$. **(4)** P-value: 0.48. **(5)** Conclusion: If the null hypothesis were true, the probability would be 0.48 of getting a test statistic at least as extreme as the value observed. There is no evidence to support that the population mean is different than 5.1 ounces. **9.39 (a)** The confidence interval does not include 0 and also indicates that coupons led to higher sales than did the outside posters. **(b)** A one-sided test might be problematic because if the population distribution is highly non-normal (such as very skewed) the method is not robust for a one-sided test. **9.41** The test statistic changes from 2.21 to 1.98, and the P-value changes from 0.04 to 0.06. The test statistic is less extreme, and the P-value > 0.05. We can no longer reject the null hypothesis. The conclusion does depend on the single observation of 20.9. **9.43 (a)** Reject H_0. **(b)** Type I: Conclude that dogs can detect urine from bladder cancer patients but they are not really able to do so better than chance guessing. **9.45 (a)** Concluding that those opposing fracking are in the minority when in fact they are not. **(b)** Saying that there is no evidence of a minority of those who oppose fracking when, in fact, they are in the minority. **9.47 (a)** Reject H_0, conclude that the population mean weight change post-therapy is greater than 0. **(b)** Type I. **(c)** Fail to reject H_0; type II. **9.49 (a)** If H_0 is rejected, we conclude that the new drug is not safe. **(b)** A Type I error would result in finding the drug is not safe when it actually is safe. **(c)** If we fail to reject H_0, we conclude that the drug is safe. **(d)** A Type II error would result in failing to find the drug not safe when it actually is not safe. **9.51 (a)** Diagnose prostate cancer when there is none; results in treatment or further testing for patient who does not need it. **(b)** Fail to diagnose prostate cancer when it is present; results in a patient not receiving needed care. **(c)** Type II error. **(d)** The 2/3 refers to the probability that someone does not have prostate cancer given that he received a positive result. The probability of a Type I error, refers to the probability that someone will receive a positive result, given that he does not have prostate cancer. **9.53 (a)** Researcher A: P-value $= 2P(z > 2.0) = 0.046$. **(b)** Researcher B: P-value $= 2P(z > 1.90) = 0.057$. **(c)** Part a leads to statistically significant result, part b does not. Results that are not different from one another in practical terms might lead to different conclusions if based on statistical significance alone. **(d)** If we do not see these two P-values, but merely know that one is statistically significant and one is not, we are not able to see that the P-values are so similar. **(e)** We can add and subtract the result of (1.96)(0.025), namely the z-score associated with a 95% confidence interval multiplied by the standard error, to the sample proportions for each of these samples to get confidence intervals of (0.501, 0.599) for Researcher A and (0.499, 0.596) for Researcher B. This method shows the enormous amount of overlap between the two confidence intervals. **9.55 (a)** $t = 0.31$ **(b)** P-value $= 0.76$. The probability of observing a test statistic this large or larger (in either direction), given the null hypothesis is true, is quite large (about 76%). It is plausible that the population mean score is 4.0. **(c)** $4.09 \pm 2.064(1.43/\sqrt{25}) = (3.5, 4.7)$ **(d) (i)** A decrease in sample size increases the P-value; **(ii)** confidence intervals become wider as sample sizes become smaller. **9.57** If we report only results that are "statistically significant," these are the only ones of which the public becomes aware. There might be many studies on the same topic that did not reject the null and did not get published, which may be misleading to the public because the published result may well be a Type I error. **9.59 (a)** No, it just means that the difference in proportions was not found to be statistically significant. No, not exactly the same, but the difference between the two population proportions is small and not relevant. **(b)** Research that suggests an impact of a therapy or drug tends to get the most media coverage if it's a very large difference. It's possible that studies that found little or no difference did not get media coverage. **9.61 (a)** $se = \sqrt{0.4(1-0.4)/50} = 0.069$; the value 1.645 standard errors below 0.4 is $0.4 - 1.645(0.069) = 0.286$. **(b)** $se = \sqrt{0.2(1-0.2)/50} = 0.0566$, $z = (0.286 - 0.20)/0.0566 = 1.52$, $p(z > 1.52) = 0.06$. Thus, P(Type II error) $= 0.06$. **9.63 (a)** $Z = \dfrac{0.405 - 0.35}{\sqrt{0.35(1-0.35)/116}} = 1.24$, P(Type II error) $= P(z < 1.24) = 0.89$. **(b)** The chances of failing to reject H_0 when the hypothesized value is close to the true value is higher than when it is far away because we are less likely to detect a difference when that difference is small. **9.65 (a)** If truly $p = 0.2$, then with 60% probability, the proposed trial will lead to a rejection of the null hypothesis H_0: $p = 0.1$ in favor of H_a: $p > 0.1$. **(b)** Not rejecting H_0: $p = 0.1$, when, in fact, $p > 0.1$. **(c)** P(Type II error when $p = 0.2$) $= 1 -$ P(not committing a Type II error when $p = 0.2$) $= 1 -$ (Power when $p = 0.2$) $= 1 - 0.60 = 0.4$. **9.67 (a)** Null. **(b)** Alternative. **(c)** Alternative. **(d)** Null. **9.69 (1)** Observed variable is categorical (correct vs. incorrect guess) and obtained through a randomized experiment (coin flips). We expect $np = 30(0.5) = 15$ successes and $n(1-p) = 30(0.5) = 15$ failures, so sample size condition is met. **(2)** H_0: $p = 0.5$, H_a: $p > 0.5$, where p = probability of her guess being correct. **(3)** $z = 1.1$ **(4)** P-value $= 0.137$ **(5)** Since the P-value is not small, there is insufficient evidence to support the claim that the probability of a correct guess is larger than 0.5 or 50%. **9.71 (a) (1)** Assumptions: The data are categorical (Brown, Whitman, someone else) and obtained through a random sample; the expected successes and failures are both at least fifteen under H_0; $np = (0.5)(650) \geq 15$, and $n(1-p) = (0.5)(650) \geq 15$. **(2)** p = population proportion of voters who prefer Brown. Hypotheses: H_0: $p = 0.50$; H_a: $p \neq 0.50$. **(3)** Test statistic: $z = \dfrac{0.554 - 0.50}{\sqrt{0.5(1-0.5)/650}} = 2.75$. **(4)** P-value: 0.006. **(5)** Conclusion: We can reject the null hypothesis at a significance level of 0.05; we do have strong evidence that the population proportion of voters who chose Brown is different from 0.50. **(b)** If the sample size had been 50, the test statistic would have been $z = \dfrac{0.56 - 0.50}{\sqrt{0.5(1-0.5)/50}} = 0.849$, and the P-value would have been 0.40. We could not have rejected the null hypothesis under these circumstances. **(c)** With a sample of size 50, the standard error can be too large to reject H_0: $p = 0.5$. With a sample of size 650, the standard error is small enough to reject H_0, even though the two samples result in roughly the same sample proportion of 0.55. **9.73 (1)** Assumptions: Observed variable is categorical (whether agree or not) and come from a random sample. Expected number of successes and failures both larger than 15. $(1690(0.5) = 845)$. **(2)** Hypotheses: H_0: $p = 0.5$, H_a: $p \neq 0.5$ where p is proportion of Americans agreeing that homosexuals should be able to marry. **(3)** Test statistic: $se_0 = \sqrt{0.5(1-0.5)/1690} = 0.0122$; $z = (0.565 - 0.5)/0.0122 = 5.35$. **(4)** P-value < 0.001 **(5)** Conclusion: At the 0.05 significance level, we have strong evidence (P-value < 0.001) that the proportion of Americans agreeing with the statement that homosexuals should have the right to marry is different from 0.5. With a sample proportion of 0.565, a clear majority now supports gay marriage. **9.75 (a)** p = proportion of people who would pick Box A; H_0: $p = 0.50$; H_a: $p \neq 0.50$. **(b)** $z = 5.06$; P-value $= 0.000$. There is very strong evidence to conclude that the population proportion that chooses Box A is not 0.50. Box A seems to be preferred. **9.77** We are testing "$p = 0.50$ versus not $= 0.50$." X is 40, the number of people in the sample who preferred the card with the annual cost. 100 is the "N," the size of the whole sample. "Sample p" of 0.40 is the proportion of the sample that preferred the card with the annual cost. "95.0% CI" is the 95% confidence interval. "Z-Value" is the test statistic. "P-Value" tells us that if the null hypothesis were true, the proportion 0.0455 of samples would fall at least this far from the null hypothesis proportion of 0.50. The majority of the customers seem to prefer the card without the annual cost. **9.79 (a)** Type I error would have occurred if we had rejected the null hypothesis, when really women were not being passed over. A Type II error would occur if we had failed to reject the null, but women really were being picked disproportionate to their representation in the jury pool. **(b)** Type I error. **9.81 (b)** Sufficient evidence to reject null and conclude that the population mean is not 0. **(c)** 0.001; we have strong evidence to conclude that the population mean is positive. **(d)** 0.999; insufficient evidence to conclude that the population mean is negative. **9.83 (a)** H_0: $\mu = 40$; H_a: $\mu \neq 40$ **(b) (i)** SE Mean = standard error of sampling distribution of sample mean = 0.455, **(ii)** T = t test statistic = 0.59 = distance (measured in standard errors) of the sample mean of 40.27 from null value of 40 hours, **(iii)** P-value = 0.55 = probability of observing a sample mean of 40.27 or more extreme (on either side) when the null hypothesis is true. This is rather large, so the sample mean is not unusually extreme if H_0 is true. No evidence to reject the null hypothesis. **(c)** Confidence interval shows that 40 is a plausible value for the hours in a workweek in the population. This is consistent with result of hypothesis test, which does not reject H_0: $\mu = 40$. **9.85 (a) (1)** Data are quantitative and have been produced randomly and have an approximate normal population distribution. **(2)** H_0: $\mu = 130$; H_a: $\mu \neq 130$. **(3)** The sample mean is 150.0 and standard deviation is 8.37; $t = 5.85$. **(4)** P-value $= 0.002$. **(5)** Strong evidence to conclude that the true mean is different from 130. **(b)** We do not know whether the population distribution is normal, but the two-sided test is robust for violations of this assumption. **9.87 (a)** Software indicates a test statistic of -5.5 and a P-value of 0.001. **(b)** For a significance level of 0.05, we would conclude that the process is not in control. **(c)** If we rejected the null hypothesis when it is in fact true, we have made a Type I error and concluded that the process is not in control when it actually is. **9.89 (1)** Data are quantitative and seem to have been produced randomly; also assume approximately normal population distribution. **(2)** H_0: $\mu = 500$; H_a: $\mu \neq 500$. **(3)** $t = -13.9$. **(4)** P-value $= 0.000$. **(5)** Extremely strong evidence that the population mean is different from 500. **9.91 (a)** We can reject the null hypothesis. **(b)** It would be a Type I error. **(c)** No, because the P value is less than 0.05; when a value is rejected by a test at the 0.05 significance level, it does not fall in the 95% confidence interval. **9.93 (a)** By choosing a smaller significance level. **(b)** It will be too difficult to reject the null hypothesis, even if the null hypothesis is not true. **9.95 (a)** $\sqrt{0.333(1-0.333)/60} = 0.061$.

(b) When P(Type I error) = significance level = 0.05, $z = 1.645$, the value 1.645 standard errors above 0.333 is 0.433. **(c)** 0.15; Type II error is larger when n is smaller, because a smaller n results in a larger standard error and makes it more difficult to have a sample proportion fall in the rejection region. **9.97** Answers will vary. **9.99 (a)** These data give us a sense of what the probability would look like in the long run. If we look at just a few games, we don't get to see the overall pattern, but when we look at a number of games over time, we start to see the long run probability of the home team winning (in this case 1359/2430). **(b)** $z = \frac{0.5592 - 0.5}{\sqrt{0.5(1-0.5)/2430}} = 5.8$. P-value = 0.000. We can add and subtract the result of (1.96)(0.0101), namely the z-score associated with a 95% confidence interval multiplied by the standard error, to the sample proportion to obtain a confidence interval of (0.54, 0.58) for the probability of the home team scoring more runs. The test merely indicates whether $p = 0.50$ is plausible whereas the confidence interval displays the range of plausible values. **9.101 (a)** After seeing the data, we know the direction of results; it is cheating to do a one-tailed test now. **(b)** If there really is no effect, but many studies are conducted, eventually someone will achieve significance, and then the journal will publish a Type I error. **9.103** The subgroups have smaller sample size, so for a particular size of effect will have a smaller test statistic and a larger P-value. **9.105** The studies with the most extreme results will give the smallest P-values and be most likely to be statistically significant. If we could look at how results from all studies vary around a true effect, the most extreme results would be out in a tail, suggesting an effect much larger than it actually is. **9.107** Just because the sample statistic was not extreme enough to conclude that the value at H_0 is unlikely doesn't mean that the value in H_0 is the actual value. A confidence interval would show that there is a whole range of plausible values, not just the null value. **9.109** Statistical significance: strong evidence that the true parameter value is not the value in H_0; practical significance: true parameter is sufficiently different from value in H_0 to be important in practical terms. **9.111** With the probability of a false-positive diagnosis being about 50% over the course of 10 mammograms, it would not be unusual for a woman to receive a false positive over the course of having had many mammograms. Likewise, if you conduct 10 significance tests at the 0.05 significance level in 10 cases in which the null hypothesis is actually true, it would not be surprising if you sometime reject the null hypothesis just by chance. **9.113** Suppose P-value = 0.057. If the significance level were any number above this, we would have enough evidence to reject the null; if it were any number below this, there would not be enough evidence. **9.115** (b). **9.117** (a). **9.119** False. **9.121** False. **9.123** False. **9.125** False. **9.127** Sample proportion = 0, standard error = 0, test statistic = infinity, which does not make sense. A significance test is conducted by supposing the null is true, so in finding the test statistic we should substitute the null hypothesis value, giving a more appropriate standard error. **9.129** Answers will vary.

Chapter 10

10.1 (a) The response variable is unemployment rate and the explanatory variable is race. **(b)** The two groups that are the categories of the explanatory variable are white and black individuals. **(c)** The samples of white and black individuals were independent. No individuals could be in both samples. **10.3 (a)** Point estimate = 0.422 − 0.212 = 0.21. We estimate the population proportion of students reporting binge drinking has decreased by 0.21 from the 1999 survey to the 2009 survey. In terms of percentages, the percent of students reporting binge drinking has decreased by 21 percentage points. **(b)** The standard error is the estimated standard deviation of the sampling distribution for the difference between two sample proportions. Using the formula, plugging in the sample proportions, $se = 0.0304$. **(c)** p_1 = proportion of student population in 1999 that binge drinks, p_2 = proportion of student population in 2009 that binge drinks **(d)** (0.15, 0.27); we are 95% confident that the proportion of the student population binge drinking in 1999 is between 0.15 and 0.27 higher than in 2009. Because the interval does not contain 0, i.e., is entirely positive, we can conclude that $p_1 > p_2$, i.e., that the proportion in 1999 was larger. **(e)** The assumptions are that the response variable is categorical (whether students binge drink) and observed in two groups (years 1999 and 2009), that the two samples are independent (the response of students sampled in 1999 is independent from the ones sampled in 2009) and obtained randomly (given), and that the two sample sizes are sufficiently large (both have at least 10 successes and 10 failures). **10.5 (a)** 0.46; 0.63. **(b)** We're 95% confident that the population proportion for females falls between 0.11 higher and 0.22 higher than the population proportion for males; 0 is not in this interval, so we conclude that females are more likely to say that they believe in miracles. Assumptions: categorical data, independent and randomly obtained samples, sufficient sample size. **(c)** The confidence interval has a wide range of plausible values, including some (such as 0.11) that indicate a moderate difference and some (such as 0.22) that indicate a relatively large difference. **10.7 (a)** H_0: $p_1 = p_2$; H_a: $p_1 \neq p_2$. **(b)** If the null were true, we would obtain a difference at least this extreme a proportion 0.14 of the time. **(c)** This study has smaller samples than the Physicians Health Study did. Therefore, its standard error was larger and its test statistic was smaller. A smaller test statistic has a larger P-value. **(d)** 0.07. **10.9 (a)** Assumptions: Categorical response variable (whether someone has unplanned sex), two groups (students samples in 1999 and students samples in 2009), samples are random and independent (given), and must have at least 10 successes and 10 failures. Notation: p_1 = population proportion of students engaging in unplanned sex in 1999, p_2 = population proportion of students engaging in unplanned sex in 2009. Hypotheses: H_0: $p_1 = p_2$, H_a: $p_1 \neq p_2$. **(b)** Pooled proportion = $\hat{p}$ = 0.252; this is the estimate of the common proportion under H_0. **(c)** $se_0 = 0.028$. $z = 2.75$. P-value = 0.006. If the null hypothesis were true, the probability of observing a test statistic as or even more extreme is 0.6%. This is a small P-value. Therefore, we have strong evidence to reject H_0 and conclude that the population proportion of students engaging in unplanned sex in 1999 differs from the population proportion in 2009. **10.11 (a)** Each sample has at least 10 outcomes of each type; data are categorical; independent random samples; p: probability someone developed cancer; H_0: $p_1 = p_2$; H_a: $p_1 \neq p_2$. **(b)** The test statistic is 1.03, and the P-value is 0.30. We do not have strong evidence that there are different results. **(c)** We cannot reject the null hypothesis. **10.13** One of the assumptions for the inference in this section is that we have two independent samples. Here, we ask the same subjects two questions, so each subject is measured twice and the responses to the two questions are not independent. Therefore, we cannot use the methods of this section (but see Section 10.4). **10.15 (a)** The response variable is the amount of tax the student is willing to add to gasoline in order to encourage drivers to drive less or to drive more fuel-efficient cars; the explanatory variable is whether the student believes that global warming is a serious issue that requires immediate action or not. **(b)** Independent samples; the students were randomly sampled so which group the student falls in (yes or no to second question) should be independent of the other students. **(c)** A 95% confidence interval for the difference in the population mean responses on gasoline taxes for the two groups, $\mu_1 - \mu_2$, is given by $(\bar{x}_1 - \bar{x}_2) \pm t_{.025}(se)$ where $\bar{x}_1$ is the sample mean response on the gasoline tax for the group who responded yes to the second question, $\bar{x}_2$ is the sample mean response on the gasoline tax for the group who responded no to the second question, t is the t-score for a 95% confidence interval and $se = \sqrt{\frac{s_1^2}{n_1} + \frac{s_2^2}{n_2}}$ is the standard error of the difference in mean responses. **10.17 (a)** The margin of error is the t value of 2.576 multiplied by the standard error of 1.20 = 3.1. The bounds are 10.0, and 16.2. **(b)** This interval is wider than the 95% confidence interval because we have chosen a larger confidence level, and thus, the t value associated with it will be higher. To be more confident, we must include a wider range of plausible values. **10.19 (a)** $se = \sqrt{s_1^2/n_1 + s_2^2/n_2} = \sqrt{0.89^2/921 + 0.85^2/754} = 0.043$ **(b)** $0.04 \pm 1.96(0.043) = (-0.04, 0.12)$. In the U.S. population, the mean number of children that women think is ideal is between 0.04 smaller and 0.12 larger compared to what men think is ideal. Because 0 is in the confidence interval, with 95% confidence, the population mean number of children that women and men think is ideal does not differ significantly between the sexes. **10.21 (a)**

$se = 0.97$. **(b)** The 95% CI $(-4.79, -0.81)$ indicates that we can be 95% confident that the population mean difference is between -4.79 and -0.81. Because 0 does not fall in this interval, we can conclude that, on average, the sexually abused students had a lower population mean family cohesion than the non-abused students. **10.23 (a) (i)** Because the mean is very close to 0; **(ii)** Those who reported inhaling had a mean score that was $2.9 - 0.1 = 2.8$ higher. **(b)** Not for the noninhalers. The lowest possible value of 0, which was very common, was only a fraction of a standard deviation below the mean. **(c)** 0.24; it's approximately the standard deviation of the difference between sample means from different studies using these sample sizes. **(d)** Because 0 is not in this interval, we can conclude that there is a difference in population mean HONC scores. **10.25 (a)** 0.36 is the standard deviation of the difference between sample means from different studies using these sample sizes. **(b)** $t = 3.30$; P-value $= 0.001$; very strong evidence that females have higher population mean HONC score. **(c)** No, because in each case the lowest possible value of 0 is less than 1 standard deviation below the mean. This does not affect the validity of our inference greatly because of the robustness of the two-sided test for the assumption of a normal population distribution for each group. **10.27 (a)** H_0: $\mu_1 = \mu_2$ versus H_a: $\mu_1 \neq \mu_2$, where μ_1 is the population mean score for clips based on male speakers and μ_2 is the population mean score for clips based on female speakers. **(b)** $t = 1.69 (df = 57.8)$, P-value $= 0.097$. If there is no difference in the population mean score for clips based on male and female speakers, then there is a 9.7% chance of observing a difference in the sample means of 11.8 or larger (or -11.8 and smaller). Compared to a 0.05 significance level, this is not small. There is insufficient evidence to conclude that the population mean scores differ. The population mean dominance score for clips based on male speakers may equal the one for clips based on female speakers. **(c)** Yes, the interval would include 0 because the significance test failed to reject H_0: $\mu_1 = \mu_2$. **10.29 (a)** Let Group 1 represent the students who planned to go to graduate school and Group 2 represent those who did not. Then, $\bar{x}_1 = 11.67$, $s_1 = 8.34$, $\bar{x}_2 = 9.10$ and $s_2 = 3.70$. The sample mean study time per week was higher for the students who planned to go to graduate school, but the times were also much more variable for this group. **(b)** $se = 2.16$. If further random samples of these sizes were obtained from these populations, the differences between the sample means would vary. The standard deviation of these values would equal about 2.2. **(c)** A 95% confidence interval is $(-1.9, 7.0)$. We are 95% confident that the difference in the mean study time per week between the two groups is between -1.9 and 7.0 hours. Since 0 is contained within this interval, we cannot conclude that the population mean study times differ for the two groups. **10.31 (a)** Let Group 1 represent males and Group 2 represent females. Then, $\bar{x}_1 = 11.9$, $s_1 = 3.94$, $\bar{x}_2 = 15.6$ and $s_2 = 8.00$. The sample mean time spent on social networks was higher for females than for males, but notice the apparent outlier for the female group (40). The data were also much more variable for females, but this may also merely reflect the outlier. **(b)** $se = 2.084$. If further random samples of these sizes were obtained from these populations, the differences between the sample means would vary. The standard deviation of these values would equal about 2.1. **(c)** A 90% confidence interval is $(-7.24, -0.17)$. We are 90% confident that the difference in the population mean number of hours spent on social network per week is between -7.2 and -0.17 for males and females. Since 0 is not quite contained within this interval, we can conclude that the population mean time spent on social networks per week differs for males and females. **10.33** With large random samples, the sampling distribution of the difference between two sample means is approximately normal regardless of the shape of the population distributions. Substituting sample standard deviations for unknown population standard deviations then yields an approximate t sampling distribution. With small samples, the sampling distribution is not necessarily bell-shaped if the population distributions are highly non-normal. **10.35 (a)** The standard error for comparing the means: $s = 6.41$, $se = 1.78$. **(b)** The confidence interval of (2.36, 9.44) indicates that we can be 95% confident that the population mean difference is between 2.36 and 9.44. Because 0 does not fall in this interval, we can conclude that, on average, the leansport athletes had a higher population mean body dissatisfaction than the nonlean sport athletes did. **10.37 (a)** $(-10.6, 6.4)$. We can be 95% confident that the population mean pain score is between 10.6 points smaller and 6.4 points larger for patients treated with the placebo procedure compared to patients treated with the lavage procedure. Because 0 falls in this interval, it is plausible that the mean pain score is the same under both procedures. **(b)** Yes, because sample standard deviations s_1 and s_2 are very similar—in fact, identical. **(c)** (1) Assumptions: independent random samples from the two groups (patients are randomly assigned to the two groups), approximately normal population distributions for each group (not crucial because sample size is large) and equal population standard deviations. (2) H_0: $\mu_1 = \mu_2$ versus H_a: $\mu_1 \neq \mu_2$. (3) t-test statistic value $= -0.49$. (4) P-value $= 0.627$. (5) If there is no difference in the population mean pain score, the probability of observing a test statistic this extreme is 0.63. This is large. There is no evidence of a difference in the population mean pain score between the placebo and lavage arthroscopic surgery procedures. **10.39 (a)** If the null hypothesis were true, the probability would be 0.06 of getting a test statistic at least as extreme as the value observed. **(b) (i)** Fail to reject; it is possible that both therapies result in the same mean improvement scores; **(ii)** Reject; Therapy 1 leads to better scores on average. **(c)** H_a: $\mu_1 > \mu_2$; P-value $= 0.03$. Since the P-value < 0.05, reject the null hypothesis and conclude that Therapy 1 has larger population mean change score than does Therapy 2. **10.41 (a)** The hypotheses that were tested: H_0: $\mu_1 = \mu_2$; H_a: $\mu_1 \neq \mu_2$. Alternatively, we could test: H_0: $\mu_1 - \mu_2 = 0$; H_a: $\mu_1 - \mu_2 \neq 0$. **(b)** The P-value is reported as < 0.05 meaning that there is $< 5\%$ chance of obtaining the observed difference or a more extreme difference in the means if we presume no difference in the population means. Thus, we reject the null hypothesis. We have strong evidence that there is a difference in population mean change scores between the two treatment types. **(c)** The pooled standard deviation is

$$s = \sqrt{\frac{(n_1 - 1)s_1^2 + (n_2 - 1)s_2^2}{n_1 + n_2 - 2}} = \sqrt{\frac{(58 - 1)1.32^2 + (59 - 1)1.29^2}{58 + 59 - 2}}$$

$= 1.305$. The standard error is $se = s\sqrt{\frac{1}{n_1} + \frac{1}{n_2}} = 1.305\sqrt{\frac{1}{58} + \frac{1}{59}}$

$= 0.241$. The t statistic is $t = 2.78$, $df = (n_1 + n_2 - 2) = 115$.

The resulting P-value is 0.006. This is statistically significant. **(d)** The mean change for whitening gel was 2.91 times the mean change for toothpaste. **10.43 (a)** The distribution of the improvement scores is the same under therapy 1 and therapy 2. **(b)** Under H_0, outcomes under each assignment are equally likely. Because there are a total of six possible assignments, each has probability 1/6. Because two assignments lead to a difference of -20, that difference occurs with probability 2/6. Differences -10 and 10 occur once, so each has probability 1/6. Difference 20 occurs twice, so has probability 2/6 of occurring. **(c)** The P-value is the probability of observing a difference as extreme or even more extreme if H_0 is true. The observed difference was 20, the most extreme possible. Because $P(20) = 2/6 = 1/3$, the P-value is 0.333. If the distribution of improvement scores is the same under therapy 1 and therapy 2, we would observe a difference of 20 or more with a probability of 0.33. This would not be considered unusual, indicating that it is plausible the two therapy distributions of improvement scores (and their means) are the same. **10.45 (a)** $\bar{x}_1 = 11.9$, $\bar{x}_2 = 15.6$, $\bar{x}_1 - \bar{x}_2 = -3.7$ **(b)** Answers will vary. We got $\bar{x}_1 = 14.6$, $\bar{x}_2 = 14.1$, $\bar{x}_1 - \bar{x}_2 = 0.49$ **(c)** Answers will vary. We got less extreme because $-3.7 < 0.49 < +3.7$ **(d)** Answers will vary slightly. We got 1498 permutations that resulted in a difference smaller than -3.7 or larger than $+3.7$ (two-sided alternative). **(e)** Based on these 10,000 random permutations, permutation P-value $= 1498/10{,}000 = 0.149$. This is not small. If truly the distribution of time spent on social network sites is the same for males and females, then the probability of observing a difference of -3.7 or more extreme (i.e., larger in absolute value) in the sample means is 0.149. This indicates that the null hypothesis is plausible. **10.47 (a)** H_0: The population distribution of ratings is the same for clips based on male and female speakers. (This implies the population means are the same.) H_a: The population mean rating is different for clips based on male and female speakers. The observed difference in sample means equals 11.8. Out of 10,000 random permutations, 980 yielded a difference at least as extreme, resulting in a permutation P-value of 0.098. (Your results might differ slightly.) Because $0.098 > 0.05$, there is no evidence of a difference in the population mean dominance rating between clips based on female and male speakers. It is plausible that the distributions are the same. **(b)** $t = 1.69(df = 57.8)$, P-value $= 0.097$. Results are comparable. The sample size is fairly large (30 in each group), and the histogram of the ratings in each group does not indicate major deviations from normality. **10.49 (a)** The same patients are in both samples. **(b)** 150; 130; 20; "before" mean minus "after" mean equals mean of the difference scores. **(c)** We can be 95% confident that the difference between the population means is between 7.6 and 32.4. **10.51 (a)** Dependent; the same students are in both samples. **(b)** No, there is quite a bit of variability, but outlying values appear in both directions. **(c)** The 95% confidence interval was obtained by adding and subtracting the margin of error (the t-score of 2.262 for $df = 9$ times the standard error of 5.11, which is 11.6) from the mean difference score of 4.0. **(d)** The test statistic was obtained as $t = \frac{\bar{x}_d - 0}{se} = \frac{4.0 - 0}{5.11} = 0.78$; the P-value is 0.45. We cannot conclude that there is a difference in attendance at movies versus sports events. **10.53 (a) (1)** Assumptions: the difference scores are a random sample from a population distribution that is approximately normal. **(2)** H_0: $\mu_1 = \mu_2$. (or population mean of difference scores is 0); H_a: $\mu_1 \neq \mu_2$. **(3)** $t = -1.62$. **(4)** P-value $= 0.14$. **(5)** Insufficient evidence to conclude that the population means are different for movies and parties. **(b)** $(-21.1, 3.5)$. We are 95% confident that the population mean number of times spent attending movies is between 21.1 less and 3.5 higher than the population mean number of times spent attending parties. **10.55 (a)** The standard deviation of the change in weight scores could be much smaller because even though there is a lot of variability among the initial and final weights of the women, most women do not see a large change in weight over the course of the study, so the weight changes would not vary much. **(b)** $se = s_d/\sqrt{n} = 2.0/\sqrt{132} = 0.174$. A 95% confidence interval given by $\bar{X}_d \pm t_{.025}(se)$ has lower endpoint $2.1 - (1.98)(0.174) = 1.76$ and upper endpoint $2.1 + (1.98)(0.174) = 2.44$. Thus, the confidence interval is (1.76, 2.44). 15 is not a plausible weight change in the population of freshmen women. The plausible weight change falls in the range from 1.76 to 2.44. **(c)** The data must be quantitative, the sample of difference scores must be a random sample from a population of such difference scores, and the difference scores must have a population distribution that is approximately normal (particularly with samples of size less than 30). **10.57 (1)** Assumptions: the differences in prices are a random sample from a population that is approximately normal. **(2)** H_0: $\mu_d = 0$ vs. H_a: $\mu_d \neq 0$. **(3)** $t = \frac{\bar{d} - 0}{s_d/\sqrt{n}} = \frac{4.3}{4.7152/\sqrt{10}} = 2.88$. **(4)** P-value $= 0.02$. **(5)** If the null hypothesis is true, the probability of obtaining a difference in sample means as extreme as that observed is 0.02. We would reject the null hypothesis and conclude that there is a significant difference in the mean price of textbooks used at her college between the two sites for $\alpha = 0.05$. **10.59 (a)** $\hat{p}_1 = 0.9895$, $\hat{p}_2 = 0.9685$. **(b)** We are 95% confident that the population proportion of correct results for GDMS is between 0.013 and 0.029 higher than the population proportion of correct results for CDHMM. **10.61 (a)** (i) 0.38, (ii) 0.43. Difference $= -0.05$. We estimate the population proportion of people buying Sanka coffee after the advertising campaign was 0.05 larger than before the campaign. In terms of percentages, we estimate 5% more people in the population bought Sanka coffee after the campaign. **(b)** With 95% confidence, the proportion of people buying Sanka coffee after the advertising campaign is between 0.01 and 0.09 larger than before it. This means that we are 95% confident that between 1% and 9% more people in the population bought Sanka coffee after the advertising campaign. **(c)** H_0: $p_1 = p_2$, where p_1 and p_2 are the (marginal) population proportions of people buying Sanka coffee before and after the advertising campaign, respectively. We have sufficient evidence (P-value of $0.02 < 0.05$ significance level) that the population proportion of people buying Sanka coffee differs before and after the advertising campaign. **10.63 (a)** 0.135. **(b) (i)** independent, random samples and sums of two counts at least 30. **(ii)** H_0: $p_1 = p_2$; H_a: $p_1 \neq p_2$; **(iii)** $z = 3.00$; **(iv)** P-value: 0.003; **(v)** Strong evidence that there is a difference between the population proportions. **10.65 (a)** This refers to an analysis of three variables, a response variable, an explanatory variable, and a control variable. The response variable is "whether or not at risk for cardiovascular disease," the explanatory variable is "whether drink alcohol moderately," and the control variables would be socioeconomic status and mental and physical health. **(b)** There is a stronger association between drinking alcohol and its effect on risk for cardiovascular disease for subjects who have a higher socioeconomic status. **10.67 (a)** The proportion of shots made is higher for Barry both for 2-point shots and for 3-point shots, but the proportion of shots made is higher for O'Neal overall. **(b)** O'Neal took almost exclusively 2-point shots, where the chance of success is higher. **10.69 (a)** Higher mean for English-speaking families (1.95) than French-speaking families (1.85). **(b)** In each case, higher mean for French-speaking families: Quebec: French (1.80); English (1.64); other provinces: French (2.14); English (1.97). **(c)** There are relatively more English-speaking families in the "other" provinces, and the "other" provinces have a higher mean regardless of language. This illustrates Simpson's paradox. **10.71** There could be no difference in the prevalence of breast cancer now and in 1900 for women of a given age. Overall, the breast cancer rate would be higher now, because more women live to an old age now, and older people are more likely to have breast cancer. **10.73 (a)** Response: opinion on fracking (favor/oppose). Explanatory: type of survey (U.S. adults/scientists) **(b)** Independent samples because each survey uses different subjects. (Highly unlikely that a subject from the scientists' survey was also included in the Pew Research Center survey.) **(c)** Dependent samples (matched pairs) because the same scientists who were asked about fracking were asked about offshore drilling. **10.75 (a)** We are 95% confident that the population proportion of females who have used marijuana is at least 0.01 lower and at most 0.09 lower than the population proportion of males who have used marijuana (when rounded). Because 0 is not in the confidence interval, we can conclude that females and males differ with respect to marijuana use. **(b)** The confidence interval would change only in sign. It would now be (0.01, 0.09) instead of $(-0.09, -0.01)$, rounded. We are 95% confident that the population proportion of males who have used marijuana is at least 0.01 higher and at most 0.09 higher than the population proportion of females who have used marijuana. **10.77 (a)** Pooled $\hat{p} = 0.796$; $se_0 = 0.017$. **(b)** $z = 4.78$; P-value $= 0.000$; we have sufficient evidence (P-value < 0.05) to reject the null hypothesis. The population proportion of females believing in an afterlife is different from the population proportion for males. **(c)** No, the decision was not an error. The proportions differed for females and males, agreeing with our decision. **(d)** Independent random samples of females and males (okay since GSS); at least 5 successes and 5 failures in each sample. **10.79 (a)** Box plots are part of answer. Female crabs have a higher median and more variability if they had a mate (right-skewed distribution) than if they did not have a mate (symmetrical). **(b)** 0.5. **(c)** $se = 0.076$. **(d)** We can be 90% confident that the difference between the population mean weights of female crabs with and without a mate is between 0.375 and 0.625 kg. **10.81 (a)** H_0: $\mu_1 = \mu_2$; H_a: $\mu_1 \neq \mu_2$. **(b)** $t = 5.25$. P-value $= 0.000$. If the population means of blacks and whites are the same, it would be extremely unusual (probability less than 0.001) to observe a test statistic as or more extreme than $t = 5.25$. **(c)** There is sufficient evidence (P-value < 0.05) to reject the null hypothesis and conclude that the population mean number of hours watching TV differs for blacks and whites. **(d)** When we reject the null hypothesis with significance level 0.05, the 95% confidence interval does not include 0. **10.83 (a)** Response: number of hours spent on the web (quantitative). Explanatory: gender (categorical) **(b)** $(-0.8, 2.5)$. With 95% confidence, the population mean number of hours spent on the web is between 0.8 hours shorter and 2.5 hours longer for males compared to females. Because 0 is in the confidence interval, there is no evidence that the population mean time on the web differs by gender. **(c) (1)** Assumptions: Independent random samples of males and females (okay since GSS), population distribution of time spent on the web should be approximately normal for each gender (less crucial because of large sample sizes in both groups). **(2)** H_0: $\mu_1 = \mu_2$ versus H_a: $\mu_1 \neq \mu_2$, where μ_1 is the mean number of hours for the population of all U.S. males and μ_2 is the mean number of hours for the population of all U.S. females. **(3)** $t = 1.03$. **(4)** P-value $= 0.30$. **(5)** If the null hypothesis of equal population means is true, observing a test statistic of 1.03 or more extreme is not unusual (probability = 0.3). At a significance level of 0.05, we do not have evidence to reject H_0. It is plausible that the population mean time spent on the web is the same for males and females. **10.85 (1)** Assumptions: the data are quantitative (child's score); the samples are independent random samples and the population distributions of scores are approximately normal for each group. **(2)** H_0: $\mu_1 = \mu_2$; H_a: $\mu_1 \neq \mu_2$ where Group 1 represents the group with the male tester and Group 2 represents the group with the female tester. **(3)** $se = 0.235$, $t = -1.28$. **(4)** P-value: 0.205. **(5)** If the null hypothesis were true, the probability would be 0.205 of getting a test statistic at least as extreme as the value observed. Since the P-value is quite large, there is not much evidence of a difference in the population mean of the children's scores when the tester is male versus female. **10.87 (a)** The 95% confidence interval is (0.6, 7.4). **(b)** It tells us the P-value = 0.02; we would expect a difference of sample means at least this size only 2% of the time if there were truly no difference between the population means. **10.89 (a)** P-value = 0.10, so there is a probability of 0.10 that we would get a test statistic at least this large if the null hypothesis is true that there is no difference between population mean change scores. **(b)** Data are quantitative; samples are independent and random; population distributions for each group are approximately normal. Based on the box plots (which show outliers and a skew to the right for the cognitive behavioral group), it would not be a good idea to conduct a one-sided test. It is not as robust as the two-sided test to violations of the normal assumption. **(c)** The lowest plausible difference between means is −0.7, a difference of less than 1 pound. The highest plausible difference between means is 7.6. **(d)** We do not reject the null hypothesis that the difference between the population means is 0, and 0 falls in the 95% confidence interval for the difference between the population means. **10.91** We can be 95% confident that the true population mean difference is between −10.8 and 5.2. **10.93 (a)** We can be 95% confident that the true population mean difference is between −0.7 and 7.6. **(b)** If the null hypothesis were true, there would be probability 0.10 of obtaining a test statistic at least this large (in absolute value). **(c)** P-value = 0.10/2 = 0.05. If the null hypothesis were true, the probability = 0.05 of getting a t statistic of 1.68 or larger. **(d)** Quantitative response variable, independent random samples, and approximately normal population distributions for each group. **10.95 (a)** Dependent samples because the same subject was measured at two occasions, before the crash and in the earlier accident-free period. **(b)** McNemar's test for comparing (marginal) proportions from matched pairs **10.97 (b)** Increase the sample size and randomizing the side the tire is put on. **10.99 (a)** (−0.1, 5.5). We are 95% confident that the difference in population mean scores is between −0.1 and 5.5. **(b)** The confidence interval gives us a range of values for the difference between the population mean scores rather than just telling us whether or not the scores are significantly different. **10.101** 95% confidence interval = (−5.9, −0.5). We are 95% confident that the population mean amount of time spent reading news stories on the Internet is between 5.9 and 0.5 hours less than the population mean amount of time spent communicating on the Internet. Since 0 is not contained in this interval, we conclude that the population means differ. The population consists of the 165 students in the course. **10.103 (a)** We can be 95% confident that the population mean difference between responses with respect to movies and TV is between −0.43 and 0.76. Because 0 falls in this interval, it is plausible that there is no difference between the population mean responses for TV and movies. **(b)** The P-value = 0.55. If the null hypothesis were true, the probability would be 0.55 of getting a test statistic at least as extreme as the value observed. It is plausible that the null hypothesis is correct and that there is no population mean difference between responses with respect to movies and TV. **10.105 (a)** No, the same sample is used for both sets of responses, we should use methods for dependent samples. **(b)** No, we would need to know the specific numbers of subjects who said that they believed in ghosts but not in astrology, and who said that they believed in astrology, but not in ghosts. **10.107 (a)** If the United States has a higher proportion of older people (who are more likely to die in both countries than are younger people), and Mexico has a higher proportion of younger people, then the death rate in the United States could be higher. **(b)** Even if older people in South Carolina are more likely to die than are older people in Maine, if Maine has far more older people and far fewer younger people, this could lead to an overall higher death rate in Maine than in South Carolina. **10.109** Answers will vary but should include: $(\hat{p}_1 - \hat{p}_2) = 0.13$; $z = 1.03$; P-value = 0.3; 95% CI = (−0.12, 0.38). Since the confidence interval contains 0 and the P-value is large, we are unable to conclude that there is a difference in the population proportion of males and females who believe in life after death. Assumptions: Independent random samples. **10.111** Answers will vary but should include: Men: $\bar{x}_1 - \bar{x}_2 = -0.2$, $t = -0.07$, P-value = 0.94, 95% CI = (−5.6, 5.2). Since the confidence interval contains 0 and the P-value > 0.05, we are unable to conclude that there is a difference in the population mean number of dates between more and less attractive men. Women: $\bar{x}_1 - \bar{x}_2 = 7.4$, $t = 1.83$, P-value = 0.07, 95% CI = (−0.7, 15.5). Since the confidence interval contains 0 and the P-value > 0.05, we are unable to conclude that there is a difference in the population mean number of dates between more and less attractive women. However, the confidence interval shows there could be a large difference. **10.113** If the population distributions are identical, the sampling distribution of $\bar{x}_1 - \bar{x}_2$ should be centered at around 0. Mean = $\sum xP(x) = (-4.67)(1/10) + (-3.83)(2/10) + (0.33)(2/10) + (1.17)(3/10) + (2.00)(1/10) + (6.17)(1/10) = 0$. **10.115 (a)** Whether obese (yes or no) and wage. **(b)** Education level; the women could be paired according to education level and then compared in obesity rates. **10.117** (d). **10.119** False. **10.121** False. **10.123** We can be 95% confident that the difference between the population mean is between 9.6 and 17.0. **10.125 (a) (i)** $\hat{p}_1 = \hat{p}_2 = 0$ because there are no successes in either group (i.e., 0/10 = 0); **(ii)** $se = 0$ because there is no variability in either group if all responses are the same (and can also see this from formula for se); **(iii)** The 95% confidence interval would be (0,0) because we'd be adding 0 to 0 (se multiplied by z would always be 0 with se of 0, regardless of the confidence level). **(b)** The new confidence interval, (−0.22, 0.22), is far more plausible than (0, 0). **10.127 (a)** From Table 10.18, $b = 162$, $c = 9$ and $n = 1314$, resulting in the null standard error $se_0 = \sqrt{(162 + 9)/1314^2} = 0.010$. **(b)** $z = \dfrac{(\hat{p}_1 - \hat{p}_2)}{se_0} = \dfrac{0.12}{0.010} = 12$ (or 11.7 if not using rounding) **10.129** Answers will vary.

Chapter 11

11.1 (a) Response: Party identification, explanatory: gender
(b)

	Political Party Identification				
Gender	**Democrat**	**Independent**	**Republican**	**Total**	***n***
Female	39.6%	37.4%	23.0%	100%	1063
Male	33.0%	43.5%	23.5%	100%	843

Women are more likely than are men to be Democrats, whereas men are more likely than are women to be Independents. **(c)** Distributions should show percentages in the party categories that are the same for men and women, such as (36%, 38%, 26%).

11.3 (a) Y given X

	Admitted		
Gender	**Yes**	**No**	
male	18.2%	81.8%	100% (3195)
female	16.9%	83.1%	100% (3658)

(b) X and Y are dependent because the probability of a student being admitted differs by gender. **11.5 (a)**

	Happiness of Marriage			
Income	**Not Too Happy**	**Pretty Happy**	**Very Happy**	***n***
Below	6	62	139	207
Average	7	125	283	415
Above	6	69	115	190

(b)

	Happiness of Marriage			
Income	**Not Too Happy**	**Pretty Happy**	**Very Happy**	n
Above	3%	30%	67%	100% (207)
Average	2%	30%	68%	100% (415)
Below	3%	36%	61%	100% (190)

The conditional distributions of marital happiness for above-average and average income are nearly identical; however, among people of below-average income, the percentage of very happy people is lower, and the percentage of pretty happy people is larger. **(c)** Across all three income categories, the percentage of very happy people is much larger for marital happiness (always over 60%) than for general happiness (always below 40%). **11.7** Answers will vary depending on the column variable selected. **11.9 (a)** H_0: Gender and happiness are independent. H_a: Gender and happiness are dependent (associated). **(b)** If the null hypothesis of independence is true, it is not unusual to observe a chi-square value of 1.04 or larger because the probability is 59% of this occurring. Hence, there is no evidence of an association between gender and happiness. **11.11 (a)** H_0: Income and marital happiness are independent. H_a: Income and marital happiness are dependent (associated). **(b)** $df = (3 - 1)(3 - 1) = 4$ **(c)** **(i)** Expected value of chi-squared statistic $= df = 4$, **(ii)** standard deviation $= \sqrt{2(4)} = \sqrt{8} \approx 2.8$. The value 4.58 is 0.2 $(= (4.58 - 4)/2.8)$ standard deviations above the expected value under independence, which is not extreme. **(d)** 9.49 **(e)** P-value > 0.25 (exact P-value $= 0.33$). There is no evidence (P-value > 0.25) of an association between income and marital happiness. **(f)** $207 \times 19/812 = 4.84$. One of the assumptions of the chi-squared test is that expected cell counts are at least 5. If not, X^2 might not have an approximate chi-squared distribution. **11.13 (a)** (61.1%, 38.9%) and (5.9%, 94.1%); suggests marijuana use much more common for those who have smoked cigarettes than for those who have not. **(b)** **(1)** Assumptions: two categorical variables (cigarette use and marijuana use), randomization, expected count at least five in all cells. **(2)** H_0: marijuana use independent of cigarette use; H_a: dependence. **(3)** $X^2 = 642.0$. **(4)** P-value: 0.000. **(5)** Extremely strong evidence that marijuana use and cigarette use are associated. **11.15 (a)** H_0: opinion about helping the environment by cutting standard of living is independent of whether someone is currently in school or retired. H_a: opinion about helping environment depends on whether someone is currently in school or retired. **(b)** $r = 2, c = 5, df = (r - 1)(c - 1) = 4$ **(c)** When $X^2 = 9.49$, P-value $= 0.05$; when $X^2 = 11.14$, P-value $= 0.025$; because $X^2 = 9.56$ is in between, it has P-value **(i)** less than 0.05 but **(ii)** larger than 0.025. **(d)** **(i)** There is evidence ($P < 0.05$) for an association between helping the environment and whether someone is in school or retired. **(ii)** There is not enough evidence ($P > 0.025$) for an association.
11.17 (a)

	Heart attack	No heart attack
placebo	28	656
aspirin	18	658

(b) **(1)** 2 categorical variables, randomization, expected count at least 5 in all cells. **(2)** H_0: whether have heart attack independent of treatment; H_a: dependence. **(3)** $X^2 = 2.1$. **(4)** P-value: 0.14. **(5)** It is plausible that treatment and heart attack incidence are independent. **11.19 (a)** H_0: The distribution of severity of fever is the same in the active and placebo group (homogeneity), H_a: The distributions differ. **(b)** $df = 2$, so we expect the chi-squared statistic to be around 2, with a standard deviation of $\sqrt{4} = 2$. 2.49 is less than half a standard deviation away from the mean, which makes it not extreme. **(c)** There is no evidence ($P = 0.287$, which is larger than any reasonable significance level) that the distribution of the severity of fewer differs between the active and placebo group. **11.21 (a)** H_0: $p = 0.75$. **(b)** $X^2 = 3.46$; $df = 1$. **(c)** P-value $= 0.06$. The probability of obtaining a test statistic at least as extreme as that observed, assuming the null hypothesis is true, is 0.06. Some evidence against the null, but not very strong. **11.23 (a)** 1/37. **(b)** 100. **(c)** 1. **(d)** $df = 36$. P-value $= 0.54$. Since the P-value is quite large, there is not strong evidence that the roulette wheel is not balanced. **11.25 (a)** False; larger X^2 might be due to larger sample size rather than stronger association. **(b)** Yes. Confidence interval for race effect covers larger values than confidence interval for gender effect, so race has the stronger association with opinion on death penalty. **11.27** There are several possible answers. The proportion of male victims murdered by females $= 0.77$. The proportion of male victims murdered by males $= 0.70$. Ratio $= 0.77/0.70 = 1.1$. Male victims are 1.1 times more likely to have been murdered by a female than by a male. (That is, relatively more females murder males than males murder males.) **11.29 (a)** The proportion with myocardial infarctions in the naproxen group was 0.003 (or 0.3 percentage points) lower than the proportion in the rofecoxib group. **(b)** The proportion with myocardial infarctions in the naproxen group is 0.2 times (or 80%) lower than the proportion in the rofecoxib group. **(c)** $1/0.2 = 5$ times more likely **11.31 (a)** The difference of proportions is $0.00135 - 0.00046 = 0.00089$. The proportion of male teenagers who die is 0.00089 higher than the proportion of female teenagers who die. **(b)** The relative risk is $0.00135/0.00046 = 2.9$. Male teenagers are 2.9 times more likely than are female teenagers to die. **(c)** The relative risk seems more useful because it shows there is a substantial gender effect, which the difference does not show when both proportions are close to 0. **11.33 (a)** The proportion of females who identify as Republican is by 0.005 smaller than the proportion for males. **(b)** The proportion of females who identify as Democrat is 0.066 higher than the proportion for males. **(c)** The proportion of females who identify as Republican is 2% lower than the proportion for males. **(d)** The proportion of females who identify as Democrat is 20% higher than the proportion for males. **(e)** Rather weak association between gender and whether identifying as Republican, as seen from parts a and c. Stronger association between gender and whether identifying as Democrat, as seen in parts b and d. **11.35 (a)** The observed count is -2.49 standard deviations below the expected one for this cell. **(b)** Both show that the observed count is much higher than the expected one (greater than 3 standard deviations). For people with above-average income, many more were very happy than what independence between income and happiness would predict. For people with below-average income, many more were not happy than what independence would imply. **(c)** Both show that the observed count is much lower than the expected one (greater than 3 standard deviations). For people with average income, many fewer were not happy than what independence would predict. For people with below-average income, many fewer were very happy than what independence would imply. **11.37 (a)** Observed count is only 0.9 standard deviations below expected count—not unusual under the null hypothesis of independence. **(b)** These are the cells with positive residuals. Consider category (very happy, very happy). The large positive residual indicates that those very happy in their marriage are more likely also to be very happy in general compared to what would be predicted under independence. **11.39** Females tend to be Democrat more often and males tend to be Democrat less often than one would expect if party ID were independent of gender.
11.41 (a)

	S	F	Total
control	2	6	8
treatment	12	0	12

(b) **(1)** There are two binary categorical variables, and randomization was used. **(2)** H_0: $p_1 = p_2$; H_a: $p_1 \neq p_2$. **(3)** Test statistic: 2. **(4)** P-value: 0.001. **(5)** Strong evidence that care and diet are associated with ability to solve a task. **(c)** Because the expected cell counts are less than 5 for at least some cells. **11.43 (a)** 0.24; no evidence for an association between nervousness and treatment **(b)** No, two cells have expected count < 5, (2.5 and 3.5, respectively) **11.45 (a)** First row: 5, 0; second row: 6, 6. **(b)** 462 out of 6188 permutations ($= 0.075$) have a first cell count as large or larger than 5. **(c)** The (exact or permutation) P-value of 0.075 ($>$ than significance level of 0.05) indicates not sufficient evidence to conclude that the probability to change study habits is larger in the STAT course.

11.47 (a)

	Y	N
Male	0.94	0.06
Female	0.94	0.06

(b) Yes; percentages of men and women who would vote for a qualified woman may be the same. **11.49 (1)** Two categorical variables, randomization, expected count at least 5 in all cells. **(2)** H_0: blood test result independent of Down syndrome status; H_a: dependence. **(3)** $X^2 = 114.4$, $df = 1$. **(4)** P-value =0.000. **(5)** Very strong evidence of an association between test result and actual status. **11.51 (a)** The chance of any particular happiness category (such as very happy) would be identical for each number of close friends. **(b)** The number of cases we'd expect in a given cell if the two variables were independent. $(169 \times 164)/1446 = 19.2$. **(c) (i)** Those with highest number of close friends; **(ii)** those with fewest close friends. **11.53 (a)** $df = 9$; chi-squared probability distribution for $df = 9$. **(b)** It is plausible that the null hypothesis is correct and that income and job satisfaction are independent. **(c)** Fail to reject the null hypothesis. No. **11.55 (a)** Table with single row of 315, 108, 101, 32 showing the counts for the four combinations RY, RG, WY, and WG **(b)** (9/16,3/16,3/16,1/16) **(c)** $312.75(= 556 \times (9/16))$, 104.25, 104.25, 34.75 **(d)** $df = 4 - 1 = 3$ **(e)** Large because the chi-square statistic of 0.47 is well below the expected value of 3, so area above 0.47 under chi-squared curve with $df = 3$ is large. **11.57 (a)** The proportion who were injured is 0.06 higher for those who did not wear a seat belt than for those who wore a seat belt. **(b)** People were 1.95 times as likely to be injured if they were not wearing a seat belt than if they were wearing a seat belt. **11.59 (a)** Relative risk $= (29/127)/(19485/26571) = 0.31$. The proportion of organic food samples with pesticide residues present was 69% (or 0.31 times) lower than the proportion of conventional food samples with pesticide residues present. **(b)** The proportion of conventional food samples with pesticide residues present was 3.2 $(= 1/0.31)$ times larger than the proportion for organic food samples with pesticide residues. **(c)** Odd ratio $= (29/98)/(19485/7086) = 0.11$. The odds of finding pesticide residues on organic food samples were 89% (or 0.11 times) lower than on conventional food samples. **(d)** The odds of finding pesticide residues on conventional food samples were 9.1 times higher than on organic food samples. **(e)** The *proportion* is only about 3.2 times larger (= relative risk), but the *odds* are more than 9 times larger. This statement confuses relative risk with the odds ratio. **11.61** Those with no or 2 or more sex partners in the previous year are much less likely to be very happy than would be expected if happiness and number of sex partners were independent. Conversely, those with 1 sex partner are much more likely to be very happy than expected under independence. **11.63 (a)** H_0: $p_1 = p_2$; H_a: $p_1 \neq p_2$; p_1: population proportion of those who are aggressive in the group that watches less than one hour of TV per day; p_2: population proportion of those who are aggressive in the group that watches more than one hour of TV per day. **(b)** 0.0001; very strong evidence that TV watching and aggression are associated. **11.65 (b)** No, many cell counts are very small, leading to expected cell counts that are less than 5. Then, the sampling distribution of X^2 may not be approximately chi-squared. **(c)** Approximate permutation P-value $= 9908/10000 = 0.9908$. This P-value is large and almost 1. There is no evidence that the clarity depends on whether the diamond's cut is good or fair. **11.67** Report could include: Contingency table of summary counts and Pearson chi-squared $= 21.4$, $df = 6$, P-Value $= 0.002$. **11.69** Answers will vary.
11.71 (a)

	Has Young Children	
Gray Hair	Yes	No
Yes	0	4
No	5	0

(b) Yes. **(c)** There often are third factors, such as age in this case, that influence an association. **11.73 (a)** Difference of proportion with United States as group 1: 0.000037; Britain as group 1: −0.000037 **(b)** Relative risk with United States as group 1: 4.6; Britain as group 1: 0.22 **(c)** Relative risk; the difference may be very small although one is many times the other. **11.75** False. **11.77** False. **11.79** True. **11.81 (a)** The chi-squared value for a right-tail probability of 0.05 and $df = 1$ is 3.84, which is the z value for a two-tail probability of 0.05 squared: $(1.96)(1.96) = 3.84$. **(b)** The chi-squared value for P-value of 0.01 and $df = 1$ is 6.63. This is (apart from rounding) the square of the z value for a two-tail P-value of 0.01, which is 2.58. **11.83** The two observed values in a given row (or column) must add up to the same total as the two expected values in that same row (or column). **11.85** For the top row the last number must be 33 because the numbers must add up to the row total of 100. For the bottom row, the numbers must add to the column totals of 40 for each column. Thus, the bottom row should read 16, 19, 28, 30, and 7.
11.87 (a)

F1, F2, F3	F1, F2, M1	F1, F2, M2	F1, F2, M3
F1, F3, M1	F1, F3, M2	F1, F3, M3	F1, M1, M2
F1, M1, M3	F1, M2, M3	F2, F3, M1	F2, F3, M2
F2, F3, M3	F2, M1, M2	F2, M1, M3	F2, M2, M3
F3, M1, M2	F3, M1, M3	F3, M2, M3	M1, M2, M3

This contingency table shows that two males were chosen (M1 and M3) and one was not (M2). It also shows that one female was chosen (F2) and two were not (F1 and F3). **(b)** 10 of the 20 tables have a first cell count of 2 or 3. Under a null hypothesis of no gender bias versus an alternative hypothesis of a preference for males, observing tables with 2 or 3 males selected (i.e., a 2 or 3 in the first cell) has a probability of 0.5, which is the P-value from Fisher's exact test **11.89 (b)** No, there are 6 cells with expected cell count below 5. The chi-squared distribution may not approximate well the actual sampling distribution of X^2. **(c)** (Answers will vary.) We got a value of 3.1, smaller than the observed 14.1. **(d)** (Answers will vary.) For us, none of the 10 permutations gave a value as large or larger than 14.1. **(e)** (Answers will vary slightly.) For us, 233 of the 10,000 permutations resulted in a chi-squared statistic as large or larger than the observed one, giving a P-value of 0.0233. This means that if there is no association between grade level and opinion, observing a test statistic as large or larger than the one we have observed is unlikely (probability of 0.02). With such a small P-value, we reject the null hypothesis and conclude that there is an association between the grade level and the opinion about voting with 16.

Chapter 12

12.1 (a) Response: mileage; explanatory: weight. **(b)** $\hat{y} = 45.6 - 0.0052x$; y-intercept is 45.6; slope is −0.0052. **(c)** For each 1000-pound increase, the predicted mileage will decrease by 5.2 miles per gallon. **(d)** No; the y-intercept is the predicted miles per gallon for a car that weighs 0 pounds. **12.3 (a)** 322.6 kg. **(b)** 117.5 kg. **(c)** The y-intercept indicates that for male athletes who cannot perform any repetitions for a fatigue bench press, the predicted max bench press is 117.5 kg. As repBP increases from 0 to 35, the predicted maxBP increases from 117.5 to 322.6 kg. **12.5** For a given x-value, there will not be merely one y value—not every elementary schoolgirl in your town who is a given height will weigh the same. **12.7 (a)** There appears to be a positive association between GPA and study time. **(b)** Predicted GPA = 2.63 + 0.0439 Study time. For every one-hour increase in study time per week, GPA is predicted to increase by about .04 points. **(c)** 3.73. **(d)** −0.13. The observed GPA for Student 2, who studies an average of 25 hours per week, is 3.6 which is 0.13 points below the predicted GPA of 3.73. **12.9 (a)** A clear trend is visible in the scatterplot, showing that phones with larger capacity tend to weigh more. One phone (number 70 with battery capacity of 3300) has a much larger battery capacity than all the others, yet its weight is about average, not following this trend. This phone is a clear outlier. **(b)** It will pull the regression line toward it. Its residual will be negative and very large in absolute value. **(c)** $\hat{y} = 66.7 + 0.0436x$. Predicted weight at capacity 1000mAh: 110g; predicted weight at 1500mAh: 132g **(d)** For every 100 mAh increase in the capacity of a cell phone's battery, the predicted weight increases by 4.3g. **12.11 (a)** 23. **(b)** −2.07 and 2.07. **(c)** 2.07.

12.13 (a) On average, the selling price of a house increases between \$64 and \$90 for every one square foot increase in size. **(b)** On average, the selling price of a house increases between \$6400 and \$9000 for every 100 square feet increase in size. **12.15 (a) (i)** Assume linear relationship between mean maximum leg press and number of 200-pound leg presses; random sample; normal conditional distribution of maximum leg press for given number of 200-pound leg presses with constant standard deviations. These data are not a random sample, so conclusions are highly tentative; **(ii)** H_0: $\beta = 0$; H_a: $\beta \neq 0$; **(iii)** $t = 9.6$; **(iv)** P-value = 0.000; **(v)** Very strong evidence that an association exists between these variables. **(b)** (4.2, 6.4). On average, maximum leg press increases between 4.2 pounds and 6.4 pounds for every additional 200-pound leg press that the athlete can do. The interval gives us a range of plausible values for the increase. The test only tells us there is strong evidence that the increase (slope) is significantly different from 0. **12.17 (a)** Having more daughters is good. **(b) (i)** Assume that there was roughly a linear relationship between variables, and that the data were gathered using randomization and that the population y-values at each x-value follow a normal distribution, with roughly the same standard deviation at each x-value; **(ii)** H_0: $\beta = 0$; H_a: $\beta \neq 0$; **(iii)** $t = 1.52$; **(iv)** P-value = 0.13. v) It is plausible that there is no association. **(c)** $(-0.1, 1.0)$. Zero is a plausible value for this slope. **12.19 (a)** Means: advertising is 2, sales is 7. Standard deviations: advertising is 2.16, sales is 2.16. **(b)** $\hat{y} = 5.286 + 0.857x$. **(c)** For H_0: $\beta = 0$; H_a: $\beta \neq 0$, $t = 2.35$, P-value = 0.14, it is plausible that there is no association between advertising and sales. **12.21** $(-0.11, -0.05)$. On average, GPA decreases by between 0.05 and 0.11 points for every additional class that is skipped. **12.23** 0.0015. **12.25** Answers will vary. **12.27 (a)** There is a strong, positive linear association between weight and percent body fat. **(b)** $r^2 = 0.78$. Using the regression equation with weight to predict percent body fat instead of predicting it with the sample mean results in a 78% reduction in the overall prediction error (the sum of the squared errors). **(c)** No. The correlation r does not depend on the units. **12.29 (a)** 650. **(b)** $x = 800$ is 3 standard deviations above the mean, so the predicted y value is $0.5(3) = 1.5$ standard deviations above the mean. **12.31 (a)** $r = 0.81$. There is a fairly strong, positive linear association between study time and GPA. **(b)** $r^2 = 0.66$. **(i)** The overall prediction error when using the regression equation with study time to predict GPA is 66% smaller compared to using the sample mean GPA. **(ii)** 66% of the variability observed in college GPA can be explained by the linear relationship with study time. **12.33** Explanatory is midterm score, response is final score. No. These students were very low to start with so the increase could have occurred because of regression to the mean. Subjects who are relatively low at one time will, on the average, be higher at a later time. **12.35** We can expect that the five leaders will, on average, have higher scores in the second round. **12.37** Correlation for the means because there will be less variability. **12.39 (a)** Positive correlation with one outlier. **(b)** The correlation drops so dramatically because it depends in magnitude on the variability in scores. Without the outlier, the range of x values is much smaller. **12.41 (a)** 105.00 = maximum bench press observed for athlete 10, 85.90 = predicted maximum bench press based on BP60 = 15, 19.10 = difference between actually observed and predicted maximum bench press = residual for athlete 10, 2.41 = standardized residual = how many standard deviations residual for athlete 10 falls above 0. **(b)** No; we would expect about 5% of standardized residuals to have an absolute value above 2.0. **12.43 (a)** Distribution of standardized residuals and hence conditional distribution of maximum bench press. **(b)** The conditional distribution seems to be approximately normal. **12.45 (a)** 448 = predicted amount spent on clothes in past year for those in 12th grade of school. **(b)** (427, 469): range of plausible values for the population mean of dollars spent on clothes for 12th grade students in the school. **(c)** (101, 795): range of plausible values for the individual observations (dollars spent on clothes) for all the 12th grade students at the school. **12.47 (a)** The square root of 1303.72 is 36.1. This is the estimated standard deviation of maximum leg presses for female athletes who can do a fixed number of 200-pound leg presses. **(b)** Standard deviation = 36.1; (277.6, 422.0). **12.49 (a)** Total SS = residual SS + regression SS, where residual SS = error in using the regression line to predict y, regression SS = how much less error there is in predicting y using the regression line compared to using $\bar{y}$. **(b)** Sum of squares around mean divided by $n - 1$ is 192,787/56 = 3442.6, and its square root is 58.7. This estimates the overall standard deviation of y-values whereas the residual s estimates the standard deviation of y-values at a fixed value of x. **(c)** The F test statistic is 92.87; its square root is the t statistic of 9.64. **12.51 (a)** MS values: 200,000, 22,580.6; F: 8.86. **(b)** H_0: $\beta = 0$ against H_a: $\beta \neq 0$.

12.53

Source	Df	SS	MS	F	P
Regression	1	13682	13682	29.24	0.000
Error	76	35560	468		
Total	77	49242			

(a) Total SS = 49242 = residual SS + regression SS = 13682 + 35560. The total SS is a measure of the overall variability in y (phone weight) but also measures the overall error when using $\bar{y}$ to predict y. The residual SS measures the overall prediction error when using $\hat{y}$ to predict y. Their difference equals the regression SS, which tells us how much the prediction error decreases when using $\hat{y}$ instead of $\bar{y}$ to predict y. **(b)** $s = 21.6$, which is the square root of 468, the mean square error. It estimates the standard deviation of cell phone weight at given battery capacity value and describes a typical value of the residual. **(c)** $s_y = 25.3$. This describes the variability in cell phone weight over the entire range of battery capacity values, not just the variability in cell phone weight at a particular capacity value. **12.55 (a)** $(1.072)^{10} = 2.0$. **(b)** $(1.10)^{10} = 2.59$; the effect here is multiplicative, not additive. **12.57 (a)** $\hat{y} = 81.14 \times 1.1339^0 = 81.14$ million; $\hat{y} = 81.14 \times 1.1339^{11} = 323.26$ million. **(b)** 1.1339 is the multiplicative effect on $\hat{y}$ for a one-unit increase in x. **(c)** This suggests a very good fit of data to model. The high correlation indicates a linear relation between the log of the y values and the x values. **12.59 (a)** 0.32 is the prediction for $\hat{y}$ when $x = 0$; 1.078 is the multiplicative effect on $\hat{y}$ for a one-unit increase in x. **(b) (i)** 1.4; **(ii)** 13.7; **(iii)** 130.2. **(c)** Every 10 years. **12.61 (a)** The exponential model because the log of y values and the x values have a larger (absolute value) correlation. **(b)** 3.35 weeks. **12.63 (a)** 0.9. **(b)** 68; $\hat{y} = 68 + 0.9(x)$. **(c)** $\hat{y} = 280 + 0.4(x)$. **12.65** Response: height of children; explanatory: height of parents. Children tend to be short but not as short as parents. Because of regression toward the mean, the value of y tends (on the average) to be not so far from its mean as the x value is from its mean. **12.67 (a)** 210,991. This house sold for \$210,991 more than would have been predicted. **(b)** This observation is 4.02 standard errors higher than predicted. **12.69 (a)** residual standard deviation of y: variability of the y-values at a particular x-value; standard deviation: variability of all of the y-values **(b)** Variability of y-values at a given x is about the same as variability of all y observations $r^2 = 0.13$. **12.71 (a)** The plausible values range from 338 to 365 for the mean of y values for all female high school athletes having $x = 80$. **(b)** For all female high school athletes with a maximum bench press of 80, we predict that 95% of them have maximum leg press between about 248 and 455 pounds. The 95% PI is for a single observation y, whereas the confidence interval is for the mean of y. **12.73 (a)** $1000 \times 2^5 = 32{,}000$. **(b)** $1000 \times 2^{10} = 1{,}024{,}000$. **(c)** 1000×2^x. **12.75 (a)** 1900: $\hat{y} = 1.424 \times 1.014^0 = 1.42$ billion; 2010: $\hat{y} = 1.424 \times 1.014^{110} = 6.57$ billion. **(b)** The fit of the model corresponds to a rate of growth of 1.4% per year because multiplying by 1.014 adds an additional 1.4% each year. **(c) (i)** The predicted population size doubles after 50 years because $1.014^{50} = 2.0$, the number by which we'd multiply the original population size; **(ii)** It quadruples after 100 years: $1.014^{100} = 4.0$. **(d)** The exponential regression model is more appropriate for these data because the log of the population size and the year number are more highly correlated ($r = 0.99$) than are the population size and the year number. **12.77 (a)** The 3 outlying points represent outliers—values more than $1.5 \times IQR$ beyond either Q1 or Q3. **(b)** From software: Diff = −9.125 + 1.178 Run; difference is positive when $-9.125 + 1.178(\text{runs}) > 0$, which is equivalent to runs > 9.125/1.178 = 7.7. **(c)** Runs, hits, and difference are positively associated with one another. Errors are negatively associated with those three variables.

	Run	Hits	Errors
Hits	0.819		
Errors	−0.259	−0.154	
Difference	0.818	0.657	−0.501

(d) From software, the P-value of 0.000 for testing that the slope equals 0 provides extremely strong evidence that DIFF and RUNS are associated. **12.79** Report would interpret results from:
high_sch_GPA = 3.44 − 0.0183 TV
S = 0.446707 R-Sq = 7.2% R-Sq(adj) = 5.6%

Source	DF	SS	MS	F	P
Regression	1	0.8921	0.8921	4.47	0.039
Error	58	11.5737	0.1995		
Total	59	12.4658			

12.81 (a) In this case, the predictions should exactly match the observations, i.e., $y = x$ which translates to the true y-intercept equaling 0 and the true slope equaling 1. **(b)** No. The P-value for testing that the true y-intercept is 0 is large, so that we are unable to conclude that the y-intercept differs from 0. **12.83** Explain how players or teams that had a particularly good or bad year tended to have results in the following year that were not so extreme (i.e., regression toward the mean). **12.85** As the range of values reflected by each sample is restricted, the correlation tends to decrease when we consider just students of a restricted range of ages. **12.87 (a)** The slope would be two times the original slope. **(b)** The correlation would not change because it is independent of units. **(c)** The t statistic would not change because although the slope doubles, so does its standard error. (The result of a test should not depend on the units we use.) **12.89 (a)** There are two parameters α and β, and so $df = n - 2$. **(b)** There is only one parameter, and therefore, $df = n - 1$. **12.91 (a)** The percentage would likely fluctuate over time, and this would not be a linear relationship. **(b)** Annual medical expenses would likely be quite high at low ages, then lower in the middle, then high again, forming a parabolic, rather than linear, relationship. **(c)** The relation between these variables is likely curvilinear. Life expectancy increases for awhile as per capita income increases, then gradually levels off. **12.93 (a)** The statement is referring to additive growth, but this is multiplicative growth. There is an exponential relation between these variables. **(b)** $\hat{y}$ = \$175,000 × 0.966^{10} = \$123,825; the percentage decline for the decade is about 29.2%. **12.95** (b). **12.97** (d). **12.99** The best response is (b). **12.101 (a)** At 0 impact velocity, there would be 0 putting distance. The line would pass through the point having coordinates (0, 0). **(b)** If x doubles, then x^2 (and hence the mean of y) quadruples; e.g., if x goes from 2 to 4, then x^2 goes from 4 to 16. **12.103** Because $r^2 = \frac{\Sigma(y - \bar{y})^2 - \Sigma(y - \hat{y})^2}{\Sigma(y - \bar{y})^2}$, and dividing each term by approximately n (actually, $n - 1$ and $n - 2$) gives the variance estimates, it represents the relative difference between the quantity used to summarize the overall variability of the y values and the quantity used to summarize the residual variability. **12.105 (a)** Error is calculated by subtracting the mean from the actual score, y. If this difference is positive, then the observation must fall above the mean. **(b)** $\epsilon = 0$ when the observation falls exactly at the mean. **(c)** Since the residual $e = y - \hat{y}$, we have $y = \hat{y} + e = a + bx + e$. As $\hat{y}$ is an estimate of the population mean, e is an estimate of ϵ. **(d)** It does not make sense to use the simpler model, $y = \alpha + \beta x$ that does not have an error term because it is improbable that every observation will fall exactly on the regression line.

Chapter 13

13.1 (a) $\hat{y} = 134.3$. **(b)** −19.3. The actual total body weight is 19.3 pounds lower than predicted. **13.3 (a) (i)** 3.80; **(ii)** 1.60; **(b)** $\hat{y} = 0.20 + 0.50x_1 + 0.002(500) = 0.20 + 0.50x_1 + 1 = 1.20 + 0.50x_1$. **(c)** $\hat{y} = 0.20 + 0.50x_1 + 0.002(600) = 0.20 + 0.50x_1 + 1.2 = 1.40 + 0.50x_1$. **13.5 (a) (i)** 18.3; **(ii)** 12.5; **(b)** When education goes up 10 = 80 − 70, predicted crime rate changes by 10 multiplied by the slope, 10(−0.58) = −5.8. **(c) (i)** $\hat{y} = 59.1 - 0.583x_1 + 0.683(0) = 59.1 - 0.583x_1$; **(ii)** $\hat{y} = 59.1 - 0.583x_1 + 0.683(50) = 93.2 - 0.583x_1$; **(iii)** $\hat{y} = 59.1 - 0.583x_1 + 0.683(100) = 127.4 - 0.583x_1$; For each fixed level of urbanization, the predicted crime rate decreases by 5.8 for every 10 percentage-point increase in education **(d) (i)** Line passing through all data points has positive slope; **(ii)** line when only considering urbanization = 50 has negative slope; when ignoring urbanization, the predicted crime rate increases with increasing education. When controlling (adjusting) for a given level of urbanization, the predicted crime rate decreases with increasing education. **13.7 (a)** $\hat{y}$ = 26,417,000 + 168,300(GIR) + 33,859(SS) − 19,784,000(AvePutt) − 44,725(Events). **(b)** Keeping all other variables constant, the predicted earnings decrease the higher the average number of putts after reaching the green (which results in a higher score and, hence, a lower ranking). **(c)** $\hat{y}$ = 26,417,000 + 168,300(60) + 33,859(50) − 19,784,000(1.5) − 44,725(20) = 7,637,450. **13.9** We don't need to control x_2 if it's not associated with x_1. Changes in x_2 will not have an impact on the effect of x_1 on y. **13.11 (a)** The relationship between price and age is linear, negative, and strong. The relationship between price and HP is less clear; it may be linear but rather weak. **(b)** Predicted Price = 19,348.7 − 1,406.3(Age) + 25.5(HP); **(i)** 10,100, **(ii)** 7,300 **(c)** No, the predicted price difference depends on the age of the two cars because each predicted price depends on it. Only if the age of the two cars is the same does the effect of age cancel out, and the predicted price difference will be 25.5(80 − 60) = 510. **13.13 (a)** Height because it is more strongly correlated with weight than are age and percent body fat. **(b)** One of the properties of R^2 is that it gets larger, or at worst stays the same, whenever an explanatory variable is added to the multiple regression model. **(c)** No, the reduction in error from using the regression equation to predict weight rather than the mean is only 1% more when adding age. **13.15 (a)** $R^2 = \frac{\Sigma(y - \bar{y})^2 - \Sigma(y - \hat{y})^2}{\Sigma(y - \bar{y})^2}$ = (222,102,253 − 69,534,753)/222,102,253 = 0.69. **(b)** Using both age and horsepower to predict used car price reduces the prediction error by 69%, relative to using the sample mean price $\bar{y}$. **(c)** 69% of the variability in used car prices can be explained by the varying age and horsepower of the cars. **13.17 (a)** The number of hits does not make much of a difference, over and above runs and errors, because its slope is so small. An increase of one hit only leads to a predicted difference 0.026 more. **(b)** A small increase in R^2 indicates that the predictive power doesn't increase much with the addition of this explanatory variable over and above the other explanatory variables. **13.19** R^2 = 25.8%; R = 0.51. Using these variables together to predict college GPA reduces the prediction error by 26%, relative to using $\bar{y}$ alone to predict college GPA. There is a correlation of 0.51 between the observed college GPAs and the predicted college GPAs. Only 25.8% of the observed variability in students' college GPA can be explained by their high school GPA and study time. The remaining 74.2% of the variability in college GPA is due to other factors. **13.21 (a)** If the null hypothesis were true, the probability would be 0.63 of getting a test statistic at least as extreme as the value observed. It is plausible that the null hypothesis is correct, and that study time does not predict college GPA, if we already know high school GPA. **(b)** (−0.02, 0.04). Because 0 falls in the confidence interval, it is plausible that the slope is 0 and that study time has no association with college GPA when high school GPA is controlled. **(c)** No. It is likely that study time and high school GPA are highly correlated and therefore it doesn't add much predictive power to the model to include study time once high school GPA is already in the model. This does not mean that study time has no association with college GPA. **13.23 (a) (1)** Assumptions: We assume a random sample and that the model holds. Here, the 57 athletes were a convenience sample, not a random sample, so inferences are highly tentative. **(2)** Hypotheses: H_0: $\beta_2 = 0$; H_a: $\beta_2 \neq 0$. **(3)** Test statistic: $t = 1.39$. **(4)** P-value: 0.17. **(5)** Conclusion: The P-value of 0.17 does not give strong evidence against the null hypothesis that $\beta_2 = 0$. It is plausible that the null hypothesis is correct, and that the number of times an athlete can perform a 200-pound leg press does not predict upper body strength if we already know the number of times she can do a 60-pound bench press. **(b)** $b_2 \pm t_{.025}(se) = 0.211 \pm 2.005(0.152) = 0.211 \pm 0.305$ or $(-0.1, 0.5)$. The small values in the interval suggest a weak impact. **(c)** When LP200 is included in the model, the P-value of the slope associated with BP60 is 0.000, very strong evidence that the slope of BP60 is not 0. **13.25 (a)** The residual standard deviation estimates the standard deviation of the distribution of maxBP at given values for BP60 and LP200. This standard deviation is assumed to be the same for any combination of BP60 and LP200 values and is estimated as 7.9. The sample standard deviation of maxBP of 13.3 shows how much maxBP values vary overall, over the entire range of BP60 and LP200 values, not over just a particular pair of values. **(b)** Approximately 95% of maxBPs fall within about $2s = 15.8$ of the true regression equation. **(c)** The prediction interval is an inference about where the population maxBP values fall at fixed levels of the two explanatory variables. **(d)** It would be unusual because 100 is not in the prediction interval. **13.27 (a)** $\mu_y = \alpha + \beta_1 x_1 + \beta_2 x_2$; where μ_y is the population mean for monthly revenue, x_1 is a given level of TV advertising and x_2 is a given level of newspaper advertising. **(b)** H_0: $\beta_1 = 0$. **(c)** H_0: $\beta_1 = \beta_2 = 0$. **13.29 (a)** $F = 9.49$, P-value ≈ 0. **(b)** H_a: At least one β parameter is not equal to 0. **(c)** The result in part a indicates only that at least one of the variables is a statistically significant predictor of mental health impairment. **13.31 (a)** H_0: $\beta_1 = \beta_2 = 0$; H_a: At least one β parameter is not equal to 0; $F = 108.60$; P-Value $= 0.000$; the P-value of 0.000 gives very strong evidence against the null hypothesis that $\beta_1 = \beta_2 = 0$. It is not surprising to get such a small P-value for this test because size and number of bedrooms are both statistically significant predictors of selling price. **(b)** The t statistic is 2.85 with a P-value of 0.0025. If the null hypothesis were true, the probability would be close to 0 of getting a test statistic at least as extreme as the value observed. The P-value gives very strong evidence against the null hypothesis that $\beta_2 = 0$. **(c)** $B_2 \pm t_{0.025}(se) = 15.170 \pm 1.97(5.330) = 15.170 \pm 10.50 = (4.67, 25.67)$: the plausible values for the slope for number of bedrooms, when controlling for house size, range from about 4.7 to 25.7.

```
The regression equation is
HP in thousands = 60.1 + 0.0630 House Size + 15.2
Bedrooms
Predictor        Coef     SE Coef       T       P
Constant        60.10       18.62    3.23   0.001
House Size   0.062983    0.004753   13.25   0.000
Bedrooms       15.170       5.330    2.85   0.005

S = 80.2707 R-Sq = 52.4% R-Sq(adj) = 52.0%

Analysis of Variance
Source            DF        SS       MS        F       P
Regression         2   1399524   699762   108.60   0.000
Residual Error   197   1269345     6443
Total            199   2668870
```

13.33 (a) The values of BP60 play a role in determining the standardized residuals against which the LP200 values are plotted. **(b)** The residuals are closer to 0 at lower values of LP200. **(c)** Without the three points with standardized residuals around -2, the data do not appear as though there is more variability at higher levels of LP200. We should be cautious in looking at residuals plots because one or two observations might prevent us from seeing the overall pattern. **13.35 (a)** U-shaped scatterplot. **(b)** U-shaped pattern, with residuals above 0 for small age and large age and residuals below 0 for medium-size age values. **13.37** The purpose of performing residual analysis is to determine if assumptions are met for tests. We cannot construct a single plot of the data for all the variables at once because such a plot would require many dimensions. **13.39 (a)** The histogram checks the assumption that the conditional distribution of y is normal, at any fixed values of the explanatory variables. Although the distribution appears mostly normal, there is an outlier with a standardized residual above 6. **(b)** This plot checks the assumption that the regression equation approximates well the true relationship between the predictors and the mean of y. The same large standardized residual (>6) is evident, but there does not appear to be a discernible pattern in the residuals. **13.41 (a)** U.S. cars: Predicted price $= 20{,}493 - 1{,}185(\text{age}) - 2{,}379(1) = 18{,}114 - 1{,}185(\text{age})$. Foreign cars: Predicted price $= 20{,}493 - 1{,}185(\text{age}) - 2{,}379(0) = 20{,}493 - 1{,}185(\text{age})$ **(b)** Both prediction equations in part a have the same slope of $-1{,}185$. For a one-year increase in the age of a car, we predict that the price drops by \$1,185. Since the slope is the same, this applies for both types of cars. **(c) (i)** Predicted price $= 20{,}493 - 1{,}185(8) - 2{,}379(1) = 8{,}634$; **(ii)** predicted price $= 20{,}493 - 1{,}185(8) = 11{,}013$. Difference in predicted price between U.S. and foreign 8-year-old car $= 8{,}634 - 11{,}013 = -2{,}379$, which is the coefficient for the indicator variable for type. **13.43 (a)** $\hat{y} = 96.3 + 0.0664\,\text{house\_size} + 12.9\,\text{condition}$; Good condition: $\hat{y} = 96.3 + 0.0665\,\text{house\_size} + 12.9(1) = 109.2 + 0.0665\,\text{house\_size}$; Not good condition: $\hat{y} = 96.3 + 0.0665\,\text{house\_size} + 12.9(0) = 96.3 + 0.0665\,\text{house\_size}$. **(c)** The difference between the predicted selling price for the two different conditions of the property, controlling for house size, is the slope for condition, 12.9. **13.45 (a)** $x_1 = 1$ if inner city; 0 if other; $x_2 = 1$ if suburbia; 0 if other. **(b)** Suburbia: $\hat{y} = 5.8 - 0.7(0) + 1.2(1) = 7.0$; interstate exits: $\hat{y} = 5.8 - 0.7(0) + 1.2(0) = 5.8$. Interstate exit restaurants have predicted sales of \$1.20 less than suburban restaurants. **13.47 (a)** The assumption of no interaction means that we are assuming that the slope for house size is the same for houses with or without a garage. **13.49 (a)** We would have two explanatory variables, one for number of people and one for location (campus = 0, and mall = 1). **(b)** We would have a model with one explanatory variable, number of people, for the campus location, and another model with one explanatory variable, number of people, for the mall location.

13.51 (a)

$$\hat{p} = \frac{e^{(-6.7+0.0175(359))}}{1 + e^{(-6.7+0.0175(359))}} = 0.397;\ \hat{p} = \frac{e^{(-6.7+0.0175(369))}}{1 + e^{(-6.7+0.0175(369))}} = 0.440.$$

(b)

$$\hat{p} = \frac{e^{(-6.7+0.0175(465))}}{1 + e^{(-6.7+0.0175(465))}} = 0.808;\ \hat{p} = \frac{e^{(-6.7+0.0175(475))}}{1 + e^{(-6.7+0.0175(475))}} = 0.834.$$

13.53 (a) $x = -\hat{\alpha}/\hat{\beta} = 2.04$. **(b)** Crabs over 2.04. **(c)** Crabs under 2.04. **13.55 (a)** $x = 50{,}000$. **(b)** (i) Above \$50,000; (ii) Below \$50,000. **(c)** 0.005. **13.57 (a)** The response variable is whether or not the student graduated (yes or no).

(b)

		Graduated		
Race	**Gender**	**Yes**	**No**	**Total**
White	Female	10,781	20,468	31,249
	Male	10,727	28,856	39,583
Black	Female	2,309	10,885	13,194
	Male	2,054	15,653	17,707

(c) Based on these estimates, white women have the highest estimated probability of graduating. The coefficient for race is positive, indicating that 1 (white) would lead to a higher estimated probability of graduating than would 0 (black). Similarly, the coefficient for gender is positive, indicating that 1 (female) would lead to a higher estimated probability of graduating than would 0 (male).

13.59 (a) $\hat{p} = \dfrac{e^{-3.596-0.868(0)+2.404(1)}}{1 + e^{-3.596-0.868(0)+2.404(1)}} = 0.233$. **(b)**

	Defendant's Race	
Victim's Race	**White**	**Black**
White	0.113	0.233
Black	0.011	0.027

Defendant's race has the same effect on the predicted probability of receiving the death penalty for both white and black victims. In both cases, black defendants are predicted to be more likely to receive the death penalty than are white defendants. **(c)**

Defendant's Race	Death Penalty Yes	No	Percent Yes
White	53	430	11.0
Black	15	176	7.9

This is an example of Simpson's paradox because the direction of association changes when we ignore a third variable. When ignoring victim's race, the predicted proportion of whites receiving the death penalty is now higher than blacks. This occurs because there are more white defendants with white victims than any other group. **13.61 (a)** $\hat{y} = 78.1$; the residual is $y - \hat{y} = 6.9$. **(b)** $\hat{y} = 64.8 + 1.33(BP60)$; the slope of 1.33 indicates that, when controlling for LP200, an increase of one in BP60 leads to an increase of 1.33 in predicted maxBP. **(c)** The additional variable does not add much predictive ability. **13.63 (a)** $\hat{y} = 517.120$; the residual is -41.1; the violent crime rate for Massachusetts is 41.1 lower than predicted from this model. **(b) (i)** $\hat{y} = -270.7 + 28.334x_1$; **(ii)** $\hat{y} = 270.9 + 28.334x_1$. As percent living in urban areas increases from 0 to 100, the intercept of the regression equation increases from -270.7 to 270.9. When poverty rate is held constant, the increase in percent living in urban areas from 0 to 100 results in an increase in predicted violent crime rate of 541.6. **13.65 (a)** -0.66. **(b)** 0.443. **(c)** 279,160. **(d)** 155,577. **(e)** 44.50. **(f)** 33.455. **(g)** -5.21. **(h)** 0.000. **13.67 (a)** Predicted GDP = 39,892 + 798(CO_2) − 399(NoInternet) **(b)** For given percentage of the population not using the internet, we predict GDP to increase by \$798,000 for every metric ton increase in CO_2 emissions. Controlling for CO_2 emissions, we predict GDP to decrease by \$399,000 for every percentage point increase in the percentage of the population not using the Internet. **13.69 (a)** Estimated probabilities are 0.51 and 0.81, an increase of 0.30. **(b) (i)** $x = 24.9$; **(ii)** above a width of 24.9; **(iii)** below a width of 24.9. **13.71 (a)** This is because the coefficients are positive for all of these explanatory variables. **(b)** Because the estimate divided by the standard error is small (equals − 0.93). **13.73** The explanations will be different for each student, but should indicate that multiple regression uses *more than one* characteristic of a subject to predict some outcome. **13.75** (a). **13.77** (a). **13.79 (a)** True. **(b)** True. **(c)** False, R^2 cannot exceed 1. **(d)** False; the predicted values $\hat{y}$ cannot correlate negatively with y. Otherwise, the predictions would be worse than merely using $\bar{y}$ to predict y. **13.81** Indicator variables for a particular explanatory variable must be binary. Here we need three variables: one for Protestant (1 = Protestant, 0 = other), one for Catholic (1 = Catholic, 0 = other), and one for Jewish (1 = Jewish, 0 = other). Using numerical scores would treat religion as quantitative with equidistant categories, which is not appropriate. **13.83** $R^2 = 1$ only when all residuals are 0 because when all regression predictions are perfect (each $y = \hat{y}$), residual SS = $\Sigma(y - \hat{y})^2 = 0$. When residual SS = 0, R^2 is total SS divided by total SS, which must be 1. On the other hand, $R^2 = 0$ when each $\hat{y} = \bar{y}$. In that case, the estimated slopes all equal 0, and the correlation between y and each explanatory variable equals 0. Under these circumstances, the residual SS would equal the total SS, and R^2 would then be 0. In practical terms, it means that R^2 is only 1 when the regression model predicts y perfectly, and it is only 0 when it doesn't predict y at all. **13.85 (a)**

```
Source          DF     SS       MS      F      P
Regression       2   1200.2   600.1   3.74   0.030
Residual Error  54   8674.4   160.6
Total           56   9874.6
```

P-value of 0.030 is less than 0.05.

(b)

```
Predictor     Coef      SE Coef     T       P
Constant    54.019      9.677     5.58    0.000
WT (lbs)     0.1251     0.1378    0.91    0.368
BF%          0.3315     0.6950    0.48    0.635
```

P-values of 0.368 and 0.635 are both larger than 0.35. **13.87** 10: Adjusted $R^2 = 0.357$; 100: Adjusted $R^2 = 0.490$; 1,000: Adjusted $R^2 = 0.499$. As the sample size increases, adjusted R^2 approaches R^2. **13.89** If we wanted to compare two groups on a given variable, we could use regression analysis. The response variable y would be the same. The explanatory variable would be the two levels of the groups; one would be assigned 0 and one would be assigned 1. $\mu_1 = \mu_2$ would correspond to $\beta = 0$. **13.91 (a)** This is a multiple regression model with two variables. If x, for example, is 5, we multiple 5 by β_1 and its square, 25, by β_2. **13.93** $p = e^{\alpha+\beta(-\alpha/\beta)}/(1 + e^{\alpha+\beta(-\alpha/\beta)}) = e^0/(1 + e^0) = 1/(1 + 1) = 0.50$

Chapter 14

14.1 (a) Response variable: performance gap; factor: which hotel the guest stayed in; categories: five hotels. **(b)** H_0: $\mu_1 = \mu_2 = \mu_3 = \mu_4 = \mu_5$; H_a: at least two of the population means are unequal. **(c)** $df_1 = g-1 = 5-1 = 4$; $df_2 = N-g = 125-5 = 120$. **(d)** From a table or software, $F = 2.45$. **14.3 (a) (i)** Assumptions: Independent random samples, normal population distributions with equal standard deviations; **(ii)** Hypotheses: H_0: $\mu_1 = \mu_2 = \mu_3$; H_a: at least two population means are unequal; **(iii)** Test statistic: $F = 2.50$ ($df_1 = 2, df_2 = 5$); **(iv)** P-value = 0.18; **(v)** Conclusion: It is plausible that H_0 is true. **(b)** The sample sizes are very small. **(c)** Observational; a lurking variable might be school GPA. Perhaps higher GPA students are more likely to have previously studied a language and higher GPA students also tend to do better on quizzes than other students. **14.5 (a)** H_0: $\mu_1 = \mu_2 = \mu_3$; μ_1 represents the population mean satisfaction rating for San Jose, μ_2 for Toronto, and μ_3 for Bangalore. **(b)** 27.6 = 13.00/0.47; $df_1 = 2$ and $f_2 = 297$. **(c)** Very small P-value of 0.000 gives strong evidence against the null; we would reject the null and conclude at least two population means differ. **14.7 (a)** μ_1 represents the population mean ideal number of kids for Protestant; μ_2 represents the population mean for Catholic; μ_3 for Jewish; μ_4 for those of Another Religion; H_0: $\mu_1 = \mu_2 = \mu_3 = \mu_4$. **(b)** Independent random samples; normal population distributions with equal standard deviations. **(c)** $F = 5.48$; P-value = 0.001. Very strong evidence that at least two of the population means differ. **(d)** No; ANOVA tests only whether at least two population means are different. **14.9 (a)** New York: mean = 21.9, sd = 1.9; London: 20.4, 2.8; Paris: 23.4, 2.8 **(b)** H_0: $\mu_1 = \mu_2 = \mu_3$, H_a: at least two population means are not equal; $F = 2.8$, P-value = 0.083. At a significance level of 0.05, we do not have sufficient evidence to reject H_0. It is plausible that the population mean ratings of French restaurants in New York, London, and Paris are equal.

14.11 (a)

```
Level        N    Mean    StDev
famchange   17    7.265   7.157
cogchange   29    3.007   7.309
conchange   26   -0.450   7.989
```

The means of these groups are somewhat different. The standard deviations are similar. **(b)** $F = 5.42$; P-value = 0.006; strong evidence that at least two population means are different. **(c)** The assumptions are that there are independent random samples and normal population distributions with equal standard deviations. There is evidence of skew, but the test is robust with respect to this assumption. The subjects were randomly assigned to treatments. Note that since this was not a random sample of subjects suffering from anorexia, the scope of inference to the population may be limited. **14.13** $(\bar{y}_1 - \bar{y}_2) \pm t_{0.25}\, s\sqrt{\frac{1}{n_1} + \frac{1}{n_2}} = (63.7 - 49.0) \pm 1.961(70.81)\sqrt{\frac{1}{440} + \frac{1}{407}} = 14.7 \pm 9.55$; which is (5.2, 24.2). Because 0 does not fall in this confidence interval, we can infer at the 95% confidence level that the population mean times are different (higher for Freshmen compared to Seniors). **14.15 (a)** Classical music and Muzak. **(b)** Because the Tukey method uses an overall confidence level of 95% for the entire set of intervals. **14.17 (a)** $x_1 = 1$ for observations from the first group and $= 0$ otherwise; $x_2 = 1$ for observations from the second group and $= 0$ otherwise. **(b)** H_0: $\mu_1 = \mu_2 = \mu_3$; H_0: $\beta_1 = \beta_2 = 0$. **(c)** For group 1, $x_1 = 1, x_2 = 0$, so predicted mean response $= 12 + 6(1) + 3(0) = 18$. For group 2:

$12 + 6(0) + 3(1) = 15$. For group 3: $12 + 6(0) + 3(0) = 12$. **14.19** **(a)** $x_1 = 1$ for observations from San Jose and $= 0$ otherwise; $x_2 = 1$ for observations from Toronto and $= 0$ otherwise. **(b)** **(i)** This is the estimated for β_1, which equals 0.5. The estimated difference between the population means for San Jose and Bangalore is 0.5. **(ii)** This is the estimated for β_2, which equals 0.7. **14.21** **(a)** Group 2 – Group 1: $(-8.7, 2.7)$, Group 3 – Group 1: $(-3.1, 7.1)$ Group 3 – Group 2: $(-0.7, 10.7)$ Because 0 falls in all three confidence intervals, we cannot infer that any of the pairs of population means are different. **(b)** Note: Statistical software such as MINITAB is needed to complete this solution. Group 2 – Group 1: $(-10.3, 4.3)$ Group 3 – Group 1: $(-4.5, 8.5)$, Group 3 – Group 2: $(-2.3, 12.3)$. Again, we cannot infer that any of the pairs of population means are different. The intervals are wider because we are now using a 95% confidence level for the overall set of intervals. **14.23** **(a)** The response variable is change in cholesterol level. The factors are dosage level and type of drug. **(b)** The four treatments are low-dose Lipitor, high-dose Lipitor, low-dose Zocor, and high-dose Zocor. **(c)** When we control for dose level, we can compare change in cholesterol level for the two types of drugs. **14.25** **(a)** Mean political ideology in adult U.S. population is identical for blacks and whites, for each of the two sexes. **(b)** $F = 36.5/2.1 = 17.4$; P-value $= 0.000$; if the null hypothesis were true, it is extremely unlikely to observe such a value for the F test statistic. We have strong evidence that the mean political ideology in the United States depends on race, for each sex. **(c)** There is no evidence (P-value $= 0.229$) that mean political ideology in the United States differs by gender, for blacks and for whites. **14.27** **(a)** The only difference between the equations for the low manure groups and the ones for the high manure groups is the addition of 1.96. **(b)** $2.11 = t_{.025}$ for 17 degrees of freedom. 0.747 is the standard error of the estimate of the manure effect. 1.96 is the estimate of the manure effect. **14.29** **(a)** Population regression model: $\mu_y = \alpha + \beta_1 x_1 + \beta_2 x_2 + \beta_3 x_3$

Recording	Length	x_1	x_2	x_3	Mean of y
Advert	10 min	1	0	1	$\alpha + \beta_1 + \beta_3$
Muzak	10 min	0	1	1	$\alpha + \beta_2 + \beta_3$
Classical	10 min	0	0	1	$\alpha + \beta_3$
Advert	5 min	1	0	0	$\alpha + \beta_1$
Muzak	5 min	0	1	0	$\alpha + \beta_2$
Classical	5 min	0	0	0	α

(b) $\hat{y} = 8.867 - 5.000\,x_1 - 7.600\,x_2 + 2.556\,x_3$; 8.867 is the estimated holding time when a customer listens to classical music repeating every five minutes (all x's $= 0$); -5.0 represents the decrease in estimated mean when an advertisement is played, and -7.6 represents the decrease in estimated mean when Muzak is played—both at each level of repeat time; 2.556 represents the increase in estimated mean when the repeat time is 10 minutes, for all types of recordings. **(c)** Note: Numbers in parentheses represent values on x_1 and x_2 for type of recording, and on x_3 for repeating time. All numbers are rounded to two decimal places.

	10 minutes (1)	5 minutes (0)
Advertisement (1,0)	6.42	3.87
Muzak (0,1)	3.82	1.27
Classical music (0,0)	11.42	8.87

(d) 2.56. This is the coefficient for x_3, the indicator variable for repeat time. **(e)** Confidence interval for β_3: $2.556 \pm 2.201(1.709) = (-1.2, 6.3)$ **14.31** **(a)** Response: hourly wage. Factors: gender and degree

(b)

	High School	College	Advanced
Male	17	33	43
Female	14	24	32

(c) **(i)** For high school graduates, males make on average \$3 more per hour than females. **(ii)** For college graduates, males make on average \$9 more per hour than females. The difference between males and females is not the same for the two types of degrees. In particular, the wage gap is much larger for graduates with a college degree compared to a high school degree. **(d)** One possibility:

	High School	College	Advanced
Male	17	33	43
Female	14	30	40

14.33 **(a)** Response: number of dates in the last three months; factors: gender and attractiveness. **(b)** Yes. There appears to be a large effect of attractiveness among women, and little to no effect among men. **(c)** The population standard deviations likely differ, based on the sample standard deviations. ANOVA is typically robust with respect to violations of this assumption. **14.35** **(a)** Let $x_1 = 1$ for beef and 0 otherwise, $x_2 = 1$ for cereal and 0 otherwise, and $x_1 = x_2 = 0$ for pork. Likewise, let $x_3 = 1$ for high-protein $x_3 = 0$ for low protein. $\mu_y = \alpha + \beta_1 x_1 + \beta_2 x_2 + \beta_3 x_3$. **(b)** Weight_gain $= 81.8 + 0.50\,x_1 - 4.20\,x_2 + 14.5\,x_3$; 14.5 is the difference in the estimate of the weight gain between low and high protein diets. **(c)** H_0: $\beta_1 = \beta_2 = 0$.

(d)

	High	Low
Beef	96.8	82.3
Cereal	92.1	77.6
Pork	96.3	81.8

We assume that the difference between the high and low protein levels is the same for each source of protein. **14.37** **(a)** **(i)** H_0: $\mu_1 = \mu_2 = \mu_3$; H_a: at least two of the population means are unequal; **(ii)** $F = 3.03$; **(iii)** P-value $= 0.049$; if the null hypothesis were true, the probability would be 0.049 of getting a test statistic at least as extreme as the value observed. We have strong evidence that a difference exists in the population mean number of friends among people going to bars very often, occasionally or never. **(b)** Yes; the sample standard deviations suggest that the population standard deviations might not be equal and the distributions are probably not normal. This is a concern especially in the "very often" group as the sample size is not that large. **14.39** **(a)** The samples are independent and random, the population distributions are normal with equal standard deviations. **(b)** H_0: $\mu_1 = \mu_2 = \mu_3$; H_a: at least two of the population means are unequal. **(c)** $F = 18.50$; $df_1 = 2$, $df_2 = 3$. **(d)** P-value $= 0.02$. **(e)** If the null hypothesis were true, the probability would be 0.02 of getting a test statistic at least as extreme as the value observed. We have strong evidence that a difference exists among the three types of bumpers in the population mean cost to repair damage.

14.41 **(a)**

	Mean	Standard Deviation
NE	70.75	5.56
NC	73.75	11.90
S	62.00	3.65
W	61.25	7.18

(b) We can denote the segregation index means for the population that these four samples represent by μ_1 for Northeast, μ_2 for North Central, μ_3 for South, and μ_4 for West. The null hypothesis is H_0: $\mu_1 = \mu_2 = \mu_3 = \mu_4$. The alternative hypothesis is that at least two of the population means are different. **(c)** $F = 2.64$; P-value $= 0.097$; there is some evidence, but not very strong, that a difference exists among the four regions in the population mean segregation index. **(d)** The ANOVA would not be valid because this would not be a randomly selected sample. **14.43** **(a)** Seems plausible given the similar sample standard deviations. **(b)** The normality assumption is not as important as the assumption that the groups are random samples from the population of interest. However, the influence of the outlier should be investigated. **(c)** The confidence interval does not include 0; we can conclude at the 95% confidence level that on the average Republicans are higher in conservative political ideology than are Democrats. **(d)** We can conclude that a difference exists among the three political parties in their political ideologies; however, we can only conclude that there is a difference between Republicans and Democrats and between Independents and Republicans. We cannot draw conclusions about differences between Independents and Democrats.

14.45

Source	DF	SS	MS	F	P-value
Quadrant	3	2700	900	180	0.000
Error	296	1480	5		
Total	299	4180			

14.47 (a) Response: ideal number of kids; Factors: gender and race. **(b)** The difference between population means for the two genders is the same for each race. One possibility

	Female	Male
Black	3.5	3.3
White	1.5	1.3

(c) H_0: no interaction; H_a: there is an interaction. $F = 1.36$; P-value $= 0.24$; if the null hypothesis were true, the probability would be 0.24 of getting a test statistic at least as extreme as the value observed. It is plausible that there is no interaction. **14.49 (a)** For both at 11 P.M. and 8 A.M., the mean time Williams College students need to complete the task is 0.39 minutes shorter when consuming an energy drink. **(b)** The mean time Williams College students need to complete the task is 2 minutes shorter at night (11 P.M.) compared to in the morning (8 A.M.), whether or not consuming an energy drink. **(c)** $\mu_y = \alpha + \beta_1 e + \beta_2 d$. β_1 needs to equal zero. **(d)** $t = -0.58$, P-value $= 0.57$. No evidence of a difference in means. **14.51** This suggests an interaction since smoking status has a different impact at different levels of age. There is a bigger mean difference between smokers and non-smokers among older women than among younger women. **14.53 (a)** The coefficient for gender, -13 (thousands of dollars), indicates that at fixed levels of race, men have higher estimated mean salaries than women. Women salaries are reduced by 13 (thousands of dollars). **(b) (i)** 109.2 (calculation: 96.2 + 13); **(ii)** 56.2 (calculation: 96.2 − 40). **14.55 (a)** $\mu_y = \alpha + \beta_1 g + \beta_2 m_1 + \beta_3 m_2$

Gender	Status	g	m_1	m_2	Mean of y
M	Single	1	1	0	$\alpha + \beta_1 + \beta_2$
M	Married	1	0	1	$\alpha + \beta_1 + \beta_3$
M	Divorced	1	0	0	$\alpha + \beta_1$
F	Single	0	1	0	$\alpha + \beta_2$
F	Married	0	0	1	$\alpha + \beta_3$
F	Divorced	0	0	0	α

(b) TV hours $= 2.78 + 0.16g + 0.41m_1 - 0.21m_2$. The mean hours of TV watching are estimated to be 0.16 hours higher for males, for each marital status. **(c)** β_2 **(d)** Find CI for β_2: $0.41 \pm 1.962 \times (0.184) = (0.05, 0.77)$. With 95% confidence, the mean number of hours watching TV for singles is by between 0.05 hours and 0.77 hours larger than the mean for divorced subjects. **14.57 (a)** Have little variability of points in each group, but large differences between means of different groups. **(b)** Have lots of variability of points in each group and similar means for different groups. **14.59** A confidence interval of 0.95 for a single comparison gives 95% confidence for only the one interval. A confidence level of 0.95 for a multiple comparison of all six pairs of means provides a confidence level of 95% for the whole set of intervals. **14.61** (d). **14.63** (c). **14.65** True. **14.67 (a)** $\Sigma(\bar{y}_i - \bar{y})^2/(g-1)$ estimates the variance σ^2/n of the distribution of the $\{\bar{y}_i\}$ values, because $\Sigma(\bar{y}_i - \bar{y})^2/(g-1)$ is essentially the formula for variance, in which each observation is a sample mean. **(b)** If $\Sigma(\bar{y}_i - \bar{y})^2/(g-1)$ estimates σ^2/n, then n times $\Sigma(\bar{y}_i - \bar{y})^2/(g-1)$ estimates σ^2. **14.69 (a)** (0.95)(0.95)(0.95)(0.95)(0.95) = 0.77. **(b)** $(0.9898)^5 = 0.95$. **14.71 (a)** Eight groups. **(b)** Let $x_1 = 1$ for the high level of nitrogen and 0 for the low level of nitrogen, $x_2 = 1$ for the high level of phosphate and 0 for the low level of phosphate, and $x_3 = 1$ for the high level of potash and 0 for the low level of potash. Then $\mu_y = \alpha + \beta_1 x_1 + \beta_2 x_2 + \beta_3 x_3$. **(c)** One possibility is $\hat{\alpha} = 6, \hat{\beta}_1 = 2, \hat{\beta}_2 = 2, \hat{\beta}_3 = -2$.

Chapter 15

15.1 (a) / **(b)**

(a) Lotion	(1,2)	(1,3)	(1,4)	(2,3)	(2,4)	(3,4)
(b) Studio	(3,4)	(2,4)	(2,3)	(1,4)	(1,3)	(1,2)
Lotion mean rank	1.5	2.0	2.5	2.5	3.0	3.5
Studio mean rank	3.5	3.0	2.5	2.5	2.0	1.5
Difference of mean ranks	−2.0	−1.0	0.0	0.0	1.0	2.0

(c) $P(-2.0) = 1/6$, $P(-1.0) = 1/6$, $P(0.0) = 2/6$, $P(1.0) = 1/6$, $P(2.0) = 1/6$. **15.3** Parts a and b together: example given for seven combinations only; there would be 20.

Treatment	Ranks						
Therapy 1	(1,2,3)	(1,2,4)	(1,2,5)	(1,2,6)	(1,3,4)	(1,3,5)	(1,3,6)
Therapy 2	(4,5,6)	(3,5,6)	(3,4,6)	(3,4,5)	(2,5,6)	(2,4,6)	(2,4,5)
Therapy 1 mean rank	2.0	2.33	2.67	3.0	2.67	3.0	3.33
Therapy 2 mean rank	5.0	4.67	4.33	4.0	4.33	4.0	3.67
Difference of mean ranks	−3.0	−2.33	−1.67	−1.0	−1.67	−1.0	−0.33

(c) Differences between mean ranks followed by probabilities: (−3.00, 1/20) (−2.33, 1/20) (−1.67, 2/20) (−1.00, 3/20) (−0.33, 3/20) (0.33, 3/20) (1.00, 3/20) (1.67, 2/20) (2.33, 1/20) (3.00, 1/20). **(d)** P-value = 0.20. If the two therapies had identical effects, the probability of a difference in the mean ranks as observed (or one even more extreme) is 0.20, which is large. There is no evidence of an effect. **15.5 (a)** The point estimate of −2.000 is an estimate of the difference between the population median birth weight for the smokers group and the population median birth weight for the nonsmokers group. **(b)** The confidence interval of (−3.300, −0.700) estimates that the population median birth weight for the smokers group is between 3.3 and 0.7 pounds below the population median birth weight for the nonsmoking group. Because 0 does not fall in the confidence interval, there is evidence that there is a difference between the population medians for the two groups. **15.7 (a)** The estimated difference between the population median weight change for the cognitive behavioral treatment group and the population median weight change for the control group is 3.05. **(b)** The confidence interval estimates that the population median weight change for the cognitive-behavioral group is between 0.6 below and 8.1 above the population median weight change for the control group. The assumption needed is that the girls were randomly assigned to the two treatment groups and that the shape of the distribution of weight change is similar in the two groups. **(c)** P-value = 0.11 for testing against the alternative hypothesis of different expected median ranks; there is not much evidence against the null hypothesis. It is plausible that the population distributions are identical. **15.9 (a)** Group 1 ranks: 2, 5, 6; Group 2 ranks: 1, 3.5; Group 3 ranks: 3.5, 7, 8. The mean rank for Group 1 = (2 + 5 + 6)/3 = 4.33. **(b)** P-value = 0.209; it is plausible that the population median quiz score is the same for each group. **15.11 (a)** Dependent; all students receive both treatments. **(b)** 0.81. **(c)** $z = 3.54$; P-value = 0.0002. Strong evidence that the population proportion of drivers who would have a faster reaction time when not using a cell phone is greater than 1/2. **(d)** Matched-pairs t test; the sign test uses merely the information about *which* response is higher and how many, not the quantitative information about *how much* higher. **15.13** H_0: $p = 0.50$. H_a: $p > 0.50$; $P(3) = (0.50)^3 = 0.125$. The evidence is not strong that walking lowers blood pressure. **15.15 (a)** H_0: population median of difference scores is 0; H_a: population median of difference scores is > 0. **(c)** P-value = 1/16 = 0.06; there is some, but not strong, evidence that cell phones tend to impair reaction times. **15.17 (a)** Bumper A: ranks are 4, 6, 5; mean is 5. Bumper B: ranks are 1, 2, 3; mean is 2.
(b)

Treatment	Ranks
Bumper A	(1, 2, 3) (1,2,4) (1,2,5) (1,2,6) (1,3,4) (1,3,5) (1,3,6) (1,4,5) (1,4,6) (1,5,6)
Bumper B	(4,5,6) (3,5,6) (3,4,6) (3,4,5) (2,5,6) (2,4,6) (2,4,5) (2,3,6) (2,3,5) (2,3,4)

Treatment	Ranks
Bumper A	(2,3,4) (2,3,5) (2,3,6) (2,4,5) (2,4,6) (2,5,6) (3,4,5) (3,4,6) (3,5,6) (4,5,6)
Bumper B	(1,5,6) (1,4,6) (1,4,5) (1,3,6) (1,3,5) (1,3,4) (1,2,6) (1,2,5) (1,2,4) (1,2,3)

(c) There are only two ways in which the ranks are as extreme as in this sample: Bumper A with 1, 2, 3 and Bumper B with 4, 5, 6, or Bumper A with 4, 5, 6 and Bumper B with 1, 2, 3. **(d)** The P-value is 0.10 because out of 20 possibilities, only two are this extreme. $2/20 = 0.10$.

15.19 (a)

Group	Ranks	Mean Rank
Muzak	1,2,4,5,3	3.0
Classical	9,8,7,10,6	8.0

(b) There are only two cases this extreme (i.e., Muzak has ranks 1–5 or Muzak has ranks 6–10). Thus, the P-value is the probability that one of these two cases would occur out of the 252 possible allocations of rankings. The probability would be 0.008 of getting a sample like we observed or even more extreme. **15.21 (a)** Kruskal-Wallis test. **(b)** All examples would have one group with ranks 1–3, one with ranks 4–6, and one with ranks 7–9. **15.23 (a) (i)** H_0: Population proportion $p = 0.50$ who use the cell phone more than Internet; H_a: $p \neq 0.50$; **(ii)** $se = \sqrt{(0.50)(0.50)/n} = \sqrt{(0.50)(0.50)/39} = 0.08$, $z = (\hat{p} - 0.50)/se = (0.897 - 0.50)/0.08 = 4.96$; **(iii)** P-value $= 0.000$; if the null hypothesis were true, the probability would be near 0 of getting a test statistic at least as extreme as the value observed. We have extremely strong evidence that a majority of countries have more cell phone usage than Internet usage. **(b)** This would not be relevant if the data file were comprised only of countries of interest to us. We would know the population parameters so inference would not be relevant. **15.25 (a)** We could use the sign test for matched pairs or the Wilcoxon signed-ranks test. **(b)** One reason for using a nonparametric method is if we suspected that the population distribution of the differences was not normal and because we have a one-sided alternative. Then, parametric methods like the paired t-test are not robust. **(c)** For the one-sided test with H_0: median difference $= 0$ vs. H_a: median difference > 0, software reports a test statistic (sum of ranks of positive differences between high school and college GPA) of 1271, with a P-value of 0.000. The P-value of 0.000 gives very strong evidence that in the population, the median high school GPA is higher than the median college GPA. **15.27 (a)** H_0: population median of difference scores is 0; H_a: population median of difference scores > 0.

Possible Samples with Absolute Difference Values of Sample

Subject	1	2	3	4	5	6	7	8	Rank of Absolute Value
1	5.5	5.5	−5.5	5.5	−5.5	5.5	−5.5	−5.5	3
2	−0.5	−0.5	−0.5	0.5	−0.5	0.5	0.5	0.5	1
3	1.5	−1.5	1.5	1.5	−1.5	−1.5	1.5	−1.5	2
Sum of Ranks for Positive Differences									
	5	3	2	6	0	4	3	1	

The rank sum is 5 one-eighth of the time, and is more extreme (i.e., 6) one-eighth of the time (values that were greater than the observed). Thus, the P-value $= 2/8 = 0.25$. If the null hypothesis were true, the probability would be 0.25 of getting a test statistic at least as extreme as the value observed. It is plausible that the null hypothesis is correct and that the population median of difference scores is not positive. **(b)** The p-value is smaller than in Example 8. Outliers do not have an effect on this nonparametric statistical method.**15.29** One example is when the population distribution is highly skewed and the researcher wants to use a one-sided test. **15.31** Kruskal-Wallis. **15.33** False. **15.35 (a)** The proportions are calculated by pairing up the subjects in every possible way, and then counting the number of pairs for which the tanning studio gave a better tan. **(b)**

Proportion	Probability
0/6	1/10
1/6	1/10
2/6	2/10
3/6	2/10
4/6	2/10
5/6	1/10
6/6	1/10

(c) The P-value would be 2/10. The probability of an observed sample proportion of 5/6 or more extreme (i.e., 6/6) is $2/10 = 0.20$. **15.37** No; we are taking the median of all slopes, and the median is not susceptible to outliers.

Index

A

B

C

D

E

F

G

H

I

J

K

L

M

Q

R

S

T

U

V

W

Y

Z

Index of Applications

S

T

U

V

W

Credits

Screenshots from Minitab. Courtesy of Minitab Corporation.
Screenshots from Texas Instruments. Courtesy of Texas Instruments.
Screenshots of Shiny Apps. Created with RStudio® and Shiny™.

COVER RunPhoto/Getty

PREFACE **p. xxiii** (from top to bottom) Alan Agresti; Christine Franklin; Sophie Klingenberg

CHAPTER 1 **p. 1** (from left to right) Ra2 Studio/Fotolia; Adimas/Fotolia; Pershing/Fotolia; Triff/Shutterstock **p. 2** Ra2 Studio/Fotolia **p. 9** S44/ZUMA Press/Newscom **p. 11** Richard Levine/Alamy **p. 13** Forestpath/Shutterstock **p. 19** Claudiodivizia/123RF

CHAPTER 2 **p. 26** Adimas/Fotolia **p. 29** Davidk79/Fotolia **p. 32** Davidk79/Fotolia **p. 35** Branislav Senic/iStock/Getty Images **p. 44** From *Internet World Stats Usage and Population Statistics.* Copyright © 2000–2011 Miniwatts Marketing Group. **p. 45** Sborisov/123RF **p. 46** Pearson Education, Inc. **p. 52** Wrangler/Shutterstock **p. 60** Andy Dean Photography/Shutterstock **p. 68** Matka_Wariatka/Fotolia **p. 73** Henryk Sadura/Shutterstock **p. 80** Pearson Education, Inc. **p. 80** Quote by John Tukey. **p. 80** © THE SCOTSMAN PUBLICATIONS LIMITED. **p. 81** BBC License Fee from *Evening Standard.* Copyright, 2 November 29, 2006 by London Evening Standard. Used by permission of London Evening Standard. **p. 83** From *Statistical Science Vol. 17,* pp. 1–5. Copyright © 2002 Institute of Mathematical Statistics. Used by permission of Institute of Mathematical Statistics.

CHAPTER 3 **p. 91** Pershing/Fotolia **p. 93** WB/Shutterstock **p. 95** Asharkyu/Shutterstock **p. 101** NetPhotos/Alamy **p. 106** Gary I Rothstein/AP Images **p. 113** Cafaphotos/Fotolia **p. 116** Bill Florence/Shutterstock **p. 119** Tupungato/Shutterstock **p. 123** Technotr/E+/Getty Images **p. 128** 4x6/Getty Images **p. 136** Jiri Foltyn/Shutterstock **p. 137** Kevin George/Dreamstime LLC. **p. 140** Originally published in *Florida Law Review.* Michael Radelet and Glenn L. Pierce, *Choosing Those Who Will Die: Race and the Death Penalty in Florida,* vol. 43, *Florida Law Review 1* (1991). **p. 146** From *African Droughts and Dust Transport to the Caribbean: Climate Change Implications*, by Joseph M Prospero, Peter J Lamb in *SCIENCE,* Vol. 302, pp. 1024–1027. Copyright © 2003 by American Association for the Advancement of Science (AAAS). Used by permission of American Association for the Advancement of Science (AAAS). **pp. 149–150** Copyright ©1996 Marilyn vos Savant. Initially Published in *Parade Magazine.* All rights reserved. **p. 150** Excerpt from *Domestic Dogs and Human Health: An Overview* by Deborah L. Wells in *British Journal of Health Psychology.* Published by John Wiley & Sons, Inc. Copyright © 2007.

CHAPTER 4 **p. 153** Triff/Shutterstock **p. 156** Monkey Business Images/Dreamstime LLC. **p. 160** Roger L Wollernberg/Newscom **p. 163** Shevelev Vladimir/Dreamstime LLC **p. 169** Pearson Education, Inc. **p. 174** Paul Matthew Photography/Shutterstock **p. 181** WavebreakmediaMicro/Fotolia **p. 182** Mihai Simonia/Shutterstock **p. 183** Rob Marmion/Shutterstock **p. 185** Dalaprod/Fotolia **p. 191** © ESPN .com (2012), (graphic feature used with permission).

CHAPTER 5 **p. 199** (from left to right) Anna Galkovskaya/E+/Getty Images; Bikeriderlondon/Shutterstock; Steve Debenport/E+/Getty Images **p. 200** Anna Galkovskaya/E+/Getty Images **p. 202** Excerpt from Ainslie's Complete Hoyle by Tom Ainslie. Published by Simon and Schuster. Copyright © 2003. **p. 204** Tomo/Shutterstock **p. 208** © The Vanguard Group, Inc., used with permission. **p. 210** Alexander Raths/Fotolia **p. 212** Jill Fromer/E+/Getty Images **p. 214** Michelle Milano/Shutterstock **p. 223** Dizzy/iStock/Getty Images **p. 226** (from top to bottom) Vlad Mereuta/Shutterstock; Zentilia/Shutterstock **p. 233** MSPhotographic/Fotolia **p. 234** Mikephotos/Dreamstime LLC. **p. 237** Angelo Giampiccolo/Fotolia **p. 241** Janet Wall/Fotolia **p. 250** Excerpt from Calculated Risks: How To Know When Numbers Deceive You by Gerd Gigerenzer. Published by Simon and Schuster. Copyright © 2002. **p. 252** Excerpt from Calculated Risks: How To Know When Numbers Deceive You by Gerd Gigerenzer. Published by Simon and Schuster. Copyright © 2002. **p. 252** Excerpt from Calculated Risks: How To Know When Numbers Deceive You by Gerd Gigerenzer. Published by Simon and Schuster. Copyright © 2002.

CHAPTER 6 **p. 254** Bikeriderlondon/Shutterstock **p. 256** Modestil/Fotolia **p. 259** Nikada/Getty Images **p. 260** Noamfein/Dreamstime LLC **p. 263** Oliveromg/Shutterstock **p. 267** Matthias Buehner/Fotolia **p. 272** Jaimie Duplass/Shutterstock **p. 275** Lightpoet/Fotolia **p. 281** Fuse/Getty Images **p. 283** Pressmaster/Fotolia **p. 286** Ilya Andriyanov/Shutterstock **p. 296** Sozaijiten

CHAPTER 7 **p. 298** Steve Debenport/E+/Getty Images **p. 301** Screenshot from Random.org. Copyright © 1998–2015 Random.org. **p. 305** Kennytong/Fotolia **p. 322** Steve Mason/Getty Images

CHAPTER 8 **p. 333** (from left to right) Blvdone/Shutterstock; Norbel/Fotolia; Matt Burgess/123RF; Alexbrylovhk/Fotolia **p. 334** Blvdone/Shutterstock **p. 339** wavebreakmedia/Shutterstock **p. 343** Justasc/Shutterstock **p. 346** Wallenrock/Shutterstock **p. 351** Pearson Education, Inc. **p. 354** Scyther5/Shutterstock **p. 362** (from left to right) Pearson Education, Inc.; Matt Burgess/123RF **p. 365** Karin Hildebrand Lau/Shutterstock **p. 369** 123RF **p. 371** Ionescu Bogdan/Fotolia **p. 375** Tab62/Fotolia

CHAPTER 9 **p. 386** Norbel/Fotolia **p. 388** Bizoo_n/Fotolia **p. 392** Jovan Nikolic/Shutterstock **p. 396** Cameron Cross/Shutterstock **p. 408** Alexey Stiop/Shutterstock **p. 421** Junial Enterprises/Shutterstock **p. 424** (from top to bottom) Christopher Halloran/Shutterstock; Kurniawan1972/Dreamstime LLC. **p. 427** Shutterstock **p. 429** Pearson Education, Inc.

CHAPTER 10 **p. 444** Alexbrylovhk/Fotolia **p. 445** Copyright © 2009 Jim Borgman. Distributed by Universal Uclick. Reprinted with permission. All rights reserved. **p. 446** Pearson Education, Inc. **p. 452** Excerpt from The Seven Warning Signs of Bogus Science. Published by The Chronicle of Higher Education, © 2003. **p. 455** CandyBox Images/Shutterstock **p. 467** Lucidwaters/Dreamstime **p. 471** Excerpt from Chelation Therapy for Ischemic Heart Disease: A Randomized Controlled Trial by Merril L. Knudtson, D. George Wyse, P. Diane Galbraith, Rollin Brant, Kathy Hildebrand, Diana Paterson, Deborah Richardson, Connie Burkart and Ellen Burgess in JAMA Vol. 287, p. 481. Published by the American Medical Association, © 2002. **p. 474** Capifrutta/Shutterstock **p. 491** Excerpt from Profiles in Driver Distraction: Effects of Cell Phone Conversations on Younger and Older Drivers by David L. Strayer and Frank A. Drews in Human Factors and Ergonomics Society, Vol. 46, pp. 640–649. Published by the Human Factors and Ergonomics Society, © 2004. **p. 492** Igor Zh/Shutterstock **p. 500** Shutterstock

CHAPTER 11 **p. 515** (from left to right) Rawpixel/Fotolia; Tyler Olson/Shutterstock; Andy Dean Photography/Shutterstock; Diego Cervo/Shutterstock; Travnikovstudio/Fotolia **p. 516** Rawpixel/Fotolia **p. 524** Andresr/Shutterstock **p. 531** Shutterstock **p. 539** Image Source/Getty Images **p. 550** Piyachok Thawornmat/Shutterstock **p. 554** B Christopher/Alamy

CHAPTER 12 **p. 566** Tyler Olson/Shutterstock **p. 574** Hxdbzxy/Shutterstock **p. 579** Jack Hollingsworth/Photodisc/Getty Images **p. 587** Michaeljung/Fotolia **p. 592** Pearson Education, Inc. **p. 596** Andres Rodriguez/Dreamstime LLC **p. 605** Adisa/Shutterstock **p. 607** From Cramming More Components Onto Integrated Circuits by Gordon E Moore in Electronics Vol. 38 No. 8, pp. 114–117. Copyright © 1965 by MDPI AG. **p. 608** Excerpt from Gordon Moore: The Man Whose Name Means Progress by Rachel Courtland. Copyright © 2015 by IEEE Spectrum. **p. 612** Excerpt from Variation in Cancer Risk Among Tissues can be Explained by the Number of Stem Cell Divisions by Cristian Tomasetti, Bert Vogelstein in Science Vol. 347 No. 6217 pp. 78–81. Published by American Association for the Advancement of Science, © 2015. **p. 615** Quote by George Edward Pelham Box.

CHAPTER 13 **p. 618** Andy Dean Photography/Shutterstock **p. 620** StockLite/Shutterstock **p. 632** Muzsy/Shutterstock **p. 651** Brenda Carson/Shutterstock **p. 656** Olli Wang/Fotolia **p. 672** Originally published in *Florida Law Review.* Michael Radelet and Glenn L. Pierce, *Choosing Those Who Will Die: Race and the Death Penalty in Florida,* vol. 43, *Florida Law Review 1* (1991).

CHAPTER 14 **p. 669** Diego Cervo/Shutterstock **p. 671** Mr.Markin/Fotolia **p. 681** Dmitry Berkut/Shutterstock **p. 690** Maksud/Shutterstock **p. 695** Auremar/Shutterstock

CHAPTER 15 **p. 710** Travnikovstudio/Fotolia **p. 714** Sandra Cunningham/Shutterstock **p. 720** Susan Montgomery/Shutterstock

Dataset Files

Chapter 1

FL student survey

Chapter 2

Alligator Food
Animals
Baseball Hitters
Central Park Yearly Temps
Cereal
Cigarette Tax
CO2 Europe & America
College Athletes
Energy Consumption
Europe CO2
FL Student Survey
GA Student Survey
Health Coverage
Heights
HS Female Athletes
HS Graduation
Hurricanes
Iris
Newnan GA Temperatures
NYY Salaries 2014
Pertussis
SAT 2010
Sharks
Teacher Salary
TV Hours
Youth Unemployment

Chapter 3

AL Team Statistics
Animals
Buchanan Butterfly Ballot
Car Weight & Mileage
Central Park Yearly Temps
Cereal
Diamonds
FL Crime
FL Student Survey
Fuel
GA Student Survey
High Jump
House Prices (FL)
HS Graduation Rates
Human Development
Internet Use
Long Jump
Mountain Bikes
Newnan GA Temps
NL Team Statistics
SAT 2010
US Statewide Crime
US Temperatures
Zagat Boston

Chapter 7

Inns

Chapter 8

Email Hours (GSS 2012)
FL Student Survey
Mountain Bikes
TV Hours (long format)
WWW Hours

Chapter 9

Anorexia
Anorexia (long format)
FL Student Survey
Number of Kids
Political Views
40-Hour Work Week (GSS 2012)

Chapter 10

Anorexia
Anorexia (long format)
FL Student Survey
Number of Kids
Cell Phone (wide format)
Cell Phone (long format)
Reaction Time (wide format)
Reaction Time (long format)
Stick Figures
Text & Graph
Time on Facebook (F, S)
TV Hours by Race
Work Week (GSS 2014)
WWW Hours

Chapter 11

Benford
Diamonds
Happiness & Income (2012)
Headache
Religiosity

Chapter 12

Car Weight & Mileage
Georgia Student Survey
HS Female Athletes
House Selling Prices FL
Male Athlete Strength
Specs Cellphones
Stemcells
Internet Use
FL Student Survey

Chapter 13

Female College Athletes
Credit Card & Income
FL Crime
Georgia Student Survey
High Jump
HS Female Athletes
House Selling Prices OR
Mental Health
Mountain Bike
Quality & Productivity
Softball
Used Cars
Fertility & Literacy
FL Student Survey

Chapter 14

Anorexia
Anorexia (long format)
Energy Drink
French Cuisine
Georgia Student Survey
House Selling Prices OR
Protein & Weight Gain
Time on Facebook (all)
TV Hours (2014)

Chapter 15

Anorexia
Anorexia (long format)
FL Student Survey
Georgia Student Survey
Reaction Time (wide format)
Reaction Time (long format)

Web Apps

Chapter 1

Sampling Distribution of a Sample Proportion

Chapter 2

Mean vs. Median
Explore Categorical Data
Explore Quantitative Data

Chapter 3

Explore Linear Regression
Fit Linear Regression
Guess the Correlation

Chapter 5

Random Numbers
Binomial Distribution

Chapter 6

Normal Distribution

Chapter 7

Sampling Distribution of a Sample Proportion
Sampling Distribution of a Sample Mean

Chapters 8 and 9

Inference for a Proportion
Illustrating Coverage
t Distribution
Inference for a Mean
Bootstrap
Errors and Power

Chapter 10

Comparing two Proportions
Comparing two Means
Permutation Test

Chapter 11

Chi-squared Distribution
Chi-squared Test
Fisher's Exact Test
Permutation Test for Independence

Chapter 14

ANOVA

To access datasets and web apps please go to www.pearsonhighered.com/AFK

A Guide to Choosing a Statistical Method

CATEGORICAL RESPONSE VARIABLE (ANALYZING PROPORTIONS)

1. If there is only one categorical response variable, use
   - Descriptive methods of Chapter 2 (Sections 2.1 and 2.2)
   - Inferential methods of Section 8.2 (confidence interval) and Section 9.2 (significance test) for proportions
2. To compare proportions of a categorical response variable for two or more groups of a categorical explanatory variable, use
   - Descriptive methods of Chapter 3 (Sections 3.1 and 3.4)
   - Inferential methods of Sections 10.1 and 10.4 for comparing proportions between two groups
   - Inferential methods of Chapter 11 for comparing two or more proportions or testing the independence of two categorical variables
3. If working with a binary response variable with quantitative and/or categorical explanatory variables (predictors), use logistic regression methods of Section 13.6

QUANTITATIVE RESPONSE VARIABLE (ANALYZING MEANS)

1. If there is only one quantitative response variable, use
   - Descriptive methods of Chapter 2
   - Inferential methods of Section 8.3 (confidence interval) and Section 9.3 (significance test) for a mean
2. To compare means of a quantitative response variable for two groups of a categorical explanatory variable, use
   - Descriptive methods of Chapter 2
   - Inferential methods of Sections 10.2 and 10.3 for independent samples
   - Inferential methods of Section 10.4 for dependent samples
   - Nonparametric tests in Section 15.1 for independent samples or Section 15.2 for dependent samples
3. To compare several means of a quantitative response variable for two or more groups of a categorical explanatory variable, use
   - ANOVA methods of Chapter 14 for independent samples, which are equivalent to regression methods with indicator variables for categorical predictors
   - Nonparametric methods from Section 15.2
4. To analyze the association of a quantitative response variable and quantitative explanatory variable, use regression and correlation
   - Descriptive methods of Chapters 3 and 12
   - Inferential methods of Chapter 12 (Sections 12.2 and 12.4)
5. To analyze the association of a quantitative response variable and several explanatory variables (predictors), use
   - Multiple regression methods of Chapter 13 (Sections 13.1–13.4) for several quantitative predictors
   - Multiple regression methods of Section 13.5 with indicator variables for categorical predictors